Societies, Networks, and Transitions

A GLOBAL HISTORY

Fourth Edition

Craig A. Lockard
University of Wisconsin—Green Bay

 CENGAGE

Australia • Brazil • Mexico • Singapore • United Kingdom • United States

Societies, Networks, and Transitions:
A Global History, **Fourth Edition**
Craig A. Lockard

Product Director: Laura Ross

Senior Product Manager: Joseph Potvin

Product Assistant: Haley Gaudreau

Marketing Director: Neena Bali

Senior Marketing Manager: Valerie Hartman

Senior Content Manager: Claire Branman

Learning Designer: Kate MacLean

Subject Matter Expert: Matt Kennedy

Senior Designer: Sarah Cole

IP Analyst: Deanna Ettinger

IP Project Manager: Nick Barrows

Production Service & Compositor: SPi Global

Text and Cover Designer: Sarah Cole

Design Credits: iStock.com/
FrankvandenBergh; iStock.com/fmajor;
Voronin76/ShutterStock.com; iStock.com/
Vectorios2016

Cover Image: HIP/Art Resource, NY

For product information and technology assistance,
contact us at
Cengage Customer & Sales Support, 1-800-354-9706
or support.cengage.com.

For permission to use material from this text or product,
submit all requests online at **www.cengage.com/permissions**.

Library of Congress Control Number: 2019920405

Student Edition:
ISBN: 978-0-357-36530-4

Loose-leaf Edition:
ISBN: 978-0-357-36543-4

Cengage
200 Pier 4 Boulevard
Boston, MA 02210
USA

Cengage is a leading provider of customized learning solutions with
employees residing in nearly 40 different countries and sales in more
than 125 countries around the world. Find your local representative at
www.cengage.com.

Cengage products are represented in Canada by
Nelson Education, Ltd.

To learn more about Cengage platforms and services, register or
access your online learning solution, or purchase materials for your
course, visit **www.cengage.com**.

Printed in the United States of America
Print Number: 01   Print Year: 2020

Brief Contents

Contents

Maps

Features

MEET THE PEOPLE

DISCOVER HISTORICAL VOICES

DEBATE THE HISTORIANS

Preface

> *"Awareness of the need for a universal view of history—for a history which transcends national and regional boundaries and comprehends the entire globe—is one of the marks of the present. Our past [is] the past of the world, our history is the first to be world history."*[1]
>
> —British historian Geoffrey Barraclough

British historian Geoffrey Barraclough wrote these words four decades ago, yet historians are still grappling with what it means to write and study world history, and why it is crucial to do so, especially to better inform today's students about their changing world and how it came to be. The intended audience for this text is students taking introductory world history courses and the faculty who teach them. Many of these students will be taking world history in colleges, universities, and community colleges, often with the goal of satisfying general education requirements or building a foundation for majoring in history or a related field. Most others will take world history in secondary schools, often as Advanced Placement courses. Like the contemporary world, the marketplace for texts is also changing. Both students, many of whom have outside jobs, and instructors, often facing expanded workloads, have increasing demands on their time. New technologies are promoting new pedagogies and a multiplicity of classroom approaches. Hence, any textbook must provide a sound knowledge base while also enhancing teaching and learning whatever the pedagogy employed.

To make this fourth edition even more accessible and reader friendly than the first three editions, we have included more human-interest material and short quotes from primary sources to liven up the narrative and convey a better sense of the diverse people of all backgrounds in world history and streamlined and shortened the narrative. Based on instructor feedback, we have kept the popular *Societies, Networks, and Transitions* essay features at the beginning of each Part in order to give them more prominence and added more human interest material to them. Like the core chapter narrative, these essays are organized by theme so that students can easily grasp the major parallels and changes that take place over the timeframe of the part. There has been considerable new scholarship since the third edition in all areas of world history and I have updated the narrative to include some of the most important findings as well as covering recent developments (see below). I believe that these changes and additions enhance the book's presentation and clarity and enable it to convey the richness and importance of world history for today's students and tomorrow's leaders while also making the teaching of the material easier for both high school and college instructors using this text.

Twenty-first-century students, more than any generation before them, live in multicultural countries and an interconnected and rapidly changing world. The world's interdependence calls for teaching a wider vision, which is the goal of this text. My intention is to create a meaningful, coherent, and stimulating presentation that conveys to students the incredible diversity of societies from earliest times to the present, as well as the ways they have been increasingly connected to other societies and shaped by these relationships. History may happen "as one darn thing after another," but the job of historians is to make it something more than facts, names, and dates. A text should provide a readable narrative, supplying a content base while also posing larger questions. The writing is as clear and thorough in its explanation of events and concepts as I can make it. No text can or should teach the course, but I hope that this text provides enough of a baseline of regional and global coverage to allow each instructor to bring her or his own talents, understandings, and particular interests to the process.

I became involved in teaching, debating, and writing world history as a result of my personal and academic experiences. My interest in other cultures was first awakened in the multicultural Southern California city where I grew up. Many of my classmates and neighbors or their parents had come from Asia, Latin America, or the Middle East. There were also substantial African American and Mexican American communities. A curious youngster did not have to search far to hear music, sample foods, or encounter ideas from many different cultures. I remember being enchanted by the Chinese landscape paintings at a local museum devoted to Asian art, and vowing to one day see some of those misty mountains for myself. Today many young people may be as interested as I was in learning about the world, since, thanks to immigration, many cities and towns all over North America have taken on a cosmopolitan flavor similar to my hometown.

While experiences growing up sparked my interest in other cultures, it was my schooling that pointed the way to a career in teaching world history. When I entered college, many undergraduate students in the United States, often as part of the general education requirement, were required to take a year-long course in Western Civilization that introduced students to Egyptian pyramids, Greek philosophy, medieval pageantry, Renaissance art, and the French Revolution, enriching our lives. Fortunately, my university expanded student horizons further by adding course components (albeit brief) on China, Japan, India, and Islam while also developing a study abroad program. I participated in both the study abroad semester in Salzburg, Austria, and a year-long student exchange with a university in Hong Kong, which meant living with, rather than just sampling, different customs, outlooks, and histories.

---

[1]Geoffrey Barraclough, *Main Trends in History* (New York: Holmes & Meier, 1979), p. 153.

More teachers and academic historians came to realize that the emphasis in U.S. education on the histories of the United States and western Europe, to the near exclusion of the rest of the world, was not sufficient for understanding the realities of the twentieth century nor is it today. For decades young Americans have been sent thousands of miles away to fight wars in countries, such as Vietnam, Afghanistan, Iraq, and Syria, that many Americans had never heard of. Newspapers and television reported developments in places such as Japan and Pakistan, Egypt and Congo, Cuba and Brazil, which had increasing relevance for Americans. Over the past sixty years graduate programs and scholarship directed toward Asian, African, Middle Eastern, Latin American, Pacific Island, and eastern European and Russian history also grew out of the awareness of a widening world, broadening conceptions of history. I attended one of the new programs in Asian Studies for my MA degree, and then the first PhD program in world history. Thanks to that program, I encountered the stimulating work of pioneering world historians from North America such as Philip Curtin, Marshall Hodgson, William McNeill, and Leften S. Stavrianos. My own approach, developed as I taught undergraduate world history courses beginning in 1969, owes much to the global vision they offered.

To bring some coherence to the emerging world history field as well as to promote a global approach at all levels of education, several dozen of us teaching at the university, college, community college, and secondary school levels in the United States and Canada came together in the early 1980s to form the World History Association (WHA), for which I served as founding secretary and later as a member of the Executive Council. The organization grew rapidly, encouraging the teaching, studying, and writing of world history not only in the United States but all over the world. The approaches to world history found among active WHA members vary widely, and my engagement in the ongoing discussions at conferences and in essays, often about the merits of varied textbooks and teaching methods, provided an excellent background for writing this text.

The Aims and Approach of the Text

Societies, Networks, and Transitions: A Global History provides an accessible, thought-provoking guide to students in their exploration of the landscape of the past, helping them to think about it in all its social and cultural diversity and interconnectedness and to see their lives with fresh understanding. It does this by combining clear writing, special learning features, current scholarship, and a comprehensive, global approach that does not omit the role and richness of particular regions.

There is a method behind these aims. For fifty years I have written about and taught Asian, African, and world history at universities in the United States and, as a visiting professor, Malaysia. A cumulative seven years of study, research, teaching, or travel in Southeast Asia, East Asia, East Africa, and Europe gave me insights into a wide variety of cultures and historical perspectives. Finally, the WHA, its publications and conferences, various academic and teaching-oriented journals devoted to world history, and the electronic listserv H-WORLD have

provided active forums for vigorously discussing how best to think about and teach world history.

The most effective approach to presenting world history in a text for undergraduate and advanced high school students, I have concluded, is one that combines the themes of connections and cultures. World history is very much about connections that transcend countries, cultures, and regions, and a text should discuss, for example, major long-distance trade networks such as the Silk Road, the spread of religions, maritime exploration, world wars, globalization, and transregional empires such as the Persian, Mongol, and British Empires. These connections are part of the broader global picture. Students need to understand that cultures, however unique, did not emerge and operate in a vacuum but faced similar challenges, shared many common experiences, and influenced each other.

The broader picture is drawn by means of several features in the text. To strengthen the presentation of the global overview, the text uses a short but innovative essay feature titled "Societies, Networks, and Transitions." Appearing at the beginning of each of the six chronological parts, this feature analyzes and synthesizes some of the wider trends of the era, such as the role of long-distance trade, human migrations, the spread of technologies and religions, gender relations and experiences, and global climate change. The objective is to introduce and amplify the wider transregional messages developed in the part chapters and help students to think about the global context in which societies are enmeshed. The essays also make comparisons, for example, between the Han Chinese, Mauryan Indian, and Roman Empires, and between Chinese, Indian, and European emigration in the nineteenth century. These comparisons help to throw further light on diverse cultures and the differences and similarities between them during the era covered. Finally, each essay is meant to show how the transitions that characterize the era lead up to the era discussed in the following part. Furthermore, six chapters largely concentrate on global or transregional rather than regional developments.

However, while a broad global overview is a strongly developed feature of this text, most chapters, while acknowledging, highlighting, and explaining relevant linkages, focus on a particular region or several regions. Most students learn easiest by focusing on one region or culture at a time. Students also benefit from recognizing the cultural richness and intellectual creativity of specific societies. From this text students learn, for instance, about Chinese poetry, Indonesian music, Arab science, Greek philosophy, West African arts, Polynesian outrigger sailing, Indian cinema, Latin American economies, French painting, Mayan city life, and Anglo-American political thought. As a component of this cultural richness, this text also devotes considerable attention to the enduring religious traditions, such as Buddhism, Christianity, Hinduism, Judaism, and Islam; issues of gender; and popular culture such as music. The cultural richness of a region and its distinctive social patterns can get lost in an approach that minimizes regional coverage. Today most people are still mostly concerned with events in their own countries, even as their lives are reshaped by transnational economies and global cultural movements.

Also a strong part of the presentation of world history in this text is its attempt to be comprehensive and inclusive. To enhance comprehensiveness, the text balances social, economic, political, and cultural and religious history, and it also devotes some attention to geographical, environmental, and climate contexts as well as to the history of ideas and technologies. At the same time, the text highlights features within societies, such as economic production, technological innovations, and portable ideas, that had widespread or enduring influence. To ensure inclusiveness, the text recognizes the contributions of many societies, including some often neglected, such as sub-Saharan Africa, pre-Columbian America, Southeast Asia, and Oceania. In particular, this text offers strong coverage of the diverse Asian societies. Throughout history, as today, the great majority of the world's population has lived in Asia.

Organizing the Text

All textbook authors struggle with how to organize the material. To keep the number of chapters corresponding to the twenty-eight or thirty weeks of most academic calendars in North America, and roughly equal in length, I have often had to combine several regions into a single chapter to be comprehensive, sometimes making decisions for conveniences sake. For example, unlike texts that may have only one chapter on sub-Saharan Africa covering the centuries from ancient times to 1500 CE, this text discusses sub-Saharan Africa in each of the six chronological eras, devoting three chapters to the centuries prior to 1500 CE and three to the years since 1450 CE. But this sometimes necessitated grouping Africa, depending on the era, with Europe, the Middle East, or the Americas. Unlike texts that may, for example, have material on Tang-dynasty China scattered through several chapters, making it harder for students to gain a cohesive view of that society, I want to convey a comprehensive perspective of major societies such as Tang and Song China. The material is divided into parts defined as distinct eras (such as the Classical and the Early Modern) so that students can understand how all regions were part of world history from earliest times. I believe that a broadly chronological structure aids students in grasping the changes over time while helping to organize the material.

Distinguishing Features

Several features of *Societies, Networks, Transitions: A Global History* will help students better understand, assimilate, and appreciate the material they are about to encounter. Those unique to this text include the following.

Introducing World History World History may be the first and possibly the only history course many undergraduates will take in college. The text opens with a short essay that introduces students to the nature of history, the special challenges posed by studying world history, and why we need to study it.

Balancing Themes Three broad themes—uniqueness, interdependence, and change—have shaped the text. They are discussed throughout in terms of three related concepts—societies, networks, and transitions; they are also clearly identified in the text via the use of icons. These concepts, discussed in more detail in "Introducing World History," can be summarized as follows:

- **SOCIETIES** Influenced by environmental and geographical factors, people have formed and maintained societies defined by distinctive but often changing cultures, beliefs, social forms, institutions, and material traits.

- **NETWORKS** Over the centuries societies have generally been connected to other societies by growing networks forged by phenomena such as migration, long-distance trade, exploration, military expansion, colonization, the spread of ideas and technologies, and webs of communication. These growing networks modified individual societies, created regional systems, and eventually led to a global system.

- **TRANSITIONS** Each major historical era has been marked by one or more great transitions sparked by events or innovations, such as settled agriculture, Mongol imperialism, industrial revolution, or world war, that have had profound and enduring influences on many societies, gradually reshaping the world. At the same time, societies and regions have experienced transitions of regional rather than global scope that have generated new ways of thinking or doing things, such as the expansion of Islam into South Asia or the European colonization of East Africa and Mexico.

Through exposure to these three ideas integrated throughout the text, students learn of the rich cultural mosaic of the world. They are also introduced to its patterns of connections and unity as well as of continuity and change.

"Societies, Networks, and Transitions" Mini-Chapters A short, thematically organized feature at the beginning of each part assists the student in backing up from the stories of societies and regions to see the larger historical patterns of change and the wider links among distant peoples. This comparative analysis allows students to identify experiences and transitions common to several regions or the entire world and to reflect further on the text themes. Additionally, the feature provides an important overview of key developments in the subsequent set of chapters.

Debate the Historians Since one of the common misconceptions about history is that it is about the "dead" past, included at the end of each part is a brief account of a debate or controversy among historians over how an issue in each of the six eras should be interpreted and what it means to us today. For example, why are the major societies dominated by males, and has this always been true? Why and when did Europe begin its "great divergence" from China and other Asian societies? How do historians evaluate contemporary globalization and its future? Reappraisal is at the heart of history, and many historical questions are never completely answered. Yet most textbooks ignore this dimension of historical study; this text is innovative in including it. The Debate the Historians essays will help show students that historical facts are anything but dead; they live and change their meaning as new questions are asked by each new generation. This feature has enjoyed especially enthusiastic support from teachers and reviewers.

Meet the People It is impossible to recount the human story without using broad generalizations, but it is also difficult to understand that story without seeing historical events reflected in the lives of men and women, prominent but also ordinary people. Each chapter contains a Meet the People feature that focuses on the experiences or accomplishments of a woman or man, to convey the flavor of life of the period, to embellish the chapter narrative with interesting personalities, and to integrate gender into the historical account. These try to show how gender affected the individual, shaping her or his opportunities and involvement in society. Several focus questions ask the student to reflect on the profile. For instance, students will examine a historian in early China, look at the spread of Christianity as seen through the life of a pagan female philosopher in Egypt, learn why Vietnamese today still honor two women rebels who lived two millennia ago, follow a fourteenth-century Moroccan's travels around Afro-Eurasia, relive the experience of a female slave in colonial Brazil, be introduced to a famed Ottoman Turkish architect, learn about an English minstrel and activist coal miner, find out about a Noble Prize-winning Kenyan environmentalist, and envision modern Indian life through a sketch of a film star.

Special Coverage This text also treats often-neglected areas and subjects. For example:

- It gives attention to several regions with considerable historical importance but often marginalized or even omitted in many textbooks, including sub-Saharan Africa, Southeast Asia, Korea, Central Asia, pre-Columbian North America, ancient Mesoamerica and South America, the Caribbean, Polynesia, Australia, Canada, and the United States.

- It includes discussions of significant groups that have transcended regional boundaries, such as the Silk Road caravan travelers and traders, Mongol empire builders, Indian Ocean maritime traders, Viking explorers, Chinese and Indian migrants to faraway lands, and contemporary humanitarian organizations such as Amnesty International and Doctors Without Borders.

- It features extensive coverage of the roots, rise, reshaping, and enduring influence of the great religious and philosophical traditions.

- It blends strong coverage of gender, particularly the experiences of women, and of social history generally, into the larger narrative, an approach praised by many reviewers and teachers.

- It devotes the first chapter of the text to the roots of human history. After a brief introduction to the shaping of our planet, human evolution, and the spread of people around the world, the chapter examines the birth of agriculture, cities, and states, which set the stage for everything to come.

- It includes strong coverage of the world since 1945 right up to 2019, a focus of great interest to many students.

- It includes increasing attention to environmental and climate change issues in the past and today.

Discover Historical Voices Many texts incorporate excerpts from primary sources, but this text also keeps student needs in mind by using up-to-date translations and addressing a wide range of topics. Included are excerpts from important Buddhist, Hindu, Confucian, and Islamic works that helped shape great traditions. Readings such as a collection of Roman graffiti, a thirteenth-century description of a Chinese city, a report on an Aztec market, and a manifesto for modern Egyptian women reveal something of people's lives and concerns. Also offered are materials that shed light on the politics of the time, such as an African king's plea to end the slave trade, Karl Marx's *Communist Manifesto*, and a recent *Arab Human Development Report*. Four new primary source readings are included in this edition, including an introduction to China's "New Silk Road" Belt and Road Initiative and an overview of the Anthropocene concept. The wide selection of document excerpts is also designed to illustrate how historians work with original documents. Unlike most texts, chapters are also enlivened by brief but numerous excerpts of statements, writings, or songs from people of the era that are effectively interspersed in the chapter narrative so that students can better see the vantage points and opinions of the people then living.

Chapter Learning Aids

The carefully designed learning aids are meant to help faculty teach world history and students actively learn and appreciate it. A number of aids have been created, including some that distinguish this text from others in use.

Chapter-Opening Features A chapter outline shows the chapter contents at a glance. The outlines include *focus questions* for each section to prepare students for thinking about the main themes and topics of the chapter. We have also added a *thought question* that asks the student to relate the material in that section of the chapter to today and often to their own lives and experiences. Chapter text then opens with a quotation from a primary source pertinent to chapter topics. An interest-grabbing vignette or sketch then funnels students' attention toward the chapter themes they are about to explore.

Thematic Icons Every major section within each chapter is now identified by helpful thematic icons that let students know which of the main themes, societies, networks, or transitions are being discussed.

Timelines To help students grasp the overall chronological picture of the chapter, timelines highlight key dates and events for each of the major regions discussed in each chapter.

Special Boxed Features Each chapter contains a *Discover Historical Voices* drawn from a primary source, and a *Meet the People* highlighting a man or woman from that era. Questions are also placed at the end of the primary source readings and profiles to help students comprehend the material.

Maps and Other Visuals Maps, photos, chronologies, and tables are amply interspersed throughout the chapters, illustrating and unifying coverage and themes. Thought questions have also been added to images and maps to give students experience in analyzing these kinds of sources.

Section Summaries At the end of each major section within a chapter, a bulleted summary helps students to review the key topics.

Chapter Summary At the end of each chapter, a concise summary invites students to sum up the chapter content and review its major points.

Key Terms and Pronunciation Guides Important terms likely to be new to the student are boldfaced in the text and immediately defined. These key terms are also listed at the end of the chapter and then listed with their definitions at the end of the text. The pronunciation of foreign and other difficult terms is shown parenthetically where the terms are introduced to help students with the terminology.

New to This Edition

In developing this new edition, I have also benefited from the responses to the first three editions, including correspondence and conversations with instructors and students who used the text.

Incorporating many of their suggestions and preferences, each of the six Parts opens with the comparative "Societies, Networks, and Transitions" essays that provide students an overview of important themes in the coming set of chapters. The chapter structure is now streamlined by combining some materials and hence eliminating superfluous headings and subheadings.

In addition to all these changes, there has been considerable new scholarship since the third edition in all areas of world history, including in recent history, and I have tried to update the narrative to include some of the most important findings. Hence, all the chapters include new information. Paleontology, archaeology, and ancient history are lively fields of study that constantly produce new knowledge, making some of the material on these fields in earlier editions obsolete or outdated. The chapters in Part I include extensive updates on subjects such as human evolution, the spread of modern humans, the rise of agriculture, the emergence of states, early human migration to and settlement in the Americas, and ancient migrations into the Indian subcontinent. Parts II–V incorporate new material on such subjects as the maturation of Hinduism, Austronesian migrations, precolonial Australian agriculture, pre-Columbian and postconquest Western Hemisphere societies, the role of pandemic diseases, environmental history, climate change throughout history, the overland and maritime Silk Roads, the "Silver Way" trans-Pacific trade, the trans-Atlantic slave trade,

Ottoman naval expansion, Native American revolts against colonialism, and the experiences of women and LGBTQ people in varied societies.

As most readers know, many important developments have occurred in the past decade, and hence the chapters in Part VI have required the most revision. Many events and processes have rapidly reshaped world politics, economies, and environments and hence of human life and international relationships. I have addressed some of the most critical, such as the rise of China and U.S.–China rivalry, the disruptive presidency of Donald Trump, trade wars, China under Xi Jinping, tensions in the South China Sea, China's Belt and Road Initiative, Russian policies and actions toward the Western nations, Brexit, right-wing populist nationalism (especially in Europe and the United States), anti-democratic movements and leaders, Narendra Modi and Hindu supremacy in India, the Saudi Arabia–Iran rivalry and its consequences, migration and refugee crises (such as the U.S.–Mexico border, Europe, and the Rohingya), growing challenges to the globalized world order, protests in many places (including Hong Kong and Iraq), local wars (such as Yemen and Ukraine), political changes in various countries (including Indonesia, South Africa, Brazil, Italy, India, and Zimbabwe), the experiences of feminists and women's rights movements around the world, the burning of tropical rain forests (especially in Brazil and Indonesia), and the effects of and dangers from global warming.

Ancillaries

A wide array of supplements accompanies this text to assist students with different learning needs and to help instructors master today's various classroom challenges.

Instructor Resources

MindTap™ for *Societies, Networks, and Transitions* is a flexible online learning platform that provides students with a relevant and engaging learning experience that builds their critical thinking skills and fosters their argumentation and analysis skills. Through a carefully designed chapter-based learning path, MindTap™ supports students as they develop historical understanding, improve their reading and writing skills, and practice critical thinking by making connections between ideas.

Students read sections of the eBook and take Check Your Understanding quizzes that test their reading comprehension and understanding of the chapter's content. They put critical thinking skills into practice to complete chapter tests that focus on important events and themes and include map- and primary-source-based questions. Students also use critical thinking skills to analyze textual and visual primary sources in each chapter through a chapter-opening, autograded image primary-source activity and a later manually graded short essay activity in which they write comparatively about primary sources. In some of the writing prompts, students use other writing formats beyond the essay (such as letters or memos) to imagine themselves as historical actors.

Beyond the chapter-level content, students can increase their comfort in analyzing primary sources through a set of twenty-six thematically organized, autograded primary-source activities that span the text and cover topics such as Westward Expansion, the Civil War, Reconstruction, the Atomic Bomb, the Cultural Cold War, and the Civil Rights Movement. They also practice synthesizing their knowledge and articulating what they have learned through responding to essay prompts that span broader themes in the book and ask them to engage with primary sources to defend their arguments.

MindTap™ also allows instructors to customize their content, providing tools that seamlessly integrate YouTube clips, outside websites, and personal content directly into the learning path. Instructors can assign additional primary-source content through the Instructor Resource Center, a database that houses hundreds of primary sources.

The additional content available in MindTap™ mirrors and complements the authors' narrative, but also includes primary-source content and assessments not found in the printed text. To learn more, ask your Cengage Learning sales representative to demo it for you—or go to www.cengage.com/mindtap.

Instructor's Companion Website The Instructor's Companion Website, accessed through the Instructor Resource Center (login.cengage.com), houses all of the supplemental materials you can use for your course. This includes a Test Bank, Instructor's Manual, and PowerPoint Lecture Presentations.

- **Test Bank** The Test Bank contains multiple-choice and true-or-false questions for each chapter and is available in **Cognero**® and within MindTap™. The Cognero® version includes essay questions. Cognero® is a flexible, online system that allows you to author, edit, and manage test bank content for *Societies, Networks, and Transitions*. With Cognero®, you can create multiple test versions instantly and deliver them through your LMS from your classroom, or wherever you may be, with no special installs or downloads required. The following format types are available for download from the Instructor Companion Site: Blackboard, Angel, Moodle, Canvas, and Desire2Learn. You can import these files directly into your LMS to edit, manage questions, and create tests.

- **PowerPoint Lectures** The PowerPoint Lectures have a new design intended to support instructor and student participation with key content coverage, images, maps, and figures from the text, new discussion questions, reflection questions, and "quick check" comprehension questions. Also available is a JPEG library of images and maps for each chapter. They are in an ADA-compliant, concise visual format suited for in-class presentations or for student review.

- **Instructor's Resource Manual** The Instructor's Resource Manual closely complements the new PowerPoint design and is focused on supporting instructors who are new to teaching or new to using *Societies, Networks, and Transitions*. It includes chapter summaries, suggested lecture topics, a listing of the in-book primary sources, discussion questions for the primary sources, and other resources for teaching a World History survey course.

Reader Program Cengage Learning publishes a number of readers, some containing exclusively primary sources, others a combination of primary and secondary sources, and some designed to guide students through the process of historical inquiry. Visit Cengage.com/history for a complete list of readers.

Custom Options Nobody knows your students like you, so why not give them a text that is tailor-fit to their needs? Cengage Learning offers custom solutions for your course—whether it's making a small modification to *Societies, Networks, and Transitions* to match your syllabus or combining multiple sources to create something truly unique. You can pick and choose chapters, include your own material, and add additional map exercises. Ensure that your students get the most out of their textbook dollar by giving them exactly what they need. Contact your Cengage Learning representative to explore custom solutions for your course.

Student Resources

Cengage Unlimited is the first-of-its-kind digital subscription that empowers students to learn more for less. One student subscription includes total access to every Cengage online textbook, platform, career and college success centers, and more—in one place. Learn across courses and disciplines with confidence that you won't pay more to access more. Available now in bookstores and online. Details at www.cengage.com/unlimited.

Formats

The text is available in a one-volume hardcover edition, a two-volume paperback edition, and as an interactive eBook. *Volume I: To 1500* includes Chapters 1–14; *Volume II: Since 1450* includes Chapters 15–31.

Acknowledgments

The author would like to thank the following community of instructors who, by sharing their teaching experiences and insightful feedback, helped shape the fourth edition and accompanying ancillary program:

Milan Andrejevich, Ivy Tech Community College
Maria Arbelaez, University of Nebraska–Omaha
Natalie Bayer, Drake University
Peter Boykin, Wayne County Community College
William Burns, George Washington University
David Burrow, University of South Dakota
Brent Carney, Eastern Gateway Community College
William Collins, Salem State University
Jeremy Cook, Northern Oklahoma College–Stillwater
P. Scott Corbett, Ventura College
John Dennehy, Massachusetts Maritime Academy
Ross Doughty, Ursinus College
Ashley Duane, Wayne County Community College
Sherrie Dux-Ideus, Central Community College–Hastings
Amy Forss, Metropolitan Community College
George Gastil, San Diego State University
Randee Goodstadt, Asheville-Buncombe Technical Community College
Aimee Harris-Johnson, El Paso Community College
Gregory Havrilcsak, University of Michigan–Flint
Michael Hinckley, Northern Kentucky University
Donna Hoffa, Wayne County Community College
Janet Jenkins, Arkansas Tech University
Kenneth Koons, Virginia Military Institute
Raymond Krohn, Boise State University
Elizabeth Littell-Lamb, University of Tampa
Chrissy Lutz, Fort Valley State University
Mary Lyons-Carmona, University of Nebraska–Omaha
John McCannon, Southern New Hampshire University
David K. McQuilkin, Bridgewater College
Kyriakos Nalmpantis, Kent State University
Jonathan O'Brien, Jamestown Community College
Victor Padilla, Wright College
Roger Pauly, University of Central Arkansas
Dave Price, Santa Fe College
Marsha Robinson, Miami University
Shelley Rose, Cleveland State University
Julie Smith, Mount Aloysius College
Michael Swope, Wayne County Community College
Kelly Thompson, Wayne County Community College
Ann Tschetter, University of Nebraska–Lincoln
Rhonda Westerhaus, Pratt Community College
James Williams, University of Indianapolis
Laura M. Wood, Tarrant County College
Bryan Wuthrich, Santa Fe College
Charles Young, Umpqua Community College

The author would also like to acknowledge the following instructors who lent their insight and guidance to the previous editions: Siamak Adhami, Saddleback Community College; Sanjam Ahluwalia, Northern Arizona University; David G. Atwill, Pennsylvania State University; Susan Autry, Central Piedmont Community College; Ewa K. Bacon, Lewis University; Brett Berliner, Morgan State University; Edward Bond, Alabama A&M University; Bradford C. Brown, Bradley University; Gayle K. Brunelle, California State University, Fullerton; Clea Bunch, University of Arkansas at Little Rock; Rainer Buschmann, California State University, Channel Islands; Jorge Canizares-Esguerra, State University of New York–Buffalo; Bruce A. Castleman, San Diego State University; Harold B. Cline, Jr., Middle Georgia College; Simon Cordery, Monmouth College; Steve Corso, Elwood-John Glenn High School; Dale Crandall-Bear, Solano Community College; Gregory Crider, Winthrop University; Cole Dawson, Warner Pacific College; Hilde De Weerdt, University of Tennessee, Knoxville; Anna Dronzek, University of Minnesota, Morris; Jodi Eastberg, Alverno College; James R. Evans, Southeastern Community College; Robert Fish, Japan Society of New York; Eve Fisher, South Dakota State University; Robert J. Flynn, Portland Community College; Gladys Frantz-Murphy, Regis University; Timothy Furnish, Georgia Perimeter College; James E. Genova, The Ohio State University; Deborah Gerish, Emporia State University; Rick Gianni, Purdue University Calumet; Kurt A. Gingrich, Radford University; Candace Gregory-Abbott, California State University, Sacramento; Paul L. Hanson, California Lutheran University; A. Katie Harris, Georgia State University; Timothy Hawkins, Indiana State University; Linda Wilke Heil, Central Community College; Mark Hoffman, Wayne County Community College District; Don Holsinger, Seattle Pacific University; Mary N. Hovanec, Cuyahoga Community College; Bram Hubbell, Friends Seminary; Jonathan Judaken, University of Memphis; Thomas E. Kaiser, University of Arkansas at Little Rock; Frances Kelleher, Grand Valley State University; Carol Keller, San Antonio College; Patricia A. Kennedy, Leeward Community College–University of Hawaii; Kim Klein, Shippensburg University; Rachel Layman, Lawrence North High School; Jonathan Lee, San Antonio College; Thomas Lide, San Diego State University; Derek S. Linton, Hobart and William Smith Colleges; David L. Longfellow, Baylor University; Christine Lovasz-Kaiser, University of Southern Indiana; John Lyons, Joliet Junior College; Mary Ann Mahony, Central Connecticut State University; Erik C. Maiershofer, Point Loma Nazarene University; Afshin Marashi, California State University, Sacramento; Laurence Marvin, Berry College; Robert B. McCormick, University of South Carolina Upstate; Patrick McDevitt, University at Buffalo SUNY; Doug T. McGetchin, Florida Atlantic University; Bill Mihalopoulos, Northern Michigan University; W. Jack Miller, Pennsylvania State University—Abington; Edwin Moise, Clemson University; Kerry Muhlestein, Brigham Young University–Hawaii; Aarti Nakra, Salt Lake Community College; Peter Ngwafu, Albany State University; Monique O'Connell, Wake Forest University; Melvin Page, East Tennessee State University; Annette Palmer, Morgan State University; Nicholas C. J. Pappas, Sam Houston State University; Craig Patton, Alabama A & M University; Patricia M. Pelley, Texas Tech University; William Pelz, Elgin Community College; John Pesda, Camden County College; Paul Philp, John Paul II HS/Eastfield Community College; Jason Ripper, Everett Community College; Pamela Roseman, Georgia Perimeter College; Paul Salstrom, St.

Mary-of-the-Woods; Sharlene Sayegh, California State University, Long Beach; Michael Seth, James Madison University; Rose Mary Sheldon, Virginia Military Institute; David Simonelli, Youngstown State University; Peter Von Sivers, University of Utah; Anthony J. Steinhoff, University of Tennessee–Chattanooga; Nancy L. Stockdale, University of Central Florida; Bill Strickland, East Grand Rapids High School; Robert Shannon Sumner, University of West Georgia; Kate Transchel, California State University, Chico; Sally N. Vaughn, University of Houston; Thomas G. Velek, Mississippi University for Women; Kurt Waters, Centreville High School; and Kenneth Wilburn, East Carolina University.

The author has incurred many intellectual debts in developing his expertise in world history, as well as in preparing this text. To begin with, I cannot find words to express my gratitude to the current editors and staff at Cengage Learning. In particular I want to thank Claire Branman, the Senior Content Manager and a patient, helpful editor indeed; Matt Kennedy, the in-house world history expert whose knowledge and suggestions greatly benefitted the project; Joseph Potvin, the Senior Project Manager for History, who helped jump start the project; Haley Gaudreau, the history team Product Assistant; and Phil Scott, Project Manager for SPi Global, who all had enough faith in this project to tolerate my occasional confusion and sometimes grumpy responses to editorial decisions or some other crisis. I also owe an incalculable debt to my development editor on the first edition, Phil Herbst, who prodded and pampered and helped me write for a student, rather than scholarly, audience. Tonya Lobato adroitly supervised the second and third editions. I also owe much to Pam Gordon, whose interest and encouragement got the first edition started, and Nancy Blaine, who skillfully oversaw the writing and revising of the first two editions. Ken Wolf of Murray State University prepared the initial drafts of several of the early chapters in the first edition and in other ways gave me useful criticism and advice. I would also like to acknowledge the inspiring mentors who helped me at various stages of my academic preparation: Bill Goldman, who introduced me to world history at Pasadena High School in California; Charles Hobart and David Poston, University of Redlands professors who sparked my interest in Asia; George Wong, Bart Stoodley, and especially Andrew and Margaret Roy, my mentors at Chung Chi College in Hong Kong; Walter Vella, Robert Van Niel, and Daniel Kwok, who taught me Asian studies at Hawaii; and John Smail and Philip Curtin, under whom I studied comparative world history in the immensely exciting PhD program at Wisconsin. My various sojourns in East Asia, Southeast Asia, and East Africa allowed me to meet and learn from many inspiring and knowledgeable scholars. I also learned much from discussions with local scholars on visits to China, Spain, Morocco, Turkey, and Cuba. I have been greatly stimulated and influenced in my approach by the writings of many fine global historians, but I would single out Philip Curtin, Marshall Hodgson, L. S. Stavrianos, William McNeill, Fernand Braudel, Eric Hobsbawm, Immanuel Wallerstein, Wang Gungwu, and Peter Stearns. Curtin, Hobsbawm, and McNeill also gave me personal encouragement concerning my writing in the field, for which I am very grateful.

Colleagues at the various universities where I taught have been supportive of my explorations in world and comparative history. Most especially I acknowledge the friendship, support, and intellectual collaboration over three and a half decades of my colleagues in the interdisciplinary Social Change and Development Department at the University of Wisconsin–Green Bay (UWGB), especially Harvey Kaye, Lynn Walter, Larry Smith, Andy Kersten, Kim Nielsen, Andrew Austin, and the late Tony Galt, as well as members of the History faculty. I have also benefited immeasurably as a world historian from the visiting lecture series sponsored by UWGB's Center for History and Social Change, directed by Harvey Kaye, which over the years has brought in dozens of outstanding scholars. My students at UWGB and elsewhere have also taught me much.

I also thank my colleagues in the World History Association (WHA), who have generously shared their knowledge, encouraged my work, and otherwise provided an exceptional opportunity for learning and an exchange of ideas. I am proud to have helped establish this organization, which incorporates world history teachers at all levels of education and in many nations. Among many others, I want to express a special thank-you to longtime friends and colleagues in the WHA from whom I have learned so much and with whom I have shared many wonderful meals and conversations. Since the mid-1960s my colleagues in the Association of Asian Studies have also stimulated and expanded my thinking in many ways. I also credit the talented history teachers and academics whom I met during a half summer's grading and discussing Advanced Placement World History exams for giving me their insights, and the various colleagues who have posted interesting, provocative, and relevant material on H-World and H-Asia as well as on Facebook.

Finally, I need to acknowledge the loving support and intellectual contributions of my wife Kathy, who patiently for the many years of the project put up with my hectic work schedule and the ever-growing piles of research materials, books, and chapter drafts scattered around our cluttered family room and sometimes colonizing other space around the house. I dedicate this edition to our son Colin and late son Chris, who have always taken an interest in my writing and career, and to our grandsons Josh and Aaron, both budding historians in the making.

About the Author

Craig A. Lockard is Ben and Joyce Rosenberg Professor of History Emeritus in the Social Change and Development Department at the University of Wisconsin–Green Bay, where from 1975 to 2010 he taught courses on Asian, African, comparative, and world history. He has also taught at SUNY-Buffalo, SUNY-Stony Brook, and the University of Bridgeport, and twice served as a Fulbright-Hays professor at the University of Malaya in Malaysia. After undergraduate studies at the University of Redlands, during which he was able to spend a semester in Austria and a year as an exchange student at Chung Chi College in Hong Kong (now part of the Chinese University of Hong Kong), Dr. Lockard earned an MA in Asian Studies at the University of Hawaii and a PhD in Comparative World and Southeast Asian History at the University of Wisconsin–Madison. His published books, articles, essays, and reviews range over a wide spectrum of topics: world history; Southeast Asian history, politics, and society; Malaysian studies; Asian emigration and diasporas; the Vietnam War; and folk, popular, rock, and world music. Among his major books are *Southeast Asia in World History* (2009); *WORLD* (2009); *Chinese Society and Politics in Sarawak: Historical Essays* (2009); *Dance of Life: Popular Music and Politics in Modern Southeast Asia* (1998); and *From Kampung to City: A Social History of Kuching, Malaysia, 1820–1970* (1987). Dr. Lockard was also part of the task force that prepared revisions to the U.S. National Standards in World History (1996). He has served on various editorial advisory boards, including the *Journal of World History, World History Connected*, and *The History Teacher*, and as book review editor for the *Journal of Asian Studies* and the *World History Bulletin*. He was one of the founders of the World History Association, served as the organization's first secretary and several terms as a member of the Executive Council. Dr. Lockard was awarded the WHA's highest honor, the Pioneer of World History award, in 2017. He has lived and traveled widely in Asia, Africa, and Europe.

Note on Spelling and Usage

Transforming foreign words and names, especially those from non-European languages, into spellings usable for English-speaking readers presents a challenge. Sometimes, as with Chinese, Thai, and Malay/Indonesian, several Romanized spelling systems have developed. Generally, I have chosen user-friendly spellings that are widely used in other Western writings (such as *Aksum* for the classical Ethiopian state and *Ashoka* for the classical Indian king). For Chinese, I generally use the *pinyin* system developed in the People's Republic over the past few decades (such as *Qin* and *Qing* rather than the older *Chin* and *Ching* for these dynasties, and *Beijing* instead of *Peking*), but for a few terms and names (such as the twentieth-century political leaders *Sun Yat-sen* and *Chiang Kai-shek*) I have retained an older spelling more familiar to Western readers and easier to pronounce. The same strategy is used for some other terms or names from Afro-Asian societies, such as *Cairo* instead of *al-Cahira* (the Arabic name) for the Egyptian city. Since the 1940s some countries have changed the well-known and long-used names of cities and states, such as *Mumbai* (the current Indian usage) instead of *Bombay* for India's largest city, and *Myanmar* instead of *Burma*. I have used the older name before Part VI. In some cases I have favored a newer spelling widely used in a region and modern scholarship but not perhaps well known in the West. For example, in discussing Southeast Asia I follow contemporary scholarship and use *Melaka* instead of *Malacca* for the Malayan city and *Maluku* rather than *Moluccas* for the Indonesian islands. Sometimes experts differ in spellings. For example, some Africa specialists use *Gikuyu* and others *Kikuyu* for the Kenyan ethnic group. In this case I use one spelling throughout. To simplify things for the reader I have tried to avoid using diacritical marks within words. Sometimes their use is unavoidable, such as for the premodern Chinese city of *Chang'an*; the two syllables here are pronounced separately. I also follow the East Asian custom of rendering Chinese, Japanese, and Korean names with the surname (family name) first (e.g., *Mao Zedong, Tokugawa Ieyasu*). The reader is also referred to the opening essay, "Introducing World History," for explanations of the dating system used (such as the Common Era and the Intermediate Era) and geographical concepts (such as Eurasia for Europe and Asia and Oceania for Australia, New Zealand, and the Pacific islands).

> *"A journey of a thousand miles begins with the first step."*
>
> —Chinese Proverb

This introduction helps you take the important "first step" toward understanding the scope and challenge of studying world history, presenting the main concepts and themes of world history to serve as your guide, while providing a foretaste of the lively debates among historians as they try to make sense of the past, and how societies' contacts with one another, and the changes they often fostered, created the interconnected world we know today.

What Do Historians Do?

History, the study of the past, looks at all of human life, thought, and behavior. The job of the historian is to both describe *and* interpret the past. Most professional historians want to make sense of historical events. Two general concepts help in these efforts: continuity and change. The legal system in the United States, for example, is unlike any other in the world, but has also been shaped in part by both English and ancient Roman legal practices.

Historians face their greatest challenges in interpreting the past. Although most strive to support their generalizations with evidence, they often disagree on how an event should be interpreted, sometimes because of political differences. In 1992 a widely publicized debate marked the 500-year anniversary of the first cross-Atlantic voyage of Christopher Columbus to the Western Hemisphere in 1492. Some historians pictured Columbus as a farsighted pioneer who made possible communication between the hemispheres, while others saw him as an immoral villain who began a pattern of exploiting and killing Native American peoples by Europeans. Similar debates raged about whether it was necessary for the United States to drop atomic bombs on Japan in 1945, killing thousands of Japanese civilians but also ending World War II. Indeed, many nations struggle with coming to terms with their history, its glories and failures. Today political leaders, scholars, and average citizens in countries like India, China, the Netherlands, Portugal, Australia, Ethiopia, South Africa, Bolivia, Canada, and the United States argue over historical events and developments that happened decades, hundreds, or even sometimes thousands of years ago. Some Europeans debate, sometimes bitterly, over how to assess the colonialism they once imposed on societies in Asia, Africa, and the Americas.

Our understanding of the past often changes as historians both acquire new information and use old information to answer new questions. Only within the past seventy years, for example, have historians studied the diaries and journals that reveal the important role of women during the American Civil War and the American Revolution against the British. Recently some historians used long neglected sources to conclude that, a millennium ago, China had the world's most dynamic economy and sophisticated technology. Similarly, historians have now discovered thousands of old books written in African languages, forcing a rethinking of literacy and scholarship in West African societies hundreds of years ago. Archaeological discoveries have now given us a better appreciation of the sophistication of various pre-Columbian American societies as well as of indigenous Aboriginal Australians..

What history "tells us" is constantly evolving. New evidence, changing interests, and the asking of new questions all add up to seeing things in a new light. No text contains the whole or final truth. **Historical revision**, or changing understanding of the past, and the difficulties of interpretation also make history controversial. In recent years heated debates about what schools should teach about history have erupted in many countries, including Japan, India, France, Egypt, Malaysia, Belgium, Britain, South Africa, and the United States.

Historians bridge the gap between the humanities and social sciences. As humanists, historians study the philosophies, religions, literatures, and arts that people generated over the ages. As social scientists, historians examine political, social, cultural, and economic patterns, though frequently asking questions different from those asked by anthropologists, economists, political scientists, and sociologists, who are generally more concerned with the present and theoretical questions. In the past several decades environmental history has become better understood and historians, including those of us who write about the world as a whole, need to pay attention to how humans affect the land, waters, plants, animals, and climate and how these in turn shape our lives. Historians also study people in their many roles and stations in life, the accomplishments of the rich and famous, as well as the struggles and dreams of common women and men.

Why Study World History?

World or global history, the broadest field of history, studies the human record as a whole and the experiences of people in all the world's inhabited regions—Africa, the Americas, Asia, Europe, and the Pacific, Atlantic, and Indian Ocean basins— and also helps us better understand individual societies by making it easier to look at them comparatively. Studying history on a global scale also brings out patterns of life, cultural traditions, and connections between societies that go beyond a particular region, such as the spread of Buddhism, which followed the trade routes throughout southern and eastern Asia. World history helps us comprehend both the "forest" ("big picture") and the "trees" (individual societies), allowing us to situate ourselves in a broader context.

This enhances our ability to understand our increasingly connected world. Decisions made in Washington, D.C., Paris, or Beijing influence citizens in Argentina, Senegal, and Malaysia, just as events elsewhere often affect the lives of people in Europe and North America. World historians use the widest angle of vision to comprehend how diverse local traditions and international trends intermingle. Western phenomena such as McDonald's, Hard Rock Cafes, French wines, Hollywood films, churches, the Internet, cell phones, and text messaging have spread around the world but so have "non-Western" products and ideas, among them Mexican soap operas, Chinese food, Japanese cars, Indonesian arts, African rhythms, and the Islamic religion. We must remember that, for all their idiosyncrasies, each society develops in a wider world.

A global perspective also highlights the past achievements of but also some of the challenges that have faced all peoples. The history of science, for example, shows that key inventions—among others printing, sternpost rudders, the compass, the wheelbarrow, gunpowder—originated in China, and the modern system of numbering came from India, reaching Europe from the Middle East as "Arabic" numerals. Indeed, various peoples—Mesopotamians, Egyptians, Greeks, Romans, Chinese, Indians, Arabs—built the early foundation for modern science and technology; their discoveries moved along the trade routes. Importers of technology and ideas often modified or improved on them. For example, Europeans made good use of Chinese, Indian, and Arab technologies, as well as their own inventions, in their quest to explore the world in the fifteenth and sixteenth centuries. The interdependence among and exchanges between peoples is a historical as well as a present reality. Furthermore, over the millennia various societies have encountered some of the same or similar challenges, such as climate change, food scarcity, epidemic diseases, invaders, and catastrophic wars. Learning how they dealt with these and perhaps overcame or adjusted to them can provide examples for us as we contend with the turmoil of today's world.

The World History Challenge

When we study world history, we examine other countries and peoples, past and present, with which we may be unfamiliar. World history helps us to recognize how some of the attitudes we absorb from the particular society and era we live in shape, and may distort, our understanding of the world and of history. Coming to terms with this mental baggage means examining such things as maps and geographical concepts and acquiring intellectual tools for comprehending other cultures.

Broadening the Scope of Our Histories

During much of the twentieth century and even in some places today, many high school and college students in North America were taught some version of a course, usually called Western Civilization, that emphasized the rise of western Europe and the European contributions to modern North American societies. This course recognized the undeniably influential role of Western nations, technologies, and ideas in the modern world, but also reflected more available data and research on Europe and North America compared with the rest of the world. This approach often exaggerated the role that Europe played in world history before modern times, pushing Asian, African,

and Native American peoples and their accomplishments into the background while underplaying the contributions these peoples made to Europe. Students usually learned little about China, India, or Islamic societies, and even less about Africa, Southeast Asia, or pre-Columbian and Latin America.

In the 1960s history teaching began to change in North America. The political independence of most Asian, African, and Caribbean nations from the colonial empires imposed by several Western nations fostered a more sophisticated understanding of African, Asian, Latin American, Native American, and Pacific island history in North America and Europe, making it easier to write a history of the entire globe. As a result, world history courses, rare before the 1960s, became increasingly common in U.S. universities, colleges, and high schools by the late twentieth century and have proliferated in several other countries, such as Australia, Canada, South Africa, China, and the Netherlands.

Revising Maps and Geography

Maps not only tell us where places are; they also create a mental image of the world, revealing how peoples perceive themselves and others. For example, for several millennia Chinese maps portrayed China as the "Middle Kingdom," the center of the world surrounded by "barbarians," reflecting and deepening the Chinese sense of superiority over neighboring peoples. Similarly, twenty-five hundred years ago, Greek maps showed Greece at the center of the inhabited world known to them.

Even modern maps can be misleading. The Mercator projection (or spatial presentation) still used in many school maps and atlases in North America and elsewhere, is based on a sixteenth-century European model that, by picturing the world as a rectangle rather than an oval, distorts the relative size of landmasses, greatly exaggerating landmasses on the northern third including Europe, North America, and Greenland while diminishing the lands nearer the equator and in the Southern Hemisphere. Hence, Africa, India, Southeast Asia, China, and South America look much smaller than they actually are. In the United States, maps using a Mercator projection have often tellingly placed the Americas in the middle of the map, cutting Asia in half, suggesting that the United States, appearing larger than it actually is, plays the central role in the world. Some alternative maps give a more accurate view of relative size. For example, the oval-shaped Eckert projection uses an ellipse that shows a better balance of size and shape while minimizing distortion of continental areas. A comparison between the Mercator and Eckert world maps is shown below, on pp. xxxi-xxxii.

Concepts of geographical features and divisions, such as continents, the large landmasses on which most people live, also shape mental images. The classical Greeks used the terms *Europe, Africa,* and *Asia* in defining the world they knew twenty-five hundred years ago; later Europeans transformed these terms into the names for continents. For centuries Western peoples have considered Europe a continent, although Europe is not a separate landmass, and the physical barriers between it and Asia are not that significant. If towering mountain ranges and other geographical barriers mark off a continent, India (blocked off by truly formidable mountains), China, or Southeast Asia make better candidates than Europe. Seeing Asia as a single continent is also a problem, given its spectacular size and geographical diversity. Today world geographers and historians often consider Europe and Asia to constitute one huge continent, Eurasia, containing several subcontinental regions such as Europe, South Asia, and East Asia.

Popular terms such as *Near East, Middle East,* or *Far East* are also misleading. They were originally formulated by Europeans to describe regions in relationship to Europe. Much depends on the viewer's position; Australians, for example, often label nearby Southeast and East Asia as the "Near North." Few Western scholars of China or Japan today refer to the "Far East," preferring the more neutral term *East Asia.* This text considers the term *Near East,* long used for western Asia, as outdated, but it refers to Southwest Asia and North Africa, closely linked historically (especially after the rise of Islam fourteen hundred years ago), as the Middle East, since that term is more convenient than the alternatives. The text also sometimes uses the term *Oceania* to refer to Australia, New Zealand, and the Pacific islands.

Rethinking the Dating System

A critical feature of historical study is the dating of events. World history challenges us by making us aware that all dating systems are based on the assumptions of a particular culture. Many Asian peoples saw history as moving in great cycles of birth, maturation, and decay (sometimes involving millions of years), whereas Westerners saw history as moving in a straight line from past to future (as can be seen in the chronologies within each chapter). Calendars were often tied to myths about the world's creation or about a people's or country's origins. Hence, the classical Roman calendar was based on the founding of the city of Rome around twenty-seven hundred years ago.

The dating system used throughout the Western world today is based on the Gregorian Christian calendar, created by a sixteenth-century Roman Catholic pope, Gregory XIII. It uses the birth of Christianity's founder, Jesus of Nazareth, around two millennia ago as the turning point. Dates for events prior to the Christian era were identified as BC (before Christ); years in the Christian era were labeled AD (for the Latin *anno domini,* "in the year of the Lord"). Many history books published in Europe and North America still employ this system, which has spread around the world in recent centuries.

The notion of Christian and pre-Christian eras has no longer been satisfactory for studies of world history because it is rooted in the viewpoint of only one religious tradition, whereas there are many traditions in the world, usually with different calendars. Muslims, for example, who consider the revelations of the prophet Muhammad to be history's central event, begin their dating system with Muhammad's journey, within Arabia, from the city of Mecca to Medina in 622 AD. The Chinese chronological system divides history into cycles

stretching over twenty-four million years. The Chinese are now in the fifth millennium of the current cycle, which corresponds more accurately than does the Gregorian calendar to the beginning of the world's oldest cities and states, between five thousand and six thousand years ago. Many other alternative dating systems exist. Selecting one over the others constitutes favoritism for a particular society or cultural tradition.

Therefore, most world historians and many specialists in Asian and African history, and some in European, U.S., and Latin American history, have moved toward a more secular, or nonreligious, concept, the Common Era. This system still accepts as familiar, at least to Western readers, the dates used in the Western calendar, but it calls the period after the transition a "common" era, since many influential, dynamic societies existed two millennia ago throughout the world, not only in the Judeo-Christian Holy Land. Two millennia ago, the beginning of the Common Era, the Roman Empire was at its height, Chinese and Indian empires ruled large chunks of Asia, and many peoples in the Eastern Hemisphere were linked by trade and religion to a greater extent than ever before. Several African and American urban societies also flourished. Hence this period makes a useful and familiar benchmark. In the new system, events are dated as BCE (before the Common Era) and as CE (Common Era, which begins in year 1 of the Christian calendar). This change is an attempt at including all the world's people.

Rethinking the Division of History into Periods

To make world history more comprehensible, historians divide long periods of time into smaller segments, such as "the ancient world" or "modern history," each marked by certain key events or turning points, a system known as **periodization**. For example, scholars of European, Islamic, Chinese, Indonesian, or U.S. history generally agree among themselves on the major eras and turning points for the region or country they study, but world historians need a system that can encompass all parts of the world since most historic events did not affect all regions. For instance, developments that were key to eastern Eurasia, such as the spread of Buddhism, did not directly affect western Eurasia and Africa in these centuries; the Americas remained isolated from the Eastern Hemisphere until about five hundred years ago.

Given the need for an inclusive chronological pattern, this book divides history into periods, each notable for significant changes around the world:

1. **Ancient (100,000–600 BCE)** The Ancient Era, during which the foundations for world history were built, can be divided into two distinct periods. During the long centuries known as Prehistory (ca. 100,000–4000 BCE), peoples who made and used stone tools and lived in small groups, survived by hunting, gathering, and scavenging food. Eventually some of them in southwest Asia began simple farming and living in villages, launching the era

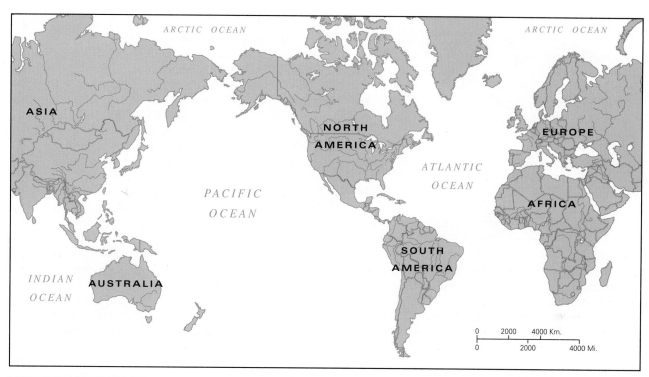

MERCATOR PROJECTION

of agrarian societies. Between 4000 and 600 BCE, agriculture became more productive, the first large cities and states were established in both hemispheres, and some societies invented writing, allowing historians to better study their experiences and ideas.

2. **Classical (600 BCE–600 CE)** The creation of more complex states and agrarian societies, the birth of major religions and philosophies, the formation of the first large empires, and the expansion of long-distance trade, which linked distant peoples, marked the Classical Era.

3. **Intermediate (600–1500 CE)** The Intermediate Era, comprising a long middle period or "Global Middle Ages" of expanding horizons that modified or displaced the classical societies, was characterized by increasing trade connections between distant peoples within the same hemisphere; the growth and spread of several older religions and of a new faith, Islam; and oceanic exploration by Asians and Europeans. Some world historians refer to these centuries as the Medieval or Post-Classical Era.

4. **Early Modern (1450–1750 CE)** During the Early Modern Era, the whole globe became intertwined as European exploration and conquests in the Americas, Africa, and southern Asia fostered the rise of a global economy, capitalism, and a trans-Atlantic slave trade while undermining American, African, and some other societies. China also built a large empire dominating much of East Asia.

5. **Modern (1750–1945 CE)** Rapid technological and economic change in Europe and North America, Western colonization of many Asian and African societies, large-scale migrations of Europeans and Asians to distant lands, political revolutions and ideologies, world wars, and a widening gap between rich and poor societies distinguished the Modern Era.

6. **Contemporary (1945–present)** In the Contemporary Era we see a more closely interlinked world, including the global spread of commercial markets, cultures, and communications; the collapse of Western colonial empires; international organizations; new technologies; struggles by poor nations to develop economically; environmental destruction; movements for and against globalization; and conflict between powerful nations.

Understanding Cultural and Historical Differences

The study of world history challenges us to understand peoples and ideas very different from our own. The past is, as one writer has put it, "a foreign country; they do things differently there."[1] As human behavior changes with the times, sometimes dramatically, so do people's beliefs, including moral and ethical standards. For example, in Asia centuries ago, Assyrians and Mongols sometimes killed everyone in cities that resisted their conquest. Some European Christians seven hundred years ago burned suspected heretics and witches at the stake and enjoyed watching blind beggars fight. Across the Atlantic, American peoples such as the Aztecs and Incas engaged in human sacrifice. None of these behaviors would be morally acceptable today in most societies.

---

[1]P. I. Harley, quoted in David Lowenthal, *The Past Is a Foreign Country* (Cambridge, UK: Cambridge University Press, 1985), xvi. The quote is on p. xxxi.

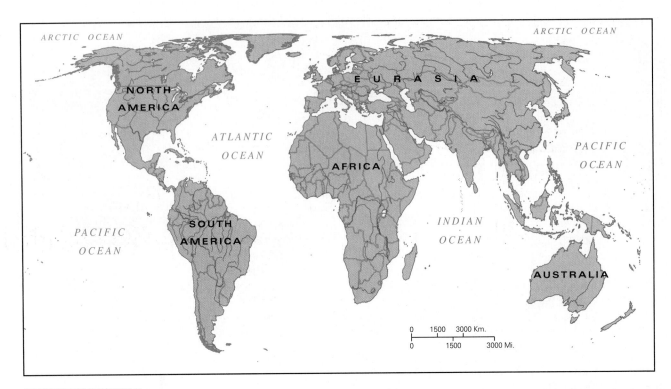

ECKERT PROJECTION

Differences in customs complicate efforts to understand people of earlier centuries. We need not approve of empire builders, plunderers, human sacrifice, and witch burning, but we should be careful about applying our current standards of behavior and thought to people who lived in different times and places and had different mindsets. We should avoid **ethnocentrism**, viewing others narrowly through the lens of one's own society and its values. Many historians perceive value-loaded words such as *primitive*, *barbarian*, *civilized*, or *progress* that carry negative or positive meanings as often matters of judgment rather than fact. For instance, soldiers on the battlefield may consider themselves civilized and their opponents barbarians. And progress, such as industrialization, often brings negative developments, such as pollution and greenhouse gases, along with the positive.

Today anthropologists use the term **cultural relativism** to remind us that, while all people have much in common, societies are diverse and unique, embodying different standards of proper behavior and thought. Hence, cultures may have very different ideas about children's obligations to their parents, what happens to people's souls when they die, or what constitutes pleasing music. We can still conclude that Mongol empire builders in Eurasia some eight hundred years ago were brutal; or that the mid-twentieth-century Nazi German dictator, Adolph Hitler, was a murderous tyrant; or that laws in some societies today that blame and penalize women who are raped are wrong. But cultural relativism discourages us from criticizing other cultures or ancient peoples just because they are or were different from us.

The Major Themes

This text uses certain themes to take maximum advantage of world history's power to illuminate both change and continuity as we move from the past to the present. Specifically, the author asked himself: What do educated students today need to know about world history to understand the globalizing era in which they live?

Three broad themes shaped around three concepts—societies, networks, and transitions—help you comprehend how today's world emerged.

1. **SOCIETIES** are broad groups of people that have common traditions, institutions, and organized patterns of relationships with each other. Societies, influenced by environmental factors, were defined by distinctive but often changing cultures, beliefs, social forms, governments, economies, and ways of life. In many cases they formed or became part of states.
2. **NETWORKS** are collections of links between different societies, such as the routes over which traders, goods, diplomats, armies, ideas, religions, and information travel. Over the centuries societies were increasingly connected to, and modified by, other societies, through growing networks forged by phenomena such as population movement, long-distance trade, exploration, military expansion, colonization, and the diffusion of ideas and technologies. Growing networks eventually fostered a global system in which distant peoples came into frequent contact.

3. **TRANSITIONS** are passages, changes, events, or movements that reshape societies and regions. Each major historical era was marked by one or more great transitions that were sparked by events or innovations that had profound, enduring influences on many societies and that gradually reshaped the world.

The first theme recognizes the importance in world history of the distinctiveness of societies. Cultural traditions and social patterns differed greatly. For example, around 2,000–2,500 years ago societies in Eurasia fostered several influential philosophical and religious traditions, including Confucianism in eastern Asia, Hinduism and Buddhism in South Asia, and Christianity, born in the Middle East and later nourished both there and in Europe. Historians often identify unique traditions in a society that go back hundreds or even thousands of years. Some historians apply the term *civilization* to larger, more complex societies such as ancient Egypt and China that left an extensive record of bureaucratic governments, monumental architecture, writings, and influential thought, but this is a controversial concept that neglects societies with less known histories. Since ancient times some peoples have seen themselves as "civilized" and criticized other societies as "barbarians." *Civilization* could also refer to any large grouping of people with a common history and traditions, such as the Arabs, Maya, or French. Thus the term is too subjective to have much value in understanding world history. It is not used in this text.

The second theme acknowledges the way societies have contacted and engaged with each other through networks to create the interdependent world we know today. The spread of technologies and ideas, exploration and colonization, and global trade across Eurasia and Africa and then into the Western Hemisphere spurred this interlinking process. Today networks such as the World Wide Web, airline routes, multinational corporations, and terrorist organizations operate on a global scale. The third theme helps to emphasize major developments that shaped world history. The most important transitions include, roughly in chronological order, the beginning of agriculture, the rise of cities and states, the birth and spread of philosophical and religious traditions, the forming of great empires, the linking of Eurasia by the Mongols, the European seafaring explorations and conquests, the Industrial Revolution, the forging and dismantling of Western colonial empires, world wars, and the invention of electronic technologies that allow for instantaneous communication around the world.

With these themes in mind, the text constructs the rich story of world history. The intellectual experience of studying world history is exciting and will give you a clearer understanding of how the world as you know it came to be.

PART I

Ancient Foundations of World History, to ca. 600 BCE

Most of us carry pictures in our minds of the world's ancient peoples and their ways of life: prehistoric cave dwellers huddling around a fire, wandering desert tribes, towering pyramids, and spectacular ruins of cities and temples. In fact, the centuries between 100,000 and 600 BCE saw the evolution of these and many other social and cultural phenomena, more complex and often more significant for us today than these mental pictures convey. These centuries also saw humans take the first steps in establishing regular contacts and exchanges, often those of trade, with one another, creating the networks that linked many societies over wide areas. World history is a record of human migrations, environmental adaptations, and social interactions over ever larger distances. People today live in the shadow of the ancient peoples who began farming, learned to work metals, and founded the first cities and states in Eurasia, Africa, and the Americas. These ancient centuries, and the transitions that marked them, constructed the foundations for much that came later, including organized societies and the growing networks that connected them. The ancient world is hotly debated and its meaning contested today. It is impossible to understand the modern world without studying the deep past.

With the first great transition in human history, the introduction of agriculture some 10,000 to 12,000 years ago, people began to deliberately cultivate plants and raise draft animals. In recent years the rise and benefits of this way of life have been the subject of often heated debate among scholars. Many now view the old notion of an Agricultural Revolution as misleading since the changes were often gradual as many people mixed both cultivation and foraging to survive. Some argue that the problems farming eventually created—such as more social inequality, hierarchy, congested cities, powerful and often oppressive states, population explosion, and soil depletion—often outweighed the benefits. Others think that this perspective romanticizes pre-farming communities as egalitarian, unspoiled utopias. Whatever the case, agriculture was the essential building block that stimulated other major developments, in particular the founding of cities and states and the invention of metalworking. We can thank early farmers in Eurasia and northern Africa for giving us valuable inventions such as pottery, cloth, and the plow. New developments then fostered other changes. For example, better means of transportation over land and sea allowed people, goods, foods, ideas, and diseases to travel longer distances in a shorter time. Bananas, first cultivated in New Guinea seven thousand years ago, eventually spread around the world, grown in many societies in both hemispheres. Expanded trade encouraged cities, and metal weapons and improved transportation allowed city rulers to build or expand states.

Transportation became the basis for networks of trade and cultural exchange linking distant societies. In turn, this wider sharing of ideas helped bring about further transformations in social and cultural patterns. Today, like the ancients, we still get our food mostly from intensive agriculture and livestock raising, work metals into useful products like tools, ride in wheeled vehicles and boats that allow us to travel over long distances, worship in religious buildings, and often live in cities, where people representing several classes and many occupations work and trade. These cities, like ancient cities, are mostly located in powerful states that are administered by bureaucratic governments and protected by military forces. The Ancient Era built the framework for much that came later.

Technological Foundations

⊂⊃ TRANSITIONS

We can credit the ancient peoples for inventing useful technologies such as metallurgy (metalworking) and for vastly improving transportation. Today we take these technologies for granted; indeed, they are basic to modern industrial life. In ancient times, however, people developed these technologies to help them solve particular problems. Once developed, they had many consequences and spurred many transitions. For example, metallurgy became a key to economic growth but also led to deforestation as forests were cut to make charcoal to fire the kilns. Bronze and, a few centuries later, iron aided agriculture, transportation, and communication (see Map I.1: Metals and Great States, ca. 1000 BCE).

The Copper and Bronze Ages

The first metal to be worked was copper. Stoneworkers discovered that heating copper reduced it to liquid form and allowed it to be shaped in a mold. As it cooled, it could be given a good cutting edge. Many peoples in both hemispheres made copper tools and weapons, and they traded copper widely.

Beginning around 3000 BCE in western Asia, metalworkers figured out how to mix copper with tin or arsenic to create bronze. This discovery launched the Bronze Age in the Eastern Hemisphere. The Sumerians were the first society known to use bronze in commerce. Between 2600 and 2000 BCE bronze technology was adopted or invented in northern Africa (Egypt and Nubia), eastern Europe, India, China, and Southeast Asia. In South America, some peoples made use of another copper-arsenic alloy, as well as silver and gold.

Bronze technology affected life. Easier to make and more durable than copper, bronze was well suited for tools, drinking vessels, and weapons. In Hebrew tradition, the formidable biblical Philistine warrior Goliath had a bronze helmet, bronze armor on his legs, and a bronze javelin. Since many regions lacked adequate tin deposits, bronze making probably spurred both trade networks and warfare. Armies were formed in part to protect or acquire mines, markets, and trade routes. Metalsmiths were so valuable that invading armies often carried them home in captivity. Finally, copper and bronze, as well as gold and silver, were used for the first coins, which gradually became the major medium of exchange.

The Iron Age

The making of iron provided the next technological break-through. Western Asia had little tin but large quantities of iron ore. Iron was much harder to work than copper: artisans needed to produce higher temperatures, and heating produced a spongy mass rather than a liquid. Eventually inventive workers, possibly in the Hittite kingdom along the Black Sea or in Palestine, discovered a completely new but laborious technology that involved repeatedly heating and hammering the iron and plunging the result into cold water.

The Iron Age began in western Asia and Egypt by around 1600 BCE. Between 900 and 500 BCE, iron technology was also adopted or invented in Greece, India, western and central Europe, Central Asia, China, Southeast Asia, and West and East Africa. Some peoples acquired iron through trade, and others through contact with ironworking peoples. Eurasians and Africans may have especially benefited from having iron-producing societies close enough to each other to regularly exchange ideas. In contrast, many thousands of miles, much of it rain forest or desert,

separated the societies of North and Mesoamerica from those in the Andes region, limiting contact. Since ironworking didn't originally develop in the Americas or Australia, these societies had no iron weapons or tools until centuries later.

Ironworking brought many advantages. The metal was cheaper to make than bronze and also more adaptable: with it people could produce better axes for cutting wood, plows for farming, wagon wheels for transport, and swords for warfare. For example, in Hebrew tradition, the Israelites could not drive the Canaanites out of the Palestinian lowland because they had iron chariots. Centuries later metalworkers learned how to add carbon to iron to make steel. But like many technologies, iron proved a mixed blessing. While it improved farming, it also made for deadlier weapons. Armies equipped with iron-tipped weapons enjoyed a strategic advantage over their neighbors. Although iron shields afforded some protection, more men may have died as warfare became more frequent.

The Rise of Cities and Population Growth

TRANSITIONS

Beginning around 3500 BCE the social and cultural forms common to hunters and gatherers began to change as more and more people settled down to farming and developed more organized societies. Gradually some farming villages became towns and then cities. Ancient cities represented a huge change in the way humans related to their environment. People had to adapt to densely populated neighborhoods full of often unfamiliar people who may have been newcomers as more migrated to cities from rural areas or other regions. A mix of different languages and customs offered possibilities for learning and expanding horizons but also suspicion and conflict. From the very beginning, ancient cities served a variety of functions. Some, like several Mesopotamian and South American cities, developed as centers for religious ceremonies. Cities in Egypt and China, by contrast, seem to have been founded chiefly as administrative centers to govern the surrounding territories. Many others, including those in India, Nubia (in Northeast Africa), and Mexico, formed around marketplaces. The shift from the relatively egalitarian ethos of hunting and gathering to a more hierarchical social organization changed people's lives. Because trade was a major city activity, merchants became prominent members of urban society, making products from near and far available in their shops and stalls. Increasingly people were divided into social classes, with the wealthier groups controlling the distribution and consumption of economic resources. The inequality between the rich and poor often became very wide.

Productive agriculture and urbanization fostered a dramatic increase in population around the world. The most densely populated ancient societies emerged where agriculture, aided by irrigation, flourished: in large river valleys, particularly the floodplains of the Nile in Egypt, the Tigris-Euphrates in Mesopotamia, the Indus in India, and the Yellow and Yangzi in China. Between 8000 and 500 BCE the world's population jumped from 5 or 10 million up to an estimated 100 million. The great majority of these people lived in Mesopotamia (the most densely populated area), Egypt,

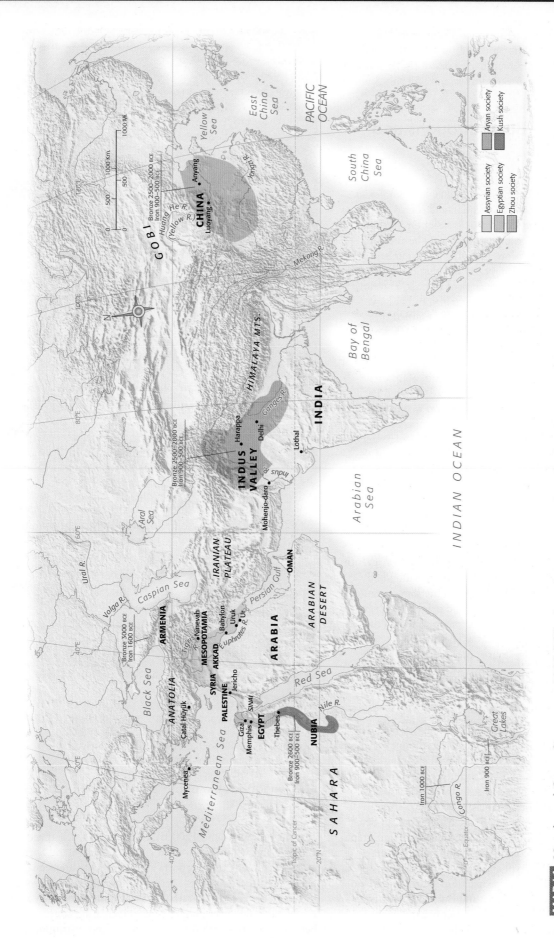

MAP I.1 **Metals and Great States, ca. 1000 BCE** The earliest states arose in river valleys—the Nile, Tigris-Euphrates, Indus, and Yellow—and these early states also worked metals, first bronze and then iron, to produce tools and weapons.

Q What does this map tell us about the spacing between the earliest states and the geographical features that encouraged or discouraged communication?

India, China, and southeastern Europe. People were also living longer than during the Stone Age, when a third died before age twenty and only a tenth lived past forty. Bronze Age peoples lived into their early forties, and probably 5 to 10 percent lived past sixty.

Transportation Breakthroughs and Human Mobility

NETWORKS

Metalworking was only one of several valuable technologies invented in ancient times. The invention and spread of wheeled vehicles and boats also made it easier for people to migrate or carry cargo over longer distances. The ancient era saw several great migrations involving large numbers of people over the centuries. Using carts and chariots, Indo-European peoples occupied large areas of Eurasia. Traveling by foot or in canoes, and also possessing iron technology, Bantu-speaking peoples from western Africa settled the forests and grasslands of the southern half of Africa. Boat sails had been invented in the Middle East by 5000 BCE, allowing wind to be harnessed to drive boats. Using seagoing boats, especially large outrigger canoes, peoples from Southeast Asia sailed to and settled most of the widely scattered Pacific islands. Increasingly better forms of transport made it easier for distant peoples to come into contact with one another and share their ways of life. Maritime trade networks, such as those linking Pacific islands with Southeast Asia and the eastern Mediterranean with northwest Europe, stretched over vast distances.

This increased travel inspired the first maps, drawn in Mesopotamia around 2300 BCE. These maps, carved onto small tablets and then baked, recognized distant relationships in portraying agricultural land, town plans, and the world as known to Babylonians. Such a map from the sixth or seventh century BCE reveals how trade and communication had expanded their horizons. The map shows the Babylonian world, including rivers, canals, cities, and neighboring states, in the center of a flat earth, with the remote lands on the fringe inhabited by legendary beasts. The mapmaker noted that his sketch showed the "four corners" of the earth.

Trade and Networks of Exchange

NETWORKS

Trade networks moving objects of value, from raw materials to luxury goods, linked major cities and even distant societies. Between 4000 and 3000 BCE traders began shipping minerals, precious stones, and other valued commodities over long distances. Goods traveled initially by riverboat and by donkey, horse caravans, or by llamas in South America. By 2000 BCE, however, sea trading in the Mediterranean Sea, Persian Gulf, and Indian Ocean had become more important. Mesopotamia became a commercial hub linking southern and Central Asia with Egypt and Italy. Its location allowed it to draw ideas, produce, and people from a huge hinterland. Similarly, Egypt connected Africa and Eurasia. The Persian Gulf has served as a contact zone for over five millennia, with various cities serving as major trade hubs.

DEA/A. DAGLI ORTI/De Agostini/Getty Images

IMAGE I.1 **Terra-Cotta Figure from Harappa** Terra-cotta figures like this one found in the ruins of Harappa show the diverse hairstyles and ornaments popular in the city. Archaeologists believe that these indicate the diversity of social classes and ethnic groups that inhabited Harappa.

Q What does the photo tell us about the lives of women in Harappa?

Beginning around 1200 BCE, the heavily urbanized Phoenicians, who lived in what is now Lebanon and Syria, established many trading ports around the Mediterranean, becoming the first known society to flourish mostly through interregional commerce rather than farming. Gradually trade routes expanded over long distances, increasing contacts between societies with different cultures and institutions.

Trade fostered other innovations. The need to guide ships or caravans to distant destinations, as well as the belief that the changing night skies could influence human activity (astrology), sparked the study of the stars. Babylonian astrological beliefs and the zodiac may have been spread by trade to western Asia and southern Europe, where they became popular. Today people in societies around the world consult astrology before making decisions. Growing trade also required the creation of currencies, without which our modern economic life would be impossible. Simple forms of money, mostly varied weights of precious metals like silver, were invented between 3000 and 2500 BCE in Mesopotamian cities. Legal codes were then written that specified fines, interest rates, and even the ideal price of some common goods. By 600 BCE the first gold coins were being struck in western Asia. Money made exchange easier, especially in cities, and it may have stimulated the development of mathematics as a tool for calculating wealth. Various ancient societies in both hemispheres developed some system of mathematics.

States, Political Hierarchies, and Warfare

TRANSITIONS

Closely related to urbanization and trade was the emergence of the first states, hierarchically organized political and bureaucratic structures that were governed by powerful elites and that often comprised many cities. States marked a major transition to more complex and organized societies. Kings and emperors, and occasionally queens, ruled, sometimes ruthlessly, over many rural peasants and city dwellers who paid taxes, in money or in agricultural products, in acknowledgment of the ruler's ability to keep order, promote justice, and protect his or her subjects from harm. According to ancient Hindu sacred writings: "Him do ye proclaim, O men as kings and father of kings, the lordly power, the suzerain of all creation…the slayer of foes, the guardian of the law."[1] Opposition to the rulers and their policies was viewed as treason and could mean death or imprisonment.

The first known states formed in Mesopotamia around 3500 BCE and in Egypt by 3000 BCE. Between 3000 and 1000 BCE states were also established in India, China, Vietnam, Nubia, and southeastern Europe, as well as in Mesoamerica and South America. Today we take for granted the notion of large political units to whom people owe allegiance, but in the ancient world they were major innovations. By 2350 BCE the first empires, formed by conquest, appeared in Mesopotamia. Among the consequences of states and empires was the rise of conflict between them as well as with nearby pastoral peoples, which resulted in increased warfare.

One of the chief tasks of the rulers was to protect and perhaps expand their state, and often rulers waged war to acquire land and people and thereby gain more resources and tax revenues. Warfare by settled peoples required a powerful state. To wage war, kings had to marshal resources such as food and metals as well as recruit soldiers. Rulers also had to discourage dissent and instill among the population a sense that warfare was worthwhile. Even today people remember the legends of great ancient warriors (real or mythical), such as Hercules at Troy. But soldiers experienced difficult lives. One Egyptian text reported that a soldier "is awakened when an hour has passed and he is driven like an ass. He works till the sun sets. He is hungry, his body is exhausted, he is dead while still alive. His body is broken with dysentery."[2]

Warfare became increasingly lethal as weaponry and strategy improved. When the powerful Assyrians, who built a great empire, swept through Mesopotamia in the ninth century BCE, their advanced cavalry and siege weaponry enabled them to level and burn the great city of Babylon. Later the Assyrians themselves experienced defeat, as their capital, Nineveh, fell to "the noise of the whip and of rattling wheels, galloping horses, clattering chariots!"[3] Even though many ancient cities were surrounded by defensive walls, they were still vulnerable to well-armed foes.

In Afro-Eurasia many wars matched states against pastoral nomads, who were attracted by the wealth of the farming societies and their cities. Often viewed by the farming peoples as pre-literate "barbarians," nomads made art, worked metals, possessed many horses or camels, and pioneered the

IMAGE I.2 **Fragments of Egyptian-Hittite Treaty** This carved stone fragment contains a treaty, signed around 1250 BCE, between Egypt and the Hittite kingdom in Anatolia that ended a war between the two states. The treaty is inscribed in the widely used cuneiform script of the Akkadian language. It eloquently demonstrates the reality of ancient warfare but also expresses the age-old quest for peace.

Q Can you speculate on what we might learn about these ancient societies if we could read the translation of the treaty?

[1]From the *Brahmanas*, quoted in F.R. Allchin, *The Archaeology of Historic South Asia: The Emergence of Cities and States* (New York: Cambridge University Press, 1995), 86–87.
[2]Quoted in Barbara Mertz, *Red Land, Black Land: Daily Life in Ancient Egypt*, rev. ed. (New York: Dodd, Mead and Company, 1978), 135–136.
[3]Nahum 3:2–3, *The Holy Bible*, New King James Version (Chicago: Thomas Nelson, 1983), 907.

development of chariot and cavalry warfare. Between 2000 and 1000 BCE nomadic peoples occasionally conquered cities and states. As an example of how warfare could spawn cultural transitions, many of these pastoralists eventually adopted some of the ways of the conquered farmers, while the urban peoples acquired the pastoralists' military technologies.

The costs of war, in treasure and people, also prompted rulers to make peace treaties with rival powers and inspired a Hebrew prophet to call for beating "their swords into ploughshares, their spears into pruning hooks; nation shall not lift up sword against nation."[4] The quest for peace was as old as the urge to wage war.

Institutionalized Religions

SOCIETIES

Institutionalized religions shaped the values and behavior of societies, just as they do most places today. While most pre-farming peoples were polytheists or animists, believing in many gods or spirits, a few, such as the Hebrews and some African societies, were monotheists, believing in one high god who presided over the universe. The rise of agriculture and then cities gradually transformed for many people the belief that nature was alive with spiritual forces to more systematic theologies and organized religious observances. These beliefs and practices gave order and meaning to people's lives and may have promoted cooperation and a sense of community. Ideas about the fate of individual humans after death as well as notions of right and wrong differed widely as societies developed unique traditions and beliefs.

Religious views spread from one society to another, at first orally, through myths or stories about the interaction of gods with the human world. These myths explained the birth of the universe, the progression of seasons, the uncertainties of agriculture, the flooding of rivers, and human dramas such as battlefield losses and victories. Religious views and myths were later captured in sacred books, and several thousand years later many millions of people still revere some of these books, such as the Hebrew Bible and the Hindu Vedas. Oral traditions and sacred texts helped Egyptian and Mesopotamian ideas, such as an afterlife, Day of Judgment, and Garden of Eden, to become influential around the Mediterranean Basin and western Asia.

Full-time religious specialists often replaced the shamans, the part-time spiritual leaders associated with earlier times. With the rise of agriculture and larger communities, a priestly class was seen as able to communicate with the gods and interpret their will. Because they provided essential services such as writing or calculating the time of the annual floods and staffing temples serving thousands of believers, priests were the first social group to be freed from direct subsistence labor.

Institutionalized religions influenced societies. Since religious ceremonies and ideas provided supernatural sanction for the social and political order, they became a powerful force for social control. Challenging the political or social system, which was seen as divinely inspired, now constituted blasphemy and condemned one to eternal punishment after death. Most of the ancient religions, led by men and worshipping chiefly male gods, supported patriarchal attitudes.

Writing and Its Consequences

SOCIETIES

Writing, which allowed for recordkeeping and improved communication, was one of the most crucial cultural innovations. It first arose in Mesopotamia around 3300 to 3400 BCE, rapidly spread to nearby western Asians, and later developed in many societies around the world, with a wide variety of scripts. Although limited to a relatively small group of people for much of history, writing was a critical invention of several early societies that increased occupational specialization, including the emergence of clerks, scribes, bureaucrats, and eventually teachers, scholars, and historians. Initially developed chiefly to keep commercial accounts, codify legends and rituals, or record political proclamations, writing later gave birth to literature, historiography, sacred texts, and other forms of learning and culture that could now be transmitted and expanded. Hence the Sumerian epic of Gilgamesh influenced both the Hebrew book of Genesis and the stories of the Greek bard Homer many centuries later. Rulers used writing to communicate over long distances with district governors and foreign leaders, and merchants used it to make arrangements with merchants in other cities, enhancing the role of communication networks.

Writing, however, had contradictory consequences. On the one hand, it clearly stimulated creativity and intellectual growth while allowing for a spread of knowledge. But writing often became a tool for preserving the social and political order, especially when literacy was restricted to a privileged elite such as bureaucrats, lawyers, or priests. For example, a soldier in ancient China complained that he and his colleagues wanted to return home, but they "were in awe of the [official] orders in the tablets."[5] Sacred literature was also frequently closed to debate, since it supposedly came from the gods.

Social Inequality, Patriarchy, and Social Life

SOCIETIES

With less equality but more people, the potential for social conflict increased. Most farming-based communities included haves and have-nots, landlords and landless, free citizens and slaves. The gap between rich and poor made crime a serious problem. Theft was common in major Mesopotamian and Egyptian cities and was addressed through harsh law codes. In societies with large enslaved populations, which included debtors and prisoners of war, revolt was a possibility. Although more pervasive in Mesopotamia than in China, Egypt, and India, slaveholding was common in all ancient agricultural societies.

Patriarchy was another source of inequality and remains a feature of life today. To protect their own privileged position and power monopoly in society, men increasingly

---

[4]Isaiah 2:4, *Holy Bible*, 683.
[5]Quoted in Herlee Glessner Creel, *The Birth of China: A Survey of the Formative Period of Chinese Civilization* (New York: Frederick Unger, 1961), 256.

sleepingpanda/Shutterstock.com

IMAGE I.3 **Bells of Marquis Yi of Zeng** Music had a key function in the court life of Zhou-dynasty China. This sixty-four-piece, two-toned bell set was found in the tomb of a regional ruler, Marquis Yi of Zeng, which also contained many flutes, drums, zithers, pan pipes, and chimes. Five men using mallets and poles were needed to play this set of bells.

Q On what kinds of occasions do you think this bell set might have been played?

believed that women were unsuited to run governments or families, and few women were allowed to do so. Social changes that required heavy physical labor in farming, warfare, and long-distance trade influenced gender and family relations. Women became known as the "weaker sex" and were often assigned chiefly domestic tasks. An ancient Chinese saying asserted that "men plow and women weave."[6] Although women continued to produce some of the pottery and most of the cloth, and some helped in family gardens and care of farm animals, they were no longer equal contributors to food needs because they now spent more time at home. In farming families, women were also encouraged to bear a larger number of children to help in the fields. In many places, men, especially rulers and the rich, had multiple wives or took concubines. Sexual options became more limited for women because men wanted to ensure that their personal wealth could be passed on to children of known paternity. For much of history the creation of new life seemed to be a mystical power that females possessed. Such terms as "Mother Nature" and "Mother Earth" are survivors from that understanding.

Most urban women led busy lives. As households began to stir each morning, they may have prepared a quick meal for husbands and sons heading out to their work, perhaps as artisans, peddlers, soldiers, or laborers. Many used pots and pans made of copper or bronze to cook and serve the food. After cleaning up the meal, many women walked through dusty streets to market stalls to buy food grown on nearby farms. As they returned home,

they may have passed children playing in the narrow alleys, perhaps watched by grandparents. In some societies, the wealthier women were increasingly restricted inside walled courtyards. The poorest women and men begged, searched through trash, or offered their services to those who were better off.

Despite the social inequality and long hours of toil, leisure activities developed that are familiar to us today. For example, the Sumerian city dwellers in Mesopotamia enjoyed dancing and music and invented beautiful, elaborate harps and lyres for their pleasure. Chinese music lovers preferred flutes and drums, and Egyptians favored metal horns. Music was used for worship, festivals, and work, but the oldest known love songs had also appeared by 2300 BCE in Egypt. Wrestling became a popular sport in many cultures.

Alcoholic drinks like beer and wine were also common, often consumed in public taverns. In many societies drinking became an integral part of leisure and social relationships. The literary figure Homer summed up the pleasures favored in early Greece: "The things in which we take a perennial delight are the feast, the lyre [a musical instrument], the dance, clean linen in plenty, a hot bath and our beds."[7] These are pleasures that most modern people share, indicating that some things have not changed much in three thousand years.

---

[6]Quoted in Merry Wiesner-Hanks, *Gender in History* (Malden, MA: Blackwell, 2001), 61.
[7]From Homer's *The Odyssey*, quoted in Rodney Castledon, *Minoans: Life in Bronze Age Crete* (New York: Routledge, 1993), 9.

The Origins of Human Societies, to ca. 2000 BCE

It takes a long time to build a mountain.

—Malay proverb

IMAGE 1.1 Tassili Archers Thousands of ancient paintings on rock surfaces and cave walls record the activities of African hunters, gatherers, and pastoralists. This painting of archers on a hunt was made in a rock shelter on the Tassili plateau of what is today Algeria, probably long before the Sahara region had dried up and become a harsh desert.

Q What does the rock painting show us about some of the animals these people had possessed or hunted?

The human story was already very old when, at Abu Hureyra (**AH-boo hoo-RAY-rah**) in the Euphrates (**you-FRAY-teez**) River Valley of what is now Syria, a group of villagers became some of the world's first farmers, thus taking a large step in shaping world history. People who hunted game and gathered vegetables and nuts occupied Abu Hureyra 13,000 years ago, when the area was wetter and blessed with many edible wild plants and herds of Persian gazelles. But a long cold spell brought a drought; to survive, the Abu Hureyra villagers began cultivating the most easily grown grains and later raised domesticated sheep and goats. By 7600 BCE they had shifted completely to farming and animal herding.

The Abu Hureyra farmers pursued a life familiar to rural folk for millennia afterward and even similar to many places today. A village was composed of several hundred people crowded into narrow lanes and courtyards, with families dwelling in multiroom mud houses with plaster floors. At night family members studied the sky and pondered the mysteries of the universe. Men did much of the farm work while women carried heavy loads on their heads, prepared meals, and ground grain in a kneeling position—activities that were hard on arms, knees, and toes. Work for both women and men called for muscle power and strong arms, and many villagers suffered from arthritis and lower back injuries. Abu Hureyra was abandoned in 5000 BCE.

Prehistory includes a vast span of time during which all living creatures appeared and developed. Humans evolved physically, mentally, and culturally over many millennia, learning to make simple tools and then spreading throughout the world. Later most societies, like the Abu Hureyra villagers, made the first great historical transition from hunting and gathering to farming and animal herding, profoundly changing the relationship between people and the environment. The rise of agriculture all over the world made possible the emergence of larger societies with cities, states, and more advanced technologies, which in turn stimulated long-distance trade and the rise of social, cultural, and economic networks linking distant societies. The ancient farmers, traders, and city folk laid the bedrock for the world we live in today.

1-1 Prehistory: The Cosmos, Earth, and the Roots of Humanity

⚟ TRANSITIONS

Ⓠ According to most scientists, what were the various stages of human evolution?

Some scholars have promoted a "big history" that places the development of human societies and networks in a much longer and more comprehensive framework. They argue that we cannot comprehend the rise of complex societies without knowledge of pre-farming peoples, human ancestors, and, before that, the beginning of life on Earth and the formation of our planet within the larger cosmic order. Recurring patterns of balance and imbalance and of order and disorder in the natural world, such as global warming and cooling, have always played a role in human history. People have speculated about the origins of the cosmos, Earth, life, and humanity for countless generations. Over the years their views have been integrated into religions.

> **CONNECTION to TODAY**
>
> How do you think that early speculations about the cosmos and the world might have influenced the beliefs of people in modern times?

1-1a Perceptions of Cosmic Mysteries

Human development on Earth constitutes only a tiny fraction of the long history of the universe, which most astronomers think began in a Big Bang explosion some 13.7 billion years ago. As the universe expanded, matter coalesced into stars, which formed into billions of galaxies. Our solar system emerged about 4.5 billion years ago out of clouds of gas. On earth the developing atmosphere kept the surface warm enough for organic compounds to coalesce into life forms. This is the story presented by modern science.

Over the centuries most human societies, to explain their existence, crafted creation and origin stories and cosmologies explaining the natural and supernatural worlds. While varying greatly, these explanations usually involved myths or legends of some divine creator or creators. The earliest known creation story developed by a farming-based society, from Mesopotamia, claimed that heaven and Earth were formed as one in a primeval sea and were separated by the gods, powerful human-like beings unperceivable to mortals. Mesopotamian beliefs influenced the seven-day creation story in the Hebrew book of Genesis.

Many cosmological traditions, however, were very different. Ancient Hindu holy books describe a universe emerging out of nothingness: "There was neither nonexistence or existence then…neither the realm of space nor the sky which is beyond. Darkness was hidden by darkness…emptiness."[1] Then a great heat formed the cosmos and generated life. The Chinese believed that the universe was created out of chaos and darkness when the creator Pan Ku fashioned the sun, moon, and stars to put everything in proper order, producing a unifying force in the universe, the "way," or dao (**DOW**). A related Chinese theory, *fengshui* (**fung-SHWAY**), suggests that the earth itself contains natural forces that people must

[1]From the *Rig Veda*, quoted in Carolyn Brown Heinz, *Asian Cultural Traditions* (Prospect Heights, IL: Waveland, 1999), 132.

	6 million BCE	5 million BCE	4 million BCE	3 million BCE	2 million BCE	1 million BCE	500,000 BCE	400,000 BCE	300,000 BCE
HUMAN EVOLUTION AND MIGRATIONS		6–5 million BCE Earliest protohumans							
			2.5 million BCE *Homo habilis*						
			2.2–1.8 million BCE *Homo erectus*						
					400,000–200,000 BCE Archaic *Homo sapiens*				
TECHNOLOGICAL DEVELOPMENTS									
URBANIZATION									

comprehend in order to properly situate buildings and graves, ideas that were recently popularized, gaining a following in some Western countries.

1-1b Early Life and Evolutionary Change

Life has a long history. Simple, single-celled life emerged by perhaps 3.5 to 3.9 billion years ago and remained dominant until about a half billion years ago, when complex life forms proliferated in incredible variety. Animal life colonized the land between 400 and 500 million years ago and evolved into many species. Volcanic and earthquake activity influenced human history, and sometimes intense volcanic eruptions dramatically altered regional and even global climates. Warmer or cooler climates helped shape human societies and sometimes undermined them. Most natural scientists, while still debating the mechanisms, agree that living things change over many generations through evolution, modifying their genetic composition to adapt to their changing biological and physical environment.

A half dozen massive species extinctions have occurred in the past 400 million years. For example, 250 million years ago gigantic volcanic eruptions produced enough climate-changing gases to rapidly warm the planet and almost wipe out all life. The best-known extinction involved the dinosaurs, which flourished for 150 million years before dying out about 65 million years ago, probably from the cooling of the planet from increasing volcanic activity combined with the cataclysmic impact of one or several large asteroids or comets smashing into the earth, destroying food sources and killing off about 70 percent of all species. This occurrence gave mammals a chance to rise, and one group eventually evolved into humans. So far humans have been lucky. Scientists estimate that 99 percent of all species eventually became extinct when conditions changed dramatically. Yet species have died rapidly over the past two hundred years, most likely because of environmental changes such as pollution, habitat removal, and global warming generated by human activity; this trend is rapidly accelerating today.

Eventually evolutionary changes among one branch of mammals led to the immediate ancestors of humans, which are part of the primate order, the mammal category that includes the apes. Over 98 percent of human DNA is the same as that of chimpanzees and bonobos, although human-chimp lines diverged sometime between five and six million years ago. By using their superior brain to gain an evolutionary edge, humans ultimately dominated other large animal species. They formed complex social organizations that emphasized cooperation for mutual benefit, developed tools, mastered fire, and learned how to use speech, all of which gave them great advantages. Ultimately they developed a more complex technology to manipulate the physical environment in many ways to meet their needs. Understanding human origins requires archaeologists and other scientists to sift through evidence from many sources, including fossils, DNA, early tools and other artifacts, caves, and campsites. New evidence is regularly discovered, fostering new understanding but also controversies. However, there is much that scholars and scientists agree on.

Hominids (HOM-uh-nids), a family including humans and their immediate ancestors, first evolved five to six million years ago from more primitive primates in Africa, where the span of human prehistory is much longer than anywhere else. The most extensive fossil evidence comes from the southern African plateau and the Great Rift Valley of East Africa, a wide, deep chasm stretching from Ethiopia south to Tanzania. Scientists vigorously debate fossil and artifact remains and whether teeth, skulls, and bones

hominids A family including humans and their immediate ancestors.

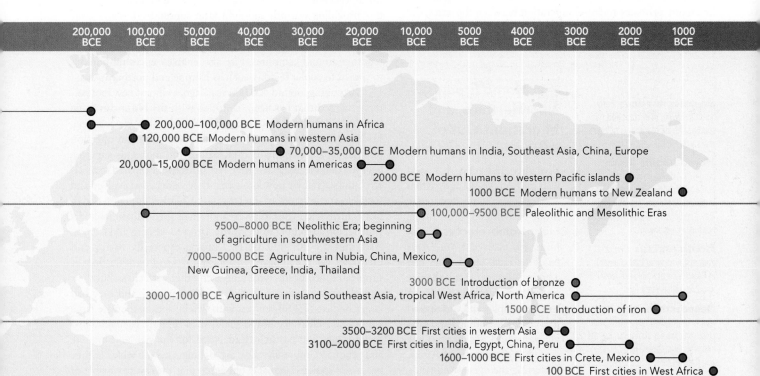

200,000 BCE	100,000 BCE	50,000 BCE	40,000 BCE	30,000 BCE	20,000 BCE	10,000 BCE	5000 BCE	4000 BCE	3000 BCE	2000 BCE	1000 BCE

200,000–100,000 BCE Modern humans in Africa
120,000 BCE Modern humans in western Asia
70,000–35,000 BCE Modern humans in India, Southeast Asia, China, Europe
20,000–15,000 BCE Modern humans in Americas
2000 BCE Modern humans to western Pacific islands
1000 BCE Modern humans to New Zealand

100,000–9500 BCE Paleolithic and Mesolithic Eras
9500–8000 BCE Neolithic Era; beginning of agriculture in southwestern Asia
7000–5000 BCE Agriculture in Nubia, China, Mexico, New Guinea, Greece, India, Thailand
3000 BCE Introduction of bronze
3000–1000 BCE Agriculture in island Southeast Asia, tropical West Africa, North America
1500 BCE Introduction of iron

3500–3200 BCE First cities in western Asia
3100–2000 BCE First cities in India, Egypt, China, Peru
1600–1000 BCE First cities in Crete, Mexico
100 BCE First cities in West Africa

belong to ancestors of humans, other hominid species who died out, or apes, but fossil discoveries and analyses of DNA sometimes recovered from them point to several stages and branches in early human evolution. A common ancestral, apelike group living in the woodlands and savannahs of East Africa developed occasional and then permanent bipedalism (walking upright on two feet), making more activity possible by leaving hands free for holding food or babies, making and manipulating objects such as tools, and carrying food back to camp. Bipeds, being higher off the ground, could also scan the horizon for predators or prey.

Diverse hominid groups apparently coexisted at the same time, but only one led to modern humans. Early hominids known as **australopithecines** (aw-strah-lo-PITH-uh-seens) lived in eastern and southern Africa four or five million years ago, with brains about one-third the size of our brains. Some 2.5 million years ago one branch of australopithecines evolved into our direct ancestor. The earth cooled, fostering the first of a series of Ice Ages, which covered large areas of northern Eurasia and North America with deep ice sheets and glaciers. As Africa and its hominid inhabitants experienced a drier climate and more open habitats, the challenges posed by this climate change encouraged increased intelligence. Our likely ancestor **Homo habilis** (HOH-moh HAB-uh-luhs) ("handy human") had a larger brain size and ability to make and use simple stone tools for hunting and gathering. Stone choppers and later hand axes made possible a more varied diet, more successful hunting, and larger groups that could cooperate to share food. The other branches of australopithecines died out.

As hominid societies developed, males increasingly became the hunters or scavengers for meat and females the gatherers of nuts and vegetables, a subsistence model often known as foraging. Although meat became a more crucial protein source, gathering still probably brought more food than hunting or scavenging. These early humans were most likely vegetarians, like many primates today. Cooperation between the sexes and group members was the key to survival and probably involved communication through gestures and vocal cries.

australopithecines Early hominids living in eastern and southern Africa four to five million years ago.

Homo habilis ("handy human") A direct ancestor of humans, so named because of its increased brain size and ability to make and use simple stone tools for hunting and gathering.

Homo erectus ("erect human") A hominid that emerged in East Africa probably between 1.8 and 2.2 million years ago.

Neanderthals Hominids who were probably descended from *Homo erectus* populations in Europe and who later spread into western and Central Asia.

1-1c *Homo Erectus, Neanderthals, and Migrations Out of Africa*

Probably between 1.8 and 2.2 million years ago, when their environment fluctuated, more advanced hominids, called **Homo erectus** ("erect human"), evolved from *Homo habilis* in East Africa. They had a brain about two-thirds the size of ours and eventually developed a more complex and widespread tool culture including hand axes, cleavers, and scrapers. They spread to other parts of Africa, preferring the open savannah.

Between one and two million years ago, as southern Eurasia developed a warmer climate, some *Homo erectus* bands migrated out of Africa, perhaps following game herds. They carried with them refined tools, more effective hunting skills, and an ability to adapt to new environments. This first great migration in human history corresponded to the ebb and flow of the Ice Ages as well as the periodic drying out of the Sahara region. Over thousands of years these hominids came to occupy northern Africa, the Middle East, South and Southeast Asia, China, Europe, and perhaps Australia.

One of the earliest and best studied non-African sites, perhaps 1.8 million years old, was found in the Caucasus (KAW-kuh-suhs) Mountains of western Asia. Bones and tools discovered in Chinese caves and skulls from the Indonesian island of Java, then connected to mainland Asia, have been dated at 1.6 to 1.9 million years ago, and one recent but controversial find in China suggests an even older date of 2.1 million. Fossils from frigid eastern Siberia date back 300,000 years, indicating how adaptable and resourceful the species had become. These hominids also lived in Spain by 800,000 BCE. However, their tool cultures differed somewhat from those of Chinese *Homo erectus*, indicating cultural diversity and perhaps major variation from the Asian species. By 500,000 years ago *Homo erectus* in China lived in closely knit groups, engaged in cooperative hunting, and used both wood and bamboo for containers and weapons. Most lived in caves, but some built simple wooden huts for shelter. Their hand axes were the Swiss army knives of their time, with a tip for piercing, thin edges for cutting, and thick edges for scraping and chipping. Scientists debate whether *Homo erectus* could use speech or make art. Finding their fossils on Indonesian islands suggest that they could build and sail primitive boats.

Discovering how to start and control fire was perhaps the most significant human invention. Where or when people first used fire or how many millennia it took for knowledge of fire to spread widely remains unclear; *Homo erectus* probably controlled fire at least one million years ago. Fire opened up many possibilities, providing warmth and light after sunset, frightening away predators, and making possible a more varied diet of cooked food, which fostered group living and cooperation as people gathered together around campfires. Fire also enabled ancestral humans to spread to cooler regions, such as Europe and northern Asia.

Beginning around 400,000 years ago, a vibrant new tool culture emerged that has been identified with the **Neanderthals** (nee-AN-der-thals), hominids probably related to *Homo erectus*. Earlier generations of scientists, obsessed with the question of what separates humans from nature and makes us superior, believed that Neanderthals were very primitive compared to modern humans, but we now know that they were just as evolved and social as, and behaved in similar ways to, modern humans, and in fact contributed genes to us. Neanderthals gradually inhabited a wide region stretching from North Africa to western and Central Asia and, by 200,000 BCE, Europe, especially Spain and Germany. We might have cartoonish images of Neanderthals as simple-minded brutes whacking each other with clubs, but their cranial capacity equaled that of modern humans, and they had larger bodies. Skillful hunters with deadly spears, they ate large animals as well as plants and shellfish. Neanderthals maintained social values, buried their dead, cared for the sick and injured, and produced impressive cave art. Scholars debate whether they possessed spoken language, but agree that they were capable of communication, used tools, made bone flutes, wore jewelry, and sailed boats to Mediterranean islands. Recent fossil discoveries in Siberia and Tibet suggest that a species related to Neanderthals, known as **Denisovans** (dun-EE-suh-vinz), may have once been widespread in eastern Eurasia before the arrival of modern humans, but their exact relationship to the Neanderthals and to modern humans is a matter of debate. Recent genetic studies suggest that Neanderthals and Denisovans also interbred with at least three other unknown early human groups as they spread across Eurasia.

Neanderthals had long lived in Palestine when modern humans arrived there from Africa and apparently shared the territory for many centuries. Around 45,000 years ago some modern, tool-using humans, known as **Cro-Magnons** (krow-MAG-nuns) after a French cave where early fossils were found, began migrating into Europe from Asia. Recent analyses have found that modern humans in Europe and Asia (but not Africa) have a small number of Neanderthal genes, suggesting some interbreeding. Many people in eastern Asia and the Pacific islands also inherited 3 to 5 percent of their DNA from Denisovans. A recent but disputed study suggests that Denosovans may have mated with modern humans as recently as 15,000 years ago. Recent finds also reveal some possible cases of Neanderthal–Denisovan mixing. Modern humans inherited some Neanderthal DNA that helps protect us from certain infections. The last Neanderthals died out by 30,000 BCE. Whether and how Neanderthals were ultimately annihilated, outnumbered, outcompeted, assimilated, or simply outlasted by the more resourceful and adaptable modern humans, who had better technology and warmer clothing, generates much debate among scholars.

1-1d The Evolution and Diversity of Homo Sapiens

The transition from *Homo erectus* to archaic forms of **Homo sapiens** ("thinking human"), a species physically close to modern humans, began around 400,000 years ago in Africa. By 200,000 years ago a more widespread, complex tool culture indicated *Homo sapiens* occupation. Eventually members of *Homo sapiens* were the only surviving hominids and humanity became a single species, despite some superficial differences. With a larger brain, Archaic (early) *Homo sapiens* were more adaptive and intelligent, able to think conceptually. They lived in fairly large organized groups, built temporary shelters, created crude lunar calendars, killed whole herds of animals, and raised more children to adulthood. Possession of language gave *Homo sapiens* an advantage over all other creatures, allowing them to share information over the generations, adjust to their environment, and overcome challenges collectively.

Scientists debate precisely how and where *Homo erectus* evolved into *Homo sapiens*, with some arguing that the evolution occurred in different parts of the Afro-Eurasian zone. The most widely supported scenario based on rich finds, called the African Origins theory, suggests that *Homo sapiens* evolved only in Africa. Until recently, the oldest known fossils of our species in East Africa dated back about 195,000 years. But fossils discovered in 2017 in Morocco, in far northeastern Africa thousands of miles from East Africa, are roughly 300,000 years old, suggesting that, if other scientists confirm the finds as *Homo*

sapiens, not just East Africa but the whole African continent might be considered the "cradle of humankind." More discoveries in the future may well deepen our knowledge but also complicate our understanding of the human past.

Whatever the case many *Homo sapiens* eventually left Africa, perhaps in several dispersals or waves likely sparked by sporadic climate change, and then spread throughout Afro-Eurasia, displacing and ultimately dooming the remaining *Homo erectus*, Neanderthals, and Denisovans. The study of genetic codes mostly supports the African Origins theory. But many mysteries about hominid evolution remain. For example, scientists debate whether a controversial 210,000-year-old skull found in Greece is Neanderthal or *Homo sapien*, raising questions about human migration from Africa. And 18,000-year-old bones of diminutive but tool-using hominids, 3 to 3.5 feet tall as adults, on the small remote Indonesian island of Flores sparked debate as to where these fossils fit into the human family tree. The Flores people (nicknamed by observers "hobbits" because of their small stature) may have been miniature versions of *Homo erectus* or *Homo sapiens* or perhaps constituted some unknown, and more primitive, human-like species. In 2019 another fossil discovery in a Philippine cave adds to the mystery. What scientists have named *Homo luzonensus* ("Luzon Man"), who seems to have had a mix of human, *Homo erectus*, *Homo floresiensis*, and australopithecus traits and may also have been small in size, lived there fifty thousand years ago and may or may not descend from *Homo erectus* or perhaps Denisovans. No land bridges ever connected Luzon or Flores to the Asian mainland, raising more questions as to how they got to the islands. These finds confirm that human evolution was highly versatile and diverse as groups adapted to unknown conditions around the world.

However and wherever the evolution into *Homo sapiens* occurred, all humans came to constitute one species that could interbreed and communicate with each other. It remains unclear whether a few differences in physical features, such as skin and hair color and eye and face shape, developed earlier or later in *Homo sapiens* evolution. Recent studies suggest that these appeared between 40,000 and 100,000 years ago. In the past, some scholars attempted to explain these physical differences through allegedly objective or scientific categories, such as the nineteenth-century concept of "race," or a large group thought to share distinctive genetic traits and physical characteristics. Attempts to organize societies by such categories have produced horrible abuses, systematic inequalities, and even genocide. But, by the late twentieth century, most experts discarded "race" as a scientific concept not only because of its inability to classify human populations and its harmful legacy, but also because "race" is now viewed as a social construct—a subjective concept created by individuals and groups to describe their identities and those of others. Such categories change with time and social context and are not scientific fact. Much genetic

Denisovans Hominids related to Neanderthals who lived in eastern Eurasia.

Cro-Magnons The first modern, tool-using humans in Europe.

Homo sapiens ("thinking human") A hominid who evolved around 400,000 years ago and from whom anatomically modern humans (*Homo sapiens sapiens*) evolved around 100,000 years ago.

SPL/Science Source

IMAGE 1.2 **The Laetoli Footprints**   Some four million years ago in Tanzania, three australopithecines walked across a muddy field covered in ash from a nearby volcanic eruption. When the mud dried, their tracks were permanently preserved, providing evidence of some of the earliest upright hominids.

Q What about our hominid ancestors do you think scientists can learn from ancient footprints?

intermixing occurred over the millennia. Observable physical attributes such as skin color reflect a tiny portion of one's genetic makeup and thus cannot predict whether two groups are genetically similar or different. For example, the earliest hunter gatherers in Britain ten thousand years ago may have had dark skin, but later arrivals, farmers from the Middle East, intermarried with them. For all of these reasons, some argue that there is no such thing as a pure "European," or anyone else, in the past or today. Scientifically speaking, humans are much more similar than different.

Sometime between 135,000 and 100,000 years ago in Africa, anatomically modern humans with slightly larger brains, known as *Homo sapiens sapiens*, developed out of *Homo sapiens*. With this biological change, language and culture expanded in new directions and developed many variations. Scholars debate whether creativity, intelligence, and even language abilities were innate to *Homo sapiens sapiens*, as suggested by advanced stone tools and wall paintings in South African caves from 75,000 to 100,000 years ago, or arose only some 50,000 years ago, possibly as a result of a genetic mutation. With this great transition humanity reached its present level of intellectual and physical development, establishing the foundation for the constant expansion of information networks to a global level.

Modern human language development made possible complex cultures with shared learning and became the main method of communication for much of history. Five or six thousand languages emerged around the globe. Some, such as English and German, have a clear common ancestry, but scholars debate the relationships and origins of most of the world's languages. Human intellectual development also included thinking in abstract, symbolic ways, revealed early in decoration and art. Ocher (**O-ker**), for example, a natural red iron oxide, was mined in various African locations and probably used for body decoration. The first gorgeous cave and rock art appeared at opposite ends of Eurasia, in southwestern Europe and Southeast Asia, around forty thousand years ago, and over the next ten thousand years became widespread in Africa, Eurasia, and Australia. This shows that art was developing about the same time across the Eastern Hemisphere. The art probably had magical, religious, or ritual purposes, such as the celebration of spirits or valued animals. But some old cave paintings in Europe represent star constellations, telling us about their concept of time and interest in the seasons or the future.

1-1e The Globalization of Human Settlement

Pushed by changing environments sparking a quest for food resources, beginning by around 120,000 years ago or perhaps even earlier, and continuing until some 12,000 years ago, restless modern humans settled much of the world. As people spread, genetic differences grew and *Homo sapiens sapiens* proved able to adapt to many environments. Some had already left Africa to settle in Palestine, where they likely encountered and perhaps interbred with Neanderthals. Eventually modern humans reached central and eastern Eurasia, from where some moved on to Australia and the Americas.

With many traveling east along or near the Indian Ocean coast, and others perhaps taking a northern route through Central Asia, modern humans crossed to the eastern half of Asia, arriving in India and Southeast Asia by 70,000 years ago and maybe earlier, China between 70,000 and 120,000 years ago, Japan by 25,000 and 30,000 BCE, Tibet by 30,000 and 40,000 years ago, Siberia 30,000 years ago, and Europe between 35,000 and 45,000 years ago (see Map 1.1). To reach Australia and New Guinea from Southeast Asia across a very shallow sea required rafts or boats, but modern humans may have settled there between 73,000 and 45,000 BCE. The peopling of the far-flung Pacific islands to the east began much later, around 2000 BCE.

Archaeologists long thought that the peopling of the Americas came very late, the earliest migration into North America occurring only 12,000 to 15,000 years ago. But recent discoveries suggest that the pioneer arrivals may have crossed from Northeast Asia, probably in very small numbers,

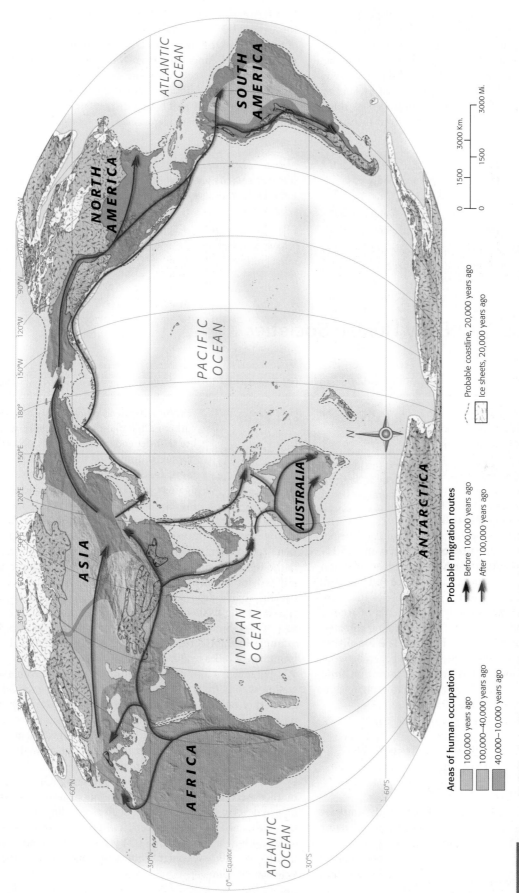

MAP 1.1 Spread of Modern Humans Around the Globe Most scholars believe that modern humans originated in Africa and that some of them began leaving Africa around 100,000 years ago. Gradually they spread out through Eurasia. From eastern Asia, some crossed to the Americas.

Q In what ways does this map suggest that migration should be considered one of the main themes of human history from our very beginnings in Africa?

as early as 15,000-20,000 or possibly, as a few disputed studies propose, even 30,000 or 40,000 years ago (see Chapter 4). At various times a wide Ice Age land bridge connected Alaska and Siberia across today's Bering Strait, and the evidence for several migrations chiefly from Asia over thousands of years is strong. The first settlers moved by land or by boat along the coast. A few highly controversial studies suggest that some Stone Age settlers arrived in eastern

North America from Spain. Gradually Asian migrants settled throughout the Western Hemisphere, becoming the ancestors of today's Native Americans. DNA research suggests that all modern Native Americans, from North America to Chile, are closely related to each other and to several peoples in eastern Siberia or the Altai region of Central Asia. Some Native American languages also have a distant but possible connection to several Siberian languages.

KEY POINTS

▶ Early hominids first evolved in Africa (most likely East Africa) four to six million years ago.

▶ Of the early hominids, our direct ancestor, *Homo habilis*, was most successful because it used simple stone tools.

▶ *Homo erectus* developed more refined tools and migrated to Eurasia and throughout Africa;

Homo sapiens had larger brains and evolved into modern humans, who developed language and spread throughout the world.

▶ Though humans from different parts of the world may have different appearances, their genetic differences are insignificant.

1-2 The Odyssey of Early Human Societies

▦ SOCIETIES

Ⓠ How did hunting and gathering shape life during the long Stone Age?

For thousands of years humans lived at a very basic level in small, usually mobile, family-based societies during what is often called the Stone Age, a misleading term because people also used other materials, such as wood and bone, to help them sustain life. This era included three distinct periods. The long **Paleolithic** (pay-lee-oh-LITH-ik) period (or Old Stone Age) began about 100,000 years ago. The **Mesolithic** (mez-oh-LITH-ik) period (Middle Stone Age) began around fifteen thousand years ago, when the glaciers from the final Ice Age receded. Major meat sources in Eurasia and North America that were adapted to Ice Age climates, such as the herds of woolly mammoths and mastodons, died out from warming climates, catastrophic disease, or hunting by humans. The **Neolithic** (nee-oh-LITH-ik) period (New Stone Age) began between 9500 and 8000 BCE in Eurasia, with the transition from hunting and gathering to simple farming.

> **CONNECTION to TODAY**
>
> Can you see any parallels between hunting and gathering by early people and the leisure activities many people enjoy today of hunting and collecting natural and organic foods in the wild?

scavenge for dead or dying animals, and gather edible plants, a subsistence way of life that depended on naturally occurring resources. Improved tools made possible more food options and better weapons against predators or rivals, and hunting became more important. When the bow and arrow were invented in Africa, Europe, and southwestern Asia at least fifteen thousand years ago, hunters could kill large animals at a safer distance. Although the main hunters, men, gained prestige, meat usually provided a small part of the diet. Some coastal peoples became skilled deep-sea fishermen by forty thousand years ago, inventing fishhooks, harpoons, fuel lamps, dugout boats, and canoes. Some also traded with neighboring groups. For example, in Eurasia treasured obsidian tools were traded over hundreds of miles by 30,000 to 40,000 years ago.

For much of history the gathering by women of edible vegetation such as fruits and nuts was probably more essential for group survival than obtaining meat, giving women status and influence. This is still true among many hunter-gatherers today. For example, among the Hadza of northern Tanzania, men are very often unsuccessful in their hunt for large animals while women, both young and old, provide the majority of calories to their families and group through gathering. Often grandmothers were the key to survival. Furthermore, women probably helped develop new technologies such as grinding stones, nets (to catch small animals), baskets, and primitive cloth. Woven cloth clothing appeared by 28,000 years ago and eyed sewing needles by 45,000 years ago. Pottery was made at least 18,000 years ago in China.

1-2a Hunting, Gathering, and Cooperation

The earliest and simplest forms of society, small groups of twenty to sixty members, depended on members cooperating to fish, hunt live animals,

Paleolithic The Old Stone Age, which began 100,000 years ago with the first modern humans and lasted for many millennia.

Mesolithic The Middle Stone Age, which began around 15,000 years ago as the glaciers from the final Ice Age began to recede.

Neolithic The New Stone Age, which began between 10,000 and 11,500 years ago with the transition to simple farming.

Although we must be cautious in comparing modern hunters and gatherers to peoples who lived many millennia ago, today's few remaining hunter-gatherers can probably reveal something about ancient pre-farming societies. Throughout history and even today many people have looked on those in less complex societies as "barbarians" or "uncivilized" because they are poor in material wealth, lack modern technology, and do not have their own highly organized governments. But many of these people may have enjoyed happy, moral, and fulfilling lives without living in richer but stressful cities and towns with competitive economic values and poor people of their own. The hunter-gatherer way of life may not have been as impoverished as we sometimes imagine. Many twentieth-century hunter-gatherers, such as the Mbuti (em-BOO-tee) of the Congo rain forest and the !Kung of the Kalahari Desert, enjoyed varied, healthy diets mixing fish, meat, and plants generally packed with nutrients and fiber. In recent years in many countries the so-called Paleolithic (Paleo) or stone-age diet has become a modern fad based on mainly eating foods presumed to have been available to early humans. But critics contend that the lifestyles and digestive abilities of people today are very different from those thousands of years ago, diminishing the diet's benefits. Hunter-gatherers generally also benefited from lots of physical activity; lack of chronic diseases like heart disease and cancer; often longer life expectancies; a rich communal life; and, for some, adequate food. Many spent only ten to thirty hours a week obtaining food, establishing camps, and doing domestic chores, and hence had plenty of time for music, dance, and socializing (see Meet the People: The !Kung Hunters and Gatherers). Yet hunter-gatherers always faced serious challenges. Early humans had to make their own weapons and clothing and construct temporary huts. For some groups, life remained precarious and many died young, since not all enjoyed access to adequate food resources and medical care was primitive.

Hunting and gathering generally encouraged cooperation, fostering closely knit communities based on kinship. Members communicated with one another and passed information from one generation to another, conveying a sense of the past and traditions. Personal relationships were paramount, while obtaining material wealth was devalued because the mostly nomadic way of life made individual accumulation of material possessions impractical. These small groups shared food resources among immediate family and friends, thus helping to ensure survival and promoting an intense social life. But harmony and mutual affection were not guaranteed. Those who violated group customs could be killed or banished, and sometimes conflicts split groups apart. Most hunter-gatherer bands had no government or leader; social responsibilities linked people together in relatively egalitarian relationships; and all members generally had equal access to resources. Yet groups often tended to reward the most resourceful members.

Women and men probably enjoyed a roughly comparable status, as they do in many hunter-gatherer societies today. Gender relations could be flexible, with the work of obtaining and preparing food sometimes based on ability and knowledge rather than gender. As key providers of food, women may have participated alongside men in group decision making. They also likely held a special place in religious practice as bearers of life. This may have been the source for concepts like Mother Nature and Mother Earth still used today. Midwives were highly respected. **Matrilineal** (mat-ruh-LIN-ee-uhl) **kinship** patterns, which trace descent and inheritance through the female line, were probably common, as they are today in these societies. But physically stronger and often more assertive men enjoyed some advantages over women. Although childbearing influenced women's roles, women were not constantly pregnant. Since it was necessary to limit group size to avoid depleting environmental resources, most societies practiced birth control and abortion. Breastfeeding an infant for several years suppressed ovulation and created longer intervals between pregnancies. Paleolithic populations grew slowly, perhaps by only 10 percent a century.

1-2b Cultural Life and Violence

Some aspects of culture that we might recognize today were taking shape, such as religious belief. As people sought to understand dreams, death, and natural phenomena, they developed both **animism** (ANN-uh-miz-um)—the belief that all creatures, as well as inanimate objects and natural phenomena, have souls and can influence human well-being—and **polytheism** (PAUL-e-thee-ism), the belief in many spirits or deities. Since spirits were thought capable of helping or harming a person, **shamans** (SHAW-mans), specialists in communicating with or manipulating the supernatural realm, became important; many shamans were women, and some biologically male shamans who assumed female roles were what today might be called *transgender*. Objects found in graves suggest some groups believed in some sort of an afterlife by 35,000 years ago or earlier. Some social activities developed early, including music, dance, making and drinking early homemade forms of beer or wine, and painting on rocks and cave walls. Primitive flutes can be traced back 45,000 years. Dancing and singing likely promoted togetherness. Perhaps the world's oldest temple, Goblekli Tepe in Turkey, was built by hunter-gatherers around 9000 BCE and used for ceremonies where people consumed meat and probably got drunk in great feasts while honoring their gods.

Egalitarian, self-sufficient societies enriched by spirituality and leisure activities may sound appealing to many modern people, but violence between and within different societies has also been a part of human culture throughout history. Predators such as bears, wolves, and lions hunted people, perhaps instilling

matrilineal kinship
A pattern of kinship that traces descent and inheritance through the female line.

animism The belief that all creatures as well as inanimate objects and natural phenomena have souls and can influence human well-being.

polytheism A belief in many spirits or deities.

shamans Specialists in communicating with or manipulating the supernatural realm.

a terror of dangerous animals, apparent in myths and folklore, such as the tale of Little Red Riding Hood, that have been passed down through countless generations. Men proved their bravery by killing predators, rivals, or enemy warriors to attract women.

Anthropologists debate whether humans are inherently aggressive and warlike or peaceful and cooperative. Today's hunter-gatherer or simple agriculture societies suggest that both patterns are common. Some peoples, such as the Hopi and Zuni of the American Southwest, the rain forest–dwelling Penan of Borneo, and many Australian Aborigines, have generally avoided armed conflict. But most societies have engaged in at least occasional violence, such as when their survival or food supply was threatened. Some societies admired military prowess. For example, the Dani of New Guinea lost a third of their men to conflicts with their neighbors. We might conclude that humans have a capacity but not a compulsion for aggressive behavior but naturally seek self-preservation, and social and cultural patterns promoting certain behaviors often arise in response to environmental conditions.

1-2c The Heritage of Hunting and Gathering

Hunting and gathering never completely disappeared. Throughout history some peoples have found this way of life the most realistic strategy for survival with remarkable success. Most recent hunter-gatherers have made only a marginal impact on the surrounding environment because of their small numbers and limited technology. Learning to live within environmental constraints, they were highly successful adapters. Hunter-gatherers in what is today Jordan were baking flat bread from wild cereals around 14,400 years ago, preceding agriculture by four thousand years and perhaps stimulating ideas for cultivating crops. Although generating little material wealth, hunting and gathering remained viable for many societies, such as Australian Aborigines, until modern times. Some Australian Aborigines relied largely on this pattern, especially in the harsh deserts, but others combined it with productively cultivating crops, sometimes intensively, suitable for their environment. Trade routes spanned the continent, and many Aborigines developed notions of land management as well as rich mythologies about their origins and their relationship to the fragile environment.

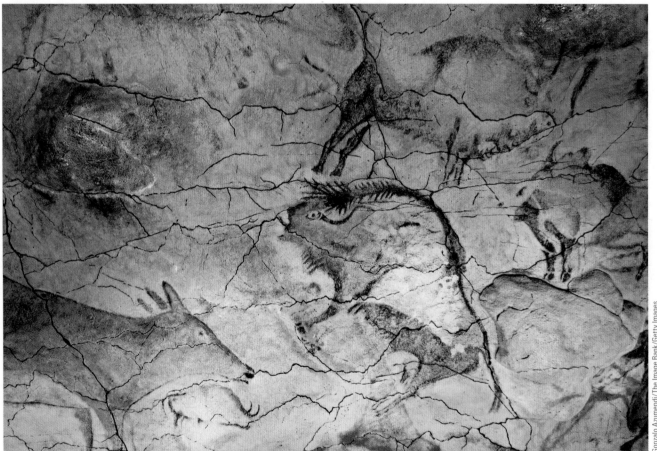

Gonzalo Azumendi/The Image Bank/Getty Images

IMAGE 1.3 **Cave Paintings in Europe** This Ice Age painting of bison and deer is from a cave in Altamira, Spain. Many paintings on cave walls have been found in France and Iberia. Paleolithic peoples all over the world painted pictures of the animals they hunted or feared as well as of each other, suggesting an increasing self-awareness.

The !Kung Hunters and Gatherers

While all societies change over time, often in response to environmental conditions, the remaining hunter-gatherer peoples today may give us a glimpse of how some prehistoric peoples lived. The !Kung, a subgroup of the Khoisan people (once disdainfully called Bushmen by European settlers), live in the inhospitable Kalahari Desert in southwestern Africa, in what is today Botswana and Namibia. Several thousand years ago the Khoisan were widespread in the southern half of Africa, and some probably adapted to desert life a long time ago. Some scholars think many Khoisan peoples may be the direct descendants of a very early dispersal of *Homo sapiens sapiens* from East Africa to southern Africa by 150,000 years ago or earlier, and their languages may be some of the world's oldest.

Over the millennia the !Kung became skilled hunter-gatherers. Women obtain between 60 and 80 percent of the food, collecting nuts, berries, beans, leafy greens, roots, and bird eggs, as well as catching tortoises, small mammals, snakes, insects, termites, and caterpillars. The men, who can follow animal tracks and other clues for many miles without rest, hunt animals, snare birds, and extract honey from beehives. The !Kung utilize some fifty species of plants and animals for food, medicine, cosmetics, and poisons. Although unfamiliar to Westerners, their food sources are highly nutritious.

The !Kung have adapted well to a harsh environment. Even during periodic drought conditions, the diversity of !Kung food sources ensures a steady supply. Furthermore, their diet is low in salt, carbohydrates, and saturated fats and high in vitamins and roughage. Combined with a relatively unstressful life, such a diet helps them avoid modern health problems like high blood pressure, ulcers, obesity, and heart disease. Living far from clinics, they die more easily from accidents and malaria. Nonetheless, !Kung life expectancy is similar to that in many industrialized countries.

ERIC LAFFORGUE/Alamy Stock Photo

IMAGE 1.4 **Modern San Family Around a Fire**
A modern San family gathers around a fire in a traditional Namibian village. Like the San in recent times, most people lived from hunting and gathering during the long centuries before the beginnings of agriculture, usually in small groups of a few families.

Q What does the photo tell us about San clothing, decoration, and housing?

Spending only fifteen to twenty hours a week in maintaining their livelihood, the !Kung have ample free time for resting, visiting friends, and playing games. Children have few responsibilities because their labor is not needed for the group's survival. The !Kung value gender interdependence and are willing to do the work normally associated with the opposite sex. Hence, fathers take an active role in childrearing. They prefer companionship to privacy, and their intense social life is symbolized by a large communal space in the midst of the camp surrounded by family sleeping huts. The !Kung strongly discourage aggressiveness. Their folk stories praise the animal tricksters who evade the use of force.

Throughout history farming peoples have affected hunter-gatherers. In recent decades the !Kung have faced many challenges that have altered the lives of many bands. Most are no longer completely self-sufficient, trading desert products to nearby farming villages for tools and food. Others have been drafted into the military, have taken up wage labor, or have been displaced because their territory has been claimed by governments or business interests. Today, forced or induced to abandon their traditional ways of life, some disoriented !Kung have moved to dilapidated, impoverished villages on the edges of towns. The future for their ancestral lifestyle is unpromising.

Reflection Questions

1. What role does the gathering by women play in the !Kung economy?
2. How does the traditional !Kung way of life promote leisure activity?
3. What problems do the !Kung face today?
4. What about traditional !Kung life do you think might appeal to people today?

But this way of life may disappear during the twenty-first century. In recent decades many societies have been disrupted or destroyed by logging, commercial fishing, plantation development, dam building, tourism, and other activities that exploit their environments, often for the financial benefit of powerful businesses, manufacturing, resource extraction, and political interests. For example, in the Amazon River Basin of South America, the burning of rain forests and opening of new land for farming or mining overwhelm many Native American groups. These peoples, along with many poor subsistence farmers, threatened by people wielding modern technology, may have to make the same transition to new survival strategies as other peoples did millennia ago. Then again, large-scale environmental destruction has and will continue to affect modern survival strategies as well.

KEY POINTS

▶ During the Paleolithic and Mesolithic eras, people lived in small groups of hunters and gatherers.

▶ In general, women gathered fruits and nuts, which provided the majority of the food, while men hunted game.

▶ Hunting and gathering groups were usually close-knit and egalitarian, though violence was not unknown.

▶ Anthropologists are undecided as to whether humans have a natural tendency toward violence or peace.

1-3 The Agricultural Transformation, 10,000–4000 BCE

⊃C TRANSITIONS

Ⓠ What environmental factors explain the transition to agriculture?

Between 10,000 and 12,000 years ago, some hunter-gatherers began to develop simple agriculture. This momentous change marked the beginning of the Neolithic period, when humans began to master the environment and alter the ecological system in unprecedented ways, cultivating the soil, selecting seeds, and breeding animals that could help them survive. The often-used term *Agricultural Revolution* is misleading because the development did not involve rapid, electrifying discoveries but occurred over hundreds of years. The shift to farming eventually changed human life all over the world, setting the stage for everything that came later, including cities, states, social classes, and long-distance trade. The transition also generates debates among historians and other scholars about whether agriculture and its consequences have ultimately been good or bad for the health of the planet and its people.

1-3a Environmental Change and the Roots of Agriculture

The first farmers did not see themselves as pioneers forging a new way of life. Even before farming began, some people were preparing themselves for permanent village life. Some, like the Abu Hureyra villagers, were settling alongside lakes or in valleys rich in easily collected wild grains. Around the world, archaeologists have discovered Neolithic period houses, baskets, pottery, pits for storing grain, and equipment for hunting, fishing, and grain preparation. However, documenting the steps to agriculture and settled life is not easy. Before 3500 BCE we have no written sources. Many material artifacts still lie buried, while others have long since turned to dust.

Most studies conclude that climate change helped trigger the shift to agriculture. After the last great Ice Age, the earth entered a long period of unusual warmth. Early agriculture may have helped accelerate global warming and prevent a return to the Ice Age. As they had for thousands of years, melting glaciers caused rising sea levels, covering about a fifth of previously available land. The spread of the Persian Gulf, the Black Sea, and the Mediterranean onto once occupied lowlands may have led to legends in the Middle East of a great flood and human expulsion from a "garden of Eden." Rising sea levels also covered many land links, including those connecting the British Isles to continental Europe and Japan to Asia. Another factor was probably population growth. Around 10,000 BCE, the world population had grown to perhaps five or ten million, and in some regions hunting and gathering could no longer meet everyone's basic needs. Soon people gravitated to areas rich in wild grains and grazing animals, some of them abandoning their nomadic ways to live permanently near these rich food sources.

1-3b The Great Transition to Settled Agriculture

The environment continued to change, posing new challenges. The earth cooled again briefly about 9000 BCE, reducing food supplies, and a drought in the Middle East presented a crisis for some hunter-gatherer societies. Responding to the challenges, some began to store food and learn how to cultivate their own fields, even experimenting with cereal grains collected in a wild state. They pioneered **horticulture**

> **CONNECTION to TODAY**
>
> Can you think of ways that farming life today has similarities to farming life several thousand years ago?

horticulture The growing of crops with simple methods and tools.

(HORE-tee-kuhl-chur), the growing of crops with simple methods and tools, such as the hoe or digging stick, eventually spurring a profound reorganization of human society. Women may well have taken the lead in domesticating plants and some animals and in molding clay for storage and cooking pots. As the chief gatherers, women knew how plants grew and sprouted from seeds and the amount of water and sunshine needed to sustain plants. Women are generally the main food producers in horticultural societies today.

www.BibleLandPictures.com/Alamy Stock Photo

IMAGE 1.5 **Oldest Known Human Statues** This anthropomorphic statue, found with several others in burial pits near Ain Ghazal in the Judean Hills of Jordan, was among the earliest large-scale representations of humans and was made in the seventh millennium BCE during the Neolithic period. About half human size, the statues were modeled in plaster around a core of bundled twigs and painted with ochre. Their eyes are marked out in bitumen. They were perhaps used in cultic ceremonies.

Q What does the statue tell us about the people and culture who made it?

One major food-producing strategy was shifting cultivation. With this strategy people cleared trees and underbrush by chopping and burning (hence the common term *slash and burn*). After clearing, people loosened the soil with digging sticks and scattered seeds around. Natural moisture such as rain helped the crops mature. But since the soil became eroded after a few years, shifting cultivators moved periodically to fresh land, returning to the original area only after the soil had recovered its fertility. This method is still used today in some parts of Africa, Latin America, and southern Asia, especially in forested areas.

Farming promoted many radical changes in the way people lived and connected with their environments. Historians debate whether agriculture made life more or less secure, predictable, and healthy than hunting and gathering. But the domestication of plants and animals increased the production of food in a given amount of land, producing a much higher yield per acre and thus supporting much denser populations. Permanent settlements also made possible the storage of food for future use, since the pots and buildings did not have to be moved periodically.

However, since farmers depended on fewer plant foods than hunter-gatherers, they were more vulnerable to disaster from drought or other natural catastrophes. The earliest farmers could probably grow enough to feed themselves and their families with three or four hours of work a day. But requiring more food to feed growing populations forced them to exploit local resources more intensively and to work harder in their fields. Farmers also recognized that they had hard lives. An ancient Chinese song reflected this reality: "We clear the grasses and trees, We plow and plow the land, Two thousand men and women scrabbling weeds, Along the low wet lands, along the dike walls, The masters, the eldest sons, The laborers, the hired servants."[2] Agriculture eventually depended on **peasants**, mostly poor farmers who worked small plots of land that were often owned by others. Hard-working peasants were the backbone of most societies before the Industrial Revolution and remain a large segment of the population in many societies. Today there is concern about the growing gap between rich and poor in most countries. But even millennia ago, with the rise of agriculture, wealth became more unequally distributed as some gained control of land and resources while others worked the land.

1-3c The Globalization and Diversity of Agriculture

The agricultural transformation eventually reached across the globe. Agriculture came first to Eurasia, where geography favored the movement of people to the east or west along the same general latitude, without abrupt climatic changes. By contrast, the Americas are constructed along a north–south axis, and northern and

peasants Mostly poor farmers who worked small plots of land that were often owned by others.

[2]From Robert Payne, ed., *The White Pony: An Anthology of Chinese Poetry* (New York: Mentor, 1947), 39.

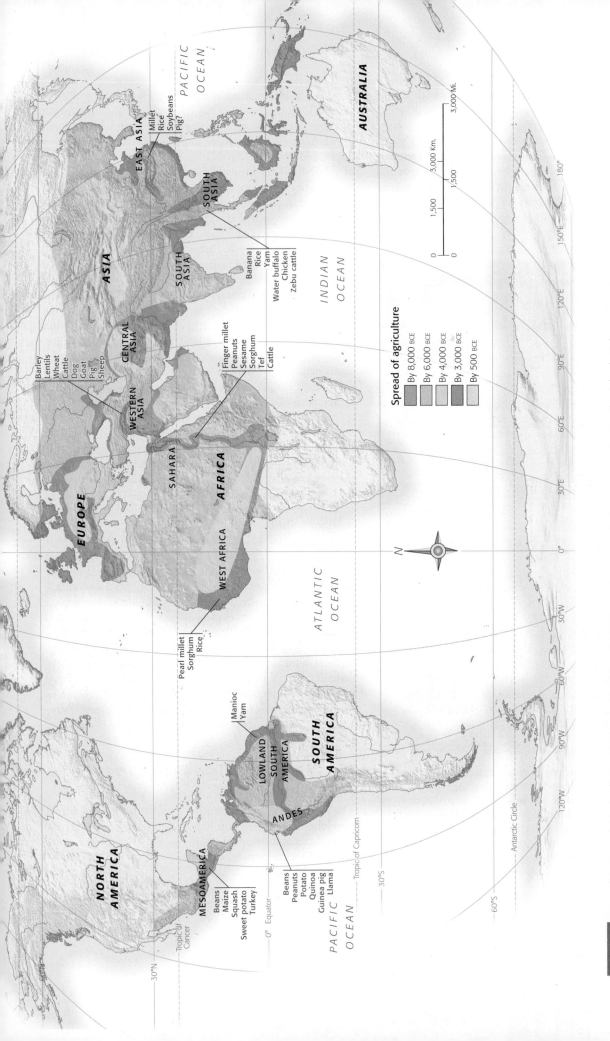

MAP 1.2 **The Origins of Agriculture** Between 11,500 and 7,000 years ago, people in western Asia, North and sub-Saharan Africa, southern Asia, East Asia, New Guinea, Mesoamerica, and South America developed agriculture independently and domesticated available animals. Later most of these crops and some of the animals spread into other regions.

Q What does this map tell us about why people today owe so many of our food choices and diets to ancient farmers all over the world?

southern temperate regions are linked only through a huge tropical zone stretching from southern Mexico to northern and eastern South America. Some peoples, such as those in Australia and the Arctic, did not or could not make a full transition from hunting and gathering food because of environmental and geographical constraints. Many societies contributed significantly to the discovery and production of the food resources we use today.

The dates for the beginning of agriculture vary considerably. The breakthrough to the earliest known farming came between 9500 and 8000 BCE in the region of southwestern Asia known as the "Fertile Crescent," encompassing what is today Iraq, Syria, central and eastern Turkey, and the Jordan River Valley, which had many fast-growing plants with high nutritional value, such as wheat, barley, chickpeas, and peas. Food growing also began independently in several other parts of the world (see Map 1.2), although we still do not know precisely when because hot, humid climates are poor for preserving plant, animal, and human remains. In eastern Eurasia crop cultivation began around 7000 BCE in China and New Guinea, 7000 or 6000 BCE in India, 5000 or 4000 BCE in Thailand, and 3000 BCE in Island Southeast Asia. Crops gradually spread to distant regions; hence, wheat and barley domesticated in the Middle East around 8000 BCE reached China a millennium later.

In the Mediterranean region, farming began in the Nile Valley between 8000 and 6000 BCE, and in Greece by 6500 BCE. Farming may have spread into Europe with migrants from Anatolia in western Asia who intermarried with or displaced local hunters and gatherers, reaching northward to Britain and Scandinavia between 4000 and 3000 BCE. Beginning around 4500 BCE some early European farmers constructed giant stone megaliths, such as Stonehenge in southern England, as ceremonial or religious centers, astronomical calendars, or for burials and funerary practices. In Africa farming in the southeast Sahara and Niger River basin may date to between 8000 and 6000 BCE and Ethiopia to 4500 BCE. In the Americas cultivation apparently began in central Mexico between 7000 and 5500 BCE and in the Andes (**ANN-deez**) highlands by 6000 BCE, if not earlier. Farming reached the Amazon River Basin by 1500 BCE, Colorado by 1000 BCE, and the southeastern part of North America by 500 BCE.

The earliest crops grown varied by local environments and needs. Millet dominated in cold North China, rice in warmer central and southern China as well as in tropical Southeast Asia, wheat and barley in the dry Middle East, yams and sorghum in West Africa, corn in upland Mesoamerica, and potatoes in the high Andes of South America. Some crops such as flax produced fiber to make clothing. Other plants had medicinal properties. Southwest Asians began making wine from grapes and beer from barley between 6000 and 3000 BCE. Over time farming became deeply ingrained in the psychology, social life, and traditions of many societies (see Discover Historical Voices: Food and Farming in Ancient Cultural Traditions). Farming technology gradually improved. People living in highlands with steep slopes, such as in Peru, Indonesia, China, or Greece, made fields on terraces, laborious to construct and maintain. Then,

as more people moved from highlands into valleys, they used water from nearby marshes or wells or built large-scale water projects such as irrigation canals.

1-3d Animal Domestication

The domestication of animals for human use developed in close association with crop raising. Animals bred in captivity were gradually modified from their wild ancestors. Men may have looked after the larger animals such as oxen and cattle, while women took charge of smaller species such as sheep and pigs. Domesticated animals supplied meat and leather, aided in farming, produced fertilizer, or supplied transportation. For example, horses and camels made long-distance travel and communication easier, and plows became more efficient tools when pulled by oxen or cattle. One disadvantage was that domesticated animals passed on diseases to humans, although living with animals eventually led to immunities among peoples in Eurasia.

Much remains unclear about the chronology and location of animal domestication. For example, dogs may have been

DEA/M. SEEMULLER/De Agostini/Getty Images

IMAGE 1.6 **Seated Goddess from Western Asia** This baked-clay figure from one of the oldest towns in western Asia, Çatal Hüyük in Anatolia, shows an enthroned female, probably a goddess giving birth, guarded on both sides by catlike animals—perhaps leopards.

Q What do you think the figure might tell us about the women of Çatal Hüyük and the goddess that they turned to for comfort?

Discover Historical Voices

Food and Farming in Ancient Cultural Traditions

As agriculture became an essential foundation for survival, it became increasingly important in the traditions and mindsets of societies around the world. The following excerpts show three examples of how food and farming were reflected in the cultural traditions of ancient societies. The first, an Andean ritual chant from South America many centuries old, is a prayer for successful harvests addressed to an ancient deity. The second is from a farmer's almanac from eighteenth-century BCE Mesopotamia that offers guidance on cultivating a successful grain crop; this excerpt deals with preparing the field and seeding. The third reading, a song collected in China around three thousand years ago, celebrates a successful harvest and explains how some of the bounty will be used.

Andean Chant

Oh Viracocha, ancient Viracocha, skilled creator, who makes and establishes
"on the earth below may they eat, may they drink" you say; for those you have established, those you have made
may food be plentiful.
"Potatoes, maize, all kinds of food may there be."

Excerpt from *Farmer's Almanac*

Keep a sharp eye on the openings of the dikes, ditches and mounds [so that] when you flood the field the water will not rise too high in it…. Let shod oxen trample it for you; after having

its weeds ripped out [by them and] the field made level ground, dress it evenly with narrow axes weighing [no more than] two thirds of a pound each…. Keep your eye on the man who puts in the barley seed. Let him drop the grain uniformly two fingers deep…. If the barley seed does not sink in properly, change your share…. Harvest it at the moment [of its full strength].

Chinese Harvest Song

Rich is the year with much millet and rice;
And we have tall granaries
With hundreds and thousands and millions of sheaves.
We make wine and sweet spirits
And offer them to our ancestors, male and female;
Thus to fulfill all the rites And bring down blessings in full.

Reflection Questions

1. Who did the Andeans believe determined the success of their harvest?
2. How did Mesopotamian farming depend on draft animals and cooperation?
3. How did ancient Chinese farmers use surplus grain and rice to fulfill obligations?
4. Can you think of ways that cultures today celebrate farmers and farming life?

Sources: Brian M. Fagan, *Kingdoms of Gold, Kingdoms of Jade* (London: Thames and Hudson, 1991), 88; Samuel Noah Kramer, *Cradle of Civilization* (New York: Time-Life, 1967), 84; William Theodore De Bary, et al., eds., *Sources of Chinese Tradition*, Vol. 1 (New York: Columbia University Press, 1960), 13.

---

domesticated from gray wolves by at least twelve thousand or perhaps fifteen thousand years ago, and possibly long before agriculture, in East Asia, Europe, or the Middle East. Dogs provided companionship, guarding, hunting assistance, and sometimes food. Cats were domesticated or domesticated themselves beginning perhaps twelve thousand years ago with the rise of farming. Sheep, goats, pigs, chickens, and cattle were all domesticated in the Middle East and southern Asia between 9000 and 7000 BCE. Some contested evidence suggests early cattle domestication in East Africa and the Sahara region. The first domesticated horses and donkeys, which date back to around 3100 to 4000 BCE in Central Asia, enabled the improved transportation that stimulated long-distance trade networks.

Zoological differences among the continents were crucial for advanced agriculture. Eurasia contained many species of large, plant-eating, herding mammals like cattle and horses whose habits and mild dispositions made their domestication into draft animals possible. Outside Eurasia, the lack of draft animals hindered agricultural development. Africa (except for cattle) and Australia lacked such animals, and most of the candidates in the Americas, such as the horse

and camel, were extinct by 10,000 BCE. The only American possibilities, the gentle llamas and alpacas of the South American highlands, were used as pack animals by 3500 BCE but were not well suited for farming.

1-3e Agriculture and Its Environmental Consequences

The resulting population growth also contributed to environmental changes, some with negative consequences such as deforestation. Indeed, human activities have had an impact on environments since the time of *Homo habilis*. Stone Age hunters in both hemispheres may have contributed to the extinction of many animal species, but intensive agriculture more radically altered the ecology, especially as technology improved. Moreover, technological innovations solved some problems but did not always prove advantageous in the long run. For example, although the plow made it easier to loosen dirt and eliminate weeds to plant seeds deeper in nutrient-rich soil, it also exposed topsoils to water and wind erosion. Similarly, vast irrigation networks provided the economic foundations for flourishing agriculture and denser settlement but required more labor than dry farming. They also tended to foster centralized governments that could allocate water resources among the people, placing more controls on people's behavior. Finally, adding water to poor soils can produce waterlogged land with a thick salt surface that ruins farming. In parts of Mesopotamia and the Americas, irrigation ultimately created deserts, contributing to the rise and fall of societies.

Various activities fostered environmental destruction. Farming and animal raising placed demands on the land. Goats, for example, caused damage by browsing on shrubs, tree branches, and seedlings, preventing forest regeneration. Cattle required much pasture. People exploited nearby forests for lumber to build wagons, tools, houses, furniture, and boats. Contemporary observers were aware of the deforestation. Twenty-four centuries ago the philosopher Plato bemoaned the deforestation of the Greek mountains: "What remains is like the skeleton of a body emaciated by disease. All the rich soil has melted away, leaving a country of skin and bone."[3] Overgrazing and deforestation in the mountains feeding the main rivers produced silt that contained harmful salt and gypsum, which moved downstream to the sea, clogging canals and dams.

The changing human–environment relationship generated new religious ideas more complex than animism and polytheism in explaining humankind's relationship to broader forces. Early sacred and philosophical texts often justified human domination over nature. For example, the authors of the Hebrew book of Genesis believed God told humans to "be fruitful and multiply; fill the earth and subdue it; have dominion over the fish of the sea,…the birds of the air, and…every living thing that moves upon the earth."[4] Many ancient thinkers saw an ordered world in which every part had a role and purpose in a divine plan, with humans the ultimate beneficiaries. These attitudes are still common today and part of debates over environmental sustainability and wildlife protection versus economic development.

KEY POINTS

▸ The shift from hunting and gathering to farming had tremendous consequences, but it occurred gradually, over hundreds of years.

▸ The end of the last great Ice Age and increased population density led people to shift from hunting and gathering to farming.

▸ Farming, which probably began in the area of Asia known as the "Fertile Crescent," could support much denser populations and allowed for food storage, but it also led to some new health problems.

▸ Irrigation and other technological advances led to larger crops but also caused great environmental damage.

1-4 The Emergence of Cities and States

TRANSITIONS SOCIETIES

Q How did farming and metallurgy establish the foundations for the rise of cities, states, and trade networks?

Farming generated more complex, multi-dimensional societies. Some western Asian people moved to fertile areas to farm, unloading their stone tools, clay pots, and plant seeds and building mud and reed huts. Families formed small villages and had more children to help in the fields. Houses had a sleeping platform, bread oven, grain silo, and a corral for domesticated animals. Older women served as religious specialists, acting as midwives, reciting myths, and composing verses. To honor a special deity the villagers built a temple. Eventually these villages with their temples grew into the first cities, establishing a foundation for the rise of states, trade networks, and writing.

1-4a The Rise of New Technologies

Many times in history people came up against a serious resource problem, such as lack of food and water, and had to overcome the challenge or perish. Their efforts often led

CONNECTION to TODAY

Why do you think cities and states have endured for several millennia as key frameworks for societies?

to some new technology with long-lasting value. One innovation, metalworking, made possible a new level of human control over resources supplied by the environment. The first metalworking was done with copper, and copper mining may have been the first real industry of the ancient world. Used in Europe for making weapons and tools as early as 7000 BCE and in the Middle East by 4500 BCE, copper was traded over considerable distances and was perhaps the first major commodity to enjoy a world market. People also used gold. These two soft metals could be fairly easily cut and shaped with stones.

Soon specialist craftsmen were mining and working metals. By 3000 BCE some specialists in western Asia had developed heating processes to blend copper together with either tin or arsenic to create bronze, and the bronze trade became a major spur to commerce in early Mesopotamia. By 1500 BCE the technology for making usable iron had also been invented, although

---

[3]From Plato's *Critas*, quoted in L.S. Stavrianos, *Lifelines from Our Past: A New World History*, rev. ed. (Armonk, NY: M.E. Sharpe, 1997), 65.
[4]Genesis 1:28, *The Holy Bible*, New King James Version (Chicago: Thomas Nelson, 1983), 2.

it took many centuries to perfect the new alloy (metal mixture) for practical use. Bronze and iron made better, more durable tools (such as plows), but also more deadly weapons. Their use shaped many societies of the ancient and classical worlds.

1-4b Urbanization and the First Cities

Agriculture fostered population growth. By using cow's milk and grain meal for infants' food, women could now breastfeed for a shorter period and consequently bear children more frequently. In the Middle East the population grew from less than 100,000 in 8000 BCE to over three million by 4000 BCE. Some farming villages grew into substantial prosperous towns. In one of the oldest, Çatal Hüyük (cha-TAHL hoo-YOOK) in central Turkey, first occupied around 7400 BCE, roughly ten thousand residents lived in cramped mud-brick buildings with paintings decorating their walls. Houses, with no doors or windows, had people entering through the roof and were home to families of five to ten people. No evidence has emerged for war or serious conflict, and the society was apparently egalitarian. Since the first toilets were not invented in Mesopotamia until the fourth millennium BCE, people before then lived in unhealthy conditions and many seem to have suffered from internal parasites. Çatal Hüyük and similar towns became centers of long-distance trade. Archaeologists found at Çatal Hüyük baskets of date palm leaves from Mesopotamia or Palestine and shells from the Red Sea or Mediterranean. By around 3700 BCE another center, Tell Hamoukar (Tell HAM-oo-kar), had grown into a town enclosed by a defensive wall. It contained both a bakery and a brewery and seems to have been ruled by a growing bureaucracy, perhaps even a king. Road networks linked the various cities of the Tigris-Euphrates Basin.

states Formal governments that controlled a recognized territory and exercised power over both people and things.

With time permanent settlements became larger, dominating nearby villages and farms. They emerged where farmers produced a food surplus and could be taxed or coerced to share their excess crops to sustain people with no time or land for farming. Priests, scribes, carpenters, and merchants increasingly congregated in the growing settlements. Cities usually contained many shops, public markets, government buildings, and religious centers.

This urban revolution constituted a major achievement perhaps as significant as the agricultural transformation, pioneering new lifestyles different from the early farming villages. In Southwest Asia, governments led by new social hierarchies dominated the first small cities emerging between 3500 and 3200 BCE. Soon cities appeared elsewhere. Small shops and makeshift stalls selling foodstuffs, household items, or folk medicines lined many streets. Hawkers peddled their wares from door to door. Craftsmen in workshops fashioned the items used in daily life, such as pottery, tools, and jewelry. Some of the goods made, mined, or grown locally were traded by land or sea to distant cities. Thus, the rise of cities reshaped societies and fostered networks of communication and exchange.

1-4c The Rise of States, Economies, and Recordkeeping

Food production and urbanization eventually led to the formation of **states**, formal governments that controlled a recognized territory and exercised power over both people and things.

muratart/Shutterstock.com

IMAGE 1.7 **Çatal Hüyük** A view of rooms and walls in one of the first known towns, Çatal Hüyük in eastern Turkey. The ruins contained many art objects, murals, wall sculpture, and woven cloth.

Q What does the photo tell us about the life of people in the town?

The people within them, often from diverse ethnic and cultural backgrounds, did not necessarily share all the same values or allegiances. Complex urban societies organized into states developed at least three thousand years ago on all the inhabited continents except Australia.

These urban societies relied on diversified economies that generated enough wealth to support a division of labor and social, cultural, and religious hierarchies. Farmers, laborers, craftsmen, merchants, priests, soldiers, bureaucrats, and scholars served specialized functions. The priests staffed the religious institutions that emerged as societies that organized and standardized their beliefs. Some states constructed monumental architecture, such as large temples, palaces, and city walls. While men dominated most of the hierarchies and heavy labor, women also played key economic roles. They made the cloth: preparing the raw materials, spinning the yarn, weaving the yarn into fabrics, and fashioning and sewing the clothing, blankets, and other useful items, while passing along their knowledge from mother to daughter. Most urban societies were connected to elaborate trade networks extending well beyond the immediate region. By 5000 BCE the first seafaring vessels had been built around the Persian Gulf. By 4000 BCE a network of merchant contacts linked India and Mesopotamia, 1,250 miles apart. Clay counting tokens used for trade had appeared by 3100 BCE, if not earlier. Various peoples in Asia and later Africa, Australia, the Pacific islands, and North America adopted some form of shell money. In the Eastern Hemisphere and Pacific islands these were most commonly whole or pieces of cowrie shells obtained from the coasts of the Indian Ocean and Southeast Asia.

The early urban societies also introduced cultural innovations such as recordkeeping and literature. A system of recordkeeping could involve a written language, such as those developed very early by the Sumerians, Egyptians, Phoenicians, Greeks, Chinese, Olmecs, and Maya, among others. In most literate societies writing was usually reserved for the privileged few until recent centuries, so knowledge of literature was not widespread. Or records could be kept by a class of memory experts, such as the professional "rememberers" among many African and South American peoples. But most societies created rich oral traditions of stories, legends, historical accounts, and poems that could be shared with all the people. For example, for many millennia Aboriginal Australians memorized vast knowledge about their environment, customs, myths, and history and passed it on to successive generations.

1-4d The Rise of Pastoral Nomadism

Not long after the rise of farming some societies adopted an alternative to agriculture and cities known as **pastoral nomadism**, an economy based on raising livestock. Both trade and conflict between pastoral nomads and settled farmers was a major theme in history. On land unsuitable for farming, some people began specializing in herding, moving their camps and animals seasonally in search of pasture and trading meat, hides, or livestock to nearby farmers for grain. Although pastoral nomadism involved dispersed rather than concentrated populations, some pastoral nomads exercised a strong influence on societies with much greater populations. Pastoral nomads

mostly concentrated in grasslands and deserts. Grasslands covered much of central and western Asia from Mongolia to southern Russia, as well as large parts of eastern and southern Africa. By 2000 BCE, the Sahara region of northern Africa was part of a great inhospitable arid zone stretching from Africa's western tip eastward through North Africa and Arabia into western and Central Asia to the frontiers of China.

Pastoralists lived very differently than farmers. They domesticated horses in Central Asia around 4300 BCE and camels in Arabia around 3000 or 2500 BCE. Although they had few material possessions, pastoralists often had humane values and a rich cultural life. Since they needed a large area to support each animal, herds had to be kept small to prevent overgrazing. Hence, herders lived in small, dispersed groups, generally organized by extended families that were often part of **tribes**, associations of clans tracing descent from a common ancestor. While some societies maintained egalitarian social structures, others were headed by chiefs. Among some Central Asians, women held a high status and even became warriors. Burial mounds in Turkestan contain the remains of what may be female warriors from 2,500 years ago, interred with daggers, swords, and bronze-tipped arrows. Some pastoralists became tough, martial peoples who were greatly feared by the farmers, and before modern times Central Asian pastoralists like the Huns and Mongols played significant roles in world history.

Particularly influential in ancient world history were the tribes known collectively as the **Indo-Europeans** (IN-dough-YUR-uh-PEE-uns), so named because their original common tongue spawned the many related languages spoken today by these peoples' descendants. Scholars vigorously debate their origins and dispersal. The original Indo-European homeland was probably located in Anatolia (modern Turkey), the nearby Caucasus Mountains, or the adjacent southern Russian/Ukrainian plains to the north of the Black Sea. Eventually, because of the spread of these strongly patriarchal tribes, most people in Europe, Iran, and northern India came to speak Indo-European languages.

Indo-European expansion apparently occurred in several waves. Some Indo-Europeans may have moved into Europe and Central Asia as early as 6500 or 7000 BCE, carrying with them not only their language but also perhaps farming technology. The culturally mixed people who resulted may have been the ancestors of the Celts and Greeks. Between 3000 and 2000 BCE many Indo-European pastoralists were driven from their western Asian homeland by some disaster, dispersing in every direction, splitting up into smaller units, and driving their herds of cattle, sheep, goats, and horses with them.

These dispersals of Indo-Europeans set the stage for profound changes across Eurasia. Encountering farming peoples, some turned to conquest. Scholars debate whether some of these people, termed by scholars the *Yamnaya*, moved into central

pastoral nomadism An economy based on breeding, rearing, and harvesting livestock.

tribes Associations of clans that traced descent from a common ancestor.

Indo-Europeans Various tribes who all spoke related languages derived from some original common tongue and who eventually settled Europe, Iran, and northern India.

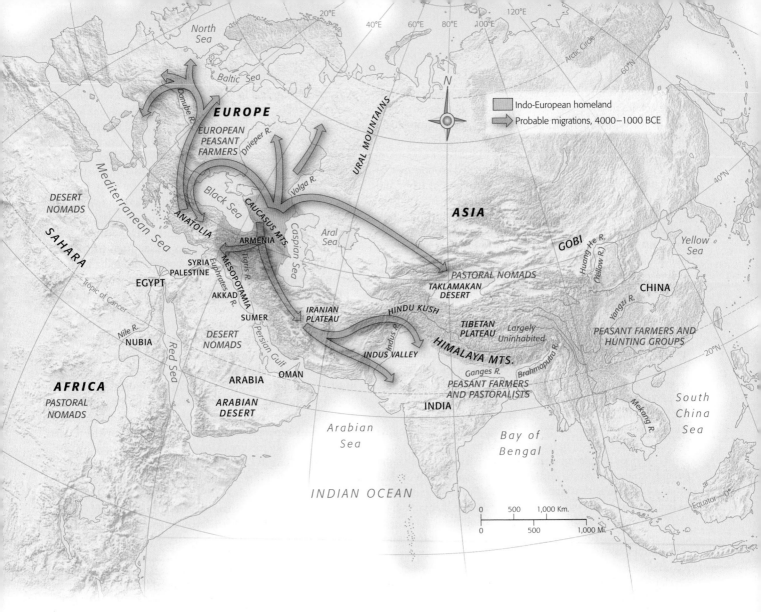

MAP 1.3 **The Indo-European Migrations and Eurasian Pastoralism** Some societies, especially in parts of Africa and Asia, adapted to environmental contexts by developing a pastoral, or animal herding, economy. One large pastoral group, the Indo-Europeans, eventually expanded from their home area into Europe, southwestern Asia, Central Asia, and India.

Q What does the map tell us about the influence of geography on the migrations and routes of the various Indo-European peoples and where their descendants in the Eastern Hemisphere live today?

and western Europe gradually or in several large waves, conquering or gradually assimilating and intermarrying with the original inhabitants. The Hittites gained dominance in Anatolia and then, around 2000 BCE, expanded their empire into Mesopotamia. Other tribes pushed on between 2500 and 1500 BCE, some to the west into Greece, some east as far as the western fringe of China, some south into Persia (Iran).

From Persia or Central Asia some tribes moved southeast through mountain passes into northwestern India. Spreading their languages and imposing their military power, they eventually absorbed or subdued other peoples. Most eventually abandoned pastoral nomadism for farming, but their dispersal opened a new chapter in the history of Europe, the Middle East, and India (see Map 1.3).

KEY POINTS

▶ Metals such as bronze and iron helped improve farming tools and weaponry.

▶ Highly productive farming allowed for the formation of the first cities, which became centers of trade.

▶ People in cities developed forms of recordkeeping and writing.

▶ Herders such as Indo-Europeans played an important role in spreading culture across Eurasia, though most eventually took up farming.

Chapter Summary

The story of humans and their societies constitutes only a tiny part of the broader 4.5-billion-year history of the earth. Some four million years ago our hominid ancestors emerged in Africa, learning to walk upright, to make and use tools, and to control fire. Eventually, evolution produced modern humans, who developed language and more complex social structures. During the long Paleolithic period, all humans, using simple technologies and living in small groups, hunted wild animals and gathered wild plants, maintaining a balance with their environment. While many such societies survived over the millennia, eventually environmental changes and other factors encouraged most peoples to adopt farming.

Beginning between 10,000 and 11,500 years ago, the climate warmed and populations increased. In a great transition, some people began to grow their own food and domesticate wild animals. Farming probably emerged first in southwestern Asia. By 2000 BCE various peoples in Eurasia, Africa, and the Americas had adopted farming, a change that led to larger populations, altered people's relationship to the environment, and set the stage for cities, states, social classes, and recordkeeping in the Afro-Eurasian zone between 3500 and 3000 BCE. The first cities and states formed in sub-Saharan Africa and the Americas between 3000 and 1000 BCE. Some people living in the grasslands and deserts became nomadic pastoralists and interacted with settled farmers. The formation of distinctive societies and increased contact between peoples inaugurated a new era of human history.

Key Terms

hominids 11
australopithecines 12
Homo habilis 12
Homo erectus 12
Neanderthals 12
Denisovans 13
Cro-Magnons 13

Homo sapiens 13
Paleolithic 16
Mesolithic 16
Neolithic 16
matrilineal kinship 17
animism 17
polytheism 17

shamans 17
horticulture 20
peasants 21
states 26
pastoral nomadism 27
tribes 27
Indo-Europeans 27

Ancient Societies in Mesopotamia, India, and Central Asia, 5000–600 BCE

" *[The goddess] Inanna filled Agade [a Mesopotamian city] . . . with gold. She filled the storerooms with barley, bronze, and lumps of lapis lazuli [a stone used in jewelry]. The ships at the wharves were an awesome sight. All the lands around rested in security.* "

—Poem praising the goddess of love and generosity, written in 2250 BCE[1]

DEA PICTURE LIBRARY/De Agostini/Getty Images

IMAGE 2.1 **Bull's Head from Sumerian Lyre** This bull's head is part of the soundbox of a wooden harp. The harp, made in Sumeria around 2600 BCE and found in the tomb of an Ur queen, is covered with gold and lapis lazuli and reflects the popularity of music in Mesopotamian society.

Q What features of this bull's head stand out?

[1]The quote is from the Oriental Institute, the University of Chicago.

Some five thousand years ago in the southern Mesopotamian (MESS-uh-puh-TAIM-ee-an) city of Uruk (OO-rook), an unknown artist carved a beautiful narrative relief on a large vase and donated it to the city's temple for the goddess of love, Inanna (ih-NON-a), the first known goddess in recorded history. The scenes of domestic and religious life celebrate a festival honoring the goddess, while an agricultural scene shows sheep, barley, and water, the staples of the area's economy. A procession of men carry foodstuffs they will present as gifts of gratitude to Inanna, possibly the female figure with a tall, horned headdress. The vase pictures for us the social order and rituals of one of the world's earliest cities.

Sometime after the people in Southwest Asia and India had become comfortable with farming technology, they began to make the next great transition by founding the first cities and states in the Indus Valley in northwestern India and all along the **Fertile Crescent**, a large semicircle of fertile land that included the valleys of the Tigris (TIE-gris) and Euphrates (you-FRAY-teez) Rivers stretching northwest from the Persian Gulf to the eastern shores of the Mediterranean Sea. Ancient South Asians (in what is today India, Pakistan, and Nepal) also established the foundations for several enduring religions.

The Mesopotamians and Indians, benefiting from contact through trade and migration networks, were among various Afro-Eurasian peoples who built the foundations to sustain large populations. For at least three millennia a large majority of the world's population has lived in an arc stretching from Egypt and Mesopotamia eastward through India to China and Japan. The people of western Asia created the first systematic use of writing, bronze, large states, institutionalized religions to worship deities like Inanna, and networks to exchange products and information by land and sea. The city of Agade (uh-GAH-duh) was visited by traders from near and far, while Southwest Asia became a crossroads between Europe, Africa, and southern Asia and a great hub for trade and communication networks extending to distant lands.

Fertile Crescent A large semicircular fertile region that included the valleys of the Tigris and Euphrates Rivers stretching northwest from the Persian Gulf to the eastern shores of the Mediterranean Sea.

2-1 Early Mesopotamian Urbanized Societies, to 2000 BCE

TRANSITIONS SOCIETIES

Q Why did farming, cities, and states develop first in the Fertile Crescent?

Around five thousand years ago, small city-states emerged in Mesopotamia, especially in the southern Tigris-Euphrates Valley, establishing a foundation for much that would come later in the region and later in world history. The connections between these diverse peoples helped their cultures change and grow. Over the centuries various peoples moved into the area, each adopting and building on the achievements of their predecessors. Their cities were dominated by religious temples, and their people were divided into elaborate social class structures. As conquerors combined city-states into empires, Mesopotamian societies were soon linked by trade to the Mediterranean and North Africa.

> **CONNECTION to TODAY**
>
> In what ways does Sumerian society seem similar to and different from our societies today?

2-1a Western Asian Environments

Life in western Asia owed much to the geographic features that brought people together. Most early urban societies began first in wide river valleys such as the Tigris-Euphrates, Indus, and Nile because they provided life-giving irrigation for crops that supported larger populations. In Mesopotamia (the Greek word for the "land between the rivers"), the flooding of the Tigris and Euphrates Rivers, which stretch from the western edge of the Persian Gulf through today's Iraq into Syria and southeastern Turkey, made possible a flourishing society. The long river valley promoted interaction, both friendly and hostile, between peoples, as well as frequent invasions through mountain passes by people living to the north and east. To the northwest is the mountainous Anatolia (**ANN-uh-TOE-lee-uh**) Peninsula (modern Turkey),

and to the east lies Iran (known through most of history as Persia), a land of mountains and deserts and the pathway to India and Central Asia. To the south the Arabian peninsula, largely desert, was characterized by oasis agriculture and nomadic pastoralism.

Ancient Mesopotamia had a climate similar to southern California today. Most rain fell in the winter, and summer temperatures in some places reached 120 degrees Fahrenheit. During the long, scorching summer, the land baked stone-hard, searing winds blew up a choking dust, and vegetation withered. The winter brought winds, clouds, and the occasional rains, while spring brought rains and melting snows from nearby mountains that swelled the rivers to flood level, sometimes submerging the plains. Still, the annual but unpredictable floods created natural levees that could be drained and planted, and the nearby swamps contained abundant fish and wildlife.

Many different peoples settled the region, some of them speaking Semitic languages, including Arabic and Hebrew, which are related to some African tongues. Speakers of Turkish tongues and of Indo-European languages such as Persian, Armenian, and Kurdish arrived later. Europeans later referred to southwestern Asia as Asia Minor or the Near East and to the region along the eastern Mediterranean coast as the Levant (**luh-VANT**) ("rising of the sun"). Geographers today use the label *Southwest Asia* and often lump the region together with Islamic North Africa under the broader concept of the "Middle East," midway between East Asia and Europe.

	6000 BCE	5500 BCE	5000 BCE	4500 BCE	4000 BCE	3500 BCE
		● 5500 BCE First Sumerian settlements				
MESOPOTAMIA						
INDIA AND CENTRAL ASIA						

The Tigris and Euphrates Rivers fostered several Mesopotamian societies. The modern city of Baghdad is midway up the Tigris, and ancient Babylon was only a few miles away on the Euphrates. Such cities arose when the farmers and herders in the nearby hills needed more food. Possibly pushed by a cooler climate, they left the hill country and created the first towns in the marshy areas near the head of the Persian Gulf, building elaborate irrigation canals to grow food after the annual floods. This irrigation had significant consequences, for it necessitated the cooperation that laid the foundations for organized societies and then cities. Yet irrigation also slowly degraded the soil, the salts it added eventually creating infertile desert.

2-1b The Pioneering Sumerians and Their Neighbors

Settling in southern Mesopotamia about 5500 BCE, the Sumerians built the first Mesopotamian cities and states (see Map 2.1). By 3500 BCE Uruk in Sumer **(soo-MUHR)** had grown into a city, eventually reaching a population of fifty thousand. Other Mesopotamian peoples, such as those in the north at Tell Hamoukar (see Chapter 1), may have also forged early states. By 3000 BCE Sumerians had created a network of city-states, urban centers surrounded by agricultural land that was controlled by the city and used to support its citizens. By 2500 BCE these Sumerian societies had grown to several million people. Uruk was surrounded by five miles of fortified walls and had influence as far north as modern Turkey. An attack by Uruk on Tell Hamoukar is the world's oldest known example of large-scale organized warfare.

The Sumerians were clearly proud of their cities and felt that their city life made them superior to other peoples.

A Sumerian myth begins with the lines "Behold the bond of Heaven and Earth, the city. Behold the kindly wall … its pure river, its quay where the boats stand … its pure canal."[2] The mud-baked brick houses of Sumerian cities were constructed around courtyards. The largest city building was the temple, or **ziggurat** (ZIG-uh-rat), a stepped, pyramidal-shaped building (almost an artificial mountain) that was seen as the home of that city's chief god. One of these temples may have inspired the later Hebrew story of the tower of Babel **(BAY-buhl/BAH-buhl)**.

2-1c Sumerian Society and Economy

The Sumerians, like later Mesopotamians, generally divided their specialized workers into full-time farmers, professional soldiers, government officials, artisans, traders, and priests. At first Sumerian cities were governed by assemblies composed of leading citizens. Whether these assemblies amounted to a kind of democratic government is a matter of scholarly debate. The assemblies seem to have appointed a city leader, sometimes a woman, with both secular and religious authority. However, the waging of wars led to more domination by rulers, priests, and nobles, and gradually women lost the right to be elected leader and serve in the assemblies. When war leaders became kings, or hereditary monarchs, the assemblies lost power.

The Sumerian nobility and priests controlled most of the land in and around the city, which was tilled by tenant farmers or slaves. A Sumerian proverb claimed that "the poor man is better dead than alive; if he has bread, he has no salt; if he has salt, he has no bread."[3] The many slaves, who included captives taken in battles and criminals, were

ziggurat A stepped, pyramidal-shaped temple building in Sumerian cities, seen as the home of the chief god of the city.

---

[2]The quote is from the Oriental Institute, the University of Chicago.
[3]Quoted in Frederick Gentels and Melvin Steinfield, *Hangups from Way Back: Historical Myths and Canons*, vol. 1, 2nd ed. (San Francisco: Canfield, 1974), 64.

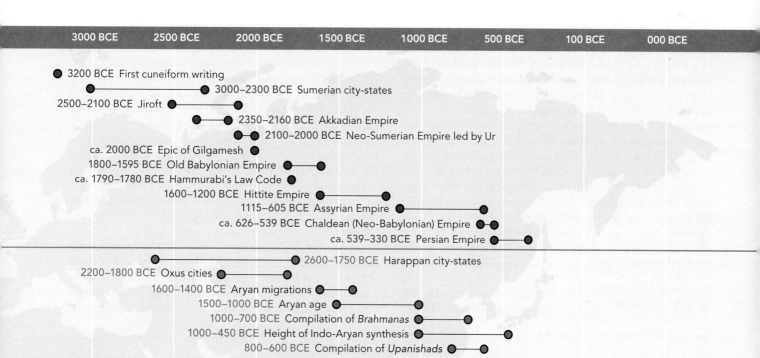

| 3000 BCE | 2500 BCE | 2000 BCE | 1500 BCE | 1000 BCE | 500 BCE | 100 BCE | 000 BCE |

3200 BCE First cuneiform writing
3000–2300 BCE Sumerian city-states
2500–2100 BCE Jiroft
2350–2160 BCE Akkadian Empire
2100–2000 BCE Neo-Sumerian Empire led by Ur
ca. 2000 BCE Epic of Gilgamesh
1800–1595 BCE Old Babylonian Empire
ca. 1790–1780 BCE Hammurabi's Law Code
1600–1200 BCE Hittite Empire
1115–605 BCE Assyrian Empire
ca. 626–539 BCE Chaldean (Neo-Babylonian) Empire
ca. 539–330 BCE Persian Empire

2600–1750 BCE Harappan city-states
2200–1800 BCE Oxus cities
1600–1400 BCE Aryan migrations
1500–1000 BCE Aryan age
1000–700 BCE Compilation of *Brahmanas*
1000–450 BCE Height of Indo-Aryan synthesis
800–600 BCE Compilation of *Upanishads*

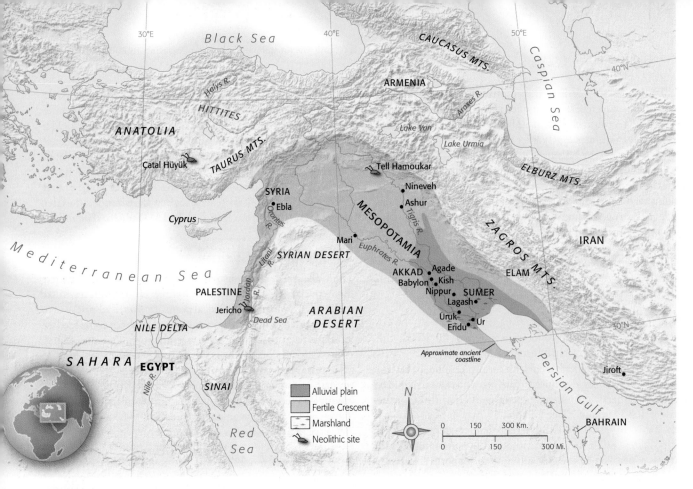

MAP 2.1 **Ancient Mesopotamia** The people of Mesopotamia and the adjacent regions of the Fertile Crescent pioneered farming. The Mesopotamians also built the first cities and formed the first states. Sumerian cities dominated southern Mesopotamia for over a millennium, only to lose power to societies from northern Mesopotamia.

Q What are some of the reasons that Mesopotamia's location in the Fertile Crescent and its particular geography, environment, and climate may have fostered the migration of peoples, agriculture, state building, and warfare?

treated as personal property but allowed to marry. Eventually royal officials, nobility, and priests controlled most of the economic life of the cities. Royal tombs in Ur show that the elite lived well but practiced human sacrifice on a large scale. When a king or queen died some members of their court, including soldiers and attendants, who may have considered it an honor, were killed in grisly rituals and buried with them. Their bodies were usually arranged neatly in the royal tomb alongside their dead sovereigns, the warriors with weapons at their side and the women in elaborate headdress. Ritual killing associated with a royal death was also practiced by some other ancient cultures.

The Sumerians introduced **patriarchy**, a system in which men largely control women and children and also shape ideas about appropriate gender behavior. Sumerian women were generally subservient to men, but they could inherit property, run their own businesses, and serve as witnesses in court. A queen enjoyed much respect as the wife of the king, and Sumerian religion allowed a woman to be the high priestess if the city divinity was female. Within family life, which was much treasured, women were important but also faced stereotypes, as this proverb suggests: "The wife is a man's future; the son is a man's refuge; the daughter is a man's salvation; the daughter-in-law is a man's devil."[4]

The trade networks involving Sumeria may have been some of the first in world history with significant consequences. Because of their lack of natural resources, the Sumerian cities formed extensive trade links with neighboring societies. They imported copper from the Caucasus Mountains to the north and then discovered how to mix it with tin to make bronze, an alloy that made for stronger weapons. This discovery began the Bronze Age in western Asia; later bronze helped shape other societies in Eurasia and North Africa. The Sumerians also imported gold, ivory, obsidian, and other necessities from Anatolia, the Nile Valley, Ethiopia, India, the Caspian Sea, and the eastern shore of the Mediterranean.

The Persian Gulf became a major waterway, with many trading ports. Bahrain (**bah-RAIN**) Island served as a transshipment point for goods flowing in from all directions and as a hub where various traders and travelers met. Mesopotamian merchants traveled there carrying textiles, leather objects, wool,

patriarchy A system in which men largely control women and children and shape ideas about appropriate gender behavior.

[4]Quoted in William H. Stiebing, Jr., *Ancient Near Eastern History and Culture* (New York: Longman, 2003), 48.

and olive oil and returned with copper bars, ivory, precious objects, and rare woods from various western Asian societies and India. Trade helped people learn and profit from each other's skills and surplus goods.

The Sumerians also had some trade and other connections with Jiroft (**JEER-oft**) in southeastern Iran, another urban-based, bronze-using farming society that emerged sometime between 3000 and 2500 BCE. Jiroft's economy was based on cultivating date palms. Its gaily decorated capital city, with lofty red brick towers, supplied craftsmen to Uruk. The ruins of Jiroft city include a two-story citadel, a Sumerian-like ziggurat, the world's oldest known board games, and staggering numbers of decorated vases, goblets, cups, and boxes, often adorned with precious stones from India and Afghanistan.

2-1d Sumerian Writing and Technology

The world's first written records were produced by the Sumerians, who were innovators in many areas. Trade and the need to keep accurate records of agricultural production and public and private business dealings led around 3200 BCE to the **cuneiform** (kyoo-NEE-uh-form) (Latin for "wedge-shaped") writing system. Temple recordkeepers, or scribes, made rough pictures (say, of an animal or fish) on soft clay with a reed stylus that made wedges in the clay and then baked the bricks on which these pictograms were scratched. Soon a stylized version of the pictogram stood for an idea, and eventually an even more abstract version with a phonetic sign described a speech sound. The oldest tablets allow us for the first time to know the names of a few ancient people. For example, a five-thousand-year-old receipt for shipments of barley revealed that Kushim was the accountant in charge of the transaction.

Writing provided a way of communicating with people over long distances and allowed rulers to administer larger states. Those who controlled the written word, like those who master electronic communication in our day, had power, prestige, and a monopoly over a society's official history. Writing also gave temple scribes and religious leaders the power to determine how

cuneiform ("wedge-shaped") Latin term used to describe the writing system invented by the Sumerians.

IMAGE 2.2 **Ruins of Early City of Uruk** Renowned for its walls, the Sumerian city was a rich source of art objects and fine architecture. Uruk's best-known king was the legendary Gilgamesh.

Ⓠ Can you envision what the city might have looked like in the fourth century BCE?

ESSAM AL-SUDANI/AFP/Getty Images

written texts attributed to the gods should be interpreted. Since writing required mastery of at least three hundred symbols, only a few people, mostly from the upper class, learned this skill. In part to produce scribes, the Sumerians created the world's first schools, where strict instructors beat students for misbehavior or sloppy work. A clay tablet describes the life of a pupil who spent twenty-four days a month in school and was frequently beaten: "My teacher said: 'Your hand [writing] is unsatisfactory.' [He] caned me. I [begin to hate] the scribal art."[5] However, because cuneiform eventually transformed pictures into phonetic sounds, it made the written word more accessible, even for people whose only goal was a good recipe for a meal of red broth and meat. The cuneiform script was so adaptable that it was used in multiple cultures over several thousand years to write a number of quite different spoken languages.

Writing became crucial in history by making it easier to express abstract ideas and create an intellectual life based on a body of literature. The oldest known signed poetry was composed by Enheduanna **(en-who-DWAHN-ah)**, a Sumerian priestess and princess living around 2300 BCE. Royal women were often authors. A written language based on clearly understood symbols also allowed communication among people who spoke different languages but understood the same written symbols. For example, the number *5* is understood today the same way by Spanish speakers, who pronounce it "cinco," and German speakers, who say "funf."

While giving a strong sense of identity to all who shared a language, writing also encouraged the spread of trade and culture, including religion, to other peoples.

Sumerians also pioneered the first use of the wheel, glass, and fertilizer, inventions that we still live with today; created some of the earliest calendars based on their observations of the movements of various celestial bodies; and introduced one of the first mathematical systems, based on the number *60*. Remnants of this system can be seen today in our sixty-minute hours and sixty-second minutes. Many other peoples eventually adopted these innovations. Humanity also inherited from the Sumerians the division of night and day into twelve hours each. Sumerian intellectual advances set a framework for scientific progress in Mesopotamia over the next two millennia, especially in astronomy. By the eighth century BCE stargazers pondered the mechanics of the heavens in order to make predictions from what they saw in the night sky. Hence, they observed the daily movement of the stars and the shape of constellations, documenting them on clay tablets and recording and predicting celestial events such as lunar and solar eclipses. Their interest in the stars also led to the nonscientific field of astrology, predicting the impact of the stars and planets on individuals, which became and remains hugely popular around the world.

Although they were not the first to convert barley into beer, the Sumerians, like us, enjoyed alcoholic beverages and designated a special goddess, called Ninkasi or "the lady who fills the

IMAGE 2.3 **The Royal Standard of Ur** This mosaic on a wooden box from around 2600 BCE, made of inlaid shells and limestone, was found in a royal tomb. It depicts various aspects of warfare in the Mesopotamian city-state of Ur. The bottom panel shows four-wheeled battle wagons drawn by a horselike animal. The middle panel features a battle scene with soldiers wearing armor and helmets on the left and captured enemy soldiers on the right. The top panel shows war prisoners being brought before the king (the tall figure in the center), with his bodyguards behind him. A companion panel illustrates peace.

Q What can you learn about the people and life in Mesopotamia, including warfare and transportation, from the photo?

[5] Quoted in Samuel Noah Kramer, *Cradle of Civilization* (New York: Time-Life Books, 1967), 122.

mouth," to supervise beer production. The many taverns fostered early drinking songs: "I will summon brewers and cupbearers to serve us floods of beer and keep it passing round! Our hearts enchanted and our souls radiant."[6]

2-1e The Akkadian Empire and Its Rivals

For centuries each Sumerian city had its own king who ruled the people in the name of the city's god. This independence ended about 2350 BCE when Sargon (**SAHR-gone**), the ruler of Akkad (**AH-kahd**), a region just north of Sumer whose capital was Agade, conquered Uruk and then united the other Sumerian cities under his family's rule. This was the world's first known empire, defined as a large state controlling other societies through conquest or domination. The Akkadians enslaved many people in Mesopotamia, and slaves constituted perhaps a third of the empire's population. Under Sargon, whose name meant "true king," trade between Mesopotamia and India reached a peak. Indeed, merchant ships from as far away as Oman (**O-mahn**) in eastern Arabia and even farther away, from India, docked at Agade's wharves, carrying copper and various exotic products.

Sargon's empire soon came into conflict with one created by another city, Ebla (**EBB-luh**) in northern Mesopotamia, whose large empire stretched from eastern Turkey to Mari (**MAH-ree**), several hundred miles north of Akkad. By the twenty-first century BCE the Akkadian Empire was destroyed, probably from a combination of internal conflicts, external attacks, and less rainfall due to a disastrous drought between 2200 and 1900 BCE that affected much of Eurasia. Indeed, Mesopotamian societies were powerless against abrupt climate change, and Sumerian legends express dread of the periodic droughts: "The famine was severe, nothing was produced. The fields are not watered. In all the lands there was no vegetation [and] only weeds grew."[7] Irrigation canals silted up, and settlements became ghost towns as people migrated.

As the Akkadian Empire collapsed, a new Sumerian dynasty led by Ur took over much of the lower valley between 2100 and 2000 BCE, forming the neo-Sumerian Empire. Some Ur kings boasted of their commitment to art and intellectual life. But a coalition of enemies eventually sacked and burned Ur along with other Sumerian cities. Ur's temples were destroyed, its populations killed or enslaved, and its treasures plundered. A surviving lamentation describes the destruction: "Ur is destroyed, bitter is its lament. The country's blood now fills its holes like hot bronze in a mould. Our temple is destroyed, the gods have abandoned us, like migrating birds. Smoke lies on our city like a shroud."[8]

The Akkadians, Eblaites, and neo-Sumerians established the first empires in history, even though their creations were short-lived and not the large bureaucratic organizations we see in later empires. They were largely collections of city-states that acknowledged one city as overlord. It soon became clear that whoever had the best army would dominate Mesopotamia.

KEY POINTS

▶ The first urban societies and states of Mesopotamia developed in the Tigris-Euphrates Basin.

▶ Sumerian society was hierarchical and patriarchal.

▶ The earliest writing system was probably the cuneiform system, developed by the Sumerians.

▶ The world's first empire, the Akkadian Empire, was founded by Sargon in an area just north of the Sumerians.

2-2 Later Mesopotamian Societies and Their Legacies, 2000–600 BCE

▦ SOCIETIES

🇶 What were some of the main features of Mesopotamian societies?

The Sumerians and Akkadians established a pattern of city living, state building, and imperial expansion. From 2000 to 539 BCE a series of peoples coming mainly from the north successively dominated Mesopotamia and created new empires, each contributing to the politics, laws, culture, and thought of the region. This pattern changed only when the entire area was incorporated into the Persian Empire.

CONNECTION to TODAY

How do you think the Mesopotamian wars and empires compared to those in the modern world?

2-2a The Babylonians and Hittites

Babylon was the first state to dominate Mesopotamia in this era. In 1800 BCE the Amorites (**AM-uh-rites**) conquered Babylon, a city about 300 miles north of the Persian Gulf and, based there, gradually extended their control. Babylon's most famous king, Hammurabi

---

[6]Quoted in Jean Bottero, *Everyday Life in Ancient Mesopotamia* (Baltimore: Johns Hopkins University Press, 2001), 71.
[7]Quoted in Brian Fagan, *The Long Summer: How Climate Changed Civilization* (New York: Basic Books, 2004), 138.
[8]Quoted in Michael Wood, *Legacy: The Search for Ancient Cultures* (New York: Sterling, 1994), 34.

(HAM-uh-rah-bee), who ruled from 1792 to 1750 BCE, had nearly three hundred laws collected to "make justice appear in the land, to destroy the evil and the wicked [so] that the strong might not oppress the weak."[9] His law of retaliation—an eye for an eye and a tooth for a tooth—remains famous today, and some of his principles appeared later in Hebrew laws. Some 3,700 years ago the Babylonians also developed the mathematical field of trigonometry, the branch of mathematics dealing with the relations or functions of the angles and sides of triangles, making it easier to do calculations in fields like astronomy, surveying, map making, and, many centuries later, artillery range finding. Their breakthrough, using a base of sixty, came fifteen hundred years before the classical Greeks created the version used today.

By 1595 BCE the Babylonian Empire had disintegrated from attacks by the Hittites (HIT-ites), an Indo-European people from central Anatolia who expanded their power until they met the equally strong Egyptians in Syria and Palestine. The Hittite Empire dominated various parts of western Asia from 1600 to 1200 BCE. By sending plague victims into enemy lands, the Hittites pioneered the first biological weapons. Later they also developed iron weapons, which were superior to those made of bronze. They treated their subjects less harshly than the Babylonians and adopted many Mesopotamian gods, establishing a tradition of religious tolerance in the region.

2-2b The Assyrian Empire and Regional Supremacy

In 1115 BCE the Assyrians (uh-SEER-e-uhns)—by creating a large, well-organized military; systematically using terror against enemies; and devising methods of bureaucratic organization that later empires imitated—began conquering an empire that was eventually larger than any before, with a population diverse in culture and geography. One of their greatest kings, Tiglath-pileser (TIG-lath-pih-LEE-zuhr) III (745–727 BCE), conquered the entire eastern Mediterranean shore, and later Assyrian rulers added Egypt to the empire. One Assyrian king described himself with some accuracy as "obedient to his gods and receiving the tribute of the four corners of the world."[10] Using iron weapons while their enemies still relied on softer bronze ones, the Assyrians launched armies of over fifty thousand men drawn from all corners of the empire and divided into a core of infantrymen aided by cavalry and horse-drawn chariots. They used battering rams and tunnels against the city walls of their enemies and employed guerrilla, or irregular hit-and-run tactics, when fighting in the forests or mountains.

Assyrian kings created a systematic bureaucracy to rule over several million people in the Tigris-Euphrates heartland, as part of a reliable and efficient communication network of "royal roads," and created an early version of the "pony express" that allowed them to send messages hundreds of miles within a week. While the rulers were notorious for their luxury, extravagance, and debauchery, some were both brutal and learned. Ashurbanipal (ah-shur-BAH-nugh-pahl) (680–627 BCE) was a ruthless but bookish despot who also founded a great library to collect tablets from all over the country. He boasted that, in school, he learned to solve complex mathematical problems and discovered the "hidden treasure" of writing. Assyrian kings were builders on a grand scale. To inaugurate a new palace, Ashurbanipal bragged that he invited some seventy thousand guests and for ten days gave them food and drink, bathed and anointed them, bringing peace and joy before sending them back to their own territories. One of their capitals, Ninevah, was a huge city by ancient standards and its temples and palaces were decorated with colossal sculptures and beautiful carved reliefs. An intricate system of aqueducts and canals watered the king's spectacular pleasure gardens and game parks. But such conspicuous consumption stressed the state treasury.

2-2c Violence and the Fall of the Assyrians

The Assyrians were most remembered, and deplored, for their brutality, which ultimately contributed to their downfall. Ashurbanipal bragged about mutilating and burning prisoners. After destroying the state of Elam in Iran, he boasted that "like the onset of a terrible hurricane I overwhelmed Elam. I cut off the head of … their braggart king. In countless numbers I killed his warriors." As to the capital city, "I destroyed it … [and] burned it with fire."[11] Soldiers routinely looted cities, destroyed crops, and impaled their enemies. To prevent revolts, the Assyrians often simply moved people to another part of the vast empire. For example, according to legends, all the inhabitants of one of the two small Hebrew kingdoms in Palestine were exiled to Mesopotamia, where they disappeared from history (see Chapter 3). Yet the Assyrians also tolerated other religions, allowing the Hebrew faith to survive the conquest of their state.

Many hated Assyria's brutal rule. Eventually Assyria was weakened by civil wars, political unrest, overpopulation, and drought caused by climate change. In 612 BCE, a coalition including the Chaldeans (kal-DEE-uhns) (also known as neo-Babylonians) captured the Assyrian capital at Nineveh (NIN-uh-vuh), burning the spectacular palaces and temples to the ground. The fall of Assyria was an iconic event, recorded by passages in the Hebrew bible and by Greek and Roman writers. They described the fall as punishment for the moral depravity of the rulers. The winners write history, but some modern writers have been kinder to the Assyrians, the greatest power of its era. Their most memorable neo-Babylonian ruler, Nebuchadnezzar (NAB-oo-kuhd-nez-uhr) II (r. 605–562 BCE), a brutal strongman, rebuilt Babylon and, according to ancient accounts, adorned it with magnificent palaces and elaborate terraced "hanging gardens." Built to please one of his wives, the gardens became famous throughout the ancient world. Some scholars

[9]Quoted in G. R. Driver and John C. Miles, eds., *The Babylonian Laws*, vol. II (Oxford, UK: Clarendon Press, 1952), 7.
[10]Quoted in N. B. Jankowska, "Asshur, Mitanni, and Arrapkhe," in *Early Antiquity*, I. M. Diakonoff, ed. (Chicago: University of Chicago Press, 1991), 256.
[11]Quoted in Kramer, *Cradle of Civilization*, 75.

doubt that the Hanging Gardens in Babylon ever existed and were a myth. But most scholars agree that Mesopotamians invented the idea of cultivating gardens purely for pleasure rather than food production and characterized them as "paradise." From there the notion spread throughout the ancient Mediterranean and much later the world, to the benefit of garden lovers today. Eventually wealthy private individuals and families, and not just kings, were cultivating private gardens in their own homes. Around 600 BCE some scribe in Babylon made a map on a clay tablet that depicted the world known to his society and centered on Babylon; it may be the oldest known effort at a world map. Nebuchadnezzar led the conquest of the remaining Hebrew kingdom in 586 BCE. The Chaldeans flourished from 626 BCE until they were conquered by the much larger Persian Empire in 539 BCE.

2-2d Mesopotamian Law and Society

Several documents tell us much about Mesopotamian life and beliefs. The eighteenth-century BCE Law Code of Hammurabi reveals the social structures of this early urban society (see Meet the People: Hammurabi the Lawgiver). Hammurabi's Code makes clear both how people were valued and how they viewed laws, government, and social norms. In noting that families were responsible for the crimes of any of their members, the Code probably reflected a high crime rate, no doubt because of the tremendous gap between rich and poor. To keep lines of inheritance clear, Hammurabi prescribed harsh punishments for sexual infidelity and incest, as did many societies. Women who violated social norms generally suffered harsher punishments than men, just as the eyes and teeth of poor men or slaves were worth less than the same body parts among the upper classes. Each slave was branded with the owner's symbol, and some endured harsh lives of forced labor. Yet some slaves also owned their own assets, carried on business, and even acquired their own slaves.

The Code also addressed economic issues. In this class-conscious society, a surgeon could lose his hand if his patient was a free man who failed to survive the operation, certainly a disincentive to take up medicine. If the patient was a slave, however, the surgeon had only to replace him or her with another slave. If a house collapsed, killing its inhabitants, the builder could be executed. The high interest rates on loans confirmed a thriving commercial class. The Code's punishments tell us how precarious life must have been in this society, where a single small break in an irrigation canal wall could spell disaster.

2-2e Mesopotamian Religion and Literature

Like most early people, the Mesopotamians believed in a host of gods and goddesses, such as Inanna, later called Ishtar (**ISH-tar**), the beautiful goddess of love who created desire. This polytheistic religion imposed no moral demands, but while the divinities came with human weaknesses, they were powerful enough to punish humans, who were created to serve them. People saw themselves as subject to the gods' whims and held ritual ceremonies in massive temples where the gods were housed. The Babylonians and later the Assyrians changed the names of some earlier gods but maintained the basic Sumerian view of the universe.

The *Epic of Gilgamesh* (**GILL-guh-mesh**), first written down about 2000 BCE but revised and retold by Mesopotamians for another 1,500 years, reveals some of their religious values and attitudes. Perhaps humanity's first epic adventure story, *Gilgamesh* echoes Hammurabi's view of the world as a dangerous place in which happiness is hard to find. While there are different versions in several languages, collectively they cover a range of attitudes and activities, among them love, greed, sex, sexual assault, responsibilities to society, and the centrality of urban culture. Although only one part of a very rich legacy of literature and mythology, *Gilgamesh* had the most enduring and widespread influence, enriching the traditions of varied Eurasian societies.

In one version of the story, the hero, modeled after a real king in Uruk about 2750 BCE and created to be two-thirds god and one-third man, engages in a series of adventures involving both the gods and men. With his friend Enkidu, Gilgamesh challenges and defeats the evil but divine giant who guards a mysterious cedar forest. Gilgamesh then rejects a proposal from Ishtar, telling her that she is fickle and recounting the disagreeable things she has done to her previous lovers, such as turning one of them into a wolf. In revenge, Ishtar causes the death of Enkidu. Reflecting on his friend's death, Gilgamesh searches for the key to eternal life, an ultimately futile quest involving many setbacks that reflects the general pessimism of Mesopotamian culture. A Uruk master scribe lamented: "Gilgamesh, what you seek you will never find. For when the Gods created Man they let death be his lot, eternal life they withheld. Let your every day be full of joy, love the child that holds your hand, let your wife delight in your embrace, for these alone are concerns of humanity."[12]

Scholars have noted the similarities between this epic and stories found in the later Hebrew book of Genesis. In both there is a paradise: the garden of Eden for the Hebrews, Dilmun for the Mesopotamians. In both a great flood destroys humankind, a man challenges the god(s), and a serpent comes between a man and immortality. However, although the writer or writers of Genesis may have been influenced by *Gilgamesh*, there are some differences in tone and attitude between the Babylonian and Hebrew versions. In the Hebrew story, God sends a flood to punish humans for evil living. In more urban Mesopotamia, where floods were frequent and destructive, the gods "decide to exterminate mankind" because "the uproar of mankind is intolerable and sleep is no longer possible." But a dissenting god causes his favorite mortal to survive by building a boat and loading it with his family and "the seed of all living creatures, the game of the field, and all the craftsmen."[13]

---

[12]Quoted in Wood, *Legacy*, 32.
[13]*The Epic of Gilgamesh*, trans. by N. K. Sandars (New York: Penguin Books, 1960), 108.

Hammurabi the Lawgiver

Hammurabi, a Babylonian king (r. 1792–1750 BCE) who was also at times a diplomat, warrior, builder of temples, digger of canals, and, most famously, lawgiver, personified Mesopotamian society. Many surviving tablets, inscriptions, and letters made the king and his era the best documented in Mesopotamian history. He seems to have been a good administrator and able general who governed fairly and efficiently. Like other Mesopotamian kings, Hammurabi probably had a chief queen and various concubines, as well as several sons and daughters.

When Hammurabi became king, Babylon was an insignificant city-state. To expand its power, Hammurabi shrewdly allied with the powerful king of Ashur and allowed him to conquer some nearby cities. For some years Hammurabi's small domain remained one of many rival states. Like other kings, Hammurabi had intelligence agents in other cities keeping him abreast of important developments such as pending alliances and troop movements. A spy for another king wrote that "whenever Hammurabi is perturbed by some matter, he … tells me whatever is troubling him, and all of the important information I continually report to my lord." After his army repulsed an invasion by rivals, a confident Hammurabi engaged in a long series of wars that added all of southern Mesopotamia and then much of the north to his kingdom. Finally, he conquered the strongest power, his former ally Ashur.

Kingship brought responsibilities. Hammurabi's letters reveal him sitting in his palace office and dictating to a secretary who recorded his orders or thoughts with a reed stylus on a clay tablet. Most letters conveyed commands to governors. His secretary also read aloud letters from officials. In his replies, Hammurabi tried to resolve problems, suggesting ways to clear a flooded shipping channel, warning delinquent tax collectors, punishing corrupt officials, or improving agricultural productivity. He also held daily audiences for petitioners seeking justice.

DEA/G. DAGLI ORTI/De Agostini/Getty Images

IMAGE 2.4 **Hammurabi Receiving the Law Code** The top of this stela, which is eight feet high, shows the powerful sun-god, Shamash, on his throne bestowing the famous Law Code to a standing King Hammurabi.

Q What does the stela suggest about clothing styles of Mesopotamian gods and leaders and the importance of law in the society?

Many decisions concerned temple property and administration, indicating the link between church and state.

Realizing the need to have uniform laws in his diverse country, Hammurabi compiled older laws, recent legal decisions, and social customs, arranged them systematically, and placed them on an eight-foot block of black basalt stone in the temple of Babylon's patron god, Marduk. At the top, an artist pictured Hammurabi receiving the symbols of kingship from Shamash, the sun-god and lawgiver. The Code of 282 laws informed citizens of their rights and demonstrated to both gods and people that the king was doing his job to uphold justice in a moral universe.

For nearly four millennia, we have been intrigued by the principles of this ancient Mesopotamian law code reflecting the harsh views of the era. It mandated two kinds of punishments, a monetary penalty and a retribution in kind, and the harshness of the punishment depended on the social class of the people involved: nobles and landowners, commoners, or slaves. Many laws discouraged burglary by prescribing instant death for those caught; mud-brick homes were not very secure. On the other hand, prostitution was legal. Some laws protected women and children from abuse and arbitrary treatment. For example, a husband who divorced his wife because she bore no sons had to return the dowry she brought into the marriage and forfeit the money he had given her parents for a bridal price. Since the Hebrews (Israelites) borrowed some of these laws, often in modified form, and also passed them into Christian and Islamic traditions, Hammurabi's legacy remains influential today.

Reflection Questions

1. How did Hammurabi increase the power of Babylon?
2. What were the purposes of his great Law Code?
3. What ideas in Hammurabi's law code do you think still influence Western laws and social values today?

Note: Quotation from William H. Stiebing, Jr., *Ancient Near Eastern History and Culture* (New York: Longman, 2003), 88–89.

The parallels between the Gilgamesh legend and Genesis remind us that the Gilgamesh story became widely known far beyond Mesopotamia. Some motifs can be found in Greek literature, such as the Homeric epics, which reappear in the much later Islamic period, such as the stories of Aladdin and Sinbad; they are still found in the folk cultures of some villages. The Gilgamesh epic became one of the many unique traditions that shaped the societies of southwestern Asia, even into modern times, and made them different from other early societies such as India and Egypt.

KEY POINTS

▶ The Babylonians, Hittites, Assyrians, and Chaldeans created empires in Mesopotamia.

▶ The Babylonian king Hammurabi created a legal framework that included harsh punishments and reflected strict class divisions.

▶ The Assyrian Empire, known for its brutality, dominated a large region but was finally defeated by a coalition of enemies.

▶ The *Epic of Gilgamesh*, which shows parallels with the book of Genesis, reflects Mesopotamian values and perspectives, including a pessimistic view of life.

2-3 The Earliest Indian and Central Asian Societies, 6000–1500 BCE

▦ SOCIETIES

Q. What were some of the distinctive features of the Harappan cities?

Modern humans arrived in South Asia by around 65,000 years ago. Thanks in part to the sporadic later migrations over millennia of people from southwest and Central Asia, and their mixing with local people, South Asia developed a society reflecting adaptation and synthesis, with cultural features vastly different from those of the Middle East, Europe, or China. Some South Asians made the transition to farming very early, and the first cities east of Mesopotamia were founded around 2600 BCE. The city-states and the widespread Bronze Age culture they shared, often called **Harappan** (HAR-up-un), were centered in the Indus (IN-duhs) River Valley and nearby rivers in what is now Pakistan and northwest India. Harappan culture eventually covered some 300,000 square miles, the largest in geographical extent of the ancient societies. Although the Harappans built no pyramids like the Egyptians or ziggurats like the Sumerians, they developed a remarkable society. To the north, an urban society also developed in Central Asia.

2-3a South Asian Environments and the Rise of Farming

River valley environments strongly shaped early South Asian societies, just as they did Mesopotamia, Egypt, and China. The Indian subcontinent, about half the size of Europe, is rimmed by the Indian Ocean and the Himalayan Mountains, which boast the half dozen highest peaks in the world, including Mount Everest at nearly thirty thousand feet. The Himalayas, which stretch some 1,500 miles east to west, inhibited regular communication between China and India. Just north of the Himalayas, the Tibetan Plateau is the source of great rivers, including the Indus and Ganges in India, the Yellow and Yangzi in China, and the Irrawaddy and Mekong in Southeast Asia, which eventually reach great plains and deltas. The highly fertile land fostered productive farming and dense settlement. Rice and wheat became the staple crops for most South and East Asians, and scavenging animals like chickens and pigs were more important food sources than beef cattle, which requires extensive pasture.

India's distinctive features resulted in part from its physical environment and climate. The fertile north Indian plains, watered by the Indus and Ganges Rivers, are relatively flat and so encouraged cultural unity, cities, and kingdoms. By contrast, mountainous south India developed more cultural diversity with different languages from those of north India. Other culturally distinct regions include Bengal, framed by the delta of the Ganges River, and the fertile island of Sri Lanka (once known as Ceylon), just off India's southern tip.

The tropical climate affected Indian life. South and northeast India enjoy high rainfall, but today much of the northwest is desert. Although the annual rains sustain life, seasonal flooding poses a chronic problem. Water has been an especially sacred commodity in Indian life, thought, and literature. With many domesticated cattle, most Indians learned to consume dairy products, including yogurt, a local invention. By 7000 to 6000 BCE many villages in the Indus region were pioneering productive farming. Thanks to surpluses of wheat and barley, by 3000 BCE the population of the Indus Valley may have reached one million, and regional trading networks emerged, setting the stage for the emergence of cities.

2-3b Harappan Cities

The long saga of early South Asian history generates much controversy in India today.

CONNECTION to TODAY

What do you see as the most and least attractive features of Harappan life?

Harappan Name given to the city-states and the widespread Bronze Age culture they shared that were centered in the Indus River Valley and nearby rivers in northwest India.

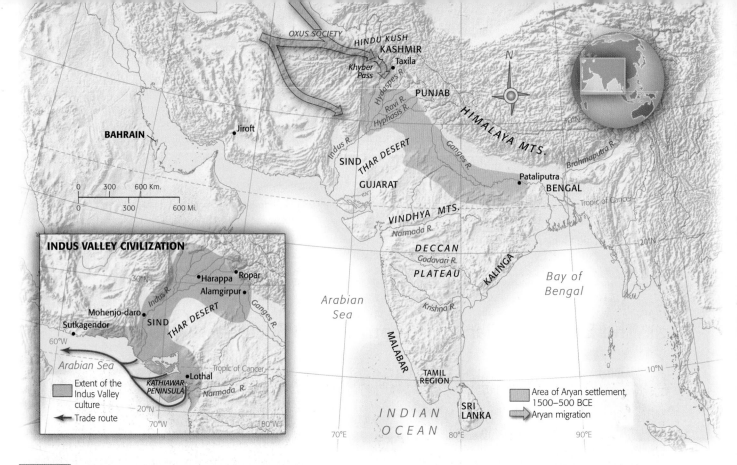

MAP 2.2 **Harappan Culture and Aryan Migrations** The Harappan culture emerged in the city-states of the Indus River Basin. They had collapsed by around 1500 BCE, when the Aryan peoples from Iran began migrating into India and setting up states.

Q What geographical and environmental features might have helped shape the generally uniform culture, vibrant economies, and foreign trade of the Harappan cities and their societies?

The most recent studies conclude that between 7000 and 3000 BCE migrants from Southwest Asia mixed with local people in northwest India, fostering agriculture and, around 2600 BCE, the first Indian urban society drawn from regional cultures in the semiarid Indus River Valley (see Map 2.2). Along the banks of the Indus, which later inspired the English term *India*, and nearby rivers, a vibrant urban-based culture thrived for hundreds of years and planted some seeds for the rich Indian culture that endures to the present. Silt spread by regular river floods served as a natural fertilizer, while nearby forests provided enough wood for baking the bricks used in building cities. Like the Nile, the flat, easily navigable Indus and its tributary rivers gave Harappan society considerable uniformity. Most of the Harappan cities were in the Punjab **(PUHN-jab)** and Sind provinces of modern Pakistan, a crossroads of major trading routes, but some were hundreds of miles to the west or east. Indeed, the Indus culture covered an area far larger than the Mesopotamian and Egyptian cultures combined. The two major Indus cities, called by archaeologists Harappa and Mohenjo-Daro **(moe-hen-joe-DAHR-oh)**, stood four hundred miles apart. The fifteen hundred Harappan cities and towns contained a total population of perhaps five million people at their zenith.

All the cities shared many common features in construction, society, government, religion, and culture, revealing a society that valued order, organization, and cleanliness. Using

the same pattern, administrators carefully laid out the cities using a north–south grid pattern with wide streets and large rectangular city blocks, separating residential and commercial districts from a smaller area for public affairs. Shops probably lined the main streets. The largest city, Harappa, some three and one-third miles in circumference, contained perhaps eighty thousand people at its height. Massive brick ramparts forty feet thick at their base partially protected it from the river waters and any potential human attackers. Large granaries provide evidence of wealth and stored voluminous supplies, perhaps of wheat for the local population, or export goods.

The Harappan people had exceptional housing for ancient times. Most buildings were made from bricks molded to a standardized size. More affluent residents lived in spacious homes constructed on strong brick foundations with interior courtyards that provided considerable privacy, but even the common people enjoyed well-built accommodations. The urban Harappans also enjoyed the ancient world's most advanced water storage and sanitation system. Most houses had a bathroom and drains to carry away the wastewater. Covered drains along city streets were more sanitary than those found in many modern cities. The close attention to providing and carrying away water and the huge public baths suggest an emphasis on washing and personal cleanliness for ritual purity, which later became important in Indian religion.

Scholars debate the identity of the Harappan people. Most scholars believe that they spoke a **Dravidian** (druh-VID-ee-uhn) language, but others consider this conclusion unsubstantiated. A 2018 study of the DNA of a male Harappan skeleton showed a mix of two populations and seems to support the Dravidian theory. But ancient South Asia was complicated and speakers of other languages may also have lived in these cities, which seem to have had cosmopolitan populations. Most modern Dravidian speakers live in southern India, where they are the great majority of the population and divided into around 80 languages and dialects.

2-3c Harappan Society and Its Beliefs

The Harappan governments, social system, and religious beliefs remain a puzzle. The available evidence for an organized monarchy is minimal, as there are no elaborate palaces, temples, or monuments glorifying leaders or prisons or slave quarters reflecting a harsh society. Each city was probably independent, perhaps governed by some powerful merchant guild or council of commercial, landowning, and religious leaders. The ruins contain few weapons, suggesting that, in contrast to Mesopotamia, war was uncommon. Many workers probably had difficult, back-breaking jobs. But there were pleasures too. Some people owned beautiful objects of personal adornment, such as necklaces and beads. The ruins also contain many toys made from clay or wood, indicating a prosperous society that valued leisure for children.

Harappan society may have had unusual gender relations for that era, different from the rigid patriarchies that characterized Mesopotamia

Dravidian A language family whose speakers are the great majority of the population in southern India.

IMAGE 2.5 **Ruins of Mohenjo-Daro** This photo shows the great bath in the city. Like modern Indians, Harappans valued bathing for hygienic and possibly religious reasons.

Luca Tettoni/Robert Harding Picture Library Ltd/Alamy Stock Photo

Q What does the photo tell us about city life in Mohenjo-Daro?

or China as governments grew more powerful. Apparently Harappan husbands moved into their wives' households after marriage, suggesting a matrilineal system. Yet to describe Harappa as mainly a peaceful, utopian realm, as some writers do, may also be misleading. Some customs harmed women. At least some Harappans may have practiced *sati* (**suh-TEE**), the custom of a widow killing herself by jumping onto the funeral pyre as her dead husband is being cremated. A controversial study concludes that some female burials show signs of traumatic injuries from possible abuse.

Harappans mixed art with religion and even commerce. They made small, square, clay seals, possibly used by merchants for branding their wares. Some seals show farming activities; others contain portraits of domesticated animals, including bulls and water buffaloes, as well as the wild tigers, elephants, and rhinoceros that inhabited the nearby forests. Small bronze statues of dancers suggest that the Harappans enjoyed dance. Most scholars argue that they created a written language, although it seems more limited than Mesopotamian, Egyptian, and Chinese writing and remains undeciphered today. The seals, pottery, and various clay tablets contained some four hundred different signs that were completely unrelated to other scripts. Most likely many of the signs represent the names of merchants, businesses, or the commodities being sold.

Some Harappan religious notions contributed to Hinduism, an eclectic religion that developed after Harappan times. For example, one seal features a human figure with multiple faces, a regular feature of later Hindu icons, sitting in a yoga-like position, oblivious to the outside world and surrounded by various animals. It may depict the great Hindu god **Shiva** (**SHEEV-uh**) in one of his major roles as "Lord of the Beasts." Harappans apparently already worshiped Shiva in his dual role as god of destruction and of fertility and the harvest. Possibly the later Hindu notions of reincarnation and yoga practice also derived from Harappan beliefs. Many small clay figurines with exaggerated breasts and hips suggest that mother-goddess worship was prominent in Harappan religious life, as it was in the Fertile Crescent and ancient Europe. Such artistic representations of voluptuous female deities remain common today in India, symbolizing earth and the life-bearing nature of women. While goddesses were mostly marginalized in or disappeared from other religions, hence reinforcing a more patriarchal theology, the persistence of a female component in Indian religion and its deities may have accorded women more respect in spiritual life, albeit within a male-dominated culture.

2-3d The Harappan Economy and the Wider World

The Harappan cities were hubs connected to southwestern and Central Asia through trade and both land and sea transportation networks that fostered extensive contact. The diverse local economy flourished from cultivating barley and wheat with sophisticated irrigation techniques and from producing cotton and metal products, helping Harappan society remain stable and prosperous for hundreds of years. Like South Asians today, the Harappans used spices in their cooking. They or their ancestors domesticated the camel, elephant, chicken, and, to aid farming, zebu (oxen) and water buffalo. These last two animals may have been worshiped, becoming the basis for the later respect accorded cows in Hinduism.

Harappans made other long-lasting contributions, among them cotton cloth and cotton textiles for clothing, one of ancient India's major gifts to the world. Skilled and aggressive Harappan traders traveled far and wide. Cotton, mostly grown in central and western India, was shipped in bulk to Mesopotamia, while metals, which were absent in the Indus Basin, were imported. Harappan sea captains had a good knowledge of navigation and monsoon winds. A huge dock, massive granaries, and specialized factories at the coastal port of Lothal reflected a high-volume maritime trade. Many Harappan seals found at the Mesopotamian city of Ur suggest a steady trade between 2300 and 2000 BCE, with Bahrain Island in the Persian Gulf functioning as a major crossroads. Some Indian exports may even have reached Egypt and Crete. The Harappans exported surplus food, cotton, timber products, copper, and gold, as well as luxury items such as pearls, precious stone products, ivory combs, beads, spices, peacock feathers, and inlay goods made from shell or bone. They imported precious stones from southern India and silver, turquoise, and tin from Persia and Afghanistan.

2-3e The Decline and Collapse of Harappan Society

Eventually Harappan society declined, for reasons not altogether clear and still debated. Sometime between 1900 and 1750 BCE a combination of factors disrupted the urban environment. By 1700 BCE most of the Harappan cities had been destroyed or abandoned, although a considerable rural population remained. Seals and writing began to disappear. The careful grid pattern for city streets was abandoned, the drainage systems deteriorated, and even home sizes were reduced. Some evidence points to violence, plundering, and banditry.

Harappan decline may have resulted from several factors. Perhaps the Harappans exhausted the land. Some evidence points to deforestation, increased flooding, excessive irrigation of marginal lands, soil deterioration, and especially drastic climate change. Apparently, rainfall decreased significantly. These catastrophes probably led to economic breakdown. The crop surpluses that had long sustained the cities disappeared, and people abandoned farms. Perhaps disease epidemics weakened the population.

The end of some of the Indus Valley cities may have been sudden, the result perhaps of an earthquake temporarily damming the rivers, unleashing an awesome flood that quickly

Shiva The Hindu god of destruction and of fertility and the harvest.

overwhelmed low-lying cities. Today as well, periodic Indus flooding remains a major problem; for example, in 2010 massive floods in Pakistan destroyed many villages and towns, displacing hundreds of thousands of people. In the Harappan case, hoards of jewelry, skeletons buried in debris, and cooking pots found strewn across kitchens indicate hastily abandoned homes. The rising floodwaters may have been accompanied by more earthquakes. Harappa, located on higher ground, and some other cities survived a while longer, although with much reduced populations.

The fate of the Harappan people and their cultures is also unclear. Some cities east of the Indus Valley remained populated for several more centuries, practicing modified forms of Harappan culture. Many Harappans may have migrated into central and southern India, mixing with local Dravidian populations and carrying with them a culture, technology, and agriculture that contributed to the Indian society to come. The calamities left the remaining Indus peoples weak and unable to resist later migrations of peoples from outside.

2-3f Central Asian Environments and Oxus Cities

Central Asia is the vast area of plains (**steppes**), deserts, and mountains that stretches from the Ural Mountains and Caspian Sea eastward to Tibet, western China, and Mongolia. Before modern times Central Asians played a role in history far greater than their relatively small populations would suggest, not only as invaders and sometimes conquerors but also as middlemen in the long-distance trade that developed between China, India, the Middle East, and Europe. They also invented chariots, horseback riding, and new types of warfare. Horses became common in Middle Eastern battles. For example, by 2000 BCE people in what are today Armenia, Kazakhstan, Tadzikistan, and the Gobi Desert painted pictographs on walls that shows they were using and probably created the first spoked-wheel chariots. Pulled by some of the first domesticated horses, the carts were much lighter, faster, and more mobile than older military vehicles such as the cumbersome Sumerian four-wheeled battle wagons pulled by donkey-like onagers around 2600 BCE. Gradually Central Asian chariots spread to China, India, Iran, western Asia, and Greece.

Much of Central Asia offered a harsh environment suitable mainly for pastoralists. It was inhabited by diverse peoples speaking Indo-European or, more commonly, Ural-Altaic languages, including various Turkish and Mongol tongues. Large-scale population movements

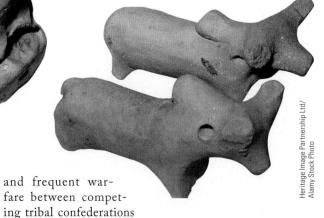

IMAGE 2.6 Harappan Art This terra-cotta cart and bullocks from the Harappan culture in the Indus valley might represent farmers or traders transporting their goods.

Q What do we learn about Harappan life from these models?

and frequent warfare between competing tribal confederations became common, as did mixing of peoples from different groups. In this dynamic melting pot people met, sharing ideas and genes. Most of the steppe societies had skilled horsemen and were led by warrior chieftains. Some attacked and occasionally conquered northern China. Over the centuries various Central Asian peoples also migrated through the mountain ranges into northwest India.

Although much of Central Asia was steppe lands, some areas supported city life, especially in Turkestan, the region from east of the Caspian Sea to Xinjiang (**SIN-john**) on China's western frontier. An early urban society, called the Oxus (**OX-uhs**), after the river that runs through the area, apparently thrived between 2200 and 1800 BCE, when the Harappan culture was also at its height. They built walled cities with mud-brick buildings and carefully designed streets, drains, and temples around desert oases in what is now Uzbekistan and Turkmenistan. Enjoying a wetter climate than now, the people grew wheat and barley, forged bronze axes, carved figurines of women from stone and ivory, and decorated pottery. A tiny stamp seal with letter-like symbols dated to 2300 BCE is evidence for writing, so far not linked to any other society. The Oxus cities, perhaps independent city-states, were situated along what later became the "Silk Road" trade routes between India and China, suggesting that this trade, perhaps originally in grain, may be older than is often thought. The cities were closely linked to the Harappans and probably traded with China, Jiroft, and Mesopotamia. Eventually the cities were abandoned and, over the centuries, buried by sand.

steppes The plains of Central Asia.

2-4 The Aryans and a New Indian Society, 1500–600 BCE

SOCIETIES

Q How did Indian society and the Hindu religion emerge from the mixing of Aryan and local cultures?

Throughout South Asia's long history, many people migrated from elsewhere into the subcontinent, some of them conquering parts of India. The assimilation of these various newcomers resulted in an increasingly diverse society. One such group, the **Aryans** (AIR-ee-unzs), Indo-European-speaking nomadic pastoralists, migrated into northwest India, expanded across northern India, and introduced new cultures. The Aryan expansion between 1500 and 500 BCE built the foundation for a new society that mixed Aryan culture with the traditions of the indigenous peoples, including the Dravidians. Over many centuries a fusion of Aryan and Dravidian cultures, what historians label the **Indo-Aryan synthesis**, forged a new social system and Hinduism, a religion of diverse beliefs. But the Aryans had a greater impact in the north than in the mostly Dravidian south, which retained its own languages and writing systems. Despite regular contact with western, Central, and Southeast Asia, the patterns that developed were distinctive and enduring.

CONNECTION to TODAY

Why do you think that scholarship and teaching about ancient Indian history and peoples would be highly controversial in India today?

2-4a The Aryan Peoples and the Vedas

Most scholars agree that the Aryans began migrating by horse-drawn chariot from Iran (the Persian word for "Aryan") or, as some recent studies conclude, Turkestan, especially Kazakhstan, into northwestern India between 1600 and 1400 BCE, well after the collapse of the Harappan cities, a time when rainfall in the Indus region was increasing again, improving economic conditions. Other Indo-Europeans had already settled in Europe, Iran, Mesopotamia, and parts of Central Asia. The early Aryan migrants to India, who brought with them mastery over horses and cultural practices such as sacrificial rituals, were probably pastoralists. In recent years the origin of the Aryans has taken on political overtones and sparked heated debates in India. Some historians and Hindu nationalists, supported by right-wing movements and the national government, argue that Aryan settlement in India was far older and that the Harappans may have been Aryans. However, most Indian and foreign scholars consider the material evidence for that claim lacking. In their view the Aryans arrived in small groups over several centuries, bringing with them a rich oral literature and unique ideas about government, society, and religion. As more arrived, the Aryans expanded throughout northern India. Furthermore, unlike the Chinese and Greeks, ancient Indians never developed a tradition of historiography, the study and writing of history, perhaps because their conceptions of time emphasized the temporary nature of existence.

Much of what we know about the ancient Aryans comes from their literature, the **Vedas** (VAY-duhs) ("books of knowledge"). This vast collection of sacred hymns to the gods and thoughts about religion, philosophy, and magic was based on oral accounts carefully preserved by bards, the memory experts of each Indo-European tribe. The principal early source of Hindu religious belief, the Vedas reflected the worldview of the priestly class and were already old when written down centuries later. We can infer that the Aryans were organized into tribes that frequently moved their settlements. Their class system consisted of warriors, priests, and commoners. They were a cattle-raising people, as is reflected in one of the hymns: "A bard am I, my father a leech, And my mother a grinder of corn. Diverse in means, but all wishing wealth, Alike for cattle we strive."[14]

A militaristic people who harnessed horses to chariots and skillfully wielded bows and arrows and bronze axes, the Aryans had fought their way through blistering deserts and snowy mountains to reach India. Some Vedas celebrate Aryan victories against fortified settlements inhabited by peoples,

Aryans Indo-European-speaking nomadic pastoralists who migrated from Iran into northwest India.

Indo-Aryan synthesis The fusion of Aryan and Dravidian cultures in India over many centuries.

Vedas The Aryans' "books of knowledge," the principal source of religious belief for Hindus: a vast collection of sacred hymns to the gods and thoughts about religion, philosophy, and magic.

---

[14]Quoted in John Keay, *India: A History* (New York: Atlantic Monthly Press, 2000), 35.

probably including Dravidians, who had darker skins than the Aryans: "For fear of thee fled the dark-hued races, scattered abroad, deserting their possessions."[15] The various Aryan tribes could unite against a common enemy, but mostly they fought against each other.

The Aryans mixed their language with those of local people, creating **Sanskrit** (SAN-skrit), the classical spoken language of north India, through which the Vedas were preserved through memorization and passed through generations. By the fourth century BCE, however, vernacular (everyday) Indo-European spoken languages were becoming more dominant in north India, and Sanskrit gradually became mostly a written language for religious and literary works. Since few Indians today learn to write or speak Sanskrit, some fear the language may eventually disappear; however, various schools and organizations are seeking to revive its popularity. Some three-quarters of Indians today speak an Indo-European language.

2-4b Early Aryan Government, Society, and Religion

Persistent military conflict marked the early Aryan political and social structure. Each tribe's autocratic male ruler, known as a *raja*, sought as much power for himself and his group as possible. The Bharata (BAA-ray-tuh) was the most powerful tribe. Later, the **Mahabharata** (MA-huh-BAA-ray-tuh) ("Great Bharata"), the world's longest poem, probably composed from collected oral traditions in the eighth or ninth century BCE but only written down around 400 to 500 BCE, spun a complex and entertaining tale of many cousins and their titanic battles for supremacy. Reflecting life around 1000 BCE, the *Mahabharata* is, like Homer's *Iliad*, drenched in the blood of endless struggles over succession and supremacy. The *Ramayana* (ruh-MA-yawn-uh) ("The Story of Rama"), another Aryan epic poem probably written down sometime between 750 and 400 BCE, may be based on the extension of Aryan power into southern India.

In the patriarchal Aryan family structure, the father dominated his wives and children. In the following centuries, both male supremacy and a hierarchy based on age became the standard Indian family pattern. The Aryans developed a living pattern known as the joint family, also common in China, in which the wives of all the sons moved into the larger patriarchal household, which included members from three or even four generations. The status of Aryan women changed with time. The early Aryans educated both daughters and sons in the Vedas. One Vedic hymn encouraged women to speak publicly, and women may have composed some of the hymns. Later women became more restricted and daughters less valued. They needed to obtain dowries (gifts for the prospective in-laws) in order to marry, could not participate in the sacrifices to gods, and did not inherit property.

Sanskrit The classical spoken language of north India but now reserved mainly for religious and literary writing.

Mahabharata ("Great Bharata") An Aryan epic and the world's longest poem.

IMAGE 2.7 **Illustrated Manuscript Page from the Ramayana** Vedic stories from millennia ago have remained popular throughout history up to the present. This scene from an illustrated manuscript made in 1649 shows the wedding procession in the epic Ramayana story.

Werner Forman Archive/Shutterstock.com

Q What do we learn about Aryan life and customs from the illustrated page?

[15]Quoted in Hermann Kulke and Dietmar Rothermund, *History of India*, 3rd ed. (New York: Routledge, 1998), 35.

The Vedas also reveal Aryan recreational interests such as horse-drawn chariot racing and gambling. Indians invented both dice and chess. Indeed, gambling features prominently in the *Mahabharata*; one raja loses his kingdom through his fondness for games of chance. The Aryans were also fond of wine and music, using such instruments as lutes, flutes, and drums. Song and dance remain an integral component of Indian religious worship and ritual.

As sacred texts, the Vedas contained considerable information about Aryan religion, the significance of various gods, and the role of priests, confirming that the Aryans' religious views were similar to those of their Hittite cousins in western Asia. Each Aryan tribe boasted its own bards, poets who were also priests who presided over sacrifices and rituals because they alone had memorized the Vedic hymns. The oldest and most important Veda, the *Rig Veda* ("Verses of Knowledge"), probably composed by various poets between 1500 and 1000 BCE but only written down by 500 BCE, contains over one thousand poems composed in Sanskrit, most of them soliciting the favor of Aryan gods.

The Aryans worshiped a pantheon of nature gods, to whom they offered sacrifices. The *Rig Veda* describes some thirty-three deities led by the thunderbolt-wielding war-god Indra (INN-druh), ever youthful, heroic, and victorious. Many poems celebrate the awesome power of the deities, as in the following tribute to the storm-gods: "You are terrible and powerful, O storm gods. You bring everlasting rain in the desert. Dark rain clouds shroud the sky, Turning day into night, drenching the earth."[16] The Rig Veda reflects an open-minded intellectual pluralism and tolerance, one poem even defending heretics and atheists. Aryan religion also included speculations on the deepest mysteries of existence. One poem, the "Hymn of Creation," is one of the most ancient expressions of questions about the creation of the universe: "Who really knows? Who will here proclaim it? Whence was this creation? The gods came afterwards, with the creation of the universe. Who then really knows whence it has arisen?"[17] This hymn also suggests a time before when there was no space or sky, night or day, life or death. Then, in a kind of Big Bang, the cosmos was created by the power of heat (see Chapter 1).

2-4c Aryan Expansion and State Building in North India

Many Aryans eventually moved eastward into the Ganges (GAN-geez) Valley between 1000 and 450 BCE, building kingdoms and mixing with local peoples. During this time they changed through conflict, cooperation, and assimilation with the peoples they encountered, eventually adopting systems of farming, village structure, and some religious concepts from local peoples, but also contributing their language, social system, and many religious beliefs to the mix.

Throughout north India, city development and economic growth encouraged political consolidation into kingdoms. By the sixth century BCE sixteen major Aryan kingdoms stretched from Bengal westward to the fringes of Afghanistan, most of them in the central Ganges region. However, kings did not have unlimited power; they were still advised by councils of warriors. No kingdom was yet strong enough to conquer all the others and create a unified government for all north India until the establishment of the Mauryan Empire in 321 BCE (see Chapter 5).

2-4d The Roots of the Caste System

The Indo-Aryan synthesis modified the social structure. Perhaps incorporating some Harappan traditions, a four-tiered class division emerged that comprised the **brahmans** (BRAH-munz), or priests; the **kshatriyas** (kuh-SHOT-ree-uhs), the warriors and landowners; the **vaisyas** (VIGH-shuhs), or merchants and artisans; and the **sudras** (SOO-druhs), mostly poorer farmers, farm workers, and menial laborers. The priests enjoyed many special privileges as guardians and interpreters of sacred knowledge. Over time the sudras, mostly of non-Aryan origins, were locked into a permanent low status and were prohibited from studying the magically potent Vedic hymns.

The Sanskrit term for a class division or ritual status—*varna* (VARN-uh)—meant "[skin] color," suggesting that the lighter-skinned Aryans wanted to maintain their domination over, and purity from "pollution" by, the darker-skinned indigenous people. Many centuries later, Portuguese visitors referred to the system as *castas* ("pure"), the origin of the Western term *caste*. Aryans used religion to justify this class system. One *Rig Veda* hymn attributed the classes to the Lord of Beings, the originator of the universe: "When they divided the Man, into how many parts did they divide him? … The brahman was his mouth, of his arms was made the kshatriya. His thighs became the vaisya, of his feet were born the sudra."[18]

Over many centuries, this four-tiered class hierarchy evolved into the immensely complex **caste system**. Eventually each hereditary social class was restricted to certain occupations, and its members were restricted in their relations with members of other castes. For example, only members of closely allied groups could intermarry. Below the caste system were a large group of outcasts (**pariahs**) or untouchables, labeled such because the higher castes considered their touch defiling. The pariahs performed tasks considered "unclean," such as tanning animal hides and removing manure. This system, probably in place in some form by 500 BCE, differed in many respects from the modern caste system. Although it was never rigid and changed over time, it provided the basic structure of Hindu society for several millennia.

brahmans The priests, the highest-ranking caste in Hindu society.

kshatriyas Warriors and landowners headed by the rajas in the Hindu caste system.

vaisyas The merchants and artisans in the Hindu caste system.

sudras The poorer farmers, farm workers, and menial laborers in the Hindu caste system.

caste system The four-tiered Hindu social system comprising hereditary social classes that restrict the occupation of members and their relations with members of other castes.

pariahs The large group of outcasts or untouchables below the official Hindu castes.

[16]William McNaughton, ed., *Light from the East* (New York: Laurel, 1978), 398.
[17]Quoted in Burton Stein, *A History of India* (Malden, MA: Blackwell, 1998), 53.
[18]Quoted in A. L. Basham, *The Wonder That Was India* (New York: Grove Press, 1959), 241.

Discover Historical Voices

Hindu Values in the *Bhagavad Gita*

The Bhagavad Gita, *a philosophical poem in the* Mahabharata, *helped shape India's ethical traditions while providing Hindus with a practical guide to everyday life. The following excerpt is part of a dialogue between the god Krishna (Vishnu) and the poem's conflicted hero, the warrior Arjuna* (**are-JUNE-ah**), *on the eve of a great battle in which Arjuna will slaughter his uncles, cousins, teachers, and friends. The reading summarizes some of Krishna's advice in justifying the battle. Krishna suggests that Arjuna must follow his destiny, for while the physical body is impermanent, the soul is eternal. The slain will be reborn. Furthermore, humans are responsible for their own destiny through their behavior and mental discipline. They also, like Arjuna, need to fulfill their obligations to society.*

The wise grieve neither for the living nor for the dead. There has never been a time when you and I and the kings gathered here have not existed, nor will there ever be a time when we will cease to exist. As the same person inhabits the body through childhood, youth, and old age, so too at the time of death he attains another body. The wise are not deluded by these changes.

When the senses contact sense objects, a person experiences cold or heat, pleasure or pain. These experiences are fleeting; they come and go. Bear them patiently…. Those who are not affected by these changes, who are the same in pleasure and pain, are truly wise and fit for immortality. Assert your strength and realize this!

The impermanent has no reality; reality lies in the eternal. Those who have seen the boundary between these two have attained the end of all knowledge. Realize that which pervades the universe and is indestructible; no power can affect this unchanging, imperishable reality. The body is mortal but he who dwells in the body is immortal and immeasurable…. As a man abandons worn-out clothes and acquires new ones, so when the body is worn out a new one is acquired by the Self, who lives within…. Death is inevitable for the living; birth is inevitable for the dead. Since these are unavoidable, you should not sorrow….

Now listen to the principles of yoga [mental and physical discipline to free the soul]. By practicing these you can break through the bonds of karma [the belief that deeds in past lives determined a person's present status]. On this path effort never goes to waste, and there is no failure…. When you keep thinking about sense objects, attachment comes. Attachment breeds desire, the lust of possession that burns to anger….

They are forever free who renounce all selfish desires and break free from the ego-cage of "I," "me," and "mine" to be united with the Lord. This is the supreme state. Attain to this, and pass from death to immortality…. Strive constantly to serve the welfare of the world; by devotion to selfless work one attains the supreme goal of life. Do your work with the welfare of others always in mind.

Reflection Questions

1. What key aspects of Hindu thought are revealed in the poem?
2. How do the attitudes toward life, death, and desire influence the behavior of individuals?
3. What are some of the viewpoints in this ancient poem that might be considered universal in their appeal even today?

Source: From *The Bhagavad Gita*, trans. by Eknath Easwaran, founder of the Blue Mountain Center of Meditation, copyright 1985. Reprinted by permission of the Nilgiri Press, P.O. Box 256, Tomales, CA 94971, easwaran.org.

2-4e Indo-Aryan Society and Economy

The Vedas and other early literature reveal some of the expectations and attitudes of ancient Indian society. For example, contained within the *Mahabharata* is a philosophical poem, the **Bhagavad Gita** (BAA-guh-vad GEE-tuh) ("Lord's Song"), the most treasured piece of ancient Hindu literature (see Discover Historical Voices: Hindu Values in the *Bhagavad Gita*). It encourages people to do their duty to their superiors and kinsmen resolutely and unselfishly. It also explains that death is not a time of grief because the concept of reincarnation makes the soul indestructible. The other great ancient epic, the *Ramayana*, resembles the *Odyssey* of the Greek Homer in that it tells of endless court intrigues and a hero's wanderings while his wife remains chaste and loyal.

The *Ramayana* illustrates the early Hindu notion of perfect manhood and womanhood through the main characters: Rama, the husband, and Sita (**SEE-tuh**), his wife, who demonstrate mutual loyalty, devotion, and self-sacrifice. But Sita is also faithful in supporting her husband and family, strongly influencing cultural expectations of womanhood, especially in north India. Women enjoyed a higher status in south India, where both matriarchal and matrilineal traditions persisted for centuries among some groups, and goddesses remained especially central to religious life.

Indo-Aryan technology derived from both foreign and local developments. The Aryans used iron, especially once they

Bhagavad Gita ("Lord's Song") A poem in the *Mahabharata* that is the most treasured piece of ancient Hindu literature.

reached iron-rich districts in the Ganges region around 1000 BCE. Soon they made the transition from a pastoral economy to a combination of pastoral and agricultural pursuits that emphasized grains like barley and wheat. One Veda prays: "Successfully let the good ploughshares' thrust part the earth, successfully let the ploughman follow the beasts of draft."[19] The use of plows and the expansion of irrigated agriculture greatly increased the available food supply and thus fostered population growth. India's population in 500 BCE has been estimated at 25 million, including 15 million in the Ganges Valley.

2-4f Hinduism: A New Religion of Diverse Roots

Although Indian religion has changed much since the Harappans, it has remained unique. Nothing in the Middle East or Europe remotely resembles basic bedrock Indian beliefs such as reincarnation. What modern Indians would clearly recognize as Hinduism had probably not fully formed until the beginning of the Common Era. The term *Hinduism* was not applied to these varied traditions until recent centuries by British colonizers, but the foundations were clearly established in ancient times. Hinduism can be seen historically as a synthesis of Aryan beliefs with Harappan and other indigenous traditions that developed over many centuries. At the most basic level, Hindus respect the authority of the Vedas and accept one of the main Hindu gods as their principle deity. As the religion became more complex, it probed ever more deeply into cosmic mysteries, resulting in ferment and questioning.

The Hindu religious system became one of the richest and most complex in the world, with gods, devotions, and celebrations drawn from various regional cultures. The Aryans gradually turned from their old tribal gods to deities of Harappan origin such as Shiva. Hence the rise of the great gods of Hinduism: *Brahma* **(BRA-ma)** (the Creator of life); *Vishnu* **(VISH-noo)** (the Preserver of life); and *Shiva* (among other functions, the Destroyer of life). Vishnu is a benevolent deity who works continually for the welfare of the world. Shiva personifies the life force and embodies both constructive and destructive power. In popular worship Vishnu and Shiva had the most devotees. The early Shiva was a meat-loving deity who consumed intoxicating drinks but, as religious views changed under brahman influence, by the eighth century CE had become a vegetarian.

Hinduism never developed a rigid core of beliefs uniting all followers; instead, it loosely linked together diverse practices and cults that shared a reverence for the Vedas. The Vedic thinkers were influenced by pre-Aryan meditation techniques and mystical practices, such as those that were later known as *yoga*. The Hindus came to believe that everyone must behave properly so that the universe can function in an orderly manner. They came to see human existence as temporary and fleeting and only the realm of the gods as eternal.

The Vedas underwent three major stages of development to become accepted as revealed literature. The earliest stage included the poems and hymns in the *Rig Veda* and several other collections. From around 1000 to 700 BCE a series of prose commentaries on the earlier Vedas appeared that also prescribed proper procedures for worshipping the gods. These commentaries, the **Brahmanas** (BRA-ma-nus), emphasize the central role of the priests, or brahmans. At this time, the prevailing religion can be termed *Brahmanism*. Later still, between 800 and 600 BCE, a third group of more philosophical ideas appeared, poetic dialogues known as the **Upanishads** (oo-PAHN-ih-shahds) ("sitting around a teacher"). These oral and later written compositions, which speculated on the ultimate truth about the creation of life, offered a striking contrast to the emphasis on ritual, devotion, and ethics in the older works because they came from an atmosphere of questioning and rebellion against priestly power. They also gave women more importance; the dialogues include the story of an exceptionally learned female.

The religious atmosphere of ancient India was dynamic, with growing tensions between competing ideas about the nature of existence and appropriate human behavior. For example, the *Ramayana* contrasts the luxury-filled decadence of the royal courts with the austere existence of hermit-sages dwelling in the forest and practicing forms of meditation and mysticism. The movements that developed out of this ferment in the first millennium BCE transformed the framework of Indian religion, fostering both Buddhism and the modified form of Brahmanism known today as Hinduism, as we shall see in Chapter 5.

Brahmanas Commentaries on the Vedas that emphasize the role of priests (brahmans).

Upanishads Ancient Indian philosophical writings that speculated on the ultimate truth about the creation of life.

KEY POINTS

▶ The Indo-European Aryans, a cattle-raising tribal people, migrated into north India 3,500 years ago, mixing with local peoples.

▶ The Vedas, written in Sanskrit, are religious writings that reveal information on the Aryan religion and their patriarchal culture.

▶ The *Bhagavad Gita*, which emphasizes one's earthly duty and the soul's immortality, became the most treasured piece of Indian literature.

▶ Hinduism developed over many centuries but never became a rigid belief structure.

---

[19]Quoted in Romila Thapar, *Early India from the Origins to AD 1300* (Berkeley: University of California Press, 2002), 116.

Chapter Summary

Mesopotamian society and early Indian society were two of humankind's first experiments with farming, cities, and states, both using technologies that were unheard of in Neolithic times. These ancient societies also developed different religious notions, social systems, and political structures. They were shaped by the challenges and opportunities of flood-prone river valleys: Mesopotamian society arose between the Tigris and Euphrates Rivers, and Harappan society arose in and around the Indus River Valley. Mesopotamians introduced the first cities and states, the cuneiform system of writing, bronze metalworking, mathematics, and science. Their many kingdoms were united under several different empires. Mesopotamia was also part of the early trade networks linking the Mediterranean Basin with India. Such connections among societies were a crucial and continuing part of history. In northwest India the Harappans built peaceful, bustling, and well-planned cities, produced cotton products, developed sophisticated sanitation systems, and participated in a trading network that reached into the Fertile Crescent and Central Asia. After the Harappan collapse, Aryan migrants established political control. The mixing of Harappan and Aryan cultures shaped a new and enduring Indian society, establishing the foundation for a caste system and the religion of Hinduism, which are still after some four thousand years prominent features of Indian society and culture today.

Key Terms

Fertile Crescent 31
ziggurat 33
patriarchy 34
cuneiform 35
Harappan 41
Dravidian 43
Shiva 44
steppes 45

Aryans 46
Indo-Aryan synthesis 46
Vedas 46
Sanskrit 47
Mahabharata 47
brahmans 48
kshatriyas 48
vaisyas 48

sudras 48
caste system 48
pariahs 48
Bhagavad Gita 49
Brahmanas 50
Upanishads 50

Ancient Societies in Africa and the Mediterranean, 5000–600 BCE

> *Behold, the heart of his majesty was satisfied with making a very great monument; never has happened the like since the beginning. He made it as an everlasting fortress. It is wrought with gold and many costly stones.*
>
> —Temple inscription at Thebes, Egypt, fourteenth century BCE[1]

GEORGE HOLTON/Science Source

IMAGE 3.1 **Abu Simbel** The great temple with its colossal statues at Abu Simbel overlooking the Nile River in Egypt was built as a monument to honor the powerful thirteenth-century BCE pharaoh Rameses the Great, who presided over empire building and economic prosperity.

Q In what ways do you think the temple reflects the power in life and death of the pharaoh and the ruling family?

---

[1]Quoted in Lionel Casson, *Ancient Egypt* (New York: Time Incorporated, 1965), 120.

Around 1460 BCE Queen Hatshepsut (**hat-SHEP-soot**), Egypt's powerful ruler, ordered a temple built on the banks of the Nile River for the glory of the highest god, Amon-Re (**AH-muhn-RAY**), with terraced gardens planted with fragrant myrrh. To obtain the myrrh, Hatshepsut ordered a naval expedition down the Red Sea to a place previously visited by Egyptians: Punt (**poont**) on the northeast African coast, probably modern Somalia (**so-MAH-lee-uh**). The new expedition returned with myrrh trees, jewels, incense, and other treasures, among them exotic animals such as giraffes, panthers, and apes. Like other Egyptian rulers, Hatshepsut commemorated these results on her magnificent new temple's walls with inscriptions and pictures: "The loading of the cargo-boats with great marvels of Punt … good woods, ebony, pure ivory, gold, monkeys…. Never were brought such things to any king, since the world was."[2] The successful expedition enhanced her reputation and popularity. To obtain such luxury products, Egyptians had become shipbuilders and sailors, connecting to a wider world. Indeed, foreign trade had made Egypt the ancient world's wealthiest society.

Among the Egyptians and some other African and eastern Mediterranean societies—including Hebrews, Minoans (**mih-NO-uhns**), Mycenaeans (**my-suh-NEE-uhns**), Phoenicians (**fo-NEE-shuhns**), and early Greeks—urban life was fostered by dramatic changes resulting from contact among different peoples. Interaction between Egypt and neighboring peoples promoted cultural development in the Nile Valley and the Mediterranean societies. Like the Tigris-Euphrates and Indus Valleys, the Nile Valley fostered population growth, social organization, large state structures, and elaborate religious systems.

Ancient peoples also created unique societies elsewhere in Africa and the eastern Mediterranean. Diverse sub-Saharan African societies developed or borrowed farming and metal technologies, and some built cities. However, unlike Egypt's spectacular pyramids, many of the sub-Saharan people's monuments and buildings were later covered by rain forest, blowing sand, or wayward rivers. Meanwhile, on eastern Mediterranean islands and shores, various peoples traded widely, built cities, and developed religious concepts that endure to this day.

---

[2]Quoted in David Phillipson, *African Archaeology*, 2nd ed. (Cambridge, UK: Cambridge University Press, 1993), 152.

3-1 The Rise of Egyptian Society

TRANSITIONS SOCIETIES

Q How did the environment shape ancient Egypt?

Many people today probably think of ancient Egypt as a place of pyramids, divine rulers, strange looking writing, and mummies. But it was much more complex, interesting, and important to history. The mixing of several different peoples in the Nile River Valley in North Africa around 3000 BCE created an Egyptian society so successful that it survived in more or less its basic form for nearly two thousand years. The river valley's location allowed the Egyptians to develop many traditions and ideas completely different from those in nearby Mesopotamia, Palestine, and Crete. Reflecting the importance of this river, the classical Greek historian Herodotus (heh-ROD-uh-tuhs) called Egypt the "gift of the Nile."

CONNECTION to TODAY

What lessons do you think modern people can learn from Egypt's astonishing two-thousand-year longevity?

3-1a North African Environments

Egypt was shaped by the environmental features of North Africa, a region stretching from Morocco in the west eastward to the Red Sea. To the north the Mediterranean Sea's maritime routes enabled the spread of products, ideas, technologies, and peoples, while the Red Sea connected Egypt to Northeast Africa, Arabia, and India. In Egypt itself, agriculture flourished only in the narrow Nile Valley; west of the Nile the vast Sahara Desert stretched all the way to Africa's western coast. In northwestern Africa (today's Tunisia, Algeria, and Morocco), mountain ranges separated the desert from the Mediterranean and Atlantic coastal plains, where farming was also possible.

The Nile River was the key to the formation of Egyptian society (see Map 3.1). By the fourth millennium BCE the grasslands and forests of earlier times had turned to desert and the silt deposited by the fall flooding had made the Nile Valley fertile. Thanks to the inhospitable deserts on both sides, the northern Nile Valley enjoyed many centuries of mostly uninterrupted development, allowing Egypt to thrive for centuries without significant outside challenges. On the navigable and slow-moving Nile, boats drifted northward with the current and used southerly winds to move south; thus the river proved a great highway promoting political stability and uniformity.

3-1b Foundations of Egyptian Society

Arising in 3100 or 3000 BCE, Egypt's urban society developed a few centuries later than the societies in Mesopotamia. With little rainfall, Egypt required irrigation works to take advantage of the rich silt. Unlike the wide Tigris-Euphrates

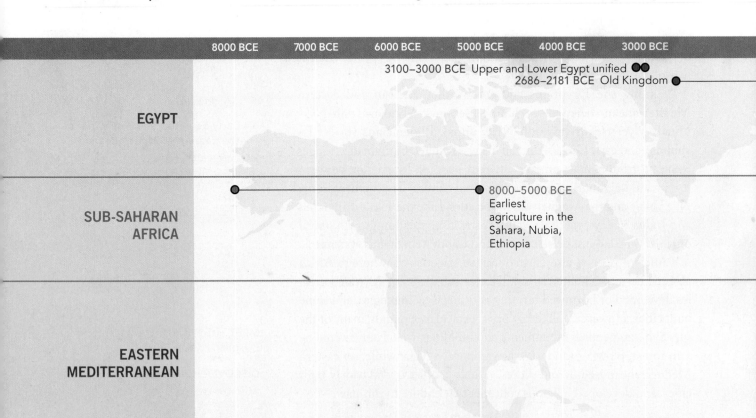

	8000 BCE	7000 BCE	6000 BCE	5000 BCE	4000 BCE	3000 BCE
EGYPT					3100–3000 BCE Upper and Lower Egypt unified ●● 2686–2181 BCE Old Kingdom ●—	
SUB-SAHARAN AFRICA		●———————————● 8000–5000 BCE Earliest agriculture in the Sahara, Nubia, Ethiopia				
EASTERN MEDITERRANEAN						

Valley, the Nile Valley was only 10 miles wide, so the population was more concentrated, and new peoples continually arrived in this area. The once fertile Sahara region began drying out by 5000 to 4000 BCE, forcing most Sahara peoples to move to western Africa grasslands, the northern coast, or into the Nile Valley. Other early migrants came from western Asia and from the Horn of Africa, southeast of Egypt. The Egyptian population eventually included peoples of Semitic, Berber (**BUHR-bur**), Ethiopian, Somali, black African, and, later, Greek origins. Egypt also enjoyed close relationships with the Nubians, black African peoples living in what is today southern Egypt and northern Sudan. Berbers dominated northwest Africa. The ancient Egyptian language belonged to the Afro-Asiatic family, which included Semitic, Berber, and many African tongues.

Unlike the Mesopotamia floods, Nile flooding came on an exact schedule. A central government organized people to prepare the cropland for the flooding, such as by building dikes to contain the floodwater used in irrigation. The backbreaking work required to maintain the irrigation canals reminds us that, for peasants at least, a complex society was a mixed blessing. If the floodwaters were not carefully channeled, little would grow. When weak governments left the dikes untended, the desert spread and famine struck the land. But with political order and dike maintenance, the valley supported a high population. By 1000 BCE, Egypt's population had reached three or four million. Given their general good fortune, it is not surprising that Egyptians saw themselves as the center of the world. As far as they knew for many centuries, they were.

In earliest times, the 100-mile-long area from the modern city of Cairo down the Nile to the fertile Nile Delta and sea was considered Lower Egypt or the northern kingdom (see Map 3.1). The area from Cairo to Aswan (**AS-wahn**), some 650 miles south, was Upper Egypt or the southern kingdom. The legendary Upper Egyptian King Menes (**MEH-neez**) united these two states about 3100 to 3000 BCE, setting the stage for three successive eras: the Old Kingdom (2686–2181 BCE), the Middle Kingdom (2040–1786 BCE), and the New Kingdom (1550–1064 BCE). During each period various dynasties ruled Egypt, while the intermediate periods were marked by disorder or foreign conquest. After 1075 BCE Egypt increasingly fell victim to the empire building of other African as well as western Asian and Mediterranean African peoples.

3-1c The Old Kingdom: Egypt's Golden Age

Most of us can picture the Old Kingdom because of the pyramids built in this splendid era, which have awed visitors for thousands of years and illustrate Egyptian self-confidence. Perhaps the greatest and most enduring of the ancient world's construction projects, they reflected a powerful government, unsurpassed organizing talent, a prosperous society, and unique values and beliefs. The largest pyramid, that of the twenty-fifth-century pharaoh Cheops at Giza, is nearly five hundred feet high, covers an area of nearly two hundred square yards, and remained the tallest building in the world until the twentieth century. Tens of thousands of workers moved the nearly six million tons of limestone into place on ramps and wooden

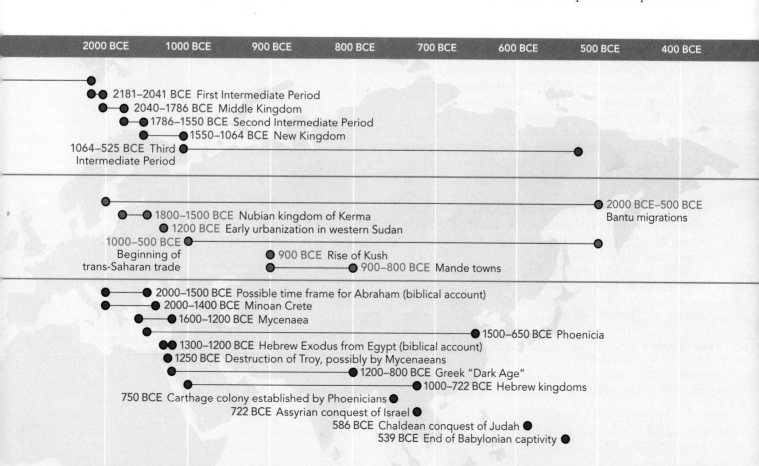

rollers without the benefit of winches, pulleys, or scaffolds. The builders of the great pyramid of Pharaoh Khufu probably had to set a block of stone in place every two minutes over a ten-hour workday for some two decades.

Most of the pyramid workers were not slaves, and many were highly skilled artisans. Workers and their families lived in villages with ample food and good housing supplied by the government. This did not prevent complaints. One disgruntled draftsman wrote to his superior: "If there is some beer, you do not look for me, but if there is work, you do look for me. I am a man who has no beer in his house."[3] Indeed, some studies suggest that worker strikes and social unrest occurred even as the rulers used propaganda campaigns to encourage acceptance of government power.

The rulers of Egypt, known as **pharaohs** (FAIR-os) (from per-o or "great house"), had immense power to order such projects because their subjects believed them to be the divine offspring of the sun-god Re, the creator of heaven, earth, and humans. Pharaohs also had soldiers and the authority of priests and religion to support their rule. Writing, invented by 3200 or 3000 BCE, enabled smooth functioning administration. The Egyptian writing system of **hieroglyphics** (hi-ruh-GLIF-iks), like Sumerian cuneiform, evolved from pictograms into stylized pictures expressing ideas. The pharaohs, considered the owners of all the land and people, governed a highly centralized state from the city of Memphis, strategically located where the Nile Valley met the delta. A chief minister supervised the administrative structure, including tax collection, grain storage in government warehouses, and salaries for government officials. Most ministers came from noble families, but occasionally pharaohs recruited for talent. One advised his son: "Do not distinguish the son of a noble man from a poor man, but take to thyself a man because of the work of his hands."[4]

The royal government expanded trade, dispatching expeditions east to Arabia, south to Nubia (NOO-bee-ah), and northeast to Lebanon, Syria, and Anatolia. Hence, around 2600 BCE forty ships brought cedar logs, probably from today's Lebanon, to make the cedar wood doors of the royal palace. Requiring huge efforts and expense, sailing expeditions to Punt to obtain exotic raw materials were much less frequent. For these expeditions, several thousand workers had to move construction materials and their supplies by donkey across 100 miles of desert from Qena, a Nile city, to a Red Sea harbor, build the 100-foot-long ship, then disassemble it plank by plank when it returned from Punt several months later, and finally trek with the materials and the cargo back to Qena.

Around 2200 BCE the Old Kingdom went into decline. The expense of the great royal tombs may have impoverished the country, the royal governors became more independent of the pharaoh, and many peasants reasoned that if the ruler's power was weakened, the gods were displeased. Furthermore, environmental change may also have

pharaohs Rulers of ancient Egypt.

hieroglyphics The Egyptian writing system, which evolved from pictograms into stylized pictures expressing ideas.

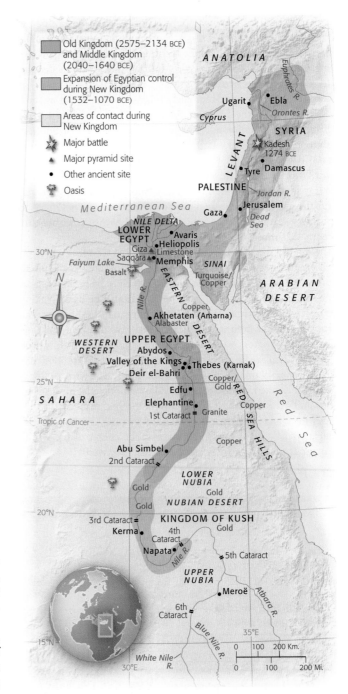

MAP 3.1 **Ancient Egypt and Nubia** The Egyptian and Nubian societies developed along the Nile River. Egypt traded with, and sometimes controlled, the peoples of the Levant on the eastern Mediterranean coast.

Q How do you think Egypt's location along both the Nile River and the Mediterranean coast shaped their society and relations with the peoples and states of sub-Saharan Africa and western Asia?

[3]Quoted in *Egypt: Land of the Pharaohs* (Alexandria, VA: Time-Life Books, 1992), 142.
[4]Quoted in Casson, *Ancient Egypt*, 95.

undermined the government. A dramatic decline in rainfall led to many years of poor harvests and starvation in upper Egypt, as some of the fertile delta turned to dust and fires swept through the valley, destroying crops, trees, and homes. The demise of the Old Kingdom led to a century of social disorder, the First Intermediate Period. One scribe lamented the consequences of this upheaval: "The son of the high-born is no longer to be recognized. Men do not sail to Byblos (**BIB-loss**) [Phoenicia] today. Gold is diminished. To what purpose is a treasure without its revenues? Laughter hath perished. It is grief that walketh through the land."[5]

3-1d The Middle Kingdom and Foreign Conquest

Eventually the pharaohs of a new dynasty restored strong government, moving the capital to Thebes in the south and establishing stronger control over the governors. This Middle Kingdom lasted for four hundred years and saw Egyptian influence extend to Palestine and, briefly, to Nubia. Amon-Re, a fusion of two great gods, now became Egypt's chief god, proclaimed the ancestor of the divine pharaoh.

However, foreign conquest and domestic disorder brought an end to the Middle Kingdom, launching the Second Intermediate Period. The Hyksos (**HICK-soes**), an iron-using Semitic people from Syria and Palestine, conquered some of Lower Egypt. Hyksos rule led to further divisions: an Egyptian dynasty ruled Upper Egypt from Thebes, and the Nubians established yet a third state. The Hyksos adopted Egyptian customs and brought several improvements to Egypt, including increased trade with the eastern Mediterranean and Mesopotamia, and military innovations, such as iron, smaller shields, body armor, powerful bows, and, especially, horse-drawn chariots.

3-1e The New Kingdom and Egyptian Expansion

In the mid-1500s BCE dynamic new rulers reestablished Egypt's regional power and fostered social and religious changes. Using the new military technology, these pharaohs began the most expansionist period of ancient Egyptian history.

WitR/Shutterstock.com

IMAGE 3.2 **Great Pyramid at Giza** Three Egyptian pharaohs from the twenty-sixth century BCE were buried in these magnificent pyramids, which symbolized the power of Old Kingdom Egypt. The rearmost pyramid, built for Pharaoh Cheops, remains the largest all-stone building ever constructed.

Ⓠ Can you imagine the feelings and thoughts ordinary Egyptians might have had when they saw these giant pyramids?

During the New Kingdom, Egypt became more active in the western Asian and Mediterranean worlds, sending armies on repeated campaigns into Palestine, Syria, the Euphrates River, and Nubia. Foreigners from as far away as Babylon served in the Egyptian court. This power derived partly from Egypt's position as the major regional supplier of gold, which it obtained mostly from Nubia and Punt.

For a few years Egypt was ruled by a female pharaoh, Hatshepsut (r. ca. 1479–1458), the daughter and wife of pharaohs. To ensure that she looked like a proper pharaoh, Hatshepsut apparently wore male clothing and the headdress and false beard that were symbols of royalty. Hatshepsut supervised military campaigns in both the north and south.

Another New Kingdom pharaoh, Amenophis (**AH-men-o-fis**) IV (r. 1353–1333), rebelled against the priests of Amon-Re and promoted the worship of a new sun-god, Aten, who he claimed was the only god (other than the pharaoh himself). Amenophis changed his name to Akhenaten (**AH-ke-NAH-tin**) ("servant of Aten") and wrote a famous hymn to Aten: "Beginner of Life. How manifold are thy works? They are hidden from the sight of men, O Sole God. Thou didst fashion the earth according to thy desire."[6] This experiment with **monotheism**, the belief in a single, all-powerful god, intrigues historians because

monotheism The belief in a single, all-powerful god.

---

[5]Quoted in Carl Roebuck, *The World of Ancient Times* (New York: Charles Scribner's Sons, 1966), 72.
[6]Quoted in *Egypt: Land of Pharaohs*, 89.

it occurred at roughly the same time that the Hebrews were developing a similar belief. Some scholars see cross-cultural influences at work, and some Hebrew psalms and proverbs are clearly derived from Egyptian writings. At Akhenaten's death, however, the priests successfully pressured his successor to return to Amon-Re worship.

The high point of Egyptian empire building was reached when Pharaoh Rameses (ram-ih-SEEZ) II (r. 1290–1224) signed a treaty with the Hittites dividing Syria and Palestine between them. Between 1250 and 1100 BCE Southwest Asia and North Africa suffered from severe drought probably caused by climate change that contributed to the downfall of several Bronze Age societies in the region. It had also brought famine to the Hittites in Anatolia. Learning of the Hittites' plight, the pharaohs had wisely anticipated the challenge and carefully planned policies that would allow them to adapt. The rulers ordered increased grain production in the more productive areas of their empire and cross-bred cattle with zebu (humped cattle) to create a more heat-resistant plow animal. These policies probably extended the life of the Egyptian empire by half a century. But ultimately the drought, combined with earthquakes and invaders, caused a collapse. In 1208 Libyan tribes invaded the Nile Delta. Although they were pushed out, Egypt began its long decline as a regional power. From about 750 to 650 BCE, a dynasty from the Kush kingdom in Nubia ruled Egypt, adopting Egyptian customs and hieroglyphics. Finally, Egypt was conquered by the Assyrians in the seventh century, followed by the Persians in the late sixth century BCE.

KEY POINTS

▶ The regular flooding of the Nile River provided the ancient Egyptians with a highly fertile valley and a dependable growing season.

▶ A strong central government allowed the Egyptians to make the most of their agricultural system.

▶ The pyramids were built by the Egyptian pharaohs of the Old Kingdom, thought to be descendants of the sun-god.

▶ The New Kingdom was a time of Egyptian expansion into western Asia and the Mediterranean, but it ended with the decline of Egyptian dominance.

3-2 Egyptian Society, Economy, and Culture

▦ SOCIETIES

Q What were some unique features of Egyptian society?

Like other ancient societies, the Egyptians had many distinctive customs, technologies, and beliefs. All social classes, blessed with many centuries of good crops, seemed to mostly view themselves as favored. One writer of the era celebrated the Nile Delta as "full of everything good—its ponds with fish and its lakes with birds. Its meadows are verdant, its melons abundant. Its granaries are so full of barley that they come near to the sky."[7] Although peasants and workers labored hard and had fewer comforts than the upper classes, they at least had a secure life and predictable routine. Women enjoyed considerable freedom. Finally, Egyptian cities grew rich by trading with distant suppliers and markets.

3-2a Society

Like other urban societies such as Mesopotamia, Egypt was divided into social classes with different responsibilities and roles. The pharaoh theoretically owned everything in the kingdom, and the pharaoh, priests, and nobles owned 80 to 90 percent of all the usable land (see Meet the People: Hekanakhte, an Egyptian Priest). The scribe, or "writing man," held an honored upper-class occupation. "Be a scribe," a young man was advised in one source. "Your limbs will be sleek. Your hands

> **CONNECTION to TODAY**
>
> How do you think the lives of ancient Egyptians compare to the lives of people today?

will grow soft. You will go forth in white clothes with courtiers saluting you."[8] Peasants maintained the irrigation works and paid high taxes. Perhaps 10 or 15 percent of the population, slaves were mostly prisoners of war and foreigners, including Nubians and people from Palestine, among them some Hebrews. Most worked in wealthy homes, palaces, or temple estates, and some were assigned to build pyramids and monuments.

Egyptians valued security and regularity more than social equality. Since planting was relatively easy in the soft soil, they did not need heavy plows. Despite occasional grueling labor on construction projects, peasants showed little sustained discontent except during the troubled intermediate periods. Although the rich ate meat and the poor had beer, bread, and beans ("beer and bread" was an ancient Egyptian greeting, much like "have a good day"), most people thought themselves lucky. Their massive tombs and mummies may seem gloomy, but their temples were once bright with paint and gold. Egyptians told bawdy and often irreverent stories; played musical instruments such as flutes, pipes, and harps; kept pet cats and monkeys; and got drunk. Both men and women used cosmetics such as eyeliner to enhance their physical attractions. In seeking beauty aids, Egyptians became the world's first chemists. Young people

---

[7]Quoted in Felipe Fernandez-Armesto, *Civilizations: Culture, Ambition, and the Transformation of Nature* (New York: Simon and Schuster, 2001), 195.
[8]Quoted in Brian M. Fagan, *People of the Earth: An Introduction to World Prehistory*, 9th ed. (New York: Longman, 1998), 407.

Hekanakhte, An Egyptian Priest

Hekanakhte (**heh-KHAN-akt**), who lived about 2000 BCE, was the ka-priest of a deceased chief government minister, Ipi. His duty was to tend the tomb of his patron, near the city of Thebes, to protect the deceased individual's guardian spirit or soul (ka). Wealthy individuals like Ipi left money or other resources to support a priest to perform these duties. If the ka were not honored with these ceremonial offerings, Egyptians feared that it would die a "second death" or be annihilated.

In addition to a large estate Ipi left to support Hekanakhte and his family, Hekanakhte also supervised other properties left to his care, visiting them much of the year. During his absences he wrote many letters to his eldest son,

only those who work should get food and urges Mersu to "make the most of my land … dig the ground deep with your noses." He also tells his son what seeds to plant and where to plant them. And he warns his son not to overpay the help or his own personal funds will be reduced. Trust between father and son seems to have been in short supply.

Hekanakhte frequently addressed family disputes. Apparently he spoiled Mersu's younger brother, Snerfu, constantly reminding Mersu to give this youngest son things he wanted. Hekanakhte decided late in life, after his wife died, to take a young concubine, Iutenhab (**YOU-ten-hob**), who disrupted the household with her many requests. The priest

Stefano Ravera/Alamy Stock Photo

IMAGE 3.3 **Measuring and Recording the Egyptian Harvest** This wall painting from a tomb in the city of Thebes shows officials and peasants figuring the size of the annual harvest.

Q What does the tomb painting tell us about the work and lives of Egyptian officials and peasants?

Mersu, who read them and then discarded them in a local tomb. The dry desert climate preserved them until they were discovered by an archaeologist in 1922. These letters reveal family life in the Middle Kingdom. Hekanakhte had a large family, including five sons, two of them married and all of them living at home. He also supported his mother, a poor female relative, and a widowed daughter.

Hekanakhte's letters give advice on cultivating and tending the grain crops. Some were written during a bad year, when inadequate Nile flooding rendered harvests slim. The priest tells his son that he is sending some food and carefully lists what each family member is to receive. He reminds family members not to complain, since "half life is better than dying together." Hekanakhte orders that

tells his son to fire a maid who had offended Iutenhab. Given the nagging tone of many of Hekanakhte's letters to his long-suffering son, it may not surprise us that one of the letters had been left unopened.

Reflection Questions

1. What were the duties of a ka-priest?
2. What do these letters tell us about family relationships in this social class?
3. In what ways are Hekanakhte's career, family life, and values similar to and different from those of modern people?

Note: Quotations from Barbara Mertz, *Red Land, Black Land: Daily Life in Ancient Egypt* (New York: Dodd, Mead, 1978), 127.

wrote sentimental poems to sweethearts. One love poem by a girl reported on a swim with her lover:

Diving and swimming with you here,
Gives me the chance I've been waiting for,
To show my looks,
Before an appreciative eye.
My bathing suit of the best material.
Nothing can keep me from my love,
Standing on the other shore.[9]

With flexible gender roles, women enjoyed more independence and legal rights than women in other ancient societies. Hatshepsut was the most famous of the several women pharaohs, although they mostly served as placeholders for the next male to take the throne. Legal distinctions also seemed to be based more on class than on gender. A woman could inherit, bequeath, and administer property; conclude legal settlements; take cases to court; initiate divorce; and testify. Some women could probably read and write, and many were involved in well-paying economic activities. Women weavers produced some of the finest cloth in world history. Wives also enjoyed rough equality with husbands and assumed the public and family responsibilities of their deceased spouses. They served as doctors and priestesses, and a few women even held administrative positions. Yet, public duties were normally reserved for men. An Old Kingdom sage advised men to "love your wife at home, as is proper. Fill her belly and clothe her back. Make her heart glad as long as you live. You should not judge her, or let her gain control."[10]

3-2b Cities, Trade, and Technology

Whereas Mesopotamian cities had long been trading centers, Egyptian cities were largely administrative centers to house tax collectors, artisans in government workshops, shopkeepers, and the priests who cared for the local temple. Unlike their Mesopotamian counterparts, Egyptian city dwellers did not think of themselves as attached to the city but were subjects of the pharaoh, and most Egyptians lived in villages.

Most of the Egyptians' wide-ranging trade involved the import of luxury goods by the wealthy. Egyptians traded with sub-Saharan Africans as far south as the Congo River Basin, with the Berber peoples of what is today Libya and Algeria to the west, with the societies along the Red Sea to the east, with Palestine, Phoenicia (a rich source of fish and wood), and Mesopotamia to the northeast, and with southeastern Europe. Gold, semiprecious stones, and such exotic things as frankincense, myrrh, ivory, ostrich feathers, and monkeys came from sub-Saharan Africa through Nubia or via the Red Sea and were exchanged for furniture, silver, tools, paper, and linen. Egyptians mined copper in the nearby Sinai (**SIGH-nigh**) Peninsula, while the Nile Delta provided papyrus and waterfowl. By 600 BCE the port city of Naukratis, in the Nile River delta, was becoming a major gateway for trade and cultural exchange, with tall tower houses and a mixed population including many Greeks. Archaeological excavations in coastal ports have uncovered jewelry, such as rings, pendants, and earrings, that had Greek and Persian influences reflecting a cosmopolitan society.

The Egyptians understood enough mathematics and physics to make the pyramids perfectly level and to match the corners of each pyramid with the four points of the compass. They also used a solar calendar that divided the year into 365 days and twelve months. In arithmetic, the Egyptians understood fractions but had no concept of zero. In medicine, Egyptians used both surgery and herbal remedies to treat illnesses. They recognized that the heart was a pump, were able to cure some eye diseases, and did some dental work. Modern observers still admire Egyptian technical skill in treating the dead, reflected in the mummies held in museums worldwide. Using a form of salt and the extremely dry climate, Egyptian morticians preserved human tissue well enough that the distinct features of individuals can be seen four thousand years later. Many aspects of Egyptian culture impressed the ancient Greeks, including mathematics, art, papyrus making, innovative sail technology, and egg hatching with egg incubators, a brilliant system of mud ovens invented over two thousand years ago. With lots of heat and moisture the oven could hatch as many as forty-five hundred fertilized eggs in two or three weeks. The incubator system is still used today.

3-2c Religion

Egyptian religious and moral beliefs included many myths, unique views of death, and some two thousand gods and goddesses, most of them benevolent. Like their Mesopotamian counterparts, the Egyptian gods explained nature but were also made in the image of humans and shared human weaknesses. The emphasis on preserving bodies indicates a chief feature of Egyptian religion, the belief that a person's soul could be united with his or her body after death, but only if the body was properly preserved. Initially only pharaohs could expect this afterlife, which mirrored life on earth. By the Middle Kingdom, all who could afford some form of mummification and whose souls passed a final moral judgment after death were candidates for immortality. People devoted vast resources to this quest.

The most dramatic and long-lived of the Egyptian myths concern Osiris (**oh-SIGH-ris**), a god-king, and his wife Isis (**EYE-sis**). Murdered by his brother, Osiris descended to the underworld, where he established justice there as he had done on Earth. A famous Egyptian drawing from the Book of the Dead, which depicts the afterlife, shows Osiris weighing the heart of a dead princess against the symbol of justice and truth. The Book of the Dead describes a confession that the dead person is to repeat as part of this judgment by Osiris indicating that he or she has not murdered or cheated anyone.

Because of the Book of the Dead, the pyramids, and the mummified remains, some scholars have viewed ancient Egyptians as preoccupied with death and the afterlife. But

---

[9]Quoted in Ezra Pound and Noel Stock, *Love Poems of Ancient Egypt* (Norfolk, CT: New Directions, 1962).
[10]Quoted in Barbara Mertz, *Red Land, Black Land: Daily Life in Ancient Egypt*, rev. ed. (New York: Dodd, Mead and Company, 1978), 56.

the Egyptians doubtless enjoyed life as much or more as other people. Many wall paintings imply that even the lower classes accepted their lot and found ways to cope. They show farmers and herders telling jokes, women bringing them their lunches, children squabbling, and shepherds asleep under a tree, a dog or flask of beer beside them. They could find solace in religion and were in awe of the pharaoh who sat, as the gods ordained, at the apex of the social pyramid.

KEY POINTS

▶ Though Egyptian society was divided into classes, with the rich enjoying lavish lifestyles, even the poor were relatively comfortable.

▶ Women had greater independence and rights in Egypt than in any other ancient society, but their roles were still quite limited.

▶ Ancient Egyptians had great technical skill in architecture, medicine, and preserving the dead.

▶ Ancient Egyptians believed they could obtain immortality if their bodies were mummified and if they passed a moral judgment after death.

3-3 Ancient Sub-Saharan African Societies

▦ SOCIETIES

Ⓠ What were some achievements of the ancient Nubian, Sudanic, and Bantu peoples?

Africa is the original homeland for all of humanity, and Egypt was only the best known and documented of the early farming societies and states that emerged on the continent. Various African societies became linked to each other and the wider world through growing networks. Like the annual Nile floods for Egypt, the environment also influenced sub-Saharan African farming and technology. While historians tend to emphasize state building and monarchs as indicating political progress, many Africans rejected political centralization, choosing public participation rather than kings and bureaucracies. However, strong states emerged in Nubia and the Sudan. Meanwhile, migrating **Bantu (BAN-too)** peoples spread farming, iron metallurgy, and their languages widely in the southern half of the continent.

CONNECTION to TODAY

What do you think modern people can learn from ancient Africans?

3-3a Sub-Saharan African Environments

Geography and climate have shaped African history. With one-fifth of the earth's landmass, Africa is the second largest continent after Eurasia and occupies more land than the United States, Europe (excluding Russia), China, and India combined. The equator bisects Africa, giving most of the continent a tropical climate. Lush rain forests have flourished along West Africa's Guinea coast and in the vast Congo River Basin in the heart of the continent. These equatorial regions are home to many insects, parasites, and bacteria that cause debilitating diseases like malaria, yellow fever, and sleeping sickness. Since the last is deadly to cattle and horses, the plow or wheel was impractical in much of equatorial Africa. Only in recent years has some progress been made in eradicating the tsetse flies that cause sleeping sickness. Most of the continent, however, is parched desert or savannah grasslands. African weather can be erratic, with fluctuating, often unpredictable rains. Rain diminishes north and south of the equator, producing a huge dry zone that is home to pastoral societies and herds of large wild animals and that receives less than 10 inches of rain a year. In some

regions the poor-quality soil has been easily eroded, fostering low agricultural productivity. Nonetheless, early farmers cultivated the grassland-covered region known as the **Sudan (soo-DAN)**, stretching along the southern fringe of the Sahara Desert from Africa's western tip to the Nile Basin.

Geography often hindered communication. Africa's eastern third includes extensive mountains and plateaus where great lakes and fertile volcanic soils permitted denser populations. The eastern highlands also produced great river systems, including the Nile, Congo, and, in the south, the Zambezi (**zam-BEE-zee**), but all these rivers have numerous rapids and waterfalls that limited boat travel. Only the Niger (**NIGH-jer**) River, which flows through West African plains, is navigable over large distances. Much of the African coast has sandbars that create great swells, making landing a boat difficult. Furthermore, there are few bays, gulfs, inland seas, or natural harbors to serve as maritime hubs. Only along the Indian Ocean, Red Sea, and Mediterranean coasts did a few protected bays and prevailing winds favor seagoing trade.

The catastrophic climatic change that created and expanded the Sahara Desert strongly shaped early African societies. In 3500 BCE the Sahara region was relatively wet, a rich grazing land with lakes and rivers occupied by hunting, gathering, fishing, and some farming societies. Ancient rock art portrays people dancing, worshipping, riding chariots, and tending horses and cattle. The paintings endow women with dignity as they raise children, gather plants, and make baskets, pottery, and jewelry. Then rain patterns shifted southward causing **desertification**, the process by

---

Bantu Sub-Saharan peoples who developed a cultural tradition based on farming and iron metallurgy, which they spread widely through great migrations.

Sudan A grassland region stretching along the southern fringe of the Sahara Desert from the western tip of Africa to the Nile Valley.

desertification The process by which productive land is transformed into mostly useless desert.

which productive land is transformed into mostly useless desert. By 2000 BCE the Sahara region was harsh desert. People contributed by overgrazing marginal lands and burning forests to create grasslands. The same desertification processes continue today on the Sahara's southern fringe. As most inhabitants migrated elsewhere, the Sahara was left largely to nomadic herders of cattle, goats, and camels. Eventually it marked a general boundary between the Berber and Semitic peoples along the southern Mediterranean coast and the darker-skinned peoples in the rest of Africa. But the desert barrier did not prevent considerable social, cultural, and genetic intermixing and exchange.

3-3b The Origins of African Agriculture

Geographical challenges did not prevent agriculture from developing early from both local and imported discoveries. Some 12,000 or 13,000 years ago, people in the eastern Sahara made pottery, probably for storing food and water, two centuries earlier than Middle Eastern people. Between 8000 and 5000 BCE, people in Nubia and the Sahara became farmers, followed by the Ethiopians. By 2500 BCE farming was widespread in West, Central, and East Africa. In West Africa almost all food crops developed from local wild African plants like sorghum, millet, yams, and African rice. Rice became a major crop in the rain forest zone. In Ethiopia, teff, a nutritious, high-protein whole grain, was the dietary mainstay for three thousand years, especially when made into a flatbread, and has become increasingly popular in North American cooking. Saharans also domesticated cotton and worked it into fabrics using spindles of baked clay, perhaps by 5000 BCE. Other crops came later from outside Africa, including wheat, barley, and chickpeas from the Middle East and bananas from Southeast Asia. But the movement went in both directions. Crops domesticated in West Africa such as sorghum and sesame reached India and China well before 2000 BCE.

Animal domestication presented a greater challenge. Cattle were probably domesticated very early from local sources in the southern Sahara and East Africa. But no other African animals were suitable for domestication, and some were dangerous predators. Rock art reveals possible attempts to domesticate giraffes, antelopes, and elephants, but most draft animals had to come from North Africa and Eurasia. Goats and sheep were brought in from the Middle East.

African peoples overcame geographical barriers in many ways. The major response to difficult climate and soils was a subsistence economy rather than the high-productivity agriculture possible in Egypt, China, India, Southeast Asia, or southern Europe. Many farmed by shifting cultivation, moving their fields around every few years and letting recently used land lie fallow for a while to regain its nutrients. If not abused, this system worked well for centuries. Only in a few fertile areas was intensive sedentary agriculture possible. Pastoral nomadism became the specialty of some groups in dry regions.

3-3c Ancient African Metallurgy

Most sub-Saharan peoples learned to make metal tools and weapons. Copper may have been mined in the Sahara by 1500 BCE. There was no pronounced bronze age, and generally

Heritage Image Partnership Ltd/Alamy Stock Photo

IMAGE 3.4 **Nubian Depictions of Egyptian Goddess** This Nubian gold and bronze depiction of the Egyptian sky goddess Hathor indicates the strength of Egyptian traditions in Nubian culture. Often depicted in the form of a cow but here in human form, Hathor holds the solar disk between the cow horns on her headdress.

Q Can you see any similarities between the Nubian depiction of Hathor and similar Egyptian ones of the era?

the use of bronze came around the same time as or later than iron. Sub-Saharan Africans were among the world's earliest ironworkers, probably making iron by at least 1000 BCE on the northern fringe of the Congo Basin. Iron smelters were built around 900 BCE in the Great Lakes region, and between 600 and 300 BCE iron was being mined, smelted, and forged widely in West, East, and Southeast Africa, with West Africans possibly influenced by iron and bronze metallurgy established on the North African coast.

Since major iron ore deposits were rare, ore and iron artifacts had to be transported over long distances. Some miners had to dig open pits or vertical shafts, backbreaking work, to reach ore deposits deep underground. Furnaces ranged from simple open holes to elaborate clay structures. Several hundred years before Europeans did so, African blacksmiths developed bellowing technology that allowed more efficient smelting by preheating iron with a mixture of hot and cold air. The craftsmen made spear blades and arrowheads for warriors and hunters; plows, hoes, sickles, axes, machetes, and knives for farmers and traders; bangles and rings for jewelry; gongs to produce music; hammers, hinges, and nails for household use; and iron bells for ceremonies and rituals. Mining and working iron were both difficult operations, and those who did them occupied a special position in the community. They still do today. For example, among the Haya (**HI-uh**) people in Tanzania (**TAN-zeh-NEE-uh**), when a new king was installed on the throne, he made a ritual visit to the blacksmith's hut, symbolizing the special relationship between the king and the ironworkers.

Agriculture and metallurgy came to various African regions at different times, depending on circumstances, spreading to the southern half of the continent last. Originally much of this region was inhabited by expert hunter-gatherers such as the !Kung (see Chapter 1), successful adapters to their environment who had little incentive to develop agriculture or ironworking. Gradually most of these groups were assimilated by or pushed farther south by iron-using farmers.

3-3d Early Urban Societies in Nubia

The first known urban African state after Egypt emerged in Nubia (see Map 3.1), today the northern half of the country of Sudan and far southern Egypt. Like Egyptians, Nubians turned to the Nile for survival. The region is mostly desert, but a thin area along the Nile was fertile; copper and gold could be mined nearby. The first Nubian kingdom may have formed as early as 3100 BCE. Egypt dominated the region for many centuries, occasionally through military occupations, and exchanged pottery and copper items for Nubian ivory, ebony, ostrich feathers, and slaves. An independent Nubian kingdom, Kerma (**CARE-ma**), appeared between 1800 and 1600 BCE. Extensive ruins of stone and mud-brick buildings, massive cemeteries, large towers, painted pottery, and copper vessels and weapons confirm a prosperous, well-organized society. Around 1500 BCE Egyptian forces occupied Nubia and destroyed the Kerma state. During the five centuries of Egyptian rule Nubian society, culture, and religion mixed with that of the rulers.

When Egyptian power declined around 900 BCE, a larger Nubian state, Kush (**koosh**), emerged, launching a golden age of trade, culture, and metallurgy. The Kushites conquered Egypt in the eighth century BCE but were pushed out by the Assyrians after a century of occupation. As a major regional trading hub, Kush was linked by overland caravan routes with the Niger and Congo Basins and with the Ethiopian highlands. It provided central and southern African goods to the Mediterranean and Red Sea regions and to markets as distant as India and China, importing Roman goblets and Chinese copper vessels.

Kush clearly benefited from its foreign contacts, adding imported ideas to Nubian traditions. For example, Egyptian and western Asian irrigation technology made farming possible in this barren area. Kushites worshipped both Egyptian and local gods and buried their kings in Egyptian-style pyramids. A sixth-century BCE inscription tells us that King Aspelta (**as-PELL-ta**), the son of the Egyptian sun-god, built a pyramid of white stone. However, while Kushite art reflected Egyptian and sometimes Greek influence, the overall effect remained distinctively Nubian. Kushite society may have also been matrilineal; some women held key political positions, including that of queen, and kings sometimes traced their descent through female ancestors.

Kush linked African and Mediterranean societies. By 600 BCE it was the major African producer of iron, giving it an even more crucial economic influence on the ancient world. The ancient Greek poet Homer described Kushites as "the most just of men; the favorites of the gods. The lofty inhabitants of Olympus (**oh-LIM-pus**) (home of Greek gods) journey to them, and take part in their feasts."[11]

3-3e The Sudanic Societies and Trade Networks

In ancient times peoples in the Sudan grasslands of West Africa also developed towns, perhaps a few small kingdoms, and long-distance trade routes including to Nubia and Egypt. By 1200 BCE farmers in Mauritania (**MORE-ee-TAIN-ee-uh**) had built over two hundred stone villages and towns in what is now mostly uninhabited desert. They may have been the ancestors of the Mande (**MAN-da**) peoples, who now occupy a large area of the western Sudan. By 900 or 800 BCE population increase had transformed walled villages into large,

Werner Forman/Art Resource, NY

IMAGE 3.5 **Nok Terra-Cotta Sculpture of Head**
Elaborate, life-size, technically complex sculptures reveal something of Nok material life in ancient Nigeria. Some figures sit on stools, carry an axe, or wear beads.

[11]Quoted in *Africa's Glorious Legacy* (Alexandria, VA: Time-Life Books, 1996), 18.

Discover Historical Voices

The Worldview of an African Society

While few primary sources survive for the ancient period in sub-Saharan Africa, contemporary oral traditions may offer some insight into ancient understandings of the natural and spiritual realms. This excerpt on the worldview of the Igbo (also spelled Ibo) people in southeastern Nigeria was compiled by an Igbo anthropologist. Many Igbo perspectives may derive from the Nok and Bantu cultures, whose ancestral homelands are near the region where the Igbo live today.

There is the world of … all created beings and things, both animate and inanimate. The spirit world is the abode of the creator, the deities, the disembodied and malignant spirits, and the ancestral spirits. It is the future abode of the living after their death…. Existence or the Igbo … involves the interaction between the material and … spiritual, the visible and … invisible, the good and … bad, the living and … dead…. The world of the "dead" is … full of activities…. The principle of seniority makes the ancestors [in the world of the "dead"] the head of the [extended kinship system in the world of man]….

The world as a natural order which inexorably goes on its ordained way … is foreign to Igbo conceptions. Rather, their world is a dynamic one— … of moving equilibrium … that is constantly threatened, and sometimes actually disturbed by natural and social calamities…. But the Igbo believe that these social calamities and cosmic forces which disturb their world are controllable and should be "manipulated" by them for their own purpose … [to maintain] … social and cosmological balance in the world…. They achieve this balance … through divination, sacrifice, and appeal to the countervailing forces

of their ancestors … against the powers of the malignant spirits…. The Igbo world is not only a world in which people strive for equality; it is one in which change is constantly expected…. Life on earth is a link in the chain of status hierarchy which culminates in … ancestral honor in the world of the dead….

They believe in a supreme god, a high god, who is all good [but a] … withdrawn god … who has finished all active works of creation and keeps watch over his creatures from a distance…. Although the Igbo feel psychologically separated from their high god, he is not too far away, he can be reached, but not as quickly as can other deities who must render their services to man to justify their demand for sacrifices…. Minor gods [can] be controlled, manipulated, and used to further human interests…. Given effective protection, the Igbo are very faithful to their gods.

Reflection Questions

1. How do the Igbo understand the relationship between the human and spiritual worlds?
2. What is the role of the supreme god in their polytheistic theology?
3. How might their beliefs about the relationship of the human and spiritual realms shape Igbo society?
4. How is Igbo religion different from, and how is it similar to, the main religious traditions in the Western world today?

Source: From Victor Uchendu, *The Igbo of Southeast Nigeria*, 1E © 1965 Wadsworth, a part of Cengage Learning, Inc. Reproduced by permission.

---

well-constructed towns. Eventually the expanding Sahara swallowed this society and the people probably moved south.

Long-distance trade, especially the caravan routes crossing the vast Sahara Desert, greatly aided the growth of Sudanic societies. While the Sahara did pose an obstacle or hindrance to humans throughout history, it also became over time a great commercial highway through which goods and people flowed back and forth between the Mediterranean coast of North Africa and the grasslands of the Sudan. The earliest caravan activity dates back to 1000 or 500 BCE. Some groups took up commerce as their primary activity, and this trans-Saharan trade depended on pack animals introduced by Berbers, initially mules and horses and later camels. First domesticated in parched Arabia, camels could endure many days of caravan travel without water. Eventually a large trade system linked the Sudanic towns with the southern Mediterranean coast and the forest zone to the south.

While each society developed distinctive notions of the cosmic order and their place within it, there were common patterns (see Discover Historical Voices: The Worldview of an African Society). Many peoples, like the Mande and Igbo

(EE-boh), believed in one divine force or supreme being, either male or female, who created the cosmos, earth, and life and then remained remote from human affairs. Africans feeling the need for immediate spiritual help appealed to secondary gods and spirits. Thus original sub-Saharan African religion became a mix of monotheism, polytheism, and animism.

African societies shaped these beliefs into complex and enduring artistic traditions. For example, in what is now central Nigeria, the Nok people, mostly farmers and herders, cultivated pearl millet by 1500 BCE and worked iron by 500 BCE. Nok artists also fashioned exquisite terra-cotta pottery and sculpture, including life-size and realistic human heads. These creations influenced the later art of several Nigerian societies.

3-3f The Bantu-Speaking Peoples and Their Migrations

Today people who speak closely related Bantu languages occupy most of Africa south of a line stretching from today's Cameroon in West-Central Africa eastward to Kenya on the Indian Ocean

MAP 3.2 **Bantu Migrations and Early Africa** The Bantu-speaking peoples spread over several millennia throughout the southern half of Africa. Various societies, cities, and states emerged in West and North Africa.

Q How do you think the Bantu migrations generated a cultural and linguistic division between people in southern Africa and those in the northern half of the continent?

coast. All of these societies can trace their distant ancestry back to the same location in West-Central Africa (see Map 3.2). In their migrations, the Bantu incorporated many of the peoples they encountered and modified their own cultures to suit local conditions. Recent scholarship suggests that the diffusion of Bantu technologies and languages, which local peoples adopted, was as important as actual human movement in expanding Bantu culture. The Bantu occupation of central, eastern, and southern Africa constitutes one of the great population

movements in world history, a saga similar to the settlement of the Pacific islands and the Indo-European migration into western and southern Eurasia. As the Bantu spread out, they gradually divided into over four hundred different ethnic groups.

The Bantu originated along the Benue (**BAIN-way**) River in eastern Nigeria and western Cameroon (**KAM-uh-roon**). But agriculture fostered overcrowding by 2000 BCE, spurring some to migrate eastward into the lands just north of the Congo River Basin. Bantu settled the Great Lakes region of East Africa between 1000 BCE and 500 BCE, and some also began moving south into the Congo River Basin. They mixed with the local peoples, exchanging technologies and cultural patterns. Eventually some would migrate into southern Africa.

The Bantu benefited from iron metallurgy and agricultural technologies, using iron tools and weapons to open new land and subdue the small existing populations. Some also adopted cattle and goat raising. By two thousand years ago some Bantu living in northeast Africa had also learned to grow domesticated bananas and plantains (large bananas) imported from Southeast Asia, as well as sorghum (SOAR-gum) from the Nile Valley. These high-yielding crops provided a spur to population growth, encouraging new migration into southern Africa.

KEY POINTS

- ▶ Small-scale agriculture flourished in Africa, though widespread disease made it difficult to domesticate animals.

- ▶ The Nubian kingdom of Kush increased in power as Egypt declined and became a major trading hub linking the peoples of Africa to the Mediterranean.

- ▶ Caravan routes through the Sahara allowed for trade and for links among widely separated African peoples.

- ▶ The Bantu spread widely throughout Africa, mixing their culture and traditions with those of local peoples.

3-4 Early Societies and Networks of the Eastern Mediterranean

▦ SOCIETIES

Q What were the contributions of the Hebrews, Minoans, Mycenaeans, Phoenicians, and Dorian Greeks to later societies in the region?

During the second millennium BCE smaller bronze- and then iron-using societies in the eastern half of the Mediterranean Basin were developing influential ideas or establishing cities and states. The Hebrews created the foundation for three major world religions, the Minoans became an economic bridge between western Asia and southeastern Europe, and the warlike Mycenaeans built the first cities in Greece. The Phoenicians created a new alphabet, established colonies in the western Mediterranean, and fostered networks connecting many ancient societies. Greeks built an influential society.

> **CONNECTION to TODAY**
>
> How do you think the ancient Mediterranean world's religions, politics, and economic patterns compare to ours today?

Italy more easily than they could establish connections with nearby inland towns. Thus the Mediterranean linked the Greeks to other peoples such as the Minoans, Egyptians, and Phoenicians.

3-4a Eastern Mediterranean Environments

The history and agriculture of eastern Mediterranean peoples were influenced by the regional climate, with its cool, rainy winters and hot, dry summers. On the northern shores, people grew grain, made bread, and planted olive trees and grape vines, and both olive oil and wine became export crops. Pastoralism was common in the drier lands of Lebanon and Palestine. Finally, the Mediterranean Sea, a mostly placid body of water, fostered boat building, maritime trade, and other contacts between diverse societies (see Map 3.3).

One of the densest populations emerged in Greece, located across the Aegean (ah-JEE-uhn) Sea from Anatolia. Unlike Mesopotamia and Egypt, where river valleys invited the creation of large political units, Greece consists of small valleys separated by mountains and has an extensive coastline with many good harbors. This geography encouraged political fragmentation and intellectual diversity. Because of this context, most Greeks in that era lived in small, independent city-states and also became a seafaring, trading people who could travel by sea east to Ionia (today western Turkey), south to Crete, or west to southern

3-4b The Hebrews and Religious Innovation

The Hebrews, a Semitic people led by powerful men known as patriarchs (from the Greek word for "rule by the father"), were one of many groups of pastoral nomads in the eastern Mediterranean. Later, as they formed states in Palestine around 1000 BCE, they preferred to be known as the Israelites and later the Jews, as they are generally called today. But due to their complicated political history, including multiple states in ancient times, there remains much complexity in the use of these terms. The Hebrew or Israelite population was small, their economic and technological developments unimpressive, and their political achievements short-lived. Their united monarchy lasted less than a century. Yet the Hebrew contribution to religious history, especially to Christian and Islamic traditions, exceeds that of either the Mesopotamians or Egyptians. The influence of their beliefs and story remains important today.

The Jews trace their ancestry back to Abraham, a patriarch who supposedly lived in Bronze Age Mesopotamia sometime between 2000 and 1500 BCE. Abraham and his two sons, Isaac and Ishmael, are considered the spiritual ancestors of three monotheistic religions—Judaism, Christianity, and Islam—often called the Abrahamic faiths and collectively having some three billion followers today. The books of the Hebrew or Jewish Bible (what Christians call the Old Testament) contain their basic laws and provide the main source for their early history.

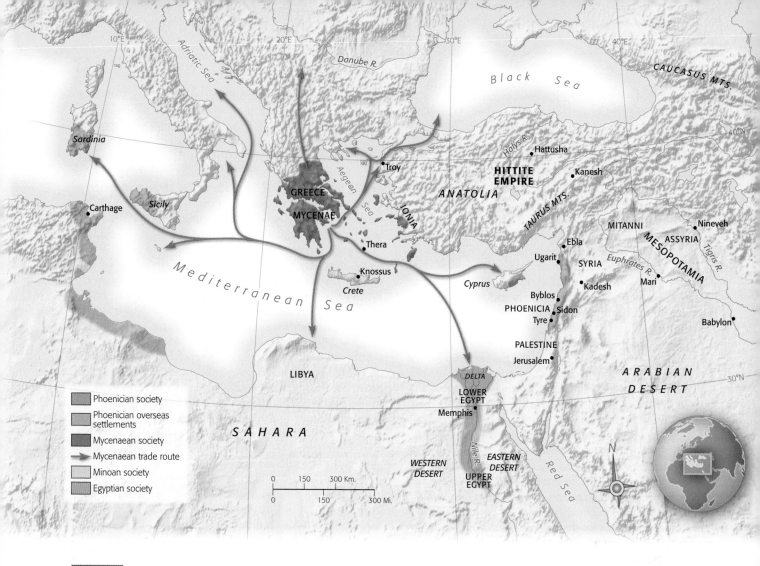

MAP 3.3 **The Ancient Eastern Mediterranean** The Hebrew, Minoan, Mycenaean, Phoenician, and Greek societies developed along the eastern shores of the Mediterranean Sea, exchanging goods and ideas with each other and with other western Asians and the Egyptians.

Q In what ways would the Mediterranean Sea facilitate communication between the peoples living along or near its shores?

Modern Israeli and Western historians and archaeologists heatedly debate the historical reliability and antiquity of the Bible, which was probably based in part on oral traditions, and even whether key figures such as Abraham, Moses, and King David were real or mythical. As archaeology cannot confirm very much of the earliest history, every newly discovered artifact is subject to heated controversy. Some scholars think some of the biblical books are quite old, others that most or all of the books were composed after 700 BCE to support rival Hebrew political or religious factions. Scholars differ on whether literacy was widespread among Hebrew elites. Some Bible stories seem based on Mesopotamian and Egyptian traditions, such as the great flood in the Epic of Gilgamesh. For example, some of the advice in the Hebrew Book of Proverbs echoes ideas in more ancient Egyptian writings. These ongoing controversies underline the importance of Hebrew religion to later history. But basing the existence of modern Israel on controversial and ancient biblical claims has also complicated that nation's relationship to the Palestinians and other Arabs, generating conflict and political crises today.

In the biblical account, Abraham led a few followers on a migration from southern Mesopotamia to Palestine. Although born into a polytheistic world, Abraham recognized one supreme god. Peoples from Palestine had long migrated, either voluntarily or as slaves, to Egypt. A group of Hebrews who had gone to Egypt and been enslaved were freed and left Egypt, probably in the thirteenth century. This "Exodus" from Egypt and eventual return to Palestine was led by Moses, whom the later Hebrews acclaimed their religion's founder. Moses gave his name to a code of laws, including the Ten Commandments.

Around 1000 BCE the Hebrews had enough unity to establish a monarchy centered in the small city of Jerusalem. But Hebrew unity proved short-lived. After the death of King Solomon in 922 BCE, the monarchy split into two kingdoms, Israel and Judah. In 722 the Assyrians conquered Israel and resettled its inhabitants elsewhere in their empire. When Assyria fell, the Israelite prophet Nahum (**NAY-hum**) expressed joy: "Nineveh [the Assyrian capital] is laid waste; who will bemoan her? All who hear the news of you will clap their hands over you."[12] In 586 the Chaldeans conquered Judah and moved its leaders to Babylon. The bitterness of the "Babylonian Captivity" was reflected in a Hebrew psalm: "By the rivers of Babylon, there we sat down, yea, we wept when we remembered Zion."[13] Some scholars think some biblical texts were written in Babylon during the exile to make a record of their history. This exile ended in 539 when the Persians conquered the Chaldeans and allowed the Israelites to return to Palestine, which later became part of the Roman Empire. The Jews were again dispersed after a revolt against Roman rule in 70 CE, and from that time until the establishment of modern Israel in 1948 CE, there was no Jewish state.

The Jews' religious history, especially their ethical code, makes them memorable in world history. Four religious concepts later influenced the Western and Islamic traditions: monotheism, morality, messianism, and meaning in history. Many ancient Hebrews worshipped a single god, Yahweh (**YA-way**), whom they believed had made a covenant with their earliest patriarchs and reinforced it when Moses received the Ten Commandments. If they would obey Yahweh, he would protect them. Gradually the Hebrews reshaped monotheism, asserting that there is only one God, Yahweh, for all peoples, as the prophet Isaiah proclaimed: "There is no other God besides Me, a just God. Look to Me, and be saved, all you ends of the earth!"[14]

Holy men known as prophets refined two other Jewish religious concepts, morality and messianism, emphasizing that following Yahweh also meant leading a moral life, refraining from lying, stealing, adultery, and persecution of the poor and oppressed. Unlike Hammurabi's Code, the law of Moses also emphasized compassion for the poor and mercy. Also, Jewish law required punishing only the wrongdoer, not members of his or her family. Another major concept, **messianism**, asserted that God had given the Jews a special mission in the world. As the Israelites faced their time of troubles after the division of Solomon's kingdom and the fall of Judah, messianism acquired a broad spiritual meaning of bringing proper ethical behavior and moral truth to all peoples. The book of Isaiah contends: "I will give you as a covenant to the people, as a light to the [nations]. To open blind eyes, to bring out prisoners from the prison, those who sit in darkness."[15] This idea later inspired Christian missionary work.

The final contribution is the idea that history itself has meaning and moves forward in a progressive, linear fashion, meaning that this earthly world was where human beings worked out their salvation by choosing good over evil. This belief gave birth later to the idea of progress, the notion that the future will be better than the past. It stood in contrast to Hindu ideas that the material world is illusory and time is cyclical.

3-4c Minoan Crete and Regional Trade

Between about 2000 and 1400 BCE an influential urban society and network hub, now called Minoan (**mi-NO-an**), thrived on the large island of Crete (**kreet**), which lies just south of the Greek peninsula. Crete's strategic location made it a center for sea trade between Egypt, western Asia, and southeastern Europe, and its achievements intrigue historians. Like Harappan cities, some Minoan cities had indoor plumbing and streets with drains and sewers. Paintings and sculptures show some Mesopotamian and Egyptian influences, but they also differ in style. Minoans apparently worshipped many female deities, including a mother goddess. The absence of fortresses or defensive walls suggests that they relied on their fleet to protect them. Yet, while many accounts portray Minoans as largely peace-loving, some recent studies find more evidence of violence, martial traditions, and warfare. Around 1630 BCE many cities were destroyed, perhaps from earthquakes following a massive volcanic explosion that blew apart the nearby island of Thera (**THER-uh**) (today's Santorini). The sinking of most of Thera and the dispersal of the survivors may have led to the legend of a lost continent, Atlantis.

The Minoans were innovators who pioneered a mixed agriculture well suited to the region's sunny, dry climate. The first great Mediterranean sea power, they traded extensively with Sicily, Greece, and the Aegean islands and sent wine, olives, and wool to Egypt and Southwest Asia. Crete also served as a meeting place connecting, through trade, western Asians and North Africans with various European societies. The Minoans possessed two writing scripts, one of possibly Mesopotamian origin and the other related to early Greek. Scholars have learned to read some of it, including accounts of goods manufactured, crops harvested, religious festivals, and war preparations.

3-4d The Mycenaeans and Regional Power

The Mycenaeans, Indo-Europeans named after the city of Mycenae (**my-SEE-nee**) in southern Greece, also became an important power between 1600 and 1200 BCE after migrating into the Greek peninsula from western Asia. Mycenaean palaces and technologies borrowed heavily from the Minoans with whom they traded, but they also introduced innovations in engineering, architecture, and military infrastructure. Bronze swords and armor in their graves indicate that they were a warrior society whose economy was tightly controlled by the king and his scribes. Eventually the Mycenaeans conquered Crete (whose Minoan society had already collapsed), all of southern Greece, and the Aegean islands, forming an empire from which they collected taxes and tribute. They dispatched ships to Sicily, Italy, and Spain and into the Black Sea and engaged in war with rivals, operating out of strong fortresses. According to legends, around 1250 the Mycenaeans conquered Troy, a prosperous Hittite trading port along the northwestern coast of Anatolia, inspiring Homer's epic story, the *Iliad*, some five hundred years later. Scholars debate whether an actual Trojan War occurred, some suspecting that the Homeric stories combine oral accounts of various conflicts, but the stories strongly influenced the later Greeks and Romans.

By 1200, however, the Mycenaeans themselves, like the Egyptians, faced collapse, perhaps from prolonged drought resulting from climate change, a possible series of earthquakes, or civil wars and attacks by warlike Indo-Europeans known as

messianism The Hebrew belief that their God, Yahweh, had given them a special mission in the world.

[12]Nahum 3:7, 19, *The Holy Bible*, New King James Version (Chicago: Thomas Nelson, 1983), 908.
[13]Psalm 137:1, *Holy Bible*, 639.
[14]Isaiah 45:21–22, *Holy Bible*, 721.
[15]Isaiah 42:6–7, *Holy Bible*, 717.

Erich Lessing/Art Resource, NY

IMAGE 3.6 **The Captivity of Israeli Women at Nineveh** This relief comes from the palace of the Chaldean king Sennacherib in Ninevah. It was probably carved at the beginning of the seventh century BCE.

Q What do we learn about transportation, clothing styles, and the mistreatment of women in Ninevah?

the Dorian Greeks, who were migrating into the peninsula. They also suffered when various groups known as "Sea Peoples" pillaged and disrupted trade throughout the Aegean and eastern Mediterranean. But eventually a creative society emerged in Greece that incorporated many influences from the Dorian Greeks, Mycenaeans, Phoenicians, and Egyptians.

3-4e The Phoenicians and Their Networks

The Phoenicians linked Mediterranean and Southwest Asian peoples by trade networks. Between 1500 and 1000 BCE this Semitic people, known to the Hebrews as the Canaanites (**KAY-nan-ites**), built the great trading cities of Tyre (**tire**), Sidon (**SIDE-en**), and Byblos (**BIB-los**) along the narrow coastal strip west of the Lebanon mountains. Tyre offered luxury goods from many societies and attracted the finest artists and craftsmen. The Hebrew prophet Ezekial denounced the rich, vibrant city and its extraordinary network of mercantile connections: "Your borders are in the midst of the seas. All the ships of the sea were in you to market your merchandise."[16]

Some historians consider the term *Phoenicia* artificial because, they conclude, the country or society was essentially a loose association of neighboring mini-states, a widespread grouping of culturally diverse people but never a nation. Whatever the case, although sometimes dominated by Egypt, Phoenician cities,

each headed by kings, were fiercely competitive and independent of each other. While the Phoenicians spoke a common language and worshipped the same gods, they never united and identified themselves with the city where they lived. Their most famous cultural achievement, the simplification of Mesopotamian cuneiform writing into a phonetic alphabet of twenty-two characters, helped spread their influence in the Mediterranean and became the basis of later European alphabets. They once had an extensive literature of philosophy, religion, law, and history but only a few tablets containing information on Phoenician government, society, and religion survive. Most of what we know comes from writings by Egyptians, Greeks, and Hebrews, peoples who admired the Phoenicians' skills as scribes, seafarers, engineers, and artisans but also denounced them as immoral profiteers and cheaters. Deserved or not, the Phoenician image as schemers survives into modern times. Our term for a shameless woman, *Jezebel*, is derived from a princess of Tyre.

Between 1000 and 800 BCE, the seafaring Phoenicians replaced the declining Mycenaeans as the leaders in Mediterranean trade with western Asia, becoming experts in new methods of dyeing cloth. They may also have sailed as far as England to get supplies of tin. Phoenicians established colonies or trading posts in Sicily, Italy, Spain, Tunisia, and beyond the Strait of Gibraltar in Morocco. Some historians think they may have reached the Canary Islands and Madeira

---
[16]Ezekial 27:3–4, 9, *Holy Bible*, 835.

PRISMA ARCHIVO/Alamy Stock Photo

IMAGE 3.7 **Wall Painting from Thera, Crete** The paintings in palaces and homes show slices of Minoan life. This portrays female boxers, hinting that women played many roles in Minoan society.

in the Atlantic Ocean. Thus the Phoenicians, ancestors of many Lebanese today, became the ancient Mediterranean's and ancient world's greatest mariners.

Between 1000 and 500 BCE, the Mediterranean Sea became a major source of goods and wealth. Solid bars of precious metals served as currency. Using their colonies for resupply and repair, the Phoenicians traveled long distances to secure iron, silver, timber, copper, gold, and tin, all valuable commodities in western Asia and Egypt. Legends suggest that around 600 BCE, under the sponsorship of the Egyptian king, a Phoenician fleet may even have sailed around Africa in a three-year expedition, but these journeys cannot be substantiated. In 650 BCE the Assyrians conquered the Phoenician home cities and brought an end to their dynamic power, but some Phoenician colonies lived on, most famously Carthage in North Africa near what is today Tunis. According to legends, in 814 BCE Dido, a princess from Tyre, fled her homicidal brother Pygmalion, who had killed her husband. Landing in North Africa with her followers she rented land from Berber tribes, choosing a strategic location commanding the trade routes. Her story and its tragic ending with a failed love affair with a fugitive from Troy, Aeneas, was memorialized centuries later by the Roman poet Virgil. Whatever the historical truth of the legend, Carthage became the capital of a major trading empire and the chief competitor to the Romans in the western Mediterranean by the third century BCE. Carthaginian sailors later explored far down the coast of West Africa.

3-4f The Eclectic Roots of Greek Society

The fall of the Mycenaeans and the Phoenicians set the stage for another seafaring people, the Greeks, to found an influential urban society. During the four centuries after the destruction of Mycenae, called the Greek "Dark Age" (1200–800 BCE), organized states and writing disappeared, and the economic and social environment changed considerably. Dorian Greeks settled much of the Greek peninsula, and many Mycenaeans dispersed, some settling the offshore islands and others crossing the Aegean Sea to Ionia, where they established cities. The Greek world scattered, as the philosopher Plato later put it, like frogs around a pond, became a mix of Mycenaean and Dorian peoples and traditions.

The Greeks were famous as both maritime traders and warriors, their respect for military strength reflected in the works of Homer, oral epics written down between the eleventh and the eighth centuries BCE that became an integral part of the Greek tradition. Whether Homer was an actual person or the collective name for several authors who compiled these epic poems into a narrative remains debated. Many themes in the epics may reflect influences from Mesopotamian literature such as the Epic of Gilgamesh, indicating the spread of ideas around the eastern Mediterranean world.

The first Homeric epic, the *Iliad*, set during an attack on Troy by some Greek cities led by their king Agamemnon **(ag-uh-MEM-non)**, emphasized valor in war but also warned its readers against excessive pride. Arrogance led the

Greeks to make some nearly fatal mistakes. For example, after a quarrel with Agamemnon the Greek hero Achilles (uh-KIL-eez) refused to fight. When Achilles' friend Patroclus (puh-TROW-klus) took Achilles' place in the battle and was killed by Hector, the Trojan leader, a remorseful Achilles then kills Hector. The poem ends when Hector's father, Priam, came to ask Achilles for his son's body. Achilles was moved by Priam's courage, and both men shared their grief. This poem and Homer's second epic, the *Odyssey*, a story of the adventures of Odysseus (oh-DIS-ee-us), or Ulysses, as he returns home after the Trojan War, portrayed the Greek gods as superheroes who intervened to help their human friends and hinder their enemies. The Homeric world measured virtue by success in combat rather than justice or mercy. Yet these great epics continue to be read even in modern times, not only because of their dramatic and often brutal war scenes, but also because they tell us something about the tragedy of human life. This emphasis on both human power and suffering remained a part of Greek literature throughout the following centuries.

The Homeric epics and belief in their gods greatly influenced the emerging Greek society. The Greeks also borrowed ideas from the Egyptians and western Asians, although the degree of outside influence on early Greek culture is debated (see the Historical Controversy for Part A). The Mediterranean provided a zone of interaction for peoples living around its rim. Phoenician ships, which had avoided a turbulent Greece for several hundred years, began to show up again, restoring Greek contact with the eastern Mediterranean and its regional trade networks. Soon the Greeks adopted and modified the Phoenician alphabet. These centuries built a foundation for a dynamic Greek society in the Classical period.

KEY POINTS

▸ The Hebrews were politically fragmented, but their religious writings—with their emphasis on monotheism, morality, messianism, and meaning in history—have had a tremendous impact on religious history.

▸ Around 1250 BCE, the Mycenaeans possibly conquered Troy; this event later inspired Homer's epic, the *Iliad*.

▸ The Phoenicians, the region's greatest maritime traders, simplified the Mesopotamian cuneiform writing into an alphabet, which served as the basis for later European alphabets.

▸ The Homeric epics, the *Iliad* and the *Odyssey*, greatly influenced the emerging Greek society, which was a synthesis of Mycenaean and Dorian Greek peoples.

Chapter Summary

Egypt is often called "the gift of the Nile" because it arose in the flood-prone Nile River Valley. The Egyptian system, led by kings, lasted for several thousand years in its basic form. In their stable and predictable environment, the Egyptians invented the hieroglyphics writing system and developed a more optimistic worldview and culture than the Mesopotamians. Egyptians also participated in trade networks linking western Asia and the Mediterranean Basin with sub-Saharan Africa and India.

Many sub-Saharan African peoples also invented or adopted agriculture and metallurgy, building the framework for cities and states. An environment of grasslands, forests, and the expanding Sahara Desert shaped their history, and the gradual drying-out of the Sahara region forced many people to migrate. Cities arose early in Nubia (along the central Nile), probably stimulated by long-distance trade and contacts with Egypt. The Sudan fostered distinctive cultures. The Bantu peoples, in one of the greatest migrations in history, spread their farming and iron-based culture and languages widely in the southern half of Africa.

The Mediterranean societies also benefited from regional connections. The trade routes of the seafaring Minoans, Mycenaeans, and Phoenicians enriched the peoples of western Asia and the Mediterranean Basin by bringing them material goods, markets, cultural contacts, and a practical new alphabet. Contact with Egyptians and Mesopotamians influenced the Hebrews' evolving understanding of their mission and of Yahweh. Some of these contributions, such as the Phoenician alphabet and Hebrew religious and ethical concepts, have influenced many peoples down to the present day. Greece arose from interaction among several Mediterranean societies in a turbulent period during which Homer wrote his great epics.

Key Terms

pharaohs 56
hieroglyphics 56
monotheism 57

Bantu 61
Sudan 61

desertification 61
messianism 68

Around the Pacific Rim: Eastern Eurasia and the Americas, 5000–600 BCE

He encouraged the people and settled them. He called his superintendent of works [and] minister of instruction, and charged them with the building of the houses. Crowds brought the earth in baskets. The roll of the great drum did not overpower [the noise of the builders].

—Chinese poem from the second millennium BCE[1]

DEA/G. DAGLI ORTI/De Agostini/Getty Images

IMAGE 4.1 **Shang Bronze Vase** The Shang made some of the ancient world's finest bronze tools and vessels. This ritual vase has an animal motif.

Q What kinds of animals and other things can you identify on the bronze vase?

[1]From the ancient Chinese *Book of Songs*, quoted in Herlee Glessner Creel, *The Birth of China: A Survey of the Formative Period of Chinese Civilization* (New York: Frederick Unger, 1937), 64.

According to Chinese tradition, beginning around

2000 BCE several legendary sage kings ruled, beginning China's history. Historians debate whether these sage kings really existed or are mythological but most agree that around 1400 BCE a later ruler named Pan Keng ordered a new capital city, Anyang (ahn-yahng), to be built in the same area on a flat plain alongside the Huan River. The king and his officials supervised the citizens as they worked to the beat of a drum. The king had high expectations for his new capital. The rich soil fostered productive farms, while the river supplied water and aided in defense. People could find timber, hunt, or seek relief from the summer heat in nearby mountains a short chariot ride away. Probably China's first planned city, Anyang was surrounded by four walls facing the points of the compass, reflecting the ancient adage that without harmony nothing lasts. Three and a half millennia later archaeologists found exquisite ritual bronzes and "dragon bones," animal bones carved with some of the earliest Chinese writing. In later centuries local chemists, not knowing their priceless historical value, ground up many of these bones to make folk medicine. But the remaining dragon bones showed that ancient China, like Mesopotamia and Egypt, had both cities and a writing system. Although Anyang's buildings crumbled with time and ruling families came and went, these ancient Chinese established a society that still retains many of its original ideas and customs.

Cities, states, agriculture, and trade networks developed on both sides of the Pacific. On the Asian side, people in China and Korea were among the earliest people to develop farming and metalworking, while Southeast Asians pioneered in maritime technology. Despite formidable geographical barriers, very early trade networks connected China and Southeast Asia to other parts of Eurasia. The same process took place on the other side of the Pacific Ocean. In the Americas, too, many people underwent the great transitions to farming, cities, regional networks of exchange, and complex social structures, although mountains, deserts, and forest barriers tended to isolate North, Central, and South American societies from each other.

4-1 The Formation of Chinese Society, 6000–1750 BCE

SOCIETIES · NETWORKS

Q How did an expanding Chinese society arise from diverse local traditions?

Societies change in part through contact with each other; while forbidding desert and mountain barriers complicated contact with China, they did not prevent some influences from crossing borders. Nevertheless, China joined Harappa, Mesopotamia, Egypt, and Minoan Crete in pioneering distinctive ways of life. Productive farming, creative cultures, and the rise of states laid the framework for a society now at least four thousand years old and still a major power in the world.

> **CONNECTION to TODAY**
>
> How do you think that China's location on the eastern edge of Asia and distant from the societies of India, the Middle East, and Europe might have helped shape attitudes toward the wider world that may still be important today?

and governments struggled to enforce centralizing policies. The Himalayas (him-uh-LAY-uhs), the high Tibetan (tuh-BET-en) Plateau, and great deserts inhibited contact with South and West Asia. However, the Chinese did have regular trade and conflict with Central Asians, Japanese, Koreans, Southeast Asians, and Tibetans, whose cultures, languages, and ways of life were very different from the Chinese. The Chinese sometimes extended political control over these peoples and sometimes were invaded and even conquered by them.

Modern China covers as much land as western and eastern Europe combined. But early China covered a much smaller area, mostly in north China. Because most people in ancient China lived in the eastern river valleys and plains rather than along the coast, maritime commerce did not develop very much until around 1000 CE. The large land area combined with many mountain

4-1a China and Its Regional Environments

The Chinese faced many challenges in communicating both with each other and with distant peoples. China's vast size, combined with a difficult topography, made transportation difficult while encouraging regional cultural and political loyalties. The early Chinese were often divided into competing states,

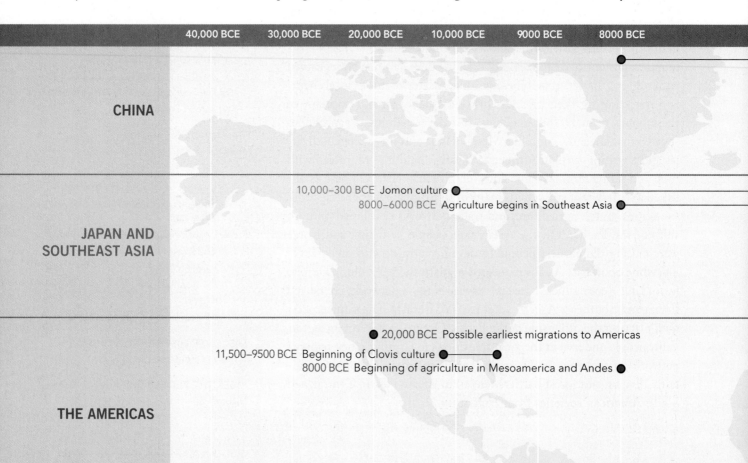

	40,000 BCE	30,000 BCE	20,000 BCE	10,000 BCE	9000 BCE	8000 BCE

CHINA

JAPAN AND SOUTHEAST ASIA

10,000–300 BCE Jomon culture
8000–6000 BCE Agriculture begins in Southeast Asia

20,000 BCE Possible earliest migrations to Americas
11,500–9500 BCE Beginning of Clovis culture
8000 BCE Beginning of agriculture in Mesoamerica and Andes

THE AMERICAS

ranges and three major river systems, which all flow from west to east and hence do not link the northern, central, and southern parts of China, helped shape Chinese regionalism. The Yellow River or Huang He (**hwang ho**), sometimes termed "China's sorrow" because of its many destructive floods, flows some three thousand miles through north China to the Yellow Sea, but it is easily navigable only in some sections. The more navigable but also flood-prone Yangzi (**yahng-zeh**), or Yangtze, River, the world's fourth-longest, flows through central China, a region of moderate climate and the densest population. The shorter West or Xijiang (**SHEE JYAHNG**) River helps define mountainous, subtropical south China.

China's neighboring regions had diverse environments and distinctive cultures. Central Asia's deserts and grasslands, with their blazing hot summers and long, cold winters, were mostly unpromising for intensive agriculture. The rugged, pastoralist Central Asian societies who lived in these areas traded with, warred against, and sometimes conquered the settled farmers of China, Korea, and India. Those who most affected Chinese history included diverse peoples speaking Turkic languages, some living in the dry Xinjiang (**SHIN-jee-yahng**) region of far western China. In contrast, the Tibetans were subsistence farmers and herders.

[2]*The Book of Songs*, translated by Arthur Waley (London: George Unwin, 1954), 162.

4-1b Early Chinese Agriculture

Agriculture in China began around 8000–7000 BCE, perhaps one thousand years later than in Mesopotamia. Neolithic settlements existed all over China, suggesting Chinese society's diverse roots. The Yellow and Wei River Valleys in north China fostered early farming, with the modest annual rainfall and frequent flooding making the region somewhat similar to the Nile, Tigris-Euphrates, and Indus Basins. Winds blowing in from the Gobi Desert of Mongolia to the northwest deposited massive amounts of dust that enriched north China soils. Initially the wheatlike, highly drought-resistant millet and later, wheat, likely imported from India or Mesopotamia, became northern China's main cereal grain. Ancient songs tell us something about the farming routine:

> They clear away the grass, the trees; Their ploughs open up the ground. In a thousand pairs they tug at weeds and roots, Along the low grounds, along the ridges. They sow the many sorts of grain, The seeds that hold moist life. How that blade shoots up, How sleek, the grown plant.[2]

Farther south, the Chinese in the Yangzi and West River Basins began cultivating rice, possibly as early as 7000 BCE.

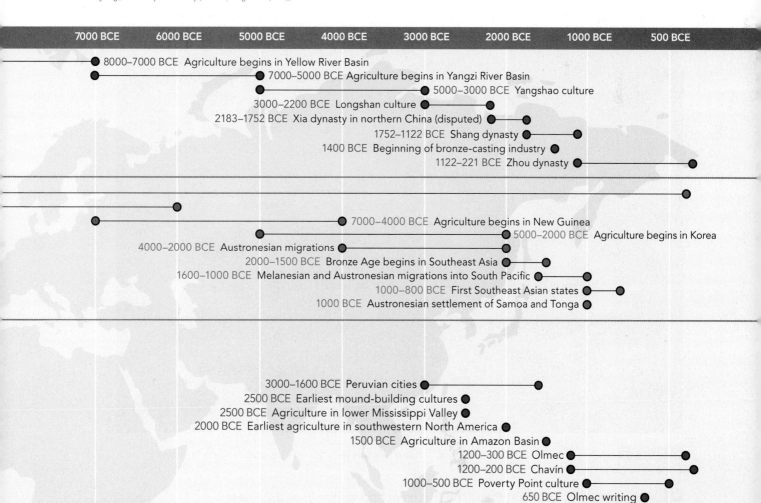

Thus very early two distinct agricultural traditions emerged. In the cooler, drier north, drought-tolerant crops like wheat, millet, pears, and apricots were mainstays. In the wetter, warmer southern half of China, irrigated rice predominated. But rice became so important that for several thousand years Chinese have greeted each other by asking, "Have you eaten rice yet?" and have described losing a job as breaking one's rice bowl.

Highly productive agriculture promoted China's success. By 3000 BCE people in the Yangzi River delta, growing weary of periodic floods that destroyed their crops, constructed one of the ancient world's largest water management projects, building canals and dams to control the water flow and prevent flooding. The work employed thousands of workers for decades. Ever since then China has been known for these kinds of massive projects to alter nature. Despite sporadic famine, the Chinese people were basically well fed and well housed throughout much of history. Productive farming also promoted population growth: China contained between two and four million people by 3000 BCE. Using chopsticks, the Chinese ate well enough that they came to perceive food as more than simple fuel. Cooking became an art form and an essential component of social life, and folk religion included a God of the Kitchen. Many regional cooking variations developed, represented by the Cantonese, Hunanese (**hoon-ahn-eez**), Mandarin (Shanghai and Beijing), and Sichuanese (**SUH-chwahn-eez**) restaurants in large cities around the world.

4-1c The Growth and Spread of Chinese Culture

Neolithic China had several distinctive traditions. The Yangshao (**YANG-shao**) ("painted pottery") culture, which emerged in the middle Yellow River region around 5000 BCE, covered an area of north China larger than Mesopotamia or Egypt. Yangshao people made fine painted pottery, used kilns, bred pigs and dogs, weaved thread, and buried their dead in cemeteries, suggesting belief in an afterlife. Houses were mostly round or square with thatched roofs arranged around a central square. Village graves suggest that some 20 percent of those buried were under fifteen years of age and that only a small minority lived past forty. Chinese also raised silkworms and fashioned the silk into clothes, and silk making became a unique Chinese activity, often handled chiefly by women, with Chinese silk eventually exported all over Eurasia. Other traditions have ancient roots as well. A seven-thousand-year-old seven-holed flute shows an early interest in music. Evidence for jade carving, for which Chinese later became famous, has been found in several regions. Copper manufacturing, which is more complex than jade working, had appeared by 3000 BCE. Since floods and earthquakes were common, the early Chinese also experimented with techniques to predict the future, including dragon bones, so they could avoid disaster.

About 3000 BCE, when the Sumerians were building their cities, an expansive Chinese culture was coalescing out of various regional traditions. As late as 2000 BCE many different cultures remained in China, and the peoples in southern China

IMAGE 4.2 Shang Era Chariots The remains of these chariots were found by archaeologists in Anyang, a Shang dynasty capital.

Q What kinds of uses might these chariots have had for the Shang Chinese?

may have been more closely related to those people settling Southeast Asia than to the Chinese of the Yellow River Basin. But gradually northern and central Chinese societies merged their traditions into a common cultural zone, with the Yellow River Basin remaining a major core of creativity.

The Longshan (**LUNG-shahn**) ("black pottery") culture (3000–2200 BCE) fostered a division of labor and social classes, built strong houses and walled villages and towns, and developed weapons. They also made pottery almost as hard as metal, carved high-quality jade, and created a simple pictographic writing. Millennia before any other society, the Chinese also used industrial diamonds to polish ceremonial ruby and sapphire axes, giving them a fine sheen. Meanwhile, in the Yangzi Basin, people produced distinctive traditions of agriculture, animal domestication, town building, and bronze metallurgy that were at least as old as those of north China.

During the first millennium BCE, Chinese identity, customs, and migrants gradually expanded into south China, displacing or absorbing most of the indigenous (**in-DIJ-uh-nuhs**) peoples (the original inhabitants) in the south, although many ethnic minorities still live there. This mixing of different peoples gradually produced a Chinese culture that encompassed many regional traditions, spoken dialects, and, at times, different states, held together by many common customs and a standardized written language. Political unity helped but was not essential to this common cultural identity. But some historians recently argued that what is today called "Chinese civilization" did not actually cohere until the eleventh century CE, when the south finally became more fully assimilated.

Population growth and shared culture made possible the first state. Chinese historians in earlier centuries labeled this state the Xia (**shya**) (**Hsia**) dynasty (2183–1752 BCE), but its existence as a real government is still debated. A city, Erlitou, built around 2000 BCE near the Yellow River, shows evidence of royal palaces and bronze casting and was perhaps the Xia capital. The Xia may have presided over an occupationally diverse society including scribes, metallurgists, artisans, and bureaucrats. Some influences also filtered in from Central Asia, including the horse and chariot and ironworking, but in general, the Chinese themselves developed the ideas and institutions that gave their society the ability to expand, grow, adapt, and coordinate large populations.

KEY POINTS

▶ Early Chinese society was concentrated inland from the sea and was frequently fragmented into various states.

▶ In the cold, dry Chinese north, crops such as wheat and millet were grown, while in the wetter, warmer south, rice was dominant.

▶ Members of the Yangshao ("painted pottery") society were skilled craftspeople who excelled at carving, weaving, and village design.

▶ As time passed, the widely diverse Chinese people began to knit themselves together in one broad society with traditions that persist to this day.

4-2 The Reshaping of Ancient Chinese Society, 1750–600 BCE

▦ SOCIETIES ⇄ TRANSITIONS

Ⓠ What were some key differences between the Shang and Zhou periods in China?

The Shang (**shahng**) dynasty established China's first powerful state and an expanding culture based on bronze technology. Under the Shang's successor, the more decentralized, iron-using Zhou (**joe**) dynasty, the Chinese improved writing and developed literature. Some enduring religious notions also appeared in these centuries. Isolation from other Eurasian states fostered a feeling of cultural superiority. The Chinese perceived themselves surrounded by less developed neighbors who either adopted Chinese customs or invaded China to enjoy its riches. Strong governments, technological developments, and writing helped make China the most influential East Asian society.

4-2a The Shang Dynasty Reshapes Northern China

The Shang (1752–1122 BCE), China's first well-documented dynasty, began around the same time that Hammurabi ruled in Babylon and the Harappan society collapsed. A people

> **CONNECTION to TODAY**
>
> What do you think are the most important and enduring contributions that the ancient Chinese have left for modern Chinese and for the world today?

from China's western fringe, the Shang, like the Aryan migrants into India, had adopted from Central Asians horse-drawn chariots for warfare. Conquering the eastern Yellow River Basin and imposing a hierarchy dominated by landowning aristocrats (see Map 4.1), they presided over a growing economy and built more cities. However, many Chinese outside Shang control maintained their own states and unique customs.

The Shang established an authoritarian state to coordinate irrigation and dam building. Shang kingship was passed on to a monarch's brother or son. Kings presented themselves as heading the country as a father did a family, claiming both political and spiritual leadership. Shang kings usually had dozens of wives, many of them probably the daughters of regional leaders allied to the monarchy. Like the Aryans and Assyrians, they emphasized military techniques, using a lethal combination of archers, spearmen, and charioteers. Throughout Chinese history, much of this military power was used to defend their northern borders against pastoral nomads,

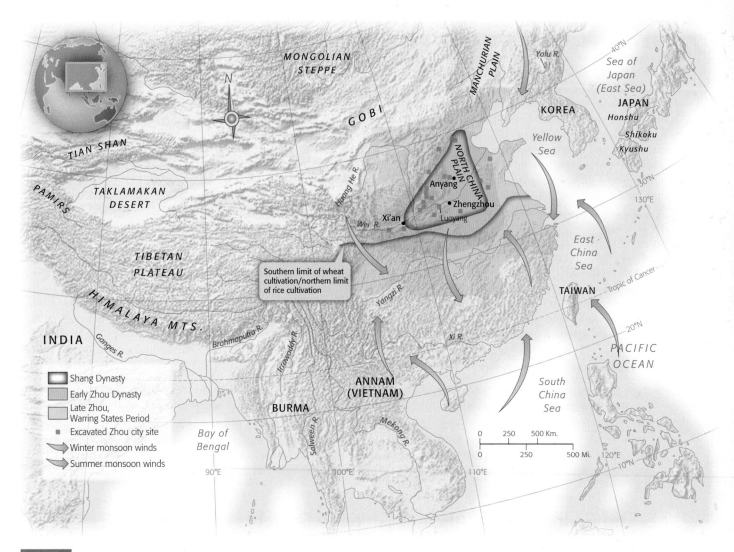

MAP 4.1 **Shang and Zhou China** The earliest Chinese states arose in north China along the Yellow River and its tributaries. The bronze-using Shang dynasty presided over the first documented state and were succeeded by the iron-using Zhou, who governed much of north and central China.

Q What geographical features on this map might have helped shape the expansion and early diversity of Chinese culture and peoples while also posing challenges to interactions with people elsewhere in Eurasia?

who were often tempted to invade the Yellow River Valley because of the relative prosperity of China in comparison to the marginal existence possible in the grasslands and deserts beyond the frontiers.

The Shang flourished economically and technologically, building many administrative and commercial cities. Anyang, the ruler Pan Keng's capital city, was surrounded by a wall thirty feet high and sixty feet wide; the city and its suburbs spread out over some ten square miles. Some ten thousand workers spent eighteen years building Anyang, a feat that reflected considerable political and social organization. Technology improved with bronze, which was introduced in 1400 BCE. Considered the most skilled bronze casters in the ancient world, the Shang produced in large quantities flawless bronze arrows, spears, sculpture, pots, and especially ritual vessels for drinking wine, partly as a display of status.

Many rich Chinese were buried together with some of their favorite bronze pieces to help them in the afterlife. They also made the glazed pottery that was the forerunner of the porcelain ("china") for which the Chinese would later become so famous.

Landowning aristocrats, many of them government officials, dominated the Shang hierarchy, enjoying luxurious surroundings and residences built on cement-like foundations. Aristocratic women held a high status. For example, Fuhao (foo-HOW), the wife of a Shang king, seems to have been appointed to protect the borders of the Shang state, governed her own territory, and led military campaigns. Leaders like Fuhao and their families were buried in elaborate royal tombs with great quantities of valuable objects. Among the vast treasure-trove buried with Fuhao were seven human sacrifices and seven dogs, 564 objects of carved bone, 110 marble objects, three ivory carvings, 500 bone

IMAGE 4.3 **Painted Shell Showing Peasant Life In China** This painted shell, from the Zhou dynasty, depicts a hunting scene of peasants and the animals they are stalking.

Q What can we learn about peasant life and hunting in China at this time?

hairpins, 755 jades, some 7,000 cowry shells (seashells, sometime strung as beads, used as money), and 3,500 pounds of bronze tools, mirrors, bells, and weapons (including two large battle-axes that honor her military exploits).

Commoners included skilled artisans, scribes, and merchants. The lower classes of farmers and laborers, including many slaves, were often mobilized by the powerful state for major building projects. The Shang were harsh masters, practicing human and animal sacrifice as part of their religious observances, often using slaves as victims.

The Shang's momentous contribution to Chinese and East Asian history was an elaborate writing system. The writing found on oracle bones was clearly the forerunner of today's Chinese writing. Hoping to predict the future, influential people wrote questions addressed to the gods on animal bones and tortoise shells, inquiring about the abundance of the next harvest, the outcome of a battle, the weather, or the birth of an heir. For example, one inquired whether "if the king hunted, whether the chase would be without mishap."[3] Some prestigious officials were experts in interpreting the future with these bones.

4-2b The Early Zhou and Their Government

As Shang power faded, a state on the western fringe of China invaded and overthrew the Shang, forming a new dynasty, the Zhou (1122–221 BCE), and a decentralized type of government differing considerably from the Shang approach. The new leader, the Duke of Zhou, supposedly urged that "we must go on, abjuring all idleness, until our reign is universal and there shall not be one who is disobedient to our rule."[4]

The Zhou's relatively weak central government ruled over small states that had considerable autonomy but owed service obligations to the king. This decentralization reflected Zhou realism. Despite their impressive military technology, the Chinese population and territory had grown considerably, making it more difficult to administer their society effectively. The royal family directly ruled the area around their capital but parceled out the rest to followers and relatives who became local lords with much local power. Hence the Zhou kings presided, however symbolically, over a much larger land area than did the Shang, from southern Manchuria to the Yangzi Basin (see Map 4.1). To encourage harmony and coexistence in society and the world order, the Zhou promoted the idea of **tianxia** (tian-sha), roughly translated as "all under heaven," meaning the earth under the sky or the whole world together under one tent. But the reality did not always match the ideal. They also began to call their country Zhongguo ("Middle Kingdom"), which endures today as the name used by the Chinese for their country.

To solidify their position, the Zhou justified their triumph over the Shang with a new concept: the **Mandate of Heaven**. According to this belief, rulers had the support of the gods ("Heaven") so long as conditions were good. However, when there was war, famine, or other hardships, Heaven withdrew its sanction and rebellion was permissible. The decadent and cruel Shang, the Duke of Zhou argued, lost their right to rule. Ever since, the Chinese have invoked the Mandate of Heaven to justify the demise of a discredited government, and over time this radical new concept was used against the Zhou and all later dynasties as well. Monarchs lost their legitimacy if their misrule led to a crisis.

Furthermore, Chinese scholars began to view their political history in terms of the **dynastic cycle**. Instead of seeing a straight line of progress in history, as the Hebrews did, the Chinese focused on dynasties of ruling families who followed the same general pattern as their predecessors. A new dynasty brought peace and prosperity. Then overexpansion and corruption led to costly government, bankruptcy, social decay, and rebellions, eventually resulting in a new dynasty. This concept shaped Chinese thinking for the next twenty-five hundred years.

Despite the tianxia concept, the Zhou system was unstable, plagued by chronic warfare between the various substates, with larger substates conquering smaller ones. As a result, by 400 BCE the seventeen hundred substates of the early Zhou years were reduced to seven that had considerable power in countering the weakening Zhou kings. Furthermore, Central Asians were obtaining faster ponies, forcing the Chinese to erect better defenses against their relentless pressure.

4-2c Early Zhou Society and Economy

Zhou government also fostered a rigid society clearly divided into aristocrats, commoners,

tianxia "All under heaven," the earth under the sky or the whole world together under one tent.

Mandate of Heaven A Chinese belief that rulers had the support of the supernatural realm as long as conditions were good, but rebellion was justified when they were not.

dynastic cycle The Chinese view of their political history, which focuses on dynasties of ruling families.

[3]From John Minford and Joseph S. M. Lau, eds., *Classical Chinese Literature: An Anthology of Translations*, vol. 1 (New York: Columbia University Press, 2000), 16.
[4]Quoted in Creel, *Birth of China*, 228–229.

Discover Historical Voices

The Poetry of Peasant Life in Zhou China

We can learn something of Zhou common folk, especially the peasants who worked the land, from The Book of Songs, a collection of 305 poems, hymns, and folk songs compiled between 1000 and 600 BCE. The songs functioned as satire, diplomacy, and moral instruction. The Book and its contents have remained hugely popular for many centuries, were performed in religious and family ceremonies, and are still beloved today, holding a status in China similar to the Greek bard Homer, who lived in the same era, in the West. One Chinese thinker called the Book the classic of the human heart and mind.

Some songs address ordinary people at their labor. Men weed the fields, plant, plow, and harvest. Women and girls gather mulberry leaves for silkworms, carry hampers of food to the men in the fields for lunch, and make thread:

The girls take their deep baskets, And follow the path under the wall, to gather the soft mulberry-leaves.

Some of the songs deal with courtship and love, sometimes revealing strong emotion, as in this song by a girl about a prospective sweetheart:

That the mere glimpse of a plain cap, Could harry me with such longing, Cause me pain so dire…. Enough! Take me with you to your house…. Let us two be one.

Within the family, the father had nearly absolute authority over his wife and children. When the family patriarch died, his wife became the family head. Children were expected to obey their parents, but some songs reveal that mutual affection and gratitude were common:

My father begot me. My mother fed me, Led me, bred me, Brought me up, reared me, Kept her eye on me, tended me, At every turn aided me. Their good deeds I would requite.

Peasant lives were filled with toil and hardship, but they could find some relief from drudgery in friendship and kinship. Entertaining relatives and friends was a major leisure activity:

And shall a man not seek to have his friends? He shall have harmony and peace. I have strained off my liquor in abundance, the dishes stand in rows, and none of my brethren are absent. Whenever we have leisure, let us drink the sparkling liquor.

Peasants faced many demands on their time and labor. Songs complain and even protest about an uncaring government and its rapacious tax collectors:

Big rat, big rat, Do not gobble our millet! Three years we have slaved for you. Yet you took no notice of us. At last we are going to leave you, And go to the happy land … where no sad songs are sung.

Some songs record abject poverty and misery:

Deep is my grief. I am utterly poverty-stricken and destitute. Yet no one heeds my misfortunes. Well, all is over now. No doubt it was Heaven's [the supernatural realm's] doing. So what's the good of talking about it!

Zhou peasants needed all the help they could get, and some songs seem to be prayers to Heaven to bless their lives:

Good people, gentle folk—Their ways are righteous…. Their thoughts constrained…. Good people, gentle folk—Shape the people of this land…. And may they do so for ten thousand years!

Reflection Questions

1. What do the songs tell us about the importance of families and friends to the Zhou Chinese?
2. What did peasants think about those who ruled them? Can you say why?
3. What are some of the sentiments expressed by ancient Chinese in their songs that people today might share or find relevant to their lives?

Source: *The Book of Songs*, translated by Arthur Waley (London: George Allen and Unwin, 1954) © copyright by permission of The Arthur Waley Estate.

---

and slaves. The nobility, owing allegiance to the king as vassals but governing their own realms, owned large estates defended by private armies and worked by slaves. The merchants enjoyed considerable freedom of action and often became rich. The majority of slaves were criminals and soldiers from rival mini-states captured in the frequent wars. Peasants were mostly bound to the soil on land owned by aristocrats (see Discover Historical Voices: The Poetry of Peasant Life in Zhou China); they were assigned work and punished if it was not done. Their songs reflected resignation: "We rise at sunrise, We rest at sunset. Dig wells and drink, Till our field and eat—What is the strength of the emperor to us?"[5] Yet there were some checks on landowner power. Many workers and slaves of the more repressive and exploitive lords migrated or absconded, depopulating the land and ruining their landlord.

Patriarchal society imposed rigid gender roles. Parents arranged all marriages. A song from this period states: "How does one take a wife? Without a matchmaker she cannot be got." Before or after marriage most women worked hard, mostly in the home preparing food, doing housekeeping, and making

[5]From Minford and Lau, *Classical Chinese Literature*, 150.

clothes. Society expected women at all levels to be submissive, enjoying no official role in public affairs. While some elite women were literate, few peasant women or men enjoyed opportunities to learn reading and writing. Both genders valued friendship and kinship, as another song illustrates: "Of men that are now, None equals a brother. When death and mourning affright us, Brothers are very dear."[6]

Zhou China nurtured many significant technological and economic developments. Ironworking reached China from Central Asia by around 700 BCE, providing better plows and tools than bronze but also improving weaponry. Newly introduced soybeans provided a rich protein source that enriched the soil, and by 600 BCE agricultural surpluses had spurred population growth to around twenty million. Trade grew, merchants became more prominent, and China developed a cash economy with copper coins.

Zhou social life often revolved around food. The ruler's Chief Cook held a high state office, and lavish feasts cemented social ties. Indeed, the banquet was a chief diplomatic tool at all levels of society, often lubricated by wine: "When we have got wine, we strain it; When we have got none, we buy it!"[7] However, the costly and complicated ceremonies enjoyed by the rich did not extend down to peasants, who had little money for anything more than basic hospitality.

4-2d The Evolution of Chinese Writing and Religion

A distinctive Chinese writing system arose to solve the special problems posed by the many, often mutually unintelligible spoken languages. Some six hundred dialects of Chinese are still spoken today, a heritage of many local cultures. Most of the Chinese north of the Yangzi River speak closely related Northern Mandarin dialects, but other Chinese, especially in the southern half of China, have vastly different dialects. Chinese from Guangzhou (**GWAHN-cho**) and Beijing (**bay-JING**) would not understand each other if they only spoke their local dialects. Another difficulty is that the monosyllabic Chinese languages are tonal: the stress placed on a sound changes its meaning. For example, depending on the tone employed by the speaker, in Mandarin the sound *ma* can mean "mother," "hemp," "horse," or "to curse" or indicate a question. To overcome these problems, the Chinese developed one written language based not on sound but on characters. The early Shang pictographs resemble crude pictures of an object, such as a man or bird. Later they evolved into complex ideographs, characters standing for ideas and concepts. Some fifty thousand new characters have been created since the Shang (see Figure 4.1). Today dictionaries contain about twenty thousand characters, highly educated Chinese manage with around eight thousand, and reading a newspaper would require perhaps three thousand. The system's practicality became apparent when modern Chinese linguists faced great difficulty converting tonal words into a Western-type alphabet.

As in Mesopotamia and Egypt, writing promoted political and cultural unity by making possible communication between

FIGURE 4.1 **Evolution of Chinese Writing** This chart shows early and modern forms of Chinese characters, revealing how pictographs, often recognizable, matured into increasingly abstract ideographs.

people speaking different dialects. Otherwise the Chinese might have split into many small countries, as occurred in India and Europe for much of history. Writing helped to create the world's largest society on Earth, unifying rather than dividing peoples of diverse ancestries, regions, and languages. The written language also gave prestige to those who mastered it. As the writing brush became the main writing instrument, writing became an art form, and every literate Chinese something of an artist. Yet the difficulty of memorizing thousands of characters, the most complex of which might require some sixty strokes to write using a brush, limited literacy mostly to the upper classes with the time and money to study. Education, scholarship, and literature became valued commodities.

Chinese ideas on the mysteries of life and the cosmic order also developed. Shang religion emphasized ancestor worship,

---

[6] The two songs are from Waley, *Book of Songs*, 68, 203.
[7] Waley, *Book of Songs*, 205.

magic, mythology, agricultural deities, and local spirits. These ideas evolved by later Zhou times into distinctive ideas, including the notion of a generalized supernatural force the Chinese called *tian* (**tee-an**), which governed the universe. The **Yijing** (**yee-CHING**) (**Book of Changes**), a collection of sixty-four mystic hexagrams and commentaries to predict future events, later became influential throughout East Asia. Its main theme was that heaven and Earth are in a state of continual change.

The *Yijing* was closely related to Chinese cosmological thinking, the theory of *yin* and *yang*, which had appeared in simple form by the Shang. Yin and yang, the two primary cosmic forces, power the universe through their interaction. Neither one permanently triumphs; rather, they are balanced, in conflict and yet complementary in a kind of cosmic symphony. Many things were correlated with these principles:

> Yang: bright, hot, dry, hard, active, masculine, heaven, sun
> Yin: dark, cold, wet, soft, quiescent, feminine, earth, moon

Given the Chinese preference for hierarchy, yang was superior to yin, and male superior to female, justifying inequalities in society. Yin–yang dualism remains important throughout East Asia. The Chinese strongly influenced their neighbors in Korea, Vietnam, and Japan, and over the centuries many Chinese ideas and institutions diffused to the peoples on their fringe. And in the late twentieth century the *Yijing* became a popular book among countercultural youth in the West.

KEY POINTS

▶ The western Shang established an authoritarian state, with the king playing the role of father to the entire country.

▶ Under the Shang, society became increasingly stratified, divided into a dominant aristocracy, a middle class, farmers and laborers, and slaves.

▶ The Zhou introduced the concepts of rule by the "Mandate of Heaven" and of the dynastic cycle, which have endured to this day.

▶ A common written language provided a unifying link for the Chinese, who spoke hundreds of different dialects (many of which are still spoken today).

4-3 Ancient Southeast and Northeast Asians

SOCIETIES   NETWORKS

Q How did the traditions developing in Southeast and Northeast Asia differ from those in India and China?

China's neighbors in Southeast and Northeast Asia also made important early contributions in farming and technology. Although influenced by China or India, they demonstrated many unique characteristics. For example, although Chinese influence was especially strong in Korea and Japan, the Koreans and Japanese had already established the foundations for complex societies before this influence began. Over the following centuries they integrated Chinese influences with their own ideas and customs, maintaining separate ethnic identities.

CONNECTION to TODAY

How does the fact that ancient societies in Southeast Asia, Japan, and Korea could both borrow ideas and technologies from India and China, but also develop their own traditions and innovations, shape these societies today?

The region's tropical climate, with long rainy seasons, fostered rain forests over much of the land. But the great rivers that flow through mainland Southeast Asia, such as the Mekong (**MAY-kawng**), Red, and Irrawaddy (**ir-uh-WAHD-ee**) Rivers, also carved out broad, fertile plains and deltas that could support dense human settlement.

The topography both helped and hindered communication. The shallow seas fostered maritime trade, seafaring, and fishing and linked the large islands such as Sumatra (**soo-MAH-truh**), Java (**JA-veh**), and Borneo (Kalimantan) to their neighbors. In contrast, the heavily forested mountains on the mainland inhibited overland travel and encouraged diverse religions, languages, and states. An Indonesian proverb well describes the mosaic of cultures that resulted: "different fields, different grasshoppers; different pools, different fish."

Some scholars think that the transition to food growing began in Thailand and Vietnam by 8000 or 9000 BCE, but most doubt that it commenced earlier than 6000 BCE. Rice was probably domesticated in south or central China first and then spread into Southeast Asia, becoming a major crop by 3000 BCE. The two regions were closely linked in Neolithic times, and the people then living in southern China were probably more closely related to the modern Thai and Vietnamese than to modern Chinese. Southeast Asians may have been the first to cultivate bananas, yams, and taro and also domesticated

4-3a Southeast Asian Environments and Early Agriculture

While historically linked by trade and migration to China and India, Southeast Asian peoples, shaped in part by geography and climate, developed in distinctive ways. Separated from the Eurasian landmass by mountain and water barriers, Southeast Asia stretches from modern Burma (or Myanmar) eastward to Vietnam and the Philippines and southward through the Indonesian archipelago.

Yijing (Book of Changes) An ancient Chinese collection of sixty-four mystic hexagrams and commentaries upon them that was used to predict future events.

Erich Lessing/Art Resource, NY

IMAGE 4.4 **Dong Son Bronze Drum** These huge Dong Son bronze drums, named for a village site in Vietnam, were produced widely in ancient Southeast Asia and confirm the extensive long-distance trade networks.

Q Do you think these drums could have been used for anything else besides music?

chickens, pigs, and perhaps even cattle very early. Farming generated rapid population growth. Between 2500 and 1000 BCE a trading network was centered on the Mekong delta of Vietnam, where imported stone was manufactured into tools and then exported hundreds of miles away.

Southeast Asians also developed or improved technologies originally from India, Mesopotamia, and China. By 1500 BCE fine bronze was being produced in northeast Thailand, where rice-growing people lived in houses perched on poles above the ground, still a common pattern in Southeast Asia today, and women made beautiful hand-painted and durable pottery. Village artists fashioned bronze and ivory jewelry, including necklaces and bracelets, and household items. The villagers seem to have been notably healthy and peaceful, with little evidence for violence. Whereas elsewhere in Eurasia the Bronze Age was synonymous with cities, kings, armies, huge temples, and defensive walls, in Southeast Asia bronze metallurgy derived from villages. For example, in Dong Son village in northern Vietnam people made huge bronze drums that were traded all over Southeast Asia. Tin mined in Southeast Asia may have reached the Indus cities, and iron was being worked by 500 BCE, several centuries later than in northern China.

4-3b Migration and New Societies in Southeast Asia and the Pacific

Gradually new societies formed from local and migrant roots. The early Southeast Asians probably included the ancestors of the present-day Vietnamese, Papuans (**PAH-poo-enz**), Melanesians (**mel-uh-NEE-zhuhns**), and Negritos (**ne-GREE-tos**).

Migrants came into Southeast Asia from China sometime before the Common Era, assimilating local peoples or prompting them to migrate eastward through the islands. Today Papuans and Melanesians are found mostly in New Guinea and the western Pacific islands, while the remaining small-statured, dark-skinned Negritos mostly live in remote mountains and islands. The newcomers probably mixed their cultures and languages with those of the remaining indigenous inhabitants, producing new peoples such as the Khmers (**kuh-MARE**) (Cambodians), who later established states in the Mekong River Basin.

Archeological, linguistic, and genetic evidence establishes that over the course of several millennia, peoples speaking Austronesian (**AW-stroh-NEE-zhuhn**) languages and possessing advanced agriculture entered Southeast Asia from the large island of Taiwan, just east of China. Some still live on the island. Beginning perhaps around 4000 BCE, Austronesians began moving south into the Philippine Islands, and by 2000 BCE into the Indonesian archipelago (see Map 4.2), settling Borneo, Java, Sumatra, and other islands. Eventually Austronesian languages became dominant in the Philippines, Indonesia, the Malay Peninsula, and the central Vietnam coast. The Austronesians brought with them domesticated pigs and dogs, grew rice and millet, and possessed a knowledge of tatooing, which became a common practice everywhere Austronesians settled and is still so today. Some early Austronesians built sophisticated ocean-going sailing vessels with multilayered hulls and maneuverable square sails. Indonesian islanders were the major seafaring traders of eastern Eurasia before the Common Era, the counterparts to the Phoenicians in the Mediterranean Basin.

There is much scholarly debate about the Austronesian migrations, which also affected other regions than Southeast Asia. The ancestors of Melanesians had already migrated eastward into the western Pacific islands beginning around 1500 or 1600 BCE, or possibly much earlier, carrying Southeast Asian crops, animals, and house styles as far east as Fiji. Some Austronesians, traveling in outrigger canoes and, later, in large double-hulled canoes, eventually sailed into the Pacific, but whether they left chiefly from Taiwan, the Philippines, and/or Indonesia is in dispute. As they migrated and settled they mixed their cultures, languages, and genes with those of the Melanesians and possibly Papuans from islands northeast of New Guinea. By around 1000 BCE Austronesian settlers had reached Samoa and Tonga. These voyages were probably intentional efforts at discovery and colonization by fearless mariners who developed remarkable navigation skills, reading the stars and the swells.

The ancient western Pacific culture known as **Lapita** emerged from a mix of Austronesian and Melanesian. It stretched some 2,500 miles from northeast of New Guinea to Samoa and Tonga and was marked by distinctive pottery and a vast trading network. In Samoa and Tonga, Polynesian culture emerged from Austronesian roots. Some Polynesians eventually reached as far east as Tahiti and Hawaii, both twenty-five hundred miles from Tonga, as well as north to eastern Micronesia. Much later they settled New Zealand. A few scholars think Polynesians might have sailed east and reached South America but there is so far no conclusive evidence to support that view.

Lapita The ancient western Pacific culture that stretched some twenty-five hundred miles from just northeast of New Guinea to Samoa.

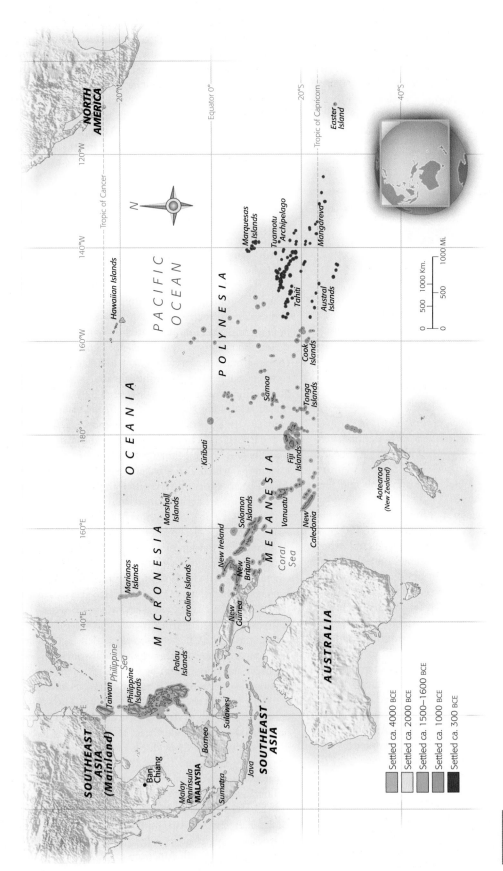

MAP 4.2 **The Austronesian Diaspora** Austronesians migrated from Taiwan into Southeast Asia, settling the islands. Later some of these skilled mariners moved east into the western Pacific, settling Melanesia. Eventually some of their descendants settled Polynesia and Micronesia.

Q What does this map reveal about the significant challenges Austronesian migrants faced?

The Austronesians, Khmer, Vietnamese, and others established societies based on intensive agriculture, fishing, and interregional commerce. By 1000 BCE Austronesian trade networks stretched over five thousand miles, from western Indonesia to the central Pacific. Using advanced boats, they were carrying out maritime trade with India by 500 BCE. Indonesian cinnamon even reached Egypt. Ancient Southeast Asia was also a world of spirits identified with locations (mountains, streams, trees, fields, stones) and ancestors. This animist heritage has by no means passed from the contemporary scene, where many people mix respect for spirits with a universal religion like Buddhism, Islam, or Christianity. The Vietnamese, who probably created the first known Southeast Asian states between 1000 and 800 BCE, believed in a god that "creates the elephants [and] the grass, is omnipresent, and has [all-seeing] eyes."[8]

4-3c The Foundations of Korea and Japan

Korea and Japan, though neighbors, were shaped by different environments (see Map 4.1). The 110 miles of stormy seas that separate them at their closest point did not prevent contact but made it sporadic. Korea occupies a mountainous peninsula 600 miles long and 150 miles wide. Japan's 3,400 islands stretched across several climatic zones, with over 90 percent of the land on three islands: densely populated Honshu (hahn-shoo), frigid Hokkaido (haw-KAI-dow) in the north, and subtropical Kyushu (KYOO-shoo) in the south. Thanks to mountains, only a sixth of Japan's land is suitable for intensive agriculture. The archipelago lacks most metals.

Koreans began farming between 5000 and 2000 BCE, by which time they were building over 100,000 large stone monuments reminiscent of the famous Stonehenge in England. Later they creatively adapted rice growing, which originated in warm southern lands, to their cool climate. As agriculture became more productive, the population grew rapidly, generating a persistent migration of Koreans across the straits to Japan. Small states based on clans emerged. In a pattern still common today, female shamans led the animistic religion. Despite centuries of contact and sometimes conquest, the neighboring Chinese never assimilated the Koreans, in part because the nontonal Korean and tonal Chinese spoken languages were very different.

Koreans imported bronze and then ironworking, probably from China and Central Asia. Shang refugees brought more Chinese culture and technology, but Koreans also created their own useful products, including fine pottery. Facing frigid winters, Koreans invented an ingenious method of radiant floor heating, still widely used today, that circulates heat through chambers in a stone floor. Much later, Chinese and Romans devised similar schemes.

The Japanese were more isolated from China than the Koreans but no less creative, producing some of the world's oldest pottery. Human settlement began perhaps forty thousand years ago, before rising sea levels separated Japan from the mainland. These early settlers were probably the ancestors of the Ainu (I-noo), who are genetically close to other East Asians despite their unusually light skin and extensive body hair. The ancestral Ainu built seaworthy boats, for they settled the Kurile (KOO-reel) Islands north of Japan and the Ryukyu Islands (including Okinawa) to the south while trading with eastern Siberia. Ainu

relics have also been found in the Aleutian (ah-LOO-shan) Islands off Alaska, suggesting some connection there in ancient times. Today the remaining few thousand Ainu, who mostly live on far northern Hokkaido and Sakhalin Islands and are a tiny minority among the millions of other Japanese, face cultural extinction.

When the non-Ainu ancestors of today's Japanese first arrived in the islands remains unclear. Most may have come from Korea beginning 3,000 or 4,000 years ago, while there are hints some Austronesians may have arrived from the south. Ainu and newcomers mixed over the millennia. Genetic studies mostly link modern Japanese to the Ainu, Siberians, and especially Koreans.

4-3d Jomon Society

The best-documented Japanese early society, called **Jomon (JOE-mon)** ("rope pattern") because of the ropelike designs on their pottery, began around 10,000 BCE and endured until 300 BCE. Probably an Ainu culture, Jomon were divided by

> **Jomon** The earliest documented culture in Japan, known for the ropelike design on its pottery.

DEA/G. DAGLI ORTI/De Agostini/Getty Images

IMAGE 4.5 Dogu Figurine Jomon fired-clay figures, like this one, typically portray women and may have been used in fertility rites. Many have a heart-shaped face and an elaborate hairstyle.

Q What does this figure tell us about the life of Jomon women?

---

[8]Quoted in Nguyen Ngoc Bich, "The Power and Relevance of Vietnamese Myths," in *Vietnam: Essays on History, Culture and Society*, ed. David P. Elliott et al. (New York: Asia Society, 1985), 62.

various languages and regional customs, a diversity perhaps reflecting the arrival of Korean migrants. Some Jomon customs, such as tatooing the body and building houses elevated above the ground on posts, hint at some Austronesian connections. However, the major, much larger migrations, which brought iron-using Korean settlers, came later, between 500 and 700 BCE. The Jomon traded with Korea and Siberia. Researchers have found very little evidence for violent behavior or death.

Living primarily from hunting, gathering, and fishing, by 5000 BCE the Jomon lived in wooden houses containing elaborate hearths, probably centers for family gatherings. Diverse foods made up their well-balanced, nutritious diet, including

shellfish, fish, seals, deer, wild boar, and yams. No evidence exists for complex agriculture until around 500 BCE.

A very different spoken language helped preserve cultural distinctiveness despite much Chinese cultural influence. Whether the Japanese language, distantly related to modern Korean, was spoken by Jomon or brought by later immigrants remains uncertain. Probably between 500 BCE and 500 CE, most of the Ainu languages were overwhelmed by a Japanese language possibly based on a Korean dialect. Perhaps in response to increasingly crowded conditions, the Japanese language promoted tact and vagueness, and the Japanese became adept at nonverbal understanding. These tendencies, which are useful in discouraging social conflict, remain part of Japan's unique heritage today.

KEY POINTS

▶ The peoples of Southeast Asia established early maritime trading networks, while inland geographical boundaries led to the development of extremely diverse cultures.

▶ Austronesian migrants from the Philippines settled much of island Southeast Asia and as expert sailors also many Pacific islands.

▶ Korea and Japan, while being strongly influenced by the Chinese, were shaped by different environments and created unique cultures and societies.

▶ Partly because of its distinct language, Korea was never assimilated into China and developed special technologies, such as radiant floor heating, to meet its needs.

▶ Japan's language promoted tact and vagueness, probably to prevent social conflict in an increasingly populated area.

4-4 Ancient Americans

SOCIETIES   TRANSITIONS   NETWORKS

Q How do scholars explain the settlement and rise of agriculture and cities in the Americas?

After the migrations of humans from Eurasia to the Americas thousands of years ago, American societies developed in isolation from those in the Eastern Hemisphere. Diverse cultures often flourished from hunting and gathering, and later some regions pioneered agriculture and, in Mexico and the Andes region, created urban societies and states. Population movement and adaptations to differing environments shaped these varied people's most ancient history, but Americans also shared some common ideas.

CONNECTION to TODAY

Why do you think there is today so much public interest in, and scholarly debate on, the origins of the ancient Americans?

4-4a Diverse American Environments

Most land in the Western Hemisphere is found on two continents, North and South America, that are linked by the long, thin strand of Central America. The Pacific coast from western Alaska down to southern Chile has many volcanoes, some quite active and occasionally destructive. A string of fertile, often volcanic islands also rings the Caribbean Sea from Florida to Venezuela. Whereas Eurasia lies on an east–west axis, the Americas lie on a north–south axis, with a large forest-covered tropical zone in Central America separating more temperate regions. Migrating peoples or long-distance travelers moving

between north and south, or east and west, encountered very different environments on their journeys.

Despite its smaller land area, the Western Hemisphere contains as much diversity of landforms and climate as the Eastern Hemisphere. Extensive tropical rainforests originally covered much of Central America, the Caribbean islands, and the vast Amazon and Orinoco (**or-uh-NO-ko**) River Basins of South America, making intensive farming difficult, although some people developed simple farming. Rain-drenched forests also once covered the northern Pacific coast, while southeastern North America had more temperate woodlands. The long winters in much of North America made hunting and gathering the most practical subsistence option. Like the Himalayas in Asia, the high Andes, which stretch nearly five thousand miles down the western side of South America, hindered travel and communication, while in North America the Rocky Mountains provided an east–west barrier. Coastal mountains running along the northern Pacific coast trap rain clouds, creating huge deserts in western North America. Both continents also have extensive grasslands. Some of the great river systems, such as the Mississippi, fostered long-distance trade.

4-4b The Antiquity and Migration of Native Americans

Native Americans' ancestry and antiquity have long generated heated scholarly debate. The peopling of the Americas seems to have been a complex process with many dramatic chapters. Most experts agree that modern Native Americans are descended from stone tool-using Asians in Siberia but scientific studies disagree on who those Siberian ancestors might be. The most recent DNA study, from 2019, suggests a complex picture involving Siberian groups who died out later or became mixed with others. Whatever the case, some migrants crossed the Bering Strait from Siberia to Alaska, probably when Ice Age conditions lowered ocean levels and created a wide land bridge. As shown by 13,000- to 14,000-year-old discoveries on islands along the Pacific coast, some migrants may have skirted the coasts by boat. Seeking game like bison, caribou, and mammoths, other migrants could have moved south through ice-free corridors in the interior. Whatever the routes, gradually they dispersed throughout the hemisphere.

Recent genetic research suggests that the earliest arrivals to Alaska split into distinct groups beginning about 15,000 to 20,000 years ago. Some groups eventually died out and were lost to history whereas others thrived, becoming the ancestors of the indigenous peoples in the region today. As some migrated southward, further divisions occurred, with some moving back north into Canada and Alaska as the ice retreated, becoming the ancestors of those speaking Athabascan languages, most of them in Canada but also including the Navajo and Apache peoples who migrated much later into southwestern North America. Others, the ancestors of most Native Americans today, kept moving south, expanding around southern North America and then into Central and South America around fourteen thousand years ago. Others reached South America later, mixing with or displacing the older arrivals. Several waves of migrants, probably in small numbers, from different cultural backgrounds in Asia might account for the over two thousand languages among Native Americans. DNA analysis suggests that the Siberian ancestors of the Inuit reached Arctic North America 5000 years ago, where they mixed with earlier arrivals.

The traditions of many Native American peoples place their origins in the areas where they lived five hundred years ago, and some may have lived in these places for many centuries or even millennia before that. For example, DNA studies link some members of present-day tribes on Canada's Pacific coast to bones from the same area dating back ten thousand years. While their origin stories, rich in spiritual meaning, deserve respect, much scientific evidence supports the notion of ancient migration from Asia. No remains of any hominids earlier than modern humans have been found in the Americas. Furthermore, the common ancestry of modern Native Americans is clear from the remarkable uniformity of DNA, blood, virus, and teeth types, which all connect them to peoples in northern Mongolia and central and eastern Siberia. A few scholars have suggested that some tool cultures in eastern North America are similar to those of Stone Age peoples who lived in Spain and France several millennia earlier, but most experts find their argument so far unconvincing.

The debate over when the first migrants arrived in and settled the Americas is continually updated with new discoveries. For many years most archaeologists traced the migration back to the **Clovis** culture some 11,500 to 13,500 years ago, named after spear points discovered at Clovis, New Mexico, but widespread in North and Central America. However, some recent skeleton and artifact discoveries in North and South America are much older, undermining the Clovis first theory. For example, Monte Verde (**MAWN-tee VAIR-dee**), a campsite in southern Chile that is over ten thousand miles from the Bering Strait, may be at least fourteen thousand years old. Monte Verde people lived in rectangular houses with log foundations and exploited a wide variety of vegetable and animal foods. Various other sites in North America, Mexico, Peru, and Brazil challenge the Clovis first theory, but none offers conclusive evidence that convinces all skeptics. For example, some researchers believe a Brazilian site could be twenty-three thousand years old, and sites in Pennsylvania, Florida, South Carolina, Texas, and Virginia may place people in southeastern North America between 15,000 and 19,000 years ago. These scattered discoveries suggest an ancient migration but also caution at drawing quick conclusions.

The earliest Native Americans, or Paleo-Indians, survived by hunting, fishing, and gathering while adapting to varied environments. For example, on the North American Great Plains, many people hunted bison on foot. Thousands of years ago skilled hunters armed with spears may have contributed to the extinction of large herbivore animals such as horses, mammoths, and camels, which disappeared from the Western Hemisphere between 9000 and 7000 BCE. But a similar die-off in Eurasia at the end of the Ice Age suggests that climate change was also a factor. The extinctions in both hemispheres likely resulted from some combination of overhunting, environmental change, and perhaps an apocalyptic disease affecting large mammals.

Some peoples flourished for many millennia. In the Pacific Northwest, coastal peoples built oceangoing boats and sturdy wood houses, while along the Peruvian coast deep-sea fishermen exploited the rich marine environment. In southern California the Chumash (**CHOO-mash**) society, like Japan's Jomon culture, lived well from a vegetation and meat diet including large marine mammals such as seals. The Chumash built large, permanent villages headed by powerful chiefs. Yet Pacific coast peoples such as the Chumash were also subject to climate change, which periodically brought drought by altering plant and animal environments. The Chumash still exist as a people.

In North America by 4000 BCE extensive long-distance trade networks linked people over several thousand miles from the Atlantic and Gulf coasts to the Great Plains and Great Lakes. Dugout canoes moved copper and red ocher from Lake Superior, jasper (quartz) from Pennsylvania, obsidian from the Rocky Mountains, and seashells from both the Gulf and East Coasts. Great Lakes copper was traded as far away as Mexico, New England, and Florida.

4-4c Early Societies and Their Cultures

Over many millennia Americans developed distinctive social and cultural patterns emphasizing cooperation within families, animistic religion, and ceremonies for such events as initiations into adult life and courtship. Most people lived in egalitarian bands linked by kinship and marriage.

Clovis A Native American culture dating back some 11,500 to 13,500 years.

Men often sought a personal guardian spirit through a visionary experience induced by fasting, enduring physical pain, or taking hallucinogenic drugs. Shamans claiming command over spirits or animal souls connected the human and spirit worlds. Most Americans revered the food-producing earth as sacred. Some also adopted creation stories widely shared with other peoples.

Some Americans organized communities around **mound building**, the construction of huge earthen mounds, often with temples on top. One of the oldest dirt mounds, the Huaca Prieta in northern Peru, dates from perhaps 6000 BCE and was probably built as a ceremonial structure. The people living there made the world's first known cotton fabric dyed blue with indigo, as well as elaborate hand-woven baskets and ingenious tools used to catch deep-sea fish like herring. The oldest mound so far discovered in North America, in Louisiana, dates to 2500 BCE. Beginning around 1600 BCE, some other hunter-gatherers in North America's eastern woodlands and Gulf coast became mound builders. One major site, Poverty Point in northeastern Louisiana, was occupied between 1000 and 500 BCE (see Meet the People: The Poverty Point Mound Builders). At its height it was about three square miles in area and home to perhaps five thousand people. Its largest mound, an effigy of a bird that can only be seen from the air, was seventy feet high, comparable to an eight-story apartment building, and seven hundred feet long and apparently built in several months. Poverty Point served as the hub of a trading system, importing goods from as far away as the Ohio and upper Mississippi River Valleys and exporting stone and clay products such as pendants and bowls to Florida, Missouri, Oklahoma, and Tennessee.

4-4d The Rise of American Agriculture

Americans were some of the earliest farmers, but they developed very different crops than the peoples of Afro-Eurasia. Population growth, long-distance trade, and changing weather conditions helped spark this great transition. Hunter-gatherers were vulnerable to devastating droughts in years when the periodic weather change known today as *El Niño* (EL NEE-nyo) shifted both rainfall patterns and the marine environment, perhaps prompting experiments with growing food. Some of the chief crops, such as maize (corn), were much more difficult to master than the big-seeded grains of the Fertile Crescent. Furthermore, with no potential draft animals, farmers needed to be creative in growing and transporting food.

Some Americans made the transition not long after Southwest Asians. In Mesoamerica (the region from northern Mexico through northern Central America), bottle gourds and pumpkins may have been raised by 8500 or 8000 BCE and maize, sweet potatoes, and beans by 3500 BCE. Andes people cultivated chili peppers and kidney beans by about 8000 BCE and later cultivated potatoes. Some Andeans, like early Eurasian farmers, built elaborate irrigation canals that created artificial garden plots. By 3000 or 2500 BCE, Peruvian coastal peoples raised cotton, squash, sweet potatoes, and maize. By 1500 BCE farming had spread to the Amazon Basin. In North America the southwestern peoples ingeniously adapted farming to their poor soils and desert conditions, growing maize, squash, beans, and corn, which eventually became mainstays from the Southwest to the northeastern woodlands, providing a nutritionally balanced diet.

Three basic farming patterns eventually shaped American societies. Mesoamerican highland and valley people relied on maize, beans, and squash. Societies in the high Andes emphasized potatoes and other frost-resistant tubers. South America's tropical forest societies grew manioc, sweet potatoes, wild rice, and root crops. These differing farming patterns proved significant for later world history because the great diversity later enriched modern food supplies. Americans domesticated a greater variety of plants than had all the Eastern Hemisphere peoples combined, including three thousand varieties of potatoes, as well as popular products like chocolate, quinine, and tobacco. People today around the world owe much of their daily diet to the ancient farmers of the Americas.

However, because they lacked draft animals, the Americans practiced less intensive agriculture than Eastern Hemisphere people. The only large herd animals available for domestication, the llama and alpaca of the Andes, were tamed by 3500 BCE, mostly for use as pack animals and wool sources. Although Americans domesticated turkeys and guinea pigs for eating, there were no surviving counterparts to horses, cattle, and oxen. With no animals to pull them, plows or wheels were useless. People innovated by creating irrigation schemes such as terraced hillsides and the floating gardens in Central Mexico, which turned swamps into productive fields, but the intensive farming that supported huge populations in China or India was impossible in the Americas.

The lack of draft animals also meant that Americans were exposed to fewer infectious diseases and epidemics. In the Eastern Hemisphere, domesticated animals passed diseases such as measles and smallpox to humans through germs and parasites, precipitating deadly outbreaks. Historians disagree over whether Americans may have been healthier than people across the oceans. Although many enjoyed long lives, many also suffered from various ailments. Furthermore, isolation from the Eastern Hemisphere left Native Americans vulnerable to the diseases brought by Europeans and Africans beginning in 1492 CE, for which they had no immunity. These diseases eventually killed the great majority of Native Americans.

4-4e Farming Societies, Cities, and States

Communal activity was essential in early villages as people cooperated for survival. Artisans in Ecuador made fine ceramic pottery by 4600–4400 BCE. In the northern Andes, people fashioned ceramics between 3000 and 2500 BCE. Institutionalized religions took shape, led by a priestly caste, and human sacrifice became common in both Mesoamerica and the Andes to honor the gods and keep the cosmos in balance. Far earlier than the more famous Egyptian mummies, some South American and North American societies developed processes for mummifying the bodies of the deceased through drying, perhaps because of religious beliefs about death and the afterlife. Some Andean and Mesoamerican societies also began building permanent structures for religious, governmental, or recreational purposes.

mound building The construction of huge earthen mounds, often with temples on top, by some ancient peoples in the Americas.

The Poverty Point Mound Builders

While the spectacular mounds at Poverty Point are the site's most striking legacy, the archaeological research has also revealed a remarkable community. The inhabitants did not need farming because their location, in a fertile valley nourished by annual Mississippi River floods, offered a benign hunting and gathering environment and a gentle climate. The people enjoyed a rich and varied diet. Men used spears, spear throwers, darts, and knives to hunt turkey, duck, deer, and rabbit and caught bass, catfish, alligator, and clams in the rivers. Women collected acorns, hickory nuts, walnuts, wild grapes, persimmons, sunflower seeds, squash, and gourds.

Probably governed by chiefs, the people lived in wood houses around a central plaza and six mounds. Men and women crafted many tools and art objects, trading some hundreds of miles away, and heated small, decorated baked-clay balls, found by the thousands in the ruins, for cooking or boiling water. Since cooking was considered women's work, women probably made these clay balls, perhaps helped by their children. Each woman apparently had her own preference for design and shape. Stoneworkers ground and polished hard stones into ornaments and useful artifacts, chipping various stones into points, blades, and cutting tools. Solid-clay female figurines, sometimes pregnant, possibly served as fertility symbols. Using red jasper, people also fashioned beautiful bead necklaces, bird-head pendants, and human effigies.

Located at the intersection of important waterways, Poverty Point was linked to trade networks that brought in Appalachian metal for bowls and platters, stone from the Ozarks and Oklahoma, and flint from as far away as Illinois and Ohio. The finely crafted red jasper items, often shaped like animals such as owls, have been found in distant settlements. Some of the Poverty Point men may have ventured out on trading expeditions or to bring home valuable stones from as far away as Missouri. Men and perhaps women undoubtedly arrived regularly in canoes full of trade goods to exchange.

At times the people were mobilized to build new mounds or rebuild old eroding ones. The complete earthworks contain an immense one million cubic yards of soil; to make them, the people probably had to transport 35 to 40 million fifty-pound basket loads to the site. Several thousand people may have participated in the construction, which was carefully planned and directed so that it followed a geometric design. The mounds perhaps aided astronomical observations as a solar calendar, or perhaps served as a regional ceremonial center for social, political, or religious purposes. Some priestly or ruling class may have lived atop the mounds, as was common in some mound-building societies around the hemisphere. At least 150 smaller satellite sites, scattered along the Mississippi for several hundred miles, all contain similar artifacts, suggesting that Poverty Point was the center of both an economic and a political network.

The culture disappeared by 500 BCE, the people having dispersed to smaller settlements. There are no signs of war or major environmental change. Perhaps some political or religious crisis disrupted society. Whatever the case, the Poverty Point people and their culture were lost to history, leaving only the badly eroded but still impressive ruins of today.

IMAGE 4.6 **Poverty Point Jasper Bead** Trade goods, such as this red jasper bead shaped like a locust, were produced at Poverty Point in Louisiana and traded over many hundreds of miles in eastern and central North America.

Gilcrease Museum/Tulsa/Oklahoma

Q What do you think would be the appeal of this bead?

Reflection Questions

1. What sort of life did the Poverty Point people experience?
2. What role did Poverty Point play in the region?
3. What in Poverty Point society seemed similar and what different from American society today?

Pacific coast and Andean cultures in South America constructed monumental architecture, including stepped pyramids, by the third millennium BCE, about the same time as Egypt, India, and China. By 5000 BCE a southern Mexico site contained a dance ground or ball court, and ceremonial ballgames involving teams of players attempting to knock a rubber ball through a high stone hoop became a fixture of Mesoamerican life for millennia. Some Mexican villages have recently revived the game.

Agriculture, monumental construction, metallurgy, population growth, and long-distance trade provided a foundation for the first cities and states in the Andes and Mesoamerica between 3000 and 1000 BCE, about the same period as in Eurasia and North Africa (see Map 4.3). People worked copper, gold, and silver to create tools, weapons, and jewelry. Growing towns with public buildings became centers of political, economic, and religious activities. Massive ceremonial centers hundreds of feet long were constructed along the Peruvian coast, and elsewhere huge mounds laid the foundation for great pyramids. Between 4000 and 1 BCE the population of the Americas grew from one or two million to around fifteen million, over two-thirds concentrated in Mesoamerica and western South America. Long-distance trade routes also became more common, moving commodities such as obsidian, mirrors, seashells, and ceramics.

4-4f South American Societies: Caral and Chavín

About the same time as the Harappan cities and the Egyptian pyramids, the first large settlements built around massive stone structures emerged around 3100 BCE in the Norte Chico region between the Andes and the Pacific coast in north-central Peru. The largest of these settlements and America's first known city, Caral, had some three thousand residents living in a 150-acre complex of plazas, pyramids, seismically resilient residential buildings, and underground ducts to keep their fires burning—innovations that interest architects today. The major pyramid, sixty feet tall and covering the equivalent of four football fields, contained an amphitheater capable of seating hundreds of spectators for civic or religious events. An elite group of priests and planners lived in large, well-kept rooms atop the pyramids. Eventually some twenty pyramid complexes occupied land for many miles around.

The Norte Chico economy was based on marine resources such as fish and on growing squash, sweet potatoes, fruits, beans, cotton, and possibly maize. The people do not seem to have made ceramics or enjoyed many arts and crafts. However, Caral was a major hub for trade routes from the Pacific coast through the Andes to the Amazonian rain forest. There is evidence for human sacrifice but few weapons. The people evidently enjoyed music, using animal bone flutes. But Caral collapsed around 1600 BCE, probably from a long drought.

Chavín (cha-VEEN), situated ten thousand feet above sea level in northwestern Peru, emerged the same time as the Olmec (discussed below), around 1200 or 1000 BCE, and collapsed by 200 BCE. The Chavín people created flamboyant sculpture and monumental architecture, developed highly

Chavín The first major urban civilization in South America (900–250 BCE).

Olmec The earliest urban society in Mesoamerica.

Nathaniel Tarn/Science Source

IMAGE 4.7 **Olmec Head** This massive head from San Lorenzo is nearly 10 feet high. The significance of such heads (and the helmets they wear) remains unclear, but they might represent chiefs, warriors, or gods.

Q What do you think this statue would have meant to the Olmecs?

original art focusing on real or mythical animals, and worked gold and silver. At its height, the main city probably had some three thousand inhabitants. Ruled by an elaborate priesthood, Chavín became a major regional power, trading widely with the coast and spreading its religion to distant peoples. The people worshipped two main deities, and their ceremonial center became a site of pilgrimage for the faithful from a wide area. Chavín also perpetuated some of the architectural and religious patterns that became common in the Andes. It became politically and economically dominant in a densely populated region that included two distinct ecological zones, the Peruvian coastal plain and the Andean foothills.

4-4g Mesoamerican Societies: The Olmec

The **Olmec** (OHL-meck), a people who lived along Mexico's Gulf coast, formed the earliest known urban society and centralized state in Mesoamerica by 1200 or 1000 BCE, flourishing

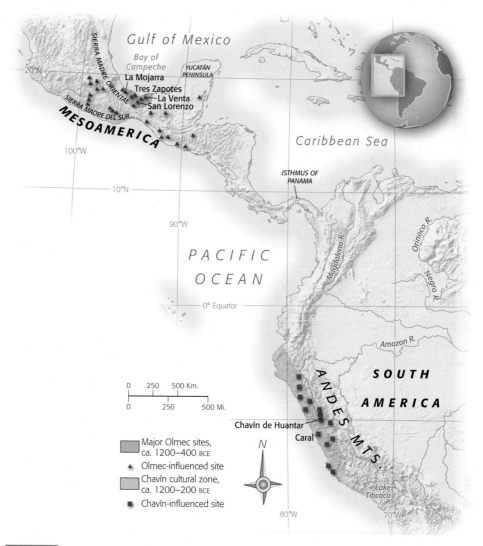

MAP 4.3 **Olmec and Chavín Societies** The earliest known American states arose in Mesoamerica and the Andes. The Olmec and Chavín states both endured for a millennium.

Q How did the geography and settlement patterns of ancient Americans hinder or help their abilities to interact with other peoples in the Western Hemisphere?

until 300 BCE (see Map 4.3). A powerful chieftain probably ruled each Olmec city. The earliest city, known today as San Lorenzo, was built on an artificial dirt platform three-quarters of a mile long, half a mile wide, and 150 feet high. Home to some twenty-five hundred people, San Lorenzo was situated above fertile but frequently flooded plains. Another Olmec city, La Venta, included huge earth mounds that required massive labor to build. The stones for Olmec sculptures and temples had to be brought from sixty miles away, and some of the blocks weigh more than forty tons. The Olmec studied astronomy to correctly orient their cities and monuments with the stars.

The Olmec created remarkable architecture, art, and a writing system. The purpose of the huge sculptured stone heads is unknown, but they might represent rulers (see Image 4.7). The Olmec built temples and pyramids in ceremonial centers and palace complexes, and their artists carved human and animal figures as well as supernatural beings in sculpture and relief. By around 650 BCE or perhaps earlier, the Olmec had also developed the first simple hieroglyphic writing in the Americas, which influenced other Mesoamerican peoples, especially the Maya. Mesoamerican writing kept records of kings, rituals, and the calendar, much as writing did in Egypt.

Commerce and the networks it created were a key to Olmec influence. The Olmec traded with Mexico's west coast and Central America, importing basalt, obsidian, iron ore, and jade, which they fashioned into ceremonial objects, masks, and jewelry. They may also have exploited cocoa trees for chocolate. Extensive communication between the Olmec and neighboring peoples contributed to some cultural homogeneity in Mesoamerica, especially in religion. Olmec religious symbols and myths emphasized fearsome half-human, half-animal supernatural beings, the prototypes of later Mesoamerican deities. Religious ceremonies requiring precise measurement of calendar years and time cycles fostered mathematics and writing. Although their society eventually disappeared, the Olmec established enduring patterns of life, thought, and kingship in Mesoamerica that influenced later peoples like the Maya (see Chapter 9).

KEY POINTS

▶ Early American peoples survived primarily by hunting, gathering, and fishing, as well as by trading over large distances.

▶ Mutual cooperation, earth worship, personal connections with guardian spirits, and shamanism were prominent features of early American cultural and spiritual life.

▶ In response to the challenges posed by different climates, American peoples domesticated a greater variety of plants than all the peoples of the Eastern Hemisphere.

▶ Lacking draft animals, Americans came up with ingenious approaches to farming.

▶ Various technological breakthroughs led to the development of urban societies in Mesoamerica and the Andes.

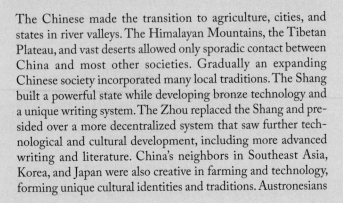

Chapter Summary

The Chinese made the transition to agriculture, cities, and states in river valleys. The Himalayan Mountains, the Tibetan Plateau, and vast deserts allowed only sporadic contact between China and most other societies. Gradually an expanding Chinese society incorporated many local traditions. The Shang built a powerful state while developing bronze technology and a unique writing system. The Zhou replaced the Shang and presided over a more decentralized system that saw further technological and cultural development, including more advanced writing and literature. China's neighbors in Southeast Asia, Korea, and Japan were also creative in farming and technology, forming unique cultural identities and traditions. Austronesians migrating into Southeast Asia were skilled mariners, and some of them settled the Pacific islands.

Scholars still debate the origin and antiquity of settlement in the Americas, but most conclude that migrants moved from eastern Eurasia by land or boat many millennia ago. For centuries, hunting, fishing, and gathering supported a viable way of life. The Americans did not have the rich farmland and draft animals common in Eurasia. Nonetheless, farming appeared nearly as early as in the Eastern Hemisphere, a result of population growth, climate change, and technological development. Americans domesticated a wide variety of crops and also forged long-distance trade networks, religious institutions, cities, and states.

Key Terms

tianxia 79
Mandate of Heaven 79
dynastic cycle 79
Yijing (Book of Changes) 82

Lapita 83
Jomon 85
Clovis 87

mound building 88
Chavín 90
Olmec 90

Patriarchy and Matriarchy in the Ancient World

Today, as in the past, men generally hold the political, economic, and religious power in most societies thanks to patriarchy, a system whereby men largely control women and children, shape ideas about appropriate gender behavior, and generally dominate society. Many people assume that patriarchal social organization springs from some innate human characteristic, symbolized by the common expression that this is a "man's world." But the situation is more complex historically. Anthropological, archaeological, and historical scholarship has shown the myriad ways that people have divided power and social functions by gender rather than stages of dominance by one gender over another. And as historian Merry Wiesner-Hanks reminds us, in searching for the origins of patriarchy and gender inequality we must first remember what anthropology, biology, history, and psychology have revealed about the ambiguity, fluidity, and instability of gender categories, since not every person or every culture was restricted to two genders and heterosexuality as the only accepted and recognized behavior.

The Problem

The prevalence of patriarchy raises three important questions. First, was there ever a time when women held equal power and status to men? Second, was matriarchy—in which women enjoy social and political dominance over, complete equality with, or strong influence on men—ever common? And third, can we identify a particular period when patriarchy triumphed? For several decades now these questions have sparked heated scholarly debates linked to social and cultural changes in modern society, especially the roles, status, and influence of women and the rise of feminism.

The Debate

The first question is the easiest to answer. Historians and anthropologists are reasonably sure that, among many peoples, women had greater equality with men during the "Stone Age" than in later eras. These small, closely knit hunter-gatherer or horticultural societies, like the !Kung of southern Africa today and similar groups in Africa, Asia, and the Americas, were often egalitarian, had leaders with limited power over others, and owned little private property to fight over. However, despite a rough equality due to women's roles, essential for a society's survival as gatherers of food and medicinal herbs, evidence that very many pre-farming societies allowed women more publicly recognized authority than men remains limited. Some peoples who practiced simple farming, such as the Iroquois, Cherokee, Hopi, and Zuni in North America, accorded women considerable influence within a matrilineal culture, even if men usually had ultimate decision-making power. Part of the debate are the varied definitions of matriarchy used by scholars. In the past matriarchy was seen narrowly as the opposite of patriarchy, with females to a large degree holding the primary power positions such as political leadership, control of property, and social privilege. It has been much harder with this definition to find pure matriarchies. Most anthropologists have found no conclusive evidence for any unambiguously matriarchal societies of this type in ancient or recent history. There were and still are numerous societies, perhaps seventeen percent, that practice matrilineal kinship (descent through the female line), matrifocal households (headed by mothers), and/or matrilocal residence (living with the wife's family), and scholars debate whether those might be considered forms of matriarchy or simply confused with it.

More recently many scholars view matriarchy in broader terms, as a gender-egalitarian society in which each gender has its own sphere of power and action. Such societies are much easier to identify but some question whether this could be considered matriarchy even though it might be a desirable form of society. Others contend matriarchy can be thought of as any society in which women's power is equal or superior to men's and the culture is centered around feminine values.

In response to the second question, beginning in the nineteenth century some scholars have argued that a "golden age of matriarchy," in which people enjoyed peace, harmony, and social stability, existed in ancient times, before the rise of urban societies and states, in Europe and the Middle East, and perhaps also in India, Japan, Southeast Asia, and the Americas. They point to the many "Venus" figurines of females, many perhaps of goddesses, unearthed at Paleolithic and Neolithic archaeological sites worldwide but especially in Europe and western Asia. Goddess worship, they believe, correlated with high female status and a woman-centered society; women were cherished for giving birth and nurturing the young, giving them a connection to the earth and spirits. Patricia Monaghan identifies more than fifteen hundred different goddesses worldwide, representing everything from mother to warrior. But some scholars suggest that they may also have been made as fertility symbols, toys, lucky charms, or images of ancestors. Today most scholars doubt the ancient "Golden Age" scenario. The controversy has divided feminists.

Perhaps the most debated recent studies supporting a "Golden Age" are by Lithuanian archaeologist Marija Gimbutas, whose writings, based on discoveries at sites such as Çatal Hüyük in Turkey, the Minoan palace at Knossos, and Stonehenge, portray ancient people in Europe and Anatolia as egalitarian and peaceful farmers led by influential women. These female-oriented societies, she claims, were destroyed around 3500 BCE by more violent Indo-European nomads from Central Asia, who brought patriarchy and a single male god with them. From then on, patriarchy spread across Europe. Gimbutas's critics accused her of a key role in constructing what they consider the "myth" of historical and universal matriarchy; they also claim that she ignored evidence that contradicted her thesis. Most archeologists disagree with Gimbutas's ideas, but she influenced many popular writers. Hence, Riane Eisler and Judith Lorber describe ancient, goddess-worshipping farming cultures in eastern and southern Europe, where men and women ruled equally, with no war or inequalities of wealth. Like Gimbutas, they contend that Indo-European new-comers imposed male governments on these earlier societies. But few scholars propose complete female control of ancient governments; Heidi Goettner-Abendroth defines these matri-archies as gender-egalitarian societies or "nonpatriarchy."

However, many scholars dispute these authors' claims about ancient matriarchies with nonviolent social orders and equal status for each gender. For example, Lotte Motz, Lucy Godison, and Christine Morris argue that goddess worship theories are unproven. Motz claims that female images are no more common in early Europe than those of men and animals. Furthermore, the figurines may have been used in fertility rites rather than revered as spiritual forces. Motz and Cynthia Eller also suggest that mother goddess theories reflect not ancient realities of polytheistic religions but modern political and cul-tural attitudes, including a feminism that challenges patriarchy and biases about women's roles. To them the "Golden Age of Matriarchy" thesis is rooted in feminist desire for a better, more equitable society, but the thesis lacks widely accepted evidence and it no longer benefits the feminist cause. Critics accuse Eller of misrepresenting matriarchal concepts. Nor can we assume that worshipping female deities actually gave real power to women. After all, the patriarchal ancient Mesopotamians and Greeks worshipped various female deities, including a god-dess of love, and many modern patriarchal cultures, such as the Chinese, Japanese, Hindu Indian, and Yoruba, include female deities in their pantheons. And although many Christians have revered the Virgin Mary over the past two millennia, men still dominate European society and the Catholic Church.

If the notion of ancient matriarchies transformed by force into patriarchies remains debatable and has been disputed by some recent historical scholarship, we are still left with the third question of how and when did patriarchy emerge. A few studies have found evidence for serious mistreat-ment of women and hence male dominance even in some pre-Neolithic societies going back 6,000 to 8,000 years. Many scholars, among them James Scott, Peter Stearns, Lauren Ristvet, and Kent Flannery and Joyce Marcus, trace social and gender inequality to the invention of agriculture, very likely by women, who had provided most plant food. With farming, men who no longer needed to spend as much time hunting largely replaced women in the fields. The growing food sup-ply also fostered population growth and hence more children. Anthropologist Sherry Ortner argues for a slow but inevitable transition from the egalitarianism of food collecting to male domination in the early cities and states. To Ortner, patriarchy derived from technological and social upheavals rather than a will to power by aggressive men. Childbearing played a role because, while women stayed home having and raising children, men could travel and engage in more paid work, warfare, and governmental, leisure, and religious activities. That development led to gender stereotypes of women in unpaid work at home and men at paid work elsewhere. Also arguing for a gradual change, anthropologist Elizabeth Barber contends that farming people needed products, such as metal ores, that had to be gained through long-distance trade. This

IMAGE 4.8 **Goddess Figure** This female figure found in France, probably a mother-goddess, was likely used in fer-tility rites. Such figures have been found in many ancient societies studied by archaeologists.

gave power to the more mobile and physically stronger men, who could travel to distant places and transport the heavy cargoes home. To be sure, knowledge of cloth making and the fiber arts gave women importance in ancient societies, since men also used products such as clothing and blankets; never-theless, patriarchy, they argue, emerged gradually as society slowly changed and began to reward strength and mobility.

There is considerable evidence that men increased their power over women in many early farming, urban, and state societies. Historian Gerda Lerner analyzed male power in the Mesopotamian city-states, where kings or male assemblies ruled, and identified property ownership and political struc-tures, as well as religion and philosophy, as key supports for patriarchy. Law codes such as Hammurabi's favored men; only women could be divorced or sold into slavery for adultery. Laws also restricted women's freedom of movement and treated them as private property. By this time, Lerner argues, gods had become more important than goddesses, and male power was legally recognized and sanctioned by religion. Lerner's work remains influential and widely respected, but she also had many critics, some of whom pointed out that her research was restricted to one society, and a literate one at that. But there were many historical patterns of gender in the world, even in western Asia and the Mediterranean. This was especially true for some nonliterate stateless societies who traditionally recognized three or four genders.

Evaluating the Debate

Until recently historians and archaeologists have neglected the role of women. When we study ancient societies, we may unknowingly be influenced by modern attitudes, as in this controversy. We are more likely to study kings and wars than the beginnings of herbal medicine, cloth production, and the role of women as negotiators in community disputes. We have not heard the last word from scholars on the question of ancient matriarchies and patriarchies, but their disputes have made us more aware of the role of women in history.

Exploring the Controversy

Some major works supporting the ancient goddess and matriarchy thesis include Marija Gimbutas, *Goddesses and Gods in Old Europe, 6500–500 BC: Myths and Cult Images* (Berkeley: University of California Press, 1982); Gimbutas, *The Language of the Goddess: Unearthing the Hidden Symbols of Western Civilization* (New York: Harper and Row, 1989); Gimbutas, *The Living Goddesses* (Berkeley: University of California Press, 1999); and Riane Eisler, *The Chalice and the Blade: Our History, Our Future* (San Francisco: Harper and Row, 1995). Heidi Goettner-Abendroth takes a more nuanced view of the thesis in *Matriarchal Societies* (London: Peter Lang, 2012) and in her edited work, *Societies of Peace: Matriarchies Past Present and Future* (London: Inanna Publications, 2009). Judith Lorber challenges basic assumptions about gender in *Paradoxes of Gender* (New Haven, CT: Yale University Press, 1994). Patricia Monaghan, *The New Book of Goddesses and Heroines* (New York: Llewellyn Publications, 1997), provides a useful reference on mythological and legendary female deities from many lands and eras.

Strong criticism of the ancient matriarchy thesis can be found in Lucy Godison and Christine Morris, eds., *Ancient Goddesses: The Myths and the Evidence* (Madison: University of Wisconsin Press, 1999); Lotte Motz, *The Faces of the Goddess* (New York: Oxford University Press, 1997); and Cynthia Eller, *The Myth of Matriarchal Prehistory: Why an Invented Past Won't Give Women a Future* (Boston: Beacon Press, 2001). Among major books on the making of patriarchy and gender roles are Elizabeth Barber, *Woman's Work: The First 20,000 Years: Women, Cloth, and Society in Early Times* (New York: W.W. Norton, 1994); Gerda Lerner, *The Creation of Patriarchy* (New York: Oxford University Press, 1986); and Sherry Ortner, *Making Gender: The Politics and Erotics of Culture* (Boston: Beacon Press, 1997). On agriculture, urbanization, state building, and patriarchy, see James Scott, *Against the Grain: A Deep History of the Earliest States* (New Haven, CT: Yale University Press, 2017); Peter Stearns, *Gender in World History* (New York: Routledge, 2000); Lauren Ristvet, *In the Beginning: World History from Human Evolution to the First States* (Boston: McGraw-Hill, 2007); and Kent Flannery and Joyce Marcus, *The Creation of Inequality: How Our Prehistoric Ancestors Set the Stage for Monarchy, Slavery, and Empire* (Cambridge, MA: Harvard University Press, 2014). For an excellent introduction to larger questions relevant to women's history, see Merry E. Wiesner-Hanks, *Gender in History: Global Perspectives*, 2nd ed. (Malden, MA: Wiley-Blackwell, 2011) and Teresa A. Meade and Merry E. Wiesner-Hanks, eds., *A Companion to Gender History* (Malden, MA: Blackwell, 2006).

Reflection Questions

1. Why can worship of a mother-goddess be understood in different ways?
2. What are the main arguments for and against the ancient matriarchies thesis?
3. Why do we need to understand patriarchy to comprehend world history and our world today?

PART II

The Classical Societies and Their Legacies, ca. 600 BCE–ca. 600 CE

The classical period, roughly the centuries between 600 BCE and 600 CE, was a formative era that saw a flourishing of societies and networks in nearly every inhabited part of the globe. In the second century BCE a Greek historian, Polybius, recognized the expanding horizons of his time and concluded that "the world's history has been a series of unrelated episodes, but from now on history becomes an organic whole. The affairs of Europe and Africa are connected with those of Asia and all events bear a relationship and contribute to a single end."[1] In his perception of increasing connections across cultures, Polybius identified a crucial transition. The era's art, literature, politics, and religion have had a lasting significance. Today's popular images of the classical Era—the Buddha meditating under a leafy tree, Greek and Chinese philosophers pondering the meaning of existence, Roman gladiators battling in the Colosseum, Mayan pyramids in Central American jungles, Polynesian mariners exploring the vast Pacific Ocean—testify to the ongoing prominence this era has held in our thought.

We live in a connected world, but twenty-five hundred years ago most people would have been unaware of much of the world outside their own community. Five hundred years later many people would have had some knowledge of a much wider world. During the classical period a vast exchange of ideas, cultures, and products grew in the Afro-Eurasian zone, while creative philosophies established new value systems or reinforced existing ones in the Mediterranean world and Asia. The Chinese sent missions into western Asia, where they met Persians and Greeks. The commercial exchanges that were carried out along the trade routes represented the first glimmerings of a world economy centered on Asia. Greek merchants traveled as far as south India. Goods from Persia and Rome reached Southeast Asia, while Romans craved Chinese silk, Arabian incense, and Indian spices. Between 350 BCE and 200 CE the Afro-Eurasian world was also transformed by large regional empires. In the wake of these empires, universal religions such as Buddhism and Christianity crossed cultural boundaries, becoming permanent fixtures of world history. Economic and social patterns changed as each society, while having its own dynamics, was also altered by contact with others. The social, economic, political, and religious or philosophical patterns of the Classical Era, some alien and some familiar to modern people, suggest both how much and how little the world has changed since that time.

The Axial Age of Philosophical Speculation

=⟨ TRANSITIONS

Between around 600 and 400 BCE, several societies of Eurasia faced a remarkably similar set of crises. People in China, India, Persia, Israel, and Greece were all challenged by chronic warfare, population movement, political disruption, and the decline of their cultural traditions. Improved ironworking technology produced better tools but also more effective weapons. Political instability was common, as rival states competed with each other for power in China, India, the Middle East, and Greece. These troubled conditions led to a climate of spiritual and intellectual restlessness, provoking a questioning of the old order. Because of the many influential and creative thinkers of this age, some scholars have called this an "axial period" or

---

[1] Quoted in Michael Wood, *Legacy: The Search for Ancient Cultures* (New York: Sterling, 1994), 192.

turning point, a crucial transition in history. Other scholars doubt the utility of this concept in explaining early Classical Era thought. They argue that the concept neglects important religious developments that occurred after 350 BCE, such as the reshaping of Hinduism, the division of Buddhism, and the rise of Christianity and Islam. Yet, the concept remains useful for linking diverse cultures to world history.

Many of the great Axial Age thinkers lived at roughly the same time, between 600 and 350 BCE. Laozi (credited by tradition as the inspiration for Daoism) and Confucius in China lived and taught in the sixth century around the same time as Buddha and Mahavira (the founder of the Jain faith) in India and the Greek thinkers Thales and Heraclitus. Other major Axial Age thinkers included the Hebrew prophets Jeremiah, Ezekiel, and the second Isaiah, as well as Socrates, Plato, and Aristotle in Greece. Although he may have lived much earlier, the teachings of the Persian Zoroaster also became more prominent in this era. The Axial Age intellectuals produced new and enduring philosophical, religious, and scientific ideas that became the intellectual underpinning of many cultural traditions and fostered ways of thinking still influential in the world today.

Several common philosophical themes can be identified in Axial Age thinking. First, especially in China and Greece, some thinkers questioned the accepted myths and gods and promoted a humanistic view of life, one more concerned with the social and natural order than the supernatural realm. In many societies including Greece, Rome, India, and China a few thinkers expressed ideas that might today be considered atheism. Second, most thinkers stressed moral conduct and values, a vision that often rejected the violent, selfish pursuit of material power they saw around them. Some, like the Buddha, Mahavira, and Laozi, were pacifists who denounced all violence. Third, Confucius, the Hebrew prophets, and several Greeks were also among the first people to think about history and its lessons for societies. Fourth, while few of these thinkers favored social equality, many argued that rulers should govern with a sense of obligation to the powerless and less fortunate. Finally, most Axial Age thinkers believed that the world could be improved, either by the actions of ethical individuals or by the creation of an ideal social order, or both. Many people today are still influenced by Laozi's advice to live in accordance with nature, the Confucian dream of an ordered

IMAGE II.1 Confucius and Laozi in Conversation Although it is unlikely that they ever actually met and Laozi may or may not have been an actual person, this picture engraved on a stone tablet in an old Confucian temple shows Confucius visiting Laozi in the ancient city of Loyang and amiably discussing with him views on ritual and music.

Q What does this picture tell us about the Chinese attitude toward their three major religious and philosophical traditions?

society based on proper ethical conduct, the Buddha's rules for ending human suffering, Mahavira's belief in absolute nonviolence, the prophetic Hebrew vision of universal justice and monotheism, the Greek emphasis on rational analysis, and the Zoroastrian notion of opposing forces of darkness and light. To pass along their ideas, leading thinkers such as Confucius and Plato took on students. Confucius reflected the passion for education: "I am not someone who was born wise. I am someone who tries to learn [from the ancients]."[2]

The consequences of the Axial Age were not only philosophical and religious but also scientific and political. Across Eurasia people raised fundamental questions about many phenomena and answered them by systematic investigation. Hebrew prophets set an ethical and moral foundation for the rise of Christianity and Islam a few centuries later. Greek thinkers such as Aristotle influenced European and Middle Eastern science, and their ideas later inspired new discoveries by Roman and Islamic scientists. Chinese influenced by Confucianism and Daoism also created another rich scientific tradition. Indians became some of the classical world's greatest mathematicians and astronomers. Together, the classical Greeks, Chinese, Indians, Romans, and the ancient Mesopotamians and Egyptians built the foundations for modern science. Axial Age ideas also became the basis for new political ideologies for building stronger states. As a result of strengthening state institutions and leaders, in China, India, Persia, and Greece the Axial Age ended in mighty empires that reflected a new order of technological and organizational planning.

[2]Quoted in Patricia Buckley Ebrey, *The Cambridge Illustrated History of China* (New York: Cambridge University Press, 1996), 46.

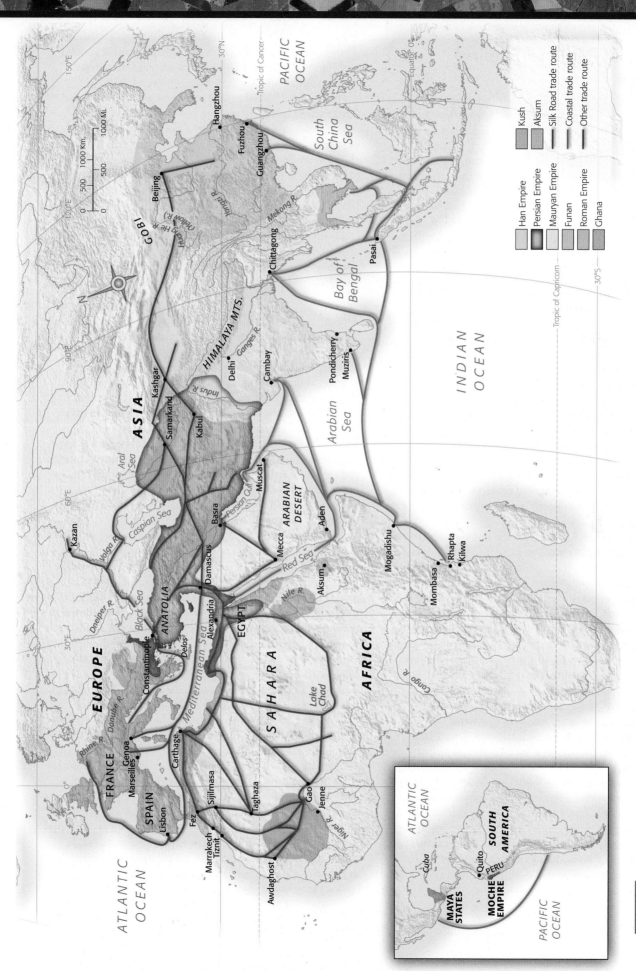

MAP II.1 **Great Empires and Trade Routes** During the classical period, great empires often dominated East Asia, India, western Asia, North Africa, and southern Europe. Extensive land and maritime trade routes linked East Asia with western Eurasia, West Africa with the Mediterranean, and East Africa with southern Asia.

Q According to the map, which regions of Afro-Eurasia were linked most closely to maritime and overland trade?

Legend:
- Han Empire
- Persian Empire
- Mauryan Empire
- Funan
- Roman Empire
- Ghana
- Kush
- Aksum
- Silk Road trade route
- Coastal trade route
- Other trade route

The Age of Regional Empires

⇄ TRANSITIONS

The empires that arose in much of Eurasia during or at the end of the Axial Age were greater in size and impact than those that had flourished in ancient times. The Persian Empire set the stage, thriving for nearly three centuries. More regional empires appeared between 350 BCE and 250 CE, from China in the East to Rome in the West, that were much grander in scale than earlier empires. The Romans conquered the Mediterranean Basin, the Parthians and then the Sassanid Persians some of western and Central Asia, the Chinese Han Empire much of East and Central Asia, and the Mauryan state much of the Indian subcontinent. Most of the empires built on the ideas of classical sages and religious leaders in organizing society. In so doing they helped resolve the crises, such as political instability, that had sparked the rise of the Axial Age reformers. Empires also appeared in sub-Saharan Africa and the Americas, but on a smaller scale than in Eurasia.

The Rise of Empires

The first great regional empires in the Eastern Hemisphere developed during the Axial Age. The Achaemenid Empire of Persia (550–334 BCE) dwarfed its Middle Eastern predecessors and was the first large empire that at its height ruled so many diverse societies, from Egypt and northern Greece to Central Asia. Persian kings had reason to brag that "they were kings of lands containing many people, of the great earth far and wide." The later Hellenistic Empire created by Alexander and the Macedonian Greeks built directly on the experiences of Persian imperial rule.

By the end of the Axial Age, in the third and fourth centuries BCE, new empires arose in Eurasia in part as a result of increased warfare, such as fighting between warring states in India, China, and the western Mediterranean. In each region one state eventually subdued its rivals. Changing social and economic conditions also helped spur the rise of these empires. Rapid economic growth due to expanding long-distance trade networks made merchants more important in all of these societies, and merchants then sought more political influence and social equality. The gap between rich and poor widened.

But the move toward empire alleviated some social conflicts by providing large, stable environments in which resources could be acquired and distributed. During this period, the growing states required extensive administrative machinery, larger armies, standardized laws, and governing philosophies. From China to Rome, provinces paid taxes and supplied soldiers to the large armies needed to sustain and expand the empires. Since everything was bigger and the stakes were higher, wars against competing states could be terribly destructive: hence, in 146 BCE, after three wars with Carthage spanning more than a century, Rome razed that great city to the ground.

Philosophical and religious beliefs maintained community standards but were also used by rulers of these large states to sustain and legitimize their power. In China, Confucian ideas urged people to respect leaders, and Legalist thinkers told leaders to exercise power ruthlessly. Thus, second-century BCE Confucian scholar Dong Zhongshu elevated the role of the emperor, arguing that "heaven, earth, and man are the source of all creatures. Heaven gives birth to them, earth nourishes them, and human beings complete them. Who else but a king could connect them all?"[3] In Mauryan India, King Ashoka enhanced his position by using Buddhist moral injunctions emphasizing peace, tolerance, and welfare to win popular support: "All men are my children, and just as I desire for my children that they should obtain welfare and happiness, so do I desire [the same] for all men."[4]

The Decline of Empires

Throughout history states rise and fall, and the classical empires did as well. While each of the great regional empires declined for different reasons, the Roman and Han Chinese Empires suffered from some of the same problems. Each empire expanded beyond its ability to support itself, weakening administrative structures and finances. Both of these empires also suffered from civil wars and growing domestic unrest. Eventually both empires, unable to acquire new wealth through further expansion, made economic cutbacks and raised taxes to sustain the imperial structure, which caused widespread resentment. A third-century CE Roman writer argued that "the World itself testifies to its own decline. . . . The loss of strength and stature must end . . . in annihilation."[5]

Climate change has affected human life and welfare since the days of our hominid ancestors. Warmer or cooler climates contributed to the rise and fall of societies around the world in ancient times and this continued in the Classical Era and indeed into later centuries as well, including our own. Both the Han and Roman Empires were plagued by environmental problems and climate change. They flourished during the peak of warmth between 200 BCE and 200 CE. With the return of a colder climate after 200 CE, however, agricultural production declined and the great empires collapsed or weakened. In addition, diseases traveled along the land and sea routes, undermining Rome and China in the second century CE.

When pastoral nomads like the Huns, pushed by climate change and population growth, began to put more pressure on the Roman and Chinese Empires, these states had been weakened so much by economic and environmental problems that they could no longer effectively resist. Various peoples eventually conquered or displaced the great empires, although they also usually adopted Roman, Indian, Persian, or Chinese culture. But the imperial ideal never died, especially in China. Hence, the imperial China of the eighteenth century CE, which incorporated many non-Chinese societies, clearly descended in recognizable form from the Han of 150 BCE.

---

[3]From Patricia Buckley Ebrey, ed., *Chinese Civilization: A Sourcebook*, 2nd ed., revised and expanded (New York: Free Press, 1993), 57–58.
[4]Quoted in Romila Thapar, *Asoka and the Decline of the Mauryas* (Delhi: Oxford University Press, 1997), 147.
[5]Cyprian, quoted in Robert P. Clark, *The Global Imperative: An Interpretive History of the Spread of Humankind* (Boulder, CO: Westview Press, 1997), 3.

Western Europeans never succeeded in reviving the Roman Empire, even though some Christian German kings centuries later claimed the title of "Holy Roman Emperor." Yet, aspects of Roman law and their republican political model endured in Western Europe and, later, North America into today.

In 535–536 CE what came to be known as the Dust Veil event or disaster, involving one or more volcanic eruptions, the largest probably in Central America and then perhaps others in or near Southeast Asia, caused the most serious global cooling episode in the past two thousand years, volcanic dust blocking the sunlight for many months across the Northern Hemisphere and precipitating panic and much colder weather for over a century, the so-called Late Antique Little Ice Age. This resulted in major problems across the Northern Hemisphere from China to Europe to North America for decades. Some places faced severe famine and pandemics, including the deadly "Plague of Justinian" that ravaged Byzantium and reached as far as England. Other regions experienced heavy snow or flooding. It can be misleading to blame everything on one catastrophic event but some historians think this instability may have contributed to or even caused varied phenomena, including mass migrations in Central Asia; abandoned villages in northern Europe; the fall of Sasanian Persia, Gupta India, Teotihuacan, and the Roman Empire; and even perhaps the rapid rise and expansion of Islam. But connecting all of these complex developments to each other and the same cooling event is controversial and hard to prove. In the 590s, another plague killed some twenty-five million West Asians, North Africans, and Europeans. To many it felt like the world was coming to an end, confirming for Christians their already apocalyptic worldviews.

Trade and Cultural Contact

NETWORKS

By stimulating commerce, communication, migration, and unprecedented population growth, the classical empires fostered the spread of ideas and technologies into neighboring societies and increased contact among distant peoples. For example, Hellenistic Greeks and Mauryan Indians encountered each other in Afghanistan, a crossroads where Eurasian peoples both fought with each other and exchanged ideas. Spurred by imperial expansion, Roman culture and then Christianity permeated the Mediterranean Basin, Hellenistic Greek culture spread in western Asia and North Africa, and China influenced Japan, Korea, Vietnam, and Central Asia.

The Diffusion of Trade, People, Ideas, and Diseases

In Eurasia trade routes grew out of transportation systems constructed to channel resources to imperial capitals. China built canals unprecedented in scale, Achaemenid Persia and Mauryan India constructed east–west highways, and the Romans developed 150,000 miles of paved roads. These roads and canals, along with seaports, became linked to long-distance trade networks, which brought many societies into closer contact with major empires.

The successful agricultural systems that these vast empires supported fostered population growth and migrations. In 4000 BCE the world population was well under 100 million. At the beginning of the Common Era there were probably 200 to 250 million people, over 70 percent living in Asia and perhaps twenty million each for Africa and the Americas. China was the largest society with around sixty million. More people lived in cities; by 1 CE Rome was the largest metropolis, with 500,000 to 1 million residents. Growing populations also led to increased movement, as people sought open lands and better opportunities. Responding to population pressures, Chinese migrants moved into central and southern China; Germanic and Turkic peoples spread into central Europe and western Asia, respectively; Bantu-speaking peoples occupied the southern half of Africa; various American groups moved around and expanded their territories; and Austronesians settled remote Pacific islands. As groups migrated, they assimilated local peoples and cultures and adapted their lives to new surroundings.

The networks of trade, like those of imperial expansion and missionary activity, linked distant peoples while spreading the influence of cultures more widely. The Greeks picked up scientific and mathematical knowledge as well as some religious notions from the Egyptians and Phoenicians. Indian cultural influences, including Buddhism, spread over the trade routes into Central, East, and Southeast Asia, reaching as far as Japan and Indonesia. Precious spices from southern Arabia, textiles from India, and gold from Malaya and West Africa found their way to the Mediterranean societies.

Trade also connected Mesoamerica with neighboring regions and fostered networks of exchange in both North America and South America. For example, copper from the North American Great Lakes reached the Gulf Coast, and Mesoamerican ball games spread far and wide. Crops like corn and tomatoes also traveled American trade routes.

Diseases began to limit population growth in the later classical period. Then as throughout history and even today mosquitoes, especially those carrying malaria, were the apex predator of humans and killed millions of people. They killed various invaders of Rome such as Huns and Visigoths but also many Romans. Networks of communication were often networks of contagion, port cities with their diverse populations and many visitors being the major hubs of transmission. Epidemics of smallpox and plague resulted from travelers unknowingly spreading new diseases into areas where people had not yet built up immunities to them. Epidemic diseases may have killed as much as 25 percent of the population of China and the Roman Empire during the second and third centuries CE. As a result of the various disease outbreaks, by 600 CE the world population remained between 200 and 240 million, similar to what it had been six centuries earlier, with the great majority concentrated in Asia, especially China. Pollution was also a problem in some places and contributed to serious health issues. The worst case may have been in Europe during Roman times. The Romans were the first society to mass-produce lead, mostly used for water pipes, sheathing the hulls of boats, making some household items, and extracting silver for coins. The mining and smelting process released toxic heavy metals into the air, which some studies conclude massively polluted the air in Europe, and possibly caused widespread lead poisoning, for about five hundred years.

The Silk Road Network

As overland trade expanded over wider areas, what European explorers in the nineteenth century popularized as the "Silk Road" linked China via Central Asia to the Middle East and Europe, becoming and remaining a major long-distance network of exchange—in effect the first transcontinental highway. There was no one major route but rather several main routes with various branches, but all of them allowed people such as diplomats, monks, artists, and craftsmen as well as goods, diseases, foods, horses, the arts, and ideas to travel thousands of miles. For example, over two thousand years ago irrigation technology from the Middle East apparently diffused to western China over the route, and many foods we consume today were transported from Central Asia to kitchens in Europe, China, and elsewehere. The huge amounts of gold and silver exported by Rome to pay for the Chinese silk and porcelain and Indian spices that traveled the route did some

IMAGE II.2 **Crossing the Pamir Mountains** The Pamir Mountains, separating the deserts of what is now western China from the deserts and grasslands of Turkestan and Afghanistan, were one of the more formidable barriers faced by camel caravans traveling the Silk Road. To avoid the blistering summer heat of the desert, the caravans often traveled in winter and thus had to maneuver through mountain snows.

Michael Fairchild/Photolibrary/Getty Images

Q What does the photo tell us about the major forms of transportation along the Silk Road in classical times and, for some travelers, even today?

damage to the Roman economy. Overland trade expanded with the growing use of camels. After the invention of an efficient saddle allowed this pack animal to be used for longer journeys across the deserts and plains of Asia and Africa, camels became the trucks of the premodern Afro-Eurasian zone. And the merchants who used the camels carried not only bullion and products but also religions, especially Buddhism, which spread along the Silk Road into Central Asia and China.

Cities grew up and flourished along the Silk Road across Central and western Asia to serve as suppliers and middlemen to the merchants, cultivating and supplying various necessities to travelers including horses and fruits such as apples, peaches, apricots, and melons. These cities, among them Kashgar in Xinjiang and Samarkand in Turkestan, became part of a contact zone linking many societies. These cities were also multireligious environments where Buddhists, Jews, Nestorian Christians, Zoroastrians, and Manicheans peacefully practiced their faiths. Samarkand opened its gates to anyone agreeing to obey the laws of trade. Samarkand's marketplace was famous for its diverse goods, with artisans known for their paper and silk manufacturing. As in many cities, slaves and drugs such as cannabis (used in mortuary rituals or as an oil seed and fiber crop) could be bought and sold. Hubs at the eastern end of the

Mediterranean served as transshipment points for goods traveling between China and Rome. This trade aided some societies. For example, the Persian-speaking, mostly Zoroastrian Sogdians dominated Central Asian trading cities. Chinese sources described the Sogdians as trained for trade: "At birth honey was put in their mouths and gum on their hands. They learned the trade from the age of five. On reaching twelve they were sent to do business in a neighboring state."[6] But there were also dangers along the route, especially in the deserts and mountains. Caravans sometimes perished in sandstorms or landslides, and travelers might be murdered by outlaws. But the lure of the opportunities and potential wealth enticed many to make the journey.

Maritime Networks

Maritime trade also flourished during this period, enriching various ports. Hence, both trade goods and cultural influences were carried by sea between eastern and western Asia, with the Straits of Melaka and the Indian Ocean as the main highway. Eventually what some modern historians have termed a vast "maritime Silk Road" linked China and Southeast Asia to India and Sri Lanka, and then stretched westward to Persia, Arabia, the East African coast, and beyond via the Red Sea and Persian

---

[6]Quoted in Frances Wood, *The Silk Road: Two Thousand Years in the Heart of Asia* (Berkeley: University of California Press, 2001), 66.

Gulf to Europe and North Africa. South Asians, Indonesians, Greeks, and Persian Gulf Arabs (more a seagoing than desert people) were all heavily involved in maritime commerce. Some cities flourished as hubs for this maritime trade. For instance, between 100 and 500 CE the Egyptian port of Berenike on the Red Sea was regularly visited by ships from India. Products from as far away as Java and Cambodia reached the markets of Berenike, and eleven different written languages, including Greek and Sanskrit, were used there. Berenike was also linked through Alexandria to the Mediterranean societies. One of the earliest written accounts of this complex trade network, written by a Greek merchant in the mid-first century CE, was the *Periplus of the Erythrean Sea*, a handbook which gave detailed information of ports along the East African and western India coasts and the products that could be bought and sold there, and the monsoon winds that facilitated the travel.

Sailing networks also connected the entire Mediterranean Basin. For several centuries one key network hub was the tiny Greek island of Delos (**DEH-los**) in the Aegean Sea, of which it was said, "Merchant, sail in and unload! Everything is as good as sold."[7] Merchants from all over, including Greeks from around the Mediterranean and Black Seas, Romans, Syrians, Jews, Phoenicians, and Arabs, flocked to Delos to trade. Some merchants developed temporary or permanent communities far from home. For example, Jews sunk roots in southwest India, Indian merchants in Southeast Asia, Indonesians and Arabs in East Africa, and Greeks all over the Mediterranean and Black Sea Basins.

In some places maritime commerce faced serious limitations. Because of formidable currents, only the strongest oars would allow a boat to pass through the Strait of Gibraltar separating Spain from North Africa. This problem inhibited trade between Mediterranean and Atlantic societies for many centuries. In the Americas some people, using balsa rafts, traded along the Pacific coast of South and Central America, while others used canoes to travel to and between Caribbean islands.

The Rise of World Religions

⥲ TRANSITIONS

Filling a vacuum created by imperial decay, political instability, and cultural decline, universal religions—Christianity, Buddhism, Hinduism, and Zoroastrianism— became more prominent in Afro-Eurasia during the later centuries of the classical period, marking another great transition that reshaped societies. Instead of the gods of the ancient world, which were mostly local and identified with particular cities or cultures, these new religions were portable and appealed across cultural boundaries. They could be carried along trade routes, attracting converts and servicing believers far from their lands of birth.

Religions spread along land and sea trade routes, as missionaries accompanied or were themselves traders, as a fourth-century CE Christian hymn in Syria acknowledged: "Travel like merchants, That we may gain the world. Fill creation with teaching."[8] About six centuries after its founding in India, Buddhism reached China via the Silk Road and Southeast Asia over the maritime trade routes. Christianity, with roots in the eastern Mediterranean, spread to Rome and the western Mediterranean, then permeated northern and eastern Europe while also establishing roots in western Asia and North and Northeast Africa. Other faiths also established a presence. Manichaeism, a mix of Christian and Zoroastrian influences, attracted believers from North Africa to China. Judaism also gained some converts in Arabia, the Caucasus, and Ethiopia. By 500 or 600 CE small Christian and Jewish communities had even been established in Central Asia, southwestern India, and northern China.

The universal religions gave people hope in the face of the political and social crises that marked the decline of the great regional empires. Sometimes these new religions merged with or incorporated existing beliefs. In East Asia, for example, Buddhism gradually blended with or accommodated Confucianism, Daoism, and Shinto, and, in northern Europe, Christianity acquired a Germanic or Celtic flavor over the centuries. Local versions of the Hindu epic *The Ramayana*, also beloved by many Buddhists, has thrilled fans from Afghanistan to Japan and Indonesia for two thousand years.

In sub-Saharan Africa and the Americas, some religious beliefs reached across many societies, becoming the counterparts to the organized Eurasian religions. The polytheistic beliefs of Sudanic peoples gradually spread to central, eastern, and southern Africa, while in the Americas the Olmec introduced gods and views of the universe that contributed to the later religious beliefs of the Maya. Some American peoples practiced human sacrifice as offerings to the gods, as did some Afro-Eurasian societies, among them the Celts, Minoan Crete, early ancient Egypt, and Shang China.

Religion and Culture

🏛 SOCIETIES

Though only one part of life and changing over time, the universal religions became a major force in shaping the societies and regions in which they became dominant, eventually creating, for example, a largely Hindu India, Buddhist Sri Lanka, and Christian Europe, identities still strong today. After the regional empires collapsed into many rival states in the Mediterranean, South Asia, and China, religious institutions often transcended political divisions, fostering cultural unity across borders. Hindus, Buddhists, and Christians often saw themselves as part of larger faith communities. As a result, Chinese Buddhist pilgrims made the long and arduous journey to India to study with Indian Buddhists, and many Christians looked to the bishops in faraway cities such as Rome for guidance. Spirituality permeated the lives of people all over the world. Religion also offered the poor the hope that they might end their suffering and low status, if not in this life then through reincarnation or in some form of heaven.

[7]Quoted in Lionel Casson, *The Ancient Mariners: Seafarers and Sea Fighters of the Mediterranean in Ancient Times*, 2nd ed. (Princeton, NJ: Princeton University Press, 1991), 166.
[8]Quoted in Richard C. Foltz, *Religions of the Silk Road: Overland Trade and Cultural Exchange from Antiquity to the Fifteenth Century* (New York: St. Martin's, 1999), 74.

All the universal religions, as well as the religions of urban American societies, had certain features, practices, and beliefs in common. They had sacred scriptures (written or oral), such as the Hindu Vedas and Christian Bible, strict moral codes, organized priesthoods, theologies laying out core beliefs, and some concept of existence after death. Most faiths also encouraged followers to treat others as they wanted to be treated themselves.

As the devout shared a belief in the universal truth of their religion, the faiths became important forces of social control. For example, Hindu ideas of reincarnation and karma underpinned the Indian caste system, encouraging people to accept their status in this life. Christians focused on attaining Heaven and were warned that questioning religious authority and beliefs might prevent salvation. Some of the religious establishments grew intolerant of dissent. For this reason, Christian bishops established a consensus on doctrine, excluding ideas considered to be heresy. Those who disagreed with orthodoxy might be banned or punished, and they were expected to face retribution after death in Hell, the abode of evil, an underworld for wicked people and disbelievers. All the religions were patriarchal to one degree or another, adding religious sanction to the growing suppression of women.

Buddhism and Jainism spawned a new social and spiritual movement, monasticism, that also became a growing component of organized Christianity by the third century CE. Buddha himself supposedly ordained the first monks as well as nuns, including his mother. Whether Christian or Buddhist, monasteries provided educational and charitable services while providing a focus for community religious life. In societies as far removed as England, Nubia, Sri Lanka, and China, a substantial number of men (and some women) joined monastic orders, abandoning the humdrum existence of everyday life for austere religious practices, including a focus on prayer, meditation, and fasting, and usually bound by a rigid code of celibacy and poverty.

King David playing the lyre, from Ethiopian d'Abbadie (vellum), Ethiopian School (15th century)/Bibliotheque Nationale, Paris, France. Photo ©AISA/Bridgeman Images

IMAGE II.3 **An Ethiopian Portrait of Hebrew King David** For centuries artists in the Christian Ethiopian kingdom, in the highlands of Northeast Africa, painted biblical figures on the pages of religious manuscripts. The artists often used Ethiopian motifs, and this painting of the Hebrew king David, adorned in rich robes and crown and playing the lyre, a harp-type instrument, resembles that of an Ethiopian king.

Q What does this painting tell us about the connections between Ethiopia and western Asia in classical times?

II-6 Social Systems and Attitudes

SOCIETIES

The social systems and attitudes of the classical period set the patterns for centuries to come. In many places gender roles hardened. Because the great empires were built and ruled through military conquest and brute force, they were very masculine in nature. Some of the new philosophies and religions gave power to older men and generally urged women to stay in the background. In addition, in the Mediterranean world the faiths that replaced Greek and Roman religions removed goddesses as objects of worship, although in southern Asia many Hindus continued to revere female deities. Although women had some legal protections in Greece and Rome, many also lived generally domestic and often secluded lives. In 195 BCE, a Roman politician complained that women should stay at home and out of politics: "women cannot partake of [local office], priesthoods, [military] triumphs, or spoils of war; elegance, finery, and beautiful clothes are women's badges; in these they find joy and take pride."[9] Women faced increasing restrictions in China and northern India, where they were expected to be obedient to men. Patriarchy was also common in Africa, the Americas, and the Pacific islands. But wherever they lived, women had varied experiences. Some were treated as property, assigned by their fathers to husbands, and many faced permanent dependency on fathers, husbands, and sons. Only a small minority of women anywhere were educated. In many societies public speaking and oratory were the exclusive practices and skills of men, and hence discouraged in women. However, a few attained great power and acclaim as queens, such as Zenobia in Palmyra, Cleopatra VII in Egypt, Theodora in Byzantium, and Amanitere of Meroe (Kush). A few female philosophers, such as Ban Zhao in China, Hypatia in Alexandria, and Hipparchia of Maroneia in Athens, gained the respect of their male peers.

Homosexuality existed in all classical societies, especially in Greece and Rome. Chinese historians reported that many emperors of the era, including the Han dynasty empire builder Wu Di, had male lovers in addition to their wives and concubines. The Chinese also accepted lesbian relationships among women in polygamous households. But in many societies official attitudes concerning gender roles and sexual behaviors became more rigid over time, pushing homosexuals to the margins of society.

Another form of repression, slavery, was practiced in many classical societies around the world. Most people saw slavery as a part of the natural order of things and essential to economic life. Slaves everywhere were bought and sold at the whim of the owner, and their lives and labor were controlled. Most slaves were poor, although some Greek and Roman slaves held high positions in society or were attached to prosperous families. In societies such as Han China, Mauryan India, and the Maya society, slaves were only one segment of the lower class, whereas in Greece and Rome they constituted a large part of the population and were used in every area of the economy, from mining and construction to prostitution and domestic work. Slavery mostly died out in China and India during the first millennium CE and became less important but not prohibited in Europe after the collapse of the Roman Empire, showing that societies do change, often dramatically, over time.

⁹Quoted in Peter Stearns, *Gender in World History* (New York: Routledge, 2000), 28.

Classical Societies in Southern and Central Asia, 600 BCE–600 CE

> "
> *The merchants used to move about in the rivers as they wished, in the forests as if in gardens and on mountains as if in their own houses. As [the King] used to protect the earth so it too gave him gems out of mines, corns from the fields, and elephants from forests.*
> "
>
> —Indian writer Kalidasa (kahl-I-Dahss-uh), fifth century CE[1]

Haruko Sheridan/Danita Delimont Stock Photography

IMAGE 5.1 Gold Coin This gold coin, showing a horseman, was made in India during the reign of King Chandragupta II, who presided over a great and prosperous Indian empire, with a dynamic economy, between 380 and 415 CE.

[1]Quoted in Jeannine Auboyer, *Daily Life in Ancient India: From 200 B.C. to 700 A.D.* (London: Phoenix, 2002), 62.

Sometime around 80 CE an unknown Greek boarded an India-bound trading ship that left the Egyptian port of Berenike **(BER-eh-nick-y)**. After braving the dangers from pirates in the Red Sea and along the Arabian coast, the ship sailed east across the Indian Ocean to reach the Indus River, where the merchants exchanged clothing, silverware, and glassware for semiprecious stones from Afghanistan, Chinese silks, and Indian textiles. Along India's west coast, they stopped near present-day Bombay (today known as Mumbai), trading silverware and Italian wine for pepper. Upon reaching the great port of Muziris **(MOO-zir-us)** in southwest India, the sailors probably haunted the waterfront dives. An Indian poet recorded the arrival of ships like this at Muziris: "The beautiful vessels stir white foam on the river, arriving with gold and departing with pepper."[2] The ship then sailed around the southern tip of India and up the east coast, stopping to collect pearls, textiles, spices, and gems. Finally it returned to Egypt, the merchants aboard hoping to make a fortune from their cargo.

From Egypt, western Asia, and East Africa ships arrived annually at Indian seaports to trade, collecting fabulous trade goods, such as pepper, cinnamon, cotton, and gems, for sale in distant markets. India also attracted sojourners and permanent settlers arriving by sea or overland. Those who arrived over the mountains from windswept Central Asia found the Indian sun a blazing fury and the drenching summer rains a shock. For newcomers, the Indian culture and religion seemed more unusual than the climate. But Indian society was adaptable and accommodating. Most immigrants found themselves gradually enfolded into Indian religions, which allowed for many paths to understanding. Resilient Hinduism bent to meet the varying needs of dissimilar people. This adaptability also helped Indian culture spread into Southeast Asia.

During this era, classical South and Southeast Asia flowered in state building, new trade networks, and religious thought, establishing many patterns that endured into modern times. Several South Asian empires forged political unity and made India a leading world power. Hinduism developed new schools of thought, while Buddhism **(BOO-diz-uhm)** arose to become a major faith in many parts of Asia. Meanwhile, various Central and Southeast Asian societies established states and social systems that differed greatly from those in India and China while becoming major participants in international trade.

---

[2]Quoted in Lionel Casson, *The Ancient Mariners: Seafarers and Sea Fighters of the Mediterranean in Ancient Times*, 2nd ed. (Princeton, NJ: Princeton University Press, 1991), 202.

5-1 The Transformation of Indian Society, Religion, and Politics

TRANSITIONS   SOCIETIES

Q How did Buddhism and the Mauryas shape Indian society?

The societies that developed in South Asia during the Ancient Era (see Chapter Two) built a foundation for the mixing of those older traditions with new influences and ideas during the Classical Era and over the centuries to follow. The results of this process proved to be enduring enough that if modern South Asians could be transported back two millennia, they would probably recognize many familiar values, religious views, and ways of life. The forging of a new society from Aryan and local traditions continued for centuries, affecting life and thought. The distinctive caste system became a key structure, and Hinduism grew more diverse and complex. Jainism and Buddhism sprouted from Axial Age religious ferment, classical Eurasia's great philosophical awakening that spawned new ways of thinking from Greece to China. India's first large centralized state, the Mauryan (**MORE-yuhn**) Empire, emerged in part from contact with peoples to the west.

> **CONNECTION to TODAY**
>
> Do you think that the Mauryan king Ashoka and his pacifist ideas would be good role models for the world today?

into thousands of subcastes known as jati ("birth groups"), each with its own rules and, frequently, occupational specialization. Each person was born into a caste that maintained a moral code stipulating such duties as family maintenance and specifying which jatis could supply marriage partners. Regulations prescribed the types of food that caste members could consume,

IMAGE 5.2 **Village Scene** In classical times most Indians lived in villages. This modern painting portrays an Indian house and villagers working, some as farmers, with the Hindu god Shiva watching over and blessing the village.

Q What does the painting tell us about Indian religion and rural life or the modern artist's perception of it?

5-1a Caste and Indian Society

The social configuration we know today as the caste system began to take formal shape in the classical period. Caste members often practiced a common occupation as priests, warriors, merchants, artisans, or farmers, while still others performed more menial tasks. Hindu values supported caste membership, including beliefs in reincarnation. But although social and religious practices eventually became similar throughout India, the caste system was never uniform and unchanging.

Over time the caste system became more fully developed and hereditary. The Code of Manu (**MAN-oo**), a moral, political, and legal document with advice for a Hindu king that was prepared around 200 BCE, formalized rules regarding caste relations. Gradually the four main castes (varna) subdivided

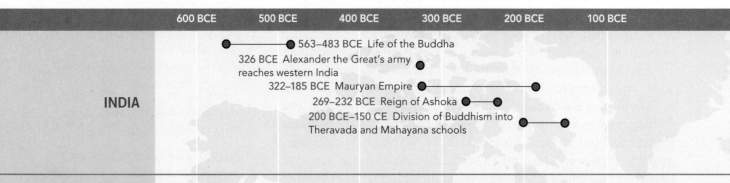

	600 BCE	500 BCE	400 BCE	300 BCE	200 BCE	100 BCE

INDIA

563–483 BCE Life of the Buddha
326 BCE Alexander the Great's army reaches western India
322–185 BCE Mauryan Empire
269–232 BCE Reign of Ashoka
200 BCE–150 CE Division of Buddhism into Theravada and Mahayana schools

SOUTHEAST ASIA

111 BCE–939 CE Chinese colonization of Vietnam

who could cook and serve the food, and who could accompany the diner. Although the ancient Aryans and some of their gods often consumed meat including beef, vegetarianism now became more common among the higher castes, with cows being protected. By 500 CE pious Hindus avoided eating beef because the cow was now considered sacred, the symbol of life and motherhood, because it gave dung for fuel and fertilizer and milk for food. Cows wandered at will, eating whatever grain they found. Scholars debate whether cows spreading disease and consuming scarce food resources outweighs their gifts to people.

Hindu ideas sanctioned the emerging caste system. The doctrine of karma held that one's status in the present life was determined by deeds in past lives. Every action had repercussions, the sum of one's karma in past lives determining one's fate in this life. Hindus considered the three top caste groupings further along the path of reincarnation, hence calling them the "twice born," while holding low-caste Indians responsible for their status because of their presumed past sins. Their only hope lay in dutifully performing their present duties and obligations. Below the formal caste system were the untouchables, or pariahs **(puh-RYE-uhz)**, some 10 percent of the population who lived largely in their own neighborhoods and were generally condemned to trades and crafts regarded as undesirable (such as carrying water to village houses) or unclean because their function involved being polluted by filth or the taking of animal life. They worked as sweepers of village streets, fishermen, butchers, gravediggers, tanners, leatherworkers, and scavengers.

Although criticized by some Hindus centuries ago as well as today for the unequal treatment of people, the caste system has functioned for the past twenty-five hundred years, providing stability, security, long-term continuity to society, and meaning and direction to Indians' lives. It has promoted mutual aid within each caste and regulated village life, as subcastes exchange goods or services with other subcastes in the village. Regional variations also developed; for example, in south India, Bengal, and northwestern India, the caste system remained less complex. Caste, village, and family became the pillars of society, contributing to a group orientation and an acceptance of authority. Although still strong in many villages in modern

times, however, the system has been breaking down in the larger cities. It is difficult to avoid close contact with members of other castes while eating in a restaurant, being confined in a hospital, or working in an office or factory.

5-1b The Shaping of Hinduism

The religion known today as Hinduism faced increasing dissent during the classical period, fostering new thinking. Some historians argue that Hinduism as a coherent religion with sacred writings and a common identity only emerged in the past few centuries under the influence of the British rulers who wanted to standardize the religion for political, administrative, and ideological purposes, including dividing and ruling the Hindus and Muslims. Some studies suggest that the term *Hindu* first appeared in a few Sanskrit texts after the twelfth century CE and was not widely used for centuries after that. For much of history, Hinduism remained a loose collection of varied beliefs, rituals, legends, practices, festivals, and shrines, with no centralized religious authority and deep knowledge of the Vedas restricted to the priestly class, the brahmins. They alone had mastered the scriptures and hymns for worship, and they alone presided over rituals. Enriched by gifts from the devout, many priests became wealthy landowners. Eventually, however, some Indians who resented priestly wealth and corruption debated the accepted wisdom. Like the Chinese and Greek philosophers, they spawned movements emphasizing new approaches to worship and spiritual fulfillment, especially meditation. Some reformist writings were collected in the Upanishads, the final portion of the vast Hindu scriptures.

Thanks to this new spirituality, Hinduism's highest ideal became escape from sensual pleasures and the material world (seen as an "illusion") and the joining of one's individual soul with **Brahman**, the Universal Soul or Absolute Reality, that fills all space and time (not to be confused with the four-faced Hindu creator-god Brahma, who fashioned the world and all its creatures). Union with the

Brahman The Universal Soul, or Absolute Reality, that Hindus believe fills all space and time.

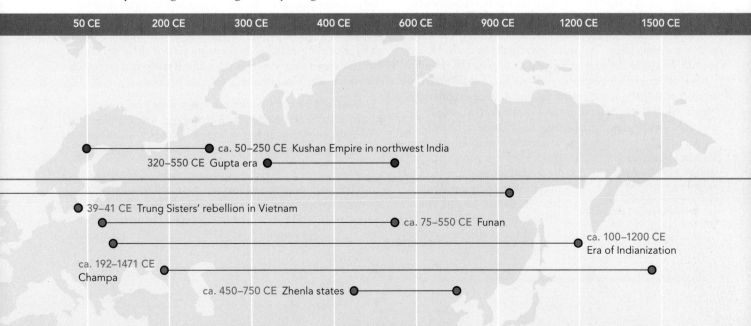

| 50 CE | 200 CE | 300 CE | 400 CE | 600 CE | 900 CE | 1200 CE | 1500 CE |

ca. 50–250 CE Kushan Empire in northwest India

320–550 CE Gupta era

39–41 CE Trung Sisters' rebellion in Vietnam

ca. 75–550 CE Funan

ca. 100–1200 CE
Era of Indianization

ca. 192–1471 CE
Champa

ca. 450–750 CE Zhenla states

Werli Francois/Alamy Stock Photo

IMAGE 5.3 **Mourning the Buddha's Death** This painting from a Nepal monastery presents the final moments of the Buddha's life as his followers mourn.

Q What in this photo conveys the spiritual greatness of the Buddha in comparison to ordinary humans?

Universal Soul meant ending the cycle of reincarnation through devotion to God, selfless action, and knowledge achieved through intense meditation. Only by escaping from one's ego by abandoning the desires and actions that prevent release from earthly lives could a person end the round of reincarnation and finally achieve the ultimate bliss of merging with Brahman, described in the Upanishads as a deep, dreamless sleep. "In thinking 'This is I' and 'That is mine,'" warned the Upanishads, "one binds himself to himself, as does a bird with a snare!"[3]

Some seekers rejected society, seeking mystical unity with the divine. Hindu holy men, greatly admired, abandoned worldly pleasures through such practices as yoga (**YOH-guh**) ("yoke" or "union"), a system of physical and mental exercises to understand the workings of the mind. Yoga emphasized breath control to promote mental concentration, calmness, and a trancelike state that produced a mystical awareness of a universal soul. In modern times yoga has become popular around the world, especially in the West, often transformed from its Indian origins into a wholesome, accessible regimen for health and well-being.

Vedanta ("Completion of the Vedas") A school of classical Indian thought that offered Hindus mystical experience and a belief in the underlying unity of all reality.

New forms of worship also stressed devotion or prayer focused on specific gods such as Vishnu or Shiva. Every home had a shrine to worship such deities, and great throngs made annual pilgrimages to sacred places such as the Ganges River. Eventually the spiritual quest led to new schools of thought such as **Vedanta** (**vay-DAHNT-uh**), meaning "completion" of the Vedas. Vedanta offered mystical experience, belief in the underlying unity of all reality, and sophisticated interpretations of the countless gods and goddesses found in popular Hinduism, a diversity often summed up by the phrase "33,000 gods." Rejecting polytheism, Vedanta viewed these deities as manifestations of the single Absolute Reality that pervades everything. The Upanishads stated that Brahman is

> *God, all gods, the five elements—earth, air, fire, water, ether; all beings, great or small, born of eggs, born from the womb, born from heat, born from soil; horses, cows, men, elephants, birds; everything that breathes, the beings that walk and the beings that walk not.*[4]

Hinduism developed a tolerant approach to religious differences. As many invaders swept into India, most of them found a place in Hinduism, which incorporated diverse beliefs, even integrating some non-Hindu figures into devotional cults.

[3]Quoted in Stanley Wolpert, *A New History of India*, 5th ed. (New York: Oxford University Press, 1997), 48.
[4]From Swami Prabhavananda and Frederick Manchester, eds., *The Upanishads: Breath of the Eternal* (New York: Mentor, 1957), 62.

Discover Historical Voices

Basic Doctrines in the Buddha's First Sermon

Buddhist tradition holds that, after achieving enlightenment, the Buddha preached his first sermon in a deer park in the Ganges city of Varanasi (Benares) around 527 BCE. One of the most important sources of belief for all Buddhists, the sermon laid out the framework of Buddha's moral message, including the Middle Way between asceticism and worldly life, the Noble Eightfold Path, and the Four Noble Truths. These are the most important concepts in all branches of Buddhism.

There are two ends not to be served by a wanderer. . . . The pursuit of desires and of pleasure which springs from desire, which is base, common, leading to rebirth, ignoble and unprofitable; and the pursuit of pain and hardship [asceticism], which is grievous, ignoble, and unprofitable. The Middle Way of the [Buddha] avoids both of these ends. It is enlightened, it brings clear vision, it makes for wisdom, and leads to peace, insight, enlightenment, and Nirvana. What is the Middle Way? It is the Noble Eightfold path—Right Views, Right Resolve, Right Speech, Right Conduct, Right Livelihood, Right Effort, Right Mindfulness, and Right Concentration. . . .

And this is the Noble Truth of Sorrow. Birth is sorrow, age is sorrow, disease is sorrow, death is sorrow; contact with the unpleasant is sorrow, separation from the pleasant is sorrow, every wish unfulfilled is sorrow—in short, all of the five components of individuality are sorrow.

And this is the Noble Truth of the Arising of Sorrow. It arises from craving, which leads to rebirth, which brings delight and passion, and seeks pleasure from here, now there—the craving for sensual pleasure, the craving for continued life, the craving for power.

And this is the Noble Truth of the Stopping of Sorrow. It is the complete stopping of the craving, so that no passion remains, leaving it, being emancipated from it, being released from it, giving no place to it.

And this is the Noble Truth of the Way which Leads to the Stopping of Sorrow. It is the Noble Eightfold Path. . . .

Reflection Questions

1. What does the Buddha mean by the Middle Way?
2. What causes suffering, and how can people stop it?
3. What conduct do these ideas promote?
4. What ideas from the Buddha do you think might appeal to people of other religions today?

Source: From *Sources of Indian Tradition*, Vol. 1, ed. William Theodore de Bary et al. Copyright © 1958 Columbia University Press. Reprinted with permission of the publisher.

Indians worshipped God in many forms. As an old Indian folk song puts it: "Into the bosom of the great sea, flow streams that come from hills on every side. Their names are various as their springs. And thus in every land do men bow down, To one great God, though known by many names."[5] Rather than a centralized church and rigidly defined theology, Hinduism developed as loosely connected sects with many variations of belief and practice. Toleration and accommodation allowed it to thrive among the better educated and villagers alike, despite the clearly inequitable divisions of caste and the burdens of karma.

5-1c Jainism and Buddhism

Perhaps influenced by the religious questioning of the Upanishads, two dissident ascetics eventually gave up on reforming Hinduism and founded movements that became separate religions, Jainism (**JANE-iz-uhm**) and Buddhism. **Jainism** derived from Mahavira (**MA-ha-VEER-a**) ("Great Hero"), the pampered son of a tribal chief who abandoned his affluent life to wander naked as an ascetic around 500 BCE. Mahavira practiced self-torture as the route to salvation, eventually starving himself to death. Jains believed that life in all forms must be protected because everything—animals, insects, and plants—has a living soul. Jain monks and nuns sweep the ground to avoid stepping on insects and some wear a cloth over the mouth to prevent inhaling them. In Mahavira's words, "All things living, all beings whatever, should not be slain, or treated with violence."[6] Most Jains became merchants and bankers, and they are prominent today in India's economic elite. Given the emphasis on austere behavior and a spartan vegetarian diet, the sect never became very large; perhaps 4.5 million Jains live in the world today. But Jainism influenced Hindu ideas of nonviolence and therefore the modern world. Twenty-five centuries after Mahavira, Mohandas Gandhi, a devout Hindu, utilized Jain ideas in developing his philosophy of nonviolence and passive resistance to oppressive rule.

More important in the long run, **Buddhism**, based on the teachings of a major Axial Age thinker, eventually spread out of India to become a major faith in

> **Jainism** An Indian religion that believes that life in all forms must be protected because everything, including animals, insects, plants, sticks, and stones, has a separate soul and is alive.

> **Buddhism** A major world religion based on the teachings of the Buddha that emphasized putting an end to desire and being compassionate to all creatures.

---

[5]C.E. Gover, *The Folk-Songs of Southern India* (London: Trubner and Co., 1872), 165.
[6]Quoted in Wolpert, *New History*, 54.

Central, East, and Southeast Asia and Sri Lanka. The religion's founder, Siddartha Gautama (si-DAHR-tuh GAUT-uh-muh) (563–483 BCE), was a prince of a small kingdom in what is now Nepal and a contemporary of Confucius, Mahavira, and several other Axial Age thinkers. As with Jesus of Nazareth and Confucius, his life and thought are known largely through his followers' written accounts. Siddartha led a privileged, self-indulgent life and was shocked when he ventured from the palace and encountered the miseries experienced by common people. He then abandoned his royal life, wife, and family to search for truth as a wandering holy man, living in the forest, practicing yoga, meditating, begging for his food, and nearly dying from fasting. He met skeptics who argued that there is no afterlife or god. Eventually Siddartha believed he understood cosmic truths and began teaching his new religion, attracting many disciples, who called him the Buddha ("The Enlightened One"). He also rejected the caste system as immoral.

Buddha emphasized the Four Noble Truths (see Discover Historical Voices: Basic Doctrines in the Buddha's First Sermon): (1) this life is one of suffering and ignorance; (2) suffering stems from desiring what one does not have and clinging to what one already has for fear of losing it; (3) to stop suffering, one must stop all desire; and (4) one does this by following the Noble Eightfold Path of correct views, intent, speech, actions, trade (or profession), effort, mindfulness, and concentration. Following this path means leading a good life that does no harm to others. To Buddhists, the world is in a constant state of flux; when mortals try in vain to stop the flow of events, they suffer. Buddhism is neither monotheistic nor polytheistic, and the Buddha was ambivalent as to whether a god or gods existed. Buddhists were encouraged to follow "the Middle Way," a lifestyle midway between austere asceticism and the real world of society. This meant living morally, non-violently, and moderately and considering the needs of others. For example, men were urged to treat their wives with respect. Asked to summarize his beliefs, the Buddha replied: "Avoid doing evil deeds, cultivate doing good deeds, and purify the mind."[7] The Buddha did not oppose acquiring wealth but believed that wealth alone did not bring happiness. He also condemned the irresponsible use of wealth, such as wasting it on drinking, gambling, and laziness rather than saving some for emergencies and donating some to worthy causes.

Although rejecting priestly power and the caste system and the Vedas as religious truth, Buddha adopted and modified many Hindu ideas. To be released from the chronic cycle of birth and rebirth, Buddhists were urged, like Hindus, to abandon all sense of self but with the goal of **nirvana** (neer-VAHN-uh) (literally, "the blowing out"), an advanced consciousness bringing everlasting peace or end of suffering through perfection of wisdom and compassion. Buddhists also avoided taking animal life if possible, many becoming vegetarians. Like Mahavira, Buddha promoted a major innovation,

nirvana ("the blowing out") For Buddhists a kind of everlasting peace or end of suffering achieved through perfection of wisdom and compassion.

monasticism The pursuit of a life of penance, prayer, and meditation, either alone or in a community of other seekers.

monasticism (muh-NAS-tuh-siz-uhm), a life of penance, prayer, and meditation. Eventually joining together in communities of other seekers, monks and nuns adopted chastity, poverty, and nonviolence; suspended family ties; followed rules of proper conduct; and practiced yoga for concentration, meditation, and self-discipline. They begged for their food, thus affirming their humility and allowing believers to gain merit by giving them food and other necessities. Eventually Buddhism became a major influence on the first great Indian imperial state, the Mauryan Empire.

5-1d Foreign Encounters and the Rise of the Mauryas

For several centuries, northwest India remained in close communication with Persia and then Hellenistic Greece. The Persians conquered much of the Indus River Valley in 518 BCE, bringing India to the attention of the Greek historian Herodotus, whose fabulous stories tantalized the young Macedonian ruler, Alexander the Great, who conquered the Greeks and then built a great empire in western Asia and North Africa (see Chapter 7). By 326 BCE Alexander's forces had reached the Indus River and soon subdued several small Aryan kingdoms east of the Indus. Impressed with the country's wealth, the Macedonian conqueror discussed religion and philosophy with Indian scholars and apparently dispatched his notes back to his own teacher, Aristotle, making some Greek thinkers aware of Buddhist and Hindu ideas. A few Indian thinkers may even have visited Athens and Alexandria. With his homesick soldiers rebellious, however, Alexander returned to Babylon, where he died in the palace occupied three centuries earlier by the Chaldean king Nebuchadnezzar II. Alexander's legacy endured in northwest India, and Greek artistic styles helped to shape Buddhist art. Furthermore, the Greek imperialists set up a powerful state in northern Afghanistan known as Bactria (BAK-tree-uh), and some Greeks also remained behind in northwest India, intermarrying with local women.

Alexander's invasion created a political vacuum filled by the military forces of Chandragupta (CHUHN-druh-GOOP-tuh) Maurya, who established the first imperial Indian state, the Mauryan Empire (322–185 BCE). Perhaps inspired by Alexander, Chandragupta transformed himself from the ruler of a Ganges state, Magadha (MAH-guh-duh), into the monarch of half the subcontinent (see Map 5.1). Eventually the Mauryan Empire included eastern Afghanistan, most of north and central India, and parts of south India. Chandragupta's war machinery was cutting edge for the time. His enormous army, mostly professional, had divisions of cavalry, infantry, chariots, and war elephants, as well as a large treasury funded by heavy taxation. The Mauryas maintained diplomatic relations with many societies, including Greece, Syria, and Egypt. Chandragupta, a cynical political realist skilled in manipulating power, was influenced by his chief adviser, Kautilya (cow-TILL-ya), who favored political centralization and compiled the initial draft of a manual for rulers on obtaining and holding power.

The classical world's most efficient government ruled the empire. A large army and secret police maintained order, with

---

[7]Quoted in Roy C. Amore and Julia Ching, "The Buddhist Tradition," in *World Religions: Eastern Traditions*, ed. Willard G. Oxtoby (New York: Oxford University Press, 1996), 230.

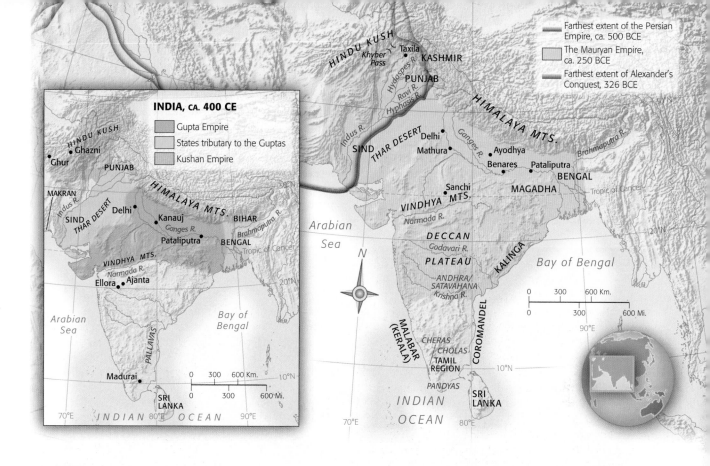

MAP 5.1 **The Mauryan Empire, 322–185 BCE** During the classical period major states arose in north India, most notably the Mauryan, Kushan, and Gupta Empires. The brief encounter with the Greek forces led by Alexander the Great, which reached the Indus River Valley in 326 BCE, may have stimulated the Mauryas to build India's first empire.

Q How do you think geography helps explain why large empires largely arose only in the northern part of South Asia during the Classical Era? Did it limit the size the empires could achieve?

spies keeping government officials under constant surveillance. An ambassador from Greece particularly admired the conscientious justice system, in which the king presided personally over court sessions and settled disputes. To maintain the expensive government, the state heavily taxed agriculture, trade, mining, herding, and other economic activities. Village councils composed of older men from leading families enjoyed considerable local autonomy, a pattern that became entrenched over the centuries. The Mauryan monarch lived in great splendor, often in seclusion and surrounded by women who cooked his food, served his wine, and in the evening carried him to his apartment, where they lulled him to sleep with music. To discourage opposition, Indian rulers had long claimed to be blessed by the gods and endowed with supernatural and magical powers. Yet the realization that excessive taxes and forced labor might drive the people into rebellion provided checks on autocratic power.

5-1e Mauryan Life, Institutions, and Networks

Many of Mauryan India's 50 to 100 million people lived in cities, the centers for a prosperous economy. With 500,000 residents, the capital, Patna (**PUHT-nuh**) (then called Pataliputra) on the Ganges River, was the world's largest city and widely celebrated for its parks, public buildings, libraries, and a great university that attracted many foreign students. The fortified timber wall around the city, which had 570 towers, was roughly twenty-one miles long, suggesting that Patna was about twice as large as Rome several centuries later.

Mauryan prosperity depended on the world's most advanced trading system and craft industries, including many skilled woodworkers, ivory carvers, stonecutters, and producers of fine cotton fabrics. Products and merchants moved along the major east–west highway stretching from near present-day Calcutta (**kal-KUHT-uh**) through the Ganges and Indus Valleys to Afghanistan. Many resident foreign merchants fostered an active trade with China, Arabia, and the Middle East. Artisan and merchant guilds supervised the private sector, while the government owned mines and forests and engaged in shipbuilding, arms manufacture, and textile production. Public granaries stored surplus food.

5-1f Ashoka and Buddhist Monarchy

The Mauryas reached their height under Chandragupta's grandson, the enlightened king Ashoka (**uh-SHOH-kuh**) (whose name means "Sorrowless"), a major political and religious figure in world history. The ambitious Ashoka (r. 269–232 BCE) rose to power through bloody campaigns of eliminating rivals and expanding into frontier lands. His early edicts, many of them carved in rocks and sandstone pillars, boast of many enemies slain and captured. Then, at some point, he experienced a spiritual conversion and became a devout Buddhist, proclaiming his remorse at past atrocities and his commitment to nonviolence. He lamented that he had killed 100,000 soldiers on the battlefield, displaced 100,000 people from their homes, and caused suffering to many noncombatants. One edict noted that Ashoka "began to follow righteousness, to love righteousness. The greatest of all victories is the victory of righteousness."[8]

Ashoka spent his remaining years promoting the Buddha's pacifist teachings, pledging to bear wrong without violent retribution, look kindly on all his subjects, and ensure the safety, happiness, and peace of mind of all living beings. He designed laws to encourage compassion, mutual tolerance, vegetarianism, and respect for all forms of life. He also sponsored hospitals and medical care paid for by the state. Although Ashoka dispatched Buddhist missions to spread the religion into Sri Lanka, Southeast Asia, and Afghanistan, he neither made Buddhism the

Borromeo/Art Resource, NY

IMAGE 5.4 **Ashoka Column** This thirty-two-foot-tall sandstone column, erected in northeast India around 240 BCE, weighs fifty tons. The inscriptions on the pillar outline Ashoka's achievements and offer advice on how citizens of the empire should behave.

Q What does the sandstone column suggest about how Ashoka communicated to the people he ruled?

---

[8]Quoted in Rhoads Murphy, *A History of Asia*, 4th ed. (New York: HarperCollins, 2003), 74.

state religion nor persecuted other faiths. While he financed the building of Buddhist temples and stupas **(STOOP-uhz)** (domed shrines), government aid was distributed to all religious groups. The king argued that "all sects deserve reverence. By thus acting a man exalts his own sect and at the same time does service to the sects of other people."[9] Ashoka styled himself "Beloved of the Gods," a semideity. The Mauryas created a political legacy of the universal emperor, a divinely sanctioned leader with a special role in the cosmic scheme of things.

Ashoka's successors were less able, and a half century after his death, the Mauryan Empire collapsed, the mounting costs of governing a large empire through a centralized bureaucracy having drained the treasury. The Mauryan Empire's demise set a political pattern different from China, where long periods of unity were the norm. In India, periods of political unity were relatively brief, followed by prolonged division into several states. But Indians possessed a strong sense of cultural unity and loyalty to the social order, including the family and caste, rather than to the state.

KEY POINTS

▶ New spiritual movements within Hinduism, such as yoga and Vedanta, challenged priestly control and emphasized the goal of escaping the ego.

▶ Jainism and Buddhism split off from Hinduism, but only Buddhism, which offered guidelines for achieving nirvana, gained wide appeal.

▶ After Alexander's retreat, Chandragupta established the first imperial Indian state, the centralized, autocratic Mauryan Empire, which included the Indus and Ganges Basins.

▶ King Ashoka, Chandragupta's grandson, became a pacifist convert to Buddhism, which he helped to spread to Sri Lanka, Southeast Asia, and Afghanistan.

5-2 South and Central Asia After the Mauryas

🏛 SOCIETIES ⚖ TRANSITIONS

Q What were some of the ways in which classical India connected with and influenced the world beyond South Asia?

The Maurya collapse in the early second century BCE launched five hundred years of political fragmentation before the rise of the next empire, that of the Guptas. These centuries saw increasing contact between South Asians and the outside world, with Indian cultural influence, especially Buddhism, spreading into Sri Lanka as well as Central and Southeast Asia. Various Central and West Asian peoples swept into northwestern India, conquering the Indus Valley and mixing with local peoples, who eventually absorbed the invaders and their ways. Substantial foreign trade and Buddhist missions to neighboring societies also occurred.

> **CONNECTION to TODAY**
>
> In what ways do you think the idea of the Maritime Silk Road might also describe world trade today?

5-2a Indians and Central Asians

India maintained constant relations with Central Asia, the area stretching from Russia eastward to China's borders. The Turkestan region north of India, where many people spoke Turkic languages, served as a key contact zone for networks stretching east to China, south to India, and west to Persia and Russia. As trade between China and western Asia increased, cities sprouted along the overland Silk Road through Turkestan, whose commerce was dominated by Sogdians **(SAHG-dee-uhns)**, Persian-speaking Zoroastrians and Buddhists with a written language and literature. A Chinese traveler described the major Sogdian city, Samarkand **(SAM-uhr-kand)**, in what is today Uzbekistan, as "a great commercial entrepot, very fertile, abounding in trees and flowers, Its

inhabitants skilled craftsmen, smart and energetic."[10]

Various Central Asian pastoralists, unable to penetrate China's defenses or pressured by Chinese expansion, moved westward, including the Huns, who developed the most effective weapon of the day, a reflex bow. Attacks by horseback-riding Huns pushed various peoples into Europe. Some Huns followed into southern Russia and Hungary and in the fourth and fifth centuries CE Huns invaded the weakened Roman Empire (see Chapter 8). Central Asian women sometimes became warriors. A popular and well-remembered story that can be traced as far back as the sixth century BCE celebrates a band of women fighters, living in the remote desert of what is today Uzbekistan, who resisted aggression by men trying to conquer them. Some experts consider the story plausible and probably based on historical fact. The heroine of the legend was Gulaim, a fifteen year old girl who rejected marriage and instead recruited forty horse-riding girls and women for her struggle. In the end the women are all killed but they had avoided submission. In possible homage to Gulaim and her brave soldiers, today teenage girls in that part of Uzbekistan begin wearing a dark blue, woven hemp "girl soldier" costume when they turn fifteen, symbolizing a fighting spirit. And in 2018 a musical mixing video and songs, called "Forty Girls", was written and performed in Uzbekistan.

Diverse Central and West Asian peoples migrated through the mountain ranges into northwest India, introducing new cultural influences. Hellenistic (Greek-influenced) Bactria in Afghanistan

---

[9]Quoted in Lucille Schulberg, *Historic India* (New York: Time-Life Books, 1968), 80.
[10]Xuan Zang, quoted in David Christian, *A History of Russia, Central Asia, and Mongolia*, vol. 1 (Malden, MA: Blackwell, 1998), 254.

was a crossroads where Greek, Persian, and Indian cultures met and mixed; Bactrian invaders reintroduced Greek influence to the Indus Basin, inspiring a Greek- and Roman-influenced form of Buddhist painting and sculpture. Eventually they became absorbed into the broad fold of Indian society.

In 50 CE the **Kushans** (KOO-shans) from Central Asia conquered much of northwest India while constructing an empire also encompassing Afghanistan and many Silk Road cities. They promoted extensive trade between India and China, the Middle East, and the eastern Mediterranean and encouraged the mix of Indian and Greco-Roman culture, even using the Greek language for administration. Some Kushan leaders embraced Buddhism and spread the religion into Central Asia, from which it then diffused to China. The Kushan king Kanishka (ka-NISH-ka) (r. 78–144 CE) patronized artists, writers, poets, and musicians and tolerated all religions. Like invaders before them, the Kushans intermarried with local people, enhancing the hybrid character of northwestern India's culture. When Kushan rule ended in 250 CE, a patchwork of competing states emerged in north India.

5-2b South India and Sri Lanka

Northwestern India's political instability was duplicated elsewhere, with frequent warfare between competing states. Some southern states flourished from maritime trade linking China to the Persian Gulf, and south India gained renown as far west as Greece and Rome for products such as gold. Both south India and the large island of Sri Lanka saw considerable political and cultural development. North Indian culture, including Aryan myths, values, rituals, and divine kingship, appealed to south Indian rulers. South Indians also adopted the caste system, although less rigidly than northerners.

Yet Aryan ideas did not destroy southern regional traditions. For example, the Dravidian-speaking Tamils, who inhabit India's southeastern corner, developed a vigorous cultural tradition esteeming poetry. They were perhaps the world's finest steel makers by the sixth century BCE, famous for their swords. Their temple-filled mountain city of Madurai (made-uh-RYE) had several colleges and became a major center of Hinduism, literature, and education. A second century CE Tamil poem describes Madurai's religious function and devout people:

> The great and famous city of Madurai, Is like the lotus
> flower of God Vishnu. Its streets are the petals of the flower.
> God Shiva's temple is the center. The citizens are the plentiful
> pollen; The poor, the crowding beetles. And in Madurai, we
> wake to the chanting of the four Vedas, Sacred sculptures
> from the tongue of Brahma, born of the lotus flower.[11]

Kushans An Indo-European people from Central Asia who conquered much of northwest India and western parts of the Ganges Basin, constructing an empire that also encompassed Afghanistan and parts of Central Asia.

Just south of India, on the island of Sri Lanka (Ceylon), a very different society emerged. As Indian migrants intermarried with local people, they formed kingdoms and eventually produced the Sinhalese (sin-huh-LEEZ) society.

Sri Lanka became a trading hub between Southeast Asia and the Middle East. By 200 BCE they were importing cloves from eastern Indonesia, which was becoming a widely popular spice in Eurasia and East Africa. In the first century BCE the Sinhalese, to improve their rice growing, also began constructing one of world history's most intricate irrigation systems, building canals dozens of miles long and artificial lakes covering thousands of acres, a water control engineering feat requiring complex hydraulic technology and comparable to that of ancient China and Mesopotamia. During Ashoka's reign, Buddhist missionaries converted most Sri Lankans, and the Sinhalese came to view themselves as protectors of Buddhism. Hindu Tamils also crossed the narrow straits and settled the northern part of the island. For the next two millennia, Sri Lanka's Sinhalese Buddhist and Tamil Hindu societies coexisted, sometimes uneasily.

5-2c Indian Encounters with the Afro-Eurasian World

Since the third millennium BCE South Asian seafarers had expert knowledge of ship building and of the Indian Ocean, including currents, wind, tides, and weather conditions. Many ports developed along the coastline from early times. The post-Maurya era stands out for its unprecedented communication with other societies and connection to exchange networks, especially by sea. Indeed, India became a central hub in a vast maritime trade system, often termed the *Maritime Silk Road* by historians today, stretching from the Roman-dominated Mediterranean Basin through Egypt and the Red Sea to southern Asia, Southeast Asia, and southern China. Even Mediterranean merchants visited India. India dispatched spices, cloth, silks, ivory, sandalwood, furniture, and art works to the Roman Empire for gold coins, silver, copper, tin, lead, and wine. The Roman writer Pliny (PLIN-ee) claimed that importing Indian goods cost the Roman treasury dearly. Around 80 CE a Greek handbook for merchants interested in trade with India described sailing routes and India's products and culture. The author recommended a south Indian port offering a large quantity of spices like cinnamon and black pepper as well as multicolored textiles, tin, copper, gems, diamonds, sapphires, fine-quality pearls, ivory, and Chinese silk. Various Indian words were incorporated into the Greek language, especially for spices such as ginger and foods like rice. By two thousand years ago a vigorous trade with Southeast Asia had also developed, led by Tamil merchants whose chief interest was in the region's gold. South Asians exported pottery, beads, textiles, glass, pearls, gems, ivory, dyes, metals, plants, forest products, and even horses eastward. In exchange, spices, gold, aromatic woods, cloves, and tin were shipped to India from Southeast Asia. But violent storms and pirates often made it a dangerous round-trip voyage. China–India trade continued along the overland Silk Road through Central Asia. Expanding foreign and domestic trade brought much wealth to India's commercial and artisan castes, and gold coins fostered banking and financial houses. But this commercial dynamism mostly occurred in cities. Foreign products did not often reach villages, where the bartering of services between farmers, craftsmen, and servants defined social and economic relations.

Indian philosophy and religious ideas reached foreign audiences. Some Indian philosophers may have visited

[11]From McNaughton, *Light from East*, 377.

western Asia, where their ideas may have influenced some religious movements. The Buddhist idea of monasticism also expanded from India to western Asia, perhaps inspiring the rise of Christian monasticism. Buddhist ideas and art also spread into Central Asia's Silk Road cities. Buddhist converts, such as the Chinese monk Faxian (fah-shee-en) (Fa-hsien), ventured to India over the Silk Road and crossed dangerous mountains to study Buddhism, visit the sites of Buddha's life, and bring back Buddhist texts to China. Thus, like Hellenistic Greek culture throughout the eastern Mediterranean and western Asia, Indian cultural influence flowed out to the world.

5-2d Religious Changes in South Asia

During the post-Mauryan centuries in India, Buddhism divided and declined, Hinduism resurged, and both Christianity and Judaism arrived. Increasingly two major schools with competing visions split Buddhism in the two centuries preceding the Common Era. Some reformers criticized the religion as being remote from the real world, atheistic in its rejection of a god, excessively individualistic, requiring too much self-discipline, and denying any afterlife. During the Kushan domination of northern India, the division into two schools, the mainstream Theravada (TEAR-eh-vah-duh) and the reformist Mahayana (MAH-HAH-YAH-nah), became complete.

Theravada ("Teachings of the Elders") remained closer to Buddha's original vision and clearly descended from Ashoka's Buddhism. To its followers the Buddha was not a god but rather a human teacher. Since the ever-changing universe had no supreme being or gods, people could only take refuge in the wise and compassionate Buddha, his teachings, and the community of monks who maintained them. Each believer was responsible for acquiring merit through devotion, meditation, and good works, such as feeding monks or supporting a temple. The only sure way to end rebirth and reach nirvana was to become a monk and abide by strict monastic rules, and many men did so for at least a few years.

The other school, **Mahayana** ("the Greater Vehicle" to salvation), was a more popularized and less demanding form of belief and practice. Mahayana developed many sects, most considering the Buddha a god. Mahayana followers found comfort in devotion to a loving deity (Buddha) and stressed charity and good works as paths toward salvation. A central concept is the **bodhisattva** (boe-dih-SUT-vuh) ("one who has the essence of Buddhahood"), a loving and compassionate "saint" who has died but has postponed his or her own attainment of nirvana to help others find salvation. In China, Mahayanists converted nirvana into an appealing heaven, with the wicked assigned to a terrifying

hell. Perhaps Mahayana ideas about achieving salvation with the help of a saint contributed to Hebrew concepts of a messiah, or the reverse. Some historians think that Persian Zoroastrianism may have influenced both Mahayana Buddhism and Christianity.

Although several Buddhist monastic orders and some believers remained, Indian Buddhism gradually assimilated into Hinduism. Perhaps Buddhism was too pessimistic, portraying life as suffering in contrast to many life-affirming Hindu gods. But Buddhism flourished abroad by providing spiritual support in times of rapid political change or instability. It spread along the trade routes, accommodating itself to local traditions and faiths. The Mahayana school eventually became dominant in Central Asia, including Tibet and Mongolia, from where it filtered into China, Korea, Vietnam, and Japan. The Theravada school became entrenched in Sri Lanka and eventually expanded into mainland Southeast Asia (see Map 5.2).

New religions also arrived in India, although our knowledge of the migrations is incomplete and based partly on each group's oral traditions. According to local legends, around 52 CE the Christian apostle Saint Thomas established Christian churches and attracted followers along southwestern India's Malabar (MAL-uh-bahr) coast. Such a trip along active maritime trade routes was certainly possible. Large Christian communities still flourish in the Malabar state of Kerala (KER-uh-luh), especially in the ancient coastal ports. Jewish settlers also came to India's west coast, establishing permanent communities in Kerala and to the north at Bombay. Local Jewish tradition in Kerala claims the first Jews arrived in 562 BCE from Judea with trading missions from King Solomon. Others may have come from Syria at the same time as St. Thomas and the Christians. Still later other Jews migrated to India. Generally the Jews faced little prejudice in a larger society composed of many religious groups, and were accepted in the local communities. In the later twentieth century CE, many Indian Jews emigrated to the new Jewish state of Israel.

Theravada ("Teachings of the Elders") One of the two main branches of Buddhism, the other being Mahayana, that arose just before the Common Era. Theravada remained closer to the Buddha's original vision.

Mahayana ("the Greater Vehicle" to salvation) One of the two main branches of Buddhism; a more popularized form of Buddhist belief and practice than Theravada. Mahayana Buddhism tended to make Buddha into a god and also developed the notion of the bodhisattva.

bodhisattva ("one who has the essence of Buddhahood") A loving and ever compassionate "saint" who has postponed his or her own attainment of nirvana to help others find salvation through liberation from birth and rebirth.

KEY POINTS

▶ Various peoples, among them the Kushans from Central Asia, invaded northwest India and adopted aspects of Indian culture.

▶ Northern Indian culture spread to the south, and Buddhism was adopted in Sri Lanka.

▶ During the post-Mauryan era, there was great demand for Indian goods among traders from western Asia and

the Mediterranean, and trade with Southeast Asia flourished.

▶ Buddhism declined in popularity in India as Hinduism adopted many of its ideas, but it spread to Central Asia, China, and Southeast Asia, where it flourished.

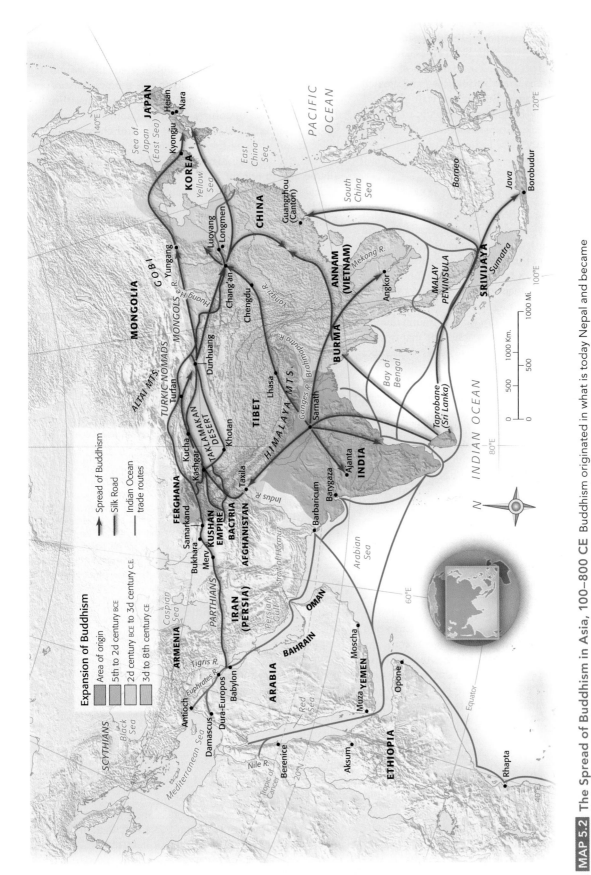

MAP 5.2 **The Spread of Buddhism in Asia, 100–800 CE** Buddhism originated in what is today Nepal and became a major religion in India during the classical period. From India it spread into Central Asia, China, Korea, Japan, and Southeast Asia as far east as Java.

From this map can you explain why in classical times Buddhism became hugely popular in eastern, southern, and Central Asia but never spread into Africa or western Eurasia?

5-3 The Gupta Age in India

SOCIETIES ⇄ TRANSITIONS

Q What were the main achievements of the Gupta era?

In the fourth century CE the great Gupta **(GOOP-tuh)** Empire brought political unity to India once again. The Gupta era (320–550 CE) was a brilliant period that saw the assimilation of both immigrants and foreign cultural influences, reshaping an ancient society. Today Indians consider the Gupta their golden age, with its prosperity, tolerant government, and major contributions in science, medicine, mathematics, and literature. In comparison with the declining Roman Empire and turbulent post-Han China, Gupta India was perhaps the world's most dynamic society, visited by travelers and pilgrims from all over Asia.

CONNECTION to TODAY

What do you think are the most valuable Gupta mathematical and scientific achievements for the world today and in your own lives?

5-3a Government and Economy

The Gupta family and their allies conquered most of north India. Like the Mauryan Empire, the Gupta Empire was decentralized, with local rulers acknowledging Gupta overlordship. The Gupta zenith came under King Chandra Gupta II (r. 375–414), one of the most revered figures in Indian history, praised as enlightened, bold, and resourceful. Internal and external trade, the widespread use of gold and silver coins, and highly productive agriculture fostered prosperity. India increasingly became the world's textile center, producing fabrics like linen, wool, and cotton; it also produced pepper and spices for export to the Middle East, Europe, China, and Indonesia. Although the Gupta government favored merchants and farmers, the rulers, like the Mauryas, operated all metal and salt mines as well as various industrial enterprises such as arms factories and textile mills.

Gupta Indians generally enjoyed domestic peace, personal freedom, and tolerance for minority views. One fifth-century Chinese Buddhist pilgrim, Faxian, was impressed by the prosperity, state services, and humane justice system: "The people are very well off. The king governs without corporal punishment. Criminals are fined according to circumstances, lightly or heavily. Even in cases of repeated rebellion, they only cut off the right hand. The people kill no living thing."[12] However, tolerance did not extend to untouchables, who still occupied a degraded status. The Gupta rulers promoted a Hindu revival but permitted no official discrimination against Buddhists or Jains, even helping, with donations from kings in foreign lands, to build a great Buddhist monastery and the world's first university at Nalanda **(na-LAN-da)** in what is today the state of Bihar. At Nalanda more than ten thousand students and two thousand teachers from all over Asia explored Buddhist subjects as well as, among other subjects, logic, medicine, Sanskrit grammar, and Hindu philosophy. The main residential seat of learning in South Asia until it was destroyed by Turkish invaders in 1193 CE, the campus contained temples, monasteries, classrooms, meditation halls, dormitories, lakes, and gardens. In 2014 the Indian government and international donors established a modern version of Nalanda University as an international graduate school near the ruins of the old campus.

The Gupta capital city, Patna, boasted hospitals providing free care to the poor and handicapped. A great university attracted ten thousand students, many from other Asian societies. One observer reported that he saw in Patna "the workshops thriving along the royal road, the river furrowed by boats, and maidens flirting with youths in the parks on the outskirts of town."[13]

5-3b Gupta Society

Indian social patterns were never stagnant. As male authority became more dominant over time, women's status gradually declined throughout northern India. By Mauryan times women enjoyed fewer opportunities to pursue intellectual or religious leadership. The Mahabharata warned men not to put "confidence in a woman or a coward, a lazybones, a violent man, a self-promoter, a thief, much less an atheist."[14] However, patriarchy remained weaker in south India. Matrilineal kinship systems remain common even today in the southwestern state of Kerala, and southern women often enjoyed more freedom than northern women. Hinduism in south India placed more emphasis than the north on goddess worship, perhaps giving women higher status. The *Kama Sutra*, a detailed sexual handbook written in the third century CE, offered ideas about gender that seem almost modern, including a liberal approach to sexual freedom and a somewhat understanding approach to homosexuality.

However, in general the Gupta age was not golden for women. Brahmans imposed their rigid views on gender relations. The Code of Manu tied women to the patriarchal family, urging that "in childhood a female must be subject to her father, in youth to her husband, and when her lord is dead, to her sons; a woman must never be independent."[15] The code restricted women's property rights and recommended early marriage to preserve chastity. Girls commonly married well before puberty, after negotiations between the senior men of the two families involved. Widows could no longer remarry, and the ancient custom of sati **(suh-TEE)**, of wives joining their late husbands on the funeral pyre, became more widespread. Many Indian writers denounced it, since families often forced an unwilling wife to agree.

5-3c Gupta Science, Mathematics, and Culture

People today owe much to the Guptas, under whose rule intellectual and cultural pursuits flourished. Gupta India became the late classical world's leading producer of scientific knowledge, planting some of the roots of modern science and mathematics.

---

[12]Quoted in John Keay, *India: A History* (New York: Atlantic Monthly Press, 2000), 145.
[13]Kalidasa, quoted in Auboyer, *Daily Life*, 117.
[14]Quoted in Stephanie W. Jamison, *Sacrificed Wife/Sacrificer's Wife: Women, Ritual, and Hospitality in Ancient India* (New York: Oxford University Press, 1996), 13.
[15]Quoted in Barbara N. Ramusack, "Women in South and Southeast Asia," in *Women in Asia: Restoring Women to History* (Bloomington: Indiana University Press, 1999), 9.

The Guptas boasted of India's "nine gems," a group of knowledge producers that included one of the world's major astronomers, mathematicians, and physicists, Aryabhata (**AR-ya-BAH-ta**) (ca. 476–550), who taught that Earth was round, rotated on its own axis, and revolved around the sun as one of a family of planets. He also correctly analyzed lunar eclipses, calculated the moon's diameter and Earth's circumference, and precisely determined the solar year at 365.36 days. In verse, Aryabhata discussed physics, including Earth's rotation and the nature of gravity. Many of these insights did not spread outside India until centuries later.

Gupta innovations in mathematics compare to the invention in western Asia of the wheel and alphabet: all pathbreaking and revolutionary in their consequences. Indians had been exploring mathematical knowledge as early as 1200 BCE, eventually creating the number system we use today. Indians probably chose 10 as a base number because it corresponded to the number of fingers. Now individual numbers were needed only for 0 through 9. By contrast, for the ancient Greeks each 8 in 888 was different. And for the Romans, 888 was written as DCCCLXXXVIII, complicating multiplication and division. The simple and logical Indian numbering system eventually reached the Middle East and later Europe, thanks to the Arabs (and hence known as "Arabic numerals"). By Gupta times Indians added to their rich legacy by introducing the concepts of zero and the decimal system while making seminal innovations to the study of trigonometry, algebra, arithmetic, and negative numbers. The great Aryabhata analyzed quadratic equations and the value of pi. Only in the fifteenth century, a thousand years after Gupta times, did European scientists and mathematicians adopt "Arabic" numerals, opening the door to modern science

and mathematics. Today South Asians account for a substantial number of world renowned mathematicians and scientists.

Remarkably creative in industrial chemistry, Gupta Indians made soap and cement, produced the world's finest tempered steel, and transformed sugar-cane juice into granulated crystals for easy storing or shipping. Europeans later adopted India's fine dyes and fabrics; *cotton*, *calico*, and *cashmere* are all Indian words. Indians also enjoyed a long tradition of medicine. Yoga practitioners promoted mental and spiritual discipline, studying posture, breath control, and pulse regulation, and Gupta physicians discovered the spinal cord's function, sketched out the nervous system structure, and expanded knowledge of physiology and herbal medicines. Gupta India had the world's best medical system, drugs, and therapeutic methods. Doctors sterilized wounds, did Caesarian deliveries, developed plastic surgery, and vaccinated patients against smallpox.

Gupta literature and performing arts flourished. Writing mostly in Sanskrit, writers produced religious works, poetry, and prose. The most popular writer, Kalidasa (**kahl-i-DACE-uh**) (ca. 400–455), rendered ancient legends and popular tales into drama and lyrics. Kalidasa's famous poem, "The Cloud Messengers," uses a passing cloud surveying the panoramic landscape to capture the heartache of lovers separated by a vast distance: "I see your body in the sinuous creeper, your gaze in the startled eyes of deer, your cheek in the moon, your hair in the plumage of peacocks, and in the tiny ripples of the river I see your sidelong glances."[16] Theater, music, and dance established the basis for the Indian performing arts of today. Imported from western Asia, instruments such as the lute, or vina (**VEE-nuh**), and zither, or sitar (**si-TAHR**), became popular. Improvisational instrumental

akg-images/Jean-Louis Nou

IMAGE 5.5 **Worship of Buddhist Relics** In the first century CE Buddhists erected a pillar containing this frieze of a stupa housing relics of the Buddha. The stupa is surrounded by throngs of worshippers and pilgrims making music and bringing offerings to honor the Buddha.

Q What does this photo tell us about reverence for the Buddha but also about the way the worshippers are portrayed?

[16]Quoted in A. L. Basham, *The Wonder That Was India: A Survey of the History and Culture of the Indian Sub-continent Before the Coming of the Muslims*, 3rd. rev. ed. (New Delhi: Rupa and Company, 1967), 420.

pieces known as ragas **(RAHG-uhz)** inspired religious and philosophical contemplation. Gupta artists also produced religious sculptures and paintings, especially on cave or temple walls.

5-3d Decline of the Guptas

Several factors may have hastened Gupta's decline and fall. Some studies suggest that massive flooding in the mid-sixteenth century, perhaps precipitated by climate change or, as some think, earthquakes that dammed several rivers, may have buried some cities and Buddhist monasteries under heavy silt and brought on a social and economic crisis. Central Asian invaders finally ended Gupta rule. In the fifth century CE Huns conquered part of northwestern India. Gupta power held them off, but the effort depleted the treasury, and other Central Asians followed the

Huns into north India. The demise of the Gupta undermined a long-flourishing Buddhism and relegated it to a marginal role in Indian life, especially in the north. The Chinese Buddhist traveler Xuanzang reported in 630 CE that the "Buddhist establishments, of which there were some hundreds, were with the exception of three or four, dilapidated and deserted, and the brethren very few."[17] When the Guptas collapsed, the varied Hindu states could not unite, and India entered a period of fragmentation, political instability, and frequent warfare that persisted for several centuries and left Indians open to conquest by Muslim peoples.

Yet India remained part of the wider world. Seafarers from the southeastern coast made piratical raids deep into Southeast Asia, while the maritime trade linking southern India with Southeast Asia and China intensified dramatically. Cargo-laden Indian fleets sailed with the monsoon winds far to the east.

KEY POINTS

▶ Under the decentralized Gupta Empire, based in northern India, the government attained prosperity while pursuing religious tolerance.

▶ During the Gupta era, science, mathematics, literature, and the arts all thrived.

▶ The Guptas formulated the numerals we use today and the concept of zero, which made the decimal system

possible and made mathematical computation infinitely more powerful.

▶ The Gupta Empire was greatly weakened by Hun invasion, and soon thereafter it collapsed and other Central Asian groups invaded India.

5-4 The Development of Southeast Asian Societies

NETWORKS SOCIETIES

Q How did Southeast Asians blend indigenous and foreign influences to create unique societies?

In the tropical lands east of India and south of China, many societies borrowed political, religious, and cultural ideas from the two neighboring regions, although the impacts of these ideas varied greatly and are much debated by historians. Southeast Asian states were products of indigenous as well as outside forces. Most of the early Southeast Asian societies were centered on coastal plains and in river valleys, where they flourished from both productive agriculture and extensive foreign trade and established enduring patterns in government, religion, and economics. Furthermore, migration of people into, out of, and around Southeast Asia was common.

CONNECTION to TODAY

How do you think Vietnam's long history of resistance to foreign invasion and rule might help us understand Vietnam's experiences in the modern world?

5-4a Austronesian Seafaring, Trade, and Migrations

Seafaring and maritime trade were major forces in the development of some Southeast Asian societies and were critical to the formation and operation of the Maritime Silk Road. One group of Austronesians **(AW-stroh-NEE-zhuhns)**, the Malays **(muh-LAYZ)**, enjoyed a strategic position for maritime commerce and cultural mixing. The Straits of Melaka **(muh-LAK-uh)**, between Sumatra **(soo-MAH-tra)** and Malaya

(muh-LAY-a), was a crossroads through which peoples, cultures, and trade passed, some taking root. The Straits remain crucial to world commerce today. These lands also provided gold, tin, spices, and forest products, some traded as far west as Rome. The prevailing climatic patterns in the South China Sea and Indian Ocean allowed ships sailing southwest and southeast to meet in the straits, where their goods could be exchanged.

Early in the Common Era small Malay trading states in the Malay Peninsula and Sumatra prospered, like the Phoenicians and Greeks, from maritime trade to distant shores. In the third century BCE, Malay ships visited China using a sail that, some historians think, may have inspired the revolutionary four-sided lateen **(luh-TEEN)** sail used later by Polynesians, Arabs, Greeks, and Romans, allowing ships to sail directly into the wind. Malays opened the maritime trade between China and India by carrying cinnamon grown on the China coast across the Indian Ocean to India and Sri Lanka. Some Austronesian sailors returned with Indian ideas about government and religion. Indonesians also introduced Southeast Asian foods (especially bananas and rice), outrigger canoes, and musical instruments (including the xylophone) to East Africa.

---

[17]Quoted in Dev Raj, "Deluge Drowned Mighty Guptas: Study," *Telegraphindia*, February 25, 2019.

Between the fourth and sixth centuries CE, instability in Central Asia disrupted the overland Silk Road, making the Indian Ocean connection linking China, India, and the Middle East more crucial. While this change benefited some Southeast Asians, the voyages held many dangers. The Chinese Buddhist pilgrim Faxian, sailing from Sri Lanka to Sumatra in 414 CE, reported that he "set sail on a large merchant ship which carried about two hundred passengers. A small boat trailed behind, for use in case the large vessel should be wrecked, as sailing on this sea was most hazardous. [We] were caught up in a typhoon [which] lasted for thirteen days. That sea is [also] infested with pirates."[18]

Austronesian seafaring also led to migration. Beginning in ancient times, other Austronesians moved from Southeast Asia into the western Pacific. Their descendants, the Polynesians (pahl-uh-NEE-zhuhns) and Micronesians (my-kruh-NEE-zhuhns), settled the central and eastern Pacific islands (see Chapter 9). The Marianas (MAR-ee-AN-uhz), including the islands of Guam and Saipan, may have been settled directly by Austronesians sailing east from the Philippines and possibly Taiwan between 1500 and 1000 BCE. Around the end of the classical age small numbers of Indonesians, mostly from southern Borneo, migrated the other way, across the Indian Ocean to settle on the large island of Madagascar (mad-uh-GAS-kuhr), off Africa's southeast coast. Eventually they mixed with African migrants to form the Malagasy people, who today comprise the majority of the island's population and speak an Austronesian language. The Malagasy also cultivate Southeast Asian crops like rice, bananas, yams, and taro and use ironworking techniques, outrigger canoes, and musical instruments originating in Indonesia. As a result of these movements, Austronesian-speaking societies stretched thousands of miles from Madagascar eastward through Indonesia, Malaysia, and the Philippines to Hawaii and Easter Island in eastern Polynesia.

5-4b Indianization and Early Mainland States

Various states developed on the Southeast Asian mainland although historians still debate the exact nature of these states during the Classical Era. The most populous societies emerged along the fertile coastal plains or in the great river valleys like the Mekong and Red, where irrigated rice cultivation was possible, providing a highly productive and labor-intensive economic mainstay that was sustainable for generations. By promoting cooperation, this economy fostered centralized kingdoms such as

Indianization The process by which Indian ideas spread into and influenced many Southeast Asian societies; a mixing of Indian with indigenous ideas.

IMAGE 5.6 **Relief of Indonesian Ship** The Indonesians were skilled mariners. This rock carving, from a Buddhist temple in central Java, depicts a sailing vessel of the type commonly used by Indonesian traders in the Indian Ocean and South China Sea in this era. These ships also carried Indonesian colonists to East Africa and Madagascar.

Q What can we learn about Indonesian ships from this relief?

Van Lang in northern Vietnam, which was ruled through a landed aristocracy who controlled rice-growing estates worked by peasants. By 500 BCE a few small bronze- and iron-using states emerged, and during the third century BCE the earliest cities with monumental architecture appeared. At Co Loa, near modern Hanoi, King An Duong built a huge citadel surrounded by a wall five miles long and ten yards wide. Urban societies also emerged among peoples such as the Khmers (kuh-MEERZ) (Cambodians).

Influences from China and India also generated change. Han China conquered northern Vietnam, imposing a colonial rule that endured for a millennium (111 BCE–939 CE) and spreading many Chinese cultural patterns. Chinese traders visited many Southeast Asian societies over the centuries. Elsewhere Indian influence fostered a very different society. Around two millennia ago, Indian traders and brahman priests began traveling the oceanic trade routes. They brought with them Indian concepts of religion, government, and the arts and settled in some states, marrying into and becoming advisors to influential families. Furthermore, Southeast Asian merchants and sailors visiting India returned with Indian ideas.

Indianization, a peaceful mixing of Indian with indigenous ideas, influenced many Southeast Asian societies about the same time as classical Greco-Roman culture spread around the Mediterranean. Some historians today question the term *Indianization*, introduced by early twentieth-century European and Indian scholars of Southeast Asia, noting that it is overly broad and that the process was collaborative rather than one way. Whatever the case, for a millennium, Southeast Asian peoples such as the Khmers in the Mekong Basin, the Chams along Vietnam's central coast, and the Javanese (JAH-vuh-NEEZ) on the fertile island of Java remained connected to India, adapting one of several

[18]From Harry J. Benda and John A. Larkin, eds., *The World of Southeast Asia: Selected Historical Readings* (New York: Harper and Row, 1967), 3–4.

Kimberley Coole/Getty Images

Indian writing systems to local but very different spoken languages. Mahayana Buddhism and Hinduism became popular, especially among the upper classes, fusing with indigenous animisms that emphasized communicating with spiritual forces. Many Southeast Asians blended outside and local religions rather than following one exclusively. In politics, Southeast Asian rulers became powerful kings claiming to possess supernatural powers and religious sanction, which made their positions difficult to challenge.

However, although borrowing helped shape Southeast Asians, they also took outside ideas that they wanted and adapted them to their own cultures, creating a distinctive synthesis. In this they followed a similar pattern as the Japanese and western Europeans. For example, the Hindu and Buddhist architecture and temples of Burma (Myanmar), Cambodia, or Java differed substantially from the South Asian models as well as from each other. Southeast Asians adopted some Indian literature, such as the Ramayana, but changed parts of the epic to reflect local customs, cultures, and environments. Today their revised versions are still performed in dance and puppet theaters and stories from them taught in many Thai and Indonesian schools.

5-4c Funan, Zhenla, and Champa

Over time productive agriculture, maritime commerce, and Indianization fostered stronger mainland states. Between 75 and 550 CE Funan (**FOO-nan**), probably populated by Khmer, Austronesians, or both peoples, flourished in the fertile Mekong Delta of southern Vietnam. Historians disagree as to whether Funan was a large and coherent state, a loosely linked set of cities, or perhaps just an important seaport controlling a small hinterland. Whatever the case, Funan's influence may have stretched into what is today Cambodia and southern Thailand. Funan traded with China, valued literacy, built complex irrigation systems to turn swamps into productive agricultural land, and apparently had some authority over Cambodia and southern Thailand (see Map 5.3). A Chinese envoy in the third century reported that the Funan king "gave three or four audiences [each day]. Foreigners and subjects offered him presents of bananas, sugar cane, turtles, and birds. . . . The king, when he travels rides an elephant."[19] Trade goods from as far away as Rome, Arabia, Central Asia, and perhaps East Africa have been found in Funan's ruins, and merchants from various countries (including India and China) lived in the major port city. A Khmer state, Zhenla, in the middle Mekong Basin, became prominent in the fifth century when Funan declined.

Meanwhile, the coastal, Austronesian-speaking Cham people of central Vietnam formed several Indianized states known collectively as Champa (**CHAM-pa**), which tried to control the coastal commerce between China and Southeast Asia. The strongly Hindu Chams gained renown as sailors, merchants, and sometimes pirates, frequently fighting the Vietnamese pushing southward. The Vietnamese finally conquered much of Champa in 1471.

5-4d Vietnam and Chinese Colonization

The long history of the Vietnamese with China, including a millennium of Chinese colonization and of sporadic conflict since then, for over two thousand years has given them a wariness

MAP 5.3 **Funan and Its Neighbors** The first large mainland Southeast Asian states emerged during the classical period. The major states included Vietnam, which became a Chinese colony in the second century BCE, Funan, Zhenla, and Champa.

Q Why do you think that the most developed and populous societies and states in classical Southeast Asia were concentrated on the mainland south of China and east of India?

toward their large and powerful northern neighbor. China's conquest and annexation of Vietnam in 111 BCE ended the kingdom's independence. The Chinese policy was to assimilate the Vietnamese and implant Chinese values, customs, and institutions, with the result that China's patriarchal family system, written language, and political ideas sank deep roots. At the same time, most Vietnamese adopted Chinese philosophies and religions like Confucianism, Daoism, and Mahayana Buddhism but mixed them with earlier ancestor and spirit worship.

While the Vietnamese adopted many Chinese patterns, they resisted cultural assimilation and sustained a hatred of Chinese rule. The survival of Vietnamese identity, language, and many customs during a millennium of colonialism constituted an unparalleled display of national determination. Many revolts, some led by women such as the Trung Sisters, punctuated the colonial period, all of them well remembered today as symbols of patriotism (see Meet the People: The Trung Sisters, Vietnamese Rebels). Before Chinese colonization ancient Vietnam had a matriarchal tradition, including worship of mother goddesses (which many still do today), and this may have helped produce feisty and dedicated female rebels. But Chinese officials harshly

---

[19]Quoted in Lawrence Palmer Briggs, *The Ancient Khmer Empire* (Philadelphia: American Philosophical Society, 1951), 22, 29.

The Trung Sisters, Vietnamese Rebels

Some of the major anti-Chinese rebellions in Vietnam were led by women such as the Trung Sisters in 39 CE. Even after two thousand years, the Vietnamese honor the two sisters and their martyrdom with annual ceremonies at cult shrines dedicated to their memory. Their revolt was prompted by Chinese attempts to raise taxes and consolidate their control over the indigenous landed aristocracy. However, our knowledge of the two sisters is limited. Some historians consider them semi-mythical rather than flesh and blood. The Trung Sisters became enshrined in images of brave and beautiful sword-bearing women mounted on elephants, leading their troops against the Chinese.

The sisters are believed to have been daughters of a prominent landowning family from near Hanoi. The older sister, Trung Trac, had married a member of another aristocratic family. When her husband protested an

Vietnam: Traditional folk painting from Dong Ho village: The Trung Sisters (Hai Ba Trung) on war elephants pursuing fleeing Chinese/PICTURES FRoM HISToRY/Bridgeman Images

IMAGE 5.7 The Trung Sisters This painting by a Vietnamese artist shows the Trung Sisters riding into battle on war elephants against the Chinese.

Q What does this illustration tell us about classical Vietnamese warfare or, since it was painted centuries later, the artist's perception of it?

increase in taxes, he was apparently executed. The spirited sisters then sparked a rebellion that rapidly spread throughout the country and involved both the elite and the peasantry. Before commencing the uprising Trung Trac reportedly began a tradition of generals writing poetry to galvanize their troops, pledging in her poem to wash away the enemy and avenge the injustices against her husband. With local Chinese officials in retreat, her followers declared Trung Trac queen of a newly independent country. The sisters abolished taxes, but, as traditionalists, they also sought to restore the pre-Chinese order dominated by landed aristocrats and protect local autonomy. Despite their aristocratic agenda, the common people joined the revolt because of their hostility to the authoritarian rule of the Chinese governors.

Han dynasty rulers, unwilling to see this valuable part of their empire secede, dispatched their most able general and his army to destroy the rebellion. As the fighting and repression grew, most of the sisters' upper-class supporters abandoned their cause. Eventually their remaining forces were defeated in 41 CE, and the sisters either committed suicide or were captured and executed. China now intensified its direct control of Vietnam and launched a more deliberate assimilation policy to integrate Vietnam politically into China proper.

Although their revolt failed, the Trung Sisters established a model for later rebels, some of them also women. Another famous anticolonial leader, the nineteen-year-old Lady Trieu in the third century CE, demonstrated a similar commitment.

When advised to marry rather than fight, she replied: "I want to ride the storm, tread the dangerous waves, win back the fatherland and destroy the yoke of slavery. I don't want to bow down my head working as a simple housewife." The Lady Trieu seems an almost modern figure in her patriotic and social defiance. She also apparently cut a grand figure on the field, carrying two swords and wearing bright yellow robes while she rode a war elephant. But in defeat, like the Trung Sisters she committed suicide rather than surrender. In the nineteenth and twentieth centuries, Vietnamese women inspired by the Trung Sisters and Lady Trieu took up arms alongside men to fight oppressive governments and invading forces, including the French and later Americans. Hence, the legacy of the Trung Sisters and other rebels from many centuries ago lives on in Vietnam today, where they are celebrated in public ceremonies and stone memorials, a link of remembrance between Vietnamese people today and their ancestors two millennia ago.

Reflection Questions

1. What sparked the rebellion led by the Trung Sisters?
2. What does the experience of the Trung Sisters tell us about Vietnamese society under Chinese rule and the role of women in that society?
3. Can you think of any other women like the Trung Sisters in world history or today who led or helped to lead rebellions and protests against unpopular governments?

Note: Quotation is from Thomas Hodgkin, *Vietnam: The Revolutionary Path* (New York: St. Martin's, 1981), 22.

retaliated against any opposition, one writing that "At every stream, cave, marketplace, everywhere there is stubbornness. Repression is necessary."[20] A long history of resistance to the Chinese, a sense of nationhood, and a desire for independence also helped the Vietnamese resist assimilation. Chinese and later foreign conquerors such as the French in the modern era found that they had to conquer each village, one by one. This history of resistance to foreign invaders meant frequent warfare. A Vietnamese Buddhist poet described the results: "War, no end to it, people scattered in all directions. How can a man keep his mind off it? The winds dark, the rains violent year after year, laying waste the land, over and over."[21] The Vietnamese eventually regained independence from China in the tenth century.

5-4e Economies, Societies, and Cultures

Despite the great differences between Southeast Asian societies, there were many commonalities. Most of the larger states had multiethnic populations, including foreign merchants. Chinese envoys described Funan's walled cities, palaces, and people who ate with silver utensils; paid their taxes with gold, silver, perfumes, and pearls; had many books and maintained well-kept archives; and used an Indian writing system. But although commerce was common, most Southeast Asians were farmers and fishermen living in self-sufficient villages held together by kinship and cooperation for mutual survival.

Many Southeast Asian family systems contrasted with those in China or India. While the Vietnamese followed a patriarchal pattern like China, others developed flexible systems incorporating both paternal and maternal kin. The Chams were matrilineal, and both men and women could have more than one spouse. In Southeast Asia women generally enjoyed a higher status and played a more active public role than they did in China, India, the Middle East, and Europe, dominating most village markets. The Southeast Asian pattern of blending religions and cultures, along with extensive trade, made Southeast Asian societies distinctive.

KEY POINTS

▶ The lands bordering the Straits of Melaka were rich in natural resources, and their peoples engaged in wide-ranging maritime trade.

▶ Austronesians settled over a wide area, from Madagascar, off the coast of Africa, to the Pacific islands of Polynesia.

▶ Southeast Asians were influenced by both Chinese and Indian culture, but they retained distinct aspects of their native cultures.

▶ Though different from each other, Southeast Asian societies tended to be multiethnic and able to blend diverse elements into cultural unity.

---

[20]Quoted in Keith Taylor, "The Rise of Dai Viet and the Establishment of Thanglong," in *Explorations in Early Southeast Asian History: The Origins of Southeast Asian Statecraft*, ed. Kenneth R. Hall and John K. Whitmore (Ann Arbor: University of Michigan Center for South and Southeast Asian Studies, 1976), 153.
[21]From Nguyen Ngoc Bich, ed., *A Thousand Years of Vietnamese Poetry* (New York: Knopf, 1975), 89.

Chapter Summary

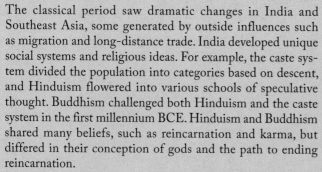

The classical period saw dramatic changes in India and Southeast Asia, some generated by outside influences such as migration and long-distance trade. India developed unique social systems and religious ideas. For example, the caste system divided the population into categories based on descent, and Hinduism flowered into various schools of speculative thought. Buddhism challenged both Hinduism and the caste system in the first millennium BCE. Hinduism and Buddhism shared many beliefs, such as reincarnation and karma, but differed in their conception of gods and the path to ending reincarnation.

India's political, economic, and intellectual life also changed. The Mauryan Empire united India, and under Ashoka the empire reflected humane and peaceful Buddhist values. The classical period also saw the forging of deeper cultural and trade connections between India and other regions, and many peoples migrated into the country from Central Asia. Buddhism spread into both Central and Southeast Asia, becoming a major world religion. During the Gupta golden age, Indians achieved new knowledge in science and mathematics that later influenced the Middle East and Europe.

The states that emerged in Southeast Asia were based on maritime trade, rice agriculture, and the blending of local and foreign influences. The Austronesian sailors fostered trade networks over vast distances, and kingdoms arose in Cambodia and Vietnam. Indian religious, political, and cultural ideas had a great impact in many parts of the region, and China's conquest of Vietnam spread Chinese influence.

Key Terms

Brahman 109	nirvana 112	Mahayana 117
Vedanta 110	monasticism 112	bodhisattva 117
Jainism 111	Kushans 116	Indianization 122
Buddhism 111	Theravada 117	

Eurasian Connections and New Traditions in East Asia, 600 BCE–600 CE

> *After the Han [dynasty] had sent its envoys to open up communications with the state of Da Xia [in today's Afghanistan], all the barbarians of the distant west craned their necks to the east and longed to catch a glimpse of China.*
>
> —Chinese diplomat Zhang Qian, reported by historian Sima Qian, ca. 100 BCE[1]

Mondadori Portfolio/Mondadori Portfolio Premium/Getty Images

IMAGE 6.1 **Fresco from Mogao Caves** The Mogao Caves, situated along the Silk Road in western China, contain many frescoes reflecting Silk Road life and the spread of Buddhism into the region. This fresco, painted in the third century CE, shows the Buddha meditating, flanked by two bodhisattvas holding lotus flowers and other goods.

Q. What does the fresco suggest about the artists' conception of the Buddha and bodhisattvas?

[1]*Records of the Historian: Chapters from the Shih Chi of Ssu-ma Ch'ien*, translated by Burton Watson (New York: Columbia University Press, 1969), 274.

In 138 BCE the Chinese emperor, Wu Di (**woo tee**), sought contact with a Central Asian group, the Yuezhi (**yueh-chih**), to forge an alliance against their mutual enemy, the Xiongnu (**SHE-OONG-noo**), Central Asians threatening China. An imperial court attendant, Zhang Qian (**jahng chee-YEN**), volunteered to undertake the dangerous diplomatic mission. A strong man known for his generosity and ability to make friends with non-Chinese, Zhang commenced the journey west with only a small escort. He was captured by the Xiongnu and held prisoner for ten years but finally escaped. He and his party continued west, following a route later known as one of the world's great trade networks: the Silk Road. Zhang crossed the Pamir (**pah-MEER**) Mountains, visiting lands in Afghanistan and Turkestan, whose people already avidly imported Chinese silk (hence the name Silk Road). Although his diplomatic mission failed, after twelve years away Zhang brought back useful products, including the grape, and informed Wu Di about the lands to the west.

For over a millennium after Zhang's journey, China connected with the lands much farther west through overland trade and travel through Central Asia. Every year merchants gathered just outside the walls of the Chinese city and often capital, Chang'an (**CHAHNG-ahn**) (today's Xian [**SEE-ahn**]), to form a caravan, loading metals, ceramics, spices, scrolls of paintings, seeds, and above all piles of silk on their horses and donkeys. These veteran Chinese and Central Asian travelers understood the dangers ahead, including blinding sandstorms and ruthless bandits, but also the fabulous profits to be made. After traveling west for weeks, skirting the Great Wall, at the last Chinese outpost, the Jade Gate, they exchanged horses and donkeys for camels, better suited to journeys through harsh deserts. After weeks of travel across waterless wastes, the caravan crossed the snow-covered Pamir Mountains. Finally, several thousand miles from Chang'an, the travelers arrived at Turkestan cities such as Samarkand to trade or sell their precious commodities. Much of this cargo was then sent on to India, western Asia, and southern Europe. In spite of great distances and immense geographical barriers, this vast network tied China to the world beyond and made peoples as far west as Rome aware of China.

China and its neighbors, Korea and Japan, being a great distance from the Middle East, India, and Europe, fostered unique technologies, governments, religions, and philosophies. But peoples, ideas, and commercial goods traveling the trade networks from Central Asia and India also influenced East Asians. The classical blossoming of East Asian cultures established frameworks for these societies in the following centuries and many of the features are still important today.

6-1 Changing China and Axial Age Thought, 600–221 BCE

TRANSITIONS

Q What were the distinctive features of Chinese philosophies that emerged during the late Zhou period?

Although Chinese technology, science, and philosophy developed largely independently from outside influences, the Chinese also responded to many of the same challenges faced by other societies. They needed ideas to explain the universe and bring order to their lives. During the late Zhou period and the Eurasian Axial Age, when changes in society and politics produced unsettled conditions, Chinese philosophers seeking to restore order spawned several schools of thought that endured for several millennia and many Chinese today still follow.

> **CONNECTION to TODAY**
>
> Can you think of philosophical ideas offered by the ancient Confucians, Daoists, and Mohists that might be valuable for countries or people to consider or adopt today?

6-1a Late Zhou Conflicts

The Zhou dynasty (see Chapter 4) endured for nearly 900 years (1122–221 BCE), but after 500 BCE it experienced rapid social and economic change and chronic warfare, known as the "Warring States Period," that was worsened through advances in iron weapons (see Map 6.1). Local lords did not challenge the Zhou king directly but increasingly ignored him, fighting instead among themselves for supremacy. This prolonged crisis fostered changes in many areas of Chinese life. For example, despite the fighting, by 250 BCE China had become Earth's most populous society, with 20 to 40 million people. Improving technology and communications fostered commerce and cities. Political and economic power gradually shifted to the eastern Yellow River Basin, while Chinese culture expanded south of the Yangzi River Basin, which became the major agricultural region because of fertility, abundant water sources, and favorable climate. Social mobility increased, as many peasants and slaves abandoned their homes and moved to open land or to the cities. The growing merchant class also gained influence. A Chinese historian recorded the situation: "The law honors farmers, yet farmers have become poorer; the law degrades merchants, yet merchants have become richer."[2]

6-1b Late Zhou Technology and Science

The late Zhou age saw many advances in Chinese technology and science. In the sixth century BCE, knowledge of ironworking filtering in from Central Asia led to the creation of iron-tipped ox-drawn plows, which improved agricultural productivity. Zhou Chinese also became the first people to manufacture cast iron, which was much easier to shape into products such as superior axes, hoes, ploughshares, picks, swords, and chariots. Chinese iron plows were the world's most efficient farm tools before the second millennium CE. In joining the Iron Age, China achieved equal technological footing with western Asia. The Chinese also improved water control and conservation. In 250 BCE, for example, to control the fickle upper Yangzi River, they constructed a vast complex of dikes, canals, and dams that is still used today. They also grew soybeans, which provided a rich protein source and enriched the soil. Late Zhou Chinese also invented the first compasses and improved mathematics, amending the Shang decimal system by adding a place for the zero in equations. While they had long produced silk from strands made by a caterpillar that fed on mulberry trees, in Zhou times the Chinese developed better methods of weaving the silk.

---

[2]Quoted in Arthur Cotterell and David Morgan, *China's Civilization: A Survey of Its History, Arts, and Technology* (New York: Praeger, 1975), 58.

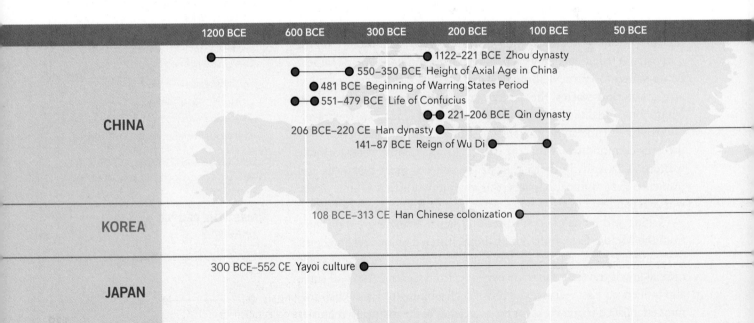

	1200 BCE	600 BCE	300 BCE	200 BCE	100 BCE	50 BCE

CHINA
- 1122–221 BCE Zhou dynasty
- 550–350 BCE Height of Axial Age in China
- 481 BCE Beginning of Warring States Period
- 551–479 BCE Life of Confucius
- 221–206 BCE Qin dynasty
- 206 BCE–220 CE Han dynasty
- 141–87 BCE Reign of Wu Di

KOREA
- 108 BCE–313 CE Han Chinese colonization

JAPAN
- 300 BCE–552 CE Yayoi culture

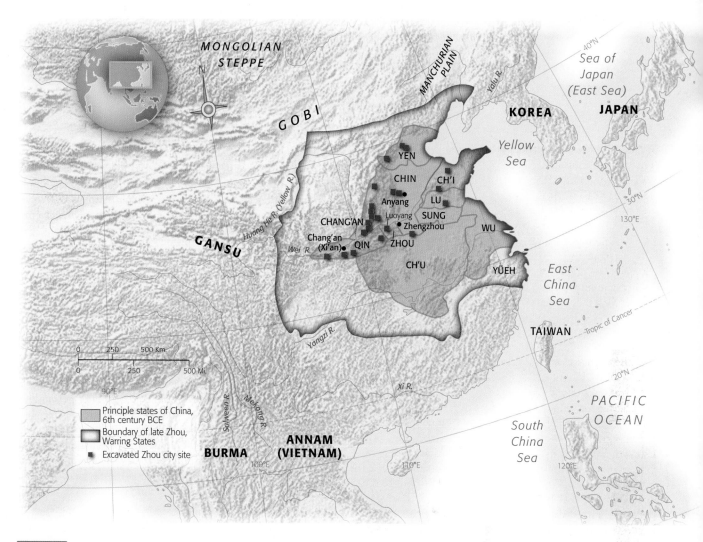

MAP 6.1 **China in the Sixth Century BCE** During the late Zhou era China was divided into competing, often warring, states, only loosely ruled by the Zhou kings. Some, such as Ch'u and Wu, were large. In the third century BCE the westernmost state, Qin, conquered the others and formed a unified empire.

Q Why do you think that China's earliest states and the heartland of Chinese society emerged in the North China plain between the two largest river systems?

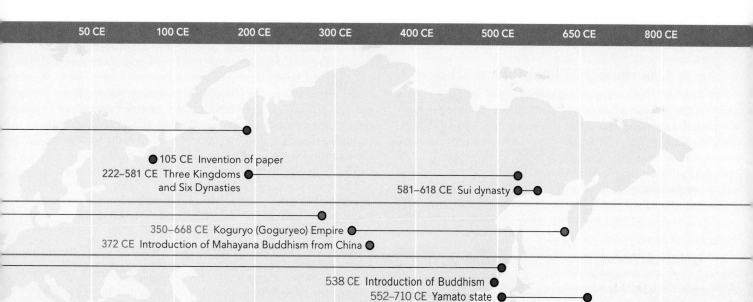

50 CE	100 CE	200 CE	300 CE	400 CE	500 CE	650 CE	800 CE

105 CE Invention of paper

222–581 CE Three Kingdoms and Six Dynasties

581–618 CE Sui dynasty

350–668 CE Koguryo (Goguryeo) Empire

372 CE Introduction of Mahayana Buddhism from China

538 CE Introduction of Buddhism

552–710 CE Yamato state

604 CE First Japanese constitution

Keren Su/Lonely Planet Images/Getty Images

IMAGE 6.2 **Confucius** Stone rubbing of a portrait of Confucius from an ancient temple. For twenty-five hundred years Confucius was the most honored and influential Chinese thinker, remembered in countless paintings, woodblock cuts, and carvings on walls.

Q What can we learn about how Confucius was perceived by the unknown artist?

6-1c One Hundred Philosophical Schools

The later Zhou era, with rising literacy and urbanization, was highly creative, a fluid, dynamic world that produced so many vigorously competing philosophies that historians refer to the "hundred schools of thought." Part of the widespread intellectual creativity in Eurasia during what some scholars term the Axial Age, this creativity in China fostered intellectual traditions that endured through the centuries. The hundred schools resulted partly from the Warring States conflicts and increased knowledge of the outside world resulting from contact with Central Asian pastoralists, who brought horses to China in exchange for grain, wine, and silks. New philosophies and widening intellectual horizons also emerged in the Mediterranean world, western Asia, and India between 600 and

Confucianism A Chinese philosophy based on the ideas of Confucius emphasizing the relations among people.

250 BCE (see Chapters 5 and 7). Hoping to restore peace and harmony, philosophers across Eurasia emphasized ethical principles, criticized political conditions, and proposed new political and social ideas. At the era's end, powerful empires emerged in China, India, and the Mediterranean.

From the late Zhou period onward, Chinese thought differed dramatically from that of other societies. The spiritual life of many Chinese in that era included magic, divination, and ancestor worship; in this latter practice Chinese families, thinking of the deceased as still with them in spirit form, honored their male ancestors, burning incense, praying, feasting, and erecting tablets in their houses listing ancestors going back many generations. As any visit to a Chinese home or temple will confirm, this is still practiced in many families today. But Chinese thinkers also generally viewed people as social and political creatures within communities and, unlike India, placed less emphasis on an afterlife and powerful gods. While Chinese thinkers did not ignore the supernatural, their main focus remained humanistic. This approach reflected the philosophers' position in society as pragmatic men who often served in government. Some also wandered from one Zhou state to another offering their services and became teachers. Their disciples collected their sayings or thoughts into the classic texts venerated by later generations, creating Confucianism, Daoism, and Legalism, all philosophies that ultimately stood the test of time and influenced China for the next two millennia. The divisions between and within the various schools were never rigid, but each had certain core ideas. Other philosophies popular at the time mostly faded after the Qin dynasty came to power in the third century BCE and tried to stamp out philosophical debate as a threat and dissent. One of these popular schools, Mohism, propounded by Mozi (c. 470–c. 391 BCE), had some ideas unusual for the time and surprisingly similar in some respects to modern liberal thought, including use of logic, rationality, respect for science, a centralized government based on meritocracy, the intrinsic moral value of all human beings, egalitarian ideas of impartiality, universal love, and the power of discussion and persuasion to address ethical problems.

6-1d Confucius and His Legacy

The most influential new philosophy, **Confucianism (kun-FYOO-shu-NIZ-um)**, based on the ideas of Confucius, emphasized relations among people and the value of hierarchical relationships and obligations to society. Although a few historians question whether he was an actual person or rather a literary creation to promote certain values, Kong Fuzi **(kong foo-dzu)** ("Master Kung"), better known in the West as Confucius, probably lived from 551 to 479 BCE. His ancestral home in Shandong province is now a museum. Because of Chinese interest in genealogy, ancestral tablets, and preserving family history, often going back many centuries, we know quite a bit about his family line and descendants. Now in the eighty-fourth generation since Confucius, they number perhaps as many as four million people today, most living in China, Taiwan, or South Korea. As with the Buddha in India or Jesus of Nazareth, we know of his life and ideas through the writings of his followers. Confucius left no direct writings that have ever been found, but his sayings were collected and

Discover Historical Voices

The Analects and Correct Confucian Behavior

The Analects is the main record of Confucius and his thought that survived the Warring States Period and the book burnings of the next dynasty. Compiled by his disciples many years after his death, it is presented largely in the form of questions from his followers and answers, short aphorisms, or long discourses by the sage. Divided into twenty chapters, the book covers many topics, mostly peoples' conduct and aspirations. It became the most important book in China from the Han dynasty down to modern times. These fragments present a few of Confucius's thoughts about the correct behavior of gentlemen (the rulers and other leaders), sons and daughters, and people in general.

[About the gentleman], Confucius said, "The gentleman concerns himself with the Way [the natural order that is also a moral order]; he does not worry about his salary. Hunger may be found in plowing; wealth may be found in studying. The gentleman worries about the Way, not about poverty. . . . The gentleman reveres three things. He reveres the mandate of Heaven; he reveres great people; and he reveres the words of the sages. Petty people . . . are disrespectful of great people and they ridicule the words of the sage. The gentleman aspires to things lofty; the petty person aspires to things base. The gentleman looks to himself; the petty person looks to other people. The gentleman feels bad when his capabilities fall short of some task. He does not feel bad if people fail to recognize him. . . ."

[About filial piety or respect for parents], Confucius said, "Nowadays, filial piety is considered to be the ability to nourish one's parents. But this obligation to nourish even extends down to the dogs and horses. Unless we have reverence for our parents, what makes us any different? Do not offend your parents. . . . When your parents are alive, serve them according to the rules of ritual and decorum. When they are deceased, give them a funeral and offer sacrifices to them according to the rules of ritual and decorum. . . . It is unacceptable not to be aware of your parents' ages. Their advancing years are a cause for joy and at the same time a cause for sorrow. . . . "

[About humanity], Confucius said, "If an individual can practice five things anywhere in the world, he is a man of humanity. . . . [These are] Reverence, generosity, truthfulness, diligence, and kindness. If a person acts with reverence, he will not be insulted. If he is generous, he will win over the people. If he is truthful, he will be trusted by the people. If he is diligent, he will have great achievements. If he is kind, he will be able to influence others. . . . When you go out, treat everyone as if you were welcoming a great guest. Employ people as if you were conducting a great sacrifice."

Reflection Questions

1. What are some of the main qualities expected of a gentleman?
2. How might Confucian views on respect for parents have influenced the family system?
3. How did the advice reflect Confucius's humanistic emphasis?
4. Which if any of these Confucian values do you think can be found in your own society today?

Source: Adapted from *Chinese Civilization and Society: A Sourcebook*, 2nd ed., revised and expanded, ed. Patricia Buckley Ebrey (New York: The Free Press, a Division of Simon & Schuster, 1993).

---

published a century or two after his death in a book called ***The Analects*** (see Discover Historical Voices: *The Analects* and Correct Confucian Behavior). Born into a modest but aristocratic family, Confucius attempted unsuccessfully to gain a government position in various states and then spent years as a teacher of dazzling ability, attracting over his career some three thousand students from all social classes. The sage claimed that he had "never refused to teach anyone, even though he came to me on foot, with nothing more to offer as tuition than a package of dried meat."[3] Maintaining that education was the key to promoting morality, Confucius stressed the study of history, philosophy, literature, poetry, and music. Considering himself not a creator of new ideas but rather a transmitter of ancient wisdom, he revived traditional ideas and with his followers reorganized them into a coherent system of thought. Hence, he promoted his idealized views of the early Zhou as a time of peace and order and extolled the past as an example for the future.

Confucianism is not primarily a religion, concerned with otherworldly issues, but a philosophy of social relations, a moral and ethical code designed to promote social stability. The Chinese never considered Confucius a god, but rather a wise sage to be honored by offerings. While Confucius accepted the notion of the world controlled by an all-powerful deity, **Tian**, and lesser deities such as the Earth god, he could be described broadly as an agnostic, arguing that, since people know little about life, they cannot know about death and the supernatural world. Like the Ionian Greeks a world away, Confucius developed a rationalist view opposed to superstition. He asserted that wisdom was working to improve society and keeping one's distance from the gods while showing them reverence. The answer to the world's problems, Confucius argued, was virtue, ethics, and, above all, benevolence and moderation in behavior. Confucius also advised people to think about the future; if they do not think about problems that are still distant, they will have to worry about them later.

Confucius advocated an autocratic but paternalistic government in which the ruler held

> **The Analects** The book of the sayings of Confucius collected by his disciples and published a century or two after his death.

[3] Quoted in H. G. Creel, *Chinese Thought from Confucius to Mao Tse-Tung* (New York: Mentor, 1953), 32.

responsibility for the people's welfare. Even distribution of goods, he argued, eliminates poverty and promotes harmony, hence ensuring stability. The family constituted the model for the state. Just as children should respect and obey their parents, a custom known as **filial piety** (FILL-eal PIE-uh-ty), so citizens should obey a fair government and play their assigned roles in a society defined by order and hierarchy: "Let the ruler be ruler, and the minister minister; let the father be father, and the son son."[4] Confucius advocated duty and obedience of inferiors to superiors: of wife to husband, son to father, younger to older, and citizen to king; but authority must be wielded justly and wisely. Government was fundamentally a matter of ethics: abusive power became illegitimate. When asked what thought should guide the conduct of both leaders and citizens, Confucius replied: "Do not do to others what you yourself do not desire."[5]

Confucian teachings have had a more enduring influence on East Asia than those of any other thinker and still do today, becoming in some form or another the official doctrine in China, Korea, Vietnam, and Japan and helping set a common pattern of compromise. As a Chinese proverb advised, people should "bend like bamboo" to avoid conflict with others. To promote harmony, Confucianism stressed rules of courtesy. For example, a late Zhou book of etiquette advised men on how to behave when visiting another man of equal status: if the host should "yawn, stretch himself, ask the time of day, order his dinner, or change his position, then [the guest] must ask permission to [leave]."[6] Ritual and etiquette maintained stability and discipline. Confucian ideas promoted social order and continuity across generations for centuries.

However, Confucian ideas, revised to some extent by followers, became increasingly rigid in application over the centuries, leading to a conservatism and inflexibility, including increasingly strict gender roles and emphasis on correct behavior, that Confucius might have condemned. Two of the sage's main followers, who lived one and a half centuries later, represented opposing schools of interpretation. Mengzi (**MUNG-dze**) (Mencius) (372–289 BCE) advocated a liberal, even permissive government, the ruler embracing benevolence and righteousness as his main goals. Believing human nature was essentially good, Mengzi was extremely optimistic about society's prospects but believed that the people could replace a very bad ruler. Xunzi (**SHOON-dze**) (Hsun Tzu) (310–220 BCE) disagreed, viewing human nature as essentially bad. Hence, the state must enforce goodness and morality. Xunzi's belief that Confucian writings were the source of all wisdom fostered dogmatism.

filial piety The Confucian rule that children should respect and obey their parents.

Daoism A Chinese philosophy that emphasized adaptation to nature.

Today the authoritarian Chinese Communist Party, which has ruled China since 1949, ignores some Confucian ethics but promotes Confucian ideas of order and obedience and an idealized past of harmony and filial piety.

6-1e Daoism and Chinese Mysticism

The second major philosophy, **Daoism** (DOW-iz-um), taught that people should adapt to nature. Legends attributed Daoism's main ideas to Laozi (**lou-zoe**) (Lao Tzu or "Old Master"), an older contemporary of Confucius and a disillusioned bureaucrat who became a wandering teacher. If such a man ever lived, he probably did not write the two main Daoist texts, which were most likely composed or compiled during the third century BCE.

Daoism was a philosophy of withdrawal for people appalled by warfare. Daoist thinkers advised people to follow the "way of the universe," or *dao*, a kind of impersonal force that underlies the cosmos, described as "unfathomable, the ancestral progenitor of all things, everlasting. All pervading, dao lies hidden and cannot be named. It produces all things. He who acts in accordance with dao becomes one with dao."[7] Convinced that people could never dominate their environment, Daoists urged allying with it, becoming simple, without desire and striving, and content with what is. A Daoist text expressed disgust with everyday life: "To labor away one's whole lifetime but never see the result, and to be utterly worn out with toil but have no idea where it is leading, is this not lamentable?"[8] Unlike Confucians, Daoists encouraged the Chinese to conform to the natural world rather than to social expectations and corrupt, oppressive governments, believing that rulers who promoted rigid, violent, aggressive, warlike, and authoritarian policies violated the natural order. One main text contended that the wise person prefers fishing on a remote stream to serving as emperor. Mystical and romantic, Daoism fostered an awareness of nature and its beauties that was reflected in Chinese poetry and landscape painting, which often recorded towering mountains, roaring waterfalls, and placid lakes.

Daoism later fragmented into several traditions. Popular Daoism became a religion of countless deities and magic, with some followers seeking an elixir of immortality, often experimenting with a wide variety of foods. By contrast, philosophical Daoism appealed to the better educated, urging individuals to turn inward and experience oneness with the universe. Daoist writers found it difficult to express their basic ideas, one claiming that "those who know do not speak; those who speak do not know."[9] Some Daoist writings contained stories filled with mysticism, unity with nature, and a humbling relativism:

> One time, Chuang-tzu dreamed he was a butterfly, flitting around, enjoying what butterflies enjoy. The butterfly did not know that it was Chuang-tzu. Then Chuang-tzu started, and woke up, and he was Chuang-tzu again. And he began to wonder whether he was Chuang-tzu who had dreamed he was a butterfly dreaming that he was Chuang-tzu.[10]

Daoists advised Confucianists to flow with the heart rather than struggle with the intellect. The active Confucian bureaucrat of the morning became the dreamy Daoist poet

[4]Quoted in Ch'u Chai and Winberg Chai, *Confucianism* (Woodbury, NY: Barron's, 1973), 45.
[5]Quoted in Dun J. Li, ed., *The Essence of Chinese Civilization* (Princeton, NJ: D. Van Nostrand, 1967), 6.
[6]From Patricia Buckley Ebrey, ed., *Chinese Civilization: A Sourcebook*, 2nd ed., revised and expanded (New York: Free Press, 1993), 43–44.
[7]Quoted in Lionel Giles, *The Sayings of Lao Tzu* (New York: E.P. Dutton, 1908), 19, 22, 25.
[8]Quoted in Creel, *Chinese Thought*, 85.
[9]Quoted in Arthur Waley, *The Way and Its Power: A Study of the Tao Te Ching and Its Place in Chinese Thought* (New York: Grove Press, 1958), 210.
[10]From William McNaughton, ed., *Light from the East: An Anthology of Asian Literature* (New York: Laurel, 1978), 132.

or nature lover of the evening. Daoism complemented Confucianism by enabling the Chinese to balance the conflicting needs for social order and personal autonomy, for responsibility and pleasure, adding enjoyment, reflection, and a sense of freedom.

6-1f Legalism and the Chinese State

Among the dozens of other competing philosophies, **Legalism** was vastly different from and strongly critical of Confucianism and Daoism. Legalists advocated that the state maintain harsh control of people and also had an enduring influence. Influenced by the Confucian Xunzi, Legalists emphasized unrestrained state power, an authoritarian government that secured prosperity, order, and stability by controlling all economic resources and instilling discipline through compulsory military duty and harsh laws. The ruler needed to be strong and disregard peoples' rights or desires. Ridiculing tradition and Confucian humanism, Legalists favored controlling people through punishments and rewards, commands and prohibitions. One of the leading Legalists, Han Feizi, wrote that the common people had about

as much understanding of what is good for them as infants and hence must be forced to do what the Legalists thought was needed: "If an infant's head is not shaved, his sores will not heal; if his boils are not lanced, his illness will worsen. Even when someone holds him and the loving mother does the shaving or lancing, he will howl without stop, for a baby cannot see that a small discomfort will result in a major improvement. Now the ruler wants people to till land and maintain pastures to increase their production but they think he is cruel. He imposes heavy penalties to prevent wickedness, but they think he is harsh.... He imposes military training on everyone in the land and makes his forces fight hard in order to capture the enemy, but they consider him violent. ... He uses means that will lead to peace but the people are not happy... ."[11]

Although Legalism influenced politics, Chinese always balanced it with the more humane ideas of Confucius and Mengzi, who stressed moral persuasion rather than coercion. Hence, many Chinese did not follow one philosophy to the exclusion of others. Despite sometimes severe laws, local officials had flexibility in implementing them, taking into account the social context.

KEY POINTS

▶ Despite chronic civil warfare, China became the most populous society on Earth; iron technologies and other breakthroughs made China competitive with western Asia.

▶ Instability resulting from military conflict led intellectuals to question basic tenets of society and government, thus creating the "hundred schools of thought."

▶ Three enduring Chinese philosophies from this period—Confucianism, Daoism, and Legalism—have influenced Chinese state and culture through two millennia.

▶ Chinese philosophies emphasized humanism rather than the supernatural or gods.

6-2 Chinese Imperial Systems and the World

⤢ TRANSITIONS   ▦ NETWORKS

Q What developments during the Han dynasty linked China to the rest of Eurasia?

More than Indian, Middle Eastern, or European societies, China has experienced cohesion, continuity, and blending of diverse influences throughout much of its history. For example, although Central Asians often attacked and even occasionally conquered China, the invaders maintained continuity by adopting Chinese culture, a process known as **Sinicization** (SIN-uh-sigh-ZAY-tion). But one major transition quickly changed the face of China: replacing the multistate Zhou system with a centralized empire. The new imperial China was forged by the harsh rulers of Qin (chin) and by the Han dynasty, which conquered a large empire, fostered foreign trade, and established enduring political patterns. Hence, China after 221 BCE set a new pattern for the centuries to follow. During these years the Chinese family matured into its basic form, dramatic economic growth affected peasant life, the Chinese examined their own history for lessons, and technology

> **CONNECTION to TODAY**
>
> Do you see any parallels in the modern world to the Qin dynasty and its brutal Legalist policies?

and science advanced, improving mathematics and health.

6-2a The Qin Dynasty

Late Zhou political turmoil ended when the Qin dynasty (221–206 BCE) conquered the other states and implemented repressive Legalist ideas, transforming the China of many states into an empire with an authoritarian central government. Advised by Legalist thinkers, Qin rulers had made their state the strongest within the Zhou system by enforcing government monopolies over many trade goods. Like Sparta in Greece, Qin's population was militarized, with men serving as citizen-warriors. Eventually

Legalism A Chinese philosophy that advocated harsh control of people by the state.

Sinicization The process by which Central Asian invaders maintained continuity with China's past by adopting Chinese culture.

---

[11] Quoted in Patricia Buckley Ebrey, *The Cambridge Illustrated History of China*, 2nd ed. (New York: Cambridge University Press, 2010), 52.

Georg Gerster/Science Source

IMAGE 6.3 **The Great Wall** This panorama from the region just north of Beijing shows a portion of the wall reconstructed in the fifteenth century CE. The wall was an attempt to mark the northern boundary of China and keep out nomadic invaders.

Q What does this photo tell us about the challenge of building, maintaining, and protecting the wall?

the Qin began conquering other Zhou states, with the brutal Legalist prime minister, Li Si **(lee SHE)** (Li Ssu), the chief deputy to the eventual first emperor of all China, arguing that those who used the past to oppose the present, meaning the Confucians, had to be exterminated. Li Si accused scholars of using records of the past to belittle the emperor's policies and undermine his popular support and demanded that history, philosophy, and other scholarly books be banned and replaced by practical manuals on subjects like medicine and farming.

In 221 BCE the Qin, after finally defeating all the remaining Zhou states, established a new government that ruled most of the Chinese people. The first Qin ruler assumed the new and imposing title of Shi Huangdi **(SHE hwang-dee)** ("first emperor"), surrounding himself with mystery and pomp to enhance his prestige while concealing himself from the consequences of his decrees. The autocrat lived in carefully guarded privacy, moving secretly from one apartment to another in his vast palaces. To reveal his movements was a crime instantly punished with death. Mandating a total reordering of China along Legalist lines, the emperor constructed a monolithic and united state that sought to control all aspects of Chinese life. The Qin sent armies to conquer much of southern China and also invaded and, for awhile, brought what is now northern

Vietnam into the empire. Chinese society eventually assimilated many southerners. Given this unification, the name *Qin* is fittingly the origin of the Western name for China.

Later Chinese historians viewed the Qin era as one of the country's most terrible periods and castigated the first emperor as a cruel, suspicious, impetuous, arbitrary megalomaniac. Common people hated the forced labor, strict laws, spies, general surveillance, and thought control that were paramount in the police state. Intellectuals despised the Qin for purging non-Legalist thought, including Confucianism and Mohism, as subversive doctrines. The Qin burned thousands of books and executed many scholars, often burying them alive, ending the intellectual creativity of the hundred schools.

Despite the repression, Shi Huangdi's policies fostered public works projects, economic growth, and social change. The Qin standardized weights and measures; unified agricultural practices; codified laws; built roads, bridges, dams, and canals; and standardized the written language so that all literate Chinese could communicate easily. To foster economic growth, the Qin established state monopolies over essential commodities like salt, raised taxes, and required forced labor on government projects. Ever since the Chinese have accepted a strong government role in economic matters. The harsh Qin laws also ended crime, as a later Chinese scholar conceded: "Nothing lost on the road was picked up and pocketed, the hills were free of bandits, men avoided quarrels at home."[12] Qin land reform also undermined the old aristocracy's power, a mighty blow to the Zhou social structure.

The most famous Qin public works project was constructing an early and limited version of a Great Wall along China's northern borders as a barrier against encroachment by Central Asian warriors. The Chinese traded with Central Asians but also fought with and feared them. A few partial earthen walls had already been built in Zhou times, but the Qin consolidated these into a more formidable structure, later known as the Great Wall. Vast numbers of conscripted laborers built the Great Wall, one of the ancient world's greatest architectural achievements. Later dynasties periodically rebuilt and added to the wall. The present brick and stone wall that so astounds tourists derives mostly from reconstruction and expansion work six centuries ago during the Ming dynasty, after which the wall stretched over fourteen hundred miles across north China. Properly manned, it could be an effective defense, but only the wealthiest emperors could afford that enormous expense. Many modern historians consider the wall to have been a major boondoggle of bad fiscal and foreign policy. Although seldom successful in curbing invaders, the wall symbolically affirmed the empire's territorial limits. For the past seven decades the Chinese communists have ruled China with a heavy hand and taken a more positive view of the Qin's authoritarian government, emphasizing the Qin policies similar to their own, such as standardization of every facet of life, economic development, social change, a very powerful central government under authoritarian leaders who harshly punished all rebellion, and opposition to freedom of thought.

But the Qin dynasty itself proved short-lived. Many hated Shi Huangdi, and his expansionist policies provoked conflict with neighboring peoples. Fearing general revolt, his inner circle kept the first emperor's death in 210 BCE secret. He was buried in a huge underground mausoleum dug under an artificial pyramid-shaped hill together with eight thousand realistic life-size terra-cotta horses and warriors, each with individual facial features and clothing, brandishing bronze weapons. Some studies suggest the terra-cotta figures may have been inspired by Greek art, perhaps from Hellenistic Greeks traveling over an early version of the Silk Road to Central Asia or even western China. It took 700,000 laborers to construct the final resting place and its contents. When news finally spread of Shi Huangdi's death, peasant revolts broke out. In 206 BCE a rebel alliance defeated the Qin forces. As various rebel groups vied for power, a former peasant led his forces to victory, establishing a new dynasty, the Han (HAHN).

harsh Legalist structure. The brilliance of Han rule and the expansion of Chinese society southward set the pattern for later dynasties, leading Chinese to call themselves the Sons of Han.

The middle classical period was the age of empires in the world, with large segments of Eurasia and North Africa dominated by large imperial structures like the Han. Built on Axial Age ideas, these empires resolved the crises that had sparked their rise. But they eventually declined as their structures and finances weakened, the conquered populations revolted, and nomadic peoples invaded the imperial heartlands. The Han and Roman Empires reached their zenith around the same time and resembled each other in population, although Rome's empire was larger in territorial size. In 2 CE the Han Empire contained at least sixty million people, most of them in China proper, and the Roman Empire ruled some fifty-five million, most of them outside Italy.

The pinnacle of Han imperial power came under the emperor Wu Di, who ruled for over half a century (141–87 BCE). After establishing control at home, Wu Di, a firm believer that the best defense is a good offense, launched bloody campaigns to counteract the encroaching pastoral nomads, especially the branch of Huns the Chinese called Xiongnu, a large tribal confederation that had constantly threatened China. As a result, some nomad groups were deflected to the west, several invading the Roman Empire.

Empire building and diplomacy soon linked China to western Eurasia, Northeast Asia, and Southeast Asia. The Han sent ambassadors such as Zhang Qian to distant Central Asians seeking allies against common enemies. Wu Di also dispatched great armies, some numbering as many as 150,000 men, to conquer southwestern China, northern Korea, Vietnam, the Xinjiang (**shinjee-yahng**) region on China's western borders, Mongolia, and parts of Turkestan. Wu Di wrote a poem about a successful military campaign that brought many horses as tribute: "The heavenly horses are coming from the Far West. They crossed the Flowing Sands, for the barbarians are conquered."[13] China ruled Korea for four centuries and Vietnam for one thousand years. Soon Chinese power extended even further, as states in Afghanistan sent tribute to Han emperors. One disgruntled Han soldier wrote a protest: "In the wilderness we dead lie unburied, fodder for crows. Tell the crows for us, 'We've always been brave men.'"[14] A Chinese army of ninety thousand men reached as far as the Caspian Sea, and a small force led by a General Gan Ying apparently traveled through Parthia to the Persian Gulf in 97 CE, the first Chinese known to reach there. On his return General Gan reported on the customs and topography of these western states, as well as information he obtained indirectly on the vast Roman Empire.

6-2b The Han Empire

The Han dynasty (206 BCE–220 CE) made China a major force in Eurasian trade, diplomacy, and imperialism. The Han built a huge empire stretching far into Central Asia (see Map 6.2); trade across this area allowed greater contact with people to the west. While building a strong state, they also modified the Qin's

6-2c The Silk Road and Eurasian Trade

The Han presence in Central Asia fostered a lively overland caravan route, known much later as the **Silk Road**, linking China with India, the Middle

Silk Road A lively caravan route through Central Asia that linked China with India, the Middle East, and southern Europe.

---

[12]Sima Qian quoted in Arthur Cotterell, *The First Emperor of China* (New York: Penguin, 1988), 106.
[13]Quoted in Frances Wood, *The Silk Road: Two Thousand Years in the Heart of Asia* (Berkeley: University of California Press, 2002), 55.
[14]From John Minford and Joseph S. M. Lau, eds., *Classical Chinese Literature: An Anthology of Translations*, vol. 1 (New York: Columbia University Press, 2000), 387.

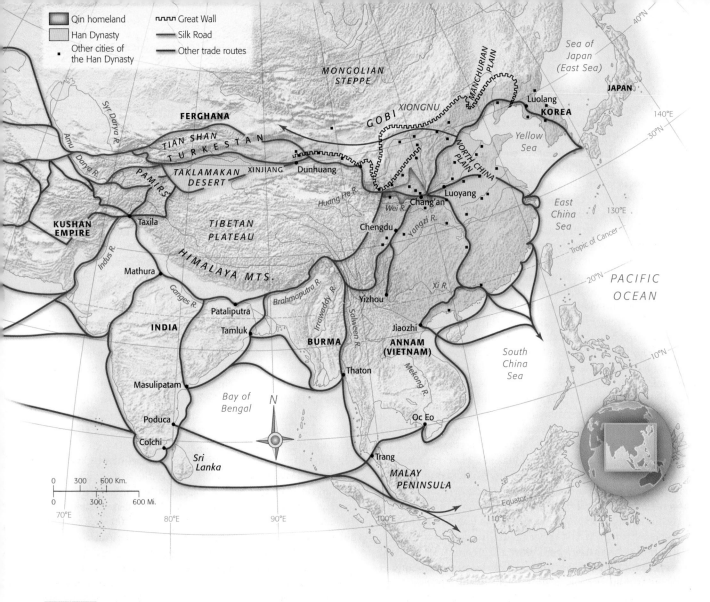

MAP 6.2 The Han Empire The Han Empire fluctuated in size but at its height controlled most of today's China, Korea, northern Vietnam, and a long corridor through Central Asia to Turkestan.

Q Why do you think the Silk Road facilitated the creation of the first great Chinese empire, the Han, and enabled China's communication with central and western Eurasia?

East, and southern Europe. Central Asian cities such as Kashgar (kahsh-gar) and Samarkand (SAM-mar-kahnd) serviced the trade and its merchants, forming an important contact zone between East and West. Chinese silk, porcelain, and bamboo moved west across the deserts and mountains to Baghdad and eastern Mediterranean ports, some eventually reaching Rome. Each westbound caravan carried lightweight, easily packed silk and then returned with horses and luxury goods such as jade from Xinjiang, Egyptian glass beads, Red Sea pearls, and Baltic amber.

The Silk Road greatly influenced participating people. To pay for Chinese luxuries, the Romans dispatched silver to China, causing a serious trade imbalance that contributed to the decline of the Western Roman Empire. Thus the Han Empire ultimately affected distant Europe politically and economically. Chinese adopted some Central and West Asian products, such as stringed musical instruments and new foods. Imperial power and foreign trade generated an economic boom and commercial

growth. Today China's leaders have introduced policies to vastly expand their foreign trade and investment by reviving the concept of the Silk Road (which they now call the "Belt and Road Initiative") to publicize and popularize the project. The term *Silk Road* was actually coined in modern times by Western travelers visiting Central Asia to describe the longstanding overland caravan trade and is hence misleading, but it does nonetheless celebrate the often significant connections between China and the lands to the west and, via the maritime route, the south during and since classical times.

6-2d Han Government and Politics

The basic Han government structure survived until the early twentieth century. Whereas the Qin sought to transform China in one brutal stroke, the more pragmatic and cautious Han softened Legalism with Confucian humanism, demonstrating that Confucian philosophy could maintain stability amidst momentous change. This mixing of Legalism with Confucianism, of power with ethics, characterized China's political system for the next two thousand years. During Han times the civil service included about one person for every 400 to 500 people, by modern standards a small number because the central government had a restricted role, mainly ensuring law, order, and border defense. Bureaucrats collected taxes, administered the legal system, and officered military forces. Yet many rebellions suggest that high taxes and demands that peasants provide military or labor service, such as rebuilding river dikes or repairing washed-out roads, generated occasional unrest.

Educated men (later called **mandarins**) staffed the Han bureaucracy. Chinese proverbs claimed that the country might be won by the sword but could be ruled only by the writing brush—by an educated elite. The Han invented the civil service examination system to select officials based on merit. These exams tested knowledge of Confucian writings, confirming Confucianism as the official state ideology while legitimizing the regime. Since they served as intermediaries between the emperor and the people, the mandarins' prestige moderated the tendency toward despotism. The emerging Han bureaucracy marked the rise of the **scholar-gentry**, a social class based on learning, officeholding, and landowning; many mandarins came from wealthy landowning families. Still, scholar-officials could not guarantee their sons' competence, and some poor men did rise by passing the civil service exams.

During the Han the concepts of the Mandate of Heaven and the dynastic cycle became ingrained in Chinese historical thinking (see Chapter 4). Premodern Chinese scholars believed that emperors ruled as deputies of the cosmic forces, but only so long as they possessed justice, benevolence, and sincerity. In each dynasty, able early rulers were succeeded by debauched incompetents indulging their pleasures, keeping harems of wives, concubines, and sometimes boys. According to the Mandate of Heaven, such imperial misrule justified rebellion. Dynastic rise and fall also correlated with economic trends: a strong new dynasty generated prosperity, luring ambitious emperors into overextending imperial power and squandering human and financial resources. The Han elite lived and died lavishly, sparing no expense to ensure their continuance. The tomb of one princess, Dou Wan, contained an astounding two-thousand-piece jade suit sown with gold wire; people thought jade could preserve a body. Two millennia later people in many countries flock to see the jade suit in visiting museum displays.

Wasteful expenditures created financial difficulties. Governments could no longer fund the large military commitment to protect the country, and some bureaucrats became corrupt. Growing deficits led to higher taxes, forcing many poorer peasants to sell their land to influential landlords, who evaded taxes. This pattern was illustrated by Han emperor Wu Di. His glorious empire came at a huge cost, straining the imperial treasury. Some Han scholars opposed military expansion as a senseless waste of lives and tax revenues, and Wu Di's

successor invited some of them to make their case before him. They did so, arguing that,

> *at present, morality is discarded and reliance is placed on military force. Troops are raised for campaigns and garrisons are stationed for defense. It is the long-drawn-out campaigns and the ceaseless transportation of provisions that burden our people at home and cause our frontier soldiers to suffer from hunger and cold.*[15]

But higher officials responded that the spending was necessary to protect the country.

The Han dynasty finally collapsed in 220 CE, not unlike the fall of Rome several centuries later. Critical factors for both empires included inadequate revenues, peasant revolts, powerful landed families contending for power, and raids by Central Asian pastoralists. Across Eurasia unusually warm conditions between 200 BCE and 200 CE came to an end, and the colder weather affected agriculture. In the second century CE both empires were also ravaged by epidemics, which killed millions and thus reduced tax revenues.

6-2e Han Society and Economy

Han social life and personal allegiance revolved around the Confucian family, which endured for over two thousand years because it provided great psychological and economic security. Each person belonged to a large family transcending time. The Chinese honored their ancestors while also considering the welfare of future generations. They idealized the joint family, three or four generations living together under one roof. But only wealthy families could support the large houses and private courtyards that made the joint family possible. Families were led by an autocratic patriarch, or senior male, who commanded respect, and the Chinese traced descent exclusively through the male line. Children were expected to respect both parents and venerate their elders, with family interests always taking precedence over individual ones. Laws held the family accountable for the actions of its members, discouraging disgraceful or criminal behavior by individuals.

This family system disadvantaged most women, requiring them to be devoted to their parents, then to their husband and sons; care of the family and children was their central preoccupation. Parents arranged marriages with the goal of linking families, and a young wife joined her husband's family and was subject to his parents' authority. Some men, especially wealthy ones, already having one wife, had one or more concubines, registered mistresses or sexual partners who were also expected to bear children. Ban Zhao (**ban chao**), an accomplished Han-era historian, astronomer, and mathematician, wrote an influential book on women's place in society in which she stressed Confucian obligations of selfless behavior, devotion, and obedience. But she also

mandarins Educated men who staffed the Chinese bureaucracy.

scholar-gentry A Chinese social class of learned officeholders and landowners that arose in the Han dynasty.

---

[15]Ebrey, *Chinese Civilization*, 61–62.

argued for teaching both boys and girls to read and write. Although many marriages were happy, the sorrows of unhappy women became a common literary theme. Many Chinese novels and plays concerned unrequited love or lovers forced to marry others. Although gender roles became more rigid than in earlier times, besides doing housework and caring for children, many women engaged in small-scale trade, worked long hours in the fields, and formed groups to spin or weave together. Yet, as a Han proverb noted, "To prick embroidery does not pay as much as leaning upon a market door."[16]

Women's experiences were never standardized, and their independence and influence depended on age, social class, and local practices. A few women like Ban Zhao achieved wide acclaim, and some elite women gained an education, a handful becoming celebrated poets. The mother of the Confucian thinker Mengzi won esteem as a model of astuteness and assertiveness, yet she was reported to have said that a "woman's duties are to cook the five grains, heat the wine, look after her parents-in-law, make clothes, and that is all!"[17] In contrast, some peasant women, who worked in the fields alongside their men, were strong-willed and exercised influence in their families and villages.

Intensive farming, especially the growing of cereal crops by peasants, dominated China's economy from the Han dynasty onward. As early as the second century BCE tea was grown and became popular among the Han elite. Later it too, like silk, would gain worldwide popularity. Landowning became the major goal of economic endeavor and investment, and peasants had to produce a food surplus for the 20 percent of the people living in towns and cities. Working fertile land, peasants achieved high yields, becoming some of the world's most efficient farmers through hard physical labor, especially in growing rice. Peasants did not lead easy lives. Fields had to be flooded with irrigation water and drained, and the rice had to be sown, transplanted, and harvested, all by hand. Peasants divided family land and movable property equally among sons, leaving some with too little land to live on. Hence, many peasants were forced into tenancy to landlords. However, slavery, an important feature of Shang and Zhou society, became less common during the Han.

Population pressure and peasant land shortage also fostered political stability. By the second century BCE, farmers had used practically all the good agricultural land in northern China. The economy's labor-intensive nature was also apparent outside agriculture. Transportation meant porters with carrying poles, men pushing wheelbarrows, and men bearing the sedan chairs of the elite. Men also walked along narrow paths pulling boats upriver through the narrow gorges of the Yangzi River. While the famous sericulture (silk-making) industry produced silks and brocades of the finest weave, producing 150 pounds of silk was hard work and required feeding and keeping clean the trays of 700,000 worms.

IMAGE 6.4 **Han Era Village House** This terra-cotta model made during the Han dynasty illustrates a fortified village house with a courtyard.

Q What does this model show us about Han era village houses?

DEA/G. DAGLI ORTI/De Agostini Picture Library/Getty Images

---

[16]Quoted in Brett Hinsch, *Women in Early Imperial China* (Lanham, MD: Rowman and Littlefield, 2002), 72.
[17]Quoted in Ebrey, *Chinese Civilization*, 73.

Sima Qian, Chinese Historian

Perhaps the greatest Han dynasty historian was Sima Qian (ca. 145–90 BCE). His dying father, a high court official and historian, begged his son on his deathbed to continue compiling a history of China and its neighbors from earliest times. "I have failed to set forth a record of all the enlightened rulers and wise lords, the faithful ministers and gentlemen who were ready to die for duty," he conceded. His dutiful son replied, "I shall not dare to be remiss," and made the project his life's work. At twenty, Sima Qian began a grand tour of the empire, examining historical sites, such as the tomb and family home of Confucius.

After receiving an official appointment, the young scholar was sent to newly conquered territories in the southwest and then far northwestern outposts, including Mongolia; he also traveled extensively with Emperor Wu Di. Like his father, Sima Qian was appointed Grand Astrologer, a post dealing with time and the heavens, and helped reform the calendar. But, being an honest man who spoke his mind, he alienated the emperor by defending a respected general whose brave attack against the Huns had failed for lack of support. As punishment Sima Qian was castrated.

Using his immense learning, combined with access to the vast imperial library containing the public records, Sima Qian produced his major book, *Records of the Grand Historian*, which covered two thousand years of history in 130 chapters, roughly ten thousand pages of text. This monumental history ranges across many topics, including astronomy, astrology, science, music, religious sacrifices, and economic patterns. Unlike most traditional Chinese historians, the sophisticated Sima Qian went beyond the usual, male-centric, emperor-focused histories by dealing with the lives of both men and some women. The *Records* offers sketches of people from many walks of life, including political and military leaders, merchants, philosophers, scholars, bureaucrats, comedians, assassins, rebels, bandits, and poets. *Records* also describes foreign peoples and lands well known to the Chinese, from Korea to Afghanistan. Because it also covers rivers and canals, we know much of Wu Di's ambitious conservation and irrigation schemes. In addition, Sima Qian was the first historian to offer a comparative appraisal of China's various philosophical traditions, in which he showed particular sympathy to Daoism.

The book is strongest on the history of his times. Because Sima Qian's castration had embittered him toward Wu Di, some chapters are filled with covert satires on the emperor and warnings about his increasing power. His most original writing came in the chapters on people and contemporary affairs. Consider this criticism of those abusing their power:

> We see that men whose deeds are immoral and who constantly violate the laws end their lives in luxury and wealth and their blessings pass down to their heirs with-out end. And there are others who expend anger on what is not upright and just, and yet, in numbers too great to be reckoned, they meet with misfortune and disaster. I find myself in much perplexity.

akg-images/Pictures From History

IMAGE 6.5 Sima Qian This modern painting, by an unknown artist, imagines what Han China's great historian, Sima Qian, might have looked like.

Q How does the artist represent the daily life and work of a Chinese scholar many centuries ago?

Sima Qian's vital narrative and lively prose made his book popular reading among Chinese scholars for many centuries. Concerned with both his literary and his moral legacy, Sima Qian concluded, in words that still stir historians: "I have assembled and arranged the ancient traditions, and if they may be handed down and communicated surely I would have no regrets," and, "those who do not forget the past are masters of the future." Sima Qian set the standard to be followed by later historians in China.

Reflection Questions

1. How did Sima Qian become a historian?
2. What does his life tell us about the pleasures and hazards of being a high official in Han China?
3. What made his historical writing so valuable to later readers?
4. Do you think that Sima Qian's career and work two thousand years ago can tell us anything about China today, which has faced some of the same challenges as the imperial Han dynasty?

Note: Quotations from Ben-Ami Scharfstein, *The Mind of China: The Culture, Customs, and Beliefs of Traditional China* (New York: Dell, 1974), 89–91; and Sima Qian, *Historical Records*, trans. Raymond Dawson (Oxford, UK: Oxford University Press, 1994), 177.

6-2f Chinese Historiography

The Chinese developed one of the greatest traditions of studying and writing about history, or historiography. Recording history was probably inevitable among a people who looked to the past for guidance in the present. Chinese history writing goes back to the Zhou dynasty, when a largely factual and chronological political history of the state of Lu, known as *The Spring and Autumn Annals*, was compiled. Confucians read into the prose a moral assessment of history. Beginning with the Han, most dynasties employed professional historians, such as the Han era's Sima Qian (**SI-mu tshen**) (see Meet the People: Sima Qian, Chinese Historian). Later Chinese historians adopted Sima Qian's belief that past events, if not forgotten, also taught about the future. They tended to favor political history, concentrating on personalities, stories, wars, and the doings of emperors while neglecting long-term social and economic trends. Most histories reflected the patriarchal society, focusing on men as the leading figures. But a book of biographies of 125 exemplary women—ranging from the wise, benevolent, chaste, principled, and righteous to the depraved, unfaithful, and scheming—compiled by the Han scholar Liu Xiang around 18 BCE, proved a notable exception. Liu based his work largely on several early Chinese histories, including work by Sima Qian. It served as a Confucianist textbook for women's moral education for the next two millennia.

The greatest Chinese historians wrote monumental works and had much in common with each other. They aimed for objectivity, carefully separating their editorial comments from the narrative text. Like all historians, they had to decide what to include and omit, focusing more on people and their foibles than on supernatural intervention. Historical literature also served as a manual for government, discussing the success and failure of past policies to achieve wisdom and promote morality.

KEY POINTS

▸ Legalism, with its strict authoritarianism and negative view of human nature, was the dominant philosophy of the brutal and authoritarian Qin rulers.

▸ The diplomatic and military expansion under the Han rulers set the stage for expanded trade, including the development of the Silk Road linking China to western Asia and Europe.

▸ The structure of government established during the Han, characterized by a blending of central and local authority and a softening of Legalism with Confucian humanism, endured until the early twentieth century.

▸ The family structure became the central social institution; its patriarchal hierarchy, codified in law, put the needs of the group above the needs of the individual.

6-3 China After the Han Empire: Continuity and Change

TRANSITIONS **NETWORKS**

Q What outside influences helped shape China after the fall of the Han?

After the collapse of the Han in 221 CE, China experienced three and a half centuries of disorder and political fragmentation known as the Three Kingdoms and Six Dynasties. During this time it was divided into several states, once as many as sixteen, some ruled by Chinese and others by invaders. Just as the incursion of new peoples shaped Europe and India in the ashes of the Roman and Mauryan Empires, so China experienced frequent incursions by pastoral nomads. In the seventh century, the Chinese restored centralized government and reaffirmed the classical tradition.

CONNECTION to TODAY

What examples of integrating and accepting foreign influences in the world today are similar to classical China's approach?

competition for good grazing land made these martial peoples scornful of but also attracted to China's richer life and milder climate. Skilled in horseback warfare, sometimes they breached the Great Wall, especially when they united in confederations under strong chiefs. These invasions produced what some historians termed the "Great Wall Complex": a natural Chinese state policy that expressed and addressed popular and official concern about border security and a perpetual fear of aggressive outsiders, especially Central Asians. In this mindset, all non-Chinese were barbarians hoping to share in China's cultural glory and material wealth. These invasions also prompted many Chinese to move south, solidifying the Chinese character of the region.

A much loved fifth-century CE ballad, perhaps based on an actual person, recalls a young woman warrior, Mulan, who disguises herself as a man to fight invading Central Asians. Only after she distinguishes herself in battle do her comrades discover her gender. The ballad makes a case for gender equality: "For the

6-3a Disunity, Invasion, and Cultural Mixing

During the troubled post-Han period, pastoral nomads attacked north China. Although chiefly livestock herders, most used bronze and iron. Brutal winters and keen

Werner Forman/Art Resource, NY

IMAGE 6.6 **Buddha Statue at Yungang** This huge statue of the Buddha, created around 290 CE, is 45 feet tall. It is one of thousands found along cliffs in western China and elsewhere along the Silk Road.

Q What does the size and sitting position of the statue tell us about how believers perceived the Buddha?

male hare has a lilting, lolloping gait, and the female hare has a wild and roving eye; But set them both scampering side by side, And who so wise could tell you 'This is he?'"[18]

Chinese learned to endure both political division and invasion by outsiders, developing a remarkable defense mechanism: assimilation. Gradually the invaders came to be Chinese and the Chinese began to have an expanded sense of themselves. Most of the conquerors eventually ruled in a Chinese way, using the Confucian bureaucracy while adapting much Chinese culture. They also eventually looked and sounded Chinese. In general the Chinese seemed to tolerate rule by foreigners who respected and protected their culture. Hence social institutions and economic patterns proved able to survive conquest. But the Chinese also learned from the invaders. This merging of cultures provided a foundation for the later rejuvenation of a China that would be greater than the empires of Qin and Han.

After the Han, China became even more connected to the world, fostering a vital, cosmopolitan culture. One fifth-century emperor loved everything foreign: dress, art works, food, beds, chairs, harps, dances. Ideas and products traveled both directions along the Silk Road and by land and sea between China and Southeast Asia, and Chinese objects from this era often showed Indian, Persian, Mesopotamian, Greek, or Roman influences. The graves of wealthy Chinese frequently contained Roman glass, Persian silver vessels, images of Greek gods, and cups made from Indonesian shells. China's openness to ideas from outside and a need for some guidance to navigate, or escape from, the disordered and disorienting era also led many Chinese to embrace an Indian religion, Buddhism, which first arrived in the later Han Dynasty. Ever since, Chinese have struggled between two approaches: embracing ideas from outside or rejecting them as foreign imports.

6-3b Buddhism and China's Eclectic Religious Tradition

During the later classical period, universal religions—faiths that appealed to people from many cultures—became more prominent in Eurasia and North Africa. The decline and collapse of

[18]Quoted in Robin R. Wang, ed., *Images of Women in Chinese Thought and Culture: Writings from the Pre-Qin Period Through the Song Dynasty* (Indianapolis, IN: Hackett, 2003), 254.

the great Afro-Eurasian empires, from China to Rome, produced political instability and social strife that challenged established ways. In response, universal religions diffused along the trade networks: Christianity from western Asia to Europe, where it soon became the dominant religion; Hinduism throughout India and into Southeast Asia; and Mahayana (mah-HAH-YAH-nah) Buddhism into Central, East, and Southeast Asia. These universal religions incorporated existing local beliefs, creating hybrid artistic forms and value systems. The most pronounced synthesis took place in East Asia as Buddhism encountered earlier belief systems such as Confucianism.

Buddhism's arrival proved a momentous transition, fostering the Buddhist Age in both Chinese and Asian history in the fourth through ninth centuries CE. Buddhism in some form became dominant in much of East, Central, Southeast, and portions of South Asia (see Chapter 5). Basic Buddhist beliefs about overcoming suffering through good deeds and thoughts derived from the sixth-century BCE teachings of the Indian sage known as the Buddha ("the Enlightened One") (see Chapter 5), but the religion later split into several rival schools. One of these, Mahayana Buddhism, was carried by merchants and missionaries along the Silk Road into Central Asia. From there it spread into western China during later Han times and was firmly established by the fourth century CE, linking China with distant India. Later the religion spread from China to Korea, Vietnam, and Japan. Buddhism preached compassion and gentleness, offering hope and meaning to people experiencing hardship, warfare, and instability. It also brought to the Chinese a spiritual outlook largely missing in Confucianism, which appealed to reason and practical ethics but said little about gods or life after death, and in Daoist mysticism, which could not explain the individual's fate in the cosmic order. Mahayana Buddhism promised salvation in an afterlife. But Buddhism also adapted to Chinese traditions. For example, the Buddhist notion of reincarnation clashed with Chinese beliefs in ancestor worship, so most Chinese never accepted this idea.

Traveling peacefully from India through Central Asia, in China Buddhism acquired a cosmopolitan outlook and Indian artistic, literary, and cultural influences, as shown by the huge Buddhist sculptures along the Silk Road and in northwestern China. Buddhist missionaries entered China. From the second through eighth centuries CE many Buddhists from Central Asia worked in China as translators of Buddhist texts, among them Sogdians and Parthians. And, just as today millions of people visit religious or historical sites around the world, several hundred Chinese pilgrims went to India overland or along the sea route through Southeast Asia, most with the goal of visiting sites of Buddha's life and bringing back Buddhist texts to China. The monk Faxian (fah-shee-en) spent fifteen years in India and also visited Buddhist centers in Southeast Asia in the fifth century CE. On their return to China the pilgrims spread knowledge of the societies they encountered.

geomancy Known in Chinese as *feng shui* ("wind and water"), a system for determining the auspicious settings of human dwellings and graves.

By the middle of the first millennium CE, an eclectic Chinese religious tradition embraced three very different viewpoints—Buddhism, Confucianism, and Daoism—sometimes known to Chinese as "the three ways." The schools mixed with each other. Hence, Buddhism influenced popular Daoism, and many Chinese could no longer clearly differentiate between them. An old but still popular Chinese story has Confucius, Laozi, and Buddha walking and talking together, debating the merits of their respective positions; as they cross a bridge, they are obscured in mist. When spotted again, only one somewhat larger figure can be seen in the distance, suggesting a merger of beliefs. Yet some distinctions were maintained. Only Buddhism developed a fully organized church, with monks and nuns. Confucianism, a philosophy of social relations rather than a true religion, had no priests. Many Chinese, not identifying themselves exclusively with any of them, saw the belief systems as different roads to the same destination, personal happiness.

Gradually a gap between the educated elite's relatively secular worldview and the common people's popular religion widened. Many intellectuals favored Confucian humanism and Daoist naturalism, with moral perfection of humankind as the ultimate goal. Since Confucianism centered on humanity rather than gods, many intellectuals viewed popular religion, with its gods, spirits, ghosts, and magic, as superstition. One Han scholar wrote that "the number of persons who have died since the world began must run into thousands of millions. If every one of them has become a spirit, there must be at least one to every yard as we walk along the road."[19] Meanwhile, although more Chinese may have been indifferent to religion than was common elsewhere, many peasants, artisans, and merchants believed devoutly in thousands of gods and goddesses of Buddhist, Daoist, or animist origin, using shamans to communicate with the spirit realm. They also accepted notions of Heaven and Hell introduced by Mahayana Buddhism, and of **geomancy** (JEE-u-MAN-see), known in Chinese as *feng shui* (fung shway) ("wind and water"), a popular Daoist-influenced system for determining the auspicious settings of buildings and graves. Geomancy is still widely employed today in East Asia. In 2019 a Beijing court ordered a media company to pay $30,000 to a real estate developer for publishing an article wrongly accusing the developer of violating law by neglecting to follow correct feng shui standards in his flashy new building and hence disrupting harmony with nature. Critics consider geomancy pseudoscience and superstition, but it has many believers. Some architects even use it to assess the suitability of modern houses and skyscrapers in North American and European cities.

6-3c Science and Technology in the Classical Period

China developed one of the world's oldest scientific and technological traditions, establishing along with the Indians, Mesopotamians, Egyptians, and Greeks the foundation for

---

[19]Quoted in Wang, *Images of Women*, 254.

modern science. Historians credit the Zhou and Han with many important breakthroughs, including porcelain ("china"), the water-powered mill, the shoulder harness for horses, the foot stirrup (possibly adapted from Central Asian models), the magnetic compass, the seismograph, the wheelbarrow, the stern-post rudder for boats, the spinning wheel, linen, and perhaps the most significant innovation, rag paper. Before paper Chinese scribes wrote with a pointed stylus on strips of wood, bamboo, or woven cloth, but these were difficult to use and store. Eventually an ingenious first-century CE artisan beat cloth into fiber and formed thin sheets. To mass-produce Buddhist texts and images and Confucian classics for students preparing for the examinations, Han craftsmen made ink rubbings on paper from stone carvings, often of entire Buddhist books. Elementary block printing was in limited use in China by the sixth century CE, and by the ninth century woodblock printing had become a major activity in East Asia. Most of these inventions did not reach western Eurasia over the trade routes until a few centuries—in some cases a millennium—later.

The Han innovated in mathematics and science. Besides making the most accurate calculation of *pi* at the time, the Chinese were many centuries ahead of the world in fractions, the concept of negative numbers, and in certain aspects of algebra and geometry. Around 190 CE they invented the *abacus*, a primitive computer and unparalleled tool for calculations, constructed by fastening balls on wires attached to a board carved with divisions; this device is still used widely in Asia today. Han astronomers compiled catalogues of stars, speculated on sunspots, and explained the causes of lunar eclipses.

Chinese science, especially medicine, owed much to the cosmological thinking exemplified in yin–yang dualism and also to Daoism, which inspired an interest in nature. An enduring medical discovery, *acupuncture*, developed from the belief that good health was the result of proper yin–yang balance in the body. Thin needles are inserted at predetermined points to alleviate pain or correct some physical condition. Experts learned the body parts and how to read a pulse. Acupuncture is still practiced today and has spread around the world. The Chinese also stressed good hygiene and preventive medicine, including a well-balanced diet and regular exercise. In their quest for the elixir of immortality, Daoist alchemists discovered many edible foods, herbs, and potions that improved health, and they developed the greatest list of pharmaceuticals in the premodern world. Doctors diagnosed gout and cirrhosis of the liver. Many ancient Chinese folk remedies remain popular today in China.

The Chinese continued to develop innovative technologies. Although never a great seafaring people like the Austronesians and Greeks, the Chinese became some of the world leaders in shipbuilding, some taking up maritime trade. Chinese ships carried trade goods back and forth to Korea, Japan, and Southeast Asia. By at least the fifth century CE the Chinese had constructed large oceangoing vessels with stern-post rudders for maneuvering, which permitted longer and farther journeys. Chinese ships and navigational skills were probably adequate to even cross the vast Pacific, although there is no compelling evidence that any did so.

6-3d The Sui Reunification of China

To a fourth-century observer it might have seemed that the Roman Empire, although visibly weakening, could endure, while the Chinese empire was overrun by "barbarian" invaders, broken apart, and turning to foreign, otherworldly religions. Yet China was eventually reunified under a powerful, centralized government, whereas Rome, facing the same kinds of challenges, fragmented and collapsed. Several factors contributed to China's reassembly. Reestablishment of a centralized state was made easier by China's large population, which by 400 CE was some fifty million, probably double Europe's population. More culturally unified than Europe's varied peoples, the Chinese could perhaps more easily absorb the nomadic invaders. Confucian ethical humanism, the merit-based civil service exams, and a writing system that transcended the many spoken languages and dialects encouraged both cultural and political unity. In contrast, India contained many very different spoken languages and writing systems, while in Europe, speakers of Romance languages based on phonetic alphabets splintered into many competing countries, never to be politically reunited.

The ruthless Sui (**sway**) dynasty (581–618 CE) played the same role in history as the Qin, reuniting China after several centuries of turmoil and division. Tyrants but also patrons of arts and letters, the Sui created the world's largest library. Like the Qin, they were builders, mobilizing six million forced workers to construct the Grand Canal linking the Yangzi and Yellow Rivers. At twelve hundred miles long, the longest human-made channel ever constructed, the canal ensured the prosperity of later dynasties, as each year huge quantities of grain were shipped north. Tree-shaded parks and inns lined the route. However, like earlier dynasties, the Sui overreached and collapsed. Exhausting campaigns of conquest temporarily extended imperial frontiers into Korea and Central Asia, but the Sui drove the Chinese too hard, causing overwork, food shortages, and soon rebellions. The victor in the ensuing struggles established the Tang (**tahng**) dynasty (618–907 CE), which launched China into its great golden age, extending over many centuries, and linked it more closely to Korea and Japan.

KEY POINTS

- ▶ Spurred by invasions of nomadic peoples from the north, the population shifted south, but the invaders were assimilated by existing Chinese government structures.

- ▶ Buddhism took root in China during this tumultuous period, spreading along the trade routes from India and melding with existing Confucian thought.

- ▶ The Chinese attitude toward religion was characterized by an easy interchange of beliefs, in which individuals drew from a variety of religious or philosophical perspectives depending on their need.

- ▶ Daoism promoted the idea of a yin–yang balance in the natural world, influencing developments in science and medicine.

6-4 Korea, Japan, and East Asian Networks

▓ NETWORKS ▓ SOCIETIES

Ⓠ How did the Koreans and Japanese assimilate Chinese influences into their own distinctive societies?

Large, densely populated China dominated East Asia for much of history. Consequently, eastern Asia did not develop the political diversity, with many rival states, that prevailed in India, western Asia, or Europe after classical times. Korea and Japan adopted intensive farming, becoming receptive to Chinese cultural influence. Although more developed than Japan for many centuries, Korea was often in China's shadow. Separated from mainland Asia by water, Japan remained more independent. Yet both Korea and Japan creatively forged distinctive societies.

> **CONNECTION to TODAY**
>
> Can you identify some modern societies that have, like classical Korea and Japan, flourished by successfully combining some foreign influences with their own unique traditions?

between 350 and 668 CE. Historians debate whether Koguryo's people had a close cultural connection to the several smaller states controlling southern Korea. Its army repulsed seven major invasions by the Sui and Tang between 598 and 655 CE, when a resurgent China was eastern Eurasia's most powerful state. In 612 CE Koguryo routed an invading Sui army of some 300,000 troops. In fact, the huge cost of the campaigns in Korea contributed to the Sui dynasty's collapse. Finally, in 668 CE, Chinese

6-4a Korea and China

As a close neighbor, Korea experienced a regular and extensive interaction with China that brought political pressures but also many advantages. Chinese cultural and technological influences permeated the peninsula. Koreans adopted iron technology from China, including advanced weapons, that later fostered agriculture-based states. However, these were soon overwhelmed by Chinese influence. In 108 BCE Wu Di's Han armies, reportedly sixty thousand troops strong, conquered northern Korea against fierce resistance. China ruled for the next four centuries, providing models to the Koreans in government structure, architecture, and city planning. Many Chinese immigrated to the peninsula. Even today, nearly two millennia later, the Confucianism promoted by Han China remains a strong influence on Korean society and culture and, in South Korea, is maintained by Confucian temples all over the country.

The end of Chinese colonization in 313 CE allowed Korean society to flower. Three native kingdoms emerged that dominated Korea between the fourth and seventh centuries, occasionally warring against each other. However, Chinese cultural influences, including the writing system and Confucianism, also spread more widely. Mahayana Buddhism, introduced in 372 CE, strongly influenced Korean painting, sculpture, and architecture and, as in China, Korean pilgrims made the long journey to India. But the Koreans never became carbon copies of the Chinese. For example, unlike in China, where family status rose or fell with dynastic change and civil service examinations, an inherited aristocracy thrived for most of Korean history. And although most Koreans adopted Buddhism, the long flourishing animism never disappeared.

Eventually one kingdom, Koguryo (Goguryeo) **(ko-GUR-yo)**, based in northern Korea and southern Manchuria, became the most influential state (see Map 6.3). In the fourth century, with China divided, Koguryo expanded far to the north and annexed much of Manchuria and southeastern Siberia, thus becoming one of Eurasia's largest states

MAP 6.3 **Korea and Japan in the Fifth Century CE** During the classical period Korea was often divided into several states. Koguryo (Goguryeo) in the north was the largest state, ruling part of Siberia. By the sixth century the Yamato state governed much of the main Japanese island, Honshu.

Ⓠ How do you think the geography and relative isolation of Korea and Japan helped shape these societies and their relations with the wider world?

armies, allied with the southern Korean state of Silla (**SILL-ah** or **SHILL-ah**), overran Koguryo. Soon Silla drove out the Chinese, reunifying much of Korea in 676.

6-4b Yayoi and Yamato Japan

Like Korea across the straits, Japan experienced dramatic change. The pottery-making Jomon culture (see Chapter 4) persisted until around 300 BCE, when a new culture, Yayoi (**ya-YOI**) (300 BCE–552 CE), emerged that was based on productive wet rice farming and had close links with Korea. Some archaeologists think Yayoi culture and rice growing may have begun on the southern island of Kyushu even earlier, perhaps by 1000 BCE. Korea remained a source of learning and population for Japan, which received a continuous flow of several million Korean and some Chinese immigrants until 900 CE, including skilled craftsmen, scribes, and artists. After Korean migrants brought horses, the armored warrior on horseback later became part of Japanese life. In this era the distinction between Korea and Japan may have been murky, but by 600 CE the Japanese people as we know them today, and the Japanese language, had coalesced from the genetic and cultural mixing over many centuries of Korean immigrants with the Jomon.

Yayoi Japan traded sporadically with China. A Chinese visitor documented Yayoi society, reporting the preoccupation with taboos, class distinctions, and especially ritual cleanliness. Like modern Japanese, the Yayoi enjoyed dancing, singing, drinking rice wine, and eating raw vegetables; experienced little crime; and revered nature. The Yayoi used the potter's wheel, were expert weavers, and mastered both bronze and iron technology, later fashioning iron into highly effective swords and armor. The Yayoi formed no centralized governments but were organized into many clans, each ruled by a hereditary priest-chieftain. During the second century CE, with Japan engulfed in conflict, Pimiko (**pih-MEE-ko**) became a powerful queen-priestess who brought peace by imposing strict laws. Chinese observers of the time were fascinated by Pimiko, one writing that: "Remaining unmarried, she occupied herself with magic and sorcery. . . . She kept one thousand female attendants, but few people saw her. . . . She resided in a palace surrounded by towers and stockade, with the protection of armed guards."[20] However, most clan elites were men who governed farmers, artisans, and a few slaves and mobilized people to build hundreds of large earthen tombs, often surrounded by moats, all over south-central Honshu Island. The tombs housed the remains of prominent leaders, buried with jewels, swords, and clay figurines.

Japan entered written history in the sixth century CE with the Yamato (**YA-ma-toe**) (552–710 CE), the first state ruling a majority of the Japanese people. The Yamato kingdom was centered in south-central Honshu, where the cities of Kyoto and Osaka now stand. Not a centralized state like Han China or Koguryo, Yamato erected a national government ruling over territorial clans headed by hereditary chiefs. Eventually it extended its influence into southern Japan while expanding its northern

IMAGE 6.7 **Prince Shotoku** This painting from the eighth century CE shows Prince Shotoku, one of the major Yamato leaders, and his sons in the Japanese-style clothing of the times. Prince Shotoku launched a period of intensive borrowing from China.

Q What are some of the features of elite male clothing and hair styles in Prince Shotoku's time?

frontier deep into Ainu territory. Like the Yayoi, the Yamato welcomed Korean and some Chinese immigrants, and some of them joined the political and cultural elite.

Yamato was headed by emperors and occasionally empresses—all ancestors of the same imperial family ruling Japan today, fifteen centuries later. Political continuity under the same royal family gave the Japanese identity and cultural unity. Japanese mythology portrayed the imperial family as descended from the Sun Goddess. This beautiful spirit, Amaterasu (**AH-mah-teh-RAH-soo**), and her male consort experienced violent mood swings and periodic conflict, perhaps an expression of the frequent storms, volcanic eruptions, and earthquakes that rock the islands. Despite her tantrums, a female creator deity might reflect the high status of

MARKA/jiarach/Alamy Stock Photo

[20]From Ryusaku Tsunoda et al., eds., *Sources of Japanese Tradition*, vol. 1 (New York: Columbia University Press, 1958), 7.

women in early Japan. Chinese visitors reported that the Yayoi made no distinction between men and women, and before the eighth century CE around half of the imperial sovereigns were women. However, patriarchy became the common pattern by 1000 CE.

6-4c Japanese Isolation and Cultural Unity

According to the myths, Amaterasu took refuge in a cave to protest the turbulent relationships she had with other gods. This story can be interpreted as Japan trying to isolate itself from its East Asian neighbors. Eventually she is lured out of the cave and rejoins the world. Throughout history Japan has experienced tensions between a desire for relative isolation and becoming an important part of the world. The Japanese forged a particularly distinctive society through a mixing of the local and the foreign. Over a hundred miles from the Eurasian mainland, Japan had only sporadic communication with Korea. Limited space and resources despite the steadily growing population on the mountainous islands fostered a tightly woven society with intense social pressures, sparking creativity. Since personal privacy became rare in this crowded land, people erected psychological walls that allowed them to "tune out" the surrounding noise and activity.

Isolation also made the Japanese expert at borrowing selectively from the outside during periods of intensive contact. Throughout their history, the Japanese borrowed from Korea, China, and, much later, the West, but they seldom left a borrowed idea in its original form. For example, they adopted the Chinese model of an exalted emperor but not the Mandate of Heaven that justified overthrowing incompetent or tyrannical dynasties. The Japanese also created much of their own culture and technology, including the classical world's best tempered steel. They created artistic forms and styles of universal appeal, such as carefully planned gardens and *bonsai* (**bon-sigh**) (miniature) trees, which are both popular in the world today, as well as ingenious solutions to chronic problems such as urban crowding and limited resources. The Japanese house, containing thick straw floor mats, sliding paper panels rather than interior walls, a hot tub for

Shinto ("way of the gods") The ancient animistic Japanese cult that emphasized closeness to nature and enjoyed a rich mythology that included many deities.

communal bathing, and charcoal-burning braziers, conserved building materials and minimized fuel needs for heating and cooking.

6-4d Japanese Encounters with China

Chinese ideas greatly influenced Japan several times in history, beginning on a large scale in the sixth century CE. Introduced around 538, Mahayana Buddhism fostered cultural change, bringing, for example, new art forms. Chinese teachers, artisans, and Buddhist monks migrated to Japan, and Japanese journeyed to Korea and China, coming back as Buddhist converts. Just as the Chinese maintained three distinct traditions of thought, in Japan Buddhism coexisted with an ancient animistic cult, centuries later known as **Shinto** (SHIN-toe) ("way of the gods"), which emphasized closeness to nature, especially water; worshipped at shrines; and enjoyed a rich mythology and many deities. Buddhists even accepted some Shinto deities and assigned them the role of protecting Buddhist temples. Many Japanese followed both faiths. Shinto hence represents one expression of the world's oldest faith (animism) and a religion unique to Japan.

A growing realization among Japanese leaders that China and Korea were much stronger politically, economically, and culturally spurred deliberate borrowing from China to reshape Japanese society. The Yamato expanded relations with Sui China and reorganized government structures, integrating Chinese writing and Confucian notions of social organization and morality. The adoption of Chinese ideas accelerated under Prince Shotoku (**show-TOW-koo**) (573–621 CE), an ardent Buddhist who sponsored temple building and promoted Confucian values. His ideas foreshadowed the later Japanese emphasis on the group: "Harmony is to be cherished, and opposition for opposition's sake must be avoided as a matter of principle,"[21] he wrote into the first Japanese constitution, issued in 604. Reflecting the Confucian emphasis on the need for ethical government and acceptance of hierarchy, the constitution emphasized cooperation and moral guidance, and Shotoku became one of the most revered figures in Japanese history. Some historians compare him to the Indian king Ashoka, who also embraced Buddhism, and the Roman emperor Constantine, who promoted Christianity. Over the next two and a half centuries many official embassies were exchanged between China and Japan, further promoting the exchange of ideas. Perhaps Amaterasu had come out of her cave and Japan was rejoining the East Asian community.

KEY POINTS

▶ Korea's proximity to China led to the adoption of Chinese writing and other technologies in Korea.

▶ Both Buddhism and Confucianism from China permeated Korean culture and were blended with the native belief system of animism.

▶ The flow of ideas and people from Korea and China to Japan introduced Buddhism, writing, and other influences

into Japan, but the Japanese culture, arts, and religion remained distinctive.

▶ The Yamato, Japan's first centralized state, began actively importing cultural and political ideas from China in the sixth century.

---

[21]From David John Lu, ed., *Sources of Japanese History*, vol. 1 (New York: McGraw-Hill, 1974), 21–22.

Chapter Summary

The classical East Asian societies were distinctive in many ways. China was large, densely populated, and an innovator in government, culture, religion, science, and technology. During the warfare and political instability of the late Zhou period, Confucius promoted ethical values and suggested how people could live in harmony with each other through a well-defined and hierarchical social structure. In contrast, the Daoists advocated a life shaped by the natural world, while the Legalists argued that a powerful government must harshly regulate society to preserve order. These classical ideas persisted in Chinese thought into modern times. The Legalist leaders of the Qin dynasty used brutal policies to transform China into a centralized imperial state. Following the short-lived Qin, the great Han dynasty established a large Asian empire and traded with western Asia and Europe across the Silk Road, becoming a major force in eastern Eurasia. The social structure became more patriarchal, and women were expected to be dutiful to their men.

After the Han collapsed, Central Asians frequently invaded and divided China politically. In this turbulent period, Mahayana Buddhism became popular in China, where it mixed with Confucianism, Daoism, and animism. Eventually the Sui dynasty reunified China, an achievement that contrasted with the Roman Empire in the West, which disintegrated into various fragments. China also became a model for neighboring societies. First the Koreans and then the Japanese adopted many Chinese ideas, including some technologies, writing, Confucianism, and Buddhism. But they also creatively blended them with their own unique traditions, creating a distinctive mix of the imported with the local.

Key Terms

Confucianism 130
The Analects 131
filial piety 132
Daoism 132

Legalism 133
Sinicization 133
Silk Road 135
mandarins 137

scholar-gentry 137
geomancy 142
Shinto 146

Western Asia, the Eastern Mediterranean, and Regional Systems, 600–200 BCE

> *Wonders are many on earth, and the greatest of these is man, who rides the ocean. He is master of the ageless earth. The use of language, the wind-swift motion of brain he learned; found out the laws of living together in cities. There is nothing beyond his power.*
>
> —Chorus in *Antigone*, by the fifth-century BCE Greek playwright Sophocles (SAHF-UH-KLEEZ)[1]

Richard Yoshida/Shutterstock.com

IMAGE 7.1 **Persepolis** During the height of their empire, Persian kings built a lavish capital at Persepolis, in today's Iran. This photo shows the audience hall, the part of the grand palace where the kings greeted their ministers and foreign diplomats.

[1]Quoted in Norman Davies, *Europe: A History* (New York: Harper, 1996), 117.

Thales (THAY-leez) and Anaximander

(uh-NAK-suh-MAN-der), pioneering Greek philosophers and scientists, grew up in prosperous Miletus (my-LEET-uhs), a commercial city on the southwestern coast of Anatolia (modern Turkey) governed by the Persian Empire, and long a regional crossroads mingling Greek and foreign cultures. Like other young men, they haunted the bustling docks and seaside bars, listening to tales of sailors returning from distant shores and of travelers from foreign lands. Some sailors brought learning from older societies such as Egypt and Mesopotamia, while Milesian merchants sent ships all over the Mediterranean carrying treasured wool developed by Milesian sheep breeders and fine furniture produced by its cabinetmakers. Around the Black Sea, Milesian settlements supplied fish and wheat, enriching the city's traders.

Miletus flourished as a great intellectual center and meeting place for the Greek and Persian worlds. This intermingling fostered new thinking about geography and cartography. Thales worked out a geometrical system to calculate a ship's position at sea, and his student, Anaximander, made the first map of the Mediterranean world and the first Greek astronomical chart. Later Hecataeus (HEK-a-TAU-us) of Miletus published a map of the world known to the Greeks, from India to Spain.

The Greeks developed a unique society on the rocky shores of the Aegean Sea. In cities such as Miletus and Athens, they introduced many ideas and institutions that endured through the centuries and are still influential in the world today. The view of humanity's greatness offered by Sophocles in the opening quotation reflects an obsession with individuality and freedom that made the Greeks role models for modern democracies. But Greek achievements are only part of the story. Connected to a wider world, Greeks benefited from regional trade, colonizing other territories and borrowing ideas from neighboring societies. Another creative society and even mightier regional power, the Persians, produced one of the great empires in history, dominating the easternmost Mediterranean and western Asia for nearly two centuries while introducing many innovations. Ultimately, the rival Greek and Persian societies were temporarily brought together in an empire mixing their two cultures.

7-1 The Persians and Their Empire

⛭ TRANSITIONS 🏛 SOCIETIES

Q How did the Persians maintain their empire?

The Persian Empire often gets modest attention in world history books compared to their neighbors the Greeks, with much of the coverage usually focused on the sometimes turbulent Greek-Persian relationship including multiple wars. Some of this may reflect a long-time fascination with the Greeks among many Western scholars and even average history buffs as well as a much smaller number of available Persian records. But the Persians merit strong coverage. Although its period of greatest political influence lasted only two centuries, the Persian Empire played an important role in world history. In a breathtaking series of conquests Persians established a larger, more multicultural empire than any people before them, encompassing Anatolian Greeks, Phoenicians, Jews,

CONNECTION to TODAY

What features of Persian state and society seem most similar to, and which most different from, modern countries?

Egyptians, Mesopotamians, and some South Asians. Domination of the east–west trade routes made the empire a major meeting ground. The Persians' wars with the Greeks and their empire building in western Asia also paved the way for an even greater imperial structure under the extraordinary Macedonian Greek Alexander the Great and his successors.

7-1a Building the Persian Empire

The Persian homeland was located on a plateau just north of the Persian Gulf, in what is now Iran (see Map 7.1). Overland routes connected Mesopotamia and Anatolia to India and

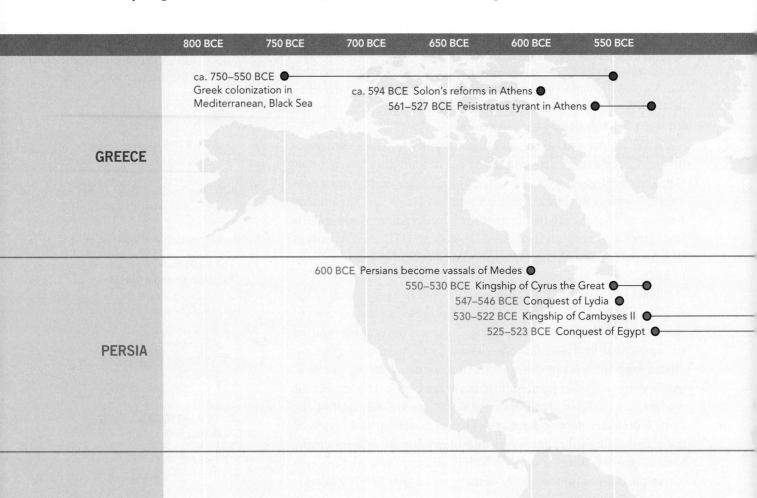

	800 BCE	750 BCE	700 BCE	650 BCE	600 BCE	550 BCE
GREECE		ca. 750–550 BCE Greek colonization in Mediterranean, Black Sea		ca. 594 BCE Solon's reforms in Athens	561–527 BCE Peisistratus tyrant in Athens	
PERSIA				600 BCE Persians become vassals of Medes	550–530 BCE Kingship of Cyrus the Great	547–546 BCE Conquest of Lydia
						530–522 BCE Kingship of Cambyses II
						525–523 BCE Conquest of Egypt
HELLENISTIC WORLD						

Central Asia through Persia's mountains and deserts, where two pastoral Indo-European societies, the Medes (**MEEDZ**) and Persians, competed for power in the early seventh century. Soon the Persians displaced the Medes.

At its peak the Persian Empire, usually known as **Achaemenid** (a-KEY-muh-nid) Persia after the ruling family, extended from the Indus Valley in the east to Libya in the west and from the Black, Caspian, and Aral (**AR-uhl**) Seas in the north to the Nile Valley in the south (see Map 7.1). King Cyrus II (Cyrus the Great) began the expansion, and his successors, Cambyses (**kam-BY-seez**) II, Darius (**duh-RY-uhs**) I, and Xerxes (**ZUHRK-seez**) I, continued the conquests. Their autocratic but culturally tolerant government established a model for later Middle Eastern empires and challenged the Greeks in the west. They also learned from their neighbors and the conquered peoples, even retaining some defeated leaders as court advisers. Hence, they learned to mint coins from the Lydians and adopted city planning from the Medes. Assessing their rule and leaders is not easy, however, since most of the written accounts of Persia that survive from twenty-five hundred years ago are by Greeks, Persia's bitter enemies. Historians still debate the nature of the Persian state, society, and culture.

After first overthrowing the Median king, by 539 Cyrus the Great (r. 550–530 BCE) had conquered Mesopotamia, Syria, Palestine, Lydia (a kingdom in western Anatolia), and all the Greek cities in Anatolia such as Miletus. As much diplomat as soldier, the pragmatic Cyrus followed moderate policies in the conquered territories, making only modest demands for tribute. After conquering Babylonia, he issued a proclamation on a cylinder that some scholars today consider the world's first charter of human rights and tolerance: "Protect this land from rancor, from foes, from falsehood, and from drought." But other scholars consider this mostly Persian propaganda. Cyrus claimed that the main Babylonian god, Marduk (**MAHR-dook**), ordered him to help the

Achaemenid The ruling family of the classical Persian Empire.

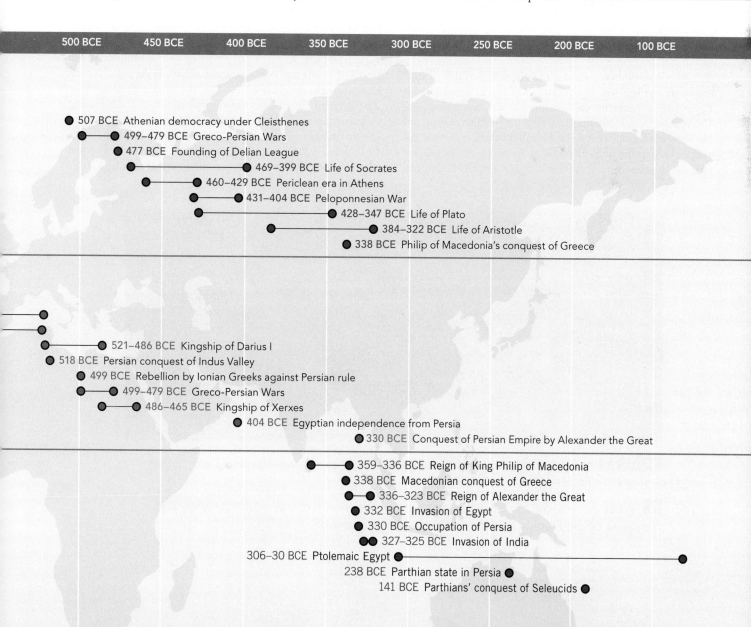

| 500 BCE | 450 BCE | 400 BCE | 350 BCE | 300 BCE | 250 BCE | 200 BCE | 100 BCE |

507 BCE Athenian democracy under Cleisthenes
499–479 BCE Greco-Persian Wars
477 BCE Founding of Delian League
469–399 BCE Life of Socrates
460–429 BCE Periclean era in Athens
431–404 BCE Peloponnesian War
428–347 BCE Life of Plato
384–322 BCE Life of Aristotle
338 BCE Philip of Macedonia's conquest of Greece

521–486 BCE Kingship of Darius I
518 BCE Persian conquest of Indus Valley
499 BCE Rebellion by Ionian Greeks against Persian rule
499–479 BCE Greco-Persian Wars
486–465 BCE Kingship of Xerxes
404 BCE Egyptian independence from Persia
330 BCE Conquest of Persian Empire by Alexander the Great

359–336 BCE Reign of King Philip of Macedonia
338 BCE Macedonian conquest of Greece
336–323 BCE Reign of Alexander the Great
332 BCE Invasion of Egypt
330 BCE Occupation of Persia
327–325 BCE Invasion of India
306–30 BCE Ptolemaic Egypt
238 BCE Parthian state in Persia
141 BCE Parthians' conquest of Seleucids

Babylonians by bringing them "justice and righteousness."[2] He also allowed the exiled Jews taken to Babylon by the Assyrians to return to Palestine and rebuild their temple, prompting a Jewish prophet to proclaim that Cyrus was favored by their god Yahweh. When Cyrus was killed while campaigning in Central Asia, his son Cambyses II (r. 530–522 BCE) subjugated Egypt, wisely presenting himself as a new Egyptian ruler who would bring, he proclaimed, stability, good fortune, health, and gladness.

Cambyses was succeeded by Darius I (r. 521–486 BCE), a usurper and arrogant man who had seized power and who boasted that "over and above my thinking power and understanding, I am a good warrior, horseman, bowman, spearman."[3] Darius crushed a revolt in Egypt and spread Persian power east and west, even annexing Afghanistan and parts of the Indus River Valley in northwestern India. As a result, today many peoples in Afghanistan and Central Asia speak languages closely related to Persian. Darius claimed that within his territories he cherished good people, rooted out the bad, and prevented people from killing each other. To promote justice and ensure his posterity as a great lawgiver, Darius fashioned a law code for Babylonia that basically reaffirmed Hammurabi's laws made almost fifteen hundred years earlier.

The Persians were among the classical world's greatest engineers and builders. For example, to forge closer links with Egypt, Darius completed the first Suez Canal, 125 miles long and 150 feet wide, that briefly connected the Mediterranean and the Red Seas. He also began building a spectacular new capital at Persepolis (puhr-SEP-uh-luhs), on whose massive stone terrace stood monumental royal buildings. Persepolis drew from Egyptian, Mesopotamian, and Greek traditions, its craftsmen and workers including Egyptians, Greeks, Hittites, and Mesopotamians.

7-1b Imperial Policies and Networks

Perhaps most crucial to their imperial success, the Persians generally treated conquered people and their social and religious institutions with respect. Cyrus the Great embraced anything in other cultures that he considered useful and contributed to cooperation and effective government. Herodotus reported that "there is no nation which so readily adopts foreign customs . . . As soon as they hear of any luxury, they instantly make it their own."[4] Unlike the earlier brutal Assyrians and Babylonians, the Persians used laws, generous economic policies, and tolerance toward the conquered to rule successfully. In Egypt, for instance, Cambyses became a pharaoh. The Persians prided themselves on their ability to unify vastly different peoples under the "king of kings," a title that respected other rulers with limited rights in their own territories. The "live and let live" tolerance was pragmatic, since Persian kings could not have realistically imposed a universal language or religion over their diverse empire. Leading citizens came from many backgrounds. Medes, Armenians, Greeks, Egyptians, and Kurds, a people living in the mountains just north of Persia and Mesopotamia, served as generals. Hence, many Greeks fought for Persia in the Greco-Persian Wars. The Persians also utilized various official languages, including Aramaic (ar-uh-MAY-ik), spoken by many peoples of varied ethnicities (including Jews) in western Asia, and later Greek. Greeks and Romans imitated some of these Persian techniques when they created even larger empires several centuries later.

IMAGE 7.2 **Bas Relief of Darius and Xerxes Holding Court** This relief was carved in one of the palaces at the Persian capital of Persepolis.

Q What can you tell from this bas relief about the throne room, clothing styles, and facial hair of the leaders and their soldiers and attendants?

[2]Quoted in Lindsey Allen, *The Persian Empire* (Chicago: University of Chicago Press, 1959), 27.
[3]Quoted in A. T. Olmstead, *History of the Persian Empire* (Chicago: University of Chicago Press, 1959), 125.
[4]From George Rawlinson, trans., *The Histories of Herodotus* (London: Dent, 1910), 1, 140.

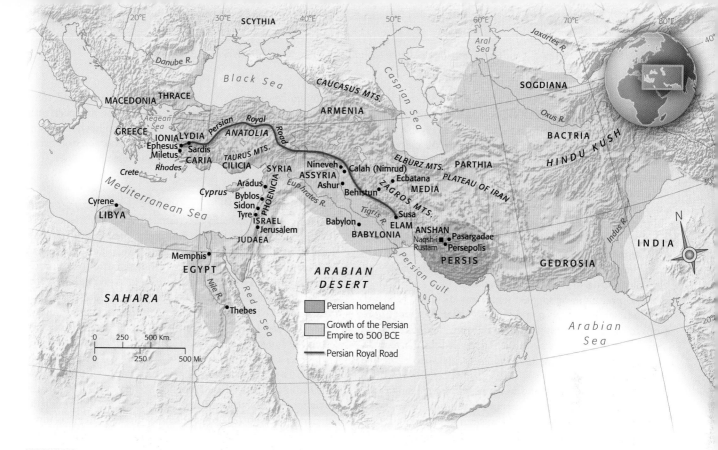

MAP 7.1 **The Persian Empire, ca. 500 BCE** At its height around 500 BCE, the Persians controlled a huge empire that included northern Greece, Egypt, and most of western Asia from the Mediterranean coast to the Indus River in India.

Q What do you consider the major challenges of governing the Persian Empire given its large size and multicultural population, as shown in this map?

Although in theory having absolute power, kings needed to consult with important nobles and judges, who were often in faraway provinces. Each provincial governor, or **satrap (SAY-trap)** ("protector of the kingdom"), ruled according to established laws and paid annual taxes to the king. Communication was aided by the "royal road" stretching seventeen hundred miles from east to west, and a king's messenger on a horse could cover this road in nineteen days. The Greek historian Herodotus marveled at the extensive, well-protected roads, writing that "neither snow, nor rain, nor heat, nor darkness of night prevents these couriers from completing their designated stages with utmost speed."[5]

The Persian Empire was strengthened by trade, which was promoted both by the highways and by the use of standard weights and measures and minted coins. A vast trade network and opportunities for extensive scientific and cultural exchanges helped attract the support of Greek cities in Anatolia. Instead of stealing their wealth, Persian rulers allowed conquered peoples to maintain their usual economic activities. Phoenicians, for example, continued their Mediterranean trade. The Persians maintained a kind of "royal navy," perhaps two thousand vessels at its height, in the eastern Mediterranean, with crews drawn from locals such as Phoenicians and Ionian Greeks. To open new trade networks, Darius sent an expedition to India that returned by sailing around Arabia to Suez, laying the foundation for conquering the Indus River Valley and opening more maritime trade.

7-1c Persian Religion and Society

The Persians made another distinct contribution to later world history by promoting **Zoroastrianism (zo-ro-ASS-tree-uh-niz-uhm)**. Some key ideas in Judaism, Christianity, and Islam are foreshadowed by, and perhaps even derived from, Zoroastrianism, which later became Persia's state religion. Its founder, Zoroaster (whose name means "With Golden Camels"), was one of the first non-Hebrew religious leaders to challenge the prevailing polytheism. Scholars debate whether he lived between 630 and 550 BCE during the Axial Age or centuries earlier, perhaps around 1000 or 1200 BCE. He may have been a priest in the early Persian religion, which was closely related to the religion of the Aryans who migrated to India.

The early Persians apparently believed in three great gods and many lesser ones, but

> **satrap** ("protector of the kingdom") A Persian official who ruled according to established laws and procedures and paid a fixed amount of taxes to the emperor each year.
>
> **Zoroastrianism** A monotheistic religion founded by the Persian Zoroaster, and later the state religion of Persia. Its notion of one god opposed by the devil may have influenced Judaism and later Christianity.

[5]Quoted in William H. Stiebing, *Ancient Near Eastern History and Culture* (New York: Longman, 2003), 303.

Zoroaster had a monotheistic vision, preaching that only one of these, **Ahura Mazda** (ah-HOOR-uh MAZZ-duh) (the "Wise Lord"), was the supreme deity in the universe, responsible for creation and the source of all goodness. A rival Satan-like entity, Angra Mainyu ("Hostile Spirit"), embodied evil and was the source of all misery, cowardice, lies, and sin. Ahura Mazda allowed humans to freely choose between himself and evil, Heaven and Hell. By serving Ahura Mazda, men and women promoted ultimate goodness and truth. At the end of time, Zoroaster believed, Ahura Mazda would win a final victory over evil and even Hell would come to an end. Zoroaster also banned the use of intoxicants and animal sacrifice. However, some Persians worshipped other gods, and several religions coexisted in Persia.

The Jews may have adopted some ideas about good and evil, God and the devil, Heaven and Hell, and a last judgment from Zoroastrians while held captive in Babylon (586–539 BCE). Christianity later incorporated such ideas, and the Zoroastrian watchwords of "good thoughts, good words, good deeds" became key ideas of several religions. Darius I publicly attributed his victories to Ahura Mazda and honored him for creating earth, sky, and humankind. While Christianity and, later, Islam eventually displaced Zoroastrianism in western Asia, the faith lives on today among small groups in Iran as well as in the wealthy Parsee (PAR-see) minority in India, descendants of Persian Zoroastrians who in the seventh and eighth centuries CE fled Islamic conquest and domination of Persia.

The Persians were not as politically diversified a society as the Greeks (see Discover Historical Voices: A Greek Account of Persian Customs). Their system was headed by nobles, many of them warriors who had been granted large estates by the king, followed by priests, merchants, and bankers. In Persian-ruled Babylonian cities these citizens made important judicial decisions in formal assemblies. Zoroastrian priests schooled noble sons to prepare for government careers. The middle class included bakers, brewers, butchers, carpenters, coppersmiths, and potters. At the bottom of the social structure, many peasant farmers were impoverished, becoming poor renters or sharecroppers bound to the land. Slaves—mainly debtors, criminals, and prisoners of war—filled various functions. Some were apprenticed in trades, while others operated small businesses.

Persian society was patriarchal and polygamous. Men believed that the greatest proof of masculinity was to father many sons, and many rich men had several wives. Persian women were usually kept secluded in harems and probably veiled themselves, an ancient practice in western Asia. But some queens and other noble women strongly influenced their husbands, and some controlled large estates. A few women became independently wealthy. For instance, one entrepreneur and landowner of commoner origins, Irdabama, controlled a large labor force of several hundred and operated her own grain and wine business.

Ahura Mazda (the "Wise Lord") The one god of Zoroastrianism.

7-1d Warfare and Persian Decline

Persia's rulers eventually encountered major resistance by Scythians and Greeks. Darius campaigned unsuccessfully against the Scythians (SITH-ee-uhnz), the warlike Indo-European pastoral nomads whose territory stretched from Ukraine to Mongolia. Skilled horsemen and master gold and bronze workers, Scythians had both fought and traded with Greek cities. The many Greeks who lived in Persian territories were also rivals for regional power. Inspired by Scythian resistance, some Greek cities on the Ionian (eye-OH-nee-uhn) coast of Anatolia rebelled against Persian control (see Map 7.1). In response Darius attacked cities on the Greek peninsula that were supporting the Ionian rebels. During this first Greco-Persian War, the tiny disunited Greek states turned back the world's most powerful empire. While the Persians failed to occupy peninsular Greece, they reclaimed the Ionian cities, brutally punishing the most rebellious. Darius then supported democratic forces in Ionian cities, a tactic that failed to inspire peninsular Greek cooperation with Persian aims.

Xerxes (r. 486–465 BCE), the son of Darius, tried again to conquer the Greeks in 480 BCE, attacking with a huge army and naval force. In this fierce two-year struggle, perhaps Xerxes's most effective ally was the Ionian Greek queen Artemisia (AHRT-uh-MIZH-ee-uh) of Helicarnassus, who was praised for her bravery as a naval commander and the wise counsel she gave the Persian king. But the Persian thrust failed. Although Xerxes still held some of the Greek world and regained control of Egypt, defeat in this second Greco-Persian War proved a turning point in Persian history.

The Persian Empire was not finally conquered until 330 BCE, when Alexander the Great's superior army defeated Persian forces. However, the seeds of decline had been planted earlier when Xerxes began imposing heavier taxes. By 424 BCE the Persian Empire suffered from civil unrest caused by fights within the Achaemenid family, disaffected satrapies, currency inflation, difficulty collecting taxes, and high interest rates and debt that ruined many merchants and landlords. Xerxes and his successors also unwisely reversed the inclusive policies of Cyrus and Darius. Some regions rebelled. Egypt ended Persian control in 404 BCE, restoring pharaonic rule. Thus support for the increasingly remote kings weakened long before Alexander the Great ended Achaemenid Persia and its once-great empire.

KEY POINTS

▶ The Persian Empire, centered on a trade crossroads, was larger than any empire that preceded it.

▶ The Persians often won the support of peoples they had conquered through their respect for native cultures and their institution of the rule of law.

▶ The monotheistic Persian religion, Zoroastrianism, may have contributed some key ideas to Judaism, Christianity, and Islam.

▶ The Persian Empire suffered several setbacks, including an unsuccessful campaign against the Scythians and repeated failure to completely conquer Greece.

▶ Though the Persian Empire was conquered by Alexander the Great in 330 BCE, it had begun to decline over a century earlier.

Discover Historical Voices

A Greek Account of Persian Customs

The Persians used several written languages, but few of their nonreligious documents have survived. Much of what we know of Persian life in this era comes from Greek sources, most of them biased against their greatest regional rival and threat. Of course, even today writers' or visitors' observations on a foreign culture may reflect their own political, cultural, and/or religious perspectives. Although his observations must be treated with caution, the Greek historian Herodotus, writing in the later fifth century BCE, had a less nationalistic and more universalistic approach than most Greeks, holding some sympathy for Persians. He was born in and traveled widely in the Persian empire, although not to the Persian heartland, and gathered considerable information, including these observations on some Persian customs.

The customs which I know the Persians to observe are the following: they have no images of the gods, no temples nor altars, and consider the use of them a sign of folly. This comes, I think, from their not believing the gods to have the same nature with men, as the Greeks imagine. Their wont, however, is to ascend the summits of the loftiest mountains, and there to offer sacrifice to Zeus [Ahura Mazda], which is the name they give to the whole circuit of the firmament. They likewise offer to the sun and moon, to the earth, to fire, to water, and to the winds. These are the only gods whose worship has come down to them from ancient times. . . .

To these gods the Persians offer [animal] sacrifice in the following manner: they raise no altar, light no fire, pour no libations; there is no sound of the flute, no putting on of chaplets, no consecrated barley-cake; but the man who wishes to sacrifice brings his victim to a spot of ground which is pure from pollution, and there calls upon the name of the god to whom he intends to offer. It is usual to have the turban encircled with a wreath, most commonly of myrtle. The sacrificer is not allowed to pray for blessings on himself alone, but he prays for the welfare of the king, and of the whole Persian people, among whom he is of necessity included. . . .

Of all the days in the year, the one which they celebrate most is their birthday. It is customary to have the board furnished on that day with an ampler supply than common. The richer Persians cause an ox, a horse, a camel, and an ass to be baked whole and so served up to them: the poorer classes use instead the smaller kinds of cattle. They eat little solid food but abundance of dessert, which is set on table a few dishes at a time; this it is which makes them say that "the Greeks, when they eat, leave off hungry, having nothing worth mention served up to them after the meats; whereas, if they had more put before them, they would not stop eating." They are very fond of wine, and drink it in large quantities. . . .

There is no nation which so readily adopts foreign customs as the Persians. Thus, they have taken the dress of the Medes, considering it superior to their own; and in war they wear the Egyptian breastplate. As soon as they hear of any luxury, they instantly make it their own: and hence, among other novelties, they have learnt unnatural lust from the Greeks. Each of them has several wives, and a still larger number of concubines. Next to prowess in arms, it is regarded as the greatest proof of manly excellence to be the father of many sons. Every year the king sends rich gifts to the man who can show the largest number: for they hold that number is strength. Their sons are carefully instructed from their fifth to their twentieth year, in three things alone—to ride, to draw the bow, and to speak the truth. Until their fifth year they are not allowed to come into the sight of their father, but pass their lives with the women. This is done that, if the child die young, the father may not be afflicted by its loss.

Reflection Questions

1. What aspects of religious beliefs and worship does Herodotus stress?
2. How was Persian culture cosmopolitan?
3. What customs made Persian society unique?
4. Can you identify some of the positive and some of the negative perceptions of Persians contained in this excerpt?

Source: William Stearns Davis, *Readings in Ancient History: Illustrative Extracts from the Sources*, vol. 2: *Greece and the East* (Boston: Allyn and Bacon, 1912), 58–61. This text is part of the Internet Ancient History Sourcebook (fordham.edu/Halsall/ancient/herodotus-persians.asp).

7-2 The Rise and Flowering of the Greeks

TRANSITIONS SOCIETIES

Q What were some features of Greek government, philosophy, and science?

When people today think of the classical Greeks, they envision the "golden age" of Athenian democracy, with thinkers pondering life's meaning and the scientific mysteries, but these were only part of a complex, innovative, and often conflicted society.

CONNECTION to TODAY

What legacies from Classical Greece do you consider the most valuable and influential today?

Historians debate how much of their culture the Greeks created and how much they adopted from others. The Mediterranean was a zone of interaction for peoples living around its rim, and by 700 BCE the Greeks were prospering through active participation

MAP 7.2 **Classical Greece, ca. 450 BCE** Greek settlements, divided into rival city-states, occupied not only the Greek peninsula but also Crete and western Anatolia. Two alliances headed by Athens and Sparta fought each other in the Peloponnesian War (431–404 BCE).

Q What geographical features of the Greek world contributed to disunity and which features promoted connections between the scattered city-states of the peninsula and Ionia?

in maritime trade. The Greeks also struggled to forge democracy. Like people today, they debated how to rule populations, choose leaders, and educate youngsters. But the ancient Greek society modern people admire was also far from egalitarian and had what many people today would consider unattractive features, including slavery and a rigid patriarchy.

polis A Greek city-state that embraces nearby rural areas, whose agricultural surplus then helped support the urban population.

7-2a The Greek City-States

Varied influences shaped the Greek world. Mountainous terrain, coastal plains, and scattered islands fostered many city-states rather than one centralized state, as well as spurring the maritime trade that brought growth and prosperity between 800 and 500 BCE. Political institutions that allowed socially diverse groups of residents in some cities to make decisions also encouraged economic growth. A growing population, too little good farmland, and commercial interests led many Greeks to emigrate, establishing new settlements along the Ionian coast, around the Black Sea, in Italy, and on the Mediterranean coasts of France and Spain (see Map 7.2). Greeks even visited and some sojourned or lived in Egypt.

Prosperity led to a new conception of the city and the citizen's role. The **polis** (POE-lis), a city-state, became the major institution of Greek life and gave citizens a sense of community, loyalty, personal identity, and meaning. Free male citizens meeting in an open assembly made all decisions, from building a new temple to making war. The worst punishment a Greek could suffer was expulsion from the polis, and some Greeks committed suicide rather than face ostracism. City-states competed fiercely with each other, including in sports events. Modern sports fans owe much to the Greeks for pioneering organized athletic competitions. In the Olympic Games, begun in the eighth century BCE as a religious festival to honor the god Zeus, each polis sent athletes who competed naked in track and field events or personal contests of strength such as wrestling. The idea was to win, even if it meant cheating.

Not all city residents were equal. Many cities developed **oligarchy** (AHL-uh-gar-kee), rule by a small group of wealthy leaders. As much as 80 percent of the population, including women, slaves, children, and resident foreigners, were not citizens and had no right to vote or hold office. Even among citizens, members of old, aristocratic families enjoyed greater respect and authority than others. By the seventh century, however, aristocratic power had weakened. Although aristocrats generally scorned trade in favor of wealth from landowning, growing trade created wealth for other citizens, allowing them to compete with the upper class. Furthermore, a new battle formation relied on infantry more than the aristocracy-dominated cavalry. The city-state of Sparta perfected the phalanx (FAY-langks), consisting of a square of soldiers moving in unison, each man protected with heavy armor and carrying a sword or spear. Greek armies became citizen-armies, not paid professional forces. As nonaristocrats risked their lives for their polis, they wanted a greater role in governing it.

The new military system, population expansion, and increased wealth from trade with the Ionian Greeks helped foster democracy. Some Greeks combined the contradictory ideas that people are politically free but also owe loyalty to their community. Some also discovered how people could live without being controlled by gods or kings, framing notions of political freedom and equality for adult male citizens. These were radical ideas for that era, or even for ours.

7-2b Reform, Tyranny, and Democracy in Athens

The most dramatic political changes occurred in Athens, a polis on the eastern Greek peninsula of Attica that became progressively more democratic. This change was partly the result of a crisis. The soil was wearing out, and farmers were going deeply into debt. As poor wheat harvests continued, farmers sold themselves and their families into slavery. The poor demanded reform. Around 594 BCE Athenians elected Solon (SOH-luhn), a general, poet, and merchant, to lead the city and rewrite the old constitution. To avoid civil war, he canceled debts, forbade enslavement for debt default, made wealth rather than birth the criterion for membership on the city's governing council, and established a Council of 400 to review issues for action by the Assembly of Citizens, a court of appeals where people, rich or poor, could bring cases to court. However, he also reduced the freedom of women by, for example, allowing fathers to sell into slavery daughters who had lost their virginity before marriage.

The Athenian path to more democracy moved from reform to tyranny to democracy. Solon's reforms failed to please either side in this social and economic struggle. The poor wanted land from the rich, while aristocrats resented their loss of power. Tensions returned, allowing Peisistratus (pie-SIS-truht-uhs) (r. 561–527 BCE) to seize power as a **tyrant**, not necessarily a brutal ruler but someone ruling outside the law. Peisistratus gave to the poor land confiscated from aristocratic estates and launched a building program, including an aqueduct to bring water directly to the city center.

In 507 BCE another aristocrat, Cleisthenes (KLICE-thuh-neez), established genuine democracy in Athens. Instead of emphasizing noble birth or wealth for citizenship, Cleisthenes created geographical units that chose people by lot (drawing names or winners by chance, usually from a container) for a new Council of 500 that submitted legislation to the Assembly, consisting of forty thousand citizens who selected city officials by lot. In the mid-fifth century aristocratic power was further reduced when lower-income citizens were allowed to become officials. Euripides (you-RIP-uh-deez) described the system in his play, *The Suppliant Woman*: "The city is free, and ruled by no one man. The people reign, in annual succession. They do not yield power to the rich; the poor man has an equal share in it."[6] Athenians believed that ordinary citizens could serve in any government positions except as military officers, choosing representatives by lot rather than by more divisive elections. However, only a small group of adult males enjoyed these rights. Moreover, many Greeks thought that democracy of any type was a bad thing.

7-2c The Spartan System

In the Peloponnese (PELL-eh-puh-NEESE) peninsula in southern Greece, the landlocked city-state of Sparta followed a course much different from that of Athens (see Map 7.2). Spartans saw military power as essential for prestige and influence. Short of land, they conquered their neighbors rather than establish overseas colonies, and they made the conquered peoples agricultural slaves with no political or human rights who could be killed almost at will. Since slaves greatly outnumbered Spartans, a rigid military state emerged, led by two kings and a Council of Elders elected for life by an Assembly of all citizens over thirty. The Assembly approved or rejected measures prepared by the Council of Elders and the kings. Thus the Spartans discouraged independent thought or behavior. Boys who seemed physically unfit were taken to a remote rural area and left to die. The other boys received rigid military training and were taught that self-discipline and courage were the highest virtues. One legend tells of a young

oligarchy Rule by a small group of wealthy leaders.

tyrant Someone who ruled a Greek polis outside the law, not necessarily a brutal ruler.

⁶From Loren J. Samons III, ed., *Athenian Democracy and Imperialism* (Boston: Houghton Mifflin, 1998), 216–217.

boy who found a small fox and concealed it under his shirt while engaged in military drill. While standing at attention, the boy suddenly fell over dead. The fox had eaten into his vital organs, but self-discipline had kept him from crying out in pain. From ages twenty to thirty, Spartan males served in the army; only after this time were they allowed to live at home with their wives.

Although enjoying no political rights, Spartan women acquired a higher status than other Greek women. Their husbands' frequent absences allowed some to acquire wealth and land. Spartan girls underwent physical training, including races and trials of strength. When grown they enjoyed reciting poetry and swigging wine. Athenian men criticized Spartan women for their independence, portraying them as greedy, licentious, and needing male control. The playwright Euripides scolded the "Spartan maidens, allowed out of doors with the young men, running and wrestling in their company, with naked thighs."[7]

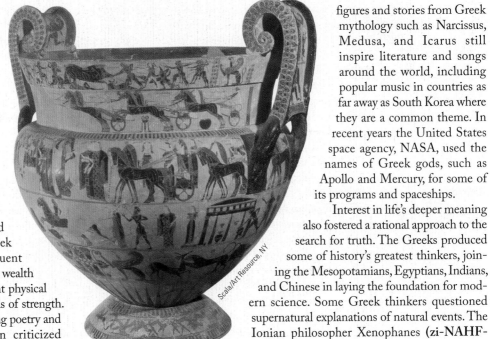

IMAGE 7.3 **Narrative Drawing on Pottery** The Francois vase, made around 570 BCE, is considered a masterpiece of narrative drawing on pottery, with fine detail and vivid coloring. It shows scenes of battle.

Q What does this vase drawing tell us about battles and weapons in early classical Greece?

7-2d Religion, Rationalism, and Science

The Greeks may have been practical people, but they also respected the supernatural realm. The many gods, legends, and myths introduced by the Homeric epics (see Chapter 3) profoundly shaped Greek thinking and values. Greek religion also owed something to Egyptian and Phoenician beliefs. Chief gods and goddesses represented various natural and human activities. Zeus, a sky-god, governed the natural and social order. Other deities included his wife, Hera (**HEER-uh**), representing marriage and the family; Poseidon (**puh-SIDE-uhn**), the lord of the sea and brother of Zeus; Athena, Zeus's favorite daughter, the goddess of wisdom; Apollo, patron of music, philosophy, and other finer things in life; Dionysus (**DIE-uh-NYE-suhs**), the god of wine; and Aphrodite (**af-ruh-DITE-ee**), goddess of love, sex, and fertility. Her reputation for inspiring lovemaking is the source for the English word *aphrodisiac*. The Greek gods indulged freely in sexual pleasure and seducing mortals. Although these deities had human virtues and vices, Greeks viewed them as immortal and more powerful than humans. Defying the gods invited disaster, whereas proper sacrifices to the gods, usually incorporated into festivals and official ceremonies, guaranteed harmony between humans and the heavens. Today,

figures and stories from Greek mythology such as Narcissus, Medusa, and Icarus still inspire literature and songs around the world, including popular music in countries as far away as South Korea where they are a common theme. In recent years the United States space agency, NASA, used the names of Greek gods, such as Apollo and Mercury, for some of its programs and spaceships.

Interest in life's deeper meaning also fostered a rational approach to the search for truth. The Greeks produced some of history's greatest thinkers, joining the Mesopotamians, Egyptians, Indians, and Chinese in laying the foundation for modern science. Some Greek thinkers questioned supernatural explanations of natural events. The Ionian philosopher Xenophanes (**zi-NAHF-uh-neez**) was skeptical of the gods:

*Mortals deem that the gods are begotten as they [humans] are, and have clothes like theirs and voice and form.... The Ethiopians make their gods black. The Thracians (**THRAY-shuhns**) say theirs have blue eyes and red hair.*[8]

Indeed, some Greeks might today be considered atheists or agnostics. The scientist Democritus (**di-MAHK-ruht-uhs**) speculated that reality consisted of nothing except fundamental particles swirling randomly in the void. Some thinkers identified God with nature. Others, like Lucretius, condemned the immorality of people who do evil acts under religious delusions. 2,500 years ago, the Ionian-born philosopher Anaxagoras (c. 510-428 BCE), reflecting a spirit of scientific inquiry, correctly determined that the moon was not a god but rather a rocky object that reflects light from the sun, which was also not a god. This enabled him to explain moonlight, lunar phases, and eclipses. However he had become friends with the Athenian leader Pericles, whose political enemies turned to persecuting those linked to him. Anaxagoras was arrested, tried, sentenced to death, and then exiled, ostensibly for breaking impiety laws while promoting his ideas about the moon and sun. But his ideas would live on to this day, and for his recognition of the moon's true nature, a lunar crater, visited by orbiting spacecraft some 2,400 years later, bears the name Anaxagoras.

Creative thought sprouted throughout the Greek world. Thales of Miletus (ca. 636–546) was the first known person to perceive the universe as orderly and to seek a natural explanation of phenomena rather than attributing them to gods. His student Anaximander of Miletus (611–547) believed the first creatures lived in water and came close to the idea, developed several

[7]Quoted in Robert Flaceliere, *Daily Life in Greece at the Time of Pericles* (London: Phoenix, 2002), 56.
[8]Quoted in Rex Warner, *The Greek Philosophers* (New York: American Library, 1958), 24.

millennia later, that human beings evolved from lower forms of life. Democritus argued that all matter was composed of tiny seeds (atoms) that moved, creating different objects. Heracleitus (**HER-uh-KLITE-uhs**) of Ephasus (**EF-uh-suhs**) in Ionia perceived the universe in a constant state of flux, with only change permanent. The Ionian Pythagoras (**puh-THAG-uh-ruhs**) helped establish modern mathematics by emphasizing the number 10 and developing the multiplication tables and major mathematical theorems.

These early thinkers laid the foundations of natural science and philosophy by emphasizing the explanatory power of human reason and evaluating evidence by human rather than divine standards. However, some Greek thinkers suggested the more troubling idea of relative rather than absolute human standards. The **Sophists** (**SAHF-uhsts**) emphasized skepticism, denying there is ultimate truth. People have struggled with this twin legacy of Greek thinkers ever since.

7-2e Axial Age Philosophy and Thinkers

Three major fifth- and fourth-century BCE Athenian thinkers helped shape world philosophy. Today in many countries students still study their work as part of classes examining the "Classics." The first two, Socrates and Plato, studied the nature of truth; the third, Aristotle (**AR-uh-staht-uhl**), examined the truth found in nature. These men participated in a philosophical and religious revolution across Eurasia between 600 and 200 BCE that historians often term the *Axial Age*. The ideas of Buddha in India, Confucius in China, several Hebrew prophets, the Persian Zoroaster (who may have actually lived much earlier), and various Greeks shaped classical societies and remained influential for many centuries.

The earliest seminal Greek philosopher, the Athenian Socrates (469–399 BCE), believed that "the unexamined life" was not worth living. Shabbily dressed, eccentric, passionate, and indifferent to money and pleasure, he asked people leading questions that helped them examine the truth of their ideas, an approach called the **Socratic Method**. Unlike the Sophists, Socrates believed in absolute truths that make people virtuous. Although considered the founder of Western moral philosophy, some of his elitist views might be unpopular even today. For example, suspicious of democracy, he favored government by the chosen few who acquired superior knowledge. Widely seen as a troublemaker for undermining the polis by asking so many, often embarrassing, questions and "corrupting the youth," Socrates was condemned to death for treason in 399 BCE. The prosecutor said of him: "Socrates is an evil doer and a curious person, searching into things under the earth and above the heavens, and making the worse appear the better, and teaching all this to others."[9] Refusing a lighter sentence or exile, Socrates chose death, making him, in modern eyes at least, a martyr for truth and free expression, although most of his contemporaries may not have viewed him this way.

Socrates's leading pupil, Plato (428–347 BCE), became disillusioned with city politics after his mentor's execution. After sojourning in Egypt, Plato founded a school in Athens called the Academy (the source of our word *academic*), where he elaborated Socrates's belief in ultimate truth, beauty, and goodness. He believed that most people, ruled by emotions, cannot see reality. Only a special class who are trained to use reason to control emotions and will, which he called the Guardians, understand ultimate truth and goodness and therefore should govern. Plato later retreated from this elitist conception, suggesting that strong laws could control democratic excesses. Some believe that Plato's thinking sanctioned dictatorships in which a few men claimed special wisdom and virtue.

The Athenian philosopher Aristotle (384–322 BCE) contributed enduring ideas, many of which might seem similar to some of ours today. The son of a Greek physician working for the king of non-Greek Macedonia, Aristotle studied philosophy with Plato and eventually founded his own school. Like Socrates, he was also charged with impiety, but he chose to go into exile. Although distrusting democracy, he encouraged people to pursue their personal desires. Rather than exploring ultimate truths, Aristotle pragmatically emphasized how human nature and physical nature worked. His writings spanned the social sciences, humanities, and natural sciences. One of the first psychologists, Aristotle described human emotions like affection, anger, bravery, fear, hate, joy, and pity. He concluded the world was round, classified and analyzed nature, dissected animals, and pioneered zoology, providing a key foundation for both Western and Islamic science. He also studied logic, ethics, and political systems. In philosophy, Aristotle speculated on **metaphysics**, the broad field that studies the most general concepts and categories underlying people and the world around them (such as "time" and "causation").

7-2f Literature

Culturally creative, Athens attracted many writers and artists because prosperity generated spending money for entertainment. Perhaps the Athenians' most enduring contribution, drama, arose from annual religious festivals during which plays, often bawdy, based on historical or mythological themes were usually performed in outdoor amphitheaters, accompanied by music. Most plays were tragedies, and the dramatists had different styles. Aeschylus (**ESS-kuh-luhs**) (525–456 BCE) emphasized traditional values, the gods, and justice issues while portraying the disasters brought on by too much pride. Sophocles (**SAUF-uh-klees**) (ca. 497–406 BCE), a humanist, stressed emotional issues. Aristophanes (**AR-uh-STAHF-uh-neez**) (448–380 BCE) wrote comedies ridiculing Athenians and their pretensions. In *The Knights*, a general tries to convince an ignorant sausage seller to unseat the Athenian leader: "To be a leader of the people isn't for learned men, or honest men, but for the ignorant and vile."[10] Some of his criticism reflected Athenian losses during a terrible war.

Sophists Thinkers in classical Greece who emphasized skepticism and the belief that there is no ultimate truth.

Socratic Method The method, introduced by Socrates, of asking people leading questions to help them examine the truth of their ideas.

metaphysics The broad field that studies the most general concepts and categories underlying people and the world around them (such as "time" and "causation").

[9]Quoted in Martyn Oliver, *History of Philosophy: Great Thinkers from 600 B.C. to the Present Day* (New York: MetroBooks, 1997), 16–17.
[10]Quoted in Mortimer Chambers et al., *The Western Experience*, vol. 1, 5th ed. (New York: McGraw-Hill, 1987), 96.

Some playwrights offered vivid images of women who refused to be silenced or abused. In *Agamemnon* (ag-uh-MEM-non), a great tragic drama by Aeschylus, the wife of Agamemnon, the hero of the Trojan War, kills him for sacrificing their daughter to the gods to get a favorable wind to sail to Troy. Some plays address questions that, twenty-five hundred years later, dominate today's headlines, such as asylum seeking, refugees, immigration, sexual violence, and treatment of foreigners. For example, in "The Suppliant Maidens" by Aeschylus, the plot involves a group of women from Egypt claiming Greek ancestry and seeking refuge in a Greek city from forced marriage back home. But although they are still seen as foreigners, the city's citizens vote in their favor and protect them.

Greek lyric poets, especially in Ionia, reflected an individualistic, intellectual approach. Hence, Archilochus (ahr-KIL-uh-kuhs) mocked the Spartan battlefield order to "return with your shield— or [carried] on it" by writing: "Some lucky Thracian has my shield, For, being somewhat flurried, I dropped it by a wayside bush, As from the field I hurried. To blazes with the shield. I'll get another just as good, When next I take the field."[11] A girl's school director and perhaps the most intensely personal poet, Sappho (SAFF-oh), from the Ionian island of Lesbos, wrote passionate love lyrics to her students: "A host of horsemen, some say, is the loveliest sight upon the earth; some say a display of soldiery; some a fleet of ships, but I say it's whomever one loves."[12] Considered Homer's equal, Sappho wrote poems that were read in the Mediterranean world long after her death. Today she is considered a lesbian artistic role model.

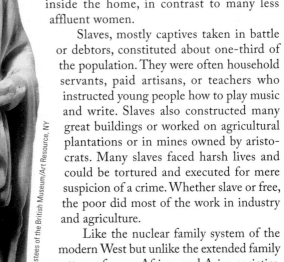

The Trustees of the British Museum/Art Resource, NY

IMAGE 7.4 Socrates This statue, made several centuries after his death, celebrates the Athenian philosopher Socrates, who had a strong influence on the thinking of Greek philosophers who came after him, including his student, Plato.

Q What does the statue suggest of how elite males dressed in fifth-century BCE Athens?

7-2g Greek Society

Pronounced differences separated social classes and genders, with freedom reserved primarily for males. Greek society consisted, from top to bottom, of free men (only some of them citizens), many resident foreigners, free women, and slaves. Most free men, if not wealthy landowners or small farmers, worked as laborers, artisans, or shopkeepers. Resident foreigners, including Phoenicians, Lydians, and Syrians, were primarily merchants, bankers, and artisans. Many became wealthy but were required to serve in the military. Free women could not vote, hold office, or serve on juries. Socrates supposedly asked a colleague: "Is there anyone of your acquaintance with whom you have less conversation than your wife?" The reply: "Hardly anyone, I think."[13] Women from elite families generally stayed inside the home, in contrast to many less affluent women.

Slaves, mostly captives taken in battle or debtors, constituted about one-third of the population. They were often household servants, paid artisans, or teachers who instructed young people how to play music and write. Slaves also constructed many great buildings or worked on agricultural plantations or in mines owned by aristocrats. Many slaves faced harsh lives and could be tortured and executed for mere suspicion of a crime. Whether slave or free, the poor did most of the work in industry and agriculture.

Like the nuclear family system of the modern West but unlike the extended family pattern of many African and Asian societies, most Greek families consisted of a husband, a wife, and children. Women's principal tasks were to feed and clothe their families and to bear and raise children. While lacking men's sexual freedom, women could own property and divorce their husbands, and they played essential roles in religious festivals. For example, the oracle at the temple of Delphi (DELL-fye), which many leaders consulted to determine the will of Apollo, spoke through a woman's voice.

But women also experienced strong prejudice in a patriarchal society. Aristotle articulated the misogynist, or antiwoman, views of many men in describing women as deformed males. A popular saying expressed male views: "Respectable women should stay at home; the street is for worthless hussies." Some women expressed their discontent, as reflected in a tragic play by Euripides: "[Men] say we lead a safe life at home. What imbeciles! I'd rather stand to arms three times than bear one child."[14] In contrast to political marginalization, Greek literature often portrayed women as powerful and capable of great anger, humor, faithfulness, and intelligence. For example, Penelope, the wife of Ulysses in Homer's *Odyssey*, ruled the state wisely until his return while outmaneuvering many men seeking to marry her. In Aristophanes's

[11]Quoted in C. Warren Hollister, *Roots of the Western Tradition: A Short History of the Ancient World*, 5th ed. (New York: McGraw-Hill, 1991), 109.
[12]From Barbara Hughes Fowler, *Archaic Greek Poetry: An Anthology* (Madison: University of Wisconsin Press, 1992), 131.
[13]Quoted in Robert Flaceliere, "Women, Marriage, and the Family," in *Everyman in Europe: Essays in Social History*, ed. Allan Mitchell and Istvan Deak, vol. 1 (Englewood Cliffs, NJ: Prentice-Hall, 1970), 53.
[14]From *Medea*, quoted in Frank J. Frost, *Greek Society*, 2nd ed. (Lexington, MA: D.C. Heath, 1980), 94.

bawdy comedy *Lysistrata* (**lis-uh-STRAH-tuh**), a group of women organize to end war by refusing to have sex with their husbands until the men stop fighting. Lysistrata tells her husband: "We women got together and decided we were going to save Greece. Listen to us and keep quiet, as we've had to do up to now, and we'll clear up the mess you've made."[15]

Some social customs might be considered controversial today. While their wives stayed home, men attended parties, sometimes enlivened by courtesans celebrated for their wit and charm. Some courtesans enjoyed high status and probably a good education. Aspasia (**ass-PAY-zhee-uh**), a vivacious, literate, and controversial Milesian, probably operated an Athens meetinghouse where educated men, including possibly Socrates, came for sex and conversation with intellectual women. Advocating gender equality, Aspasia became the mistress of the Athenian leader Pericles (**PER-eh-kleez**), whose enemies, among them dramatists, accused her of writing his speeches, violating the tradition that politics was for men only. Indeed, Greek opinion on her was so divided that it is hard to separate fact from fiction about her life and actions. Unlike some courtesans, most prostitutes were badly exploited slaves.

Homosexuality has existed in all societies from earliest times, but Greek men and some women were particularly open about their same-sex relationships. Nudity in public was accepted as normal, not shameful. Artists fashioned many naturalistic statues of naked men and women, and diverse homosexual practices and relationships were common. Yet many of these same people also pursued heterosexual relationships and marriage. Bringing up Greek boys and girls separately reduced heterosexual contact. Hence, homosexual behavior between older and younger upper-class men was accepted as part of a training or mentoring relationship for career preparation, with many famous Greeks having such relationships, among them Solon, Aeschylus, and Sophocles. In Sparta some top military units comprised homosexual couples. Female same-sex behavior was less public but likely fairly common, especially in Sparta. But the concepts of same-sex or even opposite-sex relationships or identity twenty-five hundred years ago were not necessarily the same as those in Western societies today. Men of superior status took for granted that, with or without consent, they could have intimate relations with anyone of inferior status, including

Scala/Art Resource, NY

IMAGE 7.5 **Women Fetching Water** The painting on this vase portrays everyday life in a Greek city. Women have congregated at a public fountain to fill jugs with water to be carried back home, where it will be used for drinking, cooking, and cleaning. The women's hair coverings and long robes reflect the fashion of the day.

Q What can this vase tell us about classical Greek society and culture?

servants, slaves, and foreigners. In contrast, many nonelite Greeks and some philosophers condemned homosexual relations between two adults.

KEY POINTS

▶ The mountainous, maritime geography of Greece fostered the development of multiple city-states rather than one centralized state.

▶ The polis system of governance allowed extensive political rights for some but no political rights for many.

▶ Though Greeks had a well-developed religion, they were also notable for their commitment to using reason to understand the world.

▶ Greek drama tended to focus on tragedy, as in the works of Euripides, Aeschylus, and Sophocles; writers like Aristophanes wrote comedies.

▶ Greek women were generally expected to stay at home and out of politics, but they were often featured as powerful characters in plays.

[15]From Aristophanes, *Lysistrata and Other Plays*, translated by Alan H. Sommerstein (New York: Penguin, 1973), 200–208.

7-3 Greeks, Persians, and the Regional System

▓ NETWORKS ⮂ TRANSITIONS

Ⓠ In what ways did Persians and Greeks encounter and influence each other?

During the early fifth century BCE peninsular Greek cities successfully fought a series of wars with the greatest power of western Asia, the Persian Empire. But rival Greek states also fought ruinous wars with each other. Both Greeks and Persians borrowed many ideas from neighboring peoples, including the Egyptians and western Asians, causing historians to debate the classical Greek and Persian legacies for both Europe and the Middle East.

CONNECTION to TODAY

Can you identify any parallels between Persian-Greek relations, both peaceful and violent, and similar rivalries in the world today?

7-3a The Greco-Persian Wars

The Greco-Persian conflict began in 499 BCE, when Athens supported some Greek cities in Anatolia that were rebelling against their Persian overlords. After defeating the rebels in 494, Darius I dispatched a fleet to punish the peninsular Greeks in 492, but storms destroyed his ships. He then sent a larger Persian force, which was defeated at the Battle of Marathon in northern Greece in 490 BCE. The Greeks slaughtered the Persians, many of whom drowned in the sea.

The Persians attempted again to conquer Greece in 480 BCE, when Xerxes sent a huge army and navy to engage an alliance led by Athens and Sparta. A Spartan force of three hundred fought to the death holding a strategic pass, but they were betrayed by some Greeks who showed the Persians a path around them. The Persians swept down into Athens, burning the city. Expecting final victory, they attacked the trapped Athenian fleet in the Bay of Salamis (SAL-uh-muhs), near Athens. Surprisingly, however, they were defeated. The large Persian force, far from home, proved difficult to supply and control effectively, while the Athenians had also developed the world's most advanced fighting ship, the well-armored *trireme* (**TRY-reem**), which had three banks of oarsmen and deadly bronze rams. The following year (479) the Greeks defeated the remaining Persian forces at the battle of Plataea (**pluh-TEE-uh**). Some historians argue that the Greek victory over the Persians led to a growing divide between "Europe" and "Asia," with the Greeks increasingly viewing themselves as different from, and superior to, the people to the east.

7-3b Empire and Conflict in the Greek World

The declining Persian threat reignited old rivalries between Greek cities, fostering nearly constant warfare between them. To defeat the Persians, the Greek cities had organized the **Delian** (DEE-lee-uhn) **League**, a defensive alliance led by the richest state and largest naval power, Athens. Other cities contributed funds or ships. But the Delian League changed from a defensive alliance to an Athenian empire. Athens controlled the league treasury, spending some of the money on Athenian civic improvements. Then in 467 Athens took military action to stop the island of Naxos (**NAK-suhs**) from leaving the league. Some Athenians protested that a democracy, which allows varied opinions, could not manage an empire.

Athens reached its golden age under Pericles (ca. 495–429 BCE), a visionary leader and spellbinding orator who promoted democratic legal reforms. Athenians, then numbering some 250,000 to 300,000, were justifiably proud of their city, especially of the magnificent public buildings such as the Parthenon (**PAHR-thuh-nahn**), a temple dedicated to the city's patron goddess, Athena, on a hilltop called the Acropolis (**uh-KRAHP-uh-luhs**). But while Athenians embraced self-fulfillment and individualism, some criticized unrestrained freedom, fearing that too much pride or self-expression spelled trouble. Across classical Greece, playwrights, poets, and historians argued that arrogance led to punishment by the gods and personal disaster. Despite the warnings, the Athenians' civic pride eventually brought disaster, as increasing resentment of Athenian power by rival cities generated the long **Peloponnesian War** (431–404 BCE) between Athens and Sparta-led alliances. In a famous "funeral oration" to memorialize dead Athenian soldiers, the nationalistic Pericles (r. 460–429 BCE) reportedly contrasted Athenian democratic institutions and equality before the law with Spartan discipline and lack of freedom:

> . . . *We are called a democracy, for the administration is in the hands of the many and not of the few. . . . I have dwelt upon the greatness of Athens because I want to show you we are contending for a higher prize than those who enjoy none of these privileges. For in magnifying the city I have magnified the men whose virtues made her glorious.*[16]

Pericles introduced the novel ideas that war was not just to defend hearth and home but to spread better ideas and systems, and also that free citizens had a responsibility to their community. But the assumption that their high ideals made Athenians superior to their neighbors fueled dislike by other Greek cities.

The war proved disastrous for Athens and boosted Sparta. The Athenians' plan to use their navy to combat their enemy's superior land army floundered when a deadly plague hit Athens, killing a third of the population, including Pericles. The Athenians also unwisely attempted to capture Syracuse, a Greek city in Sicily. Later the Spartans, with Persian advice, destroyed the Athenian fleet. The victorious Spartans disbanded the Athenian navy, destroyed the city walls, and killed or exiled thousands of Athenians. Although the war made

Delian League A defensive league organized by Greek cities in the fifth century BCE to defeat the Persians.

Peloponnesian War A long war between Athens and Sparta and their respective allies in 431–404 BCE that resulted in the defeat of Athens.

[16] Reported in Thucydides, quoted in L. S. Stavrianos, ed., *The Epic of Man to 1500* (Englewood Cliffs, NJ: Prentice-Hall, 1970), 120–122.

IMAGE 7.6 **The Acropolis** The Acropolis dominated the surrounding city of Athens. The marble Parthenon at the center, dedicated to Athena, was built during the time of Pericles.

Q What does this photo tell us about the centrality of the Acropolis in classical Athenian life and in Athens today?

Sparta the most powerful Greek state, decades of instability followed, and eventually the frequent conflicts between the Greek cities proved too destructive. Less than a century after the Peloponnesian War ended, Greece was conquered by neighboring Macedonia and made the base for a much greater empire.

7-3c Historiography: Universal and Critical

The Greeks developed concepts of history that are still used today, but they did so in the context of their connections to other societies. Of course, peoples before them had some sense of history. The legends passed down through oral traditions, such as the stories in the Hebrew Bible and the Homeric epics, were narratives of history, although we cannot prove their accuracy. The Chinese, most notably Sima Qian, also wrote historical accounts based on varied documentaries and other sources. But the Greeks Herodotus and Thucydides (thyou-SID-uh-deez) were the first to pursue critical, analytical, and universal history.

Sometimes called the Father of History, Herodotus (ca. 484–425 BCE) wrote history on a scale never attempted before, providing the main source about the Greco-Persian Wars. Integrating information on geography and culture, Herodotus wrote vividly about neighboring societies. He was born in a Persian-ruled Ionian city, Halicarnassus, and traveled around the Persian Empire and sojourned in Egypt, concluding that some Greek gods could be equated with Egyptian divinities. He also visited Tyre in what is today Lebanon, where he learned that Phoenicians had invented the alphabet. A sophisticated man with an inquiring mind, Herodotus lived for a time in Periclean Athens, where he met many famous men, and he portrayed the Athenians

favorably, attributing the Greeks' victory over the Persians' absolute monarchy to the Greeks' free society. Because his interests and travels went well beyond the Greek world, Herodotus might be considered the first world historian. But his writings must be used with caution since he often reported unverified, implausible, and even fanciful hearsay and failed to subject his material to enough critical scrutiny. Yet, to his credit he was something of a cultural relativist, avoiding Greek prejudices against other cultures and offering sympathetic views of Persians and criticisms of Greeks.

Our knowledge of Greek politics and wars during the fifth century BCE comes largely from a single book, *The Peloponnesian War*, written by Thucydides (ca. 460–400 BCE), a general exiled from Athens for losing an important battle. Despite his exile, Thucydides objectively evaluated the strengths and weaknesses of his home city, setting an example of careful observation. Unlike earlier writers, he added critical judgments to his narrative, such as by criticizing the Athenians for ignoring Pericles' warnings to attempt no new conquests. He also evaluated democracy's benefits and drawbacks and asked fundamental questions about the nature of power. Thucydides looked for patterns and moral lessons in the past. Whenever historians interpret the past, they are acknowledging a debt to Thucydides, a historian who was not just a teller of tales but also a teacher of wisdom.

7-3d Interregional Trade and Cultural Mixing

The Mediterranean Basin remained a vast zone of exchange in which Greeks played the commercial role once dominated by Phoenicians, trading wine and olive oil widely, establishing colonies, and spreading their culture. Like Greeks, Persians welcomed foreign traders. Port cities like Persian-ruled Miletus in Ionia prospered as regional trade hubs, and Persian gold coins were used by many societies. Persian leaders patronized Greek traders living in their domains, and in 510 BCE one of them, Scylax of Caryanda (**SKY-lax of KAR-ee-AN-da**), headed a Persian trade mission to India. Tribute flowed to the Persian capital, including Arabian and Bactrian camels, Indian gold, Scythian horses, Egyptian bulls, Anatolian leather goods, and Ionian silver.

Long-distance trade was crucial in many ways. Merchants traveling elsewhere to trade eventually evolved into what historians call a **trade diaspora**, living permanently in foreign cities or countries to do business. Most of the shipowners, traders, and moneylenders of Athens came from western Asia or Greek diaspora colonies such as Massalia (today's Marseilles) and the Crimean peninsula. Expatriate Greek merchant communities arose in Egypt, western Asia, and around the Black Sea. Trade also spurred a strong Athenian navy, helping Greeks defeat the Persians. Athens, the leading Greek commercial and financial hub, controlled rich silver mines worked by over twenty thousand slaves and imported wheat from Egypt, Sicily, and southern Russia. It gained a reputation as the most profitable and safest city to do business in, where even those of humble origins could achieve wealth.

The interlinked Mediterranean Basin fostered cosmopolitan thinking and brought together southern European, western Asian, and North African cultures. Though highly creative, Persians and Greeks also learned much from other peoples. Persians blended Ionian Greek, Mesopotamian, and Scythian art styles and motifs with their own traditions, while Greeks integrated Phoenician, Lydian, Egyptian, and Mesopotamian influences. Phoenician traders brought art forms and styles that inspired Greeks to modify their columns, pottery, statues, and ceramic styles. Greeks also adopted West Asian musical instruments and melodies, the Phoenician alphabet, and several Phoenician, Egyptian, and Anatolian gods. In addition, many Greek colonists absorbed local influences. For example, Greeks in Massalia, on the southern coast of France, had to understand local Celtic customs and language.

Greeks visited, worked in, settled in, and learned about other societies. For example, many Ionian merchants lived in Egypt. The Athenian lawgiver Solon visited Egypt as a merchant, studied with priests, and wrote poems about living along the Nile, and the influential writings of the Athenian physician Hippocrates (**hip-AHK-ruh-teez**) included some Egyptian medical ideas. Some Greeks even fought as mercenaries for Egyptian kings and worshipped Egyptian gods, while others served in Mesopotamian and Persian armies. The scientist Democritus visited Babylonia and Persia, and both Plato and Aristotle knew something about Zoroastrianism. Cosmopolitan

trade diaspora Merchants from the same city or country who live permanently in foreign cities or countries.

Ionia, where Greek and Asian cultures mixed, produced path-breaking thinking in philosophy and science, often under Persian patronage. Thales, a Lydian subject whom some scholars think was of Phoenician descent, studied geometry in Egypt and was the first Greek to inscribe a right-angled triangle and to determine the sun's course from solstice to solstice, something the Babylonians had long known how to do. The Ionian-born mathematician Pythagoras (ca. 580–ca. 500 BCE) may have visited Egypt and Babylon.

7-3e The Persian and Greek Legacies

Both Persians and Greeks left rich legacies for later societies. The Persians built the world's first large empire and flexible, tolerant multinational state, fusing traditions from many cultures while spreading learning, such as Babylonian astronomy, to peoples such as the Greeks. Persians today still revere Cyrus the Great. The Persians' Zoroastrian ideas also influenced Judaism, Christianity, and Islam, and many Persian words entered other languages; for example, the Persian word for "garden" became the English word *paradise*. Persian culture and language strongly influenced Afghanistan and Central Asia, and science and mathematics continued to develop in Ionia and Mesopotamia.

Many historians have admired the Greeks as the direct cultural, intellectual, and political ancestors of modern Europeans and North Americans, perceiving Greek society as culturally richer than any other before modern times. They view the Athenian era of Pericles, Plato, and Aeschylus as a "golden age" that launched Western literature, history, philosophy, science, and the democratic ideal. However, the view of Greece as the fountainhead of Western culture has problems and critics. Many Greek customs and social inequalities, especially their sometimes cruel treatment of women and slaves, appall people today. To critics, most Greek thinkers were not very liberal or secular, their democracy was elitist and flawed, and what Greek ideas western Europe inherited came in modified form through the Romans and later through the Arabs. Moreover, modern science is based not only on Greek but also on Chinese, Indian, and Middle Eastern discoveries. As a result, some historians believe the Romans founded the Western tradition, while others see the Greeks as more an extension of western Asian and North African rather than Western societies.

Today the Greeks seem both very strange and quite familiar, and the debate suggests how fascinating the Greeks have been to various societies over the centuries, beginning with the Romans. Middle Eastern societies also treasured Greek thinkers and science, and Greek philosophy influenced some Islamic scholars. The debate also indicates that the Greeks, however imperfect their society, fostered ideas and institutions that were unusual for their time and that have endured for over two millennia.

KEY POINTS

▶ The Persians attacked the Greeks several times, but the Greeks, against great odds, fended them off.

▶ Following the Greek victory over the Persians, Athens' growing arrogance eventually led to the Peloponnesian War between Athens and Sparta, which ended with Spartan victory.

▶ Herodotus, who wrote of the Greco-Persian Wars, and Thucydides, who wrote of the Peloponnesian War, were the first historians to write critical and analytical history.

▶ The eastern Mediterranean and western Asia were zones of intense trade and cultural mixing.

7-4 The Hellenistic Age and Its Afro-Eurasian Legacies

TRANSITIONS NETWORKS

Q What impact did Alexander the Great and his conquests have on world history?

Between 334 and 323 BCE, Alexander of Macedonia **(MASS-uh-DUHN-ia)**, a student of classical Greek ideas, created a huge empire that spread Greek culture over a wide area. Alexander's achievements established new networks of communication, and his legacy lived on for centuries in **Hellenism**, a widespread culture that combined western Asian (mainly Persian) and Greek (Hellenic) characteristics. During the Hellenistic Age, Greeks ruled over large parts of western Asia and North Africa, a domination that ended only with the rise of the Roman Empire and new Persia-based empires that continued to influence Middle Eastern history.

7-4a Alexander the Great, World Empire, and Hellenism

Greek disunity spawned by the Peloponnesian War opened the door for Macedonia, a state on the northern fringe of Greece, to conquer a vast empire. The war had so weakened all the Greek cities that no one city could unite the peninsula. Led by King Philip II (382–336 BCE), who developed a paid professional army and devised a more effective infantry phalanx, the Macedonian army conquered the Greek cities in 338 BCE.

> ### CONNECTION to TODAY
>
> Can you identify any ways in which the cosmopolitan Hellenistic world resembles the world we live in today?

But the hard-living, hard-drinking Philip had many enemies among Greeks, Persians, and Macedonian nobles. Two years later, on the eve of an expedition to Asia, Philip was assassinated.

Philip's twenty-year-old son and Aristotle's former student, Alexander (r. 336–323 BCE), became king following his father's death. A fearless and resolute megalomaniac, his ambitions for conquest were evident as a child. Alexander reportedly lamented that, with such a multitude of other countries, it was a shame that he had not yet conquered even one of them. Later, he wrote to the Persian king that he sought vengeance on Persia for its invasions of Greece a century and a half earlier. During his thirteen-year reign, this brilliant military strategist and leader of men used Macedonian, Greek, and mercenary troops to conquer the world from Greece to western India and from the Nile Valley to the Caucasus Mountains and Black and Caspian Seas.

Alexander employed ruthless tactics against enemies, sometimes destroying entire cities and slaughtering their inhabitants. In three major battles between 334 and 331, he dismantled the

> **Hellenism** A widespread culture flourishing between 359 and 100 BCE that combined western Asian (mainly Persian) and Greek (Hellenic) characteristics.

IMAGE 7.7 **Alexander Defeating Persians at Battle of Issus** In this Roman copy of an earlier Greek painting, Alexander the Great is shown on his horse in the battle that brought defeat to Persian king Darius III in 333 BCE.

Scala/Ministero per i Beni e le Attività culturali/Art Resource, NY

Q Can you see any changes in battles and weapons during the conquest of Alexander's empire and those portrayed on the Francois vase over two centuries earlier?

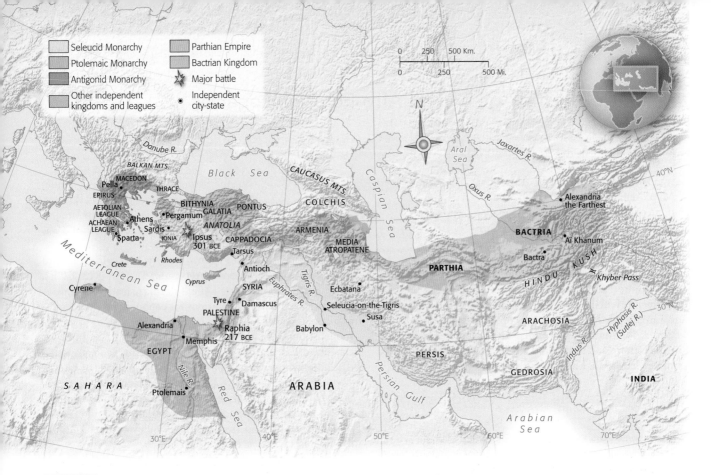

MAP 7.3 **The Hellenistic Kingdoms** The empire conquered by Alexander the Great was divided into rival Hellenistic kingdoms on his death in 323 BCE. By 140 BCE the Parthians had conquered some of the eastern territories.

Q Based on this map, how did the four major kingdoms established by Alexander's successors reflect the political geography of the old Persian Empire they displaced?

powerful Persian Empire and then burned the capital, Persepolis, reportedly after a night of drunken excess, and became not just a Greek but a Persian ruler. The burning of Persopolis symbolized the end of one era of cultural exchange and the beginning of another. His destruction of many Zoroastrian temples weakened that religion. Alexander's forces then moved through Afghanistan, fighting difficult battles with the tough and diverse peoples of that mountainous region, who chose to destroy their homes and farms than to surrender. Throughout history from ancient times until today many Afghans resisted foreign invaders and domination. Eventually many of Alexander's horses died and his grain ran out. Finally reaching the Indus Valley, the Macedonian wanted to move into India's heartland, but his exhausted, homesick troops refused, and they made a difficult desert journey back to Mesopotamia.

Alexander saw himself as a world ruler, governing all peoples. His empire incorporated most of the major ancient Afro-Eurasian societies: Egypt, Crete, Mycenae, Phoenicia, Mesopotamia, and the Indus Valley. Alexander initially organized his empire like the Persians. Although he was probably bisexual or homosexual and maintained an intimate relationship with a male adviser, Alexander married a Bactrian (northern Afghanistan) princess, encouraged his soldiers to take Asian wives, and wore the purple and white cloak and head ribbon previously worn by Persian royalty.

After Alexander died in Babylon at age thirty-three, probably from a fever acquired after a night of heavy drinking, the conquered territories retained a mixed Greek-Persian cultural

flavor for centuries under the influence of Hellenism. Ever since then, Western observers lionized Alexander, while Persians viewed him as a reckless destroyer and symbol of Western imperialism. During the Hellenistic Age the Greek legacy was passed on in a form that fifth-century BCE Greeks might not have recognized, one that emphasized individual freedom and reason less and the emotions more. Farther east, some of Alexander's soldiers settled in Afghanistan and western India, where Greek ideas had an enduring influence on the local art. For centuries afterward people as far away as Ethiopia, Nubia, and western India studied the Greek language and borrowed Greek artistic styles.

Alexander's empire soon fragmented. When asked to whom he left his empire, Alexander allegedly said: "to the strongest." By the end of the fourth century BCE, his former generals, all Macedonians, had divided Alexander's empire. A dynasty begun by Ptolemy (**TAHL-uh-mee**) controlled Egypt and the eastern Mediterranean coast; the family of Seleucus (**suh-LOO-kuhs**) controlled Persia, Mesopotamia, and Syria; and followers of Antigonus (**an-TIG-uh-nuhs**) controlled the Macedonian kingdom and northern Greece (see Map 7.3).

Seleucid dominance in Persia and Mesopotamia was ended by the Parthians (**PAHR-thee-uhnz**), Indo-European pastoral nomads who conquered large parts of Persia, Afghanistan, and Mesopotamia in the second century BCE. They expanded their empire into the Caucasus and crushed an invading Roman army in 53 BCE. Adopting many Hellenistic traditions, they made Greek the official state language. Gradually Persian influences grew stronger, and the Parthians became Zoroastrians. But frequent wars with the Romans, who replaced the other Hellenistic kingdoms, sapped their strength. A new Persian power, the Sassanians (**suh-SAY-nee-uhnz**), defeated the last Parthian ruler in 224 CE. The Sassanians ruled much of western Asia for the next four centuries, coming into frequent conflict with the Romans.

7-4b Hellenistic Cities and Economic Networks

Alexander founded many cities named after him, most famously the still-surviving city of Alexandria on Egypt's Mediterranean coast (see Map 7.3). Hellenistic cities were not independent city-states as in old Greece but part of kingdoms, their citizens enjoying little political participation. Wealthy aristocrats, professional soldiers, and bureaucrats ran the cities' governments. Although centers of Greek language and culture, which dominated elite circles, the multiethnic cities also existed in predominantly non-Greek environments and were influenced by local traditions. For example, the Ptolemaic dynasty in Egypt ruled with pharaonic pomp. While Hellenistic monarchs relied on Greeks, Persians, and others to govern, they were vastly outnumbered by their Asian and African subjects speaking their own languages.

No longer vibrant democratic communities, Hellenistic urban culture glorified hedonism. The upper classes enjoyed high living, with poets celebrating activities like horse racing, lovemaking, and drinking. A satirical Egyptian poem mocked a drunken and gluttonous harpist who showed up at weddings and festivals: "He disputes with the party-goers, shouting: 'I can't sing when I'm hungry, I can't hold my harp without my fill of wine!' And he drinks wine like two people and eats the meat of three."[17] Hellenistic cities were also cosmopolitan and ethnically diverse. Alexandria, for example, had large Egyptian, Greek, and Jewish populations and was a melting pot where many religions met, new ones sprouted up, and Zoroastrian holy books and the Hebrew Bible were translated into Greek. The Syrian Greek poet Meleager expressed the Hellenistic attitude: "Stranger, we live in the same motherland, the world."[18]

Alexander's conquests also linked the Mediterranean and western Asia in a vast trading network. Alexander had used Persian wealth to build and repair roads and harbors, and Greek colonists introduced or expanded money-based economies. Long-distance trade expanded rapidly as Chinese silk and Indian sugar were traded for Egyptian onions, Macedonian wood products, and Athenian olive oil. As caravans of vegetables and wine moved eastward, they crossed caravans of spices and other goods moving westward out of India, Arabia, and Northeast Africa. This trans-Eurasian trading network remained strong long after the Hellenistic states had disappeared.

7-4c Science, Religion, and Philosophy

Hellenistic thinkers maintained the Greek interest in scientific, religious, and philosophical questions, making outstanding contributions that still shape the world today. Scientists and mathematicians rigorously collected and evaluated data and then offered hypotheses to explain mathematical problems, natural phenomena, and the workings of the universe. Alexandria, with the ancient world's largest library (700,000 papyrus scrolls) and a famous institute with visiting scholars, was the chief research center, and Alexandrian thinkers and inventors anticipated modern scientific, mathematical, and technological developments. Here Euclid wrote his text on plane geometry, a book used for two thousand years, and Herophilus (**hair-OFF-uh-lus**) improved the understanding of the brain and the nervous system. Aristarchus (**AR-uh-STAHR-kuhs**) proposed that the sun rather than Earth was the center of the universe, an idea most Europeans rejected for the next thousand years, while the geographer Eratosthenes (**ER-uh-TAHS-thuh-neez**) calculated the circumference of Earth within about two hundred miles. The inventor Hero devised a steam turbine, although it was treated only as an amazing toy. Other major thinkers, such as the engineer and mathematician Archimedes, spent time in Alexandria (see Meet the People: Archimedes, a Hellenistic Mathematician and Engineer). Archimedes's work may have helped inspire one of the most amazing marvels of Hellenistic technology. What some have termed the world's first computer, the Antikythera, was probably invented around 100 BCE. This mechanism was a complex, whirling clockwork instrument with bronze gears bearing thousands of tiny interlocking teeth, powered by a hand crank. The machine registered the passage of time and the movement of celestial bodies with considerable precision. The only known model, which disappeared a few centuries later, was found in a shipwreck off Greece in 1901. It was not until the fourteenth century CE that the first geared clocks were invented.

Greek philosophy and religion went in new directions during the Hellenistic Age. Some thinkers put less emphasis on reason to solve problems and more on resigning oneself to life in ways that often seemed fatalistic, taking life as it comes. The school of thought known as **Cynicism**, made famous by Ionia-born Diogenes (**die-AHJ-uh-neez**) (ca. 412–ca. 323 BCE), emphasized living a simple life, shunning material things and all pretense. A famous legend of the meeting of Diogenes and a young Alexander conveys the flavor of Cynic philosophy. Diogenes asked Alexander about his greatest desire, and the Macedonian replied, "to subjugate Greece." Next, he would subjugate Southwest Asia and then the world. And after that, Alexander said, "I will relax and enjoy myself," prompting Diogenes to reply: "Why not save yourself all the trouble by relaxing and enjoying yourself now?"[19] One of the most revered Cynic thinkers was a woman, Hipparchia of Maroneia (ca. 350–280 BCE), who spent most of her life in Athens. She was married to the most famous Cynic philosopher in Greece, Crates of Thebes. Like most Cynics, her influence lies less in her writing (much of which has not survived) than in the example of choosing to live an impoverished life alongside her husband on the streets, which was usually considered unacceptable for respectable women of her day. The story

Cynicism A Hellenistic philosophy, made famous by the philosopher Diogenes, that emphasized living a simple life, shunning material things and all pretense.

---

[17]Quoted in Michael Chauveau, *Egypt in the Age of Cleopatra: History and Society Under the Ptolemies* (Ithaca, NY: Cornell University Press, 2000), 188.
[18]Quoted in Francis Chanoux, *Hellenistic Civilization* (Malden, MA: Blackwell, 2003), 319.
[19]"Diogenes," in *Biographical Encyclopedia of Philosophy* (Garden City, NY: Doubleday, 1965), 76.

Archimedes, a Hellenistic Mathematician and Engineer

Archimedes was an outstanding mathematician, the greatest engineer of the Hellenistic world, and perhaps the most wide-ranging mind of his time. Some historians consider Archimedes and Aristotle the two greatest thinkers of Greek society. Archimedes was born around 287 BCE to an influential family—his father was apparently an astronomer—in Syracuse, a Greek city on the island of Sicily. He studied in the intellectual capital of the Hellenistic world, Alexandria in Egypt, where inquisitive souls of financial means or, like Archimedes, political connections traveled widely and learned from varied cultures. In this milieu Archimedes became acquainted with famous scientists. Eventually he returned to Syracuse, where he spent the rest of his days. We know little of his personal life and do not know whether he ever married.

In mathematics Archimedes introduced many new ideas, some of which added to Euclid's geometry. He offered a new system of numerals to handle large numbers; calculated the value of *pi*, the ratio of the circumference to the diameter of a circle, more accurately than anyone before him; and discovered the laws for finding the centers of gravity of plane figures. His insights were often visionary. A book he wrote, lost for centuries but recently rediscovered, hints that eighteen hundred years before anyone else he was exploring calculus, the basis for much twenty-first-century technology. Archimedes also studied astronomy and built an ingenious instrument for measuring the movements of the sun, moon, and planets. This early clock may have inspired later timekeeping inventions.

Archimedes is equally well known for his engineering innovations but wrote much less about his applied than his theoretical studies. Nonetheless, his contributions were immense. He discovered "Archimedes' law," still tested in high school classrooms worldwide, which states that a body wholly or partly immersed in a fluid loses weight equal to the weight of the fluid displaced. This insight apparently came to him while in the public baths, as he watched water flow over the side as he entered the pool. According to his later biographer, Plutarch, he leaped from the pool and ran home naked, crying aloud: "Eureka!" ("I have found it!"). (The public nudity would not have astonished Greeks, who were used to seeing people in public without their clothes.) With such discoveries, Archimedes founded the science of hydrostatics, which involves balance and weights.

Archimedes also made other practical contributions. For instance, he supervised construction of the world's first three-masted ship, a huge combination of warship, yacht, and cargo ship that had horse stalls, fish tanks, cargo holds for wheat, and luxurious cabins. He also worked out the law of the lever and the theory of mechanical advantage, using his

IMAGE 7.8 **The Archimedes Palimpsest** In 1889 scholars discovered a crumbling, long-lost parchment containing a copy of a major work by Archimedes, the treatise called "On Floating Bodies." This work, on buoyancy, shows that he was centuries ahead of the rest of the world in his thinking on mathematics and physics, even suggesting ideas that did not reappear until the past several centuries.

Q What does the palimpsest tell us about Archimedes and his thinking?

knowledge to launch his ship with the use of compound pulleys. And he solved a major problem of the time in irrigation and mining by discovering how to move great volumes of water up a steep incline using a large pipe with a tightly fitted screw.

With Roman power on the rise, Archimedes was put in charge of Syracuse defenses. For a while Roman attackers were repulsed by his ingenious weapons, including missiles dropped from cranes that swung out over the fortified city walls and darts and balls delivered by catapults. Some legends, which many historians doubt, credit him with experimenting with mirrors to direct the sun's rays at enemy ships to set them on fire.

In 212 the Romans captured Syracuse and killed the aged Archimedes—according to one legend, as the famously absent-minded scientist was working on geometrical diagrams. This Roman triumph helped end the Hellenistic Age and begin the Roman Age in the central Mediterranean. The engineering and mathematical discoveries of Archimedes now became part of Roman and later world traditions.

Reflection Questions

1. How did Archimedes's career reflect the Hellenistic Age?
2. Why was Archimedes considered one of the major classical engineers and mathematicians?
3. If Archimedes was alive today, which STEM field or fields do you think he would find most interesting and appropriate for his skills?

of her attraction to Crates, and her rejection of conventional values, became a popular theme for later writers.

Another Hellenistic philosophy, **Stoicism** (STOH-uh-siz-uhm), emphasized cooperating with and accepting nature, as well as the unity and equality of all people. Founded by Zeno (**ZEE-noh**) (ca. 334–ca. 265 BCE) in Athens, Stoicism was cosmopolitan and optimistic and accepted cultural diversity, teaching that nature's law governing human affairs was common to all people and transcended the limited human laws created by kings. The Stoic emphasis on basic human equality survived over the centuries to influence modern lawmakers.

Hellenistic religion offered people individual happiness and eternal life. The religion of Isis, originally an Egyptian fertility goddess, promised personal salvation. **Mithraism** (MITH-ruh-iz-uhm), a very popular cult that worshipped Mithra, a Persian

sun-deity, promised salvation to people who were properly initiated into the faith. Some historians believe that these Hellenistic religions, which shared features with Christianity, help explain the appeal of the teachings and life of Jesus several centuries later. Christianity borrowed from Mithraism the concept of purgatory as well as the winter solstice and birthday of Mithra (December 25). Hellenistic ideas also influenced the Romans (see Chapter 8) and remained important in western Asia and the eastern Mediterranean for many centuries.

> **Stoicism** A Hellenistic philosophy that emphasized the importance of cooperating with and accepting nature, as well as the unity and equality of all people.

> **Mithraism** A Hellenistic cult that worshipped Mithra, a Persian deity associated with the sun; had some influence on Christianity.

KEY POINTS

▶ After the Peloponnesian War, no Greek city was strong enough to unite the rest of the Greek peninsula.

▶ King Philip II of Macedonia conquered several Greek cities, and, after he died, his ambitious son Alexander the Great established an empire that ranged from Egypt to India.

▶ Alexander's legacy included a vast trading network that linked the Mediterranean, western Asia, and India, as well

as the spread of Hellenism, a mix of Greek and Persian culture.

▶ Hellenism was marked by rigorous scientific inquiry, philosophies such as Cynicism and Stoicism that urged people to take life as it came, and mystical religions that had some influence on Christianity.

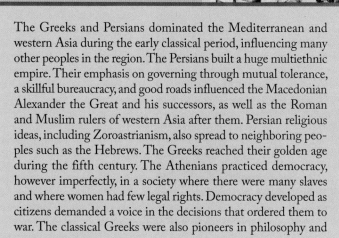

Chapter Summary

The Greeks and Persians dominated the Mediterranean and western Asia during the early classical period, influencing many other peoples in the region. The Persians built a huge multiethnic empire. Their emphasis on governing through mutual tolerance, a skillful bureaucracy, and good roads influenced the Macedonian Alexander the Great and his successors, as well as the Roman and Muslim rulers of western Asia after them. Persian religious ideas, including Zoroastrianism, also spread to neighboring peoples such as the Hebrews. The Greeks reached their golden age during the fifth century. The Athenians practiced democracy, however imperfectly, in a society where there were many slaves and where women had few legal rights. Democracy developed as citizens demanded a voice in the decisions that ordered them to war. The classical Greeks were also pioneers in philosophy and

science. Influenced by the increasing emphasis on reason, Greek thinkers like Socrates, Plato, and especially Aristotle established a foundation for critical thinking and natural science. Their legacy influenced people in both the Middle East and Europe.

The Greeks and Persians were also fierce rivals for regional power, fighting a series of destructive wars but also exchanging trade goods and ideas. The eastern Mediterranean zone fostered cultural mixing, maritime commerce, and the sharing of knowledge and products, and Alexander the Great's conquests made Greek language and culture part of the eastern Mediterranean world for several centuries after his death. The Hellenistic world mixed Greek arts and philosophy with many Persian or western Asian ideas of government. The later Roman, Christian, and then Muslim rulers in these areas retained some of this Greco-Persian heritage.

Key Terms

Achaemenid 151
satrap 153
Zoroastrianism 153
Ahura Mazda 154
polis 156
oligarchy 157

tyrant 157
Sophists 159
Socratic Method 159
metaphysics 159
Delian League 162
Peloponnesian War 162

trade diaspora 164
Hellenism 165
Cynicism 167
Stoicism 169
Mithraism 169

> *Remember, Roman, that it is for you to rule the nations. This shall be your task: to impose the ways of peace, to spare the vanquished and to tame the proud by war.*
>
> —Roman poet Virgil[1]

IMAGE 8.1 Santa Sophia The magnificent Santa Sophia Cathedral in Constantinople, rebuilt during the reign of the emperor Justinian in the sixth century CE, had interior walls covered in gold mosaics that glowed from reflected sunlight. This mosaic from the Zoe panel shows Jesus holding a Bible.

Q How do you think the mosaic portrayal of Jesus reflects Greek and Byzantine cultural and artistic influences?

---

[1]Quoted in Tim Cornell and John Matthews, *The Roman World* (Alexandria, VA: Stonehenge, 1991), 51.

Around 320 BCE Pytheas (**PITH-ee-us**), a scientist from the Greek colony of Massalia (**ma-SAL-ya**), today's city of Marseilles (**mahr-SAY**) on the Mediterranean coast of what is today France, wrote a book about his remarkable travels in Europe. According to his account, the brave and curious Pytheas reached the western coast of France, from where he sailed on a boat owned by local Celtic (**KELL-tik**) people to southwest England. Continuing north through the Irish Sea, he then ventured down Britain's east coast before exploring the North Sea coast as far as Denmark. Some of his contemporaries called him a liar. Today many scholars credit Pytheas for providing Mediterranean societies with their first eyewitness account of the then remote northern coast whose mysterious peoples they considered dangerous barbarians.

In Pytheas's time, Greeks, Etruscans (**ee-TRUHS-kuhns**), Carthaginians (**kar-thuh-JIN-ee-uhns**), the Hellenistic kingdoms including Egypt, and the upstart Romans were part of an interdependent world incorporating southern Europe, North Africa, and western Asia. They competed for economic resources and political power in the western Mediterranean, exchanging ideas and commodities. Three hundred years after Pytheas's travels, the Romans, in Pytheas's time an ambitious but still minor power, had created an empire that more closely linked these European societies. Many people today may identify classical Rome with popular stereotypes such as togas, aqueducts, gladiators, chariot races, and public baths, but their importance to history, and the ideas and institutions we inherited from them, are great.

The Romans' large empire and rich society, celebrated in the opening quote, marginalized or incorporated northern peoples while also transforming North African and western Asian politics, greatly impacting European and world history. When the Roman Empire finally ended after half a millennium, it left several legacies for later European, western Asian, and North African societies. The Romans bequeathed to later Europeans legal and governmental concepts, some derived from the Greeks. Christianity also emerged, forming the cultural underpinning of a post-Roman European society while also spreading in Asia and Africa.

Although the Roman Empire eventually declined, an eastern Mediterranean version, Byzantium (**buh-ZANT-ee-uhm**), survived, serving as a transcontinental trade center and a buffer between western Europe and West Asian states, including a revived Persian Empire. Byzantine–Persian struggles then set the stage for the rise of another society, the Arabs.

8-1 Etruscans, Carthage, Egypt, and the Roman Republic

⊐C TRANSITIONS ▓ NETWORKS

Q What were the main political and social features of the Roman Republic?

By 300 BCE the Mediterranean world was politically and culturally diverse, divided between Etruscans, Carthage, Greek city-states, various Hellenistic kingdoms including Egypt, and the rising Romans, who eventually dominated the entire region. The Romans learned much from the older Etruscan society and were influenced by Greek ideas in building their Republic. Eventually Rome conquered peoples in southern Europe and then beyond, establishing the framework of a huge empire.

CONNECTION to TODAY

Do you see any parallels between the problems leading to the demise of the Roman Republic and political, social, and economic trends in present-day democracies and republics?

8-1a European Geography, the Etruscans, and Early Rome

Geography and a mild climate shaped western Mediterranean society. Italy's geological spine, the Apennine mountain range, runs down the narrow peninsula's eastern side, while to the west and north rich plains fostered intensive agriculture. Romans exported wine and olive oil while importing grain from the nearby islands of Sicily and Sardinia (**sahr-DIN-ee-uh**) and from northern Africa. Unlike in mountainous, rocky Greece, agricultural success and easy contact

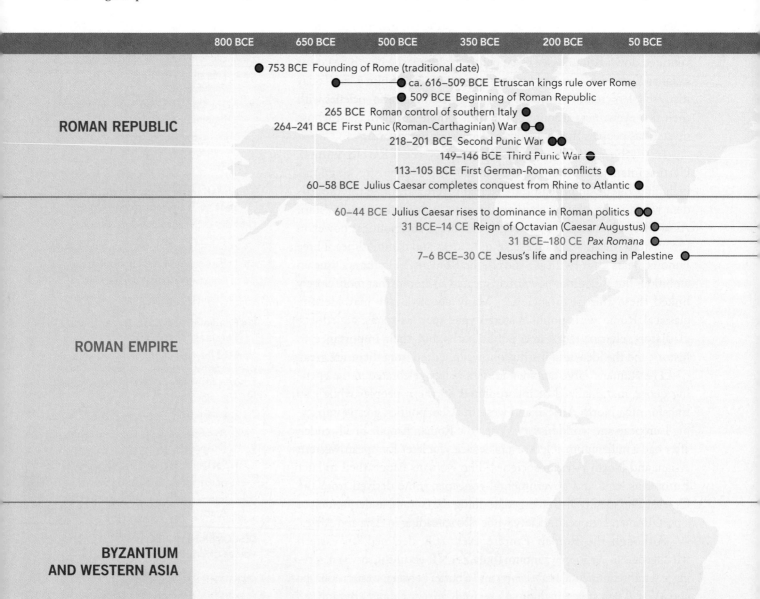

	800 BCE	650 BCE	500 BCE	350 BCE	200 BCE	50 BCE

ROMAN REPUBLIC

● 753 BCE Founding of Rome (traditional date)
● ca. 616–509 BCE Etruscan kings rule over Rome
● 509 BCE Beginning of Roman Republic
265 BCE Roman control of southern Italy ●
264–241 BCE First Punic (Roman-Carthaginian) War ●●
218–201 BCE Second Punic War ●●
149–146 BCE Third Punic War ●
113–105 BCE First German-Roman conflicts ●
60–58 BCE Julius Caesar completes conquest from Rhine to Atlantic ●

60–44 BCE Julius Caesar rises to dominance in Roman politics ●●
31 BCE–14 CE Reign of Octavian (Caesar Augustus) ●
31 BCE–180 CE *Pax Romana* ●
7–6 BCE–30 CE Jesus's life and preaching in Palestine ●

ROMAN EMPIRE

BYZANTIUM AND WESTERN ASIA

encouraged large states. Indo-European Celtic and Germanic peoples living in the forested hills and plains of western and northern Europe frequently invaded this area using passes through the Alps, a formidable mountain complex.

When Romans expanded their power beyond Italy they drew upon the natural resources of the larger Mediterranean world and beyond (see Map 8.1). Spain offered abundant silver, copper, and tin, while Egypt provided wheat. Beginning about 200 BCE, overland trade routes connected the Mediterranean with China along the Silk Road, which brought East Asian products that were bartered in return for gold, silver, precious stones, and some textiles.

The Romans were greatly influenced by the Etruscans, migrants from Anatolia who founded a dozen or so city-states in central and northern Italy by at least the eighth century BCE, and possibly much earlier. Chariot warriors, sailors, and maritime traders, Etruscans eventually dominated more of Italy and the

island of Corsica but also had contact and sometimes conflict with nearby Greek settlements. They adopted the Greek alphabet and myths, and Greek craftsmen worked in some Etruscan cities.

The Etruscan language is only partially understood, and none of its major literature, written in the Greek alphabet, survives. The Etruscans' well-decorated tombs show they were skilled artists and artisans. A good road system linked together their well-planned cities, each of which apparently had its own king. Etruscan religion, a polytheism influenced by Greek and Phoenician mythology, was the foundation of their society and played a key role in government, law, and the economy. Religious authority exercised considerable power in all walks of life. Etruscans worked iron ore into excellent iron axes, sickles, and tools. Their rigid social system included slavery, although Etruscan women apparently had a high social status, conversing with men in public, driving their own chariots,

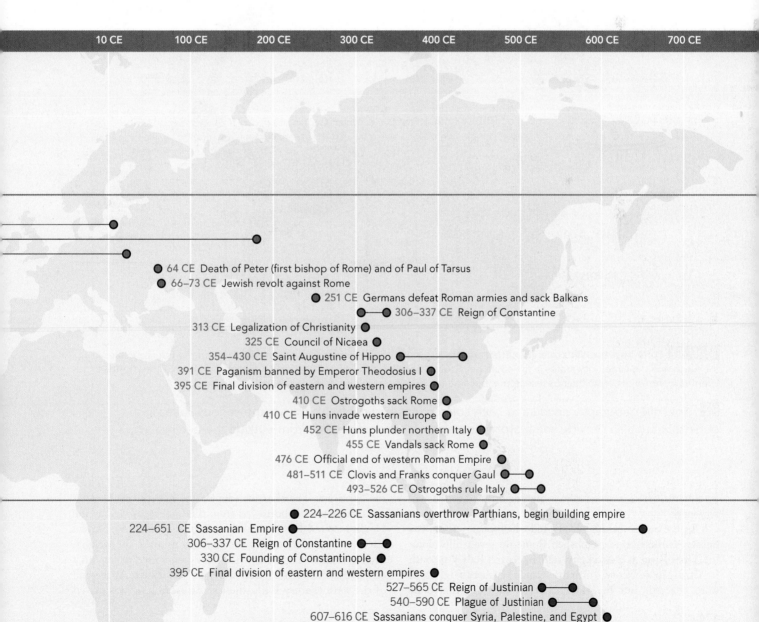

| 10 CE | 100 CE | 200 CE | 300 CE | 400 CE | 500 CE | 600 CE | 700 CE |

64 CE Death of Peter (first bishop of Rome) and of Paul of Tarsus
66–73 CE Jewish revolt against Rome
251 CE Germans defeat Roman armies and sack Balkans
306–337 CE Reign of Constantine
313 CE Legalization of Christianity
325 CE Council of Nicaea
354–430 CE Saint Augustine of Hippo
391 CE Paganism banned by Emperor Theodosius I
395 CE Final division of eastern and western empires
410 CE Ostrogoths sack Rome
410 CE Huns invade western Europe
452 CE Huns plunder northern Italy
455 CE Vandals sack Rome
476 CE Official end of western Roman Empire
481–511 CE Clovis and Franks conquer Gaul
493–526 CE Ostrogoths rule Italy

224–226 CE Sassanians overthrow Parthians, begin building empire
224–651 CE Sassanian Empire
306–337 CE Reign of Constantine
330 CE Founding of Constantinople
395 CE Final division of eastern and western empires
527–565 CE Reign of Justinian
540–590 CE Plague of Justinian
607–616 CE Sassanians conquer Syria, Palestine, and Egypt

MAP 8.1 **Italy and the Western Mediterranean, 600–200 BCE** During the early classical period the Etruscan cities in the north and the Greek city-states in the south held political power in Italy. Carthage held a similar status in Northeast Africa. Eventually the Latins, from their base in Rome, became the dominant political force in the entire region.

Q How did geography encourage both connections and conflict between the various states in the peninsula but also provide some protection against invaders coming from outside the peninsula?

owning real estate, and sometimes running businesses like pottery workshops.

In the eighth century BCE, Indo-European pastoralists known as the Latins established Rome on seven hills along the Tiber River as a small city-state in central Italy just south of Etruscan territory. Initially Roman–Etruscan relations were peaceful, but the Romans were soon dominated by the Etruscans. The Romans adopted the twenty-six-character Etruscan alphabet borrowed from the Greeks, as well as the Greek-inspired Etruscan phalanx infantry formation. Skilled Etruscan engineers taught the Romans to make the weight-bearing semicircular arch, which the Romans used to construct city walls, aqueducts to carry water, and doorways. At the end of the sixth century BCE, the last Etruscan king was driven out for his brutality, and Rome became independent. Later the Romans conquered and assimilated the Etruscans and incorporated some of their myths and deities. But the legacy of the Etruscan people did not disappear. Today the DNA of many people in central Italy shows some Etruscan ancestry.

8-1b The Roman Republic and Expansion

Using Greek political ideas, in 509 BCE the Romans established a **republic**, a state in which supreme power is held by the people or their elected representatives. Over the next three centuries, the Romans developed representative government, introducing enduring political ideas. Many modern English words taken from Latin—such as *senate, citizenship, suffrage* (the right to vote), *dictator* (a man given full power), *plebiscite* (**PLEB-i-site**) (a special vote by citizens on a political issue), and even *republic*—suggest the influence of the Romans on modern political life, including in western Europe and the United States.

Initially, the aristocratic upper class, or **patricians** (**puh-TRISH-uhnz**), held all power, controlling the Senate, a body that had previously advised the kings, the army, and the legislative body made up of soldiers, the **Centuriate Assembly**. The Senate, composed of three hundred former government officials, ratified resolutions of the Centuriate Assembly before they became law. As the Republic developed, the Centuriate Assembly elected two men each year as **consuls** with executive power.

Commoners, or **plebeians** (**pli-BEE-uhnz**), heavily outnumbered patricians. As Rome expanded, plebeian soldiers wanted to share in the wealth flowing into Rome. Years of army service had taken them away from their farms and left them in debt, and they demanded a greater political voice and economic equality. A plebeian leader expressed commoner bitterness toward those who opposed reform: "[You] realize vividly the depth of the contempt in which you are held by the aristocracy. They would rob you of the very light you see by; they grudge you the air you breathe, the words you speak."[2] Plebeians believed that political power would allow them to pass laws distributing the state's wealth more fairly.

Gradually social and political rights expanded. In 494 BCE the plebeians selected two of their number, called **tribunes**, to represent their interests in the Centuriate Assembly, much as the consuls represented patrician interests. By 471 a separate new Plebeian Assembly elected tribunes and conducted votes among plebeians, called *plebiscites*. Plebeians later gained the right to share with the patricians lands won in war, and they won full equality by 267 BCE, when their assembly became the state's principal lawmaking body.

To resolve some of its problems, in the fourth century the Roman Republic turned to **imperialism**, the control or domination by one state over another. A major defeat by the Gauls (**gawlz**), a Celtic people who plundered Rome in 390 BCE, shocked Roman leaders and prompted them to expand Roman territory and move their frontiers further from the city of Rome. As they successfully fought with other Italian city-states,

the Romans often granted either full or limited Roman citizenship to the defeated cities' inhabitants. Roman citizenship became a great honor bringing special legal treatment, an honor fathers proudly passed on to their sons. By wisely treating former enemies fairly, Romans spread their power without encouraging revolts and ensured that more men joined their army.

8-1c Carthage, Egypt, and Regional Trade

After first conquering the Etruscan cities, which had been weakened by conflicts with the Gauls, the Romans took over the Greek cities in southern Italy and Sicily in 265 BCE. Then they encountered their greatest enemy, the Carthaginians. Both Carthage and Egypt played key roles in Mediterranean trade. Carthage (**KAHR-thij**), a city-state on the North African coast near modern Tunis, was originally a Phoenician colony. In Egypt, the other great power on the Mediterranean's southern shores, the Hellenistic Greek Ptolemaic (**taw-luh-MAY-ik**) dynasty had prospered for over a century.

With a fine harbor and strategic position, Carthage grew into the wealthiest Phoenician outpost, described by a Greek as having "gardens and orchards of all kinds, no end of country houses built luxuriously, land cultivated partly as vineyards and partly as olive groves, fruit trees, herds of cattle and flocks of sheep."[3] However, the autocratic city government experienced political instability as rival leaders vied for power, and differences between the prosperous Phoenician settlers and the native Berbers created tensions. Carthaginians also fought frequent wars with their Greek commercial rivals.

Carthaginian maritime skills fostered trade networks. Around 425 BCE the Carthaginian admiral Hanno reportedly led a naval expedition through the Strait of Gibraltar and down the West African coast, seeking markets. He founded trading posts along Morocco's coast and sailed at least as far as the Senegal River. Other Carthaginian expeditions apparently reached the British Isles and perhaps several Atlantic islands off the Northwest African coast. Legends claim that a Carthaginian expedition sailed all the way around Africa but many historians doubt the story. By the third century BCE the Carthaginians had created an empire along the southern and western shores of the Mediterranean Sea, controlling a large part of Spain, much of the North African coast, and the islands of Corsica and Sardinia. In 264 BCE they

republic A state in which supreme power is held by the people or their elected representatives.

patricians The aristocratic upper class who controlled the Roman Senate.

Centuriate Assembly A Roman legislative body made up of soldiers.

consuls Two patrician men, elected by the Centuriate Assembly each year, who had executive power in the Roman Republic.

plebeians The commoner class in Rome.

tribunes Roman men elected to represent plebeian interests in the Centuriate Assembly.

imperialism Control or domination by one state over another.

[2]Livy, quoted in Frederick Gentles and Melvin Steinfield, eds., *Hangups from Way Back: Historical Myths and Canons*, vol. 1, 2nd ed. (San Francisco: Canfield, 1974), 173.
[3]Diodorus, quoted in Barry Cunliffe, *The Extraordinary Voyage of Pytheas the Greek* (New York: Penguin, 2002), 52.

IMAGE 8.2 The Roman Forum The Forum, located amidst various religious and governmental buildings, was the center of Roman political life.

Q What does the location, architecture, and layout of the Forum suggest about its importance as well as Roman construction capabilities?

moved troops to Sicily to aid several Greek cities allied with them against Rome.

The nearly three centuries of the Ptolemaic kingdom (305 to 30 BCE) was generally a prosperous time in Egypt that saw the construction of the Great Library and the Lighthouse of Alexandria. But by the second century BCE, Ptolemaic power in Egypt had become more tenuous as rulers demanded increased agricultural and craft production from workers. Egypt remained a major supplier of wheat and exported papyrus, the preferred medium for scientific, philosophical, and literary texts; textiles; pottery; and metal objects. Greek and Phoenician ships carried some of these goods to foreign ports. Despite the economic growth, many Egyptians tired of Greek occupation, hardship, and high taxes, and several bloody rebellions threatened the government. Some studies suggest that during these years periodic drought, precipitated by sporadic volcanic eruptions in Alaska, Greenland, and Russia that generated climate change, may have contributed to the challenges facing the people by lowering Nile River flows and rainfall. To maintain their own independence, Egyptian rulers sought alliances with rising Rome. In 180 BCE Cleopatra I became sole ruler, the first in a long chain of assertive queens. Then in 47 BCE an ambitious eighteen-year-old became ruler as Queen Cleopatra VII, just as poor harvests, possibly caused by a giant volcanic eruption from Mount Etna in Sicily in 44 BCE, combined with official

corruption, fostered famine, plague, and more social unrest. Her skills enabled the unstable country to maintain domestic peace and deflect Rome for nearly two decades.

8-1d The Punic Wars and Afro-Eurasian Empire

The result of Roman expansion southward was three Punic **(PYOO-nik)** Wars between the two major powers and bitter rivals, Rome and Carthage. The first Punic War (264–241 BCE) resulted in Roman naval expeditions against Carthage, finally ending with Roman occupation of Sicily, Corsica, and Sardinia. In the second conflict (218–201), the brilliant Carthaginian general Hannibal (247–182 BCE), seeking retribution for his country's loss in the first Punic War and perhaps hoping to restore control of Spain, audaciously led his thirty thousand or so troops, fifteen thousand horses, and thirty-seven elephants through Spain and France to invade Italy across the Alps, a formidable barrier, defeating every Roman army sent against them. Modern people may have images in their mind of war elephants, carefully trained to charge and terrify the enemy on the battlefield, used by Hannibal's army lumbering through the rugged mountains. But the elephants and Hannibal's troops, not used to the mountains' snow and ice, perished by the thousands, ending in their defeat in 202 BCE at the battle of Zama.

The early military success of Hannibal's force alarmed the Romans. With his supply lines overstretched, however, Hannibal could not conquer Italian cities. In contrast, having already absorbed much of Italy, Rome had considerable manpower. Hence Roman generals willingly endured staggeringly high casualties; although fifty thousand of their soldiers died in the Battle of Canae, Romans would not concede defeat. Eventually the Romans drove Hannibal's forces out and defeated Carthage, which had to surrender all its overseas possessions, including Spain. In the final Punic War (149–146), Romans laid siege to the city of Carthage and destroyed it. Northwest Africa became a Roman province, a source of copper, grain, and West African gold.

Roman victory encouraged additional imperial expansion, aimed either at punishing Carthage's allies or at restoring regional stability. In 146 BCE Romans made Greece and Macedonia into a province. Few could resist the Roman infantrymen, armed with swords and rectangular shields, or the armor-clad Roman archers, who rode in carts carrying large crossbows, among the era's most feared weapons. But Romans also employed diplomacy alongside warfare, winning some territories without force. By the mid-first century BCE the Romans had built the largest and most enduring empire in the classical world. They commanded the entire Mediterranean and its vast resources, binding together Europe, western Asia, and North Africa. The empire included most of Anatolia, Syria, and Palestine, as well as much territory in northern and western Europe. The Ptolemies still controlled Egypt, but they carefully avoided offending the Romans. The Romans also absorbed much of the Hellenistic east, with its web of international commerce. Alexandria in Egypt distributed goods from as far away as India and East Africa.

8-1e The Decline of the Republic

But imperial success also fostered major changes in Roman society, leading to the collapse of the republican system. The Roman historian Tacitus (**TASS-uh-tuhs**) believed that imperial growth increased the love of power: "It was easy to maintain equality when Rome was weak. World-wide conquest and the destruction of all rival[s] opened the way to the secure enjoyment of wealth and an overriding appetite for it."[4] Indeed, imperial expansion provoked crises that reshaped politics and undermined the Republic, turning representative institutions into window-dressing, ending participatory government, and fostering skyrocketing economic inequality. More than half of Romans died before age ten. Both contraception and infanticide were widely practiced. As warfare gave military leaders excessive power, the Senate's influence weakened, and growing Roman wealth increased the rich–poor gap. As upper-class families bought farmland from peasants impoverished by long army service, many farmers moved to Rome, where the government supported hundreds of thousands of displaced people to maintain their loyalty. The plight of the dispossessed citizen-farmers was exacerbated by a huge influx into Italy of hundreds of thousands of slaves, mostly war captives who now did much of the physical labor as well as making arts and crafts for their owners. With fewer willing soldiers, the tribune Tiberius Graccus (**tie-BIR-ee-uhs GRAK-uhs**) proposed giving public land to farmers who served in the Roman legions when needed. But when the poor gathered in Rome to support this measure, some wealthy Romans spurred a mob to club Tiberius and many to death, demonstrating rich Romans' determination to maintain power and their ability to mobilize many poor people to support one leader or another. Fraud, corruption, and bribery fostered armed and ruthless street gangs. The combative and increasingly toxic atmosphere led not to reform but to the collapse of the rules of political behavior.

Changing military power also undermined democracy, as the Senate could not control military leaders. In 107 BCE, victorious general Gaius Marius (**GAY-uhs MER-ee-uhs**) was elected consul for five straight years, violating a law limiting the officeholder to one year. Marius and his military veterans pressured the senators to vote for a law giving the veterans public land. Skillful military leaders thereafter used their armies to enhance their political power and outmaneuver civilian leaders, a pattern that resulted in civil and foreign wars. Between 78 and 31 BCE, ambitious military leaders expanded Roman territory in Europe and Asia, including Syria and Palestine, while finally destroying republican institutions within Rome itself. Many Romans welcomed the autocratic takeover for ending the chaos. Today historians fiercely debate whether the Roman Republic's demise is a warning to many nations, including the United States, that democracy can be fatally undermined by such problems as rising economic inequality, political corruption, irreconcilable political or social divisions, civic violence, foreign wars, growing military influence, demagogic politicians, disputed elections, and loss of faith in the political order.

One of the Roman leaders, the ambitious young Julius Caesar, completed the conquest of Europe from the Rhine River west to the Atlantic, sent the first Roman forces into Britain, and then won a civil war against former allies. Caesar also weakened the Senate by enlarging it to nine hundred men, too large for an effective governing body. Finally, in 44 BCE he had himself declared "perpetual dictator," an act that led to his assassination, made famous many centuries later in English author William Shakespeare's play, *Julius Caesar*.

Caesar's death led to civil war, the end of any pretense of democracy, and the conquest of Egypt. Caesar's adopted son, Octavian (**ok-TAY-vee-uhn**), fought Mark Antony, a general who had fallen in love with the Egyptian ruler Cleopatra. A Greek historian described Cleopatra, a remarkable personality who had borne a son by Julius Caesar, as someone whose "presence was irresistible; the attraction of her person, the charm of her conversation, was something bewitching. She could pass from one language to another."[5] The turmoil and the Republic ended when Octavian defeated Antony and Cleopatra at the naval Battle of Actium (**AK-tee-uhm**), in Greece, in 31 BCE. Antony and Cleopatra committed suicide and their armies surrendered to Octavian, giving Rome control of Egypt. The Romans then placed Egypt under a tight grip, imposing heavy taxes and encouraging more wheat production to feed Rome.

[4]Gentles and Steinfield, *Hangups from Way Back*, 167.
[5]From Plutarch, Life of Antony, in *Readings in Ancient History*, ed. William S. Davis, vol. 2 (Boston: Allyn and Bacon, 1913), 163–164.

8-2 The Rise and Decline of Imperial Rome

TRANSITIONS ▦ SOCIETIES ▦ NETWORKS

Q How did the Romans maintain their large empire?

Athenians had pondered whether empire and democracy were compatible, a challenge still debated in many nations today. Likewise, in Rome the clash of personal ambitions and greed created by the wealth gained through conquest led to replacing the Republic with a more autocratic and arrogant imperial system. Imperial rule saw the full development of Roman culture, including those elements such as law that became a significant legacy to European society. The Roman Empire lasted in the West for about five hundred years, ending with a long period of internal and external disorder that undermined the system. Eventually various population movements put pressure on the empire's frontiers, leading to imperial decline, division, and then collapse.

CONNECTION to TODAY

What do you see as the advantages and disadvantages of empires like Rome's?

8-2a Caesar Augustus and the *Pax Romana*

Emperors (*caesarsi*) who controlled the military and much of the government bureaucracy ruled Rome and its empire. Octavian (63 BCE–14 CE), who ruled as Caesar Augustus, a Latin term meaning "majestic, inspiring awe," was worshipped in some places during his dictatorship and deified after death. His long reign (r. 31 BCE–14 CE) established and consolidated a system in which the Senate appointed governors to the peaceful provinces while Augustus governed provinces where troops were stationed. Augustus enacted or vetoed legislation and called the Senate into session. The writer Juvenal (**JOO-vuhn-uhl**) deplored the lost popular voice and its replacement by entertainments (such as gladiator fights in the Colosseum) to divert public attention: "The people that once bestowed commands now meddles no more and longs eagerly for just two things: bread and circuses."[6]

Pax Romana The period of peace and prosperity in Roman history from the reign of Augustus through that of Emperor Marcus Aurelius in 180 CE.

The period in Roman history from Augustus through the reign of Emperor Marcus Aurelius (**aw-REE-lee-uhs**) in 180 CE is known as the **Pax Romana** ("Roman Peace"). For the first and last time, the entire Mediterranean world was controlled by one power and the Mediterranean Sea was a "Roman lake," remaining at peace for two centuries (see Map 8.2). Rome experienced few challenges from the Germanic peoples, who mostly remained east of the Rhine and north of the Danube Rivers, while in western Asia the Romans faced only a weakening Parthian kingdom in Persia and Mesopotamia. Whether in London or Paris, Vienna or Barcelona—all cities founded by the Romans—people lived under the same laws.

Peace and prosperity encouraged trade and population growth. Great fleets of ships moved goods around the Mediterranean Sea. Trade also flourished along the Silk Road between China and Rome through Central and western Asia. Thanks to this trade, and sporadic Chinese–Roman encounters in Central Asia, some Chinese scholars knew something of the Romans. One third-century CE Chinese historian, Yu Huan, even wrote a book about the Roman Empire, including observations on the popularity of Chinese silk there. Roman merchants were active many places even before the legions arrived. Rome governed a huge population, estimated at fifty-four million in the first century CE, including six million in Italy. Rome itself may have been the world's largest city, with a half million to one million inhabitants. In this diverse empire the Roman ideal, like that of the Hellenistic Greeks, was cosmopolitan. Hence, Emperor Marcus Aurelius (r. 161–180 CE) wrote: "Rome is my city and country, but as a man, I am a citizen of the world."[7] Some non-Romans joined the ruling class, and half of the Roman Senate were non-Italians. Men of wealth and military skill, whatever their ethnic background, could rise to the highest levels in the army and government. Many people migrated to Rome, bringing with them cultural forms such as musical instruments and dances. Thus the empire slowly changed into a multinational state that fostered diversity within unity. Eighteen centuries later the founders of the United States, who admired the Roman Republic model, chose a Latin slogan for their new nation: *e pluribus unum* (**EE PLUR-uh-buhs OO-nuhm**), "one from many."

Although Roman thinking owed much to Greek political and ethical philosophy, it was also distinctive, with a

---

[6]Quoted in Jerome Carcopino, *Daily Life in Ancient Rome*, 2nd ed. (New Haven, CT: Yale University Press, 1968), 202.
[7]Quoted in Norman Davis, *Europe: A History* (New York: Harper, 1998), 193.

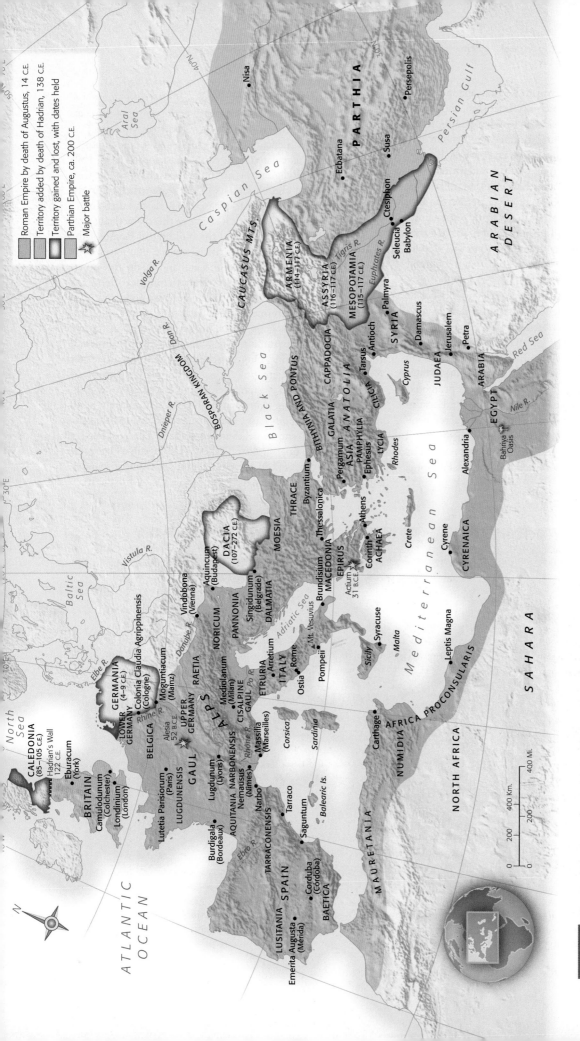

MAP 8.2 The Roman Empire, ca. 120 CE The Romans gradually expanded until, by 120 CE, they controlled a huge empire stretching from Britain and Spain in the west through southern and Central Europe and North Africa to Egypt, Anatolia, and the lands along the eastern Mediterranean coast.

Q What do you think the main challenges would be to govern such a large empire embracing many different societies, and how well do you think the Romans resolved those challenges?

practical way of looking at the world. Romans extended the meaning of some Greek ideas, such as citizenship, and developed a concept of civic virtue similar to what people today call public duty. Codified laws underpinned the Roman system, encouraging public responsibility, and several Roman legal principles survived to become part of modern national and international law. The Romans believed that all people, regardless of wealth or position, were equal before the law, and they promoted individual rather than family responsibility for one member's misdeeds. The burden of proof in a trial rested with the person making the charge, not the defendant. All of these principles can be found today in the United States and Britain.

Roman law was influenced by the Greek Stoic belief in eternal truths transcending particular cultures. Leading Roman Stoics, including the philosopher Seneca (4 BCE–65 CE), the great Roman lawyer and essayist Cicero (106–43 BCE), and the second-century emperor Marcus Aurelius, famous for his humanity and justice, believed that all people were alike in their use of reason to determine right from wrong. Stoics promoted tolerance, moderation, and acceptance of life's travails. Because of such beliefs, the Romans generally allowed conquered peoples to govern themselves and to keep their own customs and leaders so long as they paid their taxes and did not revolt. For example, kings such as Herod governed the Jews of Palestine, but with Roman oversight.

8-2b Religion and Society

Roman religion and society changed over the centuries. Romans worshipped a pantheon of gods and goddesses for practical reasons, such as to ensure good fortune, and specific gods or goddesses were associated with certain tasks, such as agriculture or thievery. Religion was an integral part of civic life, with no "separation of church and state." As state officials, priests performed public sacrifices to please the gods and ceremonies promoting the state's welfare. Reflecting these practical goals, Caesar Augustus commissioned the building in Rome of the *Ara Pacis*, or Altar of Peace, a sacrificial marble altar to celebrate the end of the wars of conquest in Gaul and Spain and, hopefully, launch a long era of peace. Not wishing to offend any divinity, Romans also adopted other people's gods and goddesses, equating the Greek deities with their own gods. Thus the leader of Greek gods, Zeus, became the Roman Jupiter, Zeus's wife Hera became the Roman Juno (**JOO-noh**), and the Greek god of wine, Dionysus, became the Roman Bacchus (**BAK-uhs**). In modern times most of the planets and dwarf planets in our solar system were named after Greek gods, many of Greek origin (Mercury, Venus, Mars, Jupiter, etc.). But underground religious faiths also appeared, such as Mithraism. In underground temples believers worshipped a deity of Persian and Zoroastrian origin called Mithra (**MITH-ruh**). The secretive religion emerged in the first century CE but disbanded during the fourth century, losing out to its rival Christianity.

Scala/Art Resource, NY

IMAGE 8.3 **Ara Pacis** The Altar of Peace, built in 9 BCE, resided in a large enclosure whose walls contain relief sculptures. This scene depicts Mother Earth and her children, with the cow and sheep at her feet representing the prosperity resulting from peace.

Ⓠ How does the altar reflect Roman culture and life?

Although there was some social mobility, Roman society remained stratified into sharply defined upper and lower classes, deeply divided by wealth. The super-rich (0.5 percent of the population) held about 80 percent of the wealth, while the poor (65 percent) lived on the edge of financial disaster. Below the upper classes, middle-class merchants and artisans ranked above the urban workers and seriously impoverished peasants. We know something of middle- and lower-class concerns and values from graffiti and tombstone memorials that they left (see Discover Historical Voices: The Voices of Common Romans).

Slaves, one-third of Italy's population, were mostly war captives, but some people were enslaved as payment for debt or criminal activity. Some slaves earned wages or ran businesses on their owner's behalf, saving until they could purchase their freedom. Others lived very hard lives, working in mines, on vast plantations growing cash crops such as olives and grapes, or as oarsmen of Roman ships. A Roman historian described slaves working in a Spanish silver mine: "The slaves secure for their masters riches which are almost beyond belief. They, however, are physically destroyed, their bodies worn down. Many die because of the excessive mistreatment they suffer. They are given no break from their toil."[8] Most gladiators who fought in the arenas to entertain the public were slaves who had trained at gladiator schools, and few lived to old age. Romans brutally crushed sporadic slave rebellions. Although they often freed slaves after years of good service, ex-slaves remained stigmatized socially.

In this patriarchal and often misogynistic society, only men had a political voice, enjoying extensive power over women, children, and slaves. A family's oldest male had the power of life and death over other family members and was even free to kill his children without fear of legal problems. Roman girls were often married by the age of thirteen or fourteen, sometimes even earlier. Wives were advised to accept their husband's extramarital sexual exploits: "Let the matron be subject to her husband." Yet, some women stepped outside expected bounds, subtly if possible to fit the ideal of the modest, obedient woman. Seneca criticized those daring women who copied "male indulgences, they keep just as late hours, and drink as much liquor; they challenge men in carousing."[9]

Adult women also eventually enjoyed some legal rights, including possession of their own property, even if married. Some acquired considerable wealth, using it for such community ends as financing public monuments. Moreover, a wife could escape her husband's legal control by spending three days and nights away from his house, and she could sue her husband if he abandoned her. For example, a woman whose husband had moved to Alexandria and married another woman asked the court to make her husband return the dowry she brought to the marriage. Roman women also had more freedom to leave their homes and travel through the city than did their Greek sisters. Finally, abortion and contraception were common until they were outlawed around 200 CE.

In the Republic's later years, Romans became free to choose their own spouse. By 17 BCE, adultery and avoidance of marriage by both genders had become serious social problems, and

some busy prostitutes earned good money. To attempt to halt a population decline among native Italians, a law was passed requiring men to marry or pay higher taxes. At the same time, Romans generally tolerated homosexual activity and did not view it as immoral. Acknowledged homosexuals, including some leading figures, participated openly in Roman life.

8-2c Economy and Trade Networks

The Romans flourished from expanding trade and industry, and Rome became a communications center for a large area of Afro-Eurasia. Industries such as mining and pottery making depended mostly on slave labor, while the wealthy invested in public displays and land rather than business or industry. The rich lived extravagantly, reflected in Roman banquets, lavish social meals that involved gastronomic excess as well as debauchery and power. The banquets live on today in popular images of men (and sometimes women) in togas reclining on couches while servants serve them copious cups of wine and heaping platters of rare and expensive foods from as far away as India, Syria, and Ethiopia, while performing troupes and poets entertained the guests. The image was probably exaggerated and embellished over the centuries, but the banquets did allow the powerful to maintain their friends and out-maneuver their enemies. Romans also built over 150,000 miles of roads, the phrase "all roads lead to Rome" reflecting this accomplishment. Even today an overview map of Europe's main roads shows most of them, whether coming from east, north, or west, converging on Rome. The Romans also mass produced lead, mostly for water pipes, sheathing boat hulls of boats, some household items, and extracting silver for coins, which caused serious air pollution in Europe for centuries.

Large merchant ships plied the Mediterranean between Egypt and Rome. The biggest Mediterranean ships were grain carriers, some capable of conveying over two thousand tons of cargo such as wheat, pickled fish, and wool. Hundreds of sunken Roman-era cargo ships discovered in the past century contained a wide variety of precious luxury goods, including glass bowls, wood and bronze couches, huge marble statues and columns, jewelry, ebony, and ivory. However, much of Roman trade depended on maritime routes that linked Rome to Asia and Africa. The Egyptian port of Berenike (**BER-eh-nick-y**), on the Red Sea, was a transfer point for fabrics, spices, gems, and other exotic goods from India and Southeast Asia, frankincense and myrrh from Arabia, and ivory, drugs, tortoise shells, and slaves from Somalia and Ethiopia. Over a hundred ships a year set off from Berenike and nearby ports for India. Archaeologists have uncovered Roman coins in India, China, and Vietnam.

Romans also traded widely over land. Roman-ruled North Africa obtained gold from West African societies across the Sahara Desert, while Central Asian and Chinese products reached Rome over the Silk Road. Romans shipped much gold and silver east in return for spices, jewelry, cut gems, glassware, and silk. But eventually the expanding Roman appetite for Chinese goods harmed Rome's economy. The historian Pliny (**PLIN-ee**) the Elder bemoaned the wealth shipped east and blamed it on Roman women's fondness for silks, pearls, and

[8]Diodorua Siculus, in Jo Ann Shelton, *As the Romans Did: A Sourcebook in Roman Social History* (New York: Oxford University Press, 1988), 175.
[9]Quoted in Henry C. Boren, *Roman Society: A Social, Economic, and Cultural History*, 2nd ed. (Lexington, MA: D.C. Heath, 1992), 279, 219.

Discover Historical Voices

The Voices of Common Romans

As with most premodern societies, we know much more from the surviving records and literature about the prominent and wealthy than about the much more numerous common people. But we can learn about the middle and lower classes from their graffiti preserved in ancient city ruins like Pompeii and tombstone epitaphs. Romans used graffiti and epitaphs to voice frank opinions on many matters and to summarize their lives. Like modern graffiti, some of the remarks address sexual activities and bodily functions or insult rivals with profanity. Perhaps centuries or millennia from now historians will study graffiti left by people today to understand today's world. The following are some examples of less profane but often humorous graffiti and epitaphs from various classical Roman cities.

Graffiti

I'm amazed, O wall, that you've not collapsed under the weight of so much written filth.

A bronze urn has disappeared from my tavern. Whoever returns it will get 65 sesterces reward. Whoever informs on the thief will get 20 sesterces, if we recover it.

Perarius, you're a thief.

No loiterers—scram!

Livia, to Alexander: "If you're well, I don't much care; if you're dead, I'm delighted."

Samius Cornelius, go hang yourself!

Stronnius is an ignoramus.

Crescens is a public whore.

Whoever doesn't invite me to dinner is a barbarian.

Whoever is in love, may he prosper. Whoever loves not, may he die. Whoever forbids love, may he die twice over!

Marcus loves Spendusa.

If you haven't seen the Venus that Apelles painted, take a look at my girl—she's just as beautiful.

Thraex makes the girls sigh.

All the goldsmiths support Gaius Cuspious Pansa for public works commissioner.

The mule-drivers support Gaius Julius Polybius for mayor. Genialis supports Bruttius Balbus for mayor. He'll balance the budget.

I ask you to support Marcus Cerrinus Vatia for public works commissioner. All the late-night drunks back him.

Epitaphs

If you wish to add your sorrow to ours, come here and shed your tears. A sad parent has laid to rest his only daughter, whom he treasured with sweet love as long as the Fates permitted. Now her dear face and form are mere shadow and her bones mere ash.

For my dearest wife, with whom I lived two years, six months, three days, and ten hours. On the day she died, I gave thanks before gods and men.

I was once famous, preeminent among thousands of strong Bavarian men. I swam across the Danube in full armor. I once shot an arrow in the air and split it with a second in midair. No Roman or barbarian ever beat me with a spear, no Parthian with the bow. This tombstone preserves the story of my deeds. But I am still unique, the first to do such things as these.

Reflection Questions

1. What do these graffiti tell us about political life?
2. What do the graffiti and epitaphs reveal about what common people valued?
3. In what ways do the sentiments seem familiar to modern readers?

Source: From *Lives and Times: A World History Reader*, Volume I, 1st edition by HOLOKA/UPSHUR. © 1985 Wadsworth, a part of Cengage Learning, Inc. Reproduced with permission. cengage.com/permissions.

---

perfumes: "India and China and [Arabia] together drain our empire. That is the price that our luxuries and our womankind cost us."[10] However, despite his gender-prejudiced criticism, which was shared by many male contemporaries, both men and women coveted imported Asian goods.

8-2d Literature, Architecture, and Technology

The remarkable achievements of Roman literary culture during the late Republic and early empire mostly reflected the views of the aristocratic elite. Virgil (70–19 BCE), Rome's greatest epic poet, promoted Roman greatness through his *Aeneid* (i-NEE-id), which described the journey of the legendary Trojan hero Aeneas (i-NEE-uhs), who, according to the poem, left Troy and eventually founded the city of Rome. The love poems of Ovid (43 BCE–17 CE) were irreverent and erotic, his treatise on the art of love advising men to indulge their sexual cravings. In disgust, the moralistic emperor Augustus eventually sent Ovid into bitter exile along the Black Sea.

Historians also made substantial literary contributions. Tacitus (56–117 CE) wrote a history of the early emperors, lamenting the end of the Republic and its more open political atmosphere and sense of equality. He also sympathetically described the Germanic tribes north of the Rhine and Danube, contrasting their sexual purity and other virtues with Roman vices. For example, the corrupt emperor Domitian "fancied that the voice of the Roman people [was] obliterated; he banished teachers of philosophy and exiled every noble pursuit, so that nothing honorable might anywhere be encountered."[11]

The Romans' quest to provide public services fostered notable architecture and engineering. The great dome of the Pantheon (PAN-thee-ahn), or temple to all the gods in Rome, has no interior-supporting pillars and forms a perfect sphere. Rome's Colosseum was the world's largest outdoor arena until the twentieth century. Another architectural wonder was aqueducts, which carried water hundreds of miles from mountains into cities. One of the Romans' most sophisticated engineering projects, public baths, became social centers containing gardens, libraries, and exercise and game rooms. A Roman writer observed that baths, sex, and wine ruin bodies but make life worth living. Wealthy Romans enjoyed many creature comforts, and some of their homes were heated from furnaces under the floor that spread heat to the house through ductwork, similar to the heating systems in Korea. The durable marine concrete piers, breakwaters, and harbors built by Romans some two thousand years ago are still in use today. Other inventions included glass windowpanes, scales with weights, chemical fertilizer, theater curtains, door keys, heavy plows, and primitive dental drills. Julius Caesar introduced a calendar creating a year of 365 days and a few minutes. His calendar had to be reformed, but not until the sixteenth century.

8-2e The Decline of the Western Roman Empire

Political and economic problems eventually undermined the empire. Roman leaders never found a good way to pass power on to a successor, and reliance on the army to decide who ruled resulted in twelve soldier-emperors between 235 and 260 CE, none dying peacefully in old age. The quality of emperors declined. Some were immoral, brutal, or mentally ill. Hence, Nero committed incest with his mother, then executed her, while Galerius was accused of feeding criminals to his pet bears as he ate meals. Not surprisingly there was frequent turnover of rulers, including five in 193 CE alone. To control their empire, the Romans spent more wealth supporting a growing bureaucracy and military, pushing the state toward bankruptcy. Paying taxes proved a particular problem in the empire's western half, where serious inflation substantially decreased real wealth. While older, larger cities provided a stronger tax base for eastern provinces, the frontier lands west of Italy consumed more than they produced. To pay for goods and food required finding more precious metals (such as gold and silver) or more slaves to sell or trade to the east for manufactured products.

The empire gradually decayed from within. Leaders were consumed by rivalries, while corruption, ineptitude, and civil wars eroded the government and made the state vulnerable to invaders. In the early third century, increasing costs and the difficulties of controlling a growing empire forced Roman rulers to end further conquests and merely defend existing frontiers, thus cutting themselves off from the income that conquest provided and further impoverishing the government. In addition, some gold and silver mines in the western lands and the fertile soil in Italy became exhausted, making goods more expensive. Romans experienced a steadily widening rich-poor gap, a serious trade deficit with China, declining literacy levels, and growing corruption, apathy, and loss of public spirit. Meanwhile, a cooler climate may have diminished crop yields. Finally, contacts with distant lands made Rome increasingly vulnerable to diseases and epidemics that killed many thousands. Reaching Europe from North Africa, a plague from 251 to 266 CE caused dramatic population decline and weakened military forces. At the epidemic's height, five thousand people reportedly died each day in the city of Rome.

8-2f Celtic and Germanic Societies and the Romans

The decline of Rome also corresponded with the rise of two northern European societies, Celts and Germans. The Celts, whose culture developed by the twelfth century BCE in the Danube River Basin north of the Alps, occupied large sections of central and western Europe, from Germany and France to

Alinari/Art Resource, NY

IMAGE 8.4 **Roman Army Camp** This carving shows a camp being built by Roman legionnaires during a military campaign. Soldiers' helmets, shields, and pikes are propped up at the right side. Some men build walls and dig ditches.

Q What does the carving tell us about Roman army life?

[11]Tacitus, Agricola, quoted in Moses Hadas, ed., *A History of Rome from Its Origins to 529 A.D. as Told by the Roman Historians* (Garden City, NY: Doubleday Anchor, 1956), 126–127.

the British Isles and Spain. The Celtic peoples resisted the expanding Romans. Powerful chiefs ruled small Celtic states, and priests, known as *druids*, organized the worship of their many gods. Many Celts lived in large fortified towns or produced a substantial agricultural surplus, and some had coins and writing. Aided by bronze and then iron technologies, they were fierce warriors and fine horsemen. By 400 BCE Celtic tribes were raiding into Italy, sacking Rome and weakening the Etruscan states. In Gaul their armies' many trumpeters and horn blowers, as well as war cries, terrified their opponents.

However, the well-drilled, disciplined Roman legions overwhelmed the Celtic fighters, which were divided by tribal rivalries, and eventually Romans colonized or Germans dislodged most of the Celts. In 225 BCE the Romans overran the Celts in northern Italy, and first Carthaginians and then Romans crushed Celtic power in Spain. Julius Caesar conquered the Celts of Gaul. In 60–61 CE, however, the Romans faced a temporary setback when Celts, resisting colonialism and led by a warrior-queen, Boudica (boo-DIK-uh) (d. 61 CE), a widow, destroyed several Roman settlements in England. Boudica had good reason to despise the Romans, who had pillaged her territory, flogged Boudica, and raped her daughters. Reflecting patriarchy, a Roman historian lamented the defeat brought by a woman, which caused the misogynistic Romans great shame since they considered women warriors as symbols of an uncivilized society. In retaliation, the Romans sent in a larger force, killing eighty thousand of Boudica's subjects. The queen committed suicide rather than surrender. Even today she remains mythologized in Britain as a feminist as well as a nationalist hero, honored by a statue in the heart of London. During Roman rule migrants from elsewhere settled in Britain, including some of African or Middle Eastern heritage.

Celtic societies and culture remained strong mostly in Ireland and the rugged hills of Wales and Scotland, where long communication and supply lines kept the Romans from extending their rule. The Roman emperor Hadrian (HAY-dree-uhn) built a remarkable seventy-three-mile-long rock wall across northern England to keep Celtic tribes out of Roman territory. Christianity, which reached Ireland in the fifth century, eventually modified Celtic culture. Today the Irish, Scottish, and Welsh people still honor their Celtic heritage, but only a small minority can speak their ancestral Celtic languages. In most of mainland Europe and England, Celtic culture gradually became Latinized and Germanized, although pockets of Celtic identity survive in Brittany (BRIT-uhn-ee) (western France) and northwest Spain.

Germanic peoples living in Scandinavia and the northern plains of Germany also pressured Rome's northern borders and eventually began migrating into the empire. No known German cities or states existed, but Germanic peoples

inflicted several defeats on Roman legions in Gaul in 113 BCE. Although the Romans ultimately crushed the Germans, fear of Germanic invasions helped prompt Roman expansion northward. Some Germans were brought into the Roman fold, often serving in the Roman army. The Roman historian Tacitus praised Germans for their hospitality, noting that they considered it a crime to turn any visitor away from their door. However, most Romans viewed Germans as dangerous "barbarians."

For the next several centuries Romans and Germans watched each other warily on the empire's fringes. When German tribes formed confederations, their combined strength made them a greater threat. Pushed by their own enemies such as westward-moving Huns from Central Asia, some Germans moved on to Roman lands, intensifying German–Roman conflict. In 251 CE Germans defeated a Roman army and plundered the Balkans. The Romans could not field enough high-quality soldiers to defeat the invaders because their shrinking population meant that men needed to farm could not be spared for the army. In 381 the Romans began drafting men, but many draftees mutilated themselves to avoid service, one of the earliest known cases of draft resistance to unpopular wars.

German expansion greatly impacted Roman society. High taxes to support the armies alienated all classes but fell primarily on poor peasants, many of whom lost their land and became workers on large landed estates. Sometimes, giving up their freedom, whole villages placed themselves under a wealthy

Gilles Mermet/Art Resource, NY

IMAGE 8.5 **Life on a Late Roman Empire Estate** The painting, of a fortified manor house and its surroundings, shows typical farming activity for each season.

Q What does the painting tell us about various farming activities and the centrality of the manor on estate lands?

landlord's protection, with men and women working their patron's land. Meanwhile, the upper classes increasingly escaped cities for their country estates. Thus Roman cities slowly but steadily shrank in size and wealth as fewer children were born and the upper classes moved away.

8-2g The Division of the Roman Empire

The mounting problems led to the empire's division. Emperor Diocletian (**DIE-uh-KLEE-shuhn**) (r. 285–305) recognized the western province's weakness and divided the empire in half, making the Adriatic Sea an east–west dividing line. He ruled the east from Nicomedia (**NIK-uh-MEED-ee-uh**) in Anatolia and appointed another man, Maximian, as western emperor. A later emperor, Constantine (r. 306–337), temporarily reunited the empire under one ruler, establishing a new capital on the Straits of Bosporus (**BAHS-puhr-uhs**), first named New Rome and then Constantinople (**cahn-stan-tih-NO-pul**)—today's Istanbul (**IS-tahn-BUL**). In 395 Constantinople became the capital of the eastern, or Byzantine, Empire, which survived the western Roman Empire by nearly a thousand years.

The worst Roman military defeats, in the fourth and fifth centuries CE, forced emperors to abandon claims to many territories, including Britain. In 410 the Germanic Ostrogoths (**AH-struh-GAHTHS**) (eastern Goths) plundered the city of Rome while a branch of the Huns, fierce horse-riding pastoralists originally from Central Asia, conquered what is today Hungary and later pushed various Germans west into Gaul, Italy, and Spain. Led by the able warrior Attila (**uh-TIL-uh**) (406–453), known to the millions who feared him as "the Scourge of God," Huns ravaged the Balkans and Greece before plundering northern Italy in 452. Hun power soon collapsed, but Rome was again sacked by another German group, the Vandals, in 455 CE. In 476, Germans deposed the last Roman emperor, marking the official end of the western empire.

Various Germanic kingdoms, including the Vandals in Northwest Africa, the Visigoths (**VIZ-uh-gahths**) in Spain, and the Ostrogoths in Italy, now ruled the western Mediterranean world. Another German group, the Franks, under their leader Clovis (**KLO-vuhs**), conquered what is now France and western Germany. Meanwhile, Germanic Angles and Saxons migrated into England. These Germanic peoples adopted a considerable amount of Roman culture, and some used local versions of Latin, forming the basis for **Romance languages** such as French, Italian, Spanish, Portuguese, and Catalan.

> **Romance languages**
> Languages that derive from Latin, such as French, Italian, and Spanish.

KEY POINTS

- ▶ The Romans set long-lasting legal standards and offered allegiance to a wide variety of gods, many of them borrowed from other peoples.

- ▶ Roman society was highly stratified; slaves performed much of the manual labor, and women, although accorded some significant legal rights, were generally subjugated.

- ▶ Rome served as a nexus for trade and communication and excelled in architecture and engineering.

- ▶ The Celts, who were fierce warriors, posed a threat to the Romans, but they were eventually conquered and Latinized except for some in rugged areas of the British Isles.

- ▶ The Roman Empire had trouble fielding enough soldiers or gathering enough money to fend off the German threat.

8-3 Christianity: From Western Asian Sect to Transregional Religion

⇌ TRANSITIONS

Q How did Christianity develop and expand?

The Christian church played a vigorous role in Roman cities even in the western empire's final decades. Christianity arose in Palestine (in western Asia) in the first century CE as a Jewish sect (see Map 8.3), and Christian religious and social institutions then accompanied Greco-Roman culture into the new Germanic kingdoms. Together they defined the culture that dominated Europe in the centuries following the classical period. The transformation of Christianity from small Jewish sect to the faith of emperors and the empire provides one of the Roman era's most dramatic legacies. To understand the history of Western societies requires analyzing Christianity's rise and values.

CONNECTION to TODAY

Can you see any influences from other religions on the rise of Christianity?

8-3a Roman Palestine and Jesus of Nazareth

Christianity was founded on the teachings of Jesus of Nazareth, a Jewish teacher in first-century CE Roman-ruled Palestine. Palestine and the surrounding region contained diverse traditions. Most people, including Jews, spoke Aramaic (**ar-uh-MAY-ik**), the later Persian Empire's official language, and most literate people wrote in Greek, a legacy of Hellenism. Various Egyptian, Mesopotamian, Phoenician, Persian, and Greek traditions undoubtedly influenced the Jewish and then Christian faiths.

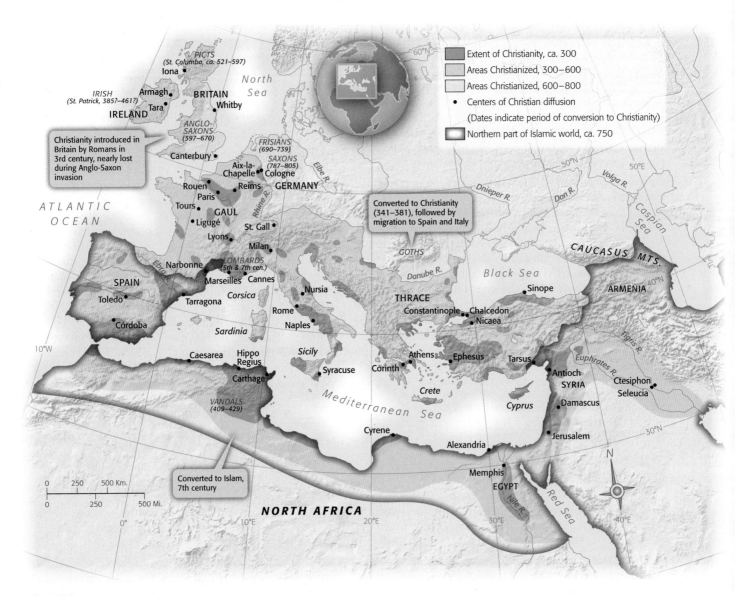

MAP 8.3 **Spread of Christianity** Christianity arose in Palestine in the first century CE and gradually gained footholds in parts of western Asia, North Africa, and southern Europe by 300 CE. Over the next five centuries Christianity became the dominant religion in much of western and Central Europe and expanded its influence in western Asia and North Africa.

Q Looking at the spread of Christianity over such a wide area in late Roman times, what seem to be the major factors that explain the success of the religion?

Palestine was one of the most restless Roman provinces and had a history of rebellion against Rome. Moreover, Jewish society had diverse beliefs and practices. Over the centuries Hebrew (or Israelite) prophets, such as Isaiah in the eighth century BCE and Jeremiah, Ezekiel, and the "Second" Isaiah during the early Axial Age, explored their relations to their God and other peoples. Some studies conclude that the prevailing Jewish expectation or hope of the time was for a messiah who would be a militaristic David-like figure to overthrow Roman rule and inaugurate "the kingdom of God," an era of justice marked by the defeat of evil and the restoration of Israel. At the same time, various mystical sects rejected both Hellenistic cosmopolitanism and the formal Jewish leadership. Jesus inherited these prophetic traditions and spoke of himself as the fulfillment of Jewish law.

For many modern theologians and historians much uncertainty surrounds the life of Jesus. Roman records report religious conflicts and instability in Palestine but make no mention of Jesus. No confirmed written eyewitness accounts of Jesus's life are known to exist. According to Christian tradition, Jesus was a Jewish carpenter, teacher, and healer who probably lived from around 7 or 6 BCE to 30 or 33 CE. As with Buddha and Confucius, our knowledge of Jesus and his career comes from his followers' writings, primarily through the four gospel (literally "good news") accounts, the centerpieces of the Christian New Testament. The earliest narrative, the Gospel of Mark, was written down around 70 CE, some forty years after Jesus died. Whether the official gospel accounts were based largely on eyewitness testimonies, oral traditions, or earlier writings since lost remains unclear. Many historians and theologians argue that the four gospels in the official canon, compiled in the mid-second century CE, were written not as historical accounts but as faith statements, a "witness" to God's power in the lives of early Jesus followers. As a result, modern theologians and historians vigorously debate the gospel accounts' historical accuracy. Scholars differ on many questions about Jesus's life, such as whether he may have been married. Several dozen other gospels or gospel fragments were excluded from the Christian Bible or have only recently been discovered, some differing considerably from the official gospels. At least one may have been written by a woman.

The official gospels describe Jesus as, among other things, a moral reformer who confronted the Jewish leaders, especially the *Pharisees* (**FAR-uh-seez**), a group emphasizing ritual purity, obeying strict ceremonial laws, and awaiting the coming of a messiah who would free them from the Romans. Jesus favored a simple life, loving others, forgiving enemies, accepting the poor and other despised groups, and opposing excessive legalism and ceremony. According to the Gospel of Matthew, Jesus summed up his teachings in two commandments: "Love God with all your heart, soul, and mind; and love your neighbor as yourself."[12] Matthew reported that Jesus angered influential Jews and Romans by advising the wealthy to give their money to the poor since rich people were unwelcome in God's kingdom. Although his followers considered Jesus much more than a teacher, modern theologians debate whether Jesus ever claimed to be divine, a "son of God," or viewed himself chiefly as a healer and wisdom teacher.

Jesus's enemies, especially the Roman governor Pontius Pilate and a few Jewish religious leaders, feared the growing civil unrest and accused Jesus of treason against Rome. It was likely Pontius Pilate, rather than the powerless Jewish high priests, who made the decision to try, convict, and execute Jesus by crucifixion. Jesus's followers, initially a few dozen people, all Jews, claimed he was revived or resurrected from death and "appeared to" his disciples. This belief in Jesus's continuing divine presence probably motivated his followers to preach his message to others and gather for worship as a special sect within the first-century CE Jewish community. Soon they numbered several thousand believers.

8-3b Paul and the Shaping of Christianity

The activities and writings of Paul of Tarsus (**TAHR-suhs**), a port city in southeast Anatolia, greatly affected the evolution of the religion of Jesus into Christianity. A first-century Romanized Jew from a Pharisee family, Paul said he was miraculously converted to belief in Jesus as a young man. He spent the rest of his life spreading this faith to non-Jews, traveling to western Asian and Greek cities before his death in a Rome prison about 64 CE. Paul's teaching emphasized Jesus as a divine being, the "son of God" who earned forgiveness for humankind's sins by his death on the cross. Accepting Jesus as the Christ (*Christus* meant "anointed one"), Paul taught, could save a person from damnation to an eternity in Hell, and a non-Jew who did not follow Jewish laws and ritual could become a follower of Jesus. By arguing that there was neither Jew nor Greek, slave nor free person, but instead a spiritual equality, he challenged Roman assumptions such as those condoning slavery, prompting

many Roman citizens to regard Christians as a threat. Paul's patriarchal views also strongly influenced Christian thinking. He valued celibacy above marriage and urged wives to be subject to their husbands and remain silent in church. Yet, some modern scholars argue that Paul's views on women and gender reflected his times, not biblical scripture. In their view, several Hebrew prophets, some biblical writings, and even an important early Christian bishop (Clement of Alexandria) had described God in gender-neutral or even feminine terms. The debate over whether God transcended gender has caused controversy in several churches in recent years.

Paul disagreed strongly with those who believed that Christians had to follow Jewish laws. His decision to exempt converts from undergoing the circumcision required by Jewish law was crucial for Christianity's success; in those days before antibiotics and anesthesia, such operations could be dangerous, which would have discouraged many. Peter, Jesus's chief disciple, finally agreed, on Paul's urging, that God made no distinction between Jews and others, and he later became the first bishop of Rome (and hence the first pope). The Emperor Nero, needing a scapegoat for his own failures that led to the charge that "Nero fiddled while Rome burned," blamed Christians for a destructive fire that many think he started. Peter was probably killed in Rome during the resulting persecution of Christians in 64 CE. Eventually, most Christians believed they were saved by faith in Jesus, not by following any Jewish tradition.

Paul's victory in convincing Peter to include non-Jews was crucial in establishing Christianity as a world religion (see Map 8.3). A Jewish revolt from 66 to 73 CE resulted in the Roman destruction of the Jewish temple in Jerusalem and the dispersion of many Jews to other lands. During the revolt the *Zealots*, a group of Jewish rebels, held out in a hilltop fort known as Masada (**muh-SAHD-uh**) overlooking the Dead Sea. Although the Romans eventually took the fort, Masada stood through history as a symbol of Jewish resistance to oppression. Jews became discredited in Roman eyes, making it fortunate that early Christians had broken with Judaism. While Jews scattered across Eurasia and North Africa, non-Jewish Christians continued to grow as the religion spread along trade networks throughout western Asia, North Africa, and southern Europe.

8-3c Christianity in the Mediterranean Zone

The Roman context shaped Christian growth and institutions. Christianity had similarities to "mystery religions," some rooted in Persian and Hellenistic traditions, that were popular in the Roman world at the same time. Like the followers of Mithra or Isis (**ICE-uhs**), Christians believed in life after death and had practices, such as a special initiation rite (baptism), that fostered religious community. But Christianity offered a greater emotional appeal by emphasizing the spiritual equality of all people and a concern for the poor. Christians used the terms *heathen* and *pagan*, which had negative connotations, for followers of polytheistic or animistic religions or the irreligious. The faith gradually

---

[12]Matthew 22:37–39, in *The Holy Bible*, King James Version (Chicago: Thomas Nelson, 1982), 957.

gained greater acceptance, and in 313 CE it became a legal religion by an edict of the Roman emperor Constantine, who believed the Christian God had helped him win a battle. The edict was the Western world's first known government document to proclaim freedom of belief. After this the organized church, loosely headed by the bishop of Rome, became more significant, and by 400 CE non-Christian faiths had been banned and Christianity had become the official Roman religion, with others eventually discouraged or suppressed. Christianity united state and church in a troubled marriage for over a millennium.

But Christians also contended with theological divisions. For example, the sect of **Arianism** (AR-ee-uh-niz-uhm) taught that Jesus was not divine but rather an exceptional human being. In 325 CE, to combat what most Christians saw as heresies and to establish core beliefs, Constantine called a church council at Nicaea (nye-SEE-uh), in Anatolia, where he ordered the bishops to resolve their doctrinal differences and determine which beliefs to follow. The **Nicene** (NYE-seen) **Creed** they produced became the official doctrine of the early church and is still recited in many denominations.

Early Christians borrowed much Greco-Roman culture but refused to acknowledge the emperor's official divine status, prompting sporadic persecution. Nevertheless, as Christianity spread, most believers were left alone to worship freely. In general, Christians adapted successfully to Roman life. Many acquired a Roman education and even celebrated Roman festivals along with the new Christian ones. For example, they celebrated Jesus's birthday on the date of the old Roman and Mithraist winter solstice festival, December 25. Early Christians also generally adopted the Greco-Roman acceptance of homosexuality. Yet tensions between Christians and non-Christians simmered, such as those leading to the gruesome murder of the philosopher Hypatia (hye-PAY-shuh) by Christian mobs in Alexandria around 416 CE (see Meet the People: Hypatia of Alexandria, a Pagan Philosopher). Some early church leaders also blamed the Jews for the death of Jesus, one calling the synagogue "a den of robbers" and dwelling of "demons". Hoping perhaps to destroy the ancient world, Christian zealots sometimes vandalized, attacked, or destroyed buildings, books, or artworks of antiquity seen as "pagan" and hence sinful. In 529 zealots decapitated a famous statue of Athena, the Greek Goddess of Wisdom.

By the early fifth century, Christians were the political and social leaders in most Roman cities, but some became troubled by their success. Followers of Jesus were supposed to focus on spiritual instead of worldly success, on heaven instead of Earth. This questioning fostered monasticism, a life of penance, prayer, and meditation, either alone or in a community of other seekers. For instance, Benedict of Nursia (ca. 480–ca. 543) became so disillusioned by hedonistic Roman life that he moved into a cave and later founded western Europe's first monastic order, the Benedictines (ben-uh-DIK-teenz). Benedict formulated monastic rules explaining how to live a spiritually fulfilling life. For many monks and nuns, the practice of **asceticism**, or austere religious practices such as intense prayer, helped to strengthen spiritual life and seek a deeper understanding of God. Some church leaders also reemphasized the superiority of virginity over marriage, a value earlier stressed in the writings of Paul.

8-3d Augustine and Roman Christianity

Christianity expanded, producing church institutions and thinkers who shaped the theology. In the empire's declining decades, the North African bishop Augustine of Hippo (354–430 CE), a city near Carthage, redefined Christianity's relation to the Roman world, and his concepts of Christian morality and history dominated western European culture for a thousand years. Augustine tried several faiths before becoming a convinced Christian, priest, and, in 395, bishop of Hippo. Like many Roman cities, Hippo had followers of many faiths, including various pagan and Persian traditions, all seen as heretical by the established church. After the Ostrogoths sacked Rome in 410, Augustine, troubled by the pagan accusation that Christians' refusal to fight (many early Christians were pacifists) and abandonment of the Roman gods caused Roman society to wither, wrote *City of God*, completed in 427. Defending Christianity against its critics, he argued that the "city of God" comprised all who followed God's laws (i.e., Christians), while the "city of man" consisted of non-Christians, who ignored God's teachings and would be damned in a final judgment at the end of time. Contending that all of history was in God's hands, he promoted a view of history as a straight line of progress from past to future, in which, at the end of history, Jesus would return to judge all humanity, living and dead.

Viewing Christian morals as superior to that of the tolerant Roman culture, Augustine urged Christian men and women to remain celibate; marriage was only for those with low self-control. He criticized sex outside of marriage, sanctioned sex within marriage only for procreation, and proclaimed men superior to women. Augustine's writings and theology strongly influenced the Roman Catholic tradition, as Christians increasingly separated themselves from hedonistic Roman practices. For example, in 498 Christian leaders introduced an annual feast day in honor of Saint Valentine to replace a holiday honoring Juno, the Roman goddess of love and marriage, and a popular, somewhat raunchy, Roman fertility festival.

Christianity filled the vacuum as Roman government collapsed and many people left cities in the fifth century. The city of Rome's population fell from some 800,000 in 300 to around 60,000 in 530, with the Christian clergy often providing the only semblance of order for those remaining. Church officials also achieved a huge boost when the Germanic Franks converted to Latin Christianity under their ruler Clovis. Then, in the late

Arianism A Christian sect that taught that Jesus was not divine but rather an exceptional human being.

Nicene Creed A set of beliefs, prepared by the council at Nicaea in 325 CE, that became the official doctrine of the early Christian church.

asceticism Austere religious practices, such as intense prayer, that were used to strengthen spiritual life and seek a deeper understanding of God; began to be used in the Christian church in the fifth and sixth centuries CE.

Hypatia of Alexandria, a Pagan Philosopher

Hypatia, a female philosopher and mathematician, lived in the Hellenistic Egyptian city of Alexandria, part of the Roman Empire. As Christianity became more influential, she followed a non-Christian polytheistic religion, making her in Christian eyes a "pagan." Perhaps nothing better shows the complex relationship between Christians and pagans, and the tension within the Christian community itself, than her murder at the hands of a Christian mob in 415 CE. To critics of religious intolerance such as the eighteenth-century English historian Edward Gibbon, Hypatia was a beautiful woman torn to pieces by a fanatic mob because she believed in the Greek spirit of reason instead of, in his view, Christianity's irrational beliefs. But it was not that simple.

Born around 355 CE, the daughter of a well-educated mathematician and astronomer, the young Hypatia studied the works of the mathematician Euclid and other great Hellenistic thinkers and became known for making geometry intelligible to students. She also studied philosophy, but not the purely rational sort Gibbon imagined. She became a neo-Platonist, viewing philosophy as almost a religion, a way to discover the hidden divine spirit within each person. She also stressed the feminine aspects of culture, arguing that women benefited from honoring goddesses. Hypatia wrote commentaries on mathematical and astronomical subjects, lived quietly as a teacher, did not publicly participate in pagan worship, and, like many Christian women of her day, practiced celibacy, although she was married to another philosopher. Women philosophers were uncommon in those days, but Hypatia's wisdom and learning became celebrated. Reflecting respect for knowledge but also gender stereotyping, admirers claimed she had "the spirit of Plato and the body of Aphrodite [the Greek goddess of love]." She taught both pagan and Christian students, one of whom became a Christian bishop in Anatolia but remained Hypatia's life-long friend.

Conditions in Alexandria changed after 391 CE, when the Roman emperor Theodosius forbade pagan worship. During the next twenty years, many Christians determined to eradicate all non-Christian religions, spurring violent attacks on Jews and pagans. Now a majority of Alexandria's population, Christians were divided into feuding factions. Tensions grew worse in the city after Cyril, a fanatic intolerant of non-Christians, won election as bishop in 412. Since Hypatia was a close friend and supporter of Orestes, the city's Christian governor, his bitter rival Cyril spread the rumor that the widely respected Hypatia was a witch and practiced black magic. He also encouraged attacks on Jews.

In 415 a semimilitary gang of young Christians allied with Cyril dragged Hypatia from her carriage, stripped off her clothes, murdered her, and burned her body. Cyril had not ordered this, but he had created a social climate that made such a crime possible. Alexandria became a more thoroughly Christian city, expelling the Jews, who had been a substantial community in Alexandria for over six hundred years. Cyril was never punished for his part in Hypatia's death.

Later critics wrongly viewed Hypatia mostly as a martyr for her non-Christian beliefs. She was also, at least partly, a victim of a jealous bishop. However, Gibbon and others correctly saw her as one of the last representatives of a tolerant paganism rooted in the Hellenistic and Roman culture's cosmopolitan ethos, now replaced by an intolerant form of Christianity. Her death also represented the displacement of philosophers from the public forum by religious men who claimed that the ideas they preached were superior because they came from God rather than from book learning.

IMAGE 8.6 **Statue of Hypatia** This statue honors the great pagan philosopher and mathematician of fifth-century Alexandria who was murdered by Christian rivals.

Ancient Art and Architecture/Alamy Stock Photo

Reflection Questions

1. What does Hypatia's career tell us about Alexandrian society?
2. What does her experience reveal about conflicts between Christians and non-Christians in the late Roman Empire?
3. Do you think Hypatia could be considered a feminist by today's standards?

Note: Quotation from Maria Dzidzka, *Hypatia of Alexandria* (Cambridge, MA: Harvard University Press, 1995), 5.

sixth century, Europe was hit by many disasters, enumerated in 599 by an alarmed Pope Gregory: "as the end of the world approaches, many things menace us which never existed before: inversions of the climate, horrors from the heavens and storms contrary to the season, wars, famine, plagues, earthquakes."[13] But the widespread mood of doom proved premature. A new age was dawning in western Europe, largely German and Christian in tone, with a Greco-Roman overlay of language and culture.

KEY POINTS	
▶ Christianity was born in Palestine, an area with a tradition of rebellion against Rome, and grew out of the Jewish prophetic tradition.	▶ In defending Christianity against its critics, Augustine distinguished between Christians, who would be saved, and non-Christians, who would be damned, and he also argued for strict standards of sexual morality that favored celibacy.
▶ Paul was instrumental in spreading and shaping Christianity after Jesus's death, as well as in arguing that one did not have to be Jewish to become a Christian.	
▶ Aided by the popularity of mystery religions similar to it and by the decline in quality of life, Christianity took hold and became the official Roman religion.	

8-4 Revival in the East: Byzantines, Persians, and Arabs

▦ NETWORKS   ▤ SOCIETIES

Q How did the flow of goods, ideas, and people between Byzantine and Sassanian Empires reinvigorate the eastern Mediterranean world?

A century after Roman emperor Constantine dedicated his new capital city, later known as Constantinople, in 330 CE, the western part of the empire fell to various German groups while the eastern empire fostered a new and distinctive society, Byzantium. Byzantium viewed itself as continuing the Roman Empire but developed a different political structure and a culture and church more Greek than Latin. By taking the brunt of attacks by resurgent western Asian peoples such as the Sassanian Persians, Byzantium gave the struggling new states in western Europe time to develop into a separate Latin Christian culture. The Persian–Byzantine conflict also helped shape the rising Arab society.

CONNECTION to TODAY

Can you see any parallels between Byzantium and modern nations?

8-4a Early Byzantium and the Era of Justinian

Byzantium emerged as the most powerful state in the eastern Mediterranean region, maintaining this status for many centuries. Constantinople straddled the narrow waterway linking the Aegean and Black Seas and separating Europe from western Asia, symbolically linking diverse peoples and traditions. As an easily accessible crossroads connecting east and west and north and south, for the centuries to follow the city attracted migrants, refugees, merchants, and others from many parts of the empire and beyond. With their city built on both sides of the Straits of Bosporus, the residents recognized no artificial division between Europe and Asia. The large eastern Roman Empire initially encompassed the Balkans, Greece, Anatolia, Syria, Palestine, and Egypt. Few emperors in Rome enjoyed the power Byzantium's government had over its people, economy, and religious institutions.

Byzantium's most important early ruler, the Emperor Justinian (juh-STIN-ee-uhn) (r. 527–565 CE), spurred on by his powerful and ambitious wife, Theodora (THEE-uh-DOR-uh), was determined to defeat the German states in the west and reunite the old Roman Empire. His armies reconquered a large part of the western territories, defeating the Ostrogothic kingdom in Italy in 563. But long years of fighting left Rome devastated, with only a few thousand impoverished, disease-ridden inhabitants. Moreover, Justinian's victories required ever higher taxes, and he was barely able to defend his own domains from Huns, Persians, and various peoples migrating into Europe. During the first half of the seventh century, Justinian's successors fought the Sassanian Persians, losing control of the eastern lands (see Map 8.4).

Justinian also established a political pattern of despotism in which Byzantine subjects treated the emperors as near-gods with absolute power over most areas of national life. They presided over a centralized and complex bureaucracy (hence our term *byzantine* for complicated and puzzling systems). Spies monitored the population. Justinian had many critics, among them the great Byzantine historian Procopius, who described the emperor as "at once villainous and amenable; as people say colloquially, a moron. He was never

---

[13]Quoted in Michael McCormick, *Origins of the European Economy: Communication and Commerce, A.D. 300–900* (New York: Cambridge University Press, 2001), 27.

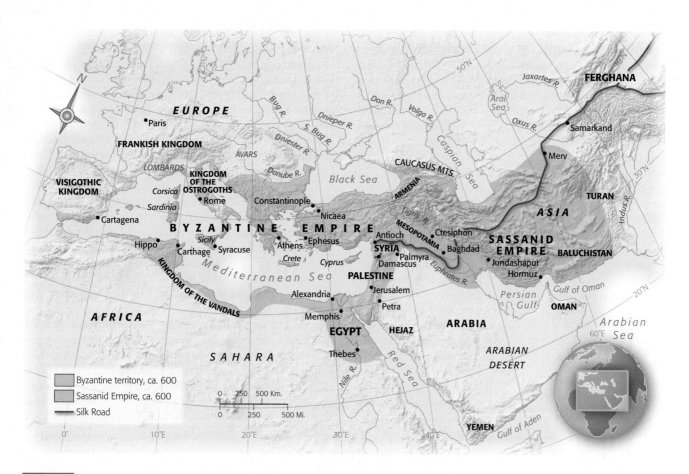

MAP 8.4 **The Byzantine and Sassanian Empires** By 600 CE the Byzantine Empire controlled much of southern Europe and the eastern end of the Mediterranean Basin, and the Sassanian Empire dominated most of the rest of western Asia, part of Turkestan, and Egypt. Various Germanic kingdoms held political sway in far western Europe, northern Europe, and northeast Africa.

Q How did the geography of the eastern Mediterranean and southwestern Asia foster both connections and conflict between Byzantium and Sassanid Persia?

truthful with anyone. His nature was an unnatural mix of folly and wickedness."[14] But Justinian and Theodora also collected all existing Roman laws into one legal code, preserving Roman legal principles for later generations. Some observers admired and others reviled Theodora, a former exotic dancer of humble origins who adopted Christianity before becoming one of the world's most powerful women. She set up a safehouse for women escaping prostitution and increased penalties for rape and pimping.

In 540 the Byzantines encountered one of the most terrible epidemics in world history, often known as Justinian's plague. The sickness, probably bubonic plague, spread along the trade routes from Egypt into western Asia before reaching Europe. At its height some ten thousand people a day perished. Ships were loaded with corpses, rowed out to sea, and abandoned. Agriculture largely halted, leaving many communities abandoned. A Christian bishop in Palestine wrote that "all the inhabitants, like beautiful grapes, were trampled and squeezed

dry without mercy."[15] The plague returned several times until 590. When Justinian died at age eighty-three, his empire was much poorer, weaker, and less populated than it had been when he took power.

8-4b Byzantine Society, Economy, and Religion

Despite its many political misfortunes, the Byzantine Empire survived for centuries because of its social and economic strengths, including more urbanization than western Europe. Constantinople grew to perhaps a million people, described by a visitor as "a splendid city, how stately, how fair. It would be wearisome to tell of the abundance of all good things."[16] The urban wealthy lived in splendor, enjoying luxury goods like silk clothes, carpets, and elegant tapestries provided by local industry. A huge gap separated them from the poor peasants, who faced unique restrictions; peasants living many

[14]From A. Atwater, trans., *Procopius: The Secret History* (Ann Arbor: University of Michigan Press, 1963), 8.
[15]Quoted in Daniel Del Castillo, "A Long-Ignored Plague Gets Its Due," *Chronicle of Higher Education*, February 15, 2002, A22.
[16]Quoted in Philip Sharrard, *Byzantium* (New York: Time-Life, 1966), 36.

years in one place were required to remain there, and they eventually became bound to the soil and controlled by powerful landlords. Despite patriarchy, urban upper-class women enjoyed influence, and some queens, like Theodora, exercised considerable power. Women could control their own property and have their dowry returned if their husbands divorced them. However, men enjoyed greater legal safeguards, and wife-beating was common. Maternal and infant mortality rates were high, pregnancy remaining hazardous and childbirth dangerous.

Byzantium had a flourishing economy. As prominent members of the urban aristocracy, merchants and bankers benefited from Constantinople's position astride the principal trade routes between Europe and Asia. The government taxed all goods passing through the capital, including spices, cotton, and copper from India and Southeast Asia; jewels, silk, gold, and silver from China and Central Asia; gold, ivory, and slaves from Africa; cotton and grain from Egypt; grains, wool, and tin from northwestern Europe; olive oil and silver from Spain and Italy; and timber, fur, copper, hides, and slaves from Russia and Scandinavia. Byzantine coins have been found as far away as China. But most trade with China and India had to go through Persian-controlled lands, and Persian–Byzantine relations alternated between uneasy peace and armed conflict.

> **Monophysites** A heretical sect that argued that Jesus had a single divine nature rather than both a divine and a human form.

> **Nestorians** A heretical Christian sect that believed that the divine and human natures of Jesus were independent of each other.

Byzantine society and culture, fundamentally Hellenistic Greek, inevitably diverged from the western Roman tradition in many ways, especially in religion and culture. Byzantines preserved and later passed on to the Latin west (often through Muslims) the works of Plato, Aristotle, Homer, Sophocles, and other Greeks. The eastern Christian church gradually separated from its Latin counterpart, evolving into the Greek Orthodox Church, with many customs and viewpoints foreign to the Roman Church. Religion permeated Byzantine life. The church, especially monasteries, gained control of considerable land and hence wealth. From the ruler, who controlled both temporal and religious affairs, to the ordinary citizen, Byzantines avidly discussed religious questions, and emperors proposed church reforms and called church councils to address what mainstream Christians considered heresies. These included the **Monophysites** (muh-NAHF-uh-sites), who argued that Jesus had a single divine nature rather than both a divine and human form; and the **Nestorians**, who believed that Jesus's divine and human natures existed independent of each other. Christianity also shaped gender relations. A goddess representing urban prosperity was replaced by the much beloved Christian image of the Holy Virgin Mary, giving women moral stature. But the church, perpetuating patriarchal stereotypes, also viewed women as weak and inferior, both physically and morally, and easily tempted by sin.

IMAGE 8.7 **Roman Ampitheater in Ancient Palmyra** The ruins of the stage and seats of the outdoor theater built in Roman times. In 2017, several years after this photo, the theater was badly damaged by Islamic State zealots during the war in Syria.

Q What does the theater tell us about life in Palmyra?

Over time theological disputes between the Greek and Latin Churches grew. In general, Greek Christians emphasized ritual and refused to accept the bishop of Rome (later known as the pope) as superior in authority to other bishops. In the eleventh century such conflicts over authority and doctrine contributed to a final split between the two churches. Meanwhile, Monophysites formed the Armenian, Coptic, and Syrian Orthodox Churches, which still exist today. Nestorians migrated to Persia, becoming the basis of the modern Chaldean and Assyrian Churches, and from Persia they spread their faith along the Silk Road into India, Mongolia, and China.

Strongly influenced by western Asian traditions, Byzantine art and architecture reflected the cultural diversity of this huge empire. The fusion of Persian and Greco-Roman influences can be seen in the great dome in Constantinople's Church of Santa Sophia (Holy Wisdom), built under Justinian. Symbolizing inner Christian spirituality in contrast to human pride, the church has a modest external appearance but a richly decorated interior that includes mosaics, marble columns, tinted glass, and gold leaf.

8-4c Sassanian Persians and Their Networks

Both the Romans and Byzantines had to deal with Persian revival under the Sassanian dynasty, which generated frequent conflict. Considering themselves the successors to the Achaemenids a half millennium earlier, the Sassanian court, based in modern Iraq, fostered a brilliant culture mixing Hellenistic and Persian influences. The Sassanians overthrew the Parthians in 224 and spent the rest of the third century building their own empire. In the east they fought with the Kushans (KOO-shans), whose Afghanistan-based empire controlled parts of western India and Central Asia. Eventually the Sassanians occupied much of Afghanistan and some of the Central Asian Silk Road cities, but they lost some territories to the Huns in the fourth century CE. To the west the Sassanians expanded into the Caucasus and Mesopotamia, creating chronic conflict with Rome in and around Syria. They also occupied parts of Arabia, including Yemen (YEM-uhn) in the south. In the sixth and early seventh centuries the Sassanians conquered the eastern Byzantine Empire, including Syria, Palestine, and Egypt (see Map 8.4). But years of war with Byzantium weakened both societies. In 651 the last Sassanian king was murdered and Arab Muslim armies gained control of all Sassanian territories.

Controlling much of the Persian Gulf, Sassanian Persia became a contact zone for international trade. Sassanian trade links stretched east as far as India, Central Asia, and China and south into Africa, and Silk Road cities used Byzantine and Sassanian coins as currency. Persians produced some of the world's finest pottery, silver plates, pearls, brocades, carpets, and glassware, exchanging these for gems, incense, perfume, and ivory.

8-4d Sassanian Religion and Culture

In contrast to the religiously tolerant Achaemenids of the earlier Persian Empire, the Sassanians mandated a state religion, Zoroastrianism, supporting the priesthood and sometimes persecuting other religions. However, state religions tend to decay. The Zoroastrian establishment became corrupt and rigid, and by the fifth century the faith's influence and followers diminished. Yet Zoroastrianism spawned various mixed religions. One of them, Mithraism, became popular in the Roman Empire and spread as far west as England. Another new religion, **Manichaeism** (man-uh-KEE-iz-uhm), founded by the Persian Mani (MAH-nee) (216–277 CE), blended Zoroastrianism, Buddhism, and Christianity, emphasizing continuing struggle between the equally powerful forces of light and dark. Although Mani was executed for heresy, his faith suppressed by both the Sassanians and Christians, Islam and some Christian sects later incorporated his religious dualism.

With Zoroastrianism less influential, the state became more tolerant of diversity, turning the capital city, Jundashapur, into a cosmopolitan intellectual center. Christian minorities such as the Armenians of the Caucasus region generally enjoyed religious freedom, and the Sassanians welcomed Nestorian Christians fleeing Byzantine repression. Foreign scholars migrated to the newly tolerant state, as did Jews and others fearing persecution in Christian Europe. The Sassanians collected scientific and literary books from many neighboring peoples, translated Greek writings, and established a renowned hospital and medical school. Sassanian Persia's multiculturalism provided a framework that enabled later Islamic governments to rule diverse peoples and faiths. But Zoroastrianism, too closely connected to Sassanian domination, became only a minor faith after Islam swept through the region.

8-4e Interregional Trade, Cities, and the Arabs

Arab culture was fostered by the ebb and flow of long-distance trade in western Asia, often influenced by Hellenistic Greek, Roman, Byzantine, and Sassanian activities. Diverse Semitic societies lived in the Arabian peninsula, whose mountains, dry plains, and harsh deserts stretch from the Jordan River and Sinai southeast to the Indian Ocean. Most Arabian peoples were traders, farmers, and pastoral nomads divided into tribes. Roman sources described the mobile pastoralists: "All alike are warriors of equal rank, ranging widely with the help of swift horses and slender camels."[17] Eventually all of these groups coalesced into the Arab society.

Arab society arose in part from the Nabataeans (NAB-uh-TEE-uhnz), who traded all over the Middle East and into Europe by land and sea and whose writing

Manichaeism A blend of Zoroastrianism, Buddhism, and Christianity, founded by Mani, that emphasized a continuing struggle between the equal forces of light and dark.

---

[17]Quoted in Patricia Crone, "The Rise of Islam in the World," in *The Cambridge Illustrated History of the Islamic World*, ed. Francis Robinson (New York: Cambridge University Press, 1966), 4–5.

system became the inspiration for Arabic script. The Nabataeans established a kingdom and in the fourth century BCE built a major trading city, Petra (**PE-truh**), in a narrow gorge in today's Jordan, astride the overland caravan routes. With a population of thirty thousand at its peak, Petra eventually flourished as a crossroads for goods moving between India, Arabia, Greece, and Egypt. Its residents developed an ingenious system of dams, pipes, channels, and underground cisterns for collecting and storing rainwater while also growing wheat, grapes, and possibly olives in this arid region. Petra's spectacular ruins, with their elaborate facades carved into rock, still astonish visitors and have been the setting for many films.

In 106 BCE the Romans occupied Petra, beginning the city's long decline as trade shifted north to Palmyra (**pal-MY-ruh**), on the Euphrates River in today's Syria. After conquering this prosperous trading city in 114 BCE, the Romans had cultivated Palmyra, to protect their eastern frontier. A vibrant trading center attracting Greeks, Romans, Jews, Persians, and Egyptians, Palmyra thrived until 273 CE, when the Romans crushed a revolt led by the shrewd and ambitious Queen Septimia Zenobia (**zuh-NO-bee-uh**), who claimed descent from Cleopatra and the Ptolemaic dynasty in Egypt. Taking advantage of Roman wars with the Goths, Zenobia sent her army into Egypt, gained control of the Roman grain supply, and then occupied much of Roman Asia. She invited Greek thinkers to Palmyra and encouraged religious tolerance. After fierce battles the Romans reoccupied Palmyra and took Zenobia to Rome, where she died. They also looted and razed the city, and most of the people left. History would repeat itself seventeen hundred years later. In 2015 the brutal, fanatically religious, and intolerant fighters of the Islamic State assaulted and occupied the ancient city. To destroy the pre-Islamic legacy, the militants killed local archaeologists, sledgehammered priceless statues, bombed temples, and bulldozed ancient buildings, assaulting humanity's knowledge of the past.

Arab culture was also shaped by successive farming-based kingdoms in Yemen in southern Arabia that had existed since the days of the fabled Queen of Sheba around 1000 BCE. Living in high, cool mountains and well-watered valleys, the Yemenites produced impressive civil engineering and architecture, abundant harvests aided by elaborate dams and terraces, and splendid cities. City-states emerged, among them Saba, possibly the Hebrew Bible's Sheba. Yemenites traded by sea with India and East Africa, as well as across Arabia with the eastern Mediterranean and Mesopotamia. The region's frankincense was prized as far away as Rome.

A recent study suggests that the Justinian plague pandemic, severe drought, and the overall decline of Byzantium and Sassanian Persia may have been due in part to the onset in the sixth century of a Little Ice Age, possibly caused in part by large volcanic eruptions elsewhere. But changing weather may

Werner Forman/Art Resource, NY

IMAGE 8.8 **Interior of Santa Sophia Cathedral** The great cathedral of Santa Sophia in Constantinople, rebuilt for Byzantine emperor Justinian, was famous for its spectacular interior.

Q What ambience or spiritual mood does the interior of this famous cathedral, often considered one of the most beautiful in the world, convey?

have brought more rain and hence more vegetation to Arabia, perhaps with political and religious consequences. The Little Ice Age continued in varying degrees of intensity until the nineteenth century. In the sixth century CE Arabian conditions also changed as political disarray, an Ethiopian invasion, and commercial depression undermined Yemenite society and power. To the north, renewed Sassanian–Byzantine conflict led both to actively seek allies in central Arabia, making Arabia a political pawn caught between Orthodox Byzantium, Zoroastrian Persia, and Coptic Ethiopia. Yet increasing overland trade fostered settlement by many Christian and Jewish merchants in desert towns like Mecca (**MEK-uh**). Some Arabs adopted these religions, and in the seventh century these trends fostered the emergence of a new Arab faith, Islam, out of classical roots and diverse traditions. Eventually Islamic armies overran most of the Byzantine Asian territories and the Sassanian Empire.

Chapter Summary

The activities and cultures of the Romans, Germans, Greeks, and Persians largely shaped the middle and late classical period in the Mediterranean world and western Asia. Romans adopted and spread some classical Greek values while also making major contributions in government, law, and architecture. For several centuries they had a republic in which some of the people had a voice in government and elected Rome's leaders. To acquire more resources and preempt challengers, the Romans gradually expanded their territory until it encompassed much of Europe, North Africa, and western Asia, in the process defeating and conquering rivals, including the Etruscans, Carthage, Egypt, and the Celts. Eventually a more autocratic system led by powerful emperors replaced the republic. Controlling far-flung territories proved expensive, however, and the Roman forces became overextended. Soon the Romans were also defending their territories against the incursions of the Germanic peoples.

New forces also developed in the eastern end of the Mediterranean Basin. Christianity arose out of Jewish society in Palestine and spread throughout the Mediterranean world, western Asia, and North Africa. The power of the Christian church rose as Roman political power declined. In the east Byzantium emerged out of the eastern Roman Empire, developing into a distinct society that incorporated Hellenistic Greek political and cultural traditions. It also fostered the Greek Orthodox Church. Meanwhile, the Sassanians reinvigorated Persian society and built a large empire, eventually putting pressure on Byzantium. These conflicts increased travel over the trade routes and generated new currents in Arab society.

Key Terms

republic 175
patricians 175
Centuriate Assembly 175
consuls 175
plebeians 175

tribunes 175
imperialism 175
Pax Romana 178
Romance languages 185
Arianism 188

Nicene Creed 188
asceticism 188
Monophysites 192
Nestorians 192
Manichaeism 193

Classical Societies and Regional Networks in Africa, the Americas, and Oceania, 600 BCE–600 CE

> *When the day dawns the trader betakes himself to his trade; the spinner takes her spindle; the warrior takes his shield; the farmer awakes, he and his hoe handle; the hunter awakes with his quiver and bow.*

—Ancient Yoruba proverb about daybreak in a West African town[1]

Werner Forman/Art Resource, NY

IMAGE 9.1 **Aksum Stele** Early in the Common Era the kings of the African state of Aksum, in what is today Ethiopia, decorated their capital city with tall, flat-sided pillars or obelisks known as steles, some nearly seventy feet high, possibly as monuments to, or markers for the underground tombs of, the royal family.

Q What do you think the false door at the bottom and multistory false windows might mean to Aksum's rulers and people?

---

[1]From *The Horizon History of Africa* (New York: American Heritage, 1971), 207.

In the classical world, few settlements were as specialized as those serving the caravans crossing the trackless sands of Africa's vast Sahara Desert, a barren landscape where scorching sun and arid soil made planting crops or trees nearly impossible. Sporadic rest stops along the routes at the few isolated oasis towns with gardens, date palms, and flocks of sheep allowed weary travelers to find fresh water and restock before resuming their journeys. The round trip of many weeks between North African coastal zone cities and those on the desert's southern fringe in West Africa held many dangers besides thirst and discomfort, including fierce raiders on horseback. Camels, the major beast of burden in the caravan trade and often called "the ships of the desert," were often uncooperative animals, waging battles of wills with their handlers, but they could travel many days without water. Thanks to these caravans and the brave men who led them, sub-Saharan African products reached a wider world while goods and ideas from North Africa and Eurasia found their way to peoples living south of the Sahara. Eventually over time the Sahara was transformed from a desert barrier in ancient and classical times to a global highway.

The diverse societies in sub-Saharan Africa, the Americas, and Oceania (the Pacific Basin) were partly shaped by their environment, whether deserts like the Sahara, rugged highlands, flood-prone river valleys, rain forests, savannahs, seacoasts, or small islands. Contacts with other peoples, whether friendly, hostile, or both, also influenced societies. Various Africans established connections with the wider world through long-distance trade, especially by the trans-Saharan camel caravans or boats around the Indian Ocean, ensuring that few societies remained completely isolated. The various societies that developed in sub-Saharan Africa, the Americas, Australia, and, thanks to intrepid mariners, the Pacific islands worshipped their own deities, created their own artistic styles, valued some products more than others, and evolved their own social and political structures, including some states. At the same time, they had much in common.

197

9-1 Classical States and Connections in Northeast Africa

SOCIETIES

Q What were some of the similarities and differences between Kush and Aksum?

Many North Americans and Europeans may have grown up with, and perhaps still have in their minds, racist images of a remote and backward "Darkest Africa." But these images were always contrary to the reality. Many Africans participated in the general trends of world history from earliest times to now, including taking up farming and trade while building sophisticated cities and forming states. During the Classical Era tropical Africa and Eurasia were connected largely through intermediaries, including North and West Africans linked together by the trans-Saharan caravan trade as well as Indian Ocean maritime traders connecting East Africa and Asia. In Northeast Africa the major societies of Kush **(koosh)** in Nubia and Aksum **(AHK-soom)** in Ethiopia became trading hubs and powerful states, both enjoying close or sporadic ties with Egypt, Arabia, western Asia, and the Greeks and Romans.

9-1a Iron, Cities, and Society in Kush

The kingdom of Kush in Nubia, along the Nile south of Egypt, existed from about 800 BCE to 350 CE, flourishing as the major African producer of iron and an important crossroads

> **CONNECTION to TODAY**
>
> Why do you think people outside of Africa today know so little about any of the early African urban societies and states except for Egypt?

for trade between sub-Saharan Africa and the Mediterranean (see Map 9.1). Its capital city, Meroë (**MER-uh-wee**), became an industrial powerhouse of the Classical world. Kush had many sources of iron ore, as evidenced by the heaps of iron slag littering the ruins of Meroë today. Kushites imported pottery, fine ceramics, wine, olive oil, and honey from Egypt and western Asia, and they exported iron and cotton cloth.

Both Greeks and Romans admired the Nubians. Some Nubians apparently visited Greece, others served in Persian armies that attacked Greece, and Africans, possibly Nubians, went to Rome to trade or work as musicians, actors, gladiators, athletes, and day laborers. A grand city of perhaps twenty-five thousand people built around a walled palace along the Nile, Meroë contained massive temples, large brick-lined pools possibly used for public baths, and rows of many spectacular pyramids, similar to those in Egypt but smaller, where kings and queens were buried in splendor. The highly skilled builders used masonry, stonework, fired brick, and mud brick. In some other Kushite towns both wealthy and powerful people and those of modest means built the pyramids. As in the Indus

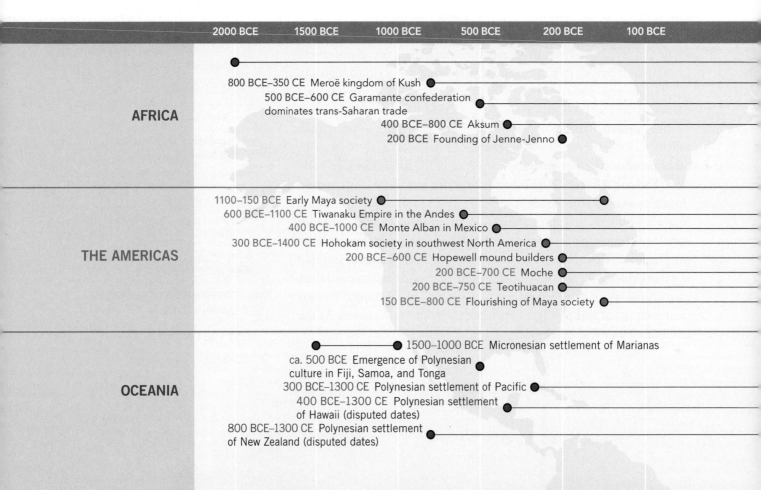

	2000 BCE	1500 BCE	1000 BCE	500 BCE	200 BCE	100 BCE

AFRICA
- 800 BCE–350 CE Meroë kingdom of Kush
- 500 BCE–600 CE Garamante confederation dominates trans-Saharan trade
- 400 BCE–800 CE Aksum
- 200 BCE Founding of Jenne-Jenno

THE AMERICAS
- 1100–150 BCE Early Maya society
- 600 BCE–1100 CE Tiwanaku Empire in the Andes
- 400 BCE–1000 CE Monte Alban in Mexico
- 300 BCE–1400 CE Hohokam society in southwest North America
- 200 BCE–600 CE Hopewell mound builders
- 200 BCE–700 CE Moche
- 200 BCE–750 CE Teotihuacan
- 150 BCE–800 CE Flourishing of Maya society

OCEANIA
- 1500–1000 BCE Micronesian settlement of Marianas
- ca. 500 BCE Emergence of Polynesian culture in Fiji, Samoa, and Tonga
- 300 BCE–1300 CE Polynesian settlement of Pacific
- 400 BCE–1300 CE Polynesian settlement of Hawaii (disputed dates)
- 800 BCE–1300 CE Polynesian settlement of New Zealand (disputed dates)

cities, washing and sanitation facilities, with many latrines, serviced Meroë's population.

Although influenced by Egypt, Kushite society and culture were distinctive. Topping the social hierarchy, absolute monarchs, including some queens, both governed and served as guardians of the state religion and temples. Besides worshipping some Egyptian gods, Kushites considered their monarchs, like Egyptian pharaohs, divine, and inscriptions testify to the rulers' piety. Roman sources report kings guided by laws and traditions:

> It is their custom that none of the subjects shall be executed, even if the person condemned to death appears to deserve punishment. Instead the king sends one of his servants bearing a symbol of death to the criminal. He upon seeing [it], immediately goes to his own house and kills himself.[2]

Queen mothers apparently played influential political roles. Below the ruler were the bureaucratic and military elite. Military officers led an army feared for both its weapons and the soldiers' appearance, as described by the Greek historian Herodotus:

> [They] were clothed in panthers' and lions' skins, and carried long bows made from branches of palm trees, and on them they laced short arrows made of cane tipped with stone. Besides this they had javelins, and at the tip was an antelope horn, made sharp like a lance; they also had knotted clubs. When they were going into battle they smeared one half of their body with chalk, and the other half with red ocher.[3]

Free peasants and slaves constituted the lower classes. Women had various economic roles, working in gold mining, farming, and craft production. They also served as priestesses, perhaps specializing in the honoring of female deities.

Kushites enjoyed a rich culture. Some Greek-speaking teachers apparently lived at Meroë, and at least one Kushite king studied Greek philosophy. Meroë artists produced highly polished, finely carved granite statues of their monarchs. Music played on trumpets, drums, harps, and flutes accompanied ceremonial and religious life, some instruments perhaps imported from Egypt and Greece. People of all classes and both genders wore jewelry. They also drank heavily, as evidenced by thousands of goblet fragments littering a ruined tavern. Finally, the presence of writing on numerous tombstones as well as graffiti suggests widespread literacy among all classes. The Kushite alphabet, **Meroitic** (mer-uh-WIT-ik), a cursive script that can only be partly read today, gradually replaced Egyptian hieroglyphics in monumental inscriptions, as Egyptian influence apparently faded over time while indigenous culture flourished.

9-1b The Legacy of Kush

After a millennium of power and prosperity, by 200 CE Kush declined. Just as widespread climate change may have hastened Han Chinese and Roman

> **Meroitic** A cursive script developed in the Classical period by the Kushites in Nubia that can only be partly read today.

[2]Quoted in Stanley Burstein, ed., *Ancient African Civilizations: Kush and Axum* (Princeton, NJ: Markus Wiener, 1998), 41.
[3]Quoted in Derek A. Welsby, *The Kingdom of Kush: The Napatan and Meroitic Empires* (Princeton, NJ: Markus Wiener, 1996), 40.

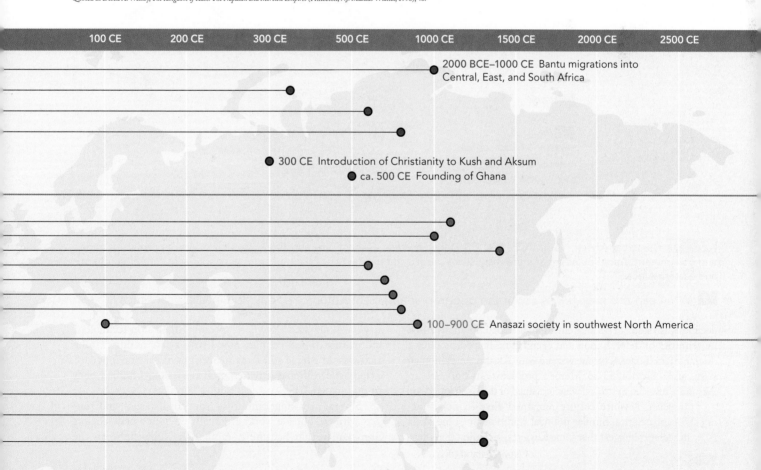

| 100 CE | 200 CE | 300 CE | 500 CE | 1000 CE | 1500 CE | 2000 CE | 2500 CE |

2000 BCE–1000 CE Bantu migrations into Central, East, and South Africa

300 CE Introduction of Christianity to Kush and Aksum

ca. 500 CE Founding of Ghana

100–900 CE Anasazi society in southwest North America

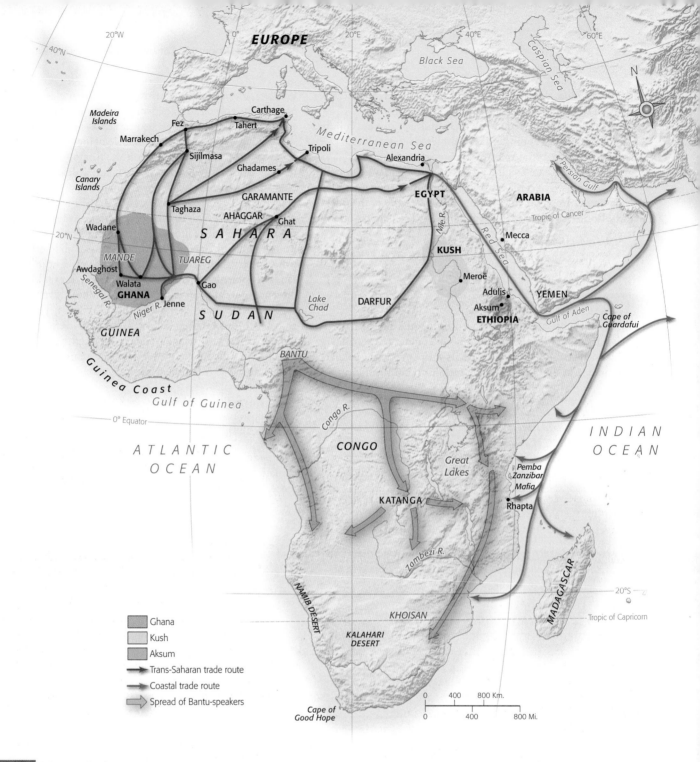

MAP 9.1 **Classical Africa, 1500 BCE–600 CE** During this era, Kush, Aksum, and Jenne were major African centers of trade and government. Trade routes crossed the vast Sahara Desert, and the Bantu-speaking peoples expanded into central, southern, and eastern Africa.

Q What can this map tell us about the geography and distribution of population in Classical Africa?

decline, Kush suffered because environmental deterioration caused by centuries of deforestation and overgrazing helped produce a drier, hotter climate. Chronic warfare with Aksum, an Ethiopian state, also contributed to Meroë's problems. In 350 CE an Aksumite invasion destroyed what remained of the Kush kingdom.

However, Kushite culture remained alive in neighboring African societies. Similar political traditions in some West African societies suggest that some Kushites, including the rulers,

may have migrated elsewhere, spreading their iron technology and culture. Some peoples now living a few hundred miles southwest of Meroë still show many signs of Kushite influence, including recreational activities (such as wrestling), fashion, body art, and material life.

Several new kingdoms arose from Kush's ashes, and contacts with the outside world eventually brought a new religion, Christianity, that became dominant in Nubia between the fourth and sixth centuries CE, during which time many churches were built. Nubian Christianity was a branch of the **Coptic (KAHP-tik) Church**, which followed Monophysite thought (see Chapter 8) and had become influential in Egypt. With its patriarchal tendencies, Christianity seems to have replaced matrilineal traditions with patrilineal ones, monarchies now passing from fathers to sons. Many Copts still live in Egypt, but Nubia's Christian kingdoms, isolated from other Christians by the Islamic conquest of Egypt in the seventh century CE, gradually faded. Around 1400 CE Muslims conquered the last Christian Nubian state, and most people converted to Islam. Today only the ruins of Christian churches and monasteries remain, along with even older Meroite pyramids, the material legacy of Kush.

IMAGE 9.2 **Queen Amanitere** Queen Amanitere ruled Meroë along with her husband, King Natakamani, around two thousand years ago. In this relief on the Lion Temple at Naqa, Kush, she holds vanquished foes by the hair while brandishing swords, thus demonstrating the power of the royal couple and the Kushite state.

Topham/The Image Works

9-1c The Aksum Empire and Society

Another literate urban African state, **Aksum**, emerged near the Red Sea in the rocky but fertile Ethiopian highlands beginning around 400 BCE. Despite an unpredictable climate and deep gorges that inhibited communication, Aksumites traded with Egypt and benefited from proximity to the Red Sea, the major maritime route linking the Mediterranean Sea and the Indian Ocean. At the Red Sea's narrowest point, only 20 miles of water separates Arabia's southern tip from Northeast Africa, and many Semitic people from Arabia crossed into Ethiopia and settled. This accessibility to Arabia greatly benefited northern Ethiopians, allowing links to the Hebrews. Ethiopian legends claim that the Queen of Sheba (**Saba**), who, according to biblical accounts, met the Hebrew king Solomon, was in fact an early Ethiopian monarch, Queen Makeda (**ma-KAY-da**), who went to Israel in search of knowledge. In the legend Makeda supposedly told her people:

> Let my voice be heard by all of you, my people. I am going in quest of Wisdom and Learning. My spirit impels me to go and find them out where they are to be had, for I am smitten with the love of Wisdom and I feel myself drawn as though by a leash toward Learning. Learning is better than treasures of gold, better than all that has been created upon earth.[4]

Semitic immigrants from Yemen, the probable location of ancient Sheba, may have brought the story with them to Ethiopia and adapted it for local needs. According to the legend, the son of Solomon and Makeda, Menelik (**MEN-uh-lik**), supposedly founded a new kingdom, Aksum. Ethiopian legends portray the young Menelik smuggling out from Jerusalem the Ark of the Covenant, which holds the holy tablets Hebrews believe God gave to Moses. Ethiopian Christians claim the Ark remains enshrined in an Aksum cathedral, with viewing restricted to only a few people. Scholars vigorously debate the historical accuracy of the stories of Sheba, Makeda, Menelik, and the Ark of the Covenant.

Aksumites, ancestors of the Amharic (**am-HAR-ik**) people who today dominate central Ethiopia, worked both bronze and iron. Between 400 BCE and 100 CE they built their first temples and palaces of masonry, as well as a city, dams, and reservoirs. Irrigation and terracing supported productive farming. The Aksumites also developed an alphabet and enjoyed close economic and cultural exchange with both southwestern Asia and eastern Africa. In about 50 CE they built an empire that dominated some of Northeast Africa and that flourished chiefly from trade. Soon Aksum eclipsed Meroë, gaining control of trade between the Red Sea and the central Nile. The Persian prophet Mani included Aksum among the world's four great kingdoms, along with Persia, Rome, and China.

The Aksumites traded all over the Middle East, eastern Mediterranean, and East Africa, and their trade networks also reached Sri Lanka and India; many Indian coins have been found at Aksum (see Discover Historical Voices: A Shopper's Guide to Aksum). Aksumites exported ivory, gold, obsidian, emeralds,

Coptic Church A branch of Christianity, based on Monophysite ideas, that had become influential in Egypt and became dominant in Nubia between the fourth and sixth centuries CE.

Aksum A literate, urban state that appeared in northern Ethiopia before the Common Era and grew into an empire and a crossroads for trade.

---
[4]From *Horizon History*, 78.

Discover Historical Voices

A Shopper's Guide to Aksum

The following account of Aksum's trade comes from the Periplus of the Erythrean Sea, *written by an unknown Greek in the second half of the first century CE. The* Periplus, *a guide prepared for merchants and sailors, outlines commercial prospects in Arabia, the Indian Ocean, and the Persian Gulf. It also describes many of the region's bustling ports. Hence, the* Periplus *provides excellent material for understanding Classical exchange networks. In this excerpt, we learn about the port city of Adulis* (**A-doo-lis**) *on the Red Sea. Now called Massawa* (**muh-SAH-wuh**), *Adulis was the chief Aksumite trade distribution center where goods from the Ethiopian interior and from faraway places such as India, Egypt, and the Mediterranean were brought for sale or transshipment.*

Adulis [is] a port . . . lying at the inner end of a bay. . . . Before the harbor lies the . . . Mountain Island, . . . with the shores of the mainland close to it on both sides. Ships bound for this port now anchor here because of attacks from the land [by bandits]. . . . Opposite Mountain Island, on the mainland, . . . lies Adulis, a fair-sized village, from which there is a three day's journey to Coloe, an inland town and the first market for ivory. From that place to the [capital] city of the . . . Aksumites there is a five day's journey more; to that place all the ivory is brought from the country beyond the Nile. . . .

There are imported into these places [Adulis], undressed cloth made in Egypt for the Berbers; robes from . . . [modern Suez]; cloaks of poor quality dyed in colors; double-fringed linen mantles; many articles of flint glass, and others of . . . [agate] made in . . . [Thebes, Egypt]; and brass, which is used for ornament and in cut pieces instead of coin; sheets of soft copper, used for cooking utensils and cut up for bracelets and anklets for the women; iron, which is made into spears used against the elephants and other wild beasts, and in their wars. Besides these, small axes are imported, and adzes and swords; copper drinking cups, round and large; a little coin for those coming to the market; wine of Laodicea [on the Syrian coast] and Italy . . . ; olive oil . . . ; for the King, gold and silver plate made after the fashion of the country, and for clothing, military cloaks, and thin coats of skin. . . . Likewise from the district of Ariaca [on the northwest coast of India] across this sea, there are imported Indian cloth [fine-quality cotton]. . . . There are exported from these places ivory, and tortoise-shell and rhinoceros-horn. The most [cargo] from Egypt is brought to this market [Adulis] from the month of January to September.

Reflection Questions

1. What were some of the societies that were linked to the trade at Adulis?
2. What does this reading tell us about the networks of exchange that connected Aksum to a wider world?
3. Can you see any similarities and differences between the market of Adulis and modern shopping centers?

Source: W. H. Schoff, trans. and ed., *The Periplus of the Erythraean Sea: Travel and Trade in the Indian Ocean by a Merchant of the First Century* (New York: Longmans, Green, and Co., 1912).

---

perfumes, and animals while importing metals, glass, fabrics, wine, and spices. They used the Greek language in foreign commerce and became the first sub-Saharan Africans to mint their own coins.

Aksum had various links to other societies. Byzantium sent envoys to the court, seeking alliances against common enemies in Arabia, and extensive ties with Yemen's Semitic peoples fostered genetic and cultural intermixing between these two peoples. The Amharic language, **Geez** (gee-EZ), blends African and Semitic influences. Hebrew culture also influenced Ethiopian literature and religion. The modern Amharic royal family, descendants of Aksumite kings, claimed ancestry from King Solomon and Queen Makeda. The Jewish communities known as *Falasha* (fuh-LAHSH-uh) have lived in northern Ethiopia for many centuries. In recent decades many of the Falasha have emigrated to Israel, where they sometimes face discrimination for their dark skin and questions about their Jewish ancestry.

Geez The classical Amharic language of Ethiopia, a mixture of African and Semitic influences.

Kings claiming a paternalistic attitude toward their people dominated Aksum's social structure. A fourth-century CE monarch left an inscription boasting that he "will rule the people with righteousness and justice, and will not oppress them."[5] Judging from their spectacular palaces, kings also enjoyed great wealth and power. A sixth-century Byzantine ambassador reported on the royal family's pomp and ceremony, noting that the king wore

a golden collar. He stood on a four-wheeled chariot drawn by four elephants; the body of the chariot was high and covered with gold plates. The king stood on top carrying a small gilded shield and holding in his hands two small gilded spears.[6]

Below the royal family, an aristocracy supplied the top government officials, a substantial middle class included many merchants, and peasants and slaves occupied the lowest tier, subject to conscription for massive building projects.

The capital city of Aksum, a wealthy and cosmopolitan trading center widely known for its monumental architecture, boasted magnificent pillars, thin stylized representations of

---

[5]Quoted in Graham Connah, *African Civilization. Precolonial Cities and States in Tropical Africa: An Archaeological Perspective* (Cambridge, UK: Cambridge University Press, 1987), 78.
[6]Quoted in Robert W. July, *A History of the African People*, 5th ed. (Prospect Heights, IL: Waveland, 1998), 45.

multistoried buildings (some over one hundred feet high), many stone platforms, and huge palaces. Making and transporting the monoliths and stone slabs required remarkable engineering skills.

9-1d The Aksum Legacy

With Christian missionaries traveling the trade routes from western Asia, Christianity became influential just as Aksum reached its height of economic and military power in the fourth century CE. The king adopted the faith, making Christianity the kingdom's official religion. According to a Roman source, he "began to search out Roman merchants [at Aksum] who were Christian and to give them great influence and to urge them to establish [churches], supplying sites for buildings, and in every way promoting the growth of Christianity."[7] The king had political reasons for conversion, since he wanted closer relations with Rome, Byzantium, and Egypt. But the Amharic population only slowly adopted the new faith. Ethiopian Christianity resembled Egypt and Nubia's

Coptic churches but also incorporated long-entrenched spirit worship and various Hebrew practices, including the Jewish sabbath and kosher food.

Aksum eventually collapsed. By 400 CE, reduced rainfall and the resulting pressure on the land had produced an ecological crisis, and political problems added to imperial decline. In addition, the conquest of southern Arabia by Aksum's enemy, Sassanian Persia, in 575 diverted the Indian Ocean commerce from the port of Adulis. Then the rapid Islamic conquests of western Asia and North Africa beginning in the mid-seventh century cut Aksum off from the Christian world. Aksum's trade withered, spawning economic stagnation, cultural decline, and political instability, and by 800 CE the Aksumites had abandoned the capital city. But unlike Kush, Ethiopian society persisted in recognizable form. Over the centuries Christianity became a deeply ingrained local religion in the Ethiopian highlands, with the unique Ethiopian church, closely connected to the monarchy, owning many landed estates. Ethiopians remained relatively isolated in their mountain fastness for the next ten centuries.

KEY POINTS

▶ The kingdom of Kush in Nubia, with its capital city of Meroë, was a major African iron producer and crossroads of trade between sub-Saharan Africa and the Mediterranean.

▶ Kush was influenced by Egypt but was also remarkable for its rich culture and its fearsome warriors and absolute monarchs.

▶ Aksum, in the Ethiopian highlands, had contact with Egypt and Arabia, may have forged links with the

Hebrews, and after a time eclipsed Meroë as the region's primary trade center.

▶ Aksum's king converted to Christianity as a means of establishing closer relationships with Rome, Byzantium, and Egypt.

▶ Like Kush, Aksum may have declined in part because of climate change, but it was also hurt by the Islamic conquest of its neighbors; unlike Kush, however, the society endured into modern times.

9-2 The Blossoming of West and Bantu Africa

NETWORKS

Q How did the spread of the Bantus reshape sub-Saharan Africa?

Complex urban societies also arose in West Africa, especially in the Sudanic region on the Sahara's southern fringe, among peoples like the Mande (**MAHN-day**), who were linked to North Africa and beyond by trade networks. Meanwhile, Bantu-speaking Africans spread their languages, cultures, and technologies widely, occupying the southern half of Africa. Some connected to trade networks linked to east coast port cities.

CONNECTION to TODAY

How do you think the trans-Saharan and Indian Ocean maritime trading systems helped create the globalized world we live in today?

economic life to the prevailing ecology. Most Sudanese became farmers in small, largely self-sufficient villages, growing vegetables and cereal crops, especially millet and sorghum, that needed little water. West Africans also grew cotton and developed richly colored cotton clothing. The food grown in a large fertile delta along the Niger (**NYE-juhr**) River helped to feed the trading cities.

Some Sudanese along the Niger River congregated in large towns and cities that reached 30,000 to 40,000 in population. The major hub, Jenne-Jeno, in today's nation of Mali, developed as early as 200 BCE. Residents built circular straw houses coated with mud and worked copper, gold, and iron obtained from mines several hundred miles away. Gold dust and small copper ingots (**IN-guhts**) apparently served as Sudanic currency. By 400 CE

9-2a Sudanic Farming, Cities, and the Trans-Saharan Networks

In the vast but dry grassland region known as the Sudan (**soo-DAN**), lying in West and Central Africa between the Sahara to the north and tropical forests to the south, societies adapted their

---

[7]Rufinus, quoted in Burstein, *Ancient African Civilizations*, 95.

Jenne-Jenno had become a crucial transshipment point for goods, including gold and copper, brought by camel or donkey caravans and Niger River boats. It flourished as a commercial center for many centuries, closely tied, like other Sudanic cities, to the trans-Sahara caravans. Eventually a wall a mile in circumference surrounded the city to protect the residents. Built upon a productive agriculture, Jenne-Jenno exported grain, fish, and animal products in exchange for metals. Historians suspect that the city and other commercial centers in the Niger Valley were probably independent city-states for most of the first millennium CE.

During the Classical Era large cities and states were less common in sub-Saharan Africa than in Eurasia, North Africa, Nubia, and Ethiopia. The African agricultural system, mostly based on shifting cultivation, suited the soils but could not generally support large settled populations. In the first century CE Africa contained perhaps between 15 and 25 million people, much less than half that of China. About half lived in Egypt, Kush, and along the Mediterranean coast. With small population densities, societies did not require a powerful state to maintain order and could be held together by social and economic ties.

Beginning well before the Common Era, various caravan routes crossing the Sahara's barren sands greatly aided Sudanic growth by fostering interregional trade. Eventually a large trade system spanned the Sahara, linking Sudanic towns with southern Mediterranean coastal societies such as Carthage. Salt moved south while gold moved north, and gold used in Carthage coins may have come from western Africa. Sudanic cities also shipped north cotton cloth, leather goods, pepper, and slaves, which the merchants in North Africa then sold to Europe.

Although largely self-sufficient, Sudanic societies needed salt mined in the central Sahara and along the West African coast. The *Garamante* tribal confederation, which inhabited a large desert region north of the Sudan, mostly controlled the salt trade. These Berber **(BUHR-buhr)** people, who created the Sahara's most elaborate urban society, dominated the caravan trade routes as intermediaries from around 500 BCE to 600 CE, managing a vast commercial network and apparently selling African slaves to the Carthaginians, Romans, and Greeks. The Garamantes used camels as pack animals and horses to pull light chariots. To the Greeks and Romans, they were warlike barbarians, but these Saharans made the parched desert livable by combining pastoral stock raising with irrigated farming. They constructed several thousand miles of underground canals to cultivate their farms, lived in walled cities and villages, built stone citadels as military outposts, and were apparently governed by royal families. Their state collapsed around the same time as the Roman Empire, the remnants later overrun by Muslims.

Ghana The first known major Sudanic state, formed by the Soninke people of the middle Niger Valley.

Mande Diverse Sudanic peoples who spoke closely related languages, shared many customs, and dominated the western Niger River Basin and adjacent areas of West Africa.

Werner Forman/Universal Images Group/Getty Images

IMAGE 9.3 **A Jenne Warrior** This statuette, about two feet tall and made of a baked clay known as terra-cotta, likely portrays a warrior in Jenne, probably of high status, although some experts believe it portrays a founding ancestor.

Q What does the statuette tell us about Jenne life and culture?

9-2b West African States and Peoples

As in Kush and Aksum, commerce stimulated state building in the Sudan and West Africa. Kingdoms apparently grew out of markets, taxing the trade in gold and other commodities. The Soninke **(soh-NIN-kay)** of the middle Niger Valley formed the first known major Sudanic state, **Ghana** **(GAH-nuh)**. Although existing by at least 700 CE, Ghana likely emerged several centuries earlier, and its probable capital city was built of stone sometime between 500 and 600 CE. Ghana reached its height as a trade-based empire in the ninth century and flourished until the thirteenth.

Diverse **Mande** **(MON-day)** peoples perhaps typified Classical Sudanic societies. The Mande spoke closely related languages, shared many customs, and dominated the western Niger River Basin and adjacent areas. Mande speakers included such ethnic groups as the Soninke (who established Ghana), Mandinka **(man-DING-goh)**, Malinke **(muh-LING-kee)**, and Bambara **(bam-BAHR-uh)**. By 900 or 800 BCE Mande farmers lived in large walled villages, and they may have built Jenne-Jenno. Later, Mande speakers dominated much of the western Sudan.

The Mande groups shared many social, political, and religious traditions. Their societies included aristocratic, warrior, and commoner classes and ritual and religious specialists. Eventually they developed theocracies with chiefs and village heads combining religious and secular duties. A respected class of oral historians and musicians known widely as **griots** (GREE-oh) memorized and recited the community's history, emphasizing leaders' deeds. Many Mande of all classes enjoyed considerable prosperity, making and trading widely their elaborate and beautiful cotton clothing. Mande and other Sudanic peoples also developed some common ideas about religion, including animism. Although they believed in a distant creator god, spirits of nature and ancestors loomed large in daily life. The Mande drew no neat line between the living and the dead while wanting to keep the favor of good spirits and avoid the hostility of bad ones.

Over time various peoples possessing new tools and agricultural techniques, including some from the Sudan, migrated into the Guinea (GIN-ee) coast, a land of forest and swamp with few edible plants or game animals that stretched some two thousand miles from modern Senegal (sen-i-GAWL) to southeastern Nigeria (nie-JEER-ee-uh). Mixing Sudanic and other traditions produced unique new societies. To survive their challenging environment, people lived mostly in small, self-sufficient villages with rich social networks, practicing subsistence agriculture, with yams and bananas as staple crops, and often working the land communally. The Guinea peoples traded with the Sudan by traveling over land or by boat up the rivers such as the Niger and Volta (VAHL-tuh), becoming linked to wider economic and cultural exchange networks. Many coastal societies practiced some common customs, including Sudanese traditions such as theocratic political systems and pronounced social-class divisions.

9-2c The Bantu-Speaking Peoples and Their Migrations

Over several thousand years, many iron-using speakers of Bantu languages migrated from their original homeland in what is today eastern Nigeria into Central and East Africa (see Chapter 3). Some scholars argue that the diffusion of Bantu culture and technology proceeded even without large numbers of migrants. During the Classical period, Bantu peoples accelerated their expansion to the south and east, some moving into the drought- and disease-prone southern Congo grasslands region known as Katanga (kuh-TAHNG-guh). South of the Congo Basin rain forest, most land is relatively arid because of irregular rainfall. Fortunately, Bantus successfully adapted sorghum and millet from the Sudan and Ethiopia to this dry southern climate. From Katanga many Bantus moved to the west, south, and east. By 200 BCE they had reached the Zambezi (zam-BEE-zee) River Basin, and by the third century CE they had entered what is now South Africa. Trade and migration networks spanning vast distances eventually connected Africa's southern third to the Sudan and the East African coast.

As Bantu migrants encountered local peoples, they incorporated new influences. Being ironworkers, Bantus possessed more effective military and agricultural technologies than many non-Bantu peoples, who were sometimes pushed into marginal economic areas suitable only for hunting and gathering. For example, the Mbuti Pygmies of the Congo region moved into thick rain forests, while many of the Khoisan (KOY-sahn) peoples in southern Africa, such as the !Kung, became desert dwellers. But many Bantus intermingled, and probably culturally assimilated, with those they met. Sudanese cultural forms carried by Bantus, such as drums and percussive music, woodcarving, and ancestor-focused religions, became widespread. The process worked both ways. For example, Xhosa (KOH-sah) and Zulu peoples, settling along the far southeastern coast, mixed their languages and cultures with local Khoisan cattle herders, incorporating Khoisan click sounds into their speech and cattle herding into their economic life.

The migrating Bantus gradually absorbed various East African societies, including pastoralists and farmers. Relationships were sometimes hostile with various ironworking pastoralists from the eastern Sudan who were also settling in East Africa, known as **Nilotes** (nie-LAHT-eez) because they speak Nilotic (nie-LAHT-ik) languages very different from Bantu tongues. Some Bantus began herding cattle and goats; others mastered new crops, including Southeast Asian foods like bananas, coconuts, sugar cane, and Asian yams brought to East Africa, along with domesticated chickens and possibly pigs, outrigger canoes, and musical instruments, by Indonesian mariners and migrants during the first millennium of the Common Era. Some Indonesians apparently established coastal trading posts and married local people. Beginning around 500 to 700 CE both Bantus and Indonesians settled the large island of Madagascar, implanting there a mixed culture and Austronesian language that still survive.

9-2d Maritime Trade and the East African Coast

Maritime trade fostered a cosmopolitan society on the East African coast. Winds and currents in the Indian Ocean reverse direction every six months, allowing boats from southwestern and southern Asia to sail to East Africa and back each year. Trading ports dotted the coast from Somalia to present-day Tanzania, and the main port, Rhapta (RAHP-ta), a metropolis and trading hub located on an island off the coast of what is today Tanzania, had a large Arab merchant community.

Coastal trade grew slowly. A first-century CE Alexandria-based Greek reported ships leaving Egypt's Red Sea ports and then visiting Adulis and Somalian ports before sailing to East African ports. In classical times Rhapta was probably the southern-most point of the Indian Ocean trade system, a place, the Greeks reported, where local people made sown boats, used dugout canoes, and behaved "each in his own

griots A respected class of oral historians and musicians in West Africa who memorized and recited the history of the group, emphasizing the deeds of leaders.

Nilotes Ironworking pastoralists from the eastern Sudan who settled in East Africa and there had frequent interactions with the Bantus.

place like chiefs."[8] Trading ships leaving Rhapta usually headed northeast to India rather than venturing farther down what they considered the mysterious southern coast and ocean. East Africa exported ivory, rhinoceros horn, metal weapons, and tortoise shell to Egypt, India, and western Asia and imported iron goods, pottery, and glass beads. Egyptian, Roman, and West

Asian coins found in the region indicate trade with Mediterranean peoples, and Persian pottery was common along the coast and inland. Eventually, coastal culture mixed Bantu and southwestern Asian ideas. But it took many centuries before any ships from the Afro-Eurasian world established contact with the Western Hemisphere, to which we now turn.

KEY POINTS

▶ The Sudan region included trading hubs such as Jenne-Jenno, but the population was not dense enough to require a powerful state; Ghana was the first state to arise, probably around 500 CE.

▶ The Garamante peoples controlled the extensive Sahara Desert caravan routes to bring salt from the African Mediterranean coast to Sudan, which exported gold in return.

▶ The Bantu peoples, equipped with iron tools, continued to migrate south and east, mixing with and sometimes pushing out other peoples, as they made their way to South Africa by the third century CE.

▶ Indonesian mariners settled on the East African coast and, to a greater extent, in Madagascar, where a mixed Indonesian-Bantu culture survives to this day.

9-3 Classical Societies and Networks in the Americas

SOCIETIES **NETWORKS**

Q How did the Mesoamerican, Andean, and North American societies compare with each other?

As in Eurasia and Africa, the first cities and states in the Americas developed during ancient times, including Mesoamerica and the Andes (see Chapter 4). Population increase helped foster more urban societies during the Classical period. By the beginning of the first century CE around fifteen million people lived in the Americas, over two-thirds of them in Mesoamerica and western South America, where several cities became centers of prosperous states. Most of these societies thrived from highly productive agriculture, developing diverse cultures, governments, and ways of life.

CONNECTION to TODAY

How did the impacts of climate change on Andean, Mesoamerican, and Native North American societies compare to the climate crises we face today?

farming of maize (corn) and other foods into tropical forests. According to Maya legends, the gods had fashioned people out of corn. Farmers built artificial platforms and terraces for growing enough crops to also support a ruling elite, and they constructed large underground reservoirs to store groundwater where rainfall was scarce.

As more productive agriculture fostered larger populations, the Maya spread southward into the mountains and coastal zones of today's Chiapas (**chee-AHP-uhs**) (Mexico), Guatemala (**GWAHT-uh-MAHL-uh**), Honduras, El Salvador, and Belize (**buh-LEEZ**).

With increasing power, Maya elites organized ambitious building projects, constructing their first pyramids and elaborate stone buildings by 600 BCE. Unlike Egyptian pyramids, which were burial tombs for top leaders, Maya pyramids were built for religious worship and ceremonies, with temples on top to house the gods. According to Maya folklore:

9-3a The Emergence of the Early Maya

In the lowland rain forests of Central America and southeast Mexico's Yucatán (**YOO-kuh-TAN**) Peninsula, the **Maya** (**MIE-uh**) became the most long-lasting and widespread Mesoamerican society, forging a literate but often brutal culture that excelled in some sciences and mathematics (see Map 9.2).

Building on earlier regional traditions, probably including the Olmec culture to the northwest, they practiced shifting cultivation agriculture and ceramic making from at least 1100 BCE. They also introduced intensive

Maya The most long-lasting and widespread of the classical Mesoamerican societies, who occupied the Yucatán Peninsula and northern Central America for almost two thousand years.

There had been five generations of people since the origin of light, of life and of humankind. And they built houses for the gods, putting these in the center of the highest part of the citadel. After that their domains grew larger and more crowded.[9]

As divine kingship notions became widespread, the Maya made stone statues and carvings of their rulers while painting sophisticated murals illustrating Maya myths.

---

[8]Quoted in Christopher Ehret, *An African Classical Age: Eastern and Southern Africa in World History, 1000 B.C. to A.D. 600* (Charlottesville: University of Virginia Press, 1998), 275.

[9]From the *Popul Vuh*, quoted in Brian M. Fagan, *Kingdoms of Gold, Kingdoms of Jade: The Americas Before Columbus* (London and New York: Thames and Hudson, 1991), 94.

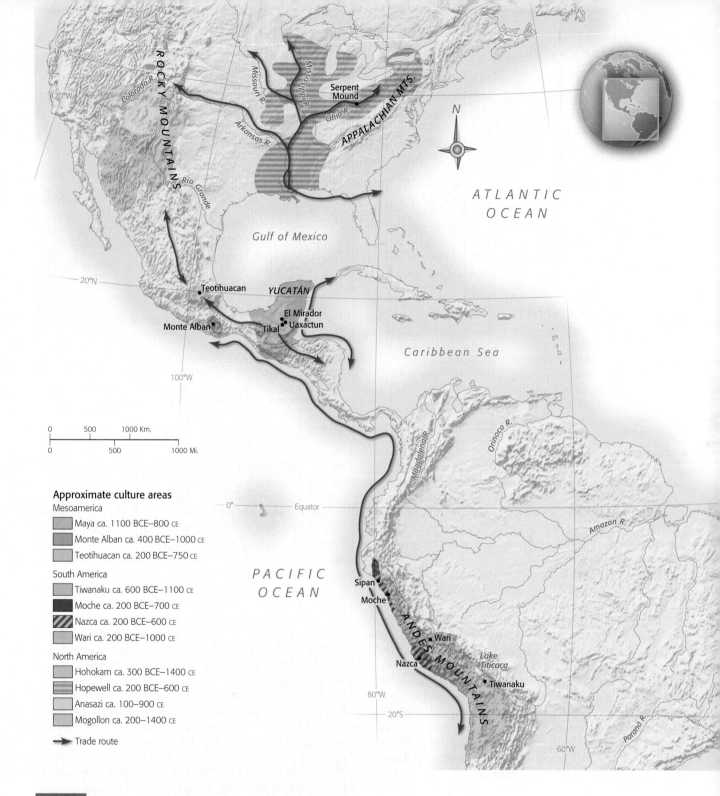

MAP 9.2 **Major Classical Societies in the Americas** Various societies in the Americas lived largely from agriculture in this era and were connected to trade networks. Some, like the Mayans and Teotihuacan in Mesoamerica and Moche, and Tiwanaku in South America, developed cities and states while various North Americans, such as the Anasazi, Hohokam, and Hopewell, lived in towns.

Q What does this map tell us about where most people lived, and how does the population distribution compare to Africa in this era (see Map 9.1)?

At their cultural height, 150 BCE to 800 CE, the Maya built many cities boasting masonry buildings, large temples, spacious plazas and pyramid complexes, and elaborate carvings. In the major early city, El Mirador, the earliest Maya writing was inscribed on pot fragments and sculpture. Influenced by Olmec models, the Maya developed the Americas' most comprehensive writing system, a hieroglyphic script used for calendars, religious regulations, many sacred books, and recordings of dynastic histories, genealogies, and military successes. A later Spanish observer admired "those who carried with them the black and red ink, the manuscripts and painted book, the wisdom, the annals, the books of song."[10] The early Maya cities also included a distinctive architecture, royal dynasties, and a highly stratified social system. In some cities, suburbs containing residences, markets, and workshops stretched for several miles out from city centers. Even the Spanish who conquered the Maya lands in the 1500s marveled at the cities. One wrote that "the buildings and the multitude of them is remarkable. So well built are they of cut stone that it fills one with astonishment."[11]

IMAGE 9.4 **Maya Codex** Only three Maya books (or codices) are known to have survived the Spanish conquest. This beautiful, illustrated folding-screen book, the Dresden Codex, compiled around 1200 CE, records astronomical calculations, tables of eclipses, and ritual detail. It is written on a long strip of bark paper coated with stucco.

Robert Michael/Stringer/AFP/Getty Images

Q What can we learn about Mayan life and thought from the codex?

Tikal (**ti-KAHL**), in eastern Guatemala, a major Maya city between 200 and 900 CE housing fifty thousand or more people at its height, contained three hundred large ceremonial buildings dominated by temple pyramids two hundred feet high that were decorated with stucco plaster carvings. The first ruler used the jaguar to symbolize kingship, military bravery, and religious authority. His descendants, King Great Jaguar Paw and General Smoking Frog, led Tikal to a great victory over the rival city Uaxactun in 378 CE, ensuring Tikal's regional supremacy for the next two hundred years. Tikal's success and survival also owed much to engineering projects, including the Maya world's largest dam, two hundred and sixty feet long and thirty-three feet high, built of stone, rubble, and dirt, to collect, store, and filter rainwater for use in periodic droughts.

9-3b Maya Politics and Trade

With Maya identity being more cultural than political, much cultural uniformity persisted among the competing cities, probably because of the region's dense population and the cities' close proximity with one another. Perhaps ten million people lived in the Maya lowlands by 600 CE, and a few cities, such as Tikal, now dominated others in the region. But no united Maya state or empire ever existed. Fortified sites with high walls, moats, watchtowers, and caches of round stones for warriors' slings, such as those discovered around Tikal, testify to a concern with defense and fear of enemies. With warfare between competing city-states over resources frequent and brutal, prisoners of war were usually enslaved or sacrificed. As in various Eastern Hemisphere and American societies, human sacrifice was common. Captured leaders from other cities faced especially agonizing deaths.

Maya ruling families were interconnected, with sons or daughters often being married into ruling families of rival cities to cement alliances or discourage attack. Cities were ruled by kings and sometimes queens who combined political, military, and religious leadership, consolidating their position by linking themselves to gods and ancestors and erecting stone monuments glorifying their deeds and ancestry. Because the scribes writing these inscriptions gained respect and influence, they might also be killed when their city-state and king lost a war.

While rulers taxed and may have distributed goods, many cities had marketplaces for traders. Many murals, carvings, and ceramic paintings depict typical market exchanges and tribute payments to Mayan kings. Maya cities were linked in networks of interregional trade forged by hacking paths through the often dense rain forests. Some Mayans, especially in Yucatán, grew enough surplus crops, such as cotton for making textiles, maize, manioc, tobacco, and chocolate, to support an active barter trade with neighbors and other people throughout Mesoamerica. By the eighth century CE woven cloth as well as chocolate in the form of dried *cacao* (kuh-COW) beans, mostly used to make a much-prized hot drink, was being used by some as a kind of money. They also traded widely with non-Maya societies, some hundreds of miles away in central Mexico or deep into Central

---

[10]Father Bernardinode Sahagun, quoted in Richard E. W. Adams, *Prehistoric Mesoamerica* (Boston: Little, Brown, 1977), 110.
[11]Frey Diego de Landa, quoted in T. Patrick Culbert, *Maya Civilization* (Washington, D.C.: Smithsonian, 1993), 23.

to the north and south. Some neighborhoods housed merchants and sojourners or settlers, many of them traders and artisans, from Maya cities a thousand miles away and other regions, and Teotihuacan merchants also traveled widely. Maya-carved jade statues were common. There may also have been close links between Teotihuacan and Maya royal families.

Eventually Teotihuacan society collapsed. Rulers became increasingly militaristic and human sacrifice more common, earning Teotihuacan enemies and harming trade. The causes of the collapse may have been environment disaster (such as a prolonged drought) or internal revolts involving disgruntled immigrants or invasions by a rival state. In 750 CE invaders burned the city down, and the population scattered. But even in ruins the city's splendor lived on. A millennium later the Aztecs who had settled the area told the Spanish conquerors of their reverence for the sacred spirit of the pyramids: "And this they call Teotihuacan, because it is where they bury the lords."[14]

9-3e Andean Societies

Other societies emerged and often flourished in South America. Chavín, the Andes state, had collapsed by 200 BCE, but some of its architectural and religious patterns spread through the Andes and into adjacent lands. **Moche (MO-che)**, a prosperous and powerful state or, as some research suggests, a grouping of affiliated communities, formed around 200 BCE in the desert along the northern Peruvian coast. In this dry region farming required maintaining irrigation canals that channeled runoff from the Andes to grow corn, beans, peppers, squash, and cotton, which Moche skillfully wove into textiles. They also exploited the abundant, protein-rich maritime resources just offshore, including fish and mollusks.

The Moche were part of a distinctive culture that built monumental architecture, with platforms and courtyards, and fashioned beautiful jewelry, mirrors, and pottery. Coastal peoples traded some of their agricultural and maritime bounty to Andes societies for potatoes and other highland crops. Eventually trade networks linked societies over western South America. Some took up seagoing trade. Between 500 BCE and the 1600s CE, the Manteno people from coastal Ecuador used balsa wood rafts equipped with sails and loaded with textiles, ceramics, precious metals, and prized shells to forge a coastal trade network stretching from Mexico to Chile. Because of these trends, coastal and interior peoples depended on each other, encouraging state formation in both places.

The well-planned Moche capital city, centered around two massive brick pyramids dedicated to the sun and moon, contained perhaps ten thousand people. Separate and perhaps hostile city-based Moche kingdoms were spread over hundreds of miles, all with similar customs, buildings, and pyramids. Burial chambers and clay pottery painted with highly realistic scenes of social activity provide knowledge of Moche society, such as the sometimes elegant, sometimes brutal life of the elite (see Meet the People: A Moche Lord). While male warrior-priests were powerful, priestess-queens seem to have occasionally ruled some cities. Enormous amounts of gold and silver artifacts were buried with dignitaries. Frequent wars helped them obtain captives who could be sacrificed in grisly ritual ceremonies.

Revealing everyday life, painted pots show midwives attending birthing mothers, women carrying babies on their backs in shawls, and men with tattooed faces. Nearly everyone wears headgear, from the elite's feathered headdresses to the common folks' decorated cotton turbans. Like most Andes peoples, Moche consumed maize beer. The paintings also portray erotic lovemaking between men and women and between gods and humans, as well as war leaders drinking their unfortunate captives' blood. While many customs shock us and may not have made them popular neighbors, the Moche should be remembered for more than bloodshed. Excellent gold workers, they also made products from a copper and gold alloy as well as silver. They created one of the world's finest ceramic traditions and apparently also developed a mathematical system based on the number *10*.

Eventually the Moche faced challenges they could not overcome, including natural disasters, among them prolonged drought, massive earthquakes, and severe *El Ñinos* (**el NEEN-yoz**), the periodic warm-water currents in the Pacific that bring higher temperatures and torrential rain. Moche leaders may have responded to the resulting food shortages with increasing warfare to obtain resources and human sacrifice to appease the gods. The ecological and political crises these disasters generated brought Moche collapse by 650 or 700 CE.

While Moche dominated the northern Peruvian coast, various states rose and fell in the Andes and along the southern Peruvian coast, a cycle often fostered by climate instability and change. In the Lake Titicaca (**tit-i-KAHK-uh**) region (in modern Bolivia and southern Peru) of the Andes highlands between 600 and 100 BCE, the ancestors of the Aymara (**AYE-muh-RAH**) people built a state and constructed impressive stone sculpture. Even in ruins, their plazas, palaces, and brightly colored temples decorated with gold-covered reliefs impressed the Spanish fifteen hundred years later; one wrote: "There is a hill made by the hands of men, on great foundations of stone. What causes most astonishment are some great doorways of stone, some made out of a single stone."[15] The capital city, Tiwanaku (**tee-wah-NA-coo**), over ten thousand feet above sea level, emerged by 100 CE and reached its height in 600 CE with a population of perhaps forty thousand, controlling much of the southern Andes. A statue of the sun-god atop a platform greeted visitors, and the city center featured a huge, sacred platform six hundred and fifty feet long and fifty feet high. The rulers staged elaborate festivals with much hallucinogenic drug and alcohol consumption to recruit labor for public works projects. Recent artifact discoveries on Lake Titicaca found spiny oyster shells from the distant Pacific coast as well as gold; both may have been used in festivals.

Tiwanaku influenced a large region of western South America. Its art and religion, probably involving human sacrifice, spread into neighboring societies. Tiwanaku's hinterland, rich in llama herds and copper mining, flourished from raised field agriculture—seeds planted on long artificial ridges separated by ditches—which

Moche A prosperous, powerful state that formed along the northern Peruvian coast from 200 BCE to 700 CE.

[14]Fra Bernardino de Sahagun, quoted in Juan Schobinger, *The First Americans* (Grand Rapids, MI: William B. Eerdmans, 1994), 97.
[15]Ciezade Leon, quoted in Fagan, *Kingdoms of Gold*, 192.

A Moche Lord

Outside of Mesoamerica, no American society left written records to help us understand individual lives. Nearly all we know of the Moche comes from recent archaeological investigations. As in Egypt, an arid climate preserved many objects, including jewelry, weapons, clothing, ceramics, and skeletons. Pottery paintings portray Moche life, and excavations at royal tombs reveal how Moche leaders lived and died, even if we do not know their names, personalities, family ties, or precise governmental functions. We can now trace the experiences of one leader, probably a warrior-priest, known to archaeologists as one of the lords of Sipan, a Moche city, who was buried in his mid-thirties around 390 CE.

Archaeologists know what Moche men and women looked like. Men were stocky, averaging about five feet three inches in height, but this lord was three inches taller. He cut his hair in bangs over his forehead, wore it long in back, pierced his ears and nose, painted his face, and tattooed his arms and legs. Moche women, such as those in the lord's family, stood about four feet seven inches tall and wore their hair long, often braided with colorful woolen strands. At ceremonies women's dress consisted of a multicolored woven smock heavily laden with long strands of beads. Women lived much longer than men, but men had far richer costumes.

Buried in all the finery he probably wore in his official and ceremonial life, the Sipan lord dressed ostentatiously, demonstrating his wealth and power. He wore a long tunic completely covered with gilded copper platelets, with copper sandals on his feet. On his wrists he sported large beaded bracelets of turquoise, gold, and shell. A beaded chest-plate and a spectacular necklace of gold and silver beads covered his chest and shoulders, probably gleaming like the sun. Around his waist a belt supported crescent-shaped bells. A crescent-shaped gold nose ornament completely covered his mouth and lower face, and his large ear ornaments were inlaid with gold and turquoise. On his head, the Sipan lord wore a large, crescent-shaped headdress ornament made of gold. In one hand he held a gold and silver scepter, signifying high rank. Moche art frequently depicted high-status men dressed like the Sipan lord.

The lord led a privileged life, but it also held many dangers. Most Moche were poor; only a few people, like the lord, lived in extreme opulence. Every valley may have had one or more royal courts connected to one another through marriage alliances and trade, like the Maya kings. Moche art frequently depicts warriors parading in front of royalty, perhaps preparing for war against rival courts. Like Maya royalty, perhaps the lord of Sipan went into battle to personally fight rival lords.

Battle was a grueling and fateful experience. Warriors used clubs to beat the enemy's heads or hurled stones and arrows with a sling. Like Roman gladiators, Moche warriors participated in hand-to-hand combat, with the ultimate goal of capturing the enemy for torture and sacrifice. Complex rules may have governed warriors' conduct on and off the field. Battles ended when one warrior caught hold of another's hair and dragged him down. The loser, stripped of his clothes and weapon, was paraded before the royalty of the winners. Painted bottles show the victorious lord presiding over a horrific sacrificial ceremony, drinking a goblet of blood drawn from the slit throats of captive enemy warriors. The lord of Sipan never suffered that fate. He was buried along with several young women, perhaps wives, concubines, or attendants; two burly men armed with shields and war clubs, possibly to protect him in the afterlife; and a dog, probably the lord's pet hound.

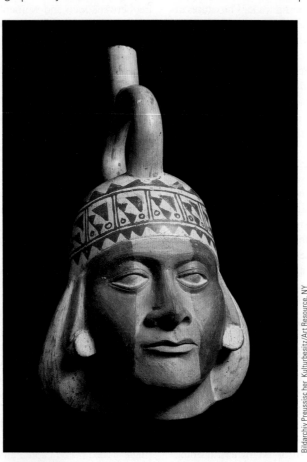

Bildarchiv Preussischer Kulturbesitz/Art Resource, NY

IMAGE 9.6 **A Moche Lord** This Moche lord, memorialized for posterity in ceramic, wears the headgear and ear ornaments common to the Moche nobility. The potter skillfully captured the lord's facial features, giving the portrait a lifelike quality.

Reflection Questions

1. How do burials and paintings on pots help us understand Moche life?
2. What do the lord's clothing and symbols of royalty tell us about Moche society?
3. What role did warfare play in the life of a Moche lord?
4. Can you identify any features of Moche society that you think might resemble practices in Peru today?

improved drainage, replaced nutrients in the poor soil, and protected crops such as potatoes from frost, making agriculture some 400 percent more productive than the region's farming today. Like other Andean peoples, the Aymara also skillfully used fibers. Weaving together reeds, they made boats to sail on the lake. But by 1100 CE the capital and surrounding fields were abandoned, perhaps because climate change generated a drought so severe that rivers dried up. The Aymara culture still exists in the region and Aymara folk music groups are frequent buskers on the streets of North America.

Little is known of Tiwanaku gender relations, but in the neighboring and rival state of Wari, women of elite status operated a mountaintop brewery, making hundreds of gallons of a light, sour corn beer called *chicha* every week that, centuries later, is still popular in Peru. Wari leaders used chicha in diplomacy to maintain control of their territories. They regularly held festivals attended by local political elites who would bring tribute and drink from three-foot-tall ceramic vessels decorated to look like Wari gods and leaders, reaffirming their affiliation with the Wari state. Hence, beer and the women brewers helped keep the Wari state together.

Another peoples, the Nazca (**NAHZ-kuh**), a decentralized agrarian society in southern Peru's harsh desert that flourished from 200 BCE to 600 CE, manufactured beautiful multicolored pottery and textiles while constructing ceremonial centers. To support farms they built an extraordinary series of underground aqueducts involving corkscrew-shaped tunnels that funneled wind into canals, carrying water from wetter districts to more arid regions. But the Nazca are most famous for creating geometric lines along their windswept plateau by clearing away surface stones to reveal the underlying rock and then laying the stones along the edges of the lines. Constructed on a huge scale, the lines depict either geometric shapes or animals such as monkeys and birds. These enigmatic markings have puzzled modern observers; scholars think they were created to mark the seasons, communicate with gods believed to dwell in the nearby mountains, or mark water sources. Or they may have just been artistic expressions of shapes and animals. Many ethnocentric Western observers, unwilling to give the Nazca credit, attributed the lines to space aliens. Now we know better.

9-3f North American Societies

Sophisticated societies also emerged in North America and had trade links with each other and, for some, with societies in Mesoamerica. Several cultural traditions and permanent towns emerged among the desert farmers of the American Southwest, including the Hohokam (**huh-HOH-kuhm**), Anasazi (**ah-nah-SAH-zee**), and Mogollon (**MOH-guh-YOHN**). By around 300 BCE the Hohokam of southern Arizona and northwest Mexico were trading extensively with other southwestern peoples and the southern California coast. Farming success depended on water, and the peoples of this arid region sought divine help to get it, as a Yuma (**YOO-muh**) legend of a creator spirit made clear: "When the people thirst, let them think of me, for I have the power to cover up the sun with a rain-cloud and to send rain every day." [16] Hohokam farmers used advanced

irrigation, dams, terraces, and other strategies to grow corn, beans, squash, and cotton. The Hohokam also built large towns; the total population in the vicinity of present-day Phoenix may have reached forty thousand. The presence of ball courts and rubber balls, as well as Mesoamerican-style platform mounds, indicates Mesoamerican influence. But no evidence for human sacrifice or warfare has been found. Eventually overpopulation, deforestation, and drier climates increased stress and conflict, and Hohokam settlements were abandoned by the fifteenth century. Their modern descendants include the Pima and Papago Indians of Arizona.

The Anasazi and closely related Mogollon culture were the direct ancestors of the Pueblo Indians in today's Arizona and New Mexico. The widespread Anasazi culture, which arose around the first century CE, reached its high point between 750 and 900 CE with towns in Arizona, Utah, and Colorado. The Mogollon culture, emerging around 200 BCE, stretched from central Arizona and New Mexico into northern Mexico. Until the fifteenth century CE these societies flourished from skillful growing and gathering of corn, which for some people may have constituted some 80 percent of the calories they consumed.

Other cultures were mound builders, following a tradition that had begun in North America around 2500 BCE (see Chapter 4). Between around 500 BCE and 400 CE, a new mound-building culture, shared by diverse ethnic groups, became even more widespread, encompassing the Mississippi, Ohio, Tennessee, and lower Missouri River Basins and their tributaries as well as the South Atlantic coast, a total area larger than India. The most prominent of these mound builders, known today as Hopewell, lived in the Ohio River region. Hopewell artistic styles, maize cultivation, religious beliefs, ceremonial traditions, and burial customs spread throughout the eastern woodlands. The Hopewell obtained valuable goods from trade with faraway societies. Without any large state, the Hopewell created extraordinary earthworks and other engineering projects. Elaborate geometric designs such as hexagons and circles marked their mounds, some of which served as burial chambers for the elite. A sophisticated geometric work, the spectacular Great Serpent Mound, built on an Ohio hilltop around two thousand years ago or possibly several hundred years earlier, was shaped like a snake, ran eight hundred feet long from head to tail, and was four feet tall and twenty feet wide. The Ortuna, a Hopewell culture in northern Florida, built twenty-foot-wide canals that allowed dugout canoes to reach both Atlantic and Gulf coasts, thus connecting them to a trading network stretching north to Ohio.

Two major economic changes supported the mound-building cultures. Agriculture became more intensive, especially after maize cultivation spread, and long-distance trade networks expanded over much of North America. Along the river trade routes moved obsidian (volcanic glass) from Wyoming and the Rocky Mountains, copper from Northern Michigan and the Great Lakes and later southern Appalachia, freshwater pearls from the Mississippi and Ohio Rivers, ceramic figurines and vessels from the lower Great Lakes, ore from Kansas, silver from Ontario, shells from the Gulf of Mexico and Florida, and

---

[16] Quoted in Brian Fagan, *The Long Summer: How Climate Changed Civilization* (New York: Basic Books, 2004), 213.

marine products from the Gulf Coast such as sharks' teeth and turtle shells. Sharks' teeth have been found in Illinois, over a thousand miles from the Caribbean.

The Hopewell culture began declining around 300 CE and collapsed by 600 CE. Overpopulation and the resulting competition for land may have stressed the environment and economic system while disrupting trade networks. The climate cooled and maize crop diminished. In addition, around 300 CE someone invented or imported the bow and arrow, altering the power balance and stimulating warfare.

9-3g Changing States and the Spread of Cultures

While Olmec and Chavín traditions remained influential in Mesoamerica and the Andes region, much change occurred over the Classical centuries, although often on a different timeline from the Eastern Hemisphere. Around 200 or 300 CE, small states such as Monte Alban, Teotihuacan, Tikal, and Tiwanaku grew into larger states, often regional empires. Long-distance trade increased, merchants became more influential, and ideas (such as Mesoamerican writing and ball games) spread more widely. Many American peoples revered the land as the source of both physical and spiritual life, with a close relationship to the supreme spirits or gods. Hence, the Maya and some North American societies considered maize sacred, a gift from the gods.

Except for the exceptionally enduring Maya and Tiwanaku, South American and Mesoamerican states rose and fell after a few centuries, perhaps because environmental and climate changes affected agriculture and fishing while fostering chronic warfare, usually over control of resources and territory. Although

establishing frameworks for later empires such as the Aztec and Inca, the Classical states did not survive in their original form, as the Chinese and Ethiopian states did.

The widespread presence of pyramids in Mesoamerica and South America has prompted some speculation about possible contacts across the Atlantic to North Africa and the Mediterranean long before the arrival of Norse Vikings around 1000 CE and, five centuries later, Spanish ships. But no firm archaeological evidence exists for any Eastern Hemisphere connections, and most specialists doubt any such contacts. Pyramids are based on practical principles of monument construction that are probably available to builders anywhere. Some American peoples built mounds nearly as early as the first Egyptian pyramids.

Pottery design, artwork, and plants along the American west coast, from California to Chile, hint at trans-Pacific contacts, provoking occasional speculation about possible Chinese, Japanese, or Polynesian voyages to the Americas. Some studies claim to find Japanese pottery (Jomon) and genes in Ecuador, Olmec hieroglyphics resembling Shang Chinese characters, Chinese artistic motifs on Mayan sculptures, Polynesian musical instruments and loan words in western South America, or Polynesian words and boat designs along the California coast. Skilled mariners, Polynesians were capable of trips over several thousand miles of uncharted ocean, and a few could have occasionally visited the American coast. This might explain South American sweet potatoes in Polynesia by 1000 CE. The plant grew wild in South and Central America and scholars vigorously debate whether plants or seeds may have been carried west to the islands by human transport or by ocean currents. However, no conclusive proof exists for any trans-Pacific contacts, and if any voyages did occur, they left no obvious long-lasting influence.

KEY POINTS

▶ The Maya society on the Yucatán Peninsula developed a comprehensive writing and numbering system, studied astronomy and devised accurate calendars, and built impressive buildings and large pyramids that served as religious centers.

▶ Teotihuacan, near present-day Mexico City, grew into one of the largest and best-designed cities in the world and had an extremely advanced infrastructure, including a complex drainage system.

▶ In the Andes, Chavín was succeeded by Moche, whose pottery depicts a violent culture of war and sacrifice but also of advanced metalwork and architecture.

▶ In the desert Southwest of North America, the Hohokam people developed extensive irrigation systems, and their cultural artifacts show some Mesoamerican influence.

▶ Supported by corn and expanded trade networks, mound-building cultures spread across eastern North America.

9-4 Populating the Pacific: Australian and Island Societies

🏛 SOCIETIES ⇄ TRANSITIONS

Q How were some of the notable features of Australian and Pacific societies shaped by their environments?

Today they are famous in the popular imagination for surfing beaches, laid-back living, and friendly people, but the history of the Pacific societies is defined far more by migration, adaptation, ingenuity, and survival in very challenging geographical and climatic environments. Although the

CONNECTION to TODAY

Which Australian Aborigine and Pacific Islander ecological practices do you find the most useful for survival in their challenging environments?

original settlers of Australia and the Pacific islands migrated from or through Southeast Asia, the societies they developed remained largely isolated from the historical currents of Eurasia for many centuries.

Australian Aborigines mastered a hostile environment and flourished from hunting and gathering. In extraordinary voyages, Austronesians bravely migrated over thousands of miles of open ocean to inhabit most of the Pacific islands, adapting to new environments, creating diverse cultures, and developing long-distance trade networks.

9-4a Australian Geography and Aboriginal Societies

Australia was settled at least fifty thousand and possibly sixty thousand years ago, people gradually spreading throughout the continent. But the when and how of the earliest migrations across open water has been a mystery and subject to debate. Several 2019 studies concluded that the first arrivals, who probably numbered a thousand to fifteen hundred people, came by boat on a deliberate rather than accidental journey, or multiple journeys, from Southeast Asia to New Guinea, and then moved on to Australia via a land bridge, but the findings are controversial. Whatever the case, by 1000 BCE Aboriginal tribes spoke some two hundred distinct languages; today there are over three hundred but most of them are endangered. Australia's environments included tropical, heavily forested north and northeast coasts, temperate southeast and southwest river basins and coasts, and harsh, dry deserts dominating much of the interior. Aboriginal life exploited many food sources such as coastal marine life and wild plants and insects. Women gathered plants and small animals, prepared family meals, ground seeds into flour, looked after children, made clothing, and built huts, while men fished, hunted large animals, and manufactured implements. Aborigines developed an intimate understanding of weather patterns, the environment, and their relationships to plants, animals, and land, knowledge used by meteorologists today.

Most Aborigines ate as well as peoples in Afro-Eurasia, with malnutrition and starvation largely unknown. But there has been considerable disagreement among scholars as to how people obtained their food before European colonization. For many years most historians contended that Aborigines lived chiefly by hunting and gathering and that agriculture never developed, largely because of mostly infertile land and erratic rains, and no native plants or animals were capable of domestication. Even today large-scale irrigation, introduced by British colonists, is required to sustain farming, but, as in Mesopotamia, it increases the groundwater's salt content, endangering fresh-water supplies. Critics have argued that the colonists' view of Aborigines as "primitive nomads" with a simple life rather than as successful land managers justified the European takeover of the best land and marginalizing the people. But recent scholarship has revealed more complex, diverse, and creative adaptations by Aborigines, including farming. Some historians now argue that some of the first accounts by Europeans exploring around Australia reported widespread and park-like grasslands and, in many regions, food production (mostly by women) of grain, yams, onions, and rice, as well as irrigation, dams, and wells, but that European settlement replaced these practices by introducing farming based on European practices, which resulted in destroying grasslands in favor of forests and shrubs.

Some recent studies show how Aboriginal societies, by cooperating with neighboring groups, had for millennia developed and maintained sophisticated and scientific systems of land management and usage that conserved their resources over thousands of years, evolving a close relationship to the earth that remained central to their customs and beliefs. This involved the deft use of fire, the natural flow of water, and the life cycle of native plants in working with and often shaping the environment, ensuring abundant plant foods and wildlife throughout the year. This fostered far more grasslands than exist today. While some moved around seasonally, others lived in large permanent settlements. Some practiced complex aquaculture. For example, beginning around 6000 BCE, one Aboriginal society, the Gunditjmara in southern Australia, built an ingenious artificial lake for operating eel farms and traded the abundant eels around southern Australia. The Gunditjmara may also have lived in a permanent town with stone houses. Hunting and gathering were likely part of the survival strategy but some peoples knew how to nourish certain food sources and even encourage wildlife.

Many Aboriginal practices made use of environmental realities. For example, fire could clear land, encouraging the regrowth of edible plants and natural ecosystem rejuvenation. Studying the night sky to help them survive the challenging landscape, they used stories to explain the tides, eclipses, the rising and setting sun and moon, and the changing positions of stars and planets throughout the year. The sky served as a calendar for when seasons changed and certain foods were available. While linguistically diverse, Aboriginal societies shared many similar customs and beliefs. Needing to move by foot with the seasons to maximize food availability, most owned few possessions, expressing pride in their mobility. Aboriginal men carried spear throwers and spears while women carried digging sticks and baskets to hold foodstuffs. They relocated to the same camps every year over regular trails. Aboriginal tribes were organized either through the patrilineal or the matrilineal line, and nuclear families operated with considerable independence and flexible relations between genders. Although few tribes had chiefs, older males exerted influence in religious and social life, while women made critical decisions about the campsite and controlled their own ceremonial life. Periodic disputes between neighboring tribes sometimes led to fighting, which was usually settled by diplomacy involving the tribal elders.

Spending only about three days a week in search of food, Aborigines had time for rituals, ceremonial expression, and religious matters, including a widely shared belief in the mythology of the **dreamtime**, the distant past when the spiritual ancestors gave order and form to the universe at the world's creation. Dreamtime myths were remarkably consistent around Australia, passed down through countless generations by a rich oral literature. Aborigines recognized an animistic world of many spirits and ghosts. Their art had a religious base, including body decoration, bark paintings, and especially rock carvings and paintings.

A complex trade system spanned the continent. Northern coast pearls and shells reached

dreamtime In Aboriginal Australian mythology, the distant past when the spiritual ancestors gave order and form to the universe at the world's creation.

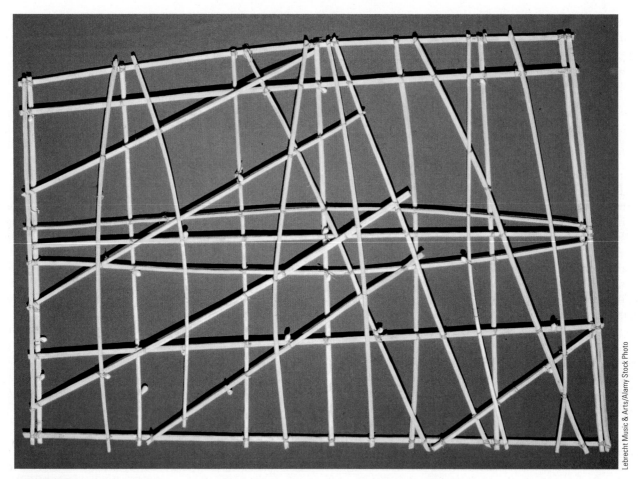

IMAGE 9.7 **Polynesian Palm-Frond Navigational Map** This nautical map, made in the Marshall Islands from palm fronds, shows distances between islands as measured by time traveled. The map may have originally had bits of shell or coral to mark islands. Polynesians and Micronesians often made such maps for their ocean voyages.

Q Can you think of ways that this map could be read by voyagers to help them navigate their journey?

southern Australia, and quartz, flint, and other tool-making stones, as well as animal skins, wood products, and ornaments, were exchanged over wide areas. By 4,000 to 5,000 years ago arrivals from eastern Indonesia may have brought Asian dogs, the ancestors of local dogs known as *dingos*. Some twenty-seven hundred years ago fine earthenware pottery was being brought by boat from Papua-New Guinea to islands off the northeastern coast, indicating a modest local maritime trade. By Classical times Indonesian trading ships probably visited the northwest coast to obtain pearls. Later, Chinese ships may have done the same. But, except for the dingos, these outside contacts had little influence on most Australian societies. Today, after two centuries of change brought by European conquest and settlement, the life that sustained Aborigines for thousands of years has largely passed. Whereas once they sang songs about their lands and history, today, largely settled on rural land reserves or in poor urban neighborhoods, Aborigines lament the loss of their traditions. Their stories still recollect tribal pasts and beliefs, but the storytellers today inhabit a very different reality, and in many ways a more challenging one, than did their ancestors.

9-4b Austronesian Expansion

Today some twelve hundred different Austronesian languages are spoken from Madagascar eastward through Indonesia, Malaysia, the Philippines, and most of the Pacific islands. No premodern peoples, including Indo-Europeans and Bantus, migrated over as wide an area in so short a time as did Austronesians. In ancient times some Austronesian-speaking peoples moved from Southeast Asia into the western Pacific islands just northeast of Australia, encountering Melanesians **(mel-uh-NEE-zhuhnz)** who had earlier migrated from Southeast Asia (see Chapter 4). Over time the two traditions and peoples mixed, and Melanesians adopted Austronesian languages. Eventually some Austronesian-speaking peoples from the western Pacific sailed farther east and north to colonize other islands, in the process fostering new groups later known as Polynesians **(PAHL-uh-NEE-zhunz)** and Micronesians **(MIE-kruh-NEE-zhunz)**. These explorations eastward from Melanesia required new technologies to meet shifting wind conditions. The wind was at the back of boats sailing east from

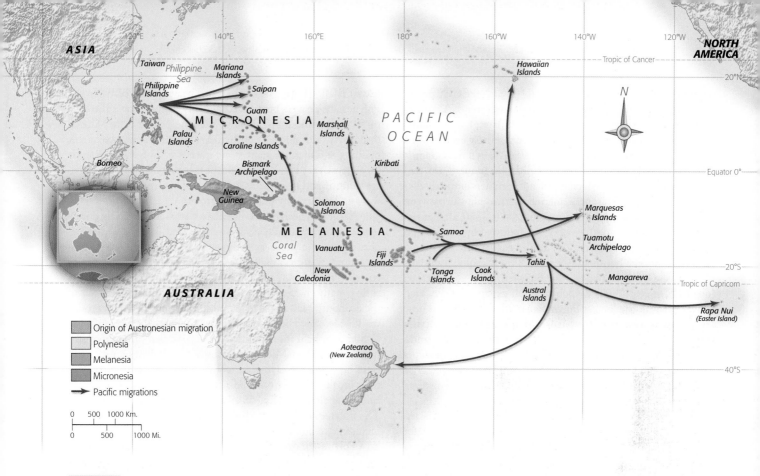

MAP 9.3 **Pacific Migrations in the Classical Era** During this era, Austronesian peoples scattered across the vast Pacific Basin, using ingenious canoes and navigation techniques to settle nearly all the inhabitable islands. From bases in Tonga and Samoa in the west, the Polynesians settled a large expanse of the basin ranging from Hawaii in the north to Easter Island in the east and New Zealand in the south.

Q What does this map tell us about the ambitions and risks of the Austronesian explorations and migrations in the Pacific?

the Solomon Islands, allowing for the settlement of Fiji, Tonga, and Samoa. But to venture further east required sails and boats able to tack against the wind. Eventually with the new technologies Polynesians would discover and settle hundreds of islands including Tahiti, Hawaii, and New Zealand.

Overpopulation on islands with limited resources, fresh water, or fertile land spurred these intentional migrations. Islanders learned to limit population growth to avoid deforestation and natural resource depletion, which would generate conflict or migration. Using only the stars, moon, sun, winds, and waves to guide them, a strategy they term "wayfinding," migrants endured the hardships of long open-sea voyages to discover new islands, some mountainous and covered by dense rain forests, others flat atolls only a few feet above sea level. Navigation and boat building were a science; voyagers spent many days selecting the right tree for their canoes because worm-ridden wood might prove disastrous at sea. An ancient Tahitian prayer reveals the voyagers' fears: "O gods! Lead us safely to land. Leave us not in the ocean. Give us a breeze. Let the weather be fine and the sky clear."[17] Excellent naval technology made these migrations possible: each double-hulled outrigger canoe, up to one hundred feet long with two hulls and

a platform lashed between them for living, cooking, work space, and storage, could carry up to eighty people, along with foods, plants, and animals.

Micronesians, who settled many central and north Pacific islands, made ingenious navigation charts from cowrie shells tied together. The Austronesian-speaking ancestors of Micronesians colonized many small islands in the central Pacific, among them the Marianas (MAR-ee-AN-uhz), including the islands of Guam and Saipan, and the Carolines. The Chamorro (cha-MOR-roe) people of the Marianas grew Asian rice, suggesting they had continuing connections with the Philippines.

9-4c Polynesian Migrations and Societies

How the Polynesians—sailing in canoes hewed with stone adzes and setting their course by the stars, winds, and ocean swells—were able to explore and colonize their island realm has long been one of the most intriguing questions about the spread of humankind on our planet. It is a thrilling saga. Polynesian culture flowered first in the neighboring Fiji, Tonga, and Samoa (suh-MO-uh) island groups around 500 BCE (see Map 9.3). Scholars vigorously debate the timing of later Polynesian

[17]Quoted in Judy Thompson and Allan Taylor, *Polynesian Canoes and Navigation* (Laie, HI: Institute of Polynesian Studies, 1980), 32.

migrations. Some contend that around 300 or 200 BCE Tongan mariners may have reached the Marquesas **(mar-KAY-suhs)** Islands and soon thereafter Tahiti **(tuh-HEE-tee)**, fifteen hundred miles east of Tonga. Other studies place these events much later, around 1000 to 1100 CE. Polynesians sailed from Samoa fifteen hundred miles north to the Kiribati **(kear-uh-BAH-tee)** Islands and then to the Marshall Islands. Scholars similarly disagree as to whether Marquesas mariners settled Hawaii between 400 and 900 CE or much later, around 1200 to 1300, after crossing over two thousand miles of ocean, followed by a migration from Tahiti twenty-five hundred miles east to Easter Island. Finally, sometime between 800 and 1300 CE, some Tahitians moved west another twenty-five hundred miles to Aotearoa **(ow-TEH-a-ROW-uh)** (which a Dutch explorer later named New Zealand), the largest Polynesian-settled landmass. These settlers, the ancestors of the Maori **(MAO-ree)** people, faced a very different climate and topography from the tropical islands, as well as new plants and animals. Conceivably Polynesian sailors also visited the Peruvian coast, perhaps explaining the presence of sweet potatoes, a South American crop, in eastern Polynesia and New Zealand for at least one thousand years.

The fact that without metal tools and writing Polynesians could develop navigational capabilities, and pass them on to later generations through oral culture, to go back and forth between distant islands, still amazes scholars. But by the twentieth century, after centuries of change including Western colonization and the introduction of modern boats and naval technology, many Polynesians had forgotten their navigation skills. In 1976, to prove that mariners from earlier times could have purposely sailed between Hawaii and Tahiti, a team of Polynesians built a traditional double-hulled voyaging canoe, the *Hokule'a*, and, led by a Micronesian, Mau Piailug, who had learned the ancient ways at his grandfather's knee, made the round trip by navigating by the stars and reading the ocean swells, as their ancestors had done. Over the next three decades the vessel made nine voyages, including to Micronesia, Japan, Canada, and the mainland United States, using centuries-old wayfaring techniques and celestial navigation. These successful journeys led to a renaissance of Austronesian voyaging and brought a sense of pride to Polynesians, especially to those in Hawaii who, under U.S. rule, had long been treated as second-class citizens on their own islands. From 2007 to 2009 the *Hokule'a* made a circumnavigation of Earth, covering forty-seven thousand nautical miles.

Polynesian agriculture emphasized Southeast Asian crops such as yams, taro, bananas, coconuts, and breadfruit and animals such as pigs, chickens, and dogs. But survival required modifications, including elaborate terracing, artificial ponds, irrigation, and exploitation of local food sources such as coconuts and of marine life in lagoons, coral reefs, and the deep sea. Cloth made from bark furnished clothing. But fragile island ecologies became easily unbalanced. Imported animals like pigs, dogs, and (unintentionally) rats consumed birds, and overhunting of local species and deforestation created problems, one of the push factors for people to sail off in search of new islands to settle. As an extreme example of environmental destruction,

Easter Island (Rapa Nui), which was heavily forested when the Polynesians arrived, became completely denuded over the centuries and, without streams or wells, the people were reduced to poverty and chronic conflict over wasting scarce resources building and moving giant stone statues. However, some studies suggest that the Rapans did in fact practice well-managed agriculture and also made good use of marine resources, but were undermined by population growth.

Early Polynesians lived in clans that were generally dominated by hereditary chiefs who controlled the lands. Conflict between rival clans over status and land led to tensions and sometimes war. Eventually the most elaborate social hierarchies emerged in Tonga, Tahiti, and Hawaii, with paramount chiefs ruling many thousands of followers and controlling much of the economy. Hawaiians invented surfing, hugely popular today worldwide, which became known as the sport of Hawaiian kings. While men held most political power, women often enjoyed a high status. Most Micronesian and some Polynesian societies were matrilineal. Polynesian women often ranked higher than their brothers in spiritual and ritual authority and, by marrying into other clans or ruling families, could help political relations. The Polynesian societies also shared many other cultural traits, including elaborate facial and body tattooing (the word *tattoo* is of Polynesian origin), myths, reverence for ancestors, and art forms such as woodcarving. Many of these customs were also common in Melanesia and Micronesia.

The huge triangle of Polynesia, anchored at the ends by Hawaii, New Zealand, and Easter Island, is one of the world's largest territorial expanses, some 800,000 square miles. One of the first outsiders to explore the area, British captain James Cook, wrote in 1774: "It is extraordinary that the same [people] should have spread themselves over all the isles in this vast Ocean, almost a fourth part of the circumference of the Globe."[18] But migration over such vast distances did not necessarily mean isolation. Thanks to a large maritime network, obsidian mined on New Britain island, northeast of New Guinea, was distributed from Borneo to Fiji, four thousand miles apart. Moreover, nearby island groups maintained trade and social links. For example, the families of Tongan and Fijian chiefs frequently intermarried. But the sailing required remarkable observation and could be dangerous, as Captain Cook reported from Tonga in 1777: "In these Navigations the Sun is their guide by day and the Stars by night; when these are obscured they have recourse to the points from whence the Wind and waves come upon the vessel. If [these] shift, they are bewildered."[19] Cook's "discoveries" of many islands as well as New Zealand and Australia owed much on Tupaia, a remarkable Tahitian chief and brilliant navigator with an encyclopedic knowledge of the Polynesian region and its languages, peoples, weather, stars, and currents. Even today Polynesian traditions honor great navigators of the past such as Moikeha and Pa'ao, who sailed back and forth between the Marquesas and Hawaii over a millennium ago, and now Mau Pialug, the Caroline Islands navigator who guided the *Hokule'a* and sparked a revival of Polynesian pride and history.

---

[18] Quoted in Peter Bellwood, *The Polynesians: Prehistory of an Island People*, revised ed. (London: Thames and Hudson, 1997), 7.
[19] Quoted in Peter Bellwood, *Man's Conquest of the Pacific: The Prehistory of Southeast Asia and Oceania* (New York: Oxford University Press, 1979), 300.

KEY POINTS

▶ Aboriginal Australians developed great understanding of natural phenomena and were very successful hunters and gatherers for thousands of years.

▶ Aborigines across Australia believed in the dreamtime of the mythic past and felt that spirits and ghosts inhabited much of the physical world.

▶ Polynesian culture probably began in Fiji, Tonga, and Samoa, but it spread out over a remarkable expanse of the Pacific Ocean.

▶ An extensive trading network developed among the Pacific islands, and, despite their isolation from each other, the islands' cultures remained quite homogenous.

Chapter Summary

During the Classical Era some sub-Saharan Africans became more closely linked by trade with North Africa and Eurasia. Kush became a center for iron production, and Aksum flourished as a trading hub. The cities and small states that emerged in West Africa's Sudanic region participated in the growing trans-Saharan caravan trade network, which linked them with the Mediterranean world. Cities also appeared along the East African coast, tied by trade networks to the Mediterranean, western Asia, and India. Bantu-speaking peoples settled the southern half of Africa, carrying with them iron technology and many Sudanic influences.

Various urban societies dominated Mesoamerica and the Andes, including the Maya, Moche, Tiwanaku, Teotihuacan, and Monte Alban. The Maya forged a particularly enduring society based on competing city-states, developed a writing system, and understood much about astronomy and mathematics. The Moche on the Peruvian coast and Tiwanaku in the highlands formed empires. In Mesoamerica, Teotihuacan became the greatest city in the Americas and a major trading hub. In North America many peoples adopted farming, built permanent towns, and took up mound building. In the Pacific, Australian Aborigines adapted well to their harsh environment, flourishing for millennia from hunting and gathering. And various Austronesian peoples, particularly the Polynesians, made spectacular migrations into the vast Pacific Ocean by using remarkable seagoing technologies and adapting to diverse island environments.

Key Terms

Meroitic 199
Coptic Church 201
Aksum 201
Geez 202

Ghana 204
Mande 204
griots 205
Nilotes 205

Maya 206
Teotihuacan 209
Moche 211
dreamtime 215

Afrocentrism, Eurocentrism, Multiculturalism, and Historians of Antiquity

For many years the writings by Western scholars about world history emphasized Europe and the West, a biased perspective known as *Eurocentrism*, a term that originated in the 1920s but became more widely used by the 1970s. In the conventional Eurocentric story line, history began in Egypt, Mesopotamia, and Palestine before moving to Greece and Rome, who were credited with inventing what was termed "Western civilization." They then passed on this legacy to northwestern Europe and eventually to North America. The rest of the world, except perhaps for India and China and sometimes Islam, constituted an exotic aside to the European mainstream. The academic fields of classics (the study of the Greco-Roman world) and Egyptology specialized in the ancient Mediterranean world, mostly excluding the rest of Africa and Asia. Before the 1970s most Western historians either ignored Africa or argued that Africa was unimportant throughout world history. Furthermore, in identifying the foundations of "Western civilization" they often minimized the multicultural nature of many ancient Mediterranean societies, the links between them, and the ways they influenced each other.

The Problem

Today a broader historical perspective incorporating Africa is common, although not universally accepted, and debates about this approach can be heated. But for much of the twentieth century many scholars agreed with an influential British historian, who wrote in 1928 that Africa had no history and that most Africans had stayed stagnant and sunk in barbarism for many centuries. In reacting to racial discrimination and lingering contempt for Africa's historical legacy, in the past six decades many historians have made a convincing case for the importance of Africa and its critical role in world history. But questions remain. Was Africa a key part of the larger ancient and Classical world? Was Egypt essentially an African or a Mediterranean society? Did Egypt and other eastern Mediterranean societies strongly influence Classical Greece? Finally, how has a more multicultural approach reshaped the debate?

The Debate

In dramatic contrast to the Eurocentrism that long dominated the field of classics and much of historical scholarship generally, an alternative approach known as Afrocentrism emphasizes Africa's, rather than Europe's, centrality in history. The more radical Afrocentrists provide a mirror image to the Eurocentric model, dismissing the older history as a lie designed to glorify European culture and perpetuate the power of white people. They assert that Africa was the fountainhead of Mediterranean culture and that a new way of understanding world history must be developed. Afrocentrists like the Senegalese Cheikh Anta Diop and the American Molefe Asante argue that black Africans, including Egyptians, originated and developed many of the arts, philosophies, and technologies of the ancient and Classical Mediterranean societies.

Critics accuse the radical Afrocentrists, like the rigid Eurocentrists, of exaggeration and selectivity in their use of historical evidence, charging that they rely on largely outdated and discredited sources. Some Afrocentrists, for example, offer unsubstantiated theories that Egyptian queen Cleopatra (a Hellenistic Greek) and Athenian philosopher Socrates were black, or that African mariners established the Olmec society of Mexico. British scholar Stephen Howe even asserts that Afrocentric writings replace outmoded Eurocentric scholarship with a misleading version that offers a fictional history.

One prong of the debate is whether ancient Egypt should be seen as essentially Mediterranean or as an African society rooted in African traditions. Most scholars now acknowledge extensive Egyptian connections to Africa, western Asia, and southeastern Europe. African ties were certainly extensive. The ancient Egyptian language was closely related to many African tongues. Some historians of Africa believe that many ideas Egyptians shared with African peoples diffused to Egypt from the south, including the notion and rituals of divine kingship that underpinned Egyptian royalty, various myths and gods, and much material culture. But Egypt's connections were diverse. Populated by migrants from all directions, Egypt produced people of many skin colors and physical features. As a trade crossroads, it maintained trade relations with Africans, Asians, and Europeans. People moved around and intermarried. Thus the Nile Valley was a zone of contact between many groups; considerable mingling of people occurred and, with that, creative cultural borrowing and invention, making it difficult to precisely identify foreign influences on Egyptian culture.

Another controversy concerns whether Egypt spread African ideas and influences to the Greek culture emerging across the Mediterranean and whether Greece should be viewed as a European society settled by Indo-Europeans who shaped the culture that was quite distinct from other eastern Mediterranean societies such as the Phoenicians, Hebrews, and Mesopotamians. In his three-volume study, *Black Athena*, British-born, U.S.-based scholar Martin Bernal contended that, until the early nineteenth century, Western historians stressed the Afro-Asiatic origins of Greek culture, acknowledging Egypt and Phoenicia as core influences. Then, he argued, because of increasing racism toward black people and rising European imperialism and nationalism, Western scholars began to stress the Greeks as being a creative source of culture rather than derivative—the pure and original source of European society. African and Middle East influences, such as those from Egypt and Phoenicia, were removed from the scenario.

To support his point, Bernal used the myths and historical writings of the Greeks themselves, including, for example, the claims by Greek historian Herodotus, who was born and raised in Persian-ruled Ionia, that Egyptians invented mathematics and that the names of Greek gods originated in Egypt. Herodotus spent time in Egypt around 450 BCE and admired the Egyptian heritage. Influenced by his views, Bernal agrees with Diop that a significant proportion of Greek religion,

IMAGE 9.8 Athena, Greek Goddess of Wisdom Some scholars suspect that some Greek deities, such as Athena, portrayed here in a Greek sculpture, were based on Egyptian deities.

Alinari/Art Resource, NY

political philosophy, architecture, science, and even language was imported from Phoenicia and Egypt. For example, Bernal suggests that Athena, the Greek goddess of wisdom and patron goddess of Athens, was a transplanted version of Neith, a goddess from the Nile Delta.

Bernal's work provoked a storm of controversy. Critics accuse Bernal of misreading and selectively using Greek myths and historical accounts. They suggest that the Greeks credited Egypt with these accomplishments because they wanted to legitimize their own position by connecting with the older and much respected Egyptian culture. Furthermore, as most historians are aware, Herodotus was entertaining but often exaggerated or relied on unreliable hearsay, and so is not always a convincing source. Reliance on Herodotus, critics charge, led Bernal to unsubstantiated links, such as one tracing the origins of Greek philosophy to Egyptian literature on wisdom, despite many differences. In one of the stronger critiques, Mary Lefkowitz links Bernal to radical Afrocentrism (an approach he criticizes), deploring his scholarship for disputing that the Greeks invented democracy, philosophy, and science.

In this debate, few classicists disagree that the Greeks admired the Egyptians and traded with them extensively. Some leading Greek thinkers, including Herodotus, Solon, Plato, Thales, and Euclid, visited or studied in Egypt. But, like Lefkowitz, many classicists believe that Bernal greatly overstates Afro-Asian influence, underestimates Greek genius, and misuses linguistic and archaeological evidence. At the same time, however, some other scholars defend Bernal or praise him for the multidisciplinary breadth of his argument, bringing out biases in classical scholarship, his inclusiveness, and stimulating and opening new vistas for needed debate. But, while they may applaud his aims, most find his methods and results disappointing. Some, including the Africanist Basil Davidson and the classicist Jacques Berlinblau, take a middle view on Bernal's work. And the controversy has also inspired more studies placing Egypt and Africa in a larger regional or world context, such as those by Schofield and Davies, Ehret, and Gilbert and Reynolds.

The debate between Afrocentrists and Eurocentrists may have recently calmed down but it has not ended. Yet, it also opened up new ways of thinking about the classical Mediterranean world through a more multicultural lens emphasizing interconnectedness. British Classicist Tim Whitmarsh argues that the classical Mediterranean world should not be viewed in strictly European or Greco-Roman terms but as part of a larger "Middle Eastern" Iraqi–Syrian–Palestinian–Egyptian complex in which Greeks borrowed various influences from the east and south, especially before the fifth century BCE. He points to such things as statuary and temple-building from Egypt and the relationship of Homer's *Iliad* to the much earlier Mesopotamian *Gilgamesh*. German scholar Johannes Haubold, noting the Middle Eastern influences on Homer's writings, posits the process as less a one-way importation than an "intertwining" of cultures. In their view, emphasizing the "uniqueness" of the Greeks is misleading since they were part of a series of networked cultures in a multivoiced conversation. Italian scholar Barbara Graziosi sees this as finding different pasts, a multicultural one in which Greeks, Romans, and Egyptians lived alongside each other and cultures were mixed rather than pure.

But multiculturalist views have been challenged by more conservative scholars like Bruce Thornton, who consider them an attempt to denigrate the Greeks' achievements. As British scholar Greg Woolf points out, it is easy to take the notion of happy multiculturalism in this era too far since there were cultural conflicts and limits to transferability, but also, he agrees, deliberate moments of hybridization, the blending of cultural influences. In the end the debate breaks away from the longtime isolation of the classics field and the study of antiquity and a bipolar conflict between Afrocentrism and Eurocentrism.

Evaluating the Debate

In modern times the Greeks and Romans have been tugged back and forth between opposing camps with different views of history and culture as part of ongoing "culture wars" and conflict over school curriculums. All sides of the debate have been accused of having a political agenda: to influence how the histories of Europe and Africa are taught in North American and European schools. Hence, the controversy illustrates the danger of what historians call "present-mindedness," the tendency to interpret the past largely in light of present social and political concerns. While we can never entirely escape this tendency, we can try to see the people of the past as they saw themselves. This means not using their experiences as ammunition in current social and political debates. Since the issues of how much Egypt contributed to Greece, how much it reflected or stimulated sub-Saharan African cultures, and whether a broader multicultural approach better addresses a complex history are legitimate subjects for historical investigation, the debates will continue.

Exploring the Controversy

Critical assessments of Eurocentric history include Samir Amin, *Eurocentrism*, 2nd ed. (New York: Monthly Review Press, 2010); James Blaut, *Eight Eurocentric Historians* (New York: Guilford Press, 2000); John M. Hobson, *The Eastern Origins of Western Civilization* (New York: Cambridge University Press, 2004); Andre Gunder Frank, *ReOrient: Global Economy in the Asian Age* (Berkeley: University of California Press, 199); and Vassillis Lambropoulos, *The Rise of Eurocentrism: Anatomy of an Interpretation* (Princeton, NJ: Princeton University Press, 1993). Afrocentric history was pioneered by Cheikh Anta Diop in *Civilization or Barbarism: An Authentic Anthropology* (Brooklyn, NY: Lawrence Hill, 1991) and *The African Origin of Civilization: Myth or Reality* (New York: Lawrence Hill, 1974). A more radical approach can be found in Molefe Asante's *Afrocentricity* (Trenton, NJ: Africa World Press, 1988) and *The Afrocentric Idea* (Philadelphia: Temple University Press, 1987).

The most significant scholarly challenge to the views of mainstream classicists can be found in Martin Bernal, *Black Athena: The Afroasiatic Roots of Classical Civilization*, 3 vols. (New Brunswick, NJ: Rutgers University Press, 1987, 1991, 2001). Bernal responds to his critics in *Black Athena Writes Back* (Durham, NC: Duke University Press, 2001). The major rebuttals to Bernal and Afrocentrism include Stephen Howe, *Afrocentrism: Mystical Pasts and Imagined Homes* (London: Verso, 1998); Mary Lefkowitz, *Not Out of Africa: How Afrocentrism Became an Excuse to Teach Myth as History* (New York: Basic Books, 1996); Mary Lefkowitz and Guy MacLean, eds., *Black Athena Revisited* (Chapel Hill: University of North Carolina Press, 1996); David Gress, *From Plato to NATO: The Idea of the West and its Opponents* (New York: Free Press, 1998); and Victor Hanson, *Who Killed Homer?: The Demise of Classical Education and the Recovery of Greek Wisdom*, with John Heath (New York: Encounter Books, 1998).

For thoughtful discussions of the Afrocentrist controversy, see Basil Davidson, *The Search for Africa: History, Culture, Politics* (New York: Times Books, 1994); and Jacques Berlinblau, *Heresy in the University: The "Black Athena" Controversy and the Responsibility of American Intellectuals* (New Brunswick, NJ: Rutgers University Press, 1999). Useful studies of Egypt and Africa in world history include Louise Schofield and W. Vivian Davies, eds., *Egypt, the Aegean and the Levant: Interconnections in the Second Millennium* (London: Trustees of the British Museum, 1995); Christopher Ehret, *An African Classical Age: Eastern and Southern Africa in World History, 1000 B.C. to A.D. 400* (Charlottesville: University of Virginia Press, 1998); and Erik Gilbert and Jonathan T. Reynolds, *Africa in World History: From Prehistory to the Present*, 3rd ed. (Upper Saddle River, NJ: Prentice-Hall, 2011). On the multicultural approach to the classical world, see Tim Whitmarsh and Stuart Thomson, eds., *The Romance Between Greece and the East* (Cambridge, UK: Cambridge University Press, 2013); Johannes Haubold, *Greece and Mesopotamia: Dialogues in Literature* (New York: Cambridge University Press, 2013); Greg Woolf, "Becoming Roman, Staying Greek: Culture, Identity, and the Civilizing Process in the Roman East," *Proceedings of the Cambridge Philological Society*, 40 (January 1994), 116–143; and Barbara Graziosi, *Homer* (New York: Oxford University Press, 2016). For a conservative critique of multiculturalism, see Bruce Thornton, *Greek Ways: How the Greeks Created Western Civilization* (New York: Encounter Books, 2002).

Reflection Questions

1. What is the Afrocentric criticism of Eurocentrism?
2. What is the classicists' criticism of Afrocentrism?
3. What are the insights and problems of Bernal's *Black Athena*?
4. How might a multicultural approach help us understand the classical Mediterranean and how it relates to the world today?

PART III

Encounters and Transformations in the Intermediate Era, ca. 600–1500

CHAPTER OUTLINE

Scholars often refer to the time frame from 600 to 1500 as the medieval period, or "the middle ages." Some older histories of Europe even referred very misleadingly to the "Dark Ages." The term *medieval* suggests societies with relatively weak governments, rigid social orders, and one dominating religion, a description that best fits Europe in this era and perhaps Japan and parts of South Asia and northeast Africa. However, the term has little relevance for China, the Islamic states, and most of Africa, Southeast Asia, and the Americas. Indeed, at various times some societies in East Asia, Southeast Asia, the Middle East, West and Southwest Africa, Mesoamerica, the Andes region, Iberia, and northwest Europe flourished in what might be termed "golden ages" in this era. In the past few years specialists on this era have introduced the non-Eurocentric concept of the Global Middle Ages, characterized in both hemispheres by porous boundaries, multiple powerful states, multiethnic empires, voluntary and forced migration, increasing trade networks, and the spread of cultural forms. *Intermediate Era* is a more neutral term to describe this creative period, which saw worldwide innovations, the emergence of new trade networks, and vigorous new cosmopolitan societies.

Historians often use the concepts of continuity and change. Most societies today are very different from those of five hundred or a thousand years ago. Yet, there are many patterns from those centuries that are still with us today. The Intermediate Era or Global Middle Ages differed from preceding eras by virtue of the increasing contacts between peoples. Thanks to the knowledge gained from these contacts, around 1467 a German monk and mapmaker, Nicolaus Germanus, published an atlas that included a remarkable map of the "known" world stretching from Greenland across Eurasia and northern Africa to Indonesia and China. Today the term *globalization* refers to the increasing interconnectedness of peoples around the world through international trade, investment, ideas, popular culture, and travel. This Part examines some early forms of globalization during the Intermediate Era, such as the spread of world religions and the social changes they fostered, long-distance trade, the spread of disease, and the connections sparked by the major transitions of the Mongol expansion, climate change, and, in the Late Intermediate Era, the acceleration of maritime exploration.

The Spread of Universal Religions

■ NETWORKS

Thanks to the expansion of universal religions over the networks of exchange, by 1500 the religious map of the Eastern Hemisphere looked very different than it had in 600. The power and reach of universal, or world, religions such as Buddhism, Christianity, and Islam increased markedly during the Intermediate Era, as millions of people embraced ideas, beliefs, and ways of life vastly different from those of their ancestors. Islam was founded and exploded onto the world stage in the seventh century and became the most widespread religion of the era, rapidly expanding through Western Asia and North Africa, eventually claiming Central Asia and parts of Europe, and finally gaining large followings in West Africa, the East African coast, South Asia, China, and Southeast Asia.

Given its wide reach across the Eastern Hemisphere, Islam fostered among some educated Muslims a vision of a wider world, as reflected in the extraordinary maps of a multicultural "medieval" world produced by the North Africa–born cartographer al-Idrisi when he worked for the Norman king of Sicily in the twelfth century. Based on information from diverse informants, his maps displayed the known world from China and Southeast Asia to Iceland and Africa's western tip. And some Muslims traveled very widely. For example, in the late 1200s and early 1300s the Somali jurist Faqih Said from Mogadishu had studied Islamic law in Mecca and Medina for fourteen years, travelled to India and China, and then settled down in southwest India working as a judge and preparing legal texts. East African Swahilis played a prominent role in making and administering Islamic law in the Indian Ocean world. Hemisphere-wide connections could also lead to cultural mixing. For example, the famous collection of *One Thousand and One Nights* from the Iraq-based Abbasid caliphate was a concoction of stories from the Arab world, Persia, South Asia, and China that were blended together from societies communicating with each other over great distances.

Older faiths also spread in this era. Theravada Buddhism became established in Sri Lanka and then expanded into mainland Southeast Asia, where it gradually displaced earlier faiths and reshaped cultures. Mahayana Buddhism became entrenched in Japan, Korea, Vietnam, Mongolia, and Tibet. Buddhist networks fostered the movement of pilgrims, such as the seventh-century Chinese monk Xuan Zang (swan tsang), who sojourned in India for several decades. By 1200 Christianity had also expanded to encompass nearly all of Europe in its fold, filtering north into the Germanic and Celtic lands and east among the Slavs. Eventually the Roman Catholic Church dominated western Europe while the Orthodox Church claimed Greece, Russia, and much of eastern Europe. Although Christianity was pushed back by Islam in western Asia, Egypt, and Ethiopia, sizable Christian communities grew and sometimes flourished in these regions, and a few southern Indians and Central Asians sustained distinctive versions of the faith.

Universal religions generally promoted moral and ethical values that helped preserve harmony in societies that were increasingly cosmopolitan. The Christian injunction to "love thy neighbor as thyself," the Buddhist emphasis on good thoughts and actions, and the Muslim ideals of social justice and the equality of believers fostered goodwill and cooperation. Nonetheless, Christians in Europe often discriminated against, condemned, segregated, imprisoned, expelled, or massacred Jews, Muslims, and the dark-skinned Romani ("Gypsies"). Some Muslim-dominated governments imposed financial penalties on Christians and Hindus and devalued peoples considered nonbelievers. Conflicts between Sunni and Shia Muslims were common. Chronic tensions arose between Christian Europe and the Islamic world, derived from political and economic conflicts as well as a clash between the strong missionary impulses of both religions. Christians and Muslims often viewed each other as barbarians. A tenth-century Arab geographer argued after visiting Europe that the manners of Christian Europeans "are harsh, their understanding dull and their tongues heavy. Those of them who are furthest to the north are the most subject to stupidity, grossness and brutishness."[1] Tensions between the

two rival faiths generated the European Crusades to regain what Christians considered the Holy Land (Palestine), which left a legacy of bitterness on both sides. Meanwhile, Muslim expansion eastward sparked sporadic conflict with Hindus and Buddhists. Some of these tensions from racial or religious differences remain powerful today.

A commonality shared by all religions was a reverence for learning, as the spread of world religions facilitated access to knowledge through the creation of libraries and various centers of scholarship including the first universities in Europe, China, and various Islamic societies. The House of Wisdom in Abbasid-ruled Baghdad attracted scholars from all over the Islamic world and beyond. Some Buddhist centers of higher education, such as the university at Nalanda in India and the monasteries in Sumatra (Indonesia), attracted students from all over Asia. In Europe, various Christian orders and thinkers encouraged the preservation of knowledge, laying the foundation for universities, such as Paris and Oxford, and spurring philosophical speculation. Eventually the European universities broadened their studies, mixing theology with secular subjects such as science and logic. But under religious influence, many societies became more patriarchal and less tolerant of lifestyles that strayed from what religious teachings deemed appropriate.

Gender Roles and Family Patterns

SOCIETIES

The expansion of universal religions, combined with increasing trade, influenced many aspects of social life, thought, and attitudes. While the status of women varied around the world, most religions had patriarchal structures. Islam incorporated many Arab and Persian customs that constrained women, including those that prescribed female seclusion and modesty. However, Islamic patriarchy was modified where pre-Islamic cultures had less rigid gender roles, as in Spain and parts of Southeast Asia and West Africa. The worldly but pious Arab traveler Ibn Battuta, for example, was astonished that, in his view, the women of Mali in West Africa wore clothing that was much too revealing and seemed to have a higher status than the men. Most Christian thinkers believed that women belonged in the home. A fifteenth-century Italian warned that "it would hardly win us [men] respect if our wife busied herself among the men in the marketplace. It also seems somewhat demeaning to me to remain shut up in the house among women when I have manly things to do among men."[2]

As Confucianism dug deeper roots in East Asia, patriarchy became a stronger force there. By the 1400s it was more common than before to seclude upper-class Chinese women, and even bind their feet. Japanese society also became more patriarchal, as the warrior culture replaced the aristocratic system in which elite women had flourished. But some Mahayana Buddhists favored gender equity, at least in principle. The Japanese Zen master Dogen (**DOE-joan**) argued that there was nothing special about masculinity:

[1]Quoted in Peter N. Stearns, *Western Civilization in World History* (New York: Routledge, 2003), 52.
[2]Leon Batista Alberti, quoted in Jeremy Brotton, *The Renaissance Bazaar: From the Silk Road to Michaelangelo* (London: Oxford University Press, 2002), 73-74.

"The elements that make up the human body are the same for a man as for a woman. You should not waste your time in futile discussion of the superiority of one sex over another."[3] In Southeast Asia, Theravada Buddhism proved a generally moderating force in gender relations, although men had more opportunity than women to acquire the merit needed to reach nirvana because only men could become monks.

Religious values shaped public roles, family patterns, and sexual attitudes. In societies as different as Byzantium, Carolingian France, West Africa, Southeast Asia, and the Inca Empire, a few favored women could still gain power as queens or as powers behind the throne. In some cases, such as the female samurai in Japanese, they gained fame as warriors. But in most societies, religious hierarchies, military organizations, and schools remained mostly male, with priesthoods, warfare, and literacy giving men more access to prestige and resources. Islam allowed men to have four wives, but polygamy for some men meant that women were unavailable to others. While Christian and Buddhist teachings favored monogamy and marriage, many men and women in both faiths joined clerical orders or for other reasons never married. And in Europe and many societies around the world, men of elite status, such as kings, often had multiple wives and concubines. Only a minority of western Europeans, mostly middle class, lived in nuclear families like those common today in the West, and only a few societies allowed women to have more than one husband.

Attitudes toward homosexuality and gender identity varied widely. Followers of Christianity, Judaism, Islam, and Confucianism all shared an aversion to homosexual relations, in part because they did not produce children. But this sexual behavior had long been practiced and even sometimes tolerated in these traditions. Christian tolerance turned to fierce repression only in the thirteenth century CE, and such repression was not a global pattern. Perhaps because there were many unmarried Muslim men and rigid segregation of the sexes, some Islamic societies ignored homosexual activity. Japanese, Chinese, and some Southeast Asian and Native American societies also tended to accept homosexuality as part of life. Gender categories could be flexible. Some Asian and American tribal peoples identified more than two genders, including homosexual or heterosexual men who lived as women and served the village as shamans.

Slavery and Feudalism

SOCIETIES

Most societies were hierarchical, and, whatever the predominant political and social system, many people lived in slavery or faced severe restrictions on their freedom. Sanctioned by various religions or simply by custom or economic necessity, slavery had long been common throughout the world and remained so in the Intermediate Era, except for East Asia, where it had once been common but had largely but not completely died out by 1000 CE. Islam permitted slavery but encouraged owners

to treat slaves well. In Arab, Persian, and Turkish societies, the availability of slaves to do the physical work made the seclusion of elite women possible. Many African societies, whether Muslim or non-Muslim, had slaves, including the West African kingdoms and East African city-states. Africans had been shipped north to Arab and Persian societies for centuries. Slaves were also transported, bought, and sold along the Silk Road land and maritime networks. Slaves were common in Southeast Asian societies such as Angkor (Cambodia) and Siam. A Persian observer wrote that, in Indonesia, the people "reckon high rank and wealth by the quantity of slaves a person owns."[4] In the Americas, various peoples, among them the Maya and Aztecs, enslaved prisoners of war, debtors, and criminals, but slavery was less common among North American tribes. After the end of the Roman Empire, slavery declined in Europe and was gradually replaced by serfdom, a less restrictive form of bondage, but the slave trade did not end. Some slaves still labored in parts of western Europe, sometimes even on lands of Christian monasteries. Among other European cities, Constantinople, Prague, and Dublin were famous slave markets, and Vikings, Italians, and Russians were some of the most active slave dealers. An active Mediterranean slave trade shipped Slavs, Greeks, and Turks from the Black Sea region to southern Europe and North Africa. Some northwestern Europeans were also sold as slaves to Mediterranean societies. Eventually Africans appeared in southern European slave markets.

Some historians consider the concept of "feudalism" misleading and applied too broadly but it is still widely accepted and used in the literature. In most feudal societies, political, military, and religious elites lived off wealth from the primary producers, such as peasants, herders, and artisans. Relations between people of different status, especially between lords and vassals, were prescribed by agreements or law, and governments were weak or decentralized. The feudal model, which included lords and knights, independent manors, serfdom, small states, and chronic warfare, was best represented by some but not all medieval western European societies between 800 and 1300. In medieval Europe the dominant Christian church encouraged people who wanted to reap rewards in Heaven to accept the social order. Hence, in 800 the Frankish king Charlemagne proclaimed that the peasant living on church and royal estates "must plow his lord's land a whole day [but not also be asked] to do handiwork service during the same week. The dependent shall not withdraw from these services and the lords shall not ask more from them."[5] Some historians also apply feudalism to Japan after 1000 C.E. under the warrior class, and others to parts of India and Southeast Asia, where many small states with rigid social orders competed for power. In both western Europe and Japan, feudalism established a basis for future change by building up intense pressures that eventually erupted. Many societies were not feudal, however. Large centralized states such as Tang and Song dynasty China, Abbasid Iraq, Mali, or the Inca Empire employed a system whereby emperors, kings, or caliphs exercised great power over the population through bureaucracies.

[3]Quoted in Peter N. Stearns, *Gender in World History* (New York: Routledge, 2000), 52.

[4]Quoted in Anthony Reid, *Southeast Asia in the Age of Commerce, 1450–1680*, Vol. 1 (New Haven, CT: Yale University Press, 1988), 1.

[5]Quoted in Adriaan Verhulst, *The Carolingian Economy* (New York: Cambridge University Press, 2002), 48.

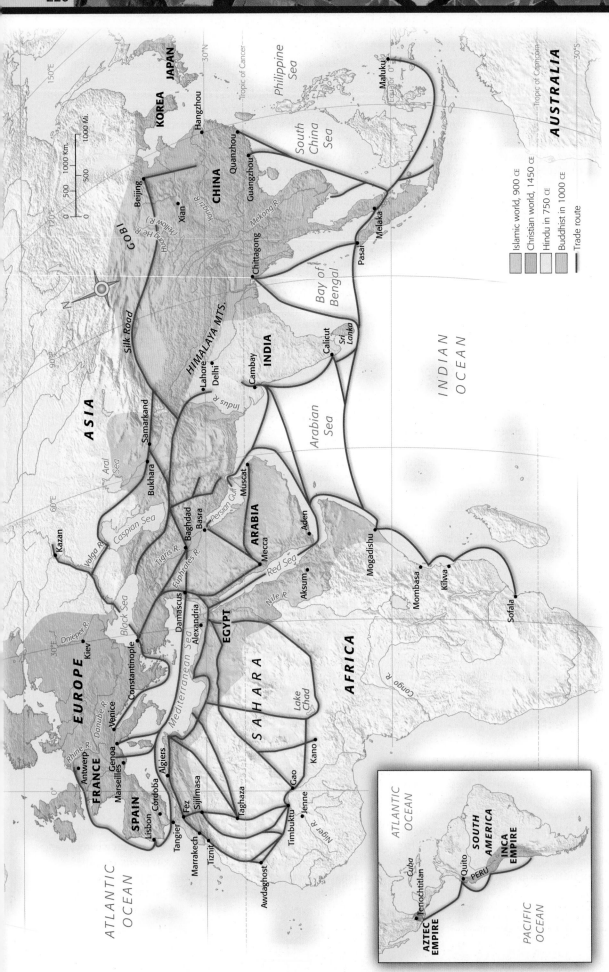

MAP III.1 **World Religions and Trade Routes, 600–1500** Much of the Eastern Hemisphere was linked by land and maritime trade routes. Along with goods and travelers, Buddhism, Christianity, and Islam spread along these trade routes, attracting believers from many societies.

Q What are some of the connections between people across Eurasia shown by this map?

Map legend:
- Islamic world, 900 CE
- Christian world, 1450 CE
- Hindu in 750 CE
- Buddhist in 1000 CE
- Trade route

IMAGE III.1 **Silk Road Travelers** The Silk Road remained a key trade route during this era. This painting, from a fourteenth-century atlas made in Spain, shows one of the horse and camel caravans that traveled between China and Central Asia.

Q What does this painting tell us about the life of travelers along the Silk Road?

Long-Distance Trade

NETWORKS

Long-distance trade had long linked faraway societies, most commonly by land. Since 200 BCE the Silk Road had allowed trade goods, ideas, religions, technologies, and people to move both ways between China and the Mediterranean basin and all points in between. For example, many Sogdians from Samarkand settled in Tang China, where some of their descendants became high government officials. Trade routes also connected West Africa and the Mediterranean across the Sahara Desert. The fabulously rich twelfth-century Mali king Mansa Musa and his large entourage used well-trod trade and pilgrimage routes to transport huge amounts of gold to Cairo before proceeding to Mecca. Peoples in the Americas traded goods over long distances by boat, foot, or, in South America, llamas. The Mongol conquests had fostered extensive trade, but with the Mongol Empire's division and demise and hence the security of overland Silk Road travel reduced, maritime trade became more crucial and naval technology improved considerably. By 1000 an increasingly lucrative maritime trade had grown in the Eastern Hemisphere, despite the dangers from pirates and storms. Much trade crisscrossed the Mediterranean, with Venice, Genoa, Constantinople, Aleppo in Syria, Alexandria, and Algiers serving as major ports. Sailing networks along Europe's Atlantic coast later linked the Baltic and North Seas to Mediterranean ports.

Farther east, the Indian Ocean routes became the heart of the most extensive maritime trade network, a "maritime Silk Road," defined by free trade and mercantile communities that moved about unconnected to specific governments. This network, which transported more people and products than the overland routes, involved the most populous societies and linked China, Japan, Vietnam, and Cambodia in the east through Malaya, Indonesia, India, and Sri Lanka to Persia, Arabia, Russia, the eastern Mediterranean, and the East African coast. Many hundreds of shipwrecks linked to this trade have been discovered in the South China Sea, Gulf of Siam, and Indian Ocean, revealing a diversity of cargoes, often very large, from the beginning of the Common Era to the nineteenth century. Over these routes the spices of Indonesia, the gold and tin of Malaya, the textiles, sugar, and cotton of India, the cinnamon of Sri Lanka, the gold and ivory of East Africa, the coffee of Arabia, the carpets of Persia, the ceramics and pots of Siam and Cambodia, and the silks, porcelain, and tea of China moved to distant markets. Europe proved a huge market for Asian spices. An English book from the early 1400s reported the popularity of black pepper, which helped disguise the bad taste of heavily salted preserved meat during the long European winter: "Pepper is black and has a good smack, And every man doth it buy."[6] The Indian Ocean network's trade dynamism depended on cosmopolitan port cities, especially hubs such as Hormuz (Persia), Kilwa (Tanzania), Cambay (northwest India), Calicut (southwest India), Melaka (Malaya), and Quanzhou **(chwan-cho)** (southern China), which all became vibrant and cosmopolitan centers of international commerce and culture drawing populations from various societies. The legacy and fame of the Silk Roads survive. Today China is utilizing both the old overland and maritime Silk Roads as the basis for its ambitious Belt and Road Initiative to expand China's economic power and reach across Afro-Eurasia, making investment and offering infrastructure loans while building highways, railroad lines, ports, factories, shopping centers, and housing developments in several dozen countries.

The Eastern Hemispheric trade system that eventually developed was primarily fueled by China and India, the great centers of world manufacturing in this era (see Historical

[6]Quoted in M. N. Pearson, "Introduction," in *Spices in the Indian Ocean World*, ed. M. N. Pearson (Aldershot, UK: Valorium, 1996), xv.

Controversy: Eastern Predominance in the Intermediate World). Today both countries are again major players in the world economy including in manufacturing. Before 1500 China and India together probably produced over three-quarters of all world industrial products. The thirteenth-century traveler Marco Polo was fascinated by the coming and going of ships at the main Chinese port, Quanzhou: "Here is a harbor whither all ships of India come, with much costly merchandise. It is also the port whither go the [Chinese] merchants [heading overseas]. There is such traffic of merchandise that it is a truly wonderful sight."[7] China exported iron, steel, silk, refined sugar, and ceramics, while India was the great producer of textiles. Their industrial products might be transported thousands of miles. Hence, the work of a cotton weaver in India might be sold in China or East Africa, and Chinese ceramics might reach Zimbabwe and Mali. The Muslim soldiers who resisted the Christian crusaders in the Middle East used steel swords smelted in India from East African iron.

Merchants from all over Afro-Eurasia—Arabs, Armenians, Chinese, Indians, Indonesians, Jews, Venetians, Genoese—traveled great distances in search of profits, fostering numerous networks and often forming permanent trade diasporas. Hence, one Cairo-based Jewish family had branches in India, Persia, and Tunisia. An Arab source reported that, thanks to their extensive travels, Jewish merchants who came to Cordoba in Moorish Spain spoke Arabic, Persian, Italian, French, and Russian. Genoese merchant networks stretched from Portugal to the Middle East and Russia. An English observer in the 1170s described the commodities offered by markets in London that reflected the city's cosmopolitan tastes, including gold from Arabia, spice from Yemen, swords from Central Asia, palm oil from Babylon, fine gems from Egypt, crimson silks from China, wines from France, and sable from Russia. Another observer noted that Mecca was one of the world's great fairs, lacking no merchandise in the world. This then was an era of globalization not unlike today, albeit on a smaller scale, and it had important consequences. The fame of Melaka, Calicut, Hormuz, and other Asian ports as commercial hubs for valuable goods reached Europe, and by the late fourteenth century some European merchants and monarchs were beginning to dream of a sea route to the East that would enable them to trade directly with China, Japan, Southeast Asia, and South Asia. This European dream of sailing to "the Indies" would lead to much more far-reaching maritime exploration in the 1400s.

The Mongol Empire

TRANSITIONS

Perhaps the greatest transition of the era was fostered by the Mongols, pastoralists and tough steppe herders of horses and camels who brutally conquered the largest land empire in world history, stretching from the western shores of the Black Sea east to China and Korea. Genghis Khan (ca. 1162–1227) was a visionary leader who effectively united the Mongol tribes. His mounted, well-armed warriors and ruthless tactics,

aided by siege weaponry and innovative military strategies of rapid attack, made a formidable fighting force. They developed a deserved reputation for merciless brutality toward their enemies and even civilian residents of conquered cities, prompting some historians to consider their behavior a form of genocide. Within the span of a century, approximately 1250 to 1350, the Mongol armies, supported by a Mongol population of less than two million, swept out of their arid Central Asian grasslands to put over 200 million people under their control. Competition for limited resources caused by ecological instability, climate change (fifteen years of heavy rain), and/or population growth may have prompted the Mongols to undertake their conquests. Whatever the reasons, the Mongol expansion, which united a large chunk of the Eurasian population and indirectly affected millions of other people, was one of the most crucial developments in world history. Mongol armies conquered Central Asia, Tibet, Russia, part of eastern Europe, Afghanistan, Persia, Iraq, Anatolia, and later China and Korea. But they also faced setbacks. In eastern Asia, using a conscripted Chinese navy, they tried but failed to conquer Java and Japan and were also unable to hold Vietnam and Burma. The Mongols were at the Danube, preparing to sweep through Hungary into western Europe, when Genghis Khan's successor died, aborting that thrust. Western Europe did not suffer the ravages experienced by other peoples and eventually benefited from the Mongols, who thus served as great equalizers.

Some world historians consider Genghis Khan the most crucial figure of the second millennium CE because, despite his brutality, the Mongol conquests he led established an early form of globalized communication characterized by technology and product transfer moving chiefly from east to west along the Silk Road. This continued even after Genghis when the empire was divided by his heirs into several parts, becoming more of a confederation of empires. During the Mongol era Chinese inventions such as the spinning wheel, medical discoveries, and domesticated fruits and plants such as the orange and lemon reached Europe and the Middle East. Some historians argue that under the Mongol aegis various overlapping circuits of trade developed between northwestern Europe and China, creating what they called a short-lived but powerful world system. The Mongols also unwittingly set in motion changes that allowed Europeans to acquire and improve Chinese technologies such as printing, gunpowder, and the magnetic compass while developing new inventions of their own. These Chinese inventions had a major impact in Europe. In the seventeenth century the English philosopher Francis Bacon noted that Chinese printing, gunpowder, and the magnet "changed the whole face and state of things" in European literature, warfare, and navigation.[8] As Europeans improved Chinese weapons such as flamethrowers and primitive guns, late medieval warfare became far deadlier, while gunpowder and Chinese military technology, coming by routes opened by the Mongols, also helped reshape Middle Eastern politics and fostered the rise of the Ottoman Empire. But while Genghis Khan conquered

---

[7]Quoted on Philip D. Curtin, *Cross-Cultural Trade in World History* (New York: Cambridge University Press, 1984), 125.
[8]Quoted in L. S. Stavrianos, *Lifelines from Our Past: A New World History*, rev. ed. (Armonk, NY: M.E. Sharpe, 1997), 58.

Ms Or 20 f.124v Mahmud ibn Sebuktegin attacks the rebel fortress of Zarang in Sijistan in 1003, miniature from the "Jami' al-Tawarikh" of Rashid al-Din, c. 1307 (vellum)/Islamic School, (14th century)/EDINBURGH UNIVERSITY LIBRARY/Edinburgh University Library, Scotland/Bridgeman Images

IMAGE III.2 **Catapults** The Mongols used advanced military technology, including catapults, to conquer cities. This battle scene, painted by a Persian artist, shows the Mongols attacking a city around 1300.

Q What can we learn about Mongol warfare and the resistance they encountered from this painting?

by arms and bravery, he ruled by commerce and religion. He created the world's greatest trading network, encouraging consumption on a continental scale, and lowered merchants' taxes, but also gave his subjects freedom of religion. Some scholars referred to his religion policy as secularism, others as pluralism, since Christian Mongol queens funded Muslim schools and the khans participated in the rituals of several religions. A Mongol government in Persia even funded the Muslim scholar Rashid al-Din of Tabriz to compile the oldest known "universal" or world history.

During Mongol times many men of talent moved from west to east, as travel from one end of Eurasia to the other became easier than ever before, fostering greater hemispheric connections. In China the Mongols relied administratively on a large number of foreigners who came to serve in the civil service. These included many Muslims from West and Central Asia and a few Europeans such as the Italian merchant Marco Polo who found their way to the fabled land the Europeans called Cathay. Polo's reports on his travels increased European interest in Asia and inspired later explorers, such as Christopher Columbus, to seek a sea route to East Asia. People moved the other way too. A Chinese Nestorian Christian monk of Turkic ancestry, Rabban Sauma, even visited Rome, France, and England in 1287 as a diplomat for the Mongol ruler of Persia, the first known visitor to western Europe from East Asia and an early example of politics on a hemispheric scale. By reopening Central Asian trade routes closed by political turmoil and by connecting with many different countries, the Mongols fostered

communication networks and the transfer of technology between once remote parts of the Eastern Hemisphere. In doing so, they were major catalysts of change, laying a foundation for the gradual transition from the Intermediate to the Early Modern Era.

Consequences of Disease in an Increasingly Global World

⟲ TRANSITIONS

The worst disease pandemic in world history, known in the West as the Black Death, changed the whole trajectory of a large part of the Eastern Hemisphere in the fourteenth century, and continued to disrupt things for over a century. Although controversial, some studies suggest that the plague bacterium, which mutated in Europe and then traveled back eastward in the following decades, may have been the source of most of the world's major plague outbreaks since then, including in East Asia in the nineteenth and twentieth centuries. It capitalized on the expanding trade networks and disrupted the complex system of interregional trade and communication that had flourished around Eurasia and northern Africa in the thirteenth and fourteenth centuries, causing unexpected economic and political transitions. In its wake agricultural and industrial production declined and financial crises and labor shortages wrecked economies from China to France. The pandemic also helped undermine Mongol rule in East Asia and the Middle East, in part because of huge population losses. Ironically, it may have resulted from the Mongol conquests, in particular the greater contact they brought between Eurasian societies. Climate change may also have been a factor. Eurasia was unusually wet during the 1300s, perhaps increasing the number of fleas and rats, through which the disease was thought to be spread.

The Black Death, which most scholars think was chiefly caused by bubonic plague, apparently originated in China or Central Asia, where it killed millions. An increasingly complex system of global networks contributed to its spread. By the mid-1300s it had been carried by merchants and soldiers along the Silk Road to southern Russia. Ships leaving the Genoese trading colony at Calfa, on the Crimean peninsula at the north end of the Black Sea, carried it unwittingly to Sicily from where it spread through the Middle East, Europe, and North Africa, raging through cities and towns. Moving along trade routes, the plague may also have had some impact in Ethiopia and parts of West Africa. In the affected societies, from China to Egypt to England and even to fishing villages in remote Greenland, perhaps a third of the total population died in the first outbreak, the higher mortality being in congested cities. Surveying the damage, the Italian writer Petrarch wrote that future generations would be "incredulous, unable to imagine the empty houses, abandoned towns, the squalid countryside, the fields littered with dead, the dreadful silent solitude which seemed to hang over the whole world. Physicians were useless, philosophers could only shrug their shoulders and look wise."[9] Millions more died as the pandemic reappeared in intervals in western Eurasia over the next century. But although the dark shadow of death was ever present, the massive death toll also created a serious labor shortage that created a demand for workers that may have helped undermine feudalism in Europe.

When the Black Death came to an end, a spurt of growth saw population levels soar from East Asia to Europe, which may have encouraged overseas explorations in search of new lands and their resources. By 1500 the world population had reached between 400 million and 600 million people, about twice the population of 1000. China accounted for a fourth of the total, and India for at least a fifth. Europe, including Russia, grew rapidly to 70 to 95 million. In contrast, sub-Saharan Africa and, unaffected by the Black Death, the Americas each probably had 60 to 80 million people by 1500.

Consequences of Climate Change

⚒ TRANSITIONS

Climate change has helped shape, and sometimes destroy, societies since the dawn of humankind and, as it accelerated in the past several centuries, has become a major issue in world and national politics and debate today. It spurred the transition to farming in western Asia ten thousand years ago, undermined the Mesopotamian and Indus societies four thousand years

ago, and hastened the decline of the Chinese Han and Roman Empires around 200 CE. Eurasian weather became more erratic during the 1200s, and the fluctuations may have helped prompt the Mongol expansion by bringing higher than normal rainfall to the grasslands, making the Mongol steppes green and verdant, hence fueling the horses that were the backbone of the empire's military. In the Americas, climate change probably contributed to the collapse of various societies, including Tiwanaku, Moche, Teotihuacan, and the southern Maya. In North America great droughts in the 1200s may have fostered decline in the Mississippi Basin societies and caused the dispersal of the Pueblo peoples of the southwestern deserts, who responded to hard times by migrating in search of wetter lands, as they said in their songs and poems: "Survival, I know this way. It rains. Mountains and canyons and plants grow. We traveled this way."[10]

Around 1300 an unusually warm period gave way to much cooler weather that lasted until 1850, sparking what scientists call the "Little Ice Age," with serious results for societies. Whatever the causes, which are still debated, longer and more frigid winters periodically affected Europe, North America, Central Asia, and China. Famine and starvation gripped southern African forests, the Russian steppes, and Ming China rice fields. Bitter cold drove the Norse Vikings out of Greenland, and Icelandic farming floundered. Severe storms and flooding in Europe were followed by drought and crop failures, causing widespread famine. As rivers and canals froze, boat traffic was inhibited. Between 1315 and 1317 perhaps 15 percent of Europe's population starved to death, and malnutrition made northern Europeans and Chinese less resistant to the Black Death. In addition, rainfall declined in India and Africa, drying up many lakes. Many people blamed governments for their misery, resulting eventually in a surge of revolts and civil wars. The North Atlantic climate became even colder from the mid-1600s to the mid-1700s, and such discomfort may have inspired some adventurous Europeans to seek greener pastures abroad, in the Americas.

Overseas Explorations

⚒ TRANSITIONS

The forces of the era, including long-distance trade, the Mongol expansion, and climate change, fostered another great transition, the great voyages of discovery. By the early 1400s the Chinese had the most advanced ships and navigational techniques. Anxious to reassert their regional influence after overthrowing the Mongol rulers, they took the initiative of exploration, dispatching unprecedented voyages of discovery. In a remarkable series of expeditions in the early 1400s, huge Chinese ships commanded by Admiral Zheng He followed long-established maritime networks as far as East Africa and Arabia, reflecting the crucial role played by Afro-Eurasian maritime commerce. However, although the voyages and Zheng He are still celebrated in China and by ethnic Chinese

[9] Quoted in Frederick F. Cartwright, *Disease and History: The Influence of Disease in Shaping the Great Events of History* (New York: Thomas Y. Crowell, 1972), 37.
[10] Quoted in Brian Fagan, *The Long Summer: How Climate Changed Civilization* (New York: Basic Books, 2004), 224.

communities in Southeast Asia today, this Chinese thrust did not have lasting effects on the world. Although they had the naval capability, the Chinese, unlike the Europeans, lacked the economic incentive and religious zeal to sail around Africa in search of Europe.

The Portuguese and then the Spanish, both peoples with long maritime traditions and coastal locations, used Chinese, Arab, and European naval technology to construct ships and equip crews for successful long-distance voyages. In search of gold, spices, slaves, and other resources as well as possible Christian African and Asian allies against Islam, Portuguese ships sailed south to West and Central Africa, where they established outposts and eventually colonies. By the end of the fifteenth century the Portuguese had rounded the Cape of Good Hope at the tip of southern Africa to reach the Indian Ocean, the East African trading ports, and finally India. The Portuguese were not the only Europeans, dazzled by Asian wealth, to seek a sea route to China, Japan, Southeast Asia, and India, this time by sailing west rather than around Africa. A historian in the early 1500s reported on another mariner and his ambitions:

> *Christopher Columbus, a Genoese, proposed to the Catholic King and Queen [of Spain] to discover the islands which touch the Indies. He asked for ships, promising not only to propagate the Christian religion, but also certainly to bring back pearls, spices and gold beyond anything imagined.*[11]

The Spanish expedition led by Columbus landed in the Americas in the 1490s. With these new networks of communication between distant societies, the history of the world was profoundly altered. An even more connected world—a great global network—and the Early Modern Era were at hand.

---

[11]Peter Martyr, quoted in Jack Turner, *Spice: The History of a Temptation* (New York: Vintage, 2004), xi.

The Rise, Power, and Connections of the Islamic World, 600–1500

> *Then came Islam. All institutions underwent change. It distinguished [believers] from other nations and ennobled them. Islam became firmly established and securely rooted. Far-off nations accepted Islam.*

—Ibn Khaldun, fourteenth-century Arab historian[1]

Apic/Hulton Archive/Getty Images

IMAGE 10.1 **Pilgrimage Caravan** Every year caravans of Muslim pilgrims converged on Islam's holiest city, Mecca, in Arabia. This painting shows such a caravan led by a band. In this era pilgrims came from as far away as Morocco and Spain in the west and Indonesia and China in the east.

Q What can you conclude about how people travelled and dressed on their journey to Mecca?

[1]From *The Muqaddimah: An Introduction to History*, trans. Franz Rosenthal and ed. N. J. Dawood (Princeton, NJ: Princeton University Press, 1967), 25-27.

In 1382 the fifty-year-old Arab scholar Abd al-Rahman Ibn Khaldun (AHB-d al-ruh-MAHN ib-uhn kal-DOON) left his longtime home in Tunis in North Africa and moved east to Egypt. He was already well traveled and renowned as a thinker; his work, like his life, reflected the expansive Islamic society's cosmopolitan nature, crossing many geographical and cultural borders. He had recently completed his greatest work, a monumental history of the world known to educated Muslims and the first attempt by a historian anywhere to discover and explain changes in societies over time. Rational, analytical, and encyclopedic in coverage, it also offered a philosophy of history rooted in the scientific method.

With roots in Arabia, Ibn Khaldun's family later migrated to Spain and several generations later to Tunis. He visited and worked in various cities of North Africa and Spain, serving diverse rulers as a jurist, adviser, or diplomat. Ibn Khaldun then settled in Cairo, Egypt, a city he praised as the "metropolis of the world, garden of the universe, meeting-place of nations, ant hill of peoples, high place of Islam, seat of power."[2] There he served as a judge and a teacher, wrote voluminously, and traveled with high Egyptian officials to Palestine, Syria, and Arabia. Six centuries after Ibn Khaldun's family left Arabia for the western Mediterranean, he could feel at home in their ancestral homeland. The Islamic world he chronicled enjoyed an extraordinary unity of time and space.

The rise of Islam that produced Ibn Khaldun was a major historical turning point that led to widespread social, cultural, and political changes over the centuries. Islamic expansion launched a thousand-year era, from the seventh to the seventeenth century, that brought many Afro-Eurasian peoples into closer contact with one another and allowed for a mixing of cultures within an Islamic framework. The Islamic world of the era was a cosmopolitan marketplace of ideas and goods. The religion originated in seventh-century Arabia and eventually spread across several continents. Today Islam is, after Christianity, the world's largest religion, embraced by about one-fifth of humanity. A dynamic faith in dialogue with, and often tolerant toward, other traditions, Islam adapted to new cultures while remaining close to its founding ideals. For nearly a thousand years Islamic peoples greatly influenced or dominated a large segment of the Eastern Hemisphere, reflecting an early form of globalization. During this period, Muslim thinkers salvaged or developed major portions of the science and mathematics that shaped later industrial society, while Muslim sailors and merchants opened or extended networks that spread goods, technologies, and ideas throughout Afro-Eurasia.

---

[2]Quoted in Albert Hourani, *A History of the Arab Peoples* (Cambridge, MA: Belknap Press, 1991), 3.

10-1 Early Islam: The Origins and Spread of a Continuous Tradition

⇄ TRANSITIONS ⛫ SOCIETIES

Ⓠ How did Islam arise and spread?

The Islamic religion was founded in the seventh century CE in the Arabian peninsula, a parched land containing a few vibrant market towns like Mecca and a fertile agricultural region in the southwest. Despite the old stereotypes still popular in the West of camel-riding desert nomads, many Arabs were city merchants, maritime sailors and traders, farmers, and poets. But the harsh desert was inhabited mainly by nomads living on the fringes of more powerful societies. The visions of one man, Muhammad (moo-HAM-mad), inspired this fervently monotheistic faith influenced by Jewish and Christian thought. Islam's explosive

CONNECTION to TODAY

How do you think Islam's roots shape its role in the world today?

energies propelled it from a small Arab sect into the dominant faith of many millions from one end of the Eastern Hemisphere to the other. Within one hundred and thirty years of Islam's birth, Arab armies and navies had conquered lands from Spain to Persia, and in the following years Islam took root in India, Central Asia, and China. These conquests and the diffusion of the new religion dramatically reshaped many societies across the Afro-Eurasian zone. Arab language and culture spread with Islam, providing a new identity for the once diverse Middle Eastern societies.

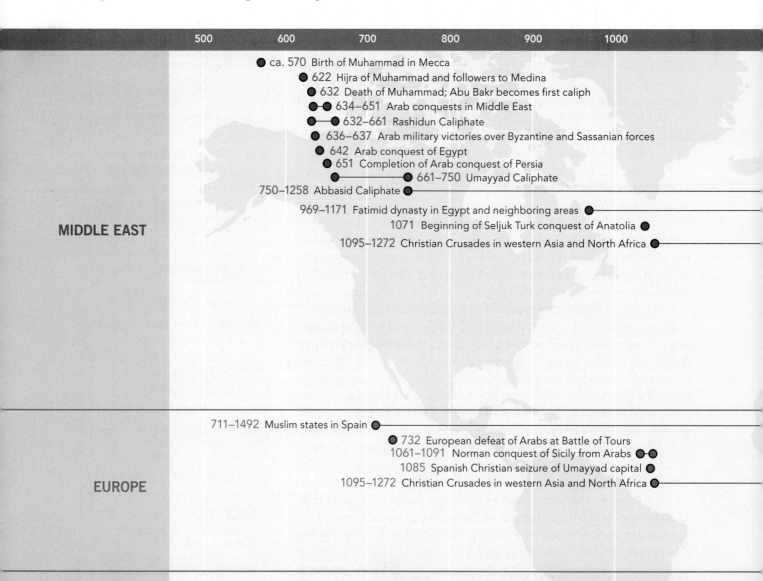

| | 500 | 600 | 700 | 800 | 900 | 1000 |

MIDDLE EAST

- ca. 570 Birth of Muhammad in Mecca
- 622 Hijra of Muhammad and followers to Medina
- 632 Death of Muhammad; Abu Bakr becomes first caliph
- 634–651 Arab conquests in Middle East
- 632–661 Rashidun Caliphate
- 636–637 Arab military victories over Byzantine and Sassanian forces
- 642 Arab conquest of Egypt
- 651 Completion of Arab conquest of Persia
- 661–750 Umayyad Caliphate
- 750–1258 Abbasid Caliphate
- 969–1171 Fatimid dynasty in Egypt and neighboring areas
- 1071 Beginning of Seljuk Turk conquest of Anatolia
- 1095–1272 Christian Crusades in western Asia and North Africa

EUROPE

- 711–1492 Muslim states in Spain
- 732 European defeat of Arabs at Battle of Tours
- 1061–1091 Norman conquest of Sicily from Arabs
- 1085 Spanish Christian seizure of Umayyad capital
- 1095–1272 Christian Crusades in western Asia and North Africa

CENTRAL ASIA

- 705–715 Arab conquests of Afghanistan and Central Asia

10-1a The Middle Eastern Sources of Islam

In Muhammad's day the Middle East—western Asia and North Africa—enjoyed great cultural diversity, a major factor in Islam's rise. The Byzantine Empire filled the vacuum left by the collapse of Roman control in western Asia and North Africa, and between 611 and 619 Sassanian Persia conquered Syria, Palestine, and Egypt. The Persians, Byzantines, and Ethiopians all interfered in Arabian politics. Many Middle Eastern people were Christians, including sects such as the Monophysites (among them the Copts of Egypt) and Nestorians, which were considered heretical by Roman Christians. These diverse traditions eventually influenced Islam.

However, Islam was produced by a distinctive Arab society and culture. Most Arabs, a Semitic people, occupied a desolate environment where only scattered oases or coastal enclaves and a few areas of fertile highlands sustained life. Some Arabs, like the Nabataeans of Petra and Palmyra, became traders who ranged widely in the Middle East. Many living along the Persian Gulf, Red Sea, and Indian Ocean were seafaring folk. Trading cities and farmers flourished in Yemen. But many Arab tribes were tent-dwelling nomadic pastoralists, known as **Bedouins (BED-uh-wuhnz)**, who wandered in search of oases and grazing lands, some raiding trade caravans. Survival in a sparsely populated environment depended on cooperation within families, clans, and tribes. A council of senior males governed each tribe, selecting a supreme elder respected for his generosity and bravery. Revering poetry, one month a year, Arabs halted raids and battles so that poets could gather and compete. The tradition was largely oral and reflected the nomadic existence of many desert Arabs. One pre-Muslim poet wrote: "Ah, but when grief assails me, straight away I ride off mounted on my

Bedouins Tent-dwelling nomadic Arab pastoralists who wandered in search of oases, grazing lands, or trade caravans to raid.

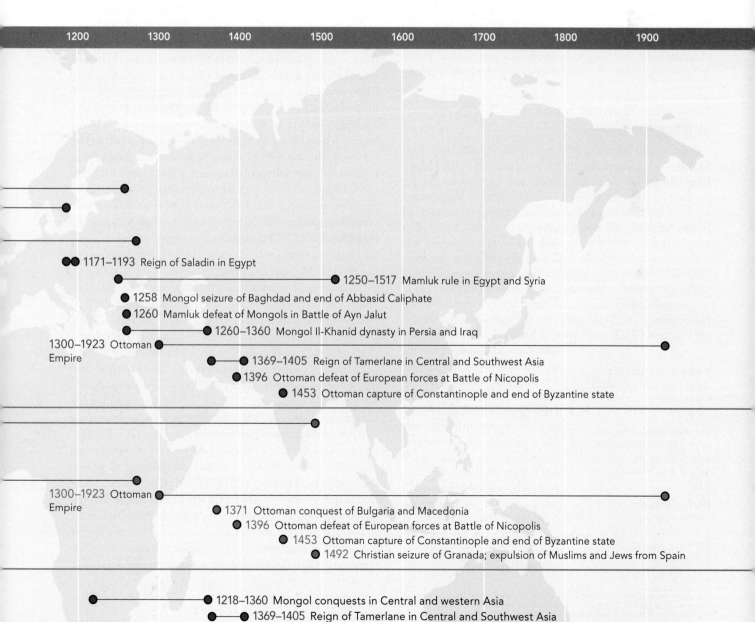

1200   1300   1400   1500   1600   1700   1800   1900

1171–1193 Reign of Saladin in Egypt

1250–1517 Mamluk rule in Egypt and Syria

1258 Mongol seizure of Baghdad and end of Abbasid Caliphate

1260 Mamluk defeat of Mongols in Battle of Ayn Jalut

1260–1360 Mongol Il-Khanid dynasty in Persia and Iraq

1300–1923 Ottoman Empire

1369–1405 Reign of Tamerlane in Central and Southwest Asia

1396 Ottoman defeat of European forces at Battle of Nicopolis

1453 Ottoman capture of Constantinople and end of Byzantine state

1300–1923 Ottoman Empire

1371 Ottoman conquest of Bulgaria and Macedonia

1396 Ottoman defeat of European forces at Battle of Nicopolis

1453 Ottoman capture of Constantinople and end of Byzantine state

1492 Christian seizure of Granada; expulsion of Muslims and Jews from Spain

1218–1360 Mongol conquests in Central and western Asia

1369–1405 Reign of Tamerlane in Central and Southwest Asia

swift, lean-flanked camel, night and day racing."[3] For many years scholars puzzled over writing, apparently in several ancient languages including Aramaic and Greek, that had been etched by ancient Arabs onto thousands of strange rocks, large and small, in what is today Jordan. Recently scholars realized how ancient Arabs ingeniously used the letters of these alphabets to transcribe their own speech by reading the sounds, which corresponded to Arabic, aloud. This became a way of preserving some of the poems. Later Christian crusaders may have taken the Arab romantic poetry tradition to Europe, where it probably influenced the chivalric love songs of medieval European performers known as troubadours.

Diverse religious traditions saturated Arabia, including Judaism, Christianity, and Zoroastrianism. Like Hebrews, Arabs believed they descended from Abraham. While some Arabs had adopted Judaism or Christianity, most were polytheistic, believing in many gods, goddesses, and spirits. Some tribes believed that the chief god was housed in a huge sacred cube-shaped structure made out of stone, known as the **Ka'ba** (KAH-buh), in Mecca, a bustling trading city in central Arabia near the Red Sea to which people made annual pilgrimages. Meccan merchants obtained hides, leather goods, spices, and perfumes in Yemen and exchanged them in Syria for textiles, olive oil, and weapons.

10-1b The Prophet Muhammad and His Revelations

The founder of Islam was Muhammad Ibn Abdullah (ca. 570–632). Just as scholars debate the historical accuracy of the Hebrew Bible and the Christian gospels, and lack adequate sources for the lives of the Buddha and Confucius, there is disagreement concerning Muhammad's life and movement, the evolution of Islamic precepts, how much Islamic thought arose out of older ideas, and the factors shaping Arab and Islamic expansion. The main sources on early Judaism, Christianity, and Islam were compiled decades, sometimes centuries, after the events described and can be interpreted by historians and believers in different ways.

In traditional accounts, Muhammad was a member of the Hashemite **(HASH-uh-mite)** clan of the prosperous mercantile Quraysh **(KUR-aysh)** tribe of Mecca. Raised by an uncle after his parents died, he became a merchant, shipping goods for a wealthy twice-widowed older woman, Khadija **(kah-DEE-juh)**, who had capitalized on opportunities that city life sometimes gave ambitious women, even in strongly patriarchal societies. They soon married. Although Muhammad's trade caravans flourished, he considered Meccan merchants greedy and materialistic, contrary to Arab traditions of generosity.

Ka'ba A huge sacred cube-shaped stone in the city of Mecca to which people made annual pilgrimages.

Quran ("Recitation") Islam's holiest book; contains the official version of Muhammad's revelations and to believers is the inspired word of God.

Hadith ("Narrative") The remembered words and deeds of Muhammad, revered by many Muslims as a source of religious guidance and law.

In seeking answers, Muhammad often meditated in the barren mountains around Mecca. In 610 he had visions in which he believed, God revealed the secrets of existence. Muhammad reported visitations by an angel bringing God's command to "recite in the name of your lord who created the human."[4] One of his wife's cousins, a monotheist, encouraged him to accept the visions as revelations from God. Fearing demonic possession, Muhammad agonized about the visions, which continued over the next twenty-three years, but he eventually accepted their authenticity largely because of his wife Khadija's support: "She believed in me when no one else did. She considered me to be truthful when the people called me a liar. She helped me with her fortune when the people had left me nothing."[5] Muhammad began preaching the new faith of Islam ("submission to God's will"). The early believers, or Muslims **(MUZ-limz)** ("those who had submitted to God's will"), mostly came from his middle-class friends, relatives, and a few other Meccans, some from lower-class backgrounds. Gradually some rich Quraysh also joined.

Probably just before or soon after Muhammad's death followers had already written down some of his visions on parchment, stone, palm leaves, and camel shoulder blades. In 650, several decades after Muhammad's death, the Caliph Abu Bakr, Muhammad's successor as leader, ordered the compilation of all his revelations into an official version, the **Quran** (kuh-RAHN), meaning "Recitation." Beloved for its beautiful poetic verses, it became Islam's holy book, to believers the inspired word of God. For many Muslims the Quran was essentially an oral experience to be recited, memorized, and revered. Today Quran recitation and knowledge competitions are regularly held in Muslim communities around the world. A second book revered as a source of religious guidance and law by most but not all Muslims, the **Hadith** (hah-DEETH), meaning "Narrative," compiled during the ninth and tenth centuries, collected the remembered words and deeds of Muhammad himself.

Muhammad insisted he was human, not divine. His followers accepted him as the last God-inspired prophet, the final voice superseding the earlier prophets Adam, Abraham, Moses, and Jesus (see Discover Historical Voices: The Holy Book, God, and the Prophet in the Quran). Muhammad's faith mixed older traditions with new understandings, many principal ideas clearly resembling some beliefs of Mecca's Christians and Jews. Muhammad's views were strictly monotheistic, putting aside all other gods, with believers assured of an afterlife. In contrast to Arab customs, Islam guaranteed women certain rights formerly denied them and promoted the equality of all believers. Muhammad advocated equality and justice, sharing all wealth, living simply, and creating a spirit of unity. Some historians contend that Muhammad's movement was ecumenical, welcoming all monotheists, including Christians and Jews, as "believers," and only after his death became more exclusive, adding new beliefs such as pilgrimage to Mecca; other scholars, while often agreeing that Islam's form gradually evolved, question this thesis.

[3]Quoted in Mohammed Munir, "The Birth of Islam in the Arabia Desert," in Claire Swisher, ed., *The Spread of Islam* (San Diego, Calif.: Greenhaven Press, 1999), 40.
[4]Quoted in Jonathan Bloom and Sheila Blair, *Islam: A Thousand Years of Faith and Power* (New Haven, CT: Yale University Press, 2002), 29.
[5]Quoted in Wiebke Walther, *Women in Islam* (Princeton, NJ: Markus Wiener, 1993), 104.

Discover Historical Voices

The Holy Book, God, and the Prophet in the Quran

The Quran is organized according to the individual chapter's length, with early and later revelations mixed together rather than a rigid organization of thoughts. English translations lose most of the nuances of the Arabic language, obscuring the beautiful, powerful, poetic writing style. In Arabic the Quran is both a scripture and an elegant literature that has inspired millions. The following brief excerpts present some basic ideas about the holy book itself, the monotheistic God's unity and power, and the recognition of Muhammad as not divine but rather a human prophet or apostle to God.

In the name of the Merciful and Compassionate God. That is the Book! There is no doubt therein; a guide to the pious, who believe in the unseen, and are steadfast in prayer, and of what we have given them expend in alms; who believe in what is revealed to thee, and what was revealed before thee, and of the hereafter they are sure. These are in guidance from their Lord, and these are the prosperous... .

God, there is no god but He, the living, the self-subsistent. Slumber takes Him not, nor sleep. His is what is in the heavens and what is in the earth. Who is it that intercedes with Him save by His permission? He knows what is before them and what behind them, and they comprehend not aught of His knowledge but what He pleases. His throne extends over the heavens and the earth, and it tires him not

to guard them both, for He is high and grand... . On Him is the call of truth, and those who call on others than Him shall not be answered at all, save as one who stretches out his hand to the water that it may reach his mouth, but it reaches it not! The call of the misbelievers is always in error... . In the name of the Merciful and Compassionate God, Say "He is God alone!"

Muhammad is but an apostle; apostles have passed away before his time; what if he die or is killed, will ye retreat upon your heels? He who retreats upon his heels does no harm to God at all; but God will recompense the thankful... . Muhammad is not the father of any of your men, but the Apostle of God, and the Seal of the Prophets; for God all things doth know!

Reflection Questions

1. What is the purpose of the Quran?
2. What are the powers of God?
3. What is the relationship between Muhammad and God?
4. What do you see as the key differences and similarities in core theology between Islam and the world's other major religions, Buddhism, Christianity, and Hinduism?

Source: Excerpts taken from Chapters 2, 3, 13, and 33 of the Quran, as reprinted in L. S. Stavrianos, ed., *The Epic of Man to 1500* (Englewood Cliffs, NJ: Prentice-Hall, 1970), 210–211.

10-1c Emigration and Triumph

Muhammad soon faced challenges that led him to leave Mecca. Mecca's political and business leaders and many Quraysh rejected Muhammad's views and followers as threatening their position, and some enemies harassed Muslims and even plotted Muhammad's murder. In 619 Khadija died, followed by the uncle who raised him, leaving Muhammad in despair. Meanwhile, the nearby city of Medina became engulfed in strife. The contending factions invited Muhammad, respected for his fairness and honesty, to come to Medina and arbitrate their disputes, and in 622 Muhammad led seventy Muslims and their families from Mecca to Medina, an event known as the **hijra** (HIJ-ruh), or "emigration." Hence, to believers, 622, which begins the Muslim calendar, represents humanity's response to God's message. In Medina the Muslims formed a new community of believers, or **umma**. Many Medinans accepted Muhammad as the Prophet, and he built his first mosque for worship and prayers.

Having a forceful personality and leadership skills, Muhammad also wisely tolerated differences, for example, by accommodating Jews and respecting the stories of their past prophets. Muhammad said their original teachings had been distorted by Jews and Christians.

In Medina Muhammad also took new wives. Because frequent warfare and raiding killed off many men, Arab men often had several wives so they could protect vulnerable women and procreate more children. Concerned for the welfare of women without husbands, Muhammad urged his men to marry widows and required that all wives be treated equally and fairly.

Muhammad's growing popularity earned him more enemies. Some Medina Jews mocked his beliefs. Muhammad urged his followers to respect sympathetic Christians and Jews, saying, "Dispute not with the People of the Book. We believe in what has been sent down to us, and what has been sent down to you; our God and your God is One."[6] But, needing strong methods to preserve his umma, he expelled two Jewish tribes and killed all the men of another suspected of aiding his opponents. Muhammad's followers won various military skirmishes, usually against much larger armies. The Muslims, mostly city-dwellers, quickly learned desert warfare. In general Muhammad proved a flexible, pragmatic leader, usually negotiating and compromising rather than shedding blood, but

hijra The emigration of Muslims from Mecca to Medina in 622.

umma The community of Muslim believers united around God's message.

[6]Quoted in Karen Armstrong, *Muhammad: A Biography of the Prophet* (San Francisco: Harper, 1992), 160.

The faithful before the Kaaba in Mecca, from the 'Siyer-i Nebi' (gouache on paper)/Turkish School, (16th century)/BILDARCHIV STEFFENS (FIRST ACCOUNT)/Topkapi Palace Museum, Istanbul, Turkey/Bridgeman Images

IMAGE 10.2 **The Pilgrimage to Mecca** This sixteenth-century Turkish painting portrays faithful pilgrims before the Ka'ba, Islam's most sacred site, in Mecca.

Q How would you describe the clothing and mood of the pilgrims in Mecca?

his brilliant military victories and shrewd diplomacy made him Arabia's most powerful man. Muhammad pardoned most of his foes and assumed power in Mecca, sharing taxes from trade with those who became Muslim.

Amidst social and economic changes in western Arabia, Muhammad's message of monotheism, community, equality, and justice proved a powerful attraction, dissolving social barriers between tribes and encouraging a larger spiritual community. In his last sermon, Muhammad told his audience to deal justly with each other, treat women kindly, and consider all Muslims as brothers. His message emphasized the one and only, all-powerful God, **Allah** (AH-luh): "He knows what is hidden and what is evident. He is the merciful lord of mercy. There is no God but him. He is the king, the holy, the

peace, the faith keeper, the preserver, the strong, the all-disposing."[7] Thanks to expanding long-distance trade, some Meccans became richer and others poorer, fostering social instability. But Muhammad, like Jesus of Nazareth, emphasized social justice, winning support among the poor.

As is the case within all large organized religions, there are fierce debates among scholars of Islam, both Muslim and non-Muslim, as to various aspects of Islamic history, although many believers reject scholarly questioning of accepted beliefs. One of the biggest controversies in Islamic studies is the question of when Muhammad died. The oldest biography by a Muslim, written over a century later, claims he died in Medina at age sixty-two in 632. But other sources—Jewish, Christian, and some Muslim—claim he died after leading the conquest of Palestine in 634 to 635. Whatever the truth, when Muhammad died the umma faced a challenge because Muhammad had left little guidance on future leadership. Disagreements arose. The four men closest to him formed a **caliphate** (KAL-uhf-uht), an imperial state headed by an Islamic ruler, or *caliph* (KAL-uhf), considered the successor of the Prophet in civil affairs. Muhammad's four consecutive successors, known later as the Rashidun ("rightly guided") caliphs, ruled from Medina between 632 and 661, but disagreements about succession continued.

10-1d Islamic Beliefs and Society

Like Christians, Muslims, considering their faith the last revealed religion, possessed a strong missionary impulse to share their faith with all people. The basic tenets provided a new worldview that changed history and a sense of community in the wider brotherhood of believers. Believers have clear duties. The "five pillars" include, first, the profession of faith: "There is no God but Allah and Muhammad is his messenger." Muhammad is not considered divine, as Christians consider Jesus, but a human teacher chosen by God to spread the notion of a monotheistic God: eternal, all powerful, all knowing, and all merciful. Second, formal worship is performed with words and action five times daily. The third pillar, assistance to the poor and disadvantaged, requires Muslims to donate a tenth of their wealth, an act that also benefits the giver. The fourth pillar, the annual fast or **Ramadan** (RAHM-uh-dahn), lasts one month, during which time Muslims abstain from eating, drinking, and having sex during daylight hours, to sacrifice for their faith and to understand hunger and poverty. Families and friends gather to eat just before sunrise and then again following sunset. Finally, if possible, at least once in their lives Muslims make a pilgrimage, or **haj** (HAJ), to Mecca, worshipping with other believers from around the world. Among other spiritual activities, pilgrims circle the great Ka'ba shrine, as Arabs had done before Islam.

Allah To Muslims the one and only, all-powerful God.

caliphate An imperial state headed by an Islamic ruler, the caliph, considered the designated successor of the Prophet in civil affairs.

Ramadan The thirty days of annual fasting when Muslims abstain from eating, drinking, and having sex during daylight hours to demonstrate sacrifice for their faith and to understand the hunger of the poor.

haj The Muslim pilgrimage to the holy city of Mecca to worship with multitudes of other believers from around the world.

---

[7]Quoted in Francis Robinson, *The Cultural Atlas of the Islamic World Since 1500* (Oxford, UK: Stonehenge, 1992), 180.

Islam places other demands on believers. A puritanical moral code prohibits adultery, gambling, usury, or the use of intoxicating liquors. Like Judaism, Islam has strict dietary laws, including a ban on pork. Muslims strive to live as God intended through effort, or **jihad (ji-HAHD)**, a spiritual, moral, and intellectual struggle to enhance personal faith and follow the Quran. However, a zealous minority has interpreted jihad as military conflict or violent struggle with nonbelievers or enemies, somewhat like the Christian crusading tradition. As with Judeo-Christian beliefs, Muslims believe in angels, heavenly servants who serve as God's helpers, and a Devil who flouts God's command; they also anticipate a last judgment where each individual is held accountable for his or her own actions. The good attain Heaven, a garden paradise, while the wicked suffer an eternity in Hell.

The search for social unity fostered what believers considered a moral and divinely guided community that regulated how people lived together, asking people to pursue justice, avoid excesses, and practice mercy. Viewing Christians and Jews as "protected peoples," Islamic laws recognized the freedom of religious minorities to worship and promoted toleration. The Quran stated: "Lo! those who believe [in Islam], and those who are Jews and Christians, whoever believeth in Allah on the last day and doeth right—surely their reward is with their Lord, and no fear shall come upon them, neither shall they grieve."[8] Some Christians and Jews, angry with the Byzantine Empire's corruption and occasional repression, aided Muslim expansion and viewed Arabs as liberators.

Islamic ideas improved the position of women in Arab culture. Before Islam, Arab women, often secluded, had few rights. Under Islam, men could have up to four wives if they could support and treat them equally and had more rights than women under divorce and inheritance rules. However, women enjoyed some legal protection, could own property and engage in business, and were considered partners before God alongside men. Scholars and theologians have debated for centuries and still do today how Muhammad viewed women's roles and what rights they should have. He enjoyed women's company, helped with household chores, listened with interest when his wives asserted their opinions, and emphasized that men should treat women kindly. He took more wives after Khadija's death; his favorite, A'isha, played a prominent political role, especially after his death. Muhammad encouraged female modesty in dress, suggesting that women draw their cloaks about them when they went out. Whether this meant full veiling of the face remains disputed. Since ancient Mesopotamia, veiling was common in Middle Eastern societies and even some Asian and European ones, and eventually it became expected of devout women. While this enforced modesty restricted women, many Muslim men and women believed that the custom protected women's dignity and virtue. This practice separated the sexes, preventing what most Muslims considered inappropriate romantic entanglements.

10-1e Arab Conquests and the Making of an Islamic World

Muslim Arabs rapidly expanded from their base in central Arabia. Between 634 and 651 Muslim armies conquered Iraq, Syria, Palestine, Egypt, and Persia, while Arab ships sailed into the Mediterranean, taking Cyprus (649), Carthage (698), Tunis (**TOO-nuhs**) (700), and then Spain (711–720). In 732 Islamic expansion in Europe was finally stopped in southern France, at the Battle of Tours (toor), by a combined Christian force. Had Arab forces won that conflict, the history of Europe might have been different. Within two centuries, Islam became the dominant religion in the Middle East and North Africa, at the expense of Christianity and Zoroastrianism. Later, it spread across the Sahara to West Africa and down the East African coast, at the expense of polytheistic and animistic traditions, and also north into Anatolia and then the Balkans, where Orthodox Christianity was dominant. Adoption of the Arabic language, identity, and Islam united diverse peoples in western Asia and North Africa by creating strong cultural ties based on Arab norms and practices.

Muslim Arabs also expanded eastward, carrying Islam with them. After completing the conquest of Sassanian Persia, they conquered Afghanistan, Sind (sind) in the lower Indus Basin, and Central Asia between 705 and 715 (see Map 10.1). By 751 Muslim Arab armies had reached the Chinese Empire's western fringes, winning a fierce engagement at the Talas River, blocking Chinese westward expansion, and turning many Central Asian Turkic peoples such as Sogdians away from China and toward the Islamic world. Muslims now controlled most Silk Road cities, such as Samarkand and Bukhara. Muslim Arabs and Persians already carried out seaborne trade with China, and some merchants settled in coastal cities there. In the eleventh century, Muslims began ruling large parts of India, and later, in the fifteenth and sixteenth centuries, Islam spread through the Southeast Asian islands. The Arabic script was now used for writing various Asian and African languages, including Urdu in India, Malay in Southeast Asia, Swahili in East Africa, and Hausa in West Africa. Even in places like Java, where spoken Arabic never displaced local languages, children were often taught to read and recite the Quran in Arabic.

Historians debate the energies involved in the rapid Muslim Arab expansion. Factors in Arabia, including long-term drought, poverty, and overpopulation, may have spurred Muslims to seek new lands. Perhaps Arab leaders needed to capture lucrative trade routes and productive lands to support their followers. The Byzantine and Sassanian Empires, exhausted from warfare and infighting, made an easy target for conquest. Furthermore, fighters were often motivated by religious faith. Yet, despite persistent myths in the West, Muslims apparently made no systematic attempt to impose their religion on the conquered. Some historians suggest that Islam was still defining itself and was not yet clearly differentiated from Judaism and Christianity. Some controversial studies even argue that Muhammad was initially viewed by some followers or observers as a preacher or prophet somewhat like those in the Hebrew tradition rather than as the founder of a new religion. Whatever the case, it eventually became clear that a new and dynamic faith was emerging.

Fragile Islamic community dynamics also provided a motive for expansion. Muhammad's death created a crisis because his followers had lost their

> **jihad** Effort to live as God intended; a spiritual, moral, and intellectual struggle to enhance personal faith and follow the Quran.

---

[8]Quoted in Henry Bucher, *Middle East* (Guilford, CT: Dushkin, 1984), 19.

MAP 10.1 **Expansion of Islam, to 750 CE** The Arabs rapidly conquered much of western Asia, North Africa, and Spain, in the process expanding Islam into the conquered territories. By 750 their empire stretched from Morocco and Spain in the west to western India and Central Asia.

Q How does the early expansion of Islam reflect the geography of the Middle East and North Africa?

charismatic spiritual leader. By providing a common cause, conquest discouraged leaving the community. Warfare also capitalized on a long tradition of tribal fighting. Arab armies were cohesive, mobile, and well led. To prevent the rise of rival factions, Muhammad's first successor, his best friend Abu Bakr **(ab-boo BAK-uhr)**, forbade people from leaving the umma and declared Muhammad God's final prophet. Abu Bakr allied with other tribes, among them the often-feuding nomadic Bedouins, whose fighting spirit could be turned against non-Arab foes. Arab fighters divided up each conquest's spoils, spreading wealth within the community, maintaining unity, and keeping the allegiance of those favoring a radical egalitarianism that challenged those with wealth and power.

By the eleventh century Islam had grown from an Arab cult into the dominant religion over a wide area of Afro-Eurasia, joining older universal religions such as Buddhism and Christianity. Late-seventh and early-eighth-century Muslims thought of themselves as carriers of a global movement and a new religion encompassing many peoples, including self-governing communities of Greek Orthodox Christians, Nestorians, Copts, Zoroastrians, Manicheans, and Jews. Rather than remaining minority rulers over non-Muslim majorities, Arab Muslims began encouraging conversion and cultural synthesis. But conversion by force was the exception rather than the rule. Many found the religion and the increasingly cosmopolitan community of believers an attractive alternative to their old traditions.

KEY POINTS

▶ Islam was born in Arabia, a harsh land where many people lived in cooperative tribes or clans.

▶ Muhammad's teachings were monotheistic (like Christianity and Judaism) and emphasized equality and mutual respect among peoples from different tribes.

▶ Islam's foundation is the five pillars: profession of faith; formal worship; charity; annual fasting, or Ramadan; and the pilgrimage, or haj, to Mecca.

▶ Islam spread extremely rapidly via Arab conquest of the Middle East, North Africa, Central Asia, and parts of India and Europe.

▶ Explanations for the rapid Arab expansion include the need for resources, the weakness of other empires, and the need for a common cause to hold the Arabs together.

10-2 Early Islamic States and Empires

⇄ TRANSITIONS

Q What were the major achievements of the Islamic states and empires?

Islamic expansion allowed powerful states to rule millions of Muslims and non-Muslims, aided by unique concepts of government and law. For over half a millennium Arabic-speaking Muslims governed a large segment of the Eastern Hemisphere. Great states and empires dominated the Middle East,

CONNECTION to TODAY

What do you think are the strengths and weaknesses of an empire comprised of diverse societies but held together by a shared religion?

and Islamic states on the fringe of Christian Europe passed on knowledge. Peoples and ideas spread widely, fostering a dynamic mix of Arab, Persian, Indian, and Greek cultures. But Islam also divided into rival sects, creating enduring tensions that influenced Middle Eastern politics for many centuries.

IMAGE 10.3 The Great Umayyad Mosque in **Damascus** This mosque, built between 709 and 715, is the oldest surviving monumental mosque.

Q What architectural features stand out on this great mosque?

Waj/Shutterstock.com

10-2a Islamic Government and Law

Since Muslims viewed government and religion as the same, Islamic states tended to punish Muslims who violated religious prohibitions. Combining political and religious power produced a theocracy headed by a caliph governing several societies or more commonly a **sultan**, a Muslim ruler of only one country or state. Such far-reaching power was easily misused, but respected religious scholars' moral authority could sometimes check political abuses. The Islamic legal code, or **Shari'a** (shah-REE-ah) ("the way to the watering hole"), regulated social and economic as well as religious life. For devout Muslims, Shari'a is the ideal realization of divine justice, a higher law that reflects God's will. Shari'a is thus more than a legal code; it is viewed as a blueprint for life, providing a comprehensive guide to issues such as divorce, inheritance, debts, and morality. But there have been a wide range of views about what Shari'a required in practice. It also evolved over time. Based chiefly on the Quran and the Hadith, augmented by Islamic legal scholarship, the Shari'a was also rooted in Arab, Persian, and Byzantine cultural traditions and customs. But conflicts over Quranic interpretation and application fostered several competing interpretative traditions that differed slightly in emphasis on such tools as reasoning and scriptural authority. Some Islamic jurists have interpreted the Shari'a as moderate, tolerant, forgiving, and rationalist; others as austere, rigid, and harsh, to be interpreted literally with strict punishments for violation of moral codes.

Religious scholars such as judges, preachers, and prayer leaders elaborated the Shari'a and sustained Islamic culture, providing a cohesion and stability that was independent of the rise and fall of rulers. Muslims valued education based on studying with renowned religious and legal scholars, and by the tenth century they had created religious boarding schools, known as **madrasas** (muh-DRAH-suhz), that were headed by religious scholars. Today thousands of these schools flourish all over the Muslim world.

10-2b Early Imperial Caliphates: Unity and Strife

Beginning with the Rashidun, imperial caliphates attempted to maintain unity but also faced

sultan A Muslim ruler of only one country.

Shari'a The Islamic legal code for the regulation of social and economic as well as religious life.

madrasas Religious boarding schools found all over the Muslim world.

challenges. After 661 Islamic political power shifted outside of Arabia with two successive imperial dynasties, the Umayyad (oo-MY-ad) and the Abbasid (ah-BASS-id), both installed by members of Muhammad's Quraysh tribe as power shifted away from Arabia. While Mecca and Medina remained spiritual hubs, reinforced by annual pilgrimages, new cities emerged as major political and economic centers.

Political conflict increased with growth. The early conquests enriched Medina and Mecca merchant clans, but criticism of the new materialism eventually prompted a full revolt against the Rashidun leadership. Dissidents murdered the unpopular third caliph, Uthman (ooth-MAHN), installing Ali (ah-LEE) (ca. 600–661), Muhammad's son-in-law, as the fourth caliph. Although well qualified, pious, and generous, Ali proved weak, and moving the capital from Medina to Kufah (KOO-fa) in Iraq provoked challenges to his leadership. The opposition to Ali, rallied by Muhammad's widow, A'isha, resulted in civil war and Ali's murder. Ali's death ended the Rashidun era, but the divisions generated a permanent split in the Islamic world. Centuries later, many Muslims viewed the Rashidun period as a golden age of simple government and righteous cause, with some calling for a new caliphate to rule the Muslim world.

The Umayyad dynasty (661–750) seized power and moved the caliphate to Damascus (duh-MAS-kuhs) in Syria. Men with no direct connection to, or descent from, the Prophet now led the Islamic empire, and large bureaucratic states with remote leaders who passed on their rule to their sons defined Arab politics. Umayyad caliphs extended the Islamic empire deep into Byzantine territory. However, rulers soon faced unrest because, although encouraging Islamic institutions and customs while calling themselves deputies of God, they ignored Islamic morality. The Umayyad leaders' legendary drinking, womanizing, and lax religious devotion generated civil war and division, which eventually led to their downfall. Umayyad opponents emphasized Muhammad's role as God's prophet, clearly setting Islam apart from rival monotheistic religions. Among the challengers, the Prophet's only remaining male heir, his grandson Husayn (hoo-SANE), attracted support from those who believed the caliph must be Muhammad's direct descendant. However, Husayn's rebellion in 680 failed, and he was killed in the Battle of Karbala (KAHR-buh-LAH), a city in Iraq, becoming, along with his murdered father Ali, a martyr against the Umayyads.

10-2c The Sunni–Shi'a Split

After Ali's death, Islam began to split into two main branches due to disagreements over the umma's nature and the full meaning of Muhammad's revelations. The main branch, **Sunni (SOO-nee)** ("The Trodden Path"), accepted the Prophet's practices and the historical succession of caliphs. In their view,

Sunni ("The Trodden Path") The main branch of Islam, comprising those who accept the practices of the Prophet and the historical succession of caliphs.

Shi'a ("Partisans" of Ali) The branch of Islam emphasizing the religious leaders descended from Muhammad through his son-in-law, Ali, whom they believe was the rightful successor to the Prophet.

governments must guarantee political independence and religious integrity. Today about 85 percent of all Muslims, including most in North Africa, Turkey, the Balkans, South and Southeast Asia, and China, as well as the majority of Arabs, are Sunni. Sunni embraces diverse opinions and practices, adhering to one of four main schools of Islamic law and a broad view of who qualifies for political power.

The other main branch began in a dispute over leadership. The **Shi'a (SHEE-uh)** ("Partisans" of Ali) revered Muhammad's family and recognized only leaders descended from Muhammad through his son-in-law, Ali, to them the Prophet's rightful successor. Karbala and nearby Najaf (NAH-jaf), where respectively Husayn and Ali are buried, became holy Shi'ite pilgrimage centers. Shi'ites provided an alternative to Sunni Islam but divided into three rival schools based on which leader after Ali should be followed. The main Shi'ite populations live today in Iran, Iraq, Lebanon, and the Persian Gulf states. Smaller minorities are scattered across Central Asia, western India, and Pakistan.

The two branches of Islam share many commonalities but, as with often-feuding Roman Catholic, Protestant, and Orthodox churches in Europe, Sunni–Shi'a differences run deep. Like Catholics, ultra-Orthodox Jews, and Hindu sects but unlike Sunnis, many Shi'ites followed strong religious leaders they considered divinely inspired. Like Catholics and Protestants in some Western countries, Sunnis and Shi'ites sometimes fought each other. Sunni majorities sometimes persecuted Shi'ite minorities, producing a Shi'ite martyrdom complex and dissent against Sunni rulers. Over the centuries Shi'ite-governed states also often ruled uneasily over Sunni majorities.

10-2d Arabian Nights: The Abbasid Caliphate

The Ummayads were replaced by the Abbasid Caliphate (750–1258), which enjoyed great power and fostered a dynamic society, surviving for half a millennium, embodying the unity of the Islamic umma, and establishing a pattern for later Muslim rulers. The Abbasids, who were Sunni Quraysh descended from Muhammad's uncle, Abbas, attracted support from both Sunnis and Shi'ites to defeat the Umayyad army. The lone Umayyad survivor fled to Spain and there established a state that flourished for three centuries. Abbasid forces expanded the empire eastward and maintained pressure against Byzantium in the west. By 800 the Abbasid Empire ruled some thirty million people and was one of the most successful states in the world (see Map 10.2).

Moving the capital to Baghdad, where the Tigris and Euphrates Rivers come closest together in Iraq, placed the Abbasid government alongside major trade routes and fertile irrigated fields. Residents called their city "the navel of the nations," the center of the world. Boasting joint-stock companies and banks, Baghdad became one of the world's greatest hubs, its bazaars filled with goods from as far away as China, Scandinavia, and East Africa. Living in a city famed for its diverse food cultures, the wealthy had access to delicacies such as spices from across Asia, sugar from India, and citrus from China. Gourmets even competed in elite cook-offs, an "Iron Chef" of the ninth century. To publicly demonstrate their piety and generosity, the Abbasids

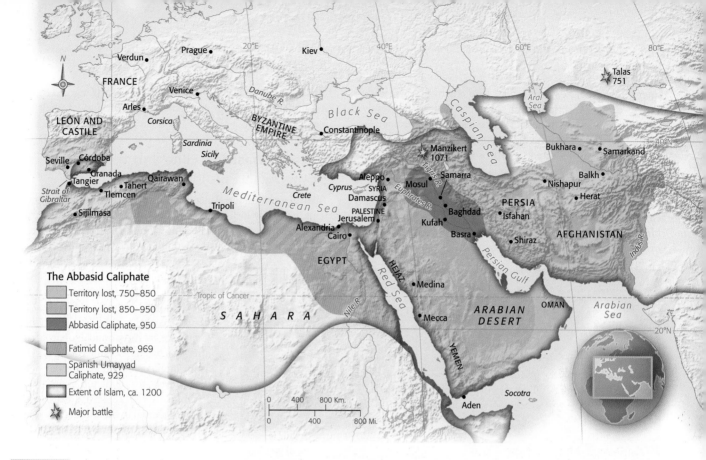

MAP 10.2 **The Abbasid Empire, CA. 800 CE** The Abbasids, a dynasty based in what is today Iraq, established the largest Muslim empire in the Early Intermediate Era, ruling lands from Central Asia to Egypt before losing most of their territories. Among other major Islamic states, the Umayyads ruled Spain and Northwest Africa and the Fatimids ruled Egypt and neighboring lands.

Q What challenges might be posed to an imperial government trying to govern such a large empire?

employed thousands to build palaces, schools, hospitals, and mosques. Some Baghdad citizens, however, openly flouted Islamic prohibitions against hedonistic behavior, and Baghdad generally reflected Islamic society's cosmopolitan flavor. In the 1160s a visiting rabbi from Muslim-ruled Spain, Benjamin of Tudela, wrote of the ethnically diverse city and its large Jewish community:

> *This great Abbasid [caliph] is extremely friendly towards the Jews, many of his officers being of that nation. Baghdad contains about one thousand Jews, who enjoy peace, comfort, and much honor. Many of the Jews are good scholars and very rich. The city contains 28 Jewish synagogues.*[9]

Islam flourished by receiving and absorbing culture from all over the Eastern Hemisphere. For example, Persian influence on the Abbasid system was strong, and many Persians occupied high government positions. The Abbasids acquired knowledge from faraway lands, such as papermaking technology from Chinese captured in the Battle of Talas of 751; by 800 Baghdad had its first paper mill. Papermaking allowed for wider distribution of the Quran, helping to spread Islam.

The height of Abbasid Baghdad conjures up the images of affluence and romance reported in *The Arabian Nights*, stories that later influenced European writers, artists, and

composers and are still popular in the world today. For example, the nineteenth-century Russian composer Nikolai Rimsky-Korsakov's **(RIM-skee KAWR-suh-kawf)** famous *Scheherazade* symphony evokes Abbasid Baghdad's atmosphere. The original *Arabian Nights* stories, augmented over several centuries, incorporated Persian, Egyptian, Indian, and other traditions and encompassed many subjects and moods, among them fantasy, comedy, piety, sex, tragedy, brutality, sentimentality, and obscenity. Some scholars perceive feminist values reflected in the proactive female characters. Some misleading images of old Baghdad, based loosely on the great literary work, come from fanciful children's books and films such as "Ali Baba and the Seven Thieves" and "Aladdin and the Magic Lamp" featuring flying carpets and genies in magic lamps, which in the original stories appeared mostly in dreams. Life under the most famous Abbasid caliph, Harun al-Rashid **(hah-ROON al-rah-SHEED)** (786–809), lacked flying carpets and magic lanterns, but it did include a large harem of wives, concubines, and slave girls numbering perhaps two thousand. These royal harems suggested a secluded world of luxury, idleness, and endless plotting for royal favor. Like some other Abbasid rulers, Harun reputedly drank heavily and pursued the temptations of the flesh.

Adopting some customs from the conquered gradually transformed Arabs from desert herders and traders into imperial

---

[9]Quoted in Manuel Komroff, ed., *Contemporaries of Marco Polo* (New York: Horace Liveright, 1928), 286-292.

rulers. The Abbasids often ruled through traditional leaders, such as Egypt's Coptic Church patriarchs. In Iraq they resolved disputes among Nestorian Christians just as the Sassanian governors had done. Like the Sassanians, the caliphs patronized a state religion, now shifted from Zoroastrianism to Islam, and lavishly supported arts and crafts. They also appointed Muslim judges and built mosques.

Urban growth followed conquests. The caliphates' administrative centers drew in surrounding people seeking work. Hence, Baghdad rapidly swelled to perhaps a million people by 900, becoming the world's largest city at the time. Like the Sassanians, the caliphs divided cities into wards marked by ethnic and occupational groups, governing them through their own leaders.

10-2e Abbasid Decline and the End of the Arab Empire

Like all empires, the Abbasids eventually faced mounting problems, gradually losing their grip on power by the tenth century. As Turkish soldiers guarding the caliphs became more powerful and disaffected Shi'ites fomented bloody revolts, the caliphate became a mere figurehead and parts of the empire broke away. Anti-Abbasid Shi'ites claiming descent from Fatima, Muhammad's daughter, established the Cairo-based Fatimid (FAT-uh-mid) Caliphate in Egypt and North Africa, after which Cairo became Baghdad's rival as an intellectual and economic center. The university founded in Cairo by the Fatimids in 970, Al-Azhar, became the most influential in the Islamic world and remains the unrivaled center of Islamic higher learning. European visitors to Fatimid Cairo were astonished by a city with a substantial middle class, general tolerance towards Christians and Jews, and luxurious clothes, magnificent silks, and elegant textiles manufactured in local workshops for export to Europe, where they became immensely popular with the upper classes. Shi'ites also ruled various smaller states in which most of the population remained Sunni or non-Muslim yet generally enjoyed religious freedom. Finally, the wealth of the Abbasid realm attracted the Mongols, Central Asian nomads who in the thirteenth century built a great regional empire stretching from East Asia to eastern Europe (see Chapter 11). In 1258 Mongol armies sacked and destroyed Baghdad and executed the last Abbasid caliph, shattering the symbolic unity of the Muslim world. Now Persians, Berbers, Kurds, Turks, and Mongols challenged Arab dominance.

Despite these setbacks, political weakness and declining cultural dynamism only become evident in the Islamic world in the sixteenth and seventeenth centuries. Yet, although few later Muslim rulers could match the power of the early Abbasids, Islam accelerated its diffusion to new peoples, and between 1258 and 1550 the territorial size of the Islamic world doubled. Scholars, saints, and mystics assumed leadership throughout this world,

julius fekete/Shutterstock.com

IMAGE 10.4 **Alhambra, Court of Lions** The Alhambra, or Palace of Lions, built in Granada in southern Spain in the fourteenth century, is one of the finest architectural treasures from Muslim Spain. It features a courtyard with a fountain.

Q What features stand out for you from the Alhambra?

establishing legal structures, dogmas, social forms, standards of piety, aesthetic sensibilities, styles of scholarship, and schools of philosophy that helped define the vital core of Islamic culture.

10-2f Cultural Mixing in Muslim Sicily and Spain

Islamic culture also flourished in Sicily and Spain, where it fostered a cosmopolitan mixed society characterized by prosperity and shared scientific knowledge. Between 825 and 900 Muslim forces conquered Sicily, the largest Mediterranean island, thus tying it closer to the Arab-dominated maritime trade system. Muslim rulers repaired long-decayed Roman irrigation works, vastly increasing agricultural production. Many Arabs, Berbers, Africans, Greeks, Jews, Persians, and Slavs gravitated to the island, mixing with local peoples. The Muslim capital, Palermo, was larger than any other European city except Constantinople. But Muslim political divisions left the island open to gradual Christian reconquest. Between 1061 and 1091 Normans, descendants of Vikings who had settled in France, replaced a Muslim government with their own, and by 1200 Christian German rulers had established a Sicilian state. The persecution of Muslims and Jews gradually brought to an end the dynamic fusion of Islamic and Christian traditions.

A more enduring Muslim society emerged in what became known as Moorish Spain, as Umayyad forces conquered much of Iberia between 711 and 720. Their capital, Cordoba (**KAWR-duh-buh**), became Europe's largest city by 1000, home to half a million people. For several centuries a famed center of culture and learning, Umayyad-ruled Spain drew scholars and thinkers from all over Europe and the Islamic world. Cordoba's library held 400,000 volumes, when Christian Europe's libraries owned only several hundred. Many historians have described a spirit of tolerance that generated a productive relationship between diverse peoples and traditions, with Christian, Muslim, and Jewish thinkers working together to share and advance knowledge. An Arab poet called Cordoba the garden of the fruits of ideas. Here intellectuals discussed ancient Greek thought and the latest astronomical discoveries and translated books from and into Arabic. This cosmopolitan intellectual culture passed on to Europe much of the Classical Greco-Roman heritage, Islamic and Indian science and mathematics, and some Chinese technology, such as papermaking. Europe also received

Arab vocal and instrumental music, important in Islamic ceremonies, pleasure, and worship. Arab folk songs and musical instruments, such as the guitar and lute, diffused northward, influencing the courtly love songs of European troubadours and, later, Western popular music.

But some historians doubt that Umayyad Spain was as enlightened, tolerant, and advanced as often assumed since there was curiosity, generosity, and creative spirit but also violence, cruelty, and greed. Whatever the case, the "golden age" came to an end by 1000 as civil wars and factionalism fostered decline, and the Umayyad government fragmented into smaller, often warring states. Intolerant Muslim Berber invaders from Morocco conquered some regions, persecuting non-Muslims and any Muslims not sharing their rigid interpretation of Islam. Many Spaniards, remaining loyal to Catholicism, provided a support base for reconquest efforts, and military force gradually brought northern Spain under Christian control. In 1085 Christian knights conquered Cordoba, the center of Islamic power. Constant Christian military pressure gradually pushed Muslim rule into southern Spain, and by 1252 Christian princes controlled much of Spain and Portugal. Finally, in 1492, Christians took the last Muslim stronghold at Granada (**gruh-NAHD-uh**). At the sultan's formal surrender of the magnificent Alhambra palace in Granada to the Catholic monarchs Ferdinand II of Aragon and Isabel I of Spain, the new rulers were accompanied by the Catholic cardinal of Spain and a retinue of courtiers and noblemen that, by some accounts, included an Italian merchant and sailor, Christopher Columbus. All the Christian royalty and knights wore Moorish dress perhaps in a gesture of respect, but it could also be seen as hostile, a symbol of Christians claiming the Moors' power and possessions. The new Christian rulers, just as militant and intolerant as the Muslim government they replaced, forced Muslims and Jews to either convert to Christianity or face expulsion. Many converted but thousands fled, usually to Muslim countries in North Africa (especially Morocco) or to the Ottoman Empire (especially Anatolia). Capitalizing on the events of 1492 Spain became one of the most powerful European countries in the sixteenth and seventeenth centuries and a pioneer in maritime exploration but also a closed, suspicious society with a sole religion and language, repressing intellectual diversity and eliminating cultural difference.

KEY POINTS

▶ Due to different views of Muhammad's teachings and the rightful succession of caliphs, Islam began to split into two branches, the Sunni majority branch and the Shi'a dissident branch.

▶ The Umayyad dynasty, which succeeded the Rashidun Caliphate, was led by men with no connection to Muhammad who extended the empire into Byzantine lands.

▶ Under the Abbasid Caliphate, which provided the setting for The Arabian Nights, Baghdad became a cosmopolitan hub of trading and culture.

▶ As they expanded, Arabs adopted the imperial ruling structures of the peoples they conquered and were targeted by numerous invaders, including the Mongols.

▶ Muslims ruled Spain and Sicily for several centuries, but Christians gradually reclaimed them and failed to maintain the tolerance of the early Muslim rulers.

10-3 Cultural Hallmarks of Islam: Theology, Society, and Learning

SOCIETIES

Q What were the major concerns of Muslim thinkers and writers?

Islamic expansion launched a thousand-year era, from the seventh to the seventeenth century, that brought many Afro-Eurasian peoples into closer contact with one another. Muslims synthesized elements from varied traditions, including Arab, Greek, Persian, and Indian, producing a durable hybrid culture rooted in theology, social patterns, literature, art, science, and learning. Several distinct strands of thought and behavior combined to produce a distinctive social system and a renowned cultural heritage. Islamic scholars contributed major scientific achievements and historical studies to the world.

10-3a Theology, Sufism, and Religious Practice

Debates over theological questions led to divergent interpretations of the Quran and diverse views about the great questions of life and death, reflecting the mixing of intellectual traditions and cultures. Some Muslim thinkers emphasized reason and free will, while others believed that Allah preordained everything. Some influential thinkers mastered several fields of knowledge. Abu Yusuf al-Kindi (a-BOO YOU-suhf al-KIN-dee) (ca. 800–ca. 870), an Iraqi Arab, praised the search for truth and popularized Greek ideas. Although stressing logic and mathematics, he also published work on science, music, medicine, and psychology. The philosopher and medical scholar Abu Ali al-Husain Ibn Sina (a-BOO AH-lee al-who-SANE IB-unh SEE-nah) (980–1037), known in the West as Avicenna (av-uh-SEN-uh), was a native of Bukhara (boo-CAR-ruh), a Silk Road city in Central Asia, who mostly worked in Persia. He believed that everyone could exercise free will but that the highest goal was communion with God. Ibn Sina's influence on Western Christian and Jewish as well as Muslim philosophy was immense. Indeed, he may have been second only to Aristotle as an inspiration for thirteenth-century European philosophy. Central Asia-born polymath Abu Nasr Muhammad al-Farabi (872–951), who worked mostly in Baghdad, made important contributions to both Aristotelian and Platonic thought, helping to preserve Greek philosophy for our modern age. Influenced by Plato's *The Republic*, al-Farabi published a book, *The Virtuous City*, in which he envisioned a city based on justice that seeks its citizens' happiness, guided by enlightened philosophers. Afghanistan-born Abu Hamid al-Ghazali (AH-boo HAM-id al-guh-ZAL-ee) (1058–1111), a Baghdad teacher, used Aristotelian logic to justify Islamic beliefs and to

Sufism A mystical approach and practice within Islam that emphasized personal spiritual experience.

> ### CONNECTION to TODAY
> What has the world of today inherited from the Intermediate-Era Muslim thinkers in philosophy, science, literature, and the arts?

try to bridge the divisions between rationalists and traditionalists, mystics and the orthodox. This rationalistic approach lost support among Sunnis from the fourteenth century onward.

Among both Sunnis and Shi'ites a mystical approach and practice called **Sufism** (SOO-fiz-uhm) gained many followers. Sufism emphasized personal spiritual experience rather than nitpicking theology, stressing the superiority of the heart over the mind and the search for communion with God. Most were peaceful and many opposed war and violence. Much as the Quran sanctioned mysticism—"Wherever ye turn there is the face of God"[10]—a famous Persian Sufi poet, Baba Kuhi, saw God in everything: "In the market, in the cloister—only God I saw; In the valley and on the mountain—only God I saw. Him I have seen beside me oft in tribulation; in favor and in fortune—only God I saw."[11] Many Sufis exchanged information with Christian, Hindu, and Jewish mystics, willingly synthesized Islam with other ideas, and considered their practices useful even for non-Muslims. Sufis were instrumental in spreading Islam to South Asia, Indonesia, and West Africa, all regions where Sufism remains strong today. But Sufism constituted a supplement rather than a challenge to conventional Islam.

Sufis congregated in orders led by masters who taught prescribed techniques. One of the most famous Sufi orders, Turkey's whirling *dervishes* (DUHR-vish-iz), practiced special exercises and methods, including trance dancing, to achieve a state of divine ecstasy. Several Sufi orders gained renown as being peace-loving and tolerant of different views and customs. As followers credited some Sufi masters with magical powers, their tombs became pilgrimage destinations. Sufis also produced most Islamic poetry. Millions revere the Persian Sufi poet Hafez (hah-FEZ) (1326–1389), who loved both God and the grape: "Here we are with our wine and the ascetics with their piety. Let us see which one the beloved [God] will take."[12] However, Sufism has remained controversial. While tolerating religious flexibility won Sufis converts, many non-Sufis condemned the suspension of Islamic biases against wine, drugs, dancing, and music in worship. In recent decades Islamic militants and fundamentalists, viewing Sufis as sinful heretics, polytheists, and not real Muslims, have attacked, flogged, and even executed Sufis and dynamited their shrines in countries like Pakistan, Iraq, Saudi Arabia, and Syria.

Spreading into diverse cultures, Islam developed several patterns of practice. Adaptationists willingly adjusted to changing conditions, providing the base for reform and modernizing movements. Conservatives, mistrusting innovation, strove to preserve established beliefs and customs, such as the rigid gender division. The most dogmatic conservatives

---

[10]Quoted in Alfred Guillaume, "Islamic Mysticism and the Sufi Sect," in *The Spread of Islam*, ed. Claire Swisher (San Diego, CA: Greenhaven Press, 1999), 153.

[11]"Baba Kuhi of Shiraz," trans. Reynold A. Nicholson. Quoted in Mary Ann Frese Witt et al., *The Humanities: Cultural Roots and Continuities*, vol. 1, 7th ed. (Boston: Houghton Mifflin, 2005), 270.

[12]Quoted in Adam Goodheart, "Pilgrims from the Great Satan," *New York Times*, March 10, 2002, A12.

argued that Muhammad's divine revelations set a permanent, unchangeable authority for judging existing conditions. Finally, some stressed personal aspects of the faith. These diverse patterns all have large followings among both Sunnis and Shi'ites, fostering political and social conflict in Muslim societies.

10-3b Social Life and Gender Relations

As Islamic culture expanded and matured, the social structure became more complex and marked by clear ethnic, tribal, class, occupational, religious, and gender divisions, especially in the Middle East. Arabs generally enjoyed a higher social status than Turks, Berbers, Africans, and others. Those claiming descent from Muhammad and his Hashemite clan held an especially honored status in Islamic societies. Many Arabs were also members of tribes. Because the first Muslims were merchants, Islam attracted people in the commercial sector, who could spiritually sanction their quest for wealth by financing pilgrimages to Mecca and helping the poor through almsgiving. However, Christian and Jewish minorities did not always have the same rights as Muslims. Because they paid higher taxes and as nonbelievers could not own weapons, they were exempt from military duty, and they enjoyed some legal protections. These communities were generally allowed to follow their own laws, customs, and beliefs and maintain their own religious institutions.

Slavery was common. Slaves served as bureaucrats and soldiers, business and factory workers, household servants and concubines, musicians, and plantation laborers. One Abbasid caliph kept eleven thousand slaves in his palace. Islamic law encouraged treating slaves with consideration, and many were eventually freed. Many slaves were war captives and children purchased from poor families or from European states like Byzantium and Venice. For over a dozen centuries, especially after 1200, an Arab-dominated slave trade brought perhaps a total of 10 to 15 million African slaves to the Middle East across the Sahara or up the East African coast. African slave soldiers were common in Egypt, Persia, Iraq, Oman (**oh-MAHN**) in eastern Arabia, Yemen, and South Asia.

Families anchored the social system, arranging marriages to cement social or business ties between two families. Although Shari'a law allowed men up to four wives at a time, this privilege remained largely restricted to the rich and powerful. Many poor men, unable to afford the large bridal gifts expected, never married at all. While divorce was theoretically easy for men, marriage contracts sometimes specified a large gift to the wife upon divorce. Parents expected children to obey and respect them, even after they became adults. Family gatherings, usually segregated by gender, often involved poetry recitations, musical performances, or Quran readings. Islamic law harshly punished homosexuality, but in practice such relationships were not uncommon, with same-sex love often reflected in poetry and literature, especially in Muslim Spain. The accepting attitudes of at least some Arabs, Persians, and Turks toward homosexual romantic relationships often shocked European visitors.

For centuries both Western and Islamic observers have debated women's status and roles in Islamic society and still do

today. Hence, the philosopher Ibn Rushd (**IB-uhn RUSHED**) (1126–1198), known in the West as Averroes (**uh-VER-uh-WEEZ**), attacked restrictions on women as an economic burden, arguing that "the ability of women is not known, because they are merely used for procreation [and] child-rearing."[13] But his views may have had more influence on Western thinkers than in the Muslim world. Although the Quran recognized certain women's rights, prohibited female infanticide, and limited the number of wives men could have to four (but only if they could support them all), it also accorded women less standing in courts of law and only half the inheritance of men. While some Muslims criticized restrictions on women in law and social custom such as modest dress as institutionalizing their social inferiority, other Muslim

Folio from a Jamshid u Khurshid, Iran, Safavid period, c.1600 (opaque watercolour, ink and gold on paper)/Persian School, (17th century)/FREER SACKLER GALLERY/Arthur M. Sackler Gallery, Smithsonian Institution, USA/Bridgeman Images

IMAGE 10.5 **Persian Women at A Picnic** This miniature from sixteenth-century Persia shows women preparing a picnic. The ability of women to venture away from home varied widely depending on social class and regional traditions.

Q What does this painting tell us about Persian social and cultural life?

---

[13]Quoted in Walther, *Women in Islam*, 40.

men and women contended that they liberate women from insecurity and male harassment. Scholars also disagreed over whether customs such as veiling and seclusion were based on Quranic mandates or patriarchal, pre-Islamic Arab, Middle Eastern, and Byzantine customs. Some Muslim communities in the Middle East, and many outside the region, never adopted these practices.

Women played diverse roles. During Abbasid times some elite women, while excluded from public life, enjoyed considerable power behind the scenes. For instance, Khayzuran, noted for her compassion and generosity, rose from a simple Yemenite slave girl to become the great love and wife of the Caliph Mahdi, dominating his harem and investing in land reclamation and charitable works. On his death, she helped smooth the transition to the rulership of her son, Harun al-Rashid. Some exceptional women circumvented restrictions. Umm Hani (also known as Mariam) in fifteenth-century Cairo studied law and religion with famous teachers, wrote poetry, owned a large textile workshop, and became a renowned teacher and scholar of the Hadith. She also had seven children by two husbands and made thirteen pilgrimages to Mecca. In the lower classes, while formal education for girls remained limited, women monopolized occupations such as spinning and weaving and worked in the fields or some domestic industries beside men. And among some Muslims, particularly sub-Saharan Africans and Southeast Asians, women often enjoyed relative independence, dressing as they liked, socializing outside the home, and earning money. Turks and Mongols were more liberal on gender issues than Arabs and Persians. Hence, gender relations varied considerably.

10-3c Pen and Brush: Writing and the Visual Arts

Although Islamic societies became identified with literacy and literature, the Arabic alphabet originated in southern Arabia long before Muhammad's time. Islam enhanced the script by emphasizing literacy, the Quran stating: "Read, and thy Lord is most generous, Who taught with the pen, Taught man what he knew not."[14] Muslims adopted the Arab poetic tradition but modified romantic ideas into praise not for a lover but for the Prophet and Allah. Thanks to the spread of literacy, an enormous number of books were published in the first three centuries of Islam.

One of the greatest Abbasid writers was the Persian astronomer and mathematician Omar Khayyam (OH-MAHR key-YAHM). In his famous poem *Rubaiyat* (ROO-bee-AHT), he noted life's fleeting nature: "One thing is certain, that Life flies; and the rest is Lies; the flower that once has blown forever dies." This led him to regret never knowing the purpose of existence:

Ah, make the most of what ye yet may spend, Before we too into the Dust descend; Dust unto Dust, and under Dust to lie, [without] Wine, Song, Singer, and End! Into this Universe, and Why not knowing, Nor Whence, like Water willy-nilly flowing; And out of it, as Wind along the Waste, I know not Whither, willy-nilly blowing.[15]

The most famous Sufi poet, the thirteenth-century Afghanistan-born Persian Jalal al-Din Rumi (ja-LAL al-DIN ROO-mee), blended liberal Sufi spirituality with humor in writings about love, desire, and the human condition. Often dancing while reciting his poems, Rumi was optimistic, joyful, and ecumenical, stating: "I am neither Christian, nor Jew, nor Zoroastrian, nor Muslim."[16] Promoting tolerance, Rumi argued that all religions pursued oneness with God. While flirting with heretical boundaries, irking local sultans and dour jurists, he also remained a devout Muslim. Every year Rumi celebration festivals are held in Konya, the cosmopolitan Turkish city and Sufi center where he lived. Over seven hundred years after his death, after his poems were translated into English (perhaps underplaying the Islamic elements), Rumi became a best-selling poet in the United States, attracting fans from many walks of life from pop stars to yoga masters.

The study of history and social sciences, especially geography, owes much to Muslim writing. With the expansion of Islam and Arab traders around Afro-Eurasia, some Muslims traveled to distant lands, and educated Muslims enjoyed reading these travelers' accounts of other countries. Modern historians are indebted to travelers such as the Moroccan jurist Ibn Battuta (IB-uhn ba-TOO-tuh) for knowledge about sub-Saharan Africa, South Asia, and Southeast Asia from the ninth to the fifteenth centuries (see Meet the People: Ibn Battuta, a Muslim Traveler). Geographers and cartographers such as Al-Idrisi (al-AH-dree-see) from Muslim Spain also produced atlases, globes, and maps.

The well-traveled North African Ibn Khaldun (1332–1406) was the first known scholar anywhere to ponder patterns and structure in history, creating theoretical models to explain the world and find universal elements. His monumental work, *Muqaddimah* ("Introduction"), connected the rise of states with a growing solidarity between leaders and their followers. His recognition of the role of "group feeling" (what today we call ethnic identity) and religion was pathbreaking. In studying other cultures, he advocated "critical examination" and in the process made the case for including the social sciences and humanities in education:

Know the rules of statecraft, the nature of existing things, and the difference between nations, regions and tribes in regard to way of life, qualities of character, customs, sects, schools of thought, and so on. [The historian] must distinguish the similarities and differences between the present and the past.[17]

While a remarkable intellectual of diverse interests and many talents—among others, politician, historian, jurist, theologian, and psychologist—Ibn Khaldun was also a man of his time, a devout Muslim and Sufi mystic, who believed in the supernatural and preferred nomads to city-dwellers. Hence he was able to put the Arab expansion into the broader flow of regional history while also explaining how people in the Muslim world of his day saw things.

[14]Quoted in Mervyn Hiskett, "Islamic Literature and Art," in *The Spread of Islam*, 120.
[15]Excerpted in John Yohannan, ed., *A Treasury of Asian Literature* (New York: New American Library, 1965), 261-262.
[16]Quoted in Jonathan P. Berkey, *The Formation of Islam: Religion and Society in the Near East, 600–1800* (New York: Cambridge University Press, 2003), 233.
[17]Quoted in Hourani, *A History of Arab Peoples* (Cambridge, MA: Belknap Press, 1991), 201.

Visual arts flourished. Since Arabic is written in a flowing style, **calligraphy** (kuh-LIG-ruh-fee), the artful writing of words, became an admired art form offering both a message and decoration. Some Muslims condemned artistic representations of natural beings, including humans, as forbidden since they might constitute idolatry (idol worship), and hence they are absent from many Islamic societies. But Islamic Persia, India, and Central Asia fostered painting, especially landscapes but also sometimes people. Muslims also produced world-class architecture, including lavishly decorated buildings such as India's Taj Mahal. Some architecture, such as mosques with domes and towers, reflected Byzantine church influence. Then as now, Muslims produced carpets and fabrics valued in many non-Muslim societies.

10-3d Science, Technology, and Learning

While many creative thinkers emerged, Muslims also borrowed, assimilated, and diffused Greek and South Asian knowledge and were familiar with some Chinese technologies. Hence, certain Classical and Hellenistic Greek traditions of philosophy and science nearly forgotten in Europe survived in the Middle East. Muslim thinkers synthesized learning from other societies with their own insights, fostering advances in science and medicine. For example, Nestorian Christians taught Greek sciences under Abbasid sponsorship. Abbasid caliphs opened the House of Wisdom in Baghdad, a research institute with schools, observatories, and a huge library, staffed by scholars who translated Greek, Syrian, Sanskrit, and Persian books on philosophy, medicine, astronomy, and mathematics into Arabic. Aristotle's writings were particularly influential. In the tenth and eleventh centuries the Shi'ite Fatimids built the House of Knowledge in Cairo with a massive library holding two million books, many on scientific subjects. Other scientific centers arose, from Spain and Morocco to Samarkand in Central Asia. Muslims also opened some of the earliest universities in Europe, first in Salerno in Muslim-ruled Sicily in 841, then in the Moorish Spain cities of Toledo, Seville, and Granada. Many students came from Christian Europe to study and graduate in these schools. The academic robes worn by university graduates in most Western countries today are based on the Arab/Muslim robes of the universities in Moorish Spain.

Arab and Persian scholars actively assimilated the imported knowledge. As the influential eleventh-century Uzbekistan-born scientist, traveler, and acute observer of other cultures and the world Al-Biruni (al-bih-ROO-nee) wrote: "The sciences were transmitted into the Arabic language from different parts of the world; by it [the sciences] were embellished and penetrated the hearts of men, while the beauties of [Arabic] flowed in their veins and arteries."[18] Al-Biruni published at least one hundred and forty-six known studies in the fields of philosophy, mathematics, astronomy, history, and ethnography (especially a pioneering study of India's history, science, religion, literature, and customs). The diversity of ideas produced an open-minded search for truth apparent in Ibn Khaldun, Ibn Sina, al-Kindi, and Ibn Rushd. For instance, the philosopher al-Kindi wrote that Muslims should acknowledge truth from whatever source it came because

nothing was more important than truth itself. Ibn Rushd (Averroes), who lived in Cordoba, influenced Christian thinkers by his writings on Aristotle and by asserting the role of reason. The Persian Shi'ite Nasir al-Din Tusi (1201–1274), an astronomer, architect, biologist, mathematician, physician, and philosopher, put forward a basic theory of evolution of species six hundred years before the British scientist Charles Darwin came up with his theories. He also translated the works of Euclid, Archimedes, Ptolemy, and other Classical Greek scientists. In the eleventh century, Christian Europe became aware of the Muslim synthesis of Greek, Indian, and Persian knowledge from libraries in Spain. But religious conservatives increasingly criticized philosophy as anti-God; Averroes was banished from Cordoba in 1195 for his views.

Muslims also advanced medicine. Although influenced by Greek ideas, medical specialists did not accept ancient wisdom uncritically, instead developing an empirical tradition. Baghdad hospitals were the world's most advanced. Muslim surgeons, using opium for anesthesia, extracted teeth and replaced them with false teeth made from animal bones. They also removed kidney stones and did colostomies. Islamic medical books translated into Latin in the twelfth century became Europe's major medical texts for the next five centuries. Two medical scientists, Abu Bakr al-Razi (a-boo BAH-car al-RAH-zee) (ca. 865–ca. 932) and Ibn Sina (Avicenna), compared Greek ideas with their own research. Al-Razi, a Persian, directed several hospitals and wrote more than fifty clinical studies as well as general medical works including the *Comprehensive Book*, an eighteen-volume medical encyclopedia used in Europe into the 1400s. Al-Razi also studied what we would today call sociological and psychological aspects of medicine; a century later Ibn Sina stressed psychosomatic medicine, treated depression, and pioneered the study of vision and eye disease, performing complicated eye operations. His medical encyclopedia provided about half of the medical curriculum in medieval European universities. Muslims also pioneered many of the apparatus, techniques, and language of chemistry later adopted in the West.

Arab and Indian mathematics made possible the later Scientific Revolution in Europe. In Baghdad the Persian Zoroastrian al-Khwarizmi (al-KWAHR-uhz-mee) (ca. 780–ca. 850) developed the mathematical procedures he called algebra, building on Greek and Indian foundations. Omar Khayyam, the Persian poet at Baghdad's House of Wisdom, and Nasir al-Din Tusi helped develop trigonometry. From Indian math books Muslims adopted a revolutionary system of numbers, today known as Arabic numerals because Europe acquired them from Muslim Spain. They were not only more convenient but also used a dot (eventually a zero) to indicate an empty column. Advances in mathematics and physics made possible improvements in water clocks, water wheels, and other irrigation apparatuses that spread well beyond the Islamic world.

Muslim astronomers combined Greek, Persian, and Indian knowledge of the stars and planets with their own observations. Applying mathematics to optics, they constructed a primitive telescope. One astronomer reportedly built an elaborate

calligraphy The artful writing of words.

[18]Quoted in Bernard Lewis, *The Arabs in History* (New York: Harper and Row, 1960), 131.

Ibn Battuta, a Muslim Traveler

Among Islamic travelers who journeyed to, and often sojourned in, distant lands, the most famous, Abdallah Muhammad Ibn Battuta, a gregarious and pious fourteenth-century Moroccan, spent thirty years tramping around the length and breadth of the Islamic world, as far east as Southeast Asia and, though some historians doubt his claim, coastal China. The Moroccan attributed his wanderlust to a dream in which a large bird took him on its wing and made a long flight toward the East, leaving him there. He was a pilgrim, judge, scholar, Sufi, ambassador, and connoisseur of fine foods and elegant architecture. Ibn Battuta's writings about his remarkable journeys, the autobiographical *Rihla* (Book of Travels), provide detailed, often unique eyewitness accounts of many societies. A collaborator compiled the *Rihla* in a literary form near the end of the adventurer's life.

Born in Tangier, Morocco, to a Berber family of scholars and trained in Islamic law, at twenty-one Ibn Battuta left home in 1325 to seek adventure and learning. His wanderlust proved difficult to quench. Expected to stay close to home and family, no woman, Muslim or otherwise, in that era could have defied gender stereotyping and social pressure to undertake such extensive travel. Traveling by camel, horse, wagon, ship, or on foot, Ibn Battuta covered between 60,000 and 75,000 miles, visiting dozens of countries, often putting himself in extreme danger. For example, he once barely escaped with his life when robbed in India by Hindu rebels who took everything but his pants. He never had a conventional family life and married several times for short periods, leaving children all over the hemisphere. The politically ambitious jurist often sojourned in a society for months or years, his longest career stint being seven years' service in the Delhi Sultanate of northern India. Wherever he went, Ibn Battuta made observations on many subjects, from cuisine and botany to political practice and Sufi mystics. For example, he reported on the "continuous series of bazaars [along the Nile] from Alexandria to Cairo. Cities and villages succeed one another without interruption." And, coming from a more patriarchal North African society, Ibn Battuta marveled at the "respect shown to women by the [Central Asian] Turks, for they hold a more dignified position than the men. Turkish women do not veil themselves."

Although he was a repeated visitor to Mecca and the Islamic heartland, Ibn Battuta's experiences in Islam's frontier regions, such as India and the Maldive Islands, Southeast Asia, the East African coast as far south as Tanzania, the western Sudan, Turkish Central Asia, Anatolia, Azerbaijan, and Mongol-ruled southern Russia, provide the most useful information, revealing an expanding, vigorous Islamic realm encountering diverse structures, peoples, and practices. For example, we learn about the sexual customs of the Maldive Islands, where he married a sultan's widow, and the Arab religious scholars, Persian merchants, and Chinese painters who gathered at Delhi "like moths around a candle."

Whereas the Christian Marco Polo a century earlier was always a stranger in his Asian travels, in most places Ibn Battuta encountered people who shared his worldview and social values. From Morocco to Central Asia and around the Indian Ocean Rim, people worshipped in mosques and used some version of Shari'a law. Ibn Battuta enjoyed the company of merchants, scholars, Sufis, and princes, conversing with them in Arabic on many topics, including developments in faraway lands. He even sometimes encountered somebody from his hometown. His knowledge of Islamic law and Arabic allowed him to work as a judge and legal scholar from Morocco to India. But, while cosmopolitan and open-minded by the era's standards, Ibn Battuta was uncomfortable in mostly non-Islamic societies such as China and Byzantium, and in frontier cultures where local custom greatly modified Islamic orthodoxy, such as Mali in West Africa. The traveler finally returned home to Tangier, where he died around 1368.

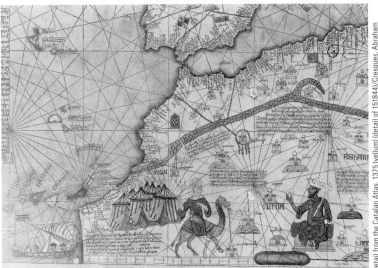

IMAGE 10.6 **The Journey to Mali** No known paintings of Ibn Battuta exist. However, this map of Africa and the Mediterranean world, made by a Jewish cartographer in Spain in 1375, features a drawing of a camel-riding Muslim traveler that some historians think represents the journey of the Moroccan to Mali.

Q What does the map tell us about West and North African geography, people, and life?

Reflection Questions

1. Why was Ibn Battuta one of the great travelers of the Intermediate Era?
2. What do his travels tell us about the values and reach of Islamic religion and culture?
3. What do Ibn Battuta's travels tell us about how different world travel was in his era from what it is today?

Notes: Quotations from Ross Dunn, *The Adventures of Ibn Battuta: A Muslim Traveller of the 14th Century* (Berkeley: University of California Press, 1986), 45, 183; Nikki R. Keddie, "Women in the Middle East Since the Rise of Islam," in *Women's History in Global Perspective*, ed. Bonnie G. Smith, vol. 3 (Urbana: University of Illinois Press, 2005), 81.

planetarium that reproduced the movement of the stars, and a remarkable observatory built at Samarkand in Central Asia in 1420 produced charts for hundreds of stars. Some astronomers noted the eccentric behavior of the planet Venus, challenging the widespread notion of an Earth-centered universe. Indeed, many Muslim astronomers accepted a round Earth. Calculating the size of Earth, Al-Biruni even postulated large unknown landmasses west of Eurasia. An unknown but well-informed scholar in eleventh-century Cairo produced an extraordinary illustrated book that guided the reader on a journey from the outermost cosmos and planets to Earth and its lands, islands, features, and inhabitants, a masterpiece of interdisciplinary learning that was only rediscovered in 2000.

Between the eighth and thirteenth centuries, Islamic societies also made agricultural innovations, expanding production in a "green revolution." Improved diets and health spurred dramatic population growth. When Arab conquests opened the door to India, the Middle Eastern peoples obtained South Asian crops such as cotton, hard wheat, rice, and sugar cane; fruits such as the coconut palm, banana, sour orange, lemon,

lime, mango, and watermelon; and vegetables such as spinach, artichokes, and eggplant. These imports from wetter lands encouraged better irrigation, including the use of enormous water wheels to supply water. The spread of agricultural products was one of the Islamic peoples' major contributions to world history. Most of these crops filtered westward to Spain, where they thrived, and cotton became a major crop in West Africa. While many crops reached Christian Europe from Spain and Sicily, they were adopted only slowly, since Europe at that time had a lower population density and limited irrigation technology. Just as tea drinkers today can thank the ancient Chinese for domesticating their favorite beverage, coffee lovers owe their morning cup to the Yemenite Arabs and Ethiopians who first cultivated it as a crop, and the Muslim merchants who between the thirteenth and seventeenth centuries spread it around the Middle East, where it became a passion of Sufi mystics, and then on to Europe and Africa. Coffee houses became a popular feature of cities in many Muslim and non-Muslim lands, but were also often condemned by religious authorities as sinful and seditious.

KEY POINTS

▶ Sufism, a mystical approach to Islam that emphasized flexibility and a personal connection with God, drew both Sunni and Shi'ite followers.

▶ Although the Quran and most Muslim societies restricted women, some Muslim societies did not, and both Muslims and non-Muslims have debated the origins and benefits of such practices as wearing a veil.

▶ Literature, especially poetry, was very important in Islamic culture, as was calligraphy, the artful writing of words.

▶ Islamic science and medicine were very advanced and pioneered such practices as anesthesia and the replacement of false teeth; Islamic mathematicians were instrumental in propelling the Scientific Revolution.

10-4 Globalized Islam and Middle Eastern Political Change

⇄ TRANSITIONS

Ⓠ Why do historians speak of Islam as a hemispheric culture?

Between the eighth and seventeenth centuries, Islam, the product of a once parochial Arab culture, expanded out of its Arabian heartland to become the dominant religion across a broad expanse of Africa and Eurasia, with Muslim minorities emerging in places as far afield as China and the Balkans. This expansion created **Dar al-Islam** (the "Abode of Islam"), the Islamic world stretching from Morocco to Indonesia and the Philippines, joined by both a common faith and trade. Islam-fostered networks reached from the Atlantic eastward to the Pacific, spreading Arab words, names, social attitudes, cultural values, and the Arabic script to diverse peoples. Eventually several powerful military states emerged that ruled over large populations of Muslims and non-Muslims. The Islamic world also faced severe challenges—expanding Turks, Christian crusaders, Mongol conquerors, and horrific pandemics—setting the stage for new political forces in the fifteenth and sixteenth centuries. Yet, the Islamic tradition was resistant, overcoming factionalism and political decay to remain creative well past the 1400s.

CONNECTION to TODAY

How does the Muslim world today reflect the globalization of Islamic society and culture and the rise of new powerful states in the Intermediate Era?

10-4a The Global Shape of Dar al-Islam

More than half of the world's nearly two billion Muslims today live outside the Middle East, the majority in South and Southeast Asia, with Arabs significantly outnumbered by non-Arab believers. After the Abbasid Caliphate's demise, Arab political power diminished, but Islam grew rapidly in both Africa and South Asia (see Chapters 12–13). Dozens of prosperous Muslim trading cities, from Tangier in Northwest Africa to Samarkand in Central Asia to Melaka in Malaya, offered goods from distant countries. Beginning in the thirteenth century, Muslims constructed a hemisphere-spanning system based on economic exchange and a shared understanding of the world and the cosmos, linked by informal networks of

Dar al-Islam ("Abode of Islam") The Islamic world stretching from Morocco to Indonesia and joined by both a common faith and trade.

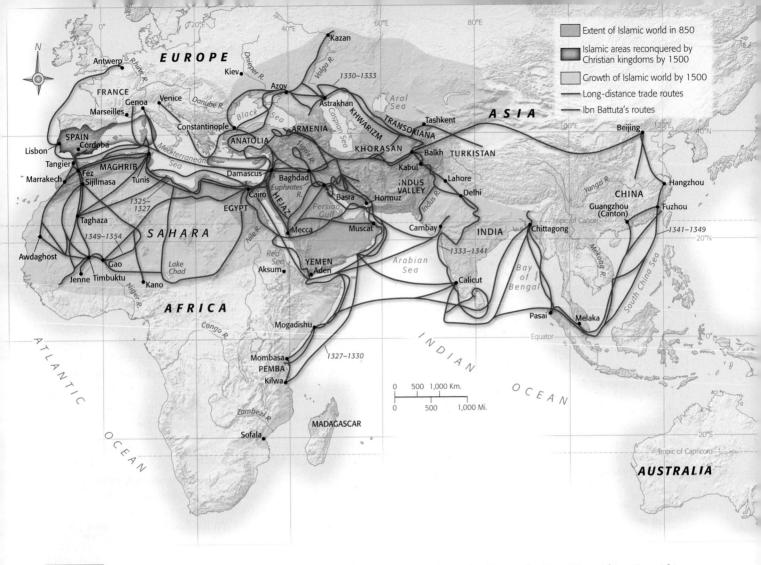

MAP 10.3 Dar Al-Islam and Trade Routes, CA. 1500 CE By 1500 the Islamic world stretched into West Africa, East Africa, and Southeast Asia. Trade routes connected the Islamic lands and allowed Muslim traders to extend their networks to China, Russia, and Europe.

Q What does this map tell us about the role and importance of trade connections in connecting Dar al-Islam?

Islamic scholars and saints. The Quran and its message of a righteous social order provided a framework for Dar al-Islam.

Islam's spread corresponded with growing Muslim-dominated long-distance trade, especially the maritime trade around the Indian Ocean Basin. Except for the Chinese, Arabs enjoyed the world's most advanced shipbuilding and navigation between 1000 and 1450. The lateen sails that Arabs devised, or perhaps adapted from Southeast Asians, later allowed European ships to undertake long-distance voyages in the 1400s. An increasingly integrated Muslim-dominated maritime trading system gradually linked the eastern Mediterranean, Middle East, East African coast, Persia, and South Asia with East and Southeast Asia (see Map 10.3). Expressing the hemispheric reach of the system, one thirteenth-century Arab merchant from the Persian Gulf with a keen knowledge of the commodity market from China to Greece stated his commercial ambitions: "I want to send Persian saffron to China, where I hear that it fetches a high price, and then ship Chinese porcelain to Greece,

Greek brocade to India, Indian iron to Aleppo [a Syrian city], Aleppo glass to the Yemen and Yemeni material to Persia."[19]

The Straits of Melaka in Southeast Asia and Hormuz (HAWR-muhz) at the Persian Gulf entrance stood at the heart of the key mercantile system of the Intermediate world. Over these sea routes, sometimes known as the Maritime Silk Road, Indonesian and East African spices, Malayan gold and tin, Indian textiles, southern African gold, and Chinese silks, porcelain, and tea traveled to distant markets. Arab and Persian merchant communities could be found as far east as Korea and China. By intermarrying with local women and practicing their faith, Muslim merchants converted others to Islam. The maritime network was already flourishing by the tenth century and was expanded by the Mongol control of East Asia in the thirteenth and fourteenth centuries and their invitation to Muslim and other traders to come to China. The maritime trade achieved its height after the Mongol era, in the fifteenth and sixteenth centuries, when Muslim economic and cultural power remained strong.

[19]Hariri, quoted in Fernand Braudel, *A History of Civilizations* (New York: Penguin, 1995), 71.

10-4b Turks and Crusaders

Between the eleventh and fifteenth centuries, a series of interventions by Turks and crusaders affected world history by reshaping Middle Eastern politics. Some historians emphasize the thrust by various Turkic peoples as a significant development that changed world history and ultimately reshaped western Asia, southeastern Europe, and North Africa. The Turks were originally pastoral nomads from Central Asia divided by tribe and dialect. For centuries these skilled horsemen intruded into Chinese, Indian, and western Asian societies, some adopting Nestorian Christianity, Judaism, or Buddhism. As they gradually drew closer to Middle Eastern cultures, most eventually embraced Islam. Some Turks sent boys to the Abbasids, where they trained to become Abbasid soldiers or administrators.

Late in the tenth century, Muslim Turks called the Seljuks (**SEL-jooks**) achieved regional power. Recruiting other Turkish tribes, they expanded from Central Asia and swept through Afghanistan and Iran into Iraq. Allied with the declining Abbasids, Seljuk forces conquered many Muslim and Christian societies in the Caucasus region, eventually creating a large empire stretching from Palestine to Samarkand. In 1071 the Seljuks seized much of Anatolia, populated largely by Greek-speaking Orthodox Christians, from the weakening Byzantine state. Even when the Seljuks' power soon diminished elsewhere and their empire crumbled, they continued to govern Anatolia.

By the eleventh century some Islamic states faced increasing challenges from European Christians. Between 1095 and 1272 Christians from various European societies launched a long series of Crusades to win back what they viewed as the Christian Holy Land from Muslim occupation (see Chapter 14). But the conflict was more complicated than a simple Muslim–Christian military confrontation. The First Crusade capitalized on Muslim weakness: feuding Muslim states could not cooperate; some states, such as Fatimid Egypt, maintained lucrative trade ties with Europe. Some historians view the Crusades as in part a conflict between the Fatimids and the Abbasid caliphate, generating shifting alliances. Some Middle Eastern societies also had substantial Christian and Jewish populations and many dissident Muslims. In some cases Muslim and Christian soldiers died next to one another fighting a common foe, as in Moorish Spain, or in the service of a European or Muslim ruler, such as the Ottoman Turkish sultan. In the thirteenth century the Holy Roman Emperor deployed thousands of Arab archers and warriors in his wars with Italian rivals, including the Pope's army. In the end, the Crusades failed to achieve the European Christian leaders' long-term goals.

The First Crusade (1095–1099) was triggered by Seljuk Turk encroachment on Byzantine territory and a Christian church division into rival branches in 1054. Roman popes, worried about Seljuk expansion and anxious to reassert primacy over the breakaway, Constantinople-based Greek Orthodox Church, promoted the idea of positive violence to defend the faith. Using untrue or exaggerated stories of Muslim atrocities against Christians in Palestine, Pope Urban II called on Christians to reclaim the Holy Land and protect Jerusalem's churches and relics. Some 100,000 European volunteers, some pious, others just hungry for booty,

responded. The crusaders fought their way to Jerusalem in 1099, taking the city and killing thousands of Muslims, Jews, and even local Christians. Some crusaders stayed on to guard the sites but also to colonize the surrounding territory, establishing four small Crusader states in what are today Israel and Lebanon. As Muslim forces regrouped, another pope dispatched the Second Crusade (1147–1149), during which the crusaders mostly slaughtered Jews in Europe and pillaged the Byzantine Empire.

Crusaders often fought each other, undermining their own power and the credibility of their religious message and goals. The Third Crusade (1189–1192) was launched when Muslims pushed back Christian forces. However, this attack was met by General Salah al-Din, or Saladin (**SAL-uh-din**) (1138–1193), an Iraqi-born Kurd who deposed Egypt's Fatimid rulers and became sultan, replacing Shi'ite with Sunni rule. Saladin led Muslim armies that stopped a crusader invasion of Egypt and then, between 1187 and 1192, captured Jerusalem and extended his power into Syria. One of his soldiers, a Syrian, praised Saladin as "The unifier of the faith, the vanquisher of the [Christians], the raiser of the banner of justice and benevolence."[20] A tolerant leader and Sufi, he spared the Christians who surrendered in Jerusalem and employed the great Cordoba-born Jewish sage and legal authority Moses Maimonides (**my-MAHN-uh-deez**) (1135–1204) as his physician. His military exploits made Saladin a hero in Muslim eyes, and he is still revered today. The final six Crusades failed to wrest control of North Africa, Jerusalem, and Anatolia from Muslim hands.

Historians still vigorously debate the Crusades. Many crusaders were undoubtedly inspired by sincere religious zeal to preserve access to Christian holy sites, but many also looted captured cities, including Orthodox Christian–dominated and ruled Constantinople. Muslim armies often showed little mercy on their enemies. Some believe that the militant Christian challenge to Islam ultimately made both religions less tolerant and more zealous, complicating relations. For centuries afterward some Muslim rulers viewed their Christian subjects as untrustworthy, while Christians persecuted the remaining Muslim populations in southern Europe. Even today, hundreds of years later, Islamic militants capitalize on lingering resentment against what they view as Western "crusaders" seeking to defeat Islam, while many in the West see Islam on the rise and a threat to Western societies. For some people today the conflicts that brought military confrontations a millennium ago never really ended or are perhaps being revived.

10-4c Mongol Conquests and the Black Death

The Mongols (**MAHN-guhlz**), Central Asian pastoral nomads, constituted a much greater short-term threat to Islam than Christian crusaders sweeping into western Asia. Led by Genghis Khan (**GENG-iz KAHN**) (ca. 1162–1227), the Mongols, prompted perhaps by environmental stress and overpopulation, began expanding out of Mongolia in the late twelfth century.

---

[20]From *An Arab-Syrian Gentleman and Warrior in the Period of the Crusades: Memoirs of Usamah Ibn-Munqidh*, translated by Philip K. Hitti (Princeton: Princeton University Press, 1987), 195.

Between 1218 and 1221 they fought their way through lands inhabited mostly by Turkic-speaking Muslims, destroying several great Silk Road cities. The Mongol attack destroyed states, created instability, and unwittingly laid the foundation for a hemisphere-wide pandemic causing much devastation and death.

Mongol atrocities became legendary, although perhaps, some historians suggest, at times exaggerated by both sides. For example, to paralyze Muslim societies with fear and to prevent opposition, the Mongols killed 700,000 mostly unarmed residents in the Persian city of Merv. Fear usually worked to quell resistance. An Arab chronicler wrote of Mongol invaders that "in the countries that have not yet been overrun by them, everyone spends the night afraid that they may appear there too."[21] After Genghis Khan's death in 1227, the Mongols turned to conquering China, Russia, and eastern Europe but also put pressure on the Caucasus and Anatolia. In 1243 they defeated the remnants of the Seljuk Turks.

In 1256 a grandson of Genghis Khan, Hulegu (hoo-LAY-goo) (1217–1275), led new attacks with more lasting consequences for the Middle East. In Iraq in 1258, Hulegu's army, faced with fierce resistance, pillaged Baghdad, burning schools, libraries, mosques, and palaces, killing perhaps a million people, and executing all the Abbasids, a fateful turning point for Arab society that ended the prosperity and intellectual glory once represented by the now-gutted city. Hulegu's forces pushed on west, occupying Damascus and destroying the great trading city of Aleppo (uh-LEP-oh). In the past few years Aleppo was again destroyed during the fighting of the Syrian civil war. The pastoralist Mongols also disrupted agriculture, returning some farms to pasture and dispersing the peasants. In some places farming never recovered.

But the Islamic tradition proved resilient. When Hulegu's armies invaded Egypt in 1260, they were defeated at the battle of Ayn Jalut by the Mamluks (MAM-looks), ex-slave soldiers of Turkish origin who had taken power there. Hulegu's Mongols stayed in Iraq and Persia, calling themselves the Il-Khanid (il-KHAN-id) dynasty, assimilating Persian culture, and eventually adopting Islam. Descendants of Mongol invaders in Russia, known as Tartars, also became Muslim. The Il-Khanids practiced religious toleration and encouraged monumental architecture, learning, and literary renaissance and scholars wrote pathbreaking world histories telling us much about the Mongol empire.

By building a large empire across Eurasia, the Mongols fostered overland trade and travel, but they also provided a path for deadly diseases to spread. Like Europe and China, the Islamic world was deeply affected by the terrible fourteenth-century pandemic known in the West as the Black Death, a catastrophic disease, probably bubonic plague, that killed quickly and spread rapidly. Initially carried into the Black Sea region from eastern Asia by fleas infesting rats that stowed away on Silk Road caravans or trading ships, the pandemic hit the Middle East repeatedly over a century, reducing Egypt and Syria's population by two-thirds. Ibn Khaldun wrote that "cities and towns were laid waste, roads and way signs were obliterated, settlements and mansions became empty. The entire inhabited world changed."[22] Ibn Khaldun felt he might be living at history's end. But by the 1400s the Middle East had stabilized and regained some economic and cultural dynamism.

10-4d The Rise of Muslim Military States

In the thirteenth and fourteenth centuries, several powerful Muslim military states arose, including the Mamluks in Egypt, the Timurids in Central Asia, and the Ottoman Turks in Anatolia. Gunpowder, a Chinese invention that moved along the Silk Road during Mongol times, forever changed warfare and also impacted politics. After 1350 firearm possession gave some states and groups advantages over rivals and led to stronger, more bureaucratic states.

The Mamluks ruled Egypt and Syria from 1250 to 1517, making Egypt the richest Middle Eastern state. After expanding into Arabia and capturing Mecca and Medina, they controlled and taxed the flow of Muslim pilgrims. They also enjoyed an active trade with Genoa and Venice, the major Italian trading cities that supplied Asian goods to Europe. Venetian merchants established trading posts around Mamluk lands, exchanging timber, metals, and gold for spices, dyes, and Indian textiles. Eventually, however, Mamluk corruption and increasing taxes prompted seafaring European merchants to seek a maritime route to the East, the fabled lands of China, Japan, Southeast Asia, and India that produced so many desirable commodities. In 1516–1517 another Turkish group, the Ottomans, defeated the Mamluks and absorbed their lands into the growing Ottoman Empire (see Map 10.4).

In Central Asia, Tamerlane (TAM-uhr-lane) (1336–1405), a ruthless Muslim prince of Turkish and Mongol ancestry who was crippled by an arrow wound as a young man but hoped to emulate Genghis Khan, made the Timurid state the dominant power for over a century. From his capital, Samarkand, Tamerlane's army rampaged through the Caucasus, southern Russia, Persia, Iraq, and Syria, killing thousands and destroying cities and farms. He then wreaked havoc in northern India (see Chapter 13). Only Tamerlane's death in 1405 halted his forces from invading China and Ottoman Turkey. Although Tamerlane protected merchants and Sufi mystics, his heritage largely consisted of smoking ruins and pyramids of human heads. However, his successors built mosques and patronized scholars, and later his grandson established a great empire in India in the early 1500s.

The Ottoman (AHT-uh-muhn) Turks established the most powerful and enduring military state. The Ottomans originated as a small Anatolian kingdom led by a chief named Osman (ohs-MAHN) (Ottoman means "followers of Osman"). Osman was influenced by Sufis dedicated to destroying Byzantium, which was reeling from temporary crusader occupation of Constantinople and weakening influence in Anatolia. Capitalizing on this vacuum, by 1300 the Ottomans had raided and then annexed remaining Byzantine strongholds in Anatolia. Using gunpowder weapons, they ultimately conquered much of the Byzantine Empire, creating a dynamic state in western Eurasia and a link between Middle Eastern Islam and European Christianity. Once great Byzantium increasingly became a shell surrounding Constantinople.

Soon the Ottomans moved into the Balkans, where they defeated Serbia, the strongest Christian power in southeastern Europe. The Ottomans favored Muslims in taxes, and many Albanian and Serb-speaking Christians adopted Islam, some for economic reasons, creating a division in the Balkans between Catholic, Orthodox, and Muslim peoples that complicates politics

[21]Ibn Al Athir, quoted in Mike Edwards, "Genghis Khan," *National Geographic* (December 1996): 9.
[22]Quoted in Francis Robinson, *The Cambridge Illustrated History of the Islamic World* (Cambridge. UK: Cambridge University Press, 1996), 198.

even today in the nations of the former Yugoslavia. At the Battle of Nicopolis (**nuh-KAHP-uh-luhs**) in 1396, the Ottomans defeated a Hungarian-led force drawn from throughout Europe to oppose Ottoman expansion. In 1453 Sultan Mehmed (**MEH-met**) the Conqueror (1432–1481) finally took Constantinople and converted the city into the Ottoman capital, which was eventually renamed Istanbul. Turkish historians today vigorously debate Mehmed. Some see him as the embodiment of Muslim piety whereas others describe him as a thoroughly secular ruler who knew Greek and Latin and was interested in European culture.

The Ottoman Empire was now the major regional power and Istanbul a major trade hub, attracting a multiethnic, multireligious population. Patronizing the arts, Mehmed the Conqueror invited famous Italian artists and architects to work in his cosmopolitan capital, by 1500 Europe's largest city. Ottoman sultans used subject peoples' administrative and military skills and promoted talented men regardless of background. Moreover, through the **millet** ("nationality") system, leaders of religious and ethnic minorities were allowed to administer their own communities. Hence, the Greek patriarch had authority over all Orthodox Christians in Ottoman territory, while Christians and Jews generally practiced their religions freely. The millet system allowed Turks to divide and hence rule diverse peoples.

A dynamic and militarily powerful Ottoman state continued to expand, by 1500 solidifying control over Greece and the Balkans (see Map 10.4). In the 1500s, Ottoman rule extended over much of western Asia as far east as Persia and North Africa from Egypt to Algeria. In the 1500s the Ottomans also played an ambitious naval role in the Indian Ocean for several

millet The nationality system through which the Ottomans allowed the leaders of religious and ethnic minorities to administer their own communities.

MAP 10.4 **The Ottoman Empire, 1566** Between 1300 and the mid-1500s the Ottoman Turks expanded out of western Anatolia to conquer a large empire in western Asia, Egypt and North Africa, and eastern Europe, making the Ottomans one of the world's largest states.

Q What areas controlled by the Ottoman Empire are still majority Muslim today?

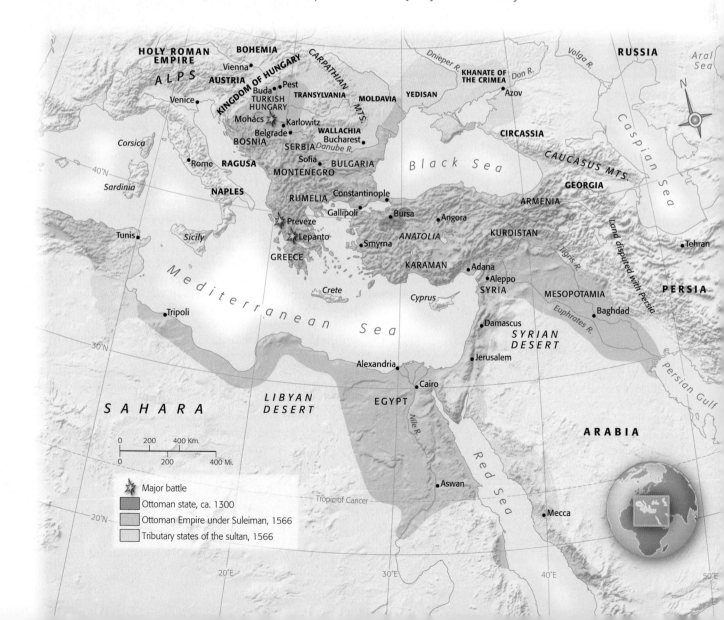

IMAGE 10.7 **Venetian Ambassadors Visiting Mamluk Damascus** Venetians and Genoese merchants, fierce rivals, regularly visited the Middle East to acquire silks, spices, and other valuable products. This painting from the 1400s shows Venetians being received by the Mamluk governor of Damascus, who wears a horned hat and sits on a low platform, in today's Syria.

Q What can we learn about the politics, economy, people, and customs of Mamluk Damascus from the painting?

decades, expanding trade and confronting Portuguese expansion while establishing an alliance with the Indonesian Muslim state of Acheh on Sumatra. Soon the empire would reach even greater heights under Sultan Suleiman the Magnificent (r. 1520–1566). But Ottoman, and Islamic, expansion in western Eurasia finally came to an end when the Ottomans were defeated while attempting to take Hungary in 1699. However, the Ottoman Empire continued until 1923.

10-4e Islamic Contributions to World History

By linking peoples of varied cultures, ideas, religions, and languages, Arab expansion fostered intellectual and artistic creativity, while the Islamic faith and culture profoundly influenced South Asian, African, and European societies. For example, the gradual Islamic conquest of much of South Asia posed an alternative to Hinduism. As Islamic influence and Arab merchants traveled south across the Sahara and along the East African coast, various African societies also adopted Islam and some Islamic customs and technologies. From the ninth through eleventh centuries, Arabs in Sicily and Spain passed on to Europe some of the advanced science, mathematics, and technology of the Middle East, India, and China. In many respects, Muslims linked the Classical Greeks

and Indians with late medieval Europeans, whose universities now studied Greco-Roman and Islamic learning. Eventually this exchange of knowledge helped spark a scientific and technological revolution in Europe as well as a questioning of the entrenched Christian church, ultimately leading to more diverse ideas within Western societies. But the exchange was not one way, as Muslims also benefited from European medicine, science, and art.

The mixture of Arab, Persian, Turkish, Byzantine, Christian, Jewish, African, Indonesian, and Indian influences created a hemispheric-wide Islamic world that connected culturally and politically diverse societies sharing a common faith and, often, values. While most Iraqis, Syrians, Egyptians, and North Africans adopted the Arabic language and called themselves Arabs, Persians and Turks maintained their own spoken languages but now wrote using Arabic script. Indeed, for many centuries Persian remained a language of government and the elite, from the Seljuk Turkish empire to various Muslim states in South and Central Asia.

Non-Muslims played key roles, especially in commerce. From the eighth through eleventh centuries Jews were the key middlemen between Christian Europe and the Muslim world. Hence, Jews from southern France traded in Spain, North Africa, and the eastern Mediterranean, many becoming fluent in Arabic. After the eleventh century Jews lost ground as intermediaries to Italians in the west and Armenian Christians in the east.

Réunion des Musées Nationaux/Art Resource, NY

By the fourteenth century Islam's center of gravity was shifting from Arab societies to Turkey, but Arab, Persian, and Turkish courts continued to attract some of the world's leading scientists and artists and remained at the cutting edge of medical advances and military technology. Muslim scholars were proud of their expansive horizons. For example, the Egyptian Jalal al-Din al-Suyuti (**juh-LALL al-din al-sue-YOU-tee**) (1445–1505) boasted that he and his books had traveled as far as West Africa and India. Yet, after the last Muslim kingdom in Spain fell in 1492, he believed the Muslim world needed intellectual and social renewal. Although the Ottoman Turks were rising, al-Suyuti could not know that, after 1500, Muslim states would also have a resurgence in Persia and South Asia, nor that various Europeans, benefiting from the encounter with Islam, would become serious rivals to Muslim power and challenge the interconnected Islamic world.

Several powerful Islamic states, including the Ottoman Empire, enjoyed political and economic influence in the sixteenth and seventeenth centuries. But, with the occasional exception of Ottoman Turkey, technological innovation, scientific inquiry, and the questioning of accepted religious and cultural ideas fell off in the Middle East. Most madrasas, while training Muslim clerics and providing spiritual guidance, had narrow, theology-based curriculums that deemphasized secular learning. These trends diminished the humanist, tolerant tradition of Islamic scholarship represented by Baghdad's House of Wisdom and the schools in Muslim Spain. Over the next three centuries, Middle Eastern peoples who had boasted innovative and cosmopolitan traditions for a millennium gradually lost military and economic power while Europeans surged. Today Islam is a growing faith and Muslim societies play a key role in world politics and the world economy, sometimes generating tense relations with each other or with Western nations.

KEY POINTS

▶ Trade routes spread Islam throughout the hemisphere, eventually creating Dar al-Islam, an Islamic world stretching from Indonesia to Morocco, in which Arabs constituted a minority of Muslims.

▶ The Mongols, led by Genghis Khan and Hulegu, ruthlessly attacked Muslims in Central Asia and sacked Baghdad, but the Islamic tradition continued throughout Mongol rule.

▶ The arrival of gunpowder from China allowed Muslim military states, such as the Mamluks and the Timurids, to gain power.

▶ The Ottoman Turks established an extremely successful empire in the territory of the former Byzantine Empire by allowing subject minorities to administer their own affairs.

▶ By conducting and preserving a great deal of scientific and philosophical learning, the Muslims contributed much to European culture.

Chapter Summary

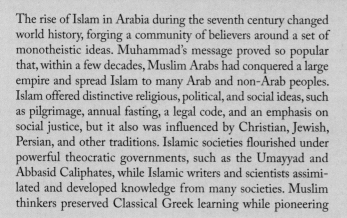

The rise of Islam in Arabia during the seventh century changed world history, forging a community of believers around a set of monotheistic ideas. Muhammad's message proved so popular that, within a few decades, Muslim Arabs had conquered a large empire and spread Islam to many Arab and non-Arab peoples. Islam offered distinctive religious, political, and social ideas, such as pilgrimage, annual fasting, a legal code, and an emphasis on social justice, but it also was influenced by Christian, Jewish, Persian, and other traditions. Islamic societies flourished under powerful theocratic governments, such as the Umayyad and Abbasid Caliphates, while Islamic writers and scientists assimilated and developed knowledge from many societies. Muslim thinkers preserved Classical Greek learning while pioneering

new ideas in astronomy, mathematics, the physical sciences, and agriculture. Arab links also contributed knowledge to medieval Europe, spurring the scientific and technological rise of the West.

The Islamic world became a cosmopolitan network of peoples linked by trade and religious scholars. While the Abbasid collapse brought some political fragmentation, Islam still expanded, overcoming several challenges in the millennium after Muhammad. By 1500 the Ottoman Turks controlled a vast empire. Stretching from western Africa and southwestern Europe eastward to Southeast Asia and western China, Islam became a hemispheric culture, even extending its influences into non-Islamic regions. After 1500, however, the Islamic Middle East began to fade as a political power and a center for intellectual inquiry.

Key Terms

Bedouins 235	caliphate 238	Sunni 242
Ka'ba 236	Ramadan 238	Shi'a 242
Quran 236	haj 238	Sufism 246
Hadith 236	jihad 239	calligraphy 249
hijra 237	sultan 241	Dar al-Islam 251
umma 237	Shari'a 241	millet 255
Allah 238	madrasas 241	

East Asian Traditions, Transformations, and Eurasian Encounters, 600–1500

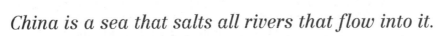

China is a sea that salts all rivers that flow into it.

—Italian traveler Marco Polo (1275 CE)[1]

Rafael Macia/Science Source

IMAGE 11.1 **Giant Japanese Buddha at Kamakura** During this era, most Japanese adopted Buddhism, some expressing their faith in art. This gigantic statue, erected in the city of Kamakura in 1252, shows the Buddha in meditation.

Q Why do you think statues of the Buddha such as this always made him look so large?

[1]Quoted in John Merson, *The Genius That Was China: East and West in the Making of the Modern World* (Woodstock, NY: Overlook Press, 1990), 14.

Early in the twelfth century the Chinese artist Zhang Zeduan, noted for his realistic drawings, painted a massive scroll of people at work and leisure throughout Kaifeng (**KIE-FENG**), then China's capital city and home to perhaps one million people. Set during the annual spring festival, the huge scroll portrays a bustling city, from its riverside suburbs to the towering city gates to the downtown business district, during one of China's most creative and prosperous eras. The scroll features people (mostly men) going about their daily activities, including foreign merchants, streetside hawkers, fortune tellers, scholars, and monks. Some people work in warehouses, iron smelters, arsenals, and shipyards. Zhang's vivid record of Kaifeng's commercial life shows building material suppliers, textile firms, drug and chemical shops, hotels, food stalls, teahouses, and restaurants. Cargo and pleasure barges cruise the river, while camels heavily laden with goods enter the city. The scroll remains a fascinating window onto the Song era, when China truly was the center of the world.

Much of the prosperous city life Zhang portrayed was familiar to Chinese of earlier and later generations, for Chinese society demonstrated considerable continuity over time. The Han's eventual succession by the Sui and then by the Tang (**tahng**) and Song (**sung**) dynasties ensured that Chinese society continued largely along traditional lines, in contrast to the dramatic changes taking place in Japan, the Middle East, India, Southeast Asia, and Europe during the Intermediate Era. Once the Tang adopted a modified version of the Han system, the ensuing millennium proved a golden age, broken only occasionally by invasion, including that of the Mongols, or disorder. Some scholars call the Intermediate Era in world history the "Chinese Centuries," with China perhaps the world's richest, most populous society, enjoying a well-organized government and economy, a flourishing artistic and literary culture, and technological and scientific creativity. Commercial and cultural networks connected China to the rest of Eurasia, influencing Korea and Japan, which adopted aspects of Chinese culture while also forging distinctive societies. China did indeed, as Marco Polo recognized, influence or awe all those with whom it came into contact.

11-1 Tang China: The Hub of the East

NETWORKS **SOCIETIES**

Q What role did Tang China play in the Eurasian world?

Many Chinese today often look back to the Tang dynasty as a Golden Age, the period in Chinese history in which they would most like to live. They have good reason to do so since during that era China was a great, influential, and respected power in the eastern half of Asia and produced some of its greatest achievements in art, literature, science, and technology. Many historians today view the Tang period as a unique conjuncture in Chinese history of power and cosmopolitanism. But China's history is not one of a never-changing essence; rather it is the story of both continuing and changing cultural traditions. The Tang came to power after replacing the harsh Sui dynasty, which ruled China for only a short time (581–618 CE) before rebellions ended the regime. The victor in the ensuing struggles between rival rebel forces established the Tang dynasty (618–907), whose three centuries of rule set a high point in many facets of Chinese life, providing a cultural and political model for neighboring societies. The only comparable power in Eurasia at that time was the Muslim Abbasid empire; India and Europe were divided into many small states often threatened by invaders. Tang models shaped China until the early twentieth century.

CONNECTION to TODAY

How might have social, cultural, and political life in Tang China been similar to and different from life today?

11-1a The Tang Empire and Eurasian Exchange

In the seventh and eighth centuries Tang China was Earth's largest, most populous society, with some 50 to 60 million people and immense influence in the eastern third of Eurasia (see Map 11.1). Like the earlier Han, the Tang launched ambitious military campaigns that brought Central Asia (as far west as the Caspian Sea), Tibet, Mongolia, Manchuria, and parts of Siberia under Chinese rule. Vietnam had long been a colony. The Koreans became a vassal state, and the Japanese established close ties. Chinese garrisons protected the Silk Road, fostering trade and migration.

As the most outward-looking Chinese dynasty, Tang China became a world market of ideas, people, and things arriving over the networks of exchange. The Tang Empire was receptive to foreign influences in many cultural practices, from literature to music, religion to medicine, clothes to food. The Silk Road across Central Asia remained a transcontinental highway for traders, adventurers, diplomats, missionaries, and pilgrims traveling east or west, carrying goods and ideas. Continuing trends that had begun several centuries earlier, Nestorian Christian, Manichean, Buddhist, and finally Muslim missionaries arrived in

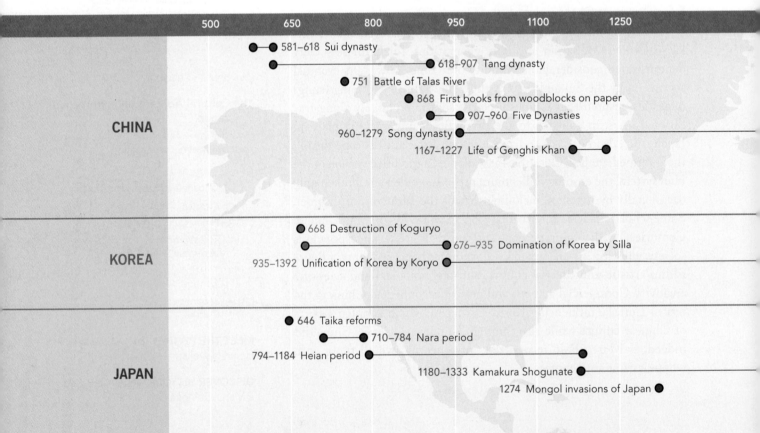

	500	650	800	950	1100	1250
CHINA		581–618 Sui dynasty				
			618–907 Tang dynasty			
			751 Battle of Talas River			
				868 First books from woodblocks on paper		
				907–960 Five Dynasties		
			960–1279 Song dynasty			
				1167–1227 Life of Genghis Khan		
KOREA			668 Destruction of Koguryo			
				676–935 Domination of Korea by Silla		
			935–1392 Unification of Korea by Koryo			
JAPAN			646 Taika reforms			
			710–784 Nara period			
			794–1184 Heian period			
				1180–1333 Kamakura Shogunate		
				1274 Mongol invasions of Japan		

China, while Chinese Buddhist monks visited India and brought back new kinds of art and literature. This inspired Chinese artisans to develop their own eclectic Buddhist art, which was then exported to other Buddhist societies. Merchants from around Asia, many coming by sea, formed communities in Chinese cities. A lively sea trade or maritime Silk Road linked China with Southeast Asia, South Asia, and the Middle East. Arab, Persian, Indian, Cambodian, and Malay immigrants and sojourners constituted perhaps two-thirds of the 200,000 residents of the southern port of Guangzhou (**gwahng-jo**), also known as Canton, which boasted both Sunni and Shi'ite mosques. Indian astronomers and mathematicians joined the Tang government as scientific officials, and several thousand people of foreign birth, mainly Central Asians including Sogdians, served as government officials or army officers. One early Tang emperor boasted that "in antiquity everyone honored Chinese and looked down upon barbarians . . . [but now he] loved them all."[2] Meanwhile, several hundred Chinese scholars visited or sojourned in India, most of them seeking Buddhist literature and knowledge.

11-1b China and the World

Tang wealth and power stimulated commerce throughout Eurasia. By land or sea, many Chinese inventions reached western Eurasia. In 753 CE a Chinese craftsman reported that, in Baghdad: "As for the weavers who make light silks, the goldsmiths who work gold and silver there, and the painters; the arts

which they practice were started by Chinese technicians."[3] Europeans and Middle Easterners prized Chinese products such as silk and porcelain, and Chinese culture also spread to Korea and Japan. Tang-era ceramics have been found as far west as Spain. This multicultural exchange benefited China. Societies such as Burma, Java, and Nepal regularly sent embassies to the Tang court bearing gifts, and renewed contacts with India and the Middle East fostered China's creativity. New products, most notably tea from Southeast Asia, appeared, first as medicine and then beverage, fostering teahouses in every marketplace. The chair, imported from the Middle East, replaced seating pads, making the Chinese East Asia's only chair users. However, some Chinese scholars criticized cosmopolitan attitudes and foreign culture.

The Eurasian exchange fostered dynamic, culturally rich cities. Tang China boasted many cities larger than any in Europe or India. The capital, Chang'an (**CHAHNG-ahn**), present-day Xi'an (**SHEE-AHN**), had two million inhabitants. The world's largest city, Chang'an reflected urban planning, its streets carefully laid out in a grid pattern, the city divided into quadrants, and broad thoroughfares crowded with visitors and sojourners from many lands, including Arabs, Persians, Syrians, Jews, Turks, Koreans, Japanese, Vietnamese, Indians, and Tibetans. Many foreign artists, artisans, merchants, and entertainers, such as Indian jugglers and Afghan actors, worked in the capital, which contained four Zoroastrian temples, two Nestorian Christian churches, and several mosques. The only contemporary cities rivaling Chang'an in size and amenities

---

[2] Quoted in Charles Holcombe, "Immigrants and Strangers: From Cosmopolitanism to Confucian Universalism in Tang China," *T'ang Studies*, 20–21 (2002–2003): 72–73.
[3] Quoted in John A. Harrison, *The Chinese Empire* (New York: Harcourt Brace Jovanovich, 1972), 239.

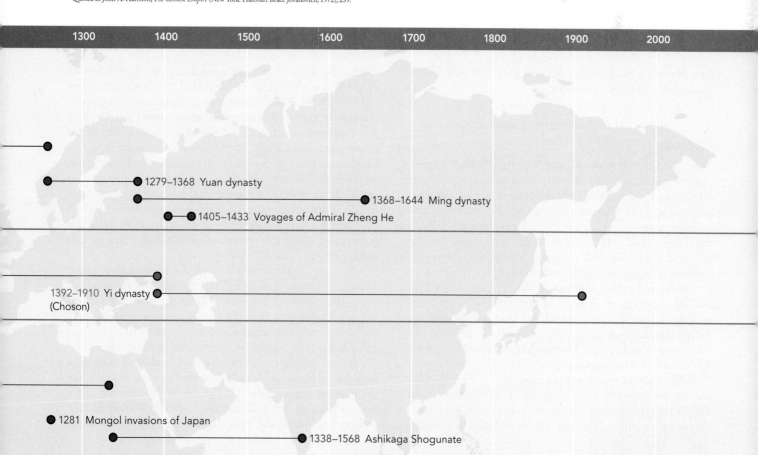

1300   1400   1500   1600   1700   1800   1900   2000

1279–1368 Yuan dynasty

1368–1644 Ming dynasty

1405–1433 Voyages of Admiral Zheng He

1392–1910 Yi dynasty (Choson)

1281 Mongol invasions of Japan

1338–1568 Ashikaga Shogunate

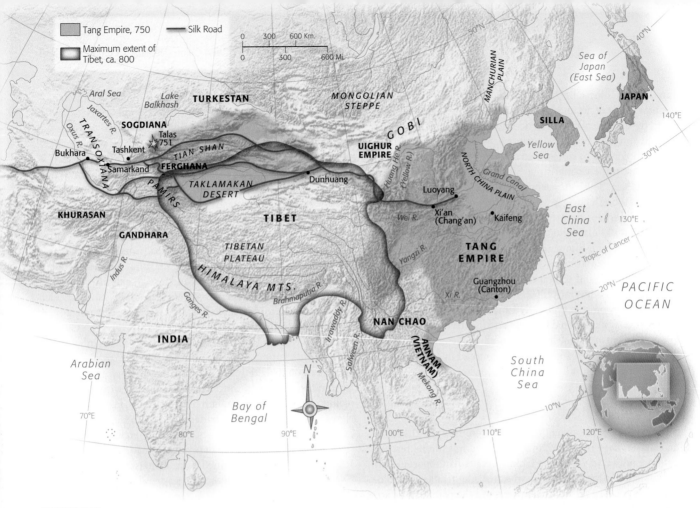

MAP 11.1 **The Tang Empire, CA. 750 CE** The Tang dynasty forged a large empire across Central Asia into Turkestan before their expansion was halted by Muslim armies at the Battle of Talas River in 751. Control of Central Asia allowed the Tang to protect the Silk Road trade route. The Tang also controlled Vietnam and dominated Korea.

Q How did the size of the Tang Empire at its height compare to the size of China today?

were Baghdad, the powerful Abbasid Caliphate's capital, and Byzantine-ruled Constantinople.

11-1c Imperial Government and Economic Growth

Tang China's centralized and highly efficient imperial government maintained one of the world's most productive economies. Despite bloody rebellions, invasions, assassinations, palace coups, and dynastic upheavals, stability marked China's political system for many centuries. Later dynasties followed the Tang model. According to Confucian theory, the state emulated the family, with the emperor serving as the people's symbolic father, governing by moral example, not physical force. Chinese considered the emperor the Son of Heaven—not divine but the intermediary between the terrestrial and supernatural realms—and the country's first scholar. During daily audiences, foreign diplomats sometimes presented gifts symbolizing their submission to his authority. In return he ceremoniously bestowed on them a title, state robes, and gifts, followed later by a banquet.

While women sometimes had power behind the throne, only one, the Empress Wu Zhao (**woo chow**) (625–705), ever officially led the government. An imperial concubine at age thirteen, she used her political skills and ruthless ambition to eventually displace the sickly emperor and maintained power for five decades. While Empress Wu generally ruled ably, Chinese scholars during and after the era, biased against strong women, considered her an evil usurper and warned future generations against women rulers.

In theory emperors held absolute power, but their actual power was circumscribed. The Censorate, an agency unique to China, monitored government workings, rooted out corruption, proposed state policy changes, and criticized government failings. Only the strongest emperors could punish the Censorate for criticism. Furthermore, the Mandate of Heaven doctrine, which gave people a right to overthrow an evil, corrupt, or ineffective government, meant that emperors had to consider their policies and behavior.

Because administering a large, diverse empire required a competent bureaucracy, the Tang revived the Han dynasty's competitive civil service exams. Believing that government officials, known as mandarins, should be the country's wisest and ablest men, they used merit-based exams to recruit talented individuals, regardless of birth, for government service. A national university and hundreds of local-level academies helped train potential officials. And yet, the Tang was also, like the Han, an age of aristocratic power, with men from great families boasting rich pedigrees dominating public life and the civil service. During the Tang and succeeding Song dynasties,

Mansell/Time Life Pictures/The LIFE Picture Collection/Getty Images

IMAGE 11.2 **Tang Empress Wu Zhao** A fanciful portrait of seventh-century Tang Empress Wu Zhao, the only woman to officially lead China's government in the Imperial period.

Q What does this portrait suggest about her appearance and clothing?

perhaps 15 percent of the mandarins did not come from upper-class backgrounds, indicating some social mobility.

The recruitment system for government service consisted of examinations at local, provincial, and national levels. Usually less than 5 percent of candidates passed and moved on to the next level. Passing the highest level earned the equivalent of a doctoral degree, a prerequisite to hold office. Largely testing knowledge of literary composition and the Confucian classics, the competitive merit exam system contributed greatly to China's long political stability, giving the ruling elite a shared Confucian ideology emphasizing ethics and loyalty. The Tang bureaucracy numbered around fifteen thousand officials, a small number for a huge country and an indication that they ruled with the people's cooperation or acquiescence. From then until the early twentieth century China's rulers governed through the bureaucracy of scholars.

Tang officials pursued economic growth, especially agricultural production. A Tang official explained the system: "Grain and cloth are produced by the [peasants], natural resources are transformed by the artisan class, wealth and goods are circulated by the merchant[s], and money is managed by the ruler."[4] The 80 percent of Chinese tilling the soil were generally able—often just

barely—to produce a food surplus for the 20 percent in towns and cities. But the Chinese also achieved better yields, becoming some of the world's most efficient farmers. To circumvent powerful landowning families, Tang officials experimented with land reform. The "equal field system" assigned each peasant family a plot of around nineteen acres, in the hope that this allotment provided enough for the family's needs. The reforms brought the peasantry some prosperity, but the system disintegrated when Tang power declined after some one hundred and twenty years. Still, throughout history some emperors and officials sought a more equitable land system.

11-1d Religion, Science, and Technology

Buddhism flourished in Central, Southeast, and East Asia during the Early Intermediate Era. Under the Tang, Mahayana Buddhism became a dominant faith, while Confucianism and Daoism also remained influential. Buddhist monks, pilgrims, and artists traveled between India and China, usually over the Silk Road, drawing the two societies into closer contact. However, competing Buddhist sects presented the Tang with problems. Furthermore, because Buddhist monasteries controlled vast tax-exempt lands and wealth, they became alternative power centers that sparked a mid-ninth-century government crackdown on Buddhist institutions. Emperor Wuzong (**woo-chong**) (840–846), desperate for more revenues, seized forty-six hundred monasteries, defrocking all monks under age fifty. Although Wuzong's successors restored the monasteries, his actions reduced the Buddhist orders' political and economic power enough to ensure they never again exercised secular power.

Some new religions moved east along the Silk Road. Nestorian Christianity, considered heretical in Byzantium, gained a small following, and Islam became strong in northwest China and parts of southwest and southern China. Jewish merchants, mostly from Persia, settled in several northern China cities, founding small but enduring Jewish communities. Unlike Wuzong, the Tang court generally took a tolerant, ecumenical view of religion, one emperor proclaiming: "The Way [truth] has more than one name. There is more than one sage. Doctrines vary in distant lands, their benefits reach all mankind."[5]

Scholars and craftsmen made scientific and technological achievements. Astronomers established the solar year at 365 days and studied sunspots, and some also argued that Earth was round and revolved around the sun, which many Europeans of the time doubted. Chinese were the first anywhere to analyze, record, and predict solar eclipses. Tang engineers also built the first load-bearing segmental arch bridge. After perfecting gunpowder, an elaboration of the firecracker, by mixing sulphur, saltpeter, and charcoal, Chinese military forces used primitive cannon and flaming rockets to protect their borders or resist rebels. Finally, the Chinese made great advances in printing. For centuries they had carved texts into stone and made ink rubbings for mass distribution of religious and Confucian texts. As demand soared, some creative men began carving texts into wooden blocks and then reproducing text on paper with ink. Koreans produced the first known woodblock print of a short text sometime

[4]Po Chu-I, quoted in William H. McNeill, *The Pursuit of Power: Technology, Armed Force, and Society Since A.D. 1000* (Chicago: University of Chicago Press, 1982), 28.
[5]Quoted in C. P. Fitzgerald, *China: A Short Cultural History* (New York: Praeger, 1961), 336.

around 751. But Chinese printed the first known paper book, a copy of an important Buddhist text, in 868. It was a massive scroll of seven sections, each section printed from a single block and stuck together to create a work more than sixteen feet in length. Woodblock printing provided texts for the civil service exams and spread Buddhist writings. Possessing an insatiable desire to classify past wisdom for use by future generations, Chinese compiled encyclopedias to record their accumulated knowledge. Woodblock printing also gave rise to a written popular culture.

11-1e The Arts and Literature

Some of China's greatest painters and sculptors lived in Tang times. Scholars and government officials avidly pursued painting and calligraphy, the beautiful rendering of Chinese characters to record a meaningful poem, quote, or passage in a refined, balanced form. Both calligraphers and painters used brush and ink on silk or paper. Chinese paintings were generally restrained, understated, and philosophical. Influenced by Daoism, many painters specialized in landscapes. An eleventh-century writer explained why: "Why does a virtuous man take delight in landscapes? That in a rustic retreat he may nourish his nature; amid the carefree play of streams and rocks, he may take delight. Haze, mist, and the haunting spirits of the mountains are what human nature seeks, and yet can rarely find."[6] But Confucian ideas were also expressed, with people and the objects they created, such as bridges or rustic retreats, and were usually a small part of the picture. Like Confucian philosophy, Chinese arts stressed order, morality, and tradition. Yet, some free-spirited artists experimented wildly; one eccentric flipped ink-soaked hair at silk, and another splashed while dancing. Artists also reflected their times. Wind-tossed bamboo and choppy water, for example, might indicate turbulent politics. Chinese also experienced art when sipping tea from nearly transparent porcelain cups, the world's most sanitary utensils at that time. China became famous for splendid lacquerware, furniture made with mother of pearl, gold and silver inlay, and luxurious brocades.

Many of China's greatest poets lived in this era. Annual literary festivals, held in Chang'an, selected prizewinners. Many poems depicted life's hardships—poverty, war, romantic love's ups and downs, the passing of time, the imminence of death. But lyrical poems explored life's wonders and the parting of friends. Chinese poems usually blended emotion with restraint, reflecting their Daoist and Buddhist influences. For example, Wang Wei **(wahng way)** expressed a Daoist appreciation of nature: "Walking at leisure we watch laurel flowers fall. In the silence of this night the spring mountain is empty. The moon rises, the birds are startled, As they sing occasionally near the spring fountains." The poem describes a changing landscape of falling laurel leaves, a quiet spring mountain, a rising moon, and birds singing, all creating Daoist feelings of peace, detachment, and purity.

The two giants of Tang poetry, their work still beloved in China today, were Li Bai **(lee pai)** (older books called him Li Po) and Du Fu **(too foo)**, close friends but very different in their personalities and styles. Born on the Western frontier, Li Bai sought a career as a civil servant but also honed his poetic craft and delighted audiences in his travels. The eccentric free spirit Li (701–762) was romantic, passionate, disrespectful of authority,

IMAGE 11.3 **Song Painting of Landscape with Imperial Travelers** This famous silk hand scroll painting from the eleventh century shows the seventh Tang Emperor Ming Huang (712–756) traveling with his attendants and officials through the mountains, but the spectacular landscape is the true star of the painting. The anonymous artist actually copied it from a Tang dynasty painting by the landscape artist Li Zhaodao, a common and accepted practice of artists in this era.

Q What kind of mood and ambience are conveyed by the painting?

and humorous but often melancholy. Influenced by Daoism, Li said that a good person must be carefree, maintaining a child's heart and mind. There is much debate about when and how he died but in popular legend he apparently drowned on a boat trip while reaching out in drunken ecstasy for the moon's reflection in the water. In "The Joys of Wine" Li wrote: "Since Heaven and Earth love wine, I can love wine without shaming Heaven. With three cups I penetrate the Great Dao. Take a whole jugful and I and the world are one. Such things as I have dreamed in wine, Shall never be told to the sober."[7] Li also occasionally wrote about public issues. He outlined the hardships of conscripted soldiers during the Tang military campaigns in Central Asia, wondering who would cultivate their fields.

A Confucian humanist, Du Fu (712–770), Li Po's opposite, was the preeminent poet of social consciousness, deeply concerned with the human condition. Du's poems held up a mirror to his times. His antiwar poems remain powerful even a millennium later: "When will men be satisfied with building a wall against the barbarians? When will the soldiers return to their native land?" He sympathized with soldiers and their families rather than with imperial aims:

The war-chariots rattle, The war-horses whinny. Each man of you has a bow and quiver in his belt. Father, mother, son, wife, stare at you going. At the border where the blood of men spills like the sea. And still the heart of Emperor Wu is beating for war. Do you know that, east of China's mountains, in two hundred districts, And in thousands of villages, nothing grows but weeds? And though strong women have bent to the ploughing, East and west the furrows are all broken down.

[6]Quoted in Derk Bodde, *China's Cultural Tradition: What and Whither?* (New York: Holt, Rinehart and Winston, 1957), 31.
[7]The Wang and Li poems are from Robert Payne, ed., *The White Pony: An Anthology of Chinese Poetry* (New York: Mentor, 1960), 154, 174.

Du also showed tenderness, celebrating everyday life's pleasures: "Clear waters wind, Around our village. With long summer days, Full of loveliness. My wife draws out, A chessboard on paper, While our little boys, Bend needles into fish hooks. What more could I wish for?"[8] Li Bai and Du Fu both transcended their times and were shaped by them.

11-1f Changes in the Late Tang Dynasty

Significant changes took place in China between the eighth and tenth centuries. The overwhelming majority of Chinese now lived in central and southern China, the fertile Yangzi Basin becoming the most productive economic region. New crop strains from Southeast Asia made possible two crops of rice a year. Combined with better transportation, this fostered more trade and increasing urban population. Crafts and merchant guilds and the world's first paper money appeared, and Chinese traders visited Southeast Asia to obtain luxury goods.

Like the Han, the Tang ultimately found its empire too expensive to maintain and difficult to defend. After a bitter defeat by Arab forces led by the Iraq-based Abbasid caliphate and their Tibetan allies at the Battle of Talas River (in present day Kyrgystan) in 751, Tang military power declined in Central Asia and they lost control of the eastern Silk Road, ending their ambitions to expand westward. Muslim forces and Islam filled the vacuum in Turkestan as well as in the Xinjiang (**shin-jee-yahng**) region on China's western frontier, which is now part of China. With Islam ascendant on the Silk Road some Central Asians, especially Sogdians, fled to China, some serving in the Tang administration and military. But during the late Tang attitudes toward the outside shifted, with more consciousness of differences between Chinese and non-Chinese. Some historians argue that this set the foundation for a less cosmopolitan Chinese identity. Instead, some recent scholarship argues, a new unified ethnocultural or ethnic definition of Chinese identity emerged and grew stronger in later dynasties. Climate change, especially a long dry spell between 840 and 940 that caused food shortages, may have contributed to Tang decline. Finally the Tang lost control of China itself. The country broke apart; in 907 Chinese rebels, spurred by famine and drought, sacked Chang'an. The Tang demise allowed Vietnam to finally free itself from Chinese rule.

For five decades, China was divided into several competing states known as the Five Dynasties. But Chinese society was now too massive and deeply rooted to tolerate centuries of anarchy; from the Tang onward the interludes of disorder between great dynasties proved brief as China recreated itself as "the central kingdom" and not a divided people. Perhaps China might have remained more innovative if smaller competing states had replaced imperial unity, which happened in western Europe in the centuries since the decline of Rome. But the Chinese deplored disunity. A proverb stated: "Just as there cannot be two suns in the sky, there cannot be two rulers in China." The centralized imperial system remained in place for nearly a millennium after the Tang. It has been partly recreated since the 1950s as China, which already included Tibet, Xinjiang, and eastern Mongolia, gained control of Hong Kong in 1997 and seeks to dominate Taiwan and the South China Sea while building and financing a transportation, commercial, infrastructure, and industrial network around Eurasia and the world modeled on the old Silk Road concept.

KEY POINTS

▶ The Tang Empire was marked by ambitious expansion, visitors and residents, and the spread of Chinese goods across Eurasia.

▶ Stability was maintained by keeping the emperor's authority somewhat in check and by rewarding high achievers through the civil service exam system.

▶ Buddhism reached its peak influence during the Tang but was greatly weakened when Emperor Wuzong seized Buddhist monasteries.

▶ During the Tang, the first books were printed using woodblocks.

▶ Poetry and other arts were very popular; while usually stressing Daoist harmony, they sometimes expressed criticism of the government.

11-2 Song China and Commercial Growth

⚍ TRANSITIONS ▥ SOCIETIES

Q Why might historians consider the Song dynasty the high point of China's Golden Age?

The next great dynasty, the Song (960–1279), presided over a sophisticated period of achievement, creating another brilliant Golden Age but one that reflected different strengths than the Tang. Although lacking the Tang's empire building and world leadership, the Song was in many respects more refined in the arts of living, technological development, and material richness. Some

CONNECTION to TODAY

Do you think the Song dynasty's impressive economic dynamism, science, technology, agriculture, and urban culture can serve as a model for China and other societies today?

historians describe the Song as premodern China's most exciting period, characterized by innovation, economic dynamism, urban sophistication, and cultural flowering. At its zenith Song China, stretching a thousand miles east to west and north to south, contained perhaps 120 million people, between a quarter and a third of the world's total.

---

[8]Du's poems are from Cyril Birch, ed., *Anthology of Chinese Literature from Early Times to the Fourteenth Century* (New York: Grove Press, 1965), 240–241; and *Tu Fu: Selected Poems* (Peking: Foreign Languages Press, 1962), 100.

11-2a Cities, Economies, and Technologies

Song China boasted the world's largest cities, at least five having populations over a million, and nearly fifty others each containing over 100,000 people. Meanwhile, once-great western Eurasian cities had fallen in population: Rome to 35,000 and Baghdad to 125,000. Chinese urban residents enjoyed a high quality of life. A modern scholar described the vibrant activity in one of these cities:

> The day started with the booming of temple bells. Peddlers began to make their way up and down the streets, calling out the foods they had for sale. Carts laden with meats and vegetables moved in toward the markets. Businesses of all kinds opened. Many . . . , such as the tailors, hairdressers, dealers in paper and brushes, and caterers, served the city's taste for luxury. As night fell, lanterns lit up taverns and restaurants, the largest of which had staffs of hundreds. In the theater district dozens of houses offered varied bills, including the latest songs, puppet shows, acrobats, wrestlers, storytellers, and comedians.[9]

In the later Song era, when nomadic invaders had pushed the government south of the Yangzi River, the capital was Hangzhou **(hahng-jo)**, a city of several million on the southern end of the Grand Canal (see Discover Historical Voices: Life in a Major Chinese City). The beauty of Hangzhou and the nearby city of Suzhou fostered a widely known proverb: "Above in Heaven there is the celestial palace, below on Earth there are Suzhou and Hangzhou."[10] A later and well-traveled Italian visitor, Marco Polo, called it unquestionably the world's greatest city. Nanjing in the fifteenth century, and Beijing from the sixteenth into the nineteenth century, followed Hangzhou as the world's largest cities.

The Song marked the high point for premodern Chinese commerce and foreign trade, making it a role model for China's aspirations today. The merchant class grew substantially, with tax revenues three times higher than for the Tang. The Grand Canal linking the Yellow and Yangzi River Basins allowed mass movement of goods between north and south. To support this commerce, China developed the world's first fully monetized economy, putting paper money and silver coins into wide use. Song China also enjoyed the world's most advanced farming. Farmers doubled the rice crop and vastly increased the growing and marketing of sugar, once a minor crop. Meanwhile, foreign trade flourished from maritime networks connecting China to the rest of Afro-Eurasia. Some historians describe the South China Sea in Song times and since as a kind of Asian version of the Mediterranean Sea, traversed by trading ships from China, Southeast Asia, and the Middle East carrying goods and people. Chinese were now as likely to import horses by sea from Arabia and Central Asia via India along the old Silk Road network. Chinese merchants regularly visited and even settled in Southeast Asia and Japan, and a few Chinese traded as far west as India. Chinese industrial and food products found markets in Persia, East Africa, and Egypt. Thousands of foreigners found their way to China, including Indonesian, Arab, Indian, Persian, and even East African merchants, and lived in the cosmopolitan southern seaports of Guangzhou (Canton) and Quanzhou (Zayton). Both cities contained numerous mosques and Hindu temples. China was hence linked to a hemispheric-wide trading network. In the later thirteenth century Persians living in Hangzhou built the Phoenix Mosque, whose grounds featured dozens of tombstones and pillars honoring various Persian, Turkish, and Syrian residents, a concrete example of a multicultural society along the southeastern coast. Indian traders including Tamils built Hindu temples in southern port cities like Quanzhou during Song times.

Song China had the world's most advanced industry, reflected in its export of manufactured goods (silks, porcelain, books) and import of raw materials (spices, minerals, horses). Chinese porcelain traded all over Asia, the Middle East, and parts of Africa, its ethereal beauty and great strength fostering a reputation for magical or spiritual power. The name *china*

Werner Forman/Art Resource, NY

IMAGE 11.4 **Scroll of Kaifeng** This segment from the scroll "Spring Festival on the River," discussed in the chapter opening, shows people thronging the Rainbow Bridge while boatmen lower their masts to pass under the cantilevered structure. Merchants sell their goods in shops and stalls along the streets and bridge.

Q What does the painting tell us about urban life in China during Song times?

[9]John Meskill, "History of China," in *An Introduction to Chinese Civilization*, ed. John Meskill (Lexington, MA: D.C. Heath, 1973), 127–128.
[10]Quoted in Yinong Xu, *The Chinese City in Space and Time: The Development of Urban Form in Suzhou* (Honolulu: University of Hawai'i Press, 2000), 15.

Discover Historical Voices

Life in a Major Chinese City

The following excerpts are from a description by Marco Polo of Hangzhou, the capital city of China during the southern Song dynasty and still an important cultural, political, and economic center during Mongol rule in the late 1200s, when Polo witnessed the city life he discusses.

There were in this city twelve guilds of the different crafts. . . . All these craftsmen had full occupation, for many other cities of the kingdom are supplied from this city with what they require. . . . The number and wealth of the merchants, and the amount of goods that passed through their hands, were so enormous that no man could form a just estimate thereof. . . . Neither . . . [the crafts masters] nor their wives ever touch a piece of work with their own hands, but live as nicely and delicately as if they were kings and queens. The wives indeed are most dainty and angelical creatures!

Inside the city there is a [large] Lake . . . and all round it are erected beautiful palaces and mansions, of the richest and most exquisite structure that you can imagine, belonging to the nobles of the city. . . . Both men and women are fair and comely, and for the most part clothe themselves in silk, so vast is the supply of that material. . . . . All the streets of the city are paved with stone or brick . . . so that you ride and travel in every direction without inconvenience. . . . The city . . . has some 3000 [hot] baths, the water of which is supplied by springs . . . , and the people take great delight in them, frequenting them several times a month, for they are very cleanly in their persons. . . .

Everything appertaining to this city is on so vast a scale, and the Great Khan's yearly revenues therefrom are so immense . . . it seems past belief. . . . The city . . . has on one side a lake of fresh and exquisitely clear water . . . , and on the other a very large river. The waters of the latter fill a number of canals of all sizes which run through the different quarters of the city, carry away all impurities, and then enter the Lake . . . , thus producing a most excellent atmosphere. By means of these channels, as well as by the streets, you can go all about the city. All the ten marketplaces are encompassed by lofty houses, and below these are shops where all sorts of crafts are carried on, and all sorts of wares are on sale, including spices and jewels and pearls. Some of these shops are entirely devoted to the sale of wine made from rice and spices, which is . . . sold very cheap.

Certain of the streets are occupied by . . . women [courtesans and prostitutes]. . . . Strangers who have once tasted their attractions seem to get bewitched, and are so taken with their blandishments and their fascinating ways that they never can get these out of their heads. Hence . . . when they return home they say they have been to . . . . the City of Heaven, and their only desire is to get back thither as soon as possible. Other streets are occupied by the Physicians, and by the Astrologers, who are also teachers of reading and writing; and an infinity of other professions have their places round about those squares. . . .

There is such a degree of good will and neighborly attachment among both men and women that you would take the people who live in the same street to be all one family. . . . They also treat the foreigners who visit them for the sake of trade with great cordiality, and entertain them in the most winning manner, affording them every help and advice on their business. . . .

Reflection Questions

1. What impression of the city do you get from Polo's account?
2. What does the reading tell us about the city's economy?
3. How does Polo evaluate the roles of men and women?
4. What does the reading tell us about Hangzhou and urban life during this era?

Source: From *The Book of Ser Marco Polo the Venetian Concerning the Kingdoms and Marvels of the East*, trans. and ed. by Henry Yule, 3rd ed. revised by Henri Cordier (London: John Murray, 1903), Vol. II, 185–193, 200–205, 215–216. This text is part of the Internet Medieval History Sourcebook (www.fordham.edu/halsall /source/polo-kinsay.asp).

became synonymous with the world's finest porcelain products. The Song were also innovators in metallurgy, inventing a new method of forging cast iron. China's iron industry, the world's largest before the eighteenth century, produced fine steel for tools, weapons, stoves, ploughshares, cooking equipment, nails, building materials, and bridges. Mass production and metal-casting techniques supplied standardized iron products to the world's largest internal market. But the use of charcoal in the iron-smelting process caused extensive deforestation. In response, Song metallurgists discovered how to produce coke from bituminous coal as a substitute for charcoal. The Song mined coal for fuel, produced salt on an industrial scale, and had the world's best maritime technology. Trade also spurred a significant shipbuilding industry. Some huge compartmentalized ships, with four decks and four to six masts, were capable of carrying five hundred sailors and extensive cargo. Thousands of cargo ships plied the rivers and canals.

In technology and science, the Chinese produced a majority of the world's major inventions between the first and fifteenth centuries CE. For example, they built the world's longest bridge (2.5 kilometers) and expanded the use of water-powered clocks and mills. Many inventions later spread throughout Eurasia, including the magnetic compass (for naval navigation), sternpost rudder, and spinning wheel. Song craftsmen also made movable type from fired clay and then tin or copper, greatly facilitating book printing. In weaponry, Song technicians developed fire lances, bamboo tubes filled with gunpowder that were the precursors of the metal-barrel gun. Fitted with missile launchers, flamethrowers, cannon, and bombs, Song ships protected the coast. Half a millennium before western Europe's Industrial Revolution,

Song engineers also invented the world's first industrial machine, a mechanized spinning process for reeling silk and later hemp thread. There were also advances in astronomy. Astronomers still use data the Song collected from observing the skies, such as on the supernova that created the Crab Nebula, and a Song calendar precisely measured the solar year (365.2425 days). In medicine, Chinese doctors inoculated against smallpox, a disease that ravaged much of Afro-Eurasia. Some Chinese medical ideas reached the Middle East and Europe by the thirteenth century.

11-2b Society and Religion

An urbane elite culture thrived. Printed books fostered the spread of education, exposing a wider audience to the social and political elite's values, and the government established schools in every district. Although only a small percentage of students ever became mandarins, a degree or some educated background brought status. The cultivated gentleman, whether or not in government service, was expected to master music (especially lute playing), chess, calligraphy, poetry, and painting.

However, women experienced more restrictions than in earlier centuries. Tang paintings and statues showed aristocratic women in swept-up hair riding horses or standing dignified in loose-fitting gowns. Now women's status declined. Fearing that new economic opportunities for women might undermine patriarchy, conservatives limited women's roles. Men more often took concubines (official mistresses) in addition to their wives, and families increasingly frowned upon widows remarrying. Yet, some women from elite families became literate, reading and writing mostly for their own pleasure. Meanwhile, peasant wives worked in the fields alongside men and were therefore crucial to the family economic livelihood. They also operated restaurants and sold fish and vegetables in markets. Still, children belonged to the father's family, and the husband's mother ruled the wife. Divorce, possible but uncommon, disgraced the woman. Poor women also faced a difficult old age, as a male writer sympathetically described:

> For women who live a long life, old age is especially hard to bear, because most women must rely on others for their existence. Some wives with stupid husbands are able to manage the family's finances. But the most remarkable are the women who manage a household after their husbands have died leaving them with young children.[11]

Another source of suffering for women, footbinding, was introduced in the tenth century and expanded during the Song among the elite and some common folk. Mothers broke and then tightly bound the feet of five- or six-year-old daughters so they looked more like hooves, preventing normal growth and crippling a girl's feet. This gave women a dainty walk that men viewed as erotic. Because they needed women's labor in homes and fields for family survival, many peasants rejected the practice as physically debilitating. However, footbinding became more widespread but not universal in later dynasties. Chinese and Western reformers in the nineteenth century criticized the custom as a symbol of backwardness and patriarchal control of women and sought to end it, but footbinding was not prohibited by law until the early twentieth century.

The Song period also saw the rise of **neo-Confucianism**, a form of Confucianism incorporating many Buddhist and Daoist metaphysical ideas that was associated particularly with Zhu Xi (**JOO shee**) (1130–1200), a child prodigy and one of China's most influential thinkers. Believing that original Confucian ideas had become rigid and misunderstood, Zhu resigned from government service in disgust at corruption and advocated rediscovering Confucianism's original essence. Daoism also influenced Zhu's rational and humane approach, which recognized a dualism between the material world and the energy the Chinese believed pervaded the universe, or **qi** (ch'i). *Tai qi* (tai ch'i) exercises were designed to build mind and body, hence harnessing qi for personal centering. Like Confucius, Zhu identified reason or principle as the unchanging law and morality for measuring all human affairs: "For every person the most important thing is the cultivation of himself as an ethical being."[12] However, Zhu's indifference to natural science diminished scientific inquiry. Although he praised accomplished women and urged them to pursue book learning at home, his writings also strengthened gender distinctions. Over time neo-Confucianism became the elites' dominant mindset and a force for stability but not innovation. At the same time, many peasants and town-dwellers, disinterested in or unaware of theological debates, revered local cults and gods, some only loosely linked to Buddhism, Daoism, or Confucianism.

11-2c The Song in World History

The Song could have proved a turning point in Chinese and world history, but their many achievements did not foster a major transition. The profound economic, technological, and urban developments remind some historians of eighteenth-century Europe at the dawn of rapid industrialization, but Song commercial and agricultural dynamism never revolutionized Chinese society. Instead, China contained and absorbed these developments. The Chinese possessed the technology to sail the seas and colonize other lands, but being largely self-sufficient, they lacked the incentive. Moreover, since the highly bureaucratic empire easily adjusted to economic change, it prevented merchants from disrupting China's social order. With productive agriculture to feed a huge population, convenient transportation by water through canals, and many natural resources, Chinese felt no need for additional mechanized technologies. The Mongol conquest of the Song, a cooler climate by the thirteenth century, and the Black Death pandemic in the fourteenth century also undermined economic dynamism. Population pressure became a growing burden as farmland filled up.

Furthermore, Confucian disdain of merchants eventually led to stagnation and allowed the imperial government to contain economic growth. Although the large number of mandarins from wealthy merchant families in this period generally supported

neo-Confucianism A form of Confucianism arising in China during the Song period (960–1279) that incorporated many Buddhist and Daoist metaphysical ideas.

qi In Chinese thought, the energizing force pervading the universe.

---

[11]Yuan Tsai, from Patricia Buckley Ebrey, ed., *Chinese Civilization and Society: A Sourcebook* (New York: The Free Press, 1981), 96.
[12]From Dun J. Li, ed., *The Essence of Chinese Civilization* (Princeton, NJ: Van Nostrand, 1967), 88.

commercial growth, many essential commodities remained government monopolies, such as iron, grain, cloth, and salt, while taxes on the wealthy financed public granaries to check famine. These monopolies over essential products enriched the state and protected the population from price and supply problems, but they also restricted merchants to handling nonessential products. One ambitious Song prime minister with socialist leanings, Wang Anshi (wahng ahn-shee) (1021-1086), experimented unsuccessfully with guaranteed state loans to farmers, fixed commodity prices, unemployment insurance, and old age pensions. He said that every family should have enough for its needs. Thus, "the state should take the entire management of commerce, industry, and agriculture into its own hands, with a view to [preventing] the working classes from being ground into the dust by the rich."[13] Wang and his ideas were a millennium ahead of their time, since various versions of socialism have been common since the nineteenth century, some of them more successful than others.

The Song, more interested in economic growth than empire, generally avoided military expansion. Prosperity, trade, and urban living made peace more attractive than conquest. Meanwhile, Central Asian pastoralists gained an edge on complacent China by importing Chinese military technologies and experts, including ironworkers and engineers. Another problem was that, although maintaining the world's largest army, the Song, unlike the Han and Tang, reduced military leaders' power so they could not threaten civilian authority, a chronic Tang problem. Hence, adopting a passive attitude toward pastoral nomads across the border, the Song attempted to appease them with generous payments. Ultimately the policy failed. In the twelfth century one group, the Jin (Chin), conquered northern China, forcing the Song court south across the Yangzi, where it continued to rule central and southern China from Hangzhou until it was invaded and conquered by the Mongols.

KEY POINTS

▶ The Song dynasty was notable for its bustling urban life, its maritime trade, and its advanced economy.

▶ Song China made great advances in the manufacture of porcelain, ships, and bridges and in the prevention of disease.

▶ During the Song, the pursuit of education and cultivation became widespread among the elite; however, the status of women declined, and footbinding began to be practiced by the elite and some commoners.

▶ The Song's achievements did not lead to a major historical transition because China at this time felt self-sufficient, was not interested in conquest, and kept merchants out of important industries; it also tried to deal with neighboring pastoral nomads peacefully, a strategy that ultimately failed.

11-3 Mongol Conquest, Chinese Resurgence, and Eurasian Connections

▱ TRANSITIONS ▦ NETWORKS ▤ SOCIETIES

Ⓠ How did China change during the Yuan and Ming dynasties?

From the thirteenth through the nineteenth centuries the Chinese way of life maintained great continuity. Three ruling houses held power between the Song downfall and the imperial system's demise in the twentieth century, an almost unprecedented record of political stability, perhaps matched only by the ancient Egyptian kingdoms. Disorder occurred chiefly during years of dynastic decline and replacement. Two of the three dynasties were conquest dynasties imposed by non-Chinese nomadic peoples riding in on horseback. The two dynasties that held power between the thirteenth and seventeenth centuries were the Yuan (yu-wenn), established by invading Mongols, and the Ming, which marked a return to Chinese rule.

CONNECTION to TODAY

How do you think the Mongol Empire compared in size, politics, religious diversity, and economic policies to other large empires since 1500 such as the Spanish, British, French, Russian, Chinese, and American (United States)?

or divide-and-rule diplomacy. Enduring Central Asian influence on China's political life resulted from the close proximity of the arid grasslands north and west of China, suitable only for mobile herding, to China's lush farmlands, with contrasting environments producing very different societies. Central Asia's pastoral economy and few resources necessitated seasonal migration and chronic poverty for the tough, self-reliant herders. When China was weak, the Great Wall proved no major barrier to peoples envious of, and anxious to share in, China's relative affluence. In the thirteenth century China's worst nightmare occurred when a confederation of warlike peoples, the Mongols, conquered all of China.

Before invading China the Mongols conquered much of Eurasia, including parts of eastern Europe and western Asia. Traditionally divided into feuding tribes, the Mongols became united under the ruthless but brilliant Temuchin (ca. 1167–1227), who defeated or co-opted his rivals and then changed his name to Genghis Khan (**GENG-iz KAHN**) ("Universal Emperor"). Of humble origins, he had simple motives: "A man's greatest

11-3a The Mongol Empire and the Conquest of China

For several millennia Chinese feared what they considered "barbarian" Central Asians who killed, looted, and took captives. The strongest rulers controlled these peoples by conquest

---

[13]Quoted in H.H. Gowan and J.W. Hall, *An Outline History of China* (New York: D. Hamilton, 1926), 142

pleasure is to defeat his enemies, . . . drive them before him, . . . take from them that which they possessed, . . . see those whom they cherished in tears, . . . to ride their horses, . . . hold their wives and daughters in his arms."[14] Skilled horse soldiers, more agile than their foes, Mongols proved formidable opponents. Their well-organized fighting units possessed powerful bows lethal at six hundred feet, disc-shaped stirrups giving the rider maneuverability, and the world's most advanced siege weaponry, including catapults. China's strength made it one of the last Mongol conquests. Genghis Khan conquered parts of northern China in 1215, and the rest of China fell fifty years after Genghis's death under his grandson, Khubilai Khan **(koo-bluh KAHN)** (r. 1260–1294), who created a new dynasty, the Yuan (1279–1368). China then became part of a great hemispheric, contiguous land empire, the largest in world history ever seen before or since and a mixing of many different societies, stretching from eastern Europe and the Black Sea to Korea (see Map 11.2).

The Mongols imposed a distinctive government and fostered new cultural forms. Khubilai Khan proved a rather enlightened ruler, less cruel and more pragmatic than most Mongol leaders elsewhere in Eurasia. He patronized Buddhism, built granaries for food storage, operated an efficient postal system, and improved the transportation network. But Chinese historians condemned Khubilai Khan for Mongol sins generally,

such as maintaining Mongol cultural identity and actively resisting assimilation into Chinese society. Later Chinese viewed the Yuan as China's darkest hour, an intolerable rule by aliens who refused to be absorbed. Khubilai Khan moved the capital to Beijing ("Northern Capital"), a provincial city close to the Great Wall and alongside major highways leading north and west. Except for brief periods since, Beijing has remained China's capital, eclipsing more ancient cities like Chang'an and Hangzhou. Reflecting his nomadic heritage, Khubilai preferred sleeping in tents, including one erected in the imperial palace gardens.

The Mongols mistrusted intellectuals but were tolerant in religion, inviting missionaries from all over Eurasia to come to the court for religious debates, including Christians of various sects (including Catholics). Khubilai Khan's mother was a Nestorian Christian of Turkish ancestry, but, like many Mongols, he adopted Tibetan Buddhism. Governing a religiously diverse society, Khubilai Khan wanted to avoid conflict. However, although a few women in the ruling family had some power, Mongols had even more rigid gender expectations and marriage practices than the Chinese, expecting widows to remain chaste and dutifully serve their parents-in-law. Chinese men now demanded that women remain at home and emphasize feminine behavior, including the growing fashion of tightly bound feet.

The Picture Art Collection/Alamy Stock Photo

IMAGE 11.5 **Khubilai Khan and His Entourage Hunting** This painting by a Chinese artist of the time shows Khubilai Khan, dressed in ermine, and Mongol colleagues, including a woman, hunting on horseback, a popular activity among Mongols.

Q What aspects of Mongol life and culture does this painting suggest?

---

[14]Quoted in H. D. Martin, *The Rise of Chingis Khan and His Conquest of North China* (Baltimore: Johns Hopkins University Press, 1950), 5.

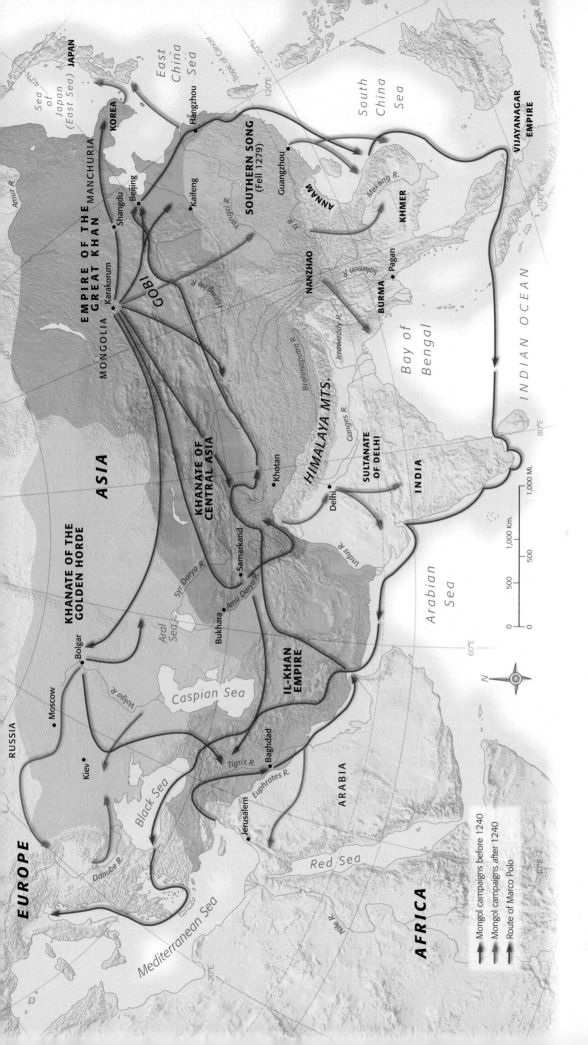

MAP 11.2 China in the Mongol Empire After the Mongols conquered much of Central Asia, western Asia, and eastern Europe, they added China and Korea to their huge empire, the largest contiguous land empire in world history. During the Mongol era many Asians and some Europeans, including the Italian Marco Polo, visited or worked in China.

Q What does this map suggest about the huge size of the Mongol Empire but also the challenges in maintaining its unity?

Mongol campaigns before 1240
Mongol campaigns after 1240
Route of Marco Polo

271

11-3b Mongol China and Eurasian Networks

The Mongols reopened China's doors to the world and protected the overland Silk Road, reviving the exchange of goods, ideas, and technologies between East and West. Chinese inventions like gunpowder, printing, the blast furnace for cast iron, silk-making machinery, paper money, and playing cards moved westward. The active maritime trade continued. Many foreigners came to Mongol China by land and sea. Although Khubilai Khan sought Chinese support by modeling his government along Chinese lines and performing Confucian rites, most scholars and bureaucrats refused cooperation. Mongols were forced to rely administratively on foreigners coming to serve in what was effectively an international civil service, including many Muslims from Central Asia, western Asia, and North Africa. For example, a Persian engineer guided the building of Khubilai's capital, Khanbaliq (now Beijing), and the first governor of Yunnan in southwest China came from the Silk Road city of Bukhara in Central Asia.

A few Europeans also found their way to "fabled Cathay," as they called China. One was the Italian merchant Marco Polo (ca. 1254–1324). Polo initially traveled to China with his father and uncle seeking trade goods but spent seventeen years there, mostly in government service. Eventually Polo returned to Italy and told of the wonders he had encountered or heard about to unbelieving Europeans who knew little about the world east of Palestine. Most dismissed Polo's account as full of lies, but it was widely read and influential in Europe, and historians confirm its general accuracy. A keen observer, he recorded Chinese resentment toward the Mongols, who once slaughtered a city's entire population for the killing of one drunk Mongol soldier. Polo wrote of China's great cities, such as Beijing and Hangzhou (see Discover Historical Voices). Standing along the shores of beautiful West Lake in Hangzhou, he wrote that "the city is beyond dispute the finest and noblest in the world in point of grandeur and beauty as well as in its abundant delights. The natives of this city are of peaceful character, thoroughly honest and truthful and accustomed to dainty living."[15] The city boasted parks, a fire department, garbage collection, a pollution-control agency, and paved streets—all things nonexistent in Polo's much smaller Venice, a major European city. Indeed, China was far more developed in many fields than the rest of Eurasia, probably enjoying the world's highest standard of living. Polo noted, for example, that the Chinese, unlike Europeans, had for a thousand years burned black stones (coal) for heat. According to his account of Hangzhou: "The streets connected with the market-squares are numerous, and in some of them are many cold baths, attended by [people] of both sexes. All [residents] are in the daily practice of washing their persons, and especially before their meals."[16] This information about regular baths probably astonished medieval Europeans, who seldom if ever bathed.

Mongol control had enormous consequences for Central Asia, the Middle East, and Europe, and the Mongols dominated regions such as Russia and Turkestan for a long time. But Mongol rule in China, lasting only a century, did not leave a deep imprint. Most Chinese hated the Mongols, whose leadership deteriorated after Khubilai Khan's death. Furthermore, after years of luxurious living in sophisticated China, Mongols lost their fighting toughness, desiring luxury more than sacrifice. As Mongols in Central Asia and Persia adopted the cultures and religions of the conquered, Mongol unity fragmented and power struggles grew rampant. Adding to these troubles, the Yellow River flooded severely, bringing famine, and a terrible plague (probably bubonic) outbreak raged. Historians still debate whether the pandemic, which killed many millions of Chinese, traveled west along the Silk Road to cause the terrible Black Death that greatly reduced the population of the Middle East and Europe in the fourteenth century (see Chapters 10 and 14). Some recent studies suggest that the Black Death plague originated in Turkestan. Soon rebellions broke out all over China. Eventually a Chinese commoner established a new dynasty, the Ming, and Mongol military forces returned to Central Asia. Today Mongols venerate Genghis Khan as their greatest leader, building memorials and even a theme park to honor the conqueror. And Chinese are still wary of the Mongols, generating sometimes hostile relations between China and Mongolia ever since then.

Detail from a vase depicting silk weaving (ceramic)/Chinese School, Ming Dynasty (1368-1644)/Golestan Palace, Tehran, Iran/Bridgeman Images

IMAGE 11.6 **Ming Silk Weaving** This detail from a Ming ceramic vase depicts women weaving silk, a craft dominated by women.

Q Does the painting tell us anything about Ming Chinese technology and women's roles in the economy?

[15]R. E. Latham, trans., *The Travels of Marco Polo* (Baltimore: Penguin Books, 1958), 184–187.

[16]Quoted in Arthur Cotterell and David Morgan, *China's Civilization: A Survey of its History, Arts, and Technology* (New York: Praeger, 1973), 190.

11-3c Ming Government and Culture

The new Ming dynasty (1368–1644) fostered orderly government, social stability, and cultural richness. The founder, Zhu Yuanzhang (**JOO yu-wen-JAHNG**) (1328–1398), a former Buddhist monk and son of an itinerant farm worker, rose, like the founder of the Han, from abject poverty through sheer ability and ruthless behavior in a time of opportunity. Ming China's people lived for nearly three centuries in comparative peace and prosperity, enjoying living standards among the world's highest and mortality rates among the lowest. During this time China more than doubled in population, from around 80 million to between 160 and 180 million.

Ming government resembled the Han and Tang but was somewhat more despotic and isolated. Perhaps because of the bitter and traumatic Mongol rule, Ming emperors exercised more power than earlier emperors and placed the bureaucracy under closer scrutiny, eliminating the office of prime minister, who had monitored the country's pulse. A more timid Censorate reduced checks on royal abuses. Like previous dynasties, some Ming emperors had male lovers as well as many wives and concubines, reflecting the tolerance of same-sex relationships among many Chinese court officials and some commoners.

Order infused the arts. Although culture in the Mongol period had proved relatively sterile, musical drama (Chinese opera) had become a popular entertainment, appealing to common folk rather than the elite. In the Ming, however, theater reached its highest level. Chinese operas included extended arias and spoken dialogue, each performance aimed at harmonizing song, speech, costume, makeup, movement, and musical accompaniment. Chinese music, mostly composed for operas or for ritual and ceremonial purposes, included string, wind, and percussion instruments, especially flutes, lutes, and zithers.

The Chinese also began writing novels in Yuan times, an elaboration of age-old storytelling. The first novelists were intellectuals who refused to work for the Mongols and made a living by writing books for a popular audience, including some of the world's first detective stories. Fiction, considered worthless by most Ming scholars, had a large audience. Most novels had a Confucian moral emphasizing correct behavior, but some offered social criticisms or satires. Perhaps the greatest Ming novel, *The Water Margin* (also known as *All Men Are Brothers*), presented heroes who were also bandits, Robin Hoods driven into crime by corrupt officials. Meanwhile, to encourage intellectual pursuits, rulers expanded the Hanlin ("Forest of Culture") Academy think tank established in the Tang, assigning some of the brightest scholars there to read and write whatever they liked. Ming scholars compiled an eleven-thousand-volume encyclopedia (with twenty thousand chapters) and a fifty-two-volume study of Chinese pharmacology.

11-3d Ming China and the Afro-Eurasian World

The early Ming rulers pursued territorial expansion, including a failed attempt to recolonize Vietnam in the early 1400s. But China was now oriented more to the sea than before. Rather than send armies far into Central Asia, the emperor dispatched a series of grand maritime expeditions to southern Asia and beyond to reaffirm China's preeminence in eastern Eurasia. Admiral Zheng He (**jung huh**) (Cheng Ho) (ca. 1371–1435), a huge man and trusted court eunuch of Muslim faith, commanded seven voyages between 1405 and 1433, a feat of seamanship that was unprecedented in world history. The largest fleet comprised sixty-two vessels carrying twenty-eight thousand men, and the largest "treasure ships," as they were known, weighed fifteen hundred tons, were four hundred and fifty feet long, boasted nine masts nearly five hundred feet high, and carried a crew of five hundred. These ships must have astounded observers when they sailed into a harbor and, although undertaking only a few military actions, perhaps intimidated them as well. By comparison, a few decades later Christopher Columbus sailed from Spain in three tiny vessels carrying a total of only about a hundred men.

Zheng He's extraordinary voyages carried the Chinese flag through Southeast Asia to India, the Persian Gulf, the Red Sea, and the East African coast (see Map 11.3). Had they continued, the fleets may have had the naval capability to sail around Africa to Europe or the Americas, if they had known those routes and places existed, but they had no incentive to do so. Some thirty-six countries in southern and western Asia officially acknowledged Chinese preeminence. The ruler of Malindi, an East African city, sent ambassadors bearing tribute, including a giraffe.

Historians still debate the reasons for Zheng's great voyages. Some point to the desire to have foreign countries reaffirm the emperor as the Son of Heaven. Zheng may also have sought a deposed boy emperor who had disappeared, possibly fleeing into exile. Others suspect the ambitious emperor wanted to demonstrate China's military capabilities. As these voyages coincided with increased activity by Chinese merchants in Southeast Asia, some historians see commercial motives as primary. Many thousands of Chinese, especially traders, visited or settled in the Philippines, Indonesia, Malaya, Siam, and Vietnam, creating a closer commercial link to China, while Yuan and Ming porcelain was sold as far west as South-Central Africa.

Zheng He's voyages may also have revitalized an imperial tribute system that during Tang times shaped China's relations with its neighbors. Historians debate the significance of the tribute system and whether it is a useful concept to understand China's historical relations to its Asian neighbors. According to the tribute system model, China considered friendly East, Southeast, and Central Asian states as vassals, granting them trade but rarely intervening to support their allies. In return tributary states sent periodic envoys bearing gifts to the emperor, confirming his superiority and playing along to gain China's goodwill and trade goods. In Ming times tribute came regularly from states in Korea, Vietnam, Cambodia, Borneo, Indonesia, South Asia, and Central Asia.

But unlike the earlier Tang, the Ming were more suspicious of foreigners migrating to China. Inevitably the Chinese saw themselves as the Middle Kingdom, surrounded by "barbarian" societies. Never recognizing any other society as equal, they felt superior not just materially but also culturally, with people considered "barbarians" and hence deemed unable to resist China's appeal, a view reinforced when other East Asians borrowed from China and others sent tribute missions. To be civilized, they believed, was to embrace Chinese culture, and a virtuous ruler irresistibly attracted "barbarians." Thus tribute-bearers performed a rite, the **kotow**, that involved prostrating themselves before the emperor, a practice from which we get the modern English word *kowtow* ("to pander to authority"). This practice, above all others, left little doubt as to who was superior and who was inferior, reflecting a Confucian sense of hierarchy.

11-3e Ming China Turns Inward

In the early Ming, China remained perhaps the world's wealthiest, most developed country. Hindu India faced Muslim conquests, Middle Eastern societies struggled to overcome setbacks, and western Europeans were just beginning to foster political and economic dynamism. Commercially vibrant and outward-thrusting, Ming China had the capability to open maritime communication between the continents and become the dominant world power. Instead, China turned

kotow The tribute-bearers' act of prostrating themselves before the Chinese emperor.

inward. The grand voyages and the commercial thrust to distant lands came to a sudden halt when the Ming emperor ordered them ended, banned construction of deep-sea vessels, and soon outlawed Chinese emigration altogether. But some Chinese continued to illegally travel or settle abroad for trade; frustrated Ming officials admitted that "powerful families traded overseas with large ships. Scoundrels secretly profited from it."[17] Foreign merchant ships still came to China, with the tribute system providing cover for extensive trade and smuggling.

The stunning reversal of official Chinese engagement with the world that, in the perspective of later history, seemed so counterproductive sparks scholarly debate. Perhaps Zheng He's voyages, which brought back few valuable resources, were too costly even for the wealthy Ming government. Unlike Christians and Muslims, the Chinese lacked missionary zeal, having little interest in spreading religion and culture except to near neighbors like Vietnam. Furthermore, despite flourishing guilds and frequent wealth, merchants generally held a low status in the

MAP 11.3 **The Voyages of Zheng He** After replacing the Mongols, the Ming reestablished a strong Chinese state, attempted to recolonize Vietnam, and rebuilt the Great Wall. Ming emperors also dispatched a series of grand maritime expeditions in the early 1400s that reached the Middle East and East Africa.

Q What does this map show about the extent of Zheng He's voyages?

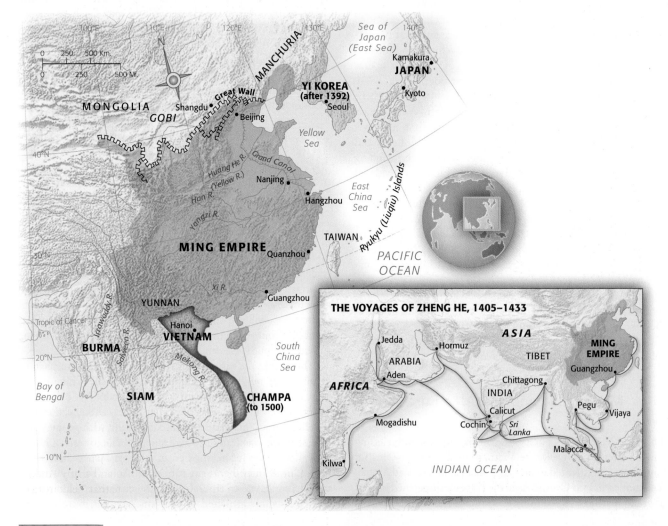

THE VOYAGES OF ZHENG HE, 1405–1433

Confucian social system. Ming leaders believed profit was evil, and mercantile interests inevitably conflicted with political ones. A later Ming scholar wrote that "one in a hundred [Chinese] is rich, while nine out of ten are impoverished. The poor cannot stand up to the rich. The lord of silver rules heaven and the god of copper cash reigns over the earth."[18] Hence, many mandarins despised merchants and opposed foreign trade. But some merchants, seeking respect and status, emulated the Confucian scholars by, for example, collecting art, engaging in philanthropy, and educating their sons.

Military factors also influenced the turn inward. With Mongols regrouping in Central Asia and memories of oppressive Mongol rule still fresh, the Ming shifted resources to defend the northern borders and the pirate-infested Pacific coast, rebuilding and extending the Great Wall. The Great Wall

sections near Beijing, enjoyed by millions of tourists every year, mostly reflect work done by the Ming. In addition, military operations along the northern border and an ill-fated invasion of Vietnam generated a fiscal crisis that weakened the government.

Finally, the catastrophe of Mongol rule made the Chinese more ethnocentric and antiforeign. Always land-based, self-centered, and self-sufficient, the Chinese now believed they needed little from outside. China remained powerful, productive, and mostly prosperous, enjoying generally high living standards, well into the eighteenth century, when profits from overseas colonies and the Industrial Revolution tipped the balance in favor of northwest Europe. By the later Ming, China had entered a period of relative isolation that was ended only by the forceful intrusion of a newly developed Europe in the early 1800s.

KEY POINTS

▶ The ancient Chinese fear of Central Asian nomads was realized when the Mongols, under Genghis and Khubilai Khan, conquered China and established the Yuan dynasty.

▶ Khubilai Khan made improvements in China's transportation system and moved the capital to Beijing.

▶ Because of lack of cooperation from Chinese scholars and bureaucrats, the Mongols established an international civil service, in which Marco Polo served.

▶ After the end of Mongol rule, the Chinese enjoyed three centuries of prosperity under the Ming dynasty, and their sense of well-being was displayed in Zheng He's grand sailing expeditions, which enhanced China's position among its neighbors.

▶ For reasons still debated, the Ming emperor suddenly ordered all overseas activity halted and China turned inward, beginning an isolation that ended only in the 1800s.

11-4 Cultural Adaptation in Korea and Japan

⇄ TRANSITIONS   🏛 SOCIETIES

Q How did the Koreans and Japanese develop their own distinctive societies?

If non-Japanese people today think about premodern Japan they may have stereotypical images of fierce samurai warriors, meditating Zen monks, enigmatic rock gardens, flower arranging, the tea ceremony, majestic Mount Fuji, and the like. Except for the samurai, those are still part of Japanese life. But while including these things, Japan's history has many more aspects. As East Asia's cultural heartland, China influenced its three large neighbors of Vietnam (see Chapter 13), Korea, and Japan. All derived considerable culture from China, including writing systems, philosophies, and political institutions. At the same time, they adapted these influences to their indigenous customs, maintaining their cultural identity. Eventually the Japanese developed a very different way of life and outlook than they had a few centuries earlier.

> **CONNECTION to TODAY**
>
> What lessons can modern people learn from the ability of Korea and Japan to borrow and adapt useful ideas from China without being overwhelmed by their large, powerful neighbor?

Chinese culture and institutions. Buddhism triumphed as many Korean Buddhist monks traveled to China, and the Tang system became the government model, with Confucianism as a political ideology. But Koreans borrowed selectively. They placed more emphasis than the Chinese did on inherited status instead of merit, and the rich–poor gap was wider. Moreover, Silla's rulers included three queens, suggesting less gender bias than in China. For example, Queen Sondok (r. 632–647) fostered science and promoted a tolerant mixing of Buddhism and shamanism. Silla women generally shared in their menfolk's social status and enjoyed many legal rights.

During the period of Silla domination (676–935), Koreans adapted Chinese writing to their own very different spoken language and created a distinctive literature in history, religion, and poetry. To mass-produce these works, Silla craftsmen developed woodblock printing as early as China, and the world's oldest extant woodblock printing, a Korean Buddhist writing, dates from 751. In astronomy, a great observatory is one of East Asia's oldest. Korea also formed connections with the wider world. Buddhist pilgrims came from India, and many Arabs traded or settled down there. One Arab wrote that "seldom has

11-4a Korea and China

Several strong states emerged on the Korean peninsula. In the mid-seventh century the southern state, Silla **(SILL-ah)**, defeated its main rival, Koguryo (Goguryeo), and eventually united most Koreans. Political unity fostered homogenization of Korean culture. Like earlier states, Silla became China's vassal, borrowing

---

[18]Zhang Tao, quoted in Timothy Brook, *The Confusions of Pleasure: Commerce and Culture in the Ming* (Berkeley: University of California Press, 1998), vii.

IMAGE 11.7 **King Sejong** This modern statue portrays the Yi dynasty King Sejong, revered by Koreans for his political, economic, and scientific achievements, such as observing stars and supervising book printing. Sejong patronized learning, supported agricultural innovations that increased crop yields, introduced humane laws, and fostered economic growth.

Q How does the statue reflect the respect accorded King Sejong by Koreans today?

a stranger who has come there from Iraq or another country left it afterwards. So healthy is the air there, so pure the water, so fertile the soil and so plentiful of all good things."[19]

Gradually Silla declined as the result of elite rivalries, corruption, and peasant uprisings. The new dominant state, Koryo (**KAW-ree-oh**), lasted for over four centuries (935–1392). Chinese influence continued in politics and philosophy, with Koreans erecting an examination system and importing neo-Confucianism. During this time the Koreans developed a publishing industry, inventing the world's first metal, movable-type printing by 1234. But they retained a distinctive political and social system. Court, military, and aristocratic landowning families influenced kings, who were never as strong as Chinese emperors. Another difference was that Korean farming relied on large estates. Women's status also changed. In contrast to Silla women, Koryo court women mainly exercised influence behind the scenes. For example, Lady Yu successfully urged her reluctant husband, Wang Kon, the Koryo dynasty founder, to seize power from a despotic ruler, arguing, "It is an ancient tradition to raise a banner of revolt against a tyrant. How can you, a great military leader, hesitate?"[20]

While most Koryo women played a lesser role in public affairs, they farmed and took full responsibility for family affairs.

Korean Buddhism, assimilating many animist elements, gradually became a powerful economic and political force. But the involvement of monks in political life fostered religious corruption and a worldly orientation, alienating some believers. Hence, although for fifteen hundred years most Koreans have been nominally Buddhist, the religion gradually lost influence.

11-4b Choson and the Yi Dynasty

When the Mongols conquered the peninsula, the Koreans resisted. The Mongols responded by devastating the land, carrying off hundreds of thousands of captives, and imposing heavy taxes. Yet, during the Mongol era closer links to trade networks brought to Korea more Chinese and western Asian learning and technology. In 1392 a new Korean dynasty, the Yi (**yee**), whose state was known as Choson (**cho-suhn**), meaning "Fresh Dawn," replaced Mongol rule and lasted five hundred and eighteen years, until 1910 (see Map 11.4).

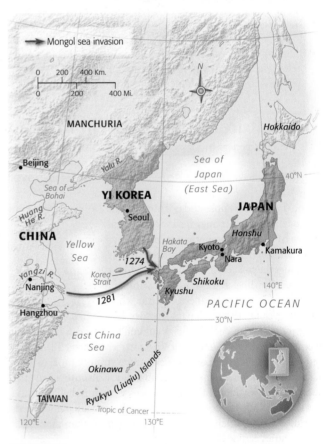

MAP 11.4 **Korea and Japan, CA. 1300** Japanese society developed in an archipelago, the major early cities rising in central Honshu. In 1274 and 1281 the Japanese repulsed Mongol invasions by sea. Throwing off the Mongols, Korea was unified under the Yi dynasty in 1392.

Q What does this map show about the relationship of Korea and Japan to China?

[19]Quoted in Bruce Cumings, *Korea's Place in the Sun: A Modern History* (New York: W.W. Norton, 1997), 37.
[20]Quoted in Yung Chung Kim, ed. and trans., *Women of Korea: A History from Ancient Times to 1945* (Seoul: Ehwa Women's University Press, 1977), 32.

Choson maintained a tribute relationship with China while expanding Chinese social and political models. Government careers required mastering Confucian scholarship, with Confucianism legitimizing government by a virtuous ruler. Education expanded to prepare students for civil service exams. Confucian influence also remade Korean social institutions such as the family. Believing Korean women had too much freedom and hence behaved immorally, the Yi encouraged women's seclusion at home, arranged marriages, face veiling when out in public, female chastity, and strict obedience to husbands and fathers. However, commoner women, needed for work in the fields, usually had more freedom of movement. Today Confucianism is arguably stronger than Buddhism, especially in rural Korea.

Choson remained among the more creative Late Intermediate societies, encouraging literature, technology, and science. For example, Koreans created the world's first rain gauges and installed them throughout the country to keep accurate rainfall records. King Sejong (**say-jong**) (r. 1418–1450), respected by Koreans for improving the economy, helping poor peasants, and prohibiting cruel punishments, strongly supported scientific progress. Sejong wrote agricultural books and formed a think tank, the Hall of Worthies, where scholars invented a phonetic system for pronouncing Chinese characters and writing the Korean language. But Koreans still used Chinese for serious scholarship.

11-4c Japan in the Nara Era

Although adopting many Chinese and Korean influences, Japan produced a robust, highly distinctive society. Influenced by Prince Shotoku's efforts, in the mid-sixth century the Japanese embarked on three centuries of deliberate cultural borrowing from China with the *Taika* (**TIE-kah**) ("Great Change") reform of 646 CE, which rulers hoped would transform Japan into a centralized empire like Tang China. The new governmental system resembled, on the surface, China's centralized bureaucracy. The Japanese now used the Chinese writing system to record their history and conduct daily activities. Adopting Buddhism also brought a rich art and architecture tradition to Japan. Meanwhile, Koreans continued to migrate to Japan.

Conscious borrowing from China peaked in the Nara (**NAH-rah**) era (710–784), named for Japan's first capital city, which was modeled on the Tang capital, Chang'an, and home to some twenty thousand people. Japan's total population at the time probably numbered 5 to 6 million. The Nara regime nationalized land in the emperor's name and, using Tang models, reallocated it on an equal basis to peasants, who then paid a land and labor tax. Abandoned as unworkable after a few decades, the system illustrated that in agrarian societies like Japan, land control supported political power.

Despite changes designed to strengthen imperial authority, the emperor never became an activist Chinese-style ruler. Powerful aristocrats controlled the bureaucracy while retaining large tax-exempt landholdings. During this era Japan was developing a system whereby the emperors held mostly symbolic political and spiritual authority, but one powerful family filled the highest government posts and exercised the most political power. Emperors lived in luxurious seclusion, guaranteeing an unbroken succession through having sons. This system of powerless

emperors remained in place, in one form or another, into the nineteenth century.

Nara leaders promoted aspects of Chinese culture, blending them with Japanese traditions. Imperial court rituals and ceremonies, largely based on Tang models and still maintained today, included stately dances and orchestral music using Japanese versions of Chinese musical instruments such as the flute, lute, and zither. Chinese writing also gained great prestige, with Chinese ideographs (characters) adapted to Japan's very different nontonal spoken language, a difficult conversion process. Chinese literary forms, including poetry and calligraphy, also became popular.

The Japanese adopted and reshaped the Chinese philosophical and religious doctrines they found appealing. They modified Confucianism's ethical and political doctrines to suit their own society and adopted Mahayana Buddhism, whose view that all things are impermanent greatly influenced their art and literature. Many artists and poets focused on the passing of time and changing seasons. Hence, one writer ruminated in 1212, "The river's waters are always changing. The foam on the pond appears, disappears. So is it in this world with men and their houses."[21] But the Japanese also retained their animist nature worship, known today as Shinto, which probably incorporated some Chinese (especially Daoist) influences as it became an official imperial religious practice. Shinto and Buddhism addressed different needs and easily coexisted. Shinto deities were not gods but beautiful natural phenomena such as Mount Fuji (**FOO-jee**), waterfalls, thunder, or stately trees. Shinto also stressed ritual purity, encouraging bathing and personal cleanliness. It offered no coherent theology, moral doctrine, or concept of death or an afterlife.

Economic unrest disrupted late Nara society. Resenting forced labor and military conscription, which often caused economic ruin, many peasants abandoned their fields and became wandering *ronin* (**ROH-neen**) ("wave people"), some of whom were hired by large landowners as workers. To stop people from becoming ronin, the government abolished compulsory service and gave responsibility for policing and defense to local officials. Eventually the ronin these officials hired as troops became the provincial warrior class, armed with bows and arrows and curved swords, who reshaped Japanese life.

11-4d Heian Cultural Renaissance

During the Heian (**HAY-en**) period (794–1184), when the capital moved from Nara to Heian, the city better known since those times as Kyoto, twenty-eight miles north, imitating and borrowing from China gradually ended and was replaced by relative isolation. Heian leaders discontinued foreign contacts in the ninth century and set about consciously absorbing and adapting imported Chinese cultural patterns under the slogan "Chinese learning, Japanese spirit." At the same time, Buddhism gradually harmonized with Shinto beliefs while generating new sects, art, and temple building. A unique court society also arose that fostered a distinctly Japanese writing system, literary styles, arts, and worldview. The development of **kana** (**KAH-nah**), a phonetic script consisting of forty-seven syllabic signs derived

> **kana** A Japanese phonetic script developed in the Heian period (794–1184) that consisted of some forty-seven syllabic signs derived from Chinese characters.

[21]Komo no Chomei, from "Hojoki: My Ten-By-Ten Hut," in William McNaughton, *Light from the East: An Anthology of Asian Literature* (New York: Laurel, 1978), 249.

from Chinese characters, allowed Japanese to write their language phonetically, especially when kana letters were combined with Chinese characters. This system is still used today.

Heian elite culture, enormously remote from us today in time, attitudes, and behavior, reached its high point around 1000 CE, flourishing among a small group of privileged families in Kyoto, a city of around 100,000. Many elite residents in Kyoto thrived from bureaucratic jobs and land ownership. This aristocracy, extraordinarily withdrawn from the outside world, created a culture governed by standards of form and beauty, making no distinction between art and life. Passionately concerned with social rank, they created some of Japan's greatest literature and art while admiring the ability to write artistically, compose a graceful poem, and create an elegant costume. They energetically created beauty, such as by putting together harmonious syllables and lines of ink on the page or perfumes on the body. The Heian period was unique for the careful attention spent in choosing an undergarment or the time taken in writing a love note, with perhaps a tastefully faded chrysanthemum to emphasize the melancholy nature of the contents. Holding superficial values, Heian aristocrats, not interested in pure intellect or social morality, were obsessed by mood, especially the sense of beauty's transience.

Women from affluent families enjoyed their highest status during Heian times, with romantic affairs and sexual promiscuity tolerated for both men and women. Aristocratic women spent their days playing games, writing, listening to romantic stories, or practicing art. Some, such as the novelist Lady Murasaki (**MUR-uh-SAH-kee**), gained a formal education and wrote poetry, fiction, prose, and diaries because, without demanding jobs, they had abundant free time and could focus on their feelings (see Meet the People: Lady Murasaki, Heian Novelist). Men were expected to compose poems in the classical Chinese style, which had more prestige, while women wrote in the phonetic Japanese alphabet. A poet might deftly turn a scene of nature into one of emotion: "The flowers withered, their color faded away, while meaninglessly, I spent my days in the world, and the long rains were falling."[22]

The Heian aristocracy saw love as an art; people wrote poems before meeting their lover and then the following morning, such as these two morning-after poems from the diary of a prominent woman writer, Izumi Shikibu:

> Woman: "painful though it were, to see you leave before dawn [to avoid discovery], better by far than when the dawn's grey light, so cruelly tears you from my side." Prince: "to leave you while the leaves are moist with dew, is bitterer by far, than if I were to say farewell at night, without a single chance to show my love."[23]

Reflecting different standards of beauty than today, Heian women wore their hair long to the ground, applied white skin powder and lipstick, plucked their eyebrows, and blackened their teeth with dye. In one novel, a lady refuses to do these things, disgusting her attendants: "Those eyebrows of hers, like hairy caterpillars, aren't they; and her teeth—like peeled caterpillars."[24] Equally concerned with their personal dress and appearance, men also used cosmetics.

However, only a tiny fraction of Japan's population could afford this hedonism so removed from real life. The common people outside Kyoto had vastly different experiences, usually working at bare subsistence levels as farmers and craftsmen. Generally illiterate and saddled by unremitting work, most knew nothing of Heian court life or Chinese literature. Heian aristocrats called the provinces "uncivilized, barbarous, wretched" places.[25] But late Heian literature also reflected a growing pessimism that the Kyoto elite's world might soon vanish. Social and economic changes were clearing the path for a more decentralized system, as powerful regional families gained wealth and built up their own warrior bands, based on kinship and vassal ties to their lord, to keep the peace. By the twelfth century, Japan was moving into a new historical phase and a much different social system.

11-4e The Warrior Class and a New Japanese Society

The provincial warrior class, who would shape Japan's future, assimilated the residue of Chinese culture from the Heian elite. As Heian governors, too fond of Kyoto life, delegated their local powers to subordinates, this warrior class gradually became the dominant force in Japanese politics and society, producing a very different culture. Rural society changed, with powerful, land-hungry, tax-exempt families and Buddhist communities often seizing land by force and increasing the tax load on peasants. Some peasants fled to remote areas or joined roving bands of unattached ronin; others signed over themselves and their lands to lords of manors, becoming bound to the soil and supplying food in exchange for protection. Thus Heian-era estates were replaced by lords ruling over the villages on their land. By around 1200 perhaps only 10 percent of the cultivated land remained taxable, and a new rural aristocracy held local power. Soldiers and ronin became military retainers to aristocratic landowning families headed by mounted warriors. As the end of conscription weakened imperial forces, political and military power dispersed to rural areas. Overpopulation also contributed to periodic fighting, with too many people competing for control of too little good land.

The warrior class fostered a social and political system more like Zhou China or medieval Europe than the centralized Tang state. Historians disagree as to when between the twelfth and fourteenth centuries the transition to a new Age of Warriors was completed, but the system continued in some form to the nineteenth century. Rights to land and lord–vassal relations lubricated military, political, and economic power. Despite many similarities between post-Heian Japan and medieval Europe, Japanese rulers were often stronger than most European kings.

The warrior class, or **samurai** (SAH-moo-rie) ("one who serves"), gradually assumed military supremacy over the emperor and the court. Rural lords and their military retainers forged a relationship based on an idealized feudal ethic later known as

samurai ("one who serves") A member of the Japanese warrior class, which gained power between the twelfth and fourteenth centuries and continued until the nineteenth.

---

[22]Quoted in Donald Keene, "Literature," in *An Introduction to Japanese Civilization*, ed. Arthur E. Tiedemann (Lexington, MA: D.C. Heath, 1974), 395.
[23]Quoted in Ivan Morris, *The World of the Shining Prince: Court Life in Ancient Japan* (New York: Kodansha, 1994), 229.
[24]Quoted in Ibid., 204.
[25]Quoted in Mikiso Hane, *Japan: A Historical Survey* (New York: Charles Scribner's, 1972), 56.

Lady Murasaki, Heian Novelist

Women produced much of the best Heian literature. Beginning around 1008, a lady-in-waiting, Lady Murasaki (Murasaki Shibiku), wrote the greatest book, *The Tale of Genji*, the first psychological novel and perhaps even the first novel written by a woman anywhere in the world. Murasaki worked as the maid to Empress Akiko, the emperor's consort and daughter of a political leader. We know only a little of Murasaki's life, much of it from a diary she kept. She was born around 978 into a leading aristocratic family steeped in literature, her grandfather being a famed poet and her father a provincial governor who, apparently lamenting she was not a boy, allowed her to study. Murasaki's writing showed familiarity with Chinese history, literature, and poetry. Indeed, she criticized young people who expected good jobs without undergoing appropriate training.

Perhaps because she avidly pursued learning, Murasaki was married late, at age twenty, but her much older husband died only a few years later from illness. She had at least two children, including a daughter who later became a well-known writer. Murasaki probably died sometime between 1025 and 1031, perhaps after several years as a Buddhist nun. Her self-description in her diary suggests an introverted woman:

> Pretty yet shy, unsociable, fond of old tales, conceited, so wrapped up in poetry that other people hardly exist, spitefully looking down on the whole world—such is the unpleasant opinion that people have of me. Yet when they come to know me they say that I am strangely gentle, quite unlike what they had been led to believe.

Combining prose with short poems, *The Tale of Genji* is much more sophisticated in language and thoughtful in sensibility than earlier Japanese literature. In *Genji* Murasaki made contemporary language rather than formal Chinese writing style an artistic medium. Even today words and phrases from *Genji* are common in Japanese language. She also had other goals, claiming that the novel should always have "a definite and serious purpose." In focusing on her characters' emotional and psychological interplay, her writing betrays a strongly feminine perspective. A treasure-trove on social history, *Genji* reveals much about the times. But it is also steeped in mystery. Scholars debate whether it is really about Prince Genji, its male hero, or chiefly about the women in his life and their struggles for love, status, and security.

The engaging story chronicles the life and amorous adventures of handsome Prince Genji, an emperor's son and model for the qualities of taste and refinement admired by the Kyoto aristocracy. Genji is an accomplished poet, painter, dancer, musician, and athlete. But his supreme gift is the art most prized: "pillowing" (lovemaking). Genji and his friends, devoting little time to their government jobs, spend their days largely searching for pleasure, attending

Culture Club/Hulton Archive/Getty Images

IMAGE 11.8 **Lady Murasaki** This eighteenth-century painting of Lady Murasaki writing *The Tale of Genji* while observing the moon reflected the styles of the artist's times but also suggests the continuing significance of the beloved Heian-era writer.

Q How does the painting portray the environment and workspace that shaped Murasaki's writing?

countless ceremonial functions, reciting poetry endlessly, and moving from one romantic affair to another. The novel's mood is subdued melancholy and nostalgia for the passing of lovely things. Both men and women freely express their emotions. Hence, Genji shows a keen sensitivity to nature: "I hope that I shall have a little time left for things which I really enjoy—flowers, autumn leaves, the sky, all those day-to-day changes and wonders that a single year brings forth; that is what I look forward to." The novel ends with Genji making plans to give up his posts and retire to a mountain village, perhaps to continue with his poetry, music, and painting while focusing more on religious knowledge. Writing fiction stories was considered frivolous and even immoral in Heian Japan, but the greatness of her work led to acceptance and acclaim. Murasaki's writing is still very popular today in Japan and with literature fans around the world.

Reflection Questions

1. What sort of background did Murasaki come from?
2. Why is *Genji* such an important work of literature?
3. Why do you think Murasaki's writing remains so popular today with audiences in Japan and other countries?

Notes: Quotations from Ivan Morris, *The World of the Shining Prince* (New York: Kodansha, 1994), 251; Ryusaku Tsunoda et al., eds., *Sources of Japanese Tradition*, vol. 2 (New York: Columbia University Press, 1958), 178–179; and Mikiso Hane, *Japan: A Historical Survey* (New York: Charles Scribner's, 1972), 56.

Bushido (boo-SHEE-doh) ("way of the warrior"), that was not completely developed until the seventeenth century. The samurai had two great ideals: loyalty to leaders and absolute indifference to all physical hardship. They enjoyed special legal and ceremonial rights and expected in return to give their lords unquestioning service. Most women from samurai families received some martial arts training to help run and defend the family estates. Some of them, known as the *onna-bugeisha* ("female martial artist"), engaged in combat alongside men, wielding some of the same weapons including swords, bows, and spears. The most celebrated female samurai in Japanese legend, Tomoe Gozen, supposedly fought in the Genpei War between two powerful clans in the 1180s. Over the centuries various plays and paintings have honored her actions in battle.

Although heading the social system, samurai constituted a small percentage of the population. If a samurai failed to do his duty or achieve his purpose, suicide was considered a purposeful and honorable act that served as conclusive evidence that here was a man who could be respected by friend and enemy alike for his physical courage, determination, and sincerity. Homosexuality was also common among the samurai, as among several other warrior castes in history, such as the Spartans in Classical Greece, perhaps because of male bonding and an ethic extolling male values. Japanese society generally tolerated same-sex relationships. Such unique cultural patterns as Zen Buddhism and the tea ceremony also rose to prominence among the samurai class.

11-4f The Shogunates and Economic Change

With Japan controlled by competing bands of feudal lords, civil war broke out between two powerful families and their respective allies. One lord, Minamoto-no-Yoritomo (MIN-a-MO-to-no-YOR-ee-TO-mo), emerged victorious and set up a military government in Kamakura (kah-mah-KOO-rah), near Tokyo (TOE-kee-oh), that lasted from 1180 to 1333. The emperor commissioned him **shogun** (SHOW-guhn) ("barbarian-subduing generalissimo"), or military dictator controlling the country in the name of the emperor, who remained in luxurious seclusion in Kyoto. Responsible for internal and external defense, the shogun could nominate his own successor. No shogun seriously attempted to abolish the imperial house, which, though politically impotent, symbolized the people and land. Kamakura shoguns, nominally subordinate to the emperors, had real power, but before 1600 the system was not very centralized. Japan now had a form of **dyarchy**, a rigid kind of dual government whereby one powerful family filled the highest government posts and dominated the emperors, whose power was mostly symbolic.

Mongols failed twice, in 1274 and 1281, to invade Japan. Khubilai Khan sent messengers imperiously demanding that Japanese leaders acknowledge a subservient tributary relationship to his regime: "You, stupid little barbarians. Do you dare to defy us by not submitting?"[26] Knowing less about Mongols than most Asians, they refused, outraging Khubilai. The 1281 attempt involved up to 150,000 men transported by over four thousand conscripted Chinese ships, some armed with ceramic bombs, the world's first known seagoing exploding projectiles. On both occasions, Mongol armies landed, met fierce resistance, and were destroyed when great storms scattered and shipwrecked their fleets. These divine winds, or *kamikaze* (KAHM-i-KAHZ-ee), convinced the Japanese of special protection by the gods, and any inferiority complex toward China ended. Japan was not successfully invaded and defeated until 1945.

In 1333 the Kamakura Shogunate collapsed through intrigues and civil wars and was replaced by a government headed by the Kyoto-based Ashikaga (ah-shee-KAH-gah) family (1338–1568). But Ashikaga shoguns never had much real power beyond the capital. Political power became increasingly decentralized as local lords struggled to obtain more land, leading to the rise of several hundred landowning territorial magnates called **daimyo** (DIE-MYO) ("great name"), whose positions somewhat resembled the lords of the manor in medieval Europe. Each daimyo monopolized local power, had his supporting samurai, and derived income from the peasants working on his land.

Between 1200 and 1500 Japan experienced rapid change in both economic and political spheres. Agriculture became more productive, and an increasingly active merchant class lived in the fast-growing towns. The Japanese developed a new interest in foreign trade, with Japanese sailors and merchants traveling to China and Southeast Asia. Chinese merchants also settled in several southern ports such as Hoian in Vietnam. These new energies strained the rigid political and social system. In the 1500s civil war and the arrival of European merchants and Christian missionaries aggravated these problems, resulting in a dramatic modification of the political system.

11-4g Japanese Society, Religion, and Culture

Shaped by the warrior class, Japanese society and culture became even more rigid than before. Inequality started in the family, which was headed by a patriarchal male: children owed obedience to their parents, and the young honored the old. Expected to be dutiful, obedient, and loyal to their menfolk, women moved into their husband's household after marriages arranged for family interests, not romantic love. Marriage became more durable and divorce more difficult, giving married women more security but fewer options. Aristocratic women dominated the imperial court staff and ran the emperor's household. As in China, group interests outweighed individual rights and freedoms.

Many Buddhist sects emerged during this time, but three became most significant in Japan and have attracted followers today in the West. The largest, the *Pure Land*, emphasized prayer and faith for salvation, stressed the equality of all believers, and rejected reincarnation, maintaining that believers went straight to nirvana; it became very popular among the lower

---

Bushido ("Way of the Warrior") An idealized ethic for the Japanese samurai.

shogun ("barbarian-subduing generalissimo") A Japanese military dictator controlling the country in the name of the emperor.

dyarchy A form of dual government that began in Japan during the Nara period (710–784), whereby one powerful family ruled the country while the emperor held mostly symbolic power.

daimyo ("great name") Large landowning territorial magnates who monopolized local power in Japan beginning with the Ashikaga period (1338–1568).

---

[26]Quoted in Lo Jung-Pang, *China as a Sea Power, 1127–1368*, ed. Bruce Elleman (Hong Kong: Kong University Press, 2012), 89.

classes and still accounts for the majority of Japanese Buddhists today. The *Nicheren* (NEE-chee-ren) sect has sometimes been compared to Christianity and Islam because of its militant pros-elytizing and concern for the afterlife. Whereas most Japanese Buddhists were peaceful and tolerant, Nicherens were angry, seeing rival views as heresy. The third major Buddhist sect, **Zen**, originating in China under Daoist influence, emphasized medi-tation, individual practice and discipline, self-control, self-understanding, and intuition. Zen practitioners believed that knowledge came from seeking deep into the mind, rather than from outside assistance. One Zen pioneer wrote, "Great is mind. Heaven's height is immeasurable but Mind goes beyond heaven; the earth's depth is unfathomable, but Mind reaches below the earth. Mind travels outside the macrocosm."[27] Zen practitioners expected enlightenment to come in a flash of understanding. Zen culture, devised to bring people in touch with their non-verbal, nonrational side, stressed simplicity and restraint, con-tending that "great mastery is as if unskillful."[28] Demanding deep mental discipline, Zen remains the smallest although probably best known of the three sects in Japan.

Zen values permeated the arts, including rock gardens, landscape gardening, and flower arrangements. Gardens, ponds, and buildings, such as the beautiful thirteenth-century Golden Pavilion of Kyoto, emphasized harmony with their natural sur-roundings. The highly formalized tea ceremony, emphasizing patience, restraint, serenity, and the beauty of simple action involving the commonplace preparing and drinking of tea, could last two hours, suggesting withdrawal from the real world. Japanese ceramics and pottery later gained world respect for their subtlety and understated beauty. Potters made cups, bowls, and vases using rough textures and irregular lines to suggest weath-ering and the effects of time, a Japanese preoccupation. An old art, painting stressed not creativ-ity or self-expression but skill and technique through self-discipline. The **Noh** drama, which included stylized gestures and spectacular masks, also appeared in this era.

> **Zen** A form of Japanese Buddhism called the meditation sect because it emphasizes individual practice and discipline, self-control, self-understanding, and intuition.

> **Noh** Japanese plays that use stylized gestures and spectacular masks; began in the fourteenth century.

KEY POINTS

▶ The Korean state of Silla was subordinate to China and borrowed a great deal from China's culture, adapting it to Korean traditions.

▶ Ruling Korea after the Mongols, the Yi sought good relations with China and instituted the Chinese educational and civil service exam system.

▶ In the Nara period, Japan borrowed heavily from Chinese culture, but its government was a dyarchy in which one powerful family dominated the emperor, and imports such

as Buddhism were melded with native cultural features such as Shinto.

▶ In the Heian period, borrowing from China ended, foreign contacts were stopped, and a small elite group, concerned almost exclusively with the pursuit of aesthetic beauty, created some of Japan's best art and literature.

▶ In Japan, the warrior class, or samurai, gradually attained supremacy over the emperor and the court, and an organization like that of medieval Europe, based on lords and vassals, became dominant.

---

[27]From Ryusaku Tsunoda et al., eds., *Sources of Japanese Tradition*, vol. 2 (New York: Columbia University Press, 1958), 236.
[28]Quoted in Noel F. Busch, *The Horizon Concise History of Japan* (New York: American Heritage, 1972), 58.

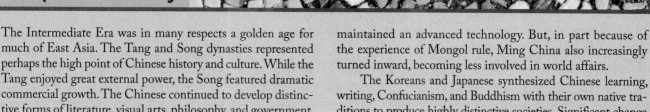

Chapter Summary

The Intermediate Era was in many respects a golden age for much of East Asia. The Tang and Song dynasties represented perhaps the high point of Chinese history and culture. While the Tang enjoyed great external power, the Song featured dramatic commercial growth. The Chinese continued to develop distinc-tive forms of literature, visual arts, philosophy, and government, as well as new technologies and scientific understandings. The Mongol conquest and brief period of rule weakened China's dynamism but extended overland trade routes that linked China even more closely to the outside world and promoted the spread of Chinese science and technology to western Eurasia. During the Ming, China briefly reasserted its transregional power and

maintained an advanced technology. But, in part because of the experience of Mongol rule, Ming China also increasingly turned inward, becoming less involved in world affairs.

The Koreans and Japanese synthesized Chinese learning, writing, Confucianism, and Buddhism with their own native tra-ditions to produce highly distinctive societies. Significant change occurred in Japan as it moved from the aristocratic court culture of Heian to a warrior-dominated culture based on large landown-ing families and their military retainers, or samurai. By the end of the 1400s the East Asian societies remained strong but faced new challenges when Europeans began to expand their power in the world.

Key Terms

neo-Confucianism 268	samurai 278	daimyo 280
qi 268	Bushido 280	Zen 281
kotow 274	shogun 280	Noh 281
kana 277	dyarchy 280	

Expanding Horizons in Africa and the Americas, 600–1500

> *A long time ago, when the Arabs arrived in Lamu [a port in today's Kenya, East Africa], they found local people there. The Arabs were received with friendliness and they wanted to stay on. The local people offered to trade land for cloths. Before the trading was finished, the Arabs had the land, and the [local people] had the cloth.*
>
> —A Lamu oral tradition[1]

Werner Forman/Universal Images Group/Getty Images

IMAGE 12.1 **Sape Ivory Saltholder** Africans had traded and carved ivory since ancient times. This magnificent ivory carving, probably made in the fifteenth century by an artist of the Sape people, who lived in what is today Sierra Leone in West Africa, was used to store salt. The carving reflected artistic influence brought to the region by the earliest Portuguese explorers and traders.

Q What features and styles in this salt holder seem to suggest Portuguese influence and what seems more African?

---

[1]Quoted in Patricia W. Romero, *Lamu: History, Society, and Family in an East African Port City* (Princeton, NJ: Markus Wiener, 1997), 14.

Around 912 the Baghdad-born Arab geographer Abdul

Hassan Ibn Ali al-Mas'udi sailed to East Africa with mariners from Oman, in eastern Arabia, on their regular trading expedition to what Arabs described as *Zanj* ("the land of black people"). The journey along the East African coast could be perilous, with reefs and strong winds generating high waves. Al-Mas'udi visited ports as far south as Sofala (so-FALL-a), in Mozambique (moe-zam-BEEK). After travels to Persia, India, and China, al-Mas'udi settled in Cairo, where he wrote scholarly books. The most influential, *Meadows of Gold and Mines of Gems*, described changing East African societies while also recording the links between these coastal towns, Arabs, and other Eurasian societies. Al-Mas'udi praised the coast's energetic traders and skilled workers, reported that the Sofala region exported abundant gold, and described how Arabs carried ivory from Zanj to Oman, from where they shipped it to India and China. He wrote that "in China the Kings and military and civil officers use ivory [to decorate furniture]. In India ivory is much sought after. It is used for the handles of daggers. But the chief use of ivory is making chessmen and backgammon pieces."[2]

Until the 1960s history textbooks and education in Western countries tended to neglect or even ignore sub-Saharan Africa and the pre-Columbian Americas before the arrival of European explorers in the fifteenth century, followed over the next several centuries by Western slave traders, conquerors, and colonizers. This neglect, reflecting both ethnocentrism and ignorance, conveyed the impression that these regions had no significant history compared to Eurasia and played minimal roles in the world. This marginalization of Africa and the Americas made for an inaccurate and limited account of world history. During the Intermediate Era many East Asians, Southeast Asians, South Asians, West Asians, North Africans, and Europeans benefited from exchanging technologies, products, religions, and ideas. As al-Mas'udi confirmed, some sub-Saharan Africans also connected to this vast network as trade expanded. African peoples like the gold producers near Sofala became integral parts of hemispheric commerce. But many sub-Saharan Africans had only indirect links, and the American societies across the Atlantic Ocean had no known links, to these busy Afro-Eurasian networks. However, like Eurasians and Africans, Americans developed agriculture, formed states, built cities, and forged technologies suitable for their needs. Despite lacking contact with each other, Africans and Americans shared some social and political patterns and challenging desert, forest, or highland environments. States and empires rose and fell. However, unlike in more densely populated areas of Eurasia, where many people lived in large, centralized states, many Africans and Americans lived in self-governing villages. Western Hemisphere geography also inhibited the growth of long-distance networks such as those linking East Africa to China. Only after 1492 did maritime exploration permanently connect African, American, and Eurasian peoples.

[2]Quoted in Esmond Bradley Martin and Chryssee Perry Martin, *Cargoes of the East: The Ports, Trade and Culture of the Arabian Seas and Western Indian Ocean* (London: Elm Tree Books, 1978), 9.

12-1 Diverse African States and Peoples

NETWORKS SOCIETIES

Q How did contact with Islamic peoples help shape the societies of West and East Africa?

In his most influential book, the provocatively titled *Meadows of Gold and Mines of Gems*, the tenth-century Arab traveler Al-Mas'udi reported on his discoveries, writing that he intended his book "to excite a desire and curiosity about its contents, and to make the mind eager to become acquainted with history."[3] This is wise advice for studying world history, including the African contributions. Several important kingdoms arose in the Sudanic region and along the Guinea coast. As in Eurasia, empires sprouted, flourished, and decayed. Scholars studied and disputed in centers of learning, and what Chinese artists accomplished with ink and Europeans with paint, African artists achieved with bronze and wood. The rise of great Sudanic kingdoms coincided with Islamic expansion and a global commerce linking West Africa with North Africa, the Mediterranean Basin, and western Asia. Along the East African coast, Islam spread in a flourishing mercantile region linked to Eurasia. The Bantus also continued to expand as they settled the vast expanses of central, eastern, and southern Africa, some building great kingdoms. Like Sudanic kingdoms, Ethiopians, various American peoples, and most Eurasian

---
[3]Quoted in Basil Davidson, *The Lost Cities of Africa* (Boston: Little, Brown, 1959), 151.

> **CONNECTION to TODAY**
>
> How do you think that the varied environments and geography influenced African societies in the Intermediate Era and still do today?

societies, some Bantu groups built cities, kept records, engaged in extensive trade, and boasted diverse social classes. Indeed, many Africans were well integrated into the hemispheric system, with people, objects, and ideas circulating within Africa as well as to and from the world outside.

12-1a Trade, State Building, and Islamic Expansion in the Sudan

For hundreds of years camel caravans transporting gold, salt, ivory, slaves, and ceramics between West and North Africa had crossed the trackless Sahara sands, where dry conditions, towering sand dunes, and searing sun conspired against crops, grasses, and trees. But the desert became more a highway than an obstacle, especially with the arrival of Islam and an increasing volume of trade after 700 CE. The trade benefited people in the Sudan, the largely grasslands region just south of the Sahara, where generally flat geography and the long but sluggish Niger River made it a meeting place of people and ideas.

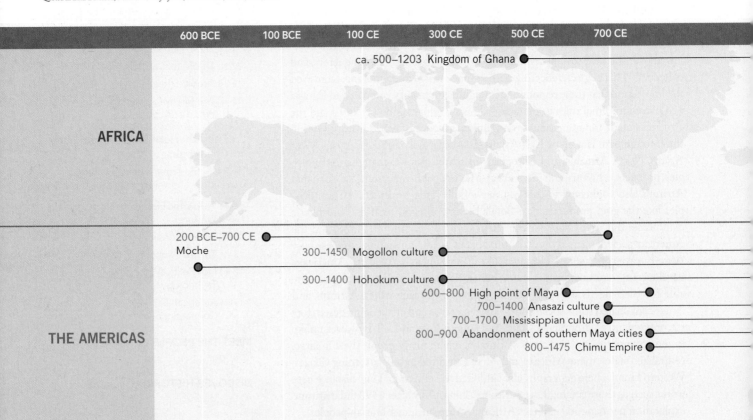

	600 BCE	100 BCE	100 CE	300 CE	500 CE	700 CE

AFRICA

ca. 500–1203 Kingdom of Ghana

THE AMERICAS

200 BCE–700 CE Moche
300–1450 Mogollon culture
300–1400 Hohokum culture
600–800 High point of Maya
700–1400 Anasazi culture
700–1700 Mississippian culture
800–900 Abandonment of southern Maya cities
800–1475 Chimu Empire

Beginning in the 800s, Islam filtered down Saharan trade routes much as it spread in Southeast Asian islands (see Chapter 13), carried peacefully by merchants, teachers, and mystics. Muslim merchants settling in Sudanic towns helped form stable governments to protect the trade, as many political and economic leaders, and eventually most Sudanic peoples, embraced Islam, introducing changes in customs, names, dress, diet, architecture, and festivals. Islamic schools spread literacy in Arabic, and the religious atmosphere promoted tolerance, by Muslims toward animists and vice versa. Still, Islamic practice was often superficial, and it took several centuries for the religion to permeate into villages.

A few kingdoms already existed before Islam reached the Sudan. Considered divine in these animist societies, kings remained aloof from the common people, ruling through bureaucracies. But elders or chiefs often played a role, electing kings and needing to approve major decisions, such as going to war. Women in royal families enjoyed some power and, in a few societies, could rule as queens. Some kingdoms became empires. But states were inherently unstable, having no fixed territorial boundaries but only fluctuating spheres of influence, and often included diverse ethnic groups.

The earliest known Sudanic kingdom was Ghana, centered on the northwestern Niger River (see Map 12.1). Mande speakers of the Soninke (**soh-NIN-kay**) ethnic group probably established Ghana around 500 CE (see Chapter 9), but it reached its golden age in the ninth and tenth centuries, prospering from controlling the trans-Saharan gold trade. Of Ghana and its profitable commerce, the Spanish Muslim traveler Abu Hamid

al-Andalusi wrote: "In the sands of that country is gold, treasure immeasurable. Merchants trade salt for it, taking the salt on camels from the salt mines. They travel on the desert as if it were a sea, having guides to pilot them by the stars or rocks."[4] Many of the twenty thousand inhabitants of Ghana's capital, Koumbi, were immigrants, including Arab and Berber merchants and some scribes who helped communicate with North Africa. Ghana's rulers converted to Islam, increasing the royal court's wealth and splendor. An Arab visitor wrote that the king's attendants had gold-plaited hair and carried gold-mounted swords, and that even guard dogs wore collars of gold and silver. Eventually mosques and Quranic schools dotted the capital. But a civil war erupted, and Berbers from North Africa attacked and destroyed the kingdom in 1203.

12-1b Mali and Songhai: Islam and Regional Power

The greatest Sudanic empire, Mali (**MAHL-ee**), was formed in 1234 by another Mande-speaking group, the Malinke (**muh-LING-kay**), led by the Keita (**KAY-ee-tah**) clan, whose leader, Sundiata (**soon-JAH-tuh**), became the **mansa** (**MAHN-suh**), or king (see Meet the People: Sundiata, Imperial Founder). Farmers and traders, the Malinke conquered much of the western Sudan, including most of the former Ghana territories.

> **mansa** ("king") Mande term used by the Malinke people to refer to the ruler of the Mali Empire.

[4]Quoted in *Africa's Glorious Legacy* (Arlington, VA: Time-Life Books, 1994), 90.

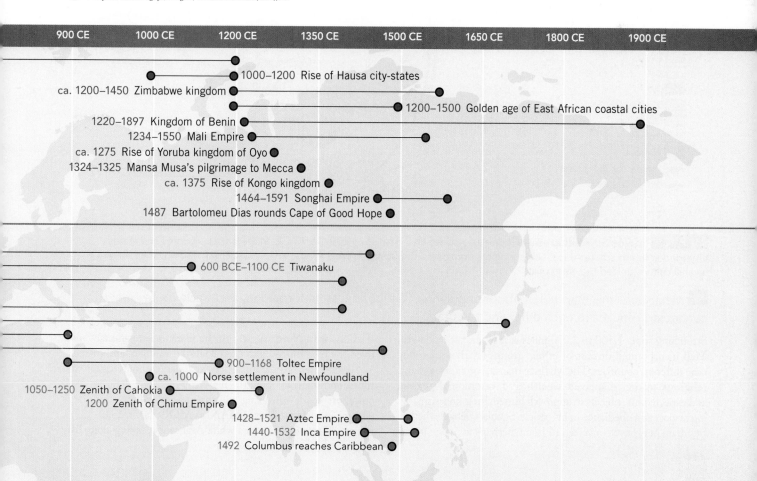

900 CE	1000 CE	1200 CE	1350 CE	1500 CE	1650 CE	1800 CE	1900 CE

1000–1200 Rise of Hausa city-states

ca. 1200–1450 Zimbabwe kingdom

1200–1500 Golden age of East African coastal cities

1220–1897 Kingdom of Benin

1234–1550 Mali Empire

ca. 1275 Rise of Yoruba kingdom of Oyo

1324–1325 Mansa Musa's pilgrimage to Mecca

ca. 1375 Rise of Kongo kingdom

1464–1591 Songhai Empire

1487 Bartolomeu Dias rounds Cape of Good Hope

600 BCE–1100 CE Tiwanaku

900–1168 Toltec Empire

ca. 1000 Norse settlement in Newfoundland

1050–1250 Zenith of Cahokia

1200 Zenith of Chimu Empire

1428–1521 Aztec Empire

1440–1532 Inca Empire

1492 Columbus reaches Caribbean

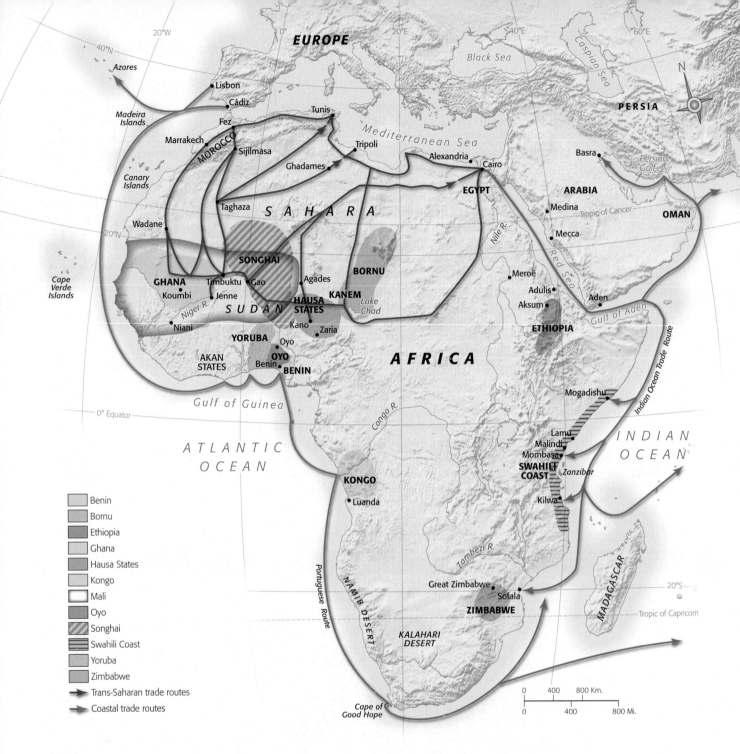

MAP 12.1 Major Sub-Saharan African Kingdoms and States, 1200–1600 CE Many large kingdoms and states emerged in Intermediate Africa. Large empires dominated the Sudan in West Africa, while prosperous trading cities sharing a Swahili culture dotted the east coast.

Q What does this map tell us about population distribution, state formation, and trade routes that connected Africans to each other and to Eurasia?

Stretching some 1,500 to 2,000 miles east to west at its height, Mali incorporated dozens of ethnic groups in what are today nine different countries. The Malinke mansa, both a secular and religious leader, displayed wealth and ceremonial regalia and expected his subjects to approach him on their knees, instilling respect and obedience in his people. Scholars debate whether Sundiata may have converted to Islam, perhaps to secure better

relations with North Africa, but he likely never seriously practiced the religion and also used Malinke animism and magic.

Increasing Islamic influence expanded communication and travel, and many adopted the new religion. Some Muslim Mali emperors made glittering pilgrimages to Mecca. Sundiata's descendant, Mansa Musa (**MAN-sa MOO-sa**) (r. 1312–1337), went to Mecca in 1324 on a white Arab horse, taking along fifty slaves bearing golden staffs, perhaps twelve thousand more slaves to carry supplies, and one thousand followers, including royal court officials, griots, entertainers, soldiers, and merchants. Then there were the one hundred camels, each loaded with three hundred pounds of gold. This opulent display, almost a city moving through the desert, was a sight to behold. Some recent scholarship suggests that Mansa Musa's major goal was geopolitical: to achieve recognition by the Mamluks who ruled Egypt as a peer in the Muslim world and hence find an ally against the Berbers in North Africa who controlled the gold trade to Europe and occasionally raided into the Sudan. An Arab official recorded Mansa Musa's visit to Egypt en route to Arabia: he "spread upon Cairo the flood of his generosity; there was no person or holder of any office who did not receive a sum of gold from him. The people of Cairo earned incalculable sums from him, whether by selling or gifts."[5]

As this account affirms, Mansa Musa was fabulously rich, a few historians even suggesting that he may have been the wealthiest man who ever lived (at least in premodern times). He probably was worth many billions of dollars in today's terms and may have controlled nearly half of the world's gold supply, the most highly valued source of wealth in the world at that time. But Mansa Musa's three-month stay in Cairo caused the price of gold to plummet for ten years, which badly damaged the economies of North Africa and West Asia. Even many Malians blamed him for wasting so much wealth. The visit and its aftermath made Mansa Musa famous in Africa and beyond and gave the Malian city of Timbuktu a mysterious reputation in Europe as a lost city of gold. He also built grand mosques in Mali (one designed by a famed poet and architect from Moorish Spain), imported Islamic jurists, and funded schools and libraries. But the majority of Mali's people remained animist and the elite were often lax in practicing Islam.

Most Malians lived in small villages, fishing, herding, and cultivating rice, sorghum, or millet. Mali also supplied most of Europe's, and two-thirds of the world's, gold supply. Men mined gold in open pits or underground passages while women extracted gold dust from the dirt dug from mines. Gold traders met salt merchants from the north and silently matched piles of gold and salt until agreeing on a fair exchange. Imports also came to Mali from as far away as China and India. The Mali trading city of Timbuktu (**tim-buk-TOO**) emerged as the major southern terminus of the trans-Saharan caravan trade. Islam's international links and trans-Saharan commerce enticed visitors and sojourners to Mali, including poets, architects, teachers, and traders from places such as Spain and Egypt, and at least one Italian merchant reached Timbuktu. The fourteenth-century Moroccan traveler Ibn Battuta (see Chapter 10), who spent months in Mali, praised Malians for their many "admirable qualities," commenting that "they are seldom unjust, and have a greater abhorrence of injustice than any other people." He also found that "neither traveler nor inhabitant in it has anything to fear from robbers or men of violence."[6] But the pious Muslim frowned on what he considered women's immodest dress and independent behavior.

Attila JANDI/Shutterstock.com

IMAGE 12.2 **The Sankore Mosque** This fourteenth-century mosque in Timbuktu was built in a traditional Sahel style of mud bricks and wooden beams. Periodic repairs can be made from ladders propped against the beams.

Q What seems unique about this mosque and how does the style differ from mosques in Middle Eastern countries?

[5]Quoted in E. Jefferson Murphy, *History of African Civilization* (New York: Dell, 1972), 120.
[6]The quotes are from E. W. Bovill, *The Golden Trade of the Moors*, 2nd ed. (London: Oxford University Press, 1970), 95.

Sundiata, Imperial Founder

According to tradition, Sundiata Keita, the "Lion Prince" of the Malinke people, founded the great Mali Empire. Separating myth from fact about his life is difficult, but, since Arab historians such as Ibn Khaldun, who surveyed Mali's history, mention him, most historians believe Sundiata did exist. Nonetheless, any account must use oral epics, which glorify his heroism and reflect a Malinke view of a glorious past.

When Sundiata was born in the early thirteenth century, Ghana was collapsing and various other groups were contending to fill the power vacuum. One of twelve sons of a Malinke king, Nare Fa Maghan, and his wife Sogolon Conde, a hunchback, Sundiata as a child was sickly and had stiff legs that made walking difficult. Hence, he was spared when a rival state, Kaniaga, under their brutal king, Sumaguru, conquered Sundiata's town, Niane, and executed all his brothers as potential threats. According to the oral epic:

> He had a slow and
> difficult childhood.
> At the age of three
> he still crawled along
> on all-fours. He had
> nothing of the great
> beauty of his father. He had a head so big that he
> seemed unable to support it. He was taciturn and
> used to spend the whole day just sitting in the
> middle of the house. Malicious tongues began
> to blab. All Niane talked of nothing but the stiff-
> legged son.

However, soothsayers predicted greatness for him. Eventually he overcame his physical problems so that "at the age of eighteen he had the stateliness of the lion and the strength of the buffalo."

As a young man Sundiata went into exile and then returned to rally his people against the tyrannical Sumaguru: "The sun will arise, the sun of Sundiata." Determined and diplomatic, he skillfully used traditional clan and kinship groups as well as a reputation for possessing magic to build and solidify his power. Persuading other Malinke chiefs to surrender their titles to him, he became his peoples' sole king, enhancing his position in preparation for war. Sundiata put together a military force, and around 1235 he triumphed over Sumaguru in the battle of Kirina, after which he conquered much of the old Ghana territories.

As king, Sundiata acquired the power to reshape Malinke government and society. According to the epics, "He left his mark on Mali for all time and his [rules] still guide men in their conduct [today]." As ruler for over two decades, Sundiata transformed his small state into the core of an imperial system based in his hometown of Niane, alongside the Niger River and near valuable gold fields. His rule brought peace, happiness, prosperity, and justice: "He protected the weak against the strong. The upright man was rewarded and the wicked one punished." The epic account is undoubtedly an idealized version of truth, but it also recorded that Sundiata punished his enemies. Malinke custom allowed high-status men to have many wives, and Sundiata, like his father, followed this practice, leaving many descendants.

Sundiata died about 1260, but his legend lived on. As the epics retold even today put it:

IMAGE 12.3 **Sundiata** This modern depiction of Sundiata Keita memorializes the legendary founder of the Mali Empire. Even today, nearly a millennium after his death, Sundiata remains a hero to Africans for his political and military skills.

MusicLive/Alamy Stock Photo

> Sundiata was unique. In his time no one equaled
> him and after him no one had the ambition to sur-
> pass him. Men of today, how small you are beside
> your ancestors. Sundiata rests but his spirit lives on
> and today the Keitas still come and bow before the
> stone under which lies the father of Mali.

Reflection Questions

1. What does Sundiata's career tell us about the personal qualities admired by the Malinke people and helpful in forging a Sudanic empire?
2. How do the epic stories told over the centuries remember Sundiata and his deeds?
3. Do you think that Sundiata should be a role model for Africans and even non-African people today? Why or why not?

Note: Quotations from D. T. Niane, *Sundiata: An Epic of Old Mali* (London: Longman, 1965), 15, 40, 47, 81, 83–85.

Mali rapidly declined in the 1400s because of internal factionalism and raids by other peoples. Soon the fringes broke away, and by 1464 Songhai (song-GAH-ee), a kingdom formed by several ethnic groups, replaced Mali as the dominant Sudanic empire. By 1550 what remained of the Mali empire had disintegrated. Some Songhai rulers were nominal Muslims, others devout. The most revered leader, Aksia (ACK-see-a) the Great (1483–1528), possibly of slave origin, was humane, pious, tolerant, and devoted to learning. The substantial imperial capital, Gao (ghow) on the Niger River, contained perhaps 100,000 people. As North African and European demand for gold and slaves increased, Songhai flourished from trans-Saharan trade, receiving glass, copperware, cloth, perfumes, and horses. Many slaves, obtained from nearby peoples and sold in the Gao slave market, were taken on the arduous journey across the Sahara to the Mediterranean societies.

Timbuktu prospered as part of the Songhai kingdom. One visiting North African noted many shops and abundant food, describing the people as "of a gentle and cheerful disposition, and spend a great part of the night in singing and dancing through all the streets of the city."[7] Timbuktu also became a major intellectual center, described by an Arab historian as "a refuge of scholarly and righteous folk, a haunt of saints and ascetics, and a meeting place for caravans and boats."[8] The city boasted a famous Islamic university that taught astronomy, astrology, medicine, history, geography, Arabic, and Quranic studies. Timbuktu attracted visiting scientists, engineers, philosophers, and poets from as far away as Arabia who came to exchange and debate ideas; some of them wrote books there in Arabic and in various African languages using Arabic script. The scripts used by many authors reflected their origins, such as the thick brushstrokes of the Hausa and the angled script from Persia. The books included works on physics, astronomy, medicine, botany, mathematics, poetry, history, geography, and jurisprudence as well as religious texts. Thinkers debated subjects like ethics, polygamy, and even advice on sex.

The city's many scholars and students, perhaps a quarter of the city's population, patronized bookstores and libraries containing thousands of books, making the city a bibliophile's paradise. In recent years over thirty thousand lost books on many subjects, hundreds of years old and revered by local people, have been found hidden underneath Timbuktu's mud houses and in nearby desert caves. When Islamic militants seized and held Timbuktu for some months in 2012–2013, they destroyed some books, but many local residents, proud of their heritage, hid most of the others again or smuggled them out for safekeeping. Songhai flourished until 1591, when Moroccans destroyed its military power.

12-1c The Central Sudan and Guinea Coast

After 1000, another dynamic Sudanic society developed farther east, in northern Nigeria, eastern Niger, and southern Chad, where the Hausa (HOUSE-uh) people formed fiercely competitive city-states, ruled by kings, that dominated some trans-Saharan trade. As its prosperity attracted non-Hausa immigrants, including Arabs and Berbers, Hausa society became increasingly Islamic. Hausa cities such as Kano (KAHN-oh) were centers for manufacturing cotton cloth and leatherwork, some sold as far away as Europe. The Hausa were also farmers, famed craftspeople, and, later, skilled traders, pursuing wealth all over West Africa. Today the Hausa language, which mixed Arab, Berber, and West African influences, remains the central Sudan's major trading language and sub-Saharan Africa's most widely spoken language.

Like many Sudanic peoples, the Hausa possessed a strong class system that was headed by royal families and aristocrats, followed by Islamic intellectuals, such as teachers, and wealthy merchants. Hausa women enjoyed a high status compared with many African women. A fifteenth-century queen, Amina, who ruled a major Hausa state, Zaria (zah-REE-uh), was praised as "like the moon at its full, like the morning star. She is a lion as precious as gold among all women."[9]

Along the Guinea coast, a region of rain forest and grasslands just south of the Sudan, Sudanic influence and trade fostered state building among societies like the Yoruba (YORE-uh-buh), who settled in what is today southwestern Nigeria around 1000 BCE. By 1275 these societies had developed a state in western Nigeria, Oyo (OY-oh) that encompassed most Yoruba. Oyo remained the area's most powerful state, flourishing until the late eighteenth century. Eventually various leaders established other Yoruba states, some linked to Oyo and each based on a large city ruled by a king or prince. While powerful and considered sacred, kings were influenced by elders and aristocrats. By modern times Yoruba identity was based more on common language and culture, including complex animistic traditions still influential today, than politics.

Many Yoruba towns served as both commercial and political centers ruled by elaborate bureaucracies, producing cloth, iron, brasswork, and terra-cotta figures. Enjoying respect, merchants were closely connected to north–south trade. Not expected to work in the fields, many Yoruba women developed wealth and influence as traders. Yoruba artists achieved fame. For example, Yoruba at Ife (EE-fay) cast beautiful bronze portraits of their rulers. Since Yoruba culture prized submissiveness to superiors and discouraged conflict, crime was rare.

East of Yoruba territory, another great kingdom, Benin (buh-NEEN), was the state of the Bini (bean-ee) people, who shared some Yoruba traditions. Benin emerged around 1220 and established an empire in the mid-1400s under King Ewuare (ee-WAHR-ee) the Great. While Ewuare was a warrior, later kings became spiritual leaders, leading secluded lives with their many wives but subject to influence by powerful local chiefs. Benin artists cast beautiful bronzes and carved ivory glorifying the king and state. Located near the Atlantic coast, Benin was one of the first African kingdoms to be visited by Europeans in the 1400s, who wrote of the prosperous society they admired.

Protected by high, thick walls, Benin city and its nearby suburbs reflected careful planning and design. The urban area included an elaborate royal palace, neat houses with verandas

---

[7]Leo Africanus, quoted in Kevin Shillington, *History of Africa*, rev. ed. (New York: St. Martin's Press, 1995), 105.
[8]Quoted in Joshua Hammer, "The Treasures of Timbuktu," *Smithsonian* (December 2006), 54.
[9]Quoted in Constance B. Hilliard, ed., *Intellectual Traditions of Pre-Colonial Africa* (New York: McGraw-Hill, 1998), 311–312.

(porches), and neighborhoods linked by straight, broad avenues. Family houses were divided into three sections, with the husband's quarters in the center, wives' to the left, and young men's to the right. The kings and nobles patronized craftsmen who cast the fine bronze art that is found today in museums all over the world. Bini merchants, trading with the Hausa, Yoruba, and Songhai, dealt in woodcarvings, foodstuffs, ironwork, farm tools, weapons, and later cloth. As producers of most of the cloth, Bini women benefited from this trade. The upper classes dressed and dined well, consuming beef, mutton, chicken, and yams, while the poor ate yams, dried fish, beans, and bananas. However, an innovative welfare system protected the poor from becoming beggars by supporting those unable to work. An early European visitor described the process: "The king being very charitable, as well as his subjects, has officers whose chief employment is, on certain days, [to carry] great quantities of provisions into the town for the use of the poor."[10] Benin began to decline in 1550 but only collapsed in 1897 when British soldiers looted and burned down Benin city. Today only a few ruins remain of the once great city and state.

12-1d The Bantu Diaspora

The expansion of Bantu peoples into eastern and southern Africa continued. Historians debate whether this involved large-scale human migration or instead small numbers of Bantu speakers, carrying advanced farming and an iron-using material culture,

IMAGE 12.4 **Benin King** This brass plaque from the royal palace depicts the Benin king on horseback, supported by two retainers.

Q What does the plaque tell us about the weapons and clothing styles of the Benin court?

who moved to a new area and mixed with local people who eventually adopted Bantu language, perhaps initially as a lingua franca. In eastern Africa migrating Bantu encountered Nilotic speakers, who had migrated from North-Central Africa. Bantus and Nilotes (**NAI-lots**) competed over good grazing land and salt, but they also traded, coexisted, and sometimes mixed together. For example, in what is today Kenya, the Bantu Gikuyu (**kee-KOO-yoo**) intermarried, traded, and sometimes fought with the Nilotic Masai (**mah-SIE**), who were mainly cattle herders.

Over time Bantu languages spread over forest, savannah, and highlands in the southern half of Africa, with the speakers developing diverse cultures, languages, political systems, and economic patterns but also maintaining many common traditions. Most Bantu-speakers remained farmers, practicing shifting cultivation where necessary but using more complex methods where possible. Bananas and sorghum became East Africa's staple crops. Some Bantus lived in towns and centralized kingdoms on the Sudanic model, especially in the Great Lakes region. But most kings had religious and ceremonial rather than real political power, and villages usually remained autonomous. Al-Masudi reported that many Bantu farmers were animists, worshipping plants, animals, metals, or whatever pleased them. But many also had a concept of a supreme deity or a great god. The port city of Sofala (in what is today Mozambique), Al-Masudi reported, was governed by a divine king, whom the people called the "son of a great god because they have chosen their king to govern them with equity." But if he became a tyrant and ruled with injustice, "he has ceased to be the son of the great god" and could be killed.[11]

12-1e East African Commerce and Swahili Culture

Expanding Islam and global commerce integrated East African coastal peoples, including many Bantus, into Dar al-Islam and the wider world. The twelve hundred miles of coast stretching from Somalia down to Mozambique proved a cultural melting pot, fostered by trade linking East Africa with societies around the rim of the Indian Ocean and bringing in diverse cultures, languages, and religions. Prevailing monsoon wind patterns, which changed direction between north and south every six months, made sailing up and down the coast relatively easy, fostering regular contact with seafaring folk from Arabia, Persia, India, and Southeast Asia. Indonesians visited East Africa for several centuries, some perhaps intermarrying with East Africans, and brought with them bananas, coconuts, and yams, which spread throughout tropical Africa. Some Indonesians also settled on Madagascar, bringing their Austronesian language, which became the main language of the island today. Eventually seafaring Arabs from the Persian Gulf, Oman, and Yemen dominated coastal trade, seeking ivory, tortoise shell, leopard skin, and later gold and copper.

As trade increased, many city-states developed, among them Mogadishu (**mo-ga-DEE-shoo**), Lamu (**LAH-moo**), Malindi (**ma-LIN-dee**), Mombasa (**mahm-BAHS-uh**),

---

[10]Quoted in John Iliffe, *Africans: The History of a Continent* (Cambridge: Cambridge University Press, 1995), 93.
[11]The quotes are in Davidson, *Lost Cities*, 156.

Zanzibar (**ZAN-zuh-bahr**), Kilwa (**KILL-wa**), and Sofala. These states governed only a small hinterland and were chiefly interested in trade rather than military expansion. Settlers came from Arabia, Persia, and India. A royal court, often claiming Persian or Arab ancestry, and powerful trading families dominated each city-state. Trade networks into the interior expanded with the discovery of gold in the Zimbabwe (**zim-BOB-way**) highlands. With access to these gold fields, Sofala at the mouth of the Zambezi (**zam-BEE-zee**) River became a wealthy city.

The coast reached its golden age from the twelfth through the fifteenth centuries as Islam became entrenched. Ships from Arabia, Persia, and India regularly visited. One passenger, the Moroccan jurist Ibn Battuta, traveled as far south as prosperous Kilwa, on an island off Tanzania, describing it as "one of the most beautiful and well-constructed towns in the world, elegantly built [with] good buildings of stone and mortar, entirely surrounded by a wall and towers."[12] With perhaps twenty thousand people, Kilwa was a collection hub for goods coming in from north, east, and south. Its upper classes built three-story stone houses with indoor plumbing and acquired large quantities of gold and silver jewelry as well as Chinese silk and porcelain. Ibn Battuta described Kilwa's Muslims as devout, chaste, and virtuous and its rulers, a family claiming Yemenite descent, as humble and pious. Still, he disliked some local customs, such as their rich diet. He approved of chicken, meat, fish, vegetables, and mangoes but not rice cooked with butter and yogurt chutney, probably of South Asian origins. His reports show East Africans closely linked to the Islamic world by trade and religion but also maintaining various local customs. In the early 1400s, as part of the grand imperial expeditions of exploration led by Admiral Zheng He, Chinese ships reached the coast and visited Kilwa, spurring a local desire for Chinese goods, especially porcelain.

East African city-states became integral to the Intermediate world's greatest maritime trading network, whose ports and trade routes linked economies around the Indian Ocean rim stretching from Indonesia and India to the Persian Gulf and East Africa. Foreign traders brought pottery, Chinese porcelain, glass beads, Indian cotton, and domesticated chickens to East Africa, trading them for iron, ivory, tortoise shell, leopard skins, gold, and slaves. The beautiful homes in coastal cities, some with tropical gardens, fountains, and pools, attested to the upper- and middle-class wealth. A visitor around 1500 noted that women from wealthy families wore fine gold jewelry, silver earrings, necklaces, bangles, and high quality silk garments.

Intermarriage and blending of Bantu, Arab, and Islamic influences in coastal cities produced a distinctive new African culture and language, **Swahili** (Arab for "people of the coast"). The Swahili language is Bantu in grammar and structure but many Arabic words have been incorporated over the centuries. While Arabic script was used to produce poetry, historical legend, religious speculation, and commercial accounts, Swahili became the coastal region's major trading language, its influence reaching as far inland as the eastern Congo River Basin. Today Swahili is second only to Hausa as a first or second language in sub-Saharan Africa.

Swahili people favored Arab architectural styles, ideas of inheritance, and dress, including long gowns for men and modest attire for women. Whereas interior Bantu peoples practiced either patrilineal or matrilineal descent, the Swahili were, like Arabs, firmly patrilineal. However, Islam only slowly penetrated the hinterland, spreading in part because it was flexible, tolerating Bantu beliefs in spirits and ancestor worship. Today Muslims are numerous in all East African countries, but five hundred years ago Islam was found mostly in coastal towns.

12-1f Zimbabwe and the Kongo

East African trading cities were only part of the wider Bantu diaspora, which also included various kingdoms in Central and southern Africa. On South-Central Africa's fertile plateau a great kingdom, Zimbabwe ("houses built of stone"), flourished from trade with the coast. Today little remains of the kingdom's monumental buildings except for dozens of impressive stone ruins dotting the landscape for hundreds of miles, constructed by the Shona (**SHO-nah**) people between the thirteenth and fifteenth centuries. The granite buildings had various functions. Some were walls enclosing towns, and others were apparently courts. In the capital city, probably containing 10,000 to 20,000 people, the largest enclosure, Great Zimbabwe, an oval space surrounded by a wall eighteen hundred feet long, thirty-two feet high, and seventeen feet thick, may have housed the royal family or perhaps served as a sanctuary where they worshipped their patron deity. The first Europeans to view Great Zimbabwe, and some even in modern times, assumed the complex, spectacular even in ruins, could not have been built by Africans, betraying their own racism and ethnocentrism. They speculated that the structure might have been built by some ancient people such as Egyptians, King Solomon, or the Queen of Sheba. Modern scholarship has substantiated the connection of Great Zimbabwe to the Shona people.

Although the Shona farmed and herded, it was mining that fostered Zimbabwe's prosperity. The Shona had migrated from the southern Congo River Basin, an area of many copper mines. After discovering gold, copper, and iron ore on the plateau, they extracted it from open-pit and occasionally underground mines and traded these minerals down the great Zambezi River to the coast. By 1500 some ten thousand Arab and Swahili traders lived along the river, buying and exporting the gold to the Middle East and India through Sofala and Kilwa. Shona exports corresponded to the rapid growth in the world demand for gold, and in return Zimbabwe received Indian textiles and Chinese ceramics. Shona artists also produced copper, bronze, and gold ornaments.

Perhaps due to overpopulation, soil exhaustion, and cattle overgrazing, in the 1400s the empire split into two rival states, and the capital city was largely abandoned by 1450. As Zimbabwe declined, trade routes and then the government may have shifted north to the upper Zambezi River Valley, but the Shona continued to export gold to the coast.

> **Swahili** Name for a distinctive people, culture, and language, a mix of Bantu, Arab, and Islamic influences, that developed during the Intermediate Era on the East African coast.

---

[12]Quoted in John Middleton, *The World of the Swahili* (New Haven, CT: Yale University Press, 1992), 40.

IMAGE 12.5 **The Great Zimbabwe Complex** Great stone enclosures, most probably used as royal residences or religious sanctuaries, were built around the Zimbabwe kingdom. This one, surrounded by high walls, was at the center of the kingdom's capital city.

Q Why do you think many historians, archaeologists, architects, and art specialists today consider this complex so impressive?

In the 1300s the Bakongo **(bah-KOHNG-goh)** people established another great kingdom, Kongo, near the Atlantic coast of northern Angola and western Congo, whose population eventually reached 2.5 million. As with Benin we know a lot about life in Kongo from Portuguese and Dutch visitors in the fifteenth and sixteenth centuries. In the capital city of Mbanga **(um-BAHN-ga)**, royal musicians bearing drums and ivory trumpets announced visitors to and ceremonies in the king's compound, which was nearly a mile around. High-status people wore finely woven cloth fabrics, beautifully dyed, that European visitors compared to velvet, silk, and brocade. Theoretically absolute and divine, the king was elected by elders and governors and had to seek advice from a council formed by heads of leading clans.

Kongo village chiefs settled disputes but referred serious quarrels or crimes to district judges. Villagers lived in houses with walls of palm matting and thatch roofs. Every day women ground millet into a white flour and stirred it in boiling water to make a stiff porridge that was eaten with peas or beans and spicy sauces made of palm oil. Meat such as chicken, fish, or game, as well as bananas, yams, and pumpkins, provided some variety. Trade flourished, with people using a seashell-based currency to buy salt, colored cloth from India, palm cloth, palm belts, and animal skins.

KEY POINTS

▶ The area south of the Sahara, known as the Sudan, benefited most from the Sahara caravan trade and gradually embraced Islam.

▶ South of the Sudan, on the Guinea coast, the Yoruba developed a balance of power between kings and aristocrats and were generally peace-loving traders and artists, and the prosperous kingdom of Benin developed an innovative welfare system.

▶ The Bantus continued to expand across eastern and southern Africa and established numerous coastal city-states that were greatly influenced by trade with Arabs.

▶ The East African coast became largely Muslim, though retaining a great deal of its native African culture along with influences from such cultures as Arabia and South Asia.

▶ Zimbabwe rose to prosperity from mining and built large granite buildings whose precise use is still debated by historians.

12-2 African Societies, Thought, and Economies

SOCIETIES   NETWORKS

Q What were some distinctive patterns of government, society, thought, and economy in Intermediate Africa?

Societies across Africa shared many common patterns of social organization, religion, culture, and economy. Nonetheless, they also varied considerably, depending on their connections to the Islamic world and whether they had centralized or village-based governments. Furthermore, as elsewhere in the world, royal families, farmers, herders, traders, and city folk, as well as men and women, experienced very different lives from each other. While intensive agriculture did not develop to the same extent as in Eurasia, eventually trade with the wider world attracted European explorers to the region.

12-2a Political and Social Patterns

Although many Africans were governed by powerful kingdoms such as Mali, Benin, and Zimbabwe, many other people lived in decentralized, stateless societies featuring self-governing villages that focused on family relationships. Here councils of elders normally assisted chiefs and applied customary law to regulate conduct. Some of these stateless societies were small and some large, but each was unique. For example, the Tiv (**tihv**) of eastern Nigeria developed an egalitarian society with kinship-based legal and economic rights. Using a form of local democracy, village elders and family heads allocated land, administered justice, and organized community activities, with custom influencing leaders' and citizens' behavior. Women controlled their own farm fields and did much of the farmwork but were aided by men in harvesting and planting. Another society, the Gikuyu, were Bantu farmers in the temperate, green highlands around Mount Kenya in East Africa who mostly lived in individual family homesteads. They had no local chiefs; instead, a senior male in each extended family represented the family to the broader society. Younger Gikuyu men formed a council that handled military affairs, while village councils elected representatives to district councils of elders. This democratic Gikuyu system relied heavily on group discussion and public opinion.

Whether living in kingdoms or stateless societies, individuals were connected to others through social networks and cooperation. An economic unit, the family frequently included all living relatives, with their spouses and children. Some societies practiced matrilineal kinship, tracing descent and inheritance through the female line. In kingdoms, the queen sister or queen mother usually enjoyed high respect. For example, the Bini people still revere Idia, an early-sixteenth-century queen mother in Benin who raised an army and used her magical powers to help her son overcome his enemies. Queen mothers often controlled access to rulers, managed treasuries, presided over court systems, and helped enthrone or depose rulers. Some queens ruled in their own right. However, women's status varied widely. Men dominated most families and often had multiple wives. With children

CONNECTION to TODAY

Which African cultural, religious, social, and economic traditions from this era do you think might have the most influence today in Africa and around the world?

the chief goal of marriage, a woman could rise in status by bearing many children. Women also looked to children rather than husbands for support in old age.

A web of associations defined socially acceptable behavior. Families were part of clans or lineages that traced descent to a common ancestor. Work or music groups, secret societies, religious cults, and age grades (men and women around the same age) promoted cooperation between people of the same generation. Most groups prized collective effort and responsibility instead of individual initiative. The *ethnic group*, often mistakenly called the "tribe" by modern observers, included people, not necessarily related by kinship ties, who spoke the same language, practiced similar customs, and lived in the same general territory. Some ethnic groups, like the Yoruba and Hausa, numbered in the millions and were divided into multiple states. Distinct cultures, languages, and religions marked off groups such as the Yoruba, Hausa, Shona, and Gikuyu.

Like many societies around the world in this era, some sub-Saharan peoples condoned slavery and traded slaves, which were often war captives or debtors. Ibn Battuta wrote that, in Sudanic cities, the wealthy "vie with one another in regard to the number of their slaves and serving-women. They never sell the educated female slaves, or but rarely and at a high price."[13] Slaves filled diverse social and economic roles: the Wolof (**WOH-lohf**) tribe of today's Senegal used them in housework, Kongo slaves worked as soldiers or plantation workers, and the Akan (**ah-KAHN**) on the Guinea coast worked their slaves in gold mines. Some Hausa slaves enjoyed a high social status as palace advisers. Some families considered slaves members of their household, and many slaves could marry and have their children freed. While slave life was often hard, African slaves often had more rights and enjoyed better treatment than slaves in most European, Islamic, Asian, and American societies. And for many their lives were likely less difficult than those of the Africans seized or bought in Africa by European slave traders between the later 1400s and mid-1800s and transported in brutal conditions to the Americas, where they were forced to work in grueling manual labor, most commonly on plantations and in mines.

12-2b Religious and Artistic Traditions

Diverse African religions included Muslim and Christian believers but also millions practicing monotheism, polytheism with many gods and spirits, animism (spirit worship), or a mix of the three. Africans often recognized a supernatural world of sorcery, magic, spirits, ancestors, and multiple gods mediated by *shamans*, male or female specialists skilled in curing disease and with knowledge about the spiritual realm. Understanding that many illnesses had spiritual and psychological as well as physical dimensions, shamans often succeeded as healers. Some

[13]Quoted in Bovill, *Golden Trade*, 96.

male elders, considered sages, collected wisdom and challenged individuals to become better and more knowledgeable. Some scholars compare these sages, in their constant probing for truth, to Classical Greek, Indian, and Chinese philosophers. Reverence toward cosmic forces blended into worship and spirituality. Many Africans believed in a life force that was part of all living and material entities. They also revered deceased family members and ancestors, who were considered present in spirit. Since most societies envisioned an unapproachable high god holding himself aloof from daily affairs, people prayed to ancestors and spirits.

The Dogon people, who live on an arid plateau in today's nation of Mali, may represent what African society and religion were like before states formed and outside religions arrived. Ruled by priest-chiefs, the Dogon work the fields collectively, center their lives on community religious festivals and arts, and bring order to their society through myths that perceive the cosmos as dualistic, mixing male and female, order and change.

Africans developed oral and written literatures. Most societies relied on **oral traditions**, verbal testimonies concerning the past that were passed through generations by professional rememberers, known as *griots* in West Africa, who served as local historians, recordkeepers, and sometimes councilors to kings and tutors to princes. Griots recounted past events and royal genealogies while updating their stories with contemporary happenings, becoming walking libraries who transmitted knowledge to their successors. As a modern griot explained: "We are vessels of speech, the repositories which harbor secrets many centuries old. We are the memory of mankind."[14] Based on oral traditions, a chronicle recognizing the reigns and genealogy of sixty-seven kings in a central Sudanic kingdom, Kanem-Borno, spans the ninth through nineteenth centuries. Many top West African writers and popular musicians today come from griot families.

Those societies that possessed written languages such as Arabic, Hausa, Amharic, and Swahili produced poetry and philosophical speculation. However, writing spread slowly because most Africans, relying on well-defined customs to maintain order, did not need written laws. With communal ownership, they also had no need to track land use and inheritance. Merchants in Sudanic and East African cities recorded large purchases or sales in Arabic or Swahili, but elsewhere writing was difficult, since paper deteriorates quickly in the tropical climate.

Africans produced a rich artistic heritage, including sculpture, dance, and music. Paleolithic Africans were among the first people anywhere to paint on rocks and cave walls. When farming developed, painting declined and sculpture in wood, clay, ivory, bronze, or gold became the major visual art form. African wooden masks for religious festivals, as well as carvings of animal, human, and spiritual figures, have influenced modern artists around the world. Music and dance, closely integrated into work, leisure, and religion, usually involved everyone's participation. Musical groups often accompanied people working in the fields, and at day's end farmers and musicians returned to the village for an impromptu party. While African musicians emphasized percussion, using many types of drums, they also played wind and string instruments. African musical traditions filtered into the Middle East, influencing Islamic music,

oral traditions Verbal testimonies concerning the past; the major form of oral literature in cultures without writing.

and beginning in the 1500s, African slaves carried their musical traditions to the Americas, blending them with European and Native American styles to foster many twentieth-century popular music forms, such as blues, jazz, rock, calypso, reggae, soca, salsa, Afro-Cuban, and samba. African influences can also be seen in recent genres like dub, dancehall, rapso, and hip-hop.

12-2c Agriculture and Trade

Sub-Saharan Africans successfully exploited their tropical environment's resources to foster farming and trade. Unlike in Eurasian societies, which had horses and oxen to pull plows and large wheeled carts, in Africa various tropical diseases or insect pests prevented breeding or maintaining these animals except in the northeast highlands, Egypt, and the dry Sudan and Sahara. With economic production and transportation relying mainly on human muscles, most Africans were small farmers who produced food primarily for their own use. With often poor soils, irregular rainfall, and no manure from draft animals for fertilizer, Africans could not match the highly productive agriculture found in China, India, and Europe. Instead, many practiced shifting cultivation, a practical adaptation to local conditions that worked well if population densities remained small. By 1500 probably some forty million people lived in sub-Saharan Africa, compared to over 100 million in China. However, where possible Africans used more sophisticated techniques such as irrigation or terracing.

Trading networks interlaced tropical Africa. Great markets emerged at Sudanic cities such as Gao and Timbuktu, where traders bought and sold ivory, ebony, and honey from the Guinea coast and books, wheat, horses, dates, cloth, and salt from the north. Tuaregs, a nomadic, camel-riding Berber people scattered around the central Sahara, were then and still are one of the main groups involved in transporting goods across the Sahara and active in the Timbuktu markets. They also had a written language that some scholars trace way back to the ancient Phoenicians in Carthage. Today Tuareg popular music, a mix of folk traditions and rock, has gained popularity even outside of Africa. In the towns and villages most market traders were women, while most traveling merchants were men. Renowned as long-distance traders, Hausa merchants traveled to the Guinea coast to buy kola nuts, a rain forest tree crop that can be made into one of the few stimulants allowed Muslims. Tropical Africans exported various items, including gold, ivory, and kola nuts, to North Africa, Asia, and Europe. Both gold and cowry (**KOW-ree**) shells, collected on the Indian Ocean coast, served as local currency. Trade also allowed for the spread of diseases. Some recent scholarship suggests that the "Black Death," a catastrophic pandemic (probably plague) that killed many millions of people in Eurasia and North Africa in the fourteenth century, may have also made its way along the trade routes to West Africa and Ethiopia, wiping out entire communities.

In local trade people bought and sold things needed for everyday life, such as salt, ironware, and copper, while women made cloth from cotton and bark. Because sources of abundant salt were rare, it commanded a high price, and traders sometimes obtained it from hundreds of miles away. Iron ore was more common. Although Africans valued copper for making bangles and bracelets, few good sources existed. The most extensive copper mining took place in the copper-belt region (today's Zambia) south of the Congo Basin and in South Africa.

---

[14]Djeli Mamoudou Kouyate, quoted in D. T. Niane, *Sundiata: An Epic of Old Mali* (London: Longman, 1965), 1.

12-2d Africans, Arab Slave Traders, and the Portuguese

Africans connected to Eurasia primarily by trade across the Sahara Desert or along the East African and Red Sea coast. For example, Arab, Berber, and African traders shipped African slaves north to be sold in North Africa, Iberia, Arabia, Persia, India, and Christian Europe. Between 650 and 1500 trans-Saharan caravans transported perhaps 2 to 4 million slaves from West Africa to Mediterranean societies, while 1 to 2 million were shipped from East Africa and 1.6 million (mostly Nubians and Ethiopians) from Red Sea ports. Though these numbers were significant, the trade was smaller in scale than the trans-Atlantic slave trade carried out by Western nations between 1500 and 1900. African slaves in the Middle East became domestic servants, laborers, soldiers, and even administrators. Perhaps 250,000 descendants of African slaves, traders, and sailors live in India and Pakistan today.

The trans-Saharan slave trade inspired western Europeans to eventually seek slaves directly in West Africa. In search of Asian spices, African gold, and slaves, well-armed Portuguese began sailing south along the West African coastline in the early 1400s, sporadically planting seven-foot-high stone pillars topped with a Christian cross, inscribed in Latin and Portuguese, to symbolize their achievements and claims to discovered lands (see Chapter 14). This exploration began a new era in African history. The Portuguese colonized the Cape Verde (**VUHRD**) Islands in the Atlantic and nearby coastal Guinea-Bissau (**GIN-ee bis-OW**) while also establishing trading forts. Some West Africans acquired artistic and religious ideas from Portuguese merchants and Christian missionaries. But these early encounters between Iberians and Africans were not just economic; they involved clashing views of diplomacy, politics, and sovereignty. The Portuguese and other Europeans based their interpretations of African cultures and politics on medieval European traditions, mindsets, and legal theories, establishing a framework of misunderstanding that would trouble Western–African relations for centuries.

In 1487 a Portuguese expedition led by Bartolomeu Dias rounded the Cape of Good Hope at Africa's southern tip and sailed into the Indian Ocean, thus opening a whole new chapter in Western exploration and intensifying Portuguese interest both in Africa and the world to the east. Even after Christopher Columbus, sailing for Spain, announced his "discovery" of what he thought was India in 1492, the Portuguese concentrated on the sea route around Africa. In 1497 Portuguese ships commanded by Vasco da Gama sailed up the East African coast to the trading city of Malindi and, engaging an Indian or Arab pilot, sailed on to southern India. Da Gama had discovered the fastest oceanic path from Europe to the Indian Ocean maritime trading network.

In the 1480s the Portuguese began a long relationship with the Kongo kingdom by sending Catholic missionaries and skilled craftsmen to that area. In 1491, after two Kongolese court officials claimed the Virgin Mary appeared to them in dreams, King Nzinga a Nkuwu (**en-ZING-a ah en-KOO-WOO**) and some aristocrats adopted Christianity and sent their children to Portugal for study. The king actually wanted Portuguese teachers, craftsmen, and weapons to use against a rival kingdom. By the early 1500s, however, after realizing the economic possibilities in the Americas, the Portuguese became far more interested in obtaining slaves than in helping Kongo's economy or treating the Kongolese as equals. In 1514 they began exporting Kongolese slaves to nearby islands and, eventually, to the Americas, beginning a new era for Africa and a direct relationship with Europe and the Americas, the region to which we now turn.

KEY POINTS

▶ Many Africans lived in "stateless societies" in which family relationships, rather than rulers or governments, organized people's lives.

▶ In addition to Muslims and Christians, many Africans were polytheistic, believers in multiple gods and spirits.

▶ In Africa the oral tradition was much stronger than the written one, and writing spread slowly because African custom did not depend on recordkeeping and important knowledge was passed down orally by griots.

▶ African agriculture faced a number of challenges, including poor soil, irregular rainfall, and the difficulty of obtaining and using draft animals.

▶ Several million African slaves were shipped to the Middle East, and the Portuguese laid the groundwork for the much larger European slave trade to the Americas.

12-3 American Societies in Transition

⊟ TRANSITIONS ▦ SOCIETIES

Q What factors explain the collapse of the Early Intermediate Era American societies?

Like Africans, most Americans creatively exploited their environments, whether in urban societies or smaller agricultural or nomadic hunter-gatherer communities. Whereas many Africans had direct or indirect contact with Eastern Hemisphere

CONNECTION to TODAY

What can people today learn from the role of climate and environmental change in the collapse of many pre-Columbian societies?

networks, Americans remained a world apart from that interconnecting zone. Furthermore, these American societies were often separated from each other by lack of large animals suitable for riding, great distances, and more geographical barriers—high mountains, harsh deserts, and thick rain forests—than their Eurasian counterparts. Yet cultures, technologies, and trade goods spread over a wide area. Powerful states with dense populations in Mesoamerica and the Andes, such as the Maya, declined or collapsed, while less centralized governments formed elsewhere, including North America.

12-3a The Collapse of the Classical States

Unlike Afro-Eurasian states such as Rome, Gupta India, and Han China, most major Classical Era American states survived into the Early Intermediate Era. Great cities such as Teotihuacan, Tikal in the Maya lands, and Tiwanaku and Wari in the southern Andes had flourished for centuries, supported by productive and innovative farming, trade, and metalworking, often combined with subduing and exploiting their neighbors. Creative plant breeders, Americans combined nutritious maize (corn) with beans, squash, and fish or game for a well-balanced, healthy diet while discovering many plant drugs, including quinine and coca, that are still used today to cure disease or alleviate pain.

However, newer centers of religious, economic, or political power now replaced older ones. In eighth-century Mesoamerica, Monte Alban declined while Teotihuacan collapsed, removing a unifying commercial and political hub. Although the Maya flourished for centuries, by 900 they had abandoned many cities. In South America, Moche collapsed around 700, Tiwanaku around 1000, and Wari around 1100. The reasons for these rapid political and economic transitions remain debated, but climate change probably played a role. In Mesoamerica and South America's Pacific coast, a warming climate baked the land as failing rains brought drought. Grassy hillsides turned brown, streams dried up, and crops withered.

12-3b The Zenith and Decline of the Maya

The Maya of Yucatán and northern Central America declined rapidly and then suddenly collapsed, allowing new powers to rise. Maya society peaked between 600 and 800, with growing populations (3 to 5 million people), creative irrigation systems, and massive monument building. Population densities reached a staggering six hundred people per square mile, similar to China today, testifying to Maya success in mastering a marginal environment for farming. Tikal may have contained fifty thousand people.

Warfare between states, mostly for royal glory and economic predominance, not conquest, was frequent, but victories were short-lived. The Maya enjoyed close commercial contact with central Mexico; for example, in Teotihuacan a whole neighborhood was reserved for Maya merchants. Maya also sometimes ventured by boat to Caribbean islands, trading jade, salt, feathers, and chocolate. Christopher Columbus described a huge trading canoe his fleet encountered off the coast of what is today Honduras; it was eight feet wide and six feet long, manned by twenty-five paddlers, and filled with valuable trade goods including copper, flint, weapons, beer, and textiles. The Maya were excellent sculptors, builders, astronomers, and mathematicians and, with a well-developed writing system that could express any thought

Quetzalcoatl The feathered serpent, a symbol that goes back deep in Mesoamerican history.

or concept, produced thousands of folding-screen books called codices, made of bark paper, although only a handful survived after the Spanish conquest. The early Maya evidently practiced forest conservation, considering certain groves of trees sacred, but they cut down forests for building large temples.

Between 800 and 900 the Maya deserted most cities in the southern lowlands, and the whole region lost perhaps two-thirds of its population. Multiple factors fostered the collapse. Climate change apparently caused a century-long drought, emptying the complex system of canals and reservoirs that collected rainwater for farming and drinking. Overpopulation prompted attempts to increase agricultural productivity on marginally fertile land, which led to soil degradation and deforestation that may have caused crop failures. Some studies suggest that population growth without finding more sustainable methods of water conservation and use not dependent on reservoirs may make the population more vulnerable during prolonged dry spells, and hence create a crisis. The Mayan elite may also have become too fond of, and dependent on, maize (corn), a drought intolerant crop, and demanded increased production from farmers. These mistakes may have undermined the Mayan economy and hence politics. Trade networks shifted from inland river-based cities to the coastal states. The Maya experienced reduced rainfall, famine, malnutrition, starvation, epidemics, and increased warfare, while increasingly unstable governments prompted revolts. Some people moved to fortified villages in remote areas. People may have lost faith in their leaders. The political and religious hierarchy of kings, aristocrats, and priests collapsed, and merchants, scribes, and craftsmen ceased their work.

These dramatic developments missed northern Maya cities on the Yucatán Peninsula such as Uxmal (oosh-MAHL), which flourished until around 1000, but more frequent warfare engulfed this region, and human sacrifice increased. The city of Chichen Itza (chuh-chen uht-SAH), founded around 800, dominated northern Yucatán between 1000 and 1250 until it was succeeded by Mayapan (MY-uh-PAHN), itself destroyed by a rebellion in 1441. By the 1500s the Yucatán Maya were fragmented into small states in chronic conflict with each other. The remnants of the Maya people, mostly reduced to subsistence farming, still lived over a wide area of Mesoamerica and Central America, and still do, but their violent but once-brilliant history was fading from memory.

12-3c The Toltecs and Chimu

As the older Mesoamerican and Andean states declined or collapsed, powerful states not unlike West African kingdoms emerged. The Toltecs (TOLL-teks), moving into Mexico's central valley from the desert north, created an empire lasting from 900 to 1168 and systematically recorded their history in writing. Their empire involved a loose military alliance of newcomers mixing with local people with roots in Teotihuacan. Toltecs adopted the cult of **Quetzalcoatl** (kate-zahl-CO-ah-tal), the feathered serpent, which goes back deep in Mesoamerican history. In Toltec tradition, Quetzalcoatl was a human leader banished to sea by war-gods, a story probably based on Topiltzin (to-PILLT-sen) (b. ca. 947), a cult high priest who succeeded his father as Toltec king but whose opposition to human sacrifice and promotion of peace angered more warlike leaders. Forced into exile, the man gradually blended into the god in myth. But the legend also said that the banished man-god,

Madrugada Verde/Shutterstock.com

IMAGE 12.6 Pyramid at Tula Each figure on this pyramid at the Toltec capital is made of fitted stone sections and represents a warrior carrying a throwing stick in one hand and a bag of incense in the other.

Q What do these figures tell us about Tula weapons and culture?

down the mountainsides. These activities helped Chimu avoid all but the most severe droughts and achieve two or three crops a year. Eventually, however, Chimu faced challenges it could not overcome. El Niño climate changes disrupted irrigation, and by the fourteenth century Chimu declined, perhaps because of overpopulation and increased soil salinization. Perhaps desperate to appease the gods and hopefully get help in response to the repeated disruptions caused by El Niño, the Chimu carried out a systematic ritual killing of some one hundred and forty children and two hundred and twenty llamas, perhaps the largest mass sacrifice in history anywhere in the world. It did not solve the crisis. A few decades later, around 1475, the Inca conquered and incorporated the Chimu into a vast Andean empire, taking the Chimu artists and craftsmen to their capital, Cusco.

12-3d Pueblo Societies

While only a few American societies formed kingdoms or built large cities, many peoples creatively farmed in challenging environments and supported towns and long-distance trade. Some of the most successful societies developed in the southwestern desert of North America, whose modern descendants are known as the Pueblo Indians because of their permanent towns, called *pueblos* in Spanish. Learning to farm this dry region, Pueblo peoples survived and sometimes flourished by selecting just the right soils for maize, growing cotton, and weaving cotton cloth. They also bred and ate turkeys, first tamed in southern Mexico 1,500 to 2,000 years ago, and used their feathers for making blankets. Without the advantages of a written language or number system, they planned and built towns, often around human-made dams, terraces, irrigation canals, and reservoirs. Even though they had to travel everywhere by foot, Pueblo peoples traded with central Mexico and the Pacific coast, mining and exchanging turquoise with Teotihuacan and the Toltecs for craft goods. Some Mesoamerican religious beliefs and customs, such as the feathered serpent tradition and ball courts and games, also filtered north.

By 700 the Hohokum and Mogollon dominated parts of southern Arizona, New Mexico, and northern Mexico (see Map 12.2). Around 1325 in Casa Grande, a town of over two thousand people in northern Mexico, the Hohokum constructed a building three stories high of thick adobe atop a platform mound. By 1000 the neighboring Mogollon people had developed masonry technology for house building. But climate change caused drought in the 1300s, and both the Hohokum and Mogollon settlements were eventually abandoned.

The Anasazi (**ah-nah-SAH-zee**), meaning "ancient ones" in the Navaho (**NAH-vuh-ho**) language, flourished between 700 and 1400, reaching their height between 900 and 1250. Anasazi towns, featuring masonry houses constructed of huge sandstone blocks, wood beams, and clay carried from distant forests, dot large sections of Arizona, Colorado, New Mexico, and Utah,

bearded and of fair complexion, would return to seek revenge. This prophecy haunted later Mesoamericans.

The Toltecs achieved wide influence, even over some northern Maya cities. Their capital city, Tula, filled with ceremonial architecture and with 30,000 to 60,000 people, was a center for obsidian mining, with Tula craftsmen producing obsidian and copper tools. The Toltecs may have established contact with Andean societies, and some Toltec trade goods reached as far north as New Mexico and Arizona. But in the twelfth century the Toltec state, weakened by long-term drought, famine, and war, collapsed, disrupting the trade routes.

Along South America's Pacific coast, the Chimu (**chee-MOO**) Empire, whose ruling class may have descended from Moche nobles, rose to prominence in the Moche valley around 800. By 1200 it was a sizable empire stretching some 600 miles north to south, with a capital, Chan Chan (**CHAHN CHAHN**), that boasted many adobe-walled royal compounds and 25,000 to 50,000 people. Chimu lords lived in magnificent walled palaces up to three stories high that included open plazas with platforms for ceremonies. They had elaborate funerals that involved the sacrifice of several hundred men and women to serve as attendants in the afterlife. Conscripted workers labored on vast construction and irrigation projects, including twenty-five-foot-wide roads. Chimu kings, who wore glittering regalia to show their power, had access to high-quality textiles made with dyed llama wool, gold- and silversmiths who made beautiful jewelry, and colorful feathers (to decorate conical-shaped crowns) from the Andes cloud forests and the Amazon jungles. To irrigate fields of maize, beans, cotton, gourds, squash, peanuts, and fruits, they constructed hundreds of miles of terraces and large storage reservoirs that controlled the water flow

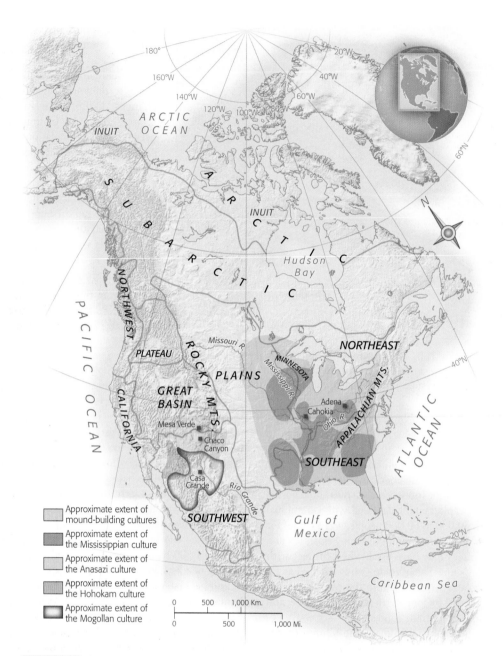

MAP 12.2 **Major North American Societies, 600–1500 CE** Farming societies were common in North America. The Pueblo peoples such as the Anasazi in the southwestern desert and the mound builders in the eastern half of the continent lived in towns. The city of Cahokia was the center of the widespread Mississippian culture and a vast trade network.

Q What does this map suggest about where the largest number of people lived and how that was influenced by geography?

including major centers at Mesa Verde and Chaco (**CHAHK-oh**) Canyon. Mesa Verde, ingeniously built into steep cliff walls, probably housed twenty-five hundred people, with another thirty thousand living in the surrounding area. In Chaco Canyon, eight adobe towns sat in or on the rim of the canyon, with multistoried houses, some six stories high, built around central plazas. In an otherwise desolate and rocky canyon the Chaco residents may have used water management to grow corn in a salty but also fertile volcanic soil. But they perhaps also needed to import corn.

Wide roads connected the Chaco pueblos with Anasazi towns a hundred miles away. Wood for Chaco homes was obtained from mountains some fifty miles away in such quantities that the mountains were eventually deforested. The Anasazi apparently traded turquoise objects to peoples in Mesoamerica for products like cacao (chocolate). Some studies suggest that the Anasazi, who probably numbered 100,000 people, were organized around houses of different sizes and varying social classes, under a powerful and wealthy elite. Others think that, like many Pueblo Indians, they lived in generally egalitarian communities. They probably practiced matrilineal kinship and matrilocal residence, with men moving into their wife's household. Women were excellent weavers and potters. They may have owned the houses, crops, and fields, but men dominated the council of elders who administered each town. Their religion apparently revolved around the belief that Earth was both a source of food and protection but also a sacred place that connected them to a Great Spirit.

Environmental challenges eventually precipitated collapse, and by 1200 Anasazi agriculture declined from severe drought. Deforestation, soil erosion, disease epidemics, and invasions or migrations by outsiders may also have been factors. Hard times fostered increased warfare between pueblos, with some pueblos, their social order undermined, possibly resorting to human sacrifice or cannibalism. By 1300 many Anasazi had moved to the Rio Grande River Valley, mixing with other newcomers to produce the Pueblo peoples of today's central and northern New Mexico, and by 1400 Anasazi culture had collapsed, with Chaco and Mesa Verde long since abandoned. Those Anasazi who survived were probably the ancestors of southwestern tribes like the Hopi (**HOH-pee**) and Zuni, who with other tribes perhaps number around seventy-five thousand people today. Most of the tribes descending from the Anasazi dislike this name for their ancestors; some prefer to have them called Ancient Puebloans.

12-3e The Mississippian and Eastern Woodlands Societies

In eastern North America's vast and fertile Mississippi and Ohio River Basins, mound-building cultures flourished that were based on trade and shifting cultivation of maize (see Chapter 9). The Mississippian culture, widespread between 700 and 1700, featured several cities, monumental architecture, social hierarchies, and religious art. The main Mississippian center, Cahokia (**kuh-HOH-kee-uh**), strategically located near the juncture of the Mississippi and Missouri Rivers near today's Saint Louis, probably contained some 30,000 to 60,000 inhabitants at its peak between 1050 and 1250, making it the North American counterpart to Teotihuacan and Tula. Perhaps spurred by a religious revival movement, people came from hundreds of miles around to live, work, and participate in mass religious ceremonies. Women did most of the farming and also creatively harvested various wild food sources such as hickory nuts and acorns. Small, flint-clay ceramic statues of women have been unearthed that may represent corn goddesses or possibly sunflower seed heads and squash. Perhaps they helped women appeal to an Earth Mother to guide their cultivation, giving them status as key players in society.

Showing Mesoamerican influences, Mississippian communities like Cahokia had central plazas with platform mounds topped by temples and elite houses, probably surrounded by markets and the wood houses with thatch roofs of commoners. The largest of many Cahokia pyramids, one thousand feet long, seven hundred feet wide, and one hundred feet tall, was larger than Egyptian pyramids and had a circumference greater than Teotihuacan's Pyramid of the Sun. Circles of standing timbers tracked the seasons by marking the sun's position. As in Mesoamerica, Cahokia's priest-rulers probably presided over lavish rituals atop the pyramids, with the chief religious cult worshipping the sun and revering mythical creatures. The Cahokians apparently divided the universe into an Upper World of spirits and ancestors, an Underworld of Earth (including water and agriculture) and animals, and a human world in between. But they were all intertwined. At a ruler's death priests sacrificed some commoners, mostly young women, to accompany him to the hereafter.

In the matrilineal Cahokia society, divided into distinct classes, a lord showed his status by riding in a flotilla of large canoes decorated with gold objects. Warfare over territory may have been common. Cahokia artisans made baskets, pottery, shell beads, leather clothes, copper ornaments, wooden utensils, and stone, flint, and copper tools, and they carved artistic images into their buildings. The major hub of a vast trade network stretching from the Great Lakes to the Rockies to the Appalachian mountains to the Gulf Coast along the Mississippi, Missouri, and Ohio Rivers, Cahokia imported Great Lakes copper to make jewelry and drinking cups, as well as marine shells, shark teeth, and barracuda jaws from the Gulf Coast. Cultural influences from Cahokia also spread through the eastern woodlands, including new strains of maize better adapted to cooler climates.

Cahokia was largely abandoned around 1300, probably from some combination of drought, massive floods, deforestation, a destructive fire around 1170, and a political-ideological crisis. Growing tensions between elites and commoners may also have undermined the political system. The greater Mississippian culture collapsed by 1550, and the Mississippi River Basin population dwindled, probably because of overpopulation, soil depletion, epidemics, and a cooling climate that damaged agriculture. By the early 1700s malaria and smallpox brought by Europeans had devastated the surviving Mississippian peoples, and French colonizers wiped out the last mound builders, the sun-worshipping Natchez people in the lower Mississippi Valley, in a battle in 1731. Reflecting the racism and ethnocentrism of the time, when the first Western explorers and settlers and even scientists came upon and studied the mostly abandoned mounds, they refused to believe that these magnificent complexes had been built by Native Americans. Instead, they attributed them to Aztecs or Eastern Hemisphere societies such as Vikings, Welshmen, and Hindus, or perhaps some mysterious race. Many years of research and scholarship have demolished these mistaken theories and myths.

In North America's eastern woodlands, few states developed, with most farming communities resembling African stateless societies such as the Tiv. Village chiefs, often elected by elders, had little authority, and every family participated in decision making. Eastern woodland farming produced abundance. An English observer visiting Massachusetts in 1614 noted that the land was "so planted with gardens and corn fields, and so well inhabited with a goodly, strong people [that] I would rather live here than anywhere."[15] While men cleared the fields, they were often gone hunting or fighting. Warfare using bows and arrows, though common, generally led to few casualties. Women, working in groups, produced most of the food and thus had high social and political status in these often matrilineal societies. Women elders often could approve or prohibit warfare, and frequently a senior clan mother known for her wisdom nominated a new chief for election or rejection by the tribe. This relative freedom fostered a stronger emphasis on romantic courtship.

[15]John Smith, quoted in Charles Mann, "The Pristine Myth," *The Atlantic Online*, March 7, 2002 (theatlantic.com/unbound/interviews/int2002-03-07.htm).

12-4 The American Empires and Their Challenges

⇄ TRANSITIONS **▦ SOCIETIES**

Q How were the Aztec and Inca Empires different, and how were they similar?

With Maya collapse and Toltec and Chimu decline, the Aztecs (**AZ-tek**) and Inca (**IN-kuh**) built the largest empires and most sophisticated states in the pre-Columbian Americas (see Map 12.3). Thanks to strong armies and well-organized governments, both empires dominated large regions but rapidly collapsed when confronted in the 1500s with Spanish military forces and the epidemic diseases they brought from the Eastern Hemisphere.

CONNECTION to TODAY

What legacies do you think the Aztecs and Incas left for Latin Americans today?

12-4a The Aztec Empire, Religion, and Warfare

Aztec society was founded by the warlike Mexica, Nahuatal (**NAH-what-uhl**)-speaking immigrants from the north. An early leader told them that "we shall conquer all peoples of the universe. I shall make you lords and kings of all that is in the world."[16] Taking pride in their warrior reputation and writing about their history, Mexica identified themselves as the Toltecs' successors, adopting many Toltec gods, rituals, and cultural forms. By 1325 they had established a strong state controlling much of the lake-filled Valley of Mexico, where Teotihuacan once flourished. There they built their capital, Tenochtitlan (**teh-noch-TIT-lan**), expanding into neighboring regions in 1428. Their greatest ruler, Moctezuma (**mock-teh-ZOO-ma**) I (1440–1468), declared that war was the major Aztec preoccupation, with its purpose to gain new territories while acquiring prisoners for sacrifice to the gods. By 1519 the Aztec Empire controlled much of central and southern Mexico, even collecting tribute from people as far south as Guatemala and El Salvador. Tribute from the conquered became an important revenue source.

Religion supported warfare. Aztecs believed the sun was a warrior-god daily battling his way across the skies to prevent the universe's destruction by the forces of darkness. To help the sun-god remain fit for this struggle, Aztecs fed the deity with blood from non-Aztec warriors captured in their frequent fighting, regularly sacrificing them in gruesome rituals. In Aztec myths,

their god Huitzilopochtli (**wheat-zeel-oh-POSHT-lee**) ("The Hummingbird Wizard") commanded them to feed him with human hearts torn from the recently sacrificed. Aztecs practiced human sacrifice on a greater scale than any other major society, sacrificing several thousand captured warriors a year in gruesome rituals, often on the same platforms used at other times by athletes and dancers. Other central Mexican people practiced blood sacrifice as well.

By 1500 the Aztecs faced growing economic, political, and military problems. The need for a regular supply of captives created a permanent state of war and terror, fostering political instability and fierce resistance. The conquered peoples paid tribute but frequently rebelled, providing an excuse to fight and obtain more captives. Brutal Aztec policies created many enemies, and some of them later proved willing to cooperate with the Spanish to invade Tenochtitlan. Even before this, Aztec leaders, haunted by bad portents, apparently felt a deepening insecurity. These worries increased in 1518, when word reached Tenochtitlan of winged towers (Spanish ships) bearing bearded white men on Mexico's east coast. Because Spanish arrival coincided with Quetzalcoatl's prophesied return, historians debate whether Emperor Moctezuma II identified Spaniards with the god and thus lost the will to resist. However, Aztec tools and weapons, still based on sharp minerals such as obsidian, were no match for Spanish guns and steel swords. Although the Spanish encountered a vigorous Aztec society, Spanish conquest and occupation in 1521 ended the Aztec era.

12-4b Aztec Economy and Society

Aztecs developed a prosperous economy and dynamic social system. Tenochtitlan (the site of today's Mexico City), on a swampy island in a large lake, was one of the world's great cities, where large palaces, temples, forty pyramids, causeways to the mainland, and diverse markets served some 150,000 to 300,000 residents. Spaniards marveled at the markets selling each kind

[16]Quoted in Richard F. Townsend, *The Aztecs*, rev. ed. (New York: Thames and Hudson, 2000), 59.

MAP 12.3 **South America and Mesoamerica, 900–1500 CE** The Maya and Aztecs in Mesoamerica and the Inca in the Andes forged the most densely populated societies, the most productive farming, and the best-organized governments. The Inca built one of the world's largest empires. Other urban societies also flourished in Mexico and South America.

Q How did geography shape the size and location of the major American empires?

of merchandise in its respective street (see Discover Historical Voices: An Aztec Market). Thousands of canoes carrying passengers or produce traversed the six major canals daily. Without pack animals the economy also depended on porters carrying loads on their backs with a strap secured to the forehead. The city awed the first Spaniards in 1519:

> And when we saw all those towns and villages built in the water, and other great towns on dry land, and that straight and narrow causeway leading to Mexico

> [Tenochtitlan], we were astounded. These great towns and buildings rising from the water, all made of stone, seemed like an enchanted vision. Indeed, some of our soldiers asked whether it was not all a dream.[17]

The leader of the Spanish forces Hernán Cortés compared the city, with its wide straight streets, to great cities in his homeland such as Cordoba and Seville.

Highly productive farming and trade underpinned the Aztec economy. The Aztecs grew their food on artificial islands,

---

[17]Quoted in Brian M. Fagan, *Kingdoms of Gold, Kingdoms of Jade: The Americas Before Columbus* (London: Thames and Hudson, 1991), 7.

called **chinampas**, that were built on the central valley lakes, a technology dating back hundreds of years. Miles of shallow canals irrigated the islands, which produced five to six crops a year. Tenochtitlan served as the core of a trade system stretching into North America and Central America, and whole villages produced copper items or textiles. Merchants enjoyed a privileged position but carefully maintained the state's goodwill, some probably serving as spies in outlying areas. Aztecs used cacao beans, cotton blankets, and quills filled with gold dust for currency.

In the Aztec system, the emperors, true despots who were considered semigods and selected by high officials, priests, and warriors, headed the hierarchical social structure. Then came the warrior-noble caste, with men divided into war lodges such as the eagle knights and jaguar knights. If captured by the enemy, they were expected to die with honor. According to an Aztec poem: "There is nothing like death in war. Far off I see it; my heart yearns for it!"[18] The priesthood, mostly celibate, played a key role, preparing calendars and most books. An Aztec remembered the priests as "sages wise in words. They watch over, they read, they lay out the books. They lead us, they tell us the way."[19] Aztecs used pictorial writing and drawings to create "codices," books made from the bark of fig trees, to produce hundreds of manuscripts, but all but eleven disappeared or were destroyed by the Spanish after conquest.

chinampas Artificial islands built along lakeshores of the central valley of Mexico for growing food.

Commoners, held in contempt by the elite, included artisans who created beautiful representations of the human figure. Indeed, Aztec sculptures, painted codex books, and murals were traded all over Mesoamerica. Many commoners worked as tenant farmers on noble-owned land. While upper classes enjoyed sumptuous meals of meat, tortillas, and tamales, followed by a chocolate drink, commoners lived on ground maize meal, beans, and vegetables; cooked with chili; and rarely ate meat. Numerous slaves, often debtors or criminals, occupied the lowliest position.

Aztec men and women led very different lives. While their menfolk served the state, elite women had two main roles: childbearer and weaver. Noble fathers advised their daughters "to learn very well the task of being a woman, which is to spin and weave. It is not proper for you to learn about herbs or to sell wood, peppers, [or] salt on the streets"[20] (like commoner women). While elite girls remained at home until their arranged marriage, when they moved into their husband's family, commoner women were freer to pursue careers such as street vendors and midwives. Many young boys learned religion, history, rhetoric, and the arts of war in schools, but girls, preparing for marriage, were taught domestic skills and religion.

12-4c The Inca Imperial System

The Inca conquered an empire in the Andes much larger than the Aztec Empire. Inca society, led by warrior chiefs, came together in central Peru around 1200. In the early 1400s a new leader, Viracocha (**VEE-ruh-KOH-chuh**) Inca, claiming to be a living god, launched campaigns of conquest with an army led by professional officers. By 1440 Viracocha's son, the pragmatic and visionary Pachacuti (**PA-cha-koo-tee**) ("World Remaker") (r. 1438–1471), the major empire builder, eventually conquered the Lake Titicaca Basin and Chimu Empire. According to legends, the sun-god told him that "you will subjugate many nations and take care to honor me and remember me in your sacrifices."[21] By 1525, after uniting both highlands and the coastal zone for the first time, the Inca dominated from southern Colombia to central Chile. Their capital city, Cuzco (**KOO-skoh**), contained between 60,000 and 100,000 people, and the empire, stretching for nearly three thousand miles, much of it above eight thousand feet in altitude, became the most politically integrated in the Americas. The Inca treated conquered peoples more generously than did the Aztecs, incorporating them into their armies, rewarding their service, and tolerating their religions and cultures. In some places far from Cuzco they erected cairn-like pillars, which apparently served calendrical, astronomical, political, and religious or ritual purposes, for example marking precise solar phenomena while also broadcasting the sacred power of the ruler.

Inca imperialism was spurred by religion and concepts of kings as divine offspring of the sun and responsible for defending the cosmic order. Kings enjoyed great wealth and pomp. According to a Spanish observer, the king in a royal procession, wearing a collar of huge emeralds, was borne on a massive gold sedan throne lined with tropical bird feathers and studded with gold and silver plates. Kings' bodies, mummified on their death, became the center of a cult. With deceased kings still considered owners of their property and land, their successors had an incentive to seek new conquests for acquiring their own property and land.

IMAGE 12.7 **The Great City of Tenochtitlan** Famous for his larger-than-life murals, the great Mexican artist Diego Rivera painted "The Great City of Tenochtitlan" in 1945 as an encyclopedic and idealized presentation of what the Aztec capital city's marketplace, with the Great Temple in the background, might have looked like five centuries earlier, including many of the products, activities, services, and people to be seen there. In Aztec times some of the products were being brought to the city as tribute from conquered peoples.

Q What does the painting tell us about the city and Aztec life as seen through Rivera's perspective?

[18]Quoted in Fagan, *Kingdoms of Gold*, 224.
[19]Quoted in Robert M. Carnack et al., *The Legacy of Mesoamerica: History and Culture of a Native American Civilization* (Upper Saddle River, NJ: Prentice-Hall, 1996), 415.
[20]Quoted in Marysa Navarro, "Women in Pre-Columbian and Colonial Latin America," in *Restoring Women to History* (Bloomington, IN: Organization of American Historians, 1988), 6.
[21]Quoted in *Incas: Lords of Gold and Glory* (Alexandria, VA: Time-Life Books, 1992), 52.

Discover Historical Voices

An Aztec Market

The wealth of foods and other trade goods available in markets in and around Tenochtitlan impressed Spanish conquistadors on their first visit in 1519, two years before their conquest. This account by Bernal Diaz del Castillo (DEE-as del kah-STEE-yoh), a Catholic priest who observed the Spanish conquest, describes the great market of Tlatelolco, near Tenochtitlan, which was thronged with as many as twenty-five thousand people every day. Special market days might have attracted twice that number.

We were astounded at the number of people and the quantity of merchandise that [the market] contained, and at the good order and control that was maintained, for we had never seen such a thing before. . . . Each kind of merchandise was kept by itself and had its fixed place marked out. Let us begin with dealers of gold, silver, and precious stones, feathers, mantles, and embroidered goods. Then there were other wares consisting of Indian slaves, both men and women. . . . Next there were other traders who sold great pieces of cloth and cotton, and articles of twisted thread. . . . There were those who shod cloths of hennequen [a tough fiber] and ropes and the sandals with which they are shod. . . .

Let us go and speak of those who sold beans and sage and other vegetables and herbs, . . . and to those who sold fowls, cocks, . . . rabbits, hares, deer, mallards, young dogs and other things of that sort in their part of the market, and let us also notice the fruiterers, and the women who sold cooked food, dough and tripe; . . . then every sort of pottery made in a thousand different forms from great water jars to little jugs; . . . then those who sold . . . lumber, boards, cradles, beams, blocks and benches. . . . Paper . . . and reeds scented with liquid [amber], and . . . tobacco, and yellow ointments. . . .

I am forgetting those who sell salt, and those who make the stone knives, . . . and the fisherwomen and others who sell some small cakes . . . [and] a bread having a flavor something like cheese. There are for sale axes of brass and copper and tin, and gourds and gaily painted jars made of wood. I could wish that I had finished telling of all the things which are sold there, but they are so numerous and of such different quality and the great market place with its surrounding arcades was so crowded with people, that one would not have been able to see and inquire about it all in two days.

Reflection Questions

1. What does the reading tell us about Aztec society and its material culture?
2. In what ways does the Aztec market remind you of a modern supermarket or department store?

Source: Bernard Diaz del Castillo, "*The Discovery and Conquest of Mexico,*" translated by A. P. Maudslay (New York: Farrar, Straus and Cudahy, 1956).

The Inca conquered or frightened into submission nearly all the farming societies, but their culture and power did not permeate far into rain forests and deserts. Deliberately resettling peoples to prevent rebellion or develop new districts, the Inca, unlike the Aztecs, faced relatively few uprisings. Many non-Inca appreciated the peace imposed after several centuries of warfare. To win support, Inca also encouraged sons of non-Inca leaders to attend school with Inca nobles in Cuzco, where they studied history, geometry, military tactics, and oratory. Goodwill and cooperation among the conquered were fostered by festivals featuring vast quantities of maize beer. While the Inca also practiced human sacrifice, they did so on a smaller scale than the Aztecs, mostly on ceremonial occasions. Several children from noble families of conquered peoples might be killed on a mountaintop as honored gifts to the mountain gods and their bodies were then mummified by the cold.

In the hierarchical and rigid Inca system, the royal family kept their bloodline undiluted by siblings marrying each other. Each ruler had many concubines and a chief queen, his sister, with her own magnificent palace and often considerable power behind the scenes. The queen headed a moon cult, led ceremonies for major goddesses, and gave birth to male heirs. Rebellions eventually became more frequent, and rivalry for the throne sometimes led to civil war. Such a conflict had just ended in 1532, weakening Inca resistance and allowing the newly arrived Spanish to triumph militarily and replace the Inca political system with Spanish rule.

12-4d Inca Political Economy, Society, and Technology

The most productive agriculture and creative technology in the Americas supported Inca society. Unlike with the Aztecs, the state, not merchants, operated the imperial economy by collecting and distributing goods, and imperial storehouses collected food for distribution as needed. The state required army service and work on state-owned farms or public works projects. Officials regularly visited villages to monitor work productivity or sanitation.

Inca society was patriarchal, with most commoners members of large extended families. Both men and women made pottery and worked in the fields, the men plowing and the women sowing the seeds. Each day peasant women spent time weaving and collecting firewood or llama dung for cooking. The ancient Andean creator-god and chief Inca deity, Viracocha, had both male and female characteristics, and the Inca worshipped several female deities, including the Earth Mother.

Whereas Aztecs mainly pursued sacrificial victims, Incas wanted control of labor and land. They built administrative centers throughout their territories, some as retreats for the elite, such as Machu Picchu (**MAH-choo PEE-choo**), a spectacular collection of buildings built high atop a narrow mountain ridge above a remote river valley. With communications a priority in ruling conquered lands, fourteen thousand miles of roads, many graded and paved with gutters for drainage, radiated out from Cuzco to link

IMAGE 12.8 **Machu Picchu** This dramatic mountaintop settlement in the high Andes was probably built as a spiritual retreat for Inca royalty, who enjoyed its well-constructed drains, baths, fountains, and administrative buildings.

Q What does this magnificent but remote complex, built on top of a high mountain in the Andes far from the capital city, tell us about Inca architecture, construction skills, planning, and transportation?

this vast empire. Inca engineers even tunneled through rocks and built suspension bridges across gorges and pontoon bridges of reeds across rivers. The road system awed the Spanish, one writing, "I believe there is no account of a road as great as this, running through deep valleys, high mountains, banks of snow, torrents of water, living rock, and wild rivers."[22] Along these roads relay runners, averaging some one hundred and fifty miles per day, conveyed administrative messages, and llama pack trains carried supplies.

Unlike Mesoamericans, the Inca had no formal writing system, but they invented an efficient, even ingenious form of record-keeping that involved different-colored knotted strings or cords, called **quipus**, to record commercial dealings, property ownership, and census data. Recent studies suggest that the complex color system and the direction of knots on the quipus contain not only numbers but also information about geography, names, stories, the tax on a particular good, and history, perhaps even as detailed as battles, speeches, and diplomatic visits. An oral literature with narrative power, including tales, prayers, and plaintive love songs, was passed down through the generations.

The Inca excelled in technology and science. Vast agricultural engineering projects, such as terraces and irrigation canals, generated widespread prosperity, surpassing most Eastern Hemisphere counterparts. Inca agriculture, far more productive than Peruvians can manage today, emphasized potatoes, maize, peanuts, and cotton. Practicing soil conservation, the Inca rarely experienced famine. They also developed sophisticated medicine and surgical techniques, including simple anesthesia procedures. Copper, bronze, and silver were fashioned into beautiful metal objects. Master cloth makers, the Inca wove luxurious woolen fabrics from alpaca fleece and made bridges from cords and roofs from fibers. Engineers built fortresses and temples with great blocks of stone so perfectly joined that even a knife could not be inserted between them. The Incas also improved on medical treatments and surgeries that had been used in the region for centuries. A study in 2019 estimated that some 83 percent of skull surgery patients in Inca times survived, a much higher rate than during the American Civil War 400 years later.

12-4e American Societies and Their Connections

Although thousands of miles of forests and mountains limited direct contact, American societies exchanged ideas and goods with each other over extended networks. Thanks to trade and conquest, many western South American peoples worshipped the same gods, shared mythologies, practiced human sacrifice, and made similar textiles, artworks, and metal products. Mesoamerican religious ideas, such as the Quetzalcoatl cult, influenced the Anasazi and even reached the Mississippi Valley, and Mesoamericans traded with the Pueblo peoples for turquoise and with Central Americans for jade. Traders known as the Manteno, from coastal Ecuador, also sailed large balsa rafts carrying cargo up and down the Pacific coast from Chile to Mexico, fostering some north–south communication.

Geographical barriers did not prevent Andean and Mesoamerican societies from developing some common social and political features. Hence, both regions had similar gender relations. Unlike in North America, where matrilineal patterns were common, these were mostly patriarchal societies, with men dominating central governments, village life, and extended family households while women prepared food, wove cloth, and ran households. Unlike kings and noble men, who might have several wives, most commoners practiced monogamy. Warfare, common but ritualized, involved much protocol, including declarations of war. Armies in close formation fought hand to hand, hoping to capture rather than kill opponents. Since most battles occurred far from cities, civilians and settlements were largely left alone.

Historians debate the size of the Western Hemisphere population in the late 1400s, but recent studies estimate 60 to 75 million, far fewer people than in the Eastern Hemisphere. Mesoamerica had the most population, perhaps 20 to 30 million, while 12 to 15 million lived in the Andes region. Perhaps seven million occupied North America, two-thirds in the eastern woodlands and southwest. Compared to inhabitants of the Eastern Hemisphere, Americans faced fewer deadly diseases, and some peoples were quite healthy. Yet, farmers and urbanites, especially Maya, experienced more health risks than hunters and gatherers. General health seems to have deteriorated for some centuries prior to the Columbian voyages. Famine caused by sporadic climate change posed a bigger problem.

quipus Different-colored knotted strings used by the Inca to record commercial dealings, property ownerships, and census data.

---

[22]Pedro Cieza de Leon, quoted in Terence N. D'Altroy, *The Incas* (Malden, MA: Blackwell, 2002), 3.

Eventually, American societies faced challenges coming from the Eastern Hemisphere. The only known European visits to the Americas before 1492 occurred in eastern Canada. Around 1000 CE a small group of Greenland-based Norse (Norwegian) Vikings, led by Leif Ericson, visited the area and established a base camp in Newfoundland (see Chapter 14). Alienating the local people, they apparently abandoned their settlement after a few years or perhaps decades, but occasional Norse trading visits may have continued for years, possibly even centuries. Recent DNA studies among Icelanders found that several long-established families carry some Native American genes, suggesting that Norse visitors may have taken at least one woman back with them. The isolated Norse did not publicize their discoveries to Europe, although Portuguese fishermen visiting Iceland may have heard some stories.

Five centuries later a more enduring trans-Atlantic connection was forged. In search of Asia, a Spanish expedition led by an Italian mariner, Christopher Columbus, ventured out in three small ships, eventually reaching the Bahamas. In later voyages Columbus visited more of the Caribbean and the South American coast. Even before 1492 some Americans had premonitions of a coming disaster. A few years earlier the Tarascan **(tuh-RAH-skuhn)** people of western Mexico, rivals of the Aztecs, forecast a time when

> *there will be no more temples or fireplaces, everything shall become a desert because other men are coming to the earth. They will spare no end of the earth, and everywhere all the way to the edge of the sea and beyond.*[23]

Despite creating technologies and ways of life that met their needs, thousands of years of isolation left Americans vulnerable to devastating diseases and the more effective steel weapons brought from more densely populated Afro-Eurasia. The new oceanic link altered American history forever, as epidemics wiped out millions of people, great empires fell, and Europeans settled and colonized the hemisphere.

KEY POINTS

▶ The Aztecs lived in a state of constant war and conquest, sacrificing thousands of enemy warriors a year, but their enemies helped the Spanish to conquer them.

▶ The Aztecs were productive farmers and active traders, with a hierarchical social structure in which priests played a central role.

▶ The Inca conquered a wide area in the Andes and had a hierarchical social structure, but they were far more inclusive and tolerant than the Aztecs.

▶ Trade in the Inca Empire was tightly controlled by the state, and an extensive irrigation system and soil conservation program yielded a consistent and abundant food supply.

▶ Despite extremely limited contact between Andean societies and Mesoamerican ones, they were similar in terms of gender relations and warfare protocols.

---

[23]"The Chronicles of Michoacan," quoted in Melvin Lunenfeld, ed., *Discovery, Invasion, Encounter: Sources and Interpretations* (Lexington, MA: D.C. Heath, 1991), 262.

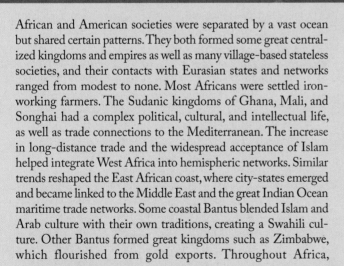

Chapter Summary

African and American societies were separated by a vast ocean but shared certain patterns. They both formed some great centralized kingdoms and empires as well as many village-based stateless societies, and their contacts with Eurasian states and networks ranged from modest to none. Most Africans were settled iron-working farmers. The Sudanic kingdoms of Ghana, Mali, and Songhai had a complex political, cultural, and intellectual life, as well as trade connections to the Mediterranean. The increase in long-distance trade and the widespread acceptance of Islam helped integrate West Africa into hemispheric networks. Similar trends reshaped the East African coast, where city-states emerged and became linked to the Middle East and the great Indian Ocean maritime trade networks. Some coastal Bantus blended Islam and Arab culture with their own traditions, creating a Swahili culture. Other Bantus formed great kingdoms such as Zimbabwe, which flourished from gold exports. Throughout Africa, however, many people lived in small stateless societies. African religion included both polytheistic and monotheistic traditions, and many people believed in diverse spirits.

Across the Atlantic in the Americas, Classical states, including the long-enduring Maya, eventually collapsed from climate change and chronic warfare and were replaced by vigorous new peoples, such as the Toltecs and Chimu. The Aztecs and Inca built the largest empires that ever existed in the Americas. The Americans also showed a pattern of continuity with the past, with both the Aztecs and Inca making use of long-established religious traditions and highly efficient agricultural techniques. The Aztecs practiced human sacrifice and commerce on a much greater scale than the Inca, while the Inca were outstanding engineers and road builders. Both empires had productive agriculture and well-organized states, but neither was prepared for the diseases and iron weapons that were brought by the Spanish.

Key Terms

mansa 285
Swahili 291

oral traditions 294
Quetzalcoatl 296

chinampas 302
quipus 304

South Asia, Central Asia, Southeast Asia, and Afro-Eurasian Connections, 600–1500

Indian government is founded on benign principles. The taxes on the people are light. Each one keeps his own worldly goods in peace. The merchants come and go in carrying out their transactions. Those whose duty it is sow and reap, plough and [weed], and plant; and after their labor they rest awhile.

—Xuan Zang, seventh-century Chinese visitor to India[1]

IMAGE 13.1 **Xuan Zang Arriving in China** A seventh-century CE Buddhist Chinese pilgrim, Xuan Zang, spent many years traveling in India, collecting Buddhist wisdom and observing Indian life. This modern Chinese painting shows him and his caravan returning to China with pack loads of Buddhist manuscripts.

Q What does this painting suggest about the spiritual and political importance of Xuan Zang's return to China?

[1]From L. S. Stavrianos, *The Epic of Man to 1500* (Englewood Cliffs, NJ: Prentice-Hall, 1970), 160, 162–163.

In 630 CE a determined Chinese Buddhist monk, Xuan Zang (**swan tsang**) (ca. 602–664), traveled the Silk Road to India on an extended pilgrimage to collect holy books, spending fifteen years visiting every corner of the subcontinent. Very observant and politically astute, he also chafed at many Indian Buddhists' perception that China was too remote to truly claim Buddhism. In a debate at the great Nalanda (**nuh-LAN-duh**) Monastery, Xuan Zang told the monks that

> *Buddha established his doctrine so that it might be diffused to all lands. Who would wish to enjoy it alone? Besides, in my country humanity and justice are highly esteemed.*[2]

Xuan Zang admired much in India, including the tolerance for diverse viewpoints. Although various Hindu traditions were dominant, Buddhism enjoyed protection and royal patronage. Xuan Zang described an Indian society with a rigid social structure but also creative and open to foreign influences, including regular contact with China, Europe, the Middle East, and Indonesia. He praised India's high standard of living, efficient governments, and generally peaceful conditions. He also criticized caste restrictions, such as confining untouchables to their own shabby neighborhoods. After traveling some 40,000 total miles, Xuan Zang returned to China in 643 with hundreds of Buddhist books to be translated into Chinese. He also became a confidant of the Tang emperor, fostering closer relations between India and China.

India's cultural diversity and openness to foreign influence resulted in part from repeated invasions by Central Asians and others that Hindu society eventually absorbed. Groups with differing customs generally lived peacefully, and Indian ideals spread to neighboring peoples. But Hindu political domination and cultural assimilation of newcomers faced a particularly severe challenge when Muslims gained control over large parts of the subcontinent. Islam's arrival constituted a turning point in India's development, comparable to the Aryan migrations into India several millennia earlier.

Southeast Asians also adopted new political systems and religions. Powerful kingdoms emerged, some strongly influenced by Indian culture. By the fifteenth century new faiths from outside, Theravada Buddhism and Islam, reshaped the political map and fostered more cultural diversity.

---

[2]Quoted in Tansen Sen, *Buddhism, Diplomacy, and Trade: The Realignment of Sino-Indian Relations, 600–1400* (Honolulu: University of Hawaii Press, 2003), 11.

13-1 Hinduism, Buddhism, and South Asian Society

TRANSITIONS SOCIETIES

Q How did Hinduism and Buddhism change in this era?

During this era no Hindu leaders recreated a longlasting empire like the Maurya or Gupta Empires. Instead, the subcontinent was shaped by political fragmentation and occasional invasion. Thanks in part to multiple migrations of diverse peoples carrying varied beliefs and customs into the subcontinent over the centuries, India encompassed many states, cultures, and languages. Despite a broad Hindu tradition and the common heritage it created, India became a collage of microcultures, with many images on the same canvas shaping one another while retaining their own distinctive character. This mixing demonstrated one of Indian history's themes: diversity in unity. Although it divided into competing schools of thought and practice, Hinduism experienced a Renaissance, growing in popularity and increasingly shaping Indian life, while Buddhism faded but found new influence in neighboring societies. Hindu culture flourished in India for half a millennium before facing the concerted challenge from Islamic peoples.

CONNECTION to TODAY

Can people today, in South Asia or elsewhere, learn any valuable lessons in how Indians in this era were able to maintain generally peaceful relations between, and learn from, diverse religions?

13-1a Unity and Disunity in Hindu India

The political disunity that followed the Gupta Empire's demise in the fifth century proved a long-term pattern. The exception was the reign of King Harsha Vardhana (600–647), who came to power at age sixteen and briefly united parts of north India, amassing a formidable army of 100,000 cavalry and 60,000 elephants. Harsha skillfully held together his small empire while cultivating close relations with Tang China. He enjoyed philosophy and renown as a poet and, while enjoying royal pomp, listened patiently to his humbler subjects' complaints. A strong Buddhist like Ashoka, he tolerated all faiths but also prevented his beloved sister, a Hindu, from committing *sati* (ritual suicide) at her husband's cremation. Harsha ruled for forty-one years, but his empire collapsed on his death.

Rajputs ("King's Sons") A Hindu Indian warrior caste formed by earlier Central Asian invaders.

Despite Harsha's brilliant reign, dozens of states proliferated in the subcontinent, and many experienced internal rivalries and conflict with neighbors. Many Hindu states were absolute monarchies whose rulers owned many economic resources, such as forests, mines, and weaving operations, and controlled outlying regions through appointed governors. Holding precarious power, they buttressed their rule by claiming a divine mission and employed brahmans (Hindu priests; see Chapter 2) as court advisers for legitimacy.

North and south India developed somewhat different political patterns. Some north Indian states were controlled by **Rajputs** ("King's Sons"), members of a Hindu warrior caste formed by varied earlier Central and West Asian invaders; Rajputs were raised in traditions of chivalry, honor, and courage not unlike Japanese samurai or medieval European knights. Their code emphasized mercy toward enemies and precise rules of conduct in warfare. However, Rajput-led kingdoms often fought each other for regional power. In contrast, many south Indian states, oriented to the sea, specialized in piracy and foreign trade. Merchants here had more political influence and

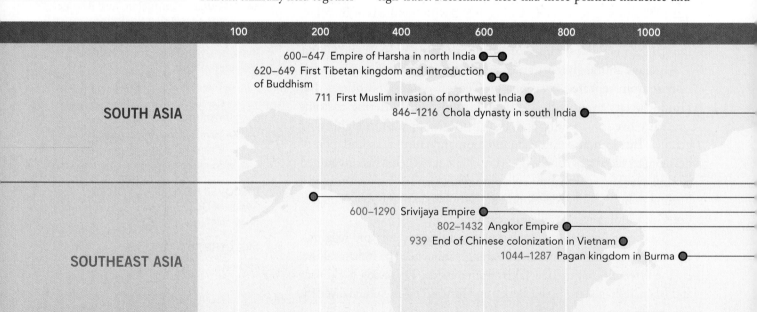

100 200 400 600 800 1000

SOUTH ASIA

600–647 Empire of Harsha in north India
620–649 First Tibetan kingdom and introduction of Buddhism
711 First Muslim invasion of northwest India
846–1216 Chola dynasty in south India

SOUTHEAST ASIA

600–1290 Srivijaya Empire
802–1432 Angkor Empire
939 End of Chinese colonization in Vietnam
1044–1287 Pagan kingdom in Burma

continued their lucrative maritime trade with Southeast Asia, China, and the Middle East. Indeed, many visited or settled in Southeast Asia, bringing with them lasting south Indian ideas on art, politics, and religion.

However fragmented were India's politics and regions, the countless villages reflected cultural continuity, remaining the basic unit of Indian life. Even today, about 70 percent of Indians live in villages. Farmers had to feed a population that reached around 100 million by 1500. Since the ruler owned all the land and was therefore entitled to tax or share the produce, the land tax remained the main source of state revenue and the main burden on villagers. By regularly meeting their tax obligations, peasants had the hereditary right to use the land they farmed. Village governments included a council elected annually from among village elders and caste leaders that dispensed local justice and collected taxes.

Villages remained largely self-sufficient and organized through the caste system, which promoted stability. Different castes lived in their own neighborhoods, but all contributed to the community's livelihood. Each village was essentially a symbiotic community, with a potter, carpenter, blacksmith, clerk, herdsman, teacher, astrologer, priest, and many farmers serving each other on a barter basis. Some modern writers romanticize traditional village life as peaceful coexistence, and certainly it offered psychological and economic security. Each villager had a recognized status, rights, and duties, a supportive caste community, and many personal relationships. When rulers maintained peace, repressed banditry, and kept the tax burden reasonable and there was adequate rainfall, most people were probably contented.

Many Indians also lived in towns and cities. Merchants helped administer the towns but, as in China, were heavily taxed and not allowed to become too independent of government. During the eighth century, to escape the Islamic conquest of Persia, some Zoroastrians fled to western India and formed the distinctive *Parsee* (Persian) community, which became known for its businessmen and manufacturers and remains very prominent in the Indian economy. Indeed, India was one of the world's leading manufacturing centers, with urban workshops producing cloth, textiles, pottery, leather goods, and jewelry for local use or export to markets as distant as China, Africa, and eastern Europe. Together, India and China provided most of the world's industrial goods before the eighteenth century, the average per capita incomes for Indians remaining high by world standards of the time.

13-1b The Hindu Social System and Scientific Traditions

Hindu society demonstrated great continuity over the centuries and, as in China, subordinated the individual to the group. Indians owed their most basic obligations to their extended family, a relationship described in an old saying as "joint in food, worship, and property." The family included several generations living together in the same household, enforcing caste regulations and collectively owning their economic assets, such as farmland. Sharing family wealth constituted an effective social security. Most families, especially in north India, were patriarchal, headed by a senior male, although older women enjoyed considerable influence. Children lived in close contact with cousins, aunts, uncles, and grandparents, making childrearing a group obligation.

Marriage customs reflected regional differences. North Indian parents arranged marriages, marrying girls off young usually to a boy in a neighboring village. Because the bride's family paid for the wedding and gave lavish presents, families preferred sons. South Indian girls often married boys they already knew, frequently a cousin. In Kerala (**CARE-a-la**) in southwestern India, one group practiced **polyandry**, marriage of a woman to several husbands. Most Indians considered divorce humiliating and shameful for the families involved.

Men enjoyed many privileges. Obsessed with social stability and controlling female sexuality, fathers of all castes taught females to avoid all men except their closest relatives after puberty. Expected to stay at

polyandry Marriage of a woman to several husbands.

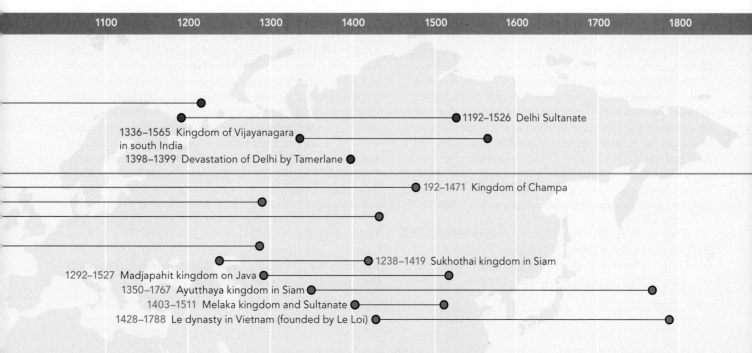

1100   1200   1300   1400   1500   1600   1700   1800

1192–1526 Delhi Sultanate

1336–1565 Kingdom of Vijayanagara in south India

1398–1399 Devastation of Delhi by Tamerlane

192–1471 Kingdom of Champa

1238–1419 Sukhothai kingdom in Siam

1292–1527 Madjapahit kingdom on Java

1350–1767 Ayutthaya kingdom in Siam

1403–1511 Melaka kingdom and Sultanate

1428–1788 Le dynasty in Vietnam (founded by Le Loi)

home, high-caste women only occasionally visited friends or family. Low-caste and untouchable women, who needed to earn incomes for family survival, enjoyed more mobility but probably had harder lives and faced more challenges. Most women led lives marked by obedience, sacrifice, and service, submitting to parents, husband, and children. Brides, usually much younger than husbands, moved into their husband's household and obeyed their new mother-in-law. Yet husbands often treated brides indulgently. Indians also revered motherhood. Bearing children (especially sons) improved the wife's status considerably, bringing more respect. Growing older and becoming a mother-in-law gained women even more influence.

Women also enjoyed some legal rights; although it was undoubtedly common, society condemned ill treatment of women. However, widowhood proved catastrophic if a woman had no son. Because Hindu custom frowned on remarriage, a young and childless widow faced a difficult situation. To avoid surviving their deceased husband, some women, especially in north India, chose or were forced to die on their husband's funeral pyre. An ancient Indian expression captures the challenge for women: "As a girl she is under the tutelage of her parents; as an adult her husband; as a widow her sons." Some women, such as actresses, singers, and prostitutes, flouted social custom and mainstream values, ensuring their low status.

Indians held diverse views about sex. Many books commended celibacy, advising married men to exercise their sexual prerogatives sparingly for better health and virtue. Yet, some Indian texts such as the *Kama Sutra*, a manual of lovemaking and related matters, reflect more worldly views. The erotic, sexually explicit paintings or carvings in many Hindu temples reflected an open portrayal of sexuality. Hindu gods and goddesses were sometimes portrayed in art and writings as highly sexual beings, even displaying their genitals and engaging in heterosexual and, for some, same-sex unions. These deities were very unlike the virginal Madonna and celibate Jesus of Christian tradition, the spiritually and morally pure Buddha, and the image of women reflected in puritanical Islamic restrictions. Some poets of both genders composed erotic explorations of sex and even female sexuality, including illicit love, in a mostly conservative and patriarchal society that closely guarded a woman's chastity. But over time South Asian culture became more puritanical under the influence of Islam and then of British colonialism.

Indians made many contributions in mathematics and science, helping to build the foundation for the technological world we live in today. In the twelfth century one of the greatest mathematicians and astronomers in history, Bhaskara (bas-CAR-a), proved that zero was infinity and designed a perpetual motion machine by filling a wheel rim with quicksilver. Bhaskara's book, translated into Arabic, later reached Europe, inspiring drawings of quicksilver wheels. His ideas also apparently influenced the first weight-driven clocks, built in Europe after 1300.

Some Indian astronomers and mathematicians found employment in Tang China, where they fostered a fruitful knowledge exchange. However, while Indians developed rational mathematics and the basis for scientific reasoning,

higher-caste indifference to applied or practical inquiry hindered scientific progress. As brahman power increased, technical expertise lost status. Some visitors reported a growing disdain among Hindu thinkers for foreign ideas. An astute Muslim observer wrote that "Hindus believe … there is no country, king, religion, [or] science like theirs."[3]

13-1c Hindu Diversity and Renaissance

Providing much of South Asians' spiritual framework before the coming of Islam, the diverse Hindu beliefs and practices accommodated all classes, personalities, and intellects, giving scholars and mystics abstract and speculative thought and the more worldly a wealth of ritual, art, and gods for every occasion. Although Hindu values permeated society, Hindus relied on no fixed and exclusive theology. As the earliest Hindu holy book, the *Rig Veda*, put it: "Reality is one; sages speak of it in different ways."[4] Concepts of spiritual power ranged from an indescribable but all-pervading, omnipotent God, to personal gods with human attributes, to demons and spirits. Some historians doubt that Hinduism existed as a cohesive religion at this time, postulating instead hundreds of competing, loosely linked devotional sects, cults, and theological strains with some common ideas such as karma. Hinduism remained undogmatic, a philosophy and way of life with no central institution or church to monitor faith or codify beliefs. Hindus even disagreed on which sacred writings were most important. It was Muslims who introduced the collective term *Hindu*, from the Persian term for "Indians," to describe the varied Indian sects and cults, and it was nineteenth-century Europeans who began referring to the diverse collection of beliefs and traditions as "Hinduism."

Hindu tolerance suggested that all approaches to God were valid, although mystics and intellectuals considered their approaches superior. For example, mother-goddess worship, common among the lower castes, especially in south India, was less popular among higher castes. Worship of the many gods and goddesses varied. Many cults, believing that the wives and consorts (companions) of the main male gods responded more to their needs, worshipped goddesses like Shiva's wife, Shakti (SHAHK-tee), who was revered as kind and beautiful but also cruel and fearsome. Most Hindus perceived the world as a collection of temporary living quarters for individual souls going through a succession of lives. The most devout sought liberation from human consciousness, which would free them from the endless cycle of birth and rebirth. But only a small minority seriously sought escape from the earthly world's pain and pleasures by becoming wandering holy men withdrawing from worldly activities, some of them living as hermits. While they admired holy men, most Hindus combined spiritual and worldly spheres, meeting social obligations to family, caste, and village while practicing moderation and temperance. The Hindu Renaissance (see below) spurred the building of flamboyant temples whose sculptural art illustrated the faith's intricate mythology. Hence, in a temple constructed in Khajuraho (kah-ju-RA-ho) dedicated to Vishnu, sculptures carved into

---

[3]Al-Biruni, quoted in Romila Thapar, *Early India: From the Origins to AD 1300* (Berkeley: University of California Press, 2002), 437.
[4]Quoted in Paul Thomas Welty, *The Asians: Their Evolving Heritage*, 6th ed. (New York: Harper and Row, 1984), 68.

the temple walls suggested delights enjoyed by the gods, including lovemaking.

Hinduism fostered a common culture throughout India. Brahmans served monarchs as advisers, standardizing political ideas and rituals. While brahmans monopolized the reading of Sanskrit scriptures, Hindu classics were available to all through storytellers. The Vedas, collections of ancient prayers and hymns, were also translated from Sanskrit into regional languages. Yet, before the eighteenth century few Indians other than brahmans and intellectuals had detailed knowledge of the Vedas and *Upanishads*. While Buddhism and Hinduism shared biases against eating animals, especially for brahmans, many Indians consumed fish, venison, and mutton.

During these centuries thinkers embellished or revitalized Hindu traditions, sparking what many historians call the Hindu Renaissance. Through itinerant preaching, debates with rivals, and written commentaries on the *Upanishads*, Shankara (**shan-kar-uh**) (788–820), a south Indian brahman child prodigy, revitalized the mystical *Vedanta* tradition, which emphasized the underlying unity of all reality and illusion of the phenomenological (material) world. To Shankara, all Hindu gods were manifestations of the impersonal, timeless, changeless, and unitary Absolute Reality, *Brahman*, and the individual soul only a tiny part of the universes' unity. While accepting Hindu scriptures as divine revelation, he tried to prove them through logical reasoning and debates with other thinkers all around India, including Buddhists, Jains, Tantrics, and atheists;

some debates lasted fifteen days. Yet Shankara also argued that all knowledge was relative because ignorance warps humankind's grasp of reality; the truth of existence is only understood through ascetic meditation. Shankara's views remain very popular among modern Indian intellectuals.

Other philosophers offered different visions. Opposing Shankara and Vedanta, Ramanuja (**RAH-muh-NOO-ja**) (b. 1017), a Tamil brahman, emphasized **bhakti**, devotional worship of a personal god, arguing that the gods should be accessible without priestly help. Somewhat like Sufism in the Islamic tradition, bhakti was a faith from the heart, bringing songs, inner peace, common participation, and even sometimes anguished protest, spread around the subcontinent by poet saints of both genders. A few centuries later some Christian reformers in Europe developed a similar notion of personal relationships with God without priestly aid. Bhakti tradition emphasized pilgrimage to holy places such as the city of Benares (**buh-NAHR-uhs**) (Varanasi), alongside the Ganges; Hindus who died in Benares hoped to have their sins washed away. Many early bhakti thinkers, most of them non-brahmans, also opposed or downplayed the caste system. The bhakti tradition appealed particularly to women, illiterates, and the lower castes. An early female poet, Antal, urged women devotees to revere Lord Krishna (an incarnation of Vishnu). Later the bhakti movement became part of mainstream Hinduism.

bhakti Devotional worship of a personal Hindu god.

IMAGE 13.2 **The Khajuraho Temple Complex** Built between 950 and 1150, these Hindu temples contain many erotic sculptures that may reflect Tantric influences.

Q What features of this temple contrast with the architecture and message of medieval Christian churches?

13-1d Transitions in Indian and Tibetan Buddhism

While Hinduism experienced resurgence, Buddhism's influence gradually declined except in northeast India, where governments patronized the religion's institutions, such as the Nalanda Monastery's university, which attracted religious students from around Asia. Pilgrims from distant lands, such as Xuan Zang from China, exemplified Buddhism's spread to Central Asia, Tibet, China, Korea, Japan, and Southeast Asia and its adaptation to different cultures. Northeast India's intellectual environment also promoted an interfaith dialogue that created new schools of Buddhist and Hindu thought. One new Buddhist school, the **Vajrayana** ("Thunderbolt"), featuring female saviors and magical powers, spread during the eighth century into Nepal and Tibet.

In Bengal the contact between Mahayana Buddhists and Hindu followers of Shiva who revered his consort, the goddess Shakti, led to **Tantrism (TAN-triz-uhm)**, which worshipped the female essence of the universe. Both Tantric and Vajrayana schools exalted female power as earth mother and divine strength, and Tantric sects developed within both Hinduism and Buddhism. Some mystical sects presented male–female sexual union as a symbolic unity between earthly and cosmic worlds, while other sects promised release from life's pain in a single lifetime to those cultivating hedonism, pleasure, and ecstasy. Tantric Hindus often opposed the caste system. But most Hindus and Buddhists denounced Tantrism as an excuse for debauchery and sexual desire, and gradually Tantrism became a minor strand in the two religions.

While Buddhism declined in India, the remote high Tibetan plateau became its refuge. The first known pre-Buddhist Tibetan state emerged when Songsten-gampo **(SONG-sten-GOM-po)** (r. 620–649 CE) unified several tribes. Interested in connecting to Asian neighbors, he established close relations with Tang China, marrying a Chinese princess. Although not a Buddhist, he allowed missionaries into his kingdom. Tibetans also made India's Sanskrit script their written language. By the eighth century Buddhism had become Tibet's dominant faith, its monasteries enjoying many legal protections and government financial support. But many Tibetans still followed the ancient folk religion, *bon*. The two faiths competed for popular support and political influence, with violent conflicts destroying the unified state.

In the thirteenth century many Buddhist monks fled to Tibet to escape Islamic persecution in India, reinvigorating both Tibetan Buddhism and state building. Political relations with the predominantly Buddhist Mongols, who had conquered China and established some control in Tibet, also boosted Tibetan Buddhism. A unified Tibetan government, reestablished in 1247 under one Buddhist sect and then by aristocratic families, persisted into the seventeenth century.

Tibet's distinctive Buddhism is often termed **Lamaism (LAH-muh-iz-uhm)** because of the centrality of monks, or *lamas* (LAH-muhz), and huge monasteries; perhaps a quarter to a third of male Tibetans became career monks. Buddhism eventually permeated every aspect of Tibetan life. Believers practiced magic, made pilgrimages to shrines, and provided generous support to monasteries and teachers. Tibetans also blended Buddhism with strong beliefs in the supernatural, including evil spirits. For example, people spun hand-held or roadside prayer wheels and carved prayers into stones, seeking the Buddha's help.

> **Vajrayana** ("Thunderbolt") A form of Buddhism that featured female saviors and the human attainment of magical powers.
>
> **Tantrism** An approach within both Buddhism and Hinduism that worshipped the female essence of the universe.
>
> **Lamaism** The Tibetan form of Buddhism, characterized by the centrality of monks (*lamas*) and huge monasteries.

KEY POINTS

▶ In the Intermediate Era, India was fragmented into many small states; the north was influenced by earlier Central Asian invaders and the south by maritime trade with Southeast Asia.

▶ In the Hindu social system, the individual was subordinate to the group and people tended to live in extended families that supported their members.

▶ Hinduism adapted itself to the needs of a wide variety of people, from the worldly to the scholarly, and helped to establish a common culture throughout India.

▶ Buddhism became the dominant religion in Tibet, where it became Lamaism, and many Indian Buddhist monks took refuge there to escape Islamic persecution.

13-2 The Coming of Islam to India and Central Asia

⚑ TRANSITIONS   ▦ SOCIETIES

Ⓠ How did Islam alter the ancient Indian pattern of diversity in unity?

The spread of Islamic religion and government in India proved a major transition, as important as the Aryan migration several millennia earlier. Having their own strongly held and organized religion, Muslims were not easily absorbed into the complex Hindu

CONNECTION to TODAY

How do you think politics in South Asia today reflect Hindu–Muslim encounters and conflicts in the earlier era?

world. With Muslims and Hindus almost exact opposites in beliefs, Islam created a great divide in South Asian society. As Al-Biruni, an eleventh-century Muslim scholar, put it: "Hindus entirely differ from us in every respect. In all manners and usages they differ from us to such a degree as to frighten their children with us."[5] For centuries Hindu society had absorbed invaders and their faiths, but Islam, a self-confident, missionary religion, could not be assimilated. Tensions between the two faiths sometimes caused conflict. However, Islam enriched Indian culture, establishing new connections with western Asia as Muslims spread Indian ideas, especially in mathematics and science, to the Middle East and Europe. Many Indians embraced the new faith, and Muslims also gained political dominance over large parts of India.

13-2a Early Islamic Encounters

Islamic forces reached Central Asia and India within a few decades of the religion's founding. Centuries before Islam's rise, Arab sailors had linked India by trade to western Asia and East Africa. The Silk Road trade had also made western Asians well aware of India's riches. Islamic rulers hoped to dominate these valuable regions.

After expanding into Afghanistan, by 673 Arab armies had moved into Silk Road cities such as Bukhara and Samarkand, dominated by Sogdian (**SOG-dee-uhn**) merchants, mostly Buddhists and Zoroastrians. Rival Central Asian city-states could not cooperate against the dynamic Arabs. Although many Sogdians resisted, by the early eighth century Arabs had conquered most of the cities. Some Sogdians fled to China. With the Arab defeat of Chinese forces at the Battle of Talas River in 751, serious

IndiaPictures/Universal Images Group/Getty Images

IMAGE 13.3 **The Kutb Minar Tower in Delhi** The 240-foot-high Kutb Minar temple in Delhi was built between the twelfth and fourteenth centuries to celebrate Muslim victory in north India.

resistance to Muslim dominance in Central Asia ended, and eventually most Central Asians adopted Islam. However, six centuries later, after Mongol rule in China ended in the 1300s, Central Asian economies suffered as the Silk Road trade declined, in part because Ming China developed more interest in maritime trade.

Islamic expansion through western and Central Asia challenged Indians. The first invasion of northwest India took place in 711. After Indian pirates plundered an Arab ship near the mouth of the Indus River, Arab armies responded by briefly conquering the western Indus Basin. But not all encounters were violent. Arab traders from Yemen also brought Islam by settling in southwestern Indian ports.

By the eleventh century Turkic peoples had formed Islamic sultanates in Afghanistan, with Ghazni (**GAHZ-nee**) the most powerful. Sultan Mahmud (**MACH-mood**) of Ghazni (r. 997–1030) led campaigns into India, as much for plunder as for conquest. Seeing the many Hindu idols and deities as an abomination to Islamic monotheism, the invaders destroyed Hindu temples while looting cities and killing Hindus. The vast wealth they took back to Ghazni helped that city become a great center of Islamic learning and arts, attracting famed scholars such as the Persian Al-Biruni.

Rajputs led opposition to Muslim invaders, maintaining a spirited Hindu resistance for many decades. Indian wars were traditionally fought largely between rulers and their respective warrior castes rather than by conscripted civilians. The caste system allowed only warriors such as Rajputs to have arms training, and they could not effectively mobilize other Indians to fight. Eventually the more mobile, horse-riding Muslims defeated Rajput armies, who also used outdated military tactics and had divided political loyalties.

The pillaging, destruction, and killing or enslaving of Hindus by early Muslim invaders fostered long-term Hindu antipathy. Even Al-Biruni concluded that Mahmud "utterly ruined [India's] prosperity. To Mahmud the Hindus were infidels, to be dispatched to hell as soon as they refused to be plundered."[6] Muslim newcomers zealously persecuted Buddhists as well, destroying monasteries and schools, including the Nalanda complex. With thousands of monks either killed or fleeing to sanctuary in the Himalayas or Tibet, Buddhism nearly disappeared from the land of its birth. In 2011 an international group of thinkers and educators announced plans to rebuild Nalanda as an ecumenical university and in 2014 it opened on a new campus near the ruins of the old monastery.

13-2b The Rise and Fall of the Delhi Sultanate

In 1191 a Turkish prince, driven by religious fervor and lust for riches, conquered most of northern India and founded the Delhi Sultanate (1192–1526), which reached its height in the 1200s and 1300s. Islamic authority and religion spread throughout north India, bringing political unity for the first time in centuries (see Map 13.1). But the unstable Delhi system experienced frequent bloodshed and treachery as leaders competed for power.

Some historians refer to the period from 1000-1765 as the Persianate Age, since India became more connected culturally and politically to Persia, Afghanistan, and Central Asia while

[5]Quoted in Lucille Schulberg, *Historic India* (New York: Time-Life Books, 1968), 11–12.

[6]Quoted in Debiprasad Chattopadhyana, *History of Science and Technology in Ancient India*, vol. 3 (Calcutta: Firma KLM Private Ltd., 1996), 60.

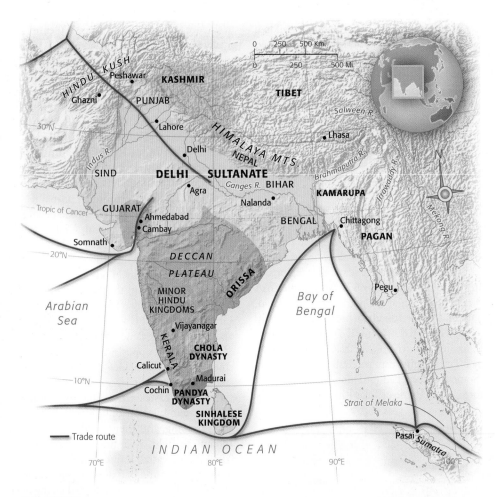

MAP 13.1 **India and the Delhi Sultanate, CA. 1300 CE** At its height, the Delhi Sultanate controlled much of northern India. South India was divided into many major states, with the Cholas and Pandyas the largest. Indian ports were connected by a vigorous maritime trade to the Middle East, East Africa, and Southeast Asia.

Q How does the political fragmentation illustrated in this map compare to South Asia during the Ancient and Classical eras?

Islam interacted in India with Sanskrit culture. This process influenced the languages, literature, art, music, cuisine, architecture, governing styles, and many other things in South Asia. Some Delhi sultans patronized the arts, supported science, treasured Greek philosophy, and built architecturally splendid structures. Many others, tyrannical and cruel, routinely killed rivals and their families. Some ruined the country with reckless spending. All employed Persian-style royal pomp, but they also styled themselves after Hindu monarchs, demanding prostration and toe-kissing from subordinates. This blending of ruling styles suggests that Muslim and Hindu cultures mixed among the elite. Some sultans expanded Delhi's power into central India and, briefly, south India, creating an empire larger than the Gupta realm. The empire attracted foreigners like the fourteenth-century Moroccan traveler Ibn Battuta, who served as a judge and diplomat for several years and noted other officials from Persia, Syria, Egypt, and Morocco. Some Africans from what are today Ethiopia, Eritrea, Sudan, and Somalia served as government and

military officials in varied South Asian states including Delhi. There were also African slave soldiers. African women were brought to India as domestic servants or concubines.

Two of the most able Delhi sultans were Iltutmish (**il-TOOT-mish**) (1211–1236), who built the most powerful north Indian state, and his remarkable daughter, Raziya (r. 1236–1240). Iltutmish kept out Genghis Khan's Mongol armies by skillful diplomacy, gradually followed more tolerant policies toward Hindus, and welcomed Muslim refugees, among them scholars and artists, fleeing the Mongols. Their large numbers helped keep Hinduism from gradually absorbing Islam. Iltutmish's chosen successor, Raziya, became the only female Muslim ruler in Indian history, praised by some historians for fostering trade, building roads, planting trees, supporting poets and artists, and opening schools. A male Muslim observer of her times described her as "a great monarch, wise, just and generous. She was endowed with all the qualities befitting a king, but she was not born of the right sex, and so in the estimation of men all these virtues were worthless."[7]

---

[7]Minhaju-s Siraj, quoted in John Keay, *A History of India* (New York: Atlantic Monthly Press, 2000), 245.

Resented as a female leader in a patriarchal society, Raziya offended Muslim conservatives by abandoning the veil, dressing in male garb, and having a close, perhaps romantic, relationship with a male personal attendant, a general originally from Ethiopia. She died defending her position from male rivals.

By the mid-fourteenth century the Delhi Sultanate went into a rapid decline, devastated by rebellion, civil war, and severe drought and famine caused in part by climate change. Meanwhile, a new Muslim threat appeared in the northwest, the Mongol and Turkic forces of Tamerlane (1336–1405). The ruthless warrior had already conquered Central Asia and Persia, creating the Timurid Empire based at Samarkand (see Chapter 10). In 1398 Tamerlane's forces invaded India, looting Delhi, killing perhaps 100,000 people, mostly Hindus, and dragging away thousands more as slaves. Tamerlane defended his actions: "although I was desirous of sparing them it was the will of God that this calamity should befall the city."[8] Tamerlane and his army returned to Central Asia, leaving Delhi's few surviving inhabitants to perish by plague or starvation. His invasion destroyed Delhi and with it political unity in north India. The Delhi Sultanate survived for several centuries in a shrunken form, but by the fifteenth century India was fragmented into dozens of Muslim and Hindu states.

13-2c Hindu Politics and Culture

Various Hindu monarchies governed parts of south and east India. Like post-Heian Japan and medieval Europe, these states featured economic self-sufficiency and political decentralization, with warriors receiving land from the monarch in exchange for military service. Commerce flourished, especially in south India. Merchants on the southwest coast, including Jews and Arabs, maintained close ties to western Asia and North Africa. An inscription from a merchant guild in 1055 boasted that they were "famed throughout the world, adorned with many good qualities. Born to be wanderers over many countries, the earth as their sack."[9] Wealthy ports such as Cochin (KOH-chin) and Calicut (KAL-ih-cut) in Kerala and Cambay (kam-BAY) in Gujarat (GOO-jur-ot) played major roles in Indian Ocean trade extending as far east as China. Ibn Battuta spent time in a Kerala port waiting to board a huge ship to China, but when a fierce storm destroyed the ship in the harbor, he sailed to the Maldive Islands instead.

The Tamil (TAA-mill) people of southeast India, controlled by a Hindu dynasty, the Cholas (CHO-luhs) (846–1216), profited from both piracy and foreign trade. The powerful Chola navy controlled the eastern Indian Ocean, conquering both Kerala and Sri Lanka (Ceylon). Chola merchant castes organized a dynamic maritime trade that brought great wealth to their society and revenue to kings. Sometimes Chola seafaring led to plunder and conquest as far away as Southeast Asia, especially Sumatra and Java. Chola rulers established close diplomatic and trade ties to Burma, Cambodia, and China.

Tamils developed an outstanding artistic tradition, including many fabulous Hindu temples featuring magnificent bronzes. Some unknown tenth-century genius created perhaps the greatest artwork, a bronze figure of Shiva portrayed as the "Lord of the Dance," ready to commence the cosmic dance of life and restore vitality to the world. For centuries artists and historians have praised this work, one writing that

> rarely has an artist achieved such perfect balance and harmony in any medium as in this metal statue, whose symbolism embraces all of Hindu civilization in its mythic power.... The workmanship of the artists was flawless in its beauty, magically transmuting metal to fleshlike texture, imparting the breath of life to their subjects.[10]

Eventually the Cholas declined, and the power vacuum was eventually filled in 1336 by another Hindu kingdom, Vijayanagara (vij-uh-yuh-NUHG-uhr-uh) ("City of Victory"). This militarily powerful state, eventually dominating much of south and central India, built a magnificent, temple-filled capital city, a massive site surrounded by huge defensive walls manned by soldiers and with broad avenues. Public rituals highlighted the state's military prowess. Some historians described Vijayanagara as a state founded to halt the advance of Muslim power and protect Hindu religion and culture. But recent scholarship challenges this, arguing that in the fourteenth century there was no concept of a unified Hinduism or of an Indian nation. Whatever the case, Vijayanagara was destroyed by rivals in 1565. The persistence of Hindu rule in parts of southern

SHAUN CURRY/Stringer/AFP/Getty Images

IMAGE 13.4 Shiva as Lord of the Dance This famous bronze statue of Shiva as Lord of the Dance was made by Chola artists in southeast India. Displaying himself as a god of many qualities, Shiva grasps the flame of destruction in one hand and the drum of creation in another. The small figure under his foot represents the illusions that Shiva undermines.

Q Why do you think this statue is considered one of the greatest works of art in world history?

[8]Quoted in Ibid., 274.
[9]Quoted in Hermann Kulke and Dietmar Rothermund, *History of India*, 3rd ed. (New York: Routledge, 1998), 245.
[10]Stanley Wolpert, *A New History of India*, 5th ed. (New York: Oxford University Press, 1997), 113.

Discover Historical Voices

The Songs of Guru Ravidas, an Untouchable Poet-Saint

Ravidas was widely considered a saint despite his humble origins. Born near Benares to an untouchable family of cobblers and shoemakers, his devotional poems and songs reflected his social reality. Some observers emphasize his protest against the unfair caste system; others contend they celebrate equality only in spiritual terms. Arguing that all can read the Vedas and worship without brahmanic mediation, Ravidas suggested that caste and gender divisions should end if people would strive together for a higher spiritual unity. His work earned respect from some brahmans and outraged others. He also influenced other bhakti poets and the founders of Sikhism, and he is revered by many Hindus and Sikhs today. The reading is excerpted from several poems.

Who could long for anything but you [God]?
My master, you are merciful to the poor;
You have shielded my head with regal parasol.
Someone whose touch offends the world
You have enveloped with yourself....
Oh well born of Benares, I too am born well known:
My labor is with leather. But my heart can boast the Lord....

A family that has a true follower of the Lord
Is neither high caste nor low caste, lordly or poor.
The world will know it by its fragrance.
Priests or merchants, laborers or warriors,
Halfbreeds, outcastes, and those who tend cremation fires—
Their hearts are all the same.
He who becomes pure through love of the Lord
Exalts himself and his family as well.
Thanks be to his village, thanks to his home,
Thank to that pure family each and every one....
No one equals someone so pure and devoted—
Not priests, not heroes, not parasolled kings.
As the lotus leaf floats above the water, Ravidas says,
So he flowers above the world of his birth.

Reflection Questions

1. How do these poems reflect Ravidas's social status?
2. How does he perceive God?
3. How do the poems foster debate over his purposes?
4. Do you think that people today in India or elsewhere might find the poem reflective of their own lives and reality?

Source: John Stratton Hawley and Mark Juergensmeyer, *Songs of the Saints of India* (New York: Oxford University Press, 1988), 24–25.

India preserved some Hindu customs and institutions disappearing or under threat in some northern areas.

13-2d Muslim Rule and the Reshaping of Indian Life

The growing number of Muslims and Islamic political power changed Indian history. Muslims and Hindus experienced chronic conflict from tensions created by their very different values still present today but now politicized. Hinduism, with its many deities, elaborate rituals, powerful priests, fondness for images, and preference for eating pork but not beef, constituted the opposite of all Islam held sacred. Hindus despised some Muslim rulers' intolerance and desperately resisted Muslim control. Muslim governments, not wanting to permanently alienate their Hindu subjects, a huge majority of the population, made some compromises. Although Muslim rulers often confiscated Hindu nobles' wealth, life in villages went on largely undisturbed. Eventually many Muslim scholars and leaders respected Hindus and the small Zoroastrian community as peoples of the book, counterparts to Christians and Jews in western Asia. But non-Muslims still faced second-class status and special tax payments.

Over the centuries many Hindus converted to Islam, especially in the Indus River Valley in the northwest and Bengal in the northeast. A much smaller proportion of southerners embraced

Islam. Converts included rich Hindus who wanted to safeguard their positions and secure government offices in Muslim-ruled states, as well as many poor Hindus who wanted to escape low or untouchable status and avoid heavier taxes on non-Muslims. Over 90 percent of today's South Asian Muslims, one-fourth of the region's population, descend from converts rather than Muslim immigrants or invaders. Sometimes Muslims, occasionally including rulers, adopted Hinduism. Sufi mystics seeking personal union with god prompted many Hindus' conversion. Bengali folk tradition celebrates a Sufi who moved to a village and built a mosque: "For the whole day [he] sat under a fig tree. His fame soon spread far and wide. Everybody talked of the occult [healing and psychic] powers he possessed."[11] People respected the Sufis' intense spiritual discipline and deep religious understanding. Perhaps the close resemblance to bhakti Hinduism, which also emphasized emotional commitment, helped the Sufi effort. Today many South Asian Muslims and some Hindus still venerate Sufi mystics of earlier centuries as saints. But in recent years dogmatic Sunni Muslim zealots in South Asia have also attacked Sufis and destroyed their shrines to saints.

Religious and cultural mixing occurred. Some Hindu and Muslim mystics came together to emphasize love of god, and some poets, honored later as saints, blended Sufi and bhakti ideals, among them Kabir (kah-BEER) (1440–1518), from a low-status caste of weavers in Benares. Although blind and illiterate, Kabir

---

[11]Quoted in Richard Eaton, "Islamic History as Global History," in *Islamic and European Expansion: The Forging of a Global Order*, ed. Michael Adas (Philadelphia: Temple University Press, 1993), 21.

composed poetry that is still revered today by both Hindus and Muslims. His writing rejects religious prejudice and the caste system while extolling love for a monotheistic god:

> *I am neither in temple nor in mosque; I am neither in Kaaba [Muslim shrine] nor in Kailash [abode of Shiva]. Neither am I in rites and ceremonies, nor in Yoga and renunciation. . . . Hari [Lord Vishnu] is in the East; Allah is in the West. Look within your heart, . . . All the men and women of the world are His Living Forms. Kabir is the child of Allah and of Ram [God].*[12]

Some revered bhakti poet-saints came from untouchable backgrounds, most notably Guru Ravidas in the fifteenth century (see Discover Historical Voices: The Songs of Guru Ravidas, an Untouchable Poet-Saint).

The cultural mixing fostered a new language still used by many Muslims in north and northwest India. Urdu **(ER-doo)** combined Persian, Turkish, Arabic, and Indian words superimposed on a Hindi grammar and written with Arabic script. In addition, Hindu social life incorporated Muslim influences, including Persian words and food, male Muslim clothing styles, and, among some north Indians, the custom of **purdah**, seclusion of women. Some intermarriage also occurred, and, at the village level, Muslims fit themselves into the caste system to some extent. Thus Muslim Indian society, like Hindu society, was not egalitarian but led by an upper class descended from immigrants or invaders.

However, despite some mixing, from the thirteenth century onward, Indian life became two distinct currents flowing side by side. Challenged by missionary Islam, Hinduism became more conservative, emphasizing tradition and priestly leadership. Refusing assimilation into Hindu culture, Muslims mostly remained disdainful of Hindus and the caste system. But, unlike Buddhism, which was centered in vulnerable monasteries like Nalanda, Hinduism's decentralized structure proved stable. Thus Hindus and Muslims mingled to some extent along the lines of contact but never formed a single stream. This persistent division greatly affected twentieth-century India, when the British colony of India (ruling most of the subcontinent) was eventually divided into separate nations, Hindu-dominated India and Muslim-dominated Pakistan. The island of Sri Lanka remained a bastion of Theravada Buddhism.

KEY POINTS

▶ Hindu warriors fended off Muslim invaders for a time, but they were outmatched and eventually defeated by their aggressive opponents.

▶ The Islamic Delhi Sultanate brought unity to north India for the first time in centuries, but its rulers ranged from the enlightened to the tyrannical.

▶ Various Hindu monarchies, including the Cholas, maintained power in southern and eastern India, while Hindu traditions died out in the north.

▶ Muslim and Hindu beliefs were radically opposed, but over time Muslim rulers came to tolerate Hindu subjects, many of whom eventually converted to Islam.

13-3 Cultural Adaptation and Kingdoms in Southeast Asia

▦ SOCIETIES

Q What political and religious forms shaped Southeast Asian societies in the Early Intermediate Era?

Southeast Asia before modern times is often neglected in general books on world history. Yet, the region's societies, many of them located along or near major maritime trade routes, played important roles in the political and economic history of the Eurasian world. Owing partly to stimuli from India and China, several great Southeast Asian kingdoms with fluctuating borders developed near the end of the first millennium CE, establishing their main centers in Cambodia, Burma, the Indonesian islands of Java and Sumatra, and Vietnam (see Map 13.2). Southeast Asian societies mixed outside influences with their own traditions.

CONNECTION to TODAY

Can you identify some of the cultural, religious, and political legacies from this era that might influence Southeast Asians today?

13-3a Indianized Kingdoms and Societies

Historians today debate the nature of first millennium CE Southeast Asian states, prompted by archaeological discoveries of the past several decades. Some suggest that the temple-building societies, known to some scholars as Indianized kingdoms or Indic states, flourished from trade but may have been more loosely organized politically and less unitary than often thought. Whatever the case, from early in the Common Era until the 1400s, many Southeast Asian societies selectively adapted Indian models to shape their political patterns, a collaborative process some historians term *Indianization*, which produced a convergence of cultures. Some rulers declared themselves god-kings, not just China-style intermediaries between the human and cosmic realms but rather reincarnated Buddhas or Shivas worthy of cult worship. By maintaining order in this world, the kings and priests claimed, they ensured cosmic harmony. Kings enjoyed enormous prestige but also faced continuous threats from neighboring states and from rivals, who often succeeded in acquiring the throne.

purdah The Indian Muslim custom of secluding women.

[12]William Theodore De Bary, ed., *Sources of Indian Tradition*, vol. 1 (New York: Columbia University Press, 1958), 355–357.

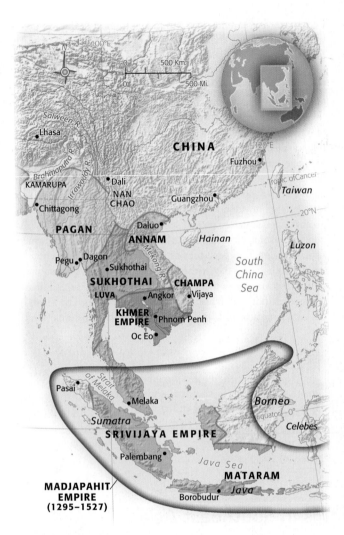

MAP 13.2 Major Southeast Asian Kingdoms, CA. 1200 CE By 1200 the Khmer Empire (Angkor), which once covered much of mainland Southeast Asia, had declined. Sukhothai, Pagan, Srivijaya, Champa, and Vietnam were other major states.

Q How does the political configuration of Southeast Asia in this era compare with that of today?

The economic foundations of Indianized kingdoms differed, with some based largely on agriculture and others, especially alongside the Straits of Melaka, dependent on maritime trade. These contrasting patterns represented skillful adaptations to differing environments. In agriculture-based economies, rice-growing technology became productive enough to sustain large centralized states, but in swampy places lacking good farmland, people maximized their access to the open sea frontier.

Migrations and mixing of peoples and cultures were significant themes in Southeast Asia, as in India, Europe, and Africa. Hence, the Burmans (**BUHR-muhnz**) in the ninth century and the Tai (**tie**) from the seventh to thirteenth centuries moved from Tibet and China into mainland Southeast Asia.

The Burmans established the dynamic state of Pagan (Bagan) (**puh-GONE**) in central Burma (1044–1287).

Religion played a central political role. While peasants chiefly remained animists, elites adopted Hinduism and Mahayana Buddhism (and in Burma Theravada Buddhism). In the twelfth century, the city of Pagan on the dusty plains of Burma (now known as Myanmar) was one of the world's architectural wonders, filled with some ten thousand magnificent temples and shrines glorifying Buddhism and Hinduism. The city of perhaps 200,000 people attracted many pilgrims and monks, as well as students who came to study philosophy, law, astrology, medicine, and Buddhist scripture. Religion in Indianized states often infused government and the arts, with Hindu priests becoming advisers on court rituals. With Hindu Indian epics such as the *Ramayana* and *Mahabharata* deeply imbedded in the cultures, Hindu kings, gods, and demons animated the arts. Many Southeast Asian written languages, such as Khmer, Burman, and Thai, used Indian scripts, fostering poetry, religious speculations, and historical chronicles, all important components of elite culture.

Southeast Asian societies shared many common features. Extensive land and maritime trade networks linked the region from earliest times, with many people specializing in local or foreign commerce. Most larger states had multiethnic populations, including foreign merchants, that encouraged a cosmopolitan attitude. Still, most Southeast Asians were farmers and fishermen, lived in villages, and cooperated for mutual survival. Differing social and cultural traditions separated the royal courts and capital cities from the villages.

Southeast Asian family patterns ranged from flexible arrangements to a few patriarchies and matriarchies. Unlike in patriarchal India and China, some women enjoyed relatively high status. A few, like the Pagan queen Pwa Saw (**pwah saw**), exercised political influence behind the scenes (see Meet the People: Pwa Saw, a Burmese Queen). Yet, in some pageantry-filled courts, women in royal harems and their many female attendants were expected to be grateful. One Javanese male poet noted: "the women's quarters seemed to radiate a shimmering light / It was as if the amazing beauty emanated from heaven."[13]

13-3b The Angkor Empire and Society

In Cambodia the Khmer people created Southeast Asia's greatest Indianized kingdom and premodern empire, Angkor (**ANG-kor**), which means "Holy City" in Sanskrit. A visionary king, Jayavarman (**JAI-a-VAR-man**) I (r. 802–834), identifying himself with the Hindu god Shiva, established the state in 802. His successors extended the kingdom, which persisted until 1431-1432. Magnificent temples still standing and popular with tourists today testify to Angkor's prosperity and organization. By the twelfth century the bustling capital, Angkor Thom (**ANG-kor tom**), contained perhaps a million people, much larger than medieval European and most Chinese and Arab cities. A massive urban network stretched out from the capital for miles, connecting satellite towns to the main temples. Although Angkor traded with China and other countries, with many Chinese merchants living in the kingdom, agriculture remained the economic foundation.

---

[13]Quoted in Helen Creese, *Women of the Kakawin World: Marriage and Sexuality in the Indic Courts of Java and Bali* (Armonk, NY: M.E. Sharpe, 2004), 44.

At its height Angkor's empire, acquired and maintained by warfare, diplomacy, and pragmatic policies, controlled much of Cambodia, Laos, Thailand, and southern Vietnam, but central power waned with distance and regional governors enjoyed considerable autonomy. The many kings who patronized art and built roads and temples bragged about their achievements, as in a monument praising a late-ninth-century king: "In all the sciences and in all the sports, in dancing, singing, and all the rest, he was as clever as if he had been the inventor of all of them"[14] Zhou Daguan (**joe ta-kwan**), China's ambassador in 1296, left vivid descriptions of Angkor, including the justice system: "Disputes of the people, however insignificant, always go to the king. Each day the king holds two audiences for affairs of state. Those of the functionaries or the people who wish to see the king, sit on the ground to wait for him."[15] The well-financed state held much power over people but supported substantial public services, including hospitals, schools, and libraries. According to temple stone inscriptions, one king ordered one hundred and twenty hospitals to be built, and another claimed that "he suffered the illnesses of his subject more than his own

because the pain of the public is the pain of kings."[16] Among other medical practices, doctors checked a patient's pulse and used butter, oil, molasses, and honey as medicine. Exhibiting some of the premodern world's most advanced civil engineering, conscripted workers constructed extensive canal and reservoir networks for efficient water distribution and storage. Craftsmen produced ceramics and metal objects. Although historians debate how much farming depended on irrigation from these canals, the Khmer had one of the world's most productive agricultures and produced three to four crops of rice a year.

The Angkor government, which resembled a theocracy, presided over a cult for god-king worship, with priestly families holding privileged positions. Numerous temples and Hindu priests controlled massive wealth. Theater, art, dance, and the many magnificent stone temples, some as huge as small mountains, reflected Hindu values. Designed to represent Hindu cosmic thinking on the gods' abode, temples also symbolized a monarch's earthly power, with construction involving amazing engineering and massive conscripted labor. Some seventy thousand workers built the premodern world's largest religious

Tim Hall/Robert Harding World Imagery

IMAGE 13.5 **Angkor Wat Temple Complex** This photograph shows the inner buildings of the Angkor Wat temple complex in northern Cambodia. The towers represented the Hindu view of the cosmos. Mount Meru, the home of the gods, rises 726 feet in the middle.

Q How do you think this famous Cambodian temple complex is different from and similar to Hindu temples in other countries?

[14]Quoted in W. Robert Moore, "Angkor, Jewel of the Jungle," *National Geographic* 117, no. 4 (April 1960): 540.

[15]Quoted in Christopher Pym, *The Ancient Civilization of Angkor* (New York: New American Library, 1968), 118.

[16]Quoted in Michelle Vachon, "Uncovering the Healthcare System of Angkor." *The Cambodia Daily* (August 22, 2015).

Pwa Saw, a Burmese Queen

Women in royal families were politically influential in many Southeast Asian states, mostly behind the scenes, but few enjoyed the influence of thirteenth-century Queen Pwa Saw of Pagan. Much of what we know about her life comes from a chronicle of the country's history compiled by Burmese scholars in the nineteenth century. Modern historians debate whether it represents more myth than fact. Whatever the accuracy, in their traditions the Burman people remember Queen Pwa Saw as witty, wise, beautiful, and instrumental in shaping politics for forty years during one of their most difficult periods.

The girl who would become queen was born to a prosperous peasant family in a remote village around 1237. According to legends, a deadly king cobra approached as she slept but failed to attack, considered a favorable omen, and a jasmine bush she tended astonished her neighbors by blooming in three colors. This unusual event drew the attention of the young King Uzana (r. 1249–1256), a playboy fond of hunting and drinking who was

IMAGE 13.6 Court Life of Pwa Saw No known paintings of Pwa Saw exist. This fresco, from the Ananda Buddhist temple at Pagan, shows rich court ladies, much like Pwa Saw herself, relaxing in an upstairs room of a magnificent Buddhist temple while, downstairs, stallholders hawk their wares to visitors.

Luca Tettoni/Robert Harding World Imagery

Q What does this fresco tell us about religious, economic, and court life as well as the varied roles of women in Pagan?

visiting the district with a large entourage of attendants. The unexpected visit of a king and his party riding on elephants spurred the villagers into frenzied preparations for a proper reception to demonstrate their respect. Infatuated with the bright, pretty, graceful, and talkative sixteen-year-old girl, Uzana took her back to Pagan as one of his many wives and appointed her a deputy queen. A short time later, Uzana died in an accident while hunting wild elephants.

With her husband's death, Pwa Saw was thrown into the royal court's schemes and rivalries as various factions maneuvered for power. Placed in a precarious position as a young bride resented by rival queens, she quickly forged an alliance with the able and wily Chief Minister Yazathingyan **(YAH-za-THING-yan)**, who feared the accession of the king's oldest son, the unpopular Prince Thitathu **(thee-TAH-thoo)**, with whom he had long quarreled. Together they convinced officials to support another son, Narathihapade **(NAR-a-THITH-a-PAH-dee)** (r. 1256–1287), as king and make Pwa Saw chief queen. But the young king proved arrogant, quick-tempered, and ruthless, alienating many at court and earning the nickname "King Dog's Dung." While the economy declined,

the king boasted that he was "the commander of 36 million soldiers, the swallower of 300 dishes of curry daily," and had three thousand concubines. His zeal to build an expensive Buddhist pagoda fostered the proverb that "the pagoda is finished and the great country ruined." Pwa Saw remained loyal but lost respect for the king.

After her ally Yazathingyan died leading royal forces to suppress a rebellion in the south, Pwa Saw skillfully survived the king's paranoid suspicions and the constant intrigues of court nobles, attendants, and other queens. Because the king trusted the widely revered queen, she could often overrule his destructive tendencies and talk him into making wiser state decisions. She also convinced the erratic king to appoint capable officials. But she had to maintain her wits. Increasingly paranoid, Narathihapade executed any perceived enemies and burned another queen to death. In the 1270s, anxious to prove himself a great leader, he rejected Pwa Saw's advice to meet Mongol demands for tribute and avoid conflict, instead escalating tensions and bringing on war, disaster, and temporary Mongol occupation of Pagan.

Even as the Pagan state declined, Pwa Saw asserted a benevolent influence. For instance, in 1271 she donated some of her lands and properties to a Buddhist temple, expressing hope that in future existences she would "have long life, be free from illness, have a good appearance, melodic of voice, be loved and respected by all men and gods, [and] be fully equipped with faith, wisdom, nobility." In 1287 one of his sons murdered the mad king. In 1289 Queen Saw and surviving ministers selected a new king, Kyawswar **(kee-YAH-swar)** (1287–1298). With that last effort to help her country, she retired in style to her home village.

Reflection Questions

1. What skills did Pwa Saw use to influence the court?
2. What does this profile tell us about the relations between queens and kings at Pagan?
3. Can you think of any queens in the past two hundred years that had the influence of Pwa Saw in politics? How do their experiences compare?

Notes: Quotations from D. G. E. Hall, *A History of South-East Asia*, 4th ed. (New York: St. Martin's Press, 1981), 169; and Michael Aung-Thwin, *Pagan: The Origins of Modern Burma* (Honolulu: University of Hawaii Press, 1985), 41.

complex, Angkor Wat (ANG-kor waht), in the twelfth century. Reliefs carved into stone at Angkor Wat and other temples illustrate daily life, showing fishing boats, midwives attending a childbirth, merchant stalls, festival jugglers and dancers, peasants bringing goods to market, crowds at a cockfight, and men playing chess.

Khmer commoners tolerated highly inequitable wealth and power distribution and substantial labor demands. Although no India-style caste system existed in the rigid social structure, each class had its appointed role: below the king were priests, and below them trade guilds. Most people were of the farmer-builder-soldier class, mostly living in small wood and thatch houses, or slaves and people in temporary servitude. Rich families lived in large houses with tiled roofs and often owned more than a hundred slaves, and merchants ten or twenty. Slaves dredged irrigation canals, rowed war boats, worked quarries, and helped build the great temples. In this matrilineal society women played a more important role in social life and politics than in most other societies, operating most retail stalls. According to Zhou Daguan: "In this country it is the women who are concerned with commerce."[17] Some royal women participated in intellectual or service activities. Jayarajadevi (JAI-ya-RAJ-adeh-vee), King Jayavarman VII's first wife, took in hundreds of abandoned girls and trained and settled them. After her death the king married Indradevi (IN-dra-deh-vee), a renowned scholar who lectured at a Buddhist monastery. Women also participated in the arts, especially as poets. They dominated the palace staff, some even serving as gladiators and warriors. Chinese visitors were shocked by the liberated behavior of Khmer women, who went out in public as they liked.

13-3c Indianized Urban Societies in Java and Sumatra

Several Indianized states developed in the Indonesian archipelago on the large islands of Java and Sumatra. Encounters in Java between Indian influence and local traditions produced a distinctive religious and political blend known as Hindu-Javanese, which perceived the earthly order mirroring and embodying the cosmic order. Hence, people must avoid disharmony and change to preserve the cosmic order, which required the god-king to prevent social deterioration and maintain order in a turbulent human world. The greatest Javanese kingdom, Madjapahit (MAH-ja-PA-hit) (1292–1527), reaching its peak in the fourteenth century under the fabled Prime Minister Gajah Mada, loosely controlled much of present-day Indonesia. As in Angkor, Javanese kingdoms like Madjapahit built capitals and palaces to imitate the cosmic order. Temple complexes such as Borobodur (BOR-uh-buh-door) in central Java, as well as shadow puppet plays, or **wayang kulit** (WHY-ang KOO-leet), based on Hindu epics like the *Ramayana* but having much local content as well, reflected Hindu-Buddhist ideas.

Social inequality permeated Hindu-Javanese society, with complex etiquette regulating relations between people of different status. Aristocrats, who administered the realm, expected deference from commoners, most of whom lived in village cultures differing substantially from royal capitals. A tradition of mutual aid fostered communal effort in village work. Peasants identified more with their village than with distant kings in their palaces.

Unlike in agricultural kingdoms on Java and in Cambodia, international trade largely shaped Sumatran coastal states. The Straits of Melaka separating Sumatra from the Malay Peninsula provided a major passageway for a complex maritime trading system linking the eastern Mediterranean, Middle East, East African coast, Persia, and India with East and Southeast Asia. Between 600 and 1290 many small trading states in the Straits region came under the loose control of Srivijaya (SREE-vih-JAI-ya), a maritime-oriented state based in southeastern Sumatra, which helped shape the region's international commerce and maintained trade relations with powerful China. Srivijaya's naval force both fought and engaged in piracy. Becoming a major center of Buddhist study, Srivijaya attracted thousands of Buddhist monks and students from many Asian countries.

13-3d International Influences and the Decline of the Indianized States

Most Indianized states declined and collapsed from internal and external challenges between the thirteenth and fifteenth centuries. Several problems challenged Angkor: military expansion overstretched resources; increased temple building spurred higher tax levies and forced labor, antagonizing many commoners; growing breakdown of the irrigation system required more labor for maintenance; and increasingly unpredictable rains due to climate change and instability, alternating between "megadroughts" and "mega monsoons" (heavy flooding), overstretched the hydraulic system. A 2019 study offers another theory, that beginning in the 1300s the ruling elites gradually abandoned the walled capital city, perhaps to move closer to the coast and the growing and lucrative maritime trade with China. In their absence floating swamp vegetation covered the moats and irrigation systems.

States also faced challenges from outsiders. Over several centuries groups from mountainous southwestern China speaking Tai languages migrated into Southeast Asia, some of them setting up states in the Mekong Basin and northern Thailand. The Tai peoples, ancestors of the closely related Siamese (SYE-uh-meez), today known as Thai, and the Lao (laow) peoples conquered or absorbed local peoples while also adopting some of their cultural traditions. Eventually they came into conflict with Angkor, repeatedly sacking the capital and seizing much of the empire's territory. The Khmer Empire soon disintegrated, with the capital city mostly abandoned although some people seem to have remained in a few neighborhoods, including around Angkor Wat. As jungles overtook the monuments to their glorious past, Khmers became pawns perched uneasily between the expanding Vietnamese and Siamese states.

> **wayang kulit** Javanese shadow puppet play based on Hindu epics like the *Ramayana* and local Javanese content.

---

[17]Quoted in David Chandler, *A History of Cambodia*, 2nd ed. updated (Boulder, CO: Westview Press, 1996), 74.

Meanwhile, Mongols threatened Angkor's neighbors. After conquering China, in 1288 they attacked Pagan, which refused to recognize Mongol overlordship. The Mongols soon withdrew, leaving instability in Burma as rival groups competed for power. Elsewhere in Southeast Asia the Mongols found mostly frustration. Although a land-and-sea invasion of Vietnam and Champa inflicted terrible damage, a temporary Vietnamese–Cham military alliance ultimately triumphed. A Vietnamese general, Tran Hung Dao, inspired resistance fighters by having his soldiers tattoo "Kill the Mongols" on their right arms. A Mongol naval expedition to Java also proved a costly failure. Southeast Asians were among the few peoples to successfully resist Mongol conquest and power.

Religion proved another force for change. By the early second millennium, Theravada Buddhism and Islam began filtering peacefully into the region. Theravada Buddhism had long influenced Burma, but a revitalized form from Sri Lanka, perhaps by way of the Pagan kingdom, provided a challenge to Indianized regimes. The Buddhist message of egalitarianism, pacifism, and individual worth proved attractive to peasants weary of war, public labor projects, and tyrannical

kings. Theravada Buddhism, a tolerant religion, coexisted with animism, with peasants honoring the Buddha while worshipping local spirits. By the fourteenth century most Burman, Khmer, Siamese, and Lao peasants had adopted Theravada Buddhism, while elites and royal families mixed the faith with older Hindu–Mahayana Buddhist traditions.

From the thirteenth through sixteenth centuries, Sunni Islam filtered in from the Middle East and India, spreading widely. Like Buddhism, Islam offered an egalitarian message and a complex theology that appealed to peasants and merchants in the Malay Peninsula, Sumatra, Java, and some other Indonesian islands. Some adopted Sunni Islam in a largely orthodox form, while others mixed it with animism or Hinduism-Buddhism. Sufism also blended well with the existing mysticism. Only a few scattered peoples maintained Indianized societies. Among the Balinese (**BAH-luh-NEEZ**) on the Indonesian island of Bali, Hinduism and other classical patterns remained vigorous, emphasizing arts like dancing, music, shadow plays, and woodcarving. Thus the throngs of visitors to Bali today glimpse patterns once widespread in the region.

KEY POINTS

▶ Most Southeast Asian states were multiethnic and influenced by immigrants and the influence of Mahayana Buddhism and Hinduism from India.

▶ The Indianized kingdom of Angkor controlled a large swath of Southeast Asia and completed advanced civil engineering projects, such as an extensive canal system and the huge temple complex of Angkor Wat.

▶ Hindu priests played a very important role in Angkor, and the social structure was extremely rigid, though an

Indian-style caste system did not take hold and women were more important in society and politics than in most places in the world.

▶ Southeast Asians fended off the Mongols, but new peoples such as the Tai invaded and destroyed Angkor, and the gradual introduction of Theravada Buddhism and Sunni Islam challenged the hierarchical order and displaced Indian influence in many states.

13-4 Buddhist, Confucian, and Islamic Southeast Asian Societies

▦ SOCIETIES

Ⓠ What was the influence of Theravada Buddhism, Confucianism, and Islam on Southeast Asia?

By the fifteenth century Southeast Asia had experienced a major transition. Less despotic states gradually replaced Indianized kingdoms, and networks of trade and religion expanded, linking the region even more closely to Afro-Eurasia. Major Southeast Asian societies diverged from earlier Indian and Chinese-influenced patterns as Theravada Buddhism, Confucianism, and Islam permeated into the countryside. By the 1400s three broad but distinctive social and cultural patterns had developed: Theravada Buddhist, Confucian-Buddhist Vietnamese, and Malayo-Muslim or Indonesian.

13-4a Theravada Buddhist Society in Siam

Siamese established several states in northern and central Thailand. Sukhothai (**SOO-ko-TAI**) (1238–1419), founded by former Angkor vassals, controlled much of Thailand's

> **CONNECTION to TODAY**
>
> In what ways do the Southeast Asian societies and cultures of the Theravada Buddhists, Muslims, and Vietnamese seem similar to and different from those of the modern West?

central plains. While some modern historians are skeptical of the stories, according to Siamese tradition, King Rama Kamkheng (**RA-ma KHAM-keng**) ("Rama the Brave"), a shrewd diplomat, established Sukhothai's glory and a tributary relationship with China. Sukhothai adopted Khmer script and incorporated Khmer influences in literature, art, and government. Siamese chronicles, which reflected elite viewpoints, portrayed Rama as a wise and popular ruler. A temple inscription tells us that

the Lord of the country levies no tolls on his subjects. If he sees someone else's wealth he does not interfere. If he captures some enemy soldiers he neither kills them nor beats them. In the [palace] doorway a bell is suspended; if an inhabitant of the kingdom has any complaint or any matter irritates his stomach and torments his mind, and he desires to expose it to the king ring the bell.[18]

This probably exaggerated his merits, but Thais credit Rama with making Theravada Buddhism the state religion and adopting humane laws. By 1350, another Siamese state with its capital at Ayutthaya (ah-YUT-uh-yuh), a few miles north of today's Bangkok, had eclipsed Sukhothai, developing a regional empire and influence extending into Cambodia and small Lao states along the Mekong River. Ayutthaya's rivalry with Burmans and Vietnamese for regional dominance occasionally led to war.

Theravada Buddhist kings, popularly viewed as semidivine reincarnated Buddhas, lived in splendor, advised by brahman Hindu priests in ceremonial and magical practices. Their many wives and sons, all possible rivals for the throne, and unclear political succession rules caused chronic instability. Despite bureaucratic government, as with most Southeast Asian states royal power lessened as distance to the capital increased.

Siamese society resembled that of other Theravada Buddhists: Khmer, Burmans, and Lao. Siamese social order—divided into a small aristocracy, many commoners, and some slaves (many of them prisoners of war)—expected deference to higher authority and respect for status differences. Unlike China or India's extended families, small nuclear families were the norm. While Theravada peoples encouraged cooperation within family and village, they also valued individualism. Although not enjoying absolute equality and expected to show their respect for men, free women enjoyed many rights, inheriting equally with men, able to initiate marriage or divorce, and operating most of village or town market stalls. The relative freedom of Siamese women shocked visitors from China, India, Europe, and the Middle East. A Muslim Persian diplomat in Ayutthaya wrote that "it is common for women to engage in buying and selling in the markets and even to undertake physical labor, and they do not cover themselves with modesty. Thus you can see the women paddling to the surrounding villages where they successfully earn their daily bread with no assistance from the men."[19]

Siamese society reflected Theravada Buddhist values, such as gentleness, meditation, and a belief in reincarnation, as well as belief in *karma*, the idea that one's actions in this life or past lives determine one's destiny. To escape the endless round of life, death, and rebirth, believers attained merit by performing generous deeds, with the ultimate goal of reaching *nirvana*, release from suffering. Many men became Buddhist monks, playing key roles in local affairs and operating village schools; consequently, Theravada societies had some of the premodern world's highest literacy rates (especially for males). Women could not gain merit as monks, although some became nuns. Most Siamese, tolerant of the less devout, believed that individuals were responsible for their own spiritual state. Peasants supported their local Buddhist temple while making offerings and prayers to placate animist spirits in the fields.

13-4b Confucianism, Buddhism, and Vietnamese Society

Vietnam, another important state, was a Chinese colony for over a thousand years, but in 939, with China in turmoil with the demise of the Tang dynasty, the Vietnamese finally pushed the Chinese out and established independence. Vietnam continued to borrow Chinese ideas and even became a vassal state, sending tribute missions. Confucians and Buddhists competed for influence. By the fourteenth century Vietnam offered a striking contrast to Theravada Buddhist societies. But historians debate how much Vietnam in those centuries should be viewed as a "smaller dragon" to China's "larger dragon," notions that emphasize the Chinese connection and downplay the Vietnamese culture and ideas in the state.

Despite Vietnam's formal subservience, Chinese forces occasionally attempted a reconquest, inspiring Vietnamese to become masters at resisting foreign invasions. In 1407 the Ming emperor sent in a large military force, which conquered Vietnam. In response to harsh Chinese repression, Le Loi (lay lo-ee) (1385–1433), a mandarin from a landowning family, organized resistance and struggled tenaciously for two decades. After finally expelling the Chinese in 1428, Le Loi founded a new Vietnamese dynasty, the Le (1428–1788). His social and economic reforms and victory over Chinese domination made him a hero of Vietnam's long struggle for independence. Le Loi told his people: "Over the centuries, we have been sometimes strong, sometimes weak; but never yet have we been lacking in heroes. In that let our history be the proof."[20] Over the centuries, common identity and national feeling greatly aided Vietnamese survival on powerful China's fringe. With peace, literature, poetry, and theater flourished.

Vietnam's imperial system was modeled on China's, with the emperor considered a "son of heaven," an intermediary between the terrestrial and supernatural realms ruling through the Mandate of Heaven. As in China, emperors governed through a bureaucracy staffed by scholar-administrators (*mandarins*) chosen by civil service examinations to recruit men of talent. The official ideology, Confucianism, stressed ethical conduct, social harmony, and hierarchy. Vietnam sought to influence or control highland peoples as well as neighboring Cham, Khmer, and Lao states.

Peasant society differed considerably from the imperial court and political elite, with religious life mixing Mahayana Buddhism, Confucianism, and Daoism, all adopted from China, with spirit and ancestor worship. Peasants had to be respected; an old proverb advised that "the scholar precedes the peasant, but when the rice runs out, it's the peasant who precedes the scholar." Another expression, "the authority of the emperor ends at the village gate," reflected the autonomy of largely self-governing villages. Villages reserved communal land for landless peasants. Despite the patriarchal social system, women dominated town and village markets, buying and selling food and crafts, and saw their influence increase with age. By the 1400s the Vietnamese also became more involved with maritime trade.

---

[18]From Ibid., 41.
[19]Ibn Muhammad Ibrahim, from Michael Smithies, *Descriptions of Old Siam* (Kuala Lumpur: Oxford University Press, 1995), 91.
[20]Quoted in Ralph Smith, *Viet-Nam and the West* (Ithaca, NY: Cornell University Press, 1971), 9.

By the tenth century, some Vietnamese, supported by imperial forces, left the overcrowded Red River Valley and Tonkin Gulf and migrated southward. In the 1440s they overran northern Cham states in central Vietnam, and by the sixteenth century, Vietnamese migrants had pushed toward the Khmer-dominated Mekong River Basin in southern Vietnam, displacing southern Cham states. With these migrations, the Vietnamese became more involved with Southeast Asia, and the central and southern dialects and cultures gradually differed from the northern Vietnamese.

13-4c Islam, Maritime Networks, and the Malay World

Southeast Asians long excelled as seafaring traders, traveling as far as East Africa. Port cities became essential intermediaries in the trade between China, India, and the Middle East. This trade fostered contact with Muslim merchants from Arabia, Persia, and India, who spread Islam along Indian Ocean trading routes. Many commercial people adopted Islam, which they viewed as a religion sanctioning wealth accumulation and preaching cooperation among believers. Some Hindu-Buddhist rulers of coastal Malay Peninsula and Indonesian states, eager to attract Muslim traders and impressed by Islam's cosmopolitan universality, embraced the faith, converting themselves into

sultans. Increasing trade spurred city growth and new maritime trading states, giving merchants more influence in local politics. As the transformed international maritime economy created unprecedented commercial prosperity and cosmopolitan culture in Southeast Asia, agricultural advances, including new crops and rice varieties, fueled population increase, migration, and more bureaucratic states.

Islamic expansion coincided with, and was spurred by, the rise of the great port of Melaka (**muh-LACK-uh**) on Malaya's southwest coast facing the Straits of Melaka. In 1403 the city's Hindu ruler, Parameswara, adopted Islam and became a sultan. Melakans blended Islamic faith and culture with older Hindu-Buddhist and animist beliefs in an eclectic cultural pattern. With regional Islam closely identified with Melaka's Malay people, some historians describe Muslim Southeast Asian societies as Malayo-Muslim. Malay identity, including the practice of Islam and the use of the Malay language, spread to many societies in Malaya, Sumatra, and Borneo.

Melaka replaced Srivijaya as the region's economic power, becoming the crossroads of Asian maritime commerce. Its rulers sent tributary missions to China and made their port a waystation for Zheng He's unprecedented Chinese voyages to the western Indian Ocean (see Chapter 11). In exchange for Melaka's service, the Ming supported the young state in regional disputes. Soon merchants from around Asia arrived,

IMAGE 13.7 **Royal Palace in Java** The kings and then sultans of the region lived on the grounds of this palace in Jogjakarta for generations, along with many retainers and functionaries.

Stefano Ember/Shutterstock.com

transforming the port into the archipelago's major trading hub and the Indian Ocean network's southeastern terminus. One of the world's major emporiums, Melaka rivaled other great trading ports such as Guangzhou (Canton), Calicut, Cambay, Hormuz, Alexandria, Genoa, and Venice. In 1468 Melaka's sultan Mansur wrote to the king of the Ryukyu Islands, "We have learned that to master the blue oceans people must engage in commerce. All the lands within the seas are united in one body. Life has never been so affluent in preceding generations as it is today."[21] Gradually, Melaka built a highly decentralized empire that dominated much of coastal Malaya and eastern Sumatra.

Melaka flourished until 1511 as a vital link in world trade. An early-sixteenth-century Portuguese visitor wrote that it had "no equal in the world," extolling Melaka's importance to peoples and trade as far away as western Europe: "Melaka is a city … made for merchandise, fitter than any other in the world. Commerce between different nations for a thousand leagues on every hand must come to Melaka."[22] Melaka enjoyed a special connection to Cambay, a northwestern Indian port nearly three thousand miles away. Every year trading ships from around the Middle East and South Asia gathered at Cambay and Calicut to make the long voyage to Melaka, carrying with them grain, woolens, arms, copperware, textiles, and opium. Goods from as far north as Korea reached Melaka.

By the late 1400s Melaka's 100,000 to 200,000 people included some fifteen thousand foreign merchants speaking some eighty-four languages, whose diversity reflected Melaka's global importance: from the west Arabs, Egyptians, Persians, Armenians, Jews, Ethiopians, Swahilis, Burmese, and Indians; from the east and north Vietnamese, Javanese, Filipinos, Japanese, Ryukyans, and Chinese. Visitors claimed that more ships crowded Melaka's harbor than any other port, attracted by a stable government and free trade policy. City shops offered Indian textiles, Middle Eastern books, cloves and nutmeg from eastern Indonesia, Javan batiks and carpets, Chinese silk and porcelain, and Philippine sugar. Gold brought from various places was so plentiful that children played with it.

From Melaka Islam spread around the Malay Peninsula and western Indonesian archipelago (see Map 13.3), spurring political change and economic growth. Some Islamic states, such as Acheh (**AH-chay**) in northern Sumatra, became regional powers. The sultanates of Ternate (**tuhr-NAH-tay**) and Tidor (**TEE-door**) in the Maluku (**muh-LUKE-uh**) (Moluccan) Islands of northeastern Indonesia prospered from producing spices (especially cloves and nutmeg) prized in Europe and the Middle East. Gradually many people, following their ruler's example, adopted Islam, joining Southeast Asia to the wider Islamic world. Sufis were prominent in spreading the religion. As in South Asia followers viewed some of them as saints and turned their graves into shrines. But many village-based societies, some still practicing animism, remained in more remote areas such as the Philippine Islands and central Borneo, with no political authority higher than local chiefs.

Various patterns of Islamic belief and practice, more diverse than elsewhere, emerged. In many cases Islam did not completely displace older customs. For example, on Java Indianized kings and courts combined Islamic beliefs with older Hindu-Buddhist ceremonies, mystical traditions, and Hindu brahman advisers. Women often retained some political influence, and Muslim courts were filled with hundreds, sometimes thousands of women, as concubines, attendants, staffers, guards, and textile workers. There were occasional Muslim women rulers, such as the fifteenth-century sisters Shi Daniang and Shi Erjie in the Sumatran city of Palembang. Of Chinese Muslim ancestry, they ruled justly, maintained peace, and stimulated the economy. Many peasants maintained mystical animist beliefs and practices under an Islamic veneer, tolerating diverse religious views, whereas others (especially merchants) adopted more orthodox beliefs, following prescribed Islamic practices and looking toward the Middle East for models. In the hierarchical Javanese social system, sultans remained aloof from common people, while aristocrats remained obsessed with practicing refined behavior rooted in mystical Hinduism. Javanese of all classes placed a great value on avoiding interpersonal conflict.

13-4d Southeast Asia and the Wider World

Southeast Asia had long been and remained a cosmopolitan region where peoples, ideas, and products from many lands met. The intrepid Italian traveler Marco Polo passed through in 1292 on his way home from his long China sojourn. His writings praising the wealth and sophistication of Champa, Java, and Sumatra aroused European interest in seeking direct trade connections with these seemingly fabulous lands. Polo wrote that, "Java is of unsurpassing wealth, producing all kinds of spices, frequented by a vast amount of shipping. Indeed, the treasure of this island is so great as to be past telling."[23] Chinese merchants played significant roles in many ports by the 1400s, often marrying local women and settling down. Their trade networks linked Southeast Asia to China, Japan, and the Ryukyu Islands. Agrarian-based societies such as Vietnam and Siam became more involved in international trade by the 1400s. In recent decades the wrecks of hundreds of trading ships and often their cargoes (often ceramic pottery) that sunk in the South China Sea or Southeast Asian waters from the tenth century to the nineteenth century have been found, suggesting the large volume and main products of the China–Southeast Asia–Indian Ocean maritime commerce.

Indeed, the Southeast Asia Marco Polo and other travelers such as the Moroccan Ibn Battuta encountered was one of the world's more prosperous and urbanized regions. Major cities like Ayutthaya, Melaka, and Hanoi (Vietnam) were as large as major European urban centers like Naples and Paris. By the 1400s, China and India's dense populations still dwarfed Southeast Asia's 15 to 20 million people. Yet, blessed with fertile land and extensive trade, Southeast Asians often enjoyed better health, more varied diets, and adequate material resources than most peoples.

[21]Quoted in Anthony Reid, *Southeast Asia in the Age of Commerce, 1450–1680*, vol. 2 (New Haven, CT: Yale University Press, 1993), 10.
[22]Tomé Pires, quoted in Paul Wheatley, *The Golden Khersonese* (Kuala Lumpur: University of Malaya Press, 1961), 313.
[23]Quoted in Kenneth R. Hall, *Maritime Trade and State Development in Early Southeast Asia* (Honolulu: University of Hawaii Press, 1985), 210.

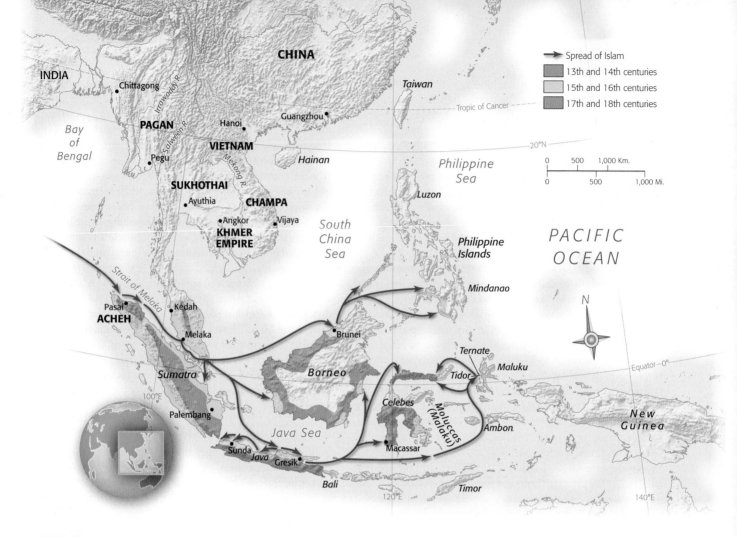

MAP 13.3 **The Spread of Islam in Island Southeast Asia** Carried by merchants and missionaries, Islam spread from Arabia and India to island Southeast Asia, eventually becoming the major faith on many islands and in the Malay Peninsula.

Q What does this map tell us about where in Southeast Asia Islam had its greatest impact and why?

Southeast Asia's connections to the wider world, as well as its famed wealth, eventually attracted less-welcome arrivals. By the beginning of the sixteenth century a few Portuguese explorers and adventurers, with deadly weapons, state-of-the-art ships, Christian missionary zeal, and desire for wealth, had reached first India and then Southeast Asia seeking "Christians and spices." Siam, Vietnam, Melaka, and Java probably enjoyed higher standards of living than Portugal, but the Portuguese previewed what became a powerful, destabilizing European presence that gradually altered the region after 1500.

KEY POINTS

▶ Siamese states such as Sukhothai and Ayutthaya were Theravada Buddhist monarchies that valued individualism and peacefulness, offered women a fair amount of freedom, and were permeated by Buddhist values.

▶ Despite gaining freedom from Chinese rule, Vietnam retained a great deal of Chinese cultural influence.

▶ Inhabitants of the Malay and Indonesian archipelagoes embraced Islam, which arrived via increasing maritime

trade, some grafting it onto Hinduism and Buddhism, to create many different patterns of Islamic belief, while native animist traditions survived to some extent in the villages.

▶ Melaka displaced Srivajaya as the center of Southeast Asian trading power and became an international crossroads.

Chapter Summary

Although many earlier patterns of life and thought persisted in India and Southeast Asia during the Intermediate Era, these regions also experienced tremendous changes. A constant stream of West Asian and Central Asian peoples into India brought more diversity to social patterns and beliefs. Although India remained politically fragmented, Hinduism enjoyed a kind of renaissance. Most people owed allegiance to their family, caste, and village. Hinduism spawned diverse ideas and cults and gradually brought some cultural unity, while Buddhism gradually lost influence in much of India. Hindu society faced its greatest challenge from Muslim conquerors, who became politically dominant in north India. Muslims would not be assimilated, although there was some mixing of Hindu and Muslim traditions. Islam added a major

new strand to India's heritage, influencing the political, religious, and cultural realms but increasing diversity at the expense of unity.

Hindu and Buddhist ideas along with various other Indian traditions diffused to Southeast Asia, where they helped foster the rise of great kingdoms. The Angkor Empire dominated much of mainland Southeast Asia by mixing Indian and local patterns. New religions and new peoples, especially the Tais, eventually reshaped Southeast Asia. Theravada Buddhism became a major influence in several societies, including Siam, while Islam became strong in peninsula and island societies such as Melaka and Java. International trade fostered economic dynamism, and Melaka served as a major international port in which many cultural traditions flourished.

Key Terms

Rajputs 308
polyandry 309
bhakti 311

Vajrayana 312
Tantrism 312
Lamaism 312

purdah 317
wayang kulit 321

Christian Societies in Medieval Europe, Byzantium, and Russia, 600–1500

> *The most Christian man beloved by God, the glorious king of the Franks, while he was building this [Christian] monastery, wished that [its] consecration and the battles which he [waged] should not be consigned completely to oblivion.*
>
> —Monastery dedication attributed to Charlemagne, ninth-century Frankish Emperor[1]

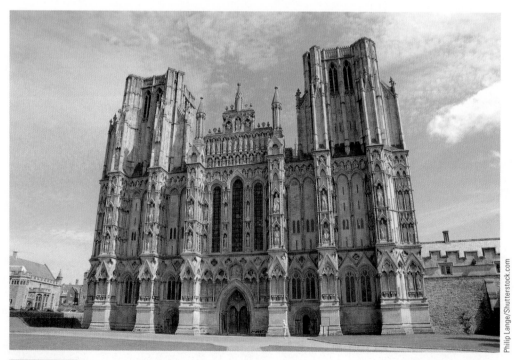

Philip Lange/Shutterstock.com

IMAGE 14.1 **Wells Cathedral** The importance of Christianity in European life was symbolized by magnificent cathedrals. This cathedral, built in the English town of Wells in the thirteenth century CE, was designed to reflect the glory of God.

Q What features in this cathedral seem to highlight the aim to reflect the glory of God?

---

[1]From a fourteenth-century legend, quoted in Amy G. Remensnyder, "Topographies of Memory: Center and Periphery in High Medieval France," in *Medieval Concepts of the Past: Ritual, Memory, Historiography*, ed. Gerd Althoff et al. (New York: Cambridge University Press, 2002), 214.

In 800 CE the city of Rome, filled with magnificent buildings and monuments, was the majestic center of western Christendom. Along one of many roads connecting the fabled metropolis to a wider Europe, the most powerful ruler in Europe, Charlemagne (**SHAHR-leh-mane**), the king of the Germanic people called the Franks, arrived from his capital of Aachen (**AH-kuhn**), some seven hundred miles away in what is today northwest Germany, to celebrate Christmas mass with Pope Leo III, Christendom's head. Wearing a Roman toga and Greek cloak, the towering Charlemagne, six feet four inches tall, entered spectacular Saint Peter's cathedral. When the Christmas service ended, the pope placed upon Charlemagne's head a golden crown encrusted with sparkling jewels while the crowd chanted, "Crowned by god, great and peace-loving Emperor of the Romans, life and victory."[2] For the first time the pope had crowned an emperor of a new, church-blessed Roman Empire. In the following centuries, complex relations between the Roman Church and diverse European states helped shape and sometimes agitate European life, as popes tried to influence secular affairs and shape monarchies, while kings worked to control the church and, like Charlemagne, used religion—even building monasteries—for their own purposes.

Fifteenth-century Italian historians first coined the term **medieval** to describe the centuries between the Classical Romans and their own time as a superstitious and ignorant "Dark Age." But the reality of what later scholars often called the "Middle Ages" in Europe was more complex. Linked by faith and culture, western Europeans combined Christianity with practices inherited from both Romans and Germanic groups like the Franks. Although mixing religion and politics went back to ancient times, in both western Europe and Byzantium, the presence of strong Christian church influences in all aspects of society, including politics, was an innovation. Medieval people perceived themselves as part of Christendom rather than Europe. As Christian culture spread into northeastern Europe and Russia, Europeans also borrowed much from other cultures, especially Islam. Finally, Europe's many tensions—including conflicts among Christian leaders, kings, and nobles for power; debates over reconciling faith and reason; and the differing priorities of the rural-based aristocracy and urban merchants—fostered a competitive spirit, helping spur overseas exploration in the fifteenth century.

medieval A term first used in the 1400s by Italian historians to describe the centuries between the Classical Romans and their own time.

[2]Quoted in *What Life Was Like in the Age of Chivalry: Medieval Europe, AD 800–1500* (Alexandria, VA: Time-Life Books, 1997), 17.

14-1 Forming Christian Societies in Western Europe

🔀 TRANSITIONS 🏛 SOCIETIES

Q How did Europeans create new societies between 500 and 1000?

People today thinking of Medieval Europe may picture in their minds spectacular but drafty castles, gallant knights clad in steel suits, jousts, elaborately dressed aristocratic women in tall, conical headwear, magnificent cathedrals, and perhaps fire-breathing dragons. Although the dragons only existed in myths and today in fantasy books and films, the others were part of medieval

CONNECTION to TODAY

Can you identify any aspects of early medieval life that helped shape or still exist in the modern world?

life but only in some places and for a few centuries. The reality was less romantic but nonetheless interesting. The western Roman Empire's disintegration in the fifth century led to political and social instability, clearing the ground for the rise of new societies between 500 and 1000 CE. The mixing of Roman and Germanic traditions as well as relations with non-European peoples spurred

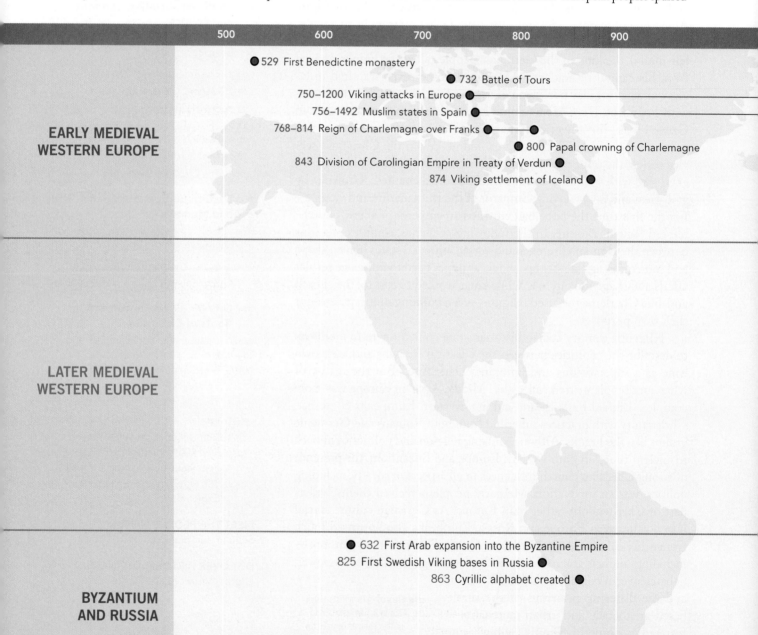

	500	600	700	800	900

EARLY MEDIEVAL WESTERN EUROPE

● 529 First Benedictine monastery
● 732 Battle of Tours
750–1200 Viking attacks in Europe ●
756–1492 Muslim states in Spain ●
768–814 Reign of Charlemagne over Franks ● ●
● 800 Papal crowning of Charlemagne
843 Division of Carolingian Empire in Treaty of Verdun ●
874 Viking settlement of Iceland ●

LATER MEDIEVAL WESTERN EUROPE

● 632 First Arab expansion into the Byzantine Empire
825 First Swedish Viking bases in Russia ●
863 Cyrillic alphabet created ●

BYZANTIUM AND RUSSIA

creativity. Diverse western European societies developed many common features, including a dominant Christian church and similar social, political, and economic systems. Economic change and technological development also fostered a new Europe.

14-1a Environment and Expanding Christianity

Climate change and disease shaped post-Roman Europe. Between 500 and 900 a cooling climate brought shorter growing seasons before warmer trends returned, while the terrible plague that devastated Europe during sixth-century Byzantine emperor Justinian's time occasionally reappeared. Given these challenges,

not surprisingly people turned to religion for support. Between 200 and 800 western Europe also suffered repeated incursions by migrating peoples. Various Germanic groups destroyed forever the western Roman Empire and culture, preventing any imperial restoration like China's, where Classical society reemerged during the Tang dynasty. Today few people study Latin, once the Mediterranean world's dominant language.

Yet, Europe's favorable geography enabled similar religious, social, economic, and political patterns to spread. Much of western and central Europe benefited from fertile, well-watered plains rich in minerals and a long coastline offering many fine harbors along the Mediterranean and Baltic Seas and the Atlantic Ocean. Long navigable rivers such as the

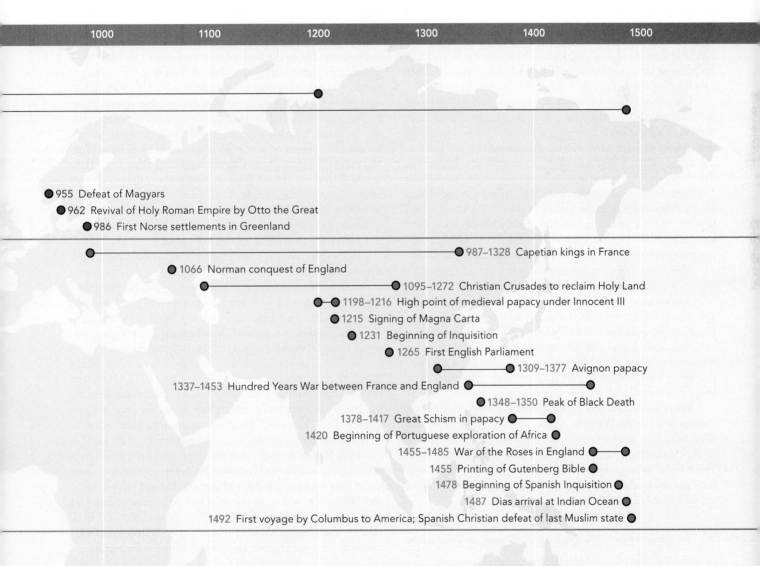

1000   1100   1200   1300   1400   1500

955 Defeat of Magyars
962 Revival of Holy Roman Empire by Otto the Great
986 First Norse settlements in Greenland

987–1328 Capetian kings in France
1066 Norman conquest of England
1095–1272 Christian Crusades to reclaim Holy Land
1198–1216 High point of medieval papacy under Innocent III
1215 Signing of Magna Carta
1231 Beginning of Inquisition
1265 First English Parliament
1309–1377 Avignon papacy
1337–1453 Hundred Years War between France and England
1348–1350 Peak of Black Death
1378–1417 Great Schism in papacy
1420 Beginning of Portuguese exploration of Africa
1455–1485 War of the Roses in England
1455 Printing of Gutenberg Bible
1478 Beginning of Spanish Inquisition
1487 Dias arrival at Indian Ocean
1492 First voyage by Columbus to America; Spanish Christian defeat of last Muslim state

988 Conversion of Vladimir of Kiev to Christianity
1054 Schism between Roman and Byzantine churches
1091 Battle of Manzikert
1237–1241 Mongol invasions of Russia and eastern Europe
1453 Ottoman Turk conquest of Constantinople
1459 Ottoman Turk defeat of Serbs

Danube (**DAN-yoob**) and Rhine, as well as accessible mountain passes through the Alps, the main mountain chain in the middle of Europe, made communication much easier than in Asia, Africa, and South America. Hence, land and sea networks linked diverse societies, fostering the movement of ideas, products, peoples, technologies, and diseases.

As Roman power melted away, the church became the major authority, with local bishops and monasteries often the only government in rural areas. Over time the Roman bishops gained authority, eventually claiming the title of pope (Holy Father) and heading the vast church apparatus. Increasingly the papacy symbolized an independent church not controlled by any one government and asserting influence over kings. Popes continued efforts to spread the faith to those Germanic peoples still following their ancient gods. Around 600 Pope Gregory I sanctioned turning pagan worship sites into churches rather than destroying them. The Anglo-Saxon kingdom of Kent in England converted and dispatched missionaries to German lands, most famously Boniface (**BON-uh-face**) (ca. 675–754), a member of the Benedictine order, who won many converts.

Christians blended German values and practices into their faith. Hence, they changed the pagan use of special amulets or charms to ward off evil to wearing Christian medals around the neck honoring Jesus or his mother. After acquiring key governmental positions, Christians often persecuted non-Christians, destroying their houses of worship or denying them government appointments. Since many church bishops came from upper-class German families, Christian leaders began valuing warriors and fighting, never a prominent feature of early Christianity. Even local church leaders often seemed more concerned with protecting their territory and family than promoting Christian values.

The church also sponsored religious orders. From Christianity's earliest centuries, some men and women tried to escape the corruptions and temptations of cities by moving to isolated places to pray and prepare for Heaven. Many monks joined monasteries, communities for men who had taken holy orders. Monasteries grew their own food, with monks clearing forests for crops, and some larger monasteries provided social services such as shelter for travelers, emergency food, and clothing for the poor. At the same time, some women joined convents for lives of service or prayer.

While monks and nuns tried to escape society, they helped create a new culture. With the slogan "to work is to pray," monks filled their lives with activity to avoid idleness, and one form of work, copying manuscripts, eventually created the bound book. The monks' willingness to serve God and their neighbors with their hands and their hearts gave manual labor a respect it never enjoyed in the Classical Mediterranean world.

14-1b The Frankish and Holy Roman Empires

Between 500 and 1000 Europe's political map changed. Muslim armies conquered North Africa, the eastern shore of the Mediterranean, and most of Spain during the seventh and eighth centuries (see Chapter 10), and Muslim bands raided Italy and France. Frankish ruler Charles Martel's victory at the Battle of Tours in France in 732 finally stopped these raids. Following this victory, the Franks created a large state in western Europe.

In 753 Pope Stephen sought their aid against the Germanic Lombard kingdom in northern Italy, which threatened papal control of central Italy. He then anointed the Frankish king Pepin (**PEP-in**) the Short as Italy's special protector, indicating the sacred nature of kingship in Christian thought and the pope's belief in his right to designate political rulers. In return, Pepin defeated the Lombards and donated land in central Italy to the pope, the foundation for small Papal States surrounding Rome that would remain under papal control for over one thousand years. Western Europe's chief religious leaders became divided between their spiritual and earthly concerns.

The papal–Frankish relationship grew during a new dynasty known as the Carolingians (**kah-roe-LIN-gee-uhnz**) after their greatest ruler, Charlemagne (r. 768–814), was crowned by the pope in Rome. Charlemagne spread Frankish power from France and northern Italy deep into the lands of another Germanic people, the Saxons, in north and central Germany, temporarily uniting the heart of western Europe (see Map 14.1). Taking great interest in his peoples' religious lives, Charlemagne promoted both education and Christianity, using the church to strengthen his empire by appointing bishops and priests, influencing ceremonies and doctrines, ordering executions for violating religious obligations, and controlling monasteries. To enhance his power, he sent diplomatic missions to Byzantium and various Islamic states. Charlemagne told Pope Leo III he would defend the church from its enemies, and the pope's only job was "to assist the success of our arms with your hands raised in prayer to God."[3] In return for protecting and promoting Christianity, Carolingians expected church leaders, from priests and bishops to monastery abbots, to be loyal to the king.

Although crowning Charlemagne "Emperor of the Romans" revived the Roman Empire symbolically, papal relations with Carolingian rulers also ensured later church–state conflict. Popes argued that lay control over church matters needed papal approval, while later German rulers wanted some political control in Italy.

Charlemagne's empire was divided among his three grandsons in the Treaty of Verdun (**vuhr-DUN**) in 843, and eventually other Germanic peoples challenged the Franks for influence. The Saxon ruler Otto I, known as Otto the Great (r. 936–973), built a new empire, establishing control over rebellious princes in Germany and leading an army into northern Italy; in 962 the pope declared Otto "Roman Emperor." From this point until 1806, rulers in Germany retained this title, eventually proclaiming their lands as the "Holy Roman Empire." But this empire had little in common with the Classical Roman Empire. Much of its territory was never under Roman control, and most Germans, Italians, Slavs, Czechs, and Hungarians within its domains had little sense of common citizenship or much awareness of politics beyond the local level. Like the Carolingians, Otto and his successors both defended and dominated the church, even appointing bishops in their lands.

14-1c Vikings and Other Invaders

Europe's heartland continued to attract other peoples seeking wealth. Norse, Danish, and Swedish Vikings—or, as many called them, Northmen—facing population pressures that led them to launch raids out of Scandinavia, a region with limited productive

---

[3]"Charlemagne's letter to Pope Leo III, 796," from C. Warren Hollister et al., *Medieval Europe: A Short Sourcebook*, 2nd ed. (New York: McGraw-Hill, 1992), 78.

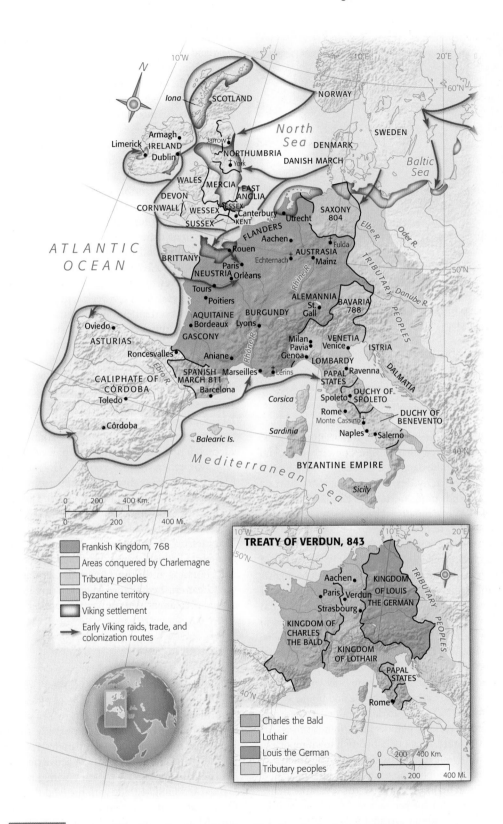

MAP 14.1 **Europe During the Carolingian Empire** At the height of their power under Charlemagne during the early Middle Ages, the Carolingian rulers of the Franks controlled much of northwestern Europe, including what is today France, the Low Countries, western and southern Germany, and northern Italy.

Q How does this map illustrate the religious and political divisions as well as the multiethnic states of the early medieval period?

Maurice ROUGEMONT/Gamma-Rapho/Getty Images

IMAGE 14.2 **Viking Longship** This longship from the ninth century, excavated from a burial mound in Norway in 1904, boasted intricate decorations and carvings. Probably used for ceremonial purposes, it became the burial chamber of a royal Viking woman.

Q What features of this longship might allow it to sail the seas as well as up rivers while also allowing for carrying enough Vikings and supplies to fulfill their mission?

farmland, posed the biggest threat. Some historians think that the growing Viking knowledge of Charlemagne's power, wealth, and expansionist policies, and the dangers it posed, may have helped stimulate their violent activities. Viking warriors burned and looted towns and monasteries in England, France, Holland, and Ireland. While rumors probably exaggerated Viking atrocities, understandably terrified people prayed: "From the violence of the men from the north, O Lord, deliver us."[4] Skilled craftsmen, Vikings built ingenious shallow-draft boats capable of both oceanic and riverine voyages. In recent years archeologists have excavated the ruins of Viking towns in Scandinavia that were home to craftsmen, artists, merchants, musicians, artists, and seafarers, evidence of sophisticated societies. DNA studies in 2018 suggest that some of the residents came from elsewhere, such as the British Isles and Ukraine. Viking burials have revealed some men interred with cooking gear, upsetting gender stereotypes or assumptions that Viking men were only warriors and merchants and women took care of the house and home.

Between 750 and 1200 various Vikings raided, traded, and settled around Europe, seeking plunder and often captives. An account of a ninth-century attack on a Scottish town reported: "They [Vikings] were four months besieging it [Strathclyde]; and at last reducing the people who were inside by hunger and thirst . . ., they broke in upon them afterwards . . . all the riches . . . were taken; a great host [of people was taken] out of it in captivity."[5] Eventually Scandinavians adopted Christianity and established the kingdoms of Denmark, Norway, and Sweden. Some Swedish Vikings moved east into Russia, establishing several states and sailing downriver to the Black Sea to trade with Byzantium and the Middle East. Danish and Norse

Vikings also established permanent settlements in coastal England, Ireland, and the islands north of Scotland, founding towns that later became cities like Dublin and York; recent DNA studies show widespread Viking ancestry in the British Isles. Other Vikings settled down in western France, in Normandy (named after Normans or Northmen). Normans descended from these Vikings conquered England in 1066.

Eventually Vikings gave up raiding for trade and farming. Those settling outside Scandinavia built towns, intermarried with local people, and adopted the local Celtic, Anglo-Saxon, Latin, Germanic, or Slavic cultures. But their heritage remains in many place names and words in local languages such as English. Vikings left other legacies as well. Among the world's greatest maritime explorers, Norse Vikings began settling Iceland in 874 and founded several settlements on Greenland in 986. Around 1000 a few Greenland Vikings established an outpost on Newfoundland, a large island off the coast of eastern Canada, staying for a few years and perhaps hoping to establish a permanent settlement. But whether because they felt threatened and outnumbered by the hostile local Native Americans or because of bitter divisions within the community, they returned to Greenland. Nonetheless, some evidence suggests that Greenlanders apparently made occasional trading visits to eastern Canada for the next several centuries. These Viking explorers also fostered a democratic ideal, as shown by the Icelanders' elected assembly, the *Althing* ("general assembly") that was created in 930 to make and administer laws. Icelanders adopted Christianity by the votes of local communities in 1000.

Two other warlike peoples, Bulgars **(BUL-gahrz)** and Magyars **(MAG-yahrz)**, migrated from Russia into central Europe. The Slavic Bulgars, contained by Byzantine armies, eventually converted to Eastern Orthodox Christianity and settled in the eastern Balkan region known as Bulgaria. Magyars, excellent horsemen speaking a Ural-Altaic language related to Turkish, moved into the Hungarian plain, threatening Germany and Italy. However, German forces under Otto the Great crushed a large Magyar army in 955; Magyars then settled permanently in Hungary, adopting Roman Christianity.

14-1d Early Medieval Trade, Moorish Spain, and Technology

While most Europeans were peasants, growing food or raising livestock, merchants traded wool hides, salt, fish, wine, and grain over long distances, often by sea or riverboat. Eastern Mediterranean trade continued briskly, tightly controlled by Byzantine rulers, and east–west trade grew dynamic. Venice, a northeast Italian port city, was an active trading center throughout the Middle Ages, competing with a northwest Italian city, Genoa, to dominate trade with the Middle East and Byzantium. Other Italian cities remained connected to the Byzantine economy. Merchants occasionally visited even remote towns, and aristocrats purchased luxury goods such as silk produced in the East. By 800, multiple networks of exchange reconnected western Europeans to each other and to eastern Europe and the increasingly Islamic western Asia and North Africa.

[4]Quoted in F. Donald Logan, *The Vikings in History*, 2nd ed. (New York: Routledge, 1991), 15.
[5]Quoted in Angelo Forte et al., *Viking Empires* (New York: Cambridge University Press, 2005), 88.

Europeans benefited from growing connections with the Muslim world, as Islamic expansion stimulated a movement of people, goods, and information, such as Asian science and Classical Greek thought, that influenced many Afro-Eurasian societies. Muslim armies had conquered much of Spain in the early eighth century and Sicily in the ninth century, which affected Europe in various ways (see Chapter 10). For example, intellectual life was enriched by the exchange of products, books, and ideas between Christian Europe and cosmopolitan Islamic (often termed Moorish) Spain and Sicily. Scholars, students, and merchants from all over the Mediterranean and the Frankish kingdom gravitated to Spanish cities such as Cordoba and Toledo, where Christian, Jewish, and Muslim traditions interacted. Hence, from these centers of learning, the philosophical, scientific, mathematical, and technological writings of many Classical Greek and South Asian as well as Persian and Arab thinkers were translated into Latin and various vernacular languages and spread among educated Europeans.

It was in twelfth-century Sicily, by then ruled by Normans from France, that the brilliant Arab cartographer, geographer, and mathematician al-Idrisi, born in North Africa, educated in Cordoba, and now an adviser to the Sicilian king Roger II, compiled an extraordinary map that depicts the world from Iceland and West Africa to China and Southeast Asia. The map resulted from a collaboration between peoples of different faiths and cultures—Arabs, Persians, Europeans, and Africans—and relied on information from many sources and countries. The map was flat but al-Idrisi was well aware that the globe was round and he calculated the circumference of Earth to within 10 percent of its real size. In the 1140s, an Italian translator of Arabic texts wrote that "it befits us to imitate the Arabs especially, for they are our teachers and the pioneers."[6] Hence, Irish physicians could read the pathbreaking medical books by the eleventh-century polymath and physician Ibn Sina in a Gaelic translation.

Various technological improvements, some originating in Asia, now came into common use in western Europe, laying the basis for European expansion after 1000. Some major technological innovations improved agriculture, spurring higher grain yields that fostered European population growth. The rugged *moldboard plow*, with a blade that dug the earth and an attached moldboard that turned over the furrow, enabled farmers to turn and drain the heavy, wet soil of northern Europe, where difficult farming conditions kept populations sparse. Horseshoes, adopted from Central Asians in the ninth century, allowed

October: sowing the winter grain, from the "Tres Riches Heures du Duc de Berry" (vellum) (for facsimile copy, see 65827), Limbourg Brothers (fl. 1400–1416)/Musee Conde, Chantilly, France/Bridgeman Images

IMAGE 14.3 **Tilling the Fields** Most medieval Europeans were peasants growing food. This French painting from the 1400s shows peasants sowing the winter grain on manor land alongside a ruler's castle.

Q How did farm life, equipment, and techniques in the Middle Ages pictured in this photo differ from today?

farmers to expand their use of horses to plow fields, especially when combined with horse collars. Invented in China, horse collars distributed the weight across the animal's shoulders so the horse could pull more weight and work longer hours. The most crucial improvement, the three-field system, replaced the Roman two-field system. Europeans divided their fields into three parts and let only one-third lie fallow each year, increasing their yield by planting winter and summer wheat in the other two fields. Increased grain consumption produced a better-balanced diet.

Other innovations fostered industry. First invented in Roman times, watermills built along rivers and streams generated power, freeing up human and animal labor for other tasks. By 1056 over 5,600 watermills in England provided power for such activities as sawing logs and grinding wheat into flour, allowing mechanization of some industries, and by the 1100s Europeans used windmills, invented in Persia, to generate power for such industries as grinding grain. The wheelbarrow also reached Europe from China.

KEY POINTS

▶ With the Roman Empire's decline, the Christian church became a power in its own right with influence over kings; monasteries created a new culture that respected manual labor.

▶ Under Germanic influence, Christians more aggressively spread their faith, assimilating "pagan" practices and transforming them into Christian ones.

▶ During this time the Papal States were created, Charlemagne's Carolingian empire temporarily united much of Europe, and Otto the Great began the tradition of calling Germany the "Holy Roman Empire."

▶ The Vikings of Scandinavia, who raided European lands for over four centuries, were also good traders and eventually settled in Iceland, Greenland, and various European territories.

▶ As merchants engaged in growing networks of exchange, trade with the expanding Muslim world and contact with Muslim Spain introduced Europeans to Classical Greek, Indian, Arab, and Persian ideas and technologies.

[6]Hugo of Santalla, quoted in Jerry Brotton, *The Renaissance Bazaar: From the Silk Road to Michelangelo* (Oxford, UK: Oxford University Press, 2002), 195.

14-2 Medieval Societies, Thought, and Politics

⊞ TRANSITIONS ⊞ SOCIETIES

Q What institutions and ideas shaped medieval European life?

Three institutions dominated medieval Europe between 800 and 1300: the papacy in religion and church–state relations, feudalism in politics and social structure, and manorialism in the economic realm. Both feudalism and manorialism developed from late Roman Empire roots, varying greatly across western Europe. The pluralism of religious, social, political, and economic institutions forged in early medieval Europe, combined with an unusually warm climate, spurred many changes between 1000 and 1300. In this period, called the "High Middle Ages," growing church and papal power fostered conflict with rulers and intellectuals. Tensions between religious and lay rulers, between Roman and Byzantine Christian leaders, and between Christians and Muslims, along with growing divergence between cities, with their merchant classes, and traditional feudal aristocrats ruling in the countryside, helped reshape European society.

14-2a The Emergence of Feudalism

Although some historians consider the concept misleading and overgeneralized, most characterize the complex and decentralized social, political, and economic system in these centuries as **feudalism**, a political arrangement in which a weak central monarchy ruled over smaller, largely autonomous states and aristocratic families that owed military and labor service obligations as **vassals** to the monarch. In turn, these nobles ruled as lords over their own vassals, the warriors and farmers on their estates. Church leaders supported this arrangement, arguing that "it is the will of the Creator that the higher shall always rule over the lower. Each individual and each class should stay in its place [and] perform its tasks."[7] This feudalistic political and social formation was strongest in France, England, and parts of Italy. Although many monarchs had little power beyond their capital and hinterland, some small states were part of a larger unit, such as the Holy Roman Empire, with their princes owing allegiance to the king but exercising power in their domains.

Despite the Christian church's role in creating a common culture and strong rulers such as Charlemagne and Otto the Great, certain forces fostered the decentralization that characterized feudalism. The old Roman roads fell into disrepair, disrupting transportation and trade, and Europe remained sparsely populated with few cities. By 1000 France, the most densely populated region, had only eight or nine million people, England a million and a half, and Europe as a whole around forty million, less than half of Song China's 100 million. With both money and talent scarce and land the source of wealth, Charlemagne rewarded his best soldiers and officials by giving them control over land. Vassals who held such land grants, called **benefices**, took an oath of personal loyalty to the king, promising him military service in exchange for a free hand governing their territory, collecting taxes from the inhabitants, and administering justice.

Feudalism also refers to legal relations between lords and vassals, including the **fief**, the thing granted in a feudal contract, usually land but occasionally something such as the right to collect tolls on a bridge. With a large enough fief of land, the vassal could subdivide it and have his own vassals. Feudalism allowed a king to rule a large country without personally administering it. Ruling through subordinates was most common in England, especially after William, Duke of Normandy, invaded in 1066, forming a feudal monarchy.

Feudal society included **knights**, armored military retainers swearing allegiance to their lord. They fought mostly on horseback while bearing the heavy expense of warhorses and elaborate armor. Knights had a rigid code of behavior, including a sense of duty and honor known as **chivalry**. A thirteenth-century French writer explained the chivalric ideal: "A knight must be hardy, courteous, generous, loyal and of fair speech; ferocious to his foe, frank and debonair to his friend. [He] has proved himself in arms and thereby won the praise of men."[8] Despite romantic images of knights wielding lances in jousts or defending maidens from fire-breathing dragons, the reality was usually more mundane. Knights wore 60 pounds of chain-mail armor and often collapsed from heat exhaustion. The formidable steel suits of armor seen in museums today were not generally used until the 1400s. Regular fights between rival states and lords kept knights busy, and successful knights might acquire wealth and marry into an aristocratic family. The stirrup, brought by Central Asians, enabled knights to stand when delivering blows, making the blows more powerful than if delivered while seated.

14-2b Manors, Cities, and Trade

The rural economy was based on **manorialism**, a system of autonomous, nearly self-sufficient agricultural estates. As Roman cities had become expensive, wealthy Romans had retreated to their large country estates and hired low-wage agricultural workers. Eventually these Roman estates and villages became manors, each supplying its own needs, from mills for grinding grain to blacksmiths for shoeing horses. Often organized around a castle, manors were owned by nobles

> **CONNECTION to TODAY**
>
> How did European societies, cultures, beliefs, political institutions, and economic life during the High Middle Ages compare to today?

feudalism A political arrangement characterized by a weak central monarchy ruling over smaller states or influential families that were largely autonomous but owed service obligations to the monarch.

vassals In medieval Europe, a subordinate person owing service to a lord.

benefices In medieval Europe, grants of land from lord to vassal.

fief In medieval Europe, the thing granted in a feudal contract, usually land.

knights In medieval Europe, armored military retainers on horseback who swore allegiance to their lord.

chivalry The rigid code of behavior, including a sense of duty and honor, of medieval European knights.

manorialism The medieval European system of autonomous, nearly self-sufficient agricultural estates.

[7]Quoted in John M. Hobson, *The Eastern Origins of Western Civilization* (New York: Cambridge University Press, 2004), 113.
[8]Quoted in Jo Ann H. Moran Cruz and Richard Gerberding, *Medieval Worlds: An Introduction to European History, 300–1492* (Boston: Houghton-Mifflin, 2004), 388.

with rights to the produce grown by hereditary **serfs**, peasants legally bound to their lord and tied to the land through the generations. Tilling the lord's fields as well as their own, serfs had use of the manor's resources, such as farming tools or crafts, and protection in the manor house or castle if the settlement was attacked. Although they could not change their status or leave without permission, they could not be dispossessed unless they failed to satisfy their obligations. Warned to work hard to receive their eventual reward in Heaven, they paid for security with a lifetime of drudgery, alleviated for many by diversions like dice games, wrestling, and bawdy jokes and stories. Occasional peasant revolts indicated some dissatisfaction.

Although serfdom became far more pervasive, slavery did not disappear altogether in Europe. Mostly farmers or domestic servants, slaves constituted perhaps 10 percent of the English population until the eleventh century, were common in Italy and Spain, and also worked papal estates and the farms of French monasteries. Leading Christian thinkers like Saint Thomas Aquinas argued that slavery was morally justified and an economic necessity. An active Byzantium-based Mediterranean slave trade acquired slaves, mostly Slavs, Greeks, and Turks, from the Black Sea region, shipping them to southern Europe and North Africa. Carolingians and Venetians also sold European slaves to Arabs, while Vikings sold English and French slaves they had seized to Byzantium and Moorish Spain. By the 1400s Arabs and Portuguese were selling enslaved West Africans in southern Europe, and by the end of the fifteenth century black Africans constituted some 40 percent of the slaves in the Spanish city of Valencia; the remainder were mostly Muslims, Russians, Greek Orthodox Christians, Canary Islanders, and Jews.

Populations, towns, and cities grew. Compared to Byzantium, China, and the Islamic world, early medieval western Europe was economically underdeveloped and had small cities: by 1000 Rome had only thirty-five thousand people; Paris, twenty thousand; and London, ten thousand. By contrast, Constantinople had three hundred thousand, Kaifeng in China had four hundred thousand, Cordoba in Moorish Spain nearly five hundred thousand, and the world's largest city, Baghdad, a million people. However, between 1000 and 1300 new methods of growing crops spurred a doubling of Europe's population to about seventy-five million, and western European cities became centers of trade and industry. Milan and Paris grew to almost one hundred thousand, and London had thirty thousand people and a problem with air pollution due to coal burning.

Some people considered cities degenerate places. An eleventh-century English monk detested London:

> I do not like that city. All sorts of men crowd together there from every country. Each race brings its own vices. No one lives in it without falling into some sort of crime. Actors, jesters, smooth-skinned lads, flatterers, effeminates, pederasts, singing and dancing girls, quacks, belly-dancers, sorceresses, extortioners, magicians, mimes, beggars, buffoons: all this tribe fill all the houses. Therefore, if you do not want to dwell with evildoers, do not live in London.[9]

Although transportation was largely limited to horses, carts, boats, and human feet, people did move around, albeit slowly.

Hence, in 1297 when the Duchess of Brabant moved with her large clothing collection from London to her new husband's home 85 miles away, it took the cart, pulled by five horses, eighteen days to complete the trip. Nevertheless, urban life and its economic opportunities attracted people. A German expression, "city air makes one free," confirmed that a serf who left the manor and spent "a year and a day" in a city without being caught was considered legally free. Thus cities increasingly operated outside the feudal social and political structure. City craftsmen and merchants organized themselves into fraternal organizations called **guilds** to protect members' economic interests and to win exemptions from feudal obligations. Eventually city charters, secured from the local lord or king who needed the wealth that city commerce and payments brought, allowed cities to have their own courts and other self-government privileges.

Although merchants benefited from cities and commercial expansion, they had to overcome social prejudices. In feudal society, people belonged to one of three categories, in order of importance: "those who prayed" (churchmen, priests, and monks), "those who fought" (aristocratic warriors, knights), and "those who worked" (peasants). Merchants and bankers had no place in this hierarchy unless they married an impoverished aristocrat's daughter and hence acquired land. But most merchants also shared society's values and Christian faith. Hence, the English merchant Godric of Pinchale (ca. 1069–1170) left home as a teenager to peddle goods in nearby villages and then traded goods by sea between England, Scotland, Denmark, and Holland. Eventually he owned a small fleet of vessels, becoming quite wealthy and making pilgrimages to Jerusalem. He never married and later in life gave away all his wealth to the poor, became a hermit, wrote religious poetry, and gained fame for his piety.

People resented merchants for selling goods for more than they paid for them and consorting with foreigners. With greed considered a serious sin, loaning money at interest was regarded as **usury**, a sin because the lender made a profit without doing any labor. But moneylending was necessary to commerce, and even popes borrowed money at interest. While Italians became renowned bankers, moneylending was often left to Jews, allowing Christians to benefit from borrowing money without committing usury. Gradually using and lending money became more acceptable.

Long-distance trade reached its peak between 1100 and 1350 as western Europeans shipped woolen textiles, flax, hemp, wines, olive oil, fruit, and timber to the East in return for luxury goods from Byzantium and Asia such as spices, silk, perfumes, and precious gems. As trade and commerce around Europe grew, prejudice against merchants declined. Cities such as Constantinople, Venice, Genoa, Bruges **(broozh)** and Amsterdam in the Low Countries, and Strassburg in the Rhineland became major commercial hubs. Italian merchants acquired goods from the Middle East and Byzantium, shipping them

serfs In medieval Europe, peasants legally bound to their lord and tied to the land through generations.

guilds In medieval Europe, collective fraternal organizations of craftsmen and merchants designed to protect the economic interests of their members.

usury The practice of loaning money at interest; considered a sin in medieval Europe, although necessary to commerce.

---

[9]Richard of Devizes, quoted in Jacques Le Goff, ed., *The Medieval World* (London: Postgate Books, 1997), 139.

IMAGE 14.4 **A Medieval Town** This fourteenth-century miniature painting shows a variety of town enterprises, including a tailor's shop, barbershop, furrier, and druggist, on a paved street in Paris.

Q In what ways does this photo resemble a commercial district today and how is it different?

14-2c Social Life and Groups

Until the past several decades we knew more about queens and female saints than average women in medieval Europe. Now we are getting a more balanced view of men and women. Medieval society was patriarchal with double standards that favored men, though family life and gender relations varied with social status and local customs. Generally, men supported their families while women ran households and raised children. Parents preferred sons, who passed on the family line, property, and name, and arranged most marriages. Society allowed men to have sex outside marriage but valued women for their virginity and faithfulness. The church considered marriage a necessary evil, with sex only for procreation, not pleasure. A leading theologian, Saint Thomas Aquinas, contended that "woman was created to help man, but only in the act of procreation, because in all other tasks he can find far better support elsewhere." One priest even warned married people to avoid sex on the Sabbath because "monsters, cripples, and all sickly children [are] conceived on Saturday nights."[10] However, rulers often flouted custom. Charlemagne enforced rigid Christian morality on his people while also marrying four times, having five mistresses, and siring eighteen children.

Today's Western middle-class model of a husband, wife, and their unmarried children living in one independent household, separate from the larger family, was the exception. Many women married late, and many men and women remained unmarried. Children often left their birth families at an early age to become apprentices in a trade, servants, or novices in religious orders. Laws favoring men spurred many women to join convents, all-female Christian communities that offered physical and social protection and leadership possibilities. A fourteenth-century treatise from an unknown man, named by historians "the Good Man of Paris," tells us something of married life. In his account we see a much younger and somewhat nervous and awkward fifteen-year-old girl married off to a man she may have scarcely known. She asked him to not speak harshly to her in front of strangers but also to help her become a good wife. He advised her to love him more than her family, be distant with other men, not be arrogant and disobedient to him, and then argued that in nature and in Christian teachings females must defer to males. However, he seems to have been a thoughtful man in the context of his time. We will never know if they had a happy marriage, but they both seemed to want to make it work.

to Belgium and Holland for woolen textiles. One French ruler, the Count of Champagne (shahm-PAHN-yuh), established the "Champagne fairs", when goods were displayed at town fairs lasting seven weeks. The wealth created fostered a commercial revolution, making merchants and bankers more influential.

Eventually commerce became more central to Europe's economy than agriculture, although the broad repercussions—the rise of capitalism; incorporation of merchants as a vital social class; stronger monarchies; and weakening of both feudalism and the Christian church—became clear only centuries later. While both popes and political leaders in Europe remained powerful, the merchant class gradually gained political and economic influence to challenge feudal nobles and eventually monarchies.

[10]The quotes are from Frederic Delouche et al., *Illustrated History of Europe: A Unique Portrait of Europe's Common History* (New York: Barnes and Noble, 2001), 170; and Georges Duby, "Marriage in Early Medieval Society," in *Love and Marriage: The Middle Ages*, trans. Jane Dunnett (Chicago: University of Chicago Press, 1994), 11.

Medieval society had contradictory views of women. Biblical gender stereotypes fostered the belief that women had to be subordinate to men, were depraved, led men into sin, and were intellectually inferior. Yet, Mary, the Virgin Mother of Jesus, became one of the most popular objects of devotion, with many cathedrals named after Notre Dame (**NO-truh DAHM**) ("Our Lady"). Furthermore, women could inherit property and were involved in the larger economy, working in many occupations, including farming, ale making, baking, small-scale trade, glassmaking, workshop management, and the textile industry. Some were seamstresses or weavers who embroidered a range of fabrics, sometimes in workshops, for family and friends but also to sell, even advertising their skills and wares. A 2018 study concluded that a few even produced medieval manuscripts, once thought to be done exclusively by monks. Some became scholars, like the tenth-century writer Lubna of Cordoba, who managed the royal library there, or accomplished in fields like medicine, such as the fourteenth-century Italian Alessandra Giliani, a respected expert in anatomy.

Probably originating in Moorish Spain, where women poets flourished, by the 1100s **courtly love** developed, a new concept of passionate but pure relationships between knights and ladies. Celebrated in song by wandering troubadours, it brought romance to male–female relations and, combined with the Virgin Mary cult, elevated aristocratic women's status. But whether courtly or not, romantic love existed mostly outside of marriage. In medieval tales, knights often sought the favors of fair maidens (usually the wife of another, perhaps their lord) who were unattainable. With adultery considered a high crime, the knight's love was usually unrequited.

Early Christian tolerance of homosexuality survived through the Early Middle Ages. Although various church leaders and rulers condemned those whom they called "sodomites," after the immoral biblical city of Sodom, public attitudes were often more accepting, with considerable homosexual fiction and poetry published in the eleventh and twelfth centuries. Several prominent bishops and English kings were thought to be homosexuals. By the thirteenth century, public attitudes shifted. Growing states promoted uniformity in social relations and religious views, fostering suspicion of those outside the mainstream. The church launched a violent campaign against heresy and unconventional behavior, often targeting suspected homosexuals. Whereas in 1250 homosexual behavior was legal and accepted in most of Europe, by 1300 it was a capital offense in many societies.

Tightly ordered medieval society was rife with tensions, with violent crime common and daily life precarious for rich and poor alike. Most Europeans disliked the Romany (or Gypsies), a wandering group originally from north India who arrived in Europe from the Middle East between 1,000 and 1,500 years ago. This prejudice still exists in many European countries. Historians debate whether skin color was important in differentiating people in this era. Prejudice and hatred certainly existed against groups seen as culturally and religiously different and therefore viewed as inferior, evil, and dangerous, such as Romany, Jews, and Muslims. This sometimes led to expulsion or sporadic violence against minorities as well as "badge of shame" laws requiring Jews to wear different clothes and live in different neighborhoods than Christians, as happened in England in 1275. Racism and racial prejudice in the West based on skin color became a bigger issue after 1500. Many tensions arose from major distinctions between Christians and "outsiders"—nonbelievers, Muslims, Jews, heretics. Christians described Muslims as "pagans," who reciprocated by calling Christians "infidels" (unbelievers). The drive to destroy all beliefs outside of the Christian mainstream eventually led to a long series of Crusades against Islam and persecution of Jews.

Many European towns had Jewish communities. Although Jews worked in many occupations, they were best known as merchants and bankers because Christians were forbidden to loan money at interest. Resentment of Jewish commercial success and moneylending made them scapegoats for hard-to-explain misfortunes, such as epidemics. While Christians mostly tolerated Jews before 1150, anti-Semitism (**AN-tee-SEM-uh-tiz-uhm**) increased dramatically as more Christians took up banking or more militantly asserted their faith. In 1182 France ordered Jews to leave, an expulsion imitated in other countries during the next three centuries. Governments also restricted Jewish businesses and residences to certain districts. Our modern term *ghetto* originally described medieval city neighborhoods where Jews were compelled to live. Many expelled Jews migrated to Poland and Byzantium, which developed large Jewish populations.

Struggling to differentiate correct belief from heresy, Christians directed disdain at alleged heretics. While some devout Christians criticized church corruption, ill-educated priests, and arrogant bishops, church leaders viewed reformers as heretics. Hence, they organized military attacks on the Albigensians (**AL-buh-JEN-shunz**), a group in southern France who criticized the church's material wealth, urged clerical poverty, and wanted the Bible translated from Latin into the vernacular languages such as French and German so that ordinary people could read it for themselves. The church destroyed the Albigensians by killing their followers and confiscating their property.

14-2d The Church as a Social and Political Force

The church enjoyed social and political power but also experienced turmoil during the High Middle Ages. Massive cathedrals with lofty spires inspired deep emotions and still do. Many Christian leaders and local priests were well respected. Medieval Christians registered births and marriages and paid taxes in the village church, and they measured the stages of their lives by sacraments such as baptism and matrimony, which priests had to administer. Able to deny someone the sacraments, considered necessary for salvation, medieval priests had enormous power. They could also **excommunicate**, or expel a person from the church and its sacraments, a psychologically devastating act.

courtly love A standard of polite relationships between knights and ladies that arose in the 1100s in medieval Europe. Courtly love was celebrated in song by wandering troubadours.

excommunicate To expel a person from the Roman Catholic Church and its sacraments.

Not all priests and bishops lived up to their responsibilities or growing expectations for celibacy. Many priests had little education and could barely recite the Latin liturgy, and some were corrupt and took bribes. Many priests and monks were also married. Reformist church leaders, believing priests should not be distracted by families and not wanting priests to pass on their parishes to their children, attempted to crack down. Nonetheless, even after the final ban on clerical marriage many priests were married, kept mistresses, or were either homosexual or assumed to be so. Many people had ambivalent attitudes toward the clergy, fearing priests because of their power and ridiculing them because of their shortcomings.

In the eleventh century, reformers attempted to change the church and end abuses by priests, monks, and high officials. New religious orders tried to restore monastic life to its original purity, insisting that all monks remain celibate. Several German rulers also appointed reform-minded popes who tried to end **simony (SIGH-muh-nee)**, a common practice whereby wealthy families paid to have their sons appointed bishops, who collected significant revenues in their territories. Attempting to keep European rulers from interfering in papal elections, the church established the College of Cardinals in 1059 to elect the pope. Churchmen made Roman law the basis of church law because it referred all matters to the person at the top, in this case the pope.

Growing papal political power became clear when a major church–state conflict erupted over the appointment of bishops. For centuries rulers had appointed leading nobles to key church offices in their states. But in 1075 Pope Gregory VII (ca. 1020–1085) excommunicated the German emperor for appointing the archbishop of Milan **(mi-LAHN)**. Gregory had a low opinion of kings, who "derive their origin from men ignorant of God who raised themselves above their fellows by pride, plunder, treachery, murder, at the instigation of the Devil."[11] In 1122 both men compromised, agreeing that both emperor and pope would invest new bishops. This dispute strengthened papal authority and weakened German emperors. As German rulers intervened in Italian politics to regain control over the church, they lost influence over their own princes at home, leading eventually to decentralized government and political warfare in German-speaking lands. Another pope, Innocent III (r. 1198–1216), dramatically extended papal authority over secular rulers, using his control over the sacraments to force King John of England to accept the pope's candidate for archbishop of Canterbury and requiring the French king to take back a wife he had divorced. He also required Jews to wear distinctive clothing and aggressively punished "heretical depravity."

The papal drive to investigate and eliminate heresy led to the **Holy Inquisition**, a church court created in 1231. Churchmen tried thousands of people with views outside the mainstream, with popes sanctioning torture and starvation to induce confessions. Those found guilty faced punishments, including penances, banishment, prison, mutilation, and death. Over two centuries several thousand people were executed. The most notorious inquisition began, under state rather than church control, in Spain in 1478 and perpetrated brutal persecution of Jews and Muslims, burning at least two thousand people at the stake. The inquisitions continued into the 1600s and included bans on books viewed as dangerous to the faith. The ban continued until the mid-twentieth century.

Christians adopted ancient Jewish ideas about nature and history, including the concept of progress. Early Christian thinkers believed that human society improved with time, an idea then foreign to most of the world. Originating with the seven-day creation story in Genesis, this linear rather than cyclical concept viewed history as moving progressively from one point to another. To many Christian thinkers, God planned the world, including the natural environment, for human benefit, an idea that necessitated exploiting nature. With no item having any purpose but to serve humans, God, they argued, wanted people to improve land by clearing forests and wetlands, which some monasteries did with enthusiasm. This attitude toward nature justified the great technological and economic development to later emerge in the West and also caused environmental problems.

Some Christian and Jewish thinkers dissented from these views and affirmed nature as God's creation that required care and stewardship. Saint Francis of Assisi (1182–1226), who renounced wealth to found a new religious order, the Franciscans **(fran-SIS-kuhnz)**, dedicated to lives of poverty, humility, and serving the urban poor, saw all creatures as part of God's plan. The twelfth-century Jewish philosopher Moses Maimonides wrote that "it should not be believed that all beings exist for the sake of the existence of man."[12] Furthermore, kings and lords often protected the forests where they enjoyed hunting.

14-2e New European States

Threatened by increasing papal power, and with growing economies reducing the need for feudal vassals, rulers sought more control over their lands (see Map 14.2). English kings were most successful at centralizing power. After conquering England, William of Normandy (1027–1087) divided the land among his chief vassals, but by the 1100s William's successors had reduced the local nobility's authority and were appointing justices and tax collectors. King Henry II (r. 1154–1189), who invaded Ireland in 1171 and established control of the island's eastern region, expanded the royal courts' power over feudal and church courts.

However, some English rulers unintentionally laid the foundations for later representative government. King John (Prince John of the Robin Hood legend), under pressure from leading barons and the Catholic Church that he had angered, weakened royal power in 1215 by signing the **Magna Carta**

simony In medieval Europe, a practice whereby wealthy families paid to have their sons appointed bishops.

Holy Inquisition A church court created in 1231 in medieval Europe to investigate and eliminate heresy; inquisitions continued into the 1600s.

Magna Carta ("Great Charter") An agreement signed by King John of England in 1215 that limited the feudal rights of the English king and his officials while protecting the rights of the church, lords, and merchants.

[11]Quoted in Cruz and Gerberding, *Medieval Worlds*, 277.
[12]Quoted in Clive Ponting, *A Green History of the World: The Environment and the Collapse of Great Civilizations* (New York: Penguin, 1991), 144.

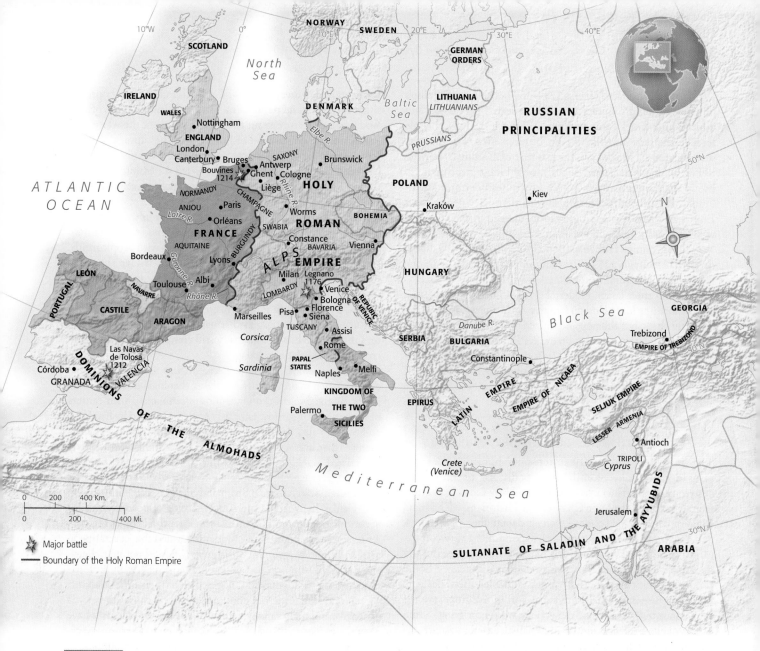

MAP 14.2 **Medieval Europe, 900–1300** During the High Middle Ages, the Holy Roman Empire, comprising dozens of smaller states, covered much of what is today Germany, Austria, eastern France, and northern Italy. France, England, Hungary, and Poland were also major states.

Q How much had the map of Europe changed in the High Middle Ages from what it was in the early Middle Ages?

(MAG-nuh KAHR-tuh) or "Great Charter," an agreement that limited the feudal and taxation rights of the king and his officials while protecting the rights of the church, lords, and merchants. The Magna Carta was later used to support the notion that rulers had to have their subjects' consent, a foundation of modern English constitutional monarchy. Another step toward representation was taken because of Henry III's (r. 1216–1272) incessant demands for taxes to fight foreign wars. In 1265, rebellious barons called together a parliament (literally, a "speaking place") including middle-class townspeople and knights to air their grievances and demand that the king consider their views. This parliament became the model for later meetings called by kings to secure approval of their policies.

Like the English kings, the Capetians (kuh-PEE-shuhnz), who succeeded the Carolingians as kings in France (987–1328), also tried to increase their power and expand their territory. King Philip II (r. 1180–1223) gained control over Normandy in northwestern France and replaced noblemen with paid officials more loyal to the crown. Louis IX, or Saint Louis (r. 1226–1270), a pious man, curbed the nobility's power while persecuting heretics and Jews. Philip the Fair (r. 1285–1314) may have had the most impact on France and Europe. To raise money for his wars, he arrested all the Jews, seizing their property before expelling them in 1306, and had the leaders of a militant religious order, the Knights Templar (TEM-plahr), burned at the stake as heretics so he could default on a loan.

341

When Pope Boniface VIII (r. 1294–1303) challenged Philip's growing power, Philip accused him of sexual perversion and murder and sent a force to Italy to arrest him. Townspeople rescued the pope by driving French troops away. For the next seventy years (1305–1377), the College of Cardinals, bowing to French pressure, elected popes, mostly French, who chose to live in Avignon (**ah-vee-NYON**), a papal territory in southern France. Philip's ruthless action showed that papal control over European rulers was ending. France emerged as the strongest western European kingdom.

The German Hohenstaufen (**HO-uhn-SHTOU-fuhn**) dynasty (1152 and 1254), in trying to control Italy while the feudal German nobility remained powerful, had less success centralizing their lands. Frederick I (r. 1154–1190) reasserted his authority as Holy Roman Emperor over the wealthy northern Italy cities, but the pope organized an Italian coalition and defeated Frederick's forces. Frederick I's successors gradually lost power to German princes. Italy divided into small papal-ruled and nonpapal states. Only seven hundred years later did Germany finally achieve the territorial unity enjoyed by France and England.

14-2f The Crusades and Intellectual Life

The religious and political tensions helped foster the Crusades, a series of military expeditions or holy wars between 1095 and 1272 to reclaim the "Holy Land," Palestine, from Muslim control (see Chapter 10). Historians—Christian, Muslim, Jewish, and secular—fiercely debate the origins, aims, and consequences of the Crusades, making this a very controversial subject today that also has religious undertones. But the debate also sometimes transcends religious differences. Some rationalize the crusades as an understandable, often idealistic Christian response to Muslim expansion into Europe, even if they concede that some of the actions were horrifying. Some others deplore the crusades as imperialistic, even racist attacks on non-Christians and non-Europeans by religious fanatics and criminals. European Christians had long made pilgrimages to Jerusalem and considered the city part of their world. Crusading began after the Byzantine emperor sought help to dislodge the Muslim Seljuk Turks, who now dominated much of western Asia, including Palestine. Medieval Christians had a militant zeal to spread their faith and destroy Islam, through the use of force if necessary, and early Christian thinkers like Augustine of Hippo sanctioned war to defend the faith. Except for Islam, no other world religion maintained a strong missionary impulse to convert the world to what its believers considered the only true faith. Religious beliefs and idealism, often mixed with lust for wealth and land, motivated crusaders. Political rivalries between European leaders also played a role.

In 1095 Pope Urban II urged Christian rulers to protect the Christian holy sites, prompting the first of nine crusades by land and sea. Citing stories of Muslim atrocities against Christians, which many historians believe to have been fabricated or exaggerated, he proclaimed that the Turks "have

completely destroyed some of God's churches. They ruin the altars with filth and defilement. They are pleased to kill others. And what shall I say about the shocking rape of the women."[13] Various kings, nobles, and bishops joined the cause. Crusaders temporarily occupied parts of the Holy Land, including Jerusalem, even establishing crusader-led states, but eventually they were forced out. Other crusaders ransacked Constantinople and Egypt.

Looting and pillaging cities, even in Europe, crusaders often slaughtered thousands of Muslims, Jews, and Byzantine Christians, burning mosques and synagogues with people inside. In Germany in 1096 crusaders slaughtered twelve thousand Jews. Many non-Christians viewed crusaders as terrorists. In response, Muslim defenders killed local Christians; Jerusalem's streets, it was said, ran ankle-deep in blood. In the thirteenth century, crusading energies dissipated, but the remaining bitter Christian–Muslim animosity still complicates political and cross-cultural relations today.

Some medieval tensions derived from robust intellectual debates, often in universities, involving theologians and philosophers. By the twelfth century, guilds of scholars formed centers of higher learning, most famously at Paris, Oxford in England, and Salerno and Bologna (**boe-LOAN-yuh**) in Italy. Whereas many earlier universities in India and the Islamic world mostly specialized in religious studies while also in some cases offering other subjects as well, European universities, perhaps influenced by universities in Moorish Spain and Sicily, taught both religion and secular knowledge, such as Aristotle's philosophy, raising eyebrows among church leaders (see Meet the People: Heloise, a French Scholar and Nun). Students learned the "seven liberal arts"—astronomy, geometry, arithmetic, music, grammar, rhetoric, and logic—before specializing in medicine, law, or philosophy. As today, students did not spend all of their time studying. When one student wrote home for money because "the city is expensive and makes many demands," his father replied: "I have recently learned that you live dissolutely, preferring play to work, and strumming your guitar while others are at their studies."[14]

Heated debates over faith and reason, often against church opposition, contributed much to later Western thought. Thomas Aquinas (**uh-KWINE-uhs**) (1225–1274), an Italian Dominican monk and professor at the University of Paris, argued that reason could determine much, even God's existence, but that eventually a believer had to accept on faith many mysteries. He also believed that God mandated human domination over nature and that women were passive and incapable of moral perfection. Some thinkers influenced by Aristotle argued that real knowledge came only from direct observation, a position that supported scientific inquiry.

Medieval literature was diverse. The *Song of Roland*, from twelfth-century France, described the great deeds of a loyal knight who died fighting in Charlemagne's army. But the epic's warlike tone contrasted with many French lyric poems and stories exalting personal happiness and romantic love in a society that generally arranged marriages. Another story, the Celtic legend of British King Arthur and his court, was addressed by

[13]Quoted in Thomas F. Madden, *A Concise History of the Crusades* (Lanham, MD: Rowman and Littlefield, 1999), 8–9.
[14]Quoted in C. Warren Hollister, *Medieval Europe: A Short History*, 8th ed. (Boston: McGraw-Hill, 1998), 296.

Heloise, a French Scholar and Nun

A scandalous love affair between two brilliant people, Abelard and Heloise, reveals much about medieval life and values, including church politics and attitudes toward sexuality. Ever since then the romance and its sad repercussions have inspired countless works of poetry, prose, and song. Often portrayed as a forbidden affair between a smitten schoolgirl and her unprincipled teacher, a famed but controversial theologian, the relationship between the two figures was far more complex.

Coming from a wealthy, influential family, Heloise (1101–1164), the niece of a high church official in Paris, had more educational opportunities than most women of her time and studed at a well-financed convent where she showed a keen intelligence. In 1117 her uncle Fulbert, a high-ranking cleric, arranged for the seventeen-year-old to study with Peter Abelard (1079–1142), a famous teacher but a nonclergyman, at the Notre Dame Cathedral school. Born into an aristocratic family in Brittany (northwest France), Abelard studied with renowned teachers and taught at several schools. Notorious for both his arrogance and intellect, he made enemies in the church by championing reason, logic, and progressive thinking on religious doctrine.

Despite a twenty-year age difference, Abelard and Heloise fell passionately in love. Abelard wrote of how they went from reading books to kissing and composing love songs and letters to each other. But their affair also reflected friendship and intellectual respect, her letters revealing good knowledge of Roman and Christian writers. The two lovers tried to keep their affair quiet and were secretly married after she became pregnant. Their son, raised by Abelard's sister, eventually became a church official. Their romance came at a time when the church was not just encouraging but mandating that clergy as well as secular teachers, such as Abelard, and students in church schools remain celibate. Abelard realized his marriage would end his current position and future church career. But Heloise's family, upon learning of the affair, sought revenge, and Fulbert hired two men to beat and then castrate Abelard. Now disgraced, Abelard joined a Benedictine monastery, and, at his encouragement, Heloise entered a convent, eventually becoming the community's director.

IMAGE 14.5 **Heloise and Abelard** This painting, from a fourteenth-century French manuscript, shows Heloise (in nun's habit) and Abelard in conversation, years after their torrid love affair had shocked church authorities.

RMN-Grand Palais/Art Resource, NY

Although separated, Heloise and Abelard continued to write to each other. Expressing her affection, Heloise wrote him that "I seek to please thee rather than [God]. Thy command brought me, not the love of God, to the [nunnery]." Strongly influenced by Aristotle's thought, Abelard restored his scholarly reputation by writing books and essays about mixing philosophy and religion, views his critics considered heresy. Later, as an abbot (head) of a large monastery, while maintaining a personal distance he helped Heloise and her nuns establish a new convent. Her ability to gain support and funding helped her convent flourish. She remained ambivalent about her career, however, writing Abelard that "I am judged religious at a time when there is little in religion that is not hypocrisy." Heloise became known for her learning, and one top male cleric praised her knowledge of the liberal arts: "You have surpassed all women and have gone further than almost every man." However, Heloise resented Abelard's desire to remain aloof from her, writing: "Of all the wretched women I am the most wretched, for the higher the ascent, the heavier the fall."

Although dying twenty years apart, the pair was buried alongside each other at the convent, a fitting conclusion to a relationship and an era. Heloise was one of the last educated churchwomen to maintain close contact with male scholars and church officials. Obsessed with celibacy, the church increasingly separated men and women engaged in religious life.

Reflection Questions

1. What does the love affair and its consequences tell us about life at this time?
2. How did the different ways in which Abelard and Heloise rebuilt their lives reflect the values of medieval people?
3. How did the culture and influence of the medieval church and its views of clergy and of relations between men and women, as reflected in the reading, compare to today?

Notes: Quotations from Barbara A. Hanawalt, *The Middle Ages: An Illustrated History* (New York: Oxford University Press, 1998), 88; Jane Slaughter and Melissa K. Bokovoy, *Sharing the Stage: Biography and Gender in Western Civilization*, vol. 1 (Boston: Houghton-Mifflin, 2003), 255, 261–262; and James Burge, *Heloise and Abelard: A New Biography* (San Francisco: HarperSanFrancisco, 2003), 271.

writers all over Europe. In some versions Arthur's wife, Guinevere (**GWIN-uh-veer**), and his best friend, Lancelot, follow their hearts, becoming doomed lovers. There was also lighter writing, such as this parody of the Christian Apostles' Creed written by a student more delighted by spirits than by the Spirit: "I believe in the tavern of my host, More than in the Holy Ghost. The tavern will my sweetheart be, and the Holy Church is not for me."[15] It could perhaps have been written by a party-loving and irreverent college student today. Some things never change.

KEY POINTS

- ▶ Feudalism was a medieval political arrangement in which a king gave nobles the right to rule over sections of his territory in exchange for their allegiance.

- ▶ Medieval society was patriarchal, considering women inferior to men; children usually left home early; and parents arranged most marriages.

- ▶ Many of the tensions in medieval society were caused by the intolerance for "outsiders": non-Christians and heretics, Muslims, and Jews, all of whom were disdained and treated harshly, killed (as in the Crusades), or expelled.

- ▶ Christians adopted the Jewish belief in progress over time and the belief that everything in the world was for the use of humans, a view that laid the ground for later industrialization in the West.

14-3 Eastern Europe: Byzantines, Slavs, and Mongols

▦ SOCIETIES

Q How did Byzantine society differ from that of western Europe?

Byzantium, and the eastern European societies it influenced, remained very distinct from western Europe. Despite Christianity and long-standing trade connections, deep political, economic, and religious differences separated them and still do. Byzantium demonstrated remarkable longevity, serving as a buffer zone protecting central and western Europe against Muslim, Slavic, and Mongol invaders, but, from the eleventh century on, it experienced steady political decline until it was finally defeated by the Ottoman Turks in 1453. Most Slavic societies in eastern Europe adopted Eastern Orthodox Christianity, and the Russians eventually created a powerful state.

> ### CONNECTION to TODAY
> Do you think that the differences between the mainly Catholic west and largely Orthodox east in medieval times are still important in Europe today and over the past century?

disagreeing on the use of icons, painted images of holy figures, and over whether the Holy Spirit proceeded from God or from both God and Jesus. Byzantine Christians refused to recognize the bishop of Rome's supremacy over other bishops. These conflicts over theology and authority spurred the final split between the Roman Catholic and Greek Orthodox Churches, which came when the pope and the patriarch of Constantinople angrily excommunicated each other in 1054.

Although the Byzantine church supported male power, a few women achieved political or intellectual influence. Empress Irene, an orphan who married an emperor, ruled Byzantium for two decades (780–802). Although her detractors considered her cruel and ruthless, Irene fostered prosperity, made peace with Muslim states, and temporarily resolved the dispute over icons. Byzantium's best-known historian, the princess Anna Comnena (1083–1148), studied literature, astronomy, medicine, and Greek philosophy.

But the state's geographical location also proved precarious. Byzantium faced nearly continuous pressure from neighboring peoples. In the sixth and seventh centuries Sassanian Persians and Byzantines fought wars, weakening both empires and making Arab conquest of their lands easier. Arabs attacked Constantinople in 673 and 717, but the Byzantines survived. For the next three and a half centuries they also faced challenges from various Slavic peoples who migrated into and settled eastern Europe, dominating this vast region of mountains, forests, and grasslands stretching north from Greece to the eastern Baltic and eastward through Russia. The major Slavic threats came from Bulgars and Serbs. The Byzantine ruler known as

14-3a Byzantium and Its Rivals

Despite many misfortunes, Byzantium's economic and religious strengths enabled it to survive for a long time. Located at a favorable location astride the principal trade routes between Europe and Asia, and the Black Sea and the Mediterranean, Constantinople's merchant class remained vital. Traders shipped eastern European slaves, including many Slavs (source of the English term *slave*) from the Black Sea region, for sale in the Mediterranean. Taxes from these goods and people as well as silk production enriched the treasury, and Byzantine coins were used around Eurasia.

With the Byzantine church and state intertwined, Christianity and its rituals influenced all aspects of society, fostering lengthy religious ceremonies and an intense prayer life. Unlike in western Europe, governments dominated the church, with rulers regularly interfering in church affairs. Byzantines also engaged in hair-splitting theological disputes, bitterly

---

[15]Quoted in Ibid., 273.

"Basil the Bulgar-Slayer" defeated a Bulgar army in 1014, blinding fifteen thousand Bulgarian prisoners of war before releasing them to return home. The Bulgar defeat opened the door to Serbs, who set up several small states in the Balkans, sparking conflict with Byzantium. After a series of wars, Ottoman Turks conquered the Serbs in 1459.

Byzantine political fortunes declined. In 1071, Norman knights drove Byzantine forces from southern Italy, and in 1091, at the Battle of Manzikert (**MANZ-ih-kuhrt**), Seljuk Turks seized eastern Anatolia. The shrunken Byzantine territories now faced regular attacks from both east and west. Turks soon completed the conquest of Anatolia, leaving Constantinople a beleaguered fortress. Desperate Byzantines requested help from western knights to defend them against the Turks; instead, crusader armies occupied Palestine and Syria between 1096 and 1200. The Byzantines also did not expect crusaders in 1204, bribed by the Venetians, Byzantine trading rivals, to use a disputed imperial succession as an excuse to conquer Constantinople itself, which they governed until forced out in 1261. Capitalizing on these disasters, expanding Ottoman Turks finally conquered Constantinople and the surrounding territory in 1453, ending the Byzantine state and transforming the capital city, which the Turks eventually renamed Istanbul.

14-3b Byzantium, Russians, and Mongols

Byzantine culture and religion spread north and east and survived the empire's defeats. Differing eastern and western versions of Christianity offered eastern European peoples a choice of which to adopt. In the ninth century, two Byzantine brothers, known later as Saints Cyril and Methodius (**mi-THO-dee-uhs**), converted many Slavs to eastern Christianity. Devising an alphabet, known as Cyrillic (**suh-RILL-ik**), for the Slavs, Cyril translated the Bible and other church writings from Greek. Bulgars, Serbs, Russians, and many Ukrainians eventually adopted Byzantine culture, including Orthodox Christianity. Russians and other

societies they influenced, including Georgians in the Caucasus, embraced ideas such as an autocratic emperor and close church–state relations, in contrast to western Europe, where church–state conflicts remained common. Other Slavs, among them Croats (**KRO-ATS**), Czechs (**checks**), Lithuanians (**lith-oo-ANE-ee-uhnz**), Poles, Slovaks (**SLO-vaks**), Slovenes (**SLO-veenz**), and many Ukrainians, adopted Roman Catholicism. Eastern and western European cultures remain distinct even today, partly because of the differences between the Greek and Roman churches of one thousand years ago.

Russian identity descended from the Rus (**roos**), whose capital was eventually at Kiev (**KEE-yev**), in today's Ukraine (**you-CRANE**). Historians debate Rus origins. Small numbers of Swedish Vikings founded trading cities in the Slavic regions and may have become the Rus ruling class while both trading with and raiding the Byzantines. Viking trade networks crisscrossed the Russian and Ukrainian plains, spreading Scandinavian cultural and linguistic influences around the region. But Slavs eventually assimilated the Vikings. From the tenth to the twelfth centuries, the Russians expanded, forming settlements as far north as Novgorod (**NOHV-goh-rod**) and shipping timber south to the Black Sea. The Rus ruler Vladimir (**VLAD-ih-mir**) I (ca. 956–1015), in Kiev, had several wives and eight hundred concubines but, hoping for political advantage, sought marriage to a Byzantine princess. After she refused to marry a pagan polygamist, he agreed to accept Orthodox Christianity in 988 and make her his only wife. Ordering his soldiers to be baptized, Vladimir guaranteed that much of eastern Europe would become Eastern Orthodox.

By the time western Europeans heard rumors about the brutal Mongols, the Russians had already encountered them. Mongol armies conquered Central Asia and parts of China and the Middle East (see Chapters 10 and 11) and repeatedly sacked Russian cities beginning in 1237. A papal envoy who visited Kiev after an attack reported, "We found lying in the fields countless

IMAGE 14.6 **St. Sophia Cathedral in Kiev** Built in the early eleventh century, possibly by Vladimir I, to rival Hagia Sophia in Constantinople, the cathedral symbolized Kiev and Rus as the "new Constantinople."

Q How does this Russian Orthodox cathedral differ from the Wells Cathedral at the beginning of the chapter?

heads and bones. [The city] has been reduced to nothing: barely 200 houses [still] stand there."[16] Until the fifteenth century most Russians remained subject to the Golden Horde, a Mongol state on the lower Volga River. Muscovy (**MUSS-koe-vee**), a Russian state centered on Moscow, benefited, since the Golden Horde treated its ruler as the senior Russian leader.

Western Europe was fortunate to escape Mongol conquest. In 1241, Mongol armies moved far into Europe, crushing Polish and Hungarian forces sent against them. Standing at the Danube, they contemplated invading German lands. But Mongol generals returned to Mongolia in 1241 when their leader, Ogodei, died, sparing Germans and Europeans farther west. There may have also been other reasons for the sudden retreat besides Mongol politics and perhaps a more effective resistance than the Mongols anticipated. A study in 2016 points to weather, with a severe winter and then rains leading to widespread spring melting, causing flooding and mud, which prevented the growth of the grasses favored by Mongol horses. Whatever the case, had the Mongol conquests continued westward, European history might have been very different.

But Europe was much less tempting than far richer China and Islamic western Asia.

Eventually Muscovy became the dominant Russian state as Mongol political power declined and the head of the Russian Orthodox Church, appointed by the Constantinople patriarch, moved from Kiev to Moscow. Under Ivan III (1440–1505), Muscovy escaped Mongol control and established domination over other Russian states. Ivan began to call himself czar (meaning "caesar"), indicating his superiority over lesser rulers, and married the last Byzantine emperor's niece. The Russian Orthodox Church broke with the patriarch of Constantinople, and Russian clergy referred to Moscow as the Third Rome, successor to Constantinople. A monastery abbot proclaimed: "The Church of old Rome fell for its heresy; the gates of the Second Rome, Constantinople, were hewn down by the axes of the infidel Turks; but the Church of Moscow, the Church of the New Rome, shines brighter than the sun in the whole universe."[17] Russians also expanded into the territories of the Catholic Lithuanians, adding religious antagonisms to political tensions between Orthodox and Catholic peoples in eastern Europe.

KEY POINTS

▶ The Byzantines were under almost constant attack by Sassanian Persians, Bulgars, Slavs, and western European Christians, but Byzantium survived until it was conquered by the Turks in 1453.

▶ Byzantium's culture and Orthodox Christianity survived because they were spread to many eastern European peoples, including the Russians, the Bulgars, the Serbs, and many Ukrainians.

▶ The Russians, who had adopted Orthodox Christianity, were attacked by the Mongols but emerged as one of the strongest societies in eastern Europe.

14-4 Late Medieval Europe and the Roots of Expansion

▷⊂ TRANSITIONS ▦ NETWORKS

Ⓠ What developments between 1300 and 1500 gave Europeans the incentive and means to begin reshaping the world after 1500?

The Late Middle Ages (1300–1500) were a period of transition. A dramatic decrease in population as a result of famine, plague, and warfare contributed to feudalism's gradual end. Royal power increased many places at the expense of the feudal nobility, while the Roman Church also lost influence as questioning of church practices and beliefs increased. Yet, the ferment fostered intellectual and cultural creativity, trade expanded, and brave mariners began exploring the world beyond Europe. These changes eventually led to the resurgence of the West.

CONNECTION to TODAY

Can you identify features of late medieval Europe that resemble or led to some features of life today in areas like disease, warfare, politics, technology, religion, intellectual trends, attitudes, and economic patterns?

caused by huge volcanic explosions, which blocked sunlight by lofting dust high into the stratosphere, combined with the sun moving into a less active phase. Sea ice expanded, ocean currents shifted, wind patterns changed, and in some places torrential rains alternated with unprecedented drought and famine. Norse farming settlements in Greenland collapsed from deforestation, expanding glaciers, and conflict with the local Inuit. The same cooler temperatures shortened Europe's growing season, causing serious food shortages and considerable starvation.

Soon after the Little Ice Age famine began to dissipate. Europe also repeatedly suffered from the Black Death, the largest pandemic (massive epidemic) in world history that crossed many regions from China to England and even apparently into sub-Saharan Africa, named for the black bruises appearing under the skin. In 1347 a Genoese trading ship coming from

14-4a The Black Death and Social Change

Late medieval Europe was an unhappy place, ravaged by famine, disease, and war. Europe's climate turned colder about 1300, fostering the "Little Ice Age," a rapid global cooling probably

[16]Quoted in Nicholas V. Riasanovsky, *A History of Russia*, 5th ed. (New York: Oxford University Press, 1993), 72.
[17]Quoted in Colin Wells, *Sailing from Byzantium: How a Lost Empire Shaped the World* (New York: Delta, 2006), 279.

Image copyright © The Metropolitan Museum of Art. Image source: Art Resource, NY

IMAGE 14.7 **Praying for Relief** This image of survivors carrying away plague victims in Rome was commissioned by a French duke for an illuminated book in the early 1400s. It illustrates the despair and devastating loss of life caused by the Black Death, especially in cities.

Q What in this image conveys the relationship of death, burials, and religion in late medieval Europe?

the Black Sea limped into a bustling Sicilian harbor, the entire crew either dead or dying from a deadly infection. Most studies have blamed the spread on fleas living on rats who had scampered aboard ship, but new research in 2018 singles out both body lice and fleas, at least in Europe. The killer was probably bubonic plague, perhaps mixed with pneumonic (**noo-MON-ik**) plague. The pandemic caused unprecedented death and terrible suffering as it spread along and disrupted trade networks all over Eurasia and North Africa. During its peak years from 1348 to 1350, it killed at least a third of all Europeans. Over 65 percent of the population in some congested cities died, greatly reducing commerce; Europe's population in the fourteenth century dropped from around 70 to 75 million to some 45 to 50 million people, most killed by either a fast-acting respiratory infection or by swelling and internal bleeding, a horrible, agonizing, and excruciating death. Pope Clement VI wrote that "the living were barely sufficient to bury the dead, or so horrified as to avoid the task. So great a terror seized nearly everyone."[18] The horrors endured in nursery rhymes: "Ring around the rosies, a pocketful of posies, ashes, ashes, we all fall down."

Those who survived developed some immunities: the Black Death, reoccurring for decades, killed fewer people each time.

The troubles reshaped social patterns, especially for the upper classes, who now faced a labor shortage. With far fewer peasants alive to till the fields or workers to labor in businesses, those remaining asked for more privileges and money. Peasant revolts demanding an end to serfdom increased, most notably in France in 1358 and in England in 1381. With the dark shadow of death always close behind, many people migrated to cities. In the years that followed middle classes began to develop. Meanwhile, some people challenged social norms. In addition to writing works of history, ethics, and poetry, the French author Christine of Pizan (1364–ca. 1430) proclaimed women equal to men, systematically disproved all negative male stereotypes of women's character, and shrewdly critiqued the patriarchal social structure. She wrote that "those who blame women out of jealousy are those wicked men who have seen many women of greater intelligence and nobler conduct than they themselves possess."[19] Some literature, such as the fiction of the fourteenth-century English writer Geoffrey Chaucer (**CHAW-suhr**), reflected changing social customs and relations (see Discover Historical Voices: A Literary View of Late Medieval People).

Death and despair influenced emotional and social life. Many people assumed the pandemic was God's punishment. Hopelessness overwhelmed people digging graves for family members before they too succumbed to death, usually within days. While famine and disease raged, aristocrats enjoyed magnificent banquets, pageants, and ostentatious clothing. The poor sought escape through prayer, meditation, and self-flagellation, imitating the torture of Jesus by beating themselves with whips until their blood flowed. In some places, people looking for scapegoats blamed outsiders for the troubles. In the mid-1300s thousands of Jews were burned alive or driven out of cities, especially in the German states.

The pandemic affected western and eastern Europe differently. Because eastern Europe had fewer cities and more villages, fewer peasants died. With eastern monarchs weaker, the aristocracy imposed serfdom on many peasants, creating large agricultural estates. In the West, however, nobles were weakened by labor shortages and higher costs. Hence, eastern Europe remained primarily an agricultural area, while western European rulers strengthened their central governments.

14-4b Warfare and Political Centralization

Chronic warfare in late medieval western Europe brought much death and misery but also strengthened kings and states (see Map 14.3). For example, the Hundred Years War (1337–1453), the longest military struggle in history, involved intermittent English–French conflict and enhanced royal power in France and, eventually, England. This war, a dynastic fight caused by the English kings' desire to hold on to their feudal lands in France, eventually resulted in French triumph. At first the English gained victories by using trained commoners and a new weapon, the longbow, that launched powerful arrows, diminishing the knights as an effective fighting force. However, aided by

[18]Quoted in Delouche, *Illustrated History*, 168.
[19]Quoted in Brotton, *Renaissance Bazaar*, 75.

Discover Historical Voices

A Literary View of Late Medieval People

The English writer Geoffrey Chaucer (ca. 1340–1400) wrote one of the best-known books of the Late Middle Ages, The Canterbury Tales, set in the time of the Black Death. A London-born cosmopolitan poet, soldier, and diplomat, Chaucer served in the English Parliament and was familiar with French and Italian intellectual and cultural trends. While strongly influencing spoken and written English, The Canterbury Tales also offered a witty and sophisticated picture of English society. This excerpt presents stereotypical and satirical views of various pilgrims on their way to visit Canterbury in southeast England, the seat of church power in England.

The knight there was, and he was a worthy man, Who, from the moment that he first began To ride about the world, loved chivalry, Truth, honor, freedom, and all courtesy. . . . Of mortal battles he had fought fifteen . . . And always won he sovereign fame for prize . . . He never yet had any vileness said [about him] in all his life. . . . He was a truly perfect, gentle knight. . . .

There was also a nun, a prioress, Who, in her smiling, modest was and coy. . . . At table she had been well taught withal, And never from her lips let morsels fall, Nor dipped her fingers deep in sauce, but ate With so much care the food upon her plate That never driblet fell upon her breast. In courtesy she had delight and zest. . . .

A monk there was, one made for mastery [and loved hunting]. . . . A manly man, to be an abbot able. Full many a blooded horse had he in stable: And when he rode men might his bridle hear A-jingling in the whistling wind as clear, Aye, and as loud as does the chapel bell Where this brave monk was of the cell. . . . This said monk let such lowly old things [strict old monastic rules] slowly pace And followed new world manners in their place. What? Should he study as a madman would Upon a book in cloister cell? Or yet, go labor with his hands and . . . sweat [as Saint Augustine commanded]?. . .

There was a merchant with forked beard, and girt. . . . Upon his head a Flemish beaver hat; His boots were fastened rather elegantly. He spoke [his opinions] pompously, Stressing the times when he had won, not lost [his profits]. . . . At money changing he could make a crown. This worthy man kept all his wits well set; There was no one could say he was in debt, So well he governed all his trade affairs. . . .

There was a good man of religion, too, A country parson, poor . . . but rich he was in holy thought and work. He was also a learned man also [a scholar] . . . who Christ's own Gospel truly sought to preach. Devoutly his parishioner's would he teach. . . . Benign he was and wondrous diligent, Patient in adverse times and well content. . . . But rather would he give . . . unto those poor parishioners about, Part of his income, even of his goods. . . . That first he wrought and after words he taught [first he practiced, then he preached]. . . .

Reflection Questions

1. What are the various clerical stereotypes presented?
2. How is the merchant portrayed?
3. How do you think Chaucer's satirical approach in portraying people, or at least their stereotypes, compares to satire and comic writing today?

Source: General Prologue to Geoffrey Chaucer's *Canterbury Tales*, electronic edition prepared by Edwin Duncan (*towson.edu/~duncan/chaucer/titlepage.htm*)

Jeanne d'Arc (**zhahn DAHRK**) (ca. 1412–1431), a sixteen-year-old peasant who believed saints' voices told her to lead troops into battle, the French broke the English siege of the city of Orleans (**or-lay-AHN**) and slowly recovered most English-held territory in France. Jeanne, captured by the English and burned at the stake, became French nationhood's most famous martyr.

During the conflict's final stages, French monarchs introduced new direct taxes, lessening their dependence on the nobility, while reorganizing royal armies by hiring more mercenary troops. In England, military defeat fostered the War of the Roses (1455–1485) between two rival royal houses. Eventually Henry VII, who founded a new Tudor dynasty, sent armies to reclaim Ireland, followed by English settlers who repressed the Celtic Irish. The Tudors established England as a world power during the 1500s.

Royal power increased during the late 1400s in Spain. In 1085 Iberian Christians began the long reconquest of the peninsula from Muslims, by 1249 reclaiming Portugal and by the 1300s displacing all of the Muslim states except Granada (**gruh-NAH-duh**) in the far south. In 1469 the marriage of King Ferdinand of Aragon (**AR-uh-gon**) to his cousin, Isabella of Castile (**kas-TEEL**), united the two largest kingdoms. These monarchs finally crushed Granada in 1492 and then, obsessed with religious uniformity, demanded that Spanish Jews and Muslims either convert to Christianity or be expelled. While many converted, some secretly maintained Jewish or Muslim practices. Jews and Muslims refusing conversion mostly emigrated to Morocco or the Ottoman Empire. Hoping to increase royal wealth, Ferdinand and Isabella also sponsored the first trans-Atlantic voyage by the Italian mariner Christopher Columbus in 1492. In the past few years, after Spain welcomed Jews back, many descendants of *conversos* (people who had hidden their Jewish attachments under a Christian facade for generations) took up the offer and have returned to settle, most from Latin America or the U.S. Southwest.

Aristocracy remained strong in the Holy Roman Empire, which encompassed many German-speaking lands and parts of Italy. After taking power in 1273, the Habsburg (**HABZ-berg**)

MAP 14.3 **Europe, 1400–1500** During this period France became western Europe's strongest kingdom, but Spanish kings gradually reunified much of the Iberian peninsula. The Holy Roman Empire remained decentralized. Meanwhile, Lithuania, Hungary, and Poland controlled much of eastern Europe.

Q What does this map tell us about whether the political configuration reflects the ethnic, cultural, and religious division of Europe today?

Spread of Roman Christendom

In 1000 CE
Added 1000–1200
Lost 1000–1200 (Regained 1200–1500)
Added 1200–1500
Lost 1200–1500
English holdings, 1360
Boundary of the Holy Roman Empire

family proved unable to create a strong centralized state. In 1356 they reduced the pope's influence over electing Holy Roman Emperors but also ratified aristocratic power. During the coming centuries imperial Habsburg rulers concentrated on increasing their family's personal territorial holdings. In the later 1400s, royal marriage alliances gave them control of the Netherlands and much of southern Italy.

14-4c Hemispheric Connections, New Intellectual Horizons, and Technology

The Late Middle Ages fostered new intellectual horizons and technologies, some derived from contacts with Asia and Africa. The Mongols did not conquer western Europe but reenergized Eurasian trade, allowing inventions and ideas to flow to Europe from China and western Asia. Some Chinese inventions, such as printing, gunpowder, and the compass, eventually revolutionized European technology. Meanwhile, Italians imported spices, carpets, silks, porcelain, glassware, and even painting supplies from Moorish Spain, Ottoman Turkey, Mamluk Egypt, and Persia. The cosmopolitan Ottoman ruler Mehmed the Conqueror (1430–1481) read and published Greek and Latin books on history and philosophy while inviting Italian merchants, craftsmen, artists, and architects to work in Istanbul (formerly Constantinople). The magnificent palaces and mosques in Islamic cities influenced some Italians, especially Venetians. By the later 1400s the Portuguese were bringing back artworks and fabrics from West Africa and the Kongo that influenced European artists.

Moral and political corruption fostered decline of papal political power and the Roman Church. Some historians argue that power tends to corrupt and the greater the power the greater the corruption. This can apply to religious organizations as well as states. Church dissidents complained about the buying of church offices, favoritism to relatives, and the absenteeism of bishops who served more than one diocese to collect extra revenue. Detractors of Cardinal Wolsey, archbishop of both Canterbury and York in England, claimed that he entered the cathedral at York only once, for his funeral. Skeptics also viewed practices such as venerating holy relics and making pilgrimages as superstition that encouraged fraud, while defenders argued that relics and pilgrimages gave people something tangible to cling to when seeking God's help.

Papal prestige declined after popes moved to Avignon in southern France (1309–1377). Avignon popes required that candidates for bishop pay a large sum to the papal treasury, hence reserving high church offices for the wealthy. When the papacy finally returned to Rome, two men claimed to be the rightful pope, with Europeans picking sides. Before this "Great Schism" (1378–1417) ended, it badly damaged the papacy's prestige. After a bishop's council tried to replace papal monarchy with church government by such councils, popes refused to call councils on church reform.

Renaissance ("Rebirth") A dramatic flowering in arts and learning that began in the Italian city-states around 1350 and spread through Europe through the 1500s.

humanism The name for the European Renaissance philosophy, which emphasized humanity, worldly concerns, and reason rather than religious ideals.

Along with church criticism, imported ideas and products contributed to the dramatic flowering of arts and learning, later known as the **Renaissance**, or "rebirth." The Renaissance began in Italian city-states around 1350 and intensified through the 1400s and 1500s, spreading to other societies. In Florence, artists and thinkers rediscovered Classical Greek and Roman ideas. Renaissance philosophy, called **humanism**, emphasized humanity, worldly concerns, and reason rather than religious ideals. The books of Dante Alighieri (**DAHN-tay ah-lee-GYEH-ree**) (1265–1321), especially *The Divine Comedy*, attacked the pope and promoted vernacular language, in this case Italian, rather than Latin. Painters in Italy, such as Sandro Botticelli (**SAHN-dro BOT-i-CHEL-ee**) (1445–1510), and in the Netherlands depicted space and the human figure realistically. Some recent studies have argued that women played a much more prominent role in the resurgence than often recognized, both as creative artists and as patrons of art and literature. For example, Isabella d'Este (1474–1539) was one of the key cultural and political figures of the Italian Renaissance as an art patron and innovative fashion leader for aristocratic and court women in Italy and France. Scholars debate whether the Renaissance undermined medieval worldviews by fostering individualism, secularism, and scientific inquiry or was mainly a cultural movement among a small, privileged elite with little impact on the larger society. Nonetheless, Renaissance artists and writers emphasized tolerance of diverse views and new ideals of beauty, weakening church influence. The Renaissance eventually spread into northern Europe in the 1500s.

Extraordinary technological development, aided by imports from other regions, also characterized late medieval Europe. European scholars translated Arab and Greek scientific writings in Muslim Spain, while Asian and Muslim technologies that reached Europe, such as the Chinese spinning wheel and loom, improved textile manufacturing. During the 1300s and 1400s western Europeans also developed better ships, improving Chinese inventions such as the compass and sternpost rudder and adapting Arab lateen sails. By the 1490s, navigation, sailing, and weaponry advances gave Europeans mastery of the oceans. They also devised time-measuring devices, including mechanical clocks, that allowed people to control and standardize units of time.

Perhaps the most crucial invention, printing by movable type, allowed information to be produced and dispersed in unlimited quantities. Knowledge of Chinese woodblock printing and movable type made of clay and metal, invented centuries earlier (see Chapter 11), may have traveled the trade routes to Europe. By the 1400s Europeans used block printing for books and playing cards, and in 1455 the German goldsmith Johann Gutenberg (**yoh-HAHN GOO-ten-burg**) (1400–1468) introduced the first known metal movable type outside of East Asia, printing a Bible. The printed word became an essential medium of mass communication and no longer the monopoly of the few who could afford expensive hand-copied volumes, undermining both feudalism and the church.

Imported technology, especially Chinese gunpowder, made for more lethal warfare. By the 1200s, the Chinese had developed primitive guns capable of ejecting flame and projectiles 40 yards. This and other weapons, reaching Europe during the

Mongol era, were then improved, making warfare far deadlier than before. Gunpowder weapons, while killing many knights and nobles in wars, also gave Europeans a huge military advantage over societies that did not have them, including those in sub-Saharan Africa and the Americas.

14-4d Population and Economic Growth

Increased agricultural development spurred a population increase of 40 to 50 percent between the tenth and fourteenth centuries, the world's highest rate. After the Black Death, Europe's population again increased rapidly, grain production doubled, and many peasants moved into eastern Europe to open lands.

Commerce also expanded. Under feudalism and manorialism, merchants mostly dealt in luxury goods for the aristocracy. Indeed, the feudal ethic opposed wealth accumulation and devalued merchants. By the 1300s, however, this feudal ethic was breaking down. As foreign trade expanded, commerce became part of everyday life. Venetian merchants, who had trading posts all around the Middle East and Black Sea, and Genoans distributed valuable spices from India and Southeast Asia. The vast quantity of merchandise, mostly from the East, in fifteenth-century Venice awed observers:

> It seems as if the whole world flocks here. Who could count the many shops so well furnished that they seem almost warehouses, with so many cloths of every make—tapestry, brocades, carpets of every sort, silks of every kind; and so many warehouses full of spices, groceries and rugs. These things stupefy the beholder.[20]

West African gold, used in coins, treasuries, and jewelry, also stimulated the economy. European merchants borrowed and used Arab trading practices and mathematics. In the early 1200s Fibonacci (fee-bo-NACH-ee), a merchant from Pisa in Italy, wrote of the Arab and Indian numerals and calculations he studied in Algeria, Egypt, and Syria. Soon Venice, Genoa, and Florence adopted his mathematical and commercial innovations.

Unlike centralized China or the Ottoman Empire, western European cities, located in a politically fragmented region, enjoyed growing political power and were able to bargain with kings for advantages and autonomy. In 1241 various north German cities and towns expanded a trade alliance, the Hanseatic (han-see-AT-ik) League, that eventually included at various times some 165-200 member cities and many trade guilds, including some in Holland, Poland, and as far northeast as Estonia, making it one of the most successful trading blocs in history. It dominated Baltic trade and also controlled its own army and navy, making it almost an independent political power. The League's innovative methods seemed almost modern and included information-sharing, lines of credit, and a kind of court of appeals for disputes. Somewhat like a much smaller, more limited, and less integrated version of the European Union today, it facilitated the flow of commodities like cloth, luxury goods, timber, corn, grain, and fish between societies in the Mediterranean region, northern Europe, and eastern Europe. However, although the League endured into the 1600s it's influence waned after 1500 as states became more powerful, religious hostilities and wars fostered instability, new Asian and American trade opportunities arose, and Dutch, Italian, and southern German trading groups became more competitive. These developments gave European merchants a status and power unique in the world. While Chinese merchants, who were often prosperous, had a low ranking in the Confucian social system, were heavily taxed, and faced many restrictions, western European merchants steadily gained influence, becoming city political leaders. Governments now supported merchants and their interests, fostering a social and institutional structure that encouraged profits. Not everyone approved. The Dutch philosopher Erasmus complained about greed, asking, "When did avarice reign more largely and less punished?"[21] Nonetheless, late medieval Europeans sparked an economic revolution that fundamentally altered western European life in the 1500s and later spread its influences around the world.

14-4e The Portuguese and Maritime Exploration

In the 1400s a few Europeans, pushed by commercial growth and taking advantage of new maritime and military technologies, began to explore the world beyond Europe by sea. The Portuguese, only recently unified in a kingdom and with a standard of living probably lower than some Africans and Asians, began sailing south seeking slaves, African gold, and other trade goods. Motivated by a missionary desire to outflank Islam and spread Christianity, as well as a compelling appetite for plunder and conquest, they enjoyed the advantage of guns, better ships, and a maritime tradition. They also had a larger strategic purpose: finding a way around Africa and sailing directly to fabled Southeast Asia, the source of spices so valued in Europe. Finally, European legends about a great Christian emperor in Africa, "Prester John," perhaps derived from the Ethiopian king, suggested to the Portuguese that they could find a possible ally against Muslims.

Hence, in search of "Christians and spices," the Portuguese began systematically exploring the West African coast in 1420. Their efforts were sponsored by Prince Henry the Navigator (1394–1460), a shipbuilding design and cartography innovator. Soon Henry's caravels, small ships that could sail on the ocean and into shallow coastal waters and rivers, discovered Madeira (muh-DEER-uh) Island and the Azores (A-zorz) and Canary Islands in the Atlantic off North Africa. By the 1480s the Portuguese had visited much of Africa's coast as far south as Angola (see Chapter 12). In 1487 Portuguese ships led by Bartolomeu Dias (DEE-uhsh) reached the Indian Ocean, intensifying Portuguese interest both in Africa and the world to the east. One of the sailors manning Portuguese ships was a Genoese immigrant to Portugal, Christopher Columbus. Columbus had lived on Madeira, where he married the daughter of the wealthy Portuguese governor, and also had visited the Canary and

---

[20]Canon Pietro Casola, quoted in Ibid., 38.
[21]Quoted in Edith Simon, *The Reformation* (New York: Time-Life Books, 1966), 71.

Cape Verde islands, England, Ireland (where he noted two bodies with "strange features" that had washed ashore in Galway Bay), perhaps Iceland, and apparently the coast of West Africa as far south as today's Ghana. Familiar with the Atlantic winds and currents, Columbus later developed an alternative strategy for reaching the East. In 1492 Columbus, under Spanish sponsorship, sailed west across the Atlantic to the Americas, changing world history forever.

KEY POINTS

▶ The Black Death killed a third of Europe's people and reduced the power of western European nobles while increasing the power of eastern European nobles.

▶ French rulers increased their power in the Hundred Years War, England's Tudor dynasty later made England a world power, and Spanish Christians gradually drove out the Muslims, while in Germany and Italy the nobility remained strong.

▶ The church declined in power and prestige as it came to be seen as corrupt, and the papacy was weakened by the Great Schism.

▶ During the Renaissance, artists and writers rediscovered Classical influences and championed worldly concerns, individualism, and realism rather than spirituality.

▶ Major technological developments, influenced in part by ideas imported from China and the Muslim world, included the printing press, which further undermined the church, and guns, which killed many in European wars.

Chapter Summary

European societies changed dramatically between 600 and 1500. By mixing Greco-Roman, Christian, and Germanic legacies between 500 and 1000, western Europeans constructed new societies based on new values and practices. These societies also acquired knowledge from and traded with the Islamic world, especially Muslim Spain. The major medieval institutions of feudalism, manorialism, and the papacy generated conflict between popes and kings, kings and nobles, nobles and merchants, cities and countryside, and Christians and outsiders. The church played a crucial social and political role in European societies. Priests dominated village life, while popes fought heresy and spurred crusades against Muslims.

The social, political, economic, and religious systems of Byzantium were different from those in western Europe. The Byzantine emperors were more powerful and had more control over the church. Eventually the Byzantine Church broke completely with the Roman Church, becoming the Greek Orthodox Church. Byzantium also passed on many traditions to various eastern European societies such as the Russians. Russia later became a strong state with a rival Orthodox Church.

Western Europeans were linked by trade networks to other societies of Eurasia and North Africa. These networks, including those formed by the Mongol expansion, allowed the movement from east to west not only of valuable goods, technologies, and ideas but also of diseases such as the Black Death. Between 1300 and 1500 western European states grew larger and, in some cases, more centralized, the church faced decline as a political force, and warfare became more deadly. Sparked in part by Afro-Asian influences, the Renaissance fostered new humanistic ideas and artistic currents, while economic growth and social change enhanced the influence of merchants. In the fifteenth century, aided by Asian and Islamic seafaring technologies, western Europeans began exploring the world.

Key Terms

medieval 329
feudalism 336
vassals 336
benefices 336
fief 336
knights 336

chivalry 336
manorialism 336
serfs 337
guilds 337
usury 337
courtly love 339

excommunicate 339
simony 340
Holy Inquisition 340
Magna Carta 340
Renaissance 350
humanism 350

Eastern Predominance in the Intermediate World

For over two centuries the prosperous and powerful nations of North America and western Europe have dominated the world economically and politically, although not without serious challenge in recent decades from China, Japan, India, and Russia. But before 1500 the world looked very different, and various societies in Asia and North Africa were much stronger and more influential than they are today, while Europe may have largely been a backwater. Some Eastern societies enjoyed power and status far beyond their borders, helping to shape much of the Eastern Hemisphere in these centuries. However, historians debate to what degree we can consider this to have been an era of Eastern predominance in Afro-Eurasia.

The Problem

Over the past two decades some historians have made the argument that from a world history perspective the rise of the West was not a long and gradual process of European advances while the rest of the world stood still. Instead, they contend that the rise to influence and prosperity of the East, especially China, India, and various Islamic societies, was a major theme of the Intermediate Era or Global Middle Ages. In their view, for most of these centuries, these Eastern peoples developed and often sustained more dynamic governments, productive economies, advanced science, and creative technologies than any other societies until around 1500, and a few (especially China) for even longer. In this era the Chinese invented paper, printing, gunpowder, the mariner's compass, paper currency, and the blast furnace while Muslim thinkers forged a great cultural synthesis bringing together ideas from Persia, India, China, Greece, and Rome. Europe remained well behind the Eastern leaders before finally surpassing them by 1700 or 1800. Hence, the "rise of the West" was a recent phenomenon, resulting partly from borrowing ideas, institutions, and technologies from other societies, especially the East. Other historians disagree, contending that after 1000 the advantage shifted to western Europeans, who laid the foundations for rapid growth and eventual world dominance. These arguments are part of a vigorous scholarly debate.

The Debate

Marco Polo was not the first Westerner to travel to Asia and return to Europe with amazing stories about a world that may have far exceeded Europe in its communication, science, military weapons (gunpowder), technology (movable-type printing), commercial life, and perhaps even arts and architecture. Many historians identify Eastern predominance in the Global Middle Ages, but they disagree on which society made the greatest contributions to the world. The largest number point to China as the Eurasian leader in the Intermediate Era and offer a variety of factors to explain China's status. S. A. M.

Adshead places the innovative and cosmopolitan Tang China at center stage in the world economy and considers it the world's best-ordered state between 600 and 900. William McNeill identifies Chinese predominance especially from 1000 to 1500, with China as the engine of the Eurasian economy. Various historians of Asia, among them Rhoads Murphey, describe a dynamic and creative Song dynasty China enjoying many of the conditions that, in the later eighteenth century, fostered industrialization in northwest Europe: urbanization, commercialization, widening local and overseas markets, rising demand, and mechanical invention. Mary Matossian labels the entire Intermediate Era the "Chinese Millennium," when China was more populous, productive, and wealthy than any other society, enjoying an orderly society and advanced technology.

Many world historians agree that Chinese innovations and commercial expansion energized Eurasian trade and contributed much to the Intermediate world. British scholar Robert Temple credits the Chinese with inventing modern agriculture, shipping, astronomical observatories, oil industries, paper money, decimal mathematics, wheelbarrows, fishing reels, multistage rockets, guns, umbrellas, hot-air balloons, chess, whiskey, and even the essential design of the steam engine. Without Chinese naval technology, he and others argue, Columbus would never have sailed to America. China and India were the two great centers of world manufacturing before 1500, their exports fueling Afro-Eurasian trade.

But China was not the only Asian powerhouse and great source of knowledge. Indians fostered two universal religions, Buddhism and Hinduism, while inventing and exporting scientific, technological, and agricultural techniques to China, the Islamic world, and later Europe in a process historian Lynda Shaffer terms "southernization." Such innovations as Indian granulated sugar crystals, the decimal system, "Arabic" numerals, and cotton plants had revolutionary implications for Eurasia. Other historians, such as Marshall Hodgson and Richard Eaton, argue for the centrality of the Islamic societies, contending that, before 1600, Islamic culture and economy were the world's most expansive, influential, and integrating force. Hodgson treated Europe as a "promontory" on the margins of what he termed the Afro-Eurasian complex. Islam was cosmopolitan, egalitarian, and flexible, allowing Muslims to rebound from the Mongol conquests and Black Death and reestablish powerful states such as Ottoman Turkey. British scholar Jerry Brotton has shown that modern Europe emerged between 1400 and 1600 during the Renaissance (which he views as a global experience) by exchanging ideas and commodities with the marketplace or bazaar of the Islamic eastern Mediterranean, especially of the Ottomans.

Still other historians think China, India, and Islam were all powerhouses in an Eastern-dominated Intermediate world. Stewart Gordon writes that, while European cultural, commercial, and intellectual life stagnated in the Global Middle Ages, Asia flourished as the world's epicenter of diplomacy and commerce, the wellspring of science, philosophy, and religion, and the axis of vast intercontinental networks of activity. Jack Goldstone emphasizes Asia's greater agricultural productivity, more refined craftsmanship, and larger variety of products from tea and spices to silk and cotton fabrics. Robert Marks argues that the Eastern Hemisphere in the 1300s and 1400s had three centers, with dynamic but linked regional systems based on China, India, and Islam. From Ottoman Turkey eastward to Japan, agricultural efficiency, consumer goods, social welfare, and civilian and military technology were generally the equal of, and often superior to, European counterparts. British scholar John Hobson believes that the rise of a dynamic East made possible the later rise of the West, the era's globalization allowing advanced Eastern inventions to flow westward, where they were gradually assimilated by Europe. Andre Gunder Frank argues that by 1400 Asian and Muslim traders dominated a global economy centered on the Indian Ocean, producing the vast majority of the world's economic output. Many historians describe Europe in this era as economically weak, with small, insignificant states, and not showing renewed vigor until 1400. Nor did Europe have, as some historians suggest, any unique cultural advantages. British anthropologist Jack Goody concludes that there were few decisive cultural differences between East and West in rationality, economic tools, family patterns, and political pluralism. In his view, the Bronze Age urban revolution, affecting China, India, and western Asia well before Europe, fostered a long-term exchange of information between East and West that generated alternating periods of dominance.

Other scholars, doubting that any Eastern societies had a great advantage in this era, strongly contend that medieval Europe was not backward compared to China, India, or Islam. David Landes, while conceding that Europe was well behind China and Islam in many areas of life in 1000, suggests that things had changed considerably five hundred years later. With many cultural and geographical advantages, Europeans, argues Landes, caught up to the East with the growth of manufacturing and trade. Landes and others describe an inventive Europe with impressive technological progress using increased nonhuman power, especially in agriculture. Joel Mokyr calls China's failure to maintain its technological supremacy the greatest enigma in the history of technology, describing a stagnation after 1400. Toby Huff favorably contrasts European science with its Chinese counterpart, especially after 1200, when restless human energy, influential merchants, and competing states made late medieval Europe dynamic. Ricardo Duchesne stresses liberal democratic culture as crucial to the rise of the West, and Rodney Stark credits the medieval Catholic Church's emphasis on reason and belief in progress for fostering economic growth, asserting that these ideas were lacking in other religions, a view many scholars have challenged. Landes and Huff also dismissed the notion of Eastern leadership, perceiving China by 1450 as overpopulated, intellectually dormant, indifferent

Vassal bringing their tributes to the Tang court, c.600–673 (ink & colour on silk)/Yan Liben (d.673) (attr. to) /DE AGOSTINI EDITORE/Bibliotheque Nationale, Paris, France/Bridgeman Images

IMAGE 14.8 **The Tang Tributary System** This satirical painting by Yan Liben (600–673) portrays representatives from vassal states bringing tribute to the Tang court.

Q What does the painting tell us about the artist's attitude toward the emperor, foreign envoys, and the tribute system?

to technology, negating commercial success, and resistant to change. Some historians of China, such as Adshead, concur that the balance of power was shifting toward Europe in the later Intermediate Era.

If several Eastern societies, and especially China, may have had some advantages and great power during much of the Intermediate Era, they lost their status between 1450 and 1800, raising the question of when and how the East declined. Some historians believe the decline of the East preceded and made possible the rise of the West. Janet Abu-Lughod describes a well-integrated hemispheric system linking Afro-Eurasia by trade for several centuries, with no single country dominant. This network declined after 1350, reducing Europe's commercial competition. Other historians blame Eastern decline on the Mongols and their heirs, who devastated western Asia and North India and ended the creative Song dynasty.

Historian L. S. Stavrianos credits what he termed the "Law of the Retarding Lead"—that nothing fails like success—for undermining China and helping underdeveloped Europe. This concept holds that the best-adapted, most successful societies have the most difficulty in changing and retaining their lead in a period of transition, losing their dynamic thrust. Conversely, less successful societies are more likely to eventually adapt and forge ahead. Hence, he argues, in the 1400s China still had an edge, with an advanced technology, efficient government, great regional power, and the world's largest commercial economy. Because these advantages seemed to work so well, they gave China a stake in preserving rather than dramatically altering its system. Indeed, some argue that the leading Eastern societies, especially China, remained successful until overtaken by a rising West between 1600 and 1800. Perhaps the leading Western nations today have suffered from a retarding lead as various "hungry" eastern societies race to catch up.

Evaluating the Debate

China, India, and the Islamic world were the major poles of global trade and technological innovation for much of this era, at least before the 1400s, but any Eastern advantage was eventually lost. We are left with tantalizing questions. What if the Mongols or Ottomans had conquered some of western Europe, or Ming admiral Zheng He had continued his voyages and headed all the way to West Africa, Europe, or the Americas? Had they occurred, these Mongol, Ottoman, or Chinese achievements might have created a world unrecognizable to us today. Perhaps China, with many prerequisites already in place and enriched by greater trade with West Africa and Europe, might have sparked an industrial revolution centuries ahead of England. It did not happen, however. Humanity stood at a crossroads in the middle of the millennium, poised between several very different futures. During the next several centuries Europe gradually forged

ahead—what some historians call "the rise of the West"—partly by assimilating Eastern technologies and science, while the Islamic societies, India, and finally China struggled, making the world after 1500 very different from the world before it. But in recent years, as the U.S. and Europe have experienced economic and political problems, China and India have borrowed ideas and technology from the West to industrialize, supply consumer goods, and challenge the West for predominance, symbolized by China's New Silk Road, the Belt and Road Initiative, to spread Chinese power and influence in the world.

Exploring the Controversy

Among books making the case for Eastern predominance and leadership are John M. Hobson, *The Eastern Origins of Western Civilisation* (New York: Cambridge University Press, 2004); Robert B. Marks, *The Origins of the Modern World: A Global and Ecological Narrative*, 3rd ed. (Lanham, MD: Rowman and Littlefield, 2015); Jack Goldstone, *Why Europe?: The Rise of the West in World History, 1500–1850* (Boston: McGraw-Hill, 2009); Stewart Gordon, *When Asia Was the World: Traveling Merchants, Scholars, Warriors, and Monks Who Created the "Riches of the East"* (Philadelphia: Da Capo Press, 2008); Andre Gunder Frank, *Reorient: Global Economy in the Asian Age* (Berkeley: University of California Press, 1998); and Jack Goody, *The East in the West* (Cambridge, UK: Cambridge University Press, 1996) and *The Eurasian Miracle* (Cambridge, UK: Polity Press, 2010). On China as the major power, see S. A. M. Adshead, *Tang China: The Rise of the East in World History* (New York: Palgrave, 2004); William H. McNeill, *The Pursuit of Power: Technology, Armed Force, and Society Since A.D. 1000* (Chicago: University of Chicago Press, 1982); Rhoads Murphey, *East Asia: A New History*, 4th ed. (New York: Pearson, 2007); Mary Kilbourne Matossian, *Shaping World History: Breakthroughs in Ecology, Technology, Science, and Politics* (Armonk, NY: M.E. Sharpe, 1997); and Robert Temple, *The Genius of China: 3,000 Years of Science, Discovery and Invention* (London: Prion Books, 1986). For Indian and Islamic influence, see Lynda Shaffer, "Southernization," *Journal of World History* 5, no. 1 (Spring 1994): 1–22; Marshall Hodgson, *Rethinking World History* (Cambridge, UK: Cambridge University Press, 1993); Edmund Burke III and Robert J. Mankin, eds., *Islam and World History: The Venture of Marshall Hodgson* (Chicago: University of Chicago Press, 2018); Richard Eaton, *Islamic History as Global History* (Washington, DC: American Historical Association, 1993); and Jerry Brotton, *The Renaissance Bazaar: From the Silk Road to Michelangelo* (New York: Oxford University Press, 2002). Among books that argue for European superiority are Toby E. Huff, *The Rise of Early Modern Science: Islam, China, and the West* (Cambridge, UK: Cambridge University Press, 1993); David S. Landes, *The Wealth and Power of*

Nations: Why Some Are So Rich and Some Are So Poor (New York: Norton, 1998); Joel Mokyr, *The Lever of Riches: Technological Creativity and Economic Progress* (New York: Oxford University Press, 1990); Ricardo Duchesne, *The Uniqueness of Western Civilization* (Boston: Brill, 2011); and Rodney Stark, *The Victory of Reason: How Christianity Led to Freedom, Capitalism, and Western Success* (New York: Random House, 2005). For broader studies of the rise and demise of the East, see Janet L. Abu-Lughod, *Before European Hegemony: The World System A.D. 1250–1350* (New York: Oxford University Press, 1989); Jonathan Daly, *Historians Debate the Rise of the West* (New York: Routledge, 2015); and Ian Morris, *Why the West Rules—For Now: The Patterns of History and What They Reveal About the Future* (New York: Picador, 2010).

Reflection Questions

1. Why do some historians emphasize China as the predominant power in this era?
2. What role did India and the Islamic societies play in the Intermediate world?
3. What points support the argument that Europe began its rise to world power in this era?
4. Why do you think that historians today might have strong views on this topic?

Connecting the Early Modern World, 1450–1750

In 1552 a Spanish historian called the landing in the Americas by a naval expedition led by Christopher Columbus "the greatest event since the creation of the world."[1] It was a claim that ignored many previous achievements, yet the permanent connecting of the hemispheres that followed Columbus in fact reshaped the world, helping to make the Early Modern Era vastly different from the Intermediate Era that preceded it. While Columbus searched for a "new world," his son found one in books. In the early 1500s Hernando Colon, the illegitimate but remarkable son of Columbus, acquired many thousands of books in many languages including Arabic and Ethiopian Ge'ez, probably the largest personal library in history to that time and a treasure-trove of information about the world and times he lived in. Colon had traveled with his father to America and widely around Europe and the Mediterranean world, acquiring a love for books, the written word, and intellectual exchange. Colon hired a staff of multilingual librarians to catalogue and summarize each volume in his vast collection. Eventually, after his death in 1539, the collection was lost to time but a recently rediscovered two-thousand-page handwritten book summarizing the library contents offers a vivid picture of Europe and the world during the transition between the late Middle Ages and the globalizing Early Modern world.

History was now painted on a larger canvas, and peoples' horizons around the world rapidly expanded. In this new global age, greatly increased communication and mobility resulted in encounters, some friendly, others hostile, between societies once remote from each other, as travel and exploration revealed the resources of the inhabited world. The exchange among societies of people, diseases, ideas, technologies, capital, resources, and products now occurred on a greater scale than ever before. Europeans forged a new world economy, while disrupting, changing, and sometimes destroying many of the societies they encountered, especially in the Americas and parts of Africa and Southeast Asia. Because of the growing contacts spanning the two hemispheres, for the first time in history an interconnected world became a reality. The links forged during the Early Modern Era laid a foundation for the building, often by force, of an even more integrated global system in the Modern Era.

New Empires and Military Power

TRANSITIONS

Increasing wealth and power, as well as more deadly weapons, allowed some Early Modern societies to build large empires that helped them acquire vast resources without relying chiefly on trade. In Eurasia Qing China, Mughal India, and the Ottomans had enormous empires and were the world's most formidable states. The Portuguese conquered the first global empire (in Africa, South Asia, Southeast Asia, and South America) and have been credited with laying the foundation for today's age of globalization. Gunpowder, an earlier Chinese invention, had spread as far west as Europe by 1241 CE. Historians characterize most of these new empires as "gunpowder empires" because they depended on bigger and better gunpowder weapons, including cannon mounted on ships, field artillery, and guns used by individual soldiers. Gunpowder empires dominated Eurasia and the Americas. Only a few European countries, however, had the means, including sea power, to envision dominating very distant societies in Africa, the Americas, Asia, and the Pacific in their quest for "gold, god, and glory."

As they spread around Eurasia and North Africa, gunpowder weapons changed warfare. In Europe—full of

[1]Francisco Lopez de Gomara, quoted in Roger Schlesinger, *In the Wake of Columbus: The Impact of the New World on Europe, 1492–1650* (Wheeling, IL: Harlan Davidson, 1996), 23.

competitive, often hostile states—no ruler had a monopoly on weapons. Hence rulers had an incentive to constantly improve their armaments, and as they did, the wars in Europe became far more deadly. The European powers used some of their weapons against each other. For example, the Dutch and Portuguese were bitter rivals for influence and territory in southern Asia and Brazil. With better ships and weapons, Europeans controlled Atlantic shipping and also gained considerable power over Indian Ocean trade, which brought them great wealth. As the English adventurer Sir Walter Raleigh recognized in 1608, "Who so commands the sea commands the trade of the world; who so commands the trade of the world commands the riches of the world."[2] But their floating flotillas of war ships armed with cannons gave Europeans more advantages at sea and at trading ports like Melaka, Kilwa, or Goa than against the well-armed Asian empires.

The maritime expansion of Europe contrasted sharply with that of the Chinese. Just as western Europeans turned outward and developed a naval technology to match that of the Chinese, the Chinese pulled back from their grand maritime expeditions of the early 1400s and turned inward, although some Chinese merchants continued to venture out to trade. China enjoyed huge budget surpluses until the late 1700s and did not need colonies or foreign trade to prosper. Moreover, the Chinese government often viewed merchants as a threat, whereas western European merchants had the support of their governments, especially in England, the Netherlands, Spain, and France. The resulting political competition between European states fostered exploration and colonization.

Unlike Europeans, Asians took the development of their gunpowder arsenals only so far. The land-oriented Mughals ruling much of India saw little gain in developing naval armaments. With gunpowder weapons, the Qing dynasty greatly expanded China's land frontier deep into Central Asia and Tibet, thereby stabilizing their border regions. After that, secure in their power, the Qing emperors had little need to increase their offensive capability or challenge the Europeans in the oceans. A Chinese military manual published in 1644 concluded that "nothing has more range than the Ottoman musket. The next best is the European one."[3] Chinese firearms were adequate for ejecting the Dutch from Taiwan and the Russians from the Amur Valley in the 1600s, but two centuries later, European military technology far surpassed that of Asian powers, dramatically changing the hemispheric balance of power.

A Polycentric World

SOCIETIES

Despite the growth of empires, the Early Modern world had varied centers of political and economic power, a situation known as polycentrism. No one country or region could dominate all other rivals. European power was on the rise but remained limited in much of Asia, the Middle East, and large parts of Africa and the Americas, and the Pacific remained untouched by European exploration. For much of the era,

the Ottoman Empire, Mughal India, and China were more politically, economically, and culturally influential in Eurasia than European societies. For example, many Muslims admired Mughal India, which became a destination for merchants, writers, and religious scholars. Hence, a Persian poet proclaimed: "Great is India, the Mecca of all in need. A journey to India is of essence to any man made worthy by knowledge and skill."[4]

The era was dynamic for many peoples. Across Eurasia varied societies experienced economic innovation, free markets, industrialization, and rising living standards. For example, cities such as Amsterdam in Holland, Isfahan (**is-fah-HAHN**) in Persia, and Ayuthia (**uh-YUT-uh-yuh**) in Siam were bustling trade crossroads, attracting merchants from all over Eurasia. Foreign merchants, such as the Dutch, Chinese, and Persians at Ayuthia, had to adapt to local customs to succeed. Sometimes, as in Siam, Tokugawa Japan, and Morocco, Europeans who disregarded local customs or threatened local governments were expelled.

The encounters between peoples fostered compromises and information exchange. Many Asians and Africans adapted ideas from other cultures to meet their own needs. Similarly, Spanish rule in the Americas survived only because the conquerors ultimately made compromises with Native American societies, including intermarriage. In the Spanish empire, as well as in other empires of the era such as the Ottoman and Mughal, laws recognized local customs, and different groups often maintained their own legal codes.

Science and technology remained creative all over Eurasia. The Chinese and British, for example, published important scientific books and invented new technologies, especially for the textile industry. New astronomical observatories were built in China, India, and the Middle East, although Europeans had by now developed a much keener interest than Asians in clocks and mathematics. Japan's fostering of schools gave it the world's highest literacy rate and an audience for a publishing industry. In addition, leaders of the European Renaissance, Reformation, and Enlightenment, Sufi mystics in the Ottoman and Mughal Empires, the Hindu bhakti (**BUK-tee**) movement in India, and some Chinese thinkers challenged accepted wisdom. Various European and Chinese philosophers emphasized reason, as did some Latin Americans. Indeed, some participants in the European Enlightenment were inspired by their growing knowledge of China, which was ruled by emperors who dabbled in philosophy. A French ambassador in 1688 praised Qing China for promoting "virtue, wisdom, prudence, good faith, sincerity, charity, gentleness, honesty [and] civility."[5]

The Emerging World Economy

NETWORKS

With the opening of the Atlantic and Pacific Oceans to regular sea travel, connections spanning not just hemispheres but also the entire world were forged during the Early Modern Era.

---

[2]Quoted in Peter J. Hugill, *World Trade Since 1430: Geography, Technology, and Capitalism* (Baltimore: Johns Hopkins University Press, 1993), vii.
[3]Quoted in Kenneth Chase, *Firearms: A Global History to 1700* (New York: Cambridge University Press, 2003), 2.
[5]Quoted in Gregory Blue, "China and Western Social Thought in the Modern Period," in *China and Historical Capitalism*, ed. Timothy Brook and Gregory Blue (New York: Cambridge University Press, 1999), 64.
[4]Quoted in Roger Savory, *Iran Under the Safavids* (Cambridge, UK: Cambridge University Press, 1980), 205.

But, as with politics, these connections produced a polycentric structure in which both Europeans and Asians played important roles. Thanks to maritime expansion, western Europeans gradually created a global network of economic and political relationships that increasingly shaped the destinies of people around the world. Rather than the luxuries of earlier times, such as silks and spices, long-distance trade increasingly moved bulk items: essential natural resources, such as sugar and silver from the Americas, and manufactured goods, such as textiles from Europe and Asia. As traders moved commodities and capital faster and more cheaply over greater distances than ever before, western Europeans became the main beneficiaries of the increased communication and travel that shaped a gradual globalization of trade. Yet, European merchants were actually only a small part of global commerce; some Asian and African merchant groups also flourished, and some Asian states, particularly China and Siam, benefited from the increasing trade.

The capitalist market economy that gradually developed was increasingly centered on northwestern Europe, especially England and the Netherlands, but a half dozen other European countries were also enriched by trade (see Map IV.1). For example, the Portuguese as well as the Dutch established regular maritime trade routes between Europe and Asia around Africa that allowed Europeans to avoid the overland routes through the Middle East, in the process harming their Muslim rivals by diminishing Persian and Ottoman commerce. The huge quantities of silver provided by the Spanish conquest of the Americas financed expansion of the European economy and, since Asian governments, especially China, valued silver, gave Europeans access to Asian markets. The Spanish establishment of a base at Manila in 1571 provided an essential economic link between eastern Eurasia and the Americas, forging a major foundation for a truly world economy and a more complex form of globalization. The discovery of a practical and less dangerous sea route across the Pacific proved a catalyst for integrating the planet. What was called "the Silver Way" because silver from Spanish America was sent to China to pay for Asian silks, tea, and other coveted products, built the basis for the first global currency. For many decades, the Spanish silver dollar greased the wheels of world trade. Much of the silver came from the Spanish colonial mining city of Potosi, 13,000 feet high in the Bolivian Andes, a center of wealth but also of pollution, crime, and brutality that some historians call the "first global city." In its main market plaza Andean and African women served maize beer and hot soup while shops displayed the world's best silk, porcelain, linen fabrics, Venetian glassware, Japanese lacquerware, Flemish paintings, and books in many languages.

But the transition to a European-dominated trading system took place over several centuries in Asia. Before the 1800s, when the transition was completed, Asia still boasted the bulk of world economic activity. The industries of China and India remained the twin pillars of Asian commerce well into the 1700s, and as late as 1775 Asians produced some 80 percent of goods. Many Asian societies imported raw materials from India (including raw cotton), China (especially silk), and Japan (copper) for production into exportable consumer goods. For example, Javanese women used beeswax and dyes to transform Indian cloth into beautiful batik clothing. The economies of India and China dwarfed those of any other country. The most economically developed regions within China, Japan, India, and northwestern Europe may have enjoyed roughly comparable standards of living, including health and income levels. (See Historical Controversy: The Great Divergence between Europe and Asia).

Asian merchants, enjoying lower overhead and shrewd business skills, could often outcompete those from Europe and also traded over long distances. In the 1600s, for example, Arab and Persian traders remained influential at the main Mughal port, Surat, while north Indian merchants were found all over the Persian Gulf and East Africa. Many wealthy Asian trading magnates had huge capital resources. The trader Virji Vohra (VEER-gee VOOR-ah) in Surat was as rich as Europe's wealthiest merchant family, the Fuggers in Germany. A European visitor to Goa in 1510 was amazed at the competition provided by fabulously rich Indian and Arab merchants: "We [Europeans] believe ourselves to be the most astute men that one can encounter, and the people here surpass in everything. And they can do better calculations by memory than we can do with the pen."[6] European merchants competed best in Asia when they were supported by military force. Moreover, European–Asian trade relations often favored Asians. Since Asians had little interest in European manufactured goods such as clothing, which they considered inferior in quality to their own goods, Europeans bought Asian goods and resources such as Chinese tea with American silver and gold. Vast amounts of American silver ended up in China, where it served as the basis of the monetary system and promoted economic growth. Meanwhile, Asian goods such as Indian textiles found a ready market around the world. Chinese goods transported from the Philippines were so much cheaper than Spanish ones in Peru that the Spanish viceroy complained it was "impossible to choke off the trade since a man can clothe his wife in Chinese silks for 25 pesos, whereas he could not provide her with clothing of Spanish silks with 200 pesos."[7]

Expanding Trade Networks

NETWORKS

The growth of long-distance trade corresponded to the expansion of trade networks operated by different commercial communities. The rise of European power allowed Dutch, English, and French merchants to establish themselves in South Asia, Southeast Asia, West Africa, eastern Europe, Russia, and the Caribbean Basin. Sephardic Jews, originally from Iberia, spread their trading networks throughout western Europe as well as in parts of South America, the Caribbean, and the Indian Ocean.

This growing commercial activity stimulated production for the market in mining and manufacturing but especially

---

[6]Quoted in Patricia Risso, *Merchants and Faith: Muslim Commerce and Culture in the Indian Ocean* (Boulder, CO: Westview Press, 1995), 96.
[7]Quoted in Robert B. Marks, *The Origins of the Modern World: A Global and Ecological Narrative* (Lanham, MD: Rowman and Littlefield, 2002), 81.

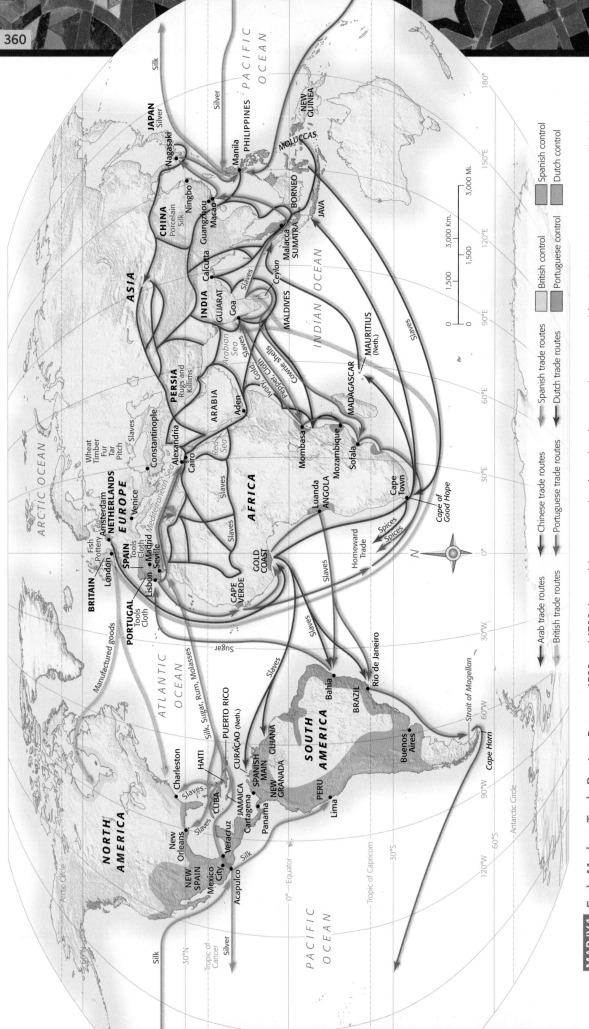

MAP IV.1 Early Modern Trade Routes Between 1500 and 1700 the world economy developed and new trade routes proliferated. Major maritime routes linked Asia and the Americas across the Pacific; Europe, Asia, and the Americas across the Atlantic; and eastern and southern Asia with Africa and Europe across the Indian Ocean.

Q What does the map tell us about trade routes and the products shipped over each of the routes?

DEA/G. DAGLI ORTI/De Agostini/Getty Images

IMAGE IV.1 **Dutch Diplomats** In this print, a Dutch delegation, eager to make an alliance with the Kongolese against the Portuguese, prostrate themselves before the Kongolese king, sitting on his throne under an imported chandelier, in 1642.

Q What can we learn from this painting about the Kongo king and royal court and the expectations for foreign envoys?

in tropical agriculture. The highly profitable plantations that sprung up around the Caribbean Basin, along the Atlantic coast of North and South America, and in the Philippines reflected the expansion of production. A growing trans-Atlantic slave trade from Africa provided cheap labor to the American plantations, enabling them to produce inexpensive calories for Europe in the form of sugar and, after 1700, abundant cotton for English textile mills. Slaves from various places also labored for Muslim enterprises in the Middle East and for European operations in southern Africa and Southeast Asia.

Groups specializing in trade were prominent in many lands. Traders of French or mixed French and Native American descent traveled deep into the North American continent contacting local peoples. Omani Arabs had a leading role in East African trade, while Muslim Hausa and Dyula Mandinka merchants traded in West Africa. Chinese remained active all over Southeast Asia, establishing permanent settlements in many cities and towns. For example, the Spanish in the Philippines depended on the large Chinese merchant class to supply many consumer goods. The Indian maritime trade network stretched westward to the Middle East and Northeast Africa and east to Southeast Asia and China. Meanwhile, South Asian overland trade networks extended across Central Asia, Afghanistan, Tibet, Persia, the Caucasus states, and much of Russia. Armenian merchants based in Persia flourished in the overland trade from India to Central Asia and the Middle East and from Persia to Russia, England, and the Baltic.

Environmental Changes

TRANSITIONS

Between 1300 and 1850 much of the world experienced a fluctuating "Little Ice Age," probably caused by a dimming sun and increased volcanic activity, that had significant consequences for many societies. In North America and Eurasia, this period brought cool temperatures, shorter growing seasons, and famine. For example, in the 1600s China often received either too much rain, which caused widespread flooding, or too little rain and late springs, which produced drought and reduced the growing season to allow for only one crop of rice rather than two. The lands bordering the North Atlantic saw much colder and wetter conditions, which diminished agricultural production and resulted in widespread starvation in much of Europe. Indeed, harsh weather conditions, combined with occasional outbreaks of bubonic plague, may have been one of the factors that spurred Europeans to seek new lands abroad. Climate change also affected tropical regions. For instance, West Africa had abundant rain until 1700, when rainfall began diminishing, allowing desert to claim much of the Sahel and pushing savannah farming southward by several hundred miles.

No environmental changes were more far-reaching than those resulting from European explorers and colonizers in the Americas and around the world. Several controversial 2019 studies contend that the colonization of the Americas in the 1500s–1600s, which resulted in massive mortality for Native American peoples and increasing migrations to the Americas by Europeans and Africans, also helped cool the world climate substantially as abandoned agricultural land reverted to forests and grasslands, lowering global surface temperatures and diminishing atmospheric carbon dioxide. The studies suggest that, because of this instability, the Anthropocene, a term or label used today by many scientists to describe the geologic era during which humans have had far more massive impacts on the earth than ever before, may have started not with the rise of industrialization in the nineteenth century or the nuclear era in the mid-twentieth, the mainstream view, but as far back as the beginning of the seventeenth century.

Nonetheless, despite the poor weather, the distribution of new food sources and other resources was widening. Seaborne trade, especially from the Americas, also provided valuable resources, especially to coastal maritime states such as the Netherlands and Britain. The increased diffusion of resources fostered population growth. Indeed, American crops such as the potato helped Europe stave off even worse climate-related famines. Around the world the expansion of farming to sustain more people came at the expense of shifting cultivators, pastoralists, and food collectors, some of whom were killed or died off.

Partly because of the spread of food crops, especially from the Americas to Afro-Eurasia, world population increased significantly, from around 500 million to 750 million; China and India accounted for about half the total. Growth put severe pressure on land and resources. Expanding settlements and farming in frontier regions displaced woodlands, grasslands, and wetlands and reduced the variety of plant and animal life. As they had for millennia, people tapped the earth for underground resources, such as coal and iron ore. For farming and light industries, Early Modern economies relied chiefly on traditional power sources, such as people, animals, water, and wind.

The Exchange of Diseases, Animals, and Crops

NETWORKS

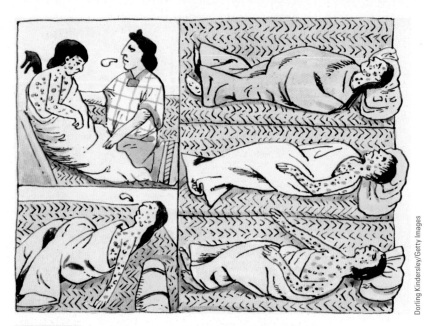

IMAGE IV.2 **Smallpox Victims in the Americas** Eurasian diseases accompanied the Europeans to the Americas, causing a catastrophic loss of life for the Native Americans, who had no immunity. As shown in this print from the 1500s, millions of people sickened and died from smallpox.

Dorling Kindersley/Getty Images

Q How does the painting portray smallpox and the victims?

As people in this era, especially Europeans and Africans, moved voluntarily or involuntarily to distant lands, they deliberately or accidentally brought with them species of animals, insects, bacteria, and plants that reshaped local ecosystems. These biological invasions, an important part of what historians have termed the Columbian Exchange, particularly accompanied the encounter between Afro-Eurasia and the Americas. The European settlers in the Americas brought with them horses and food animals—pigs, chickens, sheep, and cattle—while ships returning to Europe carried with them American turkeys, which enriched Eurasian diets.

The exchange of diseases between the Eastern and Western Hemispheres had a greater impact on the Americas than on Eurasia and Africa. Native Americans had never experienced and hence never developed immunities to many Afro-Eurasian diseases, which now devastated the Americas. Smallpox brought the greatest known demographic catastrophe in world history, killing off around 90 percent of the peoples of the Americas. The disaster emptied productive land and paved the way for Europeans to settle the Americas and to import captive Africans to labor in mining and agriculture. Only in the highlands (such as the Andes Mountains in South America) or rain forests (such as the Amazon Basin) did substantial concentrations of Native Americans survive. In contrast, only a few American diseases, especially syphilis, brought suffering to people in Europe and Africa.

Crop exchanges also proved momentous. Hence, the most American of foods, apple pie, originated in England (pies) and Central Asia (apples). Eurasian and African crops transformed some American regions. Most Native Americans had grown crops such as corn (maize) and potatoes on small plots, but settlers found that Afro-Eurasian crops such as wheat, rice, coffee, barley, and sugar were most successfully grown on large farms. Sugar had the most impact on the Americas, and vast acreage was devoted to its growth, mostly on plantations worked by African slaves and their descendants. Much of the sugar was exported to Europe for use to sweeten foods such as jam and breads, and beverages such as tea and coffee.

American crops were adopted widely in the Eastern Hemisphere. Tobacco gained popularity in China and Europe, and many imports, such as tomatoes, made the once-bland European meals more varied. Potatoes became a mainstay of the European diet and the major crop grown in several societies. Maize could be grown on marginal land and proved a boon in Africa, Southwest Asia, and China. American chilies, hotter than Asian black peppers, proved hugely popular in South and Southeast Asian cooking, adding a sharp bite to curries and other foods. Peanuts became a key crop in West Africa. The new foods offered not only a more varied diet but also a healthier one.

Population Movements and Mixing

SOCIETIES

During the Early Modern Era, the growing networks of trade, information, and technology fostered changes in societies all over the world. Improved maritime technology made it possible for people to cross vast oceans and to do so in larger numbers than ever before. Global migration brought people with very different customs and values together, not always happily.

More Europeans moved south and east to North Africa and the Middle East during the later Middle Ages and the Early Modern Era than migrants moving to Europe. Many were Jews expelled or fleeing discrimination and pogroms. The largest population movement involved Europeans settling in the Americas and bringing with them enslaved Africans but few European women. Since women comprised perhaps only a fifth of the Spanish and Portuguese who went to the Americas, men frequently sought partners among Native American and African women. Intermarriage or sexual contact between people from different ethnic groups produced new peoples with mixed cultural backgrounds, so that by 1750 in Latin America and in French colonies such as Louisiana a large part of the population blended European with Native American or African backgrounds. In turn, these groups' cultures often mixed the varying social influences, as in northeast Brazil, where people blended African religions and Catholic traditions. Unlike English North America, where any African ancestry usually meant classification as black, in much of Latin America a complex hierarchy of social categories developed based on gradations of skin color.

Migration and intermarriage also occurred in the Eastern Hemisphere. Dutch and Portuguese adventurers and merchants, most of them men, settled in southern Africa and the port cities of West Africa and South and Southeast Asia, often taking wives from the local population. For some, race was more a cultural than a physiological concept. Hence, in Java no matter their skin color a person could only be considered Dutch rather than Javanese if they spoke Dutch and followed Dutch customs, domestic arrangements, parenting styles, and moral environment. The Portuguese settlers raised their mixed-descent children as Portuguese-speaking Catholics, and Portuguese became the first language with global reach, spoken by a few million people in Brazil, coastal Africa, and southern Asia as well as Portugal. In coastal Africa the mixing of Europeans and Africans led to hybrid social groups. For example, the offspring of relations between Dutch men and African or Asian women were so common in South Africa that they became a distinct racial group, known as the Coloreds. As had been true for centuries, Arab and Indian traders also relocated to distant lands in Africa and Eurasia, often settling permanently and sometimes taking local wives. Many Chinese also moved into nearby territories such as Taiwan or settled in Southeast Asia, where they often married local women.

Changing Gender Relations

SOCIETIES

As the result of these changes, gender patterns were modified around the world. One-third of enslaved Africans taken to the Americas were women, some of whom were brought into close contact with slave-owning men, mostly white, who exercised control over their lives. The result was forced sexual activity and mixed-descent children. Since slave couples were often separated by sale, women held together many slave households, a social pattern that continued among many African Americans after the abolition of slavery. At the same time, Christian missionaries working among North American Indians often pursued policies that marginalized women in once-egalitarian cultures such as the Algonquians of eastern Canada and the Iroquois of New York. And in the parts of Africa most affected by slave trading, the absence of men in their productive years encouraged the remaining men to take multiple wives, a practice that may or may not have made life easier for women. Some women became active as slave traders, and women also played powerful roles in some of the newer kingdoms fostered by the trans-Atlantic slave trade, where they controlled access to the kings. A Portuguese missionary to one Senegambia kingdom described a powerful woman, the king's aunt, who was "so respected and obeyed that nothing of importance took place in the kingdom without her knowledge."[8]

In much of Eurasia women experienced increasing subordination by men. Hence, women generally became more restricted in Mughal India, China, and Japan as patriarchal attitudes strengthened, largely as a result of internal factors. For example, as China's leaders turned more socially conservative, they imposed harsher laws against behavior many considered deviant, such as homosexuality, and stressed the purity of women, which meant less freedom for women to leave home. More Chinese widows than ever before, forever faithful to their late husbands, frequently refused to remarry. In addition, Western missionaries and officials often sought to impose their own patriarchal prejudices on Asians. Hence, in Southeast Asia, the Spanish criticized Filipinos for tolerating adultery and premarital sex and punished those who engaged in these activities.

But there were exceptions to the growing restrictions on women. The Mughal emperor Akbar ordered that no woman could be forced by family or community pressures to immolate herself on her husband's funeral pyre, arguing that "it is a strange commentary on the magnanimity of men that they seek their own salvation by means of the self-sacrifice of their wives."[9] Many Chinese women from elite families published essays and poetry that were widely read and admired. One Chinese poet recalled how her father nurtured her talent: "Understanding that I was quite intelligent, He taught his daughters as he taught his sons, [advising us to] Develop together, support, and do not impede each other."[10]

Missionaries and Religious Change

SOCIETIES

The encounters between widely differing cultures around the world also had a religious dimension, forcing people to confront different belief systems while widening or sparking divisions in established faiths. Tensions simmering for several centuries finally fragmented Western Christianity into Catholic and diverse Protestant churches in the 1500s, spurring religious wars, militancy, and hostility toward non-Christians. Those in

[8]Balthazar Barreira, quoted in George E. Brooks, *Landlords and Strangers: Ecology, Society, and Trade in Western Africa, 1000–1630* (Boulder, CO: Westview Press, 1983), 306.
[9]Quoted in Annemarie Schimmel, *The Empire of the Great Mughals: History, Art, and Culture* (New Delhi: Oxford University Press, 2005), 113.
[10]Quoted in Susan Mann, *Precious Records: Women in China's Long Eighteenth Century* (Stanford, CA: Stanford University Press, 1997), 108.

the majority often punished dissenters as heretics. Meanwhile, mystical Sufi orders became more influential in Islamic societies from Indonesia to West Africa. But the Sufis' popularity distressed dogmatists who despised mystical practices, fostering debate on Sufism's role and value among Ottoman, Mughal, and Central Asian Muslims. Another Islamic change was the Persian shift from the Sunni to the Shi'a branch of Islam, which caused many Sunnis to emigrate. At the same time, Muslims and animists lived side by side without conflict in parts of Africa, and in some European societies Protestants and Catholics learned to live in peace.

Several religions engaged in missionary activity. Christians actively sought converts in the Americas, Africa, and Asia; however, because Christian missionaries were often intolerant of local traditions and also fought among themselves, they were expelled from Japan and China. In the Americas, one prominent Spanish clergyman strongly supported conquest and evangelization as a way of "civilizing" Native Americans, whom he described as "these pitiful men, in whom you will scarcely find any vestiges of humanness. They were born for servitude … [and] were justly conquered."[11] Despite such attitudes, Catholicism eventually triumphed in Latin America, Kongo, and the Philippines, while Protestant missionaries mostly concentrated on Catholic Europe, Southeast Asia, and North America, where they particularly targeted Native Americans and African slaves. But Christian missionary efforts had little success among Muslims, Theravada Buddhists, and Hindus. In contrast, Islam, which was not identified with unpopular Western conquest, attracted many converts in sub-Saharan Africa and southern Asia. Islam also spread into the Balkan societies under Ottoman control, and many Balkan peoples adopted the faith, forging a permanent divide between Christians and Muslims in the region. Many Muslims left Indonesia, Delhi, or Mombasa to perform the haj in Mecca or study in the Middle East, usually in Arabia or Egypt. Some of them adopted more orthodox versions of Islam and carried them home, often opening religious schools of their own.

Tensions sometimes led to secular approaches and tolerance rather than to religious zeal. To comprehend a changing world with diverse and challenging ideas, Chinese thinkers, European Enlightenment philosophers, and several Mughal emperors questioned religious dogmas and sought to broaden intellectual horizons. Theravada Buddhists generally respected all religions. Hence, when the French king, Louis XIV, sent a mission to King Narai of Ayuthia requesting that he and his people adopt Roman Catholicism, the Siamese monarch sent a letter back, arguing that God rejoiced not in religious uniformity but in theological diversities, preferring to be honored by different worships and ceremonies. And growing European knowledge of Chinese society, including Confucianism, led some thinkers to view China as an admirable, secular alternative model to the religious divisions and orthodoxies of Europe. In this way Asian ideas influenced some Europeans just as European ideas spread to some non-European peoples, a testament to an increasingly connected world.

---

[11]Juan Gimes de Sepulvida, in *1492: Discovery, Invasion, Encounter: Sources and Interpretations*, ed. Marvin Lunenfeld (Lexington, MA: D.C. Heath, 1991), 219–220.

Global Connections and the Remaking of Europe, 1450–1750

> *"O, wonder! How many goodly creatures are there here! How beauteous mankind is! O brave new world That hath such people in't!"*
>
> —Miranda, in *The Tempest* by William Shakespeare, 1611[1]

IMAGE 15.1 **Amsterdam Stock Exchange** During the seventeenth century, the Dutch port city of Amsterdam was the center of European commerce and played a key role in the world economy. The Amsterdam stock market, shown here in a painting from around 1754, attracted merchants and financiers from all over Europe.

Q What does this painting tell us about economic life and commerce in Amsterdam in this era?

[1]From "The Tempest," *The Riverside Shakespeare*, 2nd ed. (Boston: Houghton Mifflin, 1997), 1684.

European and world economies changed rapidly in the sixteenth century. Few places exemplified change more than the Flemish port city of Antwerp (**AN-twuhrp**), with its fabulous Bourse (**boors**), a huge building serving as a combination marketplace and stock exchange. The posted motto above its entrance read: "For the service of merchants of all nations and all languages." An economic boom enriched Antwerp's merchants and bankers, as well as the businesspeople from many lands who came to the Bourse to buy and sell. As many as twenty-five hundred ships from different lands anchored at one time in the harbor, many laden with gold and silver from the Americas. Every day goods went on sale in the Bourse, where bustling crowds of merchants, foreign visitors, and affluent local consumers thronged the rooms to buy Southeast Asian and Indian spices, American sugar, tin from England, Venetian glass, Spanish lace, German copper, paintings by great Flemish artists, and even the service of assassins or professional soldiers. Thus one great city linked the economies of Europe and the wider world. The Antwerp Bourse represented a post-medieval Europe shaped by overseas exploration, conquest, and expanding commerce, contributing the changes in life and thought that the English playwright Shakespeare referred to as a "brave new world."

In 1500, western Europeans were still medieval in many respects: dominated by the Roman Church, having little concept of national identity, skeptical of science, minor participants in hemispheric commerce, and barely aware of distant lands. By the mid-1700s, however, Europe had undergone a profound economic, intellectual, religious, and political transition, having conquered and settled the Americas and established colonies or trading networks in Asia and Africa. These developments were building blocks of the globalized world we live in today. Wealth flowed into Europe, fostering investment in science and technology, while new knowledge of, and influences from, non-European cultures reshaped European thinking. The Catholic Church also faced severe challenges from church critics and reformers, as well as from secular ideas, including scientific knowledge, that influenced some European thinkers. Such changes often produced long and bloody wars. By 1750 many Europeans had left their medieval institutions and beliefs behind and soon introduced even more profound changes to the world.

15-1 Overseas Expansion and Capitalism

⟐ TRANSITIONS

Ⓠ How did exploration, colonization, and capitalism increase Western power and wealth?

The late Medieval and Early Modern Eras were a crucial time in world history. In the 1400s and early 1500s European societies established the foundations for dramatic changes that would eventually affect societies around the world and shift power to various Western nations. Europe's encounter with America and its riches, the growth of a trans-Atlantic slave trade, and the opening of direct trade with Asia all increased European wealth, fostering **capitalism**, an economic system in which property, exchange, and the means of production, such as factories, are privately owned. Capitalism gradually expanded its operations to a global level, so that by the 1600s valuable Asian spices and precious American metals and plantation crops poured into Europe. The economic revolution also led to

capitalism An economic system in which property, exchange, and the means of production are privately owned.

CONNECTION to TODAY

Do you think that this era can be considered as the foundation for today's globalization and world economy? Why or why not?

stronger European states and reshaped most Europeans' daily lives.

15-1a Roots of Change

Some changes continued trends already apparent. During the 1400s, merchants flourished, cities grew larger, feudal social systems and values broke down, and commerce became part of everyday life. By 1500 cities such as Paris and London had grown to over 200,000; though still small by Asian standards, they enjoyed unique political power and autonomy, existing in a politically fragmented region rather than a centralized empire like China. City leaders could bargain with kings for advantages and autonomy. As middle classes bought more luxury goods, especially fine clothes, industries like textile manufacturing grew.

However, most Europeans were peasants working the soil, their lives organized around male-dominated households in

	1300	1350	1400
		ca. 1350–1615 Era of Renaissance ●	

CULTURAL AND INTELLECTUAL CHANGES

POLITICAL AND ECONOMIC CHANGES

which men tilled the fields while women generally had primary responsibility for the house, barn, and gardens. Although many peasants were now free or tenant farmers rather than serfs, they were still burdened by taxes and service obligations to lords and to the church. Yet, population growth and climate change also created economic change. Europe's population (excluding Russia) increased from 70 to 100 million between 1500 and 1600 and then to 125 million by 1750, fostering larger commercial markets. Global cooling began around 1300, reached its height in the late 1600s, and finally ended in the mid-1800s. This "Little Ice Age" brought winter freezing to canals and rivers, caused poor harvests and even famine, and helped motivate overseas explorers to seek better conditions and food sources, not to mention natural resources and wealth, elsewhere. Imported foods from the Americas, such as maize (corn) and potatoes, helped avert mass starvation.

More favorable attitudes toward commerce gave merchants new status and power. They now enjoyed opportunity for making profit and to establish institutions, such as banks, that favored economic growth. Blessed with these advantages, late medieval Europeans laid the foundation for an economic transition to successive forms of capitalism that fundamentally altered Western life and later influenced the wider world. In the 1400s cities such as Venice and Genoa in Italy, and Bruges (**broozh**) and Antwerp in Belgium, became centers of capitalistic enterprise. Venetians and Genoese, fierce competitors, traded all over Europe, western Asia, and North Africa. However, the Catholic Church's condemnation of usury limited early capitalism; not until after 1500 did capitalism change dramatically, allowing the Antwerp merchants to build a Bourse as a marketplace for world products.

Western European politics also began to shift in the 1500s. Medieval Europe was politically fragmented, containing some five hundred states or ministates in 1500. Unlike in China, Ottoman Turkey, or Mughal India, no single bureaucratic imperial state dominated the economy and enforced conformity. During the 1500s, however, some small states, enriched by African, American, and Asian resources, gradually became integrated monarchies. Both merchants and monarchs resented the landed aristocracy's independence and cooperated to destroy their influence in bloody wars. For the first time since the Carolingians, large but competitive centralized European states developed, particularly in England and France, that fostered dynamic but unstable political systems.

New intellectual currents also led to broader horizons, especially improvements in mapmaking. In 1375 Abraham

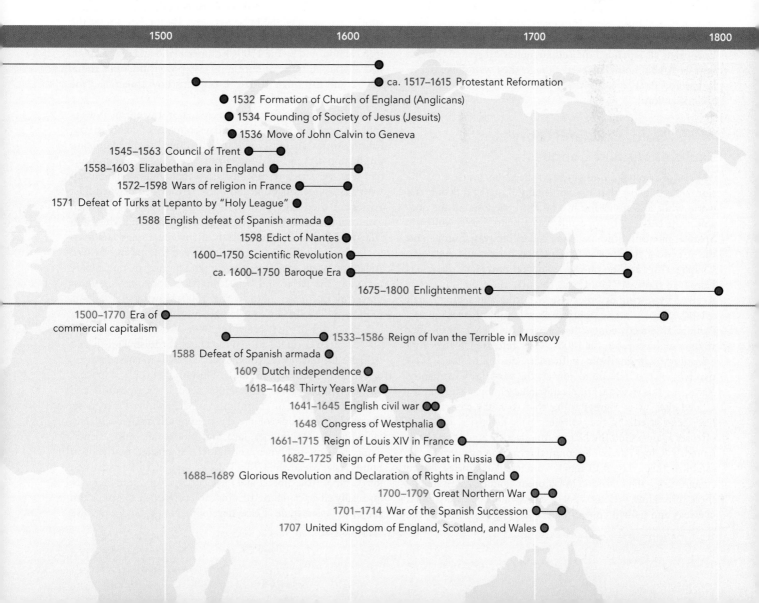

1500   1600   1700   1800

ca. 1517–1615 Protestant Reformation
1532 Formation of Church of England (Anglicans)
1534 Founding of Society of Jesus (Jesuits)
1536 Move of John Calvin to Geneva
1545–1563 Council of Trent
1558–1603 Elizabethan era in England
1572–1598 Wars of religion in France
1571 Defeat of Turks at Lepanto by "Holy League"
1588 English defeat of Spanish armada
1598 Edict of Nantes
1600–1750 Scientific Revolution
ca. 1600–1750 Baroque Era
1675–1800 Enlightenment

1500–1770 Era of commercial capitalism
1533–1586 Reign of Ivan the Terrible in Muscovy
1588 Defeat of Spanish armada
1609 Dutch independence
1618–1648 Thirty Years War
1641–1645 English civil war
1648 Congress of Westphalia
1661–1715 Reign of Louis XIV in France
1682–1725 Reign of Peter the Great in Russia
1688–1689 Glorious Revolution and Declaration of Rights in England
1700–1709 Great Northern War
1701–1714 War of the Spanish Succession
1707 United Kingdom of England, Scotland, and Wales

Cresques (**kres-kay**), a Jewish cartographer on the Spanish island of Majorca (**muh-JOR-kuh**), used Christian, Muslim, and Jewish traditions and travelers' accounts to produce a map that placed Jerusalem rather than Europe at the center of the world. Unlike Cresques, other cartographers did not decenter Europe. Flemish mapmaker Gerardus Mercator's (**muhr-KAY-tuhr**) influential 1569 world map vastly exaggerated the size of Europe and North America while diminishing the size of Africa, India, China, and South America. In spite of these distortions, Mercator's approach, which pictures Earth as a flat, uncurved rectangle intersected by straight lines for latitude and longitude, was the standard for world maps until the late twentieth century and is still widely used.

Developments in technology and mathematics, often inspired by earlier Arab, Chinese, and Indian innovations, also brought change. Between 1450 and 1550 Europe surpassed the Arabs in technology and began catching up to China, with major improvements in shipbuilding, navigation, weaponry, and printing. European ships took advantage of Arab lateen sails, Chinese sternpost rudders, and, for navigation, the Chinese magnetic compass. Facing rougher, stormier waters than the relatively placid Mediterranean, Atlantic coastal peoples built sturdier ships that gave them a naval advantage. Gunpowder weapons and printing processes, both invented in China, were improved, and the printing press disseminated knowledge to an increasingly literate audience. Europeans also blended the Indian numerical system (known now as Arabic numerals even though they were invented in India) and Arab algebra with their own insights to improve quantification.

15-1b "Gold, God, and Glory": Explorations and Conquests

The rise of Europe's world power resulted from overseas expansion and conquest that fundamentally brought together the world while also reshaping it. The Portuguese found the oceanic route between Europe and Asia around Africa, while the Spanish pioneered the maritime routes between Europe and the Americas and then between the Americas and Asia (see Chapters 16–18). The phrase "gold, god, and glory" describes European motives. "Gold" was the material gain Europeans received by seizing or otherwise acquiring and selling Asian spices, African slaves, American metals, and other resources. A desire to directly connect with Asian trade spurred the first voyages of discovery in the 1400s. "God" refers to Christianity's crusading tradition, rivalry with Islam, disdain of non-Christian religions, and desire to convert the world to Christianity. Reflecting this view, a Catholic missionary in Spanish America argued that "it is a great thing that so many souls should have been saved and that so many evils, idolatries, and great offenses against God [by Native Americans] should have been halted."[2] "Glory" describes competing monarchies seeking to establish their claims to newly contacted territories, hence strengthening their position in European politics. Motivated by these three aims, various western European peoples expanded overseas and gained control over widening segments of the globe. By the late nineteenth century Europeans dominated much of the world politically and economically.

During the 1400s seafaring Spaniards and Portuguese ventured out into the Atlantic and discovered the Azores, Madeira, Canary, and Cape Verde island chains off Northwest Africa (see Map 15.1). These Iberians enjoyed a favorable location facing the Atlantic Ocean and North Africa, deep-sea fishing traditions, a history of aggressive crusading, and possession of Europe's best ships and navigation techniques. They also had economic motives. For centuries West African gold, passed through North Africa to southern Europe, had been used for coins, treasuries, and jewelry. Furthermore, the Portuguese sought to break the Venetian monopoly over the valuable trade from southern Asia through Persia and Egypt, whose rulers the Venetians had long cultivated at their mutual profit.

Maritime exploration required new technologies. The easily maneuverable Portuguese caravel could travel long distances, and Iberian-built galleons later provided much cargo space and room for larger crews. To chart sun and star positions, Iberian sailors used the Arab astrolabe (**AS-truh-labe**). After learning how to mount weapons on ships, Europeans could overwhelm coastal defenses and defeat lightly armed ships. The Spanish in the Americas and the Portuguese in Africa and Asia, using artillery, naval cannon, and muskets, could control large territories whose inhabitants lacked guns. By the late 1500s, the English had built the most maneuverable ships and the best iron cannon, and by the 1700s European land and sea weapons had outclassed those of once militarily powerful China, India, Persia, and Ottoman Turkey. Europeans now threatened the great Asian states.

Intense competition between major European powers spurred increased exploration and a scramble for colonies, subject territories where Europeans could directly control primary production. In the 1400s the Portuguese began direct encounters with western and central Africa, including a relationship with the Kongo kingdom, and by 1497 they had reached East Africa and then sailed to India. Soon they seized key ports such as Hormuz on the Persian Gulf, Goa in India, and Melaka in Malaya. Meanwhile, the Spanish discovered a huge landmass to the west, soon named America, between Europe and Eastern Asia. Exploring the Americas and conquering many peoples, including the Aztec and Inca Empires, made Spain the most powerful European state in the 1500s. Portugal, England, France, and Holland also colonized in the Americas, sending emigrants to what they called the "New World."

First the Portuguese, then the Dutch, Spanish, French, and British, also established colonies or footholds in coastal Africa, carrying enslaved Africans to the Western Hemisphere to work on plantations growing cash crops, such as sugar, cotton, and coffee, for European consumption. Meanwhile, Portuguese, Dutch, and Spaniards colonized various Southeast Asian islands, including the Philippines, Java, and Indonesia's Spice Islands, while the British, French, and Dutch established footholds in South Asia. Meanwhile, Russia had commenced its expansion into Central Asia, Siberia, and the Caucasus. American minerals, especially silver, supported European economic expansion and access to Asian trade. These developments enabled a massive

[2]Franciscan friar Toribio de Montolinia, quoted in *1492: Discovery, Invasion, Encounter: Sources and Interpretations*, ed. Marvin Lunenfeld (Lexington, MA: D.C. Heath, 1991), 214.

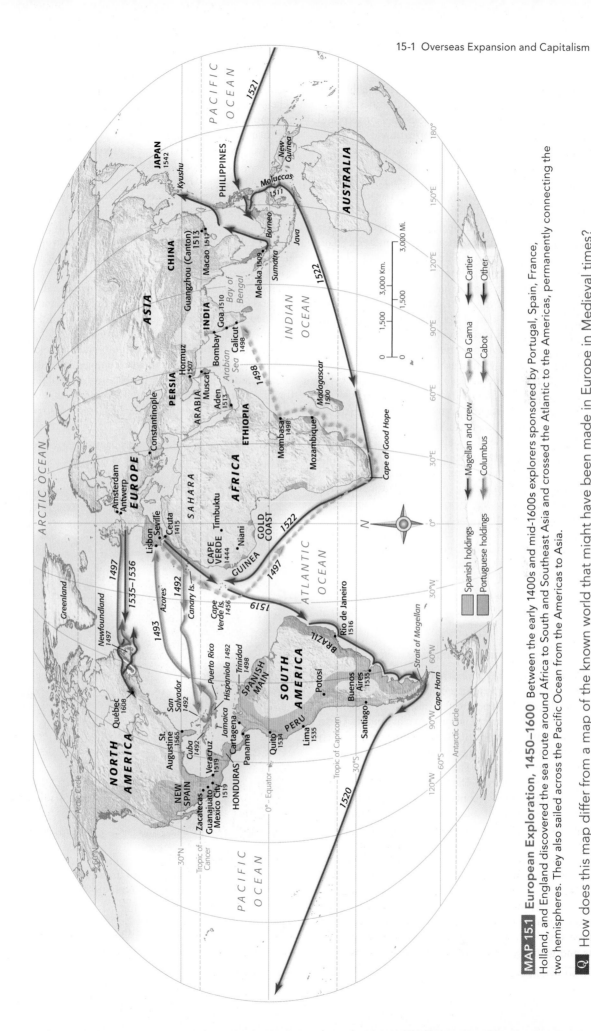

MAP 15.1 European Exploration, 1450–1600 Between the early 1400s and mid-1600s explorers sponsored by Portugal, Spain, France, Holland, and England discovered the sea route around Africa to South and Southeast Asia and crossed the Atlantic to the Americas, permanently connecting the two hemispheres. They also sailed across the Pacific Ocean from the Americas to Asia.

Q How does this map differ from a map of the known world that might have been made in Europe in Medieval times?

transfer of valuable and much coveted resources, especially silver, gold, sugar, coffee, and spices, to Europe. The fortunes of trading ports such as Venice, Genoa, Lisbon, Seville, Antwerp, and Amsterdam rose or fell depending on overseas trade.

During the Early Modern Era, Europeans began creating a globalized and increasingly integrated world. While laying the foundations for their world dominance after 1750, Portugal established the first global empire, which included scattered territories in South America (Brazil), Africa (Angola, Mozambique), and a string of Asian ports and small islands. Spain's empire became much larger in land area, encompassing most of South and Central America, Mexico, Cuba, Puerto Rico, Florida, the North American southwest from California to Texas, the Philippines, and several African footholds. Thanks to their conquests, Portugal and Spain prospered in the 1500s. In the 1600s overseas trade and the resources from their North American, Caribbean, African, and Asian colonies helped Holland, England, and France become the most powerful European countries. By providing some Europeans with valuable human labor and natural resources, overseas trade and exploitation also contributed to the growth of capitalism and world trade. But European influence remained limited in many regions, as powerful Asian and African societies such as China, Siam, Japan, and Morocco successfully resisted or ignored European demands.

Commercial trade became more complex in a globalizing world and could involve many long journeys and transactions for a single product. For example, in the 1500s Portuguese merchants shipped a clock made in Flanders (Belgium) to Lisbon, from where it was carried around Africa to Portuguese-ruled Goa in India, and then on to Melaka on the Malay Peninsula, where it was exchanged for sandalwood probably from Sri Lanka or southern India. The sandalwood was then shipped to Macao (a Portuguese enclave on the China coast) where it was sold for gold, which was carried to Nagasaki (a Japanese port) to buy a painted screen, which was then sent to Goa and eventually to Lisbon.

15-1c The Rise of Capitalism

Since its beginning in the Early Modern Era, capitalism has taken many forms and created new values around the world. Capitalism was revolutionary because, on a greater scale than before, money in the form of investment capital was used to make profits. Under capitalism, the drive for profit from privately owned, privately invested capital largely determined what goods were produced and how they were distributed. The various forms of capitalism had certain common features—the need for constant accumulation of additional capital, economic self-interest, the profit motive, a market economy of some sort, and competition—that shaped relations between people. Hence, carpenters that used to share their services on a barter basis and their profits with their guild now charged fees instead, competing for customers with other carpenters. Later capitalism included private ownership of the means of production, such as factories, businesses, and farms.

However, the profit motive, wealth accumulation, and competition contradicted some cultural values. Many cultures discouraged people from accumulating more wealth than their neighbors or working hard only to maximize income. Even today, some Asian, African, Native American (First Nation), and

Latin American cultures value cooperation, religious piety, or generosity more than acquiring great wealth. Before capitalism governments siphoned off surplus wealth, with the elite spending their resources on luxuries such as the magnificent cathedrals, palaces, and pyramids that now impress tourists. Medieval merchant and craft guilds strictly regulated economic activity for the common good. By contrast, capitalists invested some profits in further exchange or production, fostering economic expansion and transforming small-scale trade into global capitalism.

While western Europe became increasingly capitalist, eastern European nobles discouraged capitalism and preserved elements of medieval feudalism. Allied with landowning aristocracies facing labor shortages on their estates, kings in Poland, Lithuania, Prussia, and Russia mandated serfdom on the peasantries and forbade people to leave the land. Since they provided little support to merchants, capitalism did not expand and instead foreign merchants, including Dutch, Germans, Jews, and Armenians, gradually dominated eastern Europe's commerce. With chiefly agrarian economies, many once-vibrant cities declined into sleepy provincial towns, inhabited by many foreign-born merchants or their descendants. For example, many Polish and Lithuanian cities had large Jewish populations.

The Port of Seville, c.1590 (oil on canvas) (detail)/Sanchez Coello, Alonso (c.1531–88)/Museo de America, Madrid, Spain/ Bridgeman Images

IMAGE 15.2 **The Port of Seville** In the 1500s Seville became the main port for trade between Spain and its empire and a major cultural center. This view shows the busy river around 1590.

Q What does this painting tell us about port life and maritime commerce in Spain in this era?

During the 1500s capitalism took hold in northwest Europe. The English, Flemish, and Dutch developed the most dynamic capitalism and soon eclipsed Italy, shifting the economic balance of power from the Mediterranean to the English Channel and North Sea. Enriched by distributing American silver and controlling Baltic grain, Antwerp in Flanders became Europe's main financial capital. By the 1620s Amsterdam emerged as Europe's capitalist powerhouse, dominating much European and Asian trade and boasting amenities rare elsewhere, such as streetlamps. In 1728 the English writer Daniel Defoe concluded that "the Dutch are the Middle Persons of Trade, the Factors and Brokers of Europe. They buy to sell again, and the greatest part of their vast commerce consists in being supply'd from all parts of the world that they may supply the world again."[3] Instead of investing in land, people invested in business and industry; as a result, the increased production of ships, arms, and textiles created more capital while the new materialism encouraged consuming goods from tea, coffee, and sugar to clocks, china, and glassware. Based on Arab models and using coffee grown in Yemen in south Arabia or in Ethiopia, coffee houses appeared in many European cities, especially in England, in the 1600s. They served multiple social networking and informational functions as post offices, places to arrange business transactions, and venues for lively conversations and debates.

In this new capitalist era, the importation of American metals caused rising prices, which in turn meant that people needed more money. Increasing capital also encouraged the use of credit and banking. Attitudes toward charging interest for loans and seeking profit changed. Because the medieval church had denounced charging interest as usury, a mortal sin, good Christians could not become merchants or bankers, leaving this economic niche largely to Jews and later Italians. By the late 1500s, however, many rejected these church teachings, heeding the cynical saying that "he who takes usury goes to hell; he who doesn't goes to the poorhouse." Acceptance of paying and collecting interest reflected a gradual shift to an entirely different type of society.

Capitalism produced the **bourgeoisie** (BUR-swah-zee), a new urban, mostly commercial, middle class ranging from small-scale merchants to financiers. Jacob Fugger (FOOG-uhr) (1459–1525) of Augsburg in southern Germany illustrated how an ambitious commoner could prosper from capitalism. A weaver's grandson and successful textile merchant's son, Fugger built a financial empire of banks, factories, silver mines, and farmlands, becoming Europe's richest man, loaning money to royal houses, and acquiring a castle and the title of count. He praised himself as "behind no one in attainment of extraordinary wealth, in generosity, purity of morals and greatness of soul."[4] His sons published the first newsletter for merchants and bankers, tracking European political and economic developments.

Capitalism continually changed in character and expanded in scope. Under **commercial capitalism**, dominant in western Europe between 1500 and 1770, most capital was invested in commercial enterprises such as trading companies, including the world's first joint-stock companies, run by directors chosen for their experience. These precursors of today's giant multinational corporations pooled their resources by selling shares, or stocks, to merchants and bankers, mobilizing great capital. Companies invested in diversified economic activities such as real estate, mining, and industry and employed many cashiers, bookkeepers, couriers, and middlemen skilled in languages. Few Asian or African merchants could compete with this collective power.

Commercial capitalism was also shaped by cooperation between governments and big business enterprises. England, Holland, France, and Spain pursued **mercantilism**, the practice of building a nation's wealth by expanding its reserves of precious metals such as gold and silver bullion. Under this system, trade was dominated by semi-military, government-backed companies that were protected from competition. To attract other nations' bullion, these governments limited imports and increased exports. Some joint-stock companies obtained royal charters granting them monopolies and the right to colonize other lands in the state's name. In England, the English (later British) East India Company (BEIC) formed in 1600 and was allowed to recruit and use its own military and naval forces. The BEIC financed overseas exploration while supporting piracy against Spanish and French shipping. Queen Elizabeth I granted the company "exclusive" rights over trade in the "East Indies" (a misleading term for India and Southeast Asia). The BEIC was composed of aristocrats, merchants, members of the gentry, and some government officials. Spurred by mercantilism, commercial capitalism expanded into Africa, Asia, and the Americas.

bourgeoisie The urban-based, mostly commercial, middle class that arose with capitalism in the Early Modern Era.

commercial capitalism The economic system in which most capital was invested in commercial enterprises such as trading companies, including the world's first joint-stock companies.

mercantilism An economic approach that emerged in Early Modern Europe based on a government policy of building a nation's wealth by expanding its reserves of precious metals.

KEY POINTS

▸ Europe's political decentralization fostered growing cities and the development of capitalism.

▸ Despite entrenched value systems that opposed an emphasis on accumulating wealth, capitalism took hold in western Europe, while eastern European leaders resisted it and instead mandated serfdom.

▸ Amsterdam established itself as capitalist Europe's center in the 1600s.

▸ Commercial capitalists, assisted by their country's mercantilist policies, increased their world market power by pooling resources in such organizations as joint-stock companies.

[3]Quoted in Carlo M. Cipolla, *Before the Industrial Revolution: European Society and Economy, 1000–1700*, 2nd ed. (New York: W. W. Norton, 1980), 270.
[4]Quoted in Miriam Beard, *History of the Businessman* (New York: Macmillan, 1938), 239–240.

15-2 The Renaissance and Reformation

⇌ TRANSITIONS

Q How did the Renaissance and Reformation mark a crucial cultural and intellectual transition?

Two major movements, the Renaissance and Reformation, reshaped European thought and culture in the 1500s and helped foster religious and artistic approaches and trends that remain with us today. During the Renaissance, a dramatic flowering in arts and learning beginning in Italy around 1350 (see Chapter 14), new philosophical, scientific, artistic, and literary currents developed that led to more creative, secular societies. In the 1500s gold and silver imported from the Americas provided more people with money to purchase art and books. Many historians believe that the Renaissance, sparked partly by trade with Asia and North Africa, provided a bridge between medieval and modern western Europe. At the same time, the **Reformation**, a movement to reform Christianity, spawned new Christian churches that provided alternatives to the Roman Catholic Church. Both movements helped undermine medieval society's pillars and changed cultural and religious life.

15-2a Renaissance Thought, Art, and Literature

During the Renaissance, thinkers and artists rediscovered Classical Greek and Roman ideas while consuming Chinese and Islamic products and ideas. The Renaissance promoted individualism, secularism, tolerance, beauty, creativity, and a philosophy, humanism, that emphasized humanity and its creations rather than God and a troubled Catholic Church that faced a confidence crisis, including leadership and clergy abuses. Some Renaissance thinkers favored church reform. The Dutch philosopher Erasmus **(uh-RAZ-muhs)** (1466–1536) advocated a more personal spirituality that tolerated diverse beliefs and the use of living languages rather than Latin, arguing that Jesus commanded people to love one another. The French humanist writer François Rabelais **(RAB-uh-lay)** (ca. 1494–1553) was even more critical, calling monks "a rabble of counterfeit saints, hypocrites, pretended zealots, who deceive the world."[5] By encouraging freedom of thought and offering critical insights, humanists also undermined the medieval attitudes that crippled scientific investigation. But popes rejected any doctrine or institutional changes. Yet, it was Spanish monks in the sixteenth century who pioneered methods of improving life for deaf people. For centuries, going back at least as far as Roman times, the hearing impaired in Europe had been marginalized and considered damaged people useful for nothing. Then Pedro Ponce de Leon, a Spanish Benedictine possibly influenced by Native American hand language, helped invent sign language using hand gestures. This led to discovering methods to teach and learn sign language. In

CONNECTION to TODAY

Can you think of ways that the world today is still influenced by the Renaissance and Reformation?

Reformation The movement to reform Christianity that was begun by Martin Luther in the sixteenth century.

1755 a French priest, Charles-Michel de l'Epee, established a more comprehensive method of educating the deaf and founded the first public school for deaf children in Paris.

Another humanist, the Florentine thinker Niccolò Machiavelli **(MAK-ee-uh-VEL-ee)** (1469–1527), provided guidance for European leaders in his influential political manual, *The Prince*, which studied power as separate from moral doctrine. Although claiming to draw on history's lessons, Machiavelli also used his experience as a diplomat for his ideas. *The Prince* argued that the ruler must always keep the end in mind, applying ruthless policies, such as deception and violence, in pursuing vital national interests. But, he argued, rulers ignore popular moral values at their peril; although a leader need not have piety, faith, integrity, and humanity, to avoid being hated he must seem to have them.

Interested in science, some thinkers employed direct experimental methods and observation. The Florentine Leonardo da Vinci **(lay-own-AHR-doh dah VIN-chee)** (1452–1519), painter, sculptor, architect, scientist, mathematician, philosopher, inventor, and engineer, was in many ways ahead of his time and exemplified the versatile Renaissance personality and, in his knowledge about Muslim science and architecture, the Renaissance openness to varied influences. Among other contributions, he developed some of the first concepts for gliders, helicopters, parachutes, diving suits, cranes, and, though he despised war, even weapons. Da Vinci's mathematics knowledge of perspective can be seen in some of his paintings, such as in the architecture of the building in *The Last Supper*. He was also a master of visual illusions, which can be seen in the *Mona Lisa*, probably the most famous painting in history. The subject's enigmatic expression represented her inner thoughts and emotions, a novel approach in that era but common today. Polish astronomer Nicolaus Copernicus **(koh-PUR-nuh-kuhs)** (1473–1543) studied the skies and Islamic scholarship and suggested that Earth might not be the center of the universe. In 1507 Copernicus transformed astronomy and physics with his revolutionary "heliocentric," or sun-centered, theory of the solar system, refuting traditional ideas that the universe centered on Earth and the sun revolved around the planets. Fearing persecution by the church, he did not dare have his findings published until after his death.

The Renaissance spread Italian artistic influence, deepening the knowledge of humanity by more accurately representing real life in sculpture, painting, architecture, and literature. Some inspiration came from Islamic, Asian, and African artistic traditions; indeed, black Africans appeared in some paintings, including those with Christian themes. Italians such as the Venetian painter Giovanni Bellini (ca. 1430–1516) worked in or visited Muslim

[5]Quoted in H. O. Taylor, *Thought and Expression in the Sixteenth Century*, vol. 1 (New York: Macmillan, 1920), 175.

cities, spreading Italian influences but also returning with new perspectives. Rome replaced Florence as the hub of Italian art, attracting the eccentric Florentine Michelangelo Buonarroti **(mi-kuhl-AN-juh-loh bwawn-uh-RAW-tee)** (1475–1564), later famous for his realistic sculptures, paintings, and frescoes, especially the figures he painted on the ceiling of the Vatican's Sistine Chapel. Later Venice became Italy's main art center, where rich merchants and aristocrats offered artists generous financial support to produce landscapes and portraits rather than the once-common religious artworks. One Venetian, Titian **(TISH-uhn)** (ca. 1488–1576), contrary to Christian tradition, painted nudes and pre-Christian fables. Some women artists also gained a following. The Italian Artemisia Gentileschi (1593–ca. 1652), who survived rape by her art teacher and torture to test her allegations, painted heroic women from Greek mythology and the Bible. She was also known for self-portraits, including one in the guise of a saint in which her face reveals a quiet defiance and her hand rests on the instrument of her torture, a spiked wheel. In the Low Countries, Antwerp-born Pieter Bruegel **(BRU-guhl)** the Elder (ca. 1525–1569), described by some art historians as comparable to Shakespeare in literature, painted realistic landscapes and sympathetic scenes of everyday peasant and town life in all its teeming variety, a secularized vision of the world. In addition to plowed fields, village intensity, and sublime landscapes, he was also a moralist who catalogued terror and human depravity. El Greco **(ell GREK-oh)** (1541–1614), a native of Crete who studied in Italy before settling in Spain, blended Venetian, Byzantine, and Spanish traditions to create a dramatic, expressionistic style that influenced such modern movements as Expressionism and Cubism, making his work seem very contemporary.

Growing secularism and humanism had literary consequences. During Queen Elizabeth I's brilliant reign in England (1558–1603), writers replaced concern for the hereafter with stories of human passions. The most famous, William Shakespeare (1564–1616), reflected the Elizabethans' celebration of the individual person and their nation. A prosperous businessman's son, Shakespeare acted in the theater and wrote histories, comedies, and tragedies that transcended time and place. Plays such as *Othello*, *Hamlet*, and *The Merchant of Venice* commented on the world beyond England, while other plays, such as *Henry V* and *Julius Caesar*, addressed English or ancient history. One of Shakespeare's best-known characters, Hamlet, voiced Renaissance exuberance: "What [a] piece of work is a man, how noble in reason, how infinite in faculties."[6] Yet, women were essential to the professional Elizabethan theater, as company part-owners, costumers, financiers, patrons, theater-goers, occasional actors, and perhaps even playwrights (authors were often anonymous), although their contributions

The Peasant Wedding: after 1616 (oil on panel)/Brueghel, Pieter the Younger (c.1564-1638)/LUKAS - ART IN FLANDERS/Museum voor Schone Kunsten, Ghent, Belgium/Bridgeman Images

IMAGE 15.3 Bruegel's *Peasant Wedding* Painted around 1567, Pieter Bruegel's *The Peasant Wedding* celebrates the rituals of peasant life, in this case a wedding dinner for a village. The Flemish artist may also have intended the painting of the feasting villagers as a satire on self-indulgence. The bride, composed and radiant, presides over the feast under a canopy.

Q What does the wedding dinner and celebration shown here tell us about Flemish peasant life?

[6]From "Hamlet," *The Riverside Shakespeare*, 2nd ed. (Boston: Houghton Mifflin, 1997), 1204.

often went mostly unrecorded by history. Another great writer, the Spaniard Miguel de Cervantes (suhr-VAN-teez) Saavedra (1547–1616), published the great novel *Don Quixote* (kee-HO-tee), which portrayed Spain at the end of its golden age. A former steward and soldier who was once enslaved by pirates in Algiers, Cervantes became a purchasing agent and eventually was imprisoned for debt. The main character of his book, Don Quixote, sets out to battle dragons and evil men, right injustice, and defend the oppressed, but mainly makes himself a grand nuisance. While Cervantes dignified the human spirit, like some Greek playwrights, he also satirized its plight.

Growing knowledge about other cultures inspired Europeans to rethink their assumptions about the world, stimulating debate about Native American society that today might seem patronizing or prejudiced. In 1516, the English author Thomas More's (1478–1535) *Utopia* portrayed Native Americans as living in a paradise and European society as filled with poverty, injustice, hatred, and war. French writer Michel Eyquem de Montaigne (mon-TANE) (1533–1592) idealized Native American societies as "noble savages" uncorrupted by "civilization." Perhaps reflecting often-hostile encounters between English settlers and Native Americans in Virginia, Shakespeare's play *The Tempest* mocked this idea by contrasting civilized Prospero and fierce, brutal Caliban (KAL-uh-ban) (an anagram for *cannibal*).

15-2b The Reformation and Religious Change

Questioning the old order also led to the Reformation (1517–1615), which transformed Europe's religious makeup, in what some scholars call Christian civilization's civil war, and profoundly reshaped Western thought (see Map 15.2). By fragmenting the church and overturning previously accepted certainties and priorities, the movement challenged the relationship between spiritual and secular society, perceptions of the supernatural, the role of women in society and church, clerical attitudes towards sex and marriage, and understandings of the past. Critics viewed the long-dominant Roman Church as corrupt, often led by incompetent popes who intervened rashly in political affairs and by church leaders and clergy who sometimes blatantly violated celibacy and poverty requirements. At the same time, the spreading literacy inspired some to examine Christian writings for themselves. Throughout the 1500s various groups sought church reform. Some, later called **Protestants**, broke completely with the Roman Catholic Church. By 1600 almost 40 percent of non-Orthodox Europeans, mostly in the north, had renounced Catholicism and adopted some form of Protestantism. Meanwhile, English and Dutch colonists carried Protestant faiths to North America. Eventually dozens of differing Protestant churches competed with each other and with Catholics for influence.

Protestants Groups that broke completely with the Roman Catholic Church as the result of the Reformation.

Martin Luther (1483–1546), a German, launched the movement that ended Western Christianity's unity. As conflicts between the Holy Roman Emperor, princes, and cities produced widespread discontent, many Germans began to resent the pope and bishops for leading luxurious lives. Luther, an Augustinian monk and later a University of Wittenberg (WIT-n-burg) professor, believed that nothing in scripture justified papal power and church rituals, concluding that only faith, not good works, could wipe away a person's sin and ensure salvation. In 1517 Luther nailed to a door of his Wittenberg church a paper containing 95 theses attacking indulgences, clerical statements canceling punishment due for sins in exchange for lucrative cash contributions to the church. The paper prompted widespread discussion. After Pope Leo X excommunicated Luther in 1520 for refusing to retract his views, Luther translated the Bible into German and developed his doctrines, condemning Rome as "the greatest thief and robber that has ever appeared on earth or ever will. Poor Germans, we have been deceived."[7] A media pioneer, Luther spread his ideas through books, paintings, music, and prints. His pamphlets were distributed at markets and taken by cart to other cities, where they were read aloud publicly for those who were illiterate. In 1530 Lutherans formed a church rooted in the Augsburg Confession, a doctrinal statement arguing that the Bible was the only source of faith, that every believer had the freedom to interpret scripture, and that the cults of the Virgin Mary and the saints, priestly celibacy, and the monastic orders were misguided. But if people could now read the Bible for themselves and disagree about what the scriptures meant and faith required, then a foundation was being laid for diverse churches and eventually possibilities for freer political systems and intellectual inquiry.

Lutheranism spread widely in northern Germany, Scandinavia, and the eastern Baltic coast. Many German city officials, princes, priests, professors, and common people supported the reform cause. But in 1524 a major conflict split the reform movement when peasants revolted against the landowning lords and church leaders. Unsuccessfully mediating between the sides, Luther then supported the nobles, who caused over 100,000 deaths in crushing the uprisings. In the end, the Lutheran Church became closely linked to many princely governments while the Holy Roman Emperor remained staunchly Catholic.

Inspired by Luther's example, non-Germans also founded Protestant movements. Calvinism was more radical in rejecting Catholic doctrine. Its founder, John Calvin (1509–1564), having been forced to leave France, settled in Geneva (juh-NEE-vuh), Switzerland. Unlike Luther, Calvin believed not in human free will but in predestination, the doctrine that God had already determined an individual's salvation or damnation at birth. Since good behavior and faith could not guarantee reaching Heaven, Calvin concluded, governments must enforce strict morality. Calvin attacked worldly pleasures such as dancing and playing cards, and his Geneva became a theocratic society, ruled by increasingly intolerant church leaders who burned some dissenters at the stake. Calvinism spread rapidly in Switzerland, England, and Holland, and in 1561 the Calvinist John Knox founded the Presbyterian Church in Scotland, where it became the dominant church.

---

[7] Quoted in James Krokar et al., *Rhetoric and Civilization*, vol. 2 (Littleton, MA: Copley, 1988), 620.

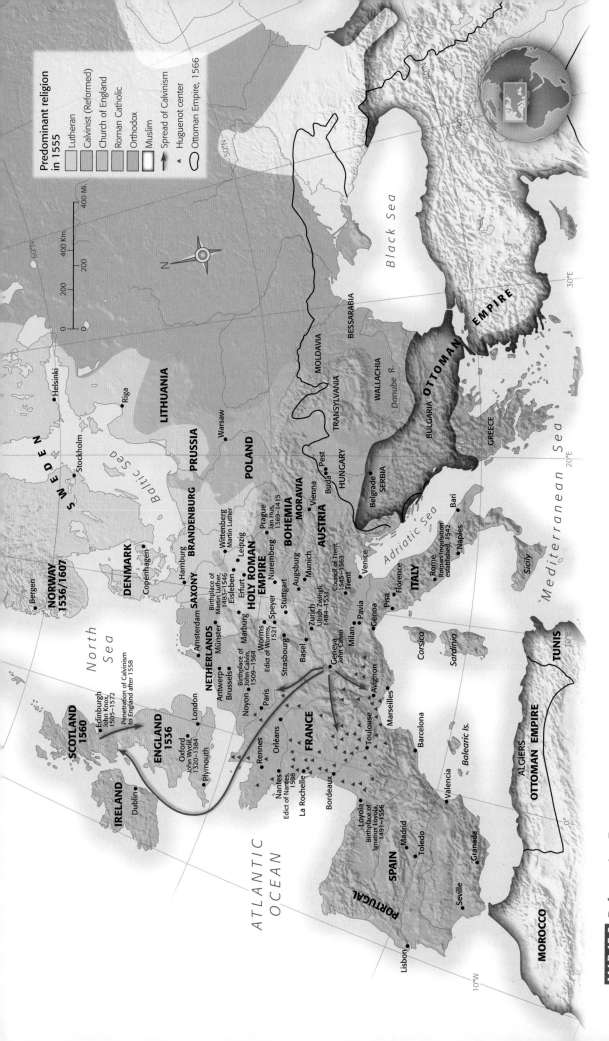

MAP 15.2 Reformation Europe The Protestant Reformation reshaped Europe's religious landscape in the 1500s and early 1600s. By the mid-1550s some form of Protestantism had become dominant in much of northern Europe, England, and Scotland. Catholicism remained predominant in the southern half of western Europe and parts of eastern Europe.

Q How different does this map look from a religious map of Europe today?

Map labels

Predominant religion in 1555
- Lutheran
- Calvinist (Reformed)
- Church of England
- Roman Catholic
- Orthodox
- Muslim
- ↑ Spread of Calvinism
- ▲ Huguenot center
- ◯ Ottoman Empire, 1566

400 Mi.
400 Km.
0   200   400

N

ATLANTIC OCEAN
North Sea
Baltic Sea
Black Sea
Adriatic Sea
Mediterranean Sea

IRELAND
Dublin

SCOTLAND 1560
Edinburgh
John Knox, 1505–1572

Penetration of Calvinism to England after 1558

ENGLAND 1536
London
Oxford
John Wyclif, 1320–1384
Plymouth

NORWAY 1536/1607
Bergen

SWEDEN
Stockholm
Helsinki

DENMARK
Copenhagen

LITHUANIA
Riga

PRUSSIA
Warsaw

POLAND

BRANDENBURG

SAXONY
Hamburg
Amsterdam

NETHERLANDS
Antwerp
Brussels

Münster
Birthplace of Martin Luther, 1483–1546
Eisleben
Martin Luther
Wittenberg
Erfurt
Leipzig

HOLY ROMAN EMPIRE
Marburg
Worms
Edict of Worms, 1521
Speyer
Nuremberg
Augsburg
Stuttgart
Munich

BOHEMIA
Prague
Jan Hus, 1369–1415

MORAVIA

AUSTRIA
Vienna

Noyon
Birthplace of John Calvin, 1509–1564
Paris
Strasbourg
Basel
Zurich
Ulrich Zwingli, 1484–1531

FRANCE
Rennes
Orléans
Nantes
Edict of Nantes, 1598
La Rochelle
Bordeaux
Toulouse
Marseilles
Avignon

Geneva
John Calvin
Milan
Pavia
Genoa
Pisa
Florence
Venice
Council of Trent, 1545–1563
Trent

ITALY
Rome
Roman Inquisition established, 1542
Naples
Bari

Corsica
Sardinia
Sicily

SPAIN
Madrid
Toledo
Loyola
Birthplace of Ignatius Loyola, 1491–1556
Seville
Granada
Valencia
Barcelona
Balearic Is.

PORTUGAL
Lisbon

MOROCCO
ALGIERS
OTTOMAN EMPIRE
TUNIS

HUNGARY
Buda
Pest
Belgrade
SERBIA

TRANSYLVANIA
WALLACHIA
Danube R.
MOLDAVIA
BESSARABIA

BULGARIA

OTTOMAN EMPIRE
GREECE

60°N
50°N
40°N

10°W   0°   10°E   20°E   30°E   40°E

In England, the initiative for religious change came from the king, Henry VIII (r. 1509–1547). Having no male heir with his wife Catherine of Aragon, a Spanish princess, Henry asked the pope to annul his marriage so he could marry Anne Boleyn (1501–1536), the much-courted daughter of English aristocrats. When Rome refused, in 1532 Henry rejected papal supremacy, announced his divorce, married Anne Boleyn, and appointed himself head of the English Catholic Church, which eventually became the Church of England. Later known as the Anglican Church, it retained much Catholic dogma and ritual. Suppressing both Calvinism and Rome-based power, Henry closed English monasteries and distributed their lands to his aristocratic and business allies. Growing disenchanted with Anne Boleyn, who bore him no sons, he had her beheaded in 1536. Eventually married four more times, Henry generated religious strife. His son and successor, who died at sixteen, was succeeded by Henry's Catholic daughter by Catherine of Aragon, Queen Mary Tudor (**TOO-duhr**) (r. 1553–1558).

Mary suppressed the Anglican Church, but it was restored when she died and was replaced by Elizabeth I (1533–1603), the daughter of Henry VIII and Anne Boleyn. Excommunicated by the Pope and fearing war with Catholic nations, Elizabeth sought diplomatic, commercial, and military ties with Muslim rulers in Morocco, Persia, and the Ottoman Empire, which all shared her antipathy for the Catholic Habsburgs who ruled diverse European states. This England–Islam connection stimulated English trade with Muslim nations, which brought to England the spices, sugar, silks, and carpets that changed what they ate, how they dressed, and how they decorated their homes. When Elizabeth died in 1603 her successor, James I, signed a peace treaty with Spain, ending England's political exile from Europe but not English trade with the Middle East and Asia. When Elizabeth's successors persecuted English Calvinists (known as Puritans), some of them emigrated to Holland. From there one Puritan group, the Pilgrims, moved to North America in 1620 to seek more religious freedom, helping plant Puritan influence in the New England colonies.

15-2c Protestantism, Capitalism, and Catholic Reaction

Protestantism's emergence had many consequences. For example, historians debate how much Protestant doctrines supplied religious underpinnings for capitalist values, what some scholars call the "Protestant ethic." Calvinists believed that citizens demonstrated their fitness for salvation by being law-abiding, industrious, thrifty, and sober, all values supporting the capitalist order. Like Protestants, capitalists favored productive labor, frugality, wealth accumulation, and individualism. Although emerging in some Catholic societies, capitalism flourished especially in Protestant Holland, England, and northern Germany. The strongest capitalist societies featured intellectual diversity and produced some secularized free thinkers. The

Counter Reformation A movement to confront Protestantism and crush dissidents within the Catholic Church.

Reformation also opened doors to democracy. Although Luther and Calvin condemned religious views other than their own, once people freely voiced their opinions on religion, they also wanted a voice in government. Similarly, women who became literate and could read the scriptures now gained some new options.

The Protestant challenge generated the **Counter Reformation**, a movement to confront Protestantism and crush Catholic Church dissidents using varied strategies, including the Holy Inquisition church court that had been formed in medieval times to combat heretical ideas (see Chapter 14). Several thousand suspected dissidents were burned at the stake in Spain, and the Congregation of the Index censored books, deciding which ones to forbid altogether. To outflank Protestantism, in 1534 the Spanish Basque former soldier, Ignatius Loyola (1491–1556), founded a highly disciplined missionary order, the Society of Jesus. One Jesuit, the Spanish Basque Saint Francis Xavier (**ZAY-vee-uhr**) (1506–1552), became a pioneering missionary in India, Southeast Asia, and Japan.

Despite harsh punitive measures, the Inquisition and Index did not suppress dissidence, prompting the pope to sponsor the Council of Trent (a city in northern Italy) to reconsider church doctrines. However, the council (1545–1563) reaffirmed most Catholic dogma—the value of both tradition and scripture, the church hierarchy and papal authority, and priestly celibacy—while imposing more papal supervision on priests and bishops and mandating that all clergy be trained in seminaries. The Trent reforms enabled Catholicism to recover some lost ground and to survive and flourish in a modified form.

But religious passions fostered intolerance. Religious minorities, such as Jews, French Protestants, and English Catholics, faced discrimination and sometimes violence. Several popes pursued anti-Jewish policies, while Luther advocated burning synagogues, arresting rabbis, and confiscating Jewish property. Facing expulsion from their countries or segregation in city ghettoes, many Jews and minority Catholics and Protestants emigrated to other European countries or the Americas.

15-2d Religious Wars and Conflicts

Europe was sporadically engulfed in conflict that made life dangerous and unsettled as religious divisions contributed to wars from the late sixteenth through early eighteenth centuries. For example, religious tensions troubled Habsburg-ruled Spain, which controlled a vast empire in the Americas, Southeast Asia, Portugal, the Low Countries, and parts of Italy. King Philip II of Spain (r. 1556–1598), known as "the most Catholic of kings," put imperial resources toward defending the Catholic cause in Europe while spreading the faith abroad.

In the Low Countries, Philip's suppression of Calvinism antagonized businessmen and the nobility, who demanded autonomy and freedom of worship. Enraged Protestants attacked Catholic churches, and the execution of dissident leaders spurred a general revolt in 1566, with both Catholics and Protestants rallying behind the Calvinist leader, the Dutchman William of Nassau

Discover Historical Voices

Queen Elizabeth I Rallies Her People

Few women ever enjoyed the power and respect of England's Renaissance queen, Elizabeth I, whose forty-five years of rule (1558–1603) marked a brilliant period for English culture, especially in literature and theater. On her death, the admiring playwright Ben Jonson wrote her epitaph: "For wit, features, and true passion, Earth, thou hast not such another." The queen may have been, as her detractors claimed, deceptive, devious, and autocratic, but her intelligence and formidable political skills helped her maneuver successfully through the snake pit of both English and European politics. One challenge was the deteriorating English–Spanish relations, which finally led to war. In 1588, as the powerful Spanish armada sailed toward the English coast, Elizabeth launched the English ships with a speech to her subjects that ironically played off her gender to reinforce her link with the English people. With the help of foul weather, the English defeated the Spanish, changing the fortunes of both countries.

My loving people. We have been persuaded by some that are careful for our safety, to take heed how we commit ourselves to armed multitudes, for fear of treachery, but I assure you, I do not desire to live to distrust my faithful and loving people. Let tyrants fear; I have always so behaved myself, that, under God, I have placed my chiefest strength and safeguard in the loyal hearts and good will of my subjects, and therefore I am come amongst you, as you see, at this time, not for my recreation and disport, but being resolved in the midst and heat of the battle, to live or die amongst you all, to lay down for my God, and for my kingdoms, and for my people, my honor and my blood, even in the dust.

I know I have the body of a weak and feeble woman; but I have the heart and stomach of a king, and of a king of England too; and I think foul scorn that…Spain, or any prince of Europe should dare to invade the borders of my realm; to which rather than any dishonor shall grow by me, I myself will take up arms, I myself will be your general, judge, and rewarder of every one of your virtues in the field.

I know already for your forwardness you have deserved rewards and crowns; and we do assure you in the word of a prince, they shall be duly paid you. In the meantime my lieutenant general shall be in my stead, than whom never prince commanded a more noble or worthy subject; no doubting but by your obedience to my general, by your concord in the camp, and your valor in the field, we shall shortly have a famous victory over those enemies of my God, of my kingdoms, and of my people.

Reflection Questions

1. How did Elizabeth justify the forthcoming battle with Spain?
2. What personal qualities did this Renaissance monarch suggest she could offer to her people in their time of peril?
3. Do you think that an appeal like this from a political leader would resonate with people today?

Source: Charles W. Colby, ed., *Selections from the Sources of English History* (Harlow, UK: Longmans, Green, 1899), 158–159. Quotation in introduction from A. L. Rowse, *The Elizabethan Renaissance: The Life of the Society* (New York: Charles Scribner's, 1971), 59.

(NAS-aw), Prince of Orange. Philip's occupation army executed over eleven hundred Protestants and sacked Antwerp. In 1579, Philip promised political liberty to the ten largely Catholic Flemish- and French-speaking southern provinces, forging the foundations of modern Belgium and Luxembourg. Then, when the English gave assistance to Low Country rebels and attacked Spanish shipping in the Americas, Philip II tried to invade England by sea in 1588, but he faced a determined foe in Queen Elizabeth I (see Discover Historical Voices: Queen Elizabeth I Rallies Her People). English ships outmaneuvered Spain's armada of one hundred and thirty ships, triumphing when a storm in the English Channel devastated Spain's once-invincible fleet. The mostly Protestant, Dutch-speaking northern provinces broke away from Spain in 1588 and became fully independent in 1609, forming the Netherlands, popularly known as Holland.

Religious conflicts also raged across France, where the powerful Bourbon family led French Calvinists, or Huguenots (**HYOO-guh-nauts**). In 1572, after the assassination of Calvinist leaders sparked Huguenot rioting in Paris, Catholic forces massacred thirty thousand Huguenots. In 1593 Henry of Bourbon (1553–1610), remarking that "Paris is well worth a mass," renounced Calvinism for Catholicism to become King Henry IV. In 1598 the Edict of Nantes (**nahnt**) recognized Catholicism as the state church but allowed Huguenots religious freedom.

Christian–Muslim conflicts also simmered, often resulting in political and military conflict. Muslim Ottoman Turks sought to expand their empire, which already included Greece, much of the Balkans, and Bulgaria (see Chapter 16). When some Balkan Christians embraced Islam, Holy Roman Emperor Charles V marshaled allies to defeat the Turks at Vienna in 1529. Later, in 1571, Spain, Rome, and Venice used advanced naval gunnery to destroy the Turkish fleet at the Battle of Lepanto (**li-PAN-toh**), off Greece, temporarily ending Turkish ambitions. In 1683, when the Turks besieged Vienna, Austria was saved by Polish intervention. Austrians pushed the Turks out of Hungary, ending Ottoman expansion in Europe and with it Christian fear of more losses to Islam.

15-3 Changing States and Politics

TRANSITIONS

Q What types of governments emerged in Europe in this era?

Capitalism, Renaissance humanism, Protestant Reformation, and encounters with the wider world fostered new institutions, beliefs, and politics. The transition unleashed forces that consumed Europe in bloody wars: kingdoms torn asunder and reconfigured, old states declining, and new states gaining influence. These states were not nations in the modern sense but multiethnic entities ruled by royal families marrying across national lines. While in some states royal absolutism flourished, a few others developed representative governments with elements of democracy.

> **CONNECTION to TODAY**
>
> Can you identify any parallels between the military conflicts, political systems, and national identities of the Early Modern Era and today?

15-3a Regional Wars and National Conflicts

Various wars raged, some prompted by religious divisions, others by tensions between rival states and within large multinational empires such as Habsburg-ruled Spain and the Holy Roman Empire. Even after religious tensions subsided, warfare remained a constant reality. Continuing the religious wars and national rivalries of the 1500s, the Thirty Years War (1618–1648), a long series of bloody hostilities, claimed millions of lives and involved many countries. It began when Czech Protestants in the Holy Roman Empire revolted against Habsburg Catholic rulers who were trying to limit religious freedom. Eventually the fighting drew in German princes and mostly Lutheran Denmark and Sweden. Finally France, although mostly Catholic, went to war against its Habsburg rivals who ruled Austria and Spain. In 1648 the conflict ended after a four-year-long congress produced the Treaty of Westphalia (**west-FALE-yuh**), which reaffirmed religious freedom but failed to end Protestant–Catholic conflict. With Spain and the Holy Roman Empire militarily exhausted, France enjoyed unrivaled prestige after 1659. The Dutch also benefited because the long struggle had weakened their former ruler, Spain. After Westphalia, Europe fought wars with well-drilled professional soldiers, large warships, and more deadly cannon and rifles.

absolutism A system of strong monarchial authority in which all power is placed in a supreme authority, a king or queen.

In the most widespread conflict, the War of the Spanish Succession (1701–1714), England, Holland, Austria, Denmark, Portugal, and some German states battled France and Spain over who would inherit the Spanish throne and how Spain's empire might be partitioned. War's human costs increased. Hence, one battle resulted in forty thousand French soldiers killed or wounded. The Treaty of Utrecht (**YOO-trekt**) ending the war transferred Spain's territory in Belgium and Italy to Austria. Once-prosperous Holland, by overextending itself, had damaged its economy. England received the most spoils, including some French territory in eastern Canada as well as the strategic Gibraltar peninsula at Spain's southern tip, which commanded the entrance to the Mediterranean Sea. Gibraltar remains a British territory today and a source of political conflict with Spain. Utrecht fostered a new European system that maintained a power balance between rival states.

15-3b Absolutist and Despotic Monarchies

These conflicts and new mindsets created diverse political patterns by the seventeenth century, among them **absolutism**, a system of strong monarchial authority with all power placed under one supreme king or queen. Hoping to avoid chaos, Spain and Habsburg-ruled Austria, the Papal States of central Italy (governed by the Vatican), and the Turk-dominated Ottoman Empire all exercised absolutist power. But French kings and Russian czars best represented this concentration of power.

For a time Europe was dazzled by the French absolute monarchy of King Louis XIV (r. 1661–1715), the envy of other rulers. French became the language of European diplomacy, and some European leaders, like Prussia's Frederick the Great, so admired aristocratic French culture that they spoke the language more than their native tongue. French art and architecture were imitated as far away as imperial Russia. By the mid-1600s France, with eighteen million people, was western Europe's largest country, self-sufficient in agriculture, and

Troops Plundering a Village during the Thirty Year' War, 1660 (oil on canvas)/Wael, Cornelis de (1592-1667)/DEUTSCHES HISTORISCHES MUSEUM/Deutsches Historisches Museum, Berlin, Germany/Bridgeman Images

IMAGE 15.4 **Troops Plundering a Village** Common people suffered along with soldiers from European wars. This 1660 painting by Cornelis de Wael shows soldiers looting a village and seizing animals during the Thirty Years War.

Q What do we learn about life in Europe during the wars in this era?

with thriving industries. The king's mercantilism fostered royal-dominated industries and companies; he also revoked the Edict of Nantes, forbade Protestant pastors to preach, and closed Protestant schools and churches; as a result, 200,000 Huguenots emigrated to England, Holland, and North America.

Louis XIV believed he was the state and that his power derived from God, making him a monarch by divine right. Known as the "Sun King" for his court's brilliant extravagance and love of glory, he demanded obedience from all. Few French kings valued marital fidelity; Louis had many mistresses and children, legitimate and illegitimate. At Versailles (**vuhr-SIGH**), a Paris suburb, some five thousand servants and courtiers lived at the Sun King's spectacular palace. Versailles became the center of French cultural life, regularly visited by French nobles and foreign leaders. Louis's brilliant finance minister, Jean Baptiste Colbert (**kohl-BEAR**), complained that "every day is one long round of dances, comedies, music of all kinds, promenades, hunts and other entertainments."[8] The king gave annual allowances to a court composer and financed playwrights and ballet dancers.

To prevent Habsburg dominance, Louis XIV caused four major wars that proved financially ruinous and fell short of their objectives. The War of the Spanish Succession sapped the

French treasury and military, enabling Austria, England, and Holland to counterbalance French power. Although France remained a major state, it lost some glory, and the French monarchy collapsed in revolution in the late 1700s.

In Russia, the czars developed a tyrannical government. After Russians freed themselves from Mongol domination, the brutal, paranoid Ivan (**ee-VON**) IV (r. 1533–1584), known as Ivan the Terrible, built a centralized state, fought wars with neighboring Poland and Sweden, conquered the Tartar states founded by Mongols and Turks, and ordered the death or torture of Russians he considered enemies. Courting the landed nobility, Muscovite czars after Ivan tightly controlled the Russian Orthodox Church and a serfdom-based rural economy. Because serfs could be sold by their lords, they were little better than slaves. Czars also began extending their sovereignty toward the Black and Baltic Seas, sparking conflict with Poles and Lithuanians.

Enlightened but despotic, Peter I the Great (r. 1682–1725), nearly seven feet tall, attempted to transform Russia into a modern state by copying Western technology and administrative techniques. He secretly toured Europe for eighteen months, visiting factories, museums, government offices, hospitals, and

[8]Quoted in *What Life Was Like During the Age of Reason* (Alexandria, VA: Time-Life Books, 1999), 18.

IMAGE 15.5 **Saint Petersburg** This painting shows the Summer Palace, built in 1744, of the imperial family in the Russian capital city of St. Petersburg, a major port that attracted many trading ships. The extravagant palace had one hundred and sixty rooms.

Q What can we learn about the Russian royal families and Russian government from this painting?

universities and even working as a carpenter in a Dutch ship-yard to view advanced industrial and military technology. Upon returning to Russia, the czar hired foreign advisers and launched ambitious political, economic, military, and educational reforms. These Westernizing policies had mixed consequences. Some, such as banning beards, were superficial and unpopular. Peter also increased royal power, often harshly, at the expense of the church and nobility. He expanded Russia's frontiers, established industries, strengthened serfdom, formed a navy to protect his Baltic flank, and developed a more efficient government. Hating gloomy, medieval Moscow, he built a new capital on the Baltic, modeled on Amsterdam and Venice, and named it Saint Petersburg.

Wanting a stronger presence on the Sweden-dominated Baltic Sea, Peter forged a secret alliance with Denmark and Poland. During the Great Northern War (1700–1709), Russia and its allies finally forced the formidable Swedes to abandon the eastern Baltic to Russia. Russian forces then pushed south toward the Black Sea and the Straits of Bosporus, seeking permanent access to the Mediterranean Sea, which was open to shipping year-round (see Map 15.3). They also began acquiring territory in Siberia and Muslim Central Asia that contained vast resources for Russians to exploit and would eventually lead to the largest contiguous land empire since the Mongols (see Chapter 16). But although Russia developed a largely self-sufficient economy, it had limited trade with western Europe,

with most czars after Peter fearing Western influence. Today Russia remains the last great land empire and rules over various non-Russian peoples.

15-3c The Rise of Representative Governments

Some European countries moved toward greater political freedom. Iceland established an elected assembly in 930, the world's oldest and longest-running legislative body. Later Switzerland formed a multilingual, decentralized, and constitutional confederation of Catholic and Protestant districts, and Venice became a self-governing republic dominated by noble and merchant families. The Netherlands and England developed the most open and accountable governments. Enriched by sea trade, wealthy businessmen and many nobles played political roles and eventually demanded more influence.

The Netherlands enjoyed a prosperous golden age in the 1600s, building and exploiting a large colonial empire in the Americas, South Africa, Sri Lanka, and Southeast Asia while dominating the Atlantic, Baltic, and Indian Ocean trade. The Dutch East India Company, a large joint-stock company formed in 1602, made huge profits monopolizing the spice trade from southern Asia; importing Chinese silks and porcelain, Japanese art, Indian cotton textiles, and precious metals; and investing in Dutch industry. Holland's climate of freedom and tolerance

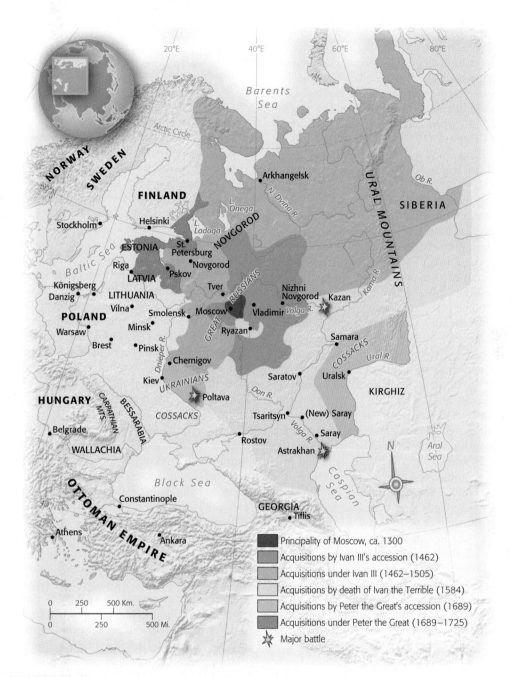

MAP 15.3 **Russian Expansion, 1300–1750** Beginning in the 1300s the Russians expanded from a small remote northern state, based in Moscow, into an empire. By the mid-1700s the Russians had spread over a wide area and gained political domination over western Siberia, the northern Caucasus, and part of what is today the eastern Baltic region and the Ukraine.

Q In what ways does this map differ from a map of Russia and Eastern Europe today?

also attracted people escaping persecution, such as Portuguese Jews, or seeking a more open intellectual atmosphere. At the same time, the wealth produced by Amsterdam, which served as a major world trade hub, fostered an innovative republican political system, as the predominantly Protestant Netherlands became a republic linked by assemblies of delegates. But tensions continued because the powerful Nassau family held the top post of Stadtholder General ("General Steward"), which controlled the army and navy and sought more authority, while the merchant elite favored provincial autonomy. Critical historians today emphasize that Holland's oppressed colonial subjects did not enjoy a "golden age."

Pursuing empire, England sent Protestant settlers to some districts in its mostly Catholic colony of Ireland and established colonies in North America and the Caribbean. Meanwhile, the English East India Company undertook commerce and conquest in Asia. Empire and growing profits from international trade fostered profound political changes.

In addition, two upheavals in the 1600s secured first a republic and then a constitutional monarchy, defining royal and parliamentary rights. After Elizabeth I died without an heir, she was replaced by the Stuarts, Scotland's royal family. With absolutist ambitions, they made Anglicanism the only recognized faith, thereby antagonizing Puritans and Presbyterians. The English civil war began in 1641, when Parliament condemned Stuart despotism. Oliver Cromwell (1599–1658), a zealous Puritan convinced he was doing God's will, led parliamentary troops who defeated royalist forces in 1645. The Stuart king Charles I was beheaded.

Parliament then abolished the monarchy and proclaimed a republican Commonwealth (1649–1660) dominated by Cromwell. The royalist defeat proved a turning point as Puritans favoring capitalism and property rights ended lingering feudalism. But the Puritan Parliamentary majority, who were fanatics determined to root out "godlessness," established laws based on the biblical edicts of Moses and, impatient with constitutional government, expelled Presbyterians from Parliament. Eventually Cromwell became dictator, imposing Puritan morality, banning newspapers, executing dissidents, and crushing a Catholic rebellion in Ireland by burning crops and massacring thousands of Irish resistors. On Cromwell's death Parliament restored the Stuarts after they accepted individual religious freedom.

However, Protestant–Catholic conflicts resumed, eventually leading to a stronger Parliament, dominated by Anglicans, that offered the kingship to Dutch Stadtholder William of Orange, a zealous Protestant. Meanwhile, riots forced pro-Catholic James II (r. 1685–1688) to flee to France. In the Glorious Revolution (1688–1689), Parliament decreed William and his wife, Mary, sovereigns after they accepted a Bill of Rights recognizing the right of petition and requiring parliamentary approval of taxes to support the monarchy and army. The Toleration Act followed, establishing freedom of religion.

Although the Glorious Revolution modified royal power, the government represented only the landed nobility, wealthy merchants, and property owners. In 1707 England, Scotland, and Wales officially combined as the United Kingdom, often known as Great Britain. English supremacy exploited ethnic minorities, for example, by clearing feisty Scottish highlanders from their lands and banning their Celtic language, Gaelic (**GAY-lik**). In colonized Ireland, Protestant English and Scottish settlers acquired land, while laws denied the majority Irish Catholics the right to education, property, and political office.

15-3d Rising New States, Declining Old States

Capitalism, religious change, warfare, and shifting political fortunes fostered several powerful new states while harming several longtime powers (see Map 15.4). Habsburg-ruled, German-speaking, Catholic Austria became a major empire after the Thirty Years War, governing Czechs, Croats, Slovenians, Hungarians, and some Italians, Romanians, and Serbs. Sweden became independent of once-mighty Denmark in 1520, forging a hereditary but not absolutist monarchy with a national assembly and Lutheranism as the state religion. Although the Swedes dominated Baltic trade, the Dutch eventually outcompeted them. Under King Gustavus Adolphus (r. 1611–1632), a brilliant military strategist, Sweden conquered parts of Poland, Prussia, and the eastern Baltic. By 1721, however, Russia and Prussia had displaced the Swedes from all their eastern Baltic possessions except Finland.

Prussia, a mostly German-speaking eastern Baltic state, became independent from Poland in 1660. Under King Frederick the Great (r. 1740–1786), an authoritarian but constitutional monarch, Prussia built a formidable standing army and rapidly expanded at the expense of Poland, Austria, and the Holy Roman Empire. A brilliant strategist, Frederick was ruthless but also a fine musician who enjoyed conversations with philosophers.

Several older states declined. Holy Roman Emperors, elected by leading princes, were figureheads who presided symbolically over some three hundred states representing assorted Germans, eastern Europeans, and Italians. The French writer Voltaire (**vawl-TARE**) mocked the incoherent entity as neither holy nor Roman nor an empire. In 1740 Austria and Prussia began a one-hundred-and-thirty-year struggle for regional dominance. Meanwhile, the pope, the Habsburgs, and the Holy Roman Empire ruled the many small Italian states. In 1569 predominantly Catholic Poland and Lithuania formed a combined republican commonwealth under elected kings and noble-dominated national and local assemblies. The commonwealth enjoyed economic prosperity and religious tolerance, and its large Jewish communities enjoyed many legal rights. But by the mid-1600s it struggled amid rebellion and invasion by Russians, who slaughtered Jews. Catholics turned on Protestants, and after 1717 Russia dominated Poland and annexed Lithuania. Catholicism became crucial to Polish and Lithuanian identity.

KEY POINTS

▶ Louis XIV of France, the archetypal absolutist monarch, lived in astounding luxury and wielded great power.

▶ Russian czars from Ivan the Terrible on exercised tight control while expanding Russia's territory, traditions that Peter the Great continued while pushing to modernize and Westernize his country.

▶ The Dutch were successful colonial merchants and instituted a decentralized republican system of government that was strained by the military power held by the Nassau family.

▶ Through a series of struggles between Parliament and monarchs, English political power became more equally shared, though it was still held largely by wealthy aristocrats and merchants.

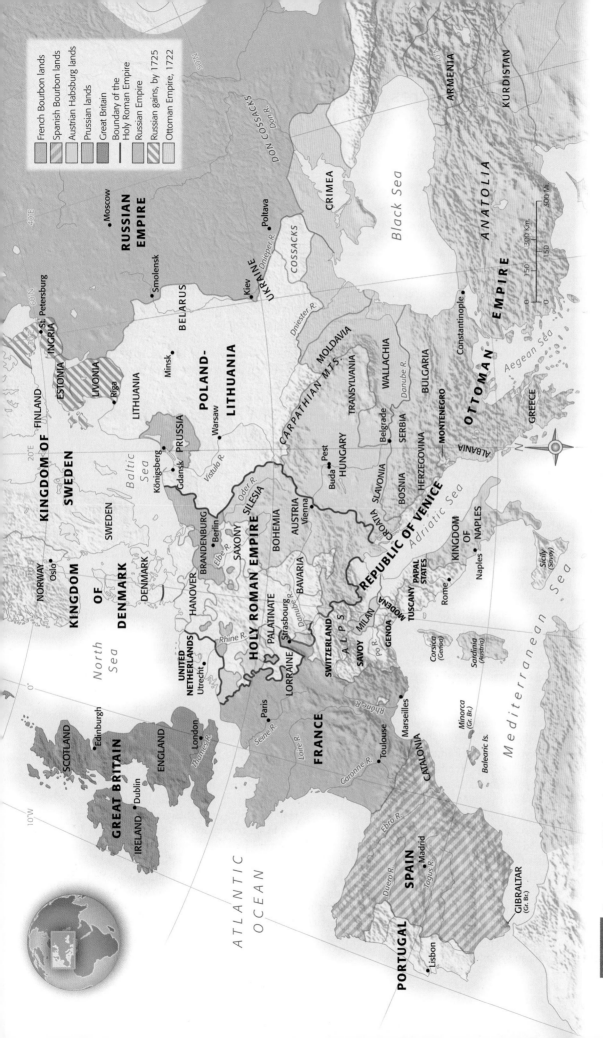

MAP 15.4 Europe in 1740 By the mid-1700s France and Great Britain were the most powerful western European states. While once powerful Spain and Portugal had lost influence and the Germans and Italians remained divided, Prussia, Sweden, Russia, and Habsburg-ruled Austria were gaining strength.

Q What states on this map have disappeared or been completely changed today?

Legend:
- French Bourbon lands
- Spanish Bourbon lands
- Austrian Habsburg lands
- Prussian lands
- Great Britain
- Boundary of the Holy Roman Empire
- Russian Empire
- Russian gains, by 1725
- Ottoman Empire, 1722

15-4 The Transformation of Cultures and Societies

TRANSITIONS   SOCIETIES

Q How did major intellectual, scientific, and social changes help to reshape the West?

Voyages of discovery and colonization altered Europeans' worldview, broadened horizons, and fostered intellectual change. In England, Scotland, Switzerland, Poland-Lithuania, and especially the Netherlands, some religious tolerance and diversity undermined barriers to free thought. Science, philosophy, and technology proceeded with fewer obstacles than elsewhere. Meanwhile, with religious or philosophical dogmatism becoming stronger in the Islamic world, China, and India, they produced fewer technological and scientific breakthroughs and innovative thinkers than before. Nevertheless, European thinkers borrowed Islamic and Asian ideas. Meanwhile, capitalism spurred by overseas expansion reshaped social patterns, creating an increasingly urban society.

15-4a Arts and Philosophy

In the 1600s the Renaissance and Reformation led to an extravagant artistic movement. One new style, the **baroque** ("contorted" or "grotesque"), shocked people by limiting restraints on expression while questioning accepted ideas. In Italy Roman sculptor Gianlorenzo Bernini **(buhr-NEE-nee)** (1598–1680) emphasized freedom through expressive, sensuous marble statues and fountains. Commercial bounty also led to Dutch artistic breakthroughs, as wealthy Dutch merchants commissioned artworks celebrating personal success, Protestant values, and the material world to decorate their houses, town halls, and guild halls. Painters catered to this taste, offering realistic pictures of everyday life, group portraits, landscapes, and the interiors of well-appointed houses. Nearly every Dutch family of means owned at least one original piece of art. Unlike earlier Renaissance artists, Dutch artists viewed their work as a capitalist enterprise, often producing for the market rather than individual patrons.

Many Dutch painters concentrated on landscapes, still lives, and domestic scenes, rejecting medieval preoccupation with religious themes. The paintings of Rembrandt van Rijn (1606-1669) and Jan Vermeer (1632–1675) conveyed emotion, immediacy, personality, and individuals' thoughts and feelings. Rembrandt's prolific and well-paid work took art beyond Renaissance traditions. Influenced by baroque interest in emotions and light, Rembrandt portrayed the pain, power, and pride of humankind by manipulating the direction, distance, and intensity of light and shadow to reveal nuances of mood and character. His portraits of churchmen, poets, rich merchants, and fashionable ladies penetrated deeply into their souls and inner feelings. Reflecting a growing world economy, some Dutch paintings

baroque An extravagant and, to many, shocking European artistic movement of the 1600s that encouraged release from restraints of thought and expression.

also showed imported foreign products such as Chinese bowls, Turkish carpets, Southeast Asian spices, and American tobacco.

Not all creative people represented baroque attitudes. German Lutheran composers George Frederick Handel (1685–1750) and Johann Sebastian Bach **(BAHCH)** (1685–1759) produced popular works that appealed to a wide audience. Settled in London, Handel wrote his famous choral work, *The Messiah*, while Bach composed pieces for both Protestant and Catholic churches. Bach's cantata about a young woman so madly in love with coffee that her father feared she would never find a husband memorialized the growing fad for such imported products.

In philosophy and science, the questioning of accepted ideas led to the greatest speculation in Europe since the Classical Greeks. For example, former English politician Francis Bacon (1561–1626) sought to eliminate intellectual restraints on science by applying reason and separating philosophy from theology. With the famous maxim "Knowledge is power," Bacon developed the scientific method: developing an idea, testing it experimentally, and drawing conclusions. These ideas, unsettling at the time, greatly influenced later thinkers.

Usually described as modern philosophy's founding father, René Descartes **(DAY-cart)** (1596–1650) rejected medieval ways of thinking and promoted a rationalist view of the world. Born in France, Descartes traveled widely and served in both Dutch and Bavarian armies. Viewing human rationality as founded on a distinction between mind and body, he wanted to sweep away traditional learning and establish a new system of knowledge. The only thing he could not doubt was his own existence, writing: "While I wanted to think everything false, it was absolutely necessary that I, who was thinking thus, must be something. I think, therefore I am."[9] Besides philosophy, Descartes studied mathematics, optics, physics, and physiology. But Descartes's reputation in history is controversial. Some recent studies suggest that his philosophical ideas were dismissed by some of his contemporaries as unoriginal and based on other thinkers, some of them women, but that nineteenth-century philosophers, with their own agendas, promoted his special place in the history of thought.

On a more somber note, the pessimistic English political thinker Thomas Hobbes (1588–1679) believed that society was not perfectible, even using reason or Christian teachings; with no government to control humanity's anarchic, power-seeking instincts, life was "solitary, poor, nasty, brutish, and short."[10] His disturbing book, *The Leviathan* **(la-VIA-thin)**, provided a new view of the relationship between the state and the individual, arguing that people needed despotic power to control them. Truth, reason, and justice were artificial attributes created by social convention and language. Although many condemned

CONNECTION to TODAY
What major features of life and thought in this era stand out as important in the world today?

Hobbes's royalist slant and apparent atheism, his idea of a social contract between citizens and rulers influenced later thinkers.

15-4b Science and Technology

The **Scientific Revolution** (ca. 1600–1750), an era of rapid advance in knowledge, particularly in mathematics and astronomy, built on the work of Bacon and Descartes to gain a new understanding of the natural and physical world. European scientists demolished the medieval view of Earth's position in the cosmos and laid the groundwork for intellectual and industrial transitions. Although religious conflicts and despotic monarchs often made it dangerous to offer new ideas, advances occurred in many areas.

The Scientific Revolution derived partly from imported Asian and Islamic ideas and technologies. European scientists were familiar with the writings of earlier Muslim thinkers and, thanks to reports from Jesuit missionaries, Chinese scientific traditions and inventions. French King Louis XIV sent a mission to China to acquire scientific and technical knowledge. As Europeans assimilated and improved imported models while creating new ones, leadership in scientific and technology gradually shifted from China and the Middle East to Europe. Some scientists gained knowledge from travel abroad. For example, Maria Sibylla Merian (1647–1717), German-born but living in Holland, managed a household and raised children but also made a successful career as an artist, botanist, and entomologist, publishing many books about insects. In 1699 she sailed to tropical Suriname in South America to research her magnum opus on plants and insects there, revealing a new insect world to fascinated Europeans. Merian was the first naturalist to bring together insects and their habitats into a single ecological study.

Astronomers made some of the most significant discoveries. While also improving telescopes, German mystic Johannes Kepler (1571–1630) used mathematics to confirm that all the planets revolved around the sun. The Italian Galileo Galilei (**gal-uh-LAY-oh gal-uh-LAY-ee**) (1564–1642) proved Copernicus's theories experimentally. By adapting spectacles, invented in Holland, in 1609 Galileo built the first telescope, with which he discovered that the moon had mountains, Jupiter had four large moons, and our solar system was but a small part of a Milky Way galaxy containing countless stars. These findings contradicting church teaching were dangerous, especially since Galileo insulted critics, mocked conventional wisdom, and criticized the biblical view of astronomy as ignorant. In 1615 the Catholic Church summoned the scientist to Rome to be tried for heresy and forced him to publicly recant his views to leave prison. When he continued writing, Inquisition officials placed him under house arrest for life.

Later, Sir Isaac Newton (1642–1727), a mathematics professor at Cambridge University, synthesized Bacon's methodologies, Descartes's mathematics, Galileo's discoveries, and other scientific findings to discover some fundamental laws of physics. A famous epitaph by the poet Alexander Pope proclaimed Newton's importance: "Nature and Nature's laws lay hidden in night; God said, 'Let Newton be!' and all was light."[11]

In 1687 Newton's book *Mathematical Principles of Natural Philosophy*, describing all the motions of the planets, the comets, the moon, and the sea, revealed the connection, especially the law of universal gravitation, that tied together varied parts of the physical world into an ordered whole. Newton's ideas dominated Western scientific thinking for the next two hundred years.

Scientific discoveries led to new technology. Useful items like the watch, the lead pencil, the thermometer, concrete, the slide rule, and the first mechanical calculator to perform multiplication, division, and much more appeared. Dutchman Christian Huygens (**HYE-guhnz**) introduced a more accurate clock. In the early 1700s, an English farmer, Jethro Tull, using a two-millennia-old Chinese model, developed a drill to sow seeds, the first step toward rural mechanization. Perhaps inspired by Chinese models, Englishman Thomas Newcomen invented the first crude steam engine to pump water from mines. Finally, by the 1730s England's textile industry efficiently produced cotton products with spinning machines that were similar to much older Chinese machines.

15-4c The Enlightenment

Another development of this era was the **Enlightenment**, often called the Age of Reason, a philosophical movement based on science and reason that rejected many traditional ideas. The Enlightenment began in 1675 and continued until 1800. Scholars debate whether it was a single movement across Europe or rather separate intellectual experiences in different countries. There are also scholars who argue that the term "Age of Reason" is misleading or even mistaken, since the movement was a diverse phenomenon, personal and intellectual rivalries were common, some thinkers also reflected passion and superstition, and both liberal and conservative currents existed. Whatever the case, the movement owed something to Bacon, Descartes, and Newton as well as to growing European knowledge of Native American societies, Islam, and secular Chinese thought. In 1687 a French observer wrote that the Confucian "moral system is infinitely sublime, simple, sensible. Never has Reason appeared so well developed with so much power."[12] In fact, some historians call Confucius the Enlightenment's patron saint. For many the Enlightenment replaced unquestioning religious faith with observed fact, suggested that objective truth could be established through reason, and took human destiny away from God and placed it in human free will. Many Enlightenment thinkers admired Christianity's moral authority but opposed organized churches' dogmatic attitudes. Some adopted **deism**, believing in a benevolent God who designed the universe but does not intercede in its affairs. Some French Enlightenment

Scientific Revolution An era of rapid European advance in knowledge, particularly in mathematics and astronomy, that occurred between 1600 and 1750.

Enlightenment A philosophical movement based on science and reason that began in Europe in the late seventeenth century and continued through the eighteenth century.

deism Belief in a benevolent God who designed the universe but does not intercede in its affairs.

---

[11]Quoted in Norman Davies, *Europe: A History* (New York: Harper, 1996), 599.
[12]Quoted in John M. Hobson, *The Eastern Origins of Western Civilisation* (Cambridge, UK: Cambridge University Press, 2004), 194.

thinkers studied and critiqued Islam along with Christianity, giving the study of Islam a new importance in Europe. While they generally reflected ethnocentric attitudes, their studies represented the beginning of the new intellectual field of comparative religion, while promoting religious tolerance. They influenced Americans like Benjamin Franklin and William Penn, who believed that Muslim theologians should have the freedom to preach their religion to the citizens of Philadelphia.

In England, France, and Scotland, new notions of tolerance, individual rights, and the citizen–state relationship emerged. The Enlightenment spread humanistic secularism, promoted critical approaches to knowledge, and addressed gender issues such as women's education and marriage equality. For example, in France Louise d'Epinay (1726–1783) condemned gender discrimination and negative female stereotypes, arguing that both women and men "struggle against pain, difficulties, obstacles [and] have the same nature."[13] Some male thinkers also favored women's education and equality. Yet, gender issues were often marginalized, with many Enlightenment thinkers accepting the era's prejudices.

empiricism An approach that stresses experience and the testing of propositions rather than reason alone in acquiring knowledge.

philosophes The intellectuals who fostered the French Enlightenment.

A major Enlightenment thinker was Englishman John Locke (1632–1704), a physician who lived for a decade in France and Holland. Locke made experimental science studies that led him to proclaim the value of **empiricism**, which stressed experience and the testing of propositions rather than reason alone to acquire knowledge. Empirical approaches later became common in the social and natural sciences. Locke's influential political theories also provided a foundation for modern democratic states and notions of human freedom. He condemned absolute monarchy and advocated defending freedom through cooperation for common goals, allowing the state only limited powers over individuals. He also stated that people had the right to oppose a state that suppressed freedom and self-government. But although Locke favored individual rights, such as separation of church and state, he also favored restricting political participation to people with property. Many of his ideas became influential not only in England but also among the founders of the United States. In the Declaration of Independence in 1776, Thomas Jefferson enshrined Locke's view that people were entitled to life, liberty, and property.

The French Enlightenment was expressed by intellectuals known as **philosophes** (fill-uh-SOHF) (philosophers). In Paris, educated women such as Madame Maria-Therese Geoffrin (JOFF-rin) (1699–1777) operated salons (sa-LAW):

IMAGE 15.6 **Madame Geoffrin's Paris Salon** The painting shows various distinguished intellectuals meeting in the living room in Madame Geoffrin's salon in Paris to read and discuss a play by Voltaire, which had been published in 1755. The play was a tragedy about Genghis Khan and his sons.

Q What can you tell from the painting about the salons and the people who attended them?

[13] From Dena Goodman and Kathleen Wellman, eds., *The Enlightenment* (Boston: Houghton Mifflin, 2004), 167.

Emilie du Chatelet, Enlightenment Scientist

Emilie du Chatelet overcame gender stereotypes and expectations to transform herself from wife, mother, and court figure into one of the French Enlightenment's more influential mathematicians and scientists. Born in Paris in 1706 to an aristocratic family that, defying the nobility's dislike of educating girls, encouraged her intellectual pursuits, she was freed by her wealth to pursue the life of the mind. Her father presided over weekly salons in their home, where she could listen to conversations between learned and talented men, and also arranged for prominent thinkers to tutor her. She became fluent in four languages (German, Italian, Latin, and Greek) and also learned riding and fencing.

In 1725 the nineteen-year-old woman married thirty-four-year-old Marquis Florent-Claude du Chatelet-Lomont, a military officer who proved a pragmatic, tolerant spouse with whom she had three children. Now with the title of marquise, she indulged avidly in court social life at Versailles, enjoying dancing, acting, opera singing, and harpsichord playing. Yet, the high-spirited, passionate, determined young woman refused to give up her intellectual pursuits, including translating Greek and Latin philosophy and plays and studying mathematics. Receiving little support from the scientific establishment because of her gender, she continuously fought prejudice. A freethinker who criticized conventional religion—the marquise considered Jesus "a pious fraud"—du Chatelet strongly advocated women's education, writing,

> I feel the full weight of the prejudice which so universally excludes us from the sciences;…there is no place where we are trained to think….Let the reader ponder why, at no time in the course of so many centuries, a good tragedy, a good poem, a respected tale, a fine painting, a good book on physics has ever been produced by women. Why these creatures whose understanding appears in every way similar to that of men, seem to be stopped by some irresistible force, this side of a barrier. Let the people give a reason, but until they do, women will have reason to protest against their education.…

In 1733, while her husband pursued his career and acquired mistresses, the marquise began a long friendship and then romantic relationship with the French Enlightenment's leading but controversial figure, Voltaire, who had recently returned from exile in England. They moved to her country house in northeastern France, where they maintained an intense intellectual collaboration. Many prominent thinkers visited the home. The collaboration and idea exchange proved fruitful for both. She published an important work in physics, including a paper on fire that explored the nature of light and infrared radiation, and a pioneering textbook that, among other subjects, explored the scientific method. The two coauthored *The Elements of the Philosophy of Newton*, introducing Newton's theories to readers who lacked knowledge of higher mathematics. Her last and greatest project, published after her death, was the grueling translation, with an insightful commentary, of Newton's seminal *Principia Mathematica* from Latin into French. Her analysis of Newton's ideas foreshadowed modern concepts of kinetic energy.

Eventually the marquise's romance with Voltaire faded. In 1748 she fell in love with the much younger courtier and poet Marquis de Saint Lambert, but she died in 1749 at age forty-three shortly after a difficult pregnancy and birth of their daughter. Remaining her close confidant, Voltaire was crushed by her death. His earlier poem memorialized her: "Here's a portrait of my Émilie: / She's both a beauty and a friend to me. / Her keen imagination is always in bloom. / Her noble mind brightens every room. / She's possessed of charm and wit…/ She has, I assure you, a genius rare."

DEA/G DAGLI ORTI/Age Fotostock

IMAGE 15.7 **Portrait of Émilie du Châtelet** The multitalented enlightenment thinker, philosopher, mathematician, and scientist was pictured here at her desk pondering her current writing or translation project.

Reflection Questions

1. How did Marquise du Chatelet become a scientist?
2. How did her relationship with Voltaire shape her career?
3. What were some of her major contributions to knowledge?
4. Do you think that du Chatelet could be a role model for women today?

Note: Quotations from Karen Frenkel, "Why Aren't More Women Physicists?" *Scientific American*, January 14, 2007, scientificamerican.com/article.cfm?id=why-arent-more-women-phys and eee.uci.edu/clients/bjbecker/RevoltingIdeas/emilie.html#divine.

elegant rooms where thinkers and artists gathered for conversation. Baron de Montesquieu (**maw-tuh-SKYOO**) (1689–1755), attacking religious dogma and arbitrary, absolutist power, proposed a republican government with checks and balances, including separation of powers between the executive, legislature, and judiciary. Colonists in North America widely discussed his ideas. The best-known philosophe, Voltaire (1694–1778), a poet, dramatist, and historian, believed that science, empiricism, and rational behavior led to happier lives. Occasionally imprisoned in France, he spent many years in England, Switzerland, and Prussia. Voltaire viewed China as an admirable model, a despotic but secular, benevolent state contrasting with absolutist France. A deist, he supported tolerance toward other views but fiercely attacked established religion and disliked the Jews for their separation, often involuntary, from mainstream society. Challenging gender discrimination, Voltaire's friend and then lover, Emilie du Chatelet (**EM-ih-lee de SHA-the-lay**) (1706–1749), wrote works on mathematics, natural philosophy, and the ideas of scientists such as Newton (see Meet the People: Emilie du Chatelet, Enlightenment Scientist).

15-4d Capitalism and Rural Society

Capitalism gradually reshaped rural society and turned many peasants into a displaced labor force. In sixteenth-century England, King Henry VIII seized Catholic Church land and distributed some to his cronies including wealthy businessmen who bought land as an investment, turning agriculture from subsistence living to commercial venture. In addition, hard-hearted landowners increased demands on peasants or shifted to more profitable sheep raising, ejecting peasants from the land. As a result, landless English peasants became tenant farmers and poor farm workers for big landlords. Some former peasants found jobs in towns, became rural craftsmen, or became rural vagabonds drifting around the countryside and resorting to any measures, including crime, to stay alive. Nursery rhymes reveal their plight and the country's negative, "blame the victim" attitudes: "Hark hark the dogs do bark, the beggars are coming to town. Some give them white bread, and some give them brown, and some give them a good horsewhip and send them out of town." While feudal people generally believed that individual well-being resulted from the inequitable manor system, under capitalism people were considered responsible for their own condition, whether wealth or poverty. Some communities imprisoned debtors and flogged the homeless.

While land loss ruined many peasant lives, it also created a labor pool for fledgling industries, giving England an advantage over the labor-short Dutch and over the French, who were reluctant to abandon feudal laws protecting peasants. Businessmen gave crafts production to displaced peasants, paying for each item they made, undermining guilds, and destroying medieval concepts of economic justice. Eventually these trends reached other western European societies. Nothing like the forced peasantry's impoverishment happened elsewhere. The Chinese and Ottoman imperial power could curb landowner and merchant greed, preventing land seizures. Thus western European

peasants, many heavily consuming alcohol as an escape, fared worse than peasants in Islamic societies.

The great rich–poor contrast, amplified by famine and devastating wars, sparked uprisings, such as the bloody 1524 peasant revolt in Germany. In England, the civil war fostered widespread discontent and radical movements such as the Levellers, led by lower-class soldiers who advocated equality, democracy, and complete religious freedom; in their 1648 manifesto, they pleaded, "May the pressing needs of our stomachs reach Parliament and the City [London]; may the tears of our starving babies be preserved; may the cries of their tender mothers begging for bread to feed them be graven in metal."[14] Life became increasingly dangerous and unhealthy. Bandits and mercenary soldiers attacked travelers, merchant convoys, and villages. Many fled to overcrowded cities, which were filled with beggars, drunks, trash-filled streets, polluted water, human waste stench, and disease. In the 1600s one-third of London's children died before the age of one. In France people said that nine-tenths of people died of hunger, one-tenth of indigestion.

15-4e Families and Gender Relations

For northern Europe's growing middle classes, the nuclear family of parents and their natural-born children, rare in medieval times, became more common, unlike southern and eastern Europe's large extended families. Societies increasingly recognized childhood as a distinct life phase, inventing toys and games while opening more schools, mostly for boys. However, at least half of children left their families by their early teens, many to become apprentices or servants with other families.

Women's economic roles and status shifted. With more consumer goods, women could now purchase rather than produce such items as cotton clothing. Men now made much higher wages than women, diminishing women's social status. Whereas many medieval women never married but worked in diverse occupations, now women were encouraged to look chiefly to marriage, motherhood, and the home. While northwest European women married in their twenties, early teenage brides were common elsewhere. Still, between 10 and 20 percent of people never married, and the Roman Catholic Church encouraged church vocations over marriage. At the Council of Trent church leaders rejected Protestantism's married clergy, denouncing the notion that "it is better and happier to be united in matrimony than to remain in virginity and celibacy."[15]

Women's experiences varied. Many Dutch women enjoyed liberated lives, some becoming merchants. Elsewhere, some women engaged in trade. German Jewish merchant Glukel of Hameln (**HAH-muhln**) (1646–1724), a mother of eight, traveled widely to trade fairs. But few women controlled financial resources. Some women wrote fiction, plays, poems, memoirs, and diaries, but most could not get their work published. A few educated French women, like Emilie du Chatelet, achieved intellectual and cultural influence. At the opposite extreme, many Russian women were, as a German visitor claimed, "most miserable; for men consider no woman virtuous unless they live at home, and be so closely guarded that she go out nowhere."[16]

---

[14]Quoted in Frederic Delouche et al., *Illustrated History of Europe: A Unique Portrait of Europe's Common History* (New York: Barnes and Noble, 2001), 247.
[15]Quoted in Diarmaid MacCulloch, *The Reformation: A History* (New York: Penguin, 2005), 609.
[16]Quoted in Robert Wallace, *Rise of Russia* (New York: Time-Life Books, 1967), 140.

Class divisions defined the social structure for men and women. Few lower-class women found paid work except as servants in affluent households. Some women faced worse problems. Millions of men and women believed in magic, astrology, prophecy, ghosts, and witches, thought to destroy crops and cause personal misfortunes. The execution or banishment from the community of thousands of women suspected of witchcraft, often after horrific ordeals, provided a diversion from wars and religious conflicts. In a Polish trial, a suspected witch was stripped naked, bound hand and foot, and suspended from the ceiling before confessing.

More restrictive views of sexuality promoted punishing women and men who defied convention. Often prompted by churches, governments regulated sexual and moral behavior to encourage family life, prosecuting adultery and premarital sex. Yet, premarital pregnancy rates ranged from 10 to 30 percent.

Condemned by Catholic and Protestant churches, homosexuals faced severe sanctions, including execution. With erratic law enforcement, especially in tolerant England and Scandinavia, male homosexuals congregated in large cities. Anti-sodomy laws in Catholic countries often ignored the nobility and clergy, some of whom advocated same-sex relationships. Some influential or famous men were possible or probable homosexuals, among them Leonardo da Vinci, Michelangelo, Francis Bacon, and several popes and kings such as Prussian Frederick the Great; many European kings had same-sex bedmates. Fewer lesbians were public. Yet, the cosmopolitan, flamboyant Swedish queen Christina (1626–1689), an outspoken supporter of the French Enlightenment and science who spoke some ten languages, had a long affair with one of her ladies-in-waiting and, after abdicating her crown, maintained an active sexual life in Rome with both men and women.

KEY POINTS

▶ The extravagant baroque style that followed the Renaissance emphasized artistic freedom, while Dutch painters eschewed religious themes for natural ones.

▶ Bacon and Descartes emphasized the role of reason in science and philosophy, respectively, while Thomas Hobbes developed a pessimistic political philosophy.

▶ Advances in astronomy, particularly those made by Galileo, greatly antagonized Catholic officials, while Isaac Newton discovered fundamental laws of physics.

▶ Locke, Montesquieu, and Voltaire were among the prominent thinkers of the Enlightenment, a movement that favored reason over unquestioning faith.

Chapter Summary

During the Early Modern Era many agrarian, feudalistic societies in Europe were reshaped and the basis for globalization was established. The Portuguese and Spanish pioneered maritime exploration and flourished from their American, African, and Asian conquests. The Dutch, English, and French also developed overseas empires that brought them considerable wealth. Meanwhile, the growth of trade, capitalism, and mercantilism created a new commercial orientation while shifting economic and political power to the countries of the Atlantic seaboard. The Renaissance, which spread humanist and secular values, and then the Reformation changed Europe's philosophical and religious terrain, challenging the Roman Church. By the mid-1500s Protestant churches dominated much of northern Europe. These challenges generated a Counter Reformation within the Catholic Church.

Wars raged during much of the era and contributed to political changes. France and Russia developed absolutist monarchies, whereas England and Holland enjoyed greater political freedom. Powerful new states such as Austria and Prussia emerged while older states such as the Holy Roman Empire declined. The discovery of new lands as well as the changing political, religious, and economic forces renewed interest in scientific discovery and a stress on individual rights, leading to the Enlightenment. The Scientific Revolution produced such revolutionary thinkers as Newton and allowed Europe to surpass China and the Middle East technologically. Capitalism made many rural peasants homeless, and family life, including the status of women, also changed.

Key Terms

capitalism 368
bourgeoisie 373
commercial capitalism 373
mercantilism 373
Reformation 374

Protestants 376
Counter Reformation 378
absolutism 380
baroque 386
Scientific Revolution 387

Enlightenment 387
deism 387
empiricism 388
philosophes 388

New Challenges for Africa and the Islamic World, 1450–1750

> *Warriors will fight scribes for the control of your institutions; wild bush will conquer your roads; your soil will crack from the drought; your sons will wander in the wilds. Yes, things will fall apart.*

—Igbo ancestral curse[1]

Janissaries and the parade musicians arriving, from 'Sur-Nama' (vellum)/Turkish School, (16th century)/DIDIER LENART/Private Collection/Bridgeman Images

IMAGE 16.1 **Ottoman Janissary Soldiers and Musicians On Parade** The Ottoman rulers periodically sponsored parades in Istanbul featuring soldiers, musicians, and various occupational groups, including storytellers, glassblowers, taxidermists, potters, merchants, and even executioners. This painting of one parade is from the 1500s.

Q What does this painting tell us about Ottoman customs, occupations, and military dress?

---

[1]Quoted in Ali Mazrui, *The Africans: A Triple Heritage* (Boston: Little, Brown, 1986), 11.

Things fell apart for many Africans in the Early Modern Era, including Ayuba Suleiman Diallo (ah-YOO-bah SOO-lay-mahn JAH-loh), both victim and beneficiary of the era's new challenges. In 1731 the thirty-year-old educated prince from Bondu, a West African kingdom, visited Senegambia, at Africa's western tip, on a trading mission. There he was captured by enemies, sold to the British as a slave, and eventually shipped to a tobacco plantation in Maryland. After he attempted to escape, Thomas Bluett, an English entrepreneur, recognized his ability to read and write Arabic and his connections to West African commercial life. Bluett emancipated Diallo, took him to London, and presented him at the royal court. The British hoped he might help their commercial activity in Senegambia. Agreeing to act as middleman in obtaining more slaves, Diallo returned to Bondu and resumed his life while profiting as a British trading partner.

Ayuba Suleiman Diallo's story represents the changing Atlantic world as Europe, Africa, and the Americas became increasingly linked in unprecedented ways. Diallo's West Africa now included English, Portuguese, Dutch, and French companies seeking gold, gum, hides, ivory, and especially slaves. Senegal's Gorée (go-ray) Island, near present-day Dakar (duh-KAHR), became a major slave collection center. Diallo's story is unique because he gained freedom quickly and eventually returned home. But the ancient Igbo curse proved prophetic for the millions of Africans shipped off as slaves who worked in wretched conditions and died far from their homeland. Meanwhile, many other Africans remained untouched by slave trading and other disruptive European activities, pursuing traditional ways of life, expanding and flourishing or declining and decaying from local conditions unrelated to European activities along the coasts.

The growing European power was also felt in Central Asia and the Islamic Middle East (western Asia and North Africa). By the 1500s Islam, the monotheistic religion originating in Arabia a millennium earlier, dominated huge chunks of Afro-Eurasia, from Africa's westernmost fringe to central Indonesia and the southern Philippines, linking widespread peoples through its political ideas, trade networks, and literary contributions. While experiencing changes, these Islamic societies maintained long-standing traditions and largely controlled their own destinies. Meanwhile, non-Islamic societies had increasing trade connections and conflicts with the powerful Ottoman Empire, which ruled much of western Asia, North Africa, and southeastern Europe, and a new Persian state, the Safavid Empire.

16-1 Sub-Saharan African Societies

SOCIETIES

Q How did the larger sub-Saharan African societies and states differ from each other in the sixteenth century?

As they had during the Intermediate Era many African societies flourished in the 1500s, forming great states and engaging in extensive long-distance trade (see Chapter 12). While many were Muslim, others mixed monotheism, polytheism, and animism. But the attraction of Europeans to African human and natural resources posed new challenges, reshaping some societies and changing Africa's relationship to the world. In the 1400s the Portuguese commenced exploratory voyages down the West African coast, foreshadowing dramatic changes to come.

> **CONNECTION to TODAY**
>
> What features of African culture and life before the dislocations of the trans-Atlantic slave trade can still be seen in Africa today?

16-1a The West African States

The last great Sudanic empire, Songhai (**song-GAH-ee**), remained strong through much of the 1500s (see Map 16.1). Based at Gao on the Niger River, Songhai's empire stretched fifteen hundred miles from east to west. Songhai's people blended Islam with local customs. For example, Arab visitors were shocked by the fact that Sudanic women enjoyed high social status and considerable personal liberty, dominating village markets. In some cities women were free to have lovers as they desired.

Within the Songhai Empire, Timbuktu became a major terminus for the trans-Saharan trade, shipping gold, ivory, and slaves to North Africa for Arab and European markets. A major center of Islamic scholarship, Timbuktu boasted schools, libraries,

well-stocked bookstores, and universities teaching theology, law, and literature. An early-sixteenth-century Arab Muslim visitor, Leo Africanus, reported that Timbuktu had "numerous judges, doctors of letters, and learned Muslims. The king greatly honors scholarship. Here too, they sell many handwritten books. More profit is had from their sale than from any other merchandise."[2] Leo Africanus was certainly qualified to praise the city. Born in Fez, Morocco, he had accompanied his diplomat uncle to Songhai. Later, kidnapped by pirates in the Mediterranean, he ended up in Rome as an assistant to the Pope. For the next several centuries his book on his travels became the most influential source of information on Africa for the Western world. From Africanus and other travelers we know that the Islamic University of Sankore at Timbuktu, employing well-known Arab scholars on its faculty, drew its student body from throughout the Islamic realm. In modern times scholars have found thousands of crumbling books, written in Arabic and several African languages, in forgotten Timbuktu storage rooms (see Chapter 12). Many were written in Ajami, a simplified Arabic-based alphabet invented by West Africans to write their own languages such as Hausa and Wolof.

Songhai's leadership deteriorated amidst succession struggles, and in 1591 a Moroccan invasion caused Songhai's collapse, ending the era of large western Sudanic empires. But several other West African societies exercised regional influence and profited from trade. For example, Sudanic kingdoms formed by the

[2]Quoted in Basil Davidson, ed., *African Civilization Revisited* (Trenton, NJ: African World Press, 1991), 118.

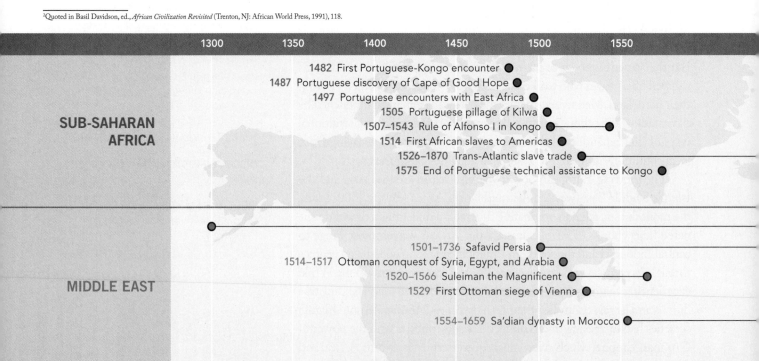

	1300	1350	1400	1450	1500	1550

SUB-SAHARAN AFRICA

1482 First Portuguese-Kongo encounter
1487 Portuguese discovery of Cape of Good Hope
1497 Portuguese encounters with East Africa
1505 Portuguese pillage of Kilwa
1507–1543 Rule of Alfonso I in Kongo
1514 First African slaves to Americas
1526–1870 Trans-Atlantic slave trade
1575 End of Portuguese technical assistance to Kongo

MIDDLE EAST

1501–1736 Safavid Persia
1514–1517 Ottoman conquest of Syria, Egypt, and Arabia
1520–1566 Suleiman the Magnificent
1529 First Ottoman siege of Vienna
1554–1659 Sa'dian dynasty in Morocco

Werner Forman/Universal Images Group/Getty Images

IMAGE 16.2 **Portuguese Visitors to Benin** This bronze plaque, one of many decorating the Benin royal palace, depicts two Portuguese men, possibly a father and son, likely traders or officials, who began visiting the kingdom in the late 1400s. The plaque was probably fashioned around 1575.

Q Does the plaque give us any insight into how the Benin artists viewed the Portuguese men and their clothing?

1600	1650	1700	1750	1800	1850	1900	1950

● 1591 Destruction of Songhai

● 1652 Dutch settlement of Cape Town

1300–1923
Ottoman Empire

1682-1699 Ottoman wars with Habsburg Austria

● 1715 Beginning of Russian conquest of Turkestan

1722 Afghan invasion of Safavid Persia ●

1736–1747 Rule of Nadir Shah in Persia ●—●

▨	Buganda
▨	Kongo
▨	Monomotapa
▨	Kingdom of Songhai, ca. 1500 CE
▨	Kingdom of Kanem-Bornu, ca. 1500 CE
▨	Hausaland
▨	Kingdom of Ethiopia
▭	Main coastal trading areas

MAP 16.1 **African States and Trade, 1500–1700** Some African states, such as Songhai, Kanem-Bornu, Benin, Lunda, Buganda, and Ethiopia, remained powerful in this era. West African coastal societies were increasingly drawn into world trade, while the East African coastal cities remained significant in Indian Ocean trade.

Q What does this map tell us about where the largest African states and regions most involved with overland and maritime trade were located in this era?

Mandinka, Bambara (**bahm-BAH-rah**), and Mossi peoples in the upper Niger Basin had effective, cavalry-based armies. The Dyula (**JOO-lah**), a Muslim mercantile clan, operated throughout West Africa, moving goods such as gold and salt with caravans of porters, canoe fleets, and donkey trains. The first European visitors tapped into these well-established trade networks and weekly

markets held in various towns. Many societies were matrilineal, with some West Africans having women chiefs or queens. Queen mothers of kings enjoyed great power, and Africans often venerated women elders for their wisdom and closeness to the ancestors.

Several strong trade-based Islamic kingdoms arose in the central and eastern Sudan. Kanem-Bornu (**KAH-nuhm-BOR-noo**),

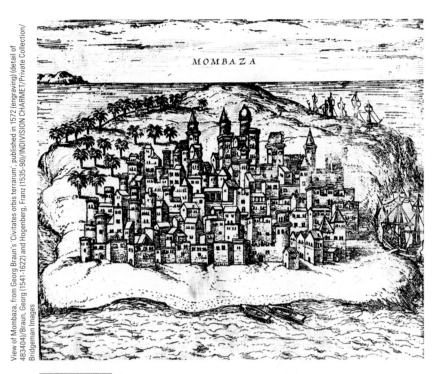

IMAGE 16.3 **The Swahili Port of Mombasa** Mombasa was one of the major port cities along the East African coast that had flourished for several centuries before the arrival of Europeans. This engraving is from 1572.

Q What do we learn about the layout and buildings of the city and its port?

centered on Lake Chad, traded slaves to North African Arabs for horses. In the late 1500s and early 1600s, King Idrus Aloma (**IH-dris ah-LOW-ma**), a devout Muslim, extended his Islamic state while importing guns and Turkish musketeers from the Ottoman Empire. Kanem-Bornu declined only in the later 1700s. Other states included the fiercely competitive Hausa city-states of what is now northern Nigeria, eastern Niger, and southern Chad. These states manufactured cotton cloth and leatherwork, some sold as far away as Europe, and Hausa merchants traded around West Africa. Although Islam gradually became the dominant faith, Hausa women, like those in other savannah states such as Songhai, played vital political and social roles. For instance, Queen Amina of Zaria (**ZAH-ree-uh**) extended her city's power while building effective walled defenses against rival states and raiders.

Non-Muslim states occupied the Guinea Coast from today's Ghana to eastern Nigeria. For example, the small Akan (**AH-kahn**) states of the Volta (**VAWL-tuh**) River Basin prospered from mining and trading gold to the north. In western Nigeria's Yoruba states, each based on a large city ruled by a king or prince, women exercised influence and could elect a representative to the chiefs' council. Oyo, the most powerful Yoruba kingdom, with a cavalry force equipped with bows, javelins, and swords, flourished until the late 1700s under able kings. Another prosperous Guinea kingdom, Benin (**buh-NEEN**) in south-central Nigeria, shared many cultural and political traditions with the Yoruba. European visitors admired the capital

city of wide streets and large wooden houses with verandas. A Dutch merchant marveled at the royal palace, which had galleries "as big as those on the Exchange at Amsterdam [supported by] wooden pillars encased with copper where their victories are depicted."[3] Benin had particularly influential queen mothers. The first and most famous was Idia, who reigned from around 1504 until 1550. She was credited with raising an army and using magic and her medical knowledge to help her son the king to overcome his enemies and handle the ambitious Portuguese, who had begun activities along the coast in the late 1400s.

16-1b Bantu Trading Cities and Kingdoms

By the sixteenth century peoples speaking closely related Bantu languages dominated much of eastern, central, and southern Africa. City-states along the East African coast from Somalia to Mozambique forged the closest ties to hemispheric networks, becoming thriving trade centers where Bantu settlers and Arab immigrants created a Swahili culture mixing African and Islamic traditions. Indonesians, Indians, Persians, and Arabs visited. And some settled in East Africa, bringing ideas, products, technologies, musical instruments, domesticated animals, and immigrants. Some cities boasted large stone and mortar buildings with terraces, towers, trees, and gardens. Prosperous Kilwa and Malindi, with their royal courts, mosques, and luxury goods, were part of the great Indian Ocean trading network dominated by seafaring Arabs and Indian Muslims. Ships from Arabia, Persia, and India regularly visited Swahili ports, which collected goods from Africa's interior, such as iron, ivory, tortoise shell, leopard skins, gold, and slaves, to be exchanged for Chinese porcelain, glass beads, and Indian cotton. Portuguese visitors to Malindi reported that the "king wore a robe of damask trimmed with green satin, and a rich turban. He was seated on two cushioned chairs of bronze, beneath a round sunshade of crimson satin attached to a pole. Two trumpets of ivory made sweet harmony."[4]

Other major Bantu states emerged inland. On the southeastern plateau bordering the Zambezi (**zam-BEE-zee**) River, the Shona people exported gold and ivory to the Middle East and India. By 1500 the once-great Shona kingdom of Zimbabwe had collapsed, replaced by competing kingdoms. By the 1700s Buganda (**boo-GON-da**), in the fertile rolling hills west of Lake Victoria in southeastern Uganda, had a well-developed bureaucracy, powerful military, and extensive trade with coastal cities. As the kingdom grew in wealth and influence, it saw a flourishing of art, poetry, dance, and philosophy. By 1500 another state, the large Kongo kingdom along the Congo River and Atlantic coast in northern Angola and western Congo, ruled 2.5 million people from a royal capital

[3]Quoted in Basil Davidson, *Africa in History* (New York: Touchstone, 1995), 176–177.
[4]Quoted in Derek Nourse and Thomas Spear, *The Swahili: Reconstructing the History and Language of an African Society, 800–1500* (Philadelphia: University of Pennsylvania Press, 1985), 82.

containing some thirty thousand residents. To the east the Luba **(LOO-buh)** and Lunda kingdoms built substantial empires in the southern Congo. Located far inland and with access to trade networks running through Central Africa, they resisted European power into the nineteenth century.

Most Bantu societies in southern Africa combined farming with cattle herding and formed small states led by chiefs. The largest, the Xhosa **(KHO-sa)** and Zulu, lived along the Indian Ocean coast. There were also scattered small cities or large towns. For example, recent research suggests that in the fifteenth century the Tswana people established Kweneng, which had perhaps 5,000 to 10,000 people, many walled family compounds, and a bustling market. The city-state was ruled by kings who regulated trade, settled disputes, and also waged war against rival cities. Around fifty thousand Khoikhoi **(KOI-KOI)**, Khoisan pastoralists Europeans later pejoratively called Hottentots **(HOT-n-TOTS)**, also lived around the Cape of Good Hope at Africa's southern tip.

16-1c Africa in the Hemispheric System

Africans had long played key roles in the hemispheric economic system but rising European power between 1450 and 1600 presented serious challenges, reshaping Africans' role in the world. Often lacking the environmental advantages and interregional connections that benefited parts of Eurasia and North Africa, sub-Saharan Africans were especially vulnerable to European and Arab power. By 1500 Eurasian and North African societies had invented or borrowed cutting-edge technologies such as printing and gunpowder weapons while developing productive economies. But few Africans encountered the Chinese technology and Indian mathematics that spurred Middle Eastern and European progress. Furthermore, much of sub-Saharan Africa had marginally fertile soils, frequent drought, scarce exploitable minerals, and few good harbors.

West and East Africans had supplied gold, ivory, and other commodities to the Middle East and Europe for centuries. Although this trade increased European interest in sub-Saharan Africa, most Europeans knew little about the region. In the Middle Ages some African slaves had been brought to North Africa and southern Europe, and an unknown number of Nubian and Ethiopian Christian soldiers had joined the European Crusaders in battling Muslims, but few Europeans and Africans had made direct contact with each other. By 1500 Islam had largely replaced Christianity in Nubia. Christianity flourished only in remote, mountainous Ethiopia, where the Amharic **(ahm-HAHR-ik)** people's state and church, related to Eastern Orthodoxy, had survived for fifteen hundred years, building splendid churches, often on steep mountainsides or canyon walls. Islamic expansion cut off the Ethiopians from Europe.

Darkest Africa Those areas of Africa least known to Europeans but, in European eyes, awaiting to be "opened" to the "light of Western civilization."

Direct contacts between Europe and sub-Saharan Africa began in the early 1400s, when Portuguese ships began exploring down West Africa's coast seeking gold, Christian allies

against Islam (based on murky recollections of Ethiopian and Nubian Christians), and a sea route to China and Southeast Asia, the sources of valuable silk and spices. Europeans' ignorance of sub-Saharan Africans and their cultures fostered the myth of **Darkest Africa** waiting to be "opened" to the "light of Western civilization." Europeans also perplexed Africans. In southern Nigeria, the first appearance of white men along the coast shocked a local fisherman, who reportedly "raced home [in a panic] and told his people what he had seen; whereupon he and the rest of the town set out to purify themselves, [to] rid themselves of the influence of the strange thing that had intruded into their world."[5]

After establishing footholds and then control in the Americas, Europeans sought large numbers of enslaved Africans to do their work. As in other world regions, slavery had existed in many African societies, and Africans had also exported slaves for centuries. Arab and Berber merchants acquired slaves in the Sudan and transported them via caravan across the Sahara to North Africa for sale to Arab or, sometimes, European owners. At the same time, an Arab-run trade from East Africa shipped slaves northward to Arabia, the Persian Gulf, Persia, and India. Over twelve centuries Arab slave traders moved perhaps 10 to 15 million enslaved Africans north. Europeans also tolerated slavery and the slave trade. Slaves from eastern Europe, particularly Russians and Greeks, had for centuries been dispatched by the Byzantines and then by the Ottomans from the Black Sea region and Balkans to Spain, Portugal, Italy, France, Central Asia, and the Middle East. Vikings and Venetians also obtained and sold slaves. By the 1400s and 1500s black slaves became increasingly common in Europe, especially Iberia (see Chapter 14). Slavery had no particular "racial" identity yet since white people could also be enslaved. But developing plantation economies in the Americas focused more attention on Africa as a slave source. Western Europeans did not invent the African slave trade, but they soon transformed it.

16-1d The Portuguese and Early African Encounters

The Portuguese had finally solved the mystery of the Atlantic winds and currents and became the first Europeans since the Classical Era to directly encounter sub-Saharan Africans. Equipped with the world's most advanced ships and gunpowder weapons, they began exploring West Africa's coastline in the early 1400s (see Chapters 12 and 14) and soon discovered and settled the uninhabited Azores and Madeira Islands. By 1471 they had reached what is today the modern nation of Ghana, where they tapped into the gold trade from Akan states, calling the region the Gold Coast. Shifting from exploration to exploitation, they then colonized the Cape Verde Islands, the nearby coastal region of Guinea-Bissau, and the small islands of Sao Tome **(tuh-MAY)** and Principe near Nigeria, establishing trading forts to obtain gold, ivory, and slaves. In the 1480s the Portuguese sent Catholic missionaries and skilled craftsmen to Kongo in South-Central Africa, thus beginning a long relationship with that prosperous kingdom. The Portuguese and Kongolese enjoyed similar standards of living and held

---

[5]Quoted in Michael Pearson, *The Indian Ocean* (New York: Routledge, 2003), 119.

similar views of government, both favoring strong monarchy. The Kongolese king, much of the elite, and some of the people adopted Christianity, blending it with their own religious concepts. But many commoners, maintaining their traditional beliefs, rejected the new religion.

In 1487 Bartolomeu Dias (ca. 1450–1500) led an expedition that sailed round Africa's southern tip into the Indian Ocean. After months at sea, he reached the Cape of Good Hope, where he and his thirsty sailors helped themselves at a watering hole without asking permission. The resident Khoikhoi threw stones, and Dias killed a herdsman with a crossbow, an encounter that foreshadowed European–African conflicts to come. But Dias's adventure intensified Portuguese interest in both Africa and Asia. Believing Dias had discovered the best route to Asia and its fabulous goods, Portugal's king rebuffed Christopher Columbus when the Italian sailor sought sponsorship to sail west. Even when Columbus returned from his first voyage in 1492 and announced, incorrectly, that he had found a sea route to India, the skeptical Portuguese pursued the route around Africa.

More Portuguese exploration followed, eventually reshaping the hemispheric trade system. In 1497 four ships commanded by Vasco da Gama (**VAS-ko dah GAH-ma**) (ca. 1469–1525), after surviving hurricanes and mutinies, sailed around the Cape and then up the East African coast, visiting the Swahili trading cities of Mozambique, Mombasa, and Malindi. There his trade goods like hats and cloaks, being of poorer quality than Asian and Arab products, failed to entice the Swahili merchants, who had no interest in his meager goods. Refocusing his attention on India, da Gama engaged a skillful pilot and sailed from Malindi to southwestern India. The Indians also told him his merchandise was unworthy and could not compete with more valuable, better-made products from India, China, Indonesia, and Persia, but da Gama had located the sea route to the East. After acquiring a small cargo of spices and precious stones, he returned home in triumph. In the following years, often using force, the Portuguese set up trading bases around the Indian Ocean, where their warships attempted to limit maritime commerce by their Arab, Ottoman, Persian, Indonesian, and Indian rivals.

KEY POINTS

▶ Songhai, the last great Sudanic kingdom with its trading city Timbuktu, produced many scholars of Islam, but its society was much more open to contributions from women than was Arab society.

▶ West African states were extremely varied and included the strict Islamic kingdom of Kanem-Bornu, the Hausa traders, the Yoruba in western Nigeria, and the prosperous kingdom of Benin.

▶ In Bantu-speaking East Africa, coastal city-states such as Kilwa and Malindi grew wealthy from the sale of goods from across Africa to Arabia, Persia, and India; the Shona

exported gold and ivory; and Buganda traded extensively with East African coastal cities.

▶ Enslavement of many people—for example, Africans by Africans, Africans by Arabs, eastern Europeans by western Europeans—was widespread when western Europeans began to obtain African slaves.

▶ The Portuguese were the first to contact sub-Saharan Africa, where they established relations with the Kongo kingdom, and to reach East Africa and India by sailing around the Cape of Good Hope.

16-2 Early European Imperialism and the Trans-Atlantic Slave Trade

SOCIETIES   NETWORKS

Q What were the consequences for Europe, Africa, and the Americas of early African–European encounters and the trans-Atlantic slave trade?

The explorations by the Portuguese and, later, other Europeans had immense, and mostly catastrophic, consequences for sub-Saharan Africans. As they made ever-longer journeys along the West African coast, Portuguese ships fostered trade but also conflict and destruction. The Portuguese eventually colonized the Kongo and became active in East Africa, undermining coastal trading cities. Meanwhile, the Dutch gained a foothold in South Africa. These activities eventually made possible the trans-Atlantic slave trade, which affected millions of Africans who were captured, transported, and sold in the Americas. Those who profited were the African states where slaves were obtained, the American societies that imported slave labor, and European and North American

CONNECTION to TODAY

In what ways do you think the European attacks, conquests, and slave trading of Africans in this era influenced the way many Western peoples view Africans today?

merchants, shippers, and planters. These experiences fostered a new global system of trade and empire that harmed some African societies. By the 1700s the gulf in wealth, power, and development, once narrow, between Africa and Eurasia had grown very wide, greatly influencing the relationship between European and African peoples.

16-2a Kongo, Angola, and the Portuguese

The Portuguese greatly impacted Kongo and the surrounding region. The Kongolese were open to foreign influence and ruled by an enlightened king and dedicated Christian, Afonso I (r. 1507–1543). A Portuguese merchant noted that, "the grandees

Discover Historical Voices

A Kongolese King Protests the Slave Trade

In the early sixteenth century Kongolese king Afonso I, who had embraced Catholicism and welcomed the Portuguese to his kingdom, wrote over twenty letters in Portuguese to Portugal's king, creating the earliest known African commentary on European activities in Africa. Some letters complained of aggressive Portuguese activities and asked that the king halt slavers from obtaining Kongolese citizens. They also requested Portuguese educational, medical, and religious assistance. The letters, usually polite in tone, revealed gradually diminished hopes as friendly early encounters turned into Portuguese plunder and exploitation. These are excerpts from several letters written in 1526.

Sir, Your Highness should know how our Kingdom is being lost in so many ways that it is convenient to provide the necessary remedy, since this is caused by the excessive freedom given by your factors and officials to the men and merchants who are allowed to come to the Kingdom to set up shop with goods and many things which have been prohibited by us....

And we cannot reckon how great the damage is, since the mentioned merchants are taking every day our natives, sons of the land and the sons of our noblemen and vassals and our relatives, because the thieves and men of bad conscience grab them wishing to have the things and wares of this Kingdom which they are ambitious of; they grab them and get them to be sold; and so great, Sir, is the corruption and licentiousness that our country is being completely depopulated, and Your Highness should not agree with this nor accept it as in your service. And to avoid it we need from...[your] Kingdoms no more than some priests and a few people to teach in schools....It is our will that in these Kingdoms there should not be any trade of slaves nor outlet

for them....And as soon as they are taken by the white men they are immediately ironed and branded with fire....

It happens that we have continuously many and different diseases which put us very often in such a weakness that we reach almost the last extreme; and the same [thing] happens to our children, relatives and natives owing to the lack in this country of physicians and surgeons who might know how to cure properly such diseases. And as we have got neither dispensaries nor drugs which might help us in this forlornness, many of those who had already been confirmed and instructed in the holy faith of Our Lord Jesus Christ perish and die; and the rest of the people in their majority cure themselves with herbs and breads and other ancient methods, so that they put all their faith in the mentioned herbs and ceremonies if they live....And this is not much in the service of God....We beg of you to be agreeable and kind enough to send us two physicians and two apothecaries and one surgeon, so that they may come with their drug-stores and all the necessary things to stay in our kingdoms, because we are in extreme need of them all.

Reflection Questions

1. What do these examples of letters tell us about Portuguese slaving activities and growing power in the Kongo?
2. What did Afonso believe his kingdom needed from the Portuguese?
3. Why were the Portuguese unlikely to grant Afonso's requests?
4. Do you think that an appeal to the world like Afonso's would make much of an impact today?

Source: Basil Davidson, ed., *African Civilization Revisited: Chronicles from Antiquity to Modern Times* (Trenton, NJ: Africa World Press, 1991), 223–226. This excerpt has been reprinted with the permission of Africa World Press in Trenton, NJ.

of the court began to dress like Portuguese, wearing mantles, capes, cloaks of scarlet silk, hats, and velvet and leather sandals."[6] Afonso, using Portuguese weapons to expand his empire, clearly wanted to modernize the kingdom along Western lines with Portuguese help. But the Portuguese became less concerned with political alliance and more interested in acquiring enslaved Kongolese, which they commenced to do in 1514. Although opposed in principle, Afonso sold slaves in exchange for goods and services he regarded as essential to his kingdom's progress. In Kongolese tradition, owners were expected to treat slaves well. However, demands for slaves multiplied as the Portuguese developed sugar plantations on Sao Tome. In their new colony in Brazil, across the Atlantic from Kongo, they set up many more plantations, multiplying the need for enslaved labor. Since Afonso and his successors permitted only a modest slave trade, the Portuguese resorted to armed raids to capture slaves.

Afonso repeatedly asked the Portuguese to halt these coercive activities, which were damaging and depopulating his country (see Discover Historical Voices: A Kongolese King Protests the Slave Trade), but his pleas were unsuccessful. Afonso grew disillusioned with the rapacious Portuguese, who halted their cooperation with the Kongo government in 1575.

Eventually the Portuguese turned to conquest. Establishing a base at Luanda (loo-AHN-duh) in 1580, they began a war against a vassal state of Kongo, Ndongo (uhn-DONG-go), whose ruler, called the Ngola, gave the name Angola (ahng-GO-luh) to the region. Like the Kongolese, Ndongo warriors were skilled but armed only with arrows and lances against Portuguese guns, cannon, and steel swords. Queen Njinga (en-JING-a) of Ndongo (1624–1663), born a slave in the royal court, proved a formidable adversary. This brilliant and pragmatic diplomat, eloquent debater, and skilled warrior who dressed as a

[6]From Roland Oliver and Caroline Oliver, eds., *Africa in the Days of Exploration* (Englewood Cliffs, NJ: Prentice-Hall, 1965), 111.

man and had a harem of men, led her troops into battle and also shrewdly negotiated to preserve her kingdom while demanding equal treatment with Europeans. Her charismatic personality rallied her people. After years of diplomacy alternating with war, the pragmatic Njinga made peace, a victim of Portugal's superior arms and ruthless quest for gold and slaves. After her death Ndongo became the foundation for Portugal's colony of Angola. Historians debate whether Njinga should be seen as an early feminist, a nationalist resisting Western power, or an opportunist who cooperated with the slave trade to increase her own power.

In the early seventeenth century both Portuguese and African mercenaries began raiding Kongo. The Christian monarchy sent moving appeals for help to the papacy, which ignored most appeals, though it pursued some with the Portuguese government. The ensuing civil wars in Kongo generated more captives for sale as slaves. Aiming to reform Kongolese political life while ending warfare and slavery, a charismatic Kongolese woman, Dona Beatriz Kimpa Vita, led a spiritual movement combining Catholic and traditional elements, but in 1706 Catholic missionaries had her burned at the stake.

Eventually most Kongolese were incorporated into Portuguese Angola, many abandoning Christianity. Angola and Kongo became deeply enmeshed in the trans-Atlantic slave trade, which, by the later 1600s, had grown much larger than the Arab and Black Sea slave trades. Angola and Kongo, the major suppliers of slaves to Brazil, became the Americas' largest source of enslaved men and women, accounting for some 35 to 40 percent of the total.

16-2b Eastern Africa and the Portuguese

Portuguese activity also extended into eastern Africa. In 1502 Vasco da Gama, leading twenty ships, occupied the cities of Mozambique and Sofala. To establish commercial control, Portuguese forces attacked, plundered, and occupied other Swahili trading cities, burning some to the ground. In Mombasa, wrote a Portuguese eyewitness, "everyone started to search the houses, forcing open the doors with axes and iron bars. A large quantity of cotton cloth, rich silk and gold embroidered clothes was seized."[7] Much of the population fled Kilwa, which the Portuguese pillaged in 1505, leaving only stone ruins. Using conquered cities as bases and ruthless methods, such as attacking and sinking Arab, Persian, and Indian ships, Portugal gradually gained partial control of the Indian Ocean maritime trading network while seizing key trading ports in the Persian Gulf, India,

The meeting of Queen Njinga of Ndongo and Joao Correia de Sousa the Portugese govenor of Luanda in 1622 (engraving)/ Dutch School, (17th century)/Private Collection/Bridgeman Images

IMAGE 16.4 **Queen Njinga** The formidable Queen Njinga of Ndongo, in Angola, meeting with the Portuguese governor of Luanda in 1622. The governor gave her a mat rather than a chair to sit on during the negotiations, an insult to someone of her royal status. Unwilling to accept the degradation, she ordered one of her servants to get on the ground and then sat on her servant's back. This illustrates her quick thinking and pragmatism in a difficult situation, which enabled her to get a peace treaty. An Italian priest, Father Cavazzi, creatively reimagined the meeting in an engraving made in 1687.

Q What do you think of Njinga's strategy in dealing with the Portuguese who were trying to annex her territories?

[7]From Basil Davidson, ed., *The African Past: Chronicles from Antiquity to Modern Times* (New York: Grosset and Dunlap, 1964), 136.

Malaya, Indonesia, and China and eastern Indonesia's Spice Islands, the main source for priceless clove and nutmeg supplies.

Portugal's East African ports never prospered, declining into poverty as many traders fled elsewhere. Fanatical Christians, the Portuguese suppressed the Islamic Swahili culture, burning books that contained epic poems, religious writings, and historical chronicles. While dominating coastal commerce for a century, their power over Indian Ocean maritime trade gradually diminished. As their influence waned all over the coast except in Mozambique, Arabs from Oman, on Arabia's northeast coast, filled the power vacuum, overrunning Portuguese settlements in the late 1600s and establishing a sultanate on Zanzibar, an island off Tanzania. Omani Arabs now supervised the lucrative slave and ivory trade to the Middle East and India, maintaining their political and commercial position into the late 1800s.

Eventually Portuguese adventurers, seeking gold on the plateau, moved up the Zambezi River to the largest Shona kingdom, Monomotapa (**MO-no-mo-TOP-a**), while gradually taking control of the lower Zambezi Valley. Because many Portuguese died from tropical diseases such as malaria, the Shona held out until 1628, when a decaying Monomotapa became a virtual Portuguese puppet state.

While trying to control the gold trade, however, the Portuguese destroyed it. Neighboring African states overrunning Monomotapa forced the Portuguese out of the plateau, but the gold fields became less productive. The Portuguese then concentrated their efforts on coastal Mozambique, with the settlers, especially in the Zambezi Valley, often marrying African women and adopting aspects of local culture and customs. Mozambique supplied slaves to the Indian Ocean islands and the Americas, but on a small scale relative to West and Central Africa. Only in the nineteenth century did Portugal gain firm control over the settlers, solidifying their Mozambique colony.

In the 1520s the Portuguese intervened briefly in Ethiopia, with its ancient Christian culture, when they sent a small force to help the Ethiopians successfully repulse an Ottoman-backed invasion by Muslim neighbors. Then in the early 1600s Portugal dispatched Jesuit missionaries to convert the king from the state Coptic church to Catholicism. He adopted the new faith and began reforming Ethiopian society and church along lines recommended by the Jesuits. In the 1630s King Susenyos persecuted the Copts but also Ethiopian free thinkers, some of whom were educated and had studied Greek philosophy. One of the free thinkers, Zera Yacob (1599–1692), developed a philosophy similar to the Enlightenment ideas beginning to percolate in Europe with figures like René Descartes. To escape persecution Yacob fled to a remote cave, where he lived for two years and codified his beliefs that no religion was more correct than any other, reason should be supreme, slavery abolished, harmony promoted, and that both men and women were created equal, ideas that today seem very modern. He published his philosophy in a remarkable book but his ideas did not gain a large following and apparently never made it to Europe. When both the Ethiopian church and much of the population resisted

Boers Dutch farming settlers in South Africa in the eighteenth century.

trekking The migrations of Boer settlers in cattle-drawn wagons into the interior of South Africa whenever they wanted to flee government restraints.

the king and his push for Catholicism, civil war erupted, the pro-Portuguese king abdicated, missionaries and other Portuguese were expelled, and Ethiopia went back to its old ways and faith. These Portuguese activities and interventions were the first of many later attempts by zealous Westerners to change an African society, often harming local people and disrupting societies.

16-2c South Africa and Dutch Colonization

European activity also affected Africa's southern tip. South Africans' social, political, and economic evolution in this era differed greatly from that of most sub-Saharan Africans. In 1652 the Dutch established a settlement, Cape Town, at the Cape of Good Hope to provision Dutch ships sailing between Europe and Dutch operations in Indonesia (see Chapter 18). Dutch farmers arrived, trading with local Khoikhoi people, but, since they had the great advantage of guns, they soon seized what they wanted. In 1659 the Khoikhoi rose against the Dutch. After crushing this resistance, the Dutch claimed Khoikhoi land and eventually enslaved or killed all the Khoikhoi. Expanding their control, the puritanical and racist Dutch settlers also imposed white supremacy rule over resident Africans. Needing labor for their farms and households, they imported slaves from Madagascar, Mozambique, and Indonesia. Masters and slaves lived close together, spawning the mixed-race (known as "Colored") population of today. But whites maintained political, legal, and economic superiority.

Continued Dutch immigration fostered rapid population growth. Some Dutch, chafing at governmental rules, looked eastward for new land. Many adopted the Bantus' pastoralism, herding cattle and sheep. As some Dutch settlers, later called **Boers** ("farmers"), expanded east seeking farmland in the 1700s, their encounters with the Xhosa and later the Zulu peoples generated bitter conflicts over land that lasted for nearly half a century. Thousands of Africans and some Boers died in the fighting. Nonetheless, Boer migrations in cattle-drawn wagons, known as **trekking**, became a tradition, occurring whenever some Boers wanted to flee government restraints. But eventually the Dutch government extended its influence into the lands settled by Boer trekkers.

16-2d The Trans-Atlantic Slave Trade

Modern relations between people of African and European ancestry have often originated in the European expansion and trade in African slaves, which forged a global distribution of power and privilege determined by skin color. The trans-Atlantic slave trade—usually dated from 1526, when the first large shipments to the Americas began, to 1870, when it was completely abolished—fostered both commerce and cultural change in the lands bordering the Atlantic Ocean (see Map 16.2). The value of plantations and mines in Europe's new American colonies created a labor market not easily filled by free men and women, European slaves and criminals, or coerced Native Americans, especially since Native American populations declined massively during European conquest and colonization. African slaves provided the lowest available cost option, creating the racial basis of trans-Atlantic slavery. This ruthless exploitation of Africans was easily rationalized by their different cultures and appearance.

In the early 1600s Portuguese, Spanish, French, Dutch, Danish, and English slavers began obtaining enslaved

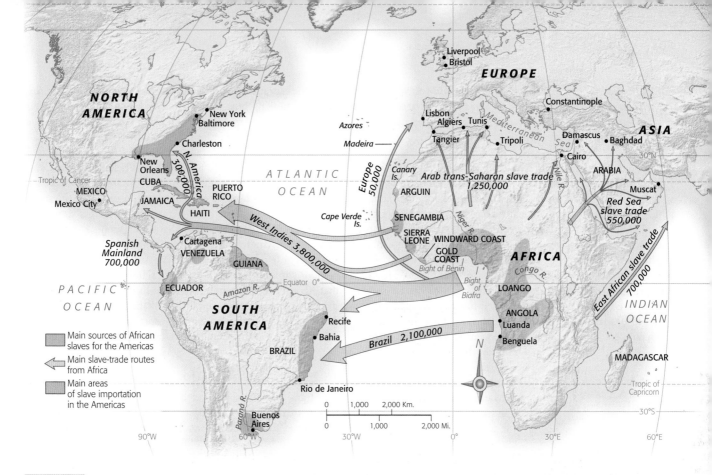

MAP 16.2 **Trans-Atlantic Slave Trade, 1526–1870** While the Arab-run slave trade from West and East Africa to North Africa and western Asia continued, the trans-Atlantic slave trade was far larger in scope. Millions of Africans were transported across the Atlantic, the greatest number ending up in Brazil and the West Indies. The majority of slaves came from what is today Angola, Congo, and Nigeria.

Q What can we learn from this map about what areas of Africa and the Americas were most impacted by the slave trade?

West Africans and shipping them across the Atlantic to meet the limitless demands of the American plantation economies, especially those in their own colonies (see Chapter 17). The commerce was often called a "triangular" trade because it was based on ships sailing from Europe to obtain slaves, transporting them to the Americas, and finally returning to Europe to await future voyages. But there was also a considerable bilateral segment of the trade, with ships from American colonies sailing to Africa to acquire slaves and then returning back with their human cargoes. And some slaves ended up in Europe. For example, by the mid-1700s there were some fifteen thousand black servants in London, many of them slaves. The West African coastal region's fragmentation into many small states precluded unified resistance, enabling European slavers to manipulate rivalries between states. Furthermore, the region's sedentary population was familiar with tropical agriculture and mining. Profits for the slavers, merchants, and planters soared as the volume of transported Africans increased. European forts to obtain, store, and ship slaves soon dotted the West African coast from Senegal down to Angola, while holding centers, such as Calabar in Nigeria, Gorée in Senegambia, and especially Luanda in Angola, processed slaves for sale. Europeans traded cotton goods, guns, iron, rum, and tobacco for slaves, often with local African chiefs' cooperation, but sometimes they acquired Africans directly by force, as in Kongo and Angola.

Perhaps some 25 to 30 million Africans were originally enslaved for the trade but half or more may never have reached the Americas. Between 9 and 12 million Africans, most between twelve and thirty years old, were landed in the Americas over four centuries, possibly a third of them women, to be sold at auction. Millions died in holding cells in West Africa or on the notorious **Middle Passage**, the slave's journey by ship from Africa to the Americas. Those surviving the Middle Passage faced a bleak future, to be sold without regard to personal or ethnic ties, mostly to sugar, cotton, or coffee plantations. The trans-Atlantic slave trade reached its peak between 1700 and 1800, with perhaps 100,000 Africans a year shipped to the Americas, some 40 percent from Angola-Kongo and 35 percent from Nigeria.

The Middle Passage lasted one or two months on notoriously overcrowded, disease-ridden slave ships. Conditions were terrible, as this description by an American observer attested:

The [naked] men were shackled two by two, the right wrist and ankle of one to the left wrist and ankle of another. The women—usually regarded as fair prey for the sailors— spent the night between decks, in a space partitioned off from that of the men. All the slaves were forced to sleep without covering on

Middle Passage The slave's journey by ship from Africa to the Americas.

bare wooden floor. In a stormy passage the skin over their elbows might be worn away to the bare bones. Every man was allowed a space six feet long by sixteen inches wide (and usually about two feet seven inches high).[8]

Olaudah Equiano (**oh-LAU-duh ay-kwee-AHN-oh**), an Igbo seized in Nigeria in the 1750s, described the intolerable stench of the hold and the floggings on the deck for misconduct, which sometimes resulted in death. The voyages' mortality rates averaged between 5 and 25 percent. Slavers debated whether cramming as many slaves as possible into the ships (known as "tight pack") or carrying slightly fewer slaves ("loose pack") would land the greater number of slaves for eventual sale. Many slaves committed suicide before reaching the Americas. Equiano remembered when two Igbos chained together jumped overboard in despair; many crews installed nets along the sides to catch jumpers. Mutinies were also frequent. In 1839 slaves seized control of a small Spanish ship, the *Amistad*, bound from Sierra Leone to Cuba. Led by a Mande chief's son, Joseph Cinque, the ringleaders picked the locks on their chains, then

racism A set of beliefs, practices, and institutions based on devaluing groups that are supposedly biologically different.

killed the captain and some crew members. After months at sea, and not knowing how to sail the ship home, they found their way to New York. Tried for mutiny in the United States, Cinque and his comrades were eventually freed by the courts.

The superiority Europeans felt toward Africans contributed significantly to the rise of **racism**, a set of beliefs, practices, and institutions based on devaluing groups that are supposedly biologically different because of skin color. To rationalize the trade, Europeans invented the cruel fiction that Africans were subhuman savages unworthy of civilized treatment. For instance, in 1589 the English adventurer Richard Hakluyt described Africans as "a people of beastly living, without a God, law, religion, or common wealth."[9] Western scholars of the era argued that Africans were naturally inferior to Europeans in intelligence. Slave traders and owners felt little guilt, believing God ordained the inequality of peoples. Some even thought slavery helped Africans by exposing them to Western values and Christianity.

16-2e The Slave Trade and African Societies

The trans-Atlantic slave trade's impact on Africa varied from region to region. Some coastal West and Central Africans succumbed to chronic raiding, kidnapping, and warfare, in an

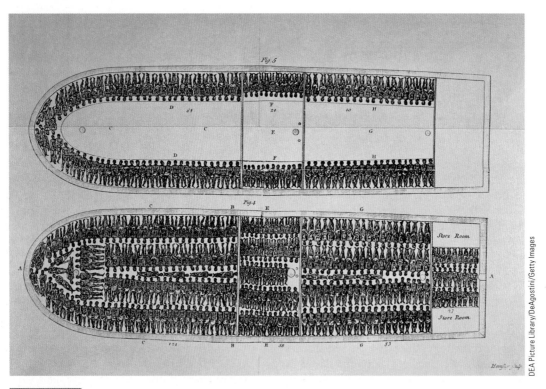

IMAGE 16.5 **The Middle Passage** This painting from the era vividly shows the overcrowded conditions on the ships that carried African slaves, packed like sardines, on the "Middle Passage" across the Atlantic to the Americas. Such brutal conditions resulted in the deaths of many slaves and eventually prompted reformers to demand the end of the slave trade.

Q What does this painting tell us about the transport of slaves and the misery and loss of life that accompanied it?

---

[8]Malcolm Cowley and Daniel Mannix, "The Middle Passage," in *The Atlantic Slave Trade*, ed. David Northrup (Lexington, MA: D.C. Heath, 1994), 99, 101.

[9]Quoted in R. A. Houston, "Colonies, Enterprise, and Wealth: The Economies of Europe and the Wider World in the Seventeenth Century," in *Early Modern Europe: An Oxford History*, ed. Euan Cameron (New York: Oxford University Press, 1999), 165.

"enslave your neighbor or be enslaved" syndrome. European guns traded for slaves resulted in plundered villages and broken families. Over three-quarters of the Africans in the Americas were Kongolese, Angolans, Yorubas, Igbos, and Akans, leaving their societies badly disrupted. In Angola, European settlers later seized land in depopulated districts. By linking Atlantic Africa closely to Europe and the Americas, the slave trade created an **Atlantic System**, a large network spanning western and Central Africa, North America's east and gulf coasts, the Caribbean Basin, and South America's Atlantic coast.

Historians vigorously debate many aspects of the slave trade. One major question involves the role of African rulers, chiefs, and merchants in facilitating the system. Some believe Africans had little choice given Western superiority in military force and other technologies. Some conclude that Africans who participated in obtaining and selling slaves did so willingly and enthusiastically. Others note that the new world economy being constructed, and the wealth created, had a coercive aspect, making it difficult not to take part. Although mainly seeking slaves, Europeans also coveted African gold and cloth. Soon Western merchants monopolized coastal trade, but some Africans and people of mixed African and European ancestry also flourished as merchants and slave traders. Other Africans refused to cooperate in slave trading, dealing with Europeans on their own terms. Hence, Benin's kings prohibited selling male slaves and instead obtained firearms needed to protect the state by trading cotton textiles, mostly made by women, as well as pepper, ivory, and beads. Some states such as Dahomey (duh-HO-mee) prospered by cooperating with the slave traders at the expense of their neighbors. Their powerful army included women soldiers, called "Amazons" by European and *mino* ("Our mothers") by local people. They were recruited as elephant hunters in the later 1600s and then bodyguards for the queen, becoming a fighting force. Along the Gold Coast, the Ashanti (a-SHAN-tee) had formed a state in the seventeenth century under their great king Osei Tutu (OH-say TOO-too), who introduced a constitution making other chiefs members of the king's advisory council. With access to gold fields, a powerful military force, and firearms acquired from Europeans, by the mid-1700s the Ashanti dominated a large area while trading gold to North Africa and slaves to the Europeans.

The slave trade fostered economic, social, and political change in Africa. The most far-reaching changes occurred along the Atlantic coast from Senegambia to Angola, sometimes reaching several hundred miles inland. Some states, such as Kongo, declined, while others, such as Ashanti, rose in power. Most West and Central African societies far from the coast, such as Kanem-Bornu, had little direct contact with European slavers or coastal states. However, Arab slave trading badly disrupted some East African regions, even reaching the eastern Congo River Basin. Meanwhile, the Sudan region supplied slaves for North Africa, while the Portuguese and Dutch colonization in southern Africa foreshadowed the division of sub-Saharan Africa by several European nations in the 1800s. In general economic terms, the trans-Atlantic slave trade, by integrating Africa into the world economy as a supplier of human and later natural resources, created imbalances that hindered local industries. Yet, the European presence also fostered the diffusion of American food crops, such as maize (corn) and peanuts, to Africa. Some African artists incorporated Western ideas and Christian symbols into their work, while some African traditions influenced Western artists. The European intrusion involved **imperialism**, the control or domination, direct or indirect, of one state or people over another. Often imperialism led to **colonialism**, government by one society over another society. The Cape Verde Islands, Angola, and parts of Senegambia, Mozambique, and South Africa became Western colonies in this era. But the full-blown Western colonial scramble for Africa only began with Europe's rapid industrialization, which accelerated the need for natural resources such as peanuts, palm oil, gold, timber, and cotton for processing into industrial or commercial products, as well as for new markets to consume these goods.

Racism made Africans and their descendants in the Americas what critics call a permanent underclass, treated with contempt. The first Europeans to encounter great African states like Benin, Kongo, and Kilwa in the late 1400s and early 1500s were awed by their prosperity and marveled at how even the poorest were treated with dignity. Yet by the 1700s Europeans and North Americans viewed Africa as in desperate need of Western tutelage, setting the stage for, and justifying, colonization. Meanwhile, the Islamic Middle East also encountered rising Western power, but, for most societies, with less dramatic consequences.

> **Atlantic System** A large network that arose with the trans-Atlantic slave trade; the network spanned western and Central Africa, the east and gulf coasts of North America, the Caribbean Basin, and the Atlantic coast of South America.

> **imperialism** The control or domination, direct or indirect, of one state or people over another.

> **colonialism** Government by one society over another society.

KEY POINTS

▶ After the Portuguese conquered both Angola and Kongo, these areas became the major source of slaves for the trans-Atlantic slave trade.

▶ Millions of West African slaves were shipped to North America because they were the cheapest form of labor available to work the farms, plantations, and mines and because the Native American population had been decimated.

▶ The conditions of the Middle Passage, from West Africa to America, were horrific, and many slaves died, committed suicide, or mutinied en route.

▶ The slave trade led to racist views, as many Europeans justified it by claiming that Africans were inherently inferior or arguing that it benefited slaves by exposing them to Western culture and religion.

16-3 The Ottomans and Islamic Imperial Revival

⇄ TRANSITIONS ▦ SOCIETIES

Q What factors made the Ottoman Empire such a powerful force in the region?

The Islamic Middle East did not experience the jarring transitions felt by many Africans. While European nations established maritime supremacy, most Islamic states remained major land powers. The greatest, the Turkish Ottoman Empire, eventually ruled much of southeastern Europe, Asia's western fringe, and much of North Africa while nearly conquering much of eastern and central Europe. By the 1700s, however, the Ottomans and other Middle Eastern states suffered from chronic warfare, poor leadership, growing rigidity, and a superiority complex toward the upstart Europeans. These Islamic societies soon became targets of European imperialism.

16-3a The Ottoman Empire, Government, and Economy

Ottoman Turks gained power over much of the once-great Byzantine Empire in the 1300s. Islamic power was conclusively demonstrated by the conquest of the Byzantine capital, Constantinople, in 1453, when the center of Orthodox Christianity was transformed into a Muslim city, later known as Istanbul. By 1512 the Ottomans controlled Anatolia and what are today Bulgaria, Greece, Albania, Serbia, and Romania. If their invasion of southern Italy had succeeded, Europe's history might have been very different. During the sixteenth century the Ottomans also defeated Persian forces, added Syria, Lebanon, Palestine, and Egypt to their domains, and controlled much of the Mediterranean.

The Ottoman golden age under Sultan Suleiman (**SOO-lay-man**) the Magnificent (r. 1520–1566), a just lawgiver but merciless conqueror, brought military expansion and a diminishing of Christian power. Suleiman's forces invaded the eastern Balkans and areas north of the Danube River, defeating the Hungarians and besieging Vienna; they also occupied Egypt and then the North African coast. After Suleiman defeated the Persians and incorporated Iraq, his empire stretched from Algeria to the Persian Gulf and from Hungary to Armenia (see Map 16.3). But the Ottomans never controlled much of the Arabian peninsula. Their conquest of Egypt in 1518 brought them into direct contact with the Indian Ocean trading world and sparked the improvement of Ottoman naval forces. During the sixteenth century they played a significant role in the Indian Ocean, launching a systematic military, commercial, and ideological challenge to the growing Portuguese Empire, which they saw as their major rivals in controlling the region's lucrative maritime trade routes. They allied with several states

janissaries ("new troops") Well-armed, highly disciplined, and generally effective elite military corps of infantrymen in the Ottoman Empire.

CONNECTION to TODAY

What similarities and what differences do you see between Turkish society and politics today and that of the Ottomans?

as far east as the Straits of Melaka, including the Acheh sultanate on Sumatra. The Ottomans eventually pulled back just as more Western states were dispatching ships to the region in search of wealth and power.

Suleiman's reign revived the Islamic glory that had faded with the Iraq-based Abbasid Empire's downfall in the 1200s. Ottoman sultans claimed to restore the caliphate, the blending of political and religious power claimed by early Islamic leaders to be ordained by God. In 1538 the Ottoman ruler boasted of his wide-ranging power: "I am God's slave and sultan of this world. I am head of Muhammad's community … who sends his fleets to the seas of Europe, the Maghrib [northwest Africa] and India."[10]

Suleiman's strategic position involved him in conflicts. Sometimes the Ottomans allied with France or with northern European Protestants against the Habsburgs, who ruled Austria and a large area of eastern Europe. Ottoman success owed much to advanced gunpowder weapons, especially cannon, that were often built and operated by Hungarian Christians in Ottoman service, as well as to an effective navy with ships often designed and crewed by Christian mercenaries. Controlling overland trade routes between Europe and the Indian Ocean, Ottomans sold spices and other products from India, Southeast Asia, and China to Venetians and other Europeans. In 1570 Suleiman's successor as sultan and Queen Elizabeth I of England entered into an unprecedented alliance that helped Protestant England circumvent the closing of its markets by Europe's Catholic states while resisting the threats from the Spanish king to take her throne. By the later 1580s thousands of English merchants, sailors, diplomats, and privateers were active from Morocco to Persia.

For decades able sultans, governing through an imperial council headed by a prime minister and officials chosen on merit, allowed Arabs and other non-Turks to serve as officials and military officers. A Habsburg envoy wrote, "No distinction is attached to birth among the Turks. Honors, high posts, and judgeships are the rewards of great ability and good services."[11] The ruling elite resided in beautiful palaces with many servants and large harems of wives and concubines.

As they recruited administrators and soldiers from Christian peoples, the sultan's agents selected Christian youth for training, essentially making them slaves required to embrace Islam. The most talented attended the palace school, where they learned to read and write Arabic, Persian, and Turkish in preparation for administration. This group produced most Ottoman prime ministers. The other conscripts joined the well-armed, well-paid, highly disciplined elite military corps of infantrymen known as **janissaries** ("new troops"), who lived in barracks and were forbidden to marry.

[10]Quoted in Halil Inalcik, *The Ottoman Empire: The Classical Age, 1300–1600* (London: Phoenix Press, 2000), 41.
[11]Quoted in Arthur Goldschmidt, Jr., *A Concise History of the Middle East*, 4th ed. revised and updated (Boulder, CO: Westview Press, 1991), 129.

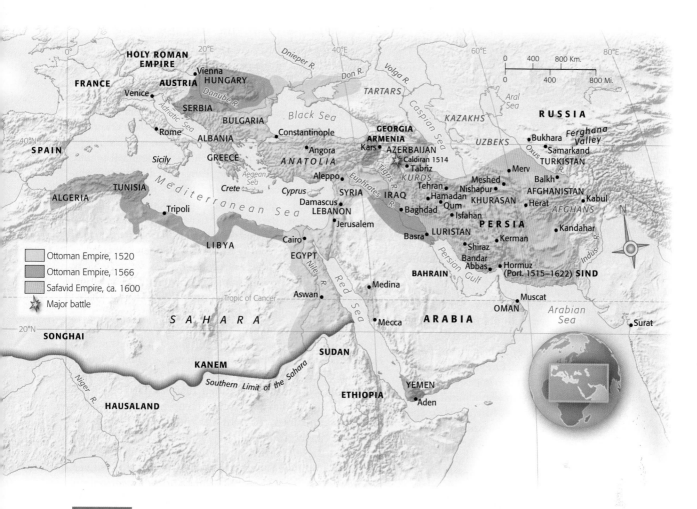

MAP 16.3 **The Ottoman and Safavid Empires, 1500–1750** By the later 1500s the Ottoman Empire included large parts of western Asia, southeastern Europe, southern Russia, and North Africa. The Ottomans' major rivals, the Safavids, controlled Persia and parts of Iraq, the Caucasus, Afghanistan, and Central Asia.

Q How does the political configuration shown on this map differ from a political map of these regions today?

The Ottoman Empire had a flourishing commercial economy. Istanbul (Constantinople), which enjoyed a particularly favorable geographic position, as well as various other major cities served as transregional trade centers where merchants from different lands bought or sold European woolens, Persian silk, Chinese porcelain, Indian spices and textiles, Arab sugar, and Anatolian iron. Artisan and merchant guilds controlled many economic activities. But international trade mostly involved luxuries, with the empire largely self-sufficient in necessities such as food.

16-3b Ottoman Society, Culture, and Thought

Ottoman society and culture were marked by diversity and prosperity. The empire's multiethnic population, about evenly divided between Christians and Muslims, contained some fifty million people at its peak, dwarfing the largest European country, France, which had perhaps fifteen million. The sultans governed sizable Jewish, Greek Orthodox, and Armenian Christian communities through their own religious leaders, laws, and courts. Although facing some legal disabilities, religious minorities generally enjoyed a toleration rare in that era. Vibrant urban social life revolved around coffeehouses, public baths, and taverns. An Ottoman observer of one coffeehouse wrote: "Some read books and fine writings, some were busy with backgammon and chess, some brought new poems and talked of literature. Pious hypocrites said: 'People have become addicts of the coffee-house; nobody comes to the mosques.'"[12] Some coffeehouses seem to have played roles for fostering intellectual conversation, not unlike the Paris salons of the French Enlightenment. Many immigrants, including Jews and Muslims fleeing persecution in Spain, brought valuable expertise and international connections. European merchants and technicians, exempted from Ottoman taxes and laws, enjoyed commercial advantages over local-born competitors.

---

[12]Ibrahim Pecevi, quoted in Philip Mansel, *Constantinople: City of the World's Desire, 1453–1924* (New York: St. Martin's, 1995), 171.

Many Christian peasants from southern and eastern Europe immigrated or welcomed Ottoman conquest, which generally brought them a better life. Some Balkan peasants said that the Turk's turban was better than the pope's tiara.

Despite patriarchy, women had a higher status in Turkish than in Arab society. Royal women exercised political clout, influencing princes brought up in royal harems while financing buildings and social service activities. Upper-class women often owned land, managed businesses, and controlled wealth. Women also took their grievances to Islamic courts, which protected their rights to inheritance and property. Having sons provided even more security. Since men usually died younger, women often headed households. Yet, men could also abuse and more easily divorce women, and sometimes families punished or killed women suspected of illicit sexual activity.

Istanbul attracted artists and artisans from all over Europe and the Middle East. For example, Suleiman the Magnificent welcomed humanist thinkers from Italy, while Sultan Mehmed II (1432–1481) had the most famous Venetian artist, Giovanni Bellini, decorate his palace with paintings. Ottoman architects, such as the innovative Pasha Sinan, designed beautiful domed mosques and other public buildings, combining form with function (see Meet the People: Pasha Sinan, Ottoman Architect). In this creative environment, Ottoman and European architects and artists influenced each other. One sultan who admired Italian art tried to woo two of the greatest talents, Michelangelo and Leonardo da Vinci, to work in Istanbul. Meanwhile, Ottoman medicine remained vibrant, while Ottoman scholars published much on astronomy, mathematics, and geography and produced world maps more sophisticated than European maps. However, by the 1700s the Ottomans had fallen behind western Europe in science, and Ottoman intellectuals remained largely disinterested in and uninformed about scientific and technological developments elsewhere. The emphasis on law and theology rather than science in higher education inhibited technological innovation.

In religious life, various mystical Sufi sects, seeking to personally experience God, had large followings. Seyh Bedreddin (SAY beh-DREAD-en), who founded an order of practitioners known as dervishes, wrote: "Ecstasy came to me, and I remained in wonderment at God's presence. The mystic who has perceived God spreads to the whole universe; he is one with the mountains and streams. There is no here or hereafter; everything is a single moment."[13] To achieve a trancelike state, dervishes danced feverishly, whirling around faster and faster while their long skirts billowed out, creating a hypnotic effect. Some Sufi sects operated with official support; critics suspected others, including the dervishes, of political disloyalty and modifying too many Islamic principles.

Perhaps as the religious establishment became closer to the state, Islam became more rigid in the Ottoman realms and Middle East. Most religious leaders emphasized memorization rather than analyzing sacred texts, punished deviation from orthodoxy, and increasingly opposed technological innovation. Meanwhile, Christian minorities flocked to schools established by Christian missionaries from Europe and North America. Some of these schools, by teaching commercial and technical subjects, exposed them to knowledge from the wider world.

16-3c Ottoman Decline and the West

Eventually the Ottomans faced new challenges that undermined the state and reduced the empire. Ottoman armies effectively battled European and Persian rivals into the 1670s, when they annexed part of the Ukraine. However, in 1683 Austria and its allies repulsed the last Ottoman attack on Vienna. Soon the Ottomans were pushed south of the Danube River, lost the Ukraine and southern Greece, and ceded Hungary to the rival Habsburgs. As its military practices and technology fell behind, reducing fear of Ottoman power, European diplomats began calling the empire "the sick man of Europe." Janissary military discipline weakened, and as officers spent winters in Istanbul, military campaigns were limited to warm-weather months. Eventually sultans eliminated the training system for young men and led campaigns personally, exhausting their energy. In addition, the Ottoman navy had once enjoyed advanced technology, but by the 1600s European ships were better armed and more maneuverable. Ottoman weaponry, especially artillery, stagnated just as European military technology rapidly improved.

Compared to China or the emerging European states, the Ottoman state was not very centralized, making imperial control difficult to maintain. Government through religious communities or provincial leaders focused peoples' loyalty on their ethnic group or region rather than the Ottoman state. Kurds, a Sunni Muslim ethnic group occupying a large region in today's eastern Turkey, northern Iraq and Syria, and northwest Iran, increasingly resented Turkish control. In addition, many Arabs and Balkan Christians who once welcomed Ottoman rule began to think of their own peoples as repressed nations. Ottoman citizens disliked higher taxes, growing corruption, bureaucratic bloat, and increasing peasant poverty. Finally, the ruling elite exercised more power over weak or incompetent sultans, some of whom were mentally unstable or despots. "Ibrahim the Mad" proved particularly tyrannical, once ordering the drowning of 280 concubines who angered him; he was deposed and executed. With weaker male leaders, senior palace women gained more influence, supporting one or another of the factions that contended for favor.

Ottoman sultans also had difficulty controlling restless provinces in North Africa and western Asia, brutally crushing occasional rebellions during the 1600s. Although formally remaining vassals of Istanbul, leaders of Ottoman descent in Algeria and Tunisia became increasingly independent. In Egypt and what is now Iraq and Syria, Ottomans ruled through local Arab leaders, who sought more autonomy. By the mid-1700s Ottoman supremacy had deteriorated, while the Russians pressured Ottoman territory north of the Black Sea.

Rising western Europeans, Habsburgs, and Russia posed not only military but also economic challenges. Western Europe's growing wealth and role in Asian trade weakened Anatolia's historic middleman position as Portuguese and Dutch ships carrying Asian resources around Africa to Europe's Atlantic ports gradually reduced trade flowing through Ottoman ports. With little official support to merchants, who were mostly Greeks, Armenians, and Jews, the once self-sufficient empire became increasingly dependent on imports from Europe.

[13]Quoted in Inalcik, *Ottoman Empire*, 189.

Western merchants also gradually controlled large sectors of the Ottoman economy. Large Western trading firms, armed with great capital and better business methods and backed by their own governments, ultimately reduced the Ottomans to a secondary power in the emerging global trade system.

The rising European power sparked fierce debates within the empire. Reformers interested in European products and customs favored importing some European technology but struggled against conservatives, who preferred the status quo and maintained a Muslim superiority complex regarding once-upstart Europeans. Many reformers looked to the era of Suleiman the Magnificent for inspiration. In this fashion the creaking Ottoman state limped into the twentieth century.

KEY POINTS

▶ The Ottoman Empire was culturally and religiously diverse; religious minorities were allowed a measure of self-governance, and many immigrants were attracted by the empire's tolerance.

▶ The Ottoman Empire attracted and encouraged a range of artists and thinkers from across Eurasia, though state support for Islam may have caused it to become more rigid and close-minded.

▶ Though the Ottoman Empire remained strong through much of the seventeenth century, its military discipline, weaponry, and political stability soon began a gradual decline.

▶ As Europeans began to trade directly with Asia, the Ottomans lost their traditional role as middlemen and became increasingly dependent on European imports.

16-4 Persia, Morocco, and Central Asia

SOCIETIES **TRANSITIONS**

Q How did the Persian and Central Asian experience differ from that of the Ottomans?

Like the Ottomans, Islamic societies from Morocco to Central Asia underwent significant changes in this era. Persian leaders, thinkers, and officials had long influenced the Islamic world, and Persian was widely spoken by Muslim elites from Istanbul to India. In the early sixteenth century a Shi'ite dynasty, the Safavids, revived Persian culture and became an internationally recognized power. In northwest Africa, Morocco developed formidable military prowess, while various Islamic societies in Central Asia struggled to maintain Silk Road trade networks while facing pressure from the expanding Russian Empire.

> **CONNECTION to TODAY**
>
> Can you think of ways that the Ottoman and Safavid Empires might be viewed as role models for Middle Eastern countries today?

religious leaders. The shift to Shi'ism took some years, with many Sunni families emigrating to India, Central Asia, or Ottoman territories. Many Persians, however, enjoyed the rich Shi'ite ceremonies and wanted to differentiate themselves from the hated Sunni Ottomans. Eventually Persians came to view Shi'ism as central to Persian identity, and today most Iranians are Shi'ites of Persian or Azeri Turkish background.

The Safavids, while establishing a strong political system, never acquired the gunpowder-based military power of the Ottomans. Safavid armies rode on horseback and viewed guns as both awkward and unmanly, an attitude that left them vulnerable to Ottoman and Portuguese gunpowder weapons. The Portuguese seized and held the strategic port of Hormuz (**hawr-MOOZ**), on Persia's southeast coast, for decades, and in 1514 the Ottomans occupied Safavid lands in Armenia and Anatolia. Battle losses to the hated Ottomans demoralized Safavid military leaders; Isma'il, unable to cope with defeat, became an alcoholic recluse in his palace. Although soon regaining their confidence, the Safavids did not attempt to expand their empire. They also adopted many governmental practices long common in the region. Like the Ottomans, they acquired slave boys, primarily from Christian peoples, especially Armenians and Georgians, for administrative or military training, and over time they adapted to local Persian customs.

Safavid rule reached its peak under Shah (king) Abbas (**ah-BAHS**) I (r. 1587–1629), who consolidated his power by manipulating or executing his enemies, including Sufi leaders. His capital, Isfahan (**is-fah-HAHN**), became a beautiful, tree-shaded city of some one million people, filled with mosques, public baths, parks,

16-4a The Safavid Empire

The Safavid dynasty in Persia was founded in 1501 by a Turkish group from Azerbaijan (**AZ-uhr-bye-ZHAHN**) in the Caucasus Mountains who belonged to a militant Shi'ite Sufi order. Led by a charismatic thirteen-year-old boy, Isma'il (1487–1524), they invaded and began conquering Persia, then a center of Sunni practice. Isma'il claimed descent from Muhammad and Sassanian princes. A Venetian diplomat described the youth as "of noble presence and a truly royal bearing, as in his eyes and brows there was something so great and commanding, which plainly showed that he would someday become a great ruler."[14] Isma'il, believing himself an agent of God, mandated the conversion of Persians to Shi'ism. Tensions between the majority Sunni and minority Shi'a had simmered since the Islamic community divided centuries earlier, and the Safavids used force when necessary on reluctant Sunnis, confiscating property and executing

---

[14]From John J. Saunders, ed., *The Muslim World on the Eve of Europe's Expansion* (Englewood Cliffs, NJ: Prentice-Hall, 1966), 35.

Pasha Sinan, Ottoman Architect

One of world history's most innovative architects, Pasha Sinan (1491–1588), served as royal architect to Ottoman sultans for fifty years, during which time he perfected the Ottoman style. Sinan's work reflected the mixing of Christian and Muslim cultures in Istanbul, the former Byzantine city of Constantinople. Thanks in part to Sinan, Istanbul's architecture symbolized the grandiose Ottoman spirit. Sinan designed over three hundred works, ranging from grand government buildings and mosques taking years to build to fountains, tombs, bridges, and baths.

Born into a Christian Greek family in central Anatolia and selected for the Ottoman military in 1512, Sinan was converted to Islam and trained as a janissary warrior, after which he fought in various military campaigns. During his military service he developed a reputation for his engineering skills. For example, he devised ways to float artillery across lakes and to quickly build a bridge across the Danube River. In 1538 the great sultan Suleiman the Magnificent appointed Sinan royal architect, based in Istanbul. In this highly visible post, Sinan developed, procured funding for, and supervised the construction of projects that are major tourist attractions today, viewed by millions and admired by architects around the world. To succeed, he needed the skills of a visionary, planner, administrator, and manager.

Istanbul was filled with inspiring architecture from Byzantine times, including the beautiful cathedral of Hagia Sophia, with its huge dome. Fascinated by these domed structures, Sinan concentrated on incorporating them into his own architecture. The Hagia Sophia church, with its ascending hierarchy of sanctity ending at the altar, had been built for the Byzantine emperor Justinian a thousand years earlier and so reflected the Byzantine worldview and Greek Orthodox Church values. Sinan sought to outdo the architects who built Hagia Sophia while adapting the dome structure to an Islamic house of worship, providing open spaces where all could face Mecca from an equal position. Sinan experimented constantly in pursuit of his vision.

Trying to incorporate Hagia Sophia's best features into an Islamic setting, Sinan designed several great mosques in Istanbul. The Suleimaniye (**SOO-lay-man-iya**) mosque, finished in 1557, sits atop a high hill, dominating the city and proclaiming Islam's triumph. A sixteenth-century English traveler, John Sanderson,

IMAGE 16.6 **Suleimaniye Mosque** Between 1548 and 1557 Sinan designed and supervised the building of one of Istanbul's most magnificent mosques, the Suleimaniye, honoring God and Sinan's patron, Sultan Suleiman the Magnificent, who was buried in the mosque. Overlooking the Straits of Bosporus, the mosque complex contains schools, shops, and a hospital.

Nickolay Vinokurov/Shutterstock.com

Q Why do you think this mosque is considered so magnificent?

believed the mosque passed "in greatness, workmanship, marble pillars, and riches all the churches of [Christian] emperors [and merited] to be matched with the 7 Wonders of the [ancient] World." The main dome is surrounded by over four hundred lesser domes. This huge complex included several of Istanbul's most elite schools.

Sinan's last great mosque, the Edirne (**eh-DURN-a**), completed in 1575, had a dome surpassing that of Hagia Sophia. Sinan considered it his masterpiece and boasted that "architects among Christians say that no Muslim architect would be able to build such a large dome. With the help of God I erected a dome higher and wider than Hagia Sophia." In designing this mosque, Sinan tried to assert what he considered the superiority of Islam over Christianity and brought Ottoman architecture to its highest point. The mosque expressed the imperial Ottoman achievement and the splendor of Islam.

Various rich Ottomans, to show their piety and provide themselves with a burial place, endowed mosques. Imperial family women and the wives of wealthy Ottoman officials also financed mosques, among other good works. Sinan designed some of these mosques and built great tombs to commemorate the powerful men and women of his day. He also designed parts of the sultan's great palace, the Topkapi Sarai (**sah-RYE**) (Abode of Felicity). This huge complex boasted beautiful interiors and contained a series of pavilions, gardens, courts, treasuries, reception halls, baths, kitchens, and other buildings. Begun by Sinan, it was constructed over several centuries with no particular master plan. The palace and the grand mosques remain as testimonies to Sinan's talents and Ottoman cultural vibrancy in the 1500s.

Reflection Questions

1. What does Sinan's career tell us about the Ottoman system?
2. How did Sinan's architecture reflect a mixing of Islamic and Christian traditions?
3. Why do you think that Sinan's mosques as well as the Hagia Sophia church have so much appeal to Western tourists and architects today?

Notes: Quotations from Andrew Wheatcroft, *The Ottomans* (New York: Viking, 1993), 143; and Aptullah Kuran, *Sinan: The Grand Old Master of Ottoman Architecture* (Washington, DC: Institute of Turkish Studies, 1987), 168–169.

and a great bazaar that one visitor described as "the surprisingest piece of Greatness in Honor of Commerce that the world can boast of."[15] The shah kept men away a few days each year so that the normally secluded women could visit the bazaars and promenade in the evening on Isfahan's spectacular main boulevard, lined with gardens, pavilions, and a water channel. Shah Abbas enjoyed visiting the city's teahouses, listening to poets and storytellers and chatting with citizens. Many peasants worked the king's land, receiving a share of the crop. Tolerant in religion, Abbas admitted Christian missionaries and maintained good relations with European powers, importing English advisers to train his military forces and manufacture modern cannon and muskets. Soon he waged successful wars against invading Ottomans and Uzbeks, and he also recaptured Hormuz from Portugal. Europeans sought Persia as an ally against their mutual Ottoman enemy.

By the eighteenth century Safavid sultans had become weaker, Shi'ite religious officials had become stronger, and the empire's economy had declined. Unable to control the Shi'ite clergy or trust their own sons plotting for the throne, later Safavid rulers often turned to alcohol and concubines for comfort, while corruption grew rampant. In 1722 Afghans seized Isfahan and then repulsed invading Ottoman forces. Isfahan was nearly destroyed. In 1736 a new Persian leader, Nadir Shah (1688–1747), drove out the Afghans, established a vigorous new state, and marched his armies into Ottoman lands and north India, plundering the major city, Delhi. But Nadir Shah proved ruthless against suspected foes while economic collapse exposed millions to famine. After ill-advised efforts to reconvert Persians back to Sunni Islam, Nadir Shah was assassinated in 1747, and his empire soon collapsed. In the decades to follow, Persia divided into smaller states while Western pressure intensified.

16-4b Persian Economy, Society, Culture, and Thought

Safavid Persia flourished economically for several centuries from long-distance trade by land and sea. Persian merchants remained active in Indian Ocean trade, operating as far away as China, Southeast Asia, and East Africa. Meanwhile, foreign merchants flocked to Isfahan's great bazaar, where artisans produced fine carpets, textiles, metalwork, and ceramics. Armenian settlers based in Persia made and exported silk while operating lucrative gold and silver crafts industries, and they also competed fiercely with Dutch, English, Portuguese, and Indian merchants in parts of Eurasia. The Armenian network radiated outward from New Julfa (**JOOL-fa**), near Isfahan, and was run by a merchants' council. Sharing a common culture and Christian religion, Armenian merchants played key roles in the overland trade from India to Central

IMAGE 16.7 **The Splendor of Safavid Isfahan** Isfahan was one of the Early Modern world's most beautiful cities. This view shows the city's central Naqsh-e Jahan Square, flanked by the Imam Mosque in the distance and the Ali Qapu Palace on the right.

Q Do you think that this scene gives us a good idea of the splendor of Isfahan in the Early Modern Era and even today?

---

[15]Quoted in Francis Robinson, *The Cultural Atlas of the Islamic World Since 1500* (London: Stonehenge, 1987), 49.

Asia and the Middle East. The New Julfa Armenian network eventually stretched eastward to India, Burma, Java, and China; westward to Venice, Marseilles, Amsterdam, and London; and northward through Russia to northern Europe. English, Dutch, and French merchants visited Persian ports, whetting European appetites for more extensive trade. By cooperating with these traders, Persians counteracted Ottoman control of overland routes.

In patriarchal Persian society, women were largely restricted to the home and were expected to veil themselves when leaving the household. Yet, they often had more influence than Arab women. Royal women in harems raised royal sons and tried to shape government policies, and some women became wealthy, owning land and businesses. Even in seclusion, they used agents to help run their enterprises and manage property or money. Poor women had no such opportunities.

Like some Muslim rulers in India, Renaissance European princes, and Chinese emperors, Safavid shahs, often themselves artists and poets, patronized art and literature. The major cities, especially Isfahan, became centers for writers, craftsmen, and artists, and Persia's style of miniature paintings spread to the Ottoman and Mughal Empires. In 1525 the Safavid sultan commissioned an ambitious, decade-long project to produce an illustrated version of an old and much-loved tenth-century epic poem, the longest ever written by a single poet and one of the world's great works of literature. The poem, by Ferdowsi, recounts the history of Persia and its kings—mythical, historical, and heroical—from the creation of the world until the arrival of Islam. Known as the *Shahnameh* ("Book of Kings"), the complete version contained fifty thousand couplets and two hundred and fifty-eight paintings by many artists. The stories are not only about battles, conquests, conspiracies, prophecies, vanities, and miracles but also about the supernatural, seeking truth, and even Alexander the Great (who defeated the Persian Empire in the fourth century BCE). Poetry thrived, with well-known Persian poets recruited by Muslim Indian courts, some using Persian as an official language. Finally, carpet weaving became both an art form and a national industry, while government-run factories produced silks, brocades, velvets, and other fabrics.

Persian Shi'ism underwent some changes. The Safavids encouraged passion plays and annual religious processions commemorating the tragic death of the prophet Muhammad's grandson, Husayn, in the Battle of Karbala in 680, which split the Islamic community. During these events, hundreds of men fulfilled vows of faith by beating their bodies with chains while chanting religious dirges. With Sufi influence gradually declining and religious teachers emphasizing their own authority over that of the Quran, Islamic leaders enjoyed greater power and more wealth than elsewhere in the Islamic world. Even the shahs claimed divine backing, giving the state a theocratic cast. But tensions over religious power between the shahs and Shi'ite leaders continued to simmer.

16-4c Moroccan Resurgence and Expansion

Cossacks Tough adventurers and soldiers from southern Russia who were descendants of Russians, Poles, and Lithuanians fleeing serfdom, slavery, or jail.

While Ottomans and Safavids in the Middle East and the Mughals in South Asia dominated much of the Islamic world, Moroccans on Africa's far northwestern fringe also forged a strong Islamic state and conquered an empire. Moroccan society comprised Berbers, Arabs, and an influential Jewish community, many of whom had migrated across the Strait of Gibraltar to Morocco as a result of the gradual Christian triumph in Iberia. Jews invigorated commercial life. Morocco traded with North Africa, West Africa, and Europe, and Venetian and Genoese ships regularly visited Moroccan ports, exchanging metals, textiles, spices, hardware, and wine for leather, carpets, wool, grain, sugar, and African slaves.

Encounters with the Portuguese brought the Sa'dians to power in Morocco. Portugal's cultivation of sugar on the Atlantic islands undermined Moroccan sugar production, and the establishment of Portuguese forts along the coast threatened the Moroccan government. In response, Sufi movements organized coalitions to resist the Portuguese. With Sufi and tribal support, in 1554 the Sa'dians, a Moroccan family claiming descent from the prophet Muhammad, conquered the country, ruling until 1659. The greatest Sa'dian leader, Sultan Ahmad al-Mansur (**man-SOOR**) (r. 1578–1603), recruited mercenary European and Turkish soldiers familiar with firearms and modern artillery. After buying ships, cannon, and gunpowder from the Netherlands and England, both Portugal's rivals, Moroccans captured the coastal Portuguese ports. Claiming to serve the Islamic world's interests, al-Mansur planned an invasion of West Africa: "The Sudan, being a very rich country and providing enormous revenues, we can now increase the size of the armies of Islam and strengthen the battalions of the faithful."[16] In 1591 Moroccan forces seized the trading city of Timbuktu in Songhai, undermining that Sudanic state, and gained control of the trans-Saharan trade. But facing disappointing profits, Moroccans withdrew in 1618.

After the Sa'dian system fragmented, a new Moroccan dynasty, the Alawis (**uh-LAH-wees**), also claiming descent from the prophet Muhammad, came to power in 1672. This dynasty still rules Morocco today. Sufi influence continued to expand, but powerful Sufi movements sometimes clashed with royal governments. Alawi-ruled Morocco traded even more heavily with Europe, North Africa, and the Sudan.

16-4d Central Asia and Russian Expansion

Russian imperial expansion into Central Asia and Ottoman territories fostered the most direct and long-lasting Muslim–European confrontations. Russians had long coveted Central Asia's dry lands, where long-distance trade flourished in Silk Road hubs such as Bukhara (**boo-CAR-ruh**) and Samarkand (**SAM-ar-kand**). Central Asia also contained large Muslim communities where Sufi masters often gained political power. As the remnants of the Mongol Empire broke up, Russia extended its power into Siberia and then into the Black Sea region and Central Asia. Seeking resources and land for possible Russian settlement, it acquired a great land-based territorial empire. This eastward and southward Russian expansion over huge distances was a saga comparable to later westward expansion by the United States and Canada across North America. Key players were the **Cossacks** (**KOS-aks**), tough, hard-drinking adventurers and fierce soldiers from southern Russia who were descended from Russians, Poles, and Lithuanians fleeing serfdom, slavery, or jail.

---

[16]Quoted in Ralph A. Austen, *Trans-Saharan Africa in World History* (New York: Oxford University Press, 2010), 58.

The expansion east across sparsely populated Siberia to the Pacific coast began in the 1500s and accelerated into the eighteenth century. In 1689 conflict with China forced Russians to temporarily abandon the Amur (**AH-moor**) River Basin north of China (see Chapter 18); however, they added other Siberian territory, often overcoming fierce local resistance. Siberia yielded the Russians furs, metals, and forest products. Seeking direct access to maritime trade routes, Russian leaders also coveted the Black Sea and the Straits of Bosporus, through which Russian ships could reach the warm Mediterranean. The southward thrust meant confronting Tartars (**TAHR-tuhrz**), Muslim descendants of Mongols. In the 1400s and 1500s Tartars, Russians, Ottoman Turks, Poles, and Lithuanians fought for control of southern Russia. After seizing the Tartar state of Kazan (**kuh-ZAN**) and slaughtering many residents, the Russians dominated the northern Caspian Sea and direct trade between the Baltic lands and Persia through Russia.

Turning toward Muslim Central Asia, settled largely by Turkic peoples and often known as Turkestan, by the early 1700s the Russians had gained territory occupied by the Kazakhs (**kah-ZAHKS**), a pastoral people, and by 1864 they controlled all Kazakh lands to the eastern border with China. They then targeted the Silk Road cities but faced formidable opponents in the Uzbeks (**OOZ-beks**), a people of mixed Turkic, Persian, and Mongol ancestry. Since they promoted Sunni Islam, Uzbek sultans were enemies of the Shi'ite Safavids. When Safavid hostility closed Persia to Uzbek trade, the Silk Road cities declined, and the Uzbeks and their neighbors earned smaller revenues while sultans lost power to tribal chiefs. In the early 1700s Persians gained control of some Uzbek territory and much of Afghanistan. But by the later 1800s an expanding Russia had conquered all of southern Turkestan, putting them well on the way to creating one of the two greatest contiguous territorial empires in world history, comparable in many ways to the Mongol Empire centuries earlier and covering some of the same territory.

KEY POINTS

▶ Under the Safavids, Persia was a major exporter of silk and remained a major conduit of trade, and its beautiful capital, built by Shah Abbas I, attracted merchants from many countries.

▶ The Safavid Empire patronized art and literature, and Safavid artists became famous for their miniature painting and their carpet weaving.

▶ Safavid religious leaders, increasingly relying on their own authority rather than that of the Quran, eventually became more influential as the power of Safavid rulers declined and then collapsed.

▶ Morocco, the far western outpost of Islam, absorbed many fleeing Iberian Muslims and grew into a powerful state that, under the Sa'dians, eventually defeated the Portuguese.

Chapter Summary

The overseas expansion of Europe affected different regions in different ways but was only one of the forces at work in most societies. Various African societies, among them Songhai, Kanem-Bornu, the Hausa states, Benin, and Buganda, remained strong in the 1500s. Eventually, however, the Europeans' arrival set in motion forces that reshaped parts of Africa, especially societies along the western and eastern coasts, and many Africans became linked more closely to Europe and the Americas. The Portuguese undermined Kongo, Angola, and the East African city-states and established the first European colonies in sub-Saharan Africa, Angola, and Mozambique. With the trans-Atlantic slave trade, which arose in the sixteenth century, various Europeans procured slaves in West and Central Africa and shipped them across the Atlantic to meet the limitless demands of the American plantations. This trade benefited a few African societies but devastated others, creating chronic conflict along the West African coast.

Several Islamic societies remained powerful, including the empires of the Ottomans, Safavids, and Morocco. The Ottomans, who were Sunni Turks, built an empire over much of western Asia, North Africa, and southeastern Europe, reuniting a large part of the Islamic world. At their zenith they had a powerful military, flourishing economy, and vibrant cultural life. The Safavids fostered a lively culture and economy in Persia and converted the Persians from Sunni to Shi'a Islam, increasing the rivalry with the Ottomans. Sa'dian Morocco repulsed the Portuguese and built a regional empire. But by the early 1700s these great Islamic states as well as Muslim societies in Central Asia experienced new challenges, some posed by Russian expansion into Muslim lands.

Key Terms

Americans, Europeans, Africans, and New Societies in the Americas, 1450–1750

> *Truly do we live on earth? Not forever on earth; only a little while here. Although it be jade, it will be broken. Although it is gold, it is crushed.*
>
> —Aztec poem on the meaning of life, ca. 1500[1]

IMAGE 17.1 **A Mestizo Family** The intermarriage of Europeans and Native Americans was common in Latin America, especially in Mexico. This Mexican painting, by the eighteenth-century artist Miguel Cabrera, shows a Spanish man, his Native American wife, and their mixed-descent, or mestizo, daughter.

Q What can you learn from this painting about the lives of an affluent colonial family in Spanish America?

---

[1]Quoted in Michael C. Meyer and William L. Sherman, *The Course of Mexican History*, 2nd ed. (New York: Oxford University Press, 1983), 86.

In the sixteenth century Spanish colonists in Mexico trained an Aztec historian, Chimalpahin Cuahtlehuanitzin (chee-MAL-pin QUAT-al-WANT-zen), how to read and write in the Western alphabet. Using this alphabet with his native Nahuatl (NAH-waht-l) language, he recorded the Mexican world just before European invaders brought change. He wrote of Aztec victories over neighboring peoples and of Aztec kings improving their great capital, Tenochtitlan (teh-noch-TIT-lan), with temple rebuilding and aqueducts to convey fresh water. But Cuahtlehuanitzin also reported ominous developments. In 1519 reports reached Tenochtitlan of pale-skinned men in huge boats arriving on the eastern coast from the sea, where gods might come from. Aztec legends claimed that, centuries earlier, a Toltec king driven into exile had become a god, Quetzalcoatl (kate-zahl-CO-ah-tal) ("the plumed serpent"), who promised to return some day and seek revenge. Dressed in metal, with unfamiliar but lethal metal weapons, and riding on large animals as tall as a house, these strange men seemed suspiciously godlike. The god's reappearance would threaten the Aztec social order. Cuahtlehuanitzin wrote that 1492 had been unusually bad, bringing an eclipse of the sun, volcanic eruptions, and widespread famine. But Aztecs were not prepared for the arriving Europeans or for a terrible and unknown disease that began killing off the people. Within two years, these men from afar, with horses, metal armor, and gunpowder weapons, had conquered the Aztec Empire, giving new meaning to the broken jade and crushed gold in the Aztec poem.

The first Europeans claimed to have discovered a "new world," but it was actually an old, long-populated one. By destroying or reshaping many long-existing societies, the exploratory voyages by Christopher Columbus and the conquests by European adventurers *created* a "new world." During the 1500s Spaniards and Portuguese conquered and colonized large areas of Latin America containing millions of people, and the English, French, and Dutch followed in North America and the Caribbean. Thanks to these incursions, few regions experienced more changes than the Americas, and the two hemispheres became closely linked. European exploration also led to encounters between Europeans and Pacific island societies. The resulting transitions affected both sides of the Atlantic, forging a complex exchange of crops and animals, peoples and cultures.

17-1 Early American–European–Pacific Encounters

NETWORKS SOCIETIES

Q How did encounters between Europe and the Americas increase in the 1500s?

Until recent decades many historians tended to use Eurocentric perspectives in discussing the pre-Columbian American societies, often in negative stereotypes, and frequently viewed the European disruption and colonization of the Western Hemisphere in this era, despite its atrocities, as progress toward a better world. This was misleading in many ways and ignored processes that were much more complex and more often destructive. A growing body of scholarship has discredited much of the Eurocentric approach to the history of the Americas and the world. American peoples had developed diverse ways of life long before European voyages of exploration permanently connected the two hemispheres. But after Christopher Columbus began the historic change in 1492, various European nations first explored and then gradually conquered and settled the entire Western Hemisphere, drawing the Americas closer to Europe. This exploration also spilled over into the Pacific Ocean.

17-1a American Societies in 1500

Before 1500, American peoples, in adapting to different environments, had developed distinctive institutions, customs, and survival strategies. Hunting, gathering, and fishing societies mostly inhabited the North American Great Plains, the Pacific

---

CONNECTION to TODAY

Can you think of reasons why Christopher Columbus, a hero to many people a generation ago, is now viewed in very negative terms by many people today?

Northwest coast, Alaska, northern Canada, and Central and South American tropical forests. Small-scale farmers were concentrated in eastern North America, parts of the North American desert and Amazon Basin, and southeastern Brazil. The most complex societies flourished from intensive farming in Mesoamerica (Mexico and northern Central America) and the Andes region of western South America (see Chapter 12). By 1500 the Aztecs of central Mexico were Mesoamerica's most powerful society, and the Inca (**IN-kuhz**), centered in central Peru, controlled most of the Andes region. Like their predecessors, the Aztecs and Inca lived in cities, farmed, and worked metals and fibers for tools, decoration, and weapons.

The Aztecs, through military conquest and well-organized government, completed their empire building in 1428. Aztec warfare relied on disciplined battle formations, shrewd tactics, and deadly weapons such as bows and arrows, stone-bladed broadswords, spears, and spear-throwers. But the Aztecs only loosely controlled their empire and faced military confrontations with rival societies, especially the Tlaxcalans (**tlax-CALL-uns**) on their eastern fringe. Cruel Aztec imperialism and extensive human sacrifice created enemies, some of whom later cooperated with the Spanish to overthrow Aztec power.

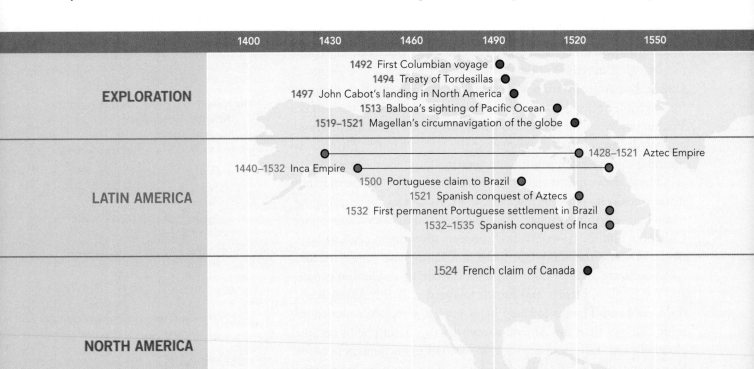

	1400	1430	1460	1490	1520	1550
EXPLORATION			1492 First Columbian voyage ●			
			1494 Treaty of Tordesillas ●			
			1497 John Cabot's landing in North America ●			
			1513 Balboa's sighting of Pacific Ocean ●			
			1519–1521 Magellan's circumnavigation of the globe ●			
LATIN AMERICA					● 1428–1521 Aztec Empire	
		1440–1532 Inca Empire ●			●	
			1500 Portuguese claim to Brazil ●			
			1521 Spanish conquest of Aztecs ●			
			1532 First permanent Portuguese settlement in Brazil ●			
			1532–1535 Spanish conquest of Inca ●			
NORTH AMERICA			1524 French claim of Canada ●			

In 1440 the Inca completed their conquest of an empire larger than the Roman or Han Chinese Empire, stretching nearly twenty-five hundred miles north to south, much of it above eight thousand feet in altitude. The Inca state was the Americas' most dynamic and integrated, geared for conquest and paternalistic regimentation. In the later 1500s the writer Garcilaso de la Vega **(GAHR-suh-LAH-so duh luh VAY-guh)**, son of a Spanish captain and Inca princess, acknowledged the misery of people colonized by the Inca but praised their highly productive farming system and generosity, which "had attained perfection. No thoughtful man can fail to admire so noble a government."[2]

Partly because of climate change, some societies had long passed their peak. The last Maya cities of southern Mexico and northern Central America had collapsed, but some 5 to 6 million Mayan-speaking people lived in villages, remnants of a once-vibrant two-thousand-year-old society. In North America, Cahokia **(kuh-HOE-key-uh)**, the main Mississippian city, was deserted by 1250, and by the 1400s the Anasazi **(ah-nah-SAH-zee)** and other southwestern desert societies had abandoned their major settlements. However, the Taino **(TIE-no)** in the Caribbean islands and the farming peoples along the Atlantic coasts of North America and Brazil had flourishing societies.

While the first European settlers wrongly considered the Americas largely empty land, by 1492 the Western Hemisphere's population probably constituted around ten percent of the world total, and numbered between 60 and 75 million people, perhaps even over 100 million, the majority in the Andes region and densely populated Mesoamerica. But European invasion changed that. Americans, isolated for many millennia from the Eastern Hemisphere, had no immunity to the diseases brought unwittingly by Europeans and later African slaves. Hence the Western explorers and colonizers brought a terrible mortality. Native Americans also had no metal swords or firearms to resist Europeans.

17-1b Bridging the Atlantic and the Columbian Voyages

The stormy Atlantic Ocean was the major barrier between the hemispheres, but a few Europeans steadily overcame the challenge. The first known contact between Americans and Europeans had no long-lasting impact. In the tenth century some Norse Vikings, sailing west from Iceland, established several small farming settlements in southern Greenland. By around 1000 a few of these hardy Norse sailed west, sighted eastern Canada, and explored the coast. They built a small village on the large island of Newfoundland, where they harvested fish and cut timber. After conflicts with Native Americans erupted, the Norse abandoned the Newfoundland settlement, but Greenland Norse apparently made occasional trading and lumbering expeditions to eastern Canada, as shown by Norse artifacts, including spun yarn, scattered across eastern Canada and the Arctic islands. Earlier scholarship suggested that the Norse may have taught spinning to the local people but we now know that some of these local people had been spinning and using yarn for a thousand years before the Norse arrived.

[2]From Lewis Hanke, ed., *History of Latin American Civilization: Sources and Interpretations*, vol. 1 (Boston: Little, Brown and Company, 1973), 64.

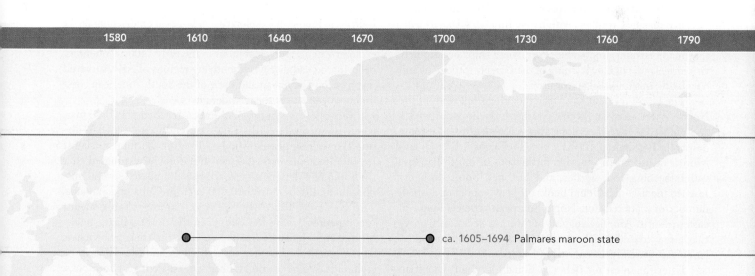

1580	1610	1640	1670	1700	1730	1760	1790

ca. 1605–1694 Palmares maroon state

1587 First English colony at Roanoke
1604 First French settlement in Acadia (Canada)
1607 First permanent English settlement in Virginia
1608 French settlement at Quebec City
1624 Dutch settlement at New York
1627 Colony of New France
1713 English control of Acadia
1739 Stono Rebellion in South Carolina
1755 Deportation of French Acadians to Louisiana
1759 English defeat of French in Quebec

Historica Graphica Collection/Heritage Image Partnership Ltd./Alamy Stock Photo

IMAGE 17.2 **Columbus Landing in the Americas** This idealized early-nineteenth-century painting by an Italian artist imagines Christopher Columbus landing in the Caribbean and presenting gifts to the first local peoples greeting him on the beach.

Q What messages does this painting convey about Columbus and his first encounter with the Taino in the Bahamas?

The Greenland settlements collapsed by 1450 as the result of factional disputes, conflicts with native Inuit (**IN-yoo-it**) people, deforestation, and colder climates during the Little Ice Age that made farming impossible. Portuguese ships occasionally visited Iceland, possibly learning of the Canada settlement and circulating this knowledge in Europe.

The Norse may not have been the only people to spot the North American coast. As cold weather brought poor harvests and reduced fish catches along Europe's Atlantic coast, some desperate Portuguese, Basque, Danish, English, Breton, and Moroccan fishermen ventured further out in North Atlantic waters seeking cod, whales, and sardines. Some probably reached the fish-rich Grand Banks off Newfoundland. A small number of scattered non-Norse European artifacts found in eastern North America suggest but do not necessarily prove that a few coastal people may have encountered Europeans, landings apparently unreported in Europe.

Later the quest for riches, national glory, and Christian converts encouraged other Europeans to explore the Atlantic (see Chapter 15). While Portuguese expeditions concentrated on the African route to the East (see Chapters 16 and 18), Christopher Columbus (1451–1506) hoped to sail westward from Europe to Asia. Contrary to myth, many educated Europeans accepted that Earth was round and hence could be circumnavigated.

The first explorer to brave the Atlantic in an attempt to reach Asia, Columbus (see Chapter 16), came under the

Spanish flag. Historians still debate Columbus, his explorations, and his role in opening the Americas to European conquest. Columbus, born in Genoa, had lived for many years in Lisbon, which had a large Genoese merchant community. His connections helped him marry Donha Felipa Moniz, the aristocratic daughter of the governor of the Portuguese-settled island of Madeira. Columbus worked in Madeira, visited the Canary and Azores Islands farther out in the Atlantic, likely was a crewman on voyages to Iceland and down the West African coast on Portuguese ships, and was probably familiar with the Norse discoveries and Portuguese fishermen's tales.

Inspired by the writings of the thirteenth-century Italian adventurer Marco Polo, who traveled in Asia and sojourned in China, Columbus, a devout Christian, hoped to find the sea route to the silk- and spice-rich lands of China and Southeast Asia and to introduce Christianity to China. But his inaccurate maps vastly underestimated Earth's size and the distance to Asia. Rebuffed in Portugal, Columbus eventually convinced the Spanish monarchs, King Ferdinand and Queen Isabella, to finance his exploration in hopes of establishing direct ties to Asia. Commanding ships far smaller than the Chinese explorer Zheng He's great junks in the early 1400s, Columbus, believing he had discovered outlying regions of Asia, surveyed much of the Caribbean and some of the South American coast in four voyages over the next decade (see Map 17.1).

On his first voyage, Columbus reached the Bahamas, where he encountered the Taino, a friendly Arawak (**AR-uh-wahk**)-speaking people who had lived on Caribbean islands for hundreds of years. A Spanish chronicler estimated that the Taino population in the Caribbean numbered several million, including perhaps 600,000 each in Cuba and Jamaica. The Bahamas Taino (the Arawak name probably meant "good people") wore few clothes in the tropical heat, shocking the straight-laced Spanish sweating in their heavy coats and trousers. Some lived in towns built around Mesoamerican-style plazas. The Taino smoked cigars, slept in hammocks, possessed a little gold, combined fishing with corn (maize) and manioc cultivation, and carried on interisland trade in large canoes capable of holding up to one hundred and fifty people. Taino women did the farming and often served as community leaders, confounding the patriarchal Spanish. Often resisting incursions by Caribs (**KAR-ibs**), a warlike group originating in South America, the Taino may have welcomed a potential ally. Columbus developed favorable views of the hospitable, patient, and peaceable Taino, seeing them as

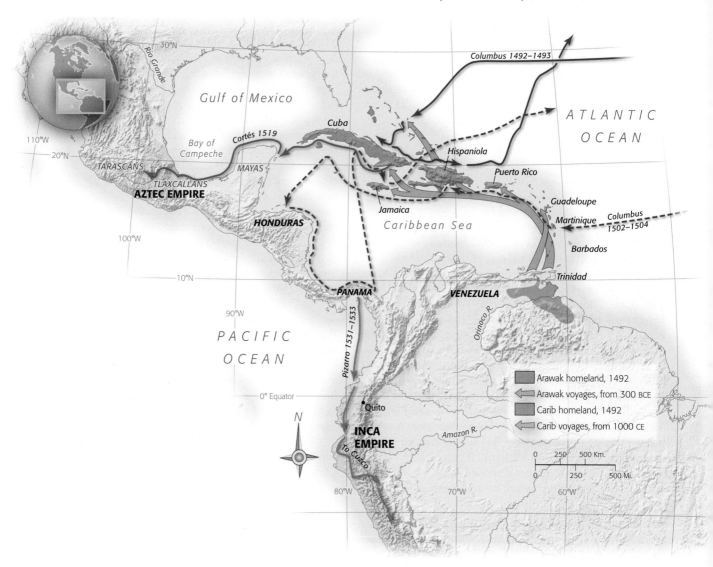

MAP 17.1 **The Americas and Early European Exploration** The several voyages across the Atlantic led by Columbus explored the Caribbean Basin and set the stage for Spanish conquest of many American societies, most notably of the Aztec and Inca Empires.

Q What does this map tell us about what parts of the Americas were explored by the Spanish adventurers and conquerors in the late 1400s and early 1500s?

innocent children of nature: "They are uncovetous people [who] love their neighbors as themselves."[3] Later, when Columbus encountered Taino noncooperation or armed resistance to Spanish demands, he changed his views.

Columbus then sailed on to the island he called Hispaniola (HIS-puhn-YO-luh), today the home of Haiti and the Dominican Republic, with a population of perhaps a million Taino. Leaving a small colony of Spaniards there, Columbus landed on Cuba. Thinking Cuba might be China, he dispatched a small party of crewmen, which included an Arabic-speaking Jew, to search for the Chinese ruler. They returned only with mysterious dried leaves called *tobacos*, which local people smoked. Later other Europeans took tobacco back to Europe,

starting a smoking fad. Taking six Taino natives to present at court, Columbus and his crew sailed back to Spain, where he was feted as a hero and promoted to admiral.

Although not finding China, Columbus launched a new era of exploration. Spanish authorities planned a second voyage and, to counteract a possible Portuguese challenge, persuaded the pope to issue the Treaty of Tordesillas (tor-duh-SEE-yuhs) in 1494 giving Spain the rights to most of the Americas; the Portuguese received Africa and Brazil. Both Iberian countries promised to evangelize and colonize the "heathen" peoples they encountered. During his four voyages, Columbus explored much of the Caribbean region. Bringing Spanish colonists with him in 1493, he established the first permanent European

[3]Quoted in Oliver Cox, "The Rise of Modern Race Relations," in *Racial Conflict, Discrimination, and Power*, ed. William Barclay et al. (New York: AMS Press, 1976), 91.

settlement in the Americas on Hispaniola, where he exploited the local Taino through forced labor and then slavery. According to a Spanish historian, Columbus stopped the baptizing of Taino so, as "heathens," they could be used or sold as slaves. As Columbus wrote, "The Indians of this island are its riches, for it is they who dig and produce the bread and other food for the [Spanish] Christians and get the gold from the mines, and perform all the services and labor of men and of draft animals."[4] Columbus also explored the Cuban and Jamaican coasts and sighted Puerto Rico. On his third voyage, in 1498, he found Trinidad and the Venezuelan coast. But his mismanagement as Hispaniola governor and his failure to discover vast riches brought disgrace, and he was ordered home under arrest.

However, Queen Isabella allowed Columbus one final voyage to find a strait leading to India. This expedition in 1502 explored the Central American coast and encountered a Maya trading raft Columbus thought might be Chinese. He now spoke of the Caribbean islands as the "West Indies," separate from the eagerly sought "East Indies" (India and Southeast Asia). After being shipwrecked for a year on Jamaica, he returned to Spain and died in 1506, a broken man.

Eventually Europeans referred to Native Americans as "Indians," confusing American peoples with those of India. The label remains controversial, and some activists prefer terms such as *Native American* or *First Nations* or *indigenous* to *Indian*. The term *America* derives from an Italian merchant, Amerigo Vespucci (ves-POO-chee) (1454–1512), who claimed to have made several voyages to the Western Hemisphere. His letters to powerful European princes described a "new world" soon known as "Amerigo's land," which became *America*.

17-1c The Continuing Search for Wealth

Exploration soon became a multinational effort involving the English, French, Portuguese, and Spanish. By 1525 European expeditions had explored the Atlantic and Caribbean coasts from eastern Canada to South America's southern tip. Some explorers sought to enrich themselves and the European monarchs who sponsored them. Others hoped to gain God's favor through Christian missionary activity. An English expedition led by another Genoese, John Cabot, and possibly financed in part by a London-based Italian bank, claimed North America's Atlantic coast in 1497, setting off a fruitless search for a northwest sea passage connecting the Atlantic Ocean through North America to the Pacific. In 1500 Portugal claimed Brazil, which fell within the longitudes awarded to it in the Treaty of Tordesillas, and began settlements. By 1511 Spain controlled Cuba, Puerto Rico, and Jamaica. In 1513 a Spanish expedition led by Vasco Nunez de Balboa (bal-BOH-uh) crossed Panama and sighted the Pacific Ocean. The French claimed eastern Canada in 1524 with a voyage led by an Italian, Giovanni da Verrazano (VER-uh-ZAH-no).

These brave explorers and their crews hoped to become rich but were just as likely to perish from violence, disease, or storms. A Spanish expedition led by a Portuguese captain, Ferdinand Magellan (muh-JELL-un) (1480–1521), finally discovered the only practical sea route to Asia via the Americas in 1520. With the Spanish monarch financing the search for a possible Pacific route to the Spice Islands via the Americas, Magellan's five ships sailed down the Atlantic, rounded South America's southern tip, and then survived a torturous trip through the stormy strait known today as the Strait of Magellan. They continued on across the Pacific, a long, difficult journey during which they spotted no inhabited islands before Guam (gwahm), the crewmen living off rat meat and boiled leather for months. Eventually the expedition reached the Philippine Islands, where Magellan tried to convert the Filipinos on several islands to Christianity but, misunderstanding local politics, enraged some chiefs and was killed in a clash with local people in 1521 (see Chapter 18). The death of Magellan and many of his crew revealed some of the Spanish overconfidence and ignorance. An excellent explorer and navigator but a poor battle tactician, Magellan believed his men and weapons were so superior that he declined help from friendly chiefs and sent only forty-nine of his crew to fight fifteen hundred local warriors. But the Spanish muskets (which took one minute to reload and fire) and armor proved worthless against skillfully wielded spears, bows, and arrows. The result was a rout. Magellan's one surviving ship, with eighteen crew members and a valuable cargo of cloves from the Spice Islands, continued on westward around Africa to Spain. Having thus gained a better idea of world geography, Europeans turned to conquering and settling the Americas.

Some explorers, greedy for quick wealth, engaged in piracy and looting. The Spanish conqueror of Aztec Mexico, Hernán Cortés (kor-TEZ), admitted that Spaniards "suffer an affliction of the heart which can only be cured by gold."[5] As governor of Hispaniola, Columbus executed the Taino who refused to supply gold. Harsh exploitation generated Taino attacks on Spaniards, prompting Columbus to enslave Taino rebels and their families and ship them to Spain in chains. Later, Spaniards raided other islands for slaves. Within thirty years all the Taino on Hispaniola, and many elsewhere, had been enslaved or killed, had died of disease or overwork, or had committed suicide because of their suffering. A Spanish priest lamented that many Caribbean islands were ruined "by men who wished to depopulate them and to kill the Indians who lived there. They were laid to waste."[6] Some Taino apparently survived in remote communities, especially in eastern Cuba; DNA suggests that some may have intermarried with Spaniards and escaped African slaves in places like Jamaica and Puerto Rico. Some Taino words—for example, *hurricane, hammock, barbecue, tobacco,* and *canoe*—survive today.

17-1d New Horizons and Exploration in the Pacific

The continued search for a sea route to Asia led to exploration of the Pacific Basin, which was inhabited by Pacific islanders, scattered across many island chains, who had developed diverse cultural and political traditions. The larger mountainous islands provided varied food sources for farming and fishing and supported states led by kings or powerful chiefs. For example, the

[4]Quoted in Herman J. Viola, "Seeds of Change," in *Seeds of Change: A Quincentennial Commemoration*, ed. Herman J. Viola and Carolyn Margolis (Washington, DC: Smithsonian Institution Press, 1991), 13.
[5]Quoted in L. S. Stavrianos, *Lifelines from Our Past: A New World History*, rev. ed. (Armonk, NY: M.E. Sharpe, 1997), 96.
[6]Alonso de Zuazo, quoted in Kathleen Deagan and Jose Maria Cruxent, *Columbus's Outpost Among the Tainos: Spain and America at La Isabela, 1493–1498* (New Haven, CT: Yale University Press, 2002), 210.

eight inhabited Hawaiian Islands, divided into four rival chiefdoms, contained perhaps 200,000 people. Some 100,000 to 200,000 Maori (**MOW-ree**), organized into chiefdoms, lived on the two main New Zealand islands. By contrast, people living on small atolls only a few feet above sea level relied chiefly on resources from the sea.

Many island societies traded over vast distances. Warfare and destruction of their fragile environments were common problems. Hence, over the centuries Polynesian settlers deforested remote Easter Island in the eastern Pacific, sparking chronic civil war for control of scarce resources. Most Pacific islanders, like indigenous Americans, had no direct contact with Asia for millennia, making them vulnerable to Eurasian diseases later brought by Europeans.

In the 1500s and 1600s Spanish, Portuguese, English, and Dutch expeditions discovered many islands and Australia, but the islands had few easily exploitable resources compared to Asia and the Americas. Although Spanish ships sailed annually between the Philippines and Mexico beginning in 1565 (see Chapter 18), Europeans made little effort to colonize the vast Pacific region. They did not locate some island chains, including Hawaii, until the later 1700s, when British settlement in Australia also began. Magellan's ships, chancing on Guam, clashed with local Chamorro (**chuh-MOR-oh**) people, the first of many unhappy Pacific Islander–European encounters. Spain colonized Guam in 1663, founding a Catholic mission. But 90 percent of the Chamorros died over the next two decades, mostly from disease. In 1671 a demoralized Chamorro chief complained to a missionary that "the Spanish would have done better to remain in their own country. We have no need of their help to live happily. They treat us as gross barbarians."[7]

KEY POINTS

▶ From 1000 on, Norse from Greenland intermittently settled in Newfoundland, and other Europeans may have crossed the Atlantic in search of fish long before Columbus discovered America.

▶ Beginning in 1492, Christopher Columbus explored the Caribbean and the South American coast under the impression that they were outlying areas of Asia, opening up exploration of the Americas.

▶ Columbus focused on the island of Hispaniola, where he enslaved the native Taino, and gradually gave up on the idea that he had discovered an Atlantic route to Asia, which was later discovered by Magellan.

▶ European nations divided up the Western Hemisphere according to the Treaty of Tordesillas, and as Europeans explored the Americas, some seeking riches and others converts, their diseases and their habit of enslaving or killing the local people decimated native populations.

17-2 The European Conquest of the Americas

⇄ TRANSITIONS   🏛 SOCIETIES

Q How did Europeans conquer and colonize the American societies and begin bringing in settlers from Europe?

Some historians use the shorthand phrase "guns, germs, and steel" to summarize the advantages that Europeans had in conquering and maintaining control of the Americas and some other parts of the world as well, bringing about the "triumph of the West." Some scholars view the phrase as useful, others as simplistic. Weapons, disease, and technology were certainly important factors but only tell part of a complex story that also includes migrations, environments, and cultures, among other factors. European explorations and the search for riches led to colonization of the Americas. Native Americans, divided into often-hostile societies, lacked guns to resist the thousands of Spanish adventurers who roamed the Americas in the 1500s, many of whom, known as **conquistadors** (**kon-KEY-stuh-dorz**), engaged in armed conquest. While Spain conquered Mexico and the Andes and the Portuguese

CONNECTION to TODAY

How do you think the brutal conquests and colonization of the Americas have influenced the societies and politics of American nations today?

annexed Brazil, the English, French, and Dutch later obtained footholds in North America, the Caribbean, and South America's northeast coast. By 1750 various European powers firmly controlled many American societies.

17-2a The Fall of the Aztec and Inca Empires

The ultimate Spanish victory in Mexico fostered a myth in which the "gallant adventurer" Hernán Cortés (1485–1547) and a few hundred plucky conquistadors overcame unbelievable odds to triumph over the enormous might of the Aztec empire and their fearsome military, a tribute to European superiority.

conquistadors The leaders of Spanish soldiers engaged in armed conquest in the Americas.

---

[7]Magá Lahen Hurao, quoted in Geoffrey C. Gunn, *First Globalization: The Eurasian Exchange* (Lanham, MD: Rowman and Littlefield, 2003), 194.

But the reality was far more complex. Spanish success owed much to a combination of factors including European diseases, Spanish weapons (guns, armor, horses), Aztec attitudes and customs, and exploiting widespread hostility toward the Aztecs.

Seeking to conquer the rich Aztec Empire, in 1519 Cortés and 550 soldiers from Spanish-controlled Cuba landed on Mexico's east coast, where they founded the settlement of Veracruz (**VER-uh-KROOZ**). Native Americans were shocked by the Spanish guns: "A thing like a ball of stone comes out its entrails; it comes out shooting sparks and raining fire. . . . If the cannon is aimed against a mountain, the mountain splits and cracks open."[8] Cortés defeated and then forged an alliance with the Tlaxcalans, longtime Aztec enemies who lived along the Caribbean coast. Impressed by Spanish power, the Tlaxcalan nobles adopted Christianity, and their soldiers joined Cortés. After defeating several other peoples, Cortés and his growing force marched west through the mountains into the Valley of Mexico, heart of an Aztec Empire of 25 million. With its gleaming temples and canal network, the Aztec capital, Tenochtitlan, astonished the Spanish. Perhaps initially confusing Cortés with Quetzalcoatl and the Spaniards with gods, the Aztec leader, Moctezuma II (**mock-teh-ZOO-ma**) (r. 1502–1520), warmly greeted them. Taking advantage of this friendliness, Cortés arrested Moctezuma. With sixty Spanish soldiers supplied with horses and guns, and many Native American allies, Cortés temporarily controlled the capital. Some historians argue that, while the Spanish religious impulse to spread Christianity was important, Spanish revulsion at Aztec human sacrifice was mainly used as a justification for their invasion.

Angered by the Spaniards' arrogant behavior and seizure of gold, Aztec mobs killed or captured some Spaniards. Either enraged Aztecs or his Spanish captors killed Moctezuma, no longer a credible leader. But the Aztecs' less deadly weapons (obsidian blades and arrows) and military goals—securing captives for sacrifice rather than killing opponents—put them at a disadvantage to the Spanish, and many died as the Spaniards fought their way out of the city. Some Spaniards, loaded down with stolen Aztec gold, fell into canals and drowned. Returning to the coast, Cortés recruited more Aztec enemies and Spanish soldiers from Cuba. Armed with deadly muskets, cannon, steel swords, crossbows, and horses, his enlarged army—around one thousand Spaniards and ten thousand Native American allies—laid siege to Tenochtitlan. The Aztecs resisted fiercely while a smallpox epidemic, inadvertently spread by the Spaniards, ravaged their population. In 1521 the Spanish occupied the city, capturing Moctezuma II's successor as emperor while revengeful Tlaxcalans massacred thousands of city residents. Aztec poets, who once addressed their violent culture in melancholy verses, now bemoaned their destruction, one lamenting that "broken spears lie in the roads; we have torn our hair in our grief. The houses are roofless now, and their walls are red with blood."[9] Within five years the epidemic wiped out some fifteen million

Codex Duran: Pedro de Alvarado (c.1485–1541) companion-at-arms of Hernando Cortes (1485–1547) besieged by Aztec warriors (vellum)/ Duran, Diego (16th century)/Biblioteca Nacional, Madrid, Spain/Bridgeman Images

IMAGE 17.3 **Codex of Aztec Resistance** Illustrations in a book published around 1580 revealed a local perspective on the Spanish conquest of the Aztec Empire. This illustration shows Aztec warriors besieging a Spanish force, commanded by a Cortés officer Pedro de Alvarado, defending a fort in Tenochtitlan and also illustrates the difference in weapons technology.

Q What are the differences in weapons and battle dress between the Aztecs and Spanish soldiers?

---

[8]Quoted in Jon T. Davidann and Marc J. Gilbert, *Cross-Cultural Encounters in Modern World History* (New York: Pearson, 2013), 16.
[9]Quoted in Jane MacLaren Walsh and Yoko Sugiura, "The Demise of the Fifth Sun," in Viola and Margolis, *Seeds of Change*, 41.

people, 80 percent of the Aztec population. Spaniards now ruled the Aztec Empire, using efficient Aztec administration to collect tribute from former Aztec subjects. In 2019 Mexico's president sent a letter to Spain's king and the Pope urging them to apologize and ask forgiveness from the indigenous people for the human rights abuses, including massacres committed "by the sword and the cross," during the conquest of the region five centuries ago. The requests, rejected by Spain, fostered some discussion in both countries of the conquest and the mixed ancestry of Mexico's population.

Seeing possibilities for wealth, Spanish conquerors pushed south from Mexico to seize Central America, Panama, and, a few years later, northern South America. Others moved north as far as New Mexico and northern California. By 1750 Spain's empire included a third of what later became the United States, stretching from San Francisco through Santa Fe and San Antonio all the way to Saint Augustine in Florida. Ten years later another conquistador, Francisco Pizarro (ca. 1476–1541), explored South America's west coast. In 1531 his forces marched into the Andes to conquer the Inca. As in Mexico, smallpox had already wiped out millions of Inca, including many leaders; in addition, the empire was divided by a civil war between two rivals for the throne. With only one hundred and sixty Spaniards but artillery and horses, Pizarro captured Atahualpa (**AH-tuh-WAHL-puh**), one of two rival claimants, and killed thousands of Inca, many unarmed. Pizarro demanded and received gold and silver for ransom, then executed Atahualpa. Ignoring pleas from Catholic priests to treat the Inca with more leniency, Pizarro retorted that he had come to take Inca gold, not spread Christianity. The conquistadors converted the Inca capital, Cuzco (**KOOZ-ko**), into a Spanish settlement and founded the city of Lima along the Pacific coast. Soon Spain gained control over much of today's Peru, Ecuador, Bolivia, and Chile, brutally crushing Native American uprisings. Pizarro and his men placed themselves at the top of the efficient Inca administrative system. Supporters of a rival Spanish leader later murdered Pizarro.

17-2b Colonization of Brazil and the Caribbean

The Portuguese established small trading posts along coastal Brazil, which was blessed by regular rainfall, striking natural beauty, and a benign climate. While the Portuguese obtained and shipped brazilwood, an excellent dye for European textiles, they initially remained more focused on exploiting African and Asian wealth than on exploiting the Americas. In 1532 the Portuguese founded a permanent colony along Brazil's southern coast and awarded land grants to private entrepreneurs. Facing not large settled societies but seminomadic food collectors and small farmers, they considered the Native Americans potential slaves who could be forced to work. Portuguese from the settlement at São Paulo (**sow PAU-low**), known as **Paulistas**, raided for slaves deep into the interior. The colonial government combatted these activities, and expanded its control in the interior, only in 1680.

In 1628 the Dutch gained control over much of northeastern Brazil, setting up plantations to grow huge quantities of sugar for the European market. Brazil was the jewel in the Dutch Atlantic crown: the most productive in wealth, largest geographically, and heavily defended. But the Portuguese eventually expelled their rivals in 1654 and took over the profitable northeast, building a city, Salvador da Bahia, at Bahia (**ba-HEE-a**).

While Spain colonized Cuba, Puerto Rico, and much of Central and South America's Caribbean coast, the Dutch, English, and French all founded Caribbean colonies. Expelled from Brazil, the Dutch moved to several small Caribbean islands and also established Dutch Guiana (**ghee-AHN-a**) (now Suriname) in northeastern South America. The French seized Haiti (**HAY-tee**), the western half of Hispaniola, where they developed plantations as a major wealth source. They also seized French Guiana and the islands of Guadeloupe (**GWAD-e-loop**) and Martinique (**mahr-ten-EEK**). Meanwhile, England made Jamaica, Barbados (**bahr-BAY-doz**), British Guiana (now Guyana), and later Trinidad their colonial linchpins.

In the Caribbean, European piracy became a major economic activity, often directed at Spanish settlements or the Spanish galleons hauling rich cargoes of silver, sugar, or imported Asian goods to Europe. In 1670 the English pirate Sir Henry Morgan led fourteen hundred men to brazenly sack Panama City, where warehouses stored wealth from Asia and Latin America. The Spanish burned the city rather than allow buccaneers to seize it. Some pirates, such as Morgan, John Hawkins, and Sir Francis Drake, became respected figures in England, celebrated for the wealth they captured from rival countries. In 1577 Drake (ca. 1540–1596) sailed from England on a secret mission for Queen Elizabeth I that eventually took him around the entire world while outflanking and plundering the Spanish Empire. Drake's fleet sailed through the Strait of Magellan and up the Pacific coast to Mexico and San Francisco Bay, and perhaps as far north as the Columbia River, looting unsuspecting Spanish settlements and treasure-laden ships along the way. Drake then sailed across the Pacific to the Spice Islands and around Africa to England. Like other explorers, he lost many crewmen to scurvy, the deadly vitamin C deficiency caused by lack of fresh fruits and vegetables; the cause was only discovered two centuries later. Drake also helped defeat the Spanish armada sent against England in 1588, a battle that decisively shifted European political power. Drake's swashbuckling career illustrated how the world had changed after 1492.

17-2c The English, French, and Indigenous Societies in North America

English and French colonizing efforts on North America's eastern seaboard undermined often matrilineal and sometimes matriarchal Native American farming societies, who generally enjoyed good health and nutritious diets. Native Americans soon disdained Europeans as unintelligent, physically weak, and smelly. While Native Americans valued personal cleanliness, the English and French seldom bathed. Nonetheless, Native Americans usually offered hospitality, traded with, and sought allies among the newcomers. But Europeans established settlements, wearing out their welcome.

Paulistas Portuguese slavers from the southern Brazilian settlement at São Paulo.

Coveting land and wanting to outflank rival countries, the English planted settlements up and down the Atlantic coast. The first, at Roanoke in Virginia in 1587, failed, but a colony established in 1607 at Jamestown in Virginia succeeded. As settlements struggled to survive in the unfamiliar land, farming families were from England. In many cases only generous Native Americans sharing knowledge or supplying food enabled colonists to survive. England also acquired the Dutch settlement at New York, which was founded in 1624 but was unable to recruit enough settlers from Holland to offset English immigration.

The French established their first settlement in Acadia (today the Canadian province of Nova Scotia) in 1604, which was followed by outposts along the Saint Lawrence River at Quebec (ke-BEK) City and Montreal, forming the basis for New France, a colony, established in 1627, that covered much of eastern Canada. French Jesuit missionaries (known as "Black Robes") traveled widely, as far west as today's Illinois, to convert Native Americans to Catholicism. Using canoes, French explorers and trappers, known as **voyageurs** (voi-uh-ZHUR), established trading outposts throughout the Great Lakes and Mississippi River Basin; decades later some of those outposts became towns and then cities. To counter English and Spanish expansion, in 1699 the French founded New Orleans, which became the base for French activities and territorial claims in Louisiana and the Mississippi Valley (see Map 17.2).

English colonies north of Maryland developed largely as agricultural economies of free white settlers. Many English and French settlers exploited two valuable commodities, fish and fur. The seas off New England and eastern Canada teamed with cod, which became a major part of European diets. As cod stocks off Europe diminished, fishermen established coastal North American bases. Later English and French settlers moved inland seeking beavers, whose fur became popular in Europe for women's and men's coats and hats. Fur remained Canadians' major export until the nineteenth century.

Both French and English settlement disrupted Native American tribes (now known as "First Nations" in Canada and to some extent in the United States). The French generally maintained better relations with local peoples, allying with tribal leaders. Nonetheless, most Native Americans, dying from disease or armed conflict, were pushed north and west or eventually forced onto reservations. In the early 1700s English colonists forced various tribes, among them the Tuscarora (tus-kuh-ROR-uh) and Delaware, to move west of the Appalachian Mountains, foreshadowing worse treatment to come.

Yet, some proved formidable opponents. The Iroquois (EAR-uh-coy) Confederation, a complex political coalition formed in the 1500s, united five once-warring longhouse-dwelling tribes living between Lake Erie and the Hudson River in what is today upstate New York. They shared a common enemy, the Huron of southern Ontario, who established a rival confederation. Around 1500 on Lake Ontario's northern shore, the Huron built the region's largest town, surrounded by a massive stockade, that housed some 1,500 to 1,800 people in around one hundred longhouses. By the 1690s, the pan-tribal Iroquois government had a council of chiefs and an oral constitution that required unanimity for any

voyageurs French explorers and trappers in North America.

MAP 17.2 **The English, French, and Spanish in North America, ca. 1700** While the English colonized much of the Atlantic coast of North America, the French concentrated on what is today eastern Canada and the interior of North America, including the Great Lakes and the Mississippi and Ohio River Basins. The Spanish colonized what is today the southwest United States and Florida.

Q Where were most of the major colonial settlements in North America and Mesoamerica located?

decision. Women had important political authority, participating in all major decision making, selecting chiefs, and having the power to veto any act of war. Some scholars credit Iroquois political ideas, such as a representative congress and freedom of speech, as influencing the later United States constitution. The effective Iroquois military alliance generally defeated rival tribes while holding off or outmaneuvering European arrivals for many years. Later it supported England in conflicts against France, which was allied with the Huron and Algonquins (al-GAHN-kwinz). Eventually the Iroquois, Huron, and Algonquins, like other Native Americans, were colonized. European Americans often developed myths about Native Americans, their lands, and their destinies, including the notions of the "Noble Savage" (innocent and virtuous), "Ignoble Savage" (violent and ignorant), the "undeveloped" wilderness (needing "development"), and the vanishing "Indian" awaiting Western "civilization."

KEY POINTS

▶ The Spanish under Cortés were able to conquer the Aztecs because of their superior weaponry, their alliances with other American peoples, and a smallpox epidemic that ravaged the Aztecs.

▶ From their base in Mexico, the Spanish pushed north and south, and Pizarro conquered the Inca, the Spanish proceeding to rule much of South America with great cruelty, using the Inca administrative system.

▶ The Spanish, Portuguese, Dutch, French, and English all struggled for colonial control of the Americas, with pirates from each country preying on other countries' ships.

▶ Many North American colonies thrived on fish and fur, while others practiced agriculture, and all eventually pushed native peoples off their lands.

17-3 The Consequences of American Colonization

NETWORKS SOCIETIES

Q What were the major consequences of European colonization of the Americas?

By the late sixteenth century Spaniards had explored and claimed an empire stretching from northern California and the Rocky Mountains to southern Chile and Argentina, forming local governments and founding cities. Meanwhile, England, France, and Holland held Caribbean Basin and North American territory. European ships crisscrossed the Atlantic, moving people, plants, animals, natural resources, and manufactured goods, while Eastern Hemisphere diseases sparked a demographic disaster for Native Americans. Despite many similarities, American colonies differed, but everywhere Native Americans suffered from the colonists' diseases, faced Christian missionary activity, and experienced violent repression of their resistance and culture. The societies spawned by colonization reflected diverse influences. Europeans, Africans, and Native Americans in Latin America and the Caribbean formed mixed cultures that differed from those in English- and French-ruled North America.

17-3a The Columbian Exchange

The **Columbian Exchange**, a useful term coined by historians, refers to the transfer of diseases, animals, and plants between hemispheres. The most catastrophic of these transfers was the transmission of virulent Eastern Hemisphere microbes to the Americas, which caused massive depopulation and suffering. Although often healthier than Eastern Hemisphere peoples, Native Americans had suffered from polio, hepatitis, tuberculosis, many intestinal parasites, and syphilis. Yet, only syphilis, a sexually transmitted disease, made any serious impact when carried to Europe, being more an unpleasant nuisance than a mass killer. In contrast, Native Americans had no immunity to Eastern Hemisphere diseases like measles, typhus, influenza, and especially smallpox, which was widespread in Europe. As a result, these diseases reduced the Native American populations by around 90 percent. No group remained untouched. A Maya writer reported that "great was the stench of the dead. The dogs and vultures devoured the bodies. We were born to die!"[10] Men died at higher rates than women, leaving widows to support households and young girls to grow up without protection by fathers and male relatives. Recent research, including a British study in 2019, concluded that the massive mortality and hence depopulation in the Americas was so catastrophic that it cooled the Earth's climate. They speculated that abandoned agricultural land was replaced by fast-growing trees and other vegetation that pulled down enough carbon dioxide from the atmosphere to chill the planet, helping intensify the worldwide Little Ice Age that began in the 1300s and ended in the 1800s But critics are unconvinced that the effect on the climate of American reforestation was that far reaching.

American population numbers began recovering as the most resistant individuals survived and immigrants from Europe and slaves brought from Africa, with some immunity, married or had relations with Native Americans, producing less susceptible children. Eventually Native American populations grew, and today descendants of Maya, Inca, and other peoples are numerous in Central and South America's highlands and forests.

The Columbian Exchange affected both hemispheres. European immigrants imported their political systems, social institutions, religious beliefs, and urban forms to the Americas as well as Eurasian plants such as wheat, orange trees, and grape vines and domesticated animals such as horses, pigs, chickens, goats, and sheep. Native Americans found some imports useful. For example, Spanish horses enabled some North American Great Plains tribes to hunt buffalo more effectively. Other arrivals were inadvertent such as insects, fungi, and weeds. Barrels of dirt carried west on English ships as ballast were dumped on arrival to make space for tobacco headed for England. The dirt carried, among other bugs, earthworms, which had been killed off in parts of North America during the Ice Age, and their tunnels helped the soil. Many invasive species such as rats came with the Europeans; facing few natural predators and exploiting new ecological niches, these plants and animals multiplied

CONNECTION to TODAY

Can you think of ways that the Columbian Exchange has influenced your life today?

Columbian Exchange
The transportation of diseases, animals, and plants between the hemispheres that resulted from European exploration and conquest.

---

[10]Quoted in Noble David Cook, *Born to Die: Disease and New World Conquest, 1492–1650* (Cambridge, UK: Cambridge University Press, 1998), vi.

rapidly and soon outcompeted and displaced many native species. The imported or invasive plants and animals remade and "Europeanized" many American environments.

Native Americans across the hemisphere had devised sophisticated agricultural systems many centuries, even millennia, before Europeans crossed the Atlantic and domesticated many food plants crucial to world diets today. Hence, American products also moved eastward across the Atlantic and later westward to Asia, including drugs such as quinine and coca and crops such as tobacco, rubber, American cotton, potatoes, sweet potatoes, tomatoes, peppers, cassava (tree root), and maize, increasing Europe's food supply. Widely grown, potatoes and corn helped end famine in Europe. Potatoes also helped generate a population boom in parts of northern Europe that paved the way for urbanization and then the Industrial Revolution. Cassava became important in African cuisine. South American chilies became mainstays of South and Southeast Asian cooking, making spicy foods even hotter. Some nutritionally neutral plants such as chocolate (cacao beans) and vanilla were hugely popular. Finally, American gold and silver financed Spain's empire and reshaped the Eurasian economy.

17-3b The Spanish Empire and New Latin American Societies

Conquered Americans paid the costs of conquest. In Spanish America and Portuguese Brazil, some Europeans made great fortunes by exploiting people, land, minerals, animals, and plants. Spanish and Portuguese seized all the riches, forced or persuaded Native Americans to adopt Christianity, destroyed their religious centers, murdered Native American leaders who refused to cooperate, and discouraged or suppressed local languages in favor of Spanish or Portuguese. While many peoples resisted, these efforts were usually futile. European settlers learned from native people how to survive and also intermarried or had sexual relations with local women, producing people of mixed descent.

While the Spanish appropriated American political structures, they also introduced their own institutions and ways. Some Spanish settlements became large cities, such as Havana, Buenos Aires, Lima, and Mexico City, the last built on the site of Tenochtitlan. Spain divided its vast empire into two smaller divisions (viceroyalties): New Spain (governed from Mexico City) and Peru (governed from Lima), each headed by a Spain-born viceroy who held great power. In 1739 Colombia, Ecuador, Venezuela, and Panama became part of the Bogota-based New Granada Viceroyalty. Smaller political units, called **audiencias**, were

audiencias Judicial tribunals with administrative functions that served as subdivisions of viceroyalties in Spanish America.

creoles People of Iberian ancestry who were born in Latin America.

mestizos Groups in Latin America that blended white and Native American ancestry.

mulattos Groups in Latin America that blended African ancestry with white or Native American ancestry or both. Mulatto is often considered a derogatory term in North America but not in Latin America or Spain.

peninsulares Europe-born residents in Latin America who monopolized wealth and power.

judicial tribunals with administrative functions. Spaniards held all key political offices, from governors down to local mayors.

Spain sometimes faced resistance. Maya Yucatán fell only in 1545 after long, bitter military struggles, and sporadic Native American resistance continued in Peru for two centuries; the last major rebellion, in 1780–1781, involved over ten thousand Inca descendants led by Tupac Amaru II **(TOO-pack ah-MAR-oo)**, named after an Inca emperor executed by the Spanish. New Mexico, with the largest sedentary Native American population north of central Mexico, became a target of Spanish slavers who raided settlements for captives to sell at auctions in village plazas to Spanish buyers. Resentment by some Pueblo peoples in New Mexico against repression of their customs, executions of protestors, and slavery by Spain and the Catholic Church led to several revolts. In 1680, a respected shaman, Popé (ca. 1630–1692), once imprisoned for suspected "witchcraft" and hoping to restore traditional culture, led a tribal coalition that pushed the Spanish out of the area. Although the Spanish returned and brutally crushed the Pueblo rebels, they adopted a more cooperative policy. In recent years many people in New Mexico have explored their roots in the mixed Native American and Spanish population.

Distinctive societies gradually emerged in Spanish America and Brazil, now called Latin America. Spanish colonial authorities, who needed to govern them, eventually created new categories informed by medieval Spanish legal distinctions that categorized people into racialist hierarchies by 'blood.' In Spanish colonial minds, **creoles** (KREE-awl), people of Iberian ancestry born in Latin America, were the key group. The mixing of peoples fostered **mestizos**, who blended white and Native American ancestry, and **mulattos**, a mix of African with white or Native American ancestry or both (see Discover Historical Voices: Spanish Men and Inca Women). Mulatto is often considered a derogatory term in North America but not in Latin America or Spain. While most creoles enjoyed high status, mixed groups held a social status between Europeans at the top and Native Americans and Africans at the bottom, and they eventually represented a sizable population in many colonies. Mexico and Peru developed large mestizo groups, while mulattos were especially prominent in Brazil and Cuba. Monopolizing wealth and power, people born in Europe (**peninsulares**) viewed creoles, mestizos, and mulattos with condescension or contempt as rustics. A Mexico-born scholar with Spanish parents complained that Europeans "think that not only the original Indian inhabitants but also those of us who were, by chance, born in [the Americas] either walk on two legs by divine dispensation or that they are hardly able to discover anything rational in us."[11]

Spanish America produced many talents, among them the creole Mexican nun Sor (Sister) Juana Inez de la Cruz (1651–1695), a renowned poet, playwright, philosopher, and scientist influenced by European Enlightenment thinkers. To pursue her intellectual interests, the well-born Sor Juana chose life in a convent over marriage, eventually collecting Mexico's largest private library. Sor Juana struggled against patriarchal customs, arguing that "like men, do women not have a rational soul? Shall they not enjoy the privilege of the enlightenment of letters? Why is she not as able to receive as much learning and science?"[12]

---

[11]From Hanke, *History of Latin American Civilization*, 388.
[12]Quoted in Jonathan C. Brown, *Latin America: A Social History of the Colonial Period* (Belmont, CA: Wadsworth, 2000), 146.

Discover Historical Voices

Spanish Men and Inca Women

In many parts of Latin America, Spaniards married or cohabitated with Native American women, fostering a mixed, or mestizo, population. In Peru some Spaniards deliberately sought to marry Inca princesses, perhaps to establish local connections in a factionalized colonial society. This account from the early seventeenth century by the Peruvian historian Garcilaso de la Vega, himself the product of such a match, describes an Inca princess unenthusiastic about her Spanish suitor, a captain from a modest background. Her ambivalent response has been viewed by some historians as representing a mixed attitude common in Latin America toward the imposition of European culture: contempt for many European customs and the brutal conquest but also admiration of some European values and Europeans' military power.

. . . a daughter of [Inca leader] Huaina Cápac and herself . . . the owner of the Indians [workers], was married to a very good soldier called Diego Hernández, a very worthy man, who was said in his youth to have been a tailor. . . . [Before the marriage] the princess learned this and refused the match, saying that it was unjust to wed the daughter of Huaina Cápac with a . . . tailor. Although the Bishop of Cuzco as well as . . . other personages who went to attend the ceremony of betrothal, begged and pleaded with her, it was all to no purpose. They then sent to fetch her brother. . . . When he came, he took his sister into a corner of the room and told her privately that it was impolitic for her to refuse the match, for by doing so she would render the whole of the [Inca] royal line odious in the eyes of the Spaniards, who would consider them mortal enemies and never accept their friendship again. She agreed, though

reluctantly, to her brother's demands, and so appeared before the bishop, who wished to honor the betrothed by officiating at the ceremony.

When the bride was asked through an Indian interpreter if she consented to become the bride and spouse of the aforesaid, the interpreter said "did she want to be the man's wife?" for the Indian language had no verb for consent or for spouse, and he could therefore not have asked anything else.

The bride replied in her own tongue:. . . . "Maybe I will, maybe I won't." Whereupon the ceremony continued . . . They were still alive and living as man and wife when I left Cuzco.

Other marriages of this kind took place throughout the empire, and were arranged so as to give allocations of Indians to [Spanish] claimants and reward them with other people's properties. Many, however, were dissatisfied, some because their income was small and others because their wives were ugly; there is no perfect satisfaction in this world.

Reflection Questions

1. What does the reading tell us about social attitudes among Inca and Spaniards in colonial Peru?
2. What do we learn about the treatment of women?
3. How might the princess's attitude be seen as a form of resistance?
4. How do attitudes concerning class and racial differences as well as intermarriage in North American societies today compare to those in sixteenth-century Spanish Peru?

Source: Based on Garcilaso de la Vega, *Royal Commentaries of the Incas and General History of Peru*, Part Two. Translated by Harold V. Livermore (Austin: University of Texas Press, 1966), 1229–1230. Copyright © 1966 by the University of Texas Press.

Despite creative, broad-minded figures like Sor Juana, Latin American culture owed more to Iberian Catholic traditions than to a western Europe reshaped by the Renaissance, Enlightenment, and Reformation. To suppress what they considered dangerous ideas, the church had to approve all printed matter entering the colonies. Universities, which trained creole men for careers as colonial officials and priests, taught largely in Latin and employed clerics as instructors. Attacking heresy, the ruthless Holy Inquisition tried suspected secret Jewish or Protestant sympathizers. *Conversos*, Jews forced to convert to Christianity in Spain, faced investigation, imprisonment, and sometimes gruesome executions. Most hid their identity, often even from their children. In recent years hundreds of Latin Americans, Mexican Americans, and Spaniards, rediscovering their converso ancestry, have embraced the Jewish identity and faith. Offering citizenship, Spain has now invited these people to migrate back and many have done so in the past several years.

Latin American writers examined the conflicted Spain–Latin America relationship, describing a mix of good and evil,

sun and shadow, as in the bullfight ring. While the elite looked toward Europe for inspiration, the majority favored preserving pre-Columbian languages, beliefs, and ways of life. Women faced the greatest dilemmas under patriarchal Spanish rule. They enjoyed new food sources, such as chickens and pigs, but they clung to their native dress and pride. Flexibility and adaptability aided survival. Since men had higher mortality rates, women often headed households. Some Native American and mestizo women engaged in commerce, worked in domestic service, tended animals, or made clothing, such as by carding, spinning, and weaving wool from sheep.

17-3c Christian Missions, the Black Legend, and Native Americans

Both Spain and Portugal pledged to spread Catholicism. Although enjoying mixed success, missionaries, frequently militant in their faith, gave Native Americans a superficial Christianity, changing local gods into Christian saints.

Sometimes missionaries altered people's settlement and economic patterns. The Spanish Franciscan missionary Fray Junipero Serra (1713–1784), traveling by foot, established mission stations along coastal California from San Diego to San Francisco. He converted many while encouraging, sometimes requiring, semi-nomadic hunters and gatherers, like the Chumash **(CHOO-mash)** near Santa Barbara, to live in towns and cultivate European crops. In recent years Serra, his mission, and its consequences for Native Americans have been the subject of heated debate between admirers and detractors.

Building forts near mission stations extended Spanish control, but missionaries often faced resistance. Many Inca women openly rejected Catholicism. A Spanish observer complained: "They do not confess, attend catechism classes, or go to mass. Returning to their ancient customs and idolatry, they do not want to serve God or the [Spanish] crown."[13] Native Americans could also put their stamp on Christianity. While some historians doubt the story, an Aztec peasant in 1531 supposedly saw a vision of the Virgin Mary at an Aztec mother-goddess shrine. Officials built a church there honoring "Our Lady of Guadalupe," and the image of the Virgin as a Native American woman became a potent symbol of Mexican nationalism.

IMAGE 17.4 **Native American Slavery** Spain's enemies publicized cases of Spanish brutality toward Native Americans, contributing to the Black Legend. This sixteenth-century engraving, by the Dutch observer Theodore de Bry, portrays the misery of Native Americans subjected to slavery and forced labor.

Q What does the engraving tell us about conditions for slaves in Spanish America?

Missionary activity sometimes proved disastrous. In Yucatán, missionaries controlled many Maya and, intolerant of non-Christian beliefs, destroyed Maya books and religious symbols. In 1562 priests, suspecting that converts still secretly worshipped Maya gods, launched a terrible inquisition, torturing 4,500 Native Americans, 158 of whom died. One witness reported that "the friars ordered great stones attached to their feet, and so they were left to hang, and if they did not admit to [worshipping] idols, they were flogged as they hung there and had burning wax splashed on their bodies."[14] The church punished the priest in charge but later appointed him bishop. Homosexuals, who were tolerated by many Native American peoples, including Maya and Caribs, were also brought before the Inquisition or sometimes executed without trial. The Spanish claimed that the widespread homosexuality they saw or heard about was bestial and justified treating Native Americans like animals.

Historians debate the mixed Spanish legacy in Latin America. Spanish actions fostered the **Black Legend** of brutality toward Native Americans, including the repression of native religions, the execution of rebels, and forced labor. Although the Black Legend exaggerated Spanish atrocities and cruelty, Spain's enemies eagerly passed along such stories. In fact, disease killed far more Native Americans than murder and brutality. Furthermore, other Europeans were often as intolerant and forceful with local peoples. And while many Spaniards saw Native Americans as savages needing to be Christianized and ruled, some Catholic clerics advocated humane policies and sought to protect them. The Dominican friar Bartolomé de las Casas **(lahs KAH-suhs)** (1474–1566), although an ardent missionary, proclaimed that Native Americans were humans like Spaniards, bemoaning their treatment. Spanish lawyer Francisco de Vitoria questioned Western colonization, suggesting that policies should always promote Native American welfare and interests and not only Spanish profits. In 1637 the Jesuits in Uruguay **(YOOR-uh-gwye)** even armed Native Americans to help protect them against slave raiders.

But intolerant people reflecting Catholic–Protestant conflict in Europe (see Chapter 15) won the battle over how to treat Native Americans. Most Spaniards considered them justly conquered and born for servitude. A Spanish scholar expressed contempt for Native Americans as "naturally lazy and vicious, in general a lying, shiftless people [whose] chief desire is to eat, drink, worship heathen idols, and commit bestial obscenities."[15]

Black Legend The Spanish reputation for brutality toward Native Americans, including the repression of native religions, execution of rebels, and forced labor.

[13]Quoted in Marysa Navarro and Virginia Sanchez-Korrol, "Latin America and the Caribbean," in *Restoring Women to History* (Bloomington, IN: Organization of American Historians, 1988), 23.
[14]Quoted in Felipe Fernandez-Armesto, *Millennium: A History of the Last Thousand Years* (New York: Scribner's, 1995), 300.
[15]Gonzalo Fernandez de Oviedo, quoted in L. S. Stavrianos, *Global Rift: The Third World Comes of Age* (New York: William Morrow, 1981), 83.

These harsh attitudes also affected women. In 1625, an Indigenous writer in Peru charged that white men exploited both women's labor and their bodies: "In the mines, Indian women are made into concubines, daughters of Indian men are kidnapped. In the villages, [Spanish men convert] single women, married women, all women into prostitutes. Parish priests have concubines. There is no one who takes these women's side."[16] This contempt and economic need led to the drafting of Native Americans to work in mines or farms. Although eventually the church treated them indulgently and paternalistically, as children needing guidance, their quality of life—health, morale, leisure, and joy—mostly declined, generating alcoholism and despair. Today many Latin American Indigenous people remain dominated politically, socially, and economically by creoles and mestizos.

17-3d English and French Colonies in North America

The English or, after the union of England and Scotland in 1707, the British and French expanded and competed in North America (see Map 17.2). By the mid-1700s the territory from New England to Georgia was divided into thirteen British colonies administered by appointed British governors. Immigration to these colonies increased, not only from England but also from Scotland, Ireland, Germany, and the Netherlands. Some from poor or criminal backgrounds arrived as indentured laborers, working on farms or in businesses, workshops, or households to repay their passage. Many affluent families in the northern British colonies had indentured white servants or African slaves to do the cooking, cleaning, child care, and other work. By 1730 the thirteen colonies contained around 500,000 whites. Although African slaves or their descendants, some 20 percent of the population, were concentrated in the South, some also lived in northern colonies.

British colonies enjoyed intellectual and religious diversity. Influenced by British and French Enlightenment thinkers, educated colonists espoused democratic ideals and reason. Many English Protestant dissenters sought religious freedom, and Puritans influenced colonial culture, implanting Calvinist values extolling work, commerce, and sobriety. In 1695 Puritan preacher Cotton Mather vigorously praised labor: "How can you ordinarily enjoy any rest at Night, if you have not been well at work in the Day? Let your Business engross the most of your time."[17] Puritans also maintained patriarchal attitudes. John Winthrop, the Massachusetts colony's first governor, argued that women lost their reason if they concentrated on reading and writing instead of household affairs. Society viewed men as public and women as private beings. Yet, colonial life also fostered gender role changes. Although deeply engrained deference to men remained and husbands had legal right to their wife's property, wages, and the couple's children, many women worked in the gardens and farm fields alongside men, and a few managed farms or plantations.

England and France clashed for decades over control of eastern Canada, part of a larger, globe-spanning English–French competition and war for access to fish and fur sources and for influence in Europe, the Caribbean, and southern Asia. In 1663 the government of New France, fearful of being swamped by the fast-growing English population to the south, addressed a gender imbalance among the three thousand mostly male French colonists (many of them priests) with an innovative plan: import and support at royal expense young French women to meet and marry male settlers and then have large families. The eight hundred women who arrived, known as "the Daughters of the King," sparked rapid French-Canadian population growth. Eventually Britain triumphed over France in North America, taking control of Acadia in 1713. In 1755 Britain deported much of the Acadian French population to the French colony of Louisiana, forming the French-speaking Cajun (KAY-juhn) community that still lives there today, maintaining some of their distinctive culture, including food, language, and music. In 1759 British forces defeated the French near Quebec City and captured

Chronicle/Alamy Stock Photo

IMAGE 17.5 **Conflicts Involving Native Americans and Europeans** This drawing from 1609 shows the French mariner, explorer, and founder of New France and Quebec City Samuel De Champlain and his Huron allies fighting Iroquois warriors, allies of the Dutch and later the English, in the Beaver Wars for control of the fur trade in the Great Lakes.

Q What does the drawing tell us about military tactics and weapons in this conflict?

---

[16]Guzman Poma de Ayala, quoted in Brown, *Latin America*, 183.

[17]Quoted in Robert Heilbroner and Aaron Singer, *The Economic Transformation of America, 1600 to the Present*, 3rd ed. (Fort Worth, TX: Harcourt Brace, 1994), 68.

Montreal, acquiring New France. But French cultural influence remained strong in Quebec, and in 1774 Britain pragmatically allowed the French in Quebec to hold public office, speak their language, and freely practice Catholicism. However, sporadic tensions over politics and national identity still complicate relations between British and French Canadians today.

Both French and British Canadians settled down to farming. French immigration to Canada largely ended in the 1760s, but the French Canadian population, especially in Quebec, increased dramatically and today totals some twelve million, one-third of Canadians. Most French Canadians today can trace their ancestry to the seventeenth- and eighteenth-century colonists, including the intrepid eight hundred "Daughters of the King." Until the mid-twentieth century the Catholic Church in Quebec encouraged early marriage and large families. French Canadians always felt threatened by the dominant British, a feeling that perhaps fostered cultural conservatism.

European–Native American relations reflected both conflict and alliance. Native Americans often fought settler occupation of their land, and the English and French had to deal carefully with the stronger tribes. But some were drawn into the English–French struggle for global influence. The Huron allied with the French, the Iroquois allied with the English, and some tribes opposed both. European–Indigenous alliances largely reflected trading partnerships. As French fur traders ventured into the interior, setting up trading posts,

they often intermarried with Native American women, producing the **Metis** (may-TEES), French-speaking people of mixed descent. Today Metis communities are scattered around Canada. In contrast, English colonists tended to immigrate as families, reducing intermarriage with Native Americans.

Encounters with Europeans reshaped and complicated Native American life, making it much more difficult. An English colonial observer, Robert Beverley, noted that "they have on several accounts to lament the arrival of the English [who] have taken away great part of their country, and consequently made everything less plenty among them."[18] Native Americans understandably mistrusted Europeans, who often broke treaties. But although often repelled by European culture, they desired European goods, especially metalwork and guns. A few tribes, like the Cherokee in the Carolinas and Georgia, adopted European influences, such as new farming methods. This change often disadvantaged women, who once enjoyed high status because they did most of the farming. Christian missionaries also brought change, although they had less success in North America than in Latin America. For example, among matrilineal societies like the Huron and Cherokee, patriarchal Christian marriage practices undermined women's power and freedom by emphasizing wives' obedience to husbands. Spousal abuse often increased as men unable to support their families turned on their wives. But some tribes responded creatively. The Cherokee still honor Sequoyah, the woman who created a Cherokee writing system.

KEY POINTS

▶ As a result of American colonization, huge numbers of Native Americans died from smallpox, and many animal and plant species were exchanged between Europe and the Americas in the Columbian Exchange.

▶ The Spanish exploited the resources of their American colonies and ruled them harshly, inspiring several rebellions and fostering the "Black Legend."

▶ In the Spanish American colonies, a recognizable culture developed, more rigidly Catholic than in Europe and featuring American-born Spanish (creoles) and mixed-race peoples (mestizos and mulattos).

▶ In their attempts to convert Native Americans to Catholicism, the Spanish and Portuguese often trampled on Native American customs and beliefs, crushing perceived resistance harshly.

17-4 New Economies, Slavery, and the Atlantic System

▓ NETWORKS ▚ TRANSITIONS

Ⓠ How were the new American economies and the trans-Atlantic slave trade connected?

The slave trade from Africa to the Americas, the realities and uses of slavery, and the consequences for the Americas, Africa, and the world are among the most examined and contentious fields of history. Today many of us live in societies and a world still shaped by slavery and its legacy. Latin America and northern English America developed different economic and social systems. In much of Latin America, the Caribbean, and the southern colonies in North America, European rule produced an inequitable

CONNECTION to TODAY

How did slavery and the economic systems of this era shape our lives today?

economic relationship between the colonizing countries and their colonies, which supplied natural resources for the growing world economy. Plantations and mines depended chiefly on slave labor mostly imported from Africa (see Chapter 16). In contrast, the northern English colonies in North America emphasized commerce and family farming, gradually moving toward economic independence. The trans-Atlantic slave trade and emerging American plantation zone linked West Africa, the Americas, and Europe into a larger Atlantic System, both a triangular and bilateral trade moving enslaved Africans to

Metis People in Canada of mixed French and Native American descent.

---

[18]Quoted in David Freeman Hawke, *Everyday Life in Early America* (New York: Harper and Row, 1988), 120.

the Americas, largely for plantation labor growing sugar, cotton, and tobacco for shipment to Europe. Millions of Africans, transported across the Atlantic against their will, now had to develop strategies to survive in often unendurable conditions. European merchants used lucrative proceeds from slave labor to purchase guns, rum, textiles, and other commodities for shipment to Africa to obtain more enslaved labor. Profits from the slave trade and the enterprises it served also influenced European economic development.

17-4a Economic Change in Latin America

Latin American colonies chiefly exported natural resources (see Map 17.3). In the Andes and Mexico, the Spaniards developed rich gold and silver mines, coercing Native Americans to do the work. These forced silver miners in the main Andean mining center, Potosi (po-tuh-SEE), Bolivia, found life difficult, "working twelve hours a day, going down to where night is perpetual, the air thick and ill smelling. When they arrive at the top out of breath, [they] find a mineowner who scolds them because they did not bring enough load."[19] By the late 1600s Mexican mines produced over half of the hemisphere's mineral wealth, and Brazilian mines, mostly worked by African slaves, supplied over half of the world's gold. While benefiting few Native Americans, mining enriched merchants, filled royal treasuries, and linked colonies to the world economy. Much of the exported gold ultimately passed through Spain and Portugal to northern Europe as payment for manufactured goods, enriching Flanders, Holland, and England. American silver also bought Europeans access to Asian markets. And a large portion of American silver was shipped to China to purchase desirable Chinese products such as silk and tea.

Cattle and horses brought from Europe made ranching a major economic activity, especially in Argentina, Brazil, and Venezuela's grasslands, providing great incomes for monarchs, merchants, and investors. As Native Americans perished, Europeans obtained good land. Vast cattle ranches, known as **haciendas**, were often over one million acres in size. To ensure profitability, Spain imposed the **encomienda** ("entrustment"), the Crown's grant to a Spanish colonist of control over a certain number of native inhabitants from whom he extracted tribute and forced labor. Clergy instructed Native Americans in Christianity in exchange for mandatory work. Defended as protecting Indigenous peoples, in reality this system fostered many abuses. A Spanish Franciscan condemned cruel mine owners who pursued profit at the expense of encomienda workers: "The Indian slaves who up to the present have died in these [gold] mines cannot be counted. Gold, in this land, was adored as a god."[20] Because of abuses, Spanish monarchs sometimes abandoned the encomienda, relenting when Spanish colonists protested. The institution was reformed but still allowed temporary conscription of Native American labor until the later 1600s.

Despite early Spanish and Portuguese successes, eventually an increasingly stagnant Latin American economy fell behind vibrant North America. Initially, Latin America enjoyed many advantages over British North America: rich mines, abundant

fertile land, and larger population. By the 1700s Latin Americans, unlike North Americans, had built a half dozen large cities and several fine universities and had produced great wealth, although it was inequitably distributed. But the rise of single-product, slave-based plantations, which, like mining or ranching, fostered specialized economic production for a world market, thwarted multidimensional development in Latin America, the Caribbean, and southern English colonies by creating **monocultures** dependent on producing and exporting one chief commodity. Monocultures depended on the colonizing country buying their resource, such as sugar, silver, or beef, in return for supplying food and other necessities. Such plantation-, mining-, or ranching-based economies cannot generate overall **development**, defined as growth in diverse economic areas that benefits the majority of people. Enriching only a minority, monocultures prosper or decline depending on world prices for their export trade commodity. Thus, with few alternative forms of employment or ways to generate wealth, plantation and mining societies in the Americas created significant poverty.

17-4b The Plantation Zone and African Slavery

Plantations became economically dominant in tropical and subtropical areas of the South American mainland, the Caribbean islands, and southeastern North America. By the later 1600s, the richest Andean and Mexican silver mines were exhausted, and plantations flourished by growing sugar, coffee, cotton, bananas, and sisal (a tough fiber used to make rope) for North America and Europe. This transition created the **plantation zone**, an area from Virginia and Kentucky southward through the West Indies and Central America to central Brazil and Peru in which economies largely relied on enslaved African labor. On Caribbean islands, sugar planting transformed whole economies. Initially European settlers founded self-sufficient farms that grew diverse crops in islands such as Jamaica, Barbados, Hispaniola, Cuba, and Puerto Rico. But in the mid-1600s sugar growing, being much more profitable, expanded. Since sugar needed plentiful land and cheap labor, slaves replaced white farmers. Whites became planters, migrated to North America, or turned to piracy.

American sugar growing fostered transitions in Europe. Europeans, especially Venetians, had earlier imported sugar from Arabs and Southeast Asia. To satisfy increasing demand,

haciendas Vast ranches in Spanish America.

encomienda ("entrustment") The Crown's grant to a colonial Spaniard in Latin America of a certain number of Native Americans from whom he extracted tribute.

monocultures An economy dependent on the production and export of one chief commodity.

development Growth in a variety of economic areas that benefits the majority of people; the opposite of monoculture.

plantation zone A group of societies with economies that relied on enslaved African labor; the plantation zone stretched from Virginia and Kentucky southward through the West Indies and the east coast of Central America to central Brazil and the Pacific coast of Colombia.

[19]Quoted in Salvador de Madariaga, *The Rise of the Spanish American Empire* (New York: Macmillan, 1947), 90–91.
[20]From Fray Toribio Motolinia, "The Ten Plagues of New Spain," in *Indian Labor in the Spanish Indies*, ed. John Francis Bannon (Boston: D.C. Heath, 1966), 45.

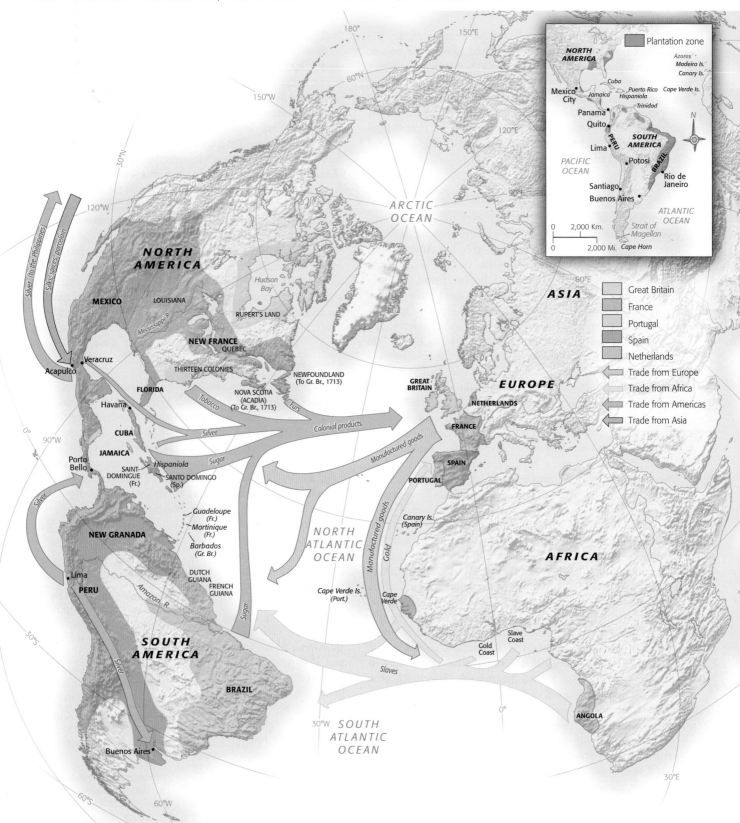

MAP 17.3 **The Atlantic Economy** The Atlantic economy was chiefly based on a triangular trade in which African slaves were shipped to the Americas to produce raw materials that were chiefly exported to Europe, where they were turned into manufactured goods and exported to Africa and the Americas.

Q What does this map tell us about which products and regions of Europe, Africa, and the Americas were most closely connected to the Atlantic economy?

the Portuguese grew sugar on small Atlantic islands such as Madeira. The search for more land for sugar production boosted the imperial appetite. American plantations and cheaper supplies transformed sugar from a rare luxury to a European dietary staple that sweetened bland foods and provided more calories for undernourished working classes. Sugar also helped foster an industrial economy in Britain because sweetened foods such as jam sandwiches and tea enabled people to take lunches to work and stay all day rather than go home for a large midday family meal.

Most Caribbean islands and some coastal districts in Brazil, the Guianas, Venezuela, Colombia, and Mexico became essentially sugar "factories," relying on mass production of raw sugar by enslaved workers. A seventeenth-century saying noted that "without sugar, no Brazil; without slaves, no sugar; without Angola, no slaves."[21] Southern English colonies of North America differed only in producing more varied crops, including cotton, rice, and tobacco as well as sugar. Enslaved people of African ancestry were numerically dominant in the plantation zone of southeastern North America, the Caribbean Basin, and coastal South America. A debilitating tropical disease spread by mosquitos, malaria had come to the Americas in the veins of African slaves, who had some degree of resistance. Hence, endemic malaria infestation tended to correlate with the plantation zone, including in North America.

The development of slavery as an institution in the Americas came to define the national character and social structure of every former slave society. In most colonies Africans, whether slave or free, occupied the bottom of the social ladder, where life was extremely harsh. On some sugar plantations, perhaps half the slaves died within two or three years of arrival. Such high mortality rates required constant importation of new slaves from Africa. Between 1500 and 1850 some 11 to 12 million Africans were brought into the Americas, especially to the plantation zone. Most went to Caribbean islands and Brazil, which today has the Americas' largest population of African descent. However, on a smaller scale African slaves were also used in northern English colonies such as New York, New Jersey, and Massachusetts and as far south as Peru and Argentina. Between 1500 and 1850 Brazil imported some 40 percent of all enslaved Africans, followed by the British Caribbean (21 percent), French Caribbean (15 percent), Spanish America (15 percent), and British North America (5 percent). About one-third of all people of African descent live in the Western Hemisphere today. Descendants of enslaved Africans constitute the large majority of people in Jamaica, Haiti, Barbados, the Bahamas, and most other Caribbean islands; half the population of Trinidad, Belize, Suriname, and Guyana; and substantial minorities in Brazil, Cuba, Puerto Rico, the Dominican Republic, Panama, Venezuela, Colombia, and the United States.

The Crusher Squeezes Juice from the Cane, Antigua, 1823 (print)/Clark, William (fl. 1823)/ BRITISH LIBRARY/British Library, London, UK/Bridgeman Images

IMAGE 17.6 **Caribbean Sugar Mill** On a West Indian plantation this windmill crushed sugar cane into juice, which was boiled down in the smoking building on the right to produce sugar granules. Such plantations were the dominant economic activity on the Caribbean islands and in parts of South America, Central America, and southeastern North America.

Q What can we learn from this painting about life on a sugar plantation?

17-4c Slave Life and African American Cultures

Marketplace imperatives, not humane considerations, governed the lives of African slaves and their unfree descendants. Unlike many African societies, colonial Americans gave enslaved people few if any legal or customary rights, treating them as cost items in the production process, bought and sold at their owner's whim. Since markets for plantation crops constantly expanded, slave owners sought maximum profit regardless of human consequences. Enslaved Africans died from mistreatment, disease, infant mortality, and disrupted family life, while slave women faced rape or sexual harassment by male owners and slaves. Encouraged by the Catholic Church to marry, many slaves formed families, even though they could be broken up by sale. In Brazil most slaves labored on sugar, coffee, and tobacco estates, and the average Brazilian sugar

---

[21]Quoted in Stuart B. Schwartz, "Brazil," in *A Historical Guide to World Slavery*, ed. Seymour Drescher and Stanley L. Engerman (New York: Oxford University Press, 1998), 101.

plantation owned between 80 and 100 slaves. Some worked as mule drivers, sugar makers, household servants, or even low-level managers, but most were field hands expected to produce three-quarters of a ton of sugar a year each. Slave owners recovered the cost of purchasing and maintaining slaves after about three years but had little incentive to maintain the health of slaves unable to work hard.

Africans and their descendants often resisted. Some, like the Brazilian slave woman Caetana, risked severe punishment by defending their interests (see Meet the People: Caetana, Slave Rebel Against Patriarchy). Some slaves, known as **maroons** in the English Caribbean, escaped from plantations and established African-type societies, often mixing varied ethnic traditions, in the interior of Brazil, Colombia, Jamaica, Haiti, Dutch Guiana, and some southern colonies in North America. Women led several of the ten major maroon societies in Brazil. For example, a woman known only as Zeferina, brought to Brazil from Angola, established a runaway slave community in Bahia and plotted an armed uprising against the white population. With colonial governments sending military forces to recapture or control maroons, some communities enjoyed only temporary independence. The largest maroon state formed in northeast Brazil, where around 1605 rebellious slaves established Palmares (**paul-MARYS**), with an African-style king and chiefs and a population of perhaps thirty thousand people. Palmares resisted nearly annual Portuguese assaults before being crushed in 1694. Slave revolts also erupted in Haiti, Mexico, the North American colonies, and elsewhere, all brutally repressed and their leaders executed. The 1739 Stono Rebellion in South Carolina, the deadliest North American uprising, largely involved recently imported Kongolese.

Some slaves were eventually freed, a process known as *manumission*. Thanks to contrasting legal codes in British North America and Latin America, manumission was rare in English colonies (and later the United States) and more common in Latin America, especially Brazil, where women, mulattos, and local-born children were most likely to be freed. In both English and Latin American colonies, a few slaves earned enough to buy their own freedom, and some slave owners gave favored slaves an inheritance. Free blacks filled niches in Latin American life, and enslaved and freed people of color constituted two-thirds of people in parts of Brazil and Cuba. While racism remained common and some places virulent, Latin Americans tended to rank people by occupation and status as well as skin color, fostering a flexible social order. In contrast, English colonies rigidly divided people largely by skin color and whether they had any African ancestry.

Harsh slave life notwithstanding, unique African American cultures emerged. Africans and their descendants frequently mixed Western and African customs, some creating hybrid religions based on both African and Christian beliefs. The ceremonies of Haitian voodoo, Cuban *santaria* (**san-tuh-REE-uh**), and Brazilian *candomblé* (**can-dum-BLAY**) involved West African practices such as animal sacrifice and worship of African spirits and gods. Yet, many followers of these faiths also revered the Christian God and saints. Combining African rhythms and instruments (such

maroons Slaves who escaped from plantations and set up African-type societies in the interior of several American colonies.

as the banjo) with local European and sometimes Native American musical traditions, African Americans laid foundations for popular twentieth-century musical forms, including North American jazz, blues, rock, and hip-hop; Caribbean salsa, Afro-Cuban, reggae, and calypso; and Brazilian samba. A few slave communities even developed new languages, such as the Gullah (**GULL-uh**) dialect of the Georgia Sea Islands, which mixes English and African words.

In addition, African American cultures influenced other American ethnic groups. African words enriched locally spoken English (such as the Mande term "okay" in the United States), French, Spanish, and Portuguese. Brazilian Portuguese, for instance, contains many Kongolese and Yoruba words. Many non-Africans also enjoyed African folktales and traditions, such as the Brer Rabbit stories of the southern United States and the Angolan-based *capoiera* martial arts of Brazil, involving music and physical movements. In agriculture and manufacturing, Africans introduced several crops, including watermelons, black-eyed peas, okra, and African rice. For example, rice brought from West Africa by slaves, mostly women who hid the grains or seeds in their hair, became a dietary mainstay and thriving crop in places as far removed as Dutch Guiana (Suriname) and South Carolina. Enslaved African chefs in white households used these and other foods to create African-derived dishes popular in American meals today like gumbo (West African stew), jambalaya (a cousin of spicy West African jollof rice with meat and vegetables), pepper pot, and okra stew. Slaves also contributed their knowledge of blacksmithing and ironworking.

African cultural forms and values probably survived most strongly in Brazil, Haiti, and Caribbean islands such as Cuba, Jamaica, and Trinidad. Especially in Brazil, the Portuguese eventually accepted the many African influences brought by thousands of African arrivals every year, creating a mixed African and European culture. In contrast, Spanish American and North American authorities often repressed African music and religion, with some success. This included Islam. Several Spanish Muslims sailed with Columbus, two decades before Protestantism began in Europe. By 1503 some Muslims were among West Africans shipped by Spain to Hispaniola. In 1522 Wolof slaves (mostly Muslim) working in Hispaniola sugar mills sparked the first slave rebellion, killing their Spanish overlords. In the early 1700s the French brought almost six thousand slaves from a heavily Muslim area to Louisiana. Many slaves came from West Africa regions with many Muslims. By some estimates up to 15 percent of slaves in the Americas, and perhaps more, came from Muslim backgrounds. Some tried to practice their faith, sometimes successfully, whereas some may have kept their beliefs private, praying in secret. Others probably adopted Christianity, which might bring them some privileges, or joined one of the syncretic African-Christian faiths.

17-4d Economic Growth in English North America

Many English North American colonies developed different economic, and eventually political, systems than monoculture colonies. Historians frequently debate this issue and its implications. Some historians contrast English culture, which was

Caetana, Slave Rebel Against Patriarchy

Thanks to a fascinating Brazilian court case in the 1830s, we learn about a remarkable female slave, Caetana, who challenged patriarchy. Caetana was born around 1818 on a large Rio Clara plantation owned by Captain Luis Mariano de Tolosa, in the Paraiba (**par-uh-EE-buh**) River Valley in southeastern Brazil. The plantation life Caetana experienced had not changed dramatically since the 1700s. At Rio Clara about half of the 134 slaves had been born in Africa while the other half, like Caetana, were Brazilian.

By 1835 coffee had become a major cash crop. Both men and women planted, maintained, and harvested the thirty thousand coffee bushes, often with children in tow. Some slaves raised other crops, tended cattle, or worked as artisans such as carpenters, blacksmiths, and stonemasons. The house slaves who worked in Tolosa's mansion did less strenuous indoor work such as cooking, cleaning, laundering and ironing clothes, carrying water, emptying kitchen slop and human waste, delivering messages, nursing infants, or taking care of the older Tolosa children. In exchange for better food and medical care than was given field hands, they were expected to be obedient and loyal.

Caetana lived in a close-knit relationship to kin, including her mother, Pulicena, and her sister, married to the free-born mulatto, Joao Ribeira da Silva, probably a supervisor of field hands. Caetana was also close to her aunt, the freed slave Luisa Jacinta, whose husband, Alexandre, served as Caetana's godfather and male authority figure. Caetana grew up speaking Portuguese with no direct knowledge of African ways or the terrible Middle Passage across the Atlantic. From a young age she served in the Tolosa house as a personal maid to the Tolosa women, including two daughters, and was trusted and allowed into their private quarters.

In 1835 Tolosa, without consulting her, ordered Caetana, then around seventeen, to marry Custodio, a slave in his mid-twenties, in a wedding blessed by the Catholic Church. Custodio was a master tailor who may have cut and sewn rough cotton clothes worn by slaves and probably also made clothes for the Tolosa family. Like many slave owners, Tolosa may have believed that slave marriages fostered social stability and diminished the threat of rebellion. Perhaps he also feared that an unmarried house slave, representing unyoked female sexuality, might be a bad influence on his two daughters, twelve and two years old, and temptation for his three adolescent sons. Most adult slave women at Rio Clara were married.

Caetana, however, refused Tolosa's order, saying, according to court records, that she felt "a great repugnance for the state of matrimony" and found Custodio especially distasteful. In the end she obeyed, succumbing to her family's pleas and fearing Tolosa's threats to punish her by assigning her to field work or selling her to another plantation. But after priests performed the ceremony and the couple moved into her aunt and uncle's house, she refused to sleep with Custodio, humiliating and enraging him.

After her uncle and godfather, Alexandre, threatened to beat her if she did not submit to her husband, and with few options, Caetana fled to Tolosa's mansion and pleaded to end the marriage. Her rebellion was apparently not against plantation slavery as such but against male authority over her. Caetana's action against the entire system of male power—slave owner, uncle, husband, church—threw Rio Clara into turmoil. After his threats to sell Caetana or reassign her to onerous field work failed, Tolosa relented, giving her protection from her husband and asking a church court to issue an annulment. In court, Caetana complained that she was "reduced to the hard necessity of obeying solely from fear of grave punishment and lasting harm." The legal case took five years, including appeals, with the church ultimately refusing the annulment request.

We do not know why, against such long odds, she rebelled, why she despised marriage, or what ultimately happened to Caetana. Perhaps she envied unmarried free women, who were often respected, or the chaste nuns in the convents. Perhaps she simply disliked or feared men or preferred to be around women, possibilities that might have been unmentioned or not recognized by officials in that era. The records do not indicate whether she continued to evade the marriage, but it seems unlikely she complied. She might have been sold to another plantation, before or after Tolosa died in 1853. What we do know is that Caetana bravely refused a demand to do something against her will.

Source: Fundacao Biblioteca Nacional, Rio de Janeiro

IMAGE 17.7 **Women Slaves In Brazil** This 1861 painting shows a personal maid, much like Caetana, instructing slave girls in making lace on a Brazilian plantation. Such slave girls often wore colorful skirts and, like the instructor, earrings.

Q What does this show about life and work for female slaves on a Brazilian plantation?

Reflection Questions

1. What does Caetana's experience tell us about life on a Brazilian plantation?
2. What does her rebellion tell us about the Brazilian system of patriarchy?
3. Do you think that Caetana should be viewed as a feminist icon for women today?

Note: Quotations from Sandra Lauderdale Graham, *Caetana Says No: Women's Stories from a Brazilian Slave Society* (New York: Cambridge University Press, 2002), 2, 57.

energized by capitalism and religious diversity, with Spain and Portugal's semi-medieval Catholic cultures, which inhibited Latin Americans because they discouraged resistance to authority, accepted poverty as God's will, and distrusted new ideas. Other historians emphasize colonial policies, pointing out that the northern English colonies enjoyed more autonomy than Spanish colonies. Others agree that both cultural and colonial patterns were influential but stress the colonial economies and social diversity they fostered. With northern English colonies lacking mines to fill galleons with gold and silver, a large Native American labor force to exploit, the soil or climate for profitable tropical crops, or open grasslands for ranching, slaves mostly worked for farms, businesses, or households. The immigrant European population, mostly farmers, artisans, and merchants, were never dependent on slave plantations and the severe social inequality they fostered.

Economic conditions fostered differing administrative policies. England allowed its colonies from New Jersey north through New England considerable freedom to build diversified economies for the local market. Being more concerned with its valuable plantation-dominated colonies such as South Carolina, Virginia, and Jamaica, the world's largest sugar producer in the 1700s, England imposed fewer restrictions on New York or Massachusetts. Merchants from Boston, Providence, and New York competed with the English in the Caribbean to obtain sugar and molasses, which was converted to rum and shipped to Africa for slaves who were brought back to the Americas for sale. Some North Americans, especially wealthy merchant families, amassed huge slave trade profits to invest in their own broad-based economies. Thus while northern English colonies moved toward development, the southern English colonies, Latin America, and the Caribbean maintained largely undiversified, monoculture economies. The result was that those colonies with the most abundant natural and human resources to exploit had the greater short-term economic growth but less long-term development than the resource-poor northern English colonies. Some highly profitable colonies, such as Haiti, Jamaica, Peru, Bolivia, and Guatemala, are now among the world's poorest countries, and northeast Brazil is one of Brazil's poorest regions, while the less profitable northern English colonies eventually became among the world's most developed regions.

17-4e The Americas, the Atlantic System, and European Wealth

As discussed in Chapter 16, increasingly close economic ties and trans-Atlantic migration, voluntary and forced, created an Atlantic System spanning western and Central Africa, North America's east and gulf coasts, the Caribbean Basin, and coastal Atlantic zones of South America. The system was defined by trans-Atlantic shipping, plantations, slavery, and the prominence of Africans and their descendants in the Americas. Ultimately, this system spurred European and North American capitalism and wealth. Slave trading and plantation economies provided enormous capital for investment to Europeans and North Americans while underpinning the prosperity of eighteenth-century cities such as Bristol and Liverpool in England and Nantes in France, as well as Boston, Providence, Charleston, Savannah, and New Orleans in North America. The slavers, cooperating African chiefs and merchants, plantation owners, shipbuilders, and other groups linked directly or indirectly to the trade, were reluctant to abandon a lucrative activity. The trade endured for four hundred years, finally ending only in the 1870s.

Historians debate how much the Atlantic System contributed to European industrialization and colonialism. Many have argued that profits from the slave trade and American plantation and mines invested in enterprises and technology in England, the Netherlands, France, and North America financed economic development and later spurred rapid industrialization in England. Some individuals and companies linked to the slave trade and plantations invested in industrial technology. For example, Glasgow merchants known as the "tobacco lords," who were tied to North American tobacco plantations, established printing companies, tanneries, and ironworks while also investing in cotton textile plants and coal mines in Britain. However, the vast profits earned from overseas commerce did not always result in substantial development. Spain and Portugal largely squandered opportunities, becoming poor countries within Europe, while the Dutch and English pursued wiser investment policies.

Spain, the most powerful European country of the 1500s, reaped vast riches from American silver mines and galleons bringing Chinese goods and tropical products from the Philippines to Mexico. But Spain used this wealth poorly, failing to promote its own economic improvement. Thus, in the end, exploitation of the Americas hurt Spain. With American bullion causing severe inflation, Spain imported lower-priced products from other European countries. Moreover, Spaniards leaving for the Americas and Asia created a labor shortage at home. Because peasants and merchants in Spain were heavily taxed for large colonial investments, Spanish investment did not spur capitalism; most Spanish merchants bought land rather than investing in trade or industry. By 1600 Spain was bankrupt. A Spanish official charged that the country had wasted its wealth on frivolous spending rather than manufacturing: "the cause of [our] ruin is that riches ride on the wind, instead of [producing] goods that bear fruit. Spain is poor because she is rich [in gold and silver]."[22] Much of the silver ended up elsewhere in Europe or in China. China benefitted initially but eventually the flood of silver caused inflation and unrest, contributing to the collapse of the Ming dynasty. Colonial wealth also tempted Spain's monarchy to pursue expensive and ultimately futile wars in Europe.

Portugal was second only to England in slave trading, and Brazil became the world's largest exporter of gold, diamonds, and sugar and a major producer of coffee and cotton. But the Portuguese also squandered their colonial wealth, building

---

[22]Gonzalez de Cellorigo, quoted in Jonathan Williams, *Money: A History* (New York: St. Martin's, 1997), 162.

magnificent churches and monasteries rather than financing local industry. As a small country with a small population, Portugal had a tiny domestic market and hence little incentive to build local industries. Investment in Brazil was more profitable.

Holland and England did much better investing their profits than the Spanish and Portuguese. Becoming a major banking center and boasting the world's largest commercial fleet, during the 1600s the Dutch earned vast profits from selling Indonesian coffee and spices to other Europeans and invested much of it in their domestic economy. Much Portuguese and Spanish wealth ended up in Holland. Replacing the Dutch as Europe's and the Atlantic system's dominant power by the end of the 1600s, England enjoyed the most long-term success, benefiting from profits earned in the Americas and India. Wealth flowed into Liverpool, Glasgow, and Bristol from the slave, tobacco, and sugar trades, enriching businessmen and bankers who could mobilize capital for investment in trade, technology, and manufacturing. These factors gave Britain unique advantages that it fully exploited in the 1700s and 1800s.

Transforming and linking the Americas to the rest of the globe reshaped world history. Conquering Native Americans, acquiring American resources, and trading slaves gave some Europeans decided economic advantages over China, India, and the Ottoman Empire. The profits from American metals, often mined by Native Americans, and American crops, chiefly grown by African slaves, shifted world economic power and added to European political and military strength. By the late 1700s , and perhaps earlier, Britain had surpassed China in wealth, living standards, and power.

KEY POINTS

▶ Using Native American labor imposed through the encomienda system, Spanish colonists became wealthy at first through ranching and mining gold and silver, but their economies eventually suffered from lack of diversification.

▶ Plantations run with African slave labor and focused on producing a single product—sugar in Latin America and the Caribbean, cotton in southeastern North America—also eventually created impoverished societies.

▶ African slaves in the Americas were treated as commodities, and resistance to slavery was rarely successful, though freed slaves had somewhat more success in Latin America than they did in North America.

▶ The slave trade and plantation economies helped spur European capitalism and were extremely profitable to Europeans and North American colonists.

Chapter Summary

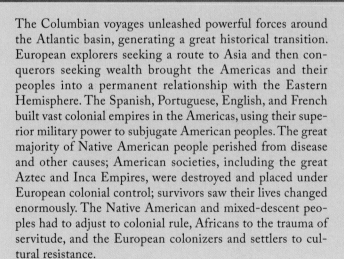

The Columbian voyages unleashed powerful forces around the Atlantic basin, generating a great historical transition. European explorers seeking a route to Asia and then conquerors seeking wealth brought the Americas and their peoples into a permanent relationship with the Eastern Hemisphere. The Spanish, Portuguese, English, and French built vast colonial empires in the Americas, using their superior military power to subjugate American peoples. The great majority of Native American people perished from disease and other causes; American societies, including the great Aztec and Inca Empires, were destroyed and placed under European colonial control; survivors saw their lives changed enormously. The Native American and mixed-descent peoples had to adjust to colonial rule, Africans to the trauma of servitude, and the European colonizers and settlers to cultural resistance.

The economic evolution of the Americas, especially mining and plantation agriculture, created a tremendous market for labor. Mine owners conscripted Native American workers, and planters exploited enslaved Africans and their descendants. The slave trade linked the Americas closely to the larger world. The emerging Atlantic System closely connected Europe, West Africa, and the Americas, mostly to the benefit of Europe and European colonists. Some colonists in English North America built more diversified economies, in contrast to the monocultures of the Caribbean and Latin America. Spain and Portugal initially prospered from their conquests but later squandered the resources they obtained, while the English and Dutch capitalized on their activities to achieve greater wealth and power. American history was thus not only a dynamic saga of local development but also the story of increasing integration into larger global processes.

Key Terms

conquistadors 421
Paulistas 423
voyageurs 424
Columbian Exchange 425
audiencias 426
creoles 426

mestizos 426
mulattos 426
peninsulares 426
Black Legend 428
Metis 430
haciendas 431

encomienda 431
monoculture 431
development 431
plantation zone 431
maroons 434

> *The Portuguese saw that Melaka was magnificent, and its port exceedingly crowded. The people gathered around to see what the Portuguese looked like, and they were all surprised by their appearance. [But] these [Portuguese] know nothing of manners.*
>
> —Malay Chronicles[1]

Japanese School (16th century)/The Art Gallery Collection/Alamy Stock Photo

IMAGE 18.1 **"Southern Barbarians"** This painting on a sixteenth-century Japanese screen, decorated with gold leaf, depicts the arrival of Portuguese ships and their crews in the port of Nagasaki. Various representatives have left the ship, with porters carrying gifts for Japanese officials and merchants.

Q What does this screen tell us about how the Japanese perceived the first Portuguese arrivals and what they brought?

---

[1]Quoted in Anthony Reid, "Early Southeast Asian Categorizations of Europeans," in *Implicit Understandings*, ed. Stuart B. Schwartz (Cambridge, UK: Cambridge University Press, 1994), 275.

Sultan Mahmud Shah (MA-mood shah) (r. 1488–1511), the Malay ruler of Melaka, the great trading state on the Malay Peninsula's southwest coast, had a problem.

In 1509 five well-armed Portuguese ships, flying banners bearing a cross and full of menacing pale-skinned men with unclear intentions, had anchored off his city on an exploratory visit prompted by Melaka's fame as a treasure-trove of Asian goods that fetched huge profits in Europe. They did not act like the peaceful Asian merchants that regularly arrived, nor did they bring the customary gifts for the sultan and his officials. Curious Melakans gathered around a Portuguese envoy, twisting his beard, taking off his hat, and grasping his hand. The Portuguese violated local customs, antagonized Melaka officials, and alarmed influential local Indian traders, who feared competition. The Portuguese considered Sultan Mahmud Shah arrogant and treacherous. Fighting between Portuguese sailors and Malays broke out. After Melakans arrested Portuguese sailors shopping in town, the remaining force, unprepared to assault the heavily defended city, sailed away, vowing revenge. Two years later forty Portuguese ships, mounted with cannon and carrying hundreds of soldiers armed with deadly muskets, returned to capture the city. The sultan led the defense mounted on his elephant. Gaining the upper hand after a bloody month-long assault, the Portuguese commander, Admiral Affonso de Albuquerque (al-ba-KER-kee), told his soldiers to expel the "Moors" (Muslims); his men then slaughtered much of the population and looted the city. This episode previewed both the conflicts and connections forged between Europeans and Asians over the next four centuries.

Many eastern and southern Asians had better success than the Melakans in deflecting the Europeans competing with each other and with Asians for markets and resources. The Portuguese in the 1500s, the Dutch in the 1600s, and the English in the 1700s established some control over the Indian Ocean maritime network and colonized a few areas, such as Melaka. But, despite their deadly gunpowder weapons, Europeans did not yet enjoy a clear military and economic advantage over the stronger Asian states. As late as 1750 China and India together still accounted for over half of world manufacturing. Asian countries could be reached only by long and dangerous voyages from Europe. Hence, most Asian societies escaped the transitions reshaping the Americas and parts of Africa in this era. Yet, by the mid-1700s most great Asian states were under stress or collapsing from internal problems and destabilizing Western activities.

439

18-1 Mughal India, South Asia, and New Encounters

⟳ TRANSITIONS ▥ SOCIETIES

Q What were the major achievements and failures of the Mughal Empire?

South Asian historians and political leaders today have diverse views of the region's history in this era, views sometimes made more divisive and passionate by the subcontinent's religious divisions and disruptive encounters with the West. Both Hinduism and Muslim conquerors shaped South Asia's culture, and the Indian subcontinent, with its multiple states, faiths, and traditions, had never been a single country for most of its history. The Mughals **(MOO-guhlz)**, Muslim Central Asians of mixed Mongol-Turkish descent, ruled much but not all of India during this era, reaching their height in the later 1500s and early 1600s. In their three centuries of rise, preeminence, and decline the Mughals remained a complex and dynamic entity. They fostered artistic and religious innovations and a prosperous economy fueled by international trade. As pressures from European states mounted in the early 1700s, however, the Mughals rapidly declined. The Mughals' significance continues to be controversial today among politicians, religious leaders, and scholars.

CONNECTION to TODAY

What are some of the developments in this era that might provoke disagreements and tensions today between Hindus and Muslims in South Asia?

18-1a The Rise and Decline of the Mughal Empire

In 1526 Babur **(BAH-bur)** (1483–1530), an ambitious, learned, and gifted poet in the Persian language who descended from Genghis Khan and Tamerlane, led twelve thousand troops from Afghanistan and conquered much of north India. The Mughal dynasty (see Map 18.1) that he formed restored India's imperial grandeur. Mughal India had few rivals in military strength, government efficiency, economic power, and arts patronage. A French visitor to the imperial court wondered whether any other monarch possessed more gold, silver, and jewels, and the English used the term *mogul* to mean someone of extreme wealth.

Like earlier Indian governments, the Mughals managed a highly diverse society. Buddhism, reduced to minor status in India, thrived in Tibet and on Sri Lanka (Ceylon). Most Indians practiced Hinduism, a religion of varied beliefs and practices, and perhaps a quarter embraced Islam. Muslim states

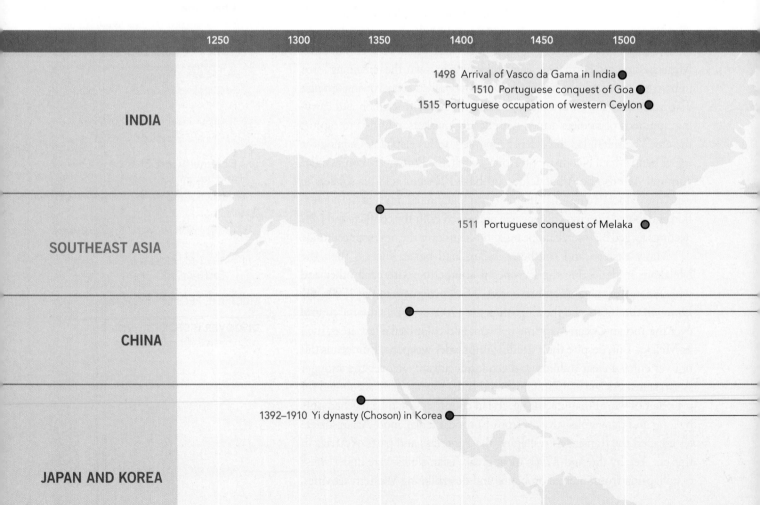

	1250	1300	1350	1400	1450	1500
INDIA						1498 Arrival of Vasco da Gama in India ● 1510 Portuguese conquest of Goa ● 1515 Portuguese occupation of western Ceylon ●
SOUTHEAST ASIA					1511 Portuguese conquest of Melaka ●	
CHINA						
JAPAN AND KOREA			1392–1910 Yi dynasty (Choson) in Korea ●			

had ruled parts of the subcontinent since the ninth century. Polytheistic Hinduism and monotheistic Islam offered starkly different visions of the cosmic and social order. But while Hindus and Muslims often disagreed, in many villages they lived side by side, sharing many customs. Indians were also divided by caste and hundreds of different regional languages, such as Bengali in the northeast and Tamil in the southeast. The adaptable Mughals used **Urdu**, a mix of Hindi, Arabic, and Persian written in the Persian script, as their language of administration. The willingness of the Mughals over several generations to adapt themselves in many ways to local culture, along with their many contributions to Indian art, food, architecture, and language, fostered an ongoing debate among historians in India today as to whether the Mughals should be seen as essentially foreigners or part of India's eclectic social, cultural, and political landscape stretching deep into the past. This debate was politicized in 2018 when India's government, spurred by militant Hindus, began "Hinduizing" the names of several cities founded by or identified with the Mughals.

Babur's grandson Akbar (**AK-bahr**) (r. 1556–1605) became the most outstanding Mughal ruler (see Meet the People: Akbar, Mughal Ruler). Akbar, whose name means "Very Great," expanded Babur's empire over all of north India and deep into south India. After winning the support of various Hindu groups, some from the Hindu warrior caste, the Rajputs (**RAHJ-putz**),

Akbar gave Hindus high government positions, removed extra taxes imposed by earlier Muslim rulers on non-Muslims, promoted religious toleration and compromise between communities, and strictly checked bribery and corruption while seeing that laws were justly administered. He tried to abolish what he considered pernicious social customs, such as *sati* (burning the wife on the husband's funeral pyre), child marriage, trial by ordeal, and enslaving prisoners of war. Akbar's India also enjoyed an enlightened criminal code; all citizens could appeal to the ruler if they believed themselves wrongly convicted or mistreated in courts. Akbar presided over what some historians consider a "golden age" of peace and prosperity, but his successors had less tolerance and wisdom.

With their many wives and concubines, Muslim rulers produced numerous ambitious male heirs to the throne and hence created unstable succession problems. Akbar was succeeded by Jahangir (**ja-HAN-gear**) ("World Seizer"), a rebellious son who poisoned Akbar and occupied the throne. Jahangir was also a man with diverse talents, a nature lover, philosopher open to many doctrines, and curious traveler. Like some other royal Mughal women, his Persian wife born in Afghanistan, Nur Jahan (**nur ja-HAN**), had considerable power at court and strongly influenced

> **Urdu** A language developed in Mughal India that mixed Hindi, Arabic, and Persian and was written in the Persian script.

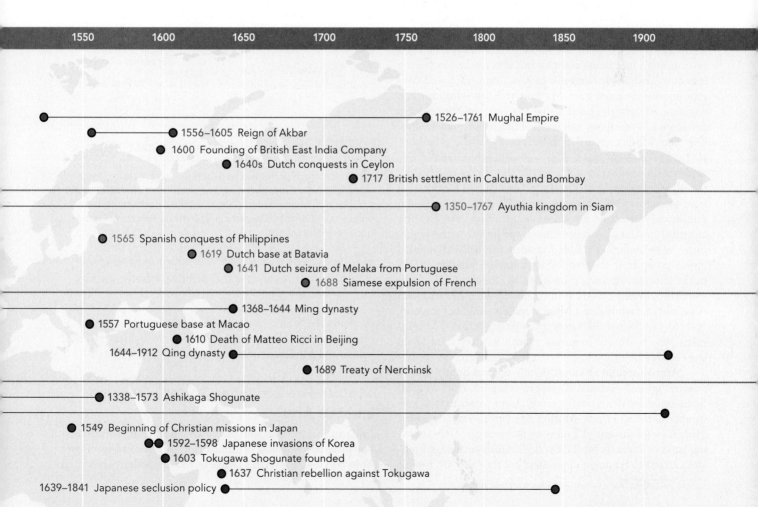

| 1550 | 1600 | 1650 | 1700 | 1750 | 1800 | 1850 | 1900 |

- 1526–1761 Mughal Empire
- 1556–1605 Reign of Akbar
- 1600 Founding of British East India Company
- 1640s Dutch conquests in Ceylon
- 1717 British settlement in Calcutta and Bombay

- 1350–1767 Ayuthia kingdom in Siam
- 1565 Spanish conquest of Philippines
- 1619 Dutch base at Batavia
- 1641 Dutch seizure of Melaka from Portuguese
- 1688 Siamese expulsion of French

- 1368–1644 Ming dynasty
- 1557 Portuguese base at Macao
- 1610 Death of Matteo Ricci in Beijing
- 1644–1912 Qing dynasty
- 1689 Treaty of Nerchinsk

- 1338–1573 Ashikaga Shogunate
- 1549 Beginning of Christian missions in Japan
- 1592–1598 Japanese invasions of Korea
- 1603 Tokugawa Shogunate founded
- 1637 Christian rebellion against Tokugawa
- 1639–1841 Japanese seclusion policy

her husband; writing that he only needed wine and meat to be happy, Jahangir handed government business over to Nur Jahan, his twentieth wife, who became essentially a co-ruler. She was a poet, innovative architect who designed public buildings, expert hunter (she once killed a rogue tiger threatening a village), philanthropist aiding poor women and orphaned girls, and patron of art and music. Male writers from Nur Janan's time and after, seeing government as a male preserve, tended to obscure or decry her role while also describing her as a power-hungry manipulator who took advantage of her husband's alleged weaknesses, including alcohol addiction. Recent studies debunk some of these charges. While Jahangir and Nur Jahan generally pursued Akbar's wise policies, his son, Shah Jahan (r. 1628–1658), promoted Islam, destroyed several Hindu temples, and assembled a harem of five thousand concubines. Sitting on his splendid jewel-encrusted Peacock Throne in Delhi, Shah Jahan doubled the tax bills, but his extensive building projects and unsuccessful military campaigns in Afghanistan and Central Asia virtually bankrupted the state. Eventually his even more intolerant son, Aurangzeb (ow-rang-ZEB) (r. 1658–1707), imprisoned Shah Jahan and greatly expanded the empire in the south while also undermining the state and its revenues.

Endless wars and extravagant royal spending finally drained the Mughals' state coffers and military strength. Once sufficient to keep Europeans and other enemies at bay, the armed forces now lacked naval power. Although the Mughal army had some one million soldiers equipped with gunpowder weapons such as muskets and field artillery that rivaled European arms, as well as thousands of battle elephants, by the early 1700s it lacked the money to match European military capabilities. Increasing taxes on both merchants and peasants also sparked increasing opposition, while Aurangzeb's ruthless, intolerant, and corrupt policies alienated both Muslims and non-Muslims. The dogmatic Aurangzeb placed higher taxes on non-Muslims and persecuted—sometimes executed—Hindu and Sikh leaders. One pious Muslim wrote that "bribery is everywhere; mean people have become governors, May God damn the tyrant! In this world he is an infidel [nonbeliever]; in the next he is in hell."[2]

Revolt eventually led to the dismantling of the Mughal state as regions broke away. Aurangzeb's imperial expansion significantly increased his already huge army's size, creating logistical problems in supplying troops just as anti-Mughal forces were becoming bolder. Marathas (muh-RAH-tuhz), a Hindu group from western India, raided the faltering empire in the later 1600s, using guns given by disenchanted Hindu merchants. When Safavid Iran conquered Mughal-controlled Afghanistan, factionalized Mughal leaders could not respond. In 1761 Hindu and Sikh insurgents finally defeated Mughal rulers, who continued to govern a small territory from Delhi until 1857.

Mughal decline and near demise opened South Asia to penetration and eventual European conquest. Anti-Mughal forces could not unite, leaving South Asia fragmented and vulnerable. Growing Hindu–Muslim divisions also facilitated the gradual establishment of European domination. After annexing parts of India in the 1700s, the English encouraged religious rivalry to fragment opposition, but they also had trouble

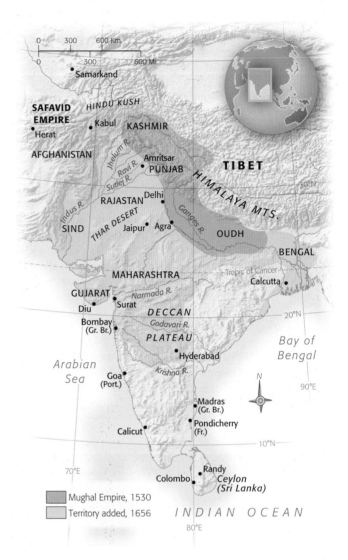

MAP 18.1 **The Mughal Empire, 1526–1761** By the mid-1600s the Mughals, a Muslim dynasty based in north India, controlled much of the Indian subcontinent. However, some ports fell under European rule. The Portuguese had a colony at Goa, and, by the early 1700s, the British had established outposts at Bombay, Calcutta, and Madras, while the French occupied Pondicherry.

Q How does the map of the Mughal Empire differ from or resemble the political configuration in South Asia today?

subduing the Sikhs. The religious divide greatly shaped contemporary South Asia, which in 1947 was divided into rival Hindu and Muslim nations.

18-1b Indian Economy, Society, Religion, and the Arts

India in this era was one of the world's major manufacturing societies. Demand continued for Indian textiles all over Eurasia and parts of Africa, while India's iron industry produced

[2]Quoted in John E. Wills, Jr., *1688: A Global History* (New York: W.W. Norton, 2001), 276.

high-quality steel and cannon. By 1750 India still accounted for one-quarter of the world's industrial output and was the largest textile producer. Efficient farming, benefiting from investments in reservoirs and irrigation, produced large yields of wheat and rice, as well as cash crops such as cotton, indigo, pepper, sugar, and opium that supplied markets at home or abroad. India's population doubled between 1500 and 1750. For centuries India had been a core of the Afro-Eurasian networks, trading fine fabrics such as cashmere and gingham to Europe and the Middle East for gold and silver. In the 1600s an influx of American silver, used by European merchants to obtain Indian products, tripled the money supply and benefited the Mughal treasury, allowing construction of ambitious but expensive buildings and imperial roads linking the empire.

Indian merchants and bankers expanded their commercial networks over vast distances, from Arabia, Persia, Northeast Africa, and the Red Sea to Malaya, Sumatra, Siam, and China. Hindu and Muslim merchants from Gujarat (**goo-juh-RAHT**) in northwest India were leading traders and financers around the Indian Ocean, including Melaka. Thousands of Indians also traded across Central Asia, Afghanistan, Tibet, the Caucasus states, and Russia, establishing, for example, commercial dominance at the Russian trading port of Astrakhan (**AS-truh-kan**) on the Caspian Sea.

Indian merchant networks enjoyed vast capital, sophisticated credit and financing arrangements, and reputations for shrewdness, often competing successfully against European and Asian rivals. Some merchants in Surat (**SOO-raht**), the main Gujarat port, were among the world's richest entrepreneurs. A Dutch diplomat wrote that merchants of Bengal were "exceptionally quick and experienced. They are always sober, modest, thrifty, and cunning in identifying the source for their profit."[3]

Caste and gender divisions divided Indian society. Most Hindu merchants belonged to various subcastes (*jati*) that moved up or down in the larger *vaisya* caste grouping, which ranked below the priests (*brahmans*) and warriors in a system that had evolved for over two thousand years. Women's influence depended on their caste and family situation. In north India both Muslim and Hindu women were often kept in seclusion, expected to be chaste and obedient to fathers and husbands in a patriarchal, patrilineal society. Yet, some Mughal court women exercised influence. Khanzada Begum (1478–1545), Babur's oldest sister, successfully interceded with rebellious brothers to end a family split and to keep Babur's son, Humayun, on the throne, avoiding bloodshed. Mughal women also had financial resources, which they often devoted to endowing mosques and supporting religious scholars.

The coming of Islam and the conversion of many Indians had dramatically changed India's religious and cultural environment. Muslims resisted assimilation into the then tolerant Hindu fold, remaining disdainful of Hindus and the caste system, and the two groups never formed a single people. Yet, many upper-caste north Indian Hindus adopted some Muslim customs, such as the veiling and secluding of women. The early Mughals, especially Akbar, mostly left Hindus free to practice their own faith and customs. However, less tolerant later rulers deepened the religious divide. At the same time, as mysticism became increasingly popular among both Muslims and Hindus, Muslim rulers welcomed Indian, Arab, and Persian Sufi masters to their courts to compose songs, poems, and sermons that facilitated communion with God. Sufis preached a personal bond between each believer and God, with some Sufi movements, such as the Chishtiya (**CHIS-tee-ya**), avoiding association with secular powers. The Indian Chishti saint Nizam al-Din Awliya (**KNEE-zam al-DIN aw-LEE-ya**) wrote that "my room has two doors. If the sultan comes through one door, I will leave through the other."[4] Akbar's and Jahangir's Sufi sympathies horrified Muslim dogmatists, who regarded mystics as heretics.

Hinduism continued to evolve. Many Hindus, particularly from lower castes, had gravitated toward the mystical bhakti (**BUK-tee**) devotional movement (see Chapter 13). Some bhakti groups opposed the caste system, ignoring high-caste brahmans and sympathizing with the poor. Often bhakti worship involved commitment to a particular Hindu god, such as Shiva or Vishnu, and many bhakti poets were women. Most famously, Mirabai (**MEERA-buy**) (ca. 1498–ca. 1546), a Rajput widowed at a young age, refused to commit sati and spent the rest of her life writing praises to Vishnu. Bhakti women like Mirabai could defy social conventions and even become saints, while Muslim women were more likely than men to honor and visit the graves of Sufi sheiks. Mysticism forged a gradual accommodation between some Muslims and Hindus venerating both Sufi and bhakti saints. Finally, between the fourteenth and seventeenth century Hindu thinkers increasingly treated diverse schools of thought, such as Vedanta, yoga, bhakti, and Shiva worship, as belonging to a single system of belief and practice, separate rivers leading to the ocean of Brahman, the absolute reality. This melding laid the foundation for the modern concept of Hinduism as a coherent religion rather than loosely connected, often rival sects and beliefs.

Other Indians blended or transcended Hinduism and Islam by forming new religions. The largest new faith, the **Sikhs** ("Disciples"), adopted elements, including mysticism, from both Hinduism and Islam. Eventually Sikhs numbered several million people, mostly living in northwest India's Punjab region. The founder, Guru Nanak (**GOO-roo NAN-ak**) (1469–1539), born a Hindu and influenced by bhakti movements, argued that devotion was not enough; people were saved by their deeds alone: "God will not ask a man his tribe or sect, but what he has done. There is no Hindu and no Muslim. All are children of God." The nine spiritual leaders who followed Nanak refined the faith during Mughal times. Arjan (1563–1606) established the holy scripture, which announced: "I do not keep the Hindu fast, nor the Muslim Ramadan. I have broken with the Hindu and Muslim. I shall put my heart at the feet of one Supreme Being."[5] Akbar granted Sikhs land for a great temple in Amritsar (**uhm-RIT-suhr**) in the Punjab.

Like Muslims, Sikhs worshipped one universal and loving God, rejected the caste system and

Sikhs Members of an Indian religion founded in the Early Modern Era that adopted elements from both Hinduism and Islam, including mysticism.

[3]Quoted in Om Prakash, *European Commercial Enterprise in Pre-Colonial India* (New York: Cambridge University Press, 1998), 4.
[4]Quoted in Francis Robinson, *The Cultural Atlas of the Islamic World Since 1500* (London: Stonehenge, 1992), 39.
[5]The quotes are from Rhoads Murphey, *A History of Asia*, 4th ed. (New York: Longman, 2002), 185; and Michael Edwardes, *A History of India* (New York: Farrar, Straus and Cudahy, 1961), 191.

Akbar, Mughal Ruler

During the early Mughal period, India was ruled by Akbar, one of history's most respected political leaders, who came to power at thirteen after his father died. A contemporary of Queen Elizabeth I of England and Shah Abbas of Persia, Akbar was also a possible epileptic (like Julius Caesar and Napoleon) and subject to bouts of depression. Rather than his ruthless military conquests, his greatness lay in his skills as an administrator and his ability to respect and blend India's diverse traditions. Always seeing himself as an Indian rather than a foreign ruler, he worked hard to accommodate all the strands of Indian culture and religion into a unified country. Although raised a Muslim, he married a Christian and two Hindu princesses, winning non-Muslim support and symbolizing acceptance of India's religious diversity.

Foreign visitors were charmed by Akbar. A Jesuit missionary who visited India in the early 1580s wrote that he was

> of a stature and type of countenance well suited to his royal dignity, so that one could easily recognize even at first glance that he is the king. He creates an opportunity almost every day for any of the common people or of the nobles to see him and converse with him. It is remarkable how great an effect this courtesy and affability has in attaching to him the minds of his subjects.

Visionary, energetic, and versatile, Akbar lived to the fullest, becoming a skilled metalworker, draftsman, polo player, and musician. Although himself illiterate, he had an insatiable love of learning and had books of all kinds read to him. His personal library included twenty-four thousand volumes. He also patronized poets, musicians, painters, and architects, even honoring his architects and artisans by having them build a new capital at Fatepuhr Sikri near Agra, where he then lived. Akbar greatly enjoyed the lovely gardens constructed around Mughal buildings in the capital and elsewhere, featuring shade trees, fountains, and pools. To show Hindus his respect, he encouraged Hindi literature and even appointed a Hindi court poet. In response to orthodox Muslims who criticized his support of Hindu court painters, some of whose subject matter violated Islamic prejudices against human images, he argued that God loved all beauty.

Although the Mughals were officially Muslims, Akbar espoused complete freedom of religion, not just for political expediency but also because he was an enlightened man with a restless, inquiring mind. Investigation of the mysteries of creation, he claimed, should be done according to the light of reason. He believed that all faiths had something truthful to offer and that all religions were untrue when they denied other religions' sincerity of purpose. Once a week, representatives of all religions held debates in the palace at his invitation; when Jesuit missionaries arrived from the West, they stayed with Akbar for several years and joined in the spirited debates. Indeed, Akbar had the Christian gospels translated into Persian and even attended the occasional mass out of curiosity.

Akbar never completely bought into any religion totally, believing that no one faith had a monopoly on truth. He remained skeptical and found some beliefs in all of them

Surjam Hada making a submission to Akbar, from the 'Akbarnama' c. 1568, Mughal, (illustrated text)/ SALLY CHAPPELL/ Victoria & Albert Museum, London, UK/Bridgeman Images

IMAGE 18.2 **Akbar** The great Mughal emperor, Akbar, enjoyed pomp and circumstance. This miniature painting shows him entertaining guests at a reception in his palace.

Q What does the painting tell us about royal life under the Mughals?

that he thought contradicted reason. Later in life he adopted the Hindu custom of vegetarianism and gave up his favorite sport of hunting. Influenced by the inclusive spirit of Sufi mysticism, in the end he created his own religion, incorporating what he saw as the best features of all religions. But, since he would not impose his views on others, Akbar's religion found few takers and died with him.

Reflection Questions

1. How did Akbar foster Indian cultural life?
2. How could Akbar afford to show so much tolerance of other religions?
3. Do you think that Akbar could be a role model today for leaders of South Asian nations and for the world?

Note: Quotation from Rhoads Murphey, *A History of Asia*, 4th ed. (New York: HarperCollins, 2003), 178.

priests, promoted egalitarianism, forbade alcohol and tobacco, and stressed discipline, hard work, and charity for the needy. Sikhs also developed distinctive customs. Observant men sported beards, wore steel bracelets, and carried a dagger or sword at all times. Prohibited from cutting their hair, many men wore a turban. Sikh women enjoyed greater freedom than Hindus and Muslims. Persistent persecution by Mughal leaders after Akbar led Sikhs, once pacifists, to become militaristic and excellent soldiers, well represented in modern India's military and police forces. The Sikhs also became skilled and practical farmers and are still among the most productive in India today.

Indian arts flourished in this period. For example, the distinctive Mughal school of miniature painting, based on Persian models, represented a synthesis between Islamic and Hindu cultures, while the Indian-Persian architectural style, known as Indo-Islamic, made lavish use of mosaics, domes, and gateways in building tombs, mosques, forts, and palaces. The Mughal elite lived in large houses with courtyards, trees, gardens, water basins, and handsome subterranean apartments furnished with large fans to escape the heat. In his spectacular Delhi palace audience hall, Shah Jahan had inscribed: "If on earth be an Eden of bliss, it is this, it is this, it is this!"[6] East of Delhi, at Agra (**AH-gruh**), Shah Jahan left another legacy, the Taj Mahal (**tahzh muh-HAHL**). Often considered the world's most beautiful building, the Taj is a marble mausoleum with pools, archways, domes, and minarets. It took twenty-two thousand workers twenty-two years to complete this final resting place for Shah Jahan's favorite wife and close political adviser, Mumtaz Mahal (**MOOM-taz muh-HAHL**).

18-1c South Asia and European Challengers

When the Mughals, the last great precolonial Indian rulers, collapsed, the power vacuum was filled by Europeans. Spurred by interest in southern Asia as a source of spices and textiles, the Portuguese sought a sea route around Africa and the Spanish sponsored the Columbian voyages across the Atlantic in search of "the Indies." The Portuguese were the first Europeans to arrive in India directly by sea around Africa. They came from a country with superior naval technology, missionary zeal, and a compelling appetite for wealth but a standard of living little if any higher than that of many Indians, Southeast Asians, and Chinese.

Following the Indian Ocean maritime trade route from East Africa, a fleet captained by Vasco da Gama (ca. 1469–1525)—using a pilot hired in East Africa, possibly a Muslim Gujarati—reached the southwestern Indian port of Calicut in 1498. Upon encountering merchants from as far away as Northwest Africa, da Gama quickly realized both Asia's economic potential and the small value of his European goods. With one military advantage over Indians—mounted cannon on his ships—he was able without force to obtain a cargo of spices, which he later sold in Europe at 3,000 percent profit. In 1500 a second Portuguese fleet returned to Calicut. After sailors fought local people who had been encouraged to resist the Portuguese by Arab merchants who used Calicut as an important base, the Portuguese bombarded Calicut to rubble and destroyed the less maneuverable Indian and Arab ships defending the city.

Like all the European powers following them to Asia, the Portuguese employed violence to enforce their power and acquire wealth. Seeking to control trade from Asia to the West, they established fortified settlements at strategic locations around the Indian Ocean, including Hormuz (**hor-MOOZ**) at the entrance to the Persian Gulf, Mombasa in East Africa, Diu (**dee-YOU**) in northwest India, Goa on India's southwestern coast, and Melaka in Malaya. In 1515 they occupied Colombo (**kuh-LUM-bow**), a Sri Lankan port that exported cinnamon. At the same time, Portuguese warships extorted payments from Ottoman, Arab, Indian, and Indonesian merchant ships in the Indian Ocean. In 1502 Vasco da Gama, using terrorism, attacked, plundered, and burned an Arab passenger ship carrying over three hundred people, including several of Calicut's richest merchants and many women and children, killing all aboard. These actions helped give Europeans a rather unsavory reputation in Asia in this era; some Asians viewed them as "pirates".

IMAGE 18.3 **The Mughal Horse Market** This eighteenth century miniature painting shows Mughal men buying and selling horses, especially valuable for military purposes.

---

[6]Quoted in Edwardes, *History of India*, 190.

But the Portuguese, while aggressive, were also often ineffectual. Despite devoting some eight hundred ships and controlling several key ports, the ambitious Portuguese found competing with Asian merchants difficult and never completely dominated Indian Ocean commerce. While Asian merchants often outmaneuvered or evaded Portuguese ships, Asian states resisted Portuguese demands. Their zealous Catholicism also caused turmoil. Da Gama had told Calicut leaders that he sought "Christians and spices," a useful shorthand for understanding Portuguese motives, and the Portuguese hostility to Islam sometimes fostered persecution of Islamic institutions and believers in Portuguese-held territories. By introducing chilies from the Americas, however, the Portuguese made a lasting contribution to South and Southeast Asian cooking, making spicy food even hotter. In Goa Portuguese and local Indians created a fiery hot dish, *vindaloo*, combining European vinegar, American potatoes, chilies, and local ingredients, that became a fixture of South Asian cuisine.

By 1750 European influence and Indian–European trade remained modest. But the Portuguese activity foreshadowed an increasingly active European presence, as Holland, France, and England all attempted to shape parts of South Asia. The overextended Portuguese struggled to sustain their power against these European rivals with larger populations and better ships and gunpowder weapons. Portuguese men settled in Goa and Colombo, marrying local women and creating mixed-descent, Portuguese-speaking Catholic communities. But Portugal later lost all its other South and West Asian footholds, retaining only Goa as a colony until 1961, when India assumed control.

In the early 1600s the Dutch, destroying most Portuguese power in South and Southeast Asia, gained partial control over the Indian Ocean commerce. With government backing, Amsterdam merchants formed the well-financed, private Dutch East India Company (or Vereenigde Oost-Indische Compagnie [VOC]) in 1602, with its own armed fleet working in conjunction with Dutch operations. In the 1600s the Dutch established trade centers in several Indian cities, which thrived until the mid-1700s when the British became dominant. But even today hints of the former Dutch presence in India survive in stray words in Bengali, old forts in Kerala, and gravestones in Surat. In the 1640s the Dutch seized some of Sri Lanka's coastal regions from the Portuguese. They remained there, often intermarrying with local people, until the British ousted them in the early 1800s and colonized Sri Lanka.

France also joined the competition, establishing a trading presence at Surat and Calcutta while building a military and commercial base at the southeast coast town of Pondicherry **(pon-dir-CHEH-ree)** in the later 1600s and early 1700s. Long-standing English–French political and commercial rivalries spilled over into conflict during the Seven Years War (1756–1763), during which the two nations fought in Europe, North America, the Caribbean, and Asia. The fierce battles for dominance in Southeast India destabilized the region's politics.

Eventually England, with a rapidly growing commercial economy, became the main threat to the Mughals, Dutch, and French. In 1600 English investors formed the English (later British) East India Company (BEIC), like the VOC, a profit-seeking trading firm with its own army. Company traders visited various ports. The English established a fort at Madras **(muh-DRAS)** (today known as Chennai) on India's southeast coast and a trading base at Surat in northwest India, where they forged a commercial alliance with the Parsis **(PAHR-seez)**, Zoroastrian descendants of Persian refugees. In 1717 the British established bases at Bombay (today called Mumbai) and Calcutta (Kolkata), both sparsely populated backwaters, for collecting and exporting textiles, indigo, and saltpeter (an ingredient for gunpowder). Many Parsis left Surat for better prospects in Bombay, again working closely with the British for their mutual benefit.

Elsewhere British officials still had to negotiate with Mughals or local princes for trading privileges. When banditry grew rapidly as Mughal authority collapsed, the law and order in British-run ports attracted Indian settlers. Competition from Indian textile imports spurred British textile manufacturers to cut costs, helping stimulate British industrialization. By the mid-eighteenth century the British were strong enough to treat local rulers with less deference and expand their control into surrounding regions, often using military force against Indian resistance. From their Calcutta base in Bengal, they began their long military conquest, continually weakening what little remained of Mughal authority and eventually controlling nearly all of South Asia except a few small enclaves, such as Portuguese Goa and French Pondicherry. Europeans judged India from their own ethnocentric and often misinformed perspective while most Indians did not understand Europeans. The Mughal emperor Shah Jahan reportedly said that Europeans might be a great people except that they follow the wrong religion, eat pork, and don't wash their private parts properly. South Asians had often been conquered by outsiders of different cultural and religious backgrounds, such as the Mughals. But now India faced a major new challenge.

KEY POINTS

▶ The Muslim Mughal Empire attained great riches and, especially under Akbar, maintained an enlightened rule over religiously diverse India, but it began to decline after the fall of Akbar.

▶ The Indian economy, already strong, expanded greatly as extensive foreign trade brought an influx of silver and enriched entrepreneurs.

▶ Tensions existed between Indian Muslims and Hindus, though some were able to bridge the gap through mysticism and others joined sects such as the Sikhs that blended or transcended the dominant religions.

▶ The Dutch, French, and British all competed with each other and with the Portuguese for dominance of trade with India, with the British growing increasingly strong by the mid-eighteenth century.

18-2 Southeast Asia and Global Connections

NETWORKS   SOCIETIES

Q How did Southeast Asia become more fully integrated into the world economy?

Diverse peoples, religions, ideas, and products had long met in cosmopolitan Southeast Asia, the crossroads region south of China and east of India. Southeast Asians participated actively in hemispheric trade, and most adopted Theravada Buddhism, Confucianism, or Islam. The Portuguese arrival at Melaka inaugurated a new era as European adventurers, traders, missionaries, and soldiers reshaped Malaya, the Philippine Islands, and parts of Indonesia. However, in most of Southeast Asia Western influence remained weak and less catastrophic than in the Americas and parts of Africa until the nineteenth century.

> ### CONNECTION to TODAY
>
> What features of the often difficult and sometimes violent encounters between Europeans and Southeast Asians in this era can be seen in Southeast Asian politics and cultures today?

18-2a Southeast Asian Transitions and Societies

Southeast Asians experienced commercial growth, political change, increasingly productive agriculture, and expansion of Islam and Buddhism in this era, opening their cultures to the outside world. Increasing connections with European, Chinese, Arab, and Indian merchants spurred commerce between the 1400s and 1700s, with Southeast Asia remaining an essential hub in maritime trade linking East Asia with India and the Middle East. Merchants from the Middle East, Central Asia, Africa, China, and India stopped in the region's ports to exchange goods or wait for monsoon winds to shift to continue their voyage or return home. Due to storms, reefs, and pirate attacks not all ships reached their destination. One study lists over 450 shipwrecks that sank in Asian waters between 1500 and 1900, their cargoes providing a rich trove of information about maritime trade.

This economic dynamism enhanced regional ports such as Melaka, Ayuthia (ah-YUT-uh-yuh) in Siam, Hoian (hoy-AHN) in Vietnam, Pegu (peh-GOO) in Burma's Irrawaddy Delta, and Banten (BAN-ten) in West Java. Thanks to increasing trade and the wealth this created, urban merchants gained political influence. Agriculture also remained a major activity, with new crops and rice varieties spurring population growth. Meanwhile, Theravada Buddhism dug deeper roots on the mainland, and Islam spread throughout the Malay Peninsula, Indonesian islands, and the southern Philippines.

Larger, more centralized states such as Burma, Siam, and Vietnam absorbed smaller neighboring states and remained vigorous (see Map 18.2). The kings of Ayuthia, a Theravada Buddhist state, governed much of Siam from 1350 to 1767, participating in maritime trade, especially with China, while expanding influence into Cambodia and several small Lao

(laow) states along the Mekong River. But Ayuthia's competition with Burma, Vietnam, and the largest Lao state, Lan Xang (lan chang), for regional dominance occasionally sparked wars. In the 1560s a Burmese army ravaged Siam and sacked Ayuthia, carrying back to Burma thousands of Siamese prisoners reflecting diverse occupational skills: actor, actress, architect, artist, blacksmith, carpenter, coiffeur, cook, coppersmith, goldsmith, lacquerware maker, painter, perfume maker, silversmith, stone carver, wood carver, and veterinarian.

Ayuthia eventually recovered and flourished. King Narai (na-RY) (r. 1656–1688) fostered a cultural renaissance, promoting literature and art, often with a Buddhist emphasis. Since Buddhist monks sponsored many village schools, Siam enjoyed one of the premodern world's highest literacy rates, providing writers an audience. For example, a long poem by Sri Mahosot (shree ma-HO-sut) describes courtship rituals of young people along the Ayuthia riverside during the evening: "O beautiful night! Excited voices on the riverbank. Couples closely embraced, they stare at each other. There is smiling, touching, singing in chorus, looking eye to eye. There is excitement, craving and longing forever."[7]

Reflecting hierarchy, the Siamese royal family and aristocracy remained aloof from commoners and a large slave class, while women operated village and town markets. But Siamese society was also relatively tolerant. In 1636 a Dutch trader contrasted Siamese Buddhist tolerance with zealous Christian and Muslim proselytizing, observing that the Siamese did not condemn any "opinions, but believe that all, though of differing tenets, living virtuously, may be saved, all services which are performed with zeal being acceptable to the great God. And the Christians [and Muslims] are both permitted the free exercise of their religions."[8] Ayuthia's openness to merchants and creative people from abroad also made it a vibrant crossroads of goods and ideas. A French visitor in the 1680s wrote that "since all nations are well received in Siam…free [to] exercise…their religion…scarcely a single nation…is not found there."[9]

However, increasing activity by English, French, and Dutch traders proved challenging. King Narai sent three diplomatic missions to Louis XIV in France to obtain Western maps and scientific knowledge while employing foreigners as officials, including a Persian Muslim as prime minister and a Greek merchant, Constantine Phaulkon (FALL-kin), as superintendent of foreign trade. After learning that the opportunistic Phaulkon and French officials planned to convert Narai to Christianity and station French troops, in 1688 Ayuthia executed Phaulkon and expelled French diplomats, missionaries,

---

[7]Quoted in Klaus Wenk, *Thai Literature: An Introduction* (Bangkok: White Lotus, 1995), 14–16.
[8]Joost Schouten, quoted in Michael Smithies, *Descriptions of Old Siam* (Kuala Lumpur, Malaysia: Oxford University Press, 1995), 19.
[9]Father Tachard, quoted in Victor Purcell, *The Chinese in Southeast Asia*, 2nd ed. (London: Oxford University Press, 1965), 90.

and merchants from Siam. The Siamese, who once welcomed foreign traders, now mistrusted Europeans. Dutch traders remained but faced fierce competition, especially from Chinese.

Trade networks fostered Islamic expansion. Southeast Asian Muslims often made the long pilgrimage to Mecca, and some sent their sons to the Middle East for study, reinforcing links between the regions. Various societies adapted Islam to their own cultures. Hence many Javanese superimposed Islam, often Sufism, on the existing Hinduism and mystical animism (spirit worship), producing an eclectic, tolerant mix. Some other peoples, including most Malays, embraced a more orthodox Islam. Muslim merchants, who preferred ports with Muslim rulers, enriched these states. Mixing Islam and maritime trade encouraged connections to the wider world. For example, Hamzah Fansuri (**HOM-sah fan-SIR-ee**), a Sufi poet from Sumatra famed for his mystical and romantic writings who once lived in Ayuthia and then Baghdad, was a follower of an earlier Spain-born mystic, Ibn al-Arabi (1165–1240), who taught, like Vedanta Hinduism, that all reality is one and everything that exists is part of the divine.

Rooted in patriarchal Arab traditions, Islam diminished women's rights and traditional independence in some Indonesian societies. Acheh (**AH-cheh**) in northern Sumatra, where four successive women ruled in the 1600s, now prohibited women from holding royal power. Yet, there were sometimes powerful queens on Java. Ratu Kali Nyamet ruled the coastal port of Jepara and its surroundings from 1549 until 1579; she is well remembered there today as an effective leader who made strategic alliances with other states, launched two attacks on the Portuguese base at Melaka, made Jepara the major port of central Java, and patronized Islamic religion and culture. Muslim royal courts on Java and other islands were filled with hundreds, sometimes thousands, of women—wives, concubines, attendants, guards, or textile workers making *batik*, the beautiful cloth produced by a wax and dying process. Batik arts later spread throughout the world.

Southeast Asia's wealth and resources, especially spices such as cloves, nutmeg, and pepper, attracted European merchants and conquerors. The process began with the Portuguese, whose occupation of Melaka began a powerful and destabilizing European presence that transformed Southeast Asia between 1500 and 1914. As the victorious admiral Albuquerque boasted: "Melaka is the source of all the spices and drugs which the [Muslims] carry every year to [the Middle East]. Cairo and Mecca will be entirely ruined, and Venice will receive no spices unless her merchants go and buy them in Portugal."[10] A few years later the Portuguese brutally conquered the Spice Islands, known as Maluku (**muh-LOO-ku**) (Moluccas), in northeast Indonesia, gaining control of the valuable spice trade to Europe. The sultanate of Acheh in northern Sumatra forged an anti-Portuguese military alliance from 1530 to 1570 with the distant Ottoman Empire, but Ottoman naval power in the Indian Ocean proved short-lived.

The Portuguese employed brutal force against rivals and challengers. Jesuit missionary Saint Francis Xavier, a Spaniard, described Portuguese behavior in the Spice Islands as little more than discovering new ways of conjugating the verb *to steal*. But,

as in India, Portuguese power proved short-lived. Like the East African ports the Portuguese occupied earlier, Melaka languished because Muslim merchants faced higher taxes and intolerance of Islam, and in 1641 the Dutch defeated and replaced the Portuguese in Melaka. However, a small Catholic, Portuguese-speaking community still lives there. For several centuries Portuguese became a trading language in some Asian coastal regions, from Basra in Iraq to Vietnamese ports, and the Indonesian and Malay languages contain some words of Portuguese origin.

Portuguese activities spurred the Spanish, Dutch, English, and French to compete for markets, resources, Christian converts, and power in Southeast Asia. The Spanish conquered the Philippines, the Dutch gained some control of Indian Ocean maritime trade and gradually conquered Java and the Spice Islands, and the English mainly sought trade relations until later in the 1700s. In the early 1600s English and Dutch traders began competing for commercial opportunities in Vietnam, which enjoyed a favorable geographic position for maritime trade. Beginning in 1615, the French also sought trade with Vietnam and also dispatched Catholic missionaries, who recruited a small Vietnamese following. The French also tried to change the Chinese-based Vietnamese writing system. To undercut Confucian influence, French missionaries created a romanized Vietnamese alphabet, and in the twentieth century this became the official writing system. Despite these influences, Southeast Asian states such as Siam, Vietnam, Burma, and Acheh were strong enough to resist over three hundred years of persistent effort by Westerners to gain complete political, social, and economic domination, which they achieved only by 1914.

18-2b The Philippines Under Spanish Colonization

The greatest Western impact before 1800 came in the Philippine Islands and it changed the world, establishing one of the foundations for today's globalization: trade between Asia and the Americas. The first Spanish ships to reach the islands in 1521, commanded by Ferdinand Magellan, were part of the first successful effort to circumnavigate the world (see Chapter 17). Magellan pressured the Filipinos he encountered to adopt Christianity, ordering a local chief to burn all his peoples' religious figures and replace them with a cross. These arrogant demands resulted in his death during a skirmish with hostile Filipinos. Today, on the Cebu Island beach where Magellan died, a memorial honors Lapulapu (**LAH-pu-LAH-pu**), the chief leading the attack, as the first Filipino to repel European aggression.

When, after visiting the Spice Islands, Magellan's ships returned to Spain, they had proved that Asia could be reached by sailing west from Europe. But Magellan had also chanced upon an archipelago inhabited by diverse peoples speaking over a hundred Malay languages and scattered across seven thousand islands, with the majority living on the two largest, Luzon (**loo-ZON**) and Mindanao (**min-duh-NOW**). The largest Filipino political units were villages led by chiefs. Muslims occupied

---

[10]Quoted in Nicholas Tarling, "Mercantilism and Missionaries: Impact and Accommodation," in *Eastern Asia: An Introductory History*, ed. Colin Mackerras, 3rd ed. (Frenches Forest, NSW, Australia: Longmans, 2000), 115.

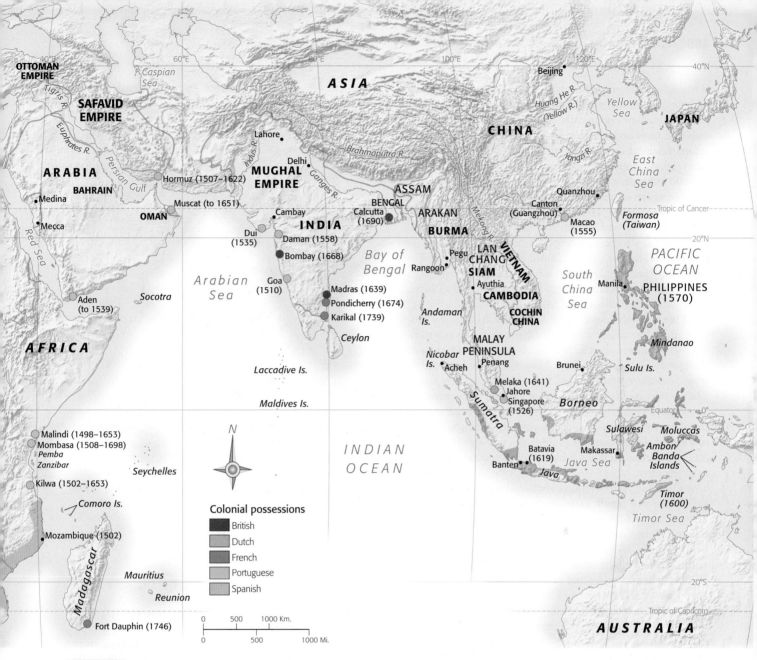

MAP 18.2 **Southeast Asia and the Indian Ocean in the Early Modern Era** Much of Southeast Asia remained independent, able to deflect European ambitions, but the Portuguese had captured the port of Melaka, Timor, and the Moluccas (Maluku), and the Spanish had colonized the Philippines. In the 1600s the Dutch displaced the Portuguese from Melaka and the Moluccas and ruled part of Java from Batavia.

Q What does this map tell us about the European presence in Southeast Asia, the Indian Ocean realm, and southern China in this era?

the southernmost islands, but most Filipinos mixed belief in one supreme being with animism; Spaniards considered them immoral devil worshippers. While little cultural influence from India or China reached these remote islands, a few hundred Chinese traders lived in major towns, and some Filipino maritime traders traveled as far as China, Melaka, and Burma. Many Filipinos used a simple writing system.

Four decades after Magellan, the Spaniards returned to conquer and evangelize the Philippines, which they renamed after their monarch, Philip II, known as "the most Catholic of kings." The militarily superior Spanish had little trouble conquering and co-opting local chiefs, but they never completely pacified the Muslims (**Moros**) in the south. Today some

southern Muslims seek independence from the Christian-dominated Philippines. As a potential base for trade with China, the Spaniards set up their colonial government in Manila, located in Luzon along a fine natural harbor. Some Spaniards dreamed of using the islands as a base for invading China. In 1576 the Governor of the Philippines naively proposed an invasion that would, he claimed, be very easy and require only a few thousand men. But Philip II denied the request, seeing good relations with China as a higher priority.

The Spanish ruled over the Philippines for nearly three centuries (1565–1898), imposing

Moros The Spanish term for the Muslim peoples of the southern Philippines.

449

Catholicism and many aspects of Spanish culture on Filipinos with a policy known as **Hispanization**. The Catholic Church governed various regions and acquired great wealth as priests collected taxes and sold crops such as sugar. With missionary efforts financed by the Spanish crown, several Catholic religious orders competed to gain the most converts. To better control and evangelize, missionaries required people to move into towns, and the church controlled what little formal education existed, emphasizing religious doctrine. As in Latin America, Spaniards destroyed nearly all pre-Spanish writings as "pagan." In recent years some Filipinos have encouraged the revival of the original Filipino alphabet, called Baybayin, and at least one community has mandated that it be used on store signs alongside English and local languages. Eventually around 85 percent of Filipinos adopted Roman Catholicism.

However, Filipinos disgusted the Spanish by incorporating their animist traditions into Catholicism, such as by transforming friendly spirits into Christian saints and magic into miracles attributed to Jesus or the Virgin Mary. Some Filipinos used religious festivals to subtly protest Spanish rule, rewriting Spanish passion plays on the life and death of Jesus into plays expressing anticolonial sentiments; for example, they presented Jesus as a social activist of humble background tormented by a corrupt ruling class. Given Spanish conquerors' contempt for the common people, few Filipinos could rise in the church hierarchy or in government.

The Philippine colonial economy, based on plantation agriculture and tenant farming, implanted a permanent gap between extraordinarily rich landowners and impoverished peasants. Emphasizing lucrative cash crops, such as sugar and hemp, for sale on the world market, Spanish officials, corporations, and Catholic orders owned most farmland, with the Filipino tenant farmers and plantation workers living almost like medieval European serfs. Peasant revolts became common. Priests and landowners told Filipinos their religious duty was to labor hard for others, receiving their just rewards later in heaven.

But although the Spanish created a country and expanded the economy, they did not construct a cohesive society; instead, regional and ethnic loyalties remained dominant. Spaniards occupied the top spots, mostly living in Manila and often in luxury, and few outside the church learned local languages. As in Latin America, many returned to Spain after acquiring wealth. Below them were Filipino families descending from chiefs, and mixed-descent mestizos, the result of unions between Spanish men with Filipinas. Chinese immigrants worked as merchants and craftsmen, some becoming rich but most remaining middle class, and many Chinese became Catholic. Chinese men frequently married Filipinas, fostering a Chinese mestizo community. As a result, many Philippine leaders today have

Hispanization The process by which, over nearly three centuries of Spanish colonial rule beginning in 1565, the Catholic religion and Spanish culture were imposed on the Philippine people.

Indios The Filipinos at the bottom of the Spanish colonial social structure, who faced many legal restrictions.

Album/Oronoz/Newscom

IMAGE 18.4 **Mestizo Family in Philippines** This painting shows three well-dressed mestizos in Manila in the eighteenth century. Mestizos of Spanish and Chinese background played key roles in colonial life.

Q What can we learn from the painting about mestizo life in the Philippines?

Chinese or Spanish mestizo ancestry. But while the Spanish needed Chinese as middlemen, they also despised, feared, persecuted, and sometimes expelled them. Spanish forces occasionally slaughtered residents of Manila's large Chinatown.

Most Filipinos, whom Spaniards called **Indios** (Indies people), occupied the lowest social status and faced many legal restrictions; hence, they were prohibited from dressing like Spaniards. While Filipinos retained close family ties, Filipinas lost their high position in pre-Spanish society because the Spanish culture and church devalued women. Female priestesses integral to Filipino animism were pushed to society's margins by Catholic priests, one of whom described the priestesses as "loathsome creatures, foul, obscene, truly damnable. My task [is] to reduce them to order."[11] But despite male prejudice and narrowing gender roles, Filipinas still controlled family finances and engaged in small-scale trade.

18-2c Indonesia and the Dutch

In the early seventeenth century the Dutch replaced Portugal as the region's dominant European power. Holland was Europe's most prosperous society during the 1600s, thanks partly to its trade and conquests in Asia, especially Indonesia. In 1595 a Dutch fleet visited the Spice Islands and returned with spices.

[11]Pedro Chirino, quoted in Carolyn Brewer, "From Animist 'Priestess' to Catholic Priest: The Re/gendering of Religious Roles in the Philippines, 1521–1685," in *Other Pasts: Women, Gender and History in Early Modern Southeast Asia*, ed. Barbara Watson Andaya (Honolulu: Center for Southeast Asian Studies, University of Hawaii at Manoa, 2000), 69.

Over the following several decades the Dutch, after bloody battles, dislodged the Portuguese from most of their scattered outposts, including Maluku. In 1641 they finally captured Portuguese-controlled Melaka, but the city never recovered its earlier glory. The Dutch sought wealth but, unlike the Portuguese and Spanish, cared little about spreading their culture and religion.

Over three hundred years the Dutch gradually gained control of the Indonesian islands, except for Portuguese-ruled Timor. They ruthlessly eliminated all competition, such as by massacring English residents on Ambon (am-BOHN) Island in 1623. In 1659, as Dutch forces attacked and occupied the prosperous trading city of Makassar (muh-KAS-uhr), in southeast Sulawesi (SOO-la-WAY-see), the city's sultan asked: "Do you believe that God has preserved for your trade alone islands which lie so distant from your homeland?"[12] Both sides sparked conflict, but the militarily superior Dutch often slaughtered their Indonesian opponents by the thousands. Well organized, resourceful, and shrewd, they allied themselves with one state against a rival state, sometimes drawing them into civil wars or sparking stiff resistance. For example, Shaikh Yusuf (ca. 1624–1699), a Sulawesi-born, Arabia-educated spiritual adviser to the sultan of Banten in western Java, led two thousand followers into an unsuccessful holy war against the Dutch in 1683.

For several centuries the Dutch East India Company, which had great capital and large resources for pursuing profit, administered the Indonesian bases. With Holland ten months away by boat, the Company had little guidance and few restraints as it pursued a trade monopoly in Southeast Asia. If Spice Islanders grew restless, Dutch forces might exterminate them or carry them off as slaves to Java, Ceylon, or South Africa, as happened in 1621 to the Banda (BAN-duh) Islands' fifteen hundred people. To increase demand and reduce supply, the Dutch sometimes chopped down spice-growing trees and bushes, leaving the population with no income.

Eventually the Dutch concentrated on the rich island of Java, which enjoyed a flourishing mercantile economy, living standards comparable to those of many western Europeans, several competing sultanates, skillful traders, and large cities with multiethnic populations drawn from throughout Asia. Javanese artisans were noted for their fine craftsmanship, and the island's smiths made perhaps the world's finest steel swords. Javanese women were prominent in business alongside the men, as an English observer noted: "It is usual for a husband to entrust his pecuniary affairs entirely to his wife. The women alone attend the markets, and conduct all the buying and selling."[13]

Capitalizing on Java's political divisions, the Dutch slowly extended their power after establishing a base at a village they renamed Batavia, on the northwestern coast, in 1619. Batavia later grew into today's Jakarta. By 1800 the Dutch controlled most of Java, ruling some districts through local aristocrats. They also invited more Chinese traders to come to Java, where they had operated for centuries. Over time, Dutch and Chinese entrepreneurs slowly displaced Javanese merchants, once major players in the Asian economy.

Soon Holland concentrated on making Indonesia a source of wealth, forcing the rice-growing peasants in the west Java and Sumatra highlands to grow coffee through annual quotas. Coffee, domesticated in Ethiopia and grown in southern Arabia, had become a popular beverage in the Middle East, Europe, and later the Americas. The Dutch made huge profits from monopolizing the world coffee trade, enough to finance much of Holland's later industrialization. Thus Westerners called coffee "java."

Inequality characterized colonial society. Europeans occupied the top layer, followed by mixed-descent Eurasians and the co-opted aristocracy, who encouraged peasants to treat aristocratic officials with great awe. The middle class was mostly Chinese. Like the Spaniards, the Dutch feared the growing Chinese community, sometimes massacring Chinese in Batavia. Denied real power, Javanese royal courts turned inward, creating more fluid, graceful, and stylized royal dances and intricate batik fabrics.

Many Dutch found Javanese culture seductive, taking local wives, owning slaves, dressing in Javanese clothes, and indulging in delicious spicy curries, now enriched by American chilies. Most Dutch lived in Batavia, which was built to resemble a city in Holland, with close-packed, stuffy houses and stagnant canals poorly suited to the tropical climate. The puritanical Dutch wore heavy woolen clothes in the tropical heat but bathed only once a week. Like many Southeast Asian cities, Batavia had a multiethnic society.

18-2d Southeast Asians and the World Economy

With the Portuguese, Dutch, and Spanish exporting luxury items and natural resources from their colonies, Southeast Asia became an even more crucial part of the world economy, reshaping global commerce. Magellan found the sea route west across the Pacific to Asia in 1520 but until 1565, despite various efforts, no ship or fleet had successfully sailed east from Asia back across the Pacific to the Americas. But an experienced Spanish navigator, Andres de Urdaneta, finally worked out the right currents and winds across the uncharted ocean, making possible two-way voyages and trade and transforming the world economy. What some called the *Ruta de la Plata* ("Silver Way"), linking Asia and the Americas, formed the lynchpin of trade routes spanning four continents and marked the first time the entire world had been connected through global trade and financial networks, the basis of our global economy today. After the Spanish founding of Manila in 1571, the first hub linking Asia and the Americas across the Pacific and soon a multicultural crossroads of the East Asian, Southeast Asian, and American markets, Asian products, including Chinese silk and porcelain, were exported directly to Mexico and from there to Europe. Spanish galleons then returned to Manila from Mexico with European goods, mail, personnel, and vast amounts of silver to pay for Asian goods, draining Spanish imperial coffers and enriching Asian treasuries. Over half the silver mined in the Americas ended up in China where it underpinned China's money supply. American silver spurred Asian economies, encouraging increased production of Philippine sugar, Chinese tea, and Indian textiles.

---

[12]Quoted in Felipe Fernandez-Armesto, *Millennium: A History of the Last Thousand Years* (New York: Scribner, 1995), 234.

[13]Thomas Stamford Raffles, quoted in Anthony Reid, *Southeast Asia in the Age of Commerce, 1450–1680*, vol. 1 (New Haven, CT: Yale University Press, 1993), 164.

The Castle of Batavia, 1661 (oil on canvas)/Beeckman, Andries (fl. 1651)/Rijksmuseum, Amsterdam, The Netherlands/Bridgeman Images

IMAGE 18.5 **Batavia** The Dutch built a port they called Batavia on the northwest coast of Java, shown in this painting from ca. 1656, which features the castle fortress. Batavia grew rapidly as the political and commercial center of the Dutch empire in Southeast Asia.

Q What kinds of activities does this painting illustrate?

In this highly speculative, "riches or ruin" Manila galleon trade, Spanish businessmen bet their fortunes that the galleons would arrive in Mexico safely. Pirates, storms, and other obstacles made voyages dangerous, and some never completed their trips. This unpredictability fostered a "get rich quick" mentality rather than a long-term strategy for Philippine prosperity.

In spite of the changes, Southeast Asians retained considerable continuity with the past. The West was not yet dominant in either political or economic spheres, except in a few widely scattered outposts such as Melaka, the Spice Islands, and the Philippines. Europeans still had to compete with Chinese, Arab, Indian, and Southeast Asian merchants. The Vietnamese, continuing their long expansion down the Vietnamese coast, annexed the Mekong Delta in the 1600s, while the Siamese forced the French to leave. Only by the eighteenth century did Southeast Asian societies, suffering from internal strife and increasingly expensive government structures, begin to collapse under the weight of accelerating Western military and economic activity.

KEY POINTS

▶ Increased trade in Southeast Asia led to greater political centralization and increased the influence of major world religions such as Islam and Buddhism.

▶ Europeans, beginning with the violent Portuguese and later including the Spanish, Dutch, English, and French, were attracted by Southeast Asia's riches and resources.

▶ The militaristic Dutch came to dominate Indonesia, particularly Java, which they turned into a highly profitable coffee exporter.

▶ As a result of European colonization, Southeast Asia entered the world economy, though European speculators often focused on making quick money rather than strengthening the region's economy for the long term.

18-3 Early Modern China and New Challenges

SOCIETIES   NETWORKS

Q What factors enabled China to remain one of the world's strongest and most dynamic societies?

Two dynasties, the Ming followed by the Qing **(ching)**, ruled China between the overthrow of the Mongols in the 1300s and the advent of a republic in 1912, together making these centuries one of the great eras of orderly government and social stability (see Map 18.3). During this time China remained one of the most industrialized societies, boasting a vibrant culture and economy. Although encounters with Europeans indicated the challenges ahead just as China experienced political and technological decay, no other country could match the size, wealth, and power of Early Modern China.

> **CONNECTION to TODAY**
>
> How was China in this era similar and how was it different than China today?

people from Manchuria just northeast of China whose forces swept into China on horseback, routing the Ming. It took several decades to occupy and pacify the country, with Ming loyalists holding out in the south and on the large offshore island of Taiwan for several decades. Increasing Chinese interest soon led to efforts to settle the island in this era, a history that helps form the basis of China's claims to Taiwan island today.

18-3a The Later Ming Dynasty

China under the Ming (1368–1644) remained dynamic. The imperial political system, administered by mandarins, was supported by highly productive agriculture and the world's largest, most diversified commercial economy. The Confucian elite shared an ambivalent attitude toward merchants. In the later 1500s a Ming official, himself from a merchant family, wrote an essay criticizing merchants as greedy, arrogant, self-serving, and pampered. However, he admired the products they supplied and thought China could benefit from lower taxes on mercantile activity. Although heavily regulated, commerce provided numerous products and services. Along with silk and tea, cotton textiles were produced and exported to Japan and Southeast Asia for silver and spices. Rebuilding of the Grand Canal facilitated shipment by barge and stimulated manufacturing. For centuries a world leader in science and technology, in the late Ming and early Qing periods China developed color woodblock printing, as well as better cotton gins, spinning wheels, and other technologies for textile and silk production.

Yet, Ming China turned somewhat inward, concentrating on home affairs and defending the northern borders. Always self-sufficient and self-centered, China became increasingly ethnocentric and uninterested in foreigners. The Ming court, viewing foreign states mainly as tribute providers and more concerned with the security of the northern border with the Mongols, ended the great maritime voyages of the early 1400s. Although some foreign merchants still came and Chinese merchants illegally went to Southeast Asia, the later Ming encouraged isolation, in contrast to earlier Tang, Song, and Yuan cosmopolitanism. Chinese were not patrolling the seas when the first Portuguese ships arrived.

Eventually misrule and other mounting problems precipitated dynastic change. Crop failures and a terrible plague tied to climate change killed millions in north China and around Eurasia. In the 1590s the treasury became depleted after Ming military forces defended their Korean vassal from Japanese invasion. Meanwhile, Japanese and Chinese pirates ravaged the southern coast and peasant revolts erupted. These problems opened the doors to the Manchus **(MAN-chooz)**, a seminomadic pastoral

18-3b Qing Empire, Society, Thought, and Culture

The new Manchu-installed Qing dynasty ruled from 1644 to 1912. The first Qing rulers, exceptionally able, governed, much like their Chinese predecessors, through the mandarin bureaucracy, patronizing Confucianism but also adding their own innovations. Although forbidding intermarriage with Chinese, the Manchus knew that to succeed they needed to adopt Chinese institutions and culture to win Chinese support. Thus, like most earlier foreign rulers, they assimilated Chinese ways and relied on scholarly degree holders educated in Confucian classics for administration. Yet, they governed with a smaller bureaucracy and lighter taxes than the Ming.

Some Qing emperors were outstanding managers, aware of their awesome responsibility. The reflective Kangxi **(kang-shee)** (r. 1661–1722), a writer and painter exemplifying the Confucian ideal of virtuous ruler, wrote that "giving life to the people and killing people—these are the powers that an emperor has. He knows that administrative errors in government bureaus can be rectified, but that a criminal who is executed cannot be brought back to life any more than a chopped string can be joined together again."[14] Kangxi toured the provinces inspecting public works and joining hunting expeditions. To bring Manchus and Chinese together, his imperial robes included elements of Manchu horse-riding attire and Chinese dragon motifs. His son and successor, Yongzheng **(young-cheng)** (r. 1723–1735), improved social conditions, ordering anyone held in hereditary servile status (slavery) anywhere in the empire to be freed.

The Manchus created the greatest Eurasian land empire since the Mongols. Qing armies reasserted Chinese control of the western and northern frontier, annexing Mongolia, Tibet (long a Chinese tributary state), and Xinjiang **(shin-chang)** ("New Dominions"), a desert region inhabited by Turkic-speaking Muslims. While Tibetans shared with Manchus and Mongols the mystical version of Buddhism called Lamaism **(LAH-muh-iz-uhm)**, they differed culturally from the Chinese. The Qing also incorporated Taiwan, which was inhabited by Austronesian peoples, and the Chinese began immigrating there in the 1600s.

---

[14]Quoted in Jonathan S. Spence, *Emperor of China: Self-Portrait of Kang-Hsi* (New York: Vintage, 1975), 29.

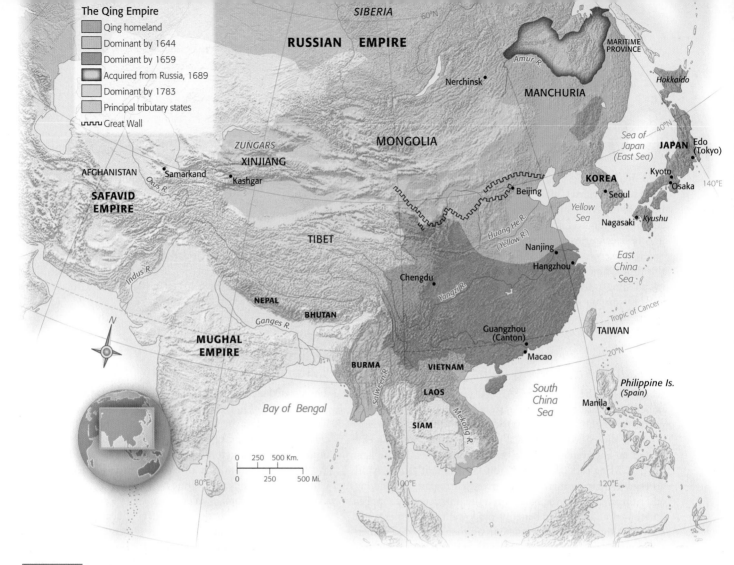

MAP 18.3 Qing China and East Asia in the Early Modern Era Qing China remained the colossus of eastern Eurasia, controlling a huge empire that included Tibet, Xinjiang, and Mongolia. Korea and Vietnam remained tributary states of China, but the Russians expanded into eastern Siberia. The Japanese partly secluded themselves from the outside world.

Q How did the configuration of the Qing Empire compare to China today?

The Qing retained China's examination system. Ming and Qing China owed their political and social stability partly to the gentry, landlords and moneylenders who dominated rural life in this agrarian-based bureaucratic empire by combining political office with land ownership. Able to afford tutors, gentry men received a formal education and held scholarly degrees. The mid-Qing novel, *The Story of the Stone* (also known as "The Dream of the Red Chamber"), revealed the expectations for gentry sons: "A boy's proper business is to read books in order to gain an understanding of things, so that when he grows up he can play his part in governing the country."[15]

Together the gentry and Manchu rulers promoted the status quo. However, some gentry could not negotiate the dynastic change. For example, the celebrated late Ming essayist, poet, historian, and degree holder Zhang Dai (**chang die**) (1597–1680), who lived a comfortable life while supporting a wife, several consorts, and eight or ten children. Zhang Dai spent his ample leisure time at a lakeside villa in Hangzhou (**hahng choh**), visiting tourist sites, collecting handcrafted lanterns, playing the lute, and participating in a crab-eating club. However, the Zhangs ran afoul of changing political winds during the dangerous Ming-Qing transition and were reduced to poverty.

Women had a complex status in patriarchal Qing society. The elite debated women's education, and some intellectuals encouraged it. Some women from gentry and merchant families, educated informally, read and even wrote literature. However, elite women were hobbled by footbinding, a custom that was introduced half a millennium earlier but that only became widespread during the Ming. In the lower classes, peasant women, usually illiterate, played key economic roles, for example, by improving and promoting spinning and weaving tools. Men planted but women picked the cotton, processed it into yarn, and wove the finished product for sale. An eighteenth-century government report observed that "whole peasant families assemble,

---

[15]Quoted in Richard J. Smith, *China's Cultural Heritage: The Ch'ing Dynasty, 1644–1913* (Boulder, CO: Westview Press, 1983), 210.

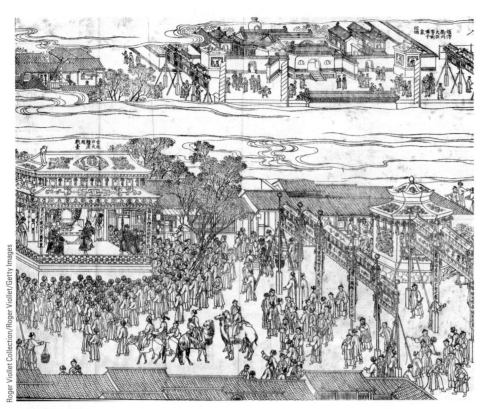

Roger Viollet Collection/Roger Viollet/Getty Images

IMAGE 18.6 **Entrance of Emperor Kangxi in Beijing** The Qing emperor Kangxi had one of the longest reigns in Chinese history. In this print of Beijing from 1670, crowds gather as Kangxi prepares for public celebrations.

Q What does this painting tell us about Beijing life and society in this era?

young and old; the mother-in-law leads her son's wives, the mother supervises her daughters; when the wicker lantern is lit and the starlight and moonlight come slanting down, still the click-clack of the spindle-wheels comes from the house."[16] But many peasant women were gradually marginalized as their menfolk or large commercial farmers, seeking greater profits, took over their livelihood. Some women in coastal villages even joined, and sometimes commanded, pirate fleets.

Chinese attitudes toward homosexuality fluctuated. Visiting Europeans were shocked by Chinese tolerance toward homosexuality, which was fiercely punished in Europe. However, some Chinese scholars, blaming the Ming downfall on lax morality, convinced the Qing to penalize homosexuality. Yet, Qing punishments were mild, and repression gradually ebbed. At least half of Qing emperors are thought to have had same-sex bedmates. Homosexual relationships also did not preclude marriage and family; one Qing emperor with a male lover fathered twenty-seven children with his wives and concubines.

Philosophy contributed to Ming and Qing stability. Most Chinese followed the eclectic mix of Confucianism, Buddhism, and Daoism that had evolved in the Classical Era. Nonetheless, during the Ming and early Qing Confucian thought enjoyed a renaissance with an interpretation of Confucianism known as neo-Confucianism, which incorporated elements of Buddhism and Daoism, stressed rational thinking, and reemphasized people's natural goodness.

Like European Renaissance and Enlightenment thinkers, Ming and Qing philosophers sought knowledge regardless of whether it conformed to religious doctrine. Like Sir Francis Bacon and René Descartes, the neo-Confucian Wang Yang-Ming (1472–1529) pondered the unity of knowledge and conduct and wondered how people know the external world, concluding that "whatever we see, feel, hear, or in any wise conceive or understand is as real as ever."[17] Like Bacon and John Locke, scholars contended that the mind is reason. Others critically studied the past. Like Enlightenment thinkers, a few Chinese scholars studied knowledge from other societies. Philosopher and poet Tai Chen made comparative studies of Chinese and Western mathematics. However, neo-Confucianism became the new orthodoxy, limiting Chinese interest in alternative ideas. Some Qing scholars argued that no more writing was needed because the truth had been made clear by ancient thinkers so people should just practice their teachings. By the 1700s, few Chinese intellectuals showed interest in practical inquiry or technological development. Thus, although neo-Confucianism contributed to the unparalleled continuity of Chinese society, it fostered an intellectual conformity that was hostile to originality or ideas from outside.

China's art and literature, in contrast, remained creative. As they had for centuries, artists painted landscapes featuring misty distances, soaring mountains, and angular pine trees. However, many innovative painters also drew on Daoist mysticism, creating fanciful, untraditional scenes. The eccentric Zhu Da (ca. 1626–1705) painted bizarre nature: huge lotuses in ponds, birds with wise-looking eyes, surging landscapes. In literature, Qing authors wrote some of China's greatest fiction. Failing the civil service examinations, some scholars became writers. *The Scholars*, by Wu Jingzi (**woo ching-see**), satirized the examination system and revealed the foibles of the pompous and ignorant. The 1,300-page *The Story of the Stone*, by Cao Xueqin (**tsao swee-chin**), used a large, declining gentry family to discuss, and sometimes satirize, Qing life. Meanwhile, Qing scholars compiled the world's greatest encyclopedia, five thousand volumes long.

---

[16]Quoted in Francesca Bray, "Towards a Critical History of Non-Western Technology," in *China and Historical Capitalism*, ed. Timothy Brook and Gregory Blue (New York: Cambridge University Press, 1999), 184.
[17]Quoted in John A. Harrison, *The Chinese Empire* (New York: Harcourt Brace Jovanovich, 1972), 335.

18-3c China and the World Economy

China had flourishing industrial production, extensive foreign trade, and the world's largest and best-integrated commercial economy. Encouraged by government taxation policies, the fertile lower Yangzi (**yahng-zeh**) Basin gradually became China's industrial heartland, commercial hub, and most prosperous region. Cities like Nanjing and Suzhou enjoyed living standards comparable to those in England and Holland, both enriched by overseas colonization. A French visitor in the early 1700s, amazed that China's internal trade vastly exceeded the commerce of all Europe, wrote that the Chinese put "merit ceaselessly in competition with merit, diligence with diligence, and work with work. The whole country is like a perpetual fair."[18] Heavy Qing investment in infrastructure, such as canals and dams, also expanded the economy.

A major force in the international economy, China exported porcelain, cotton textiles, silk, quicksilver, zinc, and tea, receiving silver from Europeans as payment. As the basis for Chinese currency, more silver fostered more investment. Tea became so popular in the world that most of the world's languages call the beverage some derivation of "tea" and "cha," both words from Chinese. While the term "cha" mostly spread along the Silk Road, the term "tea" (from Fujian on China's southeast coast) was mostly carried across the seas by the Dutch. Its resources and market for imports influenced economic decisions made in Southeast Asia, the Middle East, Europe, and the Americas. At the same time, the population grew from the introduction of American crops such as corn (maize), sweet potatoes, and peanuts, as well as from Chinese development of a new fast-growing rice. China's population numbered some 100 million in 1500 and reached 250 or 300 million by 1750, a quarter of the world total. Several major cities had over a million residents, including Nanjing (**nahn-JING**), Beijing, and Guangzhou (**gwong-joe**) (known in the West as Canton).

However, despite this economic dynamism, full-scale capitalism and industrialization did not develop. The Tang, Song, and Ming commercial revolutions and technological advances failed to foster the revolutionary changes that transformed western European feudalism into capitalism. One reason was that, unlike England and Holland, China lacked an overseas empire to provide investment capital. Another basic difference from Europe was the continuity of Chinese traditions, with successive dynasties continuing the essential Han dynasty pattern until 1912. The bureaucracy-gentry, often contemptuous of merchant values, could absorb the effects of economic growth, keeping merchants politically weak, whereas in Europe economic growth undermined the old system. With population growth, China also had no labor shortage that might spur technological innovation. China's economy satisfied basic needs well.

Unlike early modern Europe, where business enterprises increasingly influenced politics, the imperial government restricted and heavily taxed merchants. Although a wealthy Chinese merchant class existed and laws encouraged markets, the government, fearing that powerful merchants might threaten the regime, circumscribed their activities. Industrialists and merchants organized themselves into government-certified guilds responsible for their members' behavior. Although many Song dynasty mandarins had come from merchant backgrounds and protected their families and business generally, by the Qing this was no longer true. The government also maintained monopolies over producing and distributing essential commodities, including arms, textiles, pottery, salt, iron, and wine (see Discover Historical Voices: A Chinese Official's Duties).

Reflecting a centralized, agriculture-based empire, Ming emperors stopped Zheng He's overseas voyages, prohibited emigration, and ordered Chinese merchants to return home. However, some Chinese merchants, especially from mountainous Fujian (**fu-JEN**) province on the southeast coast, continued going abroad, remaining prominent in Southeast Asian and Japanese trade. Since Fujian offered poor conditions for farming, Fujian men, as a Chinese official commented, necessarily made fields from the sea. But, unlike European rivals, they received no official support and often had to bribe local Chinese officials. Thus Chinese energies focused inward at a fateful turning point in world history, leaving the world's oceans open to Western enterprise.

18-3d China's Encounters with the West

Although turning inward in the later Ming, China did not cut itself off completely from the outside world. In the 1500s and 1600s European ships seeking silk, tea, porcelain, lacquerware,

Tea Service, painted with Peonies, Chinese, Yonzheng period, 1723–35 (porcelain) (see also 120093)/Paul Freeman/Private Collection/Bridgeman Images

IMAGE 18.7 **Chinese Ceramics** China became famous for its porcelain products, much desired around the world. This tea service, painted with peonies, is from the eighteenth century.

Q What features of this porcelain might have made it so popular around the world?

18Jean-Baptiste DuHalde, quoted in Carolyn Blunden and Mark Elvin, *The Cultural Atlas of China* (Alexandria, VA: Stonehenge, 1991), 144.

Discover Historical Voices

A Chinese Official's Duties

Chen Hongmou (1696-1771) had the longest career of any official, serving the Qing dynasty as a provincial governor in various provinces. Long considered the model Qing official, he also wrote essays that were progressive for the time, for example, promoting education for all Chinese. In the following excerpts from some of his letters and other writings, he discusses the duties of an official from the perspective of Confucian ideals in a highly bureaucratic empire.

We in official service ought to look at all matters from the point of view of what is best for the people's livelihood. We must plan for the long term, rather than for the moment. We should concentrate on the substantial and practical, rather than disguising our inaction with empty words. To do otherwise would violate the court's basic principle that officials exist for the good of the people....

The way of shepherding the people involves no more than educating and nurturing them....By "nurturing" I mean construction and maintenance of irrigation works, encouragement of land reclamation, and patronage of community granaries....If the people can be made to produce a surplus, store it, and allow it to accumulate over the years, their well-being will be ensured. By "education" I mean promoting civilized behavior, diligently managing public schools, and widely distributing classical texts. Schools are the fountainheads of popular customs. If educational practice is correct, popular customs will be virtuous....

Therefore, officials must look to the long term, not the present, and in so doing put the interests of the people ahead of their own [career] concerns....In governing, good intentions and good policies alone are insufficient. There are those policies that sound admirable but that prove impossible to implement in practice....If the local official truly approaches each matter from the standpoint of the people's livelihood, in carrying out any new policy he will first thoroughly canvas local public opinion on the matter. He will then consider every aspect of its implementation, noting in which aspects it is advantageous to the people and in which aspects it will cause them hardship. If the advantages outweigh the hardships, implement it.

The court appoints officials for the benefit of the people. Officials must cherish the people and exercise their authority to the fullest in their behalf. It is no accident that the formal title of a district magistrate is "one who *knows* the district," nor that he is referred to as the "*local* official"...there should be no matter within their locality about which he does not know....Their relationship is exactly like that of a family....

I have drawn up the following list of items a local official should keep in mind in determining how to conduct himself.

1. *Maintain genuine commitment....* With genuine commitment, your energies will never flag; without it, whatever ability you possess will be wasted.
3. *Provide exemplars of civilized behavior.* Magistrates should make regular tours of the countryside, to investigate local customs, good and bad, and to meet with local community leaders to clarify for their benefit what is considered legal and proper.
6. *Keep a tight rein on your clerks.* Failure to control their predations will inevitably generate popular resentment....
8. *Prevent harassment of the people.* Evil government functionaries and local tyrants will inevitably come up with ways to harass the people...No matter how hardworking the magistrate, and how well intentioned the laws, such harassments can be prevented only through constant and diligent scrutiny....

Reflection Questions

1. What do the excerpts tell us about Confucian ideals of government?
2. How did officials promote political stability?
3. What challenges did an official confront?
4. Do you think some of his ideas could improve government officials and administrations today?

Source: *Sources of Chinese Tradition: From 1600 Through the Twentieth Century*, compiled by Wm. Theodore de Bary and Richard Lufrano, 2nd ed., vol. 2 (New York: Columbia University Press, 2000), 162–167. © 2000 Columbia University Press.

and other products reached Chinese shores. The Portuguese landed on the China coast in 1514, beginning a troubled relationship with China while earning reputations as pirates and religious fanatics. With their naval forces spread thinly around Asia and Africa, the Portuguese could not match Chinese armed junks. But in 1557, to stop the piracy, the emperor allowed the Portuguese to establish a trading base at a small unpopulated peninsula, Macao (**muh-cow**), near Guangzhou on the southeast coast. With Qing decline, Portugal transformed Macao from a trading base into the first Western colony on Chinese soil.

Christian missionaries, especially Jesuits, became active in late Ming China. In 1583 the most influential Jesuit, Italian Matteo Ricci (**ma-TAY-o REE-chee**) (1552–1610), a brilliant scholar and linguist trained in law, mathematics, and geography, arrived to study the Confucian classics and foster interest in Christianity among Confucian scholars. Impressing officials with his great learning, Ricci began training young scholars for the civil service exams. Eventually the emperor allowed Ricci and his Jesuit colleagues to settle in the capital, Beijing. Ricci became a scientific adviser to the imperial court, helping improve clocks, calendars, and astronomical observations. On Ricci's death the Chinese buried him with honors in Beijing. Yet, Ricci converted only a few to his faith.

Thanks to Jesuits, some Chinese leaders became interested in Western scientific knowledge. The emperor Kangxi wrote:

> I often worked several hours a day with [the Jesuits].
> I examined each stage of the forging of a cannon. I
> worked on clocks and mechanics. [Father] Pereira
> taught me to play a tune on the harpsichord.... I also
> learned to calculate the weight and volume of spheres,
> cubes, and cones, and to measure distance and the angles
> of riverbanks.[19]

A few Chinese even visited Europe. The Christian convert Michael Alphonsus Shen demonstrated chopstick techniques for French king Louis XIV and catalogued Chinese books in the Oxford University library. With more wealth and advanced technology than Europe, China much impressed the Italian Jesuits, whose letters describing Chinese ideas and inventions circulated widely in Europe. Jesuits lived like mandarins and wore Chinese clothing. Their admiration of Chinese traditions also led them to harmonize Christianity with Chinese philosophy, both to attract support from Chinese scholars and to avoid Christian doctrines incompatible with Confucianism.

However, despite Jesuit activity, by 1700 only some 100,000 Chinese had become Catholics, a tiny percentage of the vast population. Less tolerant missionaries who followed the early Jesuits made even less progress, and after the pope prohibited mixing Christianity and Confucianism, the faith became less appealing. Many Chinese also considered Christianity intellectually false and resented the arrogant missionary enterprise. The emperor Yongzheng asked the missionaries: "What would you say if I sent a troop of Buddhist monks into your country to preach their doctrines? You want all Chinese to become Christians. Shall we become subjects of your king? You will listen to no other voices but yours."[20] In the early 1700s the Qing banned Christianity for undermining such Chinese

traditions as ancestor worship, persecuted converts, and expelled missionaries.

Before 1800, China, being militarily and economically strong, could rebuff Western demands. But relations with the Dutch and Russians suggested trouble to come. The Dutch, who established a base on Taiwan in 1624, were expelled in 1662 by stronger Ming resistance forces that moved to the island. In 1683 the Qing took control of Taiwan and promoted Chinese settlement, but the Dutch remained active in the China trade. Meanwhile, Russian expeditions crossed sparsely populated Siberia, seeking trade with China as well as sable fur, and over time they consolidated control of the region. Russian forces fought and lost several battles to China in their quest for a gateway to the Pacific through the Amur River Valley, an area in eastern Siberia north of the Manchu homeland and under loose Qing suzerainty. But the Qing granted the Russians commercial privileges in the Treaty of Nerchinsk of 1689, the first treaty between China and a European power, symbolizing things to come. Russia maintained its ambitions in eastern Siberia, occasionally testing Qing power.

Needing little from outside, China controlled its relations with European powers before the 1800s, restricting foreign trade to a few border outposts and southern ports, especially Guangzhou (Canton), and refusing diplomatic relations with Western nations. Willing to absorb useful technologies to improve mapmaking and astronomy, the Chinese were less interested in foreign ideas like Christianity. By the mid-Qing, China was also increasingly self-centered and complacent, underestimating the Western challenge.

China's internal problems mounted just as Western economic, industrial, and military power increased; foreign pressures intensified in the later 1700s, when the West eclipsed an overconfident China within a few decades. Having lived under foreign rulers such as the Manchus, the Chinese understood political subjugation but could not comprehend foreign forces prompting them to rethink their cultural traditions, which they believed superior and which they wanted to preserve at all costs. During the later 1800s the two-thousand-year-old imperial system declined rapidly.

KEY POINTS

▶ During the Ming dynasty, China maintained its economic power, but it turned increasingly inward and antiforeign and was ultimately undermined by plague, famine, and pressures from Japan.

▶ The Qing dynasty was established by foreign Manchus, who assimilated to many Chinese ways, amassed the greatest Eurasian land empire since the Mongols, and added Taiwan to China's holdings.

▶ Chinese neo-Confucians incorporated elements of Buddhism and Daoism in their thinking and, like their

European contemporaries, emphasized reason, but over time neo-Confucianism hardened into a new orthodoxy and discouraged the growth of new ideas.

▶ China's economy remained extremely strong but never developed full-scale capitalism or industrialization, perhaps because it lacked an exploitable overseas empire, and perhaps because the government failed to encourage entrepreneurship.

[19]Quoted in Spence, *Emperor of China*, 72–73.
[20]Quoted in Joanna Waley-Cohen, *The Sextants of Beijing: Global Currents in Chinese History* (New York: W.W. Norton, 1999), 55.

18-4 Continuity and Change in Korea and Japan

⇄ TRANSITIONS 🏛 SOCIETIES

Ⓠ How did Korea and Japan change during this era?

Although neighbors, the Koreans, Japanese, and Chinese developed very different societies. Korea faced little Western pressure, with local issues and conflicts with Japan being far more important. For a brief period Japan encountered a significant European presence, but when the experience proved destabilizing, the Japanese became aloof from the West.

CONNECTION to TODAY

How does the Japan of this era seem different from the Japan of today?

18-4a Choson Korea, Ashikaga Japan, and European Encounters

Korea and Japan remained more isolated than China from the wider world. Unlike China and Japan, Korea has never received the attention it deserves from world or Asia historians. Koreans mixed Chinese influences with local traditions, adapting and modifying Chinese political models, Confucian social patterns, and Mahayana Buddhism. The Yi (**YEE**) dynasty (1392–1910), which called its state Choson (Joseon), ruled over five centuries. Strongly Confucian, Choson borrowed Chinese models and maintained close relations with China. The strong Qing support for Choson helped give the regime stability and legitimacy while Choson's willing tributary status reinforced the Manchus legitimacy as China's rulers and a great power. The early Yi era enjoyed progress in science, technology, writing, and literature. However, Choson was also damaged by factional disputes and a disastrous Japanese invasion.

The invasion occurred in 1592, when a Japanese army of 160,000 attempted to conquer the peninsula and captured the capital, Seoul (**soul**). Aided by China, the Koreans eventually prevailed by inventing the world's first ironclad naval vessels, which cut Japanese supply lines and forced Japanese withdrawal. But the invasion destroyed countless buildings, weakened the government, and generated severe economic problems.

Maintaining their power, the Yi abandoned or modified some customs borrowed from China while also modifying the rigid social class system. As agriculture became more productive, the population reached seven million by 1750. Commerce and the merchant class expanded. Yet, growing dissension fostered movements for change that grew during the 1700s.

Japan was East Asia's most unique society, exemplified by its samurai (**SAH-moo-rie**) warrior class, its distinctive mix of Buddhism, Confucianism, and Shinto, and its long history of adapting foreign influences. But by 1500 Japan under the Ashikaga (**ah-shee-KAH-gah**) Shogunate (1338–1573) was experiencing rapid economic change, population growth, and then civil war, which strained the political and social system. Ashikaga shoguns, military leaders who dominated the imperial family in Kyoto and the central government, never had much power beyond the capital.

As technological advances improved agriculture, tripling production per acre, Japan's population doubled from 16 million in 1500 to 30 million in 1750. Increased productivity stimulated trade and urban growth; by 1600 Kyoto contained some 800,000 people. Urban merchants and craftsmen organized themselves into guilds with monopoly rights to sell or make a product, earning higher status and more freedom than most Japanese enjoyed. Active merchants spurred foreign and domestic trade, with Japan supplying silver, copper, swords, lacquerware, rice wine, rice, and other goods to Asia. Only a few Japanese diplomats and Buddhist monks had ever ventured to Korea and China, but now Japanese traders and pirates visited Korea, China, and Southeast Asia. Japanese settled in Vietnam, Cambodia, Siam, and the Philippines; one even became a governor in Siam. If economic and military expansion had continued, the Japanese might have challenged Europeans for influence in Southeast Asia and perhaps even developed capitalism. But growing political turmoil and civil war turned Japan in a different direction.

Political power became increasingly decentralized, as several hundred daimyo, great territorial landowning magnates with supporting samurai forces, increasingly dominated rural Japan. The daimyo's rise precipitated a century-long civil war from the mid-1400s into the late 1500s, mostly involving hand-to-hand conflict between samurai wielding long, slightly curved, two-handed swords with great efficiency, supported by commoner spearmen. A famous poet offered a retrospective on the fleeting nature of the fighters' causes: "The summer grasses! All that is left of the warrior's dream!"[21]

Three successive shoguns, all of them both brutal warlords and devotees of the refined tea ceremony, gradually restored order. The first, Oda Nobunaga (**OH-da no-boo-NAG-ga**) (1534–1582), of daimyo background, proved a brilliant military strategist, once defeating an army of twenty-five thousand with his own small force of two thousand men. He usually performed a folk dance and then sang a delicate verse about life's transience before leading his samurai into bloody battles. Hideyoshi Toyotomi (1536–1598), of peasant origins and with ambitions abroad, dreamed of conquering China and demanded unsuccessfully that the Philippines' Spanish governor send him tribute. When Koreans refused his request to use Korea as a base for invading China, he instead attacked Korea in 1592; as already discussed, fierce Korean resistance repulsed his forces. The last of the three, Tokugawa Ieyasu (**ee-yeh-YAH-soo**) (1542–1616), one of Hideyoshi's chief generals, ended the civil war and became shogun in 1603.

During the civil war European traders and missionaries arrived in Japan, sparking cultural exchange and conflict. In 1542 the Portuguese reached Japan, causing a sensation, as we learn from a Japanese observer:

---

[21]Matsuo Basho, quoted in Noel F. Busch, *The Horizon Concise History of Japan* (New York: American Heritage, 1972), 64.

There came on a [merchant ship] a creature one couldn't put a name to, that [appeared to have] human form at first [glance], but might as well be a long-nosed goblin. Careful inquiry [revealed] that the creature was called a "Padre." The first thing one noticed was how long the nose was! It was like a wartless conch-shell.[22]

Europeans were equally astonished by Japan. An Italian Jesuit in the 1500s struggled with cultural differences:

Japan is a world the reverse of Europe. Hardly in anything do their ways conform to ours. They eat and dress differently. Their methods of doing business, their manner of sitting down, their buildings, their domestic arrangements are so unlike ours as to be beyond description or understanding.[23]

Despite mutual astonishment, Europeans had an economic, religious, and military impact. The Portuguese traded Chinese silk for Japanese gold, and soon Spanish and Dutch merchants arrived. Spanish Jesuit missionary Francis Xavier (1506–1552) began promoting Christianity in 1549. Thanks to Spanish and Portuguese missionaries, by 1600 perhaps 300,000 of the 18 million Japanese were Christians. Some daimyo on the southern island of Kyushu (KYOO-shoo) converted to gain closer relations with European traders and to acquire advanced gunpowder weapons. But many Japanese resented the missionaries' intolerance of Japanese faiths and customs, and could not comprehend the fierce competition between Portuguese and Spanish priests and between rival Catholic orders. Meanwhile, Japanese leaders viewed the Christian communities, often armed by missionaries, as posing a threat.

Thanks to the warfare, the Japanese were now more open to borrowing from outside, but they adopted what was useful to them: Western technologies. For example, they acquired, then quickly improved, Portuguese and Spanish muskets. Such European guns sharpened warfare and, since even non-samurai could obtain them, helped break down social class lines. In addition, the deadly violence resulting from guns often prompted peasants to seek solace in religion, some adopting Christianity. Japanese leaders became alarmed by this superior Western military and naval technology and the surprising effectiveness of Christian missionaries.

18-4b The Tokugawa Shogunate: Stability, Seclusion, and Society

Tokugawa Ieyasu, a great warrior, master strategist, and able administrator, but also cruel and treacherous, ended the civil war with a smashing victory in the Battle of Sekigahara, which involved at least eighty thousand soldiers on each side. After subduing his rivals, he established the Tokugawa Shogunate (1608–1868) at Tokyo, then known as Edo. Presiding over premodern Japan's most centralized state, the Tokugawa government mixed authoritarian centralization with a hierarchical social system led by samurai, somewhat resembling medieval European feudalism. A samurai scholar instrumental in developing the code of chivalry (*Bushido*; see Chapter 11) claimed that farmers, merchants, and artisans were too busy to master the warrior ways, while the samurai "is one who does not cultivate, manufacture, engage in trade. The business of the samurai consists in reflecting on his own station in life, in discharging loyal service to his master, in devoting himself to duty above all."[24] While the government and samurai ran the country, the imperial family, still based in their palace in Kyoto, remained powerless. To discourage rebellion, shoguns required some members of each daimyo family to live in Edo as hostages.

To stop the conflict between various Europeans and Catholic orders, the Tokugawa government eventually declared a seclusion policy, closing off Japan from Western pressure, ordering home Japanese traders in Southeast Asia, ejecting Western missionaries and merchants, and breaking the power of Christian communities. The shogun warned the Portuguese and Spanish that they should justly be killed, but he would spare their lives if they left Japan and never returned. When Japanese Christians rebelled in 1637, Tokugawa forces massacred thirty-seven thousand of them. But trade with China, Korea, and Southeast Asia continued, with Japan exporting its main mineral resource, silver. Meanwhile, several thousand Chinese merchants lived in Japanese ports, especially Nagasaki.

After 1639 a few Dutch traders, interested in commerce rather than Christian conversions, were allowed to keep a base on a small island, Deshima (DEH-shi-ma), in Nagasaki (nah-gah-SAH-kee) Bay. For the next two centuries Deshima served as Japan's only link to the Western world. The Dutch East Indies Company's Deshima station chief reported in 1650 that the many restrictions and humiliations they endured were worth the gains because Japan was the most profitable of the company's operations.

Tokugawa leaders believed that society could be frozen, but under the surface new social forces and tensions simmered. Even with restricted travel between cities or regions, merchants evaded the rules. Rapid population growth strained the country's resources, and peasant protests, riots, and uprisings became common. Led by Tokyo and Osaka, each with over a million inhabitants by 1800, cities became prosperous commercial centers, while merchants and their values became more influential.

Unlike some Asian women, Japanese women, never secluded, participated in community life. Some were literate, and a few became noted writers. European visitors in the 1500s were surprised that elite women had more independence than their European contemporaries. Nonetheless, the Tokugawa tried to restrict women. Women had few legal or property rights, faced arranged marriages, and were encouraged to be dependent on men. Severe laws against adultery punished only women. The Tokugawa advised peasants that "however good looking a wife may be, if she neglects her household duties by drinking tea or sight-seeing or rambling along the hillside, she must be divorced."[25]

[22]Quoted in Ronald P. Toby, "The 'Indianess' of Iberia and Changing Japanese Iconographies of Other," in Schwartz, *Implicit Understandings*, 326.
[23]Quoted in Edward Seidenstecker, *Japan* (New York: Time Inc., 1961), 58.
[24]Yamaga Soko, quoted in Conrad Totman, *A History of Japan* (Oxford, UK: Blackwell, 2000), 221.
[25]Quoted in Mikiso Hane, *Modern Japan: A Historical Survey*, 2nd ed. (Boulder, CO: Westview Press, 1992), 36.

IMAGE 18.8 **Kabuki Theater** The urban middle classes, especially the merchants and samurai, enjoyed kabuki drama. This eighteenth-century print by one of the most acclaimed artists, Moronobu, shows the audience enjoying a play about a vendetta involving two brothers.

Q What does the print tell us about the audience, stage and theater layout, and performances?

Distinctive new cultural forms emerged. In major cities entertainment districts developed that were known as the "floating world," containing restaurants, theaters, geisha houses, and brothels. A playwright described a lively district in Osaka: "Through the thronged streets young rakes were strolling, singing folk-songs as they went, reciting fragments of puppet dramas, or imitating famous actors at their dialogues. From the upper rooms of many a teahouse floated the gay plucking of a *samisen* [lute]."[26] Master artist Moronobu (**more-oh-NOH-boo**) introduced colorful woodblock prints, known as **ukiyo-e** (**oo-kee-YO-ee**), that celebrated the floating world and achieved wide distribution, making famous the actors, geishas, and courtesans portrayed. Later, landscapes, such as views of Mount Fuji, became popular woodcut themes. By the 1800s many European artists collected and were influenced by these prints.

New theater forms included the **bunraku** puppet theater and the racy **kabuki** drama, the favored entertainment of the urban merchant class. Kabuki featured gorgeous costumes, beautiful scenery, and scripts filled with violent passion. Men played all the roles. Professional female impersonators, highly honored, spent years mastering the voice, gestures, and other aspects of femininity. Seventeen-syllable **haiku** poems also became popular. Haiku portrayed the passage of time or briefly summarized some action or scene through a series of images. Hence, the samurai-turned-wanderer and greatest haiku poet, Matsuo Basho (**BAH-show**) (1644–1694), described a sudden event on a

ukiyo-e Colorful Japanese woodblock prints that celebrated the life of the "floating world," the urban entertainment districts.

bunraku The puppet theater of Tokugawa Japan.

kabuki The all-male and racy drama that became the favored entertainment of the urban population in Tokugawa Japan.

haiku The seventeen-syllable poem that proved an excellent vehicle for discussing the passage of time and the change of seasons in Early Modern Japan.

[26]Chikamatsu Monzaemon, quoted in *What Life Was Like Among Samurai and Shoguns* (Alexandria, VA: Time-Life Books, 1999), 118.

quiet pond: "An old pond. Frog jumps in. Sound of water." Another Basho poem commented on changing seasons and human emotions: "No blossoms and no moon, and he is drinking *sake* [rice wine], all alone."[27] The Japanese did not need to be lonely on a dark winter's night to appreciate Basho's delicate word art.

Tokugawa Japan largely enjoyed security, stability, and peace for two hundred and fifty years, but at a price. Although commerce thrived, Japan, like China, experienced no political transformation or social rejuvenation and thus was vulnerable to a later return of Western power. The Tokugawa had merely papered over the cracks. When the West intruded in the mid-nineteenth century, the latent tensions boiled over and the Tokugawa lost their grip on power. But Japan, unlike China, was able to respond creatively. Whereas Chinese feared cultural change more than political conquest, the Japanese were more afraid of conquest. Their history of borrowing from abroad made them uniquely prepared to assimilate Western techniques and customs to Japanese traditions, as they had done with Chinese, Korean, and Western imports in earlier eras. China and Japan eventually met the challenge from the West in very different ways.

KEY POINTS

▶ The Chinese helped Korea to rebuff a 1592 Japanese invasion, but as a result Korean culture began to liberalize and shed some customs borrowed from China.

▶ Ashikaga Japan saw tremendous economic and population growth, but it was undermined by a lengthy civil war, during which European merchants made incursions and introduced guns and Christianity, upsetting Japan's social order.

▶ The Tokugawa Shogunate ended Japan's civil war, restored strict order, and expelled European missionaries and traders, with the exception of a small group of Dutch traders who were uninterested in missionary work.

▶ Despite the Tokugawa leaders' attempt to halt change, the Japanese economy grew rapidly, tensions in Japanese society increased, and Japan's culture flourished in the urban "floating world" and in new theatrical and literary forms.

---

[27]The haiku are from Conrad Schirokauer, *A Brief History of Chinese and Japanese Civilizations*, 2nd ed. (San Diego, CA: Harcourt Brace Jovanovich, 1989), 373; and Harold G. Henderson, *An Introduction to Haiku: An Anthology of Poets from Basho to Shiki* (Garden City, NY: Doubleday Anchor, 1958), 40.

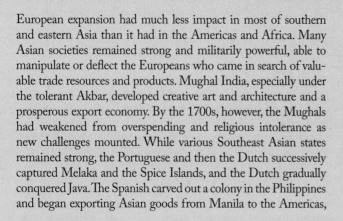

Chapter Summary

European expansion had much less impact in most of southern and eastern Asia than it had in the Americas and Africa. Many Asian societies remained strong and militarily powerful, able to manipulate or deflect the Europeans who came in search of valuable trade resources and products. Mughal India, especially under the tolerant Akbar, developed creative art and architecture and a prosperous export economy. By the 1700s, however, the Mughals had weakened from overspending and religious intolerance as new challenges mounted. While various Southeast Asian states remained strong, the Portuguese and then the Dutch successively captured Melaka and the Spice Islands, and the Dutch gradually conquered Java. The Spanish carved out a colony in the Philippines and began exporting Asian goods from Manila to the Americas, helping build a world economy. Increasing commerce more closely tied Southeast Asia to the growing world economy.

China during the late Ming and early Qing remained among the world's most powerful and prosperous countries, with outstanding leaders, extensive industry, and the world's largest commercial economy. However, while it remained creative in arts and philosophy, overpopulation and declining support for merchants eventually hindered China just as European pressures increased. Both Japan and Korea imposed policies of partial seclusion. After welcoming Western traders and missionaries, Japan restricted their access. The Tokugawa Shogunate maintained a rigid social and political system but also fostered a creative culture. Hence, European activity was only one of many factors influencing Asian societies.

Key Terms

Urdu 441	Hispanization 450	bunraku 461
Sikhs 443	Indios 450	kabuki 461
Moros 449	ukiyo-e 461	haiku 461

The Great Divergence Between Europe and Asia

In recent years historians have debated the roots of Europe's rise to world leadership, power, and wealth while other societies, especially in Asia, lost the political and economic leadership they once enjoyed (see the Debate the Historians: Eastern Predominance in the Intermediate World)—what some call "the great divergence." To many historians the surprising rise of Europe during the Early Modern Era needs explaining. It was not inevitable; history could have turned out very d ifferently. Historians have been researching and debating the question for several generations but in 2000 Kenneth Pomeranz, in his book *The Great Divergence*, introduced a new way of looking at the issue that generated a vigorous debate, perhaps the most important among specialists in Early Modern world economic history, that has continued for two decades now. Pomeranz and others raise important questions about the global economy's historical roots and how they connect to the world today.

The Problem

How, why, and when Europe, rather than a major Asian society like China, came to dominate nearly the entire world by the eighteenth or nineteenth century and foster an Industrial Revolution that transformed the world remain some of the principal questions of modern world history. If several Asian societies had an edge in power and wealth over other societies during most of the Intermediate Era, as many but by no means all historians believe, then why was the world so very different by 1800? Some western European societies, especially Britain, as well as, by the late nineteenth century, the United States, moved toward an unprecedented level of industrialization and affluence while once-influential Asian societies, including China, increasingly faced challenges from the West. And when did western Europe begin to diverge from other dynamic, commercialized economies, especially China's? The debate covers a variety of possible factors (among them culture, geography, resources, political institutions, the global economy, and colonialism) and divides into several schools of thought.

The Debate

Many historians who embrace what some consider a Eurocentric or "European exceptionalism" view argue that the great divergence began in the Intermediate Era (Middle Ages), when western Europe developed unique advantages that intensified after 1500. They contend that social, cultural, and political factors gave Europeans an advantage and a trajectory toward higher growth since the fifteenth or sixteenth century. David Landes believed Europe enjoyed a superior social and cultural heritage because its values and institutions promoted economic growth such as in the commercial revolution and rise of capitalism. In his view, European countries prospered because they were vital and open, valuing both hard work and knowledge, and these values led to increased economic productivity and positive attitudes toward change. Rodney Stark emphasizes what he considers a tradition unique to Christianity of stressing reason and progress. Offering another explanation, scholars such as E. L. Jones and Nathan Rosenberg stress the political pluralism represented by fiercely competing states. The chronic warfare between states stimulated a quest for increased revenues and more effective weapons. Furthermore, the flexibility of Western institutions, including the shift toward more representative government in England and Holland, made it easier to take advantage of overseas discoveries. Niall Ferguson contends that after 1400, western Europeans developed several "killer applications"—competition, consumerism, science, the work ethic, and modern medicine—that other societies lacked. In contrast to dynamic Europe, Landes and Jones argue, the rest of the world was static. China, in their view, had by 1700 reached an economic, political, and intellectual dead end, possessing wealth and power but introducing few inventions leading to any breakthroughs. Dutch scholar Peer Vries has reservations about both the Europe exceptionalism view and its critics, but considers the role of the state, especially in Britain, as critical for economic growth. Pomeranz and his colleagues, he argues, tend to exaggerate the resemblances between Western Europe and East Asia and neglect the role of culture and political institutions.

Historians known loosely as "the California School" (because some of the key figures, like Pomeranz, taught at universities in that state) have been critics of the traditional Eurocentric or "European exceptionalism" view of the Early Modern Era. They and other historians with similar views reject the notion of European social, cultural, and economic superiority. James Blaut and Andre Gunder Frank contended that the key to Europe's rise was not a unique culture but a polycentric world economy and European countries' acquisition of wealth, especially in precious metals, from their conquests in the Americas. Between 1500 and 1800 the colonized Americas supplied 85 percent of the world's silver and 70 percent of the gold, a huge windfall to European merchants and governments, who sold much of it to China in exchange for tea, silk, porcelain, and other valuable Chinese exports. The rise of the slavery-based plantation economy in the Americas produced additional profits for the Western colonizers. The sale of profitable American minerals and cash crops such as sugar not only stimulated European capitalism but also gave Europeans new advantages as they tapped into the lucrative Asian market. Blaut also believed that Europe benefited from being much closer than was Asia to the Americas. J. C. Sharman attributes the rise of Western empires in the Early Modern Era not to European military strength but to their deference to strong Asian and African states, disease that wiped out most of the American peoples, and maritime supremacy by default because most societies were land oriented and largely indifferent to maritime trade and war.

Many who dispute the claim that Western social and cultural traditions or the pluralistic state system provided a decisive advantage agree that Europeans capitalized on events, such as the American conquests and the acquisition of Asian and Middle Eastern technology, to foster economic growth. Scholars such as John Hobson, Alan Smith, L. S. Stavrianos, and Eric Wolf have shown that western European economies were rapidly commercializing from late medieval times and produced a full-blown commercial capitalism between 1450 and 1800 that helped generate a more widespread and powerful world economy. Nonetheless, while Europeans developed better weaponry and business organization, some historians conclude that Europe had no real advantage over China until the late eighteenth or early nineteenth centuries, when industrialization gave the British and later some other western Europeans a vastly superior technology.

Many historians disagree that China was at a dead end and in economic decline. They argue that China's commercial economy dwarfed all others, making China a major player in world trade. Chinese merchants and craftsmen were intensely competitive, hardly constrained by the Ming and Qing state. Indeed, China's commercial economy grew rapidly from the early Ming to the mid-1700s, producing abundant export products that were eagerly sought by merchants from all over Afro-Eurasia. In 1800 China still produced a third of all the world's manufactured goods and imported over half of all the silver mined in the Americas. Moreover, before 1800 Chinese in the commercialized core regions may have enjoyed as long lifespans and as high, if not higher, standards of living and per capita incomes as northwest Europeans.

In asking why sustained economic growth began first in northwestern Europe rather than in eastern Asia, Pomeranz argues that the densely populated Yangzi River Delta of China, Japan's Tokyo region, and possibly even India's Gujerat region were similar in many respects to the northwest European core regions, England and the Netherlands, in the seventeenth and eighteenth centuries, and that all these regions were facing similar ecological and demographic stress, such as overpopulation. The great divergence came sometime between 1750 and the early 1800s, he suggests, when one country, England, developed fossil fuels, especially its coal industry, for power while increasingly reaping the benefits of cheap, often slavery-produced resources from the Americas. China had used coal many centuries before Europe, but its remaining coal reserves were remote from major population centers. The availability of slave-produced American wealth and easily tapped coal reserves, Pomeranz suggests, put first England and then northwestern Europe on a completely new development path unavailable to China, Japan, and India, changing world history.

Scholars also question whether other Asian societies, including India, were in decline, even though their states were clearly weakening. By 1800 India could not match China's economy but still produced around a quarter of the world's industry, about the same as Europe. In the early Mughal era India enjoyed a far larger, more productive economy than England. Bengal in India benefitted from extensive domestic and foreign trade and highly efficient industry and agriculture, famous worldwide for shipbuilding and textile manufacturing. While many South Asian products found lucrative markets in Europe, European exports attracted few Indian buyers. Although the Mughal state was collapsing by the early 1700s and much of the subcontinent was under assault from increasing British imperialism, Indian manufactured goods still attracted a vigorous international trade. Indian historian Prasannan Parthasarathi, who disagrees with some California School findings, also views advanced regions of Europe and Asia as more alike than different and credits competition from Indian textiles and wood shortages from deforestation with prompting new spinning technologies and coal use in Britain.

With their many exports and imports, China and India remained the engines for the Eastern Hemisphere trading system well into the 1700s. Pomeranz, R. Bin Wong, Jack Goldstone, Andre Gunder Frank, and Parthasarathi suggest that eighteenth-century China, India, northwestern Europe, and perhaps Japan had comparable levels of economic development. Kavi Yasdani identifies four key areas where Asia was more advanced from the sixteenth through eighteenth centuries: China's civil service exam system, the cosmopolitan nature of the Mughal empire, better urban hygiene, and China and India mass-producing goods like porcelain and textiles. And Ottoman Egypt had a similar per capita income to France and other leading European countries in 1800. Indian scholar Amiya Kumar Bagchi agrees, stressing that western Europeans enjoyed no decisive advantage over China and India in economic production, consumption, and growth before Britain's Industrial Revolution and that China only fell behind in the 1850s. Furthermore, he argues, most Europeans saw little improvement in their lives until the late nineteenth century. But some recent studies suggest a "Little Divergence" in which England and the Low Countries separated themselves from the rest of Europe by the eighteenth century and may have had per capita incomes and wages higher than most (though not all) of the regions in China, India, Japan, and Ottoman Turkey while the rest of Europe lagged behind.

Evaluating the Debate

This debate will likely thrive for years, making thoughtful arguments on all sides. Some scholars see the rise of the West as inevitable, a result of certain advantageous trends building for centuries, while others argue that things could have turned out differently had Western nations not been able to exploit American resources and had China and perhaps India sustained their dynamism. The Industrial Revolution in Europe, beginning in the late 1700s, which gave Europeans the technology and wealth to achieve global dominance, may have been the product of long-standing

The China Tea Trade, 1790—1800 (oil on canvas)/Chinese School/PEABODY ESSEX MUSEUM/
Peabody Essex Museum, Salem, Massachusetts, USA/Bridgeman Images

IMAGE 18.9 **The Chinese Tea Trade** This fanciful painting, from the 1790s, shows tea estates in the mountains, boat transport of tea to the coastal ports, and warehouses where it was stored in chests for shipment abroad.

Q What can we learn about China and its foreign trade in the 1790s from the painting?

and unique European attitudes, or it may have resulted from a late shift in global economic power, fueled by American resources, that favored Europe and undermined China and India. Whether or not Europe was exceptionally enterprising or simply lucky in finding useful resources, the new, expanded world economy that emerged between 1500 and 1800 benefited primarily western Europe and later North America, but it eventually touched everyone, bringing about changes in many aspects of life around the world. Whatever the case, driven by globalization, for countries like China and India the great divergence turned into a great convergence by the later twentieth and early twenty-first centuries as they industrialized and raised large sections of their populations out of poverty. The great divergence debate may help us better comprehend the recent resurgence of Asia.

Exploring the Controversy

Historians emphasizing Europe's social, cultural, and political advantages include David S. Landes, *The Wealth and Power of Nations: Why Some Are So Rich and Some Are So Poor* (New York: Norton, 1998); Rodney Stark, *The Victory of Reason: How Christianity Led to Freedom, Capitalism, and Western Success* (New York: Random House, 2005); E. L. Jones, *The European Miracle: Environments, Economies and Geopolitics in the History of Europe and Asia*, 3rd ed. (Cambridge, UK: Cambridge University Press, 2003); Niall Ferguson, *Civilization: The West and the Rest* (New York: Penguin, 2012); and Nathan Rosenberg and L. E. Birdzell, Jr., *How the West Grew Rich* (New York: Basic Books, 1986). For a multifaceted view of the subject that finds problems and virtues in both approaches, see Peer Vries, *State, Economy and the Great Divergence: Great Britain and China, 1680s–1850s* (London: Bloomsbury, 2015) and *Via Peking Back to Manchester: Britain, the Industrial Revolution, and China* (Leiden, Netherlands: Leiden University, CNWS Publications, 2003).

Scholars dubious of innate European advantages include Andre Gunder Frank, *ReORIENT: Global Economy in the Asian Age* (Berkeley: University of California Press, 1998); James Blaut, *The Colonizer's Model of the World: Geographical Diffusionism and Eurocentric History* (New York: Guilford Press,

1993); Amiya Kumar Bagchi, *Perilous Passage: Mankind and the Global Ascendancy of Capital* (Lanham, MD: Rowman and Littlefield, 2005); J. C. Sharman, *Empires of the Weak: The Real Story of European Empires and the Creation of the New World Order* (Princeton, NJ: Princeton University Press, 2019); and John M. Hobson, *The Eastern Origins of Western Civilization* (New York: Cambridge University Press, 2004). On China's continuing strength, see Kenneth Pomeranz, *The Great Divergence: China, Europe, and the Making of the Modern World Economy* (Princeton, NJ: Princeton University Press, 2000) and R. Bin Wong, *China Transformed: Historical Change and the Limits of European Experience* (Ithaca, NY: Cornell University Press, 1997). On India, see Prasannan Parthasarathi, *Why Europe Grew Rich and India Did Not* (New York: Cambridge University Press, 2011) and Kaveh Yazdani, *India, Modernity and the Great Divergence: Mysore and Gujerat (17th to 19th C.)* (Leiden, Netherlands: Brill, 2017).

On the rise of the European-dominated world economy, see Alan K. Smith, *Creating a World Economy: Merchant Capital, Colonialism, and World Trade*, 1400–1825 (Boulder, CO: Westview Press, 1991); L. S. Stavrianos, *Global Rift: The Third World Comes of Age* (New York: William Morrow, 1981); Charles H. Parker, *Global Interactions in the Early Modern Age, 1400–1800* (New York: Cambridge University Press, 2010); and Eric Wolf, *Europe and the Peoples Without History* (Berkeley: University of California Press, 1983). For excellent discussions of the great divergence debate and related issues, see David D. Buck, "Was It Pluck or Luck That Made the West Grow Rich?" *Journal of World History* 10, no. 2 (Fall 1999): 413–430; Jonathan Daly, *Historians Debate the Rise of the West* (London: Routledge, 2015), and Jack Goldstone; *Why Europe?: The Rise of the West in World History, 1500–1850* (New York: McGraw-Hill, 2009).

Reflection Questions

1. What are some of the advantages many historians think Europeans possessed?
2. Why do some historians believe the great divergence between Asia and the West did not come until 1750 or after?
3. How did Western expansion into the Americas give some European countries an advantage over Asian countries in the global economy?

PART V

Global Imbalances in the Modern World, 1750–1945

CHAPTER OUTLINE

The imbalances in wealth and power between the world's societies in the nineteenth century became even wider in the early twentieth century, shaped in part by revolutions and innovations in western Europe and North America. After lengthy travels in the South Pacific, Asia, Africa, and Europe, in 1900 American writer Mark Twain, author of beloved novels about Tom Sawyer and Huckleberry Finn, became a critic of the Western imperialism that increased these imbalances, including the costly U.S. colonization of the Philippines as part of the Spanish-American War, writing in 1900 that "I left these [American] shores a red-hot imperialist. I wanted the American eagle to go screaming into the Pacific. But I have thought more since then. [Now] I am opposed to having the eagle put its talons on any other hand."[1] At the same time, Twain was being transported by the products of capitalism and industrialization, which created Western wealth and inspired new technologies such as the steamships and railroads that conveyed resources, products, and travelers like Twain over great distances.

During what some historians term the age of industrialization and globalization from the late 1700s to World War I, the combination of technological innovation, industrialization, and imperial expansion allowed the most powerful nations to build a global system more interconnected than ever before. The revolutionary changes that followed in politics, societies, and economies left few regions unaffected. Just as Spain and Portugal controlled Latin America until the early 1800s, by 1914, thanks in part to deadly new weapons, a half dozen Western nations ruled, or influenced the governments of, most Asian, African, and Caribbean peoples. Yet, other societies were not passive actors simply responding to the West. In whatever part of the world they lived, people were linked to a global system that, however imbalanced politically and economically, promoted the movement of products, ideas, institutions, technologies, and people, on a larger scale than ever before, across political boundaries. Due in part to the ravages of World War I and the Great Depression, by the 1930s people around the world, often using borrowed Western ideas such as nationalism and Marxism, were challenging Western political and economic power. The horrors and dislocations of World War II hastened the transition to a reconfigured and dynamic global system.

Global Empires

⇄ TRANSITIONS

Powerful societies had formed empires since ancient times, but over the centuries successive empires grew larger and more complex. In the mid-1700s over two-thirds of the world's people lived in one of several large, multiethnic Eurasian or American empires based largely on military power, especially gunpowder weapons. While most empires depended on agriculture, the British and Dutch empires relied more on world trade. Many of the eighteenth-century empires had crumbled by the early twentieth century. The Spanish, Portuguese, and British lost most of their territories in the Americas, and the Habsburg and Ottoman Empires, already under stress in the nineteenth century, were dismantled

---

[1]From Jim Zwick, ed., *Mark Twain's Weapons of Satire: Anti-Imperialist Writings on the Philippine-American War* (Syracuse, NY: Syracuse University Press, 1992), 3–5.

after World War I. In their place, modern empires emerged. Between 1870 and 1914, Britain and France established overseas empires on a grander scale than ever before in history, ruling colonies in Africa, Asia, and the Pacific; the Netherlands and Portugal still controlled large holdings in Southeast Asia and Africa, respectively; while Russia now controlled a vast expanse of Eurasia. On a smaller scale, Germany, Japan, and the United States also forged territorial empires. A huge portion of the globe, divided up into colonies or spheres of influence by the West, was incorporated into a Western-dominated world economic system. Influential British imperialist and author Rudyard Kipling summarized the rationale for exercising imperial power: "That they should take who have the power, And they should keep who can."[2]

Like empires throughout history, modern imperial states, whatever their democratic forms at home, harshly punished dissent in their colonies, jailing or exiling protest leaders such as Mohandas Gandhi in India, Sukarno in Indonesia, and Harry Thuku in Kenya. Sometimes protests, such as those led by Gandhi, forced Western colonizers to modify their policies, and some Western critics, like Twain, criticized colonialism. A nineteenth-century English wit, who sympathized with the colonized and often rebellious Irish, charged that "the moment the very name of Ireland is mentioned, the English seem to bid adieu to common feelings, common prudence and common sense, and to act with the barbarity of tyrants and the fatuity of idiots."[3]

Nations, Nationalisms, and Revolutions

🏛 SOCIETIES

Whether parts of empires or not, all over the world societies struggled to become nations that enjoyed self-government and a common identity. But Western peoples formed the most powerful nations, many aided by strong government structures and democratic practices that fostered debate; they also enjoyed economic dynamism, possessed advanced weapons, and engaged in fierce rivalries with each other. By the later 1800s the United States matched European capabilities and had similar imperial ambitions. Americans believed in their nation's Manifest Destiny, articulated by an influential U.S. politician: "God has marked the American people as his chosen nation to finally lead in the regeneration of the world."[4] By contrast, few people in Asian or African colonies, with often arbitrary borders, shared any sense of common identity, let alone a national mission; colonial governments were unpopular and usually viewed by the colonized as illegitimate. The ethnic diversity of most colonies—Dutch Indonesia and the Belgian Congo each contained several hundred ethnic groups—inhibited nationalist feeling and thus the formation of nationalist movements. Still, despite the barriers, nationalism spread,

often encouraged by travel, exile, or education. Venezuelan Simon Bolivar, Filipino Jose Rizal (rih-ZALL) (1861–1896), and Vietnamese Ho Chi Minh (1890–1969), all disenchanted with colonial restrictions, embraced a nationalist agenda while living in Europe. South Asian students discovered the writings of the England-born American revolutionary and exponent of liberty Tom Paine and wondered why their British rulers had ignored Paine's "rights of man" in India. Yan Fu, a Chinese student living in England in the 1870s, recalled spending "whole days and nights discussing differences and similarities in Chinese and Western thought and political institutions."[5] By 1900 Japan was a role model of nationalism and modernization for many Asians.

But nationalism was not always an imported sentiment. Many Asians had a sense of identity similar to nationalism long before the nineteenth century. People in Korea, Japan, and Vietnam, for example, had long enjoyed some national feeling based on shared religion, a common language, bureaucratic government, and the perception of one or more common enemies. Reflecting such national feeling, in 1898, Hawaii's last monarch, Queen Liliuokalani (luh-lee-uh-ohkuh-LAH-nee), pleaded with the United States not to colonize the islands, since her people's "form of government is as dear to them as yours is precious to you. Quite as warmly as you love your country, so they love theirs."[6] U.S. leaders ignored her pleas and annexed Hawaii. To resist colonial strategies, nationalists sought ways to regain the initiative and achieve independence. Indian nationalist Jawaharlal Nehru expressed the search for a successful anticolonial strategy: "What could we do? How could we pull India out of this quagmire of poverty and defeatism, which sucked her in?"[7]

Some societies needed major rebellions and revolutions to transform old discredited orders and create new nations. The American and French Revolutions of the later 1700s began an Age of Revolution and inspired people elsewhere to take up arms against unjust or outdated governments. During the mid-nineteenth century the Taiping (TIE-ping) Rebellion against China's Qing dynasty and the Indian Rebellion against the British East India Company, although they ultimately failed, provided fierce challenges to established governments in the world's two most populous societies. Early in the twentieth century, other revolutions overturned old governments and built nations in Mexico, Turkey, and China; the Chinese Revolution ended two thousand years of imperial control and established the foundation, however unstable, for a modern republic. The Russian Revolution of 1917 installed the world's first communist government, inspiring communist movements and revolutionary nationalists around the world.

The aftermath of World War I also generated new revolutionary upheavals and ideologies. Old states collapsed in eastern Europe, fascism spread in Germany and Japan in the economic shambles caused by the Great

[2]Quoted in L. S. Stavrianos, *Lifelines from Our Past: A New World History*, rev. ed. (Armonk, NY: M.E. Sharpe, 1997), 114.
[3]Rev. Sydney Smith, quoted in Frederic Delouche et al., *Illustrated History of Europe: A Unique Portrait of Europe's Common People* (New York: Barnes and Noble, 2001), 289.
[4]Senator Albert Beveridge of Indiana, quoted in Henry Allen, *What It Felt Like Living in the American Century* (New York: Pantheon, 2000), 7.
[5]Quoted in Benjamin Schwartz, *In Search of Wealth and Power: Yen Fu and the West* (New York: Harper Torchbooks, 1964), 29.
[6]Quoted in Scott B. Cook, *Colonial Encounters in the Age of High Imperialism* (New York: Longman, 1996), 100.
[7]From Clark D. Moore and David Eldridge, eds., *India Yesterday and Today* (New York: Bantam, 1970), 170.

Depression, and Spain erupted in civil war. In 1914 Marxism, the revolutionary socialist vision developed by Karl Marx (1818–1883), had relatively little influence outside of Germany and Russia, but less than two decades later in China the leader of the growing communist movement, Mao Zedong, contributed a vision of a new, unselfish socialist society. Mao believed that revolutionaries must work closely with local people, writing that "the people are the sea, we [communists] are the fish, so long as we can swim in the sea, we will survive."[8] By 1945 the ideology had mass support in many societies. Communist revolutionary movements percolated in China, Korea, Indonesia, and Vietnam.

Change in the Global System

⊨⊂ TRANSITIONS

During the Modern Era the global system expanded and changed as networks of trade and communication linking distant societies grew in number and extent. Western influence increased. For example, textbooks in French colonial schools, where the students were African, Afro-Caribbean, Arab, Asian, or Pacific Islander, celebrated the history of the French—"our ancestors the Gauls"—while children in the U.S.-ruled Philippines, a tropical and predominantly Catholic land, learned English from books showing American youngsters throwing snowballs, playing baseball, and attending Protestant church services. Americans tended to treat Filipinos indulgently, calling them "our little brown brothers." However, Western cultural influence was weak in some colonized societies, especially Muslim ones such as Egypt and northern Nigeria.

Countries gained or lost power in the global system depending on their wealth, type of government, and access to military power (see Debate the Historians: Modernization or World-System?). In 1750, Western overseas expansion, including military conquests, had already reshaped the Americas and some regions of Africa and southern Asia. Chinese, Indians, and western Europeans were the richest peoples at this time, the Chinese accounting for a third and India and western Europe each accounting for a fourth of the world's total economic production. Britain and China (or at least their more prosperous regions) may have enjoyed similar living standards, such as abundant food and long lifespans, until at least 1800. As late as the 1830s British observers reported that residents of London and the key Chinese trading city of Guangzhou (Canton) had a roughly comparable material life. By 1914, however, after a century and a half of Western industrialization, imperial expansion, and colonization, the global system had become more divided than ever before into rich and poor societies, which tended to overlap with the rulers and the ruled. Falling well behind the Western powers, India and China were now among the poorer countries. Meanwhile, a few Western nation-states—especially Great Britain, the United States, Germany, and France—had grown rich and powerful, enjoying substantial influence around the world and over the global economy. Because of their unparalleled military power, all four of these nations ruled colonial empires, from which they extracted valuable resources; played a leading role

Werner Forman/Universal Images Group/Getty Images

IMAGE V.1 **Queen Victoria as Viewed by a Nigerian Artist** This wooden mask from nineteenth-century southeastern Nigeria features a sculpture of the British monarch, to be fixed in a basketry cap and worn on the head during dance or funeral ceremonies.

Q What does the mask tell us about Nigerian customs and their perceptions of the British monarch?

in world trade; and tried to spread, with some success, their cultures and ideas. Some Western nations and Japan occupied an intermediate category. Most Western colonies in Asia, Africa, and the Caribbean and Latin American nations had little economic or political power in the world.

By 1914 living conditions and governments in rich countries differed dramatically from those in poor societies. Many Western nations boasted diversified economies, industrialization, high literacy rates, urbanization, large middle classes, independent mass media, competing political parties, and efficient, well-financed, often democratic governments. By contrast, the poor societies, especially Western colonies in Asia, Africa, and the Caribbean, where many people worked lands owned by foreign landlords or planters, were not industrialized and people earned meager wages. Few outside of the tiny local upper class—African chiefs, Indian princes, Javanese aristocrats—had access to formal education or political influence, and middle classes remained small. Economic growth was often determined by foreign investment and markets for cash crops and minerals rather than by local needs. Their general poverty and lack of options did not mean that all people in poor societies were always miserable. For

[8]Quoted in John A. Harrison, *China Since 1800* (New York: Harcourt, Brace, and World, 1967), 161.

generations many had learned how to survive despite poverty. Celebrating their survival skills in the early 1900s, the Indian writer and thinker Rabindranath Tagore found both triumph and tragedy in Indian peasant life through the ages, which "with its everyday contentment and misery, has always been there in the peasants' fields and village festivals, manifesting their … abiding humanity across all of history."[9] Western domination did not preclude cultural and scientific achievements by colonized people. For example, although their country was a British colony, various Indian writers, mathematicians, biochemists, and astrophysicists won international renown and even Nobel Prizes. For example, in Calcutta the experiments of Sir Chandrasekhara Raman (CHAHN-dra-See-ker-ah RAH-man) (1888–1970) led to significant advances in the theory of diffusion of light, for which he won the Nobel Prize in Physics in 1930. Women still faced many challenges but some were able, through talent and hard work, to overcome barriers and achieve their dreams. Hence in 1885 three women, from India, Syria, and Japan, became the first licensed female doctors in their countries after they graduated from the Women's Medical College in Pennsylvania, one of the only places in the world at that time where women could study medicine. Yet, during that era, American women could not vote and faced prejudice in attaining higher education.

Between 1914 and 1945 the global system underwent further changes. Wars were now sometimes world wars, titanic struggles that reshaped world politics, fought on a greater scale than ever before and on battlefields thousands of miles apart. World Wars I and II were the deadliest conflicts in history. And deadly pandemics could now spread around the world. Hence, the "Spanish flu" in 1918, sometimes called the greatest medical holocaust in history, killed more than double the deaths from World War I and perhaps many more than that; a third of the world's population became sick but survived. Severe economic problems in one powerful nation could also become a global disaster, as exemplified in the Great Depression of the 1930s, which had its roots in the United States but also the world economic structure; the catastrophe impacted nearly every society in one way or another. The United States became the world's richest, most powerful nation, while Germany temporarily lost wealth and power because of its defeat in World War I. Then during World War II, Germany, Italy, and Japan—all middle-ranking nations by the 1930s—challenged the rich nations—Britain, France, and the United States. Several Latin American nations and Turkey enjoyed enough economic growth and stability of government to move into the middle-ranking category by the 1940s.

The World Economy, Inequality, and Industrialization

NETWORKS

European influence on the world economy increased in the 1700s and 1800s when Western traders, supported by their governments, sought new natural resources and markets in the tropical world, thereby creating a truly global economy. By 1914 the entire world was enmeshed in a vast economic exchange that particularly benefited the more powerful nations. People often produced resources or manufactured goods—Middle Eastern oil, Indonesian coffee, British textiles, North American and South Asian cotton—for markets thousands of miles away. For instance, chocolate, whose use for over two millennia was confined to elites in Mexico, became popular among wealthy Europeans in the 1500s. Europe's Industrial Revolution, which provided manufactured goods to trade for resources, dramatically reshaped the Western economies in the 1800s but only slowly spread to other regions.

As had been the case for empires throughout history—from the Assyrian, Roman, Hellenistic, Chinese, Malian, and Inca to the Habsburg, Ottoman, Spanish, Dutch, and British—imperialism and colonialism enabled the transfer of wealth to the imperial nations to finance their own development. Many colonies developed economies that produced and exported only one or two primary resources, such as rice and rubber from French Vietnam, rubber and tin from British Malaya, sugar from Spanish Cuba, copper from British Northern Rhodesia (Zambia), and cocoa from the British Gold Coast. Most of these resource exports were transformed into consumer goods, such as rubber tires and chocolate candies, and sold in stores in Western nations to the profit of their merchants. Societies specializing in producing one or two natural resources were especially vulnerable to a changing world economy and the whims of Western consumers.

The world economy widened the wealth gap between societies. In 1500 the differences in per capita income and living standards between people in the richer regions—China, Japan, Southeast Asia, India, Ottoman Turkey, and western Europe—had probably been minor. These peoples were roughly only two to three times better off materially than the rural and city folk of the world's poorest farming societies. By 1900 the wealth gap between the richest and poorest societies had grown to about 10 to 1. This trend accelerated throughout the twentieth century, in part because the wealth produced in Western colonies seldom contributed to local development. Hence, by the 1950s the Belgian Congo still lacked all-weather roads linking the major cities and had only a few schools and health clinics for its millions of people. Unequal exchange generally came at the expense of colonized peoples, but some of them, including a few women, managed to capitalize on it. Hence in West Africa Omu Okwei (OH-moo AWK-way) (1872–1943), an Igbo, made a fortune trading palm oil for European imported goods, which she distributed widely in Nigeria through a vast network of women traders. Unequal economic exchange also fostered conflict over access to markets and resources. For example, British free trade policies sparked the Opium War with China in the mid-1800s as Britain needed to protect its opium exports from British India, which earned 20 percent of its colonial revenues from the trade. Britain's defeat of China in the war hastened China's decline.

Modern industrialization benefited Western nations. China and India had once been the world's leading manufacturing countries, and knowledge of Chinese mechanical devices probably stimulated several British inventions. Between 1750 and 1850, Britain took the lead in industrialization, and by the mid-1800s it was producing about half of the world's manufactured goods while China and India fell behind. Various other European nations, the United States, and Japan industrialized in the later 1800s. Industrialization gradually spread beyond Europe and North America, but at a highly uneven impact and pace. Western policies commonly discouraged other societies, especially colonies, from maintaining or opening industries that might compete with Western manufacturers. Hence, the British saw India not only as a market for their goods but also as a source of cash crops, such as jute and opium. In 1840 a British official boasted that his nation had "succeeded in converting India from a manufacturing country into a country exporting raw materials."[10] Although China, Persia, Egypt, the Ottoman Empire, and Mexico introduced textile industries in the nineteenth century, the British, nominally proponents of free trade, used stiff tariffs on imports to Britain to stifle many of these industries, thereby opening doors for the export of British fabrics and clothing to these countries.

Migrations

SOCIETIES

People have always been pushed to relocate by necessity or been drawn to new lands by opportunity, which often reshaped local environments and dramatically affected the societies, flora, and fauna that had occupied the land. But the rise of a modern world economy, and its constant quest for resources, markets, and labor, accelerated migration. Modern transportation networks, linked by larger and faster ships and later airplanes, facilitated the movement not only of commodities but also of people. Rapid population growth also spurred migration. Between 1800 and 1900 the world population grew from 900 million to 1.5 billion, with two-thirds of these people living in Asia. Some people escaped poverty and overcrowding by moving into nearby frontier regions, where they often mixed with local people, fostering hybrid cultures. Many others, more than 100 million between 1830 and 1914, left for distant lands. Some, such as enslaved Africans transported to the Americas, were taken from their homes unwillingly. In contrast, millions of Europeans and Asians sought, and often found, a better life in other countries, or what many of them considered "empty" frontier lands. For example, in the Americas, European settlers pushed into Native American lands, such as the Brazilian rain forests, Argentine grasslands, and North American woodlands; Native Americans were enslaved, killed, or pushed out. Similar events happened in Australia, New Zealand, South Africa, and Siberia. The settlers claimed they were bringing "progress" to "wild" areas that could be "developed." Hence, ignoring the Native Americans, the influential Benjamin Franklin wrote in 1784 about the "vast quantity of forest land we have yet to clear, and put in order for civilization."[11] But exploiting the land for "civilization" with plantations or mines often brought negative consequences such as destabilizing local cultures, deforestation, desertification, diminished diversity among local species, and climate change.

The major movement of Africans resulted from the trans-Atlantic slave trade, which reached its height between 1760 and 1800. During these years over seventy thousand people a year were herded onto crowded slave ships and shipped from Africa. Between 1800 and 1850 the annual export of Africans to the Americas ranged between 36,000 and 66,000. The great majority of Africans were landed in Brazil and the Caribbean islands, where people of African ancestry today account for a large part of the population. But the gradual abolition of slavery in the Americas eroded the trade in the 1800s. Abolition resulted in part from the efforts of some Western governments, often prompted by humanitarian organizations and Christian missionaries. Some abolitionists had themselves been slaves, such as Mary Prince, a slave from the British West Indies who was taken to London and freed; she argued eloquently in 1831: "All slaves want to be free. They work night and day, sick or well, till we are quite done up."[12] By the early 1900s slavery had declined significantly or been abolished in Africa, the Middle East, and Southeast Asia. The end of plantation slavery in the Americas opened the doors to recruitment of impoverished workers from Asia, who chiefly came voluntarily but under restrictive contracts that limited their rights by requiring them to work for years under harsh conditions.

Between 1500 and 1940 some sixty-eight million people left Europe, creating new societies in the Americas, Australia, New Zealand, and southern Africa. The largest movement came in the nineteenth and early twentieth centuries. For example, between 1820 and 1930 some thirty-two million Europeans moved to the United States, the major destination. The tendency to look toward Europe for inspiration was especially strong in Argentina, Chile, Canada, Australia, and New Zealand, where many immigrants and their descendants tended to maintain their native languages, churches, and social customs and to identify with their homeland. As a result, the numerous Italians in Argentina's capital, Buenos Aires, often spoke Italian, while Anglo-Argentines sent their children to private English-medium schools. Similarly, Canadians, Australians, and New Zealanders commonly revered the British crown. Immigrants often contributed much to their new lands. In the United States Scottish-born Andrew Carnegie (1835–1919) helped build the iron and steel industry and with his philanthropy sponsored libraries and education. Mexicans became essential to the agricultural and later the industrial economy of the United States, but often faced racism, harassment, and sometimes forced expulsion. Migrants from the Portuguese island of Madeira brought the prototype of the ukulele to Hawaii in the late 1800s, enriching Hawaiian and then world culture.

Pushed by poverty, overpopulation, or war, during this era peoples from eastern and southern Asia—Chinese, Japanese, Koreans, South Asians, Javanese, Filipinos—also emigrated in large numbers, usually by ship to distant shores. Some went voluntarily, seeking their fortunes abroad, while others were under some form of indenture, required to work for some term of years for one or another plantation, mine, or business. Many went in response to the demand among

[10]Quoted in Richard H. Robbins, *Global Problems and the Culture of Capitalism* (Boston: Allyn and Bacon, 1999), 90.

[11]Quoted in "Introduction" in Walter D. Wyman and Clifton Kroeber, eds., *The Frontier in Perspective* (Madison: University of Wisconsin Press, 1965), xviii.

[12]Quoted in Pamela Scully, "Race and Ethnicity in Women's and Gender History in Global Perspective," in *Women's History in Global Perspective*, ed. Bonnie G. Smith, vol. 1 (Urbana: University of Illinois Press, 2004), 207.

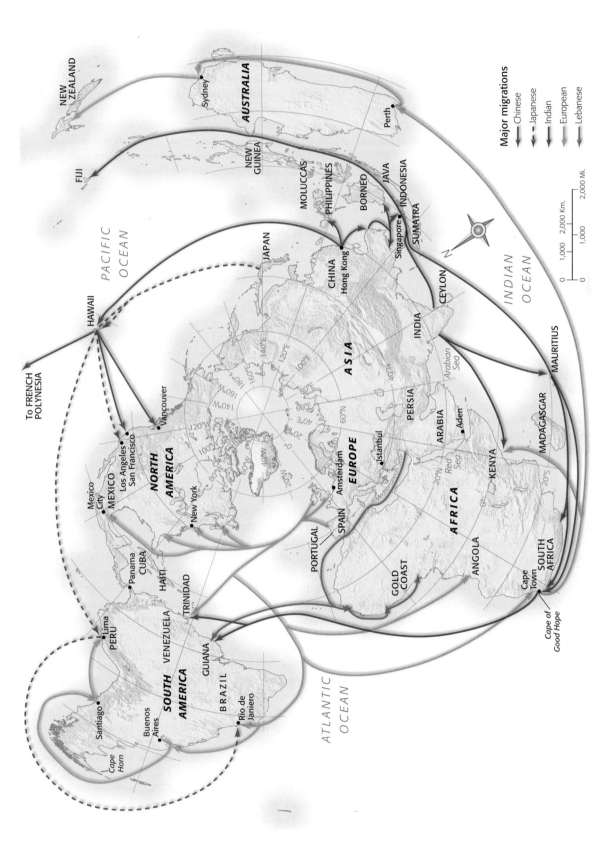

MAP V.1   Asian and European Migration, 1750–1940   During this era millions of Europeans emigrated to the Americas, South Africa, Australia, and New Zealand. Millions of Asians, especially Chinese and Indians, left their homes to work or settle in Southeast Asia, Africa, the Pacific islands, and the Americas. And millions of Africans were still being transported as slaves from west and central Africa across the Atlantic to the Americas.

Q   Which peoples had the longest and most difficult journeys, voluntary or involuntary, from their homelands to the lands where they would work or settle?

Western colonies and American nations for a labor force for the mines and plantations that supplied their wealth. As a result, Chinese mined tin in Southeast Asia and gold in California, Australia, and South Africa, while Indians worked on rubber plantations in British Malaya and sugar plantations in South Africa, Fiji in the South Pacific, Trinidad, and the Guianas in South America. Chinese also provided much of the labor to build the transcontinental railroad across the United States, where Filipinos became factory workers or farm laborers. Japanese took up farming in Brazil and California and worked on Hawaiian plantations. Immigrants often died from overwork or ill health and, as happened with Chinese in the western United States and Australia, sometimes suffered from violent attacks by local people who resented their presence. Yet, many Asians survived to raise families in their new homes. Today between 40 and 45 million Asians live outside, and often thousands of miles away from, their ancestral homelands. Chinese and Indians constituted the great majority of Asian migrants, settling in Southeast Asia while also establishing communities, often large, in the Americas, the Pacific and Indian Ocean islands, and parts of Africa. Their descendants became a vital presence in the world economy as merchants, miners, and plantation workers.

Today the majority of Chinese in Southeast Asia, the South Pacific and Indian Ocean islands, the Caribbean, and Latin America are engaged in commerce. A Chinese man who settled in New Zealand in the 1920s recalled the hard work that brought him success: "My generation really worked for a living. We had to open the shop at 7 A.M. and we closed [at] 1 A.M. Then we had to clean the shop. It was seldom before 2 A.M. before we got to bed."[13] The descendants of Chinese immigrants have constituted the most dynamic economic sector in Southeast Asia, with their money and initiative spurring the economic growth since 1970.

The Spread of Technologies

NETWORKS

The modern global system owed much to innovations in technology. Improved methods of communication and transportation allowed people, ideas, and products to travel farther and faster than ever before, enhancing networks of power and exchange. For much of history, communication over long distances had been slow, depending largely on beasts of burden carrying riders or pulling wagons, and later on sailing ships. In 500 BCE a message carried by successive riders on horses could travel the eighteen-hundred-mile length of the Persian Empire in nine days. Two millennia later, in the 1600s, it took Dutch ships some nine months to sail from Amsterdam to Dutch-ruled Java to deliver news and orders. Thanks to the Industrial Revolution, communications changed dramatically. In 1844 the first telegraph messages were exchanged between Washington and Baltimore. By 1861 submarine telegraph cables linked Britain to North America, prompting a poet to write: "Two mighty lands have shaken

hands, Across the deep blue sea; the world looks forward with new hope, Of better times to be."[14] The invention of the telephone in 1876 and radio in 1895 further increased the potential for communications. By the 1920s radio transmissions had become commonplace in industrial nations and British broadcasts could reach Canada, South Africa, India, and Australia. Radios became a major medium for entertainment and information in many households.

Some technologies conveyed people and commodities as well as messages, transforming peoples' lives around the world. Railroads carried goods and passengers, with telegraph messages smoothing their journeys by passing on traffic and weather information. By 1869 railroads connected the Pacific and Atlantic coasts of North America, and by 1903 determined travelers could ride the nine thousand miles between Paris and Siberia's Pacific coast. Steamships also linked the world. The opening of the one-hundred-five-mile Suez Canal in 1869 and the fifty-one-mile Panama Canal in 1914, both of which cost the lives of thousands of workers during their construction, greatly reduced travel times for

Photo 12/Universal Images Group/Getty Images

IMAGE V.2 **Singapore's Chinatown** By the early 1900s Singapore, a major Southeast Asian port and commercial crossroads, was predominantly Chinese in population. The bustling streets were lined by shops, workers' quarters, theaters, brothels, and street hawkers.

Q What does the photo suggest about Chinese life in Singapore in this era?

---

[13]Quoted in Ng Bickleen Fong, *The Chinese in New Zealand* (Hong Kong: Hong Kong University Press, 1959), 96.
[14]Quoted in J. R. McNeill and William H. McNeill, *The Human Web: A Bird's-Eye View of World History* (New York: W. W. Norton, 2003), 217.

many sea journeys and also made it easier and cheaper to ship resources from Asia and Latin America to Europe and North America. Now it only took a few weeks to sail from Shanghai or Singapore to New York or London. Political and economic leaders took advantage of the new travel opportunities. For example, seeking to forge diplomatic alliances and recruit laborers for his islands' plantations, in 1880–1881 Hawaii's king, David Kalakaua (**KAH-la-COW-ah**) (r. 1874–1891), sailed around the world by steamship, meeting the Japanese emperor, the Siamese king, the pope, and Britain's Queen Victoria, among others, and signing an agreement to import thousands of Japanese laborers to his kingdom. In the early 1900s motor cars and buses continued the revolution in land transportation, allowing people to more easily commute to city jobs and downtown stores or to travel between cities. After World War I thousands of middle-class Europeans and North Americans owned their own cars, and in the 1930s the first commercial air flights began, making long-distance journeys even faster.

New technologies devoted to warfare made it easier to kill more people and at a greater distance. Most of these weapons remained largely a monopoly of Western nations and Japan during this era, facilitating imperialism and contributing to the imbalances in global power. For example, white adventurers and settlers used the rifle invented by American Philo Remington (1816–1889), which was effective at fifteen hundred yards, to defeat, and seize the lands of, the Native Americans and the Australian Aborigines. In 1878 an Argentinean observed that the Remington rifle has left "the land strewn with the bodies of those [local Indians] who dared to oppose it."[15] Effective rifles also proved devastating in Africa against warriors armed only with spears and arrows. British-born American explorer Henry Stanley, working for the Belgium king, boasted of his use of repeating rifles and terrorism to destroy a hostile Congo village resisting Belgian colonizing plans: "I skirmish in their streets, drive them pell-mell into the woods beyond; with frantic haste I fire the huts, and end the scene by towing their canoes into midstream and setting them adrift."[16] Military weaponry quickly improved, including more powerful repeating guns. During World War I, since Western armies had an array of repeating weapons and field artillery as well as armored tanks and battleships, the two rival alliances in that war inflicted terrible casualties on each other. With air power in World War II, the methods of warfare were now more indiscriminate in their targets and more lethal than ever before in history. In 1945 the United States used the most deadly weapon in history, the atomic bomb, to force Japanese surrender and end World War II.

The Spread of Mass Cultures

NETWORKS

The revolution in communications and transportation technologies contributed to the creation and spread of mass cultures, popular entertainments appealing to a large audience that often crossed class divisions and national borders. People were increasingly exposed to cultural products, such as film and music, and pastimes, such as sports, that were common in other regions of their countries or imported from abroad. The media disseminated mass culture, reporting on film stars and sports events or playing popular music. As literacy rates rose, print media gained particular influence. Newspapers made available news and opinions in hundreds of languages. Popular books, from Arab detective novels to romances written in South Africa's Xhosa (**KHO-sa**) language, competed with classic works of philosophy and religion for the hearts and minds of readers.

By spreading cultural influences into other societies, mass communications and increased travel often fostered Westernization. Some organizations, such as the Red Cross, and social movements, such as feminism, crossed borders. For example, women in China, Japan, Indonesia, Egypt, and Chile, inspired in part by European and North American feminist movements, sought to adopt women's rights to their own societies. The winning of women's suffrage resulted from the efforts of women worldwide such as Emily Pankhurst in Britain, Susan B. Anthony in the United States, and Ichikawa Fusae in Japan. American film stars such as Charlie Chaplin, born in Britain, became known throughout the world, and U.S.-born jazz musicians often made a living playing the nightclubs of Europe and Asia, where they inspired local musicians to take up jazz. Many societies adopted and excelled in Western sports. For example, West Indians and South Asians became skilled in British cricket; India's Prince Ranjitsinhji (**RAHN-jeet-SING-jee**) (1872–1933) became one of the world's best players. India's field hockey team remained unbeaten in the Olympics from 1932 through 1960. European football (soccer) became an international sport, played and watched all over the world. Influences from non-Western cultures also spread, contributing to a creative cultural mixing. For example, in the eighteenth and nineteenth centuries the growing Western interest in Chinese painting, Japanese prints, Indonesian gamelan music, and African woodcarvings influenced Western arts. Hence, in the 1890s Dutch artist Vincent Van Gogh greatly admired, and was inspired by, the woodblock prints of Japanese artist

---

[15]Quoted in L. S. Stavrianos, "The Global Redistribution of Man," in *World Migration in Modern Times*, ed. Franklin D. Scott (Englewood Cliffs, NJ: Prentice-Hall, 1968), 170.
[16]Quoted in Daniel R. Headrick, *The Tools of Empire: Technology and European Imperialism in the Nineteenth Century* (New York: Oxford University Press. 1981), 116.

Hokusai and collected over five hundred Japanese prints. Many European artists, including Pablo Picasso, borrowed concepts from African masks, bronzes, and statues. Later, in the 1930s, Indian film and music became popular in Southeast Asia and the Middle East. Cuban music, a mix of African and Western traditions, developed a large following in West and Central Africa, where it blended with local styles. Hawaiian music, which mixed Polynesian and Western influences, became popular in the continental United States in the 1920s and later developed a following in Southeast Asia. People found ways to combine imported ideas, whatever their source, with their own traditions. For example, in his lyrical suite of 1930, *Bachianas Brasileiras*, Brazilian composer Heitor Villa-Lobos **(HAY-tore VEE-ya-LOW-bos)** (1887–1959) adapted the Baroque influences of German composer Johann Sebastian Bach (1685–1750) to Brazilian folk and popular music.

As people followed world events in newspapers and radio newscasts, global crises became more widely known. An avid news follower, the Trinidad calypso singer who humorously called himself Atilla the Hun appraised the devastation in the world of the later 1930s:

> *All we can hear is of unrest, riots, revolutions; There is war in Spain and China. Man using all his skill and ingenuity making weapons to destroy humanity. In the [Italian invasion of Ethiopia] it is said, over six hundred thousand maimed and dead. The grim reaper has taken a gigantic toll. Why all the bloodshed and devastation, Decimating the earth's population? Why can't this warfare cease? All that the tortured world needs is peace.[17]*

Soon after Atilla's plea, World War II raised the level of violence even further, providing a fitting end to a turbulent, violent era during which the world's people had become more closely linked into a common global system.

---

[17]Quoted in Gordon Rohlehr, *Calypso and Society in Pre-Independence Trinidad* (Port of Spain: Gordon Rohlehr, 1990), 80–81.

Modern Transitions: Revolutions, Industries, Ideologies, Empires, 1750–1914

From this foul drain the greatest stream of human industry flows out to fertilize the whole world. From this filthy sewer pure gold flows. Here humanity attains its most complete development and its most brutish.

—French writer Alexis de Tocqueville on Manchester, England, 1835[1]

IMAGE 19.1 **Crystal Palace Exposition of 1851** Attracting more than six million visitors, the Great Exhibition, held at the Crystal Palace in London in 1851, showcased industrial products and the companies that produced them from all over the world but especially from Europe. This painting shows the inauguration, opened by Queen Victoria.

Q What features of the exposition and inauguration stand out in this painting?

[1]Quoted in Eric Hobsbawm, *The Age of Revolution, 1789–1848* (New York: New American Library, 1962), 44.

On a spring day in 1851 Londoners celebrated their era's technological achievements. People of all social classes, from bankers and nobles to sailors, day laborers, and barmaids, headed for the spectacular new Crystal Palace in Hyde Park for the official opening, led by Queen Victoria, of the Great Exhibition celebrating "The Works of Industry of All Nations." The less affluent walked while the wealthy rode in horse-drawn carriages or steam-powered buses. Some came by railroad from other British cities or by steamships from France and Belgium to honor progress. The first "world's fair" featured displays by fourteen thousand firms showcasing British industrial leadership and the mineral basis such as coal and iron ore. The hall of machinery contained inventions that were revolutionizing British life: power textile looms, hydraulic presses, printing presses, marine engines, and locomotives that could attain an unimaginable sixty miles per hour. Another hall featured industrial products that British merchants sold all over the world, including fine wool, cotton, linen, and silk textiles. Manchester, condemned as a "foul drain" but praised for fostering development and progress, made many products. Nearly half of the exhibitors represented other European and North American countries, illustrating industrialization's spread.

Since its beginning three-quarters of a century earlier, industrialization was already transforming Europe's social and physical landscapes. The British, enamored with progress, considered modern industry, economic growth, and creative science humanity's triumph over the natural world. Industrialization certainly enhanced European and North American economic and military power around the world. Political revolutions and new ideologies also redefined Europe and the Americas between 1750 and 1914. Great Britain, France, Germany, and Russia emerged as the main European powers, while the United States became the strongest American country. But the trends yielded mixed blessings. The British writer Charles Dickens, commenting on the French Revolution, summed up the era: "It was the best of times, it was the worst of times. It was the age of wisdom, it was the age of foolishness, it was the season of light, it was the season of darkness, it was the spring of hope, it was the winter of despair."[2] These trends had also sparked a renewal of imperialism, with various European nations acquiring or expanding empires in Asia and Africa.

---

[2]From Charles Dickens, *A Tale of Two Cities* (New York: Bantam, 1989), 1.

19-1 The Age of Revolution

TRANSITIONS   SOCIETIES

Q How did the Caribbean and Latin American revolutions compare with those in North America and Europe?

Change has been a constant of human history but much of it was gradual. The Modern Era was a time when more dramatic transformations rocked many societies and reshaped the world. The **Age of Revolution**

Age of Revolution The period from the 1770s through the 1840s when revolutions rocked North America, Europe, the Caribbean, and Latin America.

CONNECTION to TODAY

Do you see any similarities between the revolutions of this era in Europe and the Americas and those of the twentieth century in Asia, Africa, Russia, and the Americas?

(1770s–1840s) refers to the period when violent upheavals rocked North America, Europe, the Caribbean, and Latin America as revolutionaries seized power through armed violence. While political revolutions changed governments' personnel and structure, social revolutions transformed both the political and social order. The American Revolution launched the era, ending British colonial

	1700	1750	1800

EUROPE

1770s–1840s Age of Revolution
1770s–1870s First Industrial Revolution
1774 James Watt's first rotary steam engine
1776 Adam Smith's *The Wealth of Nations*
1789–1815 French Revolution
1791–1792 Constitutional state in Poland-Lithuania
1800 British Act of Union
1804 Crowning of Napoleon as emperor of France
1810–1811 Height of Napoleon's empire
1815 Defeat of Napoleon at Battle of Waterloo; Congress of Vienna
1821–1830 Greek war of independence

THE AMERICAS

1770s–1840s Age of Revolution
1773 Boston Tea Party
1776 American Declaration of Independence
1776–1783 American Revolution
1783 Britain's recognition of U.S. independence
1787 U.S. constitutional convention; Northwest Ordinance for forming new states
1791–1804 Haitian Revolution
1808 Move of Portuguese royal family to Brazil
1810–1811 First Mexican revolution
1810–1826 Spanish-American wars of independence
1816 Argentine independence
1821 Founding of Gran Colombian republic by Bolivar
1822 Mexican independence; Dom Pedro emperor of Brazil

rule and forming a new, more democratic government. The French Revolution, the major social revolution, overthrew discredited royalty and aristocratic privilege, inspiring other peoples to seek radical changes in states, ideologies, and class structures. As in British North America, dissatisfaction with colonialism festered in the Caribbean and Spanish America, sparking revolutions and wars of independence.

These revolutions, brutal but momentous events in modern world history, had much in common. Though often well educated and from middle-class or upper-class backgrounds, revolutionary leaders mobilized disenchanted peasants and urban workers. Many revolutions, including the French, moved from moderate to more extreme actions such as purging dissidents, rivals, or opponents. Although they replaced repressive and inequitable systems, few revolutionaries satisfied their people's demands.

19-1a British Colonialism and the American Revolution

In the late 1700s Europeans and Latin Americans watched fascinated as disaffected citizens in the thirteen British colonies in North America ended colonial rule and established the United States. The struggle has taken on a mythic quality for Americans, from the Boston Tea Party and Paul Revere's ride to the Battle of Yorktown and the Declaration of Independence. But historians still vigorously debate all of the events, the causes and consequences, and whether the struggle should be viewed as a civil war between colonists, local uprising against colonial government, or a global conflict on land and sea between Britain and France on three continents, with the colonies as mainly a battlefront in a huge war. American revolutionary leaders,

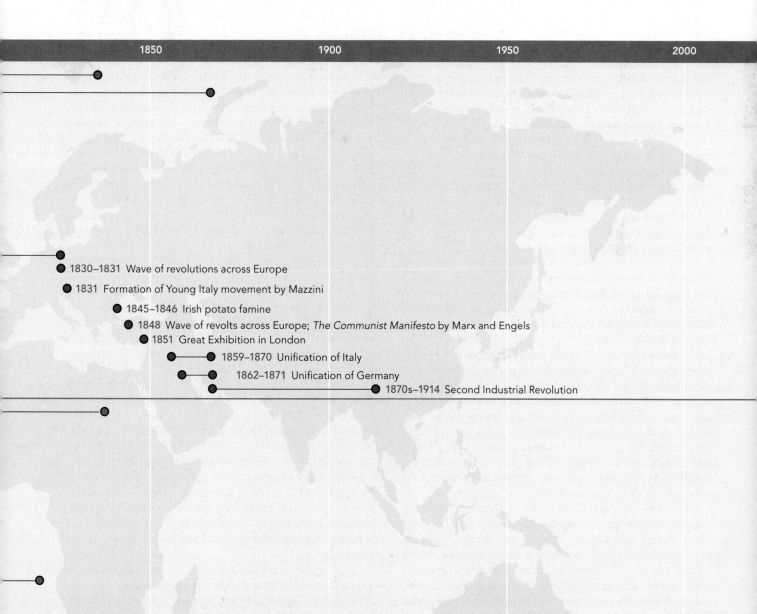

1850   1900   1950   2000

1830–1831 Wave of revolutions across Europe

1831 Formation of Young Italy movement by Mazzini

1845–1846 Irish potato famine

1848 Wave of revolts across Europe; *The Communist Manifesto* by Marx and Engels

1851 Great Exhibition in London

1859–1870 Unification of Italy

1862–1871 Unification of Germany

1870s–1914 Second Industrial Revolution

1830 Independence of Colombia, Venezuela, and Ecuador

1839 Division of Central American states

proclaiming optimistic Enlightenment political theories such as democracy and personal freedom, formed a new representative government that many hoped reflected an enlightened age of reason.

The revolution was rooted in several centuries of British and American history, including complex struggles between crown and parliament as well as between Catholics and Protestants for supremacy in the British world. In the 1600s England underwent several political transitions, from absolute monarchy to a brutal civil war and repressive republic to a constitutional monarchy (the "Glorious Revolution") and a Parliamentary act in 1689 that established people's rights and liberties and royal succession, as well as the rise of capitalism and overseas exploration, which led to English colonies on the eastern seaboard of North America and the Caribbean (see Chapter 15). In the mid-1700s Britain's hold on these colonies seemed strong. Each colony from New Hampshire to Georgia had unique institutions and economies. The southern colonies depended largely on plantation slavery, while the northern colonies had a more balanced economy that combined commerce and manufacturing with farming. Only two million persons lived in the colonies; the largest town, Boston, had twenty thousand residents. A fifth of the colonial population was African American, mostly slaves concentrated in the southern plantation zone. White American colonists, generally prosperous, enjoyed considerable self-government and religious toleration, voted for local assemblies and mayors if they were adult males with sufficient property, faced much lighter taxes than people in Britain, and eagerly consumed British culture.

But tensions increased. Some colonists considered the British king, George III, a tyrant and perhaps even insane. But while he was a much more powerful monarch than Britain has today, he was not an autocrat since he had to answer to an elected House of Commons and prime minister. Parliamentarians could, and some did, heckle British war plans, and some in the British press sided with the Americans. Many colonists, claiming the label of Americans, felt divorced from Britain and increasingly resented British policies, such as taxation without representation in the British Parliament. Some historians argue that unhappiness about the lack of representation outweighed discontent about taxes. Britain also placed more restrictions than before on local American manufacturing. Clumsy British attempts to raise taxes, enforce long-ignored laws, and reserve coveted land west of the Appalachians for Native Americans angered many colonists, prompting boycotts of British goods. In 1773, protesters of a higher tea tax, dressed as Native Americans, raided three British ships in Boston harbor and dumped their cargo of tea overboard, an event known as the Boston Tea Party.

Clashes increased between colonists favoring independence, or Patriots, and those opposed, called Loyalists. Most Patriot and Loyalist leaders were wealthy lawyers, physicians, journalists, merchants, and landowners. Patriot leaders, admiring European Enlightenment thinkers such as John Locke in England and Baron de Montesquieu in France, favored democracy and a republic. The writings of antiroyalist Englishman Tom Paine (1737–1809), an immigrant sailor and teacher turned journalist, promoted independence, church–state separation, social equality, women's rights, abolition of slavery, and other ideas then considered radical. Paine's passionate pamphlet *Common Sense*, urging Americans to oppose tyranny and forcibly free themselves to "begin the world over again," helped galvanize public opinion against unrepresentative colonial rule.

The colonies' many competing churches and schools of thought fostered intellectual diversity. Some Patriots were devout Protestants or Catholics, others free thinkers. Some, including Paine, Thomas Jefferson, James Madison, Benjamin Franklin, and George Washington, were deists, believing in an impersonal creator who left humanity alone, and were often suspicious of organized churches. Patriot leaders reflected their times: some owned slaves, disliked or feared Native Americans, smuggled, took mistresses, had illegitimate children (sometimes from enslaved women), and, like many male colonists, drank heavily.

After preliminary American–British skirmishes, delegates met, and on July 4, 1776, approved the Declaration of Independence from the British crown, written largely by Thomas Jefferson (1743–1826), a Virginia planter. The Declaration preamble stated, "We hold these truths to be self-evident, that all men are created equal, that they are endowed by their Creator with certain inalienable Rights, that among these are Life, Liberty and the pursuit of Happiness."[3] Eight of the 56 signers were born in Britain. Reflecting the prejudices of the day, the document did not mention women, slaves, or Native Americans as having rights. Indeed, the last of the twenty-seven accusations in the Declaration complained that the king "excited domestic insurrections [slave rebellions] against us" and brought on "the inhabitants of our frontiers" (Native Americans), suggesting that racial fears played a key role. A Baltimore publisher, Mary Katherine Goddard, the sole female signer of the Declaration, printed and distributed the document, ensuring its wide availability. Some historians argue that in some respects the Declaration was less a demand to George II, who was well aware of colonial discontent, than a plea for support from foreign powers, especially Britain's enemies France and Spain (both ruled by absolute monarchs). Both France and Spain did aid the Patriot cause with arms, money, volunteer soldiers, and naval power. This support made the colonies a battle front in a larger global war involving Britain, France, Spain, Holland, Jamaica, Gibraltar, and India. But perhaps a third of colonists remained Loyalists, and many others, especially less affluent whites, were neutral or apathetic. A revolutionary army organized and commanded by George Washington (1732–1799), a wealthy Virginia farmer and decorated veteran of earlier wars against France and its Native American allies, then fought the British and their allies for six bitter years, described by Tom Paine as "the times that try men's souls."

During the war, Patriot women raised funds, served as cooks and nurses in army camps, and engaged in sabotage and spying. A few, disguising themselves as men, joined the combat. Perhaps the most famous of them, Deborah Sampson, served

---

[3]From David A. Hollinger and Charles Capper, eds., *The American Intellectual Tradition: A Sourcebook*, vol. 1, 2nd ed. (New York: Oxford University Press, 1993), 131.

at least seventeen months in the Continental Army and was wounded at least twice. Britain's rivals, France and Spain, aided the Patriot cause. Many Native Americans, resenting colonists for aggressively occupying Indian lands, and some black slaves, promised their freedom by a British general, supported Britain. Some Loyalists and British officials also accused Patriots of hypocrisy, wanting their freedom while maintaining slavery and exploitation for nonwhites. But the American defeat of British forces at Yorktown, Virginia, in 1781 proved decisive, and Britain recognized American independence in 1783. Despite their democratic values, after the war Patriots treated Loyalists harshly, confiscating their land and jailing them. Ultimately 100,000 Loyalists were expelled or fled to Canada or England. The thirteen former colonies formed an independent federation, the United States of America, and the founders then debated the relative powers of states and a national government that could unite them. The first weak confederation proved unworkable. Seeking a stronger central government, in 1787 delegates approved a constitution, mostly written by James Madison (1751–1836), a well-educated Virginia planter, that established an elected president and a congress presiding over a federal system that granted the states many powers. Delegates then elected war hero Washington (g. 1789–1797), admired for his integrity and managerial skills, as the republic's first president. The first elected congress approved ten constitutional amendments, known as the Bill of Rights, enshrining Enlightenment values such as freedom of speech, assembly, press, and religion.

However, the new republic made no effort to transform the social order by challenging slavery, recognizing Native American claims to land, or expanding voting rights even to all white men, much less nonwhite men and all women. Although some Patriots, including Washington, freed their slaves and most northern states gradually abolished slavery, blacks fighting for Britain were often executed or re-enslaved. Some black loyalists left for Nova Scotia in Canada and later some of them emigrated to Sierra Leone in West Africa. Native Americans watched bitterly as free Americans claimed and settled most Native American land east of the Mississippi River after the U.S. Congress approved the Northwest Ordinance, allowing frontier settlements to join the United States. Women did not gain equal rights with men, despite sacrificing to win independence and managing their absent husbands' shops, businesses, and farms during the war. However, new laws made it somewhat easier for women, like men, to obtain a divorce.

Americans, believing they had formed a society unique to history, an idea known as American "exceptionalism," considered themselves the world's most democratic, individualistic, enterprising, prosperous, technological, and self-determining society, unhindered by history's burdens. Yet, Americans also contended that their ideas and institutions were relevant for everyone, agreeing with Puritan Massachusetts governor John Winthrop's claim in 1630 that his new society constituted a "City upon a Hill, [with] the eyes of all people upon us."[4] Jefferson declared America a standing monument and example for the world. These attitudes remained powerful in American thought.

19-1b The French Revolution

As with the American Revolution, historians have argued over the French Revolution and its results and impacts on France today. The French Revolution electrified Europe by replacing the monarchy with a republic and spreading values of liberty and social equality, but it also generated terrible violence, despotic leaders, and long years of war, reshaping Europe. The Revolution preached "liberty, equality, and fraternity" and a fairer wealth distribution, and the middle classes took over government in the name of the common people. But the Revolution also plunged Europe into a prolonged crisis and wars between France and its European rivals, who feared the spread of radical ideas and sought to restore French royal government.

The Revolution had many causes. Aiding the anti-British cause in the American War of Independence worsened long-standing financial problems rooted in an unjust economic system that badly needed reform. Exempting Roman Catholic clergy and privileged nobility from most direct taxes put the entire burden mostly on artisans and peasants. Several bad harvests, food shortages, high prices, and high unemployment spurred resentment. People believed, erroneously, that the difficulty the poor had in buying bread led Marie-Antoinette, the king's wife, to contemptuously remark: "Let them eat cake."

To calm rising passions, King Louis XVI (1754–1793) called the Estates General, a long-dormant consultative body including representatives of the clergy, the nobility, and finally a Third Estate comprising elected representatives from the middle classes and peasants. The Third Estate's leaders, representing most of the population, demanded influence reflecting their numbers. Stalemated in the Estates General, Third Estate delegates, some inspired by Enlightenment thinkers and the American Revolution, formed a rival national assembly and began writing a new French constitution. In response, the king called in the army to restore order, provoking anger and violence.

The Revolution erupted in Paris in 1789 after armed crowds stormed the Bastille, the royal prison and hated symbol of tyranny, releasing prisoners and seizing gunpowder and cannon. The date of the bloody but inspirational Bastille attack (July 14) later became France's national holiday. As both men and women took up arms, the terrified nobility fled. Third Estate members, after forming a new Constituent Assembly, adopted the Declaration of the Rights of Man and of the Citizen, which was strongly influenced by the English Bill of Rights of 1689 and the new United States constitution. The Declaration announced that all people everywhere had a natural right to liberty, property, equality, security, religious toleration, and freedom of expression, press, and association. A new constitution made the king bound by laws and subject to an elected assembly, outlawed slavery, and reorganized and weakened the church, confiscating the higher clergy's vast wealth. Dramatic French political change inspired other Europeans. In 1791 reformers in Poland-Lithuania reshaped

---

[4]Quoted in William Appleman Williams, *America Confronts a Revolutionary World, 1775–1976* (New York: William Morrow, 1976), 15, 25.

Storming of the Bastille, 14th July 1789 (oil on canvas)/French School, (18th century)/RUE DES ARCHIVES (RDA)/Musee de la Ville de Paris, Musee Carnavalet, Paris, France/Bridgeman Images

IMAGE 19.2 **Storming the Bastille** This painting celebrates the taking of the Bastille, a castle prison in Paris that symbolized hated royal rule, by armed citizens and soldiers on July 14, 1789. The governor and his officials are led out and will soon be executed.

Q What does this painting reveal about the fort and its taking?

the state, expanding voting rights. But Russia, supported by Polish nobility, crushed the reformist government.

With several European states demanding restoration of royal power, French revolutionary leaders declared war on Austria and Prussia in 1792, followed later by war with more nations including Britain, Russia, and Spain. The army recruited volunteers, identifying the defense of France with revolutionary ideals and proclaiming that "young men shall go forth in battle, married men shall forge weapons, women shall make tents and clothing, and shall serve in hospitals."[5] A national convention, elected by universal male suffrage, made France a republic, ending the monarchy. In the name of the world's people, France crusaded to end absolute monarchies and social inequality in Europe. With patriotic enthusiasm the French public rallied behind the revolutionary government, singing a song, "Marseillaise" (**mar-sye-EZ**), that was written as a call to oppose tyranny and that is now France's national anthem. In 1793 revolutionaries executed King Louis XVI for treason.

Military conflict intensified internal dissent and economic problems in

Jacobins A radical faction in the French Revolution that believed civil rights had to be set aside in a crisis and that executed thousands of French citizens.

France. Some leaders emphasized preserving the Revolution's liberal principles. However, a more radical faction, the **Jacobins** (**JAK-uh-binz**), believing these rights had to be postponed, seized the state and imposed a dictatorship to promote internal security. The Jacobins' Committee of Public Safety used terror against real or imagined opponents, often cutting off their victims' heads in public. They executed perhaps forty thousand French citizens, mostly rebellious peasants and provincial leaders, and arrested tens of thousands more, often on flimsy evidence. The Jacobins' leader, Maximilien Robespierre (1758–1794), a lawyer and once an idealistic humanist, became the most zealous promoter of terror against alleged counterrevolutionaries, some his former allies. As the violence and radicalism intensified, sowing dissention, some Jacobin leaders, including Robespierre, were executed. The terror abated when Jacobins lost power in 1795, but several constructive Jacobin policies endured, including guaranteeing all children the right to public education.

Although not all its accomplishments proved long-lasting, the Revolution created a new order that inspired generations of revolutionaries to come. Much of the vocabulary of modern politics emerged, including terms such as *conservative* and *right-wing*, referring to those who favored retaining the status quo or restoring the past, and *liberal* and *left-wing*, meaning progressives wanting faster change. Revolutionary France also transformed warfare by introducing conscription and promotion through the ranks. France turned the countries it occupied or conquered, such as Belgium, into "sister republics" where revolutionary governments promoted human rights.

But the Jacobins' terrible violence undermined personal liberty, dampening the Revolution's appeal. The French trauma of anarchy and despotism turned North Americans against revolutions. Observers also debated whether the "Rights of Man" included women. Olympe de Gouges (1748–1793), a French butcher's daughter, published a manifesto complaining that women were excluded from decision making and tried to organize a female militia to fight for France. She was executed by the Jacobins. A British campaigner for women's rights, Mary Wollstonecraft (1759–1797), wrote the *Vindication of*

[5]Quoted in Peter N. Stearns, *Life and Society in the West: The Modern Centuries* (San Diego, CA: Harcourt Brace Jovanovich, 1988), 164.

the Rights of Women in 1792, calling for equal opportunities in education and society. But despite the efforts of reformers, women remained excluded from active citizenship in France and nearly everywhere else.

19-1c The Napoleonic Era and a New European Politics

The terror and shifting war fortunes fostered a pro-monarchy resurgence. Antiroyalists turned to ambitious General Napoleon Bonaparte **(BOW-nuh-pahrt)** (1769–1821), a lawyer's son and brilliant military strategist from the French-ruled island of Corsica. A lowly artillery officer once imprisoned for alleged Jacobin ties, he rapidly rose through the ranks through political connections and charisma to command major military victories in France, Italy, Austria, and Egypt. In 1799 Bonaparte became First Consul, the most powerful political office. With many believing that only a dictator could provide stability, in 1804 Bonaparte crowned himself emperor in a regal coronation attended by the pope, an event that harkened back a millennium to Charlemagne's crowning. Quickly promoting reconciliation and economic prosperity, Bonaparte made the Revolution's core values permanent by standardizing revolutionary laws, including citizens' equality before the law. However, his dictatorial tendencies betrayed French liberty. Developing a taste for the trappings of royal power, he divorced his childless wife, the popular Empress Josephine, and married an eighteen-year-old Austrian princess, Marie-Louise, hoping for an heir.

Wars soon resumed. In 1805 Britain, the world's dominant sea power, allied with Austria, Prussia, and Russia against France. France won most land battles and occupied much of western Europe. Bonaparte's family now ruled Spain, Naples, and some German states. But armed resistance in Spain and German states, a costly invasion of Russia in 1812 resulting in a humiliating retreat, and an invasion of France by rival powers sapped Bonaparte's military strength. Bonaparte abdicated and was imprisoned on an Italian island. He escaped and regrouped his forces, but he finally lost to British and Prussian armies at Waterloo, a Belgian village, in 1815. The Bourbon family reclaimed the French throne, and Bonaparte spent his remaining years in exile on St. Helena, a tiny and remote British-ruled South Atlantic island.

With revolutionary France and Napoleon's empire defeated, the victorious allies met in 1815 at the Congress of Vienna to remold the European state system and partly restore the status quo (see Map 19.1). Europeans preferring monarchy and church–state alliance rejoiced at the French defeat. The men overthrowing French control in Naples sang, "Naples won't stay a republic. Here's an end to equality. Here's an end to liberty. Long live God and his Majesty."[6] Dominated by Austria, Britain, Russia, and the revived royalist France, the Congress reaffirmed pre-Napoleonic borders and restored most rulers displaced by revolutionaries and reformers. However, thirty-nine German states moved toward national unity, forming the German Confederation. Russia invaded Poland-Lithuania, destroying the constitutional government and partitioning the nation between Russia and Prussia.

Once the revolutionary genie was out of the bottle, however, all the established order's best efforts could not put it back again. Revolutionary ideas combined with popular discontent with despotism and frequent wars unsettled Europe as various revolutions broke out in 1830–1831. The French overthrew despotic Bourbon king Charles X and installed his more progressive cousin, Louis-Philippe (1773–1850), as a constitutional monarch, recognizing some liberties. Uprisings in several German and Italian states and Poland sought voting rights, while peasant rebellions caused by poverty and unemployment rocked Britain.

Poor harvests, rising unemployment, massive poverty, and a desire for representative government sparked even more turbulent revolts in 1848. These upheavals began in France, forcing increasingly unpopular Louis-Philippe to abdicate, and soon spread to Austria, Hungary, and many German and Italian states. German students met in city marketplaces, demanding elected parliaments and civil liberties such as free speech and a free press. Workers in some places demanded better conditions. But conservative regimes soon violently crushed these uncoordinated movements. A French observer said that "nothing was lacking" in the repression in Paris, "not grapeshot, nor bullets, nor demolished houses, nor martial law, nor the ferocity of the soldiery, nor the insults to the dead."[7] Still, the uprisings spread democratic ideas, and parliamentary power increased in countries such as Denmark and the Netherlands. To prevent revolutionary outbursts, many European governments also began considering social and economic reforms, such as higher wages, to improve people's lives.

19-1d Caribbean Societies and the Haitian Revolution

Most small Caribbean islands and the Guianas in northeast South America were British, French, or Dutch plantation colonies inhabited chiefly by slaves of African ancestry. In these colonies, Afro-Caribbean peoples mixed European cultural forms and languages with African traditions. Hence, in British-colonized Jamaica, Barbados, and Antigua, most adopted Christianity and Anglo-Saxon names. The first successful Caribbean movement to overthrow colonialism occurred in Haiti, where slaves fought their way to power.

Slave revolts in the Americas were common throughout the colonial era, but only the Haitian Revolution overthrew a regime and became both a local and global event. The majority of Haitian slaves were of Kongo-Angolan background, some probably Catholics (although mixed with local African traditions). Many had only recently been imported since Haiti's harsh plantation society produced high death rates (most died

---

[6]Quoted in Eric Hobsbawm, *Workers: World of Labor* (New York: Pantheon), 34.
[7]Quoted in Michael Elliott-Bateman et al., *Revolt to Revolution: Studies in the 19th and 20th Century European Experience* (Manchester, UK: Manchester University Press, 1974), 87.

MAP 19.1 **Europe in 1815** With the Napoleonic wars ended, the Congress of Vienna redrew the map of Europe. France, Austria, Spain, Britain, and a growing Prussia were the dominant states, but the Ottoman Turks still ruled a large area of southeastern Europe.

Q How does this map differ from maps of Europe today?

within three years of arrival) and hence constant need for more slaves. In 1791 some 100,000 Afro-Haitians, inspired by the French Revolution's slogans of liberty and equality, rose up against the oppressive society and French planters. They were led by Toussaint L'Ouverture (**too-SAN loo-ver-CHORE**) (1746–1803), a freed slave who envisioned a republic of free people and, far more than the leaders of the American and French Revolutions, asserted the primacy of human rights. Raised a Catholic, Toussaint had learned French and Latin from an older slave.

For a decade Afro-Haitians fought the French military and anti-French British and Spanish forces hoping to capitalize on the turmoil. By 1801 Toussaint's forces controlled Haiti and had freed the slaves. But Napoleon Bonaparte sent in larger forces and captured Toussaint, who died in a French prison. However, by 1803 France had lost tens of thousands of troops and was dangerously low on cash. Hence Bonaparte offered U.S. President Thomas Jefferson an opportunity to purchase French Louisiana at a bargain price. Jefferson accepted, instantly doubling the size of the country and changing U.S. history. It can be said that without the Haitian Revolution the U.S. might never have expanded west of the Mississippi River. In 1804 Afro-Haitians defeated Napoleon's army and established the Western Hemisphere's second independent nation after the United States. Around the Americas the Haitian Revolution cheered slaves and abolitionists but alarmed planters more determined to preserve slavery. The United States, still a slave-owning nation, withheld diplomatic recognition of the black republic. As French planters were either killed or fled, ex-slaves took over sugar production. But the promise of a better life and human rights for Haitians proved short-lived; Toussaint's successor, the Africa-born Jean Jacques Dessalines (**de-sah-LEEN**) (1758–1806), ruled despotically, beginning two centuries of tyranny.

19-1e Latin America's Independence Wars

Spain and Portugal ruled much larger and more populous American empires than Britain. By 1810 some eighteen million people lived under Spanish rule from California to South America's southern tip, including four million Europeans, eight million Native Americans, one million blacks, and five million people of mixed descent. Corruption ran deep, with planters, ranchers, mine owners, bureaucrats, and church officials benefiting from the Spanish government's opposition to any major political, economic, or social changes. All preferred a system that sent raw materials, such as silver and beef, to Spain rather than develop domestic institutions or markets.

Unlike British North America, Spain allowed little self-government, maintained economic monocultures, and imposed one dominant religion: Roman Catholicism. In addition, Latin American social conditions fostered disunity and inequality. American-born whites, called *creoles*, resented influential newcomers from Spain (*peninsulares*) but also feared that resistance against Spain might get out of control and threaten their position. Meanwhile, the huge underclass of Native Americans, enslaved Africans, and mixed-descent people faced growing unemployment and perhaps the world's most inequitable wealth distribution. Even thought was repressed, as a rigid Catholic Church wary of dissent discouraged intellectual diversity. The Inquisition, considering any literature espousing equality and liberty seditious, punished "heretics." Local critics accused church and state of "[keeping] thought in chains."[8]

Given these political and social inequalities, revolts punctuated Spanish colonial rule. In Mexico a Maya revolt against high taxes and church repression in 1761 spurred Spanish reprisals, and in the 1780s, a mass uprising led by the wealthy, well-educated mestizo Tupac Amaru II (1740–1781), who claimed descent from an Inca king and dressed in royal Inca clothing, spread over large areas of Peru and into neighboring Andean regions. Tupac and Michaela Bastidas, his feisty wife and brilliant strategist, organized a broad-based coalition that seized much of the colony. They sought an independent state, with Tupac as king, where Native Americans, mestizos, and creoles would live in harmony. Many peasant followers revived Inca religion and attacked Catholic churches and clergy. However, the better-armed Spanish defeated the rebel bands, executing Tupac and his family.

Eventually, dissatisfaction exploded into wars of national independence (1810–1826). Creole merchants and ranchers, criticizing Spain's commercial monopoly, increasing taxes, and colonial favoritism toward those born in Spain, also wanted a government role. Creoles often felt more loyalty to their American region than distant Spain. Some were also inspired by the Enlightenment and the American and French Revolutions. Britain, pressuring Spain and Portugal to open Latin American markets to British goods, secretly aided anticolonial groups. Meanwhile, Spain experienced domestic political problems, including French occupation during the Napoleonic wars.

With Spain refusing serious political concessions, two separate independence movements began in Venezuela and Argentina, led respectively by Simon Bolivar (**bow-LEE-vahr**) and Jose de San Martin. From a wealthy Caracas family that owned slaves, land, and mines, Bolivar (1783–1830), a charismatic Spain-educated lawyer and free thinker who admired rationalist Enlightenment thought, offered an inclusive view of his Latin American people: "We are a microcosm of the human race, a world apart, neither Indian nor Europeans, but a part of each."[9] Bolivar spent time in Haiti and Jamaica, where he gained sympathy for blacks, and in 1816 he formed an army to liberate northern South America, offering freedom to slaves who aided his cause. After many setbacks, Bolivar's forces triumphed. In 1821 the resulting republic of Gran Colombia united Colombia, Ecuador, and Venezuela. San Martin (1778–1850), a former Spanish army colonel, helped Argentina gain independence in 1816 and Chile in 1818. In 1824 San Martin and Bolivar cooperated to liberate Peru, where royalist sympathies were strongest.

As in North America, some women enthusiastically served as soldiers and nurses in the fight for liberation. For example, Policarpa Salavarrieta helped Bolivar as a spy until she was captured by the Spanish. Before her execution in Bogota's main plaza, she exclaimed: "Although I am a woman and young, I have more than enough courage to suffer this death and a thousand more."[10] Generally, however, women still lived in patriarchal societies that offered few new legal or political rights.

Although these wars for liberation were eventually successful, their aftermath was complicated. Economies were damaged while people fled the fighting. Moreover, the new creole-dominated governments often forgot promises made to the Native Americans, mestizos, blacks, and mulattos (a term widely used in Latin America for people of mixed black and white or Native American ancestry), who had constituted most of the revolutionary armies. While some slaves gained freedom, slavery was not abolished. Unlike in the United States, Latin America's new leaders also largely failed to form democratic governments. Bolivar could not hold his own

---

[8]Jose de San Martin, quoted in Edwin Early, *The History Atlas of South America* (New York: Macmillan, 1998), 76.

[9]Quoted in Carlos Fuentes, *The Buried Mirror: Reflections on Spain and the New World* (New York: Houghton Mifflin, 1992), 252.

[10]Quoted in E. Bradford Burns and Julie A. Charlip, *Latin America: A Concise Interpretive History*, 7th ed. (Upper Saddle River, NJ: Prentice-Hall, 2002), 75.

Mexico and Brazil also experienced political change, though less violently (see Map 19.2). In 1810 two progressive Mexican Catholic priests, creole Manuel Hidalgo and mestizo Jose Maria Morelos (**moh-RAY-los**), mobilized peasants and miners to launch a revolt promoting independence, abolition of slavery, and social reform. Creole conservatives and royalists suppressed that revolt, but a compromise between factions brought Mexico independence in 1822 under a creole general, Agustin de Iturbide (**ah-goos-TEEN deh ee-tur-BEE-deh**) (1783–1824), who proclaimed himself emperor. However, the anti-Spanish alliance of creoles, mestizos, and Native Americans unraveled, and a republican revolt ousted Iturbide. Central American peoples split off from Mexico, by 1839 splintering into five states. Even with independence the spirit of rebellion was not extinguished. For example, in 1847 Mayans in southeast Yucatán, many of them abused and poorly paid plantation workers, revolted against the wealthy European-descended elite in the area, beginning a lengthy and sometimes brutal conflict for political and economic control of Yucatán that came to be known as the Caste War of Yucatán (1847–1901). The Mayans set up their own state and gained recognition from, and trade relations with, Britain until 1893. In 1901 the Mexican army finally occupied the Mayan-controlled territories but the region's resentment simmered until 1915 when the Mexican government finally allowed some reforms to satisfy Mayan grievances.

By the late 1700s Brazil was the wealthiest part of the Portuguese empire, but only white plantation and gold mine owners benefited much from this wealth. Since Brazil accounted for a quarter to a third of all Africans arriving in the Americas, blacks vastly outnumbered Native Americans. Disgruntled Afro-Brazilians demanding a better life faced many setbacks, including defeat of a 1799 revolt in the northeastern state of Bahia (**buh-HEE-uh**). Yet, Brazil enjoyed a nearly bloodless transition to independence. In 1808 the Portuguese royal family and government sought refuge in Brazil to escape the Napoleonic wars, and in the coming years Brazilians increasingly viewed themselves as separate from Portugal. A royal family member, Dom Pedro (1798–1834), severed ties with Portugal completely in 1822, becoming emperor of Brazil as Pedro I. But despite a new elected parliament, most Brazilians had no vote, Pedro I governed autocratically, and Brazilian politics was dominated by merchants, landowners, and the royal family.

akg-images

IMAGE 19.3 **Simón Bolívar** The main leader of the anti-Spanish war of independence in northern South America, Bolívar came to be known as "the Liberator," a symbol of Latin American nationalism and the struggle for political freedom. Here Bolívar is pictured riding in a victory parade in Caracas after defeating a military uprising in 1829.

Q What does the painting tell us about Bolívar, military and civilian dress, and Caracas?

country together; in 1830 Gran Colombia broke into Colombia, Ecuador, and Venezuela. Meanwhile, Uruguay and Paraguay split from Argentina, and Bolivia from Peru. Disillusioned, Bolivar concluded that Latin America was ungovernable.

OREGON COUNTRY
(Joint U.S.-British occupation)

BRITISH NORTH AMERICA
(CANADA)
(Gr. Br.)

Mississippi R.

Colorado R.

UNITED STATES

New York

Philadelphia
Washington, D.C.

MEXICO
1821

Rio Grande

San Antonio

New Orleans

Charleston

Gulf of Mexico

Mexico City

Veracruz

BRITISH
HONDURAS (Gr. Br.)

GUATEMALA
Guatemala City

BAHAMA IS.
(Gr. Br.)

Havana

CUBA
(Spain)

JAMAICA
(Gr. Br.)

HAITI 1804

PUERTO RICO (Spain)

Caribbean Sea

ATLANTIC
OCEAN

N

UNITED PROVINCES OF
CENTRAL AMERICA
1823–1839

Panama

TRINIDAD (Gr. Br.)

Caracas

VENEZUELA

BR. GUIANA (Gr. Br.)

DUTCH GUIANA (Neth.)

FRENCH GUIANA (France)

Socorro

Bogotá

Magdalena R.

Orinoco R.

GRAN COLOMBIA
1819–1830

Quito

ECUADOR

Galápagos
Islands

Amazon R.

Equator 0°

PACIFIC
OCEAN

PERU
1824

Lima

BOLIVIA
1825

La Paz

Sucre

EMPIRE OF BRAZIL
1822

Salvador

Paraná R.

20°S

PARAGUAY
1811

Rio de Janeiro

São Paulo

CHILE
1817

UNITED
PROVINCES OF
THE RIO DE
LA PLATA
1816

URUGUAY
1828

Valparaíso

Santiago

ARGENTINA

Buenos Aires

Bahía
Blanca

Montevideo

PATAGONIA
(Disputed between
Argentina and Chile)

Islas Malvinas
(Falkland Islands)

80°W

60°W

0   500   1000 Km.

0   500   1000 Mi.

1811 Year independence gained

Colony

40°W

40°N

20°N

MAP 19.2 Latin American Independence, 1840 By 1840 all of Latin America except for Cuba and Puerto Rico, still Spanish colonies, had become independent, with Brazil and Mexico the largest countries. Later the Central American provinces and Gran Colombia would fragment into smaller nations, and Argentina would annex Patagonia.

Q How does this map differ from maps of the Americas today?

19-2 The Industrial Revolution and Economic Growth

TRANSITIONS SOCIETIES

Q How did industrialization reshape economic and social life?

The **Industrial Revolution**, a dramatic transformation in the production and transportation of goods, reshaped economic, political, and social patterns of Europe and later North America and Japan. In perhaps the greatest transformation since settled farming, urbanization, and the first states arose millennia ago, for the first time in history the shackles were taken off societies' productive power and people became capable of a rapid, constant, and seemingly limitless increase in goods and services. In the late 1700s Britain made breakthroughs in productivity that then crossed the English Channel to western Europe and the Atlantic to North America, eventually transforming Europe's limited power of 1750 into Western domination over much of the world by 1914. Until recently most people accepted a triumphalist story of the Industrial Revolution as generating economic and even moral progress. Economists, inventors, scientists, and statesmen were portrayed as heroes in bringing a new plateau of civilization involving wage labor, mobility, sparkling products, and increased human happiness. The story contained some truth. But today many critics stress the huge costs, arguing that the transformation made some things better but also some things worse. Among the negative consequences have been clashes over control of natural resources, a growing rich–poor gap, environmental destruction, greenhouse gases, global warming, toxic industrial sites, ruined mining land, and water and air pollution. Industrialization seems to have been at best a mixed blessing.

19-2a The Age of Machines

The Industrial Revolution had deep roots. They were planted many centuries earlier with scientific knowledge and technological inventions in varied societies, especially China, India, Mesopotamia, Greece, Rome, and the Islamic world. In Early Modern Europe the Renaissance, Reformation, Scientific Revolution, and Enlightenment generated new ways of thought and understandings of the natural and physical world, while newly discovered lands, animals, plants, peoples, and cultures stimulated curiosity about the world. At the same time, commercial capitalism and conquest overseas formed political and economic links between the Americas, the African coast, some Asian societies, and western Europe, allowing Europeans to acquire natural resources and great wealth overseas for investment in new technologies and production of more commodities for the world market.

The first nation to take advantage of these developments, Great Britain, became the world's leading trading nation. By the early 1700s British inventors had experimented with steam power and spinning machines, and accelerating world demand then spurred Britain to replace India as the world's main cotton textiles supplier. Britain had many advantages: a diverse intellectual atmosphere, a reasonably democratic political system, favorable terrain for building transportation networks, abundant raw materials like coal and iron, and many water sources to run machines. Between the 1780s and 1830s Britain dominated industrialization, thanks partly to its profits from British-controlled Caribbean islands, North American colonies, and trading posts in India. Some British companies, enriched by the trans-Atlantic slave trade and by sugar, cotton, and tobacco plantations in the Americas, often invested their excess capital in new British industries. The English Midlands east of Liverpool, a slave trade port, and northern Wales, near rich coal and iron ore fields, became the center of British industry (see Map 19.3).

Machines now produced goods and performed more human tasks, reshaping peoples' lives. Instead of things being made by hand by people, aided by simple tools, they were made by increasingly complicated chemical processes and machines moved by energy derived from steam and other inanimate sources. By tapping the earth's resources and turning them into commodities, the Industrial Revolution created both material richness and

CONNECTION to TODAY

How did life during the Industrial Revolution compare to life in industrialized societies today?

Industrial Revolution A dramatic transformation in the production and transportation of goods.

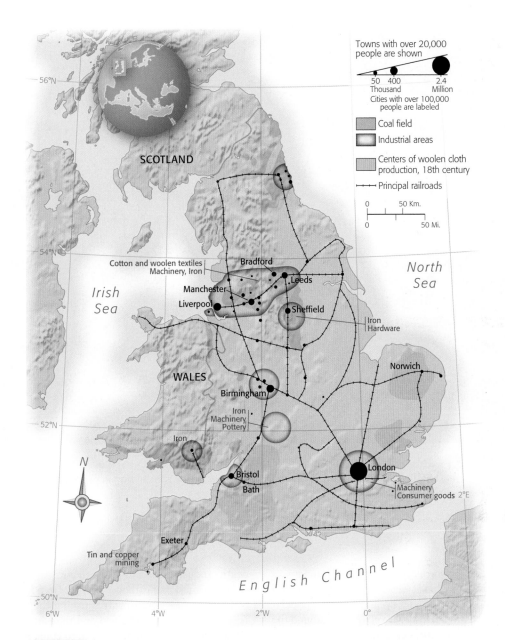

Towns with over 20,000 people are shown

50 400 2.4
Thousand Million

Cities with over 100,000 people are labeled

Coal field

Industrial areas

Centers of woolen cloth production, 18th century

Principal railroads

0 50 Km.

0 50 Mi.

SCOTLAND

Irish Sea

North Sea

Cotton and woolen textiles
Machinery, Iron

Bradford

Leeds

Manchester

Liverpool

Sheffield

Iron
Hardware

WALES

Norwich

Birmingham

Iron
Machinery
Pottery

Iron

Bristol

Bath

London

Machinery
Consumer goods 2°E

Exeter

Tin and copper mining

English Channel

N

56°N

54°N

52°N

50°N

6°W 4°W 2°W 0°

MAP 19.3 **Industrial Transformation in England** British industrialization mostly occurred near coalfields and iron ore deposits, spurring the rise of cities such as Birmingham, Leeds, Liverpool, and Manchester.

Q What does this map tell us about the location of natural resources and the location of cities and industries?

misery. Between the 1770s and 1914 sprawling and polluted industrial cities such as Manchester displaced peasant holdings, country estates, and domestic workshops, widening the gap between the few rich and the many poor. After the late 1700s Europe's material culture changed more than it had in the previous 750 years. Today industrialized societies use transportation, wear fabrics, and employ building materials inconceivable in 1750. As one measure of change, consider some English words that first appeared between 1780 and 1850: *industry, factory, middle class, working class, engineer, crisis, statistics, strike,* and *pauper.*

The Industrial Revolution triggered continual technological innovations and led to increasing economic activity, as inventions in one industry stimulated inventions in others. New cotton machines created demand for more plentiful and reliable power than that provided by water wheels and horses. The steam pump invented in 1712 was inefficient, but in 1774 Scottish inventor James Watt (1736–1819), financed by a wealthy merchant, produced the first successful rotary steam engine. Useful in many industrial activities, steam engines provided power for textile mills, iron furnaces, flour mills, and mines. In powering railroads and steamships, steam power also conquered time and space, bringing the world much closer together. Watt's backer, Matthew Boulton, claimed he had to sell steam engines to all the world to make money. Not all methods of transportation

IMAGE 19.4 **Industrial Sheffield** This mid-nineteenth-century illustration of one of the key English industrial cities, Sheffield, shows the smokestacks and factories, many specializing in producing steel and metal goods, that dominated the landscape.

Mansell/The LIFE Picture Collection/Getty Images

Q What impression does this painting convey of life in an English industrial city in this era?

were as costly. In the 1880s the bicycle as we know it today was developed in England, making it easier for average men and women to get around. A decade later, cycling became a popular sport and form of recreation. Bicycles are ubiquitous around the world today and in some countries clog the streets.

The need for more iron, steel, and coal for the new machines and engines led to improvements in mining, metalworking, and then transportation to move coal and ore. Eventually people accepted technological and economic growth as normal. British novelist William Thackeray celebrated the changes in 1860: "It is only yesterday, but what a gulf between now and then! *Then* was the old world. Stagecoaches, riding horses, pack-horses, knights in armor, Norman invaders, Roman legions. But your railroad starts a new era."[11] Mechanization also provoked fear. Between 1815 and 1830 **Luddites**, British anti-industrialization activists, most of them skilled textile workers, invaded factories and destroyed machines in a mass protest against mechanization. After British troops stopped the destruction, wrecking machines became a crime punishable by

Luddites Anti-industrialization activists in Britain who destroyed machines in a mass protest against the effects of mechanization.

death. Industrialization also affected environments. Recent studies suggest that carbon emissions from factory smokestacks and black smog were already warming the climate by melting Alpine glaciers, which helped end the Little Ice Age by 1850, a harbinger of the climate change to come as industrialization spread. But coal mining, which stoked Britain's industrial rise and at its peak employed more than a million Britons, eventually declined for economic and environmental reasons. In 2015 the last deep coal mine in England closed forever.

For decades Britain, the world's richest, most competitive nation, enjoyed a reputation as the world's workshop. Factories mass-produced goods of better quality and lower price than traditional handicrafts, giving British merchants marketable goods and incentives to sell them to the world to recoup heavy investments in machinery and materials. By the mid-1800s Britain produced two-thirds of the world's coal, half the iron, four sevenths of its steel, and half the cotton cloth and other manufactured goods. A British poet boasted that "England's a perfect World, hath Indies, too, Correct your Maps, Newcastle [a center of the coal industry] is [silver-rich] Peru."[12] No other state could threaten Britain's economic and political position.

---

[11]Quoted in John R. Gillis, *A World of Their Own Making: Myth, Ritual, and the Quest for Family Values* (New York: Basic Books, 1996), 65.
[12]Quoted in Fernand Braudel, *The Perspective of the World: Civilization and Capitalism, 15th–18th Century* (New York: Harper and Row, 1984), 553.

However, between the 1830s and 1870s the British also helped spread the Industrial Revolution by investing some profits in western Europe. Capitalizing on its mineral reserves, prosperous trading cities, and a strategic location, Belgium industrialized in the early 1800s and built a railroad system to transport coal, iron, and manufactured goods. By the 1830s the French government also helped fund industrial activity. In the German states, political fragmentation before 1870 discouraged industrialization except in several coal-rich regions, and some countries, including Portugal, Spain, and Austria-Hungary, remained largely agricultural. By 1914, however, industrialization was widespread around Europe and in North America and Japan, and large numbers of people lived in cities and worked in factories.

19-2b Industrial Capitalism and Society

Industrialization and the vast increase in manufactured goods transformed commercial capitalism, dominated by large trading companies, into industrial capitalism centered on manufacturing. European industrial firms exported manufactured goods and imported raw materials, such as iron ore, to make more goods. Since economic success depended on large, steady turnover of goods, advertising developed to create demand. Banking and financial institutions also expanded operations, while government policies supported the industrialists, bankers, and financiers, maximizing private wealth.

Economic philosophers praised and justified British-style capitalism. Scottish professor and Enlightenment supporter Adam Smith (1723–1790) helped formulate modern economics theory, known as neoclassical economics. In his book *The Wealth of Nations* (1776), Smith advocated the policy of **laissez faire**, which opposed government interference in the marketplace through laws regulating business and profits. Instead, Smith believed in self-interest, arguing that the marketplace's "invisible hand" would turn the entrepreneur's individual greed into a rising standard of living for all. He also introduced the idea of a permanently growing economy, reinforcing long-standing Western views of progress, of history leading to a better future.

In industrializing societies life seemed light-years removed from the Middle Ages. Adam Smith's free trade philosophy refuted medieval attitudes condemning mercantile activity and usury, helping end Early Modern mercantilism. Free traders believed that Britain should serve as the world's industrial center, with raw materials flowing in and manufactured goods flowing out. But Smith saw capitalism's potential for both good and evil: free enterprise did not necessarily generate prosperity for all, since the prosperity of the manufacturer and society might differ. Smith encouraged businesses to pay their employees high wages, writing that "no society can surely be flourishing and happy of which the far greater part of its members are poor and miserable. [They should be] well fed, clothed and lodged."[13]

Around 1870, the Second Industrial Revolution commenced, characterized by technological change, mass production, and specialization and led by the United States and Germany. Application of science to industry improved electrical, chemical, optical, and automotive industries, bringing new inventions such as electricity grids, radio, internal combustion engines, gasoline, and flush toilets. By 1900 Germany was Europe's main producer of electrical goods and chemicals. Assembly lines of separate specialized tasks became common; for example, an automobile worker might only install wheels. The Second Industrial Revolution promoted a shift from many competitive enterprises to giant monopolies led by fabulously wealthy tycoons.

Concentrating capital in "big business" gave a few businessmen and bankers, such as the Krupp family in Germany and the Rockefellers in the United States, vast economic power and control over many industries. Hence, Alfred Krupp (1812–1887), Europe's leading manufacturer of arms, also owned steel mills and mines. Factories, some now producing such useful innovations as aluminum and electrical power, required heavy capital investment to start, eliminating many small businesses and fostering monopolies. In the late 1800s a long depression also undermined competition, encouraging businesses to merge or cooperate and fix prices to moderate slumps. These economic changes generated a drive to colonize more of the world to ensure access to resources and markets.

The Industrial Revolution affected both men and women and all social and economic classes (see Chapter 20). Mainly agricultural a century earlier, by 1900 Europe had a greater division of labor, growing social problems, most people living in cities, and machines replacing many human workers. The factory system compelled millions to migrate from the countryside into overcrowded, unhealthy cities with high rates of alcoholism, prostitution, and crime. City people crowded into festering slums, worked long hours for low wages, and learned new lifestyles. French writer Alexis de Tocqueville (**TOKE-vill**) described the atmosphere of Manchester in 1835:

> *The footsteps of a busy crowd, the crunching wheels of machinery, the shriek of steam from boilers, the regular beat of the looms, the heavy rumble of carts, these are the noises from which you can never escape in the somber half-light of these streets. Crowds are ever hurrying this way and that, but their footsteps are brisk, their looks preoccupied, and their appearance somber and harsh.*[14]

Factories, mines, and cities reshaped European life. Many factory workers labored fourteen- or even eighteen-hour days under rigid discipline, with no insurance for accidents, ill health, or old age, and many children worked seven days a week in mines or factories. In mid-nineteenth-century English cotton mills, adult men were about one-quarter of workers, women and girls over half, with the rest boys under eighteen. Workers such as English coal miner Tommy Armstrong sometimes used songs to express their solidarity with each other and resentment of those they worked for (see Meet the People: Tommy Armstrong, Bard of the English Coal Mines).

Gradually many people considered themselves members of a social and economic

laissez faire Restriction of government interference in the marketplace, such as laws regulating business and profits.

---
[13]Quoted in Peter Gay, *Age of Enlightenment* (New York: Time, Inc., 1966), 105–106.
[14]Quoted in Peter Hall, *Cities in Civilization* (New York: Fromm International, 1998), 310.

Tommy Armstrong, Bard of the English Coal Mines

Tommy Armstrong (1849–1919) was one of the most famous song-makers from Britain's industrial working class. From a poor family and with little formal schooling, Armstrong began working in the mine pits around Durham in north England's Northumbrian region at age nine. Since the youngster was born with crooked legs, his older brother William carried him to work on his back. Working first as a trapper-boy, opening ventilation doors for coal and miners to pass through, he later went on to more demanding jobs in the pits.

In the later 1800s many miners in Durham and elsewhere composed rhymes and songs. Armstrong began writing song lyrics at age twelve. Eventually he married, but miners' wages barely covered expenses for his overworked wife and fourteen children, prompting Armstrong to seek additional money by writing songs and having them printed. He then sold single sheets with lyrics, known as broadsides, in pubs to raise money for his family and buy beer for himself. The Tyneside balladeer, as he was known, referring to the nearby Tyne River, developed a legendary thirst. His son claimed, "Me dad's Muse was a mug of beer." Armstrong engaged in song duels with rival songwriters and even made up verses about people in the houses he passed on his way home from work or the pub. His songs usually reflected social class and social criticism. One of them encouraged educating the young, in part to avoid trouble with the law: "Send your bairns [children] to school, Learn them all you can. Make scholarship your faithful friend, and you'll never see the school-board man [truant officer]." He set his songs to folk and music-hall tunes as well as to Irish melodies brought by the thousands of Irish immigrants to the mines.

Armstrong became renowned for writing songs reflecting the miners' increasingly radical views, and his ballads memorialized mining disasters, usually to raise money for union funds or relief of orphans and widows. For example, in 1882, after an explosion killed seventy-four miners, Armstrong produced a song commemorating the lost men: "Oh, let's not think of tomorrow lest we disappointed be. Our joys may turn to sorrow as we all may daily see. God protect the lonely widow and raise each dropping head; Be a father to the orphans, never let them cry for bread." Conscious of his responsibility, he claimed that "when you're the Pitman's [coalminer's] Poet and looked up for it, if a disaster or a strike goes by without a song from you, they say: What's with Tommy Armstrong? Has someone let out all the inspiration?"

Armstrong was especially productive in the last two decades of the 1800s when strikes were common and the Miners' Union grew rapidly from 36,000 to over 200,000 members.

Source: Northern Recording Company, UK

IMAGE 19.5 **Tommy Armstrong** Known as the "Pitman's (coalminer's) Poet," Armstrong worked in the coalfields around Durham, in England, and wrote many songs celebrating the miners' struggles for a better life.

Q What does this photo tell us about Armstrong and English coal miners of the era?

As struggles between miners and mine owners became more bitter, the union grew more assertive and organized. Armstrong wrote strike songs to give information and courage to miners, but also to collect money for hungry families of strikers. Some of the worst conflicts erupted in 1892, when the Durham miners were asked to take a large pay cut. When the union refused, workers were locked out of their workplaces, prompting one of Armstrong's most famous songs: "In our Durham County I am sorry for to say, That hunger and starvation is increasing every day. For want of food and coals, we know not what to do, But with your kind assistance, we will stand the battle through. Our work is taken from us now, they care not if we die, For they [the mine owners] can eat the best of food, and drink the best when dry." After months of labor strife, the union pragmatically agreed to a lower pay reduction. The songs of Tommy Armstrong and other industrial balladeers provide a chronicle of the Industrial Revolution and the ways it shaped the lives of millions of people.

Reflection Questions

1. How did Armstrong's life reflect the working conditions and often hardships imposed on workers by the Industrial Revolution?
2. What did the songs of industrial balladeers like Armstrong tell us about how working-class people confronted the realities of industrial society?
3. How do the labor union and working-class protest songs of Armstrong compare to protest, topical, and labor union songs today?

Note: Quotations from A. L. Lloyd, *Folk Song in England*. Copyright © 1967 by International Publishers. Reprinted with permission of International Publishers Co., New York.

class with interests in opposition to other classes. Working classes, such as coal miners and factory workers, were the largest group, while middle classes included businesspeople, professionals, and prosperous farmers. A salaried labor force, today known as "white-collar" workers, emerged to handle sales and paperwork. Hence, some ninety thousand British women worked as secretaries by 1901. Middle classes, proud of what

they viewed as their keen work ethic, attributed poverty to poor work habits and lack of initiative, blaming the victims for their problems. Meanwhile, in many countries beleaguered aristocrats struggled to maintain dominance over governments and churches. In this developing situation, the obvious gap between the haves and the have-nots encouraged crime, political unrest, and labor strikes.

KEY POINTS

▸ The Industrial Revolution began in England and gradually spread throughout western Europe and North America.

▸ Some people marveled at the technological changes brought by the Industrial Revolution, while others, such as the Luddites, resisted them.

▸ The Second Industrial Revolution ushered in an age of specialization and mass production and favored

monopolistic corporations that could afford enormous investments in new technology.

▸ As a result of the revolution, new classes arose—the working class; the middle classes, including a new secretarial force; and the aristocrats—and the gap between the haves and the have-nots widened.

19-3 Nationalism, Liberalism, and Socialism

SOCIETIES

Q How did nationalism, liberalism, and socialism differ from each other?

Modern Europe produced three new ideologies—nationalism, liberalism, and socialism—that still shape our world and political opinions and movements today. An **ideology** is a coherent, widely shared system of ideas about the social, political, and economic realm. Nationalism fostered unified countries, liberalism encouraged democratic governments, and socialism sparked movements to counteract industrial capitalism's power and the social dislocations generated by industrialization.

19-3a Nations and Nationalism

Nationalism, a primary loyalty to, and identity with, a nation bound by common culture, government, and shared territory, greatly influenced Europe and the Americas. Nationalists insisted that support for country transcended loyalty to family, village, church, region, social class, monarch, or ethnic group. Many peoples increasingly felt citizenship in a nation, such as France or Italy, that shared a common identity separate from, and they felt often better than, other nations. For example, a Swiss newspaper proclaimed in 1848 that the "nation [Switzerland] stands before us as an undeniable reality. The Swiss of different cantons [small self-governing states] will henceforth be perceived and act as members of a single nation."[15] Some historians perceive the nation as an "imagined community" in the minds of people living in the same society.

While nationalism provided a cement bonding all citizens to the state, it also fostered wars with rival nations. Because it united people who shared many traditions and a sense of

CONNECTION to TODAY

How do these ideologies figure into political debates and differences in the world today?

common destiny, nationalism appealed particularly to rising middle classes and intellectuals struggling for more political power; they claimed the nation included all the people, regardless of social status. The India-born English poet Rudyard Kipling captured this perception of collective identity and the nation's special nature: "If England was what England seems, An' not the England of our dreams, But only putty, brass an' paint, 'Ow quick we'd drop 'er! But she ain't!"[16]

Most historians credit modern nationalism's birth to late-eighteenth- and early-nineteenth-century France and Great Britain. French revolutionaries claimed that all sovereignty emanated from the nation, rather than individuals or groups, and the British increasingly viewed themselves as one nation composed of several peoples. Although England and Wales united in 1536 under English monarchs and were joined by Scotland in 1707, no Britain yet existed; the peoples sharing the island identified as English, Scottish, or Welsh. But the spread of English power nearly suffocated Scottish and Welsh cultures and languages. Although some Welsh and Scots remained wary of England, eventually most accepted membership in Great Britain, a linking formalized in the British Act of Union in 1800. And yet even today some Scottish nationalists, unhappy with recent British governments and their policies, promote independence for Scotland.

ideology A coherent, widely shared system of ideas about the nature of the social, political, and economic realm.

Nationalism A primary loyalty to, and identity with, a nation bound by a common culture, government, and shared territory.

---

[15]Quoted in Oliver Zimmer, *A Contested Nation: History, Memory and Nationalism in Switzerland, 1761–1891* (Cambridge, UK: Cambridge University Press, 2003), 119.
[16]Quoted in W. Raymond Duncan et al., *World Politics in the 21st Century*, 2nd ed. (New York: Longman, 2004), 311.

Culture Club/Hulton Archive/Getty Images

IMAGE 19.6 **Bismarck and German Unification** This advertisement for Liebig's Meat Extract, published in 1899, celebrates Germany's Chancellor Otto von Bismarck's proclamation of German unification in 1871, a source of German pride.

Q What does this painting tell us about Bismarck's status and German support for unification?

Nationalism also transformed Europe's political landscape. Multinational states with ethnically diverse populations dominated much of Europe in 1750. One royal family, the Vienna-based Habsburgs, ruled Austria, Hungary, the Czech lands, Belgium, and parts of Italy. Critics often described the Hapsburg Empire as the "prison of nations," but some recent scholarship views it as becoming a modern multinational state, a kind of early European Union, by the late nineteenth century. In contrast, by the mid-1800s nationalism had fostered diverse **nation-states**, politically centralized countries with defined territorial boundaries, such as France, the Netherlands, Denmark, Portugal, and even multiethnic Britain, Belgium, and Spain. By 1914 only the Russian and Habsburg-ruled Austro-Hungarian empires remained major multinational European states.

Greeks, Italians, and Germans eventually created unified nations, partly through violence. Greeks, long part of the Turkish-dominated Ottoman Empire, served in the Ottoman government and dominated commerce in Ottoman-ruled western Asia. But some Greeks sent their sons to western Europe to study. Returning home with nationalist ideas, they organized an uprising for independence in 1821, killing many Turks. The Ottomans responded by massacring Greek

nation-states Politically centralized countries with defined territorial boundaries.

villages, pillaging churches, and hanging the Greek Orthodox Church leader in Istanbul, inflaming western European opinion. When British, French, and Russian intervention helped Greece become independent in 1830, other restless Ottoman subjects were inspired. In 1862 Romania also became independent.

Unlike the Greeks, Italians, divided into many small states ruled by Habsburgs, the Holy Roman Empire, or the pope, long dreamed of unity. In 1831 the fiery Giuseppi Mazzini **(jew-SEP-pay mots-EE-nee)** (1805–1872), an exiled Genoese political philosopher, founded the Young Italy movement advocating one Italian nation. He also promoted republican government and women's rights, radical ideas in Italy. Nationalists and democrats elsewhere, inspired by Mazzini, formed organizations such as Young Poland. In 1859 nationalists began an armed struggle for Italian unity. Forces under Giuseppi Garibaldi **(gar-uh-BOWL-dee)** (1807–1882), who had nurtured his passions during years of exile in South America, created the kingdom of Italy in 1861. In 1870 Italian troops entered the last Papal State, Rome, reuniting Italy for the first time since the Roman Empire. However, Vatican City remained independent of Italy. The job of creating Italians who shared a common national vision took longer.

German unification also came in stages. In 1862 Prussian prime minister Otto von Bismarck (1815–1898) brought together many northern German states under Prussian domination. From the landed nobility, Bismarck spent his youth gambling and womanizing before beginning a rapid political ascent. Hostile to business and democratic political rights, he united the Germans through warfare, a policy of "blood and iron." Successful wars in 1866 with Austria and then Denmark and France added all the German-speaking territories west of Austria. In 1871 King William I of Prussia was declared *kaiser* (emperor) of a united Germany, now one of Europe's major powers.

Some peoples could not satisfy their nationalist aspirations. Poles frequently but unsuccessfully rebelled against their Russian and German rulers, while Jewish minorities, scattered around Europe, often had little in common. Many East European and Russian Jews, largely restricted to all-Jewish villages and urban neighborhoods known as ghettoes, often maintained conservative cultural and religious traditions. Especially in Germany, France, and Britain, many Jews moved toward assimilation with the dominant culture. Reacting against widespread anti-Semitism, other Jews gravitated to revolutionary groups or to **Zionism**, a movement founded by Hungarian-born journalist Theodor Herzl (**HERT-suhl**) (1860–1904) that sought a Jewish homeland. In 1948 Zionists formed the state of Israel in Palestine.

Another oppressed people were the Irish, whose simmering opposition to harsh, centuries-long English rule sometimes erupted in violence. England attempted to destroy the Irish language, religion, poetry, literature, dress, and music. As an Irish folk song from 1798 protested, "She's the most distressful country that ever yet was seen. [The English] are hanging men and women for the wearing of the green [Ireland's unofficial national color]."[17] Much of Ireland's farming land belonged to rich English landlords. After 1800 England mounted even more restrictive laws, deporting thousands who resisted to Australia, where Britain maintained penal colonies. In addition, the British army recruited many poor, jobless Irish men to fight in colonial wars abroad. Irish ballads memorialized men going out to fight, mothers or wives greeting their wounded men when they returned, and families grieving for those who would never return. Then during the 1840s, when the potato crop failed for several successive years because of a fungus blight, one and a half million Irish died from starvation while British policies discouraged food exports to Ireland and English landlords ejected Irish peasants, replacing subsistence food growing with more profitable sheep raising. Millions of Irish sought escape from poverty and repression by emigrating to the Americas and Australia. Recent research suggests that the potato blight that affected Ireland and Europe probably originated in South America and made its way to the United States and then Europe through potato and seed shipments, illustrating how interlinked the world was becoming from global trade.

But the Irish continued to rebel against British rule. The Fenians (**FEE-nians**), a secret society dedicated to Irish independence, were transformed by 1905 into Sinn Fein (**shin FANE**) (Gaelic for "Ourselves Alone"). Sinn Fein extremists formed the violent Irish Republican Army (IRA), which organized a rebellion on Easter Monday, 1916, during which some fifteen hundred volunteers seized key buildings in Dublin and proclaimed a republic. The proclamation by rebellion leaders, reflecting progressive values, was addressed to both "Irishmen and Irishwomen" and promised equal rights and opportunities for all citizens. English troops quickly crushed the rising in six days, killing over four hundred people (half of them civilians), executing the ringleaders, and jailing two thousand participants, but Sinn Fein, the IRA, and terrorism still bedeviled the English colonizers. They remain a problem for Britain today since they are a political party with representation in the Ireland, Northern Ireland, and British parliaments, are active in Northern Irish politics, and promote unification of that territory with the Irish republic.

19-3b Liberalism and Parliamentary Democracy

Another ideology offered a vision of democracy and individual freedom. Influenced by Enlightenment thinkers such as John Locke and Baron de Montesquieu, **liberalism** preached the emancipation of individuals from all governmental, economic, or religious restraints. Liberals, mainly of middle-class background, favored progressive goals such as representative government, the right to vote, and basic civil liberties such as freedom of speech, religion, assembly, and the press. Scottish philosopher John Stuart Mill (1806–1873) eloquently defended free expression, writing that no one should restrict what arguments a legislature or executive should hear. Liberal politicians fought against slavery, advocated religious toleration, and worked for more popular participation in government.

Democratic decision making was an old idea. Village democracies allowing many residents to voice their opinions and shape decisions had long existed in various societies in Asia, Africa, and the Americas. Classical Greeks and Romans also introduced democratic institutions, but they restricted political rights to a small minority of male citizens. By 1800 representative institutions of some sort had been established in various states including Iceland, England, Holland, Switzerland, Poland, the United States, and Canada. By the nineteenth century liberal democracy implied choice and competition, usually between contending political parties and policies, within a constitutional framework that allowed voters free choice. Eventually some nations, including Britain, adopted **parliamentary democracy**, government by representatives elected by the people. Liberalism proved particularly popular in Britain and the United States, underpinning the U.S. Constitution and Bill of Rights. To protect against tyranny, the nation's founders mandated a separation of executive, legislative, and judicial powers.

Zionism A movement that sought a Jewish homeland.

liberalism An ideology that favored emancipating the individual from all restraints, whether governmental, economic, or religious.

parliamentary democracy Government by representatives elected by the people.

---

[17]Quoted in Patrick Galvin, *Irish Songs of Resistance* (New York: Folklore Press, n.d.), 84.

British democracy gradually grew as royal power declined over several centuries. After coming to power at age eighteen, Queen Victoria (r. 1837–1901) reigned over Britain for sixty-four years, providing, with her German-born husband Prince Albert, models of morality and stability. But even the respected Queen Victoria no longer had much power and exercised influence mostly behind the scenes. Prime ministers, elected by the majority of Parliament members, now made national and foreign policy. Democracy gradually widened as the elected House of Commons exercised more power than the appointed and hereditary House of Lords. Both houses featured lively debate between political parties.

But democratic access remained somewhat limited in Britain, and reformers wanted average people to have more voice in the electoral system. The Reform Act of 1832 increased the number of voters to all upper- and middle-class males. The major working-class protest movement, Chartism, called for universal adult male suffrage, secret ballots, and salaries for Parliament members so that people without wealth could run for office. Some Chartists, led by Elizabeth Neesom, advocated women's right to participate in government. Chartists used demonstrations, strikes, boycotts, and riots to support their demands; however, because the wealthy feared radical ideas such as wealth redistribution, these actions had little success.

19-3c Socialism, Marxism, and Social Reform

While liberals favored preserving wealth and property rights while fearing radical popular movements, a third ideology encouraged protest and more widely shared wealth. In contrast to liberalism's individual liberty, **socialism** offered a vision of social equality and the common, or public, ownership of economic institutions such as factories and utilities. Socialism grew out of the painful social disruption accompanying the Industrial Revolution. Utopian socialists in Britain, France, and North America, many influenced by Christian ideals, offered visions of cooperative societies that promoted the common good. A few even founded communal villages that were based on community service and that renounced personal wealth. For example, British industrialist Robert Owen (1771–1858) founded a model factory town around his cotton mill and later established a model socialist community, New Harmony, in Indiana. Some proponents of women's rights, such as Emma Martin (1812–1851) in Britain and Flora Tristan (1801–1844) in France, stirred controversy by promoting socialism as the solution to female oppression. Clergymen opposed to feminism and socialism urged their congregations to disrupt Martin's speeches, and outraged mobs chased and stoned her.

The ideas of Karl Marx (1818–1883), known as Marxism, had the most long-lasting influence on socialist thought and became a major intellectual and political influence around the world. Marx, a German Jew with a passion for social justice, studied first law and then philosophy at the University of Berlin, but was blocked from an academic career by the wary Prussian government, who considered him a radical. Marx then worked as a journalist before settling in London. His German friend, Friedrich Engels (1820–1895), who managed his father's cotton factory in England and introduced Marx to English industrial workers' degraded conditions, collaborated in writing and editing some of Marx's books. In *The Communist Manifesto* (1848), Marx claimed that the downtrodden could redress the wrongs inflicted upon them through violent socialist revolution, seizing power from capitalists and creating a new society (see Discover Historical Voices: The Communist View of Past, Present, and Future). Marx argued that revolutionary peoples can change inequitable political, social, and economic patterns inherited from the past. He opposed nationalism, writing that working people, having common interests, needed to cooperate across borders. In 1864 Marx helped form the International Workingmen's Association to work toward those goals.

Marx was a product of his scientific age and considered his ideas as laws of history, writing in his influential, three-volume *Capital* that historical change resulted from struggle between antagonistic social classes. All social and economic systems, he argued, contain contradictions dooming them to conflict, which generates a higher stage of development. Hence, confrontation between nobles, merchants, and serfs undermined feudalism, leading to capitalism. Eventually, Marx predicted, this process would replace capitalism with socialism, where all would share in owning the means of production and the state would serve common people rather than privileged classes; and then communism, where the state would wither away and all would share the wealth, free to realize their human potential without exploitation by capitalists or governments. Such a vision of redistributing wealth and power proved attractive to many disgruntled Europeans and later around the world.

Economists and historians have debated Marxian ideas ever since, and the arguments continue unabated today. Marx believed in economic determinism, the theory that the nature of the economic system (such as feudalism with medieval manors or capitalism with factories) and technology determined all aspects of society, including religious values, social relations (such as family patterns), government, and laws. Hence, capitalism constantly destroyed older industries, transforming the instruments and means of production, and thus the whole relations of society. This caused instability. Marx also argued that religion, which he called the "opiate of the people," discouraged protest but encouraged fatalistic acceptance of life's inequalities in hopes of a better afterlife. He criticized capitalism for fostering extremes of wealth and poverty, furnishing wealth to farm, mine, factory, and business owners as well as to the urban-based, mostly commercial, middle class Marx called the *bourgeoisie*. Marx observed that the industrial working class, the **proletariat**, grew more miserable as wealth became concentrated in giant monopolies in the later 1800s.

Marxist ideas attracted a wide following, first in Europe and later in various American, Asian, and African countries, sometimes stimulating unrest. In 1871 France, following a disastrous war with Germany and election of a conservative government, Marxists, republicans, and other groups briefly gained control of Paris. The Paris Commune, as this government

socialism An ideology offering a vision of social equality and the common, or public, ownership of economic institutions such as factories.

proletariat The industrial working class.

The Communist View of Past, Present, and Future

In 1848 Karl Marx and Friedrich Engels published The Communist Manifesto as a statement of beliefs and goals for the Communist League, an organization they had founded. In this excerpt Marx and Engels outlined their view of history as founded on class struggle, stressed the formation of the new world economy, and offered communism as the alternative to an oppressive capitalist system. They ended their summary of contemporary society's problems by imploring the working class to take its future into its own hands through unity and revolution.

A specter is haunting Europe—the specter of communism. All the powers of old Europe have entered into a holy alliance to excise this specter.... Where is the party in opposition that has not been decried as communistic by its opponents in power?...The history of all hitherto existing society is the history of class struggles.... Oppressor and oppressed stood in constant opposition to one another, carried on in an uninterrupted, now hidden, now open fight, a fight that each time ended, either in a revolutionary reconstitution of society at large, or in the common ruin of the contending classes.

In the earlier epochs of history, we find almost everywhere a complicated arrangement of society into various orders, a manifold gradation of social rank. In ancient Rome we have patricians, knights, plebeians, slaves; in the Middle Ages, feudal lords, vassals, guild-masters, journeymen, apprentices, serfs; in almost all these classes, again, subordinate gradations. The modern bourgeois [middle-class] society that has sprouted from the ruins of feudal society has not done away with class antagonisms. It has but established new classes, new conditions of oppression, new forms of struggle in place of the old ones.

Our epoch, the epoch of the bourgeoisie, possesses, however, this distinctive feature: it has simplified the class antagonisms. Society as a whole is more and more splitting up into two great hostile camps, into two great classes directly facing each other: bourgeoisie and proletariat (working class)....The discovery of America, the rounding of the Cape [of Good Hope], opened up fresh ground for the rising bourgeoisie. The East Indian and Chinese markets, the colonization of America, trade with the colonies, the increase in the means of exchange and in commodities generally, gave to commerce, to navigation, to industry, an impulse never before known, and, thereby, a rapid development to the revolutionary element in the tottering feudal society.... Meantime the markets kept ever growing, the demand ever rising. Even manufacture no longer sufficed. Thereupon, steam and machinery revolutionized industrial production. The place of manufacture was taken by the giant, modern industry, the place of the industrial middle class, by industrial millionaires....

Modern industry has established the world market, for which the discovery of America paved the way....The bourgeoisie, by the rapid improvement of all instruments of production, by the immensely facilitated means of communication, draws all, even the most barbarian, nations into civilization. The cheap prices of its commodities are the heavy artillery with which it batters down all Chinese walls....It compels all nations, on pain of extinction, to adopt the bourgeois mode of production....It creates a world after its own image....

[The Communists] have no interests separate from those of the proletariat as a whole....The immediate aim of the Communists is...the formation of the proletariat into a class; the overthrow of the bourgeois supremacy; and the conquest of political power by the proletariat....The Communists disdain to conceal their views and aims. They openly declare that their ends can be attained only by the forcible overthrow of all existing social conditions. Let the ruling classes tremble at a Communistic revolution. The proletarians have nothing to lose but their chains. They have a world to win. WORKING MEN OF ALL COUNTRIES, UNITE!

Reflection Questions

1. What did Marx and Engels identify as the opposing classes in European history?
2. What developments aided the rise of the bourgeoisie to power?
3. What is the goal of the communists?
4. Can you find any ideas expressed in the reading that can be applied to the country and world you live in today?

Source: From *The Communist Manifesto*, trans. 1880. *www.anv.edu.au/polisci/marx/classics/manifesto.html*.

---

was called, experimented with socialist programs such as better wages and working conditions. The French government attacked Paris with ruthless force; in response Commune supporters (Communards) burned public buildings and killed the Catholic archbishop. French soldiers' brutality horrified a British reporter: "Paris the beautiful is Paris the ghastly, the battered, the burning, the blood-splattered."[18] When the dust cleared, thirty-eight thousand Communards had been arrested,

twenty thousand executed, and seventy-five hundred deported to French island colonies in the South Pacific. Later rebels across Europe hoisted Marxist banners for radical redistribution of power and privilege.

By promising a more equitable society, Marxism became a major world force, with socialist parties forming all over Europe in the late 1800s and early 1900s. More radical socialists soon split off and established parties calling themselves communist.

[18]Quoted in S. C. Burchell, *The Age of Progress* (New York: Time, Inc., 1966), 120.

While many poor people or industrial workers envied the rich and thought life unfair, family, religion, and social connections also inhibited them from joining radical movements or risking their lives in a rebellion that might fail. An English pub toast reflected the desires for more immediate pleasures: "If life was a thing that money could buy, the rich would live and the poor might die. Here's to oceans of wine, rivers of beer, a nice little wife and ten thousand a year."[19] North Americans had a weaker sense of social class, and Marxism never became as influential in the United States as in parts of Europe, Asia, and Latin America. Furthermore, Marx was poor at predicting the future. For example, he mistakenly believed that socialist revolution would first erupt in leading capitalist nations such as Britain and Germany. Instead, the first successful socialist revolution came, over three decades after Marx had died, in semi-feudal Russia.

In contrast to revolution, some Marxists favored a more gradual, evolutionary approach of working within constitutional governments to establish social democracy, a system mixing capitalism and socialism within parliamentary frameworks. The first Social Democratic Party, formed in Germany in 1875, criticized Marxist revolutionaries. Its leader, Eduard Bernstein (1850–1932), argued that socialists should work less for the better future and more for the better present. Shared socialist views and class backgrounds in various countries fostered the founding of the Second International Workingmen's Association by nonrevolutionary socialist parties in 1889, with the goal of world peace, justice, and social reform.

Social Democrats and Marxists actively supported labor unions and strikes to promote worker demands, including collective bargaining. Despite strong employer opposition, unions gradually gained legal recognition as worker representatives in many nations. In Britain, France, Germany, Holland, and Sweden, trade unions and labor parties acquired enough political influence to legislate for better working conditions. In the later 1800s governments implemented social reforms that laid foundations for state-run welfare systems. Many European nations legislated the length of the workday, working conditions, and safety rules. To tackle poverty, Germany and Britain introduced health and unemployment insurance and created old-age pensions. Thus, contrary to Marx's expectations, life for many European workers improved considerably by the early 1900s. But many people still worked in dangerous and unhealthy conditions or faced a ten-hour working day, and child labor continued.

Marx remains very influential but controversial today and his legacy is alive and well, reflected in countless books and discussions on him and his ideas. Many people view Marxist socialist ideas as a threat to their countries, economic systems, and ways of life. In assessing Marx's writings and thought, many scholars today have a more mixed opinion. Many agree that his analysis of how capitalism works and how a divisive class struggle largely benefits the rich and powerful is accurate in many respects. But most agree he was poor at predicting the future. While they may admire Marx's description, they disagree strongly with each other on appropriate or possible strategies for how and whether the social and economic contradictions of global capitalism he examined, in which (according to 2017 figures) the richest one percent of the world's people earn 82 percent of the world's wealth, can be addressed.

KEY POINTS

▶ With the rise of nationalism, the inhabitants of a given country came to identify with each other as distinct from, and often better than, the inhabitants of other countries.

▶ Liberalism, which favored maximizing individual liberty, was particularly influential in Britain and the United States.

▶ Socialism aimed to achieve economic equality through common ownership of industry, and its major proponent, Karl Marx, argued that history is driven by class struggle and that capitalism would inevitably be replaced first by a socialist and then a communist society.

▶ Social Democrats, who rejected Marx's revolutionary ideas and instead favored working to better the lot of workers within a capitalist democracy, managed to greatly improve working conditions by the early 1900s.

19-4 The Resurgence of Western Imperialism

⟲ TRANSITIONS   ▦ NETWORKS

Q What factors spurred the Western imperialism of the later 1800s?

Few history topics are as furiously debated in recent years as Western imperialism and colonialism, most especially that of Great Britain and the British Empire. But these debates also take place in, or are about the roles of, France, Belgium, the Netherlands, and other once imperial powers. The Industrial Revolution provided economic

CONNECTION to TODAY

Do you see any parallels between the Western imperialism of the nineteenth century and the efforts by various large nations to expand their political and economic influence and power in the world today?

incentives, and nationalism provided political incentives, for European merchants and states to exploit other lands, enriching their own nations and thwarting rival nations' ambitions. Initially Britain dominated the growing world economy. But economic, political, and ideological factors eventually fostered resurgent imperialism, leading European nations

---

[19]Quoted in Reginald Nettel, *Sing a Song of England: A Social History of Traditional Song* (London: Phoenix House, 1969), 183.

IMAGE 19.7 **Lipton Tea** European imperial expansion brought many new products to European consumers. Tea, grown in British-ruled India, Sri Lanka (Ceylon), and Malaya, became a popular drink, advertised here in a London weekly magazine.

Q What can we learn about tea growing and the tea trade from this advertisement?

to colonize and dominate much of Asia and Africa, reshaping the global system. With the entire world connected by economic and political networks, history now transcended regions and became truly global.

19-4a British Trade, Industrialization, and Empire

The quest for colonies diminished in the early Industrial Revolution, even for Great Britain, which feared no competitor in world trade and had none. British free traders, wanting neither economic nor political restrictions, viewed acquiring more colonies as too expensive. Britain already controlled or had access to valuable American, African, Asian, and Pacific territories. Although it lost its thirteen North American colonies, Britain gained French Canada, Australia, New Zealand, and later South Africa. Furthermore, Britain's Spanish and Portuguese rivals suffered graver losses; independence for their Latin American colonies opened doors for British commercial activity.

British merchants benefited from new technologies that enabled them to compete all over the world. No longer dependent on trade winds, British ships reached distant shores faster. The first steam-powered ships, in 1813, took one hundred thirteen days to travel from England around Africa to India; in contrast, sailing ships took eight or nine months. Completion of the Suez Canal linked the Mediterranean Sea and the Red Sea in 1869, dramatically cutting travel time; Britain, the canal's major shareholder, extended its influence to East Africa and Southeast Asia. By 1900 the England–India trip took less than twenty-five days, more efficiently transporting resources, goods, and people.

Although it pragmatically preferred peaceful commerce, Britain obtained some colonies between 1750 and 1870 by seizing territories or fighting wars when governments refused to trade or could not protect British commerce and its agents. For example, as states in India grew weaker and banditry increased, the British began expanding their influence and gradually gained direct control or indirect power over most of India. They also established footholds in Malaya, Burma, China, and

South Africa. But the British preferred undercutting their rivals' economic power, as they did against Spanish or Portuguese interests in Argentina, Chile, and Brazil. They flooded India with cheap manufactured goods, greatly diminishing India's crafts and industries for their own benefit. British industrialists and merchants opposed any attempts to foster rival enterprises, such as textile mills, in Asian and African states.

However, the British advantage in world markets gradually diminished as economic leadership changed during the later 1800s. Britain often invested profits earned from India and its Caribbean colonies in other nations, especially the United States, Canada, New Zealand, and Australia, all settled largely by British immigrants. This investment helped the United States become a serious competitor. Increasingly the United States and Germany gained on Britain. Because British investors earned more profits investing abroad than at home, Britain's industrial plants became increasingly obsolete. In 1860 Britain was the leading economic power, with France a distant second followed by the United States and Germany. By 1900, however, the United States was at the top, followed by Germany and then a fading Britain and France.

As industrializing Germany, France, and the United States became more competitive with Britain, their growing competition renewed the quest for colonies abroad. Domestic economies dominated by large monopolies stimulated empire building by piling up huge profits, and hence excess capital, that needed investment outlets abroad to keep growing. Furthermore, by the 1880s some wealth began filtering down to European working classes, stimulating new consumer interests in tropical products such as chocolate, tea, soap, and rubber for bicycle tires. Businessmen in Britain, Germany, Italy, France, Belgium, and the United States, seeking new opportunities to exploit Africa, Asia, and the Pacific, pressured their governments to pursue colonization.

National rivalries also motivated imperialism. Nations often seized colonies to prevent competing nations from gaining opportunities. While expanding British control in southern Africa, British imperialist Cecil Rhodes (1853–1902) remembered his Oxford University professor, the philosopher and art critic John Ruskin's, advice: "This is what England must either do, or perish: found colonies as fast and as far as [it] is able, seizing every piece of waste ground [it] can get [its] foot on."[20] National rivalries and intense competition for colonies also planted the roots of European conflict. By the early 1900s Germany and Austria-Hungary had forged an alliance, prompting Britain, France, and Russia to do likewise, setting the stage for future wars.

19-4b The Scramble for Empire and Imperial Ideologies

Conflicts between European powers fostered renewed Western imperialism between 1870 and 1914, resulting in colonialism or, less commonly, informal empire (strong Western political or economic influence). New colonies brought profits for business interests while strengthening a nation's power in competition with rival nations. The result was the greatest land grab in world history: a handful of European powers dividing up the globe among themselves. Imperial Western nations conquered or impacted millions of Africans, Asians, and Pacific islanders, bringing them into the Western-dominated world economic system. By 1914 European- and American-governed colonies accounted for 57 percent of the world's population.

Many peoples fiercely resisted conquest or foreign rule. Vietnamese, Burmese, and various Indonesian and African societies held off militarily superior European military forces for decades. Even after conquest, guerrilla forces often attacked European colonizers. For fifteen years after France annexed Vietnam, anticolonial fighters refused to surrender, preferring to fight to the death. Countless revolts punctuated colonial rule, from West Africa to India to the Philippines. Western ambitions also sometimes faced frustration. Ethiopians defeated an Italian invasion force, while Afghan slaughter of British occupiers discouraged direct colonization. The Japanese prevented Western political domination by modernizing their own government and economy, and the Siamese (Thai) deflected Western power by using skillful diplomacy and selective modernization.

Despite these efforts, by 1914 Western colonial powers controlled 90 percent of Africa, 99 percent of Polynesia, and 57 percent of Asia (see Map 19.4). The British Empire, the world's largest, included fifty-five colonies containing four hundred million people, ten times Britain's population, inspiring the boast that "the sun never sets on the British Empire." France acquired the next largest empire of twenty-nine colonies. Germany, Spain, Belgium, and Italy joined in the grab for African colonies, and between 1898 and 1902 the United States took over Hawaii, Puerto Rico, Guam, the Philippines, and several of the Samoan Islands; in 1916–1917 the U.S. purchased the Virgin Islands from Denmark. Russia also continued its Eurasian expansion begun in the Early Modern Era (see Chapter 23).

New technologies facilitated and stimulated imperial expansion. Industrialization gave Europeans better weapons to enforce their will against Asians and Africans, including repeating rifles and machine guns, such as the lightweight, quick-firing Maxim Gun. A British writer boasted: "Whatever happens we have got the Maxim Gun, and they have not."[21] The discovery of quinine to treat malaria helped European colonists and officials survive in tropical Africa and Southeast Asia. Later, better communication and transportation networks, such as steamship lines, colonial railroads, and undersea telegraph cables, helped consolidate Western control and more closely connected the world. In 1866 a speaker, praising the new trans-Atlantic cable linking Europe and North America, noted that on the statue of Christopher Columbus in Genoa,

---

[20]Quoted in Robert A. Huttenback, *The British Imperial Experience* (New York: Harper and Row, 1966), 101.
[21]Hillaire Beloc, quoted in Eric Hobsbawm, *The Age of Empire, 1875–1914* (New York: Vintage, 1987), 20.

Italy, was the inscription: "There was one world; let there be two." Now, with the cable, "There were two worlds and [now] they [are] one."[22]

Western imperialism forged globe-spanning networks of interlinked social, economic, and political relationships. Hence, decisions made by a government or business in London or Paris affected people in faraway Malaya or Madagascar, while silk spun in China was turned into dresses worn by fashionable women in Chicago and Munich. Westerners also enjoyed advantageous trade relations with, or strong influence over, countries such as China, Siam, Persia (Iran), and Argentina, known as informal empire or, more recently, neocolonialism. Western imperialism changed world power arrangements. In 1750 China and the Ottoman Empire remained among the strongest countries, but by 1914 they could not match Western military and economic power. In 1500 the wealth gap between more and less economically developed Eurasian and African societies was small, and China and India dominated world trade and manufacturing. By 1914 the gap in total wealth and personal income between industrialized societies, whether in Europe or North America, and most other societies, including China and India, had grown very wide.

Many supporters of imperialism embraced a new ideology, Social Darwinism, that was based on ideas about the natural world developed by British scientist Charles Darwin, who described a struggle for existence among species (see Chapter 20). Social Darwinists, interpreting this struggle as survival of the fittest, applied this notion to the human world of social classes and nations. Industrialized peoples considered themselves most fit and the poor or exploited less fit. A German naval officer wrote in 1898 that "the struggle for life exists among individuals, provinces, parties and states. The latter wage it either by the use of arms or in the economic field. Those who don't want to, will perish."[23]

To justify imperialism, Social Darwinists stereotyped Asian and African societies as "backward" and even "barbarian," upholding their own nations as "superior" and "civilized" peoples with the right to rule. As most Westerners took innate inequality for granted, Western racism and arrogance increased. Hence, whereas many Western observers once admired the Chinese, and Enlightenment thinkers viewed China as a secular, efficient government model, by the 1800s Europeans and North Americans pejoratively scorned "John Chinaman" and the "heathen Chinee." Intellectual and political leaders popularized these stereotypes. Cecil Rhodes boasted, "I contend that we British are the finest race in the world, and that the more of the world we inhabit the better it is for the human race."[24]

This self-proclaimed superiority legitimized "improving" other people by bringing them Western culture and religion. The French proclaimed their "civilizing mission" in Africa and Indochina, the British in India claimed they were "taking up the white man's burden," and Americans colonized the Philippines claiming condescendingly to "uplift" their "little brown brothers." Western defenders argued that colonialism gave "stagnating" non-Western societies better government and drew them out of isolation into the world market. A British newspaper in 1896 claimed that "the advance of the Union Jack means protection for weaker races, justice for the oppressed, liberty for the down-trodden."[25] However, most people in Asia, Africa, and the Pacific opposed colonialism, seeing the terrible toll on their lives. Indian nationalist leader Mohandas Gandhi, educated in Britain, reflected the resentment. When asked what he thought about "Western civilization," he reportedly replied that civilizing the West would be a good idea. The tensions, resentments, and mindsets that developed between Western colonizers and the societies they impacted can still be seen in various international disputes and even military conflicts today.

KEY POINTS

▶ Even after losing thirteen of its North American colonies, Britain continued to dominate the world economy through its other holdings and its technological advantages, but it gradually lost ground, especially to the United States.

▶ As Germany, France, and the United States became more competitive with Britain, the powers competed for colonies that could provide natural resources for their industries and power over their rivals.

▶ In the renewed scramble for colonial domination, many African, Asian, and Pacific peoples resisted Western imperialism, but the technological advantage of Western nations often proved insurmountable.

▶ Westerners rationalized imperialism and colonization as good for the colonized, who were offered the fruits of Western culture in exchange for their independence.

---

[22]Quoted in John Steele Gordon, *A Thread Across the Ocean: The Heroic Story of the Transatlantic Cable* (New York: Perennial, 2003), 215.

[23]Quoted in Winnifred Baumgart, *Imperialism: The Idea and Reality of British and French Colonial Expansion, 1880–1914* (New York: Oxford University Press, 1986), 88.

[24]Quoted in L. S. Stavrianos, *Global Reach: The Third World Comes of Age* (New York: William Morrow, 1981), 263.

[25]Quoted in Baumgart, *Imperialism*, 52.

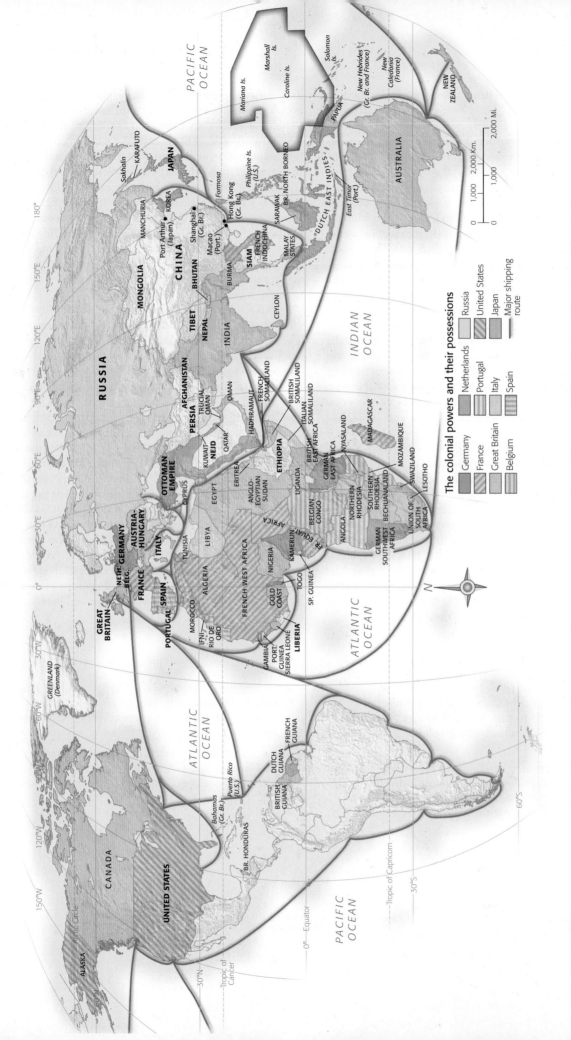

MAP 19.4 **The Great Powers and their Colonial Possessions in 1913** By 1913 the British and French controlled huge empires, with colonies in Africa, southern Asia, the Caribbean zone, and the Pacific Basin. Russia ruled much of northern Eurasia, while the United States, Japan, and a half dozen European nations controlled smaller empires.

Q From this map can we identify which countries or regions today might have the strongest resentments of the Western powers?

The colonial powers and their possessions

- Germany
- France
- Great Britain
- Belgium
- Netherlands
- Portugal
- Italy
- Spain
- Russia
- United States
- Japan
- Major shipping route

Chapter Summary

The years between 1750 and 1914 were an age when revolutions reshaped economies, governments, and social systems in Europe and the Americas. Colonists in North America overthrew British rule and established a republic that included democratic institutions. The French Revolution ended the French monarchy and brought the middle classes to power. Although the Revolution was consumed in violence and then modified by Napoleon Bonaparte's dictatorship, the shock waves reverberated around Europe, carrying with them new ideas about liberty and equality. The American and French Revolutions also inspired peoples in the Caribbean and Latin America. Haitians ended slavery and forced out the French colonial regime and planters, and in South America creoles waged successful wars of independence against Spanish rule.

The Industrial Revolution, which began in Britain in the late 1700s, transformed societies profoundly, reorienting life to cities and factories and producing goods in unparalleled abundance. Until the 1850s Britain enjoyed unchallenged economic power. With the spread of industrialization, positions of world economic leadership began to change. New ideologies contributed to the creation of new states and government structures. Nationalism introduced new ideas of the nation and provided a glue to bind people within the same nation. Liberalism promoted increasing freedom and democracy. Socialism addressed the dislocations industrialization created and sought to improve life for the new working classes by forging a system of collective ownership of economic property. Capitalism, industrialization, and interstate rivalries in the West also generated a worldwide scramble for colonies and neocolonies in the later 1800s, allowing Western businesses to seek resources and markets abroad. This imperialism brought many more societies into a global system largely dominated by the West.

Key Terms

Age of Revolution 479
Jacobins 482
Industrial Revolution 488
Luddites 490
laissez faire 491

ideology 493
Nationalism 493
nation-states 494
Zionism 495
liberalism 495

parliamentary democracy 495
socialism 496
proletariat 496

Changing Societies in Europe, the Americas, and Oceania, 1750–1914

"

Of course, some day we [Americans] shall step in. We are bound to. We shall be giving the word for everything: industry, trade, law, journalism, art, politics, and religion. We shall run the world's business whether the world likes it or not. The world can't help it, and neither can we, I guess.

"

—American millionaire in Joseph Conrad's novel *Nostromo* (1904)[1]

Brees, Samuel Charles/State Library Victoria

IMAGE 20.1 **Australian Gold Rush** The discovery of gold in southeastern Australia set off a gold rush in the 1850s. Hoping to strike it rich, miners, often from other countries such as China, flocked to the gold fields, and immigration to Australia boomed. This painting from 1856 shows a long line of Chinese gold workers walking through the gold rush town of Bendigo in Victoria, Australia, heading for the mines.

Q What does this painting tell us about the gold mining towns in Australia?

[1]Quoted in Joseph Conrad, *Nostromo* (Garden City, NY: Doubleday, Page, and Company, 1924), 77.

In 1871 a thirty-three-year-old Japanese samurai and Confucian scholar, Kume Kunitake (1839–1931), began a three-week voyage on an American steamship to San Francisco as part of an official information-gathering Japanese delegation to the United States and then Europe. Visiting factories, museums, schools, churches, public parks, and scenic mountains around the country, Kume recorded his perceptive impressions of Western life but also filtered them through Japanese cultural concepts, concluding that "customs and characteristics of East and West are invariably different." Although admiring U.S. democracy, he also perceived potential disorder, since Americans were "careless about official authority, each person insisting on his own rights." Kume recorded Americans' friendliness but also brashness, ambition, and sense of destiny, attitudes satirized four decades later by Polish-born British novelist Joseph Conrad in *Nostromo*. Traveling around Europe, Kume noted how Europeans treasured and even imitated Japanese art. He loved the cafes, theaters, and art museums of Paris. But this ardent Confucian rationalist considered Christianity irrational and the Christian Bible full of "absurd tales." Kume contrasted splendid churches with people's poverty. But he preferred Europe's constitutional monarchies to the untidy U.S. republic, viewing rapidly industrializing Germany as Japan's natural model. Returning home by ship, Kume's delegation passed through Western colonies such as Ceylon, Singapore, and Hong Kong, Kume writing that "Europeans treated the natives with arrogance and cruelty."[2]

Kume's observations reflected the revolutions, industrialization, nation building, and overseas imperialism that reshaped European and American social, cultural, and intellectual patterns in this era while also demonstrating how much more connected the world had become. By 1914 the United States, Canada, and Mexico occupied all of North America; Latin America was divided into many countries large and small; and while some Caribbean societies were independent, many remained colonies. Europeans also settled the Pacific region known today as Oceania, Australia, and New Zealand and colonized the smaller Pacific islands. Although vast distances and unique characteristics separated Europe, the Americas, and Oceania, similar patterns of capitalism, migration, and nation building shaped their societies.

---

[2]The Kume quotes are from Donald Keene, *Modern Japanese Diaries: The Japanese at Home and Abroad as Revealed Through Their Diaries* (New York: Columbia University Press, 1998), 90–115.

20-1 The Reshaping of European Societies

TRANSITIONS　SOCIETIES

Q How and why did European social, cultural, and intellectual patterns change during this era?

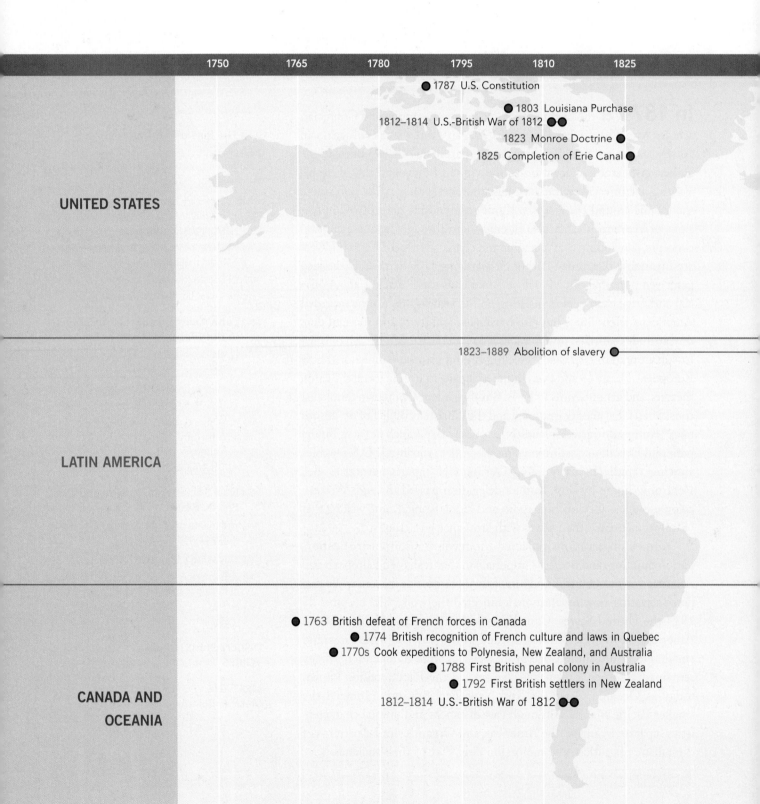

	1750	1765	1780	1795	1810	1825

UNITED STATES

● 1787 U.S. Constitution
● 1803 Louisiana Purchase
1812–1814 U.S.-British War of 1812 ●●
1823 Monroe Doctrine ●
1825 Completion of Erie Canal ●

LATIN AMERICA

1823–1889 Abolition of slavery ●

CANADA AND OCEANIA

● 1763 British defeat of French forces in Canada
● 1774 British recognition of French culture and laws in Quebec
● 1770s Cook expeditions to Polynesia, New Zealand, and Australia
● 1788 First British penal colony in Australia
● 1792 First British settlers in New Zealand
1812–1814 U.S.-British War of 1812 ●●

Thanks to destabilizing revolutions in political and economic life (see Chapter 19), modern Europeans lived in a world of cities, new occupations, and rising populations, prompting millions of people

CONNECTION to TODAY

Which of the many changes and new directions of this era do you think have influenced our world today the most?

to emigrate to the Americas, southern Africa, and Oceania seeking work and a better life. Industrialization transformed social structures and family systems. Thought, art, and science reflected and also shaped the new Europe,

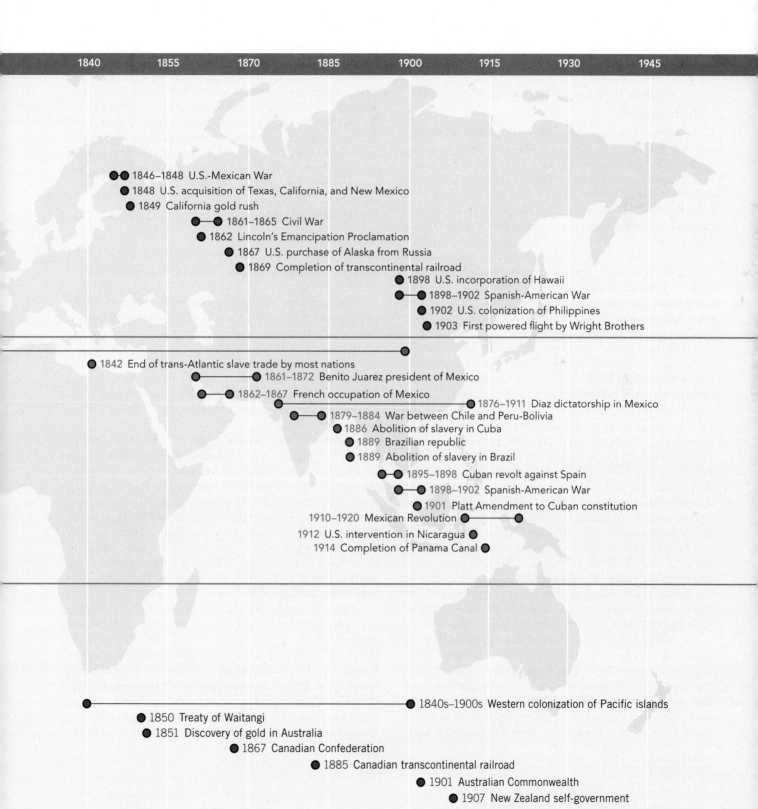

| 1840 | 1855 | 1870 | 1885 | 1900 | 1915 | 1930 | 1945 |

1846–1848 U.S.-Mexican War
1848 U.S. acquisition of Texas, California, and New Mexico
1849 California gold rush
1861–1865 Civil War
1862 Lincoln's Emancipation Proclamation
1867 U.S. purchase of Alaska from Russia
1869 Completion of transcontinental railroad
1898 U.S. incorporation of Hawaii
1898–1902 Spanish-American War
1902 U.S. colonization of Philippines
1903 First powered flight by Wright Brothers

1842 End of trans-Atlantic slave trade by most nations
1861–1872 Benito Juarez president of Mexico
1862–1867 French occupation of Mexico
1876–1911 Diaz dictatorship in Mexico
1879–1884 War between Chile and Peru-Bolivia
1886 Abolition of slavery in Cuba
1889 Brazilian republic
1889 Abolition of slavery in Brazil
1895–1898 Cuban revolt against Spain
1898–1902 Spanish-American War
1901 Platt Amendment to Cuban constitution
1910–1920 Mexican Revolution
1912 U.S. intervention in Nicaragua
1914 Completion of Panama Canal

1840s–1900s Western colonization of Pacific islands
1850 Treaty of Waitangi
1851 Discovery of gold in Australia
1867 Canadian Confederation
1885 Canadian transcontinental railroad
1901 Australian Commonwealth
1907 New Zealand self-government

resulting in innovations that influenced peoples around the world. As European immigrants settled in North America, Australia, New Zealand, and also various Latin American countries such as Argentina, Brazil, Chile, and Uruguay, they planted European institutions and ideas after largely displacing and sometimes attempting to exterminate indigenous populations. These European institutions were then modified by time, circumstances, and the cultures of indigenous peoples, such as Native Americans and New Zealand Maori, or imported peoples such as Afro-Americans, Afro-Brazilians, and Afro-Cubans.

20-1a Population Growth, Emigration, and Urbanization

In the Modern Era, expanding economies, better public health, and new crops such as American potatoes lowered mortality rates and fostered population growth, as people married earlier and in larger numbers than in Early Modern times. Europe's population (including Russia) grew from 100 million in 1650 to 190 million in 1800 and to 420 million in 1900. This growth created problems. English clergyman and economist Thomas Malthus argued in 1798 that without the checks of poverty, disease, war, and famine, the population would outgrow its means of subsistence. In some regions overpopulation indeed brought bleak poverty and underemployment, a trend that accelerated when small family farms were replaced by large farms that needed fewer workers. But urban and industrial growth also provided new employment opportunities.

Population growth and poverty spurred migration within Europe and emigration overseas. Many Poles, for example, moved to northern France and western Germany, while Irish immigrants built railroads, canals, and roads in England. Emigration cut Ireland's population by half between 1841 and 1911. In eastern Europe and Russia, Jews migrated because they became public scapegoats for unresolved problems and were sometimes subjected to violent, usually coordinated mob attacks known as *pogroms* (from the Russian word meaning "roundup"). As a result, many sought better lives in western Europe and the Americas. In all, some forty-five million Europeans emigrated to the Americas, Australia, New Zealand, Algeria, and South Africa to escape their difficulties (see Map 20.1).

Internal migration also occurred as rural people moved to industrial cities. By 1900, 90 percent of Britons lived in towns and cities, the world's highest rate. Manchester, the center of the British cotton industry, grew tenfold between 1800 and 1900, while London increased from 900,000 to 4.7 million, Paris from 600,000 to 3.6 million, and Berlin from 170,000 to 2.7 million. Urbanization fostered social problems. Rapidly expanding cities lacked social services such as sanitation, street cleaning, and water distribution. Huge numbers lived in poverty, crammed into overcrowded housing in crime-ridden slums with high disease rates, overflowing privies, and littered streets. As the English poet William Blake wrote: "Every night and every morn, some to misery are born." Most Europeans' standard of living did not rise much until the 1880s, when incomes began improving and several countries, including Britain and Germany, began building a social safety net for their citizens. By 1900 British and French workers earned nearly twice their wages in 1850. By 1914 a decline in the birthrate in much of Europe suggested that people wanted to protect their new standards of living and hence had fewer children, perhaps assisted by new forms of contraception.

Western European rural life also changed. New agricultural technology and practices fostered better yields, more mechanization, and improved animal breeding, while market agriculture largely displaced subsistence production. But peasants often earned low wages, and many small farmers lost their land to highly capitalized, mechanized operations. Occasional famines also occurred, notably in Ireland and Russia. Some feudal traditions remained influential in eastern Europe, especially Russia and Poland, where landed gentry retained authority over peasant lives.

20-1b Social Life, Families, and Gender Relations

In the Modern Era Europeans enjoyed wider social horizons than their ancestors. After 1870 mass-distribution newspapers, organized football (soccer) leagues, widespread vacation travel, and other activities connected peoples within and between nations. The world's first cinema opened in Paris in 1896, launching a film industry that became popular entertainment in Europe and then the world. People also enjoyed more options in life choices: where to live, work, or worship and whom to marry. Choice brought more personal freedom but also more social instability. Some viewed these changes as liberation; others concluded they fostered anxious uncertainty.

Industrialization reshaped sexual attitudes, particularly in Britain. The middle class, considering unbridled passion a sign of bad character, increasingly discouraged sexual activity before marriage while limiting it within marriage. In contrast, working classes experienced higher illegitimacy rates and more frequent sexual relations. Marital infidelity flourished in urban slums, fostering negative middle-class stereotypes of the poor. A British factory girl in 1909 complained, "I wanted no one to know that I was a factory girl because I was ashamed at my position. I was always hearing people say that factory girls were loose-living and corrupt."[3]

Home life and families changed. During the Early Modern Era many in Britain and Holland began living in nuclear families, usually including just parents and their children. During the 1800s nuclear families became common in northern Europe, especially among middle classes, while large extended families remained the norm in southern and eastern Europe. Unlike in earlier centuries, families now included few nonrelated members. In the 1700s western Europeans began choosing their partner and marrying for love rather than to meet family

---

[3]Quoted in Frederic Delouche et al., *Illustrated History of Europe* (New York: Barnes and Noble, 2001), 312.

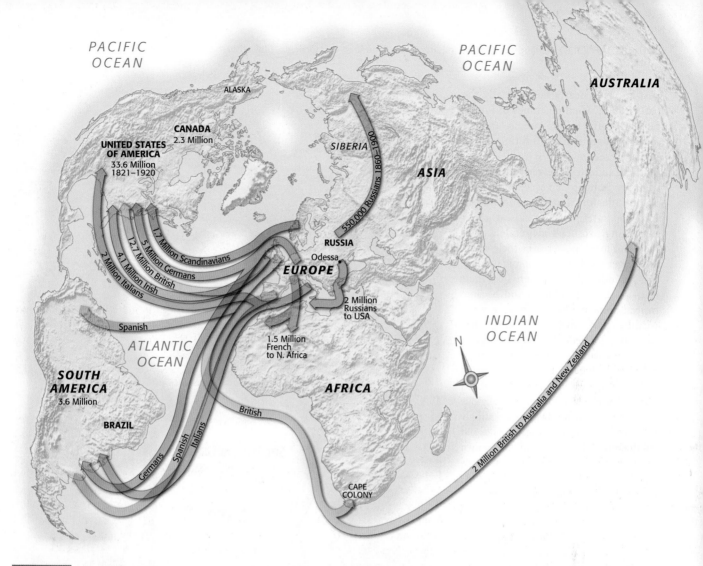

PACIFIC OCEAN

PACIFIC OCEAN

AUSTRALIA

ALASKA

CANADA
2.3 Million

UNITED STATES
OF AMERICA
33.6 Million
1821–1920

SIBERIA

550,000 Russians 1890–1900

ASIA

RUSSIA
Odessa
EUROPE

1.7 Million Scandinavians
5 Million Germans
4.1 Million British
12.7 Million Irish
2 Million Italians

2 Million
Russians
to USA

INDIAN OCEAN

Spanish

ATLANTIC
OCEAN

1.5 Million
French
to N. Africa

N

SOUTH
AMERICA
3.6 Million

AFRICA

BRAZIL

British

Germans
Spanish
Italians

2 Million British to Australia and New Zealand

CAPE
COLONY

MAP 20.1 **European Emigration, 1820–1910** Pushed by rapid population growth and poverty, millions of Europeans left their homes to settle in the Americas (especially the United States), North and South Africa, Siberia, Australia, and New Zealand. The British and Irish accounted for the largest numbers of emigrants, nearly seventeen million combined.

Q What does this map tell us about the populations of North and South America, South Africa, Australia, and Siberia today?

demands or economic need. Married men and women often spent more time with their same-sex friends than their spouses, with the line between friendships and homosexual relationships sometimes becoming murky.

Family life was also redefined. By the later 1800s some men and women, criticizing marriage as stifling and old-fashioned, lived out of wedlock with lovers. Prominent artistic and political people, such as popular French actress Sarah Bernhardt, openly had affairs or, like fiery German socialist Rosa Luxemburg, lived openly with same-sex partners. Homosexuals occupied all levels of society but often faced discrimination and persecution. The Irish poet, novelist, and playwright Oscar Wilde (1854–1900), a married father of two, was tried and imprisoned in 1895 for engaging in homosexual relationships, known as sodomy. Increasing attention to homosexuality and the first scientific studies of it sparked heated and ongoing debates as to whether the behavior

or orientation was in fact a natural phenomenon or, as some Victorian critics believed, a perversion. While in the present day the scientific consensus has long maintained that homosexuality is naturally occurring, this debate continues in many nations, mixed in with politics, pseudoscience, and differences over secular and religious viewpoints.

The industrial economy was hard on families, particularly women and children. Seldom viewed as breadwinners, women typically earned only 25 percent of men's wages. Single mothers found it especially difficult to earn a living, with some forced into prostitution for survival. Many women and children did hard manual labor in cotton mills and coal mines. In 1838 a liberal British Parliament member reported: "I saw a cotton mill, a sight that froze my blood, full of women, young, all of them, some large with child, and obliged to stand twelve hours each day. The heat was excessive in some of the rooms, the stink pestiferous. I nearly fainted."[4] By the early 1900s, when machines did more factory work, fewer women and far fewer children worked full time in the industrial sector.

The Industrial Revolution, in many cases by moving the workplace from home to factory, put men and women into separate work worlds, thereby increasing women's dependence on men and men's power over their wives. No longer needed in economic production, middle-class women lost their roles as direct producers and became instead home managers ("housewives"). Middle-class men, believing that women belonged at home as submissive helpmates, encouraged them to cultivate their beauty and social graces to please men. While men dominated political, social, economic, and religious spheres, women's roles were increasingly restricted to marriage, motherhood, and childrearing. They could not vote or own property. Often women, without legal standing, could not divorce their husbands. To be unmarried and pregnant meant deep trouble and compromised a woman's "virtue." For most of history, in many Western societies aborting an early (but not necessarily later-term) pregnancy was generally considered a private matter controlled by women and was not a crime. But by the early and mid-1800s more governments, wanting to raise birthrates as nationalism and imperialism increased tensions between countries, began to criminalize the procedure and it moved underground. Nonetheless many desperate, often poor women still opted for abortion. Meanwhile, upper- and middle-class women limited their number of children by practicing artificial birth control. By 1900, however, women enjoyed longer life expectancies and devoted fewer years to childbearing and childrearing.

In the later 1800s European women gained more legal rights and economic opportunities. Some women became secretaries, telephone operators, department store sales clerks, and occasionally professionals. The Netherlands had Europe's first woman physician in 1870, France the first woman lawyer in 1903. Leading professionals—such as Italian educator Maria Montessori (mon-ti-SAWR-ee) (1870–1952), whose innovative schools allowed children to develop at their own pace; Polish-born French scientist Marie Curie (1867–1934), who won a Nobel Prize in physics in 1903; influential German composer and pianist Clara Schumann (1819–1896); and British nurse Florence Nightingale (1820–1910), who revolutionized nursing practices—provided role models. In 1867 the University of Zurich in Switzerland began to admit women, soon followed by universities in France, Sweden, and Finland.

IMAGE 20.2 "Convicts and Lunatics" The movement for women's right to vote, or suffrage, was particularly strong in Britain. This poster, designed by the artist Emily Harding Andrews for the Artist's Suffrage League around 1908, shows a woman graduate, deprived of basic political rights, treated similarly to a convict and a mentally disturbed woman.

Q What can you learn from the poster about British customs, gender relations, and feminist protests of the era?

---

[4]Quoted in Louise A. Tilly and Joan W. Scott, *Women, Work, and Family* (New York: Holt, Rinehart and Winston, 1978), 64.

Seeking more rights, some women espoused **feminism**, a philosophy promoting political, social, and economic equality for women with men. The first feminist movements emerged in Britain and Scandinavia, where activists, later known as **suffragettes**, pressed for equal voting rights with men. In 1896 Finland introduced female suffrage. British suffragettes led by Emily Pankhurst (1858–1928) campaigned for voting rights, giving speeches, canvassing door-to-door, and demonstrating. In southern and eastern Europe, however, feminists had only a small following.

20-1c Thought, Religion, and Culture

Europe's industrial, political, and social changes fostered new intellectual and cultural directions. Philosophers such as the Germans Immanuel Kant (1724–1804) and Friedrich Nietzsche (**NEE-chuh**) (1844–1890) debated Enlightenment values. Kant believed that experience alone was inadequate because the mind ultimately shapes perceptions, imposing structure on the sensations we see. Kant doubted that a perfect society was possible, arguing that "man wishes concord, but nature, knowing better what is good for his species, wishes discord."[5] Nietzsche rejected Enlightenment notions of progress, perceiving a growing cultural decadence caused by Christian values and democratic ideas. Unlike Enlightenment thinkers, Nietzsche perceived no fundamental moral and scientific truth, but rather misconceptions developed by each culture trying to understand the world. With no absolute truth, absolute good and evil cannot exist. Later extreme nationalists and racists distorted Nietzsche's ideas to persecute ethnic minorities, while many European and North American intellectuals, seeing truth as relative, argued that all knowledge was culturally constructed.

Religion also changed with the times. Some British churches were prominent in the movement to abolish slavery; in 1833 the parliament outlawed slavery in most parts of the empire, freeing 800,000 Africans who were the legal property of Britain's slave holders in Britain and the Americas. But parliament then betrayed the former slaves by using taxpayer money to fund a massive reparation to generously compensate the 46,000 slave holders for their loss, not the slaves for their years of unfree and unpaid labor. After centuries of bitter religious strife, gradually Protestants and Catholics learned to tolerate each other. In the later 1700s and early 1800s a religious revival inspired many European Protestants to move to the United States. Evangelicals stressed personal relations with God, favored missionary activity, and condemned behavior they considered sinful, such as social dancing and drinking. Soon new churches appeared. The charismatic British Anglican preacher John Wesley (1703–1791) founded the Methodist movement, later a church. The Society of Friends, or Quakers, emphasizing nonviolence, human dignity, and individual conscience, fought against slavery and for social and political freedom and humanitarian causes.

Many middle-class Protestants sought a liberalized faith stressing social tolerance rather than the hellfire and damnation preached by some evangelicals. As religion's relevance declined, by 1851 only half of England's population attended church.

The divide between liberal and devout Europeans fostered public debates about religion's role in society. British evangelicals sought to ban alcohol and gambling and to require businesses to close on Sunday, but many Protestants and Catholics opposed these moves.

Roman Catholic and Greek Orthodox Churches also faced challenges. As a result of the French Revolution, Catholic clergy in France and Belgium lost their privileged status. France opened a public school system in the 1890s and mandated state neutrality toward religion in 1905. However, the Catholic Church strengthened dogma and organization, with popes reasserting their theological infallibility and announcing new doctrines such as the Virgin Mary's Immaculate Conception. The church remained a major spiritual force and landowner in Austria, southern Germany, Poland, Spain, Portugal, and Italy. Meanwhile, the Greek Orthodox world fragmented into national churches in Greece, Serbia, Romania, and Bulgaria.

During this era, a growing literate public with a desire for cultural products liberated writers, composers, and artists from dependence on wealthy patrons. Classical music enjoyed a golden age, producing compositions that are still enjoyed by audiences around the world. Influenced by the Enlightenment, Austrian Wolfgang Amadeus Mozart (**MOTE-sahrt**) (1756–1791) wrote thirty-five symphonies, eight operas, and many concertos. Inspired by the Age of Revolution, some thinkers and artists also adopted **romanticism**, a philosophical, literary, artistic, and musical movement that questioned rationalist Enlightenment values, instead glorifying emotions, imagination, and heroism. Some romantics celebrated great figures such as Napoleon Bonaparte. German writer Friedrich Schiller (1759–1805) offered nationalist images, such as a poem turning the story of William Tell, a legendary Swiss resistance hero, into a manifesto for German political freedom. Influenced by nationalism, one of the early operas of Italian Giuseppi Verdi (**VER-dee**) (1813–1901) begins with the refrain: "Long live Italy!" Romanticism inspired German composer Ludvig von Beethoven (1770–1827), whose much-admired *Ninth Symphony* set Schiller's poem, "Ode to Joy," to music.

Some writers and artists embraced another movement, realism, that portrayed a grimy industrial world filled with uncertainty and conflict. Liberal Spanish painter Francisco de Goya's (1746–1828) moving series on Napoleon's invasion of Spain portrayed not warfare's heroism but its horrors: orphans, pain, rape, blood, despair. British realist novelist and former factory worker Charles Dickens (1812–1870) revealed industrial life's hardships, capitalism's injustices, and the miseries of the poor. Some writers fit into no particular trend. One of these, Jane Austin (1775–1817) in Britain, wrote novels of keen wit that offered subtle

> **feminism** A philosophy promoting political, social, and economic equality for women with men.

> **suffragettes** Women who press for the same voting rights as men.

> **romanticism** A philosophical, literary, artistic, and musical movement that questioned the Enlightenment's rationalist values and instead glorified emotions, individual imagination, and heroism.

---

[5]Quoted in T. W. C. Blanning, "The Commercialization and Sacralization of European Culture in the Nineteenth Century," in *The Oxford Illustrated History of Modern Europe*, ed. T. W. C. Blanning (Oxford, UK: Oxford University Press, 1996), 147.

observations on society. Austin's books remain popular today and several have been turned into successful feature films by a filmmaker born in India.

Several significant movements reflecting Asian, African, and Pacific artistic influences shaped visual arts in the later 1800s. **Modernism** embraced progress, welcoming the future. Realistic landscape paintings, photography, and Japanese prints also contributed to the rise in France of **impressionism**, an artistic movement expressing immediate impressions aroused in momentary scenes that were bathed in changing light and color. Painters such as Claude Monet **(moe-NAY)** (1840–1926) and Pierre Renoir **(ren-WAH)** (1841–1919) achieved worldwide fame. Some French artists also rebelled against impressionism and returned to familiar shapes and compositions, including Paul Cezanne **(say-ZAN)** (1839–1906), famous for landscapes, still lifes, and portraits; Dutch-born Vincent Van Gogh **(van GO)** (1853–1890), who introduced intense primary colors and thick brushstrokes; and Paul Gauguin **(go-GAN)** (1848–1903), a French former stockbroker whose richly colored paintings often featured idyllic scenes of Polynesian life based on his long residence there, stimulating European interest in the wider world. Pablo Picasso (1881–1973), a young Spaniard in Paris, revolutionized Western art by integrating ideas from African sculpture and masks. The new art bore little resemblance to medieval art.

20-1d Science and Technology

The Modern Era saw spectacular achievements in science and technology. British naturalist Charles Darwin (1809–1882), after traveling for years around the world studying plants, animals, and fossils, formulated the theory of evolution emphasizing the natural selection of species: Individuals developed variations that helped them to compete for food and domination within their own species and to triumph over rival species. His book, *On the Origin of Species,* argued that all existing plant and animal species, including humans, evolved into their present forms over millions of years, during which time species either adapted to their environment or died out. Eventually evolution became the foundation for modern biological sciences but, while most scientists strongly

modernism A cultural trend that embraced progress and welcomed the future.

impressionism An artistic movement that sought to express the immediate impression aroused by momentary scenes that were bathed in light and color.

agree with the evolutionary approach, they still debate evolution's precise mechanisms. Although it was confirmed by many studies and accepted by most scientists, it also provoked controversy, as many churches saw evolutionary theory as degrading humans, contradicting biblical accounts of human origins, and negating religious faith. This divide between most scientists and some religious groups continues today.

Later in the Modern Era, German-born Jewish physicist Albert Einstein (1879–1955) made discoveries that rank him with Galileo, Newton, and Darwin as a pathbreaking scientist. His papers on the theory of relativity, published in the early 1900s, provided the basis for modern physics, our understanding of the universe, and the atomic age. Einstein clarified space and time, showing that distances and durations are not, as Newton thought, absolute but affected by one's motion. His proving that matter can be converted into energy and that everything is composed of atoms made possible atomic energy. Einstein taught in Swiss, Czech, and German universities before immigrating to the United States in 1934 as Germany increased discrimination against Jews.

Many other thinkers made technological discoveries that improved people's lives such as electric batteries, motors, and generators as new sources of power. Physicians introduced the first effective vaccines against deadly diseases such as smallpox that had long ravaged the world. In 1895 German physicist Wilhelm Röntgen **(RUNT-guhn)** (1845–1923) discovered x-rays, spurring progress in diagnosis and surgery. Together medical advances and improved sanitation fostered better public health. For example, thanks to cleaner water, Europe's industrial cities eradicated cholera. Meanwhile, electric batteries, motors, and generators provided new power sources. Italian Guglielmo Marconi (1874–1937) introduced wireless telegraphy and used his invention in 1901 to communicate between England and Canada, further connecting the world. Two Germans, Gottlieb Daimler and Karl Benz, became the "fathers of the automobile," producing the first petroleum-powered vehicle in the 1880s.

Meanwhile, some scientists worried about industrial pollution's effects on the environment. Observing that carbon dioxide emissions from coal-burning factories heated the atmosphere, Swedish scientist Svante Arrhenius identified a "greenhouse effect" that potentially threatened modern societies. Later scientific studies confirmed his fears. As the climate dramatically changes and the planet warms a little more nearly every year, the world still struggles with the promise but also the perils of the technologies and industrial processes developed in this era.

KEY POINTS

▶ In Europe, better crops and health care produced larger populations, which led to increasing urbanization, impoverishment, and emigration.

▶ Industrialization made men more powerful and relegated women to the home, but in the late nineteenth century women began to gain legal rights and economic opportunities.

▶ While some Protestants attempted to stamp out behavior they considered sinful, Europeans as a whole became more secular and the Catholic Church's influence declined.

▶ Artists, writers, and composers became dependent on the public marketplace rather than wealthy patrons, and artistic trends such as romanticism, realism, modernism, and impressionism became dominant.

▶ Advances in science and technology led to the theory of evolution, greater understanding of the physical world, improved medical care, new sources of energy, and new concerns about pollution and its effects.

20-2 The Rise of the United States

SOCIETIES **TRANSITIONS**

Q What impact did westward expansion, immigration, and industrialization have on American society?

After the Revolution, Americans began building their new nation, establishing new government forms, reshaping economic patterns, fostering a new culture, and moving westward. They also conquered Native Americans, acquired Mexican territory, and became involved in the wider world. By expanding its frontiers and rapidly industrializing between 1860 and 1914 the United States changed dramatically. The Civil War maintained the nation's territorial unity, ended slavery, and spurred federal government centralization, which, combined with economic protectionism, allowed the United States to duplicate the economic and political growth that mercantilism had fostered in Early Modern western Europe. Industrialization created more wealth, supported U.S. power, and reshaped American society. By 1900 the United States had a larger population than all but one European nation; boasted the world's most productive economy; owned half a continent; enjoyed a powerful, stable, democratic government; and exercised power abroad—all sustained by abundant natural resources. Now a world power, the United States extended its political and economic influence into Latin America, Asia, and the Caribbean.

20-2a The Early Republic and American Society

At first, the new American republic—weak, disunited, and surrounded by hostile neighbors in British Canada and the Spanish American Empire—found nation building challenging. Seeking to unite the diverse states, Americans ultimately forged a distinctive representative democracy while constructing an economic framework to preserve independence and encourage free enterprise. The Constitution and Bill of Rights established a relatively powerful central government, elected by voters in each state, within a federal system that recognized each member state's lawmaking powers. By the mid-1800s all white adult males could vote, but the nation maintained slavery until the end of the Civil War and excluded Native Americans and women from political activity.

Professing a love of freedom, Americans have had to constantly redefine the balance between the rights of the state and the individual and between the majority and the minority. The U.S. political system mixed liberalism, which underpinned the Bill of Rights, and fear of disorder. The founders made tyranny difficult by separating government powers into executive and legislative branches and an independent judiciary. But, wary of radicalism and shocked by the French Revolution's excesses, American leaders also discouraged attacks on the upper classes by limiting voting rights, such as through property and literacy qualifications, and by electing the president indirectly through the Electoral College, in which each state chose electors to

> ### CONNECTION to TODAY
> What do you see as the most valuable ideas, policies, and cultural forms to have developed in the United States in this era?

cast their votes. This system has produced results that have not reflected the national popular vote four times (in 1876, 1888, 2000, and 2016), when the popular vote loser won by gaining more electoral votes. The College has been polarizing among Americans since it began. Critics argue that it was established in order to give added weight and hence a political advantage to less populated rural states and the many small states at the expense of big states and city voters.

American leaders wanted a sound economic foundation. While southern plantation interests favored free trade to market their crops abroad without obstacles, many founders, insisting that economic independence was necessary to safeguard political independence, preferred self-reliance and **protectionism**, using trade barriers to shield local industries from foreign competition. The first treasury secretary, West Indian–born Alexander Hamilton (1757–1804), established a national bank, favored high tariffs to exclude competitive foreign goods, and provided government support for manufacturing. Continued conflicts with Britain sparked a temporary embargo of all foreign trade in 1807, stimulating domestic manufacturing to offset the lost imports.

Trade and border conflicts between Britain and the United States sparked the War of 1812 (1812–1814), during which the British captured the capital, Washington; burned down the White House; and repulsed a U.S. invasion of Canada. After some U.S. victories, the two sides negotiated peace. Industrialization proceeded in the Northeast, where the first large textile mills manufacturing finished cloth opened in New England. Northern industrialists favoring protectionist policies soon prevailed over southern planters wanting free trade. By the mid-1800s manufactured goods comprised about one-third of exports, and food and raw materials (especially wheat and cotton) two-thirds. To move resources and products, Americans built over 3,300 miles of canals, including the Erie Canal across New York State, linking midwestern markets and resources to New York City.

Gradually American society diverged from Britain's. French writer Alexis de Tocqueville (1805–1859), visiting the United States in the early 1830s, noted Americans' commitment to democracy, individualism, and "unbounded desire for riches."[6] But he condemned slavery and feared that too much individualism and greed undermined community. De Tocqueville admired single American women's independence, marriage as voluntarily uniting loving equals, and married women's influence in the family. Nonetheless, men who believed women's place was in the home still controlled many women's lives.

> **protectionism** Use of trade barriers to shield local industries from foreign competition.

---

[6]Alexis De Tocqueville, *Democracy in America and Two Essays on America* (New York: Penguin, 2003), xxxiii.

Discover Historical Voices

Protesting Sexism and Slavery

Sarah Grimke and her younger sister, Angelina, daughters of a wealthy slaveholding family in Charleston, South Carolina, adopted the Quaker faith, which emphasized human dignity. Rejecting their elite status, they dedicated their lives to advocating women's rights and abolition of slavery. In 1837 they moved north, where they gave lectures before large audiences, often drawing criticism from churches for violating gender expectations and speaking out so publicly. In 1838 Sarah Grimke responded by writing letters to her critics using Christian arguments to defend women's right and obligation to voice their views. The letters, published together in one volume, became the first American feminist treatise on women's rights. The following excerpts convey some of Grimke's arguments.

Here then I plant myself. God created us equal; he created us free agents; he is our Lawgiver, our King and our Judge, and to him alone is woman bound to be in subjection, and to him alone is she accountable for the use of those talents with which her Heavenly Father has entrusted her....As I am unable to learn from sacred writ when woman was deprived by God of her equality with man, I shall touch upon a few points in the Scriptures, which demonstrate that no supremacy was granted to man....[In the Bible] we find the commands of God invariably the same to man and woman; and not the slightest intimation is given in a single passage, that God designed woman to point to man as her instructor....

I hope that the principles I have asserted will claim the attention of some of my sex, who may be able to bring into view, more thoroughly than I have done, the situation and degradation of women....During the early part of my life, my lot was cast among the butterflies of the *fashionable* world; and of this class of women, I am constrained to say, both from experience and observation, that their education is miserably deficient; that they are taught to regard marriage as the one thing needful, the only notice of distinction; hence to attract the notice and win the attentions of men, by their external charms, is the chief business of fashionable girls. They seldom

think that men will be allured by intellectual acquirements, because they find, that where any mental superiority exists, a woman is generally shunned and regarded as stepping out of her "appropriate sphere," which, in their view, is to dress, to dance, to set out to the best possible advantage her person....To be married is too often held up to the view of girls as [necessary for] human happiness and human existence. For this purpose...the majority of girls are trained....[In education] the improvement of their intellectual capacities is only a secondary consideration....Our education consists almost exclusively of culinary and other manual operations....

There is another class of women in this country, to whom I cannot refer, without feelings of the deepest shame and sorrow. I allude to our female slaves....The virtue of female slaves is wholly at the mercy of irresponsible tyrants, and women are bought and sold in our slave markets, to gratify the brutal lust of those who bear the name of Christians....If she dares resist her seducer, her life by the laws of some of the slave States may be...sacrificed to the fury of disappointed passion....The female slaves suffer every species of degradation and cruelty, which the most wanton barbarity can inflict; they are indecently divested of their clothing, sometimes tied up and severely whipped....Can any American woman look at these scenes of shocking...cruelty, and fold her hands in apathy, and say, "I have nothing to do with slavery"? *She cannot and be guiltless.*

Reflection Questions

1. What do the letters tell us about the social expectations and education for white women from affluent families?
2. In what way do Grimke's letters address the issue of slavery?
3. How do Grimke's ideas and goals compare to feminist and antiracist ideas today?

Source: Sarah M. Grimke, *Letters on the Equality of the Sexes, and the Condition of Woman* (Boston: Issac Knapp, 1838).

Enslaved African Americans, mostly plantation workers, were concentrated in southern states, constantly replenished by new arrivals from Africa. Slave resistance was sometimes violent, such as the rebellion in Virginia led by Nat Turner in 1831. African Americans also created spirituals, based partly on African rhythms and song styles, that used Christian images to indirectly express a longing for emancipation. In "Go Down Moses," the refrain emphasized "let my people go," just as Moses led the Hebrews in Egypt to freedom. The abolitionists Sojourner Truth (ca. 1797–1883) and Frederick Douglass (1818–1895), both former slaves, also eloquently advocated emancipation, gender equality, and women's suffrage. Harriett Tubman (1822–1913), born a slave, rescued many escaped slaves and helped them to freedom in

the North along the Underground Railroad. She also served with the Union forces in the Civil War as a nurse and scout, becoming the first woman to lead a successful raid to free 700 slaves in South Carolina. After the war she became an outspoken supporter of women's rights and the suffrage movement. Many white Americans also wanted to eliminate slavery and other social ills. Sarah Grimke (1792–1873), a Quaker from a South Carolina slaveholding family, became an active abolitionist and feminist, rejecting the notion of different male and female natures (see Discovering Historical Voices: Protesting Sexism and Slavery). Upon discovering that their deceased brother had fathered two sons with one of his slaves, Sarah and her sister Angelina flouted custom and laws by raising and educating their nephews.

Distinctively American religious and cultural beliefs often ignored rigid doctrines and dogmatic church leaders. Many secular Americans, indifferent to organized religion, tolerated diverse ideas. Others actively sought personal, intense religious experiences. Religious dissenters, such as Quakers and Methodists, had long flocked to North America. Protestant denominations multiplied, reinforced periodically by religious revivals. Yet, Puritan and Calvinist values remained influential, promoting hard work and criticizing music, dancing, and reading for pleasure.

20-2b Manifest Destiny and Expansion

The nation gradually expanded westward, acquiring abundant fertile land and rich mineral deposits, thus providing a counterpart to European imperialism in Asia and Africa (see Chapter 19). As pioneers crossed the Appalachian Mountains seeking new opportunities, Americans embraced **Manifest Destiny**, the conviction that their country's unmatched institutions and culture gave them a God-given right to expand over the continent. This idea was the religious sanction for U.S. nationalism and the thrust outward. In 1823 Secretary of State John Quincy Adams favored transforming the United States into "a nation, coextensive with the North American continent, destined by God and nature to be the most populous and powerful people ever combined under one social compact."[7]

After acquiring the Ohio territory in 1787, the new nation extended from the Atlantic to the Mississippi River. In 1803, thanks to the Haitian Revolution and its drain on French coffers, President Thomas Jefferson (g. 1800–1809) astutely bought from France, in the Louisiana Purchase, much of the Midwest and South, doubling the country's

> **Manifest Destiny** Americans' conviction that their country's unmatched institutions and culture gave them a God-given right to take over the land.

Source: Library of Congress Prints and Photographs Division, Washington, D.C. [LC-USZC4-668]

IMAGE 20.3 **American Progress** This 1893 painting by the American artist John Gast extols progress and shows Americans, guided by divine providence, expanding across, and bringing civilization to, the forests and prairies of the Midwest and West. The painting reflects views held by many Americans of their destiny and special role in the world.

Q Do you think that Americans still hold these views today? If so, how do these views influence U.S. policies?

[7]Quoted in James Chase and Caleb Carr, *America Invulnerable: The Quest for Absolute Security from 1812 to Star Wars* (New York: Summit, 1988), 46.

size. Acquiring Florida and the Pacific Northwest added more. Some Americans crossed vast prairies, deserts, and mountains to Oregon by wagon train. In 1848, after the U.S.–Mexican War, the United States obtained Texas, New Mexico, and California from Mexico. Then in 1849 gold discoveries near Sacramento prompted over 100,000 Americans, known as "49ers," to board sailing ships or covered wagons and head west for California, hoping to strike it rich. In California these "49ers" sometimes clashed with immigrant Chinese and the long-settled Mexicans. Finally, the 1867 purchase of Alaska from Russia eliminated all European rivals from North America (see Map 20.2). By 1913 the United States had grown to forty-eight states.

On the vast North American frontier, settlers developed new ways of life and ideas. Cattle ranching on the Great Plains fostered a new occupation: cowboys on horseback who guided large herds on long, lonely drives to railroad towns for shipment east. Cowboys—whites, Mexicans, African Americans, and men of mixed descent—often learned survival skills from Native Americans. Individualists sought adventure, social equality, and a better life in the West. But frontier life was often hard, especially on women. An Illinois farm wife, Sara Price, lamented her hardship in poetry: "life is a toil and love is a trouble. Beauty will fade and riches will flee. Pleasures will dwindle and prices they double, And nothing is as I would wish it to be."[8]

Westward expansion came at the expense of Mexicans, Spaniards, and Native Americans already there. Native Americans, viewing whites as invaders, often resisted violently. To whites, what they called "Indians" represented an alien culture best restricted to reservations. The U.S. Supreme Court ruled in 1831 that Native Americans' "relation to the United States resembles that of a ward to his guardian."[9] Eventually, at the order of President Andrew Jackson, perhaps 100,000 Native Americans, even tribes living peacefully and who had adopted aspects of white culture, were forcibly removed from their native lands, what some today condemn as "ethnic cleansing"; many thousands died. The Cherokee—farmers of Georgia and the Carolinas who had an alphabet, constitution, published newspaper, and good relations with their white neighbors—were one of five tribes forced into concentration camps and finally, in 1838, sent on a twelve-hundred-mile forced march, the "Trail of Tears," to Oklahoma. Four thousand died from starvation or exposure. The government broke up some tribes such as the Delaware, who once controlled a large mid-Atlantic territory but were now scattered from Canada to Texas. Some tribes resisted removal. The Seminole (**SEM-uh-nole**) in Florida, led by Chief Osceola (**os-ee-OH-luh**) (ca. 1804–1838), fought two wars with the U.S. army, attacking with guerrilla tactics and then retreating into the Everglades swamps. After Osceola was finally captured, Seminole resistance faded, and many were exiled to Oklahoma. Further west the most powerful tribe, the warlike and adaptable Comanche, fiercely resisted European settlement. From around 1750 to 1850 they had

sphere of interest An area in which one great power assumes responsibility for maintaining peace and monopolizes the area's resources.

dominated much of the Southwest and parts of the southern Midwest, fighting other tribes and resisting Spanish, French, and American encroachment. But the slaughter by both Native Americans and American settlers and soldiers of thirty-one million buffalo between 1868 and 1881 undermined the Comanche economy, contributing to their downfall and final defeat in 1871.

The quest for resources and markets spurred territorial expansion into Latin America and the formation of an empire. In 1823 Congress approved the Monroe Doctrine, a unilateral statement warning European nations against interfering in the Western Hemisphere and affirming U.S. commitment to shape Latin America's post-Spain political future. In the early 1900s the U.S. Secretary of State reaffirmed this pattern, claiming that the U.S. "considers its own interests. The integrity of other American nations is an incident, not an end."[10] The doctrine claimed Latin America as an American **sphere of interest**, a region where one great power assumes responsibility for maintaining peace and monopolizes resources. The Monroe Doctrine forged complex links between the United States and Latin America, often provoking hostility, and set the stage for the United States as a world power. Even in recent years some U.S. leaders, seeking to interfere in Latin American affairs, still employ the Monroe Doctrine rhetoric as a justification, angering many Latin Americans.

After the U.S.–Mexican War of 1846–1848, the United States greatly expanded its national territory. Some thirty-five thousand Americans, who owned many black slaves, lived in the Mexican province of Texas, chafing at Mexican rule and its anti-slavery policies, rebelled in 1836 and pushed Mexican forces out, declaring themselves an independent republic. Soon Texans sought annexation to the United States, with proslavery southern states favoring and antislavery northern states opposed. The U.S. president and Congress moved to admit Texas to statehood in 1844, provoking Mexicans, who had never recognized Texan independence. The war that followed stirred divisive and passionate debate. Many Americans opposed the conflict. After President James Polk (1795–1849) ordered military action, a Massachusetts legislative resolution proclaimed "that such a war of conquest, so hateful, unjust and unconstitutional in its origin and character, must be regarded as a war against freedom, against humanity, against justice, against the Union."[11] The war ended when fourteen thousand U.S. troops invaded Mexico, capturing Mexico City. The United States then permanently annexed Mexican territories from Texas to California, often marginalizing the local Mexican Americans and sometimes seizing their land and property. However, the conflict had killed thirteen thousand Americans and fifty thousand Mexicans, while fostering an enduring Mexican distrust of the United States.

Many Americans supported extending Manifest Destiny to Latin America and Asia. Polk wanted to seize California to increase profitable commerce with China. In 1853 Senator William Seward placed expansion in global perspective, advising Americans: "You are already the great continental power. But does that content you? I trust that it does not. You want the commerce of the world. The nation that draws the most from

---

[8]From Peter Blood-Patterson, *Rise Up Singing* (Bethlehem, PA: Sing Out Publications, 1988), 246.

[9]Quoted in Walter L. Williams, "American Imperialism and the Indians," in *Indians in American History: An Introduction*, ed. Frederick E. Hoxie (Arlington Heights, IL: Harlan Davidson, 1988), 233.

[10]Robert Lansing, quoted in Gabriel Kolko, *Main Currents in Modern American History* (New York: Pantheon, 184), 13.

[11]Quoted in Simon Serfaty, *The Elusive Enemy: American Foreign Policy Since World War II* (Boston: Little, Brown, 1972), 13.

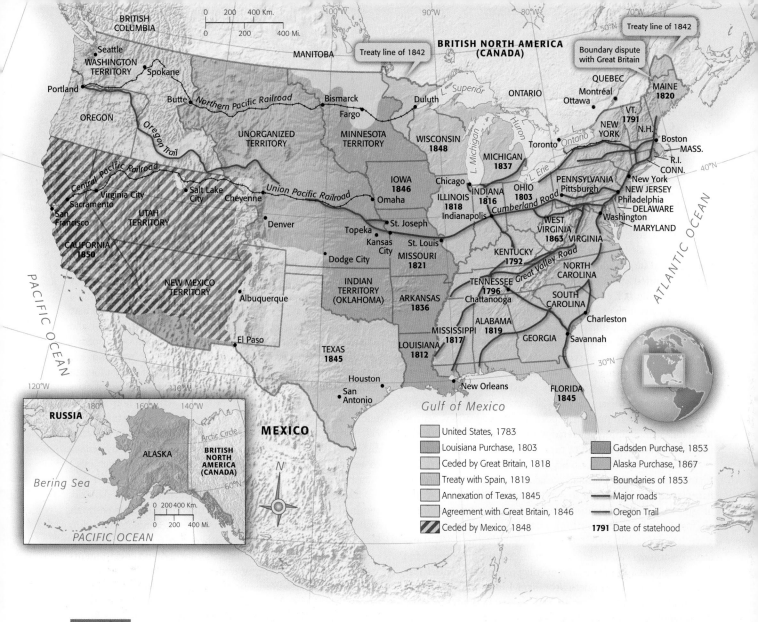

MAP 20.2 **U.S. Expansion through 1867** The United States expanded in stages after independence, gaining land from Spain, France, Britain, and Mexico until by 1867 the nation stretched from the Atlantic to the Gulf and Pacific coasts. During the same period Canadians expanded westward from Quebec to British Columbia. In both the U.S. and Canada the indigenous Native Americans were not consulted in these decisions.

Q What can we learn from this map about which parts of the United States today were once claimed by other countries and what were they?

the earth and fabricates most, and sells the most to foreign nations, must be and will be the great power of the earth."[12] Throughout the 1850s leading Americans discussed crossing the Pacific to occupy Taiwan or Okinawa as a kind of American Hong Kong (a new British colony on the China coast). American traders participated in the lucrative China trade, including opium smuggling, while the United States Navy opened up reclusive Japan. Merchants from New England ports such as Salem (Massachusetts) established, and grew rich from, operations in Asian ports such as Macao and Madras, while U.S. traders, missionaries, adventurers, diplomats, and soldiers flocked to Asia (see Chapters 22–23).

Many historians argue that, unlike Britain and Spain's territorial empires, during the nineteenth century the United States built an "informal" empire largely based on extending U.S. power through financial controls, trade, and military operations rather than formal political control. American naval forces intervened in Southeast Asia almost annually from the 1830s through the 1860s. For example, in 1832 a U.S. naval expedition bombarded a port on the Indonesian island of Sumatra, whose officials had seized a private U.S. ship for illegal activities; U.S. officials boasted that the port demolition had "struck terror," forcing release of the ship. Some leaders advocated military action to gain trade agreements, an aggressive attitude

---

[12]Quoted in William Appleman Williams, *The Contours of American History* (Chicago: Quadrangle, 1966), 284.

that increasingly influenced U.S. policies during the century. Presidents also sought to obtain nearby Cuba from Spain, even financing Cuban revolts.

20-2c The Civil War, Abolition, and Industrialization

The Civil War (1861–1865) remains a traumatic event in the American collective consciousness and reshaped U.S. society by ending slavery and preserving the union. Many Americans believed that slavery mocked liberal democracy. By the early 1800s it had largely disappeared from northern states, and in 1810 the United States outlawed the slave trade. But slavery survived in the South. By 1860, the North boasted industries, banks, and great ports such as New York, Boston, and Philadelphia. By contrast, the South, inhabited by 350,000 white families and three million black slaves, had a monocultural economy that depended on exports to survive. Some southern leaders worked to expand slavery to new states and territories. The cotton grown on the slave plantations and then transformed into yarn and cloth, mostly in northern factories, was critical to the U.S. economy as the most important export. This also made it central to an increasingly interconnected world economy, the Industrial Revolution, and the spread of capitalism to the wider world.

Some historians contend that the Civil War was in many respects a political and social revolution as the slavery-based southern plantation society tried to break free from the urbanization, industrialization, abolitionist sentiments, and social change percolating in northern states. For southern planters slave labor was still profitable and productive. In 1860–1861 eleven southern states, hostile to the federal government, seceded from the union and formed the openly pro-slavery Confederate States of America. President Abraham Lincoln (1809–1865), an Illinois lawyer, wanting to end slavery and preserve the union, mobilized the military forces of the remaining states to resist secession. In 1862 his Emancipation Proclamation freed all slaves. Lincoln was anti-slavery and pro-worker, views he shared with Karl Marx, then a crusading journalist, with whom he enjoyed a friendly correspondence. But Lincoln also reimbursed pro-Union slaveholders in Washington, D.C., who agreed to free their slaves. Their slaves were not likewise given reparations for their long captivity. The North's dynamic economy better mobilized resources for war, while northerners enjoyed a population advantage of nearly 4 to 1. After four years of bloody fighting, the North defeated the South.

It may have been the world's first industrial conflict, involving railroads, steamships, the telegraph, and mass-manufactured weaponry. Northern victory ultimately upended the plantation system, crushed southern self-determination, destroyed the South's economic link to Britain, confirmed protectionism as economic policy, and strengthened the federal government. Some 360,000 Union and 258,000 Confederate troops died, more than in all other wars combined fought by Americans, and thousands of civilians as well. The South began to enjoy balanced economic development in the mid-twentieth century, with industries largely paid for by northern investors. The death of high tariffs finally occurred during the Great Depression of the 1930s and World War II, when a now powerful U.S. no longer feared imports and became a free trade exporting nation.

But emancipation did not eliminate the disadvantages faced by African Americans and other ethnic minorities. Although African Americans made some political gains, even holding elected office, and some acquired land during the Reconstruction era that followed the war, many of these gains were eventually ended as planter-dominated southern states grabbed the land back, barred African Americans and poor whites from voting or holding office, and constructed a system of brutal "Jim Crow" racial exclusion and discrimination. Many former slaves taught themselves to read, and some opened schools, expanding opportunities. Many also left plantations, but they found job prospects chiefly limited to sharecropping or physical labor. Moreover, long after slavery ended, African Americans faced laws restricting their rights. Southern states, and some northern states, prohibited interracial marriage and, unlike Latin America, offered no separate recognition for people of mixed ancestry, who were lumped with African Americans and treated as such. Any trace of African ancestry meant automatic relegation to inferior status. Skin color determined social class, and racial segregation was imposed in schools, housing, and public facilities. Those violating these laws and customs faced jail, beatings, or executions by white vigilantes. The journalist Ida B. Wells (1862–1931), born into slavery, sparked a long movement to end mob violence, including hangings (known as "lynchings"). Nevertheless, segregation remained the norm until the 1960s.

As expansion into central and western North America resumed, more Native Americans lost control of their destinies. Whites subdued the Great Plains with new technology, including six-shooters, steel ploughs, and barbed-wire fences. Farmers and ranchers reshaped prairie and northern woodland environments. Settlers, railroad builders, fur traders, wealthy sportsmen, and the U.S. army massacred millions of bison, Great Plains tribes' chief subsistence source. As one U.S. colonel advised in the late 1860s: "Kill every buffalo you can! Every buffalo dead is an Indian gone."[13] Native Americans resisted but eventually faced defeat. In 1886 the Apache, under their chief, Geronimo (1829–1909), finally surrendered after years of fighting. In 1890, the U.S. Army's massacre of three hundred Lakota Sioux followers of the Ghost Dance, an Indigenous spiritual revival movement, at Wounded Knee in South Dakota confirmed colonization of the West. Defeated, impoverished, and decimated by epidemics, Native Americans were put on government-controlled reservations, their children prohibited from speaking their native languages or practicing tribal traditions in boarding and public schools, often far from the reservation and their families. This was a deliberate policy to assimilate Native Americans into mainstream society and eventually destroy their traditional culture and identity. But they never stopped fighting back and the assimilation policy finally began to end in 1934, when tribal communities were allowed to form their own governments and resume their own lifeways and traditions. For many Americans the stereotypes of Native Americans remain frozen in time in tomahawks, feathers, tipis, and totem poles. The struggle continues but Native Americans dodged annihilation and some are flourishing today.

Meanwhile, northern victory and protectionism improved material life and spurred great industrial growth in the later

---

[13]Quoted in J. Weston Phippen, "Kill Every Buffalo You Can! Every Buffalo Dead is an Indian Gone," *The Atlantic*, May 13, 2016.

1800s, as new food processing, textile, iron, and steel industries flourished and coal, mineral, and oil production expanded. In 1860 the United States ranked fourth among industrial nations, but by 1894 it ranked first and trailed only Britain as a world trader. Technological innovations changed economic life. Electric power and improved production methods turned out goods faster, more cheaply, and in greater quantities than ever before, increasing U.S. competitiveness. New American inventions such as typewriters, cash registers, adding machines, telegraphs, and telephones increased business productivity. Other American and European inventions—water-tube boilers, steam-powered forging hammers, portable steam engines, and internal combustion engines—revolutionized industry. Thomas Edison (1847–1931) perfected the light bulb, benefiting both the public and industry.

Improved transportation and communication networks reshaped life and population patterns. The transcontinental railroad, completed in 1869, opened western lands for settlement. Many workers who drove spikes and blasted passages through rocks and mountains for the railroad tracks were African Americans, Chinese, or Irish. In 1903 Henry Ford's (1863–1947) motor company, manufacturing the first affordable cars, refined the mass-production assembly line. Orville and Wilber Wright achieved the first powered flight in 1903, launching the aviation age.

But industrialization also facilitated monopolistic concentration of industrial and financial resources similar to Europe's, worsening inequitable wealth distribution. A few fabulously wealthy tycoons such as John D. Rockefeller and J. P. Morgan, known to their critics as "Robber Barons," influenced politicians, controlled much economic power, and paid workers subsistence wages. The Social Darwinist Rockefeller claimed that "the growth of large business is merely survival of the fittest and a law of God."[14] Many less affluent Americans also valued and hoped to acquire wealth, considering the United States a land of opportunity where anyone could succeed with hard work regardless of social background.

Industrialization reshaped the American social structure by creating new classes of workers. Although many Americans prospered, industrial workers often experienced hard lives. In

IMAGE 20.4 **Women Textile Workers** In both Europe and North America women became the largest part of the workforce in the textile industry. These women, working in a New England spinning mill around 1850, endured harsh work conditions and the boring, often dangerous, job of tending machines.

Q What does the photo suggest about working conditions for women in mills in that era?

[14]Quoted in Robert Heilbroner and Aaron Singer, *The Economic Transformation of America, 1600 to the Present*, 3rd ed. (Fort Worth, TX: Harcourt Brace, 1994), 163.

southern Appalachian and Ohio River Valley coal mines, work was dangerous, hours long, and wages low. Children worked alongside their parents, and miners often died young from breathing coal dust. Before the Civil War the New England textile industry also badly exploited women and children. Companies recruited teenage girls from poor rural families to work fourteen hours a day (5:00 A.M.–7:00 P.M.), six days a week in dark, hot mill rooms filled with cotton dust. The girls were housed in company dormitories, six to eight girls per room. By the 1880s the textile industry moved south to Virginia and the Carolinas, where wages were lower and people even more desperate for jobs.

20-2d Social Change, Thought, and Culture

Some twenty-five million Europeans immigrated to the United States between 1870 and 1916, initially largely northwestern Europeans—English, Irish, Germans, and Scandinavians—and later many southern and eastern Europeans—Italians, Greeks, Serbs, and Poles. Some businesses posted signs saying, "No Irish need apply." With many Jews fleeing persecution, by 1927 the American Jewish population totaled four million. The population of European ancestry increased from 2.5 million in 1770 to 92 million by 1910. In addition, thousands of Chinese, Japanese, Filipino, and South Asian immigrants landed on the Pacific coast, where most of them faced discrimination. Most became miners, farmers, shopkeepers, or laborers. Some twenty thousand Chinese helped build the first trans-Pacific railroad. Asian immigrants, mostly living in western states, faced harsher restrictions and sometimes violence including occasional massacres and lynchings.

Once a mostly rural nation along the Atlantic coast, the United States became a transcontinental powerhouse. The federal government encouraged migration westward, giving free land to settlers in the Midwest, where farming became dominant, pushing cattle raising westward to frontier territories. The country also became urbanized, with half the people living in cities, including metropolises such as New York and Chicago. Industrialization, urbanization, and improved transportation spawned social change. For example, before this era many Europeans and white Americans, with less mobility, often married close family members such as a fourth cousin. Now they could find suitable partners far from their homes.

These decades also saw movements for economic and social change. Since factories produced more goods than Americans could consume, by the 1890s economic depression, panics, and bloody labor conflicts had led to working-class radicalism and discontent among the big business and industrial interests. Farmers and workers resented Robber Baron wealth and powerful large corporations and railroads. Many farmers went bankrupt, losing their land to banks. As a result, popular movements, some led by women, fought those with power and privilege. Labor unions first appeared in the 1820s; by midcentury textile mill girls were campaigning for better conditions and shorter workdays. Railroad union leader Eugene Debs (1855–1926) explained in 1893 that "the capitalists refer to you

as mill hands, farm hands, factory hands. The trouble is he owns your head and your hands."[15] By the early 1900s the radical, Marxist-influenced Industrial Workers of the World (better known as Wobblies) had gained support among some industrial workers, miners, and longshoremen. Union militants such as Irish immigrant Mary Harris ("Mother") Jones (1830–1930) organized coal miners and railroad workers, fighting big business power. Employers and their political allies, disparaging union members as communists, fought their demands.

Women, often working in factories, shops, and offices while also managing their homes, also struggled for their civil rights. Religious leaders urged women to be more pious, self-sacrificing, and obedient to men. Symbolizing this submission to male expectations, women wore stiff, uncomfortable whalebone corsets that constrained movement and accentuated their figure. Many wanted more options; banners carried by striking factory workers in 1912 read, "We want bread and roses too." Women gained basic privileges only after a long, nonviolent suffrage movement for the vote that declared that "all men and women are created equal." Suffragettes opposed a system that permitted women no rights to property or even to their own children after divorce. After seven decades of marching, publicizing their cause, and lobbying male politicians, they convinced Congress to approve women's voting rights in 1920.

During these years Americans created their own distinctive literary and intellectual traditions. Journalist Walt Whitman (1819–1892) celebrated democracy, the working class, and a broadminded view of sexual affection while addressing the impact of industrialization. Whitman described his dynamic, ethnically diverse nation as "a newer garden of creation, dense, joyous, modern, populous millions, cities and farms. By all the world contributed."[16] Inspired by European realism, Mark Twain (1835–1910), a former printer and riverboat pilot turned journalist, emphasized the underside of American life and character, was skeptical about technology's value, and opposed the increasing U.S. imperial thrust in the world.

American philosophy and religion went in new directions. Leading philosophers such as William James and John Dewey, breaking with European tradition, claimed that ideas had little value unless they enlarged people's concrete knowledge of reality, an approach known as pragmatism. While many Americans embraced secular and humanist views, others sought inspiration in religion. As the Protestant missionary impulse fostered religious and moral fervor, Americans became active as Christian missionaries around the world. Religious diversity also grew. In 1776 most Americans were Protestant, often Calvinist, but by 1914 the United States contained followers of many faiths, including some Buddhist and Muslim immigrants.

Mixing black and white traditions, Americans produced unique forms of music, especially blues and jazz. Derived from black plantation life, blues songs detailed personal woes in a harsh and racist world: lost love, police brutality, jail, joblessness, and oppression. Some songs celebrated black heroes such as the legendary hand driller and black prison inmate John Henry, who allegedly died competing against a steam drill to build a railroad tunnel in the later 1800s. The blending of black

[15]Quoted in Juliet Haines Mofford, ed., *Talkin' Union: The American Labor Movement* (Carlisle, MA: Discovery Enterprises, 1997), 24.

[16]From Mark Van Doren, ed., *The Portable Walt Whitman* (New York: Penguin, 1973), 210.

blues with white folk music and popular music fostered several twentieth-century genres, including rock, rhythm and blues, and soul, that spread around the world.

20-2e American Capitalism and Empire

As in Europe, industrial capitalism led to imperialism and warfare. Repeated economic depressions from the 1870s through the 1890s, as well as difficult domestic problems, spurred demand for foreign markets and led many American businessmen, farmers, and workers to favor overseas conquests or interventions to improve national economic prospects. Others hoped to spread freedom and capitalism. The United States sent military forces to at least twenty-seven countries and territories between 1833 and 1898 to protect American economic interests or suppress piracy threatening U.S. shipping. Troops were dispatched to many Latin American nations, China, Indonesia, Korea, and North Africa, and for decades U.S. gunships patrolled several of China's rivers, protecting American businessmen and missionaries from Chinese who resented Western imperialism.

U.S. forces also brought the Hawaiian Islands, a Polynesian kingdom, into the U.S. empire. The growing American population in Hawaii of traders, whalers, planters, and missionaries resented the Hawaiian monarchy, while Queen Liliuokalani (**luh-lee-uh-oh-kuh-LAH-nee**) (1838–1917), a Hawaiian nationalist, wanted to restrict American settler political influence. Although strong, resolute, fluent in English, and beloved by her people as a songwriter, she faced economic disaster when the U.S. Congress abandoned preferential treatment for Hawaiian sugar imports. In 1893 American settlers, aided by one hundred and fifty U.S. troops, overthrew the monarchy, formed a provisional government, and sought affiliation with the United States. A heated American debate on direct colonization delayed annexation until 1898. The monarchy's end transformed the islands socially, as Japanese, Chinese, Korean, and Filipino immigrants became the main labor force, mostly working on the sugar and pineapple plantations that provided Hawaii's major exports, owned by American settlers and companies. By the 1930s, Asians constituted the large majority of Hawaii's population. In 2016 the last Hawaiian sugar mill closed, ending an era.

The major American conflict of this era, the Spanish-American War (1898–1902), which Secretary of State John Hay called "that splendid little war," pitted American against Spanish forces in several Spanish colonies and helped make the United States a major world power and empire. With President William McKinley (1843–1901) seeking foreign markets for America's surplus production, the United States coveted Spain's restless colonies: Cuba, Puerto Rico, Guam, and the Philippines. McKinley was the first president to send troops overseas and make U.S. territorial claims abroad. The war unleashed American nationalist fervor, one observer describing patriotism as oozing out of every boy old enough to feed the pigs. While the United States quickly triumphed against the hopelessly outmatched Spanish, fifty-five hundred Americans died in Cuba, mostly of disease that caused, according to one surgeon, pale faces, sunken eyes, staggering gaits, and emaciated forms. The war made a hero of Theodore Roosevelt, a major backer of U.S. imperialism who led an irregular mounted group of American soldiers, the Rough Riders, and later was elected president. Yet, many Americans, among them social and political reformers, writers, labor leaders, some national and state legislators, and even southern farmers, opposed the war and the control of the Philippines, Cuba, and Puerto Rico, albeit for a variety of reasons.

The war also changed Americans' outlook on the world as they gradually abandoned isolation for intervention. A future president, Woodrow Wilson, boasted about America's emergence as a major power: "No war ever transformed us quite as the war with Spain. No previous years ever ran with so swift a change as the years since 1898. We have witnessed a new revolution, the transformation of America completed."[17] However, to colonize the Philippines, the United States had to brutally suppress a fierce nationalist resistance by Filipinos opposing U.S. occupation, a struggle that resulted in thousands of Filipino and American deaths. Exercising power in the world proved costly, and many Americans protested the bloody U.S. invasion of distant islands (see Chapter 22). Americans considered Filipinos and Cubans unready for self-government and needing guidance. Indiana Senator Albert Beveridge argued for colonizing the Philippines to "civilize the natives" because God "has marked the American people as His chosen nation to finally lead in the regeneration of the world."[18] Colonization of the Philippines, Puerto Rico, and Guam, and economic and political domination over nominally independent Cuba, transformed the United States from an informal into a territorial empire much like the Netherlands and Portugal.

KEY POINTS

▶ Americans gradually pushed toward the West Coast, taking advantage of abundant natural resources and inflicting great suffering on Native Americans.

▶ The Monroe Doctrine announced that the United States saw Latin America as its own sphere of interest, off-limits to European powers.

▶ The bloody and divisive U.S.–Mexican War brought a large chunk of Mexican territory under American control.

▶ Millions of immigrants poured into the United States, seeking opportunity and often finding discrimination, while social movements arose seeking better treatment for workers and greater rights for women.

▶ To promote and protect American business interests, the U.S. military intervened in the affairs of many foreign countries and territories, most notably in the Spanish-American War, which brought the United States its first formal colonies.

---

[17]Quoted in Lloyd Gardner, *Safe for Democracy: The Anglo-American Response to Revolution, 1913–1923* (New York: Oxford University Press, 1984), 26.
[18]Quoted in Jackson Lears, "How the U.S. Began Its Empire," *The New York Review of Books*, February 23, 2017.

20-3 Latin America and the Caribbean in the Global System

TRANSITIONS SOCIETIES

Q What political, economic, and social patterns shaped Latin America after independence?

Brazil and most of Spain's Latin American colonies won their independence in the early 1800s, although the Caribbean islands mostly remained colonies (see Chapter 19). But the new states, failing to forge enduring democracies or significant economic change, mostly experienced political instability and regional conflicts in this era. By the 1870s expanding European markets increased demand for Latin American exports, though free trade policies also deepened economic monocultures. Black slaves gained their freedom, European immigrants changed the social landscape, and the United States increasingly exercised regional power.

20-3a New Latin American Nations

Latin Americans faced challenges in creating stable republics and political unity. While countries like Argentina, Brazil, and Mexico were large and unwieldy, others, like El Salvador and the Dominican Republic, were small and had limited resources. Some governments failed to win the allegiance of all the people, and civil wars often pitted those favoring federalism and regionalism against partisans of strong centralized government. Tensions between central governments and remote regions simmered. Meanwhile, frontier disputes led to occasional wars. After Chile fought Peru and Bolivia in 1837 and again in 1879–1884, it acquired territory from those two countries. Political instability also fostered military dictatorships. Although most countries adopted elections and U.S.-style constitutions, authoritarian governments often ignored their provisions.

Most leaders did not favor dramatic social and economic change. The upper class, mostly creoles, owned large businesses, plantations, and haciendas, while mestizos and mulattos (terms used in Latin America but controversial in North America) constituted the small middle class of shopkeepers, teachers, and skilled artisans. Over half the population, including most Native Americans and blacks, were poor. Plantation agriculture and mining-based economies, with similar, highly unequal social structures, offered limited educational opportunities. Planters, ranchers, mine owners, merchants, and military officers dominated politics, often restricting political participation by poor nonwhites. In many countries military strongmen, known as **caudillos**, acquired and maintained power through force. For example, under the dictator Juan Manuel de Rosas **(huan man-WELL deh ROH-sas)** (1793–1877) in Argentina, police and thugs beat up, tortured, or murdered opponents, often poor peasants. For their armies, caudillos and regional leaders sometimes recruited

caudillos Latin American military strongmen who acquired and maintained power through force.

gauchos Cowboys in Argentina and Uruguay who worked on large ranches and were skilled horsemen and fighters.

CONNECTION to TODAY

How do you think the rise of nationalism in Latin America, and U.S. interventions and growing power in the region in this era, influence Latin American relations with the United States today?

local cowboys, skilled horsemen and fighters known as **gauchos** in Argentina and Uruguay who worked on large ranches.

Despite these problems, most nations established some stability by the 1850s. Many countries sought both "progress and order," usually under caudillos, but a few created multiparty systems. Liberals generally favored federalism, free trade, and separation of church and state, opposing the Catholic Church's institutional power for diminishing individual liberty. Conservatives sought centralization, trade protectionism, and maintenance of church power. Conflicts between these groups were sometimes violent.

Brazil was the only nation governed by a monarchy, which largely ignored popular aspirations toward abolishing slavery and forming a republic. As tensions simmered, the army seized power in 1889, exiled Emperor Dom Pedro II, and established a republic with a federal system that highly restricted suffrage. Most Brazilians gained neither property nor civil rights, many remaining desperately poor. Brazil maintained an authoritarian tradition that was repeatedly challenged by rebellions and regionalism.

Social and economic inequalities often spurred reforms and sometimes revolutions. The Mexican republic, founded in 1824, did not bring stability to this vast country that stretched from northern deserts to southern rain forests. Between 1833 and 1855 General Antonio Lopez de Santa Anna (1797–1876) led a series of dictatorships punctuated by civil war. Santa Anna also lost half of Mexico's territory, including Texas and California, in the disastrous U.S.–Mexican War (1846–1848), a humiliation still felt by Mexicans today. Growing social problems and Santa Anna's misadventures sparked upheaval. In 1861 Mexican liberals led by Benito Juarez **(WAHR-ez)** (1806–1872), a pragmatic but determined lawyer and Zapotec, defeated conservatives and suspended foreign debt repayment, provoking a French invasion. When the first French troops arrived and marched toward the capital in 1862, a small Mexican force surprisingly defeated them on May 5, a victory that is celebrated today as "Cinco de Mayo" in Mexico and by Mexican Americans in the United States. The French defeat, although temporary, was significant for U.S. history as it stopped France from recognizing and supporting the Confederacy in the Civil War. Soon an overwhelming French force took Mexico City. A French occupation that installed a Habsburg, Maximilian of Austria (1832–1867), as Mexico's head proved short-lived. When France withdrew its troops, Maximilian's regime collapsed in 1867. Juarez again served as president until 1872, seeking social justice, fighting corruption, subordinating the church to the secular state, and assigning church and communal lands to individual peasant families. His reformist policies and Native American ancestry made Juarez Mexico's most honored leader and national symbol (see Meet the People: Benito Juarez, Mexican Reformer and President).

Benito Juarez, Mexican Reformer and President

Benito Juarez (1806–1867) was one of Latin America's most extraordinary figures, rising to great achievements and high office despite extremely humble origins. President for five terms in a turbulent era of military conflicts and political divisions (1858–1872), Juarez was the only full-blooded Native American to ever serve as Mexico's president. Sometimes called modern Mexico's founding father, he struggled to preserve Mexico as a sovereign state while breaking with the Hispanic past, but he could not heal all the nation's ills and deep divisions.

A Zapotec born into grinding poverty in a mountain village, San Pablo Guelatao, Oaxaca, in 1806, Juarez did not even speak Spanish until his teens. Orphaned at three and raised by an uncle, he worked in cornfields and as a shepherd until age twelve. Then, seeking a better life, he walked forty-one miles to the state capital, Oaxaca City, where his sister worked as a cook for an immigrant Genoese merchant, Antonio Maza. Impressed with the boy's intelligence, industriousness, tenacity, and thirst for learning, a lay Franciscan brother paid his tuition to enter a seminary. Finding himself poorly suited for clerical training, Juarez entered the Institute of Science and Art and graduated with a law degree in 1834.

After joining the Oaxaca state congress, Juarez also practiced law, often defending poor Native American villagers who challenged wealthy hacienda owners and greedy clergy. Believing that Mexico's political and social system needed structural change, he joined the Liberal movement battling conservatives to shape the country's future. In 1843 Juarez, then thirty-seven, married seventeen-year-old Margarita Mazo (1826–1871), his first employer's illegitimate daughter. Together they had ten children. After holding various local and state offices and judgeships and serving in the national congress, Juarez was elected Oaxaca governor in 1847 and served until 1852, during which time he balanced the state budget, built rural schools, and promoted girls' education. Believing in popular sovereignty, he wanted "to protect mankind in the free development of his moral and physical faculties. . . . no one individual, no sectional interest, and no class shall oppress the rest of society."

Between 1853 and 1855 Juarez and other liberal leaders, having been exiled by the returned caudillo, General Santa Anna, mostly lived in New Orleans, where he worked in a cigarette factory. When a liberal general overthrew Santa Anna, Juarez and his colleagues hurried home. While believing in God, Juarez opposed clerical power and corruption, and after being appointed secretary for justice, he sponsored legislation (known as the Juarez Law) subordinating military officers' and the clergy's traditional privileges to civil law. The law required the forced sale of church-owned lands not used for religious purposes. New laws also barred Native American villages from owning communal lands. Liberals hoped that selling and privatizing church and village lands would create a class of small private property holders, hence expanding the middle class and allowing increased tax collection.

A new constitution in 1857 proclaimed liberal ideals, guaranteeing church–state separation, secular education, abolition of slavery, equality before the law, and free speech, press, and assembly. Before this document, Catholicism was the state church and people could be jailed, even executed, for antigovernment writings. The changes provoked fierce church and conservative opposition, sparking Mexico's bloodiest civil war (1858–1861), the War of Reform, which pitted liberals against conservatives. Liberals eventually prevailed, but the fighting left Mexico exhausted, indebted, and broke. After being elected president in 1862, Juarez was forced to flee north during the French intervention (1862–1867). Led by Juarez, however, liberals eventually ousted the French puppet regime and regained control, but they now faced huge problems, including revolts, famine, and an empty treasury. From 1867 until his death at sixty-six from a heart attack in 1872, Juarez governed in an increasingly authoritarian manner, seeking improved relations with the United States while implementing educational, economic, and military reforms and conciliating enemies with an amnesty.

Today Mexicans view the tough-minded but practical Juarez as the greatest symbol of resistance to foreign intervention. He was controversial in his time and remains so today, fostering mythologies on both left and right. Supporters have celebrated a wise, visionary, strong, courageous model of patriotic integrity promoting democracy, legal equality, and rights and justice for indigenous Mexicans. Detractors have condemned Juarez as a stubborn, anti-Christian dictator who undermined valuable traditions. Always convinced he was right, Juarez offered firm leadership when his nation badly needed it. Today a city (Ciudad Juárez) and many streets, schools, and businesses are named after him. A national holiday celebrating Juarez is held every March 21.

Source: Library of Congress Prints and Photographs Division[LC-US262-7875]

IMAGE 20.5 **Mexican President Benito Juarez** Juarez promoted social, cultural, and economic liberalization and fought French invasion.

Reflection Questions

1. What factors enabled Juarez's political rise?
2. How might his background have influenced his liberal views?
3. How have his policies and actions provoked disagreement about his legacy?
4. Do you think Juarez could be a role model for Mexicans and other Latin Americans today?

Note: Quotation from Brian Hamnett, *Juarez* (London: Longman, 1994), 77.

In 1876 Porfirio Diaz **(DEE-ahs)** (1830–1915), a mestizo, became Mexico's dictator. Diaz brought stability and economic progress while allowing foreign business interests and investors to control much of Mexico's economy, doing little to help the poor majority. Under his free enterprise policies many Native Americans sold their land to large haciendas and land companies to pay off debts, intensifying rather than ending the colonial legacy of landed estates owned by a small elite. Women such as Dolores Hernandez, who led a working-class organization advocating women's empowerment, were among those opposing Diaz. The Diaz regime ended in civil war and the Mexican Revolution (1910–1920). Liberal creole Francisco Madero (1873–1913), a landowner's son educated in France and the United States, led one revolutionary faction. Another rebel leader, Pancho Villa **(VEE-uh)** (1877–1923), a former cowboy, attracted support chiefly from northern Mexican ranchers. In the south, charismatic mestizo and former peasant Emiliano Zapata **(zeh-PAH-teh)** (1879–1919) organized a peasant army, seizing haciendas and fighting the federal army.

After the defeat of Diaz, largely by Zapata's forces, the idealistic new president, Madero, was murdered by a rival, generating a free-for-all between diverse rivals. Sporadic violence engulfed Mexico, with all factions using ruthless tactics while alliances formed and collapsed. A novel recorded the confusion: "thinkers prepare the Revolution; bandits carry it out. At the moment no one can say with any assurance: 'So-and-so is a revolutionary and What's his-name is a bandit.' Tomorrow, perhaps, it will be clearer."[19] Though Zapata was assassinated by a rival in 1919, his reputation lived on, making him the most celebrated revolutionary hero.

The fighting raised expectations for social change. Women played a critical revolutionary role, cooking for and commanding troops, serving as spies and couriers, and shooting carbines and pistols. A constitution introduced in 1917 addressed women's rights, setting forth progressive goals such as an eight-hour workday and paid maternity leave. In 1920 the conflict wound down after claiming one million lives. While most Mexicans remained impoverished, former revolutionaries formed a government that brought political stability while opening opportunities for women to enter the business world and state governments.

Spanish-ruled Cuba also experienced revolt. By the later 1800s journalist and acclaimed poet Jose Marti (1853–1895), who had traveled and lived in Europe, the United States, and around Latin America, led an independence movement. Marti admired American writers and poets like Walt Whitman and Ralph Waldo Emerson as well as U.S. technology. Marti's writings promoting freedom, equality, and social justice helped inspire a Cuban revolt in 1895. Marti welcomed Afro-Cubans and women, who became the struggle's backbone. However, Marti was killed in the fighting, and U.S. intervention during the Spanish-American War sidetracked the revolution. Americans soon dominated the economy and strongly influenced Cuban governments. But even today Marti remains a source of national Cuban pride whose writings and actions shifted the national imagination and inspired faith in a dignified future.

Armed Women "Soldaderas" (b/w photograph)/Mexican Photographer, (20th century)/PETER NEWARK/Private Collection/Bridgeman Images

IMAGE 20.6 **Women Revolutionaries in Mexico** Women joined men in fighting, and sometimes dying, for one or another faction during the Mexican Revolution. Many women hoped that the revolution would bring social change and a greater emphasis on improving women's political and economic rights.

Q What image of Mexican women fighters does this photo convey?

20-3b Latin American Economic and Social Change

Like North Americans, Latin Americans debated free trade and involvement in the world economy as opposed to the protectionism and self-sufficiency implemented by the United States. As exports and investments declined, Latin American leaders maintained plantation, mining, and ranching monocultures, concentrating on exporting raw materials—Ecuadorian cocoa, Brazilian coffee, Argentine beef, Cuban sugar, and Bolivian and Chilean ores—mainly to the United States and Europe. Since earnings from minerals and cash crops ebbed and flowed with world commodity prices, Latin Americans remained vulnerable, and by the twentieth century economic conditions were linked to fluctuating "boom or bust" world prices for exports. Hence, politically unstable Central American countries whose economies could be heavily influenced by American corporations, such as the United Fruit Company, became dependent on tropical agriculture and were derisively called "banana republics" by North Americans.

---

[19] From Mariano Azuela's novel *The Flies*, quoted in Lesley Byrd Simpson, *Many Mexicos*, 4th ed. rev. (Berkeley: University of California Press, 1967), 298.

Policies fostering growth but not development widened the gap between rich and poor. The poverty of most Native Americans and blacks gave them little purchasing power to support local industries. In addition, industrialization efforts in Brazil, Colombia, and Mexico in the 1830s and 1840s failed because of competition from European imports. North American, French, and especially British merchants and financiers used their economic power to dominate banking and the import trade for industrial goods while investing in mines and plantations, so that by the mid-1800s British businessmen and bankers controlled Brazilian and Argentine imports and exports. An Argentine nationalist complained that "English capital has done what English armies could not do. Today our country is tributary to England."[20] After 1890 the United States also became a powerful economic influence in Latin America.

Foreign corporations increasingly owned plantations and mines. Latin America became a major contributor to world commodity markets, producing some 62 percent of the world's coffee, 38 percent of the sugar, and 25 percent of the rubber by World War I. With powerful families or foreign corporations owning most usable land, inequalities grew, producing political unrest in the twentieth century. In parts of rural Brazil, landed families maintained peasants in semibondage through private armies and gunmen.

Yet, the abolition of slavery facilitated social change. Some leaders freed slaves who fought in the wars of independence. Between 1823 and 1854 slavery was legally abolished in most of Latin America and the Caribbean, and most European and American countries outlawed the trans-Atlantic slave trade. Spain finally granted Cuban slaves their freedom in 1886, while Brazilian abolitionists became more outspoken. Slave resistance, growing opposition to slavery by educated Brazilians, and plans to promote European immigration finally led to abolition in 1889. However, as in the United States, emancipation did not dramatically improve economic conditions. Many Latin American and Caribbean blacks shifted from slaves to low-status sharecroppers, tenant farmers, and laborers. A popular Brazilian verse lamented: "Everything in this world changes; Only the life of the Negro [black] remains the same. He works to die of hunger."[21] For over a century after abolition few Brazilians wrote about or schools taught about black Brazilian history and slavery; only in 2003 did Brazil mandate attention to black history in schools. Latin America's population doubled between 1850 and 1900 to over sixty million, as millions of European immigrants reshaped many societies. Italians, Spaniards, Germans, Russians, and Irish sought better economic prospects, especially in Argentina, Brazil, Chile, and Uruguay. As a result, today many people in Buenos Aires, Argentina, trace their roots to Italy. Continued immigration generated markets for European products and fashions.

Immigrants also came from overcrowded Asian and Middle Eastern lands. After slavery abolition in Trinidad, British Guiana, and Dutch Guiana prompted labor-short planters to import workers from India, Indians eventually accounted for around half of these colonies' populations. Japanese settled in Brazil, Peru, and Paraguay as farmers and traders, Arab Lebanese and Syrians developed trade diasporas throughout Latin America, Indonesians (mostly Javanese) became plantation workers in Dutch Guiana, and Chinese flocked to Peru, Cuba, Jamaica, Trinidad, and the Guianas. Much cultural mixing occurred. For example, an Afro-Trinidadian might have a Spanish surname, belong to the Presbyterian Church, possess a Hindu love charm, enjoy English literature, and favor Chinese food. Moreover, people of Asian or Middle Eastern ancestry have sometimes headed Latin American or Caribbean governments, including in Brazil, Peru, Argentina, Ecuador, Honduras, Belize, El Salvador, the Dominican Republic, Jamaica, Guyana (formerly British Guiana), and Suriname (formerly Dutch Guiana).

Despite the newcomers, Latin American society generally remained more conservative than North American society. Creole elites dominated most countries, while European and Asian immigrants and mixed-descent people constituted the middle class. Many mulattos and most blacks and Native Americans remained lower class. Indians often withdrew into their village communities, limiting contact with national society. In 1865 a Mexican described the wide gap between whites and Native Americans: "The white is the proprietor; the Indian the worker. The white is rich; the Indian poor and miserable."[22] In Brazil, European, African, and mixed-descent people fostered a unique, multiracial society. Unlike in the United States, economic class and skin color did not always coincide, and intermarriage and cultural mixing were common. Millions of Brazilians of all backgrounds blended African religions with Catholicism, creating new sects. Yet blacks were also more likely to experience prejudice and poverty, as reflected in Rio de Janeiro's largely black hillside shantytowns.

20-3c Latin American and Caribbean Cultures

Latin Americans struggled to reconcile indigenous with imported European and African cultural traditions. Novelists focused on social themes. For example, Euclides da Cunha (KOO-nyuh) (1866–1909), acting as the spokesman for rising Brazilian nationalism and urban intellectuals, helped create a realistic Brazilian literature that described the life of the poor. Da Cunha's book *Rebellion in the Backlands* (1902), about a long uprising in his country's remote, impoverished northeast, challenged the nation's conscience and stimulated other authors to question accepted political wisdom. The Brazilian Joaquim Maria Machado de Assis (1839–1908), the mulatto grandson of freed slaves, became what some critics consider perhaps Latin America's greatest writer. Born into poverty and with no formal education, he wrote many novels and short stories that pulse with life and ideas. Today streets and subway stops are named after him and some of his

[20]Quoted in Stanley J. Stein and Barbara H. Stein, *The Colonial Heritage of Latin America: Essays on Economic Dependence in Perspective* (New York: Oxford University Press, 1970), 151.

[21]Quoted in E. Bradford Burns, *Latin America: A Concise Interpretive History*, 5th ed. (Englewood Cliffs, NJ: Prentice-Hall, 1990), 213.

[22]Quoted in Michael C. Meyer and William L. Sherman, *The Course of Mexican History*, 2nd ed. (New York: Oxford University Press, 1983), 416.

books are required reading in schools. Radical Chilean essayist Francisco Bilbao praised freedom and rationalism while denouncing slavery, Catholicism, and U.S. expansionism. In contrast, a cosmopolitan new French-influenced literary and artistic movement, *modernismo* ("modernism"), flourished from 1880 to World War I as Latin America's most important literary innovation. Well-traveled Nicaraguan poet Ruben Dario (1867–1916), seeking ways to express Latin American experience, gave modernism its name and definition, his free verse expressing individualism and freedom. Dario offered escapist and fantastic images while stressing beauty as an end in itself. Living at various times in Chile, Argentina, Guatemala, Spain, and France, among other countries, he expressed a vision that transcended his nation to embrace the entire Latin American and Hispanic world.

Musicians and dancers produced creative cultural innovations. Mixing African and European traditions, the sensuous tango dance emerged in working-class bars and clubs of Buenos Aires, becoming Argentina and Uruguay's most popular music. Tango rhythms derived from African drumming, and the music featured the accordion-like *bandoneon*, carried by Italian immigrants. Becoming a symbol of lower-class identity, by the early 1900s tango achieved popularity in Europe's ballrooms and nightclubs. Brazil's unique music also blended European melody and African rhythms. **Samba**, a popular music and dance developed by Afro-Brazilian women from Bahia who settled in Rio de Janeiro's hillside shantytowns, became integral to Carnival, the three-day celebration before the long Christian period of fasting and penitence known as Lent.

Caribbean peoples also mixed African and European influences. On Trinidad, British officials, fearing the black majority, prohibited African-based musics, but two traditions reflecting Afro-Trinidadian identity defied British rule. **Calypso**, a song style featuring lyrics that often addressed daily life and topical subjects, eventually became hugely popular in English-speaking eastern Caribbean islands. The second tradition, the pre-Lent Carnival, was a major festival that featured calypso songs, some of which questioned colonial policies. A song in the 1880s protested restrictions on music during Carnival: "Can't beat my drum, In my own native land. Can't have Carnival, In my native land."[23] By the 1920s informal calypso presentations in makeshift theaters had evolved into elaborate, heavily rehearsed shows.

20-3d The United States in Latin America

Latin Americans envied and feared the increasingly powerful United States, whose military forces occasionally intervened in Central America and the Caribbean. In 1856 William Walker, an American adventurer financed by influential U.S. businessmen, invaded Nicaragua with well-armed American mercenaries and

samba A Brazilian popular music and dance.

calypso A song style in Trinidad that featured lyrics addressing daily life and topical subjects.

proclaimed himself president, after which the United States granted his government diplomatic recognition. Walker introduced slavery before being forced out in 1857, becoming a hated symbol of what Latin Americans often called "Yankee imperialism." Ruben Dario expressed this hatred when, outraged by the U.S. victory in Cuba, he addressed his critique of U.S. policies to President Teddy Roosevelt:

> You are the United States, future invader of our naive America with its Indian blood, an America that still prays to Christ and still speaks Spanish....
> The United States is grand and powerful. Whenever it trembles, a profound shudder runs down the enormous backbone of the Andes. If it shouts, the sound is like the roar of a lion.[24]

The Spanish-American War turned Cuba into a U.S.-dominated informal colony. The Platt Amendment to the Cuban constitution, imposed by the United States in 1901 and only repealed in 1934, integrated Cuban and U.S. economies and required U.S. congressional approval of any treaties negotiated by Cuba. The American military governor summarized the situation: "There is little or no real independence left to Cuba. She is absolutely in our hands, a practical dependency of the United States."[25] U.S. businessmen owned much of Cuba's economy, including railroads, banks, and mills, and Americans also acquired a naval base at Guantanamo Bay. Later Cuban nationalists blamed Cuba's squalid political and economic condition not on despotic Cuban governments but on the United States. The U.S. also turned Puerto Rico into a colony without the full equality of statehood or independence and restricted foreign ships from entering Puerto Rican ports, hence monopolizing the island's resources and exports. Dependent on U.S. investment, the island remains a quasi-colony today, hampered in its ability to engage with the wider world.

The United States became deeply involved in other Central American and Caribbean states as well. To build a canal across Central America linking the Pacific and Atlantic Oceans, Americans helped Panamanians secede from Colombia in 1903. Panama then leased a 10-mile-wide zone across the isthmus in perpetuity to the United States for the canal. Several thousand workers from Panama and Caribbean islands died in ten arduous years of construction. In 1914 the Panama Canal, 51 miles long, was completed, one of history's greatest engineering feats. Ships could now sail between the oceans safely and conveniently. In another intervention in 1912, Americans overthrew Nicaragua's president, who was suspected of inviting the British to build a rival canal. But unrest followed, prompting the United States to send in a military force that remained until 1933. U.S. soldiers also occupied Haiti (1915–1933) and the Dominican Republic (1916–1924) to quell unrest or maintain friendly governments. These interventions set the stage for more active U.S. imperial policies and resentment of the United States in the region.

[23]Quoted in Lloyd Braithwaite, "The Problem of Cultural Integration in Trinidad," in *Consequences of Class and Color: West Indian Perspectives*, ed. David Lowenthal and Lambors Comitas (Garden City, NY: Anchor, 1973), 248.
[24]From *Selected Poems of Ruben Dario* by Ruben Dario, translated by Lysander Kemp, Copyright © 1965, renewed 1993. Reprinted by permission of the University of Texas Press.
[25]General Leonard Wood, quoted in Saul Landau, *The Dangerous Doctrine: National Security and U.S. Foreign Policy* (Boulder, CO: Westview Press, 1988), 80–81.

KEY POINTS

▶ After gaining independence from Spain, Latin American nations were plagued by instability, undemocratic governments, and socioeconomic inequality along racial lines.

▶ Latin American economies tended to focus on the export of one or two natural resources, which created instability and made them susceptible to foreign domination.

▶ The abolition of slavery in Latin America did not greatly improve the economic conditions of former slaves, and millions of immigrants from Europe, India, China, Japan, and elsewhere flowed into Latin American countries.

▶ The tango developed in lower-class Buenos Aires, and samba was a result of cultural mixing in Rio de Janeiro, while Caribbean calypso was a legacy of resistance to British efforts to stamp out African-based music on Trinidad.

▶ The United States became increasingly active politically and economically in the region, sometimes engaging in military conflicts.

20-4 New Societies in Canada and the Pacific Basin

🏛 SOCIETIES

Ⓠ Why did the foundations for nationhood differ in Canada and Oceania?

The United States became the most powerful and prosperous of the American and Oceanic societies settled by Europeans, but the others also fostered democracies and growing economies. Canada expanded across North America to the Pacific. Western nations also colonized the island societies scattered around the Pacific Basin. In Australia and New Zealand, Britain established settler colonies.

20-4a Making a Canadian Nation

By 1763 Britain defeated the French and gained control of eastern Canada, including the main French colony, Quebec, but it had to forge stable relations with French Canadians, who maintained their language, culture, and identity. By 1774 Britain pragmatically recognized Catholic Church influence and French civil law in Quebec, while British colonists settled chiefly along the Atlantic coast and west of Quebec in Ontario. But relations between British and French Canadians remained uneasy; a British official in the 1830s concluded that Canada was "two nations warring in the bosom of a single state."[26] French power in North America ended in 1803, when the United States acquired the vast Louisiana territory, including the Mississippi River Basin long coveted by Americans.

American leaders hoped that Canada might eventually join the United States, but in the U.S.–British treaty of 1783 following the American Revolution, the United States recognized British control north of the Great Lakes and the Saint Lawrence River. Many pro-British Loyalists moved to Canada, increasing the English-speaking population and promoting democratic reforms and representative assemblies. But relations between the United States and Canada remained tense for years. Americans feared that Canadians were aiding Native Americans who were resisting U.S. expansion in the Ohio region, where the powerful and charismatic Shawnee chief Tecumseh (1768–1813) gathered a large tribal alliance to drive the white settlers out of Ohio and reinvigorate Native American ways. Then during the War of 1812 Americans repeatedly invaded Canada but were repulsed. The war ended U.S. attempts to expand north while fostering a separate Canadian identity. In 1846 another treaty fixed the U.S.–Canada boundary in the west.

Canadians resumed building a democratic nation in peace while modifying British control. Between 1815 and 1850 Canada welcomed 800,000 British immigrants. Gradually reforms fostered a unified Canada, an elected national parliament, and waning British political influence. But fearing U.S. power, Canadians rejected complete independence in favor of self-rule within the British Empire. In 1867 leaders from Ontario, Quebec, New Brunswick, and Nova Scotia negotiated a Canadian Confederation that guaranteed provincial rights and preserved the French language wherever it was spoken. Canada became a **dominion**, a country having autonomy but owing allegiance to the British crown.

However, expansion of white settlement and political power westward fired resentment among Native Americans and mixed-descent, French-speaking Metis (**may-TEES**). Combative Metis leader Louis Riel (**ree-EL**) (1844–1885) led two rebellions before being executed for treason. Eventually Manitoba, British Columbia, Saskatchewan, and Alberta joined the Confederation. Hoping to transform the four million Canadians into a unified nation, Canada's first prime minister, Scottish-born John MacDonald (g. 1867–1873, 1878–1891), promised to build a transcontinental railroad. Completed in 1885, the railroad crossed over two thousand miles of forests, prairies, and high mountains. Putting many Native Americans on reservations allowed white settler migration to the western provinces. As in the United States, government policies toward First Nations (indigenous) people included forced migration, segregation,

dominion A country having autonomy but owing allegiance to the British crown.

---

[26]Quoted in Louis Hartz, *The Founding of New Societies* (New York: Harcourt, Brace and World, 1964), 248.

outlawing traditional cultures, no right to vote (until 1960), and separating children from parents by sending them to government-funded but church-run residential schools to be assimilated to European ways. By 1905 Canada included all the present territory except the island of Newfoundland, a British dominion which joined in 1949.

Canada's economy and ethnic structure changed between the 1860s and 1914. Wheat grown in the Great Plains replaced beaver fur and fish as the major export. Gold strikes in the northwest and free land in western Canada attracted several million immigrants, many from eastern and southern Europe as well as China, Japan, South Asia, and the Middle East, enriching the ethnic mosaic. By 1911 Canadians controlled their own foreign affairs and diplomacy. Over the next several decades Canada encouraged industrialization and established warmer relations with the United States while maintaining the British monarch as symbolic head of state.

20-4b Exploration and Colonization of the Pacific Islands

The peoples on the small mountainous islands and flat atolls scattered across the vast Pacific Ocean Basin eventually experienced European expansion, launching a new and sometimes troubling era. Spain colonized Guam, in the Marianas, in 1663,

but otherwise European contact with Pacific islanders was minimal until the mid-1700s, when Britain and France raced to explore what they considered the last frontier. They eventually colonized, along with Spain, Germany, Russia, and the United States, all the inhabited islands. English captain James Cook (1728–1779), an agricultural laborer's son, led extensive explorations. Cook reached Tahiti, in eastern Polynesia, in 1769, recruiting a Polynesian high priest, Tupaia (ca. 1725–1771), whose navigational skills and command of several Polynesian languages greatly aided Cook's expedition. A scientist with Cook concluded that Tupaia knew more of Polynesia's geography, produce, religion, laws, and customs than anyone else. Tupaia drew up the charts that helped Cook map Polynesia, including New Zealand, and the Australian coast. Cook made two more expeditions and, after becoming the first known captain to circumnavigate Antarctica, located the Hawaiian Islands in 1778. His early reports created a naive, misleading image of the South Sea islands as a "Garden of Eden" utopia with beautiful scenery and amiable people, an easy life with fruit dripping off the trees, and the practice of free love, an image still surviving in popular culture. Cook himself was killed in Hawaii after antagonizing local leaders. Diseases, guns, and alcohol accompanying the European explorers ravaged the populations of most of the Pacific islands.

European explorations spurred economic exploitation and Christian missionary activity. Russians established footholds in Alaska and the Aleutian Islands, where they hunted seals and

Hulton Archive/Stringer/Getty Images

IMAGE 20.7 **Riding the Canadian Pacific Railway** During the late nineteenth century Canadians and immigrants from many lands followed the railroad to settle the midwestern plains and western mountains. This illustration shows passengers aboard a sleeping car in 1888.

Q What can you learn about the immigrants to Canada and the trip westward from this drawing?

sea otters to near extinction for their fur. Thousands of Aleuts died from the diseases brought by these Europeans. Deep-sea whaling lasted longer, attracting Western sailors. Western traders also sought Pacific island resources such as sandalwood, greatly valued in Asia for building furniture. Soon all of Fiji's sandalwood was gone. Meanwhile, Protestant and Catholic missionaries found mixed results. Samoans welcomed them, often adopting Christianity. Fijians initially rejected missionaries but later often pragmatically blended Christianity with their own traditions. One chief, Ratu Tui Levuka, reportedly said that his right hand was Methodist, his left hand Catholic, and his body heathen. Some islanders were hostile to outside influences. For instance, New Hebrides people killed the first missionaries who reached the islands.

With traders and missionaries opening the way, Western powers colonized all of the Pacific societies between the 1840s and 1900. France acquired many island chains, such as the Society Islands (including Tahiti), while Britain colonized various others, among them Fiji. Germans and Americans divided up Samoa. Germans seized most of Micronesia, and Britain and France controlled much of Melanesia. By 1875 smallpox, measles, and venereal diseases introduced by Western visitors and settlers to Hawaii had reduced the population from 150,000 to 50,000, but American and especially Asian immigrants were reshaping the population. Hawaii remained a Polynesian kingdom until 1893, when American settlers seized control.

20-4c The Rise of Australia and New Zealand

Britain colonized and settled Australia and New Zealand (see Map 20.3 and Chapter 9). Historians, politicians, and average people still debate, often quite heatedly, this process. The Aboriginal (or indigenous) population in Australia contend that they were subject to attack, incursion, assault, plunder, conquest, subjugation, land confiscation, diseases like smallpox and tuberculosis, and sometimes massacres. Many historians agree. In 1788 the British began transporting convicts, often Irish, from overcrowded British jails to penal colonies they founded on Australia's southeast coast. Soon former convicts and discharged soldiers formed settlements and farms around Sydney. Agriculture, ranching, and mining underpinned the modern economy. The continent was eventually shared by six British colonies, with New South Wales and Victoria in the southeast having the largest populations.

British colonization disrupted the Aborigines, who were completely different from Pacific islanders in language, culture, and ways of life and whose nomadic ancestors had lived on the continent for thousands of years. Divided into hundreds of scattered tribes and languages and numbering between 500,000 and 3 million people in 1750, Aborigines lived chiefly by fishing, hunting, and gathering but some practiced forms of agriculture suited to their environment. Reflecting racism, European settlers considered them an inferior, primitive people. Many Aborigines, resisting encroachments on their land, raided British settlements. While early British settlers killed as many as twenty thousand Aborigines, European diseases such as smallpox and influenza killed the majority of Aborigines. By 1875 only 150,000 Aborigines remained, and whites forcibly settled their land. Eventually many Aborigines had little choice but to move to cities or work on white-owned cattle and sheep ranches. However, large numbers remained on tribal reservations, maintaining many of their traditions and beliefs.

Creating a common Australian identity and nationhood took over a century. Throughout the 1800s whites clung to coastal regions suitable for farming and ranching, avoiding the inhospitable desert interior. Gold discoveries in southeastern Australia in 1851 attracted settlers from Europe and Chinese and other Asians to seek their fortunes in Australia, creating resentments among whites. Violence between Europeans and Asians, especially in mining camps, prompted laws, known as the "White Australia Policy," restricting Asian immigration. Meanwhile, white women struggled for influence in the male-dominated society. By the 1880s women's movements pressed for moral reform and suffrage; white women gained the right to vote in 1902. However, Aborigines gained voting rights only in 1962.

By 1890 Britain had turned all six of its Australian colonies into self-governing states, which formed the Commonwealth of Australia in 1901 (see Map 20.3). Like Canada, Australia became a self-governing, democratic dominion maintaining close political links with Britain, but it gradually formed its own identity. A transcontinental railroad system, completed in 1917, connected the vast country. Yet most white Australians lived in or near five coastal cities. Distance from European supplies fostered some local manufacturing, including steel production.

Colonizing New Zealand's two large mountainous islands, twelve hundred miles east of Australia, came at the Polynesian Maori people's expense. They had lived on the islands, which they called Aotearoa, for hundreds of years, gradually dividing into sometimes warring tribes headed by chiefs. In 1792, when the first British settlers arrived, Maori numbered around 100,000. Some Maori used British newcomers for their own purposes. One chief, Hongi Hika (ca. 1772–1828), befriended a Protestant missionary, who took him to England. Returning with guns, Hongi and his warriors raided rival tribes. Maori intertribal warfare became more deadly, limiting cooperation to oppose the British.

As more British settlers came, territorial disputes with the Maori increased. The Treaty of Waitangi in 1850 between Britain and five hundred Maori chiefs seemingly confirmed Maori rights to their land and the authority of their chiefs while acknowledging British sovereignty. But English-language and Maori-language versions differed, the British claiming that the treaty gave them political and legal power. Disagreement over treaty provisions and British occupation of more Maori land provoked deadly wars that ended only in the 1870s. During these wars Britain skillfully exploited Maori tribal rivalries while employing heavy artillery and armored steamships. Eventually Maori resistance subsided, leading to an 1881 peace agreement that accorded Maori control over some districts.

Gradually British identity in New Zealand grew stronger. Gold discoveries in 1861 stimulated British immigration, so that by 1881 Maori comprised only 10 percent of the half-million population. High living standards, farming and sheep

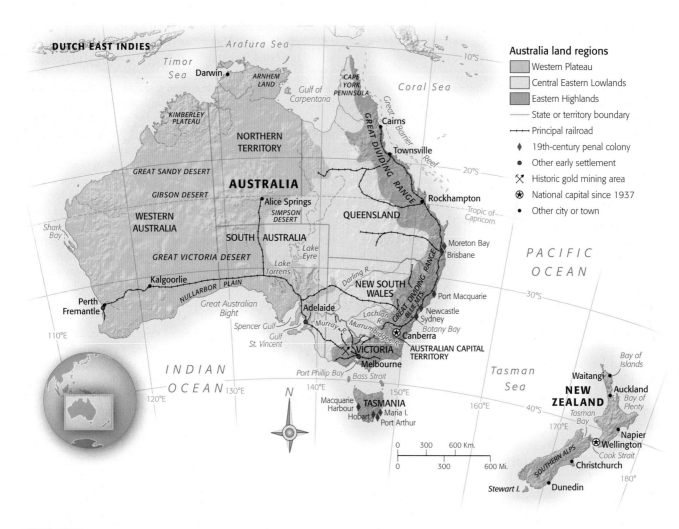

MAP 20.3 **Australia and New Zealand** The British colonized and gradually settled Australia and New Zealand between the late 1700s and 1914. In 1901 the six Australian colonies became a federation, with a capital eventually built in Canberra. The Australian Aborigines and New Zealand Maoris were not consulted in these decisions.

Q What does this map indicate about where most of the European immigrants and their descendants settled?

raising, and a growing government welfare system attracted immigrants, mostly from Europe and Polynesia but also some Chinese. New Zealand prospered after 1882, when steamships, having acquired refrigerated holds, carried lamb and dairy products to Europe. A parliamentary government including Maori representatives was formed in 1852, and by 1893 all men and women enjoyed universal suffrage. New Zealand gained self-government as a British dominion in 1907, its alliance with Britain guaranteeing security. It remained an outpost of the British Empire well into the twentieth century.

KEY POINTS

▶ Canada had to contend with the challenge of forming a unified country that included French and English speakers, as well as with the threat of the neighboring United States.

▶ Western nations, starting with Britain and France but later including Russia, the United States, and Germany, colonized the Pacific islands and exploited their natural resources.

▶ Starting as penal colonies, British settlements in Australia expanded and pushed the native Aborigines off their land and then clashed with Asians who came to mine gold.

▶ British colonizers of New Zealand clashed repeatedly with the native Maori, ultimately deceiving them into signing away the rights to their land in the Treaty of Waitangi, which led to a series of wars that ended only in the late nineteenth century.

Chapter Summary

During the Modern Era European populations grew and millions of people emigrated to the Americas and Oceania. More people lived in cities, where social problems and poverty increased. The industrial system influenced relations between men and women, as family life changed and European women lost status, fostering feminist movements. Reacting to political and social turbulence, some European thinkers abandoned Enlightenment ideas. The pace of scientific and technological innovation also increased.

Across the Atlantic, the new democratic republic in the United States gradually became a regional and then world power with a diversified economy and distinctive culture. The United States expanded westward, eventually incorporating large sections of North America, some of it acquired after war with Mexico. As Americans settled the frontier, they subdued Native Americans and fostered new social patterns. The Civil War temporarily divided the nation and ended slavery. In the aftermath, economic growth and industrialization spurred massive immigration from Europe and social movements to improve the lives of workers and women. Industrial capitalism also motivated Americans to increase their influence in the wider world, eventually leading to the Spanish-American War. The U.S. victory in that conflict made the United States a world power.

Other new nations arose in the Americas and Oceania during the Modern Era. After Latin Americans gained independence from Spain and Portugal, the new governments remained authoritarian and fostered little economic or social change. Latin American and Caribbean economies remained monocultures geared to exporting raw materials and under foreign domination. While millions of European immigrants arrived, most blacks and Native Americans remained poor. Social inequalities produced tensions and, in Mexico, a revolution. Latin American and Caribbean societies created unique cultures that reflected the mix of peoples from around the world. The United States also played an increasing role in the region, creating resentments that have lingered into the present.

Despite a division between French and English speakers, Canada expanded to the Pacific and became a nation with a self-governing democracy. Meanwhile, European powers colonized the Pacific islands. Europeans settled in Australia and New Zealand and, like Canadians, elected to remain tied to Britain even while developing their own democratic nations.

Key Terms

feminism 511
suffragettes 511
romanticism 511
modernism 512
impressionism 512

protectionism 513
Manifest Destiny 515
sphere of interest 516
caudillos 522
gauchos 522

samba 526
calypso 526
dominion 527

Africa, the Middle East, and Imperialism, 1750–1914

> *The power of these Europeans has advanced to a shocking degree and has manifested itself in an unparalleled manner. Indeed, we are on the brink of a time of [complete] corruption. As for knowing what tomorrow holds, I am blind.*

—Moroccan historian Ahmad Ibn Khalid al-Nasri, 1860[1]

iStock.com/Konstantin_Novakovic

IMAGE 21.1 **Tomb of Muhammad Ahmad in Khartoum** Muhammad Ahmad Ibn 'Abd Allah, known to history as the Mahdi ("Divinely Guided One"), used Islamic appeals to recruit a large army and lead opposition to the joint British and Egyptian rule in Sudan. He died soon after routing the British forces in 1885, but the British destroyed his tomb in the Khartoum suburb of Omdurman in 1898. They then burned his body and threw it into the Nile. In 1947 the tomb and mosque were rebuilt and remain a popular place of pilgrimage and a symbol of Muslim resistance to Western power.

Q What does the splendor and popularity of this tomb tell us about the importance of the Mahdi in Sudanese history?

---

[1]Quoted in Edmund Burke III, *Prelude to Protectorate in Morocco: Precolonial Protest and Resistance, 1860–1912* (Chicago: University of Chicago Press, 1976), xi.

Fresh from victories in Italy and Austria, in 1798

French general Napoleon Bonaparte vowed to join illustrious European conquerors who had achieved glory in the Middle East. Alexander the Great had conquered Egypt and Persia, Roman and Byzantine emperors had controlled the eastern Mediterranean, and medieval Christian crusaders had established temporary western Asia footholds. In his mind, Europe hardly deserved his talents when the rich Muslim world beckoned. He planned to invade Egypt and then reduce the Ottoman Turks and Persians to French vassals. With four hundred ships carrying fifty thousand soldiers, Bonaparte quickly controlled northern Egypt. He also brought some five hundred French scholars to study Egyptian history, society, language, and environment. In the Nile River Delta they discovered the multilanguage Rosetta stone, a tablet from 196 BCE that facilitated, for the first time, translating ancient Egyptian hieroglyphics. Seeking popular support, the French general confidently announced: "People of Egypt, I come to restore your rights; I respect God, His Prophet and the Quran. We are friends of all true Muslims. Happiness to the People!"[2] He also claimed to have liberated Egyptians from repressive Mamluk rulers. But Bonaparte's policies soon alienated Egyptians, who came to see the French as even worse. The ill-equipped French army withered in the desert heat. An attempt to conquer Syria having failed, Bonaparte left for Paris in 1799, another example of Westerners unsuccessfully attempting to control and change Muslim societies.

As Moroccan historian Ahmad Ibn Khalid al-Nasri had feared, the invasion, while unsuccessful, provided a harbinger of more conflicts resulting from European imperial thrusts in sub-Saharan Africa and the Middle East. Industrializing Europe's accelerating need for natural resources and new markets, combined with European political rivalries and powerful military technologies, sparked ruthless colonization. European colonialism generally lasted only a century or less, and sub-Saharan and North Africans often resisted Western power. Yet Western governments, technologies, and ideas reshaped African societies and their economies, cultures, and political systems while linking them closely to a European-dominated world economy. Although western Asian societies experienced less disruption, Ottomans lost their North African and European territories and, like Persians, struggled to meet challenges posed by European power.

[2]Quoted in Alan Palmer, *The Decline and Fall of the Ottoman Empire* (New York: Barnes and Noble, 1992), 58.

21-1 The Colonization of Sub-Saharan Africa

TRANSITIONS SOCIETIES

Q How did various Western nations obtain colonies in sub-Saharan Africa?

The dramatic changes of the Early Modern Era, such as the trans-Atlantic slave trade and the incursions and early colonial footholds by Western nations, had dramatically reshaped sub-Saharan Africa. By 1750 these societies barely resembled their predecessors of the Middle Ages. Dramatic changes continued during the Modern Era. Between 1750 and the later 1800s the trans-Atlantic slave trade's diminishing importance gradually changed African–European relationships. The Western impact was uneven during the slave trade, which

CONNECTION to TODAY

What do you see as the major political and economic legacies from this era that still influence African countries today?

had drawn Africa into the world economy chiefly to supply slaves while impeding most trade involving other products. As demand for slaves waned and industrialization spread, Europeans increasingly sought African agricultural and mineral resources and more territories, precipitating the full-blown quest for colonies, what a British newspaper called the "scramble for Africa." European powers divided up Africa among themselves, often against fierce resistance, accelerating economic penetration. By 1914 colonization was complete.

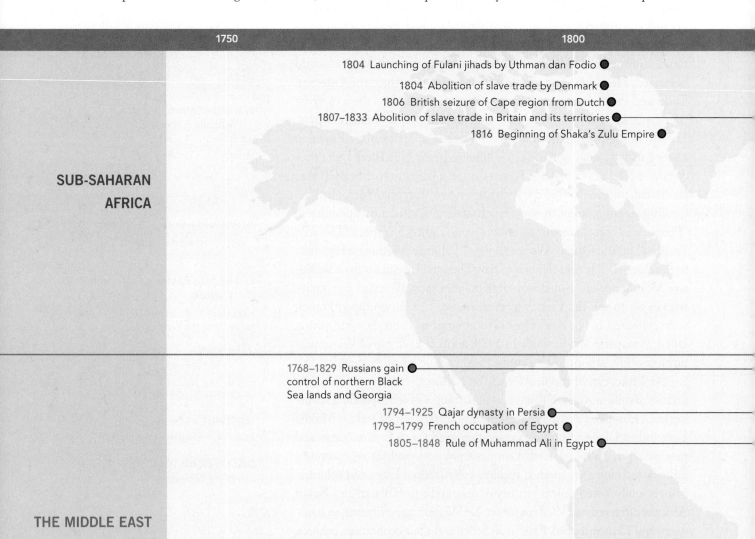

1750   1800

SUB-SAHARAN AFRICA

1804 Launching of Fulani jihads by Uthman dan Fodio ●

1804 Abolition of slave trade by Denmark ●

1806 British seizure of Cape region from Dutch ●

1807–1833 Abolition of slave trade in Britain and its territories ●

1816 Beginning of Shaka's Zulu Empire ●

THE MIDDLE EAST

1768–1829 Russians gain ●
control of northern Black
Sea lands and Georgia

1794–1925 Qajar dynasty in Persia ●

1798–1799 French occupation of Egypt ●

1805–1848 Rule of Muhammad Ali in Egypt ●

21-1a The End of the Slave Trade and African Societies

For over three centuries the trans-Atlantic slave trade (1520–1870) dominated relations between Africa, Europe, and the Americas, but humanitarian opposition and economic concerns spurred abolitionist movements. British abolitionists hoped to open Africa to both Christian missionaries and trade in diverse commodities. Abolitionists also included Christians prompted largely by moral outrage at slavery and others influenced by visions of human equality. One sympathizer wrote that people "are not objects. Everyone has his rights, property, dignity. Africa will have its day."[3]

Africans and African Americans also struggled against slavery. Olaudah Equiano (1745–1797), an Igbo (**EE-boh**) taken from Nigeria to Barbados and then Virginia, eventually purchased his freedom and campaigned in Europe for abolition. Equiano published a best-selling book chronicling his own horrific experiences and exposing self-proclaimed devout Christians mistreating their slaves. His book's riveting narrative became very influential and widely admired among opponents of the slave trade and slavery. Slave revolts in the Americas, including Haiti's successful revolution (see Chapter 19), confirmed that many slaves were risking their lives for freedom. Meanwhile, the widely read poetry and Christian writings of Phyllis Wheatley (ca. 1753–1785), a Senegal-born slave in Boston who learned Latin and Greek and eventually won her freedom, undermined widespread notions that Africans were incapable of sophisticated thought.

There were also economic reasons. The Industrial Revolution made slavery uneconomical as overseas markets for factory-made goods became more desirable than cheap labor

[3]Quoted in John Iliffe, "Tanzania Under German and British Rule," in *Zamani: A Survey of East African History*, ed. B. A. Ogot, new ed. (Nairobi: Longman Kenya, 1974), 301.

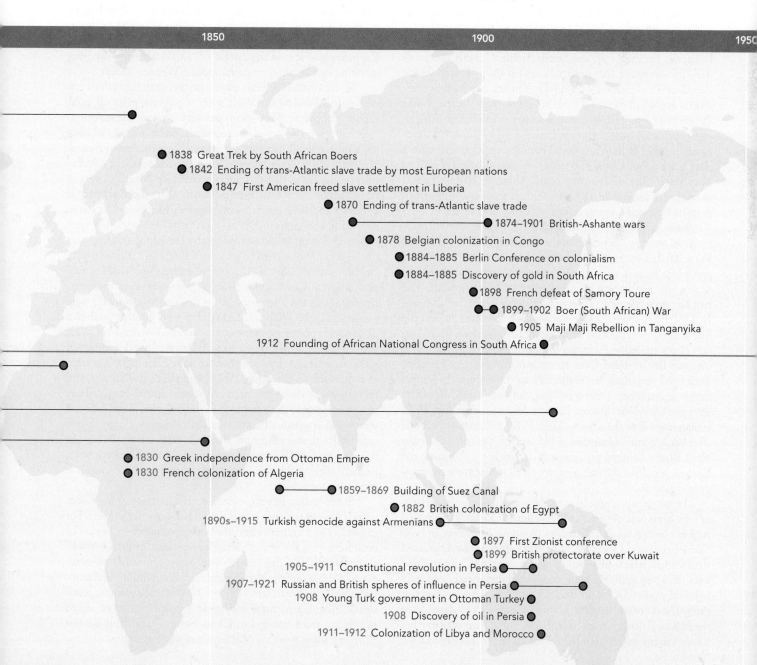

1850   1900   1950

1838 Great Trek by South African Boers
1842 Ending of trans-Atlantic slave trade by most European nations
1847 First American freed slave settlement in Liberia
1870 Ending of trans-Atlantic slave trade
1874–1901 British-Ashante wars
1878 Belgian colonization in Congo
1884–1885 Berlin Conference on colonialism
1884–1885 Discovery of gold in South Africa
1898 French defeat of Samory Toure
1899–1902 Boer (South African) War
1905 Maji Maji Rebellion in Tanganyika
1912 Founding of African National Congress in South Africa

1830 Greek independence from Ottoman Empire
1830 French colonization of Algeria
1859–1869 Building of Suez Canal
1882 British colonization of Egypt
1890s–1915 Turkish genocide against Armenians
1897 First Zionist conference
1899 British protectorate over Kuwait
1905–1911 Constitutional revolution in Persia
1907–1921 Russian and British spheres of influence in Persia
1908 Young Turk government in Ottoman Turkey
1908 Discovery of oil in Persia
1911–1912 Colonization of Libya and Morocco

for plantations. Moreover, plantations became less profitable because so many colonies producing sugar flooded the market. African states also charged more to provide slaves. Investing in manufacturing proved more profitable.

Given these moral and economic factors, the slave trade and slavery were ended in the Atlantic world in the nineteenth century. Denmark outlawed the trade in 1804, Britain in 1807, and then all British-controlled territories, including their plantation-rich Caribbean colonies, in 1833. Britain declared war on slave traders, intercepting slave ships in the Atlantic and returning the slaves to Africa. By 1842 most European and American countries made transporting slaves across the Atlantic illegal. The Civil War ended slavery in the United States in 1865. In the later 1880s Brazil and Cuba finally outlawed slavery.

The East African trade sending slaves to the Middle East and Indian Ocean islands, run chiefly by Omani Arabs, continued longer. In 1835 the Omani leader, Sayyid Sa'id (**SIGH-id SIGH-eed**) (r. 1806–1856), moved his capital to Zanzibar, an island just off the Tanzanian coast, where he built a commercial empire shipping ivory to India, China, and Europe and slaves to India, the Persian Gulf, and South Arabia. Omanis also profited from growing Indonesian cloves on slave plantations on Zanzibar. To obtain slaves and ivory, Omani and Swahili merchants expanded overland trade routes through Tanzania into the eastern Congo River Basin. During the 1860s East African ports such as Zanzibar exported some seventy thousand slaves a year. In 1873 Britain convinced the sultan to close Zanzibar's slave market, but slavers still raided African villages for men to carry huge ivory tusks to the coast. Although Britain gained control of Zanzibar in 1890, some slave trading continued in parts of East and Central Africa until the early 1900s.

Even before abolition, freed slaves who chose, or were pressured, to return to Africa from the Americas established several West African states and port cities. The states' black founders and white financiers wanted the freed slaves to run their own lives while also setting up new centers of Western trade. The two largest settlements emerged in Sierra Leone and Liberia. In 1787 Britain settled four hundred former slaves around the fort at Freetown, the core of its Sierra Leone colony. More former slaves arrived in Freetown from Britain's West Indian colonies and British-ruled Canada, many of them former Loyalists during the American Revolution. Freed slaves from the United States first reached Liberia in 1847 and were joined by others after the Civil War. One of the first African nationalists, West Indian–born Edward Blyden (1832–1912), emigrated to Liberia after being denied admission to U.S. universities because he was black. Blyden believed that, given the racism in the Americas and Europe, people of African ancestry could realize their potential only in Africa.

However, some problems remained. Although descendants of former slaves governed an independent Liberia, U.S.-owned rubber plantations dominated its economy. Moreover, in both Sierra Leone and Liberia, local Africans often resented the freed slave settlers, who were mostly English-speaking Christians and who occupied valuable land, dominated commerce, and held political power. In recent decades conflicts between the two groups have torn apart both countries. Some freed slaves from the U.S. or British Caribbean colonies found their way to what is now Ghana and Nigeria, which for some may have been their ancestral homes. Some of these returnees went into business and became part of a growing urban commercial class.

The decline of slave trading made Africa more accessible to Western explorers hoping to discover whether great rivers were navigable for commercial purposes. Scottish explorer Mungo Park (1771–1806), an English trading company doctor in West Africa, traveled along the Niger to open new sources of wealth for British industry. Obsessed with finding the source of Africa's greatest river, the Nile, adventurers finally located Lake Victoria in 1860. David Livingstone (1813–1873), a Scottish cotton mill worker turned medical missionary, spent over two decades traveling in eastern Africa, collecting information and opening the region to Christian missionary activity and Western trade. Although European adventurers claimed to have "discovered" inland African societies and geographical features, they usually followed long-established trading routes using local guides and actually "discovered" little that Africans and Arabs did not already know. Western views were shaped mostly by myths: ethnocentric stereotypes of "intrepid" white explorers "struggling in hardship" through "dangerous virgin territories." Explorers also spread the notion of "Darkest Africa" awaiting salvation by Christian missionaries and Western traders.

In the 1800s European traders began obtaining various raw materials needed by the West, such as peanuts, palm oil, gold, timber, and cotton. They competed with dynamic West African merchants who set up cash crop plantations, many producing palm oil, the main lubricant for industrial machinery in Europe before the development of petroleum.. To avoid African middlemen on the coast, British traders traveled up Nigeria's rivers to buy palm oil directly from Igbo producers. With superior financial resources and their governments' support, European companies eventually undermined African merchants and states that were reluctant to grant trade concessions; by 1890, in the trading port of Lagos, only one African merchant could still compete with British merchants. Some African traders were women. In several port cities of what is today Senegal, businesswomen known as *signares* (from the Portuguese word for "married women") were prominent in the 1700s and 1800s. They were mostly mixed-race descendants of European merchants and high-status Senegalese women. Many owned ships, managed trade networks, employed men, owned land, traded slaves, spoke several European languages as well as the local tongue, Wolof, had political influence, and found ways to thrive at a time of Western encroachment. They also wore opulent cloth fashions including colorful conical head wraps and sported intricate locally made gold jewelry. Some married European merchants. But their status greatly declined in the early 1900s as Western merchants and colonial governments limited their influence and roles. Today many Senegalese remember them as icons of negotiation.

Some major developments derived largely from forces within African societies rather than relations with the West. For example, some militancy and political expansion were caused by tensions within the Sudan's Islamic societies. Conflicts between those wanting to purge pre-Islamic customs from Islamic practice and those mixing Muslim and African traditions broke out sporadically in West Africa. By the 1790s these conflicts spread to the Fulani, a pastoral and trading people scattered across the Sudan from Senegal to Chad. Some Fulani were devout Muslims, some nominal Muslims, and some animists.

Uthman dan Fodio (AHTH-mun dahn FOH-dee-oh) (1754–1817), a respected Fulani Muslim scholar with a magnetic personality, author of over a hundred books, and a Sufi mystic who lived in the Hausa states of northern Nigeria, criticized the Hausa rulers' religious tolerance and called for the conversion of non-Muslim Fulani, making Islam central to Sudanic life. His magnetic personality and Islamic zeal attracted a Fulani and Hausa following. But Uthman's attacks on high taxes and social injustice, as well as his promise to build an Islamic government, alarmed Hausa rulers. After an attempt was made on his life, Uthman launched a jihad (holy war) in 1804, during which he conquered the Hausa states and created a caliphate based in Sokoto (SOH-kuh-toh) city. Uthman divided his empire into small, Fulani-led states led by governors known as *emirs*.

Uthman's jihad and his vision of purified Islam sparked others to form several other jihadist states, often led by Fulani religious scholars, in the Sudan. The Islamic revival, continuing into the 1880s, spread a more orthodox Islam just as Western influence increased in Africa. But by the later 1800s, the Fulani states had declined and Sokoto's power had waned. The Fulani resisted French and British expansion but eventually could not stop it; however, Islam remained a vital force in the Sudanic zone, mostly

INTERFOTO/Alamy Stock Photo

IMAGE 21.2 **African Muslim Warrior** While Western pressure on coastal societies increased, several Muslim peoples expanded their influence in the West African interior. Some military forces, having acquired Western arms in exchange for slaves and gold, conquered regional empires that flourished for a century or more. But many fighters lacked modern arms and relied on traditional weapons and strategies.

Q What does the illustration tell us about traditional West African soldiers and warfare?

as a peaceful influence. But modern politics has revived extremism. In the past several decades a few groups of West African jihadi militants associated with the Islamic State or al Qaeda have engaged in violent conflicts with secular governments in countries like Nigeria, Mali, Burkina Faso, and Niger. And a brutal jihadi group known as Al Shabab has caused turmoil in Somalia.

21-1b European Conquest and Partition

Eventually nearly all of Africa came under Western political control. Britain, France, Germany, Spain, Belgium, and Italy all acquired African colonies in the late 1800s, often through warfare or the threat of force (see Map 21.1). Several factors made this possible. Western companies sought their government's help to pressure states to admit Western merchants. In addition, advances in tropical medicine, especially the treatment of malaria with quinine, freed Europeans from high tropical mortality rates. Inventing more powerful weapons also gave Europeans huge military advantages over African forces armed only with rifles or spears. When possible, Europeans achieved conquest peacefully through deceptive treaties, bribes, division of states, and attempts to convince leaders that resistance was futile. When Africans resisted, Europeans used ruthless force.

In 1878 Belgium's King Leopold (g. 1865—1909) took the lead in colonization, hiring Henry Stanley (1841–1904), a Welsh-born American and former Confederate soldier and journalist who had earlier searched successfully in East Africa to find David Livingstone. Stanley then explored the Congo River Basin, which King Leopold now commissioned him to acquire for Belgium. Soon other European powers joined the scramble to obtain colonies. In 1884–1885 these nations held a conference in Berlin to set colonization ground rules. To have a claim recognized, the colonizer had to announce its intent and then militarily occupy the territory. Agents of European governments such as Stanley asked African chiefs, few of whom knew any Western languages, to sign treaties of friendship or protection, which actually signed over their land, or face war. But in most African traditions tribal members, not chiefs, owned the land. Fearing a slaughter or war with their neighbors, many chiefs signed. The Buganda king reflected African distress when he concluded that Europeans were coming to eat his country.

The colonial scramble came at a time of famine; rains failed, and smallpox and cholera epidemics killed millions. One French missionary reflected the despair: "wars, drought, famine, pestilence, locusts, cattle-plague! Why so many calamities in succession? Why?"[4] The military disparity in weapons and tactics played a major role. The British had the hand-cranked Gatling gun, which could fire hundreds of rounds per minute, and then the Maxim gun, a totally automatic machine gun invented in 1884. Europeans willingly slaughtered thousands. In Southwest Africa (today's Namibia), the German colonizers seized the land of the nomadic pastoralist Herero (hair-AIR-oh) people and banned them from owning cattle, threatening their whole way of life. This prompted a rebellion in 1904. In response the Germans killed all but 15,000 of the 80,000 Herero in a brutal war of extermination. They poisoned Herero wells and put thousands in concentration camps. Many died from starvation, disease, and dehydration. In Kenya, British military expeditions attacked villages for chasing

[4]Francois Coillard, quoted in John Iliffe, *Africans: The History of a Continent* (New York: Cambridge University Press, 1995), 208.

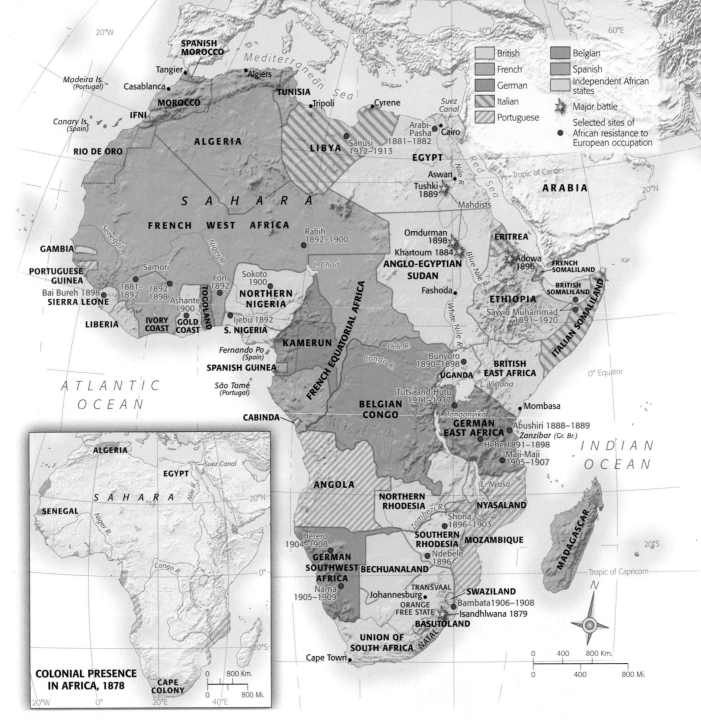

MAP 21.1 **Africa in 1914** Before 1878 the European powers held only a few coastal territories in Africa, but in that year they turned to expanding their power through colonization. By 1914 the British, French, Belgians, Germans, Italians, Portuguese, and Spanish controlled all of the continent except for Ethiopia and Liberia.

Q How do the political boundaries and nations on this map compare to a map of today?

away tax collectors or ambushing Western military patrols that intimidated potential resisters. A British officer boasted of giving orders that every living thing in a Kikuyu village, except children, should be killed without mercy because an Englishman had been killed nearby. Soldiers then burned all the huts and destroyed banana farms. They called establishing law and order, often by force, the "Pax Britannica," the Latin term for "British peace."

After centuries of rivalries and slave wars, Africans could not unite for common defense. Europeans took advantage, pitting state against state and ethnic group against ethnic group.

Various independent kingdoms and village-based stateless societies existed in the region that became Nigeria. Thanks to the slave trade, some were already unstable; Yorubas engaged in bitter civil war for much of the 1800s. Between 1887 and 1903 Britain conquered or annexed these diverse societies, creating the colony Nigeria because it occupied both sides of the lower Niger River.

By 1914 European powers, by drawing boundaries and staking claims, had divided up the entire continent except for Ethiopia and Liberia. The French empire, concentrated in North, West, and Central Africa, extended across the Sahara from Senegal to

Lake Chad, and south to the Congo basin. The British had four colonies in West Africa, including Nigeria, but built most of their empire in eastern and southern Africa. The four German colonies were scattered, while Italy concentrated on Northeast Africa, including Somalia and Eritrea, and on Libya in North Africa.

Fierce competition for territories sometimes led to the brink of war over rival claims. Britain wanted to control eastern Africa from Cairo in the north to the Cape of Good Hope, while Germans dreamed of a Central African empire. German colonization of Tanganyika spurred Britain to move into Kenya, Uganda, and Zanzibar. In South Africa, the brash British imperialist Cecil Rhodes (1853–1902), a clergyman's son who made millions in the South African diamond mining industry, led efforts to outflank Germany and Portugal by extending British influence into territories he arrogantly named Northern and Southern Rhodesia. British settlers migrated to Southern Rhodesia (today's Zimbabwe) and Kenya, solidifying Britain's domination.

Although outgunned, many Africans offered spirited resistance to conquest. Mandinka leader Samory Toure (1830–1900), in the western Sudan, resisted French invasion for a decade. An inspirational military commander, he recruited a large, well-trained army from among Muslims and animists, building a revived Mandinka state modeled on Sundiata's earlier Mali empire. Finally, France defeated Samory's brave but exhausted force in 1898 and exiled him. In 1903 many in Fulani-ruled Sokoto died in battle against the British rather than surrender. In Muslim West Africa, mystical Sufi brotherhoods sometimes rallied opposition to France or Britain. When the French tried to rule Senegal's Wolof people through their kings and chiefs, resisters turned to Muslim clerics, especially Amadu Bamba Mbacke (AH-mah-doo BOM-ba um-BACK-ee) (ca. 1853–1927), founder of a peaceful Sufi order, the *Murids* ("learners seeking God"). France exiled him for many years but eventually realized it could only rule Senegal with Murid cooperation. While Amadu Bamba acknowledged French administration, he was allowed to expand the Murids. The only decisive African military triumph came in Ethiopia, fortified in high mountains and plateaus. In 1896, reforming Emperor Menelik (MEN-uh-lik) II's (1844–1914) French-trained army of eighty thousand men defeated an invasion force of ten thousand Italian troops.

In the Gold Coast (today's Ghana), the Ashanti kingdom held off British forces for decades. Seeking to protect its coastal forts, Britain repeatedly clashed with the prosperous, powerful, expanding Ashanti. In 1874 a large British force secured the coast and looted the capital, Kumasi, but effective Ashanti resistance by forty thousand troops equipped with obsolete but serviceable muskets prevented the British from pushing further into the interior. British forces withdrew from Kumasi but forced the Ashanti to pay a large indemnity. The British then fomented civil war in Ashanti territories, but the Ashanti king refused British ultimatums to surrender. In 1896 three thousand well-armed British troops finally occupied Kumasi and exiled the king. However, resistance continued, often spurred by royal women such as queen-mother Yaa Asantewa (ca. 1840–1921).

IMAGE 21.3 Samory Toure Samory Toure, the ruler of a Mandinka state, led a military force that resisted French incursion into their West African region in the late nineteenth century, but he was eventually captured by the French. This photo shows him (front, left) in custody.

Q What can you tell about the contrasting clothing styles of the participants in the surrender?

Outraged by British demands for the golden stool that symbol-ized Ashanti kingship, she offered to lead Ashanti forces if the men would not: "Is it true that the bravery of the Ashanti is no more? I cannot believe it....We the women...will fight the white man...till the last of us falls in the battlefields."[5] Not until 1901 did the British manage to quell her rebellion, stamp out resistance, and fully incorporate the Ashanti into their Gold Coast colony.

KEY POINTS

▶ Opposed by many Europeans on humanitarian and reli-gious grounds, African slavery became less profitable than manufacturing as the Industrial Revolution gained momentum, and it was phased out by the end of the nineteenth century.

▶ With the end of the slave trade, Europeans began to explore Africa's interior and to take advantage of its vast store of natural resources.

▶ European nations rapidly colonized Africa by engaging in deceptive negotiations, by threatening and often carrying out acts of violence, and by exploiting existing rivalries among groups of Africans.

▶ By 1914, all but a small portion of Africa had been divided up among the European powers, which sometimes feuded over control of various territories and sometimes met fierce resistance from Africans such as the Ashanti.

21-2 The Colonial Reshaping of Sub-Saharan Africa

▦ SOCIETIES

Ⓠ What were some of the major consequences of colonialism in Africa?

Western colonial domination from the 1880s to the 1960s reshaped sub-Saharan Africans' politics, society, culture, and eco-nomy. Whereas the trans-Atlantic and East African slave trades had devastated parts of Africa for four centuries, colonial conquests undermined all African societies' autonomy. Colonialism created artificial states while transforming Africans into subject peoples who enjoyed few political rights. Europeans also took some land as settlers. The largest settler colony, South Africa, experienced an unusual history: over three centuries of white supremacy introduced by Dutch colonizers and perpetuated by Britain. European immigrants also settled in British East Africa, the Rhodesias, and Portuguese colonies. Asian migrants joined them, often as traders. Colonialism allowed Western business interests to penetrate the continent, integrating Africa into the global system as a supplier of valuable raw materials.

CONNECTION to TODAY

How do you think the African economies today reflect the economic policies of the colonial era?

21-2a Colonial States and African Societies

Colonial policies devised in London, Paris, Berlin, Lisbon, and Brussels introduced new kinds of governments, with each colonizing power seeking to achieve maximum control at minimum expense. France grouped its colonies into large federations, such as French West Africa, headed by one governor; Britain preferred to govern each colony, such as the Gold Coast and Nigeria, separately. Despite little under-standing of, or interest in, African cultures, Europeans always held ultimate political authority, usually supervising administra-tion; Africans had to obey decisions made by European bureaucrats. Under **direct rule**, administration was largely European down to the local level, with chiefs or kings reduced to symbolic roles. Under **indirect rule**, tradi-tional kings or chiefs enjoyed considerable local power but were subject to colonial officials. Leaving much of African society intact, indirect rule caused less disruption, but African lead-ers had to consult with local European advisers on many mat-ters. Indirect rule was inspired by pragmatism, there being too few European officials to administer large colonies. Colonizers sometimes strengthened chiefs or appointed chiefs where none previously existed, undermining village democracy.

Huge and unwieldy Nigeria, with some 250 distinct African ethnic groups, reflected both kinds of administration. Struggling to keep the largely Muslim north pacified, Britain needed coop-eration from Hausa and Fulani emirs. Lord Lugard, a British governor, proclaimed that every emir "will rule over the people as of old time but will obey the laws of the [British] Governor,"[6] hence leaving the traditional Hausa-Fulani courts and social structure largely undisturbed. By contrast, in southern Nigeria, which was chiefly governed through direct rule, greater change occurred, including the introduction of Christian missions and cash crop farming. Some southerners adapted to these changes. The Igbo, particularly receptive to Christianity, became promi-nent in Nigeria's educated middle class. The Yoruba blended their rich artistic tradition and polytheism with imported English lit-erary forms and Christianity, maintaining tolerance for divergent views. Rejecting fate and helplessness, Yoruba described their

direct rule A method of ruling colonies whereby a largely European colonial administration supervised all activity, even down to the local level, and native chiefs or kings were reduced to symbolic roles.

indirect rule A method of ruling colonies whereby districts were administered by traditional (native) leaders, who had considerable local power but were subject to European officials.

---

[5]Quoted in "Yaa Asantewaa" (Ghanaweb.com/GhanaHomePage/people/person.php?ID=175).

[6]Quoted in Iliffe, *Africans*, 200–201.

culture as a river that never rests, with swift-moving currents that can either run deep and quietly or be turbulent and overpowering.

However, many policies politically handicapped Africans. Supporters of Western colonialism claimed it provided "a school for democracy," but by 1945 only a few Africans enjoyed political rights or access to democratic institutions. A few thousand urban merchants and professionals in British Nigeria and Gold Coast voted for and served on city councils, while males in French Senegal elected members of the colonial council and a representative to the French parliament. Meanwhile, African chiefs and kings, to keep their positions, implemented colonial policies, such as supervising cash crop agriculture and recruiting people for labor and war. Africans often viewed these privileged, wealthy leaders as little better than paid colonial agents.

Misunderstanding African ethnic complexities, to simplify administration colonizers identified people of similar culture and language as "tribes," even though these peoples were actually collections of subgroups without much historical unity. In reality, African peoples such as the Yoruba, Kikuyu, Igbo, Xhosa, and Mandinka were ethnic groups, not unlike the politically divided Italians, Irish, and Poles of early-nineteenth-century Europe. Thus colonial boundaries, often ignoring traditional ethnic relationships, created artificial countries such as Nigeria, Ghana (the former Gold Coast), Congo, and Mozambique, not nations built on shared culture and identity. Colonizers ignored local interests, sometimes dividing ethnic groups between two or more colonial systems. The Kongolese, once masters of a great kingdom, were split between Portuguese Angola and the Belgian and French Congos. Rival societies were sometimes joined, creating a basis for later political instability. In Nigeria the tensions between Igbo, Yoruba, Hausa-Fulani, and other groups have fostered chronic conflict since British rule ended. Other countries also experienced ethnic conflicts that sometimes provoked violence.

Several colonies heavily restricted African civil and economic rights, particularly South Africa, Portuguese-ruled Angola, and British-ruled Kenya and Southern Rhodesia. They reserved for immigrant white farmers the best land, such as Kenya's fertile highlands once dominated by the Kikuyu, and the most lucrative crops, such as coffee. At the same time, African farmers faced barriers in obtaining bank loans. European settlers participated in government and erected rigid color bars limiting contact between whites and Africans except as employers and hired workers, perpetuating white supremacy.

Europeans viewed African culture as irrational and static, with no history of achievement. An ethnocentric British scholar argued in 1920 that "the chief distinction between the backward and forward peoples is that the former are of colored skin."[7] This prejudice translated into demeaning ideas that Africans were unfit to rule themselves and badly needed Western leadership. Racist ideology spawned the French and Belgian idea of their "civilizing mission": in their view Africans were children who could attain adulthood only by adopting the French language, religion, and culture. Europeans also imposed a color bar, excluding Africans from clubs, schools, and jobs reserved for Europeans.

Some colonies attracted Asian immigrants. Beginning in the 1890s South Asians, mostly Indians, arrived to build railroads, work on sugar plantations, or become middle-level retail traders. They became East Africa's commercial middle class and played key economic roles in South Africa, the Rhodesias, Mozambique, and Madagascar (Malagasy) as well as the Indian Ocean islands of Mauritius and Reunion. Cities such as Nairobi in Kenya, Kampala in Uganda, and Durban in South Africa had substantial Indian populations, their downtowns dominated by Indian stores and Hindu temples. In much smaller numbers Chinese went to South Africa (first as goldminers) and Mauritius. Today most are in the professions or the commercial sectors. In West and Central Africa, Lebanese and Syrians became urban shopkeepers. Black Africans resented this growing Asian influence and wealth, and after independence many governments restricted Asian economic power and some returned to their ancestral countries or emigrated to Europe or North America. However, seeking to divide and rule, Europeans hoped that Africans would focus their resentment on Asian traders rather than European officials.

21-2b Europeans and Africans in South Africa

Conflicts between European settlers and Bantu-speaking Africans shaped South Africa. From their first settlement at Cape Town, established in 1652, the Dutch settlers, known as Boers (Dutch for "farmers"), expanded while establishing white rule over nonwhites that enforced physical separation of the groups in all areas of life. White supremacy became even more rigid in the late 1700s and early 1800s. Many Boers migrated by wagon trains east along the coast and into the interior, a journey they called trekking, seeking good farmland and escaping government restrictions on their freedom of action.

Trekking sparked chronic conflicts for nearly half a century between Boers and Xhosa (**KHO-sa**) farmers and pastoralists in the eastern Cape region, during which time many Xhosa died. When fearing attack, trekkers pulled their wagons into a circle, known as a **laager**, that came to symbolize Boer resistance to new ideas and desire for separation from other peoples. The Boers' white supremacy, sanctioned they believed by their strict, puritanical Calvinist Christian beliefs, ensured them a cheap labor supply for their farms and ranches. This economy, dependent on thousands of slaves of African and Asian origin, was threatened when the British annexed Cape Colony in 1806 and then in 1807 ended South African slavery and later granted voting rights to Africans and mixed-descent people, known as coloreds. These developments prompted more Boers to migrate into the interior.

Eventually migrating Boers faced the largest Bantu group in the region, the Zulus. In the early 1800s some Zulus began expanding under an ambitious military genius, Shaka (ca. 1787–1828), who overcame the disadvantage of birth out of wedlock to gain fame as a courageous warrior and become a powerful chief. Shaka united various Zulu clans in Natal (**nuh-TELL**), along South Africa's Indian Ocean coast, into a powerful nation. Soil exhaustion, severe drought, population growth, and fears of

laager A defensive arrangement of wagons in a circle. Used by the Boers in South Africa in the eighteenth and nineteenth centuries to guard against attacks by native Africans.

---

[7]H. H. Johnston, quoted in M. E. Chamberlain, *The Scramble for Africa* (Harlow, UK: Longman, 1974), 96.

WAGGON ASCENDING THE UNCOMMOSS HILL, NATAL.

Mansell/The LIFE Picture Collection/Getty Images

IMAGE 21.4 **The Great Trek** Many Boers migrated into the South African interior in wagon trains. These migrants, known as trekkers, endured hardships but also eventually subjugated the local African peoples, taking their land for farming, pasturing, and mining.

Q What does this painting, perhaps exaggerating the challenge and heroism, suggest about the Great Trek and the people involved?

potential Boer migration may all have provoked Zulu expansion. Shaka organized a disciplined army of some forty thousand warriors and invented effective new military tactics, such as dividing his troops into regiments armed with short, stabbing spears. In 1816 he began invading other groups' territories, wreaking widespread disruption and causing the deaths of thousands of Zulus and non-Zulus. Western visitors described a desolate countryside with human bones whitening in the sun and rain. After conquering much of the mineral-rich interior plateau, Shaka grew more despotic and was assassinated by his brother, and eventually the Zulu empire fell to the Boers. Ironically, by depopulating much of the mineral-rich interior plateau, Shaka's wars made it easier for Boers to later move in. Historians still debate Shaka's wars. Some suspect that the scale of fighting and number of victims were

exaggerated by Zulu enemies, both Africans and Boers; others disagree.

Some Bantus avoided Zulu or Boer conquest. For example, amidst the regional turmoil Moshoeshoe (**UM-shway-shway**) I created a kingdom for his branch of the Sotho (**SOO-too**) people, skillfully evading colonization for half a century (see Meet the People: Moshoeshoe I, Sotho Chief and State Builder). Eventually gaining British support allowed his Sotho kingdom to remain independent until 1871, when British-ruled Cape Colony absorbed it.

British–Boer conflict intensified. In 1838 many Boers began the Great Trek, heading in well-armed wagon caravans of several hundred families with their sheep and cattle into the interior. After many hardships and fighting with Zulus, they moved into the high plateau and formed two independent Boer republics, Transvaal

Moshoeshoe I, Sotho Chief and State Builder

Moshoeshoe I (ca.1786–1870), a paramount Sotho chief, built the most successful black-ruled state in nineteenth-century southern Africa thanks to his mental toughness, pragmatism, remarkable political and military skills, diplomacy, generosity, and fairness to subjects. As a youth his cattle-raiding successes earned him the nickname "the razor" for cutting away an opponent's herds as neatly as a shave. The son of a minor chief, by thirty-four he rose to clan chief and eventually settled with his followers on a defensible flat-top mountain, surrounded by a fertile valley, from where he warded off attacks.

The Sotho peoples, farmers and herders, were divided into several often feuding chiefdoms, but when Zulu and Boer military expansion caused regional chaos, many Sotho and non-Sotho refugees sought protection with Moshoeshoe, who wisely welcomed them into his community regardless of ethnic backgrounds. In building his own state, he generally avoided warfare and coercion, preferring peaceful negotiations when possible. "Peace is like the rain which makes the grass grow," he concluded, "while war is like the wind which dries it up."

Using diverse survival strategies, Moshoeshoe sent tribute, especially cattle, to potential aggressors, among them Zulus, to avoid war and built his Basuto state around cattle exchange and an inclusive administration; some Sotho rivals, ignoring diplomacy, were defeated. He understood cattle's key economic role and rewarded supporters with captured cattle for marriage gifts. Tapping polygamous traditions, he made many marriage alliances and probably had over a hundred wives himself. But his many sons and grandsons, who all needed administrative posts, later proved a strain when they schemed against each other for power in his waning years.

Moshoeshoe encouraged people to debate civic questions in public meetings, including in a crucial decision-making state-level assembly. Chiefdoms that joined his state were bound to Moshoeshoe through political marriages and councils and kept some local autonomy, making his state more a confederation than a centralized kingdom. Refugees could maintain their chiefs and traditions and rule themselves. His community grew from about twenty-five thousand in 1833 to eighty thousand by 1848.

Moshoeshoe also looked for help elsewhere. He invited Christian missionaries to his state and used them to acquire guns and horses. French Protestants from the Paris Evangelical Society greatly aided him, advising him on, and negotiating with, his British, Boer, and colored (mixed-race) adversaries. Missionaries created a Sotho written language, built churches and schools, and educated many Sotho youth. Moshoeshoe sent his own sons to the schools but, unwilling to abandon polygamy, never became a Christian. If one of his wives converted, he granted her a divorce. He also welcomed a few British

army deserters to teach firearm skills and technologies. French missionary Eugène Casalis, the state's unofficial foreign minister, described Moshoeshoe as having "an agreeable and interesting countenance, his deportment is noble and dignified, and a benevolent smile plays upon his lips." Furthermore, Casalis wrote, "Being of a very observant disposition, he knew how to resist and how to yield at the right moment; procured himself allies, even among the invaders of his territory; set his enemies at variance with each other, and by various acts of kindness secured the respect of those even who had sworn his ruin."

For decades Moshoeshoe's state faced continuous military challenges from Zulus, Ndebeles, Sotho rivals, and Boers, but, while the attacks devastated the countryside, his forces successfully defended his bastion. Eventually Britain proved the most formidable opponent, respecting his regional power but disputing his territorial claims. In 1848 his forces beat back a British general who tried to annex his state. British forces withdrew after Moshoeshoe sent General George Cathcart a face-saving message: "I entreat peace from you—you have shown your power,—you have chastised,—let it be enough I pray you; and let me no longer be considered an enemy of the Queen." Soon recognizing his diminishing options and needing a counterweight to the encroaching Boers, Moshoeshoe humbly cultivated friendship and alliance with Britain as "fleas in the blanket of Queen Victoria." British support allowed his Sotho state to remain formally independent until 1871, when it was absorbed into Britain's Cape Colony. In 1884 it became Basutoland, a British protectorate separate from, and with more autonomy than, South Africa.

When Moshoeshoe died in 1870, his state's independence was compromised, his people were still not united, and much Sotho land was lost to Afrikaners. Yet, more skillfully than other southern African leaders facing similar challenges, he created a kingdom out of chaos and steered it to the best destiny open to it. In 1966, Basutoland gained its independence as Lesotho, and his family continued his legacy. One great-grandson became South Africa's first black Roman Catholic bishop; another, Moshoeshoe II, became Lesotho's king after independence.

IMAGE 21.5 **King Moshoeshoe** The pragmatic Sotho king built a kingdom that withstood Western pressure for decades.

Fotosearch/Archive Photos/Getty Images

Q What does the drawing tell us about the king and the royal regalia?

Reflection Questions

1. What strategies led to Moshoeshoe's state-building success?
2. Why is he considered one of Africa's great leaders?
3. Can you think of any of Moshoeshoe's qualities and policies that you admire?

Note: Quotations from Leonard Thompson, *A History of South Africa* (New Haven, CT: Yale University Press, 1990), 86 and 95; "Moshoeshoe of Lesotho, 'Africa's Greatest Leader,'" *afrol News* (afrol.com/features/35246); Donald Denoon, *Southern Africa Since 1800* (New York: Praeger, 1973), 57.

(TRANS-vahl) and Orange Free State. Seizing cattle, the Boers forced conquered Africans to work on Boer farms. They consolidated control over Africans and dedicated themselves to preserving their culture and upholding unequal relations between white "master" and African "servant." The Boers despised the British and considered black Africans an "inferior race" hostile to European values.

However, the discovery of gold and diamonds in the Boer republics spurred Britain to seek control there, leading to the South African War (1899–1902), often called the Boer War. The ensuing British victory intensified Boer resentment. The British burned farms, destroyed towns, and interned thousands, including women and children, in concentration camps, where twenty-six thousand Boers died of disease and starvation. The brutalities discredited the war in Britain. Britain relied on African troops, thousands of whom died hoping the British would be less oppressive.

But African hopes were soon dashed as they discovered that they had merely exchanged one set of white masters for another. British and Boer leaders worked out a compromise, making the South African government a collaboration between the two groups. The regime extended discriminatory laws, restricted African civil and political rights, and put many Africans on reserves, rural lands with few resources from which workers could be recruited. The white-owned economy chiefly valued Africans as cheap unskilled labor; laws limited their movement and reserved desirable neighborhoods and jobs only for whites. Facing continued African resistance, the government built a police state to enforce its racial policies. Furthermore, British–Boer tensions simmered as thousands of British settlers eventually became a third of the white population. Boers began calling themselves Afrikaners (people of Africa) and their Dutch-derived language Afrikaans.

21-2c Christian Missions and African Culture

Supported by colonial governments, Christian missionaries, seeking to reshape African culture and religious life, established most of Africa's modern hospitals and schools. Mission doctors practiced Western medicine while denouncing African folk medicine. Yet, sometimes Europeans found African expertise to praise. In 1879 a Scottish medical anthropologist witnessed a highly developed medical procedure, a caesarean section, performed by a local doctor in the precolonial kingdom of Bunyoro, now part of Uganda. He was shocked and impressed at the surgeon's skill and success using mostly traditional African methods, reporting that the young patient seemed to experience little pain and recovered within two hours. But few Europeans admired local knowledge. By teaching new agricultural methods, mathematics, reading, writing, and Western languages, mission schools gave a few Africans valuable skills for the colonial economy and administration. But critics complained that, while teaching Western values and European history, they ignored African history and derided African beliefs as superstition. Some African nationalists, themselves mission school graduates, claimed that these schools, as an Igbo writer put it, "miseducated" and "de-Africanized" them, perpetuating their status as "hewers of wood and haulers of water."[8] In addition, Africans who attended mission schools and adopted individualistic Western ways often became divorced from their village traditions, loosening their communities' social ties. Yet, before 1945

only 5 percent of children attended any government or mission school. Sierra Leone established the first modern African college in 1827, but before 1940 the few Africans who could attend a university mostly did so in Europe or the United States.

Millions of Africans adopted Christianity, some becoming devout Catholics or Protestants and others only accepting beliefs they liked while rejecting others. Africans often emphasized Bible passages calling for justice and equality. Some African churches incorporated traditional practices and beliefs, such as men having more than one wife. Yorubas often added Christian and Muslim gods to their polytheistic pantheon. Christianity also marginalized once-influential female deities and shamans, reducing women's religious roles. Moreover, Christian leaders who required men to give up multiple wives left these women without support for their children. Yet, women often welcomed monogamy and favored Christian social values such as promoting girls' education.

Europeans and missions sometimes used the law to impose their own cultural prejudices on Africans. For example, homosexuality and transgender identity had long been accepted or tolerated in some African societies going back hundreds of years or more, just as they had in various other societies around the world. But Muslims, Christians, and the British generally condemned these practices. The British campaigned against homosexual behavior and relationships and made them illegal both at home and in their African and Asian colonies. Influenced by the colonial prohibitions promoted as "modern," many African nations today have maintained and even increased this repression, often with harsh penalties, strongly supported by some Muslim and Christian religious organizations and missionaries.

21-2d Africans in the World Economy

Africa's economic transformation was as significant as its political reorganization. Extracting wealth required linking its economy closely to that of the colonizers. European businessmen now controlled the key economic institutions, including banks, import–export companies, mines, and plantations. Since subsistence food growing was unable to produce enough revenues for governments or investors, colonial policies made Africans into producers for the world market and required that taxes be paid in cash. These policies promoted the growing of cash crops such as cotton, cocoa, rubber, and palm oil and the mining of copper, gold, oil, chrome, cobalt, and diamonds. If taxation did not spur changes, authorities resorted to forced labor, most notoriously in the Belgian Congo, which required much of the population to grow rubber for Belgian planters. An American missionary reported in 1895 that the Belgian policies "reduced the people to a state of utter despair. Each town is forced to bring a certain quality [of rubber]. The soldiers drive the people into the bush. If they will not go they are shot down, and their left hands cut off. The soldiers often shoot poor helpless women and harmless children."[9] Over half the Congolese died from overwork or brutality over a twenty-year period.

Linking Africans to the world economy often left them vulnerable, subjecting their livelihoods to fluctuations in world prices for the commodities they produced, which were determined by the whims of Western consumers and corporations. Colonies became markets for Western industrial products, displacing village handicrafts, while Africans became exporters of

---

[8]Nnamdi Azikiwe, quoted in Minton F. Goldman, "Political Change in a Multi-National Setting," in *Dynamics of the Third World: Political and Social Change*, ed. David Schmitt (Cambridge, UK: Winthrop, 1974), 172.

[9]Rev. J. B. Murphy, quoted in Kevin Shillington, *History of Africa*, rev. ed. (New York: St. Martin's Press, 1995), 333–334.

PUNCH, OR THE LONDON CHARIVARI—NOVEMBER 28, 1906.

IN THE RUBBER COILS.

SCENE—*The Congo "Free" State.*

Mary Evans Picture Library Ltd/Age Fotostock

IMAGE 21.6 **Rubber Coils in Belgian Congo** The Belgians colonized the Congo hoping to exploit its resources. This critical cartoon, published in the British satirical magazine *Punch* in 1906, shows a Congolese ensnared in the rubber coils of the Belgian king Leopold in the guise of a serpent. Rubber was the major cash crop, introduced by the Belgians to generate profits.

Q What seems to be the point of view and main points of this cartoon?

cash crops they did not consume, such as cocoa and rubber, and importers of goods they did not produce. Many cash crops dominating African lives, such as peanuts and rubber from South America or cocoa from Mexico, had been introduced from outside. A growing automobile culture in the West also fostered an oil-drilling industry along the West African coast, making these societies dependent on oil exports. As a result, colonies often became economic monocultures. Hence Northern Rhodesia (now Zambia) mostly exported copper, Senegal peanuts, and Gold Coast cocoa. A local popular song from the 1960s well described Ghanaians' dependence on growing and selling cocoa: "If you want to send your children to school, build your house, marry, buy cloth [or] a truck, it is cocoa. Whatever you want to do in this world, it is with cocoa money that you do it."[10]

The colonial economy's opportunities and demands profoundly affected both men and women. Recruiting or forcing many men to migrate to other districts or colonies for mining or industrial labor established a permanent pattern of labor migration. South Africa's white-owned farms and mines recruited thousands of workers, mostly men, from Mozambique and British Central Africa on renewable one-year contracts, while men from the Sahel migrated to Ivory Coast and Gold Coast cocoa estates. These migrations disrupted family and village life. Male migrants lived in crowded dormitories or huts offering little privacy, enjoyed few amenities other than drinking beer in makeshift bars, and could visit their families back home for only a few days a year.

Many thousands of South Africans also moved to cities, especially the Transvaal mining center of Johannesburg, becoming temporarily or permanently removed from their farming villages. They experienced dreadful work conditions on white-owned factories and farms, and even worse in the mines, where safety regulations were few; hundreds of miners died each year. The Zulu poet B. W. Vilakezi described the miner's life in the early 1900s: "Roar, without rest, machines of the mines, Roar from dawn till darkness falls. To black men groaning as they labor, Tortured by their aching muscles, Gasping in the fetid air, Reeking from the dirt and sweat. The earth will swallow us who burrow. And, if I die there, underground, What does it matter? All round me, every day, I see men stumble, fall and die."[11]

In many African societies women had long played key roles as traders and farmers. As men migrated for work or took up cash crop farming, women's workload increased as they became responsible for less lucrative food production. Women's agricultural workweek in the German-ruled Cameroons increased from forty-five to seventy hours. Baule women of the Ivory Coast, who once profited from growing cotton and spinning it into thread, lost their position to Baule men when cotton became a cash crop and textiles an export item. In addition, women traders who had dominated town markets now faced competition from Indians or Lebanese. Some women responded with self-help organizations. Ashanti market women in Kumasi organized themselves under elected leaders later known as market queens, promoting cooperation and settling disputes among themselves. Thanks to education, self-help, and ambition, some African women also supported themselves as teachers, nurses, and traders. But trying to preserve their families while fulfilling their new responsibilities overwhelmed many poor women.

21-2e African Responses and the Colonial Legacy

Africans responded to colonialism in various ways. In South Africa the small educated middle class of professionals and traders found ways to oppose white supremacy. Johannesburg lawyer Pixley ka Isaka Seme (**PIX-ley ka I-sa-ka SE-me**), a graduate of Columbia University in New York, helped found the African National Congress in 1912 to promote African rights and cultural regeneration. In Nigeria many educated Igbos became cash crop farmers, merchants, professionals, or clerks. Other Africans dealt with change by enriching traditional ways. In the woodcarvings and elaborately carved doors he sculpted for Yoruba kings, the imaginative Yoruba artist Olowe of Ise (**oh-LO-way of ee-SAY**) (ca. 1875–1938) emphasized Yoruba themes and ideals and creatively added richly textured surfaces and the illusion of movement. Some Africans mixed Western and African ideas. The Black Zion movement in South Africa had

---

[10]Quoted in Dennis Austin, *Politics in Ghana* (London: Oxford University Press, 1964), 275.
[11]Quoted in Tom Hopkinson, *South Africa* (New York: Time Inc., 1964), 93.

Christian overtones, claiming that Jesus was African, but also promoted African traditions such as faith healing.

Sometimes traditional cultural forms expressed African sentiments. Combining dance and theater, Igbo women influenced their individualistic but patriarchal society by dancing and singing their grievances in a strategy known as "sitting on a man." Some dance performances encouraged noncooperation with colonial demands, such as increased taxes, or with excessive male Igbo chauvinism. When local leaders ignored dance messages, Igbo women took stronger action, including rioting. In South Africa Zulu workers reworked dance tunes to protest white domination. Sotho people transformed poetry praising influential people and ancestors into songs expressing male migrants' experiences in the mines and the women left behind in villages. And South African composers mixed Christian hymns with traditional Xhosa or Zulu choral music. The African National Congress adopted one such hymn, "God Bless Africa," as their official anthem. Later the song, with its uplifting message of hope, became the anthem of black empowerment:

> *Bless the youth, that they may carry the land with patience. Bless the wives and young girls. Bless agriculture and stock raising. Banish all famine and diseases. Fill the land with good health. Bless our effort, of union and self uplift, of education and mutual understanding.*[12]

Resistance strategies varied. Tax evasion and passive protest were rampant, especially in rural areas. Some Africans formed labor unions, which were usually illegal since colonial regimes protected Western-owned businesses. Strikes were common, especially among mine workers, but governments arrested strike leaders, jailing them along with political activists. Rebellions sparked by unpopular policies, such as new taxes or forced labor, punctuated colonial rule. The Maji Maji Rebellion in German-ruled Tanganyika in 1905 began as a peasant protest against a new cotton-growing scheme that forced people to work for only 35 cents a month. Africans' preference to grow their own food rather than be commercial farmers sparked a new religious cult, Maji Maji ("water medicine"), which used "magic water" in hopes of better crops. Sprinkling their bodies with magic water and believing it would make them immune from bullets, rebels occupied towns. Germans regained the towns with machine guns and in 1907 defeated the Maji Maji, killing twenty-six thousand Africans. However, the resistance caused the Germans to end forced labor.

Some historians contend that colonialism increased the land's productive capacity, built cities and transportation networks, brought advances in technology, and stimulated Africans to produce more wealth than ever before. Other historians disagree, arguing that colonial rulers stole land, exploited labor, gained profitable access to raw materials, shifted wealth back to Europe, limited Africa's economic growth, and created artificial, unstable countries. While colonial profits supported European industrialization and enriched businesses, Africans enjoyed little balanced economic growth that benefited the majority. One observer in the early 1900s noted that in Portuguese-ruled Mozambique a man "works…all his life under horrible conditions to buy scanty clothing for his wife and daughters. The men and boys can rarely afford proper clothing."[13] Moreover, many former colonies became economically vulnerable monocultures. Seventy-five years of Belgian colonialism in the Congo failed to build any paved road system linking the major cities or establish more than a handful of schools and medical clinics for the millions of Congolese. As a result, sub-Saharan Africa was the most impoverished region of the world at the end of the colonial era, a legacy difficult to overcome and with which some Africans still struggle.

KEY POINTS

▶ Colonizers divided Africa into countries with artificial boundaries, sometimes splitting an ethnic group into more than one country and sometimes throwing rival groups into a single country, thus creating lasting tensions.

▶ Dutch settlers of South Africa, called Boers, pursued a policy of white supremacy in spite of more liberal British policies.

▶ Christian missionary schools provided a small minority of Africans with skills they could use in the colonial world but largely ignored and often damaged the native African culture.

▶ As African economies came to depend on a single commodity desired by Europeans, colonized Africans lost their subsistence skills and were often forced to work far from home.

▶ Blacks suffered greatly in white-dominated South Africa, but many resisted through poetry, music, dance, and political organizations such as the African National Congress.

21-3 Imperialism, Reform, and the Middle Eastern Societies

⊐ TRANSITIONS ⧉ SOCIETIES

Q What political and economic impact did Europe have on the Middle East?

In earlier centuries some Muslim states enjoyed great power and vibrant economies and were among the world leaders in science and mathematics. By 1750 the "golden ages" were fading as regional and world political arrangements were being

CONNECTION to TODAY

How do you think that the political developments in the Ottoman territories, Egypt, and Persia during these years influence those countries today?

reshaped. Between 1750 and 1914 most Muslim societies suffered repeated challenges from western Europe and Russia. The Ottoman Empire remained the only significant power and, despite its remarkable ability to rejuvenate itself, fell behind

---

[12]The lyrics are in David B. Coplan, *In Township Tonite: South Africa's Black City Music and Theater* (London: Longman, 1985), 44–45.
[13]Quoted in Leroy Vail, "The Political Economy of East-Central Africa," in *History of Central Africa*, ed. David Birmingham and Phyllis M. Martin, vol. 2 (New York: Longman, 1983), 233.

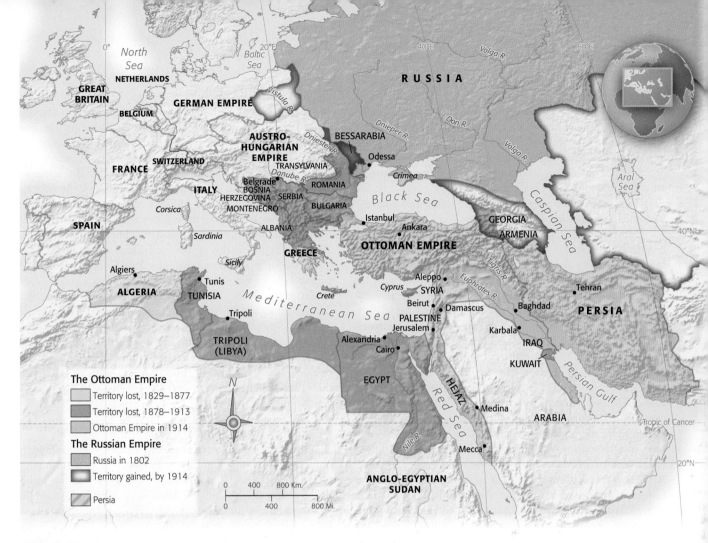

MAP 21.2 **The Ottoman Empire and Persia, 1914** The Ottoman Empire once included much of southeastern Europe, western Asia, and North Africa. By 1914, after losing most of its European, Caucasian, and North African territories, it was restricted largely to parts of western Asia.

Q How does this political map compare to maps of the Middle East and Islamic world today?

the industrializing West. As Ottomans and Persians lost territories to expanding European empires, European economic penetration and cultural influences forced diverse responses.

21-3a Challenges to the Ottoman Empire

During the Early Modern Era the Ottoman Turks forged a huge empire in southeastern Europe, western Asia, and North Africa, becoming a major world power. Many Muslims viewed the Ottoman sultan as the caliph, successor to the Prophet and the Islamic community's leader. But by 1750 Ottoman power had diminished from both conflicts with Western powers and internal problems. In the nineteenth century rising pressure from Europe and Russia undermined the empire and its more than sixty million people (see Map 21.2). The Russians had been expanding south toward the Black Sea since the 1500s. In 1768, defeating Ottoman forces, they gained partial control of the northern Black Sea coast. They later acquired the Crimean peninsula and in 1829 took over Georgia, a largely Christian Caucasus state. In 1853 Czar Nicholas I characterized the weakening Ottoman Empire as "the sick man of Europe," a reputation that would stick.

European powers schemed to outflank each other in dismantling the weakening empire. With European support, Greeks, Serbs, Romanians, and Bulgarians threw off Ottoman rule in the 1800s (see Chapter 19). An Anglo-French fleet and the Russian army intervened to aid the Greeks, shifting the military balance. The 1830 treaty ending the war recognized Greek independence and gave autonomy to Serbia and Moldavia.

Weakened by military losses, the Ottoman government had difficulty satisfying the empire's multiethnic population. Because Turks had long benefited from tapping the varied peoples to enrich their state, non-Muslim minorities played major roles in commerce, the professions, and government. Some historians argue that the Ottoman identity was cosmopolitan, ambiguous, and hybrid, a mixture contradicting the common idea of peoples and nations with fixed identities and cultural belonging. Generally tolerating minorities such as Kurds (mostly Sunni Muslims), Jews, and Arab Christians, Ottomans allowed each group to basically rule itself through its own religious establishment, such as the Greek Orthodox Church. Christians and Jews felt particularly secure in major Ottoman cities, with Jews generally enjoying more rights and prosperity than in Europe. Seeing the persecution of Jews in Christian Europe, Ottoman Jews, mostly of Sephardic background, appreciated Ottoman tolerance, had generally good relations with Turkish Muslims, and rallied around the empire in times of war. Multiethnic Istanbul was described in 1873 as "a city not of one nation but of many. Eight or nine languages are constantly spoken in the streets and five or six appear on the shop fronts."[14] Various religious sects also settled in Lebanon's mountains, maintaining their traditions.

But despite the accommodation to ethnic and religious diversity, some ethnic minorities became restless, especially in eastern Turkey and the Caucasus, where Turkish relations with Christian Armenians deteriorated. Armenians had long remained loyal Ottoman subjects, some holding high government positions, but nationalist and socialist ideas percolating in Europe inspired some to desire nationhood. With European and North American financial and moral support, Armenians founded their own schools, colleges, libraries, hospitals, presses, and charitable organizations. In the 1890s and early 1900s Ottomans responded to increasing Armenian assertiveness, including terrorist attacks, by seizing Armenian property, killing over 100,000 Armenians, and exiling thousands more. Many moved to North America. Then in 1915, during World War I, charging Armenians with supporting Russia, the government began removing Armenians from eastern Anatolia; in response Armenian nationalists declared a republic, after which the Ottoman army, aided by local Turks and Kurds, killed around a million Armenians. Many historians consider the violent assault a genocide, the singling out of one group for mass killing, but Turkish nationalists consider it an incidental side effect of war. The killings still complicate Armenian–Turkish relations. Surviving Armenians formed a small republic in the Caucasus, Armenia, that was absorbed by Russia in 1920. Today Armenia is independent but wary of neighboring Turkey.

To survive and match Western power, Ottoman sultans tried to reform and modernize, building a more secular and centralized government. However, Islamic religious leaders, the privileged Janissary military force, and the virtually independent governors of distant Arab provinces benefited from weak central authority. Gradually Ottoman leaders and thinkers recognized the need to obtain Western knowledge and aid. Reformist sultan Mahmud II (**MACH-mood**) (r. 1808–1839) tried to eliminate the Janissaries, who were once an effective fighting force but now a costly burden that resisted change. Mahmud recruited a new military force, crushed the Janissaries, and then slowly built a modern army trained by Prussian officers. His successors founded new schools that taught European learning and languages; the University of Istanbul became the Muslim world's first modern higher education institution. Replacing many older Islamic laws with laws based on French revolutionary codes, Ottoman rulers increasingly marginalized Islam and treated Islamic knowledge as irrelevant, demoralizing conservatives.

Young Turks A modernizing group in Ottoman Turkey that promoted a national identity and that gained power in the early twentieth century.

The centralized government and a modern, secular Ottoman nationality grew through the 1800s. To foster a national identity, Ottoman sultans declared all citizens equal before the law, announcing that "the differences of religion and sect among the subjects is something not affecting their rights of citizenship. It is wrong to make discriminations among us."[15] But attempts to involve the people in government largely failed; the reforms proved inadequate. In the 1880s a modernizing group, the **Young Turks**, emerged in the military and universities. Seeking to make Turkey a modern nation with a liberal constitution, in 1908 the Young Turks, espousing Turkish nationalism, led a military coup that deposed the old sultan. Under the facade of parliamentary government, they ruled as autocrats and military modernizers. During World War I, as an ally of Germany and Austria-Hungary, the Young Turks embraced a Turkish ethnic identity, secularization, and closer ties to the Western world. After defeat in World War I, the Ottoman Empire was dissolved, and Arab peoples once ruled by the Ottomans fell under British or French rule. By 1920 the Turks were struggling to hold on to their Anatolian heartland.

21-3b Egypt: Modernization and Occupation

The most extensive effort to deflect Western pressure through modernization came in Egypt, but only after minimizing Ottoman influence. The Ottomans had governed the province through the Mamluks, a Muslim caste of Turkish origin whose corruption and repression gave French general Napoleon Bonaparte an excuse to invade the country. When Bonaparte abandoned his Egyptian adventure, Muhammad Ali (r. 1805–1848), a Turkish-speaking Albanian who led Ottoman forces that helped eject the French, became ruler. After being appointed viceroy by the Ottoman sultan, Muhammad Ali made Egypt effectively independent but was forced by European powers to remain loosely bound to the weakening Ottoman state. The charming sultan impressed Europeans with his talents: "If ever a man had an eye that denoted genius, [he] was the person. Never dead nor quiescent, it was fascinating like that of a gazelle; or, in the hour of storm, fierce as an eagle's."[16]

Muhammad Ali introduced ambitious reforms to transform Egypt into a European-style industrial nation. Using government revenues from increased agricultural exports, he established foundries, shipyards, factories (textile, sugar, and glass), a conscript army trained by Western instructors, a navy, and an arms industry. He also replaced Islamic with French legal codes, sent Egyptians to study technical subjects in Europe, fostered the first Arab newspapers, and established a state educational system that trained people for the military and bureaucracy. To demonstrate and celebrate modernization, he built a grand opera house in Cairo in the 1860s. However, his programs ultimately failed to protect Egyptian independence and foster development. Unlike European nations, Egypt lacked iron and coal, and the workforce was not used to industrial regimentation. Moreover, as Muhammad Ali and his successors welcomed Western investment, they also became more shackled

[14]Quoted in Andrew Wheatcroft, *The Ottomans* (New York: Viking, 1993), 146.

[15]Quoted in Halil Inalcik, "Turkey," in *Political Modernization in Japan and Turkey*, ed. Robert E. Ward and Dankwart A. Rostow (Princeton, NJ: Princeton University Press, 1964), 57–58.

[16]Quoted in Afaf Lutfi al-Sayyid Marsot, *Egypt in the Reign of Muhammad Ali* (New York: Cambridge University Press, 1994), 28.

IMAGE 21.7 **Muhammad Ali Meets European Representatives** Muhammad Ali, the Egyptian sultan who tried to modernize his state, cultivated ties with Western nations. This painting shows the sultan in an 1839 meeting with representatives from several European governments.

Q What does the painting tell us about the sultan, his diplomacy, and the meeting?

to European finance. Finally, importing cheap British commodities stifled Egypt's textile and handicraft manufacturing. Rather than buy finished textiles, Europeans wanted Egyptian raw cotton for processing in their own mills.

Like leaders of European nations, Muhammad Ali soon sought resources and markets through conquest. Egyptian armies moved south, conquering the Sudanic lands once known as Nubia along the Nile River, and also into Ottoman-ruled Arabia, Palestine, Syria, and Greece. But this aggression alarmed European powers, who intervened to push the Egyptians back. Britain in particular sought to undermine Egypt to expand its regional influence and gain control of the Suez Canal, which was built as a French–Egyptian collaboration between 1859 and 1869. The one-hundred-mile-long canal, a magnificent technological achievement whose construction cost thousands of Egyptian lives, linked the Mediterranean and Red Seas, greatly decreasing the shipping time between Europe and Asia. British merchant and naval ships became the canal's major users. To celebrate the opening of the canal the government staged an opera by the famous Italian composer Giuseppe Verdi in the new Cairo Opera House. In 1875 Muhammad Ali's grandson

was forced by skyrocketing national debt to sell Egypt's share of canal ownership to the British government.

Egypt's bankruptcy and debt to European financiers and governments eventually led to a British takeover. While the country's political and commercial elite, including many Coptic Christians, were committed to modernization, most Egyptians, influenced by conservative Islamic ideas and leaders, opposed Western influence. To preempt other European powers' ambitions, in 1882 Britain, using local unrest and threats to European residents as an excuse, invaded the country, making Egypt part of Britain's growing worldwide empire.

Britain soon faced a challenge from the Sudanic region to Egypt's south (today the nation of Sudan). In 1881 the militant Arab Muslim Muhammad Ahmad (1846–1885) declared himself the Mahdi (**MAH-dee**) ("the Guided One") sent to restore Islam's purity and destroy the corrupt Egyptian-imposed government. He recruited an army, defeated Egyptian forces and their British officers, and then formed an Islamic state. However, the Mahdist government wasted money in wars. In 1898 British and Egyptian forces triumphed, forming a new state known as the Anglo-Egyptian Sudan, effectively a British colony.

21-3c Persia: Challenges and Reforms

More a diverse collection of tribes, ethnic groups, and religious sects than a nation, Persia, increasingly known as Iran, faced many problems. While Christian Armenians, Jews, Zoroastrians, and Sunni Kurds all sought increased autonomy, the majority of Persia's people, including Turkish-speaking Azeris in the northwest, were Shi'ites. Shi'ite clerics controlled education, law, and welfare, enjoying vast wealth from landholdings and tithes. After the Safavid collapse in 1736 and the following decades of turmoil, in 1794 one Persian tribe, the Qajars **(KAH-jars)**, established control from their base in Tehran, from where they ruled uneasily until 1925. Early Qajar rulers, unable to resolve most problems, became noted for greed, corruption, and lavish living. One extravagant shah married one hundred fifty-eight wives, fathered nearly one hundred children, and was survived by some six hundred grandchildren.

Politics and religion sometimes came into conflict. Top Shi'ite clerics engaged in power struggles with Qajar shahs. Shi'ites also persecuted as heretical the **Bahai (buh-HI)** religion. Founded in 1867 by the Persian Baha'u'llah **(bah-hah-oo-LAH)** (1817–1892) as an offshoot of Shi'ism. The son of a government official in Tehran, Baha'u'llah became a follower of a Persian merchant known as the Bab, who preached that God would soon send a new prophet similar to Muhammed and Jesus. But this assertion was a threat to the political and religious establishment, prompting the authorities to execute the Bab and thousands of his followers. Baha'u'llah fled to Baghdad in 1863, became the leader of the remaining Bab community, and claimed to be the predicted prophet bringing God's message. His views formed the basis for the tolerant Bahai faith, which called for universal peace, the unity of all religions, and service to others. He died under Ottoman house arrest after writing many books on his beliefs. Over the years Shi'ites in Persia (now Iran) have killed many Bahais and forced their leaders into exile, but the Bahai movement now has some five to eight million followers around the world including in the West.

Persia also faced continuous pressure from Russia and Britain. By the 1870s Russia had gained territory on both sides of the Caspian Sea, including the Caucasus, and between 1907 and 1921 it asserted a sphere of influence in northern Persia. At the same time, British power steadily grew in the Persian Gulf and along Arabia's Indian Ocean coast. Wanting to keep Russians away from the Persian Gulf and India, Britain asserted a sphere of influence in southeastern Persia, at the entrance to the Persian Gulf. British entrepreneurs soon monopolized Persian railroad construction and banking; the Anglo-Persian Oil Company (later British Petroleum, or BP), which struck oil in 1908, became Persia's dominant economic enterprise, with profits going chiefly to Britain. Persians considered the powerful British economic role a humiliation. Weak government combined with foreign pressure prompted reforms, and to restore central government power, some Qajar shahs rebuilt an army, established a Western-style college, introduced a telegraph system, and allowed Christian missionaries to establish schools and hospitals. But while some celebrated the reforms, they threatened the conservative Shi'ite clergy, who hoped to thwart modernization.

From 1905 to 1911 Persia enjoyed a constitutional revolution and democracy unique in the Middle East. Liberal Shi'ite clergy, allied with Tehran merchants, Armenians, and Western-educated radicals, imposed a democratic constitution that curbed royal power and provided for an elected parliament and freedom of the press. When a conservative, pro-Russian shah took power and attempted to weaken the parliament, liberal newspapers, writers, and musicians lampooned him and his allies, while troubadours performed songs about love of country, democracy, freedom, justice, and equality. However, Britain and Russia pressured Persia to grant them more influence, straining the progressive leadership. The constitutionalist forces split into pro-Western nationalists who sought separation of religious and civil power, land reform, and universal education, and Shi'ite clerics, who, alarmed at secularism, favored slower change. As violence increased in 1911, the royal government closed down the parliament, ending the democratic experiment. Aref Qazvini, a popular pro-revolution songwriter, lamented the setback: "O let not Iran thus be lost, if ye be men of truth."[17] By then, Britain and Russia, stationing troops in Persia, had reduced Persia's political and economic independence.

21-3d Western Asia, Northwest Africa, and Europe

Declining Ottoman power and growing Western activity eventually reshaped the empire's eastern Arab provinces, especially Syria and Lebanon, an ethnically and religiously diverse region whose Arab and Armenian Christians, Sunni and Shi'ite Arabs, and Sunni Kurds had mostly lived in peace. By recognizing each community's autonomy, the Ottomans promoted religious tolerance. A British writer admired Lebanon's generally stable conditions: "every man lives in a perfect security of life and property. The peasant is not richer than in other countries, but he is free."[18] However, in the 1850s poverty and a stagnant economy led to conflicts, and the densely populated region around Mount Lebanon came under Western influence. The French developed a special relationship with Maronites **(MAR-uh-nite)**, Arab Christians seeking a closer connection with the Roman Catholic Church, while American Protestant missionaries established a college in Beirut, spreading modern ideas. Economic problems also encouraged emigration, especially of Lebanese Christians to the United States, and by 1914 perhaps 350,000 Lebanese and Syrians had emigrated to the Americas. Today there may be as many as 17 to 30 million people of Middle Eastern ancestry in the Americas, mostly Christians and Muslims but also some Bahais and Zoroastrians, including 9 million in Brazil and 3.5 million in the United States. In the United States many have been elected as state governors or served in Congress or presidential cabinets. Many Lebanese and Syrians also migrated to West Africa, where they dominated the commercial sector. In the past half century

Bahai An offshoot of Persian Shi'ism that was founded in 1867; Bahai preached universal peace, the unity of all religions, and service to others.

---

[17]Quoted in Yahya Armajani and Thomas M. Ricks, *Middle East: Past and Present*, 2nd ed. (Englewood Cliffs, NJ: Prentice-Hall, 1986), 221.
[18]Quoted in Charles Issawi, *The Middle East Economy: Decline and Recovery* (Princeton, NJ: Markus Wiener, 1995), 126.

people of Lebanese, Syrian, or other Arab ancestry have served as presidents or prime ministers of several Latin American and Caribbean nations, including Argentina, Brazil, Dominican Republic, Ecuador, Belize, Honduras, El Salvador, and Jamaica.

Under Ottoman rule, Iraq, the heart of ancient Mesopotamia and the first cities and states, lacked political unity and prosperity. Ottoman Iraq included three provinces: a largely Sunni Arab and Kurdish north, a chiefly Sunni Arab center, and a mostly Shi'ite Arab south. Iraqis suffered from major floods and repeated plague and cholera epidemics. A British official described Iraq as "a country of extremes, either dying of thirst or of being drowned."[19] Iraq also lacked security, foreign capital, widespread literacy, railroads, and steamships. Pirates attacked Persian Gulf shipping, while Bedouin tribes raided land caravans. Yet, Western interest in Iraq's economic potential and strategic location grew. In 1899 Britain established a protectorate over the neighboring Persian Gulf kingdom of Kuwait (koo-WAIT), allowing it to station troops and agents. But both the British and Germans suspected that Iraq might have considerable oil, spurring Ottomans and foreign investors to pour money into Iraq.

The Ottomans never firmly controlled Arabic-speaking societies along Africa's Mediterranean coast from Libya to Algeria, and their proximity to Europe made them natural targets. In 1830 France embarked on full-scale colonization of Algeria. Abd al-Qadir (AB dul-KA-deer), using Islamic appeals, united Arab and Berber opposition to the French. His resourceful followers quickly learned how to make guns. Facing years of determined resistance, France demoralized the Algerians, driving peasants off the best land and selling it to European settlers while relocating and breaking up tribes. Yet anti-French revolts erupted until the 1880s. Ruthless French conquest cost tens of thousands of French and hundreds of thousands of Algerian lives.

France intended to impose French culture, settlers, and economic priorities on Algeria. General Bugeaud, who conquered Algeria, conceded in 1849 that "the Arabs with great insight understand very well the cruel revolution we have brought them; it is as radical for them as socialism would be for us."[20] Between the 1840s and 1914 over a million immigrants from France, Italy, and Spain poured into Algeria, erecting a racist society similar to South Africa. Algeria was incorporated into the French state with European settlers given voting rights. Vineyard cultivation and wine production displaced food crops and pasture, mocking Islamic values prohibiting alcoholic beverages.

Gradually European power in Northwest Africa increased. In Morocco, Sultan Mawlay Hassan (r. 1873–1895), to preserve the country's independence, skillfully played rival European powers against each other. However, France and Spain, attracted by Morocco's economic potential and strategic position, had divided the country between them by 1912. Tunisia long enjoyed considerable autonomy under Ottoman rule, with the port city of Tunis prospering as a trade and piracy center. In 1881 France colonized Tunisia. The Italians conquered Libya, a sparsely populated, mostly desert land between Tunisia and Egypt, in 1911–1912. Islamic orders led repeated resistance efforts, and the resulting conflicts killed one-third of Libya's people. European colonialism now dominated all of North Africa, ruling over often restless and disgruntled populations.

KEY POINTS

▶ With sultans viewed by many Muslims as the new caliphs, the Ottomans modernized their army, adopted French-style laws, and became increasingly secular, but their power began to wane under pressure from Russia and western Europe and also from the Armenians.

▶ After Napoleon left Egypt, an Ottoman-appointed governor, Muhammad Ali, attempted an ambitious and somewhat successful program of modernization; ultimately, however, Britain gained control of the Suez Canal and made Egypt a colony.

▶ Persia, fragmented under the rule of the Qajars, came to be dominated economically by Britain, and interference by both Britain and Russia helped to end a brief period of progressive rule.

▶ Westerners became increasingly influential in Syria and Lebanon, as well as in Iraq, which was undeveloped but attracted Western attention because of its economic potential.

▶ Europeans colonized Northwest Africa: first Algeria, where settlers established a racist society; then Morocco, which was shared by France and Spain; and finally Tunisia and Libya.

21-4 Middle Eastern Thought and Culture

SOCIETIES TRANSITIONS

Q How did Middle Eastern thought and culture respond to the Western challenge?

West Asians and North Africans responded to Western challenges in three ways. Some formed vibrant revivalist movements promoting a purer version of Islamic practice rooted in early Muslim tradition. Others mounted reform movements combining Islam with modernization and secularization. Early stirrings

CONNECTION to TODAY

How influential are the varied strands of Islam and nationalist thought from these years in the Middle East today?

of Arab nationalism constituted a third response. While governments stagnated or struggled, revivalist, reform, and nationalist movements pumped fresh vitality into cultures and religious life. But no movement offered an effective resistance to Western economic and military power.

---

[19] Gertrude Bell, quoted in Emory C. Bogle, *The Modern Middle East: From Imperialism to Freedom, 1800–1958* (Upper Saddle River, NJ: Prentice-Hall, 1996), 103.
[20] Quoted in Eric R. Wolf, *Peasant Wars of the Twentieth Century* (New York: Harper and Row, 1969), 209.

21-4a Islamic Revivalism

Islamic revivalism sought to purify religious practices by returning to a purer vision of Islamic society rooted in the faith's early years, embracing what followers regarded as God's word in the Quran and the Prophet Muhammad's sayings. Revivalists idealized the theocratic state of the early Mecca caliphs, which blended religion and government, and criticized as corrupt the scholarly and mystical additions from Persian, Hindu, Indonesian, African, and European cultures that over the centuries had been mixed with Islam. In many African and Southeast Asian societies, Muslims still consulted shamans skilled in magic and healing, revered Sufi saints, and permitted women to engage in trade and reject veiling. Muslim revivalists despised Sufism and its mystical practices, such as music and dance. Several Sufi brotherhoods eventually abandoned mystical beliefs and emphasized the Prophet Muhammad's original teachings.

While political leaders lost prestige and authority, revivalists allied to merchant and tribal groups seized the initiative. For example, Othman dan Fodio in West Africa and the Mahdist Army in Sudan interpreted the early Muslim idea of jihad, or struggle for the faith, as a call to wage holy war against Muslims who disagreed with them as well as non-Muslims. Carried by scholars, merchants, and missionaries, revivalist Islam spread all over the Islamic world. Many sub-Saharan African, Indian, and Southeast Asian Muslims visited, studied, or sojourned in the Middle East, often embracing revivalist ideas. These movements stiffened resistance against French colonization in Algeria and West Africa and against Dutch colonization in Indonesia.

Revivalism had its greatest impact in Arabia, where it produced a militant movement in the 1700s called **Wahhabism (wah-HAH-bi-zuhm)**. The founder, Muhammad Abd al-Wahhab **(al-wah-HAHB)** (1703–1792), led a long campaign to purify Arabian Islam. After studying Islamic theology in Medina and Iraq, al-Wahhab adopted a strict interpretation of Islamic law and promoted intolerance toward all alternative views, such as Sufism and Shi'ism, and those lax in their faith. In 1744 a key ally, Muhammad Ibn Saud **(sah-OOD)**, a tribal chief, put together a fighting force to expand their influence, and during the later 1700s Wahhabis used military force to take over parts of Arabia. Advancing into Syria and Iraq, they occupied the city of Karbala and destroyed the major Shi'ite holy site. By 1805 Wahhabis controlled Mecca and Medina, Islam's two holiest cities, where they horrified non-Wahhabis by massacring the residents and trying to destroy sacred tombs to prevent saint worship. Egypt's governor, Muhammad Ali, used his European-style army and modern weapons to push Wahhabis back from the holy cities. However, Wahhabi ideas, puritanism, and zeal spread widely during the 1800s as Western power undermined Middle Eastern governments. Yet many Muslims condemned Wahhabi intolerance, extremism, and such practices as forced veiling of women and still do today.

Islamic revivalism Arab movements that sought to purify Islamic practices by reviving what they considered to be a purer vision of Islamic society.

Wahhabism A militant Islamic revivalist movement founded in Arabia in the eighteenth century.

In 1902 al-Wahhab and Ibn Saud's descendants launched a second expansion. The head of the Saud family, Abdul Aziz Ibn Saud (1880–1953), sent Wahhabi clergy to convince Bedouins to abandon nomadic ways and join self-sufficient farming communities that adopted extreme asceticism and literal interpretation of the Islamic legal code, the Shari'a. Wahhabi clergy beat men for arriving late for prayers. In 1925 the Saud family established Saudi Arabia, a state based on the Shari'a. Oil discoveries in 1938 gave the Saud family and their Wahhabi allies the wealth to maintain their control and spread their ideas throughout the Muslim world, a thrust that continues today with Saudi-sponsored schools and mosques.

21-4b Modernist Islamic Thought

The Muslim world never had any major widespread movement similar to the Renaissance, Reformation, and Enlightenment in Europe that welcomed and generated new ideas. But by the later 1800s and early 1900s some thinkers were looking for ways to accommodate the modern world while preserving what they considered the best features of Islam. In some cases they revived the quest for knowledge pursued by innovative broad-minded Islamic philosophers and scientists in the Middle Ages like Al-Biruni, Ibn Rushd, and Ibn Sina, some of whom were also persecuted by conservatives and dogmatists in their day. Some reformist Muslim thinkers, rejecting a rigid, backward-looking vision such as Wahhabism, promoted modernization to transform Islamic society and meet the Western challenges. Intellectuals argued that Muslims should reject blind faith and welcome fresh ideas, social change, and religious moderation. Modernists detested many conservative traditions. Qasim Amin **(KA-sim AH-mean)**, a French-educated Egyptian lawyer, argued that liberating women was essential to liberating Egypt, that acquiring their "share of intellectual and moral development, happiness, and authority would prove…the most significant development in Egyptian history." Women reformers such as Bahithat al-Badiya **(buh-TEE-that al-buh-DEE-ya)** echoed these sentiments (see Discover Historical Voices: Egyptian Women and Their Rights). The radical male Iraqi poet Jamil Sidqi az-Zahawi **(ja-MILL SID-key az-za-HA-wi)** identified the veil as symbolizing female exclusion, imploring women to "unveil yourself for life needs transformation. Tear it away, burn it, do not hesitate. It has only given you false protection!"[21]

Modernists believed that introducing change would be a straightforward process, that buying weapons and machines could strengthen their armies and industries to deflect Western pressure, enrich their countries, and avoid domestic unrest. But their dreams proved impractical; visionaries were ahead of largely conservative populations. Challenges increased as Western technical and economic capabilities grew. Like European Enlightenment thinkers, some modernists struggled with reconciling faith and reason. They worried that modernization required adopting Western philosophical and scientific theories, often contrary to Islamic beliefs about society, God, and nature. Belief in equality also contradicted Muslim women's low status, while notions of popular sovereignty and the nation troubled those who believed that only God could make laws or establish standards, which the state must then administer. Some reformers doubted whether

---

[21]The quotes are from Akram Fouad Khater, ed., *Sources in the History of the Modern Middle East* (Boston: Houghton Mifflin, 2004), 75; Wiebke Walther, *Women in Islam* (Princeton, NJ: Markus Wiener, 1993), 221.

Discover Historical Voices

Egyptian Women and Their Rights

One of the leading women writers and thinkers in early-twentieth-century Egypt, Bahithat al-Badiya (1886–1918), advocated greater economic and educational rights for women in a rapidly changing society. She wrote at a time when Egyptian nationalists demanded independence from Britain and a modern state while intellectuals debated the merits of modernity as opposed to tradition. In 1909, in a lecture to an Egyptian women's club associated with a nationalist organization, Bahithat offered a program for improving women's lives. Struggling against male and Islamic opposition to women's rights, she sought a middle ground between Islamic conservatism and European secular liberalization.

Ladies, I greet you as a sister who feels what you feel, suffers what you suffer, and rejoices in what you rejoice....Complaints about both men and women are rife....This mutual blame which has deepened the antagonism between the sexes is something to be regretted and feared. God did not create man and women to hate each other but to love each other and to live together so the world would be populated....Men say when we become educated we shall push them out of work and abandon the role for which God has created us. But isn't it rather men who have pushed women out of work? Before, women used to spin and to weave cloth for clothes,...but men invented machines for spinning and weaving....In the past, women sewed clothes...but men invented the sewing machine....Women...[made bread] with their own hands. Then men invented bakeries employing men....I do not mean to denigrate these useful inventions which do a lot of our work....Since male inventors and workers have taken away our work should we waste our time in idleness or seek other work to occupy us? Of course, we should do the latter....

Men say to us categorically, "You women have been created for the house and we have been created to be breadwinners." Is this a God-given dictate?...No holy book has spelled it

out....Women in villages...help their men till the land and plant crops. Some women do the fertilizing, haul crops, lead animals, draw water for irrigation, and other chores....Specialized work for each sex is a matter of convention,...not mandatory....Women may not have to their credit great inventions but women have excelled in learning and the arts and politics....Nothing irritates me more than when men claim they do not wish us to work because they wish to spare us the burden. We do not want condescension, we want respect....

If we had been raised from childhood to go unveiled and if our men were ready for it I would approve of unveiling those who want it. But the nation is not ready for it now....The imprisonment in the home of the Egyptian woman of the past is detrimental while the current freedom of the European is excessive. I cannot find a better model [than] today's Turkish woman. She falls between the two extremes and does not violate what Islam prescribes. She is a good example of decorum and modesty....We should get a sound education, not merely acquire the trappings of a foreign language and rudiments of music. Our education should also include home management, health care, and childcare....We shall advance when we give up idleness.

Reflection Questions

1. How does Bahithat evaluate women's roles and gender relations in Egypt?
2. What does her moderate advice to Egyptian women suggest about Egyptian society and the power of patriarchy?
3. How do Bahithat's proposals compare to feminists and other supporters of women's rights and empowerment today?

Source: Bahithat al-Badiya, "A Lecture in the Club of the Umma Party, 1909," trans. by Ali Badran and Margot Badran, in *Opening the Gate: A Century of Arab Feminist Writing*, ed. by Margot Badran and Miriam Cooke (Bloomington: Indiana University Press, 1990), pp. 228–238. Copyright © 1990 by Indiana University Press. Reprinted with permission of Indiana University Press.

Islam, which idealized a universalistic, multiethnic, God-guided community, was compatible with nationalism, which emphasized unity defined by a common state. Moroccan historian Ahmad Ibn Khalid al-Nasri worried that military cadets being trained in Western weapons and tactics "want to learn to fight to protect the faith, but they lose the faith in the process of learning how."[22] What role, modernizers wondered, could clerics and the Shari'a have in a world of machines and nations?

Some Egypt-based thinkers argued about Islam's compatibility with modernization. Persia-born teacher Jamal al-Din al-Afghani (1838–1895), believing that reason and science were not contrary to Islam, argued that rigid religious interpretations, intolerance of new ideas, and the weight of local traditions

contributed to Arab backwardness. He lamented that "the Arab world still remains buried in profound darkness,"[23] while rational interpretations of Islam would free Muslims for positive change. Strongly criticizing British imperialism and Arab leaders he viewed as puppets, he moved to Paris, where he published a weekly newspaper promoting his views. Another well-traveled thinker, Muhammad Abduh (**AHB-doo**) (1849–1905), wanted to reform his native Egypt and rejuvenate Islam. Although opposing wholesale Westernization, Abduh admired major European thinkers, contending that no knowledge, whatever its origin, was incompatible with Islam. A top Islamic jurist, he promoted modernist Islam at Al-Azhar University, the Middle East's most influential higher education institution.

[22]Quoted in Burke, *Prelude to Protectorate*, 38.
[23]From Khater, *Sources*, 34.

Album/Alamy Stock Photo

IMAGE 21.8 **Portrait of Muhammad Abduh, Egyptian Reformer** Muhammad Abduh was one of the leading modernist reformers in the Islamic world in the late nineteenth century. He admired European thinkers but opposed wholesale modernization.

21-4c The Roots of Arab Nationalism and the Zionist Quest

During the 1800s an Arab national consciousness developed in response to Ottoman, British, and French domination. Some proposed a pan-Arab movement uniting Arabs from Morocco to Iraq in a common struggle for political and cultural independence. But diverse religious and group affiliations divided Arabs. Most were Sunni Muslims, but many Shi'ites lived in western Asia, and some Christians lived in Egypt, Lebanon, Syria, and Iraq. Feuding patriarchal tribes sometimes disliked rival tribes as much as their Ottoman or European overlords. Many Arabs also remained loyal to Ottoman rule. In 1876, hoping to defuse

kibbutz A Jewish collective farm in Palestine that stressed the sharing of wealth.

ethnic nationalism, the Ottomans gave Arabs seats in the national legislature.

Yet, some thoughtful Arabs envisioned self-governing Arab nations. Arab nationalism emerged from a Syrian literary and cultural movement in the later 1800s that included Lebanese Christians; one published a poem calling on Arabs to "arise and awake." Abd-al-Rahman al-Kawabiki (**AB-dul-RAH-man al-KA-wa-BIK-ee**) (1849–1903), a witty Syrian who had studied in Egypt and Mecca and hated intolerance and injustice, criticized Ottoman despotism as contrary to Islam while promoting Arab politics. Arab nationalist groups formed all over the Ottoman Empire, but before World War I they were small and had little public influence.

While Islamic societies struggled against Western power, the Zionist movement (see Chapter 19) introduced another challenge. In Jewish ghettoes of eastern Europe, especially Poland and Russia, some thinkers sought a state for their long-persecuted, widely scattered people. Prayers in Jewish synagogues for worshipping "next year in Jerusalem," the ancient Hebrew (Israelite) capital in Palestine, endured for centuries. Few European Jews spoke Hebrew, and many rejected Zionism, identifying with the country where they lived. For others, Zionism functioned like nationalism. The first Zionist conference, held in Basel, Switzerland, in 1897, identified Ottoman-ruled Palestine as the potential Jewish homeland. Jews had long visited or settled in Palestine, and perhaps twenty thousand lived there in 1870. When the Ottomans, worried about unbalancing and destabilizing a divided Palestine society that might threaten their control, prohibited Zionists from organizing a massive Jewish settlement, the Zionist leader, Hungarian-born journalist Theodor Herzl (1860–1904), proposed accepting a British offer for a temporary home in East Africa.

Soon militant Zionists promoted Jewish migration to Palestine without Ottoman permission or European governments' support. By 1914 some eighty-five thousand Jews, many newcomers from Russia and Poland, lived in Palestine alongside some 700,000 Arabs. Committed to creating a socialist society, many immigrants established Jewish collective farms, each known as a **kibbutz**, whose members shared their wealth and promoted Hebrew rather than the German-based Yiddish widely spoken by central and east European Jews. International Zionist organizations funded Palestine settlement, buying land from absentee Arab and Turkish landowners. Zionists had a flag, an anthem, and an active Jewish press but no legal recognition in Palestine, setting the stage for future conflict with Palestinian Arabs, who resented the newcomers and their plans to acquire more land for a Jewish state.

KEY POINTS

▶ One response to European pressure was Islamic revivalism, which advocated a pure form of Islam, favored a theocratic state, and sometimes used violence.

▶ Revivalism was most influential in Arabia, where militant followers of al-Wahhab and Ibn Saud took over a number of cities and eventually formed Saudi Arabia.

▶ Some intellectuals tried to modernize their religion, but modern European ideas such as equality continued to clash with Islamic practices such as the subjugation of

women, and Western nationalism was at odds with the idea of a universal brotherhood under God.

▶ Some tried to inspire Arab nationalism, but religious divisions and rivalries made this a difficult task.

▶ Muslims were also challenged by European Zionists, who moved to Palestine in spite of Ottoman objections and also in spite of the Palestinian Arabs, setting the stage for future conflict.

Chapter Summary

Sub-Saharan Africa underwent extensive changes between 1750 and 1914. Ending the trans-Atlantic slave trade opened Africa to exploration and trade by Europeans. Industrial Europe's need for resources and markets fostered a "scramble for Africa" as various Western nations colonized African societies, sometimes by military force against protracted resistance. The French colonized a vast area of West and Central Africa; Britain forged a large empire in West, Central, and East Africa; and the Germans, Belgians, and Italians also acquired African colonies. European settlers flocked to colonies in southern and eastern Africa, most notably South Africa, establishing white supremacist societies. Colonialism created artificial, multiethnic countries. It replaced subsistence agriculture with cash crop farming, plantations, and mineral exploitation while enmeshing Africa in the world economy as a supplier of natural resources. Africans mounted strikes and rebellions against colonialism, but all such efforts were eventually defeated.

The Middle East also experienced European imperialism. The Ottoman Empire attempted to stall its decline with Western-style reforms, but it still lost territory and influence. Egypt attempted an ambitious modernization program, but it proved inadequate to prevent British colonization. In Persia, Western economic and political influence sparked reforms that were later rejected by Persian conservatives. France and Italy colonized North Africa, and French settlers displaced Algerians from valuable land. In response, some Muslims, most notably Wahhabis, pursued a revivalist strategy to purify the religion and reject Western influence, while modernist reformers sought to energize Muslim societies by adapting secular Western ideas to Islam. Arab nationalist movements also arose but remained weak before World War I. Finally, Jewish Zionists posed a threat to Palestinian Arabs by beginning to settle in Palestine, where they hoped to build a Jewish state.

Key Terms

direct rule 540	Young Turks 548	Wahhabism 552
indirect rule 540	Bahai 550	kibbutz 554
laager 541	Islamic revivalism 552	

Rice fields are littered with our battle-killed; blood flows or lies in pools, stains hills and streams. [French] Troops ... grab our land, our towns, roaring and stirring dust to dim the skies. A scholar with no talent and no power, could I redress a world turned upside down?

—Protest by Vietnamese poet Nguyen Dinh Chieu against French conquest, late nineteenth century[1]

IMAGE 22.1 **Dipenegara** This painting shows Prince Dipenegara, a Javanese aristocrat who led a revolt against the Dutch colonizers in the 1820s, reading, with several attendants at hand.

Q What can we learn about aristocratic Javanese life from this painting?

[1]From Huynh Sanh Thong, *An Anthology of Vietnamese Poems from the Eleventh Through the Twentieth Centuries* (New Haven, CT: Yale University Press, 1996), 88.

In 1858, seeking to expand its empire and frustrated by the Vietnamese emperor's refusal to liberalize trade relations and protect Christian missionaries, France attacked Vietnam with military force, and over the next three decades it conquered the country against determined resistance. One of the strongest resisters was a blind poet, Nguyen Dinh Chieu **(NEW-yin dinh chew)** (1822–1888), who gave an oration honoring Vietnamese soldiers killed during a heroic battle: "You preferred to die fighting the enemy, and return to our ancestors in glory rather than survive in submission to the [Westerners] and share your miserable life with barbarians." The French retaliated, seizing Chieu's land and property. The poet, unbowed, refused to use Western products and forbade his children to learn the romanized Vietnamese alphabet developed by French Catholic missionaries. In painstakingly copied manuscripts spread throughout the land, Chieu promoted the struggle and heaped scorn on Vietnamese who collaborated with French occupiers: "I had rather face unending darkness, Than see the country tortured. Everyone will rejoice in seeing the West wind [colonialism], Vanish from [Vietnam's] mountains and rivers."[2] Chieu was to become a physician, scholar, and teacher famous for epic poems sung in the streets that extolled love of country, friendship, marital fidelity, family loyalty, scholarship, and military arts. He rejected the French offer of a financial subsidy and the return of his family land if he supported their cause. Vietnamese continue to revere his stirring poems.

Using their enhanced military, economic, and technological power (see Chapters 19–20), and motivated by greed and cultural arrogance, Britain, France, the Netherlands, and the United States colonized all of South and Southeast Asia except Thailand. Western domination proved a transforming experience, destroying traditional political systems, reorienting economies, and posing challenges for societies and their worldviews. As Asian workers produced resources that spurred Western economic growth, these regions were introduced to Western ideas and technologies and became linked more closely to a European-dominated world economy. Resentment against colonialism simmered for decades; eventually some Asians asserted their peoples' rights to self-determination.

---

[2]The poem excerpts are in Helen B. Lamb, *Vietnam's Will to Live: Resistance to Foreign Aggression from Early Times Through the Nineteenth Century* (New York: Monthly Review Press, 1972), 134, 152.

22-1 Forming British India

⊃⊂ TRANSITIONS

Ⓠ How and why did Britain extend its control throughout India?

India had been a world leader for centuries and enjoyed something of a Golden Age in the sixteenth and early seventeenth century under the early Mughal state, which ruled much of the subcontinent and boasted a strong government, impressive textile manufacturing, vibrant mixed Hindu-Muslim culture, and effective military (see Chapter 18). But by the early 1700s the Muslim Mughals

CONNECTION to TODAY

What lessons can people today learn from the British conquest of a large and densely populated society like India?

were in steep decline, challenged by both Indians and Europeans. Mughal court splendors and India's valuable exports had earlier attracted Portuguese, Dutch, French, and British adventurers, businessmen, and diplomats. But it was the British who took advantage as Mughal power declined. In the mid-1700s they began their conquest, and by the mid-1800s they controlled both India and the island of

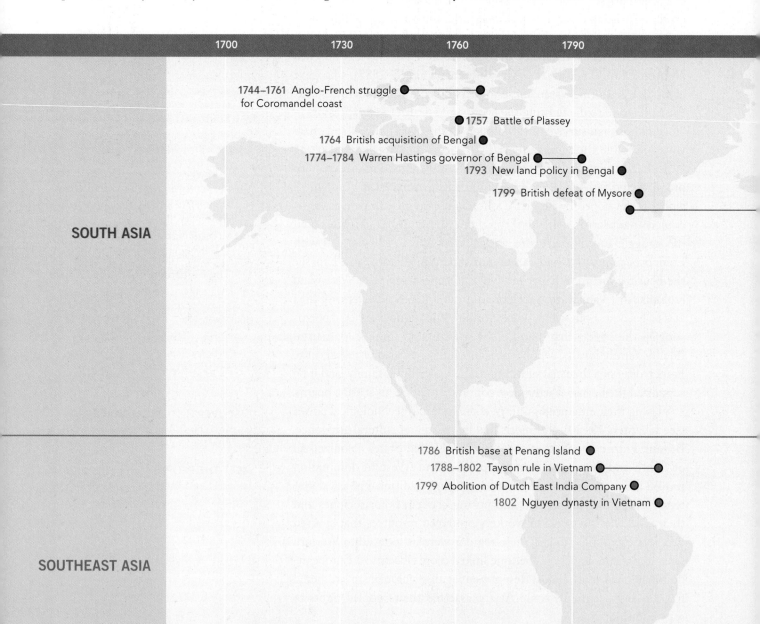

| | 1700 | 1730 | 1760 | 1790 |

SOUTH ASIA

1744–1761 Anglo-French struggle for Coromandel coast

1757 Battle of Plassey

1764 British acquisition of Bengal

1774–1784 Warren Hastings governor of Bengal

1793 New land policy in Bengal

1799 British defeat of Mysore

SOUTHEAST ASIA

1786 British base at Penang Island

1788–1802 Tayson rule in Vietnam

1799 Abolition of Dutch East India Company

1802 Nguyen dynasty in Vietnam

Sri Lanka (Ceylon). Unlike earlier conquerors from western and Central Asia, who often assimilated into Indian society, the British maintained their separate traditions while promoting Western values.

22-1a Mughal Decline and the British

Europeans had long coveted South Asia for its spices and textiles, which they had imported for many centuries. Even today, just as in olden times, small, single-masted sailing barges ply the coastline between western India, the Persian Gulf, and East Africa, ferrying merchandise with the coming and going of monsoon winds. Between 1500 and 1750 European powers controlled some of the Indian Ocean maritime trade but conquered or occupied only a few scattered outposts in

South Asia. The Dutch, after destroying Portuguese power, concentrated on Sri Lanka and Indonesia. By 1696 the British possessed three fortified trading stations in India: Calcutta (now Kolkata) in Bengal, Madras (today known as Chennai) on the southeastern coast, and Bombay (today called Mumbai) on the west coast. Today these settlements are huge metropolises and comprise three of the four largest cities in India.

By 1750 many Indians had already broken away from weak and corrupt Mughal control, and the emperors sitting on the spectacular Peacock Throne in Delhi's Red Fort enjoyed little actual power beyond Delhi. As they consoled themselves with the royal harem or opium and as Mughal factions quarreled among themselves, the countryside became increasingly

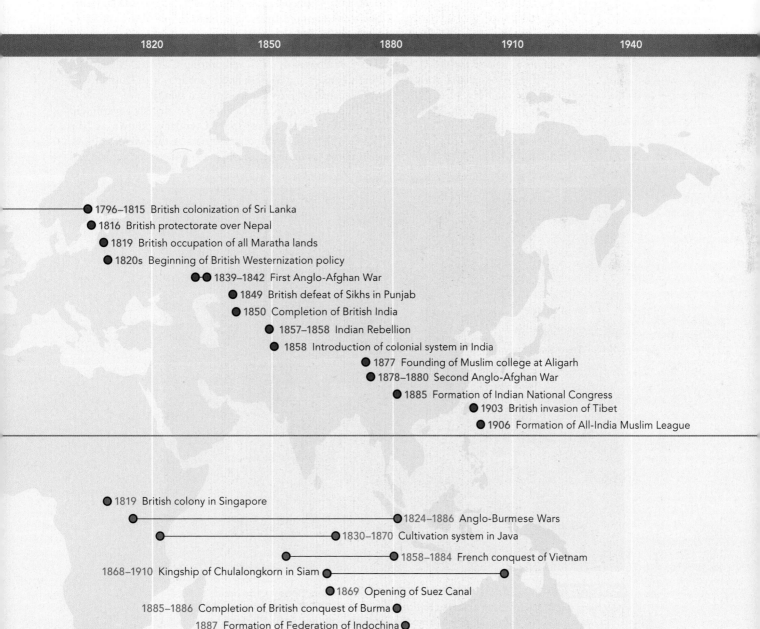

1820   1850   1880   1910   1940

1796–1815 British colonization of Sri Lanka
1816 British protectorate over Nepal
1819 British occupation of all Maratha lands
1820s Beginning of British Westernization policy
1839–1842 First Anglo-Afghan War
1849 British defeat of Sikhs in Punjab
1850 Completion of British India
1857–1858 Indian Rebellion
1858 Introduction of colonial system in India
1877 Founding of Muslim college at Aligarh
1878–1880 Second Anglo-Afghan War
1885 Formation of Indian National Congress
1903 British invasion of Tibet
1906 Formation of All-India Muslim League

1819 British colony in Singapore
1824–1886 Anglo-Burmese Wars
1830–1870 Cultivation system in Java
1858–1884 French conquest of Vietnam
1868–1910 Kingship of Chulalongkorn in Siam
1869 Opening of Suez Canal
1885–1886 Completion of British conquest of Burma
1887 Formation of Federation of Indochina
1898–1902 U.S. conquest of Philippines
1908 Dutch defeat of last Balinese kingdom

disorderly. Powerful new states arose, including those built by the **Marathas (muh-RAH-tuhs)**, a loosely knit, Hindu-led confederacy from west-central India, and the Sikh religious minority in northwest India. By 1800 Marathas ruled much of western India, while Sikhs under the dynamic Ranjit Singh **(RUN-ji SING)** (1780–1839) conquered the Punjab and Kashmir. Mounted on sturdy ponies, the feared Marathas made plundering raids deep into central India against helpless Mughal armies. Without a powerful state to unite it, this diverse Indian society could not effectively resist European encroachments. Both Britain and France attempted to fill the power vacuum in southern India, supporting their respective Indian allies in the struggle for regional advantage. Ultimately, no Indian state gained enough power or acquired enough support to repulse the West.

Britain posed the gravest challenge, and one of the key events took place in Bengal, India's richest and most populous region that was ruled by governors who mostly ignored the Mughal government. Aliverdi Khan (r. 1740–1756) had left British trade unmolested. But his successor, Siraja Dowlah **(see-RAH-ja DOW-luh)** (ca. 1732–1757), considering the British bothersome leeches on his land's riches, alienated Western merchants and in 1757 rashly attacked trading stations. After capturing Calcutta, Dowlah's forces placed one hundred forty-six captured British men, women, and children in a crowded jail known as the **Black Hole of Calcutta**. The next day only twenty-three staggered out, the rest having perished from suffocation and dehydration. The enraged British dispatched a force under General Robert Clive (1725–1774) to regain holdings. A former clerk turned daring and brilliant war strategist, the ambitious Clive had earlier military experiences in India and was well acquainted with the opposing forces and local realities. With this knowledge and some freedom from higher-ups to plot his strategy of retaliation, Clive and his thirty-two hundred well-armed and trained soldiers defeated fifty thousand Bengali troops at the Battle of Plassey in 1757, recapturing Calcutta. Allied with Hindu bankers and Muslim nobles unhappy with Dowlah, who was executed, by 1764 Clive controlled Bengal.

Pursuing a mercantilist policy the British government allowed the British East India Company (known as "the Company") to govern Indian districts as they were acquired, sharing the profits. The British, much like the former Mughal

Marathas A loosely knit confederacy led by Hindu warriors from west-central India; one of several groups that challenged British domination after the decline of the Mughals.

Black Hole of Calcutta A crowded jail in India where over a hundred British prisoners of a hostile Bengali ruler died from suffocation and dehydration in 1757. This event precipitated the beginning of British use of force in India.

AISA/Everett Collection

IMAGE 22.2 **Clive Meets Indian Leaders** In this painting, Robert Clive meets the new Bengali official, Mir Jafir, after the British victory in the 1757 Battle of Plassey. Clive supported Mir Jafir's seizure of power from the anti-British leader, Siraja Dowlah.

Q What does this painting tell us about British and Indian warfare and diplomacy in the 1700s?

rulers, expected Indians to serve them, showing a lust for riches equal to Spanish conquistadors in the Americas in the 1500s. Thanks to the BEIC's predatory behavior and what one historian calls the greatest act of corporate violence in world history, one of the very first Indian words adopted by the British was "loot," the Hindi word for plunder. As Bengal governor (1758–1760, 1764–1767), Clive sanctioned organized plunder; British merchants and officials drained Bengal's wealth while Company officials, including Clive, lived like kings. Praised by British leaders and celebrated in the press and schoolboy stories, Clive became the idol of every young Englishman dreaming of glory and wealth via India's battlefields and bazaars. Inspired by Clive's rags-to-riches story, the cry of "Go East" fueled British imperialist ambitions. But Clive was eventually accused and later cleared of corruption and fraud charges, and at the age of forty-nine, depressed, he committed suicide.

To undo Clive's economic chaos and consolidate Britain's position, the Company appointed Warren Hastings as Bengal's governor-general (1774–1784). Hastings redesigned the revenue system, made treaty alliances, and annexed nearby districts to safeguard the bases. Unlike other British officials, Hastings respected Indians and opposed colonizing all of India. Like Britons, he argued, many Indians had intellect and integrity and should enjoy equal rights with the colonizers. His successors often disregarded his advice. Hastings himself, accused of corruption and forced out of office, lived the rest of his life in disgrace.

22-1b Expanding British India

Bengal success fueled further British expansion. The Company, transforming itself from just a corporation into what some scholars consider a mighty army with a trading division, had the authority to administer all British-controlled Indian territories while also seeking profit, but not further annexation. Despite the ban, governor-generals authorized occupying more areas, often against opposition, to prevent trade disruption or to counteract European rivals. Some imperialists promoted Britain's "sacred trust" to reshape the world, viewing British authority, culture, religion, and free trade policies a great blessing for Asians. Reality often differed. In expanding, Britain mixed military force, extortion, bribery, and manipulation of India's diversity. British agents and merchants pitted region against region and Hindu against Muslim, aided by Indian collaborators, especially businessmen eager for access to the world market. Superior weapons and disciplined military forces overcame spirited resistance. British officers commanded mercenary Indian soldiers, known as **sepoys**; by 1857 Company forces comprised nearly 200,000 sepoy troops and ten thousand British officers and soldiers.

With France hoping to block British expansion, European wars involving the two nations as well as their rivalry for territory in North America were extended into a contest for India's southeastern Coromandel coast, enmeshing South Asia in a worldwide struggle that also included the American Revolution against Britain. Victory over the French in 1761 sparked British actions against other Indian states. In Mysore, a mostly Hindu

state in south-central India, Haidar Ali Khan (r. 1761–1782), a devout Muslim and brilliant military strategist who modeled his army on Western lines, warned the British, "I will march your troops until their legs swell to the size of their bodies. You shall not have a blade of grass, nor a drop of water."[3] Only in 1799, after twenty years of bloody wars, was Mysore, a French ally, defeated.

Gradually Britain controlled southern, western, central, and northern India. With the Maratha confederacy divided by rivalries, in 1805 the British occupied the Marathas' northern territories and entered Delhi, deposing the aged Mughal emperor. After taking the remaining Maratha lands in 1819, they turned to northwest India, which was dominated by Sikhs and Rajputs, a declining Hindu warrior caste. Admitting their weakness, the Rajputs now signed treaties giving Britain claims on their lands. The death of Sikh leader Ranjit Singh in 1839 shattered Sikh unity and undermined their powerful military state. In 1849, after a series of bloody British–Sikh wars, Britain finally triumphed and then stationed troops in the many small independent principalities scattered around India. By 1850, the British ruled all Indians directly or through princes who collaborated with them (see Map 22.1).

The British also coopted Indian scientific knowledge in their efforts to gain control and profit from India. South Asians had been studying the heavens for several thousand years, surveying the movements of planets and stars that could be used by astrologers and priests. Their astronomical expertise was later enriched by Persian and Arab discoveries. By the 1500s the city of Lahore, in what is now Pakistan, produced sophisticated astronomical instruments such as celestial spheres. By the early 1700s, as Mughal control faded, several local rulers in north India used astronomy to enhance their own authority as "patrons of knowledge" by building vast astronomical stations (known as *mantars*). The greatest promoter was the raja of Jaipur, Jai Singh II, who oversaw monumental observatories around his domains, which also allowed him to gain useful knowledge about the lands he ruled by comparing data from the mantars. He invited French Jesuit missionary scientists to help him build modern telescopes. The Jesuits also learned Sanskrit and translated the greatest writings of Indian astronomy. But the collaboration ended with the raja's death in 1743. When the British later took control of the mantars around India, British surveyors could calculate the exact location of towns, farms, and other sites, a first step is assessing the value of land for tax purposes. Indian science and British expertise would now serve the needs of a global empire imposing its power on subject peoples.

British expansion in India eventually fostered interventions in neighboring societies, including Sri Lanka **(Ceylon)**, the large, fertile island just south of India. Fearing that France might establish a base, in 1796 the British acquired Dutch-held territory there as an offshoot of the Napoleonic wars raging in Europe; by 1815, after conquering the last remaining Sri Lankan kingdom of Kandy, they controlled the entire island. They seized rice-growing land

sepoys Mercenary soldiers recruited among the warrior and peasant castes by the British in India.

[3]Quoted in Sinharaja Tammita-Delgoda, *A Traveller's History of India*, 2nd ed. (New York: Interlink, 1999), 154.

from peasants; established coffee, tea, and rubber plantations; and recruited Tamil-speaking workers from southeast India as laborers. A British planter had brought in the first tea plants from China in 1854. Sri Lanka became particularly famous for growing "Ceylon tea," which became popular in Europe, especially Britain, as a luxury. In the late 1800s a wealthy Scottish grocer, Thomas Lipton, bought up many unprofitable Sri Lankan coffee plantations and planted tea, increasing production while marketing the tea in a more convenient and inexpensive form. As the price fell, working class consumers vastly increased the market, making Lipton a household name for the tea, which is sold today in one hundred fifty countries by a large multinational corporation. But the Tamil laborers and their families, constituting 11 percent of Sri Lanka's population, remained poorly paid; young women did and still do most of the field labor and are housed in crowded dormitories. The Tamils maintained their own customs, language, and Hindu religion and had little contact with the Buddhist Sinhalese majority. Since many Sinhalese considered both British and Tamils unwanted aliens, Sinhalese–Tamil tensions simmered and, after independence, a demand by some Tamils for their own state sparked a long and intermittent civil war that only ended in 2009.

Fearing that the Russians, who had already conquered Muslim Central Asia, coveted South Asia, the British attempted to secure India's land borders. First they invaded Nepal, a Himalayan kingdom, defeated Nepal's Hindu ruling caste and its fierce fighters, the Gurkhas **(GORE-kuhz)**, in 1814–1816, and made Nepal a British protectorate. Britain later recruited these Nepalese soldiers to support British objectives around the world. Mountainous Afghanistan, an ethnically diverse Muslim region with little political or ethnic unity, seemed particularly vulnerable to Russian expansion despite a long history of resisting foreign incursion and domination. However, Pashtun tribes in the south possessed fighting skills to oppose conquest. The British twice invaded Afghanistan and occupied the major eastern city, Kabul, but they faltered against fierce Pashtun resistance. In the first Afghan War (1839–1842), Pashtuns massacred most of the twelve thousand retreating British and sepoy troops and the civilians, including women and children, who accompanied them. Undeterred, Britain fought the second Afghan War (1878–1880). Concluding that Afghanistan could not be annexed by military force, Britain replaced a pro-Russian Pashtun leader with a pro-British leader who gave Britain control of Afghanistan's foreign affairs. These British thrusts helped reinforce Afghans' hatred of foreign invaders and rule.

Westernization A deliberate attempt to spread Western culture and ideas.

Orientalism A scholarly interest among British officials in India and its history that prompted some to rediscover the Hindu Classical age.

22-1c India Under the East India Company

The British East India Company gradually tightened its control of India, shifting from sharing government with local rulers to administering through British officials. Sir Thomas Munro, Madras governor (1820–1827), arrogantly explained the imperial mission by claiming that British rule must continue until Indians, sometime in the distant future, abandoned their "superstitions" and became "enlightened" enough to govern themselves. In the 1820s, the Company began **Westernization**, a policy to spread Western culture and ideas. Protestant evangelism, then strong in Britain, influenced reform ideas. Disregarding Indian traditions, British officials encouraged Christian missions and tried to ban customs they disliked. Many Indians agreed with prohibiting *sati*, the practice of widows throwing themselves on their husband's funeral pyre, but disliked tinkering with Muslim and Hindu law codes.

As part of Westernization, Britain established English-medium schools. Lord Macaulay (1800–1859), a reformer and cultural chauvinist, considered it pointless to teach Indian languages, declaring in 1832 that "a single shelf of a good European library is worth the whole native literature of India and Arabia." Reflecting racist views, Macaulay proposed creating "a class of persons Indian in blood and color but English in taste, opinions, morals and intellect."[4] Many Indians considered English schools a threat to both Hindu and Muslim customs; others believed they opened students to a wider world. Indians formed the first English-medium higher education institution, the Hindu College in Calcutta, in 1818.

Not all Britons found Indian culture backward and a few even admired it. Some scholarly Britons studied India and its history, reflecting an approach later called **Orientalism**. Warren Hastings, who promoted Indian culture, languages, and literature, preferred reading the European and Asian languages he had mastered—Greek, Latin, Persian, and Urdu—to his regular duties. One official, William Jones (1746–1794), who mastered Arabic, Persian, and Sanskrit, became the most influential Orientalist scholar, but he often attempted to fit India into Western concepts of history and religion. Just as Christians and Jews considered the Bible historical truth, Jones treated ancient Vedic texts as accurate historical records rather than religious teachings and claimed that the Classical Greeks derived some ideas from the same ancient source as Classical Indian sages. Although modern scholarship has debunked many of them, Jones's views shaped scholarly understanding of Indian history and religion. Several religious movements based on Hindu concepts, such as reincarnation, also gained a small Western following. Scholars today debate whether "Hinduism" as a unified religion was "invented" during the early nineteenth century by British Orientalists, Christian missionaries, and Indian thinkers who applied Christian concepts such as sacred texts and authority figures to this ancient, diverse faith with many earthy traditions, or whether instead Hindus accommodated or reshaped new ideas. By the later 1800s British nationalism and intolerance had largely replaced Orientalist respect for India.

The India–West encounter also fostered a Hindu social reform movement and philosophical renaissance led by brilliant Bengali scholar Ram Mohan Roy (1772–1833). Seeing his

---

[4]The quotes are in Burton Stein, *A History of India* (Malden, MA: Blackwell, 1998), 265–266.

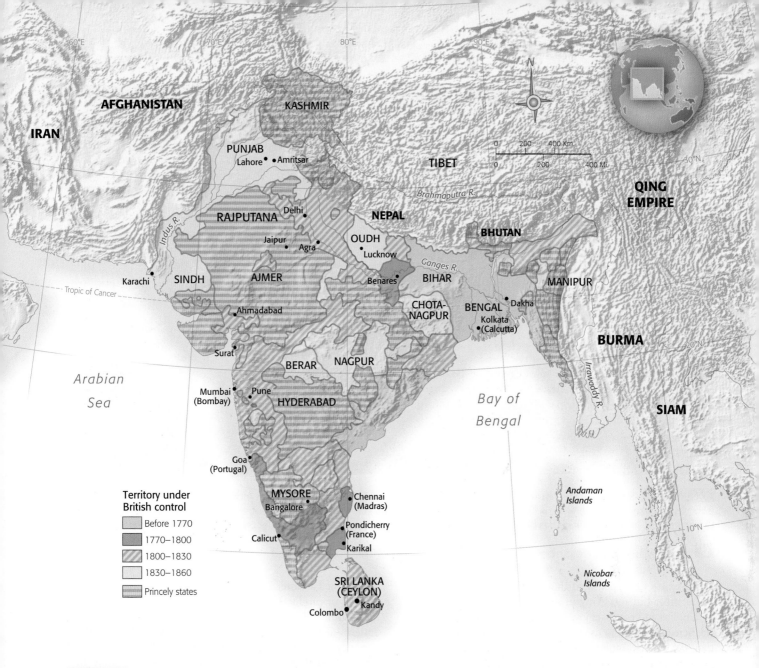

MAP 22.1 **The Growth of British India, 1750–1860** Gradually expanding control from their bases at Calcutta, Madras, and Bombay, the British completed their military conquest of the final holdout states by the 1850s.

Q How does this map of South Asia compare to a map of the region today?

sister die on a funeral pyre, and believing that customs such as *sati* and caste divisions were harmful, Roy hoped that the adoption of certain Western ways could reform and strengthen Hinduism. He cautioned against Hindu dogmatism, writing that Indian "youths [will] not be fitted to be better members of society by the Vedantic doctrines which teach them to believe that [since reality is illusion] all visible things have no real existence."[5] Roy may have been the first Hindu to describe India's eclectic religious tradition as "Hinduism." To better understand the world by studying non-Hindu religions, Roy mastered their source languages—Hebrew,

Greek, Arabic, and Persian—and thus became the first modern scholar of comparative religion. Roy and his followers tried to synthesize the best in Hinduism and Christianity; he also founded secondary schools, newspapers, and a Hindu reform organization. Admiring their knowledge and liberty, Roy wanted the British to promote modernization while also seeking Indian advice.

To make India more profitable, the Company built roads, railroads, and irrigation systems; most significantly for rural Indians, it revised land revenue collection. Britons simplistically viewed Indian rural society as stagnant, unable to provide

[5]Quoted in Sugata Bose and Ayesha Jalal, *Modern South Asia: History, Culture, Political Economy* (New York: Routledge, 1998), 83–84.

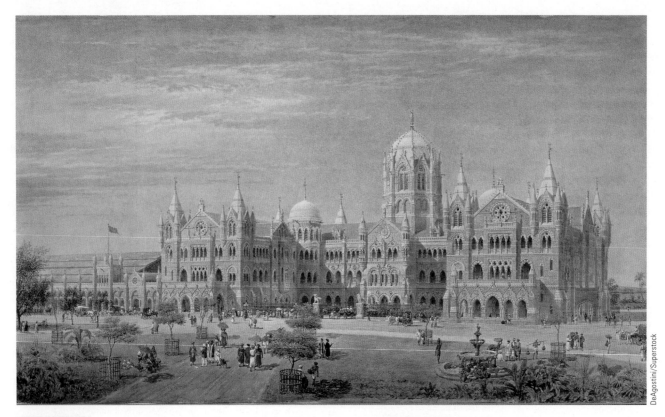

IMAGE 22.3 **British Rule in India** This painting from the later 1800s presents the Great Indian Peninsular Terminus in Bombay, also known as the Victoria Terminus Station, a massive train station but also the center of railroad administration for the British Raj. In recent years it has been renamed the Chhatrapati Shivaji Terminus to reflect a more nationalist perspective.

Q How would you describe the style and symbolism of the architecture?

tax revenues to support British administration. In precolonial times, most Indians, living in self-sufficient villages governed by families and castes, enjoyed considerable social stability and the hereditary right to use the land. One British observer wrote that "the village communities [have] everything they want within themselves. They seem to last when nothing else lasts. Dynasty after dynasty tumbles down; but the village communities remain the same."[6]

Company officials, seeking higher revenues, began mandating that farmers' taxes be collected in money rather than in a portion of the crop, as was done before. In 1793 British officials in Bengal converted Mughal revenue collectors, or **zamindars**, into landlords, thus giving them the additional rights to buy and sell land. Peasant farmers now became tenants to landlords and lost their hereditary rights to land. Many landlords sold their land rights to businessmen, absentee landlords who became enriched from the peasants' crops. In Madras, Governor Munro, mistakenly believing that peasants were or could become profit-seeking individualists like English farmers, made them deal directly with the government, paying taxes in cash but being subject to eviction for nonpayment. Both systems transformed a barter economy, with villagers exchanging their services or products with each other, into a money economy. Since some villagers earned more money, cash-based systems undermined peasant stability and security while benefiting a moneylender caste that eventually controlled much of the land. Rather than food crops, the foundation of peasant life, the Company also encouraged cash crops that could be sold on the world market such as opium, coffee, rubber, tea, and cotton, often grown on plantations.

22-1d Resistance: The 1857 Revolt

Most Indians resented the Company's Westernization and economic policies. Many once-prosperous families lost land or became indebted, while courts enforced laws based on British traditions, fueling hostility. Thanks to such grievances, local revolts were common. Furthermore, sepoys resented aggressive British attempts to convert them to Christianity. Sepoys in Bengal particularly disliked new army rifle cartridges, which had to be bitten off before being rammed down the gun barrel. A rumor, probably true, spread that the cartridges were greased with beef and pork fat, violating dietary prohibitions of both cow-revering Hindus and pork-avoiding Muslims.

zamindars Mughal revenue collectors that the British turned into landlords who were given the rights to buy and sell land.

---

[6]Charles Metcalfe, quoted in David Ludden, *An Agrarian History of South Asia* (New York: Cambridge University Press, 1999), 161.

In 1857 one revolt, which the British called the Indian Mutiny and Indian nationalists later termed the first War of Independence, spread rapidly in north and northeast India, seriously challenging British authority. The revolt began among sepoys and soon fostered peasant and Muslim uprisings. A few members of princely families, who resented British attempts to take away their local power, joined the rebel cause, including the rani (queen) of Jhansi, Laxmibai (the widow of the Maratha ruler), who led her troops into battle dressed as a man. Even when Laxmibai was a teenager she had defied many of the rules of a patriarchal society by learning to read and write, wield a sword, and ride a horse, skills that would serve her well as she trained and led her own army composed of both men and women. These actions enhanced her reputation as a social reformer and anti-colonial hero. No rebel leaders envisioned a unified Indian nation, but many Indians perceived their customs and religions threatened by British policies. Some leaders attempted to unite Hindus and Muslims against their common British enemy. A few wanted to restore the Mughal order.

The rebels captured Delhi and besieged several cities. Both sides used ruthless tactics and committed massacres. Rebels murdered a thousand British residents when they occupied the city of Kanpur, and British troops recapturing Delhi engaged in widespread raping, pillaging, and killing. Muslim poet Ghalib mourned: "Here is a vast ocean of blood before me. Thousands of my friends are dead. Perhaps none is left even to shed tears upon my death."[7] The rebels could not overcome inadequate arms, weak communications, and lack of a unified command structure or strategy. Nor did they receive support from people in other parts of India. Linguistic, religious, cultural, and regional fragmentation made a united Indian opposition impossible. When the British captured the last rebel fort, held by the rani of Jhansi, in 1858, she was killed and the rebellion collapsed, although a few small rebel groups fought skirmishes until 1860.

KEY POINTS

▶ Fragmented after the decline of the Mughals, India was unable to resist encroachment by the Portuguese, Dutch, British, and French.

▶ Though initially opposed by the French, the British East India Company gradually expanded its control over India by employing local collaborators and playing groups against each other, and by 1850 Britain controlled all of India.

▶ The British expanded into Sri Lanka, where they imported Tamils to work on the tea plantations; into Nepal, where they recruited effective soldiers; and into Afghanistan, where they met fierce resistance but ultimately installed a friendly ruler.

▶ Though some Indians supported Westernization, periodic revolts occurred, and in 1857 the sepoys began a large rebellion that led to much bloodshed and eventually Indian defeat.

22-2 The Reshaping of Indian Society

▣ TRANSITIONS ▥ SOCIETIES

Q How did colonialism transform the Indian economy and foster new ideas in India?

The 1857 revolt proved a watershed, shocking the British and prompting Britain to replace the Company government with direct colonial rule. While the British felt betrayed, some officials viewed the troubles as symptoms of deeper discontents that called for change. The 1858 Government of India Act transferred sovereignty to the British monarch. In 1876 Queen Victoria was proclaimed Empress of India and head of the British *Raj*, named for the ancient title of Hindu kings. India became the brightest "jewel in the imperial crown," a source of fabulous wealth. The policies now pursued reshaped economic, intellectual, and social patterns, eventually inspiring movements reflecting a new sense of the Indian nation.

CONNECTION to TODAY

How do you think the economic, social, cultural, religious, and intellectual changes of the era still influence South Asia today?

22-2a Colonial Government and Education

The British Raj bore many similarities to the Mughal system. Top British officials, the viceroys, lived in splendor in Delhi and then in a new capital at New Delhi, enjoying pomp and circumstance, including Mughal-style ceremonies. Despite health problems from tropical heat and diseases such as malaria, the British built palatial mansions, museums, schools, universities, and city halls and connected India with a network of roads, bridges, and railways; by 1900 India had over twenty-five thousand miles of track, the world's fourth largest rail system.

---

[7]Quoted in Tammita-Delgoda, *Traveller's History*, 167.

Although British officials mistrusted Indians after 1857, they allowed traditional princes to keep their privileges and palaces in exchange for promoting acceptance of British policies. Deliberately pitting the Hindu majority against the Muslim minority, Britons favored one or the other group in law, language, and custom, which exacerbated hatreds that remain today. For example, Hindus protested use of the main Muslim language, Urdu, in many north Indian courts and Muslims hated local bans on eating beef.

Local revenue supported a huge army of 200,000 men, mostly Indian volunteers, who were needed to keep the peace in India and fight British battles abroad. In societies like India with many poor people it was not difficult to recruit hungry and desperate men willing to serve as soldiers and fight for the colonizing power, as was also demonstrated in some Southeast Asian and African colonies. As part of the "Great Game" of strategic rivalry with Russia, Britain invaded Tibet in 1903, a formidable challenge given the difficult mountainous geography, cold climate, and thin air; Lord Curzon (viceroy from 1899 to 1905) conceded, "It would be madness for us to cross the Himalayas and to occupy it [Tibet]. But it is important that no one else should seize it."[8] The British withdrew after Tibetan leaders agreed not to concede territory to Russia or any foreign power.

Europeans typically believed that Western colonialism improved Asian and African societies. Rudyard Kipling (1865–1936), a Bombay-born, Britain-educated English poet and novelist, articulated this view: "Take up the White Man's burden—Send forth the best ye breed—Go, bind your sons in exile. To serve your captives' need."[9] Some policies reflected racism and Westernization. Much like colonized Africans, Indians were excluded from European-only clubs and parks as well as from high bureaucratic positions, enjoying no real power or influence. An expanded English-medium education system promoted British and often Christian values. But although English became the common language for educated Indians, only a privileged minority, mostly higher-caste Hindus, could afford to send their children, mostly boys, to English schools. By 1911 only 11 percent of men and 1 percent of women were literate in any language, and less than 2 percent of Indians were Christians. However, an emerging English-educated middle class, with a taste for European products and ideas, sent their sons and a few daughters to British universities. Acquiring notions like "freedom" and "self-determination of peoples" that contrasted with the nondemocratic Raj, this growing professional class organized social, professional, and political bodies concerned with improving Indian life and acquiring more political influence. Indian words had found their way into Western languages for over two millennia, spread by trade, and this process continued under British rule. Among Indian words borrowed from British India and common in English today are *bungalow*, *jungle*, *loot*, *nirvana*, *pundit*, *pajamas*, *shampoo*, *shawl*, and *thug*.

22-2b Economic Transformation

In perhaps the most momentous and enduring change, Britain transformed India's economy. Long an economic powerhouse and major cotton textile exporter, India still produced a quarter of all world manufactured goods in 1750. Two centuries later, conditions had become very different. Many Indians were harmed by British policies, which were designed to drain Indian wealth to benefit Britain. Land policies commercialized agriculture, while tax and tariff policies diminished manufacturing. The land tax system exploited the peasantry, fostering one of contemporary India's greatest dilemmas, inequitable land ownership. Many fell hopelessly into debt. With peasants growing cash crops such as cotton, jute, pepper, or opium rather than food, famine killed millions as food supplies and distribution became more uncertain. Between 1870 and 1900 millions of south Indians perished from hunger when the Raj refused to divert excess food from north India.

Other changes affected rural life. Steamships freed shipping from the vagaries of monsoon winds, and the Suez Canal, opened in 1869, made shipping raw materials from India to Europe easier and much faster. The return ships brought cheap machine goods, undermining village craftsmen such as weavers and tinkers who could compete only by lowering prices, earning too little to support families. In addition, felling forests and plowing grassland to grow more cash crops placed massive pressure on the physical environment.

Scholars vigorously debate Britain's total economic impact on colonized South Asia. Many historians, both Western and South Asian, argue that British rule and economic policies led to a decline in manufacturing. Seeking new markets abroad for its industrial products led Britain to undermine India's centuries-old industries. Britain denied India tariff protection for its more expensive handmade products, excluded Indian manufactured goods from Britain, and prohibited importing industrial machinery for Indians. Meanwhile, British products flooded India, destroying many skilled craftsmen's livelihood. Textile imports increased sixfold between 1854 and 1913, ruining millions of weavers, who, like metalworkers and glass blowers, often became farm laborers.

By the late 1800s the limits on India's industries were generating heated controversy. Indian critics alleged that tariffs protecting British industries strangled Indian competition. The British–Indian wealth gap grew. By 1895 Britain's per capita income was fifteen times higher than India's, much more unequal than two hundred years earlier. A 2019 study calculated that Britain drained (some critics would use the harsher term "stole") a staggering $45 trillion from India between 1765 and 1938, seventeen times more than the total annual gross domestic product of Britain today, largely due to the unequal trade system. Much of this money went to funding British industrialization. Defenders contended that British rule brought investment, imported goods, railroads, and law and order. But critics questioned whether these innovations, enriching British

---

[8] Quoted in Judith M. Brown, *Modern India: The Origins of an Asian Democracy*, 2nd ed. (New York: Oxford University Press, 1994), 134.
[9] Quoted in Tammita-Delgoda, *Traveller's History*, 173.

merchants, industrialists, and collaborating Indian businessmen and landlords, benefited most Indians. Indian scholars attacked "The Drain" of wealth, arguing that British policies gave India "peace but not prosperity; the manufacturers lost their industries; the cultivators were ground down by a heavy and variable taxation; and the revenues were to a large extent diverted to England."[10] By 1948, after two centuries of British influence and domination, most Indians remained poor.

Yet, industrial activity and technical innovation did not disappear completely; some Indians found ways to prosper. A few competed with British imports by manufacturing cotton textiles and initiating a modern iron and steel sector. Gujarati industrialist Jamsetji N. Tata (**JAM-set-gee TA-ta**) (1839–1904) built cotton mills, while his son, Sir Dorabji Tata (**DOR-ab-ji TA-ta**) (1859–1932), founded the Indian steel industry in 1907. Unable to get British funding, they raised money among Indian investors, later using their wealth to promote scientific education and found technical colleges. Some Indians tried to maintain India's historical importance in developing scientific knowledge. In 1895 the Bengal-born physicist and botanist Jagadish Chandra Bose, without any support from the British, sent an electromagnetic wave across 75 feet, passing through walls to remotely ring a bell and explode some gunpowder, making him the father of wireless communication. He also invented a radio wave receiver that was later used by Guglielmo Marconi to build his first transatlantic two-way radio that communicated over two thousand miles. India also produced one of the most versatile and eccentric inventors of the late nineteenth and early twentieth centuries, Shankar Abaji Bhise (1867–1935), sometimes called the "Indian Edison." Born into poverty in a Bombay slum and largely self-educated (he credited his knowledge to avidly reading *Scientific American* magazine as a boy), Bhise invented a dazzling variety of some 200 products, including kitchen gadgets, an automatically flushing toilet, an electric signboard, a device for curing headaches, a push-up bra, a liquid iodine solution, and a new revolutionary printing machine. But not all of his devices attracted investment (although he received some support from the Tatas) or succeeded in the market. However, in the tradition of Bose and Bhise, India today, with a far better educational and technological structure, has become a hub of innovation and scientific talent.

22-2c Population Growth and Indian Emigration

Population growth worsened the peasants' plight. With peace and improved sanitation and health, India's population rose from perhaps 100 million in 1700 to 300 million by 1920. Yet, average Indian life expectancy dropped by a fifth from 1870 until 1920 and many millions died in famines. While encouraging agricultural productivity, the Raj provided economic incentives to have more children to help in the fields. But whereas Europe's population increase could be absorbed by industrialization or emigration to the Americas and Australia,

India enjoyed neither industrial revolution nor increased food growing. Profiting from the cash crop system, Indian landlords discouraged innovation. In addition, growing population numbers far outstripped available food and land, creating dire poverty and widespread hunger.

This impoverishment created millions of desperately poor Indians who were recruited to emigrate to other lands. After abolition, former slaves often left American plantations, creating a market for Indian labor in Trinidad, British Guiana (today's Guyana), and Dutch Guiana (now Suriname). Plantations in Sri Lanka, Malaya, Fiji, the Indian Ocean island of Mauritius, and South Africa also wanted Indian labor. But travel was hazardous. For example, in 1884 a family of low-caste landless laborers—Somerea, a fifty-year-old widow, her two sons, a daughter-in-law, and four grandchildren—facing starvation in Bihar state, boarded a sailing ship at Calcutta bound for the distant Fiji Islands in the South Pacific. After three months the ship reached the islands, and all but fifty-six of the four hundred ninety-seven passengers had died from cholera, dysentery, typhoid, and a shipwreck. Somerea's family apparently survived the journey. Indians were also recruited to British East Africa to build railroads.

Many merchants, moneylenders, and laborers flocked to British Burma, Singapore, Malaya, and East Africa. Between 1880 and 1930 a quarter million people a year left India. Few returned. Most Indian emigrants, including Somerea's family, were indentured, having signed contracts obligating them to work for a period of years (usually three to five) to repay their passage. Somerea's family probably worked on a sugar plantation. Indenture contracts stipulated the number of days per week (six) and hours per day (usually nine to ten) to be worked. With high mortality rates and unfavorable indenture terms, critics considered the system another form of slavery. Earning only a few pennies a day, many Indian migrants could never pay off their contracts.

Indians now played key economic roles in many countries. Cities such as Nairobi in Kenya, Durban in South Africa, Rangoon (Yangon) in Burma, Georgetown in British Guiana, and Port of Spain in Trinidad had large Indian neighborhoods, and Indian trade networks reached around the Indian Ocean and Pacific Rim. The future leader of the Indian nationalist movement, India-born and British-educated Mohandas Gandhi (**GAHN-dee**), experimented with nonviolent resistance to illegitimate power while working among Indians in South Africa. Today people of Indian ancestry comprise half or more of the Mauritius, Trinidad, Guyana, Suriname, and Fiji populations and substantial minorities in Sri Lanka, Malaysia, Singapore, Burma, Kenya, and South Africa. Since the 1960s prime ministers or presidents of South Asian ancestry have been elected and served in various nations, including Guyana, Suriname, Trinidad, Mauritius, Fiji, and Ireland. Although many Indian emigrants succeeded in business or the professions, the majority still labor on plantations growing cocoa, rubber, tea, or sugar.

[10]Dadabhai Naoroji and R.C. Dutt, quoted in Ainslee T. Embree, *India's Search for National Identity* (New York: Alfred A. Knopf, 1972), 48–49.

22-2d Indian Thought, Literature, and Society

Indian intellectuals responded to British rule and ideas in several ways. A few, like Ram Mohan Roy, wanted to combine the best of East and West while reforming customs, such as removing the Hindu ban on widow remarriage, that they considered corruptions of Hinduism. Their influence waned after 1900. Another group, hostile to Western ways, sought to revive Hindu culture and emphasized the past's glories, arguing that India needed nothing from the West. Influential teacher Swami Vivekananda (**SWAH-me VIH-vee-keh-NAHN-da**) (1863–1902) wanted to end British cultural and political domination: "O India, this is your terrible danger. The spell of imitating the West is getting such a strong hold upon you. Be proud that thou art an Indian, and proudly proclaim: 'I am an Indian, every Indian is my brother.'"[11]

Also a reformer, Swami Vivekananda condemned untouchable oppression and the conditions of the poor. His writings and lectures fostered Indians' pride in their culture and helped spread Hindu thought to the West. Visiting New York in 1893, he formed the Vedanta Society, which promoted a philosophical Hinduism based on the ancient *Upanishads*. Vedanta portrayed the Hindu holy books, the Vedas, which were compiled over twenty-five hundred years ago, as the supreme source of religious knowledge, although not necessarily authored by either God or humans. Vedanta ideas contributed to another movement, **Theosophy**, that attracted some Western followers by blending Hindu notions with Western spiritualist and scientific ideas. Founded by Ukrainian-born Helen Blavatsky (1831–1891), Theosophy promoted the idea that India was more spiritual than other societies.

Like Hindus, Muslims had to rethink their values and prospects. Although Britain left many Muslim institutions untouched, Muslims resented Christian missionary activity that was supported by British officials critical of Islam. With European and Hindu values increasingly dominating India, some Muslims pursued Islamic knowledge in the Middle East, coming home with Islamic revivalist ideas; some opened schools. In the northwest frontier and Bengal, dogmatic Wahhabis (see Chapter 21) opposed to modernization clashed with other Muslims, Christians, Sikhs, and Hindus.

In contrast, Muslim modernists, led by cosmopolitan Sayyid Ahmad Khan (1817–1898), wanted Muslims to gain strength: "the more worldly progress we make, the more glory Islam gains." Believing that Islam was compatible with modern science, in 1877 he founded a college at Aligarh (**AL-ee-GAHR**) that offered Western learning within a Muslim context. Trained for government jobs, Aligarh students studied many subjects in English and learned how to play the British game of cricket. Many later studied at top British universities. A satirist observed Aligarh's secular atmosphere, where leaders "neither believe in God, nor yet in prayer. They say they do, but it is plain to see, What they believe in is the powers that

Theosophy A nineteenth-century North American and European movement that blended Hindu thought with Western spiritualist and scientific ideas.

IMAGE 22.4 **Rabindranath Tagore** Tagore was a leading thinker, poet, and writer in British India who achieved international fame. Considered one of the most striking photos of Tagore ever made, it was taken around 1917.

be."[12] Aligarh graduates dominated Muslim political activity in India until independence.

Indian literature took on a more nationalist flavor. The Tagore family, wealthy Hindus from Calcutta, worked to awaken national pride and expand literary expression. Hugely influential, Rabindranath Tagore (**RAH-bin-drah-NATH ta-GORE**) (1861–1941) was a poet, educator, patriot, and internationalist whose writings won him the Nobel Prize for literature in 1913 (see **Discover Historical Voices**: Challenging British Imperialism with Spiritual Virtues). Tagore sought a new and freer India, "where the mind is without fear and the head is held high; Where knowledge is free; where the clear stream of reason has not lost its way into the dreary desert sand of dead habit; Into that heaven of freedom, let my country awake."[13] One of his songs eventually became India's national anthem. Yet, Tagore opposed narrow and chauvinistic nationalism, arguing that he would never allow patriotism to triumph over humanity, that excessive love of country can lead to disaster.

British policies also affected society, including the caste system. Historians debate whether the elaborate modern caste system existed for centuries as a continually changing part of Indian life or was shaped by colonial-era officials seeking to classify Indians for administrative and census purposes. Before colonialism, Hindus in Bengal, Punjab, and south India generally

[11]Quoted in Clark D. Moore and David Eldridge, eds., *India Yesterday and Today* (New York: Bantam, 1970), 154–155.

[12]The quotes are in Francis Robinson, *The Cultural Atlas of the Islamic World Since 1500* (Oxford, UK: Stonehenge, 1992), 148–149.

[13]From Rabindranath Tagore, *Gitanjali: A Collection of Indian Songs* (New York: Macmillan, 1973), 49–50.

Discover Historical Voices

Challenging British Imperialism with Spiritual Virtues

On the last day of the nineteenth century Rabindranath Tagore wrote a poem in Bengali protesting the brutal imperialism of Britain's war against the Boers in South Africa, driven, Tagore believed, by British nationalism. The poem suggested that patient cultivation of India's "spiritual virtues" would become a force in the world after reckless Western imperialism, sparked by nationalism, had lost its control over humankind. He echoed the views of many Hindu nationalists and reformers that Hinduism and India had a special devotion to peace and spiritual insights that could benefit the Western world. For this poem and other influential writings, Tagore won the Noble Prize for literature in 1913.

The last sun of the century sets amidst the blood-red clouds of the West and the whirlwind of hatred.

The naked passion of self-love of Nations, in its drunken delirium of greed, is dancing to the clash of steel and the howling verses of vengeance.

The hungry self of the Nation shall burst in a violence of fury from its own shameless feeding, for it has made the world its food.

And licking it, crunching it, and swallowing it in big morsels, It swells and swells,

Till in the midst of its unholy feast descends the sudden shaft of heaven piercing its heart of grossness.

The crimson glow of light on the horizon is not the light of thy dawn of peace, my Motherland.

It is the glimmer of the funeral pyre burning to ashes the vast flesh—the self-love of the Nation—dead under its own excess.

The morning waits behind the patient dark of the East, Meek and silent.

Keep watch, India.

Bring your offerings of worship for that sacred sunrise.

Let the first hymn of its welcome sound in your voice and sing

"Come, Peace, thou daughter of God's own great suffering.

Come with thy treasure of contentment, the sword of fortitude, And meekness crowning thy forehead."

Be not ashamed, my brothers, to stand before the proud and the powerful, With your white robe of simpleness.

Let your crown be of humility, your freedom the freedom of the soul.

Build God's throne daily upon the ample barrenness of your poverty.

And know that what is huge is not great and pride is not everlasting.

Reflection Questions

1. How does Tagore perceive nationalism?
2. How does he believe India should respond to Western power?
3. How do you think that Tagore's plea for India's "spiritual values" as a positive force for the world is reflected in India's role in the world today?

Source: From *Sources of Indian Tradition*, Vol. 2, William Theodore de Bary, ed. Copyright © 1958 Columbia University Press. Reprinted with permission of the publisher.

---

placed less emphasis on formal differences among varied castes. But British policies, sharpening caste identities, classified people largely through caste affiliations, making the system more rigid and favoring higher castes to win their support. As different Indians increasingly came into contact with one another, some sought firmer social boundaries by further dividing castes. Much of India became more caste conscious than ever before; upper castes stressed their uniqueness, and lower castes emulated the upper castes to improve their social status. Envying the highest caste, other castes adopted brahmin rituals and ideas, such as vegetarianism. Hence, some untouchable leather workers joined an anti-caste movement but, like brahmins, avoided eating meat. Higher castes, trying to preserve their privileged positions, demanded that lower castes be excluded from government jobs. Meanwhile, Hindu thinkers disagreed about the caste system. Some reformers called for abolishing caste, while defenders praised the system's ideals of conduct and morality. Still others, such as Swami Vivekananda, argued that caste had a bad side but that its benefits outweighed its disadvantages.

Gender relations changed in British India. Traditionally women and men performed separate but interdependent roles within patriarchal households: men ploughed; women tended house and garden; and both did transplanting and weeding. But both men and women lost work as absentee landlords emphasized cash crops rather than food. Lower-caste men emulated upper castes, often forcing women into seclusion. But new opportunities also arose for women. More girls attended school, becoming teachers, nurses, midwives, and even doctors. By the 1870s women published biographies of their experiences and struggles. Like boys, some girls now enjoyed social gatherings separate from their families. For centuries girls had been married early with little choice of husband. Now a small minority of urban "new women" led more independent lives, marrying later, in their twenties or thirties, or sometimes not at all.

Indian and British reformers sought to improve women's lives and foster greater gender equality. A controversial marriage law in 1872 provided for both civil and cross-caste marriage. Britain also tried incremental reforms, such as allowing widow remarriage and raising the age of female consent from ten to twelve. But although reformers often supported marriages based on love, they also encouraged wives to show husbands and children self-sacrificing devotion. Some women considered progress inadequate. For example, the reformer father of the feminist scholar, educator, and activist Pandita Ramabai (1858–1922) defied tradition by educating her and declining to marry her off as a child. She then promoted education, traveling around India and urging women to take control of their lives, breaking every rule that confined an upper-caste Hindu woman of her time. Ramabai's knowledge of Sanskrit, rare for a woman, won her comparison to *Saraswati*, the Hindu goddess of wisdom, and Calcutta University proclaimed her a Pandita ("learned"). She married a lawyer of low-caste background, a shocking move for a brahmin woman. When a court sentenced a child bride to prison for refusing to have conjugal relations with a much older husband, Ramabai protested what she considered slavery: "Our only wonder is that a defenseless woman … dared to raise her voice in the face of the powerful Hindu law, the mighty British government, the 129,000,000 [Indian] men, the 330,000,000 gods of the Hindus; all these have conspired to crush her into nothingness."[14] She then studied in England, becoming a Christian, and the United States, and gave lectures in Australia and Japan. Upon returning to India, Ramabai opened a school for girls, especially child widows, and a refuge for female famine victims. The mission she founded remains active today, providing housing, education, vocational training, and medical services for widows, orphans, and the blind. Ramabai published several books, including one on the difficult widowhood for upper-caste women, and supported girls who refused to enter arranged marriages. She was the most controversial Indian woman of her times and remains so today among conservatives.

22-2e The Rise of Nationalism

British leaders viewed India as their empire's centerpiece, to be ruled into the far future, but their rule inevitably produced nationalist reactions. The Western idea of the "nation," an inclusive feeling among people living within the same state (see Chapter 19), was new for Indians, who perceived themselves joined by a common Hindu or Muslim culture rather than a centralized state. By establishing political unity, educating Indians in European ideas, but then largely excluding Indians from administration, Britain fostered national feelings but also anticolonial bitterness. Furthermore, by 1900 six hundred Indian newspapers were reporting on world events such as Irish independence struggles, the Japanese defeat of Russia, and the U.S. conquest of the Philippines, all of which inspired Indians to oppose British rule. In 1885 nationalists formed the Indian National Congress, which worked for peaceful progress toward self-government. But the Congress, scorned by Britons, mostly attracted well-educated professionals and merchants, especially Bengalis. Constitutional reforms in 1909 brought limited representative government but no true legislative and financial power.

By 1907 radical nationalists led by former journalist Bal Gangadhar Tilak (**BAL GAGN-ga-DAR TEA-lak**) (1856–1920) had transformed the Congress from a gentleman's pressure group into an active independence movement. Tilak fiercely defended Hindu orthodoxy and custom; however, many Indians disliked Tilak and remained wary of the Congress. For their part, Muslims perceived the Hindu-dominated Congress, particularly Tilak, as anti-Muslim. As Hindu–Muslim tensions increased, the All-India Muslim League, founded in 1906, sought unity for Muslims scattered around the country. Hindus constituted 80 percent of Indians; Muslims were a majority only in eastern Bengal, Sind, north Punjab, and west of the Indus Valley. Influential Muslim reformer and educator Sayyid Ahmad Khan opposed potential Hindu majority rule, arguing that "it would be like a game of dice, in which one man has four dice and the other only one."[15] The Muslim League's first great victory came in 1909, when British reforms guaranteed some seats in representative councils to Muslims. Enraged, the Congress charged divide and rule. Hindu–Muslim rivalries complicated the nationalist movement throughout the twentieth century, eventually leading to separate Hindu- and Muslim-majority nations, India and Pakistan, in 1949. But Pakistan, divided geographically into eastern and western regions with different languages and cultures, proved too unwieldly and artificial to survive. In 1972, after a bloody civil war over secession, East Pakistan (Bengal) separated from West Pakistan to become independent as Bangladesh (Bengali Nation).

KEY POINTS

▶ After 1857, the British monarchy ruled India through the British Raj, which built palatial buildings, a large railroad system, and an expanded English-language school system, thereby educating Indians about Western ideals such as nationalism and sowing the seeds for an Indian revolution against Britain.

▶ Britain stifled Indian industry by using India as a market for British industrial products, and it turned Indian peasants into tenants who had to grow cash crops for Britain rather than their own food, thus destroying the centuries-old village economy and exacerbating famine and poverty.

▶ The caste system became more rigid under British rule, with lower castes imitating upper castes, upper castes trying to strengthen their privileges, and women facing greater restrictions in some cases and expanded opportunity in others.

▶ As Indian nationalists began to unite in their opposition to the British, members of the Hindu majority formed the Indian National Congress in 1885, but it was opposed by many Muslims, who formed the All-India Muslim League in 1906.

---

[14]Quoted in Geraldine Forbes, *Women in Modern India* (New York: Cambridge University Press, 1996), 49.
[15]Quoted in John McLane, ed., *The Political Awakening of India* (Englewood Cliffs, NJ: Prentice-Hall, 1970), 46.

22-3 Southeast Asia and Colonization

⊃⊂ TRANSITIONS

Ⓠ How did the Western nations expand their control of Southeast Asia?

Like South Asians and many Africans the various Southeast Asian societies experienced colonization imposed by Western military force. And like South Asians, they resisted in whatever way they could, including using violence against colonial force where necessary and possible. During the 1800s Western challenges became more threatening, and by 1914 all the major Southeast Asian societies except Siam were under Western colonial control. Indonesia, Vietnam, and Burma, where the Dutch, French, and British, respectively, increased their power, and the Philippines, controlled by the United States beginning in 1902, faced the most changes. Thus Southeast Asian societies became tied even more to the larger world but lost their political and economic independence.

CONNECTION to TODAY

What lessons can we learn today from the violent and nonviolent resistance of Southeast Asians to the imperialist thrust of the Western nations in this era?

22-3a Colonialism in Indonesia and Malaya

Holland (the Netherlands) had commenced interventions in the Indonesian archipelago in the early 1600s (see Chapter 18) and now sought to expand their power throughout the islands. The Dutch East India Company already controlled the Spice Islands (Maluku) and Java, territories that provided great wealth. In 1799 the Dutch abolished the Company because of debts and corruption and replaced it with a formal colonial government largely focused on Java and Sumatra. In 1830 the **cultivation system**, an agricultural policy that forced farmers on Java to grow sugar on their rice land and allowed the government to pay peasants a low fixed price for sugar, even when world prices were high, enriched the Dutch but ultimately impoverished many peasants. A Dutch critic described the results: "If anyone should ask whether the man who grows the products receives a reward proportionate to the yields, the answer must be in the negative. The Government compels him to grow on *his* land what pleases *it*; it punishes him when he sells the crop to anyone else but *it*."[16] Dutch-owned plantations growing sugar and other cash crops replaced the cultivation system in the 1870s.

In the later 1800s the Dutch turned to gaining control, and exploiting the resources, of other Indonesian islands such as the southern portion of Borneo (the Indonesian region of Borneo is now known as Kalimantan) and Sulawesi, sometimes using violence to impose their rule and suppress resistance (see Map 22.2). For example, between 1906 and 1908 they crushed the small kingdoms on Bali, an island just east of Java. After valiant Balinese resistance failed, the royal family of the largest kingdom committed collective suicide by walking into Dutch guns rather than surrender, shaming the Dutch and depriving them of any sense of victory. The Dutch also united the thousands of scattered societies and dozens of states of the archipelago into the Dutch East Indies. But the diverse colony, governed from Batavia (now Jakarta) on Java, promoted little common national feeling, making it difficult later to build an Indonesian nation with a shared identity.

Meanwhile the British became more active in Malaya, eventually subjugating the varied Malay states. Seeking a naval base, the British East India Company purchased Penang **(puh-NANG)** Island, off Malaya's northwest coast, from a cash-strapped sultan in 1786. In 1819 a visionary British East India Company agent, Jamaica-born Thomas Stamford Raffles (1781–1826), capitalized on local political unrest to acquire, and become governor of, sparsely populated Singapore Island at the tip of the Malay Peninsula. Historians and Southeast Asians still debate Raffles, some viewing him as a visionary realist, free trade promoter, scholar, and stateman, and others as an incompetent administrator, bloodthirsty imperialist, and reckless adventurer who looted palaces and led military attacks during a brief British intervention in Dutch Java. Singapore had seemed to most Western observers to be a tiny, swampy backwater with limited prospects for generating wealth. But a fine harbor and strategic location on the Straits of Melaka soon made Singapore a valuable base and a great source of profit for British businessmen and government treasuries. Welcoming Chinese immigrants, Singapore became the major Southeast Asian hub for both British and Chinese economic activity and networks. By the 1860s it was mostly Chinese in population and the key crossroads of Southeast Asian commerce. After obtaining Melaka from the Dutch in 1824, Britain governed the three Malayan ports as one colony, the Straits Settlements.

Pressured by merchants, Britain soon extended its influence into the Malay states. Chinese immigrants in western Malaya contracted with Malay rulers to mine tin and gold, and Europe's growing demand for metals spurred British merchants to seek control of the mining. By the 1870s Britain, demanding order and security, threatened or forced Malay sultans to accept British advisers and then domination. Soon it achieved formal or informal control over nine sultanates, which, with the Straits Settlements, became British Malaya. The British also colonized the northern third of Borneo, creating the states of Sabah (British North Borneo) and Sarawak and imposing a protectorate over the Brunei sultanate. The historical Malay world of sultanates was now artificially divided between the British, Dutch, and Siamese.

cultivation system An agricultural policy imposed by the Dutch in Java that forced Javanese farmers to grow sugar on rice land.

---

[16]Douwes Dekker, from Harry J. Benda and John A. Larkin, eds., *The World of Southeast Asia: Selected Historical Readings* (New York: Harper and Row, 1967), 127.

MAP 22.2 The Colonization of Southeast Asia Between 1800 and 1914 the European powers gradually conquered or gained control over the Southeast Asian societies that had not been colonized in the Early Modern Era. Only Siam remained independent.

Q Which European power controlled the most territory in Southeast Asia by 1914 and which the least?

British rule changed Malaya, encouraging pepper, tobacco, oil palm, and rubber planting on the west coast while attracting many Chinese and Indian immigrants. Malayan tin was used by Europeans and North Americans to make household utensils, tin cans, and barrels for food and oil storage. Malay villagers, pressured to plant rubber, lost their self-sufficiency. Britain maintained Malay sultans and aristocrats as symbolic and privileged local leaders, fostering what sociologists term a **plural society**, a medley of peoples—Malays, Chinese, and Indians—that mixed but by and large did not blend. The different groups generally maintained their own cultures, religions, languages, schools, neighborhoods, and customs, confirming a Malay proverb: "raven with raven, sparrow with sparrow." As in Malaya, Chinese also immigrated to Sarawak and Sabah in northern Borneo, with mining and cash crop agriculture (mostly on plantations in Sabah) underpinning the economies.

plural society A medley of peoples who mix but do not blend, maintaining their own cultures, religions, languages, and customs.

22-3b Vietnam and Burma: Colonization and Resistance

Vietnam fell to French colonialism after a bitter struggle. In 1771 three brothers from southern Vietnam launched the Tayson Rebellion against the royal government. Social revolutionaries seeking a unified Vietnam and opposed to corruption and misrule, the Taysons fought against Vietnamese emperors and their French allies, using the slogan "seize the property of the rich and redistribute it to the poor."[17] In 1788

---

[17]Quoted in Truong Buu Lam, *Resistance, Rebellion, Revolution: Popular Movements in Vietnamese History* (Singapore: Institute of Southeast Asian Studies, 1984), 11.

they defeated their foes and reestablished national unity, after which they sponsored economic expansion and rallied the people against Chinese invasion.

However, Tayson policies alienated some Vietnamese. In 1802, forces led by Nguyen Anh (**NEW-yin ahn**) (1761–1820) defeated the Taysons with French assistance and established a new imperial dynasty. But the Nguyen dynasty, unable to address social inequalities, proved unpopular. *The Tale of Kieu*, a thirty-three-hundred-line poem still cherished by the Vietnamese, sympathetically portrays an intelligent, beautiful young woman, Kieu, who is forced by poverty to become a concubine and then a prostitute but maintains her sense of honor. Kieu symbolized the people mistreated by the upper-class Vietnamese and their French allies. Another critic was the outspoken, witty, sarcastic, and sometimes raunchy woman poet Ho Xuan Huong (**ho swan wan**), formerly a concubine to several high officials. Criticizing the imperial court and patriarchal Confucianism, she wrote freely about sex, championed women's rights, and attacked polygamy: "One wife gets quilts, the other wife must freeze. To share a husband … what a fate! I labor as a wageless maid."[18]

In 1858 the militarily powerful French, hoping to control the Mekong and Red River trade routes to China, began their arrogant "civilizing mission" to spread French culture and Christianity, launching bloody campaigns against determined but badly outgunned Vietnamese resistance. After first conquering the south, they moved north, facing opposition the whole way. Although victorious by 1884, the French faced prolonged, heroic resistance for another fifteen years from thousands of poorly armed rebels known as the **can vuong** (**kan voo-AHN**) ("aid-the-king"), who waged guerrilla warfare, just as their ancestors had against Chinese and Mongol invaders, often against hopeless odds. One of the rebel leaders rejected any compromise: "Please do not mention the word *surrender* any more. You cannot give any good counsel to a man who is determined to die." As a French witness admitted, the Vietnamese resisted fiercely: "We have had enormous difficulties in imposing our authority. Rebel bands disturb the country everywhere, appear from nowhere, arrive in large numbers, destroy everything, and then disappear into nowhere."[19] Rebels received food and shelter from local populations. In suppressing resistance, the French massacred thousands and executed surrendered or captured rebels. The can vuong rebels became powerful symbols of resistance for later generations of Vietnamese fighting colonialism and foreign invasion in the twentieth century, often using some of the same tactics as earlier rebels.

In 1887 France created the artificial Federation of Indochina, linking Vietnam, now divided into three separate colonies, with newly acquired Cambodia and Laos, all states with very different social, cultural, and political histories. While France maintained its rule by force, French commercial interests and settlers exploited natural resources and markets. The colonial regime destroyed the Vietnamese villages' traditional autonomy, appointing leaders and raising taxes to finance administrative costs. Many peasants lost their land, or access to communal lands, to private landowners, investors, and rubber planters, mostly French. And although powerful French enterprises prospered, Indochina proved a financial burden for French taxpayers. Meanwhile, ruling through the traditional monarchies and aristocracies, France did little to promote economic development or improve living conditions in Cambodia and Laos.

As with French Indochina, Britain devoted decades to colonizing Burma (today Myanmar) and overcoming resistance. Aiming to expand its power in India, Britain coveted Burma's rich lands and contested Burmese claims to border regions. In three wars—1824–1826, 1851–1852, and 1885–1886—the British conquered Burma, both sides suffering huge casualties. Vastly differing cultures and clashing strategic interests produced violent conflict, while the gradual loss of independence demoralized Burmans (today called Bamans), the country's majority ethnic group. In losing territory, they felt an impending doom that they expressed in frenzied cultural activity, including drama, love poetry, and music. For instance, Myawaddy (**mee-ya-WAH-dee**) (1761–1853), a government minister, soldier, scholar, and musician, tried to salvage Burmese traditions by writing plays set in villages and collecting folk songs. But the desire to preserve Burmese culture did not preclude interest in foreign ideas that might aid in the country's survival. Myawaddy appreciated Siamese music and culture, learned some Hindi (the major language of north India), and hired a Spaniard to translate English-language newspapers from India. The court, fearing that the Burmese heritage might disappear if Britain triumphed, compiled *The Glass Palace Chronicle*, a history of Burma from earliest times.

Between 1853 and 1878 a new Burmese king, the idealistic Mindon, tried to salvage his country's prospects by pursuing modernization and seeking good relations with Britain. Mindon introduced steamships, promoted foreign trade, and tried to break down barriers between the court and the people. Worried he might succeed, the British tried to humiliate Mindon, and in 1886, their conquest complete, they exiled the royal family and abolished the aristocratic system. When some resisted colonial rule, the British, calling it "pacification," destroyed whole villages and executed rebel leaders. Burma became a province of British India, a humiliating fate. For the next fifty years Britain undermined Burmese Buddhism and cultural values, established Christian mission schools, and recruited non-Burman hill peoples into the government and army.

22-3c Siamese Modernization

Burma's traditional enemies, the Siamese (Thai), were the only Southeast Asians who maintained their independence. The vigorous new Bangkok-based Chakri dynasty ruled a strong Siam in the early 1800s.

can vuong ("aid-the-king") Rebel groups who waged guerrilla warfare for fifteen years against the French occupation of Vietnam.

---

[18]From Huynh, *Anthology of Vietnamese Poems*, 214.

[19]The quotes are in Lamb, *Vietnam's Will to Live*, 229; Truong Buu Lam, *Patterns of Vietnamese Response to Foreign Intervention, 1858–1900*, Monograph Series No. 11, Southeast Asia Studies (New Haven, CT: Yale University Press, 1967), 8.

View of European shipping on the Saigon river, by T. Child, F. Beato and Charles E. Watkins, 1870s (albumen print)/BONHAMS/Private Collection/Bridgeman Images

IMAGE 22.5 **Maritime Trade in French Indochina** Under French colonialism, Vietnam became more closely tied to the world economy. This photo from the 1870s shows European cargo ships, barges, and warehouses on the Saigon River.

Q What can we learn about cargo ports in this era?

Seeing Burma's dilemma, able Chakri kings mounted a successful strategy to resist Western pressures. With Britain and France both coveting Siam but preoccupied with controlling Malaya, Burma, and Indochina, Siamese leaders had time to strengthen government institutions, improve economic infrastructure, cultivate a long-standing alliance with China, and broaden popular support. Farsighted Siamese kings, understanding changing Southeast Asian politics and rising Western power, promoted modernization, yielding to the West when necessary and consolidating what remained. They gave up claims to Laos and several Malay states. Siamese leaders also accepted commercial agreements opening the country to Western businesses. Recognizing Siamese determination and pressed by unrest in Burma and Indochina, Britain and France decided that conquering Siam would be too costly and left Siam as a buffer between British Burma and French Indochina.

Two kings and their advisers presided over Siam's policies. Scholarly, peace-loving Mongkut (**MAHN-kut**)

(r. 1851–1868) had been a Buddhist monk and teacher who studied science and learned to read Latin. Mongkut calculated that if many Western nations obtained rights in Siam, they would fight each other first. To discourage invasion, he signed treaties, often unfavorable for Siam, with Western powers, invited Western aid to modernize his kingdom, and hired Christian missionaries' wives to teach his wives and sons English. In 1859, as a show of Siamese power, Mongkut, who claimed that his dynasty descended from the once powerful Khmer Empire, hatched an ambitious plan to dismantle part of the massive Angkor Wat temple in Cambodia, built hundreds of years earlier, and steal it away to Bangkok where it would be reconstructed. But the expedition he dispatched was ambushed on their way to Angkor by Khmer soldiers and forced to retreat. As a consolation to Mongkut, a miniature Angkor Wat was built in a Bangkok temple but Mongkut had died before it was completed.

Mongkut's widely traveled son and successor, Chulalongkorn (**CHOO-lah-LONG-corn**) (r. 1868–1910), emphasized diplomacy and modernization, abolishing slavery, centralizing government services, strengthening the bureaucracy, establishing a Western-style government education system, and stimulating economic growth by encouraging Chinese immigration. Opening new land for rice production made Siam one of the world's leading rice exporters. Hence, Siam generally kept pace with its colonized neighbors in economic development, but under Siamese, not colonial, direction. When Chulalongkorn died in 1910, Siam (today Thailand) remained independent, avoiding political, cultural, and economic disaster under colonialism, and Western appetites for new colonies had waned. For many years many Thais, especially middle-class Bangkok residents, have shared in a worshipful cult around Chulalongkorn, seen as the Great Modernizer and patron saint of the Thai middle class, who laid a foundation for prosperity. The cult has faded somewhat since the economic crash of 1997 but still has many followers.

22-3d The Philippines, Spain, and the United States

As in Latin America (see Chapter 19), hostility toward corrupt, repressive, economically stagnant Spanish rule simmered for decades in the Philippines. Many educated Filipinos of Spanish, indigenous, and mixed (mestizo) background resented colonial power, privileged immigrants from Spain, and Catholic Church domination. These anti-Spanish feelings were encouraged by the Chinese mestizo poet and novelist Jose Rizal (ri-ZAHL) (1861–1896), who lived for a time in Spain and Germany. Rizal's novels satirizing the government and church earned him official condemnation as a subversive heretic, and he was publicly executed for alleged treason in 1896. Rizal had earlier prophesied that "the day the Spanish inflict martyrdom [on me] farewell Spanish government."[20] Indeed, Rizal's death united varied opposition groups, turning nationalists toward revolution. One nationalist leader, Emilio Aguinaldo (AH-gee-NAHL-doe) (1870–1964), called on Filipinos to rebel: "Filipinos! Open your eyes! Lovers of their native land, rise up in arms, to proclaim their liberty and independence."[21] Women played active roles in the movement as soldiers, couriers, spies, and nurses. Gregoria de Jesus boasted that she "learned to ride,…shoot a rifle,…manipulate other weapons…sleep on the ground without tasting food…drink dirty water from mudholes."[22] Despite such heroic efforts, Spain contained the revolution by 1897, but it failed to crush scattered resistance.

The situation changed dramatically in 1898 when a U.S. fleet sailed into Manila Bay and destroyed the Spanish navy. Having engaged in occasional naval skirmishes in Southeast Asia throughout the 1800s, Americans now sought control of its resources and markets. The United States intervened in the Philippines as part of the Spanish-American War (see Chapter 20), the first of four ground wars it would fight in East and Southeast Asia over the next eight decades. The U.S. attack on Manila rejuvenated the revolutionaries led by Aguinaldo, who, receiving American support, soon controlled much of the country, declared independence, and established a semidemocratic republican government. But the factionalized leaders disagreed in their objectives, and Americans had other plans for the islands.

The U.S. decision to remain in the Philippines as a colonizer led Americans to suppress the nationalist revolution. U.S. president William McKinley, answering British imperialist Rudyard Kipling's call to assume "the white man's burden," articulated Manifest Destiny, the notion that God supported U.S. expansion. Ignoring centuries of Filipino history and deep desire for independence, McKinley proclaimed: "It is our duty to uplift and civilize and Christianize and by God's Will do our very best by [the Filipinos]."[23]

But McKinley, admitting he could not locate the Philippines on a map, underestimated Filipino opposition to U.S. occupation. Some 125,000 American troops fought during the four-year Philippine-American War, during which over five thousand Americans and sixteen hundred Filipinos died in battle. Another 200,000 Filipinos perished from famine and disease or in guarded internment (some critics call them concentration) camps set up to keep villagers from helping the revolutionaries. Since Filipino soldiers often enjoyed active support from local people, Americans had to fight for every town. The elusive revolutionaries' guerrilla warfare demoralized American soldiers, who expected quick victory. While Americans controlled towns, revolutionaries controlled the countryside. Both sides committed atrocities, including torture. Americans destroyed whole villages, looted Catholic churches, and used waterboarding (a torture method which they called "the water cure") on captured rebels, while Filipinos killed captured Americans. U.S. general Jacob Smith ordered his men to turn Samar Island into a "howling wilderness," to "kill and burn. The more you kill and burn the better you will please me."[24]

The war and the many reports of brutal treatment of Filipinos divided Americans. Supporters coveted Philippine resources and markets, and many U.S. newspapers urged the slaughter of all Filipinos who resisted. But an organized protest movement opposed the war. In his rewriting of "The Battle Hymn of the Republic," the antiwar writer Mark Twain, who had traveled widely in Asia, satirized American economic motives: "Mine eyes have seen the orgy of the launching of the Sword; He is searching out the hoardings where the strangers' wealth is stored; He hath loosed his fateful lightnings, and with woe and death has scored; His lust is marching on."

[20]Quoted in David Joel Steinberg, *The Philippines: A Singular and Plural Place*, 3rd ed. (Boulder, CO: Westview Press, 1994), 64.
[21]Quoted in Teodoro A. Agoncillo, *A Short History of the Philippines* (New York: Mentor, 1969), 93.
[22]Quoted in Barbara Watson Andaya, "Gender, Warfare, and Patriotism in Southeast Asia and in the Philippine Revolution," in *The Philippine Revolution of 1896: Ordinary Lives in Extraordinary Times*, ed. Florintina Rodao and Felice Noelle Rodriguez (Quezon City: Ateneo de Manila Press, 2001), 11.
[23]Quoted in David Joel Steinberg et al., *In Search of Southeast Asia: A Modern History*, rev. ed. (Honolulu: University of Hawaii Press, 1987), 274.
[24]Quoted in Daniel B. Schirmer, *Republic or Empire: American Resistance to the Philippine War* (Cambridge, UK: Schenkman, 1972), 237.

American critics also rejected imperialism: "We've taken up the white man's burden, of ebony and brown; Now will you tell us, Rudyard [Kipling], how we may put it down."[25]

By 1902, with revolutionaries defeated and many wealthy Filipinos supporting U.S. rule to protect their own interests, the Philippines became an American colony. Americans reshaped the society of those they paternalistically called "our little brown brothers," establishing an elected legislature filled mostly by wealthy Filipinos. Unlike in most European colonies, the government fostered modern health care and education, producing many Filipinos fluent in English, a big advantage in today's globalizing world. But American rule ignored peasant needs while perpetuating Filipino landowners, who controlled millions of impoverished peasant tenants, and reinforcing the cash crop economy now linked to American economic needs.

KEY POINTS

▶ As the Dutch expanded their control over the Indonesian archipelago, they joined together vastly disparate cultures and disrupted the traditional economy.

▶ The British expanded control over the Malay Peninsula, which they used to supply raw materials such as tin and rubber, and Singapore, which became a key crossroads of Southeast Asian and India–China trade.

▶ After conquering Vietnam, the French faced fierce resistance from can vuong rebels, but they ultimately conquered the rebels and opened the country to exploitation by French commercial interests.

▶ As the British gradually conquered Burma, native Burmans attempted to preserve their culture, but after the British victory in 1886 the Burmese traditions were largely undermined.

▶ Siam (now Thailand) avoided colonization because of its fortunate geographical location and its farseeing leaders, who gave in to some Western demands and consolidated popular support.

▶ After defeating the Spanish in the Philippines and supporting local rebels, the U.S. government turned against the Filipinos and, after a bloody struggle, established a colony geared toward American economic needs.

22-4 The Reshaping of Southeast Asia

⮀ TRANSITIONS ⬛ SOCIETIES

Q What were the major political, economic, and social consequences of colonialism in Southeast Asia?

Colonialism in Southeast Asia resembled that in South Asia and Africa, with many common features. Although some benefited, many others experienced worsening living conditions. A chant popular among Vietnamese peasants lamented the French seizure of resources: "Ill fortune, indeed, for power has been seized by the French invaders. It's criminal to set out the food tray and find that one has nothing but roots and greens to eat."[26] From a global perspective, colonialism linked Southeast Asia more firmly to a Western-dominated world economy. But colonial policies also affected political, social, intellectual, and cultural life. Like Indians, Southeast Asians responded to the challenges in creative ways.

> **CONNECTION to TODAY**
>
> Which impacts of colonialism do you see as the most influential legacies, positive or negative, for Southeast Asians today?

limited democracy since U.S. officials had to approve its decisions. Britain allowed some influential Malayans, mostly drawn from Malay royal families and wealthy Chinese merchants, participation in local government and, in 1935, formed a Burmese legislature that included elected and appointed members. But the French and Dutch allowed little democracy. Colonialism often meant government by stodgy, autocratic, and ethnocentric European bureaucrats who frequently knew no Asian languages and little about local cultures.

Colonial governments varied widely. As in sub-Saharan Africa (see Chapter 21), direct rule, which removed traditional leaders, such as Burmese kings, or made them symbolic only, as with the Vietnamese emperors, was used in Burma, the Philippines, and parts of Vietnam and Indonesia. Under indirect rule, mostly applied in Malaya, Sarawak, Cambodia, Laos, and some parts of Indonesia, colonialists governed districts through traditional leaders, such as Malay sultans or Javanese aristocrats, who frequently supported colonial rule for

22-4a Colonial Governments and Economies

Colonialism proved a shattering experience for most Southeast Asians. The only colony with much self-government, the U.S.-ruled Philippines had an elected legislature, but there was only

---

[25]The quotes are in David Howard Bain, *Sitting in Darkness: Americans in the Philippines* (Baltimore: Penguin, 1986), 2; and Gary R. Hess, *Vietnam and United States: Origins and Legacy of War* (Boston: Twayne, 1990), 25.

[26]Quoted in Ngo Vinh Long, *Before the Revolution: The Vietnamese Peasants Under the French* (New York: Columbia University Press, 1991), v.

Chronicle/Alamy Stock Photo

IMAGE 22.6 Java Coffee Plantation This painting from the nineteenth century shows a European manager supervising barefoot laborers who are raking and drying coffee beans, a major Javanese cash crop.

Q What can we learn from the painting about social structure, work, and life on a coffee plantation in Java?

their own self-interests. Colonial authorities played one ethnic group or one region against another, creating problems that made national unity difficult after independence. As in Africa, colonial boundaries sometimes ignored traditional ethnic relationships and rivalries, fostering political instability. Countries such as Burma, Indonesia, and Laos were artificial creations rather than organic unities with culturally similar populations.

As in South Asia and Africa, colonialism transformed economic life. Since traditional subsistence food farming, practiced for many centuries, could not produce enough revenues for colonial governments or investors, it was replaced by cash crop farming, plantations, and mines, which, along with banks and import–export companies, were mostly controlled by Western businessmen. Thus the colony's economy was tied more closely to the colonizer and Western resource needs. Under these conditions, Southeast Asia became one of the world's most valuable economic areas, with colonial taxation policies encouraging the cultivation of rubber, pepper,

sugar, coffee, tea, opium, and palm oil; the cutting of timber; the mining of gold and tin; and the drilling for oil. Some key cash crops, such as rubber from Brazil and coffee from the Middle East, originated elsewhere. Many colonies became specialized monocultures emphasizing one or two major commodities—Malaya's rubber and tin, Vietnam's rubber and rice—but world prices fluctuated with unstable demand. These economic activities often harmed the natural environment, with forests cleared for plantations or logged for timber. In most colonies opium (obtained mostly from India) provided at least 10 percent (and some places like Singapore, half) of the revenues to support the colonial projects of modernity, such as schools, roads, irrigation canals, and public health clinics. But this depended on establishing government monopolies, in conjunction with local Chinese businessmen who managed them, that induced Chinese and Southeast Asians to become addicts. Similar monopolies marketed alcohol and tobacco and operated legal gambling halls.

Rubber was a key crop. As the invention of bicycles and then automobiles opened markets for rubber tires, many now depended on rubber growing for their livelihood. Britain introduced rubber to Malaya, and it soon spread to Sumatra, Borneo, southern Thailand, Vietnam, and Cambodia, grown mostly on European-owned plantations. Malaya supplied over half the world's natural rubber by 1920. Plantation workers endured long hours, strict discipline, monotonous routine, and poor food, generally arising before dawn to tend rubber trees and trying to finish before the blazing tropical sun made hard physical work unhealthy. A Vietnamese writer described rubber estate workers: "every day one was worn down a bit more, cheeks sunken, eyes hollow. Everyone appeared almost dead."[27]

Scholars debate the economic impact but most think that the economic growth benefited only a minority. Colonizers and the local officials and merchants, planters, mine-owners, and steamship companies cooperating with them gained wealth while most peasants and workers gained little. Sometimes there were short-term gains. For example, peasants on Java growing sugar and coffee initially earned new income. But costs rose faster than compensation, forcing peasants to grow more and work longer hours to earn the same profit as before. Peasants now depended on sugar or coffee profits for survival, but rising costs often impoverished them. They also faced disaster when world sugar and coffee prices declined and then, during the Great Depression in the 1930s, collapsed altogether.

22-4b Social Change

As in India, colonial policies sparked rapid population growth, from perhaps 30 to 35 million people in 1800 to around 140 or 150 million by the late 1930s. Java experienced the greatest increases, from some 10 million in 1800 to 30 million by 1900 and 48 million by 1940, creating a burden for contemporary Indonesia. Dutch policies fostered better health care, people lived longer, and economic incentives encouraged larger families to provide more labor. However, women faced more hours working in the fields as well as increased expectations for bearing more children. Fast-growing populations, especially in Java, Vietnam, and the Philippines, resulted in smaller farm plots and more landless people.

Between 1800 and 1941 millions of Chinese and South Asians immigrated to Southeast Asia to work as laborers, miners, planters, and merchants. The Chinese chiefly came from two poor, overcrowded coastal provinces in southeast China. Although some Chinese established businesses or joined relatives, many immigrated under indenture, a system that obligated them to work for years in mines, plantations, or enterprises. Chinese immigrants, mostly males, hoped to return to their native village wealthy and respected, but some remained poor, spending their lives as laborers, miners, or plantation workers. Many Chinese prospered as merchants, planters, and mine owners, often deciding to remain in Southeast Asia to maintain their businesses and raise families.

Dominating retail trade, the Chinese became the commercial middle class, operating general stores, specialty shops, and restaurants in every city and town. Some cities, such as Singapore and Kuala Lumpur (**KWAW-luh loom-POOR**) in Malaya, had largely Chinese populations but many cities had sizeable Chinatowns. Since few unmarried women emigrated from China before World War I, many Chinese married local women or brought families from China, their descendants often adopting aspects of local culture and language. By adjusting to local conditions, the Chinese became a permanent presence in Southeast Asian life, but some Southeast Asians resented them for what they perceived as their relative affluence, although many Chinese remained poor workers, fishermen, miners, or farmers.

Indian immigrants had long come to Malaya as traders, craftsmen, and workers. Beginning in the 1880s, the British imported Tamils from southeast India to work on rubber plantations. Together Chinese and Indians eventually outnumbered Malays. Britain governed the various communities through their own leaders: Malay chiefs, Chinese merchants, and urban Indian traders. But this strategy separated and discouraged cooperation between the groups. Indians also immigrated to Burma, which was administered as part of British India; most worked as professionals, merchants, or moneylenders.

The changes particularly affected women, traditionally farmers, traders, and weavers. As men took up cash crop farming, women often had the increased workload of growing the family's food. With Chinese, Indian, and sometimes Arab men increasingly monopolizing small-scale trade, many women lost their role in the local marketplace and thus their status as family income earners. Women also lost their domination of weaving, spinning, and dyeing. Although this was hard work, even drudgery, women could weave at home with friends and relatives while caring for children. But after 1850, inexpensive factory-made textiles from Europe displaced local handwoven cloth, slowly forcing women out of the textile business. A Javanese noblewoman wrote in 1909 that "little by little [women] feel that their life is no longer of such value, considered by men only as ornaments as they are no longer contributing to the household coffers."[28] Women had to find other income sources that often took them away from home and children.

Influenced by European feminism, in the late nineteenth and early twentieth centuries some women joined movements asserting their rights. Hence, Siamese feminists opposed polygamy and supported girls' education. Today many Indonesians honor an inspirational Javanese woman, Raden Adjeng Kartini, even celebrating her memory and example every year on April 21 with a "Kartini Day" in schools, government offices, and the media. Her life and writings advocating governmental reform, progress, and women's rights influenced Indonesian feminism and struck a chord with the emerging nationalist movement (see Meet the People: Kartini, Indonesian Feminist and Teacher). Although she died young, the girls' schools she founded in 1900 multiplied and still exist. Like Kartini, other women struggled to cope with the changing world.

---

[27]Tran Tu Binh, *The Red Earth: A Vietnamese Memoir of Life on a Colonial Rubber Plantation*, translated by John Spragens, Jr. (Athens: Center for International Studies, Ohio University, 1985), 26.

[28]Raden Ajoe Mangkoedimedjo, quoted in Norman Owen et al., *The Emergence of Modern Southeast Asia: A New History* (Honolulu: University of Hawaii Press, 2005), 197.

Kartini, Indonesian Feminist and Teacher

Inspirational social activist and teacher Raden Adjeng Kartini **(RAH-den AH-jeng KAR-teen-ee)** (1879–1905), usually known simply as Kartini, represented a feminist consciousness new to Indonesia while sharing the problems and facing the prejudices that Indonesian women encountered in the colonial system and their own societies. A Javanese aristocrat's daughter, she chafed against the confined lives of her social class, which expected young women to obey men, especially their fathers, without question, stay home, and train for marriage. However, Kartini's unusually liberal parents subscribed to Dutch-language newspapers, hired Dutch tutors for their sons and daughters, and then sent Kartini and her siblings to a Dutch-language primary school. Her brothers later moved on to a Dutch-language high school, and one even attended a university in Holland. A good student, Kartini keenly wanted to complete high school and study in Holland, but these experiences would have required her to leave home. Since Javanese customs discouraged aristocratic women from traveling without their families, her father would not permit it. Conforming to aristocratic custom, at puberty Kartini was restricted to the family's house and ordered to prepare for an arranged marriage by learning domestic skills but she also read novels, newspapers, and magazines.

But Kartini had larger ambitions. From her experience in Dutch school and friendships with Dutch women, she drew a model of personal freedom contrary to her Javanese society, including a commitment to educate women and give them more options in life. Eventually Kartini bowed to her parents' demands and entered an arranged marriage with a man she scarcely knew who already had two other wives; he agreed to support her plan to open a girls' school. Kartini sent a memorandum to the colonial government titled "Educate the Javanese," and then, at twenty, she opened Indonesia's first girls' school, combining Javanese and Western values.

Kartini wrote fascinating letters to Dutch friends in Java and Holland that revealed much about her thinking. Her correspondents, often nonconformist career women with socialist leanings, known in Holland as "modern girls," encouraged Kartini's educational plans and thirst for knowledge. In 1899 she told a pen-friend, the radical feminist Stella Zeehandelaar: "I have been longing to make the acquaintance of a 'modern girl,' that proud independent girl who has all my sympathy." Mixing her Dutch friends' ideas with her own, Kartini's letters asserted women's right to education and freedom from polygamy and child marriage.

Like European feminists, in her letters Kartini criticized the constraints of marriage, family, and society, revealing serious

Historic Collection/Alamy Stock Photo

IMAGE 22.7 **Raden Adjeng Kartini** This photo honors the young Javanese woman who was an Indonesian feminist pioneer and founded girls' schools that still operate in Indonesia.

Q What does this photo tell us about Kartini?

doubts about the advantages of marriage in her own society: "But we must marry, must, must. Not to marry is the greatest sin which the Muslim women can commit. And marriage among us? Miserable is too feeble an expression for it. How can it be otherwise, when the laws have made everything for the man and nothing for the woman. When law and convention both are for the man; when everything is allowed to him." She thought women repressed: "The ideal Javanese girl is silent and expressionless as a wooden doll, speaking only when it is necessary." She also condemned religious prejudice, whether by Muslims or Christians: "We feel that the kernel of all religion is right living, and that all religion is good and beautiful. But, o ye peoples, what have you made of it?" But she had hope for change: "I glow with enthusiasm toward the new time which has come. My thoughts and sympathies are with my sisters who are struggling forward in the distant West."

Kartini died in childbirth at age twenty-five. Her Dutch friends later published Kartini's letters, ensuring her fame. Thanks partly to royalties from her published letters, the schools Kartini founded multiplied after her death, educating thousands of Indonesian girls in the twentieth century. Her schools filled a great need, for which many Indonesians are grateful. Although Kartini criticized Javanese culture and admired Western ideals, in 1964 the Indonesian president named her a national heroine and honored her as the nation's *ibu* ("mother"). But Kartini left a controversial legacy for Indonesians and it has become mixed up today with political debates and power struggles involving various factions, liberals, feminists, and conservatives. Some conservatives accused her of abandoning Islam and Javanese culture. Because of her close ties to Dutch friends, her detractors labeled Kartini an apologist for colonialism; some contrasted her unfavorably to Rahma El-Yunusiah, a devout Muslim woman from Sumatra who taught Arabic and the Quran and refused any contact with the Dutch. Nonetheless, today Kartini is honored as a proponent of Indonesian women's rights and a precursor perhaps of Indonesian nationalist sentiment.

Reflection Questions

1. What does Kartini's life tell us about the challenges that faced Javanese women of her day?
2. How do Kartini's thoughts reflect the meeting of East and West?
3. Do you think that Kartini's views and life should make her a role model today for women in Southeast Asia and the larger world?

Note: Quotations from Raden Adjeng Kartini, *Letters of a Javanese Princess*, edited with an introduction by Hildred Geertz (New York: W. W. Norton, 1964), 31, 34, 42, 45, 73.

Southeast Asia already had large cities, but Western rule encouraged more rapid urbanization. Cities such as Manila, Jakarta, Rangoon (today Yangon), Singapore, Kuala Lumpur, and Saigon (today Ho Chi Minh City) grew as colonial capitals or financial and commercial centers. Attracting migrants from nearby districts and immigrants, towns and cities offered diverse food stalls and restaurants and schools catering to different ethnic groups, as well as Muslim mosques, Christian churches, and Buddhist, Hindu, and Chinese temples. While most people maintained their own culture, some descendants of Chinese, Indian, and Arab immigrants assimilated into the surrounding society; friendships and even marriages crossed ethnic lines. For example, much of Thailand's political and economic elite has mixed Chinese-Siamese ancestry. Similarly many people of pure or part Chinese background play leading roles in Filipino society.

22-4c Cultural Change

Colonial governments differed in educating people and fostering indigenous cultures. Most colonies left education to Christian missions, which taught useful skills but, as in Africa and India, emphasized Western learning and culture as well as religious knowledge. Hence, Vietnamese students studied about "our ancestors the Gauls," Filipinos learned to read with U.S. textbooks that showed children playing in the snow and celebrating Thanksgiving, and Malayan schools taught about the history of the British royal family. Some Vietnamese, Indonesians, and Chinese and many hill peoples became Christian, but few Theravada Buddhists or Muslims abandoned their faiths. A few colonies established public schools, especially in the U.S.-ruled Philippines, which enrolled 75 percent of children in elementary schools. Independent Siam made public education widely available for both boys and girls. In contrast, French Indochina spent little public money on schools. However, some communities developed alternatives to Western education. Buddhist and Muslim groups expanded schools that taught from a non-Western perspective, while other schools mixed Eastern and Western ideas. Schools run by a mystical Javanese religious organization provided an alternative to both Islamic and Christian instruction, emphasizing Indonesian arts such as music and dance but also Western self-expression and social equality.

New cultural forms developed. Indonesian musicians mixed European string instruments with largely percussion Javanese gamelan orchestra rhythms, creating a romantic new popular music, *kronchong*. In the 1800s these sentimental songs were adopted by Indonesian sailors and soldiers, as well as by disreputable young men, known as "kronchong crocodiles," who dressed flamboyantly, gambled, and drank heavily. By the early 1900s, however, kronchong had become respectable and it was eventually embraced by Indonesian nationalists as an anticolonial artistic weapon featuring topical and nationalist songs.

Cultural exchange was not one way. A few Western composers, observing performances by Javanese and Balinese gamelan orchestras, incorporated gamelan influences into their music. In most colonies, modern literature reflected alienation from colonialism and an awareness of rapid change. But since colonial regimes suppressed criticism, authors made their points indirectly to avoid censorship or arrest. Vietnamese writers used historical themes or critiques of Vietnamese society to discuss contemporary conditions, while Indonesian writers explored characters experiencing despair and disorientation because of the colonial system.

KEY POINTS

▶ Colonized Southeast Asian peoples were allowed very little autonomy and were frequently combined into countries with little ethnic or cultural unity.

▶ Economic life in colonies was reshaped to serve Western nations' needs for raw materials, especially rubber, and for markets for their goods, and in many cases this change led to destruction of the natural environment and the impoverishment of local people.

▶ Millions of Chinese immigrated to Southeast Asia, where many prospered as merchants and retailers, while Indians came to work in Malayan rubber plantations.

▶ Economic changes due to colonization forced women to grow food for their families and eliminated the market for their handmade textiles, thus taking away their traditional ability to earn an income.

▶ Education in colonies included both Western-style and more traditional schools, and cultural and artistic interchange between Westerners and colonized peoples produced new cultural forms, such as kronchong music.

Chapter Summary

Change was more obvious than continuity in South and Southeast Asia. Gradually Britain extended its control over the Indian subcontinent, using military force but also outmaneuvering rivals, forging alliances, and intimidating small states into accepting British domination. By 1850 the British East India Company controlled all of India directly or indirectly. The Company introduced policies to reshape India's economy and culture, including a Westernizing education system. The rebellion of 1857, suppressed with great difficulty, shocked Britain into replacing the Company with colonial government rule. The new British Raj allowed little Indian participation in government. British policies transformed the Indian economy by favoring landlords at the expense of peasants and by suffocating traditional industries to benefit British manufactures. Population growth and poverty fostered emigration. The encounter with the West also prompted Indian thinkers to reassess their cultural traditions. Some Indians adopted Western influences, some rejected them, and others tried to mix East and West. Finally, unpopular British policies generated a nationalist movement that challenged British rule.

The European powers finished colonizing Southeast Asia. Using military force or threats, the Dutch became dominant throughout the Indonesian archipelago, reaping its wealth in part by compelling Javanese to grow cash crops. Britain gained control of Burma through warfare but needed less force in Malaya, which proved profitable as a source of minerals and cash crops. Against strong resistance the French occupied Vietnam, exploiting and reshaping rural Vietnamese society. The Americans displaced the Spanish as the colonial power in the Philippines after suppressing a nationalist revolution. While they maintained the cash crop economic system, they also fostered some political participation. Only Siam, led by perceptive kings, avoided colonization. Colonialism reshaped social patterns, undermining the economic activities of women, fostering urbanization, and promoting immigration of Chinese, who later became the commercial class. Southeast Asians responded by forming creative schools and unique cultural activities.

Key Terms

Marathas 560
Black Hole of Calcutta 560
sepoys 561
Westernization 562

Orientalism 562
zamindars 564
Theosophy 568
cultivation system 571

plural society 572
can vuong 573

East Asia and the Russian Empire Face New Challenges, 1750–1914

> " *The sacred traditions of our ancestors have fallen into oblivion. Those who watch attentively the march of events feel a dark and wonderful presentiment. We are on the eve of an immense revolution. But will the impulse come from within or without?* "
>
> —A Chinese official, 1846[1]

IMAGE 23.1 **Treaty Between Japan and China** After an industrializing Japan defeated a declining China in a war over Japanese encroachments in Korea (1894–1895), diplomats from both nations met to negotiate a peace treaty. This painting shows the Chinese and Japanese representatives, easily identified by their different clothing styles, discussing the terms.

Q What can you tell about the meeting and negotiations from the photo?

[1]Quoted in Frederic Wakeman, Jr., *Strangers at the Gate: Social Disorder in South China, 1839–1861* (Berkeley: University of California Press, 1966), 126.

In 1820 Li Ruzhen (**LEE ju-chen**) (1763–1830) published a satiric novel boldly attacking Chinese social conditions and culture. Set in the Tang dynasty, *Flowers in the Mirror* explored a sensitive topic only superficially discussed by male Chinese writers: relationships between the sexes. Li described a trip by three men to a country in which all the gender roles followed in China for centuries have been reversed, where men suffered ear piercing and footbinding pain, and endured hours every day putting on makeup, to please the women running the country. One of the men, Merchant Lin, is conscripted as a court "lady" by the female "king":

> *His [bound] feet lost much of their original shape. Blood and flesh were squeezed into a pulp, shrunk to a dainty size. With blood-red lipstick, and powder adorning his face, and jade and pearl adorning his coiffure and ears, Merchant Lin assumed a not unappealing appearance.*[2]

Li seemed an unlikely man to address so sympathetically women's daily challenges. A conventionally educated Confucian scholar who failed the civil service examinations, Li became a writer on language, political philosophy, mathematics, and astrology. But growing Western pressure to open China's borders to foreign trade, unchecked population growth, domestic unrest, political corruption, and growing opium addiction spurred Chinese scholars such as Li to reassess Chinese traditions, such as the social inequities that prevented women from participating in China's regeneration. Growing dissatisfaction, combined with Western intervention, set the stage for the immense revolution that eventually transformed this ancient society.

Still powerful in the late 1700s, China in the 1800s experienced three military defeats, devastating rebellions, and increasing poverty. Eventually, revolutionary movements overthrew the imperial system. When Western ships forced Japan open in the 1850s, the old system fell, and Japan's new leaders launched an all-out modernization program to prevent Western domination. Meanwhile, Russia, perched on the borders of Europe, East Asia, and the Islamic Middle East and Central Asia, became Eurasia's largest territorial power.

---

[2]Quoted in Jonathan D. Spence, *The Search for Modern China*, 2nd ed. (New York: W.W. Norton, 1999), 148.

23-1 The Zenith and Decline of Qing China

NETWORKS TRANSITIONS

Q What were the causes and consequences of the Opium War?

China had been a major world society for over two millennia, during which time they had enjoyed several long "golden ages" and made major innovations in science, technology, manufacturing, philosophy, government, and the arts while being a key participant in the Eurasian and then global economy. But China faced severe challenges during the later Qing dynasty that undermined this long successful system. Established by Manchus, the Qing (ching) (1644–1912) was the last dynasty in China's two-thousand-year-old imperial history. After reaching its zenith in the eighteenth century, Qing China experienced decay in the nineteenth as several catastrophic wars resulted in unequal treaties that increased Western penetration and fostered major rebellions. As China's economy changed, increasing poverty prompted millions to seek their fortunes abroad. Qing decline had as much to do with Europe's rise as with China's failures.

> **CONNECTION to TODAY**
>
> How do you think the disasters China experienced in the nineteenth century have influenced China's foreign policies and view of the world in recent years?

23-1a Qing China in an Imperial World

Eighteenth-century China, self-sufficient and self-centered, was one of the world's most powerful, prosperous, and technologically sophisticated societies. But the Manchus were more despotic than earlier Chinese rulers and forbade intermarriage with the Chinese. While the Chinese accepted Manchu rule, as they had tolerated alien rule in the past, they resented the ethnic discrimination. The Qing built a great empire, occupying predominantly Muslim Xinjiang (**shin-jee-yahng**), a desert region west of China proper; conquering the Mongols; annexing Tibet; and adding the fertile island of Taiwan (Formosa), to which many Chinese migrated. This expansion stretched Qing military power and proved economically costly.

Yet the Qing generally maintained prosperity for nearly two centuries. New crops from the Americas, such as corn (maize), sweet potatoes, and peanuts, increased food sources,

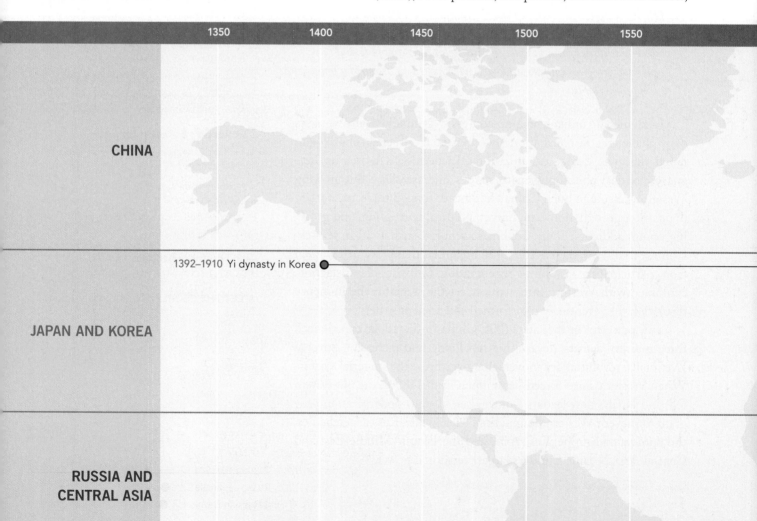

	1350	1400	1450	1500	1550

CHINA

JAPAN AND KOREA

1392–1910 Yi dynasty in Korea

RUSSIA AND CENTRAL ASIA

while expanded cash cropping of cotton, tea, and American tobacco fostered growing concentration of land ownership. In 1830, with growing domestic trade, new textile factories, and increased copper mining, China remained the world's largest commercial economy and produced a third of the world's manufacturing. In the 1850s a British observer called the Chinese the world's greatest manufacturing people. Some historians suggest that the mid-Qing commercialized economy resembled the patterns that sparked economic change in Early Modern Western Europe. Between 1700 and 1850 China's population nearly tripled, growing from 150 million to 432 million. Peasants responded to population pressure by farming marginal land and expanding their use of irrigation and fertilizer.

But population growth outstripped the expansion of the food supply, straining resources and fostering corruption and Chinese resentment of the Qing government. Although in the 1700s living standards in more developed regions of China and western Europe were probably comparable, China's living standards deteriorated in the 1800s just as several Western European societies were industrializing and becoming more powerful and aggressive in Asia. As Chinese culture and society became more conservative, the Qing prohibited books and plays considered treasonable or subversive to traditional Chinese values. Some scholars, arguing that moral laxness caused dynastic collapses, applauded the crackdown. The Qing

imposed harsher laws against homosexuality, which Chinese had generally tolerated, and increased social pressures on women to conform to gender expectations, such as by prohibiting widow remarriage. Imperial edicts emphasized Confucian moral virtues, heaping honor on filial sons, loyal officials, and faithful wives. Government-sponsored instructional books encouraged female obligations such as not laughing aloud, talking loudly, or swaying their skirts, and China's historians generally considered women to be "exemplary" only if they adhered to female virtue according to Confucian family standards. Yet, women also read popular literature, such as the satirical novel *Flowers in a Mirror*. Some historians have noted that some Qing women became writers, practicing a kind of self-empowerment to cross boundaries typically closed to women in order to gain knowledge, economic power, cultural authority, and political engagement. Women were already known for their poetry, but now some took up other writing genres such as genealogies and medical treatises. In a few Hunan province (central China) villages, peasant women wrote their communications in a secret script, *nuxu* (**noo-shoe**), probably developed by and for women sometime between the tenth century CE and the later Qing, when it reached its zenith.

China's problems were caused by both internal decay and foreign pressure. Greedy officials took bribes to allow the smuggling and sale of narcotic drugs. Local rebellions against

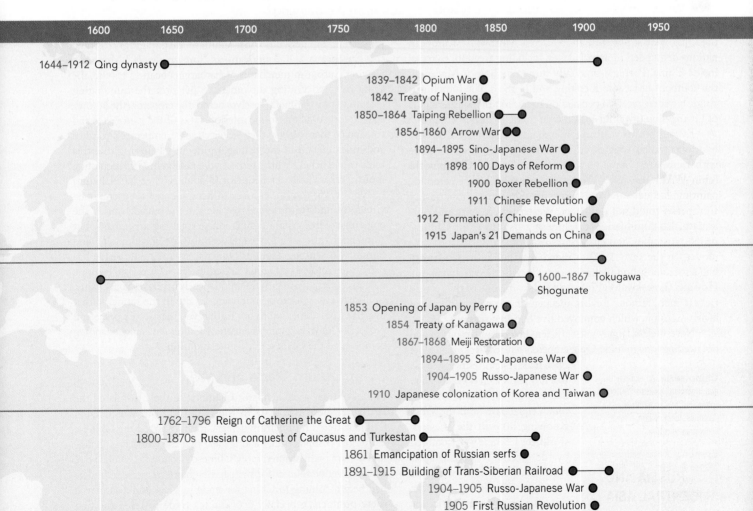

1600   1650   1700   1750   1800   1850   1900   1950

1644–1912 Qing dynasty
1839–1842 Opium War
1842 Treaty of Nanjing
1850–1864 Taiping Rebellion
1856–1860 Arrow War
1894–1895 Sino-Japanese War
1898 100 Days of Reform
1900 Boxer Rebellion
1911 Chinese Revolution
1912 Formation of Chinese Republic
1915 Japan's 21 Demands on China

1600–1867 Tokugawa Shogunate
1853 Opening of Japan by Perry
1854 Treaty of Kanagawa
1867–1868 Meiji Restoration
1894–1895 Sino-Japanese War
1904–1905 Russo-Japanese War
1910 Japanese colonization of Korea and Taiwan

1762–1796 Reign of Catherine the Great
1800–1870s Russian conquest of Caucasus and Turkestan
1861 Emancipation of Russian serfs
1891–1915 Building of Trans-Siberian Railroad
1904–1905 Russo-Japanese War
1905 First Russian Revolution

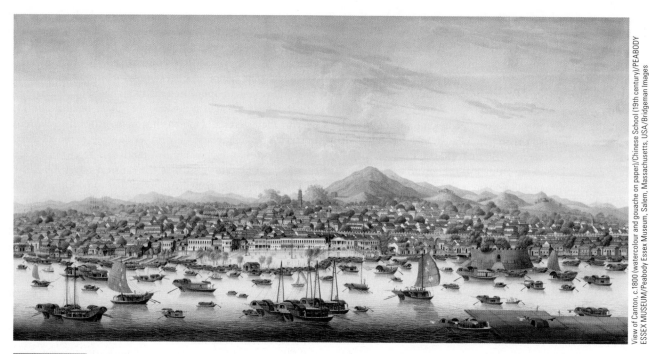

IMAGE 23.2 **Guangzhou** During the eighteenth century, the Western traders in China were restricted to one riverside district in Guangzhou (Canton), where they built their warehouses, businesses, and homes in European style.

Q What can you ascertain about the city and its trade from the painting?

the Qing were suppressed at great cost. Meanwhile, European nations demanded more privileges, including freedom to travel inside China. Portugal gradually turned its base at Macao on the southern coast into a colony, and in the 1700s Dutch and English traders received permission to trade at the southern port of Guangzhou **(gwahng-jo)** (known to the British as Canton).

Eyeing profits, Chinese merchants in coastal cities, who had long traded with Southeast Asia, often supported trade with Europeans. Some merchants specialized in **Chinoiserie (chin-WAH-zur-ee)**, a Western vogue for Chinese ceramics, painting, lacquerware, and decorative furniture whose quality Europeans could not duplicate. Western merchants and diplomats also commissioned Chinese artists to paint Chinese people, costumes, and city scenes using Western artistic techniques. In the early 1800s a merchant's guild, the **Co-hong**, had a monopoly on Guangzhou's trade with the West; its head, Howqua **(how-kwah)** (1769–1843), became one of the world's richest men, famous for his spectacular pleasure garden and lavish mansion, which employed five hundred servants.

Nevertheless, largely self-sufficient in food and resources and not needing foreign trade, Qing emperors refused to permit a more open trade system, restricting trade to a few ports such as Guangzhou and refusing diplomatic relations on an equal basis with the West. Knowing little of the Western world, the Chinese were confused by the diverse Western peoples from half a dozen different countries who did not all speak the same language or practice the

Chinoiserie An eighteenth- and nineteenth-century Western vogue for Chinese painting, ceramics, lacquerware, and decorative furniture.

Co-hong A nineteenth-century Chinese merchant's guild that had a monopoly on Guangzhou's trade with the West.

same religion and customs. Chinese disparagingly termed the Europeans and Americans as "foreign devils." Moreover, viewing European merchants as barbarians bearing tribute, the Qing required visiting diplomats to perform the humiliating custom of prostrating themselves before the emperor (the kotow), leaving little doubt as to the inferior status of the Europeans and convincing them of what they perceived as the emperor's arrogance and inflexibility. But the British, righteously believing that free trade would benefit China, sent a trade mission in 1793 requesting more access. The letter Emperor Qianlong **(chee-YEN-loong)** (r. 1736–1795) sent in response to King George III exemplified China's attitude toward foreign trade and the outside world. The emperor denied Britain permission to establish an embassy but commended the king for his respectful spirit of submission and humility in sending tribute: "Our dynasty's majestic virtue has penetrated into every country under heaven. Our celestial empire possesses all things in prolific abundance. It behooves you, O king, to display ever greater devotion and loyalty in the future, so that by perpetual submission to our throne, you may secure peace and prosperity for your country hereafter."[3] Cultural misunderstanding complicated the Chinese–British relationship.

23-1b Opium Trade and War

Half a century after Emperor Qianlong blithely dismissed the British request, two wars in the mid-1800s, in which Qing China suffered humiliating defeats, forcibly jarred the Chinese from their complacency, making clear that the world was changing. Britain badly wanted more Chinese silk and tea, which were valued revenue sources for British merchants. American traders had begun coming to China for trade in 1784 and also craved these products, especially tea. The tea trade fostered the first

[3]Quoted in Derk Bodde, *China's Cultural Tradition: What and Whither?* (New York: Holt, Rinehart and Winston, 1957), 62–63.

American millionaires (among them John Jacob Astor) and spurred American shipbuilding, including the first speedy clipper ships. But with a few exceptions (such as American ginseng) China, desiring little from the West, accepted only precious gold and silver bullion as payment. Between the 1760s and 1780s silver imports to China increased over 500 percent, presenting balance-of-payment problems for Western economies. Seeking a marketable product to alter this unfavorable trade disparity, the British turned to opium, an addictive drug grown in India and the Middle East, becoming in Chinese eyes essentially drug traffickers, an opinion shared by some modern historians.

The Chinese had used opium as a painkiller since the 1600s. By the later 1700s some smoked opium for pleasure by mixing it in a pipe with tobacco; opium dens were established where people could buy and use opium. The dreamy, relaxed experience produced by the drug temporarily relieved boredom, stress, physical pain, and depression, appealing to officials, wealthy women cooped up at home, busy clerks, anxious merchants, nervous soldiers, and overworked peasants and manual laborers. Highly addictive, it also produced severe withdrawal symptoms such as cramps and nausea.

The British grew opium as a cash crop in Bengal and soon found foreign markets around Asia. In fact, opium sales became an important revenue source for all European colonial governments in Southeast Asia; some critical historians have characterized these governments as glorified "drug cartels" with warships. British and American traders, smuggling opium into China for huge profits, ignored the terrible moral and social consequences, just as drug cartels and dealers do today. Opium trading brought wealth and prominence to various British and American companies and families, helping support universities, schools, churches, and hospitals in cities such as Bristol (England) and Salem (Massachusetts). Between 1800 and 1838 opium imports increased six-fold with 5 to 10 million Chinese becoming addicts. As the opium trade undermined Chinese society and impoverished families, one Chinese official concluded: "opium is nothing else but a flowing poison [which] utterly ruins the minds and morals of the people, a dreadful calamity."[4] Another argued that opium smokers should be strangled and the pushers and producers beheaded.

Just as today, trade disputes between China and the West led to instability and tensions. The emperor prohibited opium marketing, smuggling, and consumption, forcing British, American, and other Western traders to trade through the Co-hong merchant's guild in Guangzhou. But finding that local officials could be bribed to overlook smuggling, the British doubled opium imports during the 1830s while also pressing for trading system reform. In response, the emperor appointed the mandarin Lin Zexu **(lin tsay-shoe)** (1785–1850) to go to Guangzhou and end the opium trade. Lin, an incorruptible Confucian moralist, wrote to Britain's Queen Victoria, arguing that China provided Britain with valuable commodities including silk, tea, spices, and porcelain but the British only sent "poison" in return: "Suppose there were people from another country who carried opium for sale to England and seduced your people into buying and smoking it. Certainly you would be bitterly aroused."[5] He asked the queen to end the trade.

But Chinese and British officials had very different mindsets about international relations and economic exchange. Lin's officials raided the Western settlement, seizing and destroying twenty thousand chests of opium worth millions of dollars. Today Lin is viewed as an upright hero, albeit a tragic one, in China, Taiwan, and among Chinese communities abroad and immortalized in several films as a symbol of Chinese resistance to Western imperialism. A statue of Lin overlooks a park in New York's Chinatown. As a tribute to Lin's efforts, the day the dumping of the opium in Canton ended, June 26, is now celebrated worldwide as the International Day against Drug Abuse and Illicit Trafficking.

In support of outraged Western traders, the British commenced what they called the Opium War (1839–1842). The British public was divided and many opposed opium dealing and use as well as a war to support the drug trade. The House of Commons came within a few votes of stopping the war. A leading opponent and politician argued that "I am in dread of the judgments of God upon England for our national iniquity towards China."[6] The British fleet raided up and down the Chinese coast, blockading and bombarding ports, including Guangzhou. The Chinese fought back, often resisting against hopeless odds, but they lacked the weapons to triumph. Europeans had now greatly surpassed once powerful China in naval and military technology. A few alarmed officials recognized Chinese military inadequacy. Lin Zexu wrote to a friend that China badly needed ships and guns like the British, but most officials rejected such ideas, remaining scornful of all things Western. One official wrote to the emperor that "the English barbarians are a detestable people, trusting entirely to their strong ships and large guns."[7] Average Chinese reacted with rage. One placard in Canton in 1841 was addressed to "rebellious barbarian dogs. If we do not completely exterminate you we will not be manly Chinese able to support the sky over our heads. We are definitely going to kill you, cut your heads off, and burn your bodies in the trash."[8]

British preparations to assault a major Yangzi city, Nanjing, forced the Qing to negotiate for peace (see Map 23.1). In 1842 the Treaty of Nanjing, the first of a series of humiliatingly unequal treaties nibbling away at Chinese sovereignty, gave Britain permanent possession of Hong Kong, a sparsely populated coastal island downriver from Guangzhou; opened five ports to British trade; abolished the Co-hong and its trade monopoly; set fixed tariffs so China no longer controlled its economic policy; and gave the British **extraterritoriality**, or freedom from local laws. In addition, China was required to pay Britain's war costs. Soon other Western countries signed treaties with China giving them the same rights as Britain. Each successive treaty expanded foreign privileges. In 1848 an agent for the British East India Company spirited some high-quality tea seedlings and secrets of production out of China, using them to develop a rival tea industry in British India. As a side effect of the war, the Chinese government, to counteract the revenues lost to imported opium, began growing opium in highland areas of southern China, which made the drug even more available to an ever-growing population of

extraterritoriality Freedom from local laws for foreign subjects.

[4]Chu Tsun, quoted in Hsin-Pao Chang, *Commissioner Lin and the Opium War* (New York: W.W. Norton, 1970), 89.
[5]Quoted in Mark Borthwick, *Pacific Century: The Emergence of Modern East Asia* (Boulder, CO: Westview Press, 1992), 97.
[6]William Gladstone, quoted in Austin Ramzy, "How Britain Went to War with China Over Opium," *New York Times* (July 3, 2018).
[7]Franz Schurman and Orville Schell, eds., *Imperial China* (New York: Vintage Books, 1967), 146.
[8]Ssu-Yu Teng and John K. Fairbank, eds., *China's Response to the West: A Documentary Survey, 1839–1923* (New York: Atheneum, 1963), 26.

addicts, and part of local life at all levels of society. One American journalist wrote that "wrapped in opium dreams, the coolie sloughed off the day's fatigue in some smoky hovel and the banker forgot business cares while he enjoyed ineffable self-satisfaction in his walled compound, with a deft servant to fill his ... pipe."[9] The Opium War became to the Chinese a permanent symbol of Western imperialism and its disastrous consequences for China.

23-1c The Treaty System and Rebellion

The Opium War debacle soon sparked other wars, a treaty system opening China to the West, and rebellions. Britain remained dissatisfied with trade volume while China evaded its obligations, ensuring another conflict. When China imprisoned Chinese sailors for suspected piracy aboard a ship, *The Arrow*, registered in Hong Kong, Britain used the incident as a pretext to attack China, generating the Arrow War (1856–1860). France soon joined on Britain's side. Defeated again, China signed a new unequal treaty that opened more coastal and interior ports to Western traders, established foreign embassies in Beijing, and permitted Christian missionaries to enter interior China. Again forced to pay war costs, China fell deeper into debt. China had to abandon its claim to Vietnam, a longtime vassal state being colonized by France, and acquiesce in Russian takeover of eastern Siberia.

By restricting China's power to control its economy and make rules for Western residents, the treaty system deprived China of considerable autonomy and added to Chinese resentment and distrust of the West that are still apparent today. **International settlements**, zones in major Chinese port cities such as Guangzhou and Shanghai that were set aside for foreigners, restricted Chinese residence. Hence, a small riverfront island adjacent to downtown Guangzhou, accessible only by a footbridge, housed Western merchants, officials, and missionaries. Its mansions, warehouses, clubs, and churches served the largely British, American, and French population, with Chinese unwelcome except as servants or consumers. However, some historians question the popular notion that signs in Shanghai's international settlement warning "no dogs or Chinese allowed" really existed.

The Opium and Arrow Wars and the treaty system forced the Chinese to debate responses. Some officials understood the need to learn from the West, examine Western books, build modern ships and guns, and study science, mathematics, and foreign languages. Provincial official and reformer Zeng Guofan (zung gwoh-FAN) (1811–1872) recommended making modern weapons and steamships. But, failing to see the magnitude of the challenges, few mandarins showed interest, one conservative rejecting Western knowledge as based largely on earlier Chinese discoveries.

international settlements Special zones in major Chinese cities set aside for foreigners, where most Chinese were not allowed; arose as a result of China's defeat in the Opium and Arrow Wars.

While scholars debated, China's problems multiplied, especially in coastal provinces. To pay for wars, the Qing raised taxes, causing many peasants to lose their land; some turned to begging or banditry. Between 1800 and 1850 the Yellow River flooded twenty times and then changed course entirely, wiping out hundreds of towns and villages. Meanwhile, Western cultural influence increased. American and British Christian missionaries opened most of China's Western-type schools and hospitals, providing educational and health benefits to those with access to them. However, Christian missionaries—twenty-five hundred of them Americans by the 1920s—often lived well and were protected by Western military power, challenging Chinese religions and provoking negative opinions. Many Western residents, ethnocentric and proud of their "superior" Western civilization, mocked Chinese culture. For their part, the Chinese often distrusted the several hundred thousand Chinese Christians.

Deteriorating conditions eventually generated the Taiping Rebellion (1850–1864), the most critical of several midcentury upheavals against the Qing. Guangdong (GWAHNG-dong) province, on the southeast coast, experienced particularly severe social and economic dislocations, increasing popular unrest. Many peasant families, having no food surplus, were reduced to eating the chaff of the wheat. Economic insecurity, famine, loss of faith in government, and a desire for social change fueled rebellion. The leader of the rebellion, Hong Xiuquan (hoong shee-OH-chew-an) (1813–1864), who failed the civil service examinations four times, had received confused visions in a trance. Later reading Christian tracts, he believed himself the younger brother of Jesus, appointed by God as the new Son of Heaven to exterminate evil. Impressed by Western military power but also proudly Chinese, Hong crafted a doctrine that blended Christianity and Chinese thought, a mixing of local and Western ideas typical in Asia and Africa as a response to Western disruption.

Hong advocated a new form of government, equal distribution of goods, communal property, and gender equality: "How can it be," he proclaimed, "that this age so full of insults and violations, fighting and killing, cannot in a day be changed into a world where the strong no more oppress the weak, the many overwhelm the few, the wise delude the simple, or the bold annoy the fearful."[10] The puritanical Hong prohibited social ills including opium use, polygamy, footbinding, prostitution, concubinage, and arranged marriages. He established the Taiping (Heavenly Kingdom of Great Peace) sect, rejecting Confucian traditions and promising a God-oriented utopia where all people were equal. Many Taiping men and women were, like Hong himself, Hakkas, a south China group with a distinctive Chinese dialect and several distinctive customs whose assertive women never bound their feet. Hong organized an army and in 1850 launched a rebellion, invoking Chinese nationalism: "We raise the army of righteousness to liberate the masses for the sake of China."[11] Soon he had attracted millions of poor and disaffected supporters.

Taiping armies conquered large parts of central and southern China, but they suffered from leadership conflicts, and their hostility to traditional Chinese culture cost them popular support. Conservative Confucians disliked their espousal of women's rights, which threatened the patriarchal family system, and intellectuals accused them of opening China to Westernization. Most of the educated elite and wealthy merchants rallied to the Qing and some organized provincial armies. Westerners, while often sympathizing with the progressive Taiping social

[9]Quoted in Zheng Yangwen, *The Social Life of Opium in China* (New York: Cambridge University Press, 2005), 189.
[10]Quoted in Jonathan D. Spence, *God's Chinese Son: The Taiping Heavenly Kingdom of Hong Xiuquan* (New York: W.W. Norton, 1996), 91.
[11]Quoted in Jean Chesneaux et al., *China: From the Opium Wars to the 1911 Revolution* (New York: Pantheon, 1976), 123.

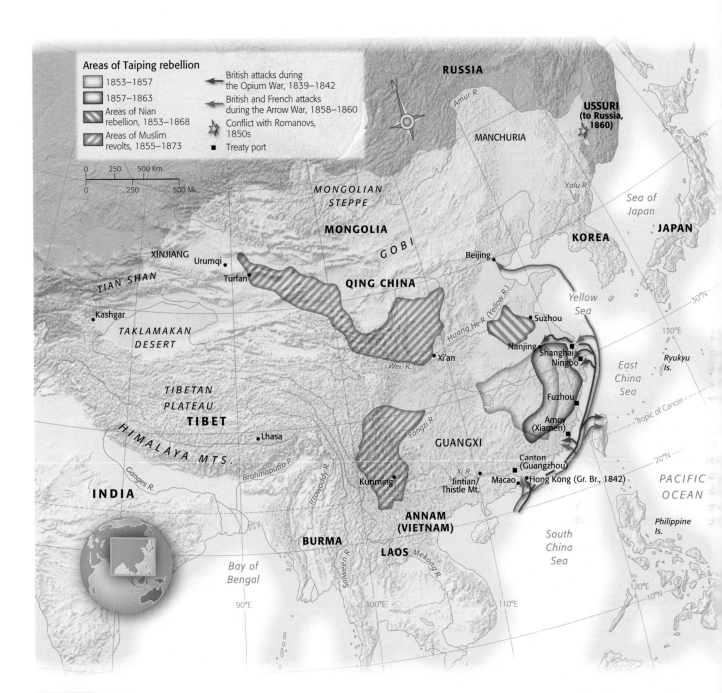

MAP 23.1 **Conflicts in Qing China, 1839–1870** During the mid-1800s Qing China experienced repeated unrest, including several major rebellions. The largest and most destructive, the Taiping Rebellion, engulfed a large part of southern and central China between 1850 and 1864.

Q What does the map tell us about living and political conditions in China in these years?

message, knew that a weak Manchu government made Western exploitation of China easier. Hence, various Western nations aided the Qing with money, arms, mercenary soldiers, and military advisers. The Taiping were defeated, and the conflict, which cost twenty million lives, left China devastated. An American missionary described the destruction: "Ruined cities, desolated towns and heaps of rubble still mark their path. The hum of busy populations had ceased and weeds and jungle cover

the land."[12] The Qing, now deeper in debt, were compelled to adopt even more conciliatory attitudes toward the West.

23-1d Economic Change and Emigration

China's encounters with the West generated economic changes. The extension of Western businesses into the interior stimulated the Chinese merchant class and small-scale Chinese-owned

[12]S. Wells Williams, quoted in John A. Harrison, *China Since 1800* (New York: Harcourt, Brace and World, 1967), 42.

Manufacture of Porcelain: Hand Modelling & Moulding (w/c and gouache on paper), Chinese School, (19th century)/ PEABODY ESSEX MUSEUM/Peabody Essex Museum, Salem, Massachusetts, USA/Bridgeman Images

IMAGE 23.3 **Manufacturing Porcelain**   This nineteenth-century painting shows Chinese artists and craftsmen making pottery and other objects, often for shipment abroad.

Q   What does the painting tell us about the workers, the factory, and their product?

industries, such as match factories and flour mills, but merchants disliked Western economic domination and the weak government. Gradually a new working class formed in mines, factories, railways, and docks. The gulf between peasants and coastal merchants and workers was vast. Unequal treaties enabled Western economic penetration, with China's economy increasingly geared to Western needs. Westerners often operated government agencies, banks, railroads, factories, and mines, guarding them with Western police, and by 1920 foreign companies controlled most of China's iron ore, coal, railroads, and steamships. Western businessmen believed in a vast China market. For example, Standard Oil's kerosene from the United States replaced locally produced vegetable oil in the lamps of China. One U.S. firm launched an advertising campaign to put a cigarette in the mouth of every Chinese man, woman, and child. It was ultimately effective and today China has one of the world's highest rates of smoking, which is a big public health problem. Imported British textiles frequently displaced Chinese women from textile production. Although continuing to weave, women earned lower incomes than before.

Some scholars contend that Western economic imperialism spurred the growth of China's domestic economy, but others believe that Western competition ruined Chinese industries such as cotton spinning and iron and steel production, hurting China's ability to compete with the West. Western businesses enjoyed greater capital and support of Western governments and military power. At the same time, competition from other Asian countries diminished China's traditional exports. By 1900 India and Sri Lanka

were the world's largest producers of tea and Japan of silk. The Qing had little money left for building economic institutions.

From the 1840s through 1930s, deteriorating economic, social, political, and environmental conditions in hard-hit southern coastal provinces prompted millions of Chinese to emigrate, usually to places where Western colonialism and capitalism were opening new economic opportunities. Several hundred thousand people a year left, usually for Southeast Asia but, in many cases, for Pacific islands such as Hawaii, Fiji, and Tahiti or for Australia, New Zealand, Peru, Cuba, the Guianas, North America, South Africa, and several Indian Ocean islands (see Chapters 20 and 22). Chinese emigrants who joined or opened businesses in these new countries formed the basis for mostly urban middle-class Chinese communities. But many left China as part of the notorious "coolie trade." Between 1801 and 1925 three million contract laborers were shipped from China. Westerners called emigrant workers, whether Chinese or Indians, "coolies," a derogatory term. Under this labor system, desperate Chinese, recruited or coerced, became indentured workers in faraway places, signing contracts that required them to labor for years in harsh conditions on plantations, in mines, or in building railroads. Unmarried Chinese women began to emigrate in significant numbers only in the 1920s.

This emigration greatly enlarged the Chinese diaspora to a global scale. The societies where Chinese settled, especially in Southeast Asia, became more closely connected to China through economic and social networks than ever before. Chinese businesses overseas often had branches in China, and families in China maintained ties to relatives abroad. While some Chinese emigrants returned to their native villages with the wealth they earned, others never earned enough to return home, and many settled permanently abroad. Many emigrants and their descendants sustained Chinese culture and language, while others mixed Chinese and local customs. Today some 30 to 40 million people of Chinese ancestry live outside China, the large majority in Southeast Asia. Some finance businesses, industries, and educational institutions in China.

KEY POINTS

▶ In the eighteenth century, Qing China was still thriving on the strength of its agriculture, trade, and manufacturing, but its rapidly growing population began to intensify internal problems such as poverty and corruption.

▶ In the nineteenth century, China faced increasing problems as well as pressure from Westerners for greater trade opportunities, but the Qing refused to allow an open trading system, thus creating a severe trade imbalance between the West and the East.

▶ To solve this imbalance, the British began smuggling opium into China, and when China resisted, the British defeated China in the Opium War and forced the Chinese to agree to highly unfavorable terms that allowed the British to trade in China.

▶ After another war, China was forced to set aside special areas exclusively for Westerners, called international settlements, and to also allow Christian missionaries into the country.

▶ Economic insecurity, famine, and Western interference eventually led to the Taiping Rebellion, a widespread and devastating revolt that was ultimately put down by the Qing with help from Western powers.

▶ Due to poverty and instability in China many Chinese emigrated, temporarily or permanently, to various societies in Southeast Asia, the Americas, several Pacific islands, and southern Africa.

23-2 From Imperial to Republican China

⇄ TRANSITIONS

Q Why did efforts at modernization by Qing reformers and self-strengtheners fail?

Rebellions, government stagnation, poverty, and growing Western demands generated a crisis for the Qing. Some Chinese still concluded that China should reaffirm traditional ways, rejecting the West. But a growing number of reformers wanted to adapt useful Western technologies to Chinese ways. However, the reforms of the imperial government in response to rebellions and wars did not foster the modernization needed to control foreign influence. As setbacks mounted, some gave up on reform and organized revolutionary movements. Eventually revolutionaries overthrew the imperial system, but they could not solve China's problems.

CONNECTION to TODAY

How do you think China would be different today if the Qing modernization policies had worked and the ideas of the liberal reformers had been implemented, perhaps avoiding the revolutions to come?

23-2a Chinese Debates and New Challenges

China's elite divided over whether China should modernize. Conservatives dominating the bureaucracy advised holding fast to Confucian traditions, opposing railroads, underground mines, and other innovations that disrupted harmony between humanity and nature and put boatmen and cart drivers out of work. One conservative wrote it was "better to see the nation die than its way of life change."[13] Conservatives believed that the new technologies undermined social, economic, and even political values. Liberals, believing China had to adopt certain Western ideas to survive, streamlined central and regional governments, set up a foreign ministry, formed a college to train diplomats, and sent some students to schools in the West, especially the United States. Some argued that Confucius favored democracy and gender equality. Few liberals, however, wanted radical transformation, preferring, naively perhaps, to try and graft on some technological innovations while rejecting most Western ideas and institutions. To most reformers, Western ideas such as political democracy and nationalism were not easily adapted to China's family-centered society, which was defined in cultural rather than in political terms. As one noted, "China should acquire the West's superiority in arms and machinery, but retain China's superiority in Confucian virtue."[14]

Reformers in the provinces, calling themselves "self-strengtheners," aimed to strengthen China by building arsenals and shipyards. By 1894 China had a better-trained army and sixty-five warships, but it was still insufficient against a fully industrialized enemy. Reforms failed to save the Qing because technological innovations generated new problems. New warships required coal to make steam power, which required improved coal-mining technology. Moving coal necessitated building railroads, which needed telegraphs to communicate train

---

[13]Hsu Tung, quoted in Joseph R. Levenson, *Confucian China and Its Modern Fate: A Trilogy* (Berkeley: University of California Press, 1968), 105.
[14]Quoted in Earl Swisher, "Chinese Intellectuals and the Western Impact, 1838–1900," *Comparative Studies in Society and History* 1 (October 1958): 35.

movements. Training workers for these new enterprises required technical schools. Furthermore, the new working class did not fit into the Confucian social categories of scholars, peasants, artisans, and merchants. Although Western advisers helped set up and manage new industries and government departments, the new enterprises were often poorly run. Costly innovations further complicated the problems of a Chinese government financing a growing debt to Western nations and banks.

China's problems grew less manageable. China was too large, overpopulated, and saddled with a poorly led, bureaucratic, and overly conservative government. From 1861 to 1908 Empress Dowager Ci Xi **(zoo shee)** (1835–1908), the old emperor's barely literate concubine, held the real power. He had chosen her to share his bed because of her respectful behavior, good looks, and ability to sing. After his death she became the regent of the new child emperor, allowing her to dominate the imperial government and the intrigue-filled, male-dominated court from behind the scenes (in this case, a screen in the throne room). Women had more freedom in Manchu than in Chinese society. Unlike Chinese, Manchu women could divorce, ride horseback, practice archery, and hunt with men and did not bind their feet. Some royal women also read books, did calligraphy, painted, and tutored the princes of the realm. Several Qing empresses had played influential roles under earlier emperors, but none were as powerful as Ci Xi. Until recently most who wrote about her were men, who tended to stereotype strong women, especially leaders, as irrational, ruthless, and power hungry. In response, several studies have argued that she was kind of a feminist, a controversial opinion. Forceful and intelligent but also covetous, irresponsible, strong-willed, and, like many at court, an opium smoker, she diverted money for building a modern navy to construct the magnificent Summer Palace, just outside Beijing, for her personal retreat. A popular tourist attraction today, it is a wonderland of beautiful lakes, wooden pavilions, and luxurious gardens, but the project's cost drained the government treasury. China's inability to deflect growing challenges fostered escapism and disenchantment among many thoughtful Chinese, expressed by a poet official: "I'll drink myself merry, Thrash out a wild song from my lute, And let the storms rage at will."[15]

Foreign economic and political pressures also placed constraints on what China could accomplish, fostering a siege mentality. By the late 1800s Western gunboats patrolled China's rivers, international settlements existed in major cities, Christian missionaries challenged Chinese values, and Westerners influenced the imperial government and economy. Some foreign powers dominated particular regions as spheres of influence, such as Britain in Guangdong and Germany in Shandong, acquiring resources, establishing enterprises, and manipulating local governments. The effects still linger in some places today. Hence, breweries in Shandong, where German influence was strong, still produce some of China's best and most popular beers.

The United States, Britain, France, and Germany exercised power through **gunboat diplomacy**, the use of superior firepower to impose a foreign country's will on local populations and governments. Western gunboats patrolled some rivers and seacoasts in the late 1800s and early 1900s, protecting Western businessmen, missionaries, and diplomats whose activities generated Chinese hostility. Ignoring sovereign Chinese rights and outrage at foreign intrusion, a notorious U.S. naval force, the Yangzi Patrol, comprising shallow-draft gunboats, destroyers, and cruisers, patrolled hundreds of miles of the Yangzi River "to make every American feel perfectly safe in coming to live or to transact business, until such time as the Chinese themselves are able to afford these guarantees."[16] This involvement in China's internal affairs helped foster China's outspoken opposition today to Western countries interfering in the affairs of China or any other country. Americans also promoted free trade, generously funded Christian missionaries, and donated to humanitarian causes such as flood relief and orphanages. Yet China never became a full Western colony such as India or Vietnam, perhaps because too many foreign powers were involved. The United States promoted an "open-door" policy that allowed equal access by all the foreign powers to China's vast markets and resources, enabling industrialized nations to avoid conflict and acquire wealth without the high political and military costs of conquering and governing China.

23-2b Wars, Reforms, and Nationalism

During the middle and late nineteenth century China lost influence over various tributary states, such as Vietnam (to France), Burma (to Britain), and the Ryukyu **(ree-OO-kyoo)** Islands (to Japan). Growing foreign challenges soon included rapidly industrializing Japan. Seeking resources and markets, in the 1890s Japan intervened in Korea. A long-time vassal state of China, Koreans pleaded for help from Japan. The resulting Sino-Japanese War (1894–1895) ended in humiliating defeat, with China forced to pay Japan an indemnity and recognize Korean independence; in 1910 Korea became a Japanese colony. The Qing were also forced by the defeat to cede to Japan the large island of Taiwan, populated largely by Chinese. The defeat by Japan damaged Chinese pride and the Qing rulers' credibility.

A group of progressive reformers began advising the young Manchu emperor, Guangxu, and in 1898 he called for dramatic changes, later known as the 100 Days of Reform, that included economic modernization. But the Empress Dowager Xi Ci and her conservative allies blocked the proposals, arrested the reformers, placed the emperor under house arrest, promoted an antiforeign atmosphere, and encouraged Chinese to organize antiforeign militias. The ensuing tensions sparked the Boxer Rebellion, a Qing-backed popular movement in 1900 to drive foreigners out of China. While the Boxers ("Righteous Harmony Fists"), a predominantly peasant, anti-Western, anti-Christian secret society, attacked foreigners in north China, occupied Beijing, and besieged the foreign embassies, the Qing declared war on the foreign powers. But the British, Americans, and French organized an international force that routed the Boxers, occupied Beijing, and forced the Qing to pay another huge indemnity and permit foreign military forces in China.

gunboat diplomacy The Western countries' use of superior firepower to impose their will on local populations and governments in the nineteenth century.

[15]Wang Pengyun, from Cyril Birch, ed., *Anthology of Chinese Literature* (New York: Grove Press, 1972), 294.
[16]Quoted in Lloyd Gardner, *Safe for Democracy: The Anglo-American Response to Revolution, 1913–1923* (New York: Oxford University Press, 1984), 318.

Source: Library of Congress Prints and Photographs Division [LC-USZ62-5972]

IMAGE 23.4 **Sun Yat Sen** The main founder of the Chinese nationalist movement, Sun challenged the Qing government and formulated the ideology of the Chinese republic.

Q What can you tell about Sun and his demeanor from the photo?

Europeans talked openly of dismantling China; Russians used the rebellion to occupy Manchuria. These actions further enraged Chinese.

The defeats generated frantic efforts at reform and modernization. Fearing China might soon be divided into colonies, the chastened Qing looked to Japan for models, abolished the two-thousand-year-old Confucian examination system, allocated more money to the military, strengthened provincial governments and former provincial and national assemblies (which met in 1909–1910), sent ten thousand students to Japan, and established modern Western-style schools. But the fifty-seven thousand state schools enrolled only a fraction of China's school-age children, and Manchus still monopolized decision making.

Reformist ideas also sparked movements among women. Some women studying in Japan formed the Encompassing Love Society, which sought to make Chinese women full participants in society. Other women worked to raise female literacy and expand economic opportunities. The feminist Zhang Zhuzhun encouraged Chinese women to emulate Western women role models such as British nurse Florence Nightingale and

American anti-slavery crusader Harriett Beecher Stowe. Later executed as a revolutionary, feminist Qin Jin **(chin jin)** (1877–1907) left her arranged marriage for study in Japan and then started a women's magazine and pursued political activity. She wrote in a poem, "Our women's world is sunk so deep, who can help us? Unbinding my feet I clear out a thousand years of poison."[17] She hoped China would one day see free women "blooming like fields of flowers."

Gradually liberals who criticized Qing reforms as too slow became more influential. Many reformers familiar with European literature and scholarship were deeply impressed by Japan's modernization. The leading liberal, scholar and journalist Liang Qichao **(Li-ANG chi-CHAO)** (1871–1929), promoted modernization that blended Confucian values and Western learning. He supported industrialization, constitutional government, and a focus on the nation instead of culture. Liang's colleague, Kang Youwei **(KANG yoo-WAY)** (1858–1928), envisioned a world government, a welfare state, and the end of nationalist strife and gender discrimination. He also campaigned against footbinding, the longtime practice that severely hampered women, as expressed by a song passed among illiterate women: "Your body is so heavy a burden for your feet that you fear you may stumble in the wind."[18]

For some Chinese nationalists, most importantly Sun Zhong Shan (1866–1925), better known in the West as Sun Yat-sen **(soon yot-SEN)**, the Boxer Rebellion fiasco showed the futility of reform from above, prompting them to organize revolution from below. Unlike liberal reformers Liang and Kang, Sun did not come from an upper-class Mandarin background. Having no commitment to the traditional system, he identified with the poor and downtrodden, calling himself a coolie's son. Born near Guangzhou to a peasant family that supported the Taipings, at age thirteen Sun joined an elder brother in Hawaii, where he studied in an Anglican high school. Later he was baptized as a Christian but rarely attended church and tended to view the faith as part of a larger modernizing and revolutionary thrust for China. After receiving a medical degree in British-ruled Hong Kong, he dressed in Western clothes and visited England, where he learned that Westerners often criticized their own governments.

Convinced the Qing system was hopeless, Sun devoted his life to politics and became the Chinese Revolution's chief architect. In 1895 he founded a secret society dedicated to replacing the imperial system with a Western-style republic, and branches of the society were formed in China, Japan, and Hawaii (see Discover Historical Voices: Planning a Revolutionary New China). Facing arrest in China for treason, Sun traveled extensively, recruiting support among Chinese merchants in Southeast Asia, North America, and the treaty ports; among Chinese students in Japan; and among sympathetic military officers. Traditionally Chinese tended to think of themselves as part of a family, village, and culture or civilization rather than as belonging to a political unit or state with fixed boundaries. But Sun and his followers considered themselves nationalists, more interested in China as a nation, like in the modern West, than as a culture.

[17]Quoted in Jonathan D. Spence, *The Gate of Heavenly Peace: The Chinese and Their Revolution, 1895–1980* (New York: Viking, 1981), 52.
[18]Quoted in Ono Kazuko, *Chinese Women in a Century of Revolution* (Stanford, CA: Stanford University Press, 1989), 30.

Discover Historical Voices

Planning a Revolutionary New China

In 1905 various radical Chinese groups, meeting in Japan, merged into one revolutionary organization, the Tongmen Hui (Chinese Alliance Association), that was led by Sun Yat-sen and based in Tokyo. Most members were drawn from the ten thousand Chinese students enrolled in Japanese universities. Unhappy with the Qing and impressed by modernizing Japan, they sought to change China through revolution. In their founding proclamation, influenced by Western thought, they set out their agenda, visionary but vague, for a three-stage passage from military to constitutional government and a more equitable society.

Since the beginning of China as a nation, we Chinese have governed our own country despite occasional interruptions. When China was occasionally occupied by a foreign race, our ancestors could always…drive these foreigners out…and preserve China for future generations….There is a difference, however, between our revolution and the revolutions of our ancestors. The purpose of past revolutions…was to restore China to the Chinese, and nothing else. We, on the other hand, strive not only to expel the ruling aliens [Manchus]…but also to change basically the political and economic structure….The revolutions of yesterday were revolutions by and for the heroes; our revolution, on the other hand, is a revolution by and for the people….everyone who believes in the principles of liberty, equality, and fraternity has an obligation to participate in it….

At this juncture we wish to express candidly and fully how to make our revolution today and how to govern the country tomorrow.

1. Expulsion of the Manchus from China….We shall quickly overthrow the Manchu government so as to restore the sovereignty of China to the Chinese.
2. Restoration of China to the Chinese. China belongs to the Chinese who have the right to govern themselves….
3. Establishment of a Republic. Since one of the principles of our revolution is equality, we intend to establish a

republic….All citizens will have the right to participate in the government, the president of the republic will be elected by the people, and the parliament will have deputies elected by and responsible to their respective constituencies….

4. Equalization of land ownership. The social and economic structure of China must be so reconstructed that the fruits of labor will be shared by all Chinese on an equal basis….

To attain the four goals…, we propose a procedure of three stages. The first…is that of military rule…[in which] the Military Government, in cooperation with the people, will eradicate all the abuses of the past; with the arrival of the second stage the Military Government will hand over local administration to the people while reserving for itself the right of jurisdiction over all matters that concern the nation as a whole; during the…final stage the Military Government will cease to exist and all governmental power will be invested in organs as prescribed in a national constitution. This orderly procedure is necessary because our people need time to acquaint themselves with the idea of liberty and equality…, the basis on which the republic of China rests….On…restoring China to her own people, we urge everyone to step forward and to do the best he can….Whatever our station in society is, rich or poor, we are all equal in our determination to safeguard the security of China as a nation and to preserve the Chinese people.

Reflection Questions

1. How does the proclamation use Western revolutionary and nationalist ideas?
2. How will revolution build a new China?
3. Do you think some of the ideas in this document could be a blueprint for China today?

Source: Pei-Kai Cheng and Michael Lestz with Jonathan D. Spence, eds., *The Search for Modern China: A Documentary Collection* (New York: W.W. Norton, 1999), 202–206.

Sun began developing his program, the "Three Principles of the People." The first principle, nationalism, involved overthrowing the Qing, restoring ethnic Chinese to power, and reclaiming China's historical greatness. His second principle, republicanism, proposed constitutional democracy with elected representative government, rather than the constitutional monarchy liberal reformers sought. The third principle, people's livelihood, envisioned an equitable economic status for all. Vague on details, Sun favored partial state control of the economy and the reshaping of China into a modern, wealthy, powerful nation. He did not support imitating Europe and the United States, but eventually, he hoped, the Chinese could look over their shoulders and find the West lagging far behind.

23-2c Chinese Revolution and Republic

Sun was raising money in the United States when, on October 10, 1911, some followers began the uprising. Soldiers in a Yangzi River city, Wuhan (**WOO-HAHN**), mutinied and were soon joined by sympathizers in other cities. Within two months revolutionary soldiers controlled provinces in central and southern China. As Qing authority crumbled outside the north, Sun returned to China for the first time in sixteen years. With wide popular support, his nationalist message spread rapidly, especially among students, military officers, and Chinese in the treaty ports. Reorganizing his anti-Manchu secret society into a political party, the Guomindang (**gwo-min-dong**) (Chinese

Nationalist Party), Sun gathered varied nationalists and liberal reformers. However, the revolutionaries agreed only on opposing the Qing, and Sun was not a forceful leader. When the Qing asked an ambitious general, Yuan Shikai (**yoo-AHN shee-KAI**) (1859–1916), to crush the revolutionaries, Yuan, in control of a large army, decided to replace the dynasty with his own rule by playing the Manchus against the revolutionaries.

Two centers of power now existed. General Yuan held power in the north and influence over Qing leaders in Beijing, while the revolutionaries, controlling the Yangzi Valley and parts of south China, made plans for a provisional government. Seeking compromise to save China from civil war, Sun made Yuan president for arranging the five-year-old Qing emperor's abdication. In February 1912 the Qing dynasty and the two-thousand-year-old imperial system ended, and a republic was established in Nanjing. Symbolizing a change of direction, the new government adopted the Western calendar. But Sun underestimated Yuan's ambitions. Hoping to restore and lead an autocratic system, Yuan moved the capital back to Beijing. On the centenary of the 1911 revolution Chinese scholars debated the causes and significance of the empire's collapse. Rather than highlighting Sun's relatively divided and weak revolutionary movement, they identified the main causes as political and socioeconomic change in China, which created new social forces and political movements that undermined dynastic legitimacy, including on the frontiers.

During the first year, the republic's leaders established liberal institutions, including a constitution written by Sun providing for a two-chamber parliament and a president. In 1913, in China's first general election, a restricted electorate chose a national assembly and provincial assemblies, while a new women's suffrage movement, influenced by European feminists, pressed for equal rights for women. But although Sun's Guomindang won a majority of seats, it lacked consensus about the directions of change. The republican system failed to bring stability and liberty, dashing Sun's hopes. Convinced that China needed a strong leader, Yuan had Guomindang leaders assassinated, bought off, or, like Sun, forced into exile. Supported by much of the army, the imperial bureaucracy, and foreign powers, who preferred a strongman to democratic uncertainties, Yuan outlawed the Guomindang, suspended parliament, and banned the women's suffrage movement. Sun and his closest followers moved to Japan, embittered and demoralized. Increasingly autocratic, Yuan announced plans to found a new dynasty.

Financial problems, constant pressure from foreign powers, and secession of regions occupied largely by non-Chinese delayed Yuan's plans. Moreover, growing nationalism made concessions to foreign powers unpopular. With China bankrupt, Yuan was forced to borrow heavily from foreign governments to keep the country afloat. In 1911 much of Mongolia declared independence and later became allied with Russia, while Tibet expelled the Chinese administration. Although China remained neutral during World War I, Japan, allied with Britain, occupied Germany's sphere of influence in the Shandong peninsula. In 1915 Japan presented Yuan with 21 Demands, including control of Shandong, more rights in Manchuria, and Japanese advisers to China's government. The 21 Demands sparked huge Chinese protests and boycotts against Japan and against Yuan for his inability to protect China's interests. His imperial restoration plans aborted, a humiliated Yuan died in 1916. The liberal reformer Liang Qiqao concluded scornfully that Yuan, by assuming that everything could be bought with gold and intimidated by the sword, caused his own downfall while ruining China. Yuan's years in power had wrecked republican institutions, and his submission to Japan's 21 Demands suggested that China was even weaker than before. After Yuan's death, China fell into the abyss of prolonged civil war.

KEY POINTS

▶ In the debate over what China should do next, conservatives thought the country should stick to its traditions, while liberals tried to modernize China, but their reforms failed to bring it to the technological and military level of the West.

▶ Sun Yat-sen, born to Chinese peasants but educated in Western schools, formed a secret society devoted to replacing imperial rule with a Western-style republic and set out three principles: nationalism, republicanism, and economic equality.

▶ A revolution inspired by Sun Yat-sen succeeded in toppling the Qing dynasty with the assistance of General Yuan Shikai.

▶ Yuan seized power after Sun Yat-sen's party won the republic's first election, but he was weakened by Japanese encroachment and the loss of influence over areas such as Mongolia and Tibet, and after his death China entered a period of civil war.

23-3 The Remaking of Japan and Korea

TRANSITIONS SOCIETIES

Q How did the Meiji government transform Japan and Korea?

In the later nineteenth century Japan met Western challenges more successfully than China and rapidly transformed itself into a powerful industrialized nation. When the first Western ships demanded to open Japan,

CONNECTION to TODAY

What legacies of the Tokugawa and Meiji eras can you perceive in Japan today?

the Japanese were as far behind the West in military and industrial technology as other Asian societies. Yet, despite serious internal problems, Japan possessed significant strengths, and its response was radically different from China's; it avoided colonialism and became the only non-Western nation to successfully industrialize before World War II. Tokugawa shoguns, or military dictators, had governed Japan since 1600, tightly controlling the country. A revolution ended Tokugawa rule and created a new government whose dramatic reforms helped Japan resist the West. By 1900 Japan had developed heavy industry, a modern military, and a comprehensive educational system and began seeking resources and markets abroad. Across the straits, Korea also faced severe challenges, eventually becoming a Japanese colony.

23-3a Late Tokugawa Japan

While China gradually lost some of its autonomy, Japan successfully met the challenge of Western intrusion, thanks partly to differences between these two ancient neighbors. Living in a geographically compact and linguistically homogeneous country, the Japanese shared a strong loyalty to the emperor as a national symbol, whereas China's vastness meant that loyalties were restricted largely to the family and local community; many Chinese held little reverence for the imperial family in distant Beijing. The Chinese slowly assimilated or modified foreign ideas, such as Buddhism, whereas the Japanese readily borrowed from outside. Hence, Japanese leaders could more easily decide to import and adopt new ideas, technologies, and institutions.

The two neighbors also had different economic, political, and military systems. Japan's assertive merchant class rapidly expanded its scope and power, whereas China's government restricted commercial energies. Unlike in China's centralized empire, Tokugawa shoguns, based in Edo (today's Tokyo), had to balance the interests of regional landowning families while keeping the Kyoto-based emperor powerless. Although the samurai had lost their fighting edge, they still held a respected and influential position. Never successfully invaded, the Japanese felt vulnerable when encountering well-armed Westerners. Unlike the Chinese, Japanese leaders prized political independence far more than cultural purity, and hence, informed by Dutch traders of Western capabilities, were far more sensitive to the threat than China's elite.

Japan also benefited from openness to new ideas. Its many schools fostered high literacy rates, and it acquired Western knowledge from Dutch traders that included sciences such as medicine, physics, and chemistry. One reformer argued that "Dutch [Western] learning is not perfect, but if we choose the good points, what harm could come? What is more ridiculous than to refuse to discuss its merits?"[19] Although women generally suffered a low status and were subject to rigid social expectations of marriage, domesticity, and motherhood, some gained an education. Poet and painter Ema Saiko (1787–1861) compared her reading with her father's: "My father deciphers Dutch books; His daughter reads Chinese poetry. Divided by a single lamp, We each follow our own course."[20] There were also some female samurai (known as *onna-bugeisha*), a tradition that began as early as 200 CE. During the Tokugawa era they

were trained in skilled combat as a method of moral discipline and learned how to protect their villages. Every year during the autumn festival Japanese girls join in a procession in memory of samurai Nakano Takeko and her all-woman army who died protecting their castle from imperial forces in 1868.

Japanese also valued hard work, thrift, saving, and cooperation—attributes that facilitated modernization. Cities such as Edo and Osaka, already among the world's largest, offered flourishing commerce and diverse entertainments. For example, a carnival in Edo in 1865 included many amusements, services, and vendors: kabuki theater, archery booths, fortune tellers, wandering balladeers, massage healers, barbershops, and peddlers of chilled water, sushi (raw fish), confectionery, stuffed fritters, dumplings, fried eel livers, toys, and lanterns.

Vigorous Tokugawa arts produced ceramics, jewelry, and furniture that achieved worldwide renown, enriching Dutch traders at Nagasaki. The Japanese also produced outstanding paintings and woodblock prints, the two greatest artists blending Japanese and imported art styles. Katsushika Hokusai (**HO-koo-sie**) (1760–1849) created thousands of paintings but was most famous for landscape prints such as the *Thirty-six Views of Mount Fuji*. He strove to improve his craft, predicting that "by ninety I will surely have penetrated the mystery of life. At one hundred, I will have attained a magnificent level and at one hundred and ten, each dot of my work will vibrate with life."[21] Ando Hiroshige (**AN-do hir-o-SHEE-gee**) (1797–1858) concentrated on Tokyo scenes and landscapes emphasizing nature (see Meet the People: Hiroshige, Japanese Artist). The Japanese treatment of atmosphere and light in color prints influenced French impressionist painters of the later 1800s (see Chapter 20), especially influential Dutch artist Vincent van Gogh. Both Japanese prints and French impressionism asked viewers to look at an everyday scene in a new way.

23-3b Growing Problems and the Opening of Japan

By the early 1800s many Japanese blamed the Tokugawa for growing problems: inflation, increasing taxes, social disorder, and gradual samurai impoverishment. As daimyo families, burdened with heavy expenses, cut salaries, their samurai borrowed money from merchants to support their own families. In the 1830s Japan also experienced widespread famine, while growing social tensions fostered urban riots, peasant revolts, and plots to depose the shogun. Finally, the growing Western presence in the region worried officials. They knew that Russians were active in Siberia and the North Pacific and that British ships were sailing along Japan's coast. The shogun ordered samurai to fire on foreign ships approaching the coast. After China's defeat in the Opium War, Japan's shocked leaders encouraged samurai to develop more effective weapons. The Japanese considered Westerners money-grubbing barbarians who did not understand proper social behavior. The samurai, vowing to resist to the death, pressured the shogun to deal firmly with the threat.

---

[19]Otsuki Gentaku, quoted in Mikiso Hane, *Modern Japan: A Historical Survey*, 2nd ed. (Boulder, CO: Westview Press, 1992), 59.

[20]Quoted in Patricia Fister, "Female *Bunjin*: The Life of Poet-Painter Ema Saiko," in *Recreating Japanese Women, 1600–1945*, ed. Gail Lee Bernstein (Berkeley: University of California Press, 1991), 109.

[21]Quoted in Matthi Ferrer, *Hokusai* (New York: Barnes and Noble, 2002), 9.

Tokugawa reforms, such as establishing a bureau to translate Western books and reducing the number of government officials to save money, failed to energize the system. Some provincial governments in the southwest attempted more daring changes, recruiting talented men to their administrations, emphasizing "Dutch studies," and even sponsoring industrial experiments, including an electric steam engine. Some samurai learned how to cast better guns and iron suitable for making modern cannon.

External threats arising in the 1850s made the need for change urgent. Americans provided the most dramatic attempt to break down Japanese seclusion. American ships occasionally visited the Dutch base at Nagasaki to trade. U.S. leaders also wanted Japan to protect shipwrecked sailors and provide fresh water and coal to ships sailing between California and China. In 1853 eleven U.S. warships commanded by Commodore Matthew Perry sailed into Tokyo Bay to deliver a letter from the U.S. president, Millard Fillmore, demanding that the shogun sign a treaty opening the country or face war when Perry returned the following year. The U.S. expedition's three steamships, known as the "black ships" and described by local observers as "giant dragons puffing smoke," shocked the Japanese with their ability to move against wind and tide. The wife of a samurai who had been ordered to prepare sea defenses wrote an anti-American poem: "If they [the Americans] stop hiding, In shadows and come into/ The light of the land/ Of the rising sun, they will melt,/ Those ships from America."[22]

The shogun, more realistic than his critics about Japan's military weakness, granted Perry's demands in the Treaty of Kanagawa (1854) and then accepted blame for the nation's humiliation. The treaty opened two ports to U.S. trade and permitted stationing of a U.S. consul. Soon, American diplomats demanded more ports, extraterritoriality, and admission of Christian missionaries. The shogun reluctantly agreed, signing similar treaties with the Dutch, British, French, and Russians. As in China and India earlier, Western merchants flooded Japan with cheap industrial goods to create markets and destroy native industries. International settlements restricted to foreigners arose in major port cities, while Westerners enjoyed ever-increasing economic and legal privileges.

Western encroachment provoked a crisis and national debate about how Japan should respond. Some Japanese, believing accommodation preferable to war, favored opening to the West. One prominent Westernizer, Fukuzawa Yukichi (FOO-koo-ZAH-wa you-KEE-chee) (1835–1901), traveled in the West and became a strong proponent of liberalism, rationalism, and political freedom, writing, "I find that Japanese civilization will advance only after we sweep away the old spirit that permeates the minds of the people."[23] To convey his enthusiasm for learning from the West Yukichi wrote many books read by millions of Japanese, published a successful newspaper, and founded a school that later became one of Japan's best universities, Keio. Although never serving in

the Meiji government, he had huge influence on the country. Others found the Western model appalling. One Confucian wrote a scathing critique of Western script, describing the writing as "confused and irregular, wriggling like snakes or larvae or mosquitoes. The straight ones are like dog's teeth, the round ones are like worms."[24] Another group, advocating complete defiance and expelling the intruders by force, argued that Americans had dishonored and might enslave Japan. Turning against the ineffective Tokugawa shoguns but not the powerless emperor who symbolized the nation, one faction proclaimed, "Revere the Emperor, Expel the Barbarians."

Shaken, the Tokugawa launched efforts at modernization. They established a shipbuilding industry, promoted manufacturing, hired two hundred Western teachers, sent a few Japanese students abroad, established an institute of Western studies, and expanded the study of foreign languages. Japanese already interested in Western science and technology, however, considered these innovations too little and too late. Now widely perceived as weak, the shogun always chose negotiation, even when Westerners badly misused their power and retaliated for any attacks on Western residents. A respected poet complained angrily: "You, whose ancestors in the mighty days, Roared at the skies and swept the earth, Stand now helpless to drive off wrangling foreigners—How empty your title, 'Queller of the Barbarians.'"[25] By the 1860s Japan seemed to be repeating China's experience, gradually losing control of its political and economic future.

23-3c Tokugawa Defeat and the Meiji Restoration

However, in a remarkable awakening, the Japanese responded to the challenges very differently than Qing China. The deteriorating situation sparked a revolution against the Tokugawa, known as the **Meiji Restoration** (1867–1868) because it was carried out in the name of the emperor, whose reign name was Meiji (MAY-gee). The revolutionaries, progressive daimyo and younger samurai from southwestern Japan, were united by hatred of the status quo but had varied goals. Generally pragmatic, some were avid Westernizers, others extreme nationalists. From privileged families, they allied with commoners, especially merchants.

Rejecting the discredited shogun, dissidents turned to the relatively powerless Meiji emperor living in seclusion in Kyoto. In 1868 anti-Tokugawa military forces seized the imperial palace and convinced the emperor to decree restoration of his own rule, ousting the Tokugawa from their land and positions, opening government to men of talent, appointing rebel leaders as imperial advisers, and announcing that "the evil customs of the past shall be broken off. Knowledge shall be sought throughout the world."[26] The

Meiji Restoration A revolution against the Tokugawa Shogunate in Japan in 1867–1868, carried out in the name of the Meiji emperor; led to the successful modernization of Japan.

[22]Kawai Koume, quoted in Donald Keene, *Modern Japanese Diaries: The Japanese at Home and Abroad as Revealed Through Their Diaries* (New York: Columbia University Press, 1998), 274–275.
[23]Quoted in John Benson and Takao Matsumura, *Japan, 1868–1945: From Isolation to Occupation* (London: Pearson, 2001), 133.
[24]Shinoya Toin, quoted in Conrad Schirokauer and Donald N. Clark, *Modern East Asia: A Brief History*, 2nd ed. (Boston: Houghton Mifflin, 2008), 149.
[25]Yanagawa Seigan, quoted in H. D. Hartoonian, *Toward Restoration: The Growth of Political Consciousness in Tokugawa Japan* (Berkeley: University of California Press, 1970), 1–2.
[26]Quoted in Paul Varley, *Japanese Culture*, 4th ed. (Honolulu: University of Hawaii Press, 2000), 238.

Hiroshige, Japanese Artist

Nineteenth-century Japanese artist Ando Hiroshige (1797–1858) gained a worldwide reputation for reflecting a distinctly Japanese vision of landscape and urban life. His work, like that of his four-decades-older contemporary, Katsushika Hokusai, portrayed old Japan on the eve of dramatic change, a Japan of rice fields, small shops, traveling peddlers, sedan chairs, samurai warriors, and dirt roads rather than the later Japan of factories, conglomerates, railroads, and steamships. By portraying scenery and diverse urban scenes, Hiroshige and Hokusai carried printmaking far beyond the early Tokugawa tradition, which emphasized life in the restaurants, teahouses, theaters, and bordellos of the "Floating World" entertainment districts.

Hiroshige was born into a samurai family in Edo (Tokyo) in 1797. Since his father was a member of the fire brigade, the family lived at the fire station. As a child, Hiroshige learned to read, write, and master martial arts, and he also developed a talent for poetry. Like other young samurai, he probably visited the Floating World to enjoy kabuki theater and patronize courtesans. In 1809 the twelve-year-old youngster succeeded to his father's position as a fireman. Underpaid and enjoying art more than firefighting, he began studying with several famous artists. From this time on he used the name Utagawa Hiroshige, a tribute to the Utagawa school of art in which he had been trained. Dutch traders at Nagasaki had introduced Western art to Japan, and Hiroshige probably assimilated ideas from imported Dutch etchings. The young artist was inspired by mountains, rivers, rocks, and trees and gained a working knowledge of different modes and techniques to use in depicting them. Influenced by Hokusai's pioneering work, Hiroshige favored rural landscapes and Edo scenes. At twenty-seven he passed on his fire brigade post to his son and pursued art full time.

Although having much in common, Hokusai and Hiroshige had different outlooks. Hokusai's landscapes divided attention between the setting and the people in it, usually workers such as weavers, carpenters, and spinners. By contrast, Hiroshige subordinated everything to the setting, especially to the mood established by weather, season, time of day, and angle of view. Influenced by Chinese art, Hiroshige portrayed the insignificance of humans against the vastness of nature. His rain and snow scenes are marvels of mood, showing mastery of light and subtle harmony, mixing fact with imagination.

Hiroshige's art often reflected his personal experiences. In 1832, while accompanying an embassy of the Tokugawa shogun to the imperial court in Kyoto, Hiroshige gathered material for his famous work, *The 53 Stations of the Tokaido*, which depicts scenes of villages, inns, and lakes along the Tokaido (Eastern Sea Route) highway connecting Tokyo and Kyoto. Hiroshige

The Road to Mount Fuji (woodblock print), Hiroshige, Ando or Utagawa (1797–1858)/ NATIONAL TRUST IMAGES/Cragside, Northumberland, UK/Bridgeman Images

IMAGE 23.5 The Road to Mount Fuji This 1856 woodblock print from Hiroshige shows Edo's Surugacho Quarter, wth a street, lined by shops, running straight to the majestic mountain.

Q What does the woodblock suggest about city life and the importance of Mount Fuji?

immortalized the highway, which skirted the Pacific coast of Honshu Island, where mountains sweep down to the sea, and then traversed inland through majestic snowcapped mountains and past beautiful Lake Biwa. A continued stream of people—daimyo and their processions, couriers, monks, pilgrims, merchants, adventurers, entertainers—traveled the well-maintained Tokaido to and from the shogun's court. Stations with inns, restaurants, brothels, and bathhouses flourished as rest stops for the bustling traffic.

Since many Japanese had money to indulge in art, Hiroshige's later collections of prints sold thousands of copies, and he remained a very popular artist. Townspeople loved this art reflecting daily life or the worldly dreams of the merchant class. Hiroshige produced some fifty-five hundred different prints, sold individually or in collections such as the *53 Stations of the Tokaido* and *One Hundred Views of Famous Places in Edo*. However, his personal life was often troubled. Hiroshige, never prospering financially, was often pressed to finance his beloved nightly cup of rice wine. He married several times and sired several children. His eldest daughter's husband, known as Hiroshige II (1826–1869), continued Hiroshige's artistic tradition. At sixty Hiroshige became a Buddhist monk, not an unusual step for aging Japanese men. In 1858 he died at sixty-two of cholera during a great epidemic. On his deathbed, he discouraged his family from holding a lavish funeral by reciting an old verse: "When I die, Cremate me not nor bury me. Just lay me in the fields, to fill the belly of some starving dog."

Hiroshige was the last of the major Japanese print masters. Shortly after he died, Westerners opened up Japan, ending the secluded world that had nourished the woodblock prints and the artists who produced them. But Hiroshige prints continued to be traded around the world, giving foreigners their most vivid impressions of Japan. When Europeans imported the pictures in the late 1800s, they proved a revelation to artists looking for new ways to portray landscapes. Hence woodblock prints, born of isolation, became one of the first major cultural links between Japan and the outside world.

Reflection Questions

1. How did Hokusai and Hiroshige's prints differ from earlier Japanese prints?
2. What do Hiroshige's life and art tell us about late Tokugawa Japan?
3. How do you think people today in Japan and other countries might respond to Japanese woodblock prints like those of Hiroshige?

Note: Quotation from Julian Bicknell, *Hiroshige in Tokyo: The Floating World of Edo* (San Francisco: Pomegranate Artbooks, 1994), 50.

Tokugawa fought back, sparking a bloody one-year civil war that cost eighty-two hundred lives. Finally Meiji forces crushed all armed resistance.

The Meiji regime's crash modernization program lasted thirty years. Japan joined the world community, agreeing to honor all treaties. Symbolically attacking tradition, the imperial residence moved from Kyoto to the much larger and more dynamic Tokyo (formerly Edo). Perceiving change as a necessary evil, Meiji leaders pragmatically sought ways to achieve national unity, wealth, defense, and equality with the West. Although influenced by Western political and economic models, Meiji reformers also incorporated Japanese traditions in building a distinctive industrial society, defusing the Western threat. Despite flaws, the Meiji system proved productive and, in recent decades, an attractive model for rapidly industrializing Eastern and Southeast Asian nations.

Meiji leaders formed a State Council to advise and control the emperor while securing popular loyalty. To defuse potential opposition, they recruited both samurais and commoners into the new bureaucracy while convincing daimyos to give up control of their land, offering generous financial settlements and often appointment as regional governors. Many newly freed peasants moved to cities seeking manufacturing or service work. The government employed thousands of Western advisers, teachers, and workers to train Japanese assistants to replace them when their contracts expired. Financing these programs through tax revenues, Japan did not need foreign loans and thus avoided the debt trap that ensnared most Latin American and Middle Eastern societies as well as China.

The new political system had some democratic trappings, but, with no tradition of political freedom, the Japanese invented a new word for the concept. A small group of men made most key decisions. Nonetheless, in 1889 a growing movement for more popular participation in decision making prompted the writing of Japan's first constitution, which established a constitutional monarchy symbolically headed by the emperor, an independent judiciary, and a two-house parliament, elected by the 450,000 tax-paying, property-holding men, that chose members for the policymaking cabinet. Former samurai formed the first political parties, which remained factionalized and weak.

Using the slogan "rich country, strong army," the government stressed the development of industries, railroads, telegraphs, and, anxious about Western imperialism, the armed forces, including a modern navy. Drafting commoners as soldiers, once a profession limited to samurai, broke down the distinction between samurai, merchant, and peasant and promoted social leveling, literacy, and nationalism. Since Western pressure gradually diminished, Meiji leaders enjoyed more freedom of action than China to strengthen the nation. Japan was also a much less inviting target, with few natural resources that could be profitably exploited. Although Westerners viewed Japan as a market for their goods, China had many more potential consumers. The Western powers, largely preoccupied elsewhere, mainly considered Japan a potential ally against each other.

23-3d Meiji Economy and Society

The Meiji created **state capitalism**, an economic system in which the state takes a leading role building business and industrial enterprises and then privatizes but regulates and closely monitors the economy. The government subsidized or purchased stock in light industries, such as textiles, and heavy industries, such as mines and steel mills, and sometimes formed new corporations that it later sold to a few companies with political connections, such as Mitsui (MIT-soo-ee), a family-owned business from Tokugawa times. The most powerful corporations, the **zaibatsu**, maintained especially close government links. They believed economic independence from the West to be patriotic: "The foreigners did not come to our country out of friendship [but] to seek profits through trade. If we allow them to monopolize our foreign trade, we are betraying our duty."[27]

State capitalism and industrial growth favored city people, who obtained capital for industrialization by squeezing rural folk through the land tax. In exchange, government spurred agricultural productivity, providing new seeds, improving land use, and supplying better irrigation. However, public investment favored cities; Fukuzawa Yukichi complained that "steel bridges glisten in the capital, and horse-drawn carriages run on the streets, but in the country the wooden bridges are so rotten one cannot cross them."[28]

Meiji era life was not easy. The new economic system perpetuated traditional Japan's group orientation and social controls, exploiting workers with low pay so that scarce capital could be devoted to building factories, shipyards, and railroads, which ultimately created new jobs and national wealth. As in the United States and Europe, textile mills mainly employed women, half below age twenty and 15 percent younger than fourteen, who were chiefly recruited from rural villages. Factory women, paid half the salary of male workers, lived in crowded, often locked dormitories, working twelve-hour shifts interrupted only by one half-hour meal break. Mill workers experienced high death rates from overwork, physical abuse from supervisors, and diseases such as tuberculosis caused by crowded working conditions.

Meiji reforms attacked the rigid Tokugawa class system. People could now change occupations and travel freely. Losing their military monopoly, some samurai became lawyers, teachers, or journalists, while disgruntled samurai joined opposition political movements. The regime constructed a universal school system, financed by both taxes and tuition, that adopted the rigorous and regimented European, especially German, examination-based educational system of that era; it also opened technical schools and universities and dispatched students to Europe and the United States. By 1900 Japan was training its own scientists, engineers, and technicians.

state capitalism An economic system in which the state takes a leading role in supporting business and industrial enterprises; introduced by the Meiji government in Japan.

zaibatsu The most powerful Japanese corporations that dominated the national economy beginning during the Meiji regime and that maintained an especially close relationship to the government.

---

[27]Quoted in Kenneth B. Pyle, *The Making of Modern Japan*, 2nd ed. (Lexington, MA: D.C. Heath, 1996), 101.
[28]Fukuzawa Yukichi, quoted in Mikiso Hane, *Peasants, Rebels, and Outcasts: The Underside of Modern Japan* (New York: Pantheon, 1982), 33.

The First Modern Mitsui Building Erected in 1872 (colour litho), Japanese School (19th century)/PETER NEWARKS PICTURES/Private Collection/Bridgeman Images

IMAGE 23.6 **The Mitsui House in Edo** This bank and corporate headquarters, built in 1872, was owned by the Mitsui family, which also owned large stores, breweries, factories, coal mines, and other enterprises. Mitsui was one of the major business conglomerates in Japan, with branches all over Asia.

Q What does the painting suggest about the business and banking district of Edo (Tokyo)?

Meiji policies stimulated debate about Japanese society. Some reformers blamed patriarchal families for discouraging personal independence; conservatives worried that the individual was replacing the family. To preserve traditional gender roles and female obedience, Meiji policies promoted the "Good Wife, Wise Mother" ideal, aimed at strengthening families by having mothers stay at home with their children. Popular Confucian books praised lifelong female obedience to men, who should make the family's decisions. With little income, married women had a low social status. Some women struggled for change. Hence, Fukuda Hideko founded a magazine in 1907 to promote feminist and socialist thought, writing that "virtually everything [for women] is coercive and oppressive, making it imperative that we women rise up and develop our own social movement."[29]

Completely eradicating old social prejudices proved impossible. The **Burakumin (boo-ROCK-uh-min)**, or "hamlet people," a poor, despised subgroup identified with jobs considered unclean and undignified, such as meat processing, undertaking, and leatherworking, probably originated from people displaced by warfare during the feudal period and still faced severe discrimination during the Tokugawa. They usually lived in their own neighborhoods and villages and were expected to show subservience to, and avoid physical contact with, people of higher status. Samurai could kill them with impunity. But as nonfarmers they didn't pay taxes and, given their monopoly over certain occupations, some succeeded economically. Despite Meiji laws giving Burakumin legal equality, the Japanese still discouraged intermarriage and banned them from temples and shrines. Such prejudices remain widespread today, although many Burakumin work in nontraditional careers and some try, and sometimes succeed, to hide their origins.

23-3e Westernization, Expansion, and the Meiji Legacy

Western philosophy, social theory, economic thought, literature, and fashions all influenced Japanese society. During the peak of the Westernization in the 1870s, the Japanese adopted the Western calendar, added European words to their language, became familiar with chairs and couches, ate more meat, wore leather shoes, attended fancy dress balls, carried umbrellas, sported watches, wore trousers, shook hands rather than bowed, and often married in Western style. The Meiji also lifted prohibitions on Christianity, though missionaries never converted more than a few thousand Japanese. Writers found that Western literary styles such as realism and romanticism allowed them freer expression. For example, Futabatei Shimei **(FOO-ta-BA-tay shi-MAI)** (1864–1909) wrote Japan's first modern novels, in colloquial language rather than the highly formal traditional language.

Japan's dramatic transformation amazed Westerners. A German doctor wrote that he felt lucky to witness the

Burakumin ("hamlet people") A despised Japanese subgroup who traditionally performed jobs considered unclean and undignified.

[29]Quoted in Conrad Totman, *A History of Japan* (Malden, MA: Blackwell, 2000), 341.

interesting experiment as Japan tried to make, in one great leap, the changes toward industrial society that took Europeans five centuries to complete. But in 1911 a Japanese novelist worried about cultural confusion causing a "nervous collapse" that would devastate society. Japan seemed neither traditional nor Western.

By the later 1880s the mania for Western fads had abated. Hoping to limit Westernization, Meiji leaders carefully synthesized old and new and reemphasized traditional values, including ancient myths and the emperor's divinity. Although the Japanese never slavishly imitated the West, the dramatic changes created tensions between Japan and other nations, ultimately fostering a more imperialistic foreign policy; some samurai advocated invading Korea to serve their nation in glory. Meiji leaders, fearful of antagonizing Western powers, followed a cautious foreign policy. Nonetheless, they sponsored a vast colonization of Hokkaido (ho-KI-do), the large northern island, to protect against potential Russian aggression. This brought them into closer contact with the Ainu, a non-Japanese people who lived for millennia on Hokkaido; they had been conquered in the 1700s. In 1899 the Meiji government imposed a policy of assimilation, ostensibly to protect them. The new laws imposed Japanese education and eliminated their traditional land rights and claims. Over time most adopted Japanese customs and language but they remain a marginalized people who mostly live in poverty today, with high levels of unemployment and a declining population (about thirteen thousand in 2017).

Eventually Meiji Japan fought two wars (see Map 23.2). In the Sino-Japanese War (1894–1895), China and Japan battled over their competing influence in Korea, which Japan had long coveted for its fertile land but now also considered a market for Japanese products. After a smashing military victory, Japan dominated Korea as well as the Chinese island of Taiwan, in 1910 transforming both into colonies. Impressed, Britain forged an alliance with Japan. Meanwhile, Britain's rival, Russia, had ambitions in Korea and a foothold in China's resource-rich Manchuria region, which Japan wanted to exploit. These rising tensions led to the Russo-Japanese War (1904–1905), during which Japan seized a Russian-held Manchurian port and then destroyed the Russian fleet sent from Europe, electrifying the world. The vision of a non-Western nation defeating a major European power gave hope to colonized societies and spurred Asian nationalisms. The triumph further enhanced Japanese pride in their nation, confirming that Japan had become a world power. Among the fruits of victory, Japan acquired some Russian holdings in Manchuria and control of the southern half of Sakhalin island, off the Siberian coast.

The Meiji era, officially ending with the Meiji emperor's death in 1912, achieved stunning successes, giving Japan national security and regional power. Although the United States, Britain, France, and Germany still had more wealth and influence, Japan was now an industrial nation with fifty million people, on a par with countries such as Russia and Italy.

Historians still debate the Meiji legacy. Some consider Meiji policies as a political and social revolution, not unlike the French Revolution in uprooting the old society. Others emphasize the longtime Japanese willingness to modify culture to strengthen the country. Some Japanese found the changes shattering; others took them in stride. One supporter proclaimed Japan's "marvelous fortune. I feel as though in a dream and can only weep tears of joy." Another enthusiast wrote that "we are no longer ashamed to stand before the world as Japanese, known by the world."[30] Years later many Japanese wistfully remembered the Meiji as a time of vitality, courage, and hope, as reflected in a poetic aphorism: "Snow is falling, Meiji recedes in the distance." But concerned that growing military power would corrupt his country, one writer called on the Japanese to open their eyes to the dangers ahead. His fears were realized three decades later in World War II, when Japan's conquest of an Asian and Pacific empire provoked U.S. retaliation, ultimately leading to Japanese military defeat and occupation by U.S. forces.

23-3f Korean Transitions

The last Korean dynasty, the Yi (YEE) dynasty (1392–1910), which ruled the state they called Choson (choh-SAN), secluded themselves from the outside world for over five centuries, earning the label "the Hermit Kingdom." However, they maintained relations with China. Korean scholars who visited China and sometimes met Westerners there criticized Korea's rigid, inequitable social system. Yet, several strong eighteenth-century kings fostered learning by printing encyclopedias and historical records, and aristocratic women wrote memoirs, diaries, and stories of court life; even some commoners wrote stories and novels.

By the early 1800s Choson, like Qing China and Tokugawa Japan, faced mounting stress from growth in the economy and population (nine million by 1800), which increased pressure on society and the land. Although French and Chinese Christian missionaries were prohibited, a few had illegally entered Korea, and, with Buddhism losing influence, some Koreans embraced Christianity. One official told the French Catholic missionaries he was expelling that they had no right to tell Koreans to abandon their ancient teachings and accept those of alien cultures. As Korea experienced recurrent famines and peasant uprisings, the government blamed and persecuted Christians and missionaries.

Korean intellectuals debated the value of Western learning, some pushing to reform the traditional system. But, worried about Russian expansion in eastern Siberia, the Yi refused direct commercial negotiations with the West and drove away French and American ships seeking to open Korea to Western trade. By the later 1800s Korea needed rejuvenation.

In 1876, Meiji Japan, adopting the American model of forcing open a reluctant nation, sent a naval expedition and bullied Korea to open five ports and sign unequal treaties giving Japan strong economic influence. Impressed by Meiji modernization, the Yi introduced reforms, such as toleration of Christianity, and signed trade agreements with Western nations. In 1886 Christians opened Korea's first modern girls' school, whose graduates later promoted women's rights. By the

[30]The quotes are from Varley, *Japanese Culture*, 272.

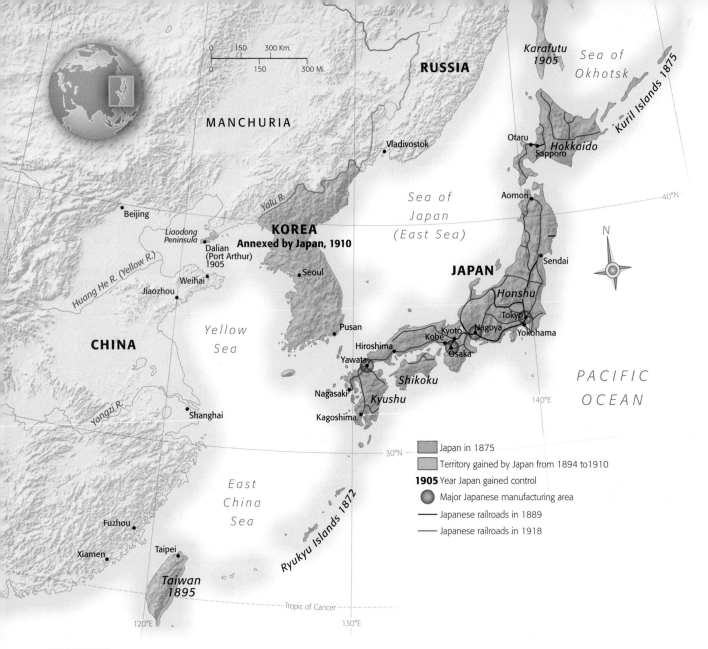

	Japan in 1875
	Territory gained by Japan from 1894 to 1910
1905	Year Japan gained control
⬤	Major Japanese manufacturing area
—	Japanese railroads in 1889
—	Japanese railroads in 1918

MAP 23.2 Japanese Modernization and Expansion, 1868–1913 Japan undertook a crash modernization in the later 1800s. By 1910 its military power had increased, and it had won a war with Russia and colonized Korea, Taiwan, and Sakhalin (then known as Karafutu).

Q What does the map tell us about industrialization and transportation growth on the main Japanese islands in these years?

mid-1890s a growing number of Westerners, among them missionaries, traders, and teachers, had moved to Korea. But both Qing China, which dominated Korean affairs between 1884 and 1894, and Meiji Japan allied with different Korean political factions as they sought to increase their influence in the country. As tensions increased many Koreans desperately sought some way to maintain their independence from their two giant neighbors and a threatening Russia to the north. Koreans referred ruefully to their precarious position between feuding and dangerous rival countries as "the breaking of a shrimp's back when caught between fighting whales."[31]

However, many peasants joined the Tonghak ("Eastern Learning"), a protest movement, not unlike the Taiping movement in China, that mixed Confucianism, Buddhism, Christianity, and hatred of Japan and the West. The movement's founder, the wandering preacher Ch'oe Che'u (1824–1864), argued that "luxury and indulgence run rampant throughout the country while ordinary people everywhere suffer deprivation. When the government and ministers are corrupt and greedy, how can the people avoid being poor and distressed?"[32] Ch'oe was arrested and executed, thus becoming a martyr to his followers. In 1894, spurred by famine, the movement grew

---

[31]Quoted in Kyung Moon Hwang, *A History of Korea* (New York: Palgrave, 2010), 132.
[32]Youngho Ch'oe et al., eds., *Sources of Korean Tradition*, vol. 2 (New York: Columbia University Press, 2000), 265.

into the nationwide Tonghak Rebellion against the government. When China sent troops to help repress the rebellion, Japan dispatched a force and captured the Korean capital, Seoul, holding the royal family hostage. This action provoked the Sino-Japanese War, which resulted in a humiliating Chinese withdrawal, a stronger Japanese presence, and the fall of the decrepit Yi dynasty. Some eighteen thousand Koreans died fighting the Japanese.

Bringing an end to the Yi dynasty, in 1910 Japan forcibly transformed Korea from the one-time "Hermit Kingdom" into a Japanese colony, which it heavily exploited and harshly ruled until 1945. One resistance leader expressed the widespread Korean despair: "I was unable to repel our nation's enemies, or hold back our 4000 year long civilization from falling to the ground."[33] Japan brutally suppressed Korean nationalism and culture, seized land for Japanese companies, and restricted civil liberties while also increasing educational opportunities and building a modern economy. In 1919 Japanese police crushed peaceful demonstrations calling for

independence, killing or injuring some twenty-four thousand demonstrators and arresting forty-seven thousand. One of the protest leaders killed, high school girl Yu Gwang-sun, has been the center of a debate in South Korea over how this history should be taught in schools, which is a politically divisive issue between liberals and conservatives. Korean resentment simmered as repressive measures, such as forcing students to speak only Japanese, increased. Some Koreans found solace in Christianity, and perhaps a fifth became Catholics or Protestants. Others turned toward Marxism, joining an underground Communist Party founded by Korean workers in China and Russia. Many Koreans, however, rejecting Western ideas, favored strengthening Confucianism. During World War II the Japanese conscripted Korean men as soldiers and workers and forced young Korean women, whom they termed "comfort women," to serve as sex slaves for Japanese soldiers. Thanks to this colonial and wartime repression and exploitation, many Koreans today maintain deep antipathy toward, and distrust of, Japan.

KEY POINTS

▶ After the Meiji Restoration, which overthrew the Tokugawa Shogunate, Japanese samurai and others, frustrated with the Tokugawa Shogunate, established a regime that was dedicated to making Japan open to and competitive with the rest of the world.

▶ The Meiji regime modernized Japan by breaking down social distinctions, pursuing industrial and military strength, and establishing a constitutional monarchy.

▶ The Meiji state supported and closely regulated industry, gave workers new rights to change occupation and travel freely but kept wages deliberately low, stripped samurai of their traditional privileges, and attempted to preserve traditional gender roles.

▶ Meiji Japan forced Korea to accept unequal trade agreements and, after defeating China in the Sino-Japanese War, turned Korea into a colony and ruled it extremely harshly, brutally suppressing dissent and exploiting its men and women during World War II.

23-4 Russia's Eurasian Empire

⇄ TRANSITIONS

Q What factors explain the expansion of the Russian Empire?

Most North Americans can probably identify Russia today as an authoritarian, powerful, and exceptionally large nation, but they may not know much about the imperial and autocratic foundation on which today's country was built. Between 1750 and 1914 Russia built a vast Eurasian empire stretching thirty-two hundred miles from the Baltic Sea to the Bering Straits, creating more intensive ties to, but also conflicts with, Asian societies. Pushing its frontiers across Siberia and into Central Asia and south toward the Black Sea made Russia a hemispheric power bordering Europe, Central Asia, and the Middle East. Shaped by autocratic

CONNECTION to TODAY

What legacies from the Russian Empire and Czarist despotism do you see in Russia today?

governments, a rural system resembling medieval feudalism, and chronic discontent, Russia nevertheless played an increasing role in Asian and European politics.

23-4a Europeanization, Despotism, and Expansionism

Russians long debated whether they shared European traditions or had a unique heritage; Russian politics reflected these debates. During her long reign, Catherine the Great (r. 1762–1796), born to a German royal family and married to the heir to the Russian

---

[33]Ch'oe Ik-hyon, quoted in Bruce Cumings, *Korea's Place in the Sun: A Modern History* (New York: W.W. Norton, 1997), 146–147.

throne, carried on Peter the Great's Europeanization campaign. She became czarina after engineering a coup by her husband's many enemies. Influenced by the Enlightenment, Catherine denounced slavery, hailed liberty, and presided over a golden age of aristocratic opulence. Wearing sumptuous gowns, the czarina gave elegant private parties and masked balls and, like many European kings, had many lovers, some twenty-one in all. Russia's elite copied royal France and learned French, increasing the huge gulf between them and peasants bound to estates as serfs. Despite her liberal views, Catherine could not encourage freedom among disgruntled common people. Because she needed the landed aristocracy's support, she extended serfdom to Ukraine and denounced the French Revolution as irreligious and immoral. Continuing Russian expansionism, Russia under Catherine's energetic foreign policy added Poland and Finland and extended the empire south to the Black Sea, annexing the Crimean peninsula in 1783.

To maintain order and their own power, the czars following Catherine often relied on the brutal despotism common in Russian history. Although alarmed by western Europe's social changes, the aristocracy opposed industrialization because it might upset serfdom. Czar Nicholas I (r. 1825–1855), fearing aristocratic alienation, suppressed restless Poles and formed a powerful secret police force to harass, imprison, or eliminate opponents. Nicholas also invaded Hungary and sought to secure Russia's grain exports through the Black Sea to the Mediterranean. In 1854 his attempts to absorb the Ottoman-held Balkans by encouraging rebellion and occupying several Ottoman provinces provoked the bloody Crimean War pitting Russia against a British–French–Ottoman alliance. With conscripted Russian serfs no match for modern British and French forces, Russia had to withdraw from Ottoman territory. Nicholas's successor, Czar Alexander II (r. 1855–1881), was oriented to western Europe and followed a reformist domestic policy, emancipating the serfs in 1861 and decentralizing the government. But discontent increased because many serfs could not pay landowners for the lands they wanted to use.

Russians became more engaged with Asia, expanding their power in Siberia, the Caucasus, and Central Asia to form the world's largest contiguous land empire (see Map 23.3). Seeking imperial glory, markets, and resources such as sable fur, Russians expanded across Siberia and reached the Pacific coast in the 1600s before losing to Chinese forces and withdrawing from the fertile Amur River Basin. By the early 1800s China had weakened and Russians occupied the Amur Basin. In 1860 China recognized Russian claims in exchange for helping end the Arrow War. Russians acquired a coastal zone on Siberia's Pacific shore, where they built a port city, Vladivostok ("Ruler of the East"), as a base for commercial and military activity in the Pacific Basin.

For several centuries Russians expanded around the Black Sea, seeking an outlet to the Mediterranean Sea. Between 1800 and the 1870s, with the Ottoman Empire weakening, Russia absorbed Armenia and Georgia, both largely Christian, and Muslim Azerbaijan (**az-uhr-bye-JAHN**) in the mountainous Caucasus, sometimes

Russification A czarist policy in the nineteenth century that promoted Russian language and culture for non-Russian peoples; created resentment among many Muslims.

facing fierce resistance. Russians needed four decades to conquer the strongly Islamic Chechens (**CHECH-uhnz**), where the resistance was led by Shamyl (1797–1871), the charismatic leader of an austere Muslim revivalist movement. Chechen men and women fought a relentless guerrilla war. The Russians only triumphed in 1859 by ravaging Chechen lands, herds, and crops and beheading their captives, fostering Chechen hatred of Russian rule that still survives today.

To gain direct access to Indian Ocean trade and to counter British influence, Russians also colonized Muslim Central Asia. By 1864 they controlled Kazakh (**KAH-zahk**) lands east of the Caspian Sea and began looking south to Turkestan's old Silk Road cities. Although the cities remained centers of Islamic learning and Sufism, only Bukhara, a strong Uzbek (**OOZ-bek**)–dominated state, maintained a thriving trade. By the 1870s Russia dominated Turkestan and coveted Afghanistan, but forbidding terrain and Afghan warriors' formidable reputation discouraged occupation. Eventually Afghanistan became a buffer between British India and Russian Central Asia.

Czarist policies in Central Asia and the Caucasus chiefly benefited Russians. Several hundred thousand Russian farmers were given Central Asian land suitable for growing cotton. Meanwhile, a policy of **Russification** promoted Russian language and culture for non-Russian peoples, sparking resentment and spiritual revival among many Muslims. But Russian expansion also brought problems. The mighty empire's sheer size hindered governance, fostered corruption, and prevented ready exploitation of the vast resources. Colonization of non-Russian lands made Russian leaders permanently fear rebellion and thus to build a huge army to maintain security. The world's longest railroad, the Trans-Siberian, built between 1891 and 1915, linked Saint Petersburg in the west with Vladivostok in the east, some six thousand miles away. The railroad facilitated Russian settlement of eastern Siberia and helped Russian traders penetrate Manchuria and Korea.

But expansion into Asia brought conflict with Japan, which also had ambitions in Korea and Manchuria. Beginning in 1897 Russia occupied Manchuria's Liaodong peninsula and built a base at Port Arthur, giving them their long-sought warm-water Pacific port, where they stationed a fleet. They also built, co-owned, and managed a Manchurian railroad as well as a new city, Harbin ("the Moscow of the Orient"). After the Boxer Rebellion in China Russia now stationed 100,000 troops in Manchuria, which was still nominally part of Qing China but increasingly resembled a Russian province. Attempts to find diplomatic solutions over Russian and Japanese rights in Manchuria and Korea failed. A Japanese attack on the Russian fleet at Port Arthur sparked the Russo-Japanese War (1904–1905), mostly fought in Manchuria and as a naval conflict in the seas around Korea and Japan. To reinforce their naval power Russia dispatched some of their Baltic fleet around the Cape of Good Hope, which took seven months to reach the war zone, by which time the Japanese had taken Port Arthur. Japan's navy wiped out the Russian fleet, including eight battleships and more than five thousand men, as they tried to reach Vladivostok to regroup. Russia's humiliating defeat and loss of confidence in its power undermined its last czar, Nicholas II (r. 1894–1917), opening the door to revolutionary movements.

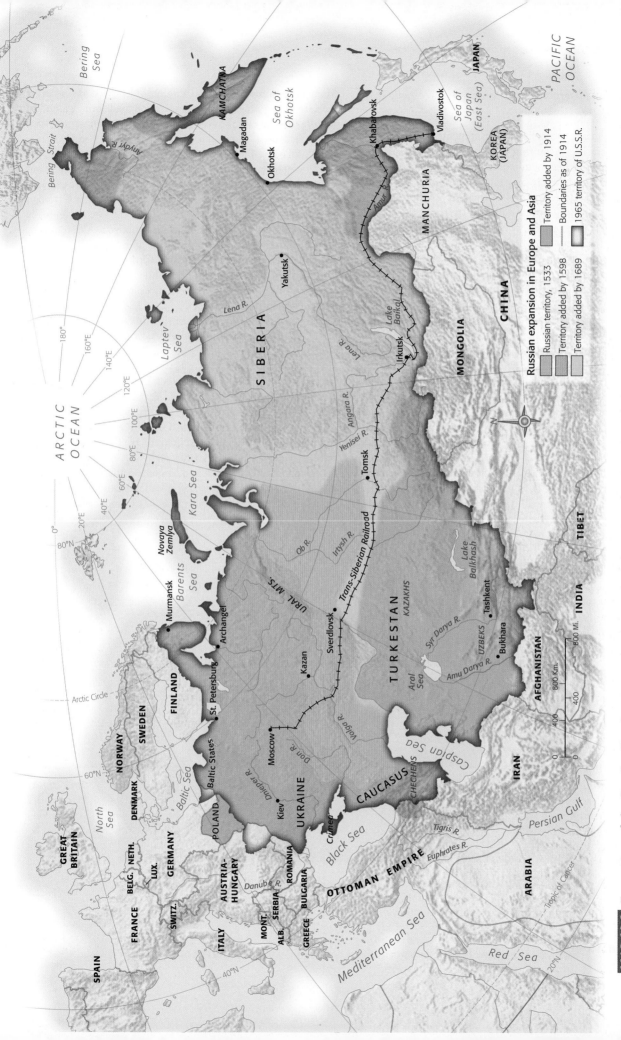

MAP 23.3 Expansion of the Russian Empire Between the 1500s and 1914 Russia gradually gained control of Siberia, Turkestan, the Caucasus, Ukraine, Poland, the Baltic states, and Finland, becoming the world's largest contiguous territorial empire.

Q How does this map compare to maps of the Soviet Union and of Russia today?

Russian expansion in Europe and Asia

- Russian territory, 1533
- Territory added by 1598
- Territory added by 1689
- Territory added by 1914
- Boundaries as of 1914
- 1965 territory of U.S.S.R.

23-4b Russian Economy, Society, and Revolution

Territorial expansion and political developments reshaped many areas of Russian life. Acquiring markets in the Caucasus and Central Asia spurred economic growth. As a result of industrialization, financed largely by western European capital and local bankers and businessmen of German or Jewish origin, by 1914 Russia's industrial power ranked fifth in the world. The factory workers on whom this power was built, whose numbers increased fivefold between 1860 and 1914, resented the fact that they were housed in crowded dormitories and expected to work thirteen hours a day. However, most Russians still lived in villages dominated by local aristocrats.

Some Russian women sought improved status. While noblewomen frequently enjoyed some public influence, most commoner women were powerless, some were beaten and abused by husbands, and laws gave men the right to control their wives and children. Peasants often spent their lives in the village where they were born. Even elite women scholars and writers had fewer rights than men. By the mid-nineteenth century, a women's movement emerged that emphasized access to higher education. Thanks to these efforts, more women earned degrees and worked as doctors, midwives, and teachers.

Russian thinkers tormented themselves over their national identity and goals.

Slavophiles Nineteenth-century Russians who emphasized Russia's unique culture and rejected Western models.

Many were Westernizers who admired rulers such as Catherine the Great who promoted modernization, and some wanted to abolish serfdom and the aristocracy. Some Russian writers, such as beloved poet Alexander Pushkin (**POOSH-kin**) (1799–1837), reflected familiarity with western European literature and thought. Pushkin came from an old aristocratic family but a paternal great grandfather was an African who had been kidnapped (possibly from Ethiopia) and shipped to the Ottoman sultan, who then sent him as a gift to Peter the Great; eventually he became a top Russian general. In contrast to Westernizers, **Slavophiles** rejected Western models and defended aspects of Russian culture such as the Russian Orthodox Church, which remained a dominant force. Slavophiles often advocated that Russians unite with other Slavs in eastern Europe and the Balkans to confront the West.

Russians were proud of their rich literary and artistic tradition. The novels of Fyodor Dostoyevsky (**dos-tuh-YEF-skee**) (1821–1881), reflecting his exile in Siberia for revolutionary activities and travels in Europe, were shaped by awareness of poverty and the troubled human soul. Leo Tolstoy (**tuhl-STOI**) (1828–1910) fought in the Crimean War. His epic work, *War and Peace* (1869), profiling two noble families during war, portrayed people as mere victims of chance. One of Russia's most honored composers, Pyotr Tchaikovsky (**chi-KOF-skee**) (1840–1893), traveled widely in Europe. Criticized by Russian nationalists for his cosmopolitan approach and by conservatives for his homosexuality, he wrote operas as well as ballets of enduring popularity around the world, especially *Swan Lake* and *The Nutcracker*.

Catherine II (1729–96) the Great, riding into one of the ports in the Crimea captured from the Turks (engraving) (b/w photo)/Baltazar, G. (18th century)/Bibliotheque Nationale, Paris, France/Bridgeman Images

IMAGE 23.7 **Catherine the Great** Resplendent in her royal robes, Catherine the Great triumphantly enters one of the ports of the Crimean peninsula recently captured from the Turks. Catherine presided over an expansion of the Russian Empire and efforts at modernization.

Q What can we learn from the painting about Catherine and the military officers accompanying her?

Increasing discontent with the autocratic system and the rising costs of empire building fostered violent resistance. To crush opposition, czars sent thousands of dissidents to remote Siberian prison camps, where many died of illness, starvation, overwork, or the harsh climate. The illegal Socialist Revolutionary Party, founded in 1898, used terror to strike against the regime. After assassinating a minister of state, the party proclaimed that "the crack of the bullet is the only possible means to talk with our ministers, until they listen to the voice of the country."[34]

In 1905 the sacrifices imposed on common people by the unsuccessful Russo-Japanese War sparked a major socialist-led revolutionary movement involving both men and women and widespread violence. One hundred thousand factory workers in the capital, Saint Petersburg, required to work longer hours to produce war supplies, went on strike and demanded legal equality, free speech, an eight-hour workday, social insurance, and other progressive goals. Russian troops opened fire on the peaceful marchers, killing some two hundred and wounding hundreds more. The violence shattered the czar's public support and fueled outrage that soon spread to the armed forces. Because the revolutionaries disagreed on their goals, the government was able to crush the uprising, execute thousands of rebels, and burn pro-rebel villages. But the czar bowed to public demands and allowed an elected national assembly with limited powers. The socialist movement fractured into hostile factions; however, conflicts simmered, and in 1917 the most militant faction, the Bolsheviks, produced the greatest upheaval in Russia's history, which ended the czarist system and would radically transform Russian society (see Chapter 24).

KEY POINTS

▶ The Russian leader Catherine the Great paid lip service to Enlightenment values, but she presided over an era of royal opulence, territorial expansion, and expanded serfdom, and she was followed by the despotic Nicholas I, who led the nation to defeat in the Crimean War.

▶ Russian expansion brought it control of eastern Siberia, Muslim Central Asia, and the Caucasus states, although some peoples, such as the Chechens, fiercely resisted.

▶ Russia's economy expanded along with its territory, creating a discontented proletariat; while many Russian thinkers embraced Western ideals, the Slavophiles argued for the superiority of traditional Russian culture.

▶ Russians, increasingly discontented with the demands of empire building and autocratic rulers, joined terrorist groups and supported a revolution in 1905, which, while put down, led to reforms.

[34]Quoted in L. S. Stavrianos, *Global Rift: The Third World Comes of Age* (New York: William Morrow, 1981), 344.

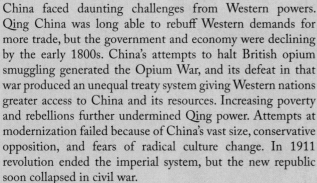

Chapter Summary

China faced daunting challenges from Western powers. Qing China was long able to rebuff Western demands for more trade, but the government and economy were declining by the early 1800s. China's attempts to halt British opium smuggling generated the Opium War, and its defeat in that war produced an unequal treaty system giving Western nations greater access to China and its resources. Increasing poverty and rebellions further undermined Qing power. Attempts at modernization failed because of China's vast size, conservative opposition, and fears of radical culture change. In 1911 revolution ended the imperial system, but the new republic soon collapsed in civil war.

While the Western challenges progressively undermined China, they prompted Japan to transform its society. The arrival of American ships demanding that Japan open itself to the West forced the issue, undermining the shogunate, which then lost power in the 1868 Meiji Restoration. Capitalizing on dynamic merchants, high literacy rates, a tradition of cultural borrowing, and national loyalties, the Meiji government launched a crash program to modernize Japan's government, military, economy, and social patterns, importing Western ideas and institutions. By 1900 the Meiji had industrialized Japan, deflected Western ambitions, and turned Japan into a world power, able to defeat China and Russia in two wars and to colonize Korea.

Despotic Russian leaders pushed Russian control across Siberia and into eastern Europe and colonized Central Asia and the Caucasus. By the later 1800s Russia dominated large parts of Eurasia, forming the world's largest contiguous land empire. But maintaining an empire against restless colonized societies strained Russian capabilities. Russia also industrialized and promoted social change, but repression of the Russian peasants ultimately brought dissent and revolutionary movements.

Key Terms

Chinoiserie 586	gunboat diplomacy 592	Burakumin 600
Co-hong 586	Meiji Restoration 597	Russification 604
extraterritoriality 587	state capitalism 599	Slavophiles 606
international settlements 588	zaibatsu 599	

World Wars, European Revolutions, and Global Depression, 1914–1945

> *My beautiful, pitiful era. With an insane smile you look back, cruel and weak, like an animal past its prime, at the prints of your own paws.*

—Osip Mandelstam, Russian poet[1]

Russian propaganda poster celebrating 1st May (colour litho)/Russian School (20th century)/IMAGE ASSET MANAGEMENT LTD/Museum of the Revolution, Moscow, Russia/Bridgeman Images

IMAGE 24.1 **Global Communism** The communist leaders of the Soviet Union hoped that their revolution in Russia in 1917 would inspire similar revolutions around the world, ending capitalism and imperialism. This poster reflects the dream of a triumphant communism.

Q Given the world today, and over the past sixty years, why do you think the goals expressed in the poster fell short of success?

---

[1] Quoted in Anne Applebaum, *Gulag: A History* (New York: Doubleday, 2003), 3.

By April 1917 the French army had fought the Germans for over two and a half years during World War I. With growing casualties and tremendous hardship on soldiers, French officers were divided over mounting a more aggressive strategy, which was likely to cause many more deaths, or a more defensive approach. Finally, a new French commander, General Philippe Pétain **(peh-TANH)** (1856–1951), advocated a strategy to minimize French casualties. A peasant's son with an aristocratic demeanor, sweeping white moustache, and many love affairs with other men's wives, Pétain was well liked by his troops because he regarded his soldiers as more than cannon fodder. But Pétain was overruled; another frontal assault on well-fortified German lines resulted in military disaster, including 120,000 deaths and a broken fighting spirit. Units mutinied in protest against the futile military strategy of suicidal assaults. Some soldiers proposed marching on Paris; twenty thousand deserted. The army executed about fifty mutineers but also granted frontline troops better food and generous rations of wine. Mutinies and overwhelming war-weariness occurred among all the combatant nations. Pétain emerged from World War I a hero but later lost his stature when he nominally headed the French government under the hated Nazi occupation in World War II. He died in prison, a broken man looking back on three tumultuous decades that brought the world so much distress and destruction.

Those decades, full of achievements and atrocities, heroism and hardship, included two great military struggles unprecedented in their geographical scope and scale of barbarity, a mighty revolution in Russia, terrible worldwide economic depression, and the rise of new ideologies. Before World War I some Europeans believed that Western democracy and peace might spread throughout the world. Liberals hoped that World War I would be the war to end all wars. But idealism was dashed by two world wars, fought partly in Europe, that challenged Enlightenment liberalism and rationalism. Dictatorship in Russia, economic collapse, and organized slaughter shattered faith in progress. The disarray in Europe damaged the political influence of all Western nations except that of the rising Western power, the United States.

1900	1910	1920

WORLD WAR I AND AFTERMATH

● 1908 Austria-Hungarian annexation of Bosnia-Herzegovina

● 1914 Outbreak of World War I

● 1916 Battle of Verdun

March 1917 Fall of czarist government in Russia ●

June 1917 U.S. intervention in World War I ●

October 1917 Bolshevik Revolution in Russia ●

March 1918 Brest-Litovsk Treaty ●

1918–1921 Russian civil war ●———●

November 1918 End of World War I ●

1919 Paris Peace Conference ●

1919–1920 First Red Scare in United States ●———●

1921 Irish Free State ●

1921 Formation of Italian fascist movement ●

1922 Formation of Soviet Union ●

1924 Death of Lenin ●

ERA OF GREAT DEPRESSION

WORLD WAR II

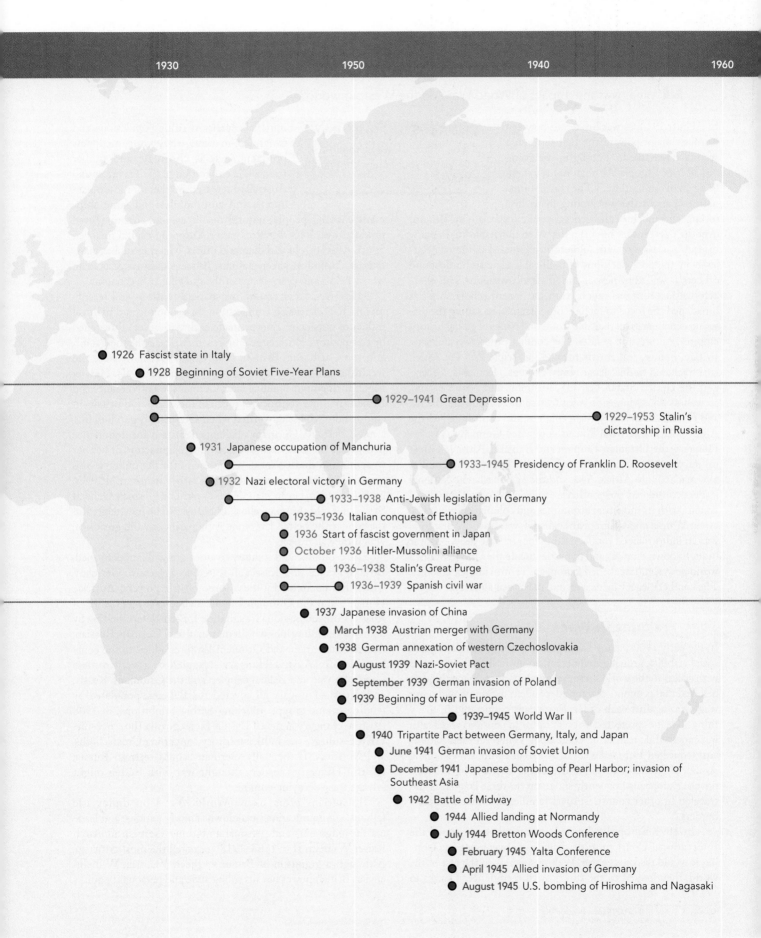

1930   1950   1940   1960

1926 Fascist state in Italy

1928 Beginning of Soviet Five-Year Plans

1929–1941 Great Depression

1929–1953 Stalin's dictatorship in Russia

1931 Japanese occupation of Manchuria

1933–1945 Presidency of Franklin D. Roosevelt

1932 Nazi electoral victory in Germany

1933–1938 Anti-Jewish legislation in Germany

1935–1936 Italian conquest of Ethiopia

1936 Start of fascist government in Japan

October 1936 Hitler-Mussolini alliance

1936–1938 Stalin's Great Purge

1936–1939 Spanish civil war

1937 Japanese invasion of China

March 1938 Austrian merger with Germany

1938 German annexation of western Czechoslovakia

August 1939 Nazi-Soviet Pact

September 1939 German invasion of Poland

1939 Beginning of war in Europe

1939–1945 World War II

1940 Tripartite Pact between Germany, Italy, and Japan

June 1941 German invasion of Soviet Union

December 1941 Japanese bombing of Pearl Harbor; invasion of Southeast Asia

1942 Battle of Midway

1944 Allied landing at Normandy

July 1944 Bretton Woods Conference

February 1945 Yalta Conference

April 1945 Allied invasion of Germany

August 1945 U.S. bombing of Hiroshima and Nagasaki

24-1 The Roots and Course of World War I

⇄ TRANSITIONS

Q What was the impact of World War I on the Western world?

In August 1914, as war broke out between Europe's major powers, the British foreign secretary remarked, "The lights are going out all over Europe. We shall not see them lit again in our lifetime."[2] The conventional narrative about the war among many historians and much of the general public (especially in Britain) over the past century has been that of an inevitable but in many respects useless war, with soldiers on all sides slaughtered needlessly by the poor decisions of political leaders and hidebound officers as well as by new and more deadly weapons. This characterization contains much truth but recent scholarship has broadened the focus to include other factors, including the differing experiences on multiple fronts and issues of global history, empires, culture, and gender. The conflict pitted two alliances. Britain, France, and Russia formed the Triple Entente, which later included Serbia, Japan, Italy, Portugal, Romania, Greece, and the United States. Canada, Australia, and New Zealand, as well as conscripted or volunteer soldiers from the British and French Asian and African colonies, also contributed on the Allies side. The Central Powers comprised Germany, Austria-Hungary, the Ottoman Empire, and Bulgaria. Although most military action occurred in and around Europe, the conflict also reached into Africa, Asia, and the Pacific islands. National leaders considered the conflict a struggle to control the global system, with its industrial economies and colonial empires. The Great War, as many Europeans called it, was history's first total war, an industrialized conflict lasting four terrible years. The war brought down empires and dynasties, made the United States a world power, and weakened Europeans' control of their colonies. The conflict's legacy made a second major war almost inevitable.

24-1a Preludes to War

In the early 1900s, many Europeans enjoyed relative affluence, social stability, growing democracy, and interlinked economies with access to the world's resources and markets. Some thinkers believed that economically interdependent nations would never wage war against each other. Europeans cooperated in many things. Treaties protected workers' rights to pensions and health insurance while restricting child labor. Whatever their nationality, educated Europeans loved Austrian composer Wolfgang Amadeus Mozart's music and Russian writer Leo Tolstoy's novels. Europeans frequently spoke two or three languages and traveled in other countries; royal families intermarried across borders.

In 1899 Europeans limited armaments and created the International Court to settle disputes between nations, hoping it would discourage war. Feeling superior to the rest of the world, they looked to the future with confidence. Thanks to

> **CONNECTION to TODAY**
>
> Can you think of ways that World War I affected your family, community, and nation?

imperial expansion, rising populations, and expanded markets, they consumed new products such as chocolate and rubber tires, while emigration to the Americas and Australia increased markets for European goods, and automobiles and large ships made moving people, natural resources, and manufactured products over long distances easier. European capital financed South African gold and diamond mines, Malayan rubber plantations, Australian sheep stations, Russian railways, Canadian wheat fields, and every sector of the growing U.S. economy.

However, other conditions sparked tensions and resentments. The increasing competition for economic and political influence outside of Europe made each nation feel threatened by competitors. With large empires in Africa, Asia, the Pacific, and the Caribbean, Britain, France, and Germany were the wealthiest, most powerful nations and fierce rivals. Having begun their empire building later, Germans resented France and Britain's political control over much of the world, and Britain, in command of the seas, worried when Germany began building a naval fleet. As Germany challenged Britain for dominance in overseas markets, each increased the manufacture of heavier weapons and drafted more young men into the military. Still considering wars necessary struggles rather than terrible evils, by 1911 leaders began planning for war. The German General Staff chief told the chancellor, "I hold war to be inevitable, and the sooner the better. Everyone is preparing for the great war, which they all expect."[3]

As economic and military rivalries grew, alliances formed. Britain, France, and Russia all feared an aggressive Germany, which felt encircled by these three hostile powers; Austria-Hungary and the Ottoman Empire shared German dislike of Russia. Growing nationalist agitation for self-determination by many ethnic minorities within multinational German, Russian, Austro-Hungarian, and Ottoman Empires added to the combustible mix. Austria-Hungary struggled to govern restless Czech, Slovak, and Balkan peoples, and the Ottomans, Russia, and Austria-Hungary all coveted the Balkans, populated by feuding ethnic groups. Blocking Serbia's ambitions, in 1908 Austria-Hungary annexed Bosnia-Herzegovina (**boz-nee-uh-HERT-suh-go-vee-nuh**), a territory containing Croats, Serbs, and Muslims. If their ally Germany could restrain Russia, Austria-Hungary's leaders thought war with Serbia might salvage their decaying empire.

Historians often blame World War I on diplomatic failures, communication breakdowns among nations, and leaders' misjudgments and personal ambitions. German monarch Kaiser Wilhelm II (r. 1888–1918) garnered the most criticism. Although a grandson of Britain's Queen Victoria, Wilhelm envied British power but his ruling style and personality quirks

[2]Quoted in S. L. Marshall, *World War I* (Boston: Houghton Mifflin, 1987), 53.
[3]Quoted in Sir Michael Howard, "Europe 1914," in *The Great War: Perspectives on the First World War*, ed. Robert Cowley (New York: Random House, 2003), 3.

played a role in his ultimate failures. Convinced of his own brilliance, he was a poor diplomat, compulsive liar, and avid speechmaker with a limited sense of cause and effect and little tolerance for critics, whom he frequently insulted. At the same time, Europe's political and military leaders underestimated the conflict's human costs and long-term consequences. Although overstating the case, a British leader later conceded that "the nations slithered over the brink into the boiling cauldron of war without a trace of apprehension or dismay."[4] Some governments hoped war might divert public attention from festering domestic problems, such as Irish resistance to English policies and German social ills. And although the general public did not pressure governments for war, neither did it restrain them. Feminists and socialists opposed war on principle but, when conflict came, often closed ranks to support their governments. While preferring war to maintaining a fragile peace, leaders also feared their people would tire of it.

24-1b The Course of the European War

The pretext for war was the assassination of Austrian archduke Franz Ferdinand (1863–1914), heir to the Habsburg throne, and his wife, Sophie, while they were riding through Sarajevo (sar-uh-YAY-vo), Bosnia-Herzegovina's capital city, during an official visit. Although the archduke was conciliatory toward the empire's Slavic minorities, to Bosnian Serb nationalists wanting to merge Bosnia with Serbia the archduke symbolized Austro-Hungarian domination. Austria-Hungary declared war on Serbia, whose leaders it believed aided the assassination. Germany supported Austria-Hungary, while Britain, France, and Russia entered the conflict against Germany. Ottoman Turkey joined the Central Powers, closing off British and French access to the Black Sea. Germany planned a quick knockout blow against France, shifting most troops east to face Russia. These plans were thwarted.

Expecting a short conflict, European leaders got a long, brutal war of attrition, the first to be fought on air, sea, and land. In the world's first fully industrialized conflict, combatants employed more efficient and indiscriminate ways of killing, including long-range artillery, poison gas, flamethrowers, and aerial bombing. A generation of men was cut down by shrapnel tearing flesh to pieces, high explosives pulverizing bone, and poison gas searing the lungs. German soldier turned writer Erich Maria Remarque remembered the "great brotherhood [caused by] the desperate loyalty to one another of men condemned to die," while British poet Wilfred Owen wrote: "By his dead [comrade's] smile I knew we stood in hell."[5] Many surviving soldiers were maimed mentally or physically and often

'Over the Top' 1st Artists' Rifles at Marcoing, 30th December 1917, 1918 (oil on canvas)/Nash, John Northcote (1893–1977)/IMPERIAL WAR MUSEUMS/Imperial War Museum, London, UK/Bridgeman Images

IMAGE 24.2 **Over the Top** This painting, by British artist John Nash, shows the trench warfare common on the western front during World War I. Here Allied soldiers leave their trenches to attack across "No Man's Land" on a snowy day.

Q What does the painting tell us about the experiences of soldiers along the front lines of battle?

[4]David Lloyd George, quoted in Holger H. Herwig, ed., *The Outbreak of World War I*, 6th ed. (Boston: Houghton Mifflin, 1997), 12.
[5]The quotes are in Michael J. Lyons, *World War I: A Short History*, 2nd ed. (Upper Saddle River, NJ: Prentice-Hall, 2000), 195; and Ian Barnes and Robert Hudson, *The History Atlas of Europe: From Tribal Societies to a New European Unity* (New York: Macmillan, 1998), 131.

suffered from shellshock, a horrific nervous condition that made normal life difficult or impossible. The war also generated disease and starvation among civilians.

The war's western front in Belgium and northern France largely involved soldiers huddling in muddy trenches, gas masks at hand, using artillery and machine guns to pound enemy troops in their trenches (see Map 24.1); sporadic attacks across barbed wire–filled ground, known as "No Man's Land," between opposing trenches generated countless casualties. Despite the sacrifices, front lines moved little in four years. The cataclysmic Battle of Verdun in northeastern France in 1916, during which the French stopped a surprise German assault, killed a million men, symbolizing the senseless slaughter, with more soldiers probably killed per square yard than in any other battle in history. Despite the carnage, Verdun had little impact on the war. By 1917 the British could put more pressure on German lines with their invention of the first armored tank, "Big Willie," which was equipped with large guns and belted treads and was able to cross over No Man's Land and German trenches.

In the east, Germany and its allies quickly overran Serbia and Romania and pushed deep into western Russia against poorly organized czarist armies. By 1917 the war had killed or wounded over seven million Russians, while Russian peasants fleeing eastward faced hunger, disease, and homelessness. Originally a German ally, Italy switched sides in 1915 but lost heavily in unsuccessful battles. In the Middle East in 1915 the Ottomans inflicted heavy losses on Allied troops, many from Australia and New Zealand, sent to invade Turkey and control Constantinople (Istanbul), hopefully knocking the Turks out of the war. But the Allies suffered a disaster at Gallipoli, the gateway to Constantinople. When naval bombardment of Turkish forts failed, British commanders ordered a land invasion, at the time the largest amphibious landing in the history of warfare. After ten months of grueling trench warfare, forty thousand British, eight thousand Australians, and sixty thousand Turks were dead, and the remaining Allied troops evacuated. But an Arab uprising in 1916 and a British invasion of Ottoman-controlled Iraq eventually forced Ottoman retreat from that area. In East Africa British and South African forces invaded Tanganyika, a German colony. Elsewhere Japan, a British ally, occupied German-held territory in China and colonies in the Pacific islands.

Although the Germans won more battles than they lost, eventually the tide turned against them, their opponents' superior wealth, better weapons, larger forces, and sea power proving decisive. Britain and Germany, the world's greatest naval powers, battled in the North Sea and eastern Mediterranean with their naval arsenal, including gigantic battleships known as dreadnoughts. German submarines broke Allied supply lines but their attacks on British and U.S. ships carrying supplies to Britain across the Atlantic enraged Americans and drew them reluctantly into the war. Before and even during the conflict many Americans, observing the horrible and futile warfare, opposed U.S. intervention. A loose coalition of socialists, politicians, industrialists (Andrew Carnegie, Henry Ford), labor unions, social reformers (such as Jane Addams and Helen Keller), women's activists, civil rights groups, clergy, and radicals of all sorts actively promoted staying out of the conflict. The movement failed because of diverse agendas, government repression of critics and leftists, and continuing German submarine warfare.

Two fateful developments in 1917—two Russian Revolutions and U.S. intervention—altered the conflict. The first Russian Revolution overthrew the czarist government; the second, led by communists, took Russia out of the war. Freed from the eastern front, German armies made breakthroughs against British and French forces in the west. But U.S. intervention, the first major U.S. interference in European affairs, eventually offset German success. The United States had remained officially neutral but President Woodrow Wilson feared a German victory would change the course of civilization; hence he did not discourage U.S. businesses and banks from aiding Britain. As German victory seemed more likely, American military leaders, munitions makers, politicians, and businessmen all pressed for intervention. U.S. companies and banks worried that British and French defeat might prevent payment on American products and investments. Eventually President Wilson, linking military actions to idealistic American values, committed the nation to war, telling Congress that "the world must be made safe for democracy. We are the champions of the rights of mankind."[6] He also introduced conscription of young men for military service. Most draftees cooperated but several million resisted or deserted.

U.S. intervention secured victory. Beginning in June 1917, over a million American troops arrived in Europe, many with high hopes. Musician and entertainer George M. Cohan provided the stirring anthem for the troops: "Send the word over there, that the Yanks are coming…we're coming over, and we won't be back till it's over, over there."[7] While many Americans struggled to comprehend European ways, others developed a taste for European culture and cities such as London and Paris. Americans helped blockade German ports, creating severe economic problems, and pushed German forces back. Beginning in January 1918 what experts consider the greatest medical holocaust in history, a terrible influenza pandemic (often called the Spanish Flu), ravaged Europe, the U.S., and much of the world, affecting maybe five hundred million and killing between 50 and 100 million people before it ebbed after four years. Perhaps twenty million Europeans perished. Some studies trace the infection to a troop transit camp and hospital in France. The misery rapidly spread around the world. By late 1918 fifty thousand had died in South Africa and forty-one thousand in Cairo. Even in remote Tahiti, trucks roamed the streets to collect the dead. The flu brought U.S. and European life to a standstill, emptying city streets, closing pool halls, saloons, churches, and theaters as people cowered behind closed doors. Soon Germany's allies began surrendering. Demoralized, its overextended army in disarray, and suffering food and fuel shortages, Germany agreed to peace in November 1918. Kaiser Wilhelm II and the Austro-Hungarian emperor both abdicated, ending two long-standing European monarchies. The peace terms dictated by the victors changed the old global order and began a new one.

[6]From L. S. Stavrianos, ed., *The Epic of Modern Man: A Collection of Readings* (Englewood Cliffs, NJ: Prentice-Hall, 1966), 354.
[7]Quoted in Michael E. Ruane, "The U.S. Joined the 'Great War' 100 Years Ago. America and Warfare Were Never the Same," *Washington Post* (April 3, 2017).

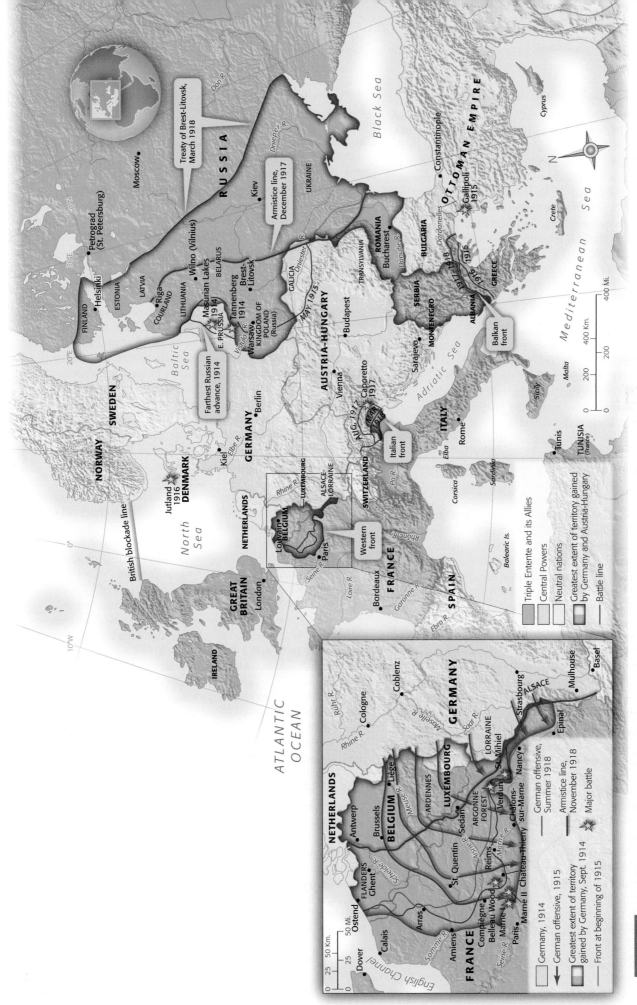

MAP 24.1 World War I World War I pitted the Triple Entente of Britain, France, and Russia, and its allies, against the Central Powers: Germany, Austria-Hungary, and the Ottoman Empire. The worst fighting occurred along the western front and in eastern Europe and Russia. The intervention of the United States in 1917 against the Central Powers proved decisive.

Q What can this map tell us about the war's geography, chronology, and participants?

24-1c Consequences of World War I

World War I undermined German power and shifted more influence to Britain, France, and the United States. The Paris Peace Conference of 1919, held in the opulent former royal palace in suburban Versailles (**vuhr-SIGH**), reshaped Europe. A complex man, U.S. president Wilson remains controversial among historians for his considerable accomplishments and crushing failures, viewed as progressive but also conservative, scholarly but uncompromising, democratic but intolerant. He hoped to use his nation's growing power to sell an agenda, the Fourteen Points, to skeptical British and French leaders. Idealistically favoring political freedom and stability, and worrying that a humiliated, crippled Germany would become chaotic, Wilson proposed conciliatory treatment of Germany. However, the French wanted to divide Germany. The final Treaty of Versailles unleashed nationalism and shaped the world for a century to come. The treaty required Germany to partly dismantle its military; abandon its Asian, African, and Pacific colonies; and shift disputed land to its neighbors, leaving three million ethnic Germans in countries such as Czechoslovakia and Poland. Germany also had to pay huge annual payments, known as reparations, to the victors to compensate for its war costs. The treaty left Germany virtually disarmed and bankrupt, planting the roots for future problems, as Wilson had feared. Germany's new leader, Friedrich Ebert, saw a troubled future: "The armistice will not produce a just peace. The sacrifices imposed on us must lead to our people's doom."[8]

The war imposed an appalling human toll. Altogether around twenty million died, including 9 to 10 million soldiers (two million Russians, two million Germans, 1.5 million French, and 117,000 Americans) and some ten million civilians. Many of the soldiers (including over half of the Americans) died from the flu rather than combat. The brutality and waste radicalized many workers and peasants, especially in eastern Europe, while leftist political parties—Socialists and Communists—gained strength. In 1914 Europeans went to war with patriotic enthusiasm; by 1918 some philosophers and writers feared the slaughter represented rejection of Enlightenment rationality, destroying the Western claim to moral leadership. Pacifist, antiwar sentiments grew, reflected by French writer and former soldier Henri Barbusse: "Shame on military glory, shame on armies, shame on the soldier's calling that changes men by turns into stupid victims and ignoble brutes."[9] Americans tend to remember the war, if they think of it at all, in a positive, even heroic light, as an episode when Americans went to Europe's rescue, but many Europeans view it as a disaster.

The war destroyed several old states and created new ones. The Russian, Ottoman, Austro-Hungarian, and German Empires collapsed, while communists gained power in Russia, launching a new political and economic system. Wilson, believing that ethnically homogeneous nation-states could prevent nationalist rivalries, promoted self-determination of European peoples. Hence, the Paris Peace Conference redrew national boundaries and gave some ethnic minorities their own states. Poland, Czechoslovakia, Yugoslavia, and Finland, carved out of the German, Austro-Hungarian, and Russian Empires, later became pawns in the Germany–Russia rivalry that helped launch World War II. Some new states placed diverse ethnic groups within arbitrary boundaries. For example, Yugoslavia was comprised of people who had fought each other for centuries and shared no common national identity, including Orthodox Serbs, Catholic Croats and Slovenes, and Muslim Slavs and Albanians. Britain, facing uprisings and civil war in its longtime colony, Ireland, was forced in 1921 to grant most counties special status as the self-governing Irish Free State. In 1937 Ireland became completely independent of the British crown, finally realizing the centuries-old Irish nationalist dream.

Yet the treaty was deeply flawed. Partly to protect Japanese immigrants to the Americas, Japan, a long time British ally, proposed a clause in the treaty that affirmed the equality of all nations, regardless of race. This would have moved the world forward on the issue of racial equality and perhaps helped forge a much different twentieth century, but, requiting unanimous support for approval, the proposal was rejected. Instead, the victorious powers ignored self-determination for their colonies. In seeking to strengthen U.S. allies Britain and France, Wilson supported preserving their Asian, African, Pacific, and Caribbean colonies. The peace settlement also transferred Germany's African colonies to Britain, France, Belgium, and South Africa and its Asian and Pacific territories to Britain, France, Australia, New Zealand, and Japan as Mandated Territories, in theory subject to the oversight of the new League of Nations but in practice regarded as colonies by another name. Britain and France acquired Middle Eastern societies formerly ruled by Ottoman Turkey but also maintained artificial borders that grouped diverse, often feuding, ethnic groups and religious sects together in unwieldy states like Iraq and Lebanon. But colonized peoples, tired of being dominated and repressed, were resentful that their aspirations and struggles were ignored, especially since thousands of Asian and African colonial subjects had been conscripted or recruited to fight for Britain, France, or Germany in the war. South Asian and African troops fighting for Britain and West Africans for France fought heroically, helping the Allies overcome horrendous battlefront losses. But they felt they had been lied to, treated as expendable and forgettable cannon fodder. Thus World War I stimulated the rise of nationalism, the desire to form politically independent nations, in the colonies between 1918 and 1941 (see Chapter 25).

Although the global system shaped by Western colonial empires and economic power survived, European prestige and influence were weakened. The war also undermined European economies, allowing the United States to leap ahead as an economic and military power. In 1916 the U.S. military numbered 130,000; by 1918 it had four million. Like nineteenth-century Britain, America, with the world's largest, most productive economy, wanted free trade and an open world to assert industrial supremacy. Having borrowed from the United States to finance the war, Europeans now owed Americans money; the United States, long a debtor nation, became a creditor nation.

[8]Quoted in A. J. Nicholls, *Weimar and the Rise of Hitler*, 2nd ed. (New York: St. Martin's, 1979), 11.
[9]Quoted in Piers Brendon, *Dark Valley: A Panorama of the 1930s* (New York: Alfred A. Knopf, 2000), 6.

By 1919 Americans produced 42 percent of the world's industrial output, more than Europe combined, replacing Britain as the world's banker and workshop. Wilson helped form a League of Nations, the first organization of independent nations to work for peace and humanitarian concerns, but could not persuade the U.S. Congress, controlled by largely isolationist Republicans, to approve U.S. membership. Hence, the only nation with power and stature to make the league work stayed outside, leaving Britain and France alone to handle European and global issues.

KEY POINTS

▶ The United States helped the French and British win the war, but U.S. president Woodrow Wilson could not prevent the French from dictating harsh settlement terms that required Germany to partially dismantle its military, abandon its colonies, give up some of its territory, and pay heavy reparations.

▶ The horrors of World War I led to the radicalization of many Europeans and a growth of antiwar sentiment.

▶ The war caused the breakup of the Ottoman and German Empires, much of which were colonized by Britain and France, and the breakup of much of the Russian and Austro-Hungarian Empires, which were carved into new countries.

▶ After the war, the United States became the dominating world power.

24-2 The Revolutionary Path to Soviet Communism

⇄C TRANSITIONS **SOCIETIES**

Q How did communism prevail in Russia and transform that country?

World War I opened a path to a world even more divided, as competing ideologies merged with national interests to stir up tensions. A key part of this transition and a major consequence of the war, the Russian Revolution erupted and shaped twentieth-century European and world history, politics, and beliefs. Some historians consider it the central event of the century. Four decades later one-third of humanity lived under governments derived from the revolution or imposed by Russians. Russia provided a testing ground for a radical ideology, communism, creating a powerful state that transformed Russian society and provided an alternative to North American and western European capitalist democracy. But the Russian model lost considerable influence by the 1990s as the communist world collapsed into pieces.

CONNECTION to TODAY

How did the Western nations' rivalry with and fear of the Soviet Union and communism shape your parents or grandparents lives?

Vladimir Lenin (**LEN-in**) (1870–1924), a middle-class lawyer who was uncompromising but a clever political strategist influenced by Marxist writings, recruited supporters with his passionate beliefs and persuasive speeches. Most Bolshevik leaders, including Lenin, had been political prisoners in harsh Siberian labor camps. Lenin had been further radicalized when the government executed his older brother for having joined an assassination plot against the czar. To avoid arrest, he lived in exile, organizing his movement.

Claiming to help downtrodden workers and peasants redress the wrongs inflicted upon them by the rich and privileged, Bolsheviks contended that revolutionary violence could create a new, classless communist society with more equitable wealth and power distribution. Lenin advocated a small, disciplined revolutionary organization embracing workers' interests in which all members had to abide by the leaders' decisions, a system known as the party line. When World War I broke out, Russia's people and even most opposition political parties, supporting a patriotic defense against hated Germany, rallied around the unpopular government. Only the Bolsheviks opposed a war they considered an imperialistic struggle over markets and colonies, in which capitalists on both sides used workers to fight other workers for the benefit of the rich. But war soon lost its allure as Russian military forces collapsed against stronger German armies.

24-2a The Roots of Revolution

The Russian Revolution had deep roots in Russian society and despotic czarism (see Chapter 23). Controlling a huge Eurasian empire, Russia had some industrialization, but powerful landed aristocrats opposed further development. Socially and economically, Russia was still somewhat feudalistic; peasants often remained subject to landowners, enjoying little social mobility or wealth. Growing discontent among intellectuals, the floundering middle class, underpaid industrial workers, and peasants, who hated the autocratic czarist system, fomented radical movements.

After the regime brutally crushed the 1905 revolution, the **Bolsheviks**, the most radical antigovernment group, transformed the revolutionary socialist views of Karl Marx into a dogmatic communist ideology. Bolshevik founder and leader

By 1917 demoralized Russians sought change, sparking two revolutions. The first, erupting in March while riots and strikes paralyzed cities, toppled the czar, imprisoned

Bolsheviks The most radical of Russia's antigovernment groups at the turn of the twentieth century, who embraced a dogmatic form of Marxism.

Sovfoto/Universal Images Group/Getty Images

IMAGE 24.3 **Lenin** The Bolshevik leader Vladimir Lenin stirred crowds with his fiery revolutionary rhetoric, helping to spread the communist message among Russians fed up with ineffective government, war, and poverty.

Q Does the photo suggest reasons why Lenin may have been successful in recruiting a mass following for his cause?

the imperial family, and established a provisional government comprised of various parties from the moderate center to the far left. Working women triggered the protests, swarming the capital, Saint Petersburg, to demand relief and food and soon gaining support from the soldiers sent to control them. The provisional government leaders, headed by lawyer Aleksandr Kerensky (1881–1970), were well-meaning urban liberals who favored progressive reform and Western-style democracy, but, having no roots among the population, they failed by refusing to provide what most Russians wanted: peace and land. Because of commitments to Russia's wartime allies Britain and France, they vowed to continue fighting, declining to redistribute land to the peasantry until the war ended and elections could be held to form a new, more representative, government.

While the increasingly discredited provisional government asked for time, radicals organized **soviets**, local action councils enlisting workers and soldiers to fight factory owners and military officers. This grassroots movement for change undermined government authority. As soviets and government jockeyed for control of Saint Petersburg, the Germans helped Lenin secretly return from

soviets Local action councils formed by Russian radicals before the 1917 Russian Revolution that enlisted workers and soldiers to fight the factory owners and military officers.

Switzerland to Russia hidden in a railroad box car. Using the slogans of "peace, bread, and land" and "all power to the soviets," Lenin built up Bolshevik influence in the soviets while refusing to support the war or compromise with the parties supporting the provisional government. Meanwhile, the weak provisional government tried to prevent peasants from seizing land and soldiers from deserting their units.

24-2b The Bolshevik Seizure of Power and Civil War

In October 1917, the Bolsheviks and their 240,000 party members, aided by the soviets, staged an uprising, seizing key government buildings in Saint Petersburg and grabbing power from Kerensky's crumbling provisional government. With a fragile hold on power, the Bolsheviks had to allow diverse parties to contest elections for an assembly, which met in January 1918. After the assembly refused to support Bolshevik leadership, Bolsheviks used troops to seize national and city governments and terrorized or executed opponents, including moderate, pro-democracy socialists. Claiming to transfer power to the working class, Lenin defended violence to build a better world, asserting that chefs cannot make an omelet without breaking eggs. The Bolsheviks, renaming themselves the Communist Party, gained popular support by pulling Russia out of the war. In the Treaty of Brest-Litovsk with Germany in March 1918, Russia gave up some of its empire in the west to Germany, abandoning the Ukraine, eastern Poland, the Baltic states, and Finland. The Bolsheviks also moved the capital from Saint Petersburg, renamed Leningrad, to Moscow much further east. In 1919, Lenin, hoping to protect Russia's revolution by promoting world revolution, organized the Communist International, or Comintern, a collection of communist parties from many countries. However, the prospect of world revolution soon faded because of U.S. aid to Europe after the war.

The Russian Revolution sparked the Russian civil war (1918–1921) (see Map 24.2). The leaders of conservative, anticommunist forces, who called themselves White Russians, included czarist aristocrats, generals angry at losing their dominance, and a few pro-Western liberals favoring democracy. Heavily funded and armed by Western nations, White Russians fought the communist Red Army for three years, mostly in fringe areas of the Russian Empire. With a cohesive party and brilliant military leadership, the communists capitalized on disunity among White Russian leaders and their Western backers. Most crucially, they received growing support from the working class and peasants, who feared the return of hated landowners with a White Russian victory. The Czarist generals leading the White army made no secret that if they were victorious they would exterminate both Bolsheviks and Jews; indeed, the Whites carried out pogroms that wiped out entire Jewish villages. Initially vulnerable, the communists eventually gained the advantage, defeating the White Russians and even reclaiming some territory lost in the Brest-Litovsk Treaty, including Ukraine.

Outside intervention by Japan, Britain, France, and the United States to roll back the Bolshevik regime added an international flavor to the civil war. Japan, concentrating on eastern

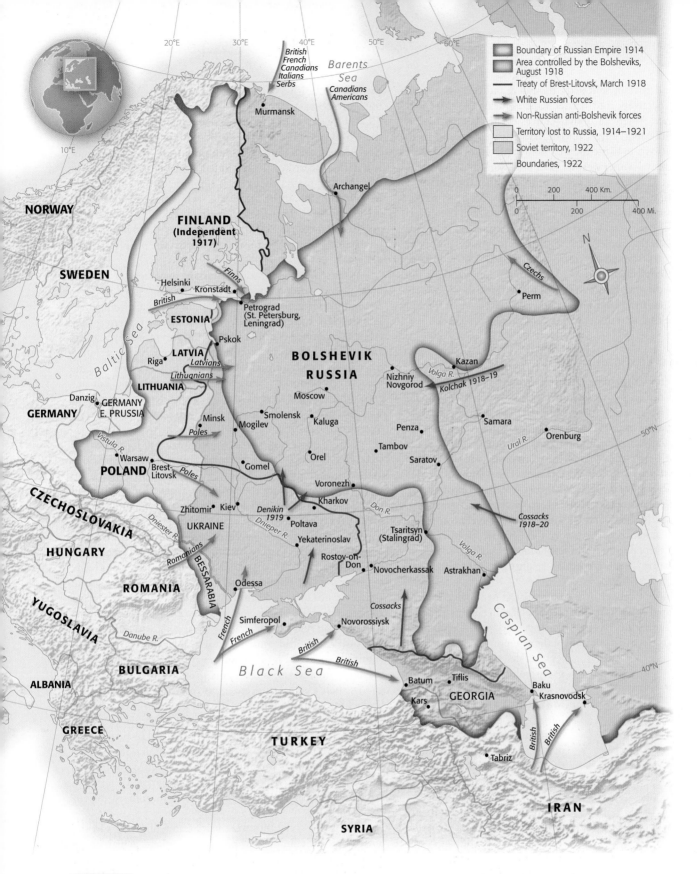

MAP 24.2 Civil War in Revolutionary Russia (1918–1921) The communist seizure of power in Russia in 1917 sparked a counteroffensive, backed by varied Western nations and Japan, to reverse the Russian Revolution. The communists successfully defended the Russian heartland while pushing back the conservative offensive.

Q What can we learn from the map about the geography of the conflict?

Siberia, and Britain sent sixty thousand and forty thousand troops, respectively, into Russia. Liberal idealist Wilson sent two separate American military forces to, he claimed, spread democratic values. Five thousand American troops went to northern Russia to battle the Red Army for control of two port cities, but brutal winter weather, poor provisions, and high casualties drove U.S. troops to near mutiny. Another contingent of ten thousand Americans entered eastern Siberia. Soon recognizing intervention as a quagmire, Wilson lamented that it was harder to get out than it was to go in, a lesson about wars and interventions that some later U.S. presidents and soldiers under their command would also learn the hard way. U.S. and other Western troops finally left in 1920. Western intervention only helped solidify the communist government, which was widely seen by Russians as fighting a nationalist war against foreign powers seeking to restore the old discredited czarist order.

24-2c Lenin, Stalin, and Dictatorship

By 1922 the Communist Party controlled much of the old Russian Empire, but the country was devastated, its people starving. The civil war made good relations with the capitalist democracies impossible while reinforcing the communists' paranoid, authoritarian, and militaristic attitudes. Meanwhile, the world's first state based on communist ideas inspired communist groups in other countries. The Union of Soviet Socialist Republics (USSR), in theory a federation of all the empire's diverse peoples—such as Kazakhs, Uzbeks, Armenians, Georgians, Chechens, and Ukrainians—was largely controlled by Russians, hence perpetuating the Russian Empire. Soon the USSR turned from world revolution to building "socialism in one country"—using coercion against reluctant citizens if necessary.

Having no model of a communist state, Soviet leaders experimented while using their secret police to eliminate opponents, including liberals and moderate socialists. Combining socialism (collective ownership of the economy) and **Leninism**,

Leninism A political system in which one party holds a monopoly on power, excluding other parties from participation.

Marxism-Leninism The basis for Soviet communism, a mix of socialism (collective ownership of the economy) and Leninism.

New Economic Policy Lenin's pragmatic approach to economic development, which mixed capitalism and socialism.

Stalinism Joseph Stalin's system of government, which included state ownership of all property, such as lands and businesses, a planned economy, and one-man rule.

a political system in which one party holds a power monopoly, Soviet leaders created **Marxism-Leninism**. Lenin initially favored centralizing all economic activity, but peasant opposition forced him to adopt the **New Economic Policy** (NEP), a pragmatic approach mixing capitalism and socialism that allowed peasants to sell their produce on the open market. The NEP brought economic recovery. However, with few consumer goods available, peasants lacked incentive to sell their produce for profit.

Dissatisfied, Lenin advocated renewal and criticized ethnic Russian chauvinism and

the bloated Bolshevik bureaucracy as socialist in appearance but not substance: "czarism slightly anointed with Soviet oil."[10] Decades later, Lenin's assessment remained accurate; the USSR never became the egalitarian society envisioned by Karl Marx. Lenin himself, combining ruthless authoritarianism with concern for the exploited, deserves some blame for constructing myths about mass support for the communist-led "dictatorship of the proletariat" while ties between political leaders and the people remained weak. The instability and divisions caused by wars made communist leaders fear unrest and therefore be unwilling to trust the people or allow dissent.

Czarist legacies of authoritarian, bureaucratic government and an obedient population fostered dictatorship. Most communist leaders were, like Lenin, intellectuals from urban middle-class backgrounds. To regenerate the economy, they eventually rejected control of farms and enterprises by workers and peasants, adopting a top-down managerial system staffed by officials chiefly of middle-class origin. The Soviet middle class, largely comprising state employees, managers, and bureaucrats who enjoyed salaries and privileges denied the masses, were dedicated to maintaining their own power. Lenin hoped to reform the party but died in 1924.

Lenin's successor, the master bureaucrat Joseph Stalin (STAH-lin) (1879–1953), reshaped Soviet communism. Born in the Caucasus province of Georgia, he studied to be a Russian Orthodox priest before the seminary expelled him. He then joined the Bolsheviks and adopted the name Stalin ("Man of Steel"). By controlling the Communist Party apparatus, Stalin outmaneuvered rivals to succeed Lenin and gained power as peasants, no longer fearing landlords, increasingly turned away from the party. Stalin urged a hard line against those resisting state policies, eliminated all his competition, and became a dictator. His system, **Stalinism**, included state ownership of all property, such as lands and businesses; a planned economy; and one-man rule.

In 1928 Stalin ended Lenin's NEP and introduced annual Five-Year Plans for future production. Formulated by state bureaucrats, these plans produced basic industrial goods, such as steel and coal, but few consumer products. Launching a crash industrialization program, Stalin withdrew the country from the global system, mobilized Russian resources, and refused foreign investment. He introduced tractors and harvesters to increase farm production and collectivized the land, turning private farms into commonly owned enterprises, destroying the wealthier small farmers, the *kulaks*, and exiling to Siberia those who refused to join collective farms.

The 1930s and 1940s were hard, terror-filled years in the Soviet Union. Stalin ordered purges to eliminate actual, imagined, and potential opponents; forced-labor camps for suspected dissidents; and widespread use of the secret police (KGB), which spied on and intimidated the people. Farming collectivization generated widespread famine and growing dissent, provoking the Great Purge of 1936–1938, which was marked by well-publicized trials of some party leaders as traitors. Stalin also deported millions to harsh Siberian forced-labor camps known as

[10]Quoted in L. S. Stavrianos, *Global Rift: The Third World Comes of Age* (New York: William Morrow, 1981), 499.

gulags (Russian shorthand for State Camp Administration). Some 4 to 5 million people were arrested and half a million executed for alleged subversion. From 1929 until 1953 some eighteen million people passed through the massive system; 4.5 million never returned home. Gulag inmates toiled, starved, and died building railroads, cutting timber, or digging canals. The repression did not spare even beloved artists, especially Jews like poet Osip Mandelstam (**MAHN-duhl-stuhm**) (1891–1938). The total dead and jailed from Stalin's repression numbered around forty million people. Beloved poet, critic, and survivor of Stalinism Anna Akhmatova (**uhk-MAH-tuh-vuh**) (1889–1966), mourning a lost generation, summarized the horror: "Madness has already covered, Half my soul with its wing. And gives to drink of a fiery wine, And beckons into the dark valley."[11]

Repression imposed high economic costs. Peasants often destroyed their equipment and livestock in protest, harming agriculture for decades, and adopted passive resistance, doing just the minimum to survive. Russia's annual food production between 1928 and 1980 was less than in 1924. Unable to use agricultural surplus to finance industrialization, the Soviets forced urban workers to labor long hours for low wages and few consumer goods. Alienated workers passively resisted, voicing their feelings in the common expression: "The government pretends they are paying us so we pretend we are working." A lack of initiative and creativity, as well as widespread alcoholism and theft, hurt the economic system.

24-2d Reshaping Russian Society

At the same time, communism fostered modernization. Crash industrialization, mobilized by Five-Year Plans, raised the gross national product (GNP), the annual total of all economic activities, to second in the world by 1932. Like Meiji Japan, the state, rather than private capital, was the main agent for change. The industrial workforce tripled between 1928 and 1937. Mass education raised the literacy rate from 28 percent in 1900 to over 90 percent by the 1980s, and better medical care raised life expectancy from thirty-two in 1914 to seventy in 1960.

Communism also reshaped social patterns. To promote social equality, Lenin tried breaking up traditional institutions, including patriarchal families. Soviet official and feminist Alexandra Kollontai (1872–1952), believing the state should fund child care and domestic work, envisioned public kitchens, laundries, and nurseries to help women work outside the home. Lenin made divorce easier, legalized homosexuality, sanctioned free love and abortion, and forbade Muslim women from wearing veils and men from having multiple wives. Reversing Lenin's policies, Stalin restored the family, made divorce more difficult, banned abortion, and persecuted homosexuals. Kollontai, whose outspoken feminism antagonized party leaders, later became ambassador to Sweden, the world's first female ambassador.

Unlike the atheistic Lenin, who considered religion spiritual oppression for postulating a better life after death, Stalin pragmatically reached accommodation with the Russian Orthodox Church while keeping it under state control. While many citizens professed atheism, at least half identified as religious in the 1936 census. Stalin also ordered writers and artists to depict Soviet life from a revolutionary perspective, a style known as **socialist realism**.

Hoping to catch up to the West, the USSR was the first society to leave the capitalist world order, industrialize rapidly under direct state control, and establish a socialist society, but at a high cost in human rights and lives. The pervasive system of political repression and state control limited its appeal to other societies. Historians debate how much of the Soviet system resulted from communism and how much from autocratic Russian traditions that despised merchants and promoted deference to state power. The USSR combined Marxist ideology, czarist despotism, and the missionary impulse derived from Christianity to spread the "true faith" to the world. Today, a century after the revolution and three decades since the disintegration of the Soviet Union, some aspects of czarist Russia (such as a powerful Russian Orthodox Church) but also some features of Soviet despotism (harassment and arrest of dissidents) have been restored to influence. Many historians note that today Russians live with a certain ambivalence toward 1917 and communist rule. While many believe that the communists wrecked the country in many ways, its symbols and laws are still a part of their daily lives. And while socialists in the early twentieth century may have held some hope that communist Russia might, in a single generation, radically transform a backward country into a developed nation that could be emulated and admired, few socialists today see Russia, then or now, as a model. Many want a society emphasizing political pluralism, diversity, and dissent.

> **gulags** Harsh forced-labor camps in Siberia.

> **socialist realism** Literary and artistic works that depicted life from a revolutionary perspective, a style first introduced in Stalin's Russia.

KEY POINTS

▶ The Bolsheviks, a group of Marxist revolutionaries led by Vladimir Lenin, were energized by the unsuccessful 1905 Russian Revolution and organized a core of professional activists devoted to violent revolution and a more equitable distribution of wealth and power.

▶ In October 1917, radical soviets, allied with the Bolsheviks, organized and seized power.

▶ In the interest of spreading the Revolution, Lenin founded the Communist International, but he was soon fighting the Russian civil war against the White Russians, who were backed by Western nations.

▶ After winning the civil war, the Bolsheviks focused on establishing Marxism-Leninism in the USSR, a one-party brand of socialism that treated opponents ruthlessly and failed to achieve a true connection between the masses and the government.

---

[11]Quoted in Brendon, *Dark Valley*, 493.

24-3 The Interwar Years and the Great Depression

TRANSITIONS SOCIETIES

Q How did the Great Depression reshape world politics and economies?

With the ashes of brutal war still smoldering, the industrialized nations turned to revival and reconstruction. Peace in Europe generated questioning of the old order, including in industrialized nations. By the early 1920s, however, western Europe had stabilized, mostly under democratically elected governments, while the United States enjoyed widespread prosperity, as did many Japanese. But the **Great Depression**, a collapse of the world economy lasting in varying degrees of severity through the 1930s, dramatically undermined Western affluence and illustrated in its global reach the world's economic interdependence. The distress, which affected both industrialized nations and societies supplying raw materials, also fostered radical political movements.

> **CONNECTION to TODAY**
>
> How did the Depression influence life in your family, community, and country?

24-3a Postwar Europe

The 1920s brought political, economic, and social change throughout western Europe. Europe's slow, painful recovery fostered opposition political movements that placed conservatives protecting the old order on the defensive. Political infighting weakened many governments. Conservative-dominated regimes usually rebuffed workers' demands for better conditions or unions, while socialist and social democratic parties, such as Britain's Labor Party, growing stronger, tried to expand workers' rights through legislation. Some countries remained politically and economically unstable. Under the post-Versailles and democratic Weimar **(VIE-mahr)** Republic, Germany struggled with high unemployment and a devastated economy. These years in Germany were marked by unstable government and economic crisis but also a vibrant cultural scene in the fields of literature, art, cinema, theater, music, and entertainment as well as science. In 1923 France occupied western Germany's industrialized Ruhr district to enforce reparations payments. But the costly reparations caused hyperinflation in Germany, fostering extremist groups. Since Europe's economy needed German prosperity, the Allies reduced reparations and the United States extended loans, but Germany still faced challenges. Multiethnic countries such as Poland, with its large German, Russian, and Ukrainian minorities, and Czechoslovakia, mixing Czechs and Slovaks with Germans, Poles, Hungarians, and Ukrainians, also experienced tensions.

Some countries enjoyed economic recovery, curbing inflation and unemployment. After Europeans borrowed U.S. mass production processes, including assembly lines pioneered at Ford Motor Company, the growing middle classes could afford cars, radios, refrigerators, vacuum cleaners, and central heating. Although the urban white-collar class largely opposed working-class socialism, labor unions gained strength, helping some workers achieve an eight-hour day. Yet Europe's economies, bound up with the world economy, lost ground to the United States and Japan.

To promote European peace and unity, some leaders emphasized common roots in Classical Greece, Rome, and Christianity. Visionary French foreign minister Aristide Briand **(bree-AHND)** (1862–1932) led efforts to renounce war among European nations, proposing a federal union and common market. His ideas were turned in to the Kellogg-Briand Pact of 1928, joined by sixty-three nations, which outlawed war, an ambitious goal. Many critics believed outlawing war to be an absurd and dangerously naive dream, and just over a decade later every nation that signed the pact (except Ireland) had gone to war. However, some historians see the pact as diminishing (but not completely eliminating) conquest, perhaps the main reason countries go to war. Briand's vision finally came to fruition (at least for Europe) two decades later, in the ashes of World War II, with the formation of the European Common Market.

Cities fostered social change. Affluent people found entertainment at nightclubs, cabarets, and dancehalls and shopped at large department stores, while U.S. culture, especially jazz, became widely popular. Religious observance declined because some felt abandoned by God on the battlefields or rejected Christianity as patriarchal, out of tune with their lives. In the 1920s and 1930s a trend that some term the "modern girl" emerged in Western societies and Japan; followers shared an affinity for consumption (especially cosmetics) while also challenging gender and class expectations. Women's fashions emphasized short hair and boyish figures, while the "new woman" sought financial independence through paid work. With the war's heavy loss of life leaving fewer young men to marry or hire, women moved into office jobs, female secretaries replacing male clerks. More women also became lawyers, physicians, and even members of parliaments. In some places women fought for and achieved suffrage. Before the war only Norway and Finland had women's suffrage. Denmark gave women the vote in 1915 and Germany in 1919, and Britain extended it to women over age thirty in 1918 and to all women over eighteen in 1928. But many countries, including France and Italy, ignored these demands.

As gender standards changed, once-shocking attitudes became common, including openness about sexuality and rejection of traditional marriage. Women now wore clothes showing off their figure, and beauty contests featured women in revealing swimsuits that were once considered scandalous. Yet, official attitudes toward homosexuality shifted toward repression. In the nineteenth century, despite anti-sodomy laws, courts usually dismissed charges; Europeans understood that some men and women had same-sex relations or emotional ties. By the early 1900s, however, the media and most

Great Depression A collapse of the world economy that lasted in varying degrees of severity through the 1930s.

churches identified LGBTQ people as different and immoral. Gay men and lesbians lived openly in cities like Paris and Berlin but suffered harassment and police raids on their clubs. Believing that same-sex love challenged mainstream values, British officials prosecuted award-winning writer Radclyffe Hall (1883–1943) for obscenity after the banning of her 1928 novel, *The Well of Loneliness*, about lesbian identity. Although Soviet Russia and Weimar Germany legalized homosexuality, these tolerant policies were later reversed. In 1934 Stalin defined homosexuality as a crime against the state, and in 1935 Nazi Germany prosecuted fifty thousand men for homosexual activity. Many European nations banned abortion and birth control.

24-3b Postwar Japan

As in Europe, industrialization, democratic politics, and liberalization reshaped Japan during the 1920s, generating prosperity and a growing urban middle class. Japan's population tripled between 1860 and 1940 to sixty million, but lack of land forced many rural people to move to cities or emigrate, often as contract laborers, to Hawaii or the Americas, especially Brazil, Peru, Canada, and the United States. A terrible earthquake in 1923 leveled Tokyo and Yokohama, killing over 100,000 people and leaving three-quarters of their populations homeless from fires and a gigantic tsunami. But, as in China and India today, cheap labor and low prices attracted foreign markets for consumer goods, especially textiles, that appealed to working-class Western and Asian consumers. Powerful business interests dominated democratic politics, with corrupt and volatile politics disillusioning many Japanese.

Japan played a visible world role. Already controlling Taiwan, Korea, and northern China footholds, during the war Japan acquired Germany's Pacific colonies, formalized as League of Nations mandates after the war, and assumed a sphere of influence in eastern China, acquisitions that created enemies. Tensions with the United States increased, fostered partly by racist American laws restricting Japanese immigrant rights and U.S. hostility to Japan's Asian and Pacific ambitions.

As in the 1870s, Western influence permeated Japan's cities. American popular culture influenced urban middle-class Japanese, and baseball became a popular sport, the first professional teams appearing in 1934. In Tokyo, young men and women, known as the "modern boy" and "modern girl," wore the latest imported styles while enjoying jazz, beer halls, and Western films. Young women avidly read mass women's magazines, and many questioned traditions of submissive females and dominant males. Many young people sought freedom to choose their own marriage partners. Non-traditional Japanese such as openly lesbian writer Yoshiya Nobuko (yo-SHE-ya no-BOO-ko) had a large following among youth (see Meet the People: Yoshiya Nobuko: Japanese Writer and Gender Rebel). Conservatives thought people like Yoshiya were leading Japan in the wrong direction. Feminist poet Yosano Akiko celebrated the emerging women's movement: "All the sleeping women, Are now awake and moving."[12] Another leading feminist, Kato Shidzue (KAH-to shid-ZOO-ee) (1897–2001), sojourned in the United States and then advocated family planning and equal political rights for women. Japanese thinkers and artists pondered traditional and modern values and cultural identity. Writer Akutagawa Ryunosuke (1892–1927), combining Western and Japanese traditions, wrote an influential short story, *Rashomon*, describing a rape and murder from several eyewitness perceptions. However, the working classes and rural population, not sharing in economic prosperity, remained alienated from Westernized urban middle-class culture, seeing little benefit in either individualistic Western thought or liberalizing customs. In 1925 a left-wing peasants' association proclaimed: "The cities grow more luxurious day by day ... while the villagers have to live on moldy salted fish and wear shopworn clothes ... the cities are living off the sweat of the farmers."[13]

24-3c U.S. Society and Politics

In the United States, anti-communism and growing middle-class prosperity bolstered conservative forces. Even before the end of the war all German-born residents had to register with the government and Americans were encouraged to spy on and report others for violating rationing programs or failure to buy war bonds. Propaganda films asked the question: "Are you 100 percent American?" To crush domestic dissent and radicalism the U.S. Congress passed the Espionage and Sedition Acts of 1917–18, which violated civil liberties and led to censoring mail, shutting down publications, and jailing critics and activists (such as labor leader and socialist Eugene Debs), sometimes just for making speeches. With Americans now hostile to socialism of any kind, especially communist ideology, hatred of Russians and communism replaced hatred of Germans. In 1919–1920 widespread public fear of communism, the "Red Scare," generated a series of government crackdowns on dissidents, freezing attitudes toward communist movements for generations; governments suppressed strikes, harassed labor unions, arrested political radicals, and deported foreigners. Some Americans worried about immigrants bringing in "foreign" cultures and values. President Calvin Coolidge's warning in the 1920s that the nation was becoming "a dumping ground" and must remain "American" reflected a long history of xenophobia. The United States also sought to isolate the USSR. A U.S. senator and critic of this policy concluded in 1925, "So long as you have a hundred and fifty million people [in the U.S.S.R.] outlawed, it necessarily follows that you cannot have peace."[14] However, the United States softened its policy and extended diplomatic recognition in 1933.

Domestic unrest challenged society. While desperate workers struck for better wages, left-wing unions fought against "big business" power. Union militants such as the charismatic Mary Harris ("Mother") Jones (1830–1930), an Irish immigrant who called herself a hell-raiser, organized coal miners and railroad workers and fought for unions and workers from the 1890s through the 1920s. In response, federal, state, and local governments

[12]Quoted in Kenneth B. Pyle, *The Making of Modern Japan*, 2nd ed. (Lexington, MA: D.C. Heath, 1996), 173.
[13]Quoted in Conrad Schirokauer and Donald N. Clark, *Modern East Asia: A Brief History*, 2nd ed. (Boston: Houghton Mifflin, 2008), 257.
[14]Senator William Borah, quoted in William Appleman Williams, *American–Russian Relations, 1781–1947* (New York: Rinehart, 1952), 164.

Yoshiya Nobuko, Japanese Writer and Gender Rebel

Yoshiya Nobuko (1896–1973), a popular writer who challenged gender roles, lived through major transitions as Japan moved from a parochial society through imperial power and world war to become an industrial powerhouse. She was born in a northern Honshu city, Niigata, just after Japan's victory over China in the Sino-Japanese War (1894–1895) and was trained by her middle-class, culturally conservative parents for the "good wife, wise mother" role expected of women in Meiji Japan. Yoshiya observed that her mother, though encouraging her to adopt traditional roles of female domesticity and obedience to men, remained in a loveless arranged marriage to Yoshiya's father.

Yoshiya began writing as a child and published her first short stories at age twelve. In 1915 she moved to Tokyo, where she began to diverge from Japanese career and gender expectations. Rising literacy opened doors to literature aimed at a popular audience, allowing writers such as Yoshiya to make a living from their work. Between 1916 and 1924 Yoshiya's short stories were serialized in a popular magazine, *Girl's Illustrated*, aimed at young, chiefly female readers. Her stories inspired a generation of women writers and made Yoshiya famous. They appealed to schoolgirls and the growing group of women not yet committed to marriage and children. According to tradition, women were supposed to be married by age twenty-four, but many young women now worked in the public jobs as clerks, cafe hostesses, ticket sellers, schoolteachers, typists, and telephone operators. Yoshiya's core audience came from this group, especially so-called "modern girls," Westernized urban women who avoided or postponed marriage. Critics accused these women of being manly and un-Japanese.

In her writing and life, the very modern Yoshiya took advantage of the new public sphere opened to women for redefining relations between them. She challenged conventions of family life, openly avowing her lesbianism. The Japanese traditionally tolerated homosexuality, including public displays of affection by people of the same gender. Now more openly passionate friendships between females became common among students, educators, civil servants, and actresses. Japanese society viewed female homosexuality as spiritual, in contrast to the popular image of the carnal male version. Gradually lesbianism developed from a phase of life among girls to an adult subculture. Despite laws requiring women to have long hair, Yoshiya was one of the first Japanese women to emulate Western fashion in the 1920s by cutting her hair short and usually dressing in a mannish style that defied gender expectations, symbolizing her maverick

IMAGE 24.4 **Yoshiya Nobuko** A prominent Japanese writer for popular audiences, especially for girls and young women, Yoshiya Nobuko represented the modern girl. She wore her hair short and usually dressed in a mannish style that defied gender expectations.

Portrait of Nobuko Yoshiya (photo)/Private Collection/Prismatic Pictures/ Bridgeman Images

Q What does the photo from 1954 tell us about Yoshiya's personality and how she reflected the "modern girl" style and attitude?

persona. In 1923 Yoshiya met her life partner, Monma Chiyo, a mathematics teacher at a Tokyo girls' school. They remained inseparable and openly lived together as a couple, writing steamy, often erotic, love letters to each other even when together. In 1957 Yoshiya adopted Monma, the only legal way for homosexual couples to share property and make medical decisions for each other. Yoshiya also flouted gender expectations in other ways. She designed her own house, was one of the first Japanese to own a car, and was the first Japanese woman to own a racehorse.

Yoshiya became one of Japan's most successful and highest-paid writers. A literary critic wrote in 1935 that "there isn't a [Japanese] woman alive who hasn't heard of Yoshiya." Her Japanese readership included many middle-class men and women, gay and straight, single and married. She published girls' fiction, social commentary, and autobiographical essays. Some literary critics criticized Yoshiya for seeking a mass audience, but her defenders argued that Yoshiya's writing broadened minds. She and Monma spent 1929 traveling in Russia, Europe, and the United States, where she was impressed by what she considered America's liberated women. After the trip, she vowed to no longer write about women "who cried a lot and simply endured their miserable lot in life."

While an ardent feminist, Yoshiya mistrusted political parties and never became active in the organized Japanese feminist movement. She also disliked the militaristic turn of the 1930s, which brought more censorship. To avoid political harassment or imprisonment, she joined a government writers' group that toured Southeast Asia and China during World War II and wrote stories and reports praising Japanese imperial ambitions. After the war she continued to publish fiction and nonfiction, winning numerous awards. She began to write historical novels to redress female stereotypes in male fiction, such as the dutiful wife, and to restore the voice of women to Japanese history. She died at home at age seventy-seven, holding Monma's hand. Yoshiya's writings remain popular in Japan today.

Reflection Questions

1. How did Yoshiya's life reflect the social changes of the era in Japan?
2. Why might her writing have attracted a large audience?
3. Do you think Yoshiya might be a successful and popular writer in the world today? Why or why not?

Note: Quotations from Jennifer Robertson, "Yoshiya Nobuko: Out and Outspoken in Practice and Prose," in *The Human Tradition in Modern Japan*, ed. Anne Walthall (Wilmington, DE: SR Books, 2002), 156, 167.

helped employers fight labor unions in Appalachian coalfields, Detroit auto plants, and South Atlantic textile mills; police broke up strikes and arrested union organizers. Many resented the U.S. Congress for passing Prohibition, which outlawed alcohol production and made obtaining liquor harder. World War I veterans, having trouble finding jobs, protested government delays in providing their back pay. Meanwhile, political leaders ignored terrorism, including lynchings by southern white racists of African Americans. Several million African Americans, escaping racist mistreatment, "Jim Crow" laws, and limited economic prospects in the South, moved to northern and western states in the 1920s, doubling the black populations of cities such as Chicago, Detroit, and New York. Lastly, the Republicans who held the presidency and dominated the federal government, oriented toward big business, neglected the country's natural and human resources, contributing to eroded croplands and fouled rivers.

The top half of Americans, including a growing middle class, considered these the "Roarin' 20s," the era of the short and sexy "flapper" dress or skirt when hedonistic high society had few inhibitions. Affluent whites, evading Prohibition, bought illegally produced liquor. Gatsby, a character in a novel by F. Scott Fitzgerald (1896–1940), exemplified optimistic American values: "Gatsby believed in the green light, the future that year by year recedes before us. It eluded us then, but that's no matter—tomorrow we will run faster, stretch out our arms farther, and one fine morning …"[15] Other changes affected all Americans. Jazz music, rooted in southern black culture, became so popular that many termed the era "the Jazz Age." Women finally won the vote in 1920, gaining a larger public role. All Americans celebrated the first nonstop flight between North America and Europe, made by Charles Lindbergh (1902–1974) in 1927, demonstrating both heroism and technological advances.

Beginning in the 1890s in some large cities gays and lesbians had space to freely pursue their lives in a flourishing social world of bars, restaurants, cabarets, and apartments, often mixing with straight customers; some became famous in the arts. But in the 1930s and the economic collapse of the Depression years, most were forced back into the closet from the widespread backlash of job losses for male breadwinners, religious opposition, and a conservative turn against cultural experimentation and non-traditional family structures and gender expectations. For example, in New York City new laws prohibited LGBTQ people from gathering in public places; hundreds of establishments were closed for tolerating gay and lesbian customers. This harassment and intolerance continued for decades.

Unlike the idealistic Woodrow Wilson, American leaders proclaimed an isolationist foreign policy but often practiced interventionism. Restless Americans sought Christian converts, commercial markets, and business investments, reflecting society's optimistic, unsettled character, free enterprise, and belief in America's political and economic model. In 1904 President Theodore Roosevelt had proclaimed that America should intervene as an international police power whenever a country, in his estimation, committed chronic wrongdoing. This view, adopted by later U.S. presidents, justified military interventions and interference to punish opponents and reward allies in Latin America. U.S. Marines remained in Nicaragua for decades (1909–1933), while El Salvador, Guatemala, Haiti, Mexico, and the Dominican Republic experienced U.S. military incursions between 1914 and 1940. These experiences intensified the instability, poverty, and hopelessness in Central America and the Caribbean that has generated the desperate migrations north to the United States in recent years.

24-3d The Great Depression

The major spur to change, the Great Depression, began in the United States in the fall of 1929, when New York Stock Exchange prices fell dramatically, ruining many investors. Historians debate whether the "crash" caused the Depression or instead intensified an economic downturn that was already in progress. Whatever the case, this crash, which ultimately precipitated a worldwide economic disaster unprecedented in intensity, longevity, and spread, lasted until 1941, affecting industrial and agricultural economies alike. The underlying cause was the wealth that had flowed into the United States, intensifying world trade and investment imbalances. Generally self-sufficient, the United States depended less on world trade than had the former world economic leader, Britain. While Britain had invested profits abroad, self-indulgent Americans mostly invested and spent at home. In addition, stiff U.S. tariff barriers against manufactured goods hurt European economies, and the nation only shifted to aggressive free trade in the 1930s. Thus the United States did not use its unmatched economic power to become the dominant force to stabilize the world economy and make the flow of spending work efficiently; this neglect helped to destabilize the world banking and credit structure. U.S. banks, anxious for profits, became overextended in loans to Britain, France, and Germany. Meanwhile, within the United States, a "get-rich-quick" philosophy fostered reckless financial practices such as risky loans and investments. The income inequality was stark: by 1929 the top 20 percent of American families earned 54 percent of the income, while the bottom 40 percent earned 12.5 percent. As more people fell into poverty, purchasing power declined even while more consumer products became available; as a result, many manufacturers could not sell enough products to stay in business or avoid layoffs.

These problems generated the stock market crash, followed later by bank failures. American banks facing ruin called in their debts from western European banks, triggering a chain reaction of bank failures. U.S. gross national product and industrial output fell by one-half in four years; unemployment rose to 25 percent by 1932. Confronting widespread misery, President Herbert Hoover (g. 1929–1933), who opposed government intervention in the economy even during a severe crisis, failed to stem the collapse or the pain. Europeans faced worse conditions. With 30 percent out of work by 1932, German industrial output declined by half. A French politician summed up the disaster: "The oceans were deserted, the ships laid up in the silent ports, the factory smokestacks dead, long lines of workless in the towns, poverty throughout the countryside. Nations were economically cut off from one another, but they shared the common lot of poverty."[16] Many Asian, African, Latin American, and Caribbean societies also

---

[15] *The Great Gatsby* (New York: Scribner's, 1925), 182.
[16] Paul Reynaud, quoted in Brendon, *Dark Valley*, 153–154.

suffered as demand for raw materials such as rubber, tin, and sugar plummeted. Only the USSR, largely outside the world economy and somewhat insulated from the dislocations, avoided major pain.

The Great Depression brought Americans severe economic distress. Banks foreclosed on homeowners and farmers, migrant workers moved around futilely seeking jobs, hungry Americans flocked to charitable organizations' breadlines and soup kitchens for food and milk, and sidewalk vendors hoped to make a few pennies selling apples. Shantytowns known as "Hoovervilles" housed the unemployed and dispossessed. Parts of the Midwest and Southwest became a **Dust Bowl**, where terrible drought and disappearing topsoil, caused by erosion and government neglect, badly unbalanced agriculture. Farm income dropped 50 percent, and 3 to 4 million people, mostly farmers, headed to the West Coast to find work after losing their land. A witness in 1932 told a congressional committee: "The roads of the West and Southwest teem with hungry hitchhikers. The campfires of the homeless are seen along every railroad track."[17] These impoverished migrants were chronicled in the novels of John Steinbeck (1902–1968), such as *The Grapes of Wrath*, and by the left-wing Oklahoma-born folksinger Woody Guthrie (1912–1967), in songs such as "Pastures of Plenty" and "Dust Bowl Refugee": "I've worked in your orchards of peaches and prunes, Slept on the ground in the light of the moon, On the edge of your city you've seen us and then, We come with the dust and we go with the wind."[18]

Panic, despair, and disillusionment seized Americans, who had no Social Security, unemployment insurance, or welfare system to turn to. In 1932, when ragged World War I veterans marched in Washington, D.C., demanding promised bonuses, federal troops dispersed them at gunpoint. Hence, the union movement and left-wing political parties such as the communists grew rapidly, while labor militancy and strikes provoked worker–police confrontations. The Depression also intensified African American poverty, their unemployment rate approaching 70 percent. During the Hoover presidency some people took out their rage on immigrants and minorities, whom they believed were taking jobs and resources away from white Americans. Around 1.8 million people of Mexican descent, perhaps sixty percent of them U.S.-born citizens, were rounded up around the country and deported to Mexico without due process, tearing apart families and communities. Some of the deportees were seized from hospitals where they were undergoing treatment for leprosy, tuberculosis, paralysis, mental illness, old age, and other health and medical problems. Historians doubt that the deportations boosted the economy since most of those expelled were hard to replace laborers and farm workers; their loss reduced demand for skilled craftsmen, managers, and salespersons, increasing unemployment. Nonetheless, the raids continued until World War II.

Dust Bowl Parts of the U.S. Midwest and Southwest during the 1930s where disappearing topsoil and severe drought threw agriculture badly out of balance.

New Deal A new U.S. government program of liberal reform within a democratic framework introduced by President Franklin Roosevelt to alleviate suffering caused by the Great Depression.

Discontent against their inaction drove Republicans from office in 1933. The new president, Democrat Franklin Delano Roosevelt (1882–1945), expressed optimism, telling Americans they had nothing to fear but fear itself. Proposing "four freedoms"—freedom of speech and worship and freedom from want and fear—Roosevelt introduced the **New Deal**, a policy of liberal reform within a democratic framework to alleviate suffering. Reforms included regulations on banks and stock exchanges to prevent future depressions, public welfare programs, and Social Security, guaranteeing retirement income for workers. Roosevelt also supported union organizing. Although it did not end the Depression, the New Deal ended the death spiral of public confidence and modified the pain, making government popular. Although some conservatives disagree, many historians conclude that, by defusing socialism and communism's appeal, Roosevelt's New Deal also saved U.S. capitalism. In the later 1930s, when recovery faltered, Roosevelt used ideas from British economist John Maynard Keynes (1883–1946), who advocated deficit spending to spur economic growth, arguing that free markets were not self-correcting and needed government regulation. The Depression finally ended when military forces and manufacturing were mobilized during World War II, creating millions of jobs.

By devastating economies, the Depression challenged weaker democratic systems. A quarter to a third of Europeans became jobless. Many Germans faced malnutrition. A French observer described Paris as an "abyss of misery, suffering, and disorder, the theaters nearly empty, factories shut, businesses bankrupt; grey faces and bad news everywhere."[19] Countries developed public works programs to create jobs; discouraging imports further reduced international trade. Some nations lacked resources for the New Deal type of reform. Burdened with World War I reparations, Germany borrowed heavily and now could not repay loans.

A few nations gradually relieved distress. Increased consumer demand and newer, rapidly growing British industries such as motor and aircraft production and electronics gradually turned around the British economy. Denmark, Norway, and Sweden had the most success, pursuing "the Middle Way," a combination of undogmatic socialist economics with long-established democratic traditions based on community action. Scandinavia's ruling Social Democratic parties, mixing free markets, welfare states, and democratic politics, increased government economic intervention, ensuring full employment and protecting people from hardship.

The Depression hit Japan harder than Europe and the United States, exposing its nearly total dependence on foreign trade. Many foreign markets closed, unemployment skyrocketed, and Japan's foreign trade was cut in half in two years, forcing one hundred million people to dramatically reduce consuming necessities such as food and fuel. With no access to resource-rich Western colonies in Southeast Asia, Japanese leaders, becoming more authoritarian, turned to radical solutions, including expansion abroad and the buildup of a heavy arms industry.

[17]Quoted in Robert Heilbroner and Aaron Singer, *The Economic Transformation of America, 1600 to the Present* (Fort Worth, TX: Harcourt Brace, 1994), 289.
[18]From Harold Leventhal and Marjorie Guthrie, eds., *The Woody Guthrie Songbook* (New York: Grosset and Dunlap, 1976), 180–181.
[19]Maurice Sachs, quoted in Brendon, *Dark Valley*, 168.

IMAGE 24.5 **Depression Breadline** During the Depression, breadlines, such as this one in New York City, were common in the United States as millions of unemployed and desperate people sought food from social service providers, including religious groups.

Q What does the photo tell us about the disconnect between life during the Depression and the idealistic aspirations and self-image of the United States?

24-3e Western Cultures, Thought, and Science

Wartime trauma and the Depression affected Western culture. Mass culture emerged in popular entertainments that appealed to large audiences and were disseminated by radio, recordings, and motion pictures. In 1930, 40 percent of U.S. families owned a radio; by 1940, 86 percent did. In North America and Europe urban middle classes found solace especially in popular music. American jazz musicians such as Louis Armstrong, Duke Ellington, and Billie Holiday had international followings, and songs by New York City–based writers, known collectively as Tin Pan Alley, reached millions around the world through radio, records, movies, and musical theater. Sophisticated and romantic songs written by Americans like Richard Rodgers and Lorenz Hart, George and Ira Gershwin, Irving Berlin, Jerome Kern, and Cole Porter buoyed peoples' spirits. Porter's song, "Anything Goes" (1934), chronicled changing fashions: "In olden days a bit of [women's] stocking, was looked on as something shocking. Now, heaven knows, anything goes." By contrast, some popular songs of the 1930s, such as "The Boulevard of Broken Dreams" and "Brother, Can You Spare a Dime?", addressed harsh reality.

Cultural vistas expanded. Painters, poets, and novelists, many settling in Paris, vigorously broke from older traditions. Innovative, versatile Spanish painter Pablo Picasso (1881–1973) helped invent **cubism**, a painting form that rejected visual reality and emphasized instead geometric shapes and forms that often suggested movement. Soon Picasso, who later joined the Communist Party, abandoned representational art entirely, seeking visual experience as transformed by the artist in his mind. Literature explored inner worlds of thought and feelings. Irishman James Joyce (1882–1941) flouted grammar rules, and his books were often banned for using obscenity. In England Virginia Woolf (1882–1941) converted the novel from narrative story into stream of consciousness, successions of images, thoughts, and emotions. Her 1929 novel, *A Room of One's Own*, championed women's growing economic independence.

Social and natural scientists developed greater understanding of human behavior and the physical world. Austrian Jewish physician Sigmund Freud **(FROID)** (1856–1939) pioneered psychoanalysis, a combination of medical science and psychology; he argued, shockingly, that thoughts of sex subconsciously shaped people's behavior. In physics, German Jew Albert Einstein (1879–1955) radically modified the Newtonian vision of physical nature and rejected absolutes of space and time, arguing that time depended on the relative motion of the measurer and the thing measured. Fleeing Nazi Germany's anti-Jewish atmosphere for the United States, Einstein helped convince President Roosevelt to sponsor atomic weapons research. He spent his later years seeking a unifying theory to explain every physical process in the universe.

cubism A form of painting that rejected visual reality and emphasized instead geometric shapes and forms that often suggested movement.

KEY POINTS

▶ After the war Germany experienced rapid inflation because of its postwar debt, Europe lost economic ground to the United States and Japan, and women entered the workforce and the political sphere.

▶ Among the factors contributing to the Great Depression were America hoarding its profits, American tariffs against European imports, risky investment practices (which helped cause the stock market crash of 1929), and uneven distribution of income.

▶ With millions of Americans jobless, homeless, and hungry, radical movements grew in power and President Franklin Delano Roosevelt instituted the New Deal.

▶ The Great Depression hit Europe and Japan even harder than the United States, rendering Germany unable to pay its heavy debts and causing Japan to become more authoritarian and expansionist, while Scandinavian nations emerged in better condition by combining social-ism, free markets, and democracy.

24-4 The Rise of Fascism and the Renewal of Conflict

⇄ TRANSITIONS

Q What were the main ideas and impacts of fascism?

The Great Depression helped spread a new ideology assaulting liberal values and rational thinking in economically devastated Germany and Japan. This ideology, **fascism**, typically involved extreme nationalism, hatred of ethnic minorities, ruthless repression of opposition groups, violent anticommunism, glorification of the state, and authoritarian government. Fascist movements often formed a party with a large membership, such as the German Nazis (National Socialist German Workers), headed by a charismatic leader. Embraced by Italy, Germany, and Japan, fascism also influenced China and several eastern European and Latin American nations.

24-4a The March to Fascism

Fascism emerged in Italy in 1921, sparked by political corruption, economic slump, unrest, unstable democratic politics, and peasants and workers demanding a fairer share of wealth. Fearing communism, upper-class conservatives in the military, bureaucracy, and industry and discouraged middle-class Italians facing economic hardships pragmatically formed an alliance. Benito Mussolini (1883–1945), a former journalist and socialist, founded the Italian fascist movement, which advocated national unity and strong government. A spellbinding orator promising a vigorous, disciplined Italy, Mussolini aroused mass enthusiasm, especially from nationalistic war veterans. An ancient Roman symbol, the *fasces*, a bundle of sticks wrapped around an ax handle and blade, symbolized the unity he promised. Landowners and industrialists funded his movement, which battered labor and peasant organizations.

Mussolini won support from the Italian king, Catholic Church, and lower middle class, from which he organized a uniform-wearing paramilitary group, the Blackshirts, who violently attacked, intimidated, and sometimes murdered opponents. In 1922 the king

fascism An ideology that typically involved extreme nationalism, hatred of ethnic minorities, ruthless repression of opposition groups, violent anticommunism, glorification of the state, and authoritarian government.

> **CONNECTION to TODAY**
>
> Do you think that fascist or Nazi-type movements or leaders could take power in any Western nations today? How and why might they be able to do so?

asked Mussolini to form a government. By 1926 Mussolini had killed, arrested, or cowed opponents, turned Italy into a one-party state with restricted civil liberties, and created a cult of personality around himself (see Discover Historical Voices: The Doctrine of Fascism). Many Italians, seeing social order restored, appreciated the efficient government; unlike before, trains ran on time.

In Germany, the Depression undermined the moderate, democratic Weimar Republic. Germany had no colonies to tap for resources and markets that might aid recovery from World War I, and Weimar leaders could not solve its severe problems. With an authoritarian political tradition and an economy in shambles, Germans also resented the treasury-draining reparation payments imposed after World War I. Preferring security to freedom, many listened to a charismatic leader who offered simplistic answers to complex problems. The upper and middle classes also feared working-class socialism.

The Nazi (National Socialist) Party, led by Adolf Hitler (1889–1945), offered a strategy for regaining political and economic strength while halting the unpopular reparations payments and controlling workers. Hitler, an Austrian-born social misfit who nurtured a hatred of Jews and labor unions, lived precariously painting signs and doing odd jobs before he joined Germany's army in World War I. In 1920 Hitler helped form the Nazi Party, which capitalized on the Great Depression to increase their strength. With economic collapse, industrial workers moved left toward the communists while the middle classes moved right toward the Nazi movement financed by big industrialists, producing a polarized society. Historians still debate how Hitler, described by a prominent German journalist in 1930 as a "pathetic dunderhead," "half-insane rascal," and "big mouth," rose to power in the land that produced Beethoven and Goethe. Some of Hitler's biographers describe an egomaniac and narcissist who only loved himself, an actor and massive liar with little self-control who gave manic speeches repeating mantra-like phrases and accusations while promising to lead Germany to a new era of national greatness. Understanding propaganda and how to use a few basic ideas, Hitler made up

Discover Historical Voices

The Doctrine of Fascism

Benito Mussolini gradually developed an ideology appealing to the Italian people's nationalistic emotions. The following excerpt comes from an essay under Mussolini's name published in an Italian encyclopedia in 1932. In fact, the true author was a Mussolini confidant, philosopher Giovanni Gentile. The essay reflected Mussolini's vision of fascism as the wave of the future, in which the individual would subordinate her or his desires to the needs of the state.

Fascism, the more it considers and observes the future and the development of humanity quite apart from political considerations of the moment, believes neither in the possibility nor the utility of perpetual peace. It thus repudiates the doctrine of Pacifism—born of the renunciation of the struggle and an act of cowardice in the face of sacrifice. War alone brings up to its highest tension all human energy and puts the stamp of nobility upon the peoples who have the courage to meet it....Fascism [is] the complete opposite of...Marxian Socialism, the materialist conception of history....Above all Fascism denies that class-war can be the preponderant force in the transformation of society...

After Socialism, Fascism combats the whole complex system of democratic ideology, and repudiates it, whether in its theoretical premises or in its practical application. Fascism denies that the majority, by the simple fact that it is a majority, can direct human society; it denies that numbers alone can govern by means of periodic consultation....The democratic regime...[gives] the illusion of sovereignty, while the real effective sovereignty lies in the hands of other concealed and irresponsible forces...

But the Fascist negation of Socialism, Democracy, and Liberalism must not be taken to mean that Fascism desires to lead the world back to the state of affairs before 1789 [the French Revolution]....Given that the nineteenth century was the century of Socialism, of Liberalism, and of Democracy, it does not...follow that the twentieth century must also be the century of Socialism, Liberalism, and Democracy: political doctrines pass, but humanity remains...

The foundation of Fascism is the conception of the State, its character, its duty, and its aim. Fascism conceives of the State as an absolute, in comparison with which all individuals or groups are relative, only to be conceived of in their relation to the State....The Fascist state is itself conscious, and has itself a will and a personality....The Fascist state is an embodied will to power and government, the Roman tradition is here an ideal of force in action....Government is not so much a thing to be expressed in territorial or military terms as in terms of morality and the spirit. It must be thought of as an Empire—...a nation which directly or indirectly rules other nations....For Fascism the growth of Empire,...the expansion of the nation, is an essential manifestation of vitality, and its opposite a sign of decadence. ... But Empire demands discipline, the co-ordination of all forces and a deeply felt sense of duty and sacrifice; this fact explains many aspects of the practical working of the regime, the character of many forces in the State, and the necessarily severe measures which must be taken against those who would oppose this spontaneous and inevitable movement of Italy in the twentieth century, and would oppose it by recalling the outworn ideology of the nineteenth century.

Reflection Questions

1. Why does fascism reject pacifism, socialism, and liberal democracy?
2. What role does the state play under fascism?
3. Can you identify any political movements or parties in the world today whose views might be considered fascist or potentially fascist?

Source: B. Mussolini, "The Political and Social Doctrine of Fascism," *Political Quarterly*, IV (July–September 1933), 341–356. Copyright © 1993 by Blackwell Publishing. Reprinted with permission by Blackwell Publishing.

"facts" to gain support. In his book *Mein Kampf* (*My Struggle*), written in 1924, he argued that "all effective propaganda has to limit itself to a very few points and to use them like slogans. A political leader must not fear to speak a lie if this might be effective."[20] Hitler developed a catchy slogan: "one people, one government, one leader." His followers believed Germany needed "a man of iron" who could shake things up. Many Germans were willing to follow him in blaming Germany's problems on unpopular minorities and foreign powers. Some historians note alarmingly that the problems Hitler addressed, however destructively and brutally, such as migration, inequality, and international capitalism, are the same ones contributing to the rise of far-right leaders and movements today.

The Nazis won the largest number of seats in the 1932 elections, and in 1933 Hitler became chancellor (prime minister). Even though Nazis won only 44 percent of votes, Hitler tightened his grip on power, immediately imposing dramatic changes. Nazis thoroughly purged schools, theater, cinema, literature, and press so they could manipulate them; outlawed leftist parties; suspended civil liberties; imposed heavy censorship; mobilized youth; told women to stay at home and take care of their husbands and children; and expanded the army. Regearing the economy toward rearmament solved high unemployment. By 1939 Germany's GNP was 50 percent higher than in 1929, mainly thanks to manufacturing heavy machinery and armaments. Nazi myths about maintaining a pure German people—termed the

---

[20]Quoted in Felix Gilbert with David Clay Large, *The End of the European Era, 1890 to the Present*, 4th ed. (New York: W.W. Norton, 1991), 263.

Hugo Jaeger/The LIFE Picture Collection /Getty Images

IMAGE 24.6 **Hitler's Motorcade** In this photo from 1938, Adolph Hitler, standing stiffly in his car, salutes members of a paramilitary Nazi group, the Brownshirts, who parade before him at a Nazi rally in Nuremburg.

Q What can we learn from this photo about the theatrical ways that Hitler attracted popular support while repressing opposition?

Aryan race, after ancient Indo-Europeans who settled Europe, Persia, and India—generated anti-Semitic laws between 1933 and 1938. Hitler banned marriage and sexual relations between Jews and so-called Aryan Germans and excluded Jews, many assimilated into German culture, from many occupations and citizenship, pushing them into urban ghettos where they could be monitored. Some were able to leave Germany for safety, mostly in Britain or the Americas, but even those escaping could face rejection. For example, polls in the United States in 1938–1939 opposed raising quotas on Jewish immigration. In 1939 a shipload of nine hundred Jewish German refugees was turned back from U.S. ports and forced to sail back to Europe, where a third of them were killed. Harsh Nazi laws also penalized homosexuals and Romany, or Gypsies, another unpopular minority.

During the 1930s Japan and Germany resembled each other, even if their fascist forms were different. Although no mass-based Fascist Party developed in Japan, fascist leaders blamed foreign nations, especially the United States and USSR, for the nation's problems. Meanwhile, big business supported military expansion. Military officers assassinated liberal politicians and fomented violence in the Chinese province of Manchuria, rich in natural resources and open land for settling Japanese. In 1931, after Japan invaded and occupied Manchuria, the League of Nations imposed no stiff penalties on Japan, helping to discredit that organization. By 1936 the military, in alliance with big business and bureaucratic interests, controlled Japan, promoting labor control, censorship, glorification of war, police repression, and

hatred of foreign powers. Schools and media taught obedience, patriarchy, and the Japanese people's sacred origins while attacking Western individualism and democracy. In 1937 a military skirmish outside Beijing provided an excuse to launch a full-scale invasion of China, and by 1938 Japan controlled most of eastern China. When Japan signed a nonaggression pact with Germany and Italy in 1940, the United States and Britain introduced strong economic sanctions, including an oil embargo, to bankrupt the country. Japan now faced economic collapse or war.

24-4b The Road to War

During the later 1930s the European nations moved toward war, forming various alliances. The United States, Britain, and France, known as the Allies, led democracies wanting to preserve Europe's state structure, the global economy, and colonialism in Asia and Africa. Fascist countries, led by Germany, Italy, and Japan, known as the Axis Powers, sought to change Europe and Asia's political map while gaining world economic dominance. Diplomatic problems, caused partly by a massive arms buildup and Axis nations' imperialism, helped spark another war. Claiming that Germany needed living space and colonies to survive, Hitler pursued an aggressive policy to dominate eastern Europe, which was home to several million ethnic Germans. In 1936 Hitler's troops occupied German territory west of the Rhine River that had been demilitarized after World War I. In 1935 Italy invaded and brutally conquered the last independent African kingdom, Ethiopia. The League of

Nations voted ineffective sanctions against Italy. While Hitler and Mussolini forged a close alliance, the later Tripartite Pact of 1940, linking Germany and Italy with Japan, was a marriage of necessity, strained and wary. Japan's participation warned the United States that opposing Japanese expansion meant facing Germany and Italy.

European tensions were heightened from civil war in Spain, which drew in foreign intervention and incorporated the competing forces raging across Europe and then the world: communism and fascism, nationalism and republicanism, anarchism and monarchism, and anticlerical reformism and Catholic conservatism. Spain had long been polarized, with liberals and conservatives struggling to shape Spanish politics. During the 1936 elections, Spain's left-wing Republicans, uniting liberals, socialists, and communists promising reforms, edged out the National Front of conservatives, monarchists, and staunch Catholics. The right, rallying around General Francisco Franco's (1892–1975) fascist military forces, launched the Spanish civil war (1936–1939), ultimately defeating the Loyalist government at a huge cost in lives. Germany and Italy helped the Spanish fascists with weapons and advice, while several thousand volunteers from North America and European nations, and the USSR, which supplied weapons, aided the Loyalist cause. But the Western Allies refused to support the Loyalists, viewing them as too radical. Both sides treated opponents brutally, committing atrocities; some 200,000 soldiers died and another 220,000 civilians were deliberately executed. The fascists were particularly ferocious, especially toward women, murdering, raping, and humiliating tens of thousands of them. Among the casualties was one of the most commanding voices of Spanish literature, poet and playwright Federico Garcia Lorca, who was murdered in 1936 by a paramilitary death squad for his antifascist beliefs and homosexuality. The German bombing of

Guernica (**GWAR-ni-kuh**), a village in northern Spain, caused an international outcry, prompting Pablo Picasso to paint a celebrated testament to the atrocity. After their victory the fascists executed twenty thousand Loyalists; tens of thousands more civilians and refugees died in prisons and concentration camps. Franco's fascist dictatorship endured until 1975. Many historians view the Spanish Civil War as the seedbed for the titanic political struggles and social upheavals that marked the turbulent decades that followed.

In the late 1930s the Allies, unprepared militarily or in public opinion for war, indecisive, politically divided, and unable to find diplomatic solutions, followed a policy of appeasement toward fascist aggression. The World War I catastrophe led many to see another war as too terrible to contemplate, even as an end to civilization. Historians debate whether the appeasement policy, which was generally supported by public opinion, was realistic, the best of available options, or a shameful betrayal whetting fascist appetites and merely postponing inevitable conflict. In 1938 Hitler succeeded through threats to merge German-speaking Austria, with many pro-Nazi citizens, into Germany and then stimulated riots by German minorities in western Czechoslovakia, which Germany claimed. To forestall war, British Prime Minister Neville Chamberlain, along with Italian dictator Benito Mussolini and French leader Édouard Daladier, visited Hitler in Munich and negotiated a peace pact. Chamberlain claimed that the Munich Agreement brought "peace for our time" but it also effectively handed over Czechoslovakia to Germany. Soon, Hitler declared: "We shall not capitulate—no never! We may be destroyed, but if we are, we shall drag a world with us—a world in flames."[21] In August 1939 Hitler and Stalin signed the Nazi–Soviet Pact, a non-aggression agreement; in September, with the Soviet threat temporarily removed, Germany invaded Poland, forcing France and Britain to declare war.

KEY POINTS

▶ The Italian fascists, led by Benito Mussolini, appealed to those upset by instability, corruption, and economic problems and viciously fought communists and any others who opposed them.

▶ Fascism, a new ideology that developed out of economic collapse, stressed extreme nationalism, an authoritarian state, and hatred of minorities and leftists.

▶ Suffering from the Depression, resentful of post–World War I reparations, and fearful of socialism, many Germans

supported Adolph Hitler's Nazi Party, which blamed problems on minorities such as the Jews and revived the economy through a military buildup.

▶ Japan became increasingly nationalistic and imperialistic, blamed its problems on foreigners, took over most of eastern China, and signed a pact with Germany and Italy.

24-5 World War II: A Global Transition

TRANSITIONS   **NETWORKS**

Q What were the costs and consequences of World War II?

Historians have sometimes viewed World War II as continuing and amplifying World War I. Both wars shared some of the same causes: nationalist rivalries, threats to Europe's balance of power, and struggles

CONNECTION to TODAY

How was your family, community, and nation affected by World War II?

to control the global economic system. But some factors differed. World War II involved an ideological contest between democracy, fascism, and communism; World War I's trench warfare was superseded by far more

---

[21]Quoted in Martin Kitchen, *A World in Flames: A Short History of the Second World War in Europe and Asia, 1939–1945* (London: Longman, 1990), vi.

lethal force and tactics, including widespread aerial bombing and mobile armies that regarded civilians as legitimate military targets. For the first two years, major battles were confined largely to Europe, the North Atlantic, and North Africa. Then the war spilled over to East and Southeast Asia and the western Pacific. The most costly war in world history—with staggering misery, fifty million deaths, one of history's worst genocides, and the deadliest weapons ever known—marked a major transition that reshaped world politics and international relations.

24-5a Cataclysmic War and Holocaust

In September 1939, Europe plunged into armed struggle. Germany and its allies overran nearly all of Europe except for Britain and neutral Switzerland and Sweden (see Map 24.3). Germany imposed puppet regimes in conquered territories, including the Vichy (**VISH-ee**) government in France headed by World War I hero, General Philippe Pétain. Occupied countries had to send raw materials and food to Germany, while millions of essentially enslaved civilians worked on German farms and in factories. But Germany failed to achieve all its strategic objectives. In a heroic resistance, Britain withstood an aerial bombing blitz in 1940, prompting Prime Minister Winston Churchill (1874–1965) to boast that it was Britain's finest hour. German submarines hampered but failed to sever Britain's maritime link with North America. Italian efforts to carve out a Mediterranean empire also faltered; Greeks pushed Italians back and the British seized parts of Italian North Africa (Libya), destroying Italy's navy. Germans had to divert military resources to confront British power in North Africa and Greece. Finally, underground movements emerged that fought Nazis all over Europe. One major resistance hero, Swedish diplomat Raoul Wallenberg (1912–ca. 1947), stationed in occupied Hungary, risked death to save some 100,000 Jews, giving them Swedish passports and smuggling many out to safety.

In June 1941 Germany, breaking its nonaggression pact, invaded Russia, in retrospect a fatal mistake. Top German military officers opposed the invasion, but Hitler obsessively feared communism and wanted Russia's rich resources, especially Caucasus oil, and open lands for German colonization. Believing himself a military genius, Hitler controlled all military operations and made many strategic blunders. Committing two-thirds of the German army to the eastern front relieved pressure on Britain. After misjudging German intentions and reeling from the invasion, Soviet leader Joseph Stalin joined the anti-Axis alliance, receiving American and British aid that helped the USSR resist. However, Western leaders, mistrusting Stalin and despising the Soviet system, expected Russia to remain a long-term threat to their interests. German forces reached Moscow's outskirts and another major city, Stalingrad (today renamed Volgagrad). Despite having superior military forces, the Germans failed to capture major Russian cities because the Red Army effectively counterattacked, exposing the invasion's folly. In February 1943, the Soviet Red Army stopped the Germans at Stalingrad. By the summer, German forces, like Napoleon Bonaparte's French army, began a long, humiliating retreat from Russia. But during their Russian occupation the Germans, joined by Ukrainian and Romanian fascists, massacred some 100,000 to 150,000 people, including thirty-four thousand Jews at Babi Yar in Kiev and fifty thousand Jews in Odessa.

German racist nationalism fostered horrific extermination campaigns against unpopular minorities and conquered peoples. The **Holocaust**, the Nazis' deliberate murder of Jews and Romany (Gypsies), one of history's worst genocides, killed some three-quarters of Europe's Jews. Seeking the "final solution," during 1942 Nazis opened death camps, such as Bergen-Belsen (**BUR-guhn-BEL-suhn**) in Germany and Auschwitz (**OUSH-vits**) in Poland, that targeted especially Germany, Poland, and Ukraine's large Jewish communities. But Jews everywhere in Nazi-occupied Europe—Vichy France, the Netherlands, Hungary, Russia—were rounded up and shipped to death camps, to be killed in gas chambers, starved, or worked to death. In addition to the six million Jews and half a million Romany (Gypsies) murdered in the Holocaust, Nazi actions killed eleven million Slavs (including over three million Poles) and many German communists, socialists, anti-Nazi Christians, homosexuals, children deemed physically or mentally unfit, and war prisoners.

Historians differ on the German people's complicity in the genocide. Some blame the brutal dictatorship that suppressed information. Nazi police chief Heinrich Himmler told his murderous special force, the SS, that "among ourselves, we can speak openly about it [the Holocaust], though we can never speak of it in public. That is a page of glory in our history that never can be written."[22] Other historians also assign responsibility to the often anti-Semitic German people. Only a few brave Germans dared resist Nazi policies. Those who did, such as the heroic Lutheran theologian Dietrich Bonhoeffer (**BON-ho-fuhr**) (1906–1945), a strong critic of anti-Semitism who supported the underground resistance, were executed.

24-5b Globalization of the War

Conflict between Japan and the United States eventually globalized the war (see Map 24.4). Many Americans opposed going to war against the Nazis, and an America First Movement, formed in 1940, recruited some 800,000 members and agitated against involvement. Roosevelt believed that war was inevitable but knew that Americans feared war. Japanese leaders, planning a new Japan-led Asian-Pacific economic order, knew they had to eliminate both Western colonial powers and the American threat. On December 7, 1941, what President Franklin D. Roosevelt called "a date which will live in infamy," Japanese planes attacked the U.S. naval base at Pearl Harbor, Hawaii, destroying much of the U.S. Pacific fleet, killing twenty-four hundred Americans, and ending U.S. neutrality. Americans understandably have focused then and now on the Pearl Harbor attack, which galvanized the nation, but this attack was only a part (and not the most deadly one) of a much larger and simultaneous Japanese military operation on December 7–8 to invade Hong Kong, Guam, Wake Island, the Philippines (where tens of thousands died), Thailand, Malaya, and Singapore, suggesting to some historians that we need a broader transnational Asian-Pacific rather than narrowly American perspective to understand these attacks and the consequences. The U.S. might

Holocaust The Nazis' deliberate murder of Jews and Romany (Gypsies), one of the worst genocides in world history.

[22]Quoted in Stephen J. Lee, *European Dictatorships, 1918–1945*, 2nd ed. (London: Routledge, 2000), 207.

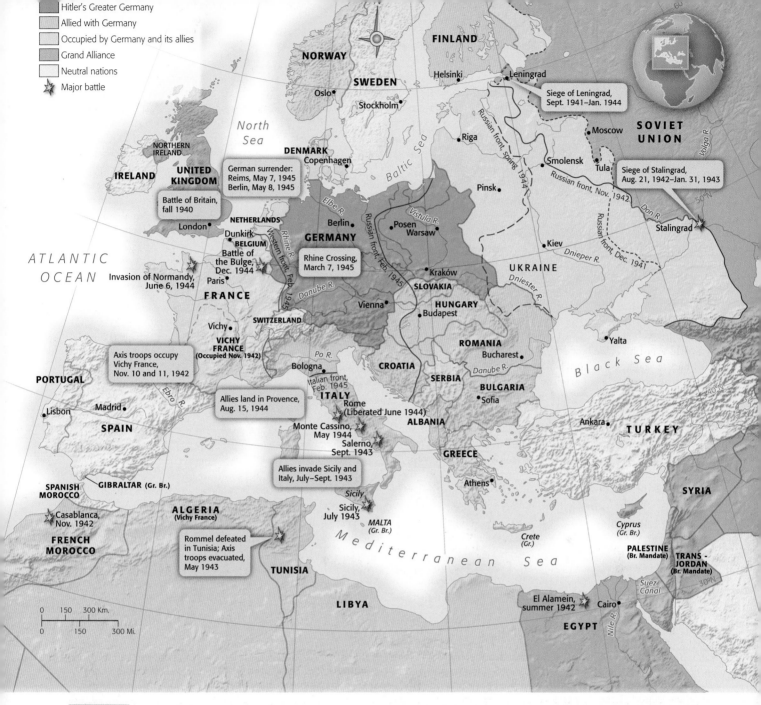

MAP 24.3 **World War II in Europe and North Africa** The Axis Powers, led by Germany and Italy, initially occupied much of Europe, and in 1941 they invaded the Soviet Union, but they were unable to hold their gains against the counteroffensive of the United States, Britain, the Soviet Union, and the Free French forces.

Q What does the map tell us about the geography, participants, and major battles of the war in the Europe–North Africa theater?

have been a lower-priority target than resource-rich Southeast Asia. Within several months Japanese forces controlled much of Southeast Asia and had imprisoned or forced Americans out of the Philippines and jailed British and Dutch residents of their colonies. Bogged down and unable to expand their occupation of China, the Japanese badly needed Southeast Asian resources, especially oil and rubber from the Dutch East Indies (Indonesia). Meanwhile, the Western powers, preoccupied with the European war and with only modest military forces left in Asia, could not resist the Japanese advance.

Japanese leaders disagreed about challenging U.S. power. Some top military officers argued against the Pearl Harbor attack, knowing that the superior U.S. military and economic power could defeat Japan if Americans mobilized to wage a prolonged war. But other leaders, impressed by Hitler's quick victories, thought they could duplicate that success by immobilizing the U.S. fleet and gaining time to consolidate control of Asia and the Pacific while forcing the U.S. to accept a political settlement. If Germany kept the United States focused on Europe, they thought Roosevelt might avoid a costly Asian

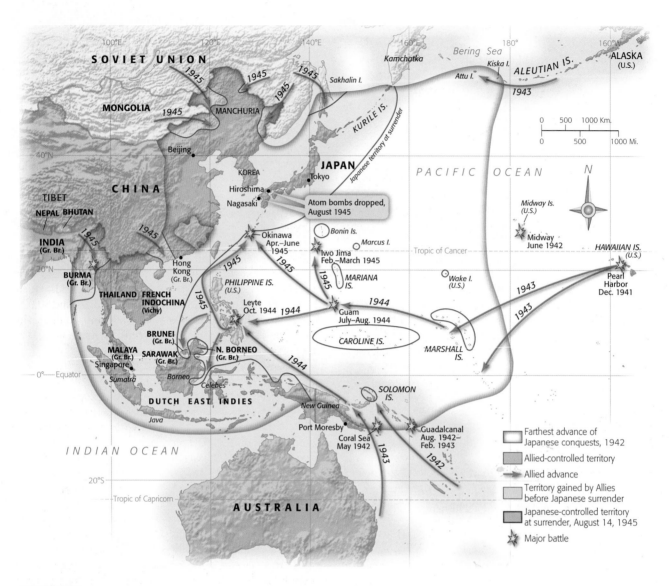

MAP 24.4 **World War II in Asia and the Pacific** After invading China in 1937, Japan disabled the U.S. fleet at Pearl Harbor in 1941 and in 1941–1942 occupied most of Southeast Asia and the western Pacific. The United States and its allies pushed back the Japanese forces from their bases in the Pacific and bombed Japan from those bases, but Japan did not surrender until 1945, when the United States dropped atomic bombs on Hiroshima and Nagasaki.

Q What does the map tell us about the geography, chronology, participants, and major battles of the war in the Asia-Pacific theater?

war. They also assumed that Americans, addicted to creature comforts, lacked the will to mobilize. But the surprise Pearl Harbor attack proved a strategic blunder, uniting Americans in support of total, unrelenting war. Admiral Isoruku Yamamoto (**EE-so-ROO-koo YAH-muh-MO-toe**), who had attended university in the United States and understood American strength, long opposed but eventually planned the attack, somberly telling colleagues: "I fear all we have done is to awaken a sleeping giant and fill him with a terrible resolve."[23] The admiral, who had predicted and feared a long war of attrition, died in 1943 when Americans shot down his plane in reprisal for Pearl Harbor.

An avowed antifascist, Roosevelt had hoped to turn U.S. public opinion toward war and end his nation's isolationism, and

Pearl Harbor served that purpose well. Historians remain divided about how much U.S. officials, including Roosevelt, knew about the forthcoming attack and whether they let it happen to shock the American public. U.S. officials anticipated military conflict with Japan but apparently expected an assault on the Philippines, an American colony, rather than on Hawaii, where Japanese Americans constituted over half of the population. U.S. military intelligence had broken some Japanese codes but probably not those ordering the attack. The United States quickly mobilized, regearing the economy for war. A patriotic wave swept the country as America entered the war on both fronts.

The war affected American society. Six million women joined the workforce, replacing the men going off to fight.

---

[23]Quoted in George Donelson Moss, *America in the Twentieth Century*, 4th ed. (Upper Saddle River, NJ: Prentice-Hall, 2000), 257.

Although many men objected, by 1943 the government encouraged women as their "patriotic duty" to take up jobs once considered unladylike, such as on factory assembly lines. A popular song celebrated "Rosie the Riveter" who was "making history working for victory." The song could have described Sybil Lewis, an African American from Oklahoma who moved to Los Angeles to work as a waitress, became a riveter making airplane gas tanks, and then worked as a shipyard welder. Anxious for workers, companies often hired African Americans, challenging prevailing racial attitudes; millions of southern blacks escaping racial segregation found jobs in northern and western cities. When the war ended, over nineteen million American women had full-time paid jobs, and the black population of many American cities had doubled. After defeating fascism, more white Americans were also sympathetic to black demands for democracy.

But racism aimed at 110,000 Japanese Americans in western states, many of them U.S.-born or naturalized citizens, fueled a great invasion of civil liberties. Many Japanese Americans joined U.S. military units to fight in Europe, suffering heavy casualties. Nevertheless, suspecting but offering little proof that some Japanese Americans might be spies or support Japan's war effort, the U.S. government seized their property and sent them to sparse, remote internment camps, such as Manzanar in the harsh California desert, for the conflict's duration. Their property was never returned. With some exceptions, German and Italian Americans did not face similar treatment.

24-5c The End of the War

The U.S. entry reshaped the conflict. Through 1942 Germany dominated much of Europe and North Africa, while Japan controlled most of Asia east of India and large areas of the western Pacific. But in 1943 the tide began to turn. The Germans were defeated in North Africa, and Allied landings knocked Italy out of the war. In June 1944, British and American forces landed on five beaches at Normandy, on France's Atlantic coast. Although German defenses caused huge casualties, the Allies, including Free French forces under General Charles DeGaulle (1890–1970), finally began pushing the Germans back in France. Meanwhile, the Soviet Red Army had regained much of Russia and Ukraine from German forces by early 1944.

Germany was finally defeated by massive Allied ground offensives and aerial bombardments that demoralized the civilian population. The British firebombed several German cities; in Hamburg, a firestorm killed thirty thousand civilians. While the Soviet Red Army pushed Germans back in the east, U.S. and British forces retook Italy, France, and other Nazi-occupied countries. By December 1944, Allied forces reached Germany and the Allies gained command of the skies. Germany's war economy collapsed. As losses mounted, Hitler lost touch with reality, giving orders to nonexistent army divisions. In spring 1945, British and U.S. armies moved into Germany from the west and the Red Army from the east; Hitler and his mistress, Eva Braun, committed suicide in their underground bunker in Berlin. Germany surrendered. Soon the liberation of concentration camps revealed the full extent of Nazi atrocities to a shocked world.

A major reason for Nazi defeat was Hitler's racist and imperialistic policies. Believing Germans racially superior to all other peoples, including conquered Slavs, Hitler brutally exploited occupied areas to supply Germany. Had the Germans patronized east Europeans and Russians, they might have won some support. Some Ukrainians, Russians, Lithuanians, and Latvians did in fact collaborate with Nazis because they hated communists more; they were pursued and punished for this collaboration after the war.

After nearly four years of bloody battles Japan's final defeat came quickly. In 1942, Americans stopped Japan's advance at the battle of Midway Island, west of Hawaii, and began isolating Japanese bases in the Pacific. By mid-1944, pushing Japanese out of most of the western Pacific islands at a heavy cost in lives, they began launching bombing raids on Japan. By early 1945, U.S., Australian, and British forces started retaking Southeast Asia and China. Increasingly desperate, the Japanese navy organized suicide pilots, known as *kamikaze*, to crash their small fighter planes into U.S. warships. The invasion of Okinawa, in the Ryukyus Islands just south of Japan's main islands, killed 12,500 American troops, 110,000 Japanese soldiers, and 80,000 civilians, warning what invading Japan's main islands might entail. The Japanese, resisting demands for total surrender, could not agree with U.S. leaders on peace negotiations.

In August 1945, the United States forever changed warfare by dropping an atomic bomb on the Japanese city of Hiroshima, demolishing the city and killing eighty thousand people; thousands more were maimed or died later from injuries or radiation. Japan's cabinet, divided on surrender, debated whether Americans had more than one bomb. Three days later, a second bomb hit Nagasaki, killing sixty thousand civilians. Japanese emperor Hirohito (1901–1989) opted for surrender, asking his people to "suffer the insufferable, endure the unendurable," and cooperate with U.S. occupation. Historians debate Hirohito's role in Japan's militarization and wars, portraying him variously as an opponent of conflict, a willing or reluctant puppet of the militarists, a timid opportunist, or an enthusiast for empire. But Japan's leaders felt it imperative that the symbol of the nation not be punished or removed; eventually U.S. diplomats agreed. For the first time in its long history, Japan was defeated and successfully invaded. Disgraced, over five hundred military officers committed suicide. But a long-imprisoned Japanese leftist celebrated defeat: "Ah, such happiness, At somehow living long enough, To see this rare day, When the fighting has ceased."[24] World War II had ended.

Historians vigorously disagree about whether dropping atomic bombs, which caused so many civilian deaths, was necessary. Many contend that the Japanese would have fiercely resisted an invasion and hence the bombs saved many American and Japanese lives. Others argue that Japan was exhausted and near surrender but that U.S. leaders misread its intentions and underestimated the growing pro-peace faction in government. Still others conclude that the United States rushed to defeat Japan because the Soviet Union was going to join the struggle to demand territory or a role in the occupation. Soviet forces had already moved into Manchuria as Japanese resistance collapsed. Furthermore, the Russians also seized the Kurile Islands and southern Sakhalin Island north of Japan; they remain in Russian hands today, complicating Russo–Japanese relations. Others point to the Soviet declaration of war, announced just after Hiroshima; Japanese leaders greatly feared communism and

---

[24]Quoted in James L. McClain, *Japan: A Modern History* (New York: W.W. Norton, 2002), 515.

AP Images /Anonymous

IMAGE 24.7 **Bombing of Nagasaki** This photo shows the awesome power of the atomic bomb dropped by the United States on the Japanese city of Nagasaki in August 1945, three days after the atomic bombing of Hiroshima. Some sixty thousand Japanese died in the Nagasaki bombing.

Q Why do you think that over seven decades later photos like this of the atomic bombings of Japan remain symbols of the horrors, destruction, and slaughter of war?

Soviet participation in occupation. Hoping to dissuade Soviet expansionism and give the U.S. diplomatic advantage, the bomb proclaimed U.S. capabilities. But some historians argue that the United States had alternatives to the horrific bombs that might have worked, including a public demonstration of the bomb or accepting a conditional rather than the unconditional Japanese surrender the U.S. demanded (which the Japanese apparently believed meant executing the emperor). Some historians argue that the Soviet entry into the war was at least as important as the atomic bombings in prompting Japan to surrender. There are also critics in Japan, the U.S., and the world who consider the bombings as unjustified and war crimes, especially the bombing of Nagasaki, often viewed as unnecessary and avoidable.

Japan lost the war primarily because of overstretched forces; failure to convert Southeast Asian resources into military and industrial products fast enough to defeat the larger, wealthier United States; and the use of authoritarian, brutal policies on subject peoples. Hence, Japanese troops, upon capturing China's capital in 1937, killed thousands of Chinese in an orgy of destruction known as the "Rape of Nanjing." Decades later the world learned that the Japanese had performed horrific medical experiments and used germ warfare on Chinese, killing

perhaps half a million people, the only documented mass use of biological weapons in modern times. They also conscripted Korean, Filipina, and Singapore Chinese women for forced prostitution and thousands of Indonesian men for forced labor. In most cases Japan's military alienated Chinese and Southeast Asians; eventually most Southeast Asians looked on Japan as perhaps even worse than Western colonizers.

24-5d The Costs and Consequences of Global War

World War II took a terrible toll: approximately fifteen million military and thirty-five million civilian deaths. Losing over twenty million people, or 10 percent of its population, Soviet Russia had one more bitter memory of invasions by countries to the west. Over 10 percent of Poles and Yugoslavs died. Britain lost 375,000 people and France 600,000. Strategic bombing blasted every major German city to rubble. Over two million Japanese military personnel and probably a million Japanese civilians died; seven million Chinese were killed or wounded. Fighting on both fronts, some 300,000 American military personnel perished.

The economic devastation cleared the way for new global economic arrangements. In 1944, at a conference held in Bretton Woods, New Hampshire, representatives of forty-four countries established the postwar world economic order, including international monetary cooperation to prevent the financial crises that caused the Great Depression. The Bretton Woods Conference established the U.S.-dominated World Bank and International Monetary Fund to provide credit to states requiring financial investment. Bretton Woods also fixed currency exchange rates and encouraged trade liberalization, benefiting the United States.

World War II transformed world politics, removing the twin threats of German Nazism and Japanese militarism. Unlike after World War I, the victors treated the vanquished more generously. But some German and Japanese political and military leaders were tried, and some executed, as "war criminals." Germany, Italy, and Japan lost their colonies and were required to adopt democratic governments. U.S. forces occupied Japan for several years, while Germany was temporarily divided into sectors controlled by Russia, Britain, France, and the United States. But the Allies gave the defeated nations massive aid and guidance, speeding recovery. In 2016 the Japanese prime minister visited Pearl Harbor to symbolize the now-friendly U.S.–Japan relationship. Meanwhile, Chinese, Korean, and Vietnamese communists capitalized on Japanese occupation to gain support. Japanese occupation undermined Western colonial rule throughout Southeast Asia. In India, nationalists jailed for opposing the wartime use of Indian troops became even more embittered against British rule (see Chapter 25). Britain had used five million soldiers from their colonies, half of them from South Asia, in the war effort, and many were killed, mostly on European battlefields. Soon devastating anticolonial or civil wars erupted in China, Korea, Indonesia, Vietnam, and Malaya.

In February 1945, Roosevelt, Churchill, and Stalin met at a conference at Yalta (**YAWL-tuh**), in Russia's Crimean peninsula, to determine the postwar political order. They proposed goals, an institutional structure, and a voting system for a new world organization, the United Nations. The Yalta Conference also divided

Europe into anticommunist and communist spheres of interest. Western leaders, drained by war and seeking postwar stability, reluctantly agreed that the Soviet Union could dominate eastern Europe, stationing troops there and influencing its governments.

Rivalry between the two emerging superpowers, the United States and the USSR, complicated the new global political order. The United States, having never fought on its own soil, emerged much less devastated than other major combatants as well as politically and economically stronger. Now the dominant world power, Americans took the lead in protecting the global system. But with the USSR a military power with imperialist ambitions, U.S. leaders realized that thwarting Soviet ambitions required reconstructing Europe and Japan to restore political stability.

World political history between 1945 and 1989 revolved around conflicts between these two competing superpowers with very different governments and economies. The USSR replaced Germany in its domination of eastern Europe, where it installed communist governments, including in eastern Germany. World War II also increased communism's appeal worldwide, fostering communist regimes in Yugoslavia and North Korea and later in China, North Vietnam, and Cuba. Both Soviet and U.S. leaders viewed the world through the lens of their World War II experience. Soviets were paranoid about any threat from the West, while Americans perceived a repeat of Hitler's aggression anywhere they identified a political threat, such as in nationalist or communist-inspired revolutions. U.S.–Soviet rivalry created a world very different from that existing before World War II.

KEY POINTS

▶ Nazi Germany deliberately killed six million Jews and a half million Gypsies in death camps, along with millions of others; historians are divided on how much the German people knew about the death camps and how responsible they were for them.

▶ After Japan attacked Pearl Harbor, the United States entered the war in both Asia and Europe, and many women and blacks found work in professions that had until then been closed to them, while Japanese Americans were put in internment camps.

▶ After the United States entered the war, the Allies slowly began to win the war in Europe, and in the spring of

1945, with U.S. forces advancing from the west and the Soviets from the east, Hitler committed suicide and Germany surrendered.

▶ After Japan refused to agree to a total surrender despite serious setbacks, the United States dropped atomic bombs on Hiroshima and Nagasaki, killing, injuring, and sickening scores of thousands.

▶ World War II killed fifty million military personnel and civilians, but in its aftermath, Germany, Italy, and Japan were aided rather than punished, and the United States and the Soviet Union emerged as the world's dominant powers.

Chapter Summary

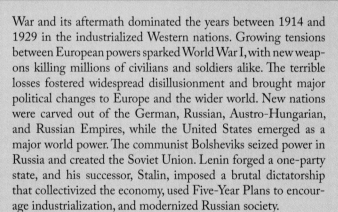

War and its aftermath dominated the years between 1914 and 1929 in the industrialized Western nations. Growing tensions between European powers sparked World War I, with new weapons killing millions of civilians and soldiers alike. The terrible losses fostered widespread disillusionment and brought major political changes to Europe and the wider world. New nations were carved out of the German, Russian, Austro-Hungarian, and Russian Empires, while the United States emerged as a major world power. The communist Bolsheviks seized power in Russia and created the Soviet Union. Lenin forged a one-party state, and his successor, Stalin, imposed a brutal dictatorship that collectivized the economy, used Five-Year Plans to encourage industrialization, and modernized Russian society.

During the 1920s much of Europe, the United States, and Japan experienced liberal democracy and middle-class prosperity. However, in the 1930s, the Great Depression generated economic collapse, a sharp decline in world trade, and millions of unemployed workers. A few wealthy nations, especially the United States, pursued recovery through liberal reform and government spending, sustaining democracy despite economic hardship. But for Germany, Italy, and Japan, economic disaster fostered fascism, an ideology that favored an authoritarian state, extreme nationalism, and repression of minorities. The increasing aggression of fascist nations, seeking lands to exploit for their resources and markets, generated World War II. During the war, Nazi brutality perpetrated genocide against Jews and other minorities. Germany initially occupied eastern Europe and much of western Europe, while Japan invaded China and Southeast Asia. With the entry of the United States into the war, the Allies eventually won. The war cost fifty million lives and devastated Europe and much of Asia. The United States emerged as the world's major superpower, with the Soviet Union as its major rival.

Key Terms

Bolsheviks 617
soviets 618
Leninism 620
Marxism-Leninism 620
New Economic Policy 620

Stalinism 620
gulags 621
socialist realism 621
Great Depression 622
Dust Bowl 626

New Deal 626
cubism 627
fascism 628
Holocaust 632

CHAPTER 2

Imperialism and Nationalism in Asia, Africa, and Latin America, 1914–1945

> *What unhappiness strikes the poor, Who wear a single worn-out, torn cloth. Oh heaven, why are you not just? Some have abundance while others are in want.*
>
> —Peasant folk song protesting colonialism in Vietnam[1]

IMAGE 25.1 **Mao Zedong Organizing Communists in China** This later artist's rendition shows the young Mao Zedong, the future Chinese communist leader, organizing a communist group in his native province, Hunan, around 1921. A portrait of Karl Marx decorates the wall.

Q What image of Mao and his leadership in the party does the artist convey?

---

[1]Quoted in James C. Scott, *The Moral Economy of the Peasant: Rebellion and Subsistence in Southeast Asia* (New Haven, CT: Yale University Press, 1976), 236.

In 1911 Nguyen Tat Thanh (NEW-win tat-tan), from an
impoverished village in French-ruled Vietnam, became a merchant sea-
man on a French ship, only returning to his homeland thirty years later.
Hating colonialism, Nguyen dreamed of an independent Vietnam:
"The people of Vietnam often wondered who would help them to
remove the yoke of French control....I saw that I must go abroad and
see for myself."[2] Nguyen visited North African and American ports,
developing a distaste for America's white racism and admiration for
its freedom. Nguyen moved to Paris, where he worked chiefly as a
photo retoucher while developing an anticolonial movement among
Vietnamese exiles. Adopting a new alias, Nguyen Ai Quoc (NEW-win
eye-kwok) ("Nguyen the Patriot"), he joined Asian nationalists and
French socialists to oppose colonialism.

Nguyen Ai Quoc became famous among Vietnamese exiles for
trying to address the Paris Peace Conference delegates about self-
determination for colonized people and changing France's treatment
of its Southeast Asian colonies, with basic freedoms and representation in government. The Western powers refused to permit his entry.
Disillusioned with Western democracy, Nguyen helped found the
French Communist Party, which promised to abolish the colonial
system. He moved to the Soviet Union and later, under a new name,
Ho Chi Minh (ho chee-min) ("He Who Enlightens"), led Vietnamese
communist forces in their long struggle against French colonialism and
then the Americans. Ho became a worldwide symbol of opposition
to Western imperialism and of sympathy for peasants suffering under
colonial policies.

Between 1914 and 1945 nationalistic Asians and Africans challenged the European imperialism, now weakened by World War I, that
had reshaped their politics and economies. From Indonesia to Egypt to
Senegal, rapid, often destabilizing change sparked nationalism aimed
at overthrowing Western domination. Similar trends influenced independent countries such as Siam (now Thailand), Persia (now Iran),
and China. During the unsettling Great Depression and World War II
nationalist movements grew stronger, making a return to the world of
the 1930s impossible.

---

[2]Quoted in William J. Duiker, *Ho Chi Minh: A Life* (New York: Hyperion, 2000), 45.

25-1 Western Imperialism and Its Challengers

SOCIETIES NETWORKS

Q What circumstances fostered nationalism in Asia, Africa, and Latin America?

The events that rocked industrialized nations—two world wars, the Russian Revolution, and the Great Depression—also affected the non- or semi-industrialized Asians, Africans, and Latin Americans. These societies, enjoying little power in the global system, also suffered from destabilizing social and economic changes resulting from colonialism. Many disenchanted Asians and Africans adopted nationalism and Marxism to struggle for power.

CONNECTION to TODAY

How do you think life in a Western-controlled colony in Asia, Africa, or the Caribbean compares to life in those societies today?

25-1a The Impact of Colonialism

Western colonialism had a major impact on Asians, Africans, and Caribbean peoples. The slaughter during World War I undermined Western credibility and whatever moral authority Western peoples claimed to possess, while the deaths of thousands of Asians and Africans conscripted or recruited as soldiers and workers to support

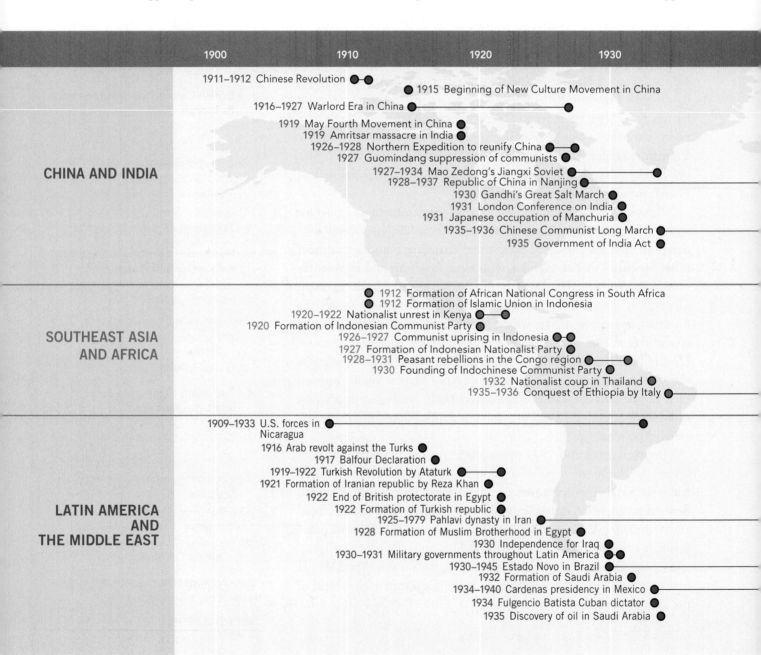

	1900	1910	1920	1930

CHINA AND INDIA

1911–1912 Chinese Revolution
1915 Beginning of New Culture Movement in China
1916–1927 Warlord Era in China
1919 May Fourth Movement in China
1919 Amritsar massacre in India
1926–1928 Northern Expedition to reunify China
1927 Guomindang suppression of communists
1927–1934 Mao Zedong's Jiangxi Soviet
1928–1937 Republic of China in Nanjing
1930 Gandhi's Great Salt March
1931 London Conference on India
1931 Japanese occupation of Manchuria
1935–1936 Chinese Communist Long March
1935 Government of India Act

SOUTHEAST ASIA AND AFRICA

1912 Formation of African National Congress in South Africa
1912 Formation of Islamic Union in Indonesia
1920–1922 Nationalist unrest in Kenya
1920 Formation of Indonesian Communist Party
1926–1927 Communist uprising in Indonesia
1927 Formation of Indonesian Nationalist Party
1928–1931 Peasant rebellions in the Congo region
1930 Founding of Indochinese Communist Party
1932 Nationalist coup in Thailand
1935–1936 Conquest of Ethiopia by Italy

LATIN AMERICA AND THE MIDDLE EAST

1909–1933 U.S. forces in Nicaragua
1916 Arab revolt against the Turks
1917 Balfour Declaration
1919–1922 Turkish Revolution by Ataturk
1921 Formation of Iranian republic by Reza Khan
1922 End of British protectorate in Egypt
1922 Formation of Turkish republic
1925–1979 Pahlavi dynasty in Iran
1928 Formation of Muslim Brotherhood in Egypt
1930 Independence for Iraq
1930–1931 Military governments throughout Latin America
1930–1945 Estado Novo in Brazil
1932 Formation of Saudi Arabia
1934–1940 Cardenas presidency in Mexico
1934 Fulgencio Batista Cuban dictator
1935 Discovery of oil in Saudi Arabia

the war effort spurred resentment. Both France and Germany drafted men, often through harsh forced labor, from their African colonies; Britain sent Africans and Indians. Some forty-six thousand Kenyans died fighting for Britain, and at least twenty-five thousand West Africans perished helping France on the front lines. Although British and French officials promised democratic reforms and special treatment for war veterans, both broke these promises. Few families of dead African soldiers ever received any compensation.

Colonialism also reshaped societies, forming artificial states that often ignored regional social, economic, and historical realities (see Chapters 21–22). Colonies such as Dutch-ruled Indonesia, British Nigeria, and the Belgian Congo incorporated diverse, often rival ethnic groups with little feeling of national unity. To cover costs, colonial governments used varied,

often unpopular methods, including higher taxes and forced labor. In Portuguese-ruled Mozambique, men and women unable to pay required taxes were assigned to plantations or mines in a system not unlike slavery. After months of labor they often received little more than a receipt saying they met their annual tax obligation. In Southeast Asia, opium and alcohol monopolies provided revenues for colonial governments. France required all Vietnamese villages to purchase designated amounts of these products, making some people opium addicts; by 1918 opium sales accounted for one-third of all the colonies' revenues. Vietnamese villages that bought too little alcohol or made their own illicit beverages were fined.

Rising birthrates and declining death rates, the result of colonial economic policies and sometimes improved health and sanitation, led to rapid population growth in colonies such as

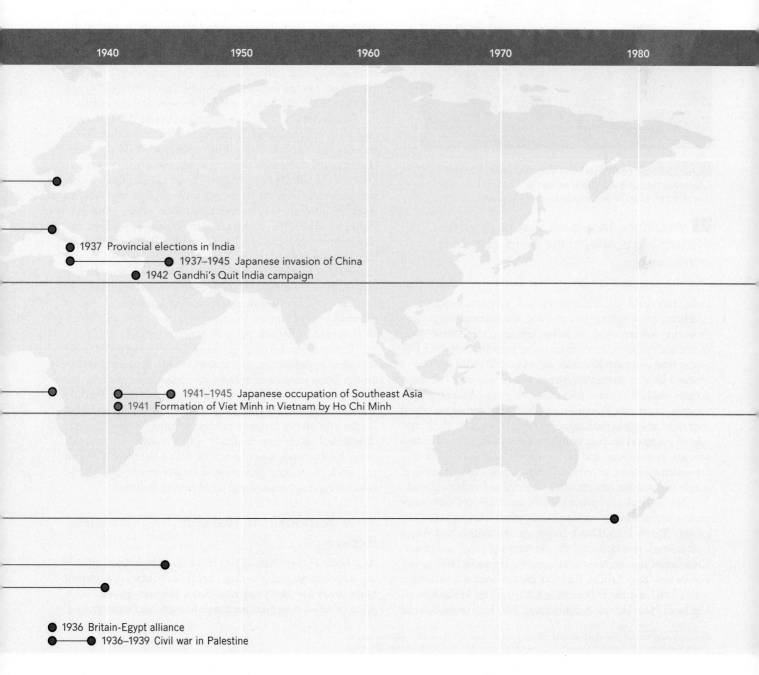

1937 Provincial elections in India
1937–1945 Japanese invasion of China
1942 Gandhi's Quit India campaign

1941–1945 Japanese occupation of Southeast Asia
1941 Formation of Viet Minh in Vietnam by Ho Chi Minh

1936 Britain-Egypt alliance
1936–1939 Civil war in Palestine

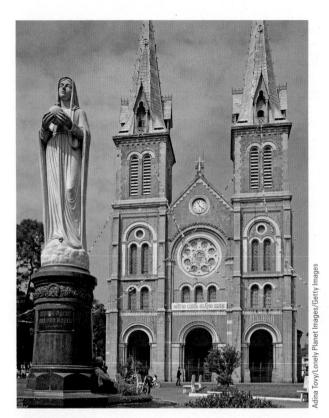

IMAGE 25.2 **Notre-Dame Cathedral in Saigon**
Colonialism spurred cultural as well as economic and political change. Many Vietnamese became Roman Catholics.

Q What does the cathedral tell us about the Westernizing policies of the French colonizers in Vietnam?

India, Indonesia, the Philippines, and Vietnam, outstripping resources, exacerbating poverty, and stimulating emigration. Producing and exporting one or two primary commodities—such as rice and rubber from Vietnam, sugar from Barbados and Fiji, copper from Northern Rhodesia, and oil from Trinidad and Iraq—retarded later economic diversification. In addition, colonized peoples disliked Western colonizers' arrogance. Assuming their societies' superiority, Europeans and North Americans enshrined their racist attitude in the League of Nations Covenant, which considered colonized peoples unable to govern themselves. Western officials, businessmen, and planters in the colonies lived in luxury—with mansions, servants, and private clubs—while many local people endured dire poverty, often underfed and underemployed.

Yet, colonial governments constructed modern communications and economic infrastructures, often spurring economic growth. British India, Dutch Indonesia, and British East Africa built railroads that facilitated the movement of goods and people. Colonialism also increased urban growth. Hence, in 1890, to service its new East African Railroad, Britain opened a settlement with a hotel and bar at Nairobi, a Kikuyu village in the Kenyan highlands. Nairobi, with its cool climate, later became the colonial

capital. Port cities founded by Western colonizers, such as Hong Kong, Jakarta in Indonesia, Singapore, Bombay (today's Mumbai), and Cape Town, became key world trade hubs. But critics questioned whether these developments benefited Asians and Africans.

Western capitalism also spurred resentment. Some non-European merchants, such as Chinese in Southeast Asia and Lebanese in West Africa, profited from the growing economic opportunities. But colonial policies, while promoting capitalist markets and expanded communications, eroded traditional political authority and also destabilized rural villages, fostering revolutionary responses in countries like Vietnam. Agricultural commercialization transformed traditional, often communal, landowning arrangements into competitive money-based private property systems, converting land into a commodity. In many colonies, among them British India, French Vietnam, and Portuguese Angola, powerful landlord classes now flourished at the expense of once-self-sufficient peasant farmers. The remaining peasant farmers had no control over fluctuating prices for their crops. Lacking money or connections to influential people, many peasants fell into dire poverty. A Vietnamese peasant later recalled the bitter colonial hardship: "My father was very poor. He and my mother, and all of my brothers and sisters, had to pull the plow. In the old days, people did the work of water buffalo."[3]

The unsettling Great Depression and World War II brought economic catastrophe and discontent to many non-industrialized societies as demand for their resources plummeted. Prices for rubber, sugar, and coffee fell in Southeast Asia and Africa, Argentina's livestock and wheat prices collapsed, and Brazilians threw nearly worthless sacks of coffee beans into the sea. To protect Western investors, international agreements restricted rubber growing to large plantations, harming small farmers, rubber workers, and shopkeepers in Malaya, Sri Lanka, and the Belgian Congo. As these exports declined, colonial revenues fell. Because rubber and tin provided most tax revenues in British Malaya, huge budget cuts undermined such activities as education and road building. During World War II many Asians and Africans were drafted or recruited to fight for their Western colonizers. Many died, often on European battlefields, generating resentment.

Unequal landowning, growing mass poverty, declining economic opportunities, and foreign economic control generated political unrest and a desire to challenge or overturn the status quo. Hence, on Trinidad, the Depression sparked strikes and labor unrest. Calypso singer Growling Tiger implored British officials not to ignore human suffering: "The authorities should deal much more leniently with the many unemployed in the colony; work is nowhere to be found but there is rent to pay while the money circulation decreases by the day."[4] Most colonial regimes harassed and jailed protest leaders.

25-1b Nationalism, Marxism, and Imperial Expansion

As a result of these hardships, ideologies of resistance, including nationalism and Marxism, became influential, fostering movements for independence. Since colonial governments jailed or exiled dissenters, nationalists organized underground.

---

[3]Quoted in James W. Trullinger, *Village at War: An Account of Conflict in Vietnam* (Stanford, CA: Stanford University Press, 1994), 18.
[4]Dick Spottswood, liner notes to the album *Calypsos from Trinidad: Politics, Intrigue and Violence in the 1930s* (Arhoolie 7004, 1991).

Nationalism appealed particularly to educated middle-class lawyers, teachers, merchants, and military officers facing white racism. The few colonial universities offered a venue for nationalist-government conflicts and campus protests. In British Burma (today's Myanmar) during the 1920s and 1930s, male and female students at the University of Rangoon repeatedly went on strike to protest British policies; student leaders were often expelled.

Nationalism promoted a sense of belonging to a nation, such as Indonesia or Nigeria, that transcended parochial differences such as social class and religion. Whereas colonialism uprooted people from villages, families, customs, and traditions, nationalists sought to help the poor, often linking capitalism with foreign control. But the "nation" sometimes existed only in people's imagination as a hopeful and maybe even unrealistic goal: In multiethnic African, Southeast Asian, and Caribbean colonies, ethnic rivalries hindered a feeling of nationhood.

Some Asians, Africans, and Latin Americans seeking radical change, such as Ho Chi Minh, mixed nationalism with Marxism, providing an alternative to colonialism, capitalism, and discredited local traditions and leaders. Some young Asians, Africans, and West Indians studying in Europe and North America adopted Marxism after facing racism in the West and bleak employment prospects and political repression at home. Some gravitated to the communism imposed on and practiced in the Soviet Union (see Chapter 24), which addressed social inequality and political powerlessness. Many found Soviet communist leader Vladimir Lenin's theories persuasive; blaming colonial societies' poverty on industrialized nations imposing a capitalist system, Lenin divided the world into imperial countries (the exploiters) and dominated countries (the exploited). Thus many nationalists who once admired Western democracies now found inspiration in Soviet Russia. Although the USSR proved capable of following blatantly imperialistic policies, many accepted Lenin's theory of capitalism-based imperialism.

In contrast, while some Muslims in societies such as Indonesia and Turkey turned to left-wing radicalism, many Muslims were less amenable to Marxism, communism, and secular nationalism. Some believed that revitalizing Islam required purging it of pre-Islamic features such as mysticism. Some adopted dogmatic and puritanical approaches such as Wahabism or its offshoot, **Salafism**, a movement, originating in nineteenth-century Egypt, that looks back to the earliest years of Islam as a model of how the modern world should be ordered. Hence, both movements rejected modernity and sought to recreate the early Muslim society of the Prophet Muhammad's time. Other Muslims emphasized Sufism and its syncretic, tolerant approaches. Better transportation, especially steamship lines, enabled more to study in the Middle East or make pilgrimages to Mecca, meeting Muslims from around the world.

While anti-imperialist feelings increased, powerful nations expanded their imperial reach after World War I, intervening in less powerful countries. Britain and France took control of former Ottoman colonies in western Asia and German colonies in West Africa; the Belgians and South Africa replaced the Germans in Central Africa and southwest Africa, respectively. Some of the colonies contained valuable resources. Australia and Japan occupied German-ruled Pacific islands. Supported by colonial governments, Europeans continued to settle in Algeria, Angola, Kenya, South Africa, and southern Rhodesia, dispossessing local people from their land. Moreover, Western military conquests in Africa had not ended. In 1935–1936 Italy invaded and brutally conquered the last independent African state, Ethiopia, killing some 200,000 Ethiopians in the process. Despite spirited defense, Ethiopians succumbed to superior Italian aerial bombing and firepower.

Meanwhile, the United States exercised influence in the Americas. Americans owned a large share of Mexico's economy, including most of the oil industry. To support these interests, President Woodrow Wilson sent thousands of U.S. troops into Mexico to restore order during the Mexican Revolution in the early 1900s. In Nicaragua U.S. Marines overthrew a hostile government and remained there from 1909 to 1933; Augusto César Sandino **(san-DEE-no)** (1895–1934) led a peasant resistance movement, becoming a hero to nationalist Central Americans. To protect U.S. investments in Central America, Americans often supported governments led by landowners and generals, such as the notoriously corrupt Nicaraguan dictator, Anastasio Somoza (1896–1956). President Franklin D. Roosevelt defended this policy, maintaining that "they may be SOBs, but they're our SOBs."[5] Repeated U.S. interventions fostered resentment against what Central Americans called "Yankee imperialism."

> **Salafism** A movement that looks back to the earliest years of Islam as a model for ordering the modern world.

KEY POINTS

▶ World War I affected colonies in Asia, Africa, and the Caribbean as thousands of colonial subjects were forced to fight and die for France, Germany, and Britain.

▶ Colonial governments imposed heavy taxes and hard labor on the colonial peoples, who often lived in poverty while their Western counterparts lived in luxury, a state of affairs that was defended by the Western idea that the colonial peoples could not yet govern themselves.

▶ Western capitalism disrupted traditional rural life in many colonies, placing formerly self-sufficient farmers at the mercy of landowners and the world economy, which led to misery, political unrest, and activism during the Great Depression.

▶ Nationalism appealed to many frustrated colonial subjects, though many multiethnic colonies struggled to develop a sense of nationhood.

▶ Despite local opposition, Western nations expanded their colonial reach between 1900 and 1945: Italy brutally conquered Ethiopia, France and Britain took over former Ottoman colonies, and the United States continued to meddle in Central America.

---

[5]Quoted in Lester Langley, *Central America: The Real Stakes: Understanding Central America Before It's Too Late* (New York: Dorsey, 1985), 23.

25-2 Nationalism and Communism in China

▷〔 TRANSITIONS　〓 SOCIETIES

Ⓠ How and why did the communist movement grow in China?

The Chinese Revolution of 1911–1912, ending the two-thousand-year-old imperial system (see Chapter 23), produced a republic Chinese hoped would foster renewed strength in the world. These hopes were soon dashed as China lapsed into warlordism and civil war, remaining nominally independent but subject to Western and Japanese forces. Alarm at China's domestic failures and continuing Western imperialism sparked resurgent nationalism, the formation of a communist party, and China's eventual reunification.

25-2a Warlords, New Cultures, and Nationalism

During the demoralizing Warlord Era (1916–1927), China was divided into territories controlled by rival **warlords**, local political leaders with their own armies that taxed and terrorized the population. Some warlords, calling themselves reformers, promoted education and industry. Others took bribes to favor merchants or foreign governments. Perhaps the most brutal, corrupt, and hated warlord, Zhang Zongchang, was known as the "Dogmeat General" because of his food preference. A children's ditty mocked his penchant for destruction and excess: "Zhang Zongchang, wicked and wasteful; Wrecks shoes, wrecks stockings, wrecks army equipment."[6] High taxes, inflation, famine, accelerating social tensions, and banditry made life difficult for most Chinese, increasing frustration.

Cities became enclaves of new intellectual, social, cultural, and economic thought. New schools and universities opened, and 4.5 million girls attended schools by 1919, although boys enjoyed more access to formal education. By the 1920s many women worked as nurses, teachers, and civil servants; however, few rural women became literate or enjoyed these new opportunities. Exposure to Western ideas in universities, many operated by Christian groups, led some students to question their own cultural traditions. Women activists and sympathetic men campaigned against footbinding, which largely disappeared except in remote areas by 1930. Chambers of commerce and labor unions also appeared.

A new movement originating at Beijing University in 1915, the **New Culture Movement**, rejected the discredited past and sprouted a literary revival. The university hired radical professors and

warlords Local political leaders with their own armies.

New Culture Movement A movement of Chinese intellectuals started in 1915 that sought to wash away the discredited past and sprout a literary revival.

May Fourth Movement A radical nationalist resurgence in China in 1919 that opposed imperialism and the ineffective, warlord-controlled Chinese government.

CONNECTION to TODAY

How do you think that the policies and attitudes in China today reflect the experiences of Chinese in these decades?

encouraged the mixing of Chinese and Western thought, and university professors published the literary magazine *New Youth*, which attacked China's traditions, including Confucianism, for promoting conformity and discouraging critical thinking. The magazine's editor, Chen Duxiu (**chen too-shoe**) (1879–1942), emphasized republican government and science. Contributors, while detesting Western imperialism, admired Western nations' liberal, open intellectual atmosphere, viewed modern science as liberation from superstition, derided the traditional Chinese family system for crushing individual rights, and advised women to seek equality with men.

Chinese rage against Western and Japanese imperialism increased in World War I's aftermath. China remained neutral until 1917 but sent 200,000 Chinese laborers to assist the Allies in France. Japan, which had occupied Germany's sphere of influence in the Shandong peninsula, in 1915 presented China with 21 Demands, including control of Shandong, increased rights in Manchuria, and appointment of Japanese advisers to China's government. The Western allies' decision to allow Japan to take over Shandong provoked a radical nationalist resurgence in 1919, the **May Fourth Movement**, that opposed imperialism and the ineffective, warlord-controlled Chinese government. Today mention the numbers 5/4 (*wu si*) and most Chinese would know the precise reference to this pivotal event, just as most Americans know the meaning of 9/11. Decrying social injustice and government inaction, thousands of outraged students and workers, including many women, mounted mass demonstrations, strikes, and boycotts of Japanese goods, igniting a new era of patriotism for a generation of young Chinese. In Beijing many gathered at the Gate of Heavenly Peace, the entrance to the Forbidden City imperial palace of the Ming and Qing dynasties. Merchants closed their businesses in sympathy. Thinking of the humiliations inflicted by the Opium War and other disasters, the protesters blamed the grasping foreign powers for mocking the new era of national "self-determination" declared by U.S. President Woodrow Wilson. They were even more upset with China's corrupt and autocratic leaders, mostly military men (warlords) who failed to protect the homeland. Capitulating to the protests, the government refused to sign the Versailles treaty. The new Soviet Union sided with China and renounced the special privileges obtained by the czars, winning Chinese admiration. New political organizations, periodicals, and study societies sprang up to discuss and criticize politics, experiment in the arts, lambast traditional values, and translate the work of Western, Russian, and Japanese thinkers representing varied strands of thought. May

[6]Quoted in James Sheridan, *China in Disintegration: The Republican Era in Chinese History, 1912–1949* (New York: Free Press, 1975), 67.

4 continues to resonate with Chinese as a symbol; however, both the current government and those protesting against it try to control the message.

In 1921 Beijing University professors and students organized the Chinese Communist Party (CCP). Some party founders, such as *New Youth* editor Chen Duxiu, were Europe- or Japan-educated reformers who admired Western science and culture. Others were nationalists who, despising Western models, believed people could liberate China if mobilized for revolution. Soviet advisers, while encouraging the party to organize the urban working class, considered the communists unlikely to become influential. But the communists formed peasant associations, labor unions, women's groups, and youth clubs, enrolling some sixty thousand members by 1927. A communist women's congress declared that "women…are still imprisoned in the yoke of the feudal ethical code and lead lives similar to prostitutes."[7]

Capitalizing on the resurgent nationalism, Sun Zhongshan, better known as Sun Yat-sen (1866–1925), whose revolutionary ideas helped overthrow the Qing dynasty (see Chapter 23), began to rebuild his Guomindang, or Nationalist Party. Receiving no help from Western nations, who benefited from China's disarray, Sun accepted Soviet advisers and military aid. In the mid-1920s Sun's Guomindang and the Chinese communists worked together, in an alliance known as the United Front, to defeat warlordism. However, Sun's ideology grew more authoritarian; he concluded that China's 400 million people—in his view just "loose sand"—were not ready for democracy. Sun died of cancer in 1925 and was replaced by his brother-in-law, Jiang Jieshi, better known in the West as Chiang Kai-shek (**CHANG kai-shek**) (1887–1975). From a wealthy landowning family, Chiang was a conservative, pro-business soldier and patriot but indifferent to social change. Developing a close relationship with the United States, Chiang began building a modern military force.

25-2b The Republic of China

Between 1926 and 1928 Guomindang forces and their communist allies reunified China with a military drive, the Northern Expedition, that defeated or co-opted warlords. Foreign powers recognized Chiang's new Republic of China. However, tensions grew between left-wing and right-wing factions. Whereas the communists and leftist Guomindang leaders sought social change and mobilization of workers, the Chiang-led right wing allied with the anti-progressive Shanghai business community. In 1927, expelling communists from the United Front, Chiang began a reign of terror, killing thousands of leftists; survivors went into hiding or fled into the interior or abroad.

From 1928 to 1937 Chiang's Republic, based at Nanjing (**nahn-JING**) along the Yangzi River, launched a modernization program. The leaders, many Western-educated Christians, built railroads, factories, a banking system, and a modern army, streamlined government, fostered public health and education, and adopted new legal codes. But while promoting monogamy and equal inheritance for women, Chiang's government lacked power to implement them. Chiang negotiated the elimination of most unequal international treaties imposed by Western nations and Japan in the 1800s. The U.S. government, closely allied with Chiang, and private Americans, feeling paternalistic responsibility, provided generous political and financial support for modernization, funding schools, hospitals, orphanages, and Christian missions. In 1940 a prominent, ethnocentric U.S. senator, believing Americans could enrich and Westernize China, proclaimed: "We will lift Shanghai up, ever up, until it is just like Kansas City."[8]

The Republic faced daunting challenges. While the elite in big coastal cities prospered, Chiang was unable or unwilling to address the peasantry's growing poverty. Agricultural commercialization shifted more land to landlords, leaving half of China's peasants unable to support their families. One 1930s academic study of rural China described the desperate peasant as "a man standing up to his neck in water, whom the slightest ripple will drown."[9] Meanwhile, Chiang tolerated government corruption, rewarding his merchant and banker financial backers. As antigovernment sentiment grew, Chiang, influenced by European fascism, built an authoritarian police state, brutally repressing dissent. Another threat to Chiang's government came from Japan. Blaming the Chinese for a railway bombing secretly perpetrated by Japanese soldiers, in 1931 Japanese forces seized Manchuria, rich in mineral resources and fertile farmland, and established a puppet government under the last Manchu emperor, Henry Pu Yi (1906–1967) (see Map 25.1). As Japan gradually extended its military and political influence southward, Chiang, with inferior military power, followed an appeasement policy. His attempts to strengthen the military diverted scarce resources from economic development, while critics considered Chiang's reluctance to fight Japan unpatriotic.

Cultural life reflected China's challenges. Disillusioned by China's weakness and continued despotism, many intellectuals lost faith in both Chiang's regime and Chinese traditions. Writer Lu Xun (**LOO shun**) (1881–1936), who studied in Japan and became proficient in several foreign languages, published satires on Chinese failures to meet challenges. Lu later formed a leftist writers' group and supported the communists. In criticizing both imperialism and greedy Chinese leaders, he argued, "Our vaunted Chinese civilization is only a feast of human flesh prepared for the rich and mighty, and China is only a kitchen where these feasts are prepared."[10] Lu became most famous for his series of satirical writings on the fictional Ah Q, a poorly educated rural peasant with no real occupation who deceives himself that he is superior to those who oppress him, and that he has won "spiritual

---

[7]Quoted in Christina Kelley Gilmartin, *Engendering the Chinese Revolution: Radical Women, Communist Politics, and Mass Movements in the 1920s* (Berkeley: University of California Press, 1995), 68–69.
[8]Kenneth Wherry of Nebraska, quoted in John Brooks, *The Great Leap: The Past Twenty-five Years in America* (New York: Harper and Row, 1966), 327.
[9]R. H. Tawney, quoted in Diane Lary, *China's Republic* (New York: Cambridge University Press, 2007), 107.
[10]Quoted in *A Pictorial Biography of Luxun* (Beijing: Peoples Fine Arts Publishing House, n.d.), 157.

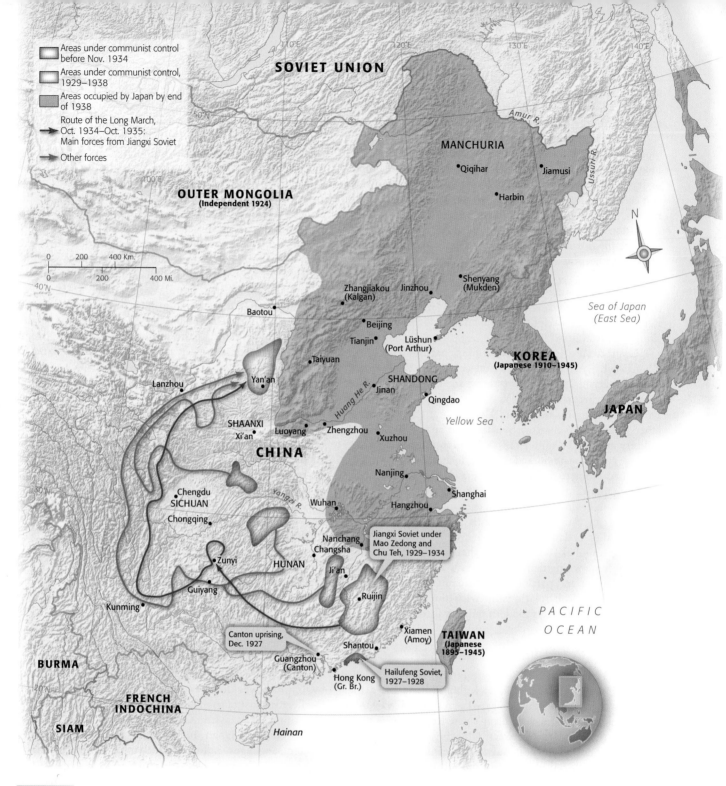

MAP 25.1 **Chinese Communist Movement and Chinese-Japanese War** Japan occupied much of northern and eastern China by 1939. In 1935–1936 the Chinese communists made the famous six-thousand-mile Long March from their base in Jiangxi in southern China to Yan'an in northwest China.

Q What does the map show us about the geography of the war, including the extent of Japanese power and the areas of communist strength?

victories" even as he mostly experiences humiliation and defeat in life. Lu presents Ah Q's many faults as representing what Lu considered the flawed Chinese national character of his day. Ding Ling (1904–1985), one of China's first feminist writers, had fled her native village to avoid an arranged marriage, participated in the May Fourth Movement, and lived a liberated city life. Her early novels and short stories featured independent women unable to find emotional or sexual satisfaction. After the Guomindang killed her politically activist husband, she dedicated her writing to the revolutionary cause but later faced communist persecution for her feminism and reluctance to follow the party line.

25-2c The Rise of Chinese Communism

As communists surviving Chiang's terror rebuilt their movement, a younger party leader, Mao Zedong (**maow dzuh-dong**) (1893–1976), pursued his own strategy to mount revolution. From a peasant family dominated by an abusive father, Mao ran away from home to attend high school and later worked in the Beijing University Library. Embracing communism, he edited a radical magazine, became an elementary school principal, and organized workers and peasants. In 1927, as Chiang eliminated communists, Mao fled to rugged mountains in Jiangxi (**kee-ON-see**) province in south-central China, established a revolutionary base, the **Jiangxi Soviet**, and organized a guerrilla army out of peasants, bandits, and former Guomindang soldiers. Rejecting Soviet advice to depend on the urban working class, Mao instead relied on China's huge peasantry (see Discover Historical Voices: Peasants as a Revolutionary Base). Mao believed that violence was necessary to oppose Chiang. Between 1928 and 1934 Mao expanded the Jiangxi Soviet, redistributing land from the rich to the poor. As Chiang's repression intensified, top communist leaders joined Mao in Jiangxi. But Mao also violently purged party rivals he labelled as "counter-revolutionaries" or "despotic landlords," using tactics such as torture, threats of execution, and endless interrogations he later employed to eliminate enemies in the years that followed.

Increasingly alarmed, Chiang's army blockaded the Soviet to keep out essential supplies, forcing Mao to reluctantly abandon his base. In 1935, seeking a safer base, 100,000 soldiers and followers broke through the blockade and began the **Long March**, an epic journey full of hardship; Mao's Red Army fought their way six thousand miles on foot and horseback through eleven provinces, crossed eighteen mountain ranges, forded twenty-four rivers, and slogged through swamps, losing 90 percent of their people to death or desertion. Finally in late 1936 the ragtag survivors arrived in a poor northwestern province and moved into cavelike homes in hills around dusty Yan'an (**YEH-nan**) city. The Long March saved the communists from elimination, making Mao the unchallenged party leader. Mao celebrated the achievement: "The Long March is the first of its kind in the annals of history [and has] proclaimed that the Red Army is an army of heroes."[11] But still vulnerable to Chiang's larger,

IMAGE 25.3 **The Long March** This idealized propaganda painting portrays Mao Zedong with Red Army soldiers in a positive light during the Long March in 1935–1936. The Long March was a military retreat to escape pressure from Guomindang forces that enabled the Red Army and communist leaders to reach a safe base in northwest China. The Red Army was the forerunner of the Peoples Liberation Army.

Q What can we learn about Mao, the Red Army soldiers, the Long March, and the role of propaganda from this painting?

better-equipped forces, they would be saved only by Japan's invasion of China in 1937, which forced Chiang to shift his military priorities to fighting the Japanese, allowing the communists to regroup and spread their message in wartime China.

25-2d Japanese Invasion and Communist Revolution

The Japanese invasion and disastrous war that followed altered China's politics as Chiang diverted modernization funds to the military. The new Sino–Japanese conflict destroyed China's major cities, devastated the countryside, undermined the economy, and ended hopes for soon building a modern society. Some 14 to 20 million Chinese died and the war instilled in many Chinese a lasting hatred and fear of Japan. Mao captured the country's patriotic mood, proposing a united front in what he called "the war of resistance" against Japan; Chiang had to agree. The Japanese soon occupied the major north China and coastal cities. When Japanese forces captured the Republican capital, Nanjing, the brutality, murders, and rapes that followed shocked the world; some 300,000, mostly civilians, died in the orgy of violence later called "the Rape of Nanjing." By the end of 1938 the Japanese

> **Jiangxi Soviet** A revolutionary base, established in 1927 in south-central China, where Mao Zedong organized a guerrilla force to fight the Guomindang.
>
> **Long March** An epic journey, full of hardship, in which Mao Zedong's Red Army fought their way six thousand miles on foot and horseback through eleven Chinese provinces to establish a safe base.

---

[11]Quoted in Stephen Uhalley, Jr., *Mao Tse-Tung: A Critical Biography* (New York: New Viewpoints, 1975), 55.

Discover Historical Voices

Peasants as a Revolutionary Base

In 1926 Mao Zedong, one of the few communist leaders from a peasant background and with experience organizing peasants, became head of the Communist Party's "Peasant Department." Returning to his native Hunan province to attend a conference of local peasants, already noted for radical activism, Mao remained for some time investigating the peasantry's revolutionary potential. The report on his findings, published in April 1927, became a key document in twentieth-century Chinese history. Although he originally thought poor peasants lacked organization, he discovered that many were already involved in peasant associations that challenged the social and economic inequities of rural life, including patriarchal power over women. Mao wanted the party to support their efforts as part of their broader struggle against the Guomindang and cultural conservatism. This excerpt includes some of Mao's best-known thoughts on revolution and the oppression of women.

I called together for fact-finding conferences experienced peasants and comrades working for the peasant movement.... And many strange things there were that I had never seen or heard before. I think these conditions exist in many other places. All kinds of arguments against the peasant movement must be speedily set right.... For the rise of the present peasant movement is a colossal event. In a very short time...several hundred million peasants will rise like a tornado or tempest, a force so extraordinarily swift and violent that no power, however great, will be able to suppress it.... They will send all imperialists, warlords, corrupt officials, local bullies, and bad gentry to their graves.... To march at their head and lead them? Or to follow at their rear, gesticulating at them and criticizing them? Every Chinese is free to choose...but circumstances demand that a quick choice be made.

All Power to the Peasant Association! The peasants attack as their main targets the local bullies and bad gentry and the lawless landlords, hitting in passing against patriarchal ideologies and institutions, corrupt officials in the cities, and evil customs in the rural areas.... The revolt of the peasants disturbed the sweet dreams of the gentry...the fact is...that the broad peasant masses have risen to fulfill their historic mission, that the democratic forces in the rural areas have risen to overthrow the rural feudal power. The patriarchal-feudal class...has formed the basis of an autocratic government for thousands of years, the cornerstone of imperialism, warlordism and corrupt officialdom. To overthrow this feudal power is the real objective of the national revolution. What Dr. Sun Yat-sen wanted to do in forty years he devoted to the national revolution but failed to

accomplish, the peasants have accomplished in a few months. This is a marvelous feat which has never been achieved in the last forty or even thousand years. It is very good indeed....

For ages these people, with power in their hands, tyrannized over the peasants and trampled them underfoot; that is why the peasants have now risen in such a great revolt... a revolution is not the same as inviting people to dinner, or writing an essay, or painting a picture, or doing fancy needlework; it cannot be anything so refined, so calm and gentle, or so mild, kind, courteous, restrained, and magnanimous. A revolution is an uprising, an act of violence whereby one class overthrows another. A rural revolution is a revolution by which the peasantry overthrows the authority of the feudal landlord class.... In the rural areas, there must be a great fervent revolutionary upsurge, which alone can arouse hundreds and thousands of the people to form a great force....

A man in China is usually subjected to the domination of three systems of authority: 1) the system of the state (political authority), ranging from the national, provincial, and country government to the township government; 2) the system of the clan (clan authority), ranging from the central and branch ancestral temples to the head of the household; and 3) the system of gods and spirits (theocratic authority)....As to women, apart from being dominated by the three systems mentioned above, they are further dominated by men (the authority of the husband). These four kinds of authority...represent the whole ideology and institutions of feudalism and patriarchy, and are the four great cords that have bound the Chinese people and particularly the peasants....In a word, then, the whole feudal-patriarchal system and ideology is tottering with the growth of the peasant's power.... The abolition of the clan system, of superstitions, and of inequality between men and women will follow as a natural consequence of victory in political and economic struggles.

Reflection Questions

1. Why does Mao believe that the peasants were angry and demonstrated revolutionary potential?
2. How does he describe the status of women and how it can be improved?
3. Do you think that Mao's portrayal of the Chinese peasants in the 1920s would describe the peasants in China today?

Source: "Report on an Investigation of the Peasant Movement in Hunan," in *Selected Works of Mao Tse-Tung*, Vol. 1 (Peking: Foreign Languages Press, 1965), 23–28, 44–46.

controlled most of eastern China, including the best farmland and major industrial cities, but, their forces overextended, they became bogged down, unable to expand control. Over ninety-five million Chinese ultimately became war refugees,

sapping the rural economy as civilians fled. War and occupation undermined Chiang's government, enabling the communists to recruit support and setting the stage for major political changes in the later 1940s.

Chiang's government, along with a mass migration of Chinese, relocated inland to Chongqing (**CHUNG-king**), a Yangzi River city protected by high mountains. Unlike cosmopolitan coastal cities, Chongqing, with a depressing climate of fog and humidity, offered no bright lights or French restaurants. Fatigue, cynicism, and inflation discouraged the Guomindang's followers. Virtually broke but needing to support an army of four to five million men, Chiang's government taxed the peasants in areas it still controlled. Militarily ineffective, politically repressive, and economically corrupt, it offered limited resistance to the Japanese, killed and imprisoned opponents, and put its leaders' personal gain above the people's economic well-being. Although supporting Chiang, the United States could supply Guomindang-held areas only by difficult, mountainous routes from Burma and India. Moreover, Chiang often ignored U.S. military and political advice. As the war wore on, Chiang lost much popular support.

Meanwhile, the communists at Yan'an improved their prospects. Used to poverty, they had a more disciplined army with higher morale. While Chiang's much larger forces had the main responsibility to fight Japan, the communists mobilized, forging a close relationship with north China peasants and mounting guerrilla bands to harass the Japanese. Their unconventional struggle, called "**people's war**," combined military action and political recruitment. In Mao's military strategy, "the enemy advances, we retreat; the enemy halts, we harass; the enemy retreats, we pursue."[12] Politically communist activists also formed village governments and peasant associations and encouraged women's rights, punishing abusive husbands.

Attracted by their message of social revolution and nationalism, thousands of Chinese, students, intellectuals, and writers such as Ding Ling flocked to Yan'an, joining the communist cause. By 1945 the party had 1.2 million members.

Communist experiences at Yan'an fostered **Maoism**, an ideology promoted by Mao that mixed Chinese ideas with Soviet Marxist-Leninism. Mao emphasized the subordination of the individual to group needs (a traditional Chinese notion), the superiority of political values over technical and artistic ones, and the belief in human will as a social force. To combat elitism, Mao introduced mass campaigns; everyone engaged in physical labor, such as building dams and roads. Sent into villages to teach literacy, intellectuals also learned from peasants. Mao expressed faith that politically educated people possessed the collective power to triumph over nature, poverty, and exploitation and build a new society.

The communists now dominated much of rural north China, where Mao's ideas on social change and economic justice gained support. When the war ended in 1945, they had improved their prospects while Chiang's Guomindang, although still a superior military force, was beset with problems and losing popular support. In 1949 the communists won a bitter civil war and established a government.

> **people's war** An unconventional struggle combining military action and political recruitment, formulated by Mao Zedong in China.
>
> **Maoism** An ideology promoted by Mao Zedong that mixed ideas from Chinese tradition with Marxist-Leninist ideas from the Soviet Union.

KEY POINTS

▸ After the end of the imperial system, rival warlords controlled China during a period of civil war, and intellectuals formed the New Culture Movement, which called for a modernized China that fostered individualism and equality rather than traditions such as Confucianism.

▸ Japan's aggressive demands after World War I enraged the Chinese, and some were attracted to communism, but Sun Yat-sen's successor, the pro-business Chiang Kai-shek, allied the nationalist movement with the United States.

▸ Chiang Kai-shek's Republic of China launched a modernization program, but it was hampered by a split with the communists, persistent rural poverty, and the Japanese seizure of Manchuria.

▸ The Chinese people lost faith in Chiang's government as it squeezed them for taxes to support a failing war against Japan, while Mao's communists instilled hope through guerrilla attacks on the Japanese and a promise of equality and progress through shared sacrifice.

25-3 British Colonialism and the Indian Response

🏛 SOCIETIES ⇄ TRANSITIONS

Q What were the main contributions of Mohandas Gandhi to the Indian struggle?

Indian resentment of British colonialism and social inequalities fueled a powerful nationalist movement. Those hoping that World War I would bring self-determination saw that British rhetoric about democracy did not apply to

> **CONNECTION to TODAY**
>
> Do you think that former colonial powers, such as the British in India, should apologize to the formerly colonized peoples?

India. Growing opposition to British rule, spurred by the Indian National Congress, led to unrest, forcing Britain to modify some policies. Nationalism also set the stage for separate Hindu and Muslim nations after World War II.

---

[12]Quoted in John Meskill, "History of China," in *An Introduction to Chinese Civilization*, ed. John Meskill (Lexington, MA: D.C. Heath, 1973), 302.

25-3a The Nationalist Upsurge and Gandhi

Nationalist opposition to the British Raj had been building for decades. During World War I the British Raj raised taxes and customs duties to finance the war, sparking several armed uprisings. Over one million Indians fought for Britain in France and the Middle East; sixty thousand were killed and seventy thousand wounded. Because of their sacrifices in a war they did not start, many Indians expected liberalization, perhaps self-government similar to Australia and Canada, both former colonies. Dashing these hopes, Britain declared it would maintain India as an integral part of its empire. However, World War I losses showed that British power was no longer unchallengeable.

With a severe economic slump heightening discontent, riots broke out and Britain clamped down on dissent, maintaining harsh wartime laws. In 1919, in the Punjab city of Amritsar, British officers, fearing a mass uprising, ordered their Indian soldiers to open fire on twenty thousand peaceful and unarmed protesters—Hindus, Muslims, and Sikhs—at an unauthorized rally in a walled field, killing four hundred to six hundred protesters and wounding around one thousand, including women and children. Indians greeted the Amritsar massacre with outrage, which intensified when the British hailed the commanding officer, General Reginald Dyer, as a national hero. Prominent Indians, many once pro-British, were appalled at the cruelty. Nobel Prize–winning writer Rabindranath Tagore (**tuh-GAWR**) (1861–1941) wrote, "The enormity of the measures taken up for quelling some local disturbances had, with a rude shock, revealed to our minds the helplessness of our position as British subjects in India."[13] In recent years Britons have debated whether the nation should formally apologize for the massacre. Both Queen Elizabeth and a prime minister have visited Amritsar and shown respect at the memorial but neither apologized. Deep political divisions and instability in Britain today make an apology unlikely anytime soon.

The unrest brought forth new nationalist leaders, most notably Mohandas K. Gandhi (**GAHN-dee**) (1869–1948) (see Meet the People: Mohandas Gandhi, Indian Nationalist). After earning his law degree in Britain, Gandhi lived for twenty-two years in South Africa, where British rulers practiced racial segregation, white supremacy, and political repression (see Chapter 21). To assert Indian immigrants' rights, Gandhi developed tactics of **nonviolent resistance**, noncooperation with unjust laws and peaceful confrontation with illegitimate authority. Influenced by his pacifist wife, Kasturbai, Gandhi adopted ideas against taking life that had been introduced twenty-five hundred years earlier by Jains and Buddhists and that were also promoted by Quakers, a pacifist Christian movement Gandhi encountered in England. Nonviolence— Gandhi often called it passive

nonviolent resistance
Noncooperation with unjust laws and peaceful confrontation with illegitimate authority, pursued by Mohandas Gandhi in India.

resistance—was, he wrote, "a method of securing rights by personal suffering; it is the reverse of resistance by arms."[14] Gandhi believed that violence was never justified. Meet the enemy with reason; if he responded with violence, this had to be endured in good spirit.

After returning to India, in 1920 Gandhi became president of the Indian National Congress, mounting nonviolent mass campaigns against British political and economic institutions. Inspired by his example, huge numbers of ordinary people— factory workers, peasants, estate laborers—joined his movement, shaking colonial rule's foundations. Gandhi made mass civil disobedience—marches, sit-ins, hunger strikes, peaceful violation of law, refusal to pay taxes, boycotts of government and businesses—an effective nonviolent strategy. His Congress colleague, Jawaharlal Nehru (**JAH-wa-HAR-lahl NAY-roo**), placed Gandhi's role in perspective: "Gandhi was like a powerful current of fresh air that made us stretch ourselves and take deep breaths, like a Whirlwind that upset many things but most of all the working of people's minds."[15]

Yet, some of Gandhi's ideas were outside mainstream nationalist thought, confounding allies. Gandhi opposed the global economic system, characterized by competitive capitalism and trade between societies with unequal power and wealth. He believed India should reject Western models and return to the self-sufficient, village-based precolonial economy, where people could spin their own cloth. He called industrialization "a machinery which has impoverished India. India's salvation consists in unlearning what she has learned during the past fifty years. The railways, telegraphs, hospitals, [and] lawyers have all to go."[16] Critics, some of them Indians, considered Gandhi's ideal of simple living a utopian fantasy, impractical, out of touch with the modern world, and unable to improve people's lives. Gandhi also insisted that society's lowest social group, untouchables, be included in political actions, distressing high-caste Hindus. Gandhi coined the term *harijans* (children of God) as a more dignified label to replace *pariahs*, the centuries-old term for untouchables. While not entirely rejecting the caste system, Gandhi wanted all people to enjoy the same dignity. In his conception, harijan toilet cleaners would have the same status as members of the priestly caste but continue cleaning toilets. Even untouchable leaders often considered Gandhi's views unrealistic and patronizing.

Thanks to Gandhi's efforts, during the 1920s the Congress developed a mass base, supported by people from all cultures, religions, regions, and social backgrounds. His tactics bewildered the British; while they claimed to uphold law, order, and Christian values, they clubbed hunger strikers, trampled nonviolent protesters with horses, and arrested Gandhi and other leaders multiple times. One Indian observer told British officials in 1930 that the Congress "has undoubtedly acquired a great hold on the popular imagination. On roadside stations where until a few months ago I could hardly have suspected that people had any politics, I have seen demonstrations and heard

---

[13]Quoted in Sinharaja Tammita-Delgoda, *A Traveller's History of India*, 2nd ed. (New York: Interlink, 1999), 189.
[14]From Clark D. Moore and David Eldridge, eds., *India Yesterday and Today* (New York: Bantam, 1970), 174.
[15]Quoted in Martin Deming Lewis, ed., *Gandhi: Maker of Modern India?* (Lexington, MA: D.C. Heath, 1965), xii.
[16]Quoted in Hermann Kulke and Dietmar Rothermund, *History of India*, 3rd ed. (New York: Routledge, 1998), 135–136.

Mohandas Gandhi, Indian Nationalist

Few individuals have had as much impact on history as Mohandas Gandhi (1869–1948), who became Indian nationalism's leading figure in the 1920s by formulating ideas of nonviolent opposition to repressive colonial rule, influencing millions both inside and outside India. Gandhi was born into an affluent vaisya family in the western state of Gujarat; although vaisyas commonly engaged in commerce, his father was a government official. Like many traditionalist, devout Hindus, his parents arranged for him to marry at thirteen to Kasturbai Kapada (**KAST-er-by ka-PO-da**) (1869–1944), a rich merchant's daughter. Kasturbai proved a courageous helpmate in his later political activities.

Gandhi wanted to study law in London, but his family feared he would be corrupted there. He vowed to live a celibate life in England and never touch meat or wine. In England he read Indian works such as the *Bhagavad Gita* and Western books including the Christian Bible. He also learned about Western nationalism and democracy.

In 1893 Gandhi joined a large Indian law firm in South Africa, where the racist government and white minority mistreated the thousands of Indians recruited as laborers and plantation workers. With his wife's encouragement, he began helping local Indians assert their rights, for which he was jailed, beaten by mobs, and almost killed by angry opponents. South Africa's British rulers raised taxes on Indians, shut down Indian gatherings, and refused official recognition of Hindu marriages. Influenced by Kasturbai's advocacy of justice and nonviolence, Gandhi developed his nonviolent resistance strategy against oppressive rule, ideas that later inspired admirers throughout the world. Gandhi spread ideas of nonviolence by leading hunger strikes, public demonstrations, and mass marches; thousands of Indians, resisting oppression, willingly risked beatings or arrest for their cause. In 1914, the colonial regime lifted the worst legal injustices. Gandhi was forty-five years old when the triumph earned him fame and the respected title of *Mahatma* (Great Soul) among Indians in South Africa and at home.

When World War I broke out, Gandhi, Kasturbai, and their four children returned to India. In 1915 Gandhi established a spiritual center in Gujarat training followers in nonviolence. Though deeply religious, he also believed everyone had to reach truth in his or her own way, writing that "there are innumerable definitions of God, because His manifestations are innumerable. But I worship God as Truth only. I have not yet found Him, but I am seeking after Him." Moved by the Indian masses' poverty and suffering, he took up their cause. The high-caste Gandhi adopted simple peasant dress and always traveled third class.

The massacre of Indian protesters at Amritsar in 1919 shook Gandhi's faith in British justice. In 1920 he became the leader of the Indian National Congress. Over the next three decades he was at times a religious figure, at other times the consummate politician, crafty and practical. He launched three great campaigns of civil disobedience, in 1920, 1930, and 1942. Each time Britain jailed him for long periods. His practice of fasting to protest oppression reflected his self-discipline, adding to his saintly image.

Gandhi's personal life was also troubled. His wife, Kasturbai, aided in his campaigns, but Gandhi was gone for long periods, neglecting her and their four children. When Gandhi took a lifelong vow of chastity in 1906, Kasturbai did also. Although both came from affluent families, the Gandhis agreed to live simply. Critics accused Gandhi of sometimes humiliating his wife by, for example, asking her to do menial tasks such as cleaning toilets. Arrested during Gandhi's "Quit India" campaign, Kasturbai, in failing health, died in her husband's lap in prison in 1944. Before passing away, she noted they had shared many joys and sorrows and asked that she be cremated in a sari (dress) made from yarn he had spun.

Gandhi helped lead India to independence from Britain. Shortly thereafter, trying to end accelerating Hindu–Muslim violence in 1948, a Hindu fanatic who opposed Gandhi's tolerant approach assassinated him (see Chapter 31). India's first prime minister, Jawaharlal Nehru, called Gandhi's death the loss of India's soul: "The light has gone out of our lives and there is darkness everywhere."

IMAGE 25.4 Gandhi Addressing Meeting Mohandas Gandhi addressed some of his followers—many women as well as men—in a mass meeting in 1931. Gandhi convened many such gatherings to recruit and sustain his goals for Indian independence. He encouraged followers to resist tyranny through mass civil disobedience founded on nonviolence.

Sueddeutsche Zeitung Photo/Scherl/Alamy Stock Photo

Reflection Questions

1. How did Gandhi's South African experiences shape his political strategies?
2. How did Gandhi's ideas and activities have a great influence in the world?
3. In what ways do you see Gandhi as a role model for India and the world today?

Note: Quotations from Judith M. Brown, *Modern India: The Origins of an Asian Democracy*, 2nd ed. (New York: Oxford University Press, 1994), 211; and Rhoads Murphey, *A History of Asia*, 4th ed. (New York: Longman, 2003), 437.

651

Congress slogans."[17] Each campaign led to British concessions and the growing realization that Britain could not hold India forever.

The Great Depression collapsed prices for cash crops and rural credit, caused distress and suffering, and sparked a new Gandhi-led campaign in 1930, the Great Salt March. Gandhi and several dozen followers marched to the west coast, where they produced salt from seawater, breaking British laws since salt production was a lucrative government monopoly. Gandhi's action and arrest caught the popular imagination, sparking demonstrations, strikes, and boycotts. In quelling the unrest, the British killed one hundred and three, injured four hundred twenty, and imprisoned sixty thousand resisters. Released a few months later, Gandhi agreed to halt civil disobedience campaigns if Britain promoted Indian-made goods and held a conference to discuss India's political future.

25-3b Social Change: Caste and Gender Relations

Nationalist politics, economic dislocations, and rapid population growth affected India's social structure. India's population grew from 255 million in 1871 to 390 million in 1940. Trends reshaping the caste system continued, including more awareness of caste identities and lower castes adopting high-caste practices such as vegetarianism. Although Gandhi urged fair treatment, stronger caste identities fostered more discrimination against untouchables, perhaps a fifth of India's population. Untouchables responded, mounting movements promoting their rights. Dr. Bhimrao Ramji Ambedkar (**BIM-rao RAM-jee am-BED-car**) (1893–1956), who rose from one of the lowest groups, sweepers who cleaned village streets, to earn a Ph.D. and law degree from major U.S. and British universities, started schools, newspapers, and political parties. Rejecting Gandhi's policies as inadequate, he successfully lobbied to offer untouchables government jobs and scholarships for higher education. Later in life, believing untouchables could never flourish within Hinduism, Ambedkar led thousands of followers to adopt Buddhism, which by then had only a small following in India.

Attitudes toward women were also changing. Hindus increasingly favored widow remarriage, once forbidden, to help offset the higher Muslim birthrate. But greater emphasis on what traditionalists considered proper female conduct largely favored male authority. While the feminist movement remained weak, many women joined the Congress, and some demanded a vote equal to men for representative institutions. In 1915 poet Sarojini Naidu (1879–1949) became the first female Congress president. With British assent, all provincial legislatures granted women the franchise between 1923 and 1930. Educated women published magazines. Rokeya Hossain (1880–1932), a Bengali Muslim raised in seclusion who opened girls' schools and campaigned for equal rights, published a utopian short story, "Sultana's Dream," portraying men confined to seclusion because of uncontrolled sexual desires while women governed. Gandhi advocated gender equality, encouraged women's participation in public life, and urged women to abandon seclusion. But Gandhi usually offered women followers more menial tasks such as picketing and cooking, promoted women's traditional roles as wives and mothers, and believed women were especially suited to passive resistance. Some militant women joined men in terrorist organizations. Pritilata Waddedar (1911–1932), a brilliant Bengali university graduate, led and died in an armed raid on a British club that reportedly boasted a sign: "Dogs and Indians not allowed."

25-3c Hindu–Muslim Division

A growing Hindu–Muslim division posed a problem for nationalists. Although some Muslims supported the largely Hindu Congress, other Muslims pondered their role in India. While Gandhi respected all religions and welcomed Muslim support, Muslim leaders, fearing independence would mean Hindu domination, mounted their own nationalist organizations to work for a potential Muslim country. In 1930 student activists in Britain called their proposed Muslim nation Pakistan ("Land of the Pure") in Urdu. Some 20 percent of British India's population and largely concentrated in the northwest and Bengal, Muslims were divided by social status, ancestry, language, and sect. The great majority were Sunnis.

While Muslim leaders envisioned a state enshrining their religious values, Congress leaders were chiefly Western-oriented Hindu intellectuals. Jawaharlal Nehru (1889–1964), who succeeded Gandhi as Congress leader in 1929, wanted a secular state that was neutral toward religion and, unlike Gandhi, a modernized India. From a wealthy brahman family, charismatic with rare public speaking skills, Nehru was a Marxist-influenced product of an elite Western education who emphasized the common people's welfare. While Gandhi wanted to reshape society, Nehru and other Congress leaders focused on political independence. Few Indian nationalists shared the Chinese communist goal of radical social transformation.

By the 1930s the Muslim League, led by Western-educated Bombay lawyer Muhammed Ali Jinnah (**jee-NAH**) (1876–1948), a dapper figure in tailored suits who always spoke English and never learned Urdu, became a mass political movement competing with the Congress. Jinnah promoted a two-nations solution, arguing that it was a naive dream that Hindus and Muslims, with different values, could ever forge a common nationality. Jinnah's claim to speak for all Muslims outraged the Congress, which, with over 100,000 Muslim members, viewed itself as a national party representing all religions and castes. But Jinnah cultivated good relations with Britain and convinced regional Muslim leaders to support the Muslim League. The Congress, trying to marginalize the Muslim League, refused to form a coalition, a mistake in the long run.

The competing Congress and Muslim League visions complicated British efforts to introduce representative government. The rival organizations clashed in 1931, when Indian leaders and British officials met in London to discuss expanded elections. Various minorities, including Muslims, Sikhs, and untouchables, demanded separate electorates to ensure they gained representation. Believing this would perpetuate British

---

[17]Sir T. P. Sapru, quoted in Judith M. Brown, *Modern India: The Origins of an Asian Democracy*, 2nd ed. (New York: Oxford University Press, 1994), 280.

divide and rule, the Congress objected, but the minorities won provincial electoral rights. The electoral agreement failed to end anticolonial unrest and British counterviolence. However, in the Government of India Act of 1935, Britain introduced a new constitution that allowed thirty-five million property-owning Indians to vote for newly formed provincial legislatures. In the 1937 elections, the Congress won 70 percent of the popular vote and the majority of seats, defeating the Muslim League even in reserved Muslim seats. Jinnah redoubled his efforts to unite Muslims against the Congress. More Indians achieved leadership positions in the army, police, and civil service. However, British officials argued that communal divisions necessitated British rule to maintain order.

25-3d World War II and India

World War II, increasing the Hindu–Muslim divide, reshaped the nationalist dialogue. Britain committed Indian troops to that conflict without consulting Congress leaders. Some two million South Asian soldiers joined the British war effort, making the sacrifices of Empire troops critical to eventual victory over Fascism. In 1942 Gandhi, fearing Britain would not end its colonial rule, mounted a campaign demanding the British

"Quit India." The British arrested the entire Congress leadership and sixty thousand party activists, jailing many for the war's duration. Meanwhile, the rural poor and urban workers suffered as prices for essential goods soared; famine in Bengal killed three to four million people. In response, Nehru's main rival for Congress leadership, militant Bengali Marxist Subhas Chandra Bose (1895–1945), allied with imperial Japan and organized an Indian National Army, recruited from the British Indian army and Indian emigrants in Southeast Asia, that invaded India from Japanese-held Burma. The invasion failed, but many Indians saw Bose as a national hero.

Meanwhile, jailing Congress leaders allowed Jinnah to strengthen his Muslim League. The British cultivated Jinnah, who joined the government and demanded a separate Muslim state based on the Muslim-majority provinces. Rejecting Muslim separatism, the jailed Gandhi unsuccessfully urged Muslims to resist what he termed the suicide of partition. After World War II, the struggle between Indian nationalists and Britain, and between Hindus and Muslims, resumed, leading to the end of British rule and creating two separate independent nations, predominantly Hindu India and chiefly Muslim Pakistan, comprised of the northwest and Bengal but divided by north India.

KEY POINTS

▶ Mohandas Gandhi, the foremost Indian nationalist leader, promoted nonviolent resistance to British rule, including strikes, boycotts, and refusal to pay taxes, and won a massive popular following for the Indian National Congress.

▶ While even his Indian supporters considered some of Gandhi's ideas naive and utopian, campaigns such as the Great Salt March were highly effective in winning concessions from the British.

▶ Leaders of the untouchables, the lowest Hindu caste, pushed for and obtained greater opportunities, and

women were allowed somewhat more freedom, though many Indian men, including Gandhi, did not see them as entirely equal to men.

▶ The British jailed tens of thousands of Indian National Congress activists after Gandhi objected to Indian troops being forced to fight in World War II.

▶ Muhammed Ali Jinnah created the Muslim League and fought for a separate country for Muslims, and eventually two countries gained independence: India and Pakistan.

25-4 Nationalist Stirrings in Southeast Asia and Sub-Saharan Africa

SOCIETIES

Q How did nationalism differ in Southeast Asia and sub-Saharan Africa?

As in India, nationalist movements and protests in Southeast Asia and sub-Saharan Africa, none as influential as the Indian National Congress, also challenged Western colonialism. In 1930 the Indonesian Nationalist Party, struggling against Dutch colonialism, urged Indonesians to zealously pursue national freedom. The plea symbolized nationalist assertions in Southeast Asia, especially French-ruled Vietnam. In sub-Saharan Africa nationalist movements, often based on ethnicity, were weaker but anti-colonialism was strongly expressed in cultural developments.

CONNECTION to TODAY

How do you think this era has shaped Southeast Asian and African countries today?

25-4a Nationalism in Southeast Asia

The first stirrings of Southeast Asian nationalism, in the Philippines in the late 1800s, were thwarted by the American occupation. The United States reduced radical sentiments by promising eventual independence and co-opting nationalist leaders into the colonial administration. By 1941 nationalists had a large following in Vietnam, British Burma, and Indonesia, all experiencing oppressive colonial rule. In French-ruled Cambodia and Laos and in British Malaya and

Borneo, all colonies enduring less social, economic, and political disruption, nationalism was weaker.

In Burma (today's Myanmar), despite limited self-government by the 1930s, most of the majority ethnic group, the Burmans (today known as Bamar), hated British rule, British favoritism toward Christian ethnic minorities, and the large, economically dominant Indian community. The colony's schools encouraged students to adopt Western ways, including clothing styles, devaluing Buddhist traditions. Nationalist leaders, using Theravada Buddhism as a rallying cry, pressed for reform; some favored women's rights. A militant student movement emerged whose members called themselves thakins ("lords"), a symbol of youthful defiance. Their leaders, such as Aung San and U Nu, would lead the struggle for independence. When the Japanese invaded Burma in 1941, many Burmans welcomed them as liberators.

Although Siam (today's Thailand) was not a colony, nationalism emerged among the rising middle class of civil servants, military officers, and professionals, who resented the royal family and aristocracy's political domination. The Great Depression forced salary and budget cuts, further fueling middle-class discontent. In 1932 military officers, calling themselves nationalists, took power in a coup against the royal government, pressuring Siam's king, whose family had ruled since the late 1700s, to become a constitutional, mostly symbolic monarch. Military leaders ran the government through the 1930s, pursuing nationalist policies, renaming the country Thailand ("Land of Free People"), and promoting modern lifestyles, including dressing in Western fashion, with hats and shoes. Allying with imperial Japan, Thailand introduced fascist policies, militarizing schools and suppressing dissent.

The most powerful nationalist movement emerged in Vietnam, destabilized by French rule. The passionately revolutionary Phan Boi Chau (**FAN boy chow**) (1867–1940), from a Mandarin family, inspired patriotism and resistance. Before dying in a French prison, he wrote, "It has been but a yearning to purchase my freedom even at the cost of spilling my blood, to exchange my fate of slavery for the right of self-determination."[18] But older Confucian scholars like Phan gradually lost influence to younger, urban, French-educated intellectuals of the Vietnamese Nationalist Party, which, with few other options, assassinated colonial officials and bombed French buildings. A premature uprising in 1930 proved a turning point, sparking greater French repression that destroyed or weakened major nationalist groups except for the better-organized communists, some of whose leadership was underground or, like Ho, living abroad.

Vietnamese communism owed much to Ho Chi Minh, a Mandarin's son turned political activist who spent many years organizing the movement among Vietnamese exiles in Thailand and China. Believing revolution was the answer to economic exploitation and political repression and that communism was the most effective strategy for promoting nationalism and development, Ho favored equality for women and improving the lives of peasants and plantation workers. In 1930 he established the Indochinese Communist Party, uniting anticolonial radicals from Vietnam, Cambodia, and Laos. Vietnamese Marxists, imbued with nationalism, linked themselves to the patriotic Vietnamese rebels who for two thousand years had resisted Chinese, Mongol, and French conquerors. As one Marxist wrote: "Behind us we have the immense history of our people. There [are] still spiritual cords attaching us."[19] In 1941 Ho established the **Viet Minh** (Vietnamese Independence League), a coalition of anti-French groups that fought both French colonizers and the Japanese, who occupied Vietnam during World War II.

Nationalist activity also emerged in the Dutch East Indies. Diverse organizations sought freedom from Dutch rule while seeking to unite the colony's hundreds of ethnic groups. Some emphasized a unifying language. Malay, the mother tongue for many peoples in western Indonesia and a trading language elsewhere, was the archipelago's **lingua franca**, a widely used common tongue among diverse groups with their own languages. Nationalist intellectuals began using Malay, calling it Indonesian, which gradually became the language of magazines, newspapers, books, and education. Indonesians also reshaped religious traditions. Traditionally many Indonesians, especially on Java, followed a tolerant, mystical, and eclectic form of Islam. But some Muslims, impressed with but also resenting Western power, sought to reform and purify their faith by eliminating older pre-Islamic influences, such as mysticism. The conservative religious organization *Muhammadiyah* ("Way of Muhammad") and its allied women's organization, *Aisyah*, criticized local customs, promoted the goal of an Islamic state, stressed Islam's five pillars, and favored segregating men and women in public, a custom most Indonesians ignored.

In 1912 Javanese batik merchants, mixing reformist religious ideas with nationalism, established the first true political movement, the Islamic Union; by 1919 it had two million members. As Marxism became influential, the colonial government arrested Marxists. Radical Marxists established the Indonesian Communist Party in 1920, attracting support from non-devout Muslim peasants and labor union members in Java. Overestimating their strength, the communists sparked a poorly planned uprising in 1926. The Dutch crushed the uprising, executing communist leaders.

Javanese aristocrats who rejected Islamic reform ideas established the Indonesian Nationalist Party in 1927, promoting a new national identity. The key founder, Sukarno (**soo-KAHR-no**) (1902–1970), from a wealthy aristocratic Javanese family, studied engineering and then dedicated his life to politics and a free Indonesia. Sukarno loved the shadow puppet stories popular on Java for centuries. Like these stories' characters, Sukarno (who had no first name)

Viet Minh The Vietnamese Independence League, a coalition of anti-French groups established by Ho Chi Minh in 1941 that waged war against both the French and the Japanese.

lingua franca A language widely used as a common tongue among diverse groups with different languages.

[18]"Phan Boi Chau's Prison Reflections, 1914," in *Major Problems in the History of the Vietnam War: Documents and Essays,* ed. Robert J. McMahon (Lexington, MA: D.C. Heath, 1990), 32.
[19]Hoai Thanh, quoted in David Marr, "Vietnamese Historical Reassessment, 1900–1944," in *Perceptions of the Past in Southeast Asia,* ed. Anthony Reid and David Marr (Singapore: Heinemann, 1979), 337–338.

brought together contradictory ideas, such as Islamic faith and atheistic Marxism. In 1941 Sukarno wrote: "What is Sukarno? A nationalist? An Islamist? A Marxist?...Sukarno is a mixture of all these isms,...a meeting place of all trends and Ideologies."[20] A spellbinding orator and nationalism's mass popularizer, he created a slogan: "one nation—Indonesia, one people—Indonesian, one language—Indonesian," designed a flag, and wrote a national anthem. Dutch authorities arrested Sukarno in 1929 and exiled him to a remote island prison for the next decade, making him a nationalist symbol. In his defense speech he stressed Indonesia's "grandiose past. Oh, what Indonesian does not feel his heart shrink with sorrow when he hears the stories about the beautiful past, does not regret the disappearance of that departed glory!"[21] With Sukarno imprisoned, the Nationalist Party and vision grew slowly throughout the 1930s.

25-4b The Japanese Occupation and Its Consequences

During World War II the Japanese occupation of much of Southeast Asia from 1941 to 1945 boosted nationalism and weakened colonialism. Before 1941 colonial authority remained strong; only Vietnamese nationalism posed a serious threat. Then everything changed. Japan had already bullied Thailand and the Vichy-controlled French colonial regime in Vietnam to allow stationing of Japanese troops. Then a rapid Japanese invasion of Southeast Asia quickly followed the Pearl Harbor bombing in 1941. Easily overwhelming colonial forces, within four months Japan controlled major cities and heavily populated regions, shattering the mystique of Western invincibility. As an Indonesian writer remembered, the occupation "destroyed a whole set of illusions and left man as naked as when he was created."[22] European and American officials, businessmen, planters, and missionaries were either in retreat or prison camps. Japanese talked of "Asia for the Asians," and some anticolonial officers sympathized with Southeast Asian nationalists. But this rhetoric also masked Japanese desire for resources, especially rubber, oil, and timber from Indonesia, British Borneo, and Malaya.

Japanese domination was brief, less than four years, yet it fostered significant changes. Conflicts between ethnic groups often increased. In Malaya, Japanese policy allowed Malay officials to keep their jobs while Chinese often faced property seizures and arrest, creating antagonisms that persisted long after the war. Some 3 to 5 percent of Singapore's population, mostly Chinese men, were executed in what the Japanese occupation officials called "cleansing through purging." Destroying the link to the world economy also caused hardship. Western companies closed, while Japanese seized natural resources and food. By 1944 living standards, crippled by food and clothing shortages, declined steeply. Japanese police harassed Southeast Asians, brutally punishing even minor violations of regulations. Japan also conscripted thousands of Southeast Asians: Javanese men became slave laborers, and Filipinas and some Singapore Chinese, termed "comfort women," were forced to serve Japanese soldiers' sexual needs. As their war effort faltered, desperate Japanese became even more repressive.

Japanese rule directly or indirectly aided some Southeast Asian nationalists. Needing experienced local help, Japanese promoted Southeast Asians into government positions once reserved for Westerners. Purging Western cultural influences, they closed Christian mission schools, encouraged Islamic or Buddhist leaders, and fostered indigenous culture and local literature. Under colonialism most nationalists were in jail or exile, hence powerless; Japan freed nationalist leaders such as Sukarno, giving them official positions, if little actual power. Nationalists used radio and newspapers to spread their beliefs. Young people, recruited into armed paramilitary forces, became the basis for later nationalist armies in Indonesia and Burma, resisting the colonizers' return.

Some Southeast Asians actively opposed Japanese rule. Vietnamese communism might never have achieved power so quickly had the occupation not discredited the French administration and imposed great hardship on millions. Ho Chi Minh led the Viet Minh, armed and trained by American advisers sent to help anti-Japanese forces. In 1944, the Viet Minh expanded their influence in northern Vietnam, attracting peasant support while attacking Japanese occupiers with guerrilla tactics. Japan exported scarce food to Japan while famine killed two million Vietnamese, spurring support for the Viet Minh, who organized local peasant-led village administrations.

As the United States gained military victories, bombing Japanese installations in Southeast Asia, Japanese encouraged Southeast Asians to resist reestablishing Western colonialism. Japanese officials helped Indonesian nationalists prepare for Indonesian independence and Burmese nationalists establish a government. Sukarno told his people: "Every city, every village, every house—yes, every heart must become a fortress [against the Dutch]."[23] Seeing Japan's prospects waning, some nationalists began secretly working with the Western Allies. Changing sides, the Burmese nationalist army helped push out Japanese forces. Tired of economic deprivation and repression, few Southeast Asians regretted Japan's defeat; some, especially in Malaya, British Borneo, and the Philippines, welcomed the renewed Western presence. Americans granted the Philippines independence under pro-U.S. leaders in 1946. But often the returning Westerners faced volatility, which produced dramatic political change in Vietnam, Indonesia, and Burma as nationalist forces successfully struggled for independence in the late 1940s and early 1950s.

25-4c Nationalism in Colonial Africa

The roots of the African struggle were planted in the interwar years, although African nationalists, lacking the Vietnamese or Indian mass base, had limited success overcoming major

[20]Quoted in J. D. Legge, *Sukarno: A Political Biography* (New York: Praeger, 1972), 341.
[21]From Harry J. Benda and John A. Larkin, eds., *The World of Southeast Asia: Selected Historical Readings* (New York: Harper and Row, 1967), 192.
[22]Sitor Situmorang, quoted in Harry Aveling, ed., *From Surabaya to Armageddon: Indonesian Short Stories* (Singapore: Heinemann, 1976), vii.
[23]Quoted in Berhard Dahm, *Sukarno and the Struggle for Indonesian Independence* (New York: Cornell University Press, 1969), 274.

barriers to widespread popular support. Few regimes prepared their colonies for political and economic independence by permitting African participation in government or producing a large educated class. No colonies offered a mass education system; only a minority of children received any formal education, and those few seeking higher education mostly had to study in Europe or North America. In addition, artificial colonial boundaries hindered nationalist organizing. Colonial regimes, using divide-and-rule strategies to govern diverse ethnic groups, made creating viable national identities and uniting all people difficult. For example, British Nigeria contained many often-rival ethnic groups. While some nationalists sought Pan-Nigerian unity, most found support only among particular regions or ethnic groups. In the 1940s a prominent Yoruba leader expressed the common fear that no Nigerian nation was really possible:

> *Nigeria is not a nation [but] a mere geographical expression. There are no "Nigerians" in the same sense as there are "English" or "French." The word "Nigerian" merely distinguish[es] those who live within the boundaries of Nigeria from those who do not.*[24]

World War I and unfulfilled expectations in its aftermath spurred nationalism. Britain, France, Belgium, and Germany all drafted or recruited Africans to serve as porters and laborers or to fight on European or African battlefields, where many thousands died. When survivors returned home, promises made about land or jobs proved empty while taxes increased. Returning Kenyan soldiers found that British settlers had seized their land. Harry Thuku (**THOO-koo**) (ca. 1895–1970), a Kikuyu, forged a diverse alliance to confront the British. When Britain arrested Thuku, rioting broke out, led by Kikuyu women; British forces killed many rioters. Anticolonial protests were also common in the Belgian Congo, sparking rebellions by peasant farmers upset at demands for unpaid labor. Women often led resistance. In Senegal Aline Sitoe Diatta (1920–1944) was exiled and later executed for leading an uprising when the French conscripted her village's rice supplies. In Nigeria in 1929, tens of thousands of Igbo women, particularly palm oil traders, rioted to protest taxes. After the British killed thirty-two women, protests escalated; restoring order took months.

In the 1920s new urban-based nationalist organizations, pressing for African participation in local government, were led by Western-educated Africans including J. E. Casely Hayford (1866–1930), a British Gold Coast lawyer and journalist influenced by Gandhi. Some like Hayford favored a Pan-African approach, seeking support across colonial borders that they rejected as the basis for nations. But neither nationalists nor Pan-Africanists could overcome ethnic divisions and, unlike Indian and Vietnamese nationalists, the city–village gap. Furthermore, some African merchants, chiefs, and kings, profiting from links to the colonizers, discouraged protests.

Even with outrage at the brutal Italian invasion and occupation of Ethiopia in 1935–1936, nationalists had modest influence before World War II. West African nationalist currents were strongest in multiethnic capital cities, where they bred the grounds of new ideas. Urban-based trade union movements sponsored occasional strikes protesting colonial policies or economic exploitation. Hence, market women in Lagos, Nigeria's largest city, protested taxation and demanded voting rights. During World War II they refused to cooperate with price controls, forcing Britain to back down. Rural people also asserted their rights. During the 1930s cocoa growers in the British Gold Coast held back their crops to protest low prices.

World War II affected Africans and spurred nationalist resentments. As in World War I, the colonial powers drafted or recruited Africans to fight in their war. Some 120,000 West and East Africans fought in Asia for Britain or France; African nurses and engineers were also sent to Asia. Another forty-six thousand West and East Africans experienced combat in

IMAGE 25.5 **South African Jazz** Jazz became very popular in South Africa during the 1930s. One of the most popular groups during those years were the Manhattan Brothers, known as South Africa's Kings of Song. Beginning their musical careers in 1934 they remained popular and active into the 1960s. In this photo they are appearing at the Bantu Men's Social Center in Johannesburg in 1955. As pioneers in the black music industry they discovered several talents, especially Miriam Makeba, who performed with them in this concert. In the 1950s through the 1970s Makeba became one of Africa's greatest and best-known performers.

---

[24]Obafemi Awolowo, quoted in Chester L. Hunt and Lewis Walker, *Ethnic Dynamics: Patterns of Intergroup Relations in Various Societies*, 2nd ed. (Holmes Beach, FL: Learning Publications, 1979), 277.

the Middle East and fifty-six thousand West Africans in East Africa. While all the troops faced openly racist attitudes and behavior from their European officers and were also poorly paid and fed, some became acquainted and shared views with others, among them Americans, Indians, Burmese, and Vietnamese, coming home with wider horizons.

New cultural trends enabled Africans to express their views, often critical, about colonial life. During the 1930s a musical style, created in the Gold Coast, spread into other British West African colonies, carried by guitar-playing Africans and West Indian sailors. **Highlife** mixed Christian hymns, West Indian calypso songs, and African dance rhythms. Later, West African musicians added Cuban, Brazilian, and American influences, especially jazz, continuing cultural links between West Africa and the Americas. Although closely tied to dance bands and parties, some highlife musicians addressed social and political issues and everyday problems. The very term *highlife* signified both envy and disapproval of Western colonizers and rich Africans living in mansions staffed by servants. Many highlife songs were sung in **pidgin English**, a broken English form mixing African and English words and grammar developed during the colonial era. Pidgin English then spread throughout British West Africa as a marketplace lingua franca among diverse urban populations.

Racial inequality and white supremacy sparked nationalism and resistance to oppression in South Africa. Early nationalists, such as the African National Congress (ANC) founders in 1912, came from the urban middle class. The ANC encouraged education and preached independence from white rule, but it did not directly confront the government until the 1950s. More militant resistance flourished in the mining industry, where strikes were endemic despite severe government repression. Resistance was often subtle, involving noncooperation or affirmation of African cultural forms. Music often expressed protest, usually veiled to avoid arrest. Knowing that few whites understood African languages, African workers filled mining camps with political music, offering messages such as "we demand freedom" and "workers unite." Road gangs worked to songs such as "We Say: Oh, the White Man's Bad." Zulu and Swazi workers, blending their traditions with Western influences, created new dances. Virile, stamping dancers laced their performances with provocative songs: "Who has taken our land from us? Come out! Let us fight! The land was ours. Now it is taken. Fight! Fight!"[25]

In South African cities jazz, adapted from African Americans, became a form of resistance and potent vehicle for protest, reflecting African rejection of racist Afrikaner culture. African American musicians such as trumpeter Louis Armstrong (1901–1971) and pianist Duke Ellington (1898–1974), popular in the 1930s, influenced South African jazz bands and new jazz-based musical styles. Educated urban Africans, envisioning a modern African culture, sometimes rejected African traditions, as one Johannesburg resident proclaimed:

Tribal music! Chiefs! We don't care about chiefs! Give us jazz and film stars, man! We want Ellington, Satchmo [Louis Armstrong], and hot dames! Yes, brother, anything American. You can cut out this junk about [rural homesteads] and folk-tales—forget it! You're just trying to keep us backward![26]

The preferred music of the small black professional and business class, jazz ultimately symbolized black nationalism in South Africa.

> **highlife** An urban-based West African musical style mixing Christian hymns, West Indian calypso songs, and African dance rhythms.

> **pidgin English** The form of broken English that developed in Africa during the colonial era.

KEY POINTS

▶ Southeast Asian nationalism was strong in places such as Burma, which experienced harsh colonial rule, and even emerged as a rallying cry in Siam, which was never colonized but where a military coup overthrew the royal government.

▶ Vietnamese resistance to French rule was continued by the terrorist Vietnamese Nationalist Party, which the French harshly repressed, and the Viet Minh, a coalition led by the communist Ho Chi Minh.

▶ A variety of groups representing Muslims, women, and communists worked toward independence for the Dutch East Indies.

▶ Although African nationalist movements were hampered by the existence of rival ethnic groups within artificial colonies, anger over the poor treatment of Africans who had fought in World War I inspired many, especially in cities, to work for independence.

▶ In South Africa, nationalists opposed the repressive white supremacist government through education, strikes, and, most pervasively, music.

---

[25]Quoted in Veit Erlmann, *African Stars: Studies in Black South African Performance* (Chicago: University of Chicago Press, 1991), 95–96.
[26]Quoted in Charles Hamm, "'The Constant Companion of Man': Separate Development, Radio Bantu and Music," *Popular Music* 10, no. 2 (May 1991): 161.

25-5 Remaking the Middle East and Latin America

Q What factors promoted change in the Middle East and Latin America?

Despite having different histories, cultures, and political systems, nationalism also influenced Middle Eastern and Latin American peoples. While North Africans experienced Western colonial rule, Turkey remained independent and Arabs in western Asian territories controlled by Ottoman Turks stagnated economically. Historians debate the nature of the Ottoman Empire in the early twentieth century. Some portray it as a decaying and rapacious relic of an earlier time. Others describe a reformist government leading a diverse and ecumenical multinational society practicing coexistence. Or perhaps both were true. Whatever the case, competing ethnoreligious nationalisms, war and oppression proved decisive in the Ottoman's fate. The transfer of Ottoman-ruled Arab territories to Britain and France as League of Nations mandates after World War I sparked nationalist resentment and reshaped Arab politics. In Latin America, two world wars and the Great Depression caused turmoil, fostered dictatorships, and spurred nationalism.

> **CONNECTION to TODAY**
>
> How do the Middle East and Latin America today reflect the developments of this era?

25-5a Reshaping the Ottoman Territories

After World War I the Turkish-dominated Ottoman Empire, Germany's ally, was dismantled. Still independent, the Turks, sharing German hatred of expansionist Russia, also dreamed of liberating Russian-controlled lands in the Caucasus and Central Asia, where many spoke languages related to Turkish. However, Caucasus peoples, especially Christian Armenians, desired independence. Suspecting them of aiding Russia, in 1915 the Turkish government turned on Armenians in eastern Anatolia (see Chapter 21), deporting more than a million, chiefly to Syria and Iraq; perhaps another 1 to 1.5 million died of thirst, starvation, or systematic slaughter by the Ottoman army. Today Turks and Armenians and historians and U.S. politicians debate whether this event should be considered a genocide (deliberate mass killing of targeted ethnic or religious groups). These sufferings created permanent Turkish–Armenian hostility.

Hardships during and after World War I also spurred Arab nationalism against Ottoman rule; hunger and disease affected millions of Arabs, with 200,000 dying in Syria alone. Syrian unrest precipitated fierce repression, during which dissidents were sent into exile or hanged for treason. The most serious challenge came in Arabia, where Sharif Hussein ibn Ali (1856–1931), the Arab ruler of the Hejaz, the western Arabia region including Mecca and Medina, shifted his loyalties from the Ottomans to Britain, who promised to support Arab independence. In 1916, at British urging, Sharif Hussein launched an Arab revolt. British officers, including the flamboyant Lt. T. E. Lawrence (famous as "Lawrence of Arabia"), advised Sharif Hussein's tribal forces as they attacked Ottoman bases and communications. Britain also invaded and occupied southern Iraq, an Ottoman province with a strategic position and potential oil wealth.

However, postwar developments crushed dreams, fostering turmoil and outrage. Arab nationalists such as Sharif Hussein were unaware that Britain, France, and Russia had made secret agreements that ignored Arab interests. The czarist Russians planned to incorporate Istanbul and nearby territories into their empire, while Britain and France agreed to partition Ottoman provinces in western Asia between them. Russian plans had to be modified after Lenin and the Bolsheviks took power and signed a peace treaty with Germany allowing the Russian-controlled Caucasus territories to be returned to the Ottomans. But with Ottoman defeat, British troops occupied much of Iraq and Palestine, French troops controlled the Syrian coast, and Russians regained control of the Caucasus, including Armenia.

The Versailles treaty dismembered the Ottoman Empire (see Map 25.2). Turkey's neighbors—Greeks, Italians, and Armenians—made claims on Anatolia and adjacent islands, while European Zionists asked for a Jewish national home in Palestine (see Chapter 21). The Allies promised eventual independence to the Kurds, a Sunni Muslim people who were distinct from both Arabs and Turks and who inhabited a large, mountainous region of western Asia, including southeast Turkey. Both Syria and Iraq declared their independence. However, the League of Nations, dominated by Western countries, awarded France control over Syria and Lebanon and gave Britain control over Iraq, Palestine, and Transjordan (today Jordan), under what the League called mandates, in theory less permanent than colonies. Considering mandates as a new colonialism, Arab nationalists in Syria proposed a democratic government; some favored granting women the vote, which few Western nations had done. Ignoring Syrian views, French forces, after facing armed resistance, exiled nationalist leaders. Despite promises, the Allies also ignored Kurdish desires for their own nation, dividing them between Turkey, Persia (Iran), Iraq, and Syria; Kurds remained the world's largest ethnic group without their own state. Some historians and international relations specialists consider the Western failure to demand an independent Kurdish state in Kurdish majority regions a major mistake because it betrayed the Kurds and established a foundation for unstable nations, disaffected Kurds, and hence unrest in the region ever since.

The Ottoman Empire's center, Turkey, saw the most revolutionary changes. Disastrous defeat and the humiliating agreements that followed left Turks helpless, bitter, and facing a Greek invasion and Arab secession. But the daring war hero and ardent nationalist later known as Kemal Ataturk (kuh-MAHL AT-uh-turk) (1881–1938) led a spectacular Turkish resurgence. In 1919 Ataturk began mobilizing military forces in eastern Anatolia into a revolutionary organization to oppose the Ottoman sultan, discredited by defeats, restore Turkish dignity, and preserve Turkish-majority areas and Kurdish

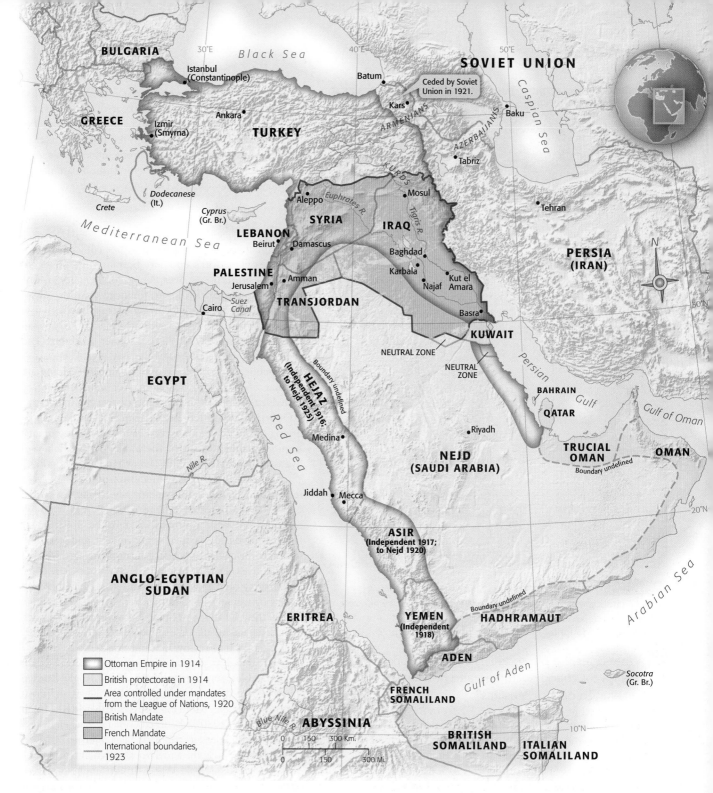

MAP 25.2 Partition of the Ottoman Empire Before 1914 the Ottoman Turks controlled much of western Asia, including western Arabia. After World War II the League of Nations awarded Iraq, Transjordan, and Palestine to Britain. Syria and Lebanon were given to France, and western Arabia was ruled by Arabs. Eventually the Saud family, rulers of the Najd, expanded their rule into western Arabia and created Saudi Arabia.

Q How does this map compare to a map of the region today?

districts in eastern Anatolia. After establishing a rival Turkish government in Ankara, a central Anatolia city, Ataturk's forces fought both the sultan's government and Greek forces moving deep into Anatolia. Ataturk finally pushed the Greeks back;

Turkey and Greece eventually agreed to transfer many Greeks living in Turkey to Greece and most Turks dwelling in Greece to Turkey. In 1922 Ataturk deposed the Ottoman sultan and founded a republic with himself as president.

Hulton Archive/Stringer/Getty Images

IMAGE 25.6 **Ataturk Wedding Dance** The Turkish leader Kemal Ataturk promoted and adopted Western fashions while defying Muslim customs. In this photo from around 1925, Ataturk dances with his daughter at her Western-style wedding.

Q What does the photo tell us about Ataturk and his agenda for changing Turkey, and how might this have alienated devout Muslims?

Ataturk was and remains a controversial figure among Turks, hugely admired by many and reviled by many others. A religious agnostic, he violated Muslim customs with sexual promiscuity and heavy public drinking. A nationalist glorifying the pre-Islamic Turkish past, Ataturk dismissed Islamic culture as outdated and favored modernization, announcing that "our eyes are turned westward. We shall transplant Western institutions to Asiatic soil. We wish to be a modern nation with our mind open, and yet to remain ourselves."[27] Ataturk claimed that secularization and women's emancipation were Turkish traditions. In the 1920s he introduced reforms challenging Muslim traditions, revamping the legal system along Western lines, replacing Arabic-based script with a Western alphabet, prohibiting polygamy, abolishing Islamic schools and courts, removing reference to Islam as the state religion from the constitution, and granting women equal rights in divorce, child custody, and

inheritance. While his government resembled a parliamentary democracy, he exercised near-dictatorial power, suppressing Kurdish language and culture. Ataturk left a deeply changed nation. While many reforms never reached villages, where Islam remained a strong influence, his secular approach remained popular with Turkish nationalists, including military officers, especially in some cities.

25-5b Modern Iran, Egypt, and Iraq

Major changes also occurred in other Middle Eastern countries. The war's end left Britain with power to impose a protectorate over Persia, forcing the government to accept British loans, financial controls, advisers, and military forces. Growing Persian opposition in 1921 prompted Britain to support General Reza Khan **(REE-za kahn)** (1877–1944), a soldier seeking to end the corrupt, ineffective royal dynasty, establish a secular republic, and address economic underdevelopment. Secular Shi'ites, long struggling for more democracy to reduce the powerful and conservative Shi'ite clergy's domination, supported Reza Khan. But in 1925, at the urging of Shi'ite clerics, Reza Khan, abandoning republican government, formed the Pahlavi **(PAH-lah-vee)** dynasty, with himself as king (known in Persia as a shah).

Reza Khan promoted modernization and in 1935 renamed his nation Iran, symbolically breaking with the past. The shah created a large national army through conscription; built railroads; established government factories producing textiles, sugar, cement, and steel; and took over the oil industry. Social changes outraged Muslim conservatives, such as introducing a Western law code, encouraging men to wear Western hats and clothes, and outlawing women's veiling in public. Women who wanted to wear the veil had to stay home. But while the modernists, merchants, and middle class supported Reza Khan's policies, poor and rural Iranians saw little improvement; the landlord class expanded at peasant expense. When Reza Khan supported Germany during World War II, Anglo-Russian forces occupied Iran. Humiliated, Reza Khan abdicated in favor of his son, Muhammad Reza Pahlavi **(REH-zah PAH-lah-vee)** (1919–1980), who ruled until 1979, when he was overthrown by Muslim leaders and nationalist reformers.

British control of Egypt and Iraq also generated nationalism. In Egypt during World War I Britain imposed martial law, drafting peasants to build roads and dig trenches in war zones. A popular song castigated British officials for carrying off the peasants' corn, camels, and cattle. After the war the leading nationalist party, the secular *Wafd*, led by Saad Zaghlul **(sod ZOG-lool)** (ca. 1857–1927), who studied under Islamic modernists and then earned a French law degree, sought independence, representative government, civil liberties, and curtailed powers for the pro-British monarchy.

In 1919 the British arrested Wafd leaders. Enraged Egyptians—rich and poor, Muslims and Coptic Christians, men and women—responded with strikes, student demonstrations, sabotaging of railroads, and murder of British soldiers,

[27]Quoted in Hans Kohn, *A History of Nationalism in the East* (New York: Harcourt, 1929), 257.

forcing the release of Zaghlul, who then went to the Paris Peace Conference to plead for national self-determination but, like Vietnam's Ho Chi Minh, was ignored. Zaghlul was arrested again, but the resulting unrest forced Britain to grant Egypt limited independence in 1922. Nationalists saw this agreement as a sham, since Britain still controlled Egypt's defense and foreign affairs. In 1936 Britain, officially ending its occupation, still kept thousands of troops along the Suez Canal and shared with Egypt administration of Sudan to the south. Resentment of the continuing British presence increased during World War II.

Britain also struggled to control Iraq, an artificial creation uniting three Ottoman provinces dominated respectively by Sunni Kurds, Sunni Arabs, and the largest group, Shi'ite Arabs. Describing their occupation as "liberation," the British promised an efficient administration, honest finance, impartial justice, and security. A plebiscite giving the appearance of popular support was manipulated to suggest pro-British sympathies. Hating occupation, in 1920 Shi'ite clerics seeking an Islamic state proclaimed holy war against the British, and various Shi'a and Sunni tribes rose in rebellion. The British, relying heavily on aerial bombing, suppressed the rebellion, killing some ten thousand Iraqis and flattening whole villages.

Shaken by the fierce resistance, Britain introduced limited self-government through an appointed Council of State. Skilled diplomacy by pro-Arab British archaeologist, writer, and diplomat Lady Gertrude Bell (1868–1926) defused tensions. Seeking a king for Iraq who would "reign but not govern" and serve as a figurehead, Britain installed a member of the Hashemite **(HASH-uh-mite)** royal family of Mecca, Sharif Hussein's son Faisal (1885–1935). In 1930 Faisal convinced Britain to grant Iraq independence, accepting continued British military bases and government advisers. By then oil discoveries made Britain unwilling to cut ties. Many Arabs considered Faisal and his successors British puppets, but Sunni Arab military autocrats influenced government more than the kings.

25-5c Islam and Zionism

European power and cultural influence concerned most Middle Eastern societies, but nationalist success came slowly. Thinkers debated how or whether to emulate Western nations. While envying industrialization and consumer goods, they disagreed about adopting Western patterns, such as freedom of thought and religion, parliamentary democracy, and women's rights. Some favored Westernization, some preservation of Islamic traditions, and still others mixing of the two. Egypt, Iraq, Lebanon, Transjordan, and Syria adopted Western-style constitutions providing civil liberties and elected parliaments that proved limited and unrepresentative. Real power remained with European officials or kings with little respect for civil liberties.

Inspired by Western modernity, Arabs made progress in education, public health, industrialization, and communications, but change came slowly. Egypt's literacy rate rose from 9 percent in 1917 to only 15 percent in 1937. Some women asserted their rights. Huda Shaarawi **(HOO-da sha-RAH-we)** (1879–1947), from a wealthy Cairo family, was married off at thirteen to a much older cousin. Finding the marriage confining, she organized nonviolent anti-British demonstrations by women after World War I, then publicly removed her veil, shocking Egyptians. The Egyptian feminist movement she founded succeeded in raising the minimum marriage age for girls to sixteen and increasing women's educational opportunities.

Debates over Westernization fostered new intellectual currents. A blind Egyptian writer, Taha Husayn (1889–1973), educated in Islamic schools but also at the Sorbonne in Paris, challenged orthodox Islam and, in 1938, proclaimed that Westernizing Arab culture fit with Egypt's traditions: "I want our new life to harmonize with our ancient glory." In contrast, the **Muslim Brotherhood**, founded in 1928 by Egyptian schoolteacher Hasan al-Banna (1906–1949), reflected popular reaction against Westernization. Al-Banna despised Western values, arguing that it "would be inexcusable for us to turn aside from the path of truth—Islam—and so follow the path of fleshly desires and vanities—the path of Europe."[28] Al-Banna favored violence against colonizers and imperialists, advocating a "jihad of the sword" rather than of the heart. The Brotherhood, while strictly interpreting the Quran, also accepted modern technology and favored a more active public role for women. Expressing widespread resentment against Western films, bars, and figure-revealing fashions, the Brotherhood developed a following in Sudan and western Asia.

The most extreme anti-Western reaction, and the one that eventually dominated Arabia, was the puritanical Wahhabi movement, which opposed women's rights, homosexuality, Shiism, Sufism, shaving beards, smoking tobacco, and drinking alcohol, seeking a return to early Islam uncorrupted by centuries of change. The Wahhabis' influence grew when their ally, tribal chief Abdul Aziz Ibn Saud **(sah-OOD)** (1902–1969), expanded Saudi family power in central and eastern Arabia (see Chapter 21). By 1932 his forces had taken western Arabia and the holy cities from the Hashemites and formed Saudi Arabia. As king, Abdul Aziz strictly enforced Islamic law, establishing Committees for the Commendation of Virtue and the Condemnation of Vice to monitor personal behavior. Policemen used long canes to enforce attendance at daily prayers, punish alcohol use and listening to music, and harass unveiled women. A militant version of Wahhabism (and to some extent Salafism) later provided the theological foundation for al Qaeda and ISIS (the Islamic State movement known in Arabic as Da'ish) since the 1980s. Yet, Saudis also welcomed Western material innovations such as automobiles, medicine, and telephones. Wealth from the world's richest oil reserves, discovered in 1935, chiefly benefited the royal family and Wahhabi clergy.

Developments in Palestine, part of Ottoman-ruled Syria with a largely Arab population, created long-term problems. Britain took over after World War I. Meanwhile, the Zionist movement, seeking a Jewish homeland, emerged in Europe's Jewish ghettoes (see Chapters 19 and 21). The Zionist slogan—"a land without a people for a people without a land"—offered a compelling vision: take long-persecuted Jewish minorities and return them to Palestine, their ancient ancestral home. To reach this goal, Zionist leaders cultivated the British

Muslim Brotherhood An Egyptian religious movement founded in 1928 that expressed popular Arab reaction to Westernization.

[28]The quotes are from Akram Fouad Khater, ed., *Sources in the History of the Modern Middle East* (Boston: Houghton Mifflin, 2004), 167, 176.

government. In 1917 the **Balfour Declaration** gave ambiguous British support for establishing Palestine as a national home for the Jewish people. But Arabs had lived in Palestine for many centuries, building cities, cultivating orchards, and herding livestock. In Arab eyes, Jewish immigrants were European colonizers planning to dispossess them.

Thousands of European Jews migrated to Palestine with British support, some fleeing Nazi Germany, so that by 1939 Palestine's population of 1.5 million was one-third Jewish. Although Jewish settlers established businesses, industries, and productive farms, Arabs feared becoming a vulnerable minority in what they considered their own land. Zionist organizations bought the best land from absentee Arab landlords who disregarded the customary rights of villagers to use it, uprooting thousands of Arab peasants. As tensions increased, violence spread, bewildering the British. Sometimes armed clashes killed hundreds of Arabs and Jews; in 1936 a three-year civil war (known as the Arab Revolt) erupted, during which Arabs demanded an independent Palestine and an end to Jewish immigration and land sales to Jews. Britain proposed a partition into two states, removing thousands of Arabs from the Jewish side, but both groups rejected the proposal. When the fighting ended, over 10 percent of the adult male Palestinian Arab population had been killed (two thousand), wounded, imprisoned, or exiled. In 1939 Britain limited Jewish immigration and banned land transfers; however, the Holocaust during World War II spurred a more militant desire for a homeland where Jews could govern themselves.

25-5d Politics and Modernization in Latin America

Latin Americans, reliant on natural resource exports such as beef, copper, coffee, and sugar, were vulnerable to global political and economic crises and sometimes foreign interventions, as when U.S. military forces occupied Nicaragua from 1909 to 1933 and Haiti from 1915 to 1934. During the Great Depression, foreign investment fell and foreign markets closed, cutting some countries' foreign trade by 90 percent; by 1932 Latin America exported 65 percent less than in 1929. Economic downturns fostered political instability and military dictators, known as *caudillos*, all over the region (see Map 25.3).

In response to the hardships and instability generated by the Great Depression, in 1930–1931 armed forces overthrew governments in a dozen Latin American nations. European fascism influenced some new governments, particularly in Argentina and Brazil. Dictators amassed huge fortunes, repressed dissent, and often increased their governments' economic roles, beginning industries to provide products normally imported. In El Salvador President Maximiliano Hernandez Martinez massacred thirty

Balfour Declaration A letter from the British foreign minister to Zionist leaders in 1917 giving British support for the establishment of Palestine as a national home for the Jewish people.

Estado Novo ("New State") A fascist-influenced and modernizing dictatorship in Brazil led by Getulio Vargas between 1930 and 1945.

thousand protesting Native American (Indigenous) peasants; praising poverty as good for common people, he claimed those who went barefoot could better receive the earth's "beneficial vibrations" than those with shoes. Some dictatorships continued for years. Collapsing sugar prices, which generated a massive Cuban strike, forced repressive right-winger Gerardo Machado (r. 1925–1933) out of office, temporarily bringing left-wing nationalists and socialists to power. But the United States, disliking the new government for reforms that hurt influential American business interests, encouraged a coup by Sgt. Fulgencio Batista (fool-HEN-see-o bah-TEES-ta) (1901–1973) in 1934; Batista dominated Cuba for the next twenty-five years as a pro-U.S. right-wing dictator.

The challenges also affected Chile, one of the most open Latin American nations. Although the military occasionally seized power for short periods, Chileans generally elected democratic governments and supported several competitive political parties. The Great Depression helped reformist parties and social movements gain support; the squabbling leftist and centrist parties, united in a Popular Front, won the 1939 elections. Their reformist government, supported by labor unions, sponsored industrialization, while a growing women's movement allied with Chile's political left brought once-forbidden ideas into the patriarchal, strongly Catholic country. Demanding respect for Chilean women and ending "compulsory motherhood," feminists lobbied for prenatal health care, child-care subsidies, birth control, and the right to abortion, which was illegal but widely practiced. But while winning some basic legal rights, women still struggled for voting rights and could not get most of their social agenda approved.

Brazil experienced political change tinged with nationalism. In the 1920s middle-class reformers, challenging a corrupt ruling class that failed to listen to common people or assert Brazil's national interests in the world, sought official recognition of labor unions, a minimum wage, restraints on child labor, land reform, universal suffrage, and expansion of education to poor children. Worker unrest fostered labor unions. But the Great Depression prompted a civilian-military coup by Getulio Vargas (jay-TOO-lee-oh VAR-gus) (1883–1954) in 1930. A pragmatic former soldier, lawyer, and government minister, Vargas launched the **Estado Novo** ("New State"), a fascist-influenced, modernizing dictatorship, ruling until 1945. An anti-Vargas businessman described him as "intelligent, extremely perceptive, but also a demagogue who knew how to manipulate the masses."[29] While using torture and censorship to repress opponents, he nationalized banks, financed industrialization, and introduced social security, an eight-hour workday, a minimum wage, the right to strike, and the vote for literate eighteen-year-olds and working women, reforms popular with the lower classes. Gradually the dictator became more populist and nationalist. After the army deposed him in 1945, tensions between right-wing and left-wing Brazilians remained.

Progressive and nationalist ideas emerged in Mexico. After the decade-long Mexican Revolution (see Chapter 20), which ended in 1920, Mexico badly needed reconstruction

[29]Severino Fama, quoted in Robert M. Levine, *The History of Brazil* (New York: Palgrave, 1999), 107.

MAP 25.3 **South and Central America in 1930** By 1930 Latin America had achieved its present political configuration, except that Britain, France, and Holland still had colonies in the Guianas region of South America and Britain controlled British Honduras (today's Belize) in Central America.

Q How much of Latin America and the Caribbean were still Western colonies or in dispute at the beginning of the Great Depression?

funds but faced sharply reduced export earnings and a deepening economic slump. A popular song noted the hardship on common Mexicans: "The scramble to be president is one of our oldest haunts. But to eat a peaceful tortilla is all the poor man wants."[30] President Plutarcho Elias Calles (**KAH-yays**) (r. 1924–1928) stabilized the political system, creating a new party that brought together various factions. Yet many saw little improvement, and women remained largely excluded from public life. In 1934 Lazaro Cardenas (**car-DAYN-es**) (r. 1934–1940), an army officer with socialist leanings, was elected president. Cynical peasants doubted political leaders' promises to supply them with land;

---

[30]From Frederick B. Pike, ed., *Latin American History: Select Problems, Identity, Integration, and Nationhood* (New York: Harcourt, Brace and World, 1969), 319.

Cardenas fulfilled this dream, assigning land ownership to *ejidos* (eh-HEE-dos), traditional agricultural cooperatives, who now apportioned land to their members. Cardenas hoped that the ejidos would build schools and hospitals and supply credit to farmers, uplifting Mexico's poorest social class. But agricultural production fell, and the promised government aid never materialized.

Other Cardenas reforms and nationalist economic policies made him popular. He encouraged a large labor confederation, allowing the working class to enjoy higher living standards and more dignity, and supported women's rights. After U.S.-owned oil companies ignored a Mexican Supreme Court order to improve worker pay, Cardenas nationalized the industry, spurring celebrations in Mexico but outraging U.S. leaders. Cardenas reorganized the ruling Party of Revolutionary Institutions around four functional groups: peasants, organized labor, military, and middle class. Thus Cardenas revitalized the Mexican Revolution, causing deep resentment among wealthy Mexican landowners and merchants and U.S. political and business leaders.

However, more moderate leaders after Cardenas reversed support for the ejidos, favoring instead individual farmers, ignored women's rights—women could not vote until 1953—and cooperated with the United States on immigration issues. While poor Mexicans had long moved to the United States, during World War II a binational agreement sent more Mexican workers north to fill industry, agriculture, and the service-sector jobs left vacant by drafted American men. The flow northward of poor Mexicans became a floodtide after the war.

25-5e Cultural Nationalism in Latin America and the Caribbean

Cultural nationalism greatly affected Latin American and Caribbean societies. A literary approach, modernism, explored Brazil's rich cultural heritage. Rather than emulating European trends, modernist writers reflected Brazil's uniqueness. Poet, novelist, and critic Mario de Andrade (1893–1945) mixed words from regional dialects and Native American, African, and Portuguese folklore into his work. The more internationalist Oswald de Andrade (1890–1954), considering Brazil a creative cultural consumer, argued that Brazilians should mix ideas from all over the world. Nationalism also shaped Brazilian music. Afro-Brazilian and Native American religious rites and urban popular music inspired unconventional composer Heitor Villa-Lobos (1890–1959). Associated with Rio de Janeiro's annual pre-Lenten carnival, *samba* music and dance became a symbol of Brazilian society while allowing the Afro-Brazilian lower classes to express themselves. Annual carnival processions grew increasingly extravagant, featuring elaborate floats, flamboyant costumes, and intricate group choreography. Professional samba groups competed for prizes, making samba a major social activity of Rio's shantytowns.

Images & Stories/Alamy Stock Photo

IMAGE 25.7 **Political Art in Mexico** This mural by the great Mexican artist Diego Rivera offers his take on the Spanish conquest of Mexico in the 1500s. Famous for his political interests and obsession with history, in this mural Rivera depicts Spanish cruelties to Native Americans.

The progressive spirit spurred literary and artistic movements. Marxist-influenced writers such as Chilean poet Pablo Neruda (ne-ROO-duh) (1904–1973) bristled with anger over economic inequalities. Sometimes governments retaliated against dissident artists; Neruda wrote some of his greatest poetry in hiding or exile. Mexican artists, glorifying the country's mixed-descent, or mestizo, heritage, addressed the remaining Native American communities' poverty and powerlessness. In this tradition, several great artists painted, usually on public building walls, magnificent murals showing Mexican history and life. Jose Orozco (1883–1949) was a realist who sharply criticized Mexico for its failings, producing a confrontational art that went against the grain. In several murals he trashed nearly every symbol of ideology common in the world of his day, including the Catholic cross, communism's hammer and sickle, and Nazism's swastika. The more romantic and better known artist was Diego Rivera (1885–1957), a Marxist who idealized Mexicans; his huge, realistic murals depicted peasants and workers struggling for dignity or emphasized conflicts between Native Americans and the Spanish colonizers. Rivera's wife, Frida Kahlo (1907–1954), a German Jewish immigrant's daughter, specialized in vivid paintings expressing women's physical and psychological pain, reflecting her own health problems and stormy personal relationships.

Caribbean intellectuals' search for an authentic West Indian identity required overcoming the reluctance to acknowledge African influences. Adopting British and French stereotypes, West Indians often associated Africa with the uncivilized. Some Afro-Caribbean intellectuals such as the Trinidadian Marxist C. L. R. James (1901–1989), rebuilding Afro-Caribbean pride by celebrating African roots, used literature, art, and music to challenge Western colonialism. James was a well-traveled historian, prolific writer, political theorist, critic, skillful cricket player, and activist in Trinidad politics, equally at home in the Caribbean, Europe, Africa, and North America, who inspired intellectuals around the world.

KEY POINTS

▶ In the post–World War I breakup of the Ottoman Empire, lands such as Iraq, Syria, and Lebanon that sought freedom were instead colonized by Britain and France, but Turkey revived under the leadership of Ataturk, who modernized the country and minimized the role of Islam.

▶ Reza Khan, the British-supported shah of Persia, attempted to modernize his country as Ataturk had Turkey, though with less success, while Britain, in reaction to violent opposition, granted Egypt and Iraq increasing measures of autonomy and independence.

▶ Vulnerable Latin American economies were greatly damaged during the Great Depression, which led to instability and the rise of military dictators in many countries, while in Chile, instability led to a progressive, pro-labor government.

▶ Impoverished and frustrated after a long revolution, many Mexicans were pleased by the rule of Lazaro Cardenas, who gave land to agricultural cooperatives, nationalized industries, and supported women's rights, but who was followed by less progressive leaders.

▶ Latin American artists, writers, and musicians used culture to present their identity and political views.

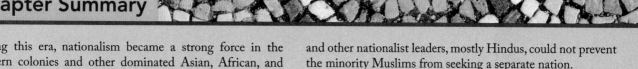

Chapter Summary

During this era, nationalism became a strong force in the Western colonies and other dominated Asian, African, and Latin American societies. Two world wars and the Great Depression destabilized local economies, capitalism reshaped rural life for millions of peasants, and many Asians and Africans resented the Western powers. Nationalism, often blended with Marxism, gained support as a strategy to oppose Western domination. Nationalists reunified China after two decades of warlord violence but could not improve rural life or halt Japanese expansion, providing an opening for Chinese communists under Mao Zedong to gain support by offering a program to transform society. In India, nationalism opposing repressive British colonialism gained a mass following. Mohandas Gandhi mounted massive, nonviolent campaigns of civil disobedience, which undermined British rule. But Gandhi and other nationalist leaders, mostly Hindus, could not prevent the minority Muslims from seeking a separate nation.

Nationalism had an uneven history in Southeast Asia, sub-Saharan Africa, and the Middle East. In Vietnam, Ho Chi Minh organized effective communist resistance to the French, while in Indonesia, Sukarno led opposition to Dutch rule. During World War II nationalists in Vietnam, Indonesia, and Burma organized to oppose a resumption of Western colonialism when the war ended. While political nationalist organizations developed in Africa and black South Africans resisted white domination, nationalism was often more influential as a cultural force, especially in music. World War I left the Middle East in turmoil, as Britain and France extended their power into Arab societies once ruled by the Ottoman Empire. But the Turks, led by Kemal Ataturk, and Iran developed modern states open to Western influences. Muslim intellectuals debated whether to adopt Western ideas or maintain Islamic traditions. Arab conservatives, including the Wahhabis, used Islam to oppose any social or cultural changes. The rise of Zionist immigration to Palestine posed another challenge to the Arabs. In many Latin American nations, while progressive social and literary movements proliferated, economic problems intensified and dictators gained power. Nationalism permeated literary, musical, and artistic expression in both Latin America and the Caribbean.

Key Terms

Salafism 643
warlords 644
New Culture Movement 644
May Fourth Movement 644
Jiangxi Soviet 647
Long March 647

people's war 649
Maoism 649
nonviolent resistance 650
Viet Minh 654
lingua franca 654
highlife 657

pidgin English 657
Muslim Brotherhood 661
Balfour Declaration 662
Estado Novo 662

Debate the Historians

Modernization or World-System?

Historians and social scientists in the West have vigorously debated which theories best explain the modern world, especially how it developed and became interconnected. One influential approach uses the concept of modernization and focuses on individual societies. Another popular approach, world-system analysis, emphasizes the links between societies. This second approach has often interested world historians.

The Problem

The attempt by historians and historically oriented social scientists to understand societies and their changes over time has led to new intellectual approaches in the past several decades. Scholars have asked why some societies in the modern world, such as the United States, Britain, and Japan, became rich and powerful while others, such as Mozambique, Haiti, and Laos, remained poor and weak. Have societies developed as they did because of their own traditions or because of their connections to the larger world? Should we study societies as separate units, as the modernization approach advocates? Or should societies be examined as part of a larger system of exchange and power, or a world-system? Or are both of these approaches inadequate?

The Debate

During the 1950s and 1960s modernization theory was developed in the United States by scholars such as C. E. Black, W. W. Rostow, David Apter, Marion Levy, and Gabriel Almond. In their classification, most societies were traditional, retaining centuries-old political and economic institutions and social and cultural values. These societies had despotic governments, extended family systems, and fatalistic attitudes. In contrast, a few dynamic societies became modern by adopting liberal democracy, secularism, flexible social systems, high-consumption lifestyles, and free market capitalism. This modernization, they argue, began in Europe between 1400 or 1500 and 1750 and reached its fullest development in the United States by the mid-twentieth century. Modernization then was linked to urbanization, industrialization, free enterprise capitalism, and the spread of education. All societies, these theorists asserted, were moving in five stages, rapidly or slowly, in the same direction toward U.S.-style modernization—some enthusiastically, others reluctantly—and this modernization was desirable. Rostow identified the fifth stage as "take-off into self-sustaining growth." And, they suggested, the United States could assist the process with aid, investment, and other guidance such as programs that were benevolent (such thinking animated diverse peacetime efforts like the Peace Corps and the Alliance for Progress in Latin America) but also tough (the controversial wartime Strategic Hamlets program in Vietnam). Modernization then was an homogenizing process.

Modernization theory was influential in the United States for several decades, but by the 1970s it began losing support among many historians. While the notion of modernity seemed helpful, critics found many flaws in the theory of modernization.

They argued that it centered history on the West as the dynamic nursery of modernization and neglected other politically and economically successful societies, such as early modern Qing China, Tokugawa Japan, and Ottoman Turkey. Although these societies had all either collapsed or struggled against Western imperialism during the nineteenth century, they had once flourished and fostered economic growth despite having few of the characteristics associated with modernity. Furthermore, critics contended, by emphasizing the individual "trees" (societies or nation-states) as the only unit of analysis at the expense of the larger "forest" (the global context of international structures and trends), the theory failed to explain the interconnections of societies through various international networks and processes constrained options and created global imbalances, such as the transfer of wealth and resources—Indonesian coffee, Iraqi oil, West African cocoa, Latin American silver, Caribbean sugar—from colonies to colonizers. Modernization theorists have also been faulted for assuming that only one single path of evolutionary development is possible for all countries, that of Western Europe and North America. Dean Tipps contended that by conflating modernization with other processes such as liberalization, democratization, and development, the term is imprecise.

Early modernization theory generally reflected the views of scholars who believed that U.S.-style individualism, democratic government, and free enterprise capitalism were the best strategies to promote personal freedom and economic growth, and who wanted to export these ideas to the world. Indeed, as historians like Nils Gilman and Michael Latham have shown, it strongly influenced U.S. foreign policies during the Cold War. Modernization theorists such as Rostow, an adviser to Presidents Kennedy and Johnson, considered challenges to U.S. influence and to capitalism, from Marxists and radical nationalists, to be diversions leading to despotic governments and an economic dead end. This view sometimes justified in their minds U.S. covert or military interventions to keep them on the proper anticommunist, pro-U.S. path. While agreeing that political and economic freedom were valuable ideas that generally benefited Western peoples, critics of this theory doubt that these freedoms are the foundation of modernity or applicable everywhere. By characterizing traditional societies as "backward" and blaming them for being this way, modernization theory, detractors believe, reflected Western prejudices about the world, such as the French "civilizing mission" and the U.S. notions of "Manifest Destiny" and "Our Little Brown Brothers" in the Philippines. These prejudices hence underpinned the expansion of Western political power and economic investment into Asia and Africa on the grounds that it fosters "progress." To some this suggested a modern version of nineteenth-century Social Darwinism. Furthermore, critics argue, most societies are a mix of "traditional" and "modern" traits. For example, the "modern" United States has been a religious society from its beginning, arguably less secular than "traditional" China. Nor have Asians and Africans always found Western social and cultural models, such as nuclear families and Christianity, to be more appealing or useful than their own traditions, although many have; some, often inspired

667

by Western ideas, have hoped to reform Muslim, Hindu, Confucian, or Buddhist traditions, but most have continued to find meaning in the beliefs and customs of their ancestors.

Challenging modernization theory's neglect of connections, scholars led by American sociologist Immanuel Wallerstein developed the concept of the "world-system," a network of interlinked economic, political, and social relationships spanning the globe. Wallerstein's views were shaped by his experiences as a research scholar in West Africa, which opened his eyes to the world's most pressing challenges and the value of using history to understand them, as well as the worldwide student-led protests of 1968, which left a short-lived but powerful legacy for young scholars like Wallerstein and others seeking social and economic change. In aiming to comprehend the problems facing recently decolonized Ghana and its connections to the wider world, he turned his attention to the rise of Western European economic and political power. To Wallerstein the world-system, originating in Europe during what he termed "the long sixteenth century" (1450–1640), arose from a crisis in feudalism. In a series of four densely researched books beginning in 1974 Wallerstein laid out his examination of what he termed the rise of the Modern World-System. At the heart of his argument was the emergence since the 1400s of a capitalist world economy that, along with rival European states and imperialism, explains the growing Western global dominance after 1500. Beginning around 1450 Spain and Portugal became the first hegemonic powers, building world empires. They were followed by the Dutch in the seventeenth century, the British in the eighteenth and nineteenth centuries, and the U.S. after World War II. By 1914 Western military expansion, colonialism, and industrialization had enriched Europe and brought other societies into the modern world-system. An Africa specialist, Wallerstein views the modern world-system as more widely spread than the more limited earlier networks, such as those of the Mongols and Arabs, that linked Afro-Eurasian societies prior to the 1400s.

For Wallerstein and his followers, world-system analysis has been a multidisciplinary, macro-scale way of thinking about history, economics, and social change that rejected many of the boundaries, approaches, and concepts that had dominated the social sciences since the nineteenth century. They identified a strong link between sociology, economics, politics, and history. Wallerstein's analysis went beyond ethnic groups, tribes, and nations in trying to understand the making of the modern world. Wallerstein's thinking was strongly shaped by Marxist concepts, such as social conflict and capital accumulation, and by the Annales School of French history, identified with Fernand Braudel, which focused on long-term processes and geo-ecological regions such as the Mediterranean world, rather than societies, as units of analysis. Wallerstein was also influenced by, but went well beyond, dependency theory, a Marxist-influenced approach that arose in the 1960s and 1970s as a reaction to modernization theory; dependency scholars argued that resources flowed from poor and underdeveloped states (the "periphery") to wealthy ones (the "core"), enriching the core societies and impoverishing the peripheral societies

even more. But it was criticized as lacking exhaustive empirical evidence and focusing more on states and too little on the international system in which the process operated. In Wallerstein's view, "modernization" involves not only changes within societies but also their changing relationship to the dominant political powers and the world economy. For example, the Ashante kingdom became a West African power in the 1700s by trading slaves to the West, but, in the late 1800s, it was conquered and absorbed into the British colony of the Gold Coast (modern Ghana). Under British rule, the Ashante chiefly grew cocoa for export and thus were dependent on the fluctuations of the world price for cocoa. To understand modern Ghana, then, requires knowledge of the Ashante relations to both British colonialism and the world economy.

To describe the world political and economic structure, Wallerstein divided the world-system and its transnational division of labor into three broad zones, or categories of

IMAGE 25.8 A Japanese View of Westerners This Japanese woodcut print records the impression of a Western family living in Japan in 1860. The mother uses a sewing machine while her husband plays with the children.

countries: the *core*, *semiperiphery*, and *periphery*. In 1914 the core included the rich and powerful nations such as Britain, France, and the United States, which all benefited from industrialization, growing middle classes, democracy, a strong sense of nationhood, and political stability. They sometimes used their armies and financial clout to assert power over other societies, even independent ones such as China, where Western powers established spheres of interest or influence patrolled by their gunboats. By 1914 Wallerstein's middle category, the semiperiphery, included countries such as Japan, Russia, and Italy, which were partially industrialized, politically independent nation-states but less prosperous and powerful than the core nations. Finally, the largest group in 1914, the periphery, comprised the colonized societies, such as French Vietnam, British Nigeria, and the U.S.-ruled Philippines, and the neocolonies such as Brazil, Thailand (Siam), and Iran (Persia). These societies were burdened with export economies based on natural resources, little or no industrialization, massive poverty, little democracy, and domination by more powerful core nations. Wallerstein rejected the popular notion of a poor, mostly non-Western "Third World," claiming there was only one world connected by a complex network of economic exchange relationships: the world economy. In this view colonialism transferred wealth from the periphery to the core, which used the wealth for its own economic development. As Wallerstein acknowledges, the world-system is not rigid, and a few societies shifted categories over the centuries. For example, the United States was semiperipheral in 1800, but by 1900 industrialization and territorial expansion had propelled it into the core. By contrast, once-powerful China fell into peripheral status after 1800. But even with some movement up or down, Wallerstein argues, the core-semiperiphery-periphery structure still characterizes the world-system today. Indeed, some recent studies confirm the relevance of world-system analysis to present-day economic flows in which trade and investment still deeply separate core and peripheries; core countries hold a higher position in the world division of labor.

If modernization analysis predicts an increasing standardization around the world toward a Western-influenced pattern, world-system analysis suggests that the core and periphery, serving different functions in the world economy, have moved in opposite directions, toward wealth on the one hand and poverty on the other. Since the economic exchange between them was unequal, the periphery became dependent on the core for goods, services, investment, and resource markets, giving core societies, which exploited the resources of the periphery, great influence. For example, the Gold Coast's cocoa growers needed British markets, and British companies provided consumer goods to the shopkeepers, often Lebanese immigrants, who served these communities. The wealth and power of a country, then, reflect its political and economic position in the world-system.

Like modernization theory, world-system analysis has provoked controversy. Some scholars embrace a world-system approach but disagree with Wallerstein's version or consider both world-system and modernization theories too rigid. Whereas Wallerstein believes a world-system began only around 1500, Christopher Chase-Dunn and Thomas Hall emphasize a longer history with diverse intersocietal networks that can be called world-systems beginning in ancient times. Andre Gunder Frank and Barry Gills identify one single world-system existing for five thousand years, since, they argue, some form of capitalism began with the earliest states, such as Sumeria, in Afro-Eurasia. Frank viewed Asia, especially China, as the center of this system. Janet Abu-Lughod postulated a thirteenth-century CE world-system stretching across Eurasia, linked together by the Mongol Empire. Russian scholar Anatoli Korotayev perceived a West Asian–based world-system stretching back to the tenth millennium BCE and the Neolithic revolution. Some critics accuse Wallerstein, like the modernization theorists, of Eurocentrism by overemphasizing the West and underestimating the key roles played by Asians in the Afro-Eurasian-American economy in the past five hundred years.

Other critics are harsher. Some charge that Wallerstein's stress on exchange between countries downplays inequitable economies and class structures within countries—such as rapacious landowners, privileged aristocrats, tyrannical chiefs, and greedy merchants—hence shifting the blame for poverty to the world economy. Others, such as Daniel Chirot, question whether exploitation of the periphery explains the economic growth of the core. Critics also wonder whether terms such as *core* and *periphery* constitute a more sophisticated version of "modernity" and "tradition," marginalizing and perhaps demeaning poor societies.

Finally, some think Wallerstein's focus on economic factors neglects politics and cultures, including religion, and places so much stress on the forest that it misses the trees. Some think world-system analysis has been too core-centric and state-centric. William I. Robinson criticized the nation-state centrism and inability to conceptualize and account for the rise of globalization, emerging transnational social forces, and the relations between them and the global institutions serving their interest. Wallerstein disagreed, viewing globalization as a product of the world-system and coterminous with the spread and development of capitalism over the past five hundred years. It can be debated whether globalization has become a more useful concept than world-system in our more complex world. Some cultural scholars regret the neglect of humanities and describe some world-system scholars of rigidity and an almost "theological omnipotence." Yet, like many world historians, even some critics find that the general concept of an interlinked, capitalism-driven global system helps explain transnational economic relations, the impact of colonialism, the background to military interventions by more powerful countries, and the political turbulence of the poorer nations today.

Evaluating the Debate

The modernization and world-system theorists launched an ongoing debate about how world history, especially modern world history, can be understood, but some wonder if either approach fully explains modern history. Many world historians consider the once-dominant modernization theory inadequate for understanding the world as a whole. Some of these are attracted to one or another version of world-system analysis but often believe that many details of Wallerstein's approach are open to challenge. Ultimately, as Wallerstein, who died in 2019, suggested, the world-system approach is not about holding this or that hypothesis about the structures and institutions of world capitalism but recognizing we are all connected across space and time—a person cannot understand what is happening in one place in the world without situating that place within a global frame, without recognizing the global nature of modern capitalism. Hence, its proponents believe that world-system analysis, albeit controversial, remains relevant today because it gives peoples the tools to make historical sense of the world economy and the turmoil raging today in many places because of economic grievances, including wealth inequality, chronic poverty, low commodity prices, substandard housing, limited employment opportunities, unpopular trade agreements, and world financial crises. While, as modernization scholars recognize, each society has unique characteristics that shape its history, perceiving some sort of global system or systems that rise and fall over time helps us understand large-scale, long-term change and explains how thousands of small hunting and gathering bands twelve thousand years ago became the contemporary global community of nation-states.

Reflection Questions

1. How do modernization and world-system approaches explain the modern world and its diverse societies differently?
2. What are the major advantages and problems of each of the two approaches?
3. Do you find one, both, or neither of the approaches helpful in explaining the world today?

Exploring the Controversy

Among the major works of modernization theory are C. E. Black, *The Dynamics of Modernization: A Study in Comparative History* (New York: Harper and Row, 1966); W. W. Rostow, *The Stages of Economic Growth: A Non-Communist Manifesto* (Cambridge: Cambridge University Press, 1960); David Apter, *The Politics of Modernization* (Chicago: University of Chicago Press, 1965); and Marion Levy, *Social Patterns and Problems of Modernization* (Englewood Cliffs, NJ: Prentice-Hall, 1967), 189–207. On a history of the approach and its political influence, see Nils Gilman, *Mandarins of the Future: Modernization Theory in Cold War America* (Baltimore: Johns Hopkins University Press, 2007); and Michael E. Latham, *Modernization and Ideology: American Social Science and "Nation-Building" in the Kennedy Era* (Chapel Hill: University of North Carolina Press, 2000). A useful critical analysis can be found in Dean Tipps, *Modernization Theory and the Comparative Study of Societies: A Critical Perspective* (New York: Free Press, 1976), 65–77.

Immanuel Wallerstein has summarized his ideas in *The Capitalist World-Economy* (New York: Cambridge University Press, 1979) and *World-Systems Analysis: An Introduction* (Durham, NC: Duke University Press, 2004). Alternative versions of the world-system concept include Christopher Chase-Dunn and Thomas D. Hall, *Rise and Demise: Comparing World-Systems* (Boulder, CO: Westview Press, 1997); Andre Gunder Frank and Barry K. Gills, eds., *The World System: Five Hundred Years or Five Thousand?* (New York: Routledge, 1996); Anatoli Korotayev, "A Compact Macro-model of World System Evolution," *Journal of World-Systems Research*, 11 (2005), 73–93; Walter Goldfrank, ed., *The World System of Capitalism: Past and Present* (New York: Monthly Review Press, 1986); and Giovanni Arrighi, *The Long Twentieth Century: Money, Power, and the Origins of Our Times*, New updated ed. (London: Verso, 2010). Daniel Chirot takes issue with much of world-system analysis in *Social Change in the Modern Era* (New York: Harcourt Brace Jovanovich, 1986). On Andre Gunder Frank's writings, see Patrick Manning and Barry K. Gills, eds., *Andre Gunder Frank and Global Development: Visions, Remembrances, and Explorations* (New York: Routledge, 2013). Excellent summaries and critiques of world-system analysis and competing ideas can be found in Thomas R. Shannon, *An Introduction to the World-System Perspective* (Boulder, CO: Westview Press, 1989); Alvin Y. So, *Social Change and Development: Modernization, Dependency, and World-System Theories* (Newbury Park, CA: Sage, 1990); Stephen K. Sanderson, ed., *Civilizations and World Systems: Studying World-Historical Change* (Walnut Creek, CA: Altamira Press, 1995); Pamela Kyle Crossley, *What Is Global History?* (Malden, MA: Polity Press, 2008); Jonathan Daly, *Historians Debate the Rise of the West* (New York: Routledge, 2015); and Thomas D. Hall, ed., *A World-Systems Reader: New Perspectives on Gender, Urbanism, Cultures, Indigenous Peoples, and Ecology* (Lanham, MD: Rowman and Littlefield, 2000); William I. Robinson "Globalization and the Sociology of Immanuel Wallerstein: A Critical Appraisal," *International Sociology*, 26, no. 6 (2011), 723–745; and D. Palumbo-Liu, N. Tanoukhi, and B. Robbins, eds., *Immanuel Wallerstein and the Problem of the World: System, Scale, Culture* (Durham, NC: Duke University Press, 2011). On dependency theory, see Samir Amin, *Unequal Development: An Essay on the Social Formations of Peripheral Calpitalism* (New York: Monthly Review Press, 1976); Cristobal Kay, "Andre Gunder Frank: From the 'Development of Underdevelopment' to the 'World System,'" *Development and Change*, 36, no. 6 (2005), 1177–1183; and Tony Smith, "The Underdevelopment of Development Literature: The Case of Dependency Theory," *World Politics*, 31, no. 2 (1979), 247–288. For a provocative critique of these debates and the rise of the world economy by an Indian scholar, see Amiya Kumar Bagchi, *Perilous Passage: Mankind and the Global Ascendancy of Capital* (Lanham, MD: Rowman and Littlefield, 2005).

PART VI

Global System: Interdependence and Conflict in the Contemporary World, Since 1945

CHAPTER OUTLINE

The world has changed dramatically since 1945. Some observers describe these years as the most revolutionary age in history, reshaping whole ways of life and worldviews. All regions of the world, opening to ideas and products from everywhere, have become part of a global village or global system. Indonesian thinker Soedjatmoko (so-jat-MOH-ko) perceived a world of collapsing "national boundaries and horrifying destructive power, expanding technological capacity and instant communication [in which] we live in imperfect intimacy with all our fellow human beings."[1] This interconnected and rapidly changing global society, and the people who shape it, have produced both great good and indescribable horrors.

The contemporary world has become a global unity within a larger diversity. Linking distant societies, globalization fostered or intensified networks of exchange and communication: international trade pacts and electronic fund transfers, jet-speed travel and the Internet. Yet, even while becoming more closely linked, nations have difficulty working together to meet the challenges facing humanity. No clear international consensus has emerged on maintaining strong local cultures in the face of global influences, correcting the widening gap between rich and poor nations, and achieving a better balance between environmental preservation and economic development.

Globalization and Its Impact

⫘ TRANSITIONS

Over recent centuries the world's people have built a human web, or networked society, characterized by transnational connections and the institutions that foster them, such as the World Bank, the Internet, and religious missionaries. Around the world people speak, with fear or enthusiasm, of globalization. Some observers see the trend as dangerous folly, others as a boon, and still others have mixed feelings.

Globalization's roots go deep into the past. A thousand years ago an Eastern Hemisphere–wide economy based in Asia and anchored by Chinese and Indian manufacturing and Islamic trade networks represented an early form of globalization. The links between the hemispheres forged after 1492, during which Europeans competed with each other and with Asians for a share of the growing trade in raw materials, created a global economy. In the nineteenth century the Industrial Revolution, which produced desirable trade goods, and European imperialism, which spurred Western colonization of much of the world, extended the connections even further, aided by technological innovations such as steamships, railroads, the telegraph, and transoceanic cables. Around thirty-six million people left Europe for the Americas, southern Africa, and Australia, and millions more departed China, Japan, and India for Southeast Asia, the Caribbean, and southern Africa, leaving countries with too many workers for countries with too few, sometimes unwillingly. The Great Depression and then World War II brought an end to that globalization. But after the war the United States led the struggle to end economic protectionism and restore immigration, urging everyone to accept that growth and development for one country might benefit all countries through increased investment and trade. This fostered a new

[1]Kathleen Newland and Kamala Chandrakirana Soedjatmoko, eds., *Transforming Humanity: The Visionary Writings of Soedjatmoko* (West Hartford, CT: Kumarian Press, 1994), 186–187.

era of globalization and a revitalized global trade system. The rise of the European Union, China, and later India added more strong pillars but also rivalries. Eventually a backlash against free trade and the mobility of capital emerged within and between nations as some countries and people were seen as winners and others as losers.

The integration of production, commerce, and financial services today is more developed than ever before, with global supply chains and financing crossing many borders. Globalization is often linked to manufacturing but actually involves a wide range of activities, services, and products. For example, discarded or "second hand" items made in the U.S. and various other countries, from clothes and books to furniture and electronics, can be found in markets and bazaars in Africa, Asia, and Latin America. Societies became more dependent on each other for everything from consumer goods and entertainments to fuels and technological innovations. All over the world people consume Chinese textiles, U.S. film, Persian Gulf oil, Colombian coffee, Indian yoga, Malaysian rubber, and Japanese electronics. Videoconferencing allows business partners in Los Angeles, Berlin, and Hong Kong to confer instantaneously with one another. Yet, while globalization affects every country to some degree, the great bulk of world trade and financial flow and activity is concentrated in, and has the largest impact on, the peoples of three huge interlinked blocs: North America, Europe, and a group of Asian nations stretching from Japan to India. Many observers have believed that globalization is unmanageable; one controversial observer wrote that: "Globalization isn't a choice. It's a reality and no one is in charge. You keep looking for someone to complain to, to take the heat off your markets. Well guess what, there's no one on the other end of the phone. The global market today is an electronic herd of anonymous stock, bond and currency traders sitting behind computer screens. Sure, this is unfair [but] there's nobody to call."[2] This impersonal globalization, operating independent of governments, has had major impacts on societies, politics, economies, cultures, and environments. Whether they are seen as positive or negative consequences depends on the observer (see Debate the Historians: Globalization: For and Against). Indeed, in the 2010s globalization has been one of the major sources of conflict within and between countries. Global financial crises (such as occurred in 2008–2009) and trade wars can wreak havoc on many countries and require years for recovery. The central premise of the rules-based trading order has been breaking down as the wealthy, more regulated but less efficient economies (such as the U.S. and the European Union) face competition from poorer, less regulated and more efficient economies (such as China and India), fomenting trade wars (such as between the U.S. and China) but also a search for new rules that serve the larger good in order to restabilize the world economy. In a world experiencing some turmoil, several historians speculate that the international rules-based system could collapse, to be replaced perhaps by smaller regional blocs and a decentralized "nation-first" world. Avoiding chaos might require developing an ethos combining national identity with a global awareness.

To adapt and flourish in an interconnected world, people have had to become aware of global conditions. International conferences have convened sporadically to discuss global issues such as human rights and climate change. In North America, activists seeking to fight inequality or preserve the environment have urged people to think globally but act locally. Thinking globally, for example, would include understanding how rapid deforestation in the tropics—especially in the Amazon and Congo Basins, where rain forests recycle vast amounts of water into the air—diminishes rainfall around the world. Acting locally, Brazilian environmental and citizens' groups work to save their rain forests, while environmentally conscious North Americans and Europeans support organizations, businesses, and political leaders committed to improving the global environment. But some politicians and business interests in many nations have opposed these movements. For example, some companies involved in mining, ranching, logging, manufacturing, and agriculture in countries like Australia, Brazil, and the U.S. have fought efforts to preserve rain forests and public lands, promote renewable energy, protect clean air and water, respect indigenous peoples, save endangered species, and combat climate change. Even the digital world has borders. Many governments dislike criticism and dissent. Since 2015 more than a quarter of countries have at some point cut off civilian access to communication tools like social media and news websites, mostly in Asia and Africa, with India, Myanmar, Zimbabwe, and Congo among the worst abusers. Claiming "cyber sovereignty" and using its "great firewall" to keep out "disruptive" information, China has banned most foreign websites and media outlets such as CNN (Cable News Network) for years. Similarly, governments, political parties, underground groups, complicit companies, and tech-savvy individuals can use covert social media campaigns to spread "fake news" or try and influence people to a particular viewpoint. This Internet warfare has become common, for example, in the U.S. elections and the Brexit referendum in 2016 and the effort by Sudan's military to undermine protests and opposition in 2019. In the future developing and mastering Big Data and artificial intelligence may be the key to national success.

The Globalization of Cultures

NETWORKS

Global forces, symbolized by advertising for foreign-made goods and satellites miles up in the sky relaying information around the world, interact with local cultures, raising questions about national and local identities. As a result, local traditions and products sometimes get replaced, and imported and local cultures blend. People around the world consume global products, from fast food to fashionable footwear to action films, but still enjoy local cultural traditions (like Thai boxing, Brazilian Carnival celebrations, or Japanese sumo wrestling) popular with earlier generations.

The inequitable relationship between the dominant West and the developing nations fostered the concept of

[2]Tom Friedman, quoted in Jan Pronk, "Globalization: A Developmental Approach," in Jan Nederveen Pieterse, ed., *Global Futures: Shaping Globalization* (London: Zed Books, 2000), 46.

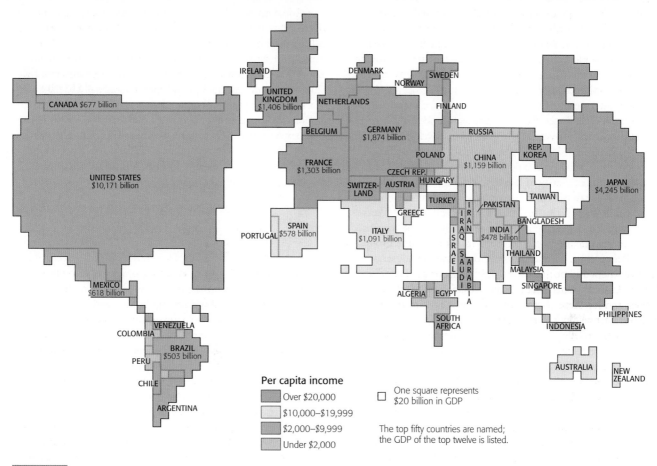

Per capita income
Over $20,000
$10,000–$19,999
$2,000–$9,999
Under $2,000

One square represents
$20 billion in GDP

The top fifty countries are named;
the GDP of the top twelve is listed.

MAP VI.1 **Global Distribution of Wealth** The countries of North America, northern Europe, and Japan have the most wealth and the world's highest per capita incomes, averaging over $20,000 per year. At the other extreme, many people in South America and most people in the poor countries of sub-Saharan Africa, South Asia, and the Middle East earn under $2,000 per year.

Q How well does the map communicate the wealth gap between the richer and poorer countries?

cultural imperialism, in which the economic and political power of Western nations, especially the United States, enables their cultural products to spread widely. Some African writers called this pattern a "cultural bomb" because, they believe, Western products and entertainments destroy local cultures. For instance, big-budget Hollywood films attract large audiences while many local films, made on small budgets, cannot compete; local film industries often die as a result. To survive, many local filmmakers adopt the formulas used by successful Hollywood filmmakers: sex and violence.

Popular culture produced in the United States, entertaining but also challenging to traditional values, emerged as the closest thing available to a global entertainment. The Monroe Doctrine—the early-nineteenth-century declaration by Congress that the United States would interfere in Latin American political developments—has now become, in the view of certain wags, the "Marilyn Monroe Doctrine," after the famous American actress who, for many non-Americans, symbolized U.S. culture in the 1950s. Some American icons, from basketball stars Michael Jordan and LeBron James to

McDonald's and Kentucky Fried Chicken, became symbols of a new global modernity and capitalism. In 1989 two young East Germans crossed the Berlin Wall and discovered their first McDonald's restaurant. One of them remembered, "It was all so modern, the windows were so amazing. I felt like a lost convict who'd just spent twenty-five years in prison. I was in a state of shock."[3] Not even the Chinese, with one of the world's most admired cuisines, were immune to the appeal of modern U.S. marketing techniques and convenience for harried urbanites. In 1993 a famous roast duck restaurant in China's capital, Beijing, sent its management staff to study the McDonald's operation in British-ruled Hong Kong and then introduced its customers to "roast duck fast food." Today McDonald's franchises are found all over China. Yet, many thousands of Chinese restaurants also flourish around the world.

Still, popular American and other Western entertainments often face opposition. Governments, from Islamic clerics running Iran to India's more democratic leaders, have attempted to halt or control the influx of what they consider destabilizing, immoral pop culture. In

---

[3]Daphne Berdahl, quoted in James L. Watson, ed., *Golden Arches East: McDonald's in East Asia* (Stanford, CA: Stanford University Press, 1997), xvii.

1995 an Islamic political party in Pakistan even demanded, unsuccessfully, that the United States turn over to them American pop stars Madonna and Michael Jackson so that they could be placed on trial as "cultural terrorists" destroying humanity. Yet the rising world culture is not uniform. No total homogenization of expression and meaning has occurred.

Anglo-American cultural forms are not the only ones to reach a global audience. Mexican, Brazilian, and Turkish soap operas, Indian (Bollywood) films, Nigerian novels, African and Caribbean pop music, and Japanese comics, animated film, and electronic games have been popular all over the globe. Thanks in part to the popularity of Jamaican singer-songwriter Bob Marley, reggae music spread around the world, as one observer marveled in the 1980s: "In Tahiti the buses all have speakers the size of foot lockers, making them moving sound systems. Their routes are jumping with the rhythms of [reggae groups] Steel Pulse, Black Uhuru, and Bob Marley. Four thousand miles away in Tokyo, there is a reggae night spot called Club 69, where local youth wear dreadlocks and dance to the beats of the Wailers. Africa has its own reggae styles and hundreds of bands."[4] The cultural traffic flow is not one-way. In North America, western Europe, and Australia, people take up Indian yoga, Chinese *tai qi*, and other Asian spiritual disciplines; patronize Thai, Indian, Chinese, Japanese, and Mexican restaurants; enjoy Brazilian and African pop music; learn Latin American dances; and master Asian martial arts, such as karate and judo. The meeting of global and local cultures fosters hybridization, the blending of two cultures, a process that can be either enriching or impoverishing. Record and CD stores in Western cities set aside some of their display space to sell a hybrid form called "world music," popular music originating largely outside of the West that mixes Western influences with local and other traditions. Just like Western pop stars, some world musicians—such as Brazilian singer-songwriter Caetano Veloso, Indian film diva Asha Bhosle (the most recorded artist in history), and Senegalese Youssou N'Dour, the descendant of griots who mixes guitars with West African talking drums—performed around the world. But not all transcultural music is hybrid. American rap and hip-hop have planted roots in many countries as a voice for discussion of social issues and even protest. And in the twenty-first century K-pop music from South Korea, featuring telegenic boy bands and girl bands, has attracted global audiences.

The North–South Gap

SOCIETIES

Globalization transcending national boundaries benefits some people but not all equally. The gap between rich and poor nations, and rich and poor people within nations, has grown and remains one of the world's major problems. In 1960 the richest fifth of the world's population had a total income thirty times the poorest fifth; by 2000 the ratio had more than doubled. Since World War II, many nations on every continent improved their living standards and per capita incomes, lowered poverty rates, and increased their stake in

the global economy, which has more than quintupled in size since 1950. But the world economy's rising tide has not lifted all ships, leaving some nations, especially in the southern lands near or below the equator, poor relative to the northern countries. Over one billion people live in extreme poverty. By 2018 the world's average wealth per person was $63,100 but for the "bottom billion" of people it was $1,079 and for the poorest nation, Central African Republic, it was $726. The country with the highest per capita wealth, Switzerland, averaged $539,657. Using a popular term for an underdeveloped nation, Jamaican reggae star Pato Banton reflected on the harshness of poverty in a 1989 song, "Third World Country":

> In a Third World country, the plants are green, it's a beautiful scene. Seems like a nice place for human beings. But there's people on the streets, no shoes on their feet. They gotta hustle to get a little food to eat. Things shouldn't be this way.[5]

The gap between the richest and poorest countries, often known as the North–South gap, has widened steadily. The difference in average per capita incomes between industrialized and nonindustrialized nations grew from 2:1 in 1850 to 10:1 in 1950 to 30:1 by 2000. A 1980s study of a farming village in a remote Bolivian valley summarized the disparity in life experiences: "In a man's lifetime he will buy only one suit, one white shirt, perhaps a hat and a pair of boots. The only things that have to be purchased in the market are a small radio-record player, the batteries to run it, plaster religious figures, a bicycle, and some cutlery."[6] Today the industrialized North contains under a quarter of the world's population but accounts for over three-quarters of its production of goods and services. Literacy rates, life expectancy, and food consumption also differ dramatically. On average, North Americans consume twice as many calories each day as Haitians and Bangladeshis. While overeating contributes to widespread obesity in industrialized nations, an eighth of the world's people are chronically malnourished, often suffering permanent brain damage because of it, and lack access to clean water. Fifteen million children die each year from hunger-related ailments. The 10 percent of people who live in the most industrialized nations consume two-thirds of the world's energy. Over 60 percent of the world's poorest people are women, who often struggle to compete with men for resources or are often prevented by local custom from working outside the home.

Building a New World Order

TRANSITIONS

The challenge of development is only a part of a larger contemporary question: how societies, working together, can forge a new, more equitable world order. The old world order, built in the eighteenth and nineteenth centuries when powerful Western nations conquered and governed much of Asia and Africa, was one in which a few rich Western nations politically and economically dominated most of the others. Even after World War II,

[4]Billy Bergman, *Hot Sauces: Latin and Caribbean Pop* (New York: Quill, 1985), 18.

[5]From Banton's album, *Visions of the World* (IRSD-82003, 1989).

[6]Frank Cajka, quoted in Peter Worsley, *The Three Worlds: Cultures and World Development* (Chicago: University of Chicago Press, 1984), xi.

decolonization, and the rise of revolutionary states such as China, a few nations, mostly in the West and East Asia, still held disproportionate power and influence in the global system. The forming of the United Nations has been one major attempt at global cooperation but has had a mixed record. The United States has played the key role and borne the major costs in managing the global system through military alliances (such as NATO), trade pacts (such as GATT), and international organizations (such as the World Bank). Some historians identify a "Pax Americana" since the 1940s as the U.S. exercised world power and helped regulate global institutions, helping limit conflict between the great powers, much like the "Pax Romana" in the Classical Era and the nineteenth century "Pax Britannica." But this leadership also sparked a nationalist populist reaction from those Americans who felt themselves left behind and helped elect the antiglobalization, antiinternationalist candidate Donald Trump as president in 2016; Trump condemned "globalism" and promised an "America First" policy to disrupt the international political and economic order. Similar political unrest has also enabled antiglobalization nationalist populists to gain influence or power in various countries in Europe, southern Asia, and Latin America. Trump's policies disrupting the world order, including retreating from global institutions and military commitments, abandoning treaties, fomenting trade wars, limiting immigration, and weakening U.S. influence in Asia and the Middle East, lead some historians and international affairs analysts to forecast the end of Pax Americana. But which nation or nations, if any, might replace America's world leadership in helping stabilize the global system remains unclear.

The prospect of fostering a more equitable sharing of world resources raises questions about the availability of resources. Experts worry that the world's resources and environment could not support a Western standard of living for all the world. If every Chinese, Indian, Angolan, Egyptian, and Peruvian, they argue, consumed the same products and calories as Americans, Swedes, or Japanese, world resources would quickly diminish. For all 7.5 billion people in today's world to live at a western European standard of living would require a 140-fold increase in the consumption of resources and energy. People in nations once poor but becoming developed, such as China, India, and Brazil, do not believe that the industrialized Western peoples have any more right to consume the world's resources than they do, and they want their fair share.

China's recent economic success shows the challenges ahead. By the early twenty-first century a China rushing toward development and with a growing and affluent middle class had become a huge consumer of the world's industrial, agricultural, and natural resources, energizing global trade but causing shortages elsewhere. For example, world oil prices have sporadically soared since 2000 in part because of China's increasing energy appetite as Chinese switch from bicycles to cars. If the Chinese consumed as much oil per capita as Americans, their demand would exceed the present world production. By 2006 Chinese consumed nearly twice as much meat and more than twice as much steel as Americans. China's living standards remain far below those of Japan and South Korea. Should they rise to that level, however, in the next decade or two, China will import vastly more resources than it does today, further stressing supplies. As occurred in the industrializing West earlier, rapid Chinese development, including the growing use of polluting fossil fuels, has also led to environmental degradation, including dangerous air and water pollution.

Building Sustainable Environments

NETWORKS

Human activity has altered environments since prehistory, sometimes with catastrophic results. Environmental collapse triggered by agricultural practices, deforestation, and/or climate change helped undermine the Mesopotamians, Harappans, Romans, and Mayans, among others. Some scientists have developed the interdisciplinary but controversial concept of the Anthropocene, a new era in Earth history when humans have more dramatically altered the environment, including climate, air, land use, and ecology. Some argue it began with the rise of agriculture some ten thousand years ago; others trace it to the Industrial Revolution of the early 1800s or perhaps to the acceleration of economic and industrial growth since 1945. Some historians propose an alternative idea, the Plantationocene, because, they argue, environmental concerns cannot be disentangled from the colonialism, capitalism, and racism of the past five centuries. In this view agricultural plantations symbolized and helped organize modern economies, environments, and social relations. Whatever we call these centuries, the Modern Era and especially Contemporary Era industrial societies, plantations, and their rapidly growing populations have encroached on their natural settings even more heavily than did earlier societies. The decades since the mid-twentieth century were unusual for the intensity of environmental deterioration and the centrality of human effort in causing it. By 2000 the challenge of a changing environment became obvious. On every continent, but especially in Eurasia and North America, gas-guzzling vehicles, passenger jets, smoky factories, coal-fired power plants, large farming operations, and burning rainforests produce large amounts of carbon dioxide, methane, chlorofluorocarbons, and other pollutants that accumulate in the atmosphere, contributing to rising average temperatures that scientists call global warming. This climate change, if it continues, may have a greater impact—possibly catastrophic—on human life than any conventional war or other destructive human activities. We can already see this today, in the obliteration of human settlements in the northern Bahamas, Puerto Rico, and the Virgin Islands in recent hurricanes (possibly made more powerful by climate change). Problems such as global warming raise the question of whether in the long term the natural environment can maintain itself and support plant, animal, and human life—a pattern known as sustainability. To sustain environmental health, a Canadian statesman argued, requires a "revolution in [our] thinking as basic as the one introduced by Copernicus who [in the 1500s] first pointed out that the earth was not the center of the universe."[7]

[7]Lester Pearson, quoted in Lester R. Brown, *World Without Borders* (New York: Vintage, 1972), ix.

IMAGE VI.1 Protesting Global Warming People in societies around the world became alarmed at the increasing environmental damage brought by modern economic activity and exploitation of resources. This demonstration by environmental activists concerned with global warming, a potentially dangerous trend caused by burning fossil fuels such as coal that produces more carbon dioxide, took place in Turkey.

Yonhap/EPA-EFE/Shutterstock.com

Q Why do you think so many people around the world are protesting the failure of their governments to adequately address global warming?

Experts have wondered whether the world's resources—minerals, wild plants, food crops, fresh water—could sustain present living standards on a long-term basis. For the past several decades scientists have been alarmed at the human consumption of natural resources faster than nature can replenish them. In the twentieth century people used more energy than had been used in all previous history. Contemporary industrial and agricultural practices contributed to, among other pressing problems, air and water pollution, disposal of hazardous waste, declining genetic diversity in crops, deforestation, and a mass extinction of plant and animal species. In the 1940s American environmentalist Aldo Leopold called for an ethic that treats the land with respect because all life belongs to a community of interdependent relationships: "Land is a fountain of energy flowing through a circuit of soils, plants, and animals, a sustained circuit, like a slowly augmented revolving fund of life."[8] With their heavy economic production and consumption, people today are borrowing from tomorrow.

In 2019 the fires burning in a vast area of the Amazon basin, the world's largest carbon sink and biodiversity reservoir, illustrated some of the challenges. The fires have mostly been deliberately set to clear "jungle" land for mining, logging, and farming. But the fire "genocide" kills countless animals, eliminates endangered plant and animal species, contributes hugely to warming the atmosphere, and destroys the lives and villages of the indigenous inhabitants, who mostly depend on the forests and survive by hunting and gathering, horticulture, or simple farming. One prominent indigenous leader in the Brazilian Amazon appealed to the world to stop the destruction: "What you are doing will change the whole world and will destroy our home—and it will destroy your home too.... Only a generation ago, many of our tribes were fighting each other, but now we are ... fighting together against our common enemy ... the non-indigenous peoples who have invaded our lands.... We call on you to stop ... your attack on the spirits of the Earth.... To live you must respect the world, the trees, the plants, the animals, the rivers and even the very earth itself. Because all of these things have spirits ... and without the spirits the earth will die.... If we don't [protect the Earth], the big winds will come and destroy the forest."[9] Some experts worry it may be too late to save the Amazon from turning from forest to savannah grasslands, which would make it a major emitter rather than an absorber of greenhouse gases.

The atmosphere faces particular dangers, including a measurable warming. Earth's climate changed little, with only minor fluctuations, between the last Ice Age, which ended ten thousand years ago, and the end of the eighteenth century, when the Industrial Revolution began in Europe, but it has been changing fast over the past two centuries. Since 1985, the world has experienced the highest average annual temperatures on record and unprecedented droughts. Blaming a greenhouse effect, human-made pollutants overheating the earth, scientists now largely agree that global warming has been increasing. For some years they debated its causes and dangers but by the 2010s there was near-unanimous agreement that it derived from human activity and that the consequences will radically disrupt and change the world we live in. In 2019 eleven thousand scientists representing diverse disciplines from 153 countries declared a "climate emergency" that required immediate action. In the pessimistic scenarios, the consequences of rising temperatures for many of the world's peoples are devastating. Earth gets baked, rich farmland turns to desert, rain comes in torrents that cause severe floods, food supplies diminish, forests wilt, Arctic and Antarctic ice and glaciers melt, and ocean levels rise, inundating low-lying islands, deltas, cities, and farm lands. Fresh water, already scarce, becomes even harder to find as lakes and streams dry up. Rising ocean temperatures damage fisheries and kill most protective coral reefs. The polar regions such as Alaska and Siberia already experience the effects, as permafrost turns to swamp, villages sink, and sea ice thins or disappears. The tropical countries, most still poor, contribute least to the problem but may experience the worst losses, with parts of Central America,

[8]Aldo Leopold, *A Sand County Almanac* (New York: Ballantine, 1966), 253.
[9]Raoni Metuktire, "We, the Peoples of the Amazon, are Full of Fear. Soon You Will Be Too," *The Guardian*, September 2, 2019.

the Caribbean, Africa, the Middle East, and southern Asia becoming unlivable, promoting millions of refugees to seek shelter in more temperate countries. Already many coastal cities are experiencing more frequent flooding, and some nations, among them Indonesia, have built or are planning new capitals inland. The oceans are warming rapidly, killing off or prompting the migration of many marine animals, as enormous ocean currents are traveling to new locations. The biggest hot spots are in the North Atlantic, North Pacific, South Pacific, and Indian Oceans, which have all warmed by at least two degrees Celsius over the past century. That is a number that scientists and policymakers identify as a red flag if the planet is to avoid catastrophic and irreversible consequences. Many experts forecast varied threats including water wars, more conflict between nations, and health harm to future generations.

The environmental challenges, such as diminishing resources, global warming, and deforestation, reinforce the scientific concept, first popularized in the 1970s, of global ecology—the world, including human societies, as a complex web in which all living things interact with each other and their surroundings. Cultural, economic, political, and social activity affects livelihoods and environmental sustainability in what some term the "humanosphere." While organizations promoting environmental sustainability proliferate, the world's leaders often disagree on ways to better balance economic growth, which all nations desire, with environmental protection. Efforts to expand renewable energy sources, such as wind and solar, remain spotty.

Understanding the Global Past

⇄ TRANSITIONS

The study of history helps us understand today's news and views as they are reported in daily newspapers, broadcast on radio and television, and disseminated on the World Wide Web. Historians often describe their work as involving a dialogue between past, present, and future. A few years ago French scientist René Dubos argued: "The past is not dead history. It is living material out of which makes the present and builds the future."[10] Current global problems have their roots in the patterns of world history: the rise of farms, cities, states, and organized religions; the expansion of trade and capitalism to global dimensions; the unprecedented mastery and altering of nature represented by the scientific, industrial, and technological revolutions; the proliferation of competitive, unequal nations; and the myriad of social, economic, political, and cultural connections between peoples encompassed in the expanding global system and globalization. American novelist William Faulkner wrote in 1951 that "the past is not dead, it is not even past." Hence, memories of the Opium War and the "century of humiliation" still color Chinese feelings toward the West, Hindus and Muslims in South Asia argue about events that happened centuries or millenia ago, some Russians still long for a restoration of the old Russian Empire, many Turks revere the long gone Ottomans, Israelis, and Arabs contest control of historic holy sites, some Southeast Asians still distrust

the Japanese because of World War II, the Dutch reconsider their seventeenth century "golden age," many Iranians view the U.S. through the lens of the overthrow of their government in 1953, the Holocaust still shapes Jewish consciousness, views toward the Civil War still affect U.S. politics, Dubai opened a spectacular themed shopping mall organized around the Afro-Eurasian journeys of the famed fourteenth century Moroccan traveler and scholar Ibn Battuta, and neo-Nazi and white supremacist groups promote their decades - or century-old racist ideas in Europe and North America. While seeking to understand how the past shaped the present, historians also speculate on how current trends may shape the future.

World historians offer several ways of understanding the world of yesterday, today, and tomorrow. One view is that contacts and collisions between different societies produce change. Whether through peaceful exchange or warfare or perhaps both, when societies encounter other societies they are exposed to different customs and ideas. Historians also emphasize continuity, the persistence of social, cultural, political, and religious ideas and patterns, as well as change, the transformations in ways of life, work, and thought. Continuities are common. For example, many millions of Christians, Muslims, Jews, Buddhists, and Hindus still look at the world through the prism of traditional religious values forged millennia ago and still meaningful today. Hundreds of thousands of Christian and Muslim missionaries spread their message around the world, often making converts. Yet changes, too, are everywhere. Hence, most people engage in activities, face challenges, and use forms of transportation and communication nonexistent a few generations ago. As a result, missionaries and clerics often use radio, television, social media, and the Internet to spread their message. Another insight offered by global historians is that great transitions, such as the agricultural and industrial revolutions or, more recently, the rise of high technology and the digital world, can turn history in new directions. Thousands of years ago farming largely displaced hunting and gathering, two centuries ago industry transformed the world economy, and today instant communication and information bring distant peoples closer together.

The experiences of most societies over the past half century reveal a mix of change and continuity. For example, Western ideas have gained even greater influence in the world since 1945 than they had before. People in many different lands have adopted Western ideas of government, such as constitutions and elections, although not necessarily the substance of democracy, along with Western-rooted ideologies and faiths: capitalism, socialism, nationalism, and Christianity. Western pop culture, from rock music and streaming video to soft drinks and blue jeans, has spread widely, leading to what critics consider the "Coca-Colazation" of the world stemming from Western economic power, including advertising. Yet influences from the West are usually strongest in large cities and penetrate less deeply into the villages in Africa, Asia, Latin America, and the Middle East, where traditional ways reflect continuity with the past. As a result, city youth in Malaysia or Tanzania may follow the latest recordings from

[10]Rene Dubos, *So Human an Animal* (New York: Scribner's, 1968), 270.

Western pop stars, but these recordings may be unknown to their rural counterparts. Yet urban youth may also share with rural youth traditional views about family and faith, and rural youth may, like their city counterparts, own motorcycles, boom boxes, and smartphones that make their lives different from those of their parents. They have access to world and national news but also extremist religious or political sources such as ISIS (the Islamic State) or neo-Nazis.

As a result of the transition to globalizing technology, culture, and commerce, the contacts between societies and their interdependence have vastly increased since 1945. In different ways nuclear weapons, multinational corporations, Earth-circling satellites, World Cup soccer, and cable news networks draw people together, willingly or not. Imperialists once claimed proudly that "the sun never set on the British Empire." By the 1990s observers noted that "the sun never sets on McDonald's." Today it never sets on smartphones or tablets and Twitter. Closer contact, of course, does not necessarily mean friendly relations and a less dangerous world; it can also bring collisions. Guided missiles and planes carrying bombs can reach ten thousand miles from their home base and cyber attacks on other countries can come from the other side of the world. Over the past several decades over sixty thousand Americans have died fighting in faraway Vietnam, Afghanistan, Iraq, and Syria in support of U.S. foreign policies. In 2019 two hundred thousand American troops were still deployed overseas.

The contacts, changes, and transitions since 1945 created a global village, a single community of exchange and interaction. Even remote societies have become part of this global village. By the 1960s, for example, people living in the once-isolated interior of the island of Borneo, divided between Indonesia and Malaysia, could access the outside world through battery-powered transistor radios and cassette players, and also by means of visiting traders, Christian missionaries, and government officials. Borneo's interior people also often left their villages to find work at logging camps, oil wells, or palm oil and rubber plantations as their rain forest environment and small farms rapidly disappeared, destroyed by international timber and mining operations that cut forests and stripped land to procure resources to ship to distant countries. As once-remote peoples are brought into the global system, and ethnic minorities are incorporated into nations, they find it harder to maintain their cultures and languages. Languages shape and reflect the cultures, values, and worldviews of their native speakers. Half of all languages are in danger of dying out over the next several decades, and less than 1 percent of languages are used on the Internet.

Toward the Future

⇄ TRANSITIONS

Women and men created the present world from the materials of the past and are now laying the foundation for the future. As a Belgian scholar wrote a few years ago, "We cannot predict the future, but we can prepare it."[11] But this raises the question of

what kind of future. The world's long history of war, inequality, and exploitation, even when seemingly offset by progress, does not foster optimism. Indeed, some respected experts predict human extinction if people do not adopt more sustainable ways, and scientific studies are more frequently pessimistic than optimistic about the future. In 2019 various studies suggested that humans had, at best, between ten and thirty years to avoid a climate catastrophe if we do not slow, stop, or reverse climate change now. One expert concluded that the climate crisis is our third world war. Worried that we face environment collapse, one study concluded: "Our generation is the first to be faced with decisions that will determine whether the earth our children inherit will be habitable."[12]

IMAGE VI.2 International Women's Day 2005 Women around the world became more willing to assert their rights. Activists from diverse Indian nongovernmental organizations interested in women's rights marched in New Delhi, India's capital, in 2005 to mark International Women's Day.

Q Do you think that these kind of marches and protests contribute to awareness about a cause such as women's rights?

[11] Ilya Prigogine, quoted in Federico Mayor and Jerome Bindé, *The World Ahead: Our Future in the Making* (New York: Zed Books, 2001), 1.

[12] Lester Brown et al., "A World at Risk," in *State of the World 1989* (New York: W.W. Norton, 1989), 20.

History is littered with "civilizations" that collapsed, probably in part from dramatic climate change, beginning with various Mesopotamians, the Egyptian Old Kingdom, Minoans, Mycenaeans, Harappans, and Caral (Peru) in the second millennium BCE. But the demise of these great societies also provided space for renewal and the formation of new societies and states. Four centuries after the end of the Han Empire the even more brilliant Tang dynasty came to power. The emergence of nation-states in western Europe was built on the downfall of the western Roman Empire several centuries earlier. And an even more prosperous western Europe and Japan emerged from the ashes of World War II, the most destructive war in history, in part with generous help from the United States. But this does not mean people today should be complacent about humanity's future prospects. There are many threats besides global warming that could disrupt our lives, from volcanic super-eruptions and asteroids to nuclear war, disease pandemics, weaponized biotechnology, super viruses, and rogue artificial intelligence. Some experts warn that today we are far more dependent on state and economic infrastructures and perhaps less resourceful with fewer survival skills than the peasants, pastoralists, and town-dwellers centuries or millennia ago. Collapsing societies usually generate severe social unrest, starvation, and political and economic turbulence.

Yet, since 1945 humanity has produced many green shoots of hope, such as institutions (like the European Union) that have created transnational unity or (like various United Nations agencies) fostered international cooperation on global problems, economic development in many once impoverished nations, nongovernmental organizations working for human rights and a healthier environment, and women elected presidents or prime ministers in over two dozen nations. A history not only of cruelty and exploitation but also of compassion and sacrifice provides hope in navigating troubled times. Remembering when people behaved magnificently may foster inspiration to answer the challenges. Historians sometimes view the past as a stream with banks. The stream is filled with people killing, bullying, enslaving, and doing other things historians usually record, while on the banks, unnoticed, women and men build homes, raise children, tend farms, settle disputes, sing songs, whittle statues, trade with their neighbors, and chat with travelers from other lands. Historians often ignore the banks for the stream, but what happens on the banks may be more reassuring.

For several decades some observers, believing that cultural differences will increasingly drive international politics, have forecast a clash of civilizations, such as between the Christian West and Islam or between the U.S. and China, which are seen as irreconcilably opposed in worldviews. But simplistic formulas miss the complexity of the global order. None of the great religions and the cultures that they shaped are monolithic, the divisions among Christians or Muslims, Westerners or Middle Easterners, being as great as their differences with other traditions. No cultures or religions have a monopoly on values such as peace, justice, charity, tolerance, public discussion, and goodwill. In any case, nations generally shape their foreign policies according to their national interests rather than ideology. Furthermore, thanks to the many available information sources, people can become informed about why past societies, such as the Mesopotamians and Mayans, destroyed their environments and collapsed, and how countries blundered into wars or failed to develop cooperative relations with their neighbors that maintained peace. These insights, if acquired, may help people today to avoid repeating the mistakes of the past and construct a better future.

Four centuries ago, English playwright William Shakespeare wrote that the past is prologue to the present. The study of world history allows us to ask questions about the global future because we understand the changing patterns of the global past, including the building of societies, their interactions through networks, and the great transitions that reshaped humanity. These have led to an increasingly connected world in the past fifteen hundred years. The contemporary age has been marked by a complex mix of dividing and unifying forces, unique societies differing greatly in standards of living and worldviews but linked into a global system of exchange. People today cannot yet know with certainty where the path will lead, but they can help build it. Nineteenth-century novelist Lewis Carroll (1832–1898) suggested a way of looking at the problem in his novel *Through the Looking Glass*, about Alice in Wonderland. Lost and perplexed, Alice asked the Cheshire Cat: "Would you tell me, please, which way I ought to go from here?" The enigmatic cat pondered the query for a few moments and then replied: "That depends a great deal on where you want to get to."[13] How nations, working together, deal with the world's many challenges will determine the shape of the future.

---

[13]Lewis Carroll, "Alice's Adventures in Wonderland," in *The Complete Works of Lewis Carroll* (New York: Modern Library, 1936), 71–72.

CHAPTER 26

The Remaking of the Global System, Since 1945

> *One heart, one destiny. Peace and love for all mankind. And Africa for Africans.*
>
> —Bob Marley, reggae superstar[1]

IMAGE 26.1 **Indonesian Environmental Activists Protest Single-Use Plastics** In July 2019 thousands of activists and supporters marched on the streets of Jakarta, Indonesia's largest city, to protest single-use plastics that pollute the environment, including rivers and oceans. They carried four-meter-tall Anglerfish plastic monsters made from various plastic wastes. The parade aimed to encourage the public to stop using single-use plastics and urged the government to immediately stop importing waste from abroad. The march reflected the globalization of social movements and political protests in the contemporary world.

Q What does the photo tell us about the concerns worldwide about pollution including plastics?

[1]Quoted in Adrian Boot and Chris Salewicz with Rita Marley as Senior Editor, *Bob Marley: Songs of Freedom* (London: Bloomsbury, 1995), 278.

In 1980, Jamaican reggae music star Bob Marley, a symbol of black empowerment, performed at Zimbabwe's celebration of independence from British rule. Marley's experience there reflected many late-twentieth-century political and cultural trends. His songs often dealt with issues such as poverty, racial prejudice, and asserting one's rights, realities for Zimbabweans, who had lived under an uncaring British colonial and then white supremacist government. But Marley's concert was disrupted by the local police, mostly whites, who used tear gas to disperse thousands of black Zimbabweans, often poor, outside the overcrowded stadium. The next night Marley, ignoring threats of violence against him, gave a free concert for forty thousand Zimbabweans. The violence and threats showed Marley that the social ills, economic inequalities, and ethnic hatreds he knew in Jamaica occurred elsewhere in the world. In Zimbabwe a black majority government would not solve them and made several of them worse.

Marley's career reflected a world interconnected as never before. An eloquent advocate of political and cultural freedom whose music was enjoyed around the world, Marley came from the slums of a small island of barely two million people; yet his music, an intoxicating mix of African, Caribbean, and North American traditions, touched hearts and minds across racial, political, religious, class, national, and cultural barriers. To the world, Marley personified reggae's progressive politics and spiritual quest.

Ancient thinkers such as the Buddha in India, Daoists in China, and the Greek philosopher Heraclitus claimed that nothing was permanent except change. Never was this more true than in the decades since 1945, when the pace of change quickened, the global economy grew dramatically, economic and cultural networks linked societies ever more closely, and ideas, technologies, and products flowed across porous borders, affecting people everywhere. Turbulent world politics reflected the conflict between the superpowers (the United States, Russia, later China) as well as African, Asian, and Latin American struggles for decolonization and development. Since 1989, when the Soviet bloc collapsed, the world has groped toward a new political configuration while dealing with mounting economic, political, climate change, and environmental problems and the turmoil they cause.

26-1 Decolonization, New States, and the Global System

TRANSITIONS   NETWORKS

Q How did decolonization change the global system?

The contemporary world derived both from Western imperialism and the resistance waged against it. Asia, Africa, and Latin America became major battlegrounds between the United States and the Soviet Union, superpowers with much more military, political, and economic might than other countries. Asian, African, and Latin American struggles to end Western domination and develop economically also shaped the postwar era. Nationalist movements proliferated, sometimes sparking interventions by Western powers or the Soviet Union (USSR), which were anxious to preserve their political and economic influence. Finally, the former colonies joined a global system marked by continued imbalances in wealth and power.

CONNECTION to TODAY

How did the global system that emerged from nationalism and decolonization shape the experiences of your family, community, and nation?

not necessarily major social and economic change. Colonial powers granted independence less reluctantly if nationalist leaders, in countries such as Nigeria and the Philippines, accepted continued Western control of mines, plantations, and other resources. In the second type, nationalist movements mounted by social revolutionaries inspired by Marxism sought both political independence and a new social order free of Western economic domination. Hence, in China the communists led by Mao Zedong reorganized Chinese society while limiting contact with the world economy and the United States. The third trend was represented by nationalist movements by long-repressed nonwhite majorities in white settler colonies such as Algeria and Zimbabwe, which struggled against domination by minority whites, who owned most land and resources.

26-1a Nationalism and Decolonization

Nationalism became a powerful force in Western colonies (see Chapter 25). Three types of nationalist movements developed. In most colonized societies, the goal was ending colonial rule, but

The Great Depression and World War II had intensified anticolonial feelings. Colonialism gradually crumbled, often after nationalist resistance led by charismatic figures such as

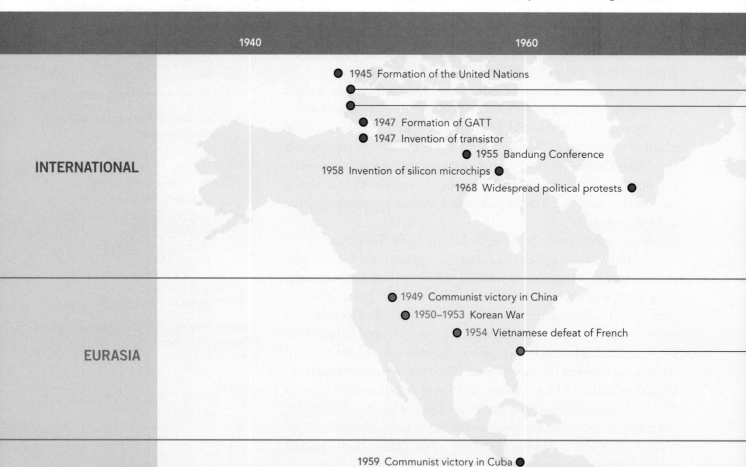

1940

1960

INTERNATIONAL

- 1945 Formation of the United Nations
- 1947 Formation of GATT
- 1947 Invention of transistor
- 1955 Bandung Conference
- 1958 Invention of silicon microchips
- 1968 Widespread political protests

EURASIA

- 1949 Communist victory in China
- 1950–1953 Korean War
- 1954 Vietnamese defeat of French

THE AMERICAS

- 1959 Communist victory in Cuba
- 1962 Cuban Missile Crisis

Mohandas Gandhi in India, Sukarno in Indonesia, and Kwame Nkrumah in Gold Coast (Ghana). Most Western colonizers realized that maintaining their control with military force against growing protests, strikes, and peasant unrest was too expensive. In 1946 the United States began the decolonization trend by granting independence to the Philippines, fulfilling a pledge made to Filipino leaders in the 1930s. Weary of suppressing nationalist resistance and political unrest, Britain gave up its rule in India and Burma. But in the process, tensions in India between Hindus and Muslims led to massive violence, killing, and land dispossession, forcing the partition of British India into two separate nations, Hindu-majority India and Muslim-majority Pakistan. In Egypt in 1952 a popular general, Abdul Gamal Nasser, led a military coup against an unpopular pro-British monarch, ending British domination. Whether peacefully or through threats or episodes of violence, between 1946 and 1975 most Western colonies in Asia, Africa, and the Caribbean achieved independence (see Map 26.1).

Some colonizers agreed to decolonization only after failing to quell nationalist uprisings. In the British white settler colony of Kenya, African nationalists supported a violent uprising known as the Mau Mau Rebellion, which targeted the white minority. The British responded by sending more troops who committed atrocities against pro-Mau Mau villages, ultimately killing ten thousand people and detaining ninety thousand

others in harsh prison camps where many died. In 1963 Kenya gained its independence. The Netherlands planned to regain Indonesia, a source of immense wealth, but battling a nationalist army proved bloody and demoralizing. Fearing regional instability, the United States pressured the Dutch to abandon their struggle in 1950. Similarly, France had no plans to abandon profitable Vietnam and Algeria, but revolutionary uprisings forced it to leave. As in Kenya, Algerian rebels supported by the Arab majority attacked white settlers while fighting five hundred thousand French troops for eight years; some two hundred-fifty thousand Algerians died until the French abandoned the fight in 1962. In Vietnam, heavy U.S. aid could not prevent humiliating French defeat by Ho Chi Minh's communist forces in 1954. The electrifying, ultimately successful anticolonial struggles by Indonesian, Vietnamese, and Algerian nationalists gave hope to colonized peoples elsewhere, warning Western powers of the heavy cost of opposing decolonization.

Both superpowers sought to capitalize on the nationalist surge. The Soviet Union generally supported nationalist movements, sometimes supplied arms to revolutionaries, and offered economic aid and diplomatic support to countries with strategic value or valuable resources, such as India, Egypt, and Indonesia. The most powerful nation, the United States, followed a mixed policy on decolonization. Wanting trade and outlets for investment in Asia and Africa, Americans encouraged the Dutch

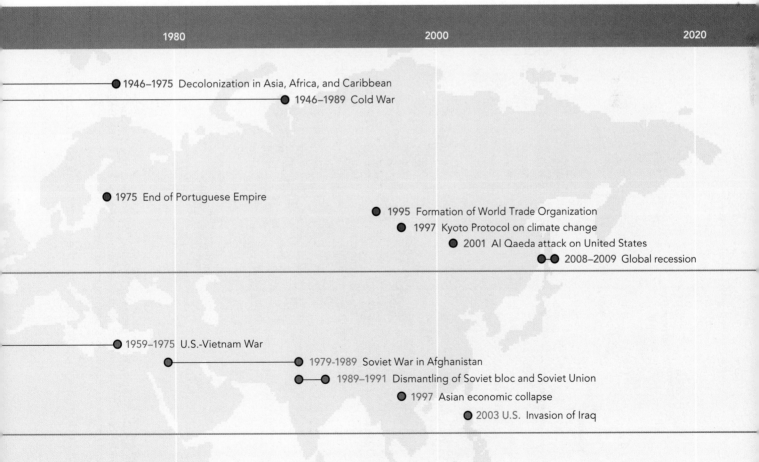

1980   2000   2020

● 1946–1975 Decolonization in Asia, Africa, and Caribbean

● 1946–1989 Cold War

● 1975 End of Portuguese Empire

● 1995 Formation of World Trade Organization

● 1997 Kyoto Protocol on climate change

● 2001 Al Qaeda attack on United States

●—● 2008–2009 Global recession

● 1959–1975 U.S.-Vietnam War

●—● 1979-1989 Soviet War in Afghanistan

●—● 1989–1991 Dismantling of Soviet bloc and Soviet Union

● 1997 Asian economic collapse

● 2003 U.S. Invasion of Iraq

● 2001 Al Qaeda attack on United States

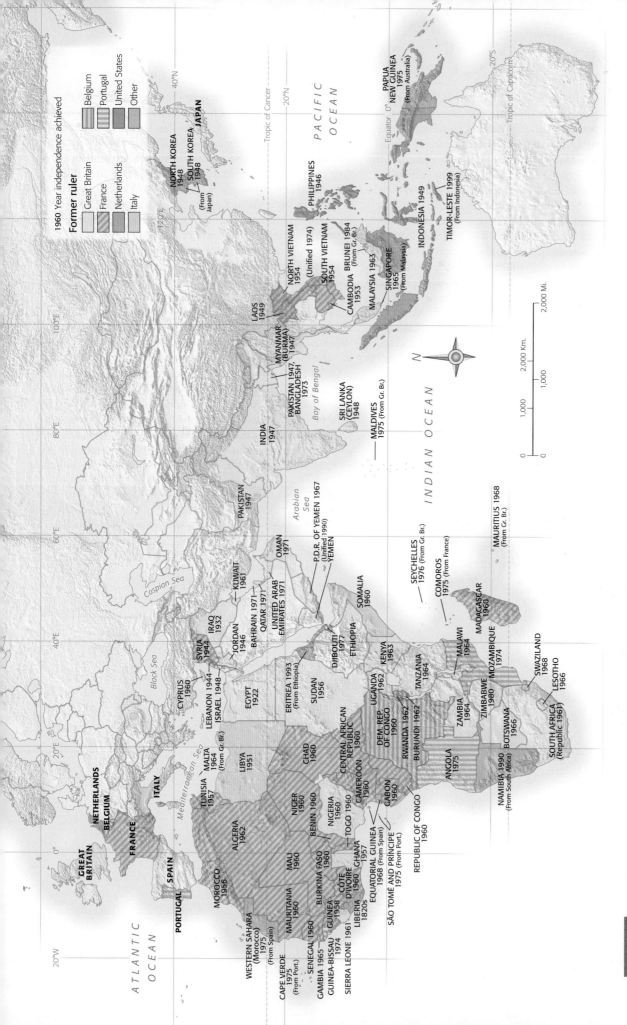

MAP 26.1 Decolonization Between 1946 and 1975 most of the Western colonies in Asia, Africa, and the Caribbean won their independence, with the greatest number achieving independence in the 1960s. The decolonization reshaped the political map, particularly of Africa, South Asia, and Southeast Asia.

Q What does the map tell us about the chronology of decolonization?

to leave Indonesia and urged independence for some British colonies in Africa, but they also opposed communism and Soviet influence. Fearing left-wing nationalism, as in French-ruled Vietnam and Portuguese-ruled Mozambique, the United States supported continued colonial power, no matter how unpopular, helping finance French and Portuguese military efforts to suppress revolutionaries. Portugal stubbornly resisted decolonization until festering African rebellions, growing demoralization at home, and the toppling of its fascist dictator forced it to abandon its African empire in 1975.

Colonialism did not completely disappear. By the 1980s the major remaining territorial empire, the USSR, strained to repress the nationalist demands of the Baltic, Caucasus, and Central Asian peoples it ruled. The Soviet Empire was largely dismantled between 1989 and 1991, when the communist system collapsed. Britain and France retained direct control of a few islands, mostly in the South Pacific, South Atlantic, and Caribbean, and some outposts such as French Guiana in South America. The United States still maintains a few territories that are mostly self-governing, including Puerto Rico and the Virgin Islands in the Caribbean and a few Pacific islands such as American Samoa and Guam.

Decolonization often produced neocolonialism, or continuing Western political and economic influence. In the Philippines, Americans maintained a major economic role, governments loyally supported U.S. foreign policies until recently, and Filipinos avidly consumed American products and popular culture such as music, film, and fashion. Similarly, the French controlled much of the economy and advised the government in Cote d'Ivoire **(COAT dee-VWAHR)** (Ivory Coast), and many Ivoirians favored French cuisine, literature, and language. A West Indian–born black writer offered a radical nationalist but oversimplified view of neocolonialism: "The colonial power says, 'Since you want independence, take it and starve' [after economic aid ends]. Other countries refuse to undergo this ordeal and agree to [accept] the conditions of the former guardian power."[2] Some Asian and African intellectuals advocated "decolonizing the mind," to escape what Bob Marley called the "mental slavery" that kept formerly colonized people in awe of Western power, wealth, and culture. This sometimes meant building a nationalist culture reflecting local traditions or abandoning Western languages in literature. For example, Kenyan novelist Ngugi wa Thiongo **(en-GOO-gey wah they-ON-go)** switched from English to his native Kikuyu.

26-1b Social Revolutionary States

During the twentieth century, revolutionary activity in Asia, Africa, and Latin America, intensified by the drive to end Western domination, often engaged peasants impoverished by loss of land or declining crop prices. Amilcar Cabral **(AM-ill-car ka-BRAWL)** (1924–1973), the revolutionary leader in Portugal's colony of Guinea Bissau **(GIN-ee bi-SOW)**, advised other Marxist intellectuals to "always bear in mind that the people are not fighting for ideas, for the things in anyone's head. They are fighting to live better, and in peace, to guarantee the future of their children."[3] Between 1949 and 1980 social revolutionaries fought their way to power in several countries or colonies including China, Vietnam, Algeria, Cuba, Nicaragua, Angola, and Mozambique. Opposed by the United States, they looked to the USSR for political, economic, and military support. Revolutionary movements were also active, although ultimately frustrated, in various other Latin American and Southeast Asian countries.

Thinkers and activists around the world, such as the West Indian–born psychiatrist and writer Frantz Fanon (1925–1961), who joined the anti-French movement while working in colonial Algeria, often romanticized the revolutionaries' promise to create more just societies. While social revolutionary governments often raised the status and living standards of the poor, they also became bureaucratic, despotic, and intolerant of dissent, frequently compiling poor human rights records. Influenced by Stalinism, they had uneven relations with capitalist nations. These states usually limited their involvement with the world economy, instead creating planned economies in which governments rather than free markets drove policies. Nevertheless, many people welcomed the end of the uncaring, often repressive governments the revolutions replaced.

Social revolutionary approaches brought mixed results. Civil wars or rebellions sidetracked some revolutions. The United States and white-ruled South Africa supported and subsidized rebels in Angola who fought the Marxist government

IMAGE 26.2 **African Independence** In 1957 the former British colony of the Gold Coast became independent. In this photo from the independence celebration in the capital, Accra, the new prime minister, Kwame Nkrumah, waves to the joyous crowd. The name Ghana derived from a great West African state and empire, which reached its zenith a millennia ago.

Q Why do you think the Ghanaians chose the name of a kingdom from the Middle Ages for their new country?

Bettmann/Getty Images

---

[2]Frantz Fanon, *The Wretched of the Earth* (New York: Grove, 1968), 97–98.
[3]Quoted in Goran Hyden, *Beyond Ujamaa in Tanzania: Underdevelopment and an Uncaptured Peasantry* (Berkeley: University of California Press, 1980), 202.

there for over two decades, a struggle that cost over two hundred thousand lives and ruined the country. In contrast, between 1949 and 1978 communist-ruled China increased its economic potential and addressed social problems, even while it severely limited personal freedom and fiercely repressed dissent. Some version of Maoism also inspired uprisings in several countries, including Cambodia and Peru, and some radicals in other countries. After market reforms in 1978 that rejected Maoist economics China sparked even more rapid growth, modifying socialism with foreign investment and some free enterprise. China's shift, followed by that of Vietnam, toward market economies and participation in the world economy suggested that revolutions could gain control of local resources from foreign interests and their local collaborators but not raise living standards to the levels of richer nations. China and Vietnam discovered that free markets created more wealth than socialism but did not necessarily foster an equitable wealth distribution, breeding explosive social tensions.

26-1c A New Global System

A new global system emerged after 1945. A few great Western powers, led by Britain and France, dominated the prewar world, ruling over vast empires in Asia, Africa, the Pacific, and the Caribbean. Decolonization and the rise of the United States and Soviet Union to superpower status modified this pattern, dividing the world, some scholars argued, into three categories characterized by different levels of economic development and power. The **First World** comprised the industrialized democracies of western Europe, North America, Australia–New Zealand, and Japan. The **Second World** referred to communist nations, led by the USSR and China. Most societies in Asia, Africa, Latin America, and the Caribbean, grouped as the **Third World**, were linked by mass poverty and Western colonization or neocolonialism. Some experts added a fourth category, the **Fourth World**, that comprised the poorest societies, with small economies and few exploitable resources, such as Laos, Afghanistan, Haiti, and Mali. However, critics contended that lumping the world's societies—with very different histories, cultures, and global connections—into a few categories was misleading. Furthermore, after the 1970s the global system changed, diminishing the descriptive value and usage of the simplistic "three worlds" concept. Countries such as Malaysia, South Korea, Dubai (doo-BYE), Brazil, and Chile, once grouped with the Third World, achieved rapid economic growth, and the communist systems often collapsed. Today some specialists group the world geographically: a highly developed North (North America, Europe, northern Asia) and the developing South.

First World The industrialized democracies of western Europe, North America, Australia–New Zealand, and Japan.

Second World The communist nations, led by the USSR and China.

Third World Societies in Asia, Africa, Latin America, and the Caribbean, which were shaped by mass poverty and a legacy of colonization or neocolonialism.

Fourth World The poorest societies, with very small economies and few exploitable resources.

Most Western nations and Japan enjoyed new heights of prosperity from the 1960s through the 1980s. After World War II the United States offered generous aid and investment to its allies (which now included defeated Japan), jump-starting a renewal of economic growth in industrialized, diversified countries that already had literate, skilled, and mostly urban populations. Hence, western Europe and Japan recovered and prospered. Japan's economy increased fivefold between 1953 and 1973, the fastest economic growth in world history. Western and Japanese businesses invested around the world, spurring international trade, and Japan and West Germany became the second and third largest capitalist economies. By the 1970s several Western nations, such as West Germany, Sweden, Canada, and Australia, had standards of living similar to those in the United States but far more income equality.

Although economic growth rates often slowed after 1990, Western prosperity relative to the rest of the world continued. Each year the United Nations issues its Human Development Report, which rates the quality of life of every country and territory by examining per capita income, health, and literacy. Over the past two decades Norway, Sweden, Australia, Canada, Iceland, Switzerland, and the Netherlands have been consistently rated among the most livable nations. A hundred years earlier Norway and Sweden were among the poorest European countries. Sweden achieved the world's lowest poverty rate, largely because the state provides each citizen free education, subsidized health care, and other welfare benefits, and the economy grew steadily. The 2018 report ranks Norway (which also topped another U.N. survey for happiness), Switzerland, Australia, Ireland, and Germany as the top five; along with Japan (19), three once-poor Asian societies made the top 25: Hong Kong (7), Singapore (9), and South Korea (22). Canada ranked 12th, the United States 13th, the United Kingdom 14th, Russia 49th, and China 86th. Of the 189 nations, colonies, and territories examined, the 2018 report ranks 38 nations, mostly in sub-Saharan Africa, as having the lowest development and quality of life—massive poverty, inadequate health care, and low literacy. The late Tanzanian president Julius Nyerere (nye-RE-re) put the gap between rich and poor nations in perspective: "While the United States is trying to reach the moon, Tanzania is trying to reach its villages."[4] Yet, in the past two decades some of the poorest African nations such as Botswana and Ghana have also enjoyed modest economic growth and become middle income nations.

In the later twentieth and early twenty-first centuries some nations had more political stability and resources to help their citizens thrive. Richer nations, usually benefiting from democracy, were nation-states with cohesive societies. However, some contained restless ethnic or religious minorities. For example, in northern Spain Basques, whose language and identity differ completely from those of the Spanish majority, as well as many Catalans, sought autonomy or independence. The two major ethnic groups in Belgium have quarreled for decades over maintaining or dividing their nation. Some French Canadians sporadically seek more autonomy or independence. Over the years some nations welcomed immigrants but in the 2010s many European countries as well as the United States, Australia,

---

[4]Quoted in Jennifer Seymour Whitaker, *How Can Africa Survive?* (New York: Harper and Row, 1988), 13.

and South Africa were engulfed in heated debates over influxes in immigrants, refugees, and asylum-seekers. But democratic governments mostly diminished social tensions, while generous social services prevented mass poverty. Many western European states, Canada, and New Zealand adopted ambitious welfare systems with comprehensive national health insurance, promoting social justice and equality. Poorer nations, having small budgets, limited resources, and often highly diverse populations, faced greater challenges in building stable nation-states. Abandoning communism and its safety net sometimes sparked violence, such as the repeated ethnic conflicts in Yugoslavia that

produced brutal atrocities and forced expulsion of minorities. Only a few non-European nations, such as Sri Lanka and oil-rich Brunei and Saudi Arabia, tried to mount welfare states with free education and health care, but they struggled to pay for them. World economic conditions can influence nations' abilities to finance their agenda. For example, the global economic crisis of 2008–2009 forced many nations to cut back spending and millions of people lost their jobs. Re-establishing economic growth and stability took some years. The trade war sparked by the United States in 2018 has also caused instability in the global system and world economy.

KEY POINTS

▶ Between 1946 and 1975, most Western colonies achieved independence, in many cases as a result of violent opposition movements, though the United States continued to oppose leftist movements and the Soviet Union's vast colonial empire endured until 1989.

▶ Western nations maintained a great deal of influence over the economy and culture of many of their former colonies, which led some intellectuals to call for "decolonizing the mind."

▶ Revolutionary regimes, often inspired by Marxism, came to power in a number of Asian, African, and Latin

American nations, though they met with mixed economic success and in some cases were embroiled in long-term civil war.

▶ The division of the world's nations into First, Second, and Third Worlds grew blurry as some Third World nations developed First World–level economies and the Soviet Union collapsed, though democratic countries tended to be more stable and offer more support to their citizens.

26-2 Cold War, Hot Wars, and World Politics

▓ NETWORKS ⇄ TRANSITIONS

Q What roles did the Cold War and superpower rivalry play in world politics?

A new global political configuration emerged after World War II and indelibly shaped the world we live in today, especially in politics, military affairs, and economics. From 1946 to 1989 the two major superpowers, the United States and the USSR, engaged in the **Cold War**, competing for allies and engaging in occasional warfare against their rival's allies rather than each other directly. Americans enjoyed much greater influence and boasted more allies. While the Cold War did not lead to direct U.S.–Soviet military conflict, it produced chronic tensions and generated covert and military interventions by each superpower seeking to block gains by the other. The globalization of the Cold War created the foundations for most of today's international conflicts. The changes that followed the end of the Cold War generated a new global system blending both Cold War and post–Cold War features.

> **CONNECTION to TODAY**
>
> How were your family, community, and nation affected by the Cold War and the wars it generated?

to influence and shape politics and economics as well as gaining allies in Eastern Europe, China, Southeast Asia, India, Africa, the Middle East, and Latin America. Americans considered the "loss of China," their long-time ally, and then Vietnam and Cuba to communism as disasters to U.S. interests. For their part the Soviets resented U.S. dominance of world resources, feared U.S. military power, and considered Soviet control of Eastern Europe to be an essential buffer against the Western nations and their liberal ideas. Americans had feared communism since the early twentieth century, sometimes leading to "red scares" that harassed or arrested left-wing Americans. From the late 1940s until the early 1960s this led to McCarthyism, with congressional investigations and harassment of people who were left-leaning, only some of them communists or pro-Soviet. U.S. schools and media promoted patriotic and anticommunist views. Soviet leaders promoted anti-U.S. views among the Soviet people and were in constant search for U.S. spies, especially during the Stalin years.

26-2a The Cold War: A Divided World

The world took on a bipolar political character, with two rival superpowers and their respective allies. Nations practicing capitalism and often democracy, led by the United States, opposed those promoting socialist authoritarianism, led by the USSR and known as the Soviet bloc. Some of the conflicts involved competition

For over four decades U.S.–USSR relations were a major factor in international

Cold War A conflict lasting from 1946 to 1989 in which the United States and the USSR competed for allies and engaged in occasional warfare against their rival's allies rather than against each other directly.

affairs. Americans sought to contain communism, whereas the USSR worked to spread communism and undercut U.S. influence. For several decades leaders of nations such as Egypt, India, and Indonesia promoted nonalignment with either superpower. In 1955 leaders from twenty-nine nonaligned Asian and African countries met in Bandung, Indonesia, to promote a Third World bloc, but they had trouble sustaining unity. The United States, the world's most powerful nation, enjoyed far greater wealth, military force, and cultural influence than any other country. In 1945, Americans already had the atomic bomb, produced half the world's industrial output, and held two-thirds of the gold. Now they assumed a heavy financial and military burden to maintain their leading role in world affairs and promote economic growth, obtaining resources and preserving profitable markets.

By 1948 the Soviets controlled all of eastern Europe and were allied with communist Mongolia and North Korea. Perceiving the USSR as rivals for world influence, Americans tried to prevent communists from controlling China and then fought the Korean War (1950–1953) to stop North Koreans from forcibly reunifying the Korean peninsula. Despite U.S. efforts, communist regimes came to power in China in 1949, North Vietnam in 1954, and Cuba in 1959. Furthermore, waging the Cold War and widely using military force, including long wars in Korea and Vietnam, cost the United States $4 to $5 trillion and some one hundred-thirteen thousand American lives, mostly soldiers, between 1946 and 1989.

Historians debate whether the USSR ever posed a serious military threat and how much each side misinterpreted its rival's motives and actions. Remembering centuries of invasions from the west and fearing the United States and its western European allies' combined military power, the USSR occupied eastern Europe as a buffer zone. Mistrusting Soviet leaders and despising communism, Americans viewed themselves as protecting freedom; the Soviets claimed they were helping the world's exploited masses and fighting imperialism. Some scholars argue that both the U.S. and the Soviet Union had much in common with each other, including views of history. Both believed that they represented in the present what the rest of the world would look like in the future, that the momentum of history was on their side. The Soviet vision (but not necessarily China's modified version) has proven wrong but whether the future looks American in a rapidly changing world remains to be seen.

Some historians believe the Cold War brought stability; others point to some eighty wars between 1945 and 1989, generating twenty million deaths and perhaps twenty million refugees. Cold War rivalries dragged in emerging nations, sparking upheavals that bankrupted economies and devastated societies. Varied small conflicts involved surrogates, governments, or movements allied to one superpower and fighting the troops from the other superpower. In Korea and Vietnam U.S. troops battled not Soviet armies but Soviet-supported local communist forces; the USSR sent military supplies and advisers to help Vietnamese communists fight

guerrilla warfare An unconventional military strategy of avoiding full-scale direct confrontations in favor of small-scale skirmishes.

first the French and then the United States, which supported a pro-Western government in South Vietnam after the French were defeated. Some historians argue that nationalism was a more important factor than communist ideology for the Vietnamese fighting the French and then the United States. Whatever the case communists controlled Vietnam by 1975. Americans also used surrogates, such as the Islamic insurgents fighting the Soviets in Afghanistan in the 1980s. Insurgencies often used **guerrilla warfare**, an unconventional military strategy of avoiding full-scale direct confrontations in favor of small-scale skirmishes, including hit-and-run attacks, sniping, land mines, and roadside bombs.

Both superpowers intervened, both covertly and militarily, to protect their interests. The USSR sent military forces into Poland, Hungary, and Czechoslovakia to crush anti-Soviet movements and into Afghanistan to support a pro-Soviet government. Some invasions proved disastrous; the heavy losses and humiliating withdrawal from Afghanistan in 1989 contributed to the Soviet system's collapse. Communist parties became a strong presence in nations like France, Italy, Indonesia, India, and Chile, at least for a time, participating openly in politics, but other communists launched unsuccessful insurgencies in countries such as Peru, Malaysia, and the Philippines. Meanwhile, the United States actively sought to shape the political and economic direction of Asian, African, and Latin American societies; Americans generously donated food, provided disaster relief and medical assistance, offered technical advice, supported democratic organizations, and sometimes promoted human rights. But other efforts destabilized or helped overthrow governments deemed unfriendly to U.S. business and political interests, including left-leaning but democratically elected regimes in Brazil, Chile, and Guatemala.

One of the earliest U.S. interventions came in 1953 in oil-rich Iran. A nationalist but noncommunist regime angered the Americans and British by nationalizing British- and U.S.-owned oil companies that sent most of their huge profits abroad and paid Iranian workers under fifty cents a day. In response, Britain and the United States imposed an economic boycott to prevent Iran from selling its oil abroad. American agents recruited disaffected military officers and paid Iranians to spark riots that paralyzed the capital, forcing the nationalists from power and installing a pro-U.S. but despotic and corrupt government under the king (shah), who returned from exile. For the first time ever the United States had overthrown a foreign government outside the Western Hemisphere. Ever since, many Iranians have hated and feared the United States.

To critics, the U.S. interventions constituted imperialism. They often proved costly as well. The U.S.-Vietnam war cost vast sums of money, killed some fifty-eight thousand Americans and several million Vietnamese on all sides, and forced Americans to negotiate for peace and withdraw, harming U.S. prestige in the world. The war also created economic problems and political divisions in the United States, reducing American willingness to exercise military power. Meanwhile, the USSR and China spent scarce resources supplying their communist allies. In 1968 the Cold War and the hot wars that it generated contributed to an outbreak of massive unrest, protests, and social movements in various countries, among them the United States, Mexico, Guatemala, Brazil, Japan, India, Tanzania, Senegal, France, Germany, Czechoslovakia, and Britain. The protesters, most of them young, were outraged by the Vietnam War, Soviet imperialism, U.S. president Richard Nixon, social and economic inequality, racism, the treatment of women, and exploitation of "Third World" countries. The unrest continued on a smaller scale into the 1970s.

The Cold War years were also marked by **terrorism**, which involves small-scale but violent attacks, often on civilian targets, that are aimed at undermining governments or demoralizing populations. Terrorist activities have expanded to global dimensions, reshaping world politics. After 1945 Palestinians under Israeli control, Basque nationalists in Spain, and Irish nationalists in Britain, among others, engaged in terrorism for their causes. Some states (such as white-ruled South Africa) sponsored terrorism against unfriendly governments or political movements. For example, the United States sponsored terrorism against leftist-ruled Nicaragua in the 1980s, helping form a military force, the *Contras*, who often attacked civilian targets such as rural schools, day care centers, and clinics. Some terrorist networks have operated on a global level, with branches in many countries. The most active, formed by militant Islamists, have capitalized on widespread Muslim anger at their own governments, U.S. foreign policies, and Israel (for its treatment of Palestinians), attacking politicians, police, Western residents and tourists, and Israeli and U.S. targets, often with suicide and car bombings.

When the Soviets intervened militarily in 1979 to support a pro-Soviet government in Afghanistan, Middle Eastern and Pakistani militants helped the Muslim Afghan resistance. In 1988 the most extreme foreign fighters came together in a jihadi organization, *Al Qaeda* ("The Base"), formed by the Saudi Osama bin Laden (1957–2011). From an extremely wealthy family and trained as an engineer, bin Laden used his wealth to support Afghan rebels, who were also funded and armed by the United States as part of its Cold War rivalry with the USSR. After the Soviets abandoned Afghanistan in 1989, bin Laden established Al Qaeda cells elsewhere, including Saudi Arabia, Egypt, and Iraq, whose governments he viewed as corrupt or as suppressing Islamic militants. To recruit, support, and communicate with members, Al Qaeda took advantage of the information superhighway—the Internet—using websites, e-mail, satellite phones, and videotapes. Bin Laden, ruthlessly willing to kill innocent people, plotted terrorism against his former Afghan resistance ally, the United States. Attacks on U.S. targets, including embassies, caused hundreds of casualties. Al Qaeda's 2001 aerial attacks in the United States prompted the U.S. to invade and wage wars in Afghanistan and then Iraq.

26-2b The Nuclear Arms Race and Global Militarization

The Cold War generated a superpower arms race and increased global militarization. Both superpowers developed first atomic and then **nuclear weapons**, explosive devices that owe their destructive power to energy released by either splitting or fusing atoms, the most deadly result of the technological surge extending back through Einstein to Newton and the Scientific Revolution of the Early Modern Era. A nuclear explosion produces a powerful blast, intense heat, and deadly radiation. The United States dropped the first atomic bombs on Japan to end World War II. Both superpowers eventually developed even more deadly nuclear warheads, placing them on missiles. The growth of nuclear arsenals represented the most dangerous part of a larger trend toward expanding war-making ability by many nations.

Since 1945 the world has lived in the shadow of nuclear weapons; a small number could reduce whole countries to radioactive rubble. Einstein, fretting that unleashed atomic power changed everything except ways of thinking, worried that leaders would create a global catastrophe by rashly using these technologies. Fortunately these weapons were never used after 1945, although the world was close to nuclear confrontations on several occasions. For example, in 1962 President John F. Kennedy (1917–1963) demanded that the USSR remove nuclear missiles secretly planted in Cuba, ninety miles from Florida, but vetoed a U.S. invasion or nuclear attack that might have sparked all-out nuclear war. His firm stance created a tense crisis, ultimately forcing the Soviets to withdraw them. Years later we learned that a Soviet submarine commander armed but did not fire a nuclear missile at Florida, averting catastrophe.

The Cold War fostered what some historians call a "balance of terror," with both superpowers unwilling to use their weapons out of fear that the other would retaliate. Historians debate whether the nuclear arms race preserved peace by discouraging all-out U.S.–USSR military confrontations or unsettled international politics, wasting trillions of dollars. Britain, France, China, India, and Pakistan also constructed or acquired nuclear bombs. Today North Korea and probably Israel have nuclear capabilities and, thanks to the U.S. withdrawal in 2017 from an international agreement to prevent a nuclear-armed Iran, that country may now develop these weapons. In 1987 the two superpowers negotiated the first of several successive treaties reducing nuclear arms, and a nuclear conflict involving the United States, Britain, Russia, and China seemed unlikely for many years. But India–Pakistan relations have remained tense and concerns grew about nuclear proliferation, especially if North Korea or Pakistan sold bombs to other countries or terrorist groups. And North Korea, isolated in world affairs, remains a wild card. Some outside the West argued that a few powerful nations' monopoly on such weapons was unfair. In 2019 the U.S. abandoned a landmark Cold War-era intermediate nuclear missile agreement with Russia, arguing that Russia had been cheating on it by developing new missiles. Russia, which had long accused the U.S. of similar cheating, followed suit. Critics of the treaty argued that the agreement did not include China or more recent missile technologies. But many experts warn that this may generate a new and very costly arms race between the U.S., Russia, and now China and make the world more dangerous.

The proportion of total world production and spending devoted to militaries grew dramatically during the Cold War.

terrorism Small-scale but violent attacks aimed at undermining a government or demoralizing a population.

nuclear weapons Explosive devices that owe their destructive power to the energy released by either splitting or fusing atoms.

By 1985, the world spent more on military forces and weapons than the combined income of the poorest half of the world's countries. The two superpowers together, with 11 percent of the world population, accounted for 60 percent of military spending, 25 percent of the armed forces, and 97 percent of nuclear weapons. They also sold conventional weapons to other countries.

Although the U.S. and the Soviet Union avoided any direct military actions against each other, the smaller wars since 1945 have caused enormous casualties, three-fourths of them civilians. For example, two million people died during China's civil war (1945–1949); eight hundred thousand during India's violent partition (1948); two million during the American-Vietnamese War; one million during the Nigerian civil war (1967); some twenty-four hundred Americans and eighty thousand Afghans and forty-five hundred Americans and two hundred-forty thousand Iraqis died in the American-led wars on Afghanistan and Iraq, respectively; and perhaps as many as half a million people in the Syrian Civil War (2011–today). Most recently at least eighteen thousand Yeminis have been killed or wounded from aerial bombing in the Yemen civil war (2015–present), which also involves Saudi Arabia, the United Arab Republic, and the U.S. supporting one side against Iran-backed rebels. Yemen today is facing the world's worst famine in the past hundred years. A U.N. study reported that twelve thousand children were killed or injured in armed conflicts around the world in 2018. Millions perished from genocide. Hence, some two million Cambodians died in the 1970s from the Cambodian civil war (which involved the U.S.), followed by mass killings by the Maoist Khmer Rouge victors. In the 1990s members of the Hutu majority slaughtered minority Tutsis in Rwanda (**roo-AHN-duh**), and extremist Serbs killed Bosnian and Albanian Muslims in Yugoslavia, in what they called "ethnic cleansing." The United States and western European nations sent in troops to restore order in Yugoslavia, punishing the worst human rights violators. Since 2015 Myanmar military forces have killed (perhaps twenty-five hundred), brutalized, raped, or forced into exile or refugee camps in neighboring countries many of the minority Muslim Rohingya. Some scholars think the ethnic or religion-based massacres in Sudan, Syria, and the eastern Congo constituted genocide.

26-2c Global Organizations and Activism

More than ever before in history, public and private organizations with a global reach and mission have promoted political cooperation and addressed various social, political, economic, and environmental issues. The largest effort to cooperate for the common good, the United Nations, founded in 1945 with fifty-one members, became a key debate forum and agency for improving global conditions. The United Nations Charter enumerated the founding principles: "To develop friendly relations among nations based on respect for … equal rights and self-determination of peoples and … strengthen universal peace." The founding members aimed to "save succeeding generations from the scourge of war, reaffirm faith in fundamental rights,

and respect international law."[5] As colonies gaining independence joined, the organization grew to nearly two hundred member states. The United Nations has also sponsored humanitarian agencies such as the World Health Organization, which monitors diseases, funds medical research, and promotes public health, and the United Nations Children Fund (UNICEF), which promotes children's welfare and education. Such programs have dramatically reduced deaths from malnutrition and infectious diseases, helping increase average life expectancy from age forty-five in 1900 to age seventy-two in 2018, and have greatly reduced the risk of mothers dying in childbirth. However, critics believe that political differences have often obstructed the United Nations' work.

The five major powers of 1945 (the United States, China, Britain, France, and the USSR) have enjoyed permanent seats with veto power in the policymaking United Nations Security Council, and both superpowers have vetoed decisions challenging their national interests. Hence, the United States vetoed resolutions aimed at penalizing Israel and until 1971 also blocked the communist government from occupying China's United Nations seat. The Security Council sometimes sent peacekeeping troops into troubled countries and discouraged, but could not prevent, states from resorting to force. To gain support for military action, nations often made their case before the Security Council and sometimes received support; a United States–led United Nations military force repulsed a North Korean invasion of South Korea as part of the Korean War. However, nations often ignored other nations' disapproval, as the United States did when it invaded Iraq in 2003. In recent years support has built, so far unsuccessfully, to give several emerging nations, such as Brazil and India, and perhaps acknowledged powers like Japan and Germany, permanent Security Council seats.

Nations have also forged international agreements and treaties. By 1975 one hundred eighty-three nations had signed a ban on biological weapons. In 1997, one hundred thirty-two nations prohibited the production, use, and export of land mines, which kill and injure civilians years after conflicts end. In 1997 most nations also signed the Kyoto Protocol, pledging to reduce the harmful gases contributing to global warming and environmental degradation, but follow-up conferences such as in Paris in 2016, while forging some modest agreement on addressing greenhouse gas emissions, adaptation, and finance, failed to impose strict regulations on the world, partly because of the strong opposition of several nations including the U.S. In 2002 a treaty established an International Criminal Court to prosecute perpetrators of genocide, war crimes, and crimes against humanity. The U.S. and several other industrial nations have consistently refused to ratify these modest efforts to reduce weapons, promote environmental stability, and establish accountability for international crimes.

Private organizations and activists have also addressed issues of peace, social justice, health, refugees, famine, conflict resolution, and environmental protection. For example, Doctors Without Borders offers medical personnel, and Amnesty International works to free political prisoners. Some religious leaders have

---

[5]The quotes are in Choi Chatterjee et al., *The 20th Century: A Retrospective* (Boulder, CO: Westview Press, 2002), 153, 306.

promoted world peace, justice, and humanitarian issues. The Dalai Lama (b. 1935), the highest Tibetan Buddhist spiritual leader, won the Nobel Peace Prize in 1989 for promoting human rights, nonviolent conflict resolution, and understanding among different religions. In 1997 he pleaded, "We all have a special responsibility to create a better world. No one loses, and everyone gains by a shared universal sense of responsibility to this planet and all living things on it."[6] The Aga Khan IV (b. 1936), spiritual leader of a largely Indian Shi'ite Muslim sect, has funded schools and clinics all over the world. The World Council of Churches, supported by diverse Protestant and Eastern Orthodox churches, has encouraged interfaith cooperation and understanding. Several Catholic popes have favored interfaith dialogue and denounced war and capital punishment, and some clergy work on humanitarian issues.

26-2d World Politics Since 1989

Between 1989 and 1991 the Soviet bloc disintegrated and communist regimes in eastern Europe and the USSR collapsed, ending the Cold War and the bipolar world it defined. Many historians conclude that no country or person "won" the Cold War, which was fueled by misconceptions and nearly bankrupted both sides. Other nations, especially Japan and West Germany, both protected by U.S. military bases, gained the most by investing heavily in economic growth. As U.S. and Soviet leaders de-escalated tensions in the later 1980s, the United States became the sole superpower. By 2019 it spent as much on defense ($649 billion) annually as the next seven biggest spenders combined and was the world's major supplier of arms. Some observers perceived a multipolar system since 1989 in which the United States, despite its power, had to share political and economic leadership with western Europe and several Asian nations, especially China, Japan, and India. Others perceive one superpower, the United States. Since 2009 five influential nations—Brazil, Russia, India, China, and South Africa—known as the BRICS, have increasingly cooperated in many areas, providing an alternative to the Western alliance. But by 2017 some experts considered the BRICS a fading force, with all but China facing serious political and/or economic problems. In 2018–2019 China has experienced slower growth but remains the engine of the world economy, second only to the U.S. in economic power. Some observers identify several informal groupings of market economies, including the "Asian Tigers" (Hong Kong, Taiwan, South Korea, Singapore) and the

Xinhua/Alamy Stock Photo

IMAGE 26.3 **The United Nations General Assembly** The United Nations General Assembly meets regularly to discuss and vote on various issues of global importance. In this photo from July 2019, the Assembly president, Maria Fernanda Espinosa Garces, addresses a meeting on observing the annual Nelson Mandela International Day. In the spirit of the late South African leader, the U.N. leaders called for actions on fighting hate speech.

Q What does the photo tell us about the diverse leadership of the General Assembly?

[6]Dalai Lama, *My Land and My People* (New York: Warner Books, 1997), x.

692 **CHAPTER 26** The Remaking of the Global System, Since 1945

MINTs (Mexico, Indonesia, Nigeria, Turkey), but their prospects ebb and flow. The more organized European Union has faced challenges but remains influential. But political and economic developments beginning in 2017, including trade wars, tensions in the Western alliance, the rise of antiglobalization and antimultilateralism forces, and U.S.–China rivalry, have unsettled and destabilized the global system, perhaps leading to some reshuffling of world leadership over the next few years.

The first major post-Cold War challenge for the United States came from Iraq's brutal dictator, Saddam Hussein (1937–2006), whose army invaded and occupied Iraq's small, oil-rich neighbor, Kuwait, in 1990. Opposing Iran's Islamic government, the United States had supported Saddam's military with weapons in the 1980s, when Iraq fought Iran. The United States organized an international coalition and, in 1991, quickly pushed the Iraqis out of Kuwait. U.S. president George H. W. Bush proclaimed a "new world order" led by the U.S. and, based on American values, envisioned the U.S. as a world policeman.

However, a new world disorder characterized the 1990s. Ethnic and nationalist conflicts exploded in violence in Yugoslavia, eastern Europe, Sri Lanka, West Africa, and Rwanda. States with weak or dysfunctional governments, among them Haiti, Liberia, Sierra Leone, Congo, Sudan, and Somalia, experienced chronic fighting and civil war. Rising tides of religious militancy or conflict between rival faiths complicated politics in countries such as India, Pakistan, Indonesia, Algeria, Egypt, and Nigeria. In particular, militant Islam demonstrated its potency in Iran, Sudan, and Afghanistan; extremists formed terrorist groups to fight moderate Islamic regimes, Israel, and Western nations. By the early 2000s Islamic radicals posed a greater challenge in southern Asia and the Middle East than declining communist movements. Aggressive dictators, such as Iraq's Saddam Hussein, and ultra-repressive North Korea, which limited contact with the outside world, fostered regional tensions. In 2008–2009 a severe global recession added to the problems; businesses closed, world trade declined, and national economies floundered. The "Arab spring" (2011–2013) displaced or challenged various authoritarian regimes but also left in its wake violence and instability, from riots and terrorism to rival militias and civil wars, in countries like Egypt, Syria, Libya, and Yemen. The new world order promise of a peaceful world moving toward democracy foundered as proliferating regional, nationalist, religious, and ethnic conflicts, combined with economic collapse, produced a context for violence.

On September 11, 2001, Al Qaeda members hijacked U.S. commercial airliners and crashed them into New York's World Trade Center, a Pennsylvania farm field, and the Pentagon near Washington, D.C., killing nearly three thousand people, mostly civilians. The attacks, shocking Americans and the world, prompted U.S. president George W. Bush to declare a war on terrorism. U.S. forces attacked Al Qaeda bases in Afghanistan and occupied the country, whose Islamist government shielded bin Laden; but Americans still faced years of resistance from Islamic militants, the Taliban. Americans finally killed bin Laden in his Pakistan hiding place in 2011. But U.S. troops were still in Afghanistan in 2019 fighting an Islamist resistance that now controls much of the country, making the conflict the longest war in U.S. history.

In 2003 the United States, claiming that Saddam Hussein's Iraq was closely linked to Al Qaeda and possessed weapons of mass destruction, invaded Iraq, removed Saddam's brutal government, and imposed a U.S. military occupation supported chiefly by Britain. However, U.S. troops found no evidence of Al Qaeda ties or weapons of mass destruction. The occupation sparked an Iraqi insurgency, unleashing sectarian divisions that hindered U.S. efforts to stabilize and rebuild Iraq. Islamists flocked to Iraq to attack Americans and destabilize the country, forming the basis for a new terrorist foe, the Islamic State (ISIS), which recruited thousands of Islamist volunteers from around the world. Eventually violence in Iraq diminished and the last U.S. combat troops withdrew in 2011. But the war alienated many U.S. allies and, like the earlier U.S. conflict in Vietnam, was unpopular around the world. Meanwhile, Al Qaeda and ISIS spawned loosely affiliated terrorist groups that launched terrorist attacks on several continents, from Spain and Britain to Indonesia, Kenya, Yemen, and Morocco. ISIS proved especially dangerous, eventually gaining control in parts of Iraq and war-torn Syria, where they killed or enslaved many captives, while also stimulating small-scale or large terrorist attacks in Afghanistan, the Middle East, Africa, Europe, and the U.S. By 2019 ISIS had lost their bases in Syria but still remained a formidable terrorist threat. In 1993 a German historian had perceptively predicted the challenges ahead in the post–Cold War world: "We are at the beginning of a new era, characterized by great insecurity, permanent crisis and the absence of any kind of *status quo*. We must realize that we find ourselves in one of those crises of world history."[7]

Yet, wars between nations, and battle deaths, became less common than in the early and middle twentieth century, thanks partly to international trade and widening prosperity. After World War II the Western nations and their allies had built what specialists have termed a liberal world order that brought seven decades of considerable peace and prosperity for many nations. Partly in its own self-interest, the U.S. led in the establishment of global norms for a rules-based international system, including promoting democracy, protecting allies, advancing free trade and free movement of goods, providing a U.S. security blanket for friendly nations, and building institutions that fostered cooperation while also legitimizing U.S. power. Despite various failures, such as not providing adequate protections for workers and the environment as well as imperfect multilateral cooperation, the system maintained global stability and prevented direct military conflict between the great powers for seventy years; there have been many wars since Korea but on a smaller or local scale. The global economy grew about sevenfold since 1960, lifting many but not all societies out of severe poverty.

But in the second decade of the twenty-first century, that liberal world order has been under threat from two forces. One is the resurgence of authoritarian leaderships as various dictators, despots, or military elites in countries like China, Russia, North Korea, Thailand, Turkey, Syria, Egypt, Pakistan, Iran, Saudi Arabia, Venezuela, Nicaragua, and Cuba repress dissent, abuse human rights, oppose political pluralism, and rig

[7]Michael Sturmer, quoted in Eric Hobsbawm, *The Age of Extremes: A History of the World, 1914–1991* (New York: Pantheon, 1994), 558.

or ignore elections. Many specialists see democracy and open societies in crisis and under siege around the world. The other threat to the world order is the rapid rise of right-wing populism, nationalist, and sometimes racist movements opposed to immigration, ethnic and religious minorities, Muslims, climate change activism, nonmainstream social behavior, and often globalization and multilateral cooperation, polarizing politics. Leaders, often demagogues, and parties with this philosophy have taken power and imposed what political scientists term "illiberal democracies" in some European nations (including Hungary, Poland, and Italy) or became influential in national politics (including among others Germany, Netherlands, Sweden, France, and Britain). Populists (mostly right-wing nationalists) have also taken power in non-European countries like the Philippines, India, Brazil and, to some degree, Australia and the U.S. The nativist rhetoric that immigrants are invading the homeland has gained increasing influence and political acceptance in Western nations amidst the dislocations generated by massive migration from Africa, the Middle East, and Latin America. Some populists model themselves on, and take inspiration from, outspoken U.S. president Donald Trump. Populist nationalism has spurred some terrorist attacks and mass killings, often against Muslim and racial minorities, by neo-Nazis and white supremacists in Europe, the United States, and New Zealand.

Some historians attribute the trend toward authoritarian or populist leadership in part to the Information Revolution that, like the Industrial Revolution two centuries ago, is transforming societies in major ways, including in spreading opinions and news, real or fake, around the world in seconds, rendering distance irrelevant. On YouTube and other digital platforms fake news and hate messages reach many millions; many are posted and spread by organized ultra-right-wing groups, some of them Russian. But while some observers see a continuing trend toward populism, in 2019 antipopulists in some countries have pushed back or protested against (Poland, Romania, Czech Republic, Georgia) or voted out (Slovakia) populist regimes or marginalized populist parties (Germany, Spain). There have also been massive protests against authoritarian regimes in Hong Kong (China), Russia, and Turkey. This backlash gives some hope to those favoring liberal democracy. Some historians also note that over the past one hundred-fifty years populism usually rises after a major financial crisis such as that in 2008-2009 and persists for around a decade before fading. But the political future remains uncertain. Indeed, in late 2019 massive civil unrest including strikes and protests, some of which resulted in violence and deaths, erupted in varied countries in the Middle East, Southeast Asia, and Latin America, generated from some combination of political and economic factors. These foreshadowed perhaps more unrest and instability to come.

The impact of these two forces has already brought changes to the global system. China and Russia have flexed their muscles. China has laid claim to much of the South China Sea and began constructing its "new Silk Road" (the Belt and Road Initiative) to establish trade connections, forge friendly ties, and influence nations all over Asia, Africa, Latin America, and even Europe, strengthening its role in the world economy. Russia has seized territory in Ukraine, re-established closer relations with some of the former Soviet republics as well as China, and made efforts (some of them successful) to influence or interfere in elections and politics in other nations, including the U.S. and Britain, to cause chaos, elect favored candidates, or support policies favorable to Russia. The British decision to leave the European Union (a controversial policy known as Brexit) was supported by right-wing populists but also weakened Western unity. The decision by U.S. president Donald Trump to begin trade wars with and impose steep tariffs on the products of many nations, including various allies and China, while taking the U.S. out of trade agreements and international treaties, also destabilized the world economic system. These actions angered allies while also, critics contend, benefiting China's quest to take over U.S. leadership in Asia. Meanwhile, the Middle East remains turbulent as Iran, Turkey, Saudi Arabia, the United Arab Emirates, and the U.S. contend for influence. The movements of migrants and refugees to Europe and North America also polarized politics. And the rapidly increasing and disruptive climate change, which contributes to global warming, and the inability or reluctance of nations to agree on solutions caused considerable alarm among those concerned about the planet's future.

KEY POINTS

▶ During the Cold War, the United States and the USSR struggled for world control, with the United States generally favoring democracy and capitalism but also seeking access to resources and foreign markets and the USSR supporting emerging communist regimes and movements.

▶ Though the United States and the USSR never fought directly, they were involved in wars in other countries, such as Vietnam, Korea, and Afghanistan, in which millions died, and they intervened in countries such as Guatemala, Iran, Poland, Hungary, and Czechoslovakia.

▶ The United States and the USSR participated in a massive arms race, spending trillions of dollars on nuclear weapons, which led to widespread fear of mass destruction, though some argue that this fear helped prevent all-out war.

▶ The United Nations was formed with the goal of promoting world peace and human rights, and various agreements have been signed to ban biological weapons and land mines, to prevent global warming, and to facilitate an international justice system, though they have encountered opposition by the United States and some other industrial nations.

▶ Terrorism was used by various groups for decades but has become more deadly since the radical Islamist group Al Qaeda attacked the United States in 2001.

▶ After World War II the liberal world system helped maintain global stability for seven decades but in the twenty-first century has been challenged by the resurgence of authoritarian governments and the rise of nationalist populist groups in many countries, fostering instability in international affairs.

26-3 Globalizing Economies, Underdevelopment, and Environmental Change

≡₵ TRANSITIONS ▦ NETWORKS

Ⓠ What were some of the main consequences of a globalizing world economy?

The world was increasingly characterized by **globalization**, a pattern in which economic, political, and cultural processes reach beyond national boundaries. This trend reduced barriers between countries, allowing for more collaboration and more closely connected societies through worldwide commercial markets, finance, telecommunications, and exchange of ideas. Some critics view globalization as displacing workers while opening borders to immigrants, which may have prompted many people to support populist and nationalist leaders and movements. Globalization also widened inequalities between the richest and poorest nations, while industrialization and economic growth produced negative environmental consequences, including increased pollution and atmospheric carbon from factories and fossil fuels and a rapidly warming climate. As a result of population growth, people expanded agriculture into semidesert areas and cut down rain forests, causing environmental deterioration and accelerating climate change.

26-3a The Transnational Economy

A world economy linking distant societies has been developing for the past twenty-five hundred years, but after 1945 globalization rapidly spread market capitalism and fostered flows of capital, goods, services, and people. The world's production of goods and services was one hundred twenty times higher in 2000 than in 1500; average personal income grew fourfold between 1900 and 2000. In the interconnected world, events occurring or decisions taken in one part of the world affect societies far away. Rising or falling prices on the Tokyo or New York stock exchanges quickly reverberate around the world, influencing stock markets elsewhere. Similarly, Western governments' sales of stockpiled rubber depress world prices, affecting rubber growers, and the businesses that supply them, in Malaysia, Sri Lanka, Brazil, and the Congo. Some transnational economic activity is illegal, especially the flow of narcotics. Heroin and cocaine smuggled into and sold in North America and Europe by transnational criminal syndicates originate largely in Asia and Latin America.

Various institutions shaped the transnational economy, especially international lending agencies formed by the Allies in 1944 to aid postwar reconstruction. The World Bank funded development projects such as dams and agricultural schemes; the International Monetary Fund (IMF) regulated currency dealings and addressed financial problems. Many Asian, African, Caribbean, and Latin American nations—not earning enough income to buy food and medicine, import luxuries, build dams, and improve ports—took out IMF or World Bank loans. Some fell deeply in debt. Moreover, the IMF, able to dictate economic policies to borrowing countries, favored Western investment and free markets rather than social services like schools and clinics. In 2013 the BRICS proposed to establish a new development bank to challenge the World Bank and IMF.

Trade agreements and trading blocs reflected unprecedented economic connectedness. Formed in 1947, the General Agreement on Trade and Tariffs (GATT) set rules for world trade, including tariffs and regulations. The World Trade Organization (WTO), founded by one hundred twenty-four nations in 1995, had stronger dispute-resolution capabilities than GATT. Regional trading blocs also formed. The European Common Market (now the European Union) eventually included most European nations. Major industrial nations cooperated to manage the global economy. By the 1990s economic officials from the seven richest industrial countries met regularly as the G7 (Group of 7), later joined by Russia to form the G8. Thanks to the 2008–2009 economic crisis and the need for concerted global action, G8 leaders permanently expanded to include twelve other countries with large economies, such as China, India, Brazil, Indonesia, South Korea, and Argentina. This new G20 grouping confirmed the changing world economic leadership, especially China's key role. But the vision of the world's financial and political elites of ever-closer commercial and political ties has been under attack from populists and leftists who want to dismantle some of the multilateral structures, darkening the global economic outlook.

Giant business enterprises, known as **multinational corporations** because they operate all over the world, have gained a leading role in the global marketplace. Some 300–400 companies, the majority U.S.-owned, dominate world production and trade and are now the world's third largest economic force, greatly influencing governments. Multinationals set the world price for various commodities, such as coffee, copper, or oil; play one country off against another to get the best deal; and move manufacturing jobs. Multinationals have also created millions of jobs in poor countries. Increasingly women are the majority in the global assembly lines of factories producing for export. Supporters argue that outsourcing—moving jobs from high-wage to low-wage countries—creates middle-class jobs and employs people with few other job prospects. Critics contend that most jobs pay low wages, require long hours, and offer little future. For example, although the U.S.-based Nike Corporation creates needed jobs in Vietnam, Vietnamese employees, mainly women, work in unhealthy conditions, face sexual harassment, and are fired if they complain.

CONNECTION to TODAY

Can you identify ideas that you have encountered or products that you use that can be linked to the globalization of economies and industries?

---

globalization A pattern in which economic, political, and cultural processes reach beyond nation-state boundaries.

multinational corporations Giant business enterprises that operate all over the world, gaining a leading role in the global marketplace.

Americans have traditionally been major globalization proponents and believe that open markets, investment, and trade lead to prosperity. By 2000 the United States produced nearly a third of the world's goods and services; Japan, the next largest economy, accounted for around a sixth. International observers described U.S. leadership metaphorically: when Americans sneeze, the rest of the world catches cold. However, economic growth and trade do not necessarily improve living conditions for everybody; well-functioning governments, legal and political rights, and health and education services are also required. Critics charge that globalization promises riches it cannot always deliver, distributing the benefits unequally.

By the 1990s the United States and China gained the most from removing trade barriers and fostering competitive markets worldwide, sucking in investment capital, aggressively acquiring natural resources, and supplying diverse products to foreign markets. Surpassing Germany and then Japan, China became the world's second largest economy, producing clothing, housewares, and other consumer goods. In the early 1990s China accounted for less than 2 percent of the global economy; by 2018 it was 15 percent and rising, growing at least three times faster than the U.S. Chinese invested in Africa, Latin America, and the Middle East and bought U.S.-based companies. But not all Chinese benefited. Some less efficient state-owned enterprises closed down, and peasants protested as their farmland was bulldozed to build foreign-owned factories, private housing developments, and golf courses for affluent Chinese. But in the past decade China's government has taken more control over many companies, a system known as "state capitalism." This has

corresponded to ambitious new initiatives to make China the world's major economic superpower. In 2013 China introduced the Belt and Road Initiative (BRI) for massive investments in infrastructure, industrialization, power generation, resource extraction, transportation, construction, and business in Central Asia, Southeast Asia, Africa, the Middle East, Latin America, and even Europe. Chinese leaders talked of the BRI as a New Silk Road and some historians have called it a return to Marco Polo's world since the main land route duplicates Polo's travels across Eurasia in the thirteenth century. Some of the BRI has involved huge loans to governments, which will have to be paid back eventually. In 2018 Sri Lanka, unable to pay back loans, ceded China control over one of their ports. Some Africans and development specialists view the influx of Chinese construction projects, businesses, merchants, workers, and especially loans as a new form of colonialism. But others argue that they benefit locals and provide new jobs. Several African governments and Malaysia have cancelled projects that they can't pay for. In 2018 four nations—the U.S., Australia, Japan, and India—opened talks for a so far unrealized alternative to the BRI.

A few other nations, such as India, Ireland, Singapore, and South Korea, capitalized on globalization, creating economic growth and becoming high-technology centers. However, Japan and some European nations struggled to compete in the globalizing economy, and some Asian, African, and Caribbean nations fell deeper into poverty. In addition, many people in developing nations—Mexican corn farmers, West African wheat growers, Pakistani textile workers—faced trade barriers and well-funded, technologically superior Western competitors. United Nations

IMAGE 26.4 **The Global Economy** Cambodian Buddhist monks, following ancient traditions, collect their food from the devout in the capital city, Phnom Penh, while advertising for American cigarettes entices Cambodians into the global economy, despite government concerns about the health danger posed by tobacco products.

Q. What does the photo tell us about the life and culture of Cambodia?

secretary general Kofi Annan (KO-fee AN-uhn), a Ghanaian, contended in 2002: "Our challenge today is to make globalization an engine that lifts people out of hardship and misery, not a force that holds them down."[8]

For most of the post–World War II era Western industrial nations and Japan generally maintained a favorable position in the global economy, controlling most of the capital, markets, and international financial institutions such as banks; moreover, their corporations own assets in other nations. As a result, Americans control many businesses, mines, and plantations in Latin America, Japanese operate factories in Southeast Asia, and the French maintain a large economic stake in West Africa. Capitalist systems in industrialized nations range from limited government interference, common in the United States, to mixed free markets and welfare states in western Europe, to close government–business relationships in Japan and South Korea. These contrast with many former colonies where power holders, often closely tied to foreign or domestic business interests, preside over largely poor populations. Hence, in the Congo, corrupt leaders protected the Belgian-owned and local corporations who fund them. Rebel movements and brutal local warlords, and outbreaks of deadly diseases such as Ebola, have added to Congolese misery for several decades.

As some once-poor countries have used the transnational economy to their advantage, some have achieved spectacular growth. The U.N. Human Development Report for 2013 focused on this century's shifting global dynamics and what they termed "the rise of the South," especially the more than forty developing countries with markedly improving quality of life. In their view, the rise is unprecedented in its speed and scale and has led to a greater diversity of voices on the world stage. A few oil-rich nations, like Kuwait and the United Arab Emirates, use revenues to improve their citizens' lives. Various Asian countries, much like Japan in the late 1800s, have combined market economies, cheap labor, and powerful governments to promote industrialization. By repressing opposition, they have ensured political stability and attracted foreign investment. Their emphasis on export-oriented growth—the production of consumer goods such as clothing, toys, electronics, and housewares for sale abroad, especially in Europe and North America—has fostered high growth rates and imported industrial jobs from Western countries or Japan. Beginning in the 1980s, China, South Korea, Taiwan, Malaysia, Thailand, Singapore, and eventually Vietnam created the world's fastest-growing economies, their major cities boasting well-stocked malls, freeways, diverse restaurants, and luxury condominiums. Elsewhere nations like Brazil, South Africa, Ghana, Turkey, and Chile enjoyed robust growth. But by 2014 some experienced slowing growth as foreign investment diminished.

Often the growing middle class and labor leaders have demanded political liberalization and a larger voice in government. By the 1990s Indonesians, South Koreans, Taiwanese, Ghanaians, Brazilians, and Chileans replaced dictatorships with democratic governments, and remain democratic today. Some Asian systems became development models by mixing capitalism, which creates wealth, with socialism, which can distribute wealth equitably. Their economic resurgence has restored the leading role some Asian societies enjoyed in the world economy for many centuries before 1800. But in the late 1990s many Asian economies crashed, then slowly rebounded until they were damaged again in 2008–2009 as the U.S. economic crisis affected Asia and the rest of the world. Factories closed and revenues declined, causing massive unemployment and hardship. By 2013 many Asian nations, including China, had reestablished strong to modest growth. Historians debate whether China or possibly India might eventually surpass the United States as the world's colossus. The success of many Asian nations led some historians to speak of the "Asian Century," during which East, South, and Southeast Asia would dominate the world economy; others define the term as embracing a new multinational system stretching from Turkey, Saudi Arabia, and Russia to Japan and Australia. But by 2019 some specialists contended that the "Asian Century" and their expectations for the future were fading due to geopolitical dangers and conflicts, domestic troubles, and stagnating economies in Asia and most of the other countries. By late 2019 world economic growth and trade was declining more rapidly. Critics argue that some of the policies of the Trump "America First" strategy, such as trade and tariff wars, abandoning agreements and treaties, alienating allies, denigrating multilateral cooperation, undermining NATO and the European Union, and destabilizing the global order may lead to an isolated U.S. with a much weaker presence in Asia and the world. Meanwhile, ten Southeast Asian nations along with China, Japan, South Korea, Australia, New Zealand and possibly India planned a possible free trade grouping, the Regional Comprehensive Economic Partnership.

26-3b The Spread of Industrialization

Industrialization spread, especially to Asia and Latin America. Entrepreneurs or state agencies in, among others, China, India, South Korea, Brazil, and Mexico built textile mills, steel mills, and automobile plants; Chinese textiles, Indian steel, and South Korean cars found markets around the world. China ranked number one in manufacturing output in 2018, with 20 percent. Meanwhile, the U.S. share of world industrial production fell from 50 percent in 1950 to 18 percent in 2018; Americans built over 75 percent of all cars in 1950 but less than 20 percent by the 1990s. Japan ranked third in manufacturing output. Together China, the U.S., and Japan produced 48 percent of the world's manufacturing output. Malaysians now drive Japanese Toyotas but also Swedish Volvos, South Korean Hyundais, and Proton Sagas manufactured locally.

Technological innovations spurred economic growth. The so-called **Third Industrial Revolution** created unprecedented scientific knowledge and new technologies, making the First and Second Industrial Revolutions seem obsolete. Nuclear power, computers, automation, and robots displaced traditional smokestack industries like steel mills. Rocketry, genetic engineering, silicon chips, and lasers became commonplace. Space technology produced the first manned trips to the moon and unmanned crafts exploring the solar system, even flying by distant Pluto and landing multiple rovers on Mars. In 2005 a probe landed on

Third Industrial Revolution The creation of unprecedented scientific knowledge and new technologies.

[8]Quoted in Peter Singer, "Navigating the Ethics of Globalization," *Chronicle of Higher Education*, October 11, 2002, p. B8.

faraway Saturn's large, mysterious moon, Titan, sending back photographs of the surface. Beside the U.S., Russia, Europe, China, and India all have active space exploration programs. More powerful telescopes increased knowledge of the solar system and the universe, by 2019 discovering over four thousand exoplanets circling other stars. British poet Archibald MacLeish observed that astronauts on space capsules circling the planet did not perceive national boundaries or international rivalries, but only oceans and lands containing people with a common planetary home: "To see the Earth as we now see it, small and blue and beautiful in that eternal silence [of space] where it floats, is to see ourselves as rulers on the Earth together."[9]

The Third Industrial Revolution has potentially dramatic consequences. One component, the **Green Revolution**, has increased agricultural output from the use of new high-yield seeds and mechanized farming. Farmers able to afford these innovations can raise more crops a year. But in countries such as India, the Philippines, and Mexico, the Green Revolution, requiring more capital for seeds and machines but fewer people to work the land, often harmed poor peasants unable to afford the investment. In many industries, including automobile manufacturing, automation has taken over production, allowing companies to fire workers. Industry became globalized and technology increasingly sophisticated. Supply chains link products built with parts from suppliers in many nations, making these products essentially collaborative. For example, an iPhone goes through five different countries for parts before it is shipped to Taiwan for assembly and then to market: Germany (accelerometer), China (battery), Japan (camera, compass, LCD screen), Switzerland (gyroscope), and the U.S. (glass screen, wi-fi and audio chips). Disruptions in trade, such as the trade and tariff war between the U.S. and China in 2018–2019, can undermine this system, hurting suppliers and consumers. By the 1990s foreign-owned factories paying low taxes and wages relocated to industrial parks around the world. Hence, factories in northern Mexico, usually U.S.-owned and making goods largely for the U.S. market, employed a half million workers, mainly women. Service and information exchange industries also grew. More people worked in service enterprises, such as fast-food restaurants.

Since 2010 technology has become increasingly sophisticated. Some historians have identified what they call the Fourth Industrial Revolution in which we use products that are connected to each other autonomously (via the "Internet of Things"); some of them are essential to navigating modern life, some like games and videos for pleasure or entertainment. Today we are living in the technological future that some twentieth-century thinkers predicted would come, marked by its own new terminologies: cyberspace, cyberwar, cyber harassment, "selfies," social media, AI, coding, smartphones, tablets, YouTube, cloud computing, virtual reality, e-commerce, smart houses, and many other creations. Responding to these trends, India, which graduates each year thousands of people fluent in English and skilled in computer technology, became a world center for offshore information and technical services. Increasingly consumers calling North American companies for computer technical support, product information, or billing questions reach people working in cubicles in India, Sri Lanka, or the Philippines. Some experts

applaud, and others fear, the prospects that the Fourth Industrial Revolution is already researching, developing, and possibly soon producing fabulously sophisticated machines: driverless cars and trucks, robots to staff factories or give legal or medical advice, fully automated supermarkets, super-smartphones for hailing Uber helicopters or planes, machines using algorithms to teach themselves cognitive tasks, floating cities, and many others. These are visions of a world remade, perhaps during the 2020s. What, critics ask, happens to the people—drivers, pilots, workers, clerks, lawyers, doctors, etc.—who once did these jobs?

Globalization came with risks. Hoping to better compete, businesses have moved factories to countries with low wages and costs. Some Western and Japanese businesses shifted operations to South Korea or Taiwan, where average workers earn in a month what American or German workers earn in a week or ten days, yet produce as much. Others established operations in Asian, African, Latin American, or eastern European nations where workers earn even less. For example, in 1990 the U.S. clothing maker Levi Strauss closed fifty-eight U.S. plants with over ten thousand workers while shifting half of its production to foreign countries. Closure of uncompetitive businesses and industrial plants still remains common today, including in the United States.

26-3c Underdevelopment and Development

Uneven economic growth has contributed to a growing gap between the richest nations and poorest undeveloped nations. The gap was already wide in 1945, thanks to colonialism; a Guyanese historian argued that "the vast majority of Africans went into colonialism with a hoe and came out with a hoe."[10] Many Asian, African, and Latin American economies grew rapidly in the 1950s and 1960s, when the world economy boomed, but most declined in the 1970s and 1980s, as the world economy soured and world prices for many exports collapsed. The world economy revived for a few years, only to experience a dramatic downturn in the later 1990s and early 2000s. In 2008–2009 the world economy went into the worst crisis since the Great Depression. Many nations were severely affected, but some Asian countries and the United States began to recover by 2010. Some countries still struggle to reboot or improve their growth and development.

Moreover, economic growth has not always fostered **development**, defined as economic growth that benefits the majority of the population. Some Asian nations have prospered from welcoming foreign investment, building schools, hospitals, and highways. Yet, foreign investment often has not created locally owned businesses. In Nigeria, for example, British enterprises still dominate banking, importing, and exporting; Western investment has gone mainly into cash crops and oil production, controlled largely by Western companies. Outraged that they gain little from the polluting oil wells around them, people in Nigeria's main oil-producing region have sabotaged operations,

> **Green Revolution** Increased agricultural output through the use of new high-yield seeds and mechanized farming.
>
> **development** Economic growth that benefits the majority of the population.

---

[9] Quoted in J. Donald Hughes, *An Environmental History of the World: Mankind's Changing Role in the Community of Life* (New York: Routledge, 2002), 206.

[10] Walter Rodney, *How Europe Underdeveloped Africa* (London: Bogle-L'Ouverture, 1972), 162.

kidnapped foreign oil workers, and resorted to armed insurgency. Furthermore, foreign investment and aid have often lined the pockets of corrupt leaders, bureaucrats, and military officers.

Scholars debate how poor countries can better profit from their connections to the world economy and spur local efforts at development. The influential Indian economist Amartya Sen (b. 1933) helped run evening schools for illiterate rural children as a youth, prompting his studies of global poverty, famine, and social and gender inequality; he won the Nobel Prize in economics in 1998. Influenced by his first wife, a writer and political activist, Sen argues that women's literacy and employment are the best predictors of both child survival and fertility rate reduction, prerequisites for development in poor villages. His views on poverty and gender inequality influenced the United Nations when, in 2000, it developed an agenda for a new millennium to address the world's pressing problems by 2020. However, few very poor countries have sufficient resources to seriously combat widespread poverty or promote women's empowerment.

Most of the poorest nations have suffered from some combination of rapid population growth, high unemployment, illiteracy, hunger, disease, corrupt or ineffective governments, and reliance on only a few exports. Hence, in Guatemala, 90 percent lived below the official poverty line; nearly half had no health care, indoor plumbing, piped water, or formal education. The income inequality grew more extreme in the twenty-first century. By 2018 the twenty-seven richest individuals in the world had an estimated combined worth of $1.4 trillion, more than the entire wealth of the poorest half of humanity, and the world's richest 1 percent possess 82 percent of the wealth. By 2018 over 100 billion of the world's people earned less than $1 per day, and another three billion under $2.50 a day; together they account for over half of the world population. One billion suffered from chronic hunger, a problem made worse during global recessions. Furthermore, despite preaching free trade, rich nations often blocked or restricted food and fiber imports from poor nations while heavily subsidizing their own farmers. Hence, wheat farmers in Mali, however industrious, cannot compete with French or U.S. wheat farmers, who enjoy financial support from their governments. In 2000 the United Nations secretary general, Kofi Annan (1938–2018), a Ghanaian, laid out the organization's challenges in a world changed dramatically since the organization's formation over five decades earlier:

> How can we say that the half of the human race which has yet to make or receive a phone call, let alone use a computer, is taking part in globalization? We cannot, without insulting their poverty.... We are plundering our children's heritage to pay for our present unsustainable practices. We must stop. Above all we need to remember the old African wisdom which I learned as a child—that the earth is not ours. It is a treasure we hold in trust for our descendants.[11]

Yet, non-Western nations can boast of many achievements. Between 1960 and 2000 they reduced infant mortality by half and doubled adult literacy rates. Among others, China, Sri Lanka, Malaysia, and Tanzania provided many social services, such as schools and clinics, to rural areas. Various countries implemented

locally based development strategies. In sub-Saharan Africa, for instance, Burkina Faso (**buhr-KEE-nuh FAH-so**) and Niger (**nee-jer**) moved away from expensive prestige projects—such as building large dams to supply hydroelectric power—to small-scale, labor-intensive projects aiding the environment, such as tree-planting campaigns; local cooperative banks provided credit to farmers. However, severe drought can still cause widespread starvation.

Women and their children face the harshest problems. Economic change has undermined the handicrafts that provide incomes for women while also fragmenting families: many men have to find work in other districts or countries, leaving their wives to support and raise the children. In Africa, men migrate each year from Burkina Faso to the Ivory Coast's cocoa plantations and logging camps and from Mozambique to South African mines. Meanwhile, women leave India, Sri Lanka, and the Philippines to work as domestic servants in the Persian Gulf states and Saudi Arabia, some facing sexual harassment or cruel employers. Asian and Latin American women work in homes and sweatshops in North America and Europe.

Development often leaves women behind because of their inferior social status in often patriarchal cultures and relative invisibility in national economic statistics. Many face social customs that accord them little influence and, in case of divorce, award their children to the father. An Indian folk song expressed the bitterness of village women who, after marriage, have no claim on their birth family's property: "To my brother belong your green fields, O father, while I am banished afar."[12] In some countries, especially in South Asia and the Middle East, women who violate social customs and rules might be killed to preserve family or village "honor." Some women do not have freedom of movement. Until the policies were changed in late 2019 Saudi Arabian women could not leave the house without a male relative's permission and requird a male guardian when they travel; only in 2019 were they allowed to drive, even as dozens of feminist activists have been jailed or killed in the country. While women do 60 percent of the world's work and produce 50 to 75 percent of the food, they own only 1 percent of the property and earn 10 percent of the income. Most of poor women's labor—food preparation, cleaning, childrearing—is unpaid and demanding. In Senegal a typical rural woman, married at a young age, gets up at 5:00 A.M. to pound millet, the staple food, for an hour. She then walks a few hundred yards or perhaps several miles to get water from a well, makes breakfast for the family, goes to the village shop, makes the family lunch, takes food to family members working in the fields, does laundry, makes supper, and then pounds millet again before bed.

Some nations help women and children through bottom-up, grassroots policies. The Grameen (**GRAH-mean**) Bank in Bangladesh, which promotes self-help, provides an outstanding model. After meeting a woman matmaker who earned four cents a day, economist Muhammad Yunus (b. 1940) concluded that conventional economics ignored rural poverty. Since few banks made loans to the poor, in 1983 Yunus opened the Grameen Bank, which makes loans under $100 on cheap terms to peasants, especially women, for buying tools they need to earn a living, like a cell phone for business or personal calls or bamboo to make chairs. By 2017 there were twenty-six hundred

---

[11]United Nations, *The Millennium Report* (*un.org/millennium/sg/report/state.htm*).
[12]Quoted in Michael H. Hunt, *The World Transformed; 1945 to the Present* (Boston: Bedford/St. Martin's, 2014), 428.

IMAGE 26.5 **Rich and Poor in Brazil** The stark contrast between the wealthy and the poor in many nations can be seen in the Brazilian city of Rio de Janeiro. Seeking jobs in expanding industries, millions of migrants flock to the city, building shantytown slums and squatter settlements on hillsides in view of luxury high-rise apartment and office buildings.

Q What does the photo tell us about life and income inequality in Rio de Janeiro?

branches in Bangladesh with nine million borrowers, 97 percent of them women. Less than 1 percent of borrowers have defaulted. The women earning an income now enjoy higher social status, and many began using contraceptives, helping to lower the Bangladesh birthrate from 3 to 2 percent a year. Muhammad Yunus won the Nobel Peace Prize in 2006. Some other nations have borrowed the Grameen model, with mixed results. Today Grameen-linked banks are in sixty-four countries, including branches in eleven U.S. cities.

26-3d Population Growth and Urbanization

Rapid population growth and overcrowded cities exemplify global imbalance. Since 1945 the world's population grew faster than ever before in history (see Map 26.2). Two thousand years ago Earth had between 125 and 250 million people; roughly ten thousand generations later, in 1830, the world population reached one billion. By 1945 the population had risen to 2.5 billion; by 2019 it had more than tripled to 7.7 billion. Some experts worried about a "population bomb" overwhelming the world's water, food sources, forests, and minerals, which Earth's resources could not support. Some experts think the bomb is still ticking. But fertility rates began dropping, especially in industrialized nations, thanks

to widespread artificial birth control, such as contraceptive pills, better health care, and more women entering the paid workforce. However, largely because of rapid African population growth, demographers now envision a world population of some 9.7 billion by 2050 and perhaps eleven billion by 2100, which will still impose a heavy burden on food supplies and services while intensifying social, economic, and environmental problems. Overpopulation and competition for limited resources have sparked sporadic violence in crowded countries such as Ethiopia, Rwanda, and El Salvador. Some studies have predicted a worldwide 50 percent rise in demand for food, 30 percent for water, and 50 percent for energy by 2030. These realities raise the question of whether Earth can sustainably support an ever-increasing population.

Most population growth in the past half century has occurred in Asia, Africa, and Latin America. China (1.43 billion) and India (1.37 billion) have the largest populations; however, India is expected to grow for several decades and surpass China, which will probably lose population. The next eleven most populous countries each contain at least 100 million people. Global fertility rates have been falling, from 3.2 births per woman in 1990 to 2.5 in 2019, and are expected to fall to 2.2 in 2050, just above the 2.1 needed for replacement of generations. Lower fertility means aging populations. While Asia continues, as it has for millennia, to

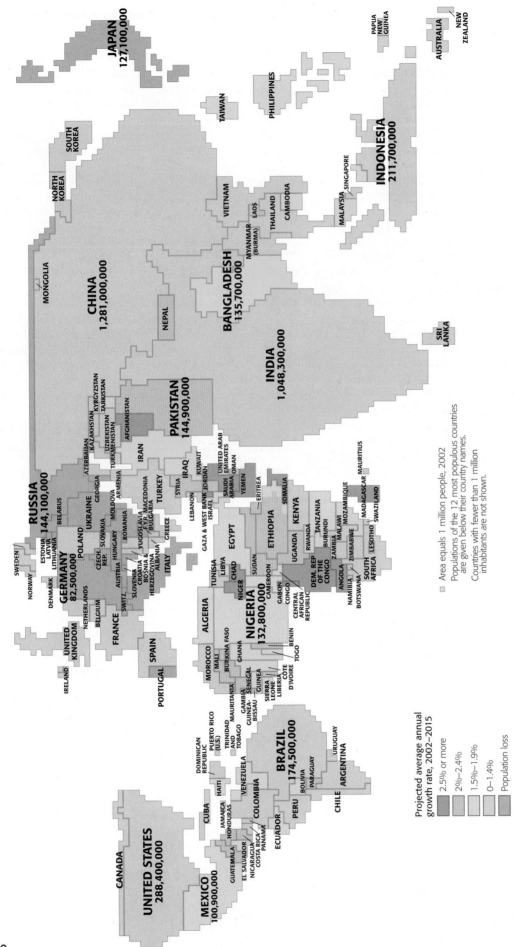

MAP 26.2 World Population Growth This map from 2015 shows dramatically which nations have the largest populations: China, India, the United States, Indonesia, and Brazil. It also shows which regions experience the most rapid population growth: Africa, South Asia, and Central America.

Q Which regions have the largest populations according to this map?

house at least 60 percent of humanity, Europe's share of population fell from a quarter in 1900 to an eighth. Because of falling birth-rates, various European nations, Russia, China, and Japan have declining and aging populations, burdening working-age people to support elderly populations. Italy and Spain, which once had high birthrates, now claim the world's lowest fertility rates. Fewer young people mean fewer taxpaying workers to finance programs aiding senior citizens. North American birthrates have also dropped, but immigration has offset the decline, although today immigration policies are controversial and subject to impassioned political debate in the United States. Between 1960 and 2009 the fertility rate in Mexico and Brazil tumbled by two-thirds. If African growth slows, as Asian and Latin American growth has, some experts forecast world population eventually falling.

Western nations, Japan, and recently China, enjoying high rates of resource consumption, including fossil fuels, harm the environment more than countries with large populations but low consumption rates. Owing to heavy energy use and metals-dependent innovations—air conditioners, central heating systems, gasoline-powered vehicles, refrigerators—the average American or Canadian consumes some twenty times, and the average Australian, German, or Japanese ten to fifteen times, more resources than the average Pakistani or Peruvian.

Rapid population growth has undermined economic development in overcrowded nations struggling with scarce food, health care, housing, and education. In countries like the Philippines, Pakistan, and Uganda, the school-age population has expanded faster than the resources to build new schools and hire teachers. Many countries cannot afford compulsory education. The increased food production caused by the Green Revolution averted mass famine, but by the 1990s harvests reached a plateau, producing only small food increases or sometimes even decreases. Fish catches have declined steeply, partly because of overfishing by high-technology Western and Japanese fleets. Providing new cropland requires massive forest clearing.

Recent advances in health and welfare could be reversed unless nations slow population growth and reduce poverty. Using harsh means, overcrowded China dramatically reduced fertility by mandating only one child per family; couples flouting the laws faced stiff fines or, sometimes, forced abortions. But in 2013, as the population aged, China modified its policy to allow some families to have two children. The most successful birth control campaigns, such as one in Thailand, targeted women, giving them better education, health care, and dignity independent of their roles as mothers. Many parents have traditionally viewed more children as insurance for their old age; in Mali the average woman had seven children, four surviving to adulthood. Economic development and affluence, including better health care to lower infant mortality, have often changed these attitudes.

Rural folk have often had to abandon their livelihoods and move to crowded cities such as Jakarta, Calcutta, Cairo, and Mexico City, where many live in shantytowns or on sidewalks. Cities held 10 percent of the world population in 1900 and 50 percent in 2000. Cairo grew from nine hundred thousand in 1897 to 2.8 million in 1947 and 20.4 million in 2018. In 1950 most of the world's ten largest metropolitan areas were Western cities, headed by New York; by 2018 Asian and Latin American cities

dominated the list. Tokyo, with 37.4 million people, was followed by Delhi (29.3 million), Shanghai, São Paulo (POU-lo), Mexico City, Cairo, Dhaka, Mumbai, Beijing, and Osaka. The largest U.S. city, New York, was ranked 36th with 8.6 million. Colossal traffic jams make driving in Bangkok, Tokyo, Mexico City, and Lagos a nightmare. Struggling to provide needed services, cities dump raw sewage into bays and rivers. Today cities consume 75 percent of the world's resources and produce 75 percent of its trash. City life reshapes traditional ways. In a Peruvian pop song, a boy who migrated to Lima complains that his girlfriend has abandoned rural values: "You came as a country girl. Now you are in Lima you comb your hair in a city way. You even say, 'I'm going to dance the twist'" [a popular dance from the United States]."[13]

26-3e Environmental and Climate Change

The last few centuries of human activity and its ever more carbon-emitting energy systems have altered our planet in many ways. As a result the climate is changing and entire land and marine ecosystems are collapsing. The fast-growing human population combined with an increasing ability to bend nature for our own benefit have precipitated multiplying changes in Earth's complex climatological and biological systems, among them altered and often devastated environments (land, air, and water), declining biodiversity, weather disasters, global warming, plastic pollution, radioactive elements from nuclear bombs, and many others. These environmental changes, which many scientists and other scholars today explain with the concept of a new epoch in Earth and human history that they term the *Anthropocene*, may ultimately threaten the viability of our modern ways of living, perhaps even of the entire human species (see Discover Historical Voices: The Anthropocene and Modern World History).

Industrialization, population growth, urbanization, and massive fossil fuel use have posed unprecedented environmental challenges; increased competition for limited resources such as oil, timber, and tin; and contributed to a much warmer, drier global climate. Over the twentieth century industrial output increased twentyfold and energy use fourteenfold. Industrialized nations and industrializing nations, such as China, South Korea, and Malaysia, paid the cost in noxious air, toxic waste, stripped forests, water pollution, and warmer climates. Discarded plastic waste, dangerous to marine life, clogs rivers and lakes while, along with many other manufactured items thrown away by humans, collects in vast floating garbage dumps in the oceans, especially what scientists call the Great Pacific Garbage Patch, hundreds of miles across. Industrial output has increased substantially in the twenty-first century.

Some environmental disasters affected large populations. In 1957 an explosion in a Russian nuclear waste dump killed some ten thousand people, contaminated one hundred fifty square miles of land, and forced the evacuation of two hundred-seventy thousand people. A Japanese nuclear plant destroyed by an earthquake and tsunami in 2011 ruined a large area with radiation. A massive die-off among frogs and some ocean species, perhaps due to pollution and ecological instability, suggested that polluted environments are increasingly dangerous to life. Sea turtle populations decreased drastically in regions as far apart as Southeast Asia, the Persian Gulf, and Central America.

---

[13]Quoted in Hobsbawm, *Age of Extremes*, 365.

Discover Historical Voices

The Anthropocene Age and Modern World History

Most of us are aware that humans have greatly reshaped our planet physically and in other ways over the course of history. Today climate change is one of the most obvious examples of how human activity is dramatically changing our world and its climate as we cut down forests and use carbon-emitting fossil fuels like coal. But many other things, from raising beef cattle to clear-cutting forests to discarding plastic items, changes the physical makeup of our planet and its varied creatures and affects our own lives. In recent years some scientists, historians, and anthropologists have developed the concept of the Anthropocene to indicate a new geological era in human and Earth history that has been dramatically reshaped by human activity. The study of this epoch is much debated, interdisciplinary, and crosses many boundaries of knowledge. Some critics, believing it is too soon to define new geological timescales that can stretch for thousands or millions of millennia, consider it premature and lacking in geological evidence. Proponents argue that the concept offers a mental framework for considering global scales of space and geological scales of time when thinking about modern human history. This excerpt from the website of the Museum of Natural History at the Smithsonian Institution explains what the Anthropocene is, when it may have started, and why it matters in helping us to understand the world we live in now and in the future. This knowledge can help us repair some of the negative effects of the Anthropocene.

Human activity has fundamentally changed our planet. We live on every continent and have directly affected at least 83% of the planet's viable land surface. Our influence has impacted everything from the makeup of ecosystems to the geochemistry of Earth, from the atmosphere to the ocean. Many scientists define this time in the planet's history by the scale of human influence, and label it as a new geological epoch called the Anthropocene.

The beginning of the Anthropocene is a subject of heated debate among geologists, anthropologists, [historians] and… the scientific community…. Some argue that the Anthropocene began with the advent of agriculture, because certain agriculture-related activities such as rice paddy irrigation and deforestation may have led to sharp rises in concentrations of CO2 and methane as early as eight thousand years ago. Many believe that it was not until the Industrial Revolution that our exploitation of fossil fuels and monumental increases of energy use and population started to push us far enough to show a discernible human influence…. A third proposed start date is [what some historians label] the Great Acceleration, or the beginning of the nuclear age in the mid-1940s. In this period, not only did our testing and use of atomic weaponry leave a distinctive radioactive signature in the sediments of Earth, but almost all human activities from water use to fertilizer consumption to globalization saw a dramatic intensification.

The concept of the Anthropocene is significant. It highlights the scale of our impact on Earth. By defining a new geological epoch, we are declaring that the impact of our activities is global and irreversible. It allows us to unite many different discussions regarding the state of the planet, from climate change to loss of biodiversity to environmental degradation, by identifying the one thing they have in common: they have all been affected by human influence.

The Anthropocene also allows us to reexamine the relationship between humans and the rest of the natural world. There has been a long-standing narrative of humanity and nature being separate; some believe that we should be the caretakers or stewards of the natural world, while others urge us to leave the environment alone and let nature run its course. But human activity is intrinsically linked to nature and is part of it. From the land we live on to the resources we use to the trash we throw away, everything we do is tied into and impacts our surroundings. The concept of the Anthropocene underlines this fact by defining the environment based on the interactive effects of our influence. The only question now becomes how we can shape our activities so our impact on the environment is intentional and leads to meaningful outcomes…. Climate change is one of the most visible parts of the Anthropocene [but] it does not paint the whole picture of our influence. Everything from damming rivers to paving roads to illuminating public spaces has changed the physical makeup of the planet in some aspect, creating a world that has truly been shaped by humans.

Reflection Questions

1. What does the excerpt identify as defining the Anthropocene?
2. When and how did it begin?
3. Using this knowledge, how can people today contribute to making and sustaining a better environment?

Source: The Age of Humans: Evolutionary Perspectives on the Anthropocene, Smithsonian Museum of Natural History (Human Origins Initiative), September 14, 2018.

Desertification, the transformation of once-productive land into useless desert, increased with government, market, and population pressure to expand agriculture onto marginal land. During the past half century, some twenty thousand square miles of African land became desert every year. To combat the resulting farming failures, Africans used more pesticides, fertilizers, and irrigation, often with negative consequences. Drier climates diminish water supplies. One of Africa's largest lakes, Lake Chad, has lost 90 percent of its water since 1975. Deforestation and desertification also cause soil erosion; with less vegetation, rains wash away fertile topsoil and cause severe flooding. A regular reality in Africa,

desertification The transformation by which productive land is transformed into mostly useless desert.

drought has forced millions to become refugees in other lands. With less rain, the Niger River in West Africa, where great trading cities once flourished, supports less farming than five centuries ago. In Nepal, farmers have stripped once-lush Himalayan mountainsides for wood. The rain then washes unimpeded down the slopes into rivers, causing, along with melting Himalayan glaciers, more destructive floods downstream in India and Bangladesh. Thanks to drought and diminishing groundwater today water taps run dry in many cities from India to Zimbabwe.

Deforestation promotes environmental destruction. In the twentieth century half of the world's rain forests were cut down; commercial loggers obtained wood for housing, farmers and large corporations converted forests into farms and plantations, and poor people collected firewood. This destruction, often by commodity-driven industrial agriculture, continues at a furious pace today, especially in Southeast Asia and South America, displacing indigenous communities and reducing or eliminating many native plant and animal species. Between 1975 and 2000 a quarter of the Central American rain forest was turned into grasslands, often to raise beef cattle for North American fast-food restaurants. Three nations hold most of the world's remaining tropical rain forests: Brazil, Congo, and Indonesia. None of them have proven responsible stewards of the land. In all of them wildfires deliberately set to clear land for agriculture or mining raged out of control in 2019. Clearing tropical land exposes thin topsoil to leaching of the nutrients by rains; after a few years the cleared land becomes unusable desert. Deforestation has enormous long-term consequences, from decreasing rainfall to losing valuable pharmaceuticals, plants, and animals. Scientists argue that protecting healthy and restoring damaged forests is urgent because it can reduce carbon emissions; trees and other vegetation currently absorb around a quarter of carbon emissions that humans add to the atmosphere.

Human activity has already annihilated wildlife on a massive sale. Populations of mammals, fish, birds, amphibians, and reptiles have declined dramatically between 1970 and 2018, which experts worry threatens the health of civilizations. A 2019 study concludes that North America has lost about 3 billion birds since 1970, a 30 percent decline, mostly from habitat loss, pesticides, and predatory cats. A 2019 U.N. report found that at least one million species (of the eight million known on the planet today) are at risk of extinction over the next few decades due to human-related causes. The list includes everything from mammals to saltwater fish to butterflies to spiders to corals to soil microbes but they are all connected in the ecosystem web of life. Some studies suggest that a quarter to half of all current species could disappear by 2100, a staggering figure.

Destroying forests, which absorb carbon dioxide, and desertification also contributed, along with industrial pollution and carbon dioxide-producing factories and fossil fuels (which power our vehicles, railroads, airplanes, and many consumer products) to the acceleration of global warming, which the vast majority of climate scientists agree is chiefly caused or at least greatly accelerated by human activity. The climate change or global warming crisis is dramatically altering and challenging the world. Carbon dioxide levels in the atmosphere are the highest in millions of years, spiking up over fifty percent since around 1960. For this reason some scholars term the era since the mid-1950s as the Great Acceleration as the pace grew more rapidly. Global temperatures today are the highest

in at least four thousand years and, according to some studies, perhaps one hundred twenty-five thousand years. Human activity has caused a 1.8 degree of warming since the 1850s. While parts of the world warmed or cooled over the past two thousand years, now it is happening everywhere in the world at about the same time, an unprecedented development. The years 2015–2018 have seen the warmest years since records began, and 2019 is on pace to be hotter still as record summer heat baked nearly all the world, including the Antarctic, Arctic, Greenland, and Siberia and Alaska (where the permafrost is melting). Antarctic ice loss today is six times greater than the 1970s while Greenland seems to be at a tipping point. If the polar and Greenland ice sheets keep melting as rapidly as they are today, ocean levels will rise substantially, flooding lowlands, river deltas, coastal cities, and small islands. Already some low-lying cities such as Miami, Jakarta, and Guangzhou experience regular flooding, disrupting life. By 2050 over 150 million people may be displaced as rising seas make low lying cities like Ho Chi Minh City (Saigon), Bangkok, Shanghai, Mumbai, Alexandria, and New Orleans unlivable. The latest predictions on sea-level rise vary, ranging from 1.5 to 3 feet by 2100, although some estimates are higher still.

The oceans are rapidly becoming warmer, greatly affecting sea life mostly in a negative way; the same is true of lakes and streams. Rising temperatures will also ruin good farmland as drought increases and make tropical regions unlivable. As global warming brings drought to Central America and fosters a disease that destroys coffee crops, desperate climate refugees migrate north to seek refuge, a part of a likely growing worldwide refugee flow from tropical lands. Some worry that the annual monsoons that bring rain and life to South Asia may diminish or shift location, undermining agriculture. Some Indian cities including Chennai already face a climate emergency, since they have no running water because extreme heat and drought drained their reservoirs. The Himalayan glaciers that feed all of South Asia's great rivers may all melt by 2100.

A landmark report in 2018 on climate change from the U.N. scientific panel (known as the IPCC) commissioned by the Paris Climate Agreement paints a far more dire picture of immediate consequences than earlier studies, based on an analysis of six thousand scientific investigations. They found that if greenhouse gas emissions continue at their current rate, the atmosphere will warm dangerously by as much as 2.7°F (1.5°C) by 2100. The results would include worsening food shortages, many more wildfires, and massive die-off of coral reefs as soon as 2040. They conclude that avoiding serious damage and avoiding a potentially catastrophic ecological tipping point requires transforming the world economy at a speed and scale that has "no documented historic precedent" by reducing greenhouse pollution by 45 percent from 2010 levels by 2030, and 100 percent by 2050. Some specialists call the climate crisis our third world war requiring a bold response. Scientists debate how many years we have to stave off a climate catastrophe, with most estimates ranging from fifteen to thirty years.

Many studies show that global warming tends to intensify weather extremes and events, and hence poses wide-ranging risks to humanity as some parts of the world may face increased climate-related crises, among them more frequent and deadly heat waves, wildfires, hurricanes, flooding, sea-level rise, drought, and shortages of food and clean water. The most pessimistic observers worry that the climate crisis, if not addressed seriously, could bring the end of human civilization by 2050 or 2100. Some worry that the annual monsoons that bring rain and life to South Asia may diminish or shift location, undermining agriculture. The most alarmed scientists suggest that in a few centuries perhaps a runaway greenhouse effect could destroy life on Earth. Some scientists have suggested measures that might limit the temperature rise, including a massive shift to renewable energy, planting huge numbers of trees and plants, piling artificial snow on the West Antarctic ice sheet, and making radical changes in Earth's diets and unfettered capitalism. A new IPCC report in 2019 calls for dramatic reforms in land use involving the way people eat, grow food, and manage forests. They urge reducing red meat and increasing plant-based food consumption. Some of the proposed solutions are technically possible today but politically and culturally unlikely. Leaders who dismiss climate change as a threat, oppose environmental protections, and favor more fossil fuel and coal use and clearing forests for farming and mining govern major greenhouse gas-producing nations such as the United States, Australia, and Brazil.

Movements and organizations to counter environmental decay and climate change have emerged. Many such as the IPCC operate under U.N. auspices. Some nongovernmental organizations, such as the Sierra Club in the United States and the Malaysian Nature Society, appeal chiefly to middle-class people. Others, such as the Chipko tree protection movement in India and the Greenbelt movement in Kenya, bring middle-class urbanites and rural peasants together. In 2004 Greenbelt leader and global environmental activist Wangari Maathai won the Noble Peace Prize (see Meet the People: Wangari Maathai, Kenyan Environmental Activist). The United Nations environmental and climate programs issue regular reports warning that environmental destruction, combined with poverty and population growth, threatens the long-term health of the planet and its people. In 2019 young people became involved in an issue that will affect their futures. An important role was played by a remarkable sixteen-year-old Swedish activist, Greta Thunberg, who campaigned tirelessly on the threat and demanding action, organizing marches, conferences, and summits, and addressing the United Nations General Assembly. In September 2019 youth-led climate protests took place around the world, often organized by girls and young women. The 2018 IPCC report articulates the rationale for action: "Limiting global warming…would reduce challenging impacts on ecosystems, human health, and well-being.… The decisions we make today are critical in ensuring a safe and sustainable world for everyone, both now and in the future."[14]

KEY POINTS

▶ Globalization has boosted world economies and has reaped great rewards for countries such as the United States and China, but it has not always benefited the lives of poor people and has also led to continued foreign domination of some groups and nations by others.

▶ Industrialization has spread throughout Asia and Latin America, the Third Industrial Revolution has created powerful new technologies, the Green Revolution has allowed for increased agricultural production, while the service and information industries have grown rapidly.

▶ Women have faced great problems in the modern economy as they have been drastically underpaid for their contributions, but grassroots programs such as the Grameen Bank have offered some increased economic opportunity.

▶ Over the past fifty years, the world population has exploded, especially in Asia, Africa, and Latin America, prompting fears that it will eventually outstrip available resources; while in more developed countries, fertility rates have dropped and populations have grown older.

▶ Economic development, industrialization, desertification, and deforestation have destroyed or harmed environments and contributed heavily to global warming, which will have a major impact on human life today and in the future.

26-4 New Global Networks and Their Consequences

▨ NETWORKS ▨ SOCIETIES

Ⓠ How did growing networks linking societies influence social, political, and economic life?

Some scholars perceive a "spaceship earth" or **global village**, an interconnected world community in which all people, regardless of nationality, share a common fate. "Global village" boundaries are fluid, the inhabitants highly mobile. Globalization has reshaped politics and cultures, fostering movement of people, diseases, cultures, and religions. Increasingly both unity

CONNECTION to TODAY

How have global networks and social media shaped you, your family, and community?

and diversity characterize the world, with common influences mixing with local traditions.

26-4a The Global Spread of Migrants, Refugees, and Disease

Human migration has been a permanent features of world history, going back to the earliest hominids. Today, many people live in

global village An interconnected world community in which all people, regardless of their nationality, share a common fate.

---

[14]IPCC, *Summary for Policymakers of IPCC Special Report on Global Warming of 1.5°C Approved by Governments* (Incheon, South Korea: Intergovernmental Panel on Climate Change, 2018), 4.

Wangari Maathai, Kenyan Environmental Activist

Wangari Maathai (**wahn-GAHR-ee muh-THIGH**), who won the 2004 Nobel Peace Prize for her environmental activism, was born in 1940 and grew up in Nyeri, a small village in Kenya, East Africa. As a young girl, fetching water from a small stream, she grew fascinated by creatures living in the stream and loved the lush trees and shrubs around her village. But over the years the stream dried up, silt choked nearby rivers, and once green land grew barren. She lamented the assault on nature. Girls in rural Kenya in the 1940s and 1950s commonly spent their youth preparing for marriage and children. But a brother convinced Wangari's parents to send the inquisitive girl to the primary school he attended.

After graduating from a Roman Catholic high school, Wangari won a scholarship to study in the United States, earning a B.A. in biology from a small Kansas college in 1964 and then completing an M.A. at the University of Pittsburgh in 1966. She credited her U.S. experience, including observations of anti-Vietnam War protests, with encouraging her interest in democracy and free speech. Returning home, she earned a Ph.D. at Nairobi University in 1971, the first East African woman to achieve that degree, and then joined the faculty to teach biological sciences. She became a dean and joined a local organization coordinating United Nations environmental programs.

Throughout her life Wangari faced and overcame gender barriers, including in her marriage to Mwangi Maathai; they had three children, but, their relationship souring, they divorced after he was elected to parliament in 1974. She attributed the breakup to gender prejudice: "I think my activism may have contributed to my being perceived as an [un]conventional [woman]. And that puts pressure on the man you live with, because he is then perceived as if he is not controlling you properly."

To stop the spread of desert in Kenya by planting trees, the dogged Wangari founded the Greenbelt movement on Earth Day 1977. Talking to women when she served on the National Council of Women, she learned they needed clean drinking water, nutritious food, and energy. Trees could provide for all these needs: stop soil erosion, help water conservation, bear fruit, provide fuel and building materials, offer shade, and also enhance the beauty of the landscape. Over ten thousand Kenyans, largely women, became involved, planting and nurturing more than thirty million trees and earning a small income for each tree planted. The movement showed Kenyans that the health of their forests and rivers mattered for both their immediate and future well-being.

IMAGE 26.6 **Wangari Maathai, Kenyan Environmentalist** Wangari Maathai, winner of the 2004 Nobel Peace Prize for her work as leader of the Green Belt movement, plants a tree at the Freedom Corner Uhuru Park in Nairobi in 2004. The Greenbelt movement has sought to empower women, improve the environment, and fight corruption in Kenya for over thirty years. Addressing the United Nations headquarters in New York in 2005 she challenged world leaders to dirty their hands by planting trees and working to stop the destruction of forests worldwide.

Q Do you think that Maathai should be considered a positive role model for African and world women?

Realizing that logging contracts enriched leaders of corrupt governments, including Kenya's repressive regime, Wangari perceived the link between environmental health and good governance. As a result, the Greenbelt Movement launched civic education programs, linking human rights, ecology, and individual activism and helping thousands of women gain more control of their lives. Women took on local leadership roles, running tree nurseries and planning community-based projects. Thanks to the movement, she said, "women have become aware that planting trees or fighting to save forests from being chopped down is part of a larger mission to create a society that respects democracy, the rule of law, human rights, and the rights of women."

Wangari and her campaign to empower and educate rural women had many critics in Kenya, including the country's dictatorial president. She was threatened by violence, harassed, sometimes severely beaten, arrested over a dozen times, and had her public appearances broken up by police. When she led protests against the building of a sixty-two-story tower that would destroy much of Nairobi's main public park in the mid-1970s, the police killed seven of her associates. Still, she continued to protest illegal forest clearing and the Kenya government's holding of political prisoners. Wangari's efforts inspired similar Greenbelt movements in the United States, Haiti, and over thirty other African countries; she became an international environmental spokesperson. In 2002, during the first fair elections in years, Wangari ran for the Kenyan parliament as a Green Party member, gaining election by a huge majority. From 2003 until 2005 she served as an Assistant Minister for Environment, Natural Resources, and Wildlife. In awarding her the Nobel Peace Prize, the Nobel committee praised Wangari for taking a comprehensive "approach to sustainable development that embraces democracy, human relations, and women's rights," saying that she "thinks globally and acts locally." She celebrated winning the Nobel Prize by planting a tree on the slopes of Mount Kenya, near her childhood home, and recommitting herself to the struggle for a better world. Wangari died of ovarian cancer in 2011.

Reflection Questions

1. How did Wangari's activities help Kenyan women?
2. How did Wangari's efforts to protect the environment also foster change in the political and social realms?

Note: Quotations from *Friends of the Greenbelt Movement North America*, gbmna.org/a.php?id.

705

nations filled with immigrants and their descendants from around the globe. Nearly 30 percent of Australians in 2016 were immigrants; many more were the children of immigrants. Thirty million people moved to labor-short western Europe between 1945 and 1975, chiefly from North Africa, West Africa, Turkey, South Asia, and the Caribbean. Similarly, since the early twentieth century millions of Mexicans, legally or undocumented, entered the United States, many filling low-wage jobs. In 2017 the 11.3 million Mexicans constituted about a quarter of the forty-five million total immigrants in the nation. Immigrants rapidly transformed cities such as Vancouver, Los Angeles, Sydney, London, and Paris into internationalized hubs of world culture and commerce. The many educated people moving to Western nations constitute a "brain drain" from poor countries. Hence, South Asian doctors and Philippine nurses play key roles in North American health care. Cosmopolitanism—the blending of peoples and cultures—flavors cities closely linked to the world economy, such as Hong Kong, Singapore, São Paulo, London, Dubai, and New York. While globalization of trade and jobs dissolves economic boundaries, governments increasingly impose tighter border controls to discourage illegal immigration, not always successfully.

The great majority of the over one hundred million voluntary migrants to foreign countries have moved for economic rather than political reasons. Many migrants—some from impoverished regions such as Central America and South Asia, others from more prosperous nations such as South Korea and Taiwan—have sought better economic opportunities in the industrialized West. Small Indian- and Pakistani-run sundry goods and grocery stores, known as corner shops, have become fixtures in British cities. Millions of Asians and Africans work in the Middle East. Especially mobile, Filipinos migrated for short periods to other Southeast Asian nations and the Middle East and more permanently to North America. Some eight million Filipinos now live abroad. A Moroccan woman whose husband worked in Europe and rarely returned home expressed her distress: "Germany, Belgium, France and Netherlands, Where are you situated? I have never seen your countries, I do not speak your language. I am afraid my love forgets me in your paradise. I ask you, give him back to me."[15]

From the 1960s to around 2010 political turbulence, wars, genocides, government repression, poverty, and famine prompted desperate people to flee nations engulfed in political violence, such as Sudan, Guatemala, Afghanistan, Somalia, Syria, Iraq, and Cambodia, and drought-plagued states like Ethiopia and Mali. Cubans, Chinese, Laotians (**lao-OH-shuhnz**), and Vietnamese escaped communist-run states that restricted their freedoms. Others, among them Haitians, Chileans, Iranians, and Congolese, escaped brutal right-wing dictatorships or corrupt despotisms. In 2018 the refugee figures were the highest since World War II, reaching seventy-one million. In recent years most refugees are escaping economic meltdown in Venezuela, repression in Myanmar, and violence and poverty in Central America, West Africa, Congo, Somalia, Yemen, Syria, and Afghanistan. But citizens in refuge countries often resented the refugees. By the 1990s many nations, especially in Europe, became more cautious in granting political asylum. Hence when many refugees made it to Europe or North America, they were not always welcome, but many others found refuge of some sort in less wealthy or even poor countries like Colombia, Turkey, Uganda, Pakistan, and Mexico, eking out an existence in refugee camps or urban slums. Millions of refugees have remained for decades, even generations, in squalid refugee camps, often fed and housed by international aid organizations. Many Palestinians have lived in refugee camps in Egypt, Jordan, and Lebanon for six or seven decades. In 2017–2019 the migrant and refugee flows to the United States and especially to Europe became a flood, upsetting politics and fueling nationalistic, right-wing populist movements that opposed accepting them.

Diseases traveling trade and migration routes have produced major pandemics, or massive disease outbreaks, throughout history. Although modern medicine has eliminated diseases long plaguing humanity like smallpox, leprosy, and polio, other diseases, such as cholera, Ebola, malaria, and HIV/AIDS, still bedevil people. Cholera, a bacterial disease, still kills several thousand people a year in poor countries; malaria, spread by mosquitoes, debilitates millions of people in tropical regions. HIV is partly spread through the increased trade and travel associated with globalization. By 2011 some thirty-four million people around the world, two-thirds in Africa, were infected with either HIV or AIDS; 1.7 million died annually, leaving millions of orphans. As much as 30 percent of the adult population of some African nations was HIV positive. AIDS victims are often rejected by their families and communities, dying alone and neglected by society. Experts worry about several viral diseases, potentially killing millions, that pass from birds, poultry, and pigs to humans. Both United Nations agencies and private organizations have worked to reduce health threats and treat victims. But the travel of migrants, tourists, businesspeople, armies, truck drivers, sailors, and others spreads diseases.

26-4b Cultures, Religions, and Societies Across Borders

Cultural products and religions have spread across national borders and creatively mixed with local traditions. Popular culture, produced for commercial purposes and spread by mass media such as radio, television, film, and, in recent years, social media, video games, and streaming services, has become part of everyday life for billions of people. Western influences have been pervasive, although often superficial. Western videos, pop music recordings, jeans, and shopping malls attract many Asian, African, and Latin American youth, but their influence on rural areas is often more limited. Some countries like China have pervasively censored Western films, books, and other media while promoting their own social media and Internet platforms. No common world culture has emerged. While the U.S. has the world's largest film industries, India, China, and Japan are also major producers of movies. India has the world's second oldest film industry. Cheap, often pirated, audio cassettes in the 1970s, videocassettes in the 1980s, and DVDs in the 1990s enabled even more people to enjoy music and film while helping political or religious groups to spread their messages. Modern media

---

[15]From Hazel Johnson and Henry Bernstein, eds., *Third World Lives of Struggle* (London: Heinemann Educational, 1982), 173.

have reshaped people's lives, especially in cities. One observer in the 1990s noted the global popularity of television:

> *Take a walk down any street, in any city or village, as the twilight fades and the darkness comes. Whether you are in London or Tokyo, Cairo or New York, Buenos Aires or Singapore, a small blue light will flicker at you from the unshuttered windows. These lights are the tiny knots in the seamless web of modern media.*[16]

By 2019 many people still watched movies and programs on television (with cable and streaming services like Netflix, Hulu, and Roku offering countless options) but many others used their computers, tablets, or smartphones. Today file sharing and social media make these products even easier to obtain. Some observers think that the once dominant sway of American popular culture is declining as more people turn to other attractive and entertaining products as well as their own cultural offerings. Hence, Bollywood (Indian) films, Turkish television soap operas (known as *dizi*), and K-pop music have huge audiences around the world and even some following in North America.

Popular music reflects cultural mixing and the spread of mass media. Some popular styles, such as American jazz and Brazilian samba, emerged well before World War II, but most appeared after 1945. Rock, jazz, and rap, inspired by or deriving from African American forms, found audiences all over the world. Vaclav Havel (**VAH-slav HAH-vel**), leader of the movement that overthrew Czech communism, credited U.S. rock musician Frank Zappa's songs with inspiring his activism. Havel even wrote songs for a Czech rock group. Rebellious youth all over the world, in cities like Manila, Cape Town, Paris, Casablanca, and São Paulo, use rap and hip-hop to express their feelings. The sudden death in 2009 of American pop musician Michael Jackson, known equally for his spectacular musical talents and bizarre lifestyle, illustrated U.S. popular culture's global influence. His passing and legacy dominated mass media in many nations for weeks, a star-studded memorial tribute was televised around the world, and millions of fans bought his recordings and memorabilia. Through their global reputations, pop stars also mount concerts to address issues like racism, political prisoners, famine, and African poverty. Bono, Irish rock band U2's lead singer, campaigns among world leaders for causes such as debt relief for poor nations.

Many musicians have mixed indigenous and imported influences, often from outside the West. Hence, Congolese popular music, which borrowed Latin American dance rhythms, gained audiences throughout Africa and Europe. Indian film music and Arab folk music influenced Southeast Asian and East African pop music. Even pop music that does not cross many borders can reflect creative blending. *Dangdut*, an Indonesian popular music, originated as a fusion of Western rock, Indian film music, and local folk music. The major dangdut star, Rhoma Irama (**ROW-muh ih-RAH-muh**), sometimes faced arrest for political protests in songs addressing poverty, human rights abuses, struggles of the underdog, Islamic moral teachings, and betrayal of nationalist promises.

Although secular thought became more popular than ever before in history, over three-quarters of the world's people identify with one or another universal religion with roots deep in the past, including in 2018 over 2.4 billion Christians (33 percent), 1.8 billion Muslims (24 percent), 1.2 billion Hindus (15 percent), five hundred twenty-one million Buddhists (7 percent), and 14.5 million Jews. Well over eight hundred million practice a local faith, such as animism or Daoism; another 1.2 million (16 percent) profess no religion, many holding secular viewpoints (see Map 26.3). Religion sometimes underlies national identity, as in Roman Catholic Poland and Ireland or Muslim Bangladesh and Pakistan. Religious leaders have debated how much, if at all, their faiths need to change to better engage the contemporary world. Pope John XXIII (pope 1958–1963) liberalized Catholic church practices, such as by having the mass in vernacular languages rather than Latin, and encouraged interfaith dialogue. Meanwhile, in the 1960s through the 1970s a controversial movement among Latin American Catholic clergy and laypeople, liberation theology, cooperated with socialist and communist groups to address poverty. Muslim liberals and militants have confronted each other over issues like the role of women, relations with non-Muslims, and basing their legal systems on Islamic law. In sub-Saharan Africa and Southeast Asia, some Muslims have become more devout, and more men have studied in the Middle East, often returning with more militant fundamentalist or radical views.

The easy spread of ideas in the globalized world has worked to the advantage of portable creeds not dependent on one culture or setting. In Africa, polytheism and animism have faded while Christianity and Islam, promoted by missionary activity, have gained wider followings. Protestants have evangelized and gained ground in predominantly Catholic Latin America. Pentacostalism, an American-born Christian tradition promoting charismatic worship and faith healing, has developed large international followings. Protestants and Catholics compete with each other, and often with Muslims, in Africa, Southeast Asia, and East Asia. Christianity increasingly has become a non-Western faith, with far more believers in Africa, Asia, and Latin America than in Europe and North America. Christian and Muslim missionaries appeal to the downtrodden, promising both spiritual health and material wealth, often recasting their messages to recognize local cultural traditions. Beginning in the nineteenth century the Hindu-linked practice of yoga began attracting some followers outside of India. In the past few decades yoga has spread all around the world, splintering into several distinct practices and appealing to many middle-class people, especially women, in Western nations and elsewhere, who see it largely as physical exercise or technique for contemplation but may know or learn little about its religious origin.

Yet, organized religion has declined in East Asia and much of the West. Communist regimes discouraged religious observance; many Japanese found neither their traditional faiths nor imported religions relevant to their lives; and church attendance and membership in Europe, Canada, and Australia fell dramatically. Religious dogmas competed with changing social attitudes. Many predominantly Catholic European nations legalized abortion and moved toward equal rights for

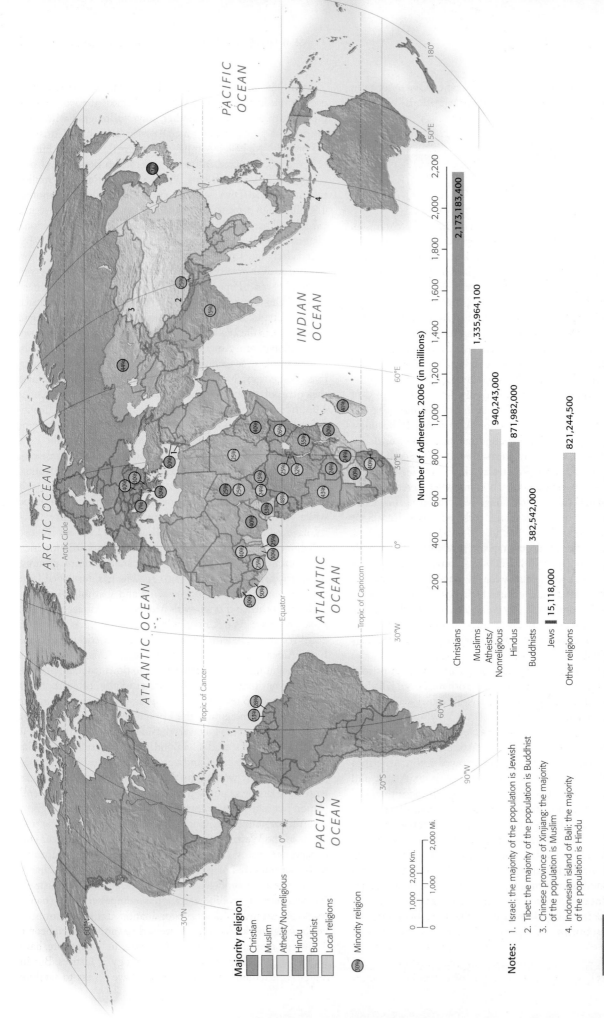

Majority religion

- Christian
- Muslim
- Atheist/Nonreligious
- Hindu
- Buddhist
- Local religions

50% Minority religion

0	1,000	2,000 Km.	
0	1,000	2,000 Mi.	

Notes:
1. Israel: the majority of the population is Jewish
2. Tibet: the majority of the population is Buddhist
3. Chinese province of Xinjiang: the majority of the population is Muslim
4. Indonesian island of Bali: the majority of the population is Hindu

Number of Adherents, 2006 (in millions)

Christians — 2,173,183,400
Muslims — 1,335,964,100
Atheists/Nonreligious — 940,243,000
Hindus — 871,982,000
Buddhists — 382,542,000
Jews — 15,118,000
Other religions — 821,244,500

MAP 26.3 World Religions Christianity has the most believers and is the dominant faith in the Americas, Oceania, Europe, Russia, and central and southern Africa. Most people in the northern half of Africa, western Asia, and Central Asia embrace Islam. Hindus are concentrated in India, and Buddhists in East and Southeast Asia.

Q What does this 2015 map tell us about the geographical spread of the major religions?

LGBTQ people, challenging church policies. Only a minority of countries have recognized and protected LGBTQ rights; in some countries, especially in Africa and Asia, homosexual behavior has been condemned by religious groups and is illegal and actively punished by shunning, harassment, imprisonment, and even death. But in the past decade same-sex marriage has become a reality in the United States, Canada, Western Europe, Australia, New Zealand, South Africa, Taiwan, and some Latin American countries such as Brazil, Mexico, and Uruguay.

Tensions remain between different faiths as some Muslims, Christians, Hindus, Buddhists, and Jews have become more militant and intolerant. Sparked by political differences, some Christians and Muslims have attacked each other in Indonesia, the Philippines, Ethiopia, Egypt, Lebanon, Yugoslavia, and Nigeria. Conflicts between Muslims and Hindus in India, Catholics and Protestants in Northern Ireland, Sunni and Shi'ite Muslims in Pakistan and western Asia, and Buddhists and Muslims in Myanmar, Sri Lanka, and Thailand have generated sporadic violence. Some Sunni regimes have discriminated against or persecuted Shi'ites. Indeed, several countries, including China, Myanmar, Saudi Arabia, and North Korea, repress and even outlaw various religious groups. Religious militancy has also grown. Some Muslim militants have turned the notion of *jihad*, or struggle within believers to strengthen their faith, into holy war against unbelievers, secular Muslims, and countries or groups they consider anti-Muslim; they hope to turn secular states into Islamic ones. Often known as Islamists or jihadis, militants appeal especially to the embittered young and poor. Jihadis unsettle politics in and terrorize Muslim countries like Pakistan, Afghanistan, Nigeria, and Mali. Many Muslims oppose market capitalism and despise the West's revealing clothing styles, open romantic behavior, independent women, LGBTQ activists, rebellious youth, and raunchy television programs and movies. At the same time, some Christians, especially in the United States, Latin America, and Africa, have turned to literal, fundamentalist interpretations of the Bible, question scientific knowledge, and promote proselytizing. Some Nigerian Protestant churches send missionaries to the United States and Europe, while South Korean Protestants evangelize in China. Conservative churches have often opposed secular culture, rejected scientific findings incompatible with biblical accounts, and condemned political and social movements promoting socialism, feminism, legalized abortion, and homosexual rights.

26-4c Global Communications and Movements

A worldwide communications network has facilitated globalization. Radio in the early 1900s was followed by tape recording, television, and then transistors, fostering miniaturization of electronics. In 1953 portable transistor radios became available and soon reached even remote villages without electricity, opening them to world news and culture. Hence, by the 1960s in remote central Borneo, a densely forested island divided between Indonesia and Malaysia, isolated villagers listened to radio broadcasts from the United States, Britain, and Australia, some learning the songs of Western pop musicians like the British rock group The Beatles.

Technological breakthroughs have generated more rapid and widespread communications, creating a networked world.

The first general-purpose computers were built in 1948; in 1958 the first silicon microchips made possible the first personal computers. By 2015 the world had nearly two billion personal computers. By 2018 some four billion Internet users (over 50 percent of humanity), 3.2 billion social media users, 5.2 billion mobile phone users, and countless web pages and blogs were all part of a vast information superhighway. Every minute millions of e-mails, texts, and tweets are dispatched instantly via computer, smartphone, or tablet, often to foreign countries. An interested reader in Hong Kong, Ghana, or Finland can access online versions of newspapers, such as the *New York Times, Al Ahram* in Cairo, or the *Deccan Herald* in India. The rise of 24-hour cable news networks reaching worldwide audiences, such as U.S.-based CNN, the BBC, and the Arab-language Al Jazeera, based in the Persian Gulf state of Qatar, widened access to diverse views. Technologically literate people send music, video, and photos around the world via electronic media.

Transnational computer companies, such as AOL, Apple, Microsoft, Amazon, and Google, have helped people use the Internet for communication and knowledge acquisition. Those anywhere with Internet access, unless restricted by governments (such as in China, Iran, and Pakistan), have had access to diverse communication networks and social media platforms, among them Facebook, Snapchat, Twitter, Whatsapp, and Instagram. But while making huge fortunes for their owners and investors, some social media companies, especially Facebook and Twitter, have been fined and heavily criticized for selling users' data and allowing fake news on their platforms, which may have affected the 2016 elections in the United States and has also prompted debate in other countries.

The rapid evolution of media and information technology has many consequences. Through fax communications, orbiting communications satellites, portable phones, electronic mail, and the World Wide Web, information can be transmitted outside governments' reach, diminishing their power to shape thinking. Hence, repressive states seeking to limit information flow, such as Iran, Cuba, Burma, and China, have banned satellite dish receivers and jammed access to controversial and dissident websites. These efforts have been only partly successful. Protesters in nations like China, Egypt, and Iran use cellphones, Twitter, and YouTube to coordinate their activities, spread their message, and circumvent government control of mass media. The U.S.-based social media site Facebook claimed 2.4 billion members and active users worldwide, the great majority of them outside the United States. Some technologies, especially the World Wide Web, have enhanced the value of education and of English, now a world language like Latin two thousand years ago and Arabic one thousand years ago. While Chinese and Spanish boast more native speakers, English has become the world's most widely spoken hyper-central or universal language. Perhaps a quarter of the world's people know some English, including up to three hundred-fifty million Chinese and at least another one hundred million Indians. For various reasons, including its dominance in science, business, and many professional fields, Anglo-American popular and mass culture has also permeated much of the world. Asian countries with many educated people fluent in English, such as India, Malaysia, and Singapore, have an advantage in attracting high-technology industries. But in the poorest nations, only a lucky few have access to satellite dishes, fax machines, and networked computers. Furthermore, many nations resent the strong U.S. influence over the Internet.

Social and political movements originating in different countries transcend borders, linking to similar movements elsewhere. Diverse transnational organizations promote issues such as political prisoners, women's rights, and anti-racism. Amnesty International, based in Britain, publicizes the plight of people imprisoned solely for their political views and activities, organizing letter-writing and pressure campaigns to seek their release. The World Social Forum, formed in 2001 and meeting annually in Brazil, brings together nongovernment organizations and activists who believe that globalization undermines workers' rights and environmental protection.

Movements or upheavals in one nation or region sometimes spread widely. During the 1960s, students, workers, and political radicals in many nations organized protests against the U.S. war in Vietnam, racism, unresponsive governments, capitalism, and other concerns. The same writers, music, and ideas often influenced young protesters. Some protesters revered leftist icons like Ho Chi Minh and Cuban revolutionary Che Guevara; others looked to non-communists or even anticommunists, such as the dissidents who opposed Poland's communist regime. After widespread youth activism in 1968, environmental, peace, workers' rights, LGBTQ rights, and feminist movements grew, especially in industrialized nations.

Women have actively sought to expand their rights, placing women's issues on the international agenda. The United

Nations periodically sponsors global conferences on women's issues such as gender equality. However, women activists, divided by culture and nationality, sometimes disagree on goals and strategies. In the United Nations' fourth World Conference on Women, held in China in 1995, the forty thousand delegates differed sharply on priorities. While delegates from rich nations favored expanding women's employment options, social freedom, and control over their bodies, Asian, African, and Latin American delegates emphasized their families' health and economic security. One Indian delegate described U.S. delegates' goals as irrelevant to Indian women: "They ask for abortion rights. We ask for safe drinking water and basic health care."[17] Abortion has become legal in most Western and many Asian nations but remains controversial. A 2017 study on closing the gender gap for one hundred forty-four countries found that Iceland, Norway, Finland, Rwanda, and Sweden had the most gender equality; fifteen of the top twenty-five were Western countries. Yemen, Pakistan, Syria, Chad, Mali, and Saudi Arabia had the least equality. The U.S. ranked 49th (mainly because of low political empowerment), just behind Peru and just ahead of Zimbabwe. The annual International Women's Day in 2019 was celebrated with marches and protests in cities around the world with the slogan #Balance for Better, with calls for a more gender-balanced world.

Despite disagreements, women have worked across borders on many issues. For example, women activists and their male supporters have fought the tradition, common in some Muslim societies, of jailing or killing women for adultery while exonerating the man responsible. In 2005 Mukhtaran Bibi (**MOOK-tahr-an BIH-bee**), an illiterate woman from an impoverished Pakistani village without electricity, gained worldwide sympathy for her resistance to male brutality. The tribal council ruled she be gang-raped to punish her family for a village dispute. Instead of following custom by ending the "disgrace" through suicide, she bravely pursued the rapists in court. They were convicted, and she used the money awarded her to start two village schools, one for boys and one for girls. When a higher court overturned the men's convictions, her courageous refusal to accept the verdict caused an international outcry. Men and women around the world, alerted by news accounts and Internet appeals, donated money and made her a symbol of the need for women's rights. Mukhtaran Bibi inspired millions everywhere with her courage and faith in education and justice.

IMAGE 26.7 **Apple Store in China** Apple computers and products have been very popular in China. This photo from 2016 shows a crowded Apple store on the popular Nanjing Road commercial district in Shanghai. Internet users in China numbered over 450 million in 2010.

Q Why do you think that computers, especially Apples, are so popular in China?

[17] Quoted in David Reynolds, *One World Divisible: A Global History Since 1945* (New York: W. W. Norton, 2000), 491.

KEY POINTS

▶ In the new global village, millions of people have immigrated to foreign countries seeking greater economic opportunity or an escape from insufferable conditions at home, including political repression, famine, and civil war.

▶ Modern medicine has eliminated many diseases, but cholera and malaria are still serious problems, and AIDS has seriously affected India, Southeast Asia, and especially Africa.

▶ Western consumer culture has spread around the world, while musical forms from different cultures have mingled and musicians and performers have expressed political and often controversial views.

▶ Worldwide communication has been facilitated by technologies such as radio, television, the Internet, and social media platforms, making a vast array of information available, even in countries such as China, Iran, and Cuba, whose governments have attempted to limit its availability.

Chapter Summary

The later twentieth century proved turbulent. Nationalism spread in Asia and Africa, leading to decolonization. During the 1950s and 1960s most of the Western colonies gained their independence through negotiations, the threat of violence, or armed struggle, and social revolutionaries gained power in some nations. However, the West maintained a strong economic presence in many former colonies. The rivalry between the United States and the USSR also shaped the global system, generating a Cold War in which the two superpowers faced each other indirectly or through surrogates. The powerful United States had a large group of allies and sometimes intervened in Asian and Latin American nations, while the USSR occupied eastern Europe. The collapse of the communist bloc and then the USSR allowed the United States to become the world's lone superpower.

The world was also shaped by globalization, with its unprecedented flow of money, products, information, and ideas across national borders. The global economy grew rapidly but did not spread its benefits equally. As industrialization spread, most Western and some Asian and Latin American nations prospered, but many poor nations struggled to escape underdevelopment and raise living standards. A billion people remained mired in deep poverty. Environmental destruction and climate change are affecting human life around the world. Meanwhile millions of people migrated, social and political movements addressed local and global problems, universal religions gained new converts, and the information superhighway and other technological innovations linked millions of people in new ways. New international terrorist networks also challenged governments and reshaped world politics.

Key Terms

First World 686
Second World 686
Third World 686
Fourth World 686
Cold War 687

guerrilla warfare 688
terrorism 689
nuclear weapons 689
globalization 694
multinational corporations 694

Third Industrial Revolution 696
Green Revolution 697
development 697
desertification 702
global village 704

East Asian Resurgence, Since 1945

Once China's destiny is in the hands of the people, China, like the sun rising in the east, will illuminate every corner with a brilliant flame, and build a new, powerful and prosperous [society].

—Mao Zedong, Chinese communist leader[1]

Sergio Azenha/Alamy Stock Photo

IMAGE 27.1 **Silk Street Market in Beijing** The East Asian nations enjoyed an economic resurgence in this era. Since the 1980s, China has boasted the world's fastest-growing economy and rapid commercial expansion. One of Beijing's most popular commercial districts, Chaoyang, is home to many shops including the vast Silk Street Market, which hosts over seventeen hundred retail vendors. It is notorious among tourists for their wide selection of counterfeit designer-brand apparel.

Q What can we learn from the photo about the shopping experience for urban Chinese and foreign visitors?

---

[1]Quoted in Jerome Chen, *Mao and the Chinese Revolution* (New York: Oxford University Press, 1967), 6.

On October 1, 1949, Mao Zedong (1893–1976), the

Chinese communist leader, was driven into Beijing accompanied by soldiers from the communist People's Liberation Army. Mao, a fifty-five-year-old peasant's son, had never been out of China and had spent the previous twenty-two years living in remote rural areas directing brutal warfare against Japanese invaders and the Chinese government. Ahead of Mao's car rolled a Sherman tank, originally donated by the United States to the Republic of China, headed by Jiang Jieshi **(Chiang Kai-shek)** (1887–1975), to help crush Mao's communist forces. But Chiang's army had lost, and the president had fled to the large offshore island of Taiwan. Mao climbed to the top of the Gate of Heavenly Peace, the entrance to the Qing emperors' Forbidden City overlooking spacious Tiananmen Square. Chinese jammed the square to hear their new ruler announce a new communist state, the People's Republic of China (PRC). Referring to a century of corrupt governments, humiliation, and domination by Western nations and Japan, Mao proclaimed: "The Chinese people have stood up. Nobody will insult us again."[2]

The People's Republic marked a watershed in Chinese and world history, ending China's severe political instability and an inability to defend against foreign imperialism. Given China's size and population, any major transition there had global significance. By the early twenty-first century Mao was long gone and many of his policies discarded, but, with a booming economy, China had reclaimed some of the political and economic status it had lost two centuries earlier.

Other East Asians also enjoyed a resurgence. By the 1980s observers referred to the **Pacific Rim**, the economically dynamic Asian countries bordering the Pacific Ocean: China, Japan, South Korea, Taiwan, and several Southeast Asian nations. The center of gravity of world economic life began moving back toward a resurgent Asia. China, Japan, and their neighbors have remained major players in the global system.

Pacific Rim The economically dynamic Asian countries on the edge of the Pacific Basin: China, Japan, South Korea, Taiwan, and several Southeast Asian nations.

---

[2]Quoted in Ross Terrill, *Mao: A Biography* (New York: Harper, 1980), 198.

27-1 Mao's Revolutionary China

⌐C TRANSITIONS ▦ SOCIETIES

Q How did Maoism transform Chinese society?

Like Chiang before him, Mao claimed that he was carrying forward Sun Yat-Sen's legacy. With Mao's portrait, rather than Chiang's, now hanging on the front of the Forbidden City and looking out over Beijing's historic district, Mao began the process of moving China in a new direction that Sun could never have envisioned. The Chinese Revolution that brought Mao and the communists to power was one of modern history's three greatest upheavals. The French Revolution (1789), extolling the common peoples' rights, destroyed lingering feudalism throughout

CONNECTION to TODAY

Can you think of reasons why some Chinese still remember Mao as a positive influence on China and others might see him as having been a disastrous leader?

western Europe; the Russian Revolution (1917) charted a noncapitalist path to industrialization. Both events swept away old social classes and ruling elites. China's revolution remade a major world society while restoring its international status. Communist government made China the world's most experimental nation, introducing innovative but often coercive policies to renovate Chinese life and overcome underdevelopment. At the same time the regime retained and even emphasized many traditional Chinese values. China's new model of economic development

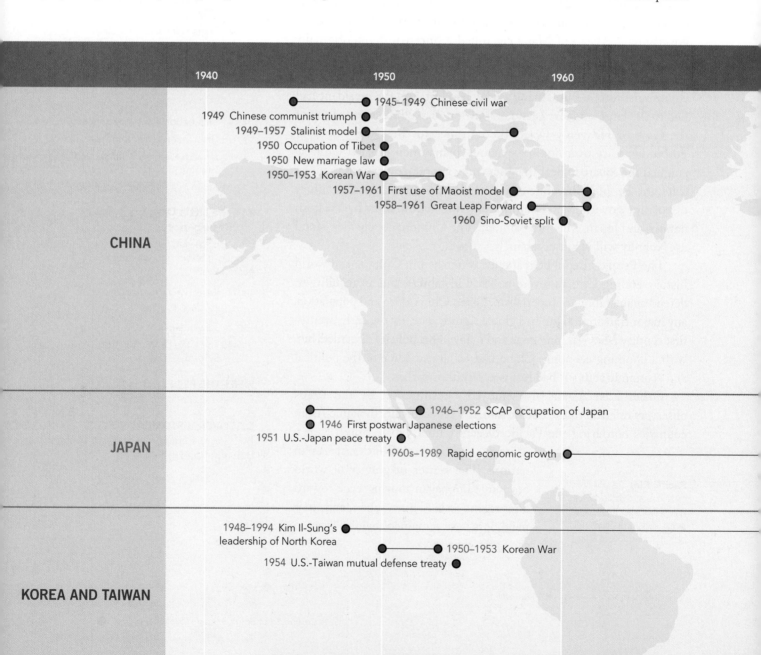

CHINA

1945–1949 Chinese civil war
1949 Chinese communist triumph
1949–1957 Stalinist model
1950 Occupation of Tibet
1950 New marriage law
1950–1953 Korean War
1957–1961 First use of Maoist model
1958–1961 Great Leap Forward
1960 Sino-Soviet split

JAPAN

1946–1952 SCAP occupation of Japan
1946 First postwar Japanese elections
1951 U.S.-Japan peace treaty
1960s–1989 Rapid economic growth

KOREA AND TAIWAN

1948–1994 Kim Il-Sung's leadership of North Korea
1950–1953 Korean War
1954 U.S.-Taiwan mutual defense treaty

differed from both Western-dominated capitalism and highly centralized Soviet communism. But conflict and repression littered its path. Furthermore, like all societies, China remained partly ancient empire, partly modern nation, its leaders often behaving much like the old emperors in autocratically exercising power.

27-1a The Communist Triumph and the New China

Japan's defeat in 1945 sparked a fierce civil war between Mao's communists and Chiang Kai-shek's nationalist government to control China. Both Mao and Chiang were patriotic, autocratic, and power hungry. Chiang's 3.7-million-man army vastly outnumbered the 900,000 communist troops. The United States lavished military aid on Chiang, providing planes and trucks to help his soldiers occupy as much

territory as possible. The communists, aided by the Soviet Union (USSR), concentrated on north China and Manchuria. Besides overstretching supply lines trying to block Mao's forces, Chiang's Republic experienced corruption and a rapid decline in the value of Chinese currency, demoralizing the population. Seeking change, many Chinese viewed the communists as a more honest alternative to Chiang's Nationalist Party.

Meanwhile, in the villages that they controlled, the communists promoted a social revolution, known as the "turning over," encouraging villagers to denounce local landlords, transferring land from richer to poorer peasants, replacing government-appointed leaders with elected village councils, and protecting battered wives. Encouraged to air their grievances, "speaking pains to recall pains" in village meetings, women warned abusive men to mend their ways or face punishment or arrest. Releasing pent-up rage against violent husbands or

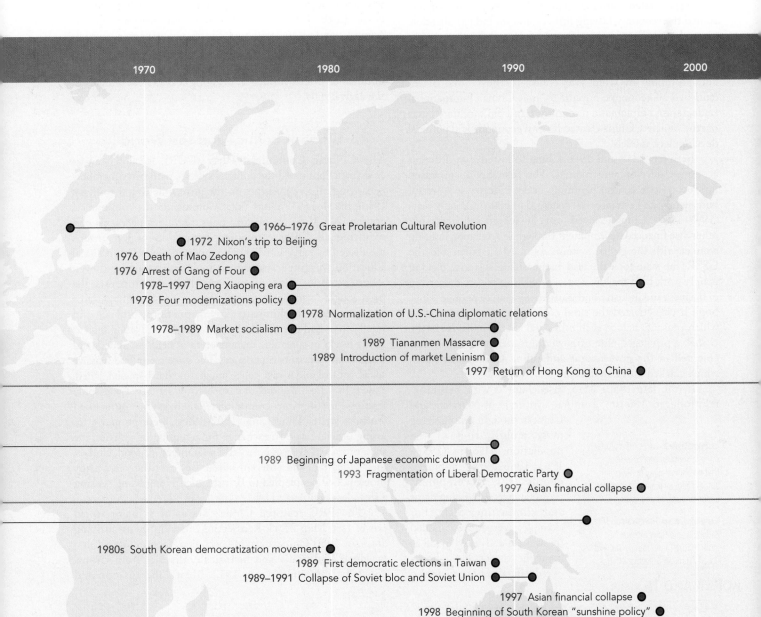

1970 — 1980 — 1990 — 2000

1966–1976 Great Proletarian Cultural Revolution

1972 Nixon's trip to Beijing

1976 Death of Mao Zedong

1976 Arrest of Gang of Four

1978–1997 Deng Xiaoping era

1978 Four modernizations policy

1978 Normalization of U.S.-China diplomatic relations

1978–1989 Market socialism

1989 Tiananmen Massacre

1989 Introduction of market Leninism

1997 Return of Hong Kong to China

1989 Beginning of Japanese economic downturn

1993 Fragmentation of Liberal Democratic Party

1997 Asian financial collapse

1980s South Korean democratization movement

1989 First democratic elections in Taiwan

1989–1991 Collapse of Soviet bloc and Soviet Union

1997 Asian financial collapse

1998 Beginning of South Korean "sunshine policy"

greedy landlords spurred excesses, such as angry crowds beating them to death.

The military and political tide turned against the Republic, and in 1948 Chiang's troops in Manchuria surrendered. The United States unsuccessfully pressured Chiang to broaden his political base with democratic reforms. Some American leaders recommended sending troops to help Chiang; others concluded that his regime had lost too much popular support to win the conflict. With the communists taking major cities, Chiang fled to the island of Taiwan in 1949, along with thousands of troops and two million supporters. But Chiang's forces had to brutally crush a popular uprising of Taiwanese who resisted his control. On Taiwan, with massive U.S. aid and military protection, the relocated Republic of China developed a successful capitalist strategy for economic growth. Meanwhile, mainland China's history now moved in a very different direction. The key question confronting PRC leaders was how to achieve rapid economic development in an overpopulated, battered country. Two decades of war had ruined the economy, leaving little capital for industrialization. China had no overseas empire to exploit, and the communists rejected loans and foreign investment that might reduce their independence. Furthermore, alarmed at Mao's policies and prompted by Cold War concerns, the United States launched an economic boycott to limit China's international trade, refused diplomatic recognition, and built military bases nearby. Isolated, China created its own economic and political development models.

Between 1949 and 1976 China followed two different economic development models. The first, Stalinism, based on Soviet-style central planning, heavy industry, a powerful bureaucracy, and a managerial system, dominated the early years (1949–1957). China received some Soviet aid and advice but otherwise financed development through self-reliance, limiting contact with the global system. As in Meiji Japan and the USSR, the state took the lead, emphasizing austerity, making people work hard for low wages, abolishing private ownership of business and industry, and transferring land to poor peasants. Soon it collectivized the rural economy into cooperatives in which peasants helped each other and shared tools. As in the USSR, a privileged elite of powerful leaders and bureaucrats emerged in the government and ruling Communist Party, which cracked down on dissent.

In the late 1950s Mao, disenchanted with Stalinism, reintroduced Maoism, a unique synthesis of Marxism and Chinese thought emphasizing mass mobilization of the population. Maoism (1957–1961, 1966–1976) mobilized people for development projects, such as building dams and eliminating pests. For example, everyone was issued fly swatters and asked to kill as many flies as possible in hopes of reducing disease; people also planted trees to reverse the ecological instability of recent centuries. Mao reorganized the rural economy into **communes**, large agricultural units that combined many families and villages into a common administrative system for pooling resources and labor. A commune could build and operate a factory, secondary school, and hospital, tasks impractical for a single village. Communes raised agricultural productivity, eliminated landlords, and promoted social and economic equality. Locating industries in rural areas also kept peasants at home rather than migrating to cities.

The most ambitious policy, the **Great Leap Forward** (1958–1961), attempted to industrialize China rapidly and end poverty through collective efforts. Farmers and workers were ordered to build small iron furnaces in their backyards, courtyards, and gardens and spend their free time turning everything from cutlery to old bicycles into steel. But the poorly conceived campaign, pushing the people too hard, nearly wrecked the economy and, along with disastrous weather, caused thirty million people to starve. One of Mao's critics in the leadership charged: "Grains scattered on the ground, potato leaves withered; Strong young people have left to smelt iron, only children and old women reaped the crops; How can they pass the coming year?"[3] These failures diminished Mao's influence, bringing less radical policies in the early 1960s.

27-1b Chinese Politics and the World

The Chinese Communist Party (CCP), led by Mao as chairman, dominated the political system, with party members occupying all key positions in the government and military. Using the slogan "Politics Takes Command," the communists emphasized ideology, making political values pervasive and requiring all Chinese to join political discussion groups monitored by party activists, who reported dissenters; political education was integrated into schools, work units, and even leisure activities. Placing group over individual interests, the party sought to eradicate inequalities and alter thought patterns and attitudes. To eliminate class distinctions, officials and intellectuals had to sporadically perform physical labor, such as laying bricks or spreading manure on farm fields, to understand workers' and peasants' experiences. The system required massive social control and a vast police apparatus that harassed, jailed, exiled, or killed millions of suspected dissenters. Even some leading or longtime communists, such as the outspoken feminist writer Ding Ling (1902–1986), were purged after losing official favor. In exchange for accepting its policies, the state promised everyone the "five guarantees" of food, clothes, fuel, education, and a decent burial. But over the years many thousands of people fled to British-ruled Hong Kong seeking a freer, less regimented life.

The PRC restored China's status as a major world power (see Map 27.1). Reasserting sovereignty in outlying areas, in 1950 Chinese troops occupied Tibet, once a Qing province. Culturally and historically distinct from China, Tibet had broken away in 1912. Most Tibetans opposed

communes Large agricultural units introduced by Mao Zedong that combined many families and villages into a common system for pooling resources and labor.

Great Leap Forward Mao Zedong's ambitious attempt to industrialize China rapidly and end poverty through collective efforts.

---

[3]Peng Dehuai, quoted in Craig Dietrich, *People's China: A Brief History*, 3rd ed. (New York: Oxford University Press, 1998), 130.

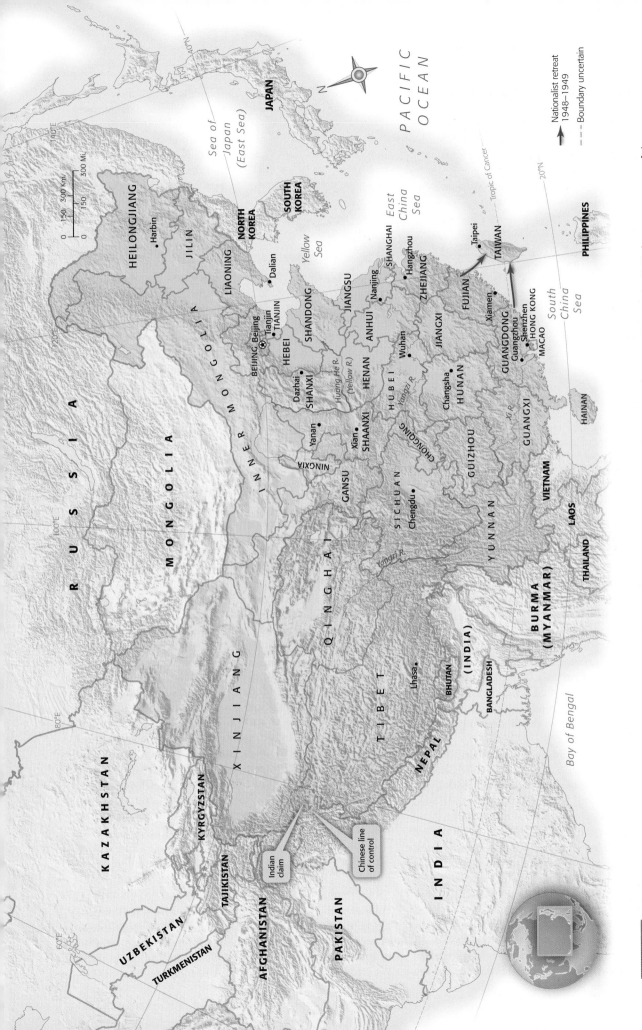

MAP 27.1 **China and Taiwan** China is a huge country, divided into many provinces, and occupies a large part of eastern Eurasia. In 1949 the government of the Republic of China, defeated by the Chinese communists, moved to the island of Taiwan, off China's Pacific coast.

Q What does the map suggest about the political and physical geography of China?

iStock.com/SeanPavonePhoto

IMAGE 27.2 **Honoring Chairman Mao** Since the beginning of communist rule in China in 1949, this giant portrait of Mao Zedong, the chairman of the Chinese Communist Party, has hung on the Gate of Heavenly Peace, the entrance to the Forbidden City of the Qing dynasty emperors, in the heart of Beijing.

Q Why do you think that Mao is still honored today by Chinese officials?

Chinese rule, sparking periodic unrest. Suppression of a Tibetan revolt led the highest Tibetan Buddhist leader, the Dalai Lama (b. 1935), to flee to India in 1959. Revered by devout Tibetans as a spiritual and political leader, he became a defiant symbol of Tibetan resistance, traveling the world to rally support for the Tibetan cause while promoting Buddhist ethics and world peace. China's leaders considered him a terrorist seeking the overthrow of Chinese rule and punished Tibetans who openly supported him. China failed to reclaim another former Qing-ruled territory, Mongolia, a communist state allied to, and protected by, the USSR; the Chinese were also irritated that Mongolians honored Genghis Khan, the founder of the Mongol Empire in the thirteenth century, as a national hero.

China faced major challenges in foreign affairs. In 1950, in support of the USSR-backed communist North Korean government, it was drawn into the Korean War (1950–1953), during which it fought United Nations forces led by the United States that were sent to defend pro-U.S. South Korea. After United Nations forces pushed North Korean forces toward China's border, the U.S. commander of these forces, General Douglas MacArthur, talked recklessly of carrying the offensive into China. Fearing a U.S. invasion, the Chinese then entered the conflict with 300,000 troops, pushing United Nations troops back south and forcing a stalemate. The war produced huge casualties, including several hundred thousand Chinese, reinforcing U.S.–Chinese hostility and mutual fear. The Korean stalemate improved China's international position, but relations with the United States remained tense. After the U.S. and the

Republic of China on Taiwan forged a mutual defense treaty, the United States maintained substantial forces in Taiwan, South Korea, Japan, Okinawa, and the Philippines, while the U.S. Navy patrolled the waters off China. Using paranoia about this formidable U.S. military presence, Mao mobilized Chinese around his programs. Many U.S. allies recognized the Republic of China on Taiwan as China's official government, and the United States continued to veto communist efforts to gain China's United Nations seat.

In the late 1950s China–USSR tensions grew. The Soviet's new "peaceful coexistence" policy with the West enraged Mao, who labeled the United States "a paper tiger." Mao also opposed Soviet leader Nikita Khrushchev's (KROOSH-chef) 1956 exposure of Stalin's brutal excesses, which questioned communist dictators' abuse of power. By 1960 the Sino–Soviet split was official; the USSR withdrew advisers, technicians, and even the spare parts for the industries it helped build. The Chinese increased their military strength, tested their first atomic bomb, and occasionally clashed with Soviet forces on their border. To counterbalance the United States and the USSR, China sought allies and influence in Asia and Africa. Yet, despite fierce anti-U.S. and anti-Soviet rhetoric, Chinese leaders generally followed a cautious foreign policy.

During the 1970s Chinese foreign policy changed dramatically, symbolized by U.S. president Richard Nixon's trip to Beijing in 1972. Both nations shared a hostility toward the USSR, and the bitter U.S. experience in Vietnam had fostered rethinking in both countries. Chinese leaders perceived Americans as stepping back from Asian commitments, and hence a diminishing threat. The United States quit blocking Chinese United Nations membership and, in 1978, normalized diplomatic relations with China. Meanwhile, China developed better relations with noncommunist nations in Southeast Asia and Africa.

27-1c Cultural Revolution and Maoist Society

Adored by millions and hated by millions, Mao was a complex figure, promoting women's rights but also sexually promiscuous, marrying several times and with many lovers. He seldom bathed or brushed his teeth. A poor public speaker, he nevertheless inspired millions to follow him. A poet and philosopher but also power hungry and ruthless, Mao made many enemies, even within the leadership. Although many of his initiatives ultimately failed or caused misery for millions, he played a powerful historical role, leading the communists to victory, reunifying China, focusing public attention on rural people, and placing his stamp on the world's most populous nation.

Dissatisfied with China's development and his diminishing influence and power after the disastrous Great Leap Forward, in the mid-1960s Mao regained his dominant status and resurrected Maoism and a Mao cult. In Mao's vision of a society comprising unselfish, politically conscious citizens, individuals inspired by the slogan "Serve the People" subordinated their own needs to the broader social order. The mass media, completely controlled by the Communist Party, reported that, illuminated by Mao's revolutionary ideas, factory workers discovered better techniques for galvanizing, a food store manager doubled watermelon sales, and farmers learned to judge the right amount of manure to fertilize their plots. In 1966 the People's Liberation Army newspaper asserted, "The most powerful ideological weapon … is the great Mao [Zedong's] thought … the highest instruction for our actions … our telescope and microscope for observing and analyzing all things.… Chairman Mao is the radiant sun lighting our minds … [and his] thought is our lifeline."[4]

Between 1966 and 1976 a radical Maoist movement convulsed and reshaped China like a whirlwind. The **Great Proletarian Cultural Revolution** represented Mao's attempt to implant his vision, promote values hostile to capitalism, destroy his enemies (including the most pragmatic leaders), crush the stifling bureaucracy, and renew revolutionary vigor. Workers and students known as **Red Guards** roamed around cities and the countryside in groups, attacking and arresting anti-Mao leaders while smashing temples, churches, and party and government headquarters. Revolutionary committees led by students, workers, and soldiers ran cities, factories, and schools. Red Guards carried a little red book containing short quotations from Mao's writings, such as his claim that understanding Marxism requires contact with workers and peasants. One observer noted that "giant portraits of [Mao] now hung in the streets, busts were in every chamber, his books and photographs were everywhere on display."[5]

During this turmoil, industrial and agricultural production was disrupted, most schools were closed for two years, and thousands of people were killed, jailed, or removed from official positions. Millions were sent to remote rural areas to experience peasant life. Anti-Mao officials, intellectuals, and people with upper-class backgrounds faced public criticism and often punishment. A Chinese journalist whose grandparents were capitalists remembered attacks on her family: "Red Guards swarming all over the house and a great fire in our courtyard onto which were thrown my father's books, my grandparent's precious traditional furniture and my toys."[6] Soon even Mao was dampening the radical fervor.

Over the first twenty-five years of the PRC the communists reshaped Chinese society. Mao, who came from a peasant family, promoted social and economic equality, known as the **Iron Rice Bowl**, in which people, especially in villages, shared resources—food, draft animals, farm equipment—and, communists claimed, peasants enjoyed dignity. Hence, Maoism often improved life for many poorer Chinese, especially in villages. Emphasizing preventive medicine, villagers trained as paramedics, known as barefoot doctors, addressed everyday health care, such as by distributing medication and setting broken bones. Where once famine and disease were common, most Chinese now enjoyed decent health care and adequate food. Mass education raised literacy rates to the levels of industrialized nations.

Trying to overturn Confucian-influenced patriarchy by raising women's status, Mao praised women for "holding up half the sky." A new marriage law abolished arranged marriages, forbade men from taking concubines, and made divorce easier; land reform empowered women, expanding their property rights. Women now enjoyed legal equality with men and greater access to education, worked for wages, and played a stronger public role, often leading local organizations. Women debated the proper balance between housekeeping and paid work and between furthering the revolution and caring for their husbands and children. Women activists sought democratic families, emphasizing love matches rather than arranged marriages; fostering closer emotional ties between husbands, wives, and children; and lessening male domination. But rural areas remained more conservative. Moreover, few women held high national positions. There has been considerable discussion in recent years about how women fared under the early revolution. Some older women did feel liberated in some ways while others had mixed feelings. One writer's grandmother, a former journalist, concluded that "the Communists did many terrible things. But they made women's lives much better."[7] Recent scholarly studies suggest a complicated picture. While women now had more job opportunities, their interests became subordinate to collective goals. Most still had the burden of childcare and housework. And the chaos of the Cultural Revolution upended many lives, marriages, and families as people were scattered around China (see Meet the People: Xue Xinran, a Chinese Voice for Women). Mao's last wife, Jiang Qing **(chang ching)** (1914–1991), a former film actress, wielded great power during the Cultural Revolution, but her radical policies made her unpopular. In 1976, after

Great Proletarian Cultural Revolution A radical movement in China between 1966 and 1976 that represented Mao Zedong's attempt to implant his vision, destroy his enemies, crush the stifling bureaucracy, and renew the revolution's vigor.

Red Guards Young workers and students who were the major supporters of the Cultural Revolution in Mao's China.

Iron Rice Bowl A model of social equality in Mao's China in which the people, especially in the villages, shared resources and the peasants enjoyed status and dignity.

[4]*The Great Socialist Cultural Revolution in China* (Peking: Foreign Languages Press, 1966), 3: 1, 17.
[5]Quoted in Maurice Meisner, *Mao's China and After: A History of the People's Republic*, 3rd ed. (New York: Free Press, 1999), 281.
[6]Xue Xinran, *The Good Women of China: Hidden Voices* (New York: Anchor, 2002), 175.
[7]Quoted in Helen Gao, "How Did Women Fare in China's Communist Revolution," *New York Times*, September 25, 2017.

Album/Alamy Stock Photo

我们心中最红最红的红太阳毛主席万岁！万万岁！

IMAGE 27.3 **Chinese Political Art** The communists used political art to rally popular support for their cause. This example celebrates the declaration establishing the People's Republic in Beijing in 1949.

Q Do you think that political art can influence people and gain support for a government or cause?

scenes of people at work, often in bright, cheerful colors conveying an optimistic tone. Part-time writers got time off from the factory to work on literary projects. A 1958 poem proclaimed: "Labor is joy, how joyful it is, Bathed in sweat and two hands full of mud. Like sweet rain, my sweat waters the land."[9] Critics considered art serving revolutionary goals to be political propaganda.

Politicization of the arts peaked during the Cultural Revolution, when elitism faced fierce attack. Red Guards sang new songs praising change and Chairman Mao, such as "The East is red, the sun has risen. China has produced a Mao Zedong; He is the great savior of the people."[10] Militant operas contained revolutionary themes, such as peasant dignity or Communist Party history. Dancers composed revolutionary ballets integrating Chinese martial arts, folk dances, and Russian ballet. For example, *The Red Detachment of Women* portrayed a company of women soldiers' experiences during the civil war.

After Mao died in 1976, the Chinese evaluated his legacy. The communists had restored China to great power status, renewing confidence after a century of imperialistic exploitation and invasion beginning with the Opium War. No longer a doormat, China even had nuclear weapons. Once again, the Middle Kingdom exercised influence in the world. Whereas a generation earlier begging and prostitution were common, now most Chinese, though enjoying little material surplus, could satisfy their basic food, housing, and clothing needs in a healthier, more broadly based economy.

Mao's policies, however, also generated failures and great political repression. Although controlling its economic destiny, China remained poor by world standards. Mao discouraged free enterprise and individual initiative; few private cars interfered with the bicycles most Chinese used to get to work or shopping. Chinese wanted better housing and more consumer goods now rather than in the distant future. With few luxuries or diversions, life was dull. Moreover, fierce punishment of dissenters and the Great Leap Forward and Cultural Revolution had ruined numerous lives. During Mao's time countless Chinese seen as "enemies of the people" were executed or jailed. Disillusioned by government coercion, unfulfilled promises, and chaotic turmoil, many blamed Mao and his radicalism. Party reformers charged that Mao had lost touch with common people's lives. Often erratic policies made people cynical, only passively cooperating and avoiding commitment to a particular line. Many Chinese were ready for change. Since 1976 Chinese have continued to debate Mao's policies and role, with various political factions using him to legitimize their own agenda or power. Even today, four decades since his death, Chinese have not fully come to terms with the man and his legacy. There are still some who worship him as half emperor and half deity, displaying posters of him in their homes or pictures in their taxis to ward off bad luck.

Mao's death, Jiang and her top party allies, the "Gang of Four," lost a power struggle and were imprisoned.

The communists often undermined traditional beliefs and culture. Calling religion a bond enslaving people, Mao controlled religious behavior and marginalized Christian churches, Buddhist monasteries, and Islamic mosques; by the 1970s a small minority openly practiced religion. Hence, organized religion could not mobilize opposition to the party. Only religious leaders who cooperated with the state maintained their positions. Mao used the arts as a weapon in the class struggle, fostering a "people's art" created by and for common people. He wrote, "In the world today all culture, all literature and art belongs to definite political lines. Art for art's sake, art that stands above the class and party do not exist in reality."[8] During the Great Leap Forward, party activists collected literature written by common people and encouraged peasants and workers to compose poetry and songs. Peasants painted

[8]From Timothy Cheek, *Mao Zedong and China's Revolutions: A Brief History with Documents* (Boston: Bedford/St. Martin's, 2002), 116.
[9]Quoted in Hu Kai-Yu, *The Chinese Literary Scene: A Writer's Visit to the People's Republic* (New York: Vintage, 1975), 227.
[10]Quoted in Orville Schell, *Discos and Democracy: China in the Throes of Reform* (New York: Anchor, 1989), 101.

27-2 Chinese Modernization

⥈ TRANSITIONS

Q What factors explain the dramatic rise of Chinese economic power in the world since 1978?

Most historians have divided China's history since 1949 into two eras, the Maoist era (1949–1978) and the Modernization era (since 1978). Now a few historians suggest that developments after 2013–2015 might have begun a new era as China became a more powerful and influential force in the world. In many ways the current decade resembles a mix of Maoism and Modernization. Time will tell if China is entering a new era, but the Modernization era certainly differed from the Maoist one in important ways. Deng Xiaoping **(dung shee-yao-ping)** (1904–1997), a pragmatic longtime Communist Party leader who often clashed with Mao and was purged during the Cultural Revolution, came to power in 1978 and changed China's direction. Deng and his allies rejected Mao's self-sufficient, ideologically pure China unlinked from the world economy, concluding that collectivized agriculture failed to raise productivity enough to finance the high technology and industry needed to make China a major power. In 1978 Deng, portraying China as at a turning point, announced the policy of four modernizations: the development of agriculture, industry, the military, and science and technology to turn China into a powerful nation by 2000. According to Deng:

> "Modernization does represent a great new revolution . . . to liberate and expand the productive forces. Without expanding the productive forces, making our country prosperous and powerful, and improving the living standards of the people, our revolution is just empty talk. We oppose the old society… because they oppressed the people and fettered the productive forces…. We do not want capitalism, but neither do we want to be poor under socialism. What we want is socialism in which the productive forces are developed and the country is prosperous and powerful."[11]

CONNECTION to TODAY

How has the rise of China in the past four decades affected you, your family, and your community?

Deng's next two successors generally followed his pragmatic policies, transforming China into an economic powerhouse and modifying Maoist society.

27-2a Market Socialism and Repression

From 1978 to 1989 Chinese leaders pursued **market socialism**, mixing free enterprise, economic liberalization, and state controls to generate economic dynamism. This pragmatic approach, unlike Mao's, emphasized economic results rather than socialist values. Deng loved a Chinese proverb: "It doesn't matter whether a cat is black or white, only if it catches mice." To Mao the color of the cat was very important. Using the market to stimulate productivity, China reentered the world economy to obtain capital investment to spur manufacturing. Like Meiji Japan, China now imported technology, foreign expertise, and capitalist ideas. Deng believed China had reached a plateau; moving to the next levels required wider international participation. Hence, he improved ties with the United States, Japan, western Europe, and noncommunist Southeast Asia. Dazzled by China's huge potential market of, as Western experts put it, one billion toothbrushes (for toothpaste) and two billion armpits (for deodorant), Western companies promoted increased trade.

Introducing capitalist ideas, such as offering workers better pay rather than just ideological slogans, Deng's reforms sparked dramatic changes, permitting small private enterprises, then larger ones; ultimately both private and state-owned enterprises competed with each other. In agriculture, Deng replaced Mao's communes with

market socialism A Chinese economic program used between 1978 and 1989 that mixed free enterprise, economic liberalization, and state controls and that produced economic dynamism in China.

[11]"We Can Develop a Market Economy Under Socialism," *People's Daily Online*, November 26, 1979, english.peopledaily.com.cn/dengxp/vol2/text/b1370.html.

the contract system, under which peasants could lease (but not buy) land to work privately. In many districts this free market generated soaring productivity; rural per capita incomes rose fourfold in the first decade. Tapping a skilled, industrious, but inexpensive labor force, many Western and Asian companies established manufacturing operations to produce goods such as shirts, underwear, and toys for export. China became a consumer society; even in small cities, shops stocked Japanese televisions and Western soft drinks. Over the next twenty-five years the economy quadrupled in size, and foreign trade increased ten times over.

Deng also loosened political and cultural controls. Intellectuals and artists enjoyed greater freedom, the press was enlivened, public debate widened, and organized religion was increasingly tolerated. Western popular culture, especially film, rock music, and discos, won a huge audience; some foreign books and magazines became available; and foreign travelers backpacked in remote areas. The sentimental recordings of Taiwan's top female singer, Deng Lijun (**deyn lee-choong**), better known in Hong Kong, Japan, and Southeast Asia as Teresa Teng, were so widely heard in homes and restaurants that people said that "the day belongs to Deng Xiaoping but the night belongs to Deng Lijun."[12] Novels and short stories addressed the suffering during the Cultural Revolution. Popular writers developed huge audiences for stories with daring sexual themes. Chinese-made films won international acclaim, but creative directors, portraying China as anything but a communist paradise, skirmished with wary government censors. Rock musicians, especially ethnic Korean Cui Jian (**sway jen**), a former Beijing Symphony trumpeter, spoke for alienated urban youth. Dressed in battered army fatigues and a Mao coat style, Cui sang: "This guitar in my hands is like a knife. I want to cut at your hypocrisy till I see some truth." Cui's songs were indirect, focusing more on bureaucratic corruption, social problems, and young people's frustrations than politics; Chinese youth easily read between the lines for hidden meanings. One fan commented that "Cui Jian says things we all feel, but cannot say."[13]

Although many Chinese applauded ideological loosening and growing economic options, market socialism hid a dark underside. Many districts enjoyed few benefits from reorganizing rural life. Chinese authorities always tended to impose one national policy rather than allowing districts and villages to find their own policy that would work with their particular social and physical environment. Furthermore, Chinese social norms stress the concept of connections or relationships (known as *guanxi*) with other people, especially influential patrons, to increase one's power and wealth, but this emphasis can lead to corruption. Villagers with better land, political connections, or entrepreneurial skills benefited more, opening a rich–poor gap. Prices rose rapidly, and corruption increased as bureaucrats and party officials lined their pockets. Moreover, intraparty tensions increased; Stalinists and Maoists feared that economic liberalization undermined one-party rule and communism. The fall of communism in eastern Europe and the USSR in 1989 alarmed hardliners. But dissidents and some reformers, believing that strong controls inhibited initiative, pushed democracy as "the fifth modernization." At a Beijing site known unofficially as the "Democracy Wall," people put up posters expressing their criticisms. In response, party hardliners called for cracking down, arresting dissidents.

In 1989 tensions reached a boiling point, generating massive protests and government repression. Thousands of unarmed protesters, led by university students and workers, took over Tiananmen Square in downtown Beijing, demanding that the most unpopular leaders resign, an end to government corruption, and the creation of a fully open political system. Smaller demonstrations erupted in several other cities. In a festive spirit, street vendors gave free food and drink to demonstrators; rock musicians entertained the throngs. Party hardliners, unwilling to compromise, decided to crack down with force; with Deng's support, they purged moderate party leaders who advocated negotiations and, declaring martial law, ordered the army to clear out the demonstrators, sparking the Tiananmen Massacre. In the chaos that followed the army killed hundreds or, according to some estimates, several thousand and injured or arrested thousands more, while horrified millions around the world watched on television. The massacre shocked the world but few China specialists were surprised. Many of them believed that the courageous Beijing protesters had overestimated their popular support and underestimated the regime's willingness to crush their movement. Since many rural Chinese valued stability more than vague promises of a better world, the protesters probably miscalculated democracy's prospects in a country with a despotic political tradition.

27-2b Economic Change and Politics Since 1989

After the Tiananmen Massacre the communists modified market socialism into **market Leninism**, with the Chinese state, obsessed with stability, asserting more power over society while also fostering an even stronger market economy. The party reestablished control in political, social, and cultural life, tolerating less dissent and debate than in the 1980s. However, the one-party state's control was not absolute and some dissenters still spoke out. Critics opposed but could not halt the environmentally damaging Three Gorges Dam project to control the Yangzi (**yahng-zeh**) River and provide electrical power, which forced several million people to move. The Chinese state, often arbitrary, has used the military and police as well as the party-controlled media and judicial system to intimidate dissidents. Assertive dissidents face arrest, dampening public debate. China has executed thousands every year, mostly criminals but also some accused of economic misbehavior or political opposition. The government also abolished hated prison labor camps, but enforcement of the reform depended on local officials who often acquired income and influence from the old system.

market Leninism A policy followed after the Tiananmen Massacre in 1989 whereby the Chinese communist state asserted more power over society while also fostering an even stronger market orientation in the economy than had existed under market socialism.

[12]Quoted in June Teufel Dreyer, *China's Political System: Modernization and Tradition* (New York: Paragon House, 1993), 345.

[13]The quotes are in Andrew F. Jones, *Like a Knife: Ideology and Genre in Contemporary Chinese Popular Music* (Ithaca, NY: East Asia Program, Cornell University, 1992), 97, 148.

China now did not fit either the pure communist or capitalist model but was essentially a form of state capitalism. The government owns many large firms and it decides which industries will receive subsidies, favorable loans, and protected markets. But private firms, less favored with state benefits, accounted for roughly 70 percent of the nation's output (gross domestic product) in 2018. In many enterprises state agencies and private entrepreneurs shared ownership; the government owned shares in many companies or entered joint ventures with foreign businessmen, often favoring state-owned or -controlled businesses in contracts. Remembering the Cultural Revolution and the 1989 unrest, the Chinese often valued political stability over individual rights, such as unfettered free speech and participation in government, especially when there was overheated economic growth. This approach was typically Chinese; for two thousand years Chinese governments had promoted social and political harmony to discourage conflict.

An aging Deng retired in 1992 and died in 1997, leaving a Communist Party (with ninety-one million members by 2019) that faced problems Mao could never have anticipated. Lacking a unifying figure like Mao or Deng, the power-sharing leadership that followed was mostly a faceless group of longtime party members who rose through the ranks not by ideology but by tapping connections and forging alliances. Once claiming to uplift the working class and poor peasants, the CCP now welcomed wealthy businessmen and professionals. Many with little faith in the communist vision have still considered party membership helpful to their career prospects. Most young Chinese, preoccupied with seeking wealth, know little about the Tiananmen Massacre. Yet, powerful provincial leaders, promoting local economic growth, increasingly ignored Beijing. Chinese leaders needed to find ways to resolve inequalities, spreading wealth more equitably, to check growing social tensions. Some pessimists in the 1990s forecast more conflicts between rich and poor Chinese, or civil war between rich and poor regions.

After 1980 China, abetted by a "get-rich-quick" mentality, generally enjoyed the world's fastest economic growth, often 10 percent a year for many years. Deng claimed that to get rich was glorious. China's exports increased fifteenfold between 1980 and 2000. The party sought popular support by offering consumer goods and wealth rather than political reform, providing shops with ample consumer goods and households with spending money. In the early reform days, people wanted the "three bigs": bicycle, wristwatch, and sewing machine. Now they coveted televisions, washing machines, video recorders, and smartphones. Clearly benefiting from the mobility of capital and products with globalization, China moved ahead of Germany in 2009 and then Japan in 2010–2011 to become the world's second largest economy; the U.S. economy was three times larger but by 2018 was only about one and a half times larger. If high annual growth rates continue, China may eventually have the world's largest economy.

Although economic reforms improved living standards for many Chinese, they produced numerous downsides. Economic dynamism has been concentrated in a few coastal provinces and special economic zones, where living standards approach those of Taiwan and South Korea. At least half of Chinese now live in cities, many boasting towering skyscrapers and huge shopping malls with upscale shops. Mocking historical preservation and often outraging residents, many sometimes dilapidated but mostly charming and historic, centuries-old neighborhoods were bulldozed, replaced by apartment blocks. Shanghai has more skyscrapers than any other world city while China can claim five of the world's ten tallest buildings. Elsewhere, conditions have often deteriorated. Cities expand and new cities are built at breakneck speed, devouring farmland and wetlands, but often accelerating environmental destruction. Flooding is common. Although laws discourage migration to another district without government permission, millions of peasants seeking jobs or a less rustic life have moved to cities, where they struggle and, considered nonresidents, have limited rights. Some find housing in small rooms or shacks but these also get demolished by local governments. Most single migrant factory workers live in crowded, company-owned dormitories, laboring twelve to fourteen hours a day, six to seven days a week. Their precarious position became clear in 2008, when the global economic crisis affected China as overseas markets collapsed. Thousands of factories closed, leaving millions of disillusioned workers without incomes and forced to return to their home villages. Yet, unlike many Western nations and Japan, China's economy still grew, albeit at a slower rate. Thanks to a huge government stimulus package and autocratic decision making, China's economy recovered and many workers found jobs. Labor shortages and worker resistance may eventually improve working conditions. Workers' activism rises when China's economy slows, mostly small-scale protests and strikes to fight reduced pay and fewer hours. The government emphasizes social stability above all else and reins in any protests.

The Chinese have become great users of world resources, such as oil and coal, and major polluters of the atmosphere. China is now the number one producer of greenhouse gases causing global warming, just ahead of the United States. Mindful of the unhealthy air pollution choking China's cities and the fouled rivers and lakes fostered by industrialization, by 2009 China had placed more emphasis on developing cleaner, greener, and renewable energy sources such as wind and solar. As the U.S. under the Trump administration retreats from green solutions China is increasing its world leadership of the industry. Yet it still relies heavily on coal-based power sources, leading the world in carbon emissions. Water supplies are badly overstretched and often polluted. With private cars clogging streets where bicycles once dominated and factories and coal-burning power plants polluting the air, smog blankets much of the country. By 2013 some local pollution emergencies, so severe and dangerous they were called "airpocalypses," paralyzed cities and closed schools and airports. But when cities ban the use of air-polluting coal (even if temporarily), factories close, costing jobs, and many poor people cannot heat their homes. Many feared consuming food produced from damaged, pesticide-saturated soils. Poorly regulated companies sell tainted food and milk. Land and energy grow more expensive.

China has devoted vast sums to infrastructure, high technology, and science. The country has built a modern transportation network, including high-speed trains, city subway systems, and superhighways. In the same time frame that California built one hundred nineteen miles of high-speed rail track, China laid sixteen thousand miles. While New York opened its latest line after a decade of construction and $4.5 million, with the same amount of money China constructed complete subway systems in more than five cities. In 2019 China unveiled its new bullet train, with a speed of up to three hundred seventy-three miles per hour, that will be the world's fastest when it begins operation in 2021. But some of the rail lines and subways are poorly built, causing accidents and collapses. China produces far more scientists and engineers than the U.S. and has now become a major innovator in some high-technology fields. In 2013 China had only two of the world's largest publicly traded tech companies; the U.S. had nine. By 2018 China and the U.S each hosted half of the top twenty. Two of the top three drone manufacturers are Chinese. Chinese companies are the world leaders in artificial intelligence (A.I.), including in computer vision/facial recognition and in speech recognition, developments that can be used for commerce but also for surveillance and social control. Indeed, the regime has systematically set up facial-recognition surveillance devices throughout cities and towns to collect and store identities and information while monitoring the population; critics consider the installation of the surveillance devices Orwellian and totalitarian.

Political and economic changes have influenced other areas of Chinese life. Newly rich entrepreneurs enjoy luxury cars, golf courses, and vacations abroad. China has several hundred thousand millionaires and some billionaires. A Chinese observer noted, "Walk around Beijing and what do you see? Buy a new Audi, look at this Rolex, you need some clothes from Gucci. Such things are simply unaffordable [for most]."[14] Party leaders' sons and daughters, known as "princelings," use their connections to advance in business or politics. Even the growing middle class, numbering over four hundred million (about a third of the population), mostly urban and often working in local or foreign businesses, enjoy a comfortable life. Some village leaders abuse their power and connections to amass wealth. The wealthy flaunt their affluence; the poor resent it. Street songs often mock the powerful: "I'm a big official, so I eat and drink, and I've got the potbelly to prove it. Beer, spirits, rice wine, love potions—I drink it all."[15] Since 2005 peasant protests against seizure of village land to build polluting factories, luxury housing, and golf courses have become frequent, numbering 180,000 annually by 2012, but most protest leaders are arrested. Meanwhile, the shift to market forces leaves millions unable to afford medical care and their children's schooling. Thanks to declining health care, especially in rural areas, between half a million and 1.5 million Chinese have HIV or AIDS. Some poorer Chinese long fondly for Mao and the Iron Rice Bowl. Yet, despite reduced job security and social services, people are now freer than before to travel, change jobs, enjoy leisure, and even complain.

In 2012 new tensions emerged as China's party elite installed a new leadership team, headed by Xi Jinping (b. 1953), the son of a top leader purged during the Cultural Revolution. As a teenager Xi himself had been sent to remote villages. Some hoped Xi's background of seeing his family punished by Mao's

regime would give him a more liberal approach, but to many he has governed more like Mao. Critics described him as a strongman with a firm grip on all levers of power and the leader of the "unfree world." Xi has inspired a Mao-like personality cult, attempted to put himself on a pedestal with Mao, rekindle a populist image, and cultivate a paternalistic but caring reputation. In 2017 party leaders agreed to bypass a rule put in place after the Cultural Revolution to prevent one-man rule and preserve a politically accountable collective leadership, allowing Xi to serve a second term, and now an indefinite one, becoming what critics call a Mao-like "Chairman of Everything for Life." Emulating the Little Red Book of Mao's thoughts, admirers touted Xi and China's mixture of merciless authoritarianism and mercantilist economic policies, the "China solution," as a model for the developing world.

Xi introduced further reforms under the concept, influenced by both Confucian and Maoist slogans, of the "Chinese Dream" that emphasized China's strength and prosperity. He also launched a far-reaching crackdown on widespread government and party corruption, but this also allowed him to arrest or sideline his competitors for leadership. Defending the rule of law, only a few brave officials dared to speak out against an anticorruption agency with sweeping powers and few checks. The arrest and conviction of a powerful but controversial regional leader for corruption revealed deep party divisions between rival leaders and between factions favoring market reforms or addressing economic inequality. While promising more influence for the market, Xi has also favored state-owned companies and a stronger role for the Communist Party. Experts debate whether Xi's policies stifle China. He has also done little to shake up the bloated state companies and farms, which suck valuable capital from the banking system. In recent years Xi and the leadership have shrugged off the worries of economists about high and increasing levels of government debt.

27-2c Chinese Society and Culture Since 1989

The government struggles to maintain social stability. Mao's China was one of the world's safest countries, but economic growth and the quest for wealth have generated a rapid increase in crime. The close connection between government and business corruption, underworld activity, and financial success led to Chinese talking about the "Five Colors," or surest roads to riches: Communist Party connections, prostitution, smuggling, illegal drug dealing, and criminal gangs. Rampant drug dealing serves the growing numbers using narcotics for escape. Maintaining Confucian and Maoist attitudes, many Chinese view wealth as corrupting and mistrust rich business interests.

Since China already had one billion people in the 1980s, a fifth of humankind, Deng Xiaoping introduced a one-child-per-family policy to stabilize the population. Critics complained that children without siblings, called "little emperors," were pampered and self-centered. The policy encouraged and

---

[14]Law professor Zhou Guanquan, quoted in Dan Levin, "China's New Wealth Gives Old Status Symbol a Boost," *New York Times*, August 10, 2011, p. A6.
[15]Quoted in R. Keith Schoppa, *Revolution and Its Past: Identities and Change in Modern Chinese History* (Upper Saddle River, NJ: Prentice-Hall, 2002), 433.

sometimes mandated abortion; since traditional attitudes favoring sons remained, killing of female babies was widespread. Raising more boys than girls has fostered serious social consequences, as many men cannot find wives. Worried that plummeting birthrates, an aging population, and a shrinking labor force might undermine the results of the economic miracle and hence political legitimacy, in 2013 the CCP relaxed the rigid one-child policy and encouraged marriage and allowing two children, even staging mass matchmaking gatherings and dating events, while shaming single women as "leftover" women; by 2018 they had closed family planning offices. But the attempt to increase China's birthrate has faltered; births fell by 630,000 in 2017 compared to 2016. China's workforce has been shrinking and aging faster than in any developing country. China will soon have a larger proportion of people over age sixty (17.3%) than the United States.

Although women's economic status has often improved, many still face restricted gender expectations. Feminist journalist Xue Xinran (**shoe shin-rahn**) argued that "Chinese women had always thought that their lives should be full of misery. Many had no idea what happiness was, other than having a son for the family."[16] Many scholars consider the long-suffering, submissive Chinese woman stereotype misleading; modern women are often strong-willed and resourceful. But women now receive little support because government policies are aimed at economic growth, not gender equality. Feminism had blossomed several times, but by 2017 it was suppressed as Xi Jinping's administration, which claims to support women's rights, enacted a patriarchal, Confucian-inspired sexist vision of "harmony" that does not tolerate dissent and advised women to look and dress in a stereotypical feminine way. A #MeToo movement emerged by 2017, particularly in universities, to fight harassment, unequal treatment, and rigid gender roles, but officials responded with persecution while prohibiting public gatherings and removing Internet posts. Meanwhile, millions of rural women migrated to cities since the 1970s for industrial and service jobs, providing much of the labor force that has helped turn China into an economic giant. Wherever they live, women commonly work long hours. Few women occupy high positions in the government, Communist Party, or top business enterprises. Trends among males also became controversial in 2018 as Chinese pop idols in film, television, and music as well as some young men favored a more androgynous, even effeminate look in clothes and grooming.

Some of the criticisms morphed into homophobic attacks on the LGBTQ community. Chinese attitudes toward that community have been mixed. LGBTQ people, who faced condemnation and discrimination under Mao, have slowly been coming out and have built an online community based on hundreds of LGBTQ-oriented websites. Gay bars are common in large cities. While many gay men have experienced discrimination and even arrest, public opinion has become more tolerant since the 1980s; lesbians face less harassment. In 2019 a Pride parade and film festival were held openly in Shanghai.

Global entertainment and consumer culture also affect China, with Western popular culture becoming a powerful force among youth. The U.S. television program *American Idol* inspired hugely popular Chinese imitators such as *Super Girl*; wary, in 2011 the party limited "vulgar" entertainment on television. Cui Jian and other rock musicians, some of whom participated in the Beijing student protest movement, now compete with heavy metal, punk, and rap musicians, and Chinese imitators of Korean and Anglo-American boy bands and girl groups enjoy a vast teen audience. But in 2018 puritanical authorities cracked down on and muzzled the fledgling rap culture as "low taste." Sometimes called the "Tolkien of Chinese literature," Jin Yong (also known as Louis Cha), China-born but Hong Kong-based, became a household name in China and in Chinese-speaking communities around Asia for his martial arts novels, which sold millions of copies and inspired TV shows, comics, and videos. Despite demolishing historical neighborhoods, the Party has used pride in the past as a resource to shape the future, refurbishing famous landmarks and buildings like the Forbidden City; financing history-themed "battles, palaces, and concubines" films; and marketing a nationalistic and retro fashion trend (known as *hanfu*) aimed at young women, of dressing in imperial Qing clothing. But in other areas the West continues to influence society. A Disney resort in Shanghai opened in 2015. Numerous McDonald's outlets (one near Mao's mausoleum), Pizza Huts, Starbucks, Hard Rock Cafes, Walmarts, and tens of thousands of Avon agents selling American beauty products serve consumers. And Chinese entrepreneurs have opened coffee shop franchises all over the country. South Korean popular culture and consumer products—music, clothing, television dramas, movies, cosmetics—have also become very fashionable among young Chinese. Much of the conversion of millions of Chinese to evangelical Christianity is due to thousands of South Korean Protestant missionaries.

More than eight hundred-twenty million Chinese have gained some access to the wider world by becoming Internet users, most of them using mobile devices, making it the world's largest Internet market. E-commerce is also becoming much more popular, used regularly by a majority of Internet users. China is years ahead of the U.S. in replacing paper money with smartphone payments. To restrict the free flow of information and crack down on cyberspace, officials created "the Great Firewall," sometimes closing down Internet cafes and preventing Internet providers—local and Western—from allowing access to banned websites. Many thousands of computer-savvy security agents monitor the Internet for any sites or discussions deemed "dangerous" to public security. But websites and blogs proliferate rapidly, making complete monitoring difficult. By 2009 the government sought even stricter controls over the Internet and electronic tools such as Twitter, Facebook, and YouTube, leaving China-based platforms like WeChat, TikTok, Tencent, and Weibo (China's Twitter) to dominate social media. In 2016 the typical WeChat user sent seventy-four messages a day. Regulators often reprimand online platforms for hosting content they deem too raunchy, creepy, flirty, weird, or politically sensitive. But Chinese users also express

---

[16]Xue Xinran, author interview in *Random House Reading Group for the Good Women of China*, randomhouse.co.uk/offthepage/guide.htm?command=Search&db+catalog/mai.

Xue Xinran, a Chinese Voice for Women

In the 1980s Xue Xinran (**shoe shin-rahn**), known professionally as Xinran, began working for a radio network and later became one of China's most successful and innovative journalists. A radio call-in show she launched in 1989 featured hundreds of poignant and haunting stories by women. Her huge audience and sensitive handling of callers made Xinran a role model and heroine for Chinese women. Her own life and career also revealed women's experiences.

Born in Beijing in 1958, Xinran had a difficult childhood complicated by the Cultural Revolution's turmoil. Her mother came from a capitalist, property-owning family. But Xinran's grandfather, although cooperating with the communists, lost his property and was imprisoned during the Cultural Revolution. Her mother joined the Communist Party and army at sixteen and was occasionally jailed or demoted in purges of those from capitalist backgrounds. Xinran's father was also from a once-wealthy family and had been imprisoned. When she was one month old, Xinran was sent to live with a grandmother, and she seldom saw her parents during childhood. Reflecting on her family, she wrote that, like many Chinese, her parents endured an unhappy marriage: "Did [my parents] love each other? I have never dared to ask." While working as an army administrator, Xinran married, had a son, and later divorced.

Eventually Xinran became a radio journalist. But she had to persuade the station to let her begin a nightly call-in program, *Words on the Night Breeze*. Since 1949 the media functioned as a Communist Party mouthpiece, ensuring that it spoke with one identical voice. However, Xinran said, "I was trying to open a little window, a tiny hole, so that people would allow their spirits to cry out and breathe after the gunpowder-laden atmosphere of the previous forty years." The question that obsessed her was: What is a woman's life really worth in a China where footbinding was a recent memory but women now lived and worked alongside men? Xinran's compassion and ability encouraged callers to talk freely about feelings. For eight groundbreaking years, women called in and discussed their lives. Broadcast all over China, the program offered an unflinching portrait of what it meant to be a woman in modern China, including expectations of obedience to fathers, husbands, and sons. Women from every social status—daughters of wealthy families, wives of party officials, children of Cultural Revolution survivors, homeless street scavengers, isolated mountain villagers—called in stories, often heartbreaking tales of sexual abuse, gang rape, forced marriages, and enforced separation of families.

Elisabetta A. Villa/Getty Images Entertainment/Getty Images

IMAGE 27.4 **Xue Xinran** Chinese journalist Xue Xinran explored the lives of Chinese women on her radio program and in her writings.

The stories did not fit the image promoted by the Communist Party of a happy, harmonious society. She told, for instance, of Jingyi and her boyfriend, Gu Da, university classmates who fell passionately in love but were sent to work in different regions. They had planned to eventually marry but lost touch during the Cultural Revolution. For forty-five years Jingyi had first longed for and then searched for Gu Da. When they finally had a reunion in 1994, Jingyi was devastated to discover that Gu Da, despairing of ever seeing Jingyi again, had married another woman. Their saga provided a window on the disrupted personal and family ties common after 1949.

In Xinran's view, "When China started to open up [to the outside world], it was like a starving child devouring everything without much discrimination." In 1997 the conflict between what Xinran knew and what she was permitted to say caused her to give up her career and leave for Britain, seeking a freer life and a global audience. She first taught at the University of London and then became a newspaper columnist. She published several nonfiction books based on the stories she learned in China. In *The Good Women of China: Hidden Voices* (2002), she revealed strong, resourceful characters who offered insights into China's past and present. Another book, *The Sky Burial* (2004), told the extraordinary story of an intrepid Chinese woman who spent thirty years searching rugged Tibet for her beloved husband, an army doctor who was reported killed. In *China Witness* (2008) and *The Promise: Love and Loss in Modern China* (2018), Xinran traced China's traumatic modern history through candid interviews with aging Chinese and with four generations of women. Her first novel, *Miss Chopsticks* (2007), explored the uneasy relationship between Chinese migrants and the cities where they work. Every year Xinran returns to China for reporting and also sponsors a charity, The Mother's Bridge of Love, that helps disadvantaged children.

Reflection Questions

1. Why did Xinran achieve such fame in China?
2. What does her journalism tell us about the experiences of Chinese women?
3. Do you think that Xinran could be a role model for Chinese women and maybe all women today?

Note: Quotations from Xue Xinran, *The Good Women of China: Hidden Voices* (New York: Anchor, 2002), 3, 126, 227.

similar concerns about their Internet privacy as Americans. The government also sometimes shuts down newspapers and magazines for daring reporting, but for a while some brave journalists and officials risked punishment by openly or subtly criticizing media micromanagement; some journalists and other writers referred to the limits imposed on them as "dancing with shackles." Today independent journalism has mostly been eliminated, and most Chinese get their information and news from government media. When liberal party members and intellectuals sign petitions and write articles protesting human rights abuses, they often lose their jobs or experience police surveillance. Yet, in 2018 some 660,000 Chinese, including children of high officials, were studying abroad. Some 350,000 of them were studying in the United States; among recent students was Xi Jinping's daughter.

Anxious to preserve national unity, the state has also repressed the sometimes-restless ethnic minorities, who constitute 8.5 percent of China's 1.42 billion in population, as well as some religious groups. Policies toward religion have been inconsistent. After 1978 the government tolerated millions of Chinese returning to their ancestral faith, but it has cracked down on movements deemed a threat or that refuse to accept official restrictions. Officials arrest and sometimes execute leaders and members of the assertive, missionary *Falun Gong* meditation sect, a Daoist–Buddhist–Christian mix, and harass or close down rapidly proliferating independent Christian churches that do not seek government approval. The communists have also strived to diminish the influence of Tibetan Buddhism, shutting down monasteries that they view as centers of dissent and resistance.

In the past few years the government has targeted some Muslims for harassment or worse, particularly repression of Muslims in Xinjiang **(shinjee-yahng)**, the far western province (with a population of twenty-four million) that has been home to Turkic peoples for many centuries. These peoples—Kazakhs, Kirghiz, and especially the more numerous Uighurs—have often seen themselves as colonized and disadvantaged by the Chinese minority, and have sought autonomy, greater religious freedom, and limits on large-scale Chinese immigration. Seething resentment periodically sparked self-immolations, riots, and interethnic violence, leaving hundreds of people dead or injured. To justify their domination the Beijing government portrays the region as part of a single Chinese nation and civilization throughout history. Prompted by sporadic separatist violence by some Islamists, China declared war on what they termed the three "evil forces" of ethnic separatism, violent terrorism, and religious extremism. One key prong was putting 1 to 1.5 million Muslims, mostly Uighurs, into prison-like political indoctrination camps in Xinjiang, to re-educate them into renouncing their religious beliefs and assimilating into Chinese culture. The process was arbitrary, with not only young and middle age men but also women, some pregnant, and elderly folks placed in the camps. Some critics called the destruction of Muslim culture and religious sites a cultural genocide. In 2019 officials began targeting the peaceful ten million ethnic Chinese Hui Muslims, demolishing mosques and banning Arabic on shop signs. Authorities also harassed Muslims elsewhere in China, using, as they did in Xinjiang and Tibet, high-tech surveillance to subdue minorities and instill fear.

27-2d China in the Global System

In October 2019 China celebrated the 70th anniversary of communist rule with glitzy cultural events, an extravagant state dinner, and a spectacular parade in Beijing, showing off 15,000 troops and advanced weapons (including five hundred-eighty tanks and one hundred-sixty fighter jets) to glorify communism, China's great power status and ambitions, and Xi's leadership. But the celebration signifying national pride and strength also came at a time when the country faced challenges and turbulence at home and abroad. Foreign observers and some Chinese worried about the consequences of China's grand ambitions or of a possible "fracture" of the U.S.-China relationship that could precipitate a world split between the two superpowers, forcing other nations to choose one or the other. The Party looked to the future but also to the past. China's relations with the wider world have been colored by humiliation from lost wars, foreign gunboats, civil wars, and Japanese invasions. Eventually the Chinese saw their nation again stand tall, strong, and increasingly rich. In 1997 they celebrated Hong Kong's peaceful return from British colonial control, rectifying the loss during the Opium War. Prosperous Hong Kong, whose towering skyscrapers, dazzling neon-lit waterfront, bustling shopping malls, and dynamic film industry symbolized East Asian capitalism, was incorporated under a "one nation, two systems" policy, with local leaders chosen or approved by China. The agreement allowed China to have sovereignty over the territory while ceding Hong Kong a "high degree of autonomy" and respecting it's open, liberal free market system. But by the early twenty-first century many young ethnic Chinese still identified as Hong Kongers (mostly Cantonese speaking) rather than citizens of authoritarian China.

A vocal and popular pro-democracy movement has charged that China's occasional interference in Hong Kong politics threatened political freedoms. Several times various policies diminishing Hong Kong identity or freedom brought thousands of protesters into the streets. The most serious challenge to the local pro-China government came in 2019 as a bill to allow extradition of Hong Kong residents to China and its party-controlled courts sparked months of unprecedented daily protests and city-wide strikes involving many thousands and sometimes up to two million people. With the support of a large segment of the city's population, protesters clogged the streets, occupied buildings, and demanded political reform including democratic elections as well as addressing problems like unaffordable housing, skyrocketing living costs, and high unemployment; the unrest complicated city life and fostered recession. Most protesters were peaceful but sporadic violence involving radicals and the police caused chaos, resulting in some deaths and over a thousand arrests. Officials in Hong Kong and China, some blaming the U.S., refused to bow to the popular demands or compromise. The China and pro-China Hong Kong media largely portray the unrest historically, through the lens of the "century of humiliation" of the Opium War, Treaty of Nanjing, and British colonial past, castigating some protest supporters for embracing "a bygone colonial fantasy." Pro-democracy, anti-Beijing candidates won a landslide victory in Hong Kong's local council elections, complicating Xi Jinping's options to end the crisis. The city's future remained uncertain. Across the Pearl River, in 1999 Portugal returned its small coastal colony of Macao to Chinese control. Macao's economy is based on gambling casinos, a lucrative enterprise that the once-puritanical communists seem happy to tolerate.

Since 1976 China has pursued a pragmatic foreign policy to win friends and trading partners but to avoid entangling alliances. China gradually improved relations with the United States and USSR and became increasingly active in the world, joining international institutions such as the World Trade Organization. Yet, China's military has also been rapidly modernizing, augmenting the world's largest army (some 2.3 million active troops and 1.1 million reserves and military police) with enhanced naval and air power. Since 2007 China dramatically increased its military budget and by 2019 ranked second in total world military spending, a third of the U.S. total.

Based on a controversial decades-old map and premodern trade routes, in 2010 China began pressing claims to much of the South China Sea, which may have vast oil reserves, and began building artificial islands with port and military facilities on the tiny reefs that dot the area. But Taiwan, Vietnam, Indonesia, Malaysia, and the Philippines also have claims in the area, including some of the reefs. Chinese naval ships and fishing vessels now occasionally challenge the ships and fishing boats of other nations in seas the world community considers international waters. Tensions simmer as the islands became a new flashpoint of world politics. The U.S. has led the opposition to China's claim; its interests are part legal, part geopolitical. Many experts consider China's maritime policies a coercive effort to establish regional military dominance.

China enjoys tremendous influence in the world economy, importing vast amounts of capital and natural resources, such as Zambian copper and Venezuelan oil, while exporting industrial products of every kind. Thousands of foreign investors from the West, Japan, Southeast Asia, South Korea, and even Taiwan have opened factories and negotiated joint ventures with Chinese firms. Meanwhile, China has supported the U.S. economy, becoming the major buyer of treasury bonds. Hundreds of Chinese enterprises buy companies in other nations or operate in Africa and Latin America, and many thousands of Chinese have followed them as workers or to open small businesses. China provides investment and loans to governments but expects cooperation in return. Thus China has become the world's most successful newly industrializing economy, buttressed by a vast resource base, a huge domestic market, and a resourceful labor force.

Yet China has met roadblocks in enhancing its global power. The communists threaten forced unification if Taiwan, enjoying a defense agreement with the United States, tries to declare a permanent break from China. Although economic and social links between China and Taiwan have increased, few in the island nation, which enjoys democracy and much higher living standards, want to merge with the mainland. Chinese relations with Japan also ebb and flow. The two nations have close economic ties but are natural rivals. The Chinese still resent Japanese brutality during World War II and fear contemporary Japanese nationalism. However, China has improved political and economic relations with once-bitter

enemies such as South Korea and anticommunist countries like Malaysia, the Philippines, and Australia, which view China as the future regional power. China is now Australia's top trading partner. In many Asian and some African and Latin American countries, many people are learning Mandarin Chinese, and some 500,000 international students studied in China in 2019. Nonetheless, historical resentment of Japan and the West stokes Chinese nationalism, sometimes resulting in anti-Japan or anti-U.S. protest demonstrations.

China's most ambitious plan to extend its influence and power to a much wider world came in 2013 when Xi introduced the Belt and Road Initiative (BRI), also known as the One Belt, One Road (OBOR) and sometimes the New Silk Road, a grandiose trillion-dollar trade and investment strategy to reconnect Eurasia and position China at the center of the global economy (see Discover Historical Voices: Building the New Silk Road and China's Belt and Road Initiative). Chinese and outside observers described it as a new maritime and overland Silk Road, an international Long March, or a Chinese version of the Marshall Plan, the massive U.S. aid and investment to renew Europe in the ashes of World War II. China would invest billions in infrastructure—including roads, bridges, railroads, ports, factories, and other development projects—in many countries. For example, China financed a string of ports around the Indian Ocean, in Sri Lanka, Pakistan, Myanmar, Malaysia, Djibouti, Kenya, and the United Arab Emirates. In Greece China bought control of the port of Piraeus and big shares of Greek utilities and fiber-optic companies. The China-linked Asian Infrastructure Bank approved $16 billion in projects in ten countries including Egypt, India, and Oman. China built rail lines in Europe and every part of Asia, allowing China to bypass U.S.-controlled sea lanes in shipping goods or resources. China's national oil corporation is now Central Asia's main energy player, displacing Russia; they pump Kazakh oil to Europe and China and natural gas from Turkmenistan to China. In extending its power and influence China has mobilized high technology; for example, they have constructed a fiber-optic network covering forty-eight African nations and a GPS-like satellite navigation system for all of Eurasia, helping them to dominate technology and trade. They have also extended operations to Latin America.

But the BRI has faced some scrutiny and resistance in the past several years, criticized by some of the nations getting the loans who now find themselves in a debt trap or worried about inadequate environmental protections. Several countries have cancelled or modified Chinese hydropower or railway projects they can't pay for. Some fear a new kind of neocolonialism and a power differential between China and the borrowers. The Kenyan president argued that if China's "win-win strategy is going to work, it must mean that, just as Africa opens up to China, China must open up to Africa."[17] Other nations worry that their influence in Asia will suffer as China soars, while the European Union fears China's ambitions in their countries, India and Japan worry about competing, and many Americans predict weakening U.S. influence in Asia and the world. These days all roads may lead to Beijing but can China deliver a "win-win" scenario not just for tycoons but for local populations?

---

[17]Uhuru Kenyatta, quoted in Peter Frankopan, "These Days, All Roads Lead to Beijing," *Huffington Post*, July 28, 2017.

Discover Historical Voices

Building the New Silk Road and China's Belt and Road Initiative

As the organizing foreign policy concept of the Xi Jinping era, in 2013 the new Chinese president announced the Belt and Road Initiative (BRI) or "new Silk Road," proposing huge development and infrastructure investments in Asian, African, and European countries. He has then rapidly turned his goals into a series of mechanisms for international cooperation, trans-regional connectivity, and a huge unified market through exchange and integration. Inspired by the overland and maritime trade routes that sporadically connected China with the Middle East and the West for over two thousand years, the BRI reestablished a twenty-first-century version. It enabled building several "belts" over which to transport goods and natural resources over vast distances across Eurasia and beyond, fostering eventual Eurasian unification and a vibrant "community of human destiny" with China at the center. The ambitious scheme has already resulted in many billions of dollars by China in infrastructure, industrial, transportation, resource extraction, power generation, and communications projects in dozens of countries, including some in Latin America. But the BRI is controversial. Defenders see it as an opportunity to spark development and bring diverse peoples together, while critics view it as a way for China to gain more power and outmaneuver the U.S. and its allies, while allowing China to capitalize on the growing debts to China these projects generate. This Chinese government document from 2015 summarizes the BRI rationale, including the historical background, the goals, and the expected benefits for the participating nations.

More than two millennia ago the diligent and courageous people of Eurasia explored and opened up several routes of trade and cultural exchanges that linked the major civilizations of Asia, Europe and Africa, collectively called the Silk Road by later generations. For thousands of years, the Silk Road Spirit—"peace and cooperation, openness and inclusiveness, mutual learning and mutual benefit"—has been passed from generation to generation, promoted the progress of human civilization, and contributed greatly to the prosperity and development of the countries along the Silk Road. Symbolizing communication and cooperation between the East and the West, the Silk Road Spirit is a historic and cultural heritage shared by all countries around the world.

In the 21st century, a new era marked by the theme of peace, development, cooperation and mutual benefit, it is all the more important for us to carry on the Silk Road Spirit in face of the weak recovery of the global economy, and complex international and regional situations....The Belt and Road Initiative...should be jointly built through consultation to meet the interests of all, and efforts should be made to integrate the development strategies of the countries along the Belt and Road.

The initiative to jointly build the Belt and Road, embracing the trend towards a multipolar world, economic globalization, cultural diversity and greater IT application, is designed to uphold ... global free trade and the open world economy in the spirit of open regional cooperation. It is aimed at promoting orderly and free flow of economic factors, highly efficient allocation of resources and deep integration of markets; encouraging the countries along the Belt and Road to achieve economic policy coordination and carry out broader...regional cooperation of higher standards; and jointly creating an open, inclusive and balanced regional economic cooperation architecture that benefits all. Jointly building the Belt and Road is in the interests of the world community. Reflecting the common ideals and pursuit of human societies, it is a positive endeavor to seek new models of international cooperation and global governance and will inject new positive energy into world peace and development.

It is open to all countries, and international and regional organizations for engagement, so that the concerted efforts will benefit wider areas. The Initiative is harmonious and inclusive. It advocates tolerance among civilizations, respects the paths and modes of development chosen by different countries, and supports dialogues among different civilizations on seeking common ground while shelving differences and drawing on each other's strengths, so that all countries can coexist in peace for common prosperity.

The Belt and Road cooperation features mutual respect and trust, mutual benefit and win-win cooperation, and mutual learning between civilizations. As long as all countries along the Belt and Road make concerted efforts to pursue our common goal, there will be bright prospects for the Silk Road Economic Belt and the 21st-Century Maritime Silk Road, and the people of countries along the Belt and Road can all benefit from this Initiative.

Reflection Questions

1. What does the document identify as the historical background of the goals of the BRI?
2. How does the report suggest that other countries will benefit by participation?
3. How do you think China will benefit from this huge investment in the world?
4. Do you think that most countries will find participation in and cooperation with the BRI to be to their advantage?

Source: Ministry of Foreign Affairs, and Ministry of Commerce of the Peoples Republic of China, National Development and Reform Commission, *Vision and Actions on Jointly Building Silk Road Economic Belt and 21st Century Maritime Silk Road*, 1st ed. March 2015.

By 2018 China faced the gravest threat to its economy as U.S. president Donald Trump, hoping to weaken what many observers believed were China's unfair or even abusive trade practices, intellectual property theft, forced technology transfers, state capitalism, and other advantages in the global system, began a trade war. In 2019 the war escalated as sporadic negotiations faltered amidst hardening hostility on both sides. By mid-2019 Trump had imposed high tariffs on nearly everything China exports to the U.S., from iPhones to sneakers to children's books. China responded by increasing their already high tariffs on U.S. exports, especially on agricultural commodities. Both countries face hardship and slower economic growth. Many American farmers have lost their largest market for many crops, including soybeans, corn, and ginseng. U.S. factories and farms losing markets or suppliers have laid off workers or shut down. Many U.S. economists criticized Trump's tariffs as poorly planned, a flawed and self-defeating strategy that, while it hurts China, hasn't benefitted the U.S., puts the world economy at risk, and suggests that the trade war may be prolonged, possibly with a deadlock for months or years to come.

Due partly to the trade war, China in 2019 is now experiencing its slowest economic growth in twenty-seven years, down to 6.2 percent, still more than double U.S. growth. Some companies have moved their operations to other countries such as Vietnam. China has too many factories making too many goods just as the huge U.S. market diminishes. Needing new markets, China has been trying to negotiate new free trade agreements. The future and ultimate consequences of the biggest trade crisis since the 1930s remain unclear but the economic clash between the two giants throws the world trade system out of balance and fosters global instability. As the rivalry between Trump and Xi to win the trade war intensifies, some specialists wonder if is too late to stop a new Cold War between China and the U.S.

In 2018 Xi told the World Economic Forum that nations must decide between "two fundamentally different outlooks," the worldview of the current U.S. administration, which represented, he argued, rising isolationism, surrendering global commitments, unilateral policies, and global fragmentation, or of China, whose model represented international cooperation, which he called "win-win development." Many found much to criticize in both of these simplistic alternatives. But the Chinese model, despite its flaws and repression, has proved attractive to many struggling countries and leaders, especially as the U.S., although still the lone superpower, seems to be pulling back from the world. In less than a generation the communists transformed China from a poor, agrarian society into an industrialized, middle-income country. Many Chinese found the trade-off of fewer political rights for greater economic and social welfare worth it. No country before ever achieved such rapid growth in such a sustained period of time, amounting to an economic miracle.

In 2018 some observers began referring to the Chinese Century. They argue that since 1990 China has driven many global trends, accounting for two-thirds of the world's decline in extreme poverty, half the total increase in patent applications, and 60 percent of the total increase in defense spending; since 2008 China produced 45 percent of the gain in world gross national product (GNP). In 1990 seven hundred-fifty million Chinese lived in extreme poverty; by 2019 only ten million did. But the gains came at a high cost, including 55 percent of the world increase in carbon emissions since 1990. China has pulled the world economy back toward Asia. Given the destructive trade war, Western opposition, and a weakening economy, some see Xi Jinping headed for failure as his reforms have been inadequate. But his "China Dream" for the "great renewal of the Chinese nation" might be considered a twenty-first-century vision of multilateral cooperation blended with a twentieth-century notion of nationalist militarism.

China has much lower overall living standards and far more overall poverty than North America, western Europe, Japan, and several industrializing Asian nations including Taiwan, South Korea, Singapore, and Malaysia. Nevertheless, its tremendous size, population, natural resources, military strength, national confidence, and sense of history make it a major global power. China, rather than the United States, led global recovery from the 2008–2009 recession. Perhaps China has returned to its historical leadership as the Asian dragon and a major engine of the global economy. Experts debate whether either China or India might replace the United States as the major world power in the next several decades. India has had advantages, such as democracy (although that has been under stress in 2019), a free press, and a sounder financial system. Yet, China, with a far superior infrastructure, might have better prospects, especially if the growing middle class fosters a more open political system (an unlikely prospect at present). Whatever the case, as during the long period of Chinese power and prosperity between 600 and 1800, China is once again a major force in world affairs.

KEY POINTS

▶ Under Deng Xiaoping, China opened up to Western economic ideas and investment, gradually introducing private ownership and competition, as well as to political, religious, and cultural currents that had been suppressed under Mao.

▶ Although many supported Deng's reforms, they led to increasing corruption and a growing gap between rich and poor.

▶ Under market Leninism, the Chinese state increased political and social control while continuing to privatize the economy, which grew briskly, though there was stagnation in many rural areas and environmental damage in others.

▶ China has enjoyed a great recovery and return to world prominence in recent decades, though it still has uncertain relations with Taiwan and Japan, and its living standard remains much lower than that of many of its rivals.

▶ Projects like China's Belt and Road Initiative have become more deeply involved in the world and a major economic power.

27-3 The Remaking of Japan

⚏ TRANSITIONS ⚎ SOCIETIES

Q How did Japan rise from the ashes of defeat in World War II to become a global economic powerhouse?

In August 1945, Japan lay in ruins, its major cities largely destroyed by U.S. bombing, its economy devastated, and its people in psychological shock. Yet, within a decade Japanese had recovered from the World War II disaster. After several decades of world history's highest economic growth rates, what some specialists called an "economic miracle," by the 1980s Japan was challenging the United States for world economic leadership. Stressing cooperation rather than individualism fostered economic and social stability in an overcrowded land (one hundred twenty-seven million in 2012). But beginning in the 1990s Japan has experienced political and economic uncertainty.

> ### CONNECTION to TODAY
>
> How have Japanese products and popular culture affected your life as well as your family and community?

27-3a Occupation, Recovery, and Politics

The U.S. post–World War II occupation aided Japan's recovery. Emperor Hirohito (**here-o-HEE-to**) (1901–1989), still a revered figure, asked the Japanese to cooperate with the Allied forces, and by and large they did. The U.S.-dominated military administration, the Supreme Command of Allied Powers (SCAP), sought to rebuild rather than punish Japan. Japan lost Korea, Taiwan, and Manchuria, while the United States took control of the Ryukyu Islands (including Okinawa), which were returned to Japan in the 1970s, and Micronesia. Hoping to democratize Japan by using the United States as a model while aiding economic recovery, SCAP dismantled the military, removed some civilian politicians, and tried and hanged seven wartime leaders as war criminals. Fearing that punishing the emperor, a member of an imperial family over fifteen hundred years old, would destabilize Japan, U.S. officials forced Hirohito to renounce his godlike aura and become a more public figure.

SCAP fostered political and social changes. Sustaining democracy required a more egalitarian society, with once-disadvantaged people sharing in the progress. A new constitution guaranteed civil liberties and, in a remarkable innovation, forever renounced war as the nation's sovereign right. But Japan and the USSR never signed a peace treaty after the war, leaving in place the Russian occupation of the Kurile Islands north of Hokkaido, long a part of Japan, in dispute. Democratic elections held in 1946 involved various competing political parties, and all adult citizens, including women, could vote. Women gained legal equality in society and marriage but were only partly freed from patriarchal expectations. New universities opened, providing greater access to higher education. The economy gradually recovered, using the same free markets mix introduced in the Meiji era, free from government intervention. Land reform subsidized the peasantry, making them strong government supporters and bringing prosperity to rural areas. Although SCAP attempted to break up entrenched economic power, large industrial–commercial–banking conglomerates still dominated manufacturing and foreign trade, making Japan more competitive in the world economy. But workers gained the right to unionize.

With the communist victory in China and then the Korean War, Americans shifted their emphasis from restructuring Japanese society to integrating Japan into the anticommunist Western alliance, symbolized by the formal U.S.–Japan peace treaty and mutual defense pact in 1951. U.S. military bases have remained in Japan ever since. The SCAP occupation officially ended in 1952; its policies were most successful where U.S. and Japanese desires coincided or when they fit with Japanese traditions. Democratic government fit both criteria. It was not without precedent; the Japanese had enjoyed several decades of democracy before the Great Depression. Borrowing from abroad also reflected tradition; the Japanese were again receptive to importing Western culture. With conditions stabilized, Japanese leaders began capitalizing on peace to strengthen the nation.

Despite stresses, Japan's democratic political system has endured. Diverse political parties—socialists, communists, liberals, center-right conservatives, Buddhists, right-wing nationalists—have competed for parliamentary seats. But the center-right Liberal Democratic Party (LDP) has dominated politics, applying generally conservative, pro-business, pro-U.S. policies. The SCAP-imposed electoral system gave greater weight to rural voters, the backbone of LDP support. But although prime ministers negotiate with opposition parties and varied LDP factions, critics believe that a political system mostly structured to favor rural voters (usually more conservative) and dominated by one party and wealthy kingmakers, who face little criticism from media largely owned by huge corporations, is at best a partial democracy.

The need to finance political careers by raising money from powerful corporations and criminal gangs has led to corruption. Bribery scandals sometimes force political leaders to resign, and a few have gone to prison. In 1993 the LDP fragmented in factional disputes but soon returned to power under a reform leader. In 2009, with Japan mired in severe recession and facing a huge national debt, the LDP experienced a huge defeat in national elections, losing power to the center-left Democratic Party, which promised reforms. But the Democrats proved unable to resolve the problems, confirming the inherent weakness of factionalized liberal and center-left political forces in Japan's politics and society. In 2013 and 2017 voters gave the LDP a smashing victory under their leader, Shinzo Abe (b. 1954), a right-wing, pro-military, anti-China nationalist but economic populist who had previously served a brief tenure as prime minister in 2006–2007. He ran under the slogan "Take Japan Back." Many hoped Abe could energize the economy and restore the nation's confidence. Although touched by several bribery scandals, Abe has remained in power since as the LDP leader. His popularity has ebbed and flowed as he introduced some measures (known as "Abenomics")

MAP 27.2 **Japan and the Little Dragons** Japan fostered the strongest Asian economy through the second half of the twentieth century, but in recent decades the Little Dragons—South Korea, Taiwan, Hong Kong, and Singapore—have also had rapid economic growth.

Q What does the map suggest about the significance of Japan, South Korea, and Taiwan in East Asian geopolitics compared to their neighbor, China?

to revive the economy, cultivated an image as a strong leader, sought a wider military reach, and promoted a nationalist agenda that glorified Japan's past.

Abe pledged to empower women and promote what he termed "womenomics," but has done little to bring them into male-dominated local or national politics. Japan has one of the world's worst records for female political representation. With women holding only 9 percent of seats in the lower house of parliament, Japan ranked 165th out of 193 countries in 2017. Abe's LDP has fielded few women but some opposition parties were much more inclusive. Over the past several decades women have led various minor parties. Among them is Yuriko Koike, one of the nation's most popular political figures, the mayor of Tokyo, and founder of the new Party of Hope. In 2018 parliament passed a "Gender Parity Law" that promotes gender equality in politics and advocates having equal numbers of male and female candidates. Women now account for half of the relatively powerless united opposition's members of the upper house but only 17.5 percent for the LDP. A Japanese political scientist concluded in 2019 that "Women are still too few and far between in Japanese politics, but a new generation of them is rising, bringing with them new concerns and new perspectives to policymaking."[18]

With a U.S. military alliance and bases for protection, Japan's military spending has long remained meager, providing more resources to the civilian economy and spurring rapid economic growth. While the Cold War superpowers invested in weapons and armies, Japan devoted its economic surplus largely to industrial development. However, leftist parties, labor unions, and militant student groups have long opposed the U.S. military presence as neocolonialism and fear that U.S. military interventions elsewhere will make Japan a potential target. Remembering World War II's horrors, especially the atomic bombings, which killed some 200,000 Japanese, many Japanese have favored pacifism. Yet, with U.S. support, Japan began increasing military spending in the 1980s, and it now has the world's ninth largest military budget, about one-fourth that of the United States. Sending soldiers to support, in noncombat activities, the U.S. war in Iraq was widely unpopular and, to critics, violated the constitutional ban against engaging in war. Seeing China as a threat, Abe, seeking a more assertive foreign policy, pledged to amend the constitution to increase Japanese military power, but his effort in 2019 aroused considerable opposition and failed in Parliament.

27-3b The Japanese Economy and Growth

Adapting capitalism to its own traditions, Japan achieved phenomenal economic growth, its goods in demand on every continent only a century after it opened to the outside world. Wartime destruction required rebuilding basic industries using

Junko Kimura/Getty Images News/Getty Images

IMAGE 27.5 **Japanese Women Commuters** A female passenger boards a train compartment reserved for women in a subway station in Tokyo. Tokyo's subways are usually jammed with passengers, and special cars allow women to travel without fear of possible sexual harassment.

Q What does the photo tell us about Japanese transportation and the lives of women?

the latest innovations. Investing in high-tech fields, Japanese became world leaders in manufacturing products such as pianos, oil tankers, and automobiles, as well as electronics such as watches, televisions, and cameras. From the 1960s through the 1980s Japan enjoyed annual growth rates three times higher than those of all other industrialized nations. An industrial giant, in 2000 Japan produced some 16 percent of the world's goods and services, half the U.S. percentage, a particularly impressive figure considering that Japan has few mineral resources, limited productive farmland, and no major rivers for hydroelectric power. Consequently, the Japanese must import the minerals needed for industry, such as iron ore, tin, and copper. Oil obtained from Alaska, Southeast Asia, and the Middle East powers Japan's transportation.

Japan became known for innovative technologies and high-quality products. A magnificent mass transit system included state-of-the-art bullet trains that carry passengers at 125–150 miles per hour and always on time. Trains of all types operate like clockwork. If a subway, suburban, or long-distance train leaves or arrives a few seconds before or after it is scheduled to, the drivers can be admonished or even punished. Electronics manufacturers such as Sony, Atari, and Nintendo invented entertainment-oriented products, among them video and handheld game systems that are now part of life everywhere,

---

[18]Mari Miura, "Japan's Leader Wants to Empower Women. Just Not in His Party," *New York Times*, July 26, 2019.

especially for youth. Millions of people, from Boston to Bogotá, Barcelona to Bombay, drive Toyotas, Hondas, Subarus, and other Japanese-made cars. Enjoying living standards equal to those of most western Europeans, Japanese became Western-style consumers, with most urbanites owning cars, televisions, washing machines, and air conditioners. One Japanese remembered his family's elation in the 1960s: "The first evening we turned on the television set we were so excited that we could not sleep. When the refrigerator arrived we kept opening and closing the door until Mother called us, and we sat transfixed watching the electric rice cooker after it was switched on. How 'high class' it was to live like this, we thought, eating bread browned in a toaster and spread with butter."[19]

The Japanese have also achieved the world's highest average life expectancy of eighty-four years, including eighty-one for men and eighty-seven for women. A more varied diet, including more meat and dairy products, has produced taller, healthier children. Western foods and beverages have become popular, and fast-food outlets such as McDonald's prove successful serving hamburgers and fries but also dishes adapted to local taste, such as teriyaki burgers and Chinese fried rice. Unlike in the 1920s, rural areas share in the prosperity; however, most rural youth have left their villages for the cities and most remaining farmers are older or even aged men and women. Many workers make do with part-time jobs offering few benefits; a small but growing underclass have no permanent jobs or homes.

Japan's capitalist economy differs in fundamental ways from that of Western industrial nations. The national government and big business work together in a cooperative relationship known as **Japan, Inc.** The government regulates business, setting overall guidelines, sponsoring research and development, and leasing the resulting products or technologies to private enterprise. Most Japanese businesses accept the guidelines, taking a longer-term view of profitability than Western business leaders. But government–business cooperation occurs chiefly in international trade, the country's lifeblood, made easier by the dominating Japanese conglomerates that own diverse enterprises such as factories, banks, and department stores. Protectionist barriers and bureaucratic hurdles impede foreign businesses but aid Japanese businesses.

Economic growth has generated new problems. As in the West, industrialization has fostered wealth but harmed the environment. Pollution of rivers and bays has wiped out coastal fishing, and smoggy air sometimes prompts city residents to cover their noses and mouths with masks to avert respiratory difficulties. Toxic waste dumped by factories has killed or sickened thousands. In 2011 a horrific earthquake and tsunami devastated a northern coastal region, leaving twenty thousand dead or missing and ruining a major nuclear power plant, which continues to poison the nearby land and sea with radioactivity, forcing reconsideration of the role and safety of Japan's many nuclear power plants.

Japan's business and factory life has contributed to success. The system capitalizes on, some say exploits, Japanese cultural values such as conformity, hard work, cooperation, thrift, and foresight, while adding innovations. While growing numbers of temporary workers and many employees in smaller businesses lack generous benefits and are vulnerable to layoffs, the 30 percent of workers in larger Japanese companies often enjoyed lifetime job security and access to generous employer-provided welfare benefits such as health insurance, recreation, housing, and car loans. Many employees enjoy company-sponsored group tours abroad or vacation retreats. Before the 1980s most workers remained with the same employer for life, but changing jobs became more common. To encourage identity with the corporate "family," employees of some companies gather together to sing the company anthem each morning before heading for their workstations. Japanese companies emphasize working in teams and "bottom-up" decision making through quality control circles and work groups; for example, a factory team that installs car engines will decide how best to undertake their tasks. Business offices are often organized around large tables, and white-collar employees work collaboratively rather than in small cubicles. The lifetime employment system has diminished considerably in the past decade as temporary contracts and job-hopping have become more common. However, businesses and factories still expect their employees to put company over personal interests, including regularly working overtime. Japan has some of the world's longest working hours, producing an increasingly common phenomenon known as *karoshi*, death attributed to overwork, that affects older and younger people alike. Declining job security has made the situation worse.

27-3c Japanese Society, Culture, and Thought

Urbanization and affluence have contributed to social change. Ninety-four percent of Japanese live in cities, with 66 percent of them in cities over one million in population. With thirty-eight million people (2016), Tokyo is the world's largest metropolitan area, and its legendary traffic jams may take police several days to untangle. With city subways convenient but overcrowded, rush hour has evolved into "crush hour"; city employees equipped with padded poles push commuters into overflowing cars to allow the train doors to close. Yet, despite notorious Mafia-like organized crime syndicates (*Yakuza*), Japan's cities are the world's safest; experts attribute the low rates of violent crime in part to strict gun control. Acquiring a gun license requires many bureaucratic steps stretching over four months, including oral and written exams on gun safety, several training sessions at gun ranges, multiple police interviews, mental health checks, past job history, and interviews of coworkers and neighbors. The system is designed to manage risks, places the burden on those who desire guns, and limits the ability of dangerous people to get guns. In 2015 the U.S. saw more than thirteen thousand non-suicide gun deaths; Japan had only one.

Japan, Inc. The cooperative relationship between government and big business that has existed in Japan after 1945.

---

[19]Ito Masanori, quoted in Peter Duus, *Modern Japan*, 2nd ed. (Boston: Houghton Mifflin, 1998), 301.

The economy has changed men's lives. Most university-educated men want white-collar office jobs in major corporations where they can become **salarymen**, urban middle-class male business employees who commit their energies and souls to the company, accepting assignments without complaint and taking few vacations. A few years ago the cover of a local book pictured a harried middle-aged salaryman eyeing the sundry items that define his work life: a computer, newspaper, lunch box, demanding boss, and subway strap. Many white-collar men are also known as "7-11 husbands," leaving for work at 7:00 A.M. and not returning until 11:00 P.M. After work they and their office mates socialize in restaurants, bars, and nightclubs while their wives take care of the home. In the 1980s one wife complained, "I don't know why Japanese men marry if they are never going to be home."[20] But given an uncertain economy, including more unstable contract jobs, more men now avoid or postpone marriage because they fear they cannot support a household; a third of men in their later 30s have never been married.

Around 70 percent of women aged fifteen to sixty-four now have jobs, but their careers are often held back by domestic burdens. While earning more money, gaining legal protections, and enjoying greater freedom, women struggle for full equality in a hierarchical society obsessed with patriarchy and seniority. They are expected to marry, work, and then retire to raise children, even though many remain in paid work. According to one young woman in the 1970s, when she graduated from a top university, "our bright appearance [for the graduation ceremonies] in vividly colored kimonos [traditional robes] was deceiving. Deep in our hearts we knew that our opportunities to use our professional education would be few."[21] Although traditional arranged marriages remain common, many men and women select their own spouse. More Japanese marry late or end unhappy marriages in divorce, but single mothers struggle with poverty and a "culture of shame." As single women discovered they could support themselves, the average marriage age for women rose from twenty-two in the 1950s to twenty-nine in 2013. In recent years, many women have avoided or postponed marriage altogether, preferring to concentrate on their careers or leisure interests and avoid what they view as domestic drudgery. Some even have weddings, attended by friends, to their "single self." In the mid-1990s only 5 percent of women had never been married by age fifty; by 2015 one in seven women were in that category. The resulting decline in marriage rates and fertility alarms politicians. Since 2000 Japan's fertility rate has fluctuated between 1.3 and 1.4 children per woman. Deaths have outnumbered births for years.

Despite popular images of timid Japanese females, assertive feminist organizations and leaders have publicized women's issues, while working women have lobbied companies for equal treatment and pay. Yet some employers, defining acceptable physical appearance, have mandated that women must wear makeup and high heels to work but are not allowed eyeglasses, prompting social media rage. Some women have moved into middle management or prestige occupations like law, journalism, college teaching, and diplomacy. Yet, women earn 60 percent less than males and largely lack political and economic power; only a few attain political or corporate leadership positions. In 2014, only 5 percent of senior managers were women, compared to 15–20 percent in Europe and North America. Gender equality activists admire former schoolteacher and journalist Ichikawa Fusae (ee-CHEE-kah-wah foo-SIGH) (1893–1981), who organized the women's suffrage movement in the 1920s and served in parliament for twenty-five years after World War II, campaigning for women's equality and human rights. Declining marriage rates make it easier for LGBTQ people to find social acceptance. Japanese society has always tolerated homosexual behavior, but now more are open about their sexual orientation. Same-sex marriage is not legally recognized but is often tolerated and many couples have been pushing for legalization. To court workers, some Japanese firms have implemented LGBTQ-friendly policies such as family benefits for couples.

Urban housing remains cramped; the elderly complain of neglect by children with no room in their small homes. Birth control and abortion were widely practiced in overcrowded Japan for centuries, and after World War II these practices, along with lower marriage rates, stabilized the population for several decades. Yet, a birthrate well below replacement standards and a rapidly aging population (20 percent over age seventy in 2018) had heavily burdened a shrinking workforce to pay for retirees' benefits and a generous health care system. Despite this problem, Japan has discouraged immigration to provide new workers. Thousands of Brazil-born Japanese who returned to their ancestral homeland, mostly to work in factories, often face resentment; those unemployed are encouraged to return to Brazil. Foreigners, mostly Chinese, Koreans, and Southeast Asians, number around 2 percent of the population (2018), in contrast to Britain (8 percent), Germany (9 percent), the United States (12 percent), and Australia (8 percent). Despite laws banning discrimination, prejudice persists against Koreans and the 1–3 million *Burakumin*, a despised underclass for centuries who traditionally did jobs considered unclean. In 2019 the government finally gave recognition as an indigenous population to the Ainu people in Hokkaido, who had endured over a century of forced assimilation and discrimination that undermined their culture.

Youth face their own pressures, including difficult exams to get into the better kindergartens, grade schools, and secondary schools; entrance exams for top universities so rigorous they are known as "exam hell"; and expectations to conform to mainstream society's values. These have encouraged youth rebellion. Some join motorcycle gangs, roaring along highways by day and neighborhood streets by night, annoying middle-class families. Others adopted counter-cultural lifestyles such as beatniks, hippies, punks, goths, metal-heads, and rappers. University students have

> **salarymen** Japanese urban middle-class male business employees who commit their energies and soul to the company, accept assignments without complaint, and take few vacations.

[20]Quoted in James L. McClain, *Japan: A Modern History* (New York: W.W. Norton, 2002), 585.
[21]Misuzu Hanikara, from Richard H. Minear, ed., *Through Japanese Eyes*, vol. 2 (New York: Praeger, 1974), 88.

The Asahi Shimbun/Getty Images

IMAGE 27.6 **Japanese Protest** Political demonstrations are common in Japanese cities. During this peaceful protest in 2012 antinuclear marchers in Tokyo opposed restarting a nuclear power plant in the aftermath of the Fukushima accident that killed many people and polluted a city and the region around it. Remembering the atomic bombings in 1945, many Japanese oppose nuclear power as unsafe and even dangerous, but governments argue that nuclear power is necessary to maintain living standards.

Q Given Japan's history of nuclear accidents, do you think that the protesters have a legitimate cause?

often supported left-wing political organizations protesting issues such as U.S. military bases or the destruction of farmland to build new airports or business developments; some others join right-wing nationalist groups. Many younger people resent the long hours and sacrifices expected of employees, especially since a high standard of living has already been achieved. But student activism has waned in recent years. Eventually, most young protesters return to the mainstream, taking jobs in the corporate or industrial world. Some who cannot conform emigrate to North America, Europe, or Latin America, seeking a more free-spirited life.

The Japanese debate the blending of traditional and modern cultures and beliefs, East and West, and its effect on cultural identity. Artists and writers ponder whether synthesizing foreign and local ideas has been the nation's salvation or bane. Some worry that Japan's adoption of foreign culture has imperiled its own distinctive legacy. Others contend that the Japanese need to become more global-minded, even encouraging immigration to create a multicultural nation.

Films, some achieving worldwide recognition, have frequently analyzed questions about Japanese identity and problems facing society. While Japan's film industry, the world's third largest, produces escapist films portraying samurai warriors, gigantic city-wrecking monsters, and anime and manga characters and stories, it also makes thought-provoking masterpieces, especially grand historical epics and introspective psychological or sociological studies. One of the most skillful directors, Kurosawa Akira (**kur-o-SAH-wa a-KEER-a**)

(1910–1998), mixed a distinctive Japanese style and setting with universal themes. *Rashomon* (1950), for example, examines the relativity of truth through varied perspectives on one event, the killing and violation of a feudal lord's wife by a bandit. Another Kurosawa film, *Ikuru* ("To Live") (1952), explores life's meaning; a Japanese bureaucrat dying of cancer overcomes endless red tape to facilitate the building of a small neighborhood park.

The Japanese have the world's highest literacy rate (99.9 percent) and the largest numbers of newspaper readers, magazine subscribers, and bookstores per capita, fostering both popular and serious literature. Kawabata Yasunari (**ka-wa-BAH-ta yah-suh-NAHR-ee**) (1899–1972) became the first Japanese novelist, in 1968, to receive the Nobel Prize for literature. Directly addressing Japanese identity, the writings of Mishima Yukio (**me-SHE-mah YOO-kee-oh**) (1925–1970) portray an effete, decadent "nation of shopkeepers" who need to renew the Tokugawa period's martial values. His best novel concerns a disturbed young man torn, like Mishima himself, between old samurai and modern Westernized values. For Mishima, a conflicted gay man and avid body builder, life became art; in 1970 he publicly committed suicide in samurai style, sacrificing himself for the "old beautiful tradition of Japan, which is disappearing day by day."[22] His action shocked the Japanese, but his message died with him; Japan continued developing a consumer society.

Continuity has long characterized Japanese popular culture. Every sport, art form, and religion appearing in the past fifteen hundred years still attracts practitioners or followers. The Japanese remain passionate about sumo wrestling, an old sport in which two large, paunchy men attempt to push each other out of a small ring. Yet, today many top wrestlers are foreigners, among them Mongolians, eastern Europeans, Turks, and Polynesians. But while kabuki or bunraku, theatrical forms appearing in the 1600s, still attract devoted audiences, and young Japanese women preparing for marriage often master the even older tea ceremony, many more Japanese follow professional and high school baseball teams (amateur competitions began in 1915); consume Japanese comics, or *manga* (**mahn-gah**), and animated films, or *anime*, which are popular worldwide; play video games; and flock to Japanese or Western films, discos, pinball palaces, and gaming arcades. Japanese creations like Transformers, Power Rangers, Hello Kitty, Pokemon, The Iron Chef, karaoke, ramen noodles, and sushi have achieved global popularity. Modern Japanese, avidly adopting foreign cultural forms, frequent nightclubs featuring, among other musical styles, local and imported versions of rock, jazz, reggae, country western, rap, and salsa.

Organized religion continues to decline, although some remain deeply religious. Militant Buddhist groups claim several million followers, and various new religions based on Buddhist or Shinto traditions, or mixing of the two, address material prosperity and family problems. Nonetheless, contemporary

[22]Mishima, quoted in Mikiso Hane, *Modern Japan: A Historical Survey*, 2nd ed. (Boulder, CO: Westview Press, 1992), 371.

Japanese are a largely secular people. In censuses, less than 15 percent report any formal religious affiliation. Despite a tiny Christian population (2 percent), millions of non-Christians ardently celebrate Christmas as an opportunity to give and receive gifts; department stores feature elaborate Christmas displays, complete with Santa Claus and brightly decorated Christmas trees. However, weak religious influence has not fostered social breakdown. The Japanese remain among the world's most law-abiding, peaceful citizens; morality mostly derives from fear of shaming the family or group rather than fear of retribution by gods or ancestors. Reluctance to disgrace the family suggests that Confucianism remains important. Yet conforming to the group and its rules has downsides. Criticizing an old saying—"the nail that sticks up gets hammered down"—Japanese liberals have sought a less conformist society that nourishes rather than inhibits individual genius.

27-3d Japan in the Global System

The Japanese have had to readjust their global views and economic expectations over the past several decades. Like their North American and European counterparts, Japanese companies, seeking cheaper labor, have established factories in Southeast Asia, South Korea, and China, a practice that has cost Japan jobs. In 1989 Japan's economy went into a severe downturn, thanks to overvalued stocks precipitating a crisis on the Tokyo Stock Exchange, global recession, and competition from newly industrializing Southeast Asia. This crisis began what observers called a "Lost Decade" of economic stagnation during the 1990s, and lingering into the 2000s, that discredited the Japan, Inc. model. Eventually policies fostering higher growth rates renewed business confidence, but the recovery remained incomplete.

Two decades later the global economic crisis of 2008–2009 undermined export-oriented Japan, causing recession, bank failures, bankruptcies, and huge drops in consumer spending abroad, even affecting leading manufacturers like Toyota and Sony. Like U.S. corporations, Japanese corporations reacted to recent foreign competition and crises by slashing salaries, cutting benefits, and even firing employees, modifying the business system that brought prosperity for a half century. Some newly unemployed men, especially office workers, ashamed to admit their humiliation to friends and families, spend each workday on park benches or in coffee houses. The economic problems have caused disenchanted voters to turn out several governments.

While comfortable as an economic powerhouse, until recently Japan remained reluctant to assert its political and military power in the world, remembering how the attempt to dominate eastern Asia brought it disaster during World War II. Japan's main concerns have been the world economy's health and access to overseas resources and markets. Hence, the Japanese people prefer peaceful rather than military solutions to world problems. Despite their strategic alliance, Japan and its main trading partner, the United States, remain keen economic rivals and sometimes engage in trade disputes. Japanese leaders have promoted peaceful exchange with China and South Korea, two countries with long memories of Japanese imperialism. However, relations with South Korea and China have often been strained; the Chinese have demanded that Japan accept responsibility for wartime atrocities. In 2012 tensions flared over ownership of tiny, uninhabited islands midway between the countries. Resurgent Japanese and Chinese nationalisms clash, fanned by opportunistic political leaders seeking to solidify popular support. As China and several other Asian nations rise economically, Japan faces more competition and the challenge of maintaining its position in the world economy. In 2019 lingering resentments between Japan and South Korea sparked a trade conflict and political standoff. South Korea's bitter memories of Japan's former colonial rule and drafting of Korean "comfort women" during World War II and other grievances increased. Japan responded by increasing controls on exporting a broad array of goods to South Korea. Relations plunged to their lowest point in decades, spooking world markets and alarming their mutual ally, the U.S.. Despite their shared fear of North Korea and efforts to renew their cooperation, the future of Japan-South Korean relations remains uncertain.

In 2018 Abe reacted to the rise of China as Asia's new top powerhouse by promoting a new vision for a vast stretch of the globe, from the Pacific to the Indian Ocean, united by trade and common political purpose. Japan's initiative, called the Free and Open Indo-Pacific, is based on principles of free trade, freedom of navigation, the rule of law, and market economies. Many perceive it as partly a counterpart to China's Belt and Road Initiative. Also wary of China, India was among potential supporters. Fearful of reviving wartime memories of Japanese imperialism, Japan has long played a generally passive role in Asian and world policies, enjoying U.S. protection. Abe's agenda staking Japan's own path suggests a shift to a more active engagement.

KEY POINTS

▶ After World War II, a U.S.-led occupation of Japan (SCAP) worked to rebuild Japan's economy while demilitarizing the country and encouraging the return of democracy.

▶ The Liberal Democratic Party dominated Japanese politics for decades, with a brief break in the 1990s, and the presence of U.S. military bases within Japan was seen by some as neocolonialism but freed up resources to help fuel the economy.

▶ Relying on innovation and collaboration between government and big business, Japan's economy has grown at a phenomenal rate.

▶ Japan's cities have become increasingly congested, men are expected to devote all their energy to work, women struggle for equality and increasingly choose work over marriage, and students face the pressure of an arduous education system.

▶ Japanese have managed to blend their traditions with modern and foreign influences and have maintained a high degree of social order in spite of low participation in organized religion.

27-4 The Little Dragons in the Asian Resurgence

⚞ TRANSITIONS ▦ SOCIETIES

Q What policies led to the rise of the "Little Dragon" nations and their dynamic economies?

In the later twentieth century many observers predicted that the twenty-first century would be the **Pacific Century**, with global economic power shifting from Europe and North America to the export-driven eastern Asian nations that were poised to dominate a post-Cold War world where economic power might outweigh military might. Although changing world politics and economic crises, especially an Asian financial collapse in 1997 and the severe global recession in 2008–2009, proved challenging, some observers still predict a Pacific or Asian Century. While China and Japan were rising to regional and global power, several of their East Asian neighbors achieved economic development. Known as the **Little Dragons** because of the strong Chinese cultural influence on these nations, South Korea, Taiwan, Singapore, and Hong Kong built rapidly growing, industrializing economies. Except for Hong Kong, a British colony until 1997 and a free enterprise bastion, these societies largely followed the Meiji Japan model of state-directed capitalism and were inspired by Japan's resurgence after World War II, which depended on participation in the world economy. Sharing a Confucian cultural heritage emphasizing hard work, discipline, cooperation, and tolerance for authoritarian governments, the Little Dragons all achieved export-oriented industrialization, raising incomes, reducing poverty, and improving health and education. For South Korea, this development followed after a brutal war, leaving a hostile, rigidly communist North Korea on the border. In China's shadow, Taiwan found its own path, while Singapore (see Chapter 31) and Hong Kong (now part of China) are city-states with largely Chinese populations.

27-4a Korean Independence and War

The Korean War (1950–1953) was rooted in Korean nationalism, which simmered, despite fierce repression, during a half century of harsh Japanese colonial rule (see Chapters 23 and 24). While introducing some economic modernization, Japan arrested or executed Korean nationalists and resistance leaders, conscripted Korean women to serve Japanese soldiers as "comfort women," relocated thousands of Korean workers to Japan, and manipulated divisions within Korean society. Christians constituted one influential group that grew in numbers; by the 1940s a fifth of Koreans were Catholics or Protestants. Another group gravitated toward communism, some escaping to the USSR to form a revolutionary movement. Most Koreans followed Buddhism and Confucianism. Although Christians, communists, and traditionalists all hated Japanese rule and worked underground to oppose it, they could not cooperate with each other, and no unified nationalist movement emerged.

Pacific Century The possible shift of global economic power from Europe and North America to the Pacific Rim in the twenty-first century.

Little Dragons South Korea, Taiwan, Singapore, and Hong Kong, which were strongly influenced by Chinese culture and built rapidly growing, industrializing economies.

CONNECTION to TODAY

How did the Korean War affect your family, community, and nation?

Japan's crushing defeat in 1945 meant Korea's political liberation and a chance to reclaim independence, free of foreign interference. But the United States quickly occupied the peninsula's southern half and the Soviet Union seized the north, bisecting Korea and making it a Cold War hostage. As the USSR and United States imposed rival governments, unification quickly became impossible. With Soviet help, communists led by the ruthless Kim Il-Sung (**KIM ill-soon**) (1912–1994) established North Korea. A clever strategist, Kim built a brutal communist system, eliminated his opponents, and reorganized rural society. But the impatient Kim disastrously overestimated the south's revolutionary potential and misjudged Americans' determination to stop spreading Soviet influence. The United States helped create and then supported a South Korean state headed by Rhee Syngman (**REE SING-man**) (1865–1965). An autocratic, politically conservative Christian from a powerful landlord family, Rhee had lived in exile in the United States for over two decades. Unpopular with the non-Christian majority, Rhee imprisoned or eliminated his opponents, sparking a leftist rebellion supported by many factory workers and peasants that American troops helped crush. Although less repressive than North Korea, Rhee's South Korea held some thirty thousand political prisoners.

The Korean War was created from the mixing of revolution and nationalism into a Cold War–driven stew (see Map 27.3). Historians still debate the origins of this conflict, which helped shape East Asian politics for over half a century. Both states, threatening to reunify Korea with military force, initiated border skirmishes. In this highly charged context, North Korea, with Soviet and Chinese approval, invaded the South in 1950. Soon South Koreans were slaughtering leftist sympathizers while North Korean sympathizers killed relatives of South Korean police and soldiers. The Western-dominated United Nations authorized a U.S.-led military intervention to support South Korea, turning the Korean crisis into a Cold War confrontation in which Americans committed the most troops, war materials, and funding. U.S. president Harry Truman secretly planned to strike North Korea with atomic weapons if the USSR entered the war. But while the Soviets gave military supplies and advice, they sent no combat troops.

United Nations troops, aided by U.S. air power, quickly pushed the North Koreans back across the north–south border. But the United Nations move into North Korea and push toward China's border sparked a massive Chinese intervention that drove back United Nations troops and turned a likely victory into a bitter stalemate. U.S. leaders had underestimated the Chinese people's willingness to fight and their military capabilities. When the war ended in 1953 with peace talks, the north–south boundary, remaining roughly where it was before the war, was now a heavily fortified zone. The war killed four hundred thousand Korean troops and 1–3 million civilians, some four hundred thousand Chinese, and forty-three thousand United Nations forces, 90 percent of them American, while generating millions of refugees who wandered the countryside, seeking

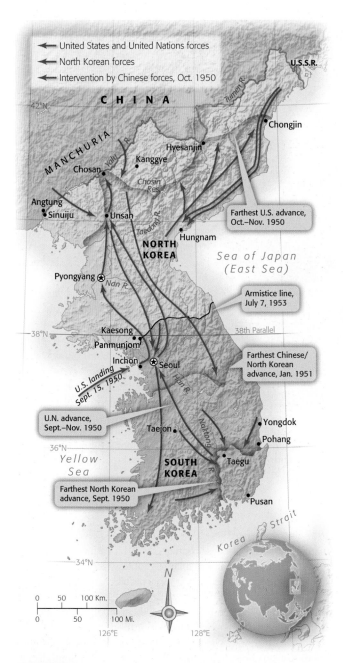

MAP 27.3 **The Korean War** In 1950, North Korean forces crossed the 38th parallel and invaded South Korea, but they were then pushed back north by United Nations forces led by the United States. The intervention of China in support of North Korea pushed the United Nations forces south and produced a military stalemate, preserving the border between North and South Korea at the 38th parallel.

Q What does the map tell us about the course of the war?

food and shelter. Both Koreas were left in economic shambles. Americans may have largely forgotten the war that ended in an unsatisfying stalemate but Koreans have not. South Koreans resent the lives lost and the terrible damage to their country but

are largely grateful for the outside world's help. North Koreans passionately hate the U.S., partly because their government's propaganda and schools have instilled a fear and loathing of "U.S. imperialism" in them for over sixty years, but also because many remember the U.S. carpet bombing of the north for three years with little concern for civilian casualties, killing some 20 percent of the population. The misery, disease, pain, suffering, starvation, and occasional atrocities (committed by both sides) affected all Koreans, leaving a debilitating legacy of the Korean War for the generations that followed and can't forget.

27-4b The Two Koreas

One of the world's poorest nations in the ashes of war, South Korea's postwar rise left North Korea lagging far behind and was nearly as dramatic as Japan's. Closely allied to the United States, South Korean governments ranged from highly repressive military dictatorships from the 1950s through the mid-1980s, to moderate semi-democracies in the later 1980s, and then to liberal democracies with free elections since the early 1990s. All regimes aimed at economic development. The dictator Park Chung Hee (1917–1979) argued in 1970, "My chief concern was economic revolution. One must eat and breathe before concerning himself with politics, social affairs, and culture."[23] Prohibited from forming unions, many South Koreans experienced brutal working conditions, especially miners and teenage girls recruited into factory work. Americans protected South Korean regimes, permanently stationing troops and supplying generous economic and military aid. Six and a half decades after the war, some thirty-eight thousand U.S. troops remained in South Korea.

South Korea enjoyed enormous economic growth, investing in the Middle East, Southeast Asia, and Russia while exporting automobiles and electronic products. By the 1990s South Korea had become the first non-Western nation since Japan to join the ranks of advanced industrial nations, and it later became a member of the G-20 grouping of industrial powers and a high-technology model. Today it is considered one of the world's most innovative nations and technology powerhouse, and the world's eleventh largest economy. Having acquired living standards they could only dream of two decades earlier, with nearly universal literacy, South Koreans now enjoy the world's fastest downloads and highest rate of high-speed Internet access: some 95 percent of households are wired and 90 percent of Koreans own mobile phones, far more than in North America and Europe. Both boys and girls receive free education through age twelve; the adult literacy rate is 98 percent. South Korean women have benefited from new job options in the professions and business, but often face harassment and discrimination. With more women in the workforce and self-supporting, marriage rates declined and average births per woman fell dramatically, from six in 1990 to 1.6 in 2005, and by 2019 the world's lowest fertility rate, 0.88 babies per woman, alarming leaders. In 2010, some national agencies and local governments began sponsoring dating parties to promote courtship.

Economic growth also fostered political change. Democracy movements, begun in the 1960s, often faced government repression. One dissident wrote that "bullets, nightsticks, and fists are not the only forms of violence. A nation with no

[23]Quoted in Frank Gibney, *The Pacific Century: America and Asia in a Changing World* (New York: Charles Scribner's, 1992), 231.

Paul Chesley/The Image Bank/Getty Images

IMAGE 27.7 **South Korean Economic Growth** One of South Korea's major, most diverse enterprises, the Hyundai Corporation, formed in 1976, engages in shipping, manufacturing, and trade, producing, among other products, chemicals, machinery, and information and telecommunications equipment. The ships in this company dry dock are being readied to carry Hyundai-made cars to distant markets around the world.

Q   What can we learn from the photo about South Korean industry?

expression of dissent is a nation in ruins."[24] In 1980 the dictatorship brutally crushed an uprising in a southern province. When some five hundred demonstrators demanded an end to martial law, paratroopers slaughtered the protesters and local people. Hundreds of thousands of enraged citizens drove the troops out of the city, only to face a much larger force that killed over two thousand people. Eventually, political tensions diminished. Governments fostered more liberalization, tolerated a freer press, and made overtures toward former Soviet and Chinese enemies. By the early 1990s, as the middle class and organized labor grew, democracy flowered, though sometimes it was sullied by political corruption. South Koreans are proud of their freedom, their bustling cities, and their popular culture's influence in both China and Japan as well as around the world. The "Korean New Wave" of popular films, television dramas, and music (K-pop), especially boy and girl bands such as Bangtan Boys (BTS) and Girls' Generation (SNSD), have gained a huge audience around the world, including in China and Southeast Asia.

But while the country and its fifty-two million people (one-quarter of them Christians) have clearly outshined repressive North Korea, problems have arisen. Many rural people and unskilled workers did not share in the prosperity, while factories expected long hours from poorly paid workers. Frustrated at their prospects, thousands, many of them middle class, emigrated, especially to the United States. The economic slowdown beginning in

1997, and then the 2008–2009 global economic crisis, which cost many jobs, also spurred discontent. By 2011 business had largely rebounded, although it was a largely jobless recovery and many young people fume at decreasing social mobility and hope for good jobs. Another problem is that while many South Koreans have welcomed U.S. bases, others consider them an affront to nationalism. Many Koreans yearn for reunification and an end to the peninsular cold war. After years of hostility, and owing partly to South Korean efforts to improve relations, North and South Korea finally achieved a wary peaceful coexistence. A dialogue known as the "sunshine policy," begun in 1998, fostered limited cross-border trade and some South Korean visits to family members in North Korea not seen since the early 1950s. Televised images of South Koreans tearfully embracing aging parents or siblings mesmerized the nation. Then in 2000 South Korean president Kim Dae-jung **(kim day-chung)** (1925–2009), a liberal reformer and former dissident, visited North Korea, an event unthinkable a decade earlier. Yet national reconciliation still remains a dream; South Koreans worry about North Korea's military capabilities and its quest to build nuclear weapons. Tensions increased after 2009, with a more conservative South Korean president skeptical of negotiations over these issues. In 2016–2017 weekends of mass "candlelight rallies" drove a scandal-ridden conservative from power. In 2017 the liberal Moon Jae-In was elected president with a reform agenda; he has sought to defuse tensions and through diplomacy develop better

[24]Cho Se-hui, quoted in Bruce Cumings, *Korea's Place in the Sun: A Modern History* (New York: W.W. Norton, 1997), 337.

relations with North Korea while following a more independent foreign policy. But he also cooperated in U.S. president Donald Trump's controversial opening to North Korean leaders, which has eased tensions but so far not halted North Korean nuclear tests or brought a peace agreement. In 2018 Moon held a summit with North Korean leader Kim Jong-Un on their border, opening new avenues of communication. In 2019, reacting to Trump's demand that South Korea massively boost spending on U.S. troops or they might be withdrawn, Moon negotiated a defense agreement with China.

North Korea's leaders chose a completely different path from South Korea. The Korean War devastated the country, though North Korea quickly recovered with Soviet and Chinese aid. From 1948 until his death in 1994, Kim Il-Sung created a personality cult around himself as the "Great Leader." North Koreans were taught that they owed everything—jobs, goods, schooling, food, military security—to Kim. To ensure loyalty and deflect blame for failures, Kim purged many communist officials and jailed or executed thousands of dissidents. Kim mixed Stalinist economic planning and central direction, emphasizing heavy industry and weapons, with Maoist self-reliance. Hence, North Koreans did not enjoy the rising living standards of South Koreans, who live about ten years longer. Although North Korea contained most of Korea's factories and mines, built during Japanese colonial times, the huge military establishment drained resources to deter enemies and intimidate South Korea.

Like nineteenth-century Korea's Confucian kings, North Korea stressed group loyalty, ultra-nationalism, and independence from foreign influence. A small political and military elite, isolated from peasants' and workers' bleak lives, enjoyed comfortable apartments and sufficient food, controlling people through regimentation and restriction of information. To monitor activities and thoughts, the government required everyone to register at a public security office and urged people to spy on their families and neighbors. To prevent contrary views, radios received only the government station. Political prisoners and people caught fleeing to China or South Korea, as thousands of people have, faced long terms in harsh concentration camps or execution. The economy declined rapidly, thanks to poor management, commodity shortages, and rigid policies. Satellite photos of the Korean peninsula at night revealed the stark differences in electrical power between brilliantly lit South Korea and completely dark North Korea. Even the capital city's lights were mostly turned off by 9:00 P.M. U.S. diplomatic and economic pressure isolated the regime, making North Korea totally reliant economically on the Soviet bloc; when it collapsed in 1989, Russia and China then demanded that North Korea pay cash for oil and other imports.

North Korea's problems increased after Kim Jong-Il **(chong-ill)** (1942–2011), known as the "Dear Leader," succeeded his deceased father in 1995. When the nation faced mass starvation, South Korea, Japan, and the United States, anxious to discourage desperate military action, sent food aid. Many people still died or were malnourished, and thousands fled to China seeking food and work. Yet the regime avoided collapse, even after inexperienced Kim Jong-Un (b. 1984), a virtual unknown, became leader after his father's death in 2011, continuing the family dynasty. Thanks to isolation and tight information control, few North Koreans traveled abroad, studied foreign languages, met foreigners, or encountered foreign publications, films, and music. Meanwhile,

a small dissident movement, risking harsh reprisals, smuggled in food from China and videotapes, books, and music from South Korea. Estimates of political prisoners, held in brutal prison camps, have ranged from 80,000 to 200,000.

North Korea worried both regional and world leaders, with its military force twice as large as South Korea's and capable of building nuclear weapons. But with both Koreas possessing lethal military forces, South Korea boasting twice the population, and U.S. nuclear weapons in South Korea, all-out war became less likely, encouraging the search for common ground. Economic disasters, especially food shortages, sometimes softened North Korea's position; after 1998 South Korea actively but sporadically sought better relations to reduce the threat from its dangerous northern neighbor and its unpredictable leaders. Indeed, isolated by its bellicose policies, North Korea relies mostly on trade with China and South Korea. A 2019 U.N. study estimated that nearly half of North Koreans are undernourished. North Korea's neighbors and the United States sought diplomatic ways to eliminate the possibility of a conventional war or a nuclear confrontation, but by 2008 tensions returned; often disapproving the regime's unpredictable behavior and bellicose rhetoric but fearing North Korean collapse, China remains the only major ally. U.S. president Trump initially threatened North Korea with "fire and fury" if it did not denuclearize, but then shifted to a policy of détente in 2018–2019, proclaiming friendship with Kim and arranging two Trump–Kim summits. South Korea cooperated in these diplomatic openings, which have diminished for now the likelihood of a disastrous war, but North Korea has continued testing nuclear weapons and missiles, still unsettling the region, and relations with South Korea remain fragile and unpredictable.

27-4c Taiwan and China

With the communist triumph on the mainland in 1949, Chiang Kai-shek and his nationalist government relocated to mountainous, subtropical Taiwan island, where they reestablished the Republic of China. Taiwan had only become a part of Chinese territory in the seventeenth and eighteenth centuries; in 1910 it became a Japanese colony. Japan ruled Taiwan less harshly than it did Korea, financing industrialization that produced higher living standards than in mainland China. After World War II China reclaimed the island, but in 1947 local resentment of Chiang's heavy-handed regime sparked an island-wide uprising. To quell the unrest, Chiang dispatched 100,000 troops that killed 30,000 to 40,000 Taiwanese, including many local leaders.

As the Republic collapsed in 1948–1949, Chiang and two million mainlanders took their government, Nationalist Party, remaining military forces, priceless national museum art collections, and China's national treasury to Taiwan. These mainlanders and their descendants eventually constituted 15 percent of the total island population, which numbered twenty-four million by 2018. Because the minority mainlanders dominated politics, the economy, and the military, the majority Taiwanese, although Chinese in culture and language, often considered the mainlanders colonizers. Hoping to retake the mainland, Chiang viewed Taiwan as a temporary refuge. After his death in 1975, many mainlanders (and their children), realizing that a return to the mainland was unlikely and that Taiwan might be their permanent home, cultivated better relations with the Taiwanese. However, two governments claiming to represent China created a long-term diplomatic problem for the world community. Both the People's Republic and the Republic on Taiwan regarded the island as an integral part of China rather than a separate nation, a "one China policy" endorsed by most of the world.

Learning from their China defeat and using generous U.S. aid, the Republic's leaders promoted rapid industrial and agricultural growth, more equitable wealth distribution, the land reform they neglected on the mainland, and access to credit facilities; as a result, the peasantry prospered. As in South Korea and Meiji Japan, Taiwan's economy mixed capitalism and foreign investment with government planning and investment. Light industry and manufacturing accounted for half the economic production and most exports. The world's third largest manufacturer of computer hardware, between the early 1970s and the late 1990s Taiwan enjoyed more years of double-digit growth than any other nation. Taiwanese companies established operations in Southeast Asia, China, Africa, and Latin America, and Taiwan's economic indicators far surpassed China's: an average annual income of $50,000, 99 percent of households owning a color television, 96 percent literacy, and a life expectancy of seventy-eight. Rapid development, however, brought environmental destruction, traffic congestion, political corruption, and a severe economic slowdown in 1997 and 2008–2009. Concrete high-rise buildings increasingly displace the lush greenery of the mountains around the capital, Taipei.

Modernization has challenged Chinese values and traditions. Small roadside cafés selling noodle soup and meat dumplings often close, unable to compete with U.S. fast-food restaurants and convenience stores selling Coca-Cola, hamburgers, and ice cream. Rampant materialism concerns those who believe that life should offer more than luxury goods and money. While Confucian values fostered material success, some worry that respect for parents and concern for community rather than the individual are threatened. Many religious and cultural conservatives opposed homosexuality but with a large and active LGBTQ community, in 2019 Taiwan recognized same-sex marriage. Yet, traditional Chinese culture remains stronger in Taiwan than on the mainland. Most Taiwanese describe themselves as Buddhists, Daoists, Confucianists, or a mix of the three; some 6 percent are Christians, while several million others infrequently attend temples or churches.

Until the later 1980s Taiwan followed the authoritarian Little Dragon political model, with a police state holding numerous political prisoners. Chiang Kai-shek made it illegal to advocate permanent independence from China, and the PRC also opposed those favoring two separate Chinese nations. For four decades Chiang's Nationalist Party ruled, but in 1989, nudged by a growing middle class seeking liberalization, the party permitted opposition candidates to run in elections. Gradually the regime recognized civil liberties, including freedom of speech and press, and direct democracy including citizen-based ballot initiatives and referendums, becoming a full democracy and one of Asia's freest societies. The 2000 elections swept into office the Democratic Progressive Party (DPP), largely supported by native Taiwanese; many party leaders supported separate Taiwan nationhood and identity, angering both nationalist leaders on Taiwan and mainland communist leaders. However, Taiwan's voters seemed less eager to confront China and in 2008 replaced the DPP government, beset by corruption, with the nationalists, who sought friendlier ties with China. In 2014 a proposed free trade pact with China enraged and energized the opposition, leading to massive protests by students and workers fearing more influence by the People's Republic over the island. In 2016 the first woman, Tsai Ing-wen, became president as the DPP returned to power, unsettling China. Tsai urged China to democratize, respect human rights, and renounce force, but China has responded with military patrols in nearby waters and reaffirming what they consider their claims to the island.

China remains Taiwan's permanent challenge. Fearing an invasion to forcibly annex the island, Taiwan lavishly funded its military, kept a large standing army, bought the latest fighter jets and gunboats, and maintained a defense alliance with the United States. But in 1978 the United States recognized the PRC as China's only government, withdrawing diplomatic recognition from the Republic but maintaining a strong economic presence and commitment to defend Taiwan. In the later 1980s Taiwan and China began improving relations. Informal trade grew substantially; many Taiwanese visited the mainland for business or family reunions, while mainland tourists and students went to Taiwan. As part of a large "brain drain" from the island, thousands of young educated people have emigrated, some to the West and some to China, which actively recruited skilled and high-tech workers. However, doubts about China's eventual liberalization and democratization, in addition to unease at occasional Chinese military exercises, precluded any serious negotiations on reunification. The shaky "one country, two systems" formula to preserve Hong Kong's autonomy, and the violent anti-China protests in that city in 2019, have made Taiwan's people even warier of reconnecting with China. Any Chinese military action against Taiwan would alarm Japan and might draw in the United States. In 2019 the U.S. agreed to sell advanced F-16 fighters to Taiwan, enraging China. Taiwan's political future remains an open question, fiercely debated by Taiwanese and their several competing political parties.

27-4d The Little Dragons in the Global System

The rise of the Pacific Rim in the late twentieth century, including China, Japan, and the Little Dragons, reshaped the global system. The quarter of the world's population living along the western edge of the Pacific Basin outpaced the West and the rest of the world in economic growth while maintaining political stability. A global economy based three decades ago on the United States, western Europe, and Japan now has to accommodate China and the Little Dragons. Using the Meiji Japan model, the Little Dragons industrialized and then diversified into high technology to make computers and other electronics products, posing an economic challenge to Japan and the West. However, the Little Dragons have recently lost market share as China manufactures competing electronic products, fueling protests against trade pacts with China in Taiwan.

Some trends suggested that the Pacific Rim nations were becoming an Asian counterpart to the European Community, the free-trade zone formed by western European nations, perhaps fostering a Pacific Century dominated economically by Asian nations rather than European and North America in the twenty-first century. Many East and Southeast Asian nations worked on closer economic cooperation, with Japan and China forming the hubs. But in 1997 and again in 2008–2009, a severe economic meltdown hit South Korea, Taiwan, Japan, and industrializing Southeast Asia. As businesses closed, unemployment soared and economies went into deep recession. Yet, many economies rebounded by 2012. Today, buffeted by China's power and destabilizing U.S. policies, various Asian nations seek ways to cooperate with each other in new trade agreements while negotiating the turbulent geopolitics and unsettling economic changes. Both the Pacific Rim countries and the United States face uncertain futures but will likely play major roles in the future. In many respects, East Asia has returned to its historical role as the key engine of the world economy. But the growing dangers as the world approaches 2020—a more assertive and repressive China, a nuclear-armed North Korea, an uneasy Japan, new Japan–South Korea tensions, a wary Taiwan, mounting uncertainty and confusion over U.S. policies, resentment over Trump's trade war, and a troubled world economy—suggests that the stability that underpinned eastern Asia's unprecedented development can no longer be assumed.

KEY POINTS

▸ South Korean governments have grown more tolerant of internal dissent and more open to relations with former enemies such as communist North Korea and China, though their primary emphasis has been on economic growth.

▸ After the Korean War, North Korea recovered with support from the USSR and China and was ruled as a repressive communist dictatorship with a centrally planned economy whose shortcomings led to widespread food shortages in the 1990s.

▸ With the communists ruling mainland China, the Nationalists took over Taiwan, which they ruled as a police state and turned into an economic powerhouse, but relations with mainland China have continued to be tense.

▸ China and the "Little Dragons" (Taiwan, South Korea, Singapore, and Hong Kong) grew rapidly in the late twentieth century, leading to predictions of a coming "Pacific Century," but several slowdowns dampened such expectations.

Chapter Summary

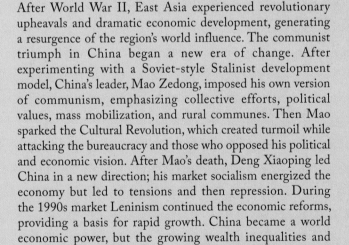

After World War II, East Asia experienced revolutionary upheavals and dramatic economic development, generating a resurgence of the region's world influence. The communist triumph in China began a new era of change. After experimenting with a Soviet-style Stalinist development model, China's leader, Mao Zedong, imposed his own version of communism, emphasizing collective efforts, political values, mass mobilization, and rural communes. Then Mao sparked the Cultural Revolution, which created turmoil while attacking the bureaucracy and those who opposed his political and economic vision. After Mao's death, Deng Xiaoping led China in a new direction; his market socialism energized the economy but led to tensions and then repression. During the 1990s market Leninism continued the economic reforms, providing a basis for rapid growth. China became a world economic power, but the growing wealth inequalities and corruption have threatened to destabilize the nation. The past decade has seen China extend its economic power into the wider world while returning to a more authoritarian mix of Maoism and modernization.

The experiences of Japan and the Little Dragons differed from China's. After the World War II defeat and U.S. occupation, Japan rapidly rose to become an economic powerhouse, based on mixing political democracy with capitalism; government and business worked together. Japanese rebuilt their industries and fostered new forms of business and production. But social change came slowly, leaving Japan hierarchical. The Little Dragon nations of South Korea and Taiwan achieved industrial growth and prosperity by borrowing the Japanese model, mixing free markets with government intervention and eventually fostering democracy. North Korea chose Stalinism and isolation from the world. The dynamism of most East Asian nations suggests that they have recovered from the disasters they experienced from the mid-1800s to the mid-1900s resulting from Western imperialism, Japanese expansion, and war, but their overall prospects remain tied to the health of the world economy.

Key Terms

Pacific Rim 713
communes 716
Great Leap Forward 716
Great Proletarian Cultural
Revolution 719

Red Guards 719
Iron Rice Bowl 719
market socialism 721
market Leninism 722
Japan, Inc. 734

salaryman 735
Pacific Century 738
Little Dragons 738

Rebuilding Europe and Russia, Since 1945

> *This [united] Europe must be born. And she will, when Spaniards say "our Chartres," Englishmen "our Cracow," Italians "our Copenhagen," and Germans "our Bruges." Then Europe will live.*
>
> —Spanish writer Salvador de Madariaga, 1948[1]

IMAGE 28.1 **Fall of the Berlin Wall** In 1989, as communist governments collapsed in eastern Europe, peaceful protesters climbed on top of the Berlin Wall, which had already been decorated with graffiti. The wall, which divided communist East and democratic West Berlin, was soon torn down.

Q What is the symbolism of this photo and event for Germans today?

---

[1]Quoted in Norman Davies, *Europe: A History* (New York: Harper, 1998), 1066.

French banker's son turned socialist politician Jacques Delors (**deh-LOW-er**) faced a challenge. Having lived through the Great Depression, World War II, and the Cold War, he now dedicated himself to building a united Europe and in 1985 became president of the European Commission, established to reconcile national loyalties with more political cooperation. In 1991, Delors convened the leaders of twelve closely linked European nations in Maastricht, Holland, a city full of historic buildings. Marshaling all his diplomatic skills, he prodded them to conclude a historic agreement for increased cooperation, affirming a dream of European unity that had long percolated among visionaries. Europeans, chastened by centuries of conflict, seemed ready to subordinate national interests to a common good. Delors asked leaders to transform the economic and political alliance begun in the late 1940s and expanded in the 1950s into a more comprehensive union.

In the same month the Soviet Union (USSR) dissolved. With their biggest communist rival no longer a threat, European leaders hoped that linking their countries would ensure a stable, peaceful future. In theory the European Union (EU) would stretch from the Atlantic to the western frontier of Russia, allowing goods and people to freely cross borders and to use a single currency, the *euro*. Voters in all member nations later ratified the Maastricht Treaty, though debates continued as new members joined. While facing road bumps, given the centuries of European strife, the European Union was a huge achievement.

From 1945 until 1990 three themes dominated European history: the Cold War shaped by the United States and the USSR, each with political and military power vastly exceeding that of all other nations; the rebirth of western European wealth and influence; and the movement toward European unity represented by Maastricht. After World War II, which left most countries in shambles, Europe became divided into mutually hostile political and military blocs. While the USSR dominated eastern Europe, much of western Europe recovered its prosperity under democratic governments. After 1989, when the communist governments collapsed, this movement accelerated, opening the way for a new, interconnected Europe. But serious economic problems, the resurgence of right-wing populism, a migration crisis, a possible British exit from the EU, and cracks in European unity have partly undermined progress, raising questions about Europe's future and identity.

28-1 Western Europe: Revival and Unity

SOCIETIES   TRANSITIONS   NETWORKS

Q What factors fostered the movement toward unity in western Europe?

After emerging from World War II economically bankrupt, western Europe rapidly recovered with American aid. Most western Europeans reestablished working multiparty democracies that guaranteed personal freedom while emphasizing consensus rather than military might. Beginning in 1947, however, Europe was split into two mutually hostile camps—western and eastern Europe—with rival military forces and different postwar reconstruction models. Eastern Europe came under Soviet domination, enduring authoritarian communist governments. Gradually West Germany, France, and Britain led a rebuilt, increasingly unified western Europe and regained world influence, while economic prosperity blunted radicalism.

> **CONNECTION to TODAY**
>
> In what ways do you think European unity has benefitted them and the rest of the world?

28-1a The Remaking of European Nations

World War II cost some fifty million lives, reduced major cities to rubble, and destroyed bridges, tunnels, and roads. Transportation, food, housing, and fuel were in short supply. Political boundaries redrawn after the war had displaced many people, including ten million Germans who were forced to leave eastern Europe and move to Germany. Emotionally traumatized by wartime atrocities, Europeans saw their prestige in tatters. War crimes trials held in Nuremberg, Germany, in 1946 condemned Nazi leaders to death and declared crimes against humanity, especially genocide, indefensible.

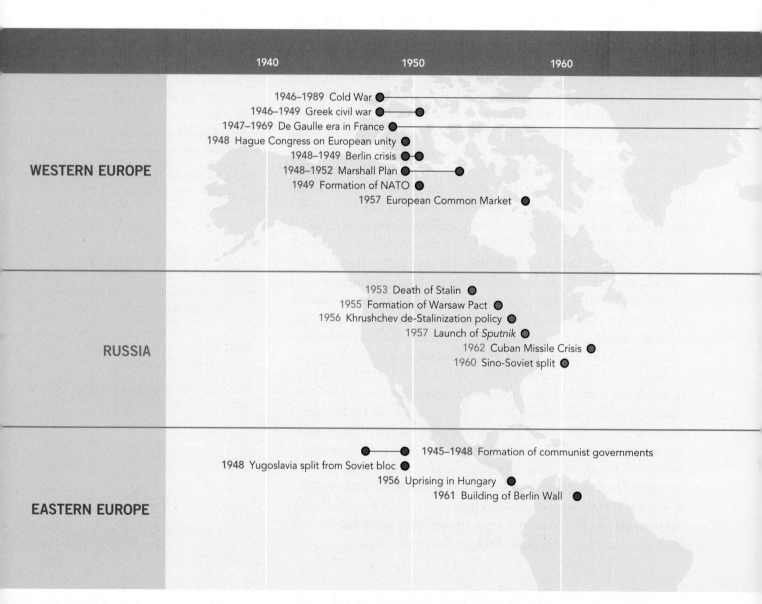

WESTERN EUROPE

1946–1989 Cold War
1946–1949 Greek civil war
1947–1969 De Gaulle era in France
1948 Hague Congress on European unity
1948–1949 Berlin crisis
1948–1952 Marshall Plan
1949 Formation of NATO
1957 European Common Market

RUSSIA

1953 Death of Stalin
1955 Formation of Warsaw Pact
1956 Khrushchev de-Stalinization policy
1957 Launch of *Sputnik*
1962 Cuban Missile Crisis
1960 Sino-Soviet split

EASTERN EUROPE

1945–1948 Formation of communist governments
1948 Yugoslavia split from Soviet bloc
1956 Uprising in Hungary
1961 Building of Berlin Wall

But economic growth fostered a new Europe. In 1947 the U.S. secretary of state, World War II general George Marshall (1880–1959), proposed that Americans help restore Europe's economic health to achieve stability and guarantee peace. The **Marshall Plan** created a recovery program to prevent communist expansion and spread liberal economic principles, such as free markets. Between 1948 and 1952 the United States provided $13 billion, half going to Britain, France, and West Germany. In exchange, American business enjoyed greater access to European markets. The Marshall Plan restored agriculture, industry, and international trade. The rapid economic resurgence from 1948 to 1965, unmatched in world history up to that time except for Japan's postwar recovery (see Chapter 27), also resulted from liberal democracy, modern production and managerial techniques, and advances in science, technology, transportation, and agriculture.

At the same time, British leader Winston Churchill (1874–1965) warned that Soviet expansionism had built "an iron curtain" across Europe, dividing western Europe from eastern Europe and pro-Western, capitalist West Germany from communist East Germany. This Cold War division stimulated western European cooperation. When delegates met in 1948 at the Hague in the Netherlands and called for a democratic economic union, Churchill urged them to "design a United Europe, where men and women of every country will think of being European as of belonging to their native land, and wherever they go in this wide domain they will truly feel 'Here I am at home.'"[2] The Hague Congress created a European assembly and human rights court, generating the "European Movement."

Western Europeans also committed to parliamentary democracy, including for the surviving constitutional monarchies—Belgium, Britain, the Netherlands, and the Scandinavian nations—where kings and queens symbolized their people but enjoyed little power. In the 1970s democrats overthrew longtime dictators in Spain, Portugal, and Greece. Britain, France, Italy, and West Germany became the most influential European nations.

Marshall Plan A recovery program created for western Europe by the United States that aimed to prevent communist expansion and to spread liberal economic principles.

[2]Quoted in ibid.

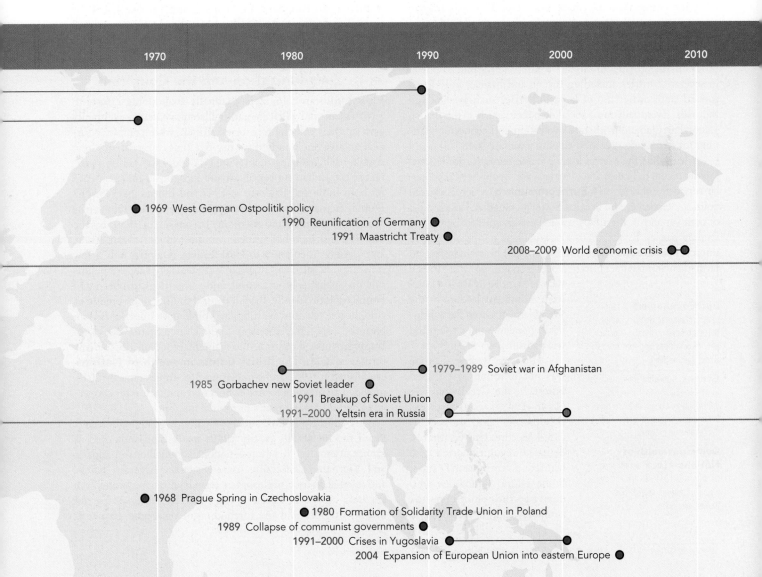

| 1970 | 1980 | 1990 | 2000 | 2010 |

1969 West German Ostpolitik policy
1990 Reunification of Germany
1991 Maastricht Treaty
2008–2009 World economic crisis

1979–1989 Soviet war in Afghanistan
1985 Gorbachev new Soviet leader
1991 Breakup of Soviet Union
1991–2000 Yeltsin era in Russia

1968 Prague Spring in Czechoslovakia
1980 Formation of Solidarity Trade Union in Poland
1989 Collapse of communist governments
1991–2000 Crises in Yugoslavia
2004 Expansion of European Union into eastern Europe

New political alignments emerged. Political stability depended on improving relations between France and Germany and helping Germany recover from war. Although Charles De Gaulle (1890–1970), the crusty general and proudly nationalist French leader (1947–1969), imagined France "like the princess in the fairy stories, as dedicated to an exalted and exceptional destiny,"[3] he made French–German reconciliation the cornerstone of French policy. Similarly, West German leaders sought a cooperative relationship. In the 1960s West German chancellor Willy Brandt (1913–1992), a fervent anti-Nazi who had fled Hitler, furthered Germany's reconciliation with its neighbors and accepted German responsibilities for the war and the new imposed borders, which awarded much German territory to Poland. Economic growth improved French–German relations. West Germany's economy was central to western European recovery; by 1960 West Germany, firmly allied with France, accounted for a fifth of the world's manufactured goods, surpassing Britain.

New political parties and movements took shape. Christian Democrats, conservatives backed by the Catholic Church who emphasized Christian values and traditional families, either formed governments or led oppositions in a half dozen countries, including West Germany and Italy. Thanks partly to corruption scandals, by the 1990s they lost considerable support; but they later regained influence in West Germany. On the left social democratic parties, favoring generous welfare programs to provide all citizens a safety net, came to power in several countries, including Britain and France, and moved toward state ownership of large industries such as steel and railroads. Eventually most social democrats, such as the British Labor Party, abandoned state ownership and economic planning for free markets combined with a welfare state.

Meanwhile, the western European communist parties declined rapidly, except in France, Italy, Portugal, and Spain. Seeking popular support, some adopted **Eurocommunism**, which embraced political democracy and rejected Soviet domination. Losing most of their support in the 1990s, communists fragmented into small feuding parties. By the 1980s a new political movement had an impact. The **Greens** rejected militarism and heavy industry and favored environmental protection over economic growth. Women such as Petra Kelly (1947–1992) were prominent leaders in the West German Green Party, helping it appeal to women voters and win parliamentary seats.

However, western Europe was not immune to political unrest. In the Greek civil war (1946–1949), conservatives supporting the monarchy, aided by the United States, defeated revolutionaries who wanted a communist state. Some ethnic minorities who desired independence or autonomy spurred violence and sometimes terrorism. For example, the Basque people, who live mostly in northern Spain and speak a language completely different from Spanish, have long sought their own nation. An underground Basque independence movement, ETA (for "Basque Homeland and Freedom"), has sporadically carried out assassinations and bombings. Many Catalans in northeast Spain have also sought their own country but are mostly nonviolent. In the 2017 regional elections, a party favoring independence for Catalonia came to power in the state, precipitating a crisis that resulted in the arrest of secessionist leaders and a federal takeover. Resentment of federal power still simmers. For decades much of the Catholic minority in Northern Ireland (Ulster), which was part of Great Britain, sought a merger with the largely Catholic Irish Republic, while the majority Protestants wanted to remain a British province. Extremist Catholic and Protestant paramilitary groups attacked each other and the British army, causing thousands of civilian deaths. But violence subsided and relations between Britain and Ireland improved after the Good Friday Agreement in 1998 between pro-British and pro-Ireland groups, which allowed for free access for people and goods across their common border. In recent years other separatist movements—Scottish nationalists in the United Kingdom; Venetians, South Tyroleans, and the Lombardy region in Italy; Flemish in Belgium—have ebbed and flowed, motivated by economic crises.

28-1b Decolonization and the Cold War

Most European colonizers, gradually abandoning efforts to quell Asian and African nationalist movements, eventually gave up their colonial territories. Britain, whose empire occupied an area one hundred twenty-five times larger than Great Britain itself, realizing that its imperial glory was fading, partitioned the Indian subcontinent and recognized independence for both India and Pakistan in 1947 and Burma in 1948. The Dutch, facing determined nationalist resistance, reluctantly abandoned their lucrative colony, Indonesia, in 1950. By the mid-1960s Britain had turned over most of its African, Asian, and Caribbean colonies to local leaders, retaining only a few tiny outposts, such as Gibraltar, a strategically valuable peninsula on Spain's southern coast, and some tiny Caribbean and South Atlantic islands. British control of Gibraltar sometimes complicates relations with Spain. While post-imperial Britain balanced a special relationship to the United States with closer European links, it continued to maintain economic ties to many former colonies. The British **Commonwealth of Nations**, established in 1931 and comprising fifty-three states by 2013, provided an ongoing formal connection and forum for cooperating and discussing issues of mutual interest.

By contrast, France and Portugal only grudgingly recognized the inevitable. In the 1940s many thousands died as France attempted to suppress nationalist rebellions in Algeria and Vietnam. Criticizing torture against Algerian rebels, anticolonial French philosopher Jean-Paul Sartre wrote: "We are sick, very sick. Feverish and prostrate, obsessed by old dreams of glory and the foreboding of its shame, France is

---

Eurocommunism A form of communism in western Europe that embraced political democracy and free elections and that rejected Soviet domination.

Greens A political movement in western Europe that rejected militarism and heavy industry and favored environmental protection over economic growth.

Commonwealth of Nations A forum, established by Britain in 1931, for discussing issues of mutual interest with its former colonies.

---

[3]Quoted in Felix Gilbert with David Clay Large, *The End of the European Era, 1890 to the Present*, 4th ed. (New York: W.W. Norton, 1991), 429.

Stefano Ravera/Alamy Stock Photo

IMAGE 28.2 **Immigrant Neighborhood in London** Many European cities such as London, Paris, and Brussels have large neighborhoods where many immigrants, often lower income, have settled. These neighborhoods have businesses, including restaurants and clothing stores, catering to various immigrant groups but also attracting other local people. This commercial street in the Deptford High Street district of London, near the dockyards along the Thames River, is a popular shopping area.

Q What sort of businesses do you think can be found along this street?

spurred formation of the North Atlantic Treaty Organization, or **NATO**. That military alliance linked nine western European countries with the United States and Canada, allowing them to coordinate defense policies against the USSR and its communist allies, the **Soviet bloc**, to repulse any potential military attack across the "iron curtain" frontier. The United States established permanent military bases in NATO countries, especially West Germany. The Soviets responded in 1955 by forming the **Warsaw Pact**, a defense alliance linking communist-ruled eastern European countries with the USSR (see Map 28.1). Europeans worried that nuclear weapons could obliterate their cities in minutes and that a U.S.–USSR nuclear conflict might inevitably destroy Europe as well. By the 1980s senior NATO and Warsaw Pact officers had spent their careers preparing for a war that fortunately never came.

The Cold War and NATO were partly generated by Germany's postwar division. The United States, Britain, France, and the USSR each had an occupation zone and also divided up the German capital, Berlin. In 1948 the three Western powers united their occupation zones. Angered, the USSR blockaded Berlin to prevent supplies from reaching the city by land through Soviet-controlled East Germany, forcing a year-long airlift of food and fuel. In 1949 the USSR allowed the creation of the Federal Republic of Germany, or West Germany, while forming the communist German Democratic Republic, or East Germany. West Germany later joined NATO.

Cold War fears gradually slackened as the danger of actual war faded; western Europeans reappraised their policies toward both superpowers. Some, especially in Britain, promoted the U.S. alliance, but many Europeans resented what they considered irresponsible U.S. foreign policies. Most opposed the American war in Vietnam and U.S. interventions to overthrow left-leaning governments in Latin America, such as Guatemala (1954) and Chile (1973). In

struggling in the grip of a nightmare it is unable either to flee or to decipher."[4] In 1954, unable to defeat communist-led revolutionaries, France withdrew from Vietnam, and in 1962 it left Algeria, causing 800,000 embittered European settlers there to flee to France. Only in 2017 did a French president acknowledge French colonialism as "a crime against humanity" and, in 2018, the use of torture against Algeria's war of independence. France retained a few small Caribbean, Pacific, and Indian Ocean islands and French Guiana. It eventually established close relations with many former colonies, including an enduring economic connection that critics considered neocolonialism because French business interests and advisers remained prominent. Meanwhile, Portugal wasted lives and wealth violently resisting African nationalist movements but, after democrats overthrew the long-standing fascist dictatorship, granted its African colonies of Angola, Guinea-Bissau, and Mozambique independence in 1975.

Beginning in 1946, the Cold War shaped European roles in the world. The USSR helped install communist governments in eastern Europe and East Germany, while the United States assumed the military burden for protecting western Europe. In 1949 strong European and U.S. fears of possible Soviet attack

NATO A military alliance, formed in 1949, that linked nine western European countries with the United States and Canada.

Soviet bloc The Soviet Union and the communist states allied with it.

Warsaw Pact A defense alliance formed in 1955 that linked the communist-ruled eastern European countries with the USSR.

---

[4]Quoted in Harold James, *Europe Reborn: A History, 1914–2000* (New York: Longman, 2001), 248.

MAP 28.1 Military Alliances and Multinational Economic Groupings, 1949–1989 Post–World War II Europe was divided by Cold War politics into communist and noncommunist blocs. Most western European nations joined the NATO defense alliance. Western Europeans also cooperated in economic matters. By 1989 the Common Market had expanded from six to eleven members. The Soviet bloc counterpart, COMECON, had eight members.

Q How does this map differ from the alliances in Europe today?

Legend:

$ Participants in the Marshall Plan

Member of NATO,* formed in 1949

Member of COMECON,** formed in 1949, and the Warsaw Pact, organized in 1955

Member of the European Common Market, formed in 1958

Iron Curtain

* North Atlantic Treaty Organization
** Council for Mutual Economic Assistance

Scale: 0 200 400 Km. / 0 200 400 Mi.

Labels on map:

ICELAND — Reykjavik — Joined Common Market, 1973

IRELAND — Dublin — Joined Common Market, 1973

UNITED KINGDOM — London — U.S. loan of $3.5 billion, 1946; Exploded first atomic bomb, 1952; Joined Common Market, 1973

NORWAY — Oslo

SWEDEN — Stockholm

FINLAND — Helsinki

DENMARK — Copenhagen — Joined Common Market, 1973

NETHERLANDS — Amsterdam

BELGIUM — Brussels

LUX.

WEST GERMANY — Bonn

FRANCE — Paris — Exploded first atomic bomb, 1960; Withdrew from NATO, 1966

SWITZ. — Bern

SPAIN — Madrid — Joined NATO, 1982; Joined Common Market, 1986

PORTUGAL — Lisbon — Joined Common Market, 1986

ITALY — Rome

AUSTRIA — Vienna — Zones of occupation ended, 1955; Joined NATO, 1955

West Berlin / East Berlin — Berlin blockade, 1948–1949

EAST GERMANY

POLAND — Warsaw

CZECHOSLOVAKIA — Prague — Communist coup, 1948; U.S.S.R. invasion, 1968

HUNGARY — Budapest — Revolution, 1956

ROMANIA — Bucharest

YUGOSLAVIA — Belgrade — Tito-Stalin schism, 1948

ALBANIA — Tiranë — Left COMECON, 1961; Withdrew from WP, 1968

BULGARIA — Sofia

GREECE — Athens — Truman Doctrine, 1947; Joined NATO, 1952; Joined Common Market, 1981

TURKEY — Ankara — Truman Doctrine, 1947; Joined NATO, 1952

CYPRUS — Nicosia

UNION OF SOVIET SOCIALIST REPUBLICS — Moscow — Exploded first atomic bomb, 1949

Volga R. / Don R. / Dnieper R. / Danube R.

Caspian Sea / Black Sea / Baltic Sea / North Sea / ATLANTIC OCEAN / Mediterranean Sea

Corsica / Sardinia / Sicily / Balearic Is.

Arctic Circle / 60°N / 40°N / 20°W / 20°E / 40°E

1969 West Germany's Social Democratic, anticommunist chancellor Willy Brandt's **Ostpolitik** ("eastern politics") policy, which sought reconciliation between West and East Germany and expanded dialogue with the USSR, fostered a thaw between West Germany and the Soviet bloc, giving hope to eastern Europeans who wanted more freedom. Gradually western Europeans rebuilt their own military forces, becoming less reliant on U.S. power. Despite the differences, the Western alliance and NATO remained strong because of mutual interests during the Cold War.

28-1c From Cooperation to European Community

Western Europe's role in the global system changed. Between the two world wars Europeans owned enterprises all over the globe, including Indian tea plantations, Malayan rubber estates, African mines, and South American railroads. But during the 1940s Europeans lost influence to the United States. Concluding they had no choice but to cooperate, in 1949 ten nations formed the Council of Europe, based on shared cultural heritage and democratic principles, which produced the European Convention on Human Rights, the root of a Europe-wide justice system and court. But some leaders wanted more. Jean Monnet (**MOAN-ay**) (1888–1979), a French economist, financier, and former League of Nations official often called the "Father of United Europe," and French prime minister Robert Schuman (1886–1963), who promoted French–German reconciliation, wanted to make war not only unthinkable but also impossible. To encourage better economic coordination, their European Coal and Steel Community (ECSC) formed in 1951 with six members, a first step for unity and peace. But some nations, including Britain, feared losing economic independence and declined to join.

The Common Market, later known as the European Community (EC) and then the European Union (EU), was formed in 1957 with six members: France, Italy, West Germany, the Netherlands, Belgium, and Luxembourg. Removing tariff barriers facilitated free movement of capital and labor across borders. Inviting others to join, the EC added Britain, Ireland, and Denmark in 1973, creating unprecedented economic unity in the world's largest free trade zone. Monnet and Schuman dreamed of a Europe united politically: societies that depend on one another, they reasoned, would not go to war. But nationalism and disagreements occasionally flared up; member nations squabbled to get the best deal for their own farmers or businesses. Some doubters, the "Euro-skeptics," believed cooperation went too far. The British, an island people proud of their distinctive traditions, periodically threatened to withdraw. Eventually, in 2016, a slim majority would vote in a referendum to do so, setting the process in motion. Yet the EC greatly reduced old national tensions. Eventually an elected European Parliament, based in Brussels, Belgium, discussed shared issues and made policies encouraging cooperation and standardization. But critics believed the arrangements marginalized both the European and national parliaments.

The EC spurred growth, creating a consumer society in western Europe (see Map 28.2). With higher wages, greater purchasing power, and more available consumer products, families bought automobiles, washing machines, refrigerators, and televisions. More people worked in the service sector and fewer in agriculture; middle classes grew rapidly, while blue-collar workers shared middle-class aspirations. Consumer markets reached from Europe's sprawling cities into remote villages. A journalist's description of an old French village in 1973 revealed the change: "The last horse trod its streets in 1968. The water mill closed down in 1952. The washing machine replaced the wash house—and broke up the community of women—in the 1960s."[5] High-speed railroads and turnpikes linked peoples together; subways and commuter trains made city life more convenient. Yet prosperity did not eliminate all poverty or regional disparities. Industrialized northern Italy remained much wealthier than largely agricultural southern Italy.

Western Europe still faced economic problems. In 1971, with the U.S. economy undermined by the war in Vietnam, President Richard Nixon devalued the U.S. dollar, the Western nations' staple currency, a move that ended its parity with gold, destabilized world trade, and triggered soaring prices and trade deficits. Then in 1973 a quadrupling of oil prices brought European economies to a standstill; this was followed by a short oil export embargo by major oil-producing nations, who were angered by Western support of Israel. Frustrated motorists waiting in long lines at gas stations showed how vulnerable prosperity could be in the global system. In addition, noxious air, toxic waste, and lakes and forests dying from acid rain—the price of industrialization—were environmental problems common to all industrial societies.

Costlier energy and growing competition from industrializing Asian nations and Japan also hurt European industries and workers. Factories built a century earlier, often decaying and inefficient, reduced operations or closed, causing high unemployment in industrial cities like Birmingham and Manchester in England. Jobless young people, living in bleak row houses or apartments and surviving on welfare payments, hung out on street corners, some turning to drugs or crime. By 1983 unemployment rates had risen to 10 percent, posing special problems to women, immigrants, and those just out of school. Some blamed their problems on immigrant workers, especially Arabs, Turks, and South Asians, whom they saw as competing with local people for jobs, boosting right-wing, anti-immigrant parties. Free market conservatives often regained political power, penalizing striking workers and weakening labor unions.

> **Ostpolitik** A West German policy, promoted by Chancellor Willy Brandt, that sought a reconciliation between West and East Germany and an expanded dialogue with the USSR.

---

[5]Quoted in Robert O. Paxton, *Europe in the Twentieth Century* (New York: Harcourt Brace Jovanovich, 1973), 576.

GDP per capita
Over $40,000
$30,000–40,000
$25,000–29,999
$20,000–24,999
$15,000–19,999
$10,000–14,999
Under $10,000

MAP 28.2 **Europe's Gross Domestic Product** The gross domestic product, or the official measure of the output of goods and services in a national economy, provides a good summary of a nation's economic production. In the early twenty-first century, Norway, Ireland, and Switzerland were the most productive European countries on a per capita basis, while former Soviet bloc nations had the weakest performance.

Q What does this map tell us about which were the richest countries and which the poorest in the mid-2010s?

KEY POINTS

▶ World War II devastated western Europe's population, infrastructure, and economy, but it enjoyed a remarkable period of growth, aided by extensive U.S. funding under the Marshall Plan.

▶ A wave of decolonization followed World War II, and Germany and France overcame centuries of mutual hatred.

▶ The Cold War shaped European politics, with eastern Europe allied with the USSR and western Europe allied

with the United States, but over time some European leaders distanced themselves from U.S. policies and advocated dialogue with the USSR.

▶ Having been surpassed economically by the United States, European countries joined together in the European Community, which became the world's largest free trade zone and led to increased prosperity.

28-2 Western European Societies and Cultures

▣ TRANSITIONS ▤ SOCIETIES

Q How did the rise of welfare states transform western European societies?

In the ashes of World War II the wartime British prime minister, Winston Churchill, wrote, "What is Europe? A rubble heap, a charnel house, a breeding ground for pestilence and hate."[6] Seeing the need for change, western European nations began reshaping their societies and improving the quality of life for all their citizens, often blending capitalism and socialism. The postwar economic boom allowed most states, influenced by socialism, to construct welfare programs that created political stability, ensured public health, and eliminated poverty for most citizens. As gender relations, family life, and sexual attitudes changed, musicians, philosophers, and churches addressed the new European cultures.

28-2a Social Democracy and Welfare States

The rise of **welfare states**, government systems offering their citizens state-subsidized health, education, and social service benefits, and the high quality of life they fostered, owed much to an influential political philosophy. Social democracy derived from early-twentieth-century socialists who favored evolutionary rather than revolutionary change, eventually promoting a mix of liberal democracy, market economies, and a safety net for workers. Between 1945 and 2010 social democratic parties governed or have been the dominant opposition in many Western countries. They usually controlled governments in the Scandinavian nations of Denmark, Finland, Norway, and Sweden; have often governed in several other nations, including Britain, France, the Netherlands, West Germany, Portugal, and Spain; and have been influential in Australia, Canada, and New Zealand.

Social democracy fostered welfare programs—a mix of free markets and government regulation, parliamentary democracy and civil liberties, and labor unions—moderating the extremes of wealth and poverty. Hence, northern and central European workers gained more rights and protections than workers enjoy anywhere else. In West Germany they received generous pensions and seats on the boards of directors of the enterprises employing them. Valuing leisure, many Europeans believed they worked to live while Americans, who earn more, lived to work. By the 1990s both white-collar and blue-collar Europeans worked many fewer hours each year than Americans and Japanese and also enjoyed four to six weeks of paid vacations per year. During the most popular vacation month, August, beach and mountain resorts were jammed; with many employees gone, stores often offered limited services. The 35-hour workweek became the norm in France and West Germany; by 2000 the average German spent around 400 fewer hours a year on the job than the average American.

CONNECTION to TODAY

What aspects of western European societies in the later twentieth century do you find most appealing?

Many Europeans receive generous taxpayer-funded benefits from the state. Free education through the university level (but with stiff university entrance exams) helps people from working-class and farming backgrounds move into the middle and upper classes. Generous unemployment insurance removes the pain of job loss. Inexpensive, widely available day care (often even for infants) allows mothers to work outside the home for wages; custodial parents receive child support payments. France made free preschool available beginning at age three. Universal health coverage, furnished inexpensively by the state or private sector, removes fear of serious illness, providing inexpensive prescription drugs and guaranteeing medical care to all citizens, greatly improving public health. Most western European nations spend much less than Americans do on health care yet often see better outcomes. Enjoying one of the world's best health care systems, the French live four years (82.5) longer than Americans (78.6). Where Europeans once looked to the extended family for support, now they expect the welfare state to care for the elderly and incapacitated. In addition, with the most equitable distributions of income in the world, northern European nations have nearly eliminated slums and deep poverty. The Scandinavian nations, poor a century ago, developed the strongest social democratic traditions and became the world's most prosperous societies. Norway achieved the world's highest living standards, thanks to North Sea oil and a generous social safety net, even thriving during the 2008–2009 global economic crisis. In Sweden, Europe's most creative country in experimenting with social change, women, youth, and even animals have more rights and protections than elsewhere. In recent decades, Sweden, with the world's most level playing field and lowest poverty rate, has often enjoyed Europe's most dynamic economy. The annual United Nations Human Development Report, which rates countries on various quality-of-life criteria, ranked eight western European nations in the top ten in 2018, headed by Norway and Switzerland, and fourteen in the top twenty. Most have variations of the social market or welfare state.

All welfare states have faced challenges, however. Funding them requires high taxes, often half of a citizen's annual income. Worker protections make it hard to fire workers, prompting companies to hire fewer people. Critics contend that workers enjoy so much security that they may not need to strive harder, which has economic costs. Losing a job is less disastrous than for Americans because the welfare state insulates people from many effects of economic slumps, promoting social stability. Yet, many people with

> **welfare states** Government systems that offer their citizens a range of state-subsidized health, education, and social service benefits; adopted by western European nations after World War II.

---

[6]Quoted in Davies, *Europe*, 1065.

modest incomes, especially immigrants, live in drab apartment blocks or houses, often far from potential jobs and the best schools. Economic problems, joblessness, and racial discrimination occasionally spark rioting and vandalism by minority youth in countries like France, Britain, and even Sweden.

Beginning in the 1980s, the welfare states experienced more problems related to sporadic downturns in the world economy. For decades governments paid for social services by borrowing against future exports, practicing deficit spending. But falling export profits, and hence revenues, stressed the welfare systems, forcing cutbacks in benefits; nations also cut defense spending. Companies downsized, putting pressure on unemployment programs. In some countries conservative parties gained power and began modifying the welfare systems. For example, in Britain, Prime Minister Margaret Thatcher (governed 1979–1990), a free market enthusiast and Europe's first woman prime minister, deeply divided Britons by cutting taxes, battling unions, and reducing health services while privatizing many industries, mass transit, and public housing; people now had to wait longer to receive medical attention. But the conservative regimes did not dismantle many welfare state institutions such as national health insurance, which remained hugely popular.

Unlike in the 1930s, these economic problems did not bring serious violence or political instability. While occasionally anti-immigrant or anti–European Union political parties gained followers, extremist right-wing and ultranationalist forces remained weak in most countries until recently. For example, the French National Front, demanding expulsion of Arab and African immigrants and secession from the EU, won 10 percent of the national vote in 1986, but its appeal faded; then the 2008–2009 economic crisis gave it new life while boosting similar parties in, among others, Britain and Greece. In general, however, the welfare state, which allows even the unemployed to receive basic necessities such as health care, provides stability. Hence, even most free market conservatives have accepted the welfare state's broad framework, although wanting to make it more efficient and cost-effective.

28-2b Social Activism, Reform, and Gender Relations

Occasional student and worker protests against capitalism, materialism, and mainstream society have erupted. In 1968, France faced widespread youth protests aimed at the aging, autocratic president Charles De Gaulle, an antiquated university education system, and the unpopular U.S. war in Vietnam, France's former colony. University students went on strike, protesters blocked traffic, and activists fought pitched battles with police, who responded with tear gas and beatings. As public sentiment shifted toward the protesters, industrial workers called a general strike, bringing some ten million workers into the streets. The protests soon spread to Italy and West Germany, where students resented conservative governments, staid bureaucracies, rigid university systems, and powerful business interests. Lacking strong public support, the protests soon fizzled, and governments did not fall. However, De Gaulle resigned a year later after the public rejected, in a referendum, his proposals to reorganize the French government.

Europeans have also dealt with social problems common to all industrialized nations, such as drug and alcohol abuse and high divorce rates. But European and American attitudes have often differed. For example, while the United States harshly punished drug use and trafficking, by the 1980s many western Europeans considered drug use and minor drug sales as social and medical rather than criminal issues. Some European countries even decriminalized marijuana use. Most nations abolished capital punishment and enacted strict gun control laws, often reducing violent crime by banning handguns.

Attitudes toward marriage and gender relations shifted. After World War II, governments tried to revitalize traditional marriage and family patterns, perceiving women as chiefly homemakers who should have many children. But in the 1960s and 1970s general access to birth control helped lead to the

IMAGE 28.3 **Swedish Father and Child** Swedes have been the most innovative Europeans in social policy, including adopting in 1975 a law requiring employers to grant parental leave. While women mainly take advantage of the law, some men, including this man with his child, take off the full allotted time.

JONATHAN NACKSTRAND/AFP/Getty Images

Q What can we learn about Swedish society and values from the photo?

sexual revolution and changed attitudes toward sexual activity. The contraceptive pill, illegal in some Catholic countries until much later, gave women control over their reproduction and sexuality. The sexual revolution upset traditionalists, such as the rural Spanish woman who regretted the ease of pursuing sex outside of marriage: "If a boy wants to be alone with a girl there's no problem; they go off alone and whatever fires they have can burn."[7]

Changing social attitudes have eliminated or moderated the social shame of divorce, extramarital sex, and unmarried cohabitation, which were challenging to cultural taboos. Although sex scandals involving politicians are not unknown, especially in Britain, public criticisms of politicians who have openly extramarital relationships or children out of wedlock, a common practice in France and Italy, are rare. But even many Italians were outraged at the sex life and corrupt practices of conservative Prime Minister Silvio Berlusconi (governed 1994–1995, 2001–2006, 2008–2011), a media tycoon who boasted of his wild "bunga bunga" parties with young prostitutes and models. With pornography and obscenity laws relaxed, long-banned works, such as British author D. H. Lawrence's racy 1920s novel *Lady Chatterly's Lover*, were published. British poet Philip Larkin satirized the changes: "Sexual intercourse began, in nineteen sixty-three (Which was rather late for me)—Between the end of the *Chatterly* ban, And the Beatles' first LP."[8]

Inspired by feminist thinkers such as philosopher Simone de Beauvoir **(bo-VWAHR)** (see Meet the People: Simone de Beauvoir, French Feminist and Philosopher), growing women's movements pressed their agendas more effectively by the 1970s. An English women's group believed that "a world freed from the economic, social and psychological bonds of patriarchy would be a world turned upside down, creating a human potential we can hardly dream of now,"[9] benefiting both men and women. Feminists sought legal divorce, easier access to birth control, abortion rights, and reform of family laws to give wives more influence. Many Protestant countries adopted their ideas. In 1973 Denmark legalized abortion on request. Scandinavian nations were often at the cutting edge of social change. For example, Swedish women have been considered especially powerful, dividing household tasks equally with their partners, and Swedish schools promoted sex education and provided free condoms. As one Swedish model and novelist wrote in 2017: "For a girl to own her sexuality meant she owned her body, she owned herself. Women could do anything men did, but they could also—when they chose to—bear children."[10] Iceland implemented policies like mandatory male–female balance on company boards, equal pay, and a ban on sexist ads. Although Pope John Paul II (pope 1978–2005) reiterated long-standing church bans on contraception, abortion, and divorce, many Catholics ignored these conservative teachings. During the 1970s and 1980s most Catholic nations, including Italy and Spain, followed France, Britain, and Germany in legalizing both divorce and abortion. Some countries decriminalized or sometimes legalized minor drug use.

Changes in work, politics, and family life affected both men and women, who now shared responsibility for financially supporting their families. By the 1980s women comprised half the workforce in Sweden, a third in France and Italy, and a quarter in conservative Ireland. Women moved into the professions, business, and, having won the right to vote by 1945, even politics. As once-powerful male-dominated institutions such as the military and church declined in influence, more women supported socialist and liberal parties guaranteeing them and their children health care and education. Women occasionally headed governments in nations such as Britain, France, Germany, Iceland, Finland, Denmark, Portugal, and Norway. Even patriarchal Ireland in 1991 elected its first woman president, social democrat Mary Robinson (b. 1944), an outspoken law professor, feminist, single parent, and supporter of LGBTQ rights. Women political activists made their voices heard. In 1976 two Northern Ireland mothers, Mairead Corrigan (b. 1944) and Betty Williams (b. 1943), jointly shared the Nobel Peace Prize for their efforts to bridge the Catholic–Protestant divide and bring peace to their troubled land. Yet, some changes came slowly. So few women had achieved high business and industry positions that, in 2006, Norway's social democratic government, outraging corporate leaders, required that 40 percent of large private companies' board members be women. The EU and several other nations have considered similar legislation. At the same time, less rigid gender roles have affected marriage patterns. In the 1970s the married heterosexual couple remained the norm; even rock stars known for their live-in girlfriends, such as Mick Jagger of the Rolling Stones, a popular British group, got married. Some celebrities, such as French rock star Johnny Halliday, changed spouses frequently. But by the 1980s more men and women remained single, often living on their own. In Scandinavia and Germany, singles accounted for between a quarter and a third of the adult population. Increasing personal independence and mobility fostered small nuclear families instead of the large extended families of old. As unhappy couples no longer needed to stay married, divorce rates more than doubled between 1960 and 1990.

LBGTQ people began to enjoy equal rights. Homosexual subcultures in European cities had been active for decades but faced discriminatory laws and attitudes. In the 1950s many governments still prosecuted LGBTQ people, including respected figures in the arts, for consensual sexual activity. Between 1953 and 1965 West Germany convicted some 99,000 men of gay and lesbian activity, jailing many of them. Although governments began eliminating anti-LGBTQ laws by the 1960s, combating prejudice took longer. Hence, in 1974 a conservative Italian leader warned that "if divorce is allowed, it will be possible to have marriages between homosexuals, and perhaps your wife will run off with some pretty young girl."[11] Eventually most societies developed tolerant attitudes. Denmark recognized domestic partnerships in 1989. Soon most of northern Europe had such laws providing legal protection, and discrimination ebbed. By 2019 sixteen nations, including Catholic Belgium, Portugal, and Spain, had legalized same-sex marriage; twelve others recognized domestic partnerships. Openly LGBTQ individuals have served as high government officials or political leaders in nations

---

[7]Quoted in Bonnie G. Smith, *Changing Lives: Women in European History Since 1700* (Lexington, MA: D.C. Heath, 1989), 509.

[8]Quoted in Richard Vinen, *A History in Fragments: Europe in the Twentieth Century* (New York: Da Capo, 2000), 370.

[9]Quoted in Bonnie S. Anderson and Judith P. Zinsser, *A History of Their Own: Women in Europe from Prehistory to the Present*, vol. 2 (New York: Harper Perennial, 1988), 334.

[10]Paulina Porizkova, "America Made Me a Feminist," *New York Times* (June 11, 2017).

[11]Amintore Fanfani, quoted in Vinen, *History in Fragments*, 493.

Simone de Beauvoir, French Feminist and Philosopher

Few thinkers had more influence on the study of women and contemporary women's movements than Simone de Beauvoir (1908–1986), the first systematic feminist philosopher and prolific writer of novels, essays, and autobiographical works. She was born in Paris to a middle-class family. Her father, a lawyer, and a devout, very traditional mother sent her to fashionable Roman Catholic girls' schools that taught her, she remembered, "the habit of obedience." She believed God expected her "to be dutiful." Her classmates aimed at marriage rather than careers.

But World War I impoverished de Beauvoir's family, pushing Simone toward a career. During her teens she battled her parents for more freedom to leave the house on her own and alarmed them by becoming an atheist.

Simone loved the liberating intellectual atmosphere at the Sorbonne in Paris, the most prestigious French university, but found that, to succeed in her studies there, she had to overcome gender stereotypes: "My upbringing had convinced me of my sex's intellectual inferiority. I flattered myself that I had a woman's heart and a man's brain." Graduating at the top of her class, she then supported herself, first as a high school teacher and then as a writer. De Beauvoir began a romantic and intellectual partnership with Jean Paul Sartre, later to become Europe's most acclaimed philosopher, whom she met at the Sorbonne, becoming a vital contributor to Sartre's ideas and books. The two maintained an intense free union, their lifelong connection providing a model of an adult male–female relationship without wedlock or exclusive commitment. Both had lovers on the side.

De Beauvoir's life reflected the transformation of a privileged woman into a feminist icon. By the late 1940s she was Europe's most famous female intellectual. Throughout her life she enjoyed the new opportunities gained by women as French society liberalized: legal equality, educational opportunities, the vote, and diverse economic roles; she also saw the limits to these freedoms. Sartre suggested she write about what difference being a woman made in her life. The result, the pioneering twelve-hundred-page study *The Second Sex*

(1949), challenged conventional thinking, becoming perhaps the most influential book on women ever written. The study, ranging through biology, history, mythology, sociology, and Marxist and Freudian theory, concluded that society's attitudes oppressed all women. Critically analyzing Western culture as dominated by males, she argued that women are not born inferior but are made to view themselves as such. De Beauvoir showed how, with their choices restricted, such as in careers, girls perceived their future differently than boys. Men took themselves as the model: "There is an absolute human type, the masculine. He is the Absolute—she is the Other." In her view, marriage denied women's individuality, becoming a contract of subjugation rather than an equal partnership. Her writings greatly influenced North American and European feminist movements. Later she addressed aging, including the way society dictated roles for the elderly.

Disillusioned by slowly changing gender relations, in 1972 de Beauvoir became a feminist activist, acknowledging her solidarity with other women and contending they had to fight to improve their social condition. She became president of the French League of Women's Rights and editor of journals calling attention to problems of violence, sexual assault, and lack of easily available contraception in Europe and the world. In 1976 she addressed the International Tribunal of Crimes Against Women, noting, "You are gathered here to denounce the oppression to which women are subjected. Talk to the world, bring to light the shameful truths that half of humanity is trying to cover up." Admired by millions, de Beauvoir died in 1986 at age seventy-eight.

IMAGE 28.4 **Simone de Beauvoir and Jean Paul Sartre** French feminist thinker Simone de Beauvoir and her partner, philosopher Jean Paul Sartre, were frequent visitors to the cafés of European cities and influential participants in the lively intellectual life of post–World War II Europe.

Francois Lochon/The LIFE Images Collection/Getty Images

Q What can we learn about de Beauvoir and Sartre from the photo?

Reflection Questions

1. How did de Beauvoir's personal life affect her ideas?
2. What were de Beauvoir's main arguments about how history and society shaped perceptions of gender?
3. Do you think that de Beauvoir should be seen as a feminist icon and leading philosopher, popular today?

Note: Quotations from Bonnie S. Anderson and Judith P. Zinsser, *A History of Their Own: Women in Europe from Prehistory to the Present*, vol. 2 (New York: Harper, 1988), 240, 169, 422; and Bonnie G. Smith, *Changing Lives: Women in European History Since 1700* (Lexington, MA: D.C. Heath, 1989), 519.

as socially different as the liberal Netherlands and conservative Ireland. A black Muslim gay peer, Lord Alli, even sits in Britain's House of Lords. In 2009 Iceland, engulfed in economic collapse, chose the openly lesbian Johanna Sigurdarlottir, a left-wing former flight attendant and trade unionist, as prime minister.

28-2c Immigration: Questions of Identity

Responding to postwar labor shortages, several million immigrants settled in various European countries as "guest workers." Poorer southern Europeans, especially Italians, Greeks, and Portuguese, migrated to northern Europe seeking better jobs and pay, and they were soon joined by Turks, Algerians, Moroccans, West Africans, and West Indians fleeing even harsher poverty. Initially many were single men who were recruited for factory work and often housed in bleak shantytowns. Later entire families arrived. Many Indians, Pakistanis, Bangladeshis, West Africans, and West Indians also sought a better life in their former imperial metropole, Britain; other people left Indonesia and Suriname, former Dutch colonies, for the Netherlands. By 2010 immigrants numbered forty-eight million and constituted nearly 10 percent of the European Union, including 12 percent in Germany, 11 percent in France, 11.5 percent in Britain, 12 percent in Spain, and 11 percent in the Netherlands. Major European cities such as Berlin, London, and Paris took on an international flavor; by 2013 nonwhites comprised half of London's population. Islamic culture flourished in cities like Hamburg (Germany) and Marseilles (France), where Arab- and Turkish-language radio stations had large audiences.

Immigrants contributed much to European societies. A large recording industry in Paris churned out music by Arab and African musicians, often for export to their homelands. Small Arab-run neighborhood grocery stores and kebab shops served vital functions in French and Spanish urban life, and Indian and Pakistani sundry goods, grocery shops, fast-food (carry-out) outlets, and restaurants became features of British and Irish city and even small-town life. Observers remarked that Indian curry was the favorite British food; many Germans treasure currywurst, a mix of German fried pork sausage, American ketchup, and South Asia curry powder. In Britain many immigrants served as mayors, officials, doctors, professors, writers, and entertainers. Immigrants have made a major impact in sports like football (soccer) and basketball. For example, stars of African, Afro-Caribbean, and Middle Eastern ancestry have been prominent on the English, French, Dutch, Belgian, and German World Cup soccer and Olympic basketball teams. People of Asian, Middle Eastern, and African descent were elected to parliaments in, among others, Britain, France, Germany, and the Netherlands. In 2007 two Muslim women, of Algerian and Senegalese background, respectively, were named to the French cabinet and in 2018 Belgium elected their first black mayor, a Congolese immigrant. Asian and African cultural forms also influenced European culture. For example, in Britain the popular **bhangra** music blended Indian folk songs with Caribbean reggae and Anglo-American styles, such as rock, hip-hop, and disco, becoming a lively dance music that was popular with both white and Indian youth. By the 1980s bhangra had spread to Indian immigrant communities in North America and the Caribbean and to India and Pakistan, sustaining Indian identity and encouraging Indian youth to have fun.

However, immigration posed problems of absorption into European society, fostering tensions between whites and non-whites. Over the years, many Turks, Arabs, Africans, Jamaicans, and Pakistanis, often doing low-paying jobs nobody else wanted, then settled down, and they and their local-born children faced discrimination and sometimes violent attack by right-wing youth gangs. Neo-Nazis in Germany sometimes set fire to immigrant apartment buildings; young toughs in England boasted of "Paki-bashing," beating up South Asians; and Greek racists harassed or assaulted immigrants. In response, many immigrants retreated into their own cultures. A British expert on Asian and West Indian immigrants noted their preference for "the novels that document the idiocies of English social snobbery, the musical forms that sustain the separate immigrant lifestyles, the ghetto life that builds up defense-mechanisms."[12] While older immigrants often clung to the cultures and attitudes brought from their Asian or Middle Eastern villages, such as a husband's authority over his wife and arranged marriages, their children struggled to reconcile their conservative family and religious traditions with materialistic, individualistic, secular Europe.

Tensions mounted further after 1989. Vanishing jobs put both immigrants and local people on unemployment rolls or competing for scarce work. Illegal immigration also increased as people fled extreme poverty or harsh repression. Boarding rickety boats, desperate Albanians headed to Italy and Africans tried to reach Spain or Italy. Later they would be joined by refugees from war-torn countries like Afghanistan, Iraq, and Syria. Hence, anti-immigrant (especially anti-Muslim) movements emerged even in famously tolerant countries like Denmark, Sweden, and the Netherlands, especially after the Islamist terrorist attacks against the United States in 2001. Facing particular hostility since 2001, some young Muslims, rejecting Western culture as immoral and criticizing the Islam their parents brought from North African, Turkish, or South Asian villages as corrupted by Sufi mysticism, became more devout and rigidly orthodox.

28-2d Reshaping Cultures, Thought, and Religion

Enriched by imports from around the world, western Europeans enjoyed a resilient cultural and intellectual life. American mass culture became widespread: cigarettes, Coca-Cola, and chewing gum symbolized postwar fashions; films and music reshaped cultural horizons. African American jazz musicians often settled in Europe, especially France and Scandinavia, to escape racism at home. In response, European governments tried to protect their languages and culture industries by mandating how much foreign music government radio stations could play. Young people also enjoyed non-Western popular entertainments, such as Caribbean reggae music, Latin American dances,

> **bhangra** A popular music that emerged in Britain from a blending of traditional folk songs brought by Indian immigrants with Caribbean reggae and Anglo-American styles, such as rock, hip-hop, and disco.

---

[12]Gordon Lewis, quoted in Chester L. Hunt and Lewis Walker, *Ethnic Dynamics: Patterns of Intergroup Relations in Various Societies*, 2nd ed. (Holmes Beach, FL: Learning Publications, 1979), 316.

and Japanese animated films. Yet Europeans often treasured entertainers that reflected local culture, such as the waiflike French singer Edith Piaf (1915–1963), known for her sad, nostalgic songs of lost love and lost youth, and the Greek composer-musician and liberal political activist Mikis Theodorakis (b. 1925).

After rock, an exciting, edgy music, emerged in the United States in the mid-1950s, it rapidly gained a huge European following, with American rock stars like Bill Haley, Buddy Holly, Elvis Presley, and Chuck Berry enjoying massive popularity. By the 1960s European musicians inspired by U.S. rock and blues, such as Francois Hardy in France and the Beatles and Rolling Stones in Britain, had reshaped local music scenes. The Beatles, young working-class men from gritty but cosmopolitan Liverpool, matured as musicians playing clubs in West Germany. "Beatlemania" reached around the world. Rock became known as "yeah yeah" music in nations as different as Brazil and Malaysia, after the Beatles lyric "she loves you yeah yeah yeah." The music and fashion of the Beatles and other rockers asserted youth identity. The Beatles' 1967 album, *Sgt. Pepper's Lonely Hearts Club Band*, became the prototype of the concept album, with a linking theme, cross-cultural musical explorations (including use of Indian instruments), and provocative lyrics, influencing popular musicians around the world.

By the mid-1970s a new style of rock, punk, expressed social protest. Although gaining a presence in North America and continental Europe, punk became especially influential in Britain, where working-class youth faced limited job options. The provocative songs of a leading punk group, the Sex Pistols, insulted the monarchy and offended British society's deeper values, delighting their fans. A leading punk magazine asserted: "[Punk] music is a perfect medium for shoving two fingers up at the establishment."[13] As punk's energy dissipated in the 1980s, many favored escapist dance music such as disco. But punk fostered creative new forms of rock in Europe and North America. To express their alienation, young people of Middle Eastern, South Asian, and Afro-Caribbean backgrounds often turned to musical forms from their ancestral countries, such as Algerian *rai* for Arabs and Jamaican dancehall and reggae for Afro-Caribbeans. Some immigrant youth adapted African American rap, writing lyrics in their own languages. For example, in France Senegalborn M. C. Solaar achieved popularity for songs chronicling the lives of young people of African ancestry. By the early twenty-first century popular music in Europe, as in North America, was fragmenting into diverse styles, from electronica to hard core to various versions of heavy metal.

Cultural life was influenced not only by cultural imports but also by local developments, especially political liberalism and growing mass media such as television and cinema. Creative cinema from France, Italy, and Sweden found a global audience by depicting the humblest lives and psychological and social dilemmas common to people in a rapidly changing

existentialism A philosophy, influential in post–World War II western Europe, whose speculation on the nature of reality reflects disillusionment with Europe's violent history and doubt that objectivity is possible.

postmodernism A European intellectual approach contending that truth is not absolute but constructed by people according to their society's beliefs.

world. Literature reflected political change. Writers known as post-colonialists challenged the worldview shaped by Western dominance. For example, India-born British writer Salman Rushdie (b. 1947), a Cambridge University–educated former actor and advertising copywriter from a Muslim family, confronted Western ethnocentrism. Remembering the prejudice he faced in British schools, Rushdie criticized Western society but also challenged what he considered Islamic culture's antimodern, antisecular sensibilities. His books *Shame* (1983), a satire on Pakistan's history, and especially *The Satanic Verses* (1988), a critical look at Islamic history, created an uproar among conservative Muslims, earning him death threats from militants.

As Europeans struggled to understand World War II's horrors, which seemed to contradict the rational thought and tolerance building in Europe since the Enlightenment, some turned to secular philosophies. Reflecting disillusionment with Europe's violent history, **existentialism** speculated on the nature of reality, doubting whether objectivity is possible. Stressing class struggle, Marxism envisioned a noncapitalist future for societies. Organized religion declined, and churches struggled to remain relevant in an increasingly secular society.

French philosopher Jean Paul Sartre **(SAHRT)** (1905–1980) and Simone de Beauvoir (1908–1986), his longtime partner, transformed little-known existential thought into a philosophy with wide appeal. Sartre argued that women and men, defined by a reality they view as fate or imposed by others, should not let others determine their lives but find their own meaning, overcoming uncertainty about the world and their place in it. People must accept responsibility for their actions, which he hoped would spark political engagement to create a better society. Sartre himself reached across political boundaries by becoming active in left-wing movements promoting world peace and banning nuclear weapons. He achieved fame unusual for a philosopher; when he died in 1980, thousands attended his funeral.

Other influential philosophies debated the nature of reality. Marxism emphasized social class and gender inequality, but as a political philosophy it lost many followers after the 1960s. Unlike Marxism's certitude about truth, an approach called deconstruction, pursued by Algeria-born Frenchman Jacques Derrida **(DER-i-dah)** (1930–2004), claimed that all rational thought could be taken apart and shown to be meaningless. Derrida questioned the entire Western philosophical tradition and whether Western civilization was superior to other cultures. Inspired by Derrida, by the 1990s **postmodernism**, contending that truth is not absolute but constructed by people according to their society's beliefs, influenced literature and scholarship. Hence, notions of different male and female aptitudes or one literary work's superiority over another are not objective but merely subjective attitudes shaped by society. Even scholars, postmodernists argue, cannot completely escape their gender, social class, ethnic, and cultural prejudices. However, many thinkers rejected postmodernist notions that truth is relative and objectivity impossible.

Organized religious life and churchgoing declined, partly because World War II and postwar materialism destroyed many people's faith, often leaving churches semi-deserted. According to opinion polls, around a quarter of Americans and western Europeans describe themselves as secular or with no religious

---

[13]*Sniffin' Glue*, quoted in Peter Wicke, *Rock Music: Culture, Aesthetics and Sociology* (New York: Cambridge University Press, 1990), 148.

affiliation. But there were differences. Whereas some two-thirds of Americans had a moderate or strong religious faith and believed in God, less than half of western Europeans did; while 40 percent of Americans regularly attended church, only 10 percent of western Europeans did. Conflicts between rival churches diminished, Protestants and Catholics no longer lived in separate worlds, and ecumenical cooperation increased. Formed in 1948, the Switzerland-based World Council of Churches brought together the main Protestant and Eastern Orthodox churches. Appalled by the Holocaust, Christian thinkers, acknowledging their faiths' relationship to Judaism, began referring to Europe's *Judeo-Christian* heritage. Although Europe's Jewish population had decreased sharply from the Holocaust and postwar emigration to Israel and the Americas, Jews remained active in public life. By the late 1900s many Jews moved back to Europe. In 2015 Spain invited the descendants of Jews expelled in 1492 and *conversos* (converted Jews) who had moved to Spanish America to return to Spain and obtain citizenship. By 2018 some sixty-four hundred people from around the world, including hundreds from the United States, have done so, in many cases to escape racism and discrimination. By 2000 immigration and conversions made Islam the second largest religion after Catholicism in France, Belgium, and Spain. Strongly religious Christians are much more likely than secular Europeans today to dislike Muslims and oppose Muslim immigration.

Protestant churches struggled to maintain their influence, often paying a price for their close ties to the state. Governments often subsidized state churches, as in Scandinavia and Britain, and church-operated schools, which did not need to actively solicit support and hence struggled to generate religious passion. This view was expressed by a popular joke about a young British man joining the army, who wrote on his enlistment form "no religion" and was told, "We'll put you down as Church of England [Anglican] then."

The Roman Catholic Church also faced challenges. As in the Americas, sexual abuse of children by priests in Europe, many revealed in the 1990s, shocked many Catholics. In Ireland, once one of the most devout and conservative Western societies, these widespread abuses helped undermine the faith of many believers, helping shift Ireland to the Left on social and cultural issues. In 2017 a prominent politician summarized the tight church control of Irish society in the past: "In the '40s and '50s, people replaced the colonialism of the Brits with a kind of colonialism of the church," a "toxic mix" of intermingled Catholicism and Irish identity.[14] The changes in Ireland were reflected in new laws in the 1990s and later, including legalization of abortion, homosexuality, same-sex marriage, gay adoption, contraception, divorce, and a pro-transgender identity law. The nation's current prime minister, Leo Varadkar (b. 1979), is the gay, biracial son of an Indian immigrant.

To deal with a changing world, reformist Pope John XXIII (pope 1958–1963) initiated convocations of church leaders, known as the Second Vatican Council (1962–1965), or Vatican II, which launched the most radical church changes since the 1500s. Reconciling the church with modernity, Vatican II gave the laity greater responsibility in worship, no longer required Latin in the liturgy, and removed blame from the Jews for the death of Jesus. The popes who followed John XXIII tended to be more conservative, supportive of traditional church dogma, and less ecumenical. Even after Vatican II, many Catholics ignored church teachings they disliked, such as banning artificial birth control. Some conservative Catholics turned to traditionalist movements opposing Vatican II, and some Catholic women, seeking more influence, advocated allowing women to become priests. As fewer European and North American men and women entered Catholic religious vocations, Asians, Africans, and Latin Americans comprised a growing share of the priesthood and religious orders. Hence, Catholic churches in Europe and North America increasingly imported parish priests from countries such as Nigeria or Mexico. Some observers predicted a Third World rather than a Western church of the future. In 2013 the elevation of the first pope from the Southern Hemisphere, the Argentine Jesuit Pope Francis (b. 1936), gave the church a more ecumenical and international perspective. Francis expressed some progressive and tolerant views that angered church conservatives. He has criticized both Marxism and capitalism as well as what he views as the mistreatment of migrants, but also maintained traditional church teachings on many issues including abortion and clerical marriage.

KEY POINTS

▶ Social democracy and the welfare state it fostered brought considerable security and stability to European life.

▶ Western Europe experienced considerable social change in this era, including the rise of feminism, influencing everything from marriage and gender relations to the world of work.

▶ Large numbers of immigrants have come to western Europe to seek work and to take advantage of the welfare state, a mix of capitalism and socialism in which citizens benefit from an extensive social safety net but pay high taxes in return.

▶ The diversity of western Europe contributes to a rich cultural and intellectual environment, though tensions have often arisen between Europeans and immigrants, leading to problems with assimilation.

▶ In 1968, a wave of radical protest swept Europe that resulted in significant social changes and ushered in the sexual revolution.

▶ Rock music, originally imported from the United States, became extremely popular among European youth, as did punk, which expressed working-class frustrations; other popular music showed Asian and African influences.

▶ Philosophies such as existentialism, which urged people to control their own lives, and postmodernism, which claimed that complete objectivity is impossible, became popular in postwar Europe, while organized religion became less influential.

---

[14]Aodhan O Riordain, quoted in "'Demise of the Church' Tilts Ireland to the Left," *New York Times* (December 3, 2017), A4.

28-3 Communism in the Soviet Union and Eastern Europe

⇄ TRANSITIONS | SOCIETIES

Q What factors contributed to political crises in the Soviet Union and eastern Europe?

Like western Europe, the Soviet Union changed after World War II. Western Europeans struggled for centuries to understand Russia; Winston Churchill called Russia a riddle wrapped in a mystery inside an enigma. For several generations during the Cold War, the USSR was the major political, military, and ideological rival to North Americans and western Europeans. They also dominated eastern Europe, where they supported and protected communist governments. The Soviets feared U.S. ambitions and NATO military power, viewing themselves as more threatened than threatening. The USSR, the last great territorial empire, enjoyed substantial natural resources while maintaining a powerful state and a planned economy. But while communism modernized society, by the 1980s the Soviet system in Russia and the satellites in eastern Europe showed signs of decay, which led ultimately to collapse in 1989–1991.

> **CONNECTION to TODAY**
>
> How did the actions of the Soviet Union in eastern Europe and the world affect your family, community, and nation in the Cold War years?

28-3a Soviet Politics and Economy

The USSR emerged from World War II as the world's number two military and economic power, no mean achievement given the war's ravages: twenty million killed, millions left homeless, cities blasted into rubble, the countryside laid waste. The trauma helps explain hostility toward the West: Russians resented the sacrifices they had been forced to make in a war they did not start and because of Germany's conflict with Britain and France. These experiences reinforced traditional Russian paranoia about the West, prompting Russians to maintain a huge defense establishment and power in eastern Europe to keep the region as a buffer zone. But the stresses in the rigid Soviet political system led to some change over the decades.

Given Russia's key role in the victory over Nazism and the Russian occupation of eastern Europe, communist leader Josef Stalin (**STAH-lin**) (1879–1953) believed that the Soviets could deal as equals with the West. Soviet armies in eastern Europe helped establish communist governments there to create the Soviet bloc of nations, which was divided from the West by heavily fortified borders. Stalin also kept control of Estonia, Latvia, and Lithuania, formerly independent Baltic nations occupied in World War II. In 1949 the USSR gained a key ally with the communist victory in China (see Chapter 27). By 1949 Soviet scientists, helped by information collected by spies in the United States, had built and tested an atomic bomb, keeping pace with the United States in the emerging arms race.

During Stalin's brutal rule, the paranoid dictator, imagining potential enemies everywhere, maintained an iron grip on power, exiling millions to Siberia; hundreds of others, including top Communist Party officials and military officers Stalin suspected of disloyalty, were convicted of treason in show trials and executed. The regime also maintained a tight rein on the arts, education, and science. Hence, party officials banned the poetry of Anna Akhmatova (**uhk-MAH-tuh-vuh**) (1888–1966), who courageously recorded the agonies of Stalin's purge victims, and detained her in a filthy hospital; they also imprisoned scientists whose research questioned theories favored by party-approved scientists in fields such as plant genetics; as a result, studies were flawed. Meanwhile, Stalin spread Russian language and culture in the empire's non-Russian regions, especially Muslim Central Asia.

Stalin's death in 1953 sparked rethinking and modest political change. Russian poet Evgeni Evtushenko remembered that "all Russia wept tears of grief—and perhaps tears of fear for the future."[15] Stalin's successor, Nikita Khrushchev (**KROOSH-chef**) (1894–1971), courageously began de-Stalinization in 1956 with a secret speech to a closed party congress session that was critical of Stalin's dictatorial ruling style, intolerance, abuse of power, and crimes. Khrushchev hoped that cleansing communism of the brutal Stalinist legacy would legitimize the system to his people and the world. The speech circulated underground throughout the Soviet bloc, stirring up dissent in eastern Europe. Suppression of a Polish strike killed or wounded hundreds, and twenty thousand Hungarians died in an abortive uprising against Soviet domination. De-Stalinization also divided the communist world—China broke its alliance with the USSR in 1960—perhaps planting the seed for the unraveling of the Soviet Empire and system three decades later.

Beginning a political thaw at home, Khrushchev promised that Soviet living standards would eventually equal those of Americans. It never happened, but Khrushchev produced some achievements. In 1957 the USSR shocked the world by launching *Sputnik*, the first artificial satellite to orbit Earth; in 1961 cosmonaut Yuri Gagaran (**guh-GAHR-un**) (1934–1968) became the first man to fly aboard a rocket ship into Earth orbit, returning a hero. In 1963, cosmonaut Valentina Tereshkova (**tare-esh-KO-va**) (b. 1937), daughter of a tractor driver and textile mill worker, became the first woman to fly in space. But Soviet repression, though less brutal than Stalin's, did not end: in 1957 Khrushchev prevented novelist Boris Pasternak (**PAS-ter-NAK**) (1890–1960) from publishing the novel *Dr. Zhivago*, a critical look at the Bolsheviks during the Russian Civil War that won a Nobel Prize after being smuggled to the West.

In 1964 Khrushchev was deposed. Leonid Brezhnev (1906–1982), a cautious bureaucrat, imposed a Stalinist system giving the state a hand in everything. Russians still found subtle ways to express their discontent, addressing their political powerlessness by passing jokes along to friends and relatives. In a popular joke, a man arrested for shouting "Brezhnev is an idiot" in Moscow's Red Square received fifteen days for hooliganism

---

[15]Quoted in Ronald Grigor Suny, *The Soviet Experiment: Russia, the USSR, and the Successor States* (New York: Oxford University Press, 1998), 387.

and fifteen years for revealing a state secret. Brezhnev led the country for two decades (1964–1982), and under him and his successors, the Soviet state, run mostly in secret by elderly, bureaucratic men, was intolerant of dissent. The secret police (KGB) monitored thought and behavior; most citizens endured Communist Party control as inevitable; and Russians learned how to avoid trouble. A few active dissidents, mostly intellectuals and artists, were often deprived of jobs and benefits; some were sent to remote Siberian prison camps, where poorly fed inmates spent their regimented days in hard labor. Many died there.

Some persecuted intellectuals had made notable achievements. In 1970 writer Alexander Solzhenitsyn (**SOL-zhuh-NEET-sin**) (1918–2008), a Red Army veteran imprisoned by Stalin, was forbidden to receive the Nobel Prize for literature because his novel, *One Day in the Life of Ivan Denisovich*, exposed the harsh labor camp life. He later fled to the United States. Another well-known dissident, Andrei Sakharov (**SAH-kuh-rawf**) (1921–1989), a physicist who helped develop the first Soviet atomic bomb but became disillusioned, was exiled to a remote city after championing human rights, democracy, and an end to the nuclear arms race. Sakharov won the Nobel Peace Prize in 1975 but was prevented from attending the ceremonies. Milovan Djilas (**JIL-ahs**) (1911–1995), a Yugoslav communist leader turned dissident, described the contrast between modern Europe's two great political movements: "Fascism is a nightmare and madness; communism is force and taboo. Fascism is temporary, communism is an enduring way of life."[16]

While the Soviets achieved notable successes, they also experienced severe economic problems. Stalin's Five-Year Plans had rapidly transformed the USSR from a backward to fairly modern society. To encourage more progress, Soviet leaders had three tools: the Communist Party, the bureaucracy, and the military. By the 1980s all three proved inadequate in directing a modern economy and society. The authoritarian party, tolerating little dissent, fostered rigidity. The cautious, overcentralized bureaucracy, anxious to preserve their perks and power, often bungled planning and management; officials planned the number of industrial products needed—from steel beams to dish pans—for five years ahead without adequate information. The military, large but inefficient and held together by brutal discipline, promoted incompetent officers and wasted resources.

Increasingly the economy struggled. The Soviets spent vast sums to achieve nuclear and military parity with the United States, building a massive defense establishment and arms industry that sucked money from other scientific and technological projects. Since Soviet factories could not supply consumer goods to meet growing demand, people often bought food and clothes through the black market from illegal vendors. Paying workers regardless of effort caused absenteeism and indifference; bored shop clerks seemed annoyed when shoppers interrupted their frequent tea breaks and gossip sessions. Failing to innovate high technology, Russians missed the personal computer revolution sweeping the West. By the 1990s few citizens or schools possessed computers. Although better off than most Asians, Africans, or Latin Americans, most Soviet citizens lived well below North American and western European standards.

Meanwhile, industrial pollution ravaged the environment, producing dying forests and lakes, toxic farmland, and poisoned air. Diverting rivers for farming and power caused the once large Aral Sea to practically dry up and diminished the world's largest inland body of water, the Caspian Sea. In 1986 the Chernobyl nuclear power station in the Ukraine exploded, causing numerous deaths and injuries, releasing radiation over Europe, and revealing the USSR's inadequate environmental protections.

When living standards rose under Krushchev in the 1950s, the Soviet people turned optimistic about communism. But Soviet leaders papered over problems, and by the 1970s fewer Soviet citizens believed in the communist future. People joked cynically: "Under capitalism man exploits man; under communism it's the other way around." In a supposedly classless society, the contrast between the party, government, and military elite's wealth and everyone else was striking. Communism fostered a favored elite that Djilas called a new class, enjoying special privileges denied to average citizens. Social decay was evident everywhere: drab working-class lives, rampant

Vyacheslav Oseledko/AFP/Getty Images

IMAGE 28.5 Aral Sea As water from the rivers that supplied it was diverted for agriculture and industry, the Aral Sea in Soviet Central Asia lost over half its water between 1960 and 2000. This photo shows a stranded boat where rich lake fisheries once existed.

Q What does this photo tell us about environmental problems in Russia and the world?

[16]Quoted in James, *Europe Reborn*, 279.

corruption and bribery, shortage of goods, widespread alcoholism, and demoralized youth seeking access to Western popular culture and consumer goods.

28-3b The Soviet Union in the Cold War

Tensions between the United States and the USSR reached a height in the late 1940s through the late 1950s. During the Korean War (1950–1953), the Soviets supplied communist North Koreans fighting the United Nations forces, mainly South Koreans and Americans. But from the late 1950s through the late 1970s, Stalin's successors promoted a less aggressive "peaceful coexistence" toward the West and tensions eased somewhat, even though Soviet-backed forces took control of North Vietnam in 1954 and Cuba in 1959. In 1961 East Germany built a high, twenty-seven-mile-long wall around West Berlin, preventing disenchanted East Germans from fleeing to the West but also symbolizing fears of exposing them to Western culture and values. In 1962 a crisis caused by secretly placing Soviet nuclear missiles in Cuba, and the U.S. demand for the missiles' removal, brought the two superpowers to the brink of nuclear war. The Soviets withdrew the missiles, easing tensions. But the Soviets helped arm communist rebel forces fighting U.S.-supported South Vietnam, Laos, and the Philippines in the 1950s and 1960s, conflicts that drew in U.S. advisers and troops.

The Soviets generally were more interested in the normal pursuit of allies, security, and political influence than in spreading communism. While supporting nationalist and revolutionary movements in Asia, Africa, and Latin America, often supplying weapons and advice, the Soviets mostly followed pragmatic policies, dispatching military forces only when their direct interests were threatened. After China broke with the USSR in 1960 and became a rival, Soviet and Chinese troops watched each other warily along their common border. Following the **Brezhnev Doctrine**, which asserted Moscow's right to interfere in the eastern European satellites to protect communist governments, the Soviets intervened militarily to suppress revolts in Poland and Hungary in the 1950s, liberalizing tendencies in Czechoslovakia in 1968, and Polish dissident movements in the 1970s and 1980s.

Eventually, military interventions proved costly. In 1979 Soviet armies invaded neighboring Afghanistan to prop up a pro-Soviet government. But the United States, along with Arab nations and Pakistan, actively aided the Afghan rebels, mostly militant Muslims, who were fighting the secular Afghan regime and Soviet occupation. Ultimately Afghanistan, where mountains and deserts made fighting difficult, proved a disaster, costing thirteen thousand Russian lives and billions of dollars; the Soviets withdrew their forces in 1989. Economic problems, restless subject peoples, and the cost of supporting a huge military and its widespread commitments contributed to major rethinking in the later 1980s.

Brezhnev Doctrine An assertion by Soviet leaders of Moscow's right to interfere in Soviet satellites to protect communist governments and the Soviet bloc.

28-3c Soviet Society and Culture

Soviet society changed over the decades. Population surged from 180 million in 1950 to 275 million by the late 1980s. Soviet citizens, far healthier, better paid, and more educated than their predecessors in 1917, enjoyed social services unimaginable fifty years earlier: free medical care, old-age pensions, maternity leaves, guaranteed jobs, paid vacations, and day-care centers. In exchange for security, however, people had to accept state power and subordination of individual rights. Moreover, state-provided benefits, often termed "cradle to grave socialism," relieved individuals of responsibility for their own lives.

Education and social services shaped women's experiences. While few served in the Soviet hierarchy, most were in the paid workforce and even constituted three-quarters of the number of doctors. Many young rural women migrated to the cities. While rural women often faced hard lives—no running water, indoor plumbing, central heating, or access to nearby shops—urban women also faced challenges. Besides working their jobs, lower-income women stood in long lines to buy food and necessities, took their kids to and from school, washed clothes and dishes in the bathroom sink, and sometimes prepared meals in communal kitchens. Because women increasingly divorced abusive husbands and abortion was legalized, families became smaller. Except in Muslim Central Asia, both birthrates and life expectancy eventually fell dramatically. Schools perpetuated stereotypes of weak, passionate women and strong, rational men. Sometimes feminist activists were harassed, arrested, or deported.

Relations deteriorated between ethnic Russians, who constituted half the Soviet population by the 1980s, and diverse minorities chafing at Russian domination. In Soviet Central Asian republics such as Kazakhstan and Uzbekistan, newly built industrial cities attracted millions of ethnic Russians, who monopolized most managerial and professional positions. Thus communism brought relatively high living standards to once impoverished Central Asia. But many Muslim peoples resented Russification of their cultures and weakening of Islamic practice. Most Baltic peoples (Estonians, Latvians, Lithuanians) hated Russian domination and the replacement of local languages with Russian; some Jews sought freedom to openly practice their religion or emigrate to Israel or North America.

The state marginalized organized religion, promoting atheism and denouncing Christianity as superstition. But the Russian Orthodox Church became an informal state agent; the clergy carefully avoided angering the Communist Party. Still, Russians often attended church and nurtured their faith; in the 1980s, when the state became more tolerant, millions returned to the church. Yet, many Russians remained skeptical of or indifferent to organized religion.

Soviet policies forced most cultural creativity underground. Intellectuals secretly exchanged copies of forbidden books and magazines, and writers published their work abroad illegally. Anti-Stalinist poets explored the breathing space between the official line and prison, while youth movements baffled Soviet and eastern European authorities. Considering Western rock degenerate, officials restricted innovative musicians, although few faced arrest. Vladimir Vysotski (**VLAD-eh-meer vih-SOT-skee**) (1938–1980), an irreverent singer-songwriter-actor-poet, expressed political disenchantment, avoiding arrest but not harassment. The urban intelligentsia admired Vysotski for songs exposing the Russian soul, extolling sex and liquor, and mocking Soviet corruption, hypocrisy, labor camps, and even politics: "But wait—let's have a smoke, better yet, let's drink to a time, when there will be no jails in Russia."[17] Cassette tapes of his unofficial concerts enjoyed wide underground distribution. After his death from cancer, hundreds of mourners left flowers at his Moscow grave every month for many years.

Young people wanted cultural liberalization. By the 1960s some modeled themselves on the Anglo-American "hippie" counterculture, wearing jeans, bell-bottom pants, miniskirts, and peace medallions and listening to the Beatles or their Soviet clones. Rock music, spread by illicit cassettes, remained the chief escape from an oppressive society; some 160,000 underground rock and jazz bands existed by the 1980s. While few musicians challenged the system directly, like Vysotski they explored the fringes, mocking the bureaucracy or the absurdity of Soviet life. Rather than seeking to change the government, rock musicians and their audience sought to live beyond the police and bureaucracy.

28-3d Eastern Europe in the Soviet System

During the late 1940s the Soviets installed communist governments in each eastern European nation, sealing the region's fate for over forty years. Political parties were abolished, churches persecuted, and nationalistic leaders purged. In 1949 COMECON (Council for Mutual Economic Assistance) more closely integrated Soviet and eastern European economies. But while communism fostered industrialization in Romania and Bulgaria, people in more industrialized Czechoslovakia, Poland, and East Germany aspired to living standards closer to those of western Europeans. To supply consumer goods and finance industrialization, governments built up huge debts. The increased industrial activity had serious environmental side effects. While the Soviets treated the satellite countries as informal colonies or neocolonies, exploiting their resources, they also had to give them generous subsidies to maintain control.

Yugoslavia followed the most independent path, breaking with the USSR entirely in 1948. In 1945 the Yugoslav Communist Party, led by Marshal Josip Broz Tito **(TEE-toe)** (1892–1980), who had led the anti-Nazi resistance, won national elections. To avoid Soviet domination, Tito cooperated with the nonaligned nations while maintaining friendly relations with the West. Tito's unique form of communism, which experimented with worker rather than manager control of factories, created enough prosperity and popular support to neutralize Yugoslavia's powerful ethnic divisions.

Resentment of Soviet domination fostered unrest. After the Soviets crushed protest demonstrations in Poland in the early 1950s, a Polish poet daringly wrote: "They [the communists] ran to us shouting, 'Under socialism, a cut finger doesn't hurt.' But they [the people] felt pain [and] lost faith."[18]

TASS/Getty Images

IMAGE 28.6 **Soviet Rock Band** The Russian rock group Kino and their lead singer Victor Tsoi, shown here in concert in Moscow, were very popular in Soviet times and after. For Soviet youth, rock music became a way of escaping the restrictions of Soviet life. The lyrics of rock bands often addressed the problems of Soviet life.

Q What does the photo suggest about the lives, styles, and musical interests of restless Soviet youth?

Poland, with its strong Catholic allegiances, was the most restless satellite, its workers demanding more public input into government. In 1956 Hungarian leaders tried to break with rigid communism, reinstating private property, inviting non-communists into government, and declaring the country neutral. In response, a Soviet bloc force occupied Hungary, crushed popular resistance, and executed anti-Soviet leaders. But even under the new pro-Soviet leaders, Hungary remained open to the West and somewhat more tolerant of dissent than other satellites. While other eastern Europeans followed the Soviet pattern of highly centralized bureaucracies, Hungary's blend of state influence and free markets, known as market socialism, created the most prosperous Soviet bloc economy.

[17]Quoted in Timothy W. Ryback, *Rock Around the Bloc: A History of Rock Music in Eastern Europe and the Soviet Union* (New York: Oxford University Press, 1990), 35.
[18]Quoted in Davies, *Europe*, 1102.

Hungarians called it "goulash communism," after their favorite dish, a mix of pasta and meat.

Other disgruntled eastern Europeans later defied Soviet power. In Czechoslovakia in 1968 the reform-minded leader Alexander Dubček (**DOOB-check**) (1927–1993) fostered the "Prague Spring" and a shift to a more liberal "communism with a human face." Alarmed, the Soviets sent in Warsaw Pact troops and replaced Dubček and his supporters with repressive Soviet puppets. In Poland, the Soviets allowed Polish-born Pope John Paul II to make a triumphant visit in 1979, which sparked an outpouring of religious and nationalist fervor. In 1980 Polish shipyard workers led by Lech Walesa (**leck wa-LEN-za**) (b. 1943), an electrical engineer, went on strike. As food prices increased, thousands of women took to the streets, shouting, "We're hungry!" When dissidents formed the Solidarity trade union, aimed at economic liberalization, the government declared martial law, banning Solidarity. Even though illegal, Solidarity, with 9.5 million members by 1981, worked for both economic and political goals. As one leader put it: "What we had in mind was not only bread, butter and sausage but also justice, democracy, truth, legality, human dignity, freedom of convicts, and the repair of the republic."[19] With political avenues closed off, young eastern Europeans used culture, especially rock music, as a protest vehicle. Government officials prohibited performances by the more daring rockers, among them the leading east German singer-songwriter Wolf Biermann (b. 1936), also a poet and novelist. Although he thought of himself as a leftist, Biermann promoted cultural liberalization and German reunification: "The German darkness descends over my spirit. It darkens overpowering in my song. It comes because I see my Germany so deeply torn."[20]

28-3e Soviet Decline and Reform

Soviet problems mounted, forcing a reappraisal of the political and economic system and the nation's place in the world. The USSR had steadily lost ground in world affairs to the United States and economic ground to Japan and West Germany, while China became a bitter rival. Conducting the Afghanistan war and subsidizing eastern European satellites drained Soviet wealth. By the mid-1980s the USSR had few close remaining allies outside the Soviet bloc, which was restless, and few Asian, African, or Latin American revolutionaries looked toward Moscow for inspiration. Soviet power was mostly military, whereas the United States and its Western allies also had cultural, economic, and technological influence. Around the world people studied English or French, not Russian; some

glasnost ("openness") The policy introduced in the Soviet Union by Mikhail Gorbachev to democratize the political system.

perestroika ("restructuring") Mikhail Gorbachev's policy to liberalize the Soviet economy using market mechanisms.

observers found more power in rock music, videos, fast food, youth fashions, and global news networks than in the Soviet Red Army. Young people from Bangkok to Buenos Aires favored blue jeans and American adventure films; few knew or cared much about Soviet life. Some scholars concluded that "soft power" such as the Beatles, McDonald's, and the Cable News Network (CNN) were at least as crucial to winning the Cold War as U.S. military power.

Declining international influence, combined with spiraling social and economic problems and a stifling bureaucracy, ultimately produced younger, reform-minded Soviet leaders who introduced dramatic change. Having more contact with the outside world, these Soviet leaders realized their growing technological backwardness. The planned economy that had transformed Russia into a superpower now seemed a burden; a Communist Party permitting no political competition and a planned economy, run from the top, left little room for individual initiative or creativity. In 1985 Mikhail Gorbachev (**GORE-beh-CHOF**) (b. 1931) became Soviet leader. Realizing that the nation, facing escalating military costs, could not win an arms race or ever match the United States as a superpower, he hoped to preserve and energize communist rule by liberalizing the economy, decentralizing decision making, and relaxing ideological controls. Gorbachev introduced a dazzling series of reforms, developed closer relations with the West, and abandoned the ideological struggle with liberal democracies. In 1987 a U.S.–USSR treaty lessened the threat of nuclear war, and both countries destroyed their short- and long-range missiles. The treaty remained in place until 2019, when the U.S., charging that Russians were cheating, ended the agreement; the Russians followed suit, sparking fear of a new arms race while unsettling Europe and the international community. With his **glasnost** ("openness") policy, Gorbachev democratized the political system, arranged for free elections and a parliament including noncommunist parties, released most political prisoners, deemphasized the Communist Party's role, loosened state control of media and the arts, and invited scholars to talk truthfully about the Soviet past. Realizing the ruinous financial costs of maintaining unpopular eastern European governments, Gorbachev did not intervene to preserve them as they collapsed or were toppled in 1989.

Admitting Soviet communism's faults, Gorbachev liberalized the economy using market mechanisms through **perestroika** ("restructuring") (see Discover Historical Voices: Restructuring Soviet Society). But the economic changes failed to take off. While many in the intelligentsia wanted democratization, the working classes mostly preferred consumer goods, which did not come. Meanwhile, top bureaucrats, including state enterprise managers, resisted changes that threatened their role. Conservatives in the Communist Party and secret police opposed reforms that might undermine their power. Soon the Soviet system collapsed.

---

[19]Quoted in James, *Europe Reborn*, 300.
[20]Quoted in Elaine Mensh and Harry Mensh, *Behind the Scenes in Two Worlds* (New York: International Publishers, 1978), 133.

Discover Historical Voices

Restructuring Soviet Society

In 1987 Mikhail Gorbachev, Soviet Communist Party and government head, published a book, Perestroika, outlining his policy of economic restructuring to transform the inefficient, stagnant Soviet economy into one based on a decentralized market similar to Hungary and China's market socialism. The new policy gave greater autonomy to local government officials and factory managers and attempted to democratize the Communist Party itself. Causing a sensation, the book was ranked by some observers as the most important publication of the late twentieth century. By the early 1990s, with Gorbachev himself removed from office, the policy was eclipsed, but the book remained a testimony to the problems that led to the Soviet system's collapse and idealistic proposals to solve them. In this excerpt, Gorbachev defines perestroika.

Perestroika means overcoming the stagnation process, breaking down the braking mechanism, creating a dependable and effective mechanism for acceleration of social and economic progress and giving it dynamism.

Perestroika means initiative. It is the comprehensive development of democracy, socialist self-government, encouragement of initiative and creative endeavor, improved order and discipline, more glasnost (openness), criticism and self-criticism in all spheres of our society. It is utmost respect for the individual and consideration for personal dignity.

Perestroika is the all-round intensification of the Soviet economy, the revival and development of the principles of democratic centralism in running the national economy, the universal introduction of economic methods, the renunciation of management by injunction and by administration methods, and the overall encouragement of innovation and socialist enterprise.

Perestroika means a resolute shift to scientific methods, an ability to provide a solid scientific basis for every new initiative. It means the combination of the achievements of the scientific and technological revolution with a planned economy.

Perestroika means priority development of the social sphere aimed at ever better satisfaction of the Soviet people's requirements for good living and working conditions, for good rest and recreation, education and health care. It means unceasing concern for cultural and spiritual wealth, for the culture of every individual and society as a whole.

Perestroika means the elimination from society of the distortions of social ethics, the consistent implementation of the principles of social justice. It means the unity of words and deeds, rights and duties. It is the elevation of honest, highly-qualified labor, the overcoming of leveling tendencies in pay and consumerism.

This is how we see perestroika today. This is how we see our tasks, and the substance and content of our work for the forthcoming period. It is difficult now to say how long that period will take. Of course, it will be much more than two or three years. We are ready for serious, strenuous and tedious work to ensure that our country reaches new heights by the end of the twentieth century.

Reflection Questions

1. What did Gorbachev mean by perestroika?
2. What problems did the policy aim to solve?
3. Do you think that Gorbachev's policy of perestroika is or should be still relevant to Russia today?

Source: Adapted from Mikhail Gorbachev, *Perestroika* (New York: HarperCollins, 1987), 34–35.

KEY POINTS

▶ Although the Soviet economy grew under communism, it suffered from lack of innovation, inept planning, and an overemphasis on the military; and it created a privileged class of Communist Party and military insiders who lived much better than the common people.

▶ U.S.–USSR relations were strained by the Cuban Missile Crisis, the Berlin Wall, and Soviet support for communist Cuba and North Vietnam.

▶ Many non-Russians in Central Asia and the Baltics resented Russian domination and the devaluing of their own cultures.

▶ Much of eastern Europe was effectively colonized by the USSR, though Yugoslavia pursued an independent communist course, and citizens of Poland, Hungary, and Czechoslovakia mounted periodic challenges to Soviet rule.

▶ With the USSR losing ground economically and culturally, Soviet leader Mikhail Gorbachev introduced reforms designed to democratize the USSR, to liberalize its economy, and to allow eastern European countries greater self-determination.

28-4 Communist Collapse: A New Russia and Europe

TRANSITIONS SOCIETIES NETWORKS

Q How did the demise of the communist system contribute to a new Europe?

For over four decades the Cold War and the iron curtain provided the context for both western and eastern European politics. The breakup of the communist bloc of nations in 1989 and the USSR in 1991 reshaped the political and economic face of Russia, former Soviet territories, eastern Europe, and western Europe, creating hope but also uncertainties. Russia struggled to rebuild and revive its power. While wars tore apart Yugoslavia and Germany was reunited, western Europe pushed toward unification, including some of eastern Europe, but still faced conflicting forces of nationalism and cooperation. Most Europeans now chose governments through multiparty elections. Europe, though no longer having imperial power, is still important in the global system.

CONNECTION to TODAY

How have you, your family, and community been affected by the changes in Europe and Russia since 1989?

28-4a A New Russia and New Post-Soviet Nations

The sudden collapse of the Soviet empire and communism in Europe was a major development of twentieth-century history. In 1985 there were five million Soviet soldiers stationed from East Germany to eastern Siberia's Pacific coast, symbolizing imperial Soviet power's reach. Six years later the USSR and its satellite nations had unraveled, mostly without violence. Though the collapse was not a complete surprise, its pace was astonishing. While outside factors, including eastern European unrest and escalating U.S. defense spending, played a role, Soviet economic decline was probably the decisive cause. The collapse showed the failure of the Soviet system, founded on Leninism and strongly shaped by Stalinism. Democratic governments and decentralized capitalism had adjusted better to global changes than communist-planned economies, while nationalist yearnings among non-Russians had sapped the empire's foundations.

Gorbachev's greatest contribution was to face up to failure. By 1991 Gorbachev, unable to control the forces unleashed, had lost his credibility and resigned in disgrace, and he was replaced by Boris Yeltsin (1931–2007), a communist bureaucrat turned reformer with strong U.S. support. Yeltsin ended seven decades of communist rule by outlawing the Communist Party. Russians welcoming the party's demise toppled statues of Lenin and restored czarist names to cities renamed during Soviet times; Leningrad once again became Saint Petersburg.

Yeltsin acquiesced in breaking up the USSR while maintaining the unity of the largest Soviet republic, Russia, which stretched from the Baltic Sea through ten time zones to Siberia's eastern tip, only a few miles from Alaska (see Map 28.3). But glasnost had opened a Pandora's box. Ethnic hatreds, long suppressed by military force or tamed by the

oligarchs Well-placed former communists who amassed enough wealth to gain control of major segments of the post-Soviet Russian economy.

safety net, soon exploded. In 1991 all the fourteen Soviet republics outside of Russia, from Lithuania and the Ukraine in the west to Kyrgyzstan (KER-giz-STAN) in eastern Turkestan, declared independence, often under former communist officials turned strongmen whose autocratic, intolerant, and often corrupt ruling style resembled the old Soviet system.

Most of the new nations struggled to achieve economic self-sufficiency and political stability. Some experienced conflict between rival ethnic or nationalist groups or fought each other over territorial claims, as did Christian Armenia and Muslim Azerbaijan. In three of the former Soviet republics—Georgia, Ukraine, and Kyrgyzstan—what observers called "colored revolutions" erupted; their proponents, pro-democracy activists, symbolized their cause with a color. With U.S. and western European encouragement, they forced out dictatorial regimes. But the leaders soon lost support by becoming less democratic or antagonizing Russia. Conflict, sometimes violent, between those favoring close ties with the West and those preferring alliance with Russia have continued to destabilize Ukraine. In Central Asia militant Muslims launched insurgencies against secular post-Soviet governments and nominal Muslims, while Islam gained support among the disenchanted and marginalized, especially jobless young men. Islamic fervor forced or prompted many women to don the headscarf or veil and to dress and behave modestly. Meanwhile, millions of ethnic Russians in the former Soviet republics faced resentment for their relative affluence and ties to the former colonizer. In Latvia, for example, the indigenous Lett people make up only half the population, while Russians constitute a third. The Latvian government now requires everyone to learn the Latvian language, which was marginalized under Soviet rule.

In Russia Yeltsin faced many problems. Taking the advice of Russian free market enthusiasts and American advisers, he introduced "shock therapy": rapid conversion of the stagnant planned economy to market capitalism. This approach, while producing more consumer goods and a growing middle class, also created other dilemmas. Soviet officials converted the enterprises they managed into private companies, becoming Russia's new capitalists, while organized crime groups and a few well-placed former communists, known as **oligarchs**, now controlled many economic assets. Oil-rich Chechnya, a largely Muslim Caucasus region, declared independence from Russia in 1994. Fearing that Chechnya's independence would encourage other secession movements, Yeltsin tried to crush the separatists, producing a persistent quagmire with thousands of casualties. Secessionist sentiments still fester in several other predominantly Muslim Caucasus regions.

Russia's economic pain was widespread. Millions of workers, especially women, lost jobs as inefficient, obsolete Soviet industries closed. Conservatives encouraged women to stay home and tend

MAP 28.3 **The Dissolution of the Soviet Union** In 1991 the leaders of Russia, who had abandoned communism, allowed the other fourteen republics to leave the Soviet Union, bringing an end to a vast federation that had endured for over seven decades. Even without the fourteen republics, Russia remained the world's largest nation in geographical size, stretching across ten time zones from the Pacific Ocean to the Baltic Sea.

Q In which of these countries is Russian influence still considerable despite political independence and which are the most hostile to Russia?

to family obligations. With free higher education ended, families devoted their funds to their sons. Factory workers, miners, and state employees, such as teachers, were often not paid for years. As Yeltsin dismantled the welfare state, health care reductions, declining incomes, heavier drinking, and illegal drug use affected public health; men's life expectancy dropped from sixty-four in 1990 to fifty-nine in 2002 but rebounded to 66.4 by 2018, ten years less than for women. By 1992 inflation was 2,500 percent, devastating people on pensions and fixed incomes. According to a popular local joke, "All the good things the communists said about communism were false, but all the bad things they said about capitalism were true."

In 2000, with the Russian economy near collapse and free markets discredited, Yeltsin resigned in disgrace and was replaced by his prime minister Vladimir Putin (b. 1952), who ended shock therapy and brought back stability after fifteen years of turbulence. A former secret police colonel who kept a portrait of Peter the Great in his office, Putin initially expressed

admiration of the West and espoused capitalism and democratic reforms, including multiparty elections. But soon, criticizing Western political forms, he pursued more authoritarian, socially conservative, and nationalist policies than Yeltsin. Critics argued that Putin sought to restore Russian pride lost in the collapse of the USSR. Political liberalism faded as Putin took control of much of the media, seizing or muffling opposition newspapers and television stations and prosecuting some oligarchs for alleged corruption. Some wealthy men were jailed; others fled into exile. But some oligarchs joined Putin's inner circle or headed powerful state-linked corporations. With the media muzzled the regime has guaranteed their victory in elections by preventing critics from getting on the ballot or intimidating the opposition. The state took over many large private companies, turning the economy into a form of state capitalism not unlike Meiji Japan. Eventually improved tax collection and higher prices for oil and natural gas exports fostered economic recovery, allowing Putin to assert Russian interests in the world. Putin outmaneuvered discredited pro-U.S. free market advocates, the rebuilt Communist Party, and extreme right-wing nationalists but also showed little patience with liberal, pro-democracy dissidents and protesters, arresting or harassing some of them.

The 2008–2009 global economic crisis caused a rapid drop in oil prices, while drastic revenue declines brought cutbacks and recession, hurting Putin's prestige and fomenting dissent. Political satire flourished, poking fun at leaders and policies even on broadcast media. Some ninety-seven million of Russia's one hundred forty-four million people had Internet access in 2019. In that same year Putin moved to bring greater censorship and government control over the Internet by cutting users off from foreign servers, what critics see as the foundation for a China-style "great firewall." As the economy rebounded, Putin's Russia became, with Brazil, China, India, and South Africa, part of the BRICS group of nations seeking an alternative to Western domination. However, during the 2010s the Russian economy dropped from the world's eighth to the twelfth largest by 2019, smaller than that of Texas. It was slowed to a standstill from a lag in foreign investment caused by resentment against endemic corruption and an expanding government economic role. Russia's power in the world is chiefly military, not economic. Meanwhile, opposition to Putin grew but remained fragmented.

Putin's Russia has mixed autocratic government with openness to the outside world and is seeking a path toward restoring Russia's imperial identity, at various times promoting concepts like the "Eurasian Commonwealth" and the "Russian World." The Russian Orthodox Church, for centuries closely connected to national identity and political power, regained influence, and even Putin claimed to be a believer. This new clout and the regime's support have allowed the church to marginalize or ban other Christian denominations. Within the church leadership, liberals promoted a tolerant and ecumenical view while the more powerful conservatives denounced ecumenism, some even supporting anti-Semitic, anti-Muslim views and a return of the monarchy. With church encouragement, Putin greatly restricted LGBTQ rights, making public support of same-sex relations a crime in 2013. He also harassed feminists and some dissidents; in 2012 members of a controversial feminist punk rock group, Pussy Riot, were sentenced to prison for a public protest in a Moscow cathedral. These repressive actions generated protests from many nations, some groups calling unsuccessfully for an international boycott of the 2014 Winter Olympics in Sochi, Russia. Yet, in many places, Muslims—who number somewhere between 7 and 15 percent of the population—and Christians live in harmony. In 2009 Russian secondary schools began teaching Alexander Solzhenitsyn's long-banned book about Stalin-era Soviet labor camps, *The Gulag Archipelago*. By the later 2010s rap music had become popular among youth, with rappers like Big Baby Tape, Oxxxymiron, and GONE.Fludd. Since pop music and access to television and radio appearances is heavily guarded by cultural officials, musicians such as rappers who crave creative independence have made the Internet the dominant force in music distribution. Hip-hop and its cosmopolitan values have spread through Russian culture with music, visual art, movies, dance, and clothing styles, worrying the Kremlin. Rappers avoid direct political references, but some songs describe the dark, alcohol-soaked reality of urban life.

Until the mid-2010s Putin sought good relations with Germany, France, the United States, and China, but he often opposed U.S. foreign policies, especially in the Middle East, and maintained alliances with authoritarian regimes such as Iran and Syria. But many problems remained. While the Russian middle class grew, the contrasts between rich and poor became stark as oil money flowed to the well connected. As young people from rural villages move to cities, the remaining farmers are mostly older. While elegantly dressed men and women in Moscow cavorted in fine restaurants and glitzy casinos, some remote towns went without heat and power. In addition, corruption, poverty, unaccountability, weak legal institutions, and the festering conflicts in the Caucasus stifled development. Russia ranks fourth in military spending, about a tenth that of the United States. Some polls have showed that a majority of Russians preferred the communist years to the new Russia, many people expressing nostalgia for Stalin and Lenin. The regime has been quietly rehabilitating Stalin, with statues in cities and a museum in his hometown in Georgia. But others remember his victims. In 2017 Putin, who has called the breakup of the USSR the "greatest geopolitical catastrophe of the twentieth century," barely acknowledged the centennial of the Russian Revolution, perhaps because, as an autocrat, he did not want a celebration of "revolution." Historians in Russia and the West still debate the Russian Revolution and the future of socialism.

28-4b The New Eastern Europe

The changes in the USSR resonated throughout eastern Europe. In the late 1980s Mikhail Gorbachev, who admired Hungarian market socialism, promoted reform because the USSR could no longer afford to subsidize these states. When it became clear that the USSR would not protect the largely unpopular eastern European governments, they fell like dominoes. Democratic movements once underground surfaced. Hungary adopted democracy, Solidarity came to power in Poland, and East Germans streamed across the border into West Germany. The world watched on television as Berliners gleefully knocked down the Berlin Wall, the symbol of Cold War division, carrying off its bricks as souvenirs. Soon the East German regime and the other communist governments collapsed or were overthrown. After massive demonstrations forced communist leaders to resign in a largely peaceful "Velvet Revolution," Czechoslovaks elected as president playwright and former rock group lyricist Václav Havel (vax-LAV hah-VEL) (1936–2011), who had been frequently arrested for his pro-democracy activities. Havel announced, "Your government, my people, has been returned to you."[21]

The new democratic or semi-democratic governments replaced planned economies with market forces; eastern Europeans took up voting enthusiastically. Yet, reformers did not anticipate the results of their policies. Ending communism

---

[21]Quoted in James Wilkenson and H. Stuart Hughes, *Contemporary Europe: A History*, 10th ed. (Upper Saddle River, NJ: Prentice-Hall, 2004), 559.

remembered communist-era free education, health care, and subsidized housing. Shops were full of attractive goods, but few people could afford to buy them. For some years only Poland and the Czech Republic enjoyed robust economic growth. While some economies gradually improved, pockets of high unemployment remained and the rich–poor gap widened. And severe pollution remained common in some countries, especially Bulgaria and Poland. The 2008–2009 world recession undermined many economies; most only slowly recovered. But, except for Russia (fifth), Poland (tenth), and the Czech Republic (twelfth), none of them are among the twenty largest economies in Europe.

Diverse political parties competed for power. Capitalizing on popular support for the social safety net, former Communist Party members, calling themselves reform communists, won some national elections, competing for power with free market advocates, pro-Western liberals, and right-wing nationalists. In a striking repudiation of the Soviet legacy, reform communists often supported joining the European Union and even NATO. Eventually most eastern European nations joined these groupings. Women have sometimes led nations, among them Croatia, Romania, Lithuania, Poland, Bulgaria, and Slovakia. Few anti-communists regretted the changes, however jarring they were. Adam Michnik, a leader of Polish Solidarity, concluded that "without the slightest hesitation it is much better to live in a country that is democratic, prosperous and thus boring."[22]

The greatest instability plagued Yugoslavia, an artificial federation of states that self-destructed in bloody civil wars (see Map 28.4). Created for political convenience after World War I, Yugoslavia contained antagonistic ethnic and religious groups. After Marshal Tito, the product of a mixed Croat–Serb marriage who kept the lid on ethnic hatreds, died in 1980, the nationalistic Orthodox Serbs tried to dominate the federation, while the Catholic Croats and Slovenians and the Bosnian and Albanian Muslims wanted independence for their regions. In 1991 the Serb-dominated Yugoslav army tried to stop Slovenia and Croatia from breaking away, but the United Nations sent in peacekeeping troops to secure their independence. In 1992 the Muslim majority in multiethnic Bosnia declared independence, opposed by minority Serbs and Croats. Bosnian Serb militias, aided covertly by the largest Yugoslav state, Serbia, massacred thousands of Muslims, using a new term for genocide, "ethnic cleansing." Western Europeans seemed more reluctant than Americans to lavish money on the military or send armed forces into combat. The United States, not Europe, led the intervention to end the killing and restore order in Yugoslavia. United Nations peacemakers and U.S. air strikes under NATO auspices forced a peace in 1995. The Bosnia conflict killed 200,000 people and generated four million refugees. In 1999 violence returned when the Albanian majority in Kosovo, Serbia's southern region, revolted; Serbs responded with ferocity, prompting another NATO-imposed settlement in 2000. Thousands of NATO troops remained in Bosnia for years and some are still in Kosovo, a symbol of unresolved challenges, but tensions still simmer.

Sovfoto/Universal Image Group/Getty Images

IMAGE 28.7 **The Velvet Revolution** Protesters, mainly high school students, took to the streets in Prague, Czechoslovakia, in 1989 to protest the communist government and demand democracy. These protests, known as the Velvet Revolution for their peaceful nature, were led by Václav Havel, pictured on the posters carried by protesters.

Q How does this protest compare with others you may have seen or read about?

uncorked ethnic hatreds and rivalries going back centuries. Slovaks seceded from the Czechs, forming their own country; Romanians repressed the large Hungarian minority; several countries persecuted or avoided providing schools to the unpopular Romany (Gypsies); and prejudice against Jews intensified.

The rapid move to capitalism, while providing abundant consumer goods, also proved destabilizing, giving shock without therapy. While millions lost work as obsolete factories closed, western European or North American companies bought many of the remaining enterprises. Dazzled by Western consumer goods, eastern Europeans may have underestimated the risks accompanying Western-style capitalism. Many people fondly

---

[22]Quoted in Vinen, *History in Fragments*, 520.

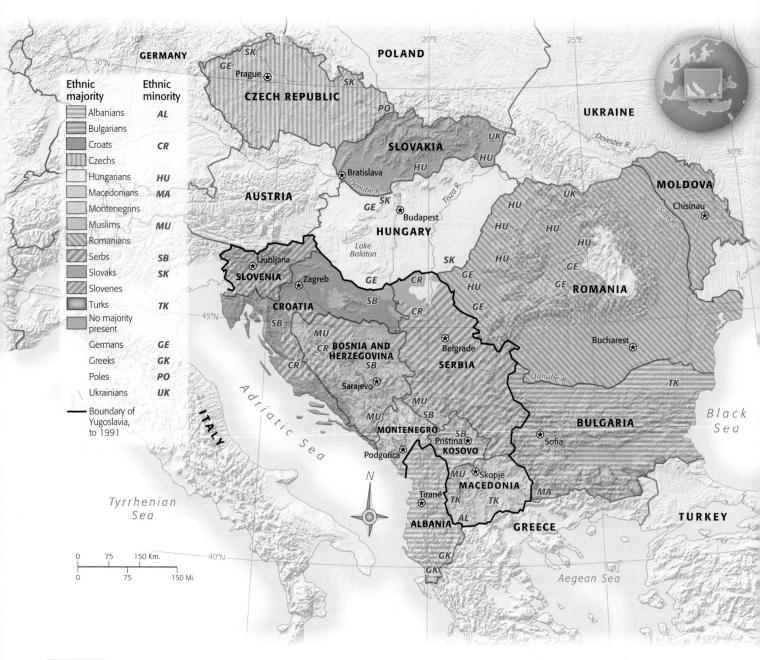

MAP 28.4 **Ethnic Conflicts in Eastern Europe** Many of the nations in central and eastern Europe contain substantial ethnic minorities, and tensions between various groups have often led to conflict. In Yugoslavia, the conflicts between the major ethnic groups—Serbs, Croats, Bosnian Muslims, and Albanians—led to violence and civil war at the end of the twentieth century.

Q Which of these countries has the greatest diversity of ethnic groups?

28-4c Toward European Unity and Disunity

Germany's reunification, the unity movement, and the 2008–2009 economic collapse dominated western Europe in the years after 1989. With the East German collapse, Germany was quickly reunified in 1990, but the results were mixed. For many East Germans, merging with prosperous West Germany offered access to a materially comfortable life. But reunification, which cost billions, threw the German economy into a tailspin. Before reunification West Germany enjoyed a long boom, but a decade later, the reunified nation was stuck

in deep recession. Since Germany has western Europe's largest economy, the slump dragged down the rest of Europe. Many East German workers lost jobs as obsolete factories were closed or sold to West Germans, who often downsized the workforce. The unemployment rate in the east was twice as high as in the west and wages much lower. As a result, some angry youth turned to right-wing, often neo-Nazi, groups that favored heavy metal rock music whose songs promoted hatred of foreigners and immigrants. Yet, Germany eventually recovered, becoming an export machine and by far Europe's largest economy, over twice the size of the second largest, the United Kingdom. By 2019 Germany had eighty-four million people. But the divide between the less affluent east, where many feel like second class citizens, and the more prosperous, cosmopolitan west has endured, raising questions of German identity and culture.

Worried by Germany's problems, western European leaders believed that hastening unification would stabilize post-communist Europe. The Maastricht Treaty, signed in 1992, proposed economic and monetary union that required budgetary and wage restraint as a prelude. Most treaty signers adopted the euro as their currency. Unity was aided by other factors. Millions of Europeans were multilingual, moving easily between cultures, and many studied in other countries. This cosmopolitanism influenced the arts. The popular Greek singer Nana Mouskeri **(NA-na mouse-KUR-ee)** gained a large international audience by recording in English, French, German, Spanish, and Greek. The Eurotunnel, stretching ninety-four miles under the English Channel, made possible a three-hour train ride from London to Paris, symbolizing the decline of political and cultural borders.

The European Union (EU) doubled its membership from twelve nations in 1993 to twenty-eight by 2019, including ten former Soviet bloc states and republics. The Czech Republic, Poland, Hungary, and Estonia had joined in 2004. The Danish prime minister told prospective new EU members: "In 1989 brave and visionary people brought about the collapse of the Berlin Wall. They could no longer tolerate the forced division of Europe. Today we are giving life to their hopes."[23] The EU became collectively the world's largest economy, a bloc of over five hundred million people encompassing most of Europe and enjoying a combined economic power of 22 percent of global GDP, slightly larger than that of the United States. Before the 2008–2009 economic collapse, Ireland, whose poverty had long spurred emigration, became known as the "Celtic Tiger" because of its rapid growth. Many thousands of migrants from Europe and Asia moved to Ireland for jobs, fostering multiethnic neighborhoods in Dublin. Many Irish emigrants also returned home.

Conducting a quarter of the world's commerce and economic production, the EU joined the United States and East Asia (especially China and Japan) in leading what some specialists called a tripolar world economy. However, critics called the EU a faceless bureaucracy with innumerable rules that compromised national independence; two of Europe's most prosperous nations, Norway and Switzerland, declined membership. The EU leaders were cautious in admitting former Soviet bloc states with weak economies and autocratic leaders. Largely Muslim Turkey long sought membership, so far unsuccessfully (due partly to a mixed human-rights record and, by the later 2010s, an increasingly authoritarian government), fostering a debate about how to define Europe that spilled over into efforts to prepare an EU constitution. Amid much controversy, the proposed constitution rejected any mention of Europe's Christian heritage. After some shocking rejections, it was modified into a treaty forming a stronger executive and European parliament while promising more democracy, transparency, and efficiency, winning most members' approval.

In the 1990s, stagnant economic conditions fostered austerity policies, unsettling politics and welfare states. Social democrats, who governed many nations in the early 1990s, now jockeyed with centrists, free market conservatives, Greens, anti-immigrant nationalists, and the fading communists for power. Attempts to roll back but not eliminate social benefits sometimes set off massive protests and long strikes. While many Europeans preferred to maintain what they termed the social market economy, even at the cost of slower economic growth, both the German and French governments replaced thirty-five-hour workweeks with forty-hour workweeks to increase their competitiveness. Despite this change, some large companies continued to downsize or export jobs. European workers have also led movements against economic globalization, which they believe destroys jobs and livelihoods. Saying the world is not for sale, in 1999 French farmer José Bové drove a tractor into a McDonald's outlet, vandalizing it to protest against large global corporations often displacing local enterprises; Bové became a hero to Europeans opposed to globalization and the institutions promoting it. Some critics compared Europe's sluggish social market economies unfavorably with the dynamic U.S. economy. Others countered that many European nations enjoyed a per capita income nearly as high as that in the United States, less inequality, universal health insurance, and a greater commitment to a high quality of life for all.

The 2008–2009 global economic crisis challenged both arguments. The crisis, the worst since the Great Depression, began in the United States with real estate, banking, and financial problems, discrediting the free-wheeling, antiregulatory U.S. economic model. But in 2009 the new Barack Obama-led U.S. administration stopped the free fall and fostered renewed growth, enabling the United States to outperform most of Europe. European economies went into steep decline, greatly stressing welfare states and demonstrating government inadequacies in resolving the problems. Germany, saddled with an indecisive coalition government, reacted slowly as deficits mounted. Iceland's economy collapsed from bank failures; as Ireland's economy rapidly plummeted, thousands of immigrants, losing jobs, returned home and many Irish emigrated. Indeed, the grim job market prompted many Arabs, Africans, and eastern Europeans to leave western European countries. As the crisis continued, Portugal, with a 14 percent unemployment rate, urged jobless citizens to emigrate to its former colonies like Brazil and Angola. Hundreds of thousands of Europeans lived in campgrounds, vehicles, and cheap hotel rooms.

Since 2009 the Mediterranean nations (except for Malta) continued to experience higher unemployment rates and public debt than the northern and eastern European nations, which also generally enjoyed higher GDP growth. Some countries, including Germany, the Netherlands, and the Scandinavian nations lowered taxes and trimmed social benefits while not abandoning the welfare state. The recovery proved short-lived in most western European nations, sparking the severe

---

[23]Quoted in Wilkenson and Hughes, *Contemporary Europe*, 590.

austerity policies pushed beginning in 2010 by Germany, now the EU's leader under moderate conservative Angela Merkel (b. 1954), an East German chemist who became chancellor in 2005. Germany's budget cuts and spending reductions generated widespread misery—cutting public-sector salaries, eliminating public works projects, but still not generating growth or jobs. Critics argue that Germany has been too obsessed with public debt, eliminating their debt in 2012 but then running surpluses. It stopped fighting unemployment and demanded spending cuts, which slowed the recovery. Consumers stopped spending. Austerity also stalled Britain's recovery; economic weakness and rising prices mixed with income stagnation fostered more poverty and hunger. Some poorer southern European economies, among them Italy, Spain, Portugal, and especially Greece, experiencing huge job losses and defunding of social services, needed EU loans and bailouts to pay their bills but had to adopt austerity and restructure to avert collapse. Some EU members wanted Greece and perhaps other troubled countries, whose problems strained other Europeans' patience and finances, expelled from the Eurozone. By 2019 most economies remained mired in problems, with high unemployment or underemployment, lower wages, and shrinking middle classes. Health care systems faltered just as chronic diseases and obesity became more common in the world, raising health care costs. In challenging times export-driven economies are most vulnerable; much of Europe relies on manufacturing, but much of the world has been experiencing a manufacturing recession.

Generally prosperous and politically stable for many years, Germany has long remained the EU's most important member but has also faced problems. Germany enjoyed a ten-year economic boom but by 2019 the economy was slowing. Economic and wage growth have been below average for over twenty years. In 2019 the German economy shrank 0.1 percent, indicating a technical recession. While unemployment is low, over a fifth of Germans have only temporary, low-wage, or marginal jobs and wealth inequality remains high and social mobility low. Poverty has been rising. The world's third largest exporter and reliant on manufacturing cars and other industrial goods, Germany is vulnerable to the uncertainties of international trade, and by 2019 was buffeted by U.S. tariffs and the British decision to exit the EU. A German economist summarized the dilemma: "We have a whole cocktail of international challenges.... They [the far-right] will say: 'Nothing works, big industry is firing employees, globalization is creating problems.'"[24] Germany was one of the world's safest and most peaceful countries, with a declining crime rate for a decade. But a recent crime spree (some of it traced to nationalist far-right supporters) has unsettled the country, as a German psychologist noted: "We are living in a time of awakening, from refugees to Brexit, Trump, [Turkish leader] Erdogan, climate change—suddenly Germans are feeling that they cannot stop time and remain in the protective bubble of prosperity that has been Germany of the past decade. This has left behind a diffuse angst about the future."[25]

While Germany weathered the stormy waters better than most, France saw anemic growth, straining the French-German alliance and forcing the French to ponder whether they can afford their comfortable way of life or become more competitive and flexible in the world economy. In 2017 the French government relaxed their labor code to try to end stagnation that many attributed to high unemployment, slow growth, and overly strong worker protections. Raising the retirement age and working hours made it easier to hire and fire workers but it also weakened unions, fostered more temporary jobs, and gave employers more power, sparking much public resistance. The most serious protests came in 2018–2019 as thousands of mostly working-class marchers, known as the Yellow Vests, targeted and sometimes violently attacked symbols of economic privilege over a proposed gas tax increase. The protests reflected a general discontent with the centrist, pro-free enterprise government of President Immanuel Macron (b. 1977), elected in 2017 as a reformer.

The economic damage from the various crises strained the EU and its monetary system. The euro, a single currency shared by many EU nations, was adapted in prosperous times but lacked institutions to make it work in harsher conditions. The crises in poorer nations like Greece and Spain stressed the euro, suggesting the need to reform the euro system. EU members debate whether to move toward further unity or step back and allow more national sovereignty and uniqueness. Thus, saddled with high joblessness and inflation, the EU's future may depend on economic recovery. A German journalist wrote in 2013 that Europe needed a new vision to cement emotional ties: "Perhaps the answer is to conceive of Europe in the flesh, with colors, smells, folklore, poetic force. And variety."[26]

The biggest challenge to the health and future of the EU came in Britain, where many right-wing and left-wing EU opponents, known as Euro-skeptics, disliked the EU's complex regulations as well as free migration between EU nations that brought in many immigrants, especially from eastern Europe. Pushed hard by the anti-EU movement (known as Brexit), which may have been secretly funded and promoted in part by Russia, the Conservative (Tory)–led government held a national referendum on whether to leave or remain in the EU. The Remain forces, who supported maintaining the customs union, single market, and free movement, won the majority of votes in London, Scotland, and Northern Ireland. But the referendum passed nationally by a narrow margin, with most of the Leave (or Brexit) voters coming from England and parts of Wales. In 2017 the Tory government headed by Theresa May invoked Britain's right under the treaty to leave, provoking a long political crisis as the divide between Leavers and Remainers deepened. A withdrawal plan negotiated with the EU by May satisfied neither side and was rejected in Parliament. Leavers split on whether the country should leave with or without a deal. Already, given the uncertainties, many EU migrants, who for years had helped keep the service, agriculture, and health care sectors functioning, were returning home, leaving farms, hotels, restaurants, and hospitals facing a labor shortage. Fearing

[24]Klaus Deutsch, quoted in "Bad News for Germany's Economy Might Be Good News for the Far Right," *New York Times* (August 6, 2019).

[25]Stephan Grunewald, quoted in "A Summer of Angst in One of the World's Safest Countries," *New York Times* (August 18, 2019).

[26]Olivier Guez, "Are There Any Europeans Left?" *New York Times* (March 13, 2013), 4.

London is losing its status as the global business crossroad, some major international businesses and banks as well as many corporate employees from EU countries have started relocating to other European cities. One major debate concerned relations between the Republic of Ireland, an EU member state, and Northern Ireland, part of the UK, which had been at peace since 1999 in part because of an open border. But a No-Deal Brexit might reimpose a hard border and reignite sectarian passions in once deeply troubled Northern Ireland, where divisions between the majority Protestants and minority Catholics run deep.

Most economists predicted significant economic problems with Brexit, including lower per capita income even with a negotiated leave, and a catastrophe for the economy generally, especially food and medical supplies, gasoline, and health care, with a No-Deal Brexit. Remainers feared the Brexiteers, who had campaigned on promises to "Fund our NHS," will instead adopt a U.S.-style "for-profit" health insurance system that leaves many people uninsured, privatizing the National Health Service and universal health insurance. The crisis deepened and debate continued after Boris Johnson, a controversial, flamboyant, and passionate No-Deal Brexiteer, became prime minister and forced his critics out of the government. As the Brexit deadline loomed, the parliament remained deadlocked, tempers flared, and EU–Britain negotiations failed to produce a new agreement that could pass Parliament. Britain remained in an unresolved crisis; some sought a second referendum but Johnson opted for new elections that he hoped to win and then implement Brexit. EU leaders feared that without Britain Europe would lapse into a full-blown recession. The crisis may also spur an already disaffected pro-EU Scotland and perhaps even Northern Ireland to seek secession from the United Kingdom. Some worry that this might revitalize longstanding movements for autonomy or secession in other EU countries such as Spain (Catalonia, the Basques), Belgium (Flanders), France (Corsica), and perhaps even Italy (Lombardy).

Europeans also faced other challenges. A century earlier overcrowded and the world's greatest exporter of people, Europe now has a declining population, due mainly to the world's lowest birthrate: 1.2 children per woman. Eastern Europe, the nations once part of Yugoslavia, and the former Soviet republics, with fifteen of the world's twenty most rapidly shrinking populations, face a serious demographic crisis. Population decline posed a long-term problem: With more people retiring from than entering the workforce, younger workers had more responsibility for financing government services for the elderly. Yet, Europeans became increasingly hostile to Middle Eastern and African immigrants, many of them unemployed young men who resented discrimination and police harassment. Tensions simmered, sometimes sparking rioting and vandalism, thus raising the issue of what sort of integration of immigrants was possible. For example, neither Britain's permissive multiculturalism nor France's ardent secularism prevented some conflict between Muslims and Christians. By the early twenty-first century, anti-immigrant parties became more influential, even in tolerant nations like Denmark and the Netherlands. As Europe is being turned into a giant political laboratory Europeans still struggled to define their place in a changing world.

IMAGE 28.8 **Protests for and Against Brexit**
Thousands of British Leave and Remain protesters gathered in London in 2019 to express their views in support and opposition to Brexit. Many Remainers advocated a second referendum as to whether Britain should leave the European Union.

Q Do you think that demonstrations like these can make a difference to political leaders or persuade the general public?

By the later 2010s European politics was in flux and saw the decline or demise of the older, once popular parties, including those of the center-left that had recognized capitalism's upsides and downsides while protecting the welfare state. Hence, the northern European Social Democrats, some plagued by infighting and desperate for new ideas in a changing world, raised the question of what replaces the old system. Several major forces have been gaining strength. The Greens movement has made a spectacular rise in several nations as voters rejected traditional parties and pressed the issue of climate change, mobilizing youth in support. Greens have made climate change, a marginal issue in the twentieth century, mainstream. German Greens want to combine climate and social justice, fostering a fierce debate between people who believe ecology and market economics are compatible against radical advocates of completely changing the growth model. Annalena Baerbock, the German Green coleader, argued that "The Green idea has been European [rather than national] from the outset, because you can't solve environmental problems within national borders."[27] For example, while the Conservatives and leftist Labor Party in Britain have

---

[27]Quoted in "Greens Are the New Hope for Europe's Center. For the Far Right, They're Enemy No. 1," *New York Times* (July 14, 2019).

maintained considerable support, the Greens, centrist Liberal Democrats, and right-wing nationalist Brexit Party gained strength. Germany's long-dominant Christian Democrats and Social Democrats lost followers to the left-leaning Greens and the far-right populist AfD (Alternative for Germany), which won 13 percent of the vote (mostly in economically depressed eastern Germany) in the 2017 federal elections. While they lack an ideological mooring, the centrists have been trying to reinvent themselves as a popular force. Hence, in France the two pillars of political life for six decades, the Socialists and center-right Republicans, collapsed, replaced by centrist Immanuel Macron's En Marche and as the main challenger, Marine Le Pen's far-right populist National Front (Rally).

By the 2010s a once marginal but increasingly powerful political force, right-wing populism mixed with nationalism, began to gain significant support in many European nations, posing a threat to the EU and the established political parties while upsetting the political order that had kept Europe stable since World War II. They have become a structural element in the political landscape, scrambling demographic boundaries and holding one hundred-fifteen of seven hundred fifty-one seats in the European parliament elected in 2019. Feeding on popular frustration with widespread unemployment and other economic challenges, the populists shared a strongly anti-immigrant and anti-Muslim agenda, Euro-skepticism, and a contempt for the political establishment and even liberal democracy. Most are opposed to environmentalism, climate change activism, multinational corporations, and globalization while defending Christian values. Some of the new populist parties had roots in neo-Nazi, fascist, and sometimes anti-Semitic movements of the past and, in many cases, a sympathy for Putin's nationalist regime in Russia and the nationalist, divisive, disruptive, and anti-immigrant, anti-Muslim politics of President Donald Trump in the United States. Among other concerns, critics worry that populists are eroding human and civil rights and constitutional principles while centralizing power. The far-right leaders of Hungary and Poland have been particularly open about their antidemocratic agenda. Some observers compare today's far-right with the fascists in Europe in the 1920s and 1930s and fear that higher unemployment, fueled in part by the U.S.–China trade war, and mass hysteria could lay the groundwork for fascist-type regimes. Calling for a united Europe, Pope Francis has repeatedly warned against extreme nationalism and argued that some recent nationalist speakers sound like "Hitler in 1934." But some conservative cardinals court the far-right.

By 2019 the populists had come to power (Hungary, Italy, Poland, Denmark) or become a major party or faction (Austria, France, Britain, Sweden, Czech Republic, Estonia, Latvia, Lithuania, Finland, Greece, Spain, Slovakia, Belgium, Bulgaria, the Netherlands) in various European nations, pushing what some called their "illiberal" agenda. For example, when the conservative-far-right coalition came to power in Austria in 2017 they closed Islamic schools, banned burkas and face coverings in public, and slashed benefits for immigrants. Italy, the Eurozone's third largest economy, struggled for years and then went into recession in 2018–2019. Continuing political crises and a very high national debt (second to Greece in the Eurozone) have

made more government aid for Italy's people difficult. The 2018 elections brought a populist coalition between the far-right League, headed by Matteo Salvini, and the quirky, antiestablishment 5 Stars Movement to power. Critics compared the ambitious, charismatic, anti-gay, anti-Muslim Salvini to Mussolini in 1922. But the coalition collapsed in mid-2019, leaving politics in disarray and Salvini's prospects unclear as various parties competed to put together new coalitions. Sweden has accepted more refugees per capita than any other European country, but this sparked an anti-immigrant backlash. Sweden's willingness to pay for a generous social safety net was tested by the refugee influx. A far-right party with neo-Nazi roots—the Sweden Democrats—captured 18 percent of the vote in the 2018 elections, assisted by an international disinformation and provocation machine, based in Putin's Russia and the U.S. far-right, devoted to cultivating and amplifying far-right anti-immigrant, anti-globalization hatred. In Germany, as the right-wing AfD gained a following, the government that had trained and placed in jobs thousands of asylum seekers began deporting them in 2019, even though labor-desperate businesses badly wanted them to stay. But in some cases, such as Slovakia in 2019, voters have turned right-wing governments out of office. Zuzana Caputova, a liberal activist and supporter of the EU, minorities, and gay rights, defeated the corrupt president and his far-right allies to become Slovakia's first woman president. She made her goals for reform clear: "I offer my expertise, emotion, and activism. I offer my mind, my heart, and my hands. I want to be the voice of those who are not heard."[28] The Slovak far-right also lost seats to the Greens but may still remain the coalition government.

28-4d Europe and Russia in the Global System

With the end of the Cold War, Russia, western Europe, and the former Soviet bloc states searched for new roles in the world. After 2000 Europe's relations with its military ally and main trading rival, the United States, became more complicated. As part of NATO and sharing the goal of combating international terrorism, some nations sent troops to Afghanistan after the 2001 terrorist attacks on the United States. But most Europeans mistrusted the U.S. decision to invade oil-rich Iraq in 2003, believing it had little to do with fighting terrorism and would destabilize the Middle East. European nations such as France and Germany criticized the U.S. invasion and occupation. Although their people strongly opposed the war, some close U.S. allies, such as Italy, Poland, and Spain, sent small token forces, but only Britain had a sizable military presence in Iraq. Along with the United States, NATO supplied aid and weapons to Libyan rebels in 2011 to successfully overthrow the autocratic Gaddafi regime, but most Europeans were reluctant to become involved in the complex Syrian civil war. In 2013 France sent troops to push back Islamist rebels in Mali.

For some years Russia sought good relations with the EU, the United States, China, and the nearby Islamic nations, such as Iran, but also acted in its own self-interest, sometimes opposing U.S. or EU policies. NATO needed to redefine its mission as it

---

[28]Quoted in "Slovakia's First Female President Takes the Helm of a Divided Country," *New York Times* (June 16, 2019), A9.

added many former Warsaw Pact nations, discomforting Russia. After Russia warned NATO against admitting former Soviet republics such as Ukraine and Georgia, it reinforced its threat in 2008 by briefly invading Georgia, a small U.S. ally and former Soviet republic in the Caucasus, to protect pro-Russian enclaves. In 2014 relations between Ukraine and Russia rapidly deteriorated after massive protests in Ukraine generated a bloodless revolution that overthrew an unpopular, autocratic pro-Russian Ukrainian president and installed in power pro-Western nationalists. Many Russian speakers in eastern Ukraine became restless. Russia armed pro-Russian separatist militias while sending Russian troops to parts of eastern Ukraine, sparking a local military confrontation that still festers. As part of the action Russian forces supported an uprising as Russian troops occupied and then annexed the strategic Crimean Peninsula, where ethnic Russians were the majority population, and the Russian Black Sea fleet was based. These actions provoked tensions with the U.S. and western Europe and more turmoil in eastern Ukraine. Since then the Crimea annexation has prevented normal relations between the two countries. In 2014 the G-8 Group of major nations expelled Russia and some Western nations imposed sanctions on Russian leaders. In 2019 U.S. President Donald Trump was accused of illegally delaying promised military aid for Ukraine's resistance to Russia in order to pressure Ukraine into helping him investigate an American political rival. This generated an impeachment inquiry in the U.S. Congress.

In the later 2010s Russia has struggled as oil prices plummeted. This has prompted Russia's turn toward, and greater reliance on, China, its longtime rival, but by 2019 China's economy was slowing. Russian propaganda attacks against the West have long derided liberal democracy as chaotic and anarchic. The regime has routinely arrested and jailed dissidents. Crackdowns in 2019 mobilized dissent. Large, well-organized public protest marches in Moscow involving over fifty thousand people, mainly youth, demanded the release of several leading dissidents and the right to vote for independent candidates in local elections. The protests were broken up with force and Putin unleashed a sweeping crackdown on dissent, arresting activists, journalists, doctors, and religious believers, raising new fears of a dysfunctional state or, worse, a revived police state. Young Russians have never known any leader except Putin; as one told reporters: "I am 20 years old, and in my entire life there has not been a single day of freedom."[29]

By the later 2010s Russian relations with many Western nations had deteriorated further, in part because of Russian use of money and the Internet to interfere in U.S., British, and perhaps other nations' internal affairs and elections. As a presidential candidate Donald Trump openly sought Russian help in his campaign to defeat the Democratic candidate, Hillary Clinton; investigations that followed his victory found various instances of Russian contacts with Trump's campaign, causing a political uproar in the United States and several convictions of Trump aides. As president, Trump has consistently sought close relations with Putin, who wanted U.S. sanctions lifted, but the U.S. Congress forced more sanctions on Russia for their interference. Russian support for countries opposed by the U.S., such as Iran, Syria, Cuba, and Venezuela, has further complicated relations. Russian relations with China, its longtime rival, have improved

since they share an antipathy toward the U.S. and support some of the same anti-U.S. nations.

Europe also felt squeezed by the U.S.–Iran dispute. The U.S., Britain, Germany, France, and China, as well as the EU, were part of the 2015 deal in which Iran would limit their nuclear program in exchange for the West lifting sanctions. But in 2017 President Trump withdrew the U.S. from the agreement and reimposed U.S. sanctions, demanding that the EU signers do the same and threatening war with Iran. But most, hoping to maintain the agreement and the stability it fostered, have been reluctant to support the U.S. agenda. NATO has also wanted to avoid an expensive new arms race. Putting in place the arms control structure of the Cold War and after had been laboriously designed over years of fraught negotiations between the two superpowers. The structure helped keep the world safe from nuclear annihilation by destroying, limiting, or monitoring tens of thousands of nuclear weapons. In 2019 the U.S. abandoned the major treaty just as new strategic competitors—China, North Korea, Iran, and perhaps Saudi Arabia—asserted themselves as regional powers. The one remaining arms treaty ends in 2021. Many experts fear a new arms race would likely foster a more dangerous and unstable environment, perhaps precipitating unwanted conflicts and demanding vastly more military spending among the biggest powers. Smaller powers could follow. With NATO's bonds already fraying, partly from U.S. demands or disinterest, Trump has threatened to pull out entirely unless the other member countries increase their military spending in an era of economic stress and divisive politics.

The trade war between U.S. and China has increasingly been creating a bipolar world, with Europe caught in the middle. The situation reminds some historians of the Cold War years, with an increasingly polarized world being split into two political and economic spheres. Many experts fear the trade war could undermine or destroy the world economic order, which, despite its flaws and inequalities, brought stability for many decades. EU relations with the U.S. have deteriorated as Trump defined the EU as a trade and regulatory foe rather than as an ally. While reluctant to antagonize the U.S., many Europeans have an interest in China as trade partner and investor. By 2019 China's Belt and Road Initiative included twelve EU members (among them Italy), and more may join. EU and German officials have worried about China's growing influence over the European economy, the high-tech firms that Chinese companies have acquired, and the ports China seeks to control. But even in Germany some cities bid for Chinese investment to build factories. As one critic noted, Europe's ambivalence toward Chinese investment could be summed up as "fear the power, love the money." Participation may come at a price. Greece has been the most willing to take on Chinese aid, investments, and loans, but they have also had to lease China a port and defend China's human rights abuses in the United Nations, alienating some EU members and international creditors.

Europeans disagreed on how best to respond to international terrorism and militant Islamic groups. Substantial Muslim immigrant populations complicated policies on the spread of militancy among some people of Arab or South Asian ancestry, especially unemployed youth. Some of the men who attacked

---

[29]Quoted in Anne Applebaum, "Hong Kong and Russia Protesters Fight for Democracy: The West Should Listen and Learn," *Washington Post* (August 16, 2019).

the United States in 2011 had studied in Europe, where Islamic militants recruited them. Deadly terrorist attacks on commuter trains in Madrid in 2004 and the London subway in 2005, which killed several hundred people, showed the potential for terrorist violence but convinced many that Middle East interventions increased terrorist threats. In 2006, riots and demonstrations that occurred when a right-wing, anti-immigrant Danish newspaper published offensive cartoons insulting the Islamic prophet Muhammad showed shocked Europeans how tense Muslim–Western relations had become. The most alienated Muslims in Europe and North America, immigrant or local-born, turned to militant jihadi groups for direction. Hundreds (mostly young) joined the Islamic State forces in Syria or carried out terrorist attacks at home. Since then dozens of attacks large and small, particularly in Britain, France, Belgium, Turkey, and Spain, killing many hundreds of people, shocked Europeans and the world. Most were perpetrated by radical Islamists linked to al-Qaeda or the Islamic State of Iraq and Syria (or ISIS), but some involved far-right militants.

Europeans played key roles in resolving world problems. Europeans took the lead in developing international treaties on issues such as climate change, biological and chemical weapons, international criminal courts, and genocide. U.S. opposition to these treaties built resentment. Like many others, Europeans have struggled to develop policies to combat global warming, which most scientists believe contributes to extreme weather such as the deadly heat waves and destructive winter storms that have walloped Europe in the later 2010s. Before the 2008–2009 economic crisis, Europeans had already identified global warming as the major world problem, and some nations strongly encouraged alternative energy strategies. Many still do. European leaders have been pondering whether the EU—the world's third largest industrial emitter of greenhouse gases and responsible for 10 percent of global emissions—can wean themselves from fossil fuels within thirty years. A large majority of people favor getting to net zero carbon emissions by 2050. So far Britain, Sweden, Finland, and Norway have set the bar highest, seeking to limit or end reliance on fossil fuels in order to reach the goal by then or earlier. If successful it will change everything from the way Europeans heat their homes to how they get to work and what food they grow and eat. Making a fast transition to renewable energy, Denmark now imports no Middle Eastern oil and aims to get 50 percent of all electricity from wind power by 2050. Half of Copenhagen residents now commute to school or work by bicycle. Scotland in the 1960s boomed from North Sea oil but after the oil bust in 2014 has turned to green power and energy, especially wind and tidal power, to revive the economy. Some nations will reach the goal by buying credits while others will develop clean power. Norway, a major oil producer but also an ally in the fight against climate change, hopes to have only electric cars by 2025 but is also looking for new oil and gas fields abroad. But some nations, especially in eastern Europe, will struggle; for example, Poland still has a powerful coal lobby.

With the closer political and economic integration that came as the Common Market morphed into the European Community and then to the European Union, which included most of the region's countries, Europe became much more than a geographical expression and a collection of separate countries sharing cultural traditions and a history. Over the years a few European leaders even envisioned a political federation, or united states of Europe, but many hurdles would have to be overcome first. However, the persisting economic problems of recent years have strained unity and raised questions about the future of the EU and the euro currency. And, as has been true for centuries, Russia remains something of a world apart, avoiding close partnership while also hoping to influence the countries to their west. Although Europeans have slowly rebuilt their shared institutions and values since 1945, nations still remain central to life. While Europe is no longer the powerhouse it had been in the nineteenth century, its peoples are carving out a new place in the world. At the end of the Cold War a respected Russian historian harked back to Peter the Great and Catherine the Great, advising Russians that, "Our future lies in openness to the entire world and in enlightenment."[30] Whether or not Russia will follow this path, many people hope that the rest of Europe would continue to embrace openness and enlightenment.

KEY POINTS

▶ The collapsing Soviet bloc and Soviet decay created problems for Mikhail Gorbachev, and he was replaced by Boris Yeltsin, who allowed independence for all the non-Russian Soviet republics, some of which ended up with authoritarian governments, and pursued a rapid shift to capitalism.

▶ With the fall of the USSR, formerly communist eastern Europe became more democratic, though many countries struggled economically and others suffered political upheaval, especially Yugoslavia, which experienced violent civil war and "ethnic cleansing."

▶ German reunification, celebrated at first, yielded mixed results, while the European Union grew to include many nations but faced questions over whether to admit non-Christian nations and over what form its constitution should take.

▶ European nations struggled to navigate the evolving world economy, to deal with Islamic terrorism, and to work out relations with each other and with the United States, whose 2003 invasion of Iraq was generally unpopular in most countries.

▶ Thanks to economic problems and a large migration of refugees from the Middle East and Africa, by the 2010s nationalist far-right populists had come to power or had influence in many countries, pushing an anti-Muslim, anti-immigrant, antiglobalization, anti-EU agenda while undermining human rights and civil liberties.

---

[30]Dimitry Likhachev, quoted in Catherine Evtuhov et al., *A History of Russia's Peoples, Legends, Events, Forces* (Boston: Houghton Mifflin, 2004), 819.

Chapter Summary

Emerging shattered from World War II, western Europeans were determined to build a new Europe. Although the Cold War divided Europe, western Europeans rebuilt democracies and began a movement to foster unity. Sparked by French–German reconciliation, they established institutions for economic cooperation that eventually became the European Union, which established a single currency and a European parliament. Stability also resulted from the rise of welfare states, which guaranteed all citizens fair access to housing, health care, and education. Social democratic parties took the lead in creating the safety net, but supporting it became more costly because of growing economic problems and unemployment rates. Gradually family and gender relations changed, while millions of immigrants reshaped European societies.

After the war the Soviet Union maintained a communist-run government and economy, with a powerful state dominating life and work. The Soviets installed communist governments in eastern Europe and brutally repressed opposition, but they failed to foster much economic dynamism and lost ground in the Cold War to a more powerful U.S.–western Europe alliance. By the 1980s the Soviet system and Soviet bloc needed reform. Although communism generated modernization and improved living standards, ethnic minorities were restless, the bureaucracy was stifling, and the economy remained stagnant. Unsettling reforms resulted in the collapse of communism and the dismantling of the Soviet Empire in 1991. Since then the former communist nations have struggled to sustain capitalism and liberal democracy. Meanwhile, most European nations joined the European Union, the world's third largest economic power. Germany struggled to make reunification work, Russia debated a new role in the world, and the European Union sought the appropriate mix of cooperation and national sovereignty.

Key Terms

Marshall Plan 747
Eurocommunism 748
Greens 748
Commonwealth of Nations 748
NATO 749
Soviet bloc 749

Warsaw Pact 749
Ostpolitik 751
welfare states 753
bhangra 757
existentialism 758
postmodernism 758

Brezhnev Doctrine 762
glasnost 764
perestroika 764
oligarchs 766

The Americas and the Pacific Basin: New Roles in the Contemporary World, Since 1945

"
It's curious. Our generals listen to the [U.S.] Pentagon. They learn the ideology of National Security and commit all these crimes [against the Argentine people]. Then the same [American] people who gave us this gift come and ask, "How did these terrible things happen?"
"

—President Raul Alfonsin of Argentina, 1984[1]

AP Images/Kiichiro Sato

IMAGE 29.1 **A Naturalization Ceremony** Seeking political freedom or economic opportunities, immigrants flock to the United States, and many become citizens. At this ceremony, eight hundred residents, representing eighty-eight countries, took the oath of citizenship in Columbus, Ohio, in April 2005.

Q What can this photo tell us about the racial and ethnic diversity of immigrants to the United States?

[1]Quoted in James D. Cockcroft, *Latin America: History, Politics, and U.S. Policy,* 2nd ed. (Chicago: Nelson-Hall, 1996), 567.

The women appeared one day in 1977 in the historic Plaza de Mayo, adjacent to the presidential palace in downtown Buenos Aires, Argentina. For several years the military government had waged a bloody campaign to eliminate dissidents, killing or abducting some thirty thousand people and arresting and torturing thousands more. Some may have belonged to outlawed leftist groups, but many simply held progressive ideas or were friends with regime critics. Initially only the feared secret police paid attention to the dozen or so frightened women who came once a week, standing in silent protest. A year later the peaceful protesters numbered more than a thousand. Wearing kerchiefs on their heads and sensible flat shoes, the mothers and grandmothers, pinning to their chests photographs of missing family members, victims of the state's terror, asked: Where were their missing children, husbands, pregnant daughters, and grandchildren? The "Mothers and Grandmothers of the Plaza de Mayo" challenged one of Latin America's most brutal tyrannies. Most were housewives fighting, as one put it, vicious armed forces, spineless politicians, complicit clergy, muzzled press, and co-opted labor unions. Their courageous protest inspired others in Argentina and around the world with hope and moral outrage at military repression. The gatherings continued weekly until 1983, when the regime fell and a civilian government could investigate the disappearances. Most never learned their loved ones' fates.

The Plaza de Mayo protest illustrates how some Latin Americans addressed the authoritarian governments they lived under, sometimes for decades. Latin American countries often shifted back and forth between dictatorship and democracy, neither system fostering widespread economic prosperity amid the stark rich–poor divide. Many Latin Americans also resented the United States, which often supported dictatorships that welcomed U.S. investment. The United States remained the hemisphere's dominant power while expanding its global influence. U.S. president Harry Truman (g. 1945–1953) argued in 1947 that American political and business practices could thrive at home only if foreign countries embraced similar practices. Hence, the United States became the global workshop and banker, preacher and teacher, umpire and policeman. Between 1946 and 1989, it enjoyed unrivaled military might, economic power, and political-ideological leadership, contested only by the Soviet Union; it remains the major superpower today. Meanwhile, U.S. society increasingly differed from the societies of its North American neighbor, Canada, and the Pacific Basin countries of Australia and New Zealand.

29-1 The United States as a Superpower

▦ NETWORKS ⇄ TRANSITIONS

Q How did the Cold War shape U.S. foreign policies?

Thanks to its size, power, and wealth, the United States has played a major world role, helping Europe and Japan recover from World War II, espousing and often promoting human rights and freedom, lavishing aid on allies, and providing

CONNECTION to TODAY

How were you, your family, and community affected by the wars involving the U.S. in countries like Korea, Vietnam, Afghanistan, and/or Iraq?

leadership in a politically fragmented world. But the U.S. could also destabilize other countries and the world. During the Cold War, competition with the Soviet bloc for allies and strategic advantage shaped U.S. policies, influencing the

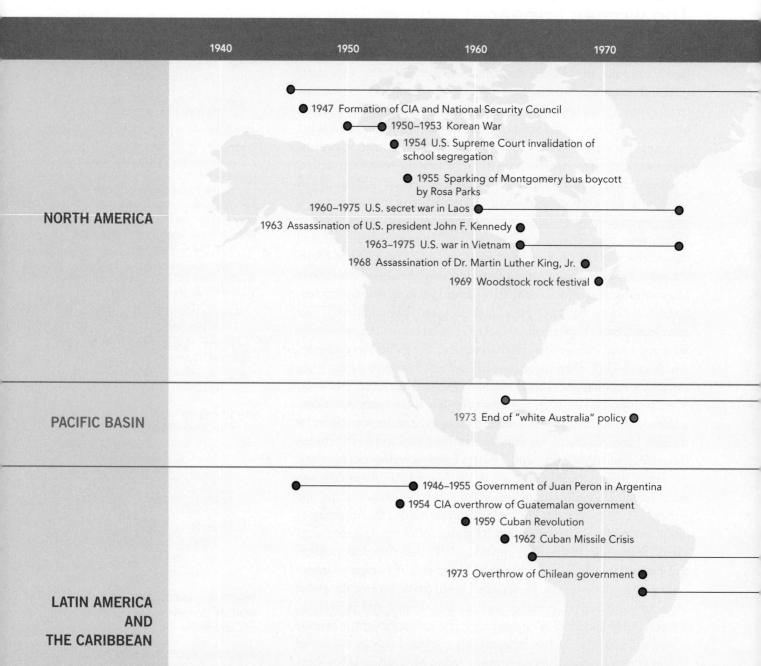

	1940	1950	1960	1970

NORTH AMERICA

1947 Formation of CIA and National Security Council
1950–1953 Korean War
1954 U.S. Supreme Court invalidation of school segregation
1955 Sparking of Montgomery bus boycott by Rosa Parks
1960–1975 U.S. secret war in Laos
1963 Assassination of U.S. president John F. Kennedy
1963–1975 U.S. war in Vietnam
1968 Assassination of Dr. Martin Luther King, Jr.
1969 Woodstock rock festival

PACIFIC BASIN

1973 End of "white Australia" policy

LATIN AMERICA AND THE CARIBBEAN

1946–1955 Government of Juan Peron in Argentina
1954 CIA overthrow of Guatemalan government
1959 Cuban Revolution
1962 Cuban Missile Crisis
1973 Overthrow of Chilean government

world's perceptions of Americans. Soviet domination of eastern Europe, communist victory in China, and the Korean War convinced Americans that communist expansion had to be thwarted. People around the world admired America's democratic ideals, prosperity, and technological ingenuity, but U.S. wars, interventions, support for often authoritarian allies, frequent neglect of human rights, and globalization of capitalism fostered widespread hostility. After the Cold War, the United States and its allies faced new challenges in South Asia, the Middle East, and East Asia and by the 2010s in Europe and the wider world.

29-1a The American Century and the Cold War

World War II was a watershed that forged Americans' vision of world politics. Increased political centralization and economic growth encouraged Americans to accept international involvements, promoting an activist foreign policy. As the global powerbroker and policeman, the United States sought to block its main rival, the Soviet Union, from gaining influence in other countries. Victory over Nazism and Japanese militarism reinforced American confidence and sense of mission. In 1941,

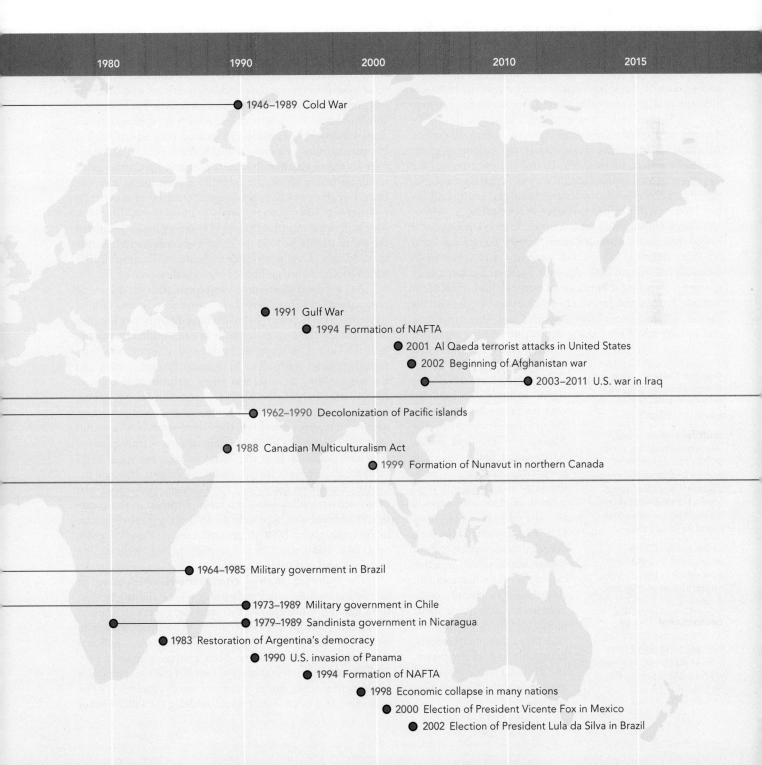

1980   1990   2000   2010   2015

1946–1989 Cold War

1991 Gulf War

1994 Formation of NAFTA

2001 Al Qaeda terrorist attacks in United States

2002 Beginning of Afghanistan war

2003–2011 U.S. war in Iraq

1962–1990 Decolonization of Pacific islands

1988 Canadian Multiculturalism Act

1999 Formation of Nunavut in northern Canada

1964–1985 Military government in Brazil

1973–1989 Military government in Chile

1979–1989 Sandinista government in Nicaragua

1983 Restoration of Argentina's democracy

1990 U.S. invasion of Panama

1994 Formation of NAFTA

1998 Economic collapse in many nations

2000 Election of President Vicente Fox in Mexico

2002 Election of President Lula da Silva in Brazil

Henry Luce, publisher of the most influential U.S. news magazine, *Time*, declared that the twentieth century would be the American Century, imposing global duties and opportunities on Americans. Luce believed that America's idealistic Bill of Rights, magnificent industrial products, and technological skills would be shared with all peoples. His view, while arrogant, reflected a longtime belief in exporting Americans' values and institutions; their nation was the world's model. But U.S.-style capitalism and democracy proved difficult to implant where they had no roots.

After World War II the United States rebuilt defeated Germany and Japan, helped establish global financial networks, lavished aid on western Europe to help stabilize democratic governments, used military forces to protect U.S. allies in Asia, and opposed radical nationalist and communist-led movements in Asia, Africa, the Caribbean, and Latin America. For several decades, as the U.S. economy soared, the American Century idea seemed realistic. But U.S. economic superiority in the 1940s and 1950s derived from unusual conditions. Among the great powers, only the United States had not been bombed or financially drained and could maintain a modern industrial system. Americans alone could mass-produce the consumer goods needed by others. In 1950, the United States accounted for 27 percent of total world economic output. Supplying the world, Americans experienced an economic boom that lasted until the late 1960s and that helped to finance an activist foreign policy.

As the United States became the world economy's engine, it forged close trade links with Canada, western Europe, and Japan while sponsoring foreign aid programs and investment, especially in Asia and Latin America. Such aid and investment spurred an economic renaissance and political stability in western Europe and Japan. However, in developing nations the aid and investment often supported cash crop agriculture and mining while reinforcing dependence on the export of natural resources promoted unbalanced growth. Later, U.S. investment developed light industry, especially textile factories, utilizing cheap labor in countries like Mexico and Thailand. Asian, African, and Latin American countries became key U.S. markets and acquired over a third of American exports by the 1990s, enriching U.S. corporations. However, American consumption of more foreign imports, from Japanese cars to Middle Eastern oil, contributed to chronic trade imbalances; Americans spent more for foreign products than they earned from exports, living beyond their means as globalization fostered outsourcing of manufacturing and jobs.

domino theory A theory that envisioned countries falling one by one to communism and that became a mainstay of U.S. policy.

multilateralism A foreign policy in which the United States sought a common front and a coordination of foreign policies with allies in western Europe, Japan, and Canada, avoiding activities that might enflame world opinion against the United States.

unilateralism A foreign policy in which the United States acted alone in its own perceived national interest even if key allies disapproved.

containment The main U.S. strategy aimed at preventing communists from gaining power, and the USSR from getting political influence, in other nations during the Cold War.

The Cold War generated long-term conflict between communism and capitalist democracy, with U.S. foreign relations shaped by the fear that the Soviet Union pursued global domination. Although the USSR, ruled by dictators, possessed formidable military might, Americans often overestimated the threat. The Central Intelligence Agency (CIA) and the National Security Council, both established in 1947, and other intelligence-gathering agencies operated in top secrecy, with little congressional oversight and ever larger budgets ($40 billion per year by the 1980s). The **domino theory**, which envisioned countries falling one by one to communism, shaped U.S. policy.

Anticommunism intensified after hard-drinking U.S. senator Joseph McCarthy (1909–1957) and his allies charged, without offering much proof, that communists had infiltrated the U.S. government and were shaping foreign policy. During McCarthyism, a campaign in the 1950s to identify suspected communists in the government, the military, education, and the entertainment industry, thousands of Americans who held left-wing or progressive political views were fired or blacklisted and condemned as "un-American." (Blacklisting prevented people from working.) For example, various university experts on Asia lost their positions for criticizing U.S. Asian policies, and some were forced to finish their careers overseas. McCarthy called hundreds before his Senate committee, from movie actors to State Department officials, and questioned them about their political activities or their friends' political views. To critics, McCarthy's investigation, a Cold War-driven hysteria, violated the Bill of Rights. In 1954 the U.S. Senate censured McCarthy for recklessly charging top military leaders with treason, after which McCarthyism's influence began to diminish.

As a broad consensus emerged around opposing communism and Soviet power, most American leaders favored an activist foreign policy that relied on military power, but they disagreed on the approach. Some favored **multilateralism**, with the United States seeking a common front to coordinate foreign policies with allies in western Europe, Japan, and Canada, avoiding activities that might enflame world opinion. In contrast, most policymakers, and the presidents they served, favored **unilateralism**: acting alone in perceived American national interests even if key allies disapproved, as most did with the U.S. war in Vietnam. Unilateralists often supported repressive allies such as the dictators who for some years ruled the Philippines, Haiti, Argentina, Nicaragua, Iran, and the Congo; those who questioned the rationale, tactics, and cost of an activist policy were sidelined. Ultimately the costly interventions abroad, especially the frustrating war in Vietnam in the 1960s and early 1970s, generated debate about the goals, operation, and impact of U.S. foreign policy, undermining consensus and increasing dissent.

The main U.S. strategy, **containment**, which aimed at preventing communists from gaining power and the Soviets from gaining influence in other nations, generated wars in Korea and Vietnam and interventions in countries seeking to weaken or escape from Western economic and political domination. An influential, top secret 1950 government report, NSC-68, provided the rationale for activist policies, painting a bleak picture of the Soviet search for world supremacy: "The issues that face us are momentous, involving the fulfillment or destruction not only of this [U.S.] Republic but of civilization itself."[2] Sanctioning any tactics in the anticommunism struggle, NSC-68 remained a foundation for U.S. military and intelligence policies abroad until the mid-1970s.

NSC-68 called for huge defense budgets and expansion of the nuclear weapons arsenal, paid for by tax increases and major reductions in spending on domestic needs such as social welfare, education, and health care; security took precedence at the expense of other priorities. The Soviets matched the U.S. military buildup, spurring costly escalation of military spending and more sophisticated weapons on both sides. Under the policy of **Mutually Assured Destruction (MAD)**, the United States and USSR used fear of nuclear weapons as deterrence. Historians debate whether MAD prevented a direct military confrontation that might have sparked World War III. As Americans reacted to that fear in the 1950s, some built bomb shelters in their basements or backyards, while schools held mock air raid drills, with students learning to "duck and cover" under their desks to protect themselves from a nuclear attack.

Defense spending reshaped the U.S. economy. U.S. World War II commander and later president Dwight Eisenhower (g. 1953–1961) warned about the growing influence of what he termed the "military–industrial complex," an alliance of military leaders and weapons producers. Defense became an enormous business, employing a fifth of the industrial workforce and a third of scientists and engineers by the 1960s and costing U.S. taxpayers hundreds of billions of dollars a year. The United States also sold weapons to allied nations, including military or civilian dictatorships, which sometimes used American weapons and police tactics against their own citizens to eliminate dissidents.

Between 1945 and 1975 U.S. power was unmatched in the world, with military bases in dozens of countries (see Map 29.1). Both the United States and the USSR intervened directly or indirectly in civil wars and revolutions to outflank the other. Americans employed military force, as in the long war in Vietnam and the invasion of the Dominican Republic in 1965, and covertly aided governments to suppress opposition or helped overthrow governments, sometimes democratically elected ones, that were considered unfriendly to U.S. economic or political interests. Some foreign observers applauded American efforts to suppress left-wing governments and movements; others criticized superpower imperialism. The U.S.–USSR rivalry persisted until many communist regimes collapsed in 1989.

U.S. power was diminished between the mid-1970s and early 1990s due to a resurgent western Europe and Japan, Soviet military strength, economic challenges from industrializing nations such as South Korea and China, damage done to the U.S. economy and prestige by the widely unpopular war in Vietnam, and the economic price for global power. With many costly military commitments, the nation's economic creativity sagged and industries became obsolete; defense spending diverted resources from the domestic economy. For over four decades Americans spent around $4 trillion on the Cold War rather than improving education and health care or meeting other needs. While the growing U.S. defense budgets helped undermine the USSR, which was unable to match the lavish spending, the ballooning federal deficits also made the United States the world's largest debtor nation. President Bill Clinton (g. 1993–2001) eliminated the budget deficits, but the debts skyrocketed again under his successors, George W. Bush (g. 2001–2009), Barack Obama (g. 2009–2017), and Donald Trump (g. 2017–present). The skyrocketing spending owed much to foreign wars (Afghanistan, Iraq), the financial crisis of 2008–2009, and large tax cuts under Bush and Trump that mostly went to the wealthy and increased the already wide income inequality to the highest level since the 1970s.

29-1b The United States, Wars, and the Developing Nations

The 1949 communist victory in longtime ally China escalated U.S. concern about communist expansion, helping spark the Korean War (1950–1953) (see Chapter 27). Comparing North Korea's invasion to Nazi aggression and influenced by Americans' anti-communist mood, U.S. president Harry S. Truman signaled adoption of an interventionist foreign policy by deploying U.S. troops to Korea. By never consulting Congress, which had constitutional responsibility to declare war, Truman also made presidents supreme in decisions to go to war, enhancing executive branch power. Furthermore, Soviet support of North Korea and Chinese intervention deepened American fear of expanding communism. Despite thirty-eight thousand Americans killed and over 100,000 wounded, the war ended in stalemate, the first time Americans failed to decisively win a war since 1812. The intervention also reflected the idealistic American desire to spread democracy and free market capitalism around the world. However, South Korea did not become a democracy until the 1980s, over three decades after the war. U.S. military bases and nearly seventy-eight thousand troops remain in South Korea and Japan today.

The domino theory, predicting a communist sweep through Southeast Asia, as well as the desire to maintain military credibility and keep valuable Southeast Asian resources in friendly hands, also fostered support for the French effort to maintain colonial control (1946–1954) in Vietnam. When that effort failed, U.S. troops eventually fought Soviet- and Chinese-armed Vietnamese communist forces (see Chapter 31). Few U.S. leaders comprehended the historical and cultural factors that motivated the Vietnamese revolutionaries and their supporters. By the mid-1960s, U.S. president Lyndon B. Johnson (g. 1963–1969) had committed military forces and launched an intensive air war in North and South Vietnam and later in neighboring Cambodia and Laos. Using domino theory rhetoric, Johnson asserted that "if we don't stop the [communists] in South Vietnam, tomorrow they will be in Hawaii and next week they will be in San Francisco,"[3] very unlikely scenarios. Between 1963 and 1975, 2.5 million

Mutually Assured Destruction (MAD) A policy in which the United States and the USSR used the fear of nuclear weapons to deter each other.

---

[2]Quoted in Marilyn B. Young, *The Vietnam Wars, 1945–1990* (New York: HarperCollins, 1991), 25.
[3]Quoted in L. S. Stavrianos, *Global Rift: The Third World Comes of Age* (New York: William Morrow, 1981), 712.

PACIFIC
OCEAN

AUSTRALIA

PACIFIC
OCEAN

NORTH
AMERICA

Panama
1989–90

Haiti
1994, 2004
Dominican
Republic
1965

Korea
1950–53

Vietnam
1954–75

SOUTH
AMERICA

Grenada
1983

Laos
1968

Cambodia
1975

ASIA

EUROPE

Pakistan
2008–
Afghanistan
2001

Bosnia/Yugoslavia
1991

Yugoslavia
1999

Iraq/Kuwait
1991, 2003–

INDIAN
OCEAN

Lebanon
1983

ATLANTIC
OCEAN

Somalia
1992–93

AFRICA

**U.S. military presence in the
world, 1945–present**

⭐ Military intervention

■ Military base

0   1,000   2,000 Km.

0   1,000   2,000 Mi.

MAP 29.1 **U.S. Military Presence in the World, 1945–Present** As the major superpower, the United States maintained
several dozen military bases outside of North America while engaging in military operations in Latin America, Africa, Asia, the
Middle East, and Europe. This map shows some of the major U.S. bases and military conflicts.

Q What does this map tell us about where U.S. military influence is the strongest and weakest?

Americans served in Vietnam; fifty-eight thousand died and
300,000 were wounded. Some three million Vietnamese died,
two-thirds of them civilians.

As public support for the war ebbed in what seemed a
quagmire, new president Richard Nixon (g. 1969–1974)
negotiated a political settlement with North Vietnam and
gradually withdrew U.S. forces. Thanks to a wartime policy
of spending lavishly on both "guns and butter"—military and
domestic needs—Americans struggled with huge deficits
and other economic problems from the later 1960s into the
1990s. According to the Pentagon the war in Vietnam cost
U.S. taxpayers $168 billion, but some estimates of the ultimate
cost run as high as $1–2 trillion. The unpopular, unsuccessful
war also made Americans wary of supporting other military
interventions that might become quagmires.

During the Cold War, decolonization, nationalism, the
U.S.–Soviet struggle, and persistent poverty combined to
make Asian, African, and Latin American societies prone
to crises. The United States often favored decolonization that
opened U.S. business opportunities, pressuring the Dutch to
abandon Indonesia and Britain to grant most of its African
colonies independence. But Americans opposed independence
for colonies, such as French-ruled Vietnam and Portuguese-
ruled Mozambique, where communists or leftists dominated
nationalist movements. After decolonization, Americans
offered generous aid to friendly nations and victims of famine
or natural catastrophes while funding the Green Revolution
in agriculture, which improved food production. However,
Cold War challenges involved Americans in long-term
confrontations with communist-led China, North Vietnam,

and Cuba and interventions, sometimes with military force, to suppress leftist insurgencies and oppose left-leaning governments.

Some U.S.-supported governments lacked widespread popular support or lost their credibility, repressing and sometimes killing domestic opponents. Some interventions also removed democratic governments, as in Guatemala and Chile, or suppressed democratic movements. Hence, President Johnson, fearing another Cuba, dispatched twenty thousand U.S. Marines into the Dominican Republic in 1965 to support a military government opposed by democratically elected leaders they had recently overthrown. Johnson consulted no other Latin American governments, and the antimilitary leaders were left-leaning but non-communist reformers. Former Dominican president Juan Bosch (1909–2001) declared that "this was a democratic revolution smashed by the leading democracy in the world."[4] The United States also provided friendly governments or anti-leftist groups with weapons, military advisers, intelligence agents, and funding. Hence, during the 1970s and 1980s it aided pro-Western but often repressive governments combating leftist insurgents in El Salvador. In Laos (1960–1975), during the CIA's "secret war" hidden from Congress and the U.S. public, Americans recruited hill peoples (especially the Hmong) to fight communist Laotian and North Vietnamese forces (see Chapter 31).

Some interventions involved covert destabilization. American agents worked underground to undermine or overthrow governments by spreading misinformation, subsidizing opposition political parties, providing weapons to the military, and facilitating assassinations of government leaders. U.S. clandestine activity undermined left-leaning democratic governments in Iran in the 1950s and Thailand and Chile in the 1970s, resulting in brutal dictatorships. Secretary of State Henry Kissinger, defending the U.S.-supported military coup against an elected Chilean government that respected civil liberties, explained, "I don't see why we [Americans] need to stand by and watch a country go communist due to the irresponsibility of its own people."[5] Only in the mid-1970s, with congressional hearings, did Americans learn of the U.S. role in Chile and other interventions, forcing debate on whether secret operations and foreign interventions unknown to the public are compatible with democracy and open, accountable government.

IMAGE 29.2 **On Patrol in Vietnam** U.S. soldiers sought out National Liberation Front fighters and supporters in the villages, rice fields, and jungles of South Vietnam. They could not easily tell friend from foe and warily dealt with local people.

Bettmann/Getty Images

Q What can we learn from the photo about the interaction of U.S. soldiers and local villagers?

29-1c The United States in the Global System After 1989

The dissolution of the Soviet bloc in 1989 and the USSR in 1991 left the United States the dominant world power, although the European Union, Japan, and rising China and India also enjoyed great influence in the global system. But the absence of a rival superpower under the *Pax Americana* ("American Peace") did not mean there were no serious challenges in a world characterized by small, deadly conflicts. During the early 1990s, for example, the United States sent a few U.S. troops, under United Nations auspices, to stabilize Somalia, a famine-racked northeast African state engulfed in civil war, but a local warlord paraded the mutilated bodies of dead U.S. soldiers through the streets, forcing a U.S. withdrawal. In the aftermath, the United States declined to intervene to stop bloody ethnic conflicts and genocides in the African states of Rwanda, Liberia, and Sierra Leone. However, working with European allies, President Bill Clinton sent U.S. forces to help end deadly civil wars in the former Yugoslavia. Clinton also established diplomatic ties and lifted the trade embargo imposed on Vietnam after 1975, improving relations.

Cold War policies sometimes came back to haunt Americans. For example, Iranians' resentment over the 1953 overthrow of their government still complicates U.S.–Iran

---

[4]Quoted in Walter LaFeber, *America, Russia and the Cold War: 1945–1992*, 7th ed. (New York: McGraw-Hill, 1993), 248.
[5]Quoted in Cockcroft, *Latin America*, 531.

relations. In another example, when the United States gave military and financial aid to Islamic rebels fighting Soviet troops and the pro-Soviet government in Afghanistan in the 1980s (see Chapter 30), some aid went to Arab volunteers fighting alongside the rebels, among them Saudi militant Osama bin Laden (1957–2011). After the defeated Soviets left Afghanistan in 1989, Muslim extremists called the Taliban ultimately took power, offering a base for bin Laden to form his global terrorist network, Al Qaeda ("the Base"). Al Qaeda plotted terrorist attacks against the United States, sometimes using leftover U.S. weapons (see Chapters 26 and 30). Iraq's ruthless dictator, Saddam Hussein, also used weapons acquired from the United States, his ally against Iran in the 1980s, to repress dissident groups and, in 1991, invaded oil-rich Kuwait. An American-led coalition pushed invading Iraqi forces out during the Gulf War. With an ever-expanding American appetite for oil, this war reflected a consistent U.S. policy to protect the oil flow from the Middle East to the West, sometimes by supporting dictatorial regimes.

The Al Qaeda terrorist attack that crashed hijacked jetliners on New York's World Trade Center, the Pentagon outside Washington, D.C., and into a Pennsylvania farm field in September 2001, which killed nearly three thousand people, mostly Americans but some from other countries, shocked the nation. The terrorists, young Islamist militants mostly from two close U.S. allies, Egypt and Saudi Arabia, attacked buildings symbolizing often-unpopular U.S. economic and military power. However, people in most countries, even if they disliked U.S. power, deplored the bombings and loss of innocent life.

The 2001 attack sparked new domestic and foreign policies. To prevent more domestic terrorism, the new U.S. president, George W. Bush (g. 2001–2009), introduced policies that critics believed infringed on civil liberties, such as preventive detention, interception of overseas phone calls, and monitoring of libraries. President Bush also declared war on international terrorism. But unlike the USSR during the Cold War, terrorist networks, having no clear command structure or military resources, could not be influenced by diplomacy. With international support, the United States invaded Afghanistan to destroy Al Qaeda terrorist bases, displacing the brutal Taliban government that tolerated their presence. Bush then announced a new doctrine of **preemptive war** sanctioning unilateral military action against potential threats: "We cannot let our enemies strike first …. The greater the threat, the greater the risk of inaction … [we] will, if necessary, act preemptively."[6] Bush named Iraq, Iran, and North Korea as an "axis of evil" threatening their neighbors and world peace. Critics considered the Bush doctrine a rationale for acquiring an American empire through military action in violation of international law and the United Nations charter.

Acting on the doctrine of preemptive war, the Bush administration resumed unilateralist U.S. foreign policies. Rejecting opposition from the United Nations and key U.S. allies, among them Canada and Germany, while still keeping thousands of U.S. soldiers in Afghanistan, in 2003 the Bush administration invaded and occupied oil-rich Iraq, ending Saddam Hussein's brutal regime. Using faulty or manipulated intelligence, Bush claimed that Iraq possessed weapons of mass destruction and aided Al Qaeda. But U.S. forces found no evidence for either claim. With poor U.S. planning for restoring stability, explosive ethnic and religious divisions threatened to explode into civil war, frustrating attempts to foster democracy. A mounting insurgency, suicide bombings, and foreign terrorists flocking to Iraq caused many thousands of U.S. casualties and complicated reconstruction, including of oil production and basic services, demoralizing Iraqis. Eventually, after forty-five hundred American and over 100,000 Iraqi deaths and some thirty-two thousand Americans wounded, in 2008 conditions stabilized, violence diminished, and political conditions improved; the last U.S. troops left in 2011. Meanwhile, the U.S.-led NATO force in Afghanistan became bogged down amidst difficult terrain, contentious Afghan politics, cultural misunderstandings, and increased resistance from Islamist fighters led by a rejuvenated Taliban; thirty-five hundred NATO coalition troops had died by 2018, including over twenty-three hundred Americans. In both Afghanistan and Iraq, U.S. forces had to return to the counterinsurgency strategy used in Vietnam. The spiraling costs of the Iraq and Afghanistan wars and occupations (ultimately some $6 trillion), combined with large tax cuts and other expenses, ballooned U.S. budget deficits and the national debt. The Iraq war, unpopular in much of the world, and the U.S. rejection of several international treaties, such as that on climate change, alienated many Western allies.

By 2014 the U.S. became involved in the Syrian civil war, using air power to support rebels against the despotic Syrian government. But Islamist militants complicated the conflict. The Islamic State of Iraq and Syria (ISIS), which had morphed out of pro-Al Qaeda militants who had fought the U.S. in Iraq, entered the conflict and also mounted attacks in Iraq. In 2015 President Obama sent in a small U.S. military force, ultimately numbering some two thousand troops, to assist Syrian Kurds and Sunni Arabs fighting both ISIS and the Russia and Iran-supported Shiite Syrian regime. Eventually the ISIS bases were captured, mostly by the U.S.-allied Kurdish militias, and the Syrian regime regained control of much of the country, but the Kurds still controlled their enclaves in the north and east. In 2019 President Donald Trump said that he planned to withdraw all the U.S. troops from Syria and many from the two-decades-long "forever war" in Afghanistan. Soon Trump endorsed a Turkish goal of using military force to push the Kurds (who the Turks viewed as terrorists) out of the border region; Trump then withdrew most of the small American Special Forces contingent advising the Kurds, who had maintained the prison camps that held tens of thousands of defeated ISIS fighters and their families.

preemptive war A U.S. doctrine, triggered by the 2001 terrorist attacks, that sanctioned unilateral military action against potential threats.

---

[6]*The National Security Strategy of the United States* (whitehouse.gov/nsc/print/nssall.html).

Soon Turkey began an air and ground offensive that displaced several hundred thousand Kurdish fighters and civilians as well as many Syrian Christians who also lived there. The U.S. withdrawal, opposed by most U.S. military leaders, national security strategists, and a majority in Congress, outraged many Americans across the political spectrum as well as European leaders; many considered it a strategic blunder and shameful betrayal of the nation's Kurdish allies (who had lost 12,000 people in the fight against ISIS) that might, they feared, destabilize the region, empower Iran and Russia, weaken U.S. credibility as a reliable ally, and allow ISIS to regroup and resume their jihad. Indeed, in the mayhem of the invasion some soon escaped the camps. Many Americans were tiring of frequent wars and global commitments. Around 1.2 million service members died in all of the wars fought by the U.S. since the nation was founded, although that is still less than the 1.5 million who died from gun-related incidents in the United States since 1968. A 2018 study concluded that the U.S. had spent six trillion dollars on wars that killed half a million people since 9/11.

Because of its unparalleled economic and military might, the United States has assumed heavy burdens, maintaining military bases and operations around the world. By 2011 its arms sales accounted for three-quarters of all arms sales to other nations. But as other nations such as Russia and France increased their sales, U.S. sales dropped to a third of the world total in 2018. While western Europeans and East Asians generally concentrated on trade relations with other nations, Americans attempted to balance trade with con-fronting the nations they perceived as dangerous. By 2018 U.S. military spending accounted for around 40 percent of all military spending worldwide and half the U.S. federal budget. A 2019 study calculated that the U.S. was spending $32 mil-lion an hour keeping the military at war while staffing eight hundred to a thousand military bases and outposts around the world and maintaining diverse intelligence agencies. While anti-U.S. sentiments grew steadily in the early twenty-first century, no major coalition of nations emerged to oppose the U.S. role. By 2012, the United States was shifting attention to eastern Eurasia, where a rising China concerned many nations in the region.

The spiraling national debt (doubling between 2001 and 2008), expensive global commitments, a housing market crisis, and overly lax regulation of banks, corporations, and the stock market generated an economic meltdown in 2008–2009 that soon spread to the rest of the world. Millions of Americans lost their jobs and homes, consumer spending dropped dramatically, stock prices plummeted, pension funds dwindled, and state and local governments faced severe budget cuts. Bailing out major banks, the distressed automobile industry, and revenue-starved states added to federal budget deficits. While the severe recession was not as catastrophic as the Great Depression, it forced debate on the free-wheeling U.S. economic model and the heavy costs of the nation's global obligations. By the 2010s historians and other specialists debated whether the United States could retain its dominance for decades or whether its growing burdens will reduce U.S. power as other nations, perhaps India or China, surge ahead. With U.S. ideological supremacy and control of the global order diminishing by the later 2010s, as the nationalist Trump administration disengaged the country from many of its alliances and multilateral cooperation, some observers have proclaimed the end of the "American Century." Thanks to the world economic crisis and the disruptive and unilateralist policies of the Trump administration, such as trade wars and threats to leave NATO—policies which were unpopular with the U.S. foreign service, many economists, and most academic experts on the world and international relations—some observers have also perceived a transition under way toward a multipolar world economy less dependent on U.S. leadership and consumption. Whatever the case, since the Romans two millennia ago, for almost seventy years no other nation had been as dominant in military, economic, political, and social realms as the United States since 1945, and especially from 1990 to 2017, forcing Americans to debate, as the Romans and Athenians did, whether democracy and imperial power are consistent with each other.

KEY POINTS

▶ For several decades after World War II, the United States enjoyed a period of economic growth and lavished economic aid on western Europe and Japan, helping them recover.

▶ During the Cold War, McCarthyism led to the persecution of many U.S. citizens for supposed communist sympathies, and defense spending became a key factor in the U.S. economy.

▶ On the basis of the domino theory, which argued that if communism wasn't stopped it would take over the world, the United States adopted an interventionist foreign policy and fought communists in Korea and Vietnam, but neither war achieved U.S. goals, and the Vietnam War severely crippled the U.S. economy.

▶ During the Cold War, the United States opposed not only communist movements but also noncommunist leftist movements in several countries, in many cases helping to replace them with brutal military dictatorships.

▶ After the Cold War ended, the United States continued to police the world and after 9/11 followed the doctrine of preemptive war, but the mixed results of its engagements and their high economic cost have raised the question of whether the United States can continue to combine democracy with interventionist foreign policies.

29-2 The Changing Societies of North America and the Pacific Basin

SOCIETIES

Q How and why are the societies of the United States, Canada, and Australia similar to and different from each other?

The United States, Canada, Australia, and New Zealand, all former British colonies with societies shaped by the many settlers from Europe, especially the British Isles, have shared a general prosperity, stable democracies, similar social patterns, and many cultural traditions. Millions of immigrants from around the world have helped to globalize their cultures, linking them more closely to other nations. But the largest and most powerful, the United States, has played a different role than the other countries, exercising more world power.

29-2a Prosperity, Technology, and Inequality in the United States

Living in the world's richest nation, many Americans have benefited from a growing economy and widespread affluence. During the 1960s, as many Americans worked in new automobile, aerospace, service, and information technology industries, production of goods and services doubled, while per capita income rose by half. By 2000 Americans produced a third of the world's goods and services and enjoyed a median annual family income over $40,000; by 2017 that had risen to $61,500. However, China had far surpassed the U.S. as the top manufacturer; by the late 2010s the U.S. produced around one-fifth of the world's goods. Americans also owned the majority of the giant multinational corporations, such as Exxon-Mobil, General Motors, and Walmart, that played ever-larger roles in the globalizing world. However, this growth had downsides. With 4.5 percent of the world's population in 2018, Americans consumed around 30 percent of all the world's resources, such as oil and iron ore, and produced a large share of the chemicals, gases, and toxic wastes that pollute the atmosphere, alter the climate, and destroy the land. Yet, Americans lagged well behind most of western Europe, Japan, and several developing nations in meeting sustainable environmental goals. Americans also worked longer hours than any industrialized people except the Japanese.

The decline of smokestack industries such as steel production and the rise of high technology reshaped the economy and workplace, realizing some of the dreams of twentieth-century science fiction writers, futurists, and TV series like *Star Trek*. Americans made innovations in medicine, space research, transportation, and electronics. Space satellites greatly improved weather forecasting, communications, and intelligence gathering; convenient and versatile, computers revolutionized life, being able to, as *Time* magazine concluded, "send letters at the speed of light, diagnose a sick poodle [and]

> **CONNECTION to TODAY**
>
> How do you think your life might be different if you lived and had grown up in another English-speaking country where people of British ancestry have strongly influenced the culture, society, and politics?

test recipes for beer."[7] By 2008 many carried pocket-sized devices, once the stuff of science fiction novels, that could make telephone calls, send text messages, take photos, play music and movies, and access news and weather. Today electronic devices, social media, and the Internet are much more advanced, with endless options.

Beginning in the 1970s, a growing economy improved life for some people, especially those trained in new technologies, but hurt millions of unskilled workers, younger workers, and children in single-parent households. Computers and robots increased efficiency but replaced workers. Industrialists won corporate bonuses for relocating factories and exporting jobs to Latin America or Asia, devastating factory-dependent communities while eliminating a quarter of manufacturing employment. By the early 2000s, although life for the majority of Americans remained comfortable compared to that in most other nations, male unemployment was the highest in five decades, and millions worked two jobs to support their families. Moreover, the United States generally ranked behind Scandinavia, Switzerland, Canada, and Australia for overall quality of life in the annual United Nations Human Development Reports; the U.S. ranked thirteenth in 2018. Some economists referred to a "winner-take-all economy" that produced ever-more millionaires—nearly six million by 2012. Thanks in part to generous tax cuts in 2017 for the wealthy and big corporations, that number doubled to nearly twelve million (6 percent of Americans) by 2019. A 2019 study found that the four hundred richest Americans, all billionaires, paid a lower federal, state, and local tax rate than any other income group, including the very poor. But many others did not share in the bounty, including a struggling middle class. More homeless people (over five hundred-fifty thousand in 2018) slept in city streets and parks. Except for the richest 1 percent, whose earnings skyrocketed, average incomes fell between 2001 and 2008. Northern European nations, Canada, and Australia fostered far more social mobility and income equality than the United States. The United States also leads the world in the percentage of its population and total number in prison.

Unlike most industrialized nations, the United States also never developed a comprehensive welfare state or national health insurance. Thus a widening gap separated the richest and poorest thirds of Americans. Wealth inequality grew dramatically after 1980 and the 2008–2009 economic crisis made things worse; by 2010 the top 1 percent of taxpayers enjoyed 93 percent of income growth, doubling their share of national income, a situation some historians and economists

---

[7]Quoted in Walter LaFeber et al., *The American Century: A History of the United States Since 1941*, 5th ed. (Boston: McGraw-Hill, 1998), 519.

compared to the wealth inequality of the Roaring Twenties that helped spark the Great Depression and delay the recovery. Meanwhile, the gap between the richest and poorest 20 percent was three times wider than in Japan, the Netherlands, Sweden, or Germany. Twelve percent of Americans lived in poverty, the industrialized world's highest rate. According to some studies, in 2017 the highest 1 percent of households owned more wealth than the bottom 90 percent. A 2018 study suggested that if the $113 trillion in assets owned by Americans was divided up equally, each person would have $343,000 worth of assets. The rich–poor gap was starkly revealed in 2005 when a devastating hurricane, Katrina, ruined New Orleans, rendered millions homeless, and killed several thousand people: Most of the victims were black and poor, unable to afford transportation out of the area. By 2019 some business leaders, fearing the inequitable system was failing under assault from right-wing populists and left-wing progressives, began to call for reforming capitalism, arguing that corporations serving customers, employees, suppliers, and communities should be as important as shareholder profits. Whether this idea becomes widely shared in the corporate world remains to be seen.

Suburbanization deepened the inequalities. Following World War II many white families with young children sought affordable housing and a better life in suburbia, bedroom communities around major cities that built shopping malls, offered well-funded schools, and seemed immune from city violence. Supporting the trend, governments subsidized real estate developers. William Levitt, who built vast suburban tracts around New York City, argued that no persons owning their own house and yard could be a communist because they were too busy working to pay the mortgage. The two-car, multi-television family symbolized affluence. Affordable automobiles and government-funded highways made long commutes from central city jobs possible. Increasing use of fossil fuels for gasoline, electricity, and heating caused pollution, while clearing land for housing and business development harmed the environment. Many jobs later moved to the suburbs, leaving the city cores to the local-born poor, often nonwhite, or immigrants. Many minorities were kept out of suburbs because of restrictive ordinances, high costs, and racial discrimination. Most suburbs lacked ethnic and cultural diversity, isolating residents from the energy and stimulation but also the problems of big-city life. Suburban living also intensified the trend toward two-parent, single-breadwinner nuclear families living apart from other relatives, encouraging mothers to stay at home. Until the mid-1960s the image of the fashionably dressed, stay-at-home suburban housewife, smiling proudly as she served breakfast to her husband and children, remained ingrained in the culture, even as more women needed to undertake paid work. Critics lambasted the conformity of life in standardized suburban tract houses, which, according to a 1950s song, resembled "little boxes. There's a green one, a pink one, a blue one and a yellow one. And they're all made out of ticky-tacky, And they all look just the same."[8]

29-2b American Political Life: Conservatism and Liberalism

Americans tended to alternate between political conservatism and liberalism. For most of the postwar years, political conservatives, allied with big-business groups favoring low taxes and religious groups who disliked social and cultural liberalization, dominated the federal government and judiciary. Liberals, influential chiefly in the 1960s, 1990s, and from 2006 until 2016, were generally supported by labor unions, environmentalists, and groups seeking social change and a stronger government safety net, such as women's, immigrant, and civil rights organizations.

The desire for stability after the Great Depression and a calamitous world war encouraged political and social conservatism throughout the 1950s; few questioned their government or prevailing social patterns. Americans who criticized U.S. foreign policy or favored social change faced harassment, expulsion from job or school, arrest, or grillings by congressional committees. More Americans than ever married, producing a "baby boom" of children born after the war. The mass media portrayed women as obsessed with bleaching their clothes a purer white and defined by kitchen, bedroom, babies, and home. Society expected LGBTQ people to remain deep in the closet; those who did not often faced taunting, beatings, or arrest, even in "liberal" big cities. The growing consumer economy emphasized pleasure and leisure activities like cocktail parties, backyard barbecues, and baseball games. Like their parents, teenagers became consumers, creating a market for youth-oriented clothes and music.

During the 1960s, many Americans became open to new ideas and lifestyles as liberalism became influential. The era saw the first people, all of them American, to walk on the moon; the Peace Corps sent idealistic young Americans to help developing nations as teachers, health workers, and agricultural specialists. Presidents John F. Kennedy (g. 1961–1963) and Lyndon B. Johnson (g. 1963–1969) launched programs to address poverty, racism, and voting rights. But the 1960s also fostered doubts, anger, and violence. Three national leaders—President John Kennedy, his brother and presidential candidate Robert Kennedy, and civil rights leader Dr. Martin Luther King, Jr.—were assassinated. War in Vietnam, the African American civil rights movement, and issues of environmental protection and women's empowerment divided the nation; pro-war "hawks" and anti-war "doves" competed for support; riots and demonstrations became common, and popular culture took on a more political tone.

During these years many young people, chiefly middle class, rebelled against the values of their parents and established society. Popular folksinger Bob Dylan (b. 1941), who later became a seminal rock icon and songwriter, sang: "Come, mothers and fathers, throughout the land, And don't criticize what you can't understand. Your sons and your daughters are beyond your command, Your old world is rapidly aging. Please get out of the new one if you can't lend your hand, For the times,

---

[8]Folksinger Malvina Reynolds, quoted in Richard O. Davies, "The Ambivalent Heritage: The City in Modern America," in *Paths to the Present: Interpretive Essays on American Society Since 1930*, ed. James T. Patterson (Minneapolis, MN: Burgess, 1975), 163.

they are a'changing."[9] High school and university students worked to change society and politics, marching against the war, registering voters, holding "teach-ins" to discuss national issues, and going door to door to spread their cause. Some youth forged a counterculture that often involved illegal drugs, such as marijuana, and casual sex, emblazoning "Make love, not war" on bumper stickers, posters, and buttons. During the "Summer of Love" in 1967 young people gathered in San Francisco to hear rock music and share comradery; the Woodstock rock music festival of 1969, which attracted over 300,000 to a New York farm to hear some of the most popular rock musicians, marked the zenith of both the youth counterculture and political activism. Many others rejected the counterculture. In contrast to liberalism, protest, and rock, country music generally leaned conservative, as reflected in Merle Haggard's 1969 song "Okie from Muskogee":

> *We don't smoke marijuana in Muskogee*
> *We don't take our trips on LSD*
> *We don't burn our draft cards down on Main Street*
> *We like livin' right, and bein' free*[10]

In the 1970s, as the war wound down, the nation returned to more conservative values and politics. With the exception of the 1990s, when the moderate Democrat Bill Clinton held the presidency, conservatives maintained their dominance of American politics and the social agenda until 2009. President Ronald Reagan (g. 1981–1989), a popular former movie star and zealous anticommunist, symbolized conservative governance, weakening the labor movement and welfare system while taking a hard line toward the USSR. Religion remained a powerful force, with Americans more likely to attend churches and profess strong Christian beliefs than Canadians or most Europeans. By the 1980s conservative Catholics and evangelical Protestants had become more influential in public life, helping elect conservatives to office. Experts debated whether Christian conservatism reflected a rejection of the Enlightenment emphasis on reason and tolerance or rather a search for personal spiritual experience and timeless rules. Many churches stressed membership in a supportive community or emphasized self-help. While Americans avidly consumed new technologies, such as cell phones and portable music players, substantial numbers mistrusted science, rejecting scientific explanations for the origins of the universe and human evolution in favor of biblical accounts. Yet, a fifth of Americans claimed no religious affiliation by 2012 and a quarter by 2019, and younger Americans increasingly identified themselves as belonging to no organized faith. Christians accounted for about 70 percent, Jews for 2 percent, and other religions for 4 percent of the U.S. population.

Observers found much to deplore and much to praise in post-1960s U.S. politics. Big corporations, billionaires, and other special interests increasingly financed political activity, fostering corruption and political apathy; generally only around half of eligible voters voted in presidential elections, far lower numbers than in most other industrial democracies. However, a free media exposed government corruption, including presidential abuses of power. President Richard Nixon, facing impeachment, resigned in 1973 for sanctioning and then covering up illegal

activities by his subordinates, and the Reagan and Clinton presidencies were marred by congressional hearings examining their misdeeds. The controversial, bitter 2000 and 2004 elections of Texas governor and Republican George W. Bush (g. 2001–2009) as president sharply divided Americans between the two major political parties and their divergent policies. The losing Democratic candidate in 2000, Clinton's Vice President Albert Gore, lost the Electoral College but won nearly a million more popular votes than Bush.

However, the apathy faded in 2008 during an exciting election campaign to replace Bush, who was widely disliked for the unpopular Iraq war, an inadequate response to Hurricane Katrina, spiraling national debt, controversial social and environmental policies, and the economic meltdown of 2008. Illinois senator Barack Obama (b. 1961), the Hawaii-born son of a black Kenyan father studying in the United States and a white mother from Kansas, won the Democratic nomination over New York senator Hillary Rodham Clinton (b. 1947), a former First Lady. Obama had lived in Indonesia for a few years as a child. Mobilizing a coalition of racial minorities, women, youth, and labor unions, Obama won the presidency; his victory as the first nonwhite U.S. president electrified the world, suggesting that U.S. society was changing. Many Americans and non-Americans hoped for a less unilateral and aggressive U.S. foreign policy. Inheriting two wars and an economic crisis, and enjoying Democratic congressional majorities, Obama introduced New Deal-like policies to generate economic recovery, withdrew U.S. troops from Iraq, ordered the operation that killed Osama bin Laden, recognized LGBTQ rights, supported immigration reform, and guided a highly controversial health coverage plan ("Obamacare") through Congress. However, while a government stimulus package averted a complete crash and the economy began modest growth, reducing unemployment proved a challenge. Furthermore, the conservative Republican opposition, which controlled the House of Representatives and the majority of states after the 2010 midterm elections, blocked many of his initiatives and vowed to repeal "Obamacare," contributing to political gridlock. Obama also continued some controversial Bush-era national security policies, including far-reaching electronic intelligence gathering at home and abroad and the use of military drones against alleged terrorists in southern and western Asia. Both policies alarmed civil libertarians and governments around the world. Obama was reelected in 2012 but the Republicans won control of both houses of Congress in 2014, enabling them to reject most of his second-term initiatives on issues like climate change and immigration and block court appointments. But the Obama economy continued to grow. In 2016 Obama, hoping to thaw long-hostile U.S.–Cuban relations, made a goodwill trip to the island, the first ever presidential visit there.

Democrats hoped that Obama's presidency had begun a new era of liberalism and economic resurgence, but the 2016 elections brought an entirely different direction, shocking the world. In a closely fought and divisive race, Republican Donald Trump, a multimillionaire property developer and reality TV star with no prior political experience, defeated the Democrat Hillary Clinton, who had been Obama's secretary of state, in

---

[9]From Peter Blood-Patterson, ed., *Rise Up Singing* (Bethlehem, PA: Sing Out Publications, 1988), 219.
[10]Merle Haggard and The Strangers, from the live album *Okie from Muskogee* (Capital Records, 1969).

the electoral college; Clinton won three million more popular votes. Describing himself as a "nationalist," Trump pledged to put "America first" and "make America great again." Promising a disruptive presidency to shake up the federal government establishment, Trump attracted disgruntled blue-collar workers, miners, ranchers, loggers, farmers, and rural people—groups that believed they were hurt by globalization and government environmental, health, and safety regulations—as well as people (including white supremacists) hostile to minorities and immigrants. Distrusting academics, experts, and science, Trump filled his administration with lobbyists and executives from powerful energy, industrial, business, timber, for profit education, and agricultural interests while understaffing most federal departments including State and Defense, hollowing out and weakening the bureaucracy. Some cabinet officials had conflicts of interest, ethical violations, or other scandals while, unlike earlier presidents, Trump also maintained ties with his own business interests and refused to release his taxes, raising for critics issues of corruption. Strongly supported by his increasingly right-wing base (including many evangelical Christians), Trump sought to undermine some protections for LGBTQ Americans.

As evidence accumulated that Russia had interfered in the 2016 presidential election to help Trump through cyberwar, fake news on social media, and contacts with the Trump campaign, a special counsel, former FBI director Robert Mueller, studied the issue for nearly two years. Mueller's final report concluded that evidence of collusion was inconclusive, despite the Trump campaign's numerous links and contacts with Russians. However, Trump was not exonerated of obstruction of justice. Government rules prevented bringing criminal charges against a sitting president. But various Trump aides and associates, including Trump's campaign chair and his national security adviser, were convicted or pled guilty to various crimes. Most Republicans, including members of Congress, supported Trump. Many other Americans wanted Trump impeached for these and other actions they viewed as compromising his presidency, such as defying congressional inquiries and ignoring presidential and constitutional precedents. In the 2018 midterms the Democrats swept to power in the House of Representatives, but the nation remained bitterly divided. In mid-2019 evidence became public that Trump may have broken the law by pressuring the Ukraine government for his own political purposes, withholding already committed military aid unless they agreed to investigate one of his Democratic challengers for president in 2020, former Vice President Joe Biden. To many observers his action invited illegal interference in U.S. elections by a foreign country and led the House of Representatives to open an impeachment inquiry about abuse of power, bribery, and other offenses; Trump refused cooperation with the probe, causing what some legal scholars called a constitutional crisis. The scandal and crisis threatened Trump's presidency.

Trump's policies, impulsive decision making, provocative language, government by tweets, and unfiltered personality made him the most controversial and perhaps most divisive president in modern U.S. history, beloved by his followers and despised by his detractors. With the Republicans controlling both houses of Congress in 2017–2018, Trump repeatedly attempted to end "Obamacare," which provided health insurance to millions of Americans, and passed through Congress a massive tax cut that

supporters hailed as an economic stimulus and critics argued chiefly benefited the wealthy and big business. The economy continued the growth trajectory of the Obama years and created more short-term job growth. A climate change denier, Trump rejected the Paris climate accord and the overwhelming scientific consensus on the catastrophic impacts of climate change on the nation and world today and in the future (see Discover Historical Voices: Confronting the Challenges of Climate Change). Hence, Trump weakened or eliminated Obama-era policies aimed at fighting global warming, such as those supporting renewable energy, curtailing greenhouse gases, and reducing reliance on fossil fuels; he also fired or forced out government scientists and researchers who opposed his actions and views. Trump's administration overturned clean air, water, and land regulations while opening public lands, national forests, national monuments, and other protected areas to mining, oil drilling, logging, and ranching.

Appealing to the anti-immigrant views of his voter base, Trump criticized Muslims and then banned travelers, immigrants, and refugees from several strife-torn Muslim countries. He also increased deportations of undocumented Hispanic residents and sought to end protections (under the DACA program) for people brought illegally to the U.S. as children. His supporters were thrilled when he ordered the building of a high wall on the long border with Mexico to try to keep out the large number of unauthorized migrants from Mexico and, more recently, a big increase in asylum-seekers from impoverished, crime-ridden and drought-stricken Central American countries. In 2018 immigration officials at the border began separating migrant families and housing many including children in prison-like camps while sending some asylum-seekers back to Mexico without a hearing, generating fierce criticism from human rights activists and many others. By later 2019 Trump made asylum seeking nearly impossible. Americans remained deeply divided on the value of immigration for the nation's future, some (including Trump) wanting more restrictions and lower numbers and others recommending even more legal immigrants to maintain an adequate future labor force and foster ingenuity. Legal immigration slowed to a trickle as Trump imposed lower quotas and demanded that arrivals prove they can support themselves.

Trump's actions in the world also generated controversy. Trump praised and openly admired longtime U.S. adversaries such as North Korea's brutal dictator Kim Jong Un, China's leader Xi Jinping, and especially Russian president Vladimir Putin while criticizing longtime allies, such as France, Germany, Mexico, and Canada, and insulting their leaders. Trump held several unprecedented summits with Kim, which diminished the tensions in East Asia but achieved no agreement on eliminating North Korea's nuclear weapons or testing. Condemning globalism and praising nationalism, as in domestic policies Trump disrupted and destabilized the globalized international cooperation on many issues, including collective security (NATO), trade agreements, and human-rights efforts. Trump also withdrew from an international agreement to keep Iran from getting nuclear weapons, but the other nations involved thought his move would further unsettle the Middle East and perhaps lead to war. Trump demanded a renegotiation of trade agreements and imposed higher tariffs on products from many allies. Although major trading partners, the U.S. and China had been at odds over trade and trade policy for

Discover Historical Voices

Confronting the Challenges of Climate Change

In November 2018 the Trump administration released the Fourth National Climate Assessment, a report that is required by law and compiled by a consortium of federal agencies including the Environmental Protection Agency, Department of Defense, and NASA. A climate change skeptic, Trump denounced and rejected the report and sidelined the scientists who prepared it. The report painted a grim picture of the U.S. already experiencing the economic and social brunt of a warming world. The report concluded that global climate change is already affecting us by contributing to the growing number and intensity of wildfires, heat waves, droughts, floods, and possibly hurricanes, and these will get worse in the future without urgent action to curb greenhouse gas emissions. Among other evidence the report notes that annual average temperatures across the U.S. have risen by nearly two degrees since 1900. They predict a catastrophic seven-degree rise in global temperatures by 2100, a damaged environment, and shrinking economy threatening agriculture and trade. The report shows that climate-related disasters have already cost the nation many billions of dollars each year. The report suggests a different approach to assessing the effects of climate change by considering how various impacts on such things as water, electricity generation, and food supplies interact with each other. This excerpt from the report comes from the Introduction to the Overview section from Volume II.

Earth's climate is now changing faster than at any point in the history of modern civilization, primarily as a result of human activities. The impacts of global climate change are already being felt in the United States and are projected to intensify in the future—but the severity of future impacts will depend largely on actions taken to reduce green-house gas emissions and to adapt to the changes that will occur. Americans increasingly recognize the risks climate change poses to their everyday lives and livelihoods and are beginning to respond....

Climate-related risks will continue to grow without additional action. Decisions made today determine risk exposure for current and future generations and will either broaden or limit options to reduce the negative consequences of climate change. While Americans are responding in ways that can bolster resilience and improve livelihoods, neither global efforts to mitigate the causes of climate change nor regional efforts to adapt to the impacts currently approach the scales needed to avoid substantial damages to the U.S. economy, environment, and human health and well-being over the coming decades...

Climate shapes where and how we live and the environment around us. Natural ecosystems, agricultural systems, water resources, and the benefits they provide to society are adapted to past climate conditions and their natural range of variability. However, the assumption that current and future climate conditions will resemble the recent past is no longer valid. Observations collected around the world provide significant, clear, and compelling evidence that global average temperature is much higher, and is rising more rapidly, than anything modern civilization has experienced, with widespread and growing impacts. The warming trend observed over the past century can only be explained by the effects that human activities, especially emissions of greenhouse gases, have had on the climate.

Climate change is transforming where and how we live and presents growing challenges to human health and quality of life, the economy, and the natural systems that support us. Risks posed by climate variability and change vary by region and sector and by the vulnerability of people experiencing impacts. Social, economic, and geographic factors shape the exposure of people and communities to climate-related impacts and their capacity to respond. Risks are often highest for those that are already vulnerable, including low-income communities, some communities of color, children, and the elderly. Climate change threatens to exacerbate existing social and economic inequalities that result in higher exposure and sensitivity to extreme weather and climate-related events and other changes. Marginalized populations may also be affected disproportionately by actions to address the underlying causes and impacts of climate change, if they are not implemented under policies that consider existing inequalities.

This report draws a direct connection between the warming atmosphere and the resulting changes that affect Americans' lives, communities, and livelihoods, now and in the future. It documents vulnerabilities, risks, and impacts associated with natural climate variability and human-caused climate change across the United States and provides examples of response actions underway in many communities. It concludes that the evidence of human-caused climate change is overwhelming and continues to strengthen, that the impacts of climate change are intensifying across the country, and that climate-related threats to Americans' physical, social, and economic well-being are rising. These impacts are projected to intensify—but how much they intensify will depend on actions taken to reduce global greenhouse gas emissions and to adapt to the risks from climate change now and in the coming decades.

Reflection Questions

1. What does the Assessment consider some of the main consequences and challenges of climate change in the United States?
2. What are some of the strategies they suggest to address climate change?
3. How does the U.S. experience of climate change compare to that in other parts of the world?

Source: Fourth National (United States) Climate Assessment 2018, Vol. II: Impacts, Risks, and Adaptation in the United States (U.S. Global Change Research Program, July 13, 2019), 33–36.

several years. In 2018–2019 Trump began a trade war with China by imposing higher tariffs on many imports; China retaliated with their own tariffs. As the fight escalated China's economy felt pain, but so did many U.S. consumers as prices for Chinese goods rose. Some U.S. farmers, companies, and industrial firms lost their important China market and many have struggled to recover it. Some U.S. experts supported a hard line on China whereas others felt Trump's policies were counter-productive. By later 2019 more U.S. factories were closing down and economic growth slowed, leading some economists to forecast a coming recession. Unless it was ratcheted down, the trade war threatened to hurt both countries and the global economy generally, alarming world leaders.

29-2c American Society and Popular Culture

Social change affected ethnic minorities, families, women, and men. African Americans, over 10 percent of the population, faced various forms of discrimination and experienced much higher rates of poverty than whites. Until the 1960s southern states maintained strict racial segregation, forcing blacks to attend separate schools and even use different public drinking fountains than whites. In northern industrial cities racism and poverty often concentrated African Americans in rundown inner-city neighborhoods, known as ghettos.

The civil rights movement, organized in the 1950s, eventually forced courts, states, and the federal government to introduce reforms. In 1954 the Supreme Court outlawed segregated schools. A year later, in Montgomery, Alabama, seamstress and community activist Rosa Parks (1913–2005) bravely refused to follow the local custom to give up her front seat on a bus to a white man, sparking a mass movement for change. Reverend Martin Luther King, Jr. (1929–1968) led a bus boycott to protest her arrest and fine. Using nonviolent resistance pioneered by Mohandas Gandhi, King led a protest movement all over the South. While leading the 1963 March on Washington to demand equal rights, he presented his vision: "I have a dream…. When we let freedom ring … all of God's children … will be able to join hands and sing in the words of that old spiritual … 'Thank God almighty, we are free at last!'"[11] King's assassination by a white racist in 1968 shocked the nation, but the African American struggle inspired similar struggles among Hispanic and Native Americans as well as elsewhere in the world, including black South Africans, Afro-Brazilians, and Australian Aborigines. African Americans gradually gained legal equality and voting rights, many moving into the middle and upper classes, although they were still more likely than whites to live in poverty, face unemployment, be imprisoned, or be harassed or shot by police; widespread outrage over these realities led to the Black Lives Matter movement in 2013 to fight violence and systematic racism. While they celebrated Obama's presidential victories as a sign of progress, they were also more likely to lose jobs and homes in the 2008–2009 recession. And over the past decade some Republican-governed states passed legislation that made voting harder, particularly for minorities, students, and the poor.

But despite these setbacks Martin Luther King and the civil rights movement had improved many black lives, as a King associate, civil rights activist, and Georgia congressman remembered on the fiftieth anniversary of the 1963 March on Washington:

> *In 1963, we could not register to vote simply because of the color of our skin. We had to pay a poll tax, pass a so-called literacy test, count the number of bubbles in a bar of soap or the number of jelly beans in a jar. Hundreds and thousands of people were arrested and jailed throughout the South for trying to participate in the democratic process.… Fifty years later we can ride anywhere we want to ride, we can stay where we want to stay. Those signs that said 'white' and 'colored' are gone. And you won't see them anymore— except in a museum, in a book, on a video. But there are still invisible signs buried in the hearts in humankind that form a gulf between us.*[12]

Others amplified King's message of equality and black worth. The inspiring novelist, essayist, teacher, and Nobel Literature Prize winner Toni Morrison (1931–2019), the granddaughter of a slave and perhaps America's greatest novelist, exposed the obscene injustices of slavery and provided a powerful rebuke to the long history that denigrated African Americans and women. Her writings called forth the spirit of trauma that, she asserted, still haunts the nation.

For three centuries the U.S. has benefited from immigration and refugees. Newcomers from around the world and their descendants occupied every occupational niche, won Noble Prizes, served in public office, founded tech companies, enriched culture, opened small businesses, and were essential to agriculture, industry, construction, and the service sector. In the past several decades, they have revitalized many towns and cities. Americans often boasted they live in a "melting pot" in which ethnic groups merged and lost their separate identities, which was often true for people of European ancestry. However, with many members of nonwhite ethnic groups maintaining their separate cultures, America increasingly became a multiracial, multicultural society. By 2018 the U.S. population of three hundred-thirty million, the world's third largest, was more diverse than ever: 76.5 percent white, 18.3 percent Hispanic, 13.4 percent black, and 5.9 percent Asian—over 14 percent were foreign-born. American life took on a cosmopolitan flavor: Spanish became widely spoken; Latin American grocery stores, Asian restaurants, and African art galleries opened in communities throughout the country. Alaska and Hawaii, both with large nonwhite populations, became states in 1959, adding to the nation's diversity.

Ethnic groups grew through both legal and illegal immigration. Some immigrants labored for meager wages in crowded sweatshops in big cities, where bosses often allowed workers only one or two breaks during their shift and ignored city safety regulations. Chinese sewed clothing in New York City; Mexicans did the same in Los Angeles. Many Native Americans lived in cities, others on isolated reservations. Some joined movements seeking a return of lands seized by white settlers

[11]Quoted in George Donelson Moss, *America in the Twentieth Century*, 4th ed. (Upper Saddle River, NJ: Prentice-Hall, 2000), 409.

[12]"Transcript: Rep. John Lewis' Speech on 50th Anniversary of the March on Washington," *Washington Post*, August 28, 2013 (washingtonpost.com/politics/transcript-rep-john-lewiss-speech-on-50th-anniversary-of-the-march-on-washington/2013/08/28/fc2d538a-100d-11e3-8cdd-bcdc09410972_story.html).

IMAGE 29.3 **The Obama Presidential Campaign** President Barack Obama addressed a large campaign rally in Las Vegas, Nevada, in November 2012, on his way to reelection for a second term.

Q What can we learn about Obama and election campaigns from the photo?

generations earlier. While a few tribes achieved prosperity by operating gambling casinos, most Native Americans remained poor. For several decades movements seeking independence, political sovereignty, or at least federal recognition for native Hawaiians became more active, some even demanding a new state constitution for the "Aloha state." By 2010 some eighty thousand of Hawaii's 1.4 million people identified as Native (indigenous) Hawaiians but another two hundred-ten claimed part-Hawaiian ancestry. Nonetheless, how sovereignty could be achieved in a diverse American state with many people from the mainland and elsewhere in the world remained to be seen.

Women's issues became more prominent. In the 1950s few women worked for high pay, colleges imposed strict quotas on female applicants, married women could not borrow money in their own names, there was no legal concept of sexual harassment, and some men joked of keeping women "barefoot and pregnant." By the early twenty-first century conditions had changed dramatically, but it took a long struggle for gender equality. Beginning in the 1960s many women joined feminist movements demanding equal legal rights with men and improved economic status. In 1963 Betty Friedan's (1921–2006) passionate book, *The Feminine Mystique*, identified women's core problem as patriarchal society and unfulfilling housework stunting their growth. With slogans such as "Sisterhood Is Powerful," women came together in groups, such as the National Organization for Women (NOW),

fighting for expanded opportunities. The number of women with paid work more than doubled between 1960 and 2000. By 2016 women workers' median income climbed to around 70 percent of men's. Women held governorships, federal cabinet posts, and United Nations ambassadorships, served in Congress, sat on the Supreme Court, and were serious candidates for president. Hillary Clinton became Obama's secretary of state, the third woman to hold that influential post. Today more women than men finish secondary school and attend universities, some joining highly paid, traditionally male occupations such as law, university teaching, engineering, and medicine. Women pursuing satisfying, well-paid careers, running for political office, and enjoying personal freedoms unimaginable to their great grandmothers owed their gains largely to the feminist movement and its male supporters. However, most employed women struggled to juggle work with family and housekeeping responsibilities. One young mother of two complained in the 1990s that "it's like twenty-four hours a day you're working. My day never ends."[13] Moreover, sexual harassment in the workplace, stalking, and rape remained serious problems. Scholars wrote of a "feminization of poverty" as many women headed single-parent families.

Some changes affected both women and men. Divorce became easier; over half of all marriages in the 1980s, and 40 percent in 2012, ended in divorce, fostering many single-parent households. As in Europe, many men and women never

---

[13]Quoted in James T. Patterson, *America Since 1941: A History*, 2nd ed. (Fort Worth, TX: Harcourt, 2000), 254.

married, often living with partners and often having children out of wedlock. Americans remained deeply divided on abortion, long common but illegal before being declared legal by the Supreme Court in 1973. Today legal abortion is widely available in many states, but many other states have made it difficult or nearly impossible to get one legally. By the 1960s gay men and lesbians actively fought harassment and legal discrimination, gaining greater acceptance; yet many, especially outside big cities, still faced hostility. Americans quarreled over allowing LGBTQ people to serve openly in the armed forces, marry, or establish legal partnerships, all patterns common in Europe and Canada but opposed by many Christian churches. By 2013 some states had legalized same-sex marriage, while many others passed laws forbidding it. In 2015 the Supreme Court legalized same-sex marriage and by 2018, either through the courts, legislation, or popular votes, it was legal everywhere. But some conservatives, viewing it as against their religious beliefs, still hope to overturn or limit the right.

Once importers of culture from Europe, Americans became the world's greatest exporters of popular culture products. U.S.-made films, television programs, books, magazines, popular music, and sports reached a global audience. Various musical styles, including the Broadway musicals of songwriters such as Richard Rodgers and Oscar Hammerstein, the blues of singer Billie Holiday and guitarist B. B. King, the jazz of saxophonist John Coltrane and trumpeter Miles Davis, and the country music of singer-songwriters Hank Williams and Dolly Parton, spread far and wide.

But no music style had the power of rock, which in the 1950s and 1960s helped spark a cultural revolution, especially among youth, in the United States and abroad. The first exhilarating blasts of rock and roll from, among others, hip-swinging white singer Elvis Presley (1935–1977) (known as "Elvis the Pelvis") and inventive black guitarist Chuck Berry (b. 1926) defied the Eisenhower era's puritanical social and political conformity, often alarming adults. Many young people accepted the invitation of popular rock and rollers Bill Haley and the Comets to "rock around the clock." Rock music broke down social barriers, challenging sexual and racial taboos by appealing across social class boundaries. Inspired by black rhythm and blues, southern white country, and gospel music, early rock proclaimed that young Americans were less divided by race than their parents. Rock became the heart of the 1960s youth movement, when albums by key rock musicians, such as poetic American singer-songwriter Bob Dylan and the British group the Beatles, seemed infused with political meaning; Dylan advised his listeners that "the answer" (to solving the nation's problems) was "blowing in the wind." Simon and Garfunkel suggested the elusive dream and promise of mid-1960s America as two lost souls struggle to navigate the highways of optimism and disillusionment, hope, and despair: "Kathy, I'm lost … empty and aching and I don't know why. Counting the cars on the New Jersey Turnpike, they've all come to look for America."[14] Rock later lost some of its political edge but, evolving into forms such as punk, grunge, heavy metal, and Indie rock, remained at the heart of U.S. popular music.

Musicians still address topical subjects. The U.S. has far more gun-related deaths and more mass killings than any other industrialized nation, with the easy availability of firearms a matter of bitter debate among Americans. Perhaps echoing Paul Simon, in 2019 eclectic pop singer Lana Del Ray, after a spate of mass shootings, went "Looking for America":

> I'm still looking for my own version of America
> One without the gun, where the flag can freely fly
> No bombs in the sky, only fireworks when you and I collide
> It's just a dream I had in mind.[15]

African American music has also addressed problems of American life. Soul music from artists like James Brown ("I'm Black and I'm Proud") and Aretha Franklin ("Respect") promoted black self-respect and unity, paralleling black pride movements. In the 1980s rap music and hip-hop culture, emerging out of urban black ghettos, became and still largely remains the cutting edge of Western pop music. An eclectic mix of rock, soul, rhythm and blues, and Caribbean music, rap expresses urban black youth's tensions, concerns, and aspirations. The boastful, often angry tone highlights conflict between white and black, rich and poor, and male and female, outraging segments of both white society and the black middle class. But it also attracted many young white fans. Perhaps no rapper has had more impact than the former street hustler Jay-Z (Shawn Carter) who assimilated his hustle, civil rights activism, and business success into his music while manifesting the quest for the "American Dream." Musicians in nations around the world adopted the rap style, often integrating it into their own traditions. Other pop and rock musical styles that emerged since the 1980s found audiences, but none had widespread appeal across racial and class lines.

29-2d The Canadian Experience

Although sharing cultural traditions and a democratic spirit with Americans, Canadians remained proudly independent of their powerful southern neighbor, nurturing differences such as two official languages—English and French. Two main parties, one liberal and one conservative, dominated national elections, but, unlike in the United States, smaller left-wing, right-wing, and regional parties also played key roles, often governing Canadian provinces. The French-Canadian nationalist Party Québécois (**KAY-be-KWAH**) often governed French-speaking Quebec, which contains a quarter of Canada's population, periodically holding votes on independence from Canada (see Map 29.2). In 1985 Quebec gained recognition as a distinct society with more provincial autonomy. By the 2010s Quebec nationalism enjoyed a revival. Several national political parties have experienced corruption or other scandals. Canadians still debate how much power to allocate to provinces and how much to the federal government.

Canadians, thirty-eight million strong by 2018, cannot ignore their proximity to the United States, which is much larger and with vastly more global power. Former prime minister Pierre Trudeau (**troo-DOE**) (g. 1968–1984), a French Canadian, complained that sharing a border with the United

[14]"America," written by Paul Simon, from Simon and Garfunkel's album *Bookends* (Columbia Records, 1968).
[15]Lana Del Ray, "Looking for America," azlyrics.com/lyrics/lanadelrey/lookingforamerica.html.

MAP 29.2 **Canada** The Canadian federation includes eleven provinces stretching from Newfoundland in the east to British Columbia and the Yukon in the west. In 1999 a large part of northern Canada, inhabited chiefly by the Inuit, became the self-governing region of Nunavut.

Q What can we learn from this map about the range of the Inuit people in Canada?

States was "like sleeping with an elephant. No matter how friendly or even-tempered the beast, one is affected by every twitch and grunt."[16] Most Canadians live within a hundred miles of the U.S. border, with easy access to the U.S. mass media. Moreover, Americans own some 20 percent of Canada's economy. Some resent U.S. domination. In 1994 the North American Free Trade Agreement (NAFTA) further bound the Canadian, Mexican, and U.S. economies. Yet, despite usually friendly relations, Canadians often opposed U.S. foreign policies, including the wars in Vietnam and Iraq.

Canadians generally enjoyed prosperity, which fostered social stability. Agricultural, industrial, and natural resource exports helped finance rising living standards, while mining vast oil reserves in tar sands enriched western provinces but also caused serious environmental damage. Hence, Canada consistently ranked among the top five nations in the annual United Nations Human Development Index of life quality. Canadians recovered better than most from the 2008–2009 global economic collapse, with lower unemployment and higher household net worth than Americans. Unlike more individualistic Americans, Canadians, influenced by social democratic ideals, built a strong social safety net, including

national health insurance. Generally more liberal on social and economic issues than Americans, they also approved same-sex marriage, banned the death penalty, and, in some provinces, decriminalized marijuana use. Organized religion's influence in public life has declined. In Quebec, where the Catholic Church once enjoyed great influence, even openly LGBTQ politicians enjoyed popular support and officials promoted secular policies. Quebec's birthrate, one of the world's highest in the 1940s, has fallen by over half, becoming one of the world's lowest.

Canadian society has become increasingly diverse, welcoming several million immigrants from all over the world, many from Asia and the Caribbean. In 2005 Haitian-born Michaëlle Jean, a Quebec television journalist, became Canada's first female governor-general, the official head of state representing the British monarch. By 2019 73 percent of Canadians were white, 5 percent Native American/ Indigenous, and 22 percent other ethnic minorities (mostly East, South, and Southeast Asians). A Canada-born Sikh, Jagmeet Singh, leads the nation's third largest political party while another Sikh, Harjit Sajjan, serves as Defense Minister for the ruling Liberal Party government of Justin Trudeau. Rather than following the American "melting pot" ideal,

---

[16]Quoted in Wayne C. Thompson, *Canada 1997* (Harpers Ferry, VA: Stryker-Post, 1997), 1.

Canadian laws, especially the Multiculturalism Act of 1988, allow ethnic minorities to maintain their cultures and languages and also recognize the rights of Native Americans, known as the "First Nations," some of whom have pressed land claims. But some Canadians resent recognition of Portuguese Canadians or Chinese Canadians. To address the desire for autonomy of the Inuit peoples of the Arctic region, in 1999 the federal government transformed much of northern Canada into the self-governing territory of Nunavut (NOO-nuh-voot). By the later 2010s the tolerant pro-immigration political consensus was fraying amidst a conservative backlash, and Quebec passed a law banning government workers, including teachers, from wearing religious symbols such as turbans and headscarves on the job. Canadians still debate how much to think of themselves as hyphenated English, French, Chinese, or Inuit Canadians and how much to live comfortably with multiple identities.

29-2e The Pacific Basin Societies

The diverse societies scattered around the Pacific Basin experienced major changes as they adjusted to a new world. In the two largest, most populous countries, Australia and New Zealand, the majority population, descended from European, mainly British and Irish, settlers, identified with western European society. Australia became one of the world's most affluent nations, known to its people as the "lucky country" because of its abundant resources and high living standards. A comprehensive system of social welfare, health care, and education helped forge a quality of life that usually places Australia near the top in the annual United Nations Human Development Reports. However, Australians have also faced chronic high unemployment and areas of persisting poverty. Like the U.S. they also have a serious opioid crisis. Feminists complain that men dominate government, business, and churches, giving women less influence than in most Western nations. Many men hold traditional views on women. Conservative prime minister, Tony Abbott (g. 2013–2015), was once asked rhetorically, in a discussion about the rarity of women in powerful positions in Australia: "What if men are, by physiology or temperament, more adapted to exercise authority or to issue command?"[17] Nonetheless, women have won considerable gender equity; Australians elected the first woman prime minister, Julia Gillard (g. 2010–2013), and Australia's richest person is mining magnate Gina Rinehart (b. 1954), by some accounts the world's richest woman.

Australia's twenty-five million people are increasingly diverse; nearly a third are foreign born and some 20 percent speak a language other than English at home. Immigrants or their descendants are prominent in most fields, including sports. In 1973 the federal government, seeking better relations with Asian nations, abandoned restrictions on nonwhite immigration—known as the "white Australia" policy—in place since 1901, stimulating immigration from Asia and the Middle East; as a result, some 13 percent of Australians have Asian ancestry and predominantly Asian neighborhoods developed in major cities. Occasional attacks on Middle Eastern and South Asian immigrants by drunken white youth have also showed that racism has not been eliminated. Newcomers from all over Europe continued to arrive. Hence, one of the major cities, Melbourne, boasted the world's largest Greek emigrant population. Race relations improved as indigenous people (Aborigines), 2.5 percent of the population, often poor and facing discrimination, gained some self-determination and land rights for their tribal territories. One group blocked a dam project in the 1990s that threatened tribal land. Yet, those Aborigines living in rundown city neighborhoods have struggled in the largely white-owned urban economy. In 2017 hundreds of indigenous leaders met and requested that their community be given some voice in Parliament and inclusion in the country's governing laws, prompting in a government agreement in 2019 to hold a constitutional recognition referendum within three years. In 2019 a ban on tourists climbing a huge rock sacred to indigenous groups went into effect. But not all Australians accepted indigenous rights. Without any public announcement, in 2019 the government of the state of Queensland unilaterally extinguished native titles over a huge tract of land so an influential Indian company could build an environmentally damaging coal mine there. The decision could see the protesting tribes forcibly removed by police from their traditional lands, including lands used for ceremonies.

Changing global conditions have forced new economic thinking. Climate change threatens Australia more than most nations, sparking even more catastrophic and frequent floods, fires, hurricanes, and droughts as well as devastating the magnificent Great Barrier Reef. Fire season itself has become nearly a year-round reality, the number of hot days has doubled in the past fifty years, and heat waves have become hotter and longer. Yet the conservative coalition that has governed Australia for most of the last two decades (1996–2007, 2013–present) has mostly embraced climate change denial and continues to expand fossil fuel use and mining. Thanks to a mining boom, Australia largely avoided recession during the global financial crisis, but growth slowed by 2013. With an economy based primarily on exporting minerals, wheat, beef, and wool, Australia needs secure outside markets. Formation of the European Union and NAFTA threatened traditional markets in Europe and North America, raising questions about the link to Britain. In a 1999 referendum, 55 percent of Australians supported remaining a constitutional monarchy under the British queen. Yet, Britain was far away, while Asia was, as Australians put it, the "near north." Torn between its European history and Asian geography, Australians established closer trade and investment links to Southeast Asia, East Asia, and the Pacific islands, fostering two decades of economic growth; by 2000, Asian nations, especially China, accounted for some 60 percent of Australia's export market. By 2018 Australia was China's sixth largest trading partner and fifth biggest supplier of imports (some 25 percent of manufactured goods) and tenth biggest customer for exports. Hence, any instability in China trade, such as the 2019 trade war with the U.S., poses difficult challenges for Australia, spurring a debate on whether the nation was becoming too close to, and susceptible to political interference from, China. A spying scandal in 2019 increased the public fears.

[17]Quoted in A. Odysseus Patrick, "Australia's Tony Abbott on Track to Win Prime Minister Post After Years in the Political Doldrums," *Washington Post*, September 3, 2013 (washingtonpost.com/world/asia_pacific/australias-tony-abbott-on-track-to-win-prime-minister-post-after-years-in-political-doldrums/2013/09/03/24aaae98-10c7-11e3-bdf6-e4fc677d94a1_story.html).

New Zealanders (five million by 2018) have long cultivated their British heritage and British patronage, but now they have also forged strategic and economic connections within the Asia-Pacific region. The economy traditionally relied heavily on tourism and export of agricultural products, mostly to Britain. But, suffering from a stumbling economy and jolted by Britain's membership in the European Community, New Zealand cultivated close relations with the United States and then with nearby Asian and Pacific countries, which by 2000 accounted for one-third of the nation's trade. By 2019 20 percent of their exports went to China. New Zealand is one of sixteen countries, including Australia, Japan, India, and China, that is working to form the world's largest free-trade zone by population, the Regional Comprehensive Economic Partnership, perhaps by 2020. While experiencing rising unemployment, New Zealanders were also helped by an elaborate social welfare system. Thanks in part to expanded educational opportunities, women gained new economic roles and served in politics. A former university professor, Labor Party leader Helen Clark (b. 1950) was the nation's first female prime minister (g. 1999–2008). In 2017 the second woman, Jacinda Ardern (b. 1980), took power after a Labor Party electoral victory. In 2013 New Zealanders approved gay marriage. Closer ties to the Pacific region fostered increased immigration from Asia and the Pacific islands. By 2018 74 percent of people were white, 15 percent Māori, 12 percent Asian, and 6 percent Pacific Islander. The government also recognized the land rights of, and worked to end discrimination against, the native Māori minority, who sought to maintain their Polynesian culture while adding modern economic skills and improving social well-being.

While Australians and New Zealanders long enjoyed independence, decolonization of many Pacific islands, spurred by the United Nations, came much later; between 1962 and 1980 nine independent Pacific nations were formed in Polynesia and Melanesia, and in 1990 the United States gave up control of some of its Micronesian territories. The new states ranged from republics such as Fiji to kingdoms like Tonga to groupings such as the Federated States of Micronesia. Not all Pacific islanders, however, became independent. Some French-ruled islands, such as Tahiti and New Caledonia, became semiautonomous French territories with representation in the French parliament, and many islanders resented what they considered disguised French colonialism. Most independent islands retained close ties to their former colonizer, as Micronesia did with the United States. Pacific islanders have remained dependent on fishing, tourism, and export of mineral and agricultural products to Japan, the United States, Australia, and New Zealand.

Islanders cooperated on common issues, forming regional organizations that promoted everything from duty-free trade to art festivals and fighting high-technology fishing fleets from industrialized nations. Opposing nuclear weapons testing, they joined with Australia and New Zealand to declare the Pacific a nuclear-free zone. The international Law of the Sea Treaty gave them more control of adjacent sea beds and their minerals. But some problems have defied solution. Thanks to rising sea levels, which threaten low-lying atolls and coastal plains, many

Kylie McLaughlin/Lonely Planet Images/Getty Images

IMAGE 29.4 **Lion Dance** In recent decades, many Asians have settled in Australia. This Chinese dragon dance, in Melbourne's large Chinatown, celebrates the Chinese New Year.

Q What does the photo suggest about the ethnic diversity of Australian cities?

islanders will have to relocate over the next century. The Tuvalu islands, with eleven thousand people and averaging only three feet above sea level, will be inundated by 2050, if not earlier, and islanders debate whether the government should begin seeking a new home, possibly in New Zealand or Australia.

Islanders have held on to some indigenous traditions while adapting to social and political change. While most became Christian, some pre-Christian customs remained important. For example, although Western Samoa, first ruled by Germany and then by New Zealand, has an elected parliament, clan chiefs still govern the villages. But poverty fostered migration to island cities, such as Suva in Fiji and Pago Pago in American Samoa, as well as emigration to Australia, New Zealand, Hawaii, and the mainland United States. More Samoans and Cook Islanders live abroad than at home; thousands of Tongans reside in California. The money migrants send back has become a valuable source of income. Some islands have experienced ethnic or regional conflict over political power and scarce land. Occasional military coups have rocked Fiji, resulting from tensions between descendants of Indian immigrants, nearly half the population, and native Fijians, who fear that Indians want to diminish traditional Fijian chiefs and challenge tribal rights to land.

KEY POINTS

▶ On average, U.S. residents are among the wealthiest in the world, yet in recent decades many industrial jobs have been moved overseas and the gap between rich and poor has grown wider, with the former often living in suburbs and the latter left behind in inner cities.

▶ After 1945 African Americans gained legal rights through the civil rights movement, immigrants made America more diverse, women increasingly entered the workforce, and gays and lesbians became more visible but still struggled for equal rights.

▶ While Canada's culture and economy are strongly influenced by the United States, in many ways Canada resembles western Europe, with a strong social safety net and a more liberal attitude on social issues.

▶ Australia and New Zealand have maintained their traditional ties with Britain but have also traded increasingly with their Asian neighbors, while many Pacific islands have gained independence from former colonizers but still face challenges such as rising sea levels, poverty, and ethnic conflict.

29-3 Political Change in Latin America and the Caribbean

▦ SOCIETIES ▦ NETWORKS

Q Why have democracy and economic development proved to be difficult goals in Latin America?

The Latin American and Caribbean peoples (see Map 29.3) had different experiences than North Americans and Pacific Basin societies. Social inequality, economic underdevelopment, and demands for change often generated revolutionary and progressive political movements in impoverished villages and shantytowns. Sometimes leftists gained power, launching reforms; only in Cuba did they remain in power for decades. A few Latin American countries and most small Caribbean islands enjoyed consistent democratic traditions; elsewhere military leaders or autocratic civilians often dominated governments. Most governments, whether democratic or dictatorial, proved unable to eliminate their nation's major problems.

CONNECTION to TODAY

How have you, your family, and community been affected by the political changes and revolutions that occurred in countries such as Cuba, Mexico, Brazil, and Venezuela in this era?

reformer who marginalized the legislature and crushed opposition. With help from his hugely popular wife, Evita Perón (1919–1952), a radio and stage actress from a poor family and a proponent of social justice, the nationalistic regime won working- and middle-class support, emphasized industrialization, and bought often foreign-owned banks, insurance companies, railroads, and shipping companies. Evita promoted women's issues. After Evita's death in 1952, corruption, growing unemployment, inflation, strikes, and human-rights abuses sparked Perón's overthrow in 1955. The military mostly ruled Argentina from the 1950s through 1983, often killing opponents. Yet Perón's followers sustained a Peronist movement, chiefly working class, that often governed Argentina after democracy was restored. In recent years economic ups and downs often determined whether Peronists or their pro–free enterprise, pro-U.S. center-right or conservative opponents came to power.

As in Argentina, right-wing and left-wing forces jockeyed for power in Latin America. From the 1950s through the late 1980s, right-wing military governments and despots ruled most countries, suppressing labor unions, student protesters, and democracy activists to maintain stability. In some Central American countries such as El Salvador and Guatemala, organized death squads assassinated dissident peasants,

29-3a Despotisms, Democracies, and the United States

Latin Americans struggled to raise living standards and expand political participation. Some paternalistic but authoritarian reformers mobilized workers and peasants for change, but they failed to empower the people or significantly improve their lives. For example, the charismatic Juan Perón (puh-RONE) (1895–1974), a former army officer, admirer of Benito Mussolini, and hypnotic public speaker, was elected Argentina's president in 1946 and proved to be an autocratic

MAP 29.3 **Modern Latin America and the Caribbean** Latin America includes the nations of Central and South America and those Caribbean societies that are Spanish-speaking, including Cuba and the Dominican Republic. Brazil, Argentina, and Mexico are the largest Latin American nations. The peoples of the small Caribbean islands, mostly English- or French-speaking, also formed independent states.

Q What are the five largest countries in Latin America?

liberal clergy, teachers, and journalists. Despite the repression, left-wing movements increased their strength. By 1979 the Sandinistas, a Marxist-led revolutionary movement, had defeated the long-standing dictatorship and gained control of Nicaragua. In 1970 the even more radical Shining Path emerged in Peru; its leaders, half of them women, mixed Maoist ideas with plans to emancipate impoverished Indians. Their

rebellion terrorized Peruvians before being crushed in the early 1990s. The president credited with crushing the Shining Path and bringing stability, Alberto Fujimori (g. 1990–2000), was the first person of Japanese ancestry to lead a Latin American country. Peru and Brazil have both had large Japanese communities since the early twentieth century. But Fujimori was forced out of office on corruption charges and later imprisoned for crimes like murder, embezzlement, and bribery while president. His daughter, Keiko Fujimori (b. 1975), also became a leading politician, heading a conservative party and running for president several times.

During the later 1980s, with right-wing rule largely discredited for not addressing mass poverty, many nations turned to democracy and free markets under centrist or moderate leftist leaders. In most cases they also could not resolve severe problems or diminish social inequalities. Some nations faced racial and ethnic tensions. Large Native American (indigenous) communities in Bolivia, Peru, Colombia, Mexico, and Guatemala, alienated from the white and mestizo elite and often allied with leftists, increasingly sought equal rights, a fairer share of wealth, and recognition of their cultures and aspirations. Hence, in 2005 Bolivia's resentful indigenous majority elected as president socialist Evo Morales (b. 1959), a former small-town soccer player who led coca farmers in fighting a white-dominated government and U.S. opposition to coca growing. At an ancient temple's ruins, Morales participated in a spiritual ceremony steeped in his Aymara peoples' pre-Inca traditions. Walking barefoot up the pyramid steps, he donned a traditional tunic and cap, accepted a gold and silver baton from Aymara priests, and promised to "seek equality and justice" for the poor and eliminate vestiges of the colonial past. However, successfully redistributing wealth and power from the white minority, reshaping the political system, and pursuing nationalistic economic policies generated conflict within Bolivia and U.S. opposition. In 2019 Bolivia fell into chaos. Morales won a disputed election but was deposed by the military and sent into exile. Right wing leaders who resented the indigenous majority, opposed socialism, and espoused conservative Christianity seized power, resulting in massive violent protests soon crushed by the army. Bolivia remains deeply polarized.

By the later 1990s, as disillusionment with capitalism increased, the left regained the political initiative, largely within a democratic context. Voters desperate for more equitable policies elected pragmatic leftist leaders in countries such as Argentina, Brazil, Chile, Ecuador, Uruguay, and El Salvador; some prosecuted or investigated human-rights violations perpetrated under military rule. But many later faced challenges. After mobilizing poor workers and peasants, in 1999 the radical former general Hugo Chavez (1954–2013) was elected president of oil-rich Venezuela, a country of thirty-two million people in 2016. Chavez introduced socialist policies to redistribute oil wealth to the poor, marginalized the congress, and controlled the courts, all actions that alienated the wealthy and middle class, who organized mass protests. Chavez called his policies the Bolivaran Revolution, linking them to the nineteenth-century, Venezuelan-born liberator. The United States moved to isolate the dictatorial, pro-Cuba Chavez regime and support the opposition. Chavez lambasted U.S. leaders and foreign policies, provided aid and oil to other Latin Americans, and tightened his grip on politics and the media, but economic problems after 2009 eroded domestic support. His allies maintained power after Chavez died of cancer soon after his 2012 reelection; his death was mourned by the poor. His successor, Nicholas Maduro, continued the populist policies, including fossil fuel subsidies,

but with disastrous results. The nation's economy collapsed, causing a crisis of hyperinflation, shortages of food and basic goods, poverty, crime, unemployment, depression, disease, malnutrition, default on national debt payments, and a violent crackdown on the opposition. The mounting problems have led to riots, irreconcilable political divisions, rigged elections, and some four million Venezuelans fleeing the country that has not abated. With China, Cuba, and Russia supporting Maduro, the Trump administration imposed an embargo, threatened military intervention, and, along with several South American nations including Brazil, Chile, and Colombia, recognized opposition leader Juan Guaidó **(GWAI DOH)** as president. But Guaido was forced into exile after an unsuccessful coup attempt encouraged by Trump, and Maduro has remained in power even while the misery for the population continues.

Latin Americans also had to deal with the United States and its powerful presence. Referring to longtime U.S. economic leverage, a leftist Nicaraguan leader lamented that his country's "function was to grow sugar, cocoa and coffee for the United States; we served the dessert at the imperialist dining table."[18] The United States acted not only as neighborhood bully at times but also as a leading trading partner, major source of investment capital, supplier of military and economic assistance, and inspiration to the region's democrats and free market enthusiasts. U.S. popular culture, particularly film and music, reached a huge audience, influencing local cultures. Moreover, millions of people seeking a better life have moved north to the United States legally or illegally.

Under the banner of Cold War-driven anti-communism, Americans often intervened in Latin American and Caribbean countries, arousing much local resentment. For example, in 1954 a CIA-organized and armed force led by exiled Guatemalan military officers overthrew a democratically elected, reformist government led chiefly by liberals and socialists who were considered communists by American leaders for implementing land reform and encouraging leftist labor unions, angering U.S. business interests. The powerful United Fruit Company, closely connected to Eisenhower administration officials, controlled much of Guatemala's economy, especially the banana plantations. The democratic regime's removal cheered wealthy Guatemalans and U.S. corporations, but Guatemala's new leaders formed death squads that killed over 200,000 people, especially poor indigenous peasants and workers, over the next three decades. By 1990, when the repression diminished, 90 percent of Guatemalans still lived in poverty, and one-third lacked adequate food. Since then politics remains a bitter contest between leftist reformers and U.S.-supported right-wingers.

U.S. leaders also used their power elsewhere, offering military assistance and advice to friendly governments against revolutionary movements in El Salvador, Honduras, and Colombia and employing covert operations to undermine or overthrow left-leaning governments in Brazil (1964), Chile (1973), and Nicaragua (1989). Most Americans were unaware of the covert activities until years later. Sometimes the United States dispatched military forces, as in the Dominican Republic (1965) and Grenada (1982). Although not inspired

---

[18]Jaime Wheelock, quoted in Kyle Longley, *In the Eagle's Shadow: The United States and Latin America* (Wheeling, IL: Harlan Davidson, 2002), 291.

by anti-communism, in 1990 U.S. troops invaded Panama to remove and arrest dictator Manuel Noriega (b. 1940), a longtime U.S. ally and well-paid CIA informant who was implicated in human-rights abuses and drug smuggling. In 1999 the United States transferred control over the Panama Canal to Panama, yet U.S. military bases remained there, symbolizing continuing regional power. Since 1990 Panama has maintained a vibrant democracy with regular changes of power and presidents. U.S. troops were also sent to Haiti in 1994 to support a reform government that replaced a brutal dictatorship, promoting stability as left-wing and right-wing forces intermittently battled for control, leaving Haitians more desperate. Little has changed since then for Haiti, with corrupt regimes, mass poverty, and sporadic destructive hurricanes. Political turbulence has been common; in 2019 deadly protests broke out against corruption, poverty, hunger, and a faltering economy, paralyzing the country for weeks.

29-3b The Legacy of Revolution: Mexico and Cuba

The early-twentieth-century Mexican Revolution inspired hopes of reducing social inequality, but the nation's leaders soon emphasized economic growth over uplifting the poor majority. Even today, in southern states where revolutionaries once promised liberty and justice, peasant men, wearing traditional white cotton pants and shirt, still use machetes to cultivate their tiny plots of corn. In Mexico's limited democracy, the Party of Revolutionary Institutions (PRI) controlled elections, often resorting to voter fraud. A broad coalition of factions led by businessmen and bureaucrats, the PRI fostered stability for decades while deflecting challenges to its power, usually by co-opting or arresting opponents. But in 1968 police fired on a large demonstration, killing hundreds of university students and other protesters.

By the 1980s the PRI began to falter as leftist and right-wing parties made some national gains. In the early 1990s a peasant revolt in a poor southern state, Chiapas, revealed starkly the PRI's failure to redress rural poverty. The 2000 election of a non-PRI president, Vicente Fox, ended the seven-decades-long PRI monopoly on federal power. Fox, a pro-U.S. rancher and free market conservative, could not foster much economic or social change, while the PRI still held power in many states and enjoyed a national power base. Gradually, however, a more open and pluralistic political system emerged, with stronger left-wing and right-wing parties contending with the PRI for support. In the 2008 elections another conservative edged out a leftist for the presidency, solidifying a multiparty system. In 2012, with sixty thousand dead from rampant violence by drug cartels, crime syndicates, and a failed war on drugs, making life dangerous in many regions, the PRI returned to power under a new president, Enrique Peña Nieto. But as the murders piled up, the economy faltered, a large movement of Central American and other refugees seeking asylum traveled through Mexico to reach the U.S. border, and U.S.–Mexico relations soured, in the 2018 elections a left-wing coalition headed by former Mexico City mayor Andrés Manuel López Obrador came to power with 50 percent of the national vote. López Obrador has pursued, with only modest success, a mix of leftist and

moderate policies and worked to find ways to cooperate with U.S. President Donald Trump, deeply unpopular in Mexico, who expressed contempt for many Mexican immigrants while demanding cooperation with his anti-immigrant policies. But as the decade nears its end recession looms, due partly to ambitious but expensive social programs but even more to the increasing economic problems faced by the nation's leading trading partner, the U.S.

Mexico's economic system also gradually opened, although corruption remained part of life. For decades the PRI mixed capitalism with a strong government role. However, with oil the major foreign revenue source, collapsing world oil prices in the 1980s damaged development prospects; open markets replaced protectionist policies. In 1994, after NAFTA helped integrate the U.S., Canadian, and Mexican economies, many U.S.-owned factories opened on Mexico's side of the border. In 2018 Trump demanded an update of the agreement that he claimed would benefit the U.S.; Mexico and Canada had little choice but to participate. The majority of new workers, poorly paid young women housed in crowded dormitories or flimsy shacks, often complained of harassment or assault by male workers or managers. Elsewhere many Mexicans lost jobs; peasant corn farmers could not compete with highly subsidized U.S. farmers. By 2000 half of the one hundred million Mexicans lived on $4 a day or less, and the bottom 20 percent of Mexicans earned only 4 percent of the country's personal income. Even the urban middle class felt the economic pain as wages stagnated. Whereas in 1980 Mexico's economy was nearly four times larger than South Korea's, by 2005 a dynamic South Korea had pushed ahead. At the same time, Mexico's population quadrupled between 1940 and 2000 but then slowed to about 1 percent a year; by 2019 there were some one hundred thirty-three million Mexicans. In recent years Mexico has become Latin America's largest exporter of manufactured products, income inequality has declined, and more people have joined the middle class. These trends attracted migrants from the United States, Asia, and Latin America; between 2000 and 2010 the foreign-born population doubled. By 2018 about 70 percent of Mexicans lived in poverty or vulnerability while the richest 20 percent of the population earned ten times as much as the poorest 20 percent. Because of poverty and overpopulation, thousands of desperate Mexicans have continued to cross the border to the United States each year, legally or illegally, in search of a better life. Others have taken up growing or smuggling illegal drugs. Mexicans have long passionately debated the Spanish conquest of Mexico. In 2019, on the 500th anniversary of that experience, a Mexican descendant of Aztec emperor Moctezuma met an Italian descendant of conquistador Hernán Cortés in Mexico City. They advocated for leaving the past behind but López Obrador wanted an apology from Spain.

Unlike Mexico, Cuba, led by Fidel Castro (1927–2016), built a society dominated by a powerful communist government. Castro, a onetime amateur baseball star nearly signed by a U.S. professional team who instead became a lawyer, came to power in 1959 in a revolution against a corrupt U.S.-supported dictator. Although a rich sugar planter's son, Castro allied with the Cuban Communist Party, pledging to introduce radical change; many thousands of affluent Cubans fled to the nearby United States.

In 1961 Americans moved to isolate and then overthrow Castro's regime by organizing a Cuban exile military force that landed on a Cuban beach, the Bay of Pigs. But the invasion, poorly planned and enjoying little popular support in Cuba, was routed—a humiliation for the United States. Castro became a firm Soviet ally, igniting even more U.S. opposition and precipitating the Cuban Missile Crisis. In 1962 U.S. air surveillance discovered Soviet ballistic missiles with a two-thousand-mile range and capable of carrying nuclear warheads. President John F. Kennedy demanded the missiles' removal, imposed a naval blockade on Cuba, and considered invading the island. With the threat of nuclear confrontation looming, the Soviets removed the missiles, defusing the crisis. In the aftermath, the United States imposed an economic boycott, supported by Cuban exiles, that cut off Cuba from sources of trade and investment.

In the 1960s and 1970s Castro tried innovative socialist policies, known as **Castroism**, to stimulate economic development while tightly controlling the population. Castro called capitalism "repugnant, filthy, gross, alienating because it causes war, hypocrisy and competition"[19]; yet his own policies generated little surplus food and few consumer goods. Despite valiant efforts, Cubans largely failed to diversify their sugar-based economy. Nonetheless, Castroism improved some aspects of life for the working classes: schools and clinics were built, literacy campaigns were mounted, and long-marginalized Afro-Cubans and women gained more equality; by 2016 women constituted 60 percent of professional and technical workers and 52 percent of the National Assembly. Yet, sexism is endemic; various forms of harassment, abuse, and violence against women as well as patriarchal attitudes persist. By the mid-1980s Cuba had the lowest infant mortality and highest literacy rates, life expectancy, and doctors per population in Latin America; its citizens lived as long as North Americans and ten years longer than Mexicans and Brazilians. Moreover, unlike in some Latin American dictatorships, no death squads murdered dissidents. However, government agencies monitored citizens and their opinions; Castro limited free expression and jailed or harassed those who defied the ban, including brave writers, homosexuals, and human-rights and free-speech advocates. Seeking political freedom, better-paying jobs, or higher living standards, nearly a million Cubans fled over the years, mostly to the United States; forty thousand of them left in 2013.

Castro exchanged dependence on the United States for dependence on the USSR, which poured billions of dollars into the country. Since the USSR's collapse, Cuba has struggled. With few foreign markets or sources of capital, the social welfare system cracked, and the economy crumbled despite some market reforms. Yet, frustrating his opponents, Castro remained in power for fifty years. In 2008 an ailing Castro turned over

IMAGE 29.5 **Castro Addressing Crowd** A spellbinding orator, the Cuban leader, Fidel Castro, often recruited support for his government and policies by speaking at large rallies. In this 2003 rally in Havana he spoke to hundreds of thousands in May Day celebrations.

Q What can this photo tell us about Castro's personality and political style?

leadership to his brother Raul Castro (b. 1931), who promised to make the revolution "prosperous and sustainable" and offered some cautious reforms, sputtering toward a market economy. Economic aid from oil-rich Venezuela helped Cubans survive. The regime tolerated mild criticism, leased some state-owned land to private farmers, and allowed small private enterprises like restaurants, pizza makers, and cobblers, often in homes or garages, while trimming the government workforce. Many of the new entrepreneurs received investment from relatives in the United States. Legal bazaars now fill streets to serve consumers. Many urban Cubans, but not the poorest residents, have access to televisions, DVDs from Miami, Internet-linked computers, cell phones, and even (often old) cars. Critics, including most U.S. allies, have opposed the U.S. embargo, arguing that it helped the Castros by reinforcing anti-U.S. feelings and discrediting dissidents. Encouraged by U.S. business and farm interests who wanted access to the Cuban market as well as many Latin American experts and younger Cuban-Americans, in 2009 U.S. president Barack Obama made it easier for U.S.-based Cubans as well as Americans to visit the island and weakened the embargo. Fidel Castro died in 2016. Raul Castro retired in 2018, replaced by the head of the National Assembly, Miguel Díaz-Canel, who was not even born when the Castros came to power. But in 2017 President Trump restored the embargo and travel ban and imposed even harsher policies, embittering many Cubans. Díaz-Canel sought to bolster his position by raising monthly

Castroism Innovative socialist policies introduced by Fidel Castro to stimulate economic development in Cuba while tightly controlling its population.

---

[19]Quoted in Sebastian Balfour, *Castro*, 2nd ed. (New York: Longman, 1995), 167.

salaries for state workers from $32 to $44. Many Cubans have resented the authoritarian rules and desired a freer system but also opposed the embargo; remembering U.S. domination from 1898 to 1959, some Cubans remain wary of the United States. Without Venezuelan aid by 2019 food shortages returned and Cuba reintroduced rationing and arrested some dissidents.

29-3c Dictatorship and Democracy: Brazil and Chile

Few Latin American nations have had as much promise and experienced as many problems as Brazil and Chile. Occupying half of South America, Brazil is Latin America's colossus, with two hundred-eleven million people (sixth in the world) and its largest economy. From the mid-1940s to the mid-1960s Brazilians, despite economic crises, maintained democracy. In 1961 João Goulart (jao joo-LART) (1918–1976), a populist reformer supported by leftists, assumed the presidency, but his efforts to organize impoverished peasants and rural workers antagonized powerful landlords. The military overthrew Goulart in 1964 and imposed a harsh dictatorship for the next two decades (1964–1985), arresting some forty thousand opponents. Fearing a communist takeover, the United States encouraged the military coup because it supported authoritarian governments that emphasized economic growth and national security. Relying on brutal repression, the generals imposed censorship, outlawed political parties, and banned strikes and collective bargaining. Right-wing vigilante groups and death squads killed up to one hundred dissidents a month and tortured countless others, including labor leaders and slum dwellers.

For a decade the capitalist economy boomed, eliciting American praise of the "Brazilian miracle" as annual growth rates averaged 10 percent between 1968 and 1974 and exports shifted from natural resources, such as coffee, to manufactured goods. Industrialization relied heavily on foreign investment, technology, and markets; the United States and international lending agencies poured in $8 billion in aid. But the "miracle" depended on low wages and redistributing income upward to the rich and middle class, confirming the local saying that there is no justice for the poor. The top 10 percent enjoyed 75 percent of the income gain, while half of all households lived below the poverty line. While many people went barefoot and dressed in rags, Brazil made and exported shoes. Brazilian governments also encouraged land speculators and foreign corporations to open up the vast Amazon Basin, the world's largest tropical rain forest and river system. Logging, farming, mining, and ranching rapidly stripped virgin forest, destabilizing the environment and displacing many of the 200,000 indigenous people living off its resources. Brazil's South American neighbors such as Peru and Bolivia are also responsible for severe deforestation in the Amazon region.

By 1980 the "miracle" had faded; Brazil experienced an inflation rate of over 100 percent, huge balance-of-payments deficits, massive foreign debt, and sagging industrial production. Meanwhile, numerous Brazilians demanded democracy, and the Catholic Church criticized human-rights violations, advocating for social justice. In 1985 democracy returned with the election of a civilian president. However, under the successive democratic governments led by moderate reformers, many problems remained unresolved; leaders feared another military coup. Inflation soared

to 2,500 percent by 1994. When landless peasants seized land, well-connected landowners hired gunmen to harass them. Social inequities such as school dropout rates, malnutrition, bankrupt public health services, homelessness, and debt slavery grew. Before 2000 Brazil maintained one of the world's most unequal income distributions: the wealthiest 1 percent earned the same percentage of national income as the poorest 50 percent. Many Brazilians became disillusioned with democracy.

Wanting further reform, in 2002 Brazilians turned to the left, electing as president socialist labor leader Luiz Inácio Lula da Silva (b. 1944), known as Lula, a former metalworker and longtime dissident. While some peasant and worker groups believed that Lula's pragmatic, moderate economic policies did too little for the poor, he had the most far-reaching policies on protecting the environment and slowing Amazon deforestation of any Brazilian president. Lula fostered such dramatic economic growth that some observers compared Brazil to dynamic Southeast Asian nations such as Malaysia, Singapore, and Thailand. Eventually Lula's center-left policies fostered a larger middle class and improved life for many. The booming economy (the world's seventh largest), growing manufacturing, and discovery of offshore oil gave Brazil regional and international clout, restoring national self-confidence. Brazil became a major player in the G-20 group of key industrial nations and joined with Russia, India, China, and South Africa to form the BRICS bloc as an alternative to the U.S.-led Western alliance. When Lula retired in 2011, still highly popular, Brazilians elected his colleague, former left-wing dissident Dilma Rousseff (b. 1947) and the nation's first female leader. But while unemployment remained low, the economy stumbled (from 7.5 percent growth in 2010 to 1 percent in 2012) and inflation increased.

In 2013 massive street protests erupted against chronic corruption, inadequate public services, police brutality, slowing economic growth, increasing violent crime, and lavish spending on facilities for the 2014 World Cup and 2016 Summer Olympics, unsettling the political landscape. Politicians from all political parties became enmeshed in tax-evasion schemes and corruption scandals. In 2016 Rousseff was impeached by the Congress for breaking budgetary laws while investigations began of lawmakers and eleven cabinet members of the conservative new president, Michel Temer, who was also arrested in 2018. In 2018 the still popular Lula, a favorite to win the presidency again, was convicted and imprisoned for corruption and money laundering. Many observers doubted his guilt, viewing his trial as political. In the 2019 elections corruption-weary Brazilians changed direction, electing a far-right nationalist government led by the avidly pro-development Jair Bolsonaro (b. 1955), who expressed contempt for feminists, LGBTQ people, indigenous groups, nonwhites (over 50 percent of the population), migrants, environmentalists, and climate-change activists while praising the military and the years under brutal junta control. An evangelical Christian, Bolsonaro and his outsized personality, unfiltered opinions, and unchecked ego are often compared to Trump. His policies are similar, patronizing ranching, agricultural, big business, and the military while promoting rapid "development" of the Amazon rain forest, nearly the size of two Indias and a cradle of biodiversity. When thousands of fires engulfed the Amazon in 2019 in Brazil (as well as Bolivia, Peru, and Colombia), most set by farmers, ranchers, and miners to clear land (often illegally) for their operations, many blamed Bolsonaro, who made little effort to mount fire-suppression efforts. Months later many fires still burned. Scientists declared this disaster an "ecocide"; they agreed that the fires, badly damaging the world's biggest carbon sink while destroying many indigenous villages as well as rare animal species and potentially medicinal plants, will accelerate and worsen global warming for the planet. Bolsonaro also established close ties to Trump, who promoted a large trade agreement between the two countries. In 2019 Brazil was on the verge of recession, partly due to slumping commodity prices. Brazilians have often shared an optimistic outlook because of the nation's size and economic potential, reflected in the saying that "God is a Brazilian." But a perennial local joke reflects cynicism: "Brazil, Country of the Future, but the future never comes."[20]

Chileans, like Brazilians, tried varied strategies, from reform to dictatorship to democracy, to foster development. Chileans enjoyed a long tradition, unusual in Latin America, of elected democratic governments sustained by a large middle class, high rates of literacy and urbanization, and multiple political parties. Nonetheless, a wealthy elite of businessmen, military officers, and landowners held political power, suppressing labor unrest. Dependent on mineral exports, especially copper, by the 1960s Chile, divided politically between the right, center, and left, had a stagnant economy in which two-thirds of Chileans earned under $200 a year. With the 1970 elections, Chileans shifted direction and elected the Popular Unity, a coalition of six liberal, socialist, and communist parties supported by small businessmen, the urban working class, and peasants. Their winning presidential candidate, medical doctor Salvador Allende (ah-YEN-dee) (1908–1973), promised a "Chilean road" to socialism, with red wine and meat pies, through constitutional means in a parliamentary democracy. His regime nationalized banks and a copper industry dominated by powerful U.S. corporations; broke up underutilized ranches and farms, dividing the land among the peasant residents; supported labor unions; and provided urban shantytowns with health clinics and better schools. Both employment and economic production soared. The Popular Unity also fostered a Chilean cultural renaissance, arguing that American magazines, recordings, and films had overwhelmed Chilean-produced cultural products. A pro-Allende cultural organization protested, "Our folklore, our history, our customs, our way of living and thinking are being strangled [by] the uncontrolled invasion [of the U.S. media and popular culture]."[21]

Although democracy flourished and Allende enjoyed growing popularity, rapid reforms produced shortages of luxury goods, fostering middle-class resentment. Allende's opponents controlled the mass media and judiciary while dominating the congress. U.S. president Richard Nixon worried about Allende's friendship with Cuba's Fidel Castro and feared that Allende's socialism without revolution could spread, threatening U.S. power and economic interests. Nixon mounted an international economic embargo on Chilean exports, while the CIA spread untrue rumors, helped assassinate pro-Allende military officers, and organized strikes to paralyze the economy.

In 1973 a U.S.-supported military coup overthrew Allende, who died defending the presidential palace. The military imposed a brutal military dictatorship led by General Augusto Pinochet (ah-GOOS-toh pin-oh-CHET) (1915–2006) that arrested 150,000 Allende supporters, detained and tortured hundreds of political prisoners for years, and murdered thousands of dissidents, sometimes in front of other prisoners held in the national stadium. Thousands fled the country. The junta forbade labor unions and strikes, prohibited free speech and political parties, restored nationalized U.S. property, and publicly burned books and records produced by leftist Chileans. Advised by U.S. economists, Pinochet installed a free enterprise economy, similar to military-ruled Brazil's, that generated growth and moderate middle-class prosperity but also a monumental foreign debt and environmental degradation. Little of this wealth trickled down to the poor, whose living standards deteriorated. By the later 1980s, unemployment had skyrocketed to 30 percent, and 60 percent of Chileans were poor. Two observers wrote that Pinochet's Chile "remained a dual society of winners and losers. The rich, roaring through traffic in their expensive sedans, seemed to mock those left behind, trapped in fuming buses."[22]

However, a severe economic crisis undermined the regime's legitimacy, and in 1989 escalating social tensions and political protests forced an election. The resulting center-left governments, often headed by presidents from Allende's Socialist Party, retained free enterprise while boosting health, housing, education, and social spending. They reduced poverty by half and lowered unemployment; tax increases and increased welfare did not stifle high annual economic growth. Chile has become the most prosperous Latin American economy and enjoys a stable democratic system, but considerable inequality persists. In 2006 Chilean voters chose pediatrician-turned-socialist-politician Michelle Bachelet (BAH-she-let), a divorced mother of three and avowed agnostic whose father was murdered while she and her mother were jailed and tortured during the Pinochet years. Striking a blow for gender equity, Bachelet filled half her cabinet positions with women, including the key defense and economy ministries. In 2010 Chileans elected their first conservative president in twenty years, Sebastián Piñera, who soon faced massive student protests, led by charismatic leftist Camila Vallejo, demanding reform of an educational system favoring the wealthy. Although the parliament refused to consider their proposals, Vallejo inspired and helped activists worldwide. In 2013 voters elected former president Michelle Bachelet on a center-left platform, defeating the conservative candidate, also a woman. But in 2017 Piñera returned to power, reversing some of Bachelet's initiatives and introducing a more right-wing agenda; one of his cabinet members praised the Pinochet dictatorship. While leaders have sought closer economic ties with the United States, many Chileans remain bitter toward the Americans for having helped perpetuate a brutal military regime. In late 2019 serious protests and rioting erupted throughout Chile, prompted by still rampant inequality, forcing the regime to consider overhauling the social and economic model and replacing the military-era constitution.

[20]The quotes are in Thomas E. Skidmore and Peter H. Smith, *Modern Latin America*, 4th ed. (New York: Oxford University Press, 1997), 147; Joseph A. Page, *The Brazilians* (Reading, MA: Addison-Wesley, 1995), 5.
[21]Quoted in David J. Morris, *We Must Make Haste—Slowly: The Process of Revolution in Chile* (New York: Vintage, 1973), 270-271.
[22]Pamela Constable and Arturo Valenzuela, *A Nation of Enemies: Chile Under Pinochet* (New York: W.W. Norton, 1991), 38.

29-4 Changing Latin American and Caribbean Societies

SOCIETIES

Q How have Latin American and Caribbean cultures been dynamic?

Latin Americans and Caribbean peoples, while facing daunting economic problems, developed social and cultural patterns different from those of North Americans. Most still exported traditional natural resources such as oil, sugar, coffee, bananas, wool, and copper. Spanish-speaking nations, Portuguese-speaking Brazil, and English-, Dutch-, and French-speaking Caribbean societies, derived from varied mixes of peoples and traditions, often have little in common with each other but have fostered dynamic cultural forms that have gained international popularity. And problems in the region have also affected the United States.

CONNECTION to TODAY

Are there any cultural forms from Latin America and the Caribbean, such as music, film, theater, and art, that you have experienced and enjoyed?

29-4a Latin American Economies

Latin Americans, while struggling to achieve the affluence common in the industrialized West or eastern Asia, often enjoyed economic growth, forged rising literacy rates, and lowered infant mortality rates. More people now own televisions, even in poor neighborhoods. Nonetheless, world prices for most of their natural resource exports have declined or fluctuated over the years. Most countries have experienced at best modest growth in per capita income and productivity. To pay the bills and import luxury items, governments took out loans, eventually owing billions to international lenders. In recent years more of those loans and investments have come from China and its Belt and Road Initiative, funding infrastructure, power generation, and resource development projects. Some sixteen nations, among them Chile, Bolivia, Cuba, Venezuela, Uruguay, Dominican Republic, El Salvador, Jamaica, and Trinidad, have accepted projects, but critics worry about the debt load, environmental consequences, and China's control over supply chains. It has also caused worries in the Trump administration in the U.S. which wants to prevent China from gaining a strategic foothold but, unwilling to increase economic assistance, has not found an effective way to do so

other than threats. For decades populations grew around 3 percent a year, adding to the social burden and causing environmental problems. Governments tried to satisfy land hunger, mineral prospecting, and timber exploitation by treating rain forests as expendable resources. Yet, population growth has dropped considerably in recent years, causing some concern to governments as populations age. Women averaged 6.0 children in 1960 and 2.0 in 2017.

Latin America has also suffered severe income inequality. By 2000 the top 10 percent earned half of all income, while 70 percent lived in poverty. Often evading taxes, the small elite class drives Rolls Royces, while the poor lack bus service. In 2000 half of Brazilians had no access to doctors; yet Rio de Janeiro became the world's plastic surgery capital catering to wealthy Brazilians and foreigners. A decade ago in Caracas, Venezuela's capital, one shopping mall serving the affluent boasted 450 stores, an amusement park, two movie theaters, and a McDonald's. But any customers coming from a slum of open sewers and tin shacks, perched a few miles away on unstable hillsides, paid half a day's wage for a Big Mac. Such inequality fueled support for leftists like Hugo Chávez. Poor peasants in some nations, their traditional crops such as coffee declining in value, turned to growing coca and opium for making cocaine and heroin. But the drug trade, largely to the U.S. market, fosters political turbulence and government corruption, profiting only a few kingpins. In recent years, violence between rival drug cartels and gangs has killed many people and unsettled life, especially in Colombia, Brazil, Mexico, and Jamaica. To reduce crime, in 2013 Uruguay became the first Latin American nation to decriminalize marijuana, sparking regional debate on drug laws. In 2018 a United Nations official suggested that, to reduce the human cost of prohibition, Latin Americans should consider legalizing drugs.

Agriculture has remained an economic mainstay. By the 1990s, 60 percent of all agricultural land was held in large

IMAGE 29.6 **U.S. Factory in Mexico** Since the 1980s growing numbers of U.S. companies have relocated industrial operations to Mexico, building many factories along the Rio Grande River that separates Mexico from Texas. In this Delphi Delco Electronics factory, in Matamoros, Mexico, the mostly female labor force makes parts for General Motors cars headed for the U.S. market.

Q What can we learn about the workforce and work environment from this photo?

estates, mostly owned by elite families and multinational corporations, and farmed inefficiently, contributing to food shortages. Modern agriculture requires large investments for machinery, fertilizers, pesticides, and fuel; growing beans and corn to feed hungry peasants supplies inadequate revenue. Vast tracts of rain forests and farms have been transformed into cattle ranches. Latin America remains a food importer, mostly from North America; malnutrition causes half of all child deaths. In Peru's major city, Lima, hundreds of poor children, known as "fruit birds," desperately compete with stray dogs for spoiled fruit.

Hardship often marks rural life. A Brazilian novel captured hopelessness in the drought-tortured northeast, where, in the 1980s, life expectancy was thirty years and only two-thirds of children attended school. The herder Fabiano understands that everything prevents his escape from endless poverty: "If he could only put something aside for a few months, he would be able to get his head up. Oh, he had made plans, but that was all foolishness. Ground creepers were never meant to climb. Once the beans had been eaten and the ears of corn gnawed, there was no place to go but to the boss's cash drawer [for a loan]."[23] Unemployment and unprofitable farms generated migration to cities and made Latin America the world's most urbanized region, growing from 30 percent of people in 1950 to over 80 percent in 2015 living in cities, often in shantytowns. Many

migrants work as shoe-shine boys, cigarette vendors, car washers, or in other poorly paid work. Half the urban population lacks adequate water, housing, sanitation, and social services.

Beginning in the 1980s, many nations adopted **neoliberalism**, an economic model, encouraged by the United States, that promoted free markets, privatization, and Western investment. But although neoliberalism generated growth for a decade, more people remained stuck in poverty because neoliberals failed to curb government corruption, install honest judicial systems, foster labor-intensive industries, reduce the power of rich elites, or decrease dependence on foreign loans and investment. A few people enjoyed fabulous wealth while most remained poor. Argentina, the most ardent neoliberalism adopter, saw its economy collapse in 1998 while unemployment soared. By 2001 half of the people lived in poverty, and neoliberalism lost credibility around the region. In 2002 Argentina defaulted on its debts. But the election of pragmatic Peronist leftists in 2003 revived the economy, which grew by 9 percent a year, and in 2006 Argentina paid back money still owed to the International Monetary Fund, symbolizing recovery and a more state-oriented economy. In 2008 Argentine economic growth dwindled and the Peronists lost

neoliberalism An economic model encouraged by the United States in the developing world that promoted free markets, privatization, and Western investment.

---

[23]Graciliano Ramos, *Barren Lives*, quoted in E. Bradford Burns, *Latin America: A Concise Interpretive History*, 5th ed. (Englewood Cliffs, NJ: Prentice-Hall, 1990), 231.

some support. But public spending by the Peronists, now led by Cristina Fernandez de Kirchner (b. 2007), elected president in 2007 and again in 2011, brought recovery from the 2008–2009 economic crisis. In 2015 a conservative pro-U.S. coalition headed by multimillionaire free market enthusiast Mauricio Macri came to power, introducing austerity to tackle inflation and deficits. But his free market policies largely failed while poverty rates, unemployment, and inflation all soared, pushing the nation into recession. In 2019 Peronists and the left returned to power. By 2014 rampant inflation and other problems had brought on another economic slide for Latin America. Thanks to economic growth and job creation, Latin America's middle classes nearly doubled to 26 percent between 2002 and 2018 while unemployment fell, but prosperity is concentrated in major cities. Corruption grew but by 2014, spurred by middle-class pressure, various nations, especially Brazil, began unprecedented crackdowns. By 2019 the movement lost momentum. A report by the United Nations in 2019 showed extreme poverty in Latin America rising, embracing about 30 percent of the region's population. The U.S.–China trade war threatened to destabilize the world economy enough to cause a severe downturn in Latin America. Venezuela, Argentina, Brazil, and Mexico, as well as the Central American nations of Guatemala, El Salvador, and Honduras (the source of most migrants and asylum seekers to the U.S. today), seemed the most endangered. In 2019 violent massive protests against unpopular regimes and neoliberalism in several nations, especially Colombia, Chile, Ecuador, Haiti, Honduras, and Peru, have resulted in some deaths and hundreds of arrests, injuries, and states of emergencies that often closed shops and schools.

29-4b Latin American Societies and Religions

Political and economic change reshaped gender relations and family life. Although men dominate governments, militaries, businesses, and the Catholic Church, women's movements have reduced gender inequality. Once considered helpless and groomed as girls to be wives and mothers, many women now do paid work, some in male-dominated trades. Millions earn money selling clothing, handicrafts, and food in small markets or from street stalls. Factories relocating from North America prefer young women, who accept lower wages and have been raised to obey. Family life has experienced strains. By the 1990s far fewer people married, especially among the poor. But divorce, banned by the Catholic Church, was difficult or impossible for centuries in some nations but is now legal everywhere, although often constrained by longstanding cultural and social customs. Men still enjoy a double standard, their extramarital affairs tolerated while women's are condemned. Although abortion is illegal in many places, Latin America has one of the world's highest abortion rates. Some nations, among them Brazil, Argentina, and Peru, allow abortions with some limitations; only Cuba, Uruguay, and Mexico City permit abortion on request.

liberation theology A Latin American movement that developed in the 1960s to make Catholicism more relevant to contemporary society and to address the plight of the poor.

In 2013 representatives of thirty-eight Latin American and Caribbean nations issued the Montevideo Consensus, urging support for safe abortion services, contraception, and same-sex marriage. For decades LGBTQ identity and behavior remained illegal and was often punished in many nations, including Castro's Cuba (where it was viewed as a remnant of the detested old regime), but attitudes have been changing. Most of Latin America no longer considers it a crime. Argentina became the first Latin American nation to legalize same-sex marriage, followed by Uruguay, Brazil, Colombia, Ecuador, and many Mexican states and cities including liberal Mexico City; Chile and Costa Rica allow civil unions. But in most of the former British West Indies, including Jamaica, old colonial laws against "the detested crime" remain on the books, punishable by up to ten years in prison. And despite antidiscrimination laws, prejudice often persists. Brazil's far-right president Jair Bolsonaro openly expressed his disdain for same-sex couples and claimed that he'd rather have a dead son than a gay one. In 2018 four hundred twenty LGBTQ people were killed across Brazil. That same year, the Inter-American Court of Human Rights ruled that the American Convention on Human Rights recognizes same-sex marriage as a human right. This will make the legalization of such unions mandatory in those countries that belong to the Court.

Gaining voting rights everywhere by 1961, women became more active in politics. In 1974 Isabel Perón (b. 1931), a former dancer who married Juan Perón after Evita's death, succeeded her late husband to become Argentina and the region's first woman president; she was ousted in a military coup in 1976. In 1990 newspaper publisher Violeta Chamorro **(vee-oh-LET-ah cha-MOR-roe)** (g. 1990–1996) was elected Nicaragua's president, and she served until 1996. Women later headed several other nations, including Brazil, Argentina, Chile, Costa Rica, Jamaica, and Trinidad. After Mexican feminists challenged inequitable laws and social practices, the legislature passed laws in 1974 guaranteeing women equal rights for jobs, salaries, and legal standing. Yet, men often resented women's empowerment; military dictatorships singled out women activists, such as Bachelet's mother, for torture and rape. Feminist activism has even been bringing changes in popular culture. In Argentina some women have been trying to make the sensuous tango less patriarchal by weakening the prescribed gender roles that critics argue privilege men and turn women into sex objects during a dance. And immensely popular Brazilian singer-dancer Daniela Mercury conveys a message of non-discrimination, tolerance, women's empowerment, human rights, democracy, and defending the environment in her music.

The religious landscape has become increasingly diverse. In the 1960s progressive Latin American Roman Catholics developed **liberation theology**, a movement to make the church more relevant to contemporary society and address poverty. Until the Vatican prohibited the movement in the 1980s, priests favoring liberation theology, especially in Brazil, cooperated with Marxist and liberal groups working for social justice. Meanwhile, the Catholic hierarchy generally remained conservative. While fewer attended church, many revered popular Catholic fiestas, pilgrimages, and family altars. The first Latin American to head the church, Pope Francis (pope 2013–), an Argentine known for his modest lifestyle, tango skills, soccer fandom, and concern for the poor, hoped to revitalize the faith in a region containing 40 percent of the world's Catholics. Protestantism, chiefly evangelical or pentecostal, grew rapidly with increased missionary efforts, attracting converts with its participatory, emotional services. By 2014 Protestants numbered 40 percent of the population in Central America, 50 percent in Guatemala and Honduras, and 26 percent in Brazil; their numbers are also growing elsewhere, including in Mexico. Protestants have served as presidents of several nations, including Brazil, Guatemala, and El Salvador. But their active evangelization has caused resentment among Catholic leaders. A top Brazilian cardinal worried: "We wonder with anxiety: how long will Brazil remain a Catholic country?"[24] Growing numbers of Latin Americans (15 percent in Brazil) are secular with no religious affiliation.

Brazil reflected the region's social changes and continuities. The urban population grew from about a quarter of Brazilians in 1920 to 87 percent in 2010. Migrants jammed into shantytowns, such as the notorious hillside shacks of Rio de Janeiro; despite recent rapid growth, poverty remained pervasive. By the 1980s three-fourths of Brazilians were malnourished, a third of adults had tuberculosis, a quarter suffered from parasitic diseases, and millions of abandoned or runaway children wandered city streets, living by their wits. Conditions remain bleak for many today. A substandard public health system that has neglected the rural and urban poor was a major cause of the massive protests in 2013, leading to the import of four thousand Cuban doctors. Yet, the shantytowns are also well organized, led by community activists and filled with hard-working residents seeking a better future for their children.

Although Brazilians have increasingly tolerated racial and cultural diversity, race remains a central social category. Like the United States, Brazil has never become a true racial "melting pot." Afro-Brazilians often condemn what they view as a racist society steeped in prejudice. Race often correlates with social status: whites (half the population) dominate the top brackets, blacks dominate the bottom, and mixed-descent Brazilians and Asians fall in between. However, Brazilians' flexible notion of race differs from North Americans' biological concept. Dark-skinned people can aspire to social mobility by earning a good income; as a popular local saying claims, "money lightens." Furthermore, Afro-Brazilian culture has increasingly influenced whites. Afro-Brazilian faiths linking West African gods or other African traditions with Roman Catholic saints and ceremonies attract over a third of Brazilians, often devout Catholics. In the 2019 Rio de Janeiro Carnival various samba troupe presentations and floats mocked the intolerance of President Bolsonaro and his supporters, who have denounced the festival, by celebrating an alternative history honoring Afro-Brazilian heroes and religious cults, indigenous groups, and women.

The mass media and professional sports have become popular entertainments and diversion from social problems for Latin Americans. Immensely popular local television soap operas dominate prime-time television viewing, with those from Brazil and Mexico gaining a large market around the world. A Brazilian anthropologist credits telenovelas, featuring affluent women with small families, for reducing fertility: "They (female characters) are all young … live well … are comfortable.…Why do they need children?"[25] Hugely popular, football (soccer) unites people of all social backgrounds. For two decades (1950s–1970s) the storied career, fluid play, and magnetic personality of Brazilian superstar Pelé (b. 1940), from a poor Afro-Brazilian family, helped make football popular globally. Brazilian national teams have enjoyed the most international success of any country, winning the World Cup championships five times between 1958 and 2002 by employing a creative, teamwork-oriented strategy known as "samba football." A playwright noted how Brazilians obsessively suspend their daily lives during the World Cup, held every four years: "The nation pauses, all of it. Robbers don't rob, ghosts don't haunt, no crimes, no embezzlements, no deaths, no adulteries."[26]

29-4c Latin American and Caribbean Cultures

Creative Latin American and Caribbean cultural forms reached a global audience. Latin American literature flourished, with writers often describing social conditions and government failures. Popular Brazilian novelist Jorge Amado (HOR-hay ah-MAH-do) (1912–2001) blended fantasy, realism, and political commitment, providing insight into Brazil's impoverished northeast. Former journalist Gabriel García Márquez (MAHR-kez) (b. 1928), a Nobel Prize–winning Colombian novelist, developed an international audience for imaginative books full of "magic realism" that represented possible events as if they were wonders and impossible events as commonplace. His most famous work, *One Hundred Years of Solitude* (1970), charts the history of a Colombian house, the family who lives in it, and the town where it was located through wars, changing politics, and economic crises. Some writers tested governments' tolerance. The greatest epic poem of the leftist Chilean writer and former diplomat Pablo Neruda (neh-ROO-da) (1904–1973), *General Song*, published in 1950, portrays the entire hemisphere's history, showing an innocent pre-Columbian America cruelly awakened by Spanish conquest. The poem romanticizes Incas, extols the liberators who ended Spanish rule, castigates foreign capitalists (often American) as exploiters, and identifies an emerging mass struggle to establish government by and for the people rather than the rich. In 1971 Neruda won the Nobel Prize for literature, cheering his admirers and distressing those who considered his radical views a threat to society.

Other art forms also developed social consciousness. Brazil's New Cinema movement, launched in 1955, tried to

[24]Cardinal Claudio Hummes, quoted in Simon Romero, "A Laboratory for Revitalizing Catholicism," *New York Times*, February 14, 2013 (nytimes.com/2013/02/15/world/americas/in-brazil-growing-threats-tocatholicism).
[25]Immacolata Vassalo de Lopes, quoted in Juan Forero, "Birth Rate Plummets in Brazil," *New York Times*, December 29, 2012.
[26]Nelson Rodrigues, quoted in Warren Hoge, "A Whole Nation More Agitated than Spike Lee," *New York Times*, June 5, 1994, p. A1.

replace Hollywood films with films reflecting Brazilian life. One of the movement's finest films, *Black Orpheus* (1959), which gained an international audience, employed a local popular music soundtrack to examine the annual pre-Lenten Carnival in Rio de Janeiro's shantytowns and the rich–poor divisions revealed in the different ways people celebrated Carnival. Brazil has also produced much vibrant and creative popular music that often found a world audience, including samba, bossa nova, MPB ("Brazil Popular Music"), and forro, as well as embracing and adapting imported genres like jazz, rock, and hip-hop. Analyzing rich musical traditions, cultural and racial mixing, as well as the many political and economic challenges, a Brazilian sociologist wrote that: "Brazil may be an absurdity, This is … all too true … but it's not deaf. Brazil has an ear for music that goes way beyond the normal."[27] **New Song**, a musical style based chiefly on local folk music and closely tied to progressive politics and protest, gained popularity in a half-dozen countries, especially Chile, in the 1960s and 1970s. Seeking an alternative to the Anglo-American popular culture favored by the elites, musicians used indigenous Andean instruments and tunes. Chilean New Song pioneers such as Violeta Parra (1918–1967) and Víctor Jara **(HAR-a)** (1932–1973) wrote or collected songs that addressed problems such as poverty and inequality (see Meet the People: Violeta Parra, Chilean New Song Pioneer). Jara used music to promote his political goals: "I don't sing for the love of singing, Or to show off my voice, But for the statements, Made by my honest guitar."[28]

Its left-wing connections made New Song vulnerable to changing political conditions. In 1970 Chilean New Song musicians joined the leftist Popular Unity coalition electoral campaign. New Song musicians promoted the new government's programs, such as land reform, and some toured abroad to gain foreign support. In 1973, Chile's military seized power, arresting, executing, or deporting most of the New Song musicians while criminalizing playing or listening to the music. Before thousands of other detainees held in the national stadium, soldiers publicly executed Víctor Jara, symbolizing the death of free expression and the military's fear of popular culture. New Song faded as a popular music in Latin America and was replaced by local forms of rock and distinctive dance-oriented hybrid music such as *salsa* (originally from Cuba and Puerto Rico) and *meringue* from Colombia.

With diverse populations of blacks, whites, and Asians, Caribbean islands fostered creative cultural development, especially in religion and music. Jamaica proved particularly fertile soil. **Rastafarianism**, a religion mixing Christian, African, and local influences that arose in 1930, attracted the urban and rural poor by preaching a return of black people to Africa. Believers revered Emperor Haile Selassie (Ras Tafari) of Ethiopia, the sole uncolonized African state in 1930. Rastafarians (Rastas) outraged Jamaica's elite by smoking ganja, an illegal drug, and sporting dreadlocked hair. Mixed with black nationalism, repatriation to Africa became more a spiritual than a physical quest. Rastafarianism became a movement of the black poor seeking to redistribute wealth.

The most influential Caribbean popular music had similar mixed origins. In the 1960s Jamaicans created **reggae**, which blended North American rhythm and blues with Afro-Jamaican traditions and which was highlighted by a distinctive beat maintained by the bass guitar. Reggae musicians, many of them Rastas, promoted social justice, economic equality, and the freedom of Rastas to live as they liked. Reggae's international popularity owed much to Bob Marley (1945–1981), a Rasta, and his group, the Wailers, the first international superstars from a developing nation (see Chapter 26). Marley's perceptions were shaped by the status of blacks in Jamaica and the wider world and the degrading conditions of the nonwhite poor. His explosive performances and provocative lyrics offered clear messages: "Slave driver, the table is turned; Catch a fire, you gonna get burned."[29] Like Chilean New Song musicians, Marley and other reggae musicians became involved in politics. Many supported socialist Michael Manley (1924–1997), whose antibusiness policies as prime minister (1972–1978) prompted crippling U.S. sanctions that caused Jamaicans hardship. After Marley's death from cancer in 1981, many reggae musicians watered down their message. Raunchy party music soon dominated Caribbean music scenes. *Reggaeton*, a hugely popular Puerto Rican-bred Spanish-language music around Latin America and among Hispanics in North America, mixed reggae with rock, rap, and Latin music.

29-4d Latin America and the Caribbean in the Global System

Latin Americans and Caribbean peoples forged closer relations with one another and increased regional economic cooperation and trade, often through trade pacts. The Southern Cone Common Market, formed in 1996, included six South American nations with over two hundred million people. Caribbean countries cooperated in the Caribbean Community and Common Market, formed in 1973, and Latin and North American leaders periodically met in summits to enhance cooperation on immigration, tariff reduction, suppression of illegal drug trafficking, and other issues. While Americans blamed Latin American drug cartels for smuggling illegal drugs, Latin Americans often resented the U.S. interventions and economic impositions they considered "Yankee imperialism." Latin American and Caribbean leaders also feared being pushed

---

New Song A Latin American musical movement based chiefly on local folk music and closely tied to progressive politics and protest; became popular in the 1960s and 1970s, especially in Chile.

Rastafarianism A religion from Jamaica that arose in 1930 and that mixed Christian, African, and local influences; Rastafarianism attracted urban slum dwellers and the rural poor by preaching a return of black people to Africa.

reggae A popular music style that began in the 1960s and that blended North American rhythm and blues with Afro-Jamaican traditions; reggae is marked by a distinctive beat maintained by the bass guitar.

---

[27]Raphael Jose de Menezes Bastos, "Music and Society in Brazil: An Introduction to Brazilian Musical Language," *Cultures*, 8(1) (1982), 68.
[28]From Jara's song "Manifiesto" ("Manifesto"). The song and the translation can be found on Jara's album *Manifiesto: Chile September 1973* (XTRA 1143, 1974).
[29]See Marley's album *Catch a Fire* (Island ILPS 9241, 1973).

Violeta Parra, Chilean New Song Pioneer

Born in 1918 to a poor school-teaching family, Violeta Parra was the key figure in the early development of New Song, a Chilean music based chiefly on local folk music, and a multitalented artist in many mediums, including poetry, filmmaking, tapestry, and painting. Despite her lower-middle-class background, the unconventional Parra lived and dressed like a peasant, wearing her hair long and almost uncombed. Restless and unsuited for marriage, she struggled to find the best outlet for her talents while supporting herself and her two children, Isabel and Angel (AHN-hell). After working as a commercial entertainer, she began collecting, writing, and singing folk music in the 1940s and eventually collected over three thousand songs. She had clear musical goals: "Every artist must aspire to unite his/her work in a direct contact with the public. I am content to work with the people close to me, whom I can feel, touch, talk and incorporate into my soul." Yet, unlike her protégés, such as Victor Jara, who was deeply engaged in left-wing movements, she never became directly active in politics.

In the early 1950s Parra began Chile's first folk music radio program and recorded her debut album, with simple guitar-accompanied arrangements. She also taught briefly at a southern Chilean university. Parra and her children introduced Andean and African American folk music to Chile after a four-year sojourn in Paris, France, where they encountered musicians from various countries. Settling with her children in Chile's capital city, Santiago, she enjoyed cooking huge pots of beans for the young Chileans who gathered around her to drink wine, discuss Chilean affairs, and exchange songs and stories. A café the Parras opened in Santiago became a meeting place for performers and other Chileans interested in New Song and leftist politics. Parra greatly influenced younger urban musicians, who began learning from her how to play traditional Andean instruments while collecting or writing their own songs; she also provided a role model for other Latin American musicians. As Cuba's top New Song musician, Silvio Rodriguez, claimed: "Violeta is fundamental. Nothing would have been as it is had it not been for Violeta."

Parra's songs displayed two essential elements of later New Song: a base in folk music and concern with Chile's social, economic, and political problems. In "Look How They

IMAGE 29.7 **Violeta Parra** An influential Chilean musician, folklorist, and artist, Violeta Parra is credited with founding the folk-music-oriented New Song movement, influencing many musicians in Chile and throughout Latin America.

EL MERCURIO/Grupo de Diarios America (GDA)/Newscom

Q Can we learn anything about Parra and her music from this photo?

Tell Us About Freedom," she critiqued the Catholic Church establishment and her nation's ills: "look how the nation's religious and political leaders brag about freedom when they are actually keeping it from us; they boast about tranquility as their power tortures us." Her music attacked such issues as police brutality, capitalism's inequalities, exploitation of Indians, and chronic conflict between Latin American governments. Yet, her songs retained an intense, highly personal, contemporary mood, both Chilean and universal.

Held in contempt by Chile's elite for her unconventional life and antiestablishment sympathies, Parra was plagued by poverty and increasing personal problems, including depression. Even her closest friends found her strong, often unpredictable personality difficult. Younger musicians began gravitating to Victor Jara and other New Song figures. Her later songs took on a more philosophical spirit. On her last album in 1966 she recorded her famous farewell, "Gracias a la Vida" (I Give Thanks to Life), a prayerlike expression of gratitude for the richness of life: "I am grateful for the life that has benefited me so much; It has given me both laughter and tears; because of this I can differentiate happiness from sadness; everybody's song is my own song." Not overtly political, the song reflected her identification with common people, becoming the underground anthem of many Latin Americans living under dictatorships. As Parra's depression deepened, she committed suicide in 1967. But her career had built a bridge between an older, peasant-based folk tradition and the developing interest of younger musicians. She may have gone, but New Song flowered in Chile and around Latin America.

Reflection Questions

1. Why did her peers consider Parra fundamental to the evolution of New Song in Latin America?
2. How did Parra's life reflect Chilean social and political conditions?
3. Do you think Violeta Parra should be considered a feminist and cultural role model for women today?

Notes: Quotations from *Studies in Latin American Popular Culture* 2 (1983): 177–178 and 5 (1986): 117; Nancy E. Morris, *Canto Porque es Necesario Cantar: The New Song Movement in Chile, 1973–1983* (Albuquerque: Latin American Institute, University of New Mexico, Research Paper Series No. 16, July 1984), 6.

aside in a world economy dominated by North American, European, and, increasingly, Asian nations. U.S. exports to Latin America nearly matched those to Europe.

Globalization influenced Latin Americans and their economies. Asian nations, especially China, Japan, Taiwan, and South Korea, captured a growing share of Latin America's traditional overseas markets while investing in, and supplying consumer goods to, Latin America and the Caribbean. Energy-hungry China sought resources such as oil from countries like Brazil and Venezuela. In a globalized economy, a hiccup in Tokyo or New York causes a stomach ache in Ecuador or El Salvador. Latin American and Caribbean economies are particularly vulnerable to ebbs and flows in the United States. When the 2001 terrorist attacks diverted U.S. attention to the Middle East, the sudden U.S. disinterest in Latin America sparked a regional economic downturn that reduced demand for Latin American exports. Economic gains made in the 1990s slipped away; the fifth of Latin Americans living in extreme poverty faced an even grimmer future; and leftists won elections in many countries. The 2008–2009 global economic crisis further damaged many Latin American and Caribbean economies as jobs disappeared, tourism declined, and many jobless migrants to North America returned home. Yet, in the twenty-first century some countries, most notably Brazil and Chile, have improved their status in the global system.

By the 2010s another crisis emanating from Latin America engaged the attention of North Americans. Mexicans had long sought a better life through temporary jobs or long-term immigration, pushing thousands of them a year to cross the border legally or illegally. Prompted by increasing violent crime, too few jobs, climate change, and unstable families, the flow increased by 2015, posing challenges to the United States. By 2017 the Mexican migrant flow diminished and migrants returning to Mexico outnumbered those leaving. Central Americans from violence-and drought-ridden Guatemala, El Salvador, and Honduras now comprised the great majority of migrants. The migrants, many seeking asylum, fled despotic governments, intimidation by rapidly increasing violent gangs, and the decline of traditional agriculture, especially coffee, as the climate warmed. Many came as families or single mothers with their children. The Trump administration responded with increasingly harsh policies, including separation of children from parents, housing thousands in jail-like camps, and eventually making immigration difficult and asylum nearly impossible. Acceding to U.S. demands, Mexico offered some cooperation, stopping migrants along well-traveled routes north and sending some back to their home countries. The border crisis became a divisive political and social issue for Americans, who disagreed about immigration generally and how the 10.5 million undocumented residents (down from 12.2 million in 2007) should be treated; around 47 percent are Mexico-born.

Buffeted by political changes and sporadic economic crises, Latin Americans search for their identity and role in a world largely dominated by other societies. But experts debate whether imported economic and political ideas from the left or right will work for Latin Americans. Calling on leaders to recognize the needs of all the people, regardless of class, ethnicity, and gender, and for both North and Latin Americans to find common ground with each other, Panamanian salsa music star, lawyer, and part-time U.S. resident Ruben Blades (**blayds**) pondered the hemisphere's destiny in song: "I'm searching for America and I fear I won't find her. Those who fear truth have hidden her. While there is no justice there can be no peace. If the dream of one is the dream of all let's break the chains and begin to walk. I'm calling you, America, our future awaits us, help me to find her."[30]

KEY POINTS

▶ Though men continue to dominate Latin American society, more women have entered the workforce, and several have become national leaders.

▶ Brazil, Latin America's largest nation, became increasingly urban and suffered widespread poverty, with a racial divide between lighter- and darker-skinned people, but Brazilians have found escape from their problems through popular sports such as soccer.

▶ In the Caribbean, the Jamaican religion of Rastafarianism promoted redistribution of wealth, while a closely related musical form, reggae, frequently included calls for social justice and freedom from police interference.

▶ Latin American and Caribbean nations forged closer relations, signed several trade pacts, and shared an uneasy economic relationship with the United States, while Asian nations also became important competitors with and investors in their economies.

▶ The migration of many migrants from Central America north through Mexico to the United States seeking asylum caused a crisis that affected the various countries involved.

---

[30]Quoted in Jan Fairley, "New Song: Music and Politics in Latin America," in *Rhythms of the World*, ed. Francis Hanly and Tim May (London: BBC Books, 1989), 90.

Chapter Summary

Having emerged from World War II as the dominant superpower, the United States soon engaged in a Cold War with the Soviet Union. The campaign to contain communism fostered the growth of a powerful military and a strong government. Americans lavished aid and investment on allies and developing nations while intervening in many nations, including some in Latin America and the Caribbean, to counter revolutionary movements or overthrow left-leaning governments. While the U.S. economy flourished for decades, American society and culture rapidly changed, as ethnic minorities and women struggled for equal rights. Although shaped, like the United States, by massive immigration from Europe, especially Britain, Canadians, Australians, and New Zealanders have more liberal attitudes on social issues and, unlike Americans, have extensive social welfare systems.

Latin American and Caribbean experiences differ from those in the United States, Canada, and the Pacific Basin. Military dictatorships dominated many Latin American nations for decades. Most nations struggled to implement and sustain democracy, which became prevalent in the 1990s, and to find the right economic mix to foster economic development. While some nations enjoyed economic growth, many people remained in dire poverty. Women and nonwhites worked to improve their status, with modest success. The Latin American and Caribbean peoples also fostered dynamic cultural forms, from innovative literatures to popular musical forms, that often expressed protest and gained worldwide audiences.

Key Terms

domino theory (782)
multilateralism (782)
unilateralism (782)
containment (782)
Mutually Assured Destruction (MAD) (783)

preemptive war (786)
Castroism (803)
neoliberalism (807)
liberation theology (808)

New Song (810)
Rastafarianism (810)
reggae (810)

The Middle East, Sub-Saharan Africa, and New Conflicts in the Contemporary World, Since 1945

> " *I saw the Berlin Wall fall, [Nelson] Mandela walk free. I saw a dream whose time has come change my history— so keep on dreaming. In the best of times and in the worst of times gotta keep looking at the skyline, not at the hole in the road.* "

—"Your Time Will Come" by South African pop group Savuka, 1993[1]

AP Images/ENRIC MARTI

IMAGE 30.1 **Modern versus Traditional** Wearing traditional clothing, including veils and head scarves, Egyptian women walk through downtown Cairo in 1998 in front of billboards promoting popular entertainers. The scene illustrates the encounter between Islamic customs and modern ideas in many Middle Eastern nations.

Q What can we learn from this photo about urban life and atmosphere in Egypt?

[1]See Savuka's album *Heat, Dust and Dreams* (EMI 9777-7-98795, 1993).

In 1987 Nigerian writer Chinua Achebe (**ah-CHAY-bay**) (1930–2013) dissected the underside of African politics in a controversial novel, *Anthills of the Savannah*, about a military dictatorship. *Anthills* illustrated the dangers of unaccountable, repressive power and portrays problems faced by average people throughout much of Africa, mercilessly depicting the dictatorship's immorality, vanity, and destructiveness. Achebe did not have to look far for examples: Nigerian military leaders who overthrew a civilian government in 1983 first arrested people well known as corrupt and then jailed anyone who questioned the regime's economic mismanagement and human rights abuses. Just as the racially integrated South African pop group, Savuka, could sing of dreams changing history and a new era with the end of white minority rule, Achebe urged people to struggle to attain a better life. He believed that no novel is ever politically neutral because even saying nothing about politics is a political statement affirming that everything is okay. *Anthills* argued eloquently that everything was not okay. Like various other creative writers, musicians, and artists who used their art to spur political and social change, Achebe had to live many years in exile from intolerant governments.

The problems Achebe vividly described—despotism, corruption, economic stagnation, combustible social tensions, failed promises of democracy—have applied to most sub-Saharan African and Middle Eastern nations. Between 1945 and 1975, country after country became independent or reduced the political power of Western domination. But unlike various Asian and Latin American nations, they often struggled just to survive. As in colonial times most countries relied on the export of natural resources such as oil, rubber, or copper. Dictatorships of long-entrenched political leaders were common. While innovative in cultural affairs, few successfully resolved their social and economic problems. For some, Islam became a rallying cry to assert political interests and preserve their culture. Meanwhile, to serve their own ends, global superpowers manipulated African and Middle Eastern governments and intervened to shape these regions. Some nations were engulfed in wars, revolutions, or rebellions, fostering instability.

30-1 The Middle East: New Nations and Old Societies

TRANSITIONS   SOCIETIES   NETWORKS

Q How have Arab–Israeli tensions and oil shaped contemporary Middle Eastern politics?

Few world regions have witnessed more turbulence since 1945 than the predominantly Muslim nations stretching from Morocco across North Africa and southwestern Asia to Iran and Afghanistan. Arabs have dominated most of these nations, but Turks, Iranians, Kurds, and Israeli Jews also influenced the region. After World War II Middle Eastern

CONNECTION to TODAY

How have the political turbulence, revolutions, Western interventions, and wars in the Middle East affected your family, community, and nation?

societies ended Western colonization and asserted their own interests, often under modernizing leaders. But they also endured dictatorial governments, chronic political instability, and centuries-old hostilities between Sunni and Shi'a Muslims. Containing the world's largest oil reserves, the region also became crucial to the global system.

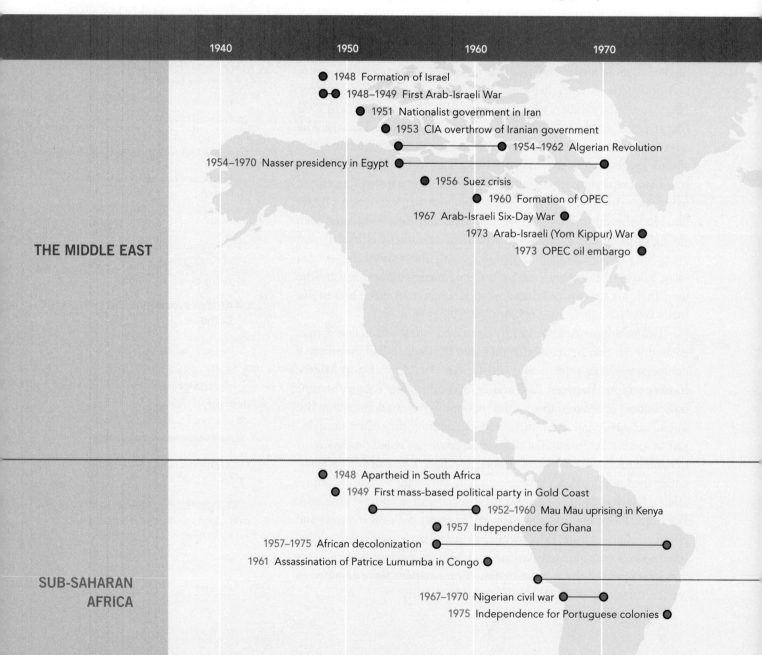

	1940	1950	1960	1970

THE MIDDLE EAST

- 1948 Formation of Israel
- 1948–1949 First Arab-Israeli War
- 1951 Nationalist government in Iran
- 1953 CIA overthrow of Iranian government
- 1954–1962 Algerian Revolution
- 1954–1970 Nasser presidency in Egypt
- 1956 Suez crisis
- 1960 Formation of OPEC
- 1967 Arab-Israeli Six-Day War
- 1973 Arab-Israeli (Yom Kippur) War
- 1973 OPEC oil embargo

SUB-SAHARAN AFRICA

- 1948 Apartheid in South Africa
- 1949 First mass-based political party in Gold Coast
- 1952–1960 Mau Mau uprising in Kenya
- 1957 Independence for Ghana
- 1957–1975 African decolonization
- 1961 Assassination of Patrice Lumumba in Congo
- 1967–1970 Nigerian civil war
- 1975 Independence for Portuguese colonies

30-1a The Reshaping of the Middle East

In the two decades after World War II, nationalist governments replaced the remaining colonial regimes. France abandoned control of Morocco, Tunisia, Lebanon, and Syria, while Italians left Libya. During the Algerian Revolution (1954–1962), nationalist guerrillas fought 500,000 French troops to bring independence to their country, which had a large European settler population. Seeing no clear end to the struggle, which killed 250,000 Algerians, France granted independence in 1962. Over five decades later, in 2017–2018, the French government finally apologized to the Algerians for colonialism and torture. But Algerians found maintaining democracy and stability a challenge and in 2019, on the 65th anniversary of the war

of independence, mass protests broke out demanding a "new revolution." Although some other nations, such as Egypt and Morocco, had a long history of national identity and unity, many states were fragile. After World War I the British formed the artificial states of Iraq, Jordan, and Palestine with arbitrary boundaries, while Afghanistan, Turkey, Lebanon, and Syria all included diverse, often feuding ethnic and religious groups.

The region's most developed and prosperous nation, Turkey, which had never been colonized and lost its own colonial empire after World War I, has sought an influential regional role and built formidable military forces. Turkey's prestige and power make it a major force in regional politics. However, Turkey has also abused human rights, arresting dissidents and restricting

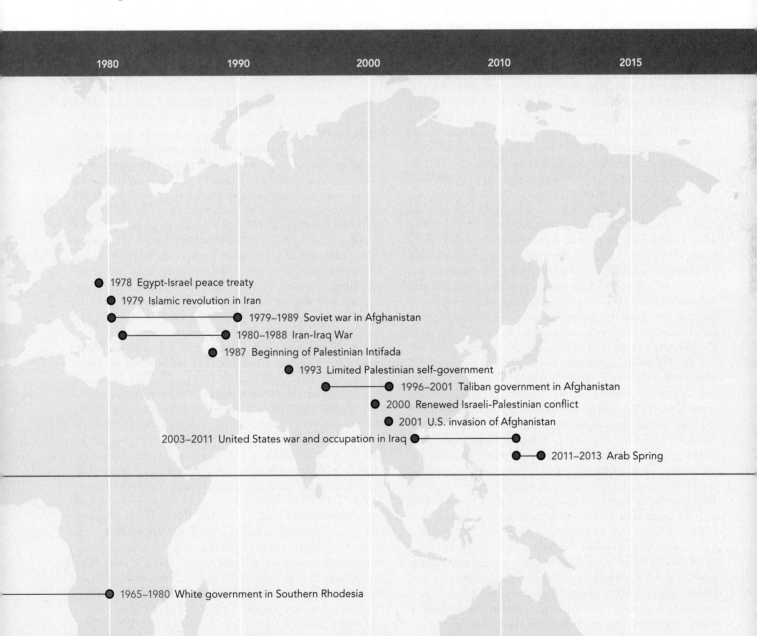

ethnic minorities. Although it shifted from military-dominated to democratically elected governments by the 1980s, it used strict internal security laws to imprison several thousand people for political offenses. Led largely by secular politicians, Turks looked increasingly westward, joining NATO (the North Atlantic Treaty Organization), hosting U.S. military bases, and applying, so far unsuccessfully, for European Union membership. But Turkey's governments, while promoting women's rights, have also suppressed the culture and language of the largest ethnic minority, the Kurds, who number between 15 and 20 percent of the population and chiefly live in southeastern Turkey. Some separatist Kurds supported an insurgency that has cost forty thousand lives.

Although Turkey's people, who numbered eighty-two million by 2018, are largely Sunni Muslim, nationalist governments had long limited political activity by groups favoring an Islamic state and discouraged conservative religious customs. However, the moderate Islamic Justice and Development Party led by Recep Tayyip Erdogan (b. 1954), which came to power in 2002 and won successive elections, loosened restrictions on Muslim practices, such as by allowing devout female students to wear head scarves, while pursuing a pro-Western policy and closer ties with Europe and, more recently, Arab states that some termed an "Ottoman Revival." The gap between largely secular urbanites and more devout rural folk is wide. A prominent secular artist and activist explained in 2012: "We don't eat the same way. … We eat at tables with ladies and men sitting together and enjoying and drinking wine and making jokes and listening to either Turkish music or Beethoven or Rolling Stones or Beatles or Edith Piaf. They sit separately with men and women. They don't drink alcohol."[2] Secular Turks revere the Ataturk era, conservatives the Ottoman Empire. While the economy has rapidly grown for over twenty years, since 2013 large protests have periodically erupted in Istanbul protesting Erdogan's controversial urban development projects, crackdown on journalists and dissenters, conservative social initiatives (such as limiting alcohol advertising and sales), allegations of corruption, and increasingly autocratic style.

In 2016 an attempted coup by anti-Erdogan generals failed. Erdogan used the unrest to declare a state of emergency and assume near dictatorial powers, purging some politicians and officers while arresting many thousands of alleged coup supporters and dissidents, including professors, teachers, journalists, bureaucrats, mayors, and military officers, while imposing an even more Islamist agenda and widening his rift with the West. These policies were symbolized by the recent makeover of Istanbul's Taksim Square, a park located in a largely secular neighborhood and a frequent locale for protests, where the regime built a huge Ottoman-style mosque which dwarfed the adjacent monument to Ataturk, founder of the secular republic. Erdogan failed to curb a currency and debt crisis in 2018 and also faced the challenge of around four million Syrian refugees from the brutal conflict there. In the 2019 regional elections the defeat of pro-Erdogan candidates in several major cities, including Istanbul and Ankara, showed widespread disaffection from his regime. Soon he would proclaim his desire for nuclear weapons and then take his nation into a more aggressive role in the Middle East by intervening in Syria to fight the Syrian Kurds, expelling thousands of Syrian refugees, and threatening to send captured Islamic State fighters and families back to their European homelands.

Outside of Turkey, hopes for development and multiparty democracy have floundered as vested interests—large landowners, military leaders, most Muslim clergy—have opposed significant changes, and many people remain mired in illiteracy, poverty, and disease. However, some semi-democratic systems have emerged. Lebanese can choose between many competing warlord- or sectarian-based parties; Iranians can vote, but the regime disqualifies candidates it dislikes. In recent years both men and women in the small Persian Gulf kingdoms of Bahrain (**BAH-rain**) and Kuwait could vote for elected parliaments, and in 2009 three Kuwaiti women won seats. Due to U.S. occupation, Iraq now has an elected, although deeply factionalized, parliament with some women deputies. In Morocco, King Muhammad VI, who claims descent from the prophet Muhammad, has used a tolerant interpretation of Islam to try to modernize his nation, granting new rights to women and recognizing Berber as an official language along with Arabic while strengthening civil liberties and the elected parliament. However, he still controls vast power, and critics believe the reforms were more cosmetic than substantive. Indeed, by 2013 the king, worried by political instability in other North African countries, veered back toward autocracy, arresting some critics.

Most Middle Eastern countries have rigged elections, weak parliaments, or rules marginalizing opposition candidates. Furthermore, during the Cold War the United States and the Soviet Union, attracted by the region's oil and strategic location along vital waterways like the Persian Gulf and Suez Canal, filled the power vacuum created by decolonization. Pan-Arab nationalism, based more on a shared cultural and linguistic background than political interests, has not overcome political rivalries and superpower meddling. Divided by rival Muslim sects and differing outlooks toward the West, Arabs have floundered in their quest for unity. Hence, the Middle East has become a highly combustible region subject to many strains.

All of these frustrations came to a boil with the "Arab Spring," when the self-immolation of a fed-up street vendor in Tunisia in 2010 sparked protests that replaced the dictatorial regime. Tunisia has largely remained a democracy since then, with regular elections and compromises between secularists and Islamists, despite rising crime, unemployment, occasional protests, and jihadist attacks. Other countries weren't so fortunate. Soon unrest spread to other nations, unleashing unpredictable forces that brought turmoil and instability to many nations and unsettled regional politics. In 2011 Libyans, with NATO help, fought and overthrew the long-established autocrat Muammar Gaddafi (g. 1969–2011). But the country was soon engulfed in a festering civil war with various rival armed warlord-led militias and tribal groups controlling their own regions and a central government in name only. The Shi'ite majority in Bahrain challenged the Sunni monarchy, and protests and insurgency forced the ruler of Yemen from office, fostering a long, complex, and deadly civil war between Shi'ites and varied Sunni factions; Iran has supported the Shi'ites while Saudi Arabia, the United Arab Emirates (UAE), and the U.S. supported one or another Sunni faction. Meanwhile, ethnically and religiously divided Syria erupted in civil war

---

[2]Bedri Baykam, quoted in Anand Giridharadas, "In Turkey, Forging a New Identity," *New York Times*, November 20, 2012.

as Sunni protests against a government supported by various minorities fostered a brutal government response and then an insurgency and civil war. Most of these uprisings evolved into bitter struggles and polarization between factions, tribes, and sects, preventing the democracy, social justice, and human rights many protesters desired. Yet the social media that spread what some called "Facebook revolutions" linked people all over the region, perhaps setting a foundation for more open societies.

30-1b Arab Nationalism and Egypt

During the 1960s and 1970s, confrontation between Arab nationalism and the world's superpowers, especially the United States and Britain, was acute in Egypt, which, with ninety-five million people (around 10 percent Christians) by 2017, is the most populous Arab country. In 1954 charismatic, anti-British general Gamal Abdul Nasser **(NAS-uhr)** (1918–1970) became Egypt's leader after a military coup ended the corrupt pro-British monarchy. Nasser's frequent childhood visits to his parents' impoverished farming village sparked his sympathy for the poor and resentment of rich landlords. As a radical student and then army officer, he developed a vision of a new Egypt, free of Western domination and social inequality.

Nasser preached modernization, socialism, and unity, and his promise to improve the lives of the poor and implement land reform made him a hero in the Arab world. To generate electric power and improve flood control, Nasser used Soviet aid to build the massive Aswan High Dam along the Nile, completed in 1970. But his nonaligned foreign policy antagonized a Cold War–obsessed United States, and his support of pan-Arab nationalism also generated wars. Accusing the West of "imperialist methods, habits of blood-sucking and usurping rights, and interference in other countries,"[3] in 1956 Egypt took over the British-operated Suez Canal, a key artery of world commerce; while foreign ownership of the canal had symbolized Egypt's subjugation to foreign powers, Europeans considered the canal the lifeline moving oil and resources to the West from Asia. Britain, France, and Israel dispatched military forces to reclaim the canal, but the United States, which disliked Nasser but feared regional instability, and the USSR forced their withdrawal. Standing up to the West made Nasser an even greater Arab hero and leader of the developing nations seeking nonalignment, or neutrality, between the two superpowers. However, Nasser was humiliated by Israel's defeat of Egypt and its allies in a brief 1967 war. Furthermore, Nasser's social and economic reforms fostered little economic development or military strength.

Nasser's successors followed pragmatic, pro-U.S. policies. In 1978 Anwar Sadat (g. 1970–1981) signed a peace treaty with Israel brokered by U.S. president Jimmy Carter (g. 1977–1981), but he was assassinated by hardline military officers. Sadat and his successor, Hosni Mubarak (1981–2012), dismantled Nasser's socialist economy, and in the coming years a few well-connected capitalists became fabulously rich while the poorest became even poorer. In Cairo, the contrast grew more dramatic between glittering rich neighborhoods, featuring luxury apartments and mansions surrounded by high walls, and poor,

overcrowded neighborhoods, where the most desperate families lived in huts on top of ramshackle apartment buildings. Hence, millions of Egyptians sought work in oil-rich Arab nations. Furthermore, climate change has become an increasing threat as farms withered in drought and coastal flooding threatens the two-millennia-old city of Alexandria and parts of the Nile delta.

Egypt boasted one of the largest economies in the Middle East and the second largest in Africa and has a modest oil industry, but few other resources than fertile Nile farmlands and popular tourist sites. Egypt suffered from high malnutrition and unemployment, low rates of literacy and public health, and a huge national debt. In elections candidates opposing long-entrenched President Mubarak (r. 1981–2012) were hampered by free speech limits, harassment, and arrest of dissidents. While liberals sought more democracy, Islamic militants like the Muslim Brotherhood, feeding on these frustrations, challenged the secular but corrupt, repressive government.

Egypt was not immune to the Arab Spring sweeping the region. In 2011 massive protests against Mubarak were met with violence, but eventually Mubarak fled and was arrested, the army stepped in, and, after a transition, in 2012 it introduced a more participatory system including freer elections. Although many of the protesters were secular liberals wanting a more open system, the Islamist Muslim Brotherhood won the elections and control of Parliament; one of their leaders, Mohammed Morsi, became president. But the Morsi government proved unable to revive a staggering economy and began imposing a more Islamic agenda, disillusioning or outraging many Egyptians. In 2013 massive protests erupted, generating violence between Islamists and secular liberals; the military then removed Morsi. In 2014 the former head of the armed forces, Abdel Fattah El-Sisi, became president, brutally repressed the Muslim Brotherhood, and instituted military rule, dashing hopes for democracy while arresting both Islamist and liberal critics of their harsh policies and the resulting civil strife and violence. A close U.S. ally, El-Sisi proved corrupt and even more despotic than Mubarak or Morsi, brutally repressing protests and all dissent, and filling the jails with several thousand political prisoners. The secular–Islamist gap made compromise difficult; many Egyptians seemed to prefer military rule to Islamist rule but discontent also grew.

30-1c Israel in Middle Eastern Politics

Israel–Arab conflict became the Middle East's most insurmountable problem, sustaining tensions for over seven decades. Zionist Jews had emigrated from Europe to Palestine since the late 1800s, building cities and forming productive socialist farming settlements, but their presence triggered occasional conflicts with the Palestinian Arab majority. The Nazis' murder of six million Jews during World War II spurred a stronger desire for a homeland free of oppression, and in the later 1940s Jewish refugees poured into Palestine. Moderate Jewish leaders asked Britain to transfer power to them in Palestine. However, Zionist extremists practiced "gun diplomacy," using bombings and assassinations against the

---

[3]Quoted in Ian J. Bickerton and Carla I. Klausner, *A Concise History of the Arab-Israeli Conflict*, 2nd ed. (Englewood Cliffs, N.J.: Prentice-Hall, 1995), 131.

British, Arabs, and moderate Jews, while Arabs, opposing an Israeli state at their expense, attacked Jews. Unable to maintain order, Britain referred the Palestine question to the new Western-dominated United Nations. As the British withdrew in 1948, Jewish leaders proclaimed the establishment of Israel. Forming a multiparty democracy, Israelis gained strong Western support, and the United States has supplied generous aid ever since.

These developments sparked full-scale war in 1948–1949 between Israel and its Arab neighbors, to whom Israel was a white settler state symbolizing Western colonialism (see Map 30.1). As some 85 percent of Palestinian Arabs fled the fighting, Israelis occupied their farms and houses. Israelis won the war against the disorganized Arabs, while many Palestinian refugees (numbering some five million by 2012) settled in overcrowded, squalid refugee camps in Egypt, Lebanon, Jordan, and Syria, nursing their hatred of Israel. Most supported the Palestine Liberation Organization (PLO), an Arab nationalist–Muslim–Christian coalition. Neither Western nations nor Israel officially recognized or would negotiate with the PLO until the 1990s, prompting it to employ terrorism, attacking public buses and rural settlements.

Israel endured chronic confrontation with its Arab neighbors and the PLO. Palestinians still in Israel, though participating in democratic politics, were disproportionally poor. Meanwhile, thousands of Jewish immigrants arrived, many from Middle Eastern countries where they had experienced discrimination or retribution. Their arrival intensified divisions between secular and devout, European and Middle Eastern Jews. Obsessed with security, well-armed Israel devoted half its total national budget to the military. A cycle of violence followed; when the PLO attacked, Israelis bombed a refugee camp in Lebanon in retaliation.

An Arab–Israeli War in 1967 further complicated regional politics, heightening conflict and reshaping Israeli society. Responding to an ill-advised attack led by Egypt and Jordan, Israel occupied the West Bank of the Jordan River; eastern Jerusalem, filled with Jewish and Islamic holy places; the Gaza Strip, a small coastal enclave of Egypt; and the Golan Heights, a Syrian plateau overlooking northeast Israel. The new Israeli-controlled lands contained a large Arab population, a combustible situation that Israel exacerbated by treating the occupied Palestinians as a colonized people, with no political rights. In 1973 another Israeli war with Egypt and Syria proved costly to all sides.

While many Israelis wanted to trade occupied land for a permanent peace settlement, others hoped to permanently annex occupied lands as part of biblical Israel. Ultranationalist and religiously conservative Israelis, with government support, began settling on Arab land, creating another problem: Jewish settlers living amid hostile Arabs. Palestinians resent the heavily fortified settlements, guarded by Israeli soldiers, that often overlook Palestinian cities and villages from nearby hilltops. Because Israel proper has remained a democracy with a vibrant free press, Israelis heatedly debate these policies and the treatment of Arabs. In

Intifada ("Uprising") A resistance begun in 1987 by Palestinians against the Israeli occupation.

1987 desperate Palestinians began a resistance, the **Intifada** ("Uprising"), against the Israeli occupation. Rising Islamic militancy in the occupied territories alarmed both the secular Fatah movement, the main PLO party, and Israelis. Negotiations led in 1993 to limited self-government under the PLO in some of the occupied territories, the basis for a possible Palestinian state, and a peace agreement between Israel and Jordan.

In 2000 violence erupted again. Moderate Israelis and Palestinians lost hope as demoralizing Palestinian suicide bombings of civilian targets, such as restaurants and public buses, and Israeli reprisal attacks on Palestinian neighborhoods made life insecure for everyone. Israel built a high security fence separating it from the West Bank that incorporated some occupied territory, enraging Palestinians. In a 2006 election, Palestinians, tired of Fatah's ineffective and corrupt regime, gave the militant Islamic Hamas movement, which sponsored terrorist attacks and refused to recognize Israel's right to exist, a majority of seats in the Palestinian parliament. Soon Hamas seized Gaza, from where militants fired rockets into Israel; Fatah controlled the West Bank. An inconclusive Israeli invasion of southern Lebanon in 2006 to stop terrorist attacks, as well as a bloody, destructive military incursion in Gaza in 2008 and a blockade in 2009, hardened Israeli and Palestinian attitudes and sparked world condemnation.

After a hardline Israeli government led by right-winger Benjamin Netanyahu (g. 1996–1999, 2009–) took power, prospects for negotiations to resolve issues ebbed and flowed. Israel, a developed nation of nine million (74 percent Jewish, 21 percent Arab, 5 percent Other) in 2019, still occupies the West Bank (home to 3.4 million people, 400,000 of them Jewish settlers), which has limited autonomy. Hamas uneasily governs Gaza but Israel (with Egyptian cooperation) maintains an air, sea, and land blockade that makes life very difficult for Gazans. While Israeli relations with Saudi Arabia have improved, tensions between Israel and Iran (Saudi Arabia's rival in the region) have increased. By later 2019 experts talked about an Israeli–Iran "shadow war" in which Israel used air power and sabotage to try and prevent Iran from providing military equipment (including missiles and drones) to its allies in Syria, Lebanon, and Yemen, setting the stage perhaps for a wider confrontation. Jewish society was increasingly divided between liberal and moderate, mostly secular Jews, concentrated especially in coastal cities, and conservative and deeply religious ultra-Orthodox and Hasidic Jews, strongest in Jerusalem and the West Bank settlements. In 2018 Netanyahu became caught up in a corruption scandal, upsetting Israeli politics; he faced criminal charges and a possible ban from political office. But his close ally, U.S. President Trump, gave him support by recognizing Jerusalem as the nation's capital as well as Israeli ownership of the Golan Heights and the right to settle the West Bank. Viewed by his political foes as an increasingly undemocratic ultra-nationalist like some of the far-right leaders in Eastern Europe, Netanyahu also announced that if he and his right-wing coalition won the 2019 elections his government would annex a large part of the West Bank, leaving the Palestinians with isolated enclaves separated from each other. With no clear victor the election proved inconclusive as leaders scrambled to put together a ruling coalition. These actions

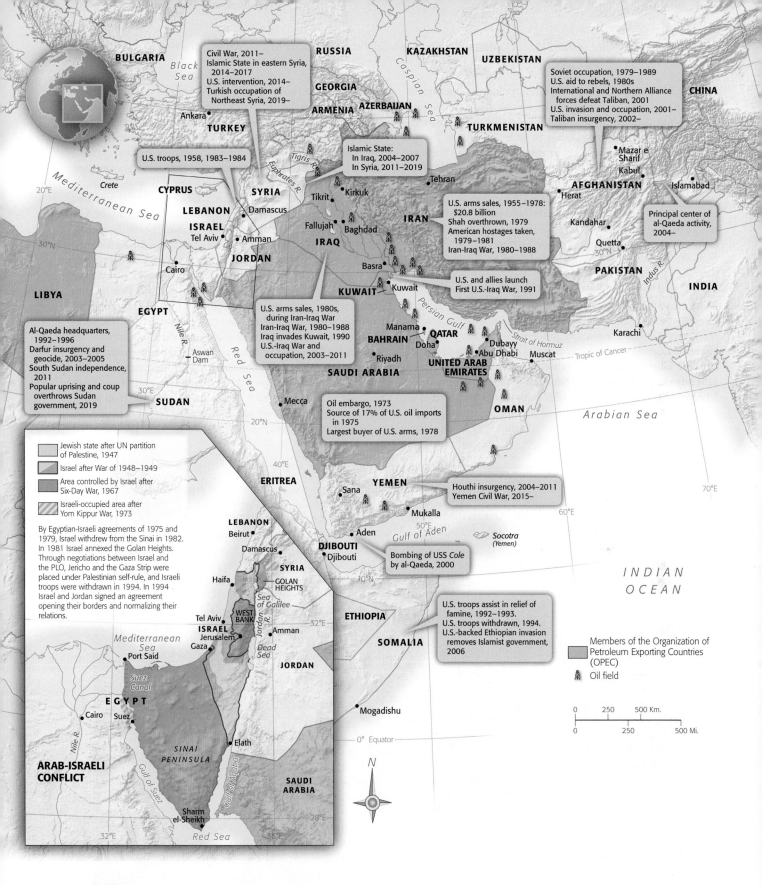

Civil War, 2011–
Islamic State in eastern Syria, 2014–2017
U.S. intervention, 2014–
Turkish occupation of Northeast Syria, 2019–

Soviet occupation, 1979–1989
U.S. aid to rebels, 1980s
International and Northern Alliance forces defeat Taliban, 2001
U.S. invasion and occupation, 2001–
Taliban insurgency, 2002–

U.S. troops, 1958, 1983–1984

Islamic State:
In Iraq, 2004–2007
In Syria, 2011–2019

U.S. arms sales, 1955–1978: $20.8 billion
Shah overthrown, 1979
American hostages taken, 1979–1981
Iran-Iraq War, 1980–1988

Principal center of al-Qaeda activity, 2004–

U.S. and allies launch First U.S.-Iraq War, 1991

Al-Qaeda headquarters, 1992–1996
Darfur insurgency and geocide, 2003–2005
South Sudan independence, 2011
Popular uprising and coup overthrows Sudan government, 2019

U.S. arms sales, 1980s, during Iran-Iraq War
Iran-Iraq War, 1980–1988
Iraq invades Kuwait, 1990
U.S.-Iraq War and occupation, 2003–2011

Oil embargo, 1973
Source of 17% of U.S. oil imports in 1975
Largest buyer of U.S. arms, 1978

Jewish state after UN partition of Palestine, 1947

Israel after War of 1948–1949

Area controlled by Israel after Six-Day War, 1967

Israeli-occupied area after Yom Kippur War, 1973

By Egyptian-Israeli agreements of 1975 and 1979, Israel withdrew from the Sinai in 1982. In 1981 Israel annexed the Golan Heights. Through negotiations between Israel and the PLO, Jericho and the Gaza Strip were placed under Palestinian self-rule, and Israeli troops were withdrawn in 1994. In 1994 Israel and Jordan signed an agreement opening their borders and normalizing their relations.

ARAB–ISRAELI CONFLICT

Houthi insurgency, 2004–2011
Yemen Civil War, 2015–

Bombing of USS *Cole* by al-Qaeda, 2000

U.S. troops assist in relief of famine, 1992–1993.
U.S. troops withdrawn, 1994.
U.S.-backed Ethiopian invasion removes Islamist government, 2006

Members of the Organization of Petroleum Exporting Countries (OPEC)

Oil field

0   250   500 Km.
0   250   500 Mi.

MAP 30.1 **Middle East Oil and the Arab–Israeli Conflict** Several Middle Eastern nations, including Saudi Arabia, Iran, Iraq, Libya, and the small Persian Gulf states, are rich in oil and active members of OPEC. Israel, founded in 1948, and the neighboring Arab countries of Egypt, Jordan, and Syria have been in chronic conflict that has resulted in four wars. Israel's victory in the 1967 war allowed it to take control of Gaza, the West Bank, and the Golan Heights.

Q What does this map indicate about the role of the United States in the Middle East since the late 1940s?

dismissed Palestinian claims and made a peace agreement even more unlikely. The possibility that a separate Palestinian state would never happen revived a bitter longstanding debate in Israel about whether Israel should be an undemocratic Jewish state with a Palestinian minority who enjoyed few rights or an inclusive, democratic, multicultural state with equal rights for all. Although in 2019 a group of liberal Arab thinkers from varied countries called for abandoning the boycotts and engaging with Israel, with conflicting visions of how Israelis and Palestinians might coexist or form two states, no consensus for ensuring long-term peace has yet emerged.

30-1d Islamic Revolution in Iran

By the end of World War II, rival European nations had interfered with Iran, rich in oil and strategically located along the Persian Gulf, for a century, and the interference continued after the war, when Iranian politics was embroiled in a conflict between the young king, Shah Mohammed Pahlavi (pah-LAH-vee) (1919–1980), and nationalist reformers opposed to foreign domination. In 1951 nationalists came to power and reduced the shah to a ceremonial role; they then nationalized the British-dominated oil industry, from which Iran had

received little revenue. Britain and its ally, the United States, considering the nationalists pro-USSR, cut off aid and launched a boycott to close oil markets, bringing Iran to near bankruptcy and fostering unrest. In 1953, American CIA agents secretly organized opposition among military leaders and riots against the nationalist government. Royalists overthrew the government, imprisoned its leaders, and restored the unpopular shah to power, embittering many Iranians. Shah Pahlavi, a ruthless, pleasure-loving man who lived extravagantly and dreamed of restoring Persia as a great power, allied himself with the United States, allowing American companies to control the oil industry.

The shah's three and a half decades of rule brought modernization, political repression, and a huge military force built with oil revenues. While his "white revolution" earned Western admiration because it promoted a market economy and women's rights while enlarging the middle class, it failed to improve most Iranians' living standards. While a corrupt elite siphoned off most of the development money and generous U.S. aid, 60 percent of peasants remained landless, and people flocked to the traffic- and smog-choked cities. Meanwhile, to increase national pride and attract Western tourists, the shah spent billions to renovate the splendid palaces and tombs of Persepolis, a city built for Persian kings twenty-four hundred years ago that

IMAGE 30.2 **Palestinian Political Rally** In 2011 after Arab media published hundreds of secret documents revealing Israeli–Palestinian peace talks, many Palestinians rallied to support president Mahmud Abbas. This rally was in Jenin, on the West Bank.

Q What can the photo reveal about Palestinian politics and Israeli–Palestinian relations?

few Iranians could afford to visit. The absolute monarch's secret police eliminated opposition, holding thousands of political prisoners. Poet Faruq Farrukhzad **(fuh-ROOK fuh-ROOK-sad)** wrote of how intellectuals, cowed into submission, retreated into "swamps of alcohol [while] the verminous mice gnawed through the pages of gilded books, stacked in ancient closets."[4] At the same time, conservative Shi'ite leaders opposed modernization, such as unveiled women and crowded bars, as threatening Muslim culture. In 1979, as the economy slumped, strikes and protests forced the shah into exile in the United States, turning Americans and Iranians into bitter foes.

An Islamic revolution then reshaped Iran. While some Shi'ite thinkers discouraged clergy from taking political action, others promoted a clergy-governed Islamic state. Militant Shi'ite clerics, led by long-exiled Ayatollah Ruhollah Khomeini **(roo-HOLE-ah KOH-may-nee)** (1902–1989), took power, eliminated leftists and moderate nationalists, overturned the shah's modernization, and mandated Islamic Shari'a law codes. Thousands fled abroad, many to the United States. Women were forced to wear veils and were prohibited from socializing with men from outside their families. They were also banned from attending sports events of men's teams, a ban only removed (at least temporarily) in 2019. The regime also restricted other personal freedoms, prompting a popular joke: "We used to drink in public and pray in private. Now we pray in public and drink in private." Like the shah, the clerics ruled by terror, suppressed ethnic minorities, such as the mostly Sunni Kurds in the northwest, and executed opponents.

The United States became a bitter enemy after Islamic militants, who hated America for its long support of the shah, seized the U.S. Embassy in 1979 and held it and U.S. diplomats for one year. Iran's Arab neighbors, fearing Iran's territorial size, large population (seventy-seven million by 2013), military strength, and regional ambitions, were also alarmed. Now they encountered Islamic militancy aimed at their more secular governments. Animosity between mostly Sunni Arabs and mostly Shi'ite Iranians fueled tensions, sparking a catastrophic war with Iraq (1980–1988) that produced 500,000 to one million Iranian casualties. An Iranian program to develop nuclear power and perhaps nuclear weapons also worried the international community and blossomed into a full-scale regional and global crisis by the 2010s.

Eventually Iran mixed theocracy with democratic trappings. Ayatollah Khomeini was succeeded as Supreme Leader by the equally hardline conservative cleric Ayatollah Ali Khamenei (b. 1939). A more open electoral process allowed opposition parties to win parliamentary seats. With the economy floundering, by 1997 moderate reformers seeking closer ties to the outside world, democratization, and loosening of harsh laws challenged the hardline clerics who controlled the judicial and electoral systems. Young people, resenting Islamic laws, increasingly confronted restrictions on personal behavior, and young women, often unveiled or wearing fashionable head scarves, began socializing again with men. But hardliners banned reformist newspapers and disqualified reformist candidates. Shirin Ebadi **(shih-RIN ee-BOD-ee)** (b. 1947), a feminist Iranian lawyer and human rights activist, won the Nobel Peace Prize in 2003 for bravely challenging the clerical leadership and favoring reformist Islam. In 2005 Iranians elected a hardline president, Mahmoud Ahmedinijad **(mah-MOOD ah-mah-DIH-nee-zhahd)** (b. 1956), who increased nuclear capabilities, restored conservative values, banned Western music from radio and television, harassed dissidents, threatened Israel, and openly defied the United States. However, as the economy declined, reformers and hardliners continued to struggle for influence. In 2009, Ahmedinijad and the hardliners won a disputed election that many Iranians considered rigged, generating massive street protests but also intensifying repression of dissidents. The brutal civil war engulfing Iran's main regional ally, Syria, complicated relations with the West. Hoping for better relations with the outside world, in 2013 Iranians elected a more moderate cleric, Hassan Rouhani **(ha-SAN roo-HAHN-ee)**, who introduced some modest reforms and negotiated a deal with the United States and the Western allies that ended Iran's controversial program to build nuclear facilities and possibly weapons in exchange for removing sanctions. But in 2017 the new U.S. president, Donald Trump, ignoring the advice of most experts but supported by Iran's bitter enemies Saudi Arabia and Israel, pulled out of the deal, causing an international crisis and increasing regional tensions as European powers worked to maintain the agreement. Trump also re-imposed tough sanctions (including on medical imports and restricting oil exports), which have made life difficult for Iranians, and threatened war on Iran. These moves undermined Rouhani, strengthened the Iranian hardliners, caused a split in the Western alliance, gave Iran an excuse to potentially resume their nuclear program, and threatened to destabilize the Middle East. But Ayatollah Ali Khamenei claimed that Iran would never develop nuclear weapons because they were forbidden in Islam. In late 2019 protests erupted in many Iranian cities over increased fuel prices, economic distress, corruption, and repression. The regime shut down the internet and responded with violence, killing hundreds of protesters. Many blamed the regime for the problems.

30-1e Civil Wars and Interventions in Afghanistan

Farther east, in Afghanistan, violence, foreign interventions, and militant Islamic movements generated instability for over three decades. From the early 1800s until 1978, kings from the largest ethnic group, the Pashtuns, loosely governed Afghanistan's diverse Sunni and Shi'a ethnic groups, which were subdivided into rival tribes. In 1978 pro-communist generals seized power, forged close ties with the Soviet Union, and introduced radical social and economic reforms that challenged Islamic traditions: land reform, women's education, and replacing Islamic law with secular family law. When conservative Islamic rebels, known as **mujahidin (moo-JAH-hi-deen)** ("holy warriors"), rebelled against the pro-Soviet regime, the USSR invaded in 1979, launching

> **mujahidin** ("holy warriors") Conservative Islamic rebels who rebelled against the pro-Soviet regime in Afghanistan in the 1970s and 1980s.

---

[4] Quoted in James Alban Bill, *The Politics of Iran: Groups, Classes and Modernization* (Columbus, OH: Charles E. Merrill, 1972), 76–77.

decades of turbulence during which the mujahidin won small victories against the 150,000 Soviet troops. Both sides were ruthless, and indiscriminate Soviet air attacks created five million refugees, turning the population against the occupation. Meanwhile, the United States, Pakistan, and Arab nations sent military and financial aid to the rebels and Islamic volunteers such as wealthy Saudi Osama bin Laden. Afghanistan became an unwinnable quagmire for Soviet forces, and they withdrew in 1989, hastening the demise of Soviet communism and the Soviet empire. As the pro-Soviet government collapsed, rival mujahidin groups fought for control. The West offered little help to reconstruct the ruined country.

Pashtun militants known as the **Taliban** ("Students"), many educated in Pakistani Islamic schools, conquered much of the Pashtun south and then seized the capital, Kabul, in 1996. Eventually they extended their influence into the north, which was mostly inhabited by anti-Taliban Tajiks and Uzbeks. The puritanical Taliban introduced an especially harsh Islamic rule. All women, including those in Kabul who once wore jeans and T-shirts, attended universities, and pursued careers, were now required to wear long black robes and stay at home. The Taliban banned women's education, alcohol, and music and film as sinful, executing people for even minor infractions. Although the streets were safe, life offered no joy. Reflecting their disdain for Afghanistan's pre-Islamic past, the Taliban also destroyed spectacular monumental Buddhas carved into a mountainside over a millennium ago, outraging the world.

Meanwhile, international jihadist terrorist groups, forming around radical Arab volunteers who fought with the mujahidin, made Taliban-controlled Afghanistan their base and used it to build training camps. Osama bin Laden, leader and chief financial backer of the largest group, Al Qaeda, called on Muslims to take up arms against Western regimes, whom he called "crusaders": "Tell the Muslims everywhere that the vanguards of the warriors who are fighting the enemies of Islam belong to them."[5]

After the Al Qaeda attacks on the United States in September 2001, Americans, enjoying widespread world support, sent military forces into Afghanistan. With local anti-Taliban allies soon displacing the Taliban from the main cities, the Americans destroyed Al Qaeda bases and installed a fragile pro-Western government. But instability ensued: Taliban and Al Qaeda leaders, including bin Laden, went into hiding (U.S. special forces killed him in Pakistan in 2011), and the victors struggled to foster development and democracy, especially after the United States shifted much of its military force and development aid to Iraq. Supported by Pakistani intelligence and military factions, the Taliban regrouped, mounted an insurgency against the pro-Western regime and the U.S.–NATO forces supporting it, and eventually controlled large sections of the Pashtun south. In 2014 NATO officially ended combat operations and, with Americans tiring of a long war, the Obama administration withdrew some combat forces but left a residual force of some nine thousand troops. The Afghan government assumed full security responsibility and competed with the Taliban to win popular support and secure territory. In 2017 Trump increased U.S. troop levels by 50 percent. Over time the Taliban splintered into a loose coalition of various, sometimes rival, factions which would fight for whichever group paid them or gained their allegiance, but they also gained more territory. Terrorism such as suicide bombings, some of it linked to even more militant jihadis, the Islamic State (ISIS), became more common. In 2018 U.S. and Taliban negotiators began talks to discuss a possible peace settlement that would allow a withdrawal of U.S. troops and give the Taliban, whose goal is an Islamic caliphate, a share of power. With Americans tiring of the long struggle, many Afghans, especially women, feared a return of the Taliban and their repression of women. As a prominent woman lawyer noted in 2019: "A Talib is a Talib. They have proven what type of people they are, what their ideology is. And if they return with the same ideology, everything will be the same again."[6] But talks broke down in late 2019 and the future of the conflict remained unclear. Many feared that the violence would intensify, the war would continue, and without a continued U.S. military presence the Taliban would ultimately triumph.

30-1f Iraq and Regional Conflicts

Iraq also proved a major source of regional instability. In 1958 the army overthrew an unpopular monarchy, beginning four decades of ruthless dictatorships that crushed all opposition. During this time the Sunni Arab minority of 20 percent ruled a nation with a restless Arab Shi'ite majority (60 percent) and a disaffected Sunni Kurdish minority (20 percent). The mostly Sunni **Ba'ath** ("Renaissance") Party, which favored socialism and Arab nationalism and strongly opposed Israel, dominated governments, fostering secular policies and some economic development and prosperity. In 1979 Saddam Hussein (1937–2006), a landless peasant's son, seized power, proving even more brutal than his predecessors.

Alarmed by the Iranian Revolution, whose leaders considered Saddam's secular regime godless, in 1980 Saddam's army invaded Iran, using poison gas against Iranian soldiers, but was unable to achieve victory. The war threatened Persian Gulf shipping lanes and hence the world oil supply. The United States, with vested interests in Iraq's oil—the world's second largest proven reserves—and hostility toward Iran, sided with Iraq, attacking Iranian shipping and arming Saddam's military. Both Iran and Iraq drafted teenagers to fight. The costs of the war were staggering: over 260,000 Iranian and 100,000 Iraqi dead, and grave damage to the Iraqi economy. The war ended in 1988 with no victor.

U.S. president George H. W. Bush (g. 1989–1993), viewing Saddam as a useful strategic ally, continued providing weapons. But in 1990 Iraq invaded prosperous, oil-rich Kuwait, ruled by an Arab royal family. Bush, worried that oil-rich Saudi Arabia

Taliban ("Students") A group of Pashtun religious students who organized a military force in the 1980s to fight what they considered immorality and corruption and to impose order in Afghanistan.

Ba'ath ("Renaissance") A political party in the Middle East that favored socialism and Arab nationalism and strongly opposed Israel.

[5]From Akram Fouad Khater, ed., *Sources in the History of the Modern Middle East* (Boston: Houghton Mifflin, 2004), 362.
[6]Quoted in "Women Fear Return of Taliban, and Old Ways," *New York Times*, July 14, 2019, A6.

might be next, launched the Persian Gulf War (1991), which drove Iraqis from Kuwait, killing perhaps thirty thousand Iraqi soldiers. The war restored Americans' faith in their military, undermined by bitter defeat in Vietnam. But Saddam remained in power, persecuting dissidents and slaughtering Shi'ites and Kurds, who rebelled with U.S. encouragement; at least thirty thousand Shi'ites and thousands of Kurds died. The United States and United Nations eventually gave the Kurds some military protection and autonomy in their northern region. But United Nations sanctions restricting Iraq's foreign income and ability to buy weapons undermined Iraq's economy; Iraqis struggled to acquire food and medical supplies, with thousands dying from the resulting shortages.

The Al Qaeda attack on the United States in 2001 and the resulting Afghan war germinated a larger conflict in Iraq. Charging that Saddam Hussein had weapons of mass destruction and was linked to Al Qaeda, U.S. president George W. Bush ordered an invasion and occupation of Iraq in 2003. Massive looting followed the quick U.S. victory, with museums, ancient historical sites, power plants, armories, and communications networks plundered. U.S. credibility suffered after claims about the Iraqi threat proved untrue. Inadequate planning for postwar reconstruction also forced Bush to shift troops and resources from Afghanistan. Fostering democracy, containing factional divisions, and restoring basic services such as electricity and clean water proved a challenge.

Although Saddam was captured and later executed, American forces struggled to maintain order against a persistent, mostly Sunni, resistance movement and terrifying suicide bombings by foreign jihadis, some of whom joined Iraqi jihadis to form a branch of al Qaeda, which morphed into the Salafist-influenced Islamic State (ISIS) in 2014. Declaring itself a worldwide caliphate, ISIS quickly gained a reputation for ruthless violence, including public beheadings of prisoners and enslaving and raping women or forcing them to cover up completely. Between 2003 and 2011 over 100,000, and by some estimates as many as half a million, Iraqis died, two million became refugees in neighboring countries, and many were forced from their neighborhoods by "ethnic cleansing." Many Iraqis, especially Shi'ites and Kurds, having hated Saddam's bloody regime, welcomed its demise, but, remembering British colonization after World War I, they also resented yet another Western occupation. While some Arab liberals hoped democracy would flower in Iraq and throughout the region, the occupation of an oil-rich Arab country, at a high cost in U.S. and Iraqi casualties, tied down the U.S. military in a quagmire. However, Iraqis then elected their own government led by Shi'ites closely tied to Iran. The new government had to handle ethnic and tribal rivalries while trying to hold the nation together and rejuvenate public services. By 2009 violence had diminished, but a large U.S. military presence remained. In some respects life returned to normal. By 2019 large public dance parties in Baghdad attracted many young Iraqi men and some women, a hodgepodge of bikers, gamers, electronic dance music enthusiasts, and varied other subcultures and featuring electronic music and hip-hop. The Shi'ites' monopoly on power and harassment of opponents alienated many Sunnis. Since the last U.S. troops withdrew in 2011, Sunni–Shia conflict

and jihadi violence have increased while the Syrian civil war next door spilled over the border, making life dangerous once again for Iraq's thirty-seven million people. In 2014 ISIS forces moved into Iraq from Syria and captured a large section of western Iraq including the major city of Mosul, carrying out terrorist attacks and massacres, especially the genocide against the Yazidis, a small religious minority. By 2017 Iraqi forces had regained most of the ISIS territory in western Iraq but spots of ISIS activism remained. By 2019 groups linked to Al Qaeda and especially ISIS, defeated in Syria, have reestablished a presence. Sectarian and ethnic tensions between Sunnis, Shi'ites, Kurds (who seek autonomy or secession), and various other minorities still fester. In late 2019 violent protests against issues that plague daily life, such as sectarian divisions, corruption, poor services, unemployment, and Iranian influence erupted in Baghdad and the south, creating a political crisis. Hundreds died and thousands were injured as the regime cracked down with force. Squeezed dangerously between the demands of Iran and the United States., who both want to maintain their influence, Iraq's future remained unclear.

30-1g Saudi Arabia, Oil, and the World

The Persian Gulf War reinforced Saudi Arabia's close connections with the United States, which had military bases and strong economic stakes in the kingdom. Mostly bleak desert, Saudi Arabia possesses the world's largest known oil reserves. Oil revenues funded modernization and the building of highways, hospitals, and universities, so that by the 1980s the Saudis had achieved high health and literacy rates for the Middle East. Glittering shopping malls offering the latest Western fashions and electronic gadgets serve affluent urbanites, who reach them in luxury cars often driven by chauffeurs. Yet, outside cities, poor Saudis often travel by camel and sleep in tents.

Despite modernization, Saudi political and social life has remained conservative. The royal family exercises absolute power, living extravagantly, quashing dissent, and maintaining traditional customs and social patterns. Modern institutions (like television) clash with a highly puritanical, patriarchal Islamic culture. With royal support, the Wahhabis impose their rigid beliefs on religious thought, life, and education. Hostile to Western and often modern ideas, Wahhabis believe that women should stay at home under male control. Hence, although some educated women desired more freedom, they could not legally drive until recently or work or study alongside men. Armed with canes, the "religious police" patrol the streets, markets, and city malls, punishing women for violating strict dress codes that require them to be covered head to foot. In the 1990s they prevented unveiled female students from fleeing a school dormitory fire, causing dozens to burn to death. Meanwhile, the Shi'ite minority, mainly concentrated on the eastern coast and despised by the Wahhabis, has enjoyed few rights, fostering tensions. Movie theaters, concerts, and most other entertainments are banned. Saudi and Western critics believe that the narrow Islam taught in Saudi schools promotes extremism and anti-Western feeling, and by 2013 calls for liberalization and

IMAGE 30.3 **Oil Wealth** Saudi Arabia contains the world's largest oil operations, mostly located on or near the Persian Gulf. A Saudi worker overlooks one of the nation's many refineries, which produces the oil exports that have brought the nation wealth.

Q What does the photo tell us about Saudi Arabia and Saudi society?

women's empowerment by some Saudi men and women had fostered some minor reforms. After a peaceful protest on Facebook, a royal edict allowed women to work as sales clerks in lingerie and cosmetic shops, a first step perhaps in expanding the female workforce. But with little public transportation, men have had to drive them to workplaces. In 2015 King Abdullah (g. 2005-2015), a cautious modernizer, allowed women to vote and be elected in municipal elections.

Saudi Arabia has strongly influenced the prices and availability of world oil. In 1960 the kingdom spurred formation of **OPEC** (Organization of Petroleum Exporting Countries), a cartel designed to give producers more power over oil prices and leverage over consuming nations. OPEC's members range from Middle Eastern nations such as Algeria, Iran, and the UAE to Mexico, Nigeria, and Indonesia. In 1973 OPEC members, angry at Western support of Israel, reduced the world oil supply to raise prices, badly discomforting industrialized nations by causing long lines at gasoline stations. After the embargo ended, the world price remained high, enriching OPEC members, while the high prices forced Americans and western Europeans to conserve fuel. For example, some nations promoted development of more fuel-efficient cars. But in the 1980s reduced oil consumption broke OPEC's power and prices plummeted, damaging most OPEC members' economies.

Saudi Arabia's status as the world's largest oil exporter ensured political support and

OPEC (Organization of Petroleum Exporting Countries) A cartel formed in 1960 to give producers more power over the price of oil and leverage with the consuming nations.

profits from industrialized nations but did not guarantee Saudi prosperity; by the 1990s the Saudi economy had soured. Between 1980 and 2000 income levels fell by two-thirds, generating government benefit cuts and climbing unemployment. Meanwhile, royal family members spent money lavishly, often violating Wahhabi restrictions by cavorting in Beirut nightclubs and European casinos. Resentment of the royal family and U.S. military bases on Saudi soil has increased. Seeing little future, frustrated young people often drink alcohol, have mixed-gender parties behind closed doors, and flirt over social media. Others have embraced militant Islam, and a few have joined terrorist groups such as Al Qaeda, including most of the young men who hijacked and crashed four U.S. airliners in 2001. Al Qaeda's leader, Osama bin Laden (1957–2011), a militant Wahhabi from a wealthy Saudi family, had long raged against the U.S. military bases in Saudi Arabia. Meanwhile, the Saudis help finance embattled Sunni groups in troubled nations like Lebanon and Syria while opposing Iranian influence. Saudis also invest heavily in the U.S. and European economies, and many Saudis have studied in the West. Thanks to oil, Saudi Arabia and the industrialized nations have remained close allies despite vastly different social and political systems.

In 2013 Crown Prince Mohammad bin Salman (b. 1985) was appointed Deputy Prime Minister and became essentially the power behind the throne. He has introduced some important reforms, including restricting the religious police, weakening male guardianship of women so they could leave the house or travel without a male relative, allowing women to drive, and introducing policies to diversify the economy. In 2018 Reema

Juffali became the first Saudi woman race car driver. Many Saudi men and women praised these innovations. But Prince Mohammad has also been an autocrat, arresting and often torturing some dissidents, human rights activists, outspoken feminists, and royal family rivals while arranging the murder of a prominent Saudi journalist living in the United States, shocking and outraging the world. In foreign policy he launched a bombing campaign against Shi'ites in Yemen and promoted diplomatic isolation of the Gulf state of Qatar. The Yemen intervention, which began in 2015 as a civil war between the Sunni government and largely Shi'ite rebels (the Houthis) for control of the country, has proven a deadly quagmire drawing in other countries including the UAE, Iran (which arms the Houthis), and the U.S. and Britain (which supply weapons including bombs to the Saudi-led coalition). The constant fighting and especially Saudi and UAE air strikes (which have killed around eighteen thousand civilians) have devastated the country including agriculture, causing widespread starvation or risk of starvation. Nearly 100,000 Yemenites have died as a result of the conflict. In 2019 a United Nations report accused the U.S., Britain, and France of complicity in potential war crimes in Yemen because of their arms transfers, but President Trump vetoed a U.S. Senate resolution to withdraw U.S. support for the Saudis. In later 2019 a drone and cruise missile attack in eastern Arabia against Saudi Arabia's major oil refineries and storage areas destroyed half of their supply, temporarily upsetting world oil markets and raising oil prices. Most of the kingdom's oil is exported to Asia (Japan, China, India, South Korea) and neighboring Jordan and Bahrain. The Houthis claimed responsibility but Saudi Arabia and the U.S. blamed Iran, ramping up Middle Eastern tensions even more. Many feared a larger, potentially devastating war that could involve the United States, which sent several thousand more troops to Saudi Arabia, and perhaps several other nations.

KEY POINTS

▶ After World War II, nationalist governments replaced many colonial regimes in the Middle East, but the region has failed to develop many working multiparty democracies.

▶ Traumatized by the Holocaust, many Jews moved to Palestine after World War II and established the state of Israel, which led to a war between Jews and Arabs, a mass exodus of Palestinians into refugee camps, and enduring tensions.

▶ After nationalists overthrew the Iranian shah, the United States helped organize a coup that returned him to power, and he ruled ruthlessly until 1979, when he was overthrown by anti-Western Islamic fundamentalists.

▶ In Afghanistan, U.S.-supported Islamic rebels and Soviet-assisted communists fought for a decade until they withdrew, after which the Taliban took over much of the country and allowed terrorist groups such as Al Qaeda to base themselves

there. After Al Qaeda's September 2001 attack on the United States, a U.S.-led invasion in Afghanistan led to significant backlash and a long war involving the U.S. and Afghan government against the Taliban.

▶ From 1958 on, Iraq was ruled by ruthless military dictatorships dominated by the Sunni minority, and in 1979 Saddam Hussein came to power, launched a costly war against Iran, and then was attacked by the United States after invading Kuwait. In 2003 the United States invaded Iraq, overthrowing Saddam but fostering sectarian tensions that increased after the U.S. withdrawal of troops in 2011.

▶ Saudi Arabia grew extremely wealthy from oil sales, but many citizens have remained poor, and Saudi society is dominated by extremely conservative religious leaders, some of whose followers resent the close relationship the Saudi royal family has forged with the United States.

30-2 Change and Conflict in the Middle East

🖳 SOCIETIES

Q What roles has Islam played in the contemporary Middle East?

In 1979 Muslims celebrated thirteen centuries of Islamic history during which they had fostered extensive trade networks, introduced and transmitted scientific knowledge, and founded powerful empires. From roughly 1850 to 1950, European powers dominated these societies, though many older traditions have remained relevant into the present. In recent decades new conflicts resulting from foreign interventions, Islamic militancy, international terrorism, and political change have unsettled the Middle East and world politics.

CONNECTION to TODAY

What aspects of Middle Eastern culture and thought do you think help them meet the challenges of modern life?

30-2a Ethnic and Religious Conflict

Ethnic and religious hostilities have led to long-term conflict in some societies. Sporadic tensions between majority Arabs and minority Berbers have sometimes complicated politics in Algeria and Morocco. And the wars in Iraq, Syria, Yemen, and Afghanistan can be attributed partly to hostilities between different ethnic and religious groups. Deeply divided societies have shaped Lebanon, Syria, and Sudan. In Lebanon competition between a dozen rival factions and sects—Christian (Greek Orthodox, Maronite-Catholic), Sunni, and Shi'ite—has sparked occasional political crises and civil war. A national government mostly existed only in name during the 1970s and 1980s, and Beirut, once a prosperous, free-wheeling mecca for trade, entertainment, and tourism, was devastated by factional fighting. Supporting various factions, Israel, Syria, Iran, and the United States were all sucked into the conflict. Syria stationed troops in the north and east, Israel in the south. In the 1980s the United States intervened to help a weak national government led by the largest, most pro-Western Christian faction. U.S. warships shelled areas around Beirut dominated by opposition, especially Shi'ite, factions while Marines secured the Beirut airport. The disastrous episode caused some five hundred U.S. deaths from suicide bombers and the holding of U.S. hostages.

In the 1990s the fighting ebbed and Lebanon regained some stability, but there was little national unity. However, the U.S. and Israeli interventions energized radical Shi'ites, who formed a militant Iran-backed organization, Hezbollah **(HEZ-bo-LAH)**, which shelled Israel. Israelis responded by invading Lebanon in 2006 to weaken Hezbollah, but the incursion was costly in lives on all sides and failed to destroy Hezbollah, which remained a strong force in the deeply polarized Lebanon politics. By 2013 the civil war in Syria, whose population is even more diverse, spilled over into Lebanon; as refugees poured in, various Lebanese factions supported the Syrian government or the rebels. Years of unstable government and a divided society followed. In 2019 massive protests against corruption, sectarianism, unresponsive leadership, Iranian influence, a financial crisis, and social dysfunction brought down the government. Some compared the rage and activism to the Arab Spring eight years earlier.

Another longtime ethnic conflict concerned Kurds, a large mostly Sunni ethnic group—over thirty million strong—that mostly inhabited mountain districts in northwest Iran, northwest Iraq, northeast Syria, and southeast Turkey. Although deeply divided by clan and factional rivalries, Kurds had long sought either their own nation or self-government within their countries of residence, generating constant conflict with central governments. Kurdish rebel groups were especially active in eastern Turkey, where the Turkish government, while building a national identity based on Turkish values and language, repressed Kurdish culture and language. Kurds were also restless in oil-rich northern Iraq, where the dictator, Saddam Hussein, made Kurds a special target of his repression, launching air raids and poison gas attacks against Kurdish villages. Today Iraqi Kurds enjoy some regional autonomy and prosperity but still have tense relations with the Arab-dominated national government, while Syrian Kurds have been caught between several seemingly irreconcilable sides in the country's complex civil war.

Syria's ethnic configuration also helped generate a violent civil war as a reaction to the "Arab Spring." Since 1970 the Assad family and the Ba'ath Party have ruled Syria with an iron fist to limit ethnic conflict and dissent while favoring the Assads' Alawite Arab community, offshoots of Shi'ism who constitute 12 percent of the Syrian population. Sunni Arabs vastly outnumber other communities, among them Christians

(10 percent), Palestinians, Kurds, and various Shi'ite groups. In 2011 Sunni anger at repressive Alawite control, a terrible drought, and high unemployment (18 percent in 2012) sparked protests and, after police repression, an uprising. As the regime had with earlier uprisings, the current dictator, Bashar al-Assad (president since 2000), responded with brutal force, attacking both civilians and insurgents. Soon the insurgency fragmented into various factions, some moderates, others Islamists or jihadis linked to Al Qaeda and later to ISIS. Fearing militant Islam, many non-Sunnis supported Assad, who used poison gas weapons. By 2019 between 370,000 and 570,000 Syrians were dead, 7.6 million displaced refugees inside, and five million refugees outside the country. The war also enflamed regional passions, with Turkey, the U.S., Saudi Arabia, Iraqi Sunnis, and the Gulf kingdoms supporting various rebel factions and Iran, Iraqi Shi'ites, Russia, and Lebanon's Hezbollah aiding Assad, raising the danger of a wider conflict. International organizations accused virtually all of the combatant factions of severe human rights violations and massacres. The war has been the deadliest conflict in the twenty-first century so far. By 2018 the Assad forces, aided by Iran and Russia, had destroyed most of the rebel factions and the regime had regained much of its territory.

Only the relatively autonomous Kurdish-led territory in the northeast, with militias supported by the U.S., remained viable. However, given the long history of Kurdish militancy in Turkey, Turkey's President Erdogan considered all Kurds to be potential terrorists and a threat; he treatened plans to create a buffer zone by destroying or pushing the Kurdish forces away from the Turkish border and deeper into Syria while settling the zone with 1–4 million Syrian refugees currently in Turkey. The Kurdish militias, supported by their U.S. allies, had helped eliminate the Islamic State bases, including seizing their capital in Raqqa. They killed or captured thousands of ISIS fighters and often their families, putting them in prison camps near the border managed and guarded by the Kurds. But although the ISIS leader was killed by a U.S. air strike, the group's influence in the restless prison camps, which held some seventy thousand ISIS supporters, along with likely sleeper cells and hidden cash reserves in Syria, suggest that ISIS was far from eliminated and still a danger. U.S. president Donald Trump announced in October 2019 that he would not oppose a Turkish invasion and then withdrew the small U.S. force supporting the Kurds, an act widely criticized by Kurds and many Americans and Europeans as a betrayal of an ally. Erdogan then sent in his powerful military, their air and artillery power augmented by pro-Turkey Syrian Arab militias, Islamist groups, and Russian assistance to clear out the Kurds and other peoples who lived in the border zone. With aerial bombing and shelling of Kurdish towns and villages, and some documented executions and beheadings of Kurds including civilians, the Turks forced several hundred thousand Kurds and other enclave residents (including many Arab Christians) to flee in what critics called an "ethnic cleansing" of the territory, creating a humanitarian crisis, throwing the region into chaos and uncertainty, and making possible settlement by the Turkey-based Syrian refugees. Protests against the Turkish invasion and Trump erupted in many European cities. During the turmoil many ISIS members escaped from

Karim Sahib/AFP/Getty Images

IMAGE 30.4 **Arab Art** The large monument of Revolution, in Baghdad, sculpted by a major modern Iraqi artist, Jawad Salim (1920–1961), occupies a central place in the city. Commissioned in 1958 after the overthrow of the monarchy, it celebrates the Iraqi struggle for justice and freedom and often provided a motif for Iraqi poets.

Q Do you think that the monument, built in the late 1950s, reflects the reality of Iraq in recent years and today?

their prisons. Abandoned by the Americans, the Kurds had few options except to cooperate with their former enemies: Russia, Iran, and the brutal Syrian regime. As a result, Kurdish leaders struck a deal for Assad's troops to replace the U.S. in the Kurdish region to counter the Turks. Turkey's future role, the fate of the Kurds, and the prospects for a larger regional war remain unclear. Whether Syria can rebuild in a way that benefits rather than punishes a large share of the population remains to be seen.

In the Sudan, the Arab Muslim-dominated government, which imposed an Islamic state, used military force to control rebellious black African Christians and animists in the south, a conflict that resulted in two million deaths. In 2005 the two sides agreed to end the conflict, but rebellion erupted in the impoverished Darfur region. Aided by local Arab militias, the government launched a genocide against African Muslim farmers, earning the world's condemnation as thousands died from

military assaults, disease, or starvation. In 2011 South Sudan became independent, but tensions with Sudan persisted over control of oil wealth. South Sudan erupted in chronic civil war between the two major ethnic groups that still festers while Sudan endured years under a corrupt and harsh Islamist dictatorship until 2019, when a popular uprising and the massacre of protesters that followed delegitimized and soon forced out the president; the military took power, agreed to share power with the pro-democracy movement, and made vague promises of future elections to choose a civilian government.

30-2b Social Change

Tradition and religion still shape gender relations and family life in the Middle East. Although four predominantly Muslim nations—Bangladesh, Pakistan, Indonesia, and Turkey—have elected women prime ministers, no Arab or Iranian women have reached this goal. Urban women operate businesses and enter the professions, especially in Turkey, Egypt, Iraq, Jordan, and Lebanon. But many women remain in the home, often secluded, their lives as daughters, wives, and mothers controlled by men. Liberals have advocated improving women's lives through education, and several nations, including Turkey, have adopted Western-influenced family laws according women divorce and child custody rights. In 2014 a new constitution in Tunisia, strongly supported by secular liberals, guaranteed gender equality. Blaming patriarchal cultural traditions for restrictions, some women activists argue that the Quran supports women's rights. For example, in 2018 the Moroccan feminist Asma Lamrabet lost her position in an Islamic think tank for challenging laws, based on Quranic verses and imposed by the "religious patriarchy," that award men much larger inheritance shares than women receive. Distant male relatives can even supersede wives, sisters, and daughters, often leaving women destitute. But conservative Muslims have prevented liberal laws in most Middle Eastern societies. Moreover, devout women have often opposed secular feminism, believing that women are best protected by strict Islamic law. Egyptian Zainab Al-Ghazali (1917–2005) founded mosques, trained female preachers, and promoted an active women's role in public life, but her staunch support of Islamic values upset both liberal feminists and modernizing President Nasser, who had her jailed and tortured. Some promoted a more open discussion about sexuality. One of mid-twentieth-century Iran's preeminent writers, Forough Farrokhzad (1935–1967), was both reviled and revered for her poetry, which often dealt with female desire. Her frank expression of feminine emotions and romantic feelings was pathbreaking in Iran. Many Iranians regarded her death at thirty-two in a car crash as a national tragedy, but the Islamic Republic that came to power in 1979 banned her writings for almost a decade. The conflict between modernizer and traditionalist has fostered gender role confusion, as an Egyptian writer noted: "Our mothers understood their situation. We, however, are lost. We do not know whether or not we still belong to the harem, whether love is forbidden or permitted."[7]

---

[7]Latifa az-Zayyat, quoted in Wiebke Walther, *Women in Islam from Medieval to Modern Times* (Princeton, NJ: Markus Wiener, 1993), 235.

Some people, especially affluent urbanites, often found ways around the conservative restrictions. Hence, in Iran by 2019 large private weddings were held, often in rural halls, where men in tuxedos and women in revealing dresses violated many of the laws regarding personal behavior, among them the mixing of the sexes, women baring flesh and failing to wear head scarves, dancing, playing pop music, and consuming alcohol. Liberal and conservative Middle Eastern Muslims have strongly disagreed on women's dress. To liberals the veil symbolizes female subjugation, and many urban middle- and upper-class women have adopted Western dress. But traditionalists praise the veil as essential to female modesty. In secular nations like Turkey and Egypt, women influenced by revivalist Islam have lobbied to wear the full veil or head scarf to demonstrate their piety. A young Egyptian, speaking for many religious women, claimed that "being totally covered saves me from the approaches of men and hungry looks. I feel more free, purer, and more respectable."[8] In fact, many independent-minded, well-educated women do not uncritically adopt Western ways. Liberal, well-traveled Moroccan sociologist and Quranic scholar Fatema Mernissi contended that Western women, obsessed with physical appearance, face their own clothing veil: "I thank you, Allah, for sparing me the tyranny of the 'size six harem.' I am so happy that the conservative male elite [in the Middle East] does not know about it. Imagine the [Muslim] fundamentalists switching from the veil to forcing women to fit size 6."[9]

Attitudes toward LGBTQ people often became more repressive. For many centuries some Muslim societies tolerated, although they did not approve, same-sex romance and sexual relations, and writings exploring same-sex experiences circulated widely. By the late 1800s gays and lesbians were forced into the closet, but in the 1990s the taboo slowly diminished in some cities. Where strict gender segregation exists, people spend most of their time, and enjoy emotional bonds, with other people of the same sex, sometimes making it easier for same-sex couples to escape notice. Yet, in many countries LGBTQ behavior, when discovered, frequently brings jail terms or even execution.

30-2c Religion and Culture

The clash between tradition and modernity has fostered creativity in religion, music, and literature. Islam remains central to life but, despite its message of peace, social justice, and community, often proves divisive (see Map 30.2), as age-old divisions—Sunni–Shi'a, liberal–conservative, secular–devout, Sufi–anti-Sufi—remain powerful. **Islamists** have become increasingly influential in many nations. Bitter rivals of secular Muslims and Sufis, they are antimodern, usually puritanical militants who seek an Islamic state. After World War I the Islamist Muslim Brotherhood spread around the region. French-educated Iranian Shi'ite Ali Shariati (**SHAR-ee-AH-tee**) (1933–1977) castigated Western democracy as subverted by the power of money but also blamed Islamic tradition for reducing women

Islamists Antimodern, usually puritanical Islamic militants who seek an Islamic state.

to, as he put it, the level of a washing machine. Egyptian writer Sayyid Qutb (**SIGH-eed ka-TOOB**) (1906–1966) sparked political Sunni Islam, redefining jihad ("struggle") as violent opposition to the West. Qutb lived for two years in the United States, where he found Americans friendly but was appalled by the anti-black racism and hedonism, such as heavy drinking and casual romantic relations. Returning to Egypt, Qutb promoted an Islamic state and joined the Muslim Brotherhood. Inspired by thinkers like Qutb, the most extreme Islamists, known as jihadists, support violence against secular Muslims, Sufis, and non-Muslims they consider obstacles to imposing their rigid beliefs. One ultra-conservative strand of Islamism, Salafism ("predecessors"), embraces seventh-century religious traditions and ways of life but tends to favor political rather than violent action. The same social media that liberals revere also allow Salafists and other Islamists to spread their message and organize. The founders of the Islamic State movement embraced a Salafist worldview but also promoted extreme violence and even enslavement of non-believers.

Resentment of repressive and corrupt governments, lack of material improvement, and Western world power have prompted a growing turn to Islam. When elections are allowed, Islamic groups with their large followings often triumph over secular parties, as happened in Palestine in 2005 and Egypt in 2012, a reason why pro-Western modernists often fear democracy. In a troubled world, the Islamic revival promises to foster tradition, personal solace, and a just political system. Devout Muslims dominated the U.S.-installed Iraqi government. While conservative activists in Iraq closed bars, harassed unveiled women, and terrorized Christians, Sunni militants in various lands attacked followers of Sufi mysticism as heretics. Some Islamists, frustrated at home, join international terrorist groups.

While Islamic militants have condemned music, dance, and other pleasures, many people—both secular and devout—enjoy popular culture, especially music. Egyptian singer Oum Kulthum (**oom KAL-thoom**) (1904–1975) symbolized Arab people's feelings. Attracting a region-wide following with emotional songs of love and abandonment, Kulthum dominated Middle Eastern popular music from the 1940s through the 1960s, becoming, with Egypt's President Nasser, one of the two most popular figures among Arabs. Her recordings were always on the radio and in film. Another hugely popular figure, Lebanese singer Fairuz (**fie-ROOZ**) (b. 1935), has been credited with symbolizing hope and community in that turbulent, civil war-plagued land. Israelis revered Yemen-born Shoshana Damari (1923–2006), whose optimistic songs encouraged Israeli unity, extolling the nation and its military forces. Some musicians challenge political and cultural taboos. The songs and concerts of Lebanese rock band Mashrou' Leila promote tolerance (including of LGBTQ people) and oppose censorship, but even in relatively open Lebanon have antagonized many devout Christian and Muslim groups who have tried to shut down their performances as "blasphemous".

In religiously dogmatic or ethnically divided states, popular music has sometimes stirred controversy. Iran's Islamic

[8]Quoted in Daniel Bates and Amal Rassam, *Peoples and Cultures of the Middle East*, 2nd ed. (Upper Saddle River, NJ: Prentice-Hall, 2001), 235.
[9]Fatema Mernissi, *Scheherazade Goes West: Different Cultures, Different Harems* (New York: Washington Square Press, 2001), 219.

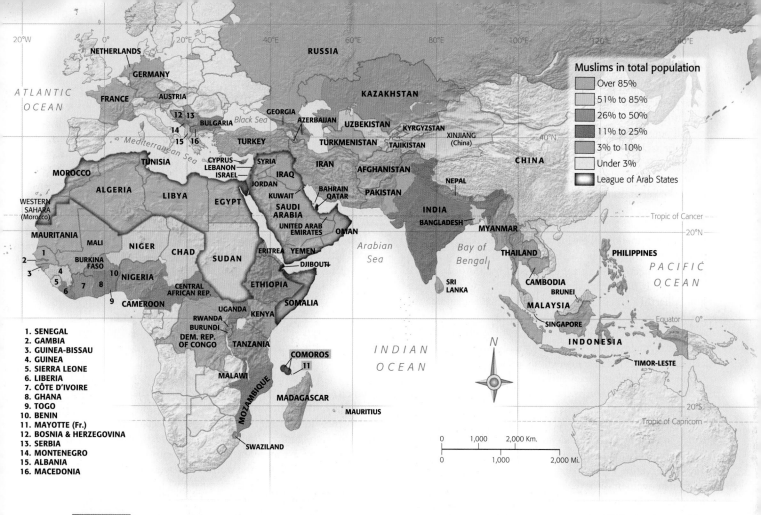

MAP 30.2 The Islamic World The Islamic world includes not only the Middle East—western Asia and North Africa—but also countries with Muslim majorities in sub-Saharan Africa, Central Asia, and South and Southeast Asia. In addition, Muslims live in most other Eastern Hemisphere nations and in the Americas.

Q What can we conclude from this map about the influence and importance of Islam in the Eastern hemisphere?

government, opposed to women performing in public, tried to silence all female singers, especially vocalist and film star Googoosh (**GOO-goosh**) (b. 1950), whose melancholic Westernized pop music had a huge audience during the 1960s and 1970s. The clerics destroyed all her recordings, posters, and films, turning Googoosh into a popular symbol against clerical rule. For many years she lived, traveled, and performed abroad before returning to Iran when the repression eased. She remains a hugely popular icon to Iranians at home and in the diaspora as well as a supporter of LGBTQ rights. Turkey's *arabesk* pop music reflects the experiences of poor Arab and Kurdish migrants to Istanbul. One observer noted that "arabesk describes a decaying city in which poverty-stricken migrant workers are exploited and abused, and calls on its listeners to pour another glass of wine and curse fate and the world."[10] Some popular styles blend Arab and foreign forms while addressing social problems. Algeria's **rai** ("opinion") music, based on local Bedouin chants, Spanish flamenco, French café songs, Egyptian pop, and other influences, often addresses forbidden themes of sex and alcohol. Appealing to urban working-class youth in

North Africa and young Arab immigrants in France, rai is despised by puritanical Islamic militants, who have forced singers into exile or even assassinated them. Rai musicians often moved their base to Paris. Rap and hip-hop also gained popularity among some, often disaffected, youth. In Turkey by 2019 rappers were releasing songs with political messages, touching a nerve in a polarized society. In the song "Susamam" ("I Cannot Stay Silent"), which received more than twenty million views on YouTube, twenty rappers and musicians took turns tackling many critical issues such as pollution, free speech, the rule of law, domestic violence, to inequality in education. One of the lyrics revealed that the rapper was "too scared to send a tweet, I've come to fear my own country's police."[11]

Middle Eastern writers have also expressed ideas forbidden in politics and religion. The novels of Egyptian Naguib Mahfuz (**nah-GEEB mah-FOOZ**) (1911–2006), a

> **rai** ("opinion") A pop music of Algeria based on local Bedouin chants, Spanish flamenco, French café songs, Egyptian pop, and other influences and featuring improvised lyrics that often deal with forbidden themes of sex and alcohol.

[10]Martin Stokes, *The Arabesk Debate: Music and Musicians in Modern Turkey* (Oxford, UK: Clarendon Press, 1992), 1.
[11]Quoted in AFP, "Turkish Rappers Get Political After Years of Stifled Dissent," *Free Malaysia Today*, September 13, 2019.

government official and journalist, addressed social problems, such as poverty, and questioned conservative religious values and blind faith, which he believed kept individuals from realizing their full potential, sparking bans on his writings in Egypt and other nations. In 1988 Mahfuz became the first Arab writer to win a Nobel Prize for Literature. The political verses of Egypt's "poet of the people," Ahmed Fouad Nagm (NEG-em) (1929–2013), skewered national leaders and Islamists, inspiring protesters from the 1970s until today. Iranian writers often risked punishment when attacking religious hypocrisy in their satires of government and business failings. One famous Iranian novel recommended opportunism for career success: "Try to establish connections with the holders of high offices. Agree with everybody, no matter what his opinion is."[12] Omani author Jokha Alharthi's acclaimed novel *Celestial Bodies* explores the space between memory and forgetting in her saga of a family spanning several generations. Arab cinema has often reflected conservative mainstream values but there have been notable exceptions, in part because many films are written and directed by women and explore social and cultural issues. For example, the 2017 film *In Between*, by the Palestinian Israeli Maysaloun Hamoud, follows three female roommates who share an apartment in Tel Aviv, where they participate, to varying degrees, in city life such as dancing, smoking, drinking, taking drugs, and even lesbian experience, subject matter that offended many conservative Palestinians; Hamoud has received death threats. The women discover that what divides them—sexual orientation, religion, degree of religiosity—is less significant than what unites them since each in her own way is struggling against a man who wants to stifle her voice.

30-2d The Middle East in the Global System

Middle Eastern nations have generally lagged behind much of Asia and Latin America in development. A Lebanese novelist wrote that dictatorial Arab regimes deprived people not only of dignity but also of air: the opportunity to discuss problems freely. The United Nations–sponsored 2016 Arab Development Report offered some hope for a better future, noting that the year 2011 may have been a tipping point as the demographic momentum for change picked up as youth ages fifteen to twenty-nine, who comprise around 30 percent of the population, began to join protests and become more politically active (see Discover Historical Voices: Improving the Lives of Arab Youth). There were other omens of progress. Regional cable networks, such as Qatar-based Al Jazeera, spur debate, spread awareness of political and social developments, and promote a modern image, such as using unveiled female news anchors. Some urbanites have access to the Internet, often at cafés, and go online to access foreign news, shop, or arrange dates; Arab and Turkish chat rooms and blogs abound. Religious and political groups also use the Web to recruit support, among them Al Qaeda and ISIS, which have been able to capitalize on a power vacuum and political instability to establish operations in countries like Iraq, Syria, Libya, and Yemen.

The region's economic record has been checkered. The Middle East has usually had the world's highest unemployment rate and, except for sub-Saharan Africa, slowest economic growth and lowest productivity. Only Turkey has fostered much industrialization and high economic growth. Nations with oil, such as Algeria, Iran, and Libya, have remained dangerously dependent on oil revenues for survival. Millions of migrant workers from other Arab countries, South Asia, and Southeast Asia work in the Gulf states; they make up the majority of the population in Bahrain and Oman, and over 80 percent in Qatar and the UAE, but as noncitizens enjoy no rights and are often treated little better than slaves, facing abuse and discrimination. Comprising around 90 percent of the workforce, most migrants are semiskilled or unskilled and work primarily in domestic work and construction. Many migrant women complain of harassment and even rape, and some have been murdered, by Arab employers. Oil wealth often fosters political corruption, spurs autocratic leaders to oppose democracy, and sometimes funds Islamist and terrorist groups. Several small Persian Gulf states have used their oil wealth to become centers of global commerce. Dubai (with the world's largest artificial port) and Abu Dhabi, two of the world's most modern, globalized cities, boast luxury hotels, towering skyscrapers, spectacular mosques, futuristic architecture, local branches of prestigious Western universities and art museums, and thousands of businessmen and workers from all over the world. They were also hurt by the 2008–2009 world economic crisis, during which many foreigners left. Yet, the Western, Japanese, and new Chinese and Indian appetite for oil ensures that oil-rich nations will profit for years to come. Meanwhile, Middle Eastern nations without oil, such as Jordan and Lebanon, struggle to build modern economies with limited resources. In the late 2010s many Middle Eastern nations have developed closer relations with China via bilateral agreements, not only in energy and economic matters but also in defense. This makes them mostly reluctant to criticize China's brutal treatment of its Muslim Uighur minority. Some Arab thinkers argue that democracy will only flourish in the Middle East if buttressed by social and economic change to improve living standards for the majority of people.

Past and present, tradition and modernity, have all been jumbled in the contemporary Middle East, whose people hope to preserve revered traditional patterns while harmonizing them with the modern world. An Egyptian novelist wrote that a Cairo resident has a split personality: "Half of him believes, prays, fasts and makes the pilgrimage [to Mecca]. The other half renders his values void in banks and courts and in the streets, the cinemas, perhaps even at home among his family before the television set."[13] The recent history of the Middle East, like that of South Asia and sub-Saharan Africa, challenges the notion that contact with the modern world automatically erodes all traditional cultures, steering people inevitably toward Western models. Older patterns of life and thought persist. Observers disagree whether this persistence constitutes a barrier to progress or gives the people an anchor to deal with the destabilizing effects of change.

---

[12]Sadiq Hidayat, in *Hajji Aqa*, quoted in Bill, *Politics of Iran*, 105.
[13]Naguib Mahfuz, quoted in Bates and Rassam, *Peoples and Cultures*, 199.

Discover Historical Voices

Improving the Lives of Arab Youth

The protests that broke out against despotism, police harassment, limited employment prospects, and poverty in several Arab countries beginning in 2011 highlighted the role of young people, who make up a major segment of the region's population. Many have been disenchanted with the narrow choices they face in a restrictive public sphere. Looking for social or personal change, some have discovered faith-based movements, peaceful or militant; others take up political or social activism. According to this 2016 United Nations report, attitudes that treat young Arabs, the region's future, as passive observers must change. Governments and societies need to understand their needs and goals so that young people can participate in shaping their own future.

Last year, world leaders adopted the 2030 Agenda for Sustainable Development as a vision for transforming global development over the next fifteen years to build a more peaceful, prosperous, sustainable, and inclusive future. The Agenda asserts that young women and men are critical agents of change and are central to achieving sustainable development. . . . [The report] calls on Arab States to invest in their youth, and to empower them to engage in development processes [and] makes two key arguments for investing in young people in the region:

First, that while young people between the ages of fifteen and 29 make up nearly a third of the region's population, another third are below the age of fifteen. This "demographic momentum" will last for at least the next two decades and offers an historic opportunity which Arab countries must seize.

Second, the report underlines that the wave of protests which has swept through a number of Arab countries since 2011 with youth at the forefront has led to fundamental transformations across the entire region. Some countries have seen new national constitutions, free and fair elections, and a widening of the public participation sphere for previously excluded groups. . . .

The report explores the many challenges which youth in the Arab region continue to face. Many continue to receive an education which does not reflect the needs of labor markets. High numbers of young people, particularly young women, are unemployed and excluded from the formal economy. Young people without livelihoods find it difficult to establish an independent home and form their own family units. The risk for these young people is that instead of exploring opportunities and discovering future prospects, they experience frustration, helplessness, alienation, and dependency.

It goes without saying that young people across the Arab States have been severely affected by the recent crises. Large numbers of them were swept onto the frontlines of conflicts they did not start. Many died, and many more have lost family members and friends, livelihoods and prospects, and hope in the future. In the face of such challenges, some have joined extremist groups. . . .

Youth empowerment requires enhancing the capabilities of young people. Delivery systems for basic services, particularly in education and health, must be improved. The opportunities available to youth must be expanded—through economies which generate decent work and encourage entrepreneurship, political environments which encourage freedom of expression and active participation, and social systems which promote equality and act against all forms of discrimination. In 2030, the Arab States will look back to assess what they have achieved over the fifteen years of the SDGs to fulfill the promise of peace, prosperity, and sustainable development for future generations. . . .

We hope that this report will galvanize decision makers, other key stakeholders, and young people themselves across the Arab States' region to ensure greater participation of youth in development. Without such participation, it will be difficult to secure progress and ensure sustainable development.

Reflection Questions

1. What does the report identify as some of the major challenges facing young people in the Arab world?
2. What does the report consider some of the actions that might improve their situation and future prospects?
3. How do the problems and challenges faced by young Arab men and women compare to the problems young people face in your country?

Source: Foreword by the Administrator, UNDP, *Arab Development Report 2016: Youth and the Prospects for Human Development in a Changing Reality* (New York: United Nations Development Programme, 2016), 5–6.

Islamic militancy taps unease with Western ideas. Many Muslims reject Western culture's materialistic, hedonistic values. The Iranian Revolution was the first successful attempt by an Islamic country to become totally independent of Western political, economic, social, and cultural influence. Many Iranians and Arabs agreed with Indian Muslim poet Muhammad Iqbal (ik-BALL) (1873–1938), who wrote in 1927: "Against Europe I protest, And the attraction of the West: Woe for Europe and her charm, Swift to capture and disarm! Earth awaits rebuilding; rise! Out of slumber deep, Arise!"[14] Militancy challenges capitalism,

---

[14]Quoted in Frances Robinson, *The Cultural Atlas of the Islamic World Since 1500* (Alexandria, VA: Stonehenge, 1982), 158.

secularism, failed governments, and Western-style democracy. But other Muslims fear militant Islamic rule, which has not delivered a better material life in countries like Iran and Sudan. In 2014 protests by secular Tunisians forced an Islamist regime to resign and reinforced multiparty democracy, sparking similar protests in several other countries including Egypt.

Interventions by outside powers, such as the USSR and the United States, reflect the region's oil wealth and strategic location among key waterways of world trade. Until cost-effective alternative power sources become common, all industrial economies need access to Middle Eastern oil, without which modern lifestyles would come to a screeching halt. The world community will not tolerate anything threatening the movement of oil tankers through the Persian Gulf. While U.S. leaders have hoped that democracy will spread, instability in Iraq, Syria, Yemen, and Egypt has unsettled the entire region, and perhaps strengthened Iran, while presenting foreign policy dilemmas for the United States, Europe, China, Japan, Russia, and other interested nations. Arab thinkers debate whether the sort of Arab unity that was common several decades ago still exists. They used to have the common cause of supporting the Palestinians against Israel but the Arab Spring uprisings of 2011, the rise of the threat from Iran, regional terrorism, and a resurgent Islamism have ruptured the traditional alliances. In late 2019 growing tensions and, many fear, a possible military confrontation between Iran and Saudi Arabia that could draw in Israel, Iraq, Turkey, Syria, the U.S., Russia, and the UAE reveal starkly that the region remains a potential tinderbox that could destabilize the world. Furthermore, few conflicts or persistent problems—including the Arab–Israeli conflict, sectarian rivalries, and Arab–Iranian tensions—seem resolvable anytime soon. These challenges make the Middle East a focus of world attention. In 2002 Arab thinkers issued an Arab Human Development Report that still seems relevant two decades later. It outlined economic and social failures, including marginalization of women and limited health and education development: "The Arab world is at a crossroads. The fundamental choice is whether its trajectory will remain marked by inertia, as reflected in much of the present institutional context, and by ineffective policies that have produced the substantial development challenges facing the region; or whether prospects for an Arab renaissance, anchored in human development will be actively pursued."[15]

KEY POINTS

▶ The Middle East has been torn by ethnic conflict, especially in Lebanon, Syria, and the Sudan, while the Kurds in various countries have struggled to gain their own home.

▶ Middle Eastern societies have been divided between Islamists and secular Muslims, and musicians and writers, popular among the people, have raised the ire of religious conservatives.

▶ Middle Eastern societies have been torn between those who feel they have failed to adapt to the modern world and those who champion tradition and urge rejection of the modern, Western values, while the region has remained extremely important to outside powers, such as the United States, because of its oil reserves.

30-3 Political Change in Sub-Saharan Africa

TRANSITIONS   NETWORKS

Q What were the main political consequences of decolonization in sub-Saharan Africa?

As in the Middle East, the rise of nationalism and the consequent wave of decolonization in Africa between 1957 and 1975 reduced Western political influence, reshaping societies and politics. Countries won political independence after the British, French, Belgians, Spanish, and eventually Portuguese came to terms with rising nationalist activity. As optimistic Africans celebrated their freedom, formed governments, and hoped for a better future, some observers proclaimed the 1960s Africa's Age of Glamor. The years since have brought rapid, though often destabilizing, change. Most Africans still struggle to find the right mix of policies to resolve their problems.

CONNECTION to TODAY

Can you think of ways that political changes in Sub-Saharan Africa affected your family, community, and nation?

30-3a Nationalism and Decolonization

Rising African nationalism sparked decolonization. European colonial powers did little to encourage national feeling, maintaining control of the diverse ethnic groups through divide and rule, while nationalists struggled to overcome the ethnic complexities within colonies with the arbitrary boundaries imposed by colonialists. The colossal slaughter in World War II undermined Western credibility, leading Africans to resent the Western powers and their pretensions of superiority, as expressed by a British official in Nigeria who argued that African "barbarism" required maintaining the "civilizing

---

[15]Arab Human Development Report 2002: Creating Opportunities for Future Generations (New York: UNDP, 2002), available online at rbas.undp.org/ahdr/press_kits2002/PRExecSummary.pdf.

mission" into the far future. While Britain and France espoused freedom and democracy, they seldom applied these values in the colonies. After the war the British encouraged African hopes by granting independence to India and Burma and introducing local government in some African colonies. Yet most colonial governments did little to prepare Africans for true political and economic independence.

The first major changes came in the British Gold Coast. In 1948 riots began after small farmers boycotted European businesses suspected of profiteering at their expense. A rising leader with British and American university degrees, Kwame Nkrumah **(KWAH-mee nn-KROO-muh)** (1909–1972), believing only socialism could save Africa, organized a political party in 1949 but was soon arrested. However, with unrest continuing, Britain allowed an election in 1951 for a legislative council, which was won by Nkrumah's party. After negotiations, in 1957 the Gold Coast became independent and was renamed Ghana, after the first great West African kingdom. The nation's first prime minister and Africa's hero, Nkrumah preached **pan-Africanism**, the goal of eventually forming some sort of united states of Africa.

Now it became impossible to stem the decolonizing tide. By 1963, after peaceful negotiations and workers' strikes, all British colonies in West Africa had become independent. France, having no plans to abandon its empire, fought brutal but unsuccessful wars in the 1950s to hold Vietnam and Algeria. Finally realizing that a peaceful transition might better maintain its economic influence, France gave its colonies the option of a complete break or autonomy within a French community of closely connected nations. Eventually all the French colonies became fully independent, though usually maintaining close political and economic ties to France.

In some colonies widespread violence preceded or accompanied independence. After both World War I and World War II, British settlers migrated to Kenya and took land from the Africans to establish farms. In 1952 many Kikuyu, Kenya's largest ethnic group and the group that had lost the most land, began an eight-year uprising known as the **Mau Mau Rebellion**, attacking British farmers and officials. British troops committed atrocities against pro-Mau Mau villages, ultimately killing ten thousand Kikuyu and detaining ninety thousand others in harsh prison camps, where many died from disease or mistreatment. Finally realizing the futility of their cause, the British released from prison the major nationalist leader, Jomo Kenyatta **(ken-YAH-tuh)** (ca. 1889–1978), a Kikuyu former herd boy who had studied anthropology in Britain. Kenya became independent in 1963, with Kenyatta the first freely elected prime minister. Britain also granted independence to its other East African colonies, Uganda and Tanzania. Many white settlers who once opposed political rights for the African majority remained in Kenya.

Stroud/Hulton Archive/Getty Images

IMAGE 30.5 Mau Mau During the 1950s Africans in Kenya, especially the Kikuyu, rebelled against British colonial rule. The British responded by detaining some ninety thousand suspected rebels and sympathizers in concentration camps such as this, where many died.

Q What does the photo tell us about the prison camps and life for the Kenyan fighters incarcerated in them?

Violence also engulfed the Belgian Congo, a vast, natural resource-rich territory containing some two hundred ethnic groups. Belgium failed to foster an educated leadership class, encourage national consciousness, or build adequate paved roads, bridges, and telephone systems. The only Congolese leader with any national following, left-leaning former post office clerk and brewery director Patrice Lumumba **(loo-MOOM-buh)** (1925–1961), opposed economic domination by Belgian business and mining interests. In 1959 widespread rioting forced the colony's first free elections, which were won by Lumumba's party. As Lumumba took power, some Congolese troops mutinied, attacking whites, while Belgian-supported, anti-Lumumba leaders in the mineral-rich Katanga region announced Katanga's secession from the country. A United Nations peacekeeping force restored order, but in 1961 Katanga leaders, with Belgian and American complicity, abducted and murdered Lumumba, whom they viewed as pro-USSR. The Congo's new leader, Belgian- and U.S.-supported General Joseph Mobutu **(mo-BOO-to)**

pan-Africanism The dream that all Africans would cooperate to eventually form some sort of united states of the continent.

Mau Mau Rebellion An eight-year uprising in the 1950s by the Gikuyu people in Kenya against British rule.

(g. 1965–1997), then became a dictator and eventually renamed the country Zaire while styling himself Mobutu Sese Seko, "Mobutu the All Powerful." Mobutu required his people to sing his praises every day at workplace or school and replaced European names and values with African ones, including exchanging Western clothes, such as ties, for traditional garb. Wearing a tie became an act of political resistance.

Meanwhile, Portugal, ruled by a fascist dictator, was reluctant to give up its empire. When revolts broke out in its three colonies—Angola, Guinea-Bissau, and Mozambique—in the 1960s, Portuguese soldiers struggled to crush them. Angola's liberation movement was divided into three rival factions based on the country's major ethnic groupings, while Marxists led the major liberation movements in Mozambique and Guinea-Bissau. Visionary Guinea-Bissau revolutionary leader Amilcar Cabral (**AH-mill-CAR kah-BRAHL**) (1924–1973), a university-educated agronomist who was assassinated in 1973, emphasized educating the people to empower them, telling his followers: "Learn from life, people, books, the experiences of others, never stop learning."[16] In 1974 Portugal's war-weary army ended Portugal's dictatorship, and the new democratic, socialist-led government granted the colonies independence in 1975. In Angola, the nationalist factions fought each other for dominance for the next two decades. Mozambique's government faced a long insurgency supported by white-ruled South Africa.

The British-ruled Rhodesias and Nyasaland in southern Africa, all containing white settlers bitterly resisting equality for Africans, struggled for independence under black majority rule. Facing largely nonviolent resistance campaigns, Britain granted independence to Zambia (Northern Rhodesia) and Malawi (formerly Nyasaland) in 1963. But Southern Rhodesia's large white settler population, declaring independence in 1965, installed a white racist government that imposed stricter racial segregation and prohibited nonwhite political activity. In response, Africans took up arms in two rival Marxist-led liberation movements. By 1980 the United States and Britain had pressured the white government to allow elections, which were won by Robert Mugabe (**moo-GAH-bee**) (1924–2019), a schoolteacher turned guerrilla leader and a former political prisoner. The country became independent as Zimbabwe.

30-3b Political Change and Conflict

A West African scholar called the term *nation* "a magical word meant to exorcise ethnic quarrels and antagonisms—and as such very precious"[17]; but the magic usually failed to overcome disunity. New African nations typically experienced political and economic challenges that generated instability: coups, civil wars, and recurring famines (see Map 30.3). Until recently, military or one-party dominance has been more common than multiparty democracy. But privileged

wabenzi ("people who drive a Mercedes Benz") A privileged urban class in Africa of politicians, bureaucrats, professionals, military officers, and businessmen who manipulate their connections to amass wealth.

military officers have often lost touch with the population; used to giving orders, they have ruled with a heavy hand and often looted treasuries. Civilian-led one-party states can minimize ethnic divisions. While some one-party states, such as the Congo (Zaire), have been despotisms, others have been relatively open, some offering multiple candidates for office. Some nations, such as Nigeria and Ghana, have shifted back and forth between authoritarian military dictatorships and ineffective, corrupt civilian governments. But the despotic governments have sometimes brutally mistreated their own people. In Uganda in 1971, a poorly educated boxer-turned-general Idi Amin (**EE-dee AH-meen**) (1925–2004), seized power in a military coup that replaced the unpopular civilian president. But Amin soon became perhaps Africa's most brutal dictator by imposing a terroristic rule that killed some 300,000 Ugandans he considered enemies, while thousands more were jailed or fled into exile. In 1979 the Tanzanian military, allied with Ugandan exiles, invaded and forced Amin into fleeing the country. But this fostered six years of violent instability before Yoweri Museveni came to power in 1986. As a strongman promising stability he has won rigged elections and remains in power as "president for life."

Western-style democracy faced tremendous odds in these artificial countries with a tiny middle class and numerous poor people. Given unstable and often deteriorating economic conditions, most governments had little money to spend on containing ethnic tensions or building schools, hospitals, and roads. The nationalist leaders and parties governing the new nations often lost their credibility and mass support after a few years. Hence, Ghana's Kwame Nkrumah was overthrown for economic mismanagement and an autocratic governing style, and he died in exile. Some leaders have been respected, farsighted visionaries, such as Tanzania's Julius Nyerere (**NEE-ya-RARE-y**) (g. 1962–1985) and Mozambique's Samora Machel (g. 1975–1986); pragmatic problem-solvers such as South Africa's first black president, Nelson Mandela; and idealistic promoters of human rights, tolerance, and the rule of law such as veterinarian-turned-politician Dawda Jawara (1924–2019), Gambia's founding president. These leaders used political office largely to improve society rather than enrich themselves. However, many leaders, emulating old Africa's despotic kings, have held on to power, rigging elections or having compliant parliaments declare them presidents for life. Some, such as Zaire dictator Mobutu (g. 1965–1997) and Nigerian military dictator Sani Abacha (g. 1993–1998), were ruthless crooks, arresting or murdering opponents and plundering the public treasury. When Abacha, hopped up on Viagra, died of a heart attack while engaging in an orgy with prostitutes, few Nigerians lamented.

Competition for personal wealth fostered political instability, conflict, and social unrest. Blatant corruption, conspicuous consumption, and smuggling in government and the business sector increased income inequalities, deepening public frustrations. In some countries, government officials were known as "Mr. 10 Percent," a reference to the share of public budgets they grab. East Africans chastised the **wabenzi**—"people who

[16] Quoted in Basil Davidson, *The People's Cause: A History of Guerrillas in Africa* (Burnt Mill, UK: Longman, 1981), 165.

[17] A. Toure, quoted in Bill Freund, *The Making of Contemporary Africa: The Development of African Society Since 1800* (Bloomington: Indiana University Press, 1984), 192.

MAP 30.3 **Contemporary Africa and the Middle East** Sub-Saharan and North Africa contain over forty nations. Six sub-Saharan African nations and Algeria in North Africa experienced anticolonial revolutions, and a dozen sub-Saharan nations have been racked by civil wars since independence.

Q Which countries have experienced revolutions or civil wars since the 1940s?

drive a Mercedes Benz"—a privileged urban class of politicians, bureaucrats, professionals, military officers, and businessmen who manipulate their connections to amass wealth. Elites have often squandered scarce resources on importing luxuries, such as fancy cars and hard liquor, confirming the continuing appeal of Western taste and consumer goods.

However, in some societies relations between governments and the governed have improved in recent years. New grassroots nongovernmental organizations have addressed issues such as

human rights and the environment. For example, by 2000 some twenty-five thousand local women's groups in Kenya pushed for improved rights and other issues, such as environmental protection. Kenyan women's rights and environmental activist Wangari Maathai **(wan-GAHR-ee MAH-thai)** (1940-2011) won the Nobel Peace Prize in 2005 (see Chapter 26). Since few Africans can afford health insurance, poor Senegalese came together to form small mutual health organizations, negotiating with local clinics to get affordable group rates for health care.

In Liberia, recovering from civil war and dictatorship, women voters helped elect economist Ellen Johnson-Sirleaf (b. 1939), a Harvard-trained banker and former United Nations official, as Africa's first woman president in 2006. Although she struggled to bring progress to a maimed nation with no piped water or electric grid and few functioning schools and hospitals, Johnson-Sirleaf promoted peace, security, and the rule of law while convincing the international community to forgive Liberia's massive debt. She also enlisted women to help her fight corruption, encourage girl's education, and rebuild the economy. She was reelected and also won the Nobel Peace Prize in 2011.

Africa's hopes and frustrations are mirrored in Nigeria, home to some two hundred-one million people in 2019, a fifth of Africa's total population. Nigeria's ethnic and religious diversity and natural wealth have been both blessing and curse. Among the two hundred fifty Nigerian ethnic groups, about two-thirds are Hausa-Fulani, Igbo (Ibo), or Yoruba. The world's twelfth largest oil producer, oil wealth has produced 80 percent of Nigeria's total revenues but has also corrupted politics and increased social inequality. Having neglected agriculture, Nigeria is now a food importer, and many Nigerians have insufficient food. Coups, countercoups, riots, political assassinations, and civil war rooted in regional and ethnic rivalries have punctuated Nigerian history. Between 1967 and 1970 a bloody civil war raged to prevent the secession of the Igbo-dominated, oil-rich southeast region. The religious divide between Christians, who dominate the south, and Muslims, who control the northern states, also complicates politics. Many northern states have imposed strict Islamic law, antagonizing non-Muslims; authorities sentenced several Muslim women to death by stoning for adultery while not punishing the men involved, causing an outcry in Nigeria and around the world. Sometimes severe Christian–Muslim fighting causes the deaths of hundreds of people. Since 2009 a militant group with probable Al Qaeda or ISIS ties seeking an Islamic state, Boko Haram ("Western learning is forbidden"), has terrorized some northern districts with kidnappings of young girls, bombings and killings, and recently acquired sophisticated drones. Such religious tensions have often generated corrupt military rule that has brought stability by suppressing opposition but pushed the people hard, alternated with periods of corrupt civilian democracy that has increased political freedom but often governed ineffectively. Since 2007 civilian regimes have held power and attempted to reduce rampant corruption.

The oil industry, while creating some prosperity, has made Nigeria dependent on oil exports. A few politicians, bureaucrats, and businessmen have monopolized oil profits, fostering corruption, sometimes outright plunder of public wealth, and inequitable wealth distribution. Roughly half the population is poor or extremely poor. By 2005 the top 20 percent received 56 percent of all the country's wealth, while the bottom 20 percent got only 4.4 percent. Impoverished people in southern oil-producing districts, watching sullenly as pipelines through their villages move oil to coastal ports for shipment to European and North American consumers, protest and sometimes sabotage oil pipelines, prompting military reprisals and sometimes execution of protest leaders. Local rebel groups harass the oil industry and fight the army. Disenchanted Nigerians refer to a "republic of the privileged and rich" and a "moneytocracy." After oil money created high expectations in the 1970s, world oil prices collapsed in the 1980s, forcing the nation to take on massive foreign debt. Oil prices have since rebounded and then in the 2010s dropped again, also affecting other oil-exporting countries such as Angola, Equatorial Guinea, and Gabon.

The combination of artificial boundaries, weak national identity, and economic collapse or stagnation has produced chronic turmoil in several African nations. Liberia and Sierra Leone, once among the more stable countries, disintegrated in the 1990s. As ethnic-based rebel groups challenged governments for power, thousands fled the slaughter and the maiming of civilians; African nations like Nigeria sent in troops to bring stability. In drought-plagued Somalia, when longtime military rule collapsed in 1991, the country fragmented into regions ruled by feuding Somali clans. As the Somali economy disintegrated, thousands starved to death. Some Americans with a United Nations humanitarian mission were killed, and the United Nations withdrew in 1994, unable to forge a unified government. Somalia remained a country in name only, controlled by warlords and, more recently, engulfed in civil war involving Islamist militias linked to Al Qaeda, a weak central government, and the Ethiopian army. Desperate young men in coastal villages turned to piracy, disrupting shipping and prompting an international naval force to police the nearby seas. Many thousands of Somalis escaped the chaos and became refugees, mostly in Kenya, Egypt, Europe, or North America. Somalia's violence spilled over into neighboring Kenya, where Somali and Kenyan Islamists mounted attacks on civilian targets, including a 2013 massacre in a downtown Nairobi mall. Ethiopia itself, an ancient society containing more than eighty ethnic groups (mostly Christian or Muslim), some of them longtime rivals for power, has experienced a long history of despotism (including a communist dictatorship from 1974 until 1991), occasional democracy or semi-democracy, and sporadic civil war aggravated by severe droughts. In 2018 a new president, Abby Ahmed, was elected and launched a series of economic and democratic reforms including ending war with neighboring Eritrea, releasing over one thousand political prisoners, restoring full access to the Internet, giving half of ministerial posts to women, encouraging tree planting campaigns, and announcing free elections; in 2019 Ahmed won the Nobel Peace Prize, but his task remained daunting as ethnic tensions, protests, and violence continued. Islamists supported by Al Qaeda also seized much of northern Mali, including historic cities like Gao and Timbuktu, in 2012–2013 but were forced out by French troops. ISIS has also become active in the Sahel, staging terrorist attacks or encouraging violent hostilities between rival ethnic groups such as Dogon farmers and Fulani pastoralists in Mali. In 2013 Christian–Muslim political tensions led to massive and continuing violence in the Central African Republic, with France once again dispatching troops to a former colony to reestablish order.

Hatreds also sparked genocide in impoverished, densely populated Rwanda, divided between majority Hutus and minority Tutsis. The Belgians had ruled through Tutsi kings, and soon after independence Hutus rebelled, slaughtering thousands of Tutsis and forcing others into exile. The remaining Tutsis faced discrimination and repression. In 1994 the extremist Hutu government began a genocide against Tutsis and moderate Hutus, murdering over 500,000 people. Tutsi exiles invaded Rwanda, forcing the Hutu leaders and their followers—over two million—into the neighboring Congo. As a result, the new Tutsi-led government continued to face militant Congo-based Hutu resistance groups, leading to Rwandan military incursions into the Congo and support for Congolese rebel groups. In recent years various warlord militias, Congolese troops, and foreign forces have terrorized the eastern Congo, killing and raping many thousands of civilians. Rwanda and Burundi remain unstable and sometimes violent as Hutus and Tutsis compete for power.

30-3c The New South Africa

From World War II to the early 1990s, South Africa remained the last bastion of institutionalized white racism. The white population, in the 1990s some 15 percent of the total and divided between an Afrikaner majority (descendants of Dutch settlers) and an English minority, ruled the black majority (74 percent) and the Indians (2 percent) and mixed-descent Coloreds (9 percent). Racial inequality became more systematic after 1948, when Afrikaner nationalists, winning the white-only elections, declared full independence from Britain. A top nationalist leader claimed: "We [whites] need [Africans] because they work for us but they can never claim political rights. Not now, nor in the future."[18] Their new policy, **apartheid** (uh-PAHRT-ate) ("separate development"), established a ruthless police state to enforce racial separation; laws required all Africans to carry ID ("pass") cards specifying where they could legally reside or visit while outlawing interracial marriage and sexual relations. Apartheid created a chilling juxtaposition of white comfort and black despair.

Apartheid expanded segregation to include designated residential areas, schools, recreational facilities, and public accommodations. Urban black men were commonly housed in crowded dormitories near mines or factories where they worked or, with their families, in shantytown suburbs. While most white families lived comfortably in well-furnished apartments or houses with swimming pools, a typical house in Soweto, a dusty Johannesburg suburb, was bleak; residents used candles or gas lamps for lighting, and most had no running water. Demoralized blacks frequented the informal bars dotting African neighborhoods.

Apartheid also created what white leaders called tribal homelands, known as **bantustans**, rural reservations where black Africans had to live if not needed in the modern economy. The system allocated whites 87 percent of the nation's land, nonwhites the other 13 percent. Every year thousands of Africans were forcibly resettled to impoverished bantustans, which contained little fertile land and few jobs, hospitals, and secondary schools and where infant mortality rates were among the world's highest. Men and women were recruited on annual contracts for jobs outside the bantustans, fracturing black families. A husband and wife recruited for jobs in the same city could not legally visit each other if their ID cards restricted each to a different neighborhood.

Rich in strategic minerals such as gold, diamonds, uranium, platinum, and chrome, South Africa became Africa's most industrialized nation with the largest economy, but it had the world's most inequitable income distribution. Whites enjoyed one of the world's highest standards of living, with well-funded schools and medical centers, while Africans and the Colored and Indian minorities enjoyed few benefits. Whites controlled two-thirds of the nation's wealth and personal disposable income, while a third of Africans were unemployed. Fearing that unrest or black majority rule might threaten their billions in investments and access to lucrative resources, several industrialized countries, including the United States, Britain, and Japan, supported South Africa.

Africans resisted, often paying a price for their defiance. The police state brutalized dissidents and had the world's highest rate of execution and prisoners. Stephen Biko (1946–1977), a former medical student whose organization encouraged black pride and self-reliance, was beaten to death in police custody. Hundreds were arrested each day for "pass law" violations and held for a few days or weeks. The police violently repressed protests; imprisoned thousands of dissidents, including numerous children, often without trial; and sometimes assassinated black leaders, such as lawyer Victoria Mxenge (ma-SEN-gee), who defended anti-apartheid activists. Nevertheless, various forms of defiance, including strikes, work interruptions, and sabotage, became common. Resistance was often subtle; Nobel Prize-winning white South African novelist and apartheid critic Nadine Gordimer (1923–2014), who was awarded the Nobel Prize for Literature in 1991, described how even domestic servants in white households protested and asserted their dignity in nonverbal ways:

> Every household in the fine suburb had several black servants—a shifting population of pretty young housemaids whose long red nails and pertness not only asserted the indignity of being undiscovered fashion models but kept hoisted a cocky guerrilla pride against servitude to whites.[19]

The African National Congress (ANC), the major opposition organization, remained multiracial, with some whites, Coloreds, and Indians serving in its leadership. In 1955, despairing of peaceful change, a more militant ANC leadership framed its inclusive vision in the

apartheid ("separate development") A South African policy to set up a police state to enforce racial separation.

bantustans Rural reservations in South Africa where black Africans under apartheid were required to live if they were not needed in the modern economy.

---

[18]Prime Minister John Vorster in 1968, quoted in L. S. Stavrianos, *Global Rift: The Third World Comes of Age* (New York: William Morrow, 1981), 759.
[19]From *Something Out There*, quoted in Jean Comaroff, *Body of Power, Spirit of Resistance: The Culture and History of a South African People* (Chicago: University of Chicago Press, 1985), vi.

Nelson Mandela, South African Freedom Fighter and President

A courageous symbol of unbroken black determination, Nelson Mandela (1918–2013) changed history in the struggle against apartheid, South Africa's policy of rigid racial separation, despite severe white supremacist repression. The inspirational Mandela represented African ambitions for several generations.

Nelson Mandela was born in the Transkei reserve near South Africa's southeast coast, the son of a Xhosa (**KHO-sa**) chief. His middle name, Rolihlahla (**ROH-lee-la-la**), meant "troublemaker." Mandela was groomed to succeed his father as chief, but, after years of hearing stories about the valor of his ancestors in war, he wanted to help with the freedom struggle. After attending a Methodist school and then earning a BA from the only college for black South Africans, he qualified as a lawyer and opened the country's first black legal practice. He also joined the African National Congress (ANC), which had, for half a century, promoted education for blacks and cautiously criticized rather than confronted the government. Mandela and his young colleagues transformed the ANC into an activist mass movement. In 1958 he married Winnie Madikizela (**MAH-dee-kee-ZEH-la**), a Xhosa nurse, but they had only a short life together before political repression separated them.

The white government tolerated little opposition. In 1960, after police opened fire on twenty thousand peaceful black protesters, killing sixty-nine of them (including women and children), the government banned the ANC and arrested black leaders. The ANC then became an underground movement committed to violence. In 1964, found guilty of sabotage and treason, Mandela was sentenced to life in prison. In his stirring statement to the court, Mandela articulated his goals: "During my lifetime I have dedicated myself to this struggle of the African people. I have fought against [both] white and black domination. I have cherished the ideal of a democratic and free society in which all persons live together in harmony and with equal opportunities. It is an ideal for which I am prepared to die."

Mandela spent most of the next three decades in the notorious Robben Island prison off Cape Town, where he was joined by dozens of other ANC leaders and members. He turned the prison experience into an ANC school, leading political discussions and studying other freedom fighters, such as Mohandas Gandhi and Jawaharlal Nehru in India. Over the years Mandela grew into an international hero. During his imprisonment Winnie Mandela campaigned ceaselessly for black rights and her husband's release, gaining an international reputation as a freedom fighter. In 1990, after secret negotiations, a realistic new South African president, F. W. de Klerk, legalized the ANC and released Nelson Mandela from prison, and in 1993 Nelson Mandela and de Klerk shared a Nobel Peace Prize. In 1994 the first all-race elections made Nelson Mandela the first black president of South Africa. At his inauguration, he told the people: "Out of the experience of an extraordinary human disaster that lasted too long must be born a society of which all humanity will be proud. Let there be justice [and] peace for all. We must act together as a united people, for the birth of a new world. God bless Africa!"

Forgiving and pragmatic, Mandela remained popular with most South Africans, white and black. His moderate, accommo-

IMAGE 30.6 Nelson Mandela A symbol of black South African aspirations for nearly thirty years in prison, Mandela led the African National Congress after his release and, in 1994, was elected the nation's first black president. Here Mandela is visiting a school and encouraging the students to learn.

Louise Gubb/Corbis Historical/Getty Images

dationist style reassured whites but also disappointed some impatient blacks for conceding too much to white business and farming interests while only slowly improving black communities. Meanwhile, his marriage to Winnie became strained, in part because of her controversial activities, legal problems, and political support for a militant ANC faction that mistrusted Nelson's conciliatory policy. In 1996 Nelson and Winnie Mandela divorced. Nelson later married Grace Machel, the widow of respected Mozambique president Samora Machel, who was killed in an airplane crash.

In 1999, at the age of eighty-one, Mandela voluntarily retired from politics and moved to his native village. But family disputes over his estate and legacy clouded his reputation. In his autobiography, he wrote, "I have walked a long road to freedom. I have tried not to falter, I have made missteps along the way. After climbing a great hill, one only finds that there are many more hills to climb. With freedom come responsibilities. I dare not linger, for my long walk is not yet ended." In 2013 South Africans watched anxiously when Mandela was hospitalized with varied ills of old age. When he died in December, national leaders and admirers from around the world traveled to Johannesburg for his memorial service, celebrating with millions of South Africans his life and achievements as the creator of a new nation. The long walk taken by Nelson Mandela did indeed change history.

Reflection Questions

1. Why did the Mandelas become international symbols of the freedom struggle?
2. How did the Mandelas change history?
3. Do you think that Nelson Mandela deserves to be a hero and role model for people today?

Note: Quotations from Kevin Shillington, *History of Africa*, rev. ed. (New York: St. Martin's, 1995), 405; Nelson Mandela, *Long Walk to Freedom: The Autobiography of Nelson Mandela* (Boston: Little, Brown, 1996), 620, 625.

Freedom Charter: "South Africa belongs to all who live in it, black and white."[20] But the government declared the ANC illegal, and the fierce repression forced it underground and toward violent resistance. Several main leaders, including Nelson Mandela (1918–2013), spent almost thirty years in prison for their political activities (see Meet the People: Nelson Mandela, South African Freedom Fighter and President). ANC women, including Mandela's wife, Winnie Mandela, often faced arrest and mistreatment.

Ultimately, international isolation, economic troubles, the need for more highly skilled black workers, and growing black unrest forced the government to relax apartheid and release Mandela from prison. Negotiations produced a new constitution requiring "one man, one vote." In 1994 white supremacy ended in the nation's first all-race elections, which installed Mandela as president and gave the ANC two-thirds of parliamentary seats. The ANC government enjoyed massive goodwill but also faced daunting challenges in healing a deeply fragmented society while restoring African pride and spirits. Mandela sought both racial reconciliation and major changes benefiting the disadvantaged black majority. He improved some services in urban black communities, such as electricity and water, and fostered a growing black upper and middle class, but critics believe he neglected addressing racial inequality while promoting racial healing. Once unified against apartheid, the African community became divided by wealth. Today Soweto reflects social and class divisions, with neighborhoods of grand mansions and flashy cars for some but shanty towns and high unemployment for many. In 1999 Mandela voluntarily retired, a still-popular figure, while the ANC retained power in free elections.

Despite these momentous changes and black Africa's second largest economy, millions of South African blacks have felt neglected, wanting better land and services and complaining about corruption and mismanagement. Whites still earn six times more income than blacks, a quarter of South Africans lack electricity and proper housing, a fifth have no proper sanitation facilities, and half live below the poverty line. South Africa has one of the world's highest rates of HIV/AIDS, crime has rapidly increased, violent protests have erupted, and poverty, income inequality, corruption, and black unemployment (about 25 percent) have remained high. About a quarter of the population live on less than US$1.25 a day. Some black activists began a movement to seize white-owned farmland without compensation, frightening white farmers. In 2009 the election of a more radical ANC leader, Jacob Zuma (b. 1942), prompted some blacks to form or join opposition parties. Zuma faced widespread discontent and strikes; in 2013, in a reminder of apartheid-era repression, the police violently crushed a strike by eighty thousand miners over low wages and poor living conditions, killing thirty-four. A union organizer charged that "the A.N.C. today is all about power.... They are supposed to be here to listen to the problems of the people.... But they are nowhere to be seen."[21] Zuma, who had become increasingly autocratic and corrupt, was forced from office in 2018 and replaced by Cyril Ramaphosa, a trade unionist and anti-apartheid activist turned wealthy businessman who promised "a new dawn" but has struggled to overcome years of corruption and mismanagement in, for example, maintaining electric power twenty-four hours a day. In the later 2010s competition over jobs, housing, and business opportunities has fostered sporadic violence and hatred against immigrants from other African countries, especially Nigeria, Mozambique, Zimbabwe, Bostwana, and Somalia. In 2019, amidst widespread violent rioting and the burning and looting of immigrant businesses, the government pondered anti-hate legislation to bolster existing bans on racism and commitment to equality. According to experts, the violence is less a spontaneous popular revolt or criminal act than a reaction to the failures of South Africa's transformation, including continuing white privilege, world-leading levels of inequality, high unemployment, erratic policing, unresponsive political leaders, and a disillusioned population. But while some of the goodwill of the Mandela years has faded, given the long history of repression and fear in South Africa, the rapid transition to multiparty democracy has been impressive. People all over Africa hope that the nation of fifty-eight million (80 percent black) succeeds in healing racial wounds while spreading the wealth to all its citizens.

KEY POINTS

- ► Most British colonies attained independence through peaceful means, but Kenya's transition was long and violent, as was that of the Belgian Congo, Angola, Guinea-Bissau, Mozambique, and Zimbabwe.

- ► After independence, many African nations were ruled by military dictatorships or corrupt civilians, many nationalist leaders lost favor over time, the gap between rich and poor widened, and some nations experienced ongoing violence, disorder, and genocide.

- ► Nigeria, home to rival ethnic and religious groups, has experienced civil war, coups, and corrupt military rule, and while its oil reserves have brought wealth to the elite, they have hardly benefited the poor, and dependence on them led to economic problems in the 1980s and deep political, economic, and religious divisions today.

- ► Under apartheid, a white minority in South Africa viciously suppressed the black majority with laws restricting their political, economic, and physical freedom, but the African National Congress, led by Nelson Mandela, resisted fiercely and ultimately won control of the government in 1994. But they have had mixed success in improving life for the majority and solving the nation's problems.

---

[20] Quoted in Gwendolen Carter, "The Republic of South Africa: White Political Control Within the African Continent," in *Africa*, ed. Phyllis Martin and Patrick O'Meara, 2nd ed. (Bloomington: Indiana University Press, 1986), 353.

[21] Teboho Masiza, quoted in Lydia Polgreen, "Killing of Strikers Alters South Africa Politics," *New York Times*, August 16, 2013.

30-4 African Economies, Societies, and Cultures

⇄ TRANSITIONS 🏛 SOCIETIES

Q What new economic, social, and cultural patterns have emerged in Africa?

Since the 1960s, achieving economic development has often seemed a desperate struggle rather than an exhilarating challenge. African nations have tried various strategies, including capitalism and socialism, to benefit the majority of people, often unsuccessfully. Economic problems have proliferated but some countries have been able to increase their wealth, largely through exploiting natural resources. Africans have also created new social and cultural forms to help deal with their problems and challenges.

30-4a Economic Change and Underdevelopment

Many African societies have experienced severe economic problems. As during colonial times, Africans mostly supplied agricultural and mineral resources, such as cocoa and copper, to the global economy, but this trade did not foster widespread wealth. Hence, in Kenya small farmers, encouraged to replace subsistence food growing with tobacco planting, found that tobacco brought in little money, required cutting down adjacent forests, and leached nutrients from the soil. In 2004, Jane Chacha, still living in the same two-room, mud-and-thatch house she and her husband built fifteen years earlier, complained that "this is a hopeless dream. Growing tobacco has been nothing but trouble."[22] Controversial research in 2017 suggested that, as in colonial times, the wealth coming to African nations with outside aid, loans, and investment is outweighed by financial flows out to foreign banks and tax havens while paying the costs of mitigating climate change mostly caused by Western nations, China, and India. The world profits more than most Africans from the continent's wealth.

Until recently only a few countries have enjoyed consistently robust economic growth, escaped reliance on one or two resources, or substantially raised living standards. Hence, sub-Saharan Africa contains most of the world's twenty poorest countries. With 1.3 billion people by 2018, Africans produce only 1 percent of the world's goods and services, about the same as Belgium, with 11.5 million people. Many sub-Saharan African countries have annual per capita incomes of under $1,000 per year, and some are under $500. Sub-Saharan Africa has also had the world's highest infant mortality and desperate poverty rates and the lowest literacy rates and average life expectancies.

The economic doldrums are linked to other problems. Until recently the region's economies generally grew slowly, but by 2017 Africa had achieved the world's second fastest growing continental economy, with average growth of around 3.4 percent. Over one-third of countries reported 6 percent or

CONNECTION to TODAY

What products of African culture such as music, film, and literature have you encountered?

higher growth. Middle classes are growing. However, Africa's population increase is now the world's highest, over 3 percent, about half the world's total, and is expected to reach 4.1 billion by 2100. Half of Africans are under age twenty-five. Since 10 to 15 percent of babies die before their first birthday, parents have had an incentive to have many children to provide for old-age security. And many Christian and Muslim religious leaders have opposed family planning as opposed to God's will. While the population may double by 2025, new jobs, classrooms, and food supplies will not keep pace. Only a few nations have enjoyed self-sufficiency in food production; most require food imports from Europe and North America. Although women grow the bulk of the food, male farmers growing cash crops receive most government aid. Millions are chronically malnourished, and several million children die each year from hunger-related ailments. Severe drought and dried-up water sources cause dehydration, starvation, or migration. In Kenya some malnourished people eat cactus. Less than half of school-age children attend school, while millions of others work in the labor force. In addition, only a quarter of Africans have access to electricity. Poverty means scraping by, physically and mentally exhausted by the struggle for survival. The inequality is dramatic. A 2019 study concluded that Africa's three richest people have more wealth than the poorest 50 percent (some 650 million people). A 2019 World Bank report forecasted that by 2030 Africa would be home to ninety percent of the world's poor, due to an expected sluggish economic growth and governments having little capital to invest in poverty-reduction programs. For several decades many Africans have sought to escape poverty, limited job prospects, or political repression by migrating to Europe, but in the 2010s, as European countries became less welcoming to new arrivals, some desperate Africans resorted to crossing the Mediterranean in rickety boats or rafts, a dangerous journey that resulted in many drownings. Some never make it that far and end up in horrific slave labor camps, brothels, or the clutches of human traffickers in North Africa (especially Libya), Yemen, or the Persian Gulf.

As Africans have sought viable strategies to achieve economic development, many have maintained close economic ties to Western nations and encouraged foreign investment and free markets, what critics call neocolonial capitalism. Countries following this strategy emphasize the cash crops and minerals that dominated the colonial economy, and Westerners, especially British and French, manage or own a substantial portion of their economies. A few countries have prospered, but the political consequences have often been negative. In the 1960s and 1970s, Ivory Coast (or Côte d'Ivoire) and Kenya, hospitable to a Western presence, were rewarded with high growth and rising incomes. Ivory Coast remained a major exporter of

---

[22]Quoted in Joe Asila, "No Cash in This Crop," in *Global Studies: Africa*, ed. Wayne Edge, 2nd ed. (Guilford, CT: Dushkin, 2006), 285.

coffee and cocoa; Kenya, with world-famous game parks, lived from tourism and exporting coffee, tea, and minerals. By the 1980s both had per capita incomes twice the African average. However, Ivory Coast rapidly logged once-verdant forests, causing less rain, and more French lived there than during colonial times, owning, along with other non-Ivoireans, most of the economy. Both countries eventually became one-party states that, while stable, grew despotic and corrupt. While their glittering capitol cities, Abidjan and Nairobi, had fancy restaurants, boutiques, and nightclubs, some rural people faced starvation. By the 1990s, as collapsing coffee and cocoa prices stressed their economies, protesters demanded more democracy, delicate ecologies became dangerously unbalanced, and crime rates soared. Economic development became a fading memory. Civil war engulfed Ivory Coast in the early 2000s, intensifying Christian–Muslim and south–north divisions. But the economy began recovering in 2014 and by the later 2010s the country had returned to civilian government. Kenyans forced out a dictator and elected a reformist government that failed to fulfill most of its promises. In 2007 a disputed Kenyan election led to riots, interethnic fighting, fifteen hundred deaths, and sixty thousand forced from their homes. Tensions between ethnic groups simmered, but, thanks partly to healthy economic growth, the 2013 election that brought Uhuru Kenyatta to the presidency remained largely peaceful but was disputed by the losing candidate. In 2017, Kenyatta won a second term in office in another disputed election but the Supreme Court annulled the results as rigged and ordered a new election, won by Kenyatta, confirming the continuing tensions caused by ethnic and regional divisions. Some critics worried that Kenya's commitment to democracy was fading, especially after the Supreme Court upheld colonial-era laws criminalizing LGBTQ activity.

The Democratic Republic of the Congo (known as Zaire between 1971 and 1997) had the most disastrous experience. A huge country, with ninety-two million people (2019) and dozens of ethnic groups, Congo enjoys a strategic location and rich mineral resources, but it became Africa's biggest failure. The United States and Belgium poured in billions of investment and aid to support President Mobutu, who looted the treasury and aid to amass a huge personal fortune—some $4–5 billion—while repressing his opponents. Mobutu built palaces for himself all over the country and in Europe while hiring top French chefs to prepare his food, spending little money on schools, roads, telephones, and hospitals. Hence, the Congo suffered one of the world's highest infant mortality rates, limited health care, and widespread malnutrition. In 1997 a long-festering rebellion gained strength, forcing Mobutu into exile, where he died. Rebels took over but have done little to foster democracy or development; elections are mostly disputed or rigged. The Congo fragmented in intractable, prolonged civil war and interethnic fighting in the center and east of the country that drew in armies from neighboring countries, with rebel groups controlling large sections of the sprawling country. Over four million Congolese died from the fighting and collapse of medical care, causing a humanitarian crisis. Today two million children risk starvation, the fighting has displaced

4.5 million people, and around 600,000 Congolese have fled to neighboring countries.

Some African nationalists pursued revolutionary or reformist strategies. Radicals argued that political institutions, businesses, and plantations inherited from colonialism, geared to transfer wealth and resources to the West, could not foster economic development; after independence more wealth still flowed out of Africa than into it. To empower Africans, they wanted to replace the colonial state with something entirely new. Various social revolutionary regimes emerged from the long wars of liberation. Looking toward China or the USSR for inspiration, Marxist revolutionary governments gained power in Angola and Mozambique. However, aided by the United States, white-ruled South Africa sponsored opposition guerrilla movements that perpetuated civil wars for several decades, leaving over 2.5 million dead in Angola and Mozambique. Blessed with coffee, diamonds, and especially oil but plagued with corruption, Angola enjoyed growth but struggled to foster development despite considerable Western investment. Since Mozambique's war ended in 1992, pragmatic Marxist leaders have introduced multiparty elections and liberalized the economy, raising per capita incomes. But regional and ethnic tensions persisted, threatening stability.

One social revolutionary state, Zimbabwe, was initially Africa's biggest success story. The Marxist-influenced government, led by liberation hero Robert Mugabe (1924–2019, g. 1987–2017), proved pragmatic for over a decade, largely respecting democracy and human rights, encouraging the white minority to stay, raising living standards and opportunities for black Zimbabweans, and exporting surplus food. But tensions between rival African ethnic groups simmered. Blacks resented continuing white ownership of the best farmland, and Mugabe became more dictatorial, using land disputes to divide the nation. The Zimbabwean president who rose to power as a champion of anticolonial struggle presided for thirty-seven years of authoritarian rule over the impoverishment and degradation of one of Africa's most promising countries. As his support waned, he rigged elections, harassed or jailed opponents, persecuted a minority ethnic group, and seized white-owned farms, awarding them to his cronies and supporters. Meanwhile, uncontrolled inflation made local currency worthless. Commercial agriculture collapsed, drought and cholera spread, life expectancy dropped sharply, food disappeared from shops, refugees fled to neighboring countries, and, in "Operation Drive Out the Trash," Mugabe's police drove poor blacks who favored the opposition out of the cities. The nation remained in precarious shape, demoralizing many Zimbabweans. The world's oldest leader at ninety-three, Mugabe was forced to resign after the army staged a coup in November 2017. Vice president and security chief Emmerson Mnangagwa, known as "The Crocodile" for his wily survival skills, became president, promising reform but there has been little and conditions have not improved much for average Zimbabweans. By 2019 severe drought dried up many water sources, causing even more misery.

Tanzania experimented with an "African" socialism compatible with African traditions, especially cooperation and mutual resource sharing. Under visionary president Julius Nyerere (1922–1999), Tanzania reorganized agriculture into cooperative villages to achieve national self-sufficiency. Nyerere encouraged some democracy in his one-party state, holding regular elections with multiple candidates running for each office or parliamentary seat. Building schools and clinics improved literacy and health to well above African norms. But Nyerere's dreams were dashed; the government became overly bureaucratic, planning proved inadequate, and many lost enthusiasm for socialism. With few imported luxury goods, life was austere compared to that in capitalist Kenya, and peasants often preferred their small family farms to collective villages. As the economy slumped, Tanzania took more foreign loans. Still admired, Nyerere retired in 1985, one of the few founding leaders to voluntarily give up power. His successors dismantled much of the socialist structure, promoted free enterprise, welcomed foreign investment and loans, and fostered a multiparty system. Yet life for most of the fifty-six million Tanzanians improved little, malnutrition became widespread, ethnic tensions intensified, and Tanzania remained a poor nation. But by 2018 the economy had improved and the nation enjoyed one of the highest growth rates on the African continent (an estimated 6 percent for 2019); this allowed the Tanzanian government to embark on a vast program of infrastructure development, particularly rail infrastructure and port improvement, some of it with Chinese investment. Critics view President John Magufuli, elected in 2015, as a populist demagogue who has jailed journalists and bloggers, repressed dissent, persecuted gays and lesbians, and denounced family planning.

The most recent showcases for economic success include Ghana and Botswana. Once a symbol of failure, Ghana has made steady progress. For several decades the country experienced a roller coaster of corrupt civilian governments interspersed with military regimes. But in the 1990s the leaders gradually strengthened democracy and adopted certain policies of the Asian Little Dragons, such as Taiwan and South Korea, mixing capitalism and socialism. Helped by newly discovered oil, Ghana and its twenty-nine million people became increasingly prosperous: by the 2010s it enjoyed one of the continent's highest annual per capita incomes, a life expectancy of fifty-nine, democratic elections, press freedom, and one of Africa's most educated populations. Botswana also made a turnaround. At its independence in 1966, it was one of the world's poorest countries, with an annual per capita income of $35. Gradually, tapping ethnic traditions and rich diamond mines, Botswanans carved out a successful democracy, while the economy, health care, education, and protection of resources all steadily improved, despite deadly droughts and a serious AIDS epidemic, which, thanks to government efforts, has diminished somewhat by 2019. Today Botswanans enjoy living standards higher than in most African and many Middle Eastern, Asian, and Latin American societies and one of Africa's highest rates of economic growth. In the past decades rapid economic growth rates have raised incomes in several other poor nations as well, among them Angola, Mozambique, and Rwanda.

30-4b Social Change

Modern Africa has experienced rapid social change. More people live in cosmopolitan cities where traditional and modern attitudes meet, mix, and clash. City life attracts rural people because it offers more variety—jobs, department stores, movie theaters, nightclubs—than village life. Cities that developed as governments and commercial centers under colonialism, such as Nairobi (Kenya), Lagos (Nigeria), and Dakar (Senegal), have grown nearly 5 percent a year since 1980. Between 1965 and 2000 the percentage of Africans living in urban areas doubled to 30 percent; by 2018 it was 40 percent. Cities grow so fast that services such as buses, water, power, police, schools, and health centers cannot meet peoples' needs. These problems are exemplified by Africa's largest city, Lagos, which grew from less than a million in 1965 to a megalopolis of some fourteen million by 2019. A journalist described the urban chaos:

> *Lagos is a vast laboratory of helter-skelter expansion … confusion and frenzy. A tiny minority of people live extremely well, in villas or plush apartments, and they go to work in gleaming skyscrapers that sit awkwardly next to traditional marketplaces. A vastly larger number of people live in appalling slums, where open sewers may run under disintegrating floorboards. The traffic jam, or "go-slow," is a fact of life. Much of the everyday commerce occurs in this city through the windows of cars, trucks, and other vehicles.*[23]

Cities also foster social changes. Interethnic mixing, even marriage, has become more common. Neighborhoods have developed their own slang, hairstyles, music, dance, art, and poetry. Institutions such as football (soccer) leagues, labor unions, and women's clubs help migrants adjust by creating a new community, replacing the villages left behind. Along sidewalks small traders hawk everything from food and drinks to cheap clothes, religious items, and music cassettes. Various nations have enjoyed international football (soccer) success, while Ethiopians and Kenyans have dominated long-distance running. Numerous Africans have played in the U.S. National Basketball Association and National Football League.

Life in cities fosters different family patterns. Smaller nuclear families have often replaced the extended family of villages, and individualism increasingly challenges village traditions. Whereas before elders largely arranged marriages, now love has become a major criterion for selecting a spouse. Traditionally village men also had an incentive to gain economic status by taking more than one wife, since women did most of the routine farm work, especially the growing of food crops. Now, since urban women have no farming option, men no longer need several wives and, enjoying more educational opportunities, men dominate wage labor in business and transportation.

Gender roles have changed as women became more independent. Growing numbers have served in governments and parliaments, and sub-Saharan Africa ranks ahead of most developing nations in the percentage of women in legislative

---

[23]Sanford Unger, *Africa: The People and Politics of an Emerging Continent* (New York: Simon and Schuster, 1985), 131–132.

positions. Reformist former businesswoman Joyce Banda of Malawi became Africa's second female president in 2012. Some women have also achieved positions as politicians, professors, lawyers, and company heads. Kenyan Grace Ogot (OH-got) (1930–2015) served in parliament while writing short stories featuring heroines who confront traditional values and change. In addition to organizations for work, savings, or worship, women have formed groups to work for society's improvement. Eka Esu-Williams (b. 1950), a Nigerian midwife's daughter who earned a PhD in immunology and became an academic, formed Women Against AIDS in 1988 to educate and empower women, who are more likely than men to get HIV, through workshops, schools, and support groups. Some women work in poorly paid occupations as teachers, nurses, and secretaries, but most women pursue low-wage self-employment, such as by hawking goods and keeping stalls in city markets, a female near-monopoly for centuries; performing domestic work as maids, cooks, or nannies; or working in hairdressing. Living Goods, an antipoverty organization in Uganda, employs women to sell health goods, such as soap, deworming pills, and fortified foods to poor families. Women in Kenya have long dominated the transporting, marketing, and overall East African trade of *khat*, a popular Somali-bred drug that is highly drought-resistant and hence offers a hedge against global warming as other crops shrivel up in the heat. Meanwhile, many men spend long hours commuting to and from work and socializing with friends after work in bars or at club meetings. Thanks to colonial anti-sodomy laws and the recent activities of antigay American Christian missionaries, LGBTQ people face severe intolerance, including imprisonment and sometimes execution, in many African countries. Homosexuality is illegal in thirty-four countries but even where not criminalized faces strong prejudice. But South African and Botswana courts legalized same-sex marriage.

30-4c African Culture and Religion

Africans have combined imported ideas with their own cultural traditions, creating works loved around the world. As Senegalese writer and president Leopold Senghor (sah-GAWR) (1906–2001) asked, "Who else would teach rhythm to the world that has died of machines and cannons?"[24] But the debate about whether to adopt Western political, economic, and cultural models or preserve indigenous traditions has never abated. The Nigerian writer Mabel Segun beautifully expressed the cultural dilemma in her poem "Conflict": "Here we stand, infants overblown, Poised between two civilizations [Europe and Africa], Finding the balance irksome, Itching for something to happen, To tip us one way or the other. Groping in the dark for a helping hand and finding none. I'm tired of hanging in the middle way—But where can I go?"[25] Urbanization, growing mass media, and the

mixing of ethnic groups and outside influences have fostered exciting new popular music styles reflecting social, economic, and political realities. World-renowned South African jazz and pop singer Miriam Makeba (muh-KAY-ba) (1932–2008), forced to spend decades in exile, described her mission: "I live to sing about what I see and know. I don't sing politics, I sing truth."[26] Popular music styles creatively blending local and imported influences have helped Africans adjust to change while affirming their cultural values. Hence, Nigeria's *juju* music reflects Yoruba traditions while adopting Western instruments, such as electric guitars. Tinariwen, Mali's Timbuktu-based "guitar gods," have earned an international audience for music mixing nomadic Tuareg traditions and Western rock, and have collaborated with famous musicians such as Robert Plant, Thom Yorke, and Bono. In Zimbabwe a pop music style known as Zimdancehall, based on Jamaican reggae and its later, more party-oriented form known as Dancehall, has attracted many young people as a vehicle for protest. The artists sing about the hard life in the impoverished townships, describing violence, poverty, water shortages, electricity blackouts, rising food prices, teenage prostitution, and widespread disillusionment with the political system.

African popular musicians perform and sell recordings around the world. Perhaps the greatest African superstar, Senegalese Youssou N'Dour (YOO-soo en-DOOR) (b. 1959), often collaborates with leading Western and Arab musicians yet remains true to his roots, living in Dakar and following his tolerant Sufi Muslim faith. Some musicians are

Jack Vartoogian/Archive Photos/Getty Images

IMAGE 30.7 **African Cultural Expression** Africans have developed diverse and vibrant popular music, often by mixing Western and local traditions. In Nigeria, juju music, played by bands such as King Sunny Ade and his band, the African Beats, seen here playing a concert in New York's Central Park in 2016, has been especially popular among the Yoruba people. King Sunny has been one of the most influential juju musicians and attracted a worldwide audience.

[24]Quoted in Richard A. Fredland, *Understanding Africa: A Political Economy Perspective* (Chicago: Burnham, 2001), 139.
[25]From James E. Miller, et al., eds., *Black African Voices* (Glenview, IL: Scott Foresman, 1970), 322.
[26]Quoted in John Follain, "Only the First Step for 'Mama Africa,'" *New Straits Times*, February 23, 1990.

highly political. Nigerian Fela Kuti (1938–1997), whose music mixed jazz, soul, rock, and Yoruba traditions, used songs as a weapon against Nigerian governments and their Western sponsors, facing frequent arrests and beatings for his protests. Like Bob Marley, Bob Dylan, and Chile's Víctor Jara, Fela gained worldwide fame for using music to attack injustice. Women have also expressed their views through music. Mali's Oumou Sangare had a massive hit with her account of a young woman torn between pleasing her parents and her loved one. In the Congo, a particularly influential (Zairean) pop music, known widely as **soukous** ("to shake"), was shaped by Cuban and Brazilian dance rhythms created by descendants of African slaves. Soukous depends heavily on the guitar as well as on traditional African songs and melodies. But some Congolese musicians, often unable to make a living or speak freely in their troubled homeland, have often sought their fortunes elsewhere. Soukous became a major dance music throughout Africa and among African immigrants in Europe. In South Africa jazz played a key role in the liberation struggle, including groups like the Jazz Epistles, whose members included pianist Dollar Brand and trumpeter Hugh Masekela, both of whom later became world famous while living in exile.

Like popular musicians, writers have combined old traditions with new influences to comment on modern society, assert African identity, and influence political change. Many write in English or French to reach an international audience. Nigerian Wole Soyinka (**WOE-lay shaw-YING-kuh**) (b. 1934), a Yoruba poet, playwright, novelist, and sometime filmmaker who won the 1986 Nobel Prize for Literature, mixed Yoruba mysticism with criticisms of Western capitalism, racism, cultural imperialism, and African failures. A former political prisoner, Soyinka denounced repressive African leaders, chastising "Nigeria's self-engorgement at the banquet of highway robberies, public executions, public floggings and other institutionalized sadisms, casual cruelties, wanton destruction."[27] Their powerful political dissent often forced both Soyinka and his Nigerian colleague Chinua Achebe to live in exile.

Writers and artists sought authentic African perspectives, among them **negritude**, a literary and philosophical movement first developed in the 1930s. Writer Léopold Senghor, later Senegal's first president after independence, attempted to balance Western rational thought with African approaches to knowledge, such as mysticism and animism. To Senghor, Africans needed to assert, rather than feel inferior about, their black skins and cultural traditions. Negritude influenced French artists and writers; philosopher Jean-Paul Sartre praised it as a weapon against all forms of oppression.

Marxism influenced one of the best-known writers in Francophone West Africa, Senegalese Ousmane Sembène (**OOS-man sem-BEN-ee**) (1923–2007). The son of a poor fisherman who was drafted into the French army during World War II, Sembène fought in Italy and Germany. After the war he worked in France as a dockworker and became a leader of the dockworkers' union; his first novel portrayed the stevedore's hard life. Returning to Senegal, Sèmbene often wrote about the colonial period, expressing resistance to Western domination and social inequality while attacking Senegal's greedy businessmen and government officials. Sèmbene also achieved international acclaim for films satirizing corrupt bureaucrats and the exploitation of the poor by the rich.

English-language literature flourished in South Africa and East Africa. Kenyan journalist-turned-university-professor Ngũgĩ wa Thiong'o (**en-GOO-gee wah thee-AHN-go**) (b. 1938) explored the relationship between colonialism and social fragmentation, showing Kikuyus struggling to retain their identity, culture, and traditions while adjusting to the modern world. Once devout, Ngũgĩ later rejected Christianity as a legacy of colonialism. His 1979 novel, *Petals of Blood*, portrays Kenya struggling to free itself from neocolonialism but also beset with corruption. His attacks on the privileged Kenyan elite allied with Western exploitation brought several jail terms and later exile. Another Kenyan writer, Binyavanga Wainaina, inspired many by openly coming out as gay in 2016, a dangerous decision in a strongly homophobic society.

Africans have maintained a triple religious heritage of animism/polytheism, Islam, and Christianity, all with many followers. Animists now account for perhaps 5 percent or less of Africans but many people mix traditional practices and beliefs with Christianity or Islam. With their links to wider worlds, Christianity and Islam are also globalizing influences, spreading Western or Middle Eastern political, social, and economic ideas. Africans often view religions in both theoretical and practical terms, adopting views that help them adjust to change.

Christianity has become Africa's largest religion, attracting over 60 percent of Africans by 2012, many of them fervent. Some countries, such as Congo, South Africa, and Uganda, are largely Christian. Christianity has proved a powerful force for social change. The Roman Catholic Church continues to expand in Africa but also faces competition from increasingly popular evangelical and Pentecostal movements. Since 1970, the percentage of African Protestants has doubled to nearly 30 percent of the population. Mission schools have educated many leaders, influencing their worldviews. However, many churches have prevented followers from practicing traditional customs. While believers often favor liberating women, many criticize progressive social views such as toleration of LGBTQ people and behavior. A growing number of independent churches, some blending African traditions into worship and theology, have no ties to older Western-based denominations. Promising to help members acquire wealth and happiness with a "prosperity gospel", some African churches have enjoyed spectacular growth, building big urban churches that attract thousands of congregants each Sunday. In a reversal of historical patterns, several evangelical churches send missionaries to revitalize Christianity in the West, establishing branches in Europe and

soukous ("to shake") A Congolese popular music that was shaped by dance rhythms from Cuba and Brazil.

negritude A literary and philosophical movement to forge distinctively African views.

---

[27]Quoted in Tejumola Olaniyan, "Narrativizing Postcoloniality: Responsibilities," *Public Culture* 5, no. 1 (Fall 1992): 47.

North America. As Christianity loses believers in Europe, the Catholic Church has recruited African priests for understaffed European parishes. Pope Francis has viewed Africa as the future face of his two- millennia-old church. A recent study estimated that by 2060 40 percent of the world's Christians will live in Africa, where 60 percent of the people today are under the age of twenty-five. Yet many other Africans have viewed Christianity as connected to Western imperialism. According to a popular nationalist saying: "When the missionaries came the Africans had the land and the Christians had the Bible. They taught us to pray with our eyes closed. When we opened them they had the land and we had the Bible."[28]

Some 30 percent of black Africans follow Islam, a fourth of all countries having Muslim majorities. Some revivalist and Wahhabi or Salafist movements have gained influence, especially in West Africa and Somalia, and some northern Nigerian states have imposed Islamic law or spawned extremist Muslim groups. These developments have sparked deadly clashes with Christian minorities and less extreme Muslims that have left several thousand dead. In 2012 jihadis linked to Al Qaeda capitalized on unrest to capture northern Mali, including ancient cities like Timbuktu, and impose harsh Islamic law while destroying ancient sites and books. Most French troops pushed them out in 2013 but Mali still experiences sporadic attacks and terrorism from jihadist groups, undermining tourism and daily life. Popular culture often bruises Christian or Muslim sensitivities. In 2019 a hugely popular TV series in mostly Muslim Senegal, *Mistress of a Married Man*, has outraged many Muslims over its frank sexuality and independent-minded women. The show addresses not just female desire but also issues of rape, male power, mental illness, and domestic violence. In Kenya the film *Rafiki* chronicled a romance between daughters of rival politicians in a virulently anti-LGBTQ country.

But most Muslims and Christians remain moderate and inclusive. While politicians use religion as a wedge issue, and although Christian–Muslim clashes have occurred in several countries, tolerant relations among Christians, Muslims, and animists are more common. Hence, Yoruba Christians and Muslims mix easily and even intermarry. One sect in Lagos mixes Islam and Christianity into a blend called "Chrislam." Ethnicity often divides people more than religion.

30-4d Africa in the Global System

The Cold War rivalry between the United States and the USSR gained some African countries aid but also fostered superpower manipulation. Countries such as Congo and Angola became pawns as superpowers helped to support or remove leaders. But with the Cold War over, the Western world often ignored Africa, providing little aid and only modest investment. The wealth gap between African countries and Western industrialized nations has grown even wider than during colonial times. In the early 2000s the gap between the richest Western and poorest African countries was around 400 to 1. When the world

economy boomed in the 1950s and 1960s, African economies showed steady growth. Between the 1970s and 2000, however, as world prices for many African exports collapsed, African economic growth rates steadily dropped. Since 2000 some countries have resumed rapid growth while others have lagged behind.

Since the 1990s Western experts have encouraged a policy of "structural adjustment" in which international lenders, such as the International Monetary Fund (IMF) and World Bank, loan nations money but require opening their economies to private investment and, to balance national budgets, reduce government spending for health, education, and farmers. The resulting hardship on average people—from eliminating money for poor children to attend village primary schools to closing local offices that aid small farmers—increases resentment both of governments and Western nations. This private investment also promotes a shift away from traditional farming to more productive modern agriculture that relies on tractors, chemical fertilizers, and new seeds, which has large environmental and social costs: marginal land is often turned into desert, and small farmers lack money to buy modern supplies. Like most of the world Africa is highly vulnerable to global warming, which intensifies drought and torrential rains. But some Africans also contribute to the problem with the shifting cultivation (slash-and-burn) agriculture that clears land for farming. In 2019 while fires were devastating the Amazon rain forest, human-set fires were also destroying forests and grasslands in central Africa, especially Angola and the Democratic Republic of the Congo.

To obtain the cars, fashionable clothes, and electronic gadgets the urban middle and upper classes desire, African nations took out loans. As a percentage of total output, African countries had the largest foreign debts in the world in the 1990s. Yet, the world prices for most of Africa's exports, such as coffee, cotton, and tobacco from Tanzania and cocoa from Ghana, steadily dropped from the 1960s to 2000 and still fluctuate. Small farmers, such as the cotton growers in Mali, cannot compete with highly subsidized Western farmers and the tariff barriers erected in Europe, North America, and Japan against food and fiber imports from Africa. The world financial institutions implemented a debt relief program in 1996 that lowered the debt burden by three-quarters and fostered reforms and dynamism, reducing debt. Prices for exports, especially minerals and oil, rebounded by 2000, spurring faster economic growth and foreign investment, but the 2008–2009 global economic crisis lowered growth rates from 6.1 percent in 2007 to 2.8 percent in 2009. Growth rebounded by 2012, but since 2013 debt has again risen rapidly. By 2019 about one-third of countries were considered in or at high risk of debt distress. Yet, most African governments, businesses, and banks remain supportive of globalization, in contrast to some more nationalist and populist governments in Europe and the Americas that are building walls and the U.S.-initiated trade and tariff war, especially with China, that challenges free trade and globalization.

---

[28]Quoted in Chinweizu, *The West and the Rest of Us: White Predators, Black Slavers, and the African Elite* (New York: Vintage, 1975), 1.

In 2019 some fifty African nations approved the African Continental Free Trade Area aimed at linking together a $3.4 trillion economic zone of some 1.3 billion people, with the goal of reducing tariffs and stimulating trade within Africa to make Africa a "food basket to the rest of the world," present a "huge consumer base" attractive to global investors, stem migration flows to Europe, and help bring political stability. But there are serious obstacles ahead to building something comparable to the European Union. The continent needs to generate a million jobs a month to satisfy the demands of a generation of young people desperate for employment and to ensure that rapid population growth does not become a dangerous liability. Africa needs around $100 billion a year in infrastructure investment, including a huge expansion of its power supply. And it needs to achieve all this while being the continent most vulnerable to the ravages of climate change; already rising sea levels are regularly flooding some coastal cities while drought devastates farmland. And, one critic notes, free trade often mostly benefits the wealthiest people, companies, and countries, and "will be great for Africa only if it reduces economic inequality and creates good quality jobs, especially for women and for our young people."[29]

Taking advantage of Western disinterest, in the past decade China, now Africa's largest trading partner, has made huge investments in African oil, refining, mining, timber, agriculture, and banking as well as constructing roads, railroads, dams, bridges, factories, and other infrastructure projects, many of them as part of China's Belt and Road Initiative to connect China with Eurasian and African countries through trade and cooperation. Bilateral trade has skyrocketed in the 2000s. Thousands of Africans, especially Nigerians, have moved to China to study in universities and others, often illegally, to establish small-scale trading operations, fostering neighborhoods informally known as "Little Africas." Perhaps a million Chinese now live and work in Africa, many running commercial operations; many African cities and towns now have Chinese stores and supermarkets featuring inexpensive Chinese products as well as restaurants. But the growing Chinese presence, including Chinese workers on construction projects, has sometimes sparked resentment, kidnappings, and riots. The Chinese activity may foreshadow a change of direction for many Africans. But as African debts to China for its investments and aid pile up, China can demand support for its foreign policies and controversial human rights record. While many Africans are grateful for China's support, others see the evolving relationship and China's growing influence as neocolonial and mainly benefitting Chinese investors and African elites.

Africa's economic problems have diverse roots. Colonial economic policies caused severe environmental destruction, such as desertification and deforestation, while incorporating Africans into the world economy as specialized producers of minerals or cash crops for export rather than food farmers.

Hence, Zambia relies on exploiting copper, Uganda coffee, Malawi tobacco, and Nigeria oil. Colonial regimes often failed to build roads, schools, and clinics. For decades bad policy decisions, poor leadership, corruption, unstable politics, and misguided advice from Western experts also contributed to the economic challenges, while the rapid spread of HIV/AIDS killed and affected millions (see Chapter 26). In some nations a third of the population had the HIV virus in the early 2010s and average life expectancy had declined. But a decade of progress has brought some optimism that the public health threat can be contained and eventually eliminated, perhaps by 2030. In eastern and southern Africa the number of people living with HIV on antiretroviral therapy has more than doubled since 2010, reaching almost 12.5 million people by 2017, while new infections have declined by a third and deaths by nearly half. But experts worry about complacency, especially among youth.

But although falling behind much of Asia and Latin America, Africans have had successes. Using foreign aid and their own resources, they have made rapid strides in literacy, social and medical services such as active birth control campaigns, and road construction. In the 1990s, some 58 percent of Africans lived on less than $1.25 per day; by 2010 the figure was 48.5 percent. But many still lived in extreme poverty. Some nations, such as South Africa and Ghana, have a feisty free press. Recent studies suggest that the great majority of Africans believe that democracy is the best form of government and that free, fair, multiparty elections are the best way to choose leaders. Nations have also worked together to resolve problems. The African Union, formed in 2000 with fifty-four members, has sent peacekeeping troops into violence-torn countries. By the 1990s Africans grew skeptical about Western models of development, which were often dependent on expensive high technology, and disillusioned with socialist governments controlling economic activity. Many nations moved toward more democratic systems and private enterprise. However, political leadership often failed to root out corruption and poverty and foster food production. Africa also suffers a particularly acute "brain drain" as academics, students, and professionals, seeking a better life, move to Europe or North America. Thus Africans have not enjoyed complete control of their destiny. In 2018 the Museum of Black Civilization opened in Dakar, Senegal, fifty-two years after Senegal's first president, Leopold Senghor, presented a postcolonial cultural vision. The museum tells a story of art, history, and the African diaspora in an attempt to finish the decolonization of knowledge pertaining to Africa. But symbolizing current African realities, the museum was built in part with financial donations from China. Ghanaian historian Jacob Ajayi (a-JAH-yee) laid out the challenge: "The vision of a new [African] society will need to be developed out of the African historical experience. The African is not yet master of his own fate, but neither is he completely at the mercy of fate."[30]

[29]Winnie Byanyima, quoted in Ishaan Tharoor, "What an African Free-Trade Deal Means for the World," *Washington Post*, September 9, 2019.

[30]Quoted in Jennifer Seymour Whitaker, *How Can Africa Survive?* (New York: Harper and Row, 1988), 197.

▶ African cities have grown rapidly and often lack necessary services, individualism has grown more common, and women have lost some of the economic value they had in agricultural villages, though some have become successful professionals.

▶ African musicians, writers, and artists have drawn on local traditions as well as influences from the West to create original forms, such as soukous, as well as works that criticize both Western encroachment and homegrown corruption.

▶ While animism has grown less influential in Africa, Christianity is the most popular religion and has undermined traditions and been seen by some as connected to Western imperialism, while Islam is followed by 40 percent of Africans.

▶ The economic gap between Africa and the industrialized West continues to grow larger, and Western attempts to help Africa through the IMF and the World Bank often include requirements that harm the environment and the poor and inspire resentment, as do tariffs against African imports and the enduring colonial legacy.

Chapter Summary

The Middle East and sub-Saharan Africa shared certain experiences, including decolonization, mass poverty, reliance on exporting natural resources, political instability, and Western intervention. Diverse developments reshaped the Middle East since 1945. Arab nationalism, especially strong in Egypt, generated conflict with the West and with Israel, which became the major Arab enemy. Arab–Israeli conflict greatly destabilized the region, while ethnic and religious divisions fostered violent struggles within nations such as Afghanistan and Iraq, fostering interventions by foreign powers including the United States. Islam proved most potent as a revolutionary political force in Iran, long a battleground for international rivalries over its oil supplies. The Middle East, especially the Persian Gulf region, provided much of the world's oil, fostering wealth but also global attention as world consumption increased. Oil-rich Saudi Arabia forged an alliance with the United States. Most Middle Eastern societies remained conservative but also fostered cultural creativity. Meanwhile, the rivalry between militant and secular Muslims, and Sunnis and Shi'ites, has provided a major cleavage in many countries.

By the 1970s long-colonized African nations achieved independence under nationalist leaders. But the hopes for a better life were soon dashed. Artificially created multiethnic nations found it difficult to sustain democracy, and dictatorial governments often gained power. Most nations remained dependent on exporting one or two resources. Ambitious development plans gave way to economic stagnation and, as commodity prices fall, increasing poverty. By the early 2000s some resumed economic growth, but most nations still struggle to raise living standards for the majority of their people. South Africa was finally transformed from a racist state to a multiracial democracy. Societies urbanized, redefined family life and gender roles, and created new music and literature. Africans still search for the right mix of imported ideas and local traditions to create better lives.

Key Terms

Intifada 820
mujahidin 823
Taliban 824
Ba'ath 824
OPEC 826

Islamists 830
rai 831
pan-Africanism 835
Mau Mau Rebellion 835
wabenzi 836

apartheid 839
bantustans 839
soukous 846
negritude 846

> *This music sings the struggle of [humanity]. This music is my life. This is the revolution we have begun. But the revolution is only a means to attain freedom, and freedom is only a means to enrich the happiness and nobility of human life.*
>
> —Hazil, the Indonesian revolutionary nationalist in Mochtar Lubis's novel *A Road with No End* (1952)[1]

PAUL ATKINSON/Shutterstock.com

IMAGE 31.1 **Commuting to Work** Vietnam has largely recovered from its decades of war and has experienced increasing economic growth. These men and women in Hanoi are commuting to work by motorcycle and motor scooter in 2017.

Q What does this photo tell us about daily life in Hanoi?

[1]Mochtar Lubis, *A Road with No End*, translated by Anthony Johns from 1952 Indonesian edition (Chicago: Henry Regnery, 1968), 9.

In 1950 several idealistic Indonesian writers published a moving declaration promoting universal human dignity: "We [Indonesians] are the heirs to the culture of the whole world, a culture which is ours to extend and develop in our own way [by] the discarding of old and outmoded values and their replacement by new ones. Our fundamental quest is [helping] humanity."[2] These writers having witnessed the Indonesian Revolution against the Dutch (1945–1950), a nationalist struggle that achieved independence, also warned against narrow nationalism. They were inspired by irreverent Sumatran poet Chairul Anwar **(CHAI-roll ON-war)** (1922–1949), who believed the revolution had made possible a new, open society. Influenced both by Western books and Indonesian sensibilities, Anwar's pathbreaking poems stretched the Indonesian language's possibilities. But Anwar had died at twenty-seven, leaving it to others, like liberal Sumatran novelist and journalist Mochtar Lubis **(MOKE-tar LOO-bis)** (1922–2004), to carry on the campaign to blend widely admired foreign ideas with Indonesian ideas, fostering change while preserving continuity.

The declaration's noble aspirations and recognition of wider world connections reflected a new sense of possibility as colonial walls were knocked down. But the writers' idealism was soon dashed by early post-World War II realities. While South and Southeast Asians longed for human dignity, more immediate goals took precedence: securing independence, building new nations, and addressing poverty and underdevelopment. But despite false starts and conflicts, Indonesians and other South and Southeast Asian nations sought, and sometimes found, answers to their challenges while increasing their links to global networks, changing dramatically without destroying tradition.

Southern Asia is the world's most densely populated region: over 2.4 billion people (more than a quarter of the world's population) live in the lands stretching from Pakistan and India to Indonesia and the Philippines. It also contains a wide array of languages, ethnic groups, religions, worldviews, governments, and levels of economic development. This region of contrasts, playing an important world role for over four millennia, continues to be a cornerstone of the world economy.

---

[2]Quoted in Anthony Johns, "Introduction," in Lubis, *Road with No End*, 4.

31-1 The Reshaping of South Asia

TRANSITIONS

Q What factors led to the political division of South Asia?

World War II undermined British colonialism, hastening independence for South Asians. Britain, economically drained and aware that maintaining control would come only at great cost, handed power over to local leaders. India's first prime minister, Jawaharlal Nehru (**JAH-wa-HAR-lahl NAY-roo**) (1889–1964), told his people: "A moment comes, which comes rarely in history, when we step from the old to the new, when an

---

CONNECTION to TODAY

How do you think that South Asian nations today reflect the struggles for independence and the conflicts that followed?

---

age ends and when the soul of a nation, long suppressed, finds utterance."[3] Yet the daunting challenges ahead tempered Nehru's idealism. India's long struggle for independence, marked by Mohandas Gandhi's (1868–1948) nonviolent philosophy, had ironically ended with Gandhi assassinated and British India divided into two separate, often hostile countries, predominantly Hindu India and largely Muslim Pakistan. Mostly

[3]Quoted in John R. McLane, ed., *The Political Awakening of India* (Englewood Cliffs, NJ: Prentice-Hall, 1970), 178.

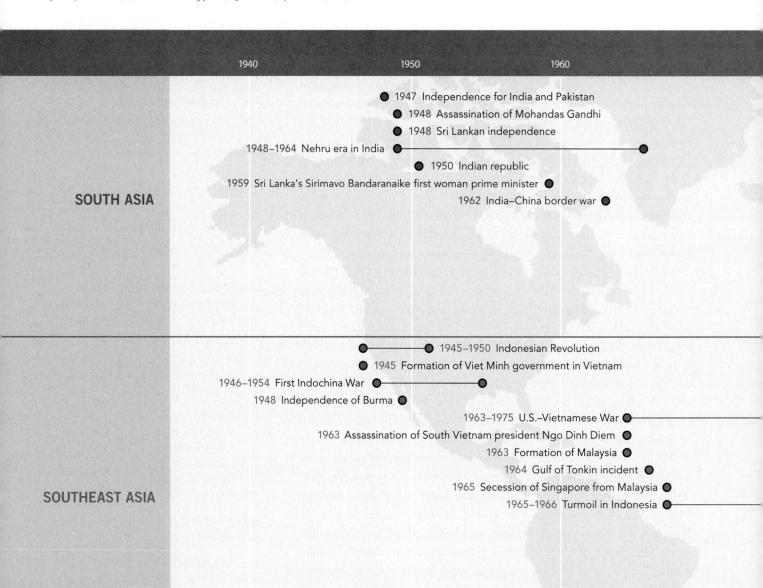

1940 **1950** **1960**

SOUTH ASIA

1947 Independence for India and Pakistan
1948 Assassination of Mohandas Gandhi
1948 Sri Lankan independence
1948–1964 Nehru era in India
1950 Indian republic
1959 Sri Lanka's Sirimavo Bandaranaike first woman prime minister
1962 India–China border war

SOUTHEAST ASIA

1945–1950 Indonesian Revolution
1945 Formation of Viet Minh government in Vietnam
1946–1954 First Indochina War
1948 Independence of Burma
1963–1975 U.S.–Vietnamese War
1963 Assassination of South Vietnam president Ngo Dinh Diem
1963 Formation of Malaysia
1964 Gulf of Tonkin incident
1965 Secession of Singapore from Malaysia
1965–1966 Turmoil in Indonesia

Buddhist Sri Lanka and, in the 1970s, largely Muslim Bangladesh also achieved independence, the latter through a violent struggle to secede from Pakistan. Each nation had achievements and failures, but the largest and most populous, India, became the regional colossus and a major player in world affairs.

31-1a Decolonization and Partition

South Asia's British-imposed regional political unity was undermined by religious divisions. During World War II relations between the British and the mainly Hindu Indian National Congress ruptured (see Chapter 25). Fearing Hindu domination, the Muslim League pressed its case for a separate Muslim nation, to be called Pakistan. As tensions increased, widespread rioting erupted; Muslims and Hindus began murdering each

other, pulling victims from buses, shops, and homes. In Calcutta alone five thousand died. With any pretense of Hindu–Muslim unity shattered, the Muslim League leader, Mohammed Ali Jinnah (1876–1948), announced that if India were not divided it would be destroyed. As violence spread, the Congress leaders and British officials realized that some sort of partition was inevitable. In 1947 the British, Congress, and Muslim League agreed to create two independent nations, India and a Pakistan formed out of the Muslim-majority areas of eastern Bengal and the northwestern provinces along the Indus River.

Addressing his new nation, Prime Minister Nehru proclaimed: "Long years ago we made a tryst with destiny, and now the time comes when we shall redeem our pledge. At the stroke of the midnight hour, when the world sleeps, India will awake to life and freedom."[4] Pakistanis had a similar mood of renewal.

[4]Quoted in B. N. Pandey, *The Break-up of British India* (New York: St. Martin's, 1969), 209.

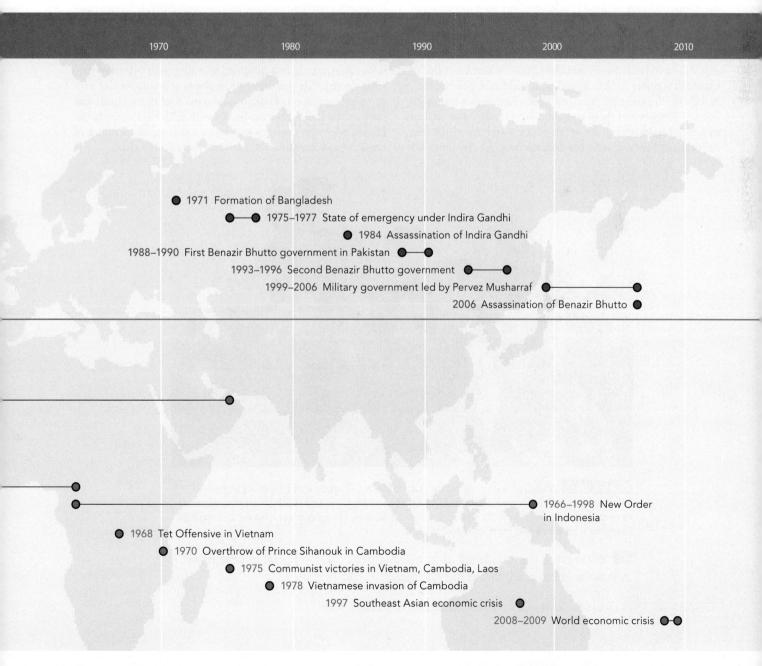

1970   1980   1990   2000   2010

1971 Formation of Bangladesh

1975–1977 State of emergency under Indira Gandhi

1984 Assassination of Indira Gandhi

1988–1990 First Benazir Bhutto government in Pakistan

1993–1996 Second Benazir Bhutto government

1999–2006 Military government led by Pervez Musharraf

2006 Assassination of Benazir Bhutto

1966–1998 New Order in Indonesia

1968 Tet Offensive in Vietnam

1970 Overthrow of Prince Sihanouk in Cambodia

1975 Communist victories in Vietnam, Cambodia, Laos

1978 Vietnamese invasion of Cambodia

1997 Southeast Asian economic crisis

2008–2009 World economic crisis

But the euphoria proved short-lived as a bloodbath ensued. Muslims and Hindus had often lived side by side, but partition sparked hatreds between members of the local majority faith, who felt empowered, and religious minorities, who feared discrimination. As violence flared, Hindus and Sikhs fled Pakistan for India, while Muslims fled India for Pakistan. Altogether some 10 to 12 million refugees crossed the India–Pakistan borders. Perhaps one million died; seventy-five thousand women were raped. Religious extremists attacked whole villages or trainloads of refugees.

Sixty-eight years old, Mohandas Gandhi labored to stop the killing. Moving into Delhi's Muslim quarter, he toured refugee camps without escort, read aloud from scriptures of all religions, including the Quran, and confronted Hindu mobs attacking mosques. Desperate, and hoping to send a message to everyone, Gandhi, who weighed only 113 pounds, began a fast until all the violence in Delhi stopped or he died. He quickly fell ill, but Gandhi's effort worked. After violence subsided, a substantial Muslim and Sikh minority remained in India and a smaller Hindu and Sikh minority in Pakistan. But partition had been shattering. A Muslim poet spoke for many disillusioned people: "This is not that long looked-for break of the day. Where did that fine breeze blow from—where has it fled?"[5] Gandhi's support for Muslim victims of Hindu violence outraged Hindu extremists, who regarded Gandhi as a traitor. In January 1948, one of them gunned down Gandhi as he walked to a meeting, shocking the whole country and the world. His death made him a martyr but Indians have argued about his

accomplishments and complex legacy ever since. Gandhi's face appears on every denomination of Indian currency and the spinning wheel he made famous occupies the center of the nation's flag. Many politicians have sought to claim or coopt his legacy, including some whose Hindu supremacist and nationalist agenda would seem to be a refutation of Gandhi's belief in a pluralistic and multifaith India. But he was also a devout Hindu who believed that religion had a place in politics. Nonetheless, some Hindu nationalists still see Gandhi as a traitor to their religion and undeserving of emulation.

Despite its bloody start, India was built on a solid political foundation. Britain bequeathed to India democratic institutions, a trained civil service, a good communications system, and an educated if Westernized elite committed to modernization. India became a republic with a British-influenced constitution, led by a prime minister chosen by the majority party in an elected parliament. However, given its huge ethnic, religious, regional, and linguistic diversity (fourteen major and hundreds of minor languages), building national unity proved difficult. In language, food preferences, and even culture Bengalis in the northeast, Punjabis in the northwest, and Tamils in the south are as different as Scots, Germans, and Italians. To accommodate the many minorities, regions, and cultures, India adopted a federal system, with elected state governments, and was officially secular with complete separation of religion and state. Kashmir, a Himalayan state on the India–Pakistan border with a Muslim majority but Hindu ruler who opted to join India, has remained a source of tension and sometimes war between India and Pakistan.

IMAGE 31.2 **Muslims Leaving India for Pakistan During Partition** As India and Pakistan split into two new nations in 1947, millions of Muslims and Hindus fled their homes to escape violence. This photo shows displaced Muslims, carrying a few meager belongings, jamming a train headed from India to Pakistan.

Q What does the photo tell us about the political and social atmosphere in India and Pakistan during the Partition?

---

[5]Faiz Ahmed Faiz, quoted in Sugata Bose and Ayesha Jalal, *Modern South Asia: History, Culture, Political Economy* (New York: Routledge, 1998), 200.

Pakistan, an artificial country with two wings separated by a thousand miles of India, confronted numerous problems. The founding leader, Jinnah, died soon after independence; his successor was assassinated. With Muslims overrepresented in the British Indian military, the army played a stronger role in Pakistan's politics than in India's. The loss of top civilian leaders, the lack of a balanced economic base, massive poverty, and geographical division made Pakistan more vulnerable than India to political instability and military rule. Pakistan and India also quarreled over issues from water use to trade to ownership of Kashmir.

31-1b Building a New India

India's first prime minister, Nehru, a British-educated lawyer and close associate of Gandhi, dominated Indian politics for a decade and a half (1948–1964). A gifted speaker, brilliant thinker, and democrat, Nehru was supported by the small and mostly secular middle class, who wanted a modern India, and the lower-class majority living in overcrowded, unhealthy urban slums or dusty villages without electricity and running water. Nehru promised to raise living standards and address the overwhelming poverty. While India lagged behind communist-ruled China in economic development, it preserved personal freedom. Promoting peaceful coexistence with neighbors, renouncing military aggression, and working to prevent a superpower nuclear conflict, Nehru became a major world figure. He helped found the Non-Aligned Movement of nations unwilling to commit to either the U.S. or Soviet camps, such as Egypt and Indonesia. As India's stature grew, the Congress Party won three smashing electoral victories.

Nehru admired Western politics, literature, and dynamism but also respected India's cultural heritage and its moral strength. Raised a Hindu brahman, Nehru was nevertheless a secularist who believed that Congress should represent and serve all religions and social groups. Like Gandhi, he opposed the caste system and fought gender inequalities. Nehru convinced parliament to approve new laws on untouchability and women's rights that penalized discrimination. Untouchables, who had preferred the designation **Dalit** ("suppressed" or "ground down" people) since the 1970s, acquired special quotas in government services and universities, while Hindu women gained legal equality with men, including the right to divorce and inheritance. To discourage child marriage, Nehru set a minimum marriage age at eighteen for males and fifteen for females. But these laws, challenging centuries of tradition, were often ignored, especially in rural areas.

Mixing capitalism and socialism in what he termed a "third way," Nehru introduced a planning system to foster modern technology. While established industries remained in private hands, new public ventures built power plants and dams, which doubled power production, and irrigation canals, increasing agricultural yields by 25 percent. In the 1960s the Green Revolution of new high-yield wheat and rice dramatically increased food production. Thanks to Nehru's five-year plans, by the 1970s India produced many industrial products, including steel, and was nearly self-sufficient in food.

But some policies proved failures. Government control of the private sector through regulations gave bureaucrats great power, fostered corruption, and shackled private enterprise. Nehru failed to cultivate good relations with Pakistan or China; in 1962 Chinese troops humiliated Indian forces during a border dispute in the Himalayas. Nehru also did not recognize that a rapidly growing population, rising from 389 million in 1941 to 434 million in 1961, undermined most of India's economic gains; he only belatedly endorsed family planning. In addition, the government built schools and universities but failed to substantially raise literacy rates. Yet, when Nehru died in 1964, millions mourned the end of an idealistic era that had earned India world respect.

Nehru fostered a family political dynasty. With his respected successor's sudden death in 1966, the Congress selected Nehru's daughter, Indira Gandhi (1917–1984), to be the nation's first woman prime minister. She had worked closely with her father while her husband (no relation to Mohandas Gandhi) served in parliament. Mrs. Gandhi enjoyed a decade and a half in power. When her support waned in the 1967 elections, she responded with policies to win back the poor, and some of her policies improved the economy. India's smashing military victory over archenemy Pakistan in 1971 also elevated her status. But mounting domestic problems precipitated increasingly harsh policies. Powerful vested interests ignored her reforms, the economy faltered, and many Indians turned against her party. In 1975 Gandhi declared a state of emergency, suspending civil rights, closing state governments, and jailing some ten thousand opposition leaders and dissidents. Meanwhile, her youngest son, Sanjay Gandhi (1946–1980), launched a controversial birth control campaign to forcibly sterilize any man with more than three children and also implemented a slum-clearance program that forced thousands out of sidewalk shanties. Both programs became deeply unpopular. In 1977 Indira lifted the emergency. After thirty years in power, the Congress Party, and with it Indira Gandhi, was voted out of office and was replaced by an uneasy coalition, including Hindu nationalists opposed to secularism. But the coalition government, solving few problems, collapsed.

When Indira Gandhi returned to power in the 1980 elections, she restored the Nehru dynasty but faced voter apathy, growing unemployment, and unrest. In 1980 Sanjay Gandhi died in a plane crash, and Indira Gandhi elevated her eldest son Rajiv (1944–1991), an apolitical airline pilot, as her heir apparent. Violence in the Punjab, India's richest state, which had a heavy Sikh population, provoked Mrs. Gandhi's final crisis. Many Sikhs, whose half-a-millennium-old religion mixes Hindu and Muslim ideas, desired autonomy from India. In 1983 armed Sikh extremists occupied the Golden Temple at Amritsar (**uhm-RIT-suhr**), the holiest Sikh shrine, and turned it into a fortress, calling for an independent Sikh homeland and murdering those, including moderate Sikhs, who opposed them. The Indian army stormed the Golden Temple and reduced the temple to rubble; over a thousand militants and soldiers died in the incident.

Sikhs were shocked by the destruction of their holiest temple, and two of her Sikh guards assassinated Indira Gandhi. In response, Hindu mobs roamed Delhi, burning Sikh shops and

Dalit The designation commonly used for untouchables since the 1970s.

killing thousands of Sikhs, often by pouring gasoline over them and setting them ablaze. Meanwhile, Rajiv Gandhi succeeded his mother but proved ineffective; in 1991 he was blown up by a young Sri Lankan woman who opposed India's support of the Sri Lankan government in its war against the Tamil secessionist group to which she belonged. Yet, despite this tumult, India remained a functioning democracy and thriving nation.

31-1c The Making of Pakistan and Bangladesh

Pakistan faced greater challenges than did India. Jinnah had pledged to make the nation happy and prosperous, but the leaders who followed had only limited success, thanks partly to tensions between ethnic groups who shared an Islamic faith but often little else. Hostilities flared between the nationalistic Bengalis, who dominated the east, and Punjabis and Sindhis, who dominated the west. The two regions differed in language, culture, and outlook. When the factionalized Pakistani parliament proved unworkable, military leaders took power in 1958. But dissatisfaction with military dictatorship sparked riots, prompting martial law. Moreover, Bengalis felt they did

not get a fair share of the nation's resources and political power. After the **Awami League**, a Bengali nationalist party, won a majority of East Pakistan's seats in national elections, in early 1971 Pakistani troops arrested party leader Sheikh Mujibur Rahman **(shake MOO-jee-bur RAH-mun)** (1920–1975). Hoping to crush Awami League support, troops opened fire on university dormitories and Hindu homes, causing hundreds of casualties.

Inspired by Sheikh Mujibur, the Awami League then declared independence. In response, West Pakistani troops poured into East Pakistan, terrorizing the Bengalis with massacres, arson, and rape. At least half a million Bengalis died, and the civil war caused ten million desperate, starving refugees to flee to India. World opinion turned against Pakistan. India appealed for support of East Pakistan, armed Bengali guerrillas, and, after an ill-advised Pakistani attack on Indian airfields, sent troops into both West and East Pakistan, rapidly gaining the upper hand. Meanwhile, Pakistan received military aid from China and the United States. By the end of 1971 Pakistani troops in Bengal had surrendered to Indian forces, and the Awami League, led by Sheikh Mujibur, established a new nation, Bangladesh (Bengali Nation) (see Map 31.1).

KEY POINTS

▶ After World War II, when majority Muslim Pakistan broke off from majority Hindu India, widespread religious violence broke out and a dispute over the territory of Kashmir set the stage for continued tension between the two countries.

▶ Nehru attempted to expand the rights of women and, through a mix of capitalism and socialism, vastly increased India's industrial and agricultural output, but the population expanded at a dangerously rapid rate and not all policies were successful.

▶ Nehru's daughter, Indira Gandhi, was prime minister for over a decade, but she treated her opposition harshly and was assassinated in the midst of clashes between Hindus and Sikhs, and her son and successor, Rajiv Gandhi, was also assassinated.

▶ East and West Pakistan were divided along ethnic lines, and a military crackdown on a Bengali nationalist party led to a bloody civil war in which India intervened on behalf of East Pakistan, which then became a separate country, Bangladesh.

31-2 South Asian Politics and Societies

SOCIETIES　TRANSITIONS　NETWORKS

Q What have been the major achievements and disappointments of the South Asian nations?

Each South Asian society forged its own political role. With 1.37 billion people by 2019 and 65 percent of the subcontinent's land, the Republic of India rose to regional dominance. In the 1990s economic liberalization stimulated growth, but in the years that followed growing Hindu nationalism, which advocates a Hindu nation ("Hindutva") based on a Hindu culture and way of life, has successfully challenged Congress Party domination, threatening its secular vision. Meanwhile, India's neighbors have struggled to achieve stability and economic development. Both Pakistan and Sri Lanka have experienced persistent political turbulence

CONNECTION to TODAY

What features of South Asian societies and cultures do you find the most interesting?

and ethnic violence, while India and Pakistan remain wary, building up military forces and nuclear weapons for possible use against the other. In each South Asian nation, ancient customs exist side by side with modern machines and ways of living.

31-2a Indian Politics and Economic Change

When India celebrated its fiftieth jubilee of independence in 1997, the president reminded his people that India's challenge was to achieve economic growth with social justice. India has generally been unable to mount the sort of concerted attack on mass poverty found in China. However, Indians have maintained one of the few working multiparty democracies outside

Awami League A Bengali nationalist party that began the move for independence from West Pakistan.

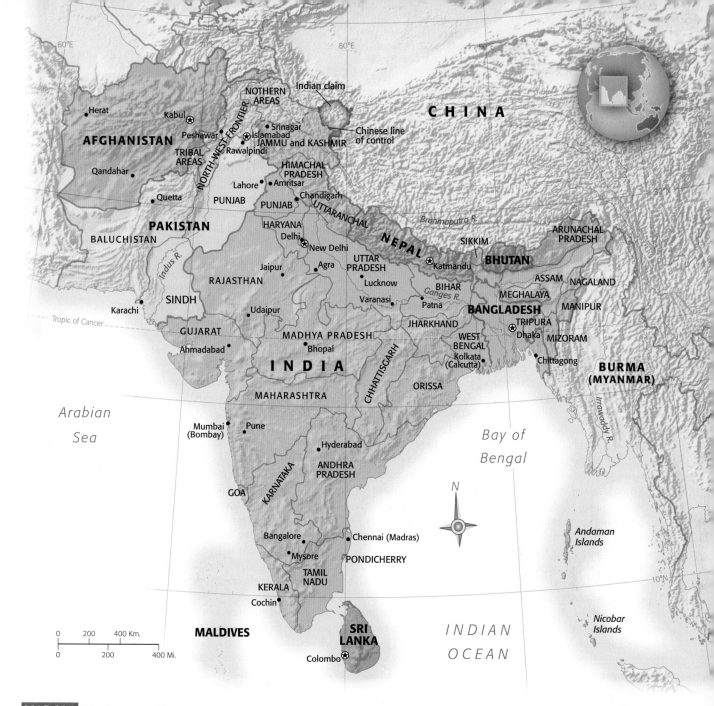

Map labels:

60°E • 70°E • 80°E • 90°E

CHINA

Indian claim

NOTHERN AREAS
Herat
Kabul
Peshawar
Srinagar
Islamabad
JAMMU and KASHMIR
Chinese line of control
AFGHANISTAN
NORTH-WEST FRONTIER
Rawalpindi
TRIBAL AREAS
HIMACHAL PRADESH
Qandahar
Lahore
Amritsar
Chandigarh
Quetta
PUNJAB
PUNJAB
UTTARANCHAL
NEPAL
Brahmaputra R.
ARUNACHAL PRADESH
PAKISTAN
HARYANA
SIKKIM
BALUCHISTAN
Delhi
New Delhi
Katmandu
BHUTAN
ASSAM
NAGALAND
UTTAR PRADESH
Jaipur
Agra
BIHAR
MEGHALAYA
MANIPUR
Indus R.
RAJASTHAN
Lucknow
Ganges R.
BANGLADESH
Karachi
Varanasi
Patna
TRIPURA
SINDH
Dhaka
MIZORAM
Tropic of Cancer
GUJARAT
MADHYA PRADESH
JHARKHAND
WEST BENGAL
Chittagong
BURMA (MYANMAR)
Ahmadabad
Bhopal
Kolkata (Calcutta)
INDIA
CHHATTISGARH
ORISSA
Irrawaddy R.
MAHARASHTRA
Arabian Sea
Mumbai (Bombay)
Pune
Bay of Bengal
Hyderabad
N
ANDHRA PRADESH
Andaman Islands
KARNATAKA
GOA
Bangalore
Chennai (Madras)
Mysore
PONDICHERRY
Nicobar Islands
10°N
TAMIL NADU
KERALA
Cochin
0 200 400 Km.
0 200 400 Mi.
MALDIVES
SRI LANKA
INDIAN OCEAN
Colombo

MAP 31.1 **Modern South Asia** India, predominantly Hindu, is the largest South Asian nation and separates the two densely populated Islamic nations of Bangladesh and Pakistan. Buddhists are the majority in Sri Lanka, just off India's southeast coast. The small kingdoms of Bhutan and Nepal are located in the Himalayan mountain range.

Q How does this map of South Asia differ from a map of early-twentieth-century British India and of sixteenth-century Mughal India?

industrialized nation-states, fostering lively debate and forcing candidates to appeal to voters. An Indian novelist described the campaign rhetoric leading up to elections: "The speeches were crammed with promises of every shape and size: promises of new schools, clean water, health care, land for landless peasants, powerful laws to punish any discrimination."[6] While such grandiose promises usually prove difficult to fulfill, millions of people vote, and changes in state and federal governments have regularly occurred. An Indian Muslim leader contrasted India

favorably with Muslim nations: "In this country there are rights. We can demand our rights, speak out. In other countries: eat, drink, and shut up. Go to Saudi Arabia…Kuwait, Dubai, Iraq, Iran….They are all dictatorships."[7]

Scholars debate whether democracy has fostered national unity by providing a flexible system for accommodating the diverse Indian population or instead intensified differences between groups. Tensions between Hindus and Muslims, between the devout and the secular, and between high-caste and low-caste

[6]Rohinton Mistry, *A Fine Balance* (London: Faber, 1996), 143.
[7]Mufti Shabbir Alam Sidiqi, quoted in Anand Giridharadas, "Once-Clear Thoughts Are Clouded," *New York Times*, June 19, 2009.

Hindus, manipulated by opportunistic politicians, have complicated political life and challenged democratic traditions. While voting has allowed the poor to put pressure on elites, elites can manipulate the system to preserve their privileges. Critics contend that democracy functions as a safety valve for popular frustration, creating the illusion of mass participation that prevents the country from attacking caste and class inequalities. Yet, lower-caste voters sometimes force officials to meet their needs, such as by paving pathways in their neighborhoods. And some state-based parties mobilize poor voters and win elections by campaigning against high-caste Hindus. Members of lower castes and Dalits serve in parliament and head state governments; one Dalit became India's president.

The Congress Party remained nationally influential but faced rivals. On the left, several communist parties often dominated politics in West Bengal and in Kerala in the southwest, repeatedly winning elections by promoting modernization and support for the poor. On the right, Hindu nationalist parties had limited success until the 1990s. In southern states various parties representing regional interests generally dominated state governments and joined federal coalitions. These regional parties, often led by local film stars, protected local languages while preserving English, understood by educated people around the country, as a national language. All parties suffered from corruption. But a free press has monitored politics, reporting on protests and violence. In 2005 a television station's investigation of corruption forced several members of parliament to resign, indicating a vibrant democracy. While older politicians still dominated government, by the 2010s some successful parliamentary candidates were younger than forty-five, and the middle class also became more assertive in politics.

Since 1989 Indian politics has become more pluralistic as the secular left declined. The major right-wing Hindu nationalist party, the **Bharatiya Janata Party (BJP)**, gained influence, especially in north India, by espousing hostility to Muslims, who they considered outsiders or foreigners even though most Muslim families had been there for many generations. The BJP also promoted state support for Hindu issues, such as having schools teach Indian history in accordance with Hindu traditions and religious writings. Some Hindu nationalists have made claims, widely debunked, that ancient Indians had modern technology such as airplanes, nuclear weapons, stem cell research, and the Internet. Many scholars ridiculed these claims as an assault on scientific rationality. The BJP slogan, "One Nation, One People, One Culture," confronts the Gandhi-Nehru vision of a tolerant multicultural state. The BJP political campaign rhetoric often reached deep into Indian history, criticizing Muslim dynasties like the Mughals and celebrating ancient Hindu stories such as *The Ramayana*. BJP-supporting Hindu militants demanded that an old Muslim mosque in the northern city of Ayodhya, which they believe is the birthplace of the God Ram, be torn down and replaced with a Hindu temple. Hindu zealots destroyed the mosque in 1992 but ownership of the land remained bitterly contested. In 2019 the Supreme Court ruled in the Hindus' favor. By the late 1990s rising political corruption, violent secessionist movements in border regions, caste conflict,

Bharatiya Janata Party (BJP) The major Hindu nationalist party in India.

and religious hostilities plagued a BJP-dominated regime. Then in 2002 major Hindu–Muslim violence left over one thousand people dead and over 100,000 terrified Muslims, burned out of their cities, huddled in tent camps. In 2004 the Congress, led by Rajiv Gandhi's Italian-born, sari-wearing widow, Sonia Gandhi (b. 1946), a Roman Catholic who met Rajiv when both were students in England, capitalized on disenchantment among the poor and Muslims and, allied with leftist parties, defeated the ruling BJP-led coalition. A Pakistan-born Sikh economist, Manmohan Singh (b. 1932), became the first non-Hindu prime minister in 2004. The Congress government, despite its short-comings, offered help for the poor, such as a controversial food subsidy program. Although India was rocked by a terrorist attack on Mumbai (Bombay) by Pakistani militants and then by the global economic crisis, in 2009 the Congress and Singh won a big electoral victory with strong support from the poor, grateful for increased spending on rural health and education.

However, by 2013, with the Congress government suffering from factionalism, corruption, ineptitude, and various scandals, the BJP regrouped under divisive but charismatic Gujarat chief minister Narendra Modi (b. 1950), a business-friendly free market enthusiast but strong anti-Muslim Hindu nationalist hated by minorities and viewed by critics as a demagogue with a xenophobic message; Modi had many wealthy and middle-class supporters. In the 2014 elections the Congress and the left were overwhelmed by the resurgent BJP and Modi, whose far-right populist, unbridled nationalist, and Hindu supremacist agenda attracted massive support from the Hindu majority, allowing the party to govern without any coalition parties. Using his personal charisma, Modi promised an economic new deal to raise living standards and to promote Hindu values to remake the nation. In 2016 Modi shocked the nation by announcing that, to end corruption, India was getting rid of most of its cash. Everyone was required to exchange or deposit their large bills within weeks or they would be worthless. The policy proved to be a disaster as long lines formed at banks while businesses, starved of payments, crumbled. Soon the government was forced by national chaos to restore the cash economy. The BJP's anti-Muslim crusade continued, as they renamed Indian cities founded by the Mughals such as Allahabad with Hindu names or the names of controversial Hindu nationalist figures. Modi intensified a government drive to take Indian citizenship, voting rights, and property rights away from, and possibly detain and deport, around two to four million Muslims in the far northeastern state of Assam with Bangladesh origins; some were migrants (called "termites" by Modi) but many others are longtime Assam residents or born there. Some BJP leaders called for officially declaring India a Hindu state, a direct repudiation of Gandhi and Nehru's inclusive vision.

Although Modi's economic policies floundered and social tensions simmered, and the BJP's anti-Muslim rabble-rousing, sporadic attacks on lower caste and Dalit people and lynchings of many Muslim cattle traders caused unease, Modi and his party were massively reelected in 2019 against a fragmented opposition. In 2019, without any democratic deliberation, Modi revoked the special status of the predominantly Muslim state of Kashmir and Jammu (and its twelve million people) in the far northwest; border tensions and occasional skirmishes with

Pakistan, as well as sometimes violent Kashmiri movements for independence or joining Pakistan, have troubled the region for years, leading to the presence of thousands of Indian troops. Modi's order led to the suspension of Kashmiri political and civil rights. As soldiers patrolled the streets, several thousand Kashmiris (including most state political leaders) were arrested, the Internet and cell phone service were shut down, and Modi hinted that he may encourage large-scale Hindu migration to the state, upsetting the delicate balance. Critics considered this the Modi government's darkest moment, a symbolic victory over Islam and a prong in the effort to make India a more Hindu nation. Modi remained hugely popular including among the large Indian diaspora. However, many liberal and secular Indians, pointing to disruptive policies, social instability, and increased BJP direct or indirect influence over the media and education, worried that India was becoming less democratic and multicultural, more authoritarian, and less respectful of civil rights and liberties. Some worried about a new dark age. While many Indians celebrated Modi's policies, critics argued that the BJP is failing to live up to the nation's founding ideals since India's secular constitution guarantees freedom of religion to maintain a robust democracy.

India has struggled to resolve economic backwardness, skyrocketing population growth, and crushing poverty for the majority. While Nehru's dream to end ignorance, poverty, and inequality of opportunity has not been fully realized, Indians can boast of many gains, especially after India changed directions economically in the 1970s. In 1956 India had to import vital foodstuffs and manufactured goods. Twenty years later it exported grain and, by 2000, made and exported its own cars, computers, and aircraft. By the 2010s India became a leader in making electric vehicles, including putting a million electric rickshaws on the streets that carry some sixty million people a day. In 2008 India sent its first robotic moon mission, which spotted evidence of water ice. In 2019 India launched a more ambitious mission to land at the Moon's south pole; the mission failed but it indicated the nation's will and technological skill to become a space explorer. Furthermore, India now grows enough wheat and rice to feed the entire population. The per capita income has grown from $200 in 1947 to about $2,200 in 2019. To spur faster growth, Indian leaders pursued reform, deregulation, and liberalization. While GDP growth averaged 6.2 percent from 1951 until 2019, it is estimated to grow perhaps 5 to 5.9 percent in 2019, a decline from 8 percent in 2018 when India was the world's fastest-growing large economy. The recent economic downturn has cost jobs. India has the world's fourth largest auto industry but it has laid off about 350,000 workers in 2019 as car sales dropped 30 percent. They join the 8.4 percent of workers already unemployed. The causes of the economic ills include a declining agricultural sector and the global economic slowdown driven by rising oil prices and the impact of the U.S.–China tariff and trade war.

Several cities, especially Bangalore and Mumbai, have become high-tech centers closely linked to global communications. Hundreds of North American and European companies, taking advantage of a growing, educated Indian middle class, especially university graduates fluent in English, have moved information and technical service jobs, such as call-in customer service and computer programming, from North America and Europe to India. Chennai (Madras), India's Detroit, ships small Fords, Nissans, and Hyundais to Africa, Europe, and Latin America. India's boom has prompted thousands of highly educated Indians living abroad to return and join its high-tech sector, often moving into spacious, newly built California-style suburbs with names like Ozone and Lake Vista. However, slower economic growth revealed structural limitations and demoralized the new middle class; unlike China or South Korea, India relies on a small skilled labor pool for call centers and high-tech jobs rather than a vast cheap, unskilled labor pool for manufacturing. And both cities and rural areas faced a growing water crisis as global temperatures rise, rains falter, groundwater sources are depleted, urbanization intensifies, and the population grows. Several major cities including Chennai (with nine million people), Delhi, and Bangalore already face severe water shortages that affect (and sometimes close) schools, businesses, hospitals, hotels, restaurants, and whole neighborhoods. At the same time rising sea levels threaten some coastal regions.

Persisting social, economic, and regional inequalities have prevented equitable food distribution. Hence, when inadequate monsoon rains cause severe drought, millions of poor farmers lose income. In 2018 some forty thousand subsistence farmers and landless peasants marched to Mumbai (Bombay) to focus public attention on the plight of tens of millions of poor rural people, who have experienced a two-decades-long agrarian crisis. Many of the marchers could not afford shoes so they wrapped their feet in tape to prevent blisters. With declining incomes many cannot afford seeds, fertilizer, and pesticides, whose distribution is mainly controlled by big, profit-hungry corporations. Climate change and too little or too much rain and water challenges their survival. Suicides among desperate, often deeply indebted small farmers, especially men, are common. Between 1991 and 2011 fifteen million people left farming. Some migrated to look for jobs in towns and cities while others joined the growing number of landless agricultural laborers. Despite the economic revival and a growing middle class—some 200 to 300 million people today—many Indians have yet to enjoy its fruits.

Compared to that of China, Malaysia, and South Korea, India still has many people left behind in poor living conditions. By the early 2010s some 25 percent (including 50 percent of children under age five) lacked an adequate diet, and half earned less than $1.25 per day. While China nears universal literacy, only 75 percent of Indians today can read and write. Despite laws against it, millions of children under age twelve, mainly girls, work full time. There has also been progress. Between 2005 and 2017 the number of people in desperate poverty fell steeply from 640 million to 366 million. Some 70 percent of households had access to electricity in 2007; by 2017 the number had improved to 93 percent. Although population growth is slowing, experts expect India to surpass China as the world's largest country by 2025, posing additional challenges because population growth eats away at national resources. Ironically, success in doubling life expectancy contributes to overpopulation, which causes overcrowded cities, lack of pure drinking water and adequate sanitation, and insufficient primary health care. India has half as many physicians per population and over twice as much infant mortality as China; Chinese live ten years longer

IMAGE 31.3 **Global Communications** A workroom in one of the hundreds of call centers in Indian cities such as Bangalore and Mumbai (Bombay). The workers, mostly well educated and fluent in English, field customer service calls from around the world for Western companies, many of them in the financial services, computer, and electronic businesses.

Q What does the photo tell us about the work atmosphere of an Indian call center?

than Indians. Lacking money, millions live in tarp and bamboo shacks in vast slums or sleep on city sidewalks. Many schools are inadequate, staffed by poorly paid teachers. While affluent Indians increasingly buy fancy imported cars to drive along newly built highways, many commuters ride on the roofs of jammed buses and trains. By 2019 India received 23 percent of its total power from renewable energy and the Modi government announced plans to build solar and wind power projects along the sun-baked, wind-whipped western border. But India's greenhouse gas emissions already account for 7 percent of global emissions and place India as the third largest emitter after China and the U.S. Experts expected emissions to increase significantly in the next two decades without drastic action. Some cities, especially Delhi, sporadically experience toxic air and smoke pollution, leaving residents gasping and their eyes burning.

The stark contrasts between modern and traditional sectors have produced development amid underdevelopment, raising questions as to who benefits from the changes. The "haves" can afford services that strapped governments cannot provide—good schools, clean water, decent health care, efficient transport, gated communities; ambitious birth control campaigns enjoy success in cities but less in the countryside. The Green Revolution has increased output but mostly benefits big landowners, who can afford the large investments in tractors and fertilizers, while per capita calorie consumption remains well below world averages. Because Indian governments have been largely unable or unwilling to challenge powerful landlords, half the rural population has become landless. Poverty fosters growing urban crime and rural banditry, and Maoist guerrillas challenge local police in some impoverished districts.

Economic growth and poverty also ravage the environment as cities encroach on farmland and villagers cut down trees for firewood. As in China, poor peasants protest, often violently, against governments for taking their land to build factories, often foreign-owned, and highways. The Chipko forest conservation movement, based on traditional and Gandhian principles and led mostly by women, is one of many groups working to protect the environment. A Chipko leader, the globe-trotting Sunderlal Bahuguna (**SUN-dur-LOLL ba-hoo-GUN-a**), stresses the place of people in the larger web of nature.

David Pearson/Alamy Stock Photo

31-2b Indian Societies and Cultures

In his will, Jawaharlal Nehru asked that his ashes be scattered in the Ganges River because it symbolized India's millennia-old culture, ever changing and yet ever the same. Ancient traditions have persisted but also been modified, especially in modern cities, where contrasts with villages, where 70 percent of Indians live, remain stark. The growing urban middle class enjoys the recreations and technologies, from golf to video games, that are available to the affluent worldwide. As young people move around the country, often on the new national highway system, they identify less with their home region and more with India, becoming cosmopolitan. Whether living in Punjab, Calcutta, or Bangalore, educated urban young people often like the same music and buy the same consumer goods. Conservatives fumed but many urbanites cheered when in 2009 Indian courts struck down laws against homosexuality, holdovers from British colonial times; other courts reinstated them in 2013, outraging those who embrace modern social change and igniting debates about cultural traditions and Western influence. In 2018 India's Supreme Court decriminalized LGBTQ behavior but many gays and lesbians, especially outside the big cities, have still faced social discrimination and disapproval rather than full acceptance.

Practices that ensure strict divisions between castes, such as avoiding physical contact or sharing food, are harder to maintain in cities than in villages. While city people often pay attention to caste, their approach to preserving it is different. Hence, many high-caste families place classified ads in national newspapers seeking marriage partners from similar backgrounds for their children, as in this example: "Suitable Brahman bride for handsome Brahman boy completing PhD (Physics). Write with biodata, photograph, horoscope."[8] Meanwhile, caste remains more firmly rooted in villages. At the bottom, untouchables (Dalits), some 20 percent of Indians, still live difficult lives, especially in villages, even though government policies to improve their status have enabled some low-caste people to succeed in high-status occupations or politics. But poor Muslims complain that they do not have access to the affirmative action programs that have helped lower-caste Hindus. The grooves of tradition run deep, particularly in rural areas; changes can bring demoralization and disorientation as well as satisfaction.

Modern life has hastened the breakup of traditional joint families, where parents lived in large compounds with their married and unmarried children and grandchildren; smaller, nuclear families have become more common. Most marriages are still arranged, but some seek family approval after selecting their own spouses. New forms of employment causing family members to move to other districts or countries have undermined family cohesion. A traditional preference for male babies continues. Today the ability of technology to determine the sex of a fetus allows many Indians preferring male children to terminate pregnancies. Experts worry that a gender-imbalanced population will experience increasing social problems.

Nehru had believed that India could progress only if women played a full part. New laws banned once-widespread customs such as polygamy, child marriage, and sati, and female literacy rose from 1 percent in 1901 to 54 percent in 2010. But some changing customs have penalized women. The requirement that new brides provide generous dowries to their in-laws, once restricted to higher castes, has become common in all castes. As a result, some families banish, injure, or kill young brides whose own families have failed to supply the promised dowries. Domestic violence and rape, including vicious and often murderous gang rapes, are also major problems. Notions of women's rights, common in cities, are less known in villages; some villages send spies to monitor young women who migrate to cities and report on their transgressions of tradition, shaming their families. In some towns police harass unmarried couples in public parks for public displays of affection; even in Bangalore, where many educated women work in high-tech jobs, conservatives sometimes harass young women who go with friends to bars and discos. One young woman complained that "India is going through a very confused phase. There are many cultures coming at us. . . . But we don't all have to wear a sari every minute of the day."[9] Furthermore, few politicians address women's issues and gender violence in their campaigns. Some politicians blame women for any violence they experience.

Nevertheless, many Indian women have benefited from education, even becoming forceful leaders in such fields as journalism, business, trade unions, and the arts. Women have been elected to parliament, are guaranteed one-third of seats on village governments, and serve as chief ministers of states. In 2009 the Congress Party challenged tradition by naming a Dalit woman, former diplomat Meira Kumar, as parliament speaker. An antipatriarchy women's movement has grown for a century. The Self-Employed Women's Association, founded by Ela Bhatt in 1972, provided low-cost credit and literacy training to some of the poorest city women: the rag pickers, in-home seamstresses, and sidewalk vendors. Outside big cities, however, women have remained largely bound by tradition, expected to demonstrate submission, obedience, and absolute dedication to their husband. Women's organizations affiliated with the Hindu nationalist BJP emphasize women as mothers who produce sons and portray Muslim men as a threat to them. AIDS has rapidly become a female health problem, due largely to women being forced into prostitution to serve the sexual needs of increasingly mobile male workers such as long-haul truckers.

Religion plays a key role in Indian life. Although Hindus form a large majority (80 percent), India's population also includes one hundred-eighty million Muslims (15 percent), over twenty million Sikhs (2 percent), some twenty million Christians, nine million Buddhists (1 percent), and 4.5 million Jains (.5 percent). In 1998 a middle-class pilgrim at a major Hindu festival explained the passion for ancient rituals: "Our technological know-how is very well, but our ancients were understanding things much better. . . . Something is there. . . which is hidden; which I may not be able to prove technically, but which I know to be there in my soul."[10] One ancient Hindu

---

[8]Quoted in Susan Bayly, *Caste, Society and Politics in India from the Eighteenth Century to the Modern Age* (New York: Cambridge University Press, 1999), 315.

[9]Quoted in Emily Cox, "A Rising Anger in India's Streets," *Washington Post*, May 1, 2009.

[10]A. K. Sharma, quoted in John F. Burns, "Ancient Hindu Festival Thrives in Computer-Age India," in *Global Studies: India and South Asia*, ed. James H. K. Norton, 4th ed. (Guilford, CT: Dushkin-McGraw-Hill, 1999), 178.

practice, yoga, has transcended its origins as a meditation vehicle to become a global phenomenon with perhaps 200 to 300 million practitioners, often as a form of exercise with little overt spiritual content. The Modi government has encouraged the trend, praising yoga as an aid to health, medicine, arts, and education. However, in India religious differences have become politicized. Polarizing election campaigns sometimes ignite sectarian violence as cynical politicians appeal to religious factions for support. These tensions have been fueled by significant poverty among all religious groups. Some upper-caste Hindus, particularly in the BJP, have used the notion of a Hindu nation to marginalize Muslims and low-caste Hindus. BJP-sponsored pop singers tour villages promoting the Hindutva message and post videos on YouTube. Violent attacks on Muslims by militant Hindus, often fundamentalists who interpret ancient Hindu religious texts literally, have caused political crises. Sometimes Muslims have initiated the violence. In 2006 Muslims protesting Danish cartoons offensive to Muslims rioted, attacking Hindu and Western targets. Yet, Muslims occupy high positions in government, business, and the professions and play key roles in cultural expression, such as film and music. India's most famous modern artist, Tyeb Mehta (1925–2009), was a Shi'ite Muslim whose works, much of which address the Hindu–Muslim divide, sell all over the world. Yet, art can stir controversy. Many Indian galleries refuse to show the works of another acclaimed Muslim artist, Maqbool Fida Husain, because some of them depict Hindu goddesses in the nude. Polarizing election campaigns sometimes ignite sectarian violence as cynical politicians appeal to religious factions for support. These tensions have been fueled by significant poverty among all religious groups.

Indians have eagerly embraced modern cultural forms. Indian-born novelists such as Arundhati Roy (**AH-roon-DAH-tee roy**) and Salman Rushdie achieved worldwide fame. India has also built the world's largest film industry, making about a thousand movies a year, many of them popular among both Indian emigrants and non-Indians in Southeast Asia, the Middle East, Africa, Europe, and the Caribbean. Mumbai's industry, known as **Bollywood**, churns out films in the major north Indian language, Hindi. But other regions make films in local languages, such as Tamil in southeast India. A pioneer actor and director of Bollywood films, Raj Kapoor, was largely responsible for the recognition of Indian cinema in the world (see Meet the People: Raj Kapoor, Bollywood Film Star). Kapoor argued that his films, which cried out against destitution and unequal wealth, found international success because young people in many countries saw in them their own sufferings, strivings, and triumphs over a world in chaos. But after Kapoor the focus in films was often on the angry young man, sometimes a gangster, with women frequently marginalized. But times are changing. Perhaps the most popular Bollywood star of the twenty-first century, Shah Ruka Khan (b. 1965), is a Muslim and a champion of social change, including the equality of women. Known as the "King of Bollywood" and "King Khan," Khan has appeared in more than eighty Bollywood films. In 2019 acclaimed actress

Bollywood The Mumbai film industry.

and feminist Tannishtha Chatterjee contended that Bollywood is undergoing a subtle shift as the work of more Indian women—and more stories about Indian women—are hitting the silver screen. These are positive signs but an overhaul of male dominance in acting, directing, and producing may take time. Many Indian films, especially musicals, portray a fantasy world that enables viewers to forget their problem-filled real world. As one fan explained: "I love to sit in the dark and dream about what I can never possibly have. I can listen to the music, learn all the songs and forget about my troubles."[11] Religious divisions are muted in Bollywood; many leading directors, writers, singers, and stars come from Muslim backgrounds. Because of their superstar status, some film stars move into state and federal politics. Voters in southern India, and more recently north India, have favored local stars as state leaders. But not all films are escapist. In 2019 popular young Bollywood star Ayushmann Khurrana caused a stir with his film *Article 15*, which tackled caste discrimination and sexual violence. Article 15 in the Indian constitution outlaws discrimination on the basis of religion, race, caste, sex, or place of birth but has been widely ignored for decades. Khurrana drew inspiration from public outrage at cases of gang rape and attacks on Dalit families.

31-2c Islamic Societies and Sri Lanka

South Asia's two densely populated Muslim countries, Pakistan and Bangladesh, struggled to develop and maintain stability while alternating between military dictatorships and elected civilian governments. With two hundred-seventeen million people, over 95 percent Sunni Muslims plus small Shia, Hindu, and Christian minorities, speaking some sixty languages, Pakistan had difficulty transforming its diverse ethnic and tribal groups into a unified nation. The longest-serving civilian leader, Zulfikar Ali Bhutto (**zool-FEE-kar AH-lee BOO-toe**) (g. 1971–1977), a Britain- and U.S.-trained lawyer from a wealthy landowning family, pursued socialist policies to help the poor. But, accusing Bhutto of corruption, the army took power and later executed him. Soviet occupation of Afghanistan in 1979 and the resulting Pakistan-supported Islamic resistance (see Chapter 30) brought more U.S. military aid to Pakistan and strengthened the military role in government. Bhutto's Oxford-educated daughter, Benazir Bhutto (**BEN-ah-ZEER BOO-toe**) (1953–2006), challenged the unpopular military regime and became prime minister in 1988, as well as later the first modern Asian leader to give birth to a child while in office. She was respected abroad but, accused of abusing power, was dismissed in 1990. Returning to power in 1993, she failed to resolve critical problems, including growing ethnic conflict and militant Sunni attacks on the small Shi'a and Christian minorities. In 1996 she was once again removed.

In 1999 the military took over and installed as president General Pervez Musharraf (**per-VEZ moo-SHAR-uff**) (g. 1999–2008), whose family had fled to Pakistan during India's partition in 1947. While introducing some economic reforms, he also largely failed to meet the persistent challenges: to halt factional violence, punish corruption, collect taxes from the wealthy, restore economic growth, solve high unemployment,

[11]Quoted in Jeremy Marre and Hannah Charlton, *Beats of the Heart: Popular Music of the World* (New York: Pantheon, 1985), 150.

Raj Kapoor, Bollywood Film Star

Raj Kapoor (1924–1988) was the first real superstar of Indian film, an accomplished actor, director, producer, and all-around showman. Kapoor skillfully combined music, melodrama, and spectacle to create a cinema with huge popular, even international, appeal, especially among the poor. He was born in Peshawar, the son of one of India's most distinguished stage and film actors, Prithviraj Kapoor. The family settled in Bombay in 1929, when the Hindi-language film industry was in a formative stage (Hindi is the major language spoken in north India). At age twenty-two Kapoor entered an arranged marriage to Krishnaji. Although he had romances with actresses, the marriage endured and the couple had five children.

Handsome and vigorous, with a talent for comedy, music, and self-promotion, the young Kapoor formed his own film company in 1948 with hopes of appealing to the common person. Over the next three decades he starred in or oversaw dozens of films, many of them commercially successful. Kapoor's greatest success came during the Nehru years from the late 1940s to mid-1960s, when Indians were optimistic and looked outward. His films, often subtitled in local languages, brought him celebrity all over South Asia and in Southeast Asia, East Africa, the Middle East, the Caribbean, and the Soviet Union. Songs from his films were sung or hummed on streets of cities and small towns thousands of miles from India, and he and his female costars became popular pin-ups in the bazaars of the Arab world and folk heroes in the Soviet lands. Kapoor, like Nehru, believed that an Indian could enjoy foreign products and influences while also remaining deeply Indian. A song from his film *The Gentleman Cheat* in 1955 reflected the hero's transnational identity: "The shoes I'm wearing are made in Japan, My trousers fashioned in England. The red cap on my head is Russian. In spite of it all my heart is Indian."

Fans saw in his characters youth, optimism about life, and revolt against authority, the little man straddling the great divides of wealth and poverty, city and village, sophistication and innocence. For example, in *The Vagabond* (1951) he portrays a rebellious youth and petty thief growing up on the streets, both daring and vulnerable, charming and reckless, surviving by his wits.

Dinodia Photos/Alamy Stock Photo

IMAGE 31.4 Raj Kapoor As the most influential male lead and director in Indian films, Kapoor could attract the top actresses to star in his films. He made many films with Nargis, the two of them shown here in a 1948 musical, *Barsaat*.

Q What can we learn about this Kapoor film from the photo?

The themes of Kapoor's films often touched on social problems or politics. They offered underdog heroes who were poor but also happy. These themes permeated some of his most popular films, such as *The Vagabond*, which broke box-office records in the USSR and the Middle East, where it was dubbed into Arabic, Persian, and Turkish. Like American comedians, especially Charlie Chaplin, Kapoor often portrayed a deglamorized tramp, the little man at odds with the world and hiding his pain behind a smiling face, a figure he thought "had a greater identity with the common man."

Kapoor's romanticism was evident in his sympathetic treatment of women. The heroine, often played by actress Nargis **(NAR-ghis)** (1929–1981), a Muslim, was always a central player in his films. Sometimes Kapoor presented women as strong and without flaws; as was his character's love interest, Nargis, in *The Vagabond*; at other times women were victims, exploited and tormented by religion and tradition. Kapoor argued, "We eulogize womankind as the embodiment of motherhood but we always give our women the worst treatment. They are burnt alive [in sati], treated as slaves [by men]." Yet, Kapoor's films presented sensuous actresses and opened the way to more sexually explicit scenes, shocking social conservatives.

Kapoor's career faded in the 1970s, when his style of romantic hero became old-fashioned. At the time of his death in 1988 he was making a film exploring the taboo subject of love across the India–Pakistan border, between a Hindu and a Muslim. His sons, all actors, tried to keep his banner alive and his grandson, Ranbir Kapoor, is a current heartthrob, but Bollywood moved in new directions, centering stories on men and their challenges rather than balancing strong male–female roles as Kapoor had done.

Reflection Questions

1. Why is Kapoor often credited with spreading Indian film to other countries?
2. What social viewpoints were expressed in his films?
3. Do you think that Kapoor's films could have been popular in your country and community? Are Bollywood films popular there today?

Notes: Quotations from Sumita S. Chakravarty, *National Identity in Indian Popular Cinema, 1947–1987* (Austin: University of Texas Press, 1993), 138, 30; and Malti Sahai, "Raj Kapoor and the Indianization of Charlie Chaplin," *East-West Film Journal* 2, no. 1 (December 1987): 64.

improve the inadequate infrastructure (such as transportation, electricity, and education), reduce rapid population growth (2.3 percent per year), and balance the demands of both militant and secular Muslims. Although Musharraf allied with the United States after the 2001 terrorist attacks and resulting U.S. invasion of Afghanistan, many Pakistanis resented America and the West. While seeking Pakistani help against international terrorism, the United States was reluctant to remove high tariff barriers against Pakistani textiles, which accounts for nearly half of all manufacturing jobs. After popular unrest forced Musharraf out in 2006, Benazir Bhutto won free elections but was soon assassinated by a Muslim zealot. Since then the government has been besieged by corruption and the rise of a Pakistani Taliban and several terrorist groups, Muslim extremists seeking a rigid theocracy; these tensions have led to terrorist attacks and Taliban-army fighting that has displaced several million refugees. The Muslim League under conservative Nawaz Sharif won the 2013 elections, promising to negotiate with rather than combat extremist groups. But corruption by the Sharif regime led to the election in 2018 of the dashing centrist Imran Khan (b. 1952), a philanthropist and former cricket star who promised change and a "new Pakistan," as prime minister. Khan is an economic liberal but also a populist, nationalist, and devout Muslim who has criticized violent Islamic extremists like the Taliban and harassment of religious minorities. His government also distanced itself from the U.S. and gave more political and economic power to military leaders but has proven unable to effectively address corruption. In late 2019 Khan warned India that its repression in Kashmir could lead to a nuclear confrontation, which might bring a catastrophic bloodbath to both sides.

Pakistani society and culture have remained conservative and deeply divided between Sufis and secular urbanites, generally moderate, and those promoting strict Islamic laws and conduct. People are prosecuted, imprisoned, or sometimes assassinated for violating strict blasphemy laws, while religious groups seen as heretics are harassed and even face violent retribution. Pakistan's cosmopolitan founding leader, Jinnah, had favored more rights for women, arguing that shutting up most Pakistani women in their houses as prisoners was a crime. But leaders sharing this view were reluctant to challenge strong opposition to women's rights, especially in rural areas. In 1979 an Islamizing military government imposed discriminatory laws making rape victims guilty of adultery, a serious offense. Women enjoyed far fewer legal rights than men and were subject to honor killings, acid attacks, rape, forced marriage, and buying and selling. Soldiers attacked women's groups courageously protesting in the streets, prompting feminist poet Saeeda Gazdar (**SIGH-ee-da GAZ-dar**) to write: "The flags of mourning were flapping, the hand-maidens had rebelled. Those two hundred women who came out on the streets, were surrounded on all sides, besieged by armed force, [repressed by] the enemies of truth, the murderers of love."[12]

Things have improved little over the years: only 16 percent of adult women are employed outside the home, and fewer than 20 percent are literate. In some districts Islamic militants have succeeded in restricting women from voting or from attending school with males. In 2012 brave and outspoken fifteen-year-old Malala Yousafzai (**MA-la-la YOU-sef-ZAI**) was shot in the face for promoting girls' schools, which Muslim extremists opposed. She survived to address the United Nations, saying the assassination attempt gave her new determination and demanding that world leaders provide free education to girls. Like another earlier Pakistani, Mukhtaran Bibi (see Chapter 26), Yousafzai inspired millions around the world. But liberal activism remained controversial. In 2019 Gulalai Ismail, a prominent women's rights activist and critic of Pakistan's human rights abuses, fled to the U.S. after facing arrest by the government for reporting rapes and abuse of many women by soldiers.

Repression exists in other areas as well. Attempts by Islamic leaders to prohibit broadcasting of music by popular singers, especially women such as disco-oriented, London-based Nazia Hassan, have fostered an ongoing debate about Westernized popular culture and women entertainers. A lively bootleg industry has provided often-banned Bollywood videos to fans. Pakistan also remains a land of villages dominated by large, politically influential landowners. Although life expectancy improved from forty-three to sixty-seven years between 1960 and 2019, 20 percent of Pakistanis and 30 percent of children suffer from malnutrition. With far too few public schools, many Pakistani youngsters attend Islamic madrasahs with narrow religious curriculums that teach few usable skills for the modern economy.

Bangladesh, overcrowded and densely packed with one hundred sixty-three million people, has also encountered barriers to development. The mostly flat land is prone to devastating hurricanes, floods, tornados, famine, and rising sea levels due to global warming. Sheikh Mujiber Rahman hoped the nation he founded—secular, democratic, and socialist—would rapidly progress, but he was assassinated by the military. None of the governments after him, military or civilian, have succeeded in resolving many problems, and all have suffered from corruption. Several leaders have been assassinated. After 1991 democracy became the main pattern, with the two largest parties led by women. Conservative, pro-capitalist Khaleda Zia (**ZEE-uh**) (g. 1991–1996, 2001–2006), widow of an assassinated leader, heads one party, while left-leaning Sheikh Hasina Wajed (**shake ha-SEE-nah WAH-jed**) (g. 1996–2001, 2009–), daughter of Sheikh Mujiber Rahman, leads the Awami League. Sheikh Hasina, who promoted education, women's empowerment, and better relations with India and Pakistan, herself escaped an assassination attempt in 2004. The two women, bitter rivals, have alternated as the nation's prime minister. In 2013–2014 the feud between the two parties intensified after Sheikh Hasina's government executed several militant Muslims after controversial war crimes trials for assisting Pakistan's invasion in 1971, leading to rioting, strikes, protests, and the Khaleda Zia-led opposition's boycott of national elections. In response, Sheikh Hasina, easily reelected thanks to the boycott, arrested some opponents, raising questions about the future of democracy in the bitterly polarized nation. However, human rights

---

[12]Quoted in Bose and Jalal, *Modern South Asia*, 232.

abuses increased under the Hasina administration, especially enforced disappearances of critics and opposition activists. Some 750,000 Bengali-speaking Rohingya refugees who took shelter in southeastern Bangladesh in 2016–2017 amid a military crackdown in neighboring Myanmar live precariously in overcrowded, squalid, and tightly controlled refugee camps with no jobs, resources, or prospects for a better future. Those Rohingya who remain in Myanmar live no better, with few rights. In 2019 the government announced plans to move most of the Rohingya to a flood-prone Bay of Bengal island often ravaged by violent storms. The 2018 Bangladeshi general election, won by Sheikh Hasina and the Awami League, was marred by allegations of widespread vote rigging, which brought criticism from foreign observers. Bangladeshi dissidents bemoaned the continuing decline of democracy.

Despite political turbulence, however, Bangladesh has pioneered programs to eliminate poverty and educate children. Due to strong domestic demand, Bangladesh also emerged as one of the world's fastest-growing economies. The Grameen Bank, which gives small loans, particularly to poor women, for starting a village business, has helped millions, earning world attention (see Chapter 26). Visionary activist Fazle Hasan Abed launched a movement to improve rural life through forming cooperatives. Bangladesh also developed a huge garment industry, with the world's lowest-paid labor force, serving many Western companies, accounting for three-fourths of export earnings; but over the years some poorly constructed factories have collapsed or caught fire, killing hundreds of workers. Despite the progress including declining poverty rates, some 10 percent of people still live below the international extreme poverty line.

Social and cultural issues have divided Bangladesh, which is officially a secular state with a large Hindu minority (10 percent). Historically Bengalis incorporated Hindu and Buddhist influences as well as Sufi mysticism, creating a tolerant Islam, but militant movements seeking an Islamic state gained strength in the 1990s, heightening divisions. Allied with Khaleda Zia's party, militants restricted women's rights. Public universities required women students to return to their dormitories by sunset to protect their chastity. Zia's government also prosecuted feminist writers such as medical doctor-turned-novelist Taslima Nasreen (b. 1962), who criticized religion and a conservative culture for holding Bengali women back, arguing that the basic division was between modern, rational values and irrational, blind faith. Muslim militants condemned Nasreen's writing as blasphemy against Islam, a capital offense. Nasreen fled to Europe to escape death threats. Since 1975 Bangladesh has improved gender equality, health, renewable energy, poverty rates, literacy (73 percent in 2018), and food production while doubling per capita income and reducing population growth. Yet, conflict and instability continue to plague the country. Responding to growing Islamist pressures to enforce blasphemy laws, the government sporadically arrested "atheist" bloggers and introduced limitations on social media.

Sri Lanka shares problems of ethnic conflict and poverty with its neighbors but has generally maintained a democracy, although sometimes shaky. In 1948 the Sinhalese, some 75 percent of the nation's twenty-one million people and mostly Theravada Buddhists, negotiated independence from Britain, inheriting a colonial economy based on rubber and tea plantations. Sinhalese-dominated governments discriminated against the language and culture of the major ethnic minority, the mostly Hindu Tamils. In 1959 Sirimavo Bandaranaike **(sree-MAH-vo BAN-dar-an-EYE-kee)** (1916–2004), widow of an assassinated leader, became the world's first woman prime minister. Her enemies derided her as a "kitchen woman" who knew all about cooking but nothing about running a country; yet she dominated politics in the 1960s and 1970s.

Successive governments promoted Sinhalese nationalism while sponsoring textile and electronics manufacturing to reduce dependence on cash crop exports. While socialist policies discouraged free enterprise, they fostered high literacy rates (93 percent), high per capita income (nearly $4,300), free education, and, by providing rice and free medical care to the poor, South Asia's longest lifespan (seventy-eight). Like India, Sri Lanka, with many English speakers, attracted outsourcing jobs by the 2000s. In 1983 some Tamils seeking independence for their northern and eastern region began a rebellion that kept the island in a constant state of tension, with assassinations of top political leaders and communal fighting. In 1994 Chandrika Kumaratunga **(CHAN-dree-ka koo-MAHR-a-TOON-ga)** (b. 1945), Bandaranaike's University of Paris-educated daughter, led her left-leaning party to victory, becoming Sri Lanka's second woman leader, but she narrowly escaped an assassination attempt in 2000.

Meanwhile, nearly sixty thousand people, many innocent civilians, died; 300,000 were displaced; and twelve thousand "disappeared" in twenty years of Tamil–Sinhalese violence. Some Buddhist clergy advocated peace and tolerance; others viewed Hindu Tamils as a threat to Buddhism. In 2009 the Sri Lankan military used brutal tactics, including killing perhaps 40,000 Tamil civilians, to finally defeat the main Tamil insurgent group, bringing hope for peace. Since the war Sri Lanka has become one of the fastest-growing economies of the world. But some Buddhists, led by charismatic monks, have abandoned the traditionally tolerant, pacifist, and peaceful tradition of the religion to embrace militant opposition to other faiths, especially Islam, which they see as an existential threat. Muslims comprise 10 percent of the population; some have reacted to discrimination and harassment by becoming disaffected while a few embraced jihadi views. On Easter Sunday 2019, a small jihadi cell carried out bombings of Christian churches in the capital, Colombo, that killed at least two hundred fifty-nine people, including forty-five foreign nationals, and injured over five hundred people. Promising security, a hardline, anti-Tamil, anti-Muslim, Sinhalese nationalist former general won the 2019 election. These new conflicts combined with bitter political and factional rivalries and an increasingly authoritarian regime, have diminished multiethnic democracy, generated human rights violations, and done little to reintegrate alienated Tamils, making long-elusive national reconciliation even more challenging.

31-2d South Asia in the Global System

Since 1945 South Asian nations have grown in geopolitical and economic stature. Along with China and Brazil, India became a major voice in the G-20 nations. Although Nehru strode the world stage, his successors lacked his international influence. However, India became an advanced technology center, importing high-tech and service jobs from the West, and one of the most industrialized non-Western nations, exporting heavy machinery, steel, and autos while producing consumer goods for local consumption. Some Indians who provide telephone technical support to users of U.S.-made computers receive training in mastering an American accent to facilitate rapport. Even with the global recession of 2008–2009, outsourcing of jobs to India has continued, although some companies now put call centers in Sri Lanka or the Philippines, both with many educated English-speakers. Every year Indian universities, some world class, turn out thousands of talented engineers and computer scientists who have built both homegrown industries and the high-tech "silicon valleys" of North America and Europe. Some of that talent has turned to innovating "green technologies" such as wind power and solar electric cars. In 2019 India launched its first locally built, semi high-speed express train, an important achievement. But its trial run was abruptly disrupted with a typical Indian traffic obstruction: it collided with a cow crossing the tracks.

Experts have debated for years whether India and/or China might eventually compete for world economic leadership with the United States. China is already challenging for the lead but some still think India has the potential. They point to India's many English-speakers, solid financial system, and vibrant democracy as advantages. However, the nation's boom added few jobs and the economy is slowing. Indians worry about China's growing power and ambitions and have sought alliances to contain it. Chinese leader Xi Jinping's 2019 visit to Nepal, a traditional India ally, to promote the Belt and Road Initiative increased the concerns. To become a world power, India needs to contain social tensions; greatly improve its transportation, communication, and education infrastructure; and find ways to better share the wealth and reduce rural poverty. In addition, diminishing water sources as Tibetan glaciers recede with global warming, as well as dam building and water diversion that threaten glacier-fed rivers, pose a danger that requires the affected nations' working together.

South Asian technology and ingenuity have sparked scientific achievements. In 1975 the Indian government launched into orbit its first satellite, named after Aryabhata (OUR-ya-BAH-ta), a major Indian scientist and mathematician over fifteen hundred years ago, and in 2013 it announced an unmanned mission to Mars. In 1998 India tested its first nuclear bomb. In response to the regional arms race, Pakistan also developed nuclear weapons, sparking international worries because Islamic militants, some with possible links to global terrorist networks, influence Pakistan's military and local and national politics. In 2004 a top Pakistani nuclear scientist admitted selling nuclear secrets to other nations.

Global and regional politics has intensified Indian–Pakistani rivalries. After 2001, when U.S. president George W. Bush justified preemptive military attacks against potential threats, ordering U.S. forces into Afghanistan and Iraq, some Indians wondered why India should not preemptively attack Pakistan: "If the United States can fly its bombs 10,000 miles to hit terrorist bases [in Afghanistan], why should India wait to knock out Pakistan's [military] bases?"[13] But while India–Pakistan relations have remained combustible, after 2000 Indian and Pakistani leaders promoted a thaw and visited each other's countries, fostering cross-border visits and sports competitions and giving hope that tensions might diminish. However, the Afghanistan conflict spilled over into Pakistan, and Islamist groups flourish among conservative Pashtuns in the tribal regions bordering Afghanistan, which was never under firm government control. Over time Islamists have extended their influence beyond the tribal areas and threaten more violence in Kashmir, alarming moderate Muslims, India, and the United States. And the BJP government in India, with its Hindu-supremacy vision, has increasingly taken a more hostile policy toward Pakistan, an effort reinforced by the suspension of state rights in Muslim-majority Kashmir and removing citizenship from many Muslims in Assam.

South Asians have made distinctive contributions to world politics. Although South Asia has maintained traditional social patterns and cultural viewpoints, at various times women have led the four major South Asian nations, all democracies some or most of the time, in a striking difference from the preference for male leaders in much of the world. Both Sri Lanka and Bangladesh have elected two different women prime ministers, although all were also from powerful political families. Hence, while women remain disadvantaged, they enjoy more high-level political power than in other nations, a part of the great complexity of this region.

KEY POINTS

▶ India's multiparty democracy has endured despite religious and caste tensions.

▶ Despite great advances in agricultural and industrial production, India still suffers from extensive poverty, and its rapidly growing population is likely to perpetuate this problem.

▶ Pakistan has alternated between civilian and military governments and has been slow to grant women equal rights, while Bangladesh has combated poverty in spite of great challenges and has generally accepted religious minorities, though militant Muslim groups have gained influence in recent years.

▶ Since it became independent, Sri Lanka has been a democracy; it elected the world's first woman prime minister, and it has nurtured a well-educated, long-lived population, despite tensions between minority Tamils and majority Sinhalese.

▶ Though women's rights are not universal in South Asia, more South Asian women have achieved positions of great power than in other areas of the world.

[13]Quoted in Stanley Wolpert, *A New History of India*, 7th ed. (New York: Oxford University Press, 2004), 462.

31-3 Revolution, Decolonization, and New Nations in Southeast Asia

TRANSITIONS   NETWORKS

Q What were the causes and consequences of the struggles in Southeast Asia?

The nationalist thrust for independence produced new nations in Southeast Asia after World War II (see Map 31.2). But the euphoria proved short-lived; building states capable of improving the lives of their people had only just begun. Indochina's peoples experienced wrenching violence as France and the United States attempted to roll back revolutionary nationalism. During the First Indochina War (1946–1954), France attempted to maintain control of Vietnam against communist-led opposition but was eventually defeated. In the second and more destructive war, the United States and its Vietnamese allies waged an ultimately unsuccessful fight against communist-led Vietnamese forces, also dragging in Cambodia and Laos. Indonesia, the Philippines, Burma, and the other new nations, while often facing violent unrest, avoided such destructive warfare but also had to overcome economic underdevelopment, promote national unity in ethnically divided societies, and deal with opposition to the new ruling groups. Economic progress but also conflict and dictatorships marked the years between 1945 and 1975. The leaders also had to forge new relationships with the former colonial powers and the new Cold War superpowers—the United States and Soviet Union—as well as with nearby China.

CONNECTION to TODAY

What do you think were the biggest impacts of the French and Americans in Southeast Asia between 1946 and 1975?

31-3a The First Indochina War and Two Vietnams

Anticolonial revolution gripped Vietnam after World War II. In 1945 the Japanese army in southern Vietnam surrendered to British forces moving into southern Vietnam to prepare for a French return to power. Meanwhile, the communist-led Viet Minh that fought the Japanese occupation captured colonial Vietnam's capital, Hanoi, and declared the end of French colonialism. Controlling much of northern Vietnam and parts of the center and south, the Viet Minh-led government, headed by Ho Chi Minh, became the first non-French regime in over eighty years. Addressing a half-million jubilant Vietnamese gathered in Hanoi's main square, Ho quoted the U.S. Declaration of Independence, adding: "It means: All the peoples on earth are equal from birth, all the peoples have a right to live and to be happy and free."[14] Both French and American observers noted that the majority of Vietnamese, especially in the north, supported the Viet Minh.

However, the French, desperate to retain their empire, quickly regrouped and reoccupied southern Vietnam. The Republic of China sent troops to disarm the remaining Japanese in northern Vietnam, alarming the Vietnamese, who feared a permanent presence by their traditional enemy. Using earthy language, Ho told his followers he had to patiently negotiate with the French because sniffing French manure for a while was better than eating China's all their lives. Americans, influenced by Cold War thinking and allied with France, and alarmed at Ho's association with the USSR and communism, shifted from supporting the Viet Minh during World War II to opposing all left-wing nationalists, including Ho and the Viet Minh.

Vietnam remained tense. As Ho negotiated with the French for recognition of Vietnamese independence, he also appealed to U.S. president Harry Truman for political and economic support, receiving no answer. French leaders, with allies among anticommunist Catholics and pro-Western nationalists, were determined to regain domination over all Vietnam. In 1946 Ho warned a French diplomat that a war would be costly and unwinnable: "You will kill ten of my men while we will kill one of yours, but you will be the ones who will end up exhausted."[15] During the First Indochina War (1946–1954) France attempted, with massive U.S. economic and military aid, to maintain its colonial grip. Meanwhile, Americans believed in the domino theory, which predicted a communist sweep through Southeast Asia, and coveted Indochina's resources. A large military force pushed the Viet Minh out of northern cities, but their brutal tactics alienated the population, while in some rural areas the Viet Minh won peasant support by transferring land to poor villagers. The French could not overcome an outgunned but determined foe with a nationalist message. As his forces became bogged down in what observers called a "quicksand war," a French general complained that fighting the Viet Minh was "like ridding a dog of its fleas. We can pick them, drown them, and poison them, but they will be back in a few days."[16] After a major military defeat in 1954, when Viet Minh forces overwhelmed a key French base in the mountains at Dien Bien Phu and took thousands of prisoners, the French abandoned their efforts and negotiated a peace settlement. After digging up the graves of their dead soldiers and dismantling some of the economic infrastructure they had built, they loaded them on ships and went home.

Peace agreements negotiated at a conference in Geneva, Switzerland, in 1954 divided the country into two Vietnams. But while northern, central, and southern Vietnamese spoke different dialects and had some cultural differences, few wanted separate nations. The agreements left the Viet Minh in control of North Vietnam and provided that elections be held in 1956 to determine whether South Vietnamese wanted to join in a unified country. Ignoring the Geneva agreements, which it had not signed, the United States helped install Ngo Dinh Diem (no dinh dee-EM) (1901–1963), an anticommunist and longtime U.S. resident, as South Vietnam's president. Believing the widely respected Ho might win, Diem refused to hold

[14]Quoted in William J. Duiker, *Ho Chi Minh: A Life* (New York: Hyperion, 2000), 323.

[15]Quoted in George Donelson Moss, *Vietnam: An American Ordeal*, 4th ed. (Upper Saddle River, NJ: Prentice-Hall, 2002), 40.

[16]Jacques Philippe Leclerc, quoted in James S. Olson and Randy Roberts, *Where the Domino Fell: America and Vietnam, 1945–1995*, 3rd ed. (St. James, NY: Brandywine, 1999), 28.

MAP 31.2 **Modern Southeast Asia** Indonesia, covering thousands of islands, is the largest, most populous Southeast Asian nation. Southeast Asia also includes four other island nations (including the Philippines and Singapore), five nations on the mainland, and Malaysia, which sprawls from the Malay Peninsula to northern Borneo.

Q How does this map differ from a map of early twentieth-century, colonial-dominated Southeast Asia and of the region in 1200 CE?

reunification elections. Some Vietnamese opposed communist ideology, backing Diem and the United States.

North and South Vietnam differed dramatically. Ho's government built a disciplined state that addressed colonial inequalities, redistributing land from powerful landlords to poor peasants. However, the government's authoritarian style and socialist policies prompted nearly a million North Vietnamese, including many Catholics, to move to South Vietnam, where President Diem, from a wealthy Catholic family, established a government in Saigon. Americans poured in economic and military aid and, to stabilize Diem's increasingly unpopular regime, sent military advisers.

The rigid Diem alienated peasants by opposing most land reform. In 1960 dissidents in South Vietnam, including former Viet Minh soldiers, formed a communist-led revolutionary movement, the **National Liberation Front (NLF)**, often known as the Viet Cong, that was armed by North Vietnam.

Diem responded with repression, murdering or imprisoning thousands of suspected rebels and other opponents. Buddhists resented the Diem government's pro-Catholic policies, while nationalists generally viewed Diem as an American puppet. Meanwhile, the NLF spread their influence in rural areas, assassinating government officials and brutalizing opponents.

By the early 1960s the NLF controlled large sections of South Vietnam, and thousands more American troops, still called military advisers, became more involved in combat. In 1963 U.S. leaders, judging Diem ineffective, sanctioned his overthrow by his own military officers, who killed him. As the situation deteriorated and North Vietnamese troops moved south, U.S. concerns about a possible communist sweep through Southeast Asia generated what Americans called the Vietnam War (1963–1975) and that many Vietnamese called the American War.

31-3b The American–Vietnamese War

In 1964 U.S. president Lyndon Johnson (g. 1963–1969) used an alleged North Vietnamese attack on a U.S. ship in the Gulf of Tonkin, which probably never occurred, to escalate the conflict into a full-scale military commitment (see Map 31.3).

National Liberation Front (NLF) Often known as the Viet Cong, a communist-led revolutionary movement in South Vietnam that resisted American intervention in the American–Vietnamese War.

When Johnson said in 1965, "I want to leave the footprints of America there [Indochina]. We can turn the Mekong into [an economically developed] Tennessee Valley,"[17] he was reflecting a longtime American mission to change the world, spreading democracy and capitalism. However, Johnson and other U.S. leaders, civilian and military, had little understanding of the nationalism and opposition to foreign occupation that shaped many of the Vietnamese, who had many historical reasons for mistrusting foreign powers on "civilizing" missions. Soon the war intensified. In 1965 Johnson ordered an air war against both South and North Vietnam targets and a massive intervention of ground troops, peaking at 550,000 Americans by 1968. The conflict also drew in other outsiders. Small numbers of Australian, South Korean, and Thai troops aided the U.S. effort, while the Soviet Union and China provided North Vietnam with military supplies. However, a series of military regimes never achieved enough credibility with the South Vietnamese majority. Military supplies and North Vietnamese troops regularly moved south through the mountains of eastern Laos and Cambodia, along what came to be called the Ho Chi Minh Trail.

Despite technological superiority, U.S. forces struggled to overcome the communists, often ignoring South Vietnamese leaders and the consequences of military actions; meanwhile, the South Vietnamese army, largely conscripts, proved somewhat ineffective. All sides committed war atrocities and abused civilians and captured soldiers. U.S. strategists measured success by counting the enemy dead and creating free fire zones from which civilians were ordered to evacuate, a strategy that made it hard to win Vietnamese "hearts and minds" and diminish considerable local support for the NLF. Vietnam became the most heavily bombed nation in history; Americans dropped twice the total bomb tonnage used in World War II. In addition, the use of chemical defoliants to clear forests and wetlands, as well as the countless bomb craters, caused massive environmental damage. Thanks in part to the toxic chemicals, Vietnam today has among the world's highest rates of birth defects and cancer.

By 1967 the United States had achieved a military stalemate, but in 1968 the **Tet Offensive**, when communist forces attacked South Vietnamese cities during the Vietnamese new year, proved a turning point. Although the communists were pushed back and suffered high casualties, Tet proved a political and psychological setback for Americans. Meanwhile, for procommunist Vietnamese, the American–Vietnamese War was a continuation of the First Indochina War to expel the French and rebuild a damaged society. When the Viet Minh humbled the hated French colonizers, they gained a popularity the United States could not overcome. The communists also gained peasant support by advocating reforms. Some U.S. policies, especially the air war, which killed thousands of innocent people, backfired. One of the thousands of women NLF fighters reported: "The first days I felt ill at ease—marching in step, lobbing grenades, taking aim with my rifle, hitting the ground. But as soon as I saw the American planes come back [to bomb], my timidity left me."[18] However, many South Vietnamese

supported the pro-U.S. government or rejected both sides. Pham Duy (**fam do-ee**), a folksinger who, like many South Vietnamese, disliked both the corrupt Saigon government and the often ruthless communists, wrote a song describing the war's impact on average Vietnamese: "The rain of the leaves is the tears of joy, Of the girl whose boy returns from the war. The rain on the leaves is bitter tears, When a mother hears her son is no more."[19]

The war, which generated huge budget deficits and other economic problems, bitterly divided Americans; by the late 1960s a majority had turned against the commitment to a seemingly endless quagmire that killed or injured Americans for uncertain goals. The United States began a gradual withdrawal of troops and negotiated peace agreements with North Vietnam. By 1973 U.S. ground forces had left Vietnam, and in 1975 the NLF and North Vietnam defeated the South Vietnamese forces, reunifying the country under communist leadership. Many South Vietnamese fled, over two million eventually settling in the United States. General Maxwell Taylor, former U.S. ambassador to South Vietnam, later concluded that Americans lost because, never understanding the Vietnamese on either side or themselves, they overestimated the effectiveness of U.S. strategies. The devastating war cost the United States fifty-eight thousand dead and 519,000 physically disabled; the Vietnamese lost around four million killed or wounded—10 percent of the total population. After the fighting ended, Vietnam turned to reconstruction.

31-3c War in Laos and Cambodia

Laos and Cambodia became pawns in the larger conflict between the United States and the North Vietnamese. Anticolonial sentiment grew during and after the Japanese occupation. In 1953 France, wearying of its Indochinese experience, granted Laos independence under a pro-French government dominated by the ethnic Lao majority. Cambodia gained its independence under young, charismatic, widely popular Prince Norodom Sihanouk (**SEE-uh-nook**) (1922–2012), who won the first free election in 1955. However, the Vietnam conflict eventually engulfed both countries, in part because of U.S. military interventions.

The U.S. intervention in Laos, which began in the late 1950s and continued until 1975, intensified conflict between three factions: U.S.-backed anticommunist right-wingers, neutralists, and the **Pathet Lao**, revolutionary nationalists allied with North Vietnam. In 1960 right-wing forces advised and equipped by the U.S. Central Intelligence Agency (CIA) seized the Laotian government as fighting intensified. Because the corrupt Laotian regime's U.S.-financed army was ineffective, Americans turned to hill peoples for recruits, among them a large faction of the Hmong.

Tet Offensive Communist attacks on major South Vietnamese cities in 1968, a turning point in the American–Vietnamese War.

Pathet Lao Revolutionary Laotian nationalists allied with North Vietnam during the American–Vietnamese War.

[17]Quoted in Thomas G. Paterson et al., *American Foreign Policy: A History Since 1900*, 3rd ed. rev. (Lexington, MA: D.C. Heath, 1991), 553.

[18]Anh Vien, quoted in Arleen Eisen Bergman, *Women of Vietnam*, rev. ed. (San Francisco: Peoples Press, 1975), 123.

[19]Quoted in Neil L. Jamieson, *Understanding Vietnam* (Berkeley: University of California Press, 1993), 290.

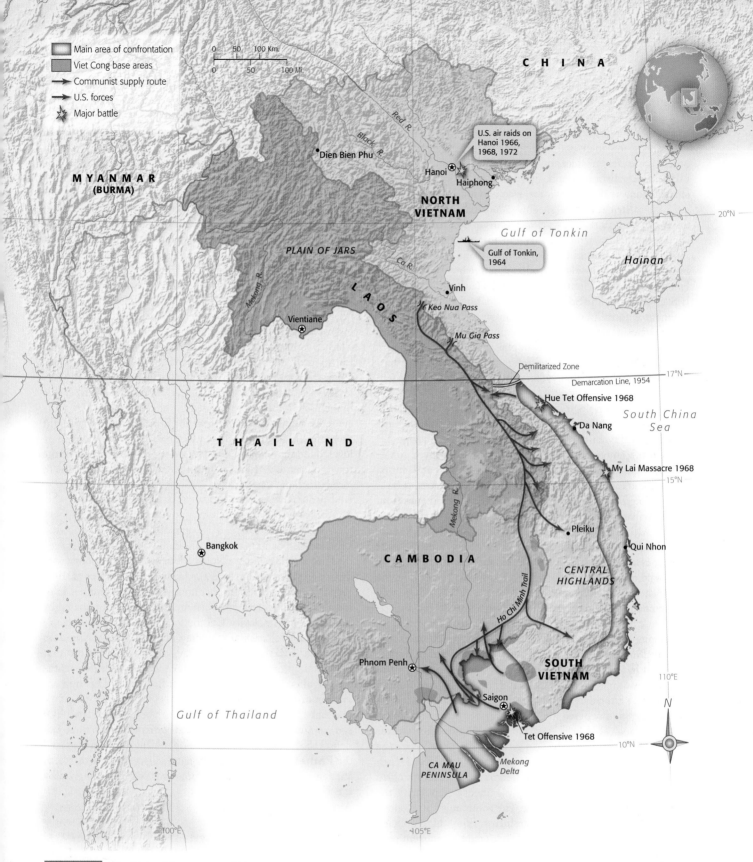

MAP 31.3 **The U.S.–Vietnamese War** From the early 1960s until 1975, South Vietnam, aided by thousands of U.S. troops and air power, resisted a communist-led insurgency aided by North Vietnam, which sent troops and supplies down the Ho Chi Minh Trail through Laos and Cambodia.

Q What can we learn about the war from this map?

Promising permanent support and protection, the CIA recruited a secret forty-five-thousand-man army, largely Hmong, that attacked North Vietnamese forces along the Ho Chi Minh Trail and fought the Pathet Lao. Ten percent of the Hmong population, some thirty thousand people, died during a conflict largely unknown to the American public. At the same time, massive U.S. bombing depopulated large areas, forcing many Laotians into refugee camps; the war killed some 100,000 Laotians. After 1975, when the Pathet Lao took full control of a war-weary Laos, thousands of anticommunist Laotians fled into Thailand, many later moving to the United States and other Western nations.

Cambodia also became embroiled in the Indochina conflict. President Prince Sihanouk ruled as a benevolent autocrat, maintaining peace while also writing sentimental popular songs, playing the saxophone, directing films, and publicizing his political views in foreign newspapers. But both the Vietnamese communists roaming the border area and the U.S. war planes bombing communist positions violated Cambodian neutrality. Sihanouk faced other problems. The **Khmer Rouge** (kmahr roozh) ("Red Khmers"), a communist insurgent group led by French-educated intellectuals seeking to overthrow Sihanouk, built support among impoverished peasants. Although Sihanouk remained popular among many peasants, military officers and big businessmen, resenting dictatorial rule, desired to share in the U.S. money and arms flowing into South Vietnam, Laos, and Thailand.

In 1970 U.S.-backed generals and civilians overthrew Sihanouk, who went into exile in China and North Korea. U.S. and South Vietnamese forces then invaded eastern Cambodia seeking Vietnamese communist bases, creating an opening for the Khmer Rouge to recruit mass support. The pro-U.S. government, dependent on U.S. aid for virtually all supplies, lacked legitimacy, while Cambodia's ineffective army suffered from corruption and low morale. To attack the Khmer Rouge, U.S. planes launched an intensive, terrifying air assault through Cambodia's agricultural heartland, killing thousands of innocent civilians. Rice production declined by almost half, raising the possibility of massive starvation. Amid the destruction, the growing Khmer Rouge recruited the displaced, shell-shocked peasants. From 1970 through 1975, between 750,000 and one million Cambodians, mostly civilians, perished from the conflict between the brutal Khmer Rouge and the brutal U.S.-backed government. In 1975 the Khmer Rouge seized the capital, Phnom Penh, and controlled the country until 1978.

31-3d Indonesia: The Quest for Freedom and Unity

Indonesian independence came through struggle in the late 1940s. During the Indonesian Revolution, the Dutch used massive force to suppress the nationalists, who fought back with great violence. Describing a brutal battle, a nationalist writer noted that, for the revolutionary soldiers, "everything blurred: the future and their heart-breaking struggle. They only knew that they had to murder to drive out the enemy and stop him trampling their liberated land. They killed [the Dutch soldiers] with great determination, spirit and hunger."[20] Some supporters of the revolution, especially writers, had more idealistic goals, such as combining the humane values of East and West shaped by Enlightenment ideals of democracy, tolerance, and free thought. But these cosmopolitan values seemed contrary to the dominant nationalist agenda. The United States, fearing regional instability, pressured the Dutch to grant independence in 1950. In 2017 the Dutch government launched an extraordinary albeit belated inquiry into the nation's violent actions during the revolution, forcing a public assessment of the legacy. They believed that the inquiry could keep alive the promise of justice for millions of other victims of war crimes. In 2019 a Dutch appeals court ruled that a lawsuit brought by five Indonesians who hold the Netherlands responsible for the execution of their fathers by Dutch soldiers in 1947 must be heard. The court said that during the conflict, Dutch soldiers executed opponents without any form of trial and tortured prisoners during interrogations.

Given the diversity of islands, peoples, and cultures, Indonesians still faced the challenge of fostering national unity and identity. Their national slogan, "unity in diversity," expressed more goal than solid reality. During the 1950s and early 1960s, the charismatic but increasingly authoritarian president Sukarno (soo-KAHR-no) (1902–1970) led Indonesia. A spellbinding, inspirational orator able to bring different factions together, Sukarno worked to create national solidarity in a huge nation where villagers on remote islands and cosmopolitan city-dwellers on Java knew or cared little about each other. Sukarno also sought a role on the world stage, sponsoring a major international conference at the Javan city of Bandung in 1955 to shape a Non-Aligned Movement, a middle way between the two rival superpowers.

However, Sukarno could not maintain stability, the multiparty parliamentary system became divisive, and regionalism grew as outer islanders resented domination by the Javanese, who constituted over half of Indonesia's population. A pro-communist Javanese novelist described post-Revolution economic failures in the early 1950s: "Jakarta [the capital city] reveals a grandiose display with no relationship to reality. Great plans, enormous immorality. [There are] no screws, no nuts, no bolts, no valves, and no washers for the machinery we do have."[21] By the early 1960s Sukarno's nationalistic but poorly implemented economic policies had generated a severe economic crisis, deepening divisions between communist, Islamic, and military forces.

By 1965 explosive social and political pressures sparked Indonesia's greatest crisis. After a small, pro-communist military faction's failed attempt to seize power, discontented generals arrested Sukarno, took over the government, and launched, with Muslim groups, a brutal campaign to eliminate all leftists, especially the large Communist Party, which was influential among poor peasants in Java. The resulting bloodbath killed perhaps half a million people, including many members of the unpopular Chinese minority. Thousands of leftists were held in remote prison camps for years. Sukarno died in disgrace in 1970.

> **Khmer Rouge** ("Red Khmers") A communist insurgent group seeking to overthrow the government in Cambodia during the 1960s and 1970s.

[20]From Idrus, "Surabaya," in *From Surabaya to Armageddon: Indonesian Short Stories*, ed. Harry Aveling (Singapore: Heinemann, 1976), 13.
[21]From Pramoedya Ananta Toer, "Letter to a Friend in the Country," in Aveling, *From Surabaya*, 72.

31-3e Making the Philippine and Malaysian Nations

The Philippines and Malaysia both became independent but troubled nations. The Philippines achieved independence on July 4, 1946, and remained closely tied to the United States politically and economically, but it soon faced problems sustaining democracy. A small group of landowners, industrialists, and businessmen manipulated elected governments to preserve their power and protect U.S. economic interests. Free elections involved so much violence, bribery, and fraud that disillusioned Filipinos complained of "guns, goons, and gold" ruling political life. Nationalists believed that the continuing U.S. influence, including several military bases, hindered a truly independent Filipino identity and culture. Referring to popular U.S. films, television programs, music, comics, and books, a prominent scholar wrote that her people "sing of White Christmases and of Manhattan. Their stereos reverberate with the American Top 40."[22] Outside influences on their culture—first Spanish, then American—were often superficial, but Filipinos struggled to create a clear national identity out of diverse local languages and regions.

Economic inequality and social divisions fueled conflict. A leftist Filipino poet portrayed the gap between rich and poor: "[For the affluent] there's pleasure and distraction, fiesta and dancing, night-long, day-long; who dares whisper that thousands have no roofs above their heads; that hunger stalks the town."[23] Only heavy U.S. assistance suppressed the communist-led Huk Rebellion (1948–1954), which capitalized on rural discontent. In the 1970s the communist New People's Army (NPA), promising radical change, controlled many rural districts, supported by rural tenant farmers and urban slum-dwellers. Religious differences have also fostered conflict. While most Filipinos became Christian in Spanish times, Muslims in the southern islands often resented domination by the nation's Christian majority, and several Muslim groups seeking autonomy or secession took up arms. In 1972 President Ferdinand Marcos (1917–1989) suspended democracy, ruling as a corrupt dictator (1972–1986) but resolving few problems.

Malayan governments proved more stable. After World War II communist-led insurgents kept the British colony on edge for a decade. In 1957, with the insurgency crushed, Malaya became independent as a federation of states led by the **United Malays National Organisation (UMNO)**, the main Malay party. However, predominantly Chinese Singapore, a major trading center and military base, remained a British colony. In Malaya the majority Malays, nearly all Muslim, dominated politics, but Chinese, a third of the population, gained liberal citizenship rights and maintained economic power. British leaders, tired of colonial burdens, forged a merger of Singapore, two northern Borneo colonies, Sabah and Sarawak, and Malaya, creating a larger independent but geographically divided federation, Malaysia, in 1963.

Malaysians struggled to create national unity out of deep regional, religious, and ethnic divisions. Singapore

United Malays National Organization (UMNO) The main Malay political party in Malaysia.

withdrew in 1965, becoming independent. To reduce political tensions, sustain economic growth, and preserve stability, the leaders of the key Malayan ethnic groups—Malays, Chinese, and Indians—cooperated through allied political parties in an UMNO-dominated ruling coalition, but below the surface ethnic tensions simmered. Street fighting between Chinese and Malays following the heated 1969 election spurred a nationwide state of emergency. After 1970 Malay-dominated governments pursued policies designed to reshape Malaysia's society and economy while sporadically detaining some dissidents and banning discussion of "sensitive" ethnic relations and religion issues.

31-3f Diversity and Dictatorship in Thailand and Burma

Thailand and Burma (known today as Myanmar) have also struggled to create national unity and stability. Although historical rivals, the two countries have shared some common patterns. The majority Thais (Siamese) and Burmans, both Theravada Buddhists, assert authority over diverse minorities, including including various hill tribes, Malay Muslims in the south, and Chinese. Both countries have also experienced insurgencies by disaffected ethnic, religious, or communist factions.

Thailand's leaders sought to build a national culture based on Thai cultural values: reverence for Buddhism and the monarchy, respect for those in authority, and social harmony. This conservatism fostered authoritarian governments and bureaucratic inertia. Various communist and Islamic insurgent groups operated during the 1960s and 1970s in ethnic minority regions. Thanks partly to unrest, Thai politics was marked by long periods of military rule, often corrupt and oppressive, followed by short-lived democratically elected or semidemocratic governments. In the 1970s opposition movements challenged the long-entrenched military regime. Many Thais also resented the United States, which supported the military regime and had military bases and some fifty thousand troops in the country. Free-spending American soldiers created a false prosperity, outraging staunch Buddhists who hated what they considered the "sleazy" bars, gaudy nightclubs, and brothels Americans patronized that often exploited poor Thai women.

In 1973 antigovernment feelings boiled over, and the military regime was overthrown following massive student-led demonstrations during which soldiers arrested protest leaders and killed or wounded over a thousand demonstrators. The collapse of military rule opened a brief era of political liberalization during which democracy and debate flourished. Progressive writers and musicians promoted what they termed "art for life," often extolling the hardworking peasants. But the fragile civilian government proved unable to resolve major problems. With society polarized between liberals and conservatives, in 1976 bloody clashes between leftist students and right-wing youth gangs sparked a military coup and martial law, during which time hundreds of students and their supporters were killed or wounded and thousands arrested. Although the crackdown reestablished order, the massacres discredited the military.

---

[22]Doreen Fernandez, "Mass Culture and Cultural Policy: The Philippine Experience," *Philippine Studies* 37 (4th Quarter, 1980): 492.
[23]"The Kingdom of Mammon," in Amado V. Hernandez, *Rice Grains: Selected Poems* (New York: International Publishers, 1966), 31.

After the destructive Japanese occupation, the British returned to Burma to reestablish their colonial control. War-weary and facing a well-armed Burmese nationalist army, they negotiated independence with charismatic nationalist leader Aung San (1915–1947) and left in 1948. But newly elected Prime Minister Aung San was assassinated by a political rival, after which U Nu (1907–1995), an idealistic Buddhist and democrat, became leader. Soon ethnic minorities, fearful of Burman (Bamar) domination, declared their secession and organized armies. For several decades the central government rarely controlled more than half the nation's territory as ethnic armies and communist insurgents, funded by opium revenues, battled the Burmese army. In 1962 the army seized control, suspended civil liberties, imposed censorship, claimed most of the government budget, discouraged foreign investment, and took over industries, banks, and commerce. By the 1980s, economic stagnation and political repression had fostered dissent; various secession movements continued, only to be largely suppressed in the 1990s.

KEY POINTS

▶ Using a questionable attack as a pretext, the United States went to war to rid Vietnam of communism, but despite vastly superior resources, the United States and its allies in South Vietnam could not triumph over the communists.

▶ In Laos the United States recruited Hmong hill people to fight the Pathet Lao revolutionaries, who took control of the country in 1975, while in Cambodia the United States bombed areas occupied by North Vietnamese and supported a weak, dependent government, which was overthrown in 1975 by the Khmer Rouge.

▶ After attaining independence, the Philippines remained strongly influenced by the United States and struggled with economic inequality and a Muslim insurgency, while Malaysia experienced intermittent tensions between the politically dominant Malays and the economically strong Chinese.

▶ Thailand alternated between long periods of military rule and short periods of democratic or semidemocratic rule, while Burma endured decades of factional fighting and, since 1962, brutal military domination.

31-4 Tigers, Politics, and Changing Southeast Asian Societies

NETWORKS   SOCIETIES

Q What role do the Southeast Asian nations play in the global system?

Southeast Asia changed dramatically after 1975, mixing influences from the past and from the wider world and reshaping life in both cities and villages. Indonesia, Malaysia, Singapore, and Thailand, with market economies geared to world commerce, gained reputations as dynamic "tigers." Governments stimulated economies and often became authoritarian to ensure social stability. When the fighting ended, the Indochinese had to rebuild their societies shattered by the turmoil. Vietnam eventually developed a tiger economy.

CONNECTION to TODAY

How have the developments since 1975 in Southeast Asian nations affected your community, state, and nation?

---

anti-Chinese violence or legal restrictions. Economic growth also had drawbacks, as the industrial activity and expansion of agriculture, mining, and logging caused widespread environmental destruction and contributed to global warming. Yet, migrants crowding into cities rubbed elbows with other peoples, encouraging cultural mixing. While governments often squashed dissent and repressed personal liberties, expanding education fostered larger middle classes who sought more political influence and fostered civil society institutions concerned with human rights. A vibrant Pacific Rim also included the "tiger" or "dragon" nations: Japan, China, Taiwan, South Korea (see Chapter 27), and eventually Vietnam. For years some have forecast a Pacific Century in which these nations as well as Southeast Asia would lead the world economically and increase their political strength. China has met the expectation so far and the other dragons are still major economic players in the world but Southeast Asians have had mixed results.

31-4a The Resurgence of Southeast Asia

Shifting their economic direction allowed several Southeast Asian nations to play greater roles in the world economy. In 1976, Indonesia, Burma, and Thailand were under military rule, Indochina's communist regimes faced monumental reconstruction, a dictator governed the Philippines, and only Malaysia and Singapore had semidemocracies. Few countries enjoyed impressive economic growth. But in the 1980s, development accelerated. Inspired by Japan's late-nineteenth-century industrialization and rapid recovery from World War II, leaders encouraged their people to "Look East," mixing capitalism and activist government to spur economic expansion. Local entrepreneurs of Chinese ancestry provided much of the initiative and capital. However, resentment by many of Chinese wealth sparked occasional

To promote growth and stability, Southeast Asian countries cooperated as never before. Founded in 1967 by Malaysia, Indonesia, Thailand, Singapore, and the Philippines, the **Association of Southeast Asian Nations (ASEAN)**

Association of Southeast Asian Nations (ASEAN) A regional economic and political organization formed in 1967 to promote cooperation among the noncommunist Southeast Asian nations; eventually became a major trading bloc.

promoted regional economic and political exchange among the noncommunist Southeast Asian nations. However, ASEAN's priorities shifted after the Indochina wars ended. As Vietnam, Cambodia, Laos, Burma, and tiny, oil-rich Brunei became members, ASEAN emerged as the world's fourth largest trading bloc while providing a forum for members to work out differences and deal with the wider world, especially in cultivating relations with China and Japan.

Many challenges remained. A rapidly growing population (six hundred sixty-five million in 2019, 8.6 percent of the world total) outstripped economic growth, burdening limited resources such as food and water, especially in the Philippines, Indonesia, and Vietnam. Half of Southeast Asians live in urban areas. But despite occasional violence, insurgencies, and political upheavals, the destructive earlier wars were not repeated. More open regimes eventually replaced dictatorships in most nations. In 1997 most countries faced a severe economic crisis, part of a broader collapse among Asian and world economies that resulted from poorly regulated banking systems, overconfident investments, and government favoritism toward well-placed business interests. The crisis eventually bottomed out, only to be rekindled in 2008–2009 by the larger world economic downturn, reducing demand for Southeast Asian products, causing massive job losses, slowing foreign investment, and calling into question a forthcoming Pacific Century. Southeast Asia is also one of the regions most threatened by global warming, which may foster erratic rains and will raise sea levels, flooding densely populated river deltas, lowlands, and cities like Hanoi, Bangkok, and Jakarta. In many places sporadic drought and diminishing ground water threaten water supplies. In 2019 Indonesia announced that, given Jakarta's overcrowding (thirty million people), pollution, and sinking, swampy ground, they will build a new capital city in sparsely populated eastern Kalimantan (Borneo). But critics noted that this move and the development that follows may accelerate dispossessing the indigenous Dayak and other peoples there of their lands as well as the destruction of the rain forest. The Thai government also suggested that they may consider moving their capital from Bangkok to a more livable and less threatened location.

31-4b New Orders in Indonesia and the Philippines

Both Indonesia and the Philippines experienced political turbulence and social instability. Indonesia, with more than seven hundred ethnic groups and two hundred seventy-one million people (2019), struggled to preserve political stability while developing economically. Between 1966 and 1998 the **New Order** government, headed by Javanese general-turned-president Suharto (1921–2008), mixed military and civilian leadership while limiting political opposition to maintain law and order. Suharto used force to repress independence movements in East Timor, a small, mostly Christian former Portuguese colony; north Sumatra, dominated by the strongly Islamic Achehnese; and West Irian (western New Guinea). However, the New Order improved Indonesia's economic position and fostered an educated urban middle class. Per capita income, life expectancy, and adult literacy increased, aided by an annual economic growth rate of nearly 5 percent by the 1990s; it remained around 5.0 to 5.2 percent by the late 2010s. Meanwhile, around 10 percent of Indonesians, mostly rural, remained desperately poor, earning less than a dollar a day. Since the 1960s creative musicians, writers, artists, and filmmakers have shaped a vibrant popular culture. For example, critical popular musicians like Islam-influenced Rhoma Irama, who helped create the rock–Arab–Malay folk fusion *dangdut* musical style, and folk rocker Iwan Fals have addressed social and political issues that sometimes challenged the status quo, earning them a mass audience, but have also at times faced official harassment for their songs.

The New Order also started some negative trends. Indonesia became dependent on exporting oil, which constituted 80 percent of foreign earnings. As a result, whenever world oil prices decline, reducing the national budget, Indonesia adds to an enormous foreign debt. The rapid development of mining, forestry, and cash crop agriculture has also badly damaged the environment. Rain forests were clear-cut so rapidly for timber and plantations that forest fires became common, often set by palm oil plantations and other agribusiness companies as well as farmers to clear the land for their own uses, polluting the air and creating a thick, unhealthy haze that spread into neighboring nations. In 2019 dozens of schools in Malaysia and Singapore were temporarily closed, and life as usual became difficult, for many weeks because of the smoke drifting in from some two thousand out-of-control fires burning in Indonesia. Meanwhile, income disparities between classes and regions widened while political and business corruption thrived. One Indonesian fiction writer satirized government officials and predatory businessmen soliciting bribes and grabbing public funds for themselves: "Indonesia, Land of Robbers. My true homeland stiff with thieves. In the future, I shall plunder while my wife shall seize."[24] The wealthy frolicked in nightclubs, casinos, and golf courses built across the street from slums or on land appropriated from powerless villages. Suharto, the son of poor peasants, became one of the world's most corrupt leaders, his family acquiring over $15 billion in assets from their business enterprises and access to public coffers.

Islam provided the chief vehicle for opposition to the New Order. Some 87 percent of Indonesians are either devout or nominal Sunni Muslims, but until recently few have supported militant Islamist movements. Given the large Christian and Hindu minorities, Suharto discouraged Islamic radicalism as a threat to national unity. However, devout Muslims have often opposed secular policies; desiring a more Islamic approach to social, cultural, and legal matters, they denounce gambling casinos, alcoholic beverages, racy magazines and films, and scantily clad female pop singers. At the same time, a progressive, democratic strand of Islamic thought has favored liberal social and political reform. Muslim liberals tap into the Javanese emphasis on harmony, consensus, and tolerance incorporated into Indonesian Islam, offering a stark contrast to the more dogmatic Islam common in Pakistan and Saudi Arabia. However, in the twenty-first century a more conservative brand of Islam

New Order The Indonesian government headed by President Suharto from 1966 to 1998, which mixed military and civilian leadership.

[24]From Taufiq Ismail's story "Stop Thief!" in *Black Clouds over the Isle of Gods and Other Modern Indonesian Short Stories*, ed. David M. E. Roskies (Armonk, NY: M.E. Sharpe, 1997), 97.

has gained many adherents, spread by charismatic television and Internet evangelists promoting conservative interpretations of the faith. Several decades ago many Indonesian women, especially in the cities, dressed in Western-style clothes, with no head scarves, but today this is much less common as people seek to overtly display their religious beliefs. This has impacted politics as well as the economy as "born-again" Muslims, seeking an "Islamic economy," develop or patronize everything that complies with sharia guidelines from housing, banking, and tourist facilities to modest fashions, cosmetics, and entertainment. And yet, on Java, where half the population lives, more and more people visit the tombs of fifteenth- and sixteenth-century Sufi "saints" or missionaries who brought the religion to the island, which suggests that some Indonesians still quietly have an alternative view to that of conservative Islamists. It is ironic that one of the most popular tombs, that of the flamboyant, homosexual eighteenth-century Prince Jimat of Madura, seems to violate the strong antigay ideology of many Indonesians today. And some women fight conservative trends and the high rates of sexual violence and child marriage. In 2019 eight hundred women began a project to produce "Mighty Girls," illustrated e-books for boys and girls with stories that smash gender stereotypes and present strong female characters.

By the 1990s Indonesian society suffered from increasing class and ethnic tensions, student protests, and labor unrest. When the economy collapsed in 1997, throwing millions out of work and raising prices for essential goods, widespread rioting resulted in Suharto's resignation. Indonesia fell into turmoil, and protests and ethnic clashes proliferated. Many among the urban middle class wanted to strengthen democracy, and in 1999 free elections were held. Later, Megawati Soekarnoputri (**MEH-ga-WHA-tee soo-KAR-no-POO-tri**), daughter of Indonesia's first president, Sukarno, became Indonesia's first woman president. Like her father, Megawati followed secular, nationalist policies but showed little faith in grassroots democracy and resolved few problems. By 2004 popular support for her regime had ebbed, and she lost to a retired Javanese general, Susilo Bambang Yudhoyono, who was re-elected in 2009 as voters decisively rejected anti-Western Islamist parties and reelected the centrist, secular government.

The disorderly democracy replacing the New Order brought unprecedented freedom of the press and speech. But removing restrictions allowed long-simmering ethnic hostilities to reemerge. East Timor, which had endured a long, unpopular Indonesian occupation, finally achieved independence in 1999 after Indonesian troops and militias killed thousands. Many people in Papua (West Irian) have opposed Indonesian rule and sought self-governance, sometimes leading to protests and violence. Muslim–Christian conflicts have also caused numerous deaths, while Islamic militants capitalized on the instability to recruit support. Several terrorist bombings of popular tourist venues added to the growing tensions. In 2005 over 100,000 Indonesians perished from earthquakes and a deadly tidal wave, or tsunami, that destroyed cities and washed away coastal villages on Sumatra. Meanwhile, assertive Muslim conservatives increasingly harass or demand punishment for people they view as behaving immorally.

In 2014 Indonesians elected the moderate Jakarta governor Joko Widodo (known as Jokowi), who emphasized infrastructure development while dealing with challenges from the military and Islamists. His economic policies raised the annual growth rate to 5.2 percent by 2019. A popular figure, Jokowi won re-election in 2019 but immediately faced severe problems that have troubled his presidency and sparked sporadic and widespread rioting and protests. Once a corruption fighter, he outraged some of the public by failing to support anticorruption and criminal code revision bills hated by wealthy business interests. Many also protested Jokowi's failure to end the wildfires destroying the nation's rain forests and punish the powerful business interests responsible; halt military action against separatists and protesters in Papua (West Irian); and reject legislation giving greater power over natural resources to companies. Liberals and students worried that his waffling on an Islamist-sponsored bill to criminalize extramarital and gay sex confirmed a slow-moving Islamization of Indonesia that threatened the traditional tolerance. The bill also prohibits pornographic and blasphemous content and "negative foreign influences" (such as K-pop), depriving artists and others of free expression. Many musicians accused Jokowi of hypocrisy since he is a well-known fan of heavy metal music. Jokowi hinted that, to defuse weeks of deadly violence, he was willing to discuss independence with Papuan separatists. While Jokowi still has considerable popular support these setbacks have raised questions about the long-term viability of Indonesian democracy.

The Philippines lagged well behind the most prosperous Southeast Asian nations in economic development. Under the Ferdinand Marcos dictatorship (1972–1986), economic conditions worsened, rural poverty became more widespread, population grew rapidly, and political opposition was limited by the murder or detaining of dissidents, censorship, and rigged elections. Marcos, his family, and cronies looted the country, amassing billions. High walls built along city freeways ensured that affluent motorists would not have to view slums along the route. A tiny minority lived in palatial homes surrounded by high walls topped with broken glass and barbed wire, with gates manned by armed guards. Across the street from the glittering pavilions of Manila's Cultural Center, homeless families slept in bushes; child malnutrition increased. A Filipino novelist described impoverished, mostly landless peasants, eking out a living on unproductive land: "Nothing in the countryside had changed, not the thatched houses, not the ragged vegetation, not the stolid people. Changeless land, burning sun."[25]

As a result of all these problems, Filipinos have often migrated, temporarily or permanently, to other Asian nations, the United States and Canada, or the Middle East. Some ten million Filipinos (11 percent of the Philippine population) lived abroad by 2018. Around five million are immigrants in North America but most of the rest are temporary workers on contracts in dozens of countries around the world. Saudi Arabia has the most temporary Filipino workers (about one million), followed by the United Arab Emirates, Malaysia, Kuwait, and Japan. About half are women, who mostly work as nurses, maids, or entertainers. About twenty-five hundred Filipinos leave the country every day for overseas work. The emigrants

[25]F. Sionel Jose, quoted in David G. Timberman, *A Changeless Land: Continuity and Change in Philippine Politics* (New York: M.E. Sharpe, 1991), xi.

have become part of what Filipinos ruefully call a "3D" culture, referring to the dirty (domestic work), the dangerous (factory work), and the difficult (entertainment). Women have been underemployed within the Philippines, where those in jobs or seeking work made up just under half of the working-age population over the last two decades. Women are held back by social expectations that they will care for homes and children. The Philippine rate of 46 percent in 2018 pushed its female labor participation below regional peers, such as Indonesia at 52 percent, Malaysia at 51 percent and Myanmar with 48 percent, which highlights the need to fight workplace stereotyping and discrimination.

The Marcos regime's failures sparked massive public protests in 1986 that restored democracy. The opposition rallied around U.S.-educated Corazón Aquino **(ah-KEE-no)** (1933–2009), whose popular politician husband had been assassinated. In a spectacular nonviolent "people's power" revolution, street demonstrations involving students, workers, businessmen, housewives, and clergy demanded justice and freedom. Marcos and his family fled into exile in the United States, which had long supported his regime. Demonstrators breaking into the presidential palace found that the dictator's wife, Imelda Marcos, a former beauty queen, owned thousands of pairs of shoes and vast stores of undergarments, symbolizing the Marcoses' waste of public resources. Mrs. Aquino became president, reestablishing democracy. Aquino negotiated a closing of U.S. military bases, although some troops remained.

But hopes that the Philippines could resolve its problems proved illusory. The new government, while open to dissenting voices, was dominated by the wealthiest Filipinos, mostly members of the hundred or so landowning families favored during U.S. colonial rule. Mrs. Aquino, who belonged to one of these families, declined reelection in 1992. Her successors had rocky presidencies; one, a former film star with a reputation for heavy drinking, gambling, and womanizing, was impeached for corruption and vote-rigging. In 2001 another woman, Gloria Macapagal-Arroyo (b. 1947), a PhD economist and daughter of a former president, became president but also faced corruption allegations; she was reelected in 2005. Powerful women are not unusual in the Philippines, where many are prominent in politics, higher education, journalism, and small business. In 2010 Benigno Aquino III, the son of Corazon Aquino, won the presidency on a reform platform and soon cracked down on corruption and tax evasion; Mrs. Macapagal-Arroyo faced criminal prosecution. Aquino began negotiations with Muslim separatists in the south for possible autonomy and, fearing China's growing power, had sought a larger American troop presence.

While many Filipinos admire the United States, others resent the continuing U.S. ties and influence. A best-selling pop song reflected the opposition to what nationalists considered neocolonialism: "You just want my natural resources, And then you leave me poor and in misery. American Junk, Get it out of my bloodstream. Got to get back to who I am."[26] While democracy returned, a free press flourished, and the economy has improved in recent years, much of the economic growth has been eaten up by rapid population growth; the nation now has

one hundred-eight million people. None of the governments have successfully addressed poverty or seemed willing to curb the activities of influential companies exploiting marine, mineral, and timber resources, often harming the environment. A local Catholic priest noted how economic exploitation and environmental destruction remained common: "A plunder economy, that's the post World War II Philippine history: plunder of seas, plunder of mines, plunder of forests."[27] At the same time, differences in access to health care, welfare, and related services have continued to reflect the great gaps in income between social classes and regions.

The nation took a new turn in 2016 when the controversial Rodrigo Duterte (b. 1945), the mayor of Davao (a Mindanao city), was elected president on a right-wing populist and nationalist platform that promised bloody wars on crime and terrorism. As mayor and then president, Duterte has pursued tough and brutal extrajudicial campaigns, including death squads, to eliminate crime and the illegal drug trade and widespread drug use while also intimidating the press and harassing or arresting some of his critics, many of them women who decry his self-proclaimed misogyny and offensive sexist comments. Duterte introduced the "Build, Build, Build" program in 2017 that aimed to foster a new "golden age" of infrastructure while creating more jobs and business opportunities to sustain the country's economic growth and accelerate poverty reduction. But by 2019 the death toll of his war on crime had reached over five thousand people, many of them probably innocent victims or minor drug users rather than major dealers. The human rights and civil liberties violations, especially the anticrime effort, outraged liberals and democrats but increased his popularity with many common people. After United Nations human rights experts criticized the death squads and killings, Duterte threatened to withdraw the Philippines from the UN and form a new organization with China and African nations. Duterte also pursued an "independent foreign policy" that distanced the Philippines from its longtime allies, the United States and European Union, and sought closer ties with China and Russia. Duterte's unwillingness to challenge China's expansionist claims to the South China Sea worried the U.S. as well as Japan and Southeast Asian nations like Vietnam and Indonesia. In 2017 five month-long battles with ISIS and Abu Sayyaf jihadi militants in Mindanao led to the destruction of a major city, Marawi, and many casualties. Negotiations for peace and a political settlement between the government and several communist insurgents and Islamic separatist groups broke down, leaving the future stability of the country unclear.

31-4c Politics and Society in Thailand and Burma

Since the 1970s the striking contrasts between prosperous Thailand and stagnant Myanmar (Burma) have increased. In the 1950s both nations had economies of similar size and growth rates, but the gap between them has become vast. While both nations have a long history of military dictatorship, by

[26] "American Junk," by the Apo Hiking Society, quoted in Craig A. Lockard, *Dance of Life: Popular Music and Politics in Southeast Asia* (Honolulu: University of Hawai'i Press, 1998), 156.
[27] Quoted in Robin Broad and John Cavanaugh, *Plundering Paradise: The Struggle for the Environment in the Philippines* (Berkeley: University of California Press, 1993), xvii.

IMAGE 31.5 **People's Power Demonstration in the Philippines** In 1986 the simmering opposition to the dictatorial government of Ferdinand Marcos reached a boiling point, resulting in massive demonstrations in Manila. Under the banner of "people's power," businesspeople, professionals, housewives, soldiers, students, and cultural figures rallied to support Corazon Aquino and topple the Marcos regime.

Q What can you tell about the participants and their enthusiasm from the photo?

the 1980s the Thais, finding the repressive atmosphere chilling, developed a more open semidemocratic system combining order and hierarchy, symbolized by the monarchy, with representative, accountable government. Although most successful political candidates came from wealthy families, often of Chinese ancestry, the rapidly growing urban middle class generally supported expanding democracy to gain more influence. A new constitution adopted in 1997 guaranteed civil liberties and reformed the electoral system, and a lively free press emerged.

Thailand and its seventy million people (2019) have generally enjoyed high rates of economic growth. Despite a growing manufacturing sector, rice, rubber, tin, and timber exports remain significant. Although the Chinese minority of some 10 percent controls much wealth, Thais enjoy high per capita incomes and standards of public health by Asian standards. Thousands of people from North America and Europe come to Thailand each year for medical treatment. Yet perhaps a quarter of Thais are very poor, especially in rural areas. The economic "miracle" was built on the backs of women and children, many from rural districts, working in urban factories, the service sector, and the sex industry. Millions of Thai women have identified with the songs of popular singer Pompuang Duangjian **(POM-poo-ahn DWONG-chen)** (1961–1992), herself the product of a poor village, which often dealt with the harsh lives of poor female migrants to the city: "So lousy poor, I just have to risk my luck. Dozing on the bus, this guy starts chatting me

up. Says he'll get me a good job."[28] With only two years of primary school education, Pompuang worked as a sugar-cane cutter before starting a music career. Much of her money was stolen by lovers, managers, and promoters, and she died at thirty-one unable to afford treatment for a blood disorder.

The economic collapses of 1997 and 2008–2009 threw many Thais out of work. The overcrowded capital, Bangkok, is one of Asia's most polluted cities, drenched in toxic matter from factories and automobiles despite efforts by local environmental groups to clean up the air. The nation's once-abundant rain forests disappear at a rapid rate, lamented by Thai musicians and poets (see Discover Historical Voices: A Thai Poet's Plea for Saving the Environment). The AIDS rate has been Southeast Asia's highest. Thais tend to accept gays as part of society but same-sex marriage is banned, although efforts to change that continue. With fewer joining the Buddhist clergy, monks complain that consumerism is now the Thai religion. But as in Sri Lanka and Burma, some monks became radicals agitating against Muslims, Western secular culture, and antimonarchy writings. An insurgency by some Malay Muslims in the deep south seeking autonomy or secession has festered for decades. In 2001 media magnate and billionaire populist Thaksin Shinawatra (b. 1949), who, like many business and political leaders, comes from an ethnic Chinese family, swept into power, supported largely by big business and discontented rural voters. Although the autocratic Thaksin's populist policies helped villagers, they

[28]Quoted in Pasuk Phongpaichit and Chris Baker, *Thailand: Economy and Politics* (Kuala Lumpur: Oxford University Press, 1995), 413-415.

also created huge budget deficits, polarizing the country and sparking massive street protests, Thaksin's removal for corruption, and a temporary return of military-aligned governments. These events resulted in several years of political turmoil between rival factions, deeply dividing the country and weakening democracy. In 2011 Thaksin's party, now headed by his pragmatic sister Yingluck Shinawatra, returned to power in free elections and energized economic growth, but the deep divide between the pro-Thaksin rural north and northeast and the anti-Thaksin Bangkok middle class remained dangerous. Devastating floods in 2011, an aging king, and controversies over the monarchy's role contributed to tensions that erupted again in 2013 with massive opposition street protests and demands that Yingluck's government resign, fostering more instability and threatening economic recovery in a deeply polarized nation.

In 2014 the army overthrew Yingluck and her government, and she fled in to exile. The new president, General Prayut Chan-o-cha, has ruled the country since, restricting civil and political rights and encouraging prosecution of people who violate laws that prohibit insulting or questioning the monarchy. The government cracked down on criticism and harassed or arrested dissenters and political opponents, sending some to "attitude adjustment" camps. King Bhumibol, the much-loved and longest-reigning Thai monarch, died in 2016, and his son Vajiralongkorn ascended to the throne. After approving a new pro-military constitution, the junta held an orchestrated national election that banned some opposition leaders and reflected the rituals but not the substance of democracy. Several opposition pro-democracy groupings contested but the military-backed party and their presidential candidate, General Prayut, won amidst allegations of election irregularities. Although some new opposition candidates and parties appeared, many Thai and foreign observers worried about more chaos and a political dead end. Some prominent dissidents have been arrested, killed, or "disappeared". Yet, Thailand still has the second largest economy in Southeast Asia (including some manufacturing), although growth declined in 2019 due in part to the U.S.–China trade and tariff war. In the long run Thais possess a talent for political compromise, and Buddhism teaches moderation, tolerance, respect for nature, and a belief in individual worth, providing the basis for a democratic spirit, more equitable distribution of wealth, and environmental ethic.

Whatever Thailand's problems, they seem dwarfed by those of Burma and its fifty-four million people (2019), which has been ruled until recently by a harsh, corrupt military regime. In one of Asia's poorest nations, few outside the ruling group have prospered, despite the country's natural riches of timber, oil, gems, and rice. Sparked by economic decline and political repression, mass protests in 1988, led by students and Buddhist monks, demanded civil liberties; soldiers killed hundreds and jailed thousands of demonstrators. In 1990 Burma, now renamed Myanmar **(my-ahn-MAH)**, under international pressure, allowed elections. Although most of its leaders were in jail, the opposition won a landslide victory. Aung San Suu Kyi **(AWNG sahn soo CHEE)** (b. 1945), the founding president's daughter and an eloquent orator, returned from England to lead democratic forces. But the military refused to hand over power, put Aung San Suu Kyi under house arrest, and jailed

thousands of opposition supporters. Aung San Suu Kyi refused to compromise to end her house arrest. A courageous symbol of principled leadership, she won the Nobel Peace Prize in 1991.

The military regime remained in power, detaining opposition leaders, until 2011. Meanwhile, many Burmese long dreamed of democracy, some exchanging illicit cassettes of protest music and opposition messages from hand to hand; others, valuing stability and fearing civil war, accommodated military rule. Eventually the government began welcoming some limited foreign investment, especially in the timber and oil industries, and diminished the willingness of other countries to punish Burma for gross human rights violations. The brutal suppression of Buddhist-led protests, a refusal of foreign assistance for the victims of a devastating hurricane, and increased military assaults on ethnic minority settlements made clear that the generals would not relax their grip or modify their isolation from the world. Yet, in 2010 the junta changed direction, releasing Aung San Suu Kyi and many political prisoners and holding new elections with opposition candidates. In 2011 the junta was dissolved and a nominally civilian government installed, albeit with many military members. Hoping for more investment for modernization, the leaders improved relations with the world, and many countries lifted sanctions. Myanmar remains a poor country with one of the widest income gaps in the world. In 2015 Aung San Suu Kyi's party swept to a landslide victory but, married to a British citizen, she was ineligible for the presidency and has governed instead as the State Counsellor (essentially the prime minister) and foreign minister. Many Burmese believed that they finally had reason to hope that the future might be much better than the past, but the government has been hemmed in by the powerful military influence embedded in the constitution.

Aung San Suu Kyi's fragile political reforms were threatened by Buddhist attacks, some led by radical monks, on minority Muslims, as well as by discontented and restless ethnic minorities, some seeking secession, and protests against unpopular dam-building and mining projects. Buddhists considered the Bengali-speaking and Muslim Rohingya people in the northwest state of Rakhine to be illegal migrants, refusing them citizenship and rights even though many of the families had lived there for decades or even several generations. These tensions had simmered for decades and sometimes led to violence. In 2012 Buddhist–Rohingya clashes resulted in hundreds of Rohingya killed or wounded, more than eighty thousand displaced, and whole villages destroyed. In 2016–2017 the military campaign (which some human rights experts consider genocide) to eliminate the Rohingya massacred resisters, destroyed villages, and forced 750,000 into Bangladesh, where they are held in refugee camps. Others have fled, often in rickety boats, to Thailand, Malaysia, or Australia, where they are mostly unwelcome and often turned away or held in detention camps. Those 660,000 remaining in Myanmar cannot own land or travel without permission and face many other restrictions as well as continued harassment and threats. Aung San Suu Kyi remains popular with many Burmese for her reforms and walking a difficult line between military demands and civilian needs, but she has lost status with many foreign governments and observers as well as Burmese liberals for persecution of journalists and her inaction

Discover Historical Voices

A Thai Poet's Plea for Saving the Environment

Angkhan Kalayanaphong (**AHN-kan KALL-a-YAWN-a-fong**) *(1926–2012), the most popular poet in Thailand for decades, also gained fame as an accomplished graphic artist and painter. His poems often addressed social, Buddhist, and environmental themes. In his long poem "Bangkok-Thailand," he examines Thailand and its problems in the 1970s and 1980s. The author pulls no punches in condemning Thai society for neglecting its heritage, skewing politicians, government institutions, big business, and the entertainment industry. In this section, Angkhan pleads for Thais to save the forest environment being destroyed by commercial logging.*

Oh, I do not imagine the forest like that
So deep, so beautiful, everything so special.
It pertains to dreams that are beyond truth. . . .
Dense woods in dense forests; slowly
The rays of half a day mix with the night.
Strange atmosphere causing admiration.
Loneliness up to the clouds, stillness and beauty.
Rays of gold play upon, penetrate the tree-tops
rays displayed in stripes, the brightness of the sun.
I stretch out my hand drawing down clouds mixing them
with brandy.
This is supreme happiness. . . .
The lofty trees do not think of reward for the scent of their
blossoms. . . .
Men kill the wood because they venerate money as in all
the world. . . .

The lofty trees contribute much to morals.
They should be infinitely lauded for it.
The trace of the ax kills. Blood runs in streams. . . .
You, trees, give the flattering pollen attended by
scents.
You make the sacrifice again and again.
Do you ever respond angrily? You have accepted your
fate which is contemptuous of all that is beautiful.
But troublesome are the murderers, the doers of future
sins.
Greedy after money, they are blind to divine work.
Their hearts are black to large extent, instead of being
honest and upright.
They have no breeding, are lawless. . . .
Thailand in particular is in a very bad way.
Because of their [commercial] value parks are "purified,"
i.e., destroyed.
Man's blood is depraved, cursed and base.
His ancestors are swine and dogs. It is madness to say
they are Thai.

Reflection Questions

1. What qualities does the poet attribute to the forest?
2. What motives does he attribute to the loggers and businessmen who exploit the forest environment?
3. How does the author's view of the environment compare to yours?

Source: Klaus Wenk, *Thai Literature: An Introduction* (Bangkok: White Lotus, 1995), 95-98. Copyright © 1995 Klaus Wenk. Reprinted with permission.

in failing to halt the anti-Muslim campaigns of radical Buddhist monks and the military. Citing the human rights violations on her watch, some critics have called for her Nobel Prize to be revoked, various cities and organizations around the world have taken back awards, and some want her tried as a war criminal, a sad commentary on the state of Myanmar today.

31-4d Diversity and Prosperity in Malaysia and Singapore

Malaysia and Singapore, both open to the world, achieved the most political stability and economic progress. Both countries successfully diversified their economies and stimulated development while raising living standards and spreading the wealth. The two nations, once joined in the same federation, share a similar mix of ethnic groups; Malays constitute 60 percent of the thirty-two million Malaysians, while Chinese (23 percent) and Indian (7 percent) are the other large communities; three-quarters of Singaporeans are Chinese. Singapore and (until recently) Malaysia have maintained limited democracies,

holding regular elections in which the ruling parties control the voting and most of the mass media. While opposition leaders sometimes face arrest or harassment, dissidents use the Internet to spread their views.

In 1969 Chinese–Malay violence in Malaysia precipitated the New Economic Policy; aimed at redistributing more wealth to Malays, it fostered a substantial Malay middle class. Televisions, stereos, cell phones, and videocassette recorders became nearly universal in cities and increasingly common in rural areas. Many Malaysians have personal computers, smart phones, and easy access to the Internet and social media. Official poverty rates dropped from some 50 percent in 1970 to around 20 percent by 2000. Nevertheless, the gap between rich and poor remains and may have widened. In the bustling capital city, Kuala Lumpur, jammed freeways, glittering malls, and high-rise luxury condominiums contrast with shantytown squatter settlements and shabbily dressed street hawkers hoping to sell enough of their cheap wares to buy a meal.

In 2008 and 2013 a multiethnic opposition coalition overcame obstacles and made electoral gains against the ruling

Malay-dominated alliance in Malaysia. In 2018 this reformist, center-left coalition, Pakatan Harapan ("Alliance of Hope"), promising a New Malaysia, surprised the nation and won a convincing victory against a long-ruling, conservative saddled with corruption scandals and widespread disenchantment with their authoritarian and divisive policies. Ninety-three-year-old Dr. Mahathir Muhammed (b. 1925), who had previously led the nation for twenty-two controversial years (1981–2003), became prime minister and appointed a multiethnic cabinet. But the Pakatan Harapan has struggled to implement some of their ambitious agenda, including to reform the economy, investigate and prosecute political corruption (including by the former prime minister and ruling party), promote more democratic participation, revive human rights and civil liberties protections, deal with East Malaysians demanding more autonomy or even secession, address environmental issues, and resolve factionalism in the four-party coalition, leading to some loss of support. The defeated parties have been regrouping, including an alliance between the two main Malay parties, UMNO and PAS (a conservative Islamist party), that espouse Malay nationalism and the protection of Malay rights and Islamic influence on society.

Religion has often divided Malaysia's Muslim majority from the Christian, Hindu, Buddhist, and animist minority. Conflict also occurs within religious traditions. Islamic movements with dogmatic, sometimes militant views have increasingly attracted some Malays, especially rural migrants to the city alienated by a Westernized, materialistic society and seeking an anchor in an uncertain world. These movements, which sometimes reject modern technology or products while strongly encouraging women to dress modestly (the majority of women now wear head scarves and can be criticized for not doing so), often alarm secular Malays and non-Muslims. In response, Malay women's rights groups use Islamic arguments to oppose the restrictions favored by conservatives. Sisters in Islam, founded by the academic Zainab Anwar (**ZEYE-nab AN-war**), espouses freedom, justice, and equality while fighting strict interpretations of Muslim family law. Numerous women hold high government positions. At the other extreme, some aimless Malay youth mock mainstream society, wearing long hair and listening to heavy metal and hip-hop music. Most Muslims and many Christians opposed LGBTQ rights, and homosexuality is against the law, although only rarely prosecuted.

Supported by abundant natural resources, such as oil and tin, economic diversification, and entrepreneurial talent, Malaysia has surpassed European nations like Portugal and Hungary in national wealth. High annual growth rates have fostered relatively high per capita income (around $10,000–11,000 in 2018) and export industries employing cheap, often female, labor to make shoes, toys, and other consumer goods. The manufacturing sector has continued to grow rapidly; Malaysians even build their own automobiles. Timber and oil have become valuable export commodities. But economic growth causes toxic waste problems, severe deforestation, and air pollution. Indeed, the clearing of land for rubber and especially oil palm estates is rapidly destroying the rain forest, especially in Sarawak and Sabah, contributing to more

global warming, depleting biodiversity, and forcing indigenous tribal groups off of their land. Like many countries Malaysians debate the balance between rapid economic development and natural resource exploitation on one hand and protection of the environment on the other.

Restricted to a tiny island, Singapore, despite few resources, joined the world's most prosperous nations, with a standard of living second only to Japan in Asia. The numerical and political predominance of ethnic Chinese makes Singapore unique in Southeast Asia. The government, efficient and ruthless, mixes free-wheeling economic policies with an autocratic leadership that tightly controls the six million people and limits dissent. People pay a stiff fine if caught spitting, littering, or even tossing used chewing gum on the street. But the regime has also curbed inequalities, redistributing pretax income. One of the healthiest societies, enjoying the world's lowest rate of infant mortality, Singapore devotes more of its national budget to education than other nations; everyone studies English in school, and world-class universities attract international faculties. In the vanguard of the information revolution, the city has become a hub of light industry, high technology, computer networking, and plans to become a global AI leader. Singapore boasts one of the world's best airlines and perhaps its most modern, user-friendly, and pathbreaking airport. Businesspeople and professionals from around the world have flocked to this globalized city, just as they flocked to Melaka centuries ago. So have lower skilled, and often poorly paid, migrant workers from around Asia, who account for a third of the population, prompting sporadic protests by local job seekers. By 2018 around a quarter of citizens and permanent residents were foreign-born. In 2011, after the political opposition had better-than-expected election results, the government pledged some modest liberalization of culture and politics. Yet, little has changed politically since then and the Peoples Action Party, which has ruled for over five decades, remains in power, harassing and sometimes arresting dissidents while keeping the opposition, who seek more democracy, ineffective. But while the U.S.–China trade war has dampened Singapore's robust economic growth, the city may benefit from the 2019 turbulence in Hong Kong, with some businesses moving to more stable Singapore.

31-4e Conflict and Reconstruction in Indochina

After years of war and destruction, Vietnam, Laos, and Cambodia began to rebuild and deal with lingering tensions. In Vietnam, socialist policies failed to revitalize the economy; the reunification of North and South Vietnam proved harsh. Because of mismanagement, natural disasters, a long U.S. economic embargo, and the war's devastation, between 1978 and 1985 half a million refugees, known as "boat people," risked their lives to escape Vietnam in rickety boats. After spending months or years in crowded refugee camps in Southeast Asia, most of the refugees were resettled in North America, Australia, or France.

In the 1980s reformists in the government, recognizing its failures, introduced free market–oriented reforms, known

IMAGE 31.6 **Kuala Lumpur** Dominated by new skyscrapers, including some of the world's tallest buildings such as the Petronas Twin Towers (in the center of the photo), and spectacular mosques, the Malaysian capital city, Kuala Lumpur, has become a prosperous center for Asian commerce and industry. Modern buildings have gradually replaced the older shop houses built decades ago. Yet, poor shantytowns have also grown apace to house the poor.

Q What kind of impression of Kuala Lumpur and Malaysian modernity does the photo convey?

as *Đổi Mới* ("Renovation"), similar to those in China favoring private enterprise and foreign investment, hence managing the transition from a planned economy to what they termed a "socialist-oriented market economy." While state influence remained strong, they encouraged private ownership of farms and factories as well as foreign investment. The reforms greatly increased agricultural and industrial productivity, facilitated export-oriented manufacturing, fostered some urban prosperity, and ended the refugee flow. Emphasizing education more than doubled the 1945 literacy rates to 95 percent of adults. Many observers have seen Vietnam as becoming another "tiger" economy. But the shift from socialism widened economic inequalities, leaving most farmers living just above the poverty line. Women's wages often fell further behind men's. Vietnamese also debated the appropriate balance between socialist and free market policies. With the global recession of 2008–2009, Vietnamese experienced the full effects of globalization. Hundreds of former farming villages producing handicrafts for export saw their income collapse as foreign consumers cut spending. But by 2019 the economy had recovered, with 6.5 percent growth, and many foreign companies were moving their operations from China to Vietnam.

Although Vietnam has remained an authoritarian one-party state, with little democracy, restrictions on cultural expression have loosened. Several former soldiers became rock or disco stars, and many writers addressed contemporary problems and the war's legacy in fiction. "The General Retires," a former North Vietnamese soldier's short story, caused a sensation by depicting the despair of an old soldier contemplating the new society's emptiness. The authoritarian government periodically jails dissenters and cracks down on social media and sometimes churches. However, beginning in the 1990s the communists have expanded ties to the West and the world economy, and the United States and Vietnam have resumed diplomatic relations. Motor scooters jam urban streets; bustling Saigon, renamed Ho Chi Minh City, has enjoyed especially dynamic economic growth and prosperity. Americans now buy shrimp and underwear imported from Vietnam, and many Americans, including former soldiers and Vietnamese refugees, visit Vietnam. Hundreds of American veterans operate businesses or social service agencies in Vietnam, sometimes in partnership with former communist soldiers. Still, the ruling communists struggle to satisfy the expectations of the ninety-seven million Vietnamese, for many of whom the war with the United States is ancient history.

In neighboring Laos, the challenge has been dealing with wartime divisions and destruction. After the Vietnam conflict, many Laotians fled into exile, among them some

300,000 Hmong who settled in the United States. The Laotian government persecuted some remaining Hmong it believed were supporting anticommunist guerillas. While Laotian leaders have sought warmer relations with neighboring Thailand, China, and the United States, they have failed to foster a more open society or energize the economy. Rigid communists still dominate the one-party state. Several places have attracted Western tourists, but most of the seven million Laotians remain poor. Laotians see a more successful development model when they look across the Mekong at the busy freeways, neon lights, and high-rise buildings in Thailand.

Cambodia has faced a more difficult challenge because the war was followed by fierce repression and mass murder; at the same time, badly disrupted agriculture raised the specter of widespread starvation. The communist Khmer Rouge leader Pol Pot (1925–1998), hardened by brutal war, achieved power in 1975 and drove the urban population into the rural areas to farm. The Khmer Rouge's radical vision of a property-less, classless peasant society, combined with violence against suspected dissenters and resisters, led thousands to flee into neighboring countries. The Khmer Rouge executed thousands in death camps and shot or starved many others, including common people such as peasants and taxi drivers, as well as Westernized and educated people. The regime was ultimately responsible for 1.5 to 2 million deaths, sparking comparisons with Nazi Germany.

In 1978 the Vietnamese, alarmed at Khmer Rouge territorial claims and the murder of thousands of ethnic Vietnamese living in Cambodia, allied with an exile army of disaffected former Khmer Rouge, invaded Cambodia, and rapidly pushed the Khmer Rouge to the Thailand border. After liberating Cambodians from tyranny, the Vietnamese installed a less brutal communist government. But military conflict continued for years as a Khmer Rouge–dominated resistance controlled some sections of the country. Cambodia proved to be for Vietnam what Vietnam had been for the United States, an endless sinkhole of conflict that drained scarce wealth and complicated Vietnam's relations with the West.

In the early 1990s a coalition government was formed under United Nations sponsorship, and the Khmer Rouge splintered and collapsed as a movement. While everyone welcomed the resulting peace, the government remained repressive and corrupt, tolerating some limited opposition but controlling the vote. Sihanouk returned from exile in 1993 to become king but served largely as a symbol of Cambodia's link to its past. Life for many Cambodians remained grim as they faced everything from high fuel prices to poor education; often using social media, some people demanded more democracy and attention to social problems. While the opposition has sometimes eroded the long-entrenched ruling party's majority in elections, it also protested what many observers considered a rigged system, corruption, the jailing or exile of leading dissidents, and low wages for workers, leading to occasional violent clashes with police. Nevertheless, the government opened the country to investment and tourism, which has brought in revenues, and has transformed Cambodia, while still haunted by past horrors, from a traumatized to a functioning society, for some years kept afloat largely by Western tourism and aid. While per capita income remains low, Cambodia today has one of the fastest-growing economies in Asia, averaging 7.6 percent over the last decade. Agriculture still dominates, but the nation enjoyed

IMAGE 31.7 Honoring Ho Chi Minh These schoolgirls, dressed in traditional clothing and parading before Ho Chi Minh's mausoleum in Hanoi, are part of an annual festival to honor the leading figure of Vietnamese communism.

Q What does the photo tell us about how many Vietnamese and their leaders view Ho Chi Minh and his role in history?

strong growth in textiles, garments, construction, and tourism, leading to increasing foreign investment and international trade. In the 2010s UN-backed war crimes tribunals convicted several Khmer Rouge leaders and sentenced them to life in prison. Over the years most of the other top leaders, including Pol Pot in 1998, have died, bringing at least a symbolic end to a horrendous and tragic era in Cambodia's long and illustrious history.

31-4f Southeast Asia in the Global System

Although Southeast Asians still export the natural resources they did in colonial times, some nations have seen major economic growth through industrialization and exploitation of other resources. Oil, timber, rubber, rice, tin, sugar, and palm oil have largely replaced the gold, pepper, and spice exports of earlier centuries. The region's world role has also changed, fostering some of the fastest-growing economies. Malaysia, Thailand, Singapore, Indonesia, and Vietnam have become major recipients of foreign investment. Meanwhile, workers produce manufactured goods like shoes, clothing, computer chips, and sports equipment for European and North American markets. Several countries elsewhere in Asia, Africa, and Latin America now borrow economic models from the Southeast Asian "tigers." Companies from China or South Korea build infrastructure projects such as dams in Laos, but this often displaces villages and destroys their livelihoods while altering the downriver environments and water flow, killing fish and draining lakes such as the once massive Tonle Sap in Cambodia. Furthermore, poorly constructed dams sometimes fail, destroying villages and killing many people. Several Southeast Asian nations also face the challenge of agricultural practices and timber, agribusiness, and mining projects that destroy the tropical rain forests, dramatically altering the environment, displacing people and wildlife, eliminating plant and insect species, and contributing to climate change. Some single out palm oil plantations in Indonesia and Malaysia for particular criticism since to clear more land the plantations involved set many of the fires that soon rage out of control, polluting the air in nearby countries. Many economists, business leaders, and politicians defend palm oil as an essential export. But by destroying the forest they destroy a culture and way of life for displaced tribal peoples. In West Kalimantan (Indonesian Borneo) one Iban village leader resisting relocation complained in 2019: "The forest means everything. Forest provides water. Water is blood, land is body, wood is breath. When we lost the forest, we lost everything. We can't pray to the god of oil palm."[29] Experts blame palm oil for 39 percent of the forest loss in Borneo between 2000 and 2019.

Recently Southeast Asians have begun shifting their focus from the United States to China, which they view as the rising world power with which they must cooperate. Cambodia and Laos are already closely allied with China. But by 2012 Chinese claims to much of the South China Sea had unsettled ASEAN, especially Vietnam and the Philippines, which also claim some of the islands, prompting closer ties with the United States as a counterweight. However, in 2016 Philippine president Duterte, seeking Chinese investment, suspended challenges to China's claims to islands near the Philippines, while in 2019

Vietnam had several facedowns with Chinese ships over oil and gas exploration in some disputed islands. This caused a rift in ASEAN over China policy. Southeast Asian observers also debated whether the U.S.–China trade war will force them to pick sides in the superpower contest, putting countries like Malaysia, which takes a neutral stance, in a tough spot. In 2019 the ten ASEAN nations joined with Japan, South Korea, China, Australia, New Zealand, and possibly India to form the Regional Comprehensive Economic Partnership.

Southeast Asians have influenced politics worldwide. The Indonesian Revolution forced a major colonial power to abandon its control, giving hope to colonized Africans. Vietnamese communists, in their ultimately successful fifty-year fight against French colonialism, Japanese occupation, and then U.S. intervention, stimulated a wave of revolutionary efforts, from Nicaragua to Mozambique, to overthrow Western domination. The Vietnamese struggle also inspired European and North American activists; in the 1960s, while protesting against war and inequality, a few of the more radical shouted slogans praising Ho Chi Minh. Women have long played an influential role in Southeast Asia, and political leaders like Indonesia's Megawati Soekarnoputri, Corazon Aquino in the Philippines, and, until recently, Burma's Aung San Suu Kyi have become inspirations to women worldwide. In the late 2010s activists in some Southeast Asian nations became among the first to demand that the Western nations stop sending their trash, especially plastic scrap, which unscrupulous local companies then put in unlicensed dumps or burn in ragtag incineration sites, causing an environmental nightmare; clogging shorelines, waterways, lakes, and city alleys; or fouling the air. But others worry this might harm the recycling industry.

Global influences and economic development have increasingly modified lives. For example, the resident of an upscale suburb of Kuala Lumpur, Bangkok, or Manila, connected through her personal technology to the information superhighway and working in a high-rise, air-conditioned office reached by driving a late-model sports car along crowded freeways, lives very differently than the peasant villager embedded in traditional society. Modern cities boast malls, supermarkets, boutiques, Hard Rock Cafes, and Planet Hollywoods. Indonesian television features many U.S.-style reality shows, which have replaced local soap operas in the ratings. Even rural areas have become more connected to wider networks by televisions, outboard motors, motor scooters, and telephones. Social media links people to influences from all over the world, including respected news sites but also fake news and propaganda sites, some purveying extremist messages to attract converts or followers and hence affecting politics directly or indirectly. Yet change has often been superficial. In poor city neighborhoods restaurants may have compact disc players or streaming services and cold beer, but they may also feature traditional music and dance and serve up fiery hot curries. For every youngster who joins the fan club for a Western or local pop star, another identifies with an Islamic, Buddhist, or Christian organization, sometimes a militant one. Many people find themselves perched uneasily between the cooperative village values of the past and the competitive, materialistic modern world.

---

[29]Mormonus, quoted in "'We Can't Pray to the God of Oil Palm,' Cry Indonesia's Indigenous Tribes," *Malaysiakini.com*, February 23, 2019, malaysiakini.com/news/492967.

KEY POINTS

- Beginning in the late 1970s, Southeast Asia experienced rapid economic growth through a Japanese-style mix of capitalism and active government involvement, though a severe economic crisis hit the region in 1997.

- Since the 1980s, Thailand has developed a semidemocratic system and has grown economically, though it has endured widespread poverty, sexual exploitation, and sporadic political crises. Burma remained a harsh military dictatorship until 2011.

- Malaysia has taken advantage of abundant natural resources to become highly successful, surpassing some European nations in wealth, while Singapore, with fewer

resources, has been even more successful through a combination of economic freedom and political restriction.

- Vietnam and Cambodia struggled after the war, but in the 1980s opened up their economies and by the 1990s had reestablished ties with the rest of the world, including the United States.

- With their rapidly growing economies, the Southeast Asian "tigers" have inspired developing nations around the world, and while most of the region has joined the modern world, tradition thrives in them as well.

Chapter Summary

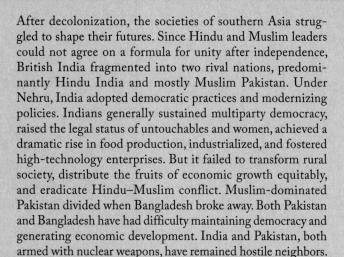

After decolonization, the societies of southern Asia struggled to shape their futures. Since Hindu and Muslim leaders could not agree on a formula for unity after independence, British India fragmented into two rival nations, predominantly Hindu India and mostly Muslim Pakistan. Under Nehru, India adopted democratic practices and modernizing policies. Indians generally sustained multiparty democracy, raised the legal status of untouchables and women, achieved a dramatic rise in food production, industrialized, and fostered high-technology enterprises. But it failed to transform rural society, distribute the fruits of economic growth equitably, and eradicate Hindu–Muslim conflict. Muslim-dominated Pakistan divided when Bangladesh broke away. Both Pakistan and Bangladesh have had difficulty maintaining democracy and generating economic development. India and Pakistan, both armed with nuclear weapons, have remained hostile neighbors.

Like South Asians, Southeast Asians also regained the independence they had lost under Western colonialism.

Vietnamese communists led by Ho Chi Minh launched a revolutionary war that eventually forced the French to leave, giving the communists control of North Vietnam. The United States, influenced by Cold War thinking, supported anticommunist South Vietnam and, in response to a growing communist insurgency, sent American troops to South Vietnam. But the United States withdrew in 1975, unable to triumph over a determined foe. The conflict caused several million casualties and major environmental damage. With the war over, Vietnam, Cambodia, and Laos, all under communist control, struggled for reconstruction. Meanwhile, Indonesia and Malaysia worked to build national unity in a complex mosaic of peoples and cultures. Burma, Thailand, and the Philippines experienced chronic unrest that often led to military or civilian dictatorships. But eventually Malaysia, Singapore, Thailand, Indonesia, and Vietnam achieved rapid economic growth, supplying natural resources and manufactured goods to the world.

Key Terms

Dalit 855
Awami League 856
Bharatiya Janata Party 858
Bollywood 862
National Liberation Front (NLF) 868

Tet Offensive 869
Pathet Lao 869
Khmer Rouge 871
United Malays National Organisation (UMNO) 872

Association of Southeast Asian Nations (ASEAN) 873
New Order 874

Globalization: For and Against

The first pictures taken from the Moon in 1969, which showed Earth as a blue oasis in the middle of nowhere, made clear that humans share a single home and an interlinked future. Different kinds of networks have increasingly connected peoples across distance, borders, supply chains, and globalization—which can be tentatively identified as the interconnections between societies, the rise in cross-border and transnational exchanges, and the creation of one world—has become a major subject of debate. Often used vaguely and inconsistently, the concept became a metaphor to explain capitalism spreading throughout the world. But to many observers, the concept has deeper meanings, describing a process that both unites and divides, creates winners and losers, and brings both new possibilities and new risks. The evidence is all around, from Disney theme parks in China and Paris to sushi restaurants in Brazil, Apple stores in Thailand, Toyota auto plants in Kentucky, Shake Shacks in Istanbul, heavy metal bands in Indonesia, reggae festivals in Japan, and Somali and Hmong refugees in Wisconsin. The debates on globalization cut across political leanings and national divisions. And some observers see trends pointing to the decline or even end of globalization and a globalized world.

The Problem

Globalization inspires passionate support and bitter opposition, generating immense discussion and disagreement. The debate focuses on five questions: What is the definition and meaning of globalization? When did globalization begin? What are the arguments in favor of it? What are some of the major opposing views? Is the trend leading the world into greater cooperation or a troubled era of increasing conflict and the demise of globalization?

The Debate

On the first question, as with any social science concept there is debate about how to define the term. Some scholars view it loosely as a complex and multifaceted process of integration of national economics and interaction among people and governments worldwide, aided by improvements in transportation and communication technologies. One American journalist offers a simple definition: the world is flat. But there are many more diverse variations. For historian Manfred Steger, globalization implies a dynamic phenomenon involving the enhancement of worldwide interdependence and growing awareness of deepening global connections. He also views it as embracing four main empirical dimensions—economic, political, cultural, and ecological—with a fifth, ideological, cutting across the others. Australian sociologist Roland Robertson postulates the compression of the world and the intensification of world consciousness as a whole. British sociologist John Giddens conceives it as the intensification of worldwide social relations that link distant localities so that local events may be shaped by developments occurring many miles or even continents away. Swedish journalist Thomas Larsson notes the reality of world shrinkage, distances getting shorter, and things moving faster. Sociologists Martin Albrow and Elizabeth King view it more broadly as all those processes by which the world's people are incorporated into a single global society. Some differentiate economic globalization from cultural globalization, which emphasizes the transmission of ideas, meanings, and values around the world, fostering more intensive and expanding social relations. All of these attempts at definition help us to understand, as Steger suggests, how globalization became one of the defining buzzwords of our time because it helps describe and explain the processes rapidly altering our experiences in the world.

The second question, the roots of globalization, remains disputed. Some scholars argue that its origins lie deep in the past, going back to the interconnections that slowly enveloped people from the dawn of cities and states in the first and second millennia BCE. Historian Andre Gunder Frank hypothesized an archaic globalization with the rise of trade between Sumer and the Indus valley, followed later by the Hellenistic-trading network stretching from Spain to India. German historians Jurgen Osterhammel and Niels Petersson trace it back a millennium or two to the Silk Road trade between China and the Mediterranean region, the sea trade between the Middle East and India, and the caravans crossing the deserts of Africa—all activities centered on the East that moved people, ideas, artwork, natural resources, goods, and coins. By contrast, Robbie Robertson argues that history changed dramatically only five hundred years ago, when the gradual linking of the world by European voyages of discovery, followed by maritime trade routes, in the Eastern and Western Hemispheres transformed societies and economic activities. A.G. Hopkins and Christopher Bayly refer to a proto-globalization between 1600 and 1800, forged by the European maritime empires and the first multinational corporations like the Dutch and British East India Companies expanding trade links and cultural exchange. Still other scholars trace it no further back than the early or mid-nineteenth century, pointing to expanding use of steamships and steam locomotives, the first permanent transoceanic telegraph cable in 1866, global social movements such as feminism, and global regulatory bodies such as the Universal Postal Union. In the later nineteenth and early twentieth centuries technology and the world economy grew quickly. The term "globalization" came into common use only in the 1970s. Some writers claim that globalization did not affect most of humanity until the 1960s or later, especially after the invention of the microchip in 1972, which generated the information revolution, and the improvement in container shipping. Whatever the roots, today a global system—defined by market capitalism, over two hundred nation-states, some four hundred international organizations, and forty thousand transnational corporations—exists with no central authority but, since the 1980s, a transnational fragmentation of supply chains as the production of goods is increasingly global, with the components of a sport utility vehicle, smartphone, or flat-screen television, for example, assembled in several different countries before becoming part of the finished product.

On the third and fourth questions, whether the effects are positive or negative, the debate has raged for years. Among the benefits attributed to globalization are higher living standards and the worldwide sharing of culture. Giddens identifies a worldwide trend toward democracy and intellectual freedom. Walter Anderson praises the opening of societies to one another, as reflected in communications satellites and the fiber-optic submarine cable system winding its way around the world. As a result, he notes, some Inuit people living in northern Alaska watch twenty-eight channels of satellite television, take courses through the Internet, and stay in touch with their families by cell phones. Free market enthusiasts, such as India-born, U.S.-based economist Jagdish Bhagwati, stress the fostering of economic freedom. Opposing antiglobalization movements as the misguided enemy of progress, many thinkers complain that newspapers and television reports focus more on shuttered textile factories, as jobs move overseas, than on the African child at the computer. Bhagwati claims that when properly governed, globalization becomes a powerful force for social good, bringing prosperity to underdeveloped nations, reducing child labor, increasing literacy, and helping women by creating jobs that increase their income and status. Another enthusiast, Thomas Friedman, considers globalization a reality, not a choice, and the principal trend of the post-Cold War world, symbolized by the Lexus, a Japanese-made luxury car sold around the world. Yet, he argues, people often prefer to hold on to meaningful traditions, symbolized by the olive tree often found at the center of an Arab village, rather than embrace new ideas. To Friedman the world has gotten flat, and this level playing field has allowed over two billion Chinese, Indians, and Russians to contemplate eventually owning a car, house, refrigerator, and toaster, increasing competition and dramatically raising the demand for the world's resources.

The contrary views on globalization stress negative consequences including a concentration of economic power, more poverty, and less cultural diversity. The challengers of economic globalization argue that powerful governments and multinational corporations bully the marketplace, control politics, and stack the deck in their favor. Historian Walter LaFeber shows how U.S. basketball star Michael Jordan, whose games were broadcast all over the world, became an international phenomenon of great commercial appeal, benefiting the international corporations who used Jordan and later LeBron James to create a demand for their expensive products, such as sneakers, often at the expense of local manufacturers making the same product. To LaFeber, the terrorist attacks on the United States, especially the World Trade Center in New York in 2001, must also be understood in the context of the growing opposition to globalization around the world as the rich become richer and the poor become poorer. Economist Joseph Stiglitz, a fan of capitalism and former World Bank official turned critic, believes that globalization can be positive and its failings fixed but that misguided policies and the economic power of industrial nations have made free trade unfair for developing nations. Looking at other aspects of globalization, political scientist Cynthia Enloe explores the often-negative effects of tourism and U.S. military bases on women, who, enjoying fewer economic options than men, often need to sell their bodies to male tourists and soldiers to survive. Historian James Mittelman argues that, experienced from below, globalization fosters the loss of local political control as power shifts upward and also a devaluation of a society's cultural achievements as foreign cultural products, such as music and film, become influential. All of these globalizing trends spur angry resistance, reflected in antiglobalization movements. Maori scholar Makere Stewart-Harawira emphasizes the impact, often negative, on indigenous groups in the evolving world order.

Experts also disagree about the fifth question, where globalization is taking the world. Some predict a growing divide both between and within societies. Political scientist Benjamin Barber, for example, analyzes the conflict between consumerist capitalism (what he calls McWorld, after McDonald's) and tribalism or religious fundamentalism (what he terms jihad, after Islamic militants). Barber dislikes both trends: the dull homogeneity of McWorld, in which everyone, moved by capitalism and advertising, has the same tastes and ideas; and the balkanized world of jihad in which rival cultures, convinced of their own superior values and disdainful of others, struggle for dominance. Other scholars also predict tensions. Giddens argues that the globalization of information, symbolized by the World Wide Web, that puts people in touch with others who think differently will promote a more cosmopolitan worldview respecting cultural differences but will also generate a backlash among narrow nationalists and religious fundamentalists who see only one path to truth. Preventing conflict between the factions and lessening the growing divide between rich and poor nations require cooperation between nations. Bhagwati, for example, supports managed rather than unfettered globalization, with world leaders discussing how to foster equality as well as growth. Taking a different approach, Mittelman doubts that globalization can be managed and calls for people around the world, rather than leaders and governments, to work together to decentralize political and economic power to build a future of greater equity. Friedman agrees that no one nation, bloc, or organization is in charge of managing globalization.

By the 2010s some experts were identifying trends that seem to be reactions to, and may spell the decline or even demise of, globalization. The economic crises of the 1990s and the near depression of the 2008–2009 crash, along with all the negative consequences noted above, soured many people in various hard-hit nations on globalization. North Americans and Europeans feared the economic challenge from Japan in the later twentieth century and even more so China's rise as a rival in the twenty-first century. Anti- or counter-globalization movements opposing and protesting corporate capitalism and neoliberalism can be found around the world. Protests against globalization's symbols, such as the World Trade Organization, International Monetary Fund, World Bank, and the World Economic Forum, have been

IMAGE 31.8 **Kuwaiti Stock Exchange** Capitalism has spread widely in the world, and with it, financial institutions such as investment banks and stock exchanges. The oil-rich, politically stable Persian Gulf sultanate of Kuwait has one of the most active stock exchanges, shown here in 2009 when it signed a deal with the U.S. NASDAQ OMX exchange for an advanced new trading technology and advisory services.

Q What does the photo tell us about the business environment in Kuwait?

common. In recent years, capitalizing on this discontent, anti-globalization, right-wing, nationalist, and populist political parties and leaders have been elected or influential in many countries, among them Hungary, Poland, Italy, Britain, Brazil, and the United States. U.S. president Donald Trump's trade wars against China and other countries as well as his criticism of multilateral organizations reflected this trend.

Some scholars now believe that globalization is dead or dying and countries need to invent a new world order. Controversial economist Michael O'Sullivan foresees a multipolar rather than multilateral world forming but believes present international institutions are unprepared for these changes such as slow growth and may become irrelevant or defunct. Hence, he suggests countries will have to adopt one of two systems: the "leveler" countries, which maintain human rights and freedoms; and the "leviathans" with state-managed growth and fewer liberties. O'Sullivan expects the replacement of global organizations with the division into three to four large regional blocs with different approaches to economic policy, liberty, warfare, society, and technology— America, the European Union, a China-centric Asia, and perhaps an India-led grouping. China has already benefitted the most from globalization and drawn much of Asia away from the United States. Mid-sized countries outside a regional bloc like Russia, Britain, Japan, and Australia might, O'Sullivan

speculates, struggle to find a place in the multipolar world and could gravitate to new but small coalitions modeled on historical models such as the Hanseatic League in the Middle Ages.

Georg Sorensen identifies a new phase of globalization with a different world order that may be neither unipolar nor multipolar but rather involves multiple stakeholders. Or it might be a heavily regionalized order. Other observers suggest that globalization is not a static force and is not dying, just evolving or slowing down. There is still dynamism and innovation in, for example, trading services such as banking and music streaming. And while the U.S. has chosen to wage a tariff war, the European Union continues to secure trade agreements that lower tariffs. Some, such as Peter Goodman, blame the United States for undermining a world trading system it helped build and disrupting international commerce. Goodman believes globalization has been such a key feature of life as to be irreversible but it may need a reset. The process of making modern goods, from medical devices to airplanes, has become immensely complex with components from multiple countries. Since 2017 the U.S. may be, as some observers think, abandoning or downsizing its world leadership and role but the global system, with all its benefits and limitations, may or may not persist in more or less the same configuration.

Evaluating the Debate

The globalization discussion, much more than an academic debate, is a disagreement about profound transformations in the world and about what ethical and institutional principles should be applied to better organize human affairs for a brighter future. Some authors engaged in the debate have proposed catchy ideas, such as the Lexus and the olive tree, jihad and McWorld, but the reality of globalization is usually more complex. Both proponents and opponents make strong points about the consequences of globalization; other scholars believe the truth may lie somewhere in between. Globalization may indeed bring great benefits, at least to a section of the world's people. While the free flow of ideas inspires some people to demand more political rights or social equality, many young women working long hours for low wages in foreign-owned factories may often prefer that life to the dead end of rural poverty. But improving the lives of those who do not benefit, as even globalization proponents Bhagwati and Friedman concede, may require action such as land reform to help poor peasants, more funding for schools, and stiffer environmental and worker protection laws to smooth the impacts on societies, cultures, and environments. Yet, the relations between business interests and their political supporters promoting globalization and the antiglobalization activists, often from worker or peasant backgrounds, remain tense. And some observers debate whether globalization is dying under attacks from nationalist and populist forces or redefining itself to meet new challenges. Local, national, regional, and global forces are intermingling in new and complex ways that may necessitate new ways of thinking.

Exploring the Controversy

Among the key historical studies are Robbie Robertson, *The Three Waves of Globalization: A History of a Developing Global Consciousness* (New York: Zed Books, 2003); Jurgen Osterhammel and Niels P. Petersson, *Globalization: A Short History* (Princeton, NJ: Princeton University Press, 2009); C.A. Bayly, *The Birth of the Modern World, 1780–1914* (Malden, MA: W.W. Norton, 2004); A. G. Hopkins, ed., *Globalization in World History* (New York: Dutton, 2003); and Andre Gunder Frank, *Re-Orient: Global Economy in the Asian Age* (Berkeley: University of California Press, 1998). Some of the major proponents are John Giddens, *Runaway World: How Globalization Is Reshaping Our Lives* (London: Routledge, 2000); Walter Truett Anderson, *All Connected Now: Life in the First Global Civilization* (Boulder, CO: Westview Press, 2001); Jagdish Bhagwati, *In Defense of Globalization* (New York: Oxford University Press, 2004); and Thomas L. Friedman, *The Lexus and the Olive Tree: Understanding Globalization* (New York: Anchor, 2000) and *The World Is Flat 3.0: A Brief History of the Twenty-First Century* (New York: Farrar, Straus, and Giroux, 2007). Skeptics questioning the benefits include Walter LaFeber, *Michael Jordan and the New Global Capitalism*, new and expanded ed. (New York: W.W. Norton, 2005);

Joseph E. Stiglitz, *Globalization and Its Discontents* (New York: W.W. Norton, 1993), *Globalization and Its Discontents Revisited: Anti-Globalization in the Era of Trump* (New York: W.W. Norton, 2017), and *Making Globalization Work* (New York: W.W. Norton, 2007); Cynthia Enloe, *Bananas, Beaches and Bases: Making Feminist Sense of International Politics*, updated ed. (Berkeley: University of California Press, 2001) and *Globalization and Militarism: Feminists Make the Link* (Lanham, MD: Rowman and Littlefield, 2007); James H. Mittelman, *The Globalization Syndrome: Transformation and Resistance* (Princeton, NJ: Princeton University Press, 2000) and *Whither Globalization?: The Vortex of Knowledge and Ideology* (New York: Routledge, 2004); and Makere Stewart-Harawiri, *The New Imperial Order: Indigenous Responses to Globalization* (London: Zed, 2005). For views of future trends, see Benjamin R. Barber, *Jihad vs. McWorld* (New York: Times Books, 1995); Michael O'Sullivan, *The Levelling: What's Next After Globalization* (New York: Public Affairs, 2019); Georg Sorensen, *Rethinking the New World Order* (London: Palgrave Macmillan, 2016); and Peter Goodman, "Globalization Is Moving Past the U.S. and Its Vision of World Order," *New York Times*, June 19, 2019. On globalization generally and the debates about it, see Thomas Hyland Eriksen, *Globalization: The Key Concepts* (New York: Berg, 2007); David Held, ed., *A Globalizing World?: Culture, Economics, Politics* (New York: Routledge, 2000); David Held and Anthony McGrew, *Globalization/Anti-Globalization: Beyond the Great Divide*, 2nd ed. (London: Polity, 2007); McGrew and Held, *Globalization Theory: Approaches and Controversies* (London: Polity, 2007); Mark Kesselman, ed., *The Politics of Globalization: A Reader* (Boston: Houghton Mifflin, 2007); George Ritzer, *Globalization: A Basic Text* (Hoboken, NJ: Wiley, 2009); Robert K. Schaeffer, *Understanding Globalization: The Social Consequences of Political, Economic, and Environmental Change*, 4th ed. (Lanham, MD: Rowman and Littlefield, 2009); Lui Hebron and John F. Stack, Jr., *Globalization*, 2nd ed. (New York: Pearson, 2010); Manfred B. Steger, *Globalization: A Very Short Introduction* (New York: Oxford University Press, 2003); Martin Albrow and Elizabeth King, eds., *Globalization: Knowledge and Society* (Newbury Park, CA: Sage, 1990); Anthony Giddens, *The Consequences of Modernity* (Cambridge, UK: Polity, 1991); Roland Robertson, *Globalization: Social Theory and Global Culture* (Newbury Park, CA: Sage, 1992); and Thomas Larrson, *The Race to the Top: The Real Story of Globalization* (Washington, DC: Cato Institute, 2001).

Reflection Questions

1. When did globalization begin?
2. What are the positive arguments for globalization?
3. What main points do opponents make?
4. Do you think globalization will disappear and be replaced by a different system or has the dynamism been enough to maintain its current shape and thrust?

Index

China, 595; France, 481; Icelandic, 334; Netherlands, 382; Russia, 618; Sumerian, 33
Assembly-line production, 491, 519, 622
Assimilation. *See* Cultural assimilation
Assyrian Empire: bureaucracy of, 38; conquests of, 38–39, 70; Egypt and, 63; Israel and, 67; metallurgy and, 3*(map)*; warfare and, 38
Astrakhan, 443
Astrolabe, 370
Astrology, 4
Astronomy: Chinese, 139, 263, 268; European, 374, 387; Hellenistic, 167, 168; Indian, 98, 310; Islamic, 245, 249; Korean, 275; Maya, 210; observatories, 249, 275, 358; Olmec, 91; telescopes and, 387, 697
Atahualpa (Inca), 423
Ataturk, Kemal, 620*(illus.)*, 658–659
Aten (sun-god), 57
Athena (goddess), 158, 162, 163*(illus.)*
Athens. *See also* Greece (Greeks): Acropolis in, 162, 163*(illus.)*; drama and literature of, 159–160; intellectual life of, 159; navy of, 162; Peloponnesian War and, 162; Persian Wars and, 156*(map)*, 162; reform, tyranny, and democracy in, 157
Atlantic system (Atlantic economy), 357; African slave trade in, 361, 393, 403*(map)*, 405, 432*(map)*, 534; Americas and, 432*(map)*; impact of, 436; plantation zone and, 432*(map)*; slave life and African-American culture, 433–434
Atomic bomb. *See also* Nuclear weapons: in France and Britain, 750*(map)*; in Soviet Union, 750*(map)*, 760, 761; United States and, 627, 688, 739; in World War II, 474, 634*(map)*, 635, 636 *and illus.*, 689, 733
Atomic energy, 512
Attila the Hun (calypso singer), 185, 475
Audiencias, in Spanish colonies, 426
Augsburg Confession, 376
Augustine of Hippo, 188, 342
Augustus Caesar (Octavian), 178–180, 182
Aung San (Burmese thinker), 654, 873
Aung San Suu Kyi (Burmese leader), 878, 883
Aurangzeb (Mughal India), 442
Auschwitz death camp, 632
Australia, 421, 797, 798; Aborigines (Indigenous Australians) of, 474, 529, 793, 797; agriculture in, 215; Britain and, 500; Chinese in, 473, 529, 580, 798*(illus.)*; European settlers in, 471,

495, 508, 509*(map)*; gold rush in, 473, 504*(illus.)*; immigration to, 504*(illus.)*, 612, 797; quality of life in, 686, 797; railroads in, 529; World War I and, 614, 616
Australia, Aborigines (Indigenous Australians) of, 18, 215–216, 474, 793, 797
Australopithecines, 12, 14*(illus.)*
Austria: Catholicism in, 384; Habsburg rule of, 385*(map)*, 406, 494; merger with Nazi Germany, 631; Ottoman expansion and, 380, 408; in War of Spanish Succession, 380, 381
Austrian Empire (Austria-Hungary): agriculture in, 491; allied with Germany, 500; Congress of Vienna and, 483, 484*(map)*; ethnic diversity in, 494, 612; in World War I, 577, 613, 615*(map)*
Austronesian languages, 83, 122, 216, 217
Austronesians, 122. *See also* Pacific Islanders; exploration and migration of, *and map*, 216–217; in Funan, 123; maritme trade of, 121
Authoritarianism (autocracy). *See also* Dictatorship; Military dictatorship: in Brazil, 522; fascist, 628; in Japan, 626, 636; in Latin America, 799, 804; in Russia, 617, 767, 768; in Singapore, 880; in South Korea, 739; in Soviet Union, 620, 621, 746; in Turkey, 548; in Vietnam, 881
Authoritarianism, in China, 78. *See also* Dictatorship
Autoimmune deficiency syndrome. *See* AIDS/HIV
Automobiles (cars), 491; German, 512; Korean, 697; Malaysian, 697; rubber for, 578; U.S., 519, 697, 789
Averroes (Ibn Rushd), 249
Avicenna (Ibn Sina), 246, 249
Avignon, papacy in, 342, 350
Awami League (Bengal), 856, 864
Axial Age (600 BCE–600 CE), 97–99. *See also* Classical Era: China, 128–132, 135; imperial China, 128–132, 135; empires of, 100; Indian religions, 108; thinkers of, 97–98, 112; trade routes in, 97, 99*(map)*
"Axis of evil" (Iran, Iraq, North Korea), 786
Axis Powers (Germany, Japan, Italy), 630, 633*(map)*
Aymara Indians, 801
Aymara people (Andes), 211
Ayn Jalut, battle of (1260), 254
Ayuthia, Siam, 364, 447; by Burma, 447; foreign merchants in, 358

Ayutthaya, Siam, 323
Azerbaijan, 409; Muslims in, 604
Azores Islands, 351, 370, 398
Aztec Empire (Aztecs), 301*(map)*, 415, 419*(map)*; economy and society of, 300–302; markets, 300, 303; mother goddess, 428; religion and warfare of, 300; slavery in, 225; Spanish conquest of, 416, 418, 419*(map)*; warrior class in, 302
az-Zahawi, Jamil Sidqi, 552

B

Ba'ath Party: in Iraq, 824; in Syria, 828
Baba Kuhi (Persian poet), 246
Babur (Mughal India), 440
Babylon (city), 33; hanging gardens of, 5, 38; Hebrews in, 67–68
Babylonia, 4. *See also* Mesopotamia; astrology in, 4; Chaldeans, 38, 68, 69*(illus.)*; laws, 38, 40 *and illus.*; map making in, 4; Persian conquest of, 38, 151, 154
Bacchus (god), 180
Bachelet, Michelle (Chilean leader), 805, 808
Bach, Johann Sebastian, 386
Bacon, Francis, 228, 387, 391, 455; scientific method and, 386
Bactria (Afghanistan), 112, 166*(map)*
Bagchi, Amiya Kumar, 464, 466
Baghdad, 33, 249, 266; Abbasid caliphate and, 242–244; House of Wisdom in, 249, 257; Mongol sack of, 244, 254; monument in, 829*(illus.)*; population of, 337; Wisdom in, 224
Bahai religion (Bahaullah), 550
Bahia, Brazil, 423, 526; revolt in, 486
Bahrain Island, 818; trade of, 34
Bahuguna, Sunderlal, 860
Bakongo people, 292. *See also* Kongo
Balance of payments: Brazilian deficit, 804; in China trade, 587
Balance of terror, in Cold War, 689
Balboa, Vasco Nunez de, 420
Balfour Declaration (1917), 661
Bali (Balinese), 571; gamelan music in, 580; Hinduism in, 322
Balkans, 334. *See also specific country*; Christian-Muslim conflict in, 364; ethnic conflict in, 612; Ottoman control of, 406, 408, 604; Ottoman expansion and, 254, 255; Serbs in, 254, 345
Ball games, Mesoamerican, 90, 209–210; Northern peoples and, 214, 297
Balsa rafts, 103; of Manteno, 211, 304
Baltic states. *See also* Estonia; Latvia; Lithuania: Russia and, 381, 385*(map)*,

Q

Qajar dynasty (Persia), 550
Qatar, cable television in, 709, 832
Qazvini, Aref (Persian songwriter), 550
Qi (ch'i), 268
Qianlong (China), 586
Qin dynasty (China, 221–206 BCE), 133–136(map)
Qing Empire (China, 1644–1912): conflicts in (1839–1870), 589(map); debates and new challenges in, 591–592; economic change and emigration, 589–591; expansion of, 358, 456, 584–585; opium trade and war, 586–588; philosopher-emperors in, 358, 455; revolution and republic, 594–595; society, thought, and culture, 453–455; Taiping Rebellion in, 588–589 and map; treaty system and, 588; wars, reforms, and nationalism, 592–594; western encounters, 456–458; world economy and, 456; zenith and decline, 584–591
Qin Jin (Chinese feminist), 593
Quakers (Society of Friends), 511, 650; abolitionism and, 514
Quality of life. See Living standards
Quanzhou (Zayton), 227, 266
Quebec, 424; autonomy in, 795; Catholicism in, 430, 527, 796
Quetzalcoatl (god), 415, 422
Quetzalcoatl cult, 296, 300, 304
Quinine, 425, 500, 537
Quipus (Inca recordkeeping), 304
"Quit India" campaign, of Gandhi, 651, 653
Quran, 239, 246, 552, 661; Islamic law and, 239, 241; Muhammad and, 236, 237; printing of, 243; women's rights in, 248, 829
Quraysh tribe, 236; caliphate and, 242
Qutb, Sayyid (Egyptian writer), 830

R

Rabban Sauma, 229
Rabelais, François (French writer), 374
Race concept, 13
Racism: African slavery and, 404; in Algeria, 551; in Australia, 797; in Brazil, 793, 809; in British-ruled India, 562, 566; in colonial Africa, 541, 544; colonialism and, 643; in Europe, 757; Japanese-Americans and, 635; minority youth in Europe, 754; in Nazi Germany, 629–630, 632, 635; Nietzsche's ideas and, 511; skin color, 363, 434, 809; Social Darwinism and, 501; in South Africa, 839–841; in United States, 518, 536, 625, 759, 793

Radio, 473, 627; in China, 726; Marconi's wireless, 512; transistors for, 678, 709
Raffles, Thomas Stafford, 571
Rahman, Sheikh Mujiber, 856, 864
Railroads, 473, 500, 854(illus.); in Australia, 529, 530(map); in Britain, 489 and(map), 490; in British East Africa, 641; in Canada, 527, 528(illus.); in Europe, 751; Eurotunnel, 771; in India, 563, 565, 641; in Indonesia, 641; in Iran, 660; in Japan, 602(map), 728; in Persia, 550; in Russia (Siberia), 473, 604, 605(map), 612; in United States, 517(map), 519, 520
Rainfall, 32, 41. See also Drought; in Egypt, 57; Indus Valley, 41; Korean records of, 277; in sub-Saharan Africa, 61; Western Asia, 32
Rain forests: in Brazil, 703, 804; clearing of, 703, 804, 806, 807, 874; in Congo, 672, 703; in Thailand, 877
Rajas, in India, 48
Rajputs (Hindu warriors), 441, 561
Rajputs (Indian warriors), 308, 313
Raleigh, Walter (English explorer), 358
Rama, 47. See also Ramayana
Ramabai, Pandita (Indian feminist), 570
Ramadan fast, in Islam, 238
Rama Kamkheng (Siam), 322
Ramanuja, 311
Ramayana, 49, 318, 321
Rameses (Egypt), 52(illus.), 52(illus.), 58(illus.)
Ranching. See Cattle (ranching)
Rangoon (Yangon), Burma, 567, 580, 643
Rani of Jhansi (Indian queen), 565
Rap music, 758, 795
Rashidun caliphate, 238, 241
Rashomon (Ryunosuke), 623; film of, 736
Rastafarianism, 810
Rationalism (reason): Confucian, 131; Enlightenment, 358, 511, 552, 616; European science and, 386; Greek, 158; in Islam, 246; Islamic modernists and, 552, 553; Roman, 180
Ratu Tui Levuka (Fiji), 529
Ravidas (Hindu poet), 317
Raw materials. See also Natural resources; specific materials: in Atlantic economy, 432(map); from colonial Africa, 546; in Great Depression, 626; industrialization and, 491; from Latin America, 524; price drop, in Great Depression, 642
Raziya, Sultan (Delhi), 314–315
Re (sun-god), 56
Reagan, Ronald (American leader), 790
Realism, in art, 511, 520
Reason. See Rationalism (reason)

Rebellion in the Backlands (Cunha), 525
Rebellions (revolts): in Afghanistan, 829; Arab, 658; against Aztecs, 300, 303; in Bahia (Brazil), 486; in British India, 468, 565; in Burma, 320; in Canada, 527; in China, 135, 137, 265, 272, 468; in colonial Africa, 546, 551; in colonial Latin America, 426, 485; in Congo, 843; in Egypt, 151, 176; by European peasants, 337, 347, 378, 390, 483; by Filipino peasants, 450, 872; in French-ruled Vietnam, 573; Inca, 303; by Ionian Greeks, 154; in Iraq, 660; in Ireland, 495; in Islam, 242, 244; in Japan, 596; by Japanese Christians, 460; in Korea, 603; by Kurds, in Turkey, 829; Mau Mau, in Kenya, 835(illus.); Maya, 296; by Mexican peasants, 802; by Native Americans, 426; in Ottoman Empire, 408; in Palestine, 186, 187; in Palmyra, 194; in Peru, 800; by Roman slaves, 181; slave, 434, 485, 535; in Sri Lanka, 865; Taiping, in China, 588–589 and map; in Texas, 516; Vietnamese, against China, 124 and illus.
Recession. See Global recession (2008–2009)
Recordkeeping, 27, 35. See also Scribes; Inca quipus, 304
Records of the Grand Historian (Sima), 140
Red Army (China), 713, 715–716; Long March and, 646(map), 647 and illus.
Red Army (Soviet Union), 762, 764, 766; in Manchuria, 596; in Russia civil war, 618, 620; in World War II, 632, 635
Red Cross, 474
Red Guards (China), 719
Red River Valley, 82, 122, 324
"Red Scare," in United States, 623
Red Sea trade: Aksum and, 201, 202; Egypt and, 53, 56 and map; ports, 103
Reform. See also Land reform: in Catholicism, 759; in Chile and Brazil, 663; in China, 592–594; Christian church, 340, 350; in Egypt, 548; in England, 496; European social democrats and, 498; in French Revolution, 481; in Great Depression, 626; in Hinduism, 562–563; in Japan, 596, 599; of Jesus, 187; in Korea, 601; in Mexico, 522, 523; Ottoman Empire, 409, 548; in Persia, 550; of Russian czars, 382, 618; of Solon (Athens), 157; in Soviet Union, 764; Taika, in Japan, 277; in Turkey, 658–660(illus.)
Reform Act (1832, Britain), 496

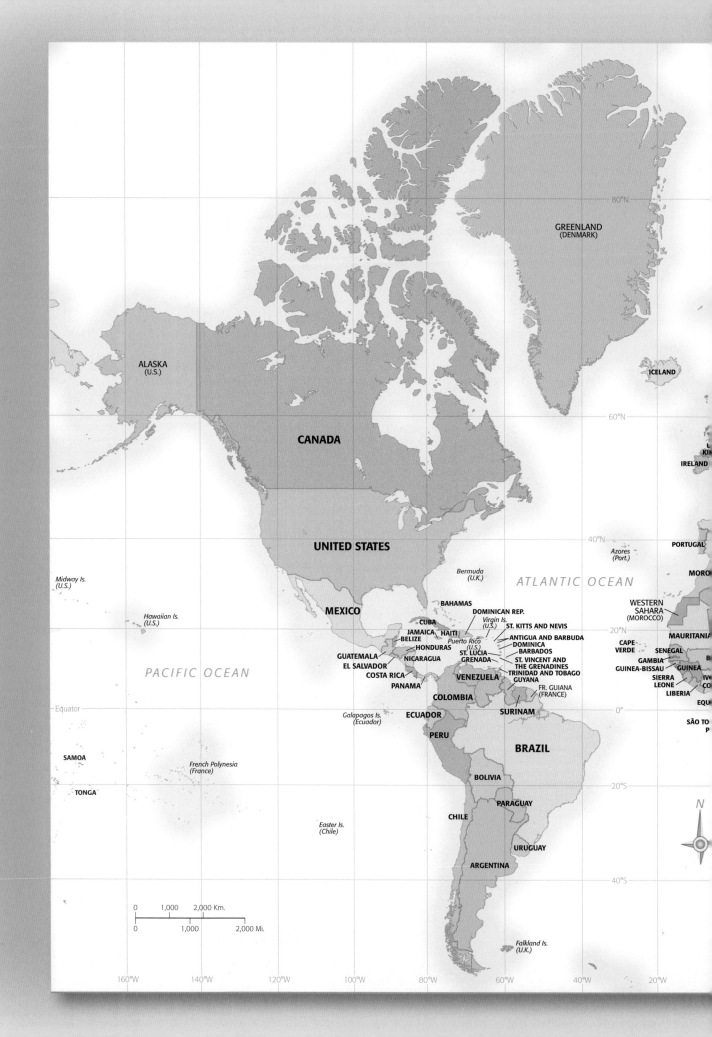

ALASKA
(U.S.)

GREENLAND
(DENMARK)

ICELAND

CANADA

UNITED STATES

80°N

60°N

40°N

PORTUGAL

Azores
(Port.)

MORO

Midway Is.
(U.S.)

Bermuda
(U.K.)

ATLANTIC OCEAN

IRELAND

KIN

Hawaiian Is.
(U.S.)

MEXICO

BAHAMAS

CUBA

DOMINICAN REP.

Virgin Is.
(U.S.)

ST. KITTS AND NEVIS

WESTERN
SAHARA
(MOROCCO)

JAMAICA
BELIZE

HAITI

Puerto Rico
(U.S.)

ANTIGUA AND BARBUDA
DOMINICA

CAPE
VERDE

SENEGAL

MAURITANIA

GUATEMALA
EL SALVADOR

HONDURAS

NICARAGUA

ST. LUCIA
GRENADA

BARBADOS
ST. VINCENT AND
THE GRENADINES
TRINIDAD AND TOBAGO

GAMBIA
GUINEA-BISSAU

B

GUINEA

PACIFIC OCEAN

COSTA RICA
PANAMA

VENEZUELA

GUYANA

SIERRA
LEONE

IV
CO

LIBERIA

COLOMBIA

FR. GUIANA
(FRANCE)

SURINAM

EQU

20°N

Galapagos Is.
(Ecuador)

ECUADOR

SÃO TO
P

Equator

PERU

BRAZIL

0°

SAMOA

French Polynesia
(France)

BOLIVIA

TONGA

PARAGUAY

20°S

CHILE

Easter Is.
(Chile)

URUGUAY

N

ARGENTINA

40°S

0   1,000   2,000 Km.

0   1,000   2,000 Mi.

Falkland Is.
(U.K.)

160°W   140°W   120°W   100°W   80°W   60°W   40°W   20°W

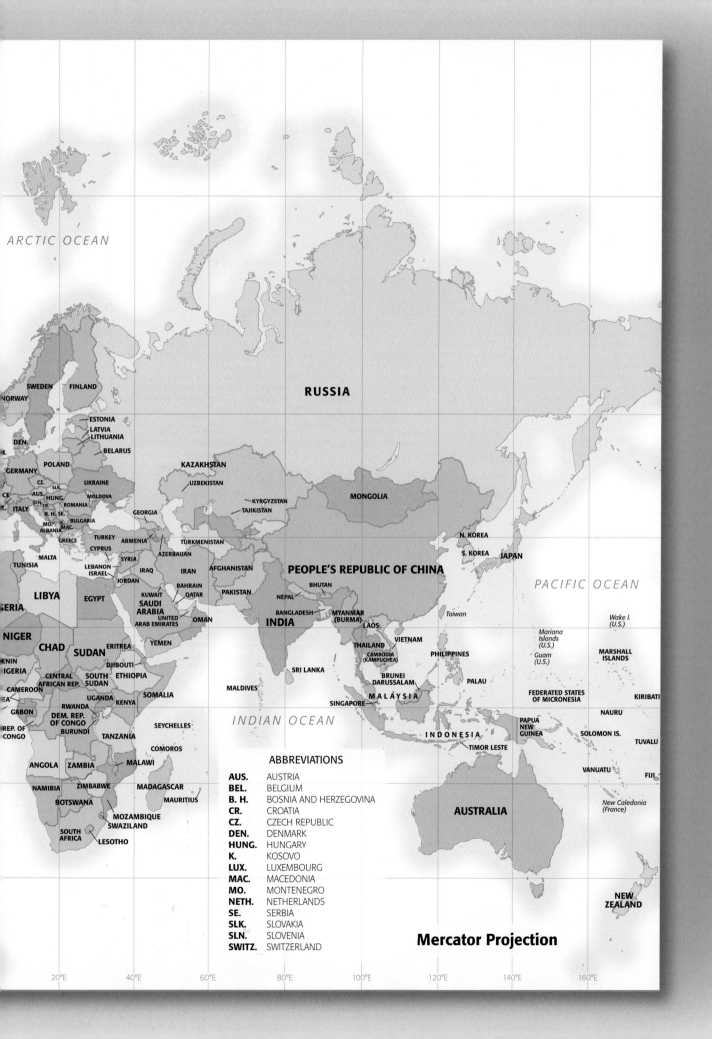

ARCTIC OCEAN

SWEDEN   FINLAND

RUSSIA

NORWAY

ESTONIA
LATVIA
LITHUANIA
DEN.
BELARUS

POLAND
GERMANY
CZ.   SLK.
AUS.
SLN.   HUNG.
CE   ITALY   ROMANIA
CR.
B. H.   SE.
MO.   MAC.
ALBANIA   BULGARIA
GREECE

KAZAKHSTAN

UZBEKISTAN

MONGOLIA

KYRGYZSTAN
TAJIKISTAN

GEORGIA

TURKEY   ARMENIA
CYPRUS
AZERBAIJAN
TURKMENISTAN

N. KOREA

S. KOREA   JAPAN

PACIFIC OCEAN

MALTA
TUNISIA
LEBANON   SYRIA
ISRAEL   IRAQ   IRAN   AFGHANISTAN
JORDAN
KUWAIT   BAHRAIN
SAUDI   QATAR
LIBYA   EGYPT   ARABIA
UNITED   OMAN
ARAB EMIRATES

PAKISTAN

PEOPLE'S REPUBLIC OF CHINA

BHUTAN
NEPAL

BANGLADESH   MYANMAR
INDIA   (BURMA)
LAOS

Taiwan

Wake I.
(U.S.)

Mariana
Islands
(U.S.)

MARSHALL
ISLANDS

GERIA

NIGER   CHAD   SUDAN   ERITREA
YEMEN

BENIN   DJIBOUTI
IGERIA   ETHIOPIA
CENTRAL   SOUTH
AFRICAN REP.   SUDAN
EA   UGANDA
CAMEROON
GABON   RWANDA   KENYA
REP. OF   DEM. REP.
CONGO   OF CONGO   BURUNDI
TANZANIA

SRI LANKA

MALDIVES

SEYCHELLES

THAILAND   VIETNAM
CAMBODIA
(KAMPUCHEA)   PHILIPPINES

Guam
(U.S.)

BRUNEI
DARUSSALAM   PALAU

MALAYSIA

SINGAPORE

FEDERATED STATES
OF MICRONESIA

KIRIBATI

NAURU

INDIAN OCEAN

COMOROS

INDONESIA

PAPUA
NEW
GUINEA

SOLOMON IS.

TUVALU

ANGOLA   ZAMBIA   MALAWI

MADAGASCAR
NAMIBIA   ZIMBABWE
BOTSWANA   MAURITIUS

TIMOR LESTE

VANUATU

FIJI

New Caledonia
(France)

MOZAMBIQUE
SWAZILAND
SOUTH
AFRICA   LESOTHO

AUSTRALIA

ABBREVIATIONS

AUS.	AUSTRIA
BEL.	BELGIUM
B. H.	BOSNIA AND HERZEGOVINA
CR.	CROATIA
CZ.	CZECH REPUBLIC
DEN.	DENMARK
HUNG.	HUNGARY
K.	KOSOVO
LUX.	LUXEMBOURG
MAC.	MACEDONIA
MO.	MONTENEGRO
NETH.	NETHERLANDS
SE.	SERBIA
SLK.	SLOVAKIA
SLN.	SLOVENIA
SWITZ.	SWITZERLAND

NEW
ZEALAND

Mercator Projection

20°E   40°E   60°E   80°E   100°E   120°E   140°E   160°E

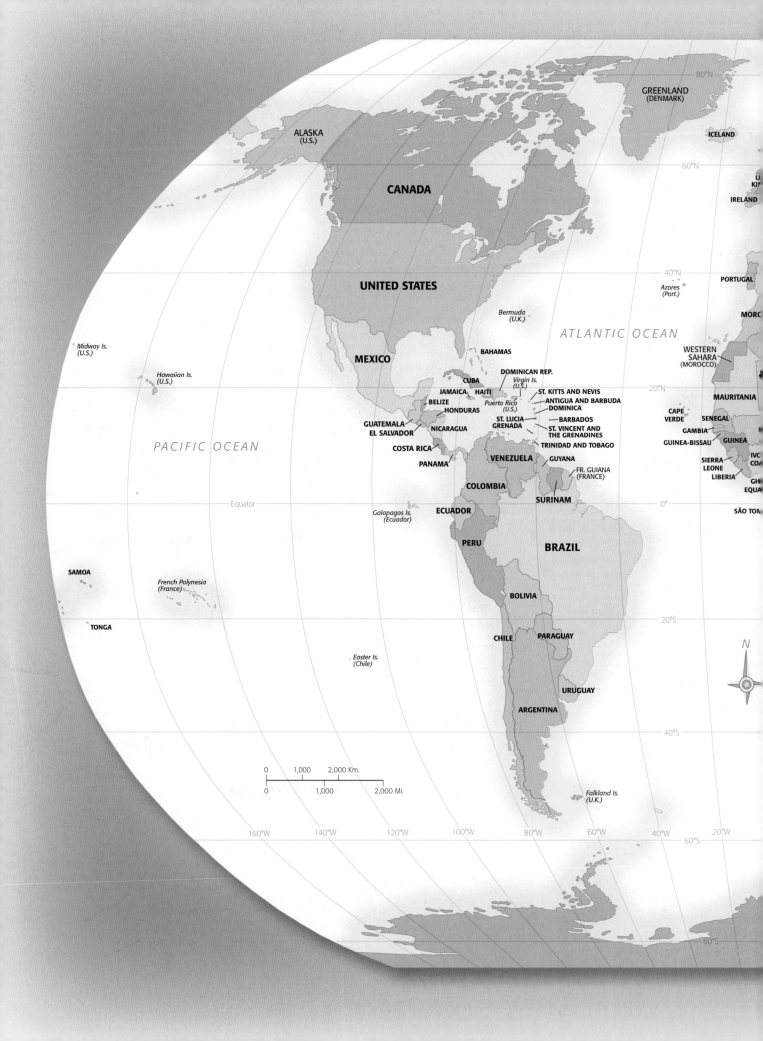

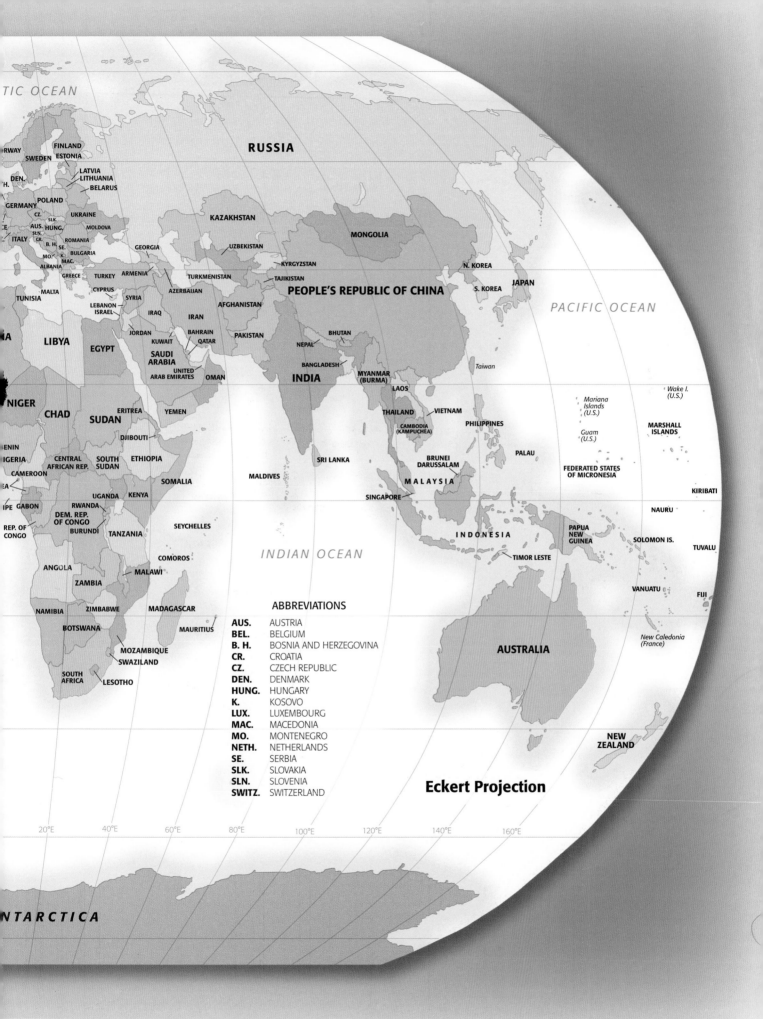

TIC OCEAN

RUSSIA

RWAY
SWEDEN
FINLAND
ESTONIA
DEN.
H.
LATVIA
LITHUANIA
BELARUS
GERMANY
POLAND
CZ.
UKRAINE
SLK.
AUS.
HUNG.
MOLDOVA
SLN.
ITALY
CR.
ROMANIA
B. H.
SE.
MO.
K.
BULGARIA
MAC.
ALBANIA
GREECE
TURKEY
ARMENIA
MALTA
CYPRUS
TUNISIA
LEBANON
ISRAEL
SYRIA
IRAQ

KAZAKHSTAN

MONGOLIA

N. KOREA

S. KOREA

JAPAN

PACIFIC OCEAN

UZBEKISTAN

KYRGYZSTAN

GEORGIA

TURKMENISTAN

TAJIKISTAN

AZERBAIJAN

PEOPLE'S REPUBLIC OF CHINA

AFGHANISTAN

IRAN

JORDAN
KUWAIT
BAHRAIN
QATAR

PAKISTAN

NEPAL

BHUTAN

BANGLADESH

Taiwan

Wake I.
(U.S.)

LIBYA

EGYPT

SAUDI
ARABIA

UNITED
ARAB EMIRATES

OMAN

INDIA

MYANMAR
(BURMA)

LAOS

Mariana
Islands
(U.S.)

NIGER

CHAD

SUDAN

ERITREA

YEMEN

THAILAND

VIETNAM

PHILIPPINES

Guam
(U.S.)

MARSHALL
ISLANDS

DJIBOUTI

CAMBODIA
(KAMPUCHEA)

ENIN

IGERIA

CENTRAL
AFRICAN REP.

SOUTH
SUDAN

ETHIOPIA

SRI LANKA

BRUNEI
DARUSSALAM

PALAU

FEDERATED STATES
OF MICRONESIA

CAMEROON

MALDIVES

MALAYSIA

KIRIBATI

EA

IPE
GABON

REP. OF
CONGO

RWANDA
DEM. REP.
OF CONGO
BURUNDI

UGANDA
KENYA

TANZANIA

SOMALIA

SEYCHELLES

SINGAPORE

INDONESIA

PAPUA
NEW
GUINEA

SOLOMON IS.

NAURU

TUVALU

COMOROS

INDIAN OCEAN

TIMOR LESTE

ANGOLA

MALAWI

ZAMBIA

NAMIBIA

ZIMBABWE

MADAGASCAR

VANUATU

FIJI

BOTSWANA

MAURITIUS

ABBREVIATIONS

MOZAMBIQUE
SWAZILAND

SOUTH
AFRICA

LESOTHO

AUS.	AUSTRIA
BEL.	BELGIUM
B. H.	BOSNIA AND HERZEGOVINA
CR.	CROATIA
CZ.	CZECH REPUBLIC
DEN.	DENMARK
HUNG.	HUNGARY
K.	KOSOVO
LUX.	LUXEMBOURG
MAC.	MACEDONIA
MO.	MONTENEGRO
NETH.	NETHERLANDS
SE.	SERBIA
SLK.	SLOVAKIA
SLN.	SLOVENIA
SWITZ.	SWITZERLAND

New Caledonia
(France)

AUSTRALIA

Eckert Projection

NEW
ZEALAND

20°E   40°E   60°E   80°E   100°E   120°E   140°E   160°E

NTARCTICA